REGNUM STUDIES IN GLOBAL CHRISTIANITY

Anthology of African Christianity

REGNUM STUDIES IN GLOBAL CHRISTIANITY

(Previously GLOBAL THEOLOGICAL VOICES series)

Series Preface

The latter part of the twentieth century witnessed a global level of change in Christian dynamics. One significant development was the rise of the churches in the global South, not only in their number but also in their engagement with their socio-cultural contexts. *Regnum Studies in Global Christianity* explores the issues that the global church struggles with, focusing particularly on churches in Africa, Asia, Latin America and Eastern Europe.

The series publishes studies that will help the global church learn not only from past and present, but also from provocative and prophetic voices for the future. The editors and the publisher particularly pray that the series as a public space will encourage the southern churches to make an important contribution to the shaping of a healthy future for global Christianity. The editors invite theological seminaries and universities from around the world to submit relevant scholarly dissertations for possible publication in the series. It is hoped that the series will provide a forum for South-to-South as well as South-to-North dialogues.

Series Editors

REGNUM STUDIES IN GLOBAL CHRISTIANITY

Anthology of African Christianity

Isabel Apawo Phiri and Dietrich Werner (Chief Editors)
Chammah Kaunda and Kennedy Owino (Associate Editors)

Editorial Committee:
Edison Kalengyo, Priscille Djomhue, Kudzai Biri, Kwabena Asamoah-Gyadu,
James Amanze, Roderick Hewitt

First published 2016 by Regnum Books International

Regnum is an imprint of the Oxford Centre for Mission Studies
St Philip and St James Church
Woodstock Road
Oxford OX2 6HR, UK
www.ocms.ac.uk/regnum

09 08 07 06 05 04 03   8 7 6 5 4 3 2 1

British Library Cataloguing in Publication Data
A catalogue record for this book is available from the British Library

ISBN: 978-1-506474-92-2

Typeset by Words by Design Ltd
www.wordsbydesign.co.uk

Cover design by Words by Design

World Council of Churches

Brot für die Welt

With financial support from the Federal Ministry for Economic Cooperation and Development

Distributed by 1517 Media in the US and Canada

I Am an African

Thabo Mbeki

I owe my being to the hills and the valleys, the mountains and the glades, the rivers, the deserts, the trees, the flowers, the seas and the ever-changing seasons that define the face of our native land.

My body has frozen in our frosts and in our latter-day snows. It has thawed in the warmth of our sunshine and melted in the heat of the midday sun. The crack and the rumble of the summer thunders, lashed by startling lightning, have been a cause both of trembling and of hope.

The fragrances of nature have been as pleasant to us as the sight of the wild blooms of the citizens of the veld.

The dramatic shapes of the Drakensberg, the soil-coloured waters of the Lekoa, iGqili noThukela, and the sands of the Kgalagadi, have all been panels of the set on the natural stage on which we act out the foolish deeds of the theatre of the day.

At times, and in fear, I have wondered whether I should concede equal citizenship of our country to the leopard and the lion, the elephant and the springbok, the hyena, the black mamba and the pestilential mosquito.

A human presence among all of these, a feature on the face of our native land thus defined, I know that none dare challenge me when I say - I am an African!

I owe my being to the Khoi and the San whose desolate souls haunt the great expanses of the beautiful Cape - they who fell victim to the most merciless genocide our native land has ever seen, they who were the first to lose their lives in the struggle to defend our freedom and independence and they who, as a people, perished in the result.

Today, as a country, we keep an inaudible and audible silence about these ancestors of the generations that live, fearful to admit the horror of a former deed, seeking to obliterate from our memories a cruel occurrence which, in its remembering, should teach us not and never to be inhuman again.

I am formed of the migrants who left Europe to find a new home on our native land. Whatever their own actions, they remain still part of me.

In my veins courses the blood of the Malay slaves who came from the East. Their proud dignity informs my bearing, their culture a part of my essence. The stripes they bore on their bodies from the lash of the slave master are a reminder embossed on my consciousness of what should not be done.

I am the grandchild of the warrior men and women that Hintsa and Sekhukhune led, the patriots that Cetshwayo and Mphephu took to battle, the soldiers Moshoeshoe and Ngungunyane taught never to dishonour the cause of freedom.

My mind and my knowledge of myself is formed by the victories that are the jewels in our African crown, the victories we earned from Isandhlwana to Khartoum, as Ethiopians and as Ashanti of Ghana, as Berbers of the desert.

I am the grandchild who lays fresh flowers on the Boer graves at St Helena and the Vrouemonument, who sees in the mind's eye and suffers the suffering of a simple peasant folk, death, concentration camps, destroyed homesteads, a dream in ruins.

I am the child of Nongqawuse. I am he who made it possible to trade in the world markets in diamonds, in gold, in the same food for which our stomachs yearn.

I come of those who were transported from India and China, whose being resided in the fact, solely, that they were able to provide physical labour, who taught me that we could both be at home and be foreign, who taught me that human existence itself demanded that freedom was a necessary condition for that human existence.

Being part of all of these people, and in the knowledge that none dares contest that assertion, I shall claim that - I am an African.

I have seen our country torn asunder as these, all of whom are my people, engaged one another in a titanic battle, the one to redress a wrong that had been caused by one to another and the other, to defend the indefensible.

I have seen what happens when one person has superiority of force over another, when the stronger appropriate to themselves the prerogative even to annul the injunction that God created all men and women in His image.

I know what it signifies when race and colour are used to determine who is human and who, sub-human.

I have seen the destruction of all sense of self-esteem, the consequent striving to be what one is not, simply to acquire some of the benefits which those who had imposed themselves as masters had ensured that they enjoy.

I have experience of the situation in which race and colour is used to enrich some and impoverish the rest.

I have seen the corruption of minds and souls as a result of the pursuit of an ignoble effort to perpetrate a veritable crime against humanity.

I have seen concrete expression of the denial of the dignity of a human being emanating from the conscious, systemic and systematic oppressive and repressive activities of other human beings.

There the victims parade with no mask to hide the brutish reality - the beggars, the prostitutes, the street children, those who seek solace in substance abuse, those who have to steal to assuage hunger, those who have to lose their sanity because to be sane is to invite pain.

Perhaps the worst among these, who are my people, are those who have learnt to kill for a wage. To these the extent of death is directly proportional to their personal welfare.

And so, like pawns in the service of demented souls, they kill in furtherance of the political violence in KwaZulu-Natal. They murder the innocent in the taxi wars.

They kill slowly or quickly in order to make profits from the illegal trade in narcotics. They are available for hire when husband wants to murder wife and wife, husband.

Among us prowl the products of our immoral and amoral past - killers who have no sense of the worth of human life, rapists who have absolute disdain for the women of our country, animals who would seek to benefit from the vulnerability of the children, the disabled, and the old, the rapacious who brook no obstacle in their quest for self-enrichment.

All this I know and know to be true because I am an African!

Because of that, I am also able to state this fundamental truth that I am born of a people who are heroes and heroines.

I am born of a people who would not tolerate oppression.

I am of a nation that would not allow that fear of death, of torture, of imprisonment, of exile or persecution should result in the perpetuation of injustice.

The great masses who are our mother and father will not permit that the behaviour of the few results in the description of our country and people as barbaric.

Patient because history is on their side, these masses do not despair because today the weather is bad. Nor do they turn triumphalist when, tomorrow, the sun shines.

Whatever the circumstances they have lived through and because of that experience, they are determined to define for themselves who they are and who they should be.

...

I am an African.

I am born of the peoples of the continent of Africa.

The pain of the violent conflict that the peoples of Liberia, and of Somalia, of the Sudan, of Burundi and Algeria is a pain I also bear.

The dismal shame of poverty, suffering and human degradation of my continent is a blight that we share.

The blight on our happiness that derives from this and from our drift to the periphery of the ordering of human affairs leaves us in a persistent shadow of despair.

This is a savage road to which nobody should be condemned. The evolution of humanity says that Africa reaffirms that she is continuing her rise from the ashes.

Whatever the setbacks of the moment, nothing can stop us now! Whatever the difficulties, Africa shall be at peace!

Part of the famous speech of the South African President Thabo Mbeki on behalf of the African National Congress, delivered in Cape Town on 8 May 1996, on the occasion of the passing of the new Constitution of South Africa.

* * * * *

Explanation for cover picture:

Explanation for cover picture: The painting of the African The Three Magi (Wise Men)/Les Rois Mages (Mt 2,1) is part of a series of 62 New Testament scenes of the life of Jesus Christ which has been published under the title 'La Vie de Jesus Mafa'. This project originated 1973 in North Cameroon, where Mafa Christian communities wanted to have an African representation of the gospel. A committee was formed to work on the project. Some important New Testament scenes were selected for liturgical and catechetical use and then adapted to be played by the village people. The sketches were photographed and then painted. After a careful and detailed study Jesus MΛFΛ paintings were carried out by a French artist chosen for her fine and deep perception of religious and African spirits.

Vie de Jésus Mafa est un ensemble cohérent de tableaux illustrant 62 scènes du Nouveau Testament. Ils sont imprimés en différentes tailles (de 10x15 à 70x100 cm) et sur une video cassette. Ces reproductions sont envoyées à travers le monde depuis plus de 30 ans, notamment dans les régions plus particulièrement concernées par un Jésus noir dans un environnement africain. Jésus ressuscité parle à chacun de nous dans son propre langage et sa propre culture. Il est devenu l'un des nôtres.

Contents

V: African Christianity and Ecumenism

VI: Issues and Themes in African Christianity

VII: The Public Role of African Christianity

VIII: Resources for the Study of African Christianity

Foreword

John S. Mbiti

Fearing for Christianity in Africa

In the 1960s and 1970s, some missionaries and church leaders in Europe and America, made much noise in writing and talking, saying frequently that: 'Christianity in Africa was (is) doomed and destined to disappear by the beginning of the 21st century'. This wave of prophecy of doom swept across the continent (with Madagascar) and some Africans believed it, assuming that it carried the full authority of western Christianity.

On the historical time-scale, these were the decades of Africa attaining independence from colonial rule. In general, from the nineteenth to the twentieth centuries, Christianity in Africa was very closely associated, or in some regions even integrated, with colonial conquest, rule, and (in some places a brutal) exhibition of western superiority. This close association between the missionary presence and colonial rule meant that the emerging Christianity was still in the 'fetters' of foreign forces.

In the struggle for political independence, there arose also a parallel but quieter struggle, for ecclesiastical independence. The movement of independent churches began in a small way at the end of the nineteenth century, but gained momentum and mushroomed in the second half of the twentieth century. These churches manifested themselves especially in Southern Africa, then Western Africa and slowly in Eastern and Central Africa. It can be affirmed that, with the independent church movement, genuine elements of African Christianity began to germinate and infiltrate missionary Christianity.

African Christianity's Search for Identity

But African Christianity still had no defined or definable identity. But then it became more than just *Christianity **in** Africa;* it was the emergence of an ***African** Christianity*. Eventually, this undefined search for identity flared up in the call for a moratorium in the 1970s and 1980s (i.e. the call for a stop to send western missionaries to Africa). Among other things, some vociferous African church leaders advocated the stopping of 'foreign aid' (in material forms and personnel) from western sources to the churches in Africa. For a short while, the moratorium debate stirred up a lot of dust in missionary and church circles, in both African and western countries.

The factors that inspired the moratorium were both ecclesiastical and political. In the churches and Christianity in general, there was on the one hand the proclamation of the gospel, with help from Africans, by western missionaries who, until the 1970s, had 'invaded' the whole continent. On the other hand, the social, economic and political realities of African peoples were calling for serious attention, and pressing for answers from Christian perspectives. These answers could not satisfactorily come (alone) from an intensely western Christianity in Africa.

That, in turn, called for a *genuine* African Christianity. But this was not attainable automatically by merely severing all ties with western Christianity. It was to be through a concerted endeavour to define itself within the framework of Biblical boundaries of the church in its African context. Around the same time – from the 1960s – *written* African theology began to develop and sketch a wide-angle view of African Christianity. It was preceded by oral theology, which has continued to prosper alongside or integrated with written theology. From the very moment the gospel is proclaimed in an African community, oral theology begins to germinate and sprout, without being systematised. African culture is primarily an oral and symbolic culture. So, oral theology emerges spontaneously, manifesting itself in conversations about the gospel, retelling and discussing Bible passages, in indigenous Christian songs, spontaneous prayers by Christians, public and family services, sermons of pastors and lay persons (many of whom do not write them down), Christians rejoicing and weeping in fellowship with one another. By the beginning of the 21st century, African theology has literally burst out in articles, books, conferences, research, symposia, and in college and university courses, both in Africa and in other continents.

Factors Contributing to the Rapid Expansion of Christianity in Africa

At the same time, the Christian faith continued to expand rapidly, due to a number of factors. We can only mention some briefly. The *missionary factor* is fundamental, since in modern times it is the missionaries that brought the gospel anew to Africa. Many were very devoted to this task, and some died in Africa spreading it and rendering its practical services – like medical care, education, and producing written materials.

The *fading of colonial rule* gave us Africans the freedom to take up seriously or reject the Christian faith, on our own terms. The majority chose to embrace it and expand it. This was in spite of the fact that the (western) Christianity that had principally mediated the faith since the nineteenth century was largely foreign on African soil (culture, worldview, lifestyle and multiplicity of languages).

The first profound factor facilitating the planting of the Christian faith was *traditional African religion and religiosity*. Almost by nature, Africans are deeply religious. However, hitherto missionaries and early converts regarded African religion and treated it as 'demonic', 'heathen' and antagonistic of the Christian faith. But beneath this surface expression of ignorance and falsification, the two religious systems were quietly interacting positively. This was particularly facilitated by the fact that African religion is fostered around a monotheistic belief in One God, the Almighty, and Creator of all things. From time immemorial this African religion has infiltrated the whole of life. It had no founders. It evolved its expressions in different ways and places, such as the names of the One God (which we find in every language and people or 'tribe'), prayers to God, and making offerings and sacrifices to God variously from place to place and time to time. People also acknowledge other spiritual realities, which are created by and subject to God. Some are personifications of natural phenomena and objects, and others are remnants of human (and animal) beings after death.

African religion acknowledges the same God who is depicted (similarly and differently) in the Bible. The attributes of God in the Bible have many parallels in African concepts of God. Adherents of African religion do not find stumbling-blocks to continuing their belief in God as presented in the Scriptures. They take the Word of God in the Bible as the Word of the same God they know through African religion. This is a complex phenomenon, taking place at profoundly spiritual, religious, mental, emotional, personal and community levels. It is both personal and public. Belief in God is a communal and integral belief that no individual can counteract or contradict. It is the total baggage with which African Christianity has entered the 21st century.

A second factor is *the work of African Christians* who both informally (mainly) and formally spread news about the Christian faith. This happens in more or less the way people share regular and ordinary news. Formal contributors are male and female, trained or untrained, literate and illiterate: catechists, evangelists, pastors, priests and church workers. They use tools and methods, including the Bible, teaching materials, radio, symbols, television, films and cassettes, and engage in personal conversations, discussions and rallies, etc. Personal witness is very effective, whereby individuals or groups tell of their conversion and joy of being Christian. This often leads to conversions and the expansion of Christian knowledge and practice. Informal spreading of the gospel takes place all the time, in family circles and communities. This is the *New* and *Good* News, and because it was previously unknown, people normally pay attention to it sooner or later. They embrace the gospel, consciously or unconsciously, feeling that it enhances their religiosity.

In the gospel, something really very new is in *the name of Jesus Christ* His life and ministry among the people of his time rings a loud bell in African life, such as in his healing of the sick, chasing out unwanted spirits, feeding the hungry, receiving people both within and on the edge of society (foreign rulers, women, children, the hungry), and preaching peace and love. Africans have fallen in love with Jesus Christ, and are formulating hundreds of Christological titles to describe him and their relationship with him. By 2015, I had collected some 170 such titles.. These speak of the people's personal experiences of Jesus and their hope in him. These can be summarised in a placard I once saw in 2013, on the back of a bus in Kenya, which read:

'Who God blesses, no man curses.
IT'S NO SECRET, I LOVE JESUS.'

A third factor is *the translation and distribution of the Bible into African languages*, in full, or the New Testament, or just a portion. By the end of 2014, these languages numbered close to 800. The Bible has had a tremendous impact upon the spreading and shaping of the Christian faith, as we, the people of Africa, hear the gospel 'in our own language'. This makes the Bible 'our Bible'. People read and hear the Bible as comprehensively describing African life – religious, cultural, social, political, economic, family life, spiritual realities, religious aspirations, world-views, historical journeys, etc.

Thus, by the beginning of the 21st century, Christianity in Africa had taken shape and established roots in all areas of African reality. It has come to stay. Therefore, we welcome Christianity afresh in Africa, where it has arrived to continue the ancient and vibrant Christianity of Egypt, Ethiopia and Eritrea. It is very appropriate that this *Anthology of African Christianity* presents, in valuable detail, this new reality that describes the African landscape in its totality. Nevertheless, it cannot exhaust the full substance of Christianity in Africa, which is becoming African Christianity without losing its ecumenical and global outreach.

Towards the end of the twentieth century, the Christian landscape had changed radically, and beyond the positive and negative expectations of many. Geographically, the southern two thirds of Africa could without qualification be defined as 'Christian Africa'. The same region had also become a politically 'independent Africa' (with South Africa to follow suit from 1994). The question of Christian survival or demise has long become outdated. Instead, it is as if the Christian faith has fallen in love with Africa and

Africa has fallen in love with the Christian faith. The two have now been destined – for some years to come – to walk hand in hand, step by step. This process seems irreversible. Christianity had not only survived but was rapidly expanding horizontally.

All this raises related questions, such as: What is Christianity doing with Africa? What kind of Christianity is defining and shaping Christian Africa? How is Africa shaping global and ecumenical Christianity? What exactly is Africa doing with the Christian faith, which is not a monopoly of any generation, land, system, island or continent?

By the beginning of the 21st century, Africa had contributed its share of martyrs. It had constructed literally millions of churches and places of worship, of every shape and size, where countless persons congregate on Saturday nights and Sundays to worship. Their worship cannot be adequately defined, as it includes shouting to the Lord, dancing to the Lord, speaking in tongues, healing the sick, driving out unwanted spirits, cleansing the defiled, soliciting success (in business, family life, examinations, politics, good rains and crops), soliciting protection against the unwelcome forces of evil (like bad dreams, curses, dwindling love, the evil eye, misfortunes, possession by unwanted spirits, sickness, sinful intentions, unclean thoughts and words, unresponsive love, witchcraft, etc.).

It is a very creative Christianity, through persons – men, women and youth: it is being heard and seen through innumerable channels and various activities and persons. These include art, Bible translations, bill boards, cassettes, catechists, choirs, dissertations, Christian education, dance, drama, DVDs, evangelistic campaigns, evangelists, films, health centres, hospitals, indigenous songs and hymns, the internet, lay preachers, leaflets, liturgies, magazines, market preachers, mobiles, music, newspapers, oral theology, photographs, planes and flying services, poetry (written and sang), prayers of the laity and clergy, publications, radio, research, sculptures, SMS, social media (Skype, Facetime, etc.), songs, story -telling, street preachers, telephone, television, thousands of students in Bible schools, colleges, and universities (church, private, and state and overseas), television, tracts, videos, etc.

Central to this African Christianity is the Bible, whose translation into African languages accelerated in the second half of the twentieth century. By the beginning of the 21st century, there were more than 800 translations of the complete Bible, the New Testament, or portions (of one or more books). African peoples are hearing the Word of God speaking in their own languages, not unlike the first Pentecost These translations are crucially powerful for the evolution of African theology in indigenous languages, which in the past century was written in European languages. We have mentioned oral African theology which has been articulated in conversations, songs, dances and musical instruments (including improvised ones like calabashes, whistles, clapping, drums, rattles with various metal and plastic pieces, etc.). Africa shows its joy at being Christian, in formal and informal, written and mainly unwritten, ways. African Christianity sings, dances, shouts, prays, heals, expels unwanted spirits, and thereby expresses praises to the Lord.

African Christianity is manifested also in practical ways. One of these is through Christian hospitals and medical centres that are often reputed to offer better medical care for the sick, and expectant mothers and babies, than many other hospitals. It is variously working for inter-ethnic reconciliation and inter-religious dialogue, especially with Islam. It is sending church workers to other ethnic groups, and to other countries of Africa, Europe, America and Asia. There are many thriving African-founded churches and congregations in America, Europe, Middle East and Asia. It is also receiving and welcoming afresh Christian workers from overseas countries in Asia, Europe, Oceania and America. Some of these serve as pastors, priests, doctors, nurses, social workers, teachers, development workers, technicians, organizers, and specialists.

Positive, Negative, and Neutral Paradoxes and Dilemmas

However, on the African scene, this Christianity exists within the paradoxes and dilemmas of African life. Many of these seem to belong to the very nature of African life {cultural, world-views, and traditions}, others are self-inflicted, but some have their roots from within and without. This pilgrim African Christianity is not separate from them. It is enveloped in them, it is entwined with them, it is part of them because they are human entities, and Christianity is a collection of human entities which carry these paradoxes and dilemmas. It is both actor (actress) and spectator.

On the negative side can be listed conflicts (economic, human greed, historical, ideological, political and religious), endemic corruption, ethnicism, exploitation, frauds, greed for money and power, health concerns, the disregard of human rights, material inequalities, harming nature and the environment, injustice, oppression (social, cultural and religious), poverty and money scams. These 'negatives' are carried out by the whole population, which includes those who are part of African Christianity.

On the positive side, African Christianity has many opportunities and facilities that foster and support it. These include all those listed just above as comprising creative Christianity. The *Anthology of African Christianity* gives us an inside view of this colossal African Christianity. It is a very welcome rainbow volume. Historically, it comes at the right time. It captures the new Christianity almost in its infancy. It points to healthy growth as part of global Christianity, confessing One Lord, under the guidance of the Holy Spirit, and is to the glory of God the Almighty and Creator of all things, visible and invisible.

We are grateful to the many learned contributors to this volume, and the editors who have conceived the idea and, with very hard work, have now put it into action. They (we) are historical witnesses to the unfolding of this rainbow Christianity of the 21st century – a blessed privilege, thanks to God.

A Pilgrim Christianity

An African proverb states: 'Cattle are born with ears; their horns grow later.' This promising and exuberant image that characterises African Christianity places it in a state of pilgrimage, born with ears but in the process of growing its horns. That accords with what both our Lord Jesus Christ and his servant the Apostle Paul, told us. At his Ascension, our Lord divulged to us that: 'It is not for you to be knowing the times *(chronos)* or the seasons *(kairos)*, which the Father has placed in his own authority *(exousia)*. But you will receive power *(dunamis)*, when the Holy Spirit comes upon you. And you will be my witnesses *(martures)* in Jerusalem, together with all Judea and Samaria, and up to the extreme end *(eschatos)* of the earth' (Acts 1:7, 8).

St Paul put this divine pilgrimage within his vision: 'But we all, who have an unveiled face, gazing like in a mirror at the glory of the Lord, are in the process of being changed into the same image, from glory *(doxas)* to glory, even as by the Spirit of the Lord' (2 Cor. 3:18).

African Christianity is a truly pilgrim Christianity. It will go no further than its eschatological completion (perfection) set in the Lord himself, as the Scriptures say: 'When all things are subjected to him, then the Son himself also will be subjected to the one who subjected all things to him, so that God may be all in all' (1 Cor. 15:28).

Amen.

John Mbiti
Former Director of Bossey Ecumenical Institute
Burgdorf, Switzerland, January 2015

Words of Greeting – AmosYong

I have often repeated, after my biblical namesake, that I am neither a prophet nor the son of one (see Amos 7:14). However in this case, let me venture the bold and audacious claim that this *Anthology of African Christianity* is a harbinger of Christian thought and practice for the third millennium. There are three interrelated reasons for my prognostications.

First, if in the last century it has become well known that the Christian centre of gravity has shifted from the Euro-American West to the global South, a case can be made that the locus of this movement is even more specific to the African continent. The fact is that, while the explosion of churches in China signals the hitherto unprecedented emergence of an Asian Christianity, the reality is both that the extremely large Chinese and Asian populations means that the percentage of Christians in Asia will stay relatively small and that the religiously pluralistic world of Asia shows no signs of abating, thus keeping the Christian faith marginal in the overall landscape. Further, even if the evangelical and pentecostal vitality across Latin America continues to intensify, it remains the case that Latin America's present 'Protestantization' unfolds within a matrix shaped by half a millennium of 'Catholicization'. What is distinctive about the African context is neither that it is devoid of Roman presence (such is not recognized as 'catholic' for nothing), nor that there are no other world religious competitors (Islam remains strong on all sides of the Saharan region), but that in terms of sheer percentages, the 'Christianization' of the African world jump-started in the nineteenth century has both gained momentum in the twentieth, and is now fed by some of the most vigorous global and transnational impulses in the contemporary ferment. In other words, the Christianity of the 21st century not only will be predominantly that of the majority world, as demographers promise, but also be most palpably coloured by African sensibilities and energies. This does not mean that Asian and Latin American voices and perspectives will be minimal, but that the African contributions will be undeniable if not central to any discussion of Christian faith in the global future.

More precisely, however (and herein my second reason), we are talking not only about the Christianization of Africa and the Africanization of world Christianity but we are also witnessing and attempting to comprehend the 'pentecostalization' and 'charismatization' of African Christianity and its diasporic influences and impacts. Thus, scholars like Cephas Omenyo, J. Kwabena Asamoah-Gyadu and Ludovic Lado, among many others, have been leading the discussion about how Protestant and Roman Catholic traditions are increasingly indistinguishable from the Spirit-type Christianities (a term coined by Allan Anderson) that have historically marked both (African) Pentecostal churches and indigenous-independent African ecclesial movements, with the result that it is precisely pneumatic forms of Christian faith that are burgeoning, regardless of denominational or other labels. Such developments are also consistent with what is happening elsewhere around the world, so again: the degree to which we understand Spirit-Christianities in the African world will be the degree to which we grasp the dynamics of world Christianity from the 'rest' back to the 'West'.

Last but not least, then, the theologian in me is eager to hear from African scholars about how to theorize – or theologize – the Christian faith, given its palpably pneumatic expressions in that context. Without jettisoning the legacy of the western theological tradition, it has by now become quaint that the received orthodoxies need to be reconsidered in view of non-western perspectives and experiences. What is most disconcerting to the western theological mentality that is beholden to modernist constructs is the pneuma-centrism of African spirituality, and it is particularly at this level that Afrocentric hermeneutic and methodological approaches will conceivably enrich, if not challenge and also subvert, the ongoing theological task. Although not intended to displace the Nicene and other ancient dogmatic traditions, starting with the Holy Spirit, as is the default springboard for the African imaginative vision, promises to not just complement but potentially transfigure and transform Christian self-understanding in the next century. The Christian theology of the third millennium, then, may finally reach the promise of a fully Trinitarian ideal, but if so, that will happen only because of the specifically pneumatological contributions and offerings from the African sphere.

Even if it turns out that I am not a prophet about the three registers of anticipations delineated here, those who attend carefully to this *Anthology of African Christianity* will be in a much better position than before to make their own projections, both historic and theological, about the nature of world Christianity for the 21st century. To the editors and contributors to this *Anthology*, we its readers are and will be immensely indebted.

Amos Yong
Asian-American Pentecostal theologian
Professor of Theology and Mission at Fuller Theological Seminary
and Director of the Fuller Theological Seminary's Center for Missiological Research

Words of Greeting – Thomas C. Oden

An enormous amount of research has flowed into the series leading to the preparation for this *Anthology of African Christianity*, especially by means of the earlier publications of the *African Handbook on Theological Education*[1] and the *Orthodox Handbook for Teaching Ecumenism.*[2] The research presented in this new volume begins with Early African Christianity and offers significant articles on a wider range of both historical periods like the colonial and post-Independence phase, as well as crucial issues like traditional African religion, religious demography and the African diaspora, presented by means of thematic, regional, denominational and national surveys, and leading towards contemporary issues of the public role of African Christianity, including issues of gender, education,, public health and conflict resolution.

The simple hypothesis I seek to set forth is this: many young African scholars on the African continent are discovering in primitive African Christianity of the earliest seven centuries, that virtually all of these public and ethical issues have been tackled in fundamental ways that still pertain to contemporary Africa (both within the African continent and also in the African diaspora): see Thomas C. Oden's *Rebirth of Orthodoxy, Bibliography* (Nashville, TN: Abingdon, 2016).[3]

The period of early African martyrdom provided the resources for courage required to confront these issues with a confidence that cannot come from the narcissistic modern West.

The depth of engagement in the understanding of Old and New Testament scripture and their relationship done on the African continent in the earliest years before Chalcedon by such brilliant writers as Clement, Origen, Tertullian, Athanasius, Augustine and Cyril the Great, significantly shaped the doctrinal consensus for world Christianity.[4] It is now ripe to be reassumed by young scholars on the continent of Africa. They will rediscover the closeness of the Spirit to the unity of the church due to their proximity to the earliest events of apostolic history.

The patterns of education first set for African Christianity by the Apostle Mark – likely born in the Libyan Pentapolis and, after ministries in Antioch, Ephesus and Rome, died in Alexandria – seeded the premises of the catechetical school in Alexandria, which formed the basis for western university education. They are still pertinent to the renewal of African colleges, universities, seminaries and churches. These

---

[1] Isabel Apawo Phiri, Dietrich Werner (eds), Chammah Kaunda, Kennedy Owino (associate eds), *Handbook on Theological Education in Africa* (Oxford: Regnum, 2013).

[2] Pantelis Kalaitzidis, Thomas Fitzgerald, Cyril Hovorun, Aikaterini Pekridou, Nikolaos Asprouklis, Dietrich Werner and Guy Liage (eds), *Orthodox Handbook on Ecumenism: Resources for Theological Education* (Oxford: Regnum, 2014).

[3] Thomas C. Oden, *The Rebirth of Orthodoxy: Signs of new life in Christianity* (San Francisco, CA: Harper, 2003).

[4] See Thomas C. Oden, *How Africa Shaped the Christian Mind: Rediscovering the African Seedbed of Western Christianity* (Downers Grove, IL: IVP, 2007); Thomas C. Oden, *African Memory of Mark: Reassessing Church Tradition* (Downers Grove, IL: IVP, 2011).

come out of Africa in their earliest stages far more than Palestine, Syria, Cappadocia or Europe. They await rediscovery.[5]

The contribution of early African Christian philosophers and theologians, from Clement and Athanasius to Marius Victorinus and Augustine, still provide for Africa today what they provided for the great intellectual tradition of African Christianity of the first seven centuries.

The earliest forms of international ecumenism are seen in the third-century conciliar movements of Carthage and Alexandria before the Nicene consensus. They shaped the central message of classic consensual Christianity in Africa before being adapted to later expressions of the international ecumenical consensus in Nicaea, Antioch, Jerusalem and Rome (see *How Africa Shaped the Christian Mind*). They remain the best hope for the recovery of depth and breadth in African Christianity today.

These are among the great gifts of early African Christianity to world Christianity. Young African scholars are rediscovering the beauty and wonder of these gifts as indigenously African and not western-dependent, to be once again offered afresh to contemporary global Christianity. They are re-entering the vault of the great African libraries in Alexandria, Sketis, Tabbenisi, Carthage and Hippo.

I congratulate the editors of the *Anthology of African Christianity* on their achievement and hope that this reference volume will encourage and facilitate more interest, research and mutual learning on African Christianity in the past, present and future, particularly the roots and ongoing significance of pre-colonial early African Christianity, both within the African continent but also in American theological schools.

Thomas C. Oden, Director
Center for Early African Christianity
(earlyafricanchristianity.com)

[5] See Thomas C. Oden, *The African Memory of Mark*, Reassessing Early Church Tradition (Intervarsity Press, 2011)

Words of Greeting – Ofelia Ortega

Spanish Version

El papa Francisco, en su reciente visita al continente africano, dijo que este 'ofrece al mundo una belleza y una riqueza natural que nos lleva a alabar al Creador'. Hoy, cuando los conflictos y el terrorismo alimentan el miedo y la desesperación, miramos a África como el continente de la esperanza, porque de ella aprendemos a valorar la existencia de sociedades multiétnicas que pueden convivir en forma armoniosa. El amor a la familia, el énfasis en la protección de la naturaleza, el respeto a la memoria de los mártires y los esfuerzos para la construcción de un orden social más justo, son valores profundamente arraigados en el alma africana.

En esta cosmovisión no hay lugar para los dualismos; vida y muerte, que son de origen divino, se entrelazan incluyendo a todo lo creado: los árboles, las plantas, la tierra y todo lo que el ser humano necesita. De manera que, porque la divinidad lo envuelve todo, se condena todo tipo de violencia contra la vida.

Todo esto conduce a enfatizar el paradigma de la interculturalidad, y a caminar en dirección de una educación teológica respetuosa de la diversidad y con una praxis pluralista, dialógica y reconciliadora.

Saludamos con orgullo esta *Antología del cristianismo africano*, que de seguro estimulará la reflexión y la praxis de iglesias e individuos a lo largo y ancho de África. Confiamos en que leer y discutir estos trabajos, ayudará también a enriquecer la teología afroamericana y a alimentar nuestra esperanza de vivir la fe y los valores del Evangelio en medio de la diversidad de culturas y las religiones.

Vayan nuestros mejores deseos para todos ustedes, que comparten con nosotros – en América Latina y el Caribe – el interés en la coexistencia pacífica, la comprensión mutua y la construcción de 'un cielo nuevo y una tierra nueva'.

English Version

In his recent visit to the African continent, Pope Francis said that it 'offers the world such natural beauty and resources that it leads us to praise the Creator'. Today, while conflicts and terrorism intensify fear and despair, we look to Africa as the continent of hope, because in it we learn to value the existence of multi-ethnic societies that can live in harmony. The love of family, the emphasis on the protection of nature, respect for the memory of martyrs, and the efforts put into the construction of a more just social order – all these are deeply rooted values in the African soul.

In this cosmo-vision there is no place for dualities; life and death, which have a divine origin, intertwine, including all that has been created: trees, plants, earth and all that a human being needs. Since divinity involves all, any kind of violence against life is condemned.

All this leads us to emphasize the paradigm of the intercultural, and to walk in the direction of a theological education respectful of diversity and with a pluralist, dialogic and reconciling praxis.

We proudly greet this *Anthology of African Christianity,* which will surely stimulate the churches' and individuals' reflection and praxis throughout the African continent. We are confident that reading and discussing these papers will help enrich Afro-American theology and nourish our hope of living the faith and the values of the gospel in the midst of the diversity of cultures and religions.

May our best wishes go with you all, who share with us – in Latin America and the Caribbean – the interest in peaceable co-existence, in mutual understanding and in the construction of 'a new heaven and a new earth'.

Ofelia Ortega Suárez
Former WCC President, Latin American Region, Cuba

Words of Greeting – Mercy Amba Oduyoye

Many have participated in the shaping of Christianity in Africa who are not 'Africans', but now we use the language of African Christianity with no apology. Many have observed the growth of Christianity in Africa but in recent times, its phenomenal growth and global impact have attracted many scholars of religion and other social scientists to its study.

This volume brings together the fruits of some of these scholars who are studying how the continent of Africa has appropriated and shaped, but most especially how it projects, an ecumenical perspective. Having been associated with the World Council of Churches and other arms of the ecumenical movement since 1966, I am especially grateful for the ecumenical perspective of this anthology. It takes a comprehensive approach to Christianity on this huge and complex continent touching some 43 countries and 27 varieties of Christianity, benefitting from the researches of over a hundred authors who have made the study of Christianity in Africa their special field of scholarship.

The editors have been careful to take an inclusive approach while at the same time ensuring persons with special and specific interests and quests can find their needs met. The sectioning of the *Anthology* makes for quick location of specific subjects. For example, there are twenty articles surveying the ecumenical movement and depicting the history of ecumenism in Africa. For the history of missions in Africa and Africa's participation in the growth of Christianity, we meet here several denominations that have found a home in Africa and those that have grown out of Africans' appropriation of Christianity. Turn to the section on issues and themes and you will find a profile of African Christianity and what makes it relevant to Africans and hence promotes its remarkable growth.

There was a time when Africans were warned to keep religion out of politics and politics out of religion. Like the rest of the world, we have grown wiser, the boundary between private and public has become porous, and the section on the public role of African Christianity attests to this. The regional surveys ensure that, wherever the ecumenical movement has touched Africa, a story is available to help us see the participation of young people, women and men in the movement.

I hail the arrival of this *Anthology* for enabling us to know where we have come from, what we have achieved, and challenging us to be relevant to the needs of this age, conscious that the future is being shaped today and we are its architects.

So, while I welcome this *Anthology*, I greet most warmly all who have made it possible. I know it has been a labour of love, but then who was going to do it if you did not do it? Well done!

Mercy Amba Oduyoye, Ghana
Former African President of WCC
Founder of the Circle of Concerned African Women Theologians

Words of Greeting – Olav Fykse Tveit

African Christianity is a marvellous gift of life given by the God of life for the life of all Africans. It is also a significant contribution to the life of the global fellowship of churches.

The World Council of Churches (WCC) is very pleased that, in its role of giving strategic leadership to the ecumenical movement, it has worked in collaboration with Bread for the World, Berlin, the All Africa Conference of Churches, the University of KwaZulu-Natal in South Africa through the Ujamaa Centre, and Trinity Theological College in Ghana in the mammoth task of producing this *Anthology of African Christianity*. This *Anthology* is a testimony to the success and recognition of the value of a previous WCC-initiated project, namely the *Handbook on Theological Education in Africa* which was published in 2013, the year in which the *Anthology* project was started. The methodology used in this project of working in collaboration with member churches and ecumenical partners is in line with the recommendation of the programme guidelines committee which was approved at the Busan 10th Assembly of the WCC in 2013, saying:

> The assembly affirms the above understanding of our future methodology in which programmatic work has a strong relational nature, and relational work strengthens programmatic work (para.16).

The WCC therefore perceives the process of producing this publication as a symbol of strengthening the visible unity of the churches and ecumenical partners, not only in Africa but also in relation to churches from other continents, especially as reflected in Part V of this publication.

The contents reflect an analysis of developments in African societies and churches, and in the ecumenical movement in Africa, including its relationships with the rest of the world. This is important because it helps the churches and the ecumenical movement in Africa to reflect on current issues. I have noted with keen interest that this publication has addressed some of the most burning issues identified by the 10th assembly of the WCC as of importance for the future of the whole of world Christianity, which include (inter-religious) peace building, sustainable economic development and climate change, health and healing, renewal and mission, and also new developments in world Christianity. With currently 94 member churches from Africa, the WCC is aware of the strategic significance of African Christianity for the future of the ecumenical movement as a whole. Certainly, this reference volume with its unique regional, denominational and national surveys on Christianity in Africa will contribute substantially to deepen ecumenical dialogue and collaboration, not only within African Christianity but also with churches from other continents.

The editorial has correctly placed this publication within the framework of the call of the 10th WCC assembly to the churches and people of goodwill to join a pilgrimage of justice and peace from 2014 to 2021. On the pilgrimage, we are called upon to engage our God-given gifts in transformative actions, together. The process of choosing who should be in the editorial, writing publishing and teams, and the choice of the themes that have been covered, are truly a manifestation of the pilgrimage of justice and peace. I foresee that this publication will be key in the 2017 focus on Africa for the pilgrimage of justice and peace which is focussing on what religions can contribute to overcoming violence.

I conclude by acknowledging the tremendous work done by the editors and editorial team in bringing this project to a successful conclusion, inspired by a rare combination of sustained ecumenical vision, a common sense of determination, and very disciplined and enduring work. We also recommend this reference volume be made available in libraries of African universities, church-related seminaries and faculties of religious or theological studies as widely as possible to stimulate ecumenical Christian leadership training as well as interreligious encounters. May the God of life lead Africa to justice and peace with dignity for all.

The Rev. Dr Olav Fykse Tveit (Norway/Switzerland)
General Secretary of the World Council of Churches

Words of Greeting – Cornelia Füllkrug-Weitzel

This *Anthology of African Christianity* is not only a unique achievement, but also an essential tool for several generations of researchers, development practitioners, church leaders and politicians to better understand the rapidly changing religious and social conditions of life in the African continent. Bread for the World, the globally active development and relief agency of the Protestant churches in Germany, is in touch with about 450 projects of local and regional partner organizations all over the African continent in the struggle against poverty, discrimination and the lack of proper educational and health standards. There are 130 active projects located in East Africa, another 190 projects in West and Central Africa, 120 projects in Southern Africa, and more than thirty projects with partners at a continental level. The majority of Bread for the World's partners come from church-related backgrounds. We are convinced that Africa has a huge potential for sustainable development. This potential can be better used if people have adequate access to health, education, quality nutrition and participation in political decision-making. A huge number of younger Africans, who long to participate in society and to give their best to create a better future for all, underline the determination of future generations to change their destiny and not to give in to fatalism or religious extremism. A proper knowledge of historical conditions, religious profiles and denominational backgrounds of the social involvement of the Christian churches, as well as of Muslim partners in Africa, is a key to engagement in local contexts. The new debate on religion and development both in UN circles as well as in the German Ministry for Development Co-operation needs the detailed expertise and scholarly insights brought together in this comprehensive volume in order to become relevant and well informed actors in African countries. This *Anthology*, written almost exclusively by African scholars themselves, offers a fascinating range of new perspectives and insights concerning social witness and engagements with the marginalized from an African perspective. We congratulate the editors for this impressive work of reference and warmly recommend this publication to churches, governments and NGOs in the African continent as well as to ACT Alliance member organizations concerned about the future of Africa. And we hope that churches in Africa can continue to become what they are called according to the demands of the gospel: ambassadors of reconciliation, advocates for the poor and representatives of credible and just African leadership in church and society!

The Rev. Cornelia Füllkrug-Weitzel
President, Bread for the World, Berlin

Words of Greeting – Mussie Hailu

The role of religions is very important in order to achieve an integrated, prosperous and peaceful Africa, driven by its own citizens and representing a dynamic force in the global arena.

Among those religions in Africa which play a critical role in the day-to-day life of the majority of Africans is Christianity, and it is one of the two most widely practised religions on the continent as well as being the largest religion in sub-Saharan Africa.

Therefore it is an idea whose time has come to have the publication of an ambitious and comprehensive *Anthology of African Christianity,* and I want to acknowledge at the outset the effort of all those people who worked tirelessly to make this publication a reality.

It is recorded fact that, in the first few centuries of Christianity, Africa produced many figures who had a major influence outside the continent, including St Augustine of Hippo, St Maurice, Origen and Tertullian. According to the Liber Pontificalis, three Roman popes – namely Pope St Victor I (c. 186-198), Pope St Miltiades (311-314) and Pope St Gelasius (492-496) were all Africans. The Biblical characters of Simon of Cyrene and the Ethiopian eunuch baptized by Philip the Evangelist were also Africans.

The earliest and best-known reference to the introduction of Christianity to Africa is mentioned in the Christian Bible's Acts of the Apostles, and pertains to the evangelist Phillip's conversion of an Ethiopian traveller in the first century AD (Acts 8:26-40).

This *Anthology of African Christianity*, the result of co-operation between leading African scholars and the World Council of Churches, Bread for the World, Berlin, and others with the aim of producing a solid and accurate self-description of all major African church families and traditions, is significant in that it presents a coherent picture and image of African Christianity written by African scholars themselves.

The *Anthology* is a crucial tool and source of knowledge for African Christianity in order for it to have an authentic self-representation and a broadened base of knowledge to understand its various facets, traditions and indigenous forms.

As this massive resource collection brings together regional surveys and shorter national profiles of Christianity for each of the 54 states within the African continent, it will be essential as a reference and research base on African Christianity for African theological education, as well as a platform for enhancing ecumenical understanding and fostering harmony and solidarity with other faith traditions on the issue of building a culture of peace, preservation of the environment, climate change and as a means of countering violent extremism. African Christianity's tasks in promoting reconciliation, constructive inter- and intra-religious dialogue, peaceful co-existence and the challenge of promoting human dignity, the ethics of sustainability and the spiritual dimension of social development have never been so immense and urgent as they are today. The role of churches and faith-based organizations for sustainable development and the achievement of the crucial goals of the African 'Agenda 2063: The Africa We Want' are all highlighted here.

I do hope that this publication will inspire African Muslims scholars to develop a similar handbook.

According to the World Book Encyclopedia, Islam is the largest religion in Africa, with 47% of the population being Muslim, accounting for a quarter of the world's Muslim population. The faith's historic roots in the continent stem from the time of the Prophet Muhammad, whose early disciples migrated (also known as the First Hegira (Arabic: هِجْرَة hijrah)) to Abyssinia (now known as Ethiopia) in fear of persecution from pagan Arabs.

The spread of Islam in North Africa came with the expansion of the Arab empire under Caliph Umar, through the Sinai Peninsula. The spread of Islam in West Africa was through Islamic traders and sailors.

Islam is the dominant religion in North Africa and the Horn of Africa. It has also become the predominant religion on the Swahili Coast as well as the West African seaboard and parts of the interior. There have been several Muslim empires in Western Africa which exerted considerable influence, notably the Mali Empire, which flourished for several centuries, and the Songhai Empire, under the leadership of Mansa Musa, Sonni Ali and Askia Mohammed.

For billions of people around Africa, faith is an essential foundation of life. Faith-based organizations (FBOs) are working actively in Africa in peace-building, reconciliation, social development, providing education and health services to communities, and environmental protection. FBOs build dialogue among different religions and ethnicities, and promote partnerships by addressing gender equality, unemployment, empowerment of youth, and peace education in schools. This fine initiative on the part of faith-based organizations needs to be recognized and encouraged by the African Union and its member-states.

The role of religious communities and FBOs is also crucial for achieving some of the visionary goals which were set out in 'Agenda 2063: The Africa We Want'.

Agenda 2063 is an approach of the African Union to formulate how the continent should effectively learn from the lessons of the past, build on progress now underway and strategically exploit all possible opportunities available in the immediate and medium term, so as to ensure positive socio-economic transformation within the next fifty years.

On the occasion of the Anniversary Solemn Declaration, the heads of state and government of the African Union (AU) rededicated themselves to the continent's accelerated development and technological progress. They laid down the vision of Agenda 2063 to serve as a beacon for the continent in the foreseeable future, translated into concrete objectives, milestones, goals, targets and actions.

Agenda 2063 is both a vision and an action plan. It is a call to action for all segments of African society to work together to build a prosperous and united Africa based on shared values and a common destiny.

The aspirations of Agenda 2063[6] reflect the voices of the African people and her diaspora, united in diversity, young and old, men and women, from all walks of life and faith traditions.

Recognizing the role of faith-based organizations in implementing and popularizing Agenda 2063, the African Union Commission (AUC), in partnership with the All Africa Conference of Churches, organized a consultation meeting with African faith-based organizations on African Agenda 2063 in the Desmond Tutu Conference Centre, 5th-6th November 2014.

After the consultation, religious leaders and representatives participating recommended among others:

- A monitoring and evaluation system be put in place to track progress at country level, and to ensure the effective implementation of Agenda 2063;
- Appropriate measures be taken to tackle challenges such as corruption, youth unemployment, land grabbing, gender inequality, religious extremism, and militarization of the state, in order that the continent achieve the aspirations of Agenda 2063;

[6] Seven key aspirations are included in Agenda 2063: 1. A prosperous Africa based on inclusive growth and sustainable development; 2. An integrated continent, politically united and based on the ideals of Pan Africanism and the vision of Africa's renaissance; 3. An Africa of good governance, democracy, respect for human rights, justice and the rule of law; 4. A peaceful and secure Africa; 5. An Africa with a strong cultural identity, common heritage, values and ethics; 6. An Africa where development is people-driven, unleashing the potential of its women and youth; 7. Africa as a strong, united and influential global player and partner. Visit the website: http://agenda2063.au.int/en/about

- The huge potential of women and youth be acknowledged and harnessed to contribute significantly towards the realization of Agenda 2063;
- Civic education be integrated with educational curricula at all levels;
- Africans in the diaspora be mobilized effectively to work actively towards the realization of Agenda 2063;
- A permanent platform be established where religious leaders and the AUC meet periodically to discuss and assess the progress of Agenda 2063.

Religions can provide what obviously cannot be attained by economic plans, political programmes or legal regulations alone. As human beings, we need social and ecological reforms, but we also need spiritual and moral renewal just as urgently. The spiritual powers of religion can offer a fundamental sense of trust, a ground of meaning, ultimate standards and a spiritual home.

It is very difficult to achieve sustainable peace, good governance, human rights, social development, positive progress or the aims of African Agenda 2063 without a fundamental consensus based on ethics, and moral and spiritual foundation.

As long as women and men are treated inhumanely, it is very difficult to achieve Agenda 2063 in Africa. In the face of all inhumanity, our religious and ethical convictions demand that every human being be treated humanely! This means that every human being, without distinction of age, sex, race, skin colour, physical or mental ability, language, religion, political view, or national or social origin, possesses an inalienable and unique dignity. And everyone, the individual as well as the state, is therefore obliged to honour this dignity and to protect it.

The fundamental principle which can provide a spiritual and ethical grounding for these values is the so-called ‘Golden Rule’ which can be found, and has persisted, in many religious and ethical traditions of humankind for thousands of years. Its content is simple and unique: What you do not wish to be done to yourself, do not do to others. In other wards: What you wish to be done to yourself, do to others! This should be the irrevocable, unconditional norm for all areas of life, for families and communities, for races, nations and religions.

Every form of egoism should be rejected in this perspective: all selfishness, whether individual or collective, whether in the form of class distinction or racism. We condemn these because they prevent humans from being authentically human. Self-determination and self-realization are thoroughly legitimate so long as they are not separated from human self-responsibility – that is, from responsibility for fellow humans and for the planet Earth.

In the great religious and ethical traditions of humankind we find the directive: You shall not kill! Or, in other words: Have respect for life! All people have a right to life, safety and the free development of personality as long as they do not injure the rights of others. No one has the right physically or psychologically to torture, injure – much less kill – any other human being. And no people, no state, no race, no religion has the right to hate or discriminate.

A human person is infinitely precious and must be unconditionally protected. But, likewise, the lives of animals and plants which inhabit this planet with us deserve protection, preservation and care. Limitless exploitation of the natural foundations of life, ruthless destruction of the biosphere, and militarization of the cosmos, are all outrages. As human beings, we have a special responsibility – especially with future generations in view – for Earth and the cosmos, for the air, water and soil. We are all intertwined together in this cosmos and we are all dependent on each other. Each one of us depends on the welfare of all. Therefore, the dominance of humanity over nature and the cosmos must not be encouraged. Instead, we must cultivate living in harmony with nature and the cosmos.

This unique and precious *Anthology of African Christianity* gives plenty of insights of how essential ethical values which undergird peace amongst peoples, peace between religions, peace between nations and peace with Mother Earth, are rooted and expressed in Christian traditions. Therefore, this volume can assist learning processes within African societies:

- To use economic and political power in the service of humanity instead of misusing it in ruthless battles for domination;
- To develop a spirit of compassion with those who suffer, with special care for children, the aged, the poor, the disabled, refugees, and the lonely;
- To cultivate mutual respect and consideration, so as to reach a reasonable balance of interests, instead of thinking only of unlimited power and competitive struggles.
- To value a sense of moderation and modesty instead of an unquenchable greed for money, prestige and consumption.

This reference volume can contribute to a transformation in the consciousness of individuals and in public life, a transformation which starts and is based in the area of ethics and values, but which also needs to be translated into transformative leadership education in African colleges and universities, using concrete and measurable criteria for African politics.

I hope that this unique reference volume will find proper attention also in African Union circles as well as in ministries dealing with higher education, with religious affairs as well as with sustainable development. It offers a huge range of insights brought together by a unique collection of voices from leading African scholars. I want to thank and congratulate all editorial team members, especially Prof. Dr Isabel Phiri and the Rev. Prof. Dr. Dietrich Werner for their unique achievement. I also want to add my appreciation and thanks to all those people and organizations that helped in the publication of this very important *Anthology of African Christianity*.

May Peace, Compassion, and Justice Prevail on Earth.

Ambassador Mussie Hailu
Regional Director of United Religions Initiative – Africa
and Special Envoy and Advisor of the African Union Economic,
Social and Cultural Council on Interfaith, Inter-religious and Inter-Cultural Issues

Editorial: Anthology of African Christianity

Africa is a continent where Christianity had already started by the middle of the first century. Contours of early Christian thought were formed in North Africa; early forms of conciliarity as well as forms of the church ministry owe their existence to the influence of early leadership in African Christianity.[7] Major forms of ancient Christianity in Africa co-existed with Islam for centuries and present an unprecedented treasure of experience of religious co-existence. Statistical data on the rapid growth of African Christianity from the *Atlas of World Christianity* has shown that, while Africa had less than 10% Christians in 1910, its population was already nearly 50% Christian in 2010, with sub-Saharan Africa well over 70% Christian. In a relatively short period, Africa has gone from having a majority of followers of indigenous, traditional religions, to being predominantly a continent of Christians and Muslims. The demographic trends on the continent predict that Africa's population of currently 1.1 billion – despite the impact and losses due to HIV and AIDS, Ebola, malaria, cholera and tuberculosis – is expected to quadruple by 2100, reaching 4.2 billion. The most populous country, Nigeria, which currently has a population of about 193 million,[8] is expected to balloon to 914 million in 2100, a more than fourfold increase. Nigeria alone would therefore surpass the population of the USA before 2050![9] This will also have vast consequences for the future of Christianity, both in a country like Nigeria (currently about 80 million Christians, predicted to rise to 155 million in 2050), as well as for Christianity in the African continent as a whole, where Christianity is predicted to grow to almost two billion followers by 2050 (1,899 million, 131% increase between 2010 and 2050).[10]

Both demographic as well as religious trends on the African continent have profound implications for its future role in global politics, for its relevance for world Christianity, as well as in the world of religions and its significance for social and political development on the continent, and for the ecumenical fellowship of churches.

Accurate knowledge on the different facets, recent trends and major shapes of African Christianity, however, remains an issue both for African governments, church leaders and academic institutions in Africa, as well as for external agencies of development co-operation and ecumenical partners outside the continent. Changing landscapes of denominational forms of Christianity, transformation processes within as well as between African countries and regions, are so fast, complex and diverse that it is difficult to keep pace and to get proper access to recent and updated sources of information. Language barriers, artificial borders and cultural divides imposed by colonialism on the African continent still make it difficult for churches and academic institutions in one part of Africa to have an exact picture of forms of Christianity in another part of the continent. It cannot be taken for granted that churches (for example) in Egypt or

[7] See the important publications of Thomas C. Oden, *How Africa shaped the Christian Mind*, and *The African Memory of Mark*: http://earlyafricanchristianity.com (accessed 13th September 2015).

[8] http://worldpopulationreview.com/countries/nigeria-population (accessed 13th September 2015).

[9] http://digitaljournal.com/article/352233 (accessed 13th September 2015).

[10] The Pew Research Centre: 'The Future of World Religions: Population Growth Projections, 2010-2050' (published 2nd April 2015): www.pewforum.org/2015/04/02/christians (accessed 13th September 2015).

Morocco have a clear understanding of the facets and trends of Christianity in Rwanda or Namibia, or vice versa.

Therefore, a group of scholars related to the World Council of Churches (WCC) and its programme on Ecumenical Theological Education (ETE) decided in 2013 to embark on a major research project under the title *Anthology of African Christianity*.

In 2013, the WCC, together with Regnum Publishers in Oxford and Cluster Publications in Pietermaritzburg, South Africa, published a major African theological handbook under the title *Handbook on Theological Education in Africa*, which brought together a first pan-African collection of foundational and contextual essays on the understanding and practice of theological education.[11] Some of the editorial committee members of this earlier project were brought together again by Prof. Dr Isabel Apawo Phiri (Geneva) and Prof. Dr Dietrich Werner (Berlin) to develop the concept for an *Anthology of African Christianity*, which was presented to an enlarged editorial committee during the first planning workshop in Nairobi, from 28th February to 1st March 2014, and then adopted in a revised form.

The group was convinced that there was a huge need for more accurate information on how African Christianity had grown and been transformed during recent decades in different African regions and traditions, and what has been its role in social and political developments and value transformation. While the editorial group was aware of several individual anthologies and research publications on some trajectories of African Christianity, as well as its general history,[12] it also affirmed that there still has not been a comprehensive volume providing accurate introduction on the current shape of African Christianity and the role of its different forms and trends for social and political development on the continent. The 'Anthology of African Christianity' research project was therefore designed, with the main goal of bringing together a major reference volume with researched essays and survey articles, mostly written by African authors, on contemporary Christianity in Africa and its role for development in all its different facets and diverse forms.

The project was formally started under the leadership of the WCC in close co-operation with the All Africa Conference of Churches (AACC) in Nairobi, Bread for the World and Church Development Services in Berlin, Trinity Theological College, Accra, and the University of KwaZulu-Natal (UKZN) in Pietermaritzburg, represented by the Ujamaa Centre. It was carried out under the leadership of Prof. Dr Isabel Apawo Phiri, Associate General Secretary of WCC, and the Rev. Prof. Dr Dietrich Werner, Senior Theological Advisor, Bread for the World, and former Director of ETE/WCC. Key members of the editorial group were: Canon Prof. Dr James Amanze, Botswana; Dr Kudzai Biri, Zimbabwe; the Rev. Prof. Dr Priscille Djomhoue, Cameroon; the Rev. Dr Chammah Kaunda, South Africa/Zambia; Prof. Dr Kwabena Asamoah-Gyadu, Ghana; Dr Kennedy Owino, South Africa/Kenya; and Prof. Dr Edison Kalengyo, Uganda/Kenya.

In the first project outline from early 2014, it was stated:

> 'It is the aim of this project to collaborate on research for a solid and accurate self-description of all major African church families and traditions in order to present a somewhat coherent picture and accurate description

[11] Isabel Apawo Phiri and Dietrich Werner (eds), *Handbook on Theological Education in Africa* (Oxford: Regnum, 2013), 1150 pages.

[12] See, for instance, Adrian Hastings, *A History of African Christianity, 1950-1975* (Cambridge: CUP, 1979); Elizabeth Isichei, *A History of Christianity in Africa: From Antiquity to the Present* (London: SPCK, 1995); Paul Gifford, *African Christianity: Its Public Role* (Hurst: London, 2001); Lamin Sanneh, *West African Christianity: The Religious Impact* (London: Hurst, 1983); Bengt Sundkler and Christopher Steed, *A History of the Church in Africa* (Cambridge: CUP, 2000); Ogbu Kalu, *African Pentecostalism*, and *African Christianity: An African Story;* J. Kwabena Asamoah-Gyadu, *Contemporary Pentecostal Christianity: Interpretations from an African Context*; Terence O. Ranger (ed), *Evangelical Christianity and Democracy in Africa* (Oxford, OUP, 2008); Elias Bongmba (ed), *Companion to African Religions* (Chichester, Sussex: Wiley-Blackwell, 2012).

of current African Christianity, which should be made available both to African theological institutions and churches (including its ecumenical organization in the form of AACC) as well as to networks of scholarly research in western theological institutions. African Christianity has come of age and needs to have an authentic self-representation and a broadened base of knowledge to inform its own various facets, traditions, rapid processes of change, its indigenous forms and its crucial contribution to social and political development.'

More specifically, the Nairobi meeting of the project planning group also agreed to structure the planned reference volume according to six major goals:

1. To bring together a couple of **general introductory essays** on the overall history of African Christianity on the continent which emphasise that African Christianity has a distinct early period of its own and cannot just be explained as the import from western Christianity during the colonial period; and a general introductory essay on understanding the crucial role of African Christianity for development on the continent.
2. To bring together **regional survey articles** on contemporary (21st-century) African Christianity and churches in Northern Africa, Western Africa, Eastern Africa and Southern Africa.
3. To bring together **denominational survey articles** on the seven major families of Christian denominations in Africa:
    - Orthodox churches
    - Roman Catholic churches
    - Churches from a historical Reformation background
    - Churches from an Evangelical background
    - Churches from a classical Pentecostal background
    - Churches from an African Independent background
    - Churches from a Neo-Pentecostal or prosperity gospel growth background
4. To bring together shorter **national profiles of Christianity** for each of the 54 states within the African continent.
5. To bring together a selection of key scholars to reflect on crucial issues relating to **future trends, challenges for African Christianity** and its **public role for development and social transformation** in its different settings in the 21st century.
6. To have a **resource section** with major links and study resources for theological education and research on African Christianity.

This original outline was then redefined, enlarged and transformed in a longer working process in order to take shape finally in the section structure of this reference volume, *Anthology of African Christianity*, with its current seven major thematic sections.

Meetings of the full editorial committee (sometimes also the smaller core committee composed of the Rev. Dr Chammah Kaunda, Dr Kennedy Owino, Prof. Dr Dietrich Werner and Prof. Dr Isabel Apawo Phiri) took place 9th-11th October 2014 at Seth Mokitimi Methodist Seminary in Pietermaritzburg, 20th-22nd February 2015 in Nairobi, 26th-29th June 2015 in Berlin, 20th-23rd August 2015 in Geneva, 19th October 2015 in Pietermaritzburg, and 8th-12th December 2015 in Pietermaritzburg. A final editorial meeting took place in spring 2016 in Geneva. Collaboration with the Ujamaa Centre of the University of KwaZulu-Natal in Pietermaritzburg, represented by the Rev. Prof. Dr Roderick Hewitt, the Rev. Prof. Dr Simanga Kumalo and Prof. Dr Gerald West, secured a smooth administrative accompaniment and institutional backing for the research project.

In the course of the working process, a number of crucial editorial issues had to be reflected on and brought to a decision, echoing both the achievements and shortcomings of this current volume, amongst which we mention as the most important:

1. The term 'African Christianity' resonates with different connotations in scholarly discourse both inside as well as outside the academic community. Some scholars, in using this term, refer mainly to the more recent non-western forms of Christianity represented by African Instituted Churches as well as some of the Charismatic forms of Christianity in the African continent, and place these in contrast to 'western' forms of Christianity on the African continent which arrived in the course of the historical mission movement of western mission agencies. Others would use the term 'African Christianity' in a more general phenomenological sense, referring to all types and branches of Christianity which can be found and which are alive on the African continent. The editors of this volume have come to the conclusion that the term as used in this *Anthology* should be understood in a broader generic sense, referring to all expressions of Christian traditions which have taken root on the African continent as well as those African Christian traditions which emerged outside Africa. They should not be overloaded with normative or judgemental aspects resulting from the debate about which forms of Christianity in Africa are more 'truly African' than others. Therefore, the editors of this volume have made the decision to give all denominational types and traditions of Christianity in Africa equal space in this volume. Part of this intention was also to keep contributions from francophone Africa in French and those from anglophone Africa in English (while we translated contributions from lusophone Africa), while we did not have the funds to have all articles translated in other languages. The intention was to allow Christian denominational traditions to present themselves in ways which resonate with their own perception, rather than to present certain traditions only from the perspectives of how they are viewed by other major Christian traditions inside and outside Africa. This follows the general interest of the WCC and the ecumenical movement – to allow churches to reflect, articulate and defend their own ecclesiological viewpoint and theological stance equally and to regard all forms of Christianity in Africa as being part of how Christian faith is shaping the future of the continent – both for the better and sometimes also for the worse.

2. The editors were aware of the fact that a lot of research on African Christianity has been done by western scholars outside the African continent. While these contributions are valued and also often referred to in many chapters as being part of the global discourse on Christianity, mission and development in the African continent, strategic planning for this *Anthology* project was done with the intention that contributors and authors assembled here should represent 'African research' on 'African realities in African Christianity'. The intention behind this decision was not to disqualify or exclude western-based research or to neglect interaction between African and western researchers, but to strengthen existing networks of African scholars, particularly also up-and-coming younger African scholars to become more visible in their vital contributions. It is hoped that this line of approach can strengthen and boost both future African research on African Christianity as well as international research and scholarly dialogue on several of the burning issues presented in this volume.

3. While having tried to be somewhat comprehensive in this volume, the editors also strongly affirm that more careful historical and research work needs to be done on several issues which this reference volume could not fully unfold and properly include, and that even thematic areas covered in several cases need more in-depth research than could be provided in these introductory surveys. Owing to limitations of space, time and work, the editors had to restrict themselves to a given set of selected topics and themes. The hope is that some of the young scholars involved in the editorial process and new generations of African scholars will complete and enlarge the work

we have started with this editorial team. (Examples are themes related to ethnicity in African Christianity, African ethics and interfaith dialogue in the African continent).

The editors are also aware that the attempt to add a section (Part IV) with chapters providing survey articles on Christianity in each African country was a very ambitious goal which could only be partially achieved, although we secured survey articles of 50 out of 54 countries. Therefore, in Part IV, certain names of countries remain without entry of articles as, despite several and sustained efforts, the editorial team could not secure a proper author or paper on the following countries before the final editorial deadline: Comoros Islands; Guinea-Conacry; Guinea-Equatorial; Mauritania; Seychelles. Again, we rely on the work of a future generation of younger African researchers and other authors to complete and enrich the picture.

4. The editorial group was also wrestling with the question of how to balance the need to have one solid reference work in one printed volume including as many national and regional survey articles as possible, with the opposite need to include as many different voices and viewpoints as possible in the overall table of contents of one and the same single volume. After careful exploration with the co-operating publishing houses for this Anthology, the editorial group came to the conclusion that the project would be best served in being published in one volume only. We only realized close to the end of our working period that publishing all material within one volume actually is possible and are grateful for careful managing of all contents by Tony Gray from Oxford.

   Realizing the difficulties involved in having appropriate distribution and marketing channels and networks within the African continent for a huge publication like this, and also being aware of high postal charges for such a book as this, the intention from the very beginning was to make these research papers available also in digital form for the whole of the interested reading community in the African continent and beyond. Therefore, we have co-operated with Globethics.net, an international foundation based in Geneva but also with a regional office in Addis Ababa, to create a thematic collection on African Christianity which basically follows the classification tree indicated in the table of contents of this reference volume. The digital collection of the essays in this reference volume can be found with the title 'Anthology of African Christianity (BI) Collection' at www.globethics.net/web/anthology-african-christianity.

5. While the editors are responsible for bringing all the selected articles together in this volume, we are aware of the fact that there can be views and convictions expressed in the articles which are in conflict with each other or sometimes also with the views of the editors. Author's arguments do not necessarily and in all details reflect the position of the editors.

We now look back in gratitude to a very demanding and challenging working process of almost three years which kept us busy day and night. The working process was facilitated by two younger and well-experienced African scholars: The Rev Dr Chammah Kaunda from Zambia and Dr Kennedy Owino from Kenya. In addition to their role as full members of the general editorial committee and as section editors, they also served as associate editors for the whole project. In this capacity, they served on the core editorial team, contributed substantially to the editing of various other sections of this volume as well as organizing the complex academic peer reviewing and language editing processes for all the 160 papers received.

The working process was also facilitated by some ecumenical advisors who gave substantial advice with regard to competent authors, selection of key topics to be addressed, and other substantial advice for the contents of this book. We express our sincere gratitude to Prof. Dr Jesse Mugambi, the Rev. Dr John Mbiti,

Prof. Dr Esther Mombo, the Rev. Dr Andre Karamaga, the Rev. Dr Simon Dossou, the Rev. Prof. Dr Simanga Kumalo, the Rev. Prof. Dr Roderick Hewitt, Prof. Dr Gerald West and Dr Samuel Johnson.

We also extend our heartfelt gratitude to several colleagues amongst the contributors who, apart from their tasks as authors, have also assisted with peer reviewing of papers which were submitted.

Several persons and colleagues have contributed greatly in doing language revision and additional assistant editorial work such as Lou Levine (Pietermaritzburg), the Rev. Dorothea Gauland (Nairobi and Frankfurt), Mrs Annett Domscheit (Berlin), Mrs Elisabeth Jeglitzka (Berlin), Nan Braunschweiger (Geneva) and Prof. Priscille Djomhoue.

We also express our gratitude to colleagues within the Boston-based Center for the Study of Global Christianity, Prof. Todd Johnson and Dr Gina Zurlo, who assisted us with making available data boxes relevant to selected details of religious demography in African countries (part of which are presented in Part II and in Part IV, with a general explanation on the nature and origin of these data in article 16a) as well as with a general survey article concerning demographic developments within Africa as seen from a global perspective (included as article 16 in Part I). Some individual authors have also referred to religious data from their own and other sources. The editors did not reconcile all religious data referred to by individual authors and their various sources with the overall religious data on African Christianity and religions as contributed by the Center for the Study of Global Christianity, Boston. The interpretation and use of different sources of religious demographic data remains an issue of continued scholarly debate and research.

We are deeply thankful for the work provided by Dr Tony Gray, senior copy editor of Regnum Publishers in Oxford, for having provided the layout for the whole volume, and to Prof. Wonsuk Ma, Director of the Oxford Centre for Mission Studies and Senior Editor of Regnum Books International, as well as to Prof. Gerald West and Nelly Melis from Cluster Publications in South Africa.

We also want to acknowledge with gratitude substantial financial support provided both for the three year's research process and the editorial as well as resource management process which has resulted in this publication: Our thanks are to Bread for the World/Protestant Development Services in Berlin/Germany. We are also grateful to the German Federal Ministry for Economic Cooperation and Development (BMZ) for their generous support of the publication. We also need to mention the Protestant Association of Churches and Mission (EMW), Hamburg, and the Africa Desk of the head office of EKD churches in Hannover, the Nagel Institute for the Study of World Christianity, Calvin College, Grand Rapids (US) and Prof. Isabel Apawo Phiri for their support for printing costs in Africa. Our gratitude includes Globethics.net, Geneva, and its current President Prof Christoph Stückelberger for enormous technical support for managing the documents.

Finally, we want to summarize some key convictions which accompany the publication of this *Anthology of African Christianity* and related hopes for the future of Africa, the role of its diverse church traditions, and the significance of Christian witness for justice, peace and the integrity of creation in the years to come:

1. The WCC during its 10th assembly in Busan, South Korea, in 2013, called on its member churches to be engaged in a *global ecumenical pilgrimage for justice and peace* in order to give witness to the God of life. We affirm that, having worked for this research project, has made us parts of this pilgrimage of learning discoveries, of sharing and of broadening our view on the realities of African Christianity. So much can be discovered in terms of what churches are doing on the African continent in giving witness to the dignity of each human individual, for justice, for peace and for human rights – both with neighbours of other Christian traditions as well as with Muslim neighbours and all people of goodwill. We wish this book to serve as an incentive for African churches to grow together and to minimize mutual mistrust, enmity and lack of co-ordination, as

we have one task founded in biblical tradition, i.e. to give witness to the God of life who has promised life in its fullness for all.

2. For becoming credible witnesses and effective tools for justice, human rights and development, *a solid knowledge of social processes, political contexts and the pastoral needs of African people today* is demanded. Churches need to become multilingual, being equally rooted in biblical and prophetic language as well as understanding the realities and secular languages of today's political, medical, social and economic challenges, rather than taking refuge in other-worldliness and religious extremism or distorting religious ideologies.[13] More *theological and political competency and pastoral training* are needed in Africa today for public theology, accountability in leadership and in anti-corruption standards, both in politics as well as in the churches. Christian traditions have a huge potential for transforming the face and fate of the African continent as long as religious literacy, pastoral literacy and political and economic literacy are combined with each other and are not played off one against the other. The Reformation Jubilee in 2017 reminds all the Christian churches that the intersection of constant renewal and reform of church life (Reformation), investment in solid and sober training and learning (Education), and the ability to effect change and capacity-building in politics and society (Transformation), are interrelated with each other.[14]

3. There is a passionate *debate on religion and development* and a renewed interest in religious development assets in international as well as many African circles, including United Nations organisations. This *Anthology* should enable and facilitate a more detailed and nuanced debate on these issues in the various contexts of the African continent. We hold that, while the African continent is certainly marked by 'religiosity' as permeating each and every aspect of everyday life for a majority of Africans, the relevance and humanizing (or dehumanizing) potential of religion is an ambivalent phenomenon. Religious traditions can contribute to grave violations of human rights, they can enslave and be misused for ethnic warfare and religious hatred, but they can also be liberative and transformative in highly promising ways, contributing to the dignity and development of each African individual and to the 2030 Agenda of Sustainable Development Goals. For African Christians and churches to become more sensitive and knowledgeable about the broad spectrum of diverse Christian traditions as well as their genuine potential for contributing to justice and peace rather than to hatred and destruction remains an ongoing task and presents the crucial priority for what can be called a *'Third African Reformation'*, an ongoing and deliberate Reformation of African Christianity towards coherent public and social responsibility and integrity of leadership in all its dimensions.[15]

---

[13] Tinyiko Sam Maluleke, in a recent article, has pointed to quite disastrous distortions of the core Christian message and the social responsibility of churches in referring to practices and teachings of certain Neo-Pentecostal churches in South Africa. See Maluleke, 'Preying on the Poor in Name of Praying', in *Sunday Independent*, 16th August 2015: www.iol.co.za/sundayindependent/preying-on-the-poor-in-name-of-praying-1.1900442#VdM3ldNjPBl (accessed 5th January 2015).

[14] See the international twin study and conference project on Reformation, Education and Transformation in 2015 and 2016: www.r-e-t.net/index.html

[15] While 'Reformation' (which could be labelled the 'first' Reformation) usually refers to the European Reformation period in the sixteenth century, much of which has also marked African Christianity by way of the missionary spread of churches from the Reformation tradition, the term 'African Reformation' (which could be labelled 'second' Reformation) was used by a number of African scholars referring to the emergence of both Pentecostal and African Instituted Churches in the twentieth century: see, for instance, Jones Darkwa Amanor, 'Pentecostalism in Ghana: An African Reformation', at: www.pctii.org/cyberj/cyberj13/amanor.pdf; Allan H. Anderson, *African Reformation: African Initiated Christianity in the 20th Century* (Trenton, NJ, and Asmara, Eritrea: Africa World Press, 2002).

4. Many articles of leading African women scholars underline the fact that the future of African Christianity will be possible only by *new ways of mutual learning between African men and African women about the relevance of the gospel for changed models of masculinity, partnership and Christian family life*. Many of the burning and difficult pastoral issues in African daily life, related to issues of HIV and AIDS, human sexuality and gender roles, would not have been brought to the common agenda and dialogue without the courageous contributions of African women theologians and scholars.

We hope that this volume can encourage and initiate new forms of dialogue, research and partnership for women and men in African theological education and for joint research projects on issues relating closely to controversial and important issues, challenging the inclusiveness and wholeness of African communities and the vulnerability of certain groups in African societies today.

The publication of this volume underlines the conviction that African Christianity in the 21st century will undoubtedly play a crucial and unique role for the future of Christianity as a whole on this planet, as was already stated once in the remarkable words of the African scholar Kwame Bediako:

> 'In view of an increasing perception of Africa as marginal to major world affairs, it becomes important to appreciate what, on the other hand, Africa's role may be as a privileged area of Christian religious, cultural, social and political engagement in the world. In that respect, Africa may not be so marginal after all in a changing world... Given Africa's significant place in Christianity's resurgence in the present century, it would be difficult to avoid the conclusion that it has played a major role in the renewal of Christianity as a non-western religion, and therefore as a world faith.'[16]

Isabel Apawo Phiri, Dietrich Werner, Chammah Kaunda, Kennedy Owino, Kwabena Asamoah-Gyadu, Priscille Djomhue, Kudzai Biri, Edison Kalengyo

[16] Kwame Bediako, *Christianity in Africa: The Renewal of a Non-Western Religion* (Edinburgh: Edinburgh University Press, 1995), ix.

List of Contributors

Aboagye-Mensah, Robert Kwasi, Most Rev., PhD (Ghana) Methodist Church of Ghana; Member, Central Committee of World Council of Churches and Executive Director, Mindolo Ecumenical Foundation, Kitwe, Zambia; former Presiding Bishop, Methodist Church, Ghana; former Vice-President for West Africa, All Africa Conference of Churches: kwasi846@gmail.com

Aboubacar, Issiaka (Niger) One of the first indigenous pastors in Niger; Maîtrise à l'Université protestante de l'Afrique de l'Ouest, Porto-Novo, Bénin.

Abuom, Agnes, PhD (Kenya) Anglican Church of Kenya; Executive Director of TAABCO Research and Development Consultants, Nairobi; former Africa President of World Council of Churches; Moderator of Central Committee of World Council of Churches: a.aboum@yahoo.com

Adjobi, Améya Philippe, MTh (Côte d'Ivoire) District Superintendent, United Methodist Church; Visiting Professor of Church History, Institut Supérieur de Théologie d'Abadjin-Doumé en Côte d'Ivoire (ISTHA): phadjobi@emu-ci.org

Adogame, Afe, Prof., PhD (Nigeria/USA) Maxwell M. Upson Professor of Christianity and Society Princeton Theological Seminary, Princeton (NY); former Professor of World Christianity and Religious Studies, School of Divinity, University of Edinburgh, UK; Secretary, African Association for the Study of Religions: afe.adogame@ptsem.edu

Amanze, James Nathaniel, Canon, Prof., PhD (Malawi/Botswana) Anglican; Professor of Systematic Theology, University of Botswana: amanzejn@mopipi.ub.bw

Arrison, Edwin, PhD (South Africa) Anglican priest and social entrepreneur; General Secretary, Kairos Southern Africa: kairossouthernafrica@gmail.com

Asale, Bruk Ayele, PhD (Ethiopia) Ethiopian Evangelical Church Mekane Yesus; Instructor, Ethiopian Graduate School of Theology and MTh Programme Co-ordinator: brukayele@gmail.com

August, Karel Thomas, Prof., PhD (South Africa) Moravian; Emeritus Professor of Theology, Department of Practical Theology and Missiology, University of Stellenbosch, South Africa: kta@sun.ac.za

Ayanga, Hazel, Prof., PhD (Kenya) Anglican; Moi University, Eldoret; East Africa Co-ordinator, Circle of Concerned African Women Theologians: hayangaus@yahoo.com

Ayegboyin, Isaac Deji, Rev. Prof., PhD (Nigeria) Pastor, Nigerian Baptist Convention; Professor, Department of Religious Studies, University of Ibadan, Nigeria; President, Nigerian Baptist Theological Seminary, Ogbomosho: dejigboyin@yahoo.com

Banda, Joshua H.K., Bishop, PhD (Zambia) Pentecostal Assembly of God Church; President of Pentecostal Assemblies of Africa - Southern Africa Region, President of International Coalition of Fellowships (ICOF) University–Zambia Campus: jhkbanda@northmeadassembly.org

Bangirana, Albert Billy (Uganda/South Africa) Catholic; PhD student, School of Religion, Philosophy and Classics, University of KwaZulu-Natal, South Africa: bangimessage@gmail.com

Baziomo, Raoul, Rev., PhD (Burkina Faso) Roman Catholic; Professeur d'Ecritures saintes, Grand Séminaire de Koumi Bobo-Dioulasso; Conférence Episcopale du Burkina-Niger: rbaziomo@gmail.com

Beyene, Tewelde, PhD (Eritrea/Italy); former Professor of Ethiopian and Eritrean History, University of Asmara, Eritrea; Professor of History of Ethiopian-Eritrean Christianity in institutions of higher education: tewahdo@lisantewahdo.org

Biyela, Fred O., (Republic du Congo-Brazzaville), candidate doctorant en anthropologie au CEPED, Faculté SHS-Sorbonne/Université Paris Descartes: fredolichet@yahoo.fr

Biri, Kudzai, Prof., PhD (Zimbabwe) Zimbabwe Assemblies of God Africa; Associate Professor, Department of Religious Studies, Classics and Philosophy, University of Zimbabwe: kudzibiri@gmail.com

Byaruhanga, Christopher, Rev. Canon Prof., PhD (Uganda) Anglican Church of the Province of Uganda; Professor of Systematic and Historical Theology, Uganda Christian University: cbyaruhanga@ucu.ac.ug

Chianeque, Luciano Chanhelela, Rev., PhD (Angola) Evangelical Congregational Church in Angola; Pastor in Bungo Parish of Luanda, Angola; Associate Professor, Catholic University of Angola; Theological Consultant, World Council of Churches's Ecumenical HIV and AIDS Initiatives and Advocacy: lcchianeque@hotmail.com

Chimhanda, Francisca Hildegardis, Sister, Prof., DTh (Zimbabwe/South Africa) Roman Catholic; Professor of Systematic Theology, University of South Africa: chimhfh@unisa.ac.za

Chirinda, Felicidade Naume, Rev., PhD (Mozambique) Igreja Presbiteriana de Moçambique; Executive Director, Scripture Union, Khovo School of Theology, Mozambique: fchirinda@teledata.mz

Chitando, Ezra, Prof., DPhil (Zimbabwe) Seventh Day Adventist; Theological Consultant, World Council of Churches's Ecumenical HIV and AIDS Initiative in Africa; Associate Lecturer, Department of Religious Studies, Classics and Philosophy, University of Zimbabwe: chitsa21@yahoo.com

de Clermont, Jean-Arnold, Rev. (France) l'Eglise Protestante Unie de France; Lecturer, Systematic Theology, Ecumenics and Ethics, United Church of Zambia University College; former President, French Protestant Federation and Conference of European Chuches (CEC): jadeclermont@gmail.com

Conradie, Ernst M., Prof., PhD (South Africa) Uniting Reformed Church in Southern Africa; Senior Professor, Department of Religion and Theology, University of the Western Cape, South Africa: econradie@uwc.ac.za

Couper, Scott Everett, Rev., PhD (South Africa/USA) United Church of Christ and United Congregational Church of Southern Africa; Senior Honorary Lecturer, School of Religion, Philosophy and Classics, University of KwaZulu-Natal; Adjunct Lecturer, Seth Mokitimi Methodist Seminary, Pietermaritzburg, South Africa; Academic Coordinator, School of International Training, Vermont, USA (Social and Political Transformation Programme, Durban, South Africa): scandsv@intekom.co.za

Coyault, Bernard, Rev., PhD (France/Morocco) Presbyterian (Eglise Evangélique au Maroc/Eglise Protestante Unie de France); Director, Institut Oecuménique de Théologie Al Mowafaqa, Rabat, Morocco; Lecturer, Sociology of Religion, Paris: bernard.coyault@gmail.com

Curpanen, James Rodney, Rev., DMin (Mauritius) Church Pastor and Supervisor for Children's Ministry, Welfare, Social Actions and Mission, Presbyterian Church of Mauritius: rcurpanen@hotmail.com

Dandala, Hamilton Mvumelwano, Rev., PhD (h.c.), DTh (h.c.) (South Africa) Methodist Church of Southern Africa; former President, Seth Mokitimi Methodist Seminary; former General Secretary, AACC: dandala@smms.ac.za

Daniels, David, Prof., PhD (USA) Henry Winters Luce Professor of World Christianity, McCormick Theological Seminary, Chicago, USA: ddaniels@mccormick.edu

Dembele, Youssouf (Mali) Global Translation Advisor, Translation Centre of Bamako, Mali: ydembele@afribonemali.net

Denis, Philippe, OP, Prof., PhD (South Africa) Member of Dominican Order; Professor of History of Christianity, School of Religion, Philosophy and Classics, University of KwaZulu-Natal, South Africa: denis@ukzn.ac.za

Diouf, Thomas (Senegal) Président de l'Eglise Luthérienne du Sénégal: revdioufthomas@yahoo.fr

Djiokou, Sadrack (Cameroon/Germany), Pastor of Eglise Evangelique du Cameroon and Evangelische Möhne-Kirchengemeinde, Westfalia/Germany, doctoral candidate University of Bochum:djiokou@yahoo.com

Djomhoue, Priscille, Rev. Prof. (Cameroun/Belgium) Eglise Evangélique du Cameroun; Professor of Greek and New Testament Studies; former Director, Family Life and Gender Justice Department, All Africa Conference of Churches: pdjomhoue@yahoo.fr

Dossou, Simon Kossi, Rev., PhD (Bénin/Togo) Methodist; Special Envoy of the All Africa Conference of Churches for West and West Africa and Regional Representative, Lomé, Togo; Chancellor, Protestant University of West Africa, Bénin: dossouksimon@gmail.com

Dube, Musa W., Prof., PhD (Botswana) United Methodist Church; Professor of Biblical Studies, University of Botswana: dubemw@mopipi.ub.bw

Duncan, Graham Alexander, Rev. Prof., PhD (Scotland/South Africa) Uniting Presbyterian Church in Southern Africa; Professor and Head of Department of Church History and Church Polity, University of Pretoria: graham.duncan@up.ac.za

Ekouaghe, Ndong, Rev. (Gabon) President, l'Eglise Evangélique du Gabon, Libreville: jacquesndongekouaghe@yahoo.fr

Eliot, Tofa, PhD (Zimbabwe/Swaziland) Senior Lecturer, Department of Theology and Religious Studies, University of Swaziland: etofa@uniswa.sz

Essono Nkoa, Samuel, Rev. (Equatorial Guinea/Cameroon) Iglesia Reformada Presbiteriana de Guinea Ecuatorial; doctoral student, Protestant University of Central Africa, Cameroon: samuel_essono@yahoo.fr

Fatokun, Samson, Rev. Prof., PhD (Nigeria) Apostolic Church; Associate Professor, Department of Religious Studies, University of Ibadan, Nigeria: samsonfatokun@yahoo.com

Frouisou, Samuel, Rev., PhD (Cameroon) Pasteur de l'Eglise Evangélique Luthérienne du Cameroun; Academic Secretary, Faculty of Protestant Theology and Religious Sciences, Protestant University of Central Africa, Cameroon: sfrouisou@gmail.com

Füllkrug-Weitzel, Cornelia, Rev. (Germany) President, Bread for the World, Berlin: Kristina.Schoger@brot-für-die-welt.de

Gathogo, Julius, Prof., PhD (Kenya) Senior Lecturer, Kenyatta University, Nairobi, and Research Fellow, University of South Africa, Pretoria: jumgathogo@gmail.com

Gatwa, Tharcisse, Prof., PhD (Rwanda), Associate Research Professor of Ethics and Missiology, Director of Research, Protestant Institute of Art and Social Science (PIASS) Butare, Rwanda; former General Secretary, Christian Council of Rwanda: tharcissegatwa@hotmail.com

Getui, Mary, Prof., PhD (Kenya) Seventh Day Adventist; Professor at Department of Religious Studies and Director of Quality Assurance Unit, Catholic University of Eastern Africa, Kenya; Chairperson, National AIDS Control Council, Kenya: mngetui@yahoo.com

Gichimu, John Njeru, Venerable, PhD (Kenya) African Independent Pentecostal Church of Africa; Co-ordinator, Programme for Theology and Ministerial Formation, Organization of African Instituted Churches: gichimu@oaic.org

Gill, Theo (Lesotho) Curator, Morija Museum and Archives, Lesotho: sgill@morijafest.com

Goddard, Allen (South Africa) Anabaptist; PhD student, University of KwaZulu-Natal, South Africa: thereIsanewcreation@gmail.com

Grobbelaar, Jan, Rev., DTh (South Africa) Dutch Reformed Church in South Africa; Research Associate, Petra Institute for Children's Ministry, South Africa; Manager, aboutchildren.net: jan@petracol.org.za

Steve de Grouchy (+), Phd, former Professor of Theology of Development, University of KwaZulu-Natal, and former Head of of the School of Theology and Theology, University of KwaZulu-Natal

Gyadu, Kwabena Asamoah-, Rev. Prof., PhD (Ghana) Methodist; Trinity Theological College, Legon, Ghana; Baeta-Grau Professor of African Christianity and Director of the Center for the Study of Christianity in Africa at Trinity Theological Seminary, Accra: kwabena.asamoahgyadu@gmail.com

Haarmann, Claudia, Rev. (Switzerland) Pastor, Sils im Domleschg, Switzerland; former Co-ordinator, Basic Income Grant Coalition and its pilot project in Namibia (2004-2009): cd.haarmann@gmx.net

Haarmann, Dirk, Rev. (Switzerland) Pastor, Sils im Domleschg, Switzerland; former Co-ordinator, Basic Income Grant Coalition and its pilot project in Namibia (2004-2009): cd.haarmann@gmx.net

Hailu, Mussi, Ambassador (Ethiopia) Regional Director, United Religions Initiative, Africa; Special Envoy and Advisor, African Union Economic, Social and Cultural Council on Interfaith, Inter-religious and Inter-Cultural Issues: mussiepeace@yahoo.co.uk

Harawa, Chimwemwe Mjisunge (Malawi) Church of Central Africa Presbyterian; Lecturer, Department of Theology and Religious Studies, University of Malawi, Chancellor College and a Co-ordinator of Board for Theological Studies, Malawi: charawa01@gmail.com

Healey, Joseph Graham, Rev., M. Chr. Sp (USA/Kenya) Roman Catholic; Lecturer, Tangaza University College, Nairobi: JGHealey@aol.com

Hedley, Robert (Ethiopia) Former Staff Member, Bread for the World, Ethiopia: bob.hedley@brot-für-die-welt.de

Hewitt, Roderick, Rev. Prof., PhD (Jamaica/South Africa) Presbyterian; Academic Leader in Higher Degrees and Research, School of Religion, Philosophy and Classics, University of KwaZulu-Natal, South Africa; former Staff Member, Council for World Mission: Hewitt@ukzn.ac.za

Iwuamadi, Lawrence Oscar Iheanyichukwu, Rev. Fr Prof., PhD (Nigeria/Switzerland) Roman Catholic; Professor of Biblical Hermeneutics, Ecumenical Institute, Bossey, Switzerland: Lawrence.iwuamadi@wcc-coe.org

Iyakaremye, Innocent, Rev., PhD (Rwanda) Free Methodist Church of Rwanda; Lecturer, Centre for Gender Studies, University of Rwanda, Butare, Southern Province, Rwanda: iyakin7@gmail.com

Johnson, Samuel Desire, PhD (Cameroon/France) Executive Secretary, CEVAA – Communaute d'Eglise en Mission; Associate Researcher, Lecturer at Theology Faculty, Montpellier, France: johnsonsamueld@yahoo.fr

Johnson, Todd, Prof., PhD (USA) Congregational; Associate Professor, Gordon-Conwell Theological Seminary, Massachusetts, USA; Director, Centre for the Study of World Christianity/Gordon-Conwell Seminary: tjohnson@gordonconwell.edu

Kalengyo, Edison, Canon Prof., PhD (Uganda/Kenya) Anglican; Associate Professor of New Testament, Bishop Tucker School of Divinity and Theology, Uganda Christian University; former Director of Theology, Ecumenical and Interfaith Department, All Africa Conference of Churches: Kalengyo@aacc-ceta.org

Kamwaria, Alex N. (Kenya) Lecturer, Department of Social Sciences, and Dean, School of Humanities and Social Sciences, Machakos University College, Kenya: akamwaria@yahoo.com

Kaoma, Kapya John, Rev. Canon, PhD (Zambia/USA) Priest of Anglican Diocese of Central Zambia; former Dean of Studies, St John's Seminary and Priest in Charge, St George's Anglican Church, Luanshya, Zambia; Senior Religion and Sexuality Researcher of Political Research Associates, MA, kaoma8john@yahoo.com

Kapere, Maria, Rev. (Namibia) African Methodist Episcopal Church; General Secretary of Council of Churches in Namibia: gs@ccnnamibia.org

Kapuma, Gertrude, Rev. (Malawi) Church of Central Africa Presbyterian; Lecturer, Zomba Theological College, Malawi: mbusaga@yahoo.com

Karamaga, André, Rev., PhD (Rwanda/Kenya) Presbyterian; General Secretary, All Africa Conference of Churches: k.andre@aacc-ceta.org

Katola, Michael T., PhD (Kenya) Senior Lecturer, Department of Philosophy and Religious Studies, Kenyatta University, Nairobi: mtkatola@yahoo.com

Kaunda, Chammah J., Rev., PhD (Zambia/South Africa) Pentecostal Assemblies of God; Post Doc in Christian Spirituality, University of South Africa, Pretoria: pastorchammah@gmail.com

Kealotswe, Obed, Rev., PhD (Botswana) United Congregational Church of Southern Africa; Senior Lecturer, Department of Theology and Religious Studies, University of Botswana: kealotsw@mopipi.ub.bw

Kgalemang, Malebogo (Botswana) Apostolic Faith Mission; Senior Lecturer, University of Botswana: kgalemang@mopipi.ub.bw

Kinda Tegwende, Leonard (Burkina Faso)**;** Secrétaire exécutif, l'AEERB et membre du comité; Directeur, ACT Alliance; ancien Président, ACT Burkina Forum.

Kiplagat, Bethuel, Ambassador, PhD (h.c.) (Kenya) Former Chancellor, Egerton University, Nairobi; former Ambassador of Kenya to France and UK); Permanent Secretary, Ministry of Foreign Affairs and International Co-operation of Kenya: bethuelkiplagat@gmail.com

Klagba, Charles, Rev. (Togo) President, l'Église Méthodiste du Togo: chaklagba@outlook.fr

Kobia, Samuel, Rev., PhD (Kenya) Methodist; former General Secretary, World Council of Churches, and Ecumenical Special Envoy for South Sudan and Sudan, All Africa Conference of Churches; Senior Advisor to Kenyan President on Peace and Conflict Resolution: kobiasam@gmail.com

Koegelenberg, Renier A., PhD (South Africa) Executive Director, Ecumenical Foundation for Southern Africa (EFSA) Institute for Theological and Interdisciplinary Research, Stellenbosch; Executive Secretary, National Religious Association for Social Development, South Africa: renier@cddc.co.za

Koopman, Nico Norman, Rev., PhD (South Africa) Uniting Reformed Church in Southern Africa; Professor of Systematic Theology and Acting Vice-Rector for Social Impact, Personnel and Transformation, and Director, Beyers Naudé Centre for Public Theology, Stellenbosch University, South Africa: nkoopman@sun.ac.za

Kombo, James, Rev., DTh (Kenya) Church of Christ in Africa; Professor of Systematic Theology and Dean of Postgraduate Studies, Daystar University, Nairobi; Lecturer for Child Development Programme at Daystar Univeersity, Nairobi: jkombo@daystar.ac.ke

Koudougueret, David, Rev. Prof., PhD (Central African Republic) Professeur des Sciences Bibliques, ancien Directeur Académique et ancien Directeur de la Recherche et de la Formation Continue de la Faculté de Théologie Evangélique de Bangui, Central African Republic: dkoudougueret@yahoo.fr

Kpobi, David N.A., Rev. Prof., PhD (Ghana) Presbyterian; Associate Professor and Director, Special Programmes, Trinity Theological Seminary, Ghana: kpobid@yahoo.com

Kurian, Manoj, Dr (Malaysia/Switzerland) World Council of Churches Programme Executive for Health and Healing: Manoj.Kurian@wcc-coe.org

Labeodan, Helen Adekunbi, PhD (Nigeria) Deacon, Grace Family International Church; Senior Lecturer, Department of Religious Studies, University of Ibadan, General Co-ordinator, Circle of Concerned African Women Theologians since 2013: kunbial@yahoo.com

Longwe, Hany, Rev., PhD (Malawi) Baptist; Senior Lecturer and Head, Theology and Religious Studies Section, Department of Humanities, Faculty of Education, University of Livingstonia, Malawi: chatupa2008@gmail.com

Longwe, Molly, PhD (Malawi) Baptist; Lecturer, University of Livingstonia, Malawi: mollylongwe@gmail.com

Lugazia, Faith Kokubelwa, Rev., PhD (Tanzania/Rwanda) Evangelical Lutheran Church in Tanzania; Lecturer in Systematic Theology, Mission and Ecumenism and Contemporary African Christianity, Protestant Institute of Arts and Social Sciences, Faculty of Theology and Religious Studies, Butare, Rwanda: flugazia001@luthersem.edu

Magesa, Laurenti, STD, Rev. Fr, Prof., PhD (Kenya/Tanzania) Catholic; Professor, Hekima College Jesuit School of Theology, Nairobi: magesapd@gmail.com

Mahamane, Addo, PhD, Prof. (Republic of Niger) Elder of the Eglise Evangélique de la République du Niger/Evangelical Church of Niger Republic; Professor and Chancellor (Recteur), Tahoua University, Niger: adomahama@yahoo.fr

Makubakube, Khosi Emmanuel, (Lesotho), former Catholic priest in the Congregation of the Oblates of Mary Immaculate; current General Secretary of Council of Churches in Lesotho: generalsecretary@ccl.org.ls

Manda, Charles Bester, PhD (South Africa) Post-doctoral Fellow, Research Institute for Theology and Religion, University of South Africa (UNISA), Expert in Pastoral Family Therapy and Trauma Healing: cmanda3@gmail.com

Manyonganise, Molly, Rev., PhD (Zimbabwe) Pentecostal Christian: mollymanyonganise@yahoo.com

Marie, Rowanne Sarojini, PhD (South Africa) Full Gospel Church of God in Southern Africa; Registrar and Academic Dean, Seth Mokitimi Methodist Seminary, Pietermaritzburg, South Africa: rowannem@smms.ac.za

Mbaya, Henry, Rev., PhD (Malawi/South Africa) Anglican; Senior Lecturer in Missiology, Stellenbosch University, South Africa: henrymbaya@webmail.co.za

Mbiti, John, Rev, PhD (Kenya/Switzerland) Former Director, Bossey Ecumenical Institute, Switzerland; Senior Scholar of African Religions and Christianity: mbiti.john@gmail.com

Messina, Jean Paul, Rev. Prof., PhD (Cameroon) Roman Catholic; Professeur d'histoire ecclésiastique et des Sciences des Religions, Correspondant du Comité Pontifical des Sciences Historiques, Université Catholique d'Afrique Centrale, Cameroon: jpaul.messina@yahoo.fr

Mombo, Esther, Prof., PhD (Kenya) Anglican; Deputy Vice-Chancellor, St Paul's University, Limuru, Kenya; Professor of African Church History and Theologies from Women's Perspective: esthermombo@yahoo.co.uk

Moyo, Herbert, Rev., PhD (Zimbabwe/South Africa) Lutheran; Lecturer in Practical Theology, University of KwaZulu-Natal, South Africa: moyoh@ukzn.ac.za

Muchimba, Felix, Rev., PhD (Zambia) Director of African Church-based Training; Member, Christian Brethren Movement: felixmuchimba@gmail.com

Müller, Retief, Rev., PhD (South Africa) Dutch Reformed Church; Senior Lecturer, Stellenbosch University, South Africa: retiefmuller@sun.ac.za

Mugambi, Jesse N.K., Prof., PhD (Kenya) Anglican; Consultant Theologian, Council of Anglican Provinces in Africa; Professor of Philosophy and Religious Studies, University of Nairobi: jnmugambi@gmail.com

Mulrain, George, Rev., PhD (Trinidad & Tobago/Jamaica) Methodist; Academic Supervisor, United Theological College of the West Indies, Jamaica: georgemulrain@hotmail.com

Murimi, Susan Wangui, PhD (Kenya) Deliverance Church of Kenya; Lecturer, Daystar University, Kenya: suemurimi@hotmail.com

Musopole, Augustine Chingwala, Rev. Prof., PhD (Malawi/Kenya) Presbyterian Church of Central Africa; Associate Professor (emeritus) at the Institute for Umunthu (Ubuntu) Studies: acmusopole@gmail.com

Mwombeki, Fidon, Rev., PhD (Tanzania/Germany) Evangelical Lutheran Church in Tanzania; former General Secretary, United Evangelical Mission; Director for Mission and Development, Lutheran World Federation: fmwombeki@hotmail.com

Naicker, Linda (South Africa) PhD student, University of KwaZulu-Natal, South Africa: w.naicker@gmail.com

Nalwamba, Kuzipa, Rev. (Zambia/South Africa) United Church of Zambia and Uniting Presbyterian Church of Southern Africa; PhD student, Faculty of Theology, Department of Dogmatics and Christian Ethics, University of Pretoria: knalwamba@gmail.com

Ndlovu, Hebron Luhlanya, PhD (Swaziland) Church of the Nazarene; Senior Lecturer, Department of Theology and Religious Studies, University of Swaziland: hlndlovu@uniswa.sz

Nell, Ian, PhD (South Africa) Associate Professor of Practical Theology, Stellenbosch University, South Africa: ianell@sun.ac.zaianell@sun.ac.za

Ngangura Manyanya, Lévi, Rev. Prof., PhD (République Démocratique du Congo) l'Eglise du Christ au Congo/ Eglises Libres de Pentecôte en Afrique (CELPA); Professeur et Doyen de la Faculté de Théologie de l'Université Libre des Pays des Grands Lacs, DR Congo: ngangura@yahoo.fr

Ngong, David Tonghou, Deacon, Prof., PhD (Cameroon/USA) Baptist; Assistant Professor of Religion and Theology, Stillman College, Alabama, USA: dvdngng@yahoo.co.uk

Njoroge, John Ngige, Rev. Fr, PhD (Kenya) Eastern Orthodox Church/Greek Orthodox Patriarchate of Alexandria and All Africa, Holy Archbishopric of Kenya; Lecturer, Kenya Methodist University: ngigenjoroge@yahoo.com

Nkansah-Obrempong, James, Prof., PhD (Ghana/Kenya) Baptist; Professor of Theology and Ethics, Africa International University and Dean, Nairobi Evangelical Graduate School of Theology; Vice-Chair, World Evangelical Alliance Theological Commission: james.nkansah@africainternational.edu

Nkomazana, Fidelis, Prof., PhD (Botswana) Seventh Day Baptist; Professor of History of Christianity, University of Botswana: nkomazaf@mopipi.ub.bw

Nupanga, Weanzana, Rev., PhD (Democratic Republic of Congo, Central African Republic and Cameroon) Evangelical Community of Christ in Congo; Lecturer and President, Bangui Evangelical School of Theology, Central African Republic: nupangaw@fateb.net

Nyawo, Sonene, PhD (Swaziland) Evangelical Church, Swaziland; Lecturer, Department of Theology and Religious Studies, University of Swaziland, Kwasuleni, Swaziland: snyawo@uniswa.sz

Nyirimana, Rose Mukansengimana, PhD (Rwanda/South Africa) Paran Christian Ministries; research fellow, Research Institute for Theology and Religion, UNISA, South Africa: rosenyirimana@ymail.com

Nyomi, Setri, Rev., PhD (Ghana) Evangelical Presbyterian Church in Ghana; former General Secretary, World Communion of Reformed Churches: nsetri@gmail.com

Obiora, Ike, Priest, PhD (Nigeria) Roman Catholic Prelate, Catholic Diocese of Enugu; Founder and Director, Catholic Institute for Development Justice and Peace, Enugu State, Nigeria; Director, Globethics.net Foundation, Geneva: obiorike@yahoo.com

Oden, Thomas, Prof., PhD (USA) Former Henry Anson Buttz Professor of Theology and Ethics, Drew University, New Jersey; Founder, Center for Early African Christianity, Pennsylvania, USA: tom@tomoden.com

Oduyoye, Mercy Amba, PhD (Ghana) Methodist Church in Ghana; Director, Institute for the Study Women in Religion and Culture, Trinity Theological Seminary, Legon, Ghana; former Deputy General Secretary, World Council of Churches; Founder, Circle of Concerned African Women Theologians: iwrcghana@yahoo.com

Oduro, Thomas A., Rev., PhD (Ghana) Baptist; President, Good News Theological College and Seminary, Accra, Ghana: taoduro@gmail.com

Olwa, Alfred, Rev. Canon, PhD (Uganda) Anglican Church of Uganda; Senior Lecturer and Dean, Bishop Tucker School of Divinity and Theology, Uganda Christian University: aolwa@ucu.ac.ug

Onyinah, Opoku, Rev., PhD (Ghana) Church of Pentecost; Chancellor, Pentecost University College, Ghana: oonyinah@hotmail.com

Ortega, Ofelia, Rev., PhD (Cuba) Presbyterian; former Rector, Matanzas Theological Seminary, Cuba; former President, World Council of Churches for Latin American Region: intre@enet.cu

Ositelu, Rufus Okikiola, Most Rev., PhD (Nigeria) Primate of Church of the Lord Worldwide, Church of the Lord (Aladura); Senior Lecturer, Aladura Theological Institute: cla.primate@gmail.com

Ouedraogo, Philippe, Rev., PhD (Burkina Faso) Vice-President, Assemblies of God; Director, Evangelical Association Supporting Development, Burkina Faso: philippe_aead@yahoo.co.uk

Owino, Kennedy, PhD (Kenya/South Africa) Anglican; Lecturer, Systematic Theology, Seth Mokitimi Methodist Seminary, Pietermaritzburg, South Africa: kennowino.76@gmail.com.

Owusu-Ansah, Sylvia (Ghana) Lecturer, School of Theology and Missions, Central University College, Accra, Ghana: sylviansah@gmail.com

Pacho, Titus Ogalo (Kenya/Germany) Catholic; Lecturer and Researcher in Philosophy and Education; PhD student, University of Hamburg, Department of Education: tituspacho@gmail.com

Phiri, Isabel Apawo, PhD, Prof. (Malawi/Switzerland) Presbyterian; Associate General Secretary, Public Witness and Diakonia, World Council of Churches; Honorary Professor, School of Religion, Philosophy and Classics, University of KwaZulu-Natal, South Africa; former General Co-ordinator, Circle of Concerned African Women Theologians: Isabel.Phiri@wcc-coe.org

Phillott-Almeida, Ralphina, PhD (Gambia) Patronal Festival Historian and Adviser, St Mary's Cathedral: ralmeida@ganet.gm

Pillay, Jerry, Rev. Prof., PhD (South Africa); Uniting Presbyterian Church in Southern Africa; Professor of Church History and Polity, University of Pretoria; President, World Communion of Reformed Churches: jerry.pillay@up.ac.za

Poucouta, Paulin, Prêtre, Prof., PhD (Congo Brazzaville/Cameroun) Catholic; Professor, University Catholique d'Afrique Centrale, Camroon: poucouta@hotmail.com

Purcell, Susan, Dr (Zimbabwe/Switzerland) Physician, Programme Executive Health and Healing Project, World Council of Churches, Geneva: Susan.Purcell_Gilpin@wcc-coe.org

Rabarijaona, Brigitte, Rev., PhD (Madagascar) Reformed Church (Church of Jesus Christ in Madagascar); Junior Lecturer in Old Testament, Faculty of Theology of Ambatonakanga, Antananarivo; Translation Consultant, United Bible Societies: rabbri@gmail.com

Ramambason, Laurent William, Rev. Prof., PhD (Madagascar) Church of Jesus Christ in Madagascar; President, Reformed University of Madagascar: lwramambason@yahoo.com

Ramos, Max Ruben (Cape Verde/Portugal) PhD student, Institute of Social Sciences, University of Lisbon: maxruben10@gmail.com

Samuel B. Reeves, Rev., PhD (Liberia) Senior Pastor, Providence Baptist Church, Member of Executive Committee Council of Churches in Liberia: providencehill2@gmail.com

Ruele, Moji, Prof., PhD (Botswana) Senior Lecturer, Department of Theology and Religious Studies, University of Botswana: ruelem@mopipi.ub.bw

Sakupapa, Teddy Chalwe, Rev. (Zambia/South Africa) United Church of Zambia; PhD student in Ecumenical Theology and Social Ethics and Lecturer at University of the Western Cape, South Africa, South Africa: tecsak@yahoo.com

Schlick, Michael, Rev. (Germany/Djibouti) Reformed Church; Director, Social Welfare Work and Development Projects, Service de Mission-Defap, Paris: m.schlick@yahoo.com

Shoko, Tabona, Prof., PhD (Zimbabwe) Professor of African Traditional Religion, University of Zimbabwe, Department of Religious Studies: shokotab@yahoo.com

Siwila, Lilian Cheelo, PhD (Zambia/South Africa) United Church of Zambia; Programme Director, Systematic Theology, University of KwaZulu-Natal, South Africa: siwila@ukzn.ac.za

Speckman, McGlory, PhD (South Africa) Professor of New Testament, University of Pretoria, South Africa: m.speckman@up.ac.za

Spitzek, Hans, PhD (Germany) Staff Member, Bread for the World, Berlin; Publisher, *Welt-sichten* (magazine on Global Development and Ecumenical Co-operation): hans.spitzek@brot-für-die-welt.de

Ssekabira, Kigoza Vincent, Fr, PhD (Uganda) Priest Professor, St Mary's Ggaba National Seminary, Kampala, Uganda: ssekabirakv@yahoo.co.uk

Suerman, Harald, PhD (Germany) Director, Missionswissenschaftliche Institut, Aachen, Germany: harald.suermann@mwi-aachen.org

Taringa, Nisbert Taisekwa, PhD (Zimbabwe) United Methodist Church; Senior Lecturer and Head of Department of Religious Studies, Classics and Philosophy, University of Zimbabwe: taisekwa64@yahoo.co.uk

Tawfik, Wedad Abbas, Prof., PhD (Egypt) Egyptian Coptic Orthodox Church; Professor of Theology, Department of Theology, Higher Institute of Coptic Studies, Cairo: wedadt@yahoo.com

Temple, Arnold C., Rt Rev. (Sierra Leone) Methodist Church; Lecturer, College of Theology and Management, Freetown, Sierra Leone; Bishop Emeritus of Methodist Church, Sierra Leone: arnoldtemple1@yahoo.com

Tengatenga, James, Rt Rev., PhD (Malawi/USA) Anglican; Chair, Anglican Consultative Council and Distinguished Visiting Professor of Global Anglicanism, School of Theology, University of the South, Tennessee, USA: tengaja@gmail.com

Tesfaye, Ayalkibet Berhanu, Deacon (Ethiopia/South Africa) Ethiopian Orthodox Tewahedo Church; PhD student, University of KwaZulu-Natal, South Africa: ayalkibet@gmail.com

Thiani, Evangelos, Fr (Kenya) Eastern Orthodox Church in Kenya; Vice-Rector, Orthodox College of Africa and Lecturer in Liturgical Studies and Public Theology, Orthodox Patriarchal Seminary, Nairobi: frevangelost@yahoo.com

Togarasei, Lovemore, Prof., PhD (Zimbabwe/Botswana) Church of Christ; Professor, Department of Theology and Religious Studies, University of Botswana: ltogarasei@yahoo.com

Toroitich, Isaiah (Switzerland) Global Advocacy and Policy Co-ordinator, ACT Alliance Office, Geneva: Isaiah.Toroitich@actalliance.org

Trimua, Dake Joseph Ekom, Rev., PhD (Togo) Professor, Université Protestante de l'Afrique de l'Ouest, Campus Atakpamé, Bénin: gamaov@yahoo.fr

Tveit, Olav Fykse, Rev., PhD (Norway/Switzerland) General Secretary, World Council of Churches, Geneva: Diana.Chabloz@wcc-coe.org

Ukah, Asonzeh, PhD, Habil. (Nigeria/South Africa) Roman Catholic; Senior Lecturer, Sociology of Religion, University of Cape Town, South Africa: asonzeh@yahoo.com

Uzochukwu, Peter Uche, Rev. Fr, PhD (Nigeria) Roman Catholic; Priest, Our Lady of Lourdes Complex, Ihiala, Anambra State, Nigeria; Senior Lecturer, St Paul's Theological School, Nnewi, Anambra State, Nigeria: uzopietro@gmail.com

Van der Water, Desmond Peter, Rev., PhD (South Africa) United Congregational Church of Southern Africa; Research Fellow, University of South Africa; former General Secretary, Council for World Mission: vanderwaters2002@aol.com

Walker-Smith, Angelique, Rev., PhD (USA) National Baptist Convention, USA; Senior Associate for Pan African Church Engagement, Indiana Wesleyan University, USA; Staff Member, Bread for the World, Washington, DC: awalker-smith@bread.org

Wandera, Joseph, Prof., PhD (Kenya) Lecturer, Department of Islam and Christian-Muslim Relations, St Paul's University, Limuru, Kenya; Co-founder, Centre for Christian-Muslim Relations, Nairobi: wandera@spu.ac.ke

W'Ehusha, Lubunga, Rev., PhD (Democratic Republic of Congo and South Africa) Bishop, Free Methodist Church of Democratic Republic of Congo and Tanzania; Post-doctoral Fellowship Researcher, Ujamaa Centre, University of KwaZulu-Natal, South Africa: lubungaw@yahoo.com

Werner, Dietrich, Rev. Prof., PhD (Germany) Lutheran Church in Northern Germany; Senior Advisor in Theology, Ecumenical Education and Research, Bread for the World – Protestant Development Service, Berlin; former Director of Ecumenical Theological Education, World Council of Churches: dietrich.werner@brot-für-die-welt.de

West, Gerald, Prof., PhD (South Africa) Anglican; Senior Professor of Old Testament and African Biblical Hermeneutics, School of Religion, Philosophy and Classics, University of KwaZulu-Natal, South Africa; Director of Ujamaa Centre: west@ukzn.ac.za

Yong, Amos, Prof., PhD (USA) Asian American Pentecostal theologian, Professor of Theology and Mission, Fuller Theological Seminary, California, USA, and Director, Fuller Theological Seminary's Center for Missiological Research: amosyong@fuller.edu

Zurlo, Gina (USA) Episcopal; Assistant Director, Center for the Study of Global Christianity, Gordon-Conwell Theological Seminary, Massachusetts, USA; PhD student in International Religious Demography, History and Sociology of Religion, Boston University: gzurlo@bu.edu

PART I

INTRODUCTION INTO AFRICAN CHRISTIANITY

(1) Introduction and Survey on Recent Research in African Christianity

Isabel Apawo Phiri

Introduction

The purpose of this chapter is twofold. First, it introduces the articles contained in Section One of this *Anthology on African Christianity.* Secondly, it gives a survey of selected research in African Christianity from 1990 to 2015. In the process of reviewing past and current literature, African theologians and scholars have proved beyond reasonable doubt that Christianity is indigenous to Africa, and not an imported faith. The voices of African scholars have not only served to explain the Christian faith in the African context and understanding alone, but they have unanimously grounded the faith deeply in the world and perception of Africans and their existential needs. The authors highlight the important observation that there has been hardly any phase or aspect of Christianity over the years without some African participation. The effort by African theologians and scholars has gone a long way to releasing Africans from depending on western interpretation of their Christianity. African theologians and scholars have domesticated and produced Christian documents that appeal to African hearts and ears, thereby addressing the very existential challenges that confront Africans today. Nevertheless, the documents produced have had a global appeal as African Christianity finds its place in global Christianity.

The authors of Section One of *the Anthology of African Christianity* provide an overview of the different contexts in which African Christianity has developed. James Tengatenga's article has reminded the reader that African Christianity has deep connections and ancient roots going back to the birth of Christianity. He demonstrates why Christianity is called an African religion. David Tonghou Ngong has demonstrated the existence of African Christianity over the centuries before the mass evangelization of Africa in the nineteenth century by missionaries from the global North. At the same time, Roderick Hewitt has drawn the attention of the reader to the fact that among the early missionaries to Africa were also Caribbeans who contributed to the evangelization of West Africa. The contribution of Africans to the development of African Christianity is well documented by Obed Kealotswe who has shown how resistance to colonialism gave birth to initiatives of different forms of African Christianity. Hebron Ndlovu, Kwabena Asamoa Gyadu, Jesse Mugambi, Afe Adogame and Asonze Ukah have given the reader a variety of interesting pictures based on analysis of the trends and development of Christianity in the context of political independence. Their analysis goes beyond the transformations and challenges of Christianity within the churches to an analysis of its contribution to public life in Africa and abroad. Their work shows Africans as agents of change in the development of African Christianity. Central to African Christianity is the place given to the Bible. The articles of Gerald West and Musa Dube take the reader into this important area of African Christianity. Musa Dube's article goes a step further in analysing how the Bible has been used in African Christianity to empower and disempower men and women in negotiating their relationships. One aspect of African Christianity is its ability to develop side-by-side with African indigenous religions and Islam. The articles of Tabona Shoko and Johnson Mbillah give the reader glimpses of this complex relationship by giving an analysis that shows co-operation and conflict. Finally, the articles of Roderick Hewitt, Jesse Mugambi, Afe Adogame and Angelique Walker-Smith show not only how African Christianity has developed in Africa due to contacts with Africans outside the continent but also how African Christians are making an impact with other Christians outside the continent.

Secondly, by attempting to survey recent research in African Christianity, this article aims to anchor the current articles in the tradition of ongoing research. Ten research projects will be cited to demonstrate international acknowledgement of African initiatives in research. The choice of the ten projects was guided by a) evidence of collaboration among African scholars across the continent, and in some cases with theologians and scholars from other continents on themes pertinent for Africa. This has meant I have left out research projects which were carried out by scholars in one country or by individual scholars. This could be a topic for further research. b) The choice of the ten projects was also guided by research projects which can be considered as forming the basis of the work presented in this section. This has meant that I have not included research projects by groups of scholars simply because the theme covered is outside the area of focus in Section One. c) As stated above, the period in question is twenty-five years. The choice of 1990 as a starting point is arbitrary and for management purposes only. This has meant that important research done before 1990 has been left out. Having outlined the parameters of this research, what follows is a presentation of ten key research projects on African Christianity:

African Indigenous Religions and Christianity

Religious Plurality in Africa: Essays in honour of John S. Mbiti[1]

As stated in the title of the book above, the project was co-ordinated by Olupona Jacob and Sulayman S. Nyang in order to honour one of Africa's leading theologians, John Mbiti. In a review of the book written by Rosalind I.J. Hackett, this is what she said about its editors: 'Olupona Jacob and Sulayman S. Nyang have assembled an impressive array of contributors in the field of African religious studies and theology to pay tribute to this influential and productive scholar and most respected person.'[2] The project addressed various themes from over three hundred publications of John Mbiti on religion in Africa. The first section was on the study of African Traditional Religion. This section focuses on issues and perspectives on religious plurality in Africa, from Westernization to Africanization, African Traditional Religion as an enduring heritage, and the encounter between traditional African healing systems versus western medicine in Southern Ghana. The project also addresses African theology by considering civil authority from the perspective of African theology, the Bible and oral tradition.

Section Two of the book addressed the issues of Africa and Christianity with a special focus on domestication of Christian values in the African Church. The project addresses the fact that the African Church/Christianity has its roots in African culture and in the tradition of healing which most Africans neglect to their disadvantage. It calls for the need to recognize the place and contribution of women in Africa, and drew attention to the importance of appreciating religious plurality in Africa instead of allowing it to be viewed as destructive of African Christianity.

Africa and some world religions are the focus of Section Three of this project. It addresses the Islamic revival in West Africa; historical perspectives and recent developments, Christian-Muslim relationships in Africa, and in retrospect, Africa and Judaism: its problems and prospects. These are timely challenges that the project raises.

Since the project is dedicated to John Mbiti, it mainstreams and criticises Mbiti's works on aspects of African religions as reflected in the perspectives of students in a British university, Mbiti's views on love and marriage in Africa, and his contribution to African philosophy.

The project was funded by the Synodal Council of the Evangelical-Reformed Church of the Canton of Berne, the Copeland Fellowship, Amherst College and the World Council of Churches (WCC), Geneva.

---

[1] Olupona Jacob and Sulayman S. Nyang (eds) 1993, *Religious Plurality in Africa: Essays in honour of John S. Mbiti.* New York and Berlin: Mouton de-Guyter.

[2] Rosalind I.J. Hackett in *The International Journal of African Historical Studies*, 28:3 (1995), 680-82.

Rites of Passage in Contemporary Africa, and the Interaction between Christianity and African Traditional Religions[3]

The project on *Rites of Passage in Contemporary Africa and the Interaction between Christianity and African Traditional Religions* addresses a variety of issues related to African indigenous and Christian rituals connected with cycle of life. Cardiff Academic Press has summarized the book by highlighting the following: 'This text demonstrates that the academic study of religion is not only responsive to developments in religious life, but is interested in actively exploring the symbolic structures expressed in Christian and traditional ritual activities. Academic understanding is shown to be interactive with the many factors which compromise meaning within human societies and religious communities.'[4] This project involved the University of Malawi, the University of Edinburgh and the University of Zimbabwe. It was sponsored by the Pew Charitable Trust. However, the scholars of religious studies who participated in this project were drawn from various parts of the continent.

The Wiley-Blackwell Companion to African Religions[5]

Elias Kifon Bongmba co-ordinated this project. As the editor of the *Wiley-Blackwell Companion to African Religions*, he stated that 'the project brings together a team of international scholars to create a single-volume resource on the religious beliefs and practices of the peoples in Africa. It offers a broad coverage of issues relating to African religions, considering experiences in indigenous, Christian and Islamic traditions across the continent. The contributors to this project are drawn from a variety of fields, ensuring the volume offers multi-disciplinary perspectives. It explores methodological approaches to religion from anthropological, philosophical and historical perspectives. It also provides insights into the historical developments in African religions, as well as contemporary issues such as the development of African-initiated churches, neo-traditional religions and Pentecostalism. It discusses important topics at the intersection of culture and religion in Africa, including the arts, health, politics, globalization, gender relations and the economy'.[6]

Biblical Studies, Theology, Religion and Philosophy[7]

The project *Biblical Studies, Theology, Religion and Philosophy* was co-ordinated by James Amanze. First, the project addresses issues concerning biblical studies. It introduces the history of interpreting the Bible and the methods involved. It gives an overview of the Old Testament and the major themes of the Old Testament. The project also introduces the survey of the New Testament and its major themes. These relate to Religion, Race, Gender and Identity as the Bible is read and understood by Africans. Biblical criticism is also introduced to create an opportunity for the voiceless to find their place in biblical interpretation.

Secondly, the project addresses theology by introducing Christian theology, its tasks and methodology. The project covers African theology with a contextual analysis of Zimbabwe. Rethinking Liberation Theology and the major themes in Black Theology are also addressed. The project includes forging a theological framework for African Women's Theology and theology of African Independent churches.

---

[3] Cox, James (ed), *Rites of passage in Contemporary Africa, Interaction between Christianity and African Traditional Religions.* Cardiff: Academic Press, 1998.

[4] https://books.google.ch/books?id=4InZAAAAMAAJ&q=review+of+Rites+of+passage+in+Contemporary+Africa,+Interaction+between+Christianity+and+African+Traditional+Religions&dq=review+of+Rites+of+passage+in+Contemporary+Africa,+Interaction+between+Christianity+and+African+Traditional+Religions&hl=en&sa=X&ved=0ahUKEwjshqOLuaTJAhXEYw8KHXdXAggQ6AEIHTAA. Accessed 21.112015.

[5] Bongmba, Elias K (eds). *The Wiley-Blackwell Companion to African Religions.* Chichester, UK: Wiley Blackwell Publication 2012.

[6] http://eu.wiley.com/WileyCDA/WileyTitle/productCd-1405196904.html (accessed 21st November 2015).

[7] Amanze, J.N. (ed), *Biblical Studies, Theology, Religion and Philosophy.* Eldoret, Kenya: Zapf Chancery, 2010.

Thirdly, the project introduces religious studies and the phenomenology of religion. It looks at African Traditional Religions in contemporary Africa; its challenges and prospects, and Christianity in Africa in the 21st century. The project also addresses philosophy from the African perspective. Finally, the project also introduces philosophy, logic, critical thinking and science. It includes epistemology, African philosophy and moral ethics.

The project was sponsored by the Ecumenical Theological Education of the World Council of Churches (WCC) in conjunction with Evangelisches Missionswerk in Germany.

The Bible in Africa

The Bible in Africa: Transactions, Trajectories and Trends[8]

This project was co-ordinated by Gerald O. West and Musa W. Dube. It involved a variety of African Bible scholars who share their own perspective of the place of the Bible in Africa. The project is about African scholars documenting and analysing African biblical scholarship. In a review by Brill, the publisher of the book that emerged from this project, it says: 'Although the arrival of the Bible in Africa has often been a tale of terror, the Bible has become an African book. This volume explores the many ways in which Africans have made the Bible their own. The essays in this book offer a glimpse of the rich resources that constitute Africa's engagement with the Bible.'[9] The book is divided into five sections: Part One is the historical and hermeneutical perspective. This section traces the historical developments of biblical interpretation in Africa. Part Two is particular encounters with particular texts. It gives examples from every region in Africa with a focus on the relationship between African biblical scholarship and scholarship in the West. Part Three decribes comparisons and translations as transactions. The history and role of vernacular translation in particular African contexts is highlighted. Part Four is about redrawing the boundaries of the Bible in Africa. The ambiguity of the Bible in Africa is explored. Part Five gives a bibliography of what is known to the editors on biblical scholarship in Africa. In doing so, this project provides African resources for reading the Bible. This project was funded by the University of Natal Research Fund and the National Research Foundation (South Africa). This project has inspired many more publications in the area of the Bible in Africa.[10]

The African Bible Commentary[11]

The project was co-ordinated by Tokunboh Adeyemo who brought together a number of African evangelical scholars. In reference to the aims of the project, Tokunboh said, 'The *Africa Bible Commentary* is a unique publishing event – the first one-volume Bible commentary produced in Africa by African theologians to meet the needs of African pastors, students and lay leaders. Interpreting and applying the Bible in the light of African culture and realities, it furnishes powerful and relevant insights into the biblical text that transcend Africa in their significance. The *Africa Bible Commentary* gives a section-by-section interpretation that provides a contextual, readable, affordable and immensely useful guide to the

[8] West, Gerald O. Dube Musa W. (eds) *The Bible in Africa: Transactions, Trajectories and Trends.* Leiden and Boston: BRILL, 2000.

[9] https://books.google.ch/books/about/The_Bible_in_Africa.html?id=4DcVuqtoEiIC&redir_esc=y accessed 21.11.2015.

[10] An example is Dube, Musa W. ed. *Other Ways of Reading: African Women and the Bible*. Atlanta/Geneva: Society of Biblical Literature/WCC, 2001 and Musa W. Dube and Musimbi Kanyoro (eds). 2004. *Grant Me Justice: HIV/AIDS & Gender Readings of the Bible*. Pietermaritzburg: Cluster Publications.

[11] Adeyemo, Tokunboh (ed). 2006. *The African Bible Commentary*. New York: Word Alive Publishers/Zondervan.

entire Bible. Readers around the world will benefit from and appreciate the commentary's fresh insights and direct style that engage both heart and mind.'

Key features of the commentary include:

- Produced by African biblical scholars, in Africa, for Africa – and for the world.
- A section-by-section interpretative commentary and application.
- More than seventy special articles dealing with topics of key importance to ministry in Africa today, but which also have global implications.
- Seventy African contributors from both English- and French-speaking countries.

Transcends the African context with insights into the biblical text and the Christian faith for readers worldwide.[12]

This project was sponsored by SIM and the Association of Evangelicals in Africa, with significant financial support from Christians worldwide.

Mission in African Christianity

African Christianity Rising[13]

This research took place over a period of ten years. It is a documentary film series telling the stories of Christianity in Ghana and Zimbabwe. It includes commentaries from renowned African theologians and church leaders such as Kwame Bediako, Peter K. Sarpong, Trevor Manhanga and Mensah Otabil. The project addresses the issue of the remarkable growth of Christianity on the African continent. Bediako argues strongly, as he has in his other publications, that Christianity is no longer the religion of the West.[14] The majority of Christians are now in the global South, while within the global South, it is in Africa where the fastest growth is taking place. Among the different traditions of African Christianity, it is in the African Indigenous Churches where church growth is very rapid. It is this background information that is informing the conversation in the film series. This is reflected through the engagement of Christianity with local culture as shown in singing, dancing, drama, healing and other rituals that speak to African contexts and realities.

Furthermore, the project also addresses how African Christianity is finding expression outside Africa. Examples are drawn from African Christianity in Holland, Norway, Sweden and Britain where African churches are expanding. It also touches on the issue of African Christian scholars taking leadership positions in academic and theological institutions in the global North. Two funders of the project have been identified as the Pew Charitable Trust and the Templeton Foundation.

African Initiatives in Christian Mission[15]

Under the leadership of M.L. Daneel and Dana L. Robert, this project has produced a series of books with the explicit purpose of highlighting the African contribution to Christian mission in Africa. It counteracts the dominant discourse that associated mission activities in Africa with only missionaries from the global

[12] https://books.google.ch/books?id=ExUm1hB1XxoC&dq=The+African+Bible+Commentary&hl=en&sa=X&ved=0ahUKEwiAlJCKzaTJAhVBtQ8KHQjCBhwQ6AEIHDAA. Accessed 21.11.2015.

[13] Ault, James (ed) *African Christianity Rising: Two Part Documentary Film* Series Stories from Ghana (77: 00) Stories from Zimbabwe (73: 00). James Ault Production, 2012. 4 DVDs http://jamesault.com/documentaries/africa-project/. Accessed 22.11.2015.

[14] Kwame Bediako, *Christianity in Africa, The Renewal of a Non-Western Religion* (Edinburgh: Edinburgh University Press/Maryknoll, NY: Orbis Books, 1995).

[15] The African Initiatives in Christian Mission Series is edited by M.L. Daneel and Dana L. Robert, published by UNISA Press. See a list of its publications at the following website: www.bu.edu/cgcm/research/africa/african-initiatives-in-christian-mission-book-series/ accessed 22.11.2015.

North. In the description of this project, it says: 'White missionaries, western mission policies, and the relationship of mission to European imperialism have dominated the discussion of African missions. Little attention has been paid by scholars to African initiatives in Christian mission, nor have missiological studies been made exclusively from the perspective of the so-called "recipients". Yet the phenomenal growth of Christianity in Africa has occurred in the twentieth century, much of it after the independence of the continent from outside control. The series *African Initiatives in Christian Mission* represents an attempt to address the reality that the spread of Christianity in Africa, its shape and character, has been the product of African Christians, both in the "mission churches" and the "African Initiated/Independent Churches (AICs)".'[16] The project was sponsored by the Center for Global Christianity and Mission.

The Dictionary of African Christian Biography[17]

The *Dictionary of African Christian Biography* started in 1995 under the leadership of Jonathan Bonk. He has this to say about the project: 'An international team of African scholars is facilitating the project. Contributors are drawn from academic, church and mission communities in Africa and elsewhere. Work began in 1995 and is expected to continue till 2020. The Center for Global Christianity and Mission at Boston University School of Theology provides technical and administrative support under the direction of Jonathan Bonk. While the growth and character of Christianity in Africa is without historical precedent, information on the major creative and innovative local figures and leaders of this growth – from local evangelists and pastors to nationally known Christian leaders – does not appear in standard historical and biographical reference works on the continent. The *Dictionary* covers the whole field of African Christianity from earliest times to the present and over the entire continent. Broadly interconfessional, historically descriptive, and exploiting the full range of oral and written records, the primary language of the *Dictionary* is English, with growing numbers of entries in the other major lingua franca of African universities: French, Portuguese and Swahili. The *Dictionary* stimulates local data-gathering and input. As a non-proprietary electronic database, it constitutes a uniquely dynamic way to maintain, amend, expand, access and disseminate information vital to an understanding of African Christianity. Being non-proprietary, it is possible for material within it to be freely reproduced locally in printed form. Being electronic, the material is simultaneously accessible to readers around the world.'[18] The project is sponsored by the Pew Charitable Trust.

The Handbook on Theological Education in Africa[19]

This project started in 2010 under the co-ordination of Isabel Apawo Phiri and Dietrich Werner. The project's focus is on the history of theological education, regional surveys on theological education, and denominational perspectives on theological education – all these in Africa. It also addresses key issues and new frontiers in African theological education, centering on mission and dialogue, Gender and HIV/AIDS, public theology, peace, justice and ecology, forms and models of theological education, selected innovative models and case studies of theological education in Africa, and networks and resources for theological education in Africa. The project addresses issues around the rapid growth of Christianity in Africa and the need for well informed and biblically sound theological education in the formation of its priests, ministers and lay church leaders. Other issues being raised in the project include the social, political and public relevance of Christian theology on the African continent.

---

[16] www.bu.edu/cgcm/research/africa/african-initiatives-in-christian-mission-book-series/ accessed 21.11.2015.
[17] Jonathan Bonk ed. *Dictionary of Africa Christian Biography*. Boston: Boston University Press.
[18] www.dacb.org/what-is-dacb.html. Accessed 21.11.2015.
[19] Isabel Apawo Phiri and Dietrich Werner. (eds) *Handbook of Theological Education in Africa*. (Oxford/Pietermaritzburg: Regnum Books International/Cluster Publication, 2013).

The project also addresses the need for working to strengthen collaboration and quality standards for theological education through the work of regional associations of theological institutions. The project calls for working to create opportunities where churches of different denominations on the continent can learn from each other as well as complementing one other.

The project is funded by the Ecumenical Theological Education (ETE) unit of the World Council of Churches, EMW Hamburg, Germany, Dan Mission Copenhagen, and Mission 21 in Basel, Switzerland.

Gender in African Christianity

While gender has been mainstreamed in most of the research projects mentioned above, the research projects of the Circle of Concerned African Women Theologians (the Circle) and Ecumenical HIV and AIDS Initiative in Africa (EHAIA) deserve special mention here because of the huge impact that their literature has had in the development of African Christianity.

The Circle of Concerned African Women Theologians

The Circle is the opportunity for women from Africa to do communal theology based on their religious, cultural and social experiences. These concerned women are engaged in theological dialogue with cultures, religions, sacred writings and oral stories that shape the African context and define the women of this continent. The mission of the Circle is to undertake research, write and publish on African issues from women's perspective. The vision of the Circle is to empower African women to contribute their critical thinking and analysis to advance current knowledge. Theology, religion and culture are the three chosen foci which are used as the framework for Circle research and publications. Between 1990 and 2015 the Circle has had five Pan-African conferences and four general co-ordinators.[20] Each Pan-African conference decides a theme for research and publications. Since the Pan-African conference of 2002, the Circle's publications has focused on women, religion and health. Among the many publications of the Circle,[21] I would highlight the following:

African Women, Religion and Health: Essays in Honour of Mercy Amba Oduyoye[22]

This book is divided into six parts that tells the story of Mercy Amba Oduyoye and deals with issues that she is very passionate about. Part 1 is entitled *Celebrating Mercy Amba Oduyoye*; Part 2 focuses on African women, the Bible and health; Part 3 on Women as Traditional Healers in Africa: Part 4 on Theological Reflections on Children and Women's Rights in Africa; Part 5 on Theological Reflection of African women's experiences of Family, Ethnicity and Sexual Health; Part 6 is a postscript, where a longstanding male friend of Mercy Oduyoye, Ogbu U. Kalu, has reflected on possible future areas of conversations between the Circle of Concerned African Women Theologians and Afro-American women theologians. The work of the Circle has been sponsored by many mission agencies including the Women's Desk, Ecumenical Theological Education, and the Ecumenical HIV/AIDS Initiative in Africa (EHAIA) of the World Council of Churches.

---

[20] Mercy Amba Oduyoye is the founder of the Circle who gave leadership of the Circle from inception of the Circle in 1989 to 1995. Musimbi Kanyoro was the Circle general coordinator during the period 1995-2002. Isabel Apawo Phiri took over from 2002 to 2007. Fulata Mbano Moyo 2007-2013. Helen Adekunbi Labeodan from 2013 to the present.

[21] Books that have been commissioned by the Circle amount to more than forty. However, Circle members in their personal capacity have written books, articles in books and journals which number over a hundred. The Circle last attempt to produce a Circle bibliography for the period 1989-2006. An updated Circle bibliography is yet to come out.

[22] Phiri, Isabel A. and Sarojini Nadar. eds. *African Women Religion and health: Essays in Honour of Mercy Amba Oduyoye.* (Maryknoll, NY: Orbis Books, 2006).

The Ecumenical HIV/AIDS Initiative in Africa (EHAIA)[23]

The EHAIA under the co-ordination of Nyambura Njoroge has done outstanding research and publications in partnership with the Circle and on its own. In my judgement, EHAIA has now taken the lead from the Circle in research and publication in addressing the issues of HIV/AIDS from a theological perspective in the context of Africa.[24] In the EHAIA Plan of Action it states that:

'WCC-EHAIA's two-pronged approach involved promoting HIV competence among churches in Africa and working with theological institutions to mainstream HIV into theological curricula. The main purpose is to transform attitudes and practices in the churches, to bring them into line with gospel values of inclusion and love.'[25] I have not singled out any one publication from EHAIA as they are all on the cutting-edge of research in African Christianity.

Conclusion

This brief survey of African theologians and scholars' contribution to African Christianity, though not exhaustive, is revealing, heart-warming and overwhelming. This leaves no-one in doubt about the fact that African theologians and scholars have done some ground-breaking work to re-root and document African Christianity, and to justify the submission that Christianity is not a religion imported to Africa and Africans, and that the Bible is an African book.

This breathtaking effort by African theologians and scholars has shown that they are focusing on issues that are of real concern to African Christians. The major concern is how much of this knowledge produced by African theologians and scholars is actually informing the theological curriculum of African theological institutions, where African church leaders are formed for the church. African theologians and scholars have a lot of work ahead of them to popularize their thinking in the African churches at grassroots level so that its impact is felt as it empowers people to eradicate some extreme social imbalances and injustices that are deeply entrenched within African societies and African Christians. One does not need a reminder that issues of gender inequality, HIV/AIDS, destructive masculinity, corruption, poverty, oppressive and repressive governance, all forms of violence against women, and socio-political and economic injustice, are all still deeply rooted in Africa. It is, therefore, hoped that the research of African theologians and scholars will contribute towards building relationships of trust in African communities.

Bibliography

Bediako, Kwame, *Christianity in Africa, The Renewal of a Non-Western Religion* (Edinburgh: Edinburgh University Press, and Maryknoll, NY: Orbis Books, 1995).

---

[23] For more information on the publications of EHAIA go to https://www.oikoumene.org/en/what-we-do/ehaia/activity_news. Accessed 22.112015.

[24] Some of the publications of EHAIA include the following: Musa W. Dube. "Culture, Gender and HIV/AIDS: Understanding and Acting on the Issues," in Musa W. Dube (ed). 2003. *HIV/AIDS and the Curriculum: Methods of Integrating HIV/AIDS in Theological Programmes*. (Geneva: World Council of Churches, 2003); Musa Dube (ed). *Africa Praying: A Handbook on HIV/AIDS Sensitive Sermon Guidelines and Liturgy*, 209-221. Geneva: WCC Publications, 2003; Ezra Chitando and Sophia Chirongoma (eds). *Justice Not Silence: Churches facing sexual and gender-based violence* (Stellenbosch: Sun Press, 2013); Ezra Chitando and Nontando Hadebe (eds). *Compassionate Circles: African Women Theologians Facing HIV*. (Geneva: WCC, 2009); Ezra Chitando, *Troubled but Not Destroyed: African Theology in Dialogue with HIV and AIDS*. (Geneva: WCC, 2009). Ezra Chitando, *Living with Hope: African Churches and HIV/AIDS*. (Geneva: WCC, 2007); Ezra Chitando, *Acting in Hope: African Churches and HIV/AIDS*. (Geneva: WCC, 2007).

[25] Plan of Action, Ecumenical HIV And AIDS Initiatives And Advocacy. Responding to the HIV and AIDS Pandemic, 2014-2021, page 6.

Chitando Ezra and Sophia Chirongoma (eds), *Justice Not Silence: Churches facing sexual and gender-based violence* (Stellenbosch, RSA: Sun Press, 2013).
Kanyoro, Musimbi R.A., and Nyambura J. Njoroge (eds), *Groaning in Faith: African Women in the Household of God* (Nairobi: Acton, 1996).
Phiri, Isabel A. and Sarojini Nadar (eds), *African Women Religion and Health: Essays in Honour of Mercy Amba Oduyoye* (Maryknoll, NY: Orbis Books, 2006).
Ranger, O. Terrence (ed), *Evangelical Christianity in Africa*. (Oxford: Oxford University Press, 2008).

(2) Early African Christianity

James Tengatenga

Introduction

In talking about African Christianity today, one hears about post-voyages-of-discovery (sic) Christianity and mostly about nineteenth-century missionary activity and its fruit in sub-Saharan Africa, and about recent movements and the phenomenal growth of the church. But until recently little was done to relate early North African Christianity to the wider story of Christianity in Africa. In recent years this deficiency has begun to be corrected. Thomas Oden, Kwame Bediako, Lamin Sanneh and Benezet Bujo have attempted the mammoth task of this recovery of the story of Christianity in Africa. Is the lack of attention because nineteenth-century mission work has some connections with the western authority over the continent and other parts of the world so that North African Christianity got little press? Was the neglect of early Christianity in Africa the result of earlier Greek and Latin authority?

The story of Christianity in Africa cannot be told and fully appreciated until we begin to appreciate the first thousand years of Christianity on the continent as part of the story of the first thousand years of Christianity. Indeed, perhaps one-tenth of all Christians in the eleventh century lived in Africa, a proportion not reached again until the 1960s.[26] Africa's relatively small contribution to today's worldwide theological discourse belies the very significant contribution of African theologians of the early church. The story of theological education as we know it cannot be fully appreciated if one does not take into account the school at Alexandria,[27] the fine theologians it produced, and the other great theologians of North Africa. Christian spirituality in its monastic form has roots in the African soil. Africa has its fair share of martyrs of antiquity as it has those of today. Church-state relations were played out on the continent from its inception, and no less a theologian than St Augustine of Hippo grappled with those relationships in his seminal *City of God*. Just as in any parts of the world where Christianity has spread, the interface of Christ and culture has always been a key, make-or-break issue in the extent of its influence.

Outline histories of the time have been written by eminent scholars, but more detailed histories that connect all of Africa have yet to be written. The aim of this essay is to highlight the themes that demonstrate the influence of early African Christianity on Christianity today and thus will help us appreciate, both now and in the future, the place and role of African Christianity in the first millennium. Africa is famous for its fervour and robustness in its expression of the Christian faith, but one rarely gets to hear of its robust engagement in theological discourse. This situation has led to a significant loss to theological language and method. If the global reality is to live up to its name, we Africans will need to rise to the challenge, claim our place, and – on the basis of our history – claim respect in worldwide Christian discourse. This outline is therefore a teaser for claiming the history and thus the pedigree of African Christianity and African theology. In order to tell this story in this brief space, I will first give a very concise historical summary. I will then proceed to outline the contribution of early African Christianity under some select themes. I believe that this approach will give context to the themes. I will conclude with a summary gleaning of the implications of early African Christianity for present-day Christianity, and particularly for African Christianity.

---

[26] P.J. Jenkins, *The Lost History of Christianity* (New York: HarperCollins, 2009), 4.

[27] The School of Alexandria in antiquity was a collection of groups of teachers who gathered students around them for teaching; over time, it developed into a formal collection of institutions.

Historical Summary[28]

> Libyan Christianity was founded in a nexus of cultures bordering on Egypt, Ethiopia and ancient Nubia, modern Sudan, ancient Darfur (part of Cush), Chad, and Roman Byzacena (southern Tunisia). Ancient Libyan Christianity had close affinities with Coptic Egypt and Ethiopia, and with the Meroe kingdom in Nubia (Sudan). They belonged intentionally to the community of worldwide believers who held to orthodox, apostolic, classical teaching.[29]

So says Thomas Oden as he begins his study of early Libyan Christianity. Such is the pedigree not only of early Libyan Christianity but of early African Christianity as a whole. In early Roman times, Africa was a set of Latin-speaking provinces in North Africa; it did not include Egypt, which was considered separate from Africa thus defined. It covered what is known today as the Maghreb. Geographically, the area under consideration is North Africa from the Red Sea to the Atlantic Ocean, and from Chad about as far south as the present tenth parallel through northern Mali to Mauritania, i.e. the area covered by the Sahara Desert. Ancient Egypt was the area that today includes Egypt, Sudan, Ethiopia, Eritrea, and Djibouti.

Roman Africa had Jews living in it who were there as refugees or traders. Some of those Jews brought in Christianity. As we know, Christianity began as a Jewish sect. We first hear of this part of Africa in the accounts of the crucifixion of Jesus, when Simon of Cyrene is made to carry Jesus' cross. In Acts 2, people from these parts are included among those present on the day of Pentecost. There were many influences from the Nile valley. The earliest recorded and extant records of Christianity in the region are documents of the persecutions in 180. This is the church of the three African catholic popes: Victor I (189-198), Melchiades or Miltiades (310/311-314), and Gelasius (492-496). It is also the church of Tertullian (160-225), Cyprian (c. 200-258), and Augustine (354-430), who taught and wrote about the faith in Latin. It was also the church in which there were Donatists and Montanists to whom these leaders responded in their writings. Because the church operated in Latin, it tended to be the church of the well-to-do, the educated, and urban dwellers, and so less the church of the common people. Most of the population was rural and spoke Berber and other local languages. Augustine is said to have valued and used some Punic.[30] In 411, the emperor (according to Marcellinus) also weighed in on the Donatist controversy in favour of the Catholics and exiled the Donatists. In 430, when the Vandals took over Carthage, they imposed their Arian form of Christianity. It was not until 533, when Emperor Justinian of Constantinople reconquered Carthage, that catholic Christianity was restored. The controversies and the domination by the elite adversely affected the strength of the church such that, when other forces arose, it was quickly overrun. The advent of Islam in the seventh century was a big blow. Prophetess Kahina resisted the invasion from the 690s until 703, when the area was lost to Islam. Her sons decided to 'convert and make common cause with the Arabs'.[31]

Egypt also had Jews, and some of them were also in Jerusalem at Pentecost. Mark the Evangelist is the one who is credited with introducing Christianity and also establishing the Christian school at Alexandria. Egypt is the place where the Septuagint (the Greek translation of the Old Testament) was produced, probably beginning around 250 BC. The earliest records of the church in Egypt are the writings of

---

[28] Thomas Oden has a helpful chronology in his *How Africa Shaped the Christian Mind* (Downers Grove, Ill.: IVP, 2007), 158-97; for much of this section I rely on Diarmaid MacCulloch, *Christianity: The First Three Thousand Years* (New York: Viking, 2009).

[29] Thomas Oden, *Early Libyan Christianity* (Downers Grove, Ill.: IVP, 2011), 21.

[30] Bengt Sundkler and Christopher Steed, *A History of the Church in Africa* (Cambridge: Cambridge University Press, 2000), 26. They make reference to W. M. Green, "Augustine's Use of Punic," in *Semitic and Oriental Studies: A Volume Presented to William Popper*, ed. Walter J. Fischel, University of California Publications in Semitic Philology 11 (Berkeley: University of California Press, 1951).

[31] Sundkler and Steed, *A History of the Church in Africa*, 29.

Demetrius of Alexandria (bishop 189-232), who in 189 claimed jurisdiction over all Egypt.[32] This is the church of Clement of Alexandria (150-215), Origen (185-254), Dionysius (d. 264), Athanasius (296-373), Cyril of Alexandria (d. 444), and Anthony the father of asceticism and monasticism (c. 251-356). The Egyptian church was a key player in the formulation of Christological and Trinitarian theology. The controversies that ensued led to the parting of ways of the Constantinopolitan church and the Coptic church. Sundkler and Steed describe the situation as follows:

> Very soon the Coptic Church could answer in kind denouncing Constantinople and the Chalcedonians as 'Diophysites' and 'Melchites' (the Emperor's men), 'running dogs of the imperial regime'. This led to renewed persecutions hitting the Unionite community. On the other hand, this outrage helped to solidify Egyptian nationalism built on the Coptic language and tradition, the Unionite doctrine and enthusiastic monastic leadership.[33]

Among other things, these controversies weakened the church to the extent that when the Islamic invasion happened in the seventh century, it could not be fully withstood. The Islamic rulers initially allowed Christians the freedom to worship as long as they paid the head tax (*jizya*), but later there were conversions under pressure. During the Crusades, Christians were of course suspect and their numbers dwindled. In 600, there were one hundred sees, in 700 only seventy, and by 1400 only forty. Currently, there are twenty-five Coptic sees in Egypt, two in Sudan, and one in Jerusalem.[34]

It was from the Alexandrian base that the church spread southwards. It is believed that monks and refugees brought Christianity to Nubia (the area covering modern Sudan and South Sudan). In 543, a priest by the name of Julian asked Theodora, Emperor Justinian's wife, to send missionaries to Nubia. She decided to send Julian there. Before long he had baptized the king and the aristocracy, and had constituted a bishopric of Philae. Thus three kingdoms of Nubia – namely, Nobatia (350-650), Makouria (570), and Alodia (580) – became Christian. Nobatia and Alodia were Unionist while Makouria was Melchite. When in 641 the Arabs attacked and defeated Nubia, an agreement was reached with the Christian kings to maintain Christianity at the cost of 360 slaves annually (later revised to every three years) to be given to the Arabs and the tending of the mosque in the capital.[35] Kings played a significant role in the maintenance of Christianity. King Merkurios (697-c 722), together with Bishop Paulos, rebuilt the cathedral at Faras. King Georgios I (860-920) was considered the protector of the Patriarch of Alexandria and the Coptic Church during the time of Arab pressure. Georgios II was approached by the Ethiopian king to send a canonically consecrated bishop to head the church there.[36] Christian influence from Nubia extended not only eastwards but also westwards to the area of modern-day Darfur.

The story in Acts about the Ethiopian eunuch comes to mind for many when Ethiopian Christianity is mentioned. It is also possible that other people brought Christianity to Ethiopia. The area referred to in the Bible is the Meroe Kingdom, which is in modern-day Sudan. Two young companions of Meropius (Frumentius and Adesius) from Tyre were rescued after a shipwreck and taken to King Ella-Amida of Aksum. They rose in rank in that society to the extent that, when the king died and his son Ezana was considered too young to rule, his mother asked these two to assist. They were Christians. When they were finally freed, they decided to go back to their home in Syria via Alexandria. Their plan was to ask Patriarch Athanasius for a bishop for Aksum. Frumentius was made bishop between 341 and 346.[37] Ezana had

[32] Harvey J. Sindima, *Drums of Redemption: An Introduction to African Christianity* (Westport, Conn.: Greenwood, 1994), 4.
[33] Sundkler and Steed, *A History of the Church in Africa*, 16.
[34] Sundkler and Steed, *A History of the Church in Africa*, 17.
[35] Sundkler and Steed, *A History of the Church in Africa*, 31-32.
[36] Sundkler and Steed, *A History of the Church in Africa*, 32.
[37] Sundkler and Steed, *A History of the Church in Africa*, 35.

embraced Christianity. Thus began the tradition of the Ethiopian bishops being appointed by Alexandria. The church spread to Tigray, where the churches were built like those at Aksum and the rock-hewn ones of Lalibela. Monasticism began when the 'Nine Saints' of Debre Damo church arrived in the area at the end of the fifth century. There was also a strong literary and liturgical movement in this church, which took Christianity to the masses. They translated patristic texts into the local language, Ge'ez. Famous among these texts were those by Cyril of Alexandria, which form the foundation of Ethiopian theology and faith. Matta Libanos (called the Apostle of Eritrea) translated the Gospel of Matthew into Ge'ez.

Kings and monks were the key agents of the spread of faith and its maintenance both locally and further afield. Between 520 and 525, King Kaleb (510-558) came to the rescue of Christian communities in southern Arabia and ruled Himyar.[38] In the eighth century, Christians moved southwards with their Ge'ez language. When Gudit, the Agew chieftainess, revolted against Aksum, Alexandria did not send bishops to Ethiopia for decades. This deficiency resulted in some decline, but the church did not disappear as it did in other parts, even though it was surrounded by Muslim states. Kings continued to play a significant role in the maintenance of the faith.

Martyrdom

As the African Tertullian said, 'The blood of the martyrs is the seed of the church.'[39] There has always been a high price to pay for living the Christian faith, if Jesus Christ himself is anything to go by. To stand for Christ has always been a costly exercise and continues to be for many who would dare challenge the status quo because of their faith. One is almost tempted to say that martyrdom is the way of Christian witness in Africa from the word go.

The early Christians of Libya and Egypt did not seek martyrdom.[40] They sought to witness to the truth that God the Father is the only true God and Jesus their only Lord. Because of this conviction, they refused to offer sacrifices to Roman gods and thus drew the ire of the emperors, whose fury spared no-one, male or female, bishop or layperson. Wave after wave of persecution began under Marcus Aurelius (161-180) and was followed by further persecution under Septimius Severus (202-203), Decius and Valerian (249-259), and Diocletian, Galerius and Maximian (303-310). Martyrdom became a way of demonstrating one's faith, but not in a 'martyr syndrome' kind of way. They could run away – as many did, including bishops. But many did eventually surrender to a martyr's death as the only way they knew to give witness to their faith. The most famous runaway was Bishop Cyprian, who ran away during the persecution by Emperor Decius and hid, but later (under Emperor Valerian) in 258 he gave himself up for martyrdom.[41] This situation caused divisions in the church, as those who glorified the courage of martyrs believed that those who ran away and/or those who handed over the Scriptures or recanted their faith to recommit to it later were traitors to the faith and were not worthy to be numbered among them. This was the controversy between those that came to be known as *Traditores*[42] and the Donatists.[43]

The account of the martyrdom of twelve North Africans about 180 is recorded in *The Acts of the Scillitan Martyrs*. It was not only leaders who faced this persecution but also ordinary citizens, both male and female, the famous ones being the well-to-do Vibia Perpetua and her servant and friend Felicitas, who

---

[38] Sundkler and Steed, *A History of the Church in Africa,* 37.
[39] Tertullian, *Apology*, 50.
[40] Oden, *Early Libyan Christianity*, 16-17.
[41] Eusebius, *Church History*, 8.13.7.
[42] *Traditores* were those who handed over the Scriptures to save themselves from martyrdom.
[43] The Donatists were those Christians who believed that only those Christians who had not handed over the Scriptures during the Diocletian persecution nor recanted their faith were true Christians. They would not accept those who then repented and came back to the faith as true saints.

were martyred together in 203. They were thrown to the animals but were finished off by gladiators' swords. During the same persecution, seven men and three other women were killed. In the fourth century, Moses the Black was martyred by Berbers when his monastery was attacked in 405.

Peter Martyr was Bishop of Alexandria from 300 to 311. He was beheaded on the orders of Emperor Maximian. Tradition has it that when the order was given, a crowd of Christians prevented the soldiers from killing him by offering themselves to die for him. It is said that he then devised a plan to be taken out of the crowd's sight for the soldiers to do it without the crowd, which they duly did.

In the seventh century, as Islam began to spread from the Middle East westwards, occasional persecutions such as that in tenth-century Egypt under Caliph el Hakim when 3,000 churches were destroyed, led many Christians to choose between recanting Christianity and embracing Islam. The weakened state of the church due to theological infighting led to fragmentation, which in turn left the church vulnerable to being overrun by more organized political forces. This fact would also suggest that, just as persecution led to the spread and strength of the church, it also led to its decline. Nevertheless, since the blood of martyrs is the seed that does not die but germinates in opportune times, persecution and even subsequent decline did not stop the renewal of the Christian faith in those lands that had been overrun. What is significant here is that the example of this early church continued to inspire African Christians in successive generations, including our own. Many Christians have given up their lives as they proclaim the gospel as evangelists, missionaries, or those who fought and continue to fight against unjust structures by speaking truth to power.

Theology (Church Fathers)

A significant contribution of early North African Christianity was in the area of theology. It should not come as a surprise to many sub-Saharan post-nineteenth-century Christians that Africans have made significant contributions to theology. Names like Augustine, Athanasius, Cyril of Alexandria, Clement of Alexandria, Tertullian, Cyprian, and Origen are like a 'Who's Who' of theological giants, and they are all Africans. The popular anti-intellectual evangelicalism prevalent in most of Africa today is alien to early African Christianity. As the faith encountered the Greek language and philosophy outside its Semitic birthplace, it came to be articulated in a different idiom. Alexandria in Egypt was the leading centre of Greek philosophical thought and learning. As such, it is no surprise that some of the early (and seminal) expressions of Christian thought in Greek philosophical language were developed here.

The Catechetical School is said to have been founded by St Mark, who appointed St Justus as its first leader. Justus later became Bishop of Alexandria. Some authorities say that the School was established in the second century. It was located in the heart of the intellectual activity in the near East where there were three other centres of learning: the Museum, the Serapeum, and the Sebastion. It thus became the first Christian school of higher learning. It dealt with the interface between Greek culture and philosophy and the Christian faith, and it taught a wide range of other subjects. We would say that it taught philosophy (both religious and moral), systematics, and biblical interpretation (the allegorical method). Clement of Alexandria and Origen both taught there. It produced many a church leader and bishop. As Philip Schaff has observed, 'There the religious life of Palestine and the intellectual culture of Greece commingled and prepared the way for the first school of theology which aimed at a philosophic comprehension and vindication of the truths of revelation.'[44] Thus it can be seen that African Christianity is not averse to intellectual pursuit and rigorous enquiry. So the idea of a university that many African churches are espousing now is like a recovery of this heritage.

[44] Quoted in "An Introduction to the School of Alexandria" on the Coptic Orthodox Network website: www.copticchurch.net/topics/patrology/schoolofalex/I-Intro/chapter1.html.

It should not come as a surprise, then, that the formulation and articulation of the Christian doctrines of God the Father, the Son and, the Holy Spirit were heavily influenced by the products of this school. Athanasius and Cyril are famous in the Christological controversies of the fourth and fifth centuries. Even the development of Mariology (especially the doctrine of the *theotokos*) is heavily influenced by Egyptian thought of the early centuries of Christianity. As such, the African imprint on the first four ecumenical councils is indisputable and should remind us of the role of African Christianity in the quest for church unity with correct doctrine. Notwithstanding the imperial (Greek and Roman) undertones of leadership in those historical processes, it is our heritage. The Coptic and Ethiopian churches were even willing to reject this leadership when proudly defending Cyril's teaching and opposing the Christological definition of the Council of Chalcedon in 451.[45]

As one follows the Christological developments of the third through the fifth centuries, one is led to an appreciation not only of African leadership and engagement in the formulation of our understanding of God but also of African contributions to the language of theology. In the new globalization it would be salutary for African Christianity to make fresh contributions to the language of theological discourse. Theology is not the domain of western thought and language only, as it was during Augustine's time. Christian theology, if it is to be truly catholic, will need to be influenced by the many languages of local Christianities, and not least by African ones.

Before moving to another aspect of early African Christianity, let me briefly highlight some of the individual theologians' contributions to Christianity as we know it. Space will not allow an in-depth discussion of those contributions. For our purposes here, it will suffice to give some bibliography and mention some theological concepts that these theologians contributed.

Clement of Alexandria (150-215) was a Christian philosopher and headed the School of Alexandria before he became Bishop of Alexandria. Among his works of note is his trilogy consisting of *Protrepticus* (exhortations intended to lead to conversion), *Paedagogus* (on Christian life and manners), and *Stromata* (miscellanies, which bear some relation to his proposed third volume *Didascalus,* on the Christian teacher), and *Quis dives salvetur?* (on Christianity and riches).

Tertullian (160-225) was a lay theologian from Roman Africa, a lawyer by training. He was an intrepid apologist for the Christian faith and defended Christianity against heretics, modalists, and pagans. He is the one who coined the term 'Trinity' to refer to the relationship among Father, Son, and Holy Spirit. In his later life he became attracted to Montanism and was influenced by it to the extent that some believed that he actually became one of them. His works include *Prescription against Heretics*, *On the Flesh of Christ*, *Against Praxeas*, and *On Baptism.*

Origen (185-254) was Clement's student at Alexandria and later succeeded him as head of the School. He was a lay theologian. Even though he was later clandestinely ordained, he did not exercise that ministry. He is considered the first theological systematician and a pre-eminent biblical scholar of the allegorical method. He embraced asceticism to the extent that he even castrated himself in order to be free from carnal desires. He was accused of subordinating the Son to the Father in his treatment of the relationships within the Godhead. Some of his works are the *Hexapla*, *Against Celsus*, and *On First Principles.* One of his famous students was Gregory Thaumaturgus of Cappadocia (c. 213-c. 270).

Dionysius of Alexandria (d. 264) was a noted administrator and biblical scholar. He was also famous for his stand against Egyptian millennialism.

Cyprian (d. 258) was a bishop theologian whose teaching shaped western understanding of the episcopacy in terms of the centrality of the office as a symbol of unity and also the idea of the collegiality of the episcopate. He is considered *the* pre-eminent Latin Christian writer after Augustine and Jerome.

---

[45] Statements on agreed Christology with the Roman Catholics in the 1970s, with Orthodoxy in the 1980s, and with Anglicans in 2014 have brought the churches closer together.

Athanasius (296-373) was yet another head of the School of Alexandria who became Bishop of Alexandria. He is most famous for his defence of the full divinity of Christ against the teaching of Arius. He taught that the Son is co-equal with the Father. His works include *Against Arius* and *On the Incarnation.*

Augustine (354-430) was Bishop of Hippo and a public theologian *par excellence*. More than anyone else he shaped western Christian thinking. 'Many of our experiential and theological categories – guilt, sin, grace, anxiety about sexuality, freedom, predestination, just war, selfhood – owe something to him.'[46] He stood against the Donatists and against other false teachings of his day. Some of his famous works are *On Christian Doctrine, Enchiridion, On the Trinity, City of God, Against Pelagius*, and *Confessions*.

Cyril (d. 444) was Bishop of Alexandria and a leading apologist for orthodoxy during the Christological controversies against Nestorius and Novatus. He was significant in expounding the understanding of Mary as *Theotokos*. He is highly honoured in the Ethiopian church, where his writings were translated and used for teaching the faith.

Leadership (African Popes)[47]

The fact that there were bishops in both Alexandria and Carthage is not much to write home about except that they were equal in status to other bishops in both the East and the West and participated as equals (if not significant leaders) in the early councils of the Church. An important point of distinction between Egypt and Carthage is that while Egypt had a Patriarch, the Libyan Church had none even though for all practical intents the bishops functioned like one and stood their ground (even against the Bishop of Rome) when needs arose. The significant fact of note during this period, is that the African Church not only produced great theologians but that it also produced three popes: Victor I (St Victor) who was Pope 189-199, Melchiades (Miltiades) from 311-314 and Gelasius from 492-496. It was an African pope from Libya who called the First Synod of Rome.

Victor I (d. 199) was the first bishop of Rome born in the Roman province of Africa. His residence was at Leptis Magna in Libya.[48] He was also the first pope to popularize the use of Latin by writing in Latin. In addition, he used papal authority to enforce conformity to the western tradition during the controversy over the date of Easter (the Quartodeciman controversy) between East and West. Victor excommunicated Theodotus for teaching that Christ was a mere human being (dynamic monarchianism).

Melchiades or Miltiades (d. 314) was of Berber descent. He was Pope when Christianity became an accepted religion in the Roman Empire. Constantine gave him the Lateran Palace as the papal residence. He condemned the Donatists and consequently alienated himself from Carthaginian Christians.

Gelasius (d. 496), who was also of Berber descent, is noted for spelling out the teaching that civil and priestly power are both of divine origin but independent of each other, and that priestly power is above civil. He is also famous for the idea that the pope is beyond criticism when he speaks from Peter's chair (*ex cathedra*). He also opposed withholding the cup from the laity at the Eucharist.

---

[46] Anthony J. Chvala-Smith, "Augustine of Hippo," in *Empire and the Christian Tradition: New Readings of Classical Theologians*, eds. Kwok Pui-Lan, Don H. Compier, and Joerg Rieser (Minneapolis: Fortress, 2007), 79.
[47] This section relies on R. P. McBrien, *Lives of the Popes* (New York: HarperCollins, 2000).
[48] Oden, *Early Libyan Christianity*, 39.

Asceticism/Monasticism[49]

Besides great bishops and theologians, the early African Church pioneered asceticism and monasticism. As history would have it, many Eastern theologians and bishops were monastics whose spirituality and apostolate are rooted in African asceticism and grew out of African desert spirituality.

Anthony, born near Memphis (c. 251) to parents of means, began the movement, having been inspired by Jesus' words in Matthew 19:21. He sold the family property, put some towards his baby sister's care, and gave the rest to the poor. He then went into the desert to lead an ascetic life. Many followed him. He visited incarcerated confessors and also walked with them to their martyrdom. He was also friends with some of the Alexandrian theologians who sought his advice, Athanasius being the most famous of them. His sister also ended up choosing the cloistered life. He died in 356.

Anthony led others to solo ascetic lives in the desert. A contemporary of his whose name was Pachomius, born in 292, founded communal monastic life, in which he lived until his death in 346. Influenced by a local monk named Palaemon, he built a monastery at Tabennisi in 325. The movement quickly grew to nine cloisters with close to 7,000 monks. As with early African Christianity in general, this movement did not grow southward beyond Ethiopia.

Another desert father worthy of note is St Moses the Black, born in 330. He was an Ethiopian who was converted from his old life as a leader of murderous bandits at Skete, near Alexandria. He lived among desert monks for years before he was ordained deacon and later priest. His life influenced other bandits to convert as well. He died during a raid on his community by Berber brigands in 405.

John Cassian (360-435) is famous for taking monasticism to southern Gaul and influencing western spirituality. He was a product of the desert monasticism at Skete. Monasticism flourished in the Near East and among the Greeks. Most of the Greek church fathers were monks. Irish spirituality also has its origins in African desert spirituality.[50]

Gospel and Culture

The question of the interface between the gospel and culture dates back to the early church of the apostles and the expansion of the church among Gentiles. As we have seen in this chapter, the Christian faith was spread to Africa through traders, refugees, and other Jews. Egypt was heavily influenced by Greek thought and language, while Carthage and the rest of Roman Africa were more influenced by Latin. The use of Berber, Punic, and other languages was very limited in the church of Roman Africa, and this limitation had an adverse effect on the spread and staying power of Christianity in those parts. For better or worse, African theologians were adept in adopting the *lingua franca* (either Greek or Latin) and becoming leading teachers in those languages.

The Alexandrian experience has multiple nuances. Apart from the fact that Greek was the *lingua franca*, there was the matter of talking about a Jewish faith using Greek philosophy. This problem was not unique to Christianity, as the Jewish philosopher Philo had become famous for using Greek philosophy to talk about the Jewish faith. So it is not just the language but also philosophical categories that have stayed with us in Christian theology. Another twist was the fact that the Egyptian church also kept the Coptic language alive and used it to do theology, by contrast with Roman Africa, where local languages did not feature in theological discourse. Part of the reason for the Christological controversy concerning the way that Egyptians talked about the natures of Christ was connected to the use of language and concepts that

---

[49] For this section see P. H. Gorg, *The Desert Fathers: Anthony and the Beginnings of Monasticism*, tr. M. J. Miller (San Francisco: Ignatius Press, 2011).

[50] See Oden, *How Africa Shaped the Christian Mind*, 73-77.

differed from the Greek Constantinopolitan ones. Further, the development of understanding Mary as *theotokos* was also influenced by Coptic culture.

Further south, the use of Ge'ez in the Ethiopian church also helped the spread of the faith and the owning of the faith by the local people. A further characteristic of the inclusion of local culture in the Ethiopian church, in addition to the use of Ge'ez and Amharic, was the adaptation of traditional open worship, the use of drums, percussion, and strings. Ethiopian and Nubian types of architecture were also featured. The links to Judaism through the story of Solomon and the Queen of Sheba also encouraged Jewish influence on Ethiopian Christianity.

Church and State

Martyrdom is an example of how the empire (state) reacted to the church in early African Christianity. The Constantinian settlement brought in a favourable state of affairs to the extent that the emperor even gave the Lateran Palace to the Pope. In addition, various emperors took a keen interest in the state of the church both for reasons of faith and for the sake of peace in the empire. This interest took the form of the emperors getting involved in mediating between different groups and even sponsoring some of the early church's councils, the Donatist controversy being one of many examples.

The establishment of Christianity in Aksum had a lot to do with the king, and in fact it was King Ezana who asked for a bishop from Alexandria. As already mentioned, in Nubia it was also the kings who were instrumental in the establishment of Christianity.

In the prevailing atmosphere of the times, with bishops and popes beginning to compete in the exercise of power, it became important for the church to spell out the relationship between church and state. Augustine took it upon himself to attempt an explication of that relationship in his *City of God*, which became in later years the basis of the concept of two kingdoms that Martin Luther and others espoused. It is the same with the 'just war' theory, which Thomas Aquinas is famous for explicating.

The seventh century came with a new phenomenon in the interface between religion and politics, and that was Islam. The new religion that had begun in the Near East began to spread through conquest, takeover, and other arrangements of coercion and assimilation. As already noted, the emergence of Islam created new dynamics of relationship. In Egypt the changed situation resulted in a minority Coptic Church. Ethiopia was surrounded by Islamic states, and most of Roman Africa was completely overrun. This is in no way an attempt to simplify the situation but rather to record the effects of the new religion that came with a political dynamic of a new kind.[51] Roman emperors had persecuted Christians on the basis of religion, and African kings of Aksum and Nubia used their power to expand the influence of the Christian faith. As has been noted, Roman emperors got involved in some of the controversies and councils of the early church. The constant evolution of church-state relations in early African Christianity continues today in ever-changing circumstances.

Conclusion

The foregoing has demonstrated that Christianity in Africa is as old as Christianity itself. There are many lessons that can be gleaned from early African Christianity for today's African Christianity. African asceticism and monasticism not only gave birth to Christian monasticism everywhere but also was influential in Islamic morality, prayer, and piety.[52]

---

[51] For the interface of Christianity with Islam, see Oden, *How Africa Shaped the Christian Mind*, 137-142; his *Early Libyan Christianity,* 44-45; and C. J. Speel II, "The Disappearance of Christianity from North Africa in the Wake of the Rise of Islam," *Church History* 29, no. 4 (1960): 379-397.

[52] Oden, *How Africa Shaped the Christian Mind*, 39.

Martyrdom, truth, and justice – speaking truth to power – have been hallmarks of Christian witness in Africa from the word go, and they continue to be. Cosiness to centres of power has had mixed effects on the church and will no doubt continue to do so. The church in Africa has to be constantly on guard against using state authority to settle matters of faith and religious authority, as Malawi knows all too well with our experience of the persecution of the Jehovah's Witnesses in the 1960s and 1970s. The Zambian experience of the Chiluba presidency, which declared Zambia a Christian nation, has to come to terms with the fact that such declarations do not negate the secular nature of modern government and do not take cognizance of the fact that we live in a religiously plural society. The public sphere is more and more a contested space in a way that we have to grapple with. Fighting within and among Christians over dogma and denominationalism creates strange bedfellows, weakens the church, and has the potential (as it did in early African Christianity) to spell the beginning of the end for the church in many parts of the continent. The fact that there continues to be a turf contest between Christianity and Islam on the continent, as it has been since the seventh century, pits two religions against each other vis-a-vis the state and the public sphere. There must be a better way, and Christianity on the continent has the wherewithal to deal with that reality. To do so will require a refusal to be enslaved to the historical evils of the relationship between the two religions.

The fact that once upon a time there were African popes and significant theologians is a matter of pride for Africa. There have been few African world leaders in Christianity, of late, however. Certainly the rise of the global village has meant that everyone has a chance to take a turn in the leadership of some world bodies. It should not come as a surprise or even be newsworthy when Africans are leaders in global Christianity.

The interface between the gospel and culture, and the employment of African languages, have always been a challenge to the African Church. The theologians we looked at all employed either Greek or Latin. Granted, those were the *linguae francae* of the day, but that situation has continued to enslave us. Coptic and Ge'ez proved to be the exception in the early church. As this history demonstrates, Africans are adept at adopting hegemonic language and becoming masters in it. Latin translations of the New Testament were in Africa before they arrived in Europe,[53] establishing Latin's pre-eminence, even apart from the way Tertullian and Augustine used the language. What we have failed to do effectively is to use some of our many African idioms to communicate Christian truth. Africa needs to rise to the challenge and bring the gifts in our languages and idiom into theological discourse. What is surprising in some of the new expressions of Christianity on the continent is the choice to use English as the medium of communication, which is counter to the lessons from early African Christianity. Could this choice lead to the same situation as happened with Latin in Roman Africa?

African idioms are relevant not only for international and ecumenical discourse but also as means to carry out mission on the continent itself. African-initiated churches have a lot to teach the mission-initiated churches in this regard. Part of the reason for the success of the new Evangelical/Pentecostal forms of Christianity may be due to the resonance of that spirituality with some residual and current African impetuous fervour that takes seriously the reality and spirituality of the meta-world.[54]

Oden observes:

> What was first firmly established in the Nile valley and the Maghreb became later widely confirmed as classic consensual Christian teaching. The seeds for the scriptural interpretations that became common Christian teaching were first woven on the African continent. *The major movement of intellectual history in the second and third centuries was South to North, Africa to Europe, Africa to Asia.* This is markedly counter-intuitive to

[53] Oden, *Early Libyan Christianity,* 39.

[54] See Sundkler and Steed, *A History of the Church in Africa,* 22, for a comment on Montanism and its similarity to recent Christian movements in Africa.

> the modern mind... African Christians today have an opportunity to see their present religion from the perspective of two thousand uninterrupted years of classic Christian teaching.[55]

There is a lot more of the history of African Christianity that has still to be told. The glaring omission continues to be that of women's stories. As we have seen, the implications and imperatives of that history are immense for today's African Christians.

Bibliography

Burns, J. Payout Jr., and Robin M. Jensen. *Roman Africa: The Development of its Practices and Beliefs.* Grand Rapids, Mich.: Eerdmans, 2014.

Faraji, S. *The Roots of Nubian Christianity Uncovered: The Triumph of the Last Pharaoh.* Trenton, N.J.: Africa World Press, 2012.

Gorg, P. *The Desert Fathers: Anthony and the Beginnings of Monasticism.* Translated by M. J. Miller. San Francisco: Ignatius, 2011.

Jenkins, P. J. *The Lost History of Christianity.* New York: HarperCollins, 2009.

MacCulloch, D. *Christianity: The First Three Thousand Years.* New York: Viking, 2009.

McBrien, R. P. *Lives of the Popes.* New York: HarperCollins, 2000.

Oden, T.C. *Early Libyan Christianity.* Downers Grove, Ill.: IVP, 2011.

Oden, T.C. *How Africa Shaped the Christian Mind.* Downers Grove, Ill.: IVP, 2007.

Sindima, H. J. *Drums of Redemption.* Westport, Conn.: Greenwood, 1994.

Sundkler, B., and S. Steed. *A History of the Church in Africa.* Cambridge: Cambridge University Press, 2000.

[55] Oden, *Early Libyan Christianity*, 38, 40; italics are in the original.

(3) AFRICAN CHRISTIANITY IN PRE-COLONIAL TIMES

David Tonghou Ngong

Introduction

African Christianity has often existed under the shadow of colonialism.[1] This is a fact that may be clouded by the way the study of African Christianity may be structured. Given that it is the experience of western colonialism that has significantly marked contemporary Africa, the study of African history in general and African Christianity in particular may be periodized based on this colonial experience. African history is sometimes studied in terms of ancient or pre-colonial, colonial, and post-colonial experiences.[2] This periodization is sometimes taken over into the study of African Christianity. In this scheme of things, early African Christianity may be seen as lying outside the colonial experience. However, as we saw in the previous chapter, early African Christianity was significantly impacted by Roman colonialism and Greek culture. As we shall see in the current chapter, what we call pre-colonial African Christianity also includes elements of western colonial experiences in Africa. It is therefore quite problematic to speak of pre-colonial African Christianity because there is very little in the history of African Christianity that has not been impacted by the colonial experience.[3]

It is perhaps because of the recognition of the complexity of speaking of a pre-colonial African Christianity that works on the subject such as Sanneh's *West African Christianity*, Isichei's *A History of Christianity in Africa*, and Sundkler and Stead's *A History of the Church in Africa* do not use this method of periodization. After dealing with the churches that emerged in Africa under Greco-Roman influences, these scholars go on to look at what they see as the first iterations of western Christianity in Africa in what Isichei, Sundkler and Stead call the 'Middle Years' or 'Middle Ages', respectively, and Sanneh calls 'The Early Pioneers'. This period includes developments that took place in North African, Nubian, Egyptian, and Ethiopian Christianity after the rise of Islam but especially focuses on the spread of the church in sub-Saharan Africa, from the late fifteenth to the eighteenth century. This period saw the arrival and fizzling of Christianity in many parts of sub-Saharan Africa. For most of sub-Saharan Africa, this period can be seen

---

[1] Colonialism is here understood not only as a situation where a foreign power rules a local population but also as a situation where the cultures of dominant foreign powers influence the cultural practices of local peoples. Colonialism therefore deals with the world historical interaction of power and culture in which the lives of local peoples are often played out at the intersection of dominant foreign powers and local cultures. Christianity in Africa has often played out at the intersection of foreign powers and cultures and their local counterparts. For the world historical understanding of colonialism, see Michael A. Polushin and Wendy Kasinec, eds., *Expanding Empires: Cultural Interaction and Exchange in World Societies from Ancient to Early Modern Times* (Wilmington, DE: Scholarly Resources Inc., 2002).

[2] See for example, the edited volumes on African history and Culture by Toyin Falola, *Africa*, 5 vols. (Durham, NC: Carolina Academic Press).

[3] The point here is not to undermine African agency in the spread of Christianity on the continent. There should be little doubt that African agency contributed significantly in the spread of Christianity in Africa, as has been pointed out by Ugbu Kalu, ed., *African Christianity: An African Story* (Asmara, Eritrea and Trenton, NJ: Africa World Press, 2007). Rather, it is to acknowledge that this agency has often been performed in the shadow of colonial experiences so that it is complex to speak of a pre-colonial African Christianity. Apart from early Ethiopian Christianity that does not appear to have been influenced by colonial experiences, Egyptian, Nubian, and early North African Christianity developed in contexts marked by the colonial experience. Perhaps, for some Ethiopians, the fact that the Abuna of the Ethiopian Orthodox Church was for a long time appointed by the Coptic Church of Egypt points to a foreign influence which is part of the colonial experience.

as stretching from the late fifteenth century to the beginnings of the modern Christian missions and the formal colonization of the continent in the late nineteenth century. Thus, if we may speak of pre-colonial African Christianity, it would designate not so much a form of Christianity in Africa untouched by elements of colonialism (as may seem to be the case when we talk of pre-colonial African indigenous cultures) but rather the state of Christianity in Africa during the period after the arrival of Islam in Northern Africa and the rise of the modern missions movement that began with the 1792 formation of the Baptist Missionary Society, culminating in the formal colonization of the continent in the late nineteenth century. This period is covered in the first part of Adrian Hastings' important work, *The Church in Africa*.[4]

The eminent historian of African history, Elizabeth Isichei, has pointed out that the history of African Christianity in this period was marked by 'the continuing life of the Coptic and Ethiopian Churches, some strikingly unsuccessful attempts to "convert" Muslim North Africa, and the history of the Catholic Churches founded in black Africa, initially by the Portuguese'.[5] This is a fine summary of some major themes in African Christianity of this period but the focus of this chapter will be on the continuing life of Ethiopian Christianity (the Ethiopian Orthodox Church) and the spread of Christianity in Black or sub-Saharan Africa, initiated by the Portuguese. The spread of Christianity in sub-Saharan Africa during this period is a very important moment in African church history but limited space is often given to it in works on the history of African Christianity perhaps because little or nothing is left of the Christianity of this period. However, this period is significant because it marks the beginnings of the appropriation of the Christian faith in sub-Saharan Africa. One of the vexing questions which has often been raised with regard to the study of this period is whether the African embrace of Christianity could be seen as genuine.[6] This is a question which has not gone away as African Christianity continues to be described even today as only 'skin-deep'.[7]

This chapter argues that African Christianity during this period was Constantinian in nature because, like the Roman Emperor Constantine's embrace of the Christian faith, those who embraced the Christian faith in sub-Saharan Africa were mostly members of the ruling classes who implicated the Christian faith in the politics of the time. They implicated the Christian faith in the politics of the time, not because they wanted to politicize the faith but rather because their understanding of religion did not preclude the political. It is perhaps this generally Constantinian nature of much of African Christianity during this period that marks it out from other periods of African Christianity. It could however be argued that it would be wrong to describe Christianity in Africa during this period, or any other period, as not genuine because it was political. Apart from the fact that there appear to be many genuine Christians among the ruling elite, the political appropriation of Christianity during this period demonstrates the understanding of the nature of religion in Africa. In much of human history, religion has often not been separate from politics because religion, like politics, is about the locus of the power that influences life. African Christianity during this period was therefore largely in the hands of rulers who used it to enhance their own power and, in some cases, the well-being of their people. Perhaps the political appropriation of the Christian faith is a theme that is characteristic of the practice of the faith in our time. A look at some of the relationships among some pastors, bishops, the Pope, and some prominent political leaders in Africa today may alert us to the fact that the Christian faith is, for good or ill, still being appropriated in political

---

[4] See Adrian Hastings, *The Church in Africa, 1450-1950* (Oxford: Oxford University Press, 1994), 3-162. This is Part I of the book dated 1450-1780. Hastings' is still the most thorough general treatment of this period in African church history.

[5] Isichei, *A History*, 45.

[6] See David Northrop, *Africa's Discovery of Europe, 1450-1850*, second edition (Oxford: Oxford University Press, 2009).

[7] See Stan Chu Ilo, *The Face of Africa: Looking Beyond the* Shadows (Bloomington, IN: Arthur House, 2006), 214.

discourses. However, during the time under investigation, the Christian faith took root, albeit only for a while in some places, when it went beyond being a palace religion but failed to take root otherwise.

Constantine in Africa

Constantine is the Roman Emperor who credited his rise to power to the Christian God and went on to tolerate the hitherto persecuted Christian movement, thus creating the condition for the faith to thrive in the Roman Empire. It could thus be argued that Christianity began to thrive in the Roman Empire in part because Constantine began to support it. Since Constantine, any form of Christianity that has tended to enjoy imperial or royal support has come to be described as Constantinian Christianity. This form of Christianity was very prominent in Africa during the time under discussion because the royal household was often the first target of those who brought Christianity to the continent and the fortunes of the Christian faith largely depended on how the royal household responded to it. We saw an early manifestation of this when the Christian faith was first brought to Ethiopia (Axum) in the fourth century. King Ezana, who embraced the faith, came to credit it with his ability to expand his territory and the cross soon came to be placed on the coins of his country.

Axum declined and, after the rise of Islam, Ethiopian Christianity was under pressure. However, Christianity was later revived by the Zagwe Dynasty that came to power in Lalibela in the twelfth century. Seen as usurpers by the Amhara, the Zagwe Dynasty was keen on legitimating its rule through establishing a new Zion (Sion) in Lalibela by constructing the magnificent rock-hewn churches that still astound us to this day. This notwithstanding, the Amharic Solomonide Dynasty replaced the Zagwe Dynasty in the thirteenth century. The Solomonide Dynasty then appropriated a myth that had existed in Ethiopia for some time in order to legitimize its own rule. This myth was written in the *Kebre Negest* and it tells of how the first Solomonide King, Menelik I, was the son of the relationship between the Queen of Sheba, who was believed to be from Ethiopia, and King Solomon, the famous wise King of Israel. The *Kebre Negest* or *Glory of the Kings* tells the story of how the Queen of Sheba heard of the wisdom of Solomon and went to visit him. During this visit, she was made pregnant by King Solomon and, upon returning to Ethiopia, she had a son. That son, Menelik I, became the first king of Ethiopia. In time, Menelik I returned to Israel to visit his father, Solomon, and upon returning to Ethiopia, he brought the Ark of the Covenant with him. Thus, this story did not only legitimize the Solomonide line but it also intimately connected Ethiopian Christianity to the Jewish faith, thus explaining why the Falashas are Jews and why the Ethiopian Orthodox Church practices rituals such as circumcision and follows dietary rules. Even more, to this day the Ethiopian Orthodox Church maintains that it is in possession of the Ark of the Covenant. Subsequent Ethiopian leaders such as Amda Sion (1314-1344) and Zar'a Yaqob would appropriate the Christian faith in their expansionist policies as they would seek to turn all whom they conquered into Christians. Amda Zion is reputed to have left those he conquered with the choices of conversion or death while Zar'a Yaqob attempted to unite his people by eliminating those who practised other religions.

This close connection between the Christian faith, king, and nation-building, would lead some Ethiopian leaders of the sixteenth and seventeenth centuries to feel indebted to the Portuguese who helped them avert almost certain conquest from a ferocious Muslim leader, Imam Ahmed, also known as Gran (1506-1543). Fed up with being under the authority of Christian kings in Ethiopia, Gran gathered fighters who went about conquering territories in Ethiopia. Many churches were destroyed and many Christians converted to Islam. However, through the intervention of the Portuguese who first arrived in the country in the sixteenth century, Gran was defeated and the Christian state was restored. Portuguese military intervention led to the sending of Portuguese missionaries to Ethiopia. Ethiopian Christians were Orthodox who were connected to the Coptic Church in Egypt but the Portuguese missionaries were Roman Catholic and wanted the Ethiopians to become Roman Catholics. The Portuguese missionary Afonso Mendez succeeded in convincing one Ethiopian King, Susenyos, who, in 1622 switched to Roman Catholicism. This switch led to a civil war in the country and the civil war only came to an end when Susenyos' son, Fasiladas, took over from his father, expelled the Portuguese missionaries from the country, and reverted to Orthodoxy.[8] Here is an example where the people resisted what was seen as a foreign religion in favour of that which they saw as a traditional or indigenous one.

Another significant political appropriation of the Christian faith in sub-Saharan Africa during this period is that of the Jolof (Senegalese) ruler Bumi Jeleen who reigned in the late fifteenth century. Jeleen was a Muslim but when he encountered the Portuguese in 1487-1488, the Portuguese attempted to convert him to Christianity but he initially rebuffed these attempts. However, when an attempt was made to overthrow him, Jeleen appealed to the Portuguese King João II (1481-1495) for help. King João however could not give Jeleen the full military help he asked for because there was a Portuguese prohibition against providing such support to rulers who were not Christians. This lack of sufficient support led to the overthrow of Jeleen who then fled for refuge at the palace of King João in Portugal. Apparently aware that he would not be granted the help he sought without converting to Christianity, he declared his conversion and was baptized on November 3, 1488. Jeleen was then given the requisite supplies he needed to go back, reclaim his throne, and convert his people to the Christian faith. This was however not to be because the Portuguese captain who was ferrying Jeleen back to Senegal, killed him and returned to Portugal.[9]

A similar saga was to take place in Benin and Warri, where the Christian faith was introduced to the ruling class but failed to take root among the general populace. The people of Benin encountered the Portuguese and the Christian faith at about the same time as the Jolof of Senegal. Portuguese missionaries first came to Benin in about 1486, with emissaries whom Oba Ewuare had sent to Portugal to learn more about the Portuguese. However, it was a succeeding Oba, Oba Ozolua, who expressed much interest in the faith, leading his son and other members of the nobility to become Christians in 1516. By 1538, however, the Christian faith had declined in Benin so much that some of the members of the nobility who had converted to it in 1516 had reverted to traditional religion. With traditional religion being so strong and the Christian faith perceived as not offering much, the nobility could not adhere to it for very long. In fact, an early eighteenth-century king who was perceived to be sympathetic to the Christian faith had a very rough tenure and was eventually exiled. Here, the Christian faith did not appear to have been helpful in politics.[10]

Things were a little different in Warri. When the Portuguese brought the Christian faith there in the second half of the sixteenth century, one of the kings (*Olu*) named Sebastian, was among the first to be converted. He appealed for more members of the clergy to be sent to his country but because this did not happen, he sent his eldest son, Domingos, to study in Portugal so that he might return and instruct the people in the Christian faith. Sebastian is himself described as instructing the people even into his old age. However, it was Domingos' son, Antonio Domingos, whom he had with his Portuguese wife after their marriage while studying in Portugal, who would do more to instruct the people in Christian ways. This enthusiasm for the gospel would however not last because an eighteenth-century *Olu* would go back to traditional religion. A fateful event, the failure of a statue of Christ to end a drought, would result in the destruction of the statue for not doing what it was supposed to do.[11] Traditional religion was apparently seen as more effective in stopping droughts than the Christian faith. What we see here is that, when the *Olu* was dedicated to the Christian faith, the faith thrived but when the king withdrew from the faith, the future of the faith was jeopardized. Thus, the faith declined in Warri partly because the ruling elite turned against it.

---

[8] Kevin Ward, "Africa" in *A World History of Christianity*, ed. Adrian Hastings (Grand Rapids, MI: Eerdmans, 1999), 197-199.

[9] See Northrup, *Africa's Discovery*, 26-29.

[10] Isichei, *A History*, 63.

[11] Isichei, *A History*, 62.

This connection of the Christian faith with the ruling elite was significantly displayed in the Kongo where the faith had a rich and glorious history during this period.[12] Apart from Ethiopia, Cape Verde and São Tomé, Christianity was perhaps nowhere more entrenched in Africa during this period than in the Kongo (present-day Angola and the Democratic Republic of Congo). In fact, the first Catholic bishop in sub-Saharan Africa would come from the Kongo during this period.[13] Christianity was introduced in the Kongo by Kongo nobles who were taken to Portugal by Diogo Cão, the first Portuguese to arrive in the Kongo in 1483. These Kongolese nobles learned the Christian faith in Portugal and upon returning home converted King Nzingaa Nkuwu (reigned 1470-1509). King Nkuwu was baptized in 1491 as João I. The King's baptism was however not without some apprehensions but these apprehensions were put to rest when two people at his court had a dream in which a beautiful woman (probably the Virgin Mary) informed them of the wisdom of the King's decision. Even more, a sacred black stone, in the form of a cross, was found at a nearby river. This further legitimized the step the King had taken.[14]

Even though Nzingaa Nkuwu was a pace-setter, it was his son, Mbemba Nzinga, baptized as Afonso I (r. 1509-1542) who did much to make Christianity a popular religion in the Kongo. Afonso I came to power after a very bitter power struggle with his half-brother who also wanted the throne. Because his half-brother adhered to traditional religion, Afonso couched the struggle as a struggle between the Christian faith and traditional religion. Formulating the struggle in this manner secured him the support of the Portuguese but it also secured the spiritual resources of the Christian faith. Afonso I attributed his victory to the intervention of the warrior Christian saint, St James. 'This narrative,' Fromont notes, 'was an ostensible attempt on the part of the new king to inscribe his reign in the historical and hagiographical tradition of Christianity.'[15]

Considering the role that the Christian faith played in his coming to power, Afonso I immediately set out to evangelize his people in a way that few African monarchs had done before and even after him. Afonso I set out opening schools to train teachers who would teach the Christian faith so that during his reign he sent teachers to other parts of his kingdom to evangelize the people. When he asked for priests from Portugal, it was mainly so that they could administer the sacraments which could not be administered by the lay teachers. When he failed to receive sufficient priests from Portugal who could administer the sacraments, he sent one of his sons, Henrique, to be trained in Portugal. Henrique was made a bishop and he returned to the Kongo where he became bishop, not of the Kongo but of a North African diocese. Because the *Patroado* system had made Portugal in charge of the evangelization of Africa, the Portuguese king wanted to maintain control over the Kongo so he appointed bishops from São Tomé over Kongo Christians. Apart from training the laity to take the gospel to his people, Afonso I was also known to have paid careful attention to studying the faith himself, studying all night and even falling asleep over his books. He was also a preacher.[16]

Afonso I's reign made Kongo famous as a Christian kingdom. Many kings after him, right into the eighteenth century, sought to maintain the strong Christian identity of the kingdom. The Christian identity of the kingdom made Kongo diplomacy run through Portugal and Spain and the Vatican, as the ruling

---

[12] See Adrian Hastings, "The Christianity of Pedro IV of the Kongo, 'The Pacific (1696-1718)" *Journal of Religion in Africa* 28, no. 2 (May 1998): 145-146.

[13] For a biography of Henrique, the first Catholic Bishop of sub-Saharan Africa, see François Bontinck, "Ndoadidiki Ne-Kinu a Mubemba, primierévêque du Kongo (c. 1495-c. 1531)," *Revue Africaine de Théologie* 3 (1979): 149-169.

[14] See Sundkler and Stead, *A History*, 50.

[15] Cécile Fromont, "Dance, Image, Myth, and Conversion in the Kingdom of Kongo, 1500-1800," *African Arts* (Winter 2011): 55. Cécile Fromont, *The Art of Conversion: Christian Visual Culture in the Kingdom of Kongo* (Chapel Hill, NC: The University of North Carolina Press, 2014).

[16] John K. Thornton, "Afro-Christian Syncretism in the Kingdom of Kongo," *Journal of African History* 54, no. 1 (March 2013): 53-77.

elites of Kongo often sent ambassadors to these places to negotiate one issue or another. One significant request that was made to the Pope was for a diocese, separate from Portugal, to be created in Kongo because successive Kongo kings wanted to be in control of the Christian faith in their kingdom. In fact, it was partly the refusal of Portugal to relinquish its control over Kongo that led to the founding of the *Propaganda Fide*, the missionary arm of the Roman Catholic Church, in 1622, taking Catholic missionary activity out of the hands of the kings and queens of Portugal and Spain. With the establishment of the *Propaganda Fide*, the Catholic Church was free to send its own missionaries to the Kongo. Slavery is another issue that was brought to the attention of the Pope in a dramatic way by the Afro-Brazilian of Kongolese descent, Lourenço Mendoza, and which led the Papacy to condemn the slave trade and call for its abolition in 1686, an act that contributed to the flowering of the abolitionist movement.[17] The embrace of Catholic Christianity in the Kongo made Kongo monarchs have very close ties to Rome even when the advances of Portugal were repelled.[18]

This close relation with Rome was perhaps nowhere more evident than during the reign of Dom Pedro IV (1696-1718) under whose reign the Antonine Movement led by Kimpa Vita Dona Beatrice developed.[19] It is only when we understand the political context of the Kongo at this time that we would better understand how not only religiously innovative but also politically inflammatory the teachings of Kimpa Vita were. Hers was a time when civil wars had laid desolate the political and religious capital of Kongo, São Salvador, the city where Kongo's Christian kings were crowned and where they were buried, a holy city. The holy city had been laid waste and deserted and there were rival claimants to the throne: Pedro IV who was holed up at Mount Kimbangu, and João II at Mbula. The dream of the people was that the holy city, like Jerusalem, be rebuilt.

It was first a lady named Mafuta who claimed to have seen a vision of the Virgin Mary who told her (Mafuta) that her (Mary's) son (Jesus) was not pleased with the fact that there was no king in São Salvador. Not long after her, Dona Beatrice Kimpa Vita came to the scene, claiming that she had been possessed by the spirit of St Anthony of Padua, a revered Franciscan saint in the Kongo, and that his spirit had instructed her to announce that the King (Pedro IV) had to go back to São Salvador, reoccupy and rebuild the city. She also preached that all fetishes should be burned; including the cross, for it was also a fetish. She is also reported to have preached that the sacraments of baptism, marriage, and confession were invalid, and that Jesus was born in São Salvador and his disciples were black. According to the Capuchin missionary, Father Bernardo, who was a very close advisor to Dom Pedro IV, Kimpa Vita's preaching was against the Catholic faith and demonstrated that she was possessed by the demon and was thus a heretic. Her call that the King should return to São Salvador was appealing to Dom Pedro but he was concerned that following her advice may validate her teachings also. While Dom Pedro was still contemplating the matter, Kimpa Vita went over to João II at Mbula and asked him to go and re-occupy and rebuild São Salvador. She even went ahead and occupied the city, accompanied by some of her followers and enemies of Pedro IV, the *Chibenga*. Pedro IV, who had attempted to solve the crisis plaguing the kingdom peacefully, decided to go to war to conquer the city. Before he went to war, however, he went over to his priest, Bernardo, who blessed him with a cross. Pedro took the cross from Bernardo, wore it, and went to war. He was victorious in the war and he attributed this victory to the cross and the protection of St Francis and St Anthony. It was in the process of his retaking of the city that Kimpa Vita was arrested and then burned at the stake in 1706.

---

[17] Richard Gray, "The Kongo Kingdom and the Papacy," *History Today* (January 1997): 44-49. Also see, Richard Gray, "A Kongo Princess, the Kongo Ambassadors and the Papacy", *Journal of Religion in Africa* 29, no. 2 (1999): 140-154.

[18] John K. Thornton, "The Kingdom of Kongo and the Counter Reformation," *Social Sciences and Missions* 26 (2013): 40-58.

[19] For this, see John K. Thornton, *The Kongolese St Anthony: Dona Beatrice Kimpa Vita and the Antonian Movement, 1684-1706* (Cambridge: Cambridge University Press, 1998).

In the end therefore the king succeeded in defeating his enemies not by burning the cross and following the teaching of Kimpa Vita but by sticking to the narrative of the Christian faith which had existed since Afonso I won his own battle against his half-brother. Pedro expected a crown from the Pope in order to further legitimize his reign but this was never granted.[20] In spite of that he still remained loyal to the Catholic faith but the disintegration that had entered the life of Kongo since the second half of the seventeenth century would hardly be reversed. The kingdom and the faith would decline.

The story of the close connection between the Christian faith and politics which we have seen in Ethiopia and some places in West and Central Africa above, was also replicated in East and Southern Africa. In East Africa the existence of Islam and the desire for political and economic power by the Portuguese led only to a brief existence of Christianity in Kilwa and Mombasa. Since the slave trade was lucrative, the Portuguese in East Africa did not baptize slaves because baptized slaves were not to be sold to Muslim traders.[21] Thus the economic opportunity stifled the evangelizing impulse. In Zambezi and Zimbabwe, the Christian faith fared a little better as both the ruling elite and ordinary people were converted but it eventually petered out.[22] South Africa is a rare exception in this period in that it was not the Portuguese Catholics who first brought the faith there but rather Protestants, especially the Dutch in the seventeenth century and the Moravians in the eighteenth century. From a sputtering start, the presence of the Christian faith in the country would be tumultuous but persistent.[23]

Concluding Observations

The close connection between Christianity and the political life of the time under consideration here has led some to question the authenticity of the conversion of some of the Christian élite: were they genuinely converted or did they choose the Christian faith for political convenience? The eminent historian of Kongo Christianity, John Thornton, has argued that addressing the question of whether or not one is an authentic Christian is something better left to the sectarians.[24] However, if being a Christian means anything, then it appears that one does not have to be sectarian in order to address the issue of authenticity. Perhaps what needs to be observed, as Adrian Hastings has pointed out, is the devotion which one has towards a certain religion.[25] This idea of being devoted may be linked with the pragmatic understanding of religion common to many African traditional cultures. Not separating the religious from the political or any other aspect of life, many Africans see religion as providing the supernatural power that enables them to navigate the intricate issues of life. Historically, therefore, many African peoples have had, not so much a *dogmatic* connection with religious beliefs as a *pragmatic* one – that religion should work.[26] Thus, people are willing to try out new religions as they navigate the problems of life. Since the problems of life often involved questions of life and death, embracing a particular religion might be temporary but hardly feigned.

Bibliography

Fromont, Cécile, *The Art of Conversion: Christian Visual Culture in the Kingdom of Kongo*. Chapel Hill, NC: The University of North Carolina Press, 2014.

---

[20] Hastings, "The Christianity of Pedro IV."
[21] Sundkler and Stead, *A History*, 69.
[22] Isichei, *A History*, 68-70; Sundkler and Stead, *A History*, 67-69.
[23] Richard Elphick and Rodney Davenport, ed., *Christianity in South Africa: Political, Social, and Cultural History* (Berkeley: University of California Press, 1997).
[24] Thornton, "Afro-Christian Syncretism", 77.
[25] Hastings, "The Christianity of Pedro IV," 157-158.
[26] Toyin Falola, *Culture and Customs of Nigeria* (Westport, CT: Greenwood Press, 2001), 35.

Hastings, Adrian. *The Church in Africa, 1450-1950*. Oxford: Oxford University Press, 1994.
Meinardus, Otto F. A. *Two Thousand Years of Coptic Christianity*. Cairo: The American University of Cairo Press, 1999.
Newitt, Malyned. *The Portuguese in West Africa, 1415-1670: A Documentary History*. Cambridge: Cambridge University Press, 2010.
Northrop, David. *Africa's Discovery of Europe, 1450-1850*. Second Edition. Oxford: Oxford University Press, 2009
Sanneh, Lamin. *West African Christianity: Its Religious Impact*. Maryknoll, NY: Orbis Books, 1983.
Sweet, James H. *Recreating Africa: Culture, Kinship, and Religion in the African-Portuguese World, 1441-1470*. Chapel Hill, NC: The University of North Carolina Press, 2003.
Thornton, John K. *The Kongolese St Anthony: Dona Beatrice Kimpa Vita and the Antonian Movement*, 1684-1706. Cambridge: Cambridge University Press, 1998.
______. *A Cultural History of the Atlantic World, 1250-1820*. Cambridge: Cambridge University Press, 2012.
Ullendorf, Edward. *Ethiopia and the Bible: The Schweich Lectures*. Oxford: Oxford University Press, 1967.

(4) The Caribbean Influences on African Christianity

Roderick R. Hewitt

Introduction

Eric Williams, a former Caribbean historian, argues that the role of British historians in writing Caribbean history was, to a great extent, a history that reflected the bias and prejudices of the historians rather than the experiences of the people.[1] The history was written within a colonial environment that did not allow mutual relationships between the colonizers and the colonized. The contemporary Caribbean region constitutes a melting pot and mosaic of blended cultures from Africa, Europe and Asia that have lived in contradiction and co-operation since the devastating effects of Spanish imperial forces under the leadership of Columbus arrived in the region. They were rescued and given hospitality by the indigenous Caribs who were unaware of their true motives.[2] Within a brief period of 163 years (1492-1655) of Spanish colonial military rule, the local population was decimated through enslavement and infections of deadly European transmitted diseases for which they had no immunity. Therefore, the European colonial history of Caribbean people is fatally flawed and calls for a re-reading and reinterpreting of the narrative that takes into account the stories and perspectives of its victims.

The focus of this article identifies and critiques *The Caribbean Influence on African Christianity*. However, the broad scope of this title demands that I limit the focus of the enquiry. First, the use of the concept 'Caribbean' will be limited to the Anglo-Caribbean countries of Barbados and Jamaica which were referred to during the colonial era as the West Indies.[3] Secondly, I will give attention to their influence on African Christianity from the mid-nineteenth to the mid-twentieth centuries. The term 'influence' will be interpreted to mean 'the extent to which the presence of mission personnel from the named Caribbean nations inspired, encouraged, gave guidance to and/or had an impact on the development of African Christianity'. Finally, I will focus on the role and influence of the Anglican, Baptist, Moravian and Presbyterian Churches that sent missions to the West African countries of Sierra Leone, Ghana, Calabar-Nigeria and Cameroon. Caribbean influences on African Christianity must be chronologically located within the phase of European colonization of sub-Saharan Africa and the consequent arrival of the Protestant missionary societies (from about 1860-1960). During this epoch of fast-changing world events is the story of a people from the Caribbean whose missional presence and action influenced the development of the identity, vocation and witness of some churches within the mosaic of West African Christianity.

Displacement and Enslavement

The landscapes of the Caribbean and Brazil have large numbers of people of African descent. Through the human trafficking trade that was well established by the Portuguese, millions of Africans were enslaved and brought to the Americas. They came primarily from the diverse tribal cultures of the West African region that stretched from Senegambia, Sierra Leone, the Windward Coast, the Gold Coast, the Bight of Benin, and Bight of Biafra to Central Africa. However, the Bight of Biafra and the Gold Coast offered the most Africans who were intentionally captured and sold as commodities to European smugglers and

---

[1] Eric Williams, *British Historians and the West Indies* (London: Andre Deutsch, 1964): 234.

[2] Eric Williams, *From Columbus to Castro* (London: Andre Deutsch, 1970): 30-45.

[3] The prescribed term 'West Indian' is misnomer used by the Spaniards and adopted by the British to describe the peoples and territories that were conquered or captured from the indigenous peoples in the Caribbean region.

traders.[4] The human tragedy of forcefully uprooting and expelling millions of Africans from their homeland to far unknown lands created severe psychological upheaval and dislocation that was made worse psychologically because they were violently removed from their homes and forcibly sent on a one-way journey to an unknown destination. They took only their memories that retained and informed their oral traditions and human dignity that kept alive their cultural traditions and institutions.

Jamaica became a colony of England in 1655 after the island was captured from Spain.[5] It was the largest British Caribbean colony, and the need to make the island economically viable led to the introduction and development of a slave-based and large-scale sugar plantation economy. This model of economic development required a large, cheap and replaceable labour force.[6] The genocide committed against the indigenous population by the Spaniards and the failure to recruit sufficient numbers of cheap European labour as a replacement led to the adoption of African slave labour. This European-designed military and economic system of colonization created the need for Africans to be violently uprooted from their homeland and be inhumanely transported in conditions unfit even for animals to the Caribbean and the wider Americas.

The desire of plantation owners to get the best productivity out of the enslaved Africans led them to invite or grant permission Protestant and Evangelical missionary societies to send missionaries to Christianize the Africans. The missionaries adopted a mission station model of evangelization through education that led to many Africans in Jamaica becoming Christians. This development laid the foundation that contributed to the emergence of 'West Indian Missions' to West Africa and therefore facilitating a small but significant influence on and advancement of Christianity within Africa.

During the period of their enslavement, Africans throughout the Caribbean engaged in active and passive resistance for their freedom. Some Africans, like the Maroons of Jamaica,[7] succeeded in their revolt and established 'independent territories' in which they established self-rule following memories of governance in their African homeland.[8] They did not regard the Caribbean lands as home but as a place of 'forced exile', and many longed for repatriation in spite of the intentional indoctrination by the colonial authorities and missionaries to present the continent of Africa as a 'land of darkness and evil' from which they had been 'rescued'. The magnetic pull of Africans in the diaspora to return to their homeland remained an indelible mark of their identity.

West African Influences in Caribbean Societies

The religious expressions that were transported and transplanted from their homeland by Africans within the Caribbean included Santeria in Cuba, Shango or Shouters in Trinidad, Voodoo in Haiti, Convince,

---

[4] Sources used: R. Lapage and D. Decamp (eds), "*Jamaican Creole". Creole Language Studies I* (London: McMillan, 1960): 61-65, 74, 84; Orlando Patterson, *The Sociology of Slavery* (London, Oxford University Press, 1967): 134-135, 137-9; Bryan Edwards, *The History of the British Colonies in The West Indies*. 2 vols. (London: J, Stockdale1793): 60-80.

[5] Hugh Sherlock, H. Bennett, *History of the Jamaican People, the Jamaican People* (Kingston: Ian Randle Publishers 1998): 77.

[6] S. Hamber and R. Greenwood, *Emancipation To Emigration* (Kingston: Macmillan Caribbean, 1979): 10-15.

[7] L.N.Erskine. *From Garvey to Marley Rastafari Theology* (Gainesville: University of Florida, 2004): 130.

[8] According to Abioseh Nico, "The first decade of the nineteenth century saw the Maroons being brought as colonists to Sierra Leone. Originally they were mostly Fantis and Ashantis captured in Ghana (then the Gold Coast) and taken to the West Indies. Some of them escaped to the mountains in Jamaica occasionally intermarrying with the local Indians. Their name was probably derived from "Cimarron" (mountain-top) rather than from their skin colour. They fought the British Government for a long time in Jamaica; some were brought to Sierra Leone where they lived in Freetown in an area extending from the Cotton Tree westwards to Wilberforce Village on the mountains".

Cumina, Pokomania and Revival in Jamaica.[9] These contextual expressions of West African religions became fully Creolized in response to the life challenges that the people experienced. Africans in the diaspora picked and used elements from folk religions and also from colonial Christianity in their ongoing search for survival. In Hamid's opinion, what worked was what gave meaning to the people and met their needs:

> … The peoples of the Caribbean and other colonised peoples of the world had not always nor wholly accepted the theology of mission or the instruction of the church. They often picked and chose what was suited to their survival. There was at work, then, a creative selectivity both of the teaching and the opportunities provided by the church.[10]

During the Spanish rule of Jamaica (1492-1655), the Roman Catholic Church was the established church. However, when the British took over in 1655, the Church of England became the established church that functioned like a chaplaincy to the colonists and did not regard the work of evangelization of the working class as a priority. However, when the economic agenda of the colonies demanded the violent abduction of millions of Africans to become enslaved labourers to enrich the Euro-American absentee owners of the economy, it incorporated religion as a tool to legitimize the socio-economic and political (dis)order. The significant shift of millions of Africans from their African homeland to become enslaved labourers also resulted in many of the British West Indian colonies like Jamaica being transformed into a majority African population. The need to ensure effective social control over the population and to condition them for a life of servitude led to strategic relationships with nonconformist evangelical missionaries, primarily from England, Scotland and Wales who engaged in the work of evangelization among the Africans. The European Protestant Missionary Christianity[11] therefore had a much earlier impact on Caribbean colonized societies before their journey into Africa. The Moravian Missionaries arrived from as early as 1760 followed by the Baptists and Methodists. The Presbyterians and Congregationalists came in 1824 and 1836.

Missionary Zeal for a Return to West Africa

The anti-slavery movement under the leadership of William Wilberforce and his evangelical Clapham Sect in England seized the political moment to mobilize for the abolition of the Atlantic Slave trade in 1807 that officially put to an end the trafficking and trading of Africans, treating them as mere commodities.[12] That was followed a few years later by the Emancipation Act of 1833 that put an official end to the enslavement of Africans in all British colonies.[13] The socio-political and economic ramification of this act triggered the latent spirit of Africans within the Caribbean but especially Jamaica to reconnect with their homeland. This vision and desire was best expressed in their mobilization to initiate and participate in the development of the so-called 'West Indian Mission' to Africa. The religious phenomenon of Mayalism[14] in 1841-42 in

---

[9] Winston Lawson, *Religion and Race* (New York: Peter Lang, 1996): 4.

[10] Edris Hamid, *Troubling of the Waters* (Trinidad: Rahaman Printery 1977): vii.

[11] The Baptist Missionary Society (BMS,1792), The London Missionary Society (LMS,1795), and the Scottish Missionary Society (SMS, 1796) that unite later with the Edinburgh Missionary Society to become Church of Scotland Mission (CSM); and the Glasgow Society and became the Free Church of Scotland Mission (FCSM) and the Methodist Missionary Society (1813), became the leading evangelical missionary organizations.

[12] Williams, *"From Columbus to Castro"*, 280.

[13] Williams, *"From Columbus to Castro"*, 280-327.

[14] Winston Lawson, "*Religion and Race"*, 8. Mayalism was an African-derived religious expression of organized cults that practised a dance ritual of 'death and resurrection' that focus on overcoming the power of evil.

particular and the Revival movement of 1860[15] played a significant role in highlighting the longing of some Afro-Jamaicans for indigenous religious symbols and meaning to inform and converse with their understanding and experience of missionary Christianity. Henry Waddell (1883), a Scottish missionary, had spent time working in West Africa before being assigned to Jamaica and was able to appreciate and appropriate the significance of spirituality that undergirded the Afro-Jamaican Christian faith. He responded to this phenomenon by affirming, challenging and channelling the missional zeal of the people to developing a mission to their ancestral West African homeland.[16]

This missionary zeal for a return to Africa constituted part of a wider socio-religious phenomenon of repatriation that was later popularized by the pan-Africanist Jamaican philosopher, Marcus Mosiah Garvey,[17] who is regarded as the early twentieth-century father of the *Back to Africa* movement and the religio-cultural movement of Rastafari that emerged from his teachings. Repatriation became an ideological form of socio-political resistance especially among Afro-Jamaicans, as a pro-active response to their experience of being forcibly, inhumanely and violently taken from their homeland into exile. The upheaval and displacement from their African context to be enslaved in an unknown world resulted in an African holocaust in which the Atlantic Ocean became the watery cemetery for millions who did not make the journey. For those that survived the brutal journey, the additional experience of colonialism and slavery bequeathed an immeasurable harm to their human dignity. However, the Africans in the diaspora were not passive recipients of the dehumanizing atrocities of European colonialism. Caribbean history, and that of Jamaica in particular, confirms numerous acts of resistance and revolt that bear witness to their non-acceptance of colonial systems of oppression.[18] There was always a strong desire for justice and liberation against oppression.

Although the popular views about African repatriation are associated with the advocacy of the modern Rastafari movement and their message that is communicated through reggae music, this paper argues that the pioneering advocates were the early Afro-Jamaicans who were enslaved on the Anglo Caribbean sugar plantations and embraced missionary Christianity with its gospel message of liberation and justice. Their allegiance to the gospel of freedom energized their desires to reconnect with their African homeland to share the good news of the gospel. The earliest organized African in the diaspora missionary movement to Africa came from the Afro-Americans who had expressed great interest in organizing their own evangelizing mission to West Africa long before the declaration of emancipation was declared in 1833.[19] Black Baptist pastors from Southern USA went to work in 1782 among those Africans who had fought with the British in the 'War of Independence' and were settled in the Canadian colony of Nova Scotia.[20] The British organized the emigration of those that wished to return to Africa, and some settled in Sierra Leone while others went to the newly created colony of Liberia for American 'free people of colour'.[21] It was the missionary enterprise of Black Baptist and African Methodist Episcopal (AME) leadership that

---

[15] It was the Great Revival of 1860 that brought this indigenous religion into direct interface with missionary Christianity. This interface of Mayalism and Christianity during the Great Revival paved the way for modern Revivalism to find a permanent home in the ministry and mission of North American- founded churches such as the Pentecostal, Church of God and African Methodist Episcopal-Zion.

[16] Henry Waddell, *Twenty-Nine Years in the West Indies and Central Africa 1829-1858* (London: T. Nelson & Sons, 1863), 34.

[17] See Hugh Sherlock, H. Bennett, *History of the Jamaican People*, *the Jamaican People,* 292-315. Garvey continued with the Jamaican revivalist tradition that viewed Africans in Jamaica as a people in exile like the children of Israel in Babylon (Jeremiah 29 & Psalm 137). Africa was seen as the Promised Land to which all Africans in the diaspora should return (Africa for Africans).

[18] Eric Williams, *From Columbus to Castro*, 193-200.

[19] J. Baur, *2000 years of Christianity in Africa- An African History 62-1992* (Nairobi: Pauline Publications, 1994): 113.

[20] J. Baur, *2000 years of Christianity in Africa- An African History.*

[21] J. Baur, *2000 years of Christianity in Africa- An African History.*

laid the foundation for the development of Christianity in West Africa and facilitated other missionary initiatives in other parts of Central and Southern and Eastern Africa.

The Baptist Mission to Cameroon

The Baptist church in Jamaica was the product of the Black American Baptist mission through the pioneering work of George Lilse and Moses Baker.[22] They first worked among the enslaved Afro-Jamaican population and empowered the oppressed people with a liberating faith that resisted state oppression. They teamed up with the British Baptist Missionary Society (BMS) in 1814 and in partnership with their missionaries, Thomas Burchell, James Phillippo and William Knibb,[23] they engaged in mass evangelization of the Afro-Jamaicans.[24] The Baptist ecclesial heritage in Jamaica evolved with two distinct missional leadership strategies. The British missionaries employed their 'mission station colonial model' of governance but the local Baptist followers preferred their indigenous 'deacon/leader system'. The mass growth of the Baptist church and its deep affirmation of embodying a strong African identity generated interest in taking the liberating gospel to their homeland from which they were stolen. It was the offerings of these people that sowed the seeds for the journey. Horace Russell argues that mission happened within the context of western economic and political interest on the continent in which Africans were traded as commodities and the consequential post emancipation interest and initiative that propelled Africans within the diaspora in the West Indies and the USA to return to the homeland for missionary work.[25]

An unsuccessful attempt was made in 1841 by the Baptist Missionary Society of Jamaica to begin missionary work among Africans who were previously enslaved at Malabo-Equatorial Guinea. Their first interest was to work in the 'Niger Delta' but eventually stopped at Fernando Po, an island close to the Cameroon mainland. The economy of this island was built on the trafficking of Africans for slave labour and oppression was rife. Their work was however short-lived because of tensions between Britain and Spain which led to the island being unsafe for them to settle there. When the exploratory mission reported to the Jamaican Baptist Church, they mobilized and sent an additional forty-two Afro-Jamaicans 'to regenerate Africa by the Bible and the plough'.[26] The British BMS, being motivated by the words of Psalm 68:32, 'Ethiopia shall stretch out her hands unto God', later decided to support the venture with personnel and financial resources.[27]

The Jamaican Baptist Church through the impact of its mission to Cameroon is recognized as having laid the foundation for the growth of the Church in that country. According to Russell the crisis in the Jamaican economy of the 1840s triggered by the collapse in sugar prices, contributed to the inability of the Jamaican Baptist Church to sustain its support for the mission in Cameroon.[28] In 1852, it gave up control to the British BMS and recalled most of its missionaries and left only a few to work for the BMS.[29] Afro-Jamaicans who had settled at Fernando Po moved and joined the mainland mission station after Spain took over control of the island from the British. They provided the mission with qualified workers, while skilled farmers gave the mission some stability. One of the famous missionaries from Jamaica was Joseph

---

[22] Jaap van Slageren, *Jamaican Missionaries in Cameroon*, Exchange Vol. 30.2 (2001), 145.

[23] Hugh Sherlock, H. Bennett, *The Story of the Jamaican People* (Kingston: Ian Randle Publishers, 1998): 206-211.

[24] Jaap van Slageren, *Jamaican Missionaries in Cameroon*, 145.

[25] J. Baur, *2000 years of Christianity in Africa- An African History*, 113.

[26] Jaap van Slageren, *Jamaican Missionaries in Cameroon*, 148.

[27] Jaap van Slageren, *Jamaican Missionaries in Cameroon*, 148.

[28] Horace Russell, *The Missionary Outreach of the West Indian Church; Jamaican Baptist Missions to West Africa in the Nineteenth Century* (New York: Peter Lang, 2000): 243-4, 260-262.

[29] Horace Russell, *The Missionary Outreach of the West Indian Church; Jamaican Baptist Missions to West Africa in the Nineteenth Century.*

Merrick. He proved to be an effective linguist who was able to quickly learn the local language and through his communication skills was able to win the confidence of the king who allowed him to build schools and houses.[30] Through his gift with languages, his translation and printing of various books of the Bible in the local language proved to be his lasting legacy and contribution to the church in Cameroon and to African Christianity. He also wrote the grammar for the Isubu language and in addition he received permission from the Bible Society for the translation of the Old Testament through which he gave priority to God's call of justice for the oppressed.[31] Another key leader in the mission was Joseph Fuller, a Jamaican of African and Jewish descent, who worked for forty years as a multi-skilled leader who was a carpenter, bricklayer, farmer, builder and instructor. After Merrick's departure from the mission, he gave leadership and served with great passion, challenging non-life-affirming traditional cultural practices in his quest to protect life.[32] He rallied and got the people in the area where he served to be vaccinated when smallpox broke out in 1877.

Many other noteworthy Jamaicans served the mission to Cameroon until the end came during the German imperial occupation of the country from 1884-1915. The mission strategy employed by the Basel Mission that took over control from the BMS was different from the 'Class system'/deacon local leadership model that was originally employed by the Jamaicans. Their continuing presence was deemed to be troublesome because the local people were taught by the Jamaican mission workers to value their local governance. This unresolved tension influenced the Jamaica Baptist Society to withdraw from Cameroon. The mission model of the Basel Mission and later the Paris Mission that replaced them in 1915, found the Jamaican mission model of giving autonomy to local church groups to be unacceptable because they wished that the entire mission stations would give their loyalty to their European mission station model. It was this competing model of governance between that which was introduced and practiced by the Jamaican mission and the Euro-centric centralized and imperial models of mission understanding and praxis that was practised by the British, Basel and Paris missions that contributed to the disunity that ultimately impacted negatively on the development of the mission work in Cameroon. The departure of the Jamaican mission from Cameroon had a lasting positive impact. Their missional legacy led to the formation of the *L'Union des Eglises Baptistes du Cameroun* (UEBC) and the *L'Eglise Evangélique du Cameroun (EEC)* formed in 1957 and The Presbyterian Church of West Cameroon (PCC) in 1957 and *L'Eglise Presbytérienne Camerounaise (EPC).*[33] The churches in Cameroon officially acknowledged the significant influence of the Jamaican mission to the development of Christianity in their country in 1995 when they celebrated 150 years of protestant mission in Cameroon. At the celebrations special attention was given to remember the legacy of the many Jamaicans that worked with the local people. As with the contributions of other West Indian missions to African Christianity, the Baptist personnel of African descent that worked among the people in Cameroon offered a mission model that was characterized by a passionate spirit of freedom from oppression that they had experienced through physical and spiritual emancipation.

The Presbyterian Church Mission to Calabar, Nigeria

The Presbyterian Church in Jamaica and Cayman was organised through the work of different British reformed missions – namely, missionaries from the colonial committee of the Church of Scotland, the Scottish Missionary Society and, finally, through the missions of the Secession and United Presbyterian Church. The Protestant missionaries brought to Jamaica an evangelical Christianity that emphasised

[30] Jaap van Slageren, *Jamaican Missionaries in Cameroon*, 150.
[31] Jaap van Slageren, *Jamaican Missionaries in Cameroon*.
[32] Jaap van Slageren, *Jamaican Missionaries in Cameroon*, 151.
[33] Jaap van Slageren, *Jamaican Missionaries in Cameroon*, 155.

preaching, instruction and observable response in word, moral behaviour and church adherence.[34] Unlike the missions of the Moravians, Baptists and Methodists, which began during slavery, the reformed missions came at the close of slavery. This meant that the issues surrounding the abolition of slavery and the creation of a new society figured highly among their reasons for starting their mission to Jamaica. The missionaries who came to Jamaica were given a model of mission and ministry that had a fourfold division of labour that consisted of teaching doctors, preaching pastors, discipling elders and deacons charged with the administration of charity.[35]

It was due to the passionate interest of the Afro-Jamaican Presbyterian members in 1839, just three years after emancipation from slavery, that one of Hope Waddell's Presbyterian congregations formed their own Afro-Jamaican Missionary Society with the objective of raising funds to finance a mission to Africa.[36] The Jamaican Presbytery passed a resolution in 1841 facilitating a mission to Africa and requested the support and facilitation of the Scottish Missionary Society to achieving its stated objectives.[37] Waddell took the cause of the Afro-Jamaican Reformed Christians and pleaded the cause before the Scottish church authorities. The Jamaica Mission Presbytery endorsed this willingness of the Afro-Jamaican to take the 'gospel back to Africa' and 'initiated a freedom offering' to launch the missionary movement. In 1941 the Jamaica Mission Council (JMC) met at Goshen in the Parish of St Mary and passed the following resolution:

> That the time seems to have arrived, and to be in an eminent degree favourable for introducing the blessed Gospel to Central Africa. That the long-neglected and critical conditions of the inhabitants of that vast country, hitherto sunk in the deepest darkness, and exposed to the deepest darkness, and exposed to all the miseries of the most iniquitous system that ever defiled or desolated the earth, together with the duty which the church owes to the Lord Jesus, to go into all the world and preach the gospel to every creature…[38]

A missio-cultural reading of the resolution text seems to suggest the following: a) The continent of Africa was 'one vast country'; b) A Eurocentric mono-cultural perception of the Africans that regarded their culture as uncivilized and in need of the civilising gift of Christianity that would take the people out of darkness into light; c) People who were different from Europeans with other religions, languages, worldviews, food and political outlook were dismissed as heathens who were living in darkness and therefore in need of the good news message of the church.

The history of the Presbyterian Church of Nigeria as told through the lens of the Church of Scotland attributes the founding of that Church to the work of its missionaries. However, from the underside of history, where the powerless workers are not the authors of that narrative, the founding of the Calabar Mission was the vision and impetus of the Afro-Jamaican Christians. The language used to motivate for the mission to Africa reflected the standard perception of the colonial mindset of the Scottish Reformed missionaries. They believed that Africa was a land in spiritual and political darkness and only the gospel that the missionaries possessed could 'save the people'. However, their understanding of salvation seemed to focus on Africans experiencing cultural change by giving up some key African traditional cultural practices and embracing and replacing them with Euro-centric values. Those Africans who were deemed to be Christians would be those that gave up traditional practices such as polygamy, human sacrifices and

---

[34] Robert Stewart, "*Religion and Society in Post Emancipation Jamaica*" (Knoxville: University of Tennessee Press 1992), xix.

[35] J. M. Barkley. *Presbyterianism* (Belfast: The Tyrone Constitution, 1956): 24-34.

[36] Henry Waddell, "*Twenty-Nine years in the West Indies and Central Africa,* 1829-1859", 160.

[37] Henry Waddell, "*Twenty-Nine years in the West Indies and Central Africa,* 1829-1859", 206-210.

[38] Elijah Obinah, *Bridging the Divide: The Legacies of Mary Slessor, 'Queen' of Calabar, Nigeria*, Studies in World Christianity 17.3 (2011): Edinburgh University Press, 278.

witchcraft. The early Scottish missionaries in Jamaica that supported the mission to Africa embraced an ideology of manifest destiny that implied Africa needed the presence of Europeans to take the leadership role in organising for their social and economic development.

The Church of Scotland officials were not enthusiastic about this proposed mission by the JMC and argued that it represented a case of 'zeal more than judgement'.[39] Their initial rejection of the Jamaican request for support for their mission to Africa was based upon their perceived inferior status as 'a dependent mission station' and therefore would lack sufficient financial and human resources to support such a mission. They also took into consideration their past experiences of the high security and health risks and economic cost for initiating previous African missions.

This negative response of the Scottish church did not kill the desire of the Jamaica Mission Council (JMC) because at their 1841 meeting in Stirling, in the parish of Westmorland, they again reaffirmed their desire and commitment to organise a mission to Africa. However, it was the initiative of two prominent missionaries, George Blyth and Peter Anderson, who lobbied on behalf of the JMC[40] to secure authorisation. Waddell raised further financial support in Scotland and the mission was adopted by The United Secession Church in 1844.[41] A pioneering team including Hope Waddell, Andrew Chisholm a carpenter, Samuel Edgerley a catechist and printer, George Miller, Edward Miller an Afro-Jamaican who was previously enslaved and who served as a doctor's assistant and George Waddell arrived in Calabar on April 10, 1846.[42]

The subsequent support and development of the mission saw Afro-Jamaican lay-leaders under the leadership of the Scottish missionaries working together in Calabar, Eastern Nigeria. The focus of the mission was on evangelism through education. The mission established a number of schools, hospitals, churches and training colleges. One of the institutions that was established was named to honour one of the pioneers of the mission, the Hope Waddell Institute, and for a number of years until close to the time of Nigeria becoming an independent nation, the Institute and other surrounding schools always had on their staff mission personnel of African descent from the Presbyterian Church of Jamaica. A number of Afro-Jamaicans served the mission as head teachers until the late 1950s when the infamous Rev. Henry Ward returned to Jamaica and this marked the end of an era.[43] Although the mission to Africa came eventually under the Scottish missions, the Presbyterian Church of Jamaica has always cherished its role in taking the initiative and offering ongoing support for the work. In order to pay honour to the pioneering role of Jamaicans in the development of this contribution to the emergence of African Christianity, a decision was taken by the mission to always have missionaries from the West Indies (meaning Jamaica) as core members of the mission personnel team in Calabar.

The continuous presence of Jamaican mission personnel on the Calabar staff therefore calls into question what was the nature of their influence and contribution to the development of African Christianity. The leadership of the mission station was unquestionably under Scottish control. Inherent within European colonial culture was the use of *race, economic, social and religious factors* to determine one's status within society. They became factors that divided rather than united peoples. With a built-in

---

[39] Elijah Obinah, *Bridging the Divide: The Legacies of Mary Slessor, 'Queen' of Calabar, Nigeria*, Studies in World Christianity 17.3 (2011): 279.

[40] Elijah Obinah, *Bridging the Divide: The Legacies of Mary Slessor, 'Queen' of Calabar, Nigeria*, Studies in World Christianity 17.3 (2011): 279.

[41] The Calabar Mission Station became part of the United Presbyterian Church in 1847 when it became united with the United Secession and Relief churches. However in 1900 the United Presbyterian Church merge with the Free Church of Scotland to form the United Free Church of Scotland which later in 1929 reunited with the Church of Scotland.

[42] Elijah Obinah, *Bridging the Divide: The Legacies of Mary Slessor, 'Queen' of Calabar, Nigeria*, Studies in World Christianity 17.3 (2011): 279.

[43] Francis J. Osborne and Geoffrey Johnston, *Coastlands and Islands: First Thoughts on Caribbean Church History*. Kingston: UTCWI (1972): 172-173.

perception that saw themselves as a superior race and culture, Europeans ranked other people hierarchically. All other cultures were deemed to be inferior and this offered justification for colonization because they viewed 'uncultured peoples' as needing European civilizing enlightenment. The presence of personnel of African descent from Jamaica on the staff of the mission was an important source of inspiration that assured the local people that the mission would one day become theirs, and their own African staff would become leaders of the different institutions that were established. The Caribbean personnel of African descent also communicated an understanding and praxis of the gospel as one that had the power to liberate from all oppression. This empowered the local Christians to be confident in their mission outreach in their communities and to face up to whatever challenges or opposition to the gospel that they faced.

The Anglican Rio Pongas Mission – Guinea and Sierra Leone

Within the British Caribbean, the island of Barbados was regarded as 'the most British' because of its small size and population, and because British influences were much more effective. The Anglican Church within the West Indies was the dominant church in Barbados. Its missional presence and work in West Africa can be traced to 1851 when Bishop Parry of the Barbados Church Society recommended during the celebration of the third jubilee of the Society for the Propagation of the Gospel (SPG)[44] that a new West Indian Church Association be formed 'for the furtherance of the Gospel in Western Africa'.

> I propose in my own diocese, and venture to suggest also to the other West Indian bishops, to commence an African Mission, if only in answer to our prayers and efforts the great Lord of the Harvest be pleased to send forth the labourers, disposing also the members of the West Indian Church to unite in the work, and others in England to assist it. I am fully aware how far from attractive is the missionary field which the Western Coasts of Africa present.[45]

There was a rider that the mission work would be carried out in partnership with the SPG as Trustees of Codrington College, their main institution of training of the clergy for Christian ministry. A sum of money for the education of missionaries and also towards the endowment of a bishopric in Sierra Leone was allocated to finance the work of the West Africa Mission.[46] The motivation for the mission project was linked with the moral dilemma of being a state church that gave its support to the British government's policy of enslavement of Africans to work for the economic development of its colonies. The West Indian Mission to Africa was therefore predicated on the notion that 'Britain owed a debt to the African race for past injustices'.[47] Therefore, the declared motivation was rooted in a quest for justice for the Africans whose ancestors' human dignity had been abused by the life denying forces of slavery. The mission to Africa became a kind of atonement and redemption for those that benefited from the evil system and they felt compelled to repay a debt and to facilitate a process of healing of a broken relationship.

In Bakary Gibba's doctoral thesis on *The West Indian Mission to West Africa: The Rio Pongas*[48] *Mission, 1850-1963* he argued that The Rio Pongo area was located in the West African state of Guinea. According to Gibba, there were earlier attempts to establish a Christian mission in the area since 1801 but for various reasons, ranging from health concerns to security risks, they were unsuccessful. Success was

---

[44] This was the Anglican Church's missionary institution within the West Indian region.

[45] SPG Digest, 1898. www.anglicanhistory.org/africa/barrow1900/01.html.

[46] M. C. F. Easmon, *Sierra Leone Doctors*, Sierra Leone Studies New Series No. 6, 81.

[47] Noel Titus "*The West Indian Mission to Africa: Its Conception and Birth*, The Journal of Negro History, Vol 65, No. 2 (spring, 1980): 93-111 published by: Association for the Study of African American Life and History, Inc.

[48] "Rio Pongo" Portuguese name meaning the mud river.

achieved with the arrival of the West Indian Mission and its contingent of members of African descent who were more adaptable to the climatic conditions of the area than Europeans. The Rev. Hamble James Leacock, a vicar and native of Barbados aged about 60, along with an evangelist, Afro-West Indian John Duport from St Kitts, were the pioneers for this mission to Rio Pongas in 1855. Their mission station model invested in establishing a school at Fallangia that was used to educate and evangelized the local people who expressed interest. The environmental challenges of the areas had a devastating impact on the health of Leacock and a number of other white missionaries that came to replace him. It was the stability of Duport's leadership over a number of years that resulted in the building of the church and the education of a number of local leaders. After Duport's departure due to ill health, he was succeeded by a number of other Afro-West Indian missionaries such as the Rev. J.B. McEwen who arrived in 1871 and the Rev. C.W. Farquhar in 1890.[49] The West Indian missionaries eventually became the main staff members of the Rio Pongas Mission and they were joined by other Sierra Leoneans in their educational project of nurturing local leadership. Their influence was best felt in the area of education where a number of key local personnel were trained at their boarding school at the Isles de Los and later became leaders of key educational institutions within the nation. The Rio Pongas Mission remained part of the diocese of Sierra Leone until the 1930s when political tensions with France led to the mission being linked with the Gambia and it became part of a separate diocese under John Daly. The key influence of this West Indian Mission to the advancement of Christianity within Africa is to be found in the contribution of the schools that it established and their impact on nation-building.

The Jamaican Moravian/Basel Mission to Ghana

Before the slave trade was abolished in 1807 throughout the British Empire, the Gold Coast (Ghana) served as a centre for human trafficking in African labourers to the Americas. Although European missionaries were in the country at that time they had little or no impact because their work was indistinguishable from the traffickers that engaged in human oppression. It was not until the arrival of the Basel Mission from Germany in 1827 that a new era in mission engagement began. However, their work to evangelize Africans in Ghana was thwarted because the people mistrusted their true motives. There was little to show for their twelve years of labour. Illness, death and lack of support from the local population almost led to the closure of the mission. The Chief of the area laid down one non-negotiable requirement for the gospel to be considered and that was that it should be read and interpreted by someone who came from among them. Since no local person had been 'converted', the Basel Mission sought the help of other partner missionary societies. The Moravian Mission in Jamaica had in the development of its mission station model used education as a method of evangelization and had built up a cadre of African educators. A group of twenty-four that included six families of farmers was recruited and sent to be the pioneers in a new evangelization strategy among the Ghanaians with a specific objective:

> They had been recruited purposely to help convince the people of the Gold Coast that the Christian religion was not reserved for Europeans alone. They had also been recruited because it was believed that they could withstand the tropical climate more than the Europeans who too easily succumbed to malaria. This was an experiment which had been tried successfully in Sierra Leone where former African slaves became the principal missionaries to the African population. The Niger Mission had also proved that Africans were best suited for the work of evangelism in Africa.[50]

---

[49] Titus Noel, "*The West Indian Mission to Africa: Its Conception and Birth*, The Journal of Negro History, Vol 65, No. 2 (spring, 1980): 93-111 .

[50] History of the Presbyterian Church of Ghana, www.pcgonline.org/index.php/about-us/history-of-pcg (accessed

They first settled at Osu and later moved to Akropong, a village about 50 km from Accra. Language learning and agricultural instruction became the two key priorities. Through the quick learning of the language by the Afro-Jamaicans, the work of evangelization was advanced. The mission facilitated the translation of the scripture into the Twi language and gave the people their first written lexicon. The Jamaican workers brought agricultural plants with them from Jamaica such as cocoa that developed into a major profitable cash crop for the mission and the local population. Within ten years of their arrival the Jamaican workers in partnership with their Ghanaian converts had succeeded in spreading their mission work throughout the country.

The Basel Mission gained a firm footing in the nation, and its work thrived until the outbreak of World War I in 1914 and after a brief respite, it was continued, but followed and interrupted again by World War II in 1945. This led to the expulsion of the Germans from the region by the British. Their work was taken over by the Church of Scotland Mission and the Moravian ethos was changed to Presbyterian and Reformed. With the changing political landscape, the Basel Mission was unable to reclaim the work that it had pioneered before the outbreak of the wars. Through their work, the Presbyterian Church of Ghana had developed into one of the leading and fastest growing churches in the country. The heirs of those first missionaries from the Caribbean are still to be found in the life and work of the church in Ghana today.

Conclusion

This article began by positing that although the Anglo-Caribbean region occupies little attention in the global history of Christianity, the influence of African-led missions from the region to the development of Christianity in West Africa constitutes an immeasurable contribution that has not yet been fully appreciated in the annals of Global Christianity. It further argued that the experience of Africans in the Caribbean of being trafficked, surviving the inhumane transportation to the Caribbean, the ordeal of forced labour, the resistance against enslavement, the embracement of missionary Christianity and the achievement of emancipation equipped those that offered to serve in the different West Indian Missions to West Africa a unique spirituality in their love of justice and freedom that came from the liberating power of the gospel. The acquisition of sound education, excellent teaching skills, farming and carpentry skills, competent evangelists and pastoral leadership made the West Indian mission personnel excellent agents that facilitated effective enculturation of the gospel within West Africa.

Bibliography

Bakary. Gibba, The West Indian Mission to West Africa: The Rio Pongas Mission, 1850-1963, https://tspace.library.utoronto.ca/bitstream/1807/31759/1/Gibba_Bakary_201111_PhD_thesis.pdf (Accessed 30/04/2015)

J. M. Barkley. *Presbyterianism* (Belfast: The Tyrone Constitution, 1956)

J Baur, 2000 years of Christianity in Africa- An African History 62-1992 (Nairobi: Pauline Publications, 1994)

P R. Dekar. American and British Baptists in West Africa, 1841-1888, Memphis Theological Seminary, Memphis, www.bwa-baptist-heritage.org/dek.htm (accessed 30/4/2015)

Bryan Edwards, The History of the British Colonies in The West Indies. 2 vols. (London: J, Stockdale, 1793)

L.N.Erskine. *From Garvey to Marley Rastafari Theology* (Gainesville: University of Florida, 2004)

S. Hamber and R. Greenwood, *Emancipation To Emigration* (Kingston: Macmillan Caribbean, 1979)

S. Hamber, S. Greenwood. *Amerindians to Africans* (Haddington: Macmillan Caribbean 2003)

1/05/2015).

Edris Hamid, *Troubling of the Waters* (Trinidad: Rahaman Printery 1977)
Roderick R. Hewitt, *Church and Culture* (Dorpspruit: Cluster Publications 2012)
R. Lapage and D. Decamp (eds.), *Jamaican Creole: Creole Language Studies I* (London: McMillan, 1960)
Winston Lawson, Religion and Race (New York: Peter Lang, 1996)
A. Nico, *West Indians in West Africa*, Sierra Leone Studies, no. 13, June 1960
Elijah Obinah, *Bridging the Divide: The Legacies of Mary Slessor, 'Queen' of Calabar, Nigeria*, Studies in World Christianity 17.3 (2011): Edinburgh University Press
Francis J. Osborne and Geoffrey Johnston, Coastlands and Islands: First Thoughts on Caribbean Church History. Kingston: UTCWI (1972)
Orlando Patterson, *The Sociology of Slavery* (London, Oxford University Press, 1967)
Horace Russell, The Missionary Outreach of the West Indian Church; Jamaican Baptist Missions to West Africa in the Nineteenth Century (New York: Peter Lang, 2000)
Jaap van Slageren, *Jamaican Missionaries in Cameroon*, Exchange Vol. 30.2 (2001)
Hugh Sherlock, H. Bennett, *History of the Jamaican People, the Jamaican People* (Kingston: Ian Randle Publishers 1998)
R. Stewart, R, *Religion and Society in Post Emancipation Jamaica* (Knoxville: University of Tennessee Press 1992)
S.P.G. Digest, 1898. www.anglicanhistory.org/africa/barrow1900/01.html
Henry Waddell, Twenty-Nine Years in the West Indies and Central Africa 1829-1858 (London: T. Nelson & Sons, 1863)
Eric Williams, *From Columbus to Castro* (London: Andre Deutch, 1970)
Eric Williams, *British Historians and the West Indies* (London: Andre Deutch, 1964)
Presbyterian Church of Ghana, *www.pcgonline.org/index.php/about-us/history-of-pcg*
A.H. Barrow *Fifty Years in Western Africa (1900)* www.anglicanhistory.org/africa/barrow1900/ 01.html

(5) African Christianity in Colonial Times

Obed Kealotswe

Introduction

A discussion of African Christianity in colonial times is a very tricky and complicated one. The complication lies in the fact that colonialism in its wide context started long before the Christian era. Christianity itself was born in a Roman colony. The argument of this chapter however is that for the purposes of a fruitful discussion, colonial Christianity should be used here to refer to the Christianity that developed after the partitioning of Africa in 1884. But this will be done after qualifying why Christianity had always been a colonial religion. Christianity first found its way into North Africa right from the time of the early church.[1] Most of the beliefs and teachings of Christianity were born in Africa through the works of Philo of Alexandria, Clement of Alexandria and Origen.[2] These great Christians of the time were Africans. This chapter argues that the Christianity which was in Africa by that time was born in a colonial situation but it was not colonial until AD 313 when Constantine made Christianity the official religion of the Roman Empire. This chapter then argues that colonial Christianity started at that time and became more prominent after 1884. The argument is that before AD 313 the state was not concerned about Christianity except for persecuting the early church because of its revolutionary teachings which were challenging all the social structures, traditions, beliefs and customs of the time. It is interesting to learn that amongst the Christian martyrs, many were women because the early church had no discrimination based on sex or gender. It propagated for human love as derived, inspired and based on faith in Jesus Christ the only Son of God. Origen even taught that all human beings including the Devil or Satan would be saved.[3] This chapter argues that early colonial Christianity reached Africa in about AD 320. This was after Constantine had declared Christianity to be the religion of the Roman Empire. The church which had been engaged in doctrinal issues was drawn into political issues as well. This led to divisions in the church which were never resolved up to today. The major division was between the East and the West followed by the Reformation of the sixteenth century which led to the breaking of the western Roman Catholic Church into many denominations which were then used by the various colonial powers to partition Africa. This chapter makes an overview of this development and makes suggestions for some possible solutions to the problems. Its theoretical framework is that the core of the Christian faith as taught by Jesus Christ, expounded by Paul and lived by the early church to AD 313, had never been taught to the Africans. The Africans need to go to the crossroads to find the core teachings and beliefs of Christianity as a religion distinct from others.

Colonial Christianity: What is It?

This is a very complicated question to answer. To attempt to answer the question this discussion will refer to the first church Council of Jerusalem in AD 49. At this Council, Paul separated from Peter and James to proclaim a gospel free from Judaism. In his letter to the Romans Chapter 8, Paul discusses the law and its

---

[1] Elizabeth Isichei, *A History of Christianity In Africa From Antiquity to the Present* (New Jersey: William B. Eerdmans Publishing Company, 1995); Williston Walker, *A History of the Christian Church* (Edinburgh: T&T Clark, 1968).

[2] Isichei, *A History of Christianity.*

[3] Isichei, *A History of Christianity.*

failure in saving people. He argues for faith as the core of the Christian faith. When pre-colonial and colonial Christianity came to Africa, it had lost this core because similar to the Jews or Israelites, the propagandists of the Christian faith did not appeal to faith but went into crusades to force not Christianity but their political interests. The conquest of Canaan by the Israelites was done through a religion which respected war as a way of forcing people to believe and have faith in Yahweh as the only God of the universe. There were no moves to convince the people about Yahweh so that they should believe in him but the people were forced to obey and recognize Yahweh as the only one God. This attitude was adopted by both the pre-colonial and post-colonial Christianity in Africa. This discussion dates back colonial Christianity to AD 313 when the Roman Emperor Constantine made Christianity the official religion of his empire. Pre-Constantinian Christianity was persecuted for being revolutionary in challenging the traditional cultures and customs of both the Romans and the Israelites and for discriminating people of other ethnicities, traditions and customs. Pauline Christianity knew no boundaries that divided people by race, gender or ethnicity. The early church was the open platform for all those who believed in Jesus Christ as their Saviour and Lord. But once Christianity came under the support of the state, it became a political movement that was used by the Emperors to rule their subjects and expand their empires. The exemption of the clergy from taxation, the building of large churches and cathedrals by the Emperors diminished the preaching of the free gospel of Jesus Christ which liberated people from all forms of bias including gender. Women began to be side-lined in decision-making in the church; issues of ethnicity arose when it came to leadership in the church. The argument of this discussion is that what is believed to be colonialism has a very long history and Christianity had always been part of colonialism and discrimination since Constantine. The despising of other people of different cultures has been characteristic of Christianity since Constantine. Pre-colonial Christianity despised African cultures and customs in favour of the colonial western cultures. It failed to recognize the Africans as human beings. Colonial Christianity forced the Africans directly and indirectly to accept Christianity which was wrapped in European culture. It is a political Christianity used by those who hold political power to force to submission all other people who are not of their race or ethnicity. Many parts of Africa south of the Sahara which is generally referred to as black Africa came into contact with Christianity in the early fifteenth and sixteenth centuries. The major aspects emerging from the contacts of Christianity with Africa, its people, customs, traditions and religious beliefs have contributed much to the manner in which Christianity was received, perceived, accepted and rejected by different African communities and societies. The years before the colonial period have showed that the major areas of concern were those of conflicts between the traditional African religious beliefs and practices and Christianity. In many parts of Africa, missionaries were either preceded by traders or they preceded traders themselves. In areas where trade came before Christianity e.g. many parts of Southern Africa, the coming of colonialism had much more serious repercussions than the areas where missionaries preceded traders. The reason was that the traders attracted their mother countries to engage in trade with Africa. By so doing they needed the protection of their mother countries. In this way, colonialism had much more serious results which were negative as opposed to those in areas where missionaries came before traders. Missionaries were more interested in developing the lives of their converts and making them to be like the Europeans from where many originated. Their establishment of educational institutions, clinics and hospitals helped very much in the social development of many African countries. In many cases, they differed from the traders who were more interested in business as opposed to developing the local people. Traders in ivory and gold had no time to develop the Africans but always wanted their countries to protect them against the rebelling Africans who did not want their resources to be diminished. In some areas, traders who had started companies helped missionaries during the colonial period when the mother-bodies of some missionaries could not afford to do so. This discussion reads and interprets African Christianity in the colonial period by looking at the present state of Christianity in Africa. The argument of this discussion is that if one studies or narrates the events of the colonial period on their own without reference to their effects in the present, the discussion does not make good sense. Colonial Christianity could only be understood with reference to the present post-colonial Christianity in Africa. This is the angle from which this discussion is approached.

Colonial Christianity in Africa

The General African Situation of Colonial Christianity

The missionaries of the nineteenth century which ushered in colonialism have been blamed from many angles as agents of colonialism. This chapter views things differently. Many historians of Africa concur that the missionaries made some great contributions to the development of Africa.[4] If one takes the year 1884 as the year that marked the beginnings of colonialism in Africa, one will realise that before that year, missionaries were regarded with respect and honour in many African countries. But the partitioning of Africa from 1884 ushered in a new picture of the missionaries and their work in Africa. The colonialism that emerged after 1884 went to the extent of destroying the good deeds of the missionaries because the new colonial administration that came had no interest in the lives of the Africans but became more concerned about trade in Africa. It could be argued in many cases that colonialism put a stop to human slavery. In many cases, preventing slavery was the major excuse used by the colonial governments to colonize many African states and partition Africa.[5] Fighting slavery made many missionary bodies invite their governments to intervene in Africa by abolishing slavery and developing good trade. By so doing, many missionary bodies became victims of their own countries because their countries forced them to accept colonialism in the guise of fighting slavery. By using conversion, many Africans were made not to resist the new governments which were coming into Africa and replacing the traditional African governments and social structures. Missionaries were equally victims of colonialism because their evangelization was also controlled by the colonial powers whose major interest was not Christianity but trade. Traders were much more favoured by the colonial governments than missionaries. It is for this reason that many missionaries became victims of colonialism. When the mother bodies of the missionaries failed to support the work of the missionaries, many missionaries became tempted to support the colonial powers in order to get help for the work of the missions. In Southern Africa, with examples from Botswana, many missionaries of the London Missionary Society (LMS) became victims of this situation. When colonialism came in the guise of Protection in 1885, the LMS began to lose control of most of its institutions, educational and medical, because the chiefs who in many cases connived with the colonial protective government were supported by the government to start national schools which were independent from missionary control.[6] These secular schools posed some great challenges to the mission schools to the extent that by the time of independence in 1966, almost all the missionary-founded institutions, hospitals, clinics and schools were taken over by government – except for a few. This phenomenon is found in many areas where the chiefs connived with the colonial governments. In areas where there was some strong

---

[4] Assa Okoth, *A History of Africa 1855-1914* (Nairobi: East African Educational Publishers, 1979).

[5] Okoth, *A History of Africa 1855-1914;* I. Tufuoh, "Relations between Christian Missions, European administration, and Traders in the Gold Coast, 1828-1874," in *Christianity in Tropical Africa: Studies Presented and Discussed at the Seventh International African Seminar, University of Ghana, April 1965 edited by* C.G. Baeta, 34-60 (London: Oxford University Press, 1968).

[6] Don Rempel Boschman, *The Conflict Between New Religious Movements and the State in the Bechuanaland Protectorate prior to 1949* (Gaborone: University of Botswana, 1994); Mutero J. Chirenje, A History of Northern Botswana 1850-1910 (London: Associated University Press, 1979); Jane M. Sales, *The Planting of the Churches in South Africa* (Michigan: William B. Eerdmans Publishing Company, 1971).

resistance to the colonial government, many missionary institutions survived for a very long time because in many parts of Africa, missionaries did not agree nor support the colonial government.

It is not an easy task to dwell on many examples on the basis of the different African countries but it suffices to follow the regional categorisation which makes things easier even if there are similarities but not identical situations. The most familiar and the most interesting is the South African situation.

The South African Colonial Christianity Situation and the Responses

In South Africa, the Dutch Reformed Church (DRC) brought Christianity as early as 1652. But it had no intention to evangelise the indigenous peoples because to the Dutch, Christianity was their culture and way of life. But the eighteenth century ushered in a period for the need of the evangelization of the indigenous peoples by the Moravians, London Missionary Society (LMS) and some DRC ministers and evangelists. The tensions between the Dutch and the English at the Cape penetrated the churches in the Cape and also made them to be divided. The first division took place in the DRC family itself. Latourette and Charles Villa-Vicencio show that the major divisions resulted in three major denominations: Nederduits Geerformeerde Kerk; Nederduits Hervormde Kerk and Gereformeerde Kerk.[7] These churches differed mainly due to their attitudes towards the evangelization of the Africans and relationships with the governments of the time. This division in the DRC family posed some serious challenges to the other churches in South Africa – Roman Catholics, Anglicans, Presbyterians, Methodists, Baptists, Lutherans, Apostolic Faith and Congregationalists. These churches were mainly English speaking. Many, such as the Congregationalists under the umbrella of the London Missionary Society (LMS) had previous good relationships with the Africans. Some of their missionaries such as John Philip and David Livingstone had pioneered the struggle for the freedom of the Africans and made some wide explorations of Africa respectively. For a long time the LMS missionaries in South Africa had fought colonial Christianity from within rather than from outside. The creation of the three Protectorates, the Kingdom of Swaziland, Basutoland and Bechuanaland were due to the work of some prominent LMS missionaries who had realised that the DRC-supported governments were aiming at taking the whole of Southern Africa under their control.

The division moved from churches into the different societies and communities. The churches found themselves entangled in many racial conflicts which led to some serious political and religious conflicts. The religious conflicts automatically divided the churches to the extent that some churches in the Dutch Reformed family took a clear stand of supporting the colonial government whilst the English-speaking churches remained neutral and ambiguous.[8] The early missionaries who had worked and lived with the indigenous peoples found themselves being separated from their people by segregational laws which divided the people into racial classes. By the end of the nineteenth century and the beginning of the twentieth, many Africans in South Africa had started some African Independent Churches (AICs) which mainly opposed the segregation laws posed by the colonial government.[9] The AICs also reacted by reverting to some of the good customs and traditions of the South African peoples by including them in their understanding of the Christian faith. In many cases they were assisted by similar cultures and traditions found in the Old Testament.[10] This discussion argues that the impact of racial segregation in

---

[7] Kenneth S. Latourette, *Christianity in a Revolutionary Age Volume 5* (New YORK: The Paternoster Press, 1962), 455.

[8] John De Gruchy, *The Church Struggle in South Africa* (Cape Town: David Philip, 1979).

[9] Bengt G.M. Sundkler, *Bantu Prophets in South Africa* (London: Oxford University Press, 1961).

[10] Sundkler, *Bantu Prophets in South Africa;* David B. Barrett, *Schism and Renewal in Africa* (Nairobi: Oxford University Press, 1968); James N. Amanze, *African Christianity in Botswana: The case of the African Independent Churches (Gweru: Mambo Press, 1998);* Obed N. Kealotswe, *"Acceptance and rejection: The traditional-healer prophet and his integration of healing methods," BOLESWA: Journal of Theology, Religion and Philosophy (BJTRP),*

South Africa was similar to the partitioning of Africa by the colonial powers. The result of this partitioning was the planting of the different denominations in Africa instead of the Christian gospel.[11] The partitioning of Africa into many regions and states controlled by western powers led to the automatic partitioning of church denominations into sects and cults. In every African state, some divisions occurred in the churches leading to many splits following the examples of colonialism. The mutual relationships which had characterized the pre-colonial church denominations deteriorated into misunderstandings and competition between church denominations fuelled by colonialism. The missionary bodies which supported colonialism found favour with the colonial powers whilst those which were not supportive felt victims of the colonial powers. This led to the birth of a fragmented church in Africa whose impacts are still felt by modern African Christianity. This discussion argues that one can only understand colonial Christianity by looking at its results as experienced in post-colonial Africa. The general African situation has been captured by Hastings[12] by approaching the subject thematically. From his observation and research he outlines African Christianity in three themes which are Church and state; the historic Churches and Independence. This categorization is supported by the present discussion because it also approaches the subject from the post-colonial stance. One can argue that steps towards independence in Africa started as early as 1950 and getting momentum in the 1960s. The twenty-five-year period studied by Hastings sheds a lot of light on colonial Christianity and post-colonial Christianity in Africa.

The Patterns of Partitioning in the Whole of Africa and the Responses

The purpose of this essay is not to go into any detailed studies of the responses to colonialism because these have been well discussed by Okoth[13] and Latourette[14] with examples from Western Africa, Central Africa, Eastern Africa and Southern Africa. The purpose of this discussion is to try to identify some common features which do characterise African Christianity in the colonial period. It must however be argued that there is no clear-cut demarcation between colonial Christianity and the Christianity of the pre-colonial period. In many African countries one identifies some developments with some continuity from pre-colonial to colonial Christianity. The general situation as discussed by Okoth and Latourette is that colonial Christianity could be understood by examining its impacts in the African continent as a whole. Latourette[15] has observed that colonial Christianity was divided into Roman Catholic and the Protestant denominations. This division was influenced by the ruling colonial authorities in the different partitions of Africa. The Protestant churches were more spread in the British colonies whilst the Roman Catholics were found in the Portuguese, French, Belgian and Spanish territories. In German colonies there was some balance between the Protestants and Roman Catholics. This paper argues that to understand the present situation of Christianity in Africa one has to be familiar with both the events of the pre-colonial and the colonial expressions of Christianity in Africa. The major thing which both pre-colonial and colonial Christianities did to Africa was the de-tribalization of many African peoples mainly through the creation of unnatural borders which separated related peoples from each other. This situation is well captured and discussed by Phiri[16] with examples from Malawi amongst the Chewa peoples. Although her focus is on

---

Vol. 1, no.1 (2005): 109-122.

[11] Gerald West, *Biblical Hermeneutics of Liberation Modes of Reading the Bible in the South African Context* (Pietermaritzburg: Cluster Publications, 1991).

[12] Adrian Hastings, *A History of African Christianity 1950-1975* (Cambridge: Cambridge University Press, 1979).

[13] Okoth, *A History of Africa 1855-1914.*

[14] Latourette, *Christianity in a Revolutionary Age.*

[15] Latourette, *Christianity in a Revolutionary Age, 449.*

[16] Isabel A. Phiri, *Women, Presbyterianism and Patriarchy Religious Experience of Chewa Women in Central Malawi* (Blantyre: Kachere Series, 1997).

women, the study reveals what has happened in many African countries regionally as Eastern, Western, Central, and Southern Africa. The de-tribalization of people led to the birth of nationalism in the twentieth century. Latourette argues that nationalism began to be strong after the two world wars which took place at the peak of colonialism. Africans who had fought in wars which were not theirs began to agitate for their freedom. They had learned that the colonial powers which involved them in their wars were actually proud of their own integrities but not aware of the fact that Africans also needed their integrity. This agitation for freedom was supported by the educational institutions of the different missionary bodies working in the different regions and areas of Africa. The very missionary-educated elites were the ones who used that education to challenge colonialism. They even challenged the expressions of Christianity as brought by the different denominations to many parts of Africa. The reaction took many forms as shall be discussed below. It is not easy to discuss region by region how colonial Christianity functioned but one example represents them all as shown by Okoth and Latourette.

The Impacts of Colonialism on Post-Colonial Christianity in Africa

The post-colonial church in Africa inherited the divisions caused by colonialism. These divisions have been caused and fuelled by the fact that when many African states became independent, they opted to be secular states which tolerate religion rather than identifying themselves with any particular religion or faith. The other factor is that many African independent states and those wanting independence became very nationalistic in their struggles for independence. Nationalism made many African political leaders resist the natural boundaries created by the colonial powers and emphasized tribal and ethnic unity. To make this possible, many independent African states co-opted for secular states rather than sacred. They did this in order to rebuild the African identities and African consciousness but at the same time taking into consideration the modern times in which globalization is taking place. The fact that many African states have not put any control on religion nor identify themselves with any one religious faith has resulted in two things which have shaped post-colonial Christianity in Africa. These are:

African creativity; and

Rebellion by various denominations in Africa against established Christianity.

African Creativity

Colonial Christianity in Africa forced many African Christians to accept teachings and beliefs which did not have meaning to them. Many just accepted the formality of being a Christian in order to benefit from the services provided by Christianity at the time. But in many cases the traditional African still remained dormant in many Africans. The first reaction has been labelled African creativity by Barrett[17] referring to the creativity that is found in the AICs and other New Religious Movements (NRMs). Many AICs which emerged during the colonial period and immediately after reacted against the manner in which the western white missionaries treated them. Barrett called the attitude of the missionaries towards the Africans as *failure in love.* This simply means that the missionaries preached a gospel of love which they never practised. The AICs then became very creative in their theology, beliefs and practices and produced their own expressions of the Christian faith which are in line with the African world view and African life. Colonial Christianity produced African Christianity. Some movements which emerged in the colonial time took some Christian guise yet they were political movements. These resulted in what Sundkler called messianic movements with black messiahs. Some much more interesting were the uprisings in Malawi by Chilembwe's movement.[18] In the Congo Simon Kimbangu[19] posed some serious challenges to the Belgian

[17] Latourette, *Christianity in a Revolutionary Age.*

[18] Okoth, *A History of Africa 1855-1914.*

colonial government. The role of women finds a classic example in Alice Lenshina in Zambia.[20] Although her movement did not oppose the colonial government but the independent one, her activities are still a result of colonial Christianity. In West Africa, the major influences came through the revivals of Prophet Harris and the Aladura.[21] In East Africa a good and classic example is that of the Luo.[22] The movements which were independent and indigenous contributed a lot to African creativity and the birth of a post-colonial church in Africa.

Rebellion by Various Denominations in Africa against Established Christianity

The use of the word rebellion to refer to what happened in some African corners might be too strong. Perhaps the much more lenient word could be apologetic. But classical apologies as written by the Greek Apologists[23] were not necessarily nice works but very challenging. Colonial Christianity produced such challenges. The first of these came from many missionaries who had the opportunity to relate to the Africans and tried to understand their worldview and their traditional religious beliefs and practices.[24]

These sympathetic works to the Africans made the western world think seriously about the conditions of the Africans. These authors studied the religious beliefs and practices of the Africans in detail in order to find some similarities with Christianity. They wanted African thought and belief to be understood instead of it being despised from lack of knowledge. Amongst the western missionaries and anthropologists works such as Parrinder[25] and Taylor[26] opened up the minds of western peoples to the world of the Africans. This led to the works by the Africans themselves such as Mbiti,[27] Idowu[28] and Setiloane[29] to mention but a few. These apologetic works were by nature rebelling against the western expressions of the Christian faith. A much clearer illustration of this rebellion against colonial Christianity which was supported by western administration is that of Luo independence as discussed by Barrett. The rebellion of the Luo people against British administration is a clear indication of the fact that colonial Christianity even disturbed the good work that was done by the pre-colonial missionaries and their relationship to the Africans. Colonial administration with its discriminative attitudes towards the Africans created a very bad image of Christianity in almost all the areas of Africa, Western, Central, Eastern and Southern Africa. The major patterns and results of colonialism are similar with very little differences as discussed by Okoth[30] and also by Baeta.[31] From his study of the Luo, Barrett found many similarities all over Africa. Although

---

[19] Martin Marie-Louise, *Kimbangu,-an African prophet and his church* (Oxford: Basil Blackwell, 1975); Marthinus L. Daneel, *Quest for Belonging: Introduction to a Study of African Independent Churches* (Gweru: Mambo Press, 1987); Daneel, *Quest for Belonging.*

[20] Hastings, *A History of African Christianity; Barrett, Schism and Renewal in Africa.*

[21] Harold W Turner, *History of an African Independent Church: The Church of the Lord (Aladura)* (Oxford: Oxford University Press, 1967).

[22] Barrett, *Schism and Renewal in Africa.*

[23] John N.D. Kelly, *Early Christian Doctrines* (London: A&C Black, 1977).

[24] Classical of these are the works of Edwin W. Smith, *Knowing the African* (London: Lutterworth Press, 1946); Henry Callaway, *The Religious System of the Amazulu* (Cape Town: Struik, 1970); William Charles Willoughby, *The Soul of the Bantu: A Study of the Sympathetic Magico-Religious Practices and Beliefs of the Bantu tribes of Africa* (London: SCM, 1928).

[25] Geoffrey E. Parrinder, *African Traditional Religion* (London: S.P.C.K., 1968).

[26] John V. Taylor, *The Primal Vision: Christian Presence Amid African Religion* (London: SCM, 1963).

[27] John S. Mbiti, *Bible and Theology in African Christianity* (Nairobi: Oxford University Press, 1986).

[28] Bolaji Idowu, *Towards an Indigenous Church* (London: Oxford University Press, 1965).

[29] Gabriel M. Setiloane, *The Image of God Among the Sotho-Tswana* (Netherlands: A.A. Balkema, 1976).

[30] Okoth, *A History of Africa 1855-1914.*

[31] Barrett, *Schism and Renewal in Africa.*

disagreements were more on religious beliefs, culture, customs and traditions, rebellion was more pronounced in areas where colonial administration was very strong.

This essay has argued that to understand colonial Christianity, one has to take a closer look at the present state of Christianity in Africa. One cannot study and understand colonial Christianity without reflecting on the present situation and then going back to the colonial period.

Modern Christianity in Africa as an Expression of Colonial Christianity

There are two major factors which have emerged in present or modern Christianity in Africa as results of colonial Christianity. These are theological creativity and the place of gender in the Christian religion. Many works have emerged which show some African theological creativity in order to make Christianity acceptable to the African worldview and by so doing making it to become African Christianity.[32]

These works and many others are reactions to colonial Christianity. To cite some of these reactions, Phiri shows how pre-colonial Chewa religion recognized the roles played by women but these were limited because patriarchy still prevailed from many angles. Amanze has done some good studies showing the roles played by women by founding churches in Botswana but still patriarchy dominated the women-founded churches. The failure of the Christian religion to make women play prominent roles in decision making and the running of churches has a long history. Starting with the Old Testament women had always been in the background. Any woman who achieved anything was regarded by men as an exception and whatever she did could not last unless a man arose to replace the woman. In the New Testament, very few women are mentioned but most of them seem to remain subjected to men in spite of their achievements. Throughout church history a few women are ever mentioned unless they are appended to men. The spread of Christianity to Europe is championed by men who fought wars to spread the gospel. When Christianity was finally established in Europe, it took a patriarchal form where women were prevented from any leadership positions as priests or ministers. The only place where they could be put because of their large numbers over men was the nunneries. The attitude towards women by western Christianity was carried to Africa by the colonial churches. This time, the attitude was not towards women but towards African men who were regarded as children to be guided by missionaries in the running of the different church denominations. Women had no place at all since the struggle remained between the white men and the black men. The reactions to this situation are now visible in post-colonial Christianity in Africa. Theologians have embarked on some serious questioning and interpretations of the Bible to suit the African situation. The works of Kwesi Dickson and Paul Ellingworth have been stated above as such examples. The re-writing the Bible project in Zimbabwe is one such project. The Association of Theological Institutions in Southern and Central Africa (ATISCA) produced its *Theology Cooked in an African Pot* in 1998. Such associations as ATIEA and ASTHEOL have also engaged themselves with theological projects which deny the theological paradigms introduced to Africa by western theologians. The rise of women's organizations such as the Circle of Concerned African Women (the Circle) in Accra, Ghana, in 1989 is one

[32] Some of the works are: James N. Amanze, Fidelis Nkomazana, Obed N. Kealotswe eds. *Biblical Studies, Theology, Religion and Philosophy an Introduction for African Universities* (Eldoret: Zapf Chancery, 2010); Appiah-Kubi Kofi and Torres Sergio eds. *African Theology En Route: Papers from the Pan-African Conference of Third World Theologians, December 17-23, 1977, Accra, Ghana* (New York: Orbis Books, 1979); C.G. Baeta, *Christianity in Tropical Africa* (London: Oxford University Press, 1968); Richard Elphick and Rodney Davenport, *Christianity in South Africa A Political, Social & Cultural History* (Cape Town: David Philip, 1997); Kwesi A. Dickson and Paul Ellingworth *eds. Biblical Revelation and African Beliefs* (New York: Orbis Books, 1969); Mercy A. Oduyoye, *Hearing and Knowing Theological Reflections on Christianity in Africa* (New York: Orbis Books, 1986); Isabel A. Phiri, *Women, Presbyterianism and Patriarchy Religious Experience of Chewa Women in Central Malawi,* Blantyre: Kachere Series, 1997); Aylward Shorter, *African Christian Theology-Adaptation or Incarnation?* (London: Geoffrey Chapman, 1975).

of the responses to colonial Christianity. The Circle is not a challenge to patriarchy as such but to the whole Bible, its set-up and its interpretation. This is not a work that is limited to women but it needs the participation of men as well. It draws the Christian faith to the crossroads where Jesus is seen all the time with his disciples composed of men and women. Jesus was compelled by the prevailing culture to have men as leaders instead of having a mixture of men and women. The core of the Christian faith has no gender, nor Jew or Greek as Paul maintained. It is a faith that should promote human, gender, sexual and racial equalities.

What then is the Future of Christianity in Africa?

The answer to this question might appear utopian to the reader. African Christianity should not be a reaction to colonial Christianity. It must go back to the crossroads, re-read the Bible, reinterpret the teachings of Jesus and establish a Christian church in Africa. The African Church must treat all its members just like Jesus who did not know racialism, tribalism or ethnicity, social status, sex or gender. Jesus mingled with all people: the despised prostitutes, the hated tax collectors, the rich and the poor – both men and women. He violated all the rules, laws, traditions and customs of his own people the Jews and those of the Greeks and Romans. His teachings were revolutionary in that they violated all the teachings of the then existing religions and even those of the other older faiths of the world. Christianity knows no walls or boundaries between people.[33] African theologians should take the Africans back to the crossroads and start building African Christianity from where Jesus and Paul left. It is not fruitful at this stage to keep on pointing out the mistakes made by the missionaries and the colonial powers in planting Christianity in Africa. The most fruitful thing is to reconstruct a theology of Christ who knew no limitations in the Christian faith. The post-colonial church should be a church for all human beings who believe in Jesus Christ regardless of their ethnicity, race or gender. It must be an African Christianity with a biblically based theology constructed by African theologians, not mimicking western theologians. The Bible does not need to be re-written but it needs to be understood from the point of Jesus Christ not from that of Moses, King David and his prophets but from Jesus Christ's point of view. All the cultures which dominated the OT and all our African cultures should be transformed by the life and teachings of Jesus Christ. This discussion argues that it is only from this standpoint that the Christian faith can have meaning in the daily lives of Africans. The achievements made by African theologians, biblical scholars and church historians already show that the colonial type of Christianity could be transformed to become African and give meaning to the African people. This is the way forward for the church in Africa.

Bibliography

Amanze, James N. *African Christianity in Botswana: The case of the African Independent Churches*. Gweru: Mambo Press, 1998.

Amanze, James N. et at. eds. Biblical Studies, Theology, Religion and Philosophy an Introduction for African Universities. Eldoret: Zapf Chancery, 2010.

Baeta, C.G. *Christianity in Tropical Africa.* London: Oxford University Press, 1968.

Barrett, David B. *Schism and Renewal in Africa.* Nairobi: Oxford University Press, 1968.

Boschman, Don Rempel. *The Conflict between New Religious Movements and the State in the Bechuanaland Protectorate prior to 1949*. Gaborone: University of Botswana, 1994.

Callaway, Henry. *The Religious System of the Amazulu.* Cape Town: Struik, 1970.

Chirenje, Mutero J. *A History of Northern Botswana 1850-1910*. London: Associated University Press,

[33] Samuel Kabue, Esther Mombo, Joseph Galgalo, and C. B. Peter, eds. *Disability, Society, and Theology Voices from Africa* (Limuru: Zapf Chancery, 2011).

1979.
Daneel, Marthinus L. *Quest for Belonging: Introduction to a Study of African Independent Churches.* Gweru: Mambo Press, 1987.
De Gruchy, John. *The Church Struggle in South Africa.* Cape Town: David Philip, 1979.
Dickson, Kwesi A. and Paul Ellingworth (eds), *Biblical Revelation and African Beliefs.* New York: Orbis Books, 1969.
Elphick, Richard and Rodney Davenport. *Christianity in South Africa A Political, Social and Cultural History*. Cape Town: David Philip, 1997.
Hastings, Adrian. *A History of African Christianity 1950-1975.* Cambridge: Cambridge University Press, 1979.
Idowu, Bolaji. *Towards an Indigenous Church.* London: Oxford University Press, 1965.
Isichei, Elizabeth. *A History of Christianity in Africa from Antiquity to the Present.* New Jersey: William B. Eerdmans Publishing Company, 1995.
Kabue, Samuel et al. eds. *Disability, Society, and Theology Voices from Africa*. Limuru: Zapf Chancery, 2011.
Kealotswe, Obed N. 'Acceptance and rejection: The traditional-healer prophet and his integration of healing methods, *BOLESWA: Journal of Theology, Religion and Philosophy (BJTRP),* Vol. 1, no.1 (2005): 109-122.
Kelly, John N.D. *Early Christian Doctrines.* London: A. & C. Black, 1977.
Kofi, Appiah-Kubi and Torres Sergio eds. *African Theology En Route: Papers from the Pan-African Conference of Third World Theologians*, December 17-23, 1977, Accra, Ghana. New York: Orbis Books, 1979.
Latourette, Kenneth S. *Christianity in a Revolutionary Age Volume 5.* New YORK: The Paternoster Press, 1962.
Marie-Loiuse, Martin. *Kimbangu,-an African prophet and his church.* Oxford: Basil Blackwell, 1975.
Mbiti, John S. *Bible and Theology in African Christianity*. Nairobi: Oxford University Press, 1986.
Oduyoye, Mercy A. *Hearing and Knowing Theological Reflections on Christianity in Africa.* New York: Orbis Books, 1986.
Okoth, Assa. *A History of Africa 1855-1914.* Nairobi: East African Educational Publishers, 1979.
Parrinder, Geoffrey E. *African Traditional Religion.* London: S.P.C.K., 1968.
Phiri, Isabel A. Women, *Presbyterianism and Patriarchy Religious Experience of Chewa Women in Central Malawi.* Blantyre: Kachere Series, 1997.
Sales, Jane M. *The Planting of the Churches in South Africa.* Michigan: William B. Eerdmans Publishing Company, 1971.
Setiloane, Gabriel M. *The Image of God among the Sotho-Tswana*. Netherlands: A.A. Balkema, 1976.
Shorter, Aylward. African Christian Theology-Adaptation or Incarnation? London: Geoffrey Chapman, 1975.
Smith, Edwin W. *Knowing the African.* London: Lutterworth Press, 1946.
Sundkler, Bengt G.M. *Bantu Prophets in South Africa.* London: Oxford University Press, 1961.
Taylor, John V. *The Primal Vision: Christian Presence Amid African Religion.* London: SCM, 1963.
Tufuoh, I. 'Relations between Christian Missions, European administration, and Traders in the Gold Coast, 1828-1874', in *Christianity in Tropical Africa: Studies Presented and Discussed at the Seventh International African Seminar, University of Ghana*, April 1965 edited by CG Baeta, 34-60. London: Oxford University Press, 1968.
Turner, Harold W. *History of an African Independent Church: The Church of the Lord* (Aladura). Oxford: Oxford University Press, 1967.
Walker, Williston *A History of the Christian Church* (Edinburgh: T. & T. Clark, 1968).
West, Gerald. *Biblical Hermeneutics of Liberation Modes of Reading the Bible in the South African Context*. Pietermaritzburg: Cluster Publications, 1991.
Willoughby, William C. *The Soul of the Bantu: A Study of the Sympathetic Magico-Religious Practices and Beliefs of the Bantu tribes of Africa*. London: SCM, 1928.

(6) African Christianity in the Post-Independence Period

Hebron L. Ndlovu

Introduction

This article aims to give a concise survey of major features, developments and trends of African Christianity in post-independence Africa, with particular references to some churches in sub-Saharan Africa. It contends, in agreement with many students of Christianity in Africa, that African Christianity in the post-independence era can be described as a multi-faceted faith tradition that has played, and still plays, a complex role in contemporary African society.[1] The article also contends that the complexity of African Christianity in post-independence Africa calls for an interdisciplinary analysis of this phenomenon; and these disciplines may include, *inter alia*, philosophy, religious studies, history, sociology and anthropology.

The article proceeds from two established premises about the place of Christianity in post-colonial African society. The first premise is that, with the notable exceptions of few African countries such as Egypt, Ethiopia, Liberia, Mozambique, Namibia, South Sudan and Zimbabwe, at the time when most of the African countries achieved their independence in the 1960s, the majority of African peoples had converted to Christianity; and Africa as a whole at that period had been classified as a Christian continent.[2]

The second premise of this article is that the conversion of most African peoples to Christianity, especially to missionary founded churches, was not simply a private spiritual affair but was part and parcel of a planned western-driven transformation of non-European societies that was accompanied by modifications of peoples, social identities, systems of morality and power relationships.[3] As a result, most of the political leaders and influential figures in post-independence African states were not only persons who professed Christianity but also individuals who had received education at mission schools or theological institutions.[4]

In keeping with the aim and scope of this article, three thematic areas will be covered in this survey, namely: 1) Features of African Christianity in post-independence Africa; 2) Major historical and religious developments; 3) Concluding Remarks: Enduring trends

---

[1] See Tinyiko Maluleke (2010). 'Of Africanised bees and Africanised churches: ten theses on African Christianity'. *Missionalia* vol. 38 (no.3), 369-380; Steven Paas (2006). *The Faith Moves South: A History of Christianity in Africa*. Kachere Series, Zomba, Malawi; Sanneh, L and Carpenter, J. A., eds. (2005). *The Changing Face of Christianity: Africa, the West, and the World*. Oxford University, Oxford.

[2] See Klaus Fiedler, *The Story of Faith Missions* (Regnum: Oxford, 1994), 364; N. I. Samwini ('African Concepts of God in both Christianity and Islam', in Kalengyo, E. M (ed), *God of Life*. (All Africa Conference of Churches: Nairobi, 2013), 49.

[3] See R. W. Hefner, 'World Building and the Rationality of Conversion', in Hefner, R. W., *Conversion to Christianity: historical and anthropological perspectives on a Great Transformation* (University of California University Press: Berkeley, Los Angeles, Oxford, 1993), 4; David Chidester, *Religions of South Africa* (Routledge: London and New York), xiii.

[4] See Adrian Hastings, *A History of African Christianity; 1950-1975* (Cambridge University Press, Cambridge, 1979) , 95; J. Webster, Bishop Desmond Tutu: *The Voice of One Crying in the Wilderness* (Mowbray and Co. Ltd, 1982), 96.

Some Features of African Christianity in the Post-Independence Era:

Although post-colonial African Christianity is an omnibus with many shapes and roles, some of its key characteristics are as follows: a) Diverse Christian denominations; b) Churches engaged in developmental issues and concerns; c) Indigenized Christianity; d) Church membership predominantly poor, oppressed and vulnerable. In what follows, the four features cited above are briefly described.

Diverse Christian denominations

African Christianity is deeply divided along confessional lines, largely because of the Christian denominationalism that had been planted by western missionary-founded churches. Like worldwide Christianity which is divided into numerous separate Christian groups that emanate from the Roman Catholic Church, Protestant Churches, Orthodox Churches and Independent Churches,[5] African Christianity in post-independence Africa is highly diversified and divided.

The causes of these divisions are many, ranging from doctrinal and cultural differences to economic, political and ideological conflicts.[6] In the context of Africa, Christian fragmentation may be attributed to a host of factors, including: material gains of church leaders, personal conflicts, theological and ecclesiastical differences, prophetic visions, search for power, monetary demands by church leaders, rapid church population growth, persecutions in the churches, family tensions, cultural tensions, social rejection, socio-political factors and magic/witchcraft accusations.[7] More often than not, these divisions along confessional lines have been heightened by cultural and political differences arising from the places of origin of the various missionary-founded churches.

Significantly, the different and separate Christian churches actually represent different Christian spiritualities, some of which are radically opposed to one another. Maluleke graphically depicts this scenario of diversity and divisions when he observes that:

> African Christianity is not homogeneous. If anything, it is a cacophonous, colourful cluster of contending Christianities – all hidden under the misleading singular name – Christianity.[8]

Thus, in post-independence Africa, beside the Coptic Orthodox Church in Egypt and the Ethiopian Orthodox Tewahedo Church which were established in the second century AD, post-independence African Christianity has consisted of different Christian traditions that include the older ecumenical churches, Evangelical/Pentecostal churches, and African-Initiated Churches. In many African countries the different church traditions are either loosely co-ordinated or not co-ordinated. In some cases, the differences and divisions between these church traditions are so deep-seated that there is animosity between them.

But the question of Christian diversity constitutes a theological and moral problem because it has both negative and positive consequences for African Christianity. Negatively, Christian fragmentation undermines the inherent unity of the Christian church since biblically there is but one holy catholic and

---

[5] See David B. Barrett, George T. Kurian, Todd M. Johnson, eds. (2001). *World Christian Encyclopedia: A Comparative Survey of Churches and Religions in the Modern World.* Second Edition. Oxford University Press, Oxford.

[6] See U. Duchrow (1981). *Conflict over the Ecumenical Movement: Confessing Christ today in the Universal Church.* WCC, Geneva; William Rusch (1985). *Ecumenism: A Movement toward Church Unity.* Fortress Press, Philadelphia.

[7] See Suzan Mbula Kikonzo (2008). 'Christian diversity and its implications to the people of Vihiga District, Kenya'. *BOLESWA Journal of Theology, Religion and Philosophy* Vol. 2 (no.2), 129-155; James Amanze, The origin and development of the Ecumenical Movement in Botswana: 1965-1994, op. cit, Frans J. Verstraelen (1998). *Zimbabwean realities and Christian responses.* Mambo Press, Gweru, Zimbabwe; Peter Kasenene (1987). Ecumenical Progress in Swaziland, Ph. D Thesis, University of Cape Town.

[8] Tinyiko Maluleke (2010). 'Of Africanised bees and Africanised churches: ten theses on African Christianity', op. cit. p. 375.

apostolic church. In the words of Amanze, Christian divisions and hostilities are problematic because Christians ought to 'consider themselves as members of the same extended Christian family with Christ as Head of the Church'.[9] In addition, a divided Christian Church in many African societies has been viewed as a catalyst for social discord, and that religious diversity frequently engendered 'unhealthy competition' that in turn 'led to hostilities which have affected community development activities'.[10]

From a positive angle, however, Christian diversity has been viewed by some as a catalyst for freedom of worship, promotion of leadership abilities, material and spiritual development, job creation, and African cultural heritage.[11] In addition, other observers have seen Christian diversity as providing African Christian avenues for the creation and development of home-grown, context-specific Christian understandings and expressions of salvation, spirituality and social responsibility. For example, Inus Daneel observes that African-Initiated Churches in Zimbabwe under the auspices of the Association of Zimbabwean Traditional Environmental Conservationists (AZTREC), embarked on a joint interfaith project with traditional African spirit mediums to appropriate and revitalize indigenous religio-ecological values with the aim of planting trees to avert deforestation in Zimbabwe.[12] Such a visionary project would have been unthinkable in former mission churches that still view western cultural values as normative for world Christianity.

Churches Engaged in Developmental Issues and Concerns

While indigenous African cultures predominantly shape the world views, values, beliefs and traditions of most African Christians in post-independence Africa,[13] Christian churches – as institutions – have been socially associated with and pre-occupied with issues pertaining to western notions of social advancement and progress. It must be recalled that, when most African countries attained or regained their political independence in the 1950-1960s, they relied heavily on Christian churches for technical and material support since they lacked material means, institutional capacity, knowledge and skills to manage their modern nation-states.[14] Because the Christianity planted by mission churches aimed at civilizing Africans in the image of western civilization, in post-independence Africa former mission churches had to play a leading role in the provision of necessary skills, knowledge and training required to manage a modern economy.[15]

Hence new African leaders had to forge diplomatic alliances with the leaders of mission churches that provided technical assistance to nation-building initiatives, notwithstanding the fact that most mission churches had previously supported European colonial states in Africa. Indeed modern bureaucratic African states and related institutions such as the civil service, colleges, health clinics, hospitals, universities and industry were led mostly by products of mission churches.[16]

As a result, the leaders of the former mission churches after independence inadvertently assumed positions of serving their respective nation-states as development partners. But because the churches themselves espoused different doctrines and theological perspectives as defined by their respective

---

[9] See James N. Amanze (1994). *The origin and development of the Ecumenical Movement in Botswana: 1965-1994.* Department of History and Department of Theology and Religious Studies, University of Botswana, Gaborone, 56.

[10] Suzan Mbula Kikonzo (2008). 'Christian diversity and its implications to the people of Vihiga District, Kenya'. *BOLESWA Journal of Theology, Religion and Philosophy* Vol. 2 (no.2), 151.

[11] See Susan Mbula Kilonzo. (2008). op. cit. 1470-151.

[12] Inus Daneel. (1998). *African Earthkeepers, Volume 1: Interfaith mission in earth-care.* UNISA, Pretoria.

[13] See Blakely, T. D., van Beek, W. E. A., Thomson, eds. (1994). *Religion in Africa.* Heinemann and James Curry, London and Portsmouth, pp. 100-106, 167-181; Jacob Olupona (2006). African Traditional Religions. In Riggs, Thomas, edit., *Worldmark Encyclopedia of Religious Practices* Vol 1. Gale Publishers, Detroit, 1-21.

[14] See William Tordoff (1984). *Government and Politics in Africa.* Second Edition. Indiana University Press, Bloomington and Indianapolis, 2.

[15] See Adrian Hastings (1979). *A History of African Christianity: 1950-1975.* Cambridge University Press, Cambridge.

[16] Adrian Hastings, op. cit.

confessional families or denominational traditions, their contributions to social development varied. The older ecumenical churches, for example, sought to address social concerns such as poverty, under-development, social injustice and human rights,[17] while Evangelical and Pentecostal churches focused on personal salvation, private morality and church planting to reach unreached souls.[18] African-Initiated Churches, on the other hand, focused on freedom to express Christian doctrines and practise the faith from African cultural perspectives unashamedly.[19]

While these kinds of church-state partnerships have been laudable, especially in the fields of education, training and social welfare, more often than not, however, such partnership would compromise the prophetic calling of the Christian church wherein the latter become the uncritical religious wing of new nation-states.[20]

Indigenized Christianity

The fact that much of African Christianity is predominantly coloured, directly and indirectly, by indigenous African world views, beliefs, values and traditions has been well documented by many observers.[21] Some cautiously view the preponderance of African cosmology, spirituality and values in African Christianity as a welcome development following many years domination of Christian theology and spirituality by western forms of Christianity.[22] Others see the indigenization of Christianity as a serious challenge to the gospel from the powers of darkness.[23]

Whether one welcomes it or not, there are strong indications that indigenized Christianity is likely to prevail on the African continent due to several related factors. First, it must be recalled that the forerunners of indigenized Christianity were African-Initiated Churches who rationalized their secessions on the grounds that Africans wished to liberate themselves from western cultural and religious domination. In 1981 AICs constituted 15% of the total Christian population in sub-Saharan Africa. At present, assuming a growth estimated at more than 2 million per year, they constitute a significant section of African Christian demography. It was not surprising, therefore, that the leaders of these churches and their followers were also supportive of various forms of political, nationalistic movements that struggled for liberation from colonial rule. In the post-independence period these African Indigenous[24] Churches played pivotal roles in nation-building through their unequivocal affirmation of core African values and beliefs such as the belief in God, the ancestors, spirit possession, divination, expressive religiosity in the form of song and dance, communal fellowship, sharing and caring, all of which helped create an African Christian spirituality that they could relate to and feel at home with.[25]

---

[17] See Dickinson, R. D. N. (1975). *To set at liberty the oppressed.* WCC, Geneva, 153ff.

[18] Klaus Fiedler (1994), op. cit 364.

[19] Mokgethi Motlhabi (2008). *African Theology/Black Theology in South Africa.* UNISA, Pretoria, 38-39; Gabriel M. Setiloane (1986). *African Theology: An Introduction.* Skotaville Press, Johannesburg.

[20] See Frans Verstraelen, op. cit. 73-74.

[21] See Tinyiko Maluleke (2010), op. cit. p. 376; Tabona Shoko (2007). *Karanga Indigenous Religion in Zimbabwe: health and well-being.* Ashgate, Farnham, UK; Jacob Olupona (2006), op. cit, 1; Adrian Hastings (1979), op. cit. 234; John Mbiti (1989). *African Religions and Philosophy.* Second Edition. Heinemann, London, 223ff.

[22] Kwesi Dickson (1984*). Theology in Africa.* Orbis, New York, 228; Gabriel Setiloane (1986), op. cit, 36; Ambrose Moyo (1996). *Zimbabwe: The Risk of Incarnation.* WCC, Geneva; John Pobee (1996). West Africa: Christ Would Be an African Too. WCC, Geneva.

[23] Byang H. Kato (1975). *Theological Pitfalls in Africa.* Evangel Publishing House, Nairobi; Steven Paas (2006), op. cit, p. 255; Heinrich Balz (2002). *Witchcraft in East and West Africa.*

[24] In the title, 'African Indigenous, Initiated and Instituted Churches' the 3 "I"s are interchangeable terms.

[25] See James Amanze (1998). *African Christianity in Botswana.* Op. cit. p.215; Inus Daneel (1998). Op. cit. p. 238; Hebron Ndlovu (1997). 'Zionist Churches and the promotion of civil society: the case of the Kingdom of Swaziland'. *Theologia Viatorum,* Vol. 24, 1-14; Gerhadus Oosthuizen (1999). Indigenous Christianity and the future of the Church

The second factor that has fostered and sustained indigenous Christianity on the African continent is the preponderance of international conventions on human rights that affirm, among other things, the right to freedom of religion, thought and conscience as well as the full recognition of the rights of indigenous communities to practice their religions. Many of these conventions have not only been ratified by many African countries, but have been incorporated into the constitutions of most (if not all) African states in sub-Saharan Africa.

Church Membership Predominantly Poor, Oppressed and Vulnerable

By international as well as regional and national standards of material welfare, Africa is arguably the poorest continent in the world, and this reality is also prevalent in African Christianity. Many observers have identified acute poverty as one of the main social challenges of African Christianity as early as the independence era.[26] But the poor Christians are largely women and dark skinned Africans, their voices are hardly heard, and they are oppressed. Tinyiko Maluleke paints a grim but accurate picture of poverty in African Christianity when he writes:

> The poor and marginalized are the overwhelming majority in African Christianity. The poor are the living face of African Christianity. They make their presence felt in worship and service... they are more silent in the theologies of African Christianity. It is their songs and their prayers that ring out and stand out... This means that African Christianity is a Christianity of the poor, the women, the black and the underclasses. It is a Christianity of irony in the sense that though boasting numbers, it is the least powerful who swell their ranks.[27]

This long citation epitomizes that challenge that poverty places on African Christian theology to address this age-old problem. Sadly, the root causes of acute poverty on the African continent are hardly addressed in a concerted manner by most of the disparate Christian groups that constitute African Christianity. Rather, either through lack of capacity or lack of moral and political will, most Christian confessional families tend to focus their energies on the provision of non-controversial poverty alleviation services such as medical services, water and sanitation, specialized skills, donations of food, fellowship, mutual assistance and support, and spiritual counselling. Yet some of the main causes of poverty on the African continent (including colonial rule and landlessness, racial discrimination, neo-imperialism, ethnic conflicts, patriarchy, dictatorships, the HIV/AIDS pandemic and endless conflicts in regions endowed with natural resources) have rarely been addressed in a collective manner by African Christian groups. Whenever these issues were addressed at all, they were tackled by liberal African Christian churches affiliated to influential international bodies such as the World Council of Churches and the United Nations.

But for many conservative evangelical Christian churches, issues pertaining to addressing social concerns such as poverty appear to be secondary to the principal mandate of preaching the gospel of eternal salvation of the soul. The mantra of many evangelical churches is that churches should refrain from attempting to resolve socio-political issues, and that political issues fall outside the ambit of the church. This view, which is held by most evangelical churches that are affiliated to the Association of Evangelicals of Africa and Madagascar as well as to the World Evangelical Fellowship, was clearly articulated by Byang Kato (1987), when he wrote:

---

in South Africa. In Walsh, T. G. and Kaufmann, F., eds., *Religion and social transformation in Southern Africa.* Paragon House, St Paul, Minnesota.

[26] Adrian Hastings (1979), op. cit. 234; Kwesi Dickson (1984). *Theology in Africa*. Orbis, New York, 225-227; Dickinson, R. D. N. (1975). *To set at liberty the oppressed.* WCC, Geneva.

[27] See Tinyiko Maluleke (2010), op. cit. 376.

> The Christian may feed all the hungry people in the world and pay all the bills of liberation movements of the society. His primary task is not done. His primary task is preaching the gospel of soul salvation.[28]

The reluctance and lack of capacity of African Christian churches to effectively confront the root causes of poverty in church and society has also been more prevalent in Independent/Indigenous churches. While the membership of these churches consists predominantly of poor, unemployed, unskilled, semi-skilled and dissatisfied workers that are acutely aware of their marginal socio-political conditions,[29] as a matter of principle, these churches tend to shy away from direct political confrontation with civil authorities over basic needs and amenities.[30] Rather, they focus their attention on providing a range of social support services to their destitute membership, drawing on African religio-ethical values of communal solidarity, harmony, sharing, caring and humanness. Oosthuizen depicts the social ministry of Indigenous Churches in modern Africa as follows:

> The AICs are in structure voluntary organizations, institutions of the poor; in the spirit of the traditional African relationships, they are prepared to assist any person in need. They constitute networks of the people which, because of their mobility and omnipresence, are deeply involved with the lot of the poor… In a situation of urban anonymity, the AICS offer emotional and spiritual help.[31]

Finally, the Charismatic and Pentecostal churches, like the Evangelical and Indigenous churches, rarely address the prevalence of abject poverty as a socio-structural problem. Many Pentecostal churches on the African continent tend to attribute poverty to the victims themselves who selected to worship false idols (of African Religion) and witchcraft, which in turn led to laziness, hatred, senseless killing of innocent people and much suffering. Vengeyi, for example, observes that for many Pentecostal churches in Zimbabwe, poverty is a curse from God:

> It is only the righteous whose needs will be met by God without fail. It is them who will not be forsaken and whose children will never beg for bread/food. In other words, according to the Pentecostals, the poor are cursed by God because they are sinners while the rich are blessed because they are righteous.[32]

As for charismatic churches, Paas (2006) observes that in many African countries charismatic preachers and evangelists avoid confrontation with oppressive regimes by attributing poverty and social injustices to the work of demons.[33] In particular, with reference to Malawi, he contends that 'Charismatics in Malawi seem to be invariably apolitical, tending to support the ruling powers of the country'.[34]

Notwithstanding these shortcomings of the social ministry of Pentecostal and charismatic churches, it must be stressed that, as elsewhere in the world,[35] these churches have played an indirect but positive role

---

[28] Byang H. Kato (1987). *Theological pitfalls in Africa*. Evangel Publishing House, Nairobi, 179.
[29] See Adrian Hastings, op. cit. pp. 251-255; Mokgethi Motlhabi, o.p. p. 27-28.
[30] See Gerhadus C. Oosthuizen (1999). *Indigenous Christianity and the Future of the Church*. op. cit. 68.
[31] Gerhadus C. Oosthuizen, ibid., 170.
[32] Obvious Vengeyi (2014). 'Blaming the victim and not the perpetrator; An African Pentecostal interpretation of Psalms 37:25 in the light of the global North-South relations'. In Kroesbergen, H., ed., *Christian identity and justice in a globalized world from a Southern African perspective*. CLF, Wellington, South Africa. 184.
[33] Steven Paas (2006). Op. cit. 233.
[34] Steven Paas (2006). Ibid. 233.
[35] Bruce Martin (1998). 'From pre- to post modernity in Latin America: the case of Pentecostalism'. In, Heelas, P., ed., *Religion, Modernity and Postmodernity*. Blackwell, Oxford.

in empowering African Christians with a sense of dignity, feeling self-worth and confidence in the face of material deprivation and marginalization.[36]

Major Historical and Religious Developments

African Christianity, as an established religion on the African continent, has been deeply influenced by rapid historical and social changes that have swept across post-independence African societies. Some of the major historical and religious changes in African Christianity that accompanied political independence were: a) assumption of church leadership by Africans; b) the emergence of African Christian theology; c) the adoption of Black Theology; d) ecumenical initiatives pertaining to social justice and human rights; e) and the mushrooming of charismatic and Pentecostal churches.

Assumption of Church Leadership by Africans

In most African societies the attainment of political independence raised higher expectations for better health, social progress and more complete realization of the aspirations of African peoples. Hence when most Christian churches, especially former missionary-founded churches, fell under the leadership of African clergy, the material, human and spiritual resources of the churches were channelled towards supporting national aspirations of African peoples as defined by heads of state.

Hastings observes, for example, that African Church leaders in Tanzania and Zambia were fully supportive of state-sponsored programmes such as the Arusha Declaration on Socialism and Self-reliance (of Tanzania), and Kaunda's programme of African Socialism under a one-party state (Zambia).[37] Similar observations were made by Sundkler, Kuper and Daneel with reference to Swaziland and Zimbabwe that African church leaders in post-independence countries tended to identify themselves with the state-initiated socio-cultural values of their countries of origin. Sundkler and Kuper show that in post-independence Swaziland several African leaders of former mission churches encouraged their members to participate in the Ncwala ritual, the Swazi annual indigenous ritual of first fruits and sacred kingship which was previously shunned by all missionary-founded churches.[38]

Daneel, with reference to indigenous churches of Zimbabwe, shows how African Church leaders joined hands with traditional chiefs and spirit mediums to embark on a forest-planting movement aimed at preventing land degradation in Masvingo Province in Zimbabwe. Daneel attributes the success of the project largely to the readiness on the part of African church leaders to interact and engage in authentic dialogue with the Zimbabwean practitioners of Shona traditional religion in the spirit of mutual respect and friendship.[39]

The Emergence of African Christian Theology

A significant by-product of the indigenization of African Christianity, African Christian theology is a contextual, African-brewed, systematic study of the Christian faith which integrates African cultural heritage with the gospel and the Christian tradition.[40] Its aim is to understand and interpret the Christian faith from a uniquely African religio-cultural perspective unashamedly and unapologetically, thereby making its own contribution to worldwide Christian spirituality. In the words of Paul Gundani, the overall

---

[36] See Richard Dickinson, op. cit. p. 45; Ogbu Kalu (2008). *African Pentecostalism: An introduction.* Oxford University Press.

[37] Adrian Hastings, op. cit. p, 184, 195.

[38] See Bengt Sundkler (1976). *Zulu Zion and Some Swazi Zionists*. Oxford University Press, London 206. Hildah Kuper (1986). *The Swazi: A South African Kingdom*. Holt, New York, 75,

[39] Daneel, M. L. (1998). Op. cit. 8.

[40] Mokgethi Motlhabi (2008), op. cit., 31.

goal of African theology is to ensure that 'African faith/spirituality has to take one distinct face in the multifaceted gem that is the Christian religion'.[41]

To be sure, many theologians have expressed serious concerns about African theology, and these include Kato and Paas. For Kato, the difficulty with African theology is that it detracts from the uniqueness of the gospel, 'the faith which was once for all delivered to the saints'.[42] And for Paas, the quest to integrate African culture and religion with Christianity can be dangerous because it compromises the gospel. He writes:

> In history many have mixed the Gospel with their traditional religion. This has weakened or taken away the witness of the Church. We can use good aspects of our culture for the expression of our faith, but glorification of humanity, superstitions, magic and witchcraft cannot be part of that.[43]

Despite these dissenting views, it appears that African theology is here to stay, considering the resilience of African religion and culture in contemporary society. For Jesse Mugambi, the fundamental premises of African theology are valid and sustainable because 'No church can survive the challenges of history unless the gospel is effectively appropriated to the cultural and religious heritage of its members – as is the case with the Coptic Church and the Ethiopian Church, which are distinctly African and trace their history to the patristic period'.[44]

The Adoption of Black Theology

The adoption of Black Theology in African Christianity emanated from historical experiences of legalized racial discrimination against Africans in European-ruled African countries such as South Africa, South West Africa (Namibia), Southern Rhodesia (Zimbabwe) and Mozambique.

Historically, Black Theology had originally been developed by James Cone, the Afro-American theologian who published his seminal work entitled *Black Theology and Black Power* (1969). The fundamental question addressed by Cone was what was the meaning of the gospel of Jesus Christ to black Christians that were oppressed because of their skin colour. His answer was categorical: God through Jesus Christ takes the side of the poor and the ill-treated. In his fourth book entitled *God of the Oppressed* (1975), Cone suggested Jesus was black, and that he identified himself with the pain and humiliation of black people, and that His aim was to liberate black people.[45] These views stimulated much debate and reflection in all Christian countries, including South Africa. By the 1970s Black Theology was formally established in South Africa.

In South Africa Black Theology was adopted by many African Christian theologians because it offered the promise of liberation, that Christ's main mission was to set at liberty the oppressed. As Motlhabi correctly observed, Black Theology in South Africa was recognized as a relevant liberation theology because:

> It recognized that blacks needed to be liberated from socio-economic and political bondage, which the church tended to ignore in favour of a pie-in-the-sky, literal interpretation of passages such as 'My kingdom is not of this world' and 'Render unto Caesar the things that are Caesar's'. They also needed to be liberated from religious

[41] Paul Gundani (1998). 'Editors' Preface'. In, eds., Fiedler, K, Gundani, P. and Mijoga, H. *Theology Cooked in an African Pot.* ATISCA, Zomba, Malawi, 3.
[42] Byang H. Kato (1987). Op. cit. 57.
[43] Steven Paas (2006), op. cit. 255.
[44] Jesse Mugambi (2010). 'African theologies of reconstruction'. In, edit., Daniel Patte. *The Cambridge Dictionary of Christianity.* Cambridge University Press, 1056.
[45] Theo Witvliet (1984). *A Place in the Sun: An Introduction to Liberation Theology in the Third World.* SCM Press, London, 70-73.

enslavement to 'heretical' churches which fashioned the Christian teaching according to their human inclinations and racial, socio-political and economic interests.[46]

Significantly, these insights from Black Theology did not only inspire South African clergy such as Desmond Tutu, Allan Boesak and Frank Chikane to fight against racial discrimination in South Africa, but they motivated many clergymen outside South Africa such as Canaan Banana who wrote his work entitled *The Gospel according to the Ghetto.*

Expansion of Ecumenical Initiatives Pertaining to Social Justice and Human Rights

Although Christian ecumenism in Africa began in the colonial era, more vigorous attempts to reconcile the divided Christian churches were carried out in the post-independence period. This was largely due to multiple socio-political challenges faced by African Christians in the different countries, and these included: under-development, ethnic conflicts, dictatorships, racial discrimination, sexism and religious intolerance. To address these challenges, African churches formed national church councils and associations through whom they forged inter-church fellowships and alliances along worldwide confessional family ties.

For example, in Botswana and Swaziland three different church organizations were formed along three broad confessional lines, namely: Evangelical/Pentecostal Churches, Ecumenical or liberal Churches, and African Indigenous Churches. In Botswana and Swaziland, the Evangelical/Pentecostal churches on one hand are affiliated to the Association of Evangelicals of Africa and the World Evangelical Fellowship. The Ecumenical Churches, on the other hand, are affiliated to the World Council of Churches and its related church organizations such as the All Africa Conference of Churches based in Nairobi, Kenya. And finally, the Indigenous Churches are affiliated to regional church bodies based in Africa such as the League of African Churches and the Organization of African Independent Churches based in Nairobi, Kenya.[47]

While these church bodies embody and reflect the polarization of the Christian fraternity in Africa, it has been under the auspices of these church organizations that African Christianity has made significant advances in addressing many of the social, moral and spiritual challenges of the Christian Church in Africa. I will cite a few examples.

Since the 1970s, African churches have partnered with the World Council of Churches (WCC) and other international organisations that aim at promoting the development of African peoples. In 1973, under the auspices of the Commission on Churches Participation in Development (CCPD), the WCC supported a number of member Churches in Cameroon and Ethiopia to promote rural development schemes. Under the Programme on Material Aid, the Scholarship Desk and the Programme to Combat Racism, the WCC provided grants for Liberation Movements in Southern Africa to cover educational, medical, agricultural and relief needs.[48]

More recently, member churches of the WCC have embarked on addressing a variety of issues such as HIV/AIDs, the promotion of gender equality, non-violence, interfaith dialogue, and social justice for people living with disabilities.[49] All these efforts have helped enhance the credibility of Christian churches as institutions that are committed to holistic salvation – a salvation that includes the personal, social, universal and cosmic dimensions of life.

---

[46] Mokkgethi Motlhabi (2008), op. cit. 23.

[47] See James Amanze (1994). Op. cit. 23-45; Marjorie Froise, ed. (1994). *Swaziland Christian Handbook*. CHRISTIA INFO, Welkom, South Africa, 31-32.

[48] Richardson Dickinson, op. cit., 47-48.

[49] Samuel Kobia (2010). 'World Council of Churches'. In Daniel Patte. *The Cambridge Dictionary of Christianity*. Cambridge University Press, 1333.

The Mushrooming of Charismatic and Pentecostal Churches

Post-independence African Christianity has seen the unprecedented exponential growth of charismatic and Pentecostal Churches across the continent. These churches are often treated together because they share common features, namely, that both churches seem to distance themselves from the conservative spirituality of African Religion and Indigenous Churches, and they attract middle class Africans and the young living in urban and peri-urban sectors.[50] They espouse a spirituality and ethic that 'put emphasis on an active engagement of the Christian faith in socio-cultural issues, thereby becoming relevant to the people'.[51] In particular, the charismatic churches, in the view of Paas, exude a sense of confidence and a positive attitude towards life:

> Charismatic groups are said to be more Spirit-centered, less hierarchical, more 'Afro-optimistic', more involved at all levels of society including education, more friendly to ruling politicians, more open to supernatural possibilities. Charismatics stress the possibilities of empowerment against evil powers, leading to transformation and freedom, including health and prosperity.[52]

Concluding Remarks: Enduring Trends

Despite the complex nature of African Christianity as evident in its diverse characteristic features, and major historical and religious developments, one can discern several enduring trends. First, the fragmentation of African Christianity appears to persist over the years – for better or for worse – and this has been reinforced by the phenomenal growth of the new Pentecostal and charismatic churches. Whether these churches may serve as a panacea for the abject poverty that is typical of African Christianity, that remains an open question.

Second, despite the diversity of Christian witness in post-independence Africa, the continuing vitality of the Christian religion as a lived and culturally standardized faith for most Africans appears to be guaranteed. That the Christian faith has continued to shape the moral actions, social fabric, ethos, aesthetics and the cosmology of many Africans since the political era seems to be another significant enduring trend.[53]

Third, the vitality and vibrancy of the Christian religion need not delude one into assuming that the indigenization of African Christianity has come to a stalemate. On the contrary there is a growing body of literature that suggests that the Christian religion continues to co-exist with African cultures and religion in more novel and nuanced ways, in many African societies.[54]

Fourth, enduring in post-independence African Christianity is the resilience of conservative rightwing Christianity in which African theologians have abandoned their prophetic ministry, and are content with

---

[50] Seven Paas (2006), op. cit. 227-232.

[51] Cephas N. Omenyo (2010). 'Charismatic and Pentecostal Movements in Africa: West Africa'. In Daniel Patte. *The Cambridge Dictionary of Christianity*. Cambridge University Press, 189-190.

[52] Steven Paas (2006), op. cit. 230.

[53] See Richard Werbner (2011), op. cit 207.

[54] See Hebron L Ndlovu (2014). 'Christian identity amid African Religion: Buganu ceremony and the creation of multiple religious identities in Swaziland'. In, Kroesbergen, H., ed., *Christian identity and justice in a globalized world from a Southern African perspective*. CLF, Wellington, South Africa, 83-95; Tinyiko Maluleke (2010). 'Of Africanised bees and Africanised churches: Ten Theses on African Christianity'. *Missionalia* vol. 38 (no.3), 369-380; Tabona Shoko (2007). *Karanga Indigenous Religion in Zimbabwe: Health and well-being*. Ashgate, Farnham, UK; Klaus, Nurnberger (2007). *Christ and the ancestors in a changing Africa.* Cluster Publications and C. B. Powell Bible Centre, Pietermaritzburg and Pretoria; Inus Daneel (1998). *African Earthkeepers, Volume 1: Interfaith mission in earth-care.* UNISA, Pretoria.

rendering to Caesar the things that are Caesar's. For example, Mokgethi Motlhabi laments this scenario in the case of post-apartheid South Africa when he writes:

> Today South African theology in general (and Black Theology in particular) seems to have lost its bearing and a sense of direction, especially since the political change that took place in the country in 1994. Black theologians, in particular, have seemingly gone into recess.... The result is that Black Theology has lost its responsiveness to and input into the new socio-economic problems that followed political change, which still need the critical and prophetic participation of black theologians and other critical church structures.[55]

Bibliography

Barrett, D. B., Kurian, G. T., Johnson, T. M. (eds) (2001). *World Christian Encyclopedia: A Comparative Survey of Churches and Religions in the Modern World.* Second Edition. Oxford University Press, Oxford.

Blakely, T. D., van Beek, W. E. A., Thomson, eds. (1994). *Religion in Africa.* Heinemann and James Curry, London and Portsmouth.

Chidester, David (1992). *Religions of South Africa.* Routledge, London and New York.

Daneel, I. (1998). *African Earth-keepers*, Volume 1: Interfaith mission in earth-care. UNISA, Pretoria.

Dickinson, R. D. N. (1975). *To set at liberty the oppressed.* WCC, Geneva.

Dickson, Kwesi (1984). *Theology in Africa.* Orbis, New York.

Duchrow, U. (1981). *Conflict over the Ecumenical Movement: Confessing Christ today in the Universal Church.* WCC, Geneva.

Fiedler, K. (1994). *The Story of Faith Missions.* Regnum, Oxford.

Fiedler, K, Gundani, P. and Mijoga, H., eds. (1998). *Theology Cooked in an African Pot.* ATISCA, Zomba.

Froise, M. ed. (1994). *Swaziland Christian Handbook.* CHRISTIA INFO, Welkom.

Gifford, P. (1998). *African Christianity: Its Public Role.* Indiana University Press.

Gundani, P. (1998). 'Editors' Preface'. In, eds., Fiedler, K, Gundani, P. and Mijoga, H. *Theology Cooked in an African Pot.* ATISCA, Zomba. Hastings, Adrian (1979). *A History of African Christianity: 1950-1975.* Cambridge University Press, Cambridge.

Hefner, W. (1993) 'World Building and the Rationality of Conversion', in Hefner, R. W., *Conversion to Christianity: historical and anthropological perspectives on a Great Transformation.* University of California University Press, Berkeley, Los Angeles and Oxford,

Kabue, Sl, Mombo, E, Galgalo, J. and Peter, C. B., eds. (2011). *Disability, society and theology*. Zapf Chancery Publishers, Limuru.

Kalu, O. (2008). *African Pentecostalism: An introduction.* Oxford University Press.

Kasenene, P. (1987). *Ecumenical Progress in Swaziland*, Ph. D Thesis, University of Cape Town.

Kato, B. H. (1987). *Theological pitfalls in Africa.* Evangel Publishing House.

Kilonzo, Susan M. (2011). Christian diversity and its implications to the people of Vihiga District, Kenya. *Journal of Theology, Religion and Philosophy* vol. 2 (no.2, 129-155.)

Kretzschmar, Louise (1986). *The Voice of Black Theology in South Africa.* Ravan Press, Johannesburg.

Kroesbergen, H., ed., *Christian identity and justice in a globalized world from a Southern African perspective*. CLF, Wellington.

Martin, B. (1998). 'From pre- to post-modernity in Latin America: the case of Pentecostalism'. In, Heelas, P., ed., *Religion, Modernity and Postmodernity.* Blackwell, Oxford.

Motlhabi, M. (2008). African Theology/Black Theology in South Africa. UNISA, Pretoria.

Milingo, Emmanuel (1984). *The world in between: Christian healing and the struggle for spiritual*

[55] Mokgethi Motlhabi (2008), op. cit. x.

survival. C. Hurst and Co., London.

Ndlovu, H. L. (2014). 'Christian identity amid African Religion: Buganu ceremony and the creation of multiple religious identities in Swaziland'. In, Kroesbergen, H., ed., *Christian identity and justice in a globalized world from a Southern African perspective*. CLF, Wellington, 83-95.

Ndlovu, H. L. (1997). 'Zionist Churches and the promotion of civil society: the case of the Kingdom of Swaziland'. *Theologia Viatorum,* Vol. 24, 1-14.

Nurnberger, K (2007). *Christ and the ancestors in a changing Africa.* Cluster Publications and C. B. Powell Bible Centre, Pietermaritzburg and Pretoria.

Olupona, J. (2006). 'African Traditional Religions'. In Riggs, Thomas, edit., *Worldmark Encyclopedia of Religious Practices* Vol 1. Gale Publishers, Detroit, 1-21.

Oosthuizen, G. (1999). 'Indigenous Christianity and the future of the Church in South Africa'. In Walsh, T. G. and Kaufmann, F., eds., *Religion and social transformation in Southern Africa*. Paragon House, St Paul, Minnesota.

Mugambi, J. (2010). 'African theologies of reconstruction'. In, edit., Daniel Patte. *The Cambridge Dictionary of Christianity*. Cambridge University Press, 1055-1057.

Rusch, W. (1985). *Ecumenism: A Movement toward Church Unity*. Fortress Press, Philadelphia.

Samwini, N. I. (2013) 'African Concepts of God in both Christianity and Islam', in Kalengyo, E. M (ed.), *God of Life*. All Africa Conference of Churches, Nairobi.

Setiloane, G. M. (1986). *African Theology: An Introduction*. Skotaville Press, Johannesburg

Shoko, T. (2007). *Karanga Indigenous Religion in Zimbabwe: Health and well-being*. Ashgate, Aldershot.

Tordoff, William (1984). *Government and politics in Africa.* Indiana University Press, Bloomington and Indianapolis.

Vengeyi, V. (2014). 'Blaming the victim and not the perpetrator; An African Pentecostal interpretation of Psalms 37:25 in the light of theoglobal North-South relations'. In, Kroesbergen, H., ed., *Christian identity and justice in a globalized world from a Southern African perspective.* CLF, Wellington, South Africa.

Verstraelen, Frans, J. (1998). *Zimbabwean realities and Christian responses*. Mambo Press, Gweru.

Webster, J. (1982). *Bishop Desmond Tutu: The voice of one crying in the wilderness*. Mowbray and Co., London and Oxford.

Werbner, Richard (2011). *Holy hustlers, schism and prophecy: Apostolic reformation in Botswana.* University of California Press, Berkeley, Los Angeles and London.

Witvliet, Theo (1984). *A place in the sun: an introduction to liberation theology in the third world.* SCM, London.

Zimmermann, Armin, ed. (2002). *Voices from Kumba: theological reflections for the Cameroon, Africa, and the world*. Presbyterian Printing Press, Limbe.

(7) GROWTH AND TRENDS IN AFRICAN CHRISTIANITY IN THE 21ST CENTURY

J. Kwabena Asamoah-Gyadu

Country	Religion	Pop_2010	Pct_2010	Pop_2025	Pct_2025	GrPct_1970_2025
Africa	Christians	502,673,000	48.1%	751,547,000	50.0%	2.7%
Africa	Independents	109,828,000	10.5%	155,266,000	10.3%	2.3%
Africa	African-initiated	97,035,000	9.3%			
Africa	Orthodox	45,175,000	4.3%	63,246,000	4.2%	2.3%
Africa	Oriental Orthodox	44,315,000	4.2%			
Africa	Protestants	192,187,000	18.4%	270,367,000	18.0%	2.3%
Africa	Anglicans	50,398,000	4.8%			
Africa	Pentecostal	34,928,000	3.3%			
Africa	Baptist	20,589,000	2.0%			
Africa	Reformed, Presbyterian	16,478,000	1.6%			
Africa	Lutheran	12,521,000	1.2%			
Africa	Adventist	9,204,000	0.9%			
Africa	Evangelical churches	9,029,000	0.9%			
Africa	United churches	8,421,000	0.8%			
Africa	Methodist	8,210,000	0.8%			
Africa	Lutheran/Reformed	5,576,000	0.5%			
Africa	Roman Catholics	178,266,000	17.1%	274,772,000	18.3%	2.9%
Africa	*Pentecostals/ Charismatics*	179,046,000	17.1%	257,931,000	17.1%	2.5%
Africa	*Evangelicals*	115,201,000	11.0%	168,819,000	11.2%	2.6%
Africa	Muslims	436,962,000	41.9%	627,440,000	41.7%	2.4%
Africa	adherents of traditional African religions	91,292,000	8.7%	106,881,000	7.1%	1.1%
Africa	Hindus	2,985,000	0.3%	3,652,000	0.2%	1.4%
Africa	Baha'is	2,149,000	0.2%	3,177,000	0.2%	2.6%
Africa	Buddhists	260,000	0.0%	314,000	0.0%	1.3%
Africa	Chinese folk religionists	133,000	0.0%	177,000	0.0%	1.9%
Africa	Jews	123,000	0.0%	106,000	0.0%	-1.0%
Africa	adherents of new religious movements	121,000	0.0%	160,000	0.0%	1.9%
Africa	Jains	95,300	0.0%	137,000	0.0%	2.4%
Africa	Sikhs	74,100	0.0%	103,000	0.0%	2.2%
Africa	Confucianists	20,600	0.0%	25,000	0.0%	1.3%
Africa	Spiritists	2,900	0.0%	3,100	0.0%	0.4%
Africa	Zoroastrians	970	0.0%	970	0.0%	0.0%
Africa	people professing no religion	7,215,000	0.7%	10,491,000	0.7%	2.5%
Africa	**Total population**	**1,044,107,000**	**100.0%**	**1,504,213,000**	**100.0%**	**2.5%**

Source: Centre for the Study of World Christianity (CSGC), Boston, Gordon-Conwell TS

This entry examines some of the changes that have taken place within world Christianity in the twentieth century focusing on developments in Africa. Developments in world Christianity over the last century include the very fact of a shift in the demographic centre of Christianity from the Northern to the Southern continents. Africa has developed into a major Christian heartland since the establishment of historic mission denominations at the beginning of the nineteenth century. In the process of growths and trends that have since taken place in the last century, Christian groups that emerged include Mission classic churches, Ethiopianist or Nationalist churches, Zionist or African Initiated/Independent/Indigenous churches (AICs), classical Pentecostal denominations of both western and indigenous origins, and more recently various

Pentecostal/charismatic churches and movements. Of Pentecostalism in particular, which has become the representative face of Christianity in Africa, Harvey Cox states that its spirituality has led to 'the reshaping of religion in the 21st century'.[1] The trends started with the African disenchantment with aspects of mission Christianity. This was the direct result of the inability of western mission Christianity to work within what was perceived as biblical and indigenous enchanted worldviews.

In responding to the presence of historic mission Christianity, the spirit world as an important African reality has informed indigenous appropriations of the faith and this also explains why pneumatic forms of Christian expression have enjoyed considerable appeal on the continent. The religious emphasis of indigenous Christians has been on the reality of supernatural evil and the power of the Holy Spirit. This has been evident not just in the rise of independent churches outside the control of mission societies but also the current formation of African immigrant churches in the former heartlands of Christianity that has been underway in the West within the last three decades. Thus as far as Christianity in Africa and African Christianity are concerned, the last century has been one of religious innovations. Endeavours in mission such as the translation of the Bible into various vernacular languages helped to facilitate the process of the expansion leading to what may be called Africa's Christian century.

Africa in World Christianity Today

In his book, *The Next Christendom,* Philip Jenkins makes it clear that we are currently living through one of the most transforming moments of religion worldwide noting that Christianity is doing very well indeed in the global south and concluding that the era of western Christianity has passed within our lifetimes, and the day of Southern Christianity is dawning.[2] This recession of Christianity in the global North has coincided with its accession in the global South with Africa emerging as one of its major heartlands. This development, occurring within the twentieth century, defied the fears of the Edinburgh 1910 World Missions Conference that Africa was going to turn Islamic by the end of that century. That the continent emerged rather as a major Christian stronghold makes it important, Kwame Bediako argues, that we 'should seek to understand what this might mean for Africa and the world'.[3] The growth of Christianity in Africa for him amounted to nothing but *The Renewal of a Non-Western Religion.*[4] This Bediako argued on the understanding that the prospects for Christian expansion and innovation in Africa were going to continue on a high note through the 21st century.

At the dawn of the 21st century, we could say that although Africa remains a religiously pluralistic continent, it has indeed emerged as a major Christian heartland. This is at a time when the faith is clearly under siege, and in some cases even being deliberately hounded out of public life, in parts of the modern West. The decline of Christian presence in the former heartlands of the faith is a process that has been underway since the era of the Enlightenment. This was the period in which rationality and science emerged as the dominant determinants in decision-making and development, leading to a deliberate courting of secularism and the creation of a morally permissive society. Africa's place as an important flag-bearer of Christianity recalls the historical biblical development in which the life of Jesus had to be preserved in Egypt because it had come under threat at the hands of Herod.

---

[1] Harvey Cox, *Fire from Heaven: The Rise of Pentecostal Spirituality and the Reshaping of Religion in the Twenty-first Century* (Reading, MA: Addison-Wesley, 1995).

[2] Philip Jenkins, *The Next Christendom: The Coming of Global Christianity. Revised and Expanded Edition* (Oxford: Oxford University Press, 2007), 2, 3.

[3] Kwame Bediako, 'Africa and Christianity on the Threshold of the Third Millennium', *African Affairs*, vol. 99, 395 (April 2000), 306.

[4] Kwame Bediako, *Christianity in Africa: The Renewal of a Non-Western Religion* (Edinburgh: Edinburgh University Press, 1995).

Development of Christianity as an African Religion

The process of transformation of Christianity from a western to a non-western religion has been gradual but certain. By confining the Kingdom of God within the protective walls of the conscious and the rational, John Taylor points out in *The Primal Vision,* it left untouched 'the great deep of the subliminal, and unredeemed the glories of the elemental energies of man'. Enlightenment Christianity, he notes, left the incalculable out of the faith and played down the supernatural leaving non-westerners with a religion that was too cerebral to touch people at the deeper levels of spirituality.[5] During the twentieth century, African Christians had to take their spiritual destiny into their own hands. Historic mission Christianity in Africa came under indigenous leadership. Translations of the Bible into various vernaculars enabled mother-tongue comprehensions and consequent spread of the message in local idioms. On the importance of the translation of the Scriptures, for example, Lamin Sanneh notes how the process bypassed Europe's Enlightenment prerequisites to connect with what he refers to as 'the pre-industrial sensibilities of hinterland populations', and 'thereby allowing the Bible to speak with authority in its own original voice'.[6]

African-initiated churches, including new forms of Pentecostalism, have over the period under consideration burgeoned with considerable speed leading to a situation where it has become impossible to talk about Africa without Christianity or Christianity without Africa. David B. Barrett had argued that given its phenomenal growth, 'African Christians might well tip the balance and transform Christianity permanently into a primarily non-western religion'.[7] During the twentieth century, Barrett surmised, the goal of world evangelization long espoused by the western churches receded from their grasp.[8] It is against this backdrop of the decline of Christianity in the West that I argue, albeit euphemistically, that the faith may have taken 'refuge' in Africa because it is under siege in its former heartlands. This decline of Christian presence in the modern West is one that according to Sanneh, carries at its heart a moral relativism that discounts Christianity's transcendent claims and resists the religion, or any religion for that matter, as a valid source of truth.[9]

In addition to all else, the experiential element around which religion revolves is very important in primal thought or preindustrial sensibilities. The neglect of the experiential dimension of Christianity was therefore problematic for many African believers. In the early 1960s, Ghanaian sociologist, Methodist lay preacher, and later Prime Minister Kofi A. Busia, expressed grave disquiet with the manner in which Europe – the main geographical source of mission work in Africa – was consciously edging God out of public life:

> There is an even more serious problem that arises. It concerns the attitude of Europe to Christianity today. It is being seriously asserted that through the advances in science and technology, man has learnt to cope with all questions of importance without recourse to God as a working hypothesis; that everything gets along without God, and that in scientific as well as human affairs generally, God has been edged out of life.[10]

---

[5] John V. Taylor, *The Primal Vision: Western Christendom and the African View of Life* (Philadelphia: Fortress Press, 1963): 21.

[6] Lamin Sanneh, *Translating the Message: The Missionary Impact on Culture.* Revised and Expanded Edition (Maryknoll, NY: Orbis Books, 2009): 57.

[7] David B. Barrett, 'AD 2000: 350 Million Christians in Africa', *International Review of Missions*, Vol. 59 (January 1970), 39-54.

[8] Barrett, '350 Million Christians in Africa': 52.

[9] Lamin Sanneh, *Encountering the West: Christianity and the Global Cultural Process: The African Dimension* (Maryknoll, NY: Orbis Books, 1993): 184.

[10] Kofi A. Busia, 'Freedom and Unity in Christ in Society', vol. LII, *International Review of Missions* (January 1963): 447.

The emergence of African immigrant Christianity in the West might be taken as a direct historical and ecclesial response to the sort of picture that Busia paints here. Today, in Europe and North America, African Christianity represented by immigrant churches contributes immensely to factors keeping the faith alive in the minds of people. We cannot talk about growth in African Christianity without reference to African Christian churches in the western diasporas. The development verifies John Mbiti's observation that the centres of the church's universality are no longer in Geneva, Rome, Athens, Paris, London, and New York, but rather in Kinshasa, Buenos Aires, Addis Ababa and Manila.[11] Much of the modern West seems to have opted for the privatization of faith, demystification of the supernatural and secularization in the process of development and the organization of public life. This means the moral imperatives of Christianity and the right to make moral judgements for example are now subordinated to liberal concepts of personal rights.[12]

Christian Europe in Africa

The Eurocentric approach to world history missed such developments in Africa as the continent's enhanced place in the modern transformation of Christianity in the world.[13] Thus an important book edited by Ogbu Kalu was entitled *African Christianity: It's an African Story.*[14] The fact is, for over five centuries, the story of Christianity had been inextricably bound up with western civilizations. The western missionary enterprise in Africa had culminated in the formation of historic mission churches from the early decades of the nineteenth century. The historic mission denominations prioritized formal education and provided health care and other social services as tools of evangelization.[15] Pastoral ministries, theological education, religious services, liturgical orders, clerical accoutrements and the architectural designs of chapel buildings with their high spires and stained-glass windows including interior set-ups and decorations, sustained models inherited from Western European Christendom traditions of the Victorian era. This was so because missionaries had a double identity as representatives of the gospel and as representatives of western cultures.[16] Vestiges of the European Christian heritage remain to varying degrees within Christianity in Africa; nevertheless, African Christianity as representing particular modes of religious expression has changed seismically.

Africa's collective response to the presence of European Christianity may be discerned through a 1955 article by E.A. Asamoa with the revealing title: 'The Christian Church and African Heritage'. It appeared at a time when the Church in Africa was still searching for relevance more than a century after missionary work began. The Church in Africa had been struggling to make Christianity relevant within a culture in which, unlike in European Enlightenment societies, supernatural realities remained real, hyperactive and important. The clash of religious cultures generated a number of important responses among Christians in Africa.

The first response came towards the end of the nineteenth century when Nationalist or Ethiopianist churches emerged under indigenous leadership in Africa south of the Sahara. David Vincent Brown of the Niger Delta was representative of this development. He formed the Native Baptist Church and, to give

---

[11] Quoted in Jenkins, Next Christendom, 2.

[12] Philip Jenkins, *God's Continent: Christianity, Islam, and Europe's Religious Crisis* (Oxford: Oxford University Press, 2007): 39, 40.

[13] For this point, see Kwame Bediako, 'Africa and Christianity on the Threshold of the Third Millennium: The Religious Dimension', *African Affairs*, 99 (2000): 303-323.

[14] Ogbu U. Kalu ed., *African Christianity*: It's an African Story (Trenton, NJ: Africa World Press, 2006).

[15] Frederick P. Keppel, 'A Comment on Christian Missions to Africa', *International Review of Missions*, vol. XVIII, 72 (October 1929): 503-508.

[16] Walls, *Missionary Movement in Christian History*, xviii.

practical expression to the African repudiation of Christianity as a western religion, he changed his name, becoming Mojola Agbebi. That was in the late 1880s. Subsequently, several Nationalist churches appeared across Africa. They did not become a mass movement as such but the Nationalist churches were important as indicators of the desire to express the Christian faith in ways that remained loyal to the Bible and indigenous religious sensibilities at the same time. The quest of the Christian Nationalists was a quest for an Africanization of the church that challenged white monopoly over ecclesial administrative structures and countered the denigration of indigenous cultures with a Nationalist anti-structure.[17]

It is the challenge thrown at the churches in Africa, beginning with the Nationalist churches that much later than the 1960s led academic theologians to start writing on African theology. There developed a fervent search for an authentic theology that would address African concerns and we find these in the writings of John S. Mbiti, E. Bolaji Idowu, Kwesi A. Dickson, Jean Marc Ela, Vincent Mulago and John S. Pobee. Mercy A. Oduyoye of Ghana later formed the Circle of Concerned African Women Theologians to reflect on religion in Africa from gender, and precisely feminine, perspectives. Subsequently a major trend in African Christianity became the importance of religion and gender on the curricula of university departments for the study of religion and theological seminaries of the Protestant type. It is important to add that the Nationalist or Ethiopianist churches differ from later religious innovations in Africa on account of their appearance as the Christian religious counterparts of local parties such as the Aborigines Rights Protection Society that initiated the agitations leading to political independence from the 1950s.

The second response to mission Christianity came through the formation of the AICs. These blazed the trail in the integration of traditional worldviews and charismatic renewal phenomena into Christian belief and practice. Additionally they championed a gender ideology that ordained women and pursued practical forms of salvation that gave pastoral attention to such issues as healing and fertility which are all, in the traditional context, matters for religion. Unlike the Nationalist churches whose main agenda was administrative and the recognition of local cultural values and languages as important vehicles for Christian expression and practice, the AICs had a much more popular agenda of reform. Their key concern was the non-recognition of the power of the Holy Spirit in historic mission church life. Discerning African Christians criticized the negative disposition of historic mission Christianity to traditional worldviews of supernatural causality and the power of witchcraft in particular. Witchcraft for example had been denied in missionary preaching and homiletics as a psychological delusion and a figment of the African imagination.

In response, Asamoa articulated a position that had long been taken on board by the AICs with their integration of charismatic experiences into Christian worship and their decisive prayers for health, wholeness, employment, marriage, business, and promotion. Their pneumatic approach to Christianity made them so popular that the Nationalist churches started to slip into oblivion. The older denominations, from which the Nationalist churches walked out, now started to lose patrons in significant numbers. The AICs served as critiques of these older denominations for clutching at the Western European missionary theological heritage that had alienated traditional worldviews as nonsensical and superstitious with no contribution to make to the appropriation of the gospel. Asamoa wrote that the dismissive approach to African worldviews would not edge out such ideas from the imagination of the people even after they came to Christ.[18]

In fact, the article was coming fifty years after the beginning of African Initiated Christianity. Indeed by the time the World Mission Conference reconvened in Le Zoute, Belgium, in 1926, indigenous charismatic prophets – Garrick Sokari Braide of the Niger Delta, Isaiah Shembe of South Africa, William Wade Harris of West Africa, and Simon Kimbangu of Central Africa – had already taken the process of evangelization to another level drawing crowds and leading to the formation of AICs across Africa. On account of their

---

[17] Ogbu U. Kalu, *African Pentecostalism: An Introduction* (Oxford: Oxford University Press, 2008): 24.
[18] Asamoa, 'The Christian Church and African Heritage', *International Review of Mission.* Vol. 44 (July 1955), 297.

disproportionate emphasis on the power of the Spirit and prayer the new AICs became known as Spiritual churches (churches of the Spirit) in Ghana and Aladura churches (churches of prayer) in Nigeria.

With the rise of Zionist, Spiritual and Aladura churches, Western European Christianity gradually ceased to be paradigmatic of the faith on African soil. The AICs emerged as embodiments of Christianity that was acclaimed as thoroughly Christian and truly African. As Lamin Sanneh observes, a process of internal change was thus initiated in which African Christians sought a distinctive way of life through mediation of the Spirit, a process that enhanced the importance of traditional religions for the deepening of Christian spirituality. He notes how the African spirit-centred movements of the early twentieth century combined the two fundamental elements of Christianity and African culture in ways that advertised their intentions without undervaluing their African credentials.[19] The new African churches, inspired by what they had read from the translated Scriptures and their own charismatic experiences, developed a strong interventionist theology that helped patrons make sense out of the spiritually precarious African world and how the name of Jesus proved capable of dealing with the fears and insecurities emanating from the African universe.

Pentecostalism in African Christianity

In Africa, contemporary forms of Pentecostal expression with their mega-size urban-centred congregations, youthful membership, and innovative uses of modern media technologies and prosperity theologies may be included in what we consider as the third response to missionary Christianity. While Ethiopianism appealed to the African Christian elite of the late nineteenth century, the new prophetic movements and AICs took on a very spirit-centred character and in the processes were able to create mass conversions that enlarged the frontiers of Christianity in Africa beyond those of the missionaries. The classical Pentecostals of the 1930s lived their ecclesial lives in somewhat parallel fashion to the independent churches. The new Pentecostals, especially their modern mega-size versions based in urban Africa have emerged within a very different socio-economic context that has usually been captured in the word 'globalization'.

The prophetic movements out of which the AICs were born laid the foundations for the rise of contemporary Pentecostalism in modern Africa.[20] In *Religious Innovation in Africa* Harold W. Turner summarized the emphases of African Christianity as mediated through the AICs in two main theological themes. The first is a pneumatological emphasis in which the Godhead is envisaged as present and powerful through the Holy Spirit, who reveals the will of God and the destiny of the individual, guides through dangers and fills men with new powers of prophecy, utterance, prayer and healing. On that account Turner even proposed that a more appropriate designation for them would be prophet-healing churches. The second is a soteriological emphasis that calls on people to turn away from the spirits and deities of the traditional pantheon, and traditional medicine-men and -women with their magical powers and techniques. They then turn towards the Christian God for their salvation that is interpreted in very practical terms, including seeking protection from the host of evil forces that inhabit the African universe.[21] To that extent, the key theological orientation of the new Pentecostal/Charismatic churches may not be markedly different from those of the AICs.

The point is that Pentecostalism in Africa has not developed as a monolithic movement. Classical Pentecostal denominations of both western missionary and indigenous kinds started in sub-Saharan Africa from the late 1920s. This means they developed alongside the AICs. This was the case until the late 1970s when new expressions of Pentecostalism started burgeoning in Africa. Contemporary Pentecostals, as I

[19] Lamin O. Sanneh, *West African Christianity: The Religious Impact* (Maryknoll, NY: Orbis Books, 1983): 180.
[20] Ogbu U. Kalu, *African Pentecostalism: An Introduction* (Oxford: Oxford University Press, 2008): x.
[21] Harold W. Turner, *Religious Innovation in Africa: Collected Essays on New Religious Movements* (Boston, MA: G.K. Hall, 1979): 98.

refer to them collectively, have manifested themselves as mega-sized urban-based independent churches; renewal movements within historic mission denominations; and as trans-denominational charismatic fellowships. The best known of the trans-denominational charismatic groups would be the Full Gospel Businessmen's Fellowship International originating from North America. Together the contemporary Pentecostals have further transformed the African Christian religious landscape. Trans-denominational charismatic fellowships for example promote a responsible church membership that makes those movements serve as conduits for charismatic renewal in non-Pentecostal churches. The new mega-size churches in particular have a tremendous appeal for Africa's youth and their innovative uses of modern media technologies and modernization of worship have contributed to their great appeal.

These churches have grown inside and outside Africa. With more than 10,000 worshippers attending its various weekly services in London alone, Pastor Ashimolowo's Kingsway International Christian Centre has taken over the territory of the Church of England as a contemporary Pentecostal Church with the single largest *active* congregation in Western Europe. Pastor Ashimolowo, aided by a vibrant media ministry, addresses more people around the world than any Protestant leader in Western Europe. The same is true of Eastern Europe where another Nigerian, Pastor Sunday Adelaja, runs a 25,000 member Church of the Embassy of the Blessed Kingdom of God for all Nations. A majority of the membership of God Embassy is white European and most of the early members of this 21-year-old church are recovered drug addicts and/or alcoholics. It is the moving testimonies of former drug and alcohol addicts and gang members and those of their grateful family members that have helped to populate God Embassy and turned their pastor, Sunday Adelaja, into a champion of Christian presence in former communist Europe. This charismatic Pentecostal church has also taken over territories that the Eastern Orthodox Church, until fairly recently, simply took for granted.

The prosperity gospel associated with contemporary Pentecostalism has often been criticized for its promotion of materialism in the name of a message of motivation and empowerment. That may well be the case if considered only against the backdrop of the flamboyant and materialistic lifestyles of some of its leaders in particular. But that is just one side of the story. The prosperity gospel has a very important empowerment and motivational dimension that often gets lost in the discussion. Within the difficult economic conditions and disappointing political leadership in Africa, many young people, through the motivational messages of contemporary Pentecostalism, have managed to take their destinies into their own hands for self-improvement. Testimonies abound of people who have returned to school to improve their employment prospects, others have started their own businesses, and for many others, simply choosing Jesus Christ has led to moral reformations that have helped to re-channel resources away from gambling, drinking, drugs and womanizing into more constructive purposes.

The Process of Transformation

The process of transformation of Christianity into a non-western religion has been inspired by several factors. Christian growth from the viewpoint of mission is inspired by the Holy Spirit who has been at work in the transformation of Christianity into a non-western religion. An important tool used by the Spirit was access to Scripture in the vernaculars. Bible translation helped to bring about a historic shift in Christianity's theological centre of gravity by pioneering a strategic alliance with local conceptions of religion.[22] In non-western Christianity, unlike in western contexts, the Bible has largely kept its place with greater respect for its authority as divinely inspired text.[23] In the hands of many western theologians, on the

---

[22] Lamin Sanneh, *Whose Religion is Christianity: The Gospel Beyond the West* (Grand Rapids and Cambridge: William B. Eerdmans, 2003): 10-11.

[23] Philip Jenkins, *The New Faces of Christianity: Believing the Bible in the Global South* (Oxford: Oxford University Press, 2006): 4.

other hand, it is now a mere textbook, which means in many cases the Bible seems to have lost its authority, holiness and respect in church and family life.

If the Bible lost its place as the source of guidance for public life and morality in the West, it did so by first losing its status as more than a sacred book through a process of biblical relativism and gradual demystification.[24] It may have been completely lost on many western Christians that St Paul writing to Timothy referred to 'all scripture' as 'God-breathed' and useful among others for teaching, rebuke and training in righteousness (2 Timothy 3:16). Unlike in many western cases, vernacular translations of the Bible were generally received in African churches as inspired by the Spirit of God. With these vernacular translations went cultural renewal that encouraged Africans to view Christianity in a favourable light.[25] Missionaries played leading roles in the translation of the Bible into the languages of societies beyond the West and, in so doing, became champions of non-western cultures.[26] Thus in the midst of the recession of the faith in its former western heartlands and its accession in Africa, the major historical contributions of Christian missions needs to be upheld and commended.

African Christianity and Politics

In many places on the continent there was a close relationship between colonial power and the mission church.[27] This was understandable as these mission agencies had their roots and financial bases in Geneva, Basel, Bremen, Rome and London. We noted earlier that mission Christianity evangelized mainly through formal education. This meant that in post-colonial Africa, the leadership of various countries, including Ghana, Liberia, the Gambia, Sierra Leone, Benin, Ivory Coast and several others, were trained in mission schools. Many of them as we noted, such as Ghana's Kofi A. Busia, remained leading churchmen and preachers well into the 1970s. The development of autocratic regimes from the late 1970s led to much insecurity in the corridors of power. In the search for protection and longevity in office, several African leaders formed alliances with founders and prophets of spiritual churches for the provision of supernatural protection against enemies using mystical means to thwart political efforts. Stephen Ellis and Gerrie ter Haar note how former President Daniel Arap Moi of Kenya visited Prophetess Mary Akatsa. Apparently, she was not the only prophet to have been sought out by politicians who considered it a matter of interest to associate with powerful spiritual leaders.[28]

In most of Africa, especially West, Central and East, coups occurred and, by the middle of the 1970s, these areas had come under military dictatorships. The leadership of many historic mission denominations was persecuted for using their academic clout to challenge the brutal regimes of military dictatorships in Ghana, Uganda and Liberia. The return to multi-party democracies from the middle of the 1980s was greatly facilitated by the Christian Councils and Catholic Bishops' Conferences with many clergymen chairing these transitions.[29] In Benin, Monsignor Isidore de Sousa who was Archbishop of Cotonou, presided over the transition to democratic rule in that country in the late 1980s. It is on record that the transitions from dictatorships to democratic governance in countries like Ghana, Togo and Benin were

---

[24] J. Kwabena Asamoah-Gyadu, 'Beyond Text and Interpretation: The Bible as a Book of Sacred Power in African Christianity', *Journal of African Christian Thought*, vol. 10, 2 (December 2007): 18-23.
[25] Sanneh, *Whose Religion is Christianity*, 18.
[26] Lamin Sanneh, *Translating the Message: The Missionary Impact on Modern Culture*. Revised and Expanded (Maryknoll, NY: Orbis Books, 2009): 30.
[27] Adrian Hastings, *A History of African Christianity 1950-1975* (Cambridge: Cambridge University, 1979).
[28] See Stephen Ellis and Gerrie ter Haar, *Worlds of Power: Religious Thought and Political Practice in Africa* (Oxford: Oxford University Press, 2004), 42, 44.
[29] See Paul Gifford, *Christianity and Politics in Doe's Liberia* (Cambridge: Cambridge University Press, 1993); *Christianity, Politics and Public Life in Kenya* (Oxford: Oxford University Press, 2009).

aided in part by especially mainline Christian denominations.[30] The developments coincided with the rise of the new Pentecostal churches. In the search for legitimacy various charismatic leaders struck new alliances with governments. The case of Frederick Chiluba of Zambia who declared his country officially Christian with the support of Pentecostal pastors is fairly well known and document in a study by Isabel Phiri.[31] There has not been one unique mode of engagement therefore between the church and the political order and establishment, but what is true is that with the massive presence of Christianity on the continent the role of the church in the state continues to be an important one in Africa.

African Christianity in Scholarship

The writings of scholars in African Christianity demonstrate the extent to which the Christian tradition has, over the past century in particular, become part of Africa. They indicate some of the distinctively African shapes that Christianity is taking following its appropriation and integration as an African religious form. Christian scholarship follows and derives from Christian mission, Andrew Walls wrote, and the demand for scholarship occurred as soon as the gospel crossed its first cultural frontier – that between Israel and the Hellenistic world.[32] Thus Christian mission from the inception of that process has been a history of scholarship and documentation and this is true also of the early planting of Christianity in Africa. Early Ethiopian Christianity developed its own distinctive literature and tradition of scholarship, using its own distinctive writing system and this, Walls notes, enabled the recovery of Ethiopian Christianity from near disaster.[33]

The tradition of Christian scholarship continued with the modern missionary movement in Africa as the missionary movement, out of its essential concern to communicate the gospel, was forced into innovative scholarship.[34] The point is that non-western Christian theology, especially when focusing on Pentecostal/charismatic Christianity, is gradually shifting to the centre as mainstream theology. There is therefore a call for Christian scholarship in Africa to realize the dawn of that new theological era, and rise to the occasion. African theological scholarship will help determine the shape and quality of world Christianity because it is only in the area of theological scholarship that leadership may shift into African hands. Authentic theological scholarship, Walls argues, must arise out of Christian mission and, therefore, from the principal theatres of mission like Africa. What this means is that, if Africa and the other continents of the South fail to develop proper capacities for leadership in theological studies, there will be, for practical purposes, no theological studies anywhere that will be worth caring about.[35]

Conclusion

Thus Africa, a continent that was minimal in Christian profession when the missionary movement began, has virtually moved to the position where it may have more professing Christians than any other

[30] Richard Joseph, "The Christian Churches and Democracy in Contemporary Africa", in John Witte, Jr. ed., *Christianity and Democracy in Global Context* (Boulder, Colorado: Worldview Press, 1993), 231, 234.

[31] Isabel A. Phiri, "President Frederick Chiluba and Zambia: Evangelicals and Democracy in a 'Christian Nation", in Terrence O. Ranger edited. *Evangelical Christianity and Democracy in Africa* (Oxford: Oxford University Press, 2008): 95-129.

[32] Andrew F. Walls, 'Christian Scholarship in Africa in the Twenty-first Century', *Journal of African Christian Thought*. Vol. 4, 2 (December 2001): 44.

[33] Walls, 'Christian Scholarship in Africa', 45.

[34] Walls, 'Christian Scholarship in Africa', 46.

[35] Walls, 'Christian Scholarship in Africa', 47.

continent.[36] This was very much the thinking of Taylor who was once a missionary to East Africa, as he observed the sort of religious innovation championed by the AICs. Impressed with their innovation, spiritual dynamism and fervour he noted:

> In Africa today it seems the incalculable Spirit has chosen to use the Independent Church Movement for another spectacular advance. This does not prove that their teaching is necessarily true but it shows they have the raw materials out of which a missionary church is made – spontaneity, total commitment, and the primitive responses that arise from the depths of life.[37]

In Pauline thought, the God of mission is said to call into being things that are not as if they were; he uses the foolish and despised things of the world to shame the wise. In choosing Africa, God would seem then to have been acting true to character by choosing the weak things of the world to shame the strong; the lowly things of this world and the despised things – and the things that are not to nullify the things that are 'so that no-one may boast before him' (1 Cor. 1:27-29). The growth and dynamism of Christianity in Africa and among Africans in the diasporas has also given the faith some new lease of life that may just ensure its survival as a world religion.

The type of Christianity and Christian theology coming from Africa would be important in understanding the current shape of world Christianity. Africa is very much a context that has been open to the work of the Spirit through various revivals and where the Bible has kept its place as containing God's prophetic voice and authority. In the end no serious study of Africa can ignore Christianity and the role it has come to play in world Christianity. To understand African Christianity however, significant attention must be given to the ways in which indigenous Christians have appropriated the faith and made it workable against the backdrop of traditional religious and cultural worldviews. It is within these cultural worldviews that people locate their identity and function as human beings in relation to the transcendent powers of the universe with the God who revealed himself in Christ at the helm and *very active* in the power of the Holy Spirit.

Bibliography

Asamoa, EA. 'The Christian Church and African Heritage', *International Review of Mission,* 44, issue 175 (July 1955): 292-301.

Asamoah-Gyadu, J. Kwabena. 'Beyond Text and Interpretation: The Bible as a Book of Sacred Power in African Christianity', *Journal of African Christian Thought,* 10, no. 2 (December 2007): 18-23.

Barrett, David B. 'AD 2000: 350 Million Christians in Africa', *International Review of Missions* 59 (January 1970): 39-54.

Bediako, Kwame. 'Africa and Christianity on the Threshold of the Third Millennium', *African Affairs,* 99, no. 395 (April 2000): 303-323.

Bediako, Kwame. *Christianity in Africa: The Renewal of a Non-Western Religion*. Edinburgh: Edinburgh University Press, 1995.

Busia, Kofi A. 'Freedom and Unity in Christ in Society', *International Review of Missions,* 52 (January 1963): 447-452.

Cox, Harvey. *Fire from Heaven: The Rise of Pentecostal Spirituality and the Reshaping of Religion in the Twenty-first Century*. Reading, MA: Addison-Wesley, 1995.

Ellis, Stephen and Gerrie ter Haar. *Worlds of Power: Religious Thought and Political Practice in Africa.* Oxford: Oxford University Press, 2004.

---

[36] Walls, *Missionary Movement in Christian History: Studies in the Transmission of Faith* (Maryknoll, NY: Orbis Books, 1996): 85.

[37] John V. Taylor, *The Go-Between God: The Holy Spirit and the Christian Mission* (London: SCM, 1972): 54.

Gifford, Paul. *Christianity and Politics in Doe's Liberia* (Cambridge: Cambridge University Press, 1993.
Gifford, Paul. *Christianity, Politics and Public Life in Kenya.* Oxford: Oxford University Press, 2009.
Hastings, Adrian. *A History of African Christianity 1950-1975.* Cambridge: Cambridge University, 1979.
Jenkins, Philip. *God's Continent: Christianity, Islam, and Europe's Religious Crisis.* Oxford: Oxford University Press, 2007.
Jenkins, Philip. *The New Faces of Christianity: Believing the Bible in the Global South.* Oxford: Oxford University Press, 2006.
Jenkins, Philip. *The Next Christendom: The Coming of Global Christianity.* Revised and Expanded Edition. Oxford: Oxford University Press, 2007.
Joseph, Richard. 'The Christian Churches and Democracy in Contemporary Africa', in *Christianity and Democracy in Global Context edited by* John Witte, Jr., 231-247 Boulder, Colorado: Worldview Press, 1993.
Kalu, Ogbu U. *African Pentecostalism: An Introduction.* Oxford: Oxford University Press, 2008.
Kalu, Ogbu U. ed. *African Christianity: It's an African Story.* Trenton, NJ: Africa World Press, 2006.
Keppel, Frederick P. 'A Comment on Christian Missions to Africa', *International Review of Missions,* XVIII, no. 72 (October 1929): 503-508.
Phiri, Isabel A. 'President Frederick Chiluba and Zambia: Evangelicals and Democracy in a 'Christian Nation', in *Evangelical Christianity and Democracy in Africa* edited by Terrence O. Ranger, 95-129. Oxford: Oxford University Press, 2008.
Sanneh, Lamin O. *West African Christianity: The Religious Impact.* Maryknoll, NY: Orbis Books, 1983.
Sanneh, Lamin. *Encountering the West: Christianity and the Global Cultural Process: The African Dimension.* Maryknoll, NY: Orbis Books, 1993.
Sanneh, Lamin. *Translating the Message: The Missionary Impact on Culture.* Revised and Expanded Edition. Maryknoll, NY: Orbis Books, 2009.
Sanneh, Lamin. *Translating the Message: The Missionary Impact on Modern Culture.* Revised and Expanded. Maryknoll, NY: Orbis Books, 2009.
Sanneh, Lamin. *Whose Religion is Christianity: The Gospel Beyond the West.* Grand Rapids and Cambridge: William B. Eerdmans, 2003.
Taylor, John V. *The Go-Between God: The Holy Spirit and the Christian Mission.* London: SCM, 1972.
Taylor, John V. *The Primal Vision: Western Christendom and the African View of Life.* Philadelphia: Fortress Press, 1963.
Turner, Harold W. *Religious Innovation in Africa: Collected Essays on New Religious Movements.* Boston, MA: G.K. Hall, 1979.
Walls, Andrew F. 'Christian Scholarship in Africa in the Twenty-first Century', *Journal of African Christian Thought* 4, no. 2 (December 2001): 217-228.
Walls, Andrew F. *Missionary Movement in Christian History: Studies in the Transmission of Faith.* Maryknoll, NY: Orbis Books, 1996.

(8) The Role of the Bible in African Christianity

Gerald West

Introduction

The Bible is both organic to Africa and a foreign artefact brought to Africa.

North Africa is part of the Mediterranean world in which the Bible was born.[1] This is evident, for example, in the presence of Africans and Africa in the Bible, and in the impact of Africa and Africans on the formation of the Bible and interpretation of the Bible. For example, among the most significant for biblical reception was the Greek translation of Hebrew scriptures, the Septuagint. The traditional story is that seventy-two or seventy (hence the shorthand 'LXX') learned Jews were sent to Egypt at the request of Ptolemy II Philadelphus (285-246 BCE) to translate the Jewish law (Torah, the Pentateuch) into Greek for the library in Alexandria.

It is not clear how and when Christianity came to Roman North Africa, but what is clear is that there were distinctive features in this form of Christianity, some of which derived from local religious and cultural traditions and some of which are directly related to their interpretation of the Bible.[2] For example, when confronted by the emissaries of the emperor Constantine, the Donatists resisted incorporation, proclaiming: 'You come with edicts of emperors, we hold nothing in our hands but volumes of scriptures.'[3]

The scriptures continued to play an important part in African receptions of the Bible through the work of North African theologians like Tertullian (ca. 160-ca. 212), Origen (185-254), Cyprian (ca. 200-258) and Augustine (354-430).[4] But these were all Africans of a particular kind, orientated as they were to the Mediterranean world. Further inland other Africans were also engaging with the Bible, including the rural regions of Egypt, with its emerging Coptic language and culture, who looked south to the desert hinterland, and whose biblical interpretation is indelibly shaped by the 'era of the martyrs' brought about by the accession of Diocletian (284).[5]

Just as the Nile facilitated the expansion of Christianity from the delta region to Upper Egypt and to the three kingdoms of Nubia, so the Rea Sea enabled contact between the Semitic peoples of the south-western Arabian coast and the northern Cushite communities of Ethiopia (or Aksum).[6] Just as trade routes carried the Bible across North Africa, so too trade routes carried the Bible to sub-Saharan Africa.

While the Bible has always, in some sense, been associated with North Africa, the same is not true for sub-Saharan Africa. The Bible was brought to these parts of Africa relatively recently, initially (1415-1787) with the wave of explorers, traders, and ecclesial representatives of the medieval Catholic Church, directed by Portugal. Slave and trade posts, with chaplains in attendance, were established at various

---

[1] Gosnell L.O.R. Yorke, "Biblical Hermeneutics: An Afrocentric Perspective," *The Journal of Religious Thought* 52(1995): 9; Keith Augustus Burton, *The Blessing of Africa* (Downers Grove, Illinois: IVP Academic, 2007), 17-55.

[2] Maureen A. Tilley, *The Bible in Christian North Africa: The Donatist World* (Minneapolis: Fortress Press, 1997), 20.

[3] Elizabeth Isichei, *A History of Christianity in Africa: From Antiquity to the Present* (Grand Rapids: Eerdmans, 1995), 37.

[4] Tilley, *The Bible in Christian North Africa*, 20-51; Bengt Sundkler and Christopher Steed, *A History of the Church in Africa* (Cambridge: Cambridge University Press, 2000), 24.

[5] Sundkler and Steed, *A History of the Church in Africa*, 10-11.

[6] Sundkler and Steed, *A History of the Church in Africa*, 34-41.

strategic sites on the African coast, circumnavigating the African continent from the Zaïre River to Ethiopia.[7]

This first wave of European mission, characterised by a particular form of imperial Christianity, was followed by a second wave, characterised at first by 'literally hundreds of European conquests of Africa',[8] and then by the more systematic European 'scramble' for Africa, precipitated by the Berlin Congress of 1885.[9] Both Roman Catholic and Protestant missions were a feature of this period.[10] This second wave, of modern nineteenth-century Catholic and Protestant missionary and imperial Christianity (1787-1919), did not find an undisturbed territory. Sub-Saharan Africa was already in flux, with large population movements and migrations across the sub-continent, propelled by the innumerable incursions from the African coast for slaves and by local African struggles for control of resources, such as the *Mfecane* in Southern Africa.[11] Not only did these movements of Africans themselves become carriers of Christianity and the Bible, the social upheavals generated both by external and internal forces produced a whole range of dislocated groups and individuals who were willing to engage with the new formations brought about by Christianity and the Bible.

The third wave (1920-1959) of missionary-colonial influence in sub-Saharan Africa is closely related to the second, but can be considered as the transition from a colonial period to that of the independent African state. Across villages and towns in sub-Saharan Africa, first the mission-educated Africans and then the Africans educated by the colonial government 'began to act as a local or regional centre of opposition'.[12] Some became the leaders of missionary-established churches, others founded African Independent Churches, while yet others founded liberation movements, each in their own diverse ways providing sites of opposition and resistance. Central to each site was a foundational vernacular book, the Bible, and through it African Christianity began 'to talk back' to power.

Though significantly diverse, there are many 'family resemblances' with respect to biblical interpretation across Mediterranean North African, as well as Coptic, Nubian, and Ethiopian North Africa, and also sub-Saharan Africa. Common to them all are a set of intersecting distinctive features.

Four Distinctive Features of African Christianities

It is clear from the above that in order to understand the role of the Bible in African Christianity, we recognise the distinctive features of African realities with which the Bible transacts. From the above brief historical and hermeneutical overview of the Bible's presence in Africa, we can discern four distinctive features that characterise the Bible's role/s in African Christianity: the Bible, Christian tradition, African culture and/as religion, and African contemporary contexts.[13]

---

[7] Isichei, *A History of Christianity in Africa*, 52-73; Sundkler and Steed, *A History of the Church in Africa*, 45-80.
[8] Sundkler and Steed, *A History of the Church in Africa*, 97.
[9] Sundkler and Steed, *A History of the Church in Africa*, 97.
[10] Sundkler and Steed, *A History of the Church in Africa*, 84.
[11] Jean Comaroff and John L. Comaroff, *Of Revelation and Revolution: Christianity, Colonialism and Consciousness in South Africa*, vol. 1 (Chicago: University of Chicago Press, 1991), 167-69.
[12] Sundkler and Steed, *A History of the Church in Africa*, 608.
[13] The work that follows incorporates the contributions of my colleague Billy Meyer, and our class in the Bible in African Christianity module, Kulekani Mpanza, Siyabonga Ntombela, Xabiso Socatsha, David Castillo, Karoline Mora, Takuze Chitsulo, and Mote Magomba.

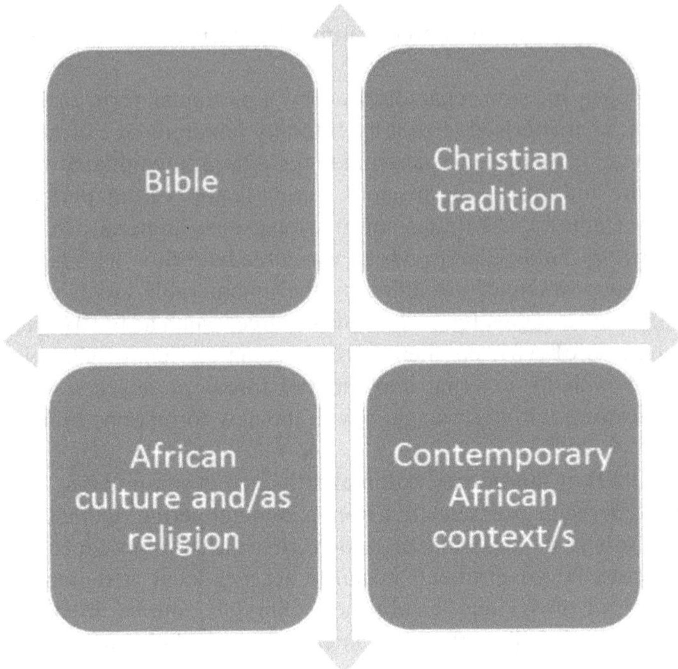

The Bible

The Bible itself has a complex identity in African Christianity. Within Coptic Christianity the Bible is a form of icon, embodying 'a rich tapestry of icons' of biblical figures. 'The Bible is understood as a witness not of deceased historical figures, but of living examples', who together with the saints are 'constantly praying for and attending to the spiritual needs of the faithful'.[14] Psalms in particular are well known, well loved, and well used in West Africa,[15] particularly in the large African Independent Churches, but also in 'mainline' missionary churches. Psalms are categorised according to local cultural concepts into protective, therapeutic, and success Psalms.[16] The Yoruba, for example, inhabited a world full of potential threat, where every material threat, such as debt or sickness, had a spiritual origin, either in one's own personal enemy (*ota*) or in an array of other local indigenous deities (*orisa*).[17] Indeed, 'the primary concern of their day-to-day prayers was to enlist the power of God for the same kind of help and protection which the *orisa* provided for their devotees'.[18] The Bible became central to this daily concern for protection, healing, and success, becoming the prime source of imprecatory potent words (*ogede*), used on their own, or recited

---

[14] J.A. (Bobby) Loubser, "How Al-Mokattam Mountain Was Moved: The Coptic Imagination and the Christian Bible," in *The Bible in Africa: Transactions, Trajectories and Trends*, ed. Gerald O. West and Musa W. Dube (Leiden: E.J. Brill, 2000), 108.

[15] Mercy Amba Oduyoye, "Biblical Interpretation and Social Location of the Interpreter: African Women's Reading of the Bible," in *Reading from This Place: Social Location and Biblical Interpretation in Global Perspective*, ed. Fernando F. Segovia and Mary Ann Tolbert (Minneapolis: Fortress Press, 1995), 34-35.

[16] David Tuesday Adamo, "The Use of Psalms in African Indigenous Churches in Nigeria," in *The Bible in Africa: Transactions, Trajectories and Trends*, ed. Gerald O. West and Musa Dube (Leiden: Brill, 2000), 337.

[17] Adamo, "The Use of Psalms in African Indigenous Churches in Nigeria," 337; J.D.Y. Peel, *Religious Encounter and the Making of the Yoruba* (Bloomington: Indiana University Press, 2000), 259.

[18] Peel, *Religious Encounter and the Making of the Yoruba*, 259.

over amulets containing various natural ingredients and/or the actual written words of a Psalm.[19] The Psalms closely resembled the traditional resources they had been instructed to abandon by the missionaries, and because the Bible was considered an iconic and aural object of power, it was readily appropriated and prescribed by African Christian practitioners. For example, Chief Ogunfuye prescribes Psalm 7 for protection against enemies and the evil one, either together with a special prayer recited every day or by writing the Psalm on parchment and putting the amulet in a special consecrated bag kept under the supplicant's pillow.[20]

The Bible is also translated text. Indeed, translation of the Bible into African indigenous languages is a very important aspect of African Christianity,[21] with vast resources allocated to Bible translation all over the African continent. The notion of 'translation' in African Christianity extends beyond the technical dimensions of translation to include the idea that 'the gospel' (usually with a capital 'G') can be translated into African languages. Implicit in this understanding of translation was the recognition that God and the gospel were already present in African communities prior to the missionaries, that African languages had the conceptual capacity to articulate the gospel, and that Africans had the capacity to do the technical translation work.[22]

The Bible in African Christianity is also full of literary, historical, and sociological detail. African Christianity tends, like other Christianities, to interpret the Bible through theological lenses (see below). But in sub-Saharan contexts, because the Bible is to some extent separable from the forms of Christianity that brought it,[23] the Bible maintains its own distinctiveness as a sacred text. And the detail of particular texts is part of this distinctiveness. So, for example, Isaiah Shembe, founder of the large and still thriving African 'church', Ibandla lama Nazaretha, the Church of the Nazarites, drew on a biblical narrative that had no previous history of interpretation in missionary Christianity (or the many African Christianities forged on the basis of missionary Christianity). The story of Jephthah's daughter in Judges 11 becomes the foundational biblical text for Shembe for a liturgical practice involving young women.[24] Alongside such forms of appropriation of particular biblical detail, African biblical scholarship has played a significant role in bringing the less familiar literary and socio-historical detail of the Bible into the public realm in helping African Christianities to engage with a host of contextual issues, like gender,[25] HIV,[26] unemployment,[27] and post-colonialism.[28]

---

[19] Adamo, "The Use of Psalms in African Indigenous Churches in Nigeria," 338-39.
[20] Adamo, "The Use of Psalms in African Indigenous Churches in Nigeria," 340-41.
[21] Ype Schaaf, *On Their Way Rejoicing: The History and Role of the Bible in Africa* (Carlisle: Paternoster Press, 1994).
[22] Lamin Sanneh, *Translating the Message: The Missionary Impact on Culture* (Maryknoll, NY: Orbis Books, 1989); Kwame Bediako, *Christianity in Africa: The Renewal of a Non-Western Religion* (Edinburgh and Maryknoll, NY: Edinburgh University and Orbis, 1995); Aloo Osotsi Mojola, "The Swahili Bible in East Africa from 1844 to 1996: A Brief Survey with Special Reference to Tanzania," in *The Bible in Africa: Transactions, Trajectories and Trends*, ed. Gerald O. West and Musa Dube (Leiden: E.J. Brill, 2000).
[23] Gerald O. West, "Early Encounters with the Bible among the Batlhaping: Historical and Hermeneutical Signs," *Biblical Interpretation* 12(2004).
[24] Gerald O. West, "The Bible and the Female Body in Ibandla Lamanazaretha: Isaiah Shembe and Jephthah's Daughter," *Old Testament Essays* 20, no. 2 (2007).
[25] Musa W. Dube, ed. *Other Ways of Reading: African Women and the Bible* (Atlanta: Society of Biblical Literature, 2001).
[26] Musa W. Dube and Musimbi Kanyoro, eds., *Grant Me Justice! HIV/Aids and Gender Readings of the Bible* (Pietermaritzburg: Cluster Publications, 2004).
[27] Gerald O. West and Sithembiso Zwane, ""Why Are You Sitting There?" Reading Matthew 20:1-16 in the Context of Casual Workers in Pietermaritzburg, South Africa," in *Matthew: Texts@Contexts*, ed. Nicole Duran Wilkinson and James Grimshaw (Minneapolis: Fortress Press, 2013).
[28] Makhosazana K. Nzimande, "Reconfiguring Jezebel: A Postcolonial *Imbokodo* Reading of the Story of Naboth's Vineyard (1 Kings 21:1-16)," in *African and European Readers of the Bible in Dialogue: In Quest of a Shared*

Christian Tradition

Though the Bible is central to African Christianities, African theologians like John Mbiti considered it essential that African Christianity must remain in continuity with 'the major traditions of Christendom' so that it was linked into 'the mainstream of ecumenical and apostolic heritage'.[29] Mbiti's position is founded on a distinction between 'Christianity', which 'results from the encounter of the gospel with any given local society', and so is always indigenous and culture-bound, and the gospel, which is 'God-given, eternal and does not change'.[30] 'We can add nothing to the gospel, for it is an eternal gift of God,' writes Mbiti.[31] For Mbiti, 'the gospel' apprehended by Africans is substantially the same as that transmitted by the missionaries. But for Kwame Bediako and Lamin Sanneh, the contribution of the African soil/soul is more distinctive. While not disputing significant continuity between what the missionaries proclaimed and what Africans appropriated, Sanneh asserts that 'the God of the Bible had preceded the missionary into the receptor-culture – so the missionary needs to discover Him in the new culture'.[32] For Sanneh, 'the gospel' is not fully understood until African voices have spoken.

The debate between Mbiti, on the one hand, and Sanneh and Bediako, on the other hand, represents, in my analysis, the difference between those forms of African Christianity that consider themselves as African forms of 'international' or 'ecumenical', or 'mainstream' Christianity and those forms of African Christianity that emphasise their break from or their discontinuity with the various forms of missionary Christianity. This distinction is expressed differently in the analysis of different scholars,[33] but can perhaps be understood as a continuum, with forms of African Christianity that are very similar to their missionary antecedents on one end and with forms of African Christianity that are very distinct from missionary manifestations of Christianity on the other end. Useful as typologies might be in providing a sketch of African Christianities in broad strokes, each particular local form of African Christianity should be analysed in its own terms rather than too quickly allocated a place within a typology.[34]

For those forms of African Christianity that locate themselves in some form of continuity with missionary Christian theological traditions, the theological frameworks from those traditions provide the

---

Meaning, ed. Hans de Wit and Gerald O. West (Leiden: EJ Brill, 2008); Musa W. Dube, Andrew M. Mbuvi, and Dora Mbuwayesango, eds., *Postcolonial Perspectives in African Biblical Interpretations* (Atlanta: Society of Biblical Literature, 2012).

[29] John S. Mbiti, *Prayer and Spirituality in African Religion* (Bedford Park: Australian Association for the Study of Religions, 1978); cited in Kwame Bediako, "John Mbiti's Contribution to African Theology," in *Religious Plurality in Africa: Essays in Honour of John S. Mbiti*, ed. Jacob K. Olupona and Sulayman S. Nyang (Berlin and New York: Mouton de Gruyter, 1993), 372.

[30] Cited in Bediako, *Christianity in Africa*, 117.

[31] John S. Mbiti, "Christianity and Traditional Religions in Africa," *International Review of Mission* 59, no. 236 (1970): 438.

[32] Lamin Sanneh, "The Horizontal and the Vertical in Mission: An African Perspective," *International Bulletin of Missionary Research* 7, no. 4 (1983): 166.

[33] In addition to the works cited above and below, see for example C.G. Baëta, ed. *Christianity in Tropical Africa* (Oxford: Oxford University Press,1968); Adrian Hasting, *African Christianity* (New York: Macmillan, 1976); Edward W. Fasholé-Luke et al., eds., *Christianity in Independent Africa* (London: Rex Collings,1978); Paul Gifford, *African Christianity: Its Public Role* (London: Hurst & Company, 1998); Éloi Messi Metogo, ed. *African Christianities*, Concilium (London: SCM Press,2006); Ogbu Kalu, *African Christianity: An African Story* (Pretoria: Dept. of Church History, University of Pretoria, 2005); Afe Adogame, Roswith Gerloff, and Klaus Hock, eds., *Christianity in Africa and the African Diaspora: The Appropriation of a Scattered Heritage* (London and New York: Continuum,2008); Ogbu U. Kalu, *Clio in a Sacred Garb: Essays on Christian Presence and African Responses, 1900-2000* (Trenton, NJ.: Africa World Press, 2008); Paul Gifford, "Trajectories in African Christianity," *International Journal for the Study of the Christian Church* 8, no. 4 (2008).

[34] James L. Cox and Gerrie Ter Haar, eds., *Uniquely African? African Christian Identity from Cultural and Historical Perspectives* (Trenton and Asmara: Africa World Press,2003); David Maxwell and Ingrid Lawrie, eds., *Christianity and the African Imagination: Essays in Honour of Adrian Hastings* (Leiden and Boston: Brill, 2013).

theological categories for interpreting the Bible. Notions of the Bible's 'authority' or 'inspiration' are theologically determined, and dogmatic or systematic theological categories are used to construct a 'biblical' theology. Theological frameworks are thus used to give a theological 'shape' to the Bible, providing a particular theological tradition's understanding of the Bible's central theological 'message'. And for those forms of African Christianity that locate themselves outside and distinct from missionary Christian theological traditions, their own theological frameworks play a similar role.

An example that does not fit easily into either of these options, demonstrating again the need for documenting and analysing each particular case of African Christianity, is that of the World Harvest Church in Nairobi, Kenya. Here the Bible is interpreted through theological categories that derive from a range of traditions, including Evangelical, Pentecostal, and Charismatic Christianity (as well as African Religion), providing a complex theological matrix. In this case, there is a strongly individualistic theological orientation, with the Bible offering a record of God's covenants and commitments to the African individual in their immediate context.[35] The biblical text itself, whichever biblical text is selected, is not dealt with in any depth. The theological framework offers the primary interpretive resources.

Though the Bible is more prominent in the church or community founded by Isaiah Shembe in South Africa in the early 1900s (see above), with no connection to any form of missionary Christianity, here too the theological categories constructed by this African indigenous 'church' provide a shape to the Bible. In the example referred to above, the Judges 11 story of Jephthah's daughter is used because it demonstrates the theological virtues of community solidarity and obedience to the 'rule' or ordinances of the community. However, there are indications that a more individual theological emphasis is finding a place in this theological tradition.[36]

In the more scholarly forms of African Christianity, such as those forms found within the Circle of Concerned African Women Theologians and South African Black Theology, ideological frameworks exert more influence on biblical interpretation than theological frameworks. Within the work of the Circle a range of feminist, womanist, and African women's theoretical and ideological conceptual resources are integrated into their theological orientations as they interpret the Bible. For example, although working within an Evangelical theological framework, Dorothy Bea Akoto-Abutiate draws deeply on a gender-based hermeneutics of suspicion in interpreting both her West African context and the biblical text.[37] Within South African Black Theology there is a similar ideological suspicion about the liberating capacity of the Bible itself, with a clear recognition that there are biblical theologies of both life and death.[38] In these cases the diversity of the Bible is not given a theologically determined unity; instead, the diversity of the Bible is recognised as forms of theological contestation within the biblical tradition itself.

African Culture and/as Religion

As is already apparent from the analysis above, African Christianities are partially constituted by African religion and African culture. My formulation, 'African culture and/as religion', indicates the difficulty of

[35] Paul Gifford, "The Bible in Africa: A Novel Usage in Africa's New Churches," *Bulletin of SOAS* 71, no. 2 (2008): 205-08.

[36] Gerald O. West, "Layers of Reception of Jephthah's Daughter (Judges 11) among the Amanazaretha: From the Early 1900s to Today," in *Reception History and Biblical Studies: Theory and Practice*, ed. William John Lyons and Emma England (London: Bloomsburg, 2015).

[37] Dorothy B.E.A. Akoto, "The Mother of the Ewe and Firstborn Daughter as the 'Good Shepherd' in the Cultural Context of the Ewe Peoples: A Liberating Approach," in *The Bible in Africa: Transactions, Trajectories, and Trends*, ed. Gerald O. West and Musa W. Dube (Leiden: Brill, 2000); see also (Durable) Dorothy Bea Akoto-Abutiate, *African Theology/ies: A Contemporary Mosaical Approach* (Bloomington: Author House, 2014).

[38] Itumeleng J. Mosala, *Biblical Hermeneutics and Black Theology in South Africa* (Grand Rapids: Eerdmans, 1989).

separating 'culture' from 'religion', and so I choose to allow these terms to mutually interact with each other.

The earliest attempts to analyse African Christianity among Africans themselves grappled with the place or role of African culture and/as religion,[39] and the discussion has continued.[40] What is clear is that the Bible is a distinctive feature of African Christianities and that there is a 'primal' connection or resonance between the culture and/as religion of biblical communities and the culture and/as religion of African communities. Because the Bible was both produced by and its texts located within what Kwame Bediako refers to as 'a primal world-view', there was a substantial resonance between large parts of the Bible and the primal world-views of Africans. Drawing on Harold Turner's characterisation of a primal world-view – including a recognition that humanity has a kinship with nature, a recognition of humanity's finitude and creatureliness, a recognition of a spiritual world of powers and beings more powerful than humanity, a recognition that humanity can enter into relationships with the spiritual world, a recognition that there is continuity between this life and the after-life, and a recognition that there is no boundary between the physical and the spiritual – Bediako argues that Africans shared a phenomenological relationship with the biblical world-view.[41] And while some African theologians have argued that this primal world-view was primarily preparatory, preparing Africans for 'the gospel'/Christianity, others like Bediako have argued that this primal world-view was/is also constitutive of African Christianity.

Because, argues Lamin Sanneh, 'language is the intimate, articulate expression of culture', the missionary decision to render the Bible in African vernaculars was 'tantamount to adopting indigenous cultural criteria for the message, a piece of radical indigenization far greater than the standard portrayal of mission as western cultural imperialism'.[42] Sanneh sees 'translation as a fundamental concession to the vernacular, and an inevitable weakening of the forces of uniformity and centralization'; translation introduces 'a dynamic and pluralist factor into questions of the essence of the religion'.[43]

We may discern two dimensions to this central argument of Sanneh's. The first dimension is the revitalisation of indigenous religion and culture. This occurs when the technical process of translation pushes indigenous respondents to re-examine their culture in order to assist the translators with appropriate language with which to translate biblical texts. This return to local culture, a culture that has often been held by missionaries and other 'civilising' forces to be inadequate at best and demonic at worst, revitalises the culture, as local respondents in the translation process reclaim aspects of their culture in order to provide a language for translation that is true to both the biblical text and their culture. And because there is so much resonance between African culture (and/as religion) and the culture (and/as religion) of biblical communities and the texts they produced, the scope for potential 'revitalisation' is substantial.

The second dimension is the potential of the receptor culture to now add its own voice to the voices of the many other communities of faith that have interpreted the Bible before them. If God really does speak the vernacular, then what is it that God is saying as understood by this new community of faith? The very act of making the Bible available in the language of the indigenous people causes the Bible to slip or be prised from the grasp of the missionaries who brought it. 'If hearers of the Word of God in their own languages may then be presumed to respond in their own (cultural and religious) terms,' argues Bediako, 'this is another way of saying that it is not others' but their own questions which they would bring to the

[39] Kofi Appiah-Kobi and Sergio Torres, eds., *African Theology En Route: Papers from the Pan-African Conference of Third World Theologians, December 17-23, 1977, Accra, Ghana* (Maryknoll, NY: Orbis Books, 1983).
[40] Rosino Gibellini, ed. *Paths of African Theology* (Maryknoll, NY: Orbis Books, 1994). See also the references in footnote 33 above.
[41] Bediako, *Christianity in Africa*, 91-108.
[42] Sanneh, *Translating the Message*, 3.
[43] Sanneh, *Translating the Message*, 53.

Bible, taking from it what they would consider to be *its* answers to their questions.'[44] To put it provocatively, what 'the gospel' is has yet to be determined, for not all African indigenous voices have yet been heard speaking for themselves. We could go further, arguing as this essay does, that what the Bible is within African Christianities has yet to be determined by reflecting more carefully on what Africans actually do with the Bible.[45]

As I have already indicated above, there are also indications that those forms of African Christianity that have traditionally rejected African culture and/as religion (being aligned to forms of missionary Christianity that have a long history of suspicion towards African culture and/as religion) are showing signs of the re-emergence of elements of African culture and/as religion. For example, the African cultural and/or religious notion of 'well-being' has been recovered in African neo-Evangelical, Neo-Pentecostal, and neo-Charismatic Christianities, albeit in a more individualistic form.[46]

And, of course, a defining feature of African Independent/Initiated/Indigenous Churches (AICs) has been African culture and/as religion as a primary resource for interpreting the Bible.

Contemporary African Context/s

Culture and/as religion is the soil and soul of African Christianity, and what is referred to here as 'contemporary African context/s' is the changing terrain of the African landscape, particularly the major 'issues' that are a part of African realities. Each African Christianity engages with a range of contextual issues, and some issues are so significant that every different form of African Christianity must 'do theology' with respect to such issues.

For example, every African Christianity is in some sense 'post-colonial', with post-colonial being understood as engagement with aspects of the colonial (and missionary) legacy. Every African Christianity is to some extent a hybrid; the very use of a term like 'African Christianity' signals this hybridity. As Gabriel Setiloane provocatively puts it, 'I am like someone who has been bewitched, and I find it difficult to shake off the Christian witchcraft with which I have been captivated.'[47] While Setiloane emphasises here the power of the Christian narrative to captivate,[48] other African Christians, like Ogbu Kalu, emphasise the agency of Africans. 'In the very process of indigenous assimilation, the decoders (ordinary African Christians) weave a new pattern following the lines of congruence, making their religious experience an organic, unified one.'[49]

HIV/AIDS is another example of a contextual issue that has left its mark on every African Christianity, even those that have not overtly dealt with the pandemic.[50] And we can add other contextual issues that call forth a theological response from African Christianities, such as cultural and political liberation, racial and economic liberation, post-liberation reconstruction, gender-based violence, patriarchy and masculinity,

---

[44] Bediako, *Christianity in Africa*, 63.

[45] Tinyiko S. Maluleke, "Black and African Theologies in the New World Order: A Time to Drink from Our Own Wells," *Journal of Theology for Southern Africa* 96 (1996): 15.

[46] Abiola Ibilola Mbamalu, *The Use of 'Abundant Life' in John 10: 10 and Its Interpretation among Some Yoruba Prosperity Gospel Preachers* (University of KwaZulu-Natal, 2010).

[47] Gabriel Setiloane, "Where Are We in African Theology?," in *African Theology En Route: Papers from the Pan-African Conference of Third World Theologians, Accra, December 17-23, 1977*, ed. Kofi Appiah-Kubi and Sergio Torres (Maryknoll, NY: Orbis Books, 1977), 64.

[48] See also Peel, *Religious Encounter and the Making of the Yoruba*, 9.

[49] Kalu, *African Christianity: An African Story*, 6.

[50] Musa W. Dube and Tinyiko S. Maluleke, "HIV/Aids as the New Site of Struggle: Theological, Biblical and Religious Perspectives," *Missionalia* 29, no. 2 (2001); Beverley G. Haddad, ed. *Religion and HIV and Aids: Charting the Terrain* (Pietermaritzburg: University of KwaZulu-Natal Press,2011). See also the comprehensive bibliography developed and maintained by the Collaborative for HIV and Aids, Religion and Theology (Chart) www.chart.ukzn.ac.za/

disability, land and ecology, leadership, sexuality, and many others. And in each case, the Bible is the first African Christian resource that African Christianity turns to in order to address such contextual demands. In an essay on 'African Biblical Interpretation', Musa W. Dube reflects on how African Christianities have interpreted the Bible in terms of contemporary African contexts. She identifies twelve 'African Bibles', including the 'Saharan Bible', the 'Enculturation Bible', the 'Black Liberation Bible', the 'Reconstruction Bible', the 'Community Bible', the 'HIV/Aids Bible', the 'Indigenous African Bible', the 'Oral Bible', the 'African Earth Bible', the 'Gendered African Bible', the 'Colonized Sub-Saharan Bible', and the 'Pentecostal Bible'.[51]

What Dube's analysis demonstrates is not only the contextual issues the African Bible has addressed, but also some of the other significant factors that shape the role of the Bible within African Christianity. But before we come to these other significant factors, it is important to reflect more fully on the intersecting relationships of the four distinctive features discussed above to each other.

Relationships between the Four Distinctive Features

The four distinctive features analysed above are the primary features that must be taken into account when reflecting on the role of the Bible in African Christianity. This matrix of four distinctive features has been gleaned from discussions by other scholars over the past sixty years.[52] What is already clear from the discussion above is that the four distinctive features overlap to some extent. For some African Christianities, for example, the Bible is difficult to separate out from the Christian tradition. This would be the case for Coptic Christianity. But for others, like the 'Christianity' of Ibandla lama Nazaretha, the Bible is entirely separate from any missionary form of the Christian tradition. It is also difficult to distinguish in particular cases between African culture and/as religion and the contemporary African context, for culture and religion are among the core issues confronting African Christianity.

In addition to recognising some overlap between the four distinctive features, we must recognise that each of the distinctive features does not carry the same weighting or influence in each of the particular forms of African Christianity. So, for example, we even have a form of African Christianity, the Johane Masowe weChishanu Church, an 'apostolic' church in Zimbabwe, which claims to be a form of African Christianity consisting of 'Christians who don't read the Bible'.[53] But for most forms of African Christianity the Bible is a decisive and central presence.

With respect to each of the other distinctive features, each form of African Christianity weights the contribution of each of these differently. As already indicated, iBandla lama Nazaretha places substantial weight on African culture and/as religion and the contemporary African context, but very little emphasis at all on the historic Christian tradition. The value of using a matrix of four distinctive features is that it offers us a useful tool to consider how each of the distinctive features is deployed in any African Christianity, and how the distinctive features each relate to biblical interpretation. In this way the matrix of four distinctive features offers a potentially useful analytical tool with which to understand the role of the Bible in African Christianities.

---

[51] Musa W. Dube, "African Biblical Interpretation," in *The Oxford Encyclopedia of Biblical Interpretation*, ed. Steven L. McKenzie (Oxford: Oxford University Press, 2013).

[52] See the references used in this essay as an example of this scholarship.

[53] Matthew Engelke, "Text and Performance in an African Church: The Book, 'Live and Direct'," *American Ethnologist* 31, no. 1 (2004); Matthew Engelke, *A Problem of Presence: Beyond Scripture in an African Church* (Berkeley, CA: University of California Press, 2007).

Other Significant Factors

We have identified three other significant factors that affect how we understand each of the distinctive factors and their relationships to each other. These are synchronic/diachronic perspectives, emic/etic perspectives, and oral/textual perspectives.

Synchronic/Diachronic Perspectives

African Christianity is not static. Indeed, what makes African Christianity a topic of considerable interest to world Christianity, as well as to scholars of religion, is that it is so dynamic. So any analysis of an African Christianity must be clear about whether its orientation is synchronic or diachronic. For example, how the Bible is used within the 'church' or congregation founded by Isaiah Shembe in the early 1900s in South Africa, Ibandla lama Nazaretha, can be analysed synchronically, focussing on a particular historical moment, such as its formation in the early 1900s.[54] But the changing contours of how the Bible has been interpreted in this congregation can also be analysed, focussing on a diachronic analysis.[55]

Diachronic forms of analysis are particularly important when considering the influence of contemporary African contexts on how the Bible is interpreted. Some historical and sociological perspective across time is important to understand how African Christianities have engaged biblically with HIV/Aids, recognising that this was facilitated because of work that had been done in the area of gender. Similarly, engaging with HIV then opened up opportunities to engage with the issues of masculinity and sexuality. These connections can only be recognised if a diachronic perspective is adopted.

Emic/Etic Perspectives

Any analysis of the role of the Bible in African Christianity must also distinguish between 'insider' (emic) perspectives on the Bible and 'outsider' (etic) perspectives. For example, while many African Christianities claim to be 'Bible-based' (an emic claim), analysis of how they actually use the Bible by scholars from outside the community (etic analysis) might find that the Bible actually plays very little part. The primary focus may in fact be on the Christian tradition of that community, which offers predetermined interpretations of almost any biblical text.[56]

Allowing emic and etic perspectives to interact and engage with each other may be a useful way forward for our analysis of the role of the Bible in African Christianity.[57]

Oral/Textual Perspectives

The Bible in African Christianity is more than a text. It is an icon and it is an oral/aural 're-membering'.[58] In understanding the role of the Bible in African Christianity the 'Oral Bible', to use Dube's term, must be taken seriously. When African Christians say, as they often do, 'The Bible says…', they are often recollecting an oral/aural version of the text. As we pay more careful attention to the role of the Bible in African Christianity, focussing on how the Bible is actually used rather than on general claims about the Bible, the textual and the oral/aural Bible will be found to interact with each other in important ways.

---

[54] Gerald O. West, "Reading Shembe 'Re-Membering' the Bible: Isaiah Shembe's Instructions on Adultery," *Neotestamentica* 40, no. 1 (2006).
[55] West, "Layers of Reception of Jephthah's Daughter; Nkosinathi Sithole, "An African Bible for African Readers: J.G. Shembe's Use of the Bible in the Sermon" *Old Testament Essays* 24, no. 1 (2011).
[56] Gifford, "The Bible in Africa: A Novel Usage in Africa's New Churches."
[57] West, "Layers of Reception of Jephthah's Daughter."
[58] Isabel Mukonyora, James L. Cox, and Frans J. Verstraelen, eds., *Re-Writing the Bible: The Real Issues* (Gweru: Mambo,1993).

Conclusion

Taken together, the four distinctive features (the Bible, Christian tradition, African culture and/as religion, and contemporary African context/s) and the three significant factors (synchronic/diachronic perspectives, emic/etic perspectives, and oral/textual perspectives) that affect how we understand each of the distinctive features, offer an analytical tool with which to understand more deeply the role of the Bible in African Christianity.

Bibliography

Adamo, David T. 'The Use of Psalms in African Indigenous Churches in Nigeria', in *The Bible in Africa: Transactions, Trajectories and Trends*, edited by Gerald O. West and Musa Dube, 336-349. Leiden: Brill, 2000.

Adogame, Afe, Roswith Gerloff, and Klaus Hock, eds. *Christianity in Africa and the African Diaspora: The Appropriation of a Scattered Heritage*. London and New York: Continuum, 2008.

Akoto, Dorothy B.E.A. 'The Mother of the Ewe and Firstborn Daughter as the 'Good Shepherd' in the Cultural Context of the Ewe Peoples: A Liberating Approach', in *The Bible in Africa: Transactions, Trajectories, and Trends*, edited by Gerald O. West and Musa W. Dube, 260-277. Leiden: Brill, 2000.

Akoto-Abutiate, (Durable) Dorothy Bea. *African Theology/ies: A Contemporary Mosaical Approach*. Bloomington: Author House, 2014.

Appiah-Kobi, Kofi and Sergio Torres, eds., *African Theology En Route: Papers from the Pan-African Conference of Third World Theologians, December 17-23*, 1977, Accra, Ghana. Maryknoll, NY: Orbis Books, 1983.

Baëta, C.G. ed. *Christianity in Tropical Africa*. Oxford: Oxford University Press,1968.

Bediako, Kwame. 'John Mbiti's Contribution to African Theology', in *Religious Plurality in Africa: Essays in Honour of John S. Mbiti*, edited by Jacob K. Olupona and Sulayman S. Nyang, 367-390. Berlin and New York: Mouton de Gruyter, 1993.

Bediako, Kwame. *Christianity in Africa: The Renewal of a Non-Western Religion*. Edinburgh and Maryknoll, NY: Edinburgh University and Orbis, 1995.

Bengt Sundkler and Christopher Steed, *A History of the Church in Africa*. Cambridge: Cambridge University Press, 2000.

Burton, Keith Augustus. *The Blessing of Africa*. Downers Grove, Illinois: IVP Academic, 2007.

Comaroff, Jean and John L. Comaroff, *Of Revelation and Revolution: Christianity, Colonialism and Consciousness in South Africa*, vol. 1. Chicago: University of Chicago Press, 1991.

Cox, James L. and Gerrie Ter Haar, eds. *Uniquely African? African Christian Identity from Cultural and Historical Perspectives*. Trenton and Asmara: Africa World Press, 2003.

Dube, Musa W. and Musimbi Kanyoro, eds. *Grant Me Justice! HIV/Aids and Gender Readings of the Bible*. Pietermaritzburg: Cluster Publications, 2004.

Dube, Musa W. Andrew M. Mbuvi, and Dora Mbuwayesango, eds. *Postcolonial Perspectives in African Biblical Interpretations*. Atlanta: Society of Biblical Literature, 2012.

Dube, Musa W. ed. *Other Ways of Reading: African Women and the Bible*. Atlanta: Society of Biblical Literature, 2001.

Éloi Messi Metogo, ed. *African Christianities*, Concilium. London: SCM Press, 2006.

Engelke, Matthew. 'Text and Performance in an African Church: The Book, "Live and Direct"', *American Ethnologist* 31, no. 1 (2004): 76-91.

Engelke, Matthew. *A Problem of Presence: Beyond Scripture in an African Church*. Berkeley: University of California Press, 2007.

Fasholé-Luke, Edward W. et al., eds., *Christianity in Independent Africa*. London: Rex Collings, 1978.

Gibellini, Rosino ed. *Paths of African Theology*. Maryknoll, NY: Orbis,1994.

Gifford, Paul. 'The Bible in Africa: A Novel Usage in Africa's New Churches', *Bulletin of SOAS* 71, no. 2

(2008): 203-219.
Gifford, Paul. 'Trajectories in African Christianity', *International Journal for the Study of the Christian Church* 8, no. 4 (2008): 275-289.
Gifford, Paul. *African Christianity: Its Public Role*. London: Hurst & Company, 1998.
Gosnell L.O.R. Yorke, 'Biblical Hermeneutics: An Afrocentric Perspective', *The Journal of Religious Thought* 52(1995): 1-13.
Haddad, Beverley G. ed. *Religion and HIV and Aids: Charting the Terrain*. Pietermaritzburg: University of KwaZulu-Natal Press, 2011.
Hasting, Adrian. *African Christianity*. New York: Macmillan, 1976.
Isichei, Elizabeth. A History of Christianity in Africa: From Antiquity to the Present. Grand Rapids: Eerdmans, 1995.
Kalu, Ogbu U. Clio in a Sacred Garb: Essays on Christian Presence and African Responses, 1900-2000. Trenton, NJ.: Africa World Press, 2008.
Kalu, Ogbu. *African Christianity: An African Story*. Pretoria: Dept. of Church History, University of Pretoria, 2005.
Loubser, J.A. (Bobby), 'How Al-Mokattam Mountain Was Moved: The Coptic Imagination and the Christian Bible', in *The Bible in Africa: Transactions, Trajectories and Trends*, edited by Gerald O. West and Musa W. Dube, 103-126.Leiden: E.J. Brill, 2000.
Maluleke, Tinyiko S. 'Black and African Theologies in the New World Order: A Time to Drink from Our Own Wells', *Journal of Theology for Southern Africa* 96(1996): 3-19.
Maxwell, David and Ingrid Lawrie, ed. Christianity and the African Imagination: Essays in Honour of Adrian Hastings. Leiden and Boston: Brill, 2013.
Mbamalu, Abiola I. *The Use of 'Abundant Life' in John 10: 10 and Its Interpretation among Some Yoruba Prosperity Gospel Preachers.* PhD thesis, Pietermaritzburg, University of KwaZulu-Natal, 2010.
Mbiti, John S. 'Christianity and Traditional Religions in Africa', *International Review of Mission* 59, no. 236 (1970): 430-440.
Mbiti, John S. *Prayer and Spirituality in African Religion*. Bedford Park: Australian Association for the Study of Religions, 1978.
Mojola, Aloo O. 'The Swahili Bible in East Africa from 1844 to 1996: A Brief Survey with Special Reference to Tanzania', in *The Bible in Africa: Transactions, Trajectories and Trends*, ed. Gerald O. West and Musa Dube, 511-523. Leiden: E.J. Brill, 2000).
Mosala, Itumeleng J. *Biblical Hermeneutics and Black Theology in South Africa*. Grand Rapids: Eerdmans, 1989.
Mukonyora, Isabel James L. Cox, and Frans J. Verstraelen, eds., *Re-Writing the Bible: The Real Issues*. Gweru: Mambo, 1993.
Musa W. Dube, 'African Biblical Interpretation', in *The Oxford Encyclopedia of Biblical Interpretation*, edited by Steven L. McKenzie. Oxford: Oxford University Press, 2013.
Musa, W. Dube and Tinyiko S. Maluleke, 'HIV/Aids as the New Site of Struggle: Theological, Biblical and Religious Perspectives', *Missionalia* 29, no. 2 (2001): 119-24.
Nzimande, Makhosazana K., 'Reconfiguring Jezebel: A Postcolonial *Imbokodo* Reading of the Story of Naboth's Vineyard (1 Kings 21:1-16)', in *African and European Readers of the Bible in Dialogue: In Quest of a Shared Meaning*, edited by Hans de Wit and Gerald O. West, 223-258. Leiden: EJ Brill, 2008.
Oduyoye, Mercy A. 'Biblical Interpretation and Social Location of the Interpreter: African Women's Reading of the Bible', in *Reading from This Place: Social Location and Biblical Interpretation in Global Perspective*, edited by Fernando F. Segovia and Mary Ann Tolbert, 33-51. Minneapolis: Fortress Press, 1995.
Peel, J.D.Y. *Religious Encounter and the Making of the Yoruba*. Bloomington: Indiana University Press, 2000.

Sanneh, Lamin 'The Horizontal and the Vertical in Mission: An African Perspective', *International Bulletin of Missionary Research* 7, no. 4 (1983): 165-171.

Sanneh, Lamin. *Translating the Message: The Missionary Impact on Culture* (Maryknoll, NY: Orbis, 1989.

Schaaf, Ype. On Their Way Rejoicing: The History and Role of the Bible in Africa. Carlisle: Paternoster Press, 1994.

Setiloane, Gabriel. 'Where Are We in African Theology?', in *African Theology En Route: Papers from the Pan-African Conference of Third World Theologians, Accra, December 17-23, 1977*, edited by Kofi Appiah-Kubi and Sergio Torres, 59-65.Maryknoll, NY: Orbis Books, 1977.

Tilley, Maureen A. *The Bible in Christian North Africa: The Donatist World.* Minneapolis: Fortress Press, 1997.

West, Gerald O. '"Layers of Reception of Jephthah's Daughter; Nkosinathi Sithole": An African Bible for African Readers: J.G. Shembe's Use of the Bible in the Sermon', *Old Testament Essays* 24, no. 1 (2011).

West, Gerald O. 'Early Encounters with the Bible among the Batlhaping: Historical and Hermeneutical Signs', *Biblical Interpretation* 12(2004).

West, Gerald O. 'Layers of Reception of Jephthah's Daughter (Judges 11) among the Amanazaretha: From the Early 1900s to Today', in *Reception History and Biblical Studies: Theory and Practice*, edited by William John Lyons and Emma England, 185-198. London: Bloomsburg, 2015.

West, Gerald O. 'Reading Shembe "Re-Membering" the Bible: Isaiah Shembe's Instructions on Adultery', *Neotestamentica* 40, no. 1 (2006): 157-184.

West, Gerald O. 'The Bible and the Female Body in Ibandla Lamanazaretha: Isaiah Shembe and Jephthah's Daughter', *Old Testament Essays* 20, no. 2 (2007): 251-281.

West, Gerald O. and Sithembiso Zwane. '"Why Are You Sitting There?" Reading Matthew 20:1-16 in the Context of Casual Workers in Pietermaritzburg, South Africa', in *Matthew: Texts@Contexts*, edited by Nicole Duran Wilkinson and James Grimshaw, 175-184. Minneapolis: Fortress Press, 2013.

(9) Christianity and Traditional African Religions

Tabona Shoko

Introduction

It is widely held that western writers took the leading part in writing about African religion, more so than indigenous writers. This is so because western writers had adequate resources such as funds to produce journals and pamphlets as well as Bibles. The advent of Christian missionaries in Africa saw the African Traditional Religions (ATRs) being largely portrayed negatively. In their writings they deliberately used derogatory terms such as 'primitive', *juju*, 'paganism', 'superstition', 'barbaric' and other terms which denote negative connotations about African Traditional Religions. Since most of these writers were missionaries and colonial administrators and agents, they wanted to convert people to their own religion and took the jurisdiction rights of the Africans. Their aim was to downplay African Traditional Religions and have many converts to Christianity. As a result, up till now, many Africans dissociate themselves from their traditional values under the guise of Christianity as if the two religions were radical opposites. However, it seems there is a meeting point between the two religions and that they are not totally opposed to one another, in fact they appear to complement one another. It is from this background that this essay seeks to explore the scholarly writings on Christianity and African Traditional Religions in Africa. The writings of scholars such as J.S. Mbiti, J.K. Olupona, D.E. Thomas, B.J. Phiri, L. Mages, R.J. Gehman and M.F.C. Bourdillon will be explored. These scholars have noted the relationship between Christianity and African Traditional Religion in Africa in different levels and terms.

Relationship between Christianity and African Traditional Religion

The interaction between Christianity and African Traditional Religion has been a subject of serious discussion amongst scholars. In fact, since setting foot upon African soil, missionaries and academics have attempted to understand and interpret African Traditional Religions. Western missiologists, religious historians and political scientists have produced numerous academic studies about the encounter between Christianity and African Traditional Religion.[1] There has been a lot of negative portrayal of African Traditional Religion. A great number of the foreign investigators used misleading terms in describing the people's beliefs of Africans. Amongst such terms are primitive, savage, fetishism, *juju,* heathenism, paganism, animism, witchcraft, idolatry, and polytheism. According to Joseph Omosade Awolalu it is obvious that these words are inappropriate in describing African religion.[2]

Positions of Relationship

A sizeable number of studies have been conducted on the relationship between African Traditional Religion and Christianity or the Bible and Biblical hermeneutics by scholars such as Musa Dube,[3] John

---

[1] Inus Daneel, *Quest for Belonging: Introduction to a Study of African Independent Churches*. Gweru: Mambo Press (1987), 30.

[2] Joseph Omosade Awolalu, "African Traditional Religion," in *Studies in Comparative Religion* 9, no.1 (1975), 35.

[3] Musa Dube, A.M. Mbuvi and Dora Mbuvayesango, *Postcolonial Perspectives In African Biblical Interpretations*. Atlanta: Soulen and Soulen (2012).

Mbiti,[4] Gerald West[5] and Lovemore Togarasei.[6] Most Biblical scholars explain the relationship between African Traditional Religion and the Bible in two ways that are closely related yet distinct. The two models are the 'dialectic' and the 'dialogic' models.[7] The dialectic accounts for the discontinuity between the Bible and African Traditional Religion while the dialogic model accounts for continuity for it facilitates dialogue between the Bible and African Traditional Religions.

There are three positions that have been established by scholars to try to explain the relationship between Christianity and African Traditional Religion. As Charles Nyamiti states, the positions are, first, the 'exclusivist' approach which argues that salvation is found only in or through the explicit knowledge and confession of Christ. The second category is 'inclusivist' which argues that salvation or truth is also found in Christ but may be mediated through the non-Christian religions or philosophies apart from any explicit knowledge of Him. The last is the 'pluralist' approach that sees Christ as simply one means of salvation and truth amongst many others. The relationship between Christianity and African Traditional Religions cannot be explained under one position; this is the reason why scholars have formulated the three key terms to explain it.[8]

Christianity and African Traditional Religion as Allies

The two religions, Christianity and African Traditional Religion, have been depicted as having some similarities, and that as allies they share some common traits, despite initial hostilities. According to John Mbiti, Christianity, the religion which puts its faith in Jesus Christ, came to Africa shortly after the death and resurrection of Jesus Christ.[9] Since then, it has spread to other parts of Africa and remained firm. Although Christianity spread so rapidly in Africa in the latter half of the twentieth century, it faced many challenges. But in the minds of the people, the religion is still associated with Europe and America for it is from there that the majority of white Christian missionaries came. At one time, overseas missionaries and their African converts condemned African Traditional Religions in the worst terms possible. But Mbiti argues that African Traditional Religions and Christianity have become allies, unofficially, one has prepared the ground for the accommodation of the other. The Christian idea of the church has parallels with African traditional life in which kinship and the extended family play a central role. African Christians seem to accommodate Christianity readily into their traditional world view. This is taking place particularly around the notion of God. They give up certain ideas, beliefs and practices in dealing with humans, as proclaimed in Christianity. There are also moral and ethical codes which Africans find similar to their traditional morals. For Mbiti, the church is the Christian family in which all are related to one another through faith and baptism in Jesus Christ. The church also includes those who died and those who are still alive.[10] This is similar to the African view of the family of both the living and the departed. In reading some aspects of the Bible, African Christianity finds many aspects that resonate with ancient Jewish life. This makes it easy to feel that the Bible belongs to them and that they belong to the Bible.[11] In this sense, African Christians then view Jesus as addressing himself to them and within their own context.

---

[4] John Samuel Mbiti, *Introduction to African Traditional Religion.* Nairobi: East African Educational Publications (1994).

[5] Gerald West, *Biblical hermeneutics of liberation: Modes of Reading the Bible in the South African Context,* Mary Knoll, NY and Pietermaritzburg: Obis Books and Cluster Publications (1995).

[6] Lovemore Togarasei, *The Bible in Context: Essay Collection,* Bamberg: University of Bamberg Press (2009).

[7] Oyekan Owomoyela, *Culture and Customs of Zimbabwe,* West Port: Greenwood Publishing Group (2002).

[8] Charles Nyamiti, "The Doctrine of God," In *A Reader in African Christian Theology*, ed John Parratt (London: SPCK, 1987) 58-68.

[9] Mbiti, *Introduction to African Traditional Religion,* 180.

[10] Mbiti, *Introduction to African Traditional Religion,* 190.

[11] Mbiti, *Introduction to African Traditional Religion,* 189.

Jesus' mission to the sick, the poor, the hungry and the oppressed becomes relevant in their hearts.[12] People feel he is concerned about them in their constant needs.

In pursuit of the amicable relationship between Christianity and African Traditional Religion, Richard Gehman refers to Mbiti who argues that African Traditional Religion should be considered a preparation for the gospel. In his argument traditional religion is fulfilled in Christianity.[13] Expounding the relationship between the two religions Gehman argues that the relationship is not merely one of perfections and imperfections nor is it merely one of promise and fulfilment. In so many ways Christianity is compatible with African Traditional Religion. In other words biblical revelation completes that which is vaguely perceived, it corrects that which was partly understood though with distortion. For Gehman the theological emphasis of African Traditional Religion and Christianity differs in that African traditional Religion focuses on humanity while biblical revelation focuses on God. African traditional Religion, he observed, is anthropocentric.[14] This means that African Traditional Religion tries to make the divine powers an instrument of humanity's personal welfare. By performing rites, humanity's aim is to compel them into God's service. According to Tokunboh Adeyemo the African people do not seek God for their own sake; they seek God in worship for what they can get out of God.[15] J.S. Mbiti says that it is a means to exploit rather than veneration. However biblical revelation is theocentric, focusing on God. God is not only the origin of humanity but God is the ultimate goal and purpose of humanity's life. The chief end of humanity is to glorify God and to enjoy God for ever. This contrast between being anthropocentric and being theocentric is not a minor difference. It strikes at the very heart of African Traditional Religion and the Christian faith.[16] This means that the central concerns of Christianity and African Traditional Religion are poles apart.

Jesse Mugambi is one prominent theologian who has made a contribution on the relationship between Christianity and African Traditional Religion. He argues that Christianity and African traditional beliefs have some similarities in which kinship and extended family plays a central role. The church thrives in the Christian family in which all are related to one another through faith and baptism in Jesus Christ. The church also indicates those who have died and those who still live in this world are similar to the African view of the family of both the living and the departed.[17] Under this notion one can add the issue of sainthood in Christianity with that of ancestorhood in African Traditional Religion. Both saints and African ancestors are the departed ones but in different religious systems.

A renowned African Christian scholar, Kwame Bediako, is of the view that God as proclaimed by the missionaries was already worshipped in African Traditional Religions. This is to say that even before the advent of Christianity in Africa, the Africans were already aware of and were worshipping the God which the missionaries thought they were introducing to Africa.[18] African theologians such as J.S. Mbiti and E.B. Idowu argue that there are many points of contact between Christianity and African Traditional Religion, including the concept of God, morality, communalism and other aspects. They criticise the foreignness of Christianity insisting that African Traditional Religions are a vital source of theology in Africa. These theologians are guided by theology of continuity, maintaining that Christianity fulfils the religious longing found in African Traditional Religions.

---

[12] Mbiti, *Introduction to African Traditional Religion,* 189.
[13] Richard Gehman, *African Traditional Religion in Biblical Perspectives.* Kampala: East African Publication Publishers (1989), 249.
[14] Gehman, *African Traditional Religion,* 253.
[15] Tokunbo Adeyemo, cited in Gehman, *African Traditional Religion*, 255.
[16] Mbiti cited in Gehman *African Traditional Religion,* 260.
[17] Jesse Mugambi, *African Theology: An Introduction.* Nairobi: East Africa Publishers (1989), 15.
[18] Kwame Bediako, *Theology and Identity: the Impact of Culture upon Christian Thought in the Second Century and in Modern Africa.* Cumbria: Regnum Books (1992), 125.

Ebolaji Idowu also stands in solidarity with those who stress continuity between Christianity and African Traditional Religion. He teaches that all worship is valid before God, that the impulse to worship comes from God and thus resulting practices of worship is Yahweh's.[19] Idowu's premise is that there is only one God who reveals himself in different ways to all creeds. All religions are therefore the result of God's loving activity among all the people of the religions. While the encounter between Christianity and African Traditional Religion has been characterised by the skewed power relationships in favour of the former, it remains possible for the religions to enter fruitful dialogue. But critics of this stance have argued that there is no common ground between the two religions. They argue that while it is possible for Christianity to be engaged in conversation with other religions of the book, African Traditional Religions do not have any sacred tests that could be consulted for clarification in the context of lofty theological debates. They would regard African Traditional Religions as a passing phase and as victims of social change.

On the relationship between Christianity and African Traditional Religion, Bizeck J. Phiri argues that the acceptance of European mission Christianity amongst the local people was justified by the various benefits of formal or European mission education. Educated Africans acquired wide knowledge of the world, were able read about western and Jewish cultures and could now compare, write, explain and be proud of their own cultures, customs and traditions.[20] The expansion of the intellectual horizon of the Africans, eased by Christianity, enhanced a new African self-understanding and self-appreciation beyond the immediate traditional circle of kinship and lineage. Also the availability of the Bible translations and other literature on local culture at a time when Africans were under foreign European domination had the inevitable consequence of arousing deep loyalties towards the indigenous cause. In other words the needs of nationalism were properly established.[21] However, there are some conflicts.

Areas of Conflict

Studies on the relationship between African Traditional Religion and Christianity have also shown that there are areas of conflict between the two religions.

John Mbiti argues that there are also conflicts between the Christian life and the life of those who follow only African Traditional Religions. Some of the areas where conflicts arise concern traditional African rituals especially those of offerings in connection with the departed, African initiation rites, marriage customs, the place of sorcery, evil magic and witchcraft in African life, and methods of dealing with disease, misfortune and suffering.[22]

The main differences between Christianity and African Traditional Religion exist in the domain of their respective claims and in their organisation. Christianity has a founder, sacred book, creeds and dogmas. African Traditional Religions are expressed through cultic rites and religious practices. Oral traditions and repetitive rituals convey beliefs in traditional religions. Mbiti holds that some of the world religions like Christianity and Islam have founders who started them which is not the case when it comes to African Traditional Religions. The traditional religions have no identifiable founder. It is believed the religions evolved slowly through many centuries, as people responded to the situations of their life and reflected upon their experiences. Above all they differ on how a human being enters a blessed eternity in the presence of a holy and just God.

Okot p'Bitek takes a critical position to those scholars who have been viewed as friendly in furthering the study of African Traditional Religions. For example, p'Bitek views such scholars as Evans Pritchard,

[19] Ebolaji Idowu, *African Traditional Religion: A Definition*. London: SCM Press (1973), 20.
[20] Bizeck Phiri, "Crises of Life in African Religion and Christianity," *Journal of Humanities* 3, no.1 (2001): 17-21.
[21] Phiri, "Crises of Life," 17-21.
[22] Mbiti, *Introduction to African Traditional Religion,* 195.

John Mbiti and other Christian missionaries and clergy as enemies of African Traditional Religions. For him, they were not truly concerned with furthering the faith or making converts to African religion; rather, they were Christian apologists who sought to show that the noble savage was capable of religious thought and that Jesus Christ was the fulfilment of their biblical allegiance.[23] p'Bitek's argument alleges that even the children of Africa are misguided by failing to view African Traditional Religions as a faith in its own right. Instead of respecting their own sacred religion and culture they denied any sacred qualities worthy of worship that exist within their culture. They are furthering the hegemonic Christian continuity which propagates the theory that Christianity is the fulfilment of all faiths. He then criticised Mbiti for what he calls 'Hellenising and Christianising the Christian deity'.[24] However, p'Bitek has since been criticised too for making a literal bombast against other scholars, and practising racism in reverse.

Another scholar, Newel Booth, pointed out that 'many western students of African historians of religions, anthropologists among others, exploit Africa for their own academic or ideological purposes'.[25] In a similar vein, Robin Horton is highly critical and suggested that the Judeo-Christian spectacles being used by several African Christian-trained scholars is 'more a bane than a boon in the study of African religion'.[26] Moreover, p'Bitek was quite categorical in his assertion that African scholars of the traditional religions are intellectual smugglers who dress up in African deities' borrowed garbs using them as mercenaries in foreign battles, none of which was in the interests of African people.[27]

One historian of religion, Jacob Olupona, also made a significant contribution on the relationship between Christianity and African Traditional Religion. According to Olupona any meeting of two different realities incurs the risk of conflict. His observation was that when Christianity came into contact and interacted with African Traditional Religion, it caused a pattern of disruption and division. As a result of its biased approach, it divided the community into two camps, with one containing the converts who looked down upon the old traditional religion and culture, and the other, loyalist adherents of African Traditional Religions. The net result therefore was a struggle between Christianity and African Traditional Religion. Due to this encounter, traditional culture was bruised and badly shaken and many Africans were Christianised to such an extent that they lampooned traditional religion and culture.[28]

Another scholar, Emmanuel Babalola, also made a contribution on the relationship between Christianity and African Traditional Religion. For him Christianity has been responsible for the erosion of African Traditional Religion. He affirms that proponents of Christianity have negatively labelled African Traditional Religion a 'non-reality'.[29] It has also been observed that many African Christians look upon African Traditional Religion with disdain. At certain historical moments, the proponents of Christian expansion into Africa operated deliberately to destroy African Traditional Religion and cultural forms that had guided the African people before the incursion of Christianity. The African evangelists worked tirelessly to propel negative myths and propaganda about African people, particularly their supposedly inherent inability to conceptualise the Deity.[30]

---

[23] Laurent Magesa, *African Religion: The Moral Tradition of Abundant Life.* Nairobi: East African Educational Publishers (1997), 5.

[24] Okot p'Bitek, *African Religions in Western Scholarship.* Nairobi: Kenya Literature Bureau (1971), 5.

[25] Newel Booth, *African Religion: A Symposium.* New York: Nok Publishers (1977), 12.

[26] Robin Horton, "Judaeo-Christian Spectacles: Boon or Bane to the Study of African Religions? *Cahiers d'etudes Africaines*, 24, no 96 (1984) 391-436.

[27] P'Bitek, African Religions, 5.

[28] Jacob Olupona, *African Traditional Religion in Contemporary Society.* New York: Paragon House (1989), 114,-128).

[29] Emmanuel Babalola, "The Impact of African Traditional Religion and Culture Upon the Aladura Churches," in *Asian Journal of Theology* 6, no 1 (1992):130-140.

[30] Babalola, "Impact of African Traditional Religion," 130-140.

Douglas E. Thomas also wrote on Christianity and African Traditional Religion. He argues that Christianity has barely touched the core of the life of most African peoples. In places such as northern Uganda at the turn of the century, 99% of families relied on their indigenous religious faith in moments of crisis. Although many African people are forced to embrace Christianity in moments of existential crisis, they immediately revert to the faith of their forebears. Okot p'Bitek states, 'The Africans' embrace of Christian religio-culture was nothing more than accepting another god into their already existing pantheon.'[31]

In the same mode of identifying the contrasting features between Christianity and African Traditional Religion, Richard Gehman also argues that African Traditional Religion beliefs in humanity and sin contrast with Christianity. For him, Scripture is clear in showing that humanity's basic problem is transgression of the law of God and rebellion against God (1 John 3:4) whereas evil in African Traditional Religion is basically that which conflicts with the interests of the community and the traditions of the past. Sin in Scripture is always related to God. Sin is sin because it is contrary to the will of God and contrary to God's very nature.[32] For Gehman, African Traditional Religion does not teach that sin is rebellion against God or the transgression of God's law. Instead, the traditional way of life is the best life which has been given by the ancestral spirits, the divinities and by God-self. There is no understanding of a spiritual new birth, a need to grow and progress in the knowledge of God. Since the *status quo* is the best life, man's primary concern is material prosperity.[33]

Richard Gehman also states that African Traditional understanding of salvation contrasts with the gospel. In biblical terms, salvation is the deliverance or release from sin and all it affects, unto a new life which is eternal in nature and duration. Salvation in biblical terms is past, present and future. In African Traditional Religion, emphasis is upon a good life here and now. The good life is abundant in vital force.[34] In African Traditional Religion good health means a large and growing family with many possessions and disruption of the *status quo* reflects displeasure of the ancestors. But life can be restored in its fullness upon requisite ritual activity. In a way the determinants of right and wrong are the dictates of society and its traditions. In a related observation made by a Zimbabwean anthropologist, Michael Bourdillon, mission churches amongst the Shona people tend to emphasise the individual rather than the family or neighbourhood groups. Christian rituals tend to break down rural communities and the social and communal aspects of traditional religion are impaired.[35]

Bizeck Phiri also expressed an element of ambivalence in the relationship between Christianity and African Traditional Religion. In his conception, Christianity introduced new modern identities to traditional African societies. Through Christianity, Africans acquired such new identities as full members of Christian churches or denominations, fully ordained priests, ministers, or bishops, teachers, catechists, elders or deacons, while many others became trained carpenters, builders as well as junior clerical workers in colonial government offices. They received a new sense of themselves as African people as well as some of the tools with which to become independent states.[36] However this is not to say that Christianity has been without what may be considered as negative effects on the local cultural identities. During the early stages of the late nineteenth-century and early twentieth-century enterprise, Christianity condemned many traditional social and religious beliefs and practices as evil or pagan, and sought to replace them with

---

[31] Okot p'Bitek cited in Douglas E. Thomas, *African Traditional Religion in the Modern Word.* London: MacFarland and Company (2005), 49.

[32] Gehman, *African Traditional Religion*, 254.

[33] Gehman, *African Traditional Religion*, 254.

[34] Gehman, *African Traditional Religion*, 254.

[35] Michael Bourdillon, *The Shona Peoples: An Ethnography of the Contemporary Shona, with Special Reference to their Religion*, Gweru: Mambo Press (1976), 285.

[36] Phiri, "Crises of Life," 17-21.

Christian-cum-European beliefs and practices. As a result, local converts to mission Christianity were frequently alienated from their own societies as they could no longer easily identify themselves with the values and meaning of their traditional societies, but neither could they identify themselves fully with the new Christian-cum-western way of life to which they had been introduced.[37]

Laurent Magesa has also contributed on the relationship between Christianity and African Traditional Religion. He states that despite the strong influence of Christianity in many areas of African life, the basic attitudes and religious philosophy of many Africans have been similar to that expressed many years ago by a Central African, Kwena Man, to David Livingstone: 'To be plain with you... we should like you much better if you traded with us and then went away without forever boring us with preaching the word of God of yours.'[38] In this light, Mbiti observed that traditional concepts still form the essential background of many African people. And one of the common complaints of Christian leaders concerns the 'duality' of African Christians' way of life, implying that African Christians do not always adhere to religious and ritual demands that are formulated and expressed by leaders of their churches. Many times they seek comfort in their own religious systems even though these may not correspond exactly to what is inculcated and expected by Christian leaders. Such African conceptions of God, the world and morality continue to penetrate Christianity in Africa. Gabriel Setiolane argues that, because of the cultural form in which it is clothed, the Christianity of the missionaries cannot be assimilated nor help African people to face up to difficult situations. Many African professors, ministers of government and members of Parliament have been known to revert in secret to the diviner or medium in order to know what lies ahead, while at the same time vigorously protesting in public that diviners are relics of by-gone primitive times and that they possess no mystical powers.[39]

Furthermore, John Parratt states that the sharp division between western missionary Christianity and pagan African culture tended to lead to a dilemma in the experience of many African Christians. Whilst some African converts were able to break completely with their traditional heritage, more frequently the adoption of the new faith produced Christians with a 'foot in two worlds', who found it difficult to reconcile their sense of belonging to their African heritage with a western form of Christianity.[40] It is argued that there are areas of African culture which throw light on aspects of the Christian faith and which may be helpful compared with them. For instance, the concept of divine life force among Africans may be seen as corresponding to the activity of the Holy Spirit in the world. Even the role of the ancestors in African Traditional Religions may throw some light on the doctrine of the communion of saints.

All the above scholars tend to agree that the relationship between Christianity and African Traditional Religion has been a mixture of 'love and hate'. But since religion is dynamic, some changes occurred that have bred the phenomenon of African Independent Churches.

African Independent Churches

The study of African Independent (or Indigenous) Churches is best understood in the religious studies depicted in the history and development of Christianity in Africa.[41] Scholars in several disciplines such as Social Science, History, Theology and Religious Studies especially in the fields of Christian History and Missiology, have produced a multiplicity of studies that explain the origins, growth and development of this new religious experience in Africa from within their respective ideologies. Adogame provides a concise survey of certain outstanding scholars who have contributed in this field such as Horton (1962,

---

[37] Phiri, "Crises of Life," 17-21.

[38] Magesa, *African Religion,* 5.

[39] Gabriel Setiolane in Magesa, *African Religion*, 8.

[40] John Parrat, *A Reader in African Theology*. London: SPCK (1987), 8.

[41] See Tabona Shoko, *Karanga Indigenous Religion in Zimbabwe*. Farnham, UK: Ashgate (2007), 164-5.

1967), Wellborn and Orgot (1966), Peel (1968) and Barrette (1968). These explain the phenomenon of African independence as signs of social and cultural change. Linton (1972) and Barber (1972) present the new churches as exemplifications of stress and adjustive phenomena. But for Blander (1953), Anderson (1958), Koebben (1960), Sundkler (1961), independent churches are sparked by political and socio-economic protest especially in the wake of colonialism and apartheid in South Africa.[42] Whilst Oosthuizen identifies the same trend in South Africa and Amanze (1988) in Botswana, M. Daneel pointed out both social, cultural, economic and political factors and above all religious grounds as causative for the sprouting of the Shona Zion churches, and as signs of theological protest caused by different doctrinal interpretations in the mainline Christian churches in Zimbabwe. It is within these broad causal explanatory models that we are able to locate the genesis and proliferation of the African Independent Churches.[43]

Some theologians have observed that worship in mission churches tended to be dull for most Africans, and this is the reason why some African Christians have broken off from mission churches and formed their own churches where they are able to incorporate more freely some traditional African customs and practices into their Christian life. According to Mbiti, this affects the form of prayers, music, hymns, songs and festivals and attitudes to dreams and visions as well as the organisation which is modified according to the ways that seem to fit the followers best. Much of the traditional worldview is retained in many of the indigenous churches. But in the course of history, Christianity and African Traditional Religions have undergone a paradigm shift that has seen a new phenomenon in the form of interreligious dialogue.

Interreligious Dialogue

Some scholars such as Ezra Chitando observed that at the formal level, Christianity has witnessed profound shifts in its attitude towards other communities of faith. Within the Catholic Church, the Second Vatican Council (1962-1965) ushered in a more positive era. The church officially acknowledged the reality of religious pluralism in the 'Declaration on the relation of the church to Non-Christian religions'.[44] African theologians have been forceful and eloquent in their plea for dialogue between Christianity and African Traditional Religion. Catholic and Protestant African theologians have maintained that until Christianity takes on an African flavour by coming to terms or dialogue with African Traditional Religions and cultural realities, it will remain a foreign religion.[45] In the same vein for E. Chitando there are many points of meeting between Christianity and African Traditional Religions, including the concept of God, morality, communalism and other aspects. They criticise the foreignness of Christianity, insisting that African Traditional Religions are a valid source of theology in Africa.[46] Other theologians argue that African Traditional Religions are a valid path to salvation and they should be treated with respect.

Chitando states that it is important to note that African communities have forced Christianity to recognise the presence and vitality of African Traditional Religions. At gatherings, steps are taken to ensure that all religious sensibilities are not wilfully trampled upon. In communities where Christians observe a certain diet, different cooking pots are used to ensure that the Christians do not feel out of place at such gatherings. In some instances Christians also participate in ceremonies to honour ancestors. When it is their turn to drink beer from the calabash that would be circulating, they ask traditionalists to stand in for

---

[42] Afe Adogame, *Celestial Church of Christ: The Politics of Cultural Identity in a West African Prophetic Charismatic Movement*, Frankfurt Am Main: Peter Lang (1999), 2.

[43] Shoko, *Karanga Indigenous Religion,* 164-5.

[44] Frans Verstraelen, *Christianity in a New Key: New Voices and Vistas through Intercontinental Communication.* Gweru: Mambo Press, 1996: 27.

[45] Parratt, Reader in African Christian Theology, 11.

[46] Ezra Chitando, "Rewrapping the Christian Faith Indigenously: A Preliminary Study of African Theology in Zimbabwe," *Journal of Theology for Southern Africa,* 2002: 3-21.

them. This tolerance is also seen in the acknowledgement of ritual specialists such as the Varemba (or Vamwenye). Members of the community allow these specialists to slaughter beasts for communal ceremonies as they observe stringent dietary regulations.[47]

Jonathan Tserayi posits that Africans have brought Christianity and African traditionalists into a dialogue by borrowing heavily from both the religions. They have sought to maximise benefits available within the two religions, without subscribing to the demonization that fundamentalist Christians seek to promote. They have brought the two religions into an ongoing dialogue, as they grapple with what it means to be 'truly African and Christian'.[48] Millions of Africans allow African Traditional Religions to whisper to them words of wisdom and encouragement. African Christians wish to embrace both religious systems because they regard African Traditional Religions as meeting real needs by procuring salvation for social ills, for the evil spirits, and for witchcraft which they experience as 'real', while Christianity is looked upon for providing salvation in the hereafter. In so doing, the African Christian feels that he or she has bought a double insurance for both salvation in time of trouble and misfortune, and salvation in heaven, by putting one foot in African Traditional Religions and the other foot in the Christian religion.[49]

Furthermore, Tserayi also states that, when confronted with problems, many African Christians tend not to exactly demonise Christianity but to shift their focus to traditional practices. When these Christians turn to the African Traditional Religion, they refer to it as 'doing the real thing'.[50] Michael Bourdillon in his book, *The Shona Peoples* (1976), carries a picture of Mr Lazarus Zonde Gwanzura, a widely respected *n'anga* (traditional healer) from Mufakose suburb in Harare. According to him, there is no discrepancy between Christianity and his way of healing. He himself is a Christian...[51] The two accounts are represented in the diviner's words that it is the diviner's conviction that Christianity and African Traditional Religion can be perfectly synchronised. If anything, according to him, these two religions complement one another; they do not, for him, conflict with one other. Their followers are the ones who have conflicts about them.

Finally, the diviner sees the unity in diversity when she or he looks at the two religions under discussion. This is of course reminiscent of Pannikar's rainbow model whose summary is the profound reality that one colour seems to exclude the other colours, when actually the others are within that colour. Given this, one can argue that there is good effect at meeting points of Christianity and African Traditional Religions.[52]

Conclusion

By way of conclusion, one can state that Christianity and African Traditional Religions have many touching points where they meet as friends. But there are also other areas where they conflict. Although Christianity has submitted itself as superior to African Traditional Religions, African theologians now portray an accurate picture that puts both religions on a par.

References

Adogame, Afe, Celestial Church of Christ: The Politics of Cultural Identity in *A West African Prophetic Charismatic Movement*, Frankfurt Am Main: Peter Lang (1999).

[47] Chitando, "Rewrapping the Christian Faith", 10.
[48] Jonathan Tserayi, "A Meeting Point for *Christianity and African Traditional* Religions," *Chiedza* (2000), 46.
[49] Tserayi, "A Meeting Point for Christianity", 46.
[50] Tserayi, "A Meeting Point for Christianity", 46.
[51] Tserayi, "A Meeting Point for Christianity", 46.
[52] Panikkar, *The Interreligious Dialogue*. New York: Paulist Press, 1978, 19-20.

Awolau Joseph Omosade, 'African Traditional Religion', in *Studies in Comparative Religion* 9, no.1 (1975).

Babalola, Emmanuel, 'The Impact of African Traditional Religion and Culture Upon the Aladura Churches', in *Asian Journal of Theology* 6, no 1 (1992):130-140.

Bediako, Kwame, *Theology and Identity: the Impact of Culture upon Christian Thought in the Second Century and in Modern Africa*. Cumbria: Regnum Books (1992).

Bitek, Okot, p', *African Religions in Western Scholarship*. Nairobi: Kenya Literature Bureau (1971).

Booth, Newel, *African Religion: A Symposium*. New York: Nok Publishers (1977).

Bourdillon, Michael, *The Shona Peoples: An Ethnography of the Contemporary Shona, with Special Reference to their Religion*, Gweru: Mambo Press (1976).

Chitando, Ezra, 'Rewrapping the Christian Faith Indigenously: A Preliminary Study of African Theology in Zimbabwe', *Journal of Theology for Southern Africa,* 2002: 3-21.

Daneel, Inus, *Quest for Belonging: Introduction to a Study of African Independent Churches*. Gweru: Mambo Press (1987).

Douglas E. Thomas, *African Traditional Religion in the Modern Word.* London: MacFarland and Company (2005).

Dube, Musa, A.M. Mbuvi and Dora Mbuvayesango, *Postcolonial Perspectives In African Biblical Interpretations.* Atlanta: Soulen and Soulen (2012).

Gehman, Richard, *African Traditional Religion in Biblical Perspectives.* Kampala: East African Publication Publishers (1989).

Horton, Robin, 'Judaeo-Christian Spectacles: Boon or Bane to the Study of African Religions?' *Cahiers d'etudes Africaines*, 24, no 96 (1984) 391-436.

Idow, Ebolaji, *African Traditional Religion: A Definition*. London: SCM Press (1973).

Magesa, Laurent, *African Religion: The Moral Tradition of Abundant Life.* Nairobi: East African Educational Publishers (1997).

Mbiti John Samuel, *Introduction to African Traditional Religion.* Nairobi: East African Educational Publications (1994).

Mugambi, Jesse, *African Theology: An Introduction.* Nairobi: East Africa Publishers (1989).

Nyamiti, Charles, 'The Doctrine of God', In *A Reader in African Christian Theology*, ed John Parratt (London: SPCK, 1987) 58-68.

Olupona, Jacob, *African Traditional Religion in Contemporary Society*. New York: Paragon House (1989).

Owomoyela, Oyekan, *Culture and Customs of Zimbabwe,* West Port: Greenwood Publishing Group (2002).

Pannikar, Raimon. *The Interreligious Dialogue*. New York: Paulist Press, 1978.

Parratt, John, *A Reader in African Theology*. London: SPCK (1987).

Phiri, Bizeck, 'Crises of Life in African Religion and Christianity', *Journal of Humanities* 3, no.1 (2001): 17-21.

Shoko, Tabona, *Karanga Indigenous Religion in Zimbabwe*. Aldershot: Ashgate (2007).

Togarasei, Lovemore, *The Bible in Context: Essay Collection,* Bamberg: University of Bamberg Press (2009).

Tserayi, Jonathan, *'A Meeting Point for Christianity and African Traditional Religions'*, *Chiedza* (2000)

Verstraelen, Frans, *Christianity in a New Key Christianity in a New Key.: New Voices and Vistas through Intercontinental Communication*. Gweru: Mambo Press, 1996.

West Gerald, *Biblical hermeneutics of liberation: Modes of Reading the Bible in the South African Context,* Maryknoll, NY: Orbis Books and Pietermaritzburg, RSA: Cluster Publications (1995).

(10) Muslim-Christian Encounters in Africa

Jacob Olupona

The historical trajectory of contact and encounter among Muslims and Christians is multifaceted, extensive, and fascinating. My central thesis and overall argument of this essay is this: Islam and Christianity must be understood as they have evolved in Africa, reflecting the conditions and aspirations of local people. Consequently, in African states where they exist side-by-side, there is potential for both co-existence and conflict. This is evident throughout the continent, reflecting conditions of various historical periods – pre-colonial, colonial, and post-colonial.

Often overlooked is the fact that Islam and Christianity contain similar themes and aspects of their trajectory, which I will highlight here only briefly. First, early Christianity and Islam took refuge in Africa, nurtured there while still fledgling and vulnerable. When King Herod intended to slay the Christ child, Joseph and Mary took him to Egypt for safety, until an angel informed them it was safe to return. In addition, in the patristic period, North Africa and Egypt in particular, stood firmly at the heart of Christianity while a significant number of early Christian converts and writings came from these areas long before Christianity took root in much of Europe.

Similarly, with respect to Islam, during the early part of his calling – often referred to as the great age of Islam – the Prophet Muhammad sent some of his followers to the Christian king of Abyssinia (Ethiopia), called the Negus, to escape persecution in Mecca. When asked to surrender the Muslim refugees, the Abyssinian king defended them on the grounds of the similarity in theology and religious practices among Christians and Muslims. Shortly afterwards, the prophet made the *hijra* (holy flight) to Medina, the City of the Prophet, where he established his first Ummah. It was then that the Muslim refugees returned safely. In addition to Africa providing safe haven for the Messiah and his family and to followers of the Prophet, this reference is often cited as proof that Christians and Muslims co-operated with each other at the earliest instance.

About a century after the death of the Prophet, Arabs expanded their territory beyond Arabia, the birthplace of Islam. They spread into North Africa where they encountered North African Christians in the Roman provinces. To establish Islam in the region, they attacked Christian Copts and Berbers who failed to resist Islamic incursions. Consequently, today Islam enjoys a strong presence in these regions outside the Holy Land, cradle of Islam, the *Hijaz*.

North Africa must be recognized as the home of great African theologians – Origen and Clement of Alexandria, Tertullian of Carthage, and of course St Augustine (354-430 AD), the Bishop of Hippo. Augustine was born in Tagaste, Numidia (now Suk Ahras), Algeria. I have always imagined the many benefits for both Christians and Muslims in keeping the home of Augustine intact for devoted pilgrims to visit. Moreover, just as North Africa was an important intellectual centre for early Christians, under Muslim rule it was also home to the earliest and most prestigious institutions of higher education, such as the famous Al-Azhar in Cairo and the Al-Qarawiyyin in Fez, the oldest university in the world. It welcomed students from the Mediterranean world, including Gerbert of Aurillac, known as Pope Sylvester II.[1]

Although certainly on the decline after the Muslim conquest of North Africa, Christianity was still practised in the region. The rising Umayyad Empire made treaties with several Christian kingdoms in present-day Sudan. The only pocket of Christianity practiced continuously until today is the Coptic Church in Egypt. However, since the early mass conversion to Islam in North Africa, Christian-Muslim

[1] Clarke, Suzanna; *A House in Fez*, 14.

relationships on the continent are more contentious and uneven. In certain regions and states where Muslims constitute a sizeable number, as in Nigeria, Sudan, and Egypt, political and religious conflicts between Muslims and Christians remain contentious. Compelling evidence suggests that these conflicts have more to do with the ways in which Muslim and Christian structures reflect political and social identities and relationships in various pre-colonial states and societies in Africa. At the same time, it must also be said that in other places – such as Senegal, which is overwhelmingly Muslim – relationships between Muslims and Christians have continued to be very amicable.

Christian and Muslim relationships have been affected historically by Africa's encounter with colonialism and the western world. One of the first important moments of contact took place through transatlantic trade, particularly in slaves, and again, both religions have had an ambivalent relationship under this dark period. Slavery was a lucrative, well-established institution in West Africa at the time of this particular trade (albeit very different from forms of American chattel slavery). Many Muslims had little problem trading slaves with Christian Europeans.

However, in 1673, a cleric named Nasr al-Din lead a brief but largely unsuccessful *jihad* to stop the sale of slaves to Europe on the coast in present-day Senegal and Mauritania.[2] From the late eighteenth century to the end of the nineteenth, the persistent abolitionist movement ultimately ended the trade in enslaved Africans. It was spearheaded by the British anti-slavery movement, articulated in Christian evangelical expression through Methodist, Baptist, and Anglican missions. Britain, the European power that brought Atlantic slavery to its zenith in the eighteenth century, was home to the abolitionist movement, leading by the end of the nineteenth century to the decline and subsequent demise of the Atlantic slave trade and slavery.

Ironically, both Christianity and Islam grew most rapidly during the colonial era. While colonial practices for some Muslims provided an opportunity for Christianity to thrive and flourish at the expense of Islam, for others, colonial authorities such as the French in Senegal or the British in northern Nigeria, advanced the power of Muslim rulers to sustain colonial power. Although not all Muslim leaders embraced European colonial powers, and some provided military resistance, many found that colonial rule provided a period of peace and infrastructure, allowing Muslims to spread their message more effectively than ever before. They reasoned that living under a Christian power permitted Muslims the free practice of Islam without violating any theological principles.

At the same time, western colonial authorities were always wary of the challenge Muslim leaders could pose to their administration. Westerners often actively worked against Islam. In some contexts Muslims inevitably equated colonialism with Christianity. New political structures certainly favoured Christian converts, and the products of Christian mission schools, as well as western military technology and medicine. Thus, many of the first presidents and prime ministers of African countries were disproportionately Christian, even when the majority of their citizens were Muslim.

Christians had a similarly ambivalent, but often much closer, relationship with colonial administrators. Western missionaries were often given resources and protection to allow them to carry out their work in conversion, education, and medicine. Western colonial authorities aligned themselves with missionaries relying on graduates of their schools to fill positions allotted to native Africans. At the same time, when the evangelical mission was at odds with the political order and profit of the colony, administrators often limited the influence of missionaries as we have seen earlier, both often at loggerheads.

Still, the general trend of both religions in Africa was to grow, and to grow rapidly. During the twentieth century, Christians grew from about 10 million to about 250 million; Muslims grew from about 34 million to approximately 300 million.[3]

---

[2] Boubacar Barry, *Le royaume de waalo*, 135-159.
[3] Encyclopedia of African History (A-G), 165.

Before the early 1960s, the Golden Age of African Independence, Christian and Muslim subjects co-existed with tolerance despite occasional skirmishes and violence. Even in predominantly Muslim countries, such as Senegal, Guinea, Burkina Faso and several parts of West Africa, peaceful relationships prevailed. At times peaceful co-existence was made possible largely through indigenous African religions and culture championed by traditional rulers, such as the sacred kings and chiefs. Africans were concerned primarily with liberating themselves from their colonial masters. They could ill afford to engage in religious wars as they focused on independence.

During the struggle for independence, a strong sense of nation-building embraced all religions – Islam, Christianity, and traditional indigenous religions – an integral but short-lived development. After independence, particularly by the 1970s following more than a decade of ineffective authoritarian regimes, religion steadily became an instrument of divisiveness in various states.

First, the military intervened in religious affairs particularly in Nigeria, where ethnicity often intersects with religion. Sha'ria (Islamic Law) was highly contested. Even Nigeria's membership in the Organization of Islamic Conference (OIC) incited protests among Christians and Muslims.

Second, radical groups of Christian and Islamic organizations queried the state over governance and power allotted to each other. Each wanted to define the nation's identity solely in their own terms. The rise of global Islam and global evangelical Christianity affected local expressions of religion, even at a grassroots level. Deterioration over the last ten years incited conflict, despite attempts by the state and the people themselves to promote peaceful co-existence.

For example, in 1958, in Ghana, a Christian-sponsored interfaith group on Muslim-Christian relations under the Islam in Africa project was established to promote peaceful co-existence and to discuss social and economic development among local communities. The initiative now labelled Programme on Christian Muslim Relations in Africa (PROCMURA) is now housed in Kenya. Underlying the skirmishes in post-independence Africa, the politics of religion and the quest of nation-states vied to define their identity largely either in religious or secular terms. During the 1960s, ethnicity was the determining, dominant factor in the contested terrain among subgroups. In the last ten years, however, the focus shifted to religious matters. Open warfare in Nigeria and the Sudan escalated when both demanded that the nation-state be organized to define economic and political power according to its own construction of the state as it competes for material goods and resources.

Adherents of both religions agree that religion is an immensely important aspect of their lives. Many believe that religion must govern the political economy. While Christians insist on a secular state government, others – including leading religious figures – make tenuous alliances with secular political figures seeking to blur the lines between church and state. Simultaneously, Muslims have put forward serious challenges to secularism, calling for a polity subjected and constructed by the law of Islam (Sha'ria). Islam is a way of life, they argue, that covers economic, political, social, and educational welfare. Subsequently, the state is caught between the two factions of faith, each fighting to possess the soul of the nation as they struggle for supremacy.

The current religious and political crises should never be underestimated. Islam and Christianity are spreading most rapidly, gaining increasing importance. Africa nurtured both religions, allowing them to flourish in their early stages. It protected them from persecution in the first instance and provided rich intellectual centres in the second, after they were firmly established. Although Islam quickly eclipsed Christianity in Northern and North-Eastern Africa after the Umayyad conquest, the two co-existed to one degree or another, even during colonial and economic exploitation. Recently, however, the two faiths struggle to gain converts and control of the state. Africa has played a crucial, often overlooked, role in the history and growth of each religion. Given current demographic trends, it will be an equally important site for vested interests in the world's two most populous religions.

Muslim-Christian Relationships and Religious Extremism

The complex Muslim-Christian relationship is linked with global religious extremism. Narratives of extreme hostility, together with uncommon co-operation, heroism, and even martyrdom abound worldwide. In the last ten years, the rise of Islamic militant groups in Africa has shattered Muslim-Christian relationships. Two groups – the Al-Shabaab militants headquartered in Somalia and Boko Haram Islamists in Nigeria – have significant influence and proliferation. Al-Shabaab has spread to the entire region, the Horn of Africa and Kenya. Al-Shabaab joined with Islamic militant groups in the Middle East, Yemen, Afghanistan, and Iraq, successfully recruiting mercenaries from these regions. Al-Shabaab has inflicted severe blows to Somalia and Kenya, as well as innocent Christian citizens of Kenya in regions close to Somalia. Similar to most militant Islamic groups in the world today, Al-Shabaab is taking over the region, declaring themselves as Islamist territories in order to practice their own form of Sha'ria. It is proven that Al-Shabaab, though an autonomous Islamic militant group, has close connections with Boko Haram Muslim extremists in Nigeria.

Boko Haram is an Islamic militant group that at its beginning operated mainly in north-eastern Nigeria, and emerged around 2010. Its official Arabic name is translated as 'People Committed to the Propagation of the Prophet's Teaching and Jihad', indicating its concern for the total emancipation of Muslims and a commitment to impose Sha'ria rule in Nigeria. Boko Haram means literally, 'Western education is forbidden' in the Hausa language, originating from the perceived hatred for western values and western education, which they believe emanates from Christian-secular tradition and society. They have launched military operations and guerrilla war in Nigeria. After its founding in northern Nigeria, Boko Haram aligned itself with worldwide Islamic movements, including ISIS. It supplies significant technological support in military logistics, ammunitions and personnel.

At its early stages, Boko Haram targeted Christian communities and churches in northern Nigeria. It quickly escalated in targeting Nigeria's state structures, particularly police and military barracks, as well as international organizations, including the United Nations. Boko Haram abducted some 300 girls from a Government school in Chibok, a most disturbing development in Nigeria's escalating crisis. Moreover, Boko Haram suicide bombers now target public areas, bus stops and markets, inflicting terror and destruction of property and human life. Although it is fair to say that both Christians and Muslims and the state are united in a campaign against Boko Haram's incursions in Nigeria, it is difficult to pinpoint why they continue to grow in strength.

Despite horrific attacks, uncommon stories of unity, love, and co-operation abound in the face of violence and terror. The dreaded Al-Shabaab attacked a bus filled with Kenyan travellers and attempted to separate Christian passengers from Muslims. Their plan was to kill the Christians, as a usual practice. Defying the terrorists, Kenyan Muslims protected their fellow Christians. Salah Fareh, a Muslim teacher, bravely refused Al-Shabaab's demand. He sustained a bullet wound in the December attack and died earlier this month.[4] In northern Nigeria, moderate Muslims remained silent out of fear when Boko Haram destroyed Christian churches. At the same time, the vast majority of victims of Boko Haram have been Muslims themselves, many because they were considered by Boko Haram to be agents of the state.

More recently, Muslim-Christian interfaith dialogues are taking place, condemning the violent acts of Boko Haram. For a while, the staunchest resistance to Boko Haram came from local vigilantes, who are overwhelmingly Muslim themselves. This fact is often overlooked with respect to groups like Boko Haram, Al-Shabaab or ISIS because they are deeply committed to what in Islam is called Takfir – the practice of condemning those who identify other Muslims as unbelievers and thus unworthy of being treated as proper Muslims. Hence, Boko Haram, Al-Shabaab or ISIS should not actually constitute a strong

[4] 'Kenyan Muslim who Shielded Christians in al Shabab dies', in: BBC News, January 19, 2016: www.bbc.com/news/world-africa.

challenge to Muslim-Christian dialogue since in many ways such movements attack the majority of Muslims in the same way that they attack Christians. Some have already come to this realization, though these horrific acts are capable of inflaming Christian-Muslim sectarianism. When viewed as a common threat, adherents of both Abrahamic faiths and the state need to stem the bloodshed by joining together.

In another context, in regions such as the Congo, political impasse pits a Christian majority against a Muslim minority over the question of who governs the state. In his recent visit to the region, Pope Francis used his visit to appeal to both groups to see themselves as members of the same Abrahamic religious family.

We should add that the aggressive invasion of evangelical Christianity worldwide – particularly Pentecostalism in Africa – has triggered a Muslim backlash, responding to the perceived Christian domination of the public sphere. Muslims in Southern Nigeria have adopted the aggressive techniques of evangelicals – keeping night vigils, organizing crusades, and engaging in public proselytization on Sundays, previously considered to be sacrosanct as a day of worship.

The competition and unhealthy religious rivalry between Christians and Muslims in places such as in Nigeria has also been played out in what for lack of a better term we may call the politics of pilgrimage. One clear example in Nigeria is over the issue of state sponsorship of pilgrimage to the holy lands in Saudi Arabia and Israel. Just as Nigeria sends the largest number of Muslim pilgrims from a non-Islamic state to perform the *hajj*, Nigeria also sends the largest number of Christian pilgrims in the world to Israel yearly. Though in principle pilgrimage in Christianity does not constitute a mandatory religious act as it is in Islam, nevertheless, it has become the most visible demonstration of Christian piety in Nigeria. Nigerian Christian pilgrims to Israel on their return bear the label JP (Jerusalem Pilgrim) after their names as a show of piety. In a similar manner, the Muslim *hajj* returnee is customarily addressed as *Alhaji/Alhaja*. Such titles apparently bestow honour on the recipients.

Today's unsavoury hostility among Christians and Muslims arises from the struggle to influence and control the state. It has triggered unnecessary and horrific skirmishes along former lines of colonial occupation. It is strengthened by disinvestment from local officials. Colonial rule destroyed states' historical socio-economic and political boundaries of language, commerce, and religion. With reckless and utter disregard for the welfare of the people, western powers carved up their colonial empires to extract enormous wealth in land, resources, and people. The fallout from colonial rule continues today in Africa as African leaders themselves have not proven to be better than the colonialists. Sadly, religion has become an open ground of struggle for competition between rival groups and Muslim and Christian communities are caught in these political and economic crises.

Bibliography

Arinze, Cardinal F. *Christian-Muslim Relations in the Twenty-First Century*. Maryknoll, NY: Orbis, 1989.

Barry, Boubacar. *Le royaume de waalo: Le Sénéga lavant la conquête*. Paris: Karthala, 1985.

Clarke, Suzanna. *A House in Fez: Building a Life in the Ancient Heart of Morocco*. New York: Pocket Books, 2007.

Comolli, Virginia. *Boko Haram: Nigeria's Islamist insurgency*. London: Hurst & Company, 2015.

Hansen, Stig J. *Al- Shabaab in Somalia: The history and ideology of a militant Islamist group, 2005 – 2012*. London: Hurst, 2013.

Hock, Klaus. 'Christian-Muslim relations in the African context', *International Journal for the Study of the Christian* Church 3, no. 2 (2003): 36–57. doi:10.1080/1474225031233 1383755.

Nielsen, Jørgen S. *The Christian-Muslim frontier: Chaos, clash or dialogue?* London: Tauris, 1998.

Rasmussen, Lissi. *Christian-Muslim relations in Africa: The cases of northern Nigeria and Tanzania compared*. London: British Academic Press, 1993.

Shillington, Kevin. *Encyclopedia of African History*. New York: Fitzroy Dearborn, 2005.

Smith, Jane I. '*Muslim-Christian relations: Historical and contemporary realities*': Accessed February 4, 2016. http://religion.oxfordre.com/view/10.1093/acrefore/9780199340378.001.0001/acrefore-9780199340378-e-11.

Smith, Mike. *Boko Haram: Inside Nigeria's unholy war*. London: I.B. Tauris, 2015.

Soares, Benjamin F. *Muslim-Christian encounters in Africa. Islam in Africa 6*. Leiden: Brill, 2006.

Umaru, Thaddeus B. *Christian-Muslim dialogue in northern Nigeria: A socio-political and theological consideration*. Philadelphia: Xlibris, 2013.

(11) THE PROFILE OF AFRICAN CHRISTIANITY AT HOME AND IN THE WEST

Jesse N.K. Mugambi

Introduction

According to the demographic survey conducted by Pew Research Centre on ageing in 2014, Africa has the youngest age profile, and will remain so at least for the next two generations. The population median age of Africa, which is the age that divides the population into two equal groups, was 19.7 in 2014 and will increase to 25.4 in 2050. Europe's age profile is the highest in the world (median age 40), and the region should retain that distinction in 2050 when it is projected to increase to the median age of 46.[1] These findings indicate that between 2010 and 2050 Africa will have the largest percentage growth of population compared with other continental regions. Depending on how the African youth are nurtured and socialized, and taking into consideration the religiosity of Africans today, projections indicate that Africa will have more Christians than any other continental region. Todd Johnson, Director of the Gordon Cornwell Centre for Global Christianity published in 2013 a Report prepared for the Pew Forum entitled 'Christianity in Global Context: Trends and Statistics':[2]

> ... Whereas in 1900 over 80% of all Christians lived in Europe and Northern America, by 2005 this proportion had fallen to under 40%, and will likely fall below 30% before 2050.... In 1900, with the exception of Brazil, the top 10 were all Western countries; by 2050, only the U.S. will make the list. It is interesting to note that, beginning in 2005, India and Nigeria are common to both lists.[3]

He continues to ask three disturbing questions arising from the projections on this unprecedented numerical growth of Christianity in the South and East:

> What might it mean for the future of Christianity that its centre of gravity continues to move south and east? Three key factors bear watching: (1) whether Southern Christians will challenge Northern Christianity's 1,000-year dominance in theology and ecclesiology by producing their own reflections and practices, hearkening back to the earliest Christian centuries when they were in the majority; (2) whether the dominant languages of Christianity will continue to shift south (already by 1980, Spanish was the leading language of church membership in the world, and Chinese, Hindi, and Swahili are increasingly important languages of Christianity); and (3) whether the closer geographic proximity between Christians and Muslims, Hindus, and Buddhists will on balance result in greater conflict or dialogue. With all three factors, the central question remains: 'How well will the new global Christianity navigate its increasingly diverse composition and southern majority?'[4]

These questions challenge African Christian scholars much more than those in other regions. During the early church, theologians based in Africa contributed immensely to the debates that shaped Christianity as we know it today. They include Augustine of Hippo, Cyprian and Tertullian of Carthage, Athanasius,

---

[1] See: www.pewglobal.org/2014/01/30/chapter-3-aging-in-major- regions-of-the-world-2010-to-2050/.
[2] See: www.pewforum.org/files/2013/04/051805-global-christianity.pdf.
[3] See: www.pewforum.org/files/2005/05/051805-global-christianity.pdf; page 1.
[4] See: www.pewforum.org/files/2005/05/051805-global-christianity.pdf; page 1.

Clement, Origen, and Peter of Alexandria, Optatus of Numidia.[5] Will African scholars in the third millennium, in their turn, rise to the task of providing exemplary apologetic leadership?

The following statistics indicate some expected demographic changes by 2050: The global demographic statistics above indicate that in 2014, 76% of the world's population lived in Asia and Oceania (61%) and Africa (15%). By 2050 more than 80% of the global population will be living in these two continental regions. Asia and Oceania will host 55% and Africa 25%. In the present and the next generation Africa will continue having the youngest population. These statistics have very significant implications for the future of Christianity globally. Are African churches prepared for this demographic shift? Will African Christianity be able to take its leading role as the most vibrant when compared and contrasted with churches in other regions? This is the challenge for the present leadership in African Christianity.[6]

The Globalization of Christianity

Christianity is no longer a predominantly 'western' religious phenomenon. Between 400 AD and 1900 AD Christianity remained European, but within a century since 1900 AD it has spread abroad through the modern missionary enterprise from Europe and North America to the whole world. Whereas in 1910 two thirds of all Christians (66.3%) were in Europe, by 2010 this percentage had shrunk to one quarter (25.9%), then to 23% in 2015, and the downward spiral continues. During the same period, adherence to Christianity among Africans rose from 1.4% in 1910 to 23.6% in 2010, and the upward spiral is sharply continuing. George Weigel in an article entitled 'World Christianity by the Numbers' (February 2015) makes the following self-explanatory observation: The most extraordinary Christian growth over the past century has come in Africa: home to 8.7 million Christians in 1900, 542 million today, and perhaps 1.2 billion by 2050, when there will be as many African Christians as Latin American and European Christians combined.

Twenty-first- century Christianity is also a far more urban reality than a century ago. In 1900, 29% of the world's Christian population lived in cities; it is 65% today, although that is projected to decline to 59% by 2050. But perhaps the most astonishing numbers in the survey involve Pentecostal and Charismatic Christians. There were 981,000 of these souls in 1900; there are 643,661,000 of them today; and there are projected to be over one billion Charismatics and Pentecostals in 2050. In raw numbers, then, Charismatic and Pentecostal Christianity is the fastest growing phenomenon in world religious history. These three phenomena – African growth, urbanization and the rise of Pentecostalism – also help contribute, perhaps, towards the greater fragmentation of Christianity worldwide. What might be called entrepreneurial Christianity – founding your own church – is very much a part of all three, and that helps explain why the number of Christian denominations grew from 1,600 in 1900 to 45,000 today, with projections of 70,000 in 2050.[7]

According to Weigel, in 1900 there were 1,600 denominations, of which only one was African – the Coptic Church. At that time there were no autonomous African denominations in tropical Africa, a vast region regarded a 'mission field' for scramble and partition by European and American missionary societies, backed and protected by their respective imperial governments. European and North American missionaries established and managed outposts of their respective denominations in Africa and elsewhere. Since 1900 the number of African denominations has risen in one century from one to thousands, and the

[5] See: www.catholic-defense.com/bios.htm.

[6] See: www.pewforum.org/2012/12/18/global-religious-landscape-christians/.

[7] See: George Weigel, *"World Christianity by the Numbers"*, dated 25 February 2015, in: www.firstthings.com/web-exclusives/2015/02/world-christianity-by-the-numbers.

rate of increase is statistically unpredictable. The Roman Catholic Church has members in every African nation.

The All Africa Conference of Churches (AACC), whose membership includes mainstream Protestant denominations, has a membership of 174 churches. African Instituted churches are in tens of thousands and the number keeps rising. It is difficult to keep abreast of their increase because many of them do not apply for registration. Increase in the number of urban-based Charismatic churches is particularly rapid, consistent with the high rate of urbanization in Africa.[8]

The 2011 Pew Research Centre Survey on Religion and Public Life indicated that although the proportion of Christianity in Africa in 1900 was insignificant as a percentage of the global aggregate, by 2010 every significant denominational thrust of western Christianity had gained a significant foothold in tropical Africa. The Pew Survey does not specifically document the statistical magnitude of African Instituted churches and Charismatic churches. Quite clearly, however, African Christians constitute a very significant proportion of all Christians globally. They may not wield comparable economic, political and ideological influence today, but this economic marginality is not permanent. The economies of some African nations are growing rapidly, and this growth is permeating into all sectors of culture including religion. Availability of surplus capital is facilitating the spread of African Christianity to other regions, particularly to Europe and North America. Some African charismatic preachers have already established themselves in various towns and cities in Europe and North America.[9]

Western Christianity in Africa

The history of western Christianity in tropical Africa dates from the voyages of European explorers around the continent of Africa in the fifteenth century. The exploratory expeditions included chaplains to care for the spiritual needs of the crews. Wherever they stopped along the African coast they erected sanctuaries, which became the initial entry points for missionaries. One such monument is the pillar constructed by Vasco da Gama at Malindi, Kenya, in early 1498, just before his departure to India.[10]

The earliest presence of western Christianity in tropical Africa is evident especially in Ghana, Angola, South Africa and Kenya. At the beginning these early initiatives were exclusively Portuguese, exploring the eastern sea route to Asia. The second phase was the Cross-Atlantic slave trade, in which European merchants procured African slaves for export to the Caribbean and the Americas. These expeditions also included chaplains, blessing the crews of the ships and the business thereof. The human merchandise (slaves) required no blessing, except, of course, in terms of the profit that would accrue to its 'owners' if it reached the Americas in 'good' enough condition to fetch the highest price from the highest bidder. When they were no longer needed, a programme to resettle them back in Africa was hatched, establishing the colonies of Sierra Leone and Liberia.

When the slave trade became no longer economically viable, a minority in the new generation of missionaries embarked on a campaign for its abolition. It was the economic argument, rather than the moral one, that persuaded perpetrators to make profit through means other than the sale and purchase of human beings.[11] David Livingstone persistently argued that it would be much more profitable for

[8] See: www.breakingchristiannews.com/articles/display_art.html?ID=10896; www.pewforum.org/2012/12/18/global-religious-landscape-christians/.

[9] See: www.pewforum.org/2011/12/19/global-christianity-traditions/; also: www.pewforum.org/2012/12/18/global-religious-landscape-christians/.

[10] See: kenyatravelsites.wordpress.com.

[11] This point is amply documented by Eric Williams in his book *Capitalism and Slavery* (University of North Carolina Press, 1944; Paperback 1994), and also in Garth Lean's *God's Politician: Wilberforce's Struggle*. (Helmers & Howard, 1987).

Europeans to promote commerce, Christianity and civilization among Africans than to sell them as goods for profit.[12]

The third phase was the establishment of colonies in Africa, a project that required missionary personnel as auxiliaries to the main project of making Africans governable. In this role missionaries provided the mediatory function between the colonial administrators and the colonial subjects. The missionaries in this phase not only endorsed and blessed the project of colonization; they were an integral part of it. During the fourth phase of western Christianity in Africa, during the colonial period, missionaries were sent from the European capitals to win African converts into the respective national churches of the imperial powers. The earliest missionary societies were Catholic, followed closely by those of the Church of England.

The Berlin Conference (1884-5) restricted the operations of these missionary initiatives after the Scramble and Partition of the continent between the imperial powers that met at the behest of Chancellor Bismarck of Germany. The provisions of the Berlin Treaty required missionaries to operate in the respective imperial spheres of influence of their home governments, but exercise freedom of movement and operation in the spheres of influence of other powers provided that they complied with the imperial law of the host imperial power. In practice, missionaries preferred to operate in the territories where their safety and security was guaranteed by their home governments. The consequence was that the dominant Christian denomination of an imperial power became also the dominant denomination in its colonies, with other denominations becoming minorities.

This colonial legacy is still evident in tropical Africa. During the colonial period, two aspects of western Christianity evolved in Africa, as follows: *a) The Western Church of the Colonizers:* One aspect was the colonial church to which the missionaries and their families belonged, normally located in the administrative centre where the colonial authorities lived. The missionaries and other expatriate personnel would conduct their rituals there, but commute to the mission outposts to supervise the native 'evangelists' doing the work on behalf of the missionary. Remnants of this colonial church are still evident. Many are cathedrals headed by African clergy, but the architecture and the relics are still hanging on the walls, on the pews and on the commemorative plaques. From an observer's perspective, there is a mismatch between the original occupants of this western church in Africa, and those who occupy it today. It remains western, and the current occupants remain African. The Dutch Reformed Church in South Africa is the most prominent in this category of Christianity, although it had variants in other colonies.

b) The Domesticated Western Church of the Colonized: The other component of this western church in Africa consists of the African denominations the missionaries introduced by winning some African converts. It was a foreign church, fashioned in the image of the missionary, according to the culture and history in which he was nurtured, socialized and ritualized. The African converts were expected to fit into this foreign church, with a liturgy that was a translation of the liturgies 'back home' – from English, French, German, Latin, Portuguese, Spanish originals. Africans awkwardly slotted themselves into the cultural garb of this western church in Africa, which was a Sunday affair, and a classroom-based form of religiosity. For the whole week they would live normal lives, until Sunday morning when they would wear their 'Sunday Best' clothes, go to church, do the Sunday ritual, then return home. They would then remove their 'Sunday Best', put on their normal clothes and resume their normal chores until the following Sunday. John V. Taylor lucidly describes this phenomenon in his book, *Christian Presence amid African Religion.*

c) Self-reliant Western Christianity in Africa: In 1963 the All Africa Conference of Churches convened its Inaugural Assembly at Kampala, bringing together the mainstream Protestant churches in Africa – Anglican, Lutheran, Methodist, and Presbyterian. This was the launching event for the modern ecumenical

---

[12] Roland Oliver describes this aspect of western Christianity in his book *The Missionary Factor in East Africa*; A.J. Temu, British Protestant Missions (London: Longman, 1972; Adrian Hastings, A History of African Christianity, 1950 – 1975 (CUP, 1979); Bengt Sundkler and Christopher Steed, *A history of the church in Africa* (CUP, 2000).

movement at the continental level in Africa. Two decades earlier, Christian councils had been formed by missionaries in various African colonies, in tandem with the modern ecumenical movement that was coalescing in Geneva. One of the focal concerns was 'Selfhood of the Church', in view of the fact that these churches were dependent on their parent denominations abroad.

In 1970, Pastor John G. Gatu, a Presbyterian church leader from Kenya, addressed a gathering at Milwaukee, Minnesota during which he stated emphatically that the time had come for missionaries to go home so that African Christians could enjoy the "selfhood of the church" here in Africa. This message was taken very negatively in the West, and precipitated what came to be called the Moratorium Debate.[13] Within the World Council of Churches this debate raged for more than a decade, especially between the Fifth Assembly (Nairobi, Kenya, 1975) and the Sixth Assembly (Vancouver, Canada, 1983). As early as 1950, Bishop Stephen Neill had been commissioned to conduct a survey on theological education for these churches. His report was less than encouraging. Despite missionary presence in Africa for decades, there was hardly anything significant to show with regard to theological preparation for African leadership.[14] A lot of recent African theological research has been done on this issue in past years.[15]

African Christianity in the West

African presence in the West began not voluntarily, but through the slave trade. European settlement in the Caribbean and the Americas was more than a double human tragedy: decimation of the native inhabitants in Africa, and the importation of Africans into the Americas as slaves to work in the plantations and the mines. African slaves on the plantations in North America and the Caribbean were forbidden to worship on their own, and the worship services organized for them by their masters were intended to 'pacify' and indoctrinate them to accept their servile condition. Attending worship sessions other than those authorized by the master would attract severe punishment, but most slaves would risk that punishment in order to worship with their fellow slaves in secret. Reading the Bible was forbidden, and most could not read. Those who were literate selected relevant verses from the Bible, and out of them the Spirituals were composed.

James H. Cone describes the theological importance of the Civil Rights Movement on the one hand, and on the other, the religiosity of enslaved Africans in North America. There was no wall separating the Spirituals and the Blues.[16] The slaves who did not feel like worshipping in a church would still get the message of liberation via the Blues in pubs where Jazz became a unique genre of African music in the Americas. The Spirituals were primarily not about *spirituality,* but about *reality* – the *reality* of suffering and the *hope* for liberation from that suffering, which only God would bring about, since nobody seemed to care. This message is summarized in the spiritual known by the title – *Nobody knows the trouble I've seen*: 'Nobody knows the trouble I've seen, Nobody knows but Jesus, Nobody knows the trouble I've seen, Glory Hallelulah!'

---

[13] The most lucid elaboration of the issue was authored by Elliott Kendall and published under the title *The End of an Era: Africa and the Missionary* (London: SPCK, 1978).

[14] This shortcoming is lucidly echoed by Professor Leslie Shyllon in the introductory Chapter of *Uniquely African: African Christian Identity from Cultural and Historical Perspectives*, edited by James L. Cox and Gerrie ter Haar, Trenton, New Jersey: Africa World Press, 2003.

[15] Laurenti Magesa, *Anatomy of Inculturation*, Maryknoll, New York: Orbis, 2004; John G. Gatu, Joyfully Christian, Truly African, Nairobi: Acton, 2005; David M. Gitari, *Responsible Church Leadership*, Nairobi: Acton, 2006; Simon Chiwanga, *The Episcopacy Reconsidered*, Nairobi: Acton, 2011.

[16] See: James H. Cone, *Black Theology and Black Power* (Catholic Foreign Mission Society America 1997, Orbis Books Maryknoll) and *The Spirituals and the Blues* (Orbis Books Maryknoll 1992).

The Civil Rights Movement of the 1950s and 1960s provided unique opportunities for creative theological reflection among some Afro-American theologians, some of which filtered into the mainstream of the modern ecumenical movement.[17] Since the 1980s, African Christian immigrants to North America and Europe have taken with them their distinctive Christian religiosity, manifested in their own worship communities where they religiously 'feel at home'.[18] African slaves took their religiosity with them, even though in their chains and handcuffs they could not carry any artefacts. On arrival in the Americas they re-constructed their material culture, some of which still survives to influence African Christianity in the West.

African Christianity in Africa

African Instituted Churches

The African Instituted Churches were formed by Africans as alternatives to the denominations introduced by missionaries in East Africa.[19] Such churches were most prevalent in colonies with settler communities, such as DR Congo, Côte d'Ivoire, Kenya, Sierra Leone, Southern Rhodesia (Zimbabwe), and South Africa. Missionaries condemned such churches as 'separatist sects', and recommended to the colonial administration that they should be banned. Some of the founders died in prison, such as Simon Kimbangu, founder of the Kimbanguist Church in DR Congo, who died in 1951 after thirty years of incarceration. Some of these churches have formed the Organization of African Instituted Churches (OAIC) as a forum to deal with their needs and concerns. This organization is parallel, not antagonistic to the All Africa Conference of Churches (AACC), whose membership is primarily from mainstream Protestant churches. There is a lot of research on African Instituted Churches in recent years.[20]

African Christianity in Africa is perhaps the most potent expression of Christian religiosity in this continent, since it is the most conscious carrier of the African self-identification with African cultural roots. Yet it is the least understood, because it has not yet nurtured enough of its own scholars to explain itself. A few representatives of this category of African Christianity have entered academia, including Solomon Waigwa, a Kenyan of the Akorino Church, currently the Chair, Department of Philosophy and Religion of

---

[17] In addition to James Cone, Gayraud Wilmore in *Black Religion and Black Radicalism* presents the broad spectrum of African religiosity under slavery in North America. Robert Hood, Must God Remain Greek? Afro-cultures and God-Talk, Minneapolis: Augsburg-Fortress, 1990. Peter Paris, *The Spirituality of African Peoples: The Search for a Common Moral Discourse*, Minneapolis: Augsburg- Fortress, 1995. Robert Beckford in his book *Dread and Pentecostal: A Political Theology for the Black Church in Britain* (London: SPCK, 2000) illustrates how culture influences social consciousness across generations and within specific historical contexts. Caribbean Christian presence in the UK bears its cultural memory from Africa via the Caribbean. It is not identical with African Christianity in the mother continent, nor is it integrated with the dominant culture of the host nation.

[18] This phenomenon has been described by various scholars, such as Gerrie ter Haar, *Half-Way to Paradise: African Christians in Europe*;(Cardiff Academic Press, 1998); Robert Beckford, *Dread and Pentecostal: A Political Theology for the Black Church in Britain* (London: SPCK, 2000). James L. Cox and Gerrie ter Haar, eds, *Uniquely African? African Christian Identity from Cultural and Historical Perspectives* (Trenton, NJ: Africa World Press, 2003).

[19] In 1965 F.B. Welbourn and Bethuel A. Ogot published a book titled *A Place to Feel at Home* (Oxford University Press) describing the emergence of AICs.

[20] See: David B. Barrett, *Schism and Renewal in Africa* (Oxford University Press, 1968); Deji Ayegboyin and S. Ademola Ishola , *African Indigenous Churches An Historical Perspective* (Grand Rapids, Michigan: Institute for Religious Research, 1997); Allan Anderson, *African Reformation* (Trenton, New Jersey: Africa World Press, 2001); Philomena N. Mwaura, *"African Instituted Churches in East Africa,"* (Studies in World Christianity, Edinburgh, Vol.10No. 2, October 2004); Samuel G. Kibicho, *God and Revelation in an African Context* (Nairobi: Acton, 2006); Berngt Sundkler, *Bantu Prophets in South Africa* (Cambridge: James Clarke, 1948). See also: http://irr.org/african-indigenous-churches-chapter-one.

Wiley College, Texas. In his blog he has written that the emergence of the Akorino Church was not influenced by any mission agency. The church was begun by 'prophetic figures, who claimed divine calling to their prophetic ministry'. Those founders were not notable figures in their former churches. Besides having been baptized in the mission churches and receiving minimal education, they had not risen beyond general church membership. The experience they received was so cataclysmically definitive that they begun to attract large crowds until their meetings were declared illegal by the colonial government by the end of the 1920s. That experience was the in-filling of the Holy Spirit.

Another representative of this category of African Christianity is Dr Thomas Asante Oduro of Christ Holy Church International and President, Good News Theological College and Seminary, Accra, Ghana, and author of *Christ Holy Church International: The Story of an African Independent Church.* The book explores and examines the history, beliefs, practices and growth of Christ Holy Church International, an African Independent Church in Nigeria, founded by Agnes Okoh, an illiterate woman who, while returning from a market in 1943, heard a voice repeatedly saying 'Matthew Ten'. How Agnes Okoh, a marginalized woman and a widow, was able to found and lead an itinerant evangelistic team of 12 members in 1947 till it developed into a church with nearly 800 congregation in 2002 in a pluralistic, multicultural and multilingual Nigeria is the focus of this book.[21]

Enculturation of Catholicism and Moratorium on Missionaries in Protestantism:

In Catholic circles, 'Enculturation' is about the domestication of western Christianity in Africa, which remains western at the core. In this third millennium the vestiges of western Christianity in Africa remain dominant, in both rural and urban churches. The oldest ones date from the colonial period, and the most recent are continually being introduced by short-term missionaries who come to 'evangelize the un-evangelized' while leaving at home their peers who have abandoned Christianity. Post-colonial Charismatic, Pentecostal missionary initiatives in Africa risk repeating the same mistakes that John V. Taylor describes in his book above, with disastrous consequences for both the missionaries and their converts.

African Christianity Evangelizing the West

Kwabena Asamoah-Gyadu in his article 'African-led Christianity in Europe: Migration and Diaspora Evangelism' has observed that African Christians in the West are participants in evangelization among their host communities, at the same time that some missionaries from the West continue to evangelize Africa:

> Today, some of the largest congregations in Europe western and eastern – are either founded by Africans or are led by people of African descent. Discussions on African immigrant Christianity usually focus on churches whose memberships tend to be constituted by Africans or people of that descent. A good example is the Kingsway International Christian Centre (KICC) in London, led by the charismatic Nigerian pastor, Matthew Ashimolowo. My research has taken me to the doors of another type of African-led church whose membership is entirely European. This means the designation of these churches in the diaspora as 'African churches' is no longer tenable. For example, Sunday Adelaja's Church of the Blessed Embassy of the Kingdom of God for all Nations is based in Kiev, Ukraine. Founded in 1994, it has a membership of approximately twenty-five thousand adults.[22]

---

[21] See: www.lutheranupress.org/pdf/announce_7.pdf.

[22] Kwabena Asamoah-Gyadu, *"African-led Christianity in Europe: Migration and Diaspora Evangelism"*, in: Lausanne World Pulse Archives 7/2008, in: www.lausanneworldpulse.com/themedarticles-php/975/07-2008.

Asamoah-Gyadu concludes that at the beginning of the 21st century Christian missionary outreach is no longer the monopoly of western missionaries going out to the rest of the world for converts, and that African Christians have become effective participants in missionary outreach abroad. Their approach to evangelization has an African cultural touch and flavour, comparable and contrastable with western approaches. According to his observation, the tasks of mission and evangelization in Africa have truly gone international. Further, Jehu Hanciles in one of his essays writes that it is often overlooked that the global South-North divide is as religious as it is economic. In western societies, the process of modernization has produced distinctive cultural changes associated with the secular ideal of liberal democracy, including: stronger individualism; a greater push for gender equality; sexual permissiveness; greater tolerance of divorce, abortion, and homosexuality; and a massive erosion of institutional religion.[23] Due to the pervasive religiosity of non-western societies, the South-to-North migration movement is essentially a religious movement. This is to say that, in addition to the economic and cultural benefits, which the new immigrants bring, they are also impacting western societies in fundamental ways related to religious life. In other words, contemporary global migrations implicate the West as a site of new religious interactions. This is particularly true of the growth of new Muslim and Christian populations; however, it is the latter that forms the focus here.[24]

Churches without Theologians and Theologians without Churches

Western Christianity has a long tradition of theological training, research and publication. As the membership declines in Europe and North America (owing to ageing, death and other factors), membership in African Christianity is inversely increasing, a trend that will continue for more than a generation, perhaps beyond 2050. The demographic statistics in preceding sections are indicative of great ecclesiastical challenges both in the West and in Africa. One of those challenges is that although there may be a surplus of theologians in the West who were trained for their respective cultural settings in the context of their respective world-views and ideological perspectives, it may be tempting for such foreign theologians (and their theologies) to be off-loaded to Africa, as happened in the nineteenth and twentieth centuries. Such a move will be catastrophic, because the Holy Spirit does not inspire retroactively.

At the same time, without adequate relevant and contextualized ministerial training, young people in Africa will continue starting unsustainable 'churches' and 'ministries' to meet the needs of their peers – moral, emotional and material. Such a scenario happened during the 1930s and 1940s when many of the African Independent churches were formed by the young of that period.

Congregations without Churches, and Churches without Congregations

Demographically, the 21st century has opened with dramatic paradoxes. In tropical Africa congregations are increasing in number and growing in membership, especially in towns and cities. Many congregations are meeting in the open, in tents or in rented halls. At the same time, in Europe and North America, some of the old churches are closing down, because there is nobody to worship in them any more. Below are the church opening and closing statistics for the UK in 2013. Peter Brierley reports that the actual number of churches increased between 2008 and 2013, and is expected to continue to do so between 2013[25] and 2020.[26]

---

[23] See: Jehu Hanciles, "The Effect of Migration and the Growing Diaspora on Evangelism Efforts: Migration, Diaspora Communities, and the New Missionary Encounter with Western Society".

[24] See: www.lausanneworldpulse.com/pdf/issues/LWPJuly2008PDF.pdf.

[25] Peter Brierley: UK Church Statistics 2: 2010-2020.

[26] See: http://www.eauk.org/church/research-and-statistics/how–many-churches-have-opened-or-closed-in-recent-

2008 – total number of churches 49,727.
2013 – total number of churches 50,660.
2020 – estimated number of churches 51,275.

Number of UK churches opening and closing 2008-2013 in each denomination

	Anglican	Baptists	Independ -ent	Methodist	New churches	Pentecostal	Presbyterian	Smaller churches
Opening	0	+1	+104	+4	+256	+640	+9	+1,937
Closing	-324	-76	-112	-813	-4	-2	-183	-38
Net Diff	-324	-75	-8	-809	+252	-638	-174	+1,899

The Table above is self-explanatory. The old churches that were responsible for the evangelization of Africa are 'dying' while new ones are emerging. The founders and members of these new churches are young, and the demographic profile includes a large percentage of immigrants. Perhaps the scenario in the 21st century is comparable with that in the first, when St Paul was writing his epistles to the Romans, Corinthians, Colossians, Ephesians, Thessalonians, Galatians and Philippians. African Christians of the present generation in the West may be paving the way for a more sustained re-evangelization of Europe and North America – but from Africa. This will not be the first time that Africa undertakes such a role. The continent seems to be entrusted with the vocation of pioneering new eras in human history since time immemorial.

years.cf.

(12) AFRICAN CHRISTIANITY AND HISTORIC AFRO-AMERICAN CHURCHES

Angelique Walker-Smith

In the book, *An Unbroken Circle*, the argument is made that 'ancient, apostolic, Orthodox Christianity has gone full circle, from continent to continent, from Christ to His Apostles, from the Apostles to ancient Africa, from Africa to America, and from Black Americans to their sons and daughters'.[1] The book proposes that there is an unbroken circle between ancient African Christianity, before the colonial period, and the Christianity of Africans who were and are Americanized.

It is in the light of this background that this paper seeks to demonstrate that the independent and indigenous historic Afro-American churches are not only expressions of American Christianity but also African Christianity by virtue of an integration of African identity in the development and evolution of such churches. While the focus of this paper is on the historic Afro-American churches in the USA, a fuller discussion of African Christianity and Afro-American churches would include other churches such as Afro-American churches associated with the Roman Catholic Church, Orthodox churches and other Afro-American churches related to predominantly white Protestant denominational bodies as well as recent African immigrant churches and a host of smaller historic and indigenous Afro-American Christian movements in the USA.

The purpose of this paper is to identify historic and spiritual trends that lead to the relationship of African Christianity and historic Afro-American churches that we have come to know as the following churches.[2] First, the National Baptist Convention USA, Incorporated which is the oldest historic Afro-American Baptist Convention that shares a historic relationship with five other Afro-American (National) Baptist churches. The first of these five churches is the Lott Carey Foreign Mission Baptist Convention that came into existence in 1897. The other four Conventions were established in the 1900s. They include the National Baptist Convention of America, Inc., Progressive National Baptist Convention, National Missionary Baptist Convention and the Full Gospel Baptist Church Fellowship. The historic Afro-American Pentecostal Church featured in this paper is the Church of God in Christ (COGIC) whose founders were former ministers with the Afro-American Baptist churches. The historic Afro-American Methodist churches are African Methodist Episcopal Church (AME), the African Methodist Episcopal Zion Church (AMEZ), and the Christian Methodist Episcopal Church (formally known as the Colored Methodist Episcopal Church). While it is important to point out that there is growing momentum today of the spread of independent Afro-American churches that have cloistered or re-organized into various types of networks, associations and denominational bodies in the USA and an increase of first and second generation immigrant African churches that have arrived or developed in the USA,[3] the focus of this paper is on the historic beginning of the oldest of the aforementioned churches since the first arrivals of African slaves.

---

[1] Father Paisius Altschul, editor, *The Unbroken Circle* (St Louis, Missouri: Brotherhood of St Moses the Black, 1997), p. back cover.

[2] C. Eric Lincoln and Lawrence H. Mamiya, *The Black Church in the African American Experience* (Duke University Press: Durham and London, 1990), 1.

[3] Wes Granberg Michaelson, *From Times Square to Timbuktu: The Post-Christian West Meets the Non-Western Church* (Eerdmans Publishing Company: Grand Rapids, Michigan), 83-84 & 86-87.

Convergences of African and Christian Identities

African Christianity and Afro-American Christianity converge historically, spiritually and through the witness of suffering and even martyrdom. These three convergences have been proposed by Albert Raboteau in the book, *An Unbroken Circle*, where he discusses the relationship between Orthodoxy, and African and Afro-American spirituality. His first argument is historical: he states: 'Ancient Christianity is not, as many think, a European religion. Christian communities were well established in Africa by the third and fourth centuries. In Egypt and Ethiopia, traditions of worship, monasticism, and spirituality have remained authentically African and authentically Christian down to the present day.' The second is spiritual: there are analogies between African Traditional Religions and Orthodox Christianity. In classic theological terms these analogies constitute a 'proto-evangelion' (Greek): a preparation for the gospel based on God's natural revelation to all peoples through nature and conscience. His third argument is about the experience of suffering Christianity. Ancient Christianity prized the gift of martyrdom, the witness through suffering – even death itself – to the truth of the Christian gospel. Paradoxically Christians throughout history have seen periods of martyrdom as periods of spiritual vitality and growth.[4]

Father Antonious Conner points out that the first resonance that is historical includes the history found in the Bible that predates Christianity and that exists during the life of Jesus and in the establishment of Christianity. He states: 'From its beginning to its end, the Bible provides information about God's dealing with numerous nations, peoples, and tongues. Of the many people who are mentioned and highlighted in the Scripture, many are black people, African people. And we too, were and are vessels whom God uses to spread His redemptive message to the world. Therefore, it is important for Afro-Americans to appreciate the presence of people of colour in the Scriptures and their contribution to Christianity.'[5] He specifically points to various Biblical persons like John Mark who was from Libya and one of the twelve apostles, Symeon, who was an African Canaanite and also Simon of Cyrene from Libya, who carried the cross of Jesus.[6]

Father Jerome Sanderson points to the importance of Afro-American churches identifying with the early African Saints of the Church, many of whom were Christian martyrs. He points to saints like Saints Perpetua and Felicity, St Cyprian of Carthage, St Athanasius the Great, St Anthony the Great, St Mary of Egypt, and St Moses the Ethiopian.[7] He states that while we may not know exactly what each looked like, we do know of their African identities. He also points to both the blessings and burdens of visual imagery from many nationalities that tend to portray Christ and the saints according to their own traditions. For example, he points to Greek art and iconography offering Greek representations. He is convinced that there is nothing wrong with this in itself but does state that European images of scripture are predominant in the West, and the typical assumption is that they are historically valid. Therefore, Christ was white, as were the Pharaohs, the Egyptians, the prophets and all the peoples in Jerusalem. He cites Acts 2:5, 6, 9-11 as one Biblical description of Jerusalem that points to a different image.[8]

In the historic Afro-American church experience, this kind of white imagery has been dominant in the USA and has contributed to a negative perception of Africans and people of African descent in the USA. This, in addition to the experience of centuries of chattel slavery, the horror of Jim Crow laws, lynching and other methods of disempowerment and disenfranchisement have contributed to the suffering and

---

[4] Altschul, *The Unbroken Circle*, 161-163.
[5] Altschul, *The Unbroken Circle*, 3.
[6] Altschul, *The Unbroken Circle*, 7.
[7] Altschul, *The Unbroken Circle*, 17-24.
[8] Altschul, *The Unbroken Circle*, 24-25.

martyrdom of Afro-American Christians in the USA. James Cone has spoken about this in his book, *God of the Oppressed*,[9] where a Black Theology has been developed as a theological response to this.

The Historic Debate

Although the aforementioned lays a foundation for understanding this paper's argument for the convergence of African identity in the evolution of Afro-American spirituality and churches, there has also been debate about this. The aforementioned perspectives and work of others cited in this paper resonate with the older works of people like the anthropologist Melville J. Herskovits, who supported the position that the slave system did not destroy the slaves' African culture and that a considerable number of Africanisms continue to define Afro-American culture in the USA.[10] People like the historian E. Franklin Frazier, however, have argued the opposite position. He argues that African retentions in the USA were negligible because the African was almost totally stripped of his culture by the process of enslavement.[11] Both arguments are important and together may offer a more balanced reading of the African slave period in the USA. At the same time, many Afro-American religious historians and theologians, since Frazier's work, have built on Herskovits's work.

Historic Convergence: African Slaves and Christianity in the USA

In the book, *From Slavery to Freedom*, John Hope Franklin, points out the following: 'The first twenty Africans were brought to Jamestown, Virginia, as indentured servants in 1619. Six years later there were only twenty-three in Virginia, and by 1650, there were only 300. The pace increased after that. By 1756 there were 120,156 Africans and 173,316 Whites and in many counties, Blacks outnumbered Whites. Trends in Virginia were matched in South Carolina, and later in other states.'[12]

Mechal Sobel continues by stating in his book, *Trabelin' On: The Slave Journey to an Afro-Baptist Faith,* the following: 'By the close of the transatlantic slave trade in 1808, there were a half million Africans and Afro-Americans (children of African slaves), and by 1860, there were 4.5 million, with almost all these additions coming by birth, not illegal importation. They were forced to migrate to the USA to provide forced labour to build up a new country founded on the principles of religious freedom, capitalism and democracy. The African immigrant was an answer to the problem of there not being enough labourers to build a new nation and prior attempts to only use the labours of Native Americans and European immigrants was not sufficient.'[13]

The African immigrants arrived from a variety of African countries but primarily from West Africa and spoke many different languages. They had many different African identities and cultures. The European immigrants who brought them were quick to dismiss such prior identities and forced another identity of slave labourer and proselyte. From the very beginning of the Atlantic slave trade, conversion of the slaves to Christianity was viewed by the emerging nations of western Christendom as a justification for enslavement of Africans. When Portuguese caravels returned from the coast of West Africa with human booty in the fifteenth century, Gomes Eannes De Azurara, a chronicler of their achievements, observed that 'the greater benefit' belonged not to the Portuguese adventurers but to the captive Africans, 'for though their bodies were now brought into some subjection, that was a small matter in comparison of their souls,

[9] James H. Cone, *God of the Oppressed* (New York: Orbis Press, 1975/1997).
[10] Melville Herskovits, *The Myths of the Negro Past* (Boston: Beacon Press, 1958), xxxiii-xxix, 20-32.
[11] E. Franklin Frazier, *The Negro Church in America* (New York: Schocken Books, 1964), 1-19.
[12] John Hope Franklin, *From Slavery to Freedom* 3rd ed (New York: Alfred A. Kempf, 1967), 73.
[13] Michael Sobel, *Trabelin' On: The Slave Journey in an Afro-Baptist Faith* (Westport, Connecticut: Greenwood Press 1979). 23.

which would now possess true freedom for evermore'.[14] Raboteau continues by stating that 'the pangs of guilt over the cruelty inherent in enslaving fellow human beings were assuaged by emphasizing the grace of faith made available to Africans, who otherwise would die as pagans'.[15] People like De Azurara believed that African slaves would not only benefit spiritually but materially from their contact with western civilization. His perspective would dominate Christian apologists for slavery for at least four centuries.

But even this zealous movement competed with the economic reasons of having African slaves in the USA. Economic dominance and prosperity by the white colonists was the primary goal and the possibility that baptism, Biblical literacy, and religious instruction would somehow suggest freedom was a value and a right for African slaves which ran directly counter to the economic interest of the colonizers. Evangelical white missionaries were faced with an ethical dilemma concerning the souls of African slaves. On the one hand, Evangelical Protestantism 'was based upon the tenet that the baptized individual was a free inner-directed person, responsible to himself, to others and to God'.[16] If the baptized Negro was a slave, however, there was one great stumbling block. He was the chattel property of another, having no personal rights nor freedom of conscience. This was intensified by the assumption that African slaves belonged to an inferior race. These assumptions were based in a system of white dominance and racism, whether represented by the white slave owners or white missionaries, and became an affront to African slaves and eventually led to a separatist movement of African Christianity defined by the original intended definition of baptism that frees persons and the persons and social history of separation by race and class rooted in the experience of chattel slavery.

Such concerns by the white colonizers and missionaries led to the development of a series of laws ensuring that religion did not run counter to their economic interest. In Virginia, by 1706 at least six colonial legislatures had passed acts denying that baptism altered the condition of a slave 'as to his bondage or freedom'.[17] The white Christian missionary and the white slave holders complemented each other's agenda of economic, racial and religious domination and oppression. Both supported the laws and structural practices that supported chattel slavery of African slaves who were considered as property of the European immigrants. As a result African slaves were subject to the horrors their owners perpetuated, including the systematic disempowerment of the African slave's ability to be human and dignified in the eyes of USA law and their slave owners. In effect, the Christian message was compromised and brought a harmful presentation that ran counter to a gospel of freedom. During the slave period, laws were created that ensured African slaves could not do the following: a) own land; b) earn income and pay taxes; c) vote; d) marry legally; e) travel freely; f) establish churches; g) build wealth; and h) own and sell slaves. Milton C. Bennett states the following in his book, *Black Religion and American Evangelicalism*, concerning what the African slave could not do: 'The black man in America was something like the unwanted child. He was part of the total society by the very fact that the Whites had brought him to America from the beginnings, and yet, because he was black, he had little claim to communal life, communal wealth, or communal freedoms. These denials of legal rights and freedoms addressed the dilemma of baptism and bondage freeing the slave. Such denial of rights made slave masters more receptive to having the gospel preached to their slaves.'[18]

---

[14] Gommes Eannes De Azurara, *Chronicle,* 1: 50-51.

[15] Albert Raboteau, *Slave Religion: The "Invisible Institution" in the Antebellum South* (Oxford: Oxford University Press 1978) 96.

[16] Raboteau, *Slave Religion: The "Invisible Institution" in the Antebellum South*, 98.

[17] Raboteau, *Slave Religion: The "Invisible Institution" in the Antebellum South,* 99.

[18] Milton C. Sernett, *Black Religion and American Evangelicalism: White Protestants, Plantation Missions, and the Flowering of Negro Christianity, 1787-1865* (Metuchen, NJ: Scarecrow Press: 1975).

Spiritual Convergence: The Invisible Years of African Identity and Slave Religion

Despite the white colonizers' and missionaries' misrepresentation of a gospel that affirmed chattel slavery and racial oppression, Charles Joyner states in his book, *Down by the Riverside*: 'Slaves did not so much adapt to Christianity (at least not to the selective Christianity evangelized to them by their masters) as adapt Christianity to themselves. Bonds people, seized and transported from Africa into a new world, selected from that world what they needed to survive as a people – the communal, expressive, mythic components of Christianity – and combined them with an African perspective, which they shared because of their common situation as slaves in America.'[19] The African perspective did not separate the sacred and secular, as had the European worldview after the Renaissance and the scientific revolution. According to Dwight Hopkins, to Africans 'nearly all experience was religious, from the naming of children to beliefs regarding when to plant and how to hunt and fish'.[20]

Albert Raboteau further points out the following in his discussion concerning catechesis and conversion. Just like Christians before the chattel slave period in the USA, African slaves appropriated Christianity on their own terms despite what they were told or not told by their slave holders and USA law. The African slaves experienced dissonance between their dignified African identities and the disempowering and undignified messaging of White colonizers and missionaries.[21]

Henry Mitchell, in his book, *Black Church Beginning: The Long-Hidden Realities of the First Years*, makes the case that during the period of 1619-1750 African slaves not only maintained their African identities but promoted their own understanding of being both African and Christian despite the consequences of chattel slavery and systematic attempts to completely strip African identity and any understanding of their Christian faith that would even hint at physical freedom from their bondage. He goes on to say that 'the progress of missionary influence among the Africans was late and slow, and managed to reach only a small percentage of the enslaved.[22] He states the following positive contributing factors for Christianity to take root among Afro-Americans: 1) the open, eclectic character of African Traditional Religion and thereby the African slaves included in some way the god strong enough to give victory to their conquerors and over their own gods and thereby anxious to learn of the white man's God and the Bible; 2) the African slaves were even more anxious when they found (often stole) and interpreted the Bible for themselves. In both the Old and New Testaments they could identify with people like Moses and Jesus; 3) the African slaves identified the impact of the commonality between the expressive culture of Africa and the unprecedented (for Whites) free expressiveness and emotion of the First Great Awakening that included parallels between African Traditional Religion and the physical.[23] Mitchell presents a very rich discussion of the varying dynamics that illustrate these contributing factors that lead to a new stream of Christendom called the Black Church and the Historic Black Churches that disassociated with the white congregations and denominations as church life matured in the USA.[24]

These aforementioned convergences have led to an important critique and hermeneutic of suspicion of white Christianity. Such a critique has been advanced by Afro-American Christians in the USA whether in Afro-American churches, in predominantly white denominations or in Historic Black Churches. In the case of the Historic Black Churches, however, a more dramatic independent, indigenous and institutional church break of protest and prophetic call to justice occurred. Such was the response of these African Christians

---

[19] Charles Joyner, *Down by the Riverside* (Campaign, Illinois: University of Illinois Press, 1985).

[20] Dwight Hopkins and George *Cummings*, eds. *Cut Loose Your Stammering Tongue* (New York: Orbis Books, 1991).

[21] Raboteau, *Slave Religion: The "Invisible Institution" in the Antebellum South*, 48-55.

[22] Henry H. Mitchell, *Black Church: The Long-Hidden Realities of the first Years* (Grand Rapids, Michigan: Eerdmans Publishing Company 2004), 25.

[23] Mitchell, *Black Church: The Long-Hidden Realities of the first Years*, 32-33.

[24] Mitchell, *Black Church: The Long-Hidden Realities of the first Years*, 46-70.

who were seeking an Afro-American expression of Christianity independent of the governance, and oppressive culture of white privilege and power of predominantly white churches.

Suffering and the Development of Historic Afro-American Churches

By the early 1790s, the first signs of a spiritual awakening not only in the general American population but also in the cause of Negro missions can be detected. According to the first federal census, in 1790 there were 757,208 Negroes – 19.3% of the total population. Nearly nine tenths of this number were slaves in the South Atlantic states. The first four decades of the nineteenth century saw a dramatic transformation in the religious configuration of the slave states.[25]

Despite the presentation of a white Christianity by white missionaries that was skewed towards maintaining a racist and exploitative slave system for the African slave, the aforementioned points to the movement of an emerging convergence between African and American Christianity. Such led to a new institutional expression of Christianity, the Black Church in America and later the Historic Black (Afro-American) Churches which chose to leave the predominantly white denominational institutions to form their own indigenous national church bodies.

C. Eric Lincoln and Lawrence H. Mamiya point out in their book, *The Black Church in the African American Experience*: 'The powerful and lasting impact of the colonies-wide revivals called the First Great Awakening and the Second Great Awakening caused an enormous increase in Africans, both enslaved and freed, making public confessions and formal commitments to the Christian faith. At first the trickle of only a few slave converts had simply been absorbed into the established white congregations. But the Great Awakenings brought an authentic religious experience to thousands. This was bound to generate additional desire among Whites and Blacks for separate worship in separate congregations. White church members were not nearly as happy as their black colleagues were with the spontaneity and free expressiveness of Great Awakening-style worship. And these churches, especially in the South, were often culturally overwhelmed in worship with sizeable and irrepressible majorities of non-voting black members.'[26]

The process that led to what became Historic Black Churches evolved from these varying aforementioned movements that wrestled with traditional and renewed African identities rooted in African spirituality and a new encounter with Christian spirituality, Biblical narrative and theology, and Christian practice. This encounter challenged the suffering of African people. It was and is an African Christianity formed in the systemic codification of white dominance and oppression of people of African descent, white privilege and racism. It was and is an expression of African Christianity that has protested injustice but that has been grounded in a conservative approach of Biblical theology and teaching.

The historic movements that led to the development of these churches began during slavery but grew to congregational expression with Afro-American separation and a measure of self-governance which varied from church to church, city to city, and region to region, with major significance given to the ratio of white to black or slave to free. The following short histories of the Historic Black Churches demonstrate how the suffering of African Christian slaves informed their agency to create their own independent and indigenous Christian churches.

---

[25] Mitchell, *Black Church: The Long-Hidden Realities of the first Years*, 32.

[26] C. Eric Lincoln and Lawrence H. Mamiya, *The Black Church in the African American Experience* (Durham, NC: Duke University Press 1990), 46.

African Methodist Episcopal Church (AME)

Mother Bethel African Methodist Episcopal (AME) Church, the first African Methodist Episcopal Church in the nation, was founded in Philadelphia in 1794 by Richard Allen, a former slave. Allen founded Mother Bethel AME after the church he had been attending, St George's Methodist Episcopal Church (MEC) in Philadelphia, began segregating its parishioners by race. The perceived need to segregate white and black parishioners at St George had its roots, ironically, in the preaching of Richard Allen who had been an itinerant preacher in a predominantly white church.[27]

Christian Methodist Episcopal Church (CME)

The Christian Methodist Episcopal Church (CME), familiarly known as the Colored Methodist Episcopal Church, was organized on December 16, 1870 in Jackson, Tennessee by 41 former slave members of the Methodist Episcopal Church, South. Composed primarily of Afro-Americans, the CME Church is a branch of Wesleyan Methodism founded and organized by John Wesley in England in 1844 and established in America as the Methodist Episcopal Church in 1784. The CME Church came into being in the tumultuous aftermath of the civil war and throes of Reconstruction. After emancipation a movement was at once inaugurated to give the Negroes a separate and independent organization.[28]

African Methodist Episcopal Zion Church (AMEZ)

Mother African Methodist Episcopal Zion (AMEZ) Church, founded in 1796, is currently located in Harlem, New York. It is the oldest Afro-American church in the state of New York and was established when black parishioners left John Street Methodist Church in that city. The group, under the leadership of Minister James Varick, had grown disillusioned with increasing segregationist practices within the Methodist church organization. Ministers James Varick, Christopher Rush, William Miller, and George Galbraith would become bishops and eventually be recognized as the founding members of the African Methodist Episcopal Zion denomination. In 1820, Zion withdrew from the predominantly white Methodist Episcopal Church and formed the African Methodist Episcopal Zion Conference denomination. Introducing black religious expression while catering to a growing population of black abolitionists, affiliate Zion churches sprang up, prompting the original church to distinguish itself as being the 'Mother' church.[29]

The National Baptist Convention, USA, Incorporated

The National Baptist Convention, USA, Incorporated[30] traces a history to Saturday, November 22, 1880 when 151 persons from 11 states met in Montgomery, Alabama and organized the Baptist Foreign Mission Convention. A yearning to see the gospel of Jesus Christ preached on the Mother Soil of Africa drove this organizing. The Rev. W.H. McAlpine of Alabama was elected as its first President. Six years later in 1886, 600 delegates from 17 states gathered at the First Baptist Church in St Louis, Missouri, and formed the National Baptist Convention of America. Seven years later in 1893, the National Baptist Education Convention was formed. None of the three Conventions thrived separately. So in 1895, the three bodies merged in a meeting held at the Friendship Baptist Church in Atlanta, Georgia. The Reverend E. C. Morris

---

[27] Lincoln and Mamiya, *The Black Church in the African American Experience*, 50-56.
[28] Lincoln and Mamiya, *The Black Church in the African American Experience*, 60-65.
[29] Lincoln and Mamiya, *The Black Church in the African American Experience*, 56-60.
[30] Lincoln and Mamiya, *The Black Church in the African American Experience*, 30-33.

from Little Rock, Arkansas, was chosen as the president of this merged body. Before 1895, nine men served as president of the Convention.

In 1897, during the Morris Administration, a group of National Baptist pastors left the convention and formed the Lott Carey Foreign Mission Convention. The separation was centred on two issues: the location of the foreign mission board and greater co-operation with White Baptists.

The second split, also during Morris' presidency, came in 1915 over ownership and operation of the Publishing Board. The Publishing Board was the most successful agency and was led by R. H. Boyd. Leaders and pastors of the Convention became suspicious of the actions of the Publishing Board when they did not receive the reports they thought due them. A debate ensued concerning the ownership. Those who supported Boyd and his view that the Board was independent of the Convention formed the National Baptist Convention of America.[31] It became known as the Unincorporated Convention (now National Baptist Convention of America, Inc.). Because of the question of incorporation, leaders who remained in the original Convention led a movement to incorporate their organization. The Constitution was amended in 1916 and the founding Convention was later incorporated, taking the name of National Baptist Convention, USA, Inc.

During the Joseph Jackson tenure, a third split occurred in the Convention. The two key issues were tenure and the lack of support of the civil rights movement. The Civil Rights Movement of the 1950s and 1960s, known for increased public activism, demonstrations and protests, was highly controversial in many Baptist churches. Often the ministers preached spiritual salvation rather than political activism. Venchael Booth formed a new Convention at the Zion Baptist Church, Cincinnati, Ohio in 1961. They named themselves as the Progressive (National) Baptist Convention.[32]

The National Missionary Baptist Convention of America (NMBCA) was formed during a meeting attended by Dr S.J. Gilbert, Sr, and Dr S.M. Wright, along with several leaders and members from the National Baptist Convention of America, Inc., and took place on November 14-15, 1988 at the People's Missionary Baptist Church, Incorporated, in Dallas, Texas.[33]

In 1992, Paul S. Morton of New Orleans, Louisiana, formed a fellowship within the convention. It was named the Full Gospel Baptist Church Fellowship. It explored spiritual gifts, speaking in tongues, prophecy, exclamatory worship, etc. The leadership of this fellowship later separated completely from the Convention.[34]

Historic Afro-American Churches and Missions in Africa

Finally, it is important to point out that each of these Historic Afro-American Churches has had historic missions to Africa and has found this work critical to their church identity. Each has their version of Foreign and Home Mission Boards, Women's Missionary Councils or Women's Auxiliaries that further this cause. This, in addition to the historic invitation of these churches to Africans to be students at Historic Black Colleges and Universities has been important. There have also been *Back to Africa* movements associated with these churches and outside these churches with a special emphasis on Liberia which was founded by such a movement and the USA government. Sierra Leone has also had a special link to these churches as well as South Africa. African slaves like George Liesle, David George, Hector Peters, and Samuel Calvert journeyed to Nova Scotia and Sierra Leone and thereby were some of the earliest African slave missionaries. Lott Carey was another famous African slave who was one of the earliest slave missionaries. Bishop Henry Turner of the AME Church encouraged mission work in Africa and Ema Delaney of the National Baptist

[31] Lincoln and Mamiya, *The Black Church in the African American Experience*, 33-36.
[32] Lincoln and Mamiya, *The Black Church in the African American Experience*, 36-39.
[33] www.nmbca.org/ Website.
[34] www.fullgospelbaptist.org/ Website.

made an impact. From 1790-1820 there were at least seventy Afro-Americans servings as missionaries to Africa.[35] Leonidas A. Johnson in her book, *The African American Church: Waking Up to God's Missionary Call*, states the following: 'The early African American missionaries believed that if Africans worshipped, obeyed and submitted to the true God and accepted the best of western culture, they would be able to control their own country, build their own nation and establish their own destiny.'[36]

By the 1800s, all the major Protestant denominations in the USA had stations in Africa and Afro-Americans were the missionaries of choice.[37] They were convinced that descendants of former Africans could better adapt to the environment and would be less likely to die of disease. The Historic Afro-American churches sent missionaries too. The golden age of Afro-American missionaries was 1890-1910 with 200 Afro-American missionaries serving in Africa and the West Indies (Caribbean).[38] By December 13-15, 1898, a mission conference[39] called the Congress on Africa was held at Gammon Theological Seminary, where the foreign mission work of the Historic Afro-American churches and Afro-Americans of the predominantly white denominations and their predominantly white leaders met in unity. It was held under the auspices of the Stewart Missionary Foundation for Africa in conjunction with the Cotton States and International Exposition.

As Europeans entered Africa, they found less use for Afro-Americans as missionaries in the predominantly white churches. They felt that Afro-Americans were unduly influenced by democracy as well as Pan African and *Back to Africa* movements of that time. There was a growing fear that they would encourage Africans to rebel against colonial authority. By the turn of the twentieth century, very few Afro-American missionaries were encouraged or sponsored to be missionaries in Africa by the predominantly white churches but the independent historic Afro-American churches continued and deepened their commitment. Afro-American missionaries that were sent by predominantly white churches were sent to places undesirable for white missionaries and settlers, and generally discouraged or prohibited to serve as missionaries in Africa. In sum, they were not treated equally. As the mission focus of the historic Afro-American churches has developed since then, the churches have integrated public policy advocacy as a form of mission priorities. Public policies like divestment in South Africa during the anti-apartheid struggle, calls for peace and reconciliation in Sudan, famine relief in Ethiopia, and today, support of the Africa Growth and Opportunities Act (AGOA) are examples of this.

Bibliography

Paisius Altschul, editor, *The Unbroken Circle* (St Louis, Missouri: Brotherhood of St Moses the Black, 1997)

Wesley Granberg-Michaelson, *From Times Square to Timbuktu: The Post-Christian West Meets the Non-Western Church* (Eerdmans Publishing Company: Grand Rapids, Michigan 2013)

Melville Herskovits, *The Myths of the Negro Past* (Boston: Beacon Press, 1958)

Leonidas A. Johnson, *The African American Church: Waking Up to God's Missionary Call* (Pasadena, California: William Carey Library 2006)

C. Eric Lincoln and Lawrence H. Mamiya, *The Black Church in the African American Experience* (Duke University Press: Durham and London, 1990)

Henry H. Mitchell, *Black Church: The Long-Hidden Realities of the first Years* (Grand Rapids, Michigan: Eerdmans Publishing Company 2004)

---

[35] Leonidas A. Johnson, *The African American Church: Waking Up to God's Missionary Call* (Pasadena, California: William Carey Library 2006), 19.

[36] Johnson, *The African American Church: Waking Up to God's Missionary Call*, 21.

[37] Johnson, *The African American Church: Waking Up to God's Missionary Call*, 19.

[38] Johnson, *The African American Church: Waking Up to God's Missionary Call*, 23.

[39] Prof. J.W.H. Bowen, *Africa and the American Negro* (Miami, Florida: Mnemosyne Publishing Inc. 1969 – First Found from Fisk University 1896 copy).

(13) African Christianity and African Diaspora Christianities outside the Continent

Afe Adogame

Introduction

On 20th May 2015, Nicolas Haque anchored the pathetic story of the 16-year-old Senegalese, Abdou, as he prepares for his perilous journey to Europe.[1] This was part of a prolonged Al Jazeera TV documentary *Desperate Journeys,* chronicling a series of woes, misery and catastrophe in which hundreds of thousands of Africans and other immigrants, hopeless but with sanguine expectations, were fleeing economic hardship, poverty, natural disasters, ethnic clashes, political oppression and unwarranted civil strife partly orchestrated by failing governments. By raising a loan of over US$3.000 to facilitate the journey organised by such agents within the migration industry, including people smugglers or human traffickers, Abdou's parents perceive their son's voyage to Europe as the only option left to salvaging family life and survival. On the fateful day that Abdou prepared to leave home, his father gave him his final words of advice and blessing with a rather brisk emotion: 'Throw your passport into the sea. Who you are doesn't matter in Europe. You are going there to work. Have faith in God. We love you.' With these brief admonitions and amid flowing tears of his parents, Abdou set out on his journey undaunted. His parent's counsel no doubt evokes some controversy arising from his sheer ignorance of life and work in Europe, his father's contentious disavowal of identity claims and dignity, an unbridled faith in God in the face of illegality and amorality, and the licentious display of desperation laced with equivocal tone of love.

Hardly a week now goes by without a 'breaking news story' of migrants, refugees, asylum-seekers from Africa or Asia drowned or rescued while trying to arrive on European shores. While it was reported that over 170,000 successfully landed in Italy in 2014 alone, at least 2,500 Africans are reported to have drowned in the Mediterranean Sea, January-April 2015. In actual fact, the numbers involved in the ongoing tragedy is staggering as no-one really knows how many people have drowned in the sea or died under harsh desert conditions. Within one week, 1,141 deaths were recorded.[2] So far, 2015 was increasingly marked by a horrific toll of hundreds of thousands of deaths by drowning in the Mediterranean Sea.[3] Historically, the Mediterranean, where Europe meets Africa and East meets West, has represented the theatre of encounters between peoples, cultures and systems. During the first decades of the 21st century, we increasingly witnessed in the Mediterranean a new encounter, both profound and dramatic, in the form of people on the move. Thus, the Mediterranean Sea has come to represent one major frontline in the

---

[1] For a full video transcript of the Al Jazeera news story, 'Desperate Journeys: Senegal Migrant Seeks better life in Europe' see: http://video.aljazeera.com/channels/eng/videos/senegal-migrant-seeks-better-life-in-europe/4246430493001.

[2] See for instance: Joe Mills, 'More than 400 people drown in Mediterranean Sea as ship carrying African migrants from Libya to Italy capsizes', April 14, 2015. Available online at: www.ibtimes.co.uk/more-400-people-drown-mediterranean-sea-ship-carrying-african-migrants-libya-italy-capsizes-1496416; Tom Kington, 'Another 41 African migrants drown making perilous crossing to Italy', April, 16, 2015; story available online at: www.latimes.com/world/europe/la-fg-italy-migrants-drowned-20150416-story.html and Patrick Kingsley, Alessandra Bonomolo and Stephanie Kirchgaessner, '700 migrants feared dead in Mediterranean shipwreck', Sunday 19 April 2015. Available online at: www.theguardian.com/world/2015/apr/19/700-migrants-feared-dead-mediterranean-shipwreck-worst-yet.

[3] See Dara Lind, '1,600 migrants have drowned in the Mediterranean this year. Europe refuses to fix the crisis', *Vox World*, 20 April, 2015. Available online at: www.vox.com/2015/4/20/8457719/mediterranean-migrant-shipwreck.

battlefield of irregular migration, where many poor, youthful, vulnerable and desperate migrants, including women and children, launch themselves on the path of tragic death in their struggle between life, survival and death. In most recent times, migrants and refugees fleeing Libya, Eritrea, Ethiopia, Somalia, Nigeria, Ghana, Mali and Senegal predominate.

I do not suggest that all immigrants are implicated in this dismal picture as that would mean simplifying the complex trajectories of African migration. Nor do African immigrants experience this precarious state only in the 'exodus from African shores'. Such contradictions are evident in internal migration within the continent itself. It is not only Europe that needs immigrants but does not want them,[4] the recurring politics of Afrophobia, xenophobic violence and hate-related incidences in South Africa[5] in April 2015, and earlier in 2008, vividly underscore the quandary immigrants now face within the theatre of international migration.

At the same time, the majority of Africans who migrate within the continent and to Europe are regular, skilled, legal, documented migrants arriving mostly through the airports and recruited into the labour force as nurses, doctors, engineers, IT specialists, sportsmen and women – or as students, diplomats, artists but also tourists. Through family reunions, many Africans have migrated to Europe. Most recently, some Africans have a mission task and have migrated or been sent by their home churches to Europe as missionaries.[6] However, we cannot deny that the African immigrant populations and African-led churches consist of those who also made it to Europe through irregular means. Migrants' travel can be clandestine through the travails of crossing the desert, sneaking onto boats and canoes, or concealment in trucks and lorries to beat the eagle-eyed surveillance of police border patrols and immigration officials. Other migrants have travelled by air and sea using other people's travel documents or using fake travel documents to exploit the ignorance of immigration entrepreneurs.

The causes and courses of the new migration are legion: economic, social, political, religious, historical, technological and more. The outcomes of a migration decision are often positive but too frequently disturbing and sometimes tragic. Zeleza[7] vividly demonstrates how the dynamics and direction of global mobility, and African participation in international migration, particularly in Western Europe and North America, has become more pronounced, notwithstanding the imposition of stringent immigration controls by these countries. The adoption of restrictive immigration policies and the regional policy harmonization has partially impeded the flow of legal immigrants and asylum-seekers, but also indirectly transformed illegal immigration.

The migration systems theory and the trans-national theory have become the preferred new analytical frameworks for understanding and contextualizing international migratory trends and processes.[8] Both theories, encapsulating several levels of analysis, account for the direction and texture of international migration as well as their complex dynamics. The basic principle of the migration systems theory is that any migratory movement can be seen as a result of interacting and intertwined macro-, meso- and micro-

---

[4] Andrew F. Walls, 'Mission and Migration: The Diaspora Factor in Christian History', *Journal of African Christian Thought*, Vol. 5/2 (December 2002), p. 10; and Adogame, Afe, *The African Christian Diaspora: New Currents and Emerging Trends in World Christianity*. London, New Delhi, New York and Sydney: Bloomsbury Academic, 2013, 182.

[5] See Cornish, Jean-Jacques. (2015). 'South Africa: Xenophobic Attacks Erupt in South Africa's Limpopo Province'. Available at: allafrica.com/stories/201503051136.html (accessed 14 April 2015); Wicks, J. (2015). 'KZN xenophobic violence spreads to KwaMashu'. Available at: www.news24.com/SouthAfrica/News/KZN-xenophobic-violence-spreads-to-KwaMashu-20150413 (accessed 14 April 2015); and Hans, B. (2015). 'King's anti-foreigner speech causes alarm'. Available at:www.iol.co.za/news/politics/king-s-anti-foreigner-speech-causes-alarm-1.1835602#.VSzaLPCROYM (accessed 14 April 2015).

[6] Adogame, Afe, *The African Christian Diaspora*, 2013.

[7] Paul Zeleza, 'Contemporary African Migrations in a Global Context', *African Issues*, XXX (1) 2002: 13.

[8] Adogame, *The African Christian Diaspora*, 2013, 6.

structures.[9] Crucial to our understanding of regular and irregular migration are the macro-structures – that is, the political economy of the world market, inter-state relationships, and the laws, structures and practices established by the states of sending and receiving countries to control migration settlement; the micro-structures embracing the networks, practices and beliefs of the migrants themselves; and the intermediate meso-structures, certain individuals, groups or institutions that take up a mediating role between migrants and political or economic institutions. The 'migration industry', including recruitment organizations, lawyers, agents, smugglers, NGOs, charitable bodies and other intermediaries that emerge, can be both helpers and exploiters of migrants. A further consideration of a new, emerging migrant population whose networks, activities and life-patterns encompass and transcend their home and host societies has produced a new body of theory on 'trans-nationalism' and 'trans-national communities'.[10] The trans-national theory in this regard captures migrants, their lives, experiences and consciousness as one that cuts across national boundaries and brings two (or more) societies into a single social field. Alejandro Portes[11] defines trans-national activities as those that take place on a recurrent basis across national borders and require a regular and significant commitment of time by participants.

The morality and politics of migration are among the most contested issues globally. However, the ethics of international migration is a relatively recent field of study in the robust literature on migration.[12] A burgeoning of the discourse on migration and ethics was witnessed in the 1970s, parallel to the globalization of migration and the increase in irregular migration during the period. Since the 1980s, following the pioneering works by Walzer[13] and Carens,[14] there has been an impressive development in ethical thinking in relation to international migration. Carens[15] illuminates one of the most pressing issues of our time: immigration poses practical problems for western democracies and also challenges the ways in which people in democracies think about citizenship and belonging, about rights and privileges, and about freedom and equality. The discourse about the ethics and morality of migration engender a realistic perspective that dwells on what is possible in the face of existing realities – and an idealistic approach that requires policy-makers to assess current reality in the light of a nation's highest ideals.[16] The investigation of ethics applied to migration concerns three areas: the right to migrate, the treatment of migrants, and the norms for a peaceful co-existence in increasingly pluralistic societies.[17] While borders are a fixed line of geography and sovereignty, they also connote ethical values. Immigration and admission do raise fundamental ethical questions. This is all the more the case at a time when restrictive migration policies lead to outcomes that are ethically or morally questionable.[18]

---

[9] Castles, Stephen and Mark Miller. *The Age of Migration: International Population Movements in the Modern World* (3rd ed.). New York: Guilford Press, 1993, 27-28.

[10] Basch, Linda, Glick-Schiller Nina and Blanc-Szanton Cristina (eds). *Nations Unbound. Transnational Projects, Postcolonial Predicaments, and Deterritorialized Nation-States*. New York: Gordon & Breach, 1994.

[11] Portes, Alejandro. 'Towards a New World – the Origins and Effects of Transnational Activities', *Ethnic and Racial Studies*, 22 (2) 1999. 464.

[12] Ricard Zapata-Barrero and Antoine Pécoud, 'New Perspectives on the Ethics of International Migration', *American Behavioral Scientist*, 56(9), 2012: 1159-1164; Zapata-Barrero, R., 'Theorizing state behaviour in international migrations: An evaluative ethical framework', *Social Research*, 77, 2010: 325-352; Christine Straehle and Patti T. Lenard, 'The Ethics of Migration: Introduction', *Journal of International Political Theory*, 8(1-2), 2012: 118-120.

[13] Walzer, M., *Spheres of Justice: A defense of pluralism and equality*. Oxford, UK: Robertson, 1983.

[14] Carens, J., 'Aliens and Citizens: The case for open borders. *Review of Politics*, 49, 1987: 251-273.

[15] Joseph H. Carens, *The Ethics of Migration*. Oxford: Oxford University Press, 2013.

[16] Ilse van Liempt and Veronica Bilger (eds) *The Ethics of Migration Research Methodology: Dealing with Vulnerable Immigrants*. Sussex: Sussex Academic Press, 2009.

[17] Graziano Battistella, 'The contributions of ethics to the management of migration', *Ciberteologia: Journal of Theology and Culture*, Issue 37, Year VIII, 2012.

[18] Parker, O., and Brassett, J., 'Contingent borders, ambiguous ethics: Migrants in (international) political theory', *International Studies Quarterly*, 49, 2005: 233-253.

The ethical discourse of migration is closely related to the theology of migration. Theologies of migration are emerging from and built around the lengthy duration of migration[19] – the home of origin as a point of departure, the transitory journey to El Dorado, the arrival at temporary and final destinations, the circumstances shaping their lived experiences of adaptation or resistance to integration, and even the imagination, illusory thoughts of return migration. William O'Neill draws biblical insights underlying the ethics of migration, focusing on three themes: the primacy of the love command, justice as covenant fidelity, and the virtue of hospitality.[20] He translates and interprets these themes for citizens of faith in a religiously pluralist polity. According to Donald Senior, 'The Christian gospel unfolds against the backdrop of exile and redemption – of Israel in Egypt and the infant Jesus in Egypt. Sharing this history of migration, the people of God, then and now, are called to particular care for the most vulnerable members of society, especially the immigrants.'[21] Christian hospitality to 'strangers and aliens' shaped the earliest understanding of disciples as fellow 'citizens with the saints' in the 'household of God' (Eph. 2:19). Hospitality is offered not only to kith and kin, but also to those whose only claim is vulnerability and need (Matt. 8:11; 22:1-14; Luke 14: 12-24). For citizens of faith, then, the urgency of basic human rights establishes the relative priority of migrants' rights as the touchstone of policy.[22]

The unwarranted waste of human bodies, mostly African immigrants desperate to cross the sea to Europe, marks an unprecedented watershed in the history and politics of regular or irregular migration to Europe. Most appalling is the somewhat international stolidity, lassitude and apathy of policy-makers and several stakeholders that has suffered many ignominies; an indifference that has perhaps encouraged the self-martyrdom and devaluing of human bodies on the Mediterranean Sea. African national governments, the African Union (AU),[23] the New Partnership for Africa's development (NEPAD), African religious institutions, the European Union (EU), European national governments, European churches and African-led churches in Europe to a greater or lesser degree, have conspired in a feat of political and socio-religious inaction, negligence and indifference that seem to further exacerbate the celerity of wasting human bodies both in desert lands and on the seas. Speaking from St Peter's Square, Pope Francis, an outspoken advocate for greater European-wide participation in rescue efforts, reiterated his call for action during mass one Sunday after learning of the latest disaster. He said, 'They are men and women like us – our brothers seeking a better life, starving, persecuted, wounded, exploited, victims of war.'[24] Besides the Vatican's voice, what is the role and position of the church in all these scenarios? It is scandalous that African and European churches are not seen to make significant public outcry and condemnation of this disaster nor call for rescue efforts.

The rest of the chapter will tease out whether, how and to what extent African-led churches in Europe are engaging (or not) in the politics of wasting bodies and unwanted migration and responding to the ethical dilemma that shapes EU immigration policies vis-à-vis their social relevance in Europe.

---

[19] Adogame, *The African Christian Diaspora*, 2013, 15.

[20] O'Neill, W., "No Longer Strangers" (Ephesians 2:19): The Ethics of Migration, *Word and World*, 29, 3, 2009: 227-233.

[21] Senior, D., "Beloved Aliens and Exiles" in Daniel G. Groody and Gioacchino Campese (eds) *A Promised Land, A Perilous Journey: Theological Perspectives on Migration*. Notre Dame, IN: University of Notre Dame Press, 2009, 23.

[22] O'Neill, "No Longer Strangers" (Ephesians 2:19): The Ethics of Migration, 231.

[23] It is beyond any imagination that the African Union waited for the loss of over 2,500 lives before tabling the issues of migration and xenophobia at their recent summit in June 2015. See: 'Migration and Xenophobia top AU Agenda at summit': http://ewn.co.za/2015/06/11/Migration-and-xenophobia-on-the-agenda-for-African-Executive-Council-meeting.

[24] See story at: www.theguardian.com/world/2015/apr/19/700-migrants-feared-dead-mediterranean-shipwreck-worst-yet.

The historiography of the new African Christian diaspora is located within recent trajectories of international migration, a dynamic process in which Africans are largely implicated as both actors and benefactors. They are not just passive recipients but active participants.

The literature of African-led churches in Europe has burgeoned since the 1980s.[25] However, not much attention has been given by scholars to the ethics and politics of African migration in Europe. How do churches in Africa and African-led churches in Europe encourage regular migration and discourage irregular ones? In what ways does regular or irregular migration impact on African Christians? How do African-led churches respond to the dehumanization, the unethical posture and policies of the EU towards African migrants? How do the religious communities engage in the discourses of identity, inclusion, exclusion and citizenship against the backlash of harsh anti-immigrant debates within the dwindling welfare economies of EU states? What methodological issues and ethical questions arise in research of irregular migration in Europe? We need a critical assessment and analysis of EU policies on irregular migration and how this may affect the place and status of African-led churches in Europe.

African Christian communities in the diaspora present a robust religious demography as they continue to mushroom across Europe. The explanations for their emergence, expansion and visibility are quintessential in understanding their spiritual worldviews and emerging theologies. As most of these religious communities are relatively new in Europe, having started within the last three decades, their evolving theologies emerge out of ongoing contestation between resilience, transformation and change. The very fluidity, insecurity and vulnerability of irregular and transit immigration affects the life, demography and mobility of African-led churches in Europe. The status of migrants are always in limbo, and susceptible to abuse, exploitation, xenophobia, deportation, incarceration, clandestine existence, and 'doing the jobs that many Europeans would normally not do'. Right-wing politics heightens the vulnerability of immigrants. The appalling experiences of African migrants in Europe shape their spirituality and theology. Before examining some of the ways in which the ethics and politics of migration affect African-led churches in Europe and how they respond, it is important to give a little flavour of EU immigration policies and the ethical dilemma it embodies.

EU Immigration Policies: An Ethical Dilemma

During the formative years of the EU in the 1950s and 1960s, immigrants were primarily an extra workforce in most Western European countries. Countries like France, Germany and the Netherlands used a permissive migration policy motivated by the need for extra labour.[26] By the late 1960s and 1970s, immigration was increasingly assuming a subject of public concern, thus marking a radical shift from the permissive immigration policy to a more control-oriented, restrictive policy. Political rhetoric increasingly linked migration with the destabilization of public order. Restrained immigration was beginning to take root all over Western Europe by the end of 1973, when labour recruiting was halted abruptly in the face of increasing social tensions and the fear of economic recession. In fact, the 'fortressization' of European immigration policy is linked with the 1973 economic recession.

A significant Europeanization of migration policy took off in the 1980s, when policy co-ordination became institutionalized in European inter-state co-operation. Since 1993, with the ratification of the Treaty of Maastricht, the European Community took a new turn. The Schengen Agreement which came into being in 1995 was a definite attempt towards harmonizing their immigration procedures and regulating flows of people. The EU set out the elements for a common EU immigration policy at the 1999 European

[25] For an extensive historiography of African-led churches in Europe and North America, see Adogame, *The African Christian Diaspora*, 2013.

[26] See Jef Huysmans, 'The European Union and the Securitization of Migration', *Journal of Common Market Studies*, vol. 38, Issue 5, 2000, 751-777.

Council in Tampere, Finland. Its adoption was confirmed by The Hague Programme in 2004. In the past three decades, EU member states moved towards further co-operation at the supranational level and introduced increasing numbers of regulations at the EU level on migration-related matters. The Europeanization of migration laws and policies is tied to wider social, political, economic and strategic dynamics. Thus, European integration process is implicated in the development of a restrictive migration and the social construction of migration into a security question.[27]

Over the past two decades, the EU not only developed a joint and coherent approach to migration but also increasingly integrated source and transit countries in its neighbourhood and beyond into its efforts. This policy is sometimes dubbed the internationalization, or externalization, of the EU's migration policy.[28] The EU and respective national governments are struggling to define attitudes and policies towards immigrants and immigration for the 21st century. This national, continental and global debate revolves surreptitiously around economic impacts and the legal status of individual or groups of immigrants more than the very welfare and well-being of migrants. EU immigration policies and strategies are hardly static or fixed. They mutate depending on the prevailing socio-political problems, national security questions, and most importantly economic needs and emergencies, especially the quest for sustained high-skilled manpower from foreign countries to complement an ageing, dwindling work force. As refugees are integral to international migration processes, legal rules on refugees constitute a significant part in the regulation of international migration.

Thus, the EU is vigorously protecting its external borders, notably against unwanted and irregular immigration. Considerable efforts are made and significant funds invested to enforce this goal.[29] Fences are erected, as in the Spanish enclaves of Ceuta and Melilla. Blue borders are patrolled by air and sea by coastguards and the navy, as in Spain, Italy, Malta and Greece. These operations are enforced by national forces but increasingly co-ordinated by the EU's border agency Frontex.[30] This focus on the external borders comes despite the fact that irregular migrants overwhelmingly enter EU territory legally and then overstay or work in breach of employment regulation.[31] Thus, the meaning attached to the security of external borders goes beyond the material. Indeed, it involves political principles, the integrity of borders, symbols, the sovereignty of the state, and the emotions and fears surrounding uncontrolled population movements.[32]

Some European national governments, such as the UK, seem to suggest that the best way to deal with the proliferation of irregular, unwanted migrants is to ignore their travails on the new frontline of migration, not to do anything by way of rescue amid the increasing loss of life on the seas and in the desert, nor accept any refugee quota – so as to serve as a natural deterrent and an acceptable way to discourage immigration. Thus, Britain has been reluctant to support a sustained EU search-and-rescue operation to preventing further mass drowning of migrants and refugees in the Mediterranean, claiming that it would contribute to more people dying needlessly on Europe's doorstep, and that it would simply encourage more people to attempt the dangerous sea crossing.[33] Ironically, the UK government stated, 'We do not support planned search-and-rescue operations in the Mediterranean; the government believed there was an unintended "pull factor", encouraging more migrants to attempt the dangerous sea crossing and thereby

[27] Ibid.
[28] Franck Düvell and Bastian Vollmer, 'Irregular Migration in and from the Neighbourhood of the EU. A comparison of Morocco, Turkey and Ukraine'. *European Commission, Clandestino*, September 2009. 5.
[29] Franck Düvell and Bastian Vollmer, 5.
[30] See Frontex, *Interceptions at EU land and sea borders during 2008*. Warsaw: Frontex, 2009.
[31] Franck Düvell, 'Paths into irregularity. The Legal and Political construction of irregular migration', *European Journal of Migration and Law*, 13, 2011, 275-295.
[32] Franck Düvell and Bastian Vollmer, 5.
[33] See Alan Travis, 'UK axes support for Mediterranean migrant rescue operation'. The *Guardian*, Monday 27 October 2014.

leading to more tragic and unnecessary deaths. The government believes the most effective way to prevent refugees and migrants attempting this dangerous crossing is to focus our attention on countries of origin and transit, as well as taking steps to fight the people smugglers who wilfully put lives at risk by packing migrants into unseaworthy boats.'[34] The British refusal came to light as the official Italian search-and-rescue operation, Mare Nostrum, was due to come to an end after contributing for over twelve months to the rescue of an estimated 150,000 people since the Lampedusa tragedies in which 500 migrants died in October 2013. Despite these efforts, more than 2,500 people are known to have drowned or gone missing in the Mediterranean in 2014 alone.

Africa appears to be the continent that matters most to EU policy-makers working on migration. The prevailing perspective of the EU concerning African migration is still focussed mainly on security and prevention. The politicization of immigration has attained an alarming proportion in which immigrants and asylum-seekers are portrayed as a challenge to the protection of national identity and welfare provisions. Thus, one main focus of the European Commission and of European Council policies and meetings has been to counter the entry of illegal migrants through EU's southern and eastern borders. The security shift in EU migration policy contradicts the so-called global approach to migration. Also witnessed is the externalisation of border controls, in which countries close to European coastlines (Morocco, Algeria, Tunisia, Libya and Turkey) have been encouraged to co-operate on specific security issues, including border management and readmission agreements. The adoption of rigid and uniform EU immigration laws has turned the coasts of southern Italy and Spain into important points of entry into continental Europe, notwithstanding the 'securitization' of migration and externalization of border controls. One consequence is that it is increasingly transforming and translating Europe into a 'fortress'.

Ethical Politics of Migration and African-led Churches in Europe

The uncertainty described above no doubt has implications for immigrants, the migratory process but also for religious communities such as African-led churches that are dominated by both regular and irregular migrants. It is within these ecologies of migration that we better understand the relevance and resilience of religion within the African immigrant and diaspora communities. These developments raise the ethics and theology of migration, both in the unethical posture of the EU towards vulnerable regular or irregular and transit immigrants, their sometimes inhuman treatment at the hands of security operatives and immigration personnel, and their maltreatment and exploitation at the hands of people smugglers, sex traffickers and all those who profit from the booming migration industry in human bodies – men, women and children. The attitude of EU countries has varied from silence, ignoring them as they drown and die, to debates of how to rescue them and give them temporary shelter, and how to deal with the people smugglers.

The 'august' visit of British Prime Minister, David Cameron to the Redeemed Christian Church of God (RCCG) Festival of Life event in April 2015, on the eve of the UK parliamentary election, best epitomizes the ambivalent stance of Tory politicians on immigration. Cameron seems to have turned into a temporary pastor-prophet while giving a disguised manifesto speech at the event. Cameron enthused and I will quote generously here:

> I want to thank you, Pastor Agu, and I'd like to thank Pastor Adeboye too – thank you, Daddy G.O. (General Overseer). It is an honour to be here, and I'm proud of this festival which started as a camp just off the Lagos expressway and set the world alight. It is now a permanent fixture here in London and I'm delighted it's getting bigger and it's getting better every year. Now, I have to say I don't envy the organisers of tonight: it must be like

[34] Lady Anelay, former Foreign Office Minister spelled out British policy in the House of Lords. See: The *Guardian*, Monday 27 October 2014.

the feeding of the five thousand, except I can see you – you are forty five thousand. You must be relieved that it's just spiritual food on the menu tonight.

Now, I remember when my good friend Boris Johnson came here to the Festival of Life a few years ago, he made some comments on the subject of aspiration. He said he believed in aspiration, and he looked out into this huge crowd and he said he knew someone would now be out there who would follow in his footsteps. Someone who would one day become Mayor of this great city of London. Well, I would go further. I believe in aspiration; I believe the only limit to someone's potential is their own ambition and talent, and I look out into this crowd and I can see someone who will hold my role and become Prime Minister of this great country… Now, for me, tonight is about one thing. It's about family. You're here with your own family: parents and children, siblings and cousins, aunts and uncles. You're united with your spiritual family; old friends, dear friends, people you've known for many years, and together we are all part of one family. As Jesus said, with his arms outstretched to his disciples, 'Here are my mother and my brothers, for whoever does the will of my Father in heaven, is my brother, my sister and my mother' – and that is what we are. As God's children, we are all one big family. Now when I was a child, I had a very specific image of what a church was. I thought: to be a church, it had to be an old grey building with a slate roof and a big spire. That it had to have pews and a pulpit, and a graveyard where the naughty boys would play hide-and-seek; but I was wrong and you proved that. You proved that church is people, church is a family, and it doesn't matter what the roof is made of because, with your energy, your devotion, your love of Jesus Christ, you raised that roof every time. Now your dedication to family – your family in blood and your family in humanity – it goes way beyond this room. I think of how many ways you love your neighbour. With care for those who are sick and lonely, with mentoring for teenagers who think they have no hope, with fund-raising for hospices, for looked-after children, for those suffering unimaginable trauma overseas. Like Jesus turning water into wine, you turn loneliness into companionship, you turn deprivation into comfort, and you turn lost lives into lives with purpose.

For years I have tried to explain to people what the 'Big Society' is. Some people were determined not to understand it. Well, I should have brought them here to the Festival of Life because this is the 'Big Society' in action, and it's as vibrant and as loud and as powerful as ever. Now, just think how great our country Britain could be if we built on that, if we had an even bigger 'Big Society' where even more people shared your family values. Values of prudence, of hard work, of looking out for those who fall on hard times. With these values, we can achieve the Britain we all want to live in. Where the oppressed are cared for, where the lonely are befriended, where it's not where you come from but it's the content of your character that really matters. Tonight, let us be proud that this is a Christian country where we stand for the freedom to practise your faith and where we stand up for Christians and all those who are persecuted anywhere in our world; they are family too. A year ago this week, 276 Nigerian schoolgirls were cruelly snatched by Boko Haram. I am a father of two young daughters, Florence and Nancy, and I have an understanding of what it's like to lose a child in tragic circumstances. So my prayer tonight is that those girls will be found soon and there will be peace in Nigeria. So thank you once again for having me here tonight with you. Thank you once again to the great Pastor Daddy G.O. Thank you to Pastor Agu and your team: thank you for what you do, thank you for making the Festival of Life such a great British tradition. So let us tonight join with our brothers and sisters here. Let us pledge to make this 'Big Society' bigger. Let us pledge to make our great country better. Let us make this Festival of Life even better, even louder and even prouder next year. Thank you and goodnight.[35]

I would need another essay to unpack the themes and threads that such a speech encumbers, yet it is ironic that the Prime Minister was speaking to a mixed audience of over 45,000 worshippers, many of whom are probably irregular or undocumented migrants. How is it that the same man who spoke very

[35] For a full transcript of Prime Minister Cameron's speech at the RCCG, Festival of Life, London, see: https://www.youtube.com/watch?v=Nt-hB1ROjjg

passionately about building a 'Big Family' and 'Big Society' – including migrants, refugees in Britain – is the same one whose government prefers immigrants to drown on the seas with reckless abandon? He leads a government that refuses to take in refugees in the EU's temporary measure to provide shelter for immigrants and refugees rescued from the Mediterranean Sea. Is it a coincidence that Cameron visited an African church event on the eve of the UK parliamentary election? The General Overseer of RCCG, Enoch Adeboye, who was attending the event from Nigeria, seized the opportunity to offer prayers for the Prime Minister. He prayed:

> Will you please stretch your hands to our Prime Minister and together pray that the Almighty God will give him wisdom – the Wisdom of Solomon. God will give him the courage of David so that, in his days and in our days, Great Britain will be great again. Let's pray together. Pray that God will grant him divine wisdom, courage, strength and special anointing from heaven. So that, in his days and in our days, Great Britain will be great again. That the entire glory of this nation will be fully restored. That there be revival in this land. So, Father Almighty, we want to thank you for our Prime Minister. Your Word says that we are to pray for those who are in authority. So in obedience, Lord, to Your commandment, we pray that you will give our Prime Minister divine wisdom, divine enablement and divine courage. So that he will rule this nation aright. That during his time and during our own days, Great Britain will be great again. Father, you are the burden-bearer, help him to carry his burdens. Please bless him, bless his family and, Lord God Almighty, bless the United Kingdom. In Jesus' mighty name we have prayed. Amen.

Tactically, neither the Prime Minister nor the General Overseer made any mention of the election that was a few days ahead. One might guess that Cameron obviously recognized this religious community as a voting constituency at a time of uncertainty of his re-election as Prime Minister. The fact that he won the election could be reinterpreted by some church members as an answer to prayers rendered during the visit. Much more striking is the fact that the Prime Minister's visit is indicative of the potentially civic relevance that African-led churches have come to assume in the UK. Some churches are playing a civic role to cushion hardships, frustration and uncertainties faced by immigrants against the backdrop of public narratives of identity and belonging. The physical, emotional and psychological trauma that many African immigrants undergo under dastardly circumstances explains why African-led churches have assumed an abode of security and community. It is within these scenarios of uncertainty, insecurity, the shattered hopes and forlorn dreams of migrants that the church appears to fill a vacuum.

The role and place of African-led churches as spiritual vacuum-fillers, as areas for socialization, and as engines for social, religious (spiritual) and capital formation, are noteworthy. African-led churches in Europe, in a limited sense, help to cushion the pains and strains of unemployment by serving both as employers and as channels of information for job opportunities at both the formal and informal economic sub-sectors of society. Some are involved in the provision of spiritual and social services, thus transforming church premises as both religious (spiritual) and social centres, where both religious rituals and non-religious activities can take place contemporaneously.

Both regular and irregular migrants employ religious resources and appropriate religious rituals through the different stages of the migration process. The role of religious and spiritual specialists such as Christian pastors, prophets and prophetesses underscore the centrality of prophecy, divination and spiritual armament in the preparatory stages of the journey. Prospective migrants and their families patronize sacred and religious sites, shrines, prayer camps and religious events to fortify themselves against the machinations of witches, sorcerers, the evil eye, envious family relatives and friends. The religious impulse and experiences encountered in the preparation and take-off stage of the potential immigrant or traveller has consequences for the journey itself, but also implications for the latter stages of the immigration process as well as their settlement. 'The immigrant condition is riddled with hope, hardship, broken dreams, and measures of success. Immigrant Christianity serves as a balm in the entire process, ranging from why and how the immigrants came to their new countries, to how they cope in the new homeland. The journey begins with prayers in Pentecostal churches and prayer camps for travel visas, to prayers in immigrant churches for everyday survival needs such as working permits, employment, and money for rent mortgage, health insurance and other bills. There is also the added pressure to accumulate money and goods to transfer home.'[36]

The lived experiences of African Christian immigrants and refugees shape their spiritual, religious lives, just as theologies are constructed from these experiences and the reservoir of indigenous religious worldviews retained by them in their 'new homes'. The ways in which immigrants' experiences shape their religious lives, and in which their spiritualities speak to and condition their day-to-day experiences and expressions, is illuminated by their narratives partly woven 'between and betwixt' themes of survival and security, adaptation and mobility. Such narratives are verbal contestations of a growing 'fortressization' of Europe characterized by the adoption of stringent, restrictive immigration policies. Immigrants' actions are to be understood in terms of their own goals, strategies established first in order to survive, and after that, to adapt or not to adapt to the new social milieu. There is a certain link between theology of hope and theology of empowerment in the diaspora.

Bibliography

Adogame, Afe, *The African Christian Diaspora: New Currents and Emerging Trends in World Christianity*. London, New Delhi, New York and Sydney: Bloomsbury Academic, 2013.

Al Jazeera news story: 'Desperate Journeys: Senegal Migrant Seeks better life in Europe': http://video.aljazeera.com/channels/eng/videos/senegal-migrant-seeks-better-life-in-europe/4246430493001(accessed 14th April 2015).

Anelay, Lady, 'Former Foreign Office Minister spelled out British policy in the House of Lords', in *The Guardian*, 27th October 2014.

Basch, Linda, Nina Glick-Schiller and Cristina Blanc-Szanton (eds), *Nations Unbound: Transnational Projects, Postcolonial Predicaments, and Deterritorialized Nation-States*. New York: Gordon & Breach, 1994.

Battistella, Graziano, 'The contributions of ethics to the management of migration', in *Ciberteologia: Journal of Theology and Culture*, 37 (2012): 346-376.

Cameron, David, 'The Prime Minister of Great Britain RT Hon David Cameron at RCCG Festival of Life, London, April 2015': https://www.youtube.com/watch?v=Nt-hB1ROjjg (accessed 14th April 2015).

Carens, J., 'Aliens and Citizens: The case for open borders', in *Review of Politics*, 49 (1987): 251-73.

Carens, Joseph H., *The Ethics of Migration*. Oxford: OUP, 2013.

Castles, Stephen and Mark Miller, *The Age of Migration: International Population Movements in the Modern World* (3rd edition). New York: Guilford Press, 1993.

Cornish, Jean-Jacques, 'South Africa: Xenophobic Attacks Erupt in South Africa's Limpopo Province': allafrica.com/stories/201503051136.html (accessed 14th April 2015).

Düvell, Franck and Bastian Vollmer, 'Irregular Migration in and from the Neighbourhood of the EU: A comparison of Morocco, Turkey and Ukraine', in *European Commission, Clandestino*, September 2009.

Düvell, Franck, 'Paths into irregularity: The Legal and Political construction of irregular migration', in *European Journal of Migration and Law*, 13 (2011): 275-95.

Hans, B., 'King's anti-foreigner speech causes alarm': www.iol.co.za/news/politics/king-s-anti-foreigner-speech-causes-alarm-1.1835602#.VSzaLPCROYM (accessed 14th April 2015).

Huysmans, Jef, 'The European Union and the Securitization of Migration', in *Journal of Common Market Studies*, 38, Issue 5 (2000): 751-77.

[36] Ogbu Kalu, *African Pentecostalism. An Introduction*. Cambridge: CUP. 2008, 282.

Kalu, Ogbu, *African Pentecostalism: An Introduction*. Cambridge: CUP, 2008.
Kingsley, Patrick, Alessandra Bonomolo and Stephanie Kirchgaessner, '700 migrants feared dead in Mediterranean shipwreck', in *The Guardian*, 19th April 2015: www.theguardian.com/world/2015/apr/19/ 700-migrants-feared-dead-mediterranean-shipwreck-worst-yet (accessed 14th April 2015).
Kington, Tom, 'Another 41 African migrants drown making perilous crossing to Italy', in *Los Angeles Times*, 16th April 2015: www.latimes.com/world/europe/la-fg-italy-migrants-drowned-20150416-story.html (accessed 14th April 2015).
Lind, Dara, '1,600 migrants have drowned in the Mediterranean this year. Europe refuses to fix the crisis', in *Vox World*: www.vox.com/2015/4/20/8457719/mediterranean-migrant-shipwreck (accessed 14th April 2015).
Mills, Joe, 'More than 400 people drown in Mediterranean Sea as ship carrying African migrants from Libya to Italy capsizes', in *International Business Times*, 14th April 2015: www.ibtimes.co.uk/more-400-people-drown-mediterranean-sea-ship-carrying-african-migrants-libya-italy-capsizes-1496416 (accessed 14th April 2015).
O'Neill, W., '"No Longer Strangers" (Ephesians 2:19): The Ethics of Migration', in *Word and World*, 29:3 (2009): 227-33.
Parker, O. and J. Brassett, 'Contingent borders, ambiguous ethics: Migrants in (international) political theory', in *International Studies Quarterly*, 49 (2005): 233-53.
Paul Zeleza, 'Contemporary African Migrations in a Global Context', in *African Issues*, Vol. XXX, No.1 (2002): 9-14.
Portes, Alejandro, 'Towards a New World – the Origins and Effects of Transnational Activities', in *Ethnic and Racial Studies*, 22, No.2 (1999): 463-77.
Senior, D., 'Beloved Aliens and Exiles', in Daniel G. Groody and Gioacchino Campese (eds), *A Promised Land, A Perilous Journey: Theological Perspectives on Migration*. Notre Dame, IN: University of Notre Dame Press, 2009.
Straehle, Christine and Patti T. Lenard, 'The Ethics of Migration: Introduction', in *Journal of International Political Theory*, 8:1-2 (2012), 118-20.
Travis, Alan, 'UK axes support for Mediterranean migrant rescue operation', in The *Guardian*, 27th October 2014.
van Liempt, Ilse and Veronica Bilger (eds), *The Ethics of Migration Research Methodology: Dealing with Vulnerable Immigrants*. Eastbourne, UK: Sussex Academic Press, 2009.
Walls, Andrew F., 'Mission and Migration: The Diaspora Factor in Christian History', in *Journal of African Christian Thought*, 5:2 (December 2002): 3-11.
Walzer, M., Spheres of Justice: A Defense of Pluralism and Equality. Oxford: Robertson, 1983.
Wicks, J., 'KZN xenophobic violence spreads to KwaMashu': www.news24.com/ SouthAfrica/News/KZN-xenophobic-violence-spreads-to-KwaMashu-20150413 (accessed 14th April 2015).
Zapata-Barrero, R., 'Theorizing state behaviour in international migrations: An evaluative ethical framework', in *Social Research*, 77 (2010): 325-52.
Zapata-Barrero, Ricard and Antoine Pécoud, 'New Perspectives on the Ethics of International Migration', in *American Behavioral Scientist*, 56:9 (2012): 1159-64.

(14) Mission Migration and African Diaspora inside the Continent

Asonzeh Ukah

The most profound and far-reaching social change in Africa in the last 150 years has been religious in nature; it is the conversion of Africans from indigenous religious practices and beliefs to Christianity and Islam. From being the continent with 7% or less of Christians in 1900, nearly one-half of the population of contemporary Africa is Christian. This transformation has radical consequences for politics, economics and social structure. Conversion to Christianity is not merely a change in the system of beliefs, ritual practice, meaning and symbols, but also the emergence of a new social force and structure that influences other aspects of societal formations.[1] Migration is at the heart of the increased religious and cultural transformation taking place in Africa. In the history of Christianity, migration played a pivotal role in its expansion.[2] In sub-Saharan Africa, European migration from the fifteenth to the mid-nineteenth century permanently altered the face and practice of Christianity;[3] through this interaction, Africans became not just Christians, but also Christian missionaries themselves. From Christianity's nascent beginnings to contemporary times, Africans have played, and continue to play, a very active role in the spread and cultural articulation of the religion. The Acts of the Apostles (ch. 2) records that Africans were present during Peter's epoch-making speech on the day of Pentecost; African Church Fathers were active in defining and articulating nascent Christian doctrines as well as combating heresies in the first four hundred years of the church. The emphasis on the contribution of Africa and Africans in the formative years of the New Testament canon as well as the New Testament church is rather a recent phenomenon.[4] Furthermore, during the European missionaries' era, particularly from the fifteenth to the nineteenth centuries – a period that parallels European imperialism and conquering colonialism[5] – African porters, translators, guides, catechists and go-betweens were prominent in the many attempts to introduce Christianity in sub-Saharan Africa.[6] During the nineteenth century specifically, Africans – either as returnee ex-slaves or local chiefs – were active in redefining the religious landscape of sub-Saharan Africa through facilitating the conversion processes of their kith and kin. Often, however, their efforts were ignored or deliberately erased from the records, which were ostensibly written and kept by Euro-American missionaries and colonial agents who were eager to report their success to their funders and home audiences. With the emergence of African-

---

[1] Martin Lindhardt, "Introduction: Presence and Impact of Pentecostal/Charismatic Christianity in Africa", in Martin Lindhardt (ed), *Pentecostalism in Africa: Presence and Impact of Pneumatic Christianity in Postcolonial Societies* (Leiden: Brill, 2015), 1-2.

[2] David Chidester, *Christianity: A Global History* (New York: Harper, San Francisco Publishers, 2000).

[3] Coptic and Orthodox Christianity in Egypt, Ethiopia and parts of Sudan (North east Africa) are older than missionary Christianity in sub-Saharan Africa. According to Dyron B. Daughrity, "About one out of ten Christians in Africa is Orthodox". European migration and missionary enterprise are not implicated in this earlier and older strand of Christianity in Africa (See Dyron B. Daughrity, "Ignoring the East: Correcting a Serious Flaw in World Christianity Scholarship", in Afe Adogame and Shobana Shankar (eds), *Religion on the Move! New Dynamics of Religious Expansion in a Globalising World* (Leiden: Brill, 2013), 41.

[4] David Tuesday Adamo, *African and Africans in the New Testament* (Lanham, Maryland: University Press of America. Inc. 2006).

[5] V.Y. Mudimbe and Susan Mbula Kilonzo describe "three different Christianities" in Africa as Apostolic, Imperial and Colonial as corresponding to "ways of figuring the epochs of religious growth" in Africa. To these three, can add two more, namely, African Indigenous Christianity and African Pentecostal-charismatic Christianity. (see V.Y. Mudimbe and Susan Mbula Kilonzo, "Philosophy of Religion on African Ways of Believing" in Elias Kifon Bongmba (ed), *The Wiley-Blackwell Companion to African Religions* (West Sussex: Wiley-Blackwell Publishers, 2012), 42.

[6] Kirsten Rüther, "Conversion to Christianity in African History before Colonial Modernity: Power, Intermediaries and Texts", *The Medieval History Journal* 12/2 (2009): 263.

Initiated Churches (AICs)[7] from the 1880s, Africans have taken the task of enculturating, interpreting, appropriating and spreading the gospel very seriously. African prophets and evangelists were at the heart of the mass revivals that swept through much of sub-Saharan Africa from West Africa to East Africa and to Southern Africa. Many of the popular movements and revivals initiated by these religious personalities still flourish, for example, in the Aladura Christian movements of West Africa[8] as well as the Zionist movements of Southern Africa.[9] These movements not only established popular mass religious trends that were trans-national in spread and appeal, but have supplied innovative, culturally relevant, doctrinal (re)interpretations that resonate with local needs and the demands of the rapidly changing social and economic circumstances of African members. The consensus of scholars is that Christian mission in Africa spread faster after independence than before, mainly through indigenous agencies. Africans have remained in the crux of the transmission and translation of the Christian message to their fellow Africans. The dynamic is still evident in the internal and intensifying migratory processes in Africa, following political, social and economic globalisation trends.

In contemporary times, and in the context of the revolutionary and dizzying popularity and runaway explosion of Pentecostal and charismatic churches and ministries, Africans are pioneering the re-evangelisation of the African continent and are actively recording their stories in their own words and deeds. Migration has a missionary component to it; and, in the context of Africa, it is a primary pathway for spreading Christianity. Christian mission is a multifaceted enterprise involving the spread and dissemination of the message of Christ's resurrection and the power therein, the expansion of the reign and kingdom of God,[10] and the conversion of non-Christians into the sphere of influence of this kingdom; mission also involves the planting of churches as the structure and context of Christian assembly and action.[11] Christian mission encapsulates coverage ('Go into all the world and proclaim the good news to the whole creation', Mark 16:15 NRSV),[12] conversion ('Go therefore and make disciples of all nations, baptizing them in the name of the Father and of the Son and of the Holy Spirit', Matt. 28:19), and congregation ('... you are Peter, and on this rock I will build my church, and the gates of Hades will not prevail against it', Matt. 16:18).

If mission means moving outwards with the intention of cultivating the gospel message where it is non-existent, migrants are especially well placed to carry out this task. In recent decades and in many African urban centres, the dynamism of migrant-driven Christian missions has achieved prominence. African migrants are the primary vectors of this energised movement of reappropriating and recontextualising Christianity in Africa during a rapidly changing – and confusing – era. Migrant missions are a central element in the processes of urbanisation in Africa.[13] As globalisation and neo-liberal capitalism spread their tentacles into the deep recesses of the continent, migrants have criss-crossed borders, often at great

[7] The "I" in AICs may also stand for Independent/Instituted/Indigenous.

[8] JDY Peel, Aladura: *A Religious Movement among the Yoruba* (London: Oxford University Press, 1968); Robert Cameron Mitchell, "Religious Change and Modernization: The Aladura Churches among the Yoruba in Southwestern Nigeria", PhD dissertation, Department of Sociology, Northwestern University (1970).

[9] Bengt G. M. Sundkler, *Bantu Prophets in South Africa*, 2nd ed. (London: Oxford University Press, 1961); David Chidester, *Christianity*, 412-433.

[10] According to David Chidester, the followers of Jesus the carpenter remembered him on three important scores, as i) a teacher of wisdom, ii) a worker of wonders, and iii) a preacher of the Kingdom of God (Chidester, *Christianity*, 14-27).

[11] Jerry Pilley, 2010. "Theological Foundations of Mission", in *Mission Continues: Global Impulse for the 21st Century*, eds. Claudia Währisch-Oblau and Fidon Mwombeki (Oxford: Regnum Books International, 2010): 11.

[12] All Bible citations come from the New Revised Standard Version, Division of Christian Education of the National Council of the Churches of Christ in the United States of America, 1989.

[13] Attempts at accounting for the changes taking place in African urban life and culture without factoring in how migrant religious organisations are irreversibly contributing to this change is only telling half the story.

personal risk, carrying with them their religious traditions and modifying these according to the political economy of their host societies. The increase in migratory processes within Africa in the late twentieth and early 21st centuries has resulted in the movement of peoples, goods, ideas and capital from one part of Africa to another. Even though there is relatively little ease in such movement – as political regulation tightens and the national borders in Africa are increasingly becoming, literally, fortresses – Africans devise means and methods in seeking for better working and living opportunities in different parts of the continent. The majority of African migrants live in other African countries; this is particularly so for western and eastern Africans, followed by central Africans. Although there are discrepancies about numbers and hard figures are rarely available now, more than fifty million Africans live in African countries different from their home countries.[14] African nations are, therefore, the largest sending nations of migrants to other African countries. The result of this is that Africans remain the largest source of migrant flow, labour as well as innovation within Africa. The two major dynamics of migrant flows – voluntary and forced – in Africa have consequences for the transformation of urban demographics, economic growth and religious and cultural ecology. Recent studies are unanimous that migration 'induces important transfers of political, cultural, sociological or behavioural norms and values between countries'.[15] In Africa, religion is *the* primary source of 'behavioural norms and values'. While the poor are the least likely to migrate, migration processes seem to embrace all classes of citizens in any African nation; when not driven by catastrophes such as wars, droughts and conflicts, the engine of migration is the desire to improve livelihoods either through better-paying jobs or through access to education. In some cases, however, religion is an important impetus for migration. Religion-driven migration induces significant culture and value transfers among African countries. This pattern is most evident in migrant-founded and -headed religious organisations. In recent years in many African countries, migrants are the most visible vectors of Christian mission where they have settled. The Nigerian diasporas within Africa illustrate this sociological fact very clearly.

Pentecostal Migrant Missions in Africa: The Nigerian Impact

Among pronounced characterisations of African migrants, founding churches is indeed a prominent and recurring one. Migrant-led Pentecostal missions have received scholarly attention in literature, particularly in Europe and North America.[16] The spread of African-initiated missions elsewhere in Africa is a strong indication of the strength and deep rootedness of African Christianity as well as its trans-local and trans-border character. However, African missions founded in other African countries have received only limited attention. What needs emphasising is the role a diverse array of internal migrants – Africans living in African countries other than their country of citizenship – play in the spread and transformation of contemporary forms of Christianity on the continent. Migrant missions not only create visible Christian

---

[14] Richard Black and others: *Migration & Development in Africa: An Overview* (Southern African Migration Project, 2006); Michael J. White "The demographic impact of migration: Evidence from Africa", UN Expert Group Meeting 3 Dec 2012 www.un.org/en/development/desa/population/migration/events/expertgroup/2012/docs/Demographic%20impact%20migration%20MJW%20UN%203Dec2012%20rev1_SH.pdf (Accessed 20.12.2014).

[15] F. Docquier, Ch. Vasilakis and D. Tamfutu Munsi, "International Migration and the Propagation of HIV in sub-Saharan Africa", *Journal of Health Economics*, vol. 35 (2014): 20.

[16] Abel Ugba, *Shades of Belonging: African Pentecostals in Twenty-First Century Ireland* (Trenton, NJ: Africa World Press 2009); Asonzeh Ukah, 2009. "Reverse Mission or Asylum Christianity? African Christian Churches in Britain", in *Africans and the Politics of Popular Cultures*, eds, Toyin Falola and Augustine Agwuele (Rochester: University of Rochester Press, 2009): 104-132; Frieder Ludwig and J. Kwabena Asamoah-Gyadu (eds) *African Christian Presence in the West: New Immigrant Congregations and Transnational Networks in North America and Europe* (Trenton, NJ: Africa World Press 2011).

communities; they also introduce innovative organisational and liturgical styles. These institutions are responsible for creating a trans-cultural religious lifestyle. Because of the global or universal outlook of Pentecostal Christianity, its activities in Africa since the late twentieth century have come with an intense missionary impetus. For many Pentecostal Christians, the first and most urgent duty of a born-again Christian is to bring others into the church of Christ. Mission has become a privileged responsibility of, not specialists, but the lay Christian who must 'always be ready to make your defence to anyone who demands from you an accounting for the hope that is in you' (1 Pet. 3: 15b-16).

African migrants to other African countries, whether displaced by communal or political strife, or by voluntary relocation, mobilise religious resources as a sure means of settling and integrating into their host societies. Recent studies indicate, for example, that refugee churches founded by the Congolese in South Africa are a formidable institution of cultural and religious life of the Congolese community in the country; they are more integrative of the refugee community than other local churches. Leaders in the refugee community address refugees' spiritual and material needs, speaking the same language and understanding the cultural context within which refugees live.[17] Similarly, Nigerian migrants in other African countries have been in the forefront of planting churches in the societies in which they live. International migration flows in Nigeria date from as far back as 1903. In the last forty years, however, multiple patterns of migration flows have been intensified by a set of diverse factors such as ease of travel, a vibrant diaspora culture, economic and political instability at home, and the search for higher education. It is estimated that, in addition to more than ten million Nigerians living as migrants in other African countries, there are 1.6 million other Nigerians living as refugees and internally displaced persons in foreign lands.[18]

Between 1996 and 2005, 14,107 Nigerians sought asylum in South Africa. Irrespective of the sibling rivalry that goes on between Nigeria and Ghana, there are over a million Nigerian nationals (and those holding dual citizenship) living and working in Ghana. In Cameroon, it is also estimated that about four million Nigerian nationals live there engaged in a variety of occupations, one of which is running religious organisations. The majority of Nigerians living and working elsewhere in Africa is Christian by religious affiliation and constitutes a formidable mission sector or means for the spread of Christianity.[19] They fan out in all directions, like the celebrated 'onward Christian soldiers', carrying with them their entrepreneurial spirit and mixing it with religious faith and enthusiasm. In addition to their known traits of being hard-working and possessing a great deal of entrepreneurial acumen, Nigerians are in the business of setting up churches, ministries and other similar religious and cultural sociabilities. In some African countries such as Liberia and South Africa, Nigerian-owned churches are some of the largest and most zealous religious organisations. The influence of Nigeria in the area of Christian mission is twofold: first, Nigerian migrants living and working in other African countries spread Christianity through building up local Christian communities; second, nationals of other African countries travel in droves to Nigeria in search of spiritual and religious support such as healing, salvation and miracles. Lagos in Nigeria has become a Christian pilgrimage centre for many citizens of other African countries such as Zambia, Lesotho

---

[17] Vedaste Nzayabino, "The Role of Refugee Established Churches in the Lives of Forced Migrants: A Case Study of Word of Life Assembly in Yeoville, Johannesburg", MA dissertation, Faculty of Arts, University of Witwatersrand, Johannesburg (2005); "Rethinking the Impact of the Church on the Dynamics of Integration of Congolese Migrants in Johannesburg: A Case Study of Yahweh Shammah Assembly", PhD. Dissertation, Faculty of humanities, University of the Witwatersrand, Johannesburg, South Africa (2011).

[18] The Nigerian diaspora as a whole is the largest of any African country, estimated in 2009 at 20 million (see: Blessing U. Mberu and Roland Pongou, "Nigeria: Multiple Forms of Mobility in Africa's Demographic giant", 30 June 2010, www.migrationpolicy.org/article/nigeria-multiple-forms-mobility-africas-demographic-giant (Accessed 22 December, 2014).

[19] "How Nigeria has Affected the Rest of Africa," www.bbc.co.uk/news/world-africa-11429067 (Accessed 22 December, 2014).

and South Africa. T.B. Joshua's Synagogue of All Nations Church, David Oyedapo's Living Faith Church Worldwide, Daniel Olukoya's Mountain of Fire and Miracles Ministries, and the Redeemed Christian Church of God, are some of the major religious attractions drawing thousands of citizens of other African countries into Lagos for conventions and healing programmes each month. Lagos is also a mission-sending centre. The remainder of this chapter will focus on Nigerian-founded churches in other African countries, principally in South Africa where their presence is ubiquitous, particularly in urban centres and cities. It will examine the dynamics of planting churches (or the proliferation of ritual spaces) and the influence of these new churches, first, among the migrant communities, and second, within local society. How do these migrant-founded and -led missions bear collective witness to the overarching Christian message in 'strange lands'?

The Nigerian Migrant Christianity in South Africa

As Andrew Walls argues, central to Christian mission is persuasion and demonstration rather than conquest and compulsion.[20] Religion is the second most important export of Nigeria; the first is crude oil. Nigerian churches are defined as Christian formations founded, headed or controlled (doctrinally, financially and organisationally) by Nigerian nationals. Nigeria not only exports Pentecostal missionaries; it also exports a significant number of Catholic clergy. Nigeria boasts the largest Catholic seminary in the world, Bigard Memory Seminary, where nearly 2,000 Catholic priests are ordained annually, many of whom are sent as missionaries to other countries. Many Nigerian Catholic clergy and religious sisters and nuns are working in South Africa among local Christians as well as among Catholic migrants (as chaplains). Nigerian migrant missions in different parts of Africa are singularly characterised by the spectacular demonstration of the power of the Holy Spirit in producing miracles, success and promotion. Ruth Marshall aptly describes this unique feature of Nigerian Pentecostal Christianity as manifesting the 'sovereignty of miracles' where faith in a miracle-producing God through 'powerful' mediators infuse and drive a range of religious activities and practices.[21] Nigerian Pentecostals accord a pivotal role to prayer as an instrument, or rather a technology, for producing miracles, which are nebulously conceptualised as divine interventions that benefit humans at a specific point in time. Similarly, miracles are conceived as the sacred insurrections that interrupt, or positively disrupt, the human order and state of affairs. Although nearly 80% of South Africans self-identify as 'Christian', Nigerian church founders in South Africa describe and understand themselves as missionaries to their host societies. Even when their religious activities mostly revolve around their compatriots, the missionary self-understanding is strong and plays a significant role in their relationship to the wider society. The missionary is the bringer of the good news, and the good news is the text of power, the bedrock of miracle. For the majority of Nigerian migrant missionaries, miracles are a diffused intensification of positive human experience rather than an interruption of the everyday experience and sense of being in a foreign land. The miraculous is that which gives them hope to smile as well as tying together the different, seemingly confusing, threads of 'life in exile'. In other words, the message that migrant missionaries advertise to their host societies is one of 'goodwill', 'blessing', 'empowerment' and 'improvement', which may be radical but not necessarily or always so. Missionaries are ostensibly the purveyors of good news and positive change, no matter how this assumption turns out in the long term. Migrant life in many African urban cities is a complex process of adjustment and contesting for scarce resources and opportunities for livelihood; migrant religious life, therefore, is both a process and a practice

[20] Andrew Walls, "Towards a Theology of Mission", in *African Christian Presence in the West: New Immigrant Congregations and Transnational Networks in North America and Europe*, eds. Frieder Ludwig and J. Kwabena Asamoah-Gyadu (Trenton, NJ: Africa World Press, 2011): 409.

[21] Ruth Marshall, "The Sovereignty of Miracles: Pentecostal Political Theology in Nigeria", *Constellations*, vol. 17, No. 2 (2010): 197-223.

of appealing to non-human resources in dealing with the angst of (re)settling in a new culture. One way of understanding this complex process is to investigate practices of mobilising miracles and prayer as a form of doing mission with limited supporting structures. Nigerian migrant Christian institutions and communities in South Africa amply exemplify this process and illustrate the functions and roles of migrant missions in a rapidly changing but fraught urban context, such as in post-apartheid South Africa.

The total figure for Nigerians living in South Africa is difficult to ascertain because many have naturalised; some are using the passports of other African countries such as Sierra Leone, Ghana and Liberia which they used in processing their asylum applications (for those who came through that system), while some are simply 'invisible'. However, it is estimated that South Africa is home to the largest Nigerian diaspora in Africa, numbering somewhere between three and four million.[22] This large diaspora community has affected the local landscape in many ways, such as entertainment, cuisine, clothing, music and intermarriage. Undoubtedly, however, the most important way in which the Nigerian community is transforming its host society is through religion, and specifically with the introduction of a new, vibrant, miracle-dominated form of Pentecostal Christianity.[23] Most of the members of the Nigerian community come from southern Nigeria, which is predominantly Christian. It is not surprising therefore that their influence has been in the production of Christian mission infrastructure, principally the formation of churches, ministries and para-church groups.

While Nigerians in South Africa do not constitute the largest ethnic foreign nationality in the country (that privilege goes to Zimbabweans), churches and Pentecostal ministries founded, owned and headed by Nigerians demonstrate numerical superiority over similar institutions founded and headed by members of other foreign nationalities. Francis Anwuzie established the first Nigerian-founded church in South Africa in 1994. In less than a decade from its establishment, the church multiplied congregations all over major South African cities. Following in the wake of his success and the further opening of the cultural and political sphere by the ANC-led national government of Nelson Mandela, many other Nigerian religious organisations joined the trail set by Anwuzie's example. The results of a research project started in 2007 ('Tradition and Innovation in South Africa's Religious Market') on migrant religious organisations in South Africa estimate that there are more than 600 distinct religious organisations founded and headed by Nigerians in South Africa. This study, which is still ongoing, seeks to map out the number, activities and demographic composition of these organisations in Johannesburg, Durban and Cape Town. By late 2009, there were well over 300 Nigerian churches in South Africa, more than half of these established in Johannesburg alone. By mid-2014, this figure had increased to over 600 discrete churches or congregations and para-church groups.

A few details will illustrate the plurality and spread of the major players in the migrant mission enterprise. The Believers Love World (BLW), better known by the moniker of Christ Embassy, is unarguably the most popular and populous of the lot – with close to 400 separate satellite parishes. In Cape Town alone, Christ Embassy has 25 satellite parishes and 72 others in Johannesburg and Pretoria combined.[24] It has attracted the largest number of South Africans across the colour line. Apart from the central doctrine and practice of healing which attracts many to Christ Embassy, the teaching of its leader and founder, Chris Oyakhilome, and his media image as a well-accomplished teacher of doctrines, appeals to a large cohort of young people – especially university students and the upwardly mobile elite. Similarly,

---

[22] Ukah, Asonzeh, "God@eBay: Nigerian Churches in South Africa", in *Creativity and Change in Nigerian Christianity*, eds. David O. Ogungbile and Akintunde E. Akinade (Lagos: Malthouse Publishing Limited, 2010), 333-348.

[23] Ukah, Asonzeh, "Prophets for Profit: Pentecostal Authority and Fiscal Accountability among Nigerian Churches in South Africa", in *Alternative Voices: A Plurality Approach for Religious Studies Essays in Honor of Ulrich Berner*, eds. Afe Adogame, Magnus Echtler & Oliver Freiberger (Göttingen: Vandenhoeck & Ruprecht, 2013), 131-159.

[24] Thanks to J.F.M. Bernard for providing the statistics on Christ Embassy (personal communication, 26.06.2014).

driven by the ideology of its leader, Enoch Adeboye – that a church be planted within five minutes' walking distance or ten minutes' driving distance in major cities of the world – the Redeemed Christian Church of God (RCCG) has established forty parishes in South Africa. Close to 40% of its membership is made up of South Africans, mainly Blacks. Living Faith Worldwide (better known as Winners Chapel) has nine large congregations in nine cities[25] while Lazarus Muoka's The Lord's Chosen Charismatic Revival Church, originally founded in Lagos in December 2002, has four branches. This church appeals mostly to the Nigerian business community. Further, Overcomers Christian Mission (originally founded in Owerri, Nigeria, in March 1985, by Alexander Ezeugo Ekewuba with the vision to 'demolish satanic strongholds and uphold the name of Jesus Christ to all men')[26] has three congregations in three cities: Johannesburg, Cape Town and Durban. The controversial but media-savvy Synagogue Church of All Nations owned by Prophet Temitope Balogun Joshua has a single congregation in South Africa that is located at Bellville in Cape Town (established in 2005). T.B. Joshua has a large following across Africa, many of whom throng his Lagos headquarters on pilgrimage and in search for salvation, miracles of healing and power – or, for politicians and business people, prophecy, victory and success. These are some of the major players in the migrant Pentecostal mission field in South Africa. There are, in addition, hundreds of start-up or storefront churches established by Nigerians jostling for a foothold in the emergent post-apartheid religious market-place.

While Pentecostal churches founded and headed by Congolese nationals in South Africa primarily target the large Congolese nationality in the country (and as a result, many of them hold their services in French and Lingala), just a few translate major sermons into English or one local language. At Ark of the Glory of the Lord[27] in Durban, headed by Prophet Joshua Bella, a Congolese national who came to South Africa in 2003 to play professional football but became a pastor when his original dream failed to materialise, membership is mainly Zulus with a few Swazi, Mozambican and Congolese congregants. According to Prophet Bella who models his church sermons and highly performative healing services after two famous Nigerian televangelists, Christopher Oyakhilome of Christ Embassy and T.B. Joshua of Synagogue of All Nations Church, of the 160 members of his congregation, 140 are South Africans, that is 87.5%. This demographic composition is consistent with his claim of divine instruction to tailor his ministry to local needs because the majority of Congolese-headed and -founded churches service Congolese migrant communities in South Africa.[28] Bella gives his sermons in English with simultaneous translation into IsiZulu by an assistant, Pinky Mhlongo. Although the Ark of the Gory of the Lord is not a Nigerian church, its religious culture is Nigerian, and illustrates the influence of Nigerian-led churches on other religious organisations and practices.

Nigerian-founded missions focus on recruiting a large spectrum of people. Church services and activities are conducted in English, and membership indicates that language is a unifying as well as an appeal factor for these organisations. It is the case, though, that many Nigerian-headed missions are dominated by Nigerians themselves, while local South Africans are the majority of the membership in some congregations, such as Christ Embassy and the Synagogue Church of All Nations. A white female

---

[25] The congregations are sited in the following cities: Johannesburg, Cape Town, Pretoria, Port Elizabeth, East London, Polokwane, Nelspruit, and Bloemfontein. A resident bishop is in charge of these and other Winners Chapel congregations in Southern Africa. He is based in Johannesburg (Personal interview with Bishop Thomas Aremu, Louise Botha Avenue, 09 March 2009).

[26] The OCM has 47 congregations in Nigeria and six congregations in four other countries, viz.: Cameroon, South Africa, the USA and Cote D'Ivoire (see: www.overcomersworld.org/aboutus.html).

[27] Bishop James Ilunga, a Congolese national, founded The Ark of the Glory of the Lord in 1996 in Cape Town. The church has congregations in many South African cities where Congolese nationals live and work as well as in Mozambique.

[28] Personal interview with Prophet Joshua Bella, Umgeni Road Congregation of Ark of the Lord Church, Durban, South Africa, 12 June 2011.

South African pastor heads the largest Christ Embassy congregation in Cape Town. Membership of this particular congregation that numbers about 1,200 is overwhelmingly non-Nigerian. For multi-congregational churches such as Winners chapel, Christ Embassy, the Redeemed Christian Church of God (RCCG), a strategy of recruiting and penetrating the local religious culture is by appointing South Africans as heads of congregations or departments that interface with state and municipal authorities and local populations. Allen Meyer, the administrator at the RCCG in Randburg in 2007-2008 was a white South African (Afrikaans) who moved from the Full Gospel Church to the Apostolic Faith Mission before migrating to the RCCG. In order for the RCCG to recruit from the local Afrikaans community, it has first to recruit and train a pastor from that community who would start a congregation within the Afrikaans neighbourhood and so depend on the community for membership. In this way, the RCCG can maintain a foothold in the local white population.[29] Congregations are built through house fellowships and evangelism in the surrounding neighbourhoods.

Because the local black population is mainly poor and poorly educated, the churches that grow from house fellowships depend on the immigrant community for its finances.[30] Recruiting local population once immigrants constitute the base of the church membership is very often challenging. Competition for the control of sensitive posts, particularly those dealing with the management of finances and prestige, often result in schisms. The rapid proliferation of congregations often compels religious leaders to recruit from among those who are already Christians instead of from the non-Christian base.

The process of gradual indigenisation has not worked in some cases. At Winners chapel, heavily reliant upon recruiting funds from the large migrant community, an attempt at installing a black South African as the head of the Johannesburg congregation met with resistance from the Nigerian community. Even though the church has a local membership of nearly 40%, when a large segment of the Nigerian membership stopped attending church services and paying their tithes, the church authority reinstalled a Nigerian head in order to maintain financial buoyancy and bring back lost membership. Successful recruitment of resources, mainly money, is therefore important in the leadership style of these migrant churches and the type of witness they provide.

Migrant mission involves service provision that transcends the numerical increase of Christians in the host society; it entails qualitative improvement or the uplift of the Christian community as a whole. The intensification of the salvific experience of migrant Christians is also a significant aspect of mission. Apart from planting churches through evangelistic efforts, there are many religious non-governmental organisations founded and headed by migrants. These religious NGOs focus their activities on both the migrant and local communities, servicing them in terms of clergy training, relief distribution and marriage counselling. Through these activities, the church is at work and engages with its host society more actively. T post-apartheid neo-liberal economy puts a great deal of stress on family cohesion; the black family is very often most adversely affected. Noah's Ark Family Web (NAFW) is one such important religious NGO established by a Nigerian couple in Pine Town, close to Durban. Recognising that the family institution is under severe stress in post-apartheid South Africa – and the family is fundamental to building a solid and stable Christian community – Isaac and Ethel Abe established NAFW on 29th January 2009 to provide family empowerment through seminars addressing the crises rocking the family from a Christian point of view.[31] The Abes are registered as Domestic Relationship Counsellors specialising in organising marriage and family conferences across KwaZulu Natal and Eastern Cape provinces. Based on the text of Revelation 22:2,[32] the Abes host a monthly seminar at different venues, mainly hotels and conference halls,

---

[29] Personal interview with Allen Meyer, RCCG National HQ, Randburg, Johannesburg, 22 March 2007.

[30] Personal Interview with Pastor Tosin Macaulay, Regional Co-ordinator of RCCG South African Region II, Randburg, Johannesburg, 15 March 2007.

[31] NAFW official brochure 2014.

[32] "In the middle of its street, and on either side of the river, was the tree of life, which bore twelve fruits, each tree

where they teach and empower mostly members of the host community in dealing with the challenges facing the family in post-apartheid South Africa.[33] Their activities and those of similar migrant-led groups put the church at work and take the church out of the church building to where its resources are most needed: repairing and building bridges, and consolidating the Christian experience and presence within their host environment. Migrant missions in Africa are partly driven by the Christian value of 'healing the nations' through the dissemination of the good news and miracles.

Conclusion

African migrant missions are harbingers of new translations of the Christian message adapted to a changing urban lifestyle; they also witness to new religious media, evangelistic methods and organisational innovation. They reframe Christianity, promote competitive diversity, and often intermingle mission enterprise with entrepreneurial activism. They contest the legitimacy of traditional religious and Christian institutions, and in so doing, generate new forms of being Christian and doing religion that takes the modern world, with all its problems and promises, as seriously as they take African cosmologies. The success of migrant missions in Africa appears to be their pragmatic approach to urban life and difficulties. Migrants generally dispense with a purpose-built form of religious worship site, preferring to rent or lease an office space that is minimally transformed into a worship hall. In this sense, methodology and pragmatism usually trump theology and orthodoxy as many of the leaders are less theologically trained but fervently zealous in building up Christian communities that respond to their charismata and vision of the Christian mission. Theological pragmatism also informs the way in which leaders relate the Christian message to the practical existential contexts of fellow migrants as well as members of the host society. Migrant missions have a tangible aural and visual imprint through new musical introductions and aesthetics. The loudness of migrant evangelical enterprise is deliberate: faith comes through hearing (Rom. 10:17). Through loud, persistent noise, music and preaching, migrants impregnate their immediate surroundings with their aural presence and contest the soundscape of the city they call home. They create a spiritual world or cocoon, albeit interpenetrative with the larger society, which sustains them through urban uncertainties and energises them in confronting the demoralising environment of strangeness with its harshness and pain. The persistent invocation or mobilisation of religion – which some term unnecessary and without justification – keeps many migrants from being despondent and falling into an urban sinkhole of drugs and crime. The spiritual energy that slips through their narratives and activities influence the people they interact with; by their energy and shouts and colourful display of religious media (posters, banners, dressing, etc.), they bear witness to a message of strength, vigour and hope that resonates with the expectations of a larger proportion of the host society. Migrant missionaries not only carry a hopeful message of the gospel; by their negotiation of the complexities of living in an unfamiliar environment, they present a hopeful expectation and disposition to their situation, and in so doing encourage those they interact with. Engaging actively with, and in, mission is a significant pathway for African migrants to adapt to and accommodate their host environment while at the same time hoping and working to make it a better place in consonance with their religious imagination.

Migrant missions face enormous challenges, such as scarcity of finance, stereotypes of migrants as parasites and criminals (drug dealers or sexual predators), limited access to worship areas, lack of quality control of mission activities, and a lack of co-operation among the various agents. The competition among the missionaries themselves *re*-presents another phase of the scandal of the fragmented gospel. These problems notwithstanding, migrant missions provide alternative worship styles, plural religious geography and social visibility for Christian organisations; they challenge existing Christian organisations to be more

---

yielding its fruit every month. The leaves of the tree were for the healing of the nations."

[33] Email interview Ethel Abel, 26 December 2014.

pro-active in evangelism. By combining entrepreneurial spirit with mission enterprise, migrant missionaries mobilise religion in contesting access to different sectors of their host societies. In some past paradigms of the missionary enterprise, the Christian church sent missionaries to foreign cultures bearing the gospel message; among migrants, the church *is* the mission. Hence, the explosion of variegated migrant-founded mission organisations in Africa is transforming and consolidating the textual nature and culture of Christianity in 21st-century Africa.

Bibliography

Adamo, David Tuesday, *African and Africans in the New Testament*. Lanham, MD: University Press of America, 2006.

Docquier, F., Ch. Vasilakis and D. Tamfutu Munsi, 'International Migration and the Propagation of HIV in Sub-Saharan Africa', in *Journal of Health Economics*, Vol. XXXV (2014): 20-33.

Ludwig, Frieder and J. Kwabena Asamoah-Gyadu (eds), *African Christian Presence in the West: New Immigrant Congregations and Transnational Networks in North America and Europe*. Trenton, NJ: Africa World Press, 2011.

Marshall, Ruth. 'The Sovereignty of Miracles: Pentecostal Political Theology in Nigeria', in *Constellations*, 17:2 (2010): 197-223.

Mitchell, Robert Cameron, 'Religious Change and Modernization: The Aladura Churches among the Yoruba in Southwestern Nigeria'. PhD dissertation, Department of Sociology, Northwestern University, 1970.

Nzayabino, Vedaste, 'The Role of Refugee Established Churches in the Lives of Forced Migrants: A Case Study of Word of Life Assembly in Yeoville, Johannesburg'. MA dissertation, Faculty of Arts, University of Witwatersrand, Johannesburg, RSA, 2005.

Nzayabino, Vedaste, 'Rethinking the Impact of the Church on the Dynamics of Integration of Congolese Migrants in Johannesburg: A Case Study of Yahweh Shammah Assembly'. PhD dissertation, Faculty of Humanities, University of the Witwatersrand, Johannesburg, RSA, 2011.

Peel, J.D.Y., *Aladura: A Religious Movement among the Yoruba*. London: Oxford University Press, 1968.

Pillay, Jerry, 'Theological Foundations of Mission', in Claudia Währisch-Oblau and Fidon Mwombeki (eds), *Mission Continues: Global Impulse for the 21st Century*, 7-17. Oxford: Regnum, 2010.

Rüther, Kirsten, 'Conversion to Christianity in African History before Colonial Modernity: Power, Intermediaries and Texts', in *The Medieval History Journal*, 12:2 (2009), 249-73.

Sundkler, Bengt G.M., *Bantu Prophets in South Africa*, 2nd edition, London: Oxford University Press, 1961.

Ugba, Abel, *Shades of Belonging: African Pentecostals in Twenty-First Century Ireland*. Trenton, NJ: Africa World Press, 2009.

Ukah, Asonzeh, 'Reverse Mission or Asylum Christianity? African Christian Churches in Britain', in: Toyin Falola and Augustine Agwuele (eds), *Africans and the Politics of Popular Cultures*, 104-32. Rochester, NY: University of Rochester Press, 2009.

Ukah, Asonzeh, 'God@eBay: Nigerian Churches in South Africa', in David O. Ogungbile and Akintunde E. Akinade (eds), *Creativity and Change in Nigerian Christianity,* 333-48. Lagos: Malthouse Publishing Limited, 2010.

Ukah, Asonzeh, 'Prophets for Profit: Pentecostal Authority and Fiscal Accountability among Nigerian Churches in South Africa', in Afe Adogame, Magnus Echtler and Oliver Freiberger (eds), *Alternative Voices: A Plurality Approach for Religious Studies Essays in Honor of Ulrich Berner,* 131-59. Göttingen, Germany: Vandenhoeck & Ruprecht, 2013.

Walls, Andrew, 'Towards a Theology of Mission', in Frieder Ludwig and J. Kwabena Asamoah-Gyadu (eds), *African Christian Presence in the West: New Immigrant Congregations and Transnational Networks in North America and Europe*, 407-17. Trenton, NJ: Africa World Press, 2011.

(15) GENDER AND THE BIBLE IN AFRICAN CHRISTIANITY

Musa W. Dube

Introduction

Gender is a crucial social category that organizes relationships and distributes power among individuals, within institutions and in all social relationships. Gender, more often than not, determines who has power to make decisions and to implement them; who has the right to speak and be heard; who has the right to own property and manage it; and who has the right to contest and hold public positions of leadership. Because most studies on gender argue that gender constructions do not distribute power equitably among females and males, all justice-seeking, peace-loving, empowerment-dreaming, salvation-preaching, deliverance-making and government-planning departments in society need to understand how gender is produced and maintained as well as how it affects the members of every community. They need to highlight gender in the implementation of their policies and programmes as well as in the monitoring and evaluation of the same. Without factoring in gender, their visions, goals and objectives will only be partially realized, if not downright frustrated. African Christianity, a vibrant institution that houses millions of females and males, preaches salvation, redemption, healing, deliverance and empowerment for its members. Unless African Christianity fully investigates how gender affects its members and the structures of the African Church, then its core business of salvation, redemption, healing and deliverance from negative powers will not be realized by all its members. It is imperative for gender-justice to be central to the message, programmes and institutions of African churches for African Christianity to deliver liberating salvation to its members and the communities they serve.

Gender is described as a 'set of behavioural, cultural, psychological and social characteristics and practices associated with masculinity and femininity'.[1] Mary Ann Tolbert asserts that 'Gender is constructed, and constructed differently, in diverse local settings'.[2] The latter definition argues that gender is not a natural trait or a divinely-given position; rather, it is a social construct. As a social construct, gender is neither permanent nor unchangeable nor uniform. Since it is a construct, every society tends to construct its members differently according to other social categories such as class, race, age, sexuality and religion, among others. This means that females and males of lower class are expected to assume different ways of behaviour, different dress, different ways of eating and attitudes to work, than those of higher class within the same society. Similarly females and males of one religion are expected to dress differently from those of another. Fashions of the younger generation and senior citizens also differ. People of other sexual orientation often find themselves forced to perform prescribed gender roles that are inconsistent with their sexual identity. I could elaborate on these differences with various social categories, but the point is made – namely, that gender is a time and culture-specific construction that is dependent on or linked with other various social categories such as class, race, ethnicity, sexuality and religion. This definition makes gender 'a fluid and shifting' category, for females and males of the same society and country will be constructed differently.

It follows that a paper on gender and the Bible in African Christianity can give only broad highlights on phenomena that can be described in a million different ways in the whole continent, given the diversities of religion, ethnicity, race, sexuality, age and class in each country and how they construct social roles for

---

[1] See Ian Buchanan, *Oxford Dictionary of Critical Theory.* Oxford: Oxford University Press, 2010, p. 198.

[2] Mary Ann Tolbert, "Gender," 99-105, in A.K.M. Adam, ed. *Handbook of Postmodern Biblical Interpretation.* St Louise: Chalice Press, 2000, 101.

their members. In her book, *Africa: Reinventing Matriarchy, Religion and Culture,* Ifi Amadiume[3] presents fieldwork-based research which shows that in most African cultures gender was not constructed as a set of binary oppositions that automatically excluded women from the public sphere and positions of power. In fact, such indigenous public economic arenas as the market-place were, in some regions, traditionally constructed as an exclusively female area, where males could have access only through female agents.[4] While Amadiume does not claim that African societies were egalitarian, she argues that gender construction was 'not monolithically masculine, that is, consisting of male symbols and masculine principles and values', but rather 'the structure of father is not as autonomous as that of mother'.[5] Amadiume argues that most, if not all, African societies have 'matriarchal roots or structures' which shape traditional ways of gender construction.[6]

Further, a paper on gender, Bible and African Christianity highlights new cultural constructions that produce other complex categories of gender for three different reasons. First, the Bible is a Jewish book that models different gender constructions, according to their cultural, religious and economic understanding. Second, the Bible is a collection of sixty-six books written or compiled over two millennia, thus presenting conflicting gender constructions. Third, African Christianity, especially sub-Saharan, is not uniform but a product of the collision of modern European Christianities, brought by different denominations (e.g. Roman Catholic, Lutheran and Methodist). The European countries brought Christianity to sub-Saharan Africa in a colonial context (laden with their own cultures)and planted it in different indigenous African cultures. In the memories of African people, the Bible is thus tied up with colonial history, as attested by the popular oral story that holds that 'when the white man came to our land, he had the Bible and we had the land. The white man said, Let us pray. But the time we had finished praying, the white man had our land and we had the Bible'.[7] The Bible is linked with land and dispossession, but is now claimed as a possession received through western colonialism. The Bible is thus described as another set of wisdom, which co-exists with pre-existing collections of African oral wisdom.[8] We do not, in other words, have one African Christianity, but several African Christianities.

This introductory background informs three 'windows' on Gender, Bible and African Christianity elaborated in this paper. The windows are not definitive or uniform for all forms of African Christianity, given the complexity of gender constructions, the diversity of biblical books and their gender constructions, or the diversity of African Christianities and their gender constructions, at different times and places. The three windows presented here are best seen as invitations to a million research projects that are time- and place-specific in the diverse contexts of the African continent. They are explored under the following sub-headings:

Gender and the Enculturation Bible in African Christianity

Gender and Translation of African Bibles

Gender and the Pentecostal African Bible

Before I briefly sketch the above windows, it is appropriate to give some brief background to Bible and gender and the institution of the Circle of Concerned African Women Theologians.

---

3 Ifi Amadiume, *Africa: Reinventing Matriarchy, Religion and Culture*. London: Zed Books, 1997.

4 See Ifi Amadiume. *Male Daughters, Female Husbands.* London: Zed Books, 139-142.

5 Amadiume, *Africa,* 36-37.

6 Ibid, 37.

7 Its oral circulation means that the text often appears in various versions.

8 See Mercy A. Oduyoye., *Beads and Strands: Reflections of an African Woman on Christianity in Africa.* Maryknoll, NY: Orbis Books, 2004, 18-34.

The Bible and Gender

The Christian Bible is a collection of sixty-six books, thirty-nine in the Hebrew Bible and twenty-seven in the New Testament. These books can be categorized into seven literary families – namely, 1. Books of the law, 2. Historical books, 3. Wisdom books, 4. Prophetic books, 5. Gospels, 6. Epistles, and 7. Apocalyptic literature. Some also have apocryphal books such as Tobit, Judith, I and II Maccabees, etc. Historical studies estimate that biblical literature was produced and evolved over a period of two millennia. Consequently, identifying authors, places of authorship and original manuscripts is generally complex and defies accuracy in most books except for a few such as the authentic letters of the apostle Paul. Narrative approach to biblical studies, however, argues that understanding the message of a story does not necessarily require historical facts, such as knowledge of the author, date and place of production, but just a complete manuscript.[9]

Studies on gender and the Bible can best be traced to Elisabeth Cady Stanton, a white suffragette, who was perturbed by the use of the Bible to exclude women from empowerment and human rights, such as voting. Her experience led her to a fundamental insight and conclusion – namely, that 'the Bible is a male book'.[10] This statement means that Cady Stanton realized that biblical texts tend to be used to support the interests of males and the subordination of females. Cady Stanton sought to produce *The Women's Bible* that would serve to empower women rather than to disadvantage them. While her project was frustrated by a lack of women trained in biblical studies and languages, in the 1960s more women began to enter biblical studies and to investigate gender construction in the Bible and its impact on biblically-based institutions, cultures, relationships and structures.[11] Their insights remained consistent with Cady Stanton – namely, that the Bible is a male book, which largely constructs cultures, social institutions and females and males who exist in the realm of its influence, from a male-centred worldview. Using various methods and theories, feminist studies sought to interrogate how gender is biblically constructed to support male interests; why and how women have allowed themselves to internalize and accept biblical perspectives that disadvantage them; and sought numerous ways to re-read the texts for empowerment of both genders.[12] Consistent with the above definition of gender as a social construction linked with various other social categories, biblical studies' analysis of biblical texts by contemporary feminists expose how class, race, sexuality, age, religion and ethnicity interpret and affect the construction of females and males in their particular communities.

The Circle of Concerned African Women Theologians

In the African continent, the Circle of Concerned African Women Theologians (henceforth, the Circle) provides an important forum for the study of the Bible and Gender in African Christianities. The Circle is a pan-African multi-religious academic association, which seeks to research and write on how religions affect the lives of women. It also seeks to find and mentor young women who are interested in studying religious tradition. The Circle was founded by Mercy Oduyoye in 1989, after realizing that religious traditions are often used to legitimise the exclusion and disempowerment of women, and that their

---

[9] See Elisabeth Struthers Malbon, "How does the Story Mean?" pp. 29-58. In S. D. Moore and J. Anderson, eds. in *Mark and Method*: *New Approaches in Biblical Studies*. Minneapolis: Fortress Press, 1992.
[10] See Ann Loades, "Elizabeth Cady Stanton's *The Women's Bible,*" pp. 307-322. In Michal Lieb, E. Mason and J. Roberts, eds. *Jesus the Light of the World: The Oxford Handbook of Reception History of the Bible*. Oxford: Oxford University Press, 2011.
[11] See Carol Newsom and Sharon Ringe, eds. *The Women's Bible Commentary*. Louisville: Westminster, 1992.
[12] See Janice Capel Anderson, "The Dancing Daughter," 111-144. In J.C. Anderson and S.D. Moore, eds. *Mark and Method: New Approaches in Biblical Studies,* 2nd ed., Minneapolis: Fortress Press, 2008, for a good summary on feminist biblical scholars at work.

interpretations are often dominated by males.[13] By seeking to create an opportunity for African women's voices to be heard, she sought for 'an African theology that flies with two wings'. The Circle currently has a continent-wide membership of about five hundred women and has produced at least a hundred books. It is structured according to regional and national chapters, which are free to identify topics and themes of study that are relevant in their particular contexts.

In its beginning, the Circle had only one biblical scholar, Teresa Okure from Nigeria. Since then, the Circle has at least sixteen African women scholars of the Bible. Within the Circle, various volumes have been produced that investigate gender constructions in the Bible from the perspectives and experiences of African women. These include: *Other Ways of Reading: African Women and the Bible* and *Grant Me Justice: HIV/AIDS and Gender Readings of the Bible*, along with numerous chapters published within other volumes of the Circle, such as *Talitha Cum: Theologies of African Women, Her Stories: Hidden Histories of Women of Faith in Africa,* among others, and in scholarly works outside the Circle, such as *Postcolonial Perspectives in African Biblical Interpretations*. Female African biblical scholars have also produced independent monographs and edited several volumes that explore gender in African Christianity. Good examples here include Musimbi Kanyoro and Madipoane Masenya's work.[14] Altogether, these volumes are crucial in providing us with sketches of gender and the Bible in African Christianity that are listed above.

Gender and the Enculturated African Bible

The Bible was received within African cultural beliefs. Sub-Saharan Christianity was thus planted in and nurtured by African oral cultural beliefs. African cultural beliefs are largely oral and diverse. Generally, they underline communal relationships. One thinks here of John Mbiti's popularized saying, 'I am because we are, and we are because I am', and the Bantu saying, *Umuntungumuntungabantu* ('a human being is only human through other human beings') to emphasise communitarian African cultures. A deeper interrogation of this communal philosophy should make no room for gender or social oppression of any kind. Indeed, it should be integral to the promotion of gender equality and liberation in general, for unless all members are respected and equally empowered, then we cannot be community. The communal African perspective is also underlined through the belief in Ancestors, who are regarded as the living dead, who continue to show interest in their surviving relatives and to intercede for them before the Divine Being (God). The Ancestors play a significant role in sustaining healthy relationships among the living, since negligence in maintaining healthy relationships is believed to result in ill health, misfortune and lack of prosperity. This is because Ancestors do not intercede for irresponsible members of the family and community. In African thinking, ill health is, therefore, first sought in one's relationships with family, the larger community and the living dead, which must be healed before medicine is administered for physical pain.

Ancestor veneration includes maintaining healthy relationships with the Earth.[15] The Earth houses both the living and the living dead, and should be kept sacred in African cultural thinking.[16] Ploughing seasons are often preceded by rituals of thanksgiving and cleansing the land of any pollution, such as the murder of human beings, unburied human bodies, aborted children, and violent crimes – for all these are held to

---

[13] See Musimbi Kanyoro, "Beads and Strands: Threading More Beads in the Story of the Circle," pp.15-38. In Isabel A. Phiri and Sarojini Nadar eds. *Her-Stories: Hidden Histories of Women of Faith in Africa.* Pietermaritzburg: Cluster, 2002.

[14] See Musimbi R. A. Kanyoro, *Introducing Feminist Cultural Hermeneutics: African Perspective*. Cleveland: The Pilgrim Press, 2002 and Madipoane Masenya, *How Worthy is the Woman of Worth: Rereading Proverbs 31:10-31 in African South Africa.* New York: Peter Land, 2004.

[15] Earth is capitalized to underline that Earth is the proto-citizen within the whole Earth community.

[16] See Laurenti Magesa, *What is not Sacred? African Spirituality.* New York: Orbis Press, 2013.

desecrate the land. The occurrence of natural disasters, such as drought, initiates a communal introspection about how human beings relate to nature and hold themselves responsible for upsetting its natural balance. Some of these perspectives can be scientifically proven to be lacking, but it cannot be disputed that human beings need to constantly evaluate how they relate to the Earth and how they negatively affect its balance. According to George Kinoti, 'Three factors in particular are harming God's creation: rapid population growth… increase in the consumption of resources… and use of polluting technologies'. These lead to the over-use of land, water pollution, climate change, loss of forests, plant and animal species, the Earth's shield, and pollution by chemicals.[17] In short, the African cultural worldview consists of the living, the living dead (Ancestors), the Earth and the highest Deity, God.[18] In this cosmology, the living and the living dead consist of both females and males. The Earth is largely regarded as female and the Divine Being is not gendered. The most crucial aspect in this cosmology is the need to maintain healthy relationships. Failure to maintain healthy relationships constitute 'sin' that requires rituals of healing and reconciliation. There was no concept of an inherently evil human being that needed a saviour in the sub-Saharan Africa cultural worldview.

The arrival of Christianity was thus planted in a pre-existing belief system. Although colonial Christianity attempted to erase African cultures by characterizing them as uncivilized, superstitious and outright evil,[19] it is not possible to erase a culture simply by introducing a new one. What results in such scenarios is the mixing of cultures: the reshaping of the incoming and the pre-existing cultures into new, hybrid identities. Planted in the cultural soil of Africa, Christianity was fed and fertilized by African cultures, but its seed would also begin to reconstitute African cultures, especially in the way that gender relations were constructed. African theological scholars have described this phenomenon of the inter-fertilization of Christianity and African cultures as 'enculturation'. According to Edward Antonio, 'enculturation can be thought of as an attempt to resolve the problem of cultural and religious "inconsumerability" entailed by the colonial insistence on the radical difference between civilized western cultures and their "irrational" African counterparts'.[20] Antonio explores the various frameworks used to construct enculturation hermeneutics and theology, pointing out that 'enculturation proceeds by making use of the cognate ideas of comparison, continuity, resemblance, similitude and synthesis'.[21] How did this new introduction and the cross-fertilization reconstitute gender?[22] I want to use the case study of Christology in the African enculturation project. This is primarily because Christianity did not introduce the concept of God to sub-Saharan Africans since they already knew God (even so, we will examine the reconstruction of God further on in this article, under translation). The concept of Christ and the biblical scriptures were the new aspects.

First, the male figure of Christ *as the one and only* intermediary to God was bound to be a major cultural shaker (emphasis mine). Jesus was no doubt a historical figure, a Jewish male, the son of Mary and Joseph, the son of David and the Son of Abraham (Matt. 1:1-2); Jesus is depicted as male, even in his spiritual status. For example, at birth, it is said, 'He will be great, and will be called the Son of the Most High' (Luke 1:31-32). At baptism, a voice from heaven said, 'This is my Son, the Beloved, with whom I am well pleased' (Matt. 3:17). His coming to the world is described as God giving his beloved son (John

[17] George Kinoti, "Christians and the Environment," in Tokunboh Adeyemo, ed., *Africa Bible Commentary*. Nairobi: Word Alive Publishers, 2006, 616.

[18] In some West African cultures their cosmology includes gods that are higher than Ancestors.

[19] See Edward P. Antonio, *Inculturation and Postcolonial Discourse in African Theology*. New York: Peter Lang, 2006, 36.

[20] Ibid, 40.

[21] Ibid, 49, African enculturation theologians have taken various angles, from the conservative to the liberal, measured by the attitude one has towards African Indigenous Religions.

[22] The work of Mercy Amba Oduyoye best addresses this question.

3:16). In John's Gospel, the sonship of Jesus is most clearly seen by the depiction of God as the Father of Jesus. The sonship of Jesus, both in the physical and spiritual realm, is therefore well attested in the gospels and throughout the New Testament. The fact that Jesus was human and acquired divine status after death is not problematic for African thinking, since it is consistent with the concept of Ancestors, as people who actually lived as members of the family and community, acting as intermediaries between God and the living, even after death.[23]

However, Jesus as the one and only intermediary was a huge shock to the African belief system and one that had serious gender implications in the spiritual and social realm. First, because colonial presentation insisted on discarding all African cultural beliefs:[24] Jesus was not presented as joining other existing Ancestors, but as erasing, invalidating and replacing all of them.[25] Second, where a whole community of the living dead acted as intermediaries, now *one single male was installed,* a move that violated the communal character of the sub-Saharan cultural cosmology. Third, this replacement had huge gender implications, for while the Ancestors included both male and female relatives, who assumed new status upon death, the installation of Jesus as the only legitimate intermediary between God and the living erased women from the spiritual realm. This was, of course, not helped by the fact that the biblical God was also well-endowed with male titles (such as Shepherd, Lord, King, Father, Mighty Warrior). Since the construction of a spiritual space has implications for the construction of social spaces, that is, God the father and Jesus, his son, sitting in the heavenly realm, also legitimize the emasculation of African social spaces.[26] Christianity has therefore entrenched patriarchy in the African social and spiritual worldview, a development that legitimizes the marginalization of African women from economic, political and social spheres of power.

Yet the African cultural worldview also cross-fertilized the biblical worldview. It was not only the biblical text that affected the African cultural worldview; the latter was actively potent. The first thing to acknowledge was that African oral cultures were pervasive "*scriptoratures*" (i.e. oral literature of sacred texts with religious content), that were embedded in the memories and members of African communities as compared with the biblical text, contained between two covers and dependent on readers. Every African person was the embodiment of African cultural beliefs, even those who were had apparently embraced the Christian faith, for as long as they belonged to African families, they remained in the cultural cosmology, naturally wired into family and communal Ancestors and to the Divine Being. The first major form of resistance, therefore, was that African oral cultures remained potent and, as Antonio points out above, 'inconsumerable'. The African oral canon would thus be brought in and read with the biblical text, as many studies on African Independent Churches attest. One such indicator would be the emphasis on the Spirit and the claim of the Spirit as the agent of empowerment.[27] The Spirit would enable women to claim positions of power, to become prophets and founders of churches, and claim to have heard God's call to the office of ordination.[28] Kimba Vita, the Congolese woman held to be the founding mother of African Independent Churches, for example, claimed that the Spirit of St Patrick was upon her, endowing her with

---

[23] See Robert J. Schreiter, ed. *Faces of Jesus in Africa*. New York: Orbis Press, 2002.

[24] See Kwesi Dickson. *Uncompleted Mission: Christianity and Exclusivism.* New York: Orbis Press, 1991.

[25] See Musa W. Dube, 'Consuming A Colonial Cultural Bomb: Translating Badimo into "Demons" in the Setswana Bible', in Stephen Moore (ed), *JSNT 73*: 1999: 33-59.

[26] See IfiAmadiume, *Male Daughters, Female Husbands*. London: Zed Books, 1987, 139-140, discussion of how Christian male symbols were accompanied by colonial intuitions, such as schools, churches, military services etc, that increasingly displaced African women from the public space by privileging males in new colonial professions.

[27] See Musa W. Dube, "Readings of *Semoya*: Batswana Women Interpretations of Matt. 15:21-28," 111-129. In *Semeia* Vol.73. Atlanta: Scholars Press, 1996b.

[28] See Goememang Tshinamo, *Women Church Leaders in Botswana: Documentation*. Gaborone: University of Botswana, 1999.

a prophetic voice against colonial Christianity that filled churches with white images of biblical characters.[29] She declared these white images as unacceptable idols, while she asserted that Jesus and his disciples were black!

In a number of studies on African Independent Churches, the realm where the Bible is read with and through African oral cultural beliefs, findings indicate that male-centred gender constructions are subverted through interpretations that call upon the oral canon. Fieldwork studies indicate that women in African who founded churches legitimized their authority to preach by creating a biblical genealogy of women Ancestors (characters), whom they invoke, together with other African women, each time they stand up to preach. As I pointed out:

> I was listening to their sermons (St John Apostolic Faith Mission women) when I realized that, when each one of them stood up to preach, they said, 'I greet Mother Mary Magdalene, Mother Mary the Mother of Jesus, Mother Martha, the holy seats of Mother Mmanku and MmaAnderson, women who wear the belt of faith…' By greeting these biblical figures prior to preaching, four things were accomplished: first, these biblical women were given the ancestral status and venerated in the church. Second, by calling this group of women prior to their teaching, they were grounding their authority to preach in these women. Third, the creative identification of African women (Mmanku and MmaAnderson) with biblical women means they do not suffer from identifying themselves with male authority to preach… What is even more significant is that by including these women, biblical and local, they have employed an African worldview to create an inclusive Christology for themselves.[30]

Second, the oral canon subverts the Bible's gender constructions, when women in the church overlook the written text by calling upon the oral canon. A good example was one woman who, when quizzed about her leadership position, which seemingly violated the deutero-Pauline injunctions against women speaking or leading in church (2 Tim. 2:8-16), the woman chose not to engage the androcentric biblical texts, but rather to stake her legitimacy on the authority of the unwritten texts. She said, 'When God spoke to me, God never opened the Bible to me.'[31] As Goememang Tshinamo's research on *Women Church Leaders in Botswana* highlights, African women's use of their indigenous oral canon is often attested by claims of seeing visions, having dreams and hearing God's voice calling them to full-time ministry.[32] African academic women scholars have appealed to the African oral canon to construct their Christology. One such article is Elisabeth Amoah and Mercy A. Oduyoye's use of the Ghanaian female legend, Eku, to construct a female Christology.[33] The African oral text is invoked and used in such a way that it bypasses the androcentric biblical text, without dismissing its authority, but rather by supplementing it.

Translating the Bible, Translating Gender, Translating African Christianity

It is undeniable that the introduction of the Christian religion and its biblical text to African cultural worldviews in a colonial context was a moment of translation. The above discussion has already indicated how it was a translation of cultural worldviews from both sides. Yet even the translation of the biblical text into African languages was not only an attempt to translate African oral cultures into written languages, but

---

[29] See John Thornton, *The Congolese Saint Anthony: Kimba Vita and the Antonian Movement 1684-1706.* New York: Cambridge University Press, 1998.

[30] Musa W. Dube, "Woman, What have I to Do with You? (John 2:1-11): A Post-colonial Feminist Theological Reflection on the Role of Christianity in Development, Peace and Reconstruction," pp. 244-258. In Isabel Phiri, Kenneth Ross and James Cox eds. *The Role of Christianity in Development, Peace and Reconstruction.* Eds. P Nairobi: AACC, 1996a, 256.

[31] Musa W. Dube, "Readings of *Semoya*" 127.

[32] Goememang Tshinamo. *Women Church Leaders in Botswana.*

[33] See Elisabeth Amoahand Mercy A. Oduyoye, "Christ for African Women," 35-46. In V. Fabella and M. A. Oduyoye, eds. *With Passion and Compassion: Third World Women Doing Theology.* New York: Orbis Press, 1990.

it was also an active agenda that translated African ways of constructing gender in the spiritual and the social realm. A number of studies have been carried out to highlight how the translation of the biblical text into African languages was also the translation of gender-inclusive spiritual and social spheres into androcentric structures. This brings us to the translation of God in African Christianity. Such studies have been carried out by Aloo Mojola with a case study of the Iraqw people of Tanzania, Seratwa Ntloedibe Kuswani in the case of the Setswana Bible translation in Botswana, and Dora Mbuwayesango in the case of the Shona Bible translation. Since Bible translation worked with a theoretical translation that insisted on privileging the so-called source text rather than the receiving culture, biblical constructions of gender could not be enriched by the gender-inclusive African spiritual realm and African languages. While Ifi Amadiume held that most African cultures leaned towards matriarchal-centred gender construction, the biblical text is patriarchal and was largely favoured by translation theories employed to impose its worldview.

AlooMajola describes the politics of Bible and gender translation of the name of God among the Iraqw of Tanzania. According to Mojola,[34] the Iraqw people of Tanzania have always regarded God as female, while evil and its forces are characterized as male. Mojola emphasizes that 'for them it is the devil who is male or masculine. It is he who has to be placated through sacrifice... God's name is believed to be Looah... She is the provider, the protector, the merciful and the giver of life'.[35] Mojola further holds that Looah 'satisfies the Christian qualities and attributes for the supreme God, such as the creator of the universe, loving, empowering and sustaining the created order, providing for all, concerned about fairness and justice, requiring mercy, moral order, etc.'[36] Yet this same people were presented with a Bible translation that presented God as male, which they found deeply unacceptable. While Looah had all the qualities that made her an acceptable equivalent of the biblical God, she had female gender! This was not consistent with the biblical God, who is endowed with characteristics associated with the male gender. To sideline Looah and enforce a masculine God, a Swahili name, Mungu, was imported into the Iraqw Bible translation. The Iraqw, shocked by this cruel inversion of their worldview, pleaded and resisted the translation. As Mojola writes as an eyewitness:

> I recall a Bible reviewers' seminar organized in Haydom, Mbulu, in 1990, where some of the Iraqw Christian leaders who were being trained to be reviewers of the ongoing Iraqw Old Testament translation strongly pleaded for a change in official church usage from God's name in Swahili to God's name i.e. from Mungu back to Looah. One leading Christian lady teacher at the Waama Bible School in Mbulu argued that she had found it difficult to do evangelism using God's name in Swahili... One Lutheran priest... is said to have rebelled by maintaining or persisting in the use of Looah in his preaching and teaching.[37]

The above citation demonstrates how the Iraqw Christians found the translation unacceptable, which leads us to ask, 'Whose interests are served in such translations?' Why are such translations carried out against the will of the communities of the concerned language and culture? But when we ask such questions, we are confronting the institutionalized theories of Bible translation that insists that the source text should not be changed, while the receiving culture can and must bend, break and be distorted to accommodate the so-called source text. This theoretical position also reflects the superiority that the biblical religion of Christianity claims for itself over other cultures, which legitimizes the violation of other

---

[34] Aloo Mojola, "How the Bible is Received in Communities: A Brief Overview with Particular Reference to East Africa," 45-69. In Philip Wickeri, ed. *Scripture, Community and Mission.* Hong Kong: Christian Conference of Asia, 2002.

[35] Ibid, 62.

[36] Aloo Mojola, "Bible Translation in Africa," 141-162. In Phillip A. Noss, ed. *A History of Bible Translation.* Roma: Edizioni di Storia e Letteratura, 2007, 159.

[37] Aloo Mojola, "How the Bible is Received in Communities," 62-63.

cultures. Because the biblical text is largely masculine in its worldview, the Christianization of many African cultures has meant the patriarchalization of relationships.

The translation of African worldviews into androcentric perspectives is also attested by Seratwa Ntloedibe,[38] who holds that the Setswana concept of the divine *Modimo* (God), the *Badimo* (Ancestors) and the *Ditaola* (divining set) were gender-neutral, until the Setswana biblical translation was begun in 1840, in the history of Christianizing Southern Africa. In the process, the Modimo of Batswana became male and the Badimo (Ancestors), who were culturally regarded as divine and venerated, were equated with demons in the Setswana Bible translation. Dora Mbuwayesanyo has studied the history and process of the Shona Bible translation in Zimbabwe, showing how *Mwari* (God) of the Shona, who used to be gender-neutral, emerged fully dressed in male garments. She asserts, 'The Shona understand Mwari to be a genderless spirit, neither male nor female. The attributes of Mwari all have to do with Mwari transcendence and creative attributes. Also, Mwari does not discriminate and can speak through women and even through objects, as well as through men.'[39]

Although more in-depth studies are needed to document how the biblical imposition of the male gender on African Christianity was received and how it has affected gender relations in general, there are indications that the oral canon of African cultures remains resistant and inconsumable. The above citation from the Iraqw example gives us an indication, by pointing out that one of the priests 'is said to have rebelled by maintaining or persisting in the use of Looah in his preaching and teaching'.[40] How about the rest of the members of this ethnic group of the Iraqw? We can assume that the rebellion of the priest is the tip of the iceberg, indicating that such a priest serves in a context where the community would find a biblically-imposed male God unacceptable (as is indeed attested in the same quote by the plea of its Christian leaders). The Iraqw priest preaches, therefore, a Christianity that is cross-fertilized by the African cultural view that views the creator God as female. It goes without saying that more research is needed on how this particular African culture – that of the Iraqw – reshapes the type of Christianity that emerges from such a context: how is the biblical text itself and its meaning translated through oral memories and readers? Much work is needed here.

Among the Batswana, where the colonial Setswana translation had included Ancestors in the Bible as demons that Jesus went around casting out, the oral canon of African cultures still prevailed. As I carried out research among women prophets of African Independent Churches, I soon discovered that they used the Bible as a divination book and carried out ancestral veneration rituals, where Jesus was among their ancestors – not over, above or as one who replaces them. Indeed:

> This usage of the Bible and method of reading is stunningly subversive to colonizing narrative designs. The AICs' readers resist the translation that turned Badimo into demons and devils in the Setswana Bible... Instead, they perceive the Bible from their own cultural perspective as a book that diagnoses relationships and promotes healing of relationships between people and divine powers... The Bible took its rightful place as one among many other divining sets. Badimo and Jesus/Holy Spirit also took their rightful place as divine powers that promoted good relationships and health where the Bible is read. This AIC's strategy of resistance entailed a method of reading the written Setswana language through and with the unwritten text of Setswana cultures.[41]

These subversive readings counteract the patriarchal perspective of the Bible. This analytical observation from my side is supported by the first readers of Setswana Bible translations, who sent a

---

[38] See Seratwa Ntloedibe-Kuswani, "The Case of Modimo in the Setswana Bible", 78-100. In Musa W. Dube (ed), *Other Ways of Reading: African Women and the Bible.* Atlanta: SBL, 2001.

[39] Dora R. Mbuwayesango, "How Local Divine Powers were Suppressed: A Case of Mwari of the Shona," 63-77. In Musa W. Dube (ed), *Other Ways of Reading: African Women and the Bible.* Atlanta: SBL, 2001, 63.

[40] Aloo Mojola, "How the Bible is Received in Communities," 63.

[41] See Musa W. Dube, "Consuming A Colonial Cultural Bomb," 33-59.

barrage of letters to the London Missionary Society newsletter, *Mahoka a Becwana,* complaining that their language had been distorted and violated in the translation. Alfred Gould, its editor, received their complaints and promised to submit their concerns to the general missionary council meeting. Upon his return, he informed them that, unfortunately, the council meeting has resolved that the language would stand as translated (and that the same language would be used for the newspaper and other prayer books) despite the concerns of Batswana. The Batswana readers charged back through the oral African cultural canon, saying to the editor, 'You should know that when we read our Bible, we change letters with our mouths'![42] Nothing better illustrates the persistent power of the oral canon of African cultures and how it shapes African Christianity.

Conclusion: African Pentecostal Christianity

It is on record that, since the 1970s, African Christianity is becoming increasingly Pentecostal. It is also documented that Pentecostal Christianity underlines the acts of the Holy Spirit and its worship seems democratic.[43] Yet the Holy Spirit in the mouths of many Pentecostal preachers is characterized as male. It is, therefore, debatable whether Pentecostal Christianity in Africa is necessarily more gender-inclusive than other forms of African Christianity. According to Mmadipoane Masenya, Pentecostal biblical reading is a two-edged sword that underlies both the patriarchal normativity of the Bible and the centrality of the Holy Spirit being poured upon all flesh.[44] Even so, Sarojini Nadar insists that the hermeneutic of the Spirit used in forms of Pentecostal Christianity in Africa needs to be subjected to a hermeneutic of suspicion, for it has on several occasions demonstrated its capacity to accommodate gender and other forms of oppression.[45] Be that as it may, the emphasis on the theology of the Spirit allows for negotiation of the spread of power among men and women, although not always successfully. More studies are needed on Pentecostal biblical interpretation and the kind of gender relations it supports.[46]

Of particular note is that Pentecostal Christianity in Africa is less accommodating of African oral beliefs, since it supposedly urges followers to 'make a complete break with the past'.[47] Other scholars insist that 'it is pertinent to note that the traditional African cosmology of evil and healing are central to the beliefs of Pentecostal and Charismatic movements in Africa'.[48] Overall, the three small windows on Gender, Bible and African Christianity in this paper underline that it is a constantly negotiated position in different forms of denominations, forms of Christianity, countries, ethnicities and times. It is, more often than not, a contested space of power between biblical texts and African oral traditions, that shape gender relations within the contact zone of two or more spiritual and social spaces. These gendered perspectives affect how power is distributed among females and males in the African Church and the communities they

[42] Mgadla, P. and S.C. Volz (translators/compilers). *Words of Batswana: Letters to Mahoka a Becwana 1883-1896.* Cape Town: Van Riesbeck Society, 2006, 33.
[43] For a comprehensive west African study , see Kwabena J. Asamoah-Gyadu, African Charismatics: Current Developments within Independent Indigenous Pentecostalism in Ghana, Brill, Leiden, 2005.
[44] Masenya Madipoane, 'The Sword that Heals! The Bible and African Women in African South African Pentecostal Churches', in I.A. Phiri & S. Nadar (eds), *On Being Church: African Women's Voices and Visions*, pp. 47-59, WCC, Geneva, 2005.
[45] Sarojini Nadar. 'On Being Pentecostal Church: Pentecostal Women's Voices and Visions,' in I.A. Phiri & S. Nadar (eds), *On Being Church: African Women's Voices and Visions,* 60-79, WCC, Geneva, 2005.
[46] See Rose Gabaitse. *Towards A Pentecostal Feminist Hermeneutic: Reading Luke-Acts With Batswana Women.* University of KwaZulu Natal PhD, 2012.
[47] B. Meyer, *Translating the Devil: Religion and Modernity Among the Ewe in Ghana*. Edinburgh University Press, Edinburgh, 1999.
[48] See Matthew A. Ojo, "Pentecostal and Charismatic Movements in Africa," 295-309. In Elias Bongmba ed. *The Wiley-Blackwell Companion to African Religions*. Oxford: Blackwell, 2012, 308.

serve. If, however, African Christianity's mandate is to spread the justice-seeking message of salvation, healing and deliverance, to their members and the communities they serve, then they must seek to emphasise gender-equity in all their structures and programmes.

Bibliography

Amadiume, Ifi. *Africa: Reinventing Matriarchy, Religion and Culture*. London: Zed Books, 1997.

Asamoah-Gyadu, Kwabena J. *African Charismatics: Current Developments within Independent Indigenous Pentecostalism in Ghana*, Brill, Leiden, 2005.

Bongma, Elias ed. *African Religions: The Wiley-Blackwell Companion.* Oxford: Wiley-Blackwell, 2012.

Dube, M. W. Ed. Other Ways of Reading: African Women and the Bible. Atlanta: SBL and Geneva: WCC, 2001.

Mbiti, John S. *Introduction to African Religion.* 2nd ed. Oxford: Heinemann Educational Publishers, 1991.

Newsom Carol and Sharon Ringe, eds. *The Women's Bible Commentary*. Louisville: John Knox Press. 1992.

Njoroge, J Nyambura and M. W. Dube, Dube, eds. *Talitha Cum: Theologies of African Women.* Natal: Cluster Publications, 2001.

Oduyoye, Mercy A. *Hearing and Knowing: Theological Reflections on Christianity in Africa*. New York: Orbis Press, 1993.

Phiri, A. I and S. Nadar (eds.), *On Being Church: African Women's Voices and Visions*. WCC, Geneva, 2005.

Phiri, A. Isabel and Sarojini Nadar eds. *Her-Stories: Hidden Histories of Women of Faith in Africa.* Pietermaritzburg: Cluster, 2002.

Yorke, Gosnell L.O.R. (ed) *Bible Translation and African Languages.* Nairobi: Acton, 2004.

(16A) RELIGIOUS DEMOGRAPHIES OF AFRICA, 1970-2025[1]

Gina A. Zurlo and Todd M. Johnson

Over the course of the twentieth century, the continent of Africa underwent profound changes in politics, culture, society and religion. Historically, Africa has been, and likely will remain, a religious continent, with over 99% of its population adhering to a religion.[2] In 1910, only 9% of Africa's population was Christian, and 80% of Christians lived in just four countries: Ethiopia, South Africa, Egypt and Madagascar. Table 1 shows that in 1970, Christians constituted 38% of the population (366 million) in Africa; this is expected to grow to 50% in 2025 (see Table 2). Over the 45-year period 1970-2025, Christianity's average annual rate of growth (3.1% p.a.) is expected to outpace those of both Islam, the second largest religion on the continent (2.6% p.a.), and the African population as a whole (also 2.6%). Muslims in Africa will grow from 148 million in 1970 (40% of the continent's population) to an expected 612 million (42%) by 2025. By 2025, Christians and Muslims together are expected to account for approximately 92% of Africa's population. Traditional African religionists (ethno-religionists) are projected to increase by about 30 million between 1970 and 2025 but to decline as a percentage of Africa's population, from 21% in 1970 to only 7% by 2025. Another surprising trend is the rise of the non-religious, who are found largely in urban centres and will number over 10 million in 2025 (with most in South Africa).

Table 1: Religious affiliation and growth in Africa, 1970-2025

Religion	*Adherents 1970*	*% 1970*	*Adherents 2025*	*% 2025*	*1970-2025 % p.a.**
Religionists	365,784,000	99.8%	1,457,481,000	99.3%	2.55%
Christians	140,657,000	38.4%	733,197,000	49.9%	3.05%
Roman Catholics	44,921,000	12.3%	268,214,000	18.3%	3.30%
Protestants	26,599,000	7.3%	191,830,000	13.1%	3.66%
Independents	19,839,000	5.4%	151,141,000	10.3%	3.76%
Anglicans	7,728,000	2.1%	73,770,000	5.0%	4.19%
Orthodox	17,782,000	4.9%	64,006,000	4.4%	2.36%
Unaffiliated Christians	25,873,000	7.1%	29,194,000	2.0%	0.22%
Muslims	148,145,000	40.4%	611,679,000	41.7%	2.61%
Ethno-religionists	74,976,000	20.5%	104,769,000	7.1%	0.61%

[1] Portions of this chapter appear as updated versions of the following: Todd M. Johnson and Gina A. Zurlo, "Religions by Continent," in *Yearbook of International Religious Demography 2015*, edited by Brian J. Grim, Todd M. Johnson, Vegard Skirbekk, and Gina A. Zurlo (Leiden/Boston: Brill, 2015); and Center for the Study of Global Christianity, *Christianity in its Global Context, 1970-2020: Society, Religion, and Mission,* June 2013. www.gordonconwell.edu/resources/documents/2ChristianityinitsGlobalContext.pdf.

[2] Helpful works on the subject include Thomas D. Blakely, Dennis L. Thomson, and Walter E. A. van Beek, *Religion in Africa: Experience and Expression* (Portsmouth, NH: Heinemann, 1994); Elizabeth Isichei, *The Religious Traditions of Africa: A History* (Westport, CT: Greenwood, 2004); Laurenti Magesa, *African Religion: The Moral Traditions of Abundant Life* (Maryknoll, NY: Orbis Books, 1997); and Benjamin C. Ray, *African Religions: Symbol, Ritual, and Community*, 2nd ed. (Upper Saddle River, NJ: Prentice-Hall, 1999).

Hindus	996,000	0.3%	3,632,000	0.2%	2.38%
Baha'is	698,000	0.2%	3,177,000	0.2%	2.79%
Buddhists	11,700	0.0%	314,000	0.0%	6.17%
Chinese folk religionists	7,300	0.0%	177,000	0.0%	5.97%
New religionists	29,500	0.0%	160,000	0.0%	3.12%
Jains	32,800	0.0%	137,000	0.0%	2.63%
Jews	202,000	0.1%	110,000	0.0%	-1.10%
Sikhs	25,900	0.0%	103,000	0.0%	2.53%
Confucianists	0	0.0%	25,000	0.0%	15.29%
Spiritists	2,300	0.0%	3,100	0.0%	0.54%
Zoroastrians	480	0.0%	970	0.0%	1.29%
Non-religionists	691,000	0.2%	10,491,000	0.7%	5.07%
Agnostics	588,000	0.2%	9,707,000	0.7%	5.23%
Atheists	103,000	0.0%	784,000	0.1%	3.76%
Total population	**366,475,000**	**100.0%**	**1,467,973,000**	**100.0%**	**2.56%**

Data source: Todd M. Johnson and Brian J. Grim (eds), *World Religion Database* (Boston and Leiden: Brill – accessed February 2015).
Numbers might not add up to 100 due to rounding.
* Average annual growth rate, per cent per year, between dates specified.

Table 2: Christianity in Africa, 1970-2025

	1970			2025				
	Population	*Christians*	*%*	*Population*	*Christians*	*%*	*Pop. rate**	*Chr. rate***
Africa	366,475,000	140,657,000	38.4%	1,467,973,000	733,197,000	49.9%	2.56%	3.05%
Eastern Africa	110,545,000	54,912,000	49.7%	511,228,000	345,729,000	67.6%	2.82%	3.40%
Middle Africa	40,472,000	29,887,000	73.8%	185,581,000	154,347,000	83.2%	2.81%	3.03%
Northern Africa	84,317,000	6,423,000	7.6%	250,981,000	10,499,000	4.2%	2.00%	0.90%
Southern Africa	25,454,000	19,286,000	75.8%	65,509,000	54,129,000	82.6%	1.73%	1.89%
Western Africa	105,686,000	30,149,000	28.5%	454,673,000	168,494,000	37.1%	2.69%	3.18%

* Average annual growth rate, per cent per year, between 1970 and 2025.
** Average annual Christian growth rate, per cent per year, between 1970 and 2025.

Roman Catholics form the largest bloc of Christians in Africa (Table 1). Between 1970 and 2025, their numbers is increasing from 45 million (12% of the population) to 268 million (18%). In 2015, the Catholic share of church members was lower than in 1970, but projections for 2025 show an increase. Independents have seen their shares of the total population and of church members decrease, although they were still higher in 2015 than in 1970. The Orthodox share of both has declined steadily since 1970, a trend that is predicted to continue. Anglicans have seen the fastest growth over the 45-year period: from 8 million in 1970 to 72 million in 2025.

Religion

Demographically, Africa experienced the greatest religious change of any continent over the twentieth century. By 1970, Muslims had replaced ethno-religionists as the largest group of religious adherents. Ironically, this occurred largely through ethno-religionists becoming Christians. This pattern – larger numbers of ethno-religionists converting to Christianity than to Islam – has continued, so that in 2015 Africa is 49% Christian, 42% Muslim, and 9% ethno-religionist.[3] The Christian and Muslim percentages are expected to increase slightly by 2025, while the ethno-religionist percentage is projected to keep declining.

Sharp regional differences exist in the distribution of religionists in Africa. Eastern Africa was home to almost half of Africa's Christians in 2015, up from about one third in 1970. Most of the rest live in Middle and Southern Africa, with Northern Africa home to the fewest (2% of the continent's 2015 total). Meanwhile, Northern Africa had 42% of Africa's Muslims in 2015, with Western Africa home to another 37% (compared with 52% and 31%, respectively, in 1970, and 39% and 40% in 2025). Southern Africa had the smallest Muslim population of any region in 2015 (less than 1% of Africa's total).

Ethno-religionists in 2015 were found mostly in Eastern and Western Africa. No other religion claims more than 1% of the continent's population in 2015 (agnostics and atheists together are closest, and most live in Southern Africa). Hindus, Jews and Buddhists are concentrated in Southern Africa as well, while most Chinese folk-religionists and Baha'is live in Eastern Africa.

Despite their large proportions of the population, Christians and Muslims in Africa have little interaction with one another, especially compared with the levels of interaction between Christians and adherents of other religions. Only 20% of Muslims in Africa knew a Christian personally in 2015, compared with 47% of ethno-religionists. Followers of many of the smaller religions on the continent, such as Baha'is and Buddhists, have the most interaction with Christians (86% and 42%, respectively).[4]

Society

Africa is the world's least-developed continent. Although individual countries have made advances towards meeting the United Nations Millennium Development Goals – notably Egypt (one of the world's most successful), Burkina Faso and Morocco – many more have had only limited progress.[5] The continent as a whole has done best in combating hunger and poverty. Addressing crises related to education, heath care (maternal and child mortality; HIV/AIDS) and clean water has been less fruitful. Religious differences tear at the social fabric of Africa as well. A Muslim-Christian 'fault line' of sorts stretches across the continent, and ideological and physical clashes between the two religions seem likely to intensify in the near future.

Eastern Africa

Eastern Africa experienced a profound transformation of its religious landscape over the twentieth century. By 1970, half of the region's population was Christian (Table 3). The Christian proportion of the region's

---

[3] All data for 2015 and data for religions by country are found in Todd M. Johnson and Gina A. Zurlo, eds. *World Christian Database* (Leiden/Boston: Brill, accessed February 2015).
[4] For more information on personal contact, see Todd M. Johnson and Kenneth R. Ross, eds. *Atlas of Global Christianity* (Edinburgh: Edinburgh University Press, 2009), 316-317. Most recent data are found in Johnson and Zurlo, *World Christian Database*.
[5] See www.unmillenniumproject.org/goals.

population increased to 62% by 2015, and it is projected to reach two thirds by 2025. At that time, Eastern Africa will be home to more than 47% of Africa's Christians (up from 39% in 1970), including 48% of Protestants, 54% of Anglicans, and 87% of all Orthodox in Africa.

	1970			*2025*				
	Population	*Christians*	*%*	*Population*	*Christians*	*%*	*Pop. rate*	*Chr. rate*
Eastern Africa	110,545,000	54,912,000	49.7%	511,228,000	345,729,000	67.6%	2.82%	3.40%
Burundi	3,457,000	2,579,000	74.6%	14,429,000	13,680,000	94.8%	2.63%	3.08%
Comoros	232,000	1,500	0.6%	954,000	5,100	0.5%	2.60%	2.24%
Djibouti	160,000	12,000	7.5%	1,023,000	18,500	1.8%	3.44%	0.79%
Eritrea	1,797,000	857,000	47.7%	8,737,000	3,810,000	43.6%	2.92%	2.75%
Ethiopia	28,415,000	15,005,000	52.8%	124,537,000	75,209,000	60.4%	2.72%	2.97%
Kenya	11,252,000	7,058,000	62.7%	59,386,000	48,880,000	82.3%	3.07%	3.58%
Madagascar	6,576,000	3,326,000	50.6%	31,741,000	19,093,000	60.2%	2.90%	3.23%
Malawi	4,530,000	2,664,000	58.8%	22,776,000	18,453,000	81.0%	2.98%	3.58%
Mauritius	826,000	296,000	35.9%	1,283,000	434,000	33.9%	0.80%	0.70%
Mayotte	37,000	360	1.0%	296,000	1,300	0.4%	3.86%	2.38%
Mozambique	9,453,000	2,611,000	27.6%	34,459,000	18,927,000	54.9%	2.38%	3.67%
Réunion	462,000	446,000	96.6%	983,000	855,000	87.0%	1.38%	1.19%
Rwanda	3,755,000	2,298,000	61.2%	15,914,000	14,748,000	92.7%	2.66%	3.44%
Seychelles	52,200	51,300	98.3%	97,300	91,600	94.1%	1.14%	1.06%
Somalia	3,445,000	4,900	0.1%	14,743,000	4,100	0.0%	2.68%	-0.30%
South Sudan	3,647,000	721,000	19.8%	15,571,000	10,074,000	64.7%	2.67%	4.91%
Tanzania	13,605,000	5,007,000	36.8%	69,329,000	39,236,000	56.6%	3.01%	3.81%
Uganda	9,446,000	6,429,000	68.1%	54,832,000	46,636,000	85.1%	3.25%	3.67%
Zambia	4,191,000	2,825,000	67.4%	21,388,000	19,082,000	89.2%	3.01%	3.53%
Zimbabwe	5,206,000	2,719,000	52.2%	18,748,000	16,491,000	88.0%	2.36%	3.33%

Source: Todd M. Johnson and Gina A. Zurlo (eds), *World Christian Database* (Leiden and Boston: Brill – accessed February 2015).
* Average annual growth rate, per cent per year, between 1970 and 2025.
** Average annual Christian growth rate, per cent per year, between 1970 and 2025.

Christians will constitute a majority of the population in fourteen of Eastern Africa's twenty countries in 2025, rising from eleven in 1970; Eritrea had a near-majority during this period. The countries in which Christians will constitute the largest share of the population in 2025 are projected to be Burundi, Seychelles, Rwanda and Zambia. By contrast, four are projected to be less than 2% Christian in 2025: Somalia, the Comoros Islands, Mayotte and Djibouti. Each of these has a Muslim majority.

Roman Catholics will continue to be the largest major tradition in the region, increasing from 17% of the total regional population in 1970 to 22% in 2015 (but 35% of all Christians in 1970 to 33% in 2015). Protestants more than doubled their share of the total population between 1970 and 2015 (from 7% to 18%), replacing Orthodox as the region's second largest major tradition. The gap is projected to widen further by 2025 (18% Protestant versus 11% Orthodox). Independents and Anglicans have seen their shares of the total population rise substantially as well (with projected 2025 population shares about 8% each, up from 4% and 3% respectively in 1970).

Religion

The growth of Christianity in Eastern Africa has been mainly at the expense of ethno-religions. The latter declined from 30% of the total population in 1970 to 11% in 2015 (placing it third, behind Islam), with a further decline to 9% expected by 2025 (Table 4). Although Muslims have experienced numerical growth over the period as well, it has been at a rate closer to that of the general population (about 3% growth per year). As a result, Muslims' share of the total population has risen only slightly, by about one percentage point in the periods 1970-2015 and 2015-2025. Though adherents of other religions are increasing in number, their combined share of the region's total population will actually decrease by 2025.

Table 4: Religious affiliation and growth in Eastern Africa, 1970-2025

Religion	*Adherents 1970*	*% 1970*	*Adherents 2025*	*% 2025*	*1970-2025 % p.a.**
Religionists	110,483,000	99.9%	509,646,000	99.7%	2.82%
Christians	54,912,000	49.7%	345,729,000	67.6%	3.40%
Roman Catholics	19,085,000	17.3%	117,794,000	23.0%	3.36%
Protestants	7,770,000	7.0%	92,087,000	18.0%	4.60%
Orthodox	12,126,000	11.0%	55,923,000	10.9%	2.82%
Independents	4,377,000	4.0%	40,658,000	8.0%	4.14%
Anglicans	3,102,000	2.8%	39,692,000	7.8%	4.74%
Unaffiliated Christians	9,159,000	8.3%	10,912,000	2.1%	0.32%
Muslims	21,579,000	19.5%	111,511,000	21.8%	3.03%
Ethno-religionists	32,879,000	29.7%	48,129,000	9.4%	0.70%
Hindus	559,000	0.5%	2,107,000	0.4%	2.44%
Baha'is	448,000	0.4%	1,763,000	0.3%	2.52%
Jains	32,800	0.0%	134,000	0.0%	2.60%
Chinese folk religionists	5,600	0.0%	102,000	0.0%	5.42%
Sikhs	21,900	0.0%	80,700	0.0%	2.40%
Buddhists	7,800	0.0%	45,900	0.0%	3.27%
Jews	35,700	0.0%	37,900	0.0%	0.11%
New religionists	1,600	0.0%	3,800	0.0%	1.62%
Zoroastrians	480	0.0%	970	0.0%	1.29%
Spiritists	300	0.0%	600	0.0%	1.27%
Non-religionists	62,300	0.1%	1,582,000	0.3%	6.06%
Agnostics	56,100	0.1%	1,404,000	0.3%	6.03%
Atheists	6,200	0.0%	179,000	0.0%	6.30%
Total population	**110,545,000**	**100.0%**	**511,228,000**	**100.0%**	**2.82%**

Data source: Todd M. Johnson and Brian J. Grim (eds), *World Religion Database* (Boston and Leiden:

Brill – accessed February 2015).
Numbers might not add up to 100 due to rounding.
* Average annual growth rate, per cent per year, between dates specified.

Each of the four countries with a Muslim majority in 2015 is at least 96% Muslim (the Comoros Islands, Djibouti, Mayotte and Somalia). In seven other countries, Muslims constitute at least 10% of the population. Ethno-religionists exceed 10% in only six countries in 2015, down from twelve in 1970. By 2025, they will exceed 10% in only three countries – Madagascar, South Sudan and Mozambique – although blending of traditional religious beliefs with Christianity is likely to continue. The only other religion having at least 10% adherence in any country is Hinduism in Mauritius. Compared with Africa as a whole, more non-Christian religionists know a Christian personally in Eastern Africa (43%, compared with the continent's 25%).

Society

Despite being home to large cities such as Addis Ababa, Nairobi and Dar es Salaam, Eastern Africa is the least-urbanized region on the continent. Urban dwellers are only 26% of the region's population in 2015, far below both the continent-wide average of 41%. In fact, globally, only Melanesia has a lower urban percentage (19%). Countries in the region continue to experience difficulty in meeting many Millennium Development Goals, such as reducing maternal and child mortality, ensuring access to safe drinking water, and combating malnutrition. How to provide for their growing populations without dependence on external assistance, especially if compounded by additional challenges brought on by urbanization, is likely to be an ongoing challenge for the region.

Middle Africa

Middle Africa experienced a drastic alteration in its religious make-up during the twentieth century. In 1910, the region was 95% ethno-religionist and only 1% Christian. Table 5 shows that by 1970, however, Christians made up 74% of the population, and ethno-religionists had fallen to 17%. This pattern has continued to the present: Christians constituted 82% of the region's population in 2015, a figure that is expected to rise to 83% in 2025.

Table 5: Christianity in Middle Africa, 1970-2025

	1970			*2025*				
	Population	*Christians*	*%*	*Population*	*Christians*	*%*	*Pop. rate*	*Chr. rate*
Middle Africa	40,472,000	29,887,000	73.8%	185,581,000	154,347,000	83.2%	2.81%	3.03%
Angola	5,928,000	4,700,000	79.3%	30,446,000	28,790,000	94.6%	3.02%	3.35%
Cameroon	6,771,000	3,152,000	46.6%	29,628,000	18,534,000	62.6%	2.72%	3.27%
Central African Republic	1,829,000	1,162,000	63.6%	5,795,000	4,388,000	75.7%	2.12%	2.44%
Chad	3,645,000	843,000	23.1%	18,185,000	6,512,000	35.8%	2.97%	3.79%
Congo	1,335,000	1,224,000	91.7%	5,970,000	5,389,000	90.3%	2.76%	2.73%
Congo DR	20,010,000	17,960,000	89.8%	92,117,000	87,740,000	95.2%	2.81%	2.93%
Equatorial Guinea	291,000	257,000	88.3%	1,023,000	903,000	88.3%	2.31%	2.31%
Gabon	589,000	517,000	87.8%	2,165,000	1,847,000	85.3%	2.39%	2.34%

São Tomé and Principe	74,300	72,200	97.2%	252,000	243,000	96.4%	2.25%	2.23%

Source: Todd M. Johnson and Gina A. Zurlo (eds), *World Christian Database* (Leiden and Boston: Brill – accessed February 2015).
* Average annual growth rate, per cent per year, between 1970 and 2025.
** Average annual Christian growth rate, per cent per year, between 1970 and 2025.

Christians form a majority of the population in eight of the region's nine countries in 2015, ranging from 96% in São Tomé and Principe to 59% in Cameroon; they are a minority only in Chad (35%). Other countries exceeding 90% Christian are DR Congo and Angola. Christian percentages are expected to rise in every country in the region except Equatorial Guinea between 2015 and 2025.

Roman Catholics are by far the largest group of Christians in the region, representing almost half of the region's population in 2025, up from 39% in 1970. No tradition could claim such a large share of any other African region's total population in the period 1970-2025, although Independents in Southern Africa are approaching it (growing from 20% of the total population there in 1970 to 38% in 2025). Catholics are also the largest Christian tradition in each country in Middle Africa, representing a majority or near-majority of Christians. Their share of Christians in the region also increased between 1970 and 2015, from 52% to 58%. Other Christian groups are experiencing even more rapid growth. For example, Protestants grew from 7% of the total population of Angola in 1970 to 26% in 2015.

Religion

Muslims currently constitute the second largest group of religious adherents in the region, growing from 9% of the total population in 1970 to 10% in 2015 and 11% in 2025 (see Table 6). They represent a majority of the population in Chad, and sizeable minorities in Cameroon and the Central Africa Republic. Ethno-religionists meanwhile declined from 17% of the region's population in 1970 to 7% in 2015, and are predicted to drop to 5% in 2025. Ethno-religionists exceed 10% of the population in only two countries in 2015: Cameroon and the Central African Republic.

Table 6: Religious affiliation and growth in Middle Africa, 1970-2025

Religion	*Adherents 1970*	*% 1970*	*Adherents 2025*	*% 2025*	*1970-2025 % p.a.**
Religionists	40,433,000	99.9%	184,263,000	99.3%	2.80%
Christians	29,887,000	73.8%	154,347,000	83.2%	3.03%
Roman Catholics	15,596,000	38.5%	87,836,000	47.3%	3.19%
Protestants	5,841,000	14.4%	35,346,000	19.0%	3.33%
Independents	5,330,000	13.2%	32,702,000	17.6%	3.35%
Unaffiliated Christians	4,026,000	9.9%	8,125,000	4.4%	1.28%
Anglicans	102,000	0.3%	878,000	0.5%	3.99%
Orthodox	8,300	0.0%	18,100	0.0%	1.43%
Muslims	3,495,000	8.6%	19,567,000	10.5%	3.18%
Ethno-religionists	6,876,000	17.0%	9,407,000	5.1%	0.57%
Baha'is	170,000	0.4%	715,000	0.4%	2.64%
Hindus	1,000	0.0%	151,000	0.1%	9.55%
New religionists	2,600	0.0%	56,200	0.0%	5.75%

Buddhists	400	0.0%	12,500	0.0%	6.46%
Chinese folk religionists	40	0.0%	6,700	0.0%	9.76%
Jews	500	0.0%	500	0.0%	0.00%
Non-religionists	38,900	0.1%	1,318,000	0.7%	6.62%
Agnostics	34,400	0.1%	1,156,000	0.6%	6.60%
Atheists	4,500	0.0%	162,000	0.1%	6.73%
Total population	**40,472,000**	**100.0%**	**185,581,000**	**100.0%**	**2.81%**

Data source: Todd M. Johnson and Brian J. Grim (eds), *World Religion Database* (Boston and Leiden: Brill, accessed February 2015).
Numbers might not add up to 100 due to rounding.
* Average annual growth rate, per cent per year, between dates specified.

Other notable populations of religionists in individual countries include Baha'is in São Tomé and Principe; atheists in Equatorial Guinea; and agnostics in Equatorial Guinea, Congo, Gabon, and São Tomé and Principe. While agnostics' share of the population has held steady in Equatorial Guinea (3% in 1970 and in 2025), it has increased noticeably in the other countries.

Middle Africa is less religiously diverse than other regions in Africa (in terms of the number of religions present). Interestingly, Middle Africa and Eastern Africa have the highest composite levels of personal contact with Christians (43% in each). Greater contact by atheists, agnostics and ethno-religionists in Middle Africa makes up for higher levels of contact among other religionists in Eastern Africa.

Society

Middle Africa is one of the most undeveloped/underdeveloped areas of the world. The United Nations Economic and Social Council classifies six of the region's nine countries as Least Developed Countries based on per capita income, human assets (which encompass many of the criteria assessed in the Millennium Development Goals), and economic vulnerability (which includes heightened susceptibility to natural disasters and changes in trade and exports, as well as sizes and remoteness of populations).[6] Several countries in the region have been among the least successful in meeting the Millennium Development Goals; in particular, DR Congo is tied for last place globally.

Northern Africa

Northern Africa is the only region in Africa to experience a decline in the percentage of Christians in the population over the period 1970-2025, continuing a trend that dates back to at least the beginning of the twentieth century. The Christian share of the regional population fell from 8% in 1970 to 5% in 2015, and is predicted to decline to 4% in 2025, despite an increase in the actual number of Christians over the period (see Table 7).

Table 7: Christianity in Northern Africa, 1970-2025

	1970			*2025*				
	Population	*Christians*	*%*	*Population*	*Christians*	*%*	*Pop. rate*	*Chr. rate*
Northern Africa	84,317,000	6,423,000	7.6%	250,981,000	10,499,000	4.2%	2.00%	0.90%

[6] See www.un.org/en/development/desa/policy/cdp/ldc_info.shtml.

Algeria	14,691,000	101,000	0.7%	46,480,000	82,100	0.2%	2.12%	-0.37%
Egypt	36,342,000	5,778,000	15.9%	96,989,000	8,208,000	8.5%	1.80%	0.64%
Libya	2,076,000	58,800	2.8%	7,145,000	210,000	2.9%	2.27%	2.34%
Morocco	15,916,000	109,000	0.7%	37,723,000	29,800	0.1%	1.58%	-2.32%
Sudan	10,233,000	318,000	3.1%	49,676,000	1,947,000	3.9%	2.91%	3.35%
Tunisia	4,983,000	27,300	0.5%	12,231,000	20,900	0.2%	1.65%	-0.48%
Western Sahara	76,900	31,600	41.1%	737,000	900	0.1%	4.19%	-6.27%

Source: Todd M. Johnson and Gina A. Zurlo (eds), *World Religion Database* (Boston and Leiden: Brill – accessed February 2015).

* Average annual growth rate, per cent per year, between 1970 and 2025.

** Average annual Christian growth rate, per cent per year, between 1970 and 2025.

Egypt was home to 90% of the region's Christians in 1970. By 2015 that figure had declined to 78%, due mainly to the dramatic increase in the Christian population of Sudan (2 million, or 19% of the regional total, up from 318,000 and 5% in 1970). That figure would be higher if not for conflict-induced migration of Christians from Sudan to South Sudan.

Immigrants and/or expatriates constitute the majority of Christians in Libya, Morocco, Tunisia and Western Sahara; they also form a sizeable minority of Christians in Sudan. Egypt has seen the Christian percentage of its population decline steadily, from 16% in 1970 to 10% in 2015 and a predicted 9% in 2025. Attacks on Christian individuals, churches and businesses in Egypt have increased in recent years. If political, economic and/or social conditions worsen, the number of Christians there could be much lower in 2025. In Western Sahara, both the number of Christians and the Christian percentage plunged between 1970 and 2015 (from over 31,000 to only 930, and from 41% to less than 1%) due to the departure of foreigners following Spanish decolonization. Algeria saw a similar drop, albeit on a much smaller scale. The Christian populations of both countries are showing growth for the period 2015-2025; in Egypt and Morocco, however, the numbers of Christians are expected to decline between 2015 and 2025.

In 1970, Orthodox constituted by far the largest Christian tradition in the region. At 6 million adherents (8% of the total population and 87% of church members), they outnumbered all other Christian traditions combined (see Table 8). By 2025, their share of all Christians will however be only 75%, due largely to an increase by Roman Catholics to 14% of church members (up from 7% in 1970). Protestants and Anglicans will see smaller gains over the period, with the Protestant share showing a continued increase. Roman Catholics are the largest tradition in every country except Algeria (Independents) and Egypt (Orthodox).

Religion

Islam is the largest religion by far in every country in the region. Over the period 1970-2015, the Muslim population rose in each country, and their percentage share of the total population rose or held steady in every country except Algeria and Libya. Other than Western Sahara, which experienced massive emigration by non-Muslims, Egypt had the highest Muslim gain in percentage share over the period, from 84% in 1970 to 89% in 2015. The biggest change between 2015 and 2025 will be in Sudan, where the Muslim percentage is expected to increase, though still only slightly.

Table 8: Religious affiliation and growth in Northern Africa, 1970-2025

Religion	*Adherents 1970*	*% 1970*	*Adherents 2025*	*% 2025*	*1970-2025 % p.a.**
Religionists	84,023,000	99.7%	248,949,000	99.2%	1.99%
Muslims	76,749,000	91.0%	237,218,000	94.5%	2.07%
Christians	6,423,000	7.6%	10,499,000	4.2%	0.90%
Orthodox	5,610,000	6.7%	7,897,000	3.1%	0.62%
Roman Catholics	437,000	0.5%	1,450,000	0.6%	2.20%
Protestants	204,000	0.2%	915,000	0.4%	2.77%
Anglicans	92,900	0.1%	557,000	0.2%	3.31%
Independents	71,400	0.1%	311,000	0.1%	2.71%
unaffiliated Christians	8,200	0.0%	49,100	0.0%	3.31%
Ethno-religionists	800,000	0.9%	1,101,000	0.4%	0.58%
Baha'is	5,200	0.0%	52,200	0.0%	4.28%
Buddhists	400	0.0%	35,100	0.0%	8.48%
Chinese folk religionists	0	0.0%	21,300	0.0%	14.95%
Jews	44,900	0.1%	10,300	0.0%	-2.64%
Hindus	0	0.0%	9,900	0.0%	13.36%
Sikhs	0	0.0%	3,000	0.0%	10.93%
Non-religionists	294,000	0.3%	2,032,000	0.8%	3.58%
Agnostics	228,000	0.3%	1,847,000	0.7%	3.88%
Atheists	66,200	0.1%	185,000	0.1%	1.89%
Total population	**84,317,000**	**100.0%**	**250,981,000**	**100.0%**	**2.00%**

Data source: Todd M. Johnson and Brian J. Grim (eds), *World Religion Database* (Boston and Leiden: Brill – accessed February 2015).
Numbers might not add up to 100 due to rounding.
* Average annual growth rate, per cent per year, between dates specified.

Not surprisingly, religious adherents in Northern Africa have significantly less interaction with Christians than in any other region in Africa, since the Christian population there is also the smallest. Of all religionists in the region, only 11% know a Christian personally.

Society

Northern Africa has been the most successful region in Africa at meeting the Millennium Development Goals, although progress is uneven. Egypt, for example, has one of the best records of any country in the world. Tunisia and Morocco also rank fairly high, while Libya is among the countries making the least progress. The full effects of the 2010 Arab Spring uprisings on the social welfare of the population remain to be seen. Of special concern to Christians is how they and other minority religionists will be treated under the Islamist governments that have gained power in many countries.

Southern Africa

Southern Africa is the smallest region in Africa in total population (58 million in 2015, less than half of next-ranked Middle Africa's 142 million) and in number of countries (five). Its demographics are dominated by South Africa, home to 85-90% of both the total and Christian populations over the period 1970-2025.

Table 9: Christianity in Southern Africa, 1970-2025

	1970			2025				
	Population	*Christians*	*%*	*Population*	*Christians*	*%*	*Pop. rate*	*Chr. rate*
Southern Africa	25,454,000	19,286,000	75.8%	65,509,000	54,129,000	82.6%	1.73%	1.89%
Botswana	693,000	255,000	36.7%	2,245,000	1,683,000	75.0%	2.16%	3.49%
Lesotho	1,032,000	841,000	81.5%	2,325,000	2,169,000	93.3%	1.49%	1.74%
Namibia	780,000	709,000	90.9%	2,830,000	2,592,000	91.6%	2.37%	2.38%
South Africa	22,503,000	17,181,000	76.4%	56,666,000	46,397,000	81.9%	1.69%	1.82%
Swaziland	446,000	300,000	67.3%	1,443,000	1,288,000	89.2%	2.16%	2.68%

Source: Todd M. Johnson and Gina A. Zurlo (eds), *World Religion Database* (Boston and Leiden: Brill – accessed February 2015).
* Average annual growth rate, per cent per year, between 1970 and 2025.
** Average annual Christian growth rate, per cent per year, between 1970 and 2025.

Southern Africa began the twentieth century with the highest Christian percentage of any African region. In 1910 the figure was at 37%, mostly by virtue of South Africa's very large Christian population. By 1970, the regional figure had increased to 76%, and only Botswana lacked a Christian majority. Swaziland, Lesotho and Namibia all had huge increases in their Christian populations; Namibia especially rose from 9% Christian in 1910 to an incredible 91% in 1970 (see Table 9). In all countries in the region, the Christian percentage was higher in 2015 than in 1970, and Botswana now has a Christian majority as well (with the exception of Namibia, which only dropped 0.1%). The percentages are projected to rise till 2025 in every country except South Africa. Protestants are dominant in Namibia, as are Roman Catholics in Lesotho. Independents are largest in Botswana, South Africa and Swaziland. These percentage shares are expected to rise in each county except Namibia till 2025.

In 1970, Protestants represented 29% of the total regional population, shrinking to 21% in 2015 and 2025, while increasing in number. Independents have grown from 20% of the region's population in 1970 to 38% in 2015. Protestants in Southern Africa represented 38% of all church members in 1970, and Independents 26%. By 2015, however, Independents (46%) had a much larger share than Protestants (25%), a trend that is expected to continue till 2025.

Religion

In 1970, adherents of four religions (Christians, ethno-religionists, Hindus and Muslims) constituted at least 1% of Southern Africa's population; most Hindus and Muslims lived in South Africa. By 2015, agnostics had risen to 5% of the population, up from less than 1% in 1970, and overtaking Hindus as the third largest group of adherents in the region. Like Hindus and Muslims (both in 1970 and currently), agnostics are found mostly in South Africa, although the number of agnostics also exceeded 1% of the total population in Namibia and in Swaziland in 2015. Meanwhile, regional percentages for Hindus and Muslims remains around 2% of the total population in 2015 and 2025.

Table 10: Religious affiliation and growth in Southern Africa, 1970-2025

Religion	*Adherents 1970*	*% 1970*	*Adherents 2025*	*% 2025*	*1970-2025 % p.a.**
Religionists	25,299,000	99.4%	61,421,000	93.8%	1.63%
Christians	19,286,000	75.8%	54,129,000	82.6%	1.89%
Independents	4,958,000	19.5%	25,047,000	38.2%	2.99%
Protestants	7,252,000	28.5%	13,725,000	21.0%	1.17%
unaffiliated Christians	3,557,000	14.0%	7,216,000	11.0%	1.29%
Roman Catholics	2,171,000	8.5%	5,747,000	8.8%	1.79%
Anglicans	1,347,000	5.3%	3,150,000	4.8%	1.56%
Orthodox	30,100	0.1%	30,100	0.0%	3.02E-05
Ethno-religionists	5,134,000	20.2%	4,290,000	6.5%	-0.33%
Hindus	433,000	1.7%	1,310,000	2.0%	2.03%
Muslims	271,000	1.1%	978,000	1.5%	2.36%
Baha'is	34,700	0.1%	369,000	0.6%	4.39%
Buddhists	2,300	0.0%	181,000	0.3%	8.31%
Jews	120,000	0.5%	59,200	0.1%	-1.28%
Chinese folk religionists	1,600	0.0%	38,200	0.1%	5.89%
Confucianists	0	0.0%	25,000	0.0%	15.29%
New religionists	10,000	0.0%	23,400	0.0%	1.56%
Sikhs	4,000	0.0%	13,400	0.0%	2.22%
Spiritists	2,000	0.0%	2,500	0.0%	0.41%
Jains	0	0.0%	2,300	0.0%	10.39%
Non-religionists	156,000	0.6%	4,089,000	6.2%	6.12%
Agnostics	151,000	0.6%	3,927,000	6.0%	6.11%
Atheists	5,100	0.0%	162,000	0.2%	6.49%
Total population	**25,454,000**	**100.0%**	**65,509,000**	**100.0%**	**1.73%**

Data source: Todd M. Johnson and Brian J. Grim (eds), *World Religion Database* (Boston and Leiden: Brill – accessed February 2015).
Numbers might not add up to 100 due to rounding.
* Average annual growth rate, per cent per year, between dates specified.

Conversely, ethno-religionists have seen their share of the regional population fall, from 20% in 1970 to 8% in 2015 and 7% by 2025. The drop has been most dramatic in Botswana (from 63% of the total population in 1970 to 29% in 2015) and Swaziland (from 31% to 9%). The only other group of religious adherents exceeding 1% of a country's population in the period 1970-2025 is the Baha'i. Although they constituted 2% of Swaziland's population in 1970, their share had fallen to less than 1% by 2015, with an actual decrease in numbers. The population has since increased but is still expected be less than 1% of the national total in 2025. The Baha'i share of the population, however, is expected to reach or exceed 1%, or exceed 1% in both Botswana and Lesotho by 2025.

Southern Africa is one of Africa's most religiously diverse regions, home to almost all of the eighteen major world religions. Of these, nearly all atheists, agnostics, Baha'i, Spiritists and new religionists personally know a Christian, but these populations are comparatively small. Significantly more ethno-religionists (the second largest religion) have personal contact with Christians (78%) than do Hindus (29%), the third largest religion.

Society

While the region has made progress in meeting some of the Millennium Development Goals, it still faces difficulties. Among the largest is the continued prevalence of HIV/AIDS in the population. HIV rates among the adult population aged 15-49 exceed 10% in every country in the region, with Swaziland having the highest rate in the world (over 25%), followed by Botswana and Lesotho. Although the incidence of HIV infection appears to be declining, the ongoing social and economic effects (such as orphaned children and lost productivity) continue to present major challenges to the countries in the region.

Western Africa

Christianity grew steadily in Western Africa for the first half of the twentieth century. The region was 29% Christian in 1970, up from 2% in 1910. Since 1970, however, growth has been more rapid. Christians expanded to 36% of the regional population in 2015, and are expected to reach 37% by 2025. The average annual growth rate of 3.2% for 1970-2025 is predicted to exceed the total population growth rate over the same period (2.7%; see Table 11).

Table 11: Christianity in Western Africa, 1970-2025

	1970			2025				
	Population	*Christians*	*%*	*Population*	*Christians*	*%*	*Pop. rate*	*Chr. Rate*
Western Africa	105,686,000	30,149,000	28.5%	454,673,000	168,494,000	37.1%	2.69%	3.18%
Benin	2,908,000	515,000	17.7%	13,891,000	6,731,000	48.5%	2.88%	4.78%
Burkina Faso	5,625,000	523,000	9.3%	23,428,000	6,529,000	27.9%	2.63%	4.70%
Cape Verde	275,000	274,000	99.5%	555,000	522,000	94.1%	1.28%	1.18%
Côte d'Ivoire	5,242,000	1,348,000	25.7%	26,414,000	9,687,000	36.7%	2.98%	3.65%
Gambia	447,000	14,500	3.2%	2,660,000	118,000	4.5%	3.29%	3.89%
Ghana	8,597,000	4,344,000	50.5%	32,509,000	21,449,000	66.0%	2.45%	2.95%
Guinea	4,209,000	55,400	1.3%	15,590,000	583,000	3.7%	2.41%	4.37%
Guinea-Bissau	683,000	66,800	9.8%	2,233,000	300,000	13.4%	2.18%	2.77%
Liberia	1,420,000	395,000	27.9%	5,716,000	2,487,000	43.5%	2.56%	3.40%
Mali	5,716,000	85,200	1.5%	22,319,000	519,000	2.3%	2.51%	3.34%
Mauritania	1,149,000	6,200	0.5%	5,097,000	10,300	0.2%	2.75%	0.93%
Niger	4,413,000	16,900	0.4%	28,477,000	88,200	0.3%	3.45%	3.05%
Nigeria	56,132,000	21,469,000	38.2%	239,874,000	113,077,000	47.1%	2.68%	3.07%

Saint Helena	4,900	4,900	99.4%	4,400	4,200	95.5%	-0.18%	-0.25%
Senegal	4,218,000	230,000	5.4%	19,415,000	1,027,000	5.3%	2.81%	2.76%
Sierra Leone	2,532,000	218,000	8.6%	7,470,000	960,000	12.8%	1.99%	2.73%
Togo	2,116,000	584,000	27.6%	9,019,000	4,402,000	48.8%	2.67%	3.74%

Source: Todd M. Johnson and Gina A. Zurlo (eds), *World Religion Database* (Boston and Leiden: Brill – accessed February 2015).
* Average annual growth rate, per cent per year, between 1970 and 2025.
** Average annual Christian growth rate, per cent per year, between 1970 and 2025.

Western Africa straddles the 'dividing line' separating the Muslim-majority north of the continent from the Christian-majority south. This divide is apparent in the Christian percentages in the various countries. Six countries, mostly in the north of the region, were less than 10% Christian in 2015. In the south, Ghana was 64% Christian in 2015, and Togo was expected to continue moving towards a majority as well, at 49% Christian. Benin, Nigeria and Liberia will all have large Christian populations in 2025, over 40% of their total populations.

The island nations of Cape Verde and Saint Helena have seen their Christian percentages shrink steadily since 1970. Their Christian percentages – as well as that for Sierra Leone (13.3% in 2015) – are forecast to decline further by 2025. Eleven of the seventeen countries in the region, however, are predicted to have a continuing increase in the Christian share of the population between 1970 and 2025.

All Christian traditions (except the unaffiliated, which are decreasing as a percentage) are predicted to grow faster than the general population at the regional level for the period 1970-2025. Roman Catholics were the largest Christian tradition in the region in 1970, representing 7% of the total population. By 2015, Independents had surpassed Roman Catholics as the largest tradition. By 2025 Protestants and Catholics are forecast to have increased their share of the total population, while the Independents' share will have shrunk.

Religion

By 1970, both Muslims (44% of the population) and Christians had passed ethno-religionists' share of the population (28% in 1970: see Table 12). These trends have continued till 2015 (Muslims 52%, ethno-religionists 12%), with similar projections for 2025. Muslims constitute a majority of the population in eight countries in 2015 (and also 2025), while by 2025 they will form a significant minority in Côte d'Ivoire, Nigeria (nearly equally split with Christians), and Guinea-Bissau. The Muslim share of the population is expected either to rise or to hold steady in every country in the region between 2015 and 2025.

Table 12 Religious affiliation and growth in Western Africa, 1970-2025

Religion	*Adherents 1970*	*% 1970*	*Adherents 2025*	*% 2025*	*1970-2025 % p.a.**
Religionists	105,546,000	99.9%	453,203,000	99.7%	2.68%
Muslims	46,051,000	43.6%	242,405,000	53.3%	3.07%
Christians	30,149,000	28.5%	168,494,000	37.1%	3.18%
Traditional African religionists	29,287,000	27.7%	41,842,000	9.2%	0.65%

Baha'is	39,700	0.0%	278,000	0.1%	3.60%
New religionists	15,300	0.0%	76,300	0.0%	2.96%
Hindus	3,000	0.0%	53,900	0.0%	5.39%
Buddhists	800	0.0%	38,900	0.0%	7.32%
Chinese folk religionists	0	0.0%	8,600	0.0%	13.06%
Sikhs	0	0.0%	5,500	0.0%	12.16%
Jews	200	0.0%	1,700	0.0%	3.93%
Non-religionists	140,000	0.1%	1,470,000	0.3%	4.37%
Agnostics	119,000	0.1%	1,374,000	0.3%	4.55%
Atheists	21,000	0.0%	95,800	0.0%	2.80%
Total population	**105,686,000**	**100.0%**	**454,673,000**	**100.0%**	**2.69%**

Data source: Todd M. Johnson and Brian J. Grim (eds), *World Religion Database* (Boston and Leiden: Brill – accessed February 2015).
Numbers might not add up to 100 due to rounding.
* Average annual growth rate, per cent per year, between dates specified.

Although ethno-religionists have declined dramatically as a percentage of the total population in most countries of the region, they continue to constitute a sizeable segment in several countries, including Guinea-Bissau, Liberia and Togo. On the other hand, the ethno-religionist share of the population has actually been rising in Cape Verde, though by 2025 it will still be only about 1% of the population. No other religion claims more than 1% of the regional population, although adherents exceed the 1% level (of the national population) in several individual countries.

Society

Progress in meeting the Millennium Development Goals has been uneven across the region. Maternal and child mortality are areas of special concern in almost every country, as is HIV/AIDS. Also of concern is the recent surge in violent activity by ethnic and religious groups in several countries in the region, including Mali, Mauritania, Niger, and Nigeria. The violence is particularly prevalent in Nigeria, where the Christian and Muslim populations are of approximately equal size.

Conclusion

The religious composition of Africa has changed dramatically since the beginning of the twentieth century, from majority traditional religionist to a competition between Christians and Muslims for adherents. Current trends are expected to continue into the future, with modest gains of both religions in many African countries. One uncertainty in the African landscape is the impact of urbanization on religious adherence. Globally, the world is becoming increasingly urban, and by 2025 over 58% of the world will live in cities. Yet Christian presence in the city is not keeping pace with urbanization rates – by 2025 Christians will represent only 38% of the global urban population. It remains to be seen whether Christians in Africa will respond to the challenges of urban living and if these urban centres will encourage a shift away from religious adherence. Nevertheless, Africa is still poised to have the most Christians of any continent in 2025, at more than 730 million.

(16B) EXPLANATORY NOTES ON RELIGIOUS DATA BOXES USED IN THE ANTHOLOGY

Gina A. Zurlo and Todd M. Johnson

The religious data boxes that appear in Section 1 in the previous article, in Section 2 above the regional survey articles, and in Section 4 at the beginning of the national survey articles of Christianity in African nations of the Anthology of African Christianity Project, are derived from the *World Christian Database* (*WCD*).[1] The *WCD* includes detailed information on 41,000 Christian denominations and religions in every country of the world. Extensive data are available on 234 countries and 13,000 ethno-linguistic peoples, as well as on 5,000 cities and 3,000 provinces. Thousands of sources are evaluated and reviewed on a weekly basis by a professional staff dedicated to expanding and updating the *WCD*, and the database is updated quarterly.

The methodology undergirding the *WCD* takes as its starting point the United Nations 1948 Universal Declaration of Human Rights, Article 18: 'Everyone has the right to freedom of thought, conscience and religion; this right includes freedom to change his religion or belief, and freedom, either alone or in community with others and in public or private, to manifest his religion or belief in teaching, practice, worship and observance.'[2] Since its promulgation, this group of phrases has been incorporated into the state constitutions of a large number of countries across the world. This fundamental right also includes the right to claim the religion of one's choice, and the right to be called a follower of that religion and to be enumerated as such.

Data Sources

Three major sources of religious demographic data are censuses, surveys and polls, and data from religious communities. National censuses are the best starting point for the identification of religious adherents, because they generally cover the entire population. In the absence of a question on religion, another helpful piece of information from a census is ethnicity or language. This is especially true when a particular ethnic group can be equated with a particular religion. For example, over 99% of Somalis are Muslim, so the number of Somalis in, for example, Sweden is an indication of a part of the Muslim community there. Similarly, a question that asks for the country of birth can use useful. If the answer is 'Nepal', there is a significant chance that the individual or community is Hindu. In each of these cases, the assumption is made (if there is no further information) that the religion of the transplanted ethnic or linguistic community is the same as that in the home country.

In the absence of census data on religion, large-scale demographic surveys, such as the MEASURE (Monitoring and Evaluation to Assess and Use Results) Demographic and Health Surveys (DHS), often include a question about the respondent's religious affiliation. In some instances, demographic surveys by groups such as UNICEF (United Nations Children's Fund) include a question on religious affiliation. Demographic surveys, though less comprehensive than a national census, have several advantages over other types of general population surveys and polls. Demographic and Health Surveys (DHS) are highly regarded by demographers and social scientists, and provide valuable nationally representative data on religion. Surveys can also be commissioned in the light of a dearth of data on a particular subject and results can be used to search for correlations between different variables.

---

[1] Todd M. Johnson and Gina A. Zurlo, eds. *World Christian Database* (Leiden/Boston, Brill, accessed January 2016), www.worldchristiandatabase.org.

[2] The full text of the UN resolution can be found in Paul M. Taylor, *Freedom of Religion: UN and European Human Rights Law and Practice* (Cambridge: Cambridge University Press, 2005), 368–72.

Religious communities also keep track of their members, using everything from simple lists to elaborate membership reports. The most detailed data collection and analysis is undertaken each year by some 43,000 Christian denominations and their 4.7 million constituent churches and congregations of believers. The latter invest over US$1.1 billion annually for a massive, decentralized and largely unco-ordinated global census of Christians. In sum, they send out around 10 million printed questionnaires in 3,000 different languages, covering 180 major religious subjects reporting on 2,000 socio-religious variables. This collection of data provides a year-by-year snapshot of the progress or decline of Christianity's diverse movements, offering an enormous body of data from which researchers can track trends and make projections.[3]

Affiliated Christians

The data presented in the tables used in this Anthology (mainly at the beginning of articles in Section 2 and in Section 4) are of 'affiliated Christians'. 'Affiliated Christians' are those known to the churches or known to the clergy (usually by names and addresses) and claimed in their statistics, i.e. those enrolled on the churches' books or records, with totals that can be substantiated. This usually means all known baptized Christians and their children, and other adherents; it is sometimes termed the total Christian community (because affiliated Christians are those who are not primarily individual Christians but who primarily belong to the corporate community of Christ), or inclusive membership (because affiliated Christians are church members). This definition of 'Christians' is what the churches usually mean by the term (and thus does the *WCD*), and statistics of such affiliated Christians are what the churches themselves collect and publish. In all countries, it may be assumed with confidence that the churches know better than the state how many Christians are affiliated to them.

All columns of absolute numbers in tables always add up exactly to the totals and sub-totals shown. However, as with all large statistical tables, a column of percentages might not always add up to exactly the total or sub-total indicated, due to rounding. Although in most cases, component percentages do in fact add up exactly to their respective totals, in a small number of cases this is not so because of the rounding feature. In addition, figures for sub-categories within Christianity might not add up to the total sum of that tradition because of the omission of certain categories from the analysis.

Evangelicals and Pentecostals/Charismatics

Evangelicalism and Pentecostalism (and Charismatics) are movements within all streams of global Christianity; that is, they cut across the other major Christian traditions (Catholics, Orthodox, Independents, Protestants). Counting Evangelicals and Pentecostals takes into consideration denominational affiliation, self-identification and theology. The results of counting these groups are directly related to denominational membership figures. Strictly speaking, denominational affiliation means official membership on a church roll.

More information about the methodology behind religious demographic data can be found in Todd M. Johnson and Brian J. Grim, *The World's Religions in Figures: An Introduction to International Religious Demography* (Malden, MA: Wiley-Blackwell, 2013).

[3] One attempt to organize a variety of source material for researchers is the website www.adherents.com, which offers thousands of figures for adherents of hundreds of religions. However, there is no attempt by its organizers to reconcile the numerous contradictions in the source material. Nonetheless, it offers an invaluable look at the amount of data researchers have at their disposal.

PART II

REGIONAL SURVEYS OF AFRICAN CHRISTIANITY

(17) CHRISTIANITY IN NORTHERN AFRICA

Bernard Coyault[1]

Country	Religion	Pop_2010	Pct_2010	Pop_2025	Pct_2025	GrPct_1970_2025
Northern Africa	Christians	9,776,000	4.8%	10,794,000	4.1%	0.7%
Northern Africa	Independents	208,000	0.1%	306,000	0.1%	2.6%
Northern Africa	African-initiated	205,000	0.1%			
Northern Africa	Orthodox	7,375,000	3.6%	7,897,000	3.0%	0.5%
Northern Africa	Oriental Orthodox	7,352,000	3.6%			
Northern Africa	Protestants	1,266,000	0.6%	1,472,000	0.6%	1.0%
Northern Africa	Roman Catholics	1,406,000	0.7%	1,450,000	0.5%	0.2%
Northern Africa	*Evangelicals*	805,000	0.4%	962,000	0.4%	1.2%
Northern Africa	*Pentecostals/ Charismatics*	756,000	0.4%	916,000	0.3%	1.3%
Northern Africa	Muslims	191,431,000	94.0%	249,837,000	94.7%	1.8%
Northern Africa	adherents of traditional African religions	1,007,000	0.5%	1,101,000	0.4%	0.6%
Northern Africa	Baha'is	42,900	0.0%	52,200	0.0%	1.3%
Northern Africa	Buddhists	26,400	0.0%	35,100	0.0%	1.9%
Northern Africa	Chinese folk religionists	17,000	0.0%	21,300	0.0%	1.5%
Northern Africa	Jews	7,600	0.0%	6,900	0.0%	-0.6%
Northern Africa	Hindus	7,300	0.0%	9,900	0.0%	2.0%
Northern Africa	Sikhs	2,200	0.0%	3,000	0.0%	2.2%
Northern Africa	people professing no religion	1,400,000	0.7%	2,032,000	0.8%	2.5%
Northern Africa	**Total population**	**203,717,000**	**100.0%**	**263,892,000**	**100.0%**	**1.7%**

Source: Centre for the Study of World Christianity (CSGC), Boston, Gordon-Conwell TS

A la différence de l'Egypte ou du Liban, l'Afrique du Nord n'a pas gardé trace vivante du christianisme qui s'y était développé durant les premiers siècles. A partir de la conquête arabe au début du septième siècle,

[1] Bernard Coyault, docteur en anthropologie (EHESS, Paris), est directeur de l'Institut œcuménique de Théologie *Al Mowafaqa* à Rabat (Maroc) où il enseigne la sociologie des religions. Il est chercheur associé au Centre Jacques-Berque de Rabat, au LEPOSHS (Université internationale de Rabat), et à l'Institut interdisciplinaire d'anthropologie du contemporain (IIAC-EHESS Paris). Ses travaux portent notamment sur les dynamiques religieuses des parcours migratoires et la pluralisation religieuse en Afrique subsaharienne et au Maghreb.

l'islam s'impose rapidement dans la région; les derniers témoignages concernant ces communautés originelles ne dépassent pas le onzième siècle.

Les acteurs européens de l'implantation du christianisme colonial en Afrique du Nord aux dix-neuvième et vingtième siècles, se réfèrent souvent à cette énigme de la disparition d'un christianisme autochtone florissant, fort d'environ 600 diocèses et d'un riche patrimoine doctrinal et spirituel, avec ses théologiens (Cyprien, Tertullien, Augustin), ses papes romains et ses martyrs.[2] Pour l'Eglise catholique qui accompagne la conquête coloniale, il s'agira ni plus ni moins d'opérer la résurrection de « l'antique Eglise d'Afrique » et de restituer à l'Afrique, après l'« éclipse spirituelle » de 12 siècles d'islam, ce christianisme qu'elle avait perdu. Le rétablissement en 1892 de l'archevêché de Carthage (Tunisie) dont l'évêque était, dans l'Antiquité, le primat des Eglises d'Afrique en est un signe éclatant. Pour les missions protestantes indépendantes (*faith missions*) qui se déploient au Maghreb à partir de la fin du 19e siècle, la cause de la disparition du christianisme originel tient au fait que la Bible n'avait pas été traduite dans les langues vernaculaires.[3] Une grande partie de leur activité d'évangélisation sera centrée sur la traduction et la diffusion de la Bible dans les langues locales (arabes dialectaux, kabyle/berbère). La page imprimée était pour le missionnaire ce '*silent preacher*'[4] qui devrait continuer le travail après son passage.

Survol Historique

Tout au long du Moyen-âge et dans la période moderne, une présence chrétienne se maintient au Maghreb, reflet des tensions entre deux univers culturels et religieux qui se font face, séparés et unis tout à la fois par la mer méditerranée. Outre les marchands et consuls, représentants des « nations chrétiennes » installés dans les ports, cette présence chrétienne est surtout composée des captifs européens, victimes des opérations de piraterie. Dès le treizième siècle des ordres religieux sont créés pour visiter et racheter les prisonniers. C'est aussi l'un des motifs de la présence des franciscains – surtout dans la zone marocaine, et dominicains à Bejaïa, Tunis ou Tripoli, à la même période. Du dix-septième jusqu'à l'aube du dix-neuvième siècle, des prêtres de différents ordres (comme les Lazaristes) sont encore envoyés auprès des captifs, à Alger, Marrakech ou Meknès. L'existence de ces « captifs chrétiens » nourrit dans l'imaginaire européen les représentations négatives d'un islam esclavagiste et cruel.

Pour la période contemporaine, l'histoire du christianisme (majoritairement catholique) en Afrique du Nord est modelée par les particularités de l'entreprise coloniale française. Selon des durées et modalités différentes, la France colonise l'Algérie en 1830, la Tunisie 50 ans plus tard et le Maroc en 1912. La même année, la Lybie passe quant à elle sous domination italienne. A la différence de l'Afrique subsaharienne, il s'agit pour l'Afrique méditerranéenne de colonies de peuplement. Le christianisme, déployé pour servir les nouveaux occupants, s'impose massivement, jusqu'à façonner le paysage avec la construction d'églises. Associé à la domination coloniale, il est perçu négativement par les populations autochtones, à l'exception des œuvres scolaires ou de santé dont elles bénéficient. L'islam – comme élément identitaire et culturel et pas seulement religieux – se constitue comme un pôle de résistance face à cette présence étrangère. Les divers efforts d'évangélisation ne portent quasiment aucun fruit: toute conversion individuelle au

---

[2] Pour le christianisme des premiers siècles en Afrique du Nord, cf. l'article de TengaTenga dans le présent ouvrage.

[3] '*The story of the conquest of Islam is well known. The people had no Christian literature in their vernacular, not even the Bible, and so no remnant of the Church remained'*, Samuel M Zwemer, "North Africa as a Mission Field", in *International Review of Mission*, 12:4 (1923), 561. Tandis que dans l'Orient ancien le Christianisme s'était développé sur le terreau des langues locales (syriaque, copte, araméen, éthiopien et, plus tard, arabe), en Afrique du Nord, seul le latin, langue de l'empire et langue liturgique était utilisé. On ne trouve aucune trace d'une traduction de la Bible ou d'une liturgie en langue amazigh (berbère) - Henri Teissier (ed), *Histoire des chrétiens d'Afrique du Nord*, Paris: Desclée (1991), 74.

[4] Willy N. Heggoy, Fifty Years of Evangelical Missionary Movement in North Africa, 1881-1931'. Senior Thesis, Hartford Seminary Foundation, 1960, 312-16.

christianisme sera perçue socialement non seulement comme une trahison à l'islam mais aussi comme une forme de collaboration avec l'envahisseur.

Durant des décennies (130 ans pour l'Algérie) le christianisme est donc l'apanage d'une grande minorité dominante. Après les indépendances, il devient celui d'une petite minorité tolérée. La désintégration de ce christianisme transplanté est tout aussi fulgurante que n'avait été son installation. Du fait de l'exode massif des Européens, les églises et écoles catholiques sont désertées, les propriétés sont cédées ou expropriées. Les nouveaux Etats acceptent néanmoins la présence des Eglises chrétiennes, puisque leurs responsables avaient choisi de soutenir le processus d'indépendance. Commence alors une nouvelle ère où ces Eglises, dépouillées de leur puissance d'antan et formées en majorité de coopérants et de religieux étrangers, inventent un autre mode de présence et de témoignage, au service des jeunes nations. Elles traversent avec elles les épreuves nationales – comme la décennie noire de l'islamisme et la guerre civile en Algérie (années 90).

Au tournant du vingt-et-unième siècle, une page nouvelle du christianisme en Afrique du Nord s'écrit avec deux phénomènes inattendus: l'africanisation des Eglises jusqu'alors à dominante européenne et l'émergence d'un christianisme autochtone. Le premier phénomène est la conséquence au niveau religieux des flux migratoires sud-nord et du développement de la coopération des Etats du Maghreb sur le continent. Le second est ta conséquence de la progression des libertés individuelles dans le monde arabe et d'un accès facilité à l'offre religieuse chrétienne par les nouveaux médias. Ce nouveau visage du christianisme participe de la pluralisation du champ religieux et de l'individualisation du croire dans les sociétés du Maghreb.

Christianisme et Colonisation: Le Grand Malentendu

La conquête militaire ou « pacification » des pays du Maghreb par l'armée française est brutale. Elle s'accompagne aussi d'une spoliation des meilleures terres. C'est sur cette violence originelle que l'Eglise catholique établit ses réseaux de paroisses pour les nouveaux arrivants. Les premiers prêtres catholiques (et plus tard quelques pasteurs) au service des colons sont les aumôniers militaires.[5] En juin 1830, ils sont seize à accompagner l'armée française qui débarque près d'Alger. C'est à leur attention que le général en chef du corps expéditionnaire déclare devant ses troupes victorieuses: « *vous venez de rouvrir avec nous les porte du christianisme en Afrique. Espérons qu'il y viendra bientôt faire fleurir la civilisation qui s'est éteinte* ».[6] En 1832, la plus grande mosquée d'Alger, la *Djemaa Ketchaoua*, est transformée de force en Eglise. Devenue cathédrale Saint Philippe d'Alger, symbole de la conquête religieuse et militaire tout au long de la période coloniale, elle sera reconvertie en mosquée à l'indépendance en 1962.

La Violence Coloniale

En Algérie, les opérations militaires menées contre les rébellions (la dernière en 1871) font des centaines de milliers de morts. Débutée dans la violence, l'occupation française se terminera 130 ans après par une guerre d'indépendance de 8 années (1954-1962) tout autant meurtrière. Cette violence coloniale se découvre ailleurs à des degrés divers. En Tunisie, les protestations et révoltes populaires contre l'invasion française d'avril 1881 et la signature en mai du traité établissant le protectorat français seront sévèrement réprimées. La ville de Sfax notamment est bombardée en juillet 1881. L'histoire du protectorat jusqu'en 1956 est ainsi émaillée de révoltes des nationalistes et de répression des autorités françaises. Au Maroc, la « pacification » s'étend de 1907 à 1934 et fera 100.000 victimes – avec notamment l'engagement

[5] C'est le cas en Algérie, mais aussi 80 ans plus tard, au Maroc avec l'établissement du protectorat en 1912: 10 prêtres franciscains aumôniers militaires désignés pour les troupes servent en parallèle les nouvelles paroisses de colons - Baida, Jamaâ et Feroldi, Vincent, *Présence chrétienne au Maroc. XIXe – XXe siècles*, Rabat: Bouregreg (2005), 39.
[6] Cité par Teissier, *Histoire des Chrétiens d'Afrique du Nord*, 118.

français dans la guerre du Rif (1921-1924) ou la campagne contre les insurrections du Haut-Atlas (1932-1934).

Dans un rapport de novembre 1911 (soit un an avant les protectorats français et espagnol) le pasteur et aumônier militaire, Jacques Pannier raconte sa première visite au Maroc, destinée à évaluer les besoins spirituels des soldats et civils protestants. Il rencontre la sympathie des troupes françaises déjà présentes, mais affronte l'hostilité des autochtones:

> « La croix en métal que je portais sur mon casque colonial (…) me fit rapidement connaître. Je me réjouis de la voir saluée militairement par beaucoup de soldats, comme équivalent à des galons d'officiers; et je vis aussi avec peine des musulmans fanatiques cracher avec mépris en détournant la tête après avoir vu le signe exécré de la religion de ceux qu'ils appellent Nazaréens »[7]

L'anecdote résume toute l'ambiguïté d'un christianisme enchainé à la conquête coloniale. Les « Musulmans fanatiques » crachent-ils leur mépris à l'encontre du casque du militaire ou à l'encontre du signe religieux chrétien ?

Eglise Coloniale *versus* Eglise Missionnaire

En Algérie où la colonisation est la plus ancienne, la création de l'évêché d'Alger en 1838 et l'installation de nombreuses congrégations religieuses entre 1840 et 1860, favorisent le développement rapide de dizaines de paroisses. Hormis quelques rares tentatives, l'évangélisation des musulmans n'est pas à l'ordre du jour, la priorité est plutôt le service des colons qui arrivent toujours plus nombreux. Les autorités, militaires (1830-1871), puis civiles, s'opposent à toute activité missionnaire, d'autant que les foyers de résistance armée ne s'éteindront que tardivement (1871, en Kabylie).

La nomination en 1868 de Charles Lavigerie (1825-1992) comme archevêque d'Alger[8] constitue un tournant. Tout en poursuivant le déploiement de l'Eglise coloniale, il élabore un vaste projet missionnaire, non seulement pour l'Afrique du Nord, mais pour le continent tout entier. Il crée en en 1868 « Les Pères de la Mission d'Afrique », appelés Pères Blancs du fait de leur habit, et en 1869, les « Sœurs missionnaires de Notre-Dame d'Afrique » ou Sœurs Blanches, deux ordres qui vont grandement contribuer au déploiement missionnaire catholique en Afrique, dès avant le traité de Berlin. Leur premier service en Algérie concerne les orphelins victimes des famines et épidémies qui sévissent alors dans le pays. La vision s'élargit ensuite aux régions limitrophes, le Sahara algérien en 1872, la Tunisie en 1875, puis l'Afrique subsaharienne où partent des « caravanes » de missionnaires formés à Alger (1878, 1892, etc.). A sa mort en 1892, il y a déjà 278 « Missionnaires d'Afrique ».[9]

Les Pères Blancs en Algérie et Tunisie, sont dédiés à l'apostolat auprès des autochtones, sans contacts avec l'Eglise coloniale servie par un clergé régulier. Ils doivent obligatoirement parler leur langue (arabe ou kabyle), manger la même nourriture et s'habiller comme eux, d'où la tenue arabe (gandoura, burnous, chechia) et leur signe religieux – un rosaire porté en collier qui rappelle le chapelet des musulmans pour l'invocation des noms de Dieu

Dans ces pays, l'Eglise est donc partagée entre deux vocations qui s'avèreront souvent antinomiques: servir la nouvelle population des colons et présenter à la population autochtone un témoignage crédible de l'Evangile.

---

[7] Rapport du Pasteur Jacques Pannier, manuscrit 33 pages, novembre 1911 (Archives EEAM), 6, 30.

[8] Devenu Cardinal par la suite, il est nommé en 1884 archevêque de Carthage et primat d'Afrique, tout en restant archevêque d'Alger

[9] Ceillier, Jean-Claude, *Histoire des missionnaires d'Afrique (Pères Blancs) - De la fondation par Mgr Lavigerie à la mort du fondateur (1868-1892),* Paris: Karthala, 2008.

La situation est identique au Maroc, où les Franciscains – espagnols pour le protectorat espagnol, français pour le protectorat français – disposent d'un quasi-monopole.[10] La majorité d'entre eux desservent les œuvres et paroisses de l'Eglise coloniale, et une infime minorité s'engage dans un apostolat parmi les populations berbères. Les autorités du protectorat par leur « politique musulmane » (Lyautey), cherchent à protéger le prestige des autorités musulmanes et du sultan. L'importance de l'apostolat auprès des autochtones est parfois évoquée, mais rarement mise en œuvre.[11] Seules les religieuses Franciscaines missionnaires de Marie, très nombreuses au Maroc,[12] sont impliquées dans des œuvres sociales bénéficiant aux Marocains.

Du côté du protestantisme, les rares initiatives de la *Société des Missions évangéliques de Paris* pour l'évangélisation des musulmans en Algérie n'aboutissent pas du fait de l'opposition des autorités ou d'obstacles internes.[13] Pour tout le Maghreb, les paroisses officielles sont soutenues par la *Société d'Evangélisation des Colonies Françaises* (fondée en 1862): composées principalement de notables, elles entretiennent généralement le même conservatisme et les mêmes préjugés coloniaux. Ce protestantisme colonial très dynamique en interne, ne s'impliquera jamais directement dans les actions d'évangélisation à destination des musulmans ou des juifs. L'action missionnaire protestante au Maghreb sera portée par des sociétés missionnaires indépendantes d'origine anglaise ou américaine (*infra*).

L'afflux de populations nouvelles dans les colonies suscite le déploiement massif d'un christianisme « à l'européenne » peu soucieux d'adaptation au contexte local. Il s'agit d'une *transplantation*, plutôt qu'une *implantation* comme dans la mission classique:

> « Les arrivants se considèrent chez eux, et ils désirent prolonger la vie qu'ils ont connue en France ou en Espagne. On bâtit des églises semblables, on crée les mêmes œuvres qu'en France, les mêmes confréries, les mêmes processions avec les bannières (…) les groupes de communiants comme en France, etc ».[14]

Depuis cette *bulle coloniale* dans laquelle évolue la société européenne, au mépris de la sensibilité religieuse et culturelle de la majorité musulmane du pays, personne ne prend vraiment la mesure de la force répulsive de ce modèle de christianisme dominant associé, comme une évidence, à la 'civilisation'.

Dans les années 1925-1935, l'alliance du colonialisme et de l'Eglise est à son apogée. La tenue du Congrès international eucharistique de Carthage (Tunisie) du 7 au 11 mai 1930 en est la plus forte illustration.[15] La date, choisie pour commémorer le 1500e anniversaire de la mort de Saint Augustin, correspondait aussi au centenaire de la présence française en Algérie. Pour les idéologues coloniaux, c'est l'action de la France qui avait permis ce grand retour de la chrétienté au Maghreb. Ce congrès international rassemble des dizaines de milliers de participants (d'Europe et d'autres continents), dont 3000 prêtres et séminaristes, une centaine d'évêques et cardinaux. Le dernier jour, une grande procession de 100.000 personnes est organisée dans les rues de Tunis. Mais c'est le jeu scénique avec 6000 enfants en tenue

---

[10] Baida et Feroldi, *Présence chrétienne au Maroc,* 18-20, 35-40. En Lybie également, la pastorale des colons est assurée par les Franciscains (Frères mineurs).

[11] Baida et Feroldi, *Présence chrétienne au Maroc,* 65-71.

[12] Baida et Feroldi, *Présence chrétienne au Maroc,* 36, 41, 91. Pour le vicariat de Rabat, elles sont 120 religieuses en 1923, 209 en 1935, s'occupant de dispensaires, orphelinats, écoles, etc. Entre 1912 et 1985, plus de 800 sœurs Franciscaines Missionnaires de Marie (FMM) ont été envoyées au Maroc - Paumard, Gabrielle Sr, *Les Franciscaines Missionnaires de Marie au Maroc. 1912-1985*, sans éditeur (355 p.), 2003, 333-348.

[13] Gadille, Jacques et Zorn, Jean-François, « Les missions chrétiennes en Afrique » in *Histoire du christianisme 11 – Libéralisme, industrialisation, expansion européenne (1830-1914)*, eds. J.-M. Mayeur, Ch. & L. Pietri, A. Vauchez A. & M. Venard (Paris: Desclée, 1995), 1023-1026.

[14] Michel Laffont, « Le père Peyriguère dans l'Église du Maroc », *Chemins de Dialogue* 36 (2010): 27-38.

[15] Nolan, Francis, *Les Pères Blancs entre les deux guerres mondiales. Histoire des Missionnaires d'Afrique (1919-1939)*, Paris: Karthala, 2015, 93-97.

blanche frappée d'une croix, semblables à des croisés, qui va susciter le plus l'indignation des Tunisiens. Ce congrès triomphaliste – vu comme une provocation chrétienne en terre d'islam – est l'une des causes de l'émergence des mouvements nationalistes qui conduiront à l'indépendance.[16]

Nationalismes et Résistance Religieuse

Ces collusions multiples entre christianisme et colonisation ont été les éléments déclencheurs des nationalismes du Maghreb qui prirent alors une coloration religieuse. Dans le rapport de force asymétrique qui caractérisait la résistance à la conquête coloniale, la référence à l'islam constituait un point de fixation identitaire tout autant qu'une force morale.

L'idéologie de la renaissance du christianisme africain semblait vouloir évacuer les douze siècles d'histoire arabe et musulmane en Afrique du Nord.

Le leader nationaliste Bourguiba, futur président de la Tunisie, déclarait que c'est l'un des discours entendu lors du Congrès de Carthage, alors qu'il était jeune avocat, qui décida de son engagement.[17]

Messaoud Boukadoum, nationaliste algérien élu député de Constantine en 1947, dénonce dans un discours à l'Assemblée nationale française le 20/8/1947 les atteintes à l'islam et à la langue arabe par la colonisation. On y trouve un réquisitoire, basé sur des citations et faits historiques précis, des ambiguïtés d'une politique d'assimilation s'appuyant sur les « valeurs » du christianisme et dénigrant l'islam.

> « La colonisation française ne s'est pas contentée de s'approprier toutes les richesses économiques de l'Algérie et de les exploiter à son unique profit. Elle s'est attaquée également au patrimoine moral et intellectuel de notre peuple. (…) C'est cette personnalité que la colonisation a voulu détruire, car elle pensait qu'un peuple vaincu par les armes, asservi économiquement et, de surcroît, privé de sa personnalité, deviendrait vite une véritable poussière d'individus, sans âme collective, et prêt à toutes les métamorphoses et à toutes les servitudes. (…) la politique de désislamisation et de désarabisation a été le fait principal de la colonisation dans notre pays. Le fait qu'elle n'ait pas réussi, malgré l'importance des moyens mis en œuvre, ne peut signifier qu'une chose, c'est que la personnalité algérienne, formée par des siècles d'histoire, est trop fortement constituée pour pouvoir être détruite par l'oppression et l'obscurantisme du colonialisme ».[18]

Le discours fait implicitement référence à l'action du Cardinal Lavigerie autour de l'évangélisation des kabyles et sa portée assimilationniste. Celui-ci voyait dans les berbères de Kabylie, avec leurs particularismes linguistiques et culturels, les descendants des chrétiens des premiers siècles. Puisqu'ils n'avaient été que superficiellement islamisés, par la contrainte et la violence, lors de la conquête arabe, ils pourraient facilement, grâce à une action d'évangélisation adaptée, abandonner l'islam (et l'arabité) et réintégrer la supposée religion de leurs ancêtres. Le mythe de l' « isolat kabyle », popularisé dans les milieux savants, tendait tout à la fois à surévaluer le rayonnement géographique du christianisme antique dans les régions rurales et montagneuses et à minimiser l'islamisation de ces mêmes espaces.[19] Il ravivait aussi le vieil antagonisme entre arabes et berbères. La Kabylie sera donc un lieu d'expérimentation de la politique d'évangélisation et d'assimilation prônée par Lavigerie. Les Pères Blancs, avec leurs d'écoles et

---

[16] Le Congrès de Carthage fut interprété dans la presse arabophone tunisienne, mais aussi égyptienne, comme la 9e croisade – Nolans, *Les Pères Blancs*, 95-96.

[17] Nolan, 95. Cité par Fulvio Grazzini, « L'Église de Tunisie », in Teissier, *Histoire des chrétiens d'Afrique du Nord*, 141.

[18] Intervention du député Messaoud Boukadoum (circonscription de Constantine) à l'Assemblée nationale française – séance du 20/8/1947.

[19] Abdelfettah Lalmi déconstruit ce mythe en montrant le rayonnement historique de l'islam à Bejaïa et dans la montagne kabyle durant le Moyen-âge musulman. Nedjma Abdelfettah Lalmi, «Du mythe de l'isolat kabyle», *Cahiers d'Études africaines*, 175 (2004): 507-531.

leurs « villages chrétiens », s'y maintiendront durablement, rejoints plus tard par les missions protestantes. La Kabylie est aujourd'hui le foyer principal du christianisme en Algérie.

Au Maroc, cette question berbère constitue également un important foyer de tension. S'appuyant sur la même idéologie d'une population berbère faiblement islamisée et arabisée, avec des particularismes culturels et raciaux, l'administration coloniale dès 1923, tente de mettre en place un réseau d'écoles franco-berbère (d'où la langue arabe est bannie). Le « dahir berbère », un décret du 16/5/1930, reconnait lui, la spécificité du droit traditionnel berbère et instaure des tribunaux coutumiers qui soustraient les populations berbères à la législation musulmane, tout en maintenant le droit français pour les affaires pénales. La stratégie sous-jacente, cautionnée par certaines publications catholiques, vise à réduire l'influence arabe et musulmane sur les Berbères pour faciliter leur assimilation, par l'action conjuguée des écoles et juridiction françaises et de la diffusion du christianisme.

La promulgation de ce dahir berbère considéré comme une atteinte à l'Islam provoque un mouvement de protestation qui s'appuie sur le réseau des mosquées: on y récite le *Latif,* la prière spéciale utilisée lors des calamités (inondation, sécheresse, etc.). L'affaire s'élargit au niveau international avec la diffusion dans les pays musulmans d'une longue *Déclaration au monde musulman sur le problème berbère au Maroc* traduite en plusieurs langues (urdu, javanais, persan, turc, etc.). Elle dénonce la connivence entre les autorités coloniales et les Eglises, pour mener à bien la dé-islamisation et l'évangélisation du Maroc, et s'achève ainsi:

> « Si les Français réussissent dans leur entreprise, leur victoire sur le Monde Musulman sera une victoire religieuse, victoire plus dure et plus amère qu'une conquête économique ou politique. Et s'ils nous barrent la route du monde d'ici-bas, ils nous interdiront aussi le monde de l'Au-delà ». [20]

L'affaire du dahir berbère est le moment fondateur du mouvement nationaliste marocain. Celui-ci remet aux autorités le 1/12/1934 un *Plan de Réformes marocaines* d'ordre politique, économique, juridique, parmi lesquelles il est aussi proposé *« d'interdire toute propagande à caractère évangélisateur parmi la population musulmane de tout le Maroc (...) de mettre un terme à l'action des missionnaires quels que soient leur nationalité et leur rite (...) de ne tolérer de leur part aucune publication portant atteinte au respect dû à l'Islam et à son Prophète ».*

Le texte visait non seulement la présence catholique mais aussi les missions protestantes indépendantes qui pratiquaient l'évangélisation directe avec des prêches en public et la distribution d'évangiles en arabe.[21]

Face à ces polémiques, l'Eglise catholique tente de se justifier des accusations et rappelle l'importance de son action sociale; elle n'en abandonne pas moins ses ambitions missionnaires « sous les plis du drapeau français ».

Finalement la présence coloniale contribue à l'émergence d'un islam d'opposition marqué par un fondamentalisme scripturaire. L'affrontement politique et économique s'est transmué en antagonisme religieux. Auparavant, *« les gens étaient musulmans de façon pour ainsi dire contingente ; à partir de ce moment- là et de plus en plus, ils en firent une politique. Ils devinrent musulmans par opposition ».*[22]

---

[20] Le texte intégral se trouve dans: Gilles Lafuente, « Dossier marocain sur le dahir berbère de 1930 », *Revue de l'Occident musulman et de la Méditerranée*, n°38 (1984): 107-111.

[21] C'est en réaction à ces activités que les nationalistes marocains lanceront à leur tour des campagnes de distribution gratuite du Coran (été 1933) - Baida et Feroldi, *Présence chrétienne au Maroc,* 85.

[22] Clifford Geertz, *Observer l'islam. Changement religieux au Maroc et en Indonésie*, Paris: La Découverte, 1992, 80. Pour Geertz, c'est à partir de là que s'opère le tournant dans l'évolution de l'islam moderne, ouvrant la voie à l'interprétation salafiste qui prône le retour aux sources fondatrices (Coran, Hadith, etc.) et la lutte contre les religiosités traditionnelles.

La résistance religieuse face aux Européens touchait également les enfants. Lilias Trotter, une missionnaire en Algérie qui travaillait auprès des femmes (*infra*), relevait ce réflexe d'auto-défense religieuse inculqué aux enfants. Elle note qu'en 1924, en Tunisie – du fait de la proximité avec l'Europe – n'importe quel enfant pris au hasard dans la rue était capable de faire l'apologie de l'islam contre le christianisme (utilisant les arguments classiques de la non-crucifixion de Jésus ou de la falsification des Ecritures)![23]

L'élan Missionnaire Catholique

Dans l'Eglise coloniale, tant du côté catholique que protestant, l'islam n'est pas une préoccupation apostolique.

Cette Eglise catholique majoritaire dédiée aux colons français, espagnols ou italiens, otage de l'entreprise coloniale et généralement conservatrice sur le plan politique et sociétal, a eu bien du mal à se positionner en dehors du moule colonial. La réflexion sur l'organisation de l'apostolat en milieu musulman a été portée principalement par les Pères Blancs d'Algérie et de Tunisie.[24] Tandis que les expériences concrètes de témoignage et de présence chrétiennes se sont développées sur le terreau d'un catholicisme et d'une spiritualité non conformistes, autour de quelques individualités, isolées et parfois contestées en leur temps.

Lavigerie, Marchal, théoriciens de l'apostolat envers les musulmans

Hormis l'expérience de la Kabylie, Lavigerie s'opposait à toute action de prosélytisme direct et à l'administration du baptême pour les musulmans. Selon lui, leur sentiment de supériorité religieuse et leur orgueil spirituel les empêchaient d'accueillir d'emblée le message chrétien. Par ailleurs, les conversions individuelles ne manqueraient pas de provoquer l'hostilité collective mettant la mission en péril. Enfin, les nouveaux convertis, marginalisés et coupés de leurs racines, risquaient de renier leur nouvelle foi du fait de la pression communautaire. Lavigerie prônait plutôt la transformation à long terme des « mentalités indigènes » vis-à-vis du christianisme. Celle-ci pourrait prendre un siècle. Les missionnaires se devaient d'abord gagner les esprits et les cœurs par la charité et, en adoptant le mode de vie de leurs interlocuteurs (langue, vêtement, nourriture, nomadisme et pauvreté), « désarmer le dédain islamique » à l'encontre des chrétiens.[25] En Kabylie comme dans les oasis du Sahara, l'évangélisation passait par les dispensaires médicaux et les écoles. Si la doctrine coloniale prônait l'assimilation des autochtones, la vision des Pères Blancs proposait une approche positive de leur culture. Dans la génération suivante, au plus fort de la domination coloniale, un autre courant avait pris le dessus prônant plutôt l'approche prosélyte et catéchuménale, et contestant l'apostolat silencieux.

Le Père Henri Marchal (1876-1957) entré chez les Pères Blancs en 1893, nommé au Sahara en 1905 puis supérieur régional de Kabylie de 1909 à 1912, avant de devenir l'assistant général des Missionnaires d'Afrique, suscite un changement d'orientation: la mission ne vise pas tant les conversions individuelles qu'à partager les valeurs essentielles au plus grand nombre et susciter ainsi un changement collectif, les

---

[23] A Lilias Trotter, "The Outlook in North Africa", *The Muslim World* Vol.14-2 (1924):131-135.

[24] On devrait citer aussi pour le Maroc, l'action novatrice du Franciscain espagnol José Maria Antonio Lerchundi (1836-1896), contemporain de Lavigerie. Envoyé à Tanger dès 1862 pour accompagner les chrétiens européens, cet érudit spécialiste de l'arabe et fin diplomate, oriente résolument son action vers la population marocaine: il crée des écoles pour garçons et filles, une imprimerie arabe-espagnol, un hôpital et une école de formation médicale ouverts aux Marocains, etc. Son approche empathique de leur culture et leur religion, sa volonté de coopération avec les Marocains pour faire progresser leur nation, tranchent avec la visée dominatrice et prédatrice de la présence européenne au Maroc à cette période. Ramon Lourido Diaz (ed), *Marruecos y el Padre Lerchundi*, Madrid: MAPFRE, 1996.

[25] Aylward Shorter, *Les Pères Blancs au temps de la conquête coloniale. Histoire des Missionnaires d'Afrique 1892-1914*, Paris: Karthala, 2011, 190.

oeuvres éducatives en constituant l'axe central. Pour Marchal, l'économie du salut ne se réduit pas à l'appartenance à l'Eglise visible. Tout en maintenant l'impératif missionnaire, il distingue trois niveaux de conversion – la conversion à Dieu, la conversion au Christ-Jésus et la conversion à l'Eglise. La vocation du missionnaire consiste d'abord à encourager cette conversion à Dieu, même à l'intérieur de l'islam, sachant que « le salut en islam ne signifie pas le salut par l'islam ».[26] Cette nouvelle approche a pour conséquence une compréhension plus positive de la langue et la culture arabo-musulmane. Marchal insiste sur la formation et crée *l'Institut des Belles Lettre Arabes* (IBLA) à Tunis en 1927 où l'on enseigne, l'arabe, le Coran et la théologie islamique et dont la bibliothèque accueille les jeunes intellectuels tunisiens. Le Père André Demeerseman (1901-1993) en sera le directeur durant des décennies contribuant à tisser des liens nouveaux entre christianisme et société tunisienne.[27] Cette ligne d'apostolat basée sur une approche positive de la religion de l'autre et une confiance dans l'œuvre du Saint Esprit dans le cœur de chaque croyant, chrétien ou non, marquera les orientations nouvelles de l'Eglise dans l'après-guerre préparant les ouvertures du Concile Vatican II (*Nostra Aetete,* 1965).

Les 'moines missionnaires': Foucauld, Peyriguère, Poissonnier.

Charles de Foucauld (1858-1916) officier de l'Armée française, géographe et explorateur, se convertit en 1886 et entre dans la vie monastique en 1890. Ses trois années en Palestine, à Nazareth, lui révèlent sa vocation d'imiter la vie cachée de Jésus à Nazareth. Devenu prêtre en 1901, il s'installe d'abord comme ermite à Beni-Abbes dans le Sahara algérien, puis se fixe à Tamanrasset plus au sud, en 1905, jusqu'à son assassinat en 1916. Il y partage la vie des Touaregs, dans une grande pauvreté, et se consacre à l'étude de leur langue pour laquelle il publiera un dictionnaire. Porteur d'une double vocation de mystique et d'apôtre, là où l'évangélisation directe est impossible, il se qualifie de « moine missionnaire », s'appuyant sur trois principes: l'imitation de vie cachée de Jésus à Nazareth, l'adoration du saint sacrement et « l'établissement parmi les peuples infidèles les plus délaissés en faisant tout ce qu'on peut pour leur conversion ».[28] Par cet apostolat de la présence, incognito, l'ermite entend 'défricher' le terrain avant l'annonce de l'Evangile. De Beni-Abbes il écrit: « *Je veux habituer tous les habitants, chrétiens, musulmans, juifs, à me regarder comme leur frère, le frère universel* ». Ill s'agit pour lui de « prêcher l'Evangile en silence », de montrer le Christ par l'amour et la bonté. Dans sa compréhension de l'eucharistie, la présence eucharistique du Christ rayonne et sanctifie les personnes qui vivent à proximité, fussent-elle non chrétiennes.

Albert Peyriguère (1883-1959), d'origine modeste et ordonné prêtre en 1906, est mobilisé en 1914 comme brancardier sur le front, puis hospitalisé et blessé de guerre jusqu'en 1919. Prêtre en Tunisie de 1920 à 1926, il découvre l'œuvre de Charles de Foucauld et souhaite s'engager comme lui dans la vie d'ermite. Peyriguère arrive au Maroc en 1927 où il est nommé prêtre à Marrakech. En juillet 1928, il s'installe à El-Kbab, village de la tribu berbère des Aït-Ichqern, dans le Moyen-Atlas. La zone est encore sous surveillance militaire. Il restera à El-Kbab jusqu'à sa mort en 1959, partageant le quotidien et la langue de ses habitants. Il y mène tout à la fois une vie contemplative et le service d'un dispensaire où il soigne jusqu'à 2000 patients par mois. Dans une lettre du 1/2/1929 il écrit:

---

[26] Shorter, *Les Pères Blancs*, 199.

[27] Nolan, *Les Pères Blancs*, 97-111. Un *Centre d'Etudes Berbères* (CEB) est créé en Kabylie en 1930 (Teissier, *Histoire des Chrétiens*, 183). D'autres centres catholiques de formation ou de documentation, signe de cette nouvelle approche, ouvriront dans l'après-guerre en Algérie et au Maroc. Le synode de l'Eglise réformée de France à Alger étudie en synode en novembre 1959 la création d'un « Centre Protestant d'Etudes Maghrébines en Afrique du Nord » mais le projet ne verra pas le jour.

[28] George Gorrée et Germain Chauvel, *D'autres récolteront... Foucauld, Peyriguère, moines missionnaires*, Lyon: Mame, 1965, 105.

> « Le Christ glorieux ne peut plus revenir sur terre; nous nous «offrons» à lui (...) nous lui «donnons» notre pauvre humanité pour que, vivant en elle, il puisse, après que nous nous sommes faits Berbères avec les Berbères nous-mêmes, en nous et par nous être Berbère lui-même, et que le Père, qui seul peut mener au Fils, regarde, aime et sauve les Berbères en lui ».[29]

Spécialiste de la culture berbère, Peyriguère est aussi l'héritier et le porte-parole de la spiritualité missionnaire du Père de Foucauld, qu'il récapitule dans le concept de *pré-mission*. Pour lui, tous les humains appartiennent au Christ par le fait qu'il les a tous assumés par l'Incarnation. Là où on ne peut prêcher le christ ouvertement, le pré-missionnaire, « porte-christ », le rend présent par la célébration de l'eucharistie et la pratique de la charité. Il fait l'expérience d'être la 'première chrétienté ethnique d'une race'.

> « Sa tâche missiologique est de penser cette chrétienté ethnique, sa tâche missionnaire, d'en être le premier adepte, le premier témoin, la vivre totalement. Le prémissionnaire est celui qui a l'obsession de ne pas occidentaliser ou orientaliser, mais de christianiser. Il a été envoyé à une race, à une civilisation, pour incarner le christianisme dans cette race, dans cette civilisation. Qu'elles reconnaissent, à travers lui, que le christianisme veut commencer par être leur christianisme, pour être plus sûr d'être le christianisme de l'universelle chrétienté ».[30]

Cet engagement absolu auprès des populations berbères n'est pas reçu par tous. Tout comme le père Charles-André Poissonnier (1897-1938), jeune prêtre franciscain arrivé au Maroc en 1929, disciple du père de Foucauld et immergé lui aussi en milieu berbère (à Tazert au sud du Maroc), le Père Peyriguère se sent incompris dans son action. On leur reproche à tous deux de sacrifier inutilement leur vie pour les populations indigènes tandis que l'Eglise des colons a besoin de forces nouvelles. Le Père Poissonnier mourra prématurément du typhus à l'âge de 40 ans en 1938. On retrouve chez lui aussi cette participation mystique à la destinée du peuple qu'il sert:

> « C'est au nom de tous ceux qui m'entourent que je prie, que j'adore. Devenu en quelque sorte marocain par mon incorporation à ce peuple auquel je vie très mêlé, et par ailleurs devenu membre du Christ par ma foi, j'ai l'impression qu'en moi le Christ s'est fait marocain, aime à prier lui-même pour ses frères marocains ».[31]

Cette identification totale et ce non-conformisme spirituel des moines missionnaires porte aussi une dimension de contestation vis-à-vis de l'autorité coloniale. Peyriguère qui approuve l'instrumentalisation coloniale de la question berbère dans ses écrits d'avant-guerre, opère ensuite un renversement complet: « *Homme chrétien et prêtre, j'ai dû prendre parti contre une administration qui n'était qu'injustice et que déloyauté* » (30/1/1951). Après avoir subi plusieurs menaces d'expulsion, il écrit:

> « L'on voudrait qu'un missionnaire fut conformiste servilement comme un fonctionnaire. (...) s'il aime son pays autant que d'autres qui pour le servir, lui ont demandé d'abord d'être leur vache à lait, le missionnaire est au service du christianisme. Et le christianisme n'est pas au service des impérialismes: il les juge et il a le devoir de les juger, même si ce sont les impérialismes de son propre pays » (19/2/1952).[32]

A la même période, le futur archevêque de Rabat, Mgr Lefèvre – signe annonciateur du changement d'attitude de l'Eglise catholique – publie une recommandation « Exigences de la présence chrétienne au

---

[29] Cité par George Gorrée, *Au-delà du père de Foucault, le père Peyriguère,* Paris: Centurion, 1960, 61-62.
[30] Albert Peyriguère, « Testament », cahier spécial des *Mardis de Dar el Salam*, 217.
[31] Cité par Jean-Pierre Flachaire, « Le monastère Notre-Dame de l'Atlas au Maroc », *Collectanea Cisterciensia* 68 (2006), 156.
[32] Albert Peyriguère, *Aussi loin que l'amour. Lettres du Maroc (1933-1957)*, Paris: Cerf, 1970, 68, 72.

Maroc » (15/2/1952) où il invite les catholiques à réviser leurs rapports avec les musulmans dans une exigence de justice et de solidarité.[33]

Les Missions Evangéliques au Maghreb

Le trait caractéristique de l'activité missionnaire protestante en Afrique du Nord à la fin du dix-neuvième siècle et jusqu'aux indépendances, tient au fait qu'elle n'a pas été initiée par des missions protestantes officielles mais qu'elle est a été le l'œuvre d'organisations évangéliques indépendantes, basées sur des initiatives individuelles. Les fondateurs et les ouvriers de ces *Faith Missions* étaient issus des milieux revivalistes anglais ou américains. Tout en fondant leur action sur des services médicaux ou éducatifs, ces missions privilégiaient l'annonce explicite du salut chrétien. L'origine étrangère des missionnaires (avec les soupçons d'espionnage qui pesaient sur eux)[34] de même que leur prosélytisme très actif, suscitèrent la méfiance et l'hostilité tant des autorités coloniales que des autorités religieuses traditionnelles. Le fait qu'ils ne côtoyaient pas les cercles coloniaux mais résidaient auprès des populations autochtones a contribué encore à leur marginalisation. Le rôle important qu'ils ont joué dans l'histoire religieuse et politique du Maghreb contemporain reste aujourd'hui encore trop méconnu.[35]

L'engagement des missions protestantes officielles est minime. En Algérie, au début de la conquête de 1830, la *Société des Missions évangéliques de Paris* préparait l'envoi de deux missionnaires mais le projet fut stoppé du fait de l'interdiction de toute évangélisation par les autorités militaires. Seule la petite Eglise méthodiste française organisa une mission à Il-Maten en Kabylie de 1887 à 1919.[36] En 1919, la station passe sous l'administration de la *Mission en Afrique du Nord de l'Église méthodiste épiscopalienne américaine*. C'est la seule grande Eglise protestante d'envergure internationale avec des pasteurs formés qui établira une mission durable au Maghreb.[37] En 1886, la *Presbyterian Church to England* envoie le Dr Robert Kerr, pasteur et médecin, à Rabat (Maroc) pour l'évangélisation des juifs, mais le soutien s'interrompt rapidement et le missionnaire fonde alors la *Central Morocco Mission*, dépendant désormais de soutiens privés.

La *North African Mission*

Parmi les missions indépendantes qui s'établissent au Maghreb l'initiative la plus durable et la mieux structurée est *The mission to the Kabyles and other Berber Races* (1881) qui prend le nom, à partir de 1888 de *North African Mission* (NAM). Elle est l'initiative de George Pearse (1815-1902), un riche chrétien anglais qui visitant l'Algérie en 1876 pour y établir un ministère parmi les soldats français, découvre la situation tragique des kabyles décimés par la famine et les épidémies. Il fonde alors une mission encouragé par le Dr H. Grattan Guinness célèbre prédicateur irlandais. La première station est ouverte en novembre 1881 à Djemma Sahridj en Kabylie et dirigée un temps par Edward Glenny, co-fondateur de la mission

[33] Louis Amédée Lefèvre, *Église du Maroc. Quelques directives (1950-1957)*, Rabat: Faits et Idées, 1959, 28-35.

[34] En Algérie, les autorités françaises mènent régulièrement des campagnes de dénigrement contre ces missionnaires étrangers soupçonnés d'activités antipatriotiques. (Heggoy, *Fifty Years*, 132-147).

[35] Deux travaux déjà anciens mais essentiels, permettent d'en prendre la mesure: Heggoy, *Fifty Years*, et pour le seul contexte marocain, Jean-Louis Miege, « Les missions protestantes au Maroc (1875-1905) », *Hespéris*, XLII (1955):153-192.

[36] Zohra Ait Abdelmalek, *Protestants en Algérie. Le protestantisme et son action missionnaire en Algérie aux xix*[e] *et xx*[e] *siècles*, Lyon: Olivetan, 2004, 23. Cf. aussi Gadille et Zorn, « Les missions chrétiennes en Afrique », 1023-1026.

[37] En 1920, cette mission possède 7 stations, 2 en Tunisie, 5 en Algérie. Elle ambitionne de rassembler chrétiens d'origine arabe ou kabyle et chrétiens d'origine européenne. Heggoy, *Fifty Years*, 229-249. Cf. aussi H. L Aurbakken, Willy Normann-Heggoy, Paul Bres, *Les Pierres crieront*, Alger: imp. Baconnier, 1960, 18.

avec Pearse. D'autres implantations vont suivre en Algérie (Alger, 1883, Constantine, 1886; etc.), puis la mission se déploie au Maroc (Tanger, 1883; Fès, 1888), en Tunisie (Tunis, 1885), en Lybie (Tripoli, 1889) et même en Egypte (Alexandrie, 1892). En 1900, la NAM était présente dans 6 pays, avec un total de 302 missionnaires (123 hommes, 179 femmes – épouses ou célibataires) et 468 assistants locaux.[38] L'objectif de la mission est ainsi défini: « *To carry the Gospel to the Berbers, Arabs, Moors and other native races in Morocco, Algeria, Tunis, Tripoli, Egypt and Arabia, as well as to Jews and Europeans in those countries* »; avec les méthodes utilisées pour l'atteindre: « *Preaching the Gospel publicly and from house to house, Medical Missions, Mission Work among Women, Itinerating and Distribution of the Scriptures* ». Le Maroc est l'un des pays où la mission connait le plus de succès, en particulier à Tanger avec l'établissement d'un petit hôpital moderne (1887), l'un des premiers du pays, qui restera en service jusqu'en 1974.[39] A Fès, la mission qui comporte aussi un dispensaire, est dirigée par Miss Emma Herdman (1844-1899).[40] Associée à deux autres femmes (Miss Copping, infirmière, et Miss Reed), elle établit en quelques années un vaste réseau de colporteurs bibliques marocains couvrant le centre du pays. Dans ce Maroc précolonial, les missionnaires – souvent des femmes, et qui sont aussi les premiers Européens en contact avec les autochtones – rencontrent un accueil plutôt bienveillant, y compris dans les classes élevés de la société traditionnelle marocaine.

La *North African Mission* témoignera d'une grande longévité puisqu'en dépit des oppositions et difficultés administratives, elle se maintiendra, jusqu'après les indépendances dans les pays concernés. Les missionnaires, jugés trop prosélytes, sont progressivement expulsés à la fin des années 1960. L'action de la NAM se poursuit au travers des ondes par la production d'émissions radio et de cours bibliques.[41]

Cette oeuvre pionnière va constituer un modèle de développement pour d'autres organisations – *Faith Missions* – qui s'installent en Afrique du Nord à la fin du 19e siècle. L'une des plus connues est la *Gospel Missionary Union* (GMU), qui après une tentative ratée d'implantation au Soudan débute au Maroc en 1894, sur l'initiative de l'américain George S. Fisher du Kansas. Elle s'y maintiendra, localisée surtout autour de Fès et Meknès jusqu'en 1969 (les missionnaires sont aussi expulsés). Contrairement aux autres missions, la GMU n'a pas de dispensaires médicaux et se consacre seulement à l'évangélisation et la formation.

En Algérie, la riche anglaise Miss Lilias Trotter (1853-1928), évangéliste, écrivain et dessinatrice, et deux autres femmes indépendantes et fortunées, fondent en 1888 une mission à Alger destinée en particulier aux femmes et aux enfants. Devenue *The Algiers Mission Band* (1907), la mission grandit et emploie, en 1920, 30 évangélistes répartis dans 15 sites différents, jusque dans le Sahara. Miss Trotter qui

---

[38] J. Rutherford and H. Edward Glenny, *The Gospel in North Africa, in two parts*, London, Percy Lund, Humphies & Co., 1900, 246.

[39] Après 86 années d'activité (1888-1974), le *Tulloch Memorial Hospital* est fermé par les autorités marocaines et la propriété de la NAM expropriée. Francis R Steele, *Not in Vain. The Story of North Africa Mission*, Pasadena: William Carey Library, 1981, 59-67.

[40] Emma Herdman née en Irlande du Nord est issue d'une famille aisée. Ayant étudié et voyagé en Europe, elle parle couramment six langues et a étudié le latin, le grec et l'hébreu. Après avoir servi dans plusieurs Eglises en Angleterre, elle s'associe à la Société biblique en France, avec le projet de travailler en Algérie. Du fait d'une épidémie de choléra qui sévissait à Alger, elle s'oriente plutôt vers Tanger où elle arrive en 1884. Sa fortune personnelle lui permettra de financer en grande partie son action missionnaire au Maroc - Albert A. Isaacs, *A Biographical Sketch Relative to the Missionary Labors of Emma Herdman in the Empire of Morocco,* London: S.W. Partridge, 1900. Cf. aussi Steele, *Not in Vain*, 28-30.

[41] Steele, *Not in Vain,* 75-80 et Jozef Martinus Strengholt, "Gospel in the Air: 50 Years of Christian Witness Through Radio in the Arab World", PhD,Utrecht University, 2008, 637-680 (NAM-AWM) et 739-783 (GMU). En 1987, la NAM devient *Arab World Ministries.* Le département média se développe encore après la période des émissions de radio: en 1999, production de programmes en arabe pour les chaines TV satellites; en 2002, lancement d'un site internet avec ressources par pays (www.maarifa.org), en 2007, développement des médias interactifs pour la génération numérique, etc.

parle parfaitement l'arabe, invente de nouvelles méthodes de transmission du message,[42] écrit des recueils de paraboles, prône l'utilisation des chants bibliques rimés et de la musique traditionnelle, etc. La mission diffuse une grande quantité de littérature d'évangélisation en arabe, notamment *The Seven Fold Secret* (basé sur les sept « *Je suis* » de Jésus dans l'Evangile de Jean). écrit par Miss Trotter spécialement à destination des mystiques musulmans. Publié en 1926 en arabe algérien (puis traduit dans d'autres langues) le livre circule dans les confréries soufis du Sahara.[43]

Faith Missions et Radicalisme Missionnaire

Ces *Faith Mssions* à l'oeuvre en Afrique du Nord pendant près de 100 ans, ont chacune une histoire particulière mais présentent néanmoins des caractéristiques communes:[44]

Comme leur nom l'indique, elles reposent sur le plan financier sur une absolue confiance en la providence divine (manifestée au travers des dons privés). Les missionnaires devaient trouver leurs propres soutiens dans le pays d'origine. La situation matérielle des missions et des individus est donc parfois précaire et incertaine.

elles sont interdénominationnelles (ou non-dénominationelles), et ne fonctionnent pas comme une Eglise, mais plutôt comme des groupements de croyants centrés sur l'impératif missionnaire, avec une approche assez individualiste de la foi. La compréhension et la pratique des sacrements (baptême et sainte cène) y est fluctuante.

les missionnaires sont en grande majorité des laïcs n'ayant pas reçu de formation pastorale ou théologique approfondie. Généralement issus de classes moyennes, sans grand bagage intellectuel,[45] ils ont une approche littéraliste de la Bible, avec une théologie centrée sur la conversion individuelle (repentance des péchés et sacrifice expiatoire du Christ). Influencés par les courants millénaristes, poussés à l'exaltation par un quotidien missionnaire difficile, en butte à l'échec et à l'absence de conversions, ils portent souvent une vision négative du monde, sous l'emprise du diable et des forces du mal.[46] Cette diabolisation concerne en premier lieu l'islam.

les fondateurs de ces *Faith Missions* visent en priorité les zones et les groupes humains non encore atteints par l'Evangile. Cette géographie de l'urgence missionnaire basée sur une stricte théologie du salut et de la perdition et teintée de ferveur millénariste, conduit les missionnaires à s'installer dans des localités isolées et à s'exposer à des situations dangereuses. L'urgence de l'annonce pour

---

42 Lisa M. Sinclair, "*The Legacy of Isabella Lilias Trotter*", *International Bulletin of Missionary Research*, 26:1 (2002), 34.

43 Miriam Huffman Rockness, *A Passion for the Impossible: The life of Lilias Trotter*, Grand Rapids: Discovery House Publishers, 2003, 221, 261, 271-272.

44 Klaus Fiedler, *The Story of Faith Missions. From Hudson Taylor to present day Africa,* Oxford: Regnum Books International, 1994 et Willy N. Heggoy, *Fifty Years*, 257-280.

45 "*It is true that most of the early faith missionaries came from the 'neglected forces of Christianity'. Most of them would not have been acceptable ot as classical mission*" (Fiedler, "The Story", 137). Mais à côté de ces recrues ordinaires, et surtout parmi les leaders des missions, on compte aussi des personnes très qualifiées, professeurs, médecins, théologiens, etc., dont certaines fortunées et influentes.

46 Glenny, responsable de la *North African Mission*, écrit en 1900: "*Mohammedanism, Romanism, and infidelity are the great anti-Christian forces we have to face. These are not merely systems of error, but system of error specially devised to obstruct and overthrow the Gospel. (...). In going to evangelise the peoples of North Africa we were sent to attack an entrenched foe – a foe who, knowing something of the power of the Gospel, had constructed his entrenchments with a view of resisting it to the uttermost (...) Added to these religious difficulties are the political ones, which the zealously religious, whether Moslem, Romanist, infidel, or Jew, are ever ready to call to their aid.(...) Moorish, French, and Turkish Governments are ever suspicious that the missionary is merely a political agent in a religious disguise, and are therefore inclined to hamper, if not to hinder him, from a sense of fear*." Rutherford and Glenny, *The Gospel in North Africa*, 242.

sauver les âmes perdues prime toujours sur les œuvres sociales que la mission entretient pour gagner la confiance des populations.[47]

Baldwin et la mission selon Matthieu 10

Les pratiques d'évangélisation de ces *Faith Mission* radicales et exaltées sont souvent controversées. L'une des « affaires » qui bouscula le monde des missions protestantes d'alors est provoquée par un missionnaire de la *North African Mission*, E.F.Baldwin, pasteur baptiste, arrivé à Tanger en 1884 avec sa famille. Il conçoit une vision radicale de la mission basée sur le texte de Matthieu 10.7-10 où Jésus envoie ses disciples sans argent ni provisions, leur demandant de compter sur l'hospitalité des populations. L'insuccès des missions modernes – pensait Baldwin – tenait au fait que ces principes de la mission apostolique n'étaient pas respectés.

Après 3 ans à la NAM, Baldwin démissionne et s'établit comme missionnaire indépendant à Fès où il met en pratique sa vision. Dix jours après son arrivée, il baptise un *sherif*, descendant du prophète. Il fait paraitre une série d'articles dans l'hebdomadaire *The Christian* de Londres, déployant les cinq « vraies principes bibliques » du travail missionnaire: 1° pas de salaire assuré, 2° pas de possessions, 3° pas de provisions pour les besoins physiques, 4° pas de facilités pour les voyages, 5° refus des amitiés naturelles. La publication suscitera des polémiques dans les cercles européens. Plusieurs revues missionnaires d'Angleterre, Allemagne et France se saisissent de la question.[48]

En 1889, Baldwin se voit confier la formation des nouveaux candidats de la *Southern Morocco Mission* nouvellement implantée à Marrakech. C'est l'occasion pour lui de tester sa « méthode ». Deux convertis Marocains sont envoyés en tournée selon les principes de Matthieu X. Ils sont logés et nourris dans les mosquées des villages. Après trois mois de tournées, on compte déjà 45 convertis baptisés. Mais la polémique enfle et les rapports s'avèrent mensongers. Plusieurs ironisent sur les exagérations de Baldwin,[49] lequel, devenu *persona non grata* aux yeux des autorités marocaines, quitte le Maroc pour la Syrie en 1890.

La traduction et la diffusion de la Bible

Le travail le plus méconnu de ces missionnaires est sans doute la vaste entreprise de traduction de la Bible qu'ils déploient. Certains consacrent des années à acquérir la maitrise de la langue tout en travaillant avec leurs assistants marocains ou algériens à la traduction des textes. Les Evangiles, le Nouveau Testament et parfois toute la Bible sont ainsi traduits dans plusieurs dialectes berbères du Maroc et d'Algérie et dans diverses variantes de l'arabe dialectal (y compris le judéo-arabe de Tunisie). Ce sont d'abord des extraits, morceaux d'Evangiles, psaumes, qui sont traduits pour les besoins de la predication,[50] puis les livres en

---

[47] Dans un rapport de1886, le docteur Churcher de la *North African Mission* à Tanger, insistant sur cette priorité de l'annonce du salut, décrit ainsi sa mission médicale: "medical mission, healing for soul and body, calculated pre-eminently to remove prejudice and opposition, and prepare good ground for the sowing of the Gospel seed. Over a thousand cases have been treated during the year, medicines and advice being given free, linked together with the Bread of life, the Gospel in all simplicity, and therefore in power. The number of patients has not been limited for want of applicants, but in order not to crowd out spiritual work among those who are seen, the study of the language, etc., many have been sent away" – F.T. Haig, *Daybreak in North Africa. An account of how Work for Christ Begun in Morocco, Algeria, Tunis and Tripoli*, London: Partridge & Co, 1890, 71.

[48] Heggoy, *Fifty Years*, 83-94.

[49] Ainsi, le docteur Kerr (*Central Morocco Mission*): "*The great Matthew X movement under Mr Baldwin at Mogador in 1889 was characterized by a marvellous outcome. Numbers flocked to him and were baptized, believing that if they became Christian they would enjoy European protection. He preached to men on Friday, baptized them on Saturday, admitted them to the Lord's Table on Sabbath, and sent them forth as messengers for the Cross to convert their fellow-countrymen on Monday*" - Robert Kerr, *Morocco, After Twenty-Five Years,* 213.

[50] Quelques mois après leur arrivée à Tanger en Janvier 1995, Nathan et Hammer, missionnaires de la *Gospel*

entiers. Le débat porte aussi sur le niveau d'arabe utilisé. Certains missionnaires (ceux de la *North African Mission*) considèrent que l'arabe classique – l'arabe du Coran – serait le seul digne d'être utilisé pour un message divin. L'usage de l'arabe dialectal risquerait de dévaloriser le message chrétien aux yeux des locuteurs. Les missionnaires traducteurs de la *Gospel Missionary Union* plaident au contraire pour les variantes dialectales, accessibles au plus grand nombre.[51] Durant des décennies, La *British and Foreign Bible Society* (BFBS) implantée dès 1884 au Maroc puis en Algérie, encourage et finance en partie, la traduction et la publication de ces extraits bibliques en langue populaire.[52] Chaque mission en assure la diffusion par le colportage, avec cette conviction unanimement partagée, que la page imprimée (tracts, évangiles, etc.) une fois distribuée, se frayait d'elle-même un chemin dans les maisons ou dans les cœurs, et continuait de « proclamer l'Evangile » efficacement après le départ du missionnaire ou quand les portes se fermaient.[53] Le missionnaire James Haldane de la *Southern Morocco Mission* (Marrakech), arrivé au Maroc en 1912, raconte avoir personnellement visité un millier de villages marocains, avec l'objectif constamment suivi de prêcher l'Evangile dans chacun et d'y laisser dans les mains de quelqu'un capable de lire, au moins une copie de la Bible complète ou du Nouveau Testament.[54] Cette croyance dans l'efficacité *per se* du texte biblique imprimé influence les nombreuses actions de diffusion de littérature biblique menées par les missions évangéliques. Ces distributions des Ecritures, relayées désormais par l'Internet ou les chaines TV par satellite[55] sont ressenties comme de la propagande invasive par le public musulman.

Une empreinte durable

Sur le terrain, ces missionnaires évangéliques établissent des relations durables avec les autochtones. Ils vivent dans leur voisinage, s'habillent comme eux, les visitent et les soignent. Durant les mois d'été, les missionnaires (surtout au Maroc) effectuent de longues tournées d'évangélisation dans les montagnes berbères.

Les femmes, qui sont les plus nombreuses, sont autorisées à pénétrer dans l'intimité des foyers. A Fès, en 1889, Miss Herdman et ses collaboratrices sont habillées et voilées comme les femmes *fasi* lorsqu'elles

---

Missionary Union traduisent 4 chapitres de l'Ev. de Jean et 4 Psaumes (1, 23, 100 et 121) pour les besoins immédiats de leur tournée missionnaire effectuée dans les villages de la région durant l'été 1995. Dennis H. Phillips, "The American Missionary in Morocco", *The Muslim World*, LXV-1 (1975), 8.

[51] Heggoy, *Fifty years*, 313-315. Cf. aussi, Heather J. Sharkey, "The Gospel in Arabic Tongues: British Bible Distribution, Evangelical Mission, and Language Politics in North Africa," in *Cultural Conversions: Unexpected Consequences of Christian Missions in the Middle East, Africa, and South Asia*, ed. by Heather J. Sharkey (Syracuse: Syracuse University Press, 2013). 210-216.

[52] William Canton, *A History Of The British And Foreign Bible Society* (Vol.V), London: John Murray, 1910, 1-18. En 1887: Evangile de Matthieu en Rifain (berbère du Nord) traduit par Mackintosh (BFBS). 1888: Ev. de Matthieu en arabe tunisien par Jocelyn Bureau (NAM). 1902: publication de l'Ev. de Luc en arabe marocain, complété en 1906 par les 4 évangiles, Actes et Romains – traduits par George Reed (GMU). 1908?: Ev. de Matthieu en arabe algérien avec caractères hébraïques par William Pope (NAM). 1906: traductions des Ev. de Jean et Matthieu en Tamazight (berbère du Centre) par G. Reed et Enyart (GMU). 1906: traduction de l'Ev. de Jean en Tachelhit (berbère du Sud) par Nair et Nuir (*Southern Morocco Mission*). Sur la valeur linguistique de cette dernière traduction, cf. Naïma Affif, « A propos de l'Evangile selon Saint Jean de la British and Foreign Bible Society en berbère tachelhit (Maroc) », *Babelao* 3 (2014), 109-125.

[53] Le Dr Samuel Zwemer (1867-1952) islamologue et arabisant, mais surtout propagandiste infatigable de la mission évangélique face à l'islam voyait dans la « page imprimée » l'élément-clé de l'évangélisation des Musulmans: « (it) *finds an entrance into many doors closed to the living witness and can proclaim the Gospel persistently, fearlessly and effectively* », Il appelait les pages imprimées « The leaves for the healing of the nations » (en référence à Ap. 22.2) - J. Christy Wilson,. *Apostle to Islam: a biography of Samuel M. Zwemer*, Grand Rapids: Baker, 1952, 186-187, 13.

[54] James Haldane, *Trekking Among Moroccan Tribes*, London: Pickering & Inglis, 1948, 17.

[55] Christian Bonnet, « Ouvrez les écluses du ciel ! La télévision par satellite, outil d'évangélisation en direction du monde musulman », *Perspectives Missionnaires*, n°57 (2009): 49-57.

se déplacent à l'extérieur.[56] L'intégration tient aussi à la bonne maitrise des langues (dialectes berbères et arabes), que les missionnaires ont l'obligation d'apprendre.[57] Les conditions de vie sont difficiles même en milieu urbain, où ils sont installés dans les quartiers indigènes. Plusieurs d'entre eux, surtout dans les premières décennies (avant la 1ère guerre mondiale), meurent du typhus ou d'autres maladies. Quelques-uns sont assassinés.[58]

Cette consécration missionnaire est souvent celle de toute une vie. Cuthbert Nairn, de la *Southern Morocco Mission*, écossais issu d'une famille de fermiers, arrivé à Marrakech en 1888, y dirige un dispensaire médical durant 55 ans. Il est assassiné en 1944. William Reid, de la *North African Mission* arrive en 1892 à Tripoli (Lybie) encore sous domination turque. Il y exerce son ministère (dispensaire et prédication) durant 44 ans et sera expulsé en 1936 par les fascistes italiens.[59] Maud Carey (1878-1967) de la *Gospel Missionary Union* sert à Meknès au Maroc de 1901 à 1955.

Ce réseau des missions évangéliques en Afrique du Nord dans l'entre-deux guerres est à la fois impressionnant de vitalité et d'une grande fragilité. En 1931, il compte 293 missionnaires en activité (168 en Algérie, 96 au Maroc, 28 en Tunisie, 1 en Lybie).[60] Mais les missions ne sont pas coordonnées entre elles et vivent dans une instabilité constante du fait des modes de financement et de recrutement. Il n'y a pas de planification stratégique à l'échelle des pays et l'absence de soutien officiel des grandes Eglises à l'international nuit aussi à leur visibilité et leur crédibilité. Cette coopération se mettra progressivement en place, mais toujours de manière confidentielle, dans les années 1930 et après la 2ème guerre mondiale dans les pays du Maghreb.[61]

Comparativement aux efforts déployés, l'impact religieux des missions s'est avéré toujours minime, surtout s'il est mesuré au nombre des conversions. La résistance culturelle et religieuse des populations cibles était inévitablement renforcée par la vision négative et réductrice de l'islam portée par les *Faith Missions* (jusqu'à aujourd'hui). Celles-ci n'en ont pas moins réussi, mieux que les missions classiques qui avaient abandonné le terrain missionnaire, à mobiliser, en Europe et aux Etats-Unis, un grand nombre d'hommes et de femmes de toutes couches sociales pour une cause qui les attachera profondément et de manière durable aux personnes et aux pays du Maghreb.

L'Expérience Ambivalente de la Mission

Missionnaires évangéliques et « moines missionnaires » (et autres religieux et religieuses catholiques), ont en commun la radicalité de leur engagement chrétien. Les théologies et spiritualités divergent mais ces

---

[56] "*We go out clothed in a white woollen burnoos, the hood fastened round the head with a white silk cord. Mouth and nose are covered with one piece of white muslin and the forehead with another, both tied round the head under the burnoos, the eyes alone are visible. I am known by my spectacles, otherwise the disguise is perfect. Fez not having mixed with Europeans do not think any woman unveiled respectable. They will learn in time*" - Haig, *Daybreak*, 86.

[57] Miss Herdman écrit dans son journal (vers 1887 ?): « it was the daily habit in Fez, after our early evening prayers, to read aloud four or five chapters of the Arabic Bible. With dictionaries at hand, we searched out and discussed new words, and as the years went on we found that we had read through the whole Bible, quite a number of times" Albert A. Isaacs, *A Biographical Sketch Relative to the Missionary Labors of Emma Herdman in the Empire of Morocco,* London: S.W. Partridge, 1900, 117.

[58] Pour la *North African Mission*: David J. Cooper à Fès en 1902 et le Docteur Charles Leach et sa famille à Sfax (Tunisie) en 1896.

[59] Heggoy, *Fifty Years*, 154-157. L'objectif initial de cette implantation de la NAM en Lybie était d'en faire une base de départ pour atteindre les tribus Touareg du Sahara. L'œuvre médicale de la NAM à Tripoli va se poursuivre jusqu'en 1969, avec l'arrivée du régime du Colonel Kadhafi, qui met fin à toute activité missionnaire – cf. Steele, *Not in Vain*, 67, 91-95.

[60] Heggoy, *Fifty Years*, 249-256. L'effectif total cumulé sur les décennies 1880-1960 serait plus impressionnant encore.

[61] Heggoy, *Fifty Years*, 346; Evelyn Stenbock, *"Miss Terri!" The Story of Maude Cary, Pioneer GMU Missionary in Morocco*, Lincoln, NE: Back to the Bible Broadcast, 1970, 96-98.

vocations missionnaires vécues en marge de la société coloniale, se font mutuellement écho à bien des égards.

A première vue, beaucoup d'éléments séparent les deux communautés missionnaires, catholique et protestante. La concurrence religieuse tout d'abord, comme en Kabylie où certains fidèles des Pères Blancs se convertissent au protestantisme.[62] Les Pères Blancs d'Algérie ou les Franciscains du Maroc critiquent aussi la diffusion massive de littérature biblique, tout en admirant parfois le zèle qu'y consacrent les protestants.[63] Sur le plan missiologique, c'est surtout le rapport à l'islam qui va peu à peu marquer le point de rupture. Alors que les catholiques évoluent – surtout après la 2e guerre mondiale – vers une position d'ouverture, les missions évangéliques maintiennent un rapport très conflictuel à l'islam, jugé diabolique. La problématique pré-missionnaire d'un Peyriguère, oriente vers une *théologie de l'accomplissement,* de type *inclusive*, tandis que l'évangélisme à tendance *polémique*, porte une *théologie de la rupture*, de type *exclusive.*[64]

Néanmoins sur le terrain, les clivages ne sont pas toujours aussi marqués. Des Pères Blancs s'inscrivent résolument dans une pratique d'apostolat direct (avec conversions et baptêmes) tandis que des missionnaires protestants apprécient la profondeur spirituelle des musulmans qu'ils rencontrent, en particulier les soufis.[65]

Leurs expériences convergent surtout sur le plan existentiel: l'intensité des relations tissées avec les populations dont les missionnaires parlent la langue[66] et partagent l'existence durant des années, voire des décennies; l'exaltation spirituelle d'un engagement total dans la prière et l'action associé à une forme de précarité matérielle, tout autant que les phases de découragement face aux échecs et à l'absence de fruits visibles de leur mission.

Au constat de leur impuissance, et comme une façon de transcender tous les obstacles de la mission, catholiques et protestants se rejoignent dans la même conception quasi magique d'un Dieu qui agit « tout

---

[62] Dans les années 1925, 1929 (Heggoy, *Fifty Years*, 341-342).

[63] Ainsi, ce témoignage en 1927 du Père Henri Koehler, l'une des figures franciscaines au Maroc, trouvé dans un bulletin de liaison entre missionnaires, non officiel, à tirage et usage confidentiels. Koehler reconnait l'apport des protestants dans la mission et la traduction biblique et semble appeler à des formes de collaboration: « *Il est utile grandement qu'on s'entraide pour cette œuvre d'évangélisation indigène du Nord d'Afrique islamique et berbère. Partager ses vues, ses méthodes est puissamment fructueux. Quand je considère les protestants et que je vois la peine qu'ils se donnent à traduire tous nos livres saints dans tous les dialectes de notre Afrique du Nord, puis leur zèle à les répandre partout, cela me donne à réfléchir et je vois pour ma part ici au Maroc combien ils sont actifs. Il faut dire pour être juste qu'ils sont ici depuis longtemps et qu'ils font plutôt œuvre superficielle, ils vont peu au fond des âmes. La civilisation chrétienne non catholique aide beaucoup à relever les indigènes mais aussi elle amène ceux-ci à s'infatuer de leur petit « moi (...). Toutefois les protestants ont une précieuse qualité qui nous manque: ils sont audacieux et ne sont pas retenus par la crainte du voisin qui nous paralyse souvent, nous Français.»* - R.P.K, ofm, *in «En Terre d'Islam»* 1927 – exemplaire ronéotypé, sans titre et sans pagination (Archives Institut *Al Mowafaqa*, Rabat).

[64] Un missionnaire écrit en 1951 (après 25 ans passés au Maroc): « *Islam is the Devil's reply to Calvary and Pentecost. Our blessed Lord had not long ascended before the early Church found itself facing the issue upon which the whole argument of Mohammedanism is constructed: 'Who is a liar but he that denieth that Jesus is the Christ ? He is antichrist, that denieth the Father and Son'(1 Jean 2.22) The Moslems acknowledge that Jesus is the Christ, but definitely deny His Sonship and deity »*. Eric G. Fisk, *The Prickly Pear*, Chicago: Moody Press, 1951, 21-22.

[65] Zwemer, généralement négatif sur l'islam, valorise la profondeur du mysticisme musulman. En 1923, il fait même cette suggestion étonnante que l'organisation des confréries soufies pourrait servir de modèle pour la formation d'une Eglise de croyants d'arrière-plan musulman: *"The moslem brotherhoods are a challenge to the Christian brotherhood and to the formation of a Christian church, which will have all the elements of strength of Moslem mystic union without its vagaries and lawlessness"* - Zwemer, "North Africa", 562.

[66] L'importance accordée à l'apprentissage de la langue – comme point d'entrée dans la culture de l'autre et élément d'acculturation du missionnaire - est aussi un point commun aux missionnaires catholiques et évangéliques. En comparaison, très peu de prêtres ou pasteurs des paroisses coloniales n'accédaient à la langue et donc à l'univers des autochtones.

seul », au travers des médiations symboliques que sont le Saint sacrement pour les uns, la distribution des portions de Bible pour les autres. L'un et l'autre supports sont supposés irradier la présence du Christ et toucher les cœurs des non croyants.

De par leur non conformisme social et spirituel, les deux groupes missionnaires partagent aussi l'expérience de l'incompréhension et du rejet du milieu colonial. Ils déplorent le contre témoignage des colons européens.

Le pasteur Paul Gounelle, premier titulaire à partir de 1915 de l'Eglise protestante française de Casablanca, donne dans une conférence de 1920 une fine analyse de la résistance des musulmans face au « modèle » européen:

> « La répulsion des musulmans pour le christianisme est quelque chose de structurel pour la société marocaine: les Marocains sont difficilement influençables. Leur élite, très polie, écoute avec bienveillance ce qu'on leur dit, car il serait inhospitalier de discuter les idées de son hôte, mais se garde bien d'en retenir quoi que ce soit. Elle est fière du monothéisme très pur de sa religion, et celle-ci joue dans sa vie un plus grand rôle que notre foi dans notre propre vie. Le grand mal c'est qu'ils ont connu notre civilisation, ses vices et ses crimes bien avant notre christianisme. (...) Seule pourra les atteindre la mission qui se livrera à eux sans se couvrir d'aucune protection officielle et se dressera la première contre la civilisation prétendue chrétienne qui les exploite, sans accepter aucun compromis avec elle. »[67]

Le rôle joué par les femmes dans l'oeuvre missionnaire – rôle-clé et facteur de réussite – constitue un autre point de convergence. Du côté catholique, pour l'Algérie et la Tunisie les statistiques de 1931 montrent que les Sœurs Blanches (303) sont presque trois fois plus nombreuses que les Pères Blancs (133).[68] La proportion est plus forte encore au Maroc où les Sœurs Franciscaines (246 en 1935) ont la responsabilité de presque toutes les œuvres indigènes (14 ateliers ou orphelinats), tandis que les Frères Franciscains (83) sont cantonnés dans les paroisses coloniales.[69] Du côté protestant, plusieurs des missions ou stations missionnaires sont dirigées par des femmes.[70] L'exemple de Lilias Trotter fondatrice et directrice de l'*Algiers Mission Band* en est l'illustration la plus frappante. Zwemer dans sa tournée en Afrique du Nord de 1922 relève que sur les 80 missionnaires toutes agences confondues recensés au Maroc, 58 sont des femmes célibataires, soit près de trois-quarts des effectifs![71] Leur activité est largement centrée sur la conversion des femmes musulmanes. S'étant affranchies elles-mêmes du carcan victorien qui enfermait la femme dans la sphère domestique, les missionnaires anglaises ou américaines qui infiltrent l'espace réservé des femmes arabes, participent à l'ébranlement des structures traditionnelles concernant la place et le rôle des femmes.[72]

L'échec missionnaire et la question des convertis

Les missionnaires catholiques et protestants ont dû chacun à leur manière affronter cette double difficulté: d'une part la rareté ou l'absence des conversions sur leur champ de mission et d'autre part, la responsabilité de l'accompagnement des quelques convertis qui les rejoignaient.

Les rapports rédigés à l'attention des donateurs européens sont remplis de chiffres et d'anecdotes relatifs aux « progrès » de la mission – aux individus, familles, quartiers, villages touchés par l'action des

---

[67] Conférence donnée en avril 1920 au Temple de l'Oratoire à Paris (document manuscrit – archives de l'EEAM).
[68] Heggoy, *Fifty Years*, 359-360.
[69] Baïda & Feroldi, *Présence chrétienne*, 90-91, 206-212.
[70] Heggoy, *Fifty Years*, 296-301, 306-311.
[71] Zwemer, "North Africa", 565.
[72] Cf. Patricia R., Hill, *The World Their Household: The American Woman's Foreign Mission Movement and Cultural Transformation, 1870-1920* (Ann Arbor: The University of Michigan Press, 1985), 3-7. Hill évoque justement le contexte marocain.

missionnaires. Tout en réalisant leur objectif premier qui était, dans la perspective des *Faith Missions*, d'atteindre les populations non atteintes (*reach the unreached*), les missionnaires prennent la mesure de l'imperméabilité de l'islam. Les conversions rapportées sont rares et les comptes-rendus les plus honnêtes évoquent les difficultés et découragements tant des missionnaires que de leurs convertis. Certains missionnaires, à Marrakech, Tripoli ou Tunis, exercent leur activité durant des années sans accueillir un seul converti. Quant à ceux-là, devenus généralement leurs collaborateurs sur le champ de mission, les conséquences de leur choix religieux, requalifié socialement en apostasie, sont parfois tragiques. Les témoignages de persécutions (voire d'assassinats) nourrissent à leur tour les rapports des missionnaires.

Dans les décennies précédant le protectorat au Maroc (années 1885-1910), là où le traumatisme de la domination coloniale ne s'était pas encore fait sentir, l'action d'évangélisation semble néanmoins obtenir quelques résultats durables. L'activité du réseau de colporteurs marocains mis en place par Miss Herdman de Fès (*supra*) eut un impact, localisé mais réel, dans plusieurs couches sociales. Autre contexte, la Kabylie (Algérie), qui s'avèrera elle aussi, et sur la longue période (de 1850 à 2015), un terrain réceptif aux diverses propositions religieuses du christianisme.

Sans prétendre accéder à l'impénétrable sanctuaire du for intérieur, ces chemins de conversion religieuse, empruntés par quelques fortes individualités non-conformistes (tout comme l'étaient leurs missionnaires) ont pu constituer le moyen d'effectuer une conversion culturelle et « civilisationnelle » au sein de ces sociétés traditionnelles du Maghreb qui vivaient l'irruption de la modernité. Quant aux missionnaires, agents de ces conversions, l'urgence millénariste et la certitude d'œuvrer pour le salut du monde qui les habitaient, les ont rendus incapables de penser sérieusement l'accommodation culturelle de leur ethos et de leur message.[73] Du fait de cette cécité culturelle des missionnaires, sous-estimant d'une part la prégnance de l'islam comme système social et religieux auto-suffisant et d'autre part la mort civile qu'entrainait la sortie de ce bloc, les nouveaux convertis se sont souvent trouvés dans des impasses existentielles.[74]

Dans les stations de la *Gospel Missionary Union* on demandait à ces convertis, pour évaluer la sincérité de leur démarche, de ne pas pratiquer le jeûne durant le mois de Ramadan.[75] D'autres missionnaires, conscients de l'enjeu de la mort sociale des convertis déclarés, acceptaient le principe des conversions secrètes. James Haldane, missionnaire de la *Southern Morocco Mission* (Marrakech, 1912-1951) écrit en 1936:

> « A number of men and women, however, have made open confession, and boldly accepted the consequences attaching to it. But many more are hidden believers who have not been daring enough to announce publicly their break from Islam (…) Would not their secret testimony and the influence of their Christian lives, even if muffled, be more effective, mingling with their fellows than if made openly within the circumscribed limites of the mission house? »[76]

---

[73] Makdisi Ussama, *Artillery of Heaven: American Missionaries and the Failed Conversion of the Middle East*, Ithaca-New York: Cornell University Press, 2008.

[74] Cette « impasse existentielle » concerne par exemple le sort des kabyles convertis au catholicisme au début du 20e siècle: « En devenant chrétiens, les habitants des villages kabyles se coupaient de façon quasi irrémédiable de leurs congénères.(…) Sortis des couches sociales désavantagées ils s'étaient dissociés de leurs origines et avaient profité de leurs études à la française (…) Adopter une attitude apostolique envers leurs semblables qui les méprisaient et qu'ils regardaient peut-être de haut était pratiquement impossible. On peut donc comprendre qu'ils aient adopté envers leurs voisins musulmans une attitude défensive » - Nolan, *Les Pères Blancs*, 117-118.

[75] Phillips, «The American Missionary», 13.

[76] James Haldane, *Missionary Romance in Morocco*, London: Pickering & Inglis, 1936, 50.

L'histoire du christianisme du vingtième siècle au Maghreb devrait s'écrire aujourd'hui en restituant (à partir des archives écrites et de la mémoire orale) les parcours et la complexité de ces figures de convertis dont certains jouèrent un rôle social et religieux important.

Du côté de l'Eglise catholique, l'échec missionnaire (quantitatif et qualitatif) a conduit missionnaires et théologiens en contact avec des intellectuels musulmans, à remettre en question non seulement les méthodes missionnaires, mais plus profondément la compréhension du monde musulman qui était en vigueur depuis des siècles. Il s'agissait aussi « d'inventer un nouveau cadre pour la présence de l'Eglise en terre d'islam »: « *la mission auprès des musulmans, par son échec, a permis à la théologie catholique du salut d'évoluer et de préparer la phase du dialogue dans les années 1960.* »[77]

Pour les protestants évangéliques, conformément à la ligne exclusiviste d'une théologie de rupture, l'expérience de l'échec missionnaire était transmutée en veille eschatologique. La persévérance dans l'épreuve, tant des missionnaires que des convertis, la continuation de l'activité missionnaire assortie d'une prière constante pour faire tomber la « forteresse de l'islam » et libérer ceux qu'elle emprisonne – en un mot, les « semences », devaient, au temps de Dieu, produire la moisson attendue. Les mêmes schèmes d'interprétation sont activés pour expliquer le phénomène actuel des conversions au christianisme (*infra*).

Les missionnaires étrangers comprennent que l'établissement durable d'un christianisme autochtone au Maghreb ne pourra se faire sans la prise en main de l'œuvre par les chrétiens locaux, avec des petits groupes de croyants décidant eux-mêmes de leur organisation. C'est le vœu qu'exprime Haldane en 1936:

> « The feeling gains ground among all who have thought over the problem seriously that the evangelisation of the country waits for the ministry of a native church. (…) until native converts are sufficiently strong and numerous to launch an offensive against this stronghold of Islam. The secret believers expect our prayers and sympathy rather than our censure for what we may too easily call their cowardice. Real freedom is on the way, and when it arrives Islam will be driven out of its last stronghold.»[78]

Les Eglises au Maghreb depuis les Indépendances

En l'espace de deux décennies, de 1950 à 1970, l'affranchissement des pays du Maghreb de la tutelle européenne et leur accès à l'indépendance entrainent l'effondrement de l'Eglise coloniale. C'est le début d'une nouvelle ère où les Eglises chrétiennes expérimentent de nouvelles modalités de présence et de témoignage.

L'aggiornamento catholique

Le départ des populations européennes a parfois été rapide et brutal, comme en Algérie où durant l'été 1962, environ un million d'Européens – y compris la population juive d'Algérie – quittent le pays, et avec eux, les Algériens musulmans qui n'avaient pas opté pour l'indépendance (dont beaucoup de kabyles chrétiens). L'Eglise est réduite au dixième de ses effectifs et passe de 146 paroisses à une quinzaine. Monseigneur Louis-Etienne Duval (1903-1996), évêque de Constantine puis archevêque d'Alger en 1955 au début de la guerre, avait pris parti pour l'autodétermination du peuple algérien. « Mohamed Duval », comme l'appelaient ses adversaires, décide que l'Eglise catholique sera algérienne, au service de la jeune nation. Lui-même en acquiert la nationalité en 1965. Il demande aux congrégations et paroisses d'ouvrir leurs établissements pour l'éducation de la jeunesse. C'est à elle que le système éducatif catholique est

[77] Oissila Saaïdia, « La conversion des musulmans: mission impossible ? », in *Les résistances à l'évangélisation. Interprétations historiques et enjeux théologiques*, edited by Jean PIrotte, Paris, Karthala, 2004, 269-271.

[78] Haldane, *Missionary Romance*, 55-56. On se souviendra que le leitmotiv du Cardinal Lavigerie était que l'oeuvre missionnaire durable (tant au Maghreb qu'en Afrique subsaharienne) ne pourrait être accomplie que « par les Africains eux-mêmes, devenus chrétiens et apôtres ».

désormais dédié. L'expérience des Pères Blancs et Sœurs Blanches qui géraient des institutions de formation au service des populations musulmanes sert de référence. En 1976, la vague de nationalisations et l'algérianisation des postes d'enseignants privent l'Eglise catholique de toutes ses œuvres éducatives et médicales.[79] En Lybie (indépendante depuis 1951), suite à la prise du pouvoir du Colonel Kadhafi en septembre 1969, des milliers colons italiens sont expulsés du pays durant l'été 1970 et tous leurs biens sont confisqués. La plupart des institutions catholiques sont fermées et expropriées et les religieux et religieuses chassés. La cathédrale de Tripoli, inaugurée en 1928, est transformée en mosquée.[80]

Pour les deux autres pays, indépendants depuis 1956, l'évolution est plus douce. En Tunisie, la nationalisation des terres des colons, intervenue en 1964, entrainera de nombreux départs. Entre 1953 et 1964, la population catholique, divisée par vingt, n'est plus servie que par douze paroisses.[81] Le *Modus Vivendi* de 1964 entre la République tunisienne et le Vatican autorise la liberté de culte pour les catholiques et le maintien des œuvres scolaires ou médicales à destination des Tunisiens, à l'exclusion de tout acte de prosélytisme. La plupart des biens fonciers et immobiliers de l'Eglise sont nationalisés.[82]

Au Maroc, Monseigneur Amédée Lefèvre (1890-1968), vicaire apostolique de Rabat en 1947 et nommé archevêque en 1955, avait approuvé l'évolution du pays vers l'indépendance (*supra*). Le Sultan Mohammed Ben Youssef (Mohammed V), rendant hommage aux chrétiens ayant soutenu l'émancipation du peuple marocain, accorde aux Eglises une pleine liberté de culte dans le royaume. En janvier 1956, lors des journées nord africaines de Casablanca auxquelles participe le Pasteur Marc Boegner, président de la Fédération protestante de France, le souverain s'adresse à lui en ces termes:

> « Comme les frères catholiques, vous avez été aux côtés du peuple marocain dans sa lutte pour le triomphe de la Justice, de la Vérité et du Droit. Vous restiez ainsi fidèle à vos origines et aux idées de vos grands réformateurs, Calvin et Luther. Vous êtes à même de saisir le sens de la lutte du Peuple marocain pour son émancipation; car l'histoire du Protestantisme est une longue lutte jalonnée de sacrifices et de souffrances. Comme vous, le Peuple marocain n'a jamais été ému par des sentiments de haine ou de vengeance ».[83]

Au Maroc comme ailleurs, L'Église connait une forte érosion de ses membres, paroisses et œuvres au gré des départs des Européens. Les Sœurs franciscaines restent néanmoins très actives dans le pays et les Ecoles catholiques accueillent désormais une population scolaire uniquement composée d'élèves marocains.[84]

C'est sur ces bases d'une liberté de culte accordée aux chrétiens étrangers, mais sous surveillance et assortie de diverses contraintes et contrôles, de l'interdiction de toute prosélytisme, avec au passage la confiscation de certains biens et propriétés, que les pays du Maghreb rétablissent des relations diplomatiques avec le Vatican: en 1972 pour l'Algérie et la Tunisie, et en 1976 pour le Maroc.

Privées progressivement de leurs moyens humains et matériels, les Eglises catholiques se recentrent sur le service des pays qui les accueillent. Devenues des Eglises dialoguantes, elles s'inscrivent dans le sillage du concile Vatican II.[85]

---

[79] Teissier, *Histoire des Chrétiens d'Afrique du Nord*, 234-240.
[80] Teissier, *Histoire des Chrétiens d'Afrique du Nord*, 244-246.
[81] La population catholique passe à 10.000 fidèles environ. En 1953, on comptait en Tunisie 80 paroisses, 156 annexes, 215 prêtres et 250.000 catholiques - Teissier, *Histoire des Chrétiens d'Afrique du Nord*, 142,
[82] Teissier, *Histoire des Chrétiens d'Afrique du Nord*, 225-230.
[83] Sa Majesté Mohammed V, *Le Maroc à l'heure de l'indépendance , Tome 1: 1955-1957*, traduit de l'arabe, Publication du Ministère de l'Information et du Tourisme, Rabat, 1957, 87-88.
[84] La bienveillance générale du Maroc à l'égard de l'Eglise catholique n'empêche pas certaines polémiques. En 1968 et dans la décennie suivante, des journaux marocains dénoncent régulièrement le « danger que représente l'enseignement dans les écoles de missionnaires'.(Baïda et Feroldi, *Présence chrétienne au Maroc*, 148-149).
[85] La visite du Pape Jean-Paul II au Maroc le 19 août 1985, à l'invitation du Roi Hassan II, constitue aussi une

La Lettre pastorale de la Conférence Episcopale de la Région Nord de l'Afrique (CERNA) – « Serviteurs de l'Espérance », publiée le 1er décembre 2014 fait état cet aggiornamento réalisé en quelques décennies:

> « Au Maghreb, notre présence trouve son sens plénier dans notre relation avec les croyants de l'Islam. Nous ne pouvons pas rester fermés sur nous-mêmes, sous peine de rester en un vase clos, et de mourir d'étouffement. Nous n'avons pas à 'subir' cette situation (…) nous la choisissons comme un don de Dieu (§ 3.3) (…) Notre Église, fidèle au souffle du Concile Vatican II, aime en conséquence se penser, au Maghreb comme ailleurs dans le monde, comme une Église 'citoyenne'. Au moment des indépendances, l'Église catholique, dans chacun de nos pays, a fait le choix de 'rester', avec la volonté de prendre une part active à la naissance de nations nouvelles. Être une Église presque «sans peuple», immergée dans une société musulmane, a permis de déployer d'une façon particulière en Afrique du Nord la vocation 'diaconale' de l'Église universelle: celle du service gratuit et du témoignage de vie au milieu d'un peuple » (§3.5).

L'ensemble de la lettre témoigne de l'influence de la pensée théologique et spirituelle des Pères de Foucauld et Peyriguère sur les Eglises catholiques du Maghreb (*supra*). Leur engagement, porté par l'espérance la « fraternité universelle », s'appuie sur un fort soubassement spirituel, enraciné dans une compréhension inclusive de l'eucharistie:[86]

> « En «ambassade pour le Christ» (cf. 2 Co 5,20) au Maghreb, nous y avons une vocation particulière à la prière. Cette vocation est à la fois un témoignage et une responsabilité. (…) L'eucharistie célébrée, ne fût-ce que par un prêtre seul dans une région des plus reculées, acquiert une valeur d'universalité et d'éternité. Comme à chaque messe, il présente en effet, avec le pain et le vin, toute l'existence de ceux qui l'entourent. Ses bras ouverts à l'autel en sont le symbole, embrassant au plus intime du sacrifice eucharistique, non seulement l'Église, présente ou non, visible ou non, mais aussi toute la densité d'amour vécue par les hommes et les femmes qui ne connaissent pas nécessairement l'Évangile, mais qui cherchent droitement à servir Dieu et à aimer » (§ 3.6).

Le cheminement théologique et spirituel sur le sens de la mission, initié par les « moines missionnaires », aboutit finalement à un changement de paradigme, qui s'exprime autour du récit évangélique de la Visitation – la rencontre en Marie et Elisabeth (Luc 1,39-56):

> « Loin de toute conquête, la mission est une Visitation. Comme Marie, portant Celui qui nous porte, nous allons visiter nos frères et soeurs pour les aider et chaque rencontre est comme une effusion d'Esprit Saint, une Pentecôte. Comme dans le récit de la Visitation, l'Esprit est le maître d'oeuvre de la rencontre, ouvrant à l'action de grâce (…) L'histoire de nos Églises est l'histoire de ces rencontres d'humanité. La grâce 'd'aller vers' nous fait expérimenter une joie semblable à celle jaillie lors de la rencontre entre Élisabeth et Marie. Les trésors que portent l'une et l'autre tressaillent au-dedans d'elles-mêmes » (§ 4.1).

Les perspectives sont renversées entre missionnaire et missionné:

> « La mission ne naît pas d'un surplus que nous aurions à communiquer aux autres, elle naît d'un manque de l'autre sans lequel, sans la rencontre de qui je ne pourrai jamais libérer mon Magnificat » (§ 4.2).

Ce stade ultime de valorisation de l'altérité religieuse (où la vérité de l'autre croyant me permet d'accéder à ma propre vérité – de « libérer mon Magnificat ») semble disqualifier toute perspective

---

ouverture inédite vers le monde musulman, dans la ligne de la mission nouvelle des Eglises du Maghreb. Cf. « Le Discours de S.S. Jean-Paul II lors de sa rencontre avec les jeunes musulmans à Casablanca le 19/8/1985», *Islamochristiana* 11 (1985):191-200.

[86] Cette *Lettre pastorale de la Conférence Episcopale de la Région Nord de l'Afrique (CERNA)* est d'ailleurs intentionnellement promulguée le 1/12/2014, « en la fête du Bienheureux Charles de Foucauld ».

d'annonce classique et s'accorde mieux avec l'interdit légal de l'évangélisation. Cette évolution théologique majeure,[87] va donner naissance à de nouvelle initiatives de rencontres et de réflexion dans les pays du Maghreb comme par exemple le lancement du réseau du GRIC (*Groupe de recherches islamo-chrétien*) en 1977.

L'évolution des diocèses catholiques du Maghreb après les indépendances est aussi caractérisée par une collaboration œcuménique renouvelée avec les Eglises protestantes, lesquelles – minorités dans la minorité – étaient restées tout au long de la période coloniale dans l'ombre d'un catholicisme majoritaire et peu dialoguant. Cette expérience de fraternité intra-chrétienne a pour enjeu principal la crédibilité d'un témoignage chrétien commun vis-à-vis des Musulmans.

La présence chrétienne au Maghreb à l'époque postcoloniale s'exprime aussi au travers de quelques implantations monastiques. Au Maroc, dans le Moyen-Atlas, le monastère bénédictin de Tioumliline fondé en 1952, connait un important rayonnement spirituel et intellectuel: outre les pèlerinages de jeunes, des rencontres internationales d'été y sont organisées de 1957 à 1964, rassemblant des dizaines d'intellectuels progressistes d'Europe et du Maghreb. Le monastère est fermé en 1968.[88] En Algérie, le monastère trappiste de Tibhirine (Médéa), fondé en 1937 dans les montagnes de l'Atlas devient en 1947 l'abbaye Notre-Dame de l'Atlas. En 1996, durant la décennie noire du terrorisme islamiste, les moines de Tibhirine sont enlevés et assassinés. Le Prieuré de Notre-Dame de l'Atlas est alors transféré au Maroc, à Fès (où une petite communauté cistercienne existait déjà depuis 1988) puis à Midelt depuis1997.[89]

Les martyrs chrétiens

Ce choix des Églises de vivre des relations fraternelles avec la population du pays d'accueil, est confronté aux évolutions internes de ces sociétés et aux bouleversements à l'échelle mondiale. La volonté de dialogue n'est pas forcément partagée du côté musulman. Les formes contemporaines du fondamentalisme islamiste et le repli dans l'irréductible de la religion, reflètent comme par le passé (colonial) la méfiance et les peurs à l'égard de forces hégémoniques extérieures (culturelle, économique, politique, etc.) porteuses de multiples effets de déstructuration sociale et culturelle auxquels on tente ainsi de résister.

L'irruption de l'islamisme en Algérie et la décennie de guerre civile qui s'en est suivie ont placé les religieux étrangers devant le choix crucial de rester ou partir. De 1994 à 1996, dix-neuf membres de l'Église catholique d'Algérie – six religieuses, douze religieux et un évêque – tous européens, sont assassinés par fidélité à leur engagement de « rester » aux côtés d'une population algérienne elle-même traumatisée par la peur, la violence et les morts. le pape Jean-Paul II évoquera pour eux la qualité de martyrs, après le meurtre en 1996 du dernier d'entre eux, Mgr Pierre Claverie, évêque d'Oran. Le fait le plus marquant sera l'assassinat des sept moines trappistes de Tibhérine en 1996. L'alliance avec le peuple algérien, comme scellée par le sang du martyre, a créé une nouvelle perception du christianisme dans ce pays et au-delà:

> « Le témoignage du plus grand amour, "donner sa vie pour ses amis", est comme le sceau qui vient authentifier tous les gestes d'amitié et de service accomplis jusque-là. Elle (l'Eglise d'Algérie) devient ainsi "signe des

---

[87] Sur les évolutions du dialogue islamo-chrétien dans la « Méditerranée francophone » après le concile Vatican II, cf. l'ouvrage-clé de Rémi Caucanas, *Relations islamo-chrétiennes en Méditerranée. Entre dialogue et crispation*, Rennes, Presses universitaires de Rennes, 2015.

[88] Elisabeth des Allues, *Toumliline. A la recherche de Dieu, au service de l'Afrique*, Paris, Cerf, 1961. Baida et Feroldi, *Présence chrétienne au Maroc,* 133-136.

[89] Cf. Flachaire, « Le monastère Notre-Dame de l'Atlas ». En Algérie, un premier monastère cistercien avait été implanté de 1843 à 1904 à Staouéli, près d'Alger.

temps" pour un plus grand nombre d'hommes et de femmes, chrétiens et musulmans. Son témoignage déborde les frontières du pays et du monde chrétien. »[90]

Cet impact est attesté, en Algérie même, par les témoignages exprimés après les assassinats des moines et de Mgr Claverie:

> « Qui sont ces moines sinon nos frères en Dieu (...) Personne ne nous a soutenus.... Excepté vous... Je pense que c'est Dieu qui veut la présence de l'Église chrétienne algérienne sur notre terre d'islam. Vous êtes une bouture sur l'arbre d'Algérie qui si Dieu veut s'épanouira vers la lumière de Dieu. »[91]

Vingt années après l'Algérie, la Lybie est le théâtre d'une autre expérience tragique de martyre touchant cette fois des chrétiens africains et non plus européens. Dans un pays tombé dans le chaos après la chute de son dictateur en octobre 2011, les milices islamistes persécutent les chrétiens présents dans le pays surtout les membres des communautés coptes (travailleurs égyptiens, éthiopiens et érythréens) et les groupes informels de chrétiens subsahariens. L'Église catholique et l'Église anglicane sont aussi contraintes de réduire leurs activités. Plusieurs cas de violences ou d'exécutions individuelles commis entre 2012 et 2014 sont passés sous silence. Le 15 février 2015, les fanatiques de l'*Etat Islamique* exécutent sur une plage libyenne 21 chrétiens (20 Égyptiens coptes et un Ghanéen). Les images de ce crime qui feront le tour du monde devaient marquer les esprits du sceau de la peur. Peu après, l'Eglise copte d'Egypte accorde à ces chrétiens le statut de martyrs, et les inscrit au synaxaire du calendrier copte (le 15 février).[92]

Deux mois après, le 21 avril 2015, un nouvel assassinat de 28 chrétiens éthiopiens enlevés en Lybie est perpétré par l'Etat Islamique avec la même mise en scène. A cette occasion, le pape François fait une déclaration concernant tous les martyrs:

> « Cela ne fait aucune différence que les victimes soient catholiques, coptes, orthodoxes ou protestantes. Leur sang est unique et égal dans leur confession du Christ ! Le sang de nos frères et de nos sœurs chrétiens est un témoignage qui crie pour se faire entendre de tous ceux qui savent encore distinguer le bien du mal. Et ce cri doit être écouté surtout par ceux qui ont entre leurs mains le destin des peuples ».[93]

La portée spirituelle du martyre de ces chrétiens africains au Maghreb échappe à l'analyse de l'historien. Il est en revanche l'un des signes d'une mutation de la population chrétienne vivant en Afrique du Nord.

Le Nouveau Paysage du Christianisme au Maghreb au début du 21e Siècle

L'africanisation des Eglises

La vision catholique d'une « Eglise sacrement de la rencontre » s'est largement construite sur une démographie déclinante – celle d'une « Eglise presque sans peuple ». Or, à partir des années 1990, la courbe démographique va s'inverser, et les Eglises du Maghreb, tant catholique que protestantes accueillent une nouvelle population, toujours plus nombreuse, de chrétiens originaires d'Afrique subsaharienne. Ceux-ci sont désormais majoritaires dans toutes les Eglises du Maghreb.

---

[90] Jean-Jacques Pérennès, "Inventing a new way of being Christian in a Muslim country: the case of the 19 martyrs of the Church of Algeria (1994-1996)", *Studia Historiae Ecclesiasticae*, 38-1 (2012): 72-73.

[91] Témoignages d'une Algérienne cité par Henri Teissier, « Une source majeure d'inspiration pour un témoignage évangélique parmi les musulmans », *Se comprendre*, N° 13/06 (2013), 7-8.

[92] Leur mort ayant été filmée attestait directement de leur martyre sans passer par une cause en canonisation.

[93] www.news.va/fr/news/la-douleur-du-pape-pour-les-coptes-ethiopiens-assa.

Au Maroc par exemple, l'Eglise protestante officielle (*Église évangélique au Maroc*) ne comptait plus dans les années 1980, qu'un seul pasteur pour 2 ou 3 lieux de culte réguliers desservant quelques dizaines de membres – des cadres et enseignants sous contrat, des conjointes de Marocains, etc. Trente ans après, la même Église, dépassant les effectifs et le rayonnement de l'époque coloniale, comprend 12 lieux de culte situés dans les villes universitaires et une quinzaine de pasteurs ou pasteurs stagiaires. Ce phénomène n'est pas seulement lié à la présence des migrants et réfugiés en transit vers l'Europe, il est aussi, et surtout, la conséquence du développement d'une coopération multiforme (universitaire, économique, militaire, médicale, etc.) du Maroc avec les pays d'Afrique subsaharienne. La nouvelle population des Églises, tant catholique que protestante, à 90 ou 95% africaine, est composée d'étudiants, mais aussi de cadres, de fonctionnaires arrivés au Maroc dans le cadre de ces programmes de coopération. Les sociologues mettent en évidence une tendance à la sédentarisation de ces populations, y compris celle des migrants.[94]

En marge des Eglises officielles, se constitue également un réseau informel d'Églises de maison (congolaises, nigérianes) encore plus important numériquement. Sans existence légale mais tolérées par les autorités pourvu qu'elles restent discrètes, elles reconstituent dans les quartiers populaires de Rabat ou de Casablanca une partie du paysage religieux multiforme et concurrentiel des mégapoles africaines, avec en particulier les nouvelles Églises pentecôtistes et charismatiques d'initiative africaine.[95] Les migrants et étudiants transportant avec eux leur pratique religieuse et leurs spécificités confessionnelles contribuent à la pluralisation du christianisme au Maghreb.

Ce double phénomène de revitalisation des Eglises officielles assorti de l'émergence de réseaux informels de communautés de maison est particulièrement marqué au Maroc mais toutes les Églises catholiques et protestantes du Maghreb connaissent – peu ou prou – la même évolution/révolution sociodémographique.[96] Pour les paroisses catholiques, l'internationalisation ne s'opère pas seulement du côté africain mais aussi par l'apport des communautés asiatiques, en particulier philippines.

La lettre « Serviteurs de l'Espérance » de la CERNA, mentionne aussi cette évolution tout en rappelant la primauté du dialogue avec les musulmans sur la pastorale chrétienne (§ 2.1).

Après avoir durant plus d'un millénaire construit leurs représentations du christianisme en relation avec les velléités de conquête des puissances européennes du Nord (y compris l'expérience coloniale des dix-neuvième et vingtième siècles), les musulmans du Maghreb sont exposés désormais à un christianisme africain venu du Sud, dégagé de toute culture de domination et porteur de connivences culturelles et religieuses inédites. Ce christianisme, sans moyens ni pouvoir, se déploie à bas-bruit dans les marges des sociétés du Maghreb, en périphérie des villes, par exemple dans les quartiers où séjournent les migrants. Les habitants de l'Afrique méditerranéenne, non dénués de préjugés raciaux, découvrent peu à peu cet autre visage du christianisme porté par les habitants de l'Afrique subsaharienne, étudiants, migrants ou travailleurs qui en sont les témoins au milieu d'eux.

[94] Bernard Coyault, « L'africanisation de l'Église évangélique au Maroc: revitalisation d'une institution religieuse et dynamiques d'individualisation », *L'Année du Maghreb*, 11 (2014): 81-86.

[95] Coyault, « L'africanisation », 92-95. Cf. aussi Bernard Coyault, « Les Églises de maison congolaises de Rabat: la participation du secteur informel à la pluralisation religieuse au Maroc », in *Migrants au Maroc: Cosmopolitisme, présence des étrangers et changements sociaux*, edited by Nadia Khrouz & Nazarena Lanza (Konrad-Adenauer-Stiftung E.V., Bureau du Maroc, 2015), 55-64.

[96] Cette évolution concerne aussi l'origine des responsables religieux: le pourcentage des prêtres, pasteurs, religieux et religieuses d'origine européenne présents au Maghreb tend à diminuer tandis que les Africains occupent de plus en plus le terrain. « *Maintenant les chrétiens du Maroc désoccidentalisent leur Église. La grande importance numérique de la communauté des Africains le favorise* »- Laffont, « Le père Peyriguère », 38.

L'émergence d'un christianisme autochtone

A l'exception de la Kabylie (Algérie), les activités missionnaires menées par les missionnaires étrangers (*Faith Missions* et Pères Blancs) tout au long du vingtième siècle ont échoué à constituer des communautés stables de chrétiens autochtones. Les conversions sont restées des phénomènes résiduels dans les sociétés du Maghreb. Depuis les années 1990 et 2000, on observe un mouvement important d'affiliations au protestantisme évangélique. Il est tout à la fois le fruit de la progression des libertés individuelles dans le monde arabe et la conséquence d'un accès facilité à l'offre religieuse chrétienne au travers des nouveaux médias d'évangélisation (chaines TV satellites, internet); des médias qui permettent d'échapper au contrôle social et renforcent la tendance à l'individualisation du choix religieux.

Rumeurs, controverses et lois répressives

Ces conversions alimentent rumeurs, campagnes de presse et débats publics tant au Maroc qu'en Algérie,[97] suscitant aussi diverses mesures légales pour tenter de les contrecarrer ou les canaliser. Ainsi la loi de mars 2006 promulguée en Algérie qui visait à réglementer l'exercice du culte autre que musulman (par un système d'autorisations), et à réprimer par des peines de prison et amendes les tentatives de conversion d'un musulman par des 'moyens de séduction'. Au-delà des motifs religieux et d'identité nationale, la résistance d'Etat aux conversions revêt un caractère plus politique: celles-ci sont perçues comme une contestation de l'ordre établi.

La rumeur concernant les activités missionnaires clandestines – 'la main de l'étranger' – est un motif récurrent qui repose sur des éléments réels mais sur-interprétés. Lorsqu'à la fin des années 1960, les missions évangéliques n'ont plus été autorisées à exercer leur activité au Maroc[98] ou en Algérie, elles n'en ont pas pour autant cessé leur mission. Les missionnaires étaient désormais envoyés sous couvert d'emplois de coopérants (ingénieurs, médecins).[99] Les inquiétudes autour de ces activités secrètes et les conversions supposées s'en suivre ont suscité à intervalles réguliers des campagnes de presses.[100] Lors de l'époque coloniale, les rumeurs visaient la collusion entre christianisme et autorité coloniale. En régime postcolonial, la perspective s'élargit et c'est l'impérialisme américain dans le monde arabe, avec ses volets économique, militaire, religieux (l'évangélisation) qui est vilipendé. Le phénomène s'intensifie dans les décennies 1990 et 2000 du fait de l'actualité internationale (les guerres et l'invasion de l'Irak, l'attentat du 11 septembre 2001). La réalité, plus inoffensive et moins connotée politiquement est que sur une période longue d'une cinquantaine d'années les conversions au christianisme dans tout le Maghreb n'ont sans doute pas dépassé quelques dizaines de milliers d'individus.

Les législations concernant le changement de religion dans les pays du Maghreb sont relativement uniformes. Les chrétiens d'origine étrangère bénéficient partout d'une pleine liberté de culte mais sont soumis à une surveillance étroite concernant d'éventuelles activités d'évangélisation. Le cas échéant, celles-ci sont sanctionnées par une expulsion du territoire.[101] En Algérie et en Tunisie, le cadre légal,

---

[97] Karima Direche, « Mondialisation des espaces néo-évangéliques au Maghreb », *Méditerranée* 116 (2011), 59-65. Cf. aussi Nadia Marzouki, "Purifying the Soul and Healing the Nation: Conversions to Evangelical Protestantism in Algeria", in *Religious Conversions and Nationalism in the Mediterranean World*, ed. Nadia Marzouki and Olivier Roy (Houndmills, UK: Palgrave Macmillan, 2013), 28-42.

[98] Les missionnaires de la North African Mission et de la Gospel Missionary Union ont été expulsés du Maroc entre 1967 et 1969. Steele, *Not in Vain*, 75, Stembock *Miss Terry,* 139.

[99] « *New missionaries had to get some type of employment as individuals in order to secure resident permits* ». Steele, *Not in Vain*. 66. Les motivations de la mission *Avant Ministries*, héritière de la GMU, restent étonnamment proches de la vision d'origine: « *We are passionate about establishing nationally led reproducing churches in the unreached areas of the world* » (avantministries.org).

[100] Comme au Maroc en 2005: Coyault, « Africanisation », 83-84.

[101] Le Maroc est régulièrement le théâtre de vagues d'expulsions. En 2010, en l'espace de quelques semaines, 150 chrétiens accusés de prosélytisme, originaires de 19 pays différents, sont arrêtés et expulsés du pays. Parmi eux se

quoique restrictif, permet aux nationaux d'adhérer à la foi chrétienne et de la pratiquer librement. Soit ils rejoignent les Eglises catholiques et protestantes officielles fréquentées aussi par les étrangers, soit ils constituent des communautés autochtones tentant d'obtenir leur reconnaissance légale.[102] C'est le cas de l'*Eglise Protestante d'Algérie* (enregistrée en 1974 et définitivement légalisée en 2011). Autrefois composée d'étrangers, l'EPA fédère en 2014 une quarantaine d'Eglises locales algériennes (28 en 2011). Au Maroc la conversion et la pratique de la foi chrétienne ne sont pas permises pour les sujets du Roi, « commandeur des croyants (musulmans) ».[103] Les Eglises officielles s'interdisent d'accueillir la petite minorité des Marocains chrétiens sous peine de contrevenir à la loi interdisant le prosélytisme (art. 220 du code pénal). Sans existence légale, ceux-ci sont donc contraints de se réunir clandestinement, quand bien même leur existence est connue et tolérée des autorités.

Les dispositions légales mises en place par les États ne sont pas toujours appliquées strictement. En outre, elles n'ont que peu d'impact sur les motifs de conscience qui sous-tendent toute conversion. Même si ces adhésions individuelles au christianisme continuent de susciter diverses formes de rejet ou d'exclusion sociale, petit à petit, à bas bruit, le pluralisme religieux s'installe dans les sociétés du Maghreb. Il contribue, sur fond de sécularisation et d'individualisation du religieux, à la dédramatisation des changements de religion :

> « La mobilité des hommes et des idées qui caractérise les temps présents et le pluralisme qui marque la culture moderne font qu'aucune des grandes religions n'est plus tout à fait autre ou entièrement externe. Cela contribue au fait que la mobilité 'inter-identitaire' ou la conversion religieuse n'a plus la dimension de rupture extraordinaire, ni le caractère dramatique qu'elle revêtait dans le passé ».[104]

Un christianisme émergent: exemple de la Kabylie

L'*Eglise protestante du plein évangile de Tizi Ouzou* (EPPETO) est un exemple frappant de la vitalité de ce christianisme maghrébin emergent.[105] Créée en 1999, cette Eglise de sensibilité pentecôtiste charismatique rassemble environ 1200 fidèles, tous nouveaux chrétiens; Elle est l'une des quinze Églises évangéliques que compterait la ville de Tizi Ouzou. Rattachée à l'Eglise Protestante d'Algérie, l'EPPETO est dirigée par deux pasteurs aidés de neuf prédicateurs laïcs: ils assurent les cultes hebdomadaires et le suivi des activités de semaine; En 2014, l'Eglise a effectué 200 baptêmes d'adultes (52% de femmes et 48% d'hommes), avec un total de 940 baptêmes en 7 ans (2007-2014).

Si la Kabylie constitue une exception en Algérie et au Maghreb quant à l'impact du christianisme sur les populations, ces adhésions nouvelles au christianisme n'en constituent pas moins un élément nouveau et durable dans le paysage du christianisme d'Afrique du Nord. Tout en cultivant une forme de marginalisation sociale et un discours critique à l'égard des autorités qui restreignent leurs libertés, ces

---

trouve également un religieux catholique.

[102] Le critère linguistique (arabe/berbère ou français/ anglais) est un élément important dans ce choix.

[103] Stricto sensu, les constitutions des 3 pays (Algérie, Maroc, Tunisie) n'accordent pas la liberté de changer de religion, mais elles ne l'interdisent pas non plus textuellement; les conversions sont donc théoriquement possibles et non condamnables pénalement. Les difficultés légales concernant le volet de la liberté religieuse proviennent des lois condamnant le prosélytisme non musulman. Cf. Mustapha Oukacha, « La protection juridique des non-musulmans au Maghreb », *Histoire, monde et cultures religieuses*, n°28 (2013), 115-124.

[104] Janjar, Mohamed Sghir, « Prosélytisme et / ou Da'wa. Réflexions sur le cas de l'islam », *Histoire, monde et cultures religieuses* n° 28 (2013): 152.

[105] Les données présentées ici sont tirées du site internet de l'Eglise *www.eppeto-algerie.com/* (y compris les statistiques de baptêmes année par année) et de l'enquête de Samia Sahari, *Etude des pratiques et des conduites religieuses chez les convertis au Christianisme en Kabylie*, mémoire de magister, Université Mouloud Mammeri de Tizi Ouzou, 2012, 75-102.

chrétiens ultra-minoritaires se considèrent néanmoins investis d'une mission quasi messianique de relèvement et de guérison de la nation toute entière.[106]

L'Eglise catholique, à l'échelle de tout le Maghreb, est également concernée par ce mouvement. Contrairement aux textes produits dans les décennies précédentes, la lettre pastorale « Serviteurs de l'espérance » (CERNA, 2014) évoque ouvertement la présence de ces « nouveaux disciples » et la mission qu'ils sont appelés à tenir:

> « Leur présence est un rappel du libre choix de Dieu et de la dimension universelle de l'appel de l'Évangile. Ils ont pleinement leur place dans nos Églises, ils les soutiennent par leur prière et leur exemple, ils en partagent l'espérance, acteurs au quotidien d'une inculturation du message de l'Évangile par le rayonnement de la vie » (§ 2.2.4)

Prenant acte de cette évolution, Mgr Teissier, archevêque d'Alger de 1988 à 2008, évoque avec finesse la nécessité pour l'Eglise catholique de ne pas se restreindre à cet entre soi des convertis qui la couperait d'un contact vivifiant avec la majorité musulmane de la population:

> « Ces chrétiens sont la joie de notre Église. Mais cela veut-il dire que l'immense majorité des habitants du pays, qui restent dans leur tradition musulmane, n'ont pas droit à une rencontre avec les chrétiens et, à travers eux, avec le Christ ? Est-ce que, nous-mêmes, nous n'avons pas, aussi, à tirer profit de leur rencontre dans leur identité religieuse, comme Jésus l'a fait avec le centurion romain ou avec la femme syro phénicienne ? Et c'est l'autre versant de la relation interreligieuse ».[107]

Le visage de ce christianisme minoritaire au Maghreb au début du vingt-et-unième siècle apparaît donc riche et multiforme. Il va poursuivre sa métamorphose et sa diversification, porté par cette triple dynamique de la recontre avec l'islam et des christianismes subsahariens et maghrébins émergents. L'interaction entre ces trois mouvements suscitera à son tour de nouvelles configurations religieuses. La situation géographique du Maghreb, aux confins tout à la fois de l'Afrique et de l'Europe, à la jonction des pays du Sud et des pays du Nord, sur la zone de rencontre (ou de fracture) entre christianisme et islam, en fait indéniablement une aire stratégique où se jouent les grands équilibres du monde et où peuvent se rencontrer et se nouer des réseaux religieux et humains distincts.

Sur cet horizon complexe et incertain, l'expérience concrète de la rencontre et des solidarités vécues entre chrétiens et musulmans est le préalable à toute réflexion sur le sens de la présence chrétienne au Maghreb. Cette rencontre, qui commence par le dialogue de la vie, dans les interactions au quotidien entre croyants ordinaires, n'est ni une infidélité à la mission, ni une 'dé-mission', elle est une forme particulière du témoignage chrétien.[108] Elle favorise une expression apaisée et non conflictuelle des identités religieuses, qui tout en dissipant les méfiances et préjugés hérités de la période coloniale, contribue à la construction de la société et promeut la liberté religieuse comme l'un des droits humains fondamentaux.

Bibliographie

Abdelfettah Lalmi, Nedjma, « Du mythe de l'isolat kabyle », *Cahiers d'Études africaines*, 175 (2004), 507-531.

Affif, Naïma, « A propos de l'Evangile selon Saint Jean de la British and Foreign Bible Society en berbère tachelhit (Maroc) », *Babelao* 3 (2014), 109-125.

Ait Abdelmalek, Zohra, *Protestants en Algérie. Le protestantisme et son action missionnaire en Algérie aux xix*[e] *et xx*[e] *siècles*, Lyon: Olivetan, 2004.

---

[106] Marzouki, "Purifying the Soul", 33-34.

[107] Teissier, « Une source majeure d'inspiration », 10. On a ici une articulation intéressante entre la spiritualité de la *Visitation* (*supra*) et les parcours de convertis accueillis dans l'Eglise.

[108] Teissier, « Une source majeure d'inspiration », 9.

Allues (des), Elisabeth, *Toumliline. A la recherche de Dieu, au service de l'Afrique*, Paris, Cerf, 1961.

Aurbakken, H. L, Heggoy, Willy Normann, Bres Paul, *Les Pierres crieront*, Alger: imp. Baconnier, 1960.

Baida, Jamaâ et Feroldi, Vincent, *Présence chrétienne au Maroc. XIXe – XXe siècles*, Rabat: Bouregreg. 2005.

Bonnet, Christian, « Ouvrez les écluses du ciel ! La télévision par satellite, outil d'évangélisation en direction du monde musulman », *Perspectives Missionnaires*, n°57 (2009): 49-57.

Boukadoum Messaoud, intervention à l'Assemblée nationale française le 20/8/1947 www.ism-france.org/analyses/Messaoud-Boukadoum-la-colonisation-s-est-attaquee-au-patrimoine-moral-et-intellectuel-de-notre-peuple--article-16360 (accessed 1 August, 2015)

Canton, William, *A History Of The British And Foreign Bible Society* (Vol.V), London: John Murray, 1910.

Caucanas, Rémi, *Relations islamo-chrétiennes en Méditerranée*, Rennes, Presses universitaires de Rennes, 2015.

Ceillier, Jean-Claude, *Histoire des Missionnaires d'Afrique (Pères Blancs). De la fondation par Mgr Lavigerie à la mort du fondateur (1868-1892)*, Paris: Karthala, 2008.

CERNA (Conférence des Evêques de la Région Nord de l'Afrique), *Les Églises du Maghreb en l'an 2000*, Alger, janvier 2000 (www.eglise-catholique-algerie.org/images/archives/les_Eglises_du_Maghreb_en_2000.pdf) (accessed 17 April 2015).

CERNA, *Serviteurs de l'Espérance. L'Église Catholique au Maghreb aujourd'hui*, Lettre pastorale du 1/12/2014 www.africamission-mafr.org/Serviteurs_de_l_Esperance_CERNA.pdf) (accessed 1 August 2015).

Coyault, Bernard, « L'africanisation de l'Église évangélique au Maroc: revitalisation d'une institution religieuse et dynamiques d'individualisation », *L'Année du Maghreb*, 11 (2014): 81-103. https://anneemaghreb.revues.org/2243 (accessed 1 August, 2015)

Coyault, Bernard, « Les Églises de maison congolaises de Rabat : la participation du secteur informel à la pluralisation religieuse au Maroc », in *Migrants au Maroc. Cosmopolitisme, présence d'étrangers et transformations sociales*, edited by Nadia Khrouz and Nazarena Lanza, 55-64. Konrad-Adenauer-Stiftung E.V., Bureau du Maroc, 2015.

Diaz, Ramon Lourido (ed.), *Marruecos y el Padre Lerchundi*, Madrid: MAPFRE, 1996.

Direche Karima, « Mondialisation des espaces néo-évangéliques au Maghreb », *Méditerranée* 116 (2011): 59-65.

Fiedler, Klaus, *The Story of Faith Missions. From Hudson Taylor to present day Africa*, Oxford: Regnum Books International, 1994.

Fisk, Eric G., *The Prickly Pear. Mission stories form Moslem Lands*, Chicago: Moody Press, 1951.

Flachaire, Jean-Pierre, « Le monastère Notre-Dame de l'Atlas au Maroc », *Collectanea Cisterciensia* 68 (2006), 147-166.

Gadille, Jacques et Zorn, Jean-François, « Les missions chrétiennes en Afrique, Asie, Australie et Océanie L'Afrique » (7ème partie, chap.I) in *Histoire du christianisme 11 – Libéralisme, industrialisation, expansion européenne (1830-1914)*, edited by J.-M. Mayeur, Ch. and L. Pietri, A. Vauchez A. and M. Venard, 1003-1052. Paris: Desclée, 1995.

Geertz, Clifford, *Observer l'islam: Changements religieux au Maroc et en Indonésie*, Paris: La Découverte, 1992 (in English: *Islam observed: Religious Development in Morocco and Indonesia)*, New Haven: Yale University Press, 1968.)

Gorrée, George, *Au-delà du père de Foucault, le père Peyriguère*, Paris: Centurion, 1960.

Gorrée, George et Chauvel, Germain, *D'autres récolteront… Foucauld, Peyriguère, moines missionnaires*, Lyon: Mame, 1965.

Haig, F. T., *Daybreak in North Africa. An account of how Work for Christ Begun in Morocco, Algeria, Tunis and Tripoli*, London: Partridge & Co, 1890.

Haldane, James, *Missionary Romance in Morocco*, London: Pickering & Inglis, 1936.

Hill Patricia R., *The World Their Household: The American Woman's Foreign Mission Movement and Cultural Transformation, 1870-1920,* Ann Arbor: The University of Michigan Press, 1985.

Heggoy, Willy N., '*Fifty Years of Evangelical Missionary Movement in North Africa*, 1881-1931', Senior Thesis, The Hartford Seminary Foundation, 1960.

Isaacs, Albert Augustus, *A Biographical Sketch Relative to the Missionary Labors of Emma Herdman in the Empire of Morocco,* London: S.W. Partridge, 1900.

Jean-Paul II, « Le Discours de S.S. Jean-Paul II lors de sa rencontre avec les jeunes musulmans à Casablanca (Maroc) le 19 août 1985 », *Islamochristiana* 11 (1985): 191-200.

Kerr, Robert, *Morocco, After Twenty-Five Years. A Description of the Country, Its Laws and Customs, and the European Situation*, London: Murray and Evenden, 1912.

Kidd Thomas S., *American Christians and Islam. Evangelical Culture and Muslims from the Colonial Period to the Age of Terrorism*, Princeton NJ: Princeton University Press. 2009.

Lourido Diaz, Ramon, ed. *Marruecos y el Padre Lerchundi*, Madrid: MAPFRE, 1996.

Laffont, Michel, « Le père Peyriguère dans l'Église du Maroc », *Chemins de Dialogue* 36 (2010): 27-38.
Lafuente, Gilles, « Dossier marocain sur le dahir berbère de 1930 », *Revue de l'Occident musulman et de la Méditerranée*, N°38 (1984): 83-116.
Lefèvre, Louis Amédée, *Église du Maroc. Quelques directives (1950-1957)*, Rabat: Faits et Idées, 1959.
Makdisi Ussama, *Artillery of Heaven: American Missionaries and the Failed Conversion of the Middle East*, Ithaca-New York: Cornell University Press, 2008.
Marzouki, Nadia, "Purifying the Soul and Healing the Nation: Conversions to Evangelical Protestantism in Algeria", In *Religious Conversions and Nationalism in the Mediterranean World*, edited by Nadia Marzouki and Olivier Roy, 28-42, Houndmills, UK: Palgrave Macmillan, 2013.
Miege, Jean-Louis, « Les missions protestantes au Maroc (1875-1905) », *Hespéris*, T. XLII, 1er/2e trim. (1955):153-192.
Mohammed V, *Le Maroc à l'heure de l'indépendance , Tome 1: 1955-1957*, traduit de l'arabe, Publication du Ministère de l'Information et du Tourisme, Rabat, 1957.
Nolan, Francis, *Les Pères Blancs entre les deux guerres mondiales. Histoire des Missionnaires d'Afrique (1919-1939)*, Paris: Karthala, 2015.
Oukacha, Mustapha, « La protection juridique des non-musulmans au Maghreb », *Histoire, monde et cultures religieuses*, n°28 (2013), 115-124.
Paumard, Gabrielle Sr, *Les Franciscaines Missionnaires de Marie au Maroc. 1912-1985*, 355 p. sans éditeur, 2003.
Pérennès, Jean-Jacques, *Pierre Claverie, un Algérien par alliance*, Paris: Cerf, 2000.
Pérennès, Jean-Jacques, "Inventing a new way of being Christian in a Muslim country: the case of the 19 martyrs of the Church of Algeria (1994-1996)", *Studia Historiae Ecclesiasticae*, 38-1 (2012): 61-74. http://uir.unisa.ac.za/handle/10500/5822 (accessed 1 August, 2015)
Peyriguère, Albert, *Aussi loin que l'amour. Lettres du Maroc (1933-1957*), Paris: Cerf, 1970.
Peyriguère, Albert, « Testament spirituel », 'Cahier Foucauld-Peyriguère' Cahier spécial des *Mardis de Dar el Salam* (1959): 155-218.
Phillips, Dennis H., "The American Missionary in Morocco", *The Muslim World*, LXV-1 (1975): 1-20.
Rockness, Miriam Huffman, *A Passion for the Impossible: The life of Lilias Trotter*, Grand Rapids: Discovery House Publishers, 2003.
Rutherford J. and Glenny, H. Edward, *The Gospel in North Africa, in two parts*, London: Percy Lund, Humphies & Co., 1900.
Saaïdia, Oissila, « La conversion des musulmans: mission impossible ? », in *Les résistances à l'évangélisation, Interprétations historiques et enjeux théologiques*, edited by Jean PIrotte, 257-271, Paris, Karthala, 2004.
Sahari, Samia, *Etude des pratiques et des conduites religieuses chez les convertis au Christianisme en Kabylie*, mémoire de magister, Université Mouloud Mammeri de Tizi Ouzou, 2012. www.ummto.dz/IMG/pdf/memoire_final-10.pdf (accessed 1 Aug., 2015)
Sharkey, Heather J., "The Gospel in Arabic Tongues: British Bible Distribution, Evangelical Mission, and Language Politics in North Africa", In *Cultural Conversions: Unexpected Consequences of Christian Missions in the Middle East, Africa, and South Asia*, edited by Heather J. Sharkey 203-221, Syracuse: Syracuse University Press, 2013.
Shorter, Aylward, *Les Pères Blancs au temps de la conquête coloniale. Histoire des Missionnaires d'Afrique 1892-1914*, Paris: Karthala, 2011 (traduit de l'anglais) [*Cross and Flag in Africa: The 'White Fathers' during the colonial Scramble (1892-1914)*, Maryknoll (NY): Orbis Books, 2006.]
Sinclair, Lisa M., "The Legacy of Isabella Lilias Trotter", *International Bulletin of Missionary Research*, 26:1 (2002), 32-35.
Steele, Francis R., *Not in Vain.The Story of North Africa Mission*, Pasadena: William Carey Library, 1981.
Stenbock, Evelyn, *'Miss Terri!' The Story of Maude Cary, Pioneer GMU Missionary in Morocco*, Lincoln, NE: Back to the Bible Broadcast, 1970.
Strengholt, Jozef Martinus, *Gospel in the Air: 50 Years of Christian Witness Through Radio in the Arab World*, PhD, Utrecht University, 2008
Teissier, Henri, ed., *Histoire des chrétiens d'Afrique du Nord*, Paris: Desclée, 1991.
Teissier, Henri « Chrétiens et Musulmans: cinquante ans pour approfondir leurs relations », I*slamochristiana* XXVI (2000): 33-50.
Teissier, Henri, « Une source majeure d'inspiration pour un témoignage évangélique parmi les musulmans », *Se comprendre*, N° 13/06 (2013),
Trotter, A Lilias, "The Outlook in North Africa", *The Muslim World,* Vol.14-2 (1924):131-135.
Zwemer, Samuel M., "North Africa as a Mission Field", *International Review of Mission*, Vol. 12- 4 (1923): 556-566.
Wilson, J. Christy, *Apostle to Islam: a biography of Samuel M. Zwemer*, Grand Rapids: Baker, 1952.

(18) Christianity in Western Africa

Isaac Deji Ayegboyin and Samson Adetunji Fatokun

Country	Religion	Pop_2010	Pct_2010	Pop_2025	Pct_2025	GrPct_1970_2025
Western Africa	Christians	110,757,000	36.0%	166,033,000	36.3%	2.7%
Western Africa	Independents	37,699,000	12.2%	52,823,000	11.6%	2.3%
Western Africa	African-initiated	34,915,000	11.3%			
Western Africa	Orthodox	97,400	0.0%	137,000	0.0%	2.3%
Western Africa	Protestants	60,190,000	19.5%	79,850,000	17.5%	1.9%
Western Africa	Anglicans	20,440,000	6.6%			
Western Africa	Pentecostal	14,761,000	4.8%			
Western Africa	Evangelical churches	6,255,000	2.0%			
Western Africa	Baptist	5,768,000	1.9%			
Western Africa	Methodist	4,316,000	1.4%			
Western Africa	United churches	3,350,000	1.1%			
Western Africa	Reformed, Presbyterian	1,856,000	0.6%			
Western Africa	Roman Catholics	36,188,000	11.8%	55,788,000	12.2%	2.9%
Western Africa	*Pentecostals/ Charismatics*	64,592,000	21.0%	96,811,000	21.2%	2.7%
Western Africa	*Evangelicals*	42,532,000	13.8%	62,412,000	13.7%	2.6%
Western Africa	Muslims	158,898,000	51.6%	246,130,000	53.8%	3.0%
Western Africa	adherents of traditional African religions	37,040,000	12.0%	42,975,000	9.4%	1.0%
Western Africa	Baha'is	200,000	0.1%	278,000	0.1%	2.2%
Western Africa	adherents of new religious movements	56,100	0.0%	76,300	0.0%	2.1%
Western Africa	Hindus	39,900	0.0%	53,900	0.0%	2.0%
Western Africa	Buddhists	30,000	0.0%	38,900	0.0%	1.7%
Western Africa	Chinese folk religionists	5,800	0.0%	8,600	0.0%	2.6%
Western Africa	Sikhs	3,800	0.0%	5,500	0.0%	2.5%
Western Africa	Jews	1,600	0.0%	1,700	0.0%	0.1%
Western Africa	people professing no religion	951,000	0.3%	1,470,000	0.3%	2.9%
Western Africa	**Total population**	**307,982,000**	**100.0%**	**457,071,000**	**100.0%**	**2.7%**

Source: Centre for the Study of World Christianity (CSGC), Boston, Gordon-Conwell TS

Defining the Scope

West Africa, which is the westernmost sub-region of the African continent, consists of eighteen countries. Along the coast are Mauritania, Senegal, the Gambia, Guinea Bissau, Guinea, Sierra Leone, Liberia, Côte d'Ivoire, Ghana, Togo, Benin and Nigeria. Landlocked countries include Burkina Faso, Mali and Niger. The three island nations are Sao Tome and Principe, Cape Verde and Saint Helena.

Developmental Process and Effects of Christian Faith

Appraising the development, expansion and effects of Christian faith in West Africa is an intricate undertaking because of the uneven nature in the advancement of Christianity in this sub-region. Peter Falk overlooks some nuances in his classification and distinguishes three broad categories: first, countries with minority churches but with a Christian presence (Senegal, Gambia, Guinea and Portuguese Guinea); second, countries with older churches but many unbaptized members (Sierra Leone and Liberia); and third are all others which are said to have growing churches but with new challenges.[1]

When did Christianity Start in West Africa?

It is pretty difficult to fix exact dates for the early advances of Christian faith in West Africa. Some anthropologists and archaeologists excavated a variety of ornamental crosses in the artwork of the Tuareg, a tribal people of the Sahara, some of whom still live in the counties of Mali, Burkina Faso and Niger. Some scholars hold that the crosses discovered are a resounding corroboration of an early Christian presence in West Africa, while others contend that the crosses unearthed merely represent the four directions of the magnet or needle compass. Be that as it may, whatever Christian influence on the Tuareg apparently then existed has become extinct. Today, nearly all the people in that region of the Sahara are Muslims.

Early Christian Outreach in West Africa

As one scans through the history of the development of Christianity in North Africa, one comes to grips with the fact that Christianity is not foreign to the African continent because the active influence of Christianity on the continent dates back to the early centuries of the Ancient Christianity period. Incidentally, there are no indications whatsoever that the influence of the celebrated North African Church extended to West Africa. It is obvious that, by the time the Catholic missionaries who introduced Christianity in some parts of West Africa arrived in the fifteenth century, they had to contend with the challenges of converting the adherents of African indigenous religions and Islam.

Phase One: The Portuguese Mission to West Africa

Portugal was the first western nation to introduce Christianity to West Africa. Some Catholic missionaries accompanied a team of over six hundred Portuguese explorers in pursuit of Prince Henry the Navigator's dream of discovering a sea route to the locale of gold deposits in West Africa and the site of spices in India. After a series of expeditions between 1422 and 1445, some of the explorers and missionaries reached the Senegal River on the West African Coast in 1445. From this time, Portuguese trading ships made steady voyages down the coast of West Africa. They established outposts in Shama in 1471 and another in Elmina where, on 20th January 1482, they celebrated mass and prayed for the conversion of the native peoples to Christianity and also for the prosperity of the church which they intended to establish in that region. Indeed, one of the motives of Prince Henry was to establish what Pobee called *Republica Christiana* in which the mission lands would become the common property of all Christian countries.[2] It is important however to mention that the Christian mission zealously embarked upon by Prince Henry and his emissary came as a package with diverse motives, the others of which were as valuable to Portugal as evangelism. In fact, some scholars assert that the primary motive of the Portuguese was not to evangelize the people of West Africa, but to engage them in trade. Undoubtedly, shortly before then, news had

[1] Peter Falk, *The Growth of the Church in Africa*, Bukuru: ACTS, 1997, 313-62.

[2] John S Pobee, *AD 2000 and After The Future of God's Mission in Africa* Accra: Asempa 1991, 4.

reached Europe that gold was flourishing around Timbuktu and the Wangara areas down the western coast. That ostensibly explains why the King of Portugal, with the help of the Pope, ensured that Portugal had not only the spiritual but also the political and economic monopoly of the Guinea Coast trade and the sea route to India. In order to ward off all possible competitors from the lucrative traffic in gold and later in slaves, the King of Portugal built a fort at Elmina. As the discovery of lands along the West African coast and the fame of Portugal increased, Pope Nicholas V granted the Portuguese the right of *Patroado.* By this papal decree, Portugal was given the highest recognition to have sovereignty over all lands discovered in her expeditions. In 1494, Pope Alexander VI not only validated the privileges of *Patroado* given to the Portuguese but also shored it up with the Treaty of Tordesillas. This agreement made the Prince of Portugal responsible for the financial support and sustenance of the missionaries and gave him exclusive rights to all ecclesiastical appointments and revenues in Africa and parts of Brazil.[3] The enterprise was intended to help Portugal seize political and economic control of Africa from the Muslims. Within the vast lands allotted to Portugal, Catholic priests embarked on missionary ventures in four major areas in West Africa: Sao Tome and Principe, Elmina, Benin and Warri.

MISSIONARY VENTURES IN CAPE VERDE, SAO TOME AND PRINCIPE (1470-1707)

The two island nations – Cape Verde in the far west and Sao Tome and Principe farther south – were discovered and colonized by the Portuguese. Before the arrival of the Portuguese, the islands were sparsely populated. Soon, African slaves were imported there to work on the cotton and sugar plantations.[4] Sao Tome soon became an economic and spiritual centre. Huge amounts of sugar were exported from there to Europe. The two islands were created bishoprics in 1533 and 1534 respectively. Some Africans on the islands were converted, while a few were ordained. Several attempts were made by these bishoprics to introduce Christianity in the hinterland of the sub-region.

MISSIONARY ENTERPRISE AT ELMINA: (1482-1576)

Inside the Castle at Elmina, a church was built. From here, efforts were made by the priests to convert the inhabitants of Elmina. Apparently the King of Elmina and a handful of people were baptized. Diego d'Alvarengo's treatise to the King of Portugal further disclosed that, about twenty years after the diminutive conversion at Elmina, there was a mass conversion at Efutu. Regrettably, about a decade after these seemingly promising responses, nothing was left of these conversions at Elmina and Efutu.[5] The Roman Catholic work came to a halt in the Gold Coast in 1637 with not much to show for their efforts.

MISSIONARY PURSUITS IN BENIN CITY (1485-1707)

The earliest sphere of a Christian mission in Nigeria, in the fifteenth century, was in Benin, and it was pioneered by the missionaries who came with the Portuguese traders. In 1486, diplomatic ties were established between *Oba* Uzolua of Benin[6] and Joao Alfonso d'Aveiro on behalf of the King of Portugal. Consequently, the *Oba* allowed the Portuguese to build a trading post at Gwato. Relations between Benin

---

[3] The other side of the globe was allotted to Spain. The line of demarcation was the 45^0 west longitude through the Atlantic and Brazil.

[4] John Baur, *2000 Years of Christianity in Africa*, Nairobi: Pauline Publications, 2009, 49.

[5] See J. K. Ekem, *Priesthood in Context*, Hamburg: Verlag an der Lottbek, 1994, 58; Lamin Sanneh *West African Christianity: The Religious Impact*, London, C. Hurst, 1983, 25.

[6] The Oba of Benin, or Omo N'Oba, Emini mini mini is the traditional ruler of the Edo people and head of the historic Eweka dynasty of the Great Benin Empire - a West African empire centered on Benin City, in modern-day Nigeria.

and Portugal grew stronger and trade in gold, palm oil, ivory and pepper in exchange for glassware, liquor, salt and manufactured goods increased. The Portuguese priests seized the opportunity which these positive developments brought in order to attempt the conversion of the king, hoping that the subjects would follow the king's example robotically. The attempts to convert the *Oba* of Benin met with failure. The *Oba* Uzolua and his successors demonstrated that they were interested only in commercial activities and in firearms and, in fact, had no serious intention of adopting a new religion which would undermine their sacred position within their own society. During the reign of *Oba* Orhogbua, a few conversions were made, but Christianity remained a minority religion restricted to the king's palace. A few attempts made in succeeding years also failed.

Mission in Warri (1555-1807)

In 1555, the Bishop of Sao Tome, the Augustinian Gasper Cao, sent a mission to Warri.[7] The Augustinian monks called upon the *Olu* (King) of Warri who embraced Christianity to the point of allowing his son and heir to the throne not only to be baptized but also to adopt the name Sebastiao (Sebastine). When Sebastine succeeded his father as the *Olu*, he reinforced the relationship between Roman Catholicism and the palace by sending one of his sons, Domingo, to Portugal to be trained for the priesthood. Domingo did not remain celibate: after his ten years' stay in Portugal, he arrived in Warri with a Portuguese wife. But Domingo remained devoted to the faith. When Domingo's son, Antonio, became the *Olu*, he bolstered further the affinity between Roman Catholicism and the royal household. Indeed, for the next century and a half or so (1570-1733), Warri rulers were proclaimed as professing Christians. However, this royal household faith did not seem to have had much effect upon the common people. In any case, by the middle of the eighteenth century, Roman Catholicism had practically disappeared from Warri. The only fragments which then suggested that Christianity was ever known in the region were religious objects of art like crucifixes, statues of Christ, images of the Blessed Mary and some sacred vessels. Later, most of these were also brought out of the region by the slave trade.

Factors Responsible for the Failure of the Second Missionary Enterprise

The fundamental question to ask is: why did the attempts to plant Christianity in these initial prospective Christian centres fail?

Apart from the marginal success stories found in the Islands of Cape Verde and Sao Tome, the Portuguese mission enterprise, by and large, failed. Enduring missionary enterprise in West Africa had to wait until the nineteenth century. A number of factors were responsible for the failure of this mission. First, in the whole missionary adventure there were personal interests at play on the part of the Europeans as well as of the Africans. The missionaries worked with a lot of zeal and enthusiasm initially but soon their interest in trade outstripped their interest in missions. The Portuguese built a trade empire and claimed that it was by divine intervention that they were brought to trade in gold, in liquor and in slaves. It is extraordinary to learn that the state Council, *Mesa de consciencia e ordens*, advised King Felipe that 'priests should be brought to Warri on trading vessels but that they should support themselves by trading in slaves'. Second, the earliest missionaries adopted a militant stance. With the ideology called *Requerimiento*, the Portuguese attempted to coerce the Africans into converting or facing hostilities.[8] Consequently, a number of people who accepted the faith possibly did so under duress. Third, the Europeans exhibited a negative attitude towards African culture and they suppressed indigenous religions. They taught that Christianity and European culture were coterminous (one always alongside the other), and

---

[7] The Kingdom of Warri is a traditional state based on the town of Warri in Delta State, Nigeria.

[8] See J. S. Pobee, *Skenosis: Christian Faith in an African Context*. Gweru: Mambo Press, 1992, 12.

they therefore created a so-called Christian community composed of their mixed-blood descendants and converts from the lower strata of society. African Christians were segregated so that they could leave their 'heathen' ways and imbibe approved 'civilized' ways. For many, the missionaries were seen to symbolize an extension of intolerable Portuguese interference in local affairs. Fourth, they adopted a faulty strategy: The Portuguese attempted to spread the faith by first converting the kings, believing that their subjects would thereby follow robotically. In most cases there was no mass conversion outside the palace. Along with this, they adopted the 'package deal' by which they offered European goods in exchange for acceptance of Christianity.[9] Fifth, numerous tropical diseases took their toll on personnel sent to the coast of West Africa. In fact, most of the earliest missionaries sent to the coast died young. Others were compelled to return to Europe on account of ill health. Consequently, there was the problem of stability and continuity. Important, also, was the fact that the territory granted by the Holy See to the King of Portugal to oversee, through the accord of P*atroado,* was too large and beyond the capacity of the human and material resources available. Finally, the presence of strong Muslim population and the challenges posed by Muslim missionaries, who were spreading Islamic civilization about this time, served as obstacles to the Portuguese missionary enterprise. Incidentally, Islam accommodated some of the practices of the Africans, such as polygyny, which the Portuguese rejected.

Phase Two: European and American Missionary Enterprise in West Africa

Enduring and successful missionary enterprise began in West Africa in the nineteenth century. This time, the initiative was dominated by the Protestant churches of Europe and America. The Catholics joined in the expedition almost half a century later. Three major factors contributed to the influx of the European and American missionaries into West Africa. The first was the abolition of the ***Atlantic slave trade***. The second had to do with the ***resettlement of freed slaves in Sierra Leone*** (1787) *and* ***Liberia*** (in 1822). The third was the ***Evangelical Revival*** and the consequent establishment of missionary societies.

The ***Trans-Saharan slave trade***. Historically, the Portuguese initiated the transatlantic slave trade during the conclaves mission in 1441. In course of this mission, a Portuguese explorer, named Gon, captured some African slaves whom he presented to Prince Henry as gifts. Henry received these 'gifts', apparently with the intention of using them as a method of propagating the gospel. To demonstrate his aversion to the slave trade, Henry placed a ban on the further importation of slaves. However, after the death of Prince Henry, the ban on slave importation was lifted by his successors who were favourably disposed towards the trade. For almost a century or so, the Portuguese monopolized the obnoxious traffic which was later embraced by other European nations. The evils and sad effects of slavery and the slave trade have been well documented. It is important to note however that the campaign against slavery, embarked upon by Evangelical groups such the Clapham Sect, inspired the formation of overseas missionary bodies which planted Christianity in Africa. Bearing in mind that evangelism would be meaningless to slaves, the Clapham Sect saw the abolition of the slave trade and of slavery as necessary for the evangelism of Africa, and therefore fought for it tooth and nail.

The ***foundation of Sierra Leone***. One of the significant achievements of the Evangelical Revival was the founding of Sierra Leone, the first West African country to be evangelized, which was founded as a home for freed slaves in 1787. By 1850, more than 50,000 former slaves, originally from many different parts of Africa, had resettled there. The uniqueness of this country stemmed from the fact

[9] K.J. Agbeti, *West African Church History: Christian Missions and Church Foundation 1482-1919*, Leiden: E.J. Brill 1986, 3.

that it served as the nursery and the mother of the church in West Africa. Among those liberated as former African slaves was a fairly large number of Christians who had a passion for missionary activity. They kept the fires of the gospel burning while they were in Sierra Leone. Quite a number of missionary societies, like the Church Missionary Society, the Methodist Missionary Society and the American Board of Commissioners for Foreign Missions, used Sierra Leone as their mission headquarters in West Africa for several years. Sierra Leone also became the training base for Christianity in West Africa. Owing to the heavy mortality rate among Europeans, some of the more visionary European missionaries pressed for leadership training for Africans. Later, Christian institutions – like the famous Fourah Bay College in 1827 – were founded to assist and teach the Africans. Thus Sierra Leone, as the leader of church organization in West Africa, was the first to change from the system of a European monopoly on missions to the system of African-controlled missions, which was eventually assimilated by some African churches in West Africa. Samuel Ajayi Crowther, J.F. Schoen and S.W. Koelle remained pillars of Christianity in Sierra Leone due to their production of a grammar and the translation of the scriptures into West African languages.

The ***establishment of Liberia (Land of the Freed)*** is not unconnected with the history of the abolition of the slave trade. British success in resettling freed slaves in Sierra Leone encouraged the Americans to follow suit. Through this, the Americans hoped that the Negroes would be saved from humiliation and degradation which they were currently suffering in America, and at the same time make them serve as the instruments by which 'civilization' and Christianity would spread to the 'darkest' parts of Africa.[10] The first group of settlers, which consisted of 88 people, arrived at Shebro Island in 1820. For the next seventy years. (1821-1891), nearly 17,000 freed slaves from the USA settled along the coast of Liberia. Missionaries moved into the hinterland of these settlements, where they converted thousands of indigenous Liberians to the Christian faith. The introduction of Christianity and education in Liberia marked a great turning point in the political life of the Liberians. They ushered in a great political awareness among Africans. No wonder Liberia has won the distinction of being the foremost independent state in West Africa. A notable achievement of Liberia was the establishment of the radio station ELWA which was established by the Sudan Interior Mission (SIM), broadcasting gospel programmes in over forty languages to all parts of Africa and the Middle East. Another remarkable achievement of the Liberian church was the exploits of the prophet William Harris, the impact of whose ministry was felt more in Ivory Coast and Western Ghana. Some of the ecumenical organizations in Liberia are the Liberia Evangelical Fundamental Fellowship and the Christian Rural Fellowship.

The Evangelical Revival and the Activation of Vibrant Missionary Enterprise in West Africa

The Protestant revival movements in Europe and America were the results of a new religious and moral awakening which swept through the Protestant countries of Europe and America towards the close of the eighteenth century. This Protestant revival was popularly known as *Pietism* in Germany, the *Evangelical Movement* in Britain, and the *Great Awakening* in the USA. In religious spheres, these revivals gave rise to a strong and active desire to spread the gospel to the non-Christian peoples of Asia and Africa. The result was the formation of a number of missionary societies in Europe and America. These sent missionaries out to West Africa and other parts of the world. Before Evangelicals took to the stage, there were only three missionary societies, namely, the Society for the Propagation of the Gospel in New England (1649), the Society for Promoting Christian Knowledge (1698), and the Society for the Propagation of the Gospel in Foreign Parts (1701).

[10] Lamin Sanneh, *West African Christianity*, 90.

Towards the end of the eighteenth century, the Evangelical Revival led to the founding of more than ten broad-based Protestant missionary societies. These included the Baptist Missionary Society (1792); William Carey, on a voluntary basis, served as its first representative abroad. The year 1793, when Carey set out for India to proclaim the gospel, is generally held to be the outset of the era of modern missions. Among others was the London Missionary Society, which was organized as an ecumenical effort by the Anglicans, Methodists and Scottish Presbyterians in 1795. The society's vigorous strategy spread to India, China, Africa, Madagascar and the West Indies. Another mission was the Glasgow and Edinburgh Society (later, the Scottish Missionary Society), which was formed as an interdenominational missionary society in 1796. The Church Missionary Society was established in April 1798 by some members of the Evangelical wing of the Church of England to serve Africa and the East. Its first field of action was Sierra Leone in West Africa. The British and Foreign Bible Society was formed in 1804 with the aim of the wide distribution of the Bible in order that converts might have easy access to the Scriptures. Stimulated by the examples of the British societies, the Americans focused more attention on the formation of missionary societies of their own, based on the London Missionary Society. Among those which emerged was the American Board of Commissioners for Foreign Missionaries which was founded in 1810. Many others soon followed. The most influential was the American Baptist Missionary Society and the General Missionary Convention (later known as the American Baptist Foreign Mission Society), both founded in 1814. In the UK, the Wesleyan Methodist Missionary Society which was born and directed by the Wesleyan Methodist Conference in 1813, began its very dynamic West African work in The Gambia in 1821. Quite a number of missionary societies sprang up on the continent of Europe. Prominent among them was the Basel Evangelical Missionary Society, better known as Basel Mission, founded in Switzerland in 1815, with the main aim of training missionaries for overseas mission. Another effective mission was the North German Missionary Society, commonly known as the Bremen Mission, founded in the city of Bremen in 1836. The Bremen Mission was well known for its unique interest in the training of local leadership and the effective use of local languages.

Turning to Roman Catholic Missionary Societies, we see that, motivated by Protestant Evangelical fervour, the Roman Catholic Church also formed in this way own missionary societies in France and other parts of Europe. The Holy Ghost Fathers emerged as an Evangelical or missionary movement in 1841. This was followed by the formation of the *Societas Missionum ad Afros*, also known as the Society for African Missions (SMA) – founded in 1858 by Bishop Marion Bresillac, with intention of forming a society of young missionaries who would devote their lives to the conversion of Africans. This society started its work in Serra Leone in 1859, went to Dahomey (Benin) in 1860, Nigeria in 1867, and the Gold Coast in 1880.

All these societies and others formed later in Europe and America took seriously the evangelization of Africa and other lands. Their untiring efforts laid the foundation for the permanent establishment of the Christian faith in West Africa after the initial failure of the Portuguese missionary enterprise.

The Impact

Protestant influence may be discussed under three strands. The first was marked by the arrival of Protestant nations in Africa. Soon after the British made their incursion into West Africa, many other European countries like the Dutch, the Danes, the French, the Germans and the Swedes registered their presence. The French and the British gained the most ground during the 'Scramble for Africa'. Britain administered Nigeria, Ghana, The Gambia and Sierra Leone throughout the colonial era. France, on the other hand, integrated Senegal, Guinea, Mali, Burkina Faso, Benin, Ivory Coast and Niger into French West Africa. Germany initially controlled Togoland, but after World War I and the consequent Treaty of Versailles, their land was divided into two between France and Britain. Only Liberia retained its independence – at the price of major territorial concessions. The second strand was the multiplication of missionary agencies from Europe and America that established themselves. Most of the European nations mentioned above attempted missionary work. Some of them could a measure of success while others failed through a lack of focus. The third strand of Protestant influence was the training of national Christians to participate in mission. These contributed significantly to the establishment of the church, particularly in the hinterland of Africa. They propagated the gospel in their mother tongues and gave an African flavour to the spread of the Christian message on the continent. They also helped in developing grammars for indigenous languages which became the bedrock of the development and training of local leaders for the church.[11] In most cases, Africans proved more suitable for evangelistic work than their European counterparts.

The Taxonomy of Churches in West Africa

The Gold Coast (today's Ghana)**:** Early efforts by Protestant churches to establish enduring mission stations failed. Anglican missionaries from England, sponsored by the Society for the Propagation of the Gospel in Foreign Parts, initiated missionary work in the middle of the eighteenth century when the Rev. Fr Thomas Thompson was sent to the Gold Coast in May 1751.He made some effort to go beyond chaplaincy confines to evangelise in the towns of Anomabu, Winneba and Tantum. Some of his Fante converts were ordained and trained in Europe as ministers. Jacobus Capitein and Philip Quaque are two of the better-known figures. Quaque served as an Anglican chaplain of the Colonial Forts for 55 years. He is claimed to have laid the foundation of Anglicanism which gave birth to some churches in other sectors later. Jacob Capitein also served as a key figure in the team of the first Bible translation project in the region. In spite of these apparent successes, it is generally held that, in missionary terms, these Fante missionaries did not achieve very much. The Anglican Church had to wait until the beginning of the twentieth century before it reactivated its evangelization work in the Gold Coast. The Basel Mission consequently became the first Protestant group to establish an enduring mission in the Gold Coast. Its first set of missionaries arrived at Osu, in Accra, on 18th December 1828. All four of these missionaries died. The challenges of malaria and adverse climatic conditions compelled the survivor of second batch of three, Andreas Riis, to relocate to Akropong in Akwapim, about 35km from Accra, where the Basel Mission established their remarkable mission station.[12] From 1843, the Basel Mission made tremendous strides when it engaged very effectively some freed African slaves from Jamaica in its wide evangelistic efforts. The Mission established a model Christian community called Salem as experimental encampments for their converts at Akropong and later in Osu. These quarters had their levels of authority and a code of social and religious behaviour. The Mission embraced the name Presbyterian Church of Gold Coast in 1926. At independence, the name was changed to the Presbyterian Church of Ghana (PCG). Today, the PCG is one of the notable providers of sound formal education in Ghana. It is also heavily involved in overseas mission, especially in The Netherlands, Germany, and Austria. The Basel Mission was followed by the Wesleyan Methodists who were invited by a Fante study group in 1834. The Methodist Conference in Britain appointed Joseph Dunwell as a missionary to serve as spiritual guide for the Bible and prayer fellowship and he arrived on 1st January 1835. Within six months, membership rose to over 100 in Cape Coast and almost 70 in Anomabo. Dunwell died after just six months' work in the Gold Coast. He was succeeded by George Wrigley, who also died after fourteen months there. The third missionary, Thomas Birch Freeman, a "*mulatto*" (person born of one white parent and one black parent), initiated a vibrant native ministry through in-service training. This effort produced some early Methodist ministers and assistants, who embarked on hinterland mission in the Gold Coast, Dahomey, Togo and Nigeria. Freeman's missionary zeal for the well-being of the native population, as well as his long and distinguished career, earned him the

---

[11] Agbeti, *West African Church History,* Vol. 1, 6.

[12] See D.N.A. Kpobi, *Mission in Ghana*: *The Ecumenical Heritage*, Accra: Asempa, 2008, 70-3.

well deserved recognition as the 'Father of Ghanaian Methodism'.[13] The North German Missionary Society (Bremen Mission) sent some missionaries to Gabon. When the mission there failed, they made a detour to the Eweland where they founded the Ewe Presbyterian Church in 1847. The Mission changed its name to Evangelical Presbyterian Church when its evangelistic outreach extended beyond Eweland. The African Methodist-Episcopal (AMEZion) Mission (an Afro-American group) founded her church also among the Ewes in Keta on the east coast of the Gold Coast in 1898.[14] There are two versions of the story of the emergence of the Baptist Convention in the Gold Coast. The first is that some Nigerian Baptists, particularly the Yoruba, established churches in the towns where they settled in order to trade. Indeed, there are quite a number of such churches, some dating back to the early 1920s in Kumasi, Cape Coast, Accra, Techiman, Sefwi-Bekwai and Tamale, to name just a few. The second version relates to the National Baptist Church which was founded by the Rev. Christian Mark Hayford. He became a Baptist while he spent time in Nigeria. Hayford established the Native Baptist Church in Cape Coast and Accra as part of the West African church movement proposed by Wilmot Blyden. Unlike the Yoruba Baptists, Hayford's church stood for self-reliance and independence, in line with nationalistic aspirations. After his death in 1935, not much was heard about the National Baptist Church until quite recently when a church in Accra was named after him. The churches established by the Yoruba, on the other hand, with the collaboration of the Southern Baptist Convention and the indigenous Baptist churches, metamorphosed into the Ghana Baptist Convention in 1964. The Salvation Army, which was founded in Great Britain in 1865, established a branch at Agona Duakwa in 1922, and soon afterwards founded a relatively larger church in Accra.

Nigeria: The Wesleyan Methodist Missionary Society was the first to sow the seeds of Christianity in the country. The Methodist pioneer Freeman, from the Gold Coast as already mentioned, arrived in Badagry on September 23rd 1842. Hot on the heels of the Methodists came the Anglican mission which was sponsored by the Church Missionary Society. The CSM missionary, Henry Townsend, arrived at Badagry in December 1842. The Church of Scotland Mission followed in its tracks when it dispatched the Rev. Hope Masterdon Waddell to pioneer the United Presbyterian Mission in Old Calabar among the Efik people in 1846.[15] The Rev. T.J. Bowen of the Southern Baptist Mission arrived at Badagry in 1850 as the leader of the fourth missionary society. The Roman Catholic Church, through the *Société des Mission Africaines* (SMA) launched a second, successful, attempt between 1860 and 1868, and its impact was felt in Lagos, Onitsha and Kaduna. In order to solidify their gains, the SMA established an experimental Christian community in Topo – a narrow piece of land outside Lagos. In 1887, the Qua Iboe Mission, a Congregationalist assemblage, was founded by a Scottish missionary, Samuel Bill, in the neighbourhood of the Qua Iboe River and Etinam. In 1893, the Sudan Interior Mission (SIM) sent three ministers – Walter Gowans, Thomas Kent and Rowland Bingham – to the northern region of Nigeria. Attempts by the SIM to establish churches in this region in the nineteenth century failed. However, a third attempt in 1901 resulted in the establishment of some churches in northern Nigeria. SIM-related churches were later designated Evangelical Churches of West Africa (ECWA).[16] In 1904, the Sudan United Mission (SUM) was formed to assist the SIM in meeting the challenge of reaching the tribes in northern Nigeria.

---

[13] C. B. Essamuah, *Genuinely Ghanaian: A History of the Methodist Church*, Ghana, 1961-2000, Trenton: AWP, 2010, 11.

[14] Kpobi, *Mission in Ghana*, 70-3.

[15] See E.A. Ayandele, *The Missionary Impact on Modern Nigeria,* 1642-1914, 7: In September 1875, Mary Mitchell Slessor arrived in Calabar as a Presbyterian missionary from the Church of Scotland Mission to strengthen the efforts of Waddell. She fought hard and bravely to abolish many cruel customs and traditions.

[16] The SIM changed her name in the 1950s to the Evangelical Church of West Africa (ECWA) See A. Ijagbemi, *Christian Missionary Activity in Nigeria: The Work of the SIM among the Yoruba 1908-1967*, Lagos, 1988.

In Senegal: The Wesleyan Methodists pioneered missions in this area in 1821. Owing to adverse weather and disease, which depleted the number of white missionaries who ventured into Senegal, few achievements can be ascribed to them. Another principal challenge was the influx of North Africans who settled in Senegal and converted the native peoples to Islam. Consequently, Senegal is one of the places where, exceptionally, Christians are in the minority. A recent and reliable census shows that the entire Christian community of Senegal is only about 3% of the population. Most of these Christians live in the south among the Serer and Mandingo peoples. In recent times, the *Eglise de Dakar* and the Roman Catholics have recorded some breakthroughs. The *Eglise de Dakar* has supported some African medical missionaries who have offered clinical assistance and embarked on youth work. The Roman Catholic missions' successful agricultural ventures have also augmented the Christian presence in Senegal.

The Gambia: The great majority of the people are Muslims. That is not because the influence of the Evangelical Revival was not felt there. An Anglican chaplain arrived in 1816 and the Wesleyan Methodist Church attempted to establish a foothold in that country as early as in 1821. The efforts of the Methodists were, however, stalled because of the climate. Other protestant missions who tried to establish their mission stations were discouraged by the overwhelming allegiance of many Gambians to Islam and failed to make progress in the country. In the late nineteenth and early twentieth centuries, some missionaries, like the Anglicans under the supervision of the USPG and a team from the Roman Catholic Church under the auspices of the Holy Ghost Fathers, also made many attempts, none of which yielded very encouraging results.

Guinea: The majority of the population, about 70%, are also Muslims, and only about 5% are Christians, while most of the people in the forest regions are adherents of African indigenous religions. A small party from the Baptist Missionary Society undertook a missionary enterprise in 1795. The following year, the Glasgow Missionary Society and the LMS made great efforts to establish their mission stations in the country. These efforts did not produce a large harvest of souls because of the climate and the high mortality rate of Christian workers. Towards the end of the nineteenth century, the CMS from the West Indies and some Roman Catholic missionaries were able to register a marginal Christian presence in this area through their medical and educational institutions. In the twentieth century, the Christian and Missionary Alliance started work at Baro in the Niger Valley. In the 1930s, the CMA was able to establish its headquarters in Kankan where it still has some schools and a thriving printing press.

Portuguese Guinea: Most of the native population is Muslim. The Worldwide Evangelization Crusade started work there in 1939, and in 1973 they had five workers. The Protestant community numbered about 1,320. Generally, in this area it is not a thriving Christian mission.

Ivory Coast: The Christian church in Ivory Coast is in a minority; most people are strong adherents of traditional religion and Islam. The effects of William Wade Harris's movement[17] is still felt in Ivory Coast. Harrism is very strong in the rural areas, especially among the Ebire and Attie living in the south-east of Ivory Coast. Roman Catholics also exercise much influence in secular matters due to their legacy of educational institutions.

Mali: As in a number of regions in West Africa, Christians are in the minority in Mali. Until very recently, Christianity was strongly resisted by the indigenous Dogon people, but later a few of them embraced Christianity. Statistics show that, in spite of this effort, Christians constitute less than 1% of the population.

Burkina Faso: Almost half the population of Burkina Faso are Muslims, while less than 20% are Christians. Most of the Christians are Mossi and mainly Roman Catholics. The Catholics and a few

[17] William Wade Harris (1860-1929), the so-called Black Elias of West Africa, was a Liberian Grebo evangelist, who preached in Liberia, Côte d'Ivoire and Ghana.

Protestants who have ventured into the country have complained of adverse ecology and the people's insensitivity to the Christian mission.

Benin: The Spanish Capuchins and Thomas Birch Freeman made some efforts to evangelize Dahomey in the seventeenth century. Their efforts produced few results due to the unfavourable disposition of the King of Dahomey and persecution of the converts. Even the resilience of Father Borghero, which resulted in the establishment of a Christian community, was strongly opposed by traditional worshippers. Today, more than half of the Beninoise maintain that they are adherents of traditional religious beliefs, chiefly *Vodun* (a belief in spirits). It is claimed that about 25% are Christians, with the majority of them Roman Catholics.

Niger: 98% of the population of Niger are said to be Muslims. Missionaries from France tried, on a number of occasions, to establish their mission outposts in Niger. Most of the Christians – who are foreigners – constitute less than 1% of the population. The main challenge has to do with the indifferent disposition of the indigenous Christians towards reaching out to the adherents of indigenous religions with the gospel.

Togo: The Bremen Mission recorded much success in Togo, particularly in founding schools for children and catechists since 1847. The Bremen workers consolidated their mission with their successful involvement of the indigenous people in the Mission and the subsequent establishment of indigenous Christianity. The Wesleyan Methodist Mission Society also registered some missionary presence through the missionary efforts of Freeman and his team. The Roman Catholic Church is the third mission which is making successful waves in the country through its educational and medical enterprises.

Phase Three: The Nativist or Ethiopian Churches

Ethiopia occupies a very important position in the history of African politics and religion. The Psalmist's proclamation: 'Ambassadors will come from Egypt, Ethiopia will stretch out her hands to God' (Ps. 68:31) is understood to be a prediction of the entry of black Africans into the household of God. J.S. Pobee explains that this prophecy is construed by some Africans to mean a shift of Christianity's centre of gravity from the North (Euro-America) to the South (Africa).[18]

In Nigeria, the first of a long list of Ethiopian churches was the Native Baptist Church, which severed her relationship with the Southern (American) Baptist Church in March 1888. A couple of years later, a multi-denominational congregation, the United Native Church (UNA), was founded in Lagos. It celebrated its first anniversary in December 1902 with the dedication of its first chapel: the African Church, Bethel. The origins of the United African Methodist Church *Eleja* (UAMC) are traced to the high-handedness of the Rev. D.H. Loko who had the support of the Rev. G.O. Griffin, Chairman of the Lagos District, to excommunicate from the church worshippers who were known to be polygamists. Sixty-five polygamists who were excommunicated resolved to establish a separate 'organization which will not be governed or controlled by the missionaries'.[19]

In the Gold Coast, there were not less than four groups that may be described as precursors of African Indigenous Churches (AICs). One was motivated by the desire to achieve a purer Christian way of life. Three others seemed to have been inspired by nationalistic feelings. They aimed to achieve complete independence from European authority and standards of conduct. The first sect, the Methodist Society or *Akonomnsu* (Water Drinkers), which had its base at Anomabu, broke away from the Methodist congregation in 1862. The date suggests that this was the first secession from any mission establishment in Africa south of the Sahara. The sect, though claiming to strive for a purer form of Christianity, had a curious mixture of traditional religious ideas, both pseudo-Christian and anti-Christian. Apart from their

---

[18] J.S. Pobee, *AD 2000 and After: The Future of God's Mission in Africa*. Accra: Asempa, 1991, 53-61.

[19] See Deji Ayegboyin and Ademola Ishola, *African Indigenous Churches*, Greater Heights, 1997.

rigid stand against the drinking and selling of liquor, they pulled their children out of mission schools. They refused to pay church dues, and they also maintained that it was wrong for Christians to sweep the house or to cultivate the ground on which the palm tree grows, because wine and brooms came from that tree. The *Akonomnsu* Society had a rather short existence for, after a decade or so, the Methodist Church tried to deal with the accusation. In 1874, the church authorities took a firm stand against the buying and selling of liquor among the its members. Thus, the *Akonomnsu's* justification for breaking away was dealt with and virtually nothing henceforth was heard about the society. The first church which was founded in Ghana with a nationalistic undertone was the National Baptist Church (referred to above). The main significance of this church is that it maintained a link with other separatist movements in West Africa. After the death of Hayford in 1935, not much was heard about the it. The Nigritian Church started as a congregation of some forty members of the Anomabu Methodist Church who dared to raise their voices against the Methodist authority's ruling regarding participation in singing bands. The dissidents felt that there was nothing wrong with Christians taking part in the *Fante* custom of dancing to the tune of singing bands. In 1907, when the Methodist ministers maintained their position and went ahead to carry out their threat to excommunicate the dissidents, they separated and went by the name 'The Nigritian Church'. The establishment of the African Methodist Episcopal Zion Church (AMEZ) was influenced by the AMEZ, which started in New York as a dissident group in 1796. It was introduced to Ghana in 1898 by John Bryan Small who served as a sergeant in the West African Regiment, stationed in the Gold Coast before he went to the USA to be ordained. Bishop Small's church seemed to have been primarily interested in awakening colour consciousness. AMEZ was a totally black people's congregation and entirely governed by Africans.

It is important to note that these Ethiopian or African churches had no scruples over their manner of worship, nor were they motivated to fully indigenize Christianity. Consequently, they took over the structure and patterns of worship which they inherited, without modification from their parent mission churches. Those who see classifications of churches in Africa in terms of reactions to white people's cultural domination and power in the church refer to Ethiopianism as the first response.[20]

Phase Four: African Indigenous Churches (AICs)

The most dynamic phenomenon in African Christianity in the twentieth century was the growth of the AICs. They are the churches that made concerted efforts to adapt Christianity to the African condition rather than accept the foreign structure of western missionary religion.[21] The most widely accepted terms now are 'African Instituted Churches', 'African Indigenous Churches', 'African Initiatives in Christianity' and, most recently, 'African Initiated Christianity'.[22] They emerged from within the mainstream (or mission-planted) churches after the 1920s.

In Nigeria, the churches in this category are Christ Apostolic Church, the Cherubim and Seraphim Movement, Church of the Lord: (*Aladura*), Celestial Church of Christ, and the splinter groups which broke away from the four primary assemblages to set up their own places of worship.[23]

In the Gold Coast, the first prophetic movement with the most far-reaching impact was the one started by William Wade Harris between 1913 and 1915. His itinerary and working area covered mostly Ivory Coast and the Gold Coast. Even though he had a large following, he did not establish a church. After his death, the onus fell on his adherents, John Nackabah and Grace Tani, who established the Twelve Apostles Church which continues to spread Harris's teachings. The *Musama Disco Christo* Church (MDCC) is one

---

[20] See Ogbu Kalu, "The Third Response: Pentecostalism and the Reconstruction of Christian Experience in Africa, 1970-1995", *Journal of African Christian Thought* Vol. 1(2) 1993, 3.

[21] N. Smart, *The World's Religious: Old Traditions and Modern Transformations*, Cambridge: CUP, 1989, p. 524.

[22] J.S. Pobee and Gabriel Oshitelu, *African Initiatives in Christianity*: The Growth, Gifts and Diversities of Indigenous African Churches: A Challenge to the Ecumenical Movement. Geneva: WCC, 1998.

[23] See Ayegboyin and Ishola, *African Indigenous Churches.*

of the oldest indigenous churches in West Africa. This church, like most other independent movements, began as a prayer group within the Methodist Church at Gomoa Oguan in 1919. The founder, Joseph Egyanka Appiah, Akaboa I, introduced a system of communal living for his followers in a new settlement called *Muzano* (God's own town) in the Central Region of Ghana. Other notable indigenous *sunsum sore* (spiritual churches)[24] include: *Odifo* (Prophet) Kwame Nkansa's African Faith Tabernacle which specializes in deliverance from the oppression of witchcraft and demonology, the Prophet Samuel Brako's Saviour's Church at Akim Osiem. In addition, Charles Komla Nutonuti 'Wovenu' founded the Apostles' Revelation Society near Keta in 1945 as a faith healing movement which enjoys much patronage.

The churches in this group have discernible characteristics in their historical context of emergence, doctrine, style of leadership and social impact which mark them out from the historic churches and later Pentecostal movements.

Phase Five: Pentecostalism

Another significant landmark in Christianity in the twentieth century was the emergence of the Pentecostals. The claim by some scholars that Pentecostalism was 'imported' into Africa has been contested.[25] It is obvious, at least, in the case of Nigeria, Ghana and Liberia, that some Pentecostal-like indigenous movements appeared in the second decade of the twentieth century as unprompted and autonomous prophetic mass organizations. A foremost example is the revivalist movement started by William Wade Harris in Liberia which had resounding impact in Ivory Coast and Ghana. Another one was led by prophet Garrick Braide in Nigeria. The Christ Army Church which emerged from Braide's movement is reputedly known as the first Pentecostal denomination in Nigeria. At least four strands of Pentecostalism may be distinguished in West Africa.

Classical Pentecostals: These churches are the institutionalized foreign Pentecostal organizations. They originated from Europe and America. In Nigeria, The Faith Tabernacle of Philadelphia, which was the first such organization, stamped her influence through contact with the leaders of *Okuta Iyebiye* (The Diamond Society) in 1923. Even though their influence on the indigenous Diamond Society was for only four years, some Faith Tabernacle churches, which were established in pockets of Nigeria, retained their designation. The second is the Apostolic Church, from Bradford (UK), whose delegation arrived in September 1931 by invitation from the indigenous leaders of the Faith Tabernacle who were being persecuted by the colonial authorities. The third – the Assemblies of God – was born in Nigeria when a group of indigenous Christians who went by the name 'The Church of Jesus Christ' in Umuahia, requested the Assemblies of God in Springfield, Missouri, to send them a resident missionary. In June 1939, the Rev. and Mrs William Shirer met with the pastors and congregation of the Church of Jesus Christ. The agreement of affiliation, sanctioned in August 1939, resulted in the renaming of the Church of Jesus Christ as Assemblies of God. Others include: the Apostolic Faith and the International Church of the Foursquare Gospel.

In Ghana during this period, a number of foreign Pentecostal churches from North America and Europe established their missions in the country. Notable among them are the Assemblies of God (AG), the Apostolic Church, the Elim Pentecostal Church (EPC), the Lutheran Church of Ghana and the Foursquare Gospel Church (FGC).

These churches, which were founded overseas in the early twentieth century, generally maintain four cardinal doctrines: instant salvation[26] (referred to as the finished work of Calvary doctrine), but with progression through life in a process of continual sanctification; an emphasis on baptism with (or in) the Holy Spirit as an endowment of power subsequent to conversion; *glossolalia* as the biblical evidence of

---

[24] See C.G. Baeta, *Prophetism in Ghana*, London: SCM, 1962.

[25] See eg. Paul Gifford, "Prosperity: A new and Foreign Element in African Christianity" *Religion*, Vol. 20 (1990) 382.

[26] Indeed, there are Second Work Pentecostals who hold on to the three acts of grace: conversion, sanctification and baptism in the spirit. In this group are: the Church of God in Christ and the Pentecostal Holiness Church.

receiving baptism of the Holy Spirit, and the continuing validity of spiritual gifts mentioned in 1 Corinthians 12:8-10. In practice, the Classical Pentecostals, by contrast with the New Pentecostals, have a blend of extremist Wesleyan and Keswick views. They emphasize maturing into perfection after conversion, along with strict moral and dress codes.

Indigenous Pentecostal Groups: In Nigeria, there are home-grown Pentecostal groups, dating from the 1950s and 1960s. These were not set up under the auspices of foreign Pentecostal missions. The first in this group is the *Ogo Oluwa* Society, which blossomed into the Redeemed Christian Church of God in 1952. This church was founded by the Rev. Josiah Olufemi Akindayomi who initially belonged to the Cherubim and Seraphim Society. The founder of the church said he was warned in a vision not to affiliate with any 'foreign church'.[27] Others in this group include the Victory Gospel Church in Lagos, which was founded in 1958 by Pastor J.O. Olatunji; the Gospel Pentecostal Assembly, founded in Lagos in 1958 by Pastor Badejo; the Evangel Faith Mission (1962); The Gospel Faith Mission which was a merger of the Apostolic Faith Mission, the Gospel Mission (1962) and a few others.

In Ghana, the most significant development in indigenous Pentecostal missions occurred with the movement begun by Apostle Anim in 1927. Just as happened in Nigeria, Anim solicited the support of the Apostolic Church, England, which sent a delegation led by Pastor and Mrs James McKeown in 1937. Later, the schism in the classical movement formed, resulting in the springing up of three distinct groups, namely, the Apostolic Church (TAC), the Christ Apostolic Church (CAC), and the blossoming and growing indigenous Church of Pentecost (COP).

Charismatic and the New Pentecostal Churches: Some scholars of new religious movements prefer to use the term 'Charismatic' to describe contemporary Pentecostal movements. Ojo,[28] for example, prefers characterizing the religious awakening of the late 1960s and 1970s as 'Charismatic revival'. Hackett[29] uses 'Charismatic' and 'Pentecostal' interchangeably. Ruth Marshall agrees with Ojo to position the genesis of this charismatic revival in Nigeria in the early 1970s.[30] Asamoah-Gyadu restricts 'Charismatic' to Pentecostal renewal movements that operate within historic mission denominations or mainstream churches.[31]

The Charismatic movement is a spiritual renewal rooted partly in the earlier wave of Pentecostalism, the origins of which historically demarcate Classical Pentecostalism from New Pentecostalism. The Charismatic movements resemble traditional Pentecostalism, manifesting such elements as *glossolalia*, prophecy, healing and deliverance. In the USA, the movements started in the 1950s first among Protestant churches, and later among Roman Catholics. Parrinder contends that it was from here that the movement spread outwards to Europe and other continents.[32]

The immediate background of charismatic movements in Nigeria was the evangelical awakening which erupted in the country's higher institutions in the 1970s. This was as a result of an intense incursion of charismatic Pentecostal ideas into university fellowships. These ideas later made inroads into the historic church bodies. The penetration was facilitated by the sporadic contacts which Pentecostal ministers and leaders had with university fellowships. With more mobility, greater prosperity and an increased

---

[27] See *Redemption Light Magazine*, Vol. 5(8) September 2000. 3-5.

[28] See Ojo M.A. "Deeper Life Bible Church of Nigeria" in P. Gifford (ed) *New Dimensions in African Christianity*, Ibadan: Sefer Books, 1992.

[29] Hackett, R.I.J. "Charismatic/Pentecostal Appropriation of Media Technologies in Nigeria and Ghana", *Journal of Religion in Africa*, XXVIII/3 (1998).

[30] Ruth Marshall "God is Not a Democrat": Pentecostalism and Democratisation in Nigeria" in P. Gifford (ed) *Christianity and Africa's Democratisation*, Leiden: Brill Pub. 1995.

[31] J. Kwabena Asamoah-Gyadu, "born of Water and The Spirit, Pentecostal/Charismatic Christianity in Africa" in Ogbu Kalu (ed) *African Christianity: An African Story*, Pretoria: UP 389.

[32] G. Parrinder, "Charisma", *Encyclopedia of Religion*, Vol. 3, N.Y: S & S Macmillan.

circulation of Pentecostal literature, notably from Europe and America, a greater interest and acceptance of Pentecostal indoctrination became apparent in several organized student Christian bodies. Before the end of the 1970s, several multi-denominational Evangelical movements, Charismatic organizations as well as Bible study and prayer fellowships had sprouted all over Nigeria. Some of the earliest trans-denominational groups include The Hour of Freedom Evangelistic Association, in Onitsha (1970), The World Action Team for Christ (1970), The Soul Harvesters, in Warri (1971), Christ Ambassadors, Evangelistic team (1971), The Masters' Vessels Group, in Umuahia (1972), The Deeper Christian Life Fellowship, in Lagos (1973); The Grace of God Mission (1973), in Onitsha, and The Maranatha Evangelical Christian Ministry (1973) The attempts by some of these fellowships to initiate radical changes in the liturgy, Bible study and prayer meetings in the historic churches were violently rebuffed. Consequently, a few charismatic renewal movements left the historic churches. During the 1980s, a noticeable trend in charismatic advancement was the remodelling of a number of multi-denominational fellowships into denominational charismatic churches. Probably the first in this group was the *Ole-Ezi* (Prayer for the Spirit) Charismatic movement which became independent of the Anglican Church in the middle of 1970s. Another was Pastor W.F. Kumiyi's Deeper Life Bible Church which was inaugurated at Gbagada, Lagos, in 1982.

The social setting of the 1980s gave birth to a plethora of Pentecostal groups, ministries, churches and para-churches competing for church membership. All over West Africa, churches evolved with so many complex varieties that they defy classification. Some are Signs and Wonders movements and quite a number are Healing and Deliverance ministries. A few which came out of the old-style Pentecostal congregations have a holiness emphasis. A number of these ministries are so recent that they lack institutionalized structures and management. Quite a number of the founders or leaders of these movements base their claims to authority on charismatic qualities. Most of these, as Marshall observes, are 'notoriously schismatic, owing partly to the struggle for clients in a competitive religious market'.[33] In Nigeria, we may list the following: Bishop David Oyedepo's Living Faith World Outreach (Winners chapel) which started at Kaduna in 1984; the Rev. George Adegboye's Rhema Chapel International Ministries at Ilorin in 1988, Bishop Francis Wale Oke's Christ Life Church, inaugurated at Ibadan in 1989. Others include the Rev. Kayode Olukoya's Mountain of Fire and Miracle Ministries, Lagos, in 1989; Bishop Mike Okonkwo's Redeemed Evangelical Mission, and so on. Another interesting phenomenon during this period, which led to the rapid proliferation of Pentecostal Charismatic churches, was the rapidity with which schisms took place within the movement. The most notable ones include the Rev. Paul Jinadu's New Covenant Church which seceded from the International Foursquare Gospel Church, Pastor Ayo Oritsejafor's Word of Life Bible Church which separated from Archbishop Idahosa's Church of God (Mission), and Dr Tunde Bakare's Latter Rain Assembly which broke away in 1989 from the Redeemed Christian Church of God.

In Ghana, the evangelical revivals of late 1950s and 1960s, coupled with the activities of students in Scripture Union (SU) and graduates of the Ghana Fellowship of Evangelical Students (GHAFES) in the 1960s and 1970s led to the evolution of many Christian Urban Fellowships and formation of para-church organizations. As in Nigeria, some of the leaders of these fellowships encouraged their members from mainstream churches to take the lead in the revival of their own churches This trend significantly affected the growth of charismatic movements in the mainstream churches. Some of the early non-denominational revival movements[34] include the Ghana Evangelical Society (GES), led by Enoch Agbozo, the Hour of Visitation Choir and Evangelistic Association (HOVCEA), led by Brother Isaac Ababio; Youth Ambassadors for Christ (YAFCA), co-ordinated by Brother Owusu Afriyie, and Christian Outreach Fellowship (COF). Today, some of the celebrated new Pentecostal churches include Bishop Nicholas

[33] Ruth Marshall, "Pentecostalism in Southern Nigeria: An Overview" in P. Gifford (ed) *New Dimensions in African Christianity*, Ibadan: Sefer Book 1992, p. 19.

[34] See C.N. Omenyo, *Pentecost outside Pentecostalism*, Amsterdam: Boekencentrun, 2002, 95-6.

Duncan-Williams' Christian Action Faith Ministries International (CAFM – 1980), Dr Mensah Otabil's Central Gospel Church (ICGC – 1984); Charles Agyin Asare's Word Miracle Church International (WMCI- 1987), and Lighthouse Chapel International (LHI – 1991), founded by Dag Heward-Mills.[35]

Neo-Prophetism: The latest strand of Pentecostalism which came under the purview of Gifford's discourse is Neo-Prophetism.[36] He mentions two movements in Ghana which are from Nigeria – namely, Abraham Chigbundu's Mark of Christ Ministries from Benin City, and the sprawling Prophet T.B. Joshua's Synagogue of All Nations, which has a branch in Accra. The most prominent Neo-Prophetic movements in Ghana include Prophet Salifu Amoako's Alive Chapel International.(ACI-1994), Isaac Anto's International Christian Miracle Centre (ACMI-1999), Abubakar Bako of the Logos Rhema Foundation, and Most Senior Prophet Odeyifoò Philip K Acquah's Church of Bethesda at Anyaa in Accra. These are prophetic movements which indulge in copious rituals with either water or 'holy' oil, or both, in their deliverance ministrations.

Conclusion

Enduring and successful missionary enterprise began in West Africa in the nineteenth century. The concerted efforts of the Protestant churches of Europe and America laid the foundation for the permanent establishment of the Christian faith in West Africa after the initial failure of the Portuguese missionary enterprise. The roles of indigenous leadership and African initiatives in strengthening and proliferating the churches have been astounding. Today, the African initiatives are known to be not only Christian, but also truly evangelical, spiritual, Pentecostal and ecumenical with a both local and international appeal.

Bibliography

Agbeti, K.J. ,*West African Church History: Christian Missions and Church Foundation 1482-1919*, Leiden: E.J Brill 1986

Asamoah-Gyad, J. K., *African Charismatics*, Leiden: Brill 2005

Asamoah-Gyadu, J. K., *Contemporary Pentecostal Christianity: Interpretations from an African Context*, Oxford: Regnum, 2013

Ayegboyin Deji and Ishola S, Ademola, *African Indigenous Churches.* Bukuru: ACTS, 2013

Baeta, C.G., *Prophetism in Ghana*, London: SCM, 1962

Baur, J., *2000 Years of Christianity in Africa*, Nairobi: Pauline Publications, 2009

Ekem, J.K., *Priesthood in Context*, Hamburg: Verlag an der Lottbek, 1994

Essamuah, C.B., *Genuinely Ghanaian: A History of the Methodist Church*, Ghana, 1961-2000, Trenton, NJ: Africa World Press, 2010,

Falk, P., *The Growth of the Church in Africa*, Bukuru: ACTS, 1997,

Ishola Ademola and Ayegboyin Deji (eds) *Rediscovering and Fostering Unity in the Body of Christ: The Nigerian Experience,*2000

Gifford, P. (ed), *New Dimensions in African Christianity*, Ibadan: Sefer Book 1992,

Gifford, P., *Ghana's New Christianity*, Bloomington, IUP 2004,

Hackett, R.I.J., 'Charismatic/Pentecostal Appropriation of Media Technologies in Nigeria and Ghana',

[35] For a detailed discussion of Pentecostal phenomenon in Ghana, see J. Kwabena. *Asamoah-Gyadu, African Charismatics*, Leiden: Brill 2005; Paul Gifford, Ghana's New Christianity, Bloomington, IUP 2004, C. Omenyo, *Pentecost outside Pentecostalism;* E.K Larbi, *Pentecostalism - the Eddies of Ghanaian Christianity,* Accra; CPCS 2001.

[36] P. Gifford, Ghana's New Christianity, 83-111. See also very detailed discussion on the phenomenon in C.N. Omenyo and Abamfo Atiemo, Claiming Religious Space: The Case of Neo-Prophetism in Ghana. *Ghana Bulletin of Theology*, Vol 1 (10 July 2006, 55-68).

Journal of Religion in Africa, XXVIII/3, 1998

Kalu, O., (ed) *African Christianity: An African Story*, Pretoria: Dept of Church History, University of Pretoria, 2005

Kpobi, D.N.A., *Mission in Ghana: The Ecumenical Heritage*, Accra: Asempa, 2008

Larbi, E.K., *Pentecostalism – the Eddies of Ghanaian Christianity,* Accra; CPCS 2001

Omenyo C.N., *Pentecost outside Pentecostalism*, Amsterdam: Boekencentrun, 2002

Parrinder, G., 'Charisma', *Encyclopedia of Religion*, Vol. 3, N.Y: S and S Macmillan

Pobee, J.S., *AD 2000 and After the Future of God's Mission in Africa* Accra: Asempa

Pobee, J.S., *Skenosis: Christian Faith in an African Context*. Gweru: Mambo Press, 1992,

Sanneh, L., *West African Christianity: The Religious Impact*, London, C. Hurst, 1983

(19) Christianity in Eastern Africa

Alfred Olwa

Country	Religion	Pop_2010	Pct_2010	Pop_2025	Pct_2025	GrPct_1970_2025
Eastern Africa	Christians	225,497,000	65.8%	347,594,000	67.8%	2.9%
Eastern Africa	Independents	27,259,000	8.0%	41,058,000	8.0%	2.8%
Eastern Africa	African-initiated	21,912,000	6.4%			
Eastern Africa	Orthodox	37,658,000	11.0%	55,163,000	10.8%	2.6%
Eastern Africa	Oriental Orthodox	36,911,000	10.8%			
Eastern Africa	Protestants	90,795,000	26.5%	132,227,000	25.8%	2.5%
Eastern Africa	Anglicans	25,878,000	7.6%			
Eastern Africa	Baptist	12,482,000	3.6%			
Eastern Africa	Pentecostal	12,098,000	3.5%			
Eastern Africa	Lutheran	9,594,000	2.8%			
Eastern Africa	Adventist	6,308,000	1.8%			
Eastern Africa	Reformed, Presbyterian	5,952,000	1.7%			
Eastern Africa	Lutheran/Reformed	5,576,000	1.6%			
Eastern Africa	United churches	3,990,000	1.2%			
Eastern Africa	Nondenominational	3,532,000	1.0%			
Eastern Africa	Roman Catholics	74,746,000	21.8%	117,635,000	22.9%	3.1%
Eastern Africa	*Pentecostals/ Charismatics*	57,264,000	16.7%	86,883,000	16.9%	2.8%
Eastern Africa	*Evangelicals*	53,356,000	15.6%	80,235,000	15.6%	2.8%
Eastern Africa	Muslims	73,068,000	21.3%	110,238,000	21.5%	2.8%
Eastern Africa	adherents of traditional African religions	40,087,000	11.7%	49,109,000	9.6%	1.4%
Eastern Africa	Hindus	1,611,000	0.5%	2,128,000	0.4%	1.9%
Eastern Africa	Baha'is	1,144,000	0.3%	1,763,000	0.3%	2.9%
Eastern Africa	Jains	93,300	0.0%	134,000	0.0%	2.5%
Eastern Africa	Chinese folk religionists	70,900	0.0%	102,000	0.0%	2.5%
Eastern Africa	Sikhs	57,000	0.0%	80,700	0.0%	2.3%
Eastern Africa	Jews	37,400	0.0%	37,900	0.0%	0.1%
Eastern Africa	Buddhists	31,300	0.0%	45,900	0.0%	2.6%
Eastern Africa	adherents of new religious movements	3,200	0.0%	3,800	0.0%	1.0%
Eastern Africa	Zoroastrians	970	0.0%	970	0.0%	0.0%
Eastern Africa	Spiritists	600	0.0%	600	0.0%	0.1%
Eastern Africa	people professing no religion	1,042,000	0.3%	1,582,000	0.3%	2.8%
Eastern Africa	**Total population**	**342,743,000**	**100.0%**	**512,821,000**	**100.0%**	**2.7%**

Source: Centre for the Study of World Christianity (CSGC), Boston, Gordon-Conwell TS

In this account, Christianity in East Africa is surveyed at a broad level. We commence with a brief explanation of three major streams of Christianity in East Africa and a general look at five aspects of it: (1) Its historical origins, (2) Its increasing growth, (3) The encounter between politics and the gospel, (4) The way it represents Christianity in the market-place, and (5) The way in which it changed indigenous cultural practices. We then highlight the nature and shape of Christianity in the major denominational families as well as noting some major challenges it currently faces. We consider briefly also the question of ecumenism before some concluding remarks.

Explaining Three Streams of Christianity in East Africa

Christianity in East Africa, according to my categorization for the purpose of this essay, exists in three main streams. My choice of the expression 'streams' is deliberate. I use this word in the sub-title of this section to mean the 'outflow of Christianity in East Africa'. The three streams refer to (1) Mainline denominations – Catholic, Anglicans, Lutheran and Greek Orthodox. This stream includes the largest group; (2) Pentecostal and Charismatic denominations – Africa Inland Church, Baptist Church, Full Gospel, Pentecostal Assemblies of God, Presbyterian Church, Salvation Army, and the Seventh Day Adventists, among others. These groups constitute the fastest growing Christian denominations; and (3) African Instituted churches[1] – Chosen Evangelical Revival, Church of the One Almighty God (Abamalaki), African Brotherhood Church, African Church of the Holy Spirit, African Divine Church, Maria Legio of Africa, and the Nomiya Luo Church, among others. In the third stream of churches there are some Christian bodies with only one or just a few congregations. These include Power of Jesus, Wokofu African Church, and the Holy Spirit Church of Zayun, among others. The reason we give a brief sketch of these three streams is to show that East Africa has become very much a Christian belt in Africa.

More may be said about these streams of churches. With the exception of the African Instituted Churches, the first and second streams usually have strong ties with their historical roots in the western world. However, from 2005, parts of the Anglican churches in East Africa have rejected teachings from their counterparts in the West which are questioning the authority of Scripture. Henry Luke Orombi, the Anglican Archbishop of Uganda (2002-2010), epitomizes such rejection. At the peak of his leadership when he rallied resistance against disobedience to the authority of Scripture by some churches in the West, he wrote:

> The Bible cannot appear to us a cadaver, merely to be dissected, analysed and critiqued, as has been the practice of much modern higher biblical criticism. Certainly we engage in biblical scholarship and criticism, but what is important to us is the power of the Word of God precisely as the *Word* of God – written to bring transformation in our lives, our families, our communities and our culture. For us, the Bible is 'living and active, sharper than a double-edged sword; it penetrates to dividing soul and spirits, joints and marrow; it judges the thoughts and attitudes of the heart' (Heb. 4:12). The transforming effect of the Bible on Ugandans has generated so much conviction and confidence that believers were martyred in the defence of the message of salvation through Jesus Christ that it brought.[2]
>
> For the Ugandan church to compromise God's call of obedience to the Scriptures would be the undoing of more than 125 years of Christianity through which African life and society have been transformed.

---

[1] For a more fuller list of these churches of African Initiated Churches originating in Kenya, see Dr. Philomena N. Mwaura of Kenyatta University, assisted by Rev. Bernard Nyabwari, in: *Dictionary of African Christian Biography*, www.dacb.org/history/aics-kenya.htmi. Accessed 18 March 2015.

[2] Henry Luke Orombi, 'What Is Anglicanism?' in 2007 First Things. www.firstthings.com/author/archbishop-henry-luke-orombi. Accessed 19 March 2015.

Historical Developments

In most of East Africa, Christianity had its origins and growth tied in with socio-political factors of the region during the missionary era. On a broad scale across East Africa, the best introduction to this subject is perhaps still Ronald Oliver's classic, *The Missionary Factor in East Africa*.[3] It was out of the humble dedicated work of missionaries as objectively discussed by Oliver that Christianity in East Africa was planted.

Once Christianity was planted in East Africa during the missionary era, it grew and spread to different parts of the region; however, this growth was not uniform: some mission stations were established fairly quickly while others struggled. For instance, in the case of Uganda, Baganda evangelists embraced the gospel introduced by CMS missionaries and soon they were dedicated to spreading the gospel within Uganda and beyond. Kevin Ward in 1991 wrote:

> Missionaries arrived first at the court of Kabaka Muteesa in 1877; almost a century after the missionary impetus from Europe had begun. And yet, within 25 years, Uganda had become one of the most successful mission fields in the whole of Africa.[4]

While the CMS missionaries arrived on 30th June 1877, the Roman Catholic Archbishop Lavigerie's missionary order – the White Fathers – arrived in Buganda in June 1879, much to the consternation of the Protestants. The CMS missionary, Alexander Mackay, brought with him invaluable practical skills and he preached with much passion, which the early converts in the Kabaka's palace liked very much. But when the While Fathers arrived, Mackay's match was to be found in Simeon Lourdel in his debating skills.[5]

In Kenya, at the end of the fifteenth century, the Portuguese had established their presence and some rulers were converted to Catholicism; however, Portuguese meddling caused hatred as, with the dwindling of Portugal's power, Christianity declined.[6] In 1844, it was the CMS missionary Ludwig Kraft who arrived in Mombasa with his pregnant wife in order to renew the Christian presence against decline. He had been expelled from Ethiopia for attempting to win over the Orthodox Church. In 1862, Bishop Tozer established a second Anglican mission station in Tanzania, at Zanzibar. David Livingstone's advocacy brought about the Universities' Mission to Central and East Africa (UMCA). In the fight against slave trade, it was more innovative than Kraft.

The UMCA's most impressive missionary was Frank Weston who arrived in Zanzibar in 1898, was made bishop in 1908, and fought for *the abolition of Serfdom in East Africa*; by the 1920s he was a leading figure in the Anglican Communion and his death at 53 was felt deeply.[7] Over time, the most remarkable missionary work was the German Lutheran ministry among the Chagga of the Mount Kilimanjaro region. By the 1870s, CMS had already established in Mpapwe, Dodoma and Mwanza as part of their supply route from the cost to Uganda. CMS Australia assumed responsibility in 1929 and, ironically, Mwita Akiri (at the time of writing, bishop of the diocese of Tarime in Tanzania), in his thesis 'The Growth of Christianity in Ugogo and Ukaguru',[8] makes the case that, in Tanzania, Catholic mission experienced to be joined by many Protestants.

---

[3] Ronald A. Oliver, *The Missionary Factor in East Africa* (London: Longmans, 1952).

[4] Kevin Ward, 'A History of Christianity in Uganda' in Nthamburi Z (ed), *From Mission to Church* (Nairobi: Uzima, 1991), 81-112.

[5] Kevin Ward, *A History of Global Anglicanism*, Cambridge: Cambridge University Press, 2006, 166.

[6] G. S. P. Freeman-Grenville, *The Mombasa Rising Against the Portuguese, 1631* (Oxford: Oxford University Press, 1980), 163.

[7] H. Maynard Smith, Frank, *Bishop of Zanzibar* (London: SPCK, 1926).

[8] Mwita Akiri, 'The Growth of Christianity in Ugogo and Ukguru', Ph.D dissertation, University of Edinburgh, 1999.

The success of the planting and growth of Christianity in East Africa were also experienced in Congo, Rwanda and Burundi. The vigour of the churches in these countries arose out of the evangelistic inspiration of the East African Revival which started in Uganda, moved to Rwanda, was reinforced with a vibrant thrust back into Uganda and then spread beyond Uganda. A challenge remains for the Anglican Church in Rwanda with the genocide that took place between the Hutu and Tutsi in 1994: what do they understand by Christian discipleship?[9]

Despite the success of the planting and spread of Christianity in the missionary era in East Africa, there were pockets of resistance to the missionaries and the gospel they preached by some groups. Among these groups in Uganda was the society of the One Almighty God (the *Abamaki*).[10] In 1924, they came into contact with the people of north-western Tanzania and established their branches in Tanzania, resenting the CMS. A similar indigenous group was *Nomiya* ('I have received'), which started in Kenya and spread to Tanzania – also a result of secession from CMS.[11]

More is yet to be said about resistance to missionary Christianity. Actually, in Kenya there are several more independent Christian churches that have broken ties with other Protestant denominations. The largest of these is the Nomiya Luo Church, whose founder, Johana Owalo, was an early convert to Christianity in 1900. It is believed that in 1907 he had a vision in which the angel Gabriel took him to heaven. While in heaven, he claims to have seen that Europeans and Asians, and even popes, were not allowed to enter heaven. However, later Owalo converted to Islam and began to preach against mission churches – and that mission churches were opposed to traditional beliefs. It is striking that Owalo's mix of Christian, Anglican and traditional practices attracted many followers. While missionaries encountered resistance from native peoples such as the Owalo in their work in East Africa, their labour in the gospel was not in vain; it would emerge more visibly in the 1970s and continue to the present.

As with other parts of Africa, there is some consensus among scholars that the nature and shape of Christianity in Africa in this century will be determined by events and processes that take place outside a western context.[12] Indeed, Andrew Walls helpfully observes that the distinguishing dogmas, worship, moral instructions and social practices of Christianity and new schemas for theology will progressively be those noticeable in Africa,[13] raising questions of historical development as well as the nature and shape of Christianity in East Africa.

In this survey, we ask: why is it that across the different denominations in East Africa there is a general sense in which every believer in the Lord Jesus Christ has a deep feeling of being a missionary. And, what implication does this feeling have for the public face of Christianity in East Africa? It continues to take on a volcanic dimension – not only in the increasingly explosive growth of its adherents – but also in many other aspects, including its indigenous leadership and cultural, political, and economic dimensions. What is behind these developments? To these questions we now turn.

---

[9] See discussion on this challenge in Meg Guillebaud, *Rwanda: The Land God Forgot? Revival, Genocide and Hope* (London: Monarch, 2002).
[10] John Iliffe, *A Modern History of Tanganyika* (Cambridge: University of Cambridge, 1979), 363.
[11] Iliffe, *A Modern History of Tanganyika*, 363.
[12] These scholars include Kwame Bediako, *Christianity in Africa: The Renewal of Non-Western Religion* (Edinburgh: Edinburgh University Press, 1995). He argues that African Christianity is to be seen as 'the renewal of a non western religion'; Philip Jenkins, *The New Christendom* (Oxford: Oxford University Press, 2001). He argues that in the 'new Christendom' Africa was a key player.
[13] Andrew F. Walls, *The Cross-Cultural Process in Christian History* (Maryknoll, N.Y: Orbis Books, 2002), 85.

Increasing Growth

As Christianity in East Africa multiplied from the mid-twentieth century, a significant increase in its profile was noticed across the denominations from the 1970s. For example, in Table 1 below, by 1970, the percentage of the population of Christians in East Africa was 49.4%. It increased by 65.9% by 2010, while by 2020 it is projected to reach 67.0%. This projection shows a clear increase in Christian numbers: nearly 45% of Africa's Christians will be found in East Africa, an increase of approximately 39% since 1970. However, numbers tell us nothing of the depth and extent of maturity of the Christian faith in East Africa.

Although out of sequence with this discussion of increasing growth, Paul Gifford, a Catholic historian, focusing on Christianity in Ghana in his *Ghana's New Christianity*, the new kind of Christianity that he describes is clearly rising across East Africa: it is a type of Christianity that is deeply engaged with the context of life in modern East Africa, engaging East Africans culturally, politically and economically.[14]

Table 1: Christianity in East Africa, 1970-2020

	1970			2020			
County	**Population**	**Christians**	**%**	**Population**	**Christians**	**%**	**Rate***
Eastern Africa	111,412,000	55,009,000	49.4	431,818,000	289,235,000	67.0	3.38
Burundi	3,513,000	1,500	0.6	933,000	4,500	0.5	2.62
Kenya	11,252,000	7,058,000	62.7	52,564,000	43,068,000	81.9	3.68
Rwanda	3,749,000	2,292,000	61.1	14,042,000	12,964,000	92.3	3.53
South Sudan	3,785,000	858,000	22.7	13,181,000	8,405,000	63.8	4.67
Tanzania	13,605,000	5,007,000	36.8	61,081,000	34,028,000	55.7	3.91
Uganda	9,446,000	6,429,000	61.8	45,424,000	38,310,000	84.3	3.63

- Rate = average annual Christian growth rate, per cent per year 1970-2020

Note: This table has been adopted from 'Christianity in its Global Context, 1970-2020: Society, Religion and Mission': 24-25, *Centre for the Study of Global Christianity, Gordon Conwell Theological Seminary*, June 2013: 1-92. It was modified by this writer, extracting only data that suits our definition of East Africa (so omitting data on countries outside the current protocol of the East African community).

The Encounter between Politics and the Gospel

In allowing Christianity in East Africa to influence everything else around our way of life, clearly East African Christians are being honest and clear about their existence: they are being true to themselves; there is no putting on of masks. Take a recent but important example from the practice of Christianity and politics as exhibited by the President of the Republic of Uganda; Lieut-General Yoweri Kaguata Museveni will suffice to illustrate a practice that is currently spreading across East Africa.

President Museveni made a prayer on the eve of the National Day of the celebration of Uganda's Independence Jubilee on 8th October 2012, at an overnight prayer meeting at the Nelson Mandela National Stadium.[15]

---

[14] Paul Gifford, *Ghana's New Christianity: Pentecostalism in a Globalizing African Economy* (Bloomington: Indiana University Press, 2004), 23.

[15] The event was organized by Uganda Jubilee Network a loose coalition of Christian leaders, Pastors and organisations together with the Covenant Nations Church (whose pastor is the President's daughter).

> Father God in heaven, today we stand here as Ugandans, to thank you for Uganda. We are proud that we are Ugandans and Africans. We thank you for all your goodness to us. I stand here today to close the evil spiritual past and especially in the last fifty years of our national leadership history and at the threshold of a new dispensation in the life of this nation.
>
> I stand here on my own behalf and on behalf of our past leaders to repent. We ask for your forgiveness for our own sins, and those of our past leaders. We confess these sins, which have greatly hampered our national cohesion and delayed our political, social and economic transformation: sins of idolatry and witchcraft, so rampant in our land; sins of shedding innocent blood; sins of political hypocrisy, dishonesty, intrigue and betrayal; sins of pride, tribalism and sectarianism; sins of laziness, indifference and irresponsibility; sins of corruption and bribery that have eroded our national resources; sins of sexual immorality, drunkenness and debauchery; sins of un-forgiveness, bitterness, hatred and revenge; sins of injustice, oppression and exploitation; sins of rebellion, insubordination, strife and conflict.
>
> These and many others have characterised our past leadership, especially the last fifty years of our history. Lord, forgive us, and give us a new beginning. Give us a heart to love you, to fear you and to seek you. Remove far from us all the above sins. We pray for national unity. Unite us as Ugandans and eliminate all forms of conflict, sectarianism and tribalism. Help us to see that we are all your children, children of the same Father; help us to love and respect one another and to appreciate unity in diversity.
>
> We pray for prosperity and transformation. Deliver us from ignorance, poverty and disease. As leaders, give us wisdom to help lead our people into political, social and economic transformation. We want to dedicate this nation to you so that you will be our God and guide. We want Uganda to be known as a nation that fears God, a nation whose foundations are firmly rooted in righteousness and justice.
>
> Blessed is the nation whose God is the Lord – a people you have chosen as your own (Ps. 33:12). I renounce all the evil foundations and covenants that were laid in idolatry and witchcraft. I renounce all the satanic influence in this nation. And I hereby covenant Uganda to you, to walk in your ways and experience all your blessing for ever. In the Name of the Father, the Son and the Holy Spirit, Amen.

The above prayers said by President Museveni, a politician with the background of the influence of the Revival Movement, show the hard facts of political leadership and the real content of daily life that politicians and Christian leaders deal with in East Africa. Although this prayer also acknowledges the significance of Christianity as lived by politicians, some Christian politicians in East Africa have used texts such as Proverbs 11:10 which state that 'when the righteous prosper, the city rejoices'. But in this prayer the president used the Scripture from Psalm 33:12: 'Blessed is the nation whose God is the Lord. A people you have chosen as your own.' It is helpful to understand the President's prayer within the broader socio-political historical context of Uganda. It reinforces the significance of the question as to what place Christianity and daily living has done or used to do in East Africa, in structuring political power.

Furthermore, the fact that the President prayed it on the eve of the celebration of Uganda's Independence Jubilee that was organized by a section of the religious community – including a section of the Christian community – in Uganda highlights the interplay between politics and Christianity in Uganda today. As much as the interplay between politics and Christianity is very real in the case of Uganda, the same is true in the rest of East Africa. And the content of the prayer by President Museveni – notably, the cleansing of the 'evil spiritual past and especially in the last fifty years of our national leadership history and at the threshold of a new dispensation in the life of this nation', is quite telling: the evils mentioned – and not mentioned; and the acknowledgement that Uganda is faced with a transition which is familiar all over East Africa.

Christianity in the Market-place

Across the different major Christian denominations in East Africa, there are Christian institutions as well as Christian men and women motivated by a desire to be Christ's representatives in the market-place of higher education as well as business as forms of Christian mission. They are pitched in doing business in a missional way: bringing the gospel to bear in their working life. The institutions of the major denominations include Kenyatta Methodist University, Kenya; Catholic University of East Africa, Kenya; St Paul's University, Kenya; the Lutheran University of Tumaini University, Tanzania; Uganda Pentecostal University, Uganda; and Uganda Christian University (UCU), Uganda, among others.

In 1997, the Anglican Church in Uganda founded Uganda Christian University. Our founding Vice-Chancellor, Prof Stephen Noll, writing on 'Higher Education as Mission: The Case of Uganda Christian University' observed that the university as a tool for mission in the hands of the Church of Uganda would be 'an authentically Christian university, not only in name but in substance'.[16] This meant two things which rings true across all Christian institutions of the different denominations spread across East Africa. First, it exposed an obvious need of the denominations to continue in actively spreading the gospel in the modern context of East Africa through higher education. Scholars in the region agree that this pattern is on the rise. One such Anglican priest-turned-academic and university administrator is James Kombo of Kenya.[17] In his article, 'The Past and Presence of Christian Theology in African Universities', he observed that much as Christianity in Africa is on the rise, it must 'embrace creativity and innovation in theological education, while avoiding the mistakes of North America and Europe, and incorporating some of the best practices in modern universities'.[18] Although his observation was made of Africa generally, whilst living and practising in East Africa, Kombo's observation makes perfect sense in East Africa for the different denominations involved in spreading Christian education at university, and not just theological education. Christian education has become increasingly popular in East Africa. The different denominations have realized that this precious way of education is not to be eschewed in their institutions if they are to remain representatives for Jesus Christ in the market-place.

Secondly, it means that for a market-place like UCU, morning devotions and community prayers are held twice during the week in the university. In doing this, the Christian denominations are continuing for students and employees from a Christian background a natural activity for the different issues in life that Christianity addresses through worship and biblical teaching. Moreover, for people who have no Christian background, both students and employees, a new Christian foundation is laid. At some of the Christian institutions, employees are requested to fast and pray for their institution once every semester to avoid losses and or bankruptcies in the case of Christian corporations.[19] Often spiritual reasons are given for the success or failure of these institutions. Besides the institutions above, there are Christian companies with branches spread across East Africa. One such company working largely with churches in the region is the Equity Bank. Their business is run on Christian principles. Besides a manager, the company has appointed a bishop as a spiritual overseer for the life of the organization. Their spiritual activities are run just as they

---

[16] Stephen Noll, 'Higher Education as Mission: The Case of Uganda Christian University': 913-918, 913, in Isabel Apawo Phiri and Dietrich Werner (eds), *A Handbook of Theological Education in Africa*, Dorpspruit, South Africa: Cluster Publications, 2013.

[17] Professor James Kombo is Deputy Vice Chancellor Academic Affairs at Daystar University, Nairobi, Kenya; currently he is our External Examiner in the Bishop Tucker School of Divinity and Theology. But he is also an Ordained Anglican Priest in the Anglican Church of Kenya.

[18] James Kombo, 'The Past and Presence of Christian Theology in African Universities': 100-107, 107, in Isabel Apawo Phiri and Dietrich Werner (eds), *A Handbook of Theological Education in Africa*, Dorpspruit, South Africa: Cluster Publications, 2013.

[19] A day of prayer and fasting for the University is fixed on the Semester Rotas. The theme of the prayers is simply: prayer and fasting as taught in the Bible.

would be in church and other sacred places. In doing so, they remain on course as representing Jesus Christ in the market-place in East Africa.

Changing Indigenous Cultural Practices

On the cultural front, the rise of Christianity in East Africa has also changed the landscape significantly. It has fast-tracked a culture that was already religious into become something even more recognizably so. It has, however, controlled the religious zeal in ways that directed and transformed people's spiritual energies according to the message from God as revealed in Christian tradition. Now, instead of consulting the diviner in times of drought, sickness or natural calamity, Christians, led by their politicians, fill a national stadium to pray to the Christian God for answers to such issues. Many believe that this Christian God was with them in East Africa before the missionaries came and introduced Christianity. The language they use to name their children, especially among the brethren in the East African Revival, are imported from Christianity.[20]

As the culture itself became more Christian, many of the traditions that were seen as secular in East Africa have been reclothed in a Christian outfit - or have simply disappeared. For instance, in the northern part of Uganda, in the area covered by the Anglican dioceses of Lango and of West Lango, the traditional initiation rite – called *Kayo cogo* – used to prepare newly married young women into a new clan, have totally disappeared in the late 1990s.[21] This tradition was central to the process of gaining acceptance in the clan (among the Langi of Uganda) when a woman is married, but Christians in the 1980s and the 1990s publicly rejected the practice, preaching against it and calling it a pagan and secular tradition that was not sanctioned by biblical teaching. The Revival sects, *Gwara* (Trumpeters) and *Nico* (Re-awakened) in the diocese (at that time, the Diocese of Lango), continued preaching against it and members of these sects would not eat in the homes of anyone who openly condoned it, causing tension in families until the practice disappeared.

With the general picture of Christianity in East Africa, we now turn to look broadly at the nature and shape of Christianity in the three major streams of Christianity in t region.

Mainline Denominations

Within the mainline denominations, as elsewhere in Africa,[22] at the heart of the churches there lies the Christian message: the gospel is public and relevant to the individual as well as to society. Given that the Christian message is ever-expanding across the different denominations since the missionary era, it is an indication in part of its coming of age in East Africa. This is precisely what is happening in the mainline denominations. It is also remarkable that new congregations emerge every week, and there are numerous changes of names and relocation of places of worship. Why? A key reason for the emergence of new

[20] See Manuel Muranga, 'The Revival's Impact on the Naming Traditions of the Peoples of East Africa, with Special Reference to Kigezi and Ankole': 65-80, in William Rukirande, Joan Hall, Zabuloni Kabaza, Elisabeth Traill, Apolo Nsibambi, Medard Birungi, Manuel Muranga, Medard Rugyendo, *The East African Revival Through Seventy Years (1935-2005)* Kampala, Uganda: Logik Media, 2005.

[21] At the funeral of the late Muzee Aleny Ketitic, Aboke, Kole district Bishop Melchizedek Otim while officiating at the funeral was challenged by one of the tradition clan leaders in Lango, lamenting the Christianity in the diocese has wiped out the traditional rite: *Kayo cogo*! Kayo cogo is a primitive cultural practice where newly married woman is ushered into the clan of her husband. She is made to sit naked on a cow that all the legs are tied together until the cow is dead. There is great celebration at the occasion.

[22] See Chapter 10, 'The East African Revival', 169-188, in Mark Noll, *The New Shape of World Christianity: How American Experience Reflects Global Faith*, Downers Grove: IVP Academic, 2009.

congregations every week and for the relocation of worship place is partly the rapid growth of the Christian faith. Growth comes with some changes and some pain.

The growth in the mainline denominations is directly linked with leadership and the working of the Holy Spirit. Leadership in the mainline denominations has become predominantly non-white, especially in the Anglican Church, Africa Inland Church, the Baptist Church, and even in the Catholic Church as it is fast becoming less dominated by foreign ministers. Closely connected with leadership in the mainline churches is denominational management. Denominationally, Christianity in East Africa has become indigenised. We may illustrate this with the benefit of hindsight in the history of Uganda when Bishop Alfred Tucker came in 1913 to offer leadership to the local Anglican church. At the outset of his ministry, Tucker proposed to set up a theological college at Namirembe to train Ugandans to lead the church. Tucker's vision became a reality as observed by scholars who studied the work of local Christians in the mainline churches. Among these scholars are Louis Pirouette who referred to the native peoples as 'Black Evangelists'.[23] Pirouette took great care to show how Christianity in the mainline churches in Uganda had been carried forward at great personal cost to the native peoples who were converted to Christianity.

This dedication is true, not only of the mainline churches in Uganda but across East Africa. And, in the early 1970s, a Ugandan historian-turned-developer and priest, Tom Tuma, produced a work that gave credit to the Basoga Catechist.[24] However, there was a second reason why early missionaries like Bishop Tucker supported the work of the native peoples in spreading the gospel: the high mortality rates among the missionaries. Once the native peoples led the mainline churches, the churches across the different denominations have learned to support themselves financially. A good example is the Lutheran church in Tanzania which was a real success story. Nearly every Sunday together with worship there is fund-raising in every church in order to sustain and grow church activities.

Pentecostals and Charismatic Churches

One of the features of Christianity in East Africa is the face of Pentecostalism. Pentecostalism in East Africa is charismatic in its nature. The Pentecostal church churches in East Africa is growing fast, a characteristic not unique to East African Christianity but true all over Africa. This has become increasingly so since the 1990s. The Pentecostal churches in East Africa date back to the late 1800s but for many reasons they really took off in the 1970s. Pentecostalism is now at the heart of church growth of Christianity in East Africa. What are the reasons for this? The worldviews of Africans that comprehend the spirit world and how it influences daily life are part of this. Bishop Festo Kivengere of Uganda, perhaps the greatest evangelist from that country in the twentieth century tells in his 'Testimony' of how he worshipped God through the agents of the spirits of his dead ancestors before his conversion to Christianity:

> Being the firstborn, my father introduced me to this worship very early. He taught me by example. He took me to the worship. We sacrificed together. And yet we never found that god… He remained a distant god – someone too far to help you when you needed him. That is where I grew.[25]

---

[23] Louis Pirouette, *Black Evangelist* (Yet to complete the citation)

[24] The Rev Canon Dr Tom Tuma taught history at Makerere University after graduating with a PhD in history from the London School of Oriental studies. Later he became Ordained and worked as Co-ordinator of Planning, Development, and Rehabilitation Officer of the Church of Uganda. He is a priest of Busoga Diocese.

[25] Festo Kivengere, 'Testimony'. Pages 416-417 in *Let the Earth Hear His Voice: Official Reference Volume, Papers and Responses*. Edited by J. D Douglas Minneapolis: World Wide Publications, 1975.

This telling testimony, seemingly so far from biblical Christianity, includes the religious background that influenced his conversion and belief in the Christian God. Later, in an interview with his biographer, Anne Coomes, he confessed that belief in the Christian God was a settled matter, but the real problem was found in the question: 'How can we know him?' Indeed, the worldview in which he was raised facilitated his understanding of the Christian God. This was nothing unique to Kivengere: it is common to all Africans – including East Africans!

Additionally, any expression of the gospel that embraces the manifestation of the power of the Holy Spirit connects immediately with the spirit-centred culture of the African people and their traditional religions.[26] In 2010, Todd Johnson, Kenneth Ross and Sandra Lee, in their book, *Atlas of Global Christianity, 1910-2010*, indicate that Pentecostals, not only in East Africa, but also all over Africa are still growing rapidly.[27] Indeed, when charismatic Christians are placed together with the Pentecostals, then their numbers are significant. A striking feature of the Pentecostal movement in East Africa today is this: when you move in the region, it is hard to find aspects of society that are not touched by it. For example, all over in Uganda, you find radio ministries, healing programmes, and now there is a move to capture power in the region!

In Tanzania, a Pentecostal pastor proudly told me: 'If the mainline churches cannot get rid of the Pentecostals, then just work with them.' This is not perhaps the view of the Pentecostal church but the expression of an attitude from within the Pentecostal movement towards the mainline churches. A closer look at the profile of the Pentecostals reveals its attraction for the young, educated and enterprising affluent classes in urban society. In Uganda today, this class of urban Pentecostals enjoys a great sense of influence in the nation.

In East Africa, the *Balokole* ('saved ones') as well as the Pentecostals have enjoyed the missionary trait of the East African Revival brethren, which itself has links with the missionary traits of the Keswick movement of the 1870s. A good example of this is found in Kivengere's style of preaching in which he combines in one sermon what the Keswick leaders would preach in a week at their conference, and on the last day they preach and make an appeal for believers to reach out in mission.[28] They preach the gospel with a sense of urgency and spread it from 'everywhere to everywhere'.[29] They explicitly believe in the work of the Holy Spirit in individuals and communities. According to them, God can speak to any individual who is following the lead of the Holy Spirit by opening him or her to spreading their faith all over East Africa. Their theology assures them that the Holy Spirit can use anyone to do missionary work as long as they have the calling of God.

But more striking are their eschatological convictions of the immanent rapture and tribulation, judgement and hell, which make it imperative for them to reach the world and to bring salvation to many. I have heard heated debates in my preaching classes,[30] drawing students from all over East Africa. One Pentecostal pastor expressing that 'he is living on bonus time' and so, like Richard Baxter, said, 'I preach like a dying man to dying men'. At which, another from Tanzania shot back, 'I have preached throughout overnight prayers and I "lost his voice" because I am living in the end times.' These heated conversations

[26] Harvey C. Kwiyani, 'The Holy Spirit in African Theology', *Transformed* 1, no. 1 (2001).

[27] Todd M Johnson, Kenneth R. Ross, and Sandra S. K. Lee, *Atlas of Global Christianity, 1910-2010* (Edinburgh: Edinburgh University Press, 20019), 110-11.

[28] Alfred Olwa, *Missionary of Reconciliation: The Role of the Doctrine of Reconciliation in the Preaching of Festo Kivengere of Uganda between 1971-1988,* Carlisle: Cumbria: 2013, 100-101.

[29] The expression is my critical appreciation of Michael Nazir Ali, *Mission is From Every Where to Every where.*

[30] I teach Homiletics, Evangelism, and Christian Communication to BD2 and Master of Divinity 2; and, Expository Preaching to Doctor of Ministry. The profile of the preaching classes is a broad range of students coming from different Christian denominations. However, the majority are Anglicans.

made the class lively! But these attitudes lie behind their missionary convictions that have brought about much outreach and enabled their churches to grow.

While interacting with my theology students in our discipleship group,[31] a fascinating feature has been the observation that there are Pentecostal pastors who from their background have no experience of the mainline churches. Their experiences are different, especially those who have converted to Christianity in the late 1980s and worked with the Miracle Centre in Kampala. They have found it difficult to stay in the mainline churches and live out their faith but, interestingly, often at the end of their BD course, they have still sought ordination within the Anglican Church and then have brought about a great transformation in their ministry to young people.

Pentecostal and Charismatic churches are used to freedom in worship – long praise and worship songs, loud singing, spontaneity and long sermons; they have coined a name for 15-minute sermons: *amala*, a kind of appetizer! Of course, this hunger for the word is not found only in Pentecostal churches. At St Francis Chapel at Makerere University, I once preached a 15-minute sermon under the strict supervision of my English tutor and I was challenged by a Christian physics professor for a short sermon: a ten-minute sermon is like a period for kindergartens whose concentration span is short. We are adults. Don't starve us!

Moreover, Pentecostals and Charismatics find it difficult to settle under the structured leadership of the mainline churches. The spirituality of these faithful ones is shaped by the word of God. Jesus is their Lord and Saviour and Friend who they commune with daily. Their pastors are referred to by expressions like 'man of God' or 'woman of God', and they speak prophetically into the situation and lives of individuals. Prayer with passion and fervour is central to their ministry and way of life. However, their understanding of prophecy in the sense of *forth*telling and *fore*telling is incomplete. They tend to emphasize *fore*telling rather than *forth*telling. In most of the Pentecostal churches in East Africa, 'feeling welcome', 'feeling appreciated', 'feeling loved' and 'feeling at home' are expressions commonly used and are also the reason why Pentecostals prefer to stick with their Pentecostal churches when they visit or move from one place to another in East Africa.

African Instituted Churches

'African instituted churches' in East Africa are known variously as African 'independent' churches or African 'initiated' churches. A closer look at the etymology of the terms describing these churches reveal some degree of ambiguity. For instance, the terms 'instituted', 'initiated' and 'independent', when used in a broad sense, may also refer to the numerous Pentecostal and Charismatic churches of East Africa.[32] However, here we take only a brief look at a few AICs. These are native spiritual churches spread all over East Africa but founded by foretelling and far-sighted spiritual leaders.

In their practice of Christianity, AICs depict a spirit-filled style of worship combined with a strong emphasis on the show of spiritual power of their leaders in the form of miraculous healing and exorcisms. Within East Africa, especially in the mainline churches, they are branded as syncretistic, as sects or cults. However, this perception is considered negative in the eyes of AICs. For the AICs, they are very much part

[31] See Alfred Olwa, 'Discipleship Groups: Philosophy and Purpose in the Context of Bishop Tucker School of Divinity and Theology Training': 1-4, presented to the Bishop Tucker School of Divinity and Theology, Easter Semester 2014. Unpublished paper.

[32] The list of Pentecostal and Independent Churches in East Africa, see Barrett, *Kenya Churches Handbook: The Development of Kenya Christianity 1498-1973*, Kisumu, Kenya: Evangel Publishing House.

of the Christian church. Why? They can only explain their argument in terms of their defence of Jesus Christ.[33]

Members of AICs largely often be recognized by their dress code: usually a long white *sultana* robe accompanied by sandals. Although in the rural areas, due to their poverty, most people walk barefoot, it has become a general for most members of AICs in rural areas to go without shoes. And most of their men wear beards. In East Africa, the most numerous and most popular AICs are to be found in Kenya. Among these is the Celestial Church (Kenya) which is also found throughout East Africa. The Aladura type of AICs has transformed itself from being seen as a quasi-spiritual sub-group to being a vibrant Christian church accepted by World Council of Churches. A good example of this is the Redeemed Christian Church of God.

Their denomination's charismatic founders also know most AICs for their firm loyalty. This loyalty – some argue – sometimes seems to supersede even their commitment to Jesus Christ. For instance, in Gulu in Northern Uganda, there is an AIC called Evangelist Yustu Otunu's Chosen Evangelical Revival (CER), with branches in Lango, Teso, Masindi, Hoima, Mukono, Tororo, West Nile, South Sudan (Kejokeji) and Kitgum. As its founder, this evangelist led the denomination until his death in exile in the USA.[34] His followers know him as their father (Baba/Daddy) and follow him with undivided loyalty. When he went to their monthly fellowship gathering, he would be carried shoulder-high and not allowed to walk, and would be accompanied with drumming and praise songs. According to Lead Ejon, renowned lay evangelist, the title 'Baba' defines his role as their spiritual father, leader and teacher of everything for the denomination. Unlike other AICs denominations, he had deputies or assistants, while women also shared in leadership.

With the opening up of increasingly better transport facilities and business opportunities in East Africa, AICs of this nature are fast multiplying all over the region and beyond its immediate hinterland. Most AICs in East Africa originate in Kenya and have most of their headquarters there. AICs in Uganda have opened congregations in Congo. But most AICs find themselves at odds with missionary Christianity. Why? Their theologies and practices reflect strong influence by the same African culture that the missionaries of the nineteenth century worked hard to evangelize.

Consequently, traditional churches in East Africa are suspicious of them. A striking feature of AICs that hold them back include worship styles involving massive celebration with dancing, loud music and speaking immense volumes of words in a short time. Their dress code resembles Muslim dress: the *sultans* and the *kaftans*. The Chosen Evangelical Revival (CER) are so focused on evangelising everyone that they do not think of themselves as citizens of one place but simply as Children of God (*Otino Obanga*). John Kamdini, a leader of CER in Lango, believes that the entire world is their mission field, which they need to evangelize faithfully, irrespective of where they are; and so they carry trumpets made out of old cooking oil tin, flattened and moulded in the shape of a trumpet (*Gwara*), and preach to any group of people. However, this urgent missionary mindset does not bear fruit: fruit that lasts. This is because of their method and also because of how they live out their faith, especially in relating to youth.

The presence and growth of AICs in East Africa has thrived on deep allegiance to their founder-leaders and their charismatic leadership. It has also thrived under the umbrella of the explosive growth and spread of Christianity in the region. How long will this growth last? It is hard to tell for many reasons. However, our projection for the immediate future is hopeful. Since Christianity in East Africa is no longer a white

---

[33] See Olupona and Gemingnani, *African Immigrant Religion*, 107. Allan Anderson, *African Reformation: African Initiated Christianity in the 20th Century* (Trenton, NJ: Africa World Press, 2001). Allan Anderson, *Moya: The Holy Spirit in An African Context*, Manuala Didactica 13 (Pretoria: University of South Africa, 1991).

[34] George Piwang, Archbishop Janani Luwum martyrdom and Biography: A Political Theology of Peace, Justice Healing and Reconciliation in Uganda & The Great Lakes Region', pages 15-16, a Unpublished paper delivered at the East Africa and Burundi Annual Conferences of the united Methodist church meeting in Mukono, Uganda, 26th-29th August 2014.

man's religion, as is argued by Kwame Bediako in his book, *Christianity in Africa: The Renewal of Non-Western Religion,*[35] the impact of African Christianity in East Africa will need careful attention.

AICs in East Africa are a phenomenon linked with the resistance to colonization and decolonization as hinted earlier in the section on the historical development of Christianity in East Africa. AICs have had little to do with the traditional churches of East Africa. Their growth is largely the work of God. However, since the AICs are founded by native peoples and they seem likely to be around for the foreseeable future, traditional churches will do well to recognize them. Will they fully recognize them as of God's making? If the growth and spread of AICs continue, Christianity will increasingly become a non-western religion in East Africa. But one serious question remains for the AICs to reckon with before they are accepted by the traditional churches is how to overcome their low theological profile and biblical depth, both in the leadership and among their congregations. John Njeru Gichimu, writing on 'Theological Education in African Independent Churches in East Africa' observed that 'from 2000, a number of AICs have attempted to start theology training programmes', adding: 'However, most of these churches have been struggling with registrations of their institution.'[36] He is spot on with the need for AICs to increase the depth of theological education for their leaders, and hence their Christians. It seems risky to belong to a church with little or no theological depth.

Ecumenism

In East Africa, ecumenical relations have remained very significant. However, in this section we give only a brief survey of Ecumenism. The work of Stephen Candia, 'East African Contribution to the Ecumenical Movement: A Catholic Perspective', is a survey of the historical attempts made in Eastern Africa to foster Christian unity, especially from the Catholic point of view.[37] However, within the Pentecostal denominations, there seems to be at a national level in each of the East African countries, an ecumenical body that brings them together; yet at the grassroots much work is still to be done on this front to make it real.

For many years, the mainline denominations have formed joint Ecumenical Councils. In Uganda, there is the Uganda Joint Christian Council formed in 1963, in Kenya there is Kenya National Council of Churches, and in Tanzania there is the Tanzania Council of Churches. These denominations have formed joint councils against a background of religious diversity in their respective countries. In Uganda, there was some inappropriate teaching on guilt that discouraged joint ecumenical meetings. This mentality has discouraged Christians to maintain proper ecumenical relations and even in other East African countries is responsible for some bloody religious wars in our history. However, on a positive note, lately there have been some improvements concerning good ecumenical relations. In 1963, the Church of Uganda, along with the Catholic and Orthodox Churches, founded the Uganda Joint Christian Council. This Council provided some excellent services in the areas of education, health care, Bible translation and distribution, printing presses and local relations, and has also monitored national elections and provided civic education for the masses.

In Tanzania, the Tanganyika Missionary Council was formed in 1936, which made possible co-operation among the denominations. In 1948, it became the Christian Council of Tanganyika and in 1964 was renamed the Christian Council of Tanzania. Members include the Lutherans, Anglicans, Monrovians, Salvation Army and the Baptists. In the 1960s, conversations were held for the unification of

---

[35] Kwame Bediako, *Christianity in Africa: The Renewal of Non-Western Religion* (*Studies in World Christianity*, Edinburgh: Edinburgh University Press, 1995.

[36] John Njeru Gichimu, *Theological Education in African Independent Churches in East Africa*, 420-422.

[37] Stephen Candia, *East African Contribution to the Ecumenical Movement: A Catholic Perspective* (Peter Lang, 2004).

the churches but in 1968 it failed. Despite this negative picture, the Roman Catholic Church has established good contacts with the various Protestant churches. A good example of inter-confessional co-operation is the shared leadership of religious broadcasting.

Additionally, there is an agreed curriculum for religious teaching in schools. And, at large religious celebrations, there are shared services of worship. President Julius Kambarage Nyerere (1964-85), Tanzania's first President after independence and an active Catholic, mediated for the churches. The Education Act of 1969, which gave the government of Tanzania oversight of all schools, was the result of an upturn in ecumenical co-operation in Tanzania. The bishops' conference meets frequently to discuss matters of mutual interest. Moreover, ecumenical co-operation in Tanzania is even visible at the level of village congregations.[38]

The Pentecostal denominations across East Africa have also come together in ecumenical co-operation. In Uganda, they have celebrated over fifty years of the Association of Pentecostal Churches in Uganda. This co-operation is true of the other East African countries. There also is the Interreligious Council of Uganda, which includes Muslim representatives. The Interreligious Council brings together the different religious groups in matters of politics, education seminars and discussions of topical issues like the absence of peace in a region. Interreligious Councils are determined to bring unity, peace and harmony to the people of God in East Africa. We project that, as time moves on, there will continue to be a positive religious presence in the region. In the universities of East Africa, study and research are done on different aspects of religion in the region. In the process, the fruits of these studies will enhance peace between the different religious groups of the region.

Conclusion

The impact of Christianity in East Africa goes far deeper than I have surveyed here. Other scholars have paid attention to some of these themes. However, we do need also to sound a note of caution that the depth of the impact of Christian faith on African society varies from place to place in East Africa. Not all cultures were open to the planting and spread of the gospel. Missionary work connected and continues to connect with the native peoples at different levels in different places through the various denominations. Nevertheless, the story of the planting and spread of Christianity in East Africa continues to be a success. In East Africa, the majority of the population now is Christian. However, it is equally important that ecumenical relations in the region are strengthened.

Bibliography

Alfred Olwa, 'Discipleship Groups: Philosophy and Purpose in the Context of Bishop Tucker School of Divinity and Theology Training': 1-4, presented to the Bishop Tucker School of Divinity and Theology, Easter Semester 2014. Unpublished paper.

______. *Missionary of Reconciliation: The Role of the Doctrine of Reconciliation in the Preaching of Festo Kivengere of Uganda between 1971-1988*, Carlisle: Cumbria: 2013.

Allan Anderson, Moya: *The Holy Spirit in An African Context*, Manuala Didactica 13, Pretoria: University of South Africa, 1991.

Andrew F. Walls, *The Cross-Cultural Process in Christian History* (Maryknoll, N.Y: Oribs Books, 2002).

Barrett, *Kenya Churches Handbook: The Development of Kenya Christianity 1948-1974*, Kisumu: Evangel

[38] At Kerekekere, Bunda, Tanzania, November 2014, I went to supervise a student on Block Placement, Rev Johannes Mark Onyango. The village churches located in the same school, Pentecostal Assembly of God and Methodist Church invited me to go and preach in their churches soon after preaching at the Anglican Church. There was a clear sense of Ecumenism among the churches at village level.

Publishing House, 1973.
Philomena N. Mwaura of Kenyatta University, assisted by Rev. Bernard Nyabwari, in Dictionary of African Christian Biography, www.dacb.org/history/aics-kenya.htmi. Accessed 18 March 2015.
Festo Kivengere, 'Testimony'. Pages 416-417 in J. D Douglas, ed., *Let the Earth Hear His Voice: Official Reference Volume, Papers and Responses*, Minneapolis: World Wide Publications, 1975.
G. S. P. Freeman-Grenville, *The Mombasa Rising Against the Portuguese, 1631*, Oxford: Oxford University Press, 1980.
H. Maynard Smith, Frank, *Bishop of Zanzibar*, London: SPCK, 1926.
Harvey C. Kwiyani, 'The Holy Spirit in African Theology', *Transformed* 1, no. 1 (2001).
James Kombo, 'The Past and Presence of Christian Theology in African Universities': 100-107, 107, in Isabel Apawo Phiri and Dietrich Werner (eds.), *A Handbook of Theological Education in Africa*, Dorpspruit, South Africa: Cluster Publications, 2013.
John Liffe, *A Modern History of Tanganyika*, Cambridge: University of Cambridge, 1979.
John Njeru Gichimu, *Theological Education in African Independent Churches in East Africa*, 420-422, in Isabel Apawo Phiri and Dietrich Werner (eds.), *A Handbook of Theological Education in Africa*, Dorpspruit, South Africa: Cluster Publications, 2013.
John S. Mbiti, *African Regions and Philosophy*, Garden City, NY: Anchor Books, 1970, 1.
Kevin Ward, 'A History of Christianity in Uganda': 81-112, in Nthamburi, Z. (ed.), *From Mission to Church*, Nairobi: Uzima, 1991
______. *A History of Global Anglicanism*, Cambridge: Cambridge University Press, 2006.
Kwame Bediako, *Christianity in Africa: The Renewal of Non-Western Religion*, Edinburgh: Edinburgh University Press, 1995.
Pirouette Louise, *Black Evangelists: The Spread of Christianity in Uganda*, Rex Collings, London, 1978.
Manuel Muranga, 'The Revival's Impact on the Naming Traditions of the Peoples of East Africa, with Special Reference to Kigezi and Ankole': 65-80, in William Rukirande, Joan Hall, Zabuloni Kabaza, Elisabeth Traill, Apolo Nsibambi, Medard Birungi, Manuel Muranga, Medard Rugyendo, *The East African Revival Through Seventy Years (1935-2005)*, Kampala, Uganda: Logik Media, 2005.
Guillebaud, Meg, *Rwanda: The Land God Forgot? Revival, Genocide and Hope*, London: Monarch, 2002.
Musana, Paddy, 'Pentecostals and Politics in Uganda', in Paddy Musana, Angus Crichton and Caroline Howell, eds., *The Ugandan Churches and Centres of Political Power: Proceedings of the First Ngoma Writers' Workshop*, 2015.
Mwita Akiri, 'The Growth of Christianity in Ugogo and Ukguru', Ph.D dissertation, University of Edinburgh, 1999.
Olupona and Gemingnani, *African Immigrant Religion*, 107, in Allan Anderson, *African Reformation: African Initiated Christianity in the 20th Century*, Trenton, NJ: Africa World Press, 2001.
Paul Gifford, *Ghana's New Christianity: Pentecostalism in a Globalizing African Economy*, Bloomington: Indiana University Press, 2004.
Philip Jenkins, *The New Christendom*, Oxford: Oxford University Press, 2001.
Ronald A. Oliver, *The Missionary Factor in East Africa*, London: Longmans, 1952.
Stephen Noll, 'Higher Education as Mission: The Case of Uganda Christian University': 913-918, in Isabel Apawo Phiri and Dietrich Werner (eds.), *A Handbook of Theological Education in Africa*, Dorpspruit, South Africa: Cluster Publications, 2013.
Todd M Johnson, Kenneth R. Ross, and Sandra S. K. Lee, *Atlas of Global Christianity, 1910-2010*, Edinburgh: Edinburgh University Press, 2009.
Tuma T. A. D and Mutibwa, *A Century of Christianity in Uganda 1877-1977*, Nairobi: Uzima Press, 1978.

(20) Christianity in Central Africa

Jean Paul Messina

Country	Religion	Pop_2010	Pct_2010	Pop_2025	Pct_2025	GrPct_1970_2025
Middle Africa	Christians	107,953,000	82.7%	170,610,000	84.2%	3.1%
Middle Africa	Independents	22,358,000	17.1%	34,802,000	17.2%	3.0%
Middle Africa	African initiated	18,547,000	14.2%			
Middle Africa	Orthodox	14,200	0.0%	18,100	0.0%	1.6%
Middle Africa	Protestants	24,482,000	18.7%	38,994,000	19.3%	3.2%
Middle Africa	Pentecostal	5,290,000	4.1%			
Middle Africa	Reformed, Presb	4,707,000	3.6%			
Middle Africa	Evangelical churches	2,354,000	1.8%			
Middle Africa	Baptist	2,174,000	1.7%			
Middle Africa	Congregational	1,627,000	1.2%			
Middle Africa	Methodist	1,614,000	1.2%			
Middle Africa	Adventist	1,599,000	1.2%			
Middle Africa	Disciples	1,089,000	0.8%			
Middle Africa	Brethren	1,056,000	0.8%			
Middle Africa	Lutheran	734,000	0.6%			
Middle Africa	Roman Catholics	60,812,000	46.6%	94,153,000	46.5%	3.0%
Middle Africa	*Pentecostals/ Charismatics*	29,897,000	22.9%	44,947,000	22.2%	2.8%
Middle Africa	*Evangelicals*	12,643,000	9.7%	18,812,000	9.3%	2.7%
Middle Africa	Muslims	12,657,000	9.7%	20,257,000	10.0%	3.2%
Middle Africa	adherents of traditional African religions	8,526,000	6.5%	9,407,000	4.6%	0.7%
Middle Africa	Baha'is	467,000	0.4%	715,000	0.4%	2.9%
Middle Africa	Hindus	94,000	0.1%	151,000	0.1%	3.2%
Middle Africa	adherents of new religious movements	43,600	0.0%	56,200	0.0%	1.7%
Middle Africa	Buddhists	7,500	0.0%	12,500	0.0%	3.5%
Middle Africa	Chinese folk religionists	5,000	0.0%	6,700	0.0%	2.0%
Middle Africa	Jews	430	0.0%	500	0.0%	1.1%
Middle Africa	people professing no religion	845,000	0.6%	1,318,000	0.7%	3.0%
Middle Africa	**Total population**	**130,598,000**	**100.0%**	**202,533,000**	**100.0%**	**3.0%**

Source: Centre for the Study of World Christianity (CSGC), Boston, Gordon-Conwell TS

Contexte

Du point de vue géographique, l'Afrique centrale comprend le Tchad, le Cameroun, la République Centrafricaine, le Congo-Brazzaville, le Gabon, la Guinée Equatoriale, Sao-Tomé et Principe. Cet espace géographique couvre une superficie de 1 152 936 km² pour une population estimée à 40 966 201 habitants.

Cette population est essentiellement composée des Bantou, sauf pour le Tchad où les Soudano-nilotiques sont majoritaires. Dans l'ensemble de cette sous-région, le taux l'urbanisation se situe entre 30 et 40%. Et les villes se *cosmopolitisent* à cause d'une part, du phénomène l'exode rural, et d'autre part, de l'activité économique qui a tendance à se diversifier dans les secteurs secondaire et tertiaire et qui, parle fait même, attire la main d'œuvre des l'arrière-pays et des pays voisins. La ville, en Afrique centrale, est le lieu de brassage d'une nouvelle culture où la religion joue un rôle prépondérant. Bien plus, la ville ici, du fait de ses fonctions politico-administratives, est le point de rencontre des personnes issues des différentes ethnies des pays concernés. Libreville, Brazzaville, Bangui, Yaoundé, Douala, Malabo, pour ne citer que ces grandes cités, ont perdu leur identité traditionnelle et se présentent aujourd'hui comme des espaces multiculturels et multi-religieux. La population étrangère est généralement constituée des ressortissants des anciennes métropoles coloniales qui, pour des raisons économiques, ont obtenu le statut de résident. Dans les pays francophones à savoir le Tchad, la Centrafrique, le Cameroun, le Congo-Brazzaville et le Gabon: ces étrangers sont essentiellement des Français. En Guinée Equatoriale, on trouve majoritairement des Espagnols; et à Sao Tomé et Principe, des Portugais. Au demeurant on rencontre un peu partout des commerçants libanais et d'avantage des Chinois qui, en plus du commerce, ont tendance à s'orienter vers les Affaires, dont le bâtiment et la construction des infrastructures de communication.

Du point de vue religieux, on rencontre en Afrique centrale trois principaux groupes, à savoir les Religions Traditionnelles Africaines (RTA), l'islam et le christianisme dans ses variantes confessionnelles. Des infiltrations des cercles ésotériques et initiatiques sont de plus en plus observées dans les centres urbains où on parle des Rose-croix, de la Franc-maçonnerie et d'autres mouvements du genre. Bénéficiant d'un cadre juridique qui préconise la liberté religieuse et de conscience, la religion est au cœur de l'activité de l'homme, et on assiste à un phénomène de démultiplication qui rend de plus en plus complexe le paysage religieux en Afrique centrale. Au sein du christianisme, cette démultiplication est encore plus forte au point que, pour certains observateurs, il serait plus convenable de parler des christianismes en lieu et place du christianisme.

Le Christianisme en Afrique Centrale

En parlant du christianisme comme religion, l'attention ici est portée sur les Églises protestantes, l'Église catholique, l'Église orthodoxe et les nouvelles Églises dites de réveil.

D'une manière générale, le christianisme en Afrique centrale compte 25 993 188 fidèles pour une population de 40 966 201 habitants, soit un pourcentage de 64%. Le christianisme est donc la religion de la majorité des habitants de cette sous-région d'Afrique. La répartition par pays est la suivante:[1]

Pays	Population	Chrétiens	Pourcentage Total
Cameroun	19 522 000	13 655 000 Catholiques: 39% Protestants: 26%	70%
Centrafrique	4 422 000	3 550 866 Catholiques: 29% Protestants et autres: 51%	80,3%

[1] Voir J.P. Messina, Archives privées- 1990 – 2010, Yaoundé.

Congo Brazzaville	3 683 000	3 163 697 Catholiques: 48% Protestants et autres: 38%	85,9%
Gabon	1 389 201	100 225	72%
Guinée Equatoriale	676 000	667 000 Catholiques: 95% Protestants: 3,6%	98,6%
Tchad	11 274 000	3 946 000 Catholiques: 20% Protestants: 15%	35%
Sao Tomé et Principe	160 000	121 931 Catholiques: 80% Protestants: 10%	88,4%

Histoire de l'Évangélisation de l'Afrique Centrale

Le pays le plus anciennement touché par le christianisme est Sao Tomé et Principe, marqué de longue date par la colonisation portugaise. L'histoire de l'évangélisation de Sao Tomé et principe est associée à la grande aventure portugaise qui a conduit à la christianisation de l'ancien royaume du Kongo aux Temps Modernes, à partir du *patroado* que Rome avant concédé au roi du Portugal. Sao Tomé (Saint Thomas) est une île découverte par le Portugal, probablement le 21 décembre 1470 (fête de saint Thomas). La Mission portugaise à Sao Tomé est liée au siège épiscopal de Funchal, érigée dans l'île de Madère en 1514.

En 1534, Sao Tomé se détache de Funchal et devient, dans le Golfe de Guinée, le «centre ecclésiastique le plus important».[2] En effet, depuis 1534, un évêque y réside et Sao Tomé se présente déjà à cette période comme un diocèse. La population noire est alors majoritairement constituée d'esclaves convertis au christianisme.

La position névralgique de Sao Tomé et Principe se perd avec la découverte de Luanda qui, à partir du XVIIe siècle, est devenu le port privilégié de la côte occidentale d'Afrique en direction du Brésil. Le siège épiscopal, le plus ancien au Sud du Sahara, passe alors sous contrôle de Luanda et ne sera rétabli à Sao Tomé et Principe qu'en 1984. Aux XIXe et XXe siècles, les missionnaires clarétains ont assuré l'évangélisation du pays. Mais le siège épiscopal sera occupé par un évêque spiritain d'origine portugaise. La colonisation portugaise, la plus longue et la plus sévère en Afrique prend fin à Sao Tomé et Principe en 1975. Depuis 1984, le diocèse de Sao Tomé fait partie de la Conférence Episcopale d'Angola. Les chrétiens de Sao Tomé sont encore marqués par les blessures de l'esclavage et de la colonisation portugaise.

La Mission protestante est introduite à Sao Tomé à partir de l'Angola au cours de la première moitié du XXe siècle. Les protestants sont encore ici très minoritaires.

Le Gabon

Le Gabon est le pays francophone d'Afrique centrale le plus anciennement évangélisé au XIXe siècle. Les missionnaires protestants y arrivent en 1842, dans le cadre de la lutte contre la Traite des Noirs. Parmi ceux-ci, il y a les Presbytériens Américains. À partir du Gabon, la Mission Presbytérienne Américaine va gagner l'île de Corisco en Guinée Equatoriale (en 1847). Les Presbytériens s'établissent en 1865 à Baraka, au Gabon. Ceux de Corisco s'associent à eux en 1871 pour constituer une seule Mission Presbytérienne. Avant cette fusion, les missionnaires Presbytériens arrivent en 1866 au Sud-Cameroun, venant de l'île de Corisco. Au XIXe siècle, l'action missionnaire presbytérienne est triangulaire. Elle est à cheval sur trois pays: la Guinée Equatoriale (Corisco), le Gabon septentrional et le Sud-Cameroun.

[2] J. Baur, *2000 de christianisme en Afrique une histoire de l'Église africaine,* Kinshasa, 2001, 46.

La Mission catholique pénètre au Gabon dans le cadre du vicariat des Deux Guinées, érigé le 28 septembre 1842 et confié à Mgr Edward Barron. Ce vicariat qui s'étendait du fleuve Sénégal au fleuve Orange, le long de la côte Atlantique sur près de 8000 km, n'avait pas de frontières précises. Face aux difficultés que vont rencontrer la dizaine des missionnaires spiritains mis à la disposition de ce vicariat en Afrique de l'Ouest, à Cape Palmas notamment, le Père Jean Bessieux se rend au Gabon où il crée, en 1844, la Mission Sainte Marie, à côté d'un petit port militaire français qui prendra le nom de Libreville. Cette Mission Sainte Marie desservait à la fois la côte gabonaise et la côté camerounaise. Mais la Mission ne réussit pas à toucher la côte camerounaise. En 1863, la Mission Sainte Marie est érigée en vicariat apostolique du Gabon et sa juridiction s'étendait toujours sur la côte camerounaise sans pour autant que les missionnaires puissent s'engager au-delà du territoire gabonais.

Les pères spiritains à qui le vicariat du Gabon est confié restent confinés à la côte atlantique jusqu'au début du XXe siècle. À partir de 1884, Mgr le Berre, vicaire apostolique du Gabon, commence à s'intéresser à la côte camerounaise, plus particulièrement à la région de Douala, mais il se heurte à la présence coloniale allemande qui, au mois de juillet de la même année, fait échec à cette première tentative d'évangélisation du territoire camerounais.

Malgré une évangélisation qui affronte les sociétés secrètes des *Banziés* de l'ethnie Fang, qui ici sont considérés comme des initiés, l'Église catholique au Gabon a pris corps et se positionne à l'indépendance, en 1960, comme la première institution religieuse du pays, comptant plus de la moitié des habitants, et 18% des protestants de la Mission Évangélique.[3] La conversion du Président gabonais, Albert Bongo, à l'islam en 1973, sous l'influence de Khadaffi, n'a pas été suivie par le peuple chrétien. La hiérarchie catholique du Gabon, jusqu'en 1961, est restée liée à celle du Congo-Brazzaville. Avec la création de l'archidiocèse de Libreville en 1961, l'Église catholique au Gabon a constitué sa propre Conférence Episcopale. Cette Église compte aujourd'hui six diocèses: Libreville (archidiocèse), Franceville, Mouila, Oyem, Port-Gentil, Makokou.

Le Congo-Brazzaville

Le Congo-Brazzaville est évangélisé par les missionnaires du Saint-Esprit. À l'appel du roi Enrique du Kongo pour avoir des missionnaires dans ce royaume dont l'évangélisation avait commencé aux Temps Modernes. Les missionnaires spiritains prennent possession de la préfecture apostolique du royaume, en 1865. Mais ils n'arriveront pas à atteindre la capitale, São Salvador, à cause des difficultés avec les Portugais qui n'apprécient pas l'arrivée des Français sur ce territoire considéré comme leur chasse gardée, et à cause de l'hostilité des populations autochtones.

Finalement, les spiritains se replient dans l'enclave de Cabinda, au lieu dit Landana, en 1873. L'intérieur du Congo restait encore à conquérir, surtout que Mgr Prosper Augouard, évêque spiritain responsable de cette évangélisation, se méfiait de la présence des protestants, en l'occurrence, les Baptistes qui ont poussé l'audace de se frayer un chemin jusqu'à São Salvador (Mbanza Kongo). Profitant de l'exploration de l'intérieur du territoire congolais par Stanley, les spiritains ouvrent un poste à Boma en 1880. En 1883, Mgr Prosper Augouard réussit à fonder la Mission Saint Joseph de Linzolo, dans le voisinage de ce qui deviendra Brazzaville, ancienne localité connue sous le nom de Mfoa.[4] L'évangélisation du Congo Brazzaville est liée à l'expansion coloniale. Mgr Prosper Augouard bénéficie de l'appui des deux plus grands explorateurs coloniaux de l'époque, Stanley et Savorgnan de Brazza. La première juridiction ecclésiastique qui parle du 'Congo Français', confiée à Mgr Antoine Carrie, est érigée le 28 mai 1886. Divisée le 14 octobre 1890, elle donne naissance au vicariat apostolique de Brazzaville à la

[3] La Mission Évangélique, d'obédience française, à cause du contexte colonial, a réduit à sa simple expression la Mission Presbytérienne Américaine.

[4] J. Delcourt, *Au Congo, avec Brazza et Stanley, Mgr Carrie,* Versailles, Imprimerie Saint Paul, 1993, 49.

tête duquel est porté Mgr Prosper Augouard, et au vicariat du Bas-Congo Français qui, en 1907 devient vicariat du Loango, puis le 14 septembre 1955, diocèse de Pointe Noire.

L'Église catholique, au Congo-Brazzaville, doit son expansion, relativement rapide, à la politique scolaire et aux œuvres socio-caritatives des missionnaires spiritains. C'est un prêtre catholique, l'abbé Fulbert Youlou, qui est le premier Président de la République du Congo indépendant, le 15 août 1960. Bien que Fulbert Youlou ne fût pas soutenu par son évêque, Michel Bernard, spiritain français, sa fonction politique à la tête de l'État congolais a donné au catholicisme une forte influence sur la nouvelle société en construction. L'Église catholique compte aujourd'hui 7 diocèses: Brazzaville (archidiocèse), Kinkala, Likouala, Nkayi, Ouesso, Owando, Pointe Noire.

La Mission évangélique suédoise arrive au Congo-Brazzaville à partir du Congo belge, au début du XXe siècle. Elle est partie de l'autre rive du grand fleuve qui sépare Léopoldville (actuelle Kinshasa) de Brazzaville. Mais son évolution a été moins rapide que celle de l'Église catholique.

Dès 1963, le nouveau régime politique du Congo Brazzaville dirigé par Massemba Débat, à la suite d'un soulèvement populaire contre Fulbert Youlou, engage le pays dans la voie du marxisme léniniste. Toutefois le christianisme, catholique et protestant, résiste à ce tourbillon politique, pour avoir imprégné les masses populaires de ses valeurs et pour avoir assuré aux jeunes une éducation moderne, même si au temps du marxisme, les écoles confessionnelles ont été nationalisées ou fermées.

Le Tchad

Le Tchad est le pays de la sous-région d'Afrique centrale qui a le moins d'affinités avec les autres, au plan géographique et anthropologique. L'évangélisation du Tchad, pays à majorité musulmane, a été inaugurée au début du XXe siècle par les Missions protestantes, parmi lesquelles la Mission Baptiste qui a formé la première élite intellectuelle du pays. Ce qui a permis, qu'à l'heure de l'indépendance, le pays soit dirigé par un protestant, François Tombalbaye. Les Églises luthériennes ont contribué à cette évangélisation, notamment dans la région méridionale, essentiellement peuplée de non musulmans.

Les premiers missionnaires catholiques qui visitent le Tchad sont les spiritains en 1928 et les Capucins en 1938. Ces derniers (les capucins) viennent de l'Éthiopie d'où ils ont été chassés. C'est dans le cadre de la Mission Tchad/Cameroun, en 1946, que Rome fait entreprendre une évangélisation plus systématique du Tchad, en l'attribuant officiellement aux oblats de Marie Immaculée. En 1947, Rome procède à la répartition des tâches au Tchad, les capucins reçoivent le Sud-Est; les oblats de Marie Immaculée, le Sud-Ouest; les jésuites, la région de Ndjamena et la partie septentrionale du pays. La carte religieuse due Tchad présente un Sud chrétien comportant des adeptes des Religions Traditionnelles et un Nord presque exclusivement musulman. L'Église catholique du Tchad compte 8 diocèses: Ndjamena (archidiocèse), Pala, Doba, Goré, Laï, Mongo, Moundou, Sarh.

Face à une écrasante majorité musulmane, plus de 90%, le christianisme tchadien est dans une dynamique de dialogue interreligieux. Mais des courants intégristes, animés par des mouvements qui se disent musulmans, alors qu'ils n'ont rien de commun avec l'islam qui enseigne la paix et la fraternité, menacent la vie religieuse au Tchad. C'est le cas de Boko-Haram qui, depuis le Nigéria voisin, sème la terreur au sein de la communauté des croyants vivant aux abords du Lac Tchad, par des actes de violence.

La Centrafrique

La Centrafrique, anciennement appelée Oubangui-Chari parce qu'encadrée par deux grands cours d'eau qui se jettent l'un dans le fleuve Congo, l'Oubangui; l'autre dans le Lac Tchad, le Chari. Pays continental, la Centrafrique n'a pas d'accès à la mer et ceci peut expliquer son évangélisation plus tardive.

À la différence du Tchad et des autres pays d'Afrique centrale, la majorité chrétienne en Centrafrique est restée protestante (voir le tableau). Les Missions protestantes que nous avons rencontrées au Tchad sont ici les plus actives à partir de 1920. La Mission Baptiste qui tente de conquérir l'intérieur de l'Afrique centrale est à la pointe de l'évangélisation de ce pays. L'un des objectifs affirmés est de lutter contre la pratique de l'esclavage qui sévit dans cette partie d'Afrique à cause des conflits interethniques. Les Missions américaines participent à cette épopée évangélisatrice avec la détermination de faire libérer les populations les plus vulnérables des chaînes d'oppression des forces tyranniques.

Les missionnaires catholiques, en l'occurrence les spiritains, arrivent dans le voisinage de Bangui en 1894, venant du Congo où l'évangélisation était déjà avancée. Cette présence spiritaine est d'ailleurs liée à la poussée évangélisatrice du vicariat apostolique du Haut-Congo. La préfecture apostolique de l'Oubangui-Chari est érigée le 8 mai 1909. Elle devient vicariat apostolique le 2 décembre 1937. Divisé le 28 mai 1940, ce vicariat apostolique donne naissance à la préfecture de Berbérati, et plus tard en 1954, à la préfecture de Bangassou. L'œuvre missionnaire spiritaine, en Centrafrique, a fait surgir une Église qui, compte actuellement 9 diocèses: Bangui (archidiocèse), Alindao, Bambari, Bangassou, Berberati, Bossangoa, Bouar, Kaga-Bandono, Mbaïki.

Depuis quelques années, la crise politique qui secoue la Centrafrique avec la prise du pouvoir par les *Seleka* et le limogeage politique de François Bozizé, le christianisme centrafricain est affecté dans ses rapports avec les musulmans, à cause des affrontements violents et sanglants entre ces *Seleka* prétendument musulmans et les *Antibalaka* soi-disant chrétiens. Cette dimension religieuse du conflit est d'autant plus curieuse qu'aucun des groupes en présence ne respecte les consignes de sa hiérarchie en vue d'une coexistence pacifique.

Le Cameroun

La dimension historique de l'évangélisation du Cameroun est plus complexe que celle des autres pays d'Afrique centrale. Ancien protectorat allemand en 1884, territoire sous mandat français et britannique au temps de la Société des Nations, territoire sous-tutelle en 1946, avec la création du Conseil de Tutelle de l'ONU, l'évangélisation du Cameroun a subi les contre coups de l'évolution coloniale.

Les premiers missionnaires chrétiens au Cameroun sont des protestants. La Société Missionnaire Baptiste de Jamaïque, installée dans l'île de Fernando Poo, non loin de Douala, a été la première à entreprendre l'évangélisation de la côte camerounaise. En 1843, la Mission Baptiste de Londres se joint aux Jamaïcains pour répondre efficacement à l'appel missionnaire dans la région côtière du Cameroun. Le résultat le plus remarquable de cette évangélisation, qui commence avant l'annexion du territoire camerounais par l'Allemagne, est la traduction de la Bible en langue douala par Alfred Saker, baptiste britannique: le Nouveau Testament en 1862 et l'Ancien Testament en 1872.

La signature du Traité germano-douala, le 12 juillet 1884, change le contexte de cette Mission. La Mission de Bâle, d'obédience suisse allemande, s'engage elle-aussi à l'évangélisation du Cameroun, en tentant de remplacer les Baptistes anglais, pour mieux servir les intérêts de la Métropole allemande. Dans la foulée des tractations et négociations coloniales, une Église protestante locale va naître: la Native Baptist Church où un Camerounais, du nom de Lotin à Samé, va jouer un rôle très important. S'estimant légitime héritière de l'œuvre missionnaire baptiste, cette Église est née en s'opposant à la succession des baptistes par les bâlois du fait des manœuvres coloniales allemandes.

Dans la patrie méridionale du Cameroun, la Mission Presbytérienne Américaine, venant de la Guinée Équatoriale et du Gabon, pénètre sur le sol camerounais en 1866. Cette Mission, en accédant à son autonomie en 1957, change de dénomination et s'identifie désormais sous le nom d'Église Presbytérienne Camerounaise.

Au Nord-Cameroun, les Églises Fraternelles Luthériennes sont à pied d'œuvre dès 1920. Elles précèdent ici la Mission Catholique et s'occupent de l'éducation des jeunes, ainsi que de la santé des populations.

La Mission catholique au Cameroun, que tente de créer Mgr Le Berre, vicaire apostolique, échoue en 1884. Le vicaire apostolique du Gabon, a voulu ouvrir une station à Douala, mais à cause de l'annexion du territoire camerounais par l'Allemagne, cette initiative a essuyé une fin de non recevoir de la part des colons allemands. Le 18 mars 1890, Rome crée la préfecture apostolique du Cameroun et la confie aux missionnaires pallottins allemands. Celle-ci est érigée en vicariat apostolique le 22 décembre 1904. Mais du fait que les Allemands ont perdu la campagne camerounaise de la Première Guerre mondiale en 1916, les missionnaires pallottins sont expulsés du territoire camerounais. Ils sont remplacés par les spiritains français en 1922.

Le 27 juin 1911, Rome autorise les prêtres du Sacré-Cœur de Jésus à se rendre dans la partie occidentale du Cameroun. Cette nouvelle Mission en terre camerounaise aboutit à l'érection de la préfecture apostolique de l'Adamaoua le 28 avril 1914, qui devient, le 11 juin 1923, préfecture apostolique de Foumban, puis vicariat apostolique de Foumban, le 28 mai 1934.

> Dans le British Cameroon, les missionnaires de Saint Joseph de Mill Hill (Saint Joseph's Foreign Missions), déjà à pied d'œuvre en Ouganda, arrivent en 1921. Le Père John Campling est nommé à la tête de cette Mission qui, le 12 juin 1923, donne naissance à la préfecture apostolique de Buea, puis au vicariat apostolique, le15 mars 1939. Le 18 avril 1950, Buea est érigé en diocèse. C'est le premier diocèse du Cameroun. Il a à sa tête Mgr Peter Rogan, missionnaire de Mill Hill.

Au Nord-Cameroun, la Mission Tchad/Cameroun inaugurée par les Oblats de Marie Immaculée, en 1946, connaît une évolution rapide. Le 9 janvier 1947, est créée la préfecture apostolique de Garoua qui devient vicariat le 24 mars 1953.

L'Église catholique au Cameroun est aujourd'hui la plus importante en Afrique centrale, du point de vue des structures, du nombre des fidèles et des diocèses. Elle comprend cinq Provinces Ecclésiastiques et 25 diocèses.

PROVINCES ECCLESIASTIQUE DE YAOUNDE

Yaoundé (archidiocèse), Mbalmayo, Bafia, Obala, Sangmélima, Ebolowa, Kribi.

PROVINCES ECCLESIASTIQUE DE DOUALA

Douala (archidiocèse), Bafoussam, Nkongsama, Edéa, Eséka, Bafang.

PROVINCES ECCLESIASTIQUE DE BAMENDA

Bamenda (archidiocèse), Buéa, Kumbo, Mamfé.

PROVINCES ECCLESIASTIQUE DE BERTOUA

Bertoua (archidiocèse), Doumé/Abong-Mbang, Batouri, Yokadouma.

PROVINCES ECCLESIASTIQUE DE GAROUA

Garoua (archidiocèse), Maroua- Mokolo, Yagoua, Ngaoundéré.

Il convient, en ce qui concerne le Cameroun particulièrement, de signaler la présence de l'Église orthodoxe grecque, la plus importante en Afrique centrale, dont la création remonte en 1949, à la suite de la vague migratoire qui a permis de constituer une communauté grecque dans ce pays dès 1900. La désignation d'un archimandrite, en la personne de Nicodimos Galliatsatos, en 1949, a été le point de départ de la Mission grecque orthodoxe au Cameroun. Longtemps fermée sur elle-même, cette Mission a commencé à s'ouvrir aux Africains et à s'étendre territorialement à partir des années 1970. De nouvelles juridictions ont été ouvertes au Tchad, en Centrafrique, en Guinée Équatoriale, au Gabon et au Congo-Brazzaville. Le culte, traditionnellement célébré en grec, s'ouvre progressivement aux langues officielles locales. Mais la liturgie est diversifiée, cinq rites sont célébrés: byzantin, arménien, antiochien, chaldéen et alexandrin. La communauté orthodoxe, au Cameroun et dans les autres pays d'Afrique centrale, est dans l'ensemble minoritaire, par rapport aux autres chrétiens. Ils'agit d'une minorité en croissance qui, au Cameroun particulièrement, s'est inscrite dans le champ du dialogue œcuménique et interreligieux. Et la spécificité du christianisme au Cameroun, c'est d'avoir créé, en 2004, une structure associative du dialogue interreligieux, connue sous l'appellation de *Association Camerounaise pour le Dialogue Interreligieux*, en abrégé ACADIR. Cette structure rassemble les musulmans, les catholiques, les protestants et les orthodoxes. Son principal objectif est de construire la paix sur des bases religieuses solides en luttant contre les intégrismes d'où qu'ils viennent et en faisant valoir au sein de la société camerounaise les valeurs morales autour de la vie qui est un don de Dieu et bien commun de l'humanité tout entière. Dans ce dialogue interreligieux, les Églises dites pentecôtistes ou de réveil ne sont pas exclues, mais on a l'impression qu'elles ont peur de diluer leurs identités dans une structure où elles vont se retrouver avec les Églises anciennes, dont elles dénoncent la tiédeur évangélique.

Quelques Aspects du Christianisme en Afrique Centrale

Le christianisme, en Afrique centrale, malgré une vision marxiste qui l'associe aux forces d'aliénation et de domination coloniale ou néocoloniale, a beaucoup contribué à l'émancipation sociopolitique des pays de la sous-région, à travers l'œuvre scolaire et sanitaire, la promotion des femmes et les œuvres de développement social. La cartographie de l'Afrique centrale a été mieux dessinée à partir de l'expansion missionnaire dans l'arrière pays. Il n'est aujourd'hui aucun esprit sérieux et objectif qui puisse ne pas reconnaître cette réalité. Et à ce sujet, E. Mveng a judicieusement observé:

> 'On se trompe à croire qu'une mise en question totale du christianisme soit encore possible en Afrique, sans remettre en question l'existence même de l'Afrique. Et c'est évidemment ignorer la loi élémentaire de tout progrès que de penser que l'on puisse repartir de zéro et construire l'Afrique comme si elle n'était pas chrétienne'.[5]

Il est curieux de constater que certains intellectuels africains se servent d'une soi-disant *Lettre du roi des Belges*, Léopold II, qui, en 1883, demanderait aux missionnaires de soutenir son œuvre coloniale, sans s'interroger sur l'authenticité de ce document qui n'existe dans aucun service d'archives connu, en dehors de l'internet.

Dans la recherche d'une meilleure articulation entre foi et culture africaine, le christianisme est en dialogue permanent avec les traditions locales et avec la modernité pour permettre aux fidèles de donner les meilleures réponses possibles aux défis du salut, ainsi qu'à ceux du développement social dans la paix et la justice. Dans ce sens, les travaux des théologiens de la place sont très édifiants, qu'il s'agisse des travaux du Père Engelbert Mveng, s.j., chantre de l'inculturation, de Jean Marc Ela, apôtre de la libération, de Meinrad Hebga, s.j., ecclésiologue africain, de Eboussi Boulaga, libérateur du *Muntu*, nous sommes là dans une quête permanente d'un christianisme plus en osmose avec le milieu social local. Les Églises protestantes et catholiques sont à l'avant-garde de cette quête.

Le phénomène des Églises pentecôtistes ou de réveil est récent. La plupart viennent des Etats-Unis. La variété des dénominations est telle qu'il est difficile de les classer. Mais dans l'ensemble, leur point commun est de revitaliser la foi, disons, de la rendre plus vivante en la mettant au service des besoins de la

[5] E. Mveng, *Histoire du Cameroun*, Tome II, Yaoundé, CEPER, 1985, 219.

société. Aussi, le ministère de la guérison ou de la délivrance se trouve ici en ligne de pointe. Leurs églises et chapelles sont souvent bondées. Certains chrétiens les fréquentent sans avoir réellement rompu avec leurs Églises d'origine, on est là dans la logique de transhumance spirituelle. Le vrai problème se situe au niveau des rapports entre ces Églises de réveil et les autres Églises chrétiennes. La suspicion qui les caractérise met à mal le dialogue œcuménique qui devrait promouvoir le rapprochement. Mais les Églises de réveil présentes dans tous les pays d'Afrique centrale jouent un rôle non négligeable dans l'encadrement pastoral de proximité de ceux qui recourent à leurs services et offices. Cette proximité avec les fidèles consonne avec la chaleur familiale qui manque tant aujourd'hui à beaucoup d'Africains, victimes de l'économie monétaire qui développe l'individualisme dans les centres urbains. Et c'est certainement là une des clefs de succès des pentecôtistes. Et de fait leur apostolat s'épanouit plus en ville que dans les villages. Mais la dispersion et l'émiettement de leurs églises est un handicap pour une pastorale organique et organisée.

Entre les Églises catholiques et protestantes et les Églises de réveil, il y a les Églises indépendantes africaines, nées le plus souvent de la contestation des prosélytismes missionnaires et de la colonisation. La plus importantes de ces Églises est celle de Simon Kimbangu. Cette Église vient du Congo belge (République Démocratique du Congo) où elle a vu le jour en 1921 grâce au prophète Simon Kimbangu. Elle a vite franchi le fleuve Congo pour se développer à Brazzaville. En 1969, l'Église kimbanguiste est admise au Conseil Mondial des Églises. C'est la preuve de son dynamisme apostolique. Mais le caractère héréditaire de la fonction de chef hiérarchique continue d'être une pomme de discorde au sein de la communauté kimbanguiste. D'autres mouvements prophétiques, parmi les mieux connus d'Afrique centrale, sont nés au Congo-Brazzaville au début du XXe siècle, il y a le matsouanisme (André Matsoua), la croix koma de Victor Malanda en 1964, le lassyisme (Dieu de la bougie). Au Gabon, le Bwiti est passé du statut de religion traditionnelle à celui d'une Église chrétienne intégrant Jésus-Christ que les initiés de cette religion ne connaissaient pas. Ce mouvement a connu une percée missionnaire au Sud-Cameroun où il est connu sous le nom d'Eboka. La difficulté majeure de ces Églises et mouvements prophétiques africains se situe au niveau du syncrétisme. Exception faite de l'Église kimbaguiste, dont les progrès spirituels sont réels, les autres mélangent les éléments de spiritualité traditionnelle avec la spiritualité chrétienne.

Relations Eglises – Etat

Depuis la période coloniale, les Églises missionnaires ont eu à affronter le gouvernement pour des raisons diverses. Si d'une manière générale, les rapports entre missionnaires et administrateurs coloniaux étaient harmonieux (le cas de Mgr Prosper Augouard avec Savorgnan de Brazza et certainement aussi celui de Mgr Vieter, 1er vicaire apostolique du Cameroun, membre du Conseil du gouvernement colonial allemand), il y a eu des situations de contestation de nature à rompre cette harmonie. Au Cameroun, Mgr Vogt, 2e vicaire apostolique, affronte l'administration coloniale sur la question des travaux forcés. Autorisés par l'administration coloniale française, ces travaux étaient critiqués par le vicaire apostolique du Cameroun parce que non conformes à la morale chrétienne et à la dignité humaine. En réalité, l'administration coloniale française ne respecte même pas la loi de séparation de 1905 et veut imposer aux Églises missionnaires la conduite à tenir dans les colonies. La règle qui prévaut ici est celle de la primauté de l'État sur la religion. C'est cet héritage colonial qui va marquer les rapports entre les Églises chrétiennes et l'État dans l'Afrique postcoloniale.

En Guinée Équatoriale, le dictateur Francisco Macias Nguema a imposé son nom pour le signe de croix à l'école primaire, voulant ainsi se faire reconnaître comme fils de Dieu. Il est chassé du pouvoir en 1979 par Théodore Obiang Nguema. Au Congo-Brazzaville, l'avènement du marxisme a amené l'État à nationaliser les écoles chrétiennes en 1964. Dans ce même pays, suite à l'assassinat du commandant

Marien Ngouabi, chef de l'Etat, le cardinal Emile Biayenda est enlevé et tué dans des circonstances qui n'ont pas encore été éclaircies. L'avènement de la démocratie en 1991, dont la Conférence Nationale Souveraine a été l'articulation majeure, présidée par un évêque congolais, le jésuite Ernest Kombo, du diocèse d'Owando, a décrispé les relations entre l'Église etl'État.

En Centrafrique, l'abbé Barthélémy Boganda, mort dans un accident d'avion à la veille de l'indépendance, n'occupera pas le fauteuil de chef d'État qui aurait pu lui revenir sans difficulté. Mais son influence dans le pays est telle que les Églises chrétiennes ont toujours été respectées parles hommes politiques. Même le flirt spiriruel entre Bokassa et Khadaffi n'a pas réussi à entamer cette influence. Mais la crise politique actuelle qui exploite le religieux à travers l'affrontement entre les Seleka (musulmans) et les Antibalaka (chrétiens) révèlent les faiblesses de l'État à faire respecter les principes fondamentaux de lalaïcité et sa volonté manifeste de vouloir instrumentaliser la religion à des fins politiques.

Au Cameroun, l'affaire Ndongmo en 1969 / 1970 a montré que le dialogue doit toujours prévaloir entre l'État et les Églises, et qu'un manque de discernement peut engendrer de graves crises. Mgr Albert Ndongmo, évêque de Nkongsamba depuis 1964, voulant protéger les maquisards upécistes, s'est retrouvé au banc des accusés pour tentative de renversement du Président Ahmadou Ahidjo. Condamné à mort, il est gracié mais exilé au Canada où il meurt en 1992. Il faut cependant souligner, d'une manière générale, que le président Ahmadou Ahidjo (1960-1982) et, à sa suite, Paul Biya (depuis 1982), se sont montrés courtois vis-à-vis des Églises chrétiennes et des autres institutions religieuses du Cameroun, jusqu'à ce jour.

En Afrique centrale, le poids du christianisme dans la vie sociopolitique des États impose du respect. Mais par moments, la prise de position des Églises chrétiennes par rapport aux événements politiques majeurs dans ces États, vient rompre l'accalmie, lorsque cette position est critique vis-à-vis des gouvernants. Et comme les peuples font généralement confiance aux autorités des Églises chrétiennes, celles-ci doivent éviter de compromettre leur mission face aux États et faire prévaloir le dialogue avec les pouvoirs publics pour le bien et la cohésion de la nation.

Les Institutions Chrétiennes Sous-Régionales

Chez les protestants, nous rencontrons des institutions purement internationales comme le Conseil Œcuménique des Églises, fondé en 1948; la Communion Mondiale des Eglises Réformées, née aux Etats-Unis en 2010 et la Fédération Luthérienne Mondiale, créée en 1947. Il y a également des institutions sous-régionales, ou inter-ecclésiales, c'est le cas du Centre de Littérature Évangélique, connu sous le nom d'éditions CLE, fondé à Yaoundé le 28 mars 1963, l'Alliance biblique; la Faculté de Théologie Protestante devenue Université Protestante d'Afrique Centrale. Yaoundé au Cameroun est le siège de ces institutions sous-régionales.

Chez les catholiques, il y a deux principales institutions sous-régionales. L'Association des Conférence Episcopales de la Région d'Afrique Centrale (ACERAC) regroupe les conférences épiscopales des six pays, que sont le Tchad, la Centrafrique, le Congo-Brazzaville, le Gabon, la Guinée Equatoriale et le Cameroun. Son siège est à Brazzaville. Initiée à l'ouverture du concile Vatican II en 1962, l'ACERAC a pris son visage actuel en 1987. L'Université Catholique d'Afrique Centrale a été créée en 1989 et inaugurée en 1991. Elle célèbre bientôt ses 25 ans. Le rectorat et les principaux établissements universitaires sont basés à Yaoundé. Elle s'efforce actuellement de créer des établissements spécialisés dans chacun des différents pays de l'ACERAC, étant donné que cette université comme fondateurs institutionnels les Églises membres de l'ACERAC.

* * *

En conclusion, le christianisme en Afrique centrale marque de manière indélébile le paysage religieux de cette sous-région. Sa contribution à l'émergence et au progrès spirituel, intellectuel et sociopolitique de cette partie d'Afrique est indéniable. Mais ce christianisme pour continuer à bien jouer son rôle ici a deux défis majeurs à relever: le dialogue œcuménique et l'auto-prise en charge de ses structures techniques et pastorales.

Bibliographie

Baur, J., *2000 ans de christianisme en Afrique. Une histoire de l'Eglise Africaine*, Kinshasa, Paulines, 2001.

De Benoist, J.R., *Deux millénaires du christianisme en Afrique*, Paris, Cerf, 1991.

Delcourt, J., *Au Congo, avec Brazza et Stanley, Mgr Carrie*, Paris, Saint Paul, 1993.

Dessare, E., *L'Afrique noire chrétienne,* Paris, Spes, 1960.

Eboussi Boulaga, F., *A contretemps. L'enjeu de Dieu en Afrique*, Paris, Karthala, 1991.

Ela, J.M., *Le cri de l'homme africain,* Paris, L'Harmattan, 1980;

______, *Ma foi d'Africain*, Paris, Karthala, 1985;

______, *Repenser la théologie africaine. Le Dieu qui libère,* Paris, Karthala, 2005.

Hastings, A., *A History of African Christianity,1450- 1950*, Oxford, Oxford University Press, 1994.

Hebga, M., *Emancipation d'Eglises sous tutelle,* Paris, Présence Africaine, 1976.

Hunnermann, F., *Histoire des Missions. Sous le soleil africain*, vol. III, Paris-Tournai, Castermann-Salvator, 1963.

Messina, J.P., Van Slageren, *Histoire du christianisme au Cameroun, des origines à nos jours,* Paris-Yaoundé, Karthala-Clé, 2005.

Messina, J.P., *Jean Zoa, prêtre et archevêque de Yaoundé,* Paris, Karthala, 2000.

Mveng, E., *L'Afrique dans l'Eglise. Paroles d'un croyant,* Paris, L'Harmattan, 1986.

(21) Christianity in Southern Africa

Philippe Denis

Country	Religion	Pop_2010	Pct_2010	Pop_2025	Pct_2025	GrPct_1970_2025
Southern Africa	Christians	48,691,000	82.4%	56,516,000	83.2%	1.0%
Southern Africa	Independents	22,304,000	37.8%	26,277,000	38.7%	1.1%
Southern Africa	African-initiated	21,456,000	36.3%			
Southern Africa	Orthodox	30,500	0.1%	30,100	0.0%	-0.1%
Southern Africa	Protestants	15,454,000	26.2%	17,825,000	26.3%	1.0%
Southern Africa	Reformed, Presb	3,688,000	6.2%			
Southern Africa	Anglicans	3,014,000	5.1%			
Southern Africa	Pentecostal	2,576,000	4.4%			
Southern Africa	Lutheran	1,819,000	3.1%			
Southern Africa	Methodist	1,507,000	2.6%			
Southern Africa	United churches	1,080,000	1.8%			
Southern Africa	Roman Catholics	5,113,000	8.7%	5,747,000	8.5%	0.8%
Southern Africa	*Pentecostals/ Charismatics*	26,537,000	44.9%	28,375,000	41.8%	0.4%
Southern Africa	*Evangelicals*	5,864,000	9.9%	6,397,000	9.4%	0.6%
Southern Africa	adherents of traditional African religions	4,633,000	7.8%	4,290,000	6.3%	-0.5%
Southern Africa	Hindus	1,233,000	2.1%	1,310,000	1.9%	0.4%
Southern Africa	Muslims	909,000	1.5%	978,000	1.4%	0.5%
Southern Africa	Baha'is	295,000	0.5%	369,000	0.5%	1.5%
Southern Africa	Buddhists	165,000	0.3%	181,000	0.3%	0.6%
Southern Africa	Jews	75,500	0.1%	59,200	0.1%	-1.6%
Southern Africa	Chinese folk religionists	34,600	0.1%	38,200	0.1%	0.7%
Southern Africa	Confucianists	20,600	0.0%	25,000	0.0%	1.3%
Southern Africa	adherents of new religious movements	18,300	0.0%	23,400	0.0%	1.7%
Southern Africa	Sikhs	11,100	0.0%	13,400	0.0%	1.2%
Southern Africa	Spiritists	2,300	0.0%	2,500	0.0%	0.4%
Southern Africa	Jains	2,100	0.0%	2,300	0.0%	0.7%
Southern Africa	professing no religion	2,978,000	5.0%	4,089,000	6.0%	2.1%
Southern Africa	**Total population**	**59,067,000**	**100.0%**	**67,897,000**	**100.0%**	**0.9%**

Source: Centre for the Study of World Christianity (CSGC), Boston, Gordon-Conwell TS

Introduction

Whether the object of this chapter is the history of Christianity in Southern Africa, a geographical area located in the southern part of the African continent, or Southern Africa, a formal or informal federation of states or churches united by geography and culture, is unclear. As Neil Parsons observed, 'Big "S" or small "s", there are no hard definitions of the region; they expand or contract with political expediency'.[1] The Southern African Development Community (SADC) includes the Democratic Republic of Congo and leaves out Madagascar. If the Inter-Regional Meeting of Bishops of Southern Africa (IMBISA), a regional structure of the Catholic Church, includes the episcopal conferences of Angola and São Tome, Mozambique, Namibia, Zimbabwe, Lesotho and 'Southern Africa' – an area encompassing South Africa, Botswana and Swaziland – Zambia and Malawi are members of the Association of Member Conferences in Eastern Africa (AMECEA). Following the example of Bengt Sundkler, the author, with Christopher Steed, of a monumental *History of the Church in Africa*,[2] we shall apply the term 'Southern Africa' to the area south of Katanga, Angola included.[3] Thus defined, Southern Africa encompasses ten post-colonial countries: Angola, Botswana, Lesotho, Madagascar, Malawi, Mozambique, South Africa, Swaziland, Zambia and Zimbabwe.

Political boundaries, in Africa especially, are often artificial but, with time, they take on a firmness that makes them override other identity markers such as topography, ethnicity, language or religion. When looking at the history of the ten countries considered to be part of Southern Africa, one observes a range of socio-economic, cultural and religious historical developments which give the region a certain specificity. The first is the episode of warfare, destruction and migration known as Mfecane which led to the displacement of essentially Nguni-speaking people from Zululand to modern-day Swaziland, Zimbabwe, Zambia and Malawi between 1815 and 1840, in a context marked by the ascendency of the Zulu kingdom and interferences from British and Portuguese traders and adventurers in African politics. Another trans-national factor was the slave trade or, rather, the efforts made by traders and missionaries in the nineteenth century to eradicate slavery while creating space for imperial conquest. Angola, Mozambique and Madagascar, the areas least influenced by Britain, resisted until the early twentieth century. Through his campaigns against the slave trade, David Livingstone, the champion of Christianity, commerce and civilisation, laid the foundations of flourishing mission fields throughout Southern Africa.

Equally important, from the late nineteenth century to the recent times, was migrant labour, with movements of population from countries as far apart as Zimbabwe, Lesotho, Mozambique and Malawi to the mines and factories of the Northern Cape and the Transvaal, not to mention internal migration movements within South Africa itself. Migrant labour undermined the traditional family structure and created an enduring culture of violence, but it also facilitated the propagation of Christianity. In Lesotho, in southern Mozambique and in the former Eastern Transvaal, migrant workers converted by chance at their place of work were the first to preach the gospel, long before missionaries from abroad institutionalised the Christian communities they had established.[4] Until the time of their independence, South Africa and, to a certain extent, the neighbouring colonies were the place in Africa with the highest density of missionary presence. Islam, one should add, is marginal and Hinduism only represented in the KwaZulu-Natal Province. Today, Southern Africa is and remains overwhelmingly Christian.

Several, though not all, Southern African countries have another experience in common. If, by and large, all countries in West Africa, Central Africa and East Africa became independent, more or less peacefully, in the early 1960s, Great Britain, France and Belgium having voluntarily relinquished their

---

[1] Neil Parsons, "Towards a Broader Southern African History: Backwards, Sideways, and Upside-Down," *South African Historical Journal*, 66 (2014), 219.

[2] Bengt Sundkler and Christopher Steed, *A History of the Church in Africa* (Cambridge: Cambridge University Press, 2000), 974-999.

[3] Sundkler and Steed list Angola under "West-Central Africa".

[4] For a suggestive example, see Jan Van Butselaar, *Africains, missionnaires et colonialistes. Les origines de l'Eglise presbytérienne du Mozambique (Mission Suisse) 1880-1896* (Leiden: Brill, 1984); Patrick Harries, *Butterflies and barbarians: Swiss missionaries and systems of knowledge in South-East Africa* (Johannesburg: Wits University Press, 2007).

colonial empires, in Angola, in Mozambique, in Zimbabwe, in Namibia and in South Africa the road to independence was longer and required more sacrifices. In all these countries lengthy wars of liberation, accompanied by civil wars and violations of human rights, took a toll on civil populations. White settlers and the regimes they put in place held on to power for long periods of time: until 1975 in Angola and Mozambique, 1980 in Zimbabwe, 1990 in Namibia and 1994 in South Africa. These episodes of war, resistance and liberation had a profound impact on the Christian churches, as we shall see.

This chapter spans five centuries. The time divisions are based, with a few modifications, on that posited by Adrian Hastings in one of his books.[5] It considers four turning-points:

First Portuguese expeditions in Southern Africa (circa 1500).

First missionary societies in England and first missions in Southern Africa (circa 1790).

Military defeats of African chiefs and establishment of a colonial administration in South Africa and the neighbouring countries (circa 1890).

Access to independence in most African countries (circa 1960) and establishment of local churches throughout the continent.

The *Padroãdo* Era

The period of the first evangelisation of sub-Saharan Africa – also called the *padroãdo* period because of the patronage exercised by the Portuguese throne over missionary work in Portuguese-held territories – began in 1458 when Diogo Gomez, the leader of an expedition sponsored by the Portuguese king, converted Nomimansa, a Gambian prince, and sent for a Portuguese priest, the abbot of Soto de Casa, to come and baptise him. Subsequently, Portuguese men married indigenous women and built villages on the European model, each with a church. Twelve priests from the Cape Verde Islands visited them on a regular basis. At the same time, a convent was established at Cachau on the Rio Grande.[6]

This pattern was duplicated, with small variations, in the kingdom of Kongo in the most northern part of present-day Angola where the first Catholic priests arrived in 1491; in Luanda on the Atlantic coast where the evangelisation started in the mid-seventeenth century; in the territory between Sofala and the island of Mozambique on the Indian Ocean coastline where the Portuguese established their first fort in the early sixteenth century; along the Zambezi River and in the kingdom of Monomotapa in present-day Zimbabwe where they were received in the last years of the sixteenth century.

In geographical terms, Christian penetration under the Portuguese was limited to a few points on the perimeter of the African continent. There were, however, two exceptions, both in Southern Africa: the kingdom of Kongo, where a wave of Christian missions unfurled in the seventeenth century, and in south-east Africa, where during the same period an extensive network of missionary stations was established by the Dominicans and the Jesuits. In 1619, the bishop of Saõ Salvador, the capital of the kingdom of Kongo, could count on the support of eighty priests and the canons chanted services 'according to the custom in Europe'. Between 1645 and 1820, no less than 434 Capuchins, mainly Italian, ministered in present-day Congo and Angola. By the middle of the seventeenth century, the Dominican Order had thirteen priories, houses and missionary stations along the Indian Ocean coast, on the banks of the Zambezi River and in the kingdom of Monomotapa. Following a liberal revolution in Portugal, the last missions had to close in Angola and in south-east Africa in 1835.

Accounts of this early wave of evangelisation are scanty. The combined effect of illnesses, irregular funding, difficulties of communication, compromises struck between the church and political powers, and

[5] Adrian Hastings, *The Church in Africa 1450-1950* (Oxford: Clarendon Press, 1994). Some parts of this chapter are based on an earlier essay, which also followed Hastings' time divisions. See Philippe Denis, "African indigenous Christianity in a geo-historical perspective," *Studia Historiae Ecclesiasticae*, 38/2 (2012), 1-22.

[6] Sundkler and Steed, *History*, 45.

the acceptance of slavery to staff mission stations ruined any chance of lasting development. The influence of Christianity in the regions penetrated by the missionaries was minimal. Its true impact was felt in syncretism. In Angola, along the Indian Ocean and in the Zambezi valley, new religious forms came into being, combining elements of African Traditional Religion with the mysteries of Christian dogma.

Very significant, from that point of view, is the story of Kimpa Vita, called Dona Beatriz, in the ancient kingdom of Kongo. In 1704 this twenty-year-old woman began to burn crosses and claimed that she died every weekend, to be reborn on Sundays. She maintained that she was a reincarnation of St Anthony, a figure who had become popular as a result of the Capuchins' sermons. She began a movement of religious and political restoration, claiming that Jesus Christ was born in Saõ Salvador, the capital of the kingdom. The venture came to an end in 1706 when it was discovered that she was pregnant. She was arrested by the king's soldiers, interrogated by a priest and burned alive. But she was remembered in the region far beyond the eighteenth century.[7]

Unlike in Senegal, in Ivory Coast and in Benin, where French priests had been active since the seventeenth century, in Southern Africa the missionary effort relied almost exclusively on the Portuguese, even though they received, after the foundation of the Roman Congregation for the Propagation of the Faith in 1622, reinforcements in the form of Italian Capuchins. The only exception was Madagascar where, in the footsteps of Portuguese Jesuits from Goa, a group of French Lazarists made a brave though unsuccessful attempt to start a mission in the mid-seventeenth century.[8]

Apart from a handful of Danes and Hollanders in Gold Coast forts in the eighteenth century,[9] the only Protestants living in Africa during the time of the first evangelisation were the employees of the Dutch East India Company in Cape Town and the Dutch and Huguenot settlers occupying farms inland from the coast. For them, Christian status and European descent were closely identified, with the result that no serious effort was made to evangelise the indigenous population. There were only four converts to Christianity from the Khoikhoi in the seventeenth century, one of them being Eva, a woman converted by Maria van Riebeeck, the wife of the commander, who died as a drunk convict, rejected by all, after the death of her European husband.[10] Dutch Reformed Church ministers like Johan Van Arckel or Michiel Christiaan Vos, who reached out to the Khoikhoi, were the exception. Company slaves of mixed parentage were normally baptised, in Cape Town at least, because, being partly white, they were considered Christians. Private slave owners, on the other hand, refused to baptise their slave children because of a Company rule stipulating that converts should be set free.

The breakthrough came with the arrival of Georg Schmidt, a member of the United Brethren, or Moravians, a Pietist movement within the Lutheran Church in Germany, in 1737. He learned the language of the Khoikhoi and shared their lives but when the neighbouring *predikanten* heard that he had baptised five of them in August 1741, they complained to the authorities and he was deported. His work had not been in vain, though. When a group of Moravian missionaries came back to Genadendal, the place of Schmidt's mission, fifty years later, they found an old woman, called Lena, holding religious services under a pear tree.[11]

---

[7] John Thornton, *The Kongolese Saint Anthony: Dona Beatriz Kimpa Vita and the Antonian Movement, 1684-1706*, Cambridge: Cambridge University Press, 1998.
[8] Sundkler and Steed, *History*, 501.
[9] *Ibid.*, 46-47.
[10] Jonathan Gerstner, "A Christian Monopoly: The Reformed Church and Colonial Society under Dutch Rule," in Richard Elphick and Rodney Davenport, eds, *Christianity in South Africa. A Political, Social and Cultural History*, Oxford: James Currey, 1997, 25-28.
[11] *Ibid.*, 27-29.

Failed Attempts and Missionary Breakthroughs

With few rare exceptions, the first mission establishments in sub-Saharan Africa, whether Portuguese or French, were those of the Catholic faith. This situation changed in the last decade of the eighteenth century with the foundation, in the wake of the emerging colonial movement, of several Protestant missionary societies, English at first, then German, French, Scandinavian and North American. A wide range of denominations – Congregationalist, Presbyterian, Anglican, Methodist, Lutheran, Reformed and Baptist – were represented. Up until the beginning of the twentieth century, Catholic missions, albeit present, were less numerous than those of their Protestant rivals.

In 1799, Johannes Theodorus Van der Kemp, the first representative of the London Missionary Society (LMS), an evangelically-minded interdenominational body, landed in the Cape where the English had just gained a foothold. Inspired by the Moravians, he established a settlement for displaced Khoikhoi and mixed-race people in Bethelsdorp near modern-day Port Elizabeth and married a Khoi woman. Some of Van der Kemp's converts ran their own missions, not without clashes with the missionaries. In 1801 William Edwards, a LMS missionary, and Jan Matthys Kok, a man of mixed Khoi-Dutch descent, arrived among the Batlhaping, preparing the way for Robert Moffat, who came ten years later to found the mission station of Kuruman from where missionary expeditions to Botswana, Zambia, Malawi and Zimbabwe would depart in subsequent years. Meanwhile, in 1804, the LMS established a station in Warmland in southern Namibia, thus expanding its outreach to the north.

It soon became clear that the LMS did not have the manpower to cover all the missionary needs. Already Wesleyan Methodists had moved into Namibia in 1816 and among the Xhosa in 1820. The Scot John Philip, who arrived in Cape Town in 1816, is mostly known for having taken the defence of Khoikhoi abused by white masters and lobbied in favour of the abolition of the slave trade. But, as LMS superintendent, he also contributed to the shaping of the missionary scene in Southern Africa. It was at his suggestion that the Society of Evangelical Missions of Paris went to Lesotho in 1833, the American Board of Commissioners for Foreign Missions to Natal in 1834 and the Rhenish Missionary Society to Namibia in 1844. Other missionary societies followed, particularly in Natal.[12]

Further north it was not until 1857 that an evangelist trained in Kuruman, Sehunelo, settled in Shoshong, Botswana, among the BamaNgwato. A group of Hermannsburg Society missionaries soon followed, but they did not last long because they were suspected of spying for the Boers. A permanent mission, this time entrusted to the LMS, was established in 1861 at the invitation of the BaNgwato.[13]

Following the same road, Moffat made four visits to King Mzilikazi, the founder of the Matabele kingdom in modern-day Zimbabwe, culminating in his journey of 1858 to the court at Bulawayo when he received land for a LMS mission in Inyati, north of Bulawayo. During the following two decades no less than twenty-one expeditions, mostly led by African evangelists or people of mixed race, were sent to Zimbabwe by missionary societies in South Africa, following a more easterly route. The initiators were the Society of Evangelical Missions of Paris in Lesotho, the Swiss Mission in the Eastern Transvaal, the Berlin Missionary Society in Venda and a Dutch Reformed Church minister pastoring a mixed-race community in the Soutpansbergen. They prepared the spirits for future missionary work. The situation changed when, with the support of the British government, businessman Cecil Rhodes carved out for his British South Africa Company a vast territory in Mashonaland, Matebeleland, Zambia and Malawi. In 1890 his 'Pioneer column' invaded Mashonaland and, in subsequent years, two rebellions, in Matebeleland and in

[12] Elizabeth Elbourne and Robert Ross, "Combating Spiritual and Social Bondage: Early Missions in the Cape Colony," in Elphick and Davenport, *Christianity in South Africa*, 31-50; Sundkler and Steed, *History*, 323-344.
[13] Fidelis Nkomazana, "The First Missionary Encounter among the Batswana: A Case Study of the BaNgwato of Shoshong, 1857-1871," in Fidelis Nkomazana and Laurel Lanner, eds, *History of the Church in Botswana*, Pietermaritzburg: Cluster Publications, 2007, 55-56.

Mashonaland, were quashed. The Jesuits, whose attempts to set foot in Zimbabwe had been unsuccessful until then, a group of Dominican Sisters, an Anglican bishop and a canon of the same church arrived in Zimbabwe under Rhodes' patronage and protection. A new era had begun.[14]

A few years before, in 1884, François Coillard, a member of the Society of Evangelical Missions of Paris in Lesotho, had made his way to Barutsoland, in western Zambia, with the encouragement of the LMS. His task was facilitated by the fact that the Lozi, who occupied the area, had learned Sesotho from populations having migrated from South Africa.[15] In subsequent years, in Livingstone's footsteps, the LMS, the Primitive Methodists, the Presbyterians and the Church of England's Universities Mission to Central Africa established mission stations in Zambia and in Malawi.

If we put aside Madagascar, where a group of LMS missionaries arrived directly from Britain in 1820 to establish a lasting presence despite heavy religious persecution during Queen Ravalona's twenty-six-year reign,[16] all the missionary routes followed by Protestants in Southern Africa started from South Africa. The LMS, the first missionary society in the region, played a pioneering role in this regard by sponsoring Livingstone's first wave of explorations and by encouraging, from Kuruman or elsewhere, missions to Namibia, Botswana, Zimbabwe, Zambia and Malawi throughout the nineteenth century. Methodist, Reformed, Presbyterian, Lutheran and Anglican missionary societies chose similar itineraries.

Because of a longer presence in the region, of the earlier arrival in central Africa of missionary congregations such as the Holy Ghost Fathers and the White Fathers and of the co-ordinating role of the Roman Congregation for the Propagation for the Faith, the Catholic missionaries functioned somewhat differently. It is true that, as with their Protestant counterparts, their first implantation in Southern Africa was in South Africa. Until 1875, they failed to make African converts, *de facto* restricting their ministry to white settlers. It was in Lesotho that the Oblates of Mary Immaculate, the first Catholic congregation in the region, encountered their first major success, King Moshoeshoe being keen to counterbalance the influence of the Protestant missionaries. In the 1880s and 1890s, by placing emphasis on agricultural development and skills training, the Trappists developed a remarkable network of mission stations and schools in Natal and the Transkei under the leadership of Abbot Franz Pfanner and his successors.[17] This being said, except for the Jesuits and the Dominican Sisters in Zimbabwe and Zambia, the missionary impulse towards other parts of Southern Africa did not come from South Africa.

A case in point is Angola. In 1866, after a stint in Senegal and Gabon, Charles Duparquet, one of the most dynamic members of the Congregation of the Holy Spirit in the nineteenth century, endeavoured to evangelise Angola, which, notwithstanding the *padroãdo* regime, had been *de facto* abandoned by the Catholic Church of Portugal. The first mission was established in Lândana in the Cabinda Province. Between 1866 and 1940 no less than 284 Holy Ghost Fathers, mostly from France but also from Portugal and from Goa, exercised the ministry in Angola. It was there that Luís de Gourlay, the first African Catholic priest in modern times (apart from Senegal), was ordained in December 1892. In 1884 Duparquet headed further south to Amboland in Namibia, where he founded a mission. A Catholic prefecture was established in Namaqualand in 1888.[18]

---

[14] John Weller and Jane Linden, *Mainstream Christianity to 1980 in Malawi, Zambia and Zimbabwe*, Gweru, Mambo Press, 1984, 52-84; Chengetai Zvogbo, *A History of Christian Missions in Zimbabwe*, Gweru: Mambo Press, 1996; Sundkler and Steed, *History*, 445-451.

[15] Weller and Linden, *Mainstream Christianity*, 26-31.

[16] Sundkler and Steed, *History*, 487-501.

[17] Joy Brain, "Moving from the Margins to the Mainstream: The Roman Catholic Church," in Elphick and Davenport, *Christianity in South Africa*, 195-200.

[18] Lawrence Henderson, *A Igreja em Angola*, Lisbon, Além-Mar, 1990, 41-44; Sundkler and Steed, *History*, 318-319; 443-444.

Likewise, it was from the north that the Missionaries of Africa, also called White Fathers, who had been in Uganda and Tanzania since 1879, came to evangelise Malawi and Zambia. Joseph Dupont, the founder of these missions, had to rely on the Portuguese to set foot in Mpanda, on the southern shore of Lake Malawi, in 1885. He soon received reinforcements from the Montfort Fathers, another French missionary congregation. The Catholics' primary aim, at the time, was to oppose the Protestants in the region. From Mpanda, Dupont moved in 1895 to Mambwe in Zambia, where a Bemba chief gave him hospitality. Currently Catholics are in significant numbers in Malawi and Zambia.[19] They also dominate in Mozambique, where after several decades of pastoral neglect, the Jesuits came in 1881 to resume a missionary presence interrupted a century earlier.[20]

Colonialism and Mission

Until the late nineteenth century, the majority of African populations escaped the colonial grasp whether they were governed by indigenous chiefs or belonged to leaderless societies with different degrees of cohesion. There were few missionaries and those who were there lived at great distance from each other. Still rare, conversions implied a transition to the European way of life. African evangelists, as Volz showed with the Tswana, played a key role in the early phase of the evangelisation process and, in doing so, they demonstrated a high degree of agency. They used Christianity and its connection with Europeans to enhance their status and that of their family or, if they belonged to subordinate families, they took refuge in mission stations to find employment and recognition. However, with time, they fell prey to what Volz called 'ecclesiastical tyranny' and their pastoral autonomy gradually disappeared.[21]

In the wake of the Berlin Congress of 1885, which paved the way for the sharing of sub-Saharan Africa between various European powers, a colonial order gradually came into being and military, administrative, economic, educational and medical infrastructures were installed in every corner of the African territory. The missionary societies benefited enormously from the new situation. As long as African chiefs had maintained their hold over their tribes, support for Christianity had posed a problem because it entailed abandoning indigenous culture for which the chiefs had been responsible. Once the chiefs' power was broken, nothing prevented the rapid diffusion of Christianity. Joining the church took on a new meaning. Local populations demonstrated an eagerness to adapt to the new order, which in future would dominate, by making the most of colonial innovations such as teaching, health care and the care of orphans, whilst simultaneously, in hidden or overt ways, maintaining areas of autonomy. For the subjects in the new empires, being baptised implied the possibility of finding a new position, albeit inferior, in modern society.

In a famous though controversial two-volume study entitled *Of Revelation and Revolution*, Jean and John Comaroff made the point that, by inducing their converts to change their eating, dressing and housing codes and accept, albeit unconsciously, the commands of modernity, the missionaries 'colonised their consciousness' and brought about 'hegemonic' relations which could only, when the colonised became aware of them, lead to resistant behaviours, as attested by the multiplication of independent churches and prophetic movements from the late nineteenth century to the present day.[22] Relying almost exclusively on missionary narratives, this thesis has been criticised for overemphasising the role of missionaries in the expansion of mission Christianity, for downplaying the agency of African evangelists and teachers, for

---

[19] Weller and Linden, *Mainstream Christianity*, 100-102, 153-155.

[20] José Augusto Alves de Sousa, *Os Jesuítas em Moçambique 1541-1991*, Braga: Livraria Apostolado da Imprensa, 1991, 32-34; Sundkler and Steed, *History*, 482.

[21] Stephen Volz, *African Teachers on the Colonial Frontier. Tswana Evangelists and their Communities during the Nineteenth Century*, New York: Peter Lang, 2011.

[22] Jean and John Comaroff, *Of Revelation and Revolution*, 2 vol., Chicago: University of Chicago, Press, 1991 and 1997.

ignoring the diversity and changeability of pre-colonial indigenous worldviews and for insufficiently taking into account the socio-economic factors explaining the rise of independent church movements.[23] As suggested by Landau,[24] there is no doubt that in order to understand the complex relationship between colonialism and mission, one should consider the religious factor on its own and not only as the expression of a cultural phenomenon.

During the colonial era, the relations between missionaries and indigenous populations underwent a profound evolution. In the early years, for lack of other company, the missionaries and their families shared the living conditions of the indigenous people and fluently spoke their language. Later on, the development of an urban colonial society, of which they became dignitaries, took them away from grassroots work which was entrusted to the catechists. The institutionalisation of the missions with their churches, schools, hospitals and orphanages made them administrators rather than evangelists, giving rise to what some have called 'verandah Christianity'.[25] Yet, missionary presence was maintained in remote posts not only by catechists, but also by priests, pastors and members of western religious congregations.

Although they were imbued with colonial prejudices and, in daily life, associated with colonial officials, the missionaries maintained a certain distance from colonial institutions. Even though the majority of them avoided being totally identified with the colonial administration, the Christians on the mission stations regarded them as representatives of the government. In some cases, such as during the genocide of the Herero by the German army in 1904, they justified the actions of colonial forces against African people.[26] Their staunch opposition to polygamy, bride price, circumcision and other traditional customs reinforced the impression that they were associated with the colonial conquest venture.[27]

The colonial period witnessed the development of centrifugal movements resulting in the creation of African Independent Churches. In many instances, the development of an indigenous clergy strengthened frustrations and tensions because the priests and pastors were better educated than other converts and were therefore a better gauge of the distance which separated Christian discourse, which was fundamentally egalitarian, from the racial prejudices and discriminatory practices of colonial society.[28]

The first ordination of a black minister in Southern Africa, that of Tiyo Soga, a Presbyterian convert from the Eastern Cape who married a Scottish woman and foreshadowed in his writings the Black Consciousness movement, took place in Glasgow in 1856.[29] By the beginning of the twentieth century the Methodists had the largest group of black ministers in South Africa followed by Anglicans, Congregationalists and, late comers to the idea that Africans could be ordained as ministers, Lutherans. The movement towards the ordination of indigenous priests and pastors speeded up at the beginning of the

---

[23] J. D. Y. Peel, "For Who Hath Despised the Day of Small Things? Missionary Narratives and Historical Anthropology", *Comparative Studies in Society and History*, 37 (1995), 585-589; Derek Peterson and Jean Allman, "New Directions in the History of Mission in Africa", *Journal of Religious History*, 23 (1999), 1-3; Paul Landau, Hegemony and History in Jean and John Comaroff's *Of Revelation and Revolution,*" *Africa*, 70 (2000), 501-519.

[24] Paul Landau, *Popular Politics in the History of South Africa,* 1900-1948, Cambridge: Cambridge University Press, 2012, 74-75.

[25] Hastings, *The Church in Africa*, 563.

[26] Carl-J Hellberg, *Mission, Colonialism, and Liberation: The Lutheran Church in Namibia, 1840-1966*, Windhoek: New Namibia Books, 1997, 119.

[27] For a South African example, see "Missionaries, Xhosa Clergy and the Suppression of Traditional Customs," in Henry Bredenkamp and Robert Ross, eds., *Missions and Christianity in South African History*, Johannesburg: Witwatersrand University Press, 1995, 151-171.

[28] Richard Elphick, *The Equality of Believers: Protestant Missionaries and Racial Politics of South Africa,* Pietermaritzburg: University of KwaZulu-Natal Press, 2012.

[29] David Atwell, "The transculturation of the enlightenment: The *Journal* of Tiyo Soga Joanne Ruth Davis," in Rewriting Modernity. Studies in Black South African Literary History", Athens: Ohio University Press, 2005, 27-50; "Tiyo Soga: man of four names", unpublished PhD thesis, University of Pretoria, 2012.

twentieth century, firstly in the Protestant churches and then later in the Catholic Church. According to the *World Christian Handbook* the number of ministers ordained in sub-Saharan Africa grew from 1200 in 1900 to 4208 in 1957.

The development of African Independent Churches dates from the end of the nineteenth century. The movement began simultaneously, but apparently without mutual influence, in South Africa and Nigeria, two regions which were colonised and occupied by the English and which came under Protestant influence. The first known break-away movement in South Africa occurred in 1883, under the leadership of Nehemiah Tile, one of the first ordained Methodist ministers in the country. He founded an ethnic church, the Tembu National Church, which did not last long. The following decade, other secessionist movements appeared in the region of Pretoria and in Natal. Political differences and financial problems played a role in the decision to break away. The leaders of the new churches belonged for the most part to the Methodist Church but there were also Anglicans, Presbyterians and Congregationalists. One of the most famous was Mangena Mokone, who founded the Ethiopian Church in 1892. With the help of James Dwane – who would soon leave him to create, within the Anglican Church, a semi-independent church body called the Order of Ethiopia – he developed ties with the American Methodist Episcopal Church (AME Church), an Afro-American church which had been founded at the beginning of the nineteenth century in the USA.[30] In Malawi, Charles Domingo, an elder of the Livingstonia Mission, started, in 1908, a break-away church called the Seventh Day Baptists. 'Livingstonia,' Hasting commented, 'continued to regard itself, and to be generally regarded, as an exceptionally progressive mission. But Scottish progressivism, here as at Lovedale (in South Africa) or Blantyre was not incompatible with a deeply, almost racist, authoritarian treatment of those it was determined to uplift.'[31]

In subsequent years the most important – in numbers and in size – African Independent Churches in Southern Africa were those which Bengt Sundkler called Zionist – by contrast with Ethiopian – and which were characterised by Africanised forms of beliefs and worship and a strong emphasis on healing.[32] By 1950 there were at least twenty-three million Christians in sub-Saharan Africa. Of these roughly eleven million were Catholics, ten million Protestant and two million members of independent churches.

Post-Independence Christianity

Up until the 1950s all the sub-Saharan countries of Africa fell under colonial domination either as colonies or as protectorates. The independence movement speeded up in 1960 and in the following years. The last countries to gain independence were Angola and Mozambique (1975), Zimbabwe (1980), Namibia (1990) and South Africa (1994).

These political changes radically modified the role of Christian churches. Under the colonial regime, the majority of white missionaries were apolitical. They accepted the legitimacy of a benevolent colonialism. The attitude of the first African political leaders towards Christianity was ambiguous. They resented the racial prejudices of the missionaries, while appreciating their support at the same time. Most of them had been educated in Christian schools. Kenneth Kaunda and Hastings Banda, respectively the presidents of Zambia and Malawi, had been Presbyterian before changing to the African Methodist Episcopal Church for a while. Joshua Nkomo, the founder of the Zimbabwe African People's Union (ZAPU), was a Methodist and Robert Mugabe, the president of Zimbabwe, a Catholic. Nelson Mandela, his South African

[30] Hastings, *The Church in Africa,* 479-481; Philippe Denis, "Financial management and economic agency in the early history of the African Independent Churches", *Studia Historiae Ecclesiasticae,* 37/2 (2011), 29-49.

[31] Hastings, *The Church in Africa*, 484.

[32] Bengt Sundkler, *Bantu Prophets in South Africa*, 2nd ed., London: Oxford University Press, 1961.

counterpart, had been educated in Methodist schools before studying law at Fort Hare, a black university established by Protestant missionaries.[33]

When liberation movements were fighting for freedom, the churches were divided. A portion, sometimes significant, of the clergy and the faithful supported the rebels; the remainder stood firm behind the colonial power. After the granting of independence, the churches, which were now separated from the missions and managed by bishops or indigenous synods, adopted an attitude of critical loyalty towards the new governments. The weaker the state, the more powerful the church became, particularly with regard to matters such as education, health care, communication and development. Some churches opposed the new political power when it became authoritarian and corrupt. In Malawi the process of terminating President Banda's rule began with the 1992 Lenten pastoral letter of the Catholic bishops on multi-party democracy. The same year, the Council of Malagasy Churches played a key role in the Comité des Forces Vives, which led to the ousting of President Ratsikara in Madagascar.[34]

In countries led by white regimes, the polarisation was even stronger. In South-West Africa, two Lutheran church leaders, Bishop Auala of Ovamboland and Moderator Gowaseb of Windhoek published an 'Open Letter' to John Vorster, the South African prime minister, on the injustices practised in the country in 1971, a week after the International Court of Justice had declared illegal South Africa's presence in the territory.[35] During Zimbabwe's war of independence, Catholic priests, sisters and catechists fed, clothed, healed and protected Mugabe's guerrilla fighters.[36] Two decades later, however, it was the Catholic Justice and Peace Commission which denounced, with the support of episcopal conference, the atrocities committed by the Zimbabwean army's Fifth Brigade in Matebeleland in the 1980s.[37] In South Africa, Christian opposition to apartheid, at first limited to Beyers Naudé's Christian Institute and university students inspired by the Black Consciousness Movement, gathered strength in the 1980s leading to the arrest of hundreds of Christian activists during the two states of emergency. A grassroots-based confession of faith, the *Kairos Document*, declared the government illegitimate. In response, the regime called Archbishop Desmond Tutu, a critic of the status quo, a communist and bombed the headquarters of the South African Council of Churches in Johannesburg and of the Southern African Catholic Bishops' Conference in Pretoria.[38]

This high degree of political mobilisation has since subsided. The mainline churches are rather muted in their criticism of the new government's failure to tackle corruption and reduce poverty. As Frederick Chiluba had done in the 1990s when he declared Zambia a 'Christian nation',[39] Jacob Zuma, the South African president, woos the Pentecostal constituency whose 'gospel of prosperity' fits better the needs of the political elites than the mainline churches' call for social justice. The relationship between the African National Congress and the South African Council of Churches, its former ally, is at an all-time low.[40]

Internally, profound changes affected the Christian churches of Southern Africa in the post-independence period. The missionary societies, at work in the region since the early nineteenth century, handed over control to the local churches and the European and North American churches gradually

---

[33] Adrian Hastings, *A History of African Christianity 1950-1975* (Cambridge: Cambridge University Press, 1979), 95, 97, 141.

[34] Paul Gifford, *African Christianity. Its Public Role* (London: Hurst, 2001), 21.

[35] Hasting, *History of African Christianity*, 209.

[36] Janice McLaughlin, *On the Frontline, Catholic Missions in Zimbabwe's Liberation Wars* (Harare: Baobab Books, 1996).

[37] Catholic Commission for Justice and Peace in Zimbabwe, *Report on the 1980s Disturbances In Matabeleland and the Midlands*, March 1997.

[38] John de Gruchy, *The Church Struggle in South Africa*, rev. ed., Minneapolis, Fortress, 2005.

[39] Gifford, *African Christianity*, 197-198.

[40] Qaanitah Hunter and Mmanaledi Mataboge, "Churches forsake the ANC", *Mail and Guardian*, vol. 30, n°52 (23 December 2014), 2.

stopped sending missionaries to Africa. This policy was faster and more clear-cut in the Protestant churches where a call for a moratorium on foreign missionaries and foreign funds was issued in the early 1970s.

As we move further into the 21st century, Christianity remains, culturally, economically and politically, a force to reckon with in Southern Africa, where it is, and by far, the dominant religion. It is, however, more diversified and decentralised than ever, even in countries of Catholic culture like Lesotho, Angola, Mozambique and Madagascar. In South Africa the Pentecostal and African Independent Churches – two categories not always easy to differentiate – carry more weight, numerically, than the mainline churches, Protestant and Catholic combined. Similar evolutions are observed, though to a lesser degree, in the other Southern African countries.

Bibliography

Bredenkamp, Henry, and Ross, Robert, eds., *Missions and Christianity in South African History* (Johannesburg: Witwatersrand University Press, 1995).

Comaroff, Jean and John, *Of Revelation and Revolution*, 2 vol. (Chicago: University of Chicago, Press, 1991 and 1997).

Elphick, Richard, and Davenport, Rodney, eds, *Christianity in South Africa. A Political, Social and Cultural History* (Oxford: James Currey, 1997).

Elphick, Richard, *The Equality of Believers: Protestant Missionaries and Racial Politics of South Africa.* (Pietermaritzburg: University of KwaZulu-Natal Press, 2012).

Gifford, Paul, *African Christianity: Its Public Role* (London: Hurst, 2001).

Hastings, Adrian, *A History of African Christianity 1950-1975* (Cambridge: Cambridge University Press, 1979).

Hastings, Adrian, *The Church in Africa 1450-1950* (Oxford: Clarendon Press, 1994).

Henderson, Lawrence, *A Igreja em Angola* (Lisbon, Além-Mar, 1990).

Landau, Paul, *Popular Politics in the History of South Africa,* 1900-1948 (Cambridge: Cambridge University Press, 2012).

Nkomazana, Fidelis, and Lanner, Laurel, eds, *History of the Church in Botswana* (Pietermaritzburg: Cluster Publications, 2007).

Sundkler, Bengt and Steed, Christopher, *A History of the Church in Africa* (Cambridge: Cambridge University Press, 2000).

Sundkler, Bengt, *Bantu Prophets in South Africa*, 2nd ed. (London: Oxford University Press, 1961).

Volz, Stephen, *African Teachers on the Colonial Frontier. Tswana Evangelists and their Communities during the Nineteenth Century* (New York: Peter Lang, 2011).

Weller, John and Linden, Jean *Mainstream Christianity to 1980 in Malawi, Zambia and Zimbabwe* (Gweru, Mambo Press, 1984).

PART III

DENOMINATIONAL SURVEYS OF AFRICAN CHRISTIANITY

(22) An Introduction into the Typology of African Christianity

J. Kwabena Asamoah-Gyadu

Christianity has, since the middle of the twentieth century, developed as a non-western and non-white religion. In the meantime, Africa, as we indicate in these anthological essays, has emerged as one of its major heartlands. The essays in this section of the *Anthology to African Christianity* provide a bird's eye view of the different strands, trajectories and developments regarding how this has happened. An important dimension of the section is that the historic mission denominations that have been virtually neglected in the study of Christianity in Africa are represented here. At the beginning of the twentieth century, the fear of the Edinburgh 1910 World Missionary Conference was that Islam was going overwhelm the rest of the continent from the north, and sub-Saharan Africa was going to become what was referred to then as a 'Muhammadan' enclave. One hundred years later in 2010, the world was faced with a different scenario when another missionary conference met in the same facilities that had housed the 1910 event. The non-western presence could not be ignored. The continent had, perhaps to the surprise of many observers, emerged as a Christian one. The surprise element lies in the fact that following the evangelization efforts of the west, African initiatives in Christianity now dominate the landscape and this is set to continue well into the future.

Today, Christianity in Africa is offered as a major course in seminaries and universities across the globe and this constitutes an important reason for the production of such a volume. Readers and researchers can follow up the issues raised for further study. Across the world, many have set up schools and institutes for the study of World Christianity with a major focus on the faith as it has developed in Africa. In almost every case, studies in World Christianity give primacy of place to Africa alongside Asia and Latin American as fertile soil for Christian faith. Additionally, a number of writings have emerged that draw attention to the importance of Africa in the fortunes of World Christianity today, with Andrew Walls even suggesting that it is now impossible to talk about Christianity without Africa and to talk about Africa without Christianity.[1] The development of Christianity as a world religion, Kwame Bediako wrote, has given the faith a new lease of life in the non-western world. What these contexts have in common is that they have retained affinities with the living world of the Bible and of the experience of the reality and actuality of the Living God, as Jesus and the apostles experienced them and as recorded in the Scriptures.[2] The name 'Christian' as applied in Africa, as indeed in other parts of the world, covers a considerable diversity of entities and phenomena. It encapsulates churches of both local and foreign origins, as well as para-church movements of different persuasions and liturgical orientations. Western denominational specificities that were inherited from the early missionary eras are no longer paradigmatic for many African ecclesiological traditions.

In the development of Africa as a major heartland of Christianity therefore, it is important to note that that the faith has not developed as a monolithic ecclesial institution. In spite of the influence of western missionaries, Christianity has never been alien to the African experience. Historically, it is impossible to talk about Christianity in Africa without reference to the naming of Libya and Egypt among the nations that participated in the biblical Pentecost (Acts 2). Much later, the Acts of the Apostles records the

---

[1] See J. Kwabena Asamoah-Gyadu, "Turning That which is Already There Towards Christ: The Contribution of Andrew F. Walls to Understanding African Christianity", in William R. Burrows, Mark R. Gornick and Janice A. Maclean ed., *Understanding World Christianity: The Vision and Work of Andrew F. Walls* (Maryknoll, NY: Orbis Books, 2011), 195-210.

[2] Kwame Bediako, "The Emergence of World Christianity and the Remaking of Theology", *Journal of African Christian Thought,* vol. 12, 2 (2009), 50.

encounter between Philip and an Ethiopian eunuch who comes to faith and experiences baptism at the hands of the Apostle. That biblical record explains the iconic status of Ethiopia in African Christianity. The modern missionary era may therefore in a sense be considered a period not just of re-evangelization but also of the institutionalization of Christianity in terms of denominations. In western Christian thought, it often makes sense to categorize the presence of Christian churches and movements in terms of Roman Catholic, mainline Protestant, Evangelical, Pentecostal, Charismatic, and so on. Such typologies have very limited application today, given the ways in which Christian religious innovations in Africa have developed and influenced each other.

The Roman Catholic Church remains a distinct and centrally governed Christian church throughout Africa. Post-Vatican II 'reformations' in the liturgy however means that the oldest Christian denomination in Africa, except for that of Ethiopia, has also changed considerably. An important work that looks at the liturgical innovations of Ghanaian Catholicism led by Archbishop Emeritus Peter K. Sarpong of the Kumasi Diocese and entitled *Asante Catholicism*, is representative of some of the changes that have taken place in that otherwise highly liturgical tradition. Additionally, the ministry of exorcism led by the former Catholic Archbishop of Lusaka, Emmanuel Milingo, enables us to appreciate how the sort of innovations occurring through the incorporation of the African traditional religious worldview into the independent church traditions have not been limited to those churches.

With its highly revered papal authority and clearly defined episcopal governance structure, the Catholic Church remains strong and its influence is seen in the numbers of basic, secondary and high schools and universities established on the continent. Additionally, the Catholic Relief Services is recognized as an important religious outfit in places where natural disasters and famine have occurred. The Church's credibility took a battering during the genocidal wars in Rwanda and Burundi but on the whole this is a denomination that has quite a respectable following in Africa. The Catholic Church shares with the historically older Protestant mission denominations the description 'mainline churches' in Africa. That description now makes sense only in terms of historical establishment but no longer in terms of numerical strength. The most popular and recognizable historic mission Protestant denominations in Africa would include the Presbyterian, Methodist and Anglican churches. These denominations established by various western mission bodies from London, Basel and Bremen have existed in Africa for close to two centuries. East and Southern African Methodists have churches that can trace their roots to both the UK and the USA, such as the United Methodist Church with its mild episcopal tradition. Similarly, Anglican churches in Africa exist in both 'high' and 'low' versions. Together the historic mission denominations, as I like to call the mainline churches, have been at the forefront in the provision of formal education and medical care in Africa. The collaboration with indigenous agents of the Protestant tradition in the translation of the Bible into various vernaculars has had a direct bearing, not just on the growth of Christianity but also in opening the way for Africans to introduce innovations into Christianity that bridged the biblical and African worlds.

The first African responses to missionary work in Africa came at the end of the nineteenth century when Nationalist or Ethiopianist churches were established. A century after the nineteenth-century missionary enterprise established its roots, a Black Nationalist elite group dubbed 'Ethiopianists' in Southern Africa and 'Nationalists' in West Africa seceded from their historic Protestant mission denominations to set up independent churches under indigenous leadership. On the whole, they retained much of the liturgical structures of the historic mission denominations but they were new in two important respects. First, Ethiopianist churches were under indigenous leadership, and secondly, they favoured the use of the vernacular in worship as part of the protest against European ecclesial leadership. One of the most popular Ethiopianist or Nationalist churches was pioneered by David Vincent Brown of the Niger Delta, who became known as Mojola Agbebi in the attempt to shed part of his colonial heritage acquired through the church in the usage of so-called baptismal or Christian names like 'David'. The Ethiopian or Nationalist churches did not develop into mass movements but they are significant as the first known group of indigenous religious initiatives in Africa.

The second response was what became known as the African Independent/Initiated/Indigenous churches (AICs) of the early twentieth century. Indigenous charismatic prophets like William Wade Harris, Isaiah Shembe and Simon Kimbangu did much to inspire new initiatives in African Christianity. These AICs, *Aladura* (people of prayer) or Spiritual churches, were the first group of mass Christian religious movements to transform the religious landscape in Africa. Their major contribution to Christianity in Africa was the integration of charismatic experiences, particularly healing and prophecy, into Christian life. They recognized the leadership role of women in church life, and indeed many founders of independent churches were women. Until the early 1970s, when their activities seemed to have started plummeting, the AICs, for the best part of the twentieth century, would be considered the representative face of Christianity on the continent. During the period of the rise of the AICs, several classical Pentecostal denominations also emerged across Africa with many having roots in similar traditions from the West. Perhaps the most popular of these would be the Assemblies of God but there are many other churches sharing the designation 'Apostolic' that belong to this tradition of classical Pentecostalism.

At the end of the 1970s, Africa experienced a third major response in Christian innovation. This new form of independent churches is a hybrid of the older independents and North American contemporary Pentecostal traditions. Like the older independent churches, they emphasize charismatic renewal and create ritual contexts for the exercise of prophetic ministries and healing and deliverance. They are a bit more 'trendy' in outlook and perhaps their main theological emphasis is the fact that God is a God of prosperity. Their periodic campaigns and conventions frequently use secular themes that teach young people about how to make money and be successful in life. Although it is not preached in the same way by all its leaders, the attraction that this movement holds for Africa's upwardly mobile youth therefore include 'the prosperity gospel'. Their expressive and exuberant styles of worship, motivational messages of success and possibilities and extensive use of modern media have endeared them to many young people in Africa. In the words of Ogbu Kalu, with the rise of this third wave in African Initiated Christianity 'we are witnessing the implosion of a third force, moved by the wind of the Third Person of the Trinity in the triple task of the re-evangelization, intensification and reconstruction of Christian experience in contemporary Africa'.[3]

The church in Africa is a virtual religious zoo with all kinds of Christian wildlife. There are multitudes of different churches and denominations that are difficult to place neatly in the categories identified here. Thus, for example, we need to take account of the many interdenominational, non-denominational and ecumenical churches that exist in urban Africa. These consist mostly of middle class public servants who for one reason or another are uncomfortable with the historic mission denominations in particular and therefore come together to find a 'middle way' to worship in terms of liturgy. It is not uncommon to find members of these churches who still hold allegiance in their historic mother mission denominations and claim that heritage when required.

We started this introduction to Christianity in Africa with reference to the work of the historic mission denominations and their evangelization efforts. These churches, products of the evangelical missionary enterprise in Europe, are said to have failed at the meeting point of liturgy and proclamation to provide people with new materials that would 'fund, feed, nurture, nourish, legitimate and authorize a counter-imagination to the world'.[4] The result was the rise of various independent churches that took the spirit world seriously and forged a new type of spirituality that remained loyal to both the biblical and African worlds. The Christian religious landscape in Africa is not simple to negotiate and the essays in this section

---

[3] Ogbu U. Kalu, "The Third Response: Pentecostalism and the Reconstruction of Christian Experience in Africa, 1970-1995", *Journal of African Christian Thought,* vol. 1, 2 (1998), 3.

[4] Kalu, "Third Response", 4.

should help somewhat to appreciate the different ecclesiological ways in which the body of Christ has transformed the African religious environment.

Bibliography

William R. Burrows, Mark R. Gornick and Janice A. Maclean ed., *Understanding World Christianity: The Vision and Work of Andrew F. Walls* (Maryknoll, NY: Orbis Books, 2011)

Kwame Bediako, "The Emergence of World Christianity and the Remaking of Theology", *Journal of African Christian Thought*, vol. 12, 2 (2009)

Ogbu U. Kalu, "The Third Response: Pentecostalism and the Reconstruction of Christian Experience in Africa, 19701995", *Journal of African Christian Thought*, vol. 1, 2 (1998)

(23) Oriental Orthodox Churches in Africa

Ayalkibet Berhanu Tesfaye

Worldwide, there are six Oriental Orthodox Churches, all of which are in full communion with each other. These churches are the:

- Coptic Orthodox Church of Alexandria,
- Ethiopian Orthodox Tewahedo Church,
- Armenian Apostolic Church,
- Syriac Orthodox Church of Antioch (also known as Syrian Orthodox Church),
- Indian Orthodox Church, and
- Eritrean Orthodox Tewahedo Church.

These six churches indicated above accept the dogmatic position that was taken in the first three ecumenical councils of Nicea (AD 325), Constantinople (AD 381) and Ephesus (AD 431). They ultimately rejected the nature of the Christological formula which was put forth by the Council of Chalcedon (AD 451).[1] The reason for their rejection was that the Council of Chalcedon (AD 451) held that Jesus has two natures – one divine and the other human. Although these natures are inseparable, this Council maintained that they act as one *hypostasis* (i.e. one nature who shares two distinct natures).[2] To the spiritual epistemologists who were led by St Cyril of Alexandria and those who supported his Christological formula, the position that was taken at the Council of Chalcedon (AD 451) was tantamount to accepting Nestorianism. Doctrinally, this idea of the two natures of Christ was previously rejected by the Council of Ephesus (AD 431).[3]

In response to the Council of Chalcedon (AD 451), the counter-argument was effectively advanced by St Cyril of Alexandria who maintained that the Incarnation was more important than all other dogmatic considerations. He expressed his position as follows: 'Incarnation is a divine mystery. The two natures of Godhead and Manhood are perfectly united and Christ is thus one person and one Nature from two natures.'[4] An elaboration on this argument maintained that: 'By the union of the nature in the Incarnation the two natures become one nature, the natures being united without separation, without confusion, and without change.'[5] This union of humanity and divinity of Christ was achieved in the Virgin Mary's womb and is inseparable and indivisible. Consequently, it follows that Christ is completely divine and human at all times and in all actions, just as he is simultaneously fully God and fully human. The Oriental Orthodox churches are, therefore, often labelled by others as monophysite churches. However, this label is rejected by the Oriental churches as it is a misnomer which, at best, represents a gross misunderstanding of the Oriental Orthodox churches' Christological formula. Monophysite is associated with Eutychian Monophysitism,[6] 'who denied the union of the human by divine, and is believed to have taught that in Christ the human Nature was absorbed by the divine nature. They also do not accept the Dyophysite teachings of Nestorius'.[7] Understandably, therefore, the Oriental Orthodox churches prefer to be called

---

[1] Desta, Alemayehu. *Introduction to the Ethiopian Orthodox Faith.* (Bloomington: Author House, 2012), 69.
[2] What is Coptic Christianity, and what do Coptic Christians believe? www.gotquestions.org/Coptic-Christianity.html.
[3] Wondmagegnehu, Aymro and Motovu, Joachim. *The Ethiopian Orthodox Church* (Addis Ababa: Ethiopian Orthodox Mission,1970), 121.
[4] Wondmagegnehu, Aymro and Motovu, Joachim. *The Ethiopian Orthodox Church*, 95.
[5] Wondmagegnehu, Aymro and Motovu, Joachim. *The Ethiopian Orthodox Church,* 95.
[6] Denying the two natures of Christ. www.gotquestions.org/Coptic-Christianity.html.
[7] Wondmagegnehu, Aymro and Motovu, Joachim. *The Ethiopian Orthodox Church,* 98.

'non-Chalcedonian' or 'miaphysite' churches (i.e. believing in one composite or conjoined nature from two).[8]

The Oriental Orthodox churches are heirs to some of the richest and most ancient traditions in Christendom in that they are hierarchically independent. These churches use ancient languages in their liturgy and calendar. In the cases of Ethiopia and Eritrea, they operate on the basis of the Julian calendar. The Coptic Church has its own calendar which 'begins with the year 248 (it corresponds to 1 "Anno Martyrum", AM or in the "Year of the Martyrs")'.[9] Other traditional practices pertain. For instance, in the case of the Coptic Church, they use the Coptic language and in Ethiopia's case, the Ge'ez language and modern Amharic. Similarly, in the Eritrean Orthodox Church, both Ge'ez and Tigrinya are used. These churches' long tradition of monastic spirituality has produced considerable religious literature and their own iconographic tradition. Moreover, since their earliest days, the Oriental Orthodox churches have developed their own forms of liturgy, art and literature.[10]

Each of the six churches traces its origins to apostolic missions of the first century. For instance, Saints Thaddeus and Bartholomew are believed to have been martyred in Armenia; St Mark is referred to as the first bishop of Alexandria; St Philip is said to have baptized an Ethiopian eunuch (*Bakos*), who had gone on a pilgrimage to Jerusalem and who returned home to spread the faith in African lands, particularly in Ethiopia; Antioch is mentioned in the book of Acts as the place where the term 'Christian' was first used; and St Thomas is believed to have been martyred in South India.[11] These significant manifestations of belief by ancient Christians who were willing to accept martyrdom indicate the spiritual strength of the *kerygma* to which they were responding.

Historically, the division between the ancient Oriental Orthodox Churches and other Churches can be traced back to the years after the Council of Chalcedon in AD 451, whose Christological teaching was not accepted by the Oriental Orthodox Churches. In arguing the merits of the Church's unity, scholars maintain that 'the whole Christian world is fully aware of the fact that there had been a universal church until Chalcedon (451) and believes that it is still invisibly one since Christ is one and the church is one'.[12] Complementing this argument is Archbishop Yesehaq of the Ethiopian Orthodox Church who attests that:

> It is necessary, therefore, for all Christian (Churches) to admit that God is not a Roman Catholic or a protestant. He is neither Monophysite nor Dyophysite or any other kind of indicated denomination that refers to political authorities and nationalistic ideas which are contrary to the high principles of equality, unity and Christian love. But Jesus Christ, Our Lord and God, is one Creator, one Saviour, for all (human)kind, who has the blood of all races in His veins, as he is the universal redeemer.[13]

In his book 'Timherte Melekot' (the Amharic version), Asrat Gebremariam, an Ethiopian Orthodox Tewahedo Church writer of the twentieth century, carefully examined the contentious theological argument that took place between the Oriental Orthodox and Roman Catholic Churches at Chalcedon in 451 and the current retrospective assessment of its divisive arguments. His evaluation of what transpired was that 'the

---

[8] What is Coptic Christianity, and what do Coptic Christians believe? www.gotquestions.org/Coptic-Christianity.html.
[9] de Gruchy, John, "From Cairo to the Cape: The significance of Coptic Orthodoxy for African Christianity." *Journal of Theology for Southern Africa*, no.99 (1997), 29. Coptic Orthodox Church, http://pluralism.org/affiliates/student/allen/Oriental-Orthodox/Coptic/CopticChurch.html.
[10] Michael S. Allen (2005). An Introduction to the Oriental Orthodox Churches http://pluralism.org/affiliates/student/allen/Oriental-Orthodox/Home.html.
[11] Michael S. Allen (2005). An Introduction to the Oriental Orthodox Churches. http://pluralism.org/affiliates/student/allen/Oriental-Orthodox/Home.html.
[12] Makarios, Abuna, et al. *The Ethiopian Orthodox Tewahedo Church Faith, Order of Worship, and Ecumenical Relations* (Addis Ababa: Tensae Publishing House, 1996), 143.
[13] Yesehaq, Abuna. *The Ethiopian Tewahedo Church* (New York: Vantage Press, 1989), 101.

Oriental Orthodox Church as it condemned Nestorius, it also condemns the heresy of Eutyches. Similarly, the Roman Catholic Church as it condemned Eutyches, it also condemns the teaching of Nestorius. Therefore, this is common ground on which the original unity of Christ's church could be restored as long as both church bodies good-heartedly strive for unity'.[14] This argument is consistent with Christ's teachings when he prayed for his followers' unity, '...that they may all be one' (John 17:21).

African Indigenous (Authentic) Christianity

Contrary to what may be viewed as conventional wisdom, Christianity in Africa was not introduced by nineteenth-century missionaries. On the contrary, Africa's piety was manifested in its hosting the Holy Family into Egypt after the birth of Jesus[15] and the baptism of an Ethiopian eunuch,[16] as was indicated above. The antecedent to these developments was the premier position that Ethiopia held in religion in general which saw it being referred to as a metaphor for Africa in Psalm 68:31 which said: 'Princes shall come out of Egypt; Ethiopia shall soon stretch out her hands unto God.' In the Christian era, Egypt and Ethiopia are the centres of Christianity's beginning and defenders of its original teachings. These churches, along with the Eritrean Church, are representatives of the '...One, Holy, Universal and Apostolic Church founded by Jesus Christ'.[17] They are called the Oriental Orthodox Churches.

Three of the six sees of the Oriental Orthodox churches are based in Africa. These are the Coptic Orthodox Church of Alexandria, in Cairo; the Ethiopian Orthodox Tewahedo Church, in Addis Ababa; and the Eritrean Orthodox Tewahedo Church, in Asmara. The first two of these churches were founding members of the World Council of Churches (WCC).[18] The Eritrean Orthodox Tewahedo Church was originally under Ethiopia when the Ethiopian Orthodox Church became a founding member of the WCC. Since its autocephaly[19] in 1993, the Eritrean Orthodox Tewahedo Church officially became a member of WCC in 2003. It is important that these three churches are examined on an individual basis in order that their historical backgrounds be clearly understood.

The Coptic Orthodox Church

Although it was historically located in Alexandria, the Coptic Orthodox Church is presently centred in Cairo, Egypt. Along with Jerusalem, Antioch, Rome and Constantinople, Alexandria was one of the five patriarchal thrones of early Christendom.[20] Founded by St Mark the Evangelist, the Coptic Church traces its history back to Egypt. St Mark's apostolic mission to Egypt in AD 61 went via the Libyan desert.[21] On his prior missionary journeys he accompanied the apostles St Peter, St Paul and St Barnabas to many locations.[22] St Mark was also known from gospel teachings as one of the seventy apostles who were chosen

[14] Gebeemariam, Asrat. *Timherte Melekot,* 2nd book (Addis Ababa, 1999), 164.
[15] What does scripture tell us about Mary's life? http://campus.udayton.edu/mary/questions/faq/faq02.html.
[16] See: Acts 8,26-40 Tewahedo.
[17] Wondmagegnehu and Motovu, *The Ethiopian Orthodox Church*, 96.
[18] World Council of Churches: Oriental Orthodox. www.oikoumene.org/en/church-families/orthodox-churches-oriental/oriental-orthodox-churches
[19] Autocephaly means the self-headed status of a hierarchical Christian church whose head bishop does not report to any higher-ranking bishop. See: https://en.wikipedia.org/wiki/Autocephaly.
[20] Michael S. Allen (2005). An Introduction to the Oriental Orthodox Churches. http://pluralism.org/affiliates/student/allen/Oriental-Orthodox/Home.html.
[21] Michael S. Allen (2005). Coptic Orthodox Church. http://pluralism.org/affiliates/student/allen/Oriental-Orthodox/Coptic/CopticChurch.html.
[22] Michael S. Allen (2005). Coptic Orthodox Church. http://pluralism.org/affiliates/student/allen/Oriental-Orthodox/Coptic/CopticChurch.html.

by Jesus Christ (Luke 10:1). He was also the first patriarch of Alexandria, was martyred in AD 68 and the first church in Egypt was named after him.[23] The unbroken hierarchy of the Coptic Patriarchal See continues up until today with its 118th Patriarch, His Holiness Tawadros II.

One of the greatest legacies of the Coptic Church is the monastic tradition, described by Coptic scholar Aziz Atiya as 'the gift of Egypt to Christendom'.[24] As early as the second or third century, Christians desiring to devote themselves entirely to a life of prayer and fasting began to retreat to the solitude of the Egyptian desert. Paralleling this development is the generally accepted fact that St Anthony the Great is regarded as the father of monasticism, though it was his younger contemporary, St Pachomius, who first organized a formal, communal style of monastic life.[25] From Egypt, the monastic movement spread throughout the Christian world, despite challenges from Islam. It has began to experience a revival in the late twentieth century. Currently, there are several hundred monks and nuns both in Egypt and abroad who have devoted their lives to monasticism. In essence, therefore, the Coptic Orthodox Church is rightly referred to '...as the Cradle of Monasticism...(as it) had a role in laying the bases for... Christian Theology'.[26]

Another significant contribution made by the Coptic Church to Christianity is its theological education through 'The Theological Catechetical School of Alexandria (the First Seminary)'.[27] This partially explains why Alexandria became a renowned centre of learning, especially in theology. It follows, therefore, that many of the early church fathers flourished in Christian Egypt. Notable among them were Clement of Alexandria and his successor Origen who headed the Catechetical School at Alexandria, one of the most famous institutions of learning in antiquity.[28] Other towering figures were St Athanasius the Great, a defender of orthodoxy at the First Ecumenical Council (325), and St Cyril of Alexandria, the most influential voice at the Third Ecumenical Council (431). The works of St Cyril, who vehemently rejected Nestorius's apparent separation of Christ's humanity from his divinity, are often cited by Oriental Orthodox theologians as a foundation for the rejection of the Council of Chalcedon (451). Coptic Church membership is now estimated to be 16 million in Egypt and abroad.[29]

The Ethiopian Orthodox Tewahedo Church (EOTC)

Historiographically, as has been attested in the Old and New Testaments, Ethiopia is the first African nation to have adhered to the Jewish religion (900 B.C.)[30] and subsequently the Christian religion from its inception, beginning with the apostolic era. With respect to the former, monotheism was concretized between the time of the Queen of Sheba of Ethiopia and King Solomon of Israel. With respect to Christianity, it was first brought to Ethiopia in AD 34 as a result of an Ethiopian eunuch who was baptized

---

[23] Michael S. Allen (2005). Introduction to our Coptic Orthodox Church. http://stmarkcharlotte.org/wp/the-coptic-church/.

[24] Michael S. Allen (2005). An Introduction to the Oriental Orthodox Churches. http://pluralism.org/affiliates/student/allen/Oriental-Orthodox/Home.html.

[25] Michael S. Allen (2005). An Introduction to the Oriental Orthodox Churches. http://pluralism.org/affiliates/student/allen/Oriental-Orthodox/Home.html.

[26] Tawfik, Wedad. "Theological education in the Coptic Orthodox Church (the Church of Alexandria)". In *Handbook of Theological Education in Africa*, edited by Isabel Apawo Phiri and Dietrich Werner (ed), 263-269 (Pietermaritzburg: Cluster Publications, 2013), 265.

[27] Tawfik, Wedad, *Theological education in the Coptic Orthodox Church,* 267.

[28] Michael S. Allen (2005). An Introduction to the Oriental Orthodox Churches. http://pluralism.org/affiliates/student/allen/Oriental-Orthodox/Home.html.

[29] Coptic Orthodox Church of Alexandria, http://en.wikipedia.org/wiki/Coptic_Orthodox_Church_of_Alexandria

[30] Ethiopian Orthodox Tewahedo Church, "Historical perspective on the Christian religion in Ethiopia". http://eotc.faithweb.com/orth.html

by the Apostle Philip, and then introduced this faith to his own country (Acts 8:26-40). Following this development, St Matthew, the evangelist, and later St Andrew, also came to Ethiopia and continued this missionary activity of spreading the Christian faith.[31] This evidence leads to the inescapable fact that not only was there a transformation from Judaism to Christianity, but also the EOTC can rightly be regarded as an African Indigenous Church and one of the earliest apostolic churches in the world. This phenomenon has been described thus:

> The Ethiopian Orthodox Church's uniqueness implies that she is not a copy of either the Coptic (meaning Egyptian) or any other church in the world but original, i.e. the Orthodox Church of Ethiopia. She… occupies a remarkable place in the country's history. The long history of indigenization of the Church has enabled her to develop unique features which show that she is (quintessentially) African…. (So profound was this adherence to uniqueness that) African Churches which were founded between 1880 and 1920, established new religious organizations that were run by Africans as religious protest movements, based on the idea of Ethiopianism….[32]

The foregoing accurately describes Ethiopia's unique Christian identity. This was initiated by the visit of the Queen of Sheba (Queen Makeda) of Ethiopia, to King Solomon of Israel as a result of her having been intrigued by his legendary wisdom. That visit brought about a remarkable outcome for Ethiopia and by extrapolation for Africa. What follows are the main elements:

1. The birth of the Solomonic Dynasty in Ethiopia began with Emperor Menelik I, Solomon's first born,[33] whose mother was the Queen of Sheba. The significance of this development is that the… *Kebra Nagast* (The Glory of the Kings), a medieval work usually cited as the textual source for the monarchical tradition, records the intriguing legend relating to Menelik. It has been maintained that he was sent to Jerusalem to visit his father, King Solomon. While he was there, he was anointed in anticipation of returning to Ethiopia. This return on Menelik's part resulted in the Ark of the Covenant (arguably, the most sacred relic in both Judaism and Christianity) being brought from Jerusalem to Ethiopia in approximately 900 B.C.[34] There are many who believe that the Ark is still there (in Ethiopia) to this day, carefully guarded in a sanctuary near the Church of St Mary of Zion in Axum.[35] However, the Solomonic dynasty ended with the overthrow of Emperor Haile Selassie I of Ethiopia in 1974.[36]
2. Accompanying this most sacred of relics were members of each of the twelve tribes of Israel, including members of the Levite clergy. They brought with them the Old Testament books.[37] The assembling of this body of relics facilitated Ethiopians in their worship of the monotheistic God.

---

[31] Tesfaye, Ayalkibet. "The Ethiopian Orthodox Tewahedo Church and its traditional theological education system." In *Handbook of Theological Education in Africa*, edited by Isabel Apawo Phiri and Dietrich Werner (ed), 281-291 (Pietermaritzburg: Cluster Publications, 2013), 283.

[32] Tamene, Getnet. "Features of the Ethiopian Orthodox Church and the Clergy". *Journal of Asian and African Studies*, no. 7 (1998), 90.

[33] Tamene, Getnet, "Features of the Ethiopian Orthodox Church and the Clergy", 92.

[34] Shahid, *"The Solomonides"*. In *The Worlds of Eastern Christianity, 300-1500 Volume 4: Languages and Cultures of Eastern Christianity: Ethiopian,* edited by Alessandro (ed), 146-178 (Farnham, UK: Ashgate, 2012),157. Hancock, Graham, *The sign and the seal: the explosively controversial international best seller: a quest for the lost Ark of the Covenant.* (London: Arrow Books, 1992), 450.

[35] Ethiopian Orthodox Tewahedo Church, http://pluralism.org/affiliates/student/allen/Oriental-Orthodox/Ethiopian/EthiopianChurch.html.

[36] Tamene, Getnet, "Features of the Ethiopian Orthodox Church and the Clergy", 87. www.aepress.sk/aas/full/aas198h.pdf.

[37] Gerima, Abuna et al., *The Ethiopian Orthodox Tewahedo Church History from the Birth of Christ up to 2000*: Ethiopia Stretches out her hands to God (2008), 9-11.

3. Ethiopians began to practise circumcision which was a Jewish tradition and as such, expressed their relationship with God. What started as a religious phenomenon has now been acknowledged as a healthful anti-HIV and sexually-transmitted infection preventative. All the above-mentioned phenomena combined in effecting Ethiopia's transformation from being a nation whose religion was based on natural law (law of consciousness) to one that was based on Covenant law.[38]
4. *Axum* (Ethiopia's ancient capital) was founded by *Axsumawi* the great grandson of Ham and descendent of Noah.[39]
5. In the fourteenth century, Emperor Dawit or David (1380-1410) of Ethiopia brought from Jerusalem iconic relics that many maintain are authentic: (a) a part of the True Cross on which Jesus was crucified; and (b) an icon known today as 'Kure'at Reesu' that depicts Christ's Crown with the thorns, and other important Christian relics (including St Mary's image that was painted by St Luke).[40]

Coupled with the twelfth to thirteenth-century construction of 'the rock-hewn church buildings',[41] the heritage mentioned above, its liturgy, history, ancient manuscripts and enchanting musical compositions, Ethiopia has seen a significant influx of scholars, writers and tourists from all over the world. Between A. D. 330 when St Frumentius was ordained by St Athanasius of Alexandria and the Ethiopian Church's autocephaly in 1950, Coptic bishops were assisting the Ethiopian Church solely in ordination. Other administrative matters and evangelization were the sole responsibility of Ethiopian scholars.[42] His Holiness Mathias I is the sixth patriarch of the EOTC. The EOTC has 'more than 45 million members, 40,000 churches and monasteries, and about 500,000 clergymen, mainly in Ethiopia. It has been the dominant church in Ethiopia since the fourth century and is also the largest Oriental Orthodox Church in the world'.[43]

The Eritrean Orthodox Tewahedo Church

Despite the geographical and nationalistic differences between Eritrea and Ethiopia, there is a symbiotic relationship in their religious traditions, which has existed for almost three millennia. This is manifested in the fact that there are no significant differences between the Eritrean Orthodox Tewahedo Church and the Ethiopian Orthodox Tewahedo Church on any level or manifestation.[44] This relationship can be explained by the fact that until its independence in 1993, Eritrea was one of the dioceses of the Ethiopian Orthodox Church Synod.[45] Because traditionally the Church and the Ethiopian state were twin institutions which

---

[38] When we say the law of consciousness, it is believed that worship of the one True God (the God of Noah) had been in existence in the early times, but it was confined to a limited number of families, and that the Sun God was widely known in Axum, one of Ethiopia's earliest kingdoms.

[39] Yesehaq, Abuna, *The Ethiopian Tewahedo Church,* 3.

[40] Melaku, L, *History of the Ethiopian Orthodox Tewahedo Church: From the Reign of Emperor Caleb to the end of Zagwe Dynasty and from the Classical (Golden) Age to the Present: Part Two and Three.* (Addis Ababa, 2010), 84-85. http://kweschn.wordpress.com/2012/09/26/meskel-festival-the-finding-of-the-true-cross/ www.adoremus.org/0800-Sheila.html https://ethiopiantimes.wordpress.com/2011/09/27/ethiopian-christians-celebrate-the-discovery-of-the-true-cross/.

[41] Wondmagegnehu, Aymro, *The Oriental Orthodox churches Addis Ababa conference* (Addis Ababa: Artistic Printers,1965), 48.

[42] Gebreamanuel, Berhanu et al., *The church of Ethiopia past and present* (Addis Ababa: Commercial Printing Enterprise, 1997), 15.

[43] Gerima, Abuna, et al., *The Ethiopian Orthodox Tewahedo Church History from the Birth of Christ up to 2000*, xxi.

[44] Michael S. Allen (2005), *Eritrean Orthodox Tewahedo Church.* http://pluralism.org/affiliates/student/allen/Oriental-Orthodox/Eritrean/EritreanChurch.html.

[45] Abbink, Jon., *A Bibliography on Christianity in Ethiopia* (2003), 1. www.ascleiden.nl/pdf/workingpaper52.pdf.

complemented each other, the *abuna* (bishop) was the most influential person in the Ethiopian nation. So much was this the case that in ancient times, the abuna had the power to crown the emperor as well as effect excommunication in consultation with the emperor. This relationship explains why it was maintained that 'the state and the church are two faces of the same book. This book is Ethiopia'.[46]

Eritrea's independence emanated from a protracted civil war in Ethiopia which lasted for more than a decade. One aspect of this war was Eritrea's opposition group to the *Derg* (or military government which deposed Emperor Haile Selassie in 1974) as well as its desire for independence from Ethiopia. Once this independence was achieved, the new Eritrean government insisted that the Eritrean Orthodox Tewahedo Church also be independent of the Ethiopian Synod.[47] These developments culminated in the Eritrean church electing its first patriarch, Philipos I, in 1998 who was consecrated by Pope Shenouda III, Patriach of the Coptic Church, Egypt.[48]

The two neighbouring country's churches' relationship is somewhat strained, in the sense that Church leaders in both countries cannot meet each other in either country.[49] However, they remain in full communion with one another as well as with the other Oriental Orthodox churches. Both the Eritrean and the Ethiopian Orthodox Tewahedo Churches share a common heritage of liturgy and art, along with other oriental Orthodox churches, a relationship which is at least fifteen hundred years old.[50] This theological and ecclesiological relationship has been cemented by the fact that both Churches always sided with non-Chalcedonian Christology, 'which teaches that Christ has but one, undivided nature, at once human and divine'. In celebration of this doctrine, the Ethiopian and Eritrean Orthodox Churches also refer to themselves as *Tewahedo*, or 'unity/made one' churches'.[51] Eritrean Orthodox Church membership is now estimated to be 3 million.[52] His Holiness Dioskoros is the fourth patriarch of the Eritrean Orthodox Tewahedo Church.

Oriental Orthodox Christianity and its African Ethos

The ethos of the Oriental Orthodox Churches is instructive in informing us about original Christianity in Africa. This was inevitable as through the process of acculturation, African elements became an integral part of the Oriental Orthodox Church practices. Such elements as drumming, night vigil, the clapping of hands, appealing to one's ancestors for intercession on one's behalf (which may be viewed as, at least, tangentially related to making a similar request of Saints),[53] and spirit possession are all elements of African religiosity. In elaborating these phenomena, de Gruchy maintains that:

---

[46] Wondmagegnehu and Motovu, *The Ethiopian Orthodox Church*, 113.
[47] The Eritrean Orthodox Church www.cnewa.org/default.aspx?ID=10&pagetypeID=9&sitecode=HQ&pageno=1.
[48] The Eritrean Orthodox Church www.cnewa.org/default.aspx?ID=10&pagetypeID=9&sitecode=HQ&pageno=1.
[49] The Eritrean Orthodox Church http://pluralism.org/affiliates/student/allen/Oriental-Orthodox/Eritrean/EritreanChurch.html.
[50] The Eritrean Orthodox Church http://pluralism.org/affiliates/student/allen/Oriental-Orthodox/Eritrean/EritreanChurch.html.
[51] Michael S. Allen (2005). *An Introduction to the Oriental Orthodox Churches.* http://pluralism.org/affiliates/student/allen/Oriental-Orthodox/Home.html. About Orthodox Faith and Eritrean Orthodox Church, www.eritreanorthodox.org/id6.html.
[52] Eritrean Orthodox Tewahedo Church, http://en.wikipedia.org/wiki/Eritrean_Orthodox_Tewahedo_Church.
[53] The worship of Saints is expressly forbidden by the Church; however, asking for their intercessions is not forbidden. Any (Orthodox) Church is named after a Patron Saint. Among all Saints, the Virgin St Mary (Theotokos) occupies a special place in the heart of all (Orthodox Christians). www.touregypt.net/featurestories/copticchristians.htm Read more: www.touregypt.net/featurestories/copticchristians.htm#ixzz3T3Up77qX.

> …monks and priests, to say nothing of lay people, expect miracles to happen in a way which not only reflects the world of the Bible, but also the world of Africa. In the same way, things such as prayer and fasting, pilgrimage to holy places, baptism and immersion in holy water, the use of holy oil in healing, a liturgy in which time stands still (as priests celebrate the sacred mysteries behind the iconostasis within the 'Holy of Holies', moving around the square altar shrouded in clouds of incense), and, of course, the use of drums in the Ethiopian Orthodox Church, are all Hebraic and African in their ethos and significance, yet undeniably Christian of the most Orthodox kind. Who needs European theology or Western Christianity?[54]

Furthermore, from an architectural perspective, Africans believe that the beauty of the place of worship parallels the celestial beauty and holiness of the transcendent God (Lev. 20:26, 1 Pet. 1:16). It is also arguable, however, that the most important aspect of Ethiopian Orthodox Church worship is its liturgy.[55]

This liturgical expression is best expressed in the work of St Yared, a sixth-century Ethiopian scholar, musician, ecclesiastic and a saint in the Ethiopian Orthodox Church. In assessing his multi-faceted cultural work, one famous scholar observed that his –

> contributions to the cultural life of the country can be divided into three categories – education, literature, and music. The educational system he developed remained in use, unchanged, until modern times. It stressed the need to adapt teaching to the pace of development of a young intellect, and also held that pupils should not only be taught but should also be diverted from idleness, by means of a stick if necessary. In literature, his work occupies the highest position, and his collection of hymns, *Mazgaba Degwa* ('Treasury of Hymns') is the oldest literary work written in Ge'ez. It is said that before Yared there was no music in Ethiopia, the liturgies and chants being murmured in a low voice; he is therefore believed to be the first Ethiopian composer. He stated that he was inspired by God in his composition, and presented his music in three modes – 'Ge'ez' (the simplest plain chant, used on ordinary days), 'Ezel' (a slow and dignified heavy-sounding mood, usually associated with fasts and funerals), and 'Araray' (the most complex mood, freer and lighter, with musical embellishments, sung on great festivals).[56]

This quotation partially explains why 'the Ethiopian Orthodox Church… is still exerting a powerful influence on the lives of millions'.[57] Influenced by a long tradition of monastic spirituality, this church has produced considerable religious literature and has its own iconographic tradition. So profound has been the influence of the Ethiopian Orthodox Church that, along with Egypt, Ethiopia played a crucial role '… both for the liberation of Africa from slavery and its independence from colonialism'.[58] The EOTC has also accommodated elements of the 'Ras Tafari Movement' which has its roots in Jamaica, West Indies.

With its roots firmly grounded in Garveyism,[59] Rastafarianism represented a rejection of idealized whiteness and as such, regarded Africa in general and Ethiopia in particular as '… that land that would best meet their real needs… a place to belong where they could be themselves without seeking approval from

---

[54] de Gruchy, John, "From Cairo to the Cape", 35.

[55] The Liturgy of the Ethiopian Church www.ethiopianorthodox.org/english/church/englishethiopianliturgy.pdf.

[56] Hable-Selassie, Sergew, et al. *The Church of Ethiopia: a Panorama of History and spiritual life.* (Addis Ababa: Ethiopian Orthodox Church, 1997). "Yared (Saint) 6th century Orthodox Ethiopia" www.dacb.org/stories/ethiopia/yared2.html. The sources of St Yared's music are the Bible and the works of the Church Fathers. He praises Almighty God in His different forms of creation. His music refers to "spring, summer, autumn, and winter… and green trees, flowers, fruits, the summer sun and its heat, rain and clouds of winter, lightening and sunder (thunder), spring water, rivers, plants, and all nature in general. Yared's music also includes hymns in tribute to the Virgin Mary, the holy Angels, holy martyrs and saints in general (Tesfaye, 2013:286).

[57] Tamene, Getnet, "Features of the Ethiopian Orthodox Church and the Clergy", 90.

[58] de Gruchy, John, "From Cairo to the Cape", 33.

[59] Yesehaq, Abuna, *The Ethiopian Tewahedo Church*, 221-222.

the white world'.[60] Hewitt maintains that 'the two fundamental tenets of the Rastafarian religion call for the salvation of Afro-Jamaicans through repatriation to Ethiopia and an acceptance of the divinity of Haile Selassie I, King of Kings and the Conquering Lion of Judah and Emperor of Ethiopia'.[61] The foregoing complements Ethiopia's long and illustrious history in its struggle against various forms of oppression (including Italian invasions), which further enhanced its reputation as an iconic anti-repression state.

Indeed, 'Ethiopia evokes a sense of African identity untrammelled by European or any other foreign power, and thereby is the symbol of African independence'.[62] Understandably, therefore, with such an illustrious history, to Rastafarians and many non-Rastafarians alike, 'Ethiopia' and 'Ethiopianism' became the generic term for African nationalism in its struggle against colonialism.[63] Paralleling this phenomenon, a large religious group broke away from Anglicanism in South Africa and joined the Ethiopian Orthodox Tewahedo Church at the end of the nineteenth century.[64] Currently, there are about 25 Ethiopian Orthodox Tewahedo Church parishes with their own native South African clergy and many laity in the Eastern Cape and Western Cape Provinces of South Africa.

In AD 284, Roman Emperor Diocletian continued the longstanding position of persecuting Christians. This practice was reversed by Emperor Constantine in AD 313. Nevertheless, following their conquest of Egypt in AD 639, the Arab Moslems continued to persecute Christians. In Ethiopia's case, Yodit, a ninth-century Jewish leader, and Ahmed Gragn (or Ahmed the left-handed) in the sixteenth century hindered Christian expansion in Southern and Western Africa. However, some missionary activities, coupled with pastoral care for the diaspora, resulted in Ethiopian and Eritrean Orthodox Churches' outreach from their Sees into many African countries. Pastoral care for the diaspora is an integral part of their undertakings. The Coptic Orthodox Church goes one step farther and incorporates missionary activities and the diaspora pastoral care in its ministry. Bishop Antonius Markos of the Coptic Church, based in Johannesburg, is symbolic of this type of multi-faceted undertaking.

Coptic Orthodox Churches are found in Kenya, Uganda, Tanzania, the Democratic Republic of Congo, Ghana, Gabon, Togo, Côte d'Ivoire (Ivory Coast), Zambia, Zimbabwe, Namibia, Botswana and South Africa.

In the diaspora, the Ethiopian Orthodox Tewahedo Church has established branches in Egypt, Sudan (Khartoum), South Sudan, Djibouti, Kenya, Uganda and South Africa.

In January 2015, the Eritrean Orthodox Tewahedo Church established a branch for its diaspora in South Africa.

Both the Coptic and Ethiopian Orthodox Tewahedo Churches have one monastery each in South Africa. In the case of the former, it is St Mark and St Samuel the Confessor Coptic Orthodox monastery in Klipfontein, District of Cullinan, in Gauteng. In the case of the latter, it is the Ethiopian Orthodox Tewahedo Church Holy Trinity and St Yared monastery in Bloemfontein, Free State.

In response to the *Zeitgeist,* the theological school in Alexandria of the Coptic Church, together with Holy Trinity University College of the Ethiopian Orthodox Tewahedo Church in Addis Ababa, now includes female students. The Coptic and the EOTC churches now accommodate the participation 'of women in all fields of ministry, except priesthood'. Some women have acquired '... advanced degrees in Theology and (in the Coptic church) teach Theology in the Seminaries and Theological Colleges...'[65]

---

[60] Yesehaq, Abuna, *The Ethiopian Tewahedo Church*, 144.
[61] Hewitt, R.R. *Church and Culture: An Anglo-Caribbean Experience of Hybridity and Contradiction* (Pietermaritzburg: Cluster Publications, 2012), 143.
[62] de Gruchy, John, "From Cairo to the Cape", 33.
[63] de Gruchy, John, "From Cairo to the Cape", 33.
[64] See: https://en.wikipedia.org/wiki/Ethiopian_movement.
[65] Tawfik , Wedad, *Theological education in the Coptic Orthodox Church,* 271.

Bibliography

Abbink, Jon. *A Bibliography on Christianity in Ethiopia*, 2003. www.ascleiden.nl/pdf/workingpaper52.pdf

de Gruchy, John. 'From Cairo to the Cape: The significance of Coptic Orthodoxy for African Christianity' *Journal of Theology for Southern Africa*, no.99 (1997): 24-39.

Desta, Alemayehu. *Introduction to the Ethiopian Orthodox Faith.* Bloomington: Author House, 2012.

Gebeemariam, Asrat. *Timherte Melekot* 2nd book. Addis Ababa, 1999.

Gerima, Abuna, et al. *The Ethiopian Orthodox Tewahedo Church History from the Birth of Christ up to 2000*: *Ethiopia Stretches out her hands to God*, 2008.

Gebreamanuel, Berhanu, et al. *The church of Ethiopia past and present.* Addis Ababa: Commercial Printing Enterprise, 1997.

Hable-Selassie, Sergew, et al. *The Church of Ethiopia: a Panorama of History and spiritual life.* Addis Ababa: Ethiopian Orthodox Church, 1997.

Hancock, Graham. 1992. *The sign and the seal: the explosively controversial international best seller: a quest for the lost Ark of the Covenant.* London: Arrow Books.

Hewitt, R.R. *Church and Culture: An Anglo-Caribbean Experience of Hybridity and Contradiction.* Pietermaritzburg: Cluster Publications, 2012

Melaku, L. *History of the Ethiopian Orthodox Tewahedo Church: From the Reign of Emperor Caleb to the end of Zagwe Dynasty and from the Classical (Golden) age to the Present: Part Two and Three.* Addis Ababa, 2010.

Mekarios, Abuna. et al. *The Ethiopian Orthodox Tewahedo church. Faith, Order of Worship and Ecumenical Relations.* Addis Ababa: Tensae Publishing House, 1996.

Shahid, '*The Solomonides'.* In: 'The Worlds of Eastern Christianity, 300-1500 Volume 4: Languages and Cultures of Eastern Christianity: Ethiopian', edited by Alessandro (ed), 146-178. England: Ashgate Publishing Limited, 2012.

Tamene, Getnet. 'Features of the Ethiopian Orthodox Church and the Clergy'. *Journal of Asian and African Studies*, no. 7 (1998):87-104.

Tesfaye, Ayalkibet. 'The Ethiopian Orthodox Tewahedo Church and its traditional theological education system'. In: *Handbook of Theological Education in Africa*, edited by Isabel Apawo Phiri and Dietrich Werner(ed), 281-291. Pietermaritzburg: Cluster Publications, 2013.

Twafik, Wedad. '*Theological education in the Coptic Orthodox Church (the Church of Alexandria)*'. In *Handbook of Theological Education in Africa*, edited by Isabel Apawo Phiri and Dietrich Werner (ed), 263-269. Pietermaritzburg: Cluster Publications, 2013.

Wondmagegnehu, Aymro and Motovu, Joachim. *The Ethiopian Orthodox Church.* Addis Ababa: Ethiopian Orthodox Mission, 1970.

Wondmagegnehu, Aymro. *The Oriental Orthodox churches Addis Ababa conference*. Addis Ababa: Artistic Printers, 1965.

Yesehaq, Abuna. *The Ethiopian Tewahedo Church: An Integrally African Church.* New York: Vantage Press, 1989.

(24) Eastern Orthodox Churches in Africa

John Ngige Njoroge

Introduction

This article will focus on the Eastern Orthodox Churches in Africa. Before that however, it is important to clarify the meaning of the Eastern Orthodox Churches' and how it will be used in this article. The phrase 'Eastern Orthodox Churches' means those Orthodox Churches that agreed to the resolutions of the fourth ecumenical council held in Chalcedon in AD 451. These churches are the Patriarchate of Constantinople, Alexandria, Jerusalem, Antioch and Rome. This distinguishes the named churches from the non-Chalcedonian or Oriental Orthodox Churches who decided not to follow the Chalcedon Council on the two natures of Christ, thus on how the divine and the human natures are united in the person of Jesus Christ. It is at this juncture that the Coptic Orthodox Church and the Ethiopian Orthodox Church belonging to the Alexandrian church did not agree with the resolutions of the council, and for centuries these two churches have remained separate from the Greek Patriarchate of Alexandria. However, through the encountering of both the Eastern and Oriental Orthodox families in the World Council of Churches (WCC), they have managed to hold a series of four unofficial conversations after 1,500 years of being separate. As a result of these consultations, a solid Christological agreement was reached.[1] Therefore, the phrase 'Eastern Orthodox Churches' will refer to Orthodox Churches under the jurisdiction of the Greek Patriarchate of Alexandria and All Africa. According to the administrative structures of the Orthodox Churches under the Greek Orthodox Patriarchate of Alexandria and All Africa, churches in Africa are grouped as either Archdiocese or Diocese. Currently, there are twenty-one archdioceses and five dioceses. An Archdiocese is under the leadership of an archbishop and a diocese under a bishop.

All Eastern Orthodox Churches in Africa are under the Greek Orthodox Patriarchate of Alexandria and All Africa. The headquarters are in Alexandria, Egypt and the current Patriarch is Pope Theodoros II. It serves the Eastern Orthodox Churches, which consists of Greek- and Russian-speaking Orthodox faithful, mainly living and working in major African cities as well as native African Orthodox communities. The Greek Orthodox Patriarchate of Alexandria and All Africa is ecclesiastically in communion with all Eastern Orthodox Patriarchates, as well as with autocephalous and autonomous churches in the world. It is a member of the World Council of Churches, All Africa Conference of Churches and Middle East Council of Churches.[2]

Eastern Orthodox Churches in Africa can be categorized into three main categories. This is mainly because of their sources of origin.

Orthodox Churches in Northern Africa

The Orthodox Churches in the northern part of Africa includes both the Eastern and Oriental Orthodox Churches. The origin of the Orthodox Church in Alexandria is from the evangelization of Apostle and Evangelist Mark. According to Eusebius 'Church History' (AD 320) and keeping with the tradition of both

---

[1] See the resolutions of a meeting held at Ana Bishop monastery in Egypt in 1989 and in Chambery 1993 respectively. Also see Dictionary of the Ecumenical Movement (Geneva: WCC Publications, 2002), 859-61.

[2] Njoroge John, Article: *The Ecumenical Dialogue in the Perspective of the Greek Orthodox Patriarchate of Alexandria All Africa* in the Orthodox Handbook on Ecumenism Resources for Theological Education (Volos: Volos Academy Publications in cooperation with WCC publication and Regnum Books International, 2014), 327-332.

the Greek Orthodox Patriarchate of Alexandria and all Africa and the Coptic-based Orthodox Patriarchate of Alexandria, St Mark the Evangelist, a missionary companion of St Peter, the apostle to the Jew (Gal. 2:8), evangelized Alexandria between AD 43-63 and after him Anianos took over this See serving between AD 62-82.[3] Alexandria being a home of the largest Jewish community in diaspora, made it possible for Peter to have sent Mark his spiritual son (1 Peter 5:13) to visit Alexandria. It could be true that Alexandria had been evangelized by AD 53 because of a story of a Christian Jew from Alexandria by the name of Apollos, who was evangelizing in Ephesus (Acts 18:24; 1 Cor. 3:4-7) at the time of St Paul. As noted above, the Alexandrian church has continuously confessed St Mark the Evangelist as its founder and from the fourth century AD, the See of Alexandria has been called Cathedra Marci ('the throne of Mark'). His symbol is a lion, an emblem used on the flag of the Greek Orthodox Patriarchate of Alexandria and All Africa. His feast day is 25th April when a liturgical rite attributed to him is supposed to be celebrated in the churches of Alexandria.[4]

After the establishment of the church in Alexandria, Christianity spread in the region and beyond where it continued with its apostolic mission of witnessing to the world the gospel of Jesus Christ so that the world may believe (John 17:21). Throughout history, the Orthodox Church in Northern Africa has been known for its active involvement with and contribution to world Christianity. First and foremost, the Alexandrian church did not only participate in the ecumenical councils but greatly contributed to the formation of the Christian doctrines through its bishops like Athanasius the Great (AD 298-373). The formation of the Nicene-Constantinopolitan creed and Christian doctrines like that of the incarnation has offered to the ecumenical church solutions to the heresies of the time.[5] Secondly the Alexandrian church has given to world Christianity the profound allegorical method of interpreting the Holy Scriptures through its famous catechetical school. One can argue that the Alexandrian catechetical school produced the first Christian thinkers like Clement of Alexandria and Origen who successfully explained the biblical faith philosophically and systematically. Thirdly, the Alexandrian church is known for its monasticism. Ordinary Christians like Antony the Great (251-356), the father of monasticism, took a total commitment to the following of Christ by enacting Matt. 19:17-21 and took to the desert to live a life of asceticism and contemplation. Monasticism inspired many people like St Pachomius (292-346) who developed the cenobitical or communal monastic way of life. The flourishing of monasticism in the Egyptian desert brought pilgrims from all over the world and at the same time the desert become the place of encounter between the Christian monks and the Nubian traders along the river Nile. Apparently, through this encounter, the historical kingdom of Nubia became Christian.

Although right from the beginning, the Alexandrian church witnessed the gospel of Christ as one united church, the fourth ecumenical council AD 451 and the AD 640 Arabic conquest have affected the unity, growth and prosperity of this church. During the fourth ecumenical council, the Alexandrian church encountered a division between the 'non-Chalcedonian' churches or the Oriental Orthodox Churches and the Chalcedonian Churches or the Eastern Orthodox Churches. It is at this juncture that the Coptic Orthodox Church and the Ethiopian Orthodox Church belonging to the Alexandrian church did not agree with the resolutions of the Chalcedonian council on the two natures of Christ, thus on how the divine and human natures are united in the person of Jesus Christ. On the other hand, what is now the Greek Orthodox Patriarchate of Alexandra remained faithful to the Chalcedonian family together with the Patriarchates of Constantinople, Jerusalem, Antioch and Rome who fully participated in the next three ecumenical councils.

---

[3] Baur, John, *2000 Years of Christianity in Africa: An African Church History* (Nairobi: Paulines Publications) 21. Also see Greek Orthodox Patriarchate of Alexandria and All Africa office website "Previous Patriarchs" available at: www.patriarchateofalexandria.com. Lastly accessed 1/01/15.

[4] Groves C.P., *The Planting of Christianity in Africa*, Vol. 1 (London: Lutterworth Press, 1964) 35.

[5] Heresies such as Arianism that was introduced by Arius; a Christian priest of Alexandria, Egypt, whose teachings affirmed the created, finite nature of Christ.

For centuries, these two Orthodox families have remained in separation, and only recently through WCC initiatives have they entered into informal and formal theological dialogues.[6]

The Arabic conquest in AD 640 marked a turning point in the history of the church in Egypt.[7] For many Egyptians, the coming of the Arabs was liberation from the Roman yoke. However, the implementation of Islamic policy was discriminative to the minority who opted to remain Christians. These kinds of legislative policies affected also the Greek Orthodox Patriarchate of Alexandria and All Africa, and because of persecutions, the Patriarch and a large number of members fled Egypt and went either back to Greece or to other parts of the world. However, after the immigration of Turks reached Egypt in 1517, a new era dawned for the Egyptian Christians. Persecutions were over and the Patriarchate re-opened with only a few Greek-speaking followers.

The Greek-speaking communities are mainly in the cities of Alexandria and Cairo although there are a few Greek-speaking communities in other cities in North African countries. The communities are found in the following archdioceses: i) The Holy Archdiocese of Ermoupolis with its headquarters in Tanta, Egypt; ii) The Holy Archdiocese of Cyrene which includes in its jurisdiction the area of Marsa and Matrouh in Egypt; iii) The Holy Archdiocese of Ptolemais includes in its jurisdiction the area of Upper Egypt, Luxor, Aswan, Minia, Fayum, Assiut and Beni Suef with its headquarters in Minia, Egypt; iv) The Holy Archdiocese of Leontopolis has in its jurisdiction the areas of Ismailia, Suez and Zagzik in Egypt with its headquarters in Ismailia, Egypt; v) The Holy Archdiocese of Carthage which was established by Patriarchal and Synodal Decree in 1931 and includes in its jurisdiction the countries of Tunisia, Algeria, Mauritania and Morocco. Its headquarters are in Tunis, Tunisia; vi) The Holy Archdiocese of Tripoli which was established by Patriarchal and Synodal Decree in 1866. In 1959 it was joined to the Holy Metropolis of Carthage. On 27th October 2004, it was re-organized again by Patriarchal and Synodal Decree and its jurisdictional areas include the country of Libya. Its headquarters are in Tripoli, Libya; and vii) The Holy Archdiocese of Aksum which has in its jurisdiction the areas Ethiopia, Eritrea, Djibouti and Somalia. It has its headquarters in Addis-Ababa, Ethiopia.[8]

Under the spiritual authority of the Patriarch of Alexandria are the St Athanasios catechetical school and the monasteries of St George in Old Cairo, St Savvas in Alexandria, the patriarchal library and the patriarchal printing house.

Greek, Russian and other Immigrant Orthodox Communities

As already mentioned, the Greek Orthodox Patriarchate of Alexandria and All Africa extends its jurisdiction all over Africa. Its extension started in 1921 when the Patriarchate of Constantinople renounced all claims to jurisdiction in any part of Africa.[9] This means that all Greek- and Russian-speaking communities who had settled in Africa as immigrants or traders automatically fell under the Greek Orthodox Patriarchate of Alexandria and All Africa. Initially, these communities were under the Patriarchate of Constantinople which was responsible for those Orthodox Christians who were beyond any other Orthodox jurisdiction.[10]

---

[6] *Dictionary of the Ecumenical Movement* (Geneva: WCC Publications, 2002), 859-61.

[7] Baur, *2000 Years of Christianity in Africa*, 25.

[8] See the official website of the Greek Orthodox Patriarchate of Alexandria and All Africa. www.patriarchateofalexandria.com/index.php?module=content&cid=004001. Also see A. Tillyridis (Archbishop Makarios of Kenya) article, The Greek Orthodox Patriarchate of Alexandria and All Africa offices (Yearbook and Review 2012) 74-78.

[9] A. Tillyridis (Archbishop Makarios of Kenya) article, *Chronology* in the Yearbook and Review 2012 , 48.

[10] See Hayes Stephen article: *A History of the Orthodox Mission in Tropical Africa*; (originally published in Missionalia, the journal of the Southern African Missiological Society) available at:

Before the Greek and Russian communities were received in the Greek Orthodox Patriarchate of Alexandria and All Africa, they had already organized themselves to meet their cultural, educational and spiritual needs. They had constructed schools, cultural centres and churches. For example, the first Greek community to sub-Saharan Africa settled in Mozambique in 1899 where they built a church and school in Beira.[11] These communities were receiving clergy to minister to them either directly from their countries of origin or from the Patriarchate of Constantinople. For example in 1908 such a priest, Father Nicodemus Sarikas, was sent to a Greek community of immigrants in Johannesburg, South Africa.[12]

For years, these communities have been closed to themselves, meaning they were reluctant to open up to African societies as well as to the mission of the Greek Orthodox Patriarchate of Alexandria and All Africa. This is so for a number of reasons. As a matter of fact, these communities and especially the immigrants fostered a situation that favours social connection and cultural cohesion amongst themselves and their countries of origin. As a result, their schools were meant only for their children and even teachers were sent and funded from Greece. Churches served as places for spiritual nourishment as well as places for preservation of cultural and national heritage. This promoted a strong sense of belonging and togetherness of immigrants who shared the same story and ambitions being far away from home. This is the reason why the Greek language was used in schools and churches. Currently, there are strong Greek Orthodox Communities in South Africa, Zambia and Zimbabwe. There are also a few Greek communities in other major cities in Africa. The largest Russian speaking communities are found in Mozambique and South Africa. In recent years these communities have flourished and enjoyed assistance from their respective governments back home through the embassies and consulates.

Over the decades a very slow movement towards more integration of these communities and the rest of African society can be observed. This has made the Orthodox faith in Africa look as if it is only a faith of immigrants. One could argue that the time these communities have been in Africa was not sufficient to witness the Orthodox faith to native African communities. However, this being the case in many parts of Africa, other cases can be identified where individuals from some of these communities have opened up and created deliberate interest in order to evangelize African native communities. This has taken place in two ways: i) through intermarriage between Greeks and Africans as well as Russians and Africans: through intermarriage, some Africans have been introduced to the Orthodox faith. ii). A Greek priest by the name of Fr Nikodemos Sarikas co-operated with Fr Ruben Mukasa Spartas of Uganda and enabled Ugandan students to join a Greek school belonging to a community of sisal farmers in Moshi, Tanzania. Later, some of these students went to Greece to study theology either in the university of Athens or Aristotle University of Thessaloniki. Their presence in Greek churches caused enthusiasm for Greek church mission in Africa. In fact, their presence rekindled a forgotten or inactive aspect of Orthodox missionary work.[13]

In recent years, the Greek and Russian communities have on the one hand tried not to stay in isolation while on the other hand they are declining in numbers for different reasons. One recommendable thing as far as these communities are concerned is that they have remained united under the Greek Orthodox Patriarchate of Alexandria and All Africa. This means that they are not divided according to national lines and attached to churches abroad in the country of origin like Greece, Romania, Serbia and Russia as witnessed in West Europe or America. This has made the pastoral and missionary work of the patriarchate simple and focused. This has also contributed to creating interest among individual Africans for joining the

---

www.orthodoxytz.com/OrthodoxMission.asp lastly accessed 20th January 2015.

[11] Njoroge John article; *Theological Training and Formation in the Eastern Orthodox Churches in Africa at the Handbook of Theological Education in Africa*: Regnum Books International for South Africa 292.

[12] See Hayes Stephen article: *A History of the Orthodox Mission in Tropical Africa*; (originally published in *Missionalia*, the journal of the Southern African Missiological Society) available at: www.orthodoxytz.com/OrthodoxMission.asp lastly accessed 20th January 2015.

[13] Kallistos Timothy Ware (Metropolitan of Diokleia), *The Orthodox Church* (London: Penguin Books, 1997), 190.

Orthodox Church and therefore opening mission opportunities for the patriarchate. Such cases are witnessed in Zambia, Malawi, South Africa, and Zimbabwe. For example, in South Africa, the church of St Nicholas of Japan has become a mission church where services are done in English language. This church is served by a Kenyan priest named Fr Athanasius Akunda and a South African deacon named Stephen, who are also in charge of reaching out to mission communities within the Archdiocese. In the Archbishopric of Zambia there is a growing native Orthodox community in Malawi being evangelized by Fr Ermolaos Iatrou.

Finally, it should also be mentioned that on the African continent there are other Balkan and Middle Eastern Orthodox Christian Communities such as from Romania, Bulgaria, Syria, Lebanon and elsewhere who do not speak Greek or Russian and who created joint or separate Orthodox communities.

Native African Orthodox Communities

Apart from the Northern African and Greek and Russian Orthodox communities, there are vibrant and rapidly growing native African Eastern Orthodox communities. The origin of these churches is through the initiatives of the Africans themselves. According to Bishop Timothy Ware, the Orthodox Church in East Africa, for example, was originated through the search by the native peoples and not through missionary preaching from the traditional Orthodox lands.[14] This came about when native communities disagreed with the protestant missions and their evangelizing methodologies and colonization patterns. The disagreements brought about the African Independent Churches (AICs) some of which later became Orthodox Churches.[15] The best examples are the Orthodox churches in East Africa and Ghana.

There is, for instance, the example of Kenya and Uganda where the birth, rising and spread of the Orthodox Church was contextual, based on the presence of Christian mission churches and the colonial upheavals of the 1920s to the 1960s. The rhythms of political, economic and cultural-religious changes, and mostly enhanced by the colonial government, settlers and Christian missionaries affected local communities. The forces of colonization, land alienation, forced labour and hut taxation, paternalism and devaluing of African culture and ethos met fierce resistance from the native peoples. Consequently, the native peoples started demanding independent churches and schools.[16] For example in Kenya the church led by Arthur George Gathuna, refused to pledge their loyalty to the mission rejecting female initiation and membership to Kikuyu Central Association (KCA) and formed their own schools and Churches.[17] Within a few years they started looking for ecclesial identity. The quest for such identity was to authenticate their self-understanding as a new community of faith, a new people of God who wanted to have the gospel of Christ incarnated to reflect the African worldview and lifestyle. This made the leaders of those communities look for affiliation with churches that were not involved in colonization.

---

[14] Ware, *The Orthodox Church*, 189.

[15] Njoroge John, Article, *The Orthodox Church in Kenya and the Quest Enculturation: A Challenging mission Paradigm in Today's Orthodoxy*, St, Vladimir's Theological Quarterly Vol. 55 N0.4, 2011, 405-438.

[16] When members of Kikuyu community left Church Scottish Mission (CSM) at in 1930, they referred to themselves as Kikuyu Karinga, which in kikuyu language means pure or orthodox. Traditionally, this term was used with the kikuyu initiation guild to stand for cultural purity and identity. After breaking from the missionaries, it took a political and religious implication, to implying those kikuyu people who opposed the missions and colonial authorities. See also Wentink D. E., "The Orthodox Church in East Africa", The Ecumenical Review Vol.20 (Geneva: WCC Publications, 1968, 33.

[17] Kikuyu Central Association (KCA) was a political party that opposed the missionaries on abolition of the Kikuyu customs, championed Kikuyu cultural patriotism and continuously presented Kikuyu's grievances on the issues pertaining to land, labour and oppression by the settlers. Mzee Jomo Kenyatta, the first President of Kenya was its secretary representing KCA in London in 1946. Almost of the Karing'a members were party supporters.

At first they were affiliated with the African Orthodox Church. This church had come to Africa through Archbishop Daniel William Alexander a primate of the African Orthodox Church in America in the Province of South Africa.[18] The African Orthodox Church in America (AOC) is an Afro-American denomination which had been started by Archbishop George Alexander McGuire in 1922. He formed the African Orthodox Church in America due to social segregation and racial discrimination he had experienced as a priest in the Protestant Episcopal Church (PEC).[19] Daniel William Alexander and a number of clergymen had broken from the Anglican Church in South Africa and joined the Independent African Church. Being dissatisfied with the administration of the Independent African Church, they established an independent church for Black Christians that would be more responsive to their own social-religious needs and to those of their parishioners. In due course, William Alexander connected to the African Orthodox Church in America. An article outlining the beginning of the Orthodox Church in South Africa reads:

> On 6th October 1924, the Rev. D.W. Alexander organised an African Orthodox church in Beaconsfield, and on affiliating with the mother church in America on 25th September 1925, he (D.W. Alexander) was appointed by the Most Rev. Alexander McGuire, Archbishop and Primate of the AOC, and endorsed by Metropolitan-Archbishop Vilatte, Vicar Apostolic for the province of South Africa.[20]

After Alexander was consecrated bishop he returned to Kimberley and his parish church of St Augustine of Hippo. This parish became the centre of African Orthodox Church activity in South Africa although with full contact with the Orthodox Church in America till he received a letter informing him of McGuire's death in 1935. At Kimberley, Alexander organised a seminary to educate his priests and annual synod meetings to discuss church issues. At the same place, he organized mission activities of the African Orthodox Church, which extended to Rhodesia, Kenya and Uganda where he was invited by the locals and where he trained priests and baptized communicants.[21]

In 1934, Archbishop Daniel William Alexander went to Kenya, following an invitation by members of the Kikuyu Independent School Association (KISA).[22] This invitation had materialized after Mr James Beauttah, one of the KISA adherents working in Mombasa and Parmenas Githendu Mukeri of the KCA had the chance to meet Archbishop William Daniel Alexander in 1932, while on his way back to South Africa coming from Uganda where he had ordained Reuben Mukasa Spartas and Obadiah Kabanda Basajakitalo, the founders of the Orthodox Church in Uganda into the priesthood.[23] During his time in Kenya, Archbishop William Daniel Alexander baptised, consecrated churches and trained and ordained priests. One of those whom he trained and ordained into the priesthood was Fr George Arthur Gatungu Gathuna of *Agîkûyû Karing'a* who initiated the growth and spreading of the Orthodox Church in Kenya.

---

[18] See an article outlining the beginning and the Apostolic Succession of the African Orthodox Church in South Africa found in the archives of the African Orthodox Church in Pitts Theological Library U.S.A

[19] JSTOR: *Journal of the Negro History*: Vol. 57 No.1 , 38-39.

[20] See an article outlining the beginning and the Apostolic Succession of the African Orthodox Church in South Africa found in the archives of the African Orthodox Church in Pitts Theological Library U.S.A.

[21] Fr. Stephen Hayes article on Gabellah, Elliot Mdutshwa 1923 to 1988 African Orthodox Church / The Gospel of God Church South Africa / Zimbabwe found at: http//: www. Elliot Mdutshwa Gabellah, South Africa Zimbabwe, African Orthodox Church the Gospel of God Church.html. Lastly accessed 20/1/15.

[22] Kikuyu Independent School Association (KISA) was one of the formal bodies that were created in 1933 to formulate policies on education, facilitate independent's schools interests and objectives as well as seeking government support.

[23] J.R. Kigogno Dam-Tibajjwa, Article on the Life of Archpriest Reverend Father Spartas R.S. Ssebanja Mukasa, Founder of The African Orthodox Church in Uganda, Politician and Educationalist.

Affiliation with the Greek Greek Orthodox Patriarchate of Alexandria and All Africa

The search for building up Eastern Orthodoxy in East Africa was the result of relentless efforts of Reuben Mukasa Spartas and Obadiah Kabanda Basajakitalo of Uganda, George Arthur Gatungu Gathuna of Kenya, Nikodemos Sarikas of Greece and Danie William Alexander of South Africa. Reuben Mukasa Spartas and Obadiah Kabanda Basajakitalo had separated from the Anglican Church of Uganda and progressively had formed a Christian community free from mission control and paternalism. Just as in the independent churches in Kenya, Africans such as Spartas and Basajakitalo had to quench their thirst for bringing Christianity 'home', meaning to play its saving and liberating role for the Africans and by the Africans. For the two Ugandan's inspirations to turn into reality, they had to search for a church that would satisfy their people's needs to overcome social-religious and economic-political dissatisfaction experienced in their former mission churches. As a head teacher and a librarian at the Bishop's school library, Spartas had ample opportunity to access information regarding different Christian denominations. It is from here that Spartas came across church history where he learned about the Orthodox Church. In 1925 Spartas contacted Archbishop George Alexander McGuire the primate of AOC who in reply in 1928 connected him (Spartas) to the then newly consecrated Archbishop Daniel William Alexander of the AOC in South Africa. In 1932 the Orthodox Church in Uganda was established under the leadership of Reuben Mukasa Spartas and Obadiah Kabanda Basajakitalo who were then ordained into the priesthood by Archbishop William Daniel Alexander as mentioned above.

The tremendous growth of the Orthodox Church in Kenya at the time of Fr George Gathuna and that of Fr Reuben Spartas and Fr Obadiah Basajakitaloin in Uganda demanded an ecclesiastical recognition that would enable the communities to appear as authentic local Eastern Orthodox Churches. This has to be understood from the point of view that Archbishop William Alexander had left these churches without any clear ecclesial identity. Likewise he had practised a liturgical service which was not actually Eastern Orthodox.[24] This made Fr Spartas continue searching for the Eastern Orthodox faith. As a result of his searching, he met Fr Nicodemus Sarikas of the Greek community in Moshi, Tanzania.[25] Consequently, Fr Nicodemus Sarikas advised Fr Spartas to connect to the Greek Orthodox Patriarchate of Alexandria and All Africa.

Fr Spartas communicated with Patriarch Meletios, who in return donated English liturgical books to the Ugandan Orthodox community. Receiving books in English made it easier for Fr Spartas to translate the liturgy of St John Chrysostom into the Luganda language. The liturgical books to be printed in Luganda through the efforts of Fr Spartas appeared in May 1935.[26] Following this development, Fr Spartas decided to give his community a new name – the African Greek Orthodox Church (AGOC). This was an indication that it was no longer an African Orthodox Church under the leadership of Archbishop William Daniel Alexander. Henceforth, Fr Sparta kept his relationship with Fr Sarikas who was offering catechetical training to young Ugandan boys who were later sent for theological training in Alexandria. Some of those who went to Alexandria were offered chances to further their studies in Athens and Thessaloniki respectively.

---

[24] See a copy of Liturgical Service that was written by Alexandra McGuire of the Africa Orthodox Church in America in 1922. The copy is found in the archives of the African Orthodox Church in Pitts Theological Library Emory University U.S.A.

[25] A. Tillyrides Makarios (Archbishop); *Greek Orthodox Patriarchate of Alexandria and All Africa;* Orthodox Archbishopric of Kenya and Irinoupolis (Year Book Review 2002) p. 152. Also see Kigogno, Article on The Life of Archpriest Reverend Father Spartas R.S. Ssebanja Mukasa, and founder of The African Orthodox Church in Uganda, Politician and Educationalist.

[26] Kigogno, Article on The Life of Archpriest Reverend Father Spartas R.S. Ssebanja Mukasa, and founder of The African Orthodox Church in Uganda, Politician and Educationalist.

In 1937, the newly-elected Patriarch Nicolaos was ambitious for Christian mission and he started a process of recognizing Fr Spartas' community by bringing it fully under the spiritual leadership of the Patriarchate of Alexandria and All Africa. Fr Spartas extended Patriarch Nicolaos' mission intentions to Kenya. Fr Spartas visited Fr George Gathuna with whom he discussed the necessity of joining the Greek Orthodox Patriarchate of Alexandria. The relationship between the two churches was enhanced in 1939 when the two leaders signed a merger and got a new church constitution. Due to that merger, there has been a very close relationship between the two churches. For example, after the decree of the Emergency Regulation in 1952, a period in which Fr Gathuna was also detained, and so was unable to tend his flock. His Ugandan comrades were forced to send a replacement for Fr Gathuna and Fr Obadiah Kabanda Basajakitalo of Uganda, who only managed to serve the western part of Kenya due to the liberation war there, allowing him to spiritually lead the 119 Orthodox congregations.[27]

The Alexandrian mission to accept Orthodox communities in East Africa was enhanced when Patriarch Christophoros II assigned Metropolitan Nicolaos of Axoum (Ethiopia) to visit Uganda and report his findings to the Holy Synod. Metropolitan Nicolaos started his mission in 1942 and he compiled a report that was reported to the synod in March 1943. Fr Spartas characterized the presence of Metropolitan Nicolaos in Uganda after 14 years of waiting as having the key of salvation, opening the door and ushering them into the One, Holy, Catholic and Apostolic Church. It was the metropolitan's duty to bring to the pen the lost one and present it as a clean sacrifice to God.[28] In his conclusion, Metropolitan Nicholaos observed and reported:

> There is a field of action for our church mainly in Uganda and secondly in Kenya, if our church ever wishes to extend her action in Africa beyond the limit and formal servicing of the religious needs for her Greek children who are spread there. This field exists… the natives' persistence, however, is irreversible. Therefore we do not have an organization that is formed within its own traditions and views, which is seeking to adjust to our own through unification. On the contrary, we are observing a movement towards our church, which, without any dogmatic or administrative conditions, is asking to enter into the bosom of our church and only nourishes the hope that under her protection it will realize its prospects and create a formally organized 'Orthodox Eastern African Church', as Spartas' organisation is called today, with its own hierarchy and clergy.[29]

Consequently, in 1946, the Holy Synod officially recognized the Orthodox communities both in Uganda and Kenya. Fr Spartas was invited to the synod where he received the title of the Patriarchal Vicar General to AGOC.[30] Fr Spartas continued to minister in Uganda and together with Fr Obadiah they opened new communities extending to the town of Bukoba in Tanzania, and to western Kenya among the Luhya and Nandi peoples.

During the Kenyan emergency, 1952-1958, the expansion of the Orthodox Church was brought to a standstill. Orthodox Churches and schools were banned by the colonial government for having been involved in fighting for freedom, giving refuge to the Mau Mau and supporting the Kikuyu Central Association (KCA). Most of its members and priests, including Fr George Gathuna, were persecuted and detained.[31] D.E. Wentink reports that members of the Orthodox Church were involved in the struggle for

---

[27] Wentink, "The Orthodox Church in East Africa", *The Ecumenical Review Vol.20* p.35.

[28] Mission report written by His Eminence metropolitan Nicolaos of Axum to His Beatitude Pope and Patriarch of Alexandria Christophoros.

[29] His Eminence Metropolitan Nicolaos of Axum, Mission report to His Beatitude Pope and Patriarch of Alexandria Christophoros and to the Holy Synod.

[30] Kigogno, Article on *The Life of Archpriest Reverend Father Spartas R.S. Ssebanja Mukasa*, and founder of The African Orthodox Church in Uganda, Politician and Educationalist.

[31] Njoroge John, *The Orthodox Church in Africa and the Quest for Enculturation: A Challenging Mission paradigm in Today's Orthodoxy*, St Vladimir's Theological Quarterly Journal Vol.55 No.4, 2011, 423.

independence for Kenya and have paid with their lives for the independence of the country.[32] Fortunately, the Orthodox Church in Kenya reopened in 1965 within the Holy Archbishopric of Kenya and Irinopolis established by the patriarchal and synodal decree of 1958. This archbishopric served Orthodox churches in Kenya, Uganda and Tanzania. Over a period of time, the latter two have been separated from the former and now they are under the Holy Archdioceses of Kampala and Irinopolis respectively, while Kenya gave birth to Bukoba, now Archdiocese of Mwanza in Eastern Tanzania.

The situation in West Africa, and especially in Ghana and Nigeria, was almost the same as in East Africa. According to Stephen Hayes, in Ghana there were some independent non-canonical Orthodox Churches. These churches traced their origin to the *episcopus vagans* Rene Joseph Vilatte who introduced the Orthodox faith to the Ghanaian group leader, Bressi-Ando whom he met in Europe.[33] It happened that, in 1974, there was a World Council of Churches meeting being held in the University of Ghana in Accra, and Joseph Kwame Labi and Gottfried Mantey, leaders of the Orthodox Youth Organization (OYO), decided to go and met the Orthodox representatives. They met Fr John Meyendorff, Fr Thomas Hopko, and Professor Nicolas Lossky, all from St Vladimir Orthodox Seminary in New York, and Alexandrian Patriarchate representative Dr Parthelus. As a result of this meeting, Joseph Kwame Labi was granted a scholarship to study at St Vladimir's Orthodox Seminary. He was later ordained, worked in the World Council of Churches and is now serving as a priest in Ghana. In 1982 in a town called Larteh, Archbishop Irenaeus of the Greek Patriarchate of Alexandria officially received the Ghanaian Orthodox communities of about 1,500 faithful into canonical Orthodoxy through Holy Baptism and Chrismation. During the same occasion, he ordained into priesthood the Revs Kyriakos Edonu, Gregory Labi, Samuel Adjei-Kumi and Joseph Kwame Labi and into office of a deacon, Fr Daniel Aidoo, Fr Jacob Sey and Fr Emmanuel Bruce. Archbishop Irenaeus continued performing more baptisms in other locations bringing the total of Ghanaians received into the Orthodox Church to nearly 3,000 after several years.[34] Currently, the Orthodox Church in Ghana is under the Holy Archdiocese of Ghana which was established by the Patriarchal Synod in 1997. In its jurisdiction it includes the countries of Ghana, Ivory Coast, Burkina Faso and Mali. Its headquarters are in Accra, Ghana.[35]

In Nigeria, there was a well-established community calling itself the 'Greek Orthodox Church'. According to Stephen Hayes, it was started by an America by the name Abuna Abraim and it was officially received in the Greek Orthodox Patriarchate of Alexandria and All Africa by Archbishop Irenaeus in 1985.[36] Currently, the Orthodox Church in Nigeria is under the Holy Archdiocese of Nigeria which was established by the Patriarchal Synod in 1997. In its jurisdiction it includes the countries of Nigeria, Benin, Togo and Niger. Its headquarters are in Lagos, Nigeria.[37] Statistically, there are 29 local churches and nine communities served by 22 priests and two deacons.[38]

---

[32] Wentink "The Orthodox Church in East Africa", 37.

[33] see Hayes Stephen article: *A History of the Orthodox Mission in Tropical Africa*; (originally published in Missionalia, the journal of the Southern African Missiological Society) available at: www.orthodoxytz.com/OrthodoxMission.asp. Lastly accessed 20th January 2015.

34 Andrew J. Anderson, project on Orthodox Church in Ghana, available at: www.orthodoxresearchinstitute.org/articles/church_history/anderson_ghana.htm. Lastly accessed 20th January 2015.

[35] See the official website of the Greek Orthodox Patriarchate of Alexandria and All Africa. www.patriarchateofalexandria.com/index.php?module=content&cid=004001. Lastly accessed 20th January 2015.

[36] See Hayes Stephen article: *A History of the Orthodox Mission in Tropical Africa*; (originally published in Missionalia, the journal of the Southern African Missiological Society) available at: www.orthodoxytz.com/OrthodoxMission.asp. Lastly accessed 20th January 2015.

[37] See the official website of the Greek Orthodox Patriarchate of Alexandria and All Africa. www.patriarchateofalexandria.com/index.php?module=content&cid=004001. Lastly accessed 20th January 2015.

[38] See the official website of the Holy Archbishopric of Nigeria available at: www.orthodoxnigeria.org/. lastly accessed 20th January 2015.

Mission Engagements

The acceptance of the native African Orthodox communities into the Greek Orthodox Patriarchate of Alexandria and All Africa is a sign of how the patriarchate was ready to rekindle, seemingly, the forgotten active mission aspect of the One, Holy, Catholic and Apostolic church. Receiving the native African communities led by Fr Reuben Mukasa of Uganda and Fr George Gathuna of Kenya, had a tremendous impact on the entire Orthodox world. After East African countries attained independence, and once-banned Orthodox churches re-opened with enthusiasm, the churches of Greece, Cyprus, America, Finland and Australia have been engaged in missionary work in Africa. Through the blessings of the primates of the Alexandrian church, these churches sent missionary personnel into Africa. The best examples of such persons are Fr Chrysostomos Papasarantopoulos from Greece, Fr Johannes Eko from Finland, Mrs Stavrista Zachariou from America and Fr Cosmas Grigoriatis from Mt Athos Greece. The four are just an example of many individual Orthodox missionaries who have sacrificed themselves to work with the Africans unceasingly in terms of building churches and supporting the local priests and finally, leaving their bones buried in the missionary field.

The presence of the Orthodox churches in East Africa has resulted in the opening of mission organizations and fraternities in traditional Orthodox countries. These organizations and fraternities have enhanced mission awareness among the faithful, who in return have become engaged in praying for mission and offering financial support. For example, in Greece, missionary organizations such as the Apostolic Diakonia of the church of Greece, formally Πορευθέντες, and the Orthodox Missionary Fraternity of Thessaloniki (formerly known as ΟίΦίλοιτής Ούγκαντα Βορείου Ελλαδος, translated as 'Friends of Uganda, Northern Greece') were formed. Following the visits of Fr Theodore Nankyamas of Uganda to America in 1965 and later to Finland many parishes and more of the youth groups were motivated for pledging themselves to prayer and financial help. It is through his appeal that the Orthodox Christian Mission Center (OCMC) in the USA and the mission desk of the Church of Finland were formed.

The presence of Orthodox churches in East Africa has also resulted in the opening of an Orthodox theological seminary, by the name of Orthodox Patriarchal Ecclesiastical School: Archbishop Makarios III of Cyprus, in Nairobi, donated by the Archbishop and President of Cyprus, Makarios, during his three-day official church visit in 1971. Archbishop Makarios of Cyprus stated:

> The seminary will greatly contribute, I believe, to the promotion of the missionary work in East Africa. The seminary will cater for the African youth, who once educated in the Orthodox religion, will subsequently serve as priests and missionaries on the African continent and the existence of a very wide field for Christians in Africa is also evidenced by the fact that Africans have joined the Orthodox Church in large numbers.[39]

Since then, the seminary has remained as the spiritual and training centre for Orthodox priests and catechist for the whole African continent. Currently, there are seventy students who are studying Orthodox theology in Nairobi with the aim that, after returning to their respective countries, they will be able to enhance the Orthodox faith through their priesthood and also teaching in minor seminaries in their respective countries.

Following the coming of the Greek missionaries to Kenya and Uganda, more Orthodox churches have opened up in other parts of Africa. The best examples are in Central Africa, Madagascar and Sierra Leone. In today's Congo there is a very vibrant and rapidly growing Orthodox church. The mission was started by Fr Chrysostom Papasarantopoulos, a Greek missionary, who had previously worked in Kenya and Uganda for more than ten years. Later, Fr Chrysostom was joined by Fr Cosmas Grigoriatis, from the Monastery of

---

[39] A. Tillyrides (Metropolitan Makarios), article, *Makarios Legacy in Kenya.* Available at www. Orthodoxresearchinstitute.org/articles/church_history/makarios_tillyrides_makarios_legacy.htm, lastly accessed 20th January 2015.

St Gregory in Mount Athos, Greece.[40] Since the death of Fr Cosmas in 1989, his monastery has continued to support his mission in Congo. A mission office was also opened in Thessaloniki dedicated to Fr Cosmas and the faithful are donating money and offering prayers to assist in the continuation of mission work in Zaïre and beyond. Today, the mission is located within the Holy Diocese of Katanga which was established by the Patriarchal and Synodal decree on 1st November 2006, originally called the Holy Diocese of Kolwezi; its name was changed on 9th October 2009 to Diocese of Katanga. Its jurisdiction includes the great area of Katanga in the Congo. Its headquarters are in Lubumbashi, Congo.

Following the rapid growth of the Orthodox Church in East Africa, the Orthodox Church in Australia has so far sent two missionaries to Africa. One is Archimandrite Nectarios Kellis who started evangelizing in Madagascar in 1994. The mission there is under the Holy Archdiocese of Madagascar which was established by Patriarchal and Synodal Decree on 23rd September 1997 as the Diocese of Madagascar but later became an Archdiocese. It includes in its jurisdiction Madagascar and the Islands of Mauritius, Réunion, Comores and Maillot. Its headquarters are in Antananarivo, Madagascar. The second missionary from Australia is Archimandrite Themistoclis Adamopoulos, who worked for several years in Kenya before going to Freetown, Sierra Leone. The mission there is under the Holy Archdiocese of Guinea which was established by Patriarchal Synodal Decree on 10 October 2010; originally it was the Holy Diocese of Sierra Leone. On 21st November 2012 it was elevated to the Archdiocese of Guinea, and includes in its jurisdiction the countries of Sierra Leone, Liberia, Guinea, Guinea Bissau, Gambia, Senegal and Cape Verde. Its headquarters are in Conakry, Guinea.

As the Eastern Orthodox Church continues to grow in Africa, the Patriarchate of Alexandria and All Africa has continued to open new dioceses. The most recent dioceses are the Holy Dioceses of Burundi and Rwanda established 2009, Botswana established 2010 and Brazzaville and Gabon established 2010.

Conclusion

Out of missionary work of the worldwide Orthodox Church, the Eastern Orthodox churches in Africa have received theological training and ordinations of local priests, translation of liturgical and spiritual books, church buildings, schools, orphanages and hospitals. This is a ground prepared for a crucial and constructive dialogue between Orthodoxy and African cultures. This means imbuing the Orthodox faith with an African ethos, in order to transform African society. This would be possible if the Orthodox Church and the Greek Orthodox Patriarchate of Alexandria and All Africa strengthens its presence in Africa and lets its rich liturgical tradition, theology and spirituality give answers to social, economic and even political problems that are affecting African people. This can be achieved through an integrated theological training, and the Orthodox seminary in Nairobi can play this role. This suggests that much more is waiting to be done as far as Orthodoxy in Africa is concerned. First, a comprehensive study is recommended that will bring out a clear statistical number of Orthodox adherents in Africa. This can be done by archdiocese or diocese. Second, it is necessary for graduates from either universities and/or theological schools to undertake research and identify areas where Orthodoxy can connect with African lifestyle and worldview. This is an area of importance because most of the Orthodox churches in East Africa started as a means of searching for and quenching the African thirst for having the gospel of Christ enculturated in order to reflect the African worldview and lifestyle. Third, African Christianity has widely spread but it is often only shallow theologically, causing imbalances in African society. Therefore, Orthodox churches in Africa need to venture into methods of mission and evangelism that will facilitate the deepening of Christian faith in Africa. Fourth, Africa is a home of many religions and different Christian

---

40 Aslanidis Demetrios and Damascene Grigoratis, *Apostle to Zaire; The Life and Legacy of Blessed Cosmos of Grigoriou* (Thessaloniki: UNCUT Mountain Press 2001) 34-105.

denominations, and it is therefore important for the Orthodox churches to continue engaging in ecumenism. To facilitate this better, ecumenical studies can be introduced into the Orthodox seminary schools' curriculum.

Bibliography

Aslanidis Demotrios and Damascene Grigoratis, *Apostle to Zaïre; The Life and Legacy of Blessed Cosmos of Grigoriou*, UNCUT Mountain Press, Thessaloniki 2001

Dictionary of the Ecumenical Movement, WCC Publications, Geneva 2002

Groves, C.P., *The Planting of Christianity in Africa,* Vol. 1, Lutterworth Press, London 1964.

Baur, John, *2000 Years of Christianity in Africa: An African Church History*, Pauline Publications, Nairobi 1994.

Ware, Kallistos Timothy (Metropolitan of Diokleia), *The Orthodox Church*, Penguin Books, London 1997.

Journals, Articles and E-Sources

Andreas Tillyrides (Metropolitan Makarios), article, Makarios Legacy in Kenya: www.Orthodoxresearchinstitute.org/articles/church_history/makarios_tillyrides_makarios_legacy.htm (accessed 20th January 2015).

______, Chronology in the Yearbook and Review 2012

Anderson, Andrew J., *Project on Orthodox Church in Ghana*: www.orthodoxresearchinstitute.org/articles/church_history/anderson_ghana.htm (accessed 20th January 2015).

Hayes, Stephen (article) *A History of the Orthodox Mission in Tropical Africa*; (originally published in Missionalia, the journal of the Southern African Missiological Society): www.orthodoxytz.com/OrthodoxMission.asp (accessed 20th January 2015).

Njoroge, John, *The Ecumenical Dialogue in the Perspective of the Greek Orthodox Patriarchate of Alexandria All Africa* in the Orthodox Handbook on Ecumenism Resources for Theological Education, Volos Academy Publications, in co-operation with WCC Publications, Regnum and Volos, 2014.

______, *Theological Training and Formation in the Eastern Orthodox Churches in Africa* in the Handbook of Theological Education in Africa: Regnum Books International for South Africa, 2013

______, *The Orthodox Church in Africa and the Quest for Enculturation: A Challenging Mission paradigm in Today's Orthodoxy*, St Vladimir's Theological Quarterly Journal Vol.55 No.4, 2011

Wentink D.E., *The Orthodox Church in East Africa*, The Ecumenical Review Vol.20, WCC Publications, Geneva, 1968.

(25) The Roman Catholic Church in Africa

Lawrence Iwuamadi and Raoul Baziomo

Introduction

The history of Catholicism in Africa is complex, owing to two major factors. First, Catholicism in Africa can be traced back to the beginnings of Christianity. Therefore one is faced with almost 2000 years of history. Second, this long period of time does not come across in a linear manner and so requires great care to avoid missing salient points and at the same time to resist the temptation of making ambiguous claims. The primary focus of this work is to highlight the stages of development and growth of Catholicism in Africa.[1]

In order to be comprehensive, this work presents Catholicism in Africa starting from the Biblical time and early Church, through the period of Christianity in North Africa before and under the Arabs, to the beginning of the fourteenth and fifteenth-century missionary strides of the Portuguese. The last part will focus on the current situation of the Catholic Church in Africa.[2]

Biblical Origins of the History of Catholicism in Africa

The basis of the Catholic claims of biblical origins of its history in Africa may also be true for other early Christian traditions on the continent, like the Copts and the Ethiopians. The presence of the Infant Jesus and the Holy Family of Nazareth in Africa (cf. Matt. 2:13-15) forms the point of departure of any Christian history on the continent. The second important New Testament reference to Christianity in Africa would be the conversion and baptism of the first non-Jewish Christian, the Ethiopian eunuch (Acts 8:26-40).[3]

Early Catholicism in Africa

Africa played a significant role both in early Christianity and early Catholicism. Though Christianity generally flourished in North Africa, the region could be divided into North Eastern and North Western African Christianity. The North Eastern African Christianity was predominantly under Greek Alexandria, while the North Western Christianity was under the Latin Rome. The North Eastern part would consist of the Copts in Egypt which were spread through the banks of the Nile to Ethiopia. These churches will become part of what is designated as Oriental Orthodox Christianity after the Council of Chalcedon (AD 451).

North Western African Christianity, with allegiance to the Pope in Rome, covered the area known today as the Maghreb, and played a significant role in the life of the early Catholic Church. The important centres

---

[1] It is not feasible within the number of pages assigned to this work to offer a detailed history of Catholicism in Africa. There are a number of history books on Christianity in North Africa and on the evangelization of sub-Saharan Africa. The focus of this work is to highlight the various stages of the development and growth of Catholicism in Africa and to present the current overview of the Catholic Church.

[2] Most of the data used in this part are based on the *Pontificio Annuario 2014*, Città Del Vaticano, Editrice Vaticana, 2014.The "*Pontificio Annuario*" is the annual official statistic publication of the Catholic Church. The 2014 edition is updated to the 31 December 2012.

[3] This is contrary to the view that Cornelius was the first non-Jewish convert to Christianity because the story of the Ethiopian Eunuch (Acts 8) precedes that of Cornelius (Acts 10).

of this region included Carthage (present-day Tunisia), Hippo or Hippo Regius (present-day Annaba in Algeria), Numidia (present-day Algeria and a small part of Tunisia) and Mauretania (the ancient first-century region which consisted of the present-day northern part of Morocco and Algeria). These centres produced great Catholic theologians like Tertullian (c. AD 160-225) who is reckoned to be the founder of western theology,[4] and who wrote extensively on varied theological themes including the Trinity, the Eucharist, Baptism, Apostolicity, among other subjects.

Another eminent theologian of Carthage was St Cyprian. Beyond his theological contributions, he oversaw at least three important councils and synods as the Metropolitan of Carthage. The third council of Carthage defined the books that constitute the canon of the Bible on 28th August 397. Cyprian wrote extensively and his works include those on the unity of the Church (*De Unitate Ecclesiae*) and his treatise on baptism.

St Augustine of Hippo, the great philosopher theologian whose teaching will be a guiding line of Catholic doctrines, is regarded as the greatest Latin theologian of all time. Augustine's teachings touched on almost every aspect of Catholic theology including Trinity, Ecclesiology, Creation, Christian Anthropology, Mariology, Freewill, Original Sin, Grace. He wrote extensively against heresies, such as Arianism, Pelagianism, Manicheanism, Donatism. He wrote commentaries of some books of the Bible, and among his most popular works are *The Confessions* and *The City of God*.

As well as the great theologians of this era, early African Catholicism produced at least three popes: Pope Victor (c. 189-199), a Berber and the first pope whose surviving encyclicals are all in Latin; Pope Miltiades (311-314) under whose pontificate Constantine gave the Pope the Lateran palace and signed the Edict of Milan (313), and he presided over the Lateran Synod, which condemned the Donatist heresy; and Pope Gelasius (492-496). This same period produced a number of African saints and saints with links to Africa who are revered in the universal Church. These include Saints Perpetua and Felicity, St Monica, St Augustine, St Cyprian, St Zeno, the Bishop of Verona who comes from Africa.[5]

Catholicism in Africa: From Arab Conquest to the Middle Ages

It is known that while North Eastern African Christianity (Coptic and the Ethiopian Churches) resisted and survived Arab conquests, the Latin western part was decimated. However, it is an overstatement to suggest that Catholicism was totally wiped out from the continent. Historians have indicated the apparent presence of Catholicism up to the twelfth, fourteenth and even eighteenth centuries in South Tunisia.[6] According to Virginie Prevost, Catholicism continued to exist in certain small quarters of this region. There were two letters of Pope Leo IX of 1053, which clearly indicated that there were at least five bishops, two of whom are those of Carthage and Mahdiyya/Gummi. Also, in 1076, Pope Gregory VII pointed to the existence of at least two bishops in Africa.[7]

---

[4] Justo L. Gonzáles, *The Story of Christianity: The Early Church to the Dawn of the Reformation,* Volume 1, New York: HarperCollins Publishers, 2010, 91-93.

[5] There are no less than 973 saints coming from Africa or whose lives are closely linked with Africa. See Catholic Online, "Black/African Saints", www.catholic.org/saints/black.php.

[6] Virginie Prevost, "Les dernières communautés chrétiennes autochtones d'Afrique du Nord." *Revue de l'histoire des religions* 4 (2007): 477.

[7] Prevost, "Les dernières communautés chrétiennes", 472. "Dans deux lettres datées de 1053, le pape Léon IX déplore, en pleine crise arabe, l'affaiblissement considérable de l'Église d'Afrique; il n'y subsiste que cinq évêques et les deux principaux, celui de Carthage et celui de Mahdiyya/Gummi, se disputent l'archevêché. Les trois autres diocèses évoqués par le pape sont sujets à discussion; il pourrait peut-être s'agir de Gabès ou de Gafsa. En 1076, le pape Grégoire VII regrette que l'on ne trouve plus en Afrique les trois évêques nécessaires à l'ordination d'un nouvel évêque: il ne reste plus que celui de Carthage et celui de Bougie, récemment nommé à la demande du souverain ḥammâdide al-Nâṣir pour sa nouvelle capital."

It is thought that some of the reasons for the collapse of Catholicism at that point were the inability of North African Catholicism to take into adequate consideration the culture of the people and to make use of local languages in liturgy and Bible translations, the persecution of the Vandals, the effects of Donatism and the Arab invasion.[8] It would take missionaries following the colonial merchants through the Atlantic Ocean to bring the Catholic faith into the other parts of Africa in the fourteenth century.

Catholicism in the Sub-Saharan Africa

The formal commitment towards implanting Catholicism in sub-Saharan Africa may be traced to about 1493 when Pope Alexander VI 'divided the world, assigning the West to Spain and the East, including Africa, to Portugal'.[9] The drive for colonization in search of gold and for the spiritual crusade of winning souls for Christ brought Portuguese merchants and missionaries into different parts of the coastal lands of Africa. However, earlier contact had already been established in the areas of Cape Verde (1445) 'where Fr Polono de Lagos celebrated the first Mass in West Africa'[10] and the Gambia region around 1458,[11] from where the spread continued along the western coasts to Wolof of Senegambia, Guinea, Saõ Tomé, Warri, Benin, the Gold Coast, etc. And a bishopric see was erected in Cape Verde in 1553. At the same time the Portuguese missionaries took Catholicism to Zaïre. The contacts, which took place around 1483, led to the conversion of prominent kings that paved the way to massive acceptance of the Catholic faith.[12] In 1597, Sao Salvador was raised to a bishopric see. The faith in the latter half of the sixteenth century reached other areas like Luanda and in the east to Mozambique, which St Francis Xavier visited on his way to Asia. Catholicism was brought to Madagascar at about the same time. Though South Africa had early contact with Catholicism, the faith was proscribed by Dutch and British rules until the nineteenth and twentieth centuries.

However, these early missionary drives did not survive much into the nineteenth century. This was as a result of the problems arising from the Portuguese domination of the mission fields on account of its *Patroado* (patronage) privileges granted by the Popes.[13] They insisted on their prerogative in Africa when indeed they were unable to handle the increasing demands of evangelization on the continent.

In 1622, Pope Gregory XV created the Congregation for the Propagation of the Faith – *de Propaganda Fide* – to direct mission churches. This congregation, now known as the Congregation for the Evangelization of Peoples, co-ordinated a number of religious orders in the mid-nineteenth century to resume a more organized missionary thrust in Africa. This phase of evangelization saw an impressive growth of the number of Catholics and a rise among Africans that accepted the vocation to the priesthood. The presence of African born missionaries energized the spread of Catholicism on the continent. If the nineteenth century was about the beginning of a committed acceptance of Catholicism in Africa, the twentieth century saw it flourishing. There has been a consistent increase in the number of African Catholics, African religious, priests and bishops, as well as the number of ecclesiastical jurisdictions in Africa.

---

[8] Philip Jenkins, *The Lost History of Christianity*. New York: HarperCollins (2008) 227-230.

[9] Bengt Sundkler – Christopher Steed, *A History of The Church in Africa*. Cambridge: Cambridge University Press (2000), 44.

[10] Joseph Kenny, O.P., *The Catholic Church in Tropical Africa, 1445-1850*. Ibadan: Ibadan University Press (1983), 1.

[11] Kenny, *The Catholic Church in Tropical Africa*, 45.

[12] Philip Jenkins, *The Next Christendom, The Coming of Global Christianity*, New York: Oxford Press (2002) 29-30, 47-51.

[13] The Patroado mission implied that mission was the task of the civil government: The King exercised the patronage over the church and the missions in early Portugues mission.

Catholicism in Africa in the 21st Century

According to the *Annuario Pontificio 2014*, Catholics in Africa make up 18.63% of the total African population. While Catholics in Africa were less than 1% of the global Catholic population in 1910, in 2012 they constituted 16% of Catholics in the world numbering over 198 million, with a 4.92 million increase between 2011 and 2012 alone.

The Catholic Church in Africa is organised according to the traditional Catholic structures of parishes within dioceses, metropolitan sees (archdioceses) with suffragan dioceses, and provincial and national episcopal conferences. According to the *Agenzia Fides* of the *Pontificie Opere Missionarie*, Africa had, on 8th October 2014, 91 Metropolitan Sees and 387 Dioceses that make a total of 478. There were 22 Apostolic Vicariates, two Apostolic Prefectures, one Mission *Sui Iuris*, and three Military Ordinariates that are under the Congregation for the Evangelization of Peoples: *de Propaganda Fide*. Outside these, there were about fifteen churches directly subject to the Holy See.[14] Africa had, on 31st December 2012, 534 Ecclesiastical Circumscriptions, 528 Mission Stations with resident priest, and 73,936 Mission Stations without resident priest.[15]

Clergy and Lay Apostolates

Africa has through history produced 42 cardinals coming from: Benin (1); Burkina Faso (2); Cameroon (1); Cape Verde (1); Democratic Republic of the Congo (3); Egypt (3) ; Ethiopia (2); Ghana (2); Guinea (1); Côte d'Ivoire (3); Kenya (2); Madagascar (3); Mauritius (1); Mozambique (2); Nigeria (4); Republic of the Congo (1); Senegal (2); South Africa (2); Sudan (1); Tanzania (2); Uganda (2); Zambia (1). Two African cardinals are members of the Roman Curia: Cardinal Robert Sarah of Guinea, the Prefect of the Congregation for Divine Worship and the Discipline of the Sacraments, and Cardinal Peter Kodwo Appiah Turkson of Ghana, President of the Pontifical Council for Justice and Peace. On 13th April 2013, Pope Francis named Cardinal Monsengwo Pasinya Laurent of the Congo (DRC) as a member of the *Council of Cardinals* whose task is to assist the Pope in the governance of the Universal Church and to reform the Roman Curia.[16] Two other African Cardinals who served in the Roman Curia were Cardinal Francis Arinze of Nigeria and late Cardinal Bernadin Gantin of Benin. With the creation of new Cardinals on February 14, 2015, Africa has 21 living Cardinals,16 of whom are Cardinal electors.

As of 31st December 2012, Africa had a total number of 700 Bishops (506 diocesan bishops and 194 religious bishops), and of these 91 were archbishops of the metropolitan sees.[17] A steady increase in the number of vocations to the priesthood, to the religious life and a greater involvement of the faithful in lay apostolates have become a remarkable aspect of Catholicism in Africa. The tables below show the details:[18]

African Population – Catholics

Population	Catholics	Percentage
1,066,140,000	198,587,000	18.63% (=)

---

[14] *Pontificio Annuario 2014,* 1099-1105.

[15] *Pontificio Annuario 2014,* 1099-1105.

[16] Vatican, "Chirograph by which a Council Of Cardinals is Established to Assist the Holy Father in the Governance of the Universal Church and to Study Possible Revisions of the Apostolic Constitution "Pastor Bonus" on the Roman Curia", http://w2.vatican.va/content/francesco/en/letters/2013/documents/papa-francesco_20130928_chirografo-consiglio-cardinali.html.

[17] Agenzia Fides, "Catholic Church Statistics", October 19, 2014. www.africamission-mafr.org/STATISTICHE_2014_eng.pdf.

[18] Agenzia Fides, "Catholic Church Statistics", October 19, 2014. www.africamission-mafr.org/STATISTICHE_2014_eng.pdf.

Bishops

Total Bishops	Diocesan Bishops	Religious Bishops
700	506	194

Priests

Total Priests	Diocesan priests	Religious priests
40,133	27,493	12,640

Persons/Catholics per Priest

Persons per priest	Catholics per priest
26,565	4,948

Permanent Deacons

Total Permanent deacons	Diocesan Permanent deacons	Religious Permanent deacons
419	387	32

Brothers and Women Religious

Brothers	Women Religious
8,645	68,590

Members of Secular Institutes

Members of secular institutes: Male	Members of secular institutes: Female
77	851

Lay Missionaries and Catechists

Lay missionaries	Catechists
7,195	393,580

Major Seminarians – Diocesan and Religious

Total Major Seminarians	Diocesan Major seminarians	Religious Major seminarians
27,728	18,713	9,015

Minor Seminarians – Diocesan and Religious

Total Minor seminarians	Diocesan Minor seminarians	Religious Minor seminarians
53,085	47,295	5,790

Schools, Hospitals, Charity Works and Welfare

The Catholic Church in Africa drew from the spirit of the early missionaries the strength of engaging actively in temporal, spiritual and social works that are geared towards the development of the human person and society. Organized around the diocesan structures and under the supervision of the local ordinaries, the Catholic Church in Africa has been engaging in education, health care and other forms of charity work. The official church statistics of 2014 show that there were about 14,711 Catholic Infant Schools with 1,444,069 pupils in Africa. There were also 36,613 Catholic primary schools with over 16 million pupils and 12,060 Catholic secondary schools with about five million pupils. In recent years, there has been an increase in the number of Catholic institutions of higher learning and universities.

The Catholic commitment to health care and concern for those who are defenceless is evident in the number of hospitals, dispensaries, homes for the elderly, etc., that have continued to provide for those in special need. The table below gives the numbers:

Hospitals	Dispensaries	Leprosy centres	Homes for the elderly, chronically ill, disabled	Orphanages	Nursery schools	Marriage Counselling centres	Other institutes
1,298	5,256	229	632	1,398	2,099	1,728	2,556

Eastern Catholic Churches in Africa

The Catholic Church in Africa is largely of the Latin Rite Catholics, but there is also a significant presence of the Catholic Churches of the Eastern Rite commonly known as the Eastern Catholic Churches. The Eastern Catholic Churches have 'institutions, liturgical rites, ecclesiastical traditions and the established standards of the Christian life'[19] similar to the Eastern and Oriental Churches, but they are in full communion with the Pope. There are about 22 Eastern Catholic Churches who together with the Latin rite Catholics make up the Catholic Church. In Africa, however, those with relevant presence are the Armenian Catholic Church, the Chaldean Catholic Church, the Coptic Catholic Church, the Maronite Catholics, the Melkite Greek Catholics and the Syrian Catholic Church in Egypt and Ethiopia. There are also the Ethiopian and the Eritrean Catholic Churches. On January 13, 2014, the Holy Father Pope Francis erected a new Apostolic Exarchate for the Maronite Catholic Church of the Antiochian Tradition in West and Central Africa in Nigeria.[20]

Special Assembly of the Synod of Bishops for Africa and African Catholicism

The spirit of Catholicism in Africa is reflected in the two Special Assemblies of the Synod of Bishops for Africa. The solemn opening of the first Special Assembly on the theme *THE CHURCH IN AFRICA AND HER EVANGELIZING MISSION TOWARDS THE YEAR 2000: 'You will be my witnesses' (Acts 1:8)* was celebrated in St Peter's Basilica on 10th April 1994. The fruit of this Synod was the post-synodal Apostolic Exhortation *Ecclesia in Africa*, issued by Saint Pope John Paul II. The Second Special Assembly of the Synod for Africa convoked by Pope Benedict XVI took place, 4th-25th October 2009, with the theme *THE CHURCH IN AFRICA IN SERVICE TO RECONCILIATION, JUSTICE AND PEACE, 'You are the salt of the earth... You are the light of the world' (Matt.5:13-14).*

These two Synods highlighted the specific elements of Catholicism in Africa, as well as the challenges facing the church.

Lay Apostolates and Spirituality

The Synods for Africa called for greater participation and involvement of the lay Catholic faithful in the life of the Church. Catholicism in Africa is marked by the existence of many and different Sodalities and Pious Prayers groups including those devoted to Jesus, Mary and the Saints, such as *the Confraternity of the Most Blessed Sacrament*; *the Sacred Heart of Jesus*; *the Legion of Mary*; *Guild of St Anthony of Padua*; *St Theresa of the Child Jesus*; *St Vincent de Paul*; *Blessed Iwene Tansi Sodality,* etc. Others are dedicated

---

[19] Vatican II, "*Orientalium Ecclesiarum*, Decree on the Catholic Churches of the Eastern Rite", *The Conciliar and Post Conciliar Documents*, Austin Flannery, ed., Northport: Costello Publishing Company (1998), no 3.

[20] *Pontificio Annuario 2014,* 1099-1105.

to particular spiritualities, such as *the Catholic Bible Society* and *the Catholic Charismatic Renewal Movement*.

There are also a number of clergy and lay faithful engaged in other movements; organizations and institutions in the Catholic Church, such as the *Focolare Movement*; *the St Egidio*; *the Communion and Liberation*; *the Prelature of the Holy Cross and Opus Dei*, etc. Regular and active participation in one or more of these constitute an integral part of Catholicism in Africa.

The Bible and the Biblical Apostolate

The Sacred Scriptures play a significant role in Catholicism in Africa. The Bible has been translated into several local languages to encourage active participation in liturgy and grassroot evangelization.[21] With the growing number of African Catholic biblical scholars and priests who are well prepared from the seminaries, Bible studies are encouraged in families and in small Christian communities.

Church Structures and Organization: National, Regional and Continental

On the local level, a number dioceses are grouped together under a metropolitan Archbishopric See to form the Bishops' Conference of an Ecclesiastical Province. Different Provincial Bishops' Conferences of a particular nation come together to form a National Episcopal Conference while national episcopal conferences of a particular region would form Regional Episcopal Conferences.

The Symposium of Episcopal Conferences of Africa and Madagascar (SECAM)

The Symposium of Episcopal Conferences of Africa and Madagascar (SECAM) is the body that gathers the different national and regional episcopal conferences of Africa and Madagascar, and aims at preserving and fostering communion, collaboration and joint action among all the Episcopal Conferences of Africa and the Islands. According to its mission, the Symposium through the Episcopal Conferences promotes: (i) Propagation of Faith, (ii) Human Development, (iii) Ecumenism, (iv) Formation, (v) Consultation.[22]

The Episcopal Conferences that constitute the SECAM are:

English-Speaking:

1. ETHIOPIA AND ERITREA: The Assembly of The Catholic Bishops' Conference Of Ethiopia And Eritrea (ACBEE)
2. GHANA: Ghana Catholic Bishops' Conference (GCBC)
3. KENYA: Kenya Episcopal Conference (KEC)
4. LESOTHO: Lesotho Catholic Bishops' Conference (LCBC)
5. LIBERIA: Catholic Bishops' Conference of Liberia (CABICOL)
6. MALAWI: The Episcopal Conference of Malawi (ECM)
7. NAMIBIA: Namibian Catholic Bishops' Conference (NCBC)
8. NIGERIA: Catholic Bishops' Conference of Nigeria (CBCN)
9. SOUTHERN AFRICA (BOTSWANA, SWAZILAND, SOUTH AFRICA): Southern African Catholic Bishops' Conference (SACBC)
10. SUDAN: Sudan Catholic Bishops' Conference (SCBC)

---

[21] II Special Assembly for Africa, *The Church in Africa in Service to Reconciliation, Justice and Peace. "You are the salt of the earth... You are the light of the world" (Mt 5: 13, 14)*, Instrumentum Laboris, Vatican: Vatican Press (2009), no. 19.

[22] SECAM, "SECAM Mission", www.secam-sceam.org/mission.html.

11. TANZANIA: Tanzania Episcopal Conference (TEC)
12. THE GAMBIA, SIERRA LEONE: Inter-Territorial Catholic Bishops' Conference of The Gambia And Sierra Leone (ITCABIC)
13. ZAMBIA: Zambia Episcopal Conference (ZEC)
14. ZIMBABWE: Zimbabwe Catholic Bishops' Conference (ZCBC)

French-Speaking:

1. EGYPT: Assemblée de la Hiérarchie Catholique d'Egypte (AHCE)
2. BENIN: Conférence Episcopale Nationale du Benin
3. BURKINA NIGER: Conférence Episcopale du Burkina/Niger
4. BURUNDI: Conférencedes Evêques catholiques du Burundi
5. CAMEROUN: Conférence Episcopale Nationale du Cameroun
6. CEDOI: (OCEAN INDIEN-COMORES, MAURITIUS, SEYCHELLES)
7. CERNA: Conférence Episcopale Régionaledu Nord de l'Afrique
8. CONGO BRAZZAVILLE: Conférence Episcopale du Congo Brazzaville
9. COTE D'IVOIRE: Conférence Episcopale Nationale de la Côte d'Ivoire
10. GABON: Conférence Episcopale du Gabon
11. GUINEE CONAKRY: Conférence Episcopale de la Guinée
12. GUINEE EQUATORIALE: Conférence Episcopale de la Guinée Équatoriale
13. MADAGASCAR: Conférence Episcopale de Madagascar
14. MALI: Conférence Episcopale du Mali
15. REPUBLIQUE CENTRAFRICAINE: Conférence Episcopale Centrafricaine (CECA)
16. REPUBLIQUE DEMOCRATIQUE DU CONGO: Conférence Episcopale Nationale du Congo (CENCO)
17. RWANDA: Conférence des Evêques catholiques du Rwanda (C. Ep. R)
18. SENEGAL/MAURITANIA/CAP-VERT/GUINEE BISSAU: Conférence des Evêques du Sénégal, de la Mauritanie, du Cap-Vert et de la Guinée Bissau
19. TCHAD: Conférence Episcopale du Tchad (CET)
20. TOGO: Conférence Episcopale du Togo (CET)

Portuguese-Speaking:

1. ANGOLA E SAO TOME E PRINCIPE: Conferencia Episcopal De Angola e Saõ Tomé (CEAST)
2. MOZAMBIQUE: Conferencia Episcopal De Moçambique (CEM)

Regional Episcopal Conferences:

1. ACEAC: Association des Conférences Episcopales de l'Afrique Centrale
2. ACERAC: Association des Conférences Episcopales de la Région de l'Afrique Centrale
3. AHCE: Assemblée de la Hiérarchie Catholique d'Egypte
4. AMECEA: Association of Member Episcopal Conferences in Eastern Africa
5. CEDOI: Conférence Episcopale de Madagascar et de l'Océan Indien
6. CERNA: Conférence Episcopale Régionale du Nord de l'Afrique
7. IMBISA: Inter-Regional Meeting of Bishops of Southern Africa
8. RECOWA-CERAO: Regional Episcopal Conferences of West Africa

Relationship with Other Christians

The commitment to ecumenism is an important aspect of the Catholic Church in Africa. However, the intensity of the ecumenical experience and collaboration differs from country to country and from region to region. In some countries, Catholics are members of the National Christian Councils or Associations. In most parts of the continent Catholics and other Christians together celebrate the Week of Prayer for Christian Unity. On other occasions, translating the Bible into local languages with the United Bible Societies has fostered dialogue among Christians of all confessions in Africa.[23]

Relationship with African Traditional Religions

The Catholic Church in Africa approaches the followers of African Traditional Religion with an open-mind to study this religion and enter into truthful dialogue with the culture. The intention is to seek out the good elements 'which Christianity can adopt, while purifying those judged incompatible with the gospel, so as to forge a culture of reconciliation, justice and peace'.[24] Bishops of dioceses and episcopal conferences give particular guidelines for this respectful relationship.

Relationship with Islam

As in the question of ecumenism, the intensity of the dialogue with the followers of the Islamic religion differs from countries and places. In some places Christians live harmoniously with Muslims, while in others there is an atmosphere of mistrust, hostility and prejudices on both sides, which creates a difficult environment for them to work together. However, the Catholic Church in African favours dialogues and collaborations in the face of these situations. There are occasions where 'Muslims have readily welcomed the documents of episcopal conferences. At the same time, the structures of the Church have sometimes served Muslim communities in the distribution of goods to the poor and needy....'[25]

Political Influence

The Catholic Church in Africa exercises notable influence in the politics of their particular countries through the prophetic voices of Bishops' Conferences that seek always to challenge bad governance, injustice, violation of human rights and wrong political ideologies working against the development of a healthy society. The Catholic position in social issues is always guided by the social teachings of the Church. The Catholic Church in Africa has always, therefore, stood in resolute defence of human life, which should be protected from the moment of conception until natural death occurs. Hence it condemns abortion and euthanasia, and pursues the promotion of the dignity of women[26] and the rights of children. The family occupies a place of priority in the Catholic Church in Africa. It strongly believes and teaches that marriage can only be a union between a man and a woman[27] and therefore opposes gay marriage, social acceptance of homosexuality and same-sex relationships. The Church however teaches that homosexual persons deserve respect.[28]

---

[23] II Special Assembly for Africa, *The Church in Africa*, no.99.
[24] II Special Assembly for Africa, *The Church in Africa*, no. 101.
[25] II Special Assembly for Africa, *The Church in Africa*, 102.
[26] Benedict XVI, *Africae Munus, Post-Synodal Apostolic Exhortation to The Bishops, Clergy, Consecrated Persons and the Lay Faithful on the Church in Africa in Service to Reconciliation, Justice And Peace*, «You are the salt of the earth... You are the light of the world' (Mt. 5: 13-14), Libreria Editrice Vaticana, 2011, Nos 55-59.
[27] Vatican, *Catechism of the Catholic Church, Second Edition*. Libreria Editrice Vaticana, 2012, no.2202.
[28] Vatican, *Catechism of the Catholic Church,* 2357-2358.

The relationship with the African Union is another important aspect of the Catholic Church in Africa. While the Holy See is an accredited non-member state to the African Union, SECAM has recently intensified efforts towards having a representation.[29] It is hoped that this will enhance the Catholic voice at the Union.

Challenges to the Catholic Church in Africa

The Special Assemblies of the Synod of Bishops for Africa not only demonstrate the vibrancy, but also highlight the internal and external challenges facing Catholicism on the continent. Prominent among these is the challenge of globalization, which seeks to import and impose cultures, ideologies, values that are neither coherent with the gospel message nor with African traditional value system. Others include the struggle for self-sufficiency, which is impeded by unjust global economic structures and high-level corruption among politicians and leaders of nations. Another great challenge is the situations of war, civil unrest, insecurity, religious extremism and terrorism. There is the challenge to build a strong platform favouring reconciliation, justice and peace. This entails a continuous process of healing of memories and working together in alleviating the pitiable humanitarian situations caused by wars, migration, famines, etc.

Other challenges are in the area of ecumenism, where there is still room for greater collaboration among Christians on the continent. This can be enhanced by greater efforts to reflect the activities of the Pontifical Council for the Promotion of Christian Unity in Rome. On the question of dialogue with cultures, there is the challenge of ensuring the genuine enculturation of African values without compromising the deposit of the faith.

Another important challenge is the pursuit and promotion of the dignity of women in Africa and the protection of children against abuse. Finally, the church in Africa has to keep abreast of the use of modern technology in living the faith, including the adequate use of the mass media and social media in evangelization and in challenging the ills of society.

Conclusion

The Catholic Church in Africa is old but still young. It is obviously a growing Church with roots in the traditional teachings of the Catholic magisterium. It is a Church that offers hope to the future of Catholicism in the world, with its growing numbers and vocations to ministerial priesthood and religious life. It is also a Church that defines itself according to the family model and earnestly hopes for a better Africa under the maternal care of the Most Holy Mary, Our Lady Queen of Africa.

Bibliography

Benedict XVI, *Africae Munus, Post-Synodal Apostolic Exhortation to The Bishops, Clergy, Consecrated Persons and the Lay Faithful on the Church in Africa in Service to Reconciliation, Justice And Peace, «You are the salt of the earth... You are the light of the world» (Matt. 5:13-14)*, Libreria Editrice Vaticana, 2011.

Bengt Sundkler – Christopher Steed, *A History of The Church in Africa.* Cambridge: CUP, 2000.

Joseph Kenny, OP, *The Catholic Church in Tropical Africa, 1445-1850*. Ibadan: Ibadan University Press, 1983.

[29] A first step towards having a representative of the Catholic Church at the African Union began in February 2015 with the appointment of the head of relations between SECAM and African Union in Addis Ababa who has the task of facilitating "the signing of an *Entente Cordiale Memorandum* for a SECAM Status of Observer to the African Union".

Justo L. Gonzáles, *The Story of Christianity: The Early Church to the Dawn of the Reformation, Volume 1*, New York: HarperCollins Publishers, 2010.

Philip Jenkins, *The Next Christendom, The Coming of Global Christianity*, New York: Oxford Press, 2002.

Philip Jenkins, *The Lost History of Christianity*. New York: HarperCollins, 2008.

Vatican, *Pontificio Annuario 2014*, Città Del Vaticano, Editrice Vaticana, 2014.

Vatican II, *The Conciliar and Post Conciliar Documents*, Austin Flannery, ed., Northport: Costello Publishing Company, 1998.

Vatican, *II Special Assembly for Africa, The Church in Africa in Service to Reconciliation, Justice and Peace. 'You are the salt of the earth... You are the light of the world' (Mt 5: 13, 14),* Instrumentum Laboris, Vatican: Vatican Press, 2009.

Vatican, *Catechism of the Catholic Church*, Second Edition. Libreria Editrice Vaticana, 2012.

Virginie Prevost, 'Les dernières communautés chrétiennes autochtones d'Afrique du Nord'. *Revue de l'histoire des religions* 4 (2007): 461-483.

Online resources

Agenzia Fides, 'Catholic Church Statistics', October 19, 2014. www.africamission-mafr.org/STATISTICHE_2014_eng.pdf

Catholic Online, 'Black/African Saints', www.catholic.org/saints/black.php

SECAM, 'SECAM Mission', www.secam-sceam.org/mission.html

Vatican, 'Chirograph by which a Council Of Cardinals is Established to Assist the Holy Father in the Governance of the Universal Church and to Study Possible Revisions of the Apostolic Constitution 'Pastor Bonus' on the Roman Curia', http://w2.vatican.va/content/francesco/en/letters/2013/documents/papa-francesco_20130928_chirografo-consiglio-cardinali.html

(26) PRESBYTERIAN CHURCHES IN AFRICA

Isabel Apawo Phiri

Introduction

The purpose of this essay is to tell briefly the stories of Presbyterian churches in Africa with a focus on tracing their historical background. The Presbyterian witness in Africa traces its roots to the foreign missionary initiatives predominantly from the nineteenth century. Similar to all mission churches, the stories of the Presbyterian churches in Africa are very rich and varied. First, they are stories of expansion initiated by local and foreign missionaries, evidenced by the establishment of new churches, which has continued to the present. Second, they have many splits within churches due to controversies over interpretation of scripture, racism,[1] sexism,[2] church discipline, perception of African culture[3] and ethnicity.[4] Third, they are stories of hardships due to: colonization which in some cases contributed to splits in the churches; struggles in holding the tension between finding indigenous identities and still remaining Presbyterian after becoming autonomous from missionary control; and finding and exercising their prophetic voice when living in a context where abuse of human rights by indigenous political leaders is rampant. Fourth, they are stories of separated churches coming together to form new United (Uniting) Churches with other Presbyterians and in some cases with other church families. Fifth, they demonstrated how to remain socially relevant in their societies through establishment and provision of education[5] at all levels, health care, agricultural projects and media. Sixth, they are involved in ecumenism. For example, there are eighteen Presbyterian churches in Africa who are members of the World Council of Churches (WCC). Forty-one Presbyterian churches in Africa are members of the World Communion of Reformed Churches (WCRC) and form its Africa region sector known as the African Communion of Reformed Churches (ACRC). Twenty-one Presbyterian churches in Africa are not members of WCC and WCRC but only of the All Africa Conference of Churches (AACC). Twenty-one Presbyterian churches in Africa are members of the World Reformed Fellowship (WRF). Yet there are others who are not listed in any of the other ecumenical families. In some cases, decisions to belong to some ecumenical organisation have led to church splits. The issues outlined above as besetting Presbyterian churches in Africa are a reflection of the stories of Presbyterian churches worldwide. In the next section, I briefly locate the historical and theological roots of the Presbyterian churches globally.

---

[1] John W. De Gruchy, *Liberating Reformed Theology: A South African Contribution to an Ecumenical Debate*. (Cape Town, David Philip Publishers, 1991) 3-4.
[2] Isabel Apawo Phiri, *Women, Presbyterianism and Patriarchy: Religious Experiences of Chewa Women in Central Malawi*. Blantyre: CLAM, 1997; Isabel Apawo Phiri, 'Marching, Suspended and Stoned: Christian Women in Malawi' in Kenneth R. Ross (ed) *God, People and Power in Malawi: Democratisation in Theological Perspective*. Gweru: Mambo Press, 1996, 63-105.
[3] Isabel Apawo Phiri. "The Initiation of Chewa Women of Malawi: A Presbyterian Woman's Perspective" in James Cox ed. *Rites of Passage: The Interaction between Christianity and African Traditional Religions*. Edinburgh: Cardiff Press, 1997, 129-145.
[4] Kwame Bediako, *Christianity in Africa: The Renewal of a Non-Western Religion* (Edinburgh: Edinburgh Univ. Press; Maryknoll, N.Y.: Orbis Books, 1995). See also Gatu, John G. Joyfully Christian and Truly African. (Acton Publishers: Nairobi, 2006).
[5] Isabel Apawo Phiri. "Theological Education in Presbyterian Churches in Africa". In *Handbook of Theological Education in Africa*. eds. Isabel Apawo Phiri and Dietrich Werner. Oxford: Regnum Books International, 2013, 345-353.

Global Historical and Theological Context of Presbyterian Churches

The story of the Presbyterian churches begins with reforming further the Protestant Reformation that started with Martin Luther in 1517. The French/Swiss John Calvin (1509-1564) based in Geneva, Switzerland, is credited with starting reformed theology and the Presbyterian form of church government. From Switzerland, reformed theology spread to the neighbouring regions of southern France and western Germany under the leadership of different key church figures.[6] For example in the Presbyterian history, John Knox, a Scotsman who studied with Calvin in Geneva, Switzerland, took Calvin's teachings back to Scotland and successfully developed Presbyterianism which later became the state church up to the present. Others went further to Western European countries of England, Ireland and the Netherlands and also to eastern European countries such as Poland, Hungary, Bohemia and Transylvania.[7] As the Scottish, Irish, English and the French emigrated to North America; they took with them the Presbyterian Church.

What makes the Presbyterians different from other churches is a key question. First, it is the form of government of the churches which was introduced by John Calvin. The leadership of the church at congregation level is in the hands of two types of elders: the teaching elder who is called the 'Reverend' and the ruling elders who are ordained laypersons. The importance of elders is seen in the name of the denomination because the word 'Presbyterian' comes from the Greek word for elder. Congregations form Presbyteries, which in turn form Synods. Different synods form one General Synod. The second unique aspect is the adherence to reformed theology developed by Calvin. He agreed with Luther on the doctrines of original sin, justification by faith alone, the priesthood of all believers, and the sole authority of the Scriptures. He differentiates himself theologically from Luther largely with the doctrines of predestination and eternal security.[8]

Although Presbyterians have the same beliefs as described above, there is some internal diversity based on context and confessions. The Apostles Creed and the Westminster confession of faith are the basics. For a diversity of reasons some Presbyterian churches may add any or all the following: Athanasian Creed, Nicene Creed, Heidelberg Catechism, Second Helvetic Confession.[9] These differences would make one Presbyterian Church very conservative and another very liberal. The Presbyterians are also known for their emphasis on hard work, discipline, the salvation of souls and the building of a better world.[10] During the time of Calvin, and even now, they stand for and are heavily involved in education, health and issues of justice and peace.

Having outlined the six characteristics of the Presbyterian churches in Africa earlier in the introduction, and having located the connection with Presbyterian history and theology, I now focus on very brief histories of the Presbyterian churches in Africa, giving examples of four countries per region.

North Africa

The major countries in North Africa with Presbyterian churches are in Egypt, Ethiopia, Eritrea and Sudan. What these churches have in common is that they are located in countries which are predominantly Muslim and where the majority of the Christians are Orthodox. Their major contribution to society has been in education, health and peace-building. What follows is what is distinct about each country.

---

[6] http://reformation.edu/colleges/pages/ref-wall.htm. accessed 12 November 2013.

[7] Odair Pedroso Mateus, "Reformed Churches" in *The Cambridge Dictionary of Christianity*. Edited by Daniel Patte (New York: Cambridge University Press, 2010), 1059.

[8] http://christianity.about.com/od/presbyteriandenomination/a/presbyhistory.htm accessed 28062014.

[9] See 'Know your Church" on www.angelfire.com/ex/pcnuyoparish/INDEX1.HTM accessed 20/03/2012.

[10] http://christianity.about.com/od/presbyteriandenomination/a/presbyhistory.htm accessed 02062012.

Egypt

The American Mission of the United Presbyterian Church of North America (UPCNA) founded the Evangelical Church of Egypt (ECE) (Synod of the Nile) (also called the Evangelical Presbyterian Church in Egypt (EPCE), Arabic الكنيسة الإنجيلية :*El-Kanisah El-Injiliyah*) in 1854.[11] It is also referred to as the Coptic Evangelical Church of Egypt. It is now the largest protestant denomination in the Middle East and in North Africa. The EPCE became autonomous from the American missionaries in 1958. The church is a member of the Evangelical Church of Egypt.[12] and the Egypt Council of Churches. Its partners are the Presbyterian Church in the USA (PC (USA)), the Church of Scotland, and the Gustav-Adolf-Werk (GAW) as the Evangelical Church in Germany Diaspora.[13] Despite the Arab uprising in Egypt since 2011 which has affected the relationship between Christians and Muslims, the EPCE has continued to remain relevant to the Egyptian community.

South Sudan

There are three Presbyterian churches in South Sudan. These are: the Presbyterian Church of the Sudan (PCS), Sudan Evangelical Presbyterian Church (SEPC) and the Sudanese Reformed Presbyterian Churches (SRPC).

The American Mission of the United Presbyterian Church of North America (UPCNA) based in Egypt established the PCS or also the Presbyterian Church of the South Sudan (PCSS) in the 1890s. Their first church was in Khartoum but by 1902 they moved to found churches in the South. The first mission station was established in Malakal. In 1962 the missionaries were expelled from Sudan, but the church spread rapidly under local leadership. It is the third largest denomination in Sudan after the Episcopal and the Roman Catholic Church. Partner churches are the Church of Scotland, the Presbyterian Church in Ireland, the Presbyterian Church of Australia, the PC (USA). It became a member of WCC in 1965.[14] It is also a member of AACC, WCRC and ACRC.[15]

The Sudan Evangelical Presbyterian Church (SEPC) was started by missionaries from the Presbyterian Church in the USA who were based in Egypt. Their focus was northern Sudan. The Missionaries were expelled from Sudan in 1964. The SEPC has grown in both Sudan and South Sudan under local leadership. Its partner church is the Reformed Church in America.[16]

The Sudanese Reformed Presbyterian Churches (SRPC) is a unified body of the small reformed and Presbyterian churches in Sudan. It started in Khartoum in 1992. Among the churches there are four congregations in Khartoum (Dar el Salam Sudanese Reformed Presbyterian Church, Abuja Sudanese Reformed Presbyterian Church, Soba Sudanese Reformed Presbyterian Church, Khartoum Sudanese Reformed Presbyterian Church), four congregation in Juba, Southern Sudan (Kator Sudanese Reformed Presbyterian Church, Munuki Sudanese Reformed Presbyterian Church, Lologu Sudanese Reformed Presbyterian Church, Hai Malakal Sudanese Reformed Presbyterian Church), as well as Churches in Renk and Malakal, Southern Sudan. It is a member of the WCRC and WRF. It is in partnership with the reformed churches in South Africa.[17]

---

[11] https://en.wikipedia.org/wiki/United_Presbyterian_Church_of_North_America accessed 02032015.
[12] https://en.wikipedia.org/wiki/Evangelical_Church_of_Egypt_(Synod_of_the_Nile) – cite_note-4WCRC
[13] https://en.wikipedia.org/wiki/Evangelical_Church_of_Egypt_(Synod_of_the_Nile) accessed 02032015.
[14] Huibert van Beek *A Handbook Of Churches And Councils*: *Profiles of Ecumenical Relationships*. Geneva: 2006, 185-6.
[15] https://en.wikipedia.org/wiki/Presbyterian_Church_in_Sudan accessed 02032015.
[16] https://en.wikipedia.org/wiki/Sudan_Evangelical_Presbyterian_Church accessed 02032015.
[17] https://en.wikipedia.org/wiki/Sudanese_Reformed_Presbyterian_Churches accessed 02032015.

Ethiopia and Eritrea

The Reformed Presbyterian Church in Ethiopia (RPCE) was established by missionaries of the Orthodox Presbyterian Church USA in 1998.[18] They also established the Mehrete Yesus Evangelical Presbyterian Church in 1995.[19]

West Africa

Space does not allow me to discuss the following: the Reformed Presbyterian Church of Equatorial Guinea (in Spanish: Iglesia Reformada Presbiteriana de Guinea Ecuatorial, IRPGE); the Presbyterian Church in Guinea-Bissau; the Evangelical Presbyterian Church in Ivory Coast and the Presbyterian Church in Liberia (PCL). Instead I will give the following examples: Cameroon, Ghana and Nigeria.

Cameroon

The Presbyterian Church *in* Cameroon (PCC) and the Presbyterian Church *of* Cameroon (PCOC) have a complicated mission history which was heavily influenced by political events of the day. In the case of the PCC, its roots are with the Baptist Missionary Society (UK) who began their mission work in 1845 in Ntanfoang, Bali. At the Berlin Conference of 1884, where Africa was partitioned among the European countries, the area where the Baptist Missionary Society (UK) was operating was given to the Germans. As a result, in 1886 the European Missionary Societies responded by requesting that the Basel Mission of the *Evangelical Missionary Society of Basel* in Switzerland take over from the Baptist Missionary Society (UK). The new church was called *Basel Mission Church in Kamerun.* However the missionary activities in this church were seriously affected during the WW1 when the country came under British rule and the Swiss missionaries were expelled. Fortunately the church continued to grow under predominantly African leadership. In 1957, the church became autonomous and its name changed to the Presbyterian Church *in* Africa.[20] The PCC became a member of the WCC in 1961, and soon after there was a theological split within the church in their understanding of the work of the WCC. Those who broke away formed the Orthodox Presbyterian Church in Cameroon (OPCC) (Eglise Presbytérienne Initiale) under the leadership of the Rev. Jean Andjongo.

While more has been written about the PCC, there is a dearth of literature on the Presbyterian Church of Cameroon. The PCOC was founded by the American Presbyterian Mission at the same time that the Baptist Missionary Society of the UK started work in Cameroon. During World War I, the Basel Mission was also involved in the running of this church. It became autonomous in 1957.[21] Although this church is also spread throughout Cameroon, its greatest impact is felt in Northern Cameroon which is predominantly Muslim.[22] Both churches have been very active in the ecumenical movement. The OPCC was registered with the government in 1970. The OPCC is supported by the Free Presbyterian Church of Ulster from the USA.[23] It joined the WCC in 1963 and managed to keep the church together. Since then, the PCC and the PCOC have joined other ecumenical bodies like the AACC, Council of Protestant Churches of Cameroon, WCRC and ACRC.

---

[18] https://en.wikipedia.org/wiki/Reformed_Presbyterian_Church_in_Ethiopia accessed 02032015.
[19] www.lakeopc.net/evangelical.htm accessed 02032015.
[20] van Beek *A Handbook Of Churches And Councils:* Geneva: 2006, 124.
[21] https://en.wikipedia.org/wiki/Presbyterian_Church_in_Cameroon accessed 05042015.
[22] https://en.wikipedia.org/wiki/Presbyterian_Church_of_Cameroon.
[23] https://en.wikipedia.org/wiki/Orthodox_Presbyterian_Church_in_Cameroon accessed 04052015.

Ghana

The Presbyterian Church of Ghana (PCG) is associated with the Basel Mission which arrived in the Gold Coast in 1828 and African and Scottish missionaries from Jamaica and Antigua in the West Indies who arrived in 1843.[24] The Basel missionaries left the Gold Coast due to WW1 in 1917. The PCG became independent in 1918 and called the Scottish Mission to work with the local church leaders. It became a member of the WCC in 1952. It also became a member of the Christian Council of Ghana, AACC, WCRC and ACRC.[25]

The Evangelical Presbyterian Church, Ghana (*Ewe:Presbyteria Nyanyui Hame le Ghana*), widely known as the 'EP Church' traces its origins to the work of the missionaries from the North German Mission Society (*Norddeutsche Mission, Bremen*) who started work among the Ewe people in 1847. The mission work expanded into Ewe land (now known as the Volta Region of Ghana) which was a British colony and into Togoland (the south of the present-day Republic of Togo) which was a Germany colony.[26] After World War I, Togoland was divided into two: the eastern side came under French rule while the western came under the British. In 1922, Scottish missionaries began working in British Togoland. The church in French Togoland was run by the Paris Mission. This led to separate developments of the two halves though both churches share the same constitution. They also hold a common synod meeting every four years.[27] In 1953, the Ghana part of the church changed its name from Ewe Presbyterian Church, Ghana, to Evangelical Presbyterian Church, Ghana, to acknowledge the fact that the church had now become national. In 1960, the Evangelical Presbyterian Church of Togo became autonomous. EPC joined WCC in 1963. It holds membership of the Christian Council of Ghana, AACC, WCRC and ACRC.

Nigeria

The Presbyterian Church of Nigeria (PCN) traces its origins to the missionary work of freed slaves from Jamaica, Scottish missionaries and the kings of Calabar starting from 1846. The church initially operated as a presbytery of Biafra, with its constitution in 1858, then as a synod of Biafra with its constitution of 1921, and following that as the Presbyterian Church of Biafra with the constitution of 1945. In 1952 the name was changed to Presbyterian Church of Eastern Nigeria, and with Nigerian independence in 1960, it became the Presbyterian Church of Nigeria.[28] It has the following synods: Synod of Akwa, Synod of Calabar, Synod of the East, Synod of East Central, Synod of Mid-East, Synod of North, Synod of South Central, Synod of Upper Cross River and Synod of West.[29] The headquarters of the church is in Ogpor Hill in Abia State in south-east Nigeria. It has a Mission Presbytery in the Republics of Benin and Togo. It became a member of the WCC in 1961. It is also a member of the AACC, the Christian Council of Nigeria, the WCRC, the Alliance of Reformed Churches in Africa (ARCA) and the Reformed Ecumenical Council of Nigeria.[30] The partner churches of PCN are the Church of Scotland, the Presbyterian Church in Canada, the PC (USA) and the Protestant Church of the Netherlands.[31]

---

[24] www.akropongcpc.faithweb.com/history.htm accessed 04052015.
[25] van Beek *A Handbook Of Churches And Councils.* Geneva: 2006, 150.
[26] http://globalevangelicalchurch.net/article/3-history accessed 04052015.
[27] https://en.wikipedia.org/wiki/Evangelical_Presbyterian_Church,_Ghana accessed 04052015.
[28] van Beek A Handbook Of Churches And Councils, 2006, 183.
[29] van Beek A Handbook Of Churches And Councils, 2006, 183.
[30] https://en.wikipedia.org/wiki/Presbyterian_Church_of_Nigeria accessed 24062015.
[31] van Beek A Handbook Of Churches And Councils, 2006, 183-4.

East Africa

Uganda Presbyterian churches have a very interesting history but I will only mention them here: Presbyterian Church in Uganda (PCU); the Reformed Presbyterian Church; Evangelical Free Church in Uganda; the Orthodox Presbyterian Churches in Uganda; the Calvary Reformed Church, formerly known as the Presbyterian Evangelical Fellowship and the Evangelical Presbyterian Church. Examples are given from Democratic Republic of Congo, Kenya and Rwanda.

Democratic Republic of Congo

The Church of Christ in Congo Presbyterian Community in Congo (PCC) was created by the American Presbyterian Congo Mission under an initial predominantly Afro-American leadership[32] in 1891. The PCC became autonomous from missionary control in 1959. After that the church went through internal and external struggles due to theological and ethical differences which resulted in the formation of two breakaway churches. The first breakaway happened in 1967 due to ethnic tensions and the Presbyterian Community in Eastern Kasai (PCEK) was formed.[33] The PCEK too suffered a split due to theological and ethnic reasons which led to the formation of the Reformed Community of Presbyterians (RCP). All three churches are members of the WCRC and have relationships with thc PC (USA).[34]

In 1982 there was a second split in the PCC which led to the establishment of the Presbyterian Community in Western Kasai (PCWK). The reason for the second split was precipitated by the request of the Church of Christ in Zaïre to the PCC to change from a Presbyterian polity to an episcopal one. This was rejected by the PCC except for Pastor Jean Bakatushipa who accepted to be made bishop. This act led to his excommunication from the PCC. He took with him members from Western Kasai to form PCWK.[35]

In addition to founding the PCC, the American Presbyterian Congo Mission also established the Church of Christ in Congo – Presbyterian Community in Kinshasa (Eglise du Christ au Congo-Communauté Presbytérienne de Kinshasa (CPK) in 1955. However, this church has its origins in the PCC because it was its members working in Leopoldville who saw the need to have an autonomous Presbyterian church in Kinshasa. The CPK was the first protestant church to be registered with the colonial government in May 1960. Then its official name was Church of Christ in Congo – Presbyterian Section of Leopoldville and this was changed to the current name in 1970.[36] CPK became a member of the WCC in 1996. It is also a member of the AACC, WCRC and ACRC. It has continued to maintain partnership with the PC (USA).[37]

Kenya

The biggest Presbyterian Church in Kenya is the Presbyterian Church of East Africa (PCEA). Its headquarters is in Nairobi. The church traces its origins to the formation of the 'East African Scottish Mission' in 1891. The first temporary church was built at Kibwezi under Dr James Stewart in 1892. From 1898 the name of the mission changed to 'Church of Scotland Mission' (CSM). It spread to Kikuyu and Tumutumu (1908), Chuka, and Mwimbi, Chogoria (1915). In 1936 the General Assembly of the Church of Scotland separated the overseas Presbytery of Kenya to serve the colonial and continental work. The

[32] Dworkin, Ira 'On the Boarders of Race, Mission and the State: African Americans and the American Presbyterian Congo Mission'. In Steven van Wolputte (ed), Borderlands and Frontiers in Africa, *African Studies* Vol. 40, LIT Verlag, Berlin 2013

[33] https://en.wikipedia.org/wiki/Presbyterian_Community_in_Eastern_Kasai accessed 04072015.

[34] https://en.wikipedia.org/wiki/Presbyterian_Community_in_Congo accessed 04072015.

[35] J Gorden Melton 'Church of Christ in Congo- Community of Presbyterians'. In *Religions of the World: A comprehensive Encyclopaedia of Beliefs and Practices.* J Gordon Melton and Martin Baumann eds. Santa Barbara: 2010, 886.

[36] van Beek *A Handbook Of Churches And Councils.* Geneva: 2006, 133.

[37] https://en.wikipedia.org/wiki/Presbyterian_Community_in_Kinshasa accessed 04072015.

Gospel Missionary Society (GMS), an American-oriented church based at Kambui in Kiambu, joined the overseas Presbytery of Kenya in 1946. In 1956 the Synod of the Presbyterian Church of East Africa and the overseas Presbytery of Kenya merged and adopted one constitution under the name the Presbyterian Church in Eastern Africa. The denomination has currently 54 presbyteries, divided into five regions, these are the Eastern Region, Central Region, Nairobi Region, Mount Kenya Region and Rift Valley Region. Since 1950, it began work in Tanzania where it has two Presbyterian Churches. It became a member of the WCC in 1957. It is also a member of the AACC, National Council of Churches in Kenya, WCRC and ACRC. It also has partnerships with PC (USA), Presbyterian Church in Ireland, Church of Scotland, United Church of Canada, Presbyterian Church in Canada, Presbyterian Church of Korea, Mission Africa.[38]

The Independent Presbyterian Church in Kenya was started in 1948 by missionaries of the Bible Presbyterian Church (USA). The split in the Bible Presbyterian Church (USA) in 1962 also led to a split in the Independent Presbyterian Church in Kenya. The bigger group retained the name and in 1964 the church became independent. The minority group became the Africa Evangelical Presbyterian Church which started from Mwingi District in 1962 under the World Presbyterian Mission of the Evangelical Presbyterian Church in America (1961). The Africa Evangelical Presbyterian Church has spread from Mombasa on the Indian Ocean to Nakuru in the Rift Valley. It also has churches in the DRC, Burundi, Tanzania and Bulawayo in Zimbabwe.[39] It is a member of WRF.

The Bible Christian Faith Church was formed in 1980 when fifteen congregations separated from the Africa Inland Church due to theological and leadership reasons. It has ties with the Free Presbyterian Church in Ulster in the USA.[40] It is not clear whether the Bible Presbyterian Church in Kenya is a breakaway of the Bible Christian Faith.[41]

Rwanda

The Presbyterian Church in Rwanda (or Eglise Presbytérienne au Rwanda) was established by German Bethel Missions in 1906. After the departure of the German missionaries in 1916 due to WW1, they were replaced by Swiss, Belgian and later Dutch missionaries. Until 1957, the church activities were concentrated in Kirinda, Rubengera, Remera. The church became independent in 1959 as the Evangelical Presbyterian Church in Rwanda, which was later changed to the Presbyterian Church in Rwanda with its headquarters in Kigali. The church lost many of its leaders and members during the 1994 genocide. It maintains close relations with churches in Switzerland, Belgium, Netherlands, Germany and other countries in Africa. It became a member of the WCC in 1981. It is also a member of the AACC, WCRC, ACRC, United Evangelical Mission (UEM) and the Protestant Council of Rwanda.[42][43]

Southern Africa

The Presbyterian churches that are only mentioned here are: the Presbyterian Church of Mauritius; the Presbyterian Church of Mozambique (PCM) (Igreja Presbiteriana de Moçambique); the Renewed Presbyterian Church in Mozambique; the Free Presbyterian Church of Scotland in Zimbabwe; The Church of Central Africa Presbyterian (CCAP) – Harare Synod; The Reformed Church in Zimbabwe; The United Church in Zambia (UCZ) and the Church of Central Africa Presbyterian (CCAP) – Synod of Zambia. Examples will be given of churches in Angola, Malawi and South Africa.

---

[38] https://en.wikipedia.org/wiki/Presbyterian_Church_of_East_Africa accessed 04072015.
[39] https://en.wikipedia.org/wiki/Africa_Evangelical_Presbyterian_Church accessed 04072015.
[40] https://en.wikipedia.org/wiki/Bible_Christian_Faith_Church accessed 04072015.
[41] https://en.wikipedia.org/wiki/Bible_Presbyterian_Church_in_Kenya accessed 04072015.
[42] https://en.wikipedia.org/wiki/Presbyterian_Church_in_Rwanda accessed 04072015.
[43] van Beek, *A Handbook Of Churches And Councils*, 2006, page 187-8.

Angola

The Presbyterian Church in Angola (in Portuguese the Igreja Presbiteriana de Angola or IPA) began on 9th June 1984 under the leadership of Pastor Antonio Neves Massaqui and in collaboration with the Presbyterian Church of Brazil. Its activities are predominantly found in Luanda and the Uige region. The IPA merged with the Independent Presbyterian Church in Angola and the Christian Presbyterian Church in Angola in 2011. The three merged churches are now known as the Presbyterian Church in Angola. It is this merged church that is a member of the WRF. In addition, it is important to note the existence of the Renewed Presbyterian Church in Angola which was founded by Brazilian missionaries of the Renewed Presbyterian Church in Brazil in the late 1990s.[44] The IPA's wish is to merge Presbyterians and form one large Presbyterian community in Angola.

Malawi

There are six Presbyterian churches in Malawi namely: the Church of Central Africa, Presbyterian (CCAP), the Presbyterian Church of Malawi (PCM), the Blackman's Church of Africa Presbyterian (BCAP), the Evangelical Presbyterian Church of Malawi (EPCM), the Reformed Presbyterian Church of Malawi (RPCM) and the Renewed Presbyterian Church in Malawi (RPCM).

The Church of Central Africa, Presbyterian (CCAP) consists of five synods with different mission history and emphasis in confessions adopted: there are three in Malawi – Livingstonia Synod in the north of the country, Nkhoma Synod in the centre,[45] and Blantyre Synod in the south. Then there is Zambia Synod in Zambia and Harare Synod in Zimbabwe. The CCAP is the largest Protestant denomination in Malawi. Following the arrival of David Livingstone, in 1875, the Free Church of Scotland established itself in northern Malawi with headquarters in Livingstonia. In 1876, the Church of Scotland set up a mission in Blantyre. In 1889, the Cape Synod of the Dutch Reformed Church in South Africa began work in central Malawi. Initially its base was Mvera, but it later relocated to Nkhoma. Blantyre and Livingstonia missions joined in 1924 to form CCAP, and the Nkhoma Mission joined in 1926. The Harare Synod joined in 1965 and the Lundazi Synod (now called the Zambia Synod) joined in 1984. In 1998, some charismatic members split from the CCAP Blantyre Synod to form the Presbyterian Church of Malawi (PCM). Besides the differences in mission history, each of the synods has a different emphasis in confessions adopted which also influences their ecumenical engagement. For example, it is only the CCAP Blantyre Synod which became a member of WCC in February 2014, not the PCM. The Blantyre and the Livingstonia Synods are members of AACC and all of them are members of WCRC and ACRC. The Nkhoma Synod is a member of the Reformed Ecumenical Council.

The Blackman's Church of Africa Presbyterian was founded in 1933 by the Rev. Yesaya Zerenje Mwase as a breakaway of the Livingstonia Synod due to tensions over African leadership and culture.[46]

There is a dearth of literature on the historical background of the Evangelical Presbyterian Church of Malawi. It is a very young church which is located in Southern Malawi. It is a member of the WRF.[47]

The Reformed Presbyterian Church of Malawi was founded in 1985 by the mission work of the Free Presbyterian Church of Scotland.[48] The Restored Reformed Missionary from the Netherlands replaced the Scottish Free Presbyterian Church's missionaries in 2006. As a young church it mainly operates in rural areas of central and southern Malawi.

---

[44] https://en.wikipedia.org/wiki/Renewed_Presbyterian_Church_in_Angola accessed 31072015.
[45] https://en.wikipedia.org/wiki/Church_of_Central_Africa,_Presbyterian accessed 31072015.
[46] https://en.wikipedia.org/wiki/Blackman%27s_Church_of_Africa_Presbyterian accessed 31072015.
[47] https://en.wikipedia.org/wiki/Evangelical_Presbyterian_Church_of_Malawi accessed 20072015.
[48] https://en.wikipedia.org/wiki/Reformed_Presbyterian_Church_of_Malawi accessed 20072015.

The Renewed Presbyterian Church in Malawi was founded by the Renewed Presbyterian Church in Brazil. There is a dearth of literature on its mission history and location of activities in Malawi. It is mainly located in Southern Malawi.[49]

South Africa

I have left out the Uniting Presbyterian Church in Southern Africa (UPCSA) because it is covered in another article in this publication.[50]

The Evangelical Presbyterian Church in South(ern) Africa (EPCSA) was previously known as Tsonga Presbyterian Church (TPC). It traces its origins to the Swiss missionaries in 1875 who worked among Tsonga people. From Valdezia it spread to the eastern and northern part of Transvaal, Gauteng, Orange Free State and KwaZulu-Natal. In 1962 the EPCSA became independent. It joined WCC in 1983.[51] It is also a member of WCRC, AACC, ARCA and the South African Council of Churches (SACC).[52]

The Free Church in Southern Africa (FCSA) traces its origins to the Glasgow Missionary Society (c. 1823), and after 1843 came under the missionaries of the Free Church of Scotland. Initially the mission was mainly to the Xhosa-speaking people in the Eastern and Western Cape regions. The FCSA became autonomous in 1982. The FCSA is a member of the International Conference of Reformed Churches. It has partnerships with the Free Church of Scotland, and the reformed churches in South Africa.[53]

The Presbyterian Church of Africa (PCA) was founded in 1898 by the Rev. James Mzimba, who broke away from the Free Church of Scotland Mission due to racial and leadership disputes. The first Synod was constituted in Alice, Cape Colony. It has now spread throughout South Africa and to Malawi, Zambia and Zimbabwe. It has nine presbyteries. It became a member of the WCC in 1981. [54] It is also a member of the WCRC, ARCA, AACC and SACC.[55]

Conclusion

It is very interesting to follow the continuing reformation of the Presbyterian churches in Africa. Areas for further study include Presbyterian responses to the following challenges: the Pentecostal and Charismatic presence; ecumenism; enculturation; the ordination of women; human sexuality; and political, economic, ecological and gender justice.

Bibliography

Bediako, Kwame. *Christianity in Africa: The Renewal of a Non-Western Religion* (Edinburgh: Edinburgh Univ. Press; Maryknoll, N.Y.: Orbis Books, 1995).

De Gruchy, John W. *Liberating Reformed Theology: A South African Contribution to an Ecumenical Debate.*(Cape Town, David Philip Publishers, 1991).

Dworkin, Ira. 'On the Boarders of Race, Mission and the State: African Americans and the American Presbyterian Congo Mission' in *Borderlands and Frontiers in Africa*. Steven van Wolputte ed. (Zurich: LIT Verlag Muster, 2013).

Gatu, John G. Joyfully Christian and Truly African. (Acton Publishers: Nairobi, 2006).

[49] https://en.wikipedia.org/wiki/Renewed_Presbyterian_Church_in_Malawi accessed 2007.

[50] Pillay. J. Uniting and United Churches in Africa.

[51] van Beek *A Handbook Of Churches And Councils*, 2006, 198.

[52] https://en.wikipedia.org/wiki/Evangelical_Presbyterian_Church_in_Southern_Africa accessed 20072015.

[53] https://en.wikipedia.org/wiki/Free_Church_in_Southern_Africa accessed 20072015.

[54] van Beek *A Handbook Of Churches And Councils*, 2006, 198.

[55] https://en.wikipedia.org/wiki/Presbyterian_Church_of_Africa accessed 20072015.

Mateus, Odair Pedroso. 'Reformed Churches' in *The Cambridge Dictionary of Christianity.* Daniel Patte ed. (New York: Cambridge University Press, 2010).

Melton, J Gordon. 'Church of Christ in Congo: Community of Presbyterians'. In *Religions of the World: A comprehensive Encyclopaedia of Beliefs and Practices.* J Gordon Melton and Martin Baumann eds. (Santa Barbara: ABC-CLOI, LLO, 2010).

Phiri, Isabel Apawo. 'Marching, Suspended and Stoned: Christian Women in Malawi' in Kenneth R. Ross (ed.) *God, People and Power in Malawi: Democratisation in Theological Perspective.* Gweru: Mambo Press, 1996, 63-105.

Phiri, Isabel Apawo. 'Theological Education in Presbyterian Churches in Africa'. In *Handbook of Theological Education in Africa.* eds. Isabel Apawo Phiri and Dietrich Werner. Oxford: Regnum Books International, 2013, 345-353.

Phiri, Isabel Apawo. *Women, Presbyterianism and Patriarchy: Religious Experiences of Chewa Women in Central Malawi.* Blantyre: CLAM, 1997.

Phiri, Isabel Apawo. 'The Initiation of Chewa Women of Malawi: *A Presbyterian Woman's Perspective' in* James Cox ed. Rites of Passage: The Interaction between Christianity and African Traditional Religions. Edinburgh: Cardiff Press, 1997, 129-145.

van Beek, Huibert, *A Handbook of Churches and Councils*: *Profiles of Ecumenical Relationships*. Geneva: 2006.

(27) CONGREGATIONAL CHURCHES IN AFRICA

Desmond P. van der Water

Origins and Spread

The story of Congregationalism in Africa traces its origins back to a coffee house in London in 1794. Every Tuesday morning, a handful of Christian ministers from different church denominations met at Bakers Coffee House 'as a place for chat and the interchange of news by the London Ministers.'[1] In 1795, this group of ministers and others who had joined them formed 'The Missionary Society', later to be called the 'London Missionary Society' (LMS). The LMS declared its only purpose of its existence as follows:

> The sole object is to spread the knowledge of Christ among heathen and other unenlightened nations.[2]

It is significant that the LMS, as a fundamental principle, established itself as an *ecumenical* mission body, intentionally setting out to avoid replicating British denominationalism in Africa, and wherever else in the world they ventured to proclaim the gospel. It is to be noted therefore that it was by default rather than by design that the LMS became predominantly Congregational. This 'accident of history' was simply due, in the course of time, to the other participating Churches founding their respective missionary societies. Notwithstanding this development, the LMS commitment to ecumenism remained a key element in the shaping of Congregationalism worldwide. A year after its establishment, the first LMS missionaries went to the South Sea island of Tahiti, to be followed a year later by a contingent to Sierra Leone. The first LMS expedition to African soil, however, ended in disappointment. Richard Lovett sums up:

> The mission at once began to feel the effects of two factors which have exerted a powerful influence… the quality of the workers, and the deadly nature of the climate. Within half a year, three of the six missionaries were dead, a fourth had to be recalled, and the other two were able to pursue their labour for only a brief period.[3]

Not to be discouraged by this failure, in 1799 the LMS sent a Dutchman by the name of Johannes Theodorus van der Kemp to the Cape to do missionary work and to plant churches – a move which effectively *signalled the birth of Congregationalism in Africa*, and within Southern Africa in particular. Although van der Kemp landed in Cape Town,[4] the first churches and mission stations were to be established in the Eastern Cape, to be followed soon after in the Northern Cape. It was in this latter part of Southern Africa that another LMS missionary, Robert Moffat, arrived in 1824 and established a mission station at Kuruman, where he also set-up the first printing press in Africa, and where the first translation of the Bible into an African language, namely Setswana, saw the light of day in 1857.[5] The Kuruman Moffat

---

[1] Richard Lovett, "The History of the London Missionary Society 1795-1895", Vol. 1 (London, Oxford University Press, 1899), 30.
[2] Lovett, "History of the London Missionary Society", 30.
[3] Lovett, "History of the London Missionary Society", 480.
[4] The ship in which van der Kemp arrived in Cape Town, known as the *Hillsborough*, mainly carried convicts bound for Australia. But it also brought other passengers who disembarked at this stage of the voyage, amongst whom were the LMS missionaries van der Kemp, Jakobus Kircherer, John Edmonds and William Edwards (Esther Johnson, "Cape Town: The establishing of Congregationalism in southern Africa" in Steve de Gruchy (ed), *Changing Frontiers: The mission story of the UCCSA* (Gaborone, Pula Press, 1999) 19).
[5] Lovett, "History of the London Missionary Society", 599.

Mission, which is one of the oldest mission stations in Africa, is still active and thriving in mission and ministry to this day. From the Northern Cape, Congregationalism spread northwards out into what is today Botswana and Zimbabwe. As the Eastern Cape, which represents the first strand of Congregationalism in Southern Africa, became more settled and less of a 'frontier', the LMS handed church ownership and authority to the local people who had been converted to Christianity, and turned its resources to the work in the north.

Robert Moffat was later joined by David Livingstone, who in 1841 reached Kuruman. During the nineteenth century, Livingstone and Moffat were among the best known LMS missionaries, opening up work among the Batswana and Ndebele peoples. Notwithstanding his substantial missionary enterprises, Livingstone is better remembered globally for his famous journeys of exploration into Central Africa and his 'discovery' of the Zambezi in 1851.[6] On the strength of his expeditions for God and country, to his credit, Livingstone certainly paved the way for other missionary societies in Central Africa. The first strand of Congregationalism and Congregational churches in Africa traces its origins in the sterling missionary work done by LMS personnel.

A second strand of Congregationalism to Southern Africa came from the USA, through the American Board of Commissioners for Foreign Missions (ABCFM), which arrived in South Africa at the invitation of the LMS. Following their charter in 1812, the ABCFM dispatched their first personnel in 1835 to work among the Zulu people of the Natal colony, and the Ndebele in Zimbabwe. With the discovery of gold in 1886, the work of the LMS and ABCFM spread to the Witwatersrand. The early missionaries were not simply intent on founding new churches. From the start, they fought for the rights of the indigenous peoples, and established educational institutions. The ABCFM was also committed to local church autonomy and sought ways to cease being 'mission' and to become 'church'. For several reasons this proved to be a difficult process 'bedevilled by issues relating to leadership, authority, finance, culture, property and power.'[7] By 1964 however, the Bantu Congregational Church was formally constituted and the transition from American-led 'mission' to Zulu-led 'church' was achieved.

The third strand in which Congregationalism emerged in Southern Africa was, as Steve de Gruchy points out, 'not a missionary movement, but rather a *settler movement*' whereby 'English settlers – traders, miners, soldiers, teachers – arrived in both the Cape and Natal colonies.'[8] By the 1960s, there were three distinct forms of Congregationalism in five Southern African countries, namely Namibia, Zimbabwe, Mozambique, Botswana and South Africa. On 3rd October 1967 these three strands of Congregationalism *united* to become the United Congregational Church of Southern Africa (UCCSA). At the united act of worship, the Congregationalists entered into solemn covenant with these words:

> We covenant to worship, work and witness together in the fellowship of the United Congregational Church of Southern Africa for the building up of the Body of Christ and the manifestation of the Kingdom of God on earth.[9]

---

[6] Lovett, "History of the London Missionary Society", 615.

[7] Steve de Gruchy, "Towards a Congregationalist Theology of the Land", *International Congregational Journal*, Vol. 2, No. 2 (August 2002), 232.

[8] Steve de Gruchy, "Towards a Congregationalist Theology of the Land", 232.

[9] D Roy Briggs, "A Covenant Church: Studies in the Polity of the United Congregational Church of Southern Africa in terms of Its Covenant" (Gaborone, Pula Press, 1996), 23.

The Nature of Congregationalism in Africa

Centrality of Covenant Principle

True to its origins, the fundamental nature of Congregationalism in Africa, for over two hundred years to the present time, never changed from its foundational principle, namely that of being a church *united by a covenantal bond.* This centrality of covenant in Congregationalism's identity harks back to its foundation when the first synod of Congregational Churches in England articulated the following definition of Congregationalism:

> A Congregational Church is by the institution of Christ a part of the militant-visible church, consisting of a company of saints by calling, united into one body by a *holy covenant* for the mutual edification one of another, in fellowship of the Lord Jesus.[10]

Congregational churches in Africa consistently maintained all the major hallmarks of classical English Congregationalism in its understanding of church, with the *covenant principle* at the heartbeat of its life, work and witness. Roy Briggs suggests that there are 'intriguing points of contact between the biblical concept of the covenant…and the traditional African idea of *ubuntu.*'[11] Referring to Hebrews 11:29-39, in which the author speaks about the heroes and heroines of faith during the Old Testament period, of whom is said 'only *with us* should they reach perfection' (italics added), Briggs inverts the statement to suggest that 'only *with them* should we reach perfection' (italics added), concluding that 'this is the equivalent of the African dictum: *Umuntu ngumuntu ngabantu.*'[12]

Due to the geographical areas in which the LMS and ABCFM missionaries worked, Congregationalists in Africa – in Southern Africa in particular – are mainly concentrated amongst the so-called Coloured people and the black African communities. Given the cultural and traditional contexts of these communities there were going to be different notions of church, community and family from that which was obtained in Europe and the USA. This is particularly the case with the distinctive ideas of kinship and community, as Briggs asserts, which 'differ radically from Western notions of individualism, socialism and collectivism'.[13]

With regard to the understanding of family as the basic unit in society within the African context, family includes the 'extended' family, namely grandparents, aunts, uncles, etc. Like the family, the kinship system as a whole has a vertical dimension as well, which includes the living-dead and the tribe's unborn offspring. The kinship concept expands from the clan or tribe to include the nation and humankind as a whole. The idea of the 'extended' family in its horizontal and vertical dimensions, in the present, past and future, represents a distinct parallel to the Christian doctrine of the communion of saints. The expansion of the concept into the clan, the tribe, and the nation where the sense of community is fully maintained, can be directly related to the understanding of the covenant within African Congregational churches. Similarly, the importance *ubuntu* ascribes to solidarity among the members of the clan, the tribe, the nation, is arguably identical with the emphasis the covenant lays on unity among covenant members. It is precisely against this background that the Congregationalist principle of covenant finds a natural home within African beliefs, culture, customs and practices. Within Congregational churches in Africa therefore, the theology and practice of covenant does not, generally speaking, come as a foreign imposition.

---

[10] Joseph Wing, "Pilgrimage of Faith", 56.
[11] Briggs, "A Covenant Church", 29.
[12] Briggs, "A Covenant Church", 29.
[13] Briggs, "A Covenant Church", 26.

Commitment to Ecumenism

The union of the three strands of Congregationalism in 1967 to form the UCCSA – true to the ecumenical principle of its founder, the LMS – proved not to be static. The Congregationalist impulse towards greater unity within the Body of Christ was further strengthened by the merger of the UCCSA, in 1972, with the South African Association of the Disciples of Christ. At the Covenant Service on 23rd September 1972 to celebrate this additional union, the Presbyterian representative introduced his fraternal greetings by saying: 'You've done it again! The first church in Southern Africa to pull off two mergers in the space of five years!'[14] Even before this latter union materialised, the UCCSA was in conversation with the Presbyterian Church of Southern Africa (PCSA) to move towards becoming a united church through merging the Congregationalist and Presbyterian denominations. Although this intended union at denominational level did not materialise,[15] various schemes were embarked upon such as the establishment of new local churches which would be united and the mutual eligibility of members and ministers from the two churches concerned.

The Congregational churches' passion for and commitment to ecumenism is reflected in the leadership the UCCSA has given to the ecumenical movement in Southern Africa. For instance, a Congregationalist, Brian Bailey was the first General Secretary of the Botswana Christian Council (BCC). Under his leadership the BCC soon took on joint action for mission, service and development in Botswana. In South Africa, John F. White, until his untimely death in 1960, was an ecumenical driving force, active in the work of the Christian Council of South Africa. Congregationalists were secretaries of the Church Unity Commission for the first twenty-one years of its life (1968-89). John Thorne, as president of the South African Council of Churches during the mid-1970s, led the church in South Africa prophetically and courageously during turbulent political times, being detained, tried and sentenced for his identification with the victims of apartheid. Although ecumenism, church unity and Christian co-operation in Zimbabwe were somewhat slow to get going, under the dynamic leadership of Congregationalists such as Joshua Danisa, James Pelling and Owen Lloyd, things improved significantly with the momentum that they provided.

The designation 'united' in the official title of the UCCSA represents an ongoing commitment of Congregationalism in Africa to unity, ecumenism and non-sectarianism. At the newly united church's inaugural Assembly in 1967, John Huxtable, in his sermon, challenged the UCCSA towards greater union:

> We are now more ready for unity, not less. The will of the great Head of the church has been made known in this matter. He wills for the church to be one…Our part is to understand how we can more perfectly express it…[16]

Commitment to Political Freedom and Justice in Society

Since the arrival of the early LMS missionaries in 1799, Congregationalism and Congregational leadership has aligned itself with the cause of the poor, the deprived and oppressed people in their struggle for justice and freedom. When LMS missionary John Philip, for instance, was accused by the authorities of meddling in politics, instead of confining himself, as a minister, to spiritual matters, he replied:

> If a minister is guilty of dereliction of his duty in advocating the cause of the oppressed, or in relieving the necessities of the destitute, I plead guilty to the charge.[17]

---

[14] Joseph Wing (ed), "Pilgrimage of Faith: Confirmation Training Handbook" (Cape Town, UCCSA, 1987), 62.

[15] It remains a sad chapter in the history of the UCCSA that the union with the PCSA did not take place, especially as both constituencies had worked so hard to achieve union.

[16] John Huxtable, extract from sermon preached at the Covenant service to inaugurate the UCCSA on 03/10/67, as quoted in D Roy Briggs and Joseph Wing, "The Harvest and The Hope: The Story of Congregationalism in Southern Africa" (Johannesburg, UCCSA, 1970), 316.

Throughout the long association of the LMS with Botswana, the missionaries had shown a concern for the political development of the country and had advised and assisted the chiefs in many ways, notably in the initiative which resulted in Bechuanaland being proclaimed a Protectorate in 1895. It was then just a matter of time before colonial rule would end, and with the advent of self-government, Seretse Khama's conviction that democratic structures based on universal franchise were the right form of government for his country Botswana, received full vindication.

In other Southern Africa countries, such as South Africa, the influence of Congregationalism has been clearly demonstrated within the leadership of the liberation movements, such as with the African National Congress (ANC). It is of no small significance that the ANC's first president was a Congregational Minister, in the person of John Dube. Of more international renown, another prominent leader in the ANC's early years[18] and the first African Nobel Peace Prize Laureate, Chief Albert Luthuli, was member and a lay leader in the Congregational Church at Groutville, KwaZulu-Natal. Chief Luthuli, whose name is enshrined in the UCCSA's Roll of Honour, is reported to have uttered these salutary words:

> I only pray to the Almighty to strengthen my resolve so that nothing may deter me from striving, for the sake of the good name of our beloved country, to make a true democracy and a true union of all the communities in the land.[19]

Given the nature and thrust of political leadership within Congregational churches from its early years in Africa, the UCCSA had taken a clear and consistent stance against the racist and oppressive system of apartheid. Under the decisive leadership of people like Joseph Wing, Bonganjalo Goba and John de Gruchy the UCCSA played an important role in critical initiatives, such as the formation of the South African Council of Churches, the statement of the *Message to the Peoples of South Africa,*[20] the *Call to Prayer for the End to Unjust Rule*[21] and the publication of the *Kairos Document.*[22] Together with other churches within the ecumenical movement, the UCCSA positioned itself at the forefront of the struggle against apartheid right up until the time when South Africa, under the leadership of Nelson Mandela, transitioned into a non-racist, non-sexist democracy in 1994.

Commitment to Education and Medical Work

Congregationalism boasts a rich legacy of the establishment of educational institutions and medical facilities in Southern Africa. The school at the Kuruman Moffat Mission, for instance, which was started by Moffat in 1829, represents the 'mother of all educational work of the LMS among the Batswana, Kalanga and Matabele peoples'.[23] Over a hundred primary schools were established in the old Rhodesia

---

[17] John Philip, quoted in Joseph Wing (ed), "Pilgrimage of Faith", 123.

[18] Chief Luthuli became President of the ANC from December 1952.

[19] Albert Luthuli, quoted in Joseph Wing (ed), "Pilgrimage of Faith", 123. See also Luthuli, "Let My People Go: The Autobiography of the Great South African Leader" (Glasgow: Fontana, 1987); and Scott Couper, "Albert Luthuli: Bound by Faith" (Pietermaritzburg, University of KwaZulu-Natal, 2010).

[20] In the wake of the Sharpeville Massacre in South Africa in 1960, the English-speaking churches voiced their opposition and protest through, amongst others, the *Message to the Peoples of South Africa.* In many ways, the *Message*, which declared apartheid a 'false gospel' anticipated the declaration in 1982 of 'Apartheid is a Heresy' by the World Alliance of Reformed Churches.

[21] Issued by the South African Council of Churches in 1985.

[22] The *Kairos* Document was published in 1985 (Braamfontein, Skotaville) by an activist group dubbed as the '*Kairos* Theologians'. The Document, which described its purpose as a 'Challenge to the Church', sharply critiqued 'State Theology' and 'Church Theology', calling for a decisive move towards 'Prophetic Theology'.

[23] Joseph Wing, "Water from the Rock", in *Gales of Change: Responding to a Shifting Missionary Context: The Story of the London Missionary Society, 1945 – 1977*, ed. Bernard Thorogood (Geneva, WCC Publications, 1994), 31.

and South Africa together with four institutions of higher learning, namely at Tiger Kloof[24] (South Africa), Inyati, Hope Fountain and Dombodema (all in the former Rhodesia).

With regard to medical establishments, the Scottish Livingstone Hospital at Molepolole, Botswana which was staffed and maintained by the United Free Church of Scotland in association with the LMS and the UCCSA had begun a period of expansion when its new maternity wing was opened in 1951. This hospital became renowned throughout Botswana as a place of healing and evangelism, with a special ministry among the Bakwena tribe and the remote villages of the Kalahari. The Livingstone Hospital was subsequently transferred to the Ministry of Health of the Republic of Botswana, but the institution has retained a Christian ethos which had been such a marked feature of its life and work.

Other Features of Congregationalism

All the other theological, ecclesiological and ecclesiastical features of Congregationalism in its original design and purpose remain present within the life, work and witness of Congregational churches in Africa. These are, inter alia:

LORDSHIP OF JESUS CHRIST IN CHURCH AND WORLD

The confession of faith, namely 'Jesus is Lord', is the only essential condition for membership within a Congregational Church. There is the clear understanding within Congregational circles that though we are amenable to other credal statements and articles of faith, once they are made conditions of membership, the local church which insists upon them ceases to be Congregational.

AUTHORITY OF THE SCRIPTURES OF THE OLD AND NEW TESTAMENTS

Scripture is the primary witness to God's revelation – the only basis on which we can know God's will in Christ. Scripture rightly understood and interpreted in the Church and in the individual Christian's life leads to faith, obedience and practice. Within Congregationalism, each member of the Church has the right and responsibility to study Scripture, and the mind of Christ is revealed as the Christian community gather together for prayer, reflection and action.

THE NONCONFORMIST CONSCIENCE AND INDEPENDENCE FROM ANY STATE OR EPISCOPAL CONTROL

In Congregationalism, the roots of the 'Nonconformist Conscience' is, according Joseph Wing, 'to be found not in a kind of negative attitude which is always against the government, but in the great principle enunciated by St Paul in his letter to the Romans 12:2: "Be not conformed to the world, but be transformed by the renewing of your mind. Then you will be able to discern the will of God, what is good and pleasing to him".'[25]

RELATIVE AND TRANSIENT AUTHORITY OF CREEDS, CONFESSIONS AND AFFIRMATIONS

The authority of creeds, confessions and affirmations in Congregationalism is never absolute or definitive or without need for further explanation. This is partly so because, at every critical stage in its history, the Church encounters new situations to which it has to respond. As such, the church is compelled to

[24] The Tiger Kloof Institution counts among its alumni Sir Seretse Khama and Sir Ketumile Masire, the first two Presidents of Botswana.

[25] Joseph Wing, "The Nonconformist Conscience", in *Jesus in Lord in Church and World: Studies in the Nature of Congregationalism* (Braamfontein, UCCSA, 1980), 37.

reformulate its faith statements and confessions which again in time became outdated and in some cases irrelevant. For this reason, the Congregational Church is, in this sense, not a confessional but a covenantal church.

The Church's Exercise of a Ministerial and not a Magisterial Authority in all Matters of Faith, Order and Discipline

In Congregationalist polity and practice, the 'courts' of the church have a responsibility, just as the gathered church, to discern the mind of Christ in order to enable faith and obedience among its members and adherents. The biblical promise 'where two and three are gathered in my name' means, in Congregationalist understanding, that Christ is present through the Word and Spirit to guide the church according to God's will. Accordingly, church government in Congregationalism is not democratic – in the sense of the Westminster System – it is church government under the guidance and authority of Christ. Authority in the church is Christ's authority. Consequently, the church cannot exercise *lordship* – which belongs rightly to Christ alone. Therefore, the church exercises ministerial and not magisterial authority.

Freedom of Individual Conscience and the Right to Dissent

Congregationalism was born in dissent, when the founding members refused to accept the authority of the state as expressing the mind of Christ for them. At the same time, Congregationalists believe in tolerance and respect for others who hold diverse and even conflicting views.

The Importance of the Gathered Church, and that Each Local Church is a Gathered Company of Believers who Discern the Mind of Christ and the Will of God

An understanding of the church as a group of believers who have acknowledged Jesus Christ as Lord, and have covenanted with God and with one another to walk in the ways of the Lord made known and yet to be made known, undergirds Congregational ecclesiology. In addition Congregationalists universally hold to the principle of the independence and autonomy of the local church from external control in all matters of worship, witness and governance. At the same time, there exists a creative tension of independence and inter-dependence in the relationship between all church constituencies.

African Congregationalism and African Congregational churches, locate themselves very firmly within the global family of reformed churches, and within the ethos of the international ecumenical movement as represented especially by the World Communion of Reformed Churches, the World Council of Churches and the Council for World Mission. Theologically and ecclesiologically, African Congregationalism traces its roots back to the Reformation teachings of John Calvin, in conjunction with the radical Anabaptist tradition that developed on the European continent and in England during the sixteenth and seventeenth centuries.

Epilogue: A Brief Critical Appraisal

It is universally recognised that the LMS was a pioneering and ground-breaking nineteenth century Christian missionary organisation. As shown in the chapters above, the passion, commitment and enterprise demonstrated by the organisation's missionary personnel are second to none in that era. However, like all other colonial mission bodies, the LMS approach, understanding and practice of mission and evangelism were not free from the influences of colonialism, cultural imperialism and paternalism. The negative impact and consequences of colonial-era mission, and the criticisms of the mission bodies and missionaries are well documented in a whole body of literature.[26]

The features of Congregationalism exported by the LMS and the ABCFM to Africa therefore came with the inevitable global North's ideological and ecclesiological baggage. For instance, in terms of its polity, Congregationalism is rather prone to defacement, whereby freedom under Christ so easily degenerates into freedom 'to do and to believe as we please'. This negative tendency is, almost inevitably, also ingrained within the fabric of African Congregationalism, resulting all too often in the undermining of unity within Congregational churches on the continent. In the same way, an over-emphasis on local church autonomy leads to self-imposed isolationism.

On the challenge of 'voice and voicelessness' within global mission, Mokhele Madise and Itumeleng Mothoagae observe that 'the African continent continues to be an echoing voice amidst the dominant discourse'.[27] Ashley Smith, a Caribbean missiologist, poses a sharp question about the rootedness of Christianity in the Caribbean in his seminal text entitled 'Potted Plants or Real Roots?'[28] Smith argues that the modern missionary movement bequeathed to the Caribbean context churches that are schizophrenic, because they were not allowed to be themselves. Does this same critique apply to African Christianity and African Congregational churches? Western Congregationalism seems to have found a comfortable home in Africa. Only time, however, will tell whether this home becomes a permanent dwelling place!

Bibliography

Books

Briggs, D Roy. *A Covenant Church: Studies in the Polity of the United Congregational Church of Southern Africa in terms of Its Covenant*. Gaborone: Pula Press, 1996.

Briggs, D Roy and Wing, Joseph. *The Harvest and the Hope: The Story of Congregationalism in Southern Africa*. Johannesburg: UCCSA, 1970.

De Gruchy, John, ed. *The London Missionary Society in Southern Africa*. Cape Town: David Philip, 1999.

Ferguson Geo P., *CUSA: The Story of the Churches of the Congregational Union of South Africa*. Paarl: A.H. Fisher & Sons, 1940.

Lovett, Richard. *The History of the London Missionary Society 1795-1895, Vol. 1*. London: Oxford University Press, 1899.

Smith, Ashley. *Real Roots or Potted Plants*, Jamaica: Mandeville Publishers, 1984.

Wing, Joseph, ed. *Pilgrimage of Faith: Confirmation Training Handbook*. Cape Town: UCCSA, 1987

Chapters in an Edited Book

Johnson, Esther. 'Cape Town: The establishing of Congregationalism in Southern Africa'. In *Changing Frontiers: The mission story of the UCCSA*, edited by Steve de Gruchy 19-22. Gaborone: Pula Press, 1999.

---

[26] The full list is too numerous to mention. For related publications during more recent decades, see Jesse Mugambi, "Christian Heritage and Contemporary Christianity" (Nairobi: Nairobi University Press, 1989); Kwame Bediako, "Jesus and the Gospel in Africa: History and Experience" (Maryknoll, NY: Orbis Books, 2004); David Bosch, "Transforming Mission" (Maryknoll, NY: Orbis Books, 1991); Ogbu Kalu, "African Christianity: an African story" (Trenton, NJ: Africa World Press, 2007); Desmond van der Water, "Postcolonial Mission: Power and Partnership in World Christianity" (Charleston: Sopher Press, 2010); Jonathan Ingleby, "Beyond Empire: Postcolonialism & Mission in a Global Context" (Milton Keynes: Authorhouse, 2010).

[27] Mokhele J.S. Madise and Itumeleng D. Mothoagae (Guest Editors), "Editorial", *Missionalia: South African Journal of Missiology*, Vol. 40, No. 3 (November 2012): 188.

[28] Ashley Smith, "Real Roots or Potted Plants" (Jamaica, Mandeville Publishers, 1984).

Wing, Joseph. 'Water from the Rock'. In *Gales of Change: Responding to a Shifting Missionary Context: The Story of the London Missionary Society, 1945 – 1977,* edited by Bernard Thorogood, 19-49. Geneva: WCC Publications, 1994.

Wing, Joseph. 'The Nonconformist Conscience'. In *Jesus in Lord in Church and World: Studies in the Nature of Congregationalism,* edited by Joseph Wing, 36-41. Braamfontein: UCCSA, 1980.

Journal Articles

De Gruchy, Steve. 'Towards a Congregationalist Theology of the Land', *International Congregational Journal* 2, no. 2 (2002):229-242.

Mokhele J.S. Madise and Itumeleng D. Mothoagae. 'Editorial', *Missionalia: South African Journal of Missiology* 40, no. 3 (2012): 188.

(28) REFORMED CHURCHES IN AFRICA

Retief Müller

Introduction

When considering the role of Reformed churches in Africa, one's attention is immediately and inexorably drawn to the Nederduitse Gereformeerde Kerk/Dutch Reformed Church of South Africa, and its role within the political history of that country. This is an important story to tell and to remember, but in a contribution such as this, the reader should also be aware of the fact that the Reformed presence and legacy in Africa reach far wider than this otherwise dominant theme. This wider Reformed legacy is in many respects partly the result of missionary efforts instituted by the South African Dutch Reformed Church into wider Africa. But there are also other Reformed presences in Africa that trace their history back to French, Swiss and American Reformed churches and missionary societies, perhaps most notably in what are today Lesotho, Madagascar, Nigeria, Cameroon and elsewhere. One might expand the scope, and one properly should, in order to include also the legacy of Presbyterian missions and churches. However, I leave these out of the present discussion, because I believe they are covered elsewhere in this volume.

Early Reformed History

I begin with the Dutch Reformed presence at the Cape where, with the arrival of the Dutch East India Company/(VOC) in 1652, a long and contentious history of church-state involvement took root on African soil. The VOC considered the Dutch Reformed Church as its official religious body and, controlled by the Classis of Amsterdam[1], it became the established church at the southern tip of Africa. Roman Catholicism was forbidden despite the fact that Portuguese sailors had reached the territory more than a century before the Dutch.[2] All colonists at the Cape were more or less considered to be part of this Dutch Reformed Church, which meant that the Lutheran church, for example, was unable to practise its faith officially until the VOC had granted such permission. Their first congregation in Strand Street, Cape Town, was founded in 1780.[3]

A particular feature of the Dutch Reformed Church as it took root in African soil was its close entanglement with Afrikaner identity and politics. As a result of the contributions of some of its office-bearers who, especially in the late nineteenth and early twentieth centuries represented some of the most educated members among the citizenry, the Dutch Reformed Church became involved in the first and second Afrikaans language movements, which successfully codified their local version of simplified Dutch as a literary language. This culminated in the first Afrikaans translation of the Bible in 1933.[4]

Another aspect pertaining to the formation of Afrikaner identity was the Great Trek, starting in the 1830s, which was an expansion of Dutch frontier colonists into the central, northern and eastern interior. In

---

[1] The Classis of Amsterdam was the regional assembly for local church boards of the Dutch Reformed Church in the region of Amsterdam

[2] John W. De Gruchy, *The Church Struggle in South Africa* (Fortress Press, 2005), 1.

[3] See Georg Scriba, "A chronology of the history of the Lutheran Church in South Africa (1652-1928)" in Hanns Lessing, *The German Protestant Church in Colonial Southern Africa: The Impact of Overseas Work from the Beginnings until the 1920s* (Cluster Publications, 2012), 272.

[4] See Richard Elphick, *The Equality of Believers: Protestant Missionaries and the Racial Politics of South Africa* (Charlottesville Va.: University of Virginia Press, 2012), 239.

the preceding decades, the Cape Colony had come under the control of the British Empire after the demise of the Batavian Republic in 1806. Britain sought to extend newly instituted anti-slavery policies to its colonies abroad, an idea which did not sit well with the rural landholding class of mainly Dutch settlers. The Great Trek ensued and although this exodus from the Cape was in contravention of the official stance of the Cape Dutch Reformed Church, the Trek itself, and particularly events surrounding the murder of Trekker leader Piet Retief at the behest of the Zulu king Dingane and the subsequent Battle of Blood River, would later become mythologised in Afrikaner lore and in the popular and official religiosity of the Dutch Reformed Church.[5] This would especially be the case in the areas occupied by the descendants of the Voortrekkers, i.e. Natal, the Orange Free State and Transvaal. For the next century and a half, the battle and ultimate Voortrekker victory would be annually commemorated on the so-called Day of the Vow (*Geloftedag/Dingaansdag*) every 16th of December in the form of church services in remembrance of the promise made by Voortrekker leaders on the eve of the original battle that their descendants would remember the day as a Sabbath.[6]

Through this day and its religious celebration within the Afrikaner Reformed churches, the developing nationalist discourse increasingly became inseparable from Reformed ideas of election and predestination. In this case, the Afrikaner identity was conceived as an elect nation with a special vocation of having been granted the tutelage or trusteeship (*voogdyskap*) of the indigenous population.[7] In this respect, mission and missionary policies increasingly played an important role in terms of the ways in which policies of supposedly equal separation were instituted on different levels in the South African societal landscape, but starting from a policy of racial segregation within churches, and especially around the Communion table.[8]

Before proceeding further, the year 1857 should be mentioned because this was the year when the Synod of the Dutch Reformed Church adopted the motion that, in spite of the fact that it was scriptural and desirable to include black converts into existing congregations, the 'weakness of some' bigoted white Christians made it necessary to institute segregated communities of worship. This was the first step towards the eventual institution of the Dutch Reformed Mission Church (DRMC) in 1881, as a so-called 'daughter' church of the Dutch Reformed Church for congregants of colour.[9] As the racial categorisation developed under apartheid, more daughter churches were spawned: i.e. the Dutch Reformed Church in Africa for black Africans, and the Reformed Church in Africa for those of Asian background. Meanwhile, the DRMC became a church exclusively for so-called 'Coloureds' (those of mixed racial background who spoke either Afrikaans or English as their language of preference).

Although the Dutch Reformed Church itself is often described in fairly monolithic cultural and ethnic terms, mostly as a result of its own self-identification over a period of time, it is important to point out the fact that this church had already, from early on in its existence at the Cape, received an impetus from the side of French Huguenots who had arrived at the Cape via the VOC as refugees from Europe. Yet more significant, in terms of their religious influence, would be the inclusion of a group of influential Scottish clergymen into the Dutch Reformed Church from the 1920s onwards. The best-known of this group was Andrew Murray Senior, originally from Aberdeen, who would be superseded in terms of personal

---

[5]June Goodwin and Ben Schiff, *Heart of Whiteness: Afrikaners Face Black Rule In the New South Africa* (Scribner, 1995), 22.

[6] See Christoph Marx, *Oxwagon Sentinel: Radical Afrikaner Nationalism and the History of the "Ossewabrandwag"* (LIT Verlag Münster, 2009).

[7] See T. Dunbar Moodie, *The Rise of Afrikanerdom: Power, Apartheid, and the Afrikaner Civil Religion* (University of California Press, 1975).

[8] Elphick, *The Equality of Believers,* 39ff.

[9] See Plaatjies-van Huffel, "Reading the *Belhar Confession* as a Historical Text", in Mary-Anne Plaatjies and Robert Vosloo, eds., *Reformed Churches in South Africa and the Struggle for Justice: Remembering 1960-1990,* First edition (Stellenbosch: Sun Media, 2013), 329-345.

influence by two of his sons, Andrew Junior, who would become a world-renowned author of evangelical revivalist literature, and John who, together with a couple of other Dutch Reformed Church ministers, founded the Dutch Reformed Church theological seminary in Stellenbosch, and who became one of the first professors to teach there. The Scottish ministers had a profound influence, not only on theological education but also in consideration of the budding foreign missionary enterprise, which the Dutch Reformed Church would launch in the latter part of the twentieth century.[10]

Dutch and American Reformed Missionary Enterprises

The Dutch Reformed Church sent missionaries to several different parts of Africa, most notably to what today are Malawi, Zambia, Zimbabwe, Nigeria and Botswana.[11] Additionally, many Afrikaans people settled over time in what was declared the protectorate of South West Africa, after the defeat of the former colonisers, the German empire, in World War I. Consequently, there is a strong Dutch Reformed Church presence also in contemporary Namibia. Similarly, one should mention the Reformed Church of East Africa, which was founded in 1944 partly as a result of a Dutch Reformed Church presence in Kenya. The Dutch Reformed Church also made a small-scale attempt, against much adversity, to establish a mission in Portuguese East Africa in the early twentieth century. The Reformed Church in Mozambique is the continuing result of this work.

The most extensive missionary projects of the Dutch Reformed Church occurred in Malawi, where close co-operation with Scottish Presbyterians eventually resulted in the formation of the Church of Central Africa Presbyterian (CCAP) in 1924.[12] The CCAP also has a synod in Zambia and another in Zimbabwe, but in terms of Malawi it was constituted on the basis of the three synods of Blantyre, Nkhoma and Livingstonia. This sub-division is in reference to the original mission stations that served as centres for the Southern, Central and Northern regions of Malawi. It is noteworthy that the CCAP (Nkhoma Synod) retained a distinct 'Dutch' identity in terms of theology and forms of worship. In different respects, it appears more conservative than brethren to the North and South –for example, in not ordaining women to the ministry in contradistinction to the other two synods.

The Dutch Reformed Church missionary project among the Tiv people in Nigeria also resulted in ecumenical co-operation with another missionary church from abroad, in this case with the Christian Reformed Church (CRC) from the USA. Dutch Reformed Church missionaries had been active in the area from about 1912, serving as the only Protestant group among the Tiv, but from 1950 they transferred parts of their missionary enterprise to the CRC.[13] The Christian Reformed Church of Nigeria would emerge out of these activities, after changing its name on a couple of occasions.

According to online sources, the American CRC also has connections with the Christian Reformed Church in Eastern Africa, which is a denomination that seceded from the above-mentioned Reformed Church of East Africa with a presence in Uganda, Tanzania and Kenya, as well as more recently the Democratic Republic of the Congo.

---

[10] See Retief Muller, "Evangelicalism and Racial Exclusivism in Afrikaner History: An Ambiguous Relationship," *Journal of Reformed Theology* 7, no. 2 (January 1, 2013): 204-32, doi:10.1163/15697312-12341296.

[11] See H. T. Gonin, "Missions of the Dutch Reformed Church in South Africa," *International Review of Mission* 42, no. 2 (April 1, 1953): 172-77, doi:10.1111/j.1758-6631.1953.tb03731.x.

[12] C. M. Pauw (Christoff Martin), *Mission and Church in Malawi : The History of the Nkhoma Synod of the Church of Central Africa, Presbyterian* (Thesis DTh – University of Stellenbosch, 1980).
June Goodwin and Ben Schiff, *Heart of Whiteness: Afrikaners Face Black Rule In the New South Africa* (Scribner, 1995).

[13] Edgar H. Smith, *Nigerian Harvest* (Grand Rapids: Baker, 1972), 159.

Church and State in South African Reformed Christianity

Before making a few comments on developments between Reformed Christianity and politics in South Africa during the mid to late twentieth century, it will be necessary to give some commentary on a couple of schisms occurring among the all-white sectors of Reformed Christianity in Southern Africa. The first occurred in 1853 in the Transvaal when the Nederduitse Hervormde Kerk (NHK) broke away from the Cape-controlled Dutch Reformed Church. The NHK had aspirations of becoming the state church of the Transvaal, but its reasons for breaking away from the mainstream Dutch Reformed Church included an objection to mission work among black people, and also in dissatisfaction against the British influence executed through imperial control of the Cape Colony on the Cape-based church.[14] A second schism occurred when the ultra-Calvinist Gereformeerde Kerk (GK) seceded from the Dutch Reformed Church in 1859.[15] One of the reasons for the schism was that these 'Doppers', as they became popularly known, objected to the singing of evangelical hymns as introduced by the increasingly revivalist Cape Dutch Reformed Church. Despite some internal differences on matters relating to mission, politics and doctrine among these three so-called 'sister churches', as they now increasingly referred to themselves, they were united in their adherence to the Canons of Dort, the Heidelberg Catechism and the Belgic Confession.

They were furthermore united in their near-universal adherence to notions of white supremacy, and all three churches contributed to the core support base of the National Party and its policy of apartheid that defined South Africa for much of the twentieth century. When the National Party came to power in 1948, it was under the leadership of Daniel Francois Malan, a former minister in the Dutch Reformed Church, who had also, subsequent to his departure from his position in the church, served as editor of the Afrikaans daily, *Die Burger*.

The policy of apartheid itself had in fact had its genesis as a mission policy of the Dutch Reformed Church in the 1930s, which politicians such as Malan then adapted to fit the secular and national discourse.[16] All the National Party leaders, prime ministers and state presidents in subsequent decades were members of the 'sister churches', and in most cases of the Dutch Reformed Church, often with close ties to its top ecclesiastical structure. This was most notably observable during the term of B.J. Vorster who was Prime Minister of South Africa 1966-1978. His brother, Koot Vorster, was a formidably conservative Dutch Reformed Church clergyman who served as moderator of the church 1970-1974 with a strong hand in terms of overseeing the theological education on offer at the seminary in Stellenbosch.[17] The final apartheid-era State President, F.W. de Klerk, as a member of the Gereformeerde Kerk, was something of an anomaly. This church has typically been understood to be even more conservative than the larger Dutch Reformed Church, and this is partly the reason why de Klerk's about-turn regarding apartheid shortly after his elevation to the seat of power in 1990 came as such a shock and surprise to insider and outside observers alike.

It is important to describe also the other side of the story, which concerns the fact that not only support for apartheid, but also some of the most vehement opposition to this policy and its dehumanising tendencies came from Reformed circles. The name of Beyers Naudé is well known as an anti-apartheid activist. After he was forced out of his pastoral position within the Dutch Reformed Church because of his anti-apartheid ideas in 1963, he increasingly continued his political and social activities within the ecumenical Christian Institute. However, he simultaneously remained anchored within the Reformed

---

[14] Robert Benedetto and Donald K. McKim, *Historical Dictionary of the Reformed Churches*, Second Edition (Scarecrow Press, 2009), 283.
[15] Ibid.
[16] See Elphick, *Equality of Believers,* 222ff.
[17] See Abdulkader Tayob, Wolfram Weisse, Carel Aaron Anthonissen, Wolfram Weie, *Maintaining Apartheid or Promoting Change?* (Waxmann Verlag, 2004), 156.

tradition where he continued to serve within the Dutch Reformed Church in Africa, which later in 1994 joined with the Dutch Reformed Mission Church to form the Uniting Reformed Church of Southern Africa (URCSA).[18] Another influential figure to be mentioned within this latter church formation would be Allan Aubrey Boesak who, along with the Anglican Archbishop Desmond Tutu and a few others, were among the leading anti-apartheid voices in the 1970s and 1980s.[19] From the ranks of the URCSA also emerged the 'Belhar Confession' that rejected apartheid as a heresy. Boesak played a pivotal role in the theological formation of this confession of faith, which has subsequently been adopted by different Reformed and Presbyterian churches around the world, but not yet by the Dutch Reformed Church. The URCSA has constantly insisted on the Dutch Reformed Church's acceptance of Belhar as a precondition for reunification to occur within these formerly racially divided churches. Although much has changed in terms of the Dutch Reformed Church's leadership and its official perspectives on race and ecumenical matters, its leadership has not yet been able to convince the majority of its members and regional synods of the need to adopt Belhar officially as actual evidence that they have rejected their racist past and, as such, to show themselves ready to meet sisters and brothers within their wider Reformed confession in a non-racial, united church body.

Brief References to Other Reformed Churches in Africa

Elsewhere on the continent, Reformed churches and missions played influential roles although it is in some cases difficult to extrapolate a distinctly Reformed impetus within plural ecumenical and inter-church ventures. A case in point is the Basel Mission which was jointly staffed by Lutheran and Reformed missionaries and which contributed much to the evangelisation of the Ga and Twi people of what is today Ghana.[20] Their first missionaries arrived there in 1828. They prioritised education as of primary concern. After World War I, the Basel missionaries left and were replaced by Scottish Presbyterians. The church that emerged out of these ventures is now known as the Presbyterian Church of Ghana.

The Basel Mission was similarly active in Cameroon from the 1880s onwards.[21] The work these missionaries had started there was taken over and continued by the Presbyterian Church in Cameroon. Swiss Reformed missionaries were also responsible for the founding of the Evangelical Reformed Church in Angola.

The Lesotho Evangelical Church is a Reformed church that traces its history to the Paris Evangelical Mission which commenced work among the Southern Sotho in 1833.[22] The steady progress and missionary success they achieved may in large part be ascribed to the personal friendship established between one of the French missionaries, Eugène Casalis, and the Basotho king, Moshoeshoe. Over time, Casalis became something of an unofficial minister of foreign affairs to the king.[23]

The Paris Evangelical Missionary Society also contributed to the formation of the Evangelical Church of Gabon which achieved independence in 1961.[24] Furthermore, Togo, Senegambia and Madagascar were evangelised by missionaries representing this society.

---

[18] Mary Anne Plaatjies van Huffel, "The Uniting Reformed Church in Southern Africa's Enactment on Church Judicial and Legal Issues", *NGTT* 54, no. 0 (July 20, 2013): 101-13: 102.

[19] See Eugene Fortuin, "Allan Boesak and the Dutch Reformed Mission Church between 1976-1990", in Mary-Anne Plaatjies-Van Huffel and Robert Vosloo (eds) *Reformed Churches in South Africa and the Struggle for Justice: Remembering 1960-1990*(Stellenbosch: SUN Press, 2013), 303-315.

[20] Bengt Sundkler and Christopher Steed, *A History of the Church in Africa* (Cambridge University Press, 2000).

[21] Ibid., 263ff.

[22] Ibid., 375ff.

[23] Ibid., 376.

[24] Ibid., 964.

Conclusion

To conclude, it should be obvious that this is a very brief overview of the Reformed churches in Africa. As expected, the major focus, especially in terms of the narrative thread, concerns South Africa. This is not only because of the disproportionately large influence this country has had on world and African affairs, nor is it entirely due to the fact that Reformed churches have been fairly large and influential in South Africa, but also because of the interesting, problematic, and even prophetic, public roles assumed by individuals associated with the Reformed tradition in that country over the course of time.

Of course, this contribution is nowhere near exhaustive, nor is it representative of every Reformed church on the continent. Historical denominational identities have certainly been in flux, and African realities have resulted in diverse syntheses as a result of various ecumenical, cultural and doctrinal factors. This means that indigenous churches of Reformed extraction might, as a result of contextualisation, have very little to differentiate them from Methodists, Baptists, Congregationalists and others. Reformed identity with respect to Africa is therefore, I suggest, very much a historical designation, and this is how I have attempted to present the case here.

Finally, I offer the explanation that I have purposefully avoided referencing numbers in terms of membership of the churches described here, because, in my opinion, head-counting is fundamentally foreign to classical Reformed epistemology. The Reformed Confession is however a tradition that takes its public role and history seriously. For better or for worse, this contribution will hopefully do a measure of justice to the aspects of that history discussed here.

Bibliography

Benedetto, Robert, and McKim, Donald K. *Historical Dictionary of the Reformed Churches*. Second Edition. Scarecrow Press, 2009.

De Gruchy, John W. *The Church Struggle in South Africa*. Fortress Press, 2005.

Elphick, Richard. *The Equality of Believers: Protestant Missionaries and the Racial Politics of South Africa*. Charlottesville Va.: University of Virginia Press, 2012.

Fortuin, Eugene. 'Allan Boesak and the Dutch Reformed Mission Church between 1976-1990', Mary-Anne Plaatjies-Van Huffel and Robert Vosloo (Eds.) *Reformed Churches in South Africa and the Struggle for Justice: Remembering 1960-1990* (Stellenbosch: SUN Press, 2013), 303-315.

Gonin, H. T. 'Missions of the Dutch Reformed Church in South Africa'. *International Review of Mission* 42, no. 2 (April 1, 1953): 172-77. doi:10.1111/j.1758-6631.1953.tb03731.x.

Goodwin, June, and Ben Schiff. *Heart of Whiteness: Afrikaners Face Black Rule In the New South Africa*. Scribner, 1995.

Gruchy, John W. De. *The Church Struggle in South Africa*. Fortress Press, 2005.

Lessing, Hanns. *The German Protestant Church in Colonial Southern Africa: The Impact of Overseas Work from the Beginnings until the 1920s*. Cluster publications, 2012.

Marx, Christoph. *Oxwagon Sentinel: Radical Afrikaner Nationalism and the History of the 'Ossewabrandwag'*. LIT Verlag Münster, 2009.

Moodie, T. Dunbar. *The Rise of Afrikanerdom: Power, Apartheid, and the Afrikaner Civil Religion*. University of California Press, 1975.

Muller, Retief. 'Evangelicalism and Racial Exclusivism in Afrikaner History: An Ambiguous Relationship'. *Journal of Reformed Theology* 7, no. 2 (January 1, 2013): 204-32. doi:10.1163/15697312-12341296.

Pauw, Christoff Martin. *Mission and Church in Malawi : The History of the Nkhoma Synod of the Church of Central Africa, Presbyterian*. Thesis DTh – University of Stellenbosch, 1980.

Plaatjies-van Huffel, M. A. 'Reading the *Belhar Confession* as a Historical Text', Plaatjies, Mary-Anne, and Vosloo, Robert (eds). *Reformed Churches in South Africa and the Struggle for Justice: Remembering 1960-1990*. First edition. Stellenbosch: Sun Media, 2013.

______. 'The Uniting Reformed Church in Southern Africa's Enactment on Church Judicial and Legal Issues'. *NGTT Is Now Stellenbosch Theological Journal (STJ)* 54, no. 0 (July 20, 2013): 101-13.

Scriba, Georg, 'A chronology of the history of the Lutheran Church in South Africa (1652-1928)', Lessing, Hanns (ed). *The German Protestant Church in Colonial Southern Africa: The Impact of Overseas Work from the Beginnings until the 1920s*. Cluster publications, 2012.

Smith, Edgar H. *Nigerian Harvest.* Grand Rapids: Baker, 1972.

Sundkler, Bengt and Steed, Christopher. *A History of the Church in Africa*. Cambridge University Press, 2000.

Tayob, Abdulkader, Wolfram Weisse, Carel Aaron Anthonissen and Wolfram Weie. *Maintaining Apartheid or Promoting Change?* Waxmann Verlag, 2004.

(29) Moravian Churches in Africa

Karlie August

The Origins of the Moravian Church[1]

The history of the Moravian Church in sub-Saharan Africa goes back to the founding of the first protestant Church in Bohemia in March, 1457.[2] Followers of the teachings of Huss and Peter of Chelsic did not feel at home in the Roman Catholic Church any more, due to the immorality and secular lives of the priests and, very importantly, the fact that lay people could not drink out of the cup at the Eucharist. Subsequently, they broke away from the church to form a movement under Gregory the Patriarch. Gregory founded a settlement with his faithful friends on the northeast-border of Bohemia in the village of Kunwalde in 1457.[3] Many people from all over Moravia and Bohemia came to Kunwalde – nobility, academics and peasants, who longed to be at peace and to follow their Master Jesus Christ and him alone.

In 1467, they met in the first synod at Lhota[4] and chose three persons from their midst as the first ministers of the newly-founded church called the Jednota Batrska, translated into Latin as the Unitas Fratrum (The Unity of the Brethren).[5] From amongst the three, a bishop was elected, in the person of Michael.[6] Consecration was sought at the ancient order of the Waldensians who were regarded as coming from the Primitive Church of the Apostolic Fathers.[7] This episcopal succession was believed to be unbroken since the Apostolic Church. At long last, the Unity of the Brethren was a true apostolic and Old Catholic Church. For their constitution, they took the Sermon on the Mount.[8] It became the only rule of faith and life – in business, in pleasure, in civil duties. What made the Brethren's Church shine so brightly in Bohemia before Luther's days was not their doctrine, but their lives, not their theory, but their practice, not their opinion, but their discipline. It called forth the admiration of Calvin, and drove Luther to despair. In later years they were known as Fratres Legis Christi – Brothers of the Law of Christ. This 'legalistic spirituality' fortunately changed in the time of Luke of Prague.[9]

The church grew to a 100,000-strong membership within a short space of time. Unfortunately, the thirty years' religious wars (1620-1650) broke out and almost wiped out the church.[10] Many of them fled into Poland and other parts of Europe, while only a 'hidden seed' remained, who worshipped secretly in caves and forests. It was these members that a fellow son of the soil, Jan Amos Komensky (Bishop of the Unitas

---

[1] Karel. Th. August, *Mustard Seeds For The Lord: Our Heritage, Our Legacy* (Cape Town: K.Th. August , 2015): 1-12.

[2] Nielsen, W. Sigurd, *The Twin Blossom of the Pear tree bears fruit, The History of the Moravian Church Eastern Province in South Africa.* Port Shepstone: W. Sigurd Nielsen (1999):.20-22. Cf. Krüger, Bernhard, *The Pear Tree Blossoms, A History of the Moravian Mission Stations in South Africa 1737-1869.* Genadendal: Provincial Board of the Moravian Church in South Africa (W.C.P) (1966):13-17.

[3] Hutton, J.E., *A History of the Moravian Church,* London: Moravian Publication Office. (1909):46-49.

[4] Hutton, J.E., *A History of the Moravian Church* (1909): 52.

[5] Holmes, John, *History of the Protestant Church of the United Brethren.* London: Holms John.(1825): 44-45

[6] Hutton, *A History of the Moravian Church,*:54-55.

[7] Holmes, *History of the Protestant Church,* 52-53.

[8] Hutton, *A History of the Moravian Church,* 55.

[9] Hutton, *A History of the Moravian Church,* 59-60.

[10] Holmes, *History of the Protestant Church,* 121-127; cf. Hutton, *A History of the Moravian Church,* 151-155.

Fratrum), referred to as the 'Hidden Seed', and for whom he prayed that the Lord would preserve them and restore his church.[11]

The Renewed Moravian Church

The church was renewed in 1727 after Christian David,[12] a member from Moravia, succeeded in finding asylum for the Moravian refugees in 1722 on the estate of a German nobleman, Count von Zinzendorf, who was a Pietist within the Lutheran Church.[13] A village was laid on, called Herrnhut, and many fugitives, mostly from Moravia and Bohemia, came to live at Herrnhut; from there the name Herrnhuters or Moravians comes from.[14]

Zinzendorf actually hid the Moravians of Herrnhut under the Lutheran Church according to the pietist conventical idea (*ecclesiola in ecclesia*) for the territory was Lutheran and therefore only Lutherans could worship there. However, Zinzendorf's life became so entwined with that of his tenants that he was drawn more and more into the centre of their religious and communal life. He even started to minister to them and to do house visitations.[15] After having read writings by Komensky, he was so overwhelmed by the virtual death wish of the former bishop of the Unitas Fratrum, that he felt called to serve the Old Catholic Church totally.[16] Up till then, Zinzendorf never thought of the Moravian Church as a separate church, but wanted it to become the umbrella body (the Ark) for all God's children out of the other denominations (his ecumenical idea). However, their strong convictions and tradition gained the upper hand when, in 1727, the community experienced a renewal known as the Moravian Pentecost and the ancient church was reborn.[17] Zinzendorf later even became a bishop of the Renewed Moravian Church, which he faithfully served with his life and possessions.[18]

From 1732, the Moravian Church became the first church after the Middle Ages to send out missionaries into the world – they were sent to the West Indies (amongst the Negro slaves), Greenland (amongst the Eskimos), the Cape (amongst the Khoi-khoi) and East Africa (Tanzania), among others....[19]

From Mission Outreach to Church Formation in South Africa

Georg Schmidt and the Beginning of the Moravian Church in South Africa

In 1737, a missionary of Moravian decent, Georg Schmidt, was sent from Holland to convert the Khoi. He started off amongst the Khoi in 1738 in Zoetenmelksvlei in the valley of the Zondereind River.[20] He later

[11] Holmes, *History of the Protestant Church* 127-145; Hutton, *A History of the Moravian Church*,:54-55
[11] Holmes, *History of the Protestant Church*, 52-53, and 156-172.
[12] Hutton, *A History of the Moravian Church*, 192-196 (for the history of Christian David (1690-1722).
[13] Hutton, *A History of the Moravian Church*, 197.
[14] Hutton, *A History of the Moravian Church*, 198
[15] Hutton, *A History of the Moravian Church*, 206-226.
[16] According to Hutton (1909: 172) it was the reading of the Ratio Disciplinae that "fired Zinzendorf's soul with love for the Brethren's Church".
[17] Hutton, *A History of the Moravian Church*, 229-231.
[18] Cf. Hutton, 1909: 238-241 for the process that led to the Count's consecration in Berlin on May, 20th, 1737 by Bishop Jablonsky, grandson of Bishop Komensky (Lat. Comenius); see also Hamilton, JT and Hamilton, KG, 1967, History of the Moravian Church, Bethlehem: Moravian Church, p. 67.
[19] Hutton, *A History of the Moravian Church*, 237-239 (240-246).
[20] Krüger, "The Peartree Blossoms", 15.

(April 1738) moved to Baviaanskloof where soon afterwards his flock counted twenty-eight. He taught them to read and write in Dutch, encouraged them to make gardens and allotted them plots.[21]

From the beginning, Schmidt's mission was full of hardships and tribulation. A pastoral letter written by the Church Council of Amsterdam in 1738 branded the Herrnhuters as a 'mystical society spreading dangerous opinions detrimental to the pure doctrine under the cover of evangelical simplicity'.[22] Fortunately for Schmidt, four dominees (clergy members) of Amsterdam protested against the letter and wrote to the Cape to counteract the open letter.[23] The farmers, however, in the surroundings of his mission settlement were embittered because the governor forbade them to trade cattle with the Khoi. In learning that Schmidt even had success with the teaching of the Khoi, this turned their initial ridicule into enmity. To make things even worse, the dominees were against him and the acting governor wanted him out of the country.[24] When Schmidt baptized five of his converts on account of a written permission from Zinzendorf and Bishop Von Watteville, the combined church council of the three Cape congregations protested heavily against Schmidt's work to the Classis in the Netherlands, since he was not ordained in the prescribed manner. They requested that Schmidt be deported for he might even proceed to baptize the children of the simple colonist on the other side of the mountains which was not in easy reach of the dominees.[25] Everything taken into account, they must take the blame for asserting their racial superiority and ecclesiastical authority over the Khoi, without making any missionary attempt on their behalf. Their negative attitude in this respect reflected the feelings of the colonist at the time at the Cape. When Schmidt left in 1744 he listed a twenty six-member congregation.[26]

During the fifty years after Schmidt's departure, the work was continued by Magdalena (Vehetga Tekoa), one of Schmidt's converts.[27] Even after 1756 they gathered the others occasionally under the pear tree in Schmidt's garden, reading from the New Testament and praying together. From later records, we learn that many of his flock taught their children to read and write, as well as praying in a very simple way. They continued to live in the neighbourhood, waiting for the return of Schmidt.[28]

The Continuation of the Mission Work under Marschveldt, Schwinn and Kuhnel

In 1793, the Moravian Mission work was restarted amongst the Khoi at Baviaanskloof, when the Mission Board in Herrnhut sent Marschveldt, Schwinn and Kuhnel.[29] They found the Khoi living in the same manner as they had done fifty years earlier, but they had become poorer, having lost much of their cattle.[30] This time the mission work enjoyed official recognition in that the governor publicly notified the civilians that Khoi who wanted to go to Baviaanskloof must not be held back.[31] Thus a new and hopeful beginning had been made for the follow up of Schmidt's arduous, pioneering labours. Subsequently, many Khoi-Khoi flocked to Baviaanskloof, amongst them also the descendants of Schmidt's converts. This showed that a whole group of people had been deeply and permanently influenced by him, revelling and abiding in his teachings, unaided over a period of fifty years.

---

[21] Krüger, "The Peartrea Blossoms", 21.
[22] Krüger, "The Peartree Blossoms", 23.
[23] Krüger, "The Peartree Blossoms", 25.
[24] Krüger, "The Peartree Blossoms", 24.
[25] Krüger, "The Peartree Blossoms", 33-36.
[26] Krüger, "The Peartree Blossoms", 42.
[27] Vehetge is today honoured as the first indigenous evangelist in Southern Africa.
[28] Krüger, "The Peartree Blossoms", 45, 47.
[29] Krüger, "The Peartree Blossoms", 49.
[30] Krüger, "The Peartree Blossoms", 52.
[31] Krüger, "The Peartree blossoms", 53.

Unfortunately, the Moravian mission settlement had no security of tenure and no fixed boundaries. Thus, the rush of people to Baviaanskloof led to incessant difficulties from the start with regard to gardening plots, grazing and other movements of the community. The problems with the farmers continued. The farmers, whose economic position was threatened by the shortage of farmhands, blamed it on the mission settlement. Some farmers in the interior envied the Khoi and Coloureds for their education while they were still illiterate. Over and above that the problems with the Dutch Reformed Church continued. The dominees at Stellenbosch questioned the capacity and authority of the missionaries and even ridiculously complained about the ringing of the church bell at Baviannskloof.[32]

Genadendal and the Expansion of the Work

In 1806, after Governor Jansen was defeated at Blaauwbergstrand by the British, he consented (as one of his last official tasks) to Kohrhammer, the superintendent of the Moravian Mission at the time, that a name change for Baviaanskloof to Genadendal could take place.[33]

Life at Genadendal changed for the inhabitants. From that time onwards overseers were elected by the people to enforce the Brotherly Agreement that regulated the life of the inhabitants. Together with the missionaries they took responsibility for the everyday life in the settlement. People were trained as artisans and had to work for their living. Strict moral codes were enforced. Every family had to have their own dwelling.[34]

In 1810, another mission settlement at Groenekloof (later Mamre), north-east of Cape Town, was accepted by the mission. The Khoi captain Klupmuts was not at all satisfied with this arrangement by the governor because the concession included his property as well.[35]

When the British Government took measures against slavery by prohibiting the trading of slaves in 1807, two slaves were offered to the mission as apprentices for 14 years. The conference of elders of the Mission however declined the offer on the ground that only voluntary confessional followers of the Saviour were gathered into their flock.[36]

Contrary to general belief not only Khoi, but also European soldiers, sailors and others came to live on the mission settlements and got married to indigenous wives. Also Ama-Xhosa came to live on the mission settlements. When in 1809 the governor legislated that the Fish River would be the boundary of the Colony, all Nguni, if they wanted to remain in the colony, had to move to the mission settlement of the Moravians; many Nguni moved to Genadendal and Mamre.[37] Among those who came was a Xhosa woman who was one of three wives of a Settler, called Buys, who lived in the Langkloof. She was baptized Wilhelmina and became the nurse-maid of the missionaries' children. She fervently desired that the missionaries would proclaim the gospel amongst her people. She started to teach the missionary children the fundamentals of her language. One of the children, Johann Adolph Bonantz in fact became a pioneer of the Moravian African mission outreach in the Eastern Cape amongst the Nguni.[38]

The Work under Hallbeck[39]

By 1818, another mission settlement was founded by the new superintendent Hallbech in the Eastern Cape in the Sunday River valley on the recommendation of the governor. This settlement, named Enon, was

[32] Krüger, "The Peartree Blossoms", 61.
[33] Krüger, "The Peartree Blossoms", 99.
[34] Krüger, "The Peartree Blossoms", 100.
[35] Krüger, "The Peartree Blossoms", 101-103.
[36] Krüger, "The Peartree Blossoms", 104.
[37] Krüger, "The Peartree Blossoms", 105.
[38] Krüger, "The Peartree Blossoms", 105.
[39] For a short background to Hallbeck see Krüger, 1966: 130-131.

established with inhabitants from Genadendal amongst who was Wilhelmina Stompies.[40] The aim of the mission was to bring the gospel nearer to the Nguni people. Of course, the governor's intention was to have a civilized outpost nearer to the border. The governor even suggested to the Xhosa chief, Ghaika, who reigned east of the Fish River, to send his children to a Moravian school. Of course his intention was politically based.[41]

In 1824, the Mission at the Cape bought its own property for the first time. Until then all the settlements were 'grant stations'.[42] A farm, Vogelstruiskraal in the Strandveldt near Cape Agulhas, was bought and named Elim.[43] From now on, every newcomer would know that they settled on Mission property. Bonatz, the missionary, endeavoured from the beginning to give the congregation an ecumenical outlook. Farmers, Khoi, slaves and other Europeans from the neighbourhood regularly attended services. The children of the neighbouring farmers even attended Sunday school with those of the settlement.[44]

In 1828, the Moravians extended their activities to the African tribes beyond the Fish River. A mission settlement was established amongst the Tembu at the request of the Chief, Bawana.[45] Hallbech was conscious of the fact that Bawana had no longing for the gospel, even although it was high fashion amongst the African chiefs to boast about having a missionary.[46] The governor, for his part, supported the project mainly for political reasons. However, he considered that the Lord had opened the door by using human ambition and fear for his purpose. Lemmertz, Hoffmann, Wilhelmina[47] and a number of Khoi and African inhabitants of Enon agreed to start the first Moravian mission settlement along the Klipplaat, later named Shiloh.[48] In 1832, Johann Adolph Bonatz arrived back in the Colony having completed his studies in Europe and was called to Shiloh, where he was further instructed in Xhosa by his nanny, Wilhelmina. Remaining in Shiloh for twenty-six years, he became the real pioneer of the Moravian Mission amongst the Xhosa people.[49]

Under Hallbeck's management, Genadendal became the centre for education and industry. The school was enlarged and indigenous teachers were trained. An infant school was started. All the mission settlements were supplied with a school, a mill, a shop and the inhabitants trained as artisans. Some became masons, carpenters, tanners, thatchers, cartwrights, dressmakers, tailors, cobblers, black- and silver-smiths. Others got engaged in the agricultural industry.[50] On 12th September 1838, a two-storey training school was dedicated for the training of teachers. People from different places came to be trained at the first indigenous teachers' training school in South Africa. From amongst the first graduates, the first indigenous minister, Carl Jonas, was ordained after many years of faithful service.[51]

The mission settlements also played a major role in harbouring the freed slaves in 1838. A special thanksgiving service was held at Genadendal for the 818 people that were integrated into the mission settlements. At Elim even a monument was erected for the liberation of the slaves.[52]

---

[40] Krüger, "The Peartree Blossoms," 132.
[41] Krüger, "The Peartree Blossoms," 134.
[42] This concept meant land allocated by the government for Moravian mission settlements under the quitrent system.
[43] Krüger, "The Peartree Blossoms," 152.
[44] Krüger, "The Peartree Blossoms," 154-155.
[45] Krüger, "The Peartree Blossoms," 166.
[46] Krüger, "The Peartree Blossoms," 169.
[47] So Wilhelmina Stompie became the first evangelist in the Eastern Cape amongst the Xhosas, assisting to European missionaries in their work.
[48] Krüger, "The Peartree Blossoms," 170-171.
[49] Krüger, "The Peartree Blossoms," 174.
[50] Krüger, "The Peartree Blossoms," 177.
[51] Krüger, "The Peartree Blossoms," 184-185.
[52] Krüger, "The Peartree Blossoms," 195-197. This could very well be the only monument in Africa for the freedom of the slaves.

By 1868 the mission work had expanded tremendously in the West as well as in the East. So much so, that there were twelve congregations with a total membership of 8,815, twenty-five missionaries, nineteen indigenous assistants and eighteen schools.[53]

The Division of the Work

At the General Synod, which gathered at Herrnhut in 1869, decisions were taken that had far-reaching implications for mission work in South Africa:[54]

The creation of self-supporting churches, ministered to by their own workers;

The differentiation between the Mission and its employees, which had to decrease, and the indigenous church and its workers, which had to increase;

The division of the Cape Mission into two Provinces.

The latter was motivated by the following realities:

Geographical distances incurred great expenses;

More effective administration could be ensured from Shiloh for the East;

The East felt that the work amongst the Xhosa-speaking section had a character different from that of the West;

Language was also a major factor in the division.

The congregations of Clarkson and Enon that were geographically part of the East, chose to join the West because they spoke Dutch; but it was rather more an ethnic than a racial division, for the Fingos in the Tsitsikamma were ministered to by Clarkson and the coloured members of Shiloh remained part of the East.

The older Western Province would advance more quickly towards self-support, free from the financial responsibility for the young and still expanding Eastern Province.[55]

Henceforth, each of the two Provinces followed its own course.

An Autonomous Church

The Moravian Church (SA Western Province) stood at the threshold of a new dispensation at its second synod in 1959. It had been a long and sometimes arduous way from the first missionary phase under Georg Schmidt, to a Church with 29,166 baptized members, of which 10,623 were communicants and 15,271 children, which was recognized by the first post-war General Synod (1957) as a 'Synodal Province' of the Unitas Fratrum.[56] It was resolved that 'the General Synod of 1957 authorise...the Unity Board to consider the application by the SA Western Province, for recognition as a Unity Province, and to grant such recognition at any time after January 1960, whenever the conditions...contained in the "Church Order of the Unitas Fratrum"... have been met'. What were the conditions laid down by the Unity Synod in 1957? The General Order set them out as follows:

> A Unity Province is one which has developed its spiritual, material and human resources to the point at which it can assume full responsibility for its own life and work, and can make an effective contribution to... the calls of the whole Church.
>
> It orders its own affairs and holds and administers its property independently but subject to the general principles which set the standard for the whole Unitas Fratrum.

---

[53] Krüger, "The Peartree Blossoms," 196; 289.
[54] Krüger, "The Peartree Blossoms," 288.
[55] Krüger, "The Peartree blossoms," 289.
[56] August, Karel Th., The Quest for being Public Church – The South African Challenge to the Moravian Church in context (1737-2004). Cape Town: K.Th. August, (2005), 180.

It is responsible to the Unity Synod for carrying out these general principles.

It supplies and sustains completely its own ministry, irrespective of the race or colour of the individual minister.

It provides for the establishment and maintenance of educational institutions including a theological seminary.

Each Unity Province works for the extension of the Kingdom of God.

It is fully self-supporting financially.

It has the responsibility of proving leadership in community, industrial and professional life, in meeting social problems, and in making positive contributions to the general welfare.[57]

These sections of the church order describe in a few words the standard achieved by the Province of South Africa-West by 1960. Even the last criterion was at least partially fulfilled, despite the small numbers and restricted opportunities of its members.

The second phase of development, when the decreasing Mission and the increasing Moravian Church worked alongside each other, had come to an end. The Mission was fully integrated into the church. The missionaries and the indigenous ministers worked under exactly the same conditions of service and remuneration. The church was truly self-supporting and truly Moravian, the ministers served as brothers amongst brothers, their wives as sisters amongst sisters and the bishop was a spiritual helper and not a high administrator of the church.

At the Synod in 1962, the chairperson of the Church Board could report as follows to the members: 'Our Unity Province is alive and developing. We are a self-reliant Church, this means that every member must be self-reliant, every congregation must assist in the work and extend it.'

The church also realized that it had to do mission work, because it saw proclaiming the gospel as a permanent task for each member, each congregation. To do so in every respect was the task of the new Unity Province![58]

A United Church

Since the introduction of the apartheid policy by the South African Nationalist government in 1948 and the Homelands structures, an increased awareness developed among members that the two autonomous regions as they had predominantly developed along racial lines were irreconcilable with the rich Moravian heritage and Biblical foundation of the church. Although the 1869 decision was well founded, the division caused deep-rooted long-term problems of alienation, separate structures, partition, suspicion, etc.[59]

This longing to become a truly unified Moravian Church and Province in South Africa soon developed into a determination that was no longer implied, but was expressed and manifested in the following specific steps:

A combined synod was held in 1956 where it was decided that the two Provincial Boards should meet as the South African Board where they could discuss and make recommendations regarding steps for closer unity. They were to report to the synods of the two Provinces.[60]

In 1969 the South African Board mapped out a three-phase unity plan, viz.

Consultation;

Federation;

[57] August, "The Quest", 181. These requirements as laid out by the Church order of the Unitas Fratrum (COUF, 1995 #200-215)the Tanzanian provinces also had to abide to in order to become a Unity Autonomous Provinces.
[58] August, "The Quest", 182-183.
[59] August, "The Quest", 194-195.
[60] August, "The Quest", 195.

Unity.[61]

This entailed the incorporation of congregations within the same geographical area, the seconding of personnel, the starting of a salary fund, the starting of a Stewardship and Educational Programme and the election of a Unity Commission.

Looking at all these decisions taken at synod it is obvious that the Church wanted to overcome the obstacles in its way on the road towards unity. Progress on the way towards unity has, however, been retarded by the fact that not all the decisions made at Provincial Synod were executed and that the unity debate that was conducted at the provincial synod level often did not reach the members on local congregation level.

The federal constitution accepted at Gelvandale, Port Elizabeth in 1975 which, although hoped to be able to facilitate the process of growing together, proved that it did not satisfy the desires for closer unity in East and West. It, however, did succeed in preparing the church for the next phase, which would be the total unification of the Moravian Church in South Africa.[62]

In 1986, the Provincial Synod appointed a Unity Commission with the main aim of making an in-depth study of all the implications involved for the two regions in becoming one Moravian Church in South Africa in all respects.[63]

The Commission submitted reports to the regional synods in 1988 and to the following Provincial synod in 1990. Synod then decided to

> Accept the report; and Adjourn till September 1991 to complete the discussions on the recommendations of the Unity Commission.[64]

In 1992, Synod accepted the Unity Resolutions for one Moravian Church which enabled the church in South Africa to meet as truly one church at the Provincial Synod of 1994 on the ground of one confession and one constitution – truly one Province of the Unitas Fratrum that was constituted in a distant land, the spiritual motherland, at that first synod in 1467.[65]

The Moravian Church in Tanzania[66]

The first missionaries of the Moravian Church came to Tanzania in the late nineteenth century after Germany assumed control of the territory. The first Moravian mission station was established by German missionaries from Herrnhut,[67] Germany, at Rungwe in Southern Tanzania[68] in 1891.[69]

---

[61] August, "The Quest", 237.
[62] August, "The Quest", 237.
[63] August, "The Quest", 239-240.
[64] August, "The Quest", 240.
[65] August, "The Quest", 241.
[66] Boytler, J.H, Ecclesiology and culture in the Moravian Church, PhD dissertation, University of Aarhus (2009):13. "In the case of Tanzania, one will look in vain for a complete contemporary historical account of the Moravian Church. It is certainly possible to find information concerning the work and development of the Tanzanian MC in magazines and pamphlets, but mostly in the form of ad hoc information on ongoing matters."
[67] The first missionaries were Theodore Meyer (superintendent), Theophil Richard, George Martin and Johannes Häfner. Cf. Hamilton, J. Taylor and Hamilton, Kenneth G., History of the Moravian Church, Bethlehem, Pa: Interprovincial Board of Christian Education Moravian Church in America (1967):597.
[68] A desire to avoid the unpromising Coastal with its Muslim Swahili, together with the problem of expensive land transport to the interior, led the (Moravians and the Lutherans) to prefer the north Nyasa region….(cf. C.P Groves, The Planting of Christianity in Africa, Vol. II, London: Lutterworth Press (1964).
[69] Cf. Musomba, Angetile, The Moravian Church in Tanzania Southern Province, Nairobi: French Institute for Research In Africa (2005), 5; Hamilton, "History of the Moravian Church", 597, Periodical Account, Second Century,

Another mission station, called Urambo in Unyamwesi in western Tanzania,[70] was handed over to the Moravian Board in Herrnhut, by the London Missionary Society in 1896.[71] As a result of active evangelism work, these two sister stations grew and became big churches, extending over large areas in the southern and western parts of Tanzania. Each one constituted a Province of its own.

The need to establish co-operation between the two newly established Provinces was felt right from the beginning of their establishment. The founding missionaries had established communication through correspondence as early as 1899.[72] Later they started meeting and exchanging experiences and the two Provinces established co-operation on various matters.[73] In 1965, it was agreed to establish formally a joint board to discuss and agree on matters common to both Provinces.[74] In 1968, the two Provinces decided to establish a Moravian theological college as a joint venture for the training of ministers. In 1976, the Southern Province was divided into two, and the same was done to the Western Province in 1986. Since then the Moravian presence in Tanzania has consisted of four Provinces.[75]

With the creation of the new Provinces, the need to establish the Moravian Church in Tanzania as a national body to co-ordinate and unify the work became greater.[76] The Moravian Church in Tanzania would run and oversee joint ventures and programmes and represent the Provinces inside and outside Tanzania. On 4th August 1986, delegates from the four Moravian Provinces met at Sikonge and resolved to formally establish the Moravian Church in Tanzania (MCT) as a church to unite all Moravians in Tanzania. On 23rd November 1986, the MCT was officially inaugurated and, in April 1987, it was registered by the government.[77] The MCT was formally recognized by the Unity Synod of the Unitas Fratrum at its meeting in Antigua, West Indies in 1988.[78]

The Moravian Church in Tanzania co-ordinates and oversees the development and growth of the theological college, which has become, since 2004, Bishop Kisanji University. It is responsible for the publication of church literature produced by the Moravian Theological Commission. It represents the Provinces before the government, other churches, agencies and ecumenical organizations. Above all, its major responsibility is, through the Provinces, to preach the holy gospel of salvation within and outside the church.[79]

Since its establishment in 1986, the MCT[80] (which is only a structure for co-ordinating certain designated areas of work and is not a church) has grown into seven autonomous Provinces with a membership of over 500,000 in Tanzania alone:[81]

London: Moravian Church, 1890.

[70] In 1898, the Edmund Dahls, the Konrad Meiers and the Rudolf Sterns started the mission in the Unyamwesior Western Tanganyika area (Hamilton, "History of the Moravian Church", 609).

[71] Hamilton, "History of the Moravian Church", 609.

[72] Musomba, Angetile, "The Moravian Church in Tanzania", 83.

[73] In 1900 there was the first General Mission Conference held at Rungwe, which many missionaries attended Hamilton, "History of the Moravian Church," 600-601. It was also decided at this conference to open a training school for the indigenous workers for evangelism as the mission field was too large for the German missionaries. The school was opened in 1903 with eleven students.

[74] Musomba, Angetile, "The Moravian Church in Tanzania", 84.

[75] Church Order of the Moravian Church (COUF), paragraph 802, Eagan: Digital House, 1988.

[76] World Council of Churches, Moravian Church in Tanzania. https:// www.oikoumene.org/en/member-churches/moravian-church-in-Tanzania (accessed 20 October, 2015).

[77] World Council of Churches, Moravian Church in Tanzania. https:// www.oikoumene.org/en/member-churches/moravian-church-in-Tanzania (accessed 20 October, 2015).

[78] COUF, par. 218 listed the MTC as a province and "Church," 1995.

[79] World Council of Churches, Moravian Church in Tanzania. https:// www.oikoumene.org/en/member-churches/moravian-church-in-Tanzania (accessed 20 October, 2015).

[80] It was resolved at the Unity Synod of 2002 to eliminate MTC as a listed province in order that MTC would only indicate a geographical coordinating secretariat which would be responsible to deal with issues of common concern as

Tanzania (Eastern Province)
Tanzania (Lake Tanganyika Province)
Tanzania (Northern Province)
Tanzania (Rukwa Province)
Tanzania (Southern Province)
Tanzania (South Western Province)
Tanzania (Western Province)[82]

Through the sterling evangelism work of the MCT, churches were also established in the Congo (DR Congo), Malawi and in Zambia (Moravian Church in Zambia),[83] whilst mission Provinces[84] have been established in the following countries and regions:

Burundi
Zanzibar
Iringa
Uganda
Rwanda
Eastern Congo (Sud Kivu)
Angola[85]

Today, the Moravian Church in Tanzania is the largest church of the Moravian fellowship in the world and a truly missional church.

Conclusion

The Moravian Church on the continent of Africa is an ecumenical Protestant church and is affiliated to the national church bodies in the respective countries as well as to the AACC. Globally, it is affiliated to the LWF and WCC.

As Provinces of the Unitas Fratrum, it co-operates as an African regional conference.[86]

As Unity Provinces, the African Provinces meet every seven years together with the other Unity Provinces of the Unitas Fratrum in the Unity Synod.[87]

The Moravian Church acknowledges that the Lord Jesus Christ calls his church into being so that it may serve him on earth until he comes. It is therefore aware of its being called in faith to serve humanity by proclaiming the gospel of Jesus Christ. It recognizes this call to be the source of its being and the inspiration of its service. As is the source, so is the aim and end of its being, based upon the will of its Lord.[88]

---

directed by all provinces of Tanzania and /or their synods, COUF par. 802, 2002. This overarching Church structure should actually be called the Union of Moravian Provinces in Tanzania.

[81] UNITAS FRATRUM, Directory of Unity provinces. http//: www.unitasfratrum.org/index.php/unity=provinces (accessed 20 October 2015).

[82] Church Order of the Moravian Church, par. , London, 2010.

[83] Unitas Fratrum, Unity Provinces. www.unitasfratrum.org/index.php/unity=provinces (accessed 20 October 2015).

[84] A "mission province" is the responsibility of a Province to whom the administration is assigned (cf. COUF, par 800.1. All these Mission provinces are assigned to the Moravian Churches (provinces) in Tanzania. Cf. http//: www.unitasfratrum.org/index.php/unity=provinces (accessed 20 October 2015).

[85] Unitas Fratrum, Unity Provinces. www.unitasfratrum.org/index.php/unity=provinces (accessed 20 October 2015). The status and responsibility of a Mission province is spelt out in COUF par.800.2, 2002.

[86] COUF, par.856 (b) (4), 2002.

[87] COUF, par. 269, 2002.

[88] COUF, par.1, 2002.

Bibliography

August, Karel Th., *The Quest for being Public Church – The South African Challenge to the Moravian Church in context (1737-2004)*. Cape Town: K.Th. August, 2005

August, Karel Th. *Mustard Seeds for the Lord, Our Heritage, Our Legacy*, Cape Town: Moravian Printing Press, 2015

Boytler, J.H, *Ecclesiology and culture in the Moravian Church*, PhD dissertation, University of Aarhus, 2009

Church Order of The Unitas Fratrum (Moravian Church), Eagan: Digital House, 2002

Groves, C.P, The Planting of Christianity in Africa, Vol. II, London: Lutterworth Press, 1964.

Hamilton, J. Taylor and Hamilton, Kenneth G., *History of the Moravian Church,* Bethlehem, Pa: Interprovincial Board of Christian Education Moravian Church in America, 1967

Holms, John, *History of the Protestant Church of the United Brethren*. London: Holms John, 1825

Hutton, J.E., *A History of the Moravian Church,* London: Moravian Publication Office, 1909

Krüger, Bernhard, *The Pear Tree Blossoms, A History of the Moravian Mission Stations in South Africa 1737-1869*. Genadendal: Provincial Board of the Moravian Church in South Africa (W.C.P), 1966

Musomba, Angetile, *The Moravian Church in Tanzania Southern Province*, Nairobi: French Institute for Research In Africa, July 2005

Nielsen, W. Sigurd, *The Twin Blossom of the Pear tree bears fruit, The History of the Moravian Church Eastern Province in South Africa.* Port Shepstone: W. Sigurd Nielsen, 1999

Unitas Fratrum, Unity Provinces. Periodical Account, Second Century, London: Moravian Church, 1890.

Unitas Fratrum: www.UnitasFratrum.org/index.php/unity=provinces (accessed 20 October 2015).

World Council of Churches, Moravian Church in Tanzania: https://www.oikoumene.org/en/member-churches/moravian-church-in-Tanzania (accessed 20 October, 2015)

Suggested Reading

Barz, Gregory F, *Performing Religion Negotiating Past and Present in Kwaya Music of Tanzania,* Rodopi: Amsterdam, 2003.

Fahlbusch, Erwin, *The Encyclopedia of Christianity*, Grand Rapids: Michigan, 1992

Höschele, Stefan, *Christian Remnant – African Folk Church 1903-1980*, Leiden: Brill.

Kamwela, Leonard, *The History of the Moravian Church from Germany to Southern Tanzania, Mbeya: Moravian Church in Tanzania* 1992.

Muneja, Mussa Simon, *HIV/AIDS and the Bible in Tanzania,* Bamberg: University of Bamberg Press, 2012.

Otiso, Kefa M, *Culture and Customs of Tanzania*, Oxford: Greenwood Press, 2013.

Pedersen, Martha, *Joy Cometh In The Morning,* London: British Mission Board, 1962

Wright, Marcia, *German Missions in Tanganyika, 1891-1941: Lutherans and Moravians in the Southern Highlands,* Oxford: Clarendon Press, 1971.

(30A) Lutheran Churches in Africa

Faith Kokubelwa Lugazia

Introduction

Lutheran churches in Africa, as elsewhere in the world, owe their theological and ecclesiastical tradition to the sixteenth-century reformer Martin Luther (1483-1546). Those convinced by Luther's view on doctrinal teachings of the church of reformation later became the Lutheran church family.

This article will provide a brief history of Lutheranism in African Christianity,[1] an introduction into major theological profiles and marks of the Lutheran Church in Africa and the special ways in which Lutheran churches contribute to social witness, development and *diakonia* in the African continent. While it is not possible in this paper to give data on work done by every Lutheran church in Africa, some actual examples of work done in different Lutheran churches on the continent will be referred to. We are beginning by clarifying some crucial terms.

Lutheranism

Historically, the term 'Lutheran' originally was used as a belittling term in polemics against Luther by John Maier von Eck during the Leipzig debate in July 1519.[2] Since Eck followed traditional Roman Catholic teachings, and Luther formulated his teachings against the prevailing medieval Roman Catholic positions, it followed that all who identified with the theology of Martin Luther, were later labelled as 'Lutherans'. Lutherans believe that human beings are saved by grace through faith and this grace is obtained by being in Christ. Lutheran churches practise the two sacraments of Baptism (Matt. 28:18-20) and Holy Communion (Matt. 26:29-29) and also insist that faith, doctrines, confessions and the order of worship are built on the foundations as rooted in the living word of God.

Confessions

The Lutheran Reformation has produced confessions, which are writings by the reformers which articulate the core biblical teachings in which the beliefs of Lutheran Christians find their expression. Carl Braaten would add that 'The true intent of the Lutheran confessional heritage is to settle for nothing less than a theonomous vision of a church with an evangelical heart beating in a Catholic body'.[3] These Confessional Writings are documented in the Book of Concord.

Social Witness

In the context of this paper the term 'social witness' is referring to the participation of the church in society in different activities aiming at transforming and improving the living conditions of people.

---

[1] African Context in this work is confined with African Lutheranism found in the south of the Sahara.

[2] Jack E. Linquist, Lutheranism" in *An Introductory Dictionary of Theology and Religious Studies,* eds. Espin, Orlando O. and Nickoloff, James B (Collegeville, Minnesota: Liturgical Press), 792.

[3] Carl E. Braaten, *Principles of Lutheran Theology.* 2nd. ed. (Minneapolis: Fortress Press, 2007), 37.

Development

Development is a complex term. The meaning of the term is changing according to time and context depending on the needs of the community. After World War II, the term 'development' often was used as synonymous with economic 'growth' and was closely associated with expectations concerning political freedom, new technology and the role of science.[4] Towards the end of the twentieth century when much of the world was suffering from poverty, environmental destruction and social disintegration, the term came to be defined as:

> … a process by which the members of a society increase their personal and institutional capacities and manage resources to produce sustainable and justly distributed improvements in their quality of life consistent with their own aspirations.[5]

In the African context, the term 'development' often is used to point to the use of resources available in a given place to uplift and equip communities to deal with social and economic problems of their time. Understanding development in the African context is always related to the concerns for human dignity as far as production and consumption habits, human relations and social compassion are concerned.[6] The term 'development' can be summarized in African perspectives as a process of empowering people through and with resources available for the positive transformation of their lives and communities.

Diakonia

For Luther, *diakonia* is the ministry of caring for the body, a work which requires men to distribute material goods[7] and to assist with the uplifting of the poor.[8] Today in Lutheran understanding, 'Diakonia is the embodiment, through human actions, of God's love for the world'.[9] The practical implications are thus described: 'Diakonia is a call to action, as a response to challenges of human suffering, injustice and care for creation.'[10] The LWF global consultation on 'The Diaconal ministries of the Lutheran Churches' which met in Sao Leopoldo, Brazil, 2nd-7th November 2005, defined *diakonia* as:

> … the core component of the essence of the church and its mission in the world. Diaconal ministry is the manifestation of diakonia in the life of the church in which every Christian is called to participate through baptism in daily life as an expression of the priesthood of all believers.[11]

---

[4] Richard, D.N. Dickinson. "Development" in *Dictionary of the Ecumenical Movement*, eds. Nicholas Lossky, José Miguez Bonino, et al. 2nd. edition (Geneva: WCC Publications, 2002) 298-303.

[5] David C. Korten, *Getting to the 21st Century. Voluntary Action and the Global Agenda.* (West Hartford: Kumarian Press,1990), 97.

[6] Molefe, Tsele. "Current Issues in Africa." *Africa Moving Towards the Eighth Assembly, Harare,* ed. John S. Pobee (Geneva: WCC Publications, 1998), 15-20.

[7] *Luther's Works,* ed. Hilton C. Oswald Vol.28 (St Louis: Concordia Publishing House, 1973), 693

[8] Oswald., *Luther's Work,* 694.

[9] Ishmael, Noko, "Foreword" in *Diakonia in Context: Transformation, Reconciliation, Empowerment. A Lutheran Contribution to the Understanding and Practice of Diakonia.* Ed. Kjell Nordstokke (Geneva: LWF Publications, 2009). 5.

[10] Kjell Nordstokke "Introduction" in *Diakonia in Context: Transformation, Reconciliation, Empowerment. A Lutheran Contribution to the Understanding and Practice of Diakonia.* Ed. Kjell Nordstokke (Geneva: LWF Publications, 2009), 8.

[11] "The Diaconical Ministry in the Lutheran Churches" in *Diaconical Ministry in the Mission of the Church, ed,* Reinhard Boettcher (Geneva: LWF Document, 2006), 82.

This paper explains *diakonia* as the work of the church and her members in responding to God's love by serving others in words and deeds.

We now turn to some general perspectives on the history of Lutheran churches in Africa:

History of Lutheranism in Africa

Lutheranism was introduced in Africa in the nineteenth century by different missions from Europe, the USA, Africa and other parts of the globe.[12]

The United Lutheran Church of America started to work in Liberia in 1860.[13] Lutherans of German background from both the Lutheran Mission Hermannsburg and the Neukirchen Mission started their mission in Kenya in the late 1880s.[14] Lutherans also came to today's Tanzania in 1886 from Germany under the umbrella of the Evangelical Mission Society for East Africa (German: *Evangelische Missionsgesellschaft für Deutsch-Ostafrika*, also known as 'Berlin III' or the Bethel Mission).[15] North Westerners from Tanzania became Lutherans only after the Church of Sweden and the Danish Mission Society started their mission activities, while others were more influenced by the Berliner Mission. While the Leipziger Mission in Tanzania was Lutheran (from Saxony) the Bethel Mission was shaped by Prussian tradition, which was united according to the Prussian Union and therefore not purely Lutheran.[16] Lutheran brethren arrived in Cameroon in 1918 to help the Paris Mission in the development of their work. They were joined in 1920 by the Brethren Church Mission from the USA.[17]

In the late twentieth century, Lutheranism was also introduced into the continent through African initiatives. For example, several other African Lutheran churches (like Kenya Evangelical Lutheran Church and the Lutheran churches in Uganda, Congo, Malawi, Rwanda and Burundi) were born through initiatives of missionary outreach originating from the Evangelical Lutheran Church of Tanzania (ELCT).[18]

While analyzing how Lutheranism came into function in the north-western part of Tanzania, Josiah Kibira said, 'We have become Lutheran by grace. It was not by literal spoon-feeding by foreigners but through the revelation and help of the Holy Spirit and by the study of the part of local Christians.'[19] Kibira's analysis can be supported as the contextualized versions of Lutheranism show equal input from both indigenous African as well as from western sources and factors, being embedded with both western and African cultures. There is a great variety of forms of Lutheranism in Africa, and there are different emphases in the interpretation of the doctrine of justification by faith or structures of leadership within Lutheran churches in Africa, which therefore are not always in complete conformity with the original

---

[12] Faith K. Lugazia, "The Relevance of 'Smacaldian Articles' in Tanzanian Context: A Lutheran View", an unpublished paper presented at the Smalkadian Conference, Germany, 23rd June 2012.

[13] Jonathan Hildebrandt, *History of the Church in Africa: A Survey* (Achimota: African Christian Press,1981), 110.

[14] W.B. Anderson, *The Church in East Africa 1840-1974* (Dodoma: Central Tanganyika Press, 1977), 62.

[15] S. Von Sicard, *The Lutheran Church of the Coast, Tanzania 1887-191* ,(Lund: Lund Printing Press, 1970), 55; Cf. Wilson Niwagila, *From the Catacomb to a Self-Governing Church: A Case Study of the African Initiative and the Participation of the Foreign Missions in the Mission History of the North-Western Diocese of the Evangelical Lutheran Church in Tanzania 1890-1965,* 2nd ed. (Hamburg: Verlagan der Lottbek,1991) , 98; Also Carl-Eric Sahlberg, *From Krapf to Rugambwa: A Church History of Tanzania* (Nairobi: Evangel Publishing House, 1986), 59. Carl-Eric Sahalberg differs with Von Sicard and Niwagila on the arrival of Berlin 111, for him these missionaries arrived in 1887.

[16] Comment given by Dr. Fidon Mwombeki (9th January, 2015).

[17] Hildebrant, *History of the Church,* 211.

[18] *Full Gospel: History of the Evangelical Lutheran Church in Tanzania 1963-2013.eds.Godson S. Maanga, Wilson Niwagila et al* (Moshi: Moshi Lutheran Printing Press, 2013), 133-141.

[19] Josiah M. Kibira, "Has Luther Reached Africa: The Testimony of a Confused Lutheran," In *African Theological Journal 12*, No. 1 (1983): 6-15.

teachings of Martin Luther – just as history and context have also transformed Lutheran teachings in certain contexts.[20]

Lutheran Christianity planted in Africa is therefore not a direct mirror or re-run of the theological positions, debates and arguments of the sixteenth century Reformation, but was moulded by different African cultures and a process of reinterpretation which took place as an integral part of the missionary spread of the gospel as expressed in the Lutheran tradition.

Major Theological Profiles and Marks of the Lutheran Churches in Africa

Certainly, the insistence on the Word of God being preached rightly and the two sacraments of Baptism and Holy Communion being administered correctly are still common elements underlining the key features of Lutheran churches in Africa.

The teaching on justification by faith through grace has always been a major concern close to the heart of Lutheran confessional identity. These marks of the Lutheran churches are expressed in key chapters of the Lutheran Confessional Writings,[21] are found in the Book of Concord, and are always interpreted together with ancient creeds of the Christian faith. Lutheran confessional writings have always understood themselves as pointing to the central message of the scriptures as a whole, not changing anything important in apostolic teachings, but renewing a clear focus on the core of the gospel as understood in relation to the Reformation principles of *sola fide, sola gratia, sola scriptura, solus Christus.*[22]

The Contribution of Lutheran Churches to Social Witness, Development and Diakonia

The Lutheran churches in Africa, like other churches in Africa, are in a transition period concerning a clear understanding of their relevant contribution to society as there is a constant process of 'self-criticism, self-motivation and self-contextualizing'.[23] In the process, there are also critical voices arguing that Lutheran churches have not yet fully attended to their call as still there is much poverty, bad leadership, corruption, hunger, disease, and a high rate of illiteracy. Others affirm the positive nature of the realized social contribution of Lutheran churches in Africa, as many of them are embarking on 'bringing good news to the poor, proclaiming the release of the captives, recovering the sight of the blind, letting the oppressed go free, and proclaiming the year of the Lord' (Luke 4:18-20). The positive voices are represented, for instance, by Martin Shao when he said, 'There are so many concrete success stories of churches working with their people to overcome poverty and other challenges.'[24]

Probably both perspectives and voices are correct, depending on which context you are looking at. There are contexts which are marked by intense suffering, HIV/AIDS, Ebola, starvation, poverty, ethnic wars, corruption and violence, but also, even in the midst of all this, many positive examples can be found

---

[20] Martin, Luther, "The Augsburg Confession Article VII: The Church" in *The Book of Concord: The Confessions of the Lutheran church,* eds. Theodore Tappert, Jaroslav Pelikan, et al (Philadelphia: Fortress Press,1959), 32.

[21] For the sake of clarity, these confessions will be elaborated briefly in this paper.

[22] David G. Tuemper, "The Lutheran Confessional Writings and the Future of the Lutheran Theology" in *The Gift of Grace: The Future of the Lutheran Theology,* eds. Niels Henrik Gregersen, Bo Holmetal. (Minneapolis: Fortress Press,2005). 131-144.

[23] Stan Nussbaum, "Africa Independent Churches and a Call of r New Three-Self Formula for Mission" in *Freedom and Independence, ed.* S. Nussbaum. Nairobi, OAIC, 1994), 1-8.

[24] Martin, Shao, "A Response to Zephaniah Kameeta" in "*So the Poor Have Hope, and Injustice Shuts its Mouth" Poverty and Mission of the Church in Africa,* eds. Karen Bloomquist and Musa Panti Filibus, Geneva: LWF Document, 2007), 71-72.

in which African people feel and appreciate the social contribution of the church, and particularly of the Lutheran church in social witness and service. Fidon Mwombeki has argued that:

> The Church (and the cross) in Africa has, from its genesis, had as part of its mission the alleviation of suffering and human pain wherever it is found. The church takes the lead in feeding the hungry, healing the sick, raising the downtrodden, fighting for the weak, and so on.[25]

On a similar line of thought, the LWF scholar Kenneth Mtata has argued that there was a unique contribution of Lutheran churches in education and health services and that the education provided by the church through missionaries helped not only the spread of general literacy but also gave Africans critical tools with which to challenge colonialism.[26] Paul John Isaak has shown how the Lutheran Church in Africa, in collaboration with other religious institutions, has fought against unjust political oppression, arguing that 'we marched against the evils of apartheid, sexism and colonialism'.[27] Tenagne Negusse, Elieshi Mungure, and Sarojini Nadar, to mention but a few, have documented Lutheran churches in Africa playing a significant role in upholding African cultural values where they were contributing to positive aspects of human dignity and challenging African cultural practices where they were oppressive, especially for women. They have stated that, 'now as society is changing, women are on the administrative committees of the synods and also more women on executive committees'.[28] According to Sarojini Nadar, 'critical interpretation of the Bible leads to transformation because… access of the word of God to the believer in the Lutheran tradition helped women to re-read and reinterpret the scriptures and discover its potential for transforming traditional practices and taboos'.[29] Thus it is becoming clear that Lutheran churches in Africa are still in a process of actualizing their critical potential, their motivation and their contextualization call; they are in a process of continued reformation.

Participation of Lutheran Churches for Social Witness and Diakonia

The Lutheran churches in Africa in their prophetic role of comforting the afflicted and afflicting the comfortable have been advocating for the rights of Africans wherever they have been deprived by powers and principalities of this world. For example, Lutheran churches in Africa with the collaboration of other churches in Africa have spoken out to remove oppressive powers in their countries in periods of racist governments or military rule. A Namibian bishop has affirmed in looking back at the history of his own country:

> We have won the political struggle for independence and democracy and the church can proudly say that it has kept the light of hope for justice, peace and liberation throughout difficult times… Despite great suffering, we did so, and won.[30]

---

[25] Fidon, Mwombeki, "The Theology of the Cross: Does it Make Sense to Africans" in *The Gift of Grace: The Future of the Lutheran Theology, eds,* Niels Henrik Gregersen, Bo Holm, et al (Minneapolis: Fortress Press, 2005), 101-114.

[26] Kenneth, Mtata. "Religion and Development: Friends or Foes?" in *Religion: Help or Hindrance to Development?* , ed. Kenneth Mtata (Leipzig: Evangelische Verlagsanstalt, 2013), 23-35.

[27] Paul, John Isaak, "The Church's Prophetic Witness: Social, Economic, and Political Engagement" in *Theological Practices that Matter,* ed. Karin L Bloomquist (Minnesota: Lutheran University Press, 2009), 143-152.

[28] Tenagne, Negusse, "The on Going Discussion" in *"Our Journey in Faith" Lutheran Women in Africa Speak* compiler. Musimbi, R.A. Kanyoro (Geneva: LWF Document, 1991), 6-10.

[29] Elieshi ,Mungure, "Narratives of Sexuality and Hope: An African Woman Perspective" in *Theological Practices that Matter,* ed. Karen L Bloomquist (Minnesota: Lutheran University Press, 2009), 71-78.

[30] Kameeta, "The Church and Poverty", 65-70.

Bishop Kameeta's voice highlights the social role Lutheran churches have played in witness and *diakonia* in different fields. The role is also enabled by deliberate efforts to make lay people participate in church leadership and decision-making: An example can be cited from ELCT in Tanzania, where 'the active layman is becoming more and more a reality… the politician taking full part in the church and in the Synodical Council; the prisons commander as the churchwarden'.[31] The Executive Council of Evangelical Lutheran Church in Tanzania, which is the high decision-making body, has 52 voting members, out of which 24 are lay.[32] Research, educational programmes and advocacy on human rights have been constant concerns in the social witness of the church. In relation to poverty reduction, a specific action plan from Lutheran churches was the 'Arusha Action Plan', which is an outcome of the consultation strategy for confronting poverty.[33] The Lutheran Church in Namibia has implemented the fight against poverty by:

> … having started a training for lay people to do research on the living conditions in the first growing informal settlements, in towns and villages, developed a social security manual for information on how to access support from the government. And a Bishop's Office Development Committee (BODC) was installed whose task is to find ways to ensure the future financial sustainability of the church.[34]

With regard to political issues, Lutheran churches together with other churches in Africa have been in the front line to fight against the apartheid system in South Africa. Also one could refer to the protest of Lutheran churches against the repressive communist government in Ethiopia, especially by the outspoken Lutheran general secretary of the Mekane Yesus Church, the Rev. Gudina Tumsa who, when asked to escape, renounced, saying:

> Here is my Church and my Congregation. How can I, as a Church leader, leave my flock at this moment of trial? I have again and again pleaded with my pastors to stay on… quoting 2 Corinthians 5:15: 'Christ died for all – that those who live should no longer live for themselves but for him who died for them and was raised again. Never ever will I escape.'[35]

It will always be remembered that Tumsa's advocacy later led him into death and he became one of the martyrs of African Christianity.

In several countries, Lutheran churches have launched educational programmes on human rights and responsibilities emphasizing the need of church members to participate in programmes for the transformation of society. This included educative seminars and workshops on election rights especially for the countries which adopted multi-party systems. One of the key intentions of Lutheran churches has been to create an awareness among Christians of their rights in elections and also the need for full participation in electoral processes.

Participation of Lutheran Churches in Diaconical Ministry

In the past, *diakonia* was often performed as charity for health and healing through medical services, prayers, pastoral care and counselling. Today, following the renewal of a more broad-based understanding of participation of the church in the *Missio Dei*, Lutheran churches in Africa have expanded diaconical

---

[31] Josiah M. Kibira, *Church, Clan and the World.* (Uppsala: Almquist and Wiksell,1974), 71.

[32] Information obtained from the 2015 Calendar of the ELCT, entitled: *Kalenda 2015: Kanisa la Kiinjili la Kilutheri Tanzania.* (Mtwara: Ndanda Mission Press, 2014), 13-15.

[33] "Confronting Poverty and injustice in Africa: A Message from the LWF Consultation on Poverty and the Mission of the Church in Africa. Arusha, Tanzania. 4-8 September, 2008".

[34] Kameeta, "The Church and Poverty…", 65-70.

[35] Gudina Tumsa: www.dacb.org/stories/ethiopia/gudina_tumsa.html.

ministries to include actions of solidarity and justice. Not only have hospitals, clinics and centres for people with disabilities, orphans and old people have been founded and constructed by Lutheran churches, but also advocacy and prophetic public voices on issues of justice and solidarity with the disadvantaged have become a regular phenomenon in several churches. Lutheran churches have medical schools and nursing schools for preparing those going to serve in the community in many countries. Concerning the deadly epidemic of Ebola, the Lutheran Church in Liberia, in collaboration with other churches and the government of Liberia, and under the umbrella 'ACT Alliance' (Action of Churches Together), has been going out to every hospital and health centre around the country to distribute Ebola preventives and medical supplies. According to the Bishop of the Lutheran Church in Liberia, 'This act had been part of efforts to demonstrate the love and care of God to his people'.[36]

Lutheran churches also have pioneered to work against HIV/AIDS through different programmes of counselling to both the infected and affected, delivering material services, fighting for the rights of HIV/AIDS orphans, widows and widowers through the work of their human rights desks. Nowadays educational programmes on HIV/AIDS issues are offered in almost all colleges and universities of Lutheran churches.

Participation of Lutheran Churches in Development

One key to understand the participation of Lutheran churches in Africa for social and economic development is the whole area of education. Many informal and formal education programmes have explored different tools and methodologies for economic development in Africa. Local Lutheran parishes, for instance, often provide educational seminars on how to start and sustain small local development projects and skills training. SACCOS (Savings And Credit Co-operative) is a network in which people are taught to save money collectively, to get loans and return loans accordingly. Several churches have also opened banks with the aim of empowering people by getting capital and being enabled to run economic businesses and create jobs.[37] The Lutheran churches in Tanzania in 2005 opened a commercial bank, the objective of which is to reduce poverty through loans to individuals and small business initiatives. During the first year of operation, 35 savings and credit co-operative societies were established under the banks' outreach programme.[38] Improved approaches to sustainable agriculture with modern technologies have also resulted as part of the impact of this project.

The basis of all participation in development work in Lutheran churches is education; therefore Lutheran churches are marked by a sustained commitment for formal education, ranging from pre-primary, vocational, secondary schools, and colleges to universities. It is important to note that the vocational schools and universities of different faculties prepare people of different religions and ideologies to serve the church and community, not only Lutheran church members.[39]

Theological institutions like Tumaini University Makumira or educational institutions of the Ethiopian Evangelical Church Mekane Yesus, together with the Bible schools in almost all 54 Lutheran churches in Africa have produced thousands of native pastors and evangelists who nowadays communicate the gospel in ways appropriate to their cultural traditions thereby leading to more indigenization of Lutheran churches in Africa.

---

[36] Jensen Seyenkulo, "Ebola Not God's Punishment", eds. Revina Judah and Bridget Milton, "Umoja Newsletter", 1 issue 3 (2014).

[37] Dawson Maanga, "The Role of the Church in Development" in *Society and Church in African Christianity,* ed. Benjamin Simon, (Erlangen: Erlanger Reihe Für Mission und Ökumene,2006),98-132.

[38] Shao, "A Response", 71-72.

[39] "First objective of the University", *Tumaini University Makumira Main Campus: Prospectus 2012-2015.*

One important tool for more indigenization of Christianity and the promotion of the social witness of Lutheran Christians is a special programme devoted to the creation of 'cell fellowships', where Small Christian Communities (SCC) emerge[40] which contribute to localizing Lutheran theology. Small Christian base groups like this read the Bible together and interpret it in a way which fits their questions of life and context. They also share their concerns related to living together in the local church or local community and thereby develop a new sense of sharing social responsibilities as one family.

Conclusion

It can therefore be affirmed that Lutheran churches have contributed significantly to the development of the continent in Africa. While there are convincing examples that Lutheran churches have become something like the 'garden of Eden' on the continent, there are also examples and contexts in which the opposite holds true. Lutheran churches, even amongst themselves and within in their own midst, are still facing challenges of being divided into rich and poor, and are struggling with bad leadership, with corruption and the violation of basic human rights.[41] Church members therefore still need more education and training on the 'ownership' of their church, and on participation in social witness, *diakonia* and prophetic public theology. The contextualization of the Lutheran tradition to be relevant and correspond with the African context is therefore an ongoing and an unfinished process. Lutheran churches in Africa are no exception to the principle of *Ecclesia semper reformanda*, which takes shape in continued efforts for self-criticism, self-motivation and self-contextualization.

Bibliography

Anderson, W.B. *The Church in East Africa 1840-1974.* Dodoma: Central Tanganyika Press, 1977.

AMECEA Bishops.' Guidelines for the Catholic Church in Eastern Africa in the 1980s', in *African Ecclesiastical Review* 16, nos. 1, 2 (1974): 9-10

Bagonza, Benson. 'Prophetic Voice of the Church' in *Our Unity and identity: A Collection of Basic Teachings About Our Unity and Identity in the Evangelical Lutheran Church in Tanzania.*65-85. Moshi: Moshi Printing Press, 2013.

Braaten, Carl. E. *Principles of Lutheran Theology.* 2nd. ed, Minneapolis: Fortress Press, 2007.

'Confronting Poverty and injustice in Africa: A Message from the LWF Consultation on Poverty and the Mission of the Church in Africa. Arusha, Tanzania. 4-8 September, 2008.'

Dickinson, Richard, D.N. in 'Development' *Dictionary of the Ecumenical Movement*, edited by Nicholas Lossky, José Miguez Bonino, et al. 2nd ed. 298-303. Geneva: WCC Publications, 2002.

Erwin, Fahlbusch, and Bromiley, Geoffrey William. *The Encyclopedia of Christianity,*Vol.3. Grand Rapids, Michigan: Eerdmaans, 2003.

'First objective of the University', *Tumaini University Makumira Main Campus: Prospectus.*2012-2015.

Forde, Gerhard. *Justification by Faith: A Matter of Death and Life.* Reprint: Mifflintown, Pa.: Siggler Press, 1999.

Full Gospel: History of the Evangelical Lutheran Church in Tanzania 1963-2013. Edited by Godson S. Maanga, Wilson Niwagila et al, Moshi: Moshi Lutheran Printing Press, 2013.

---

[40] SCC is an initiative started by the Association of Member Episcopal Conference of Eastern Africa (AMECEA) as a solution for the participation of local church in the life and work of mission and evangelization. Cf. AMECEA Bishops, "Guidelines for the Catholic Church in Eastern Africa in the 1980s" in *African Ecclesiastical Review* 16 no.1, 2 (1974); 9-10.

[41] *Tackling Poverty, Food Insecurity and Hunger: Guidelines and Tools for Participatory Poverty Studies by Churches in Africa. Poverty and mission of the church in Africa, ed. Elieshi Ayo Mungure* (Moshi: Moshi Lutheran Printing Press,2013), v.

Hildebrandt, Jonathan. *History of the Church in Africa: A Survey.* Achimota, Ghana: Africa Christian Press, 1981.

Isaak, Paul John. 'The Church's Prophetic Witness: Social, Economic, and Political Engagement', In *Theological Practices that Matter.* edited Karin L Bloomquist, 143-152. Minnesota: Lutheran University Press, 2009.

Isichei, Elizabeth. *A History of Christianity in Africa: From Antiquity to Present.* Grand Rapids, Michigan: African World Press, 1995.

Kalenda 2015: Kanisa la Kiinjili la Kilutheri Tanzania. 13-15.Mtwara: Ndanda Mission Press,2014.

Kameeta, Zacharia. 'The Church and Poverty in Africa' in *So the Poor Have Hope, and Injustice Shuts its Mouth: Poverty and the Mission of the Church in Africa.* edited by Karen Bloomquist and Musa Filibus, 65-70. Geneva: LWF Document, 2007.

Kibira Josiah M. *Church, Clan and the World.* Uppsala: Almquist and Wiksell, 1974.

Kibira, Josiah M. 'Has Luther Reached Africa? The Testimony of a Confused Lutheran', In *African Theological Journal 12*(1983):6-15.

Korten, David C. *Getting to the 21st Century. Voluntary Action and the Global Agenda.* West Hartford: Kumarian Press, 1990.

Kudidje, Joshua. 'The Strength and Weaknesses of Present Forms of Diakonia' in *Towards Abundant Life: Official Report of the African Consultation on Diakonia. Nairobi,31st March-7th April,1989.* edited by Joshua A. Kudidje and Kakule Molo, 76-77. Geneva: WCC, 1989

Linquist, Jack E. 'Lutheranism' in *An Introductory Dictionary of Theology and Religious Studies, edited by* Espin, Orlando O. and Nickoloff, James B *792,* Collegeville, Minnesota: Liturgical Press, 2008.

Laizer, Naaman. 'The Communion of God and Man in the Holy Spirit: A Study of the Concept of the Holy Spirit in Contemporary Lutheran Thinking'. ThD. Diss., Hamburg, 1981.

Lugazia Faith K. 'The Relevance of 'Small Lutheran churches in Africa. Articles' in Tanzanian Context: A Lutheran View'. An unpublished paper presented at the Smalkadian Conference, German. June 23rd, 2012.

Luther's Works, edited by Hilton C. Oswald Vol.28. St Louis: Concordia Publishing House, 1973

Maanga, Dawson. 'The Role of the Church in Development' in *Society and Church in African Christianity,* edited by Benjamin Simon, 98-132. Erlangen: Erlanger Fur Mission und Okumene,2006.

Mishkir Japhet Mallum. 'Nigeria: The Lutheran Church of Christ in Nigeria', In *Diaconical Ministry in the Mission of the Church,* edited by Reinhard Boettcher, 99-100. Geneva: LWF Document, 2006

Mtata, Kenneth. 'Religion and Development: Friends or Foes?' in *Religion: Help or Hindrance to Development?* edited by Kenneth Mtata, 23-35. Leipzig: Evangelische Verlagsanstalt, 2013.

Mungure, Elieshi Ayo. 'Narratives of Sexuality and Hope: An African Woman Perspective' in *Theological Practices that Matter, edited by* Karen L Bloomquist, 71-78 Minnesota: Lutheran University Press, 2009.

Mungure, Elieshi Ayo. *Tackling Poverty, Food Insecurity and Hunger: Guidelines and Tools for Participatory Poverty Studies by Churches in Africa. Poverty and mission of the church in Africa,* edited by Elieshi Mungure, Moshi: Moshi Lutheran Printing Press, 2013.

Mwombeki, Fidon. 'The Theology of the Cross: Does it Make Sense to Africans?' in *The Gift of Grace: The Future of the Lutheran Theology.* edited by Niels Henrik Gregersen, Bo Holm et al, 101-114. Minneapolis: Fortress Press, 2005.

Nadar, Sarojini. 'Who's Afraid of Bible Believing Christians?' *in Lutheran Respond to Pentecostalism,* edited by Karen L. Bloomquist, 63-80. Minnesota: Lutheran University Press, 2008.

Negusse, Tenagne. 'The Ongoing Discussion', in *'Our Journey in Faith': Lutheran Women in Africa Speak* compiled by Musimbi R.A. Kanyoro, 6-10. Bulawayo: Baptist Publishing House, 1991.

Niwagila, Wilson. *From the Catacomb to a Self-Governing Church: A Case Study of the African Initiative and the Participation of the Foreign Missions in the Mission History of the North-Western Diocese of the Evangelical Lutheran Church in Tanzania 1890-1965.* 2nd. ed. Hamburg: Verlagan der Lottbek, 1991.

Noko, Ishmael. 'Foreword' in *Diakonia in Context: Transformation, Reconciliation, Empowerment. A Lutheran Contribution to the Understanding and Practice of Diakonia,* edited by Kjell Nordstrokke.5. Geneva: LWF Publications, 2009

Nordstokke, Kjell, 'Introduction' in '*So the Poor Have Hope, and Injustice Shuts its Mouth': Poverty and Mission of the Church in Africa,* edited by Karen Bloomquist and Musa Panti Filibus, 13-14. Geneva: LWF Document, 2007.

Nussbaum, Stan. 'Africa Independent Churches and a Call of the New Three-Self Formula for Mission' in *Freedom and Independence,* edited by S. Nussbaum, 1-8.Nairobi:OAIC,1994.

Olotu, Angela, 'Who is a Lutheran?' in *Our Unity and identity: A Collection of Basic Teachings About Our Unity and Identity in the Evangelical Lutheran Church in Tanzania,* 59-64.Moshi: Moshi Lutheran Printing Press, 2013.

Radio Voice of the Gospel, http://en.wikipedia.org/wiki/Radio_Voice_of_the_Gospel(Accessed January 12th,2015

Sahlberg, Carl-Eric. *From Krapf to Rugambwa: A Church History of Tanzania.* Nairobi: Evangel Publishing House, 1986.

Seyenkulo, Jensen. 'Ebola Not God's Punishment', edited by Revina Judah and Bridget Milton, 'Umoja Newsletter', 1 (2014):3.

Shao Martin,, 'A Response to Zephaniah Kameeta' in '*So the Poor Have Hope, and Injustice Shuts its Mouth': Poverty and Mission of the Church in Africa,* edited by. Karen Bloomquist and Musa Panti Filibus, 71-72. Geneva: LWF Document, 2007.

Shenk, W.R. *Henry-Venn – Missionary Statesman*: Maryknoll. Orbis Books, 1983.

Sicard, S. Von. *The Lutheran Church of the Coast Tanzania 1887-1914.* Lund: Lund Printing Press, 1970.

Tackling Poverty, Food Insecurity and Hunger: Guidelines and Tools for Participatory Poverty Studies by Churches in Africa, edited by Elieshi Ayo Mungure, Moshi: Moshi Lutheran Printing Press,2013

The Book of Concord: The Confessions of the Lutheran church, edited and translated by Theodore G. Tappert, Jarislov Pelikan et al, Philadelphia: Fortress Press, 1959.

'The Diaconical Ministry in the Lutheran Churches' in *Diaconical Ministry in the Mission of the Church,* edited by Reinhard Boettcher, 81-85. Geneva: LWF Document, 2006.

Tsele, Molefe. 'Current Issues in Africa', in *Africa Moving Towards the Eighth Assembly, Harare, edited by* John S. Pobee, 15-20. Geneva: WCC Publication, 1998.

Tuemper, David G. 'The Lutheran Confessional Writings and the Future of the Lutheran Theology' in *The Gift of Grace: The Future of the Lutheran Theology,* edited by Niels Henrik Gregersen, Bo Holm et al, 131-144. Minneapolis: Fortress Press, 2005.

Vähäkangas, Mika. 'On the (Ir)Relevance of Lutheran Theology: Teaching Lutheran Theology in Tanzania', Dialogue: *A Journal of Theology* 47 (2008): 173-175.

(30B) Visages Actuels du Lutheranisme en Afrique

Samuel Frouisou

Introduction

Selon les statistiques récemment publiées par la Fédération Luthérienne Mondiale (FLM), sur son site web, trente une (31) Eglises sur cent quarante cinq (145), y compris deux (02) Eglises membres associées de cette grande famille luthérienne, se trouvent en Afrique. Ces Eglises sont reparties dans vingt trois (23) pays sur les cinquante quatre (54) que compte le continent africain.

Concernant les membres, vingt millions sept cent cinquante deux mille (20 752 000) fidèles sur les soixante douze millions (72 000 000) que comptent les Eglises membres de la FLM vivent en Afrique de nos jours.

Sur le plan de l'action sociale de l'Eglise dans le monde, ces mêmes statistiques indiquent qu'il y a actuellement trente sept (37) projets de développement qui sont soutenus par la FLM, en Afrique. Ce chiffre représente plus de la moitié de tous les projets de développement que la FLM soutient dans le monde entier.

Par ailleurs, il est aussi important de noter que le luthéranisme en Afrique, à l'instar de celui des autres continents, ne saurait se limiter aux seules Eglises membres de la FLM. C'est ainsi qu'en consultant le site web de l'Eglise Luthérienne du Synode de Missouri, dans le cadre de la rédaction de ce supplément à l'article, nous avons dénombré vingt neuf pays en Afrique où cette Eglise de confession luthérienne est active dans le champ de mission, depuis plusieurs décennies. Ce qui suppose que certaines Eglises luthériennes en Afrique sont issues ou partenaires de l'Eglise Luthérienne du Synode de Missouri, et par conséquent, ne font pas nécessairement partie de la FLM.[1]

Mais quelles peuvent être les attentes des lecteurs potentiels d'un article sur 'Les visages actuels du Luthéranisme en Afrique', en ce début du vingt unième siècle, où les grandes convulsions politiques et économiques mondiales affectent tout particulièrement la situation religieuse des pays africains? En d'autres termes, quelle contribution la connaissance des Eglises luthériennes en Afrique peut-elle apporter à la restauration d'une humanité encline aux maux dont elle souffre?

Telle nous semble être la principale préoccupation à laquelle nous tenterons de donner sinon une réponse, du moins une explication, à la lumière de l'article en Anglais de Faith Kokubelwa Lugazia, portant sur le thème de: 'Lutheran Churches in Africa' (Les Eglises luthériennes en Afrique).

Situation actuelle des Eglises luthériennes en Afrique, une duplication des Eglises missionnaires occidentales?

Les Eglises luthériennes d'Afrique sont héritières des divisions du christianisme missionnaire de l'Occident.

Dans son ouvrage intitulé *Manuel Biblique de Halley*, Henry H. Halley écrit: 'Il est impossible de comprendre la situation actuelle de la chrétienté en faisant abstraction de l'éclairage de l'histoire. Mais

[1] Parmi les Eglises luthériennes d'Afrique, plusieurs se réclament ou sont nées de l'engagement missionnaire international de l'Eglise luthérienne du Synode de Missouri, aux Etats-Unis d'Amérique.

malheureusement, l'ignorance quant à l'histoire de l'Eglise est encore plus généralisée que l'ignorance quant à la Bible».[2]

Les Eglises luthériennes d'Afrique auxquelles nous nous intéressons dans ce supplément d'article sont des Eglises issues pour la plupart, sinon toutes, des Sociétés des Missions occidentales, elles-mêmes fondées suite aux mouvements de réveil datant de la fin du dix-neuvième siècle et du début du vingtième siècle.

Il s'agit, en fait, des très jeunes Eglises assez tardivement nées de l'éveil de l'esprit et de l'action missionnaires parmi les luthériens, membres des Eglises historiques d'Allemagne, des pays Scandinaves et d'Alsace, ainsi que des Eglises de migrants, nées de l'implantation de colons venus d'Europe en Amérique du Nord, en Amérique latine, en Australie et même en Afrique australe (Afrique du Sud et Namibie).

Ainsi, des œuvres d'évangélisation et d'action sociale provenant des pays dits 'chrétiens' de confessions luthériennes, sont nées des jeunes Eglises luthériennes totalement dépendantes des 'Eglises mères' sur tous les plans.

Les compromissions certainement stratégiques de ces 'Eglises mères' avec les régimes coloniaux, en vue d'implanter des nouvelles Eglises en Afrique, ont souvent condamné ces Eglises ou Sociétés des Missions fondatrices à reproduire en terre africaine des idéologies de domination des 'Eglises mères' sur les 'jeunes Eglises'. En d'autres termes, les Eglises ou Sociétés des Missions occidentales fondatrices, des Eglises luthériennes d'Afrique, ont pour la plupart transféré leurs rivalités nationales, sociologiques, linguistiques voire doctrinales en Afrique, favorisant ainsi l'émergence des Eglises luthériennes complètement déconnectées des réalités locales, à l'instar des jeunes nations africaines dont les indépendances politiques furent octroyées par les nations colonisatrices comme un cadeau empoisonné.[3]

Dans ces conditions, faut-il s'étonner que partout dans ces Eglises luthériennes en Afrique, on entende parler des querelles, des divisions et des luttes de leadership, qui prennent parfois une tournure tribaliste ou régionaliste ? La plupart de ces conflits naissent des incompréhensions entre leaders de ces Eglises sur le sens de la mission de l'Eglise chrétienne dans le monde. Il faut le relever pour le déplorer que ces conflits qui rendent les fidèles mal à l'aise dans les Eglises luthériennes en Afrique sont généralement sans lien avec l'essentielle de la mission de l'Eglise universelle qui est de faire des hommes et des femmes 'de toute nation, de toute tribu, de tout peuple et de toute langue»,[4] de disciples du Christ ?

Les questions cruciales des divisions qui déchirent les Eglises chrétiennes en général et les Eglises luthériennes d'Afrique, en particulier, rendent de plus en plus difficile l'accomplissement de la mission holistique de l'Eglise en terre africaine, de nos jours. Car, dans l'ordre missionnaire du Ressuscité de Pâques qui fonde toute mission chrétienne: 'Allez donc, de toutes les nations faites des disciples, les baptisant au nom du Père, du Fils et du Saint-Esprit, leur apprenant à garder tout ce que je vous ai prescrit', cf. Matthieu 28: 20, tout être humain, quel qu'il soit et quelle que soit son origine, doit faire l'objet de considération de la part de l'Eglise, et être ainsi traité comme digne créature de Dieu et potentiel citoyen du royaume à venir.

C'est dans ce sens que, dans la Bible, on n'hésite pas à regarder avec amour et considération sans feinte, tous ceux et toutes celles qui ne connaissent pas le vrai Dieu Libérateur et son plan du salut révélé en son Fils Jésus-Christ, mais, qui pour une raison ou une autre, se trouvent impliqués dans l'accomplissement du plan de Dieu pour le salut de l'humanité tout entière. Aussi, le roi perse Cyrus, fut-il salué comme envoyé de Dieu pour libérer les captifs d'Israël de l'oppression babylonienne, au sixième siècle avant JC.[5]

---

[2] Henry H. Halley, Manuel Biblique de Halley, Editions VIDA, Miami, Florida, 1982, p. 855.

[3] Quand on considère les relations conflictuelles entre anciennes métropoles et leurs colonies, on est en droit de penser que les nations colonisatrices n'étaient pas prêtes à rompre les liens de vassalité qu'ils ont entretenus avec leurs colonies pendant plusieurs siècles.

[4] Apocalypse de Jean, 7:9.

[5] Esaie, 44:28-45:5.

Les stratégies des sociétés des missions protestantes occidentales mises en place entre les dix-huitième et dix-neuvième siècles, qui ont consisté en la division des terres de mission, et donc de l'Afrique, en zones d'implantation de nouvelles Eglises, tout en en suivant rigoureusement les systèmes politiques coloniaux qui visaient, de façon implicite, l'extension des cultures nationales dans les pays à évangéliser, ont favorisé la naissance des Eglises à tendances tribalistes et régionalistes en Afrique.

Mais, de nos jours, compte tenu des relations généralement tendues que vivent certaines Eglises luthériennes d'Afrique[6] avec leurs 'Eglises mères' devenues 'partenaires», depuis les années 1990, il est très difficile d'apprécier ce qui se fait dans ces Eglises de nos jours. Depuis le retrait des missionnaires de la gestion des jeunes Eglises d'Afrique, les lieux de rencontre entre ces Eglises ne se limitent plus seulement aux réunions de Consultation bilatérale, mais s'étendent aux Assemblées générales des organismes regroupant plusieurs Eglises nationales, à l'instar de la FLM. Aujourd'hui, il apparait clairement que la mission authentique de l'Eglise en Afrique ne peut plus se contenter de relations paternalistes qui ont souvent caractérisé les relations entre les 'Eglises mères' de l'Occident et les 'jeunes Eglises' d'Afrique.

Sur le plan purement ecclesial,[7] l'objectif principal de toute entreprise missionnaire, bien que souvent ternie par d'autres préoccupations telles que l'exploitation des ressources naturelles ou l'action colonisatrice en territoires conquis par l'impérialisme international, reste la création d'une Eglise locale, là où les nouveaux membres se regroupent pour persévérer dans la prière et dans la communion fraternelle, selon qu'il est écrit dans le livre des Actes 2: 42-47. Parmi les missionnaires luthériens qui ont œuvré sur le continent africain, on en a vu qui étaient tellement préoccupés par cet objectif spirituel que l'évolution sociale ou matérielle des populations évangélisées était considérée comme une œuvre diabolique.

Cette attitude des missionnaires luthériens fut l'objet d'une critique sévère de la part des chrétiens luthériens africains. Mais quoi qu'on en dise, les résultats sont là et parlent d'eux-mêmes: de l'action des missionnaires luthériens en Afrique sont nées des Eglises luthériennes, dirigées par les Africains eux-mêmes de nos jours.

Au sujet de savoir comment se portent ces Eglises aujourd'hui, et quelle en est l'action, tant sur le plan national qu'international, c'est une autre question que nous nous proposons de traiter dans le point suivant portant sur le luthéranisme africain et le dialogue interreligieux.

Le luthéranisme et le dialogue interreligieux en Afrique

La culture et la religion sont les deux domaines dans lesquels l'être humain s'exprime et se situe vis-à-vis de la nature et du créateur. Pour les Africains, les deux domaines sont si liés qu'on peut affirmer, sans grand risque de se tromper, que la culture africaine est religieuse et que la religion africaine est spirituelle. Ainsi, 'longtemps considérées avec une certaine condescendance, et même comme des simples survivances, (…) les religions se sont révélées, depuis le début du troisième millénaire, comme l'un des défis les plus formidables lancés à la civilisation économiste et technocrate qui semble dominer le monde aujourd'hui».[8]

---

[6] Certaines Eglises luthériennes d'Afrique, à l'instar de l'Eglise Fraternelle Luthérienne du Cameroun (EFLC), de l'Eglise Evangélique Luthérienne du Cameroun (EELC), de l'Eglise Evangélique Luthérienne en République Démocratique du Congo (EEL/RDC), pour ne citer que celles-ci, toutes membres de la FLM, vivent des situations des schismes depuis les années 1990, suite aux retraits du personnel missionnaire de la gestion des biens meubles et immeubles de ces Eglises.

[7] Il convient de noter que l'article de Faith K. LUGAZIA dont nous rédigeons ici un supplément, porte sur « Les Eglises luthériennes d'Afrique'.

[8] Jean Paul Messina et Jaap van Slageren, Histoire du christianisme au Cameroun Des origines à nos jour Approche œcuménique, Editions Karthala et CLE, Paris et Yaoundé, 2005, 15.

Pour ce qui concerne la pastorale dans les Eglises luthériennes d'Afrique, les pasteurs africains, à la suite de leurs 'pères-missionnaires' comprennent leur rôle, avant tout, comme des guides spirituels et dispensateurs des grâces divines au peuple de Dieu dont ils sont les bergers. Mais, pour plusieurs parmi nous[9] aujourd'hui, le ministère pastoral est un business qui se fait au dépens des chrétiens. C'est vrai que, dans la plupart des cas d'abus d'autorité ou de mauvaise gestion relevés chez les pasteurs luthériens, on remarque souvent ceux-ci y sont poussés par des mauvaises structures de gestion, elles-mêmes résultant des systèmes d'organisation des Eglises luthériennes qui ne favorisent l'esprit du partage fraternel, de la solidarité africaine et de la collégialité ministérielle telle que définie à travers les saintes Ecritures (voir 1 Corinthiens 12).

Plusieurs exemples des conflits qui déchirent les Eglises luthériennes en Afrique aujourd'hui impliquent des pasteurs qui servent des intérêts égoïstes et partisans, au détriment des intérêts de toute la communauté, et surtout de ceux des plus faibles dans l'Eglise.

Mais quel devrait être le rôle des Eglises luthériennes dans un contexte de pluralité religieuse en Afrique aujourd'hui?

Pour que les Eglises luthériennes d'Afrique aujourd'hui jouent, de manière efficiente et efficace, leur rôle de libératrices de l'être humain créé à l'image de Dieu, mais vite pris en otage par les forces destructrices du mal, elles doivent éviter, au maximum, de suivre la voie empruntée par les missionnaires occidentaux au cours du dix-neuvième siècle pour évangéliser les peuples africains. Elles doivent adopter une approche qui prenne en considération les aspirations profondes de la société africaine dans sa globalité. Car, selon le Chef de services de la communication de African Enterprise, une organisation chrétienne engagée aux cotés des Eglises chrétiennes d'Afrique dans la proclamation de l'Evangile dans les grandes villes africaines, Sello Kau,[10] les premiers missionnaires venus de l'Europe et de l'Amérique pour évangéliser les Africains ont manqué d'utiliser le moyen le plus indiqué qu'est l'héritage culturel des Africains pour leur donner l'opportunité de se libérer eux-mêmes.

A l'analyse, les églises chrétiennes doivent prendre au sérieux la manière avec laquelle elles présentent l'Evangile aux Africains de nos jours. La prédication de l'Evangile en Afrique doit premièrement viser à restaurer à l'Africain sa dignité totale et, deuxièmement, l'amener à affirmer son identité africaine longtemps perdue à cause d'une fausse et inadéquate annonce de l'Evangile par des messagers qui étaient soit mal intentionnés ou alors mal informés sur la vie culturelle et religieuse des Africains.

Mais, malheureusement, dans la plupart des Eglises luthériennes engagées dans l'évangélisation de l'Afrique aujourd'hui, la tendance est d'utiliser les méthodes employées par les mouvements charismatiques qui pullulent en Amérique ou dans certains pays d'Europe, mouvements qui souvent naissent dans ces pays, en réaction contre une sécularisation envahissante qui ne laisse aucune place à l'expression de la foi chrétienne, dans ces sociétés matérialistes. Les responsables des Eglises luthériennes d'Afrique, engagés dans cette œuvre de mission holistique de l'Eglise aujourd'hui, ne font malheureusement aucun effort pour adapter ces méthodes aux besoins spécifiques des communautés africaines, et le résultat que cette imitation servile produit, ce sont les divisions observées partout dans ces Eglises issues des Sociétés des Missions luthériennes occidentales.

Comme l'a si bien relevé Sello Kau, l'Eglise en Afrique aujourd'hui a besoin de former 'des cadres qui sont authentiquement Africains et qui n'aspirent pas de devenir Européens ou Américains à la peau noire, des cadres qui comprennent leur identité africaine et qui s'engagent à restaurer à leurs peuples leur pouvoir spirituel, intellectuel et économique qui leur a été arraché, afin que cesse chez nous cette culture de dépendance'.[11]

[9] Je fus moi-meme consacré comme pasteur dans l'Eglise Evangélique Luthérienne du Cameroun, le 13 Mai 1993, á Ngaoundéré.

[10] "What is the role of the Church in the African Renaissance?" by Sello Kau, AE, Pietermaritzburg, October, 2000.

[11] Kau Sello, "What is the role of the Church in the African Renaissance?", AE, Pietermaritzburg, October, 2000.

Vu le contexte actuel de la multiplication des conflits internes dans les Eglises luthériennes en Afrique, on peut sans grand risque de se tromper, affirmer que les Eglises luthériennes en Afrique sont mal préparées à l'exercice du dialogue interreligieux. Car, pour la plupart coupés des réalités de la vie sociale et économique du continent, et préoccupés par la défense des intérêts égoïstes d'ordre tribal et régional, la majorité des leaders des Eglises luthériennes en Afrique, sont incapables d'impacter les grandes décisions qui visent à résoudre les crises multidimensionnelles liées aux problèmes de sécurité, de la paix et du développement durable auxquels l'humanité tout entière fait face de nos jours.

Les Eglises luthériennes d'Afrique et la problématique du développement durable

Dans les sociétés postmodernes, la notion du développement durable est devenue une priorité des priorités, une nécessité impérieuse qui affecte tous les domaines de la vie humaine. Mais les mobiles qui y conduisent sont multiples et varient selon le domaine où l'on se positionne. Pour certains, seul compte l'apport des sciences dites exactes ou expérimentales, pour arriver à bon port. Priorité devrait être donnée dans ce cas à l'apport des spécialistes du béton armé.[12]

Pour d'autres, toutes les contributions, de quel que domaine que ce soit sont les bienvenues dans la bataille pour le développement durable. Il s'agit donc ici de savoir quelle peut être ou quelle doit être la contribution des Eglises luthériennes d'Afrique dans ce combat pour un mieux-être, d'abord en Afrique, et ensuite dans le monde?

Aujourd'hui, chaque fois qu'on parle de l'Afrique, nous voyons d'emblée un continent en mal de changement. Le visage que le continent africain offre au reste du monde n'est rien d'autre que celui d'un continent acculturé, déculturé même, et à cheval entre une tradition dont personne ne se souvient avec exactitude et une postmodernité qui échappe même à ses propres inventeurs-propagateurs.

L'Afrique apparait en réalité comme un dépotoir des vieilles idéologies occidentales qui maintiennent ses populations dans le statut quo, et ceci sur tous les plans économique, politique, culturel et religieux. C'est ainsi que sous l'occupation étrangère, plusieurs fois centenaire, les peuples africains ont perdu la faculté de disposer d'eux-mêmes, tant sur le plan économique, politique, culturel que religieux. Dans ce sens, quelle doit être la contribution des communautés chrétiennes, à l'instar des Eglises luthériennes d'Afrique?

La réponse à cette interrogation n'est certes pas facile à donner vu le contexte dans lequel évoluent les Eglises luthériennes de nos jours, contexte dans lequel la question du bien-être ou du développement est perçue exclusivement sur le plan matériel.

Mais si le développement signifie aussi: 'promesse et projet d'humanisme, promotion de la dignité de l'homme lié à l'intention créatrice même de Dieu»,[13] le besoin et la nécessité pour les Eglises chrétiennes en général, et les Eglises luthériennes d'Afrique en particulier se confirment et se font plus que jamais. Car dans ce contexte d'aliénation et d'oppression de toutes sortes, rien ne parait plus urgent que le fait d'être reconnu comme être humain créé à l'image de Dieu. Redonner à l'être humain sa véritable dimension qui le place par le fait même, au centre de tout processus de développement durable, devrait être la priorité des priorités de toute action chrétienne digne de ce nom.

---

[12] C'est une position largement justifiée par les politiques gouvernementales en matière d'octroi des bourses d'études supérieures et le mépris que ces mêmes gouvernements coloniaux et néocoloniaux réservent aux études des sciences sociales telles que la théologie qui forme les pasteurs des Eglises chrétiennes comme agents développeurs des communautés chrétiennes locales.

[13] Penoukou E. J., Eglises d'Afrique: Propositions pour l'avenir, Karthala, Paris, 1984.

Conclusion

En guise de conclusion, nous dirons que la crise multidimensionnelle que traverse le monde aujourd'hui est avant tout une crise d'ordre moral et spirituel. Par conséquent, la responsabilité des institutions religieuses, à l'instar des Eglises luthériennes, en vue de contribuer positivement à la résolution de cette crise, est vivement attendue.

Mais la pertinence des solutions proposées par les confessions religieuses pour résoudre cette crise dépend dans une large mesure de la capacité des leaders de ces institutions religieuses à intégrer dans leurs méthodes de travail des éléments positifs de la culture de tous les peuples du monde.

De l'analyse des situations actuelles des Eglises luthériennes en Afrique, il ressort que le christianisme dans son enveloppe occidentale tel qu'il se présente dans la vie des Eglises luthériennes, elles-mêmes victimes des multiples divisions en leur sein, n'est pas la voie indiquée pour contribuer au rayonnement du témoignage chrétien en Afrique et dans le monde de nos jours.

En fin de compte, la contribution attendue des Eglises luthériennes pour un développement du monde ne peut se faire que par la prédication de l'Evangile à l'Homme tout entier, être culturel fait de corps, d'âme et d'esprit. Car l'Evangile n'est pas seulement libérateur d'une oppression historique qui trouve son origine dans la chute de l'Homme au jardin d'Eden (Genèse 3), mais il est aussi et surtout, le plan de Dieu pour le renouvellement de toutes choses en son Fils, Jésus-Christ (2Corintiens 5: 17-19).

Bibliography

La Bible en français et en anglais publiée sous le titre Bible Edition bilingue, Alliance Biblique Universelle, Nairobi, 2010.

HALLEY H., Henry, Manuel Biblique de Halley, Editions VIDA, Miami, Florida, 1982.

KAU, Sello, 'What is the role of the Church in the African Renaissance?', AE, Pietermaritzburg, October, 2000.

PENOUKOU, E. Julien, Eglises d'Afrique: Propositions pour l'avenir, Karthala, Paris, 1984.

MESSINA J. Paul et SLAGEREN van Jaap, Histoire du christianisme au Cameroun Des origines à nos jour Approche œcuménique, Editions Karthala et CLE, Paris et Yaoundé, 2005.

Websites:

www.lutheranworld.org

www.lcms.org

www.clba.org

(31) ANGLICAN CHURCHES IN AFRICA

Henry Mbaya

Anglicanism: General Characteristic Features

The Anglican Church is officially known as the 'Anglican Communion', with its Catholic, Protestant, and Liberal elements. In its modern form, it can be said to have definitively developed (arguably, continues to develop in the 21st century)[1] during the various phases of the Reformation in the mid-sixteenth century in England.[2] One distinctive feature that symbolically and historically serves to unite the Anglican Churches in Africa and worldwide is the See of Canterbury.[3] Acknowledged as the most senior Anglican cleric in the Anglican Communion, the incumbent Archbishop of Canterbury occupies the esteemed position of the 'first amongst equals', *primus inter pares*.[4] More significantly, it is the Anglican bishops' worldwide consultation at the Archbishop's Lambeth Palace in London every ten years that appears to express a more visible sense of unity and purpose[5] of the Anglican Churches.

Much like the Roman Catholic Church, Anglican ministry rests on the three Holy Orders of deacon, priest and bishop,[6] which it cherishes as a legacy from the Primitive Church. The episcopate defines its polity. Richard Norris asserted, 'In the office of bishop, the apostolic function of oversight, which includes and indeed derives from the power of ordination, is continued... (and) is normative for the government of the Church.'[7] The Anglican Church believes in sacerdotal priesthood. Yet like all other Reformation churches, the Anglican Church believes in the priesthood of all believers and affirms the sufficiency and primacy of the 'Scripture' in its ministry.[8] Unlike Roman Catholicism where the Papacy is the magisterium, the teaching authority in the Anglican Church is the episcopate and by extension the priesthood.

The *Book of Common Prayer* (BCP),[9] originally written and compiled by Thomas Cranmer, the Archbishop of Canterbury, continues to be an important nexus between the Anglican Churches on the African continent and global Anglicanism. It is translated into almost all local African languages – in some respects adapted, yet still retaining English texture. To a greater extent, the BCP continues to define Anglican liturgical and spiritual life worldwide.[10]

---

[1] Paul Avis, Ch. 3, "What is Anglicanism?" in Steven Sykes and John Booty (eds) *The Study of Anglicanism*, Ch. 3.
[2] Avis, "What is Anglicanism", 413.
[3] WSFS Pickering, "The sociology of Anglicanism" in Steven Sykes and John Booty (eds) *The Study of Anglicanism*, 364-375., esp. 363.
[4] Pickering, "Sociology of Anglicanism", p. 364-375. esp. 363.
[5] Pickering, "Sociology of Anglicanism", p. 364-375, esp. 363.
[6] Paul Bradshaw, "Ordinals" in Steven Sykes and John Booty (eds), *The Study of Anglicanism*, 143-153, esp. 147.
[7] Richard Norris, "Episcopacy" in Steven Sykes and John Booty (eds), *The Study of Anglicanism*, 269-309, esp. 303-304.
[8] RH Puller, "Scripture" in Steven Sykes (eds), *The Study of Anglicanism*, 79-89.
[9] W Taylor Stevenson, "Lex Orandi – Lex Credendi" in Steven Sykes and John Booty (eds), *The Study of Anglicanism*, 174-188.
[10] John Pobee, "Newer Dioceses of the Anglican Communion – Movement and Prospect" in Steven Sykes and John Booty (eds), *The Study of Anglicanism*, 393-404, esp. 395-396.

Anglicanism on the Continent

The Anglican Church came to and spread on the continent largely through British colonial expansion in the late nineteenth and twentieth centuries. Besides displaying some of the features just noted, modern Anglicanism on the African continent manifests itself in various shades and colours. These range from Anglo-Catholic ('High Church'), those that seek to preserve traditions very much akin to Roman Catholic to Evangelical, to 'Low Church', such as those churches that originated from the work of the Church Missionary Society (CMS)[11] and (since the 1980s) the 'Pentecostal' and 'Charismatic' churches.[12] For instance, in the Anglican province of Southern Africa (South Africa, St Helena, Lesotho, Swaziland, Namibia, Mozambique and Angola) it was the Society for the Propagation of the Gospel in Foreign Parts (SPG) and in Central Africa the Universities' Mission to Central Africa (UMCA) who planted Anglo-Catholic spirituality and doctrine. For the rest of the continent it was dominated by 'Evangelical' spirituality, a legacy of the CMS. Thus Anglicanism closely associated with British colonialism has been an enduring legacy that, in various degrees, albeit more symbolically, continues to define faces of Anglicanism on some parts of the continent.

The socio-cultural, religious and political upheavals which have been taking place in the societies of the northern hemisphere since the 1980s have not left the Provinces in Africa unscathed. The ordination of women has been a point of difference between some Anglican Churches in the northern hemisphere and some in Africa.[13] More enduring has been the issue of human sexuality which has been a cause of controversy and acrimony, consequently plunging the Anglican Communion into disarray.[14] Devising the Covenant for member churches to subscribe to and the Windsor Report has been one way in which the Anglican Church has sought to respond to the crisis.[15] On international, regional and local levels, the Anglican Church has always been involved in ecumenical schemes.[16]

Regional Surveys of the Anglican Churches

The Church of the Province of Central Africa

Unlike East African Provinces, where national states constitute independent provinces, a conglomeration of national states makes up the Church of the Province of Central Africa (CPCA): Malawi, Zambia, Zimbabwe and Botswana. The Anglican Church in Malawi traces its origins to the work of the UMCA missionaries who were inspired by David Livingstone in 1857.[17] Initially, it started a mission station at Magomero in Southern Malawi in 1861. Short-lived, the mission was re-established more permanently, this time at Likoma in Malawi, started with initiatives from Zanzibar in 1885.[18]

---

[11] Perry Butler, "From the Early Eighteenth Century to the Present Day" in Stephen Sykes and Booty (eds) *The Study of Anglicanism,* 28-47, esp. 32-35.

[12] Personal experience.

[13] See http://blogs.telegraph.co.uk/news/timstanley/100190726/women-bishops-the-anglican-church-is-paralysed-by-its-conflicting-obsessions-of-equality-and-consensus/

[14] Miranda Katherine Hassett, *Anglican Communion in crisis: how Episcopal dissidents and their African allies are reshaping Anglicanism*, Princeton: Princeton University Press, 2007.

[15] www.anglicancommunion.org/commission/covenant/

[16] Butler, "From the Early Eighteenth Century to the Present Day", *The Study of Anglicanism*, 28-47, esp. 44.

[17] See John Weller and Jane Linden, *Mainstream Christianity to 1980 in Malawi, Zambia and Zimbabwe*, Gweru: Mambo Press, 1984.

[18] Weller and Linden, *Mainstream Christianity*, 127.

From 1910, its work extended from Malawi to Eastern and Central Zambia, and eventually to the rest of the country.[19] The Anglican Church in Zimbabwe and in Botswana derive from the work of missionaries from South Africa at the end of the nineteenth century.[20] Networks of schools, hospitals and other institutions established by the missionaries continue to play a vital role in the life of these communities.[21]

Unlike other Provinces in Africa which have fixed archiepiscopal sees, the CPCA has a rotating archiepiscopal see.[22] Perhaps partly because of the differences in political situations in different national states, the bishops have not been able to speak collectively on crucial issues affecting member states.[23] However, the dioceses in the province have all stood in solidarity with the main section faction of the Church in Zimbabwe persecuted by the renegade and deposed bishop Norbert Kunonga with his faction.[24]

The Anglican Church of Southern Africa (ACSA)

Anglican missionary work started more earnestly in the Cape with the arrival of Bishop Robert Gray (1809-72) who was instrumental in establishing the Anglican Church in Southern Africa (ACSA) in 1847.[25] Himself influenced by Anglo-Catholic spirituality, Gray chose an Anglo-Catholic missionary society, the Society for the Propagation of the Gospel (SPG), rather than the evangelical CMS which operated in East and West Africa. In this respect, the religious orders, one of the fruits of the Oxford Movement, played an important part in Gray's scheme of evangelisation.[26] From the start, Gray desired the church to develop a synodical government, the conceptualisation of the church as 'Primitive' and 'Apostolic', dubbed as the bastion of Anglo-Catholicism.[27] In 1853, bishops for Grahamstown and Natal were appointed. To these, St Helena was added in 1859. In 1853, Cape Town was elevated to a metropolitan see with Gray becoming a metropolitan bishop.[28] The John Colenso (Bishop of Natal) controversy, trial and finally his deposition triggered moves towards establishing the legal autonomy of the Anglican Church in South Africa.

The Provincial Synod in 1870 legally established the Anglican Church in South Africa as autonomous.[29] 'As the established church in England, the Anglican Church sought a prominent position for itself in Cape Town, just as it did in other colonial capitals.'[30] The presence of a much larger white settler population in South Africa, as compared with any other territory on the continent, placed the missionary church in a position where it would seem that almost from the start the race issue became more conspicuous in its missionary endeavour. Various incumbents of the archiepiscopal See of Cape Town (and of other sees) have been in the forefront in the protest against apartheid injustices towards black people. In many respects, in this role, the leadership of the Archbishops of Cape Town appear to have been acknowledged by other ecumenical church leaders. 'In some parts of the Anglican Communion, as in South Africa or Uganda, there has been outright condemnation of the policies and actions of governments.'[31]

---

[19] Weller and Linden, *Mainstream Christianity*, 167.
[20] Weller and Linden, *Mainstream Christianity*, 65.
[21] Weller and Linden, *Mainstream Christianity*, 71-75.
[22] Personal knowledge.
[23] Personal knowledge.
[24] Personal knowledge.
[25] Cecil Lewis and G B Edwards, *Historical Records of the Church of the Province of South Africa*, London: SPCK, 1934, 31.
[26] Peter Hinchliff, *The Anglican Church in South Africa*, London: Darton, Longman and Todd, 1963, 226.
[27] Frank England, "Tracing Southern African Anglicanism", in Frank England and Torquil Paterson (eds), *Bounty in Bondage*, Johannesburg: Ravan Press, 1989, 21-22.
[28] Neill, *Anglicanism*, 303.
[29] Lewis and Edwards, *Historical Records of the Church of the Province of South Africa*, 1934, 90-91.
[30] Richard Elphick and Rodney Davenport eds., *Christianity in South Africa*, Los Angeles, Berkeley: California Press, 1997, 329.
[31] Hinchliff, *History of the Anglican Church in South Africa*, 363.

Just like other missionary churches in South Africa, in ACSA a network of its private schools and hospitals and other tertiary institutions in some cases run by the members of the religious orders, like St Peter's College, Rosettenville, and subsequently, St Peter's, a constituent college of the Federal seminary in Alice (and to a much lesser extent St Paul's in Grahamstown and St Bede's in Mthatha) became critical seed-beds which nurtured incipient socio-political consciousness.[32] A network of its hospitals, schools and orphanages and churches have equally played a very important role in the mission of the church.

In the 1960s, the national trend for independence and indigenization paved the way for the consecration of African bishops. Starting with Alpheus Zulu in 1966, the pace increased from 1976. The ensuing years saw other Africans being elevated to episcopal position, notably Desmond Tutu, who subsequently became the first Black Archbishop of Cape Town in 1987.[33] Ndungane styled his episcopacy on the fight against social issues such as poverty.[34] The Province also established the Fikelela AIDS Project to fight HIV/AIDS.[35]

The Provinces of East Africa

The Church of Uganda

The start of the Anglican Church in Uganda is associated with Henry Morton Stanley who, on 14th April 1875, brought Uganda to the attention of the British through a letter that is said to have been written to the *Daily Telegraph* appealing for teachers by Kabaka Mutesa I, King of Buganda.[36] Consequently in 1877 the first group of CMS arrived at the Ugandan capital.[37] With the arrival of the Scottish Engineer Alexander Mackay in 1878, CMS started to take root.[38] Almost from the start in 1879 the church in Uganda was embroiled in rivalry and competition between the CMS missionaries and the White Fathers and the Muslims.[39]

Following the accession of the vicious and weak King Mwanga in 1884, bitter persecution followed and thirty Roman Catholic and Anglican converts were martyred.[40] Meanwhile, approaching Uganda from the East, Bishop James Hannington was speared to death, together with some of his company.[41] A civil war raged in 1892 between CMS and the White Fathers, which in fact entailed the pro-British and pro-French parties. It ended with the proclamation of the Protectorate in 1894.[42]

The Diocese of Uganda was established in 1899 and Tucker became the first Bishop of Uganda.[43] The first Ugandans were ordained in 1893, and Buganda was established as the centre of evangelisation in the Great Lakes Area. Though the idea to form a province first came up in 1927, its implementation stalled, for

[32] See OM Suberg, *The Anglican Tradition in South Africa, A Historical Overview*, UNISA: Pretoria, 1999, 67.
[33] Suberg, *The Anglican Tradition in South Africa, A Historical Overview*, 100-102.
[34] http://wbi.worldbank.org/wbi/content/archbishop-njongonkulu. Accessed 29/01/15.
[35] www.fikelela.org. Accessed 21/01/15.
[36] Neill, *Anglicanism*, 345.
[37] Holger Bernt Hansen, *Mission, Church and State in a Colonial Setting. Uganda 1890-1925*.New York: St Martin's Press, 1984, 12.
[38] Neill, *Anglicanism*, 345.
[39] Neill, *Anglicanism*, 345-346.
[40] Timothy Yates, "Anglicans and Missions" in Stephen Sykes and John Booty (eds), *The Study of Anglicanism*, London: SPCK/ Fortress Press, 1988, 429-441.
[41] Neill, *Anglicanism*, 346.
[42] Neill, *Anglicanism*, 346.
[43] www.wdl.org/en/item/9947/.

one reason: the evangelical dioceses of CMS could not envisage themselves being part of the very strongly Anglo-Catholic dioceses of the UMCA.[44]

At the turn of the twentieth century, the Anglican Church in Uganda experienced considerable growth and education was its most notable achievement. In 1913, the first Bishop Tucker Theological College was established in Mukono, which has transformed into the Uganda Christian University.[45] In 1897, the CMS took a lead in public health with the establishment of the Mengo Hospital.

In the 1950s, the emerging local church leadership began to replace the expatriate hierarchy. 'The consecration of four African assistant bishops in Uganda by the Archbishop of Canterbury on 15 May in 1955 drew worldwide attention to the progress that had been made.'[46] Like other churches in the region, the Ugandan Church was affected by the great Revival movement.[47] In spite of its close association with the state, the Anglican Church in Uganda has been outright in its condemnation of the policies and actions of the government.[48]

The Anglican Church of Kenya (ACK)

Currently, thirty-one dioceses constitute the Anglican Church of Kenya. Initial Anglican missionary activity in the area is associated with Dr Johann when he landed in Mombasa, Kenya in 1844.[49] The Anglican Church in Kenya was formally founded as part of the diocese of Eastern Equatorial Africa (Uganda, Kenya and Tanzania) in 1884, with James Hannington as the first bishop. In 1898, the diocese was split into two, with the new diocese of Mombasa governing Kenya and Northern Tanzania. Like other churches associated with the colonial power, the Anglican missions in Kenya enjoyed a privileged position. Northern Tanzania became a separate province in 1927.[50] The first Christian vocational centre was established in 1959.[51]

Previously part of the Province of East Africa, Kenya became a separate Province in 1970. Manasses Kuria was the Archbishop of Kenya from 1980 to 1994.[52] Since its inception, the Anglican Church of Kenya has been politically active. In the 1950s, the Anglican clergy condemned the Mau Mau rebellion.[53] In the 1980s, when President Daniel Arap Moi rose to consolidate his position by restricting political opposition, Anglican leaders spoke in defence of civil rights.[54] Bishop David Gitari's condemnation of the control of elections in his sermon in 1987 provoked criticism from Moi's supporters, while other church leaders joined Gitari's criticisms.[55] The Church is involved in a number of social activities such as the Nicholas Development Centre and the Board of Social Services that seeks to address justice, peace and reconciliation.[56]

Following criticism by Bishops Henry Okullu and Alexander Muge of the handling of the investigation into the murder of the foreign minister Robert Ouko, Muge was killed in suspicious circumstances,

---

[44] Neill, *Anglicanism*, 347.
[45] www.newvision.co.ug/news/661376-from-a-humble-start-ucu-leaps-forward.html, accessed 14/05/14.
[46] Neill, *Anglicanism*, 347.
[47] Hinchliff, *Anglicanism*, 351-363, esp. 363; Neill, *Anglicanism*, 347.
[48] Hinchliff, *Anglicanism*, 351-363, esp. 363.
[49] www.oikoumene.org/en/member-churches/anglican-church-of-kenya, accessed 14/05/2014.
[50] www.oikoumene.org/en/member-churches/anglican-church-of-kenya.
[51] www.ackenya.org/ack/history.html.
[52] http://uir.unisa.ac.za/bitstream/handle/10500/3252/dissertation_kagema_d.pdf.
[53] http://uir.unisa.ac.za/bitstream/handle/10500/3252/dissertation_kagema_d.pdf.
[54] http://asq.africa.ufl.edu/files/Adar-Munyae-Vol-5-Issue-1.pdf.
[55] http://publishing.cdlib.org/ucpressebooks/view?docId=ft9h4nb6fv&chunk.id=d0e3551&toc.id=d0e3551&brand=ucpress.
[56] www.ackenya.org/institutions/st_nicholas.html.

following government's threats.[57] This made Bishop Gitari and others more determined to be critical of Moi's leadership and fight for multi-party democracy.[58] Since he became Archbishop in 1995, Gitari continued to fight for civil rights. Using this position, he promoted constitutional changes such as presidential term limits and fairer elections.[59]

The Anglican Church of Tanzania (ACT)

The Anglican Church of Tanzania (ACT) is unique because it holds two contrasting church traditions, Anglo-Catholic and Evangelical.[60] The Anglo-Catholic missionaries of the UMCA planted the Church in Southern Tanganyika in the mid-nineteenth century. The rest of the country was evangelised by CMS. The Anglican Church of Tanzania came into being as an autonomous body in 1970.[61] 'It covers the geographical area of the United Republic of Tanzania with 18 dioceses in the mainland and one in the Islands of Zanzibar and Pemba.'[62]

The ACT runs several organisations including the Mothers Union, the Tanzania Anglican Youth Organization, and the Anglican Evangelistic Association. Some of its prominent institutions include the theological colleges (St Philip's located at Kongwa and St Mark's in Dar es Salaam), Mtumba Rural Women's Training Centre, Vocational Training Centre, Central Tanganyika Press and the Literature Organization (also known as the Dar es Salaam Bookshop).[63] It is involved in various social welfare and health projects as well as youth training and retreat centres.[64] It also runs programmes on HIV/AIDS, tuberculosis and malaria, and community development.[65]

The Episcopal Church of the Sudan

The Episcopal Church of the Sudan owes its origins to two events. Firstly, indirectly through the initial contacts of the first CMS missionary party to Uganda in 1878 with Charles Gordon, the Governor of Equatoria (a region in the south of present-day South Sudan) at a time when the Comboni Roman Catholic Missionaries were establishing themselves.[66] Secondly, following the death of Gordon at the hands of the Mahdi, CMS in London set up a mission named the CMS Gordon Memorial Sudan Mission. Later known as the Northern Sudan Mission, it was first administered as part of the Egyptian Mission.[67]

Llewellyn Gwynne, appointed to pioneer the mission, arrived in Sudan in 1899, the centenary of CMS.[68] The CMS principle of self-governing, self-supporting and self-propagating was put into place. The Bible Churchman's Missionary Society (today called Crosslinks), a smaller missionary organisation, broke away from CMS in 1922, claiming that the CMS had become too liberal. It worked in Kapoeta (1933-41) and Opari (1935-40).[69]

Gwynne had his mandate to work in Northern Sudan amongst the Arabs, in spite of his desire to work in the south. He worked almost exclusively amongst the settler communities (of the British and others). He

---

[57] http://faculty.vassar.edu/tilongma/Sabar.html.
[58] http://uir.unisa.ac.za/bitstream/handle/10500/6620/Parsitau.pdf?sequence=.
[59] http://uir.unisa.ac.za/bitstream/handle/10500/6620/Parsitau.pdf?sequence=.
[60] www.tarlings.com/anglican_church_of_tanzania.htm.
[61] www.oikoumene.org/en/member-churches/anglican-church-of-tanzania.
[62] www.oikoumene.org/en/member-churches/anglican-church-of-tanzania.
[63] www.oikoumene.org/en/member-churches/anglican-church-of-tanzania.
[64] www.tarlings.com/maternity_wing_progress_report_(phase_5).htm#cookhouse_store_and_laundry.
[65] www.oikoumene.org/en/member-churches/anglican-church-of-tanzania.
[66] Samuel E. Kayanga and Andrew C Wheeler, *But God is Not Defeated: Celebrating the Centenary of the Episcopal Church of the Sudan 1899-1999*,Paulines Publications: Nairobi, 1999, 52.
[67] Kayanga and Wheeler, *But God is Not Defeated*, 52.
[68] Kayanga and Wheeler, *But God is Not Defeated*, 52.
[69] Kayanga and Wheeler, *But God is Not Defeated*, 51.

put up important structures, one of which was the Cathedral of All Saints in Khartoum in 1912, very close to his residence. From the 1940s on, the Southern Sudanese and some Nuba came to the north, seeking work and education. They became members of these congregations.

However, in 1901 and 1902 he conducted exploratory journeys in the south, during which time the Catholics and the Presbyterian American Missionaries were establishing themselves.[70] In 1905, a team of missionaries arrived to open a mission in the south at Bor in 1906.[71] Following some difficulties they abandoned it and then relocated it to Malek in 1908. Slow but steady progress established Malek as the foundation of the Episcopal Church of Sudan.[72] The first unbaptised convert was in 1916. However, it was in 1917 that a convert, Jon Aruore Thon, was baptised.[73]

From 1906, when they established the first station at Malek, till 1947, twelve more major mission stations were established, which in the meantime led to other offshoots. The results of Paul Gibson developing an indigenous ministry in the 1930s at Yei bore fruit when in 1941 Bishop Morris Gelsthorpe ordained Daniel Deng Atong and Andarea Avurusi Apaya as the first deacons.[74] Bishop Oliver retired as bishop of Sudan in 1974 and was succeeded by Elinana. In 1976 Elinana was elected the first Sudanese archbishop.[75] In 1976, the ECS became an independent province from Canterbury, and four dioceses were created.[76] The Anglican Church in South Sudan has been involved in brokering peace between the government and rebels.[77]

West Africa

The Church of the Province of West Africa

The Anglican Church in Nigeria started in 1846 among the Yoruba when Henry Townsend (CMS) and Adjai Samuel Crowther entered Abeokuta.[78] Following the award of an honorary degree, an audience with the Queen and consecration in Canterbury, the freed slave, Samuel Adjai Crowther, was elevated to the episcopate in 1864,[79] becoming the first indigenous (missionary) bishop in the modern period to his native land, and worked among the Yoruba. 'A great Christian pioneer, translator and pastor, became not so much the sign that Africans were ready for leadership (as Venn had intended) as a symbol of the supposed failure of African leadership… It was another example of an Anglican desire for an indigenous church and ministry.'[80]

With the Treaty of Lagos in 1852 that guaranteed protection to the missionaries, the Rev. Charles Gollmer moved to Lagos. Soon the church spread into the neighbouring territories. 'The progress in Abeokuta, Lagos and Ibadan was so encouraging that the CMS formally established its Yoruba Mission on 3 October 1852.' Initially started at Abeokuta in 1853, the teacher training institution was transferred to Lagos in 1867.[81]

---

[70] Kayanga and Wheeler, *But God is Not Defeated*, 53.
[71] Kayanga and Wheeler, *But God is Not Defeated*, 63.
[72] Kayanga and Wheeler, *But God is Not Defeated*, 64.
[73] Kayanga and Wheeler, *But God is Not Defeated*, 65.
[74] Kayanga and Wheeler, *But God is Not Defeated*, 100.
[75] Kayanga and Wheeler, *But God is Not Defeated*, 168.
[76] Kayanga and Wheeler, *But God is Not Defeated*, 190.
[77] https://geoconger.wordpress.com/category/anglican-church-news/episcopal-church-of-the-sudan, Accessed 21/01/15.
[78] C.O. Taiwo, *Diocese of Ijebu, A Commemorative Brochure, 25 years Silver Jubilee, 1976-2001*, 47.
[79] Neill, *Anglicanism*, 340.
[80] Timothy Yates, "Anglicans and Missions" in Stephen Sykes and John Booty (eds), *The Study of Anglicanism*, London: SPCK/ Fortress Press, 1988, 435.
[81] Taiwo, *Diocese of Ijebu, A Commemorative Brochure, 25 years Silver Jubilee,1976-2001*, 48.

A significant development in the work of CMS itself was the founding of the CMS Training Institution at Oyo on 18th March 1896, as the institution by the same name which was phased out in Lagos. Oyo became a great attraction to Ijebu primary school leavers to train as teachers and catechists. When the Institution offered advanced courses, Ijebu students went there for courses leading to the ordained ministry and to an LTh at the University of Durham.[82] 'That institution, now known as St Andrew's College of Education, Oyo, has made a considerable contribution to the church and state in Nigeria.'[83]

The West African Province was established in 1951 in Freetown, Sierra Leone, by the Archbishop of Canterbury. With the exception of the Missionary District of Liberia, itself supported by the American Church, the five dioceses of British origin constituted a Province.[84] In February 1979, the new Church of Nigeria became a separate Province while the Dioceses of Accra, Kumasi, Liberia, Gambia, Guinea and Sierra Leone (later Freetown) continued in the Province of West Africa. To enhance evangelism and to ease administration ten provinces were created in 2003.

The Episcopal Church of Burundi

The Anglican Church of Burundi currently has five dioceses, with a sixth one in the process of being created. It owes its origins to the work of the Church Missionary Society who had come from Rwanda in the 1930s. Its rapid growth has been attributed to the East African Revival and medical and educational work. The CMS set up its first mission stations at Buhiga and Matana in 1935 and Buye in 1936. The diocese of Buye, covering the whole country, was created in 1965 and the first local bishop was consecrated that year.

In 1975 and 1985 new dioceses were created. They formed part of the Francophone Province of Burundi, Rwanda and Boga-Zaïre. In 1989, it was resolved to divide the province into three: Burundi, Rwanda, and Zaïre (now Democratic Republic of Congo). The resolution led to the creation of the Province of the Episcopal Church of Burundi in 1992. Since 2005 the official name is the *Province of the Anglican Church of Burundi*. Among its main concerns are peace and reconciliation, repatriation of refugees and displaced people, community development, literacy and education, and HIVAIDS. There are at least an estimated 900,000 Anglicans out of an estimated population of just over 9 million in Burundi.[85]

The Anglican Church has played an important role in reconciliation after the 1994 genocide. Speaking during a visit to Bujumbura in 2014, the Archbishop of Canterbury, Justin Welby said, 'The Anglican Church of Burundi sets before its people an inspiring vision of what can be achieved with the rebuilding of the country and the rebuilding of communities. We are committed to working with you for the long-term stability of the nation to enable real development to take place.'[86]

The Province of Rwanda

The Anglican Church in Rwanda owes its origins to the work of two missionary doctors of the CMS, Arthur Stanley Smith and Leonard Sharp, during their trips to the Eastern area of Gisaka in Rwanda in 1914-1916 from Uganda.[87] In 1922, they reached Rukira via Kigali, and Geoffrey Holmes, a British army captain, laid the foundations of the mission hospital at Gahini in 1925.[88] In 1926, Reverend Harold Guillebaud baptized the first converts at Gahini. Guillebaud started the translation of Christian literature

---

[82] Taiwo, *Diocese of Ijebu, A Commemorative Brochure, 25 years Silver Jubilee, 1976-2001,* 48.
[83] Taiwo, *Diocese of Ijebu, A Commemorative Brochure, 25 years Silver Jubilee, 1976-2001,* 49.
[84] Neill, *Anglicanism*, 341.
[85] www.anglicanburundi.org.
[86] www.archbishopofcanterbury.org/articles.php/5239/archbishop-justin-in-burundi-anglican-church-of-burundi-offers-inspiring-vision, Accessed 210/01/15.
[87] www.ear-acr.org, accessed 20 July 2014.
[88] www.ear-acr.org, accessed 20 July 2014.

into Kinyarwanda.[89] Other missions were started in 1931 by the Rev. Geoffrey Holmes at Kigeme and the Rev. Cecil Verity and Dr Tarbot at Shyira. From 1935 to 1936, there was a spiritual revival that started at Gahini and expanded to East Africa, Europe and other parts of the world, including India.[90]

In just over 26,340 square kilometres there are over one million Anglicans, out of a rapidly growing population of 8.7 million.[91] The former Ruanda Mission established its first station at Gahini in 1925 and grew through the revival of the 1930s and 1940s, with the first Rwandan bishop appointed in 1965.[92] Eight dioceses have up to forty parishes, which in turn consist of 15-20 congregations. Like all strata of Rwandan society, the church suffered through the 1994 genocide, and it is a major priority of the church to replace clergy through training.[93]

The Anglican Church in Zaïre/Congo

The start of the Anglican Church of Congo, *Eglise Anglicane du Congo* (EAC) in Zaïre is certainly unique in Africa in that it did not originate from the efforts of the white missionaries, but rather from the ministry of the Ugandan evangelist Apolo Kivebulaya in 1896 and other Ganda people who had become Christians through the work of the CMS. The church reached the Shaba region in 1955, but evangelization did not progress on a large scale until the 1970s.[94] For a decade since 1910, it was a small church with close ties with the Church of Uganda and the episcopalian Churches of Rwanda and Burundi.[95] From 1960 onwards, the EAC experienced growth to a greater extent due to migration of members from Uganda. The first diocese in Congo was established in 1972.[96] Its headquarters was in Boga, with its CMS bishop, Philip Ridsdale.

In 1976, the churches in Nord-Kivu came under the jurisdiction of a new diocese based on Bukavu. Their bishop was Bezaleri Ndahura.[97] By 1975, the EAC was present in most of the towns in Nord-Kivu and Irumu.[98] Following independence, the Church expanded and formed dioceses as part of the Province of Uganda, Burundi, Rwanda, and Boa-Zaïre. The new Province was inaugurated in 1992 and changed its name in 1997.[99] 'By 2000 the EAC had spread through Ituri, Kivu, Maniema, Katanga and the Kasais and around Kisangani and Kinshasa, from where it spread to Brazzaville.'[100] The EAC is a constitutive member of the Protestant 'umbrella' organisation, *the Eglise du Christ au Congo* (ECC). In a country where 85% of schools and health centres are run by religious institutions, the EAC provides agriculture, health and educational services.[101]

Bibliography

Paul Avis, 'What is Anglicanism?' in Steven Sykes and John Booty (eds.)*The Study of Anglicanism*, London: SPCK/ Fortress Press, 1988.

Paul Bradshaw, 'Ordinals' in Steven Sykes and John Booty (eds.), *The Study of Anglicanism*, London:

---

[89] www.ear-acr.org, accessed 20 July 2014.

[90] www.ear-acr.org, accessed 20 July 2014.

[91] www.anglicancommunion.org/tour/province.cfm?ID=R, accessed 20 July 2014.

[92] www.anglicancommunion.org/tour/province.cfm?ID=R, accessed 20 July 2014.

[93] www.anglicancommunion.org/tour/province.cfm?ID=R, accessed 20 July 2014.

[94] www.anglicancommunion.org/tour/province.cfm?ID=C4, accessed 20 July 2014.

[95] Emma Wild-Wood, *Migration and Christian Identity in Congo (DRC)*, Leiden, Boston: Brill, 2013, 14.

[96] Wild-Wood, *Migration and Christianity*, 74.

[97] Wild-Wood, *Migration and Christianity*, 74.

[98] Wild-Wood, *Migration and Christianity*, 49.

[99] www.anglicancommunion.org/tour/province.cfm?ID=C4, accessed 8 August 2014.

[100] Wild-Wood, *Migration and Christianity*, 14-15.

[101] Wild-Wood, *Migration and Christianity*, 15.

SPCK/ Fortress Press, 1988.
Perry Butler, 'From the Early Eighteenth Century to the Present Day', in Steven Sykes and John Booty (eds.), *The Study of Anglicanism*, London: SPCK/ Fortress Press, 1988.
Richard Elphick and Rodney Davenport eds., *Christianity in South Africa*, Los Angeles, Berkeley: California Press, 1997.
Frank England, 'Tracing Southern African Anglicanism', in Frank England and Torquil Paterson (eds.), *Bounty in Bondage*, Johannesburg: Ravan Press, 1989.
Holger Bernt Hansen, *Mission, Church and State in a Colonial Setting Uganda 1890-1925*, New York: St Martin's Press, 1984.
Miranda Katherine Hassett, *Anglican Communion in crisis: how Episcopal dissidents and their African allies are reshaping Anglicanism*, Princeton: Princeton University Press, 2007.
Peter Hinchliff, *The Anglican Church in South Africa*, London: Darton, Longman and Todd, 1963.
Samuel E. Kayanga and Andrew C Wheeler, *But God is Not Defeated, Celebrating the Centenary of the Episcopal Church of the Sudan 1899-1999*, Nairobi: Pauline Publications, 1999.
Cecil Lewis and G B Edwards, *Historical Records of the Church of the Province of South Africa*, London: SPCK, 1934.
Stephen Neill, *Anglicanism*, Middlesex: Harmondsworth/Penguin, 1958.
Richard Norris, 'Episcopacy' in Steven Sykes and John Booty (eds.), *The Study of Anglicanism,* London: SPCK/ Fortress Press, 1988.
W.S.F.S. Pickering, 'The sociology of Anglicanism' in Steven Sykes and John Booty (eds.),*The Study of Anglicanism,* London: SPCK/ Fortress Press, 1988.
John Pobee, 'Newer Dioceses of the Anglican Communion – Movement and Prospect' in Steven Sykes and John Booty (eds.), *The Study of Anglicanism*, London: SPCK/ Fortress Press, 1988.
R.H. Puller, 'Scripture' in Steven Sykes (eds.), *The Study of Anglicanism,* London: SPCK/ Fortress Press, 1988.
W. Taylor Stevenson, 'Lex Orandi – Lex Credendi' in Steven Sykes and John Booty (eds.), *The Study of Anglicanism,* London: SPCK/ Fortress Press, 1988.
O.M. Suberg, *The Anglican Tradition in South Africa, A Historical Overview*, UNISA: Pretoria, 1999.
C.O. Taiwo, *Diocese of Ijebu, A Commemorative Brochure, 25 Years Silver Jubilee, 1976-2001.*
John Weller and Jane Linden, *Mainstream Christianity to 1980 in Malawi, Zambia and Zimbabwe*, Gweru: Mambo Press, 1984.
Emma Wild-Wood, *Migration and Christian Identity in Congo (DRC),* Leiden, Boston: Brill, 2013.
Timothy Yates, 'Anglicans and Missions' in Stephen Sykes and John Booty (eds.), *The Study of Anglicanism*, London: SPCK and Fortress Press, 1988.

For Further Reading

A.M. Allchin and Colin Craston, *Open to the spirit: Anglicans and the experience of renewal,* London: Published for the Anglican Consultative Council by Church House, 1987.
Gregor Cuthbertson and H.L. Pretorius, *Frontiers of African Christianity: essays in honour of Inus Daneel,* Pretoria: University of South Africa, 2003.
Miranda Katherine Hassett, *Anglican Communion in crisis: how Episcopal dissidents and their African allies are reshaping Anglicanism*, Princeton: Princeton University Press, 2007.Mark Noll, *Clouds of Witnesses: Christian voices from Africa and Asia,* Nystrom, Carolyn, Downers Grove, Ill.: IVP Books, 2011.
Ian S. Markham, *The Wiley-Blackwell Companion to the Anglican Communion*, Chichester, West Sussex, UK: Malden, MA: Wiley-Blackwell, 2013.
J.W.C. Wand, *The Anglican Communion; a survey*, London, New York: Oxford University Press, 1948.
Kevin Ward, *A History of Global Anglicanism,* Cambridge, New York: Cambridge University Press, 2006.

(32) Methodist Churches in Africa

Kennedy Owino and Mvume H. Dandala

Introduction

This chapter presents a study of Methodism and Methodist churches in Africa. We describe the understanding of 'Methodism' and its central theological beliefs concentrating on key regions within Africa. This chapter briefly traces the historical background of Methodism, its development and spread into Africa, highlighting the main strands and some implications of the Methodist witness in Africa.

Historical and Theological Setting of Methodism as a Movement

The history of Methodism is often traced back to eighteenth-century England through the work of the Wesley brothers and their four Oxford friends.[1] Although this position is not contested by many modern historiographers, Davies strongly argues that it is quite wrong to think of Methodism as coming into existence in the time of the Wesleys because it was already a 'recurrent form of Christianity'[2] in other regions. Overall, what is undisputable is the central place of John Wesley in the Methodist story[3] with the name 'Methodist' having its origins with the Wesley brothers and their friends. The earlier expressions of occurrences known as Pietism can be traced from German-speaking Europe alongside similar 'revivals' in the early seventeenth century. These were characterised by different groups who claimed experiences of spiritual rebirth, as Charles and John Wesley would later speak of in 1738.[4] Generally, the Wesleys gave Methodism its expansion and permanence.[5]

Theologically, the key characteristics of a Methodist were given by John Wesley in his definition:

> By Methodists, I mean a people who profess to pursue (in whatsoever measure they have attained) holiness of heart and life, inward and outward conformity in all things to the revealed will of God; who place religion in a uniform resemblance of the great object of it; in a steady imitation of Him they worship, in all His imitable perfections; more particularly in justice, mercy and truth, or universal love filling the heart, and governing the life.[6]

A concise combination of particular theological beliefs and practices are therefore accepted as key Methodist doctrines and teaching. These include:[7]

---

[1] Holden, William Clifford. *A brief history of Methodism and of Methodist missions in South Africa* (London: Wesleyan-Methodist Book-Room, 1887), 37; John Wesley *A Short History of Methodism* (London: Sold at the Foundry, 1765), 367-372.
[2] Rupert E. Davies, *Methodism*. (London: Epworth Press, 1976), 11-12.
[3] Kenneth Cracknell and Susan J. White. *An Introduction to World Methodism* (Cambridge: Cambridge Press, 2005), 5
[4] William J. Abraham and James Kirby (eds), *The Oxford Handbook of Methodist Studies* (Oxford: Oxford University Press, 2009), 11.
[5] Davies, "*Methodism*", 11.
[6] John Wesley, *The Works of John Wesley* (Volume VIII) (Grand Rapids: Zondervan Publishing House, 1872), 352. See also summary on what is distinctive about Methodism in Barrie W. Tabraham, *The Marking of Methodism*. (London: Epworth Press, 1995), 173-178.
[7] See Methodist Conference, *The Message and the Mission of Methodism*. (London: Epworth Press, 1943), 18-28 and Thomas Langford A. *Practical Divinity: Theology in the Wesleyan Tradition.* (Nashville: Abingdon Press, 1983).

Salvation by faith as knowledge of the love of God that brings the assurance of a restored relationship between humankind and God.

Assurance as the 'knowing' of the divine forgiveness and that a believer is in a right relationship with God.

Holiness as a processes (goal) towards Christian perfection which Wesley termed 'perfect love' (sanctity).

Fellowship, understood as the definition of church expressed through life in worship, prayer, Holy Communion, and band and class meetings.

For Wesley, with these key theological beliefs, doctrine, spirit and discipline must be located within 'a burning passion, deep, faithful, unbounded passion for the authentic Christ'.[8]

Major Developments and Spread of Methodism

The rise and spread of early Methodism (1725-1739) can be sketched in three stages.[9] These are summarised as: the initial rise of Methodism was in Oxford; the second rise had its origin in 'Oxford Methodism' of the 1720s[10] mainly characterised by the spiritual search for salvation. This was during Wesley's time in Georgia and was launched in a Moravian context,[11] which became key to the development of Wesley's concept of the church in mission to the world.[12] The third rise was in London, where Wesley acquired and established models for both personal spiritual renewal and corporate organizational developments in Methodism.[13] The eighteenth century therefore establishes the numerical explosion and denominational separation of Methodism from the then established Anglican Church.[14] It is from later Methodist religious societies that Methodism developed from what was understood as a mass movement into features of a 'great Church' worldwide. The two centuries following the death of John Wesley saw the spread, splits and reunions of the Methodist movement, bringing a spread of Methodism from a small group of devoted believers into Christian churches worldwide.[15]

The task of the Methodist Church as part of the One, Holy and Catholic Church is to proclaim the love of God in the person of Jesus Christ. In other words, Methodism was 'raised up to spread "Scriptural holiness" (a life of communion with God expressed in perfect love to God and others), throughout the land (worldwide)'.[16] With such understanding, Marquardt notes that the two main channels by which Methodism spread were through mission: first, by being faithful and serving in love and second, by stating mission initiatives done by intentional planning and preparing.[17]

---

[8] Purity Malinga and Neville Richardson (eds), *Rediscovering Wesley for Africa* (Silverton: Methodist Church of Southern Africa, 2006), 5.

[9] Richard P. Heitzenrater, *Wesley and the People Called Methodists.* (Nashville: Abingdon Press, 1995), 33.

[10] Methodism as it later emerged in England goes back to the 'Oxford Methodists' (a group of young men led initially by Charles Wesley), from whom the Wesleys took habits and customs into what later became Methodism proper. Various labels such as 'The Enthusiasts,' 'The Bible Moths,' and 'The Holy Club' were attached to the group by sarcastic undergraduates. The one nickname that stuck was 'The Methodists,' probably given because of the remarkably methodical way of life which they followed. See Davies, *Methodism,* 44.

[11] Frederick Dreyer. *The Genesis of Methodism.* (London: Associated University Presses, 1999), 29.

[12] Heitzenrater, "*Wesley and the People Called Methodists*", 60.

[13] Heitzenrater, "*Wesley and the People Called Methodists*", 77.

[14] For a detailed study of the eighteenth-century early Methodism's context See Abraham and Kirby, "*The Oxford Handbook of Methodist Studies*", 4-29.

[15] Abraham and Kirby, "*The Oxford Handbook of Methodist Studies*", 85.

[16] Methodist Conference, "*The Message and the Mission*", 17.

[17] Abraham and Kirby, "*The Oxford Handbook of Methodist Studies*", 90.

Methodist migrants therefore became carriers of the Christian gospel with mission initiatives moving in the ways and courses of Anglo-American colonization, civilization and European influence, starting from Britain and North America, with the West Indies, then Gibraltar and Sierra Leone; Australia and South Africa becoming the first expanses where Methodist missions took roots.[18] Today, one will find Methodist churches of all typologies in almost all countries in Africa. In the section that follows, we briefly look at the arrival and spread of Methodism in Africa. We apply a regional approach for this task.

Methodism in Africa

Methodism in Africa is not monolithic. It is therefore important to take note of the main divisions of the Methodist family in Africa who consider themselves heirs of the Wesleyan tradition. These groupings have included: Methodist churches with their origins from British Wesleyan Methodism or the United Methodist Church (UMC) (with its roots in American Methodism), or the African Methodist Episcopal (Zion) tradition.[19] The West Africa Central Conference of the UMC includes the United Brethren in Christ started in Sierra Leone mission in 1855, Liberia (1816) and Nigeria. The African Methodist Episcopal Church (which also forms part of the global African Methodist Episcopal Church) goes back to a mission in 1820. Today, it encompasses conferences in Sierra Leone, Liberia, Ghana, Nigeria, and Ivory Coast. The Africa Central Conference of the United Methodist Church includes annual conferences in Eastern and Western Angola (established in 1885), East Africa (Burundi, established in 1984), Mozambique (1890) and Zimbabwe (1897). The Methodist churches deriving from American Methodist mission work include the Congo Central Conference and Districts, Zimbabwe, and Mozambique and Southern Africa.[20]

North Africa

The work of Methodism in North Africa was started towards the end of the nineteenth century by missionaries from the USA.[21] It is believed that the Holiness Movement Church in Egypt started in 1899 and united with the Free Methodist Church in 1959 to serve several churches and missions in various African countries in the Middle East.[22] The United Methodist churches are mainly in Algeria and Tunisia (and have become a part of the Protestant Church of Algeria since 1972), mainly belonging to the Central Conference of Southern and Central Europe.[23] It was then that the Methodist Church merged with most of the other Protestant denominations to form the Protestant Church of Algeria, and Methodist work in North Africa became reorganized as a district of the Annual Conference Switzerland-France-North Africa.[24] Before Algeria's independence in 1962, the Methodist Church in North Africa became organized as an annual conference, enjoying a period of peace, and owning mission stations, schools and clinics.[25] Eight years after independence, the events that followed dispersed Christians with half the Methodist missionaries deported, children's homes and boarding schools were forced to close, and church properties taken over by the state.[26] Today, the district of North Africa also includes the Methodist presence in Tunis and Tunisia, consisting of five congregations with four clergy, serving 185 members.[27]

---

[18] Abraham and Kirby, "*The Oxford Handbook of Methodist Studies*", 90.
[19] Abraham and Kirby, "*The Oxford Handbook of Methodist Studies*", 701.
[20] Abraham and Kirby, "*The Oxford Handbook of Methodist Studies*", 90.
[21] United Methodist Churches. North Africa. www.umc-europe.org/north_africa_e.php (Accessed 27-08-2015).
[22] Abraham and Kirby, "*The Oxford Handbook of Methodist Studies*", 91.
[23] Abraham and Kirby, "*The Oxford Handbook of Methodist Studies*", 91.
[24] United Methodist Churches, "North Africa", (Accessed 27-08-2015.
[25] United Methodist Churches, "North Africa", (Accessed 27-08-2015).
[26] United Methodist Churches, "North Africa", (Accessed 27-08-2015).
[27] United Methodist Churches, "North Africa," (Accessed 27-08-2015).

West Africa

The inauguration of a 'Christian experiment' in Sierra Leone between the years 1787 and 1792 brought opportunity for mission outreach in West Africa, and as Sanneh argues, Sierra Leone's 'explicit evangelical matrix' was Methodist in nature.[28]

SIERRA LEONE

In Sierra Leone, most settlers were Protestant Christians who were generally Baptists or Methodist.[29] It is noted that an early community of African Methodists was first introduced in Sierra Leone by a group of liberated slaves (often referred to as Krio) from London and Nova Scotia who then settled in Freetown in Sierra Leone in 1792.[30] These ex-slaves (mainly Methodist lay people), formed themselves into organised religious classes and were later joined by British Methodist preachers in 1811 who strongly supported the building of the Methodist Church in Sierra Leone.[31] Even though the Methodist Church in Britain and Ireland assisted in the development of Methodism in all the provinces with established representation in all sections of Sierra Leone,[32] the contributions of lay Methodist people must never be underestimated in the spread of Methodism in Africa as a whole. Sierra Leone holds the oldest Christian Church in tropical Africa, followed by Liberia and the Gambia, yet records the most discouraging church growth.[33] Out of a population of 75,000 in Sierra Leone in the 1900s, 55% were Christians. The Methodist church remained part of the British Conference, and only became autonomous in 1967. Today the family of the Methodist churches in Sierra Leone has a membership of over 50,000 in 244 congregations with more than 85 ordained ministers.[34]

GHANA

The Methodist Church in Ghana emerged from a Christian study group (school) formed in 1831 and owes its beginnings to a Ghanaian priest – Philip Quaque.[35] Between 1835-1838, the Rev. Joseph R. Dunwell arrived at the Gold Coast (Ghana) with several other British Methodist missionaries; from who Thomas Birch Freeman (a Wesleyan missionary of Anglo-African pedigree widely recognised as the 'father of West African Methodism') was the only survivor. He later became the founder of the first Methodist Church along the Gold Coast, Ghana, between the years 1838-1890. Mission work later extended to Lagos and Badagry, in Nigeria[36] with the first Methodist Societies established among the Asante and Yoruba people.[37] According to Bartels, the seventeen fellowships (Societies – *my addition*) with seven hundred Christians (converts) that Freeman had founded by 1850 became the nucleus of Ghanaian Methodism

---

[28] Abraham and Kirby, "*The Oxford Handbook of Methodist Studies,*" 197.

[29] John Baur. *2000 Years of Christianity in Africa: An African Church History* (Second Revised edition). (Nairobi: Paulines Publications, 1998), 110.

[30] Abraham and Kirby, "*The Oxford Handbook of Methodist Studies,*" 701.

[31] Abraham and Kirby, "*The Oxford Handbook of Methodist Studies,*" 90.

[32] World Council of Churches. "*Methodist Churches in Sierra* Leone." https://www.oikoumene.org/en/member-churches/methodist-church-sierra-leone (Accessed 17 August 2015).

[33] Baur. "*2000 Years of Christianity in Africa,*" 265.

[34] World Council of Churches. "*Methodist Churches in Sierra* Leone." (Accessed 17 August 2015).

[35] Elizabeth Isichei. *A History of Christianity in Africa* (Grand Rapids: William B. Eerdmans Publishing Company1995), 167-168.

[36] See Freeman, Thomas Birch, 1809 to 1890 Methodist Ghana/Nigeria. In *Dictionary of African Biography.* www.dacb.org/stories/ghana/freeman_t.html (Accessed 15 August 2015); and The Methodist Church Ghana, www.methodistchurch-gh.org/index.php/the-church/beginning-of-methodism (Accessed 17 August 2015).

[37] Baur, "*2000 Years of Christianity in Africa,*" 117.

which successfully established Circuits which were locally-run in modern Africa.[38] With the help of the British Methodist missionaries, the Methodist Church Ghana has developed over a period of 130 years and gained its autonomy from the British Methodist Conference in 1961.[39] Looking at the consolidation of Methodism in the Ghanaian context, Essamuah highlights how Methodism in Ghana has developed its own Ghanaian identity through contextualisation by 'accepting Methodism on their own terms' thereby reworking the Methodist tradition 'to fit their needs'.[40] Currently, the Methodist Church Ghana is one of the leading churches in the country, with a total membership of over 600,000. The church has 3,814 societies making 17 dioceses, with 1,066 pastors, 15,920 local preachers and 24,100 Lay Leaders.[41]

NIGERIA

The arrival of Wesleyan Methodist Church missionaries responding to the request made for missionaries by freed slaves who had returned to Nigeria from Sierra Leone marked the establishment of Christianity in Nigeria in 1842.[42] Although Methodism arrived in Nigeria at a period when many of its southern kingdoms like the Yoruba were involved in civil wars,[43] mission stations were established in Badagry and Abeokuta and the Methodist church spread to various parts of the country with time. The west of the River Niger and part of the north was known as the Western Nigeria District. The East of the River Niger and another part of the north was referred to as the Eastern Nigeria District. Both of these Districts existed independently of each other until 1962 when they combined to form the Conference of Methodist Church Nigeria.[44] Currently, the Methodist Church Nigeria has over 3.5 million adherents with over 2,000 congregations. The church is headed by the prelate, who presides over the conference consisting of eight archdioceses. Each archdiocese is composed of not less than four dioceses over which an archbishop presides at the archdiocesan council meetings. There are 44 dioceses, each made up of a number of circuits and headed by a bishop who presides over the annual synod.[45] It is important to recognise the efforts made in establishing 'indigenous' assemblies of Methodist models of Christianity in Nigeria. This brought the rise of various movements such as the African Methodist Episcopal Church (Zion), founded on the Gold Coast in 1898, by a Jamaican, Bishop B.J. Small, who first came to West Africa as a sergeant in the West India regiment.[46] Several Methodist revolutionists and nationalists joined the church and they today consider themselves 'Methodist' rather than 'Independent.'[47] Further secession from the Methodist Church occurred

---

[38] See Francis Lodowic Bartels, *The Roots of Ghana Methodism*. Cambridge: University Press, 1965; Baur, *2000 Years of Christianity in Africa,* 117.

[39] For a comprehensive study of mission history of the Methodist Church in post-colonial Ghana see Casely B. Essamuah, *Genuinely Ghanaian: A History of the Methodist Church* Ghana, 1961-2000. Trento: Africa World Press, 2010).

[40] Essamuah, "*Genuinely Ghanaian,*" xxix.

[41] The Methodist Church Ghana, www.methodistchurch-gh.org/index.php/the-church/beginning-of-methodism (Accessed 17 August 2015).

[42] World Council of Churches, *Methodist Church, Nigeria*, Website: https://www.oikoumene.org/en/member-churches/methodist-church-nigeria (Accessed 17 August 2015).

[43] Abraham and Kirby, "*The Oxford Handbook of Methodist Studies,*" 705.

[44] World Council of Churches, *Methodist Church, Nigeria*, https://www.oikoumene.org/en/member-churches/methodist-church-nigeria (Accessed 17 August 2015).

[45] World Council of Churches, *Methodist Church, Nigeria*, https://www.oikoumene.org/en/member-churches/methodist-church-nigeria (Accessed 17 August 2015).

[46] Isichei. "*A History of Christianity in Africa,*" 181.

[47] Isichei. "*A History of Christianity in Africa,*" 181.

in Lagos in 1917 with the formation of the United African Methodist Church (UMAC) that argued for polygamy to be permitted 'as a basic social and economic institution in Africa'.[48]

East Africa

The Methodist missions in East and Central Africa trace their beginnings to 1858 through David Livingstone's influential speech at the University of Cambridge which begged attention to be directed to Africa.[49] Following Livingstone's appeal, it was not Wesleyan Methodists who responded but the United Methodist Free Church under the British Methodists who gave particular attention to missionary work in East and Central Africa, entering Kenya in 1862.[50] Initial attempts to establish mission stations in early 1862-1864 failed following the return to Europe of two Swiss missionaries.[51] Fortunately, the labours of Thomas Wakefield (1836-1901) in Mombasa brought Methodism to the people of Galla in 1866 and in 1870 and baptised their first twenty-one converts in Kenya.[52] Wakefield extended mission work by planting stations among the Mijikenda and the Duruma people of Kenya which led to Methodists establishing two outpost stations at Lamu and Kau in 1884, with three local Christians (Mr During, a Sierra Leonian missionary, Aba Shora and Matthew Shakala) taking oversight.[53] The spread of Methodism is also traced in Central Kenya, with Methodist mission taking place in Meru under the work of J.B. Griffith in 1895.[54] Important to consider is the work of African initiatives in Methodism with specific reference to the Rev. Filio Minoti of Meru in Kenya, who was an exceptional Methodist leader and pastor.[55] Minoti's prominence as leader is seen in his attempt to bridge the gap between Methodism and Meru traditional rituals.[56]

Today, the Methodist Church is well established in most parts of Kenya, as well as in Uganda and Tanzania. Currently, the Methodist Church in Kenya which became autonomous in 1967 is led by a Presiding Bishop with a total of twelve Synods led by bishops, extending to Tanzania Synod and a new Uganda Synod created during the 2015 annual Conference.[57] The Methodist Church in Kenya has over 125 Circuits counting a membership of over 450,000 (and is still growing), with over 919 Societies under 400 ordained ministers for word and sacrament,[58] with missions extending as far as South Sudan, Uganda, Burundi, Rwanda and the Democratic Republic of Congo.

Central Africa

Methodist work in Central Africa began in 1889 through mission work that sought the gospel to speak to the whole person – through churches, schools and clinics. This mission expanded to then north-western Zimbabwe through the work of Edwin Smith who advocated for missionaries in Africa to endeavour to make converts as African Christians and not European Christians.[59] The spread of the United Methodist Church continued through American interest in East and Central Africa, thereby establishing the Congo

---

[48] See Peter B. Clarke, *West Africa and Christianity* (London: Edward Arnold, 1986), 163.
[49] Cracknell and White. "*An Introduction to World Methodism*," 76.
[50] World Council of Churches, *Methodist Church Kenya*. https://www.oikoumene.org/en/member-churches/methodist-church-in-kenya (Accessed 27 August 2015).
[51] William B. Anderson, *The Church in East Africa (1840-1974)* (Nairobi: Uzima Press, 1977), 6-9.
[52] Anderson, "*The Church in East Africa*", 7.
[53] Anderson, "*The Church in East Africa*", 7.
[54] Cracknell and White. "*An Introduction to World Methodism*", 77.
[55] Anderson, "*The Church in East Africa*", 102.
[56] Anderson, "*The Church in East Africa*", 103.
[57] Methodist Church Kenya, https://www.methodistchurchkenya.org (Accessed 24 September 2015).
[58] World Council of Churches, *Methodist Church Kenya* (Accessed 27 August 2015).
[59] Cracknell and White. "*An Introduction to world Methodism*," 78.

Mission Conference in 1896, with a chain of other mission Conferences in Zimbabwe and in neighbouring Mozambique.[60]

Southern Africa

The Methodist Church of Southern Africa (MCSA) has been described as 'One African Church in six countries'[61] with its work and history covering not only South Africa but also Lesotho, Namibia, Swaziland, Botswana and Mozambique.[62] The MCSA therefore stands as one of the largest Wesleyan Methodist Conference in Africa with a huge adherence particularly in South Africa[63] although with a limited presence in Mozambique.[64]

The Methodist community in South Africa numbered just over 2 million in 2005,[65] with the fist record of Methodist conversion and witness in Southern Africa attributed to an Irish soldier – John Irwin, stationed at the Cape in 1795.[66] Overall, early Methodism in South Africa is attributed to Sgt George Middlemiss, a soldier of the 72nd regiment of the British army who became the first (lay) Methodist preacher in Southern Africa in 1806 at the Cape of Good Hope.[67] Hence, Methodism in Southern Africa finds its roots in British Methodism. The first Methodist society in South Africa was established between 1802 and 1807 at the Cape by lay people (Christian soldiers) professing to be Methodists. By 1812, John Kendrick was leader of the small Society in the Cape Colony[68] who thereafter made a request to Britain to send a minister. It was not until 1816 that the first English Methodist missionaries to Southern Africa, Barnabas and Jane Shaw, arrived and established chains of mission stations that saw the spread of Methodism into the interior north.[69] By 1822, Shaw had trained indigenous pastors/evangelists like Jacob Links. The contribution of local laymen and women as Methodist converts who took upon themselves to undertake evangelism strongly established the growth of Methodism in South(ern) Africa. The arrival of the Rev. William Shaw in 1820 at the Eastern Cape[70] enhanced mission work there. He established the first station, Wesleyville, which evolved later into six other stations along the coast;[71] moving further inland among the Xhosa people, to the Natal region by 1842.[72]

Overall, the expansion of Methodism in Southern Africa cannot be completely attributed to the Wesleyan Methodist Missionary Society without taking into account the initiatives of indigenous converts who played a magnificent part in promoting the spread of Methodism into the interior parts of South Africa and its neighbouring South African territories. Following the establishment of the first South African Conference in 1883,[73] later expansion of the Methodist Church followed, led by men such as Samuel

---

[60] Cracknell and White. "*An Introduction to world Methodism*," 78.

[61] The Methodist Church of Southern Africa. www.methodist.org.za/# (Accessed 20 August 2015).

[62] The Methodist Church of Southern Africa. www.methodist.org.za/# (Accessed 20 August 2015).

[63] M. J. S Madise and L. M. Taunyane, *The Methodist Church in Africa*. (Pretoria: UNISA, 2012), 1.

[64] See the entire story on the spread of Methodism into interior South Africa and its territories in Donald Cragg and Joan Millard. *Open Doors: Methodism in South Africa 1883-1933.* (Cape Town: Methodist Publishing House, 2013).

[65] Cracknell and White. "*An Introduction to world Methodism*," 77.

[66] Wessel Bentley and Dion Forster (eds), *Methodism in Southern Africa: A celebration of Wesleyan Mission* (Edleen: AcadSA Publishing, 2008), 23.

[67] Daryl M. Balia, *Black Methodists and White Supremacy in South Africa* (Durban: Midiba Publications, 1991), 14.

[68] See Gordon Mears, *Methodism in the Cape: An Outline*. (Cape Town: Methodist Publishing House, 1973).

[69] See A. E. F. Garrett (ed), *South African Methodism: Her Missionary Witness* (Cape Town: Methodist House, No Date).

[70] Kenneth Cracknell. 'The Spread of Wesleyan Methodism,' in *The Cambridge Companion to John Wesley*, eds. Randy L. Maddox and Jason E. Vickers (Cambridge: Cambridge University Press, 2010), 252.

[71] Baur, "*2000 Years of Christianity in Africa,*" 190.

[72] The Methodist Church of Southern Africa. www.methodist.org.za/# (Accessed 20 August 2015).

[73] Cracknell. 'The Spread of Wesleyan Methodism' 253; and Donald Cragg, *A Spark of Grace: The Wesleyan Methodist Mission in South Africa 1816- 1883.* (Cape Town: Methodist Publishing House, 2011).

Mathabathe, Hans Aapje, David Magatha, Silas Molema, Robert Mashaba, Thomas Gebuza, Daniel Nhlannhla Msimang, Richard Giddy and Robert Ndevu Mashaba, to mention a few.

Within its Southern African context, the spread of Methodism into Namibia was through the Rev. Joseph Wood who went to that country in 1914 as a chaplain. The Rev. Owen Watkins' initiatives on church planting pressed on towards Botswana through the Mahikeng Methodism, and further north towards Zimbabwe and east into Swaziland, with the Rev. John White often considered the father of Methodism in Zimbabwe.[74] The first Methodist missionaries to Swaziland were the Rev. James Allison and Richard Giddy in 1844, whose labours did not yield many fruits. Daniel Nhlanhla Msimang later returned to Swaziland in 1880 and is rightly regarded as the founder of Methodism in Swaziland, greatly commended for having have linked the Swazi style of worship to the gospel.[75] With the influence of Methodism in his early life, the Rev. Robert Ndevu Mashaba (a native of Mozambique) is hailed as the founder of the Methodist Church in Mozambique in 1904 following his conversion in Port Elizabeth and graduation at Lovedale, Alice.[76]

As a member of the World Methodist Council (an association of the churches in Methodist tradition throughout the world), the MCSA is episcopal in nature and is referred to as a 'Connexion' in terms of its organisation. The Connexion is led by a Presiding Bishop and a Connexional executive who also take leadership oversight of the Conference which meets annually as the body that makes key decisions. Currently, the MCSA is made up of twelve District Synods, each led by a bishop. Modelled in the form of early Methodist tradition, the MCSA has over 700 active ministers, 360 Circuits at a local level, with over 3,000 Societies.

Due to socio-economic, ecclesio-political and cultural reasons, there have been several breakaways from mainstream Methodism in Southern Africa leading to formation of African Independent Churches (who longed for a more 'African' style of worship) but still hold onto their Wesleyan roots and traditions. The earliest of such breakaways are those of Nehemiah Tile in 1884 who left to form the Thembu National Church and Mangena Mokone and James Dwane in 1892 forming the Ethiopian Church. Later, the 'Bantu Methodist Church' or 'Donkey Church' (now the Methodist Church in Africa) was formed from a split in 1933, centering on a controversy around money.[77]

Beyond Methodist hymns, prayer meetings, class gatherings and the sacraments, the broad impact of the Methodist movement in Africa can also be seen in its contributions to education and nation-building.

Methodist Influence in Education

It is rightly argued that wherever Methodism has been, its significant contribution to education becomes evident. For example, from the very beginnings of early Methodist missions in Southern Africa, evangelism has gone hand-in-hand with education. As early as 1816, the Rev. Barnabas Shaw trained African youths for leadership, teaching, evangelism and industrial occupations.[78] Flourishing educational centres under Methodist inspiration were later to be seen beginning at Wesleyville, Mount Coke, Morley, Clarkebury and Buntingville which became leading educational centres where thousands were taught, with manual and industrial instructions given.[79] Nelson Mandela is one supremely significant example of a South African Methodist who portrays the influence of the Methodist Church on education and life as 'just

---

[74] See Cragg and Millard. "*Open* Doors," 147-165.
[75] Cragg and Millard, "*Open Doors*."
[76] See the establishment of Methodism in Mozambique in Cragg and Millard. "*Open Doors*".
[77] For a detailed reference on splits in the MCSA see Balia, "*Black Methodists and White Supremacy in South Africa*" (1991); Madise and Taunyane, "*The Methodist Church in Africa*" (2012); Cragg and Millard, "*Open Doors*" (2013).
[78] Garrett (ed), "*South African* Methodism," 74.
[79] Garrett (ed), "*South African Methodism*", 75.

an ordinary person trying to make sense of the mysteries of life'.[80] Mandela's address to the Methodist Conference in 1998, Durban, points out how education has been central to the Methodist mission. He observed:

> Were it not for the mission schools at a time when those who governed had no interest in the educational development of the African people, many of us would have died unknown and locked up in our villages.[81]

Today, the same story can be said of other African countries such as Ghana, Nigerian and Kenya regarding the legacy of Methodism and formal education within Wesleyan religious tradition. There are records of hundreds of Methodist schools and institutions of higher learning all over Africa contributing to the education of the African people at all levels.

Methodist Influence in Nation-State Building

In several parts of Africa, Methodism was at the forefront in educating young people who later played a pivotal role in the liberation struggle and leadership of their countries. It is doubtful if the Methodist Church had in mind, as its intentional mission, education outreach. But the impact of its products on the political, social and economic spheres is unquestionable. The high quality of education is noted to have produced future leaders for developing African nation-states. It is argued that church schools such as Healdtown, Lovedale, St John's and, later, Fort Hare University are institutions that took the same kind of role that groomed Africans in Southern Africa to take up leading political positions (with a mission for life) as Oxford and Cambridge did in England.[82] Key to Methodism in Ghana was its strong involvement in Ghanaian nationalism, a process that Baur credits the Methodist Church with seeking to 'impregnate' the Ghanaian nationalism 'with Christian principles'[83] (which formed part of the struggle against colonialism in Nigeria).

Conclusion

The story of Methodism in Africa is an exciting story that continues to influence many parts of Africa for the Kingdom of God. The diverse presence of Methodism and Methodist churches with a Wesleyan tradition is significant for African Christianity. Evidently, the social creed tradition of Methodism has played a major role in strengthening the approach of the Methodist churches in public theology. From this emanates the belief that Christianity must affect all of life. Hence, Methodism in Africa continues to seek the well-being of all.

Bibliography

Abraham, William J. and Kirby, James E. (eds), *The Oxford Handbook of Methodist Studies*. Oxford: University Press, 2009.

Anderson, William B. *The Church in East Africa (1840-1974)*. Nairobi: Uzima Press, 1977.

Balia, Daryl M. *Black Methodists and White Supremacy in South Africa*. Durban: Midiba Publications, 1991.

[80] Cracknell and White. "*An Introduction to world Methodism*", 77.

[81] Mvume H. Dandala "Conference Proceedings," *The Methodist Church of Southern Africa* (Durban, 1998).

[82] Andre Odendaal, *The Founders: The Origins of the ANC and the Struggle for Democracy in South Africa.* (Sunnyside: Jacana Media, 2012), 34.

[83] Baur, *2000 Years of Christianity in Africa,* 118.

Bartels, Francis L. *The Roots of Ghana Methodism*. Cambridge: University Press, 1965.
Baur, John. *2000 Years of Christianity in Africa: An African Church History* (Second Revised edition). Nairobi: Paulines Publications, 1998.
Bentley, Wessel and Forster, Dion. *Methodism in Southern Africa: A celebration of Wesleyan Mission,* Edleen: AcadSA Publishing, 2008.
Birch, Freeman, Thomas 1809 to 1890 Methodist Ghana/Nigeria. In *Dictionary of African Biography*. www.dacb.org/stories/ghana/freeman_t.html (Accessed 15 August 2015).
Clarke, Peter B. *West Africa and Christianity*. London: Edward Arnold, 1986.
Clifford, Holden W. *A brief history of Methodism and of Methodist missions in South Africa*. London: Wesleyan-Methodist Book-Room, 1887.
Cracknell, Kenneth and White, Susan J. *An Introduction to world Methodism*, Cambridge: Cambridge Press, 2005.
Cracknell, Kenneth. 'The Spread of Wesleyan Methodism', in *The Cambridge Companion to John Wesley*, eds. Randy L. Maddox and Jason E. Vickers, Cambridge: Cambridge University Press, 2010), 245-261.
Cragg, Donald and Millard, Joan *Open Doors: Methodism in South Africa 1883-1933.* Cape Town: Methodist Publishing House, 2013.
Cragg, Donald. *A Spark of Grace: The Wesleyan Methodist Mission in South Africa 1816- 1883.* Cape Town: Methodist Publishing House, 2011.
Dandala, Mvume H. 'Conference Proceedings', *The Methodist Church of Southern Africa.* Durban 1998.
Davies, Rupert E. *Methodism*. London: Epworth Press, 1976.
Dreyer, Frederick. *The Genesis of Methodism*. London: Associated University Presses, 1999.
Essamuah, Casely B. *Genuinely Ghanaian: A History of the Methodist Church Ghana*, 1961-2000. Trento: Africa World Press, 2010.
Garrett A. E. F. (ed.), *South African Methodism: Her Missionary Witness.* Cape Town: Methodist House, No Date.
Heitzenrater, Richard P. *Wesley and the People Called Methodists.* Nashville: Abingdon Press, 1995.
Hewson, Leslie A. *An Introduction to South African Methodism.* Cape Town: The Standard Press, 1950.
Isichei, Elizabeth. *A History of Christianity in Africa*, Grand Rapids: William B. Eerdmans Publishing Company1995.
Madise, M. J. S and Taunyane, L. M. *The Methodist Church in Africa*. Pretoria: UNISA, 2012.
Malinga, Purity and Richardson, Neville (eds.), *Rediscovering Wesley for Africa*. Silverton: Methodist Church of Southern Africa, 2006.
Mears, Gordon *Methodism in the Cape: An Outline*. Cape Town: Methodist Publishing House, 1973.
Methodist Conference, *The Message and the Mission of Methodism*. London: Epworth Press, 1943.
Methodist Church Kenya, https://www.methodistchurchkenya.org (Accessed 24 September 2015).
Methodist Church Ghana, www.methodistchurch-gh.org/index.php/the-church/beginning-of-methodism (Accessed 17 August 2015).
Methodist Church of Southern Africa. www.methodist.org.za/# (Accessed 20 August 2015).
Methodist Church of Southern Africa archives. Rhodes University. https://www.ru.ac.za/corylibrary/collections/methodistchurcharchives/ (Accessed 20 August 2015).
Langford, Thomas A. *Practical Divinity: Theology in the Wesleyan Tradition.* Nashville: Abingdon Press, 1983.
Luccock, Halford E. and Hutchison, Paul. *The Story of Methodism*. New York: The Methodist Book Concern, 1926.
Odendaal, Andre. *The Founders: The Origins of the ANC and the Struggle for Democracy in South Africa.* Sunnyside: Jacana Media, 2012.
Tabraham, Barrie W. *The Marking of Methodism*. London: Epworth Press, 1995.
Tuttle, Robert G. *John Wesley: His Life and Theology.* Grand Rapids: Paternoster Press, 1978.

United Methodist Churches. *North Africa.* www.umc-europe.org/north_africa_e.php (Accessed 27-08-2015).

Wesley, John. *A Short History of Methodism*. London: Sold at the Foundry, 1765.

______. John. *The Character of a Methodist*. Bristol: Felix Farley, 1742.

______. John. *The Works of John Wesley* (Volume VIII). Grand Rapids: Zondervan Publishing House, 1872.

World Council of Churches. '*Methodist Churches in Sierra* Leone': https://www.oikoumene.org/en/member-churches/methodist-church-sierra-leone (Accessed 17 August 2015).

World Council of Churches, *Methodist Church, Nigeria*. https://www.oikoumene.org/en/member-churches/methodist-church-nigeria (Accessed 17 August 2015).

(33) UNITED AND UNITING CHURCHES IN AFRICA

Jerry Pillay

Introduction

John Baur, author of 2,000 years of Christianity in Africa has argued: 'The picture of the church in Africa after thirty years of ecumenical history is disappointing. What has been achieved is a general peaceful co-existence, but little co-operation and much less congruence. Almost nobody feels the urgency to go further, and it would be difficult to distribute the blame for this lethargy.'[1] Whilst this might be true about Africa's ecumenical history, yet there is evidence of United and Uniting Churches going beyond 'peaceful co-existence' to become fully integrated in the truly African sense of building community (*ubuntu*). United churches are those which have been formed through the fusion of two or more separate churches, of different or the same confession. There are some 50 united churches today, found in all regions of the world.[2] It should be noted that some already United Churches describe themselves as 'Uniting' to stress their commitment to further union, for example, the Uniting Reformed Church in Southern Africa and the Uniting Presbyterian Church in Southern Africa. This article will focus on the United and Uniting Churches in Africa. Our aim is twofold: first, to offer a brief history of these churches and second to look at their contributions to transforming society. We shall conclude this article by drawing together some of the common features of United Churches.

Overview of United (Uniting) Churches in Africa

There has always been a desire for Christian unity, as a consequence of Christ's admonition to spiritual unity in John 17: 11-21. Such spiritual unity is perceived by many as a preparation for organisational unity.[3] It is thus not surprising that many Churches today are talking about possibilities of union or are already in such processes. This is no less true for Africa. However, in this section we shall only mention some, especially those connected to the World Council of Churches.

Church of Christ in Congo (DRC)

The DRC, formerly known as Zaïre, is emerging from colonial oppression under Belgium (1908-1960), a ruthless dictatorship under Mobutu (1965-1997), and a five-year war that killed 5.4 million people and involved eight African countries and 25 armed groups.[4] Driven in part by multinational interest in the DRC's fabulous mineral wealth, conflict continues to this day, particularly in the mineral-rich eastern

---

[1] John Baur, *2000 Years of Christianity in Africa: An African History 1962-1992* (Nairobi: Paulines Publications 1994), 560f, cited in Isabel Apawo Phiri and Dietrich Werner (eds), *Handbook of Theological Education in Africa* (South Africa: Cluster Publications, 2013), 70.

[2] Many of these incorporate churches that were themselves formed from earlier unions, so that the total number of "uniting actions" may be as many as 150. Uniting churches are those presently engaged in a formal process towards union. At present a total of some 40 churches are involved in at least 15 such processes worldwide.

[3] Pass, S, The Faith Moves South: *A History of the Church in Africa*, Assemblies of God Press, Malawi, 2006, p.179.

[4] From 1998 until 2003 the DRC was in the grip of civil war, in which neighbouring countries Rwanda, Uganda and Burundi intervened, supporting rebel factions, while Angola and Zimbabwe took the side of the government. According to a UN report, several million people were killed, many were displaced, and all parties committed large-scale plundering of natural resources.

provinces. With the help of South Africa, an inter-Congolese dialogue was conducted, and in 2003 a coalition government was formed.

The DRC is the home of the Kimbanguist Church, one of the largest African Instituted Churches. There are many other independent churches, and a small indigenous Orthodox Church under the Patriarchate of Alexandria. However, the Catholic Church is the largest church in the DRC. This is primarily because of the support given by King Garcia II who is said to have favoured the Dutch in commerce, but in religion he favoured Roman Catholicism, thus diminishing Dutch Protestant influence.[5] It is thus not surprising that when the Portuguese retained their position in the Congo in 1648, Protestant literature spread by the Dutch was collected and made into a bonfire.[6] Despite this, the Protestants today form a considerable number in the DRC.

Formed in 1922, the Protestants and the Anglicans are organized in the Church of Christ in Congo (the Eglise du Christ au Congo or ECC), which is composed of 62 churches called 'Communities' with around 35% of the population belonging to an ECC-affiliated Church.[7] The Catholic Church and the Church of Christ in Congo played a key role in the inter-Congolese dialogue, and several of their clergy were given high positions in the coalition government. The great majority of the people live in dire poverty and struggle daily for survival.

The Eglise du Christ au Congo provides leadership, services, and hope as the Congolese people struggle to rebuild after decades of dictatorship and devastating war.[8] With much of the country's infrastructure in ruins, the ECC operates hospitals, schools, urban food programmes, training centres for women, theological schools, and agricultural projects. The ECC is working towards both long-term development and meeting the basic needs of those most affected by the continuing crisis, including orphans and women who have been raped.

Sexual assault is being used as a weapon against thousands of women by armed groups in the eastern regions where mineral wealth is located. The ECC's Department for Women and the Family is helping women reclaim their dignity, strength, and economic ability when they are cut off from their families after being raped. The United Church of Canada has been partnered with the ECC since 1974.[9] ECC has initiated Extra Measures projects relating to Promoting Health and Well-being and Caring for Children. In the midst of continuous struggle this church attempts to engage relevant ministry.

Church of Jesus Christ in Madagascar

The Church of Jesus Christ in Madagascar, known as FJKM, from the initials in its Malagasy name, is the Reformed Church in Madagascar. After eighteen years of negotiations, the Church of Jesus Christ in Madagascar was founded in 1968 through the union of three churches which arose out of the work of the London Missionary Society, the Paris Missionary Society and the Friends Foreign Mission Association.[10] These historic links continue in a new sense of partnership in mission through the church's membership of

---

[5] Steven Pass, *The Faith Moves South A History of the Church in Africa* (Malawi: Assemblies of God Press, 2006), 63.

[6] Pass, 63. Cited in Richard Gray, *Black Christians and White Missionaries* (London: Yale University Press, 1990), 37.

[7] See www.seiyaku.com/customs/crosses/congo.html.

[8] Some examples of the participating churches are: Presbyterian, Baptist, Anglican, Evangelical, Mennonite, Presbyterian Community of Kinshasa, Protestant Baptist Church in Africa/ Episcopal Baptist Community in Africa and Community of Disciples of Christ in Congo.See*www.oikoumene.org/en/member-churches/africa/democratic-republic-of-congo.*

[9] See United Church of Canada website:www.united-church.ca/partners/global/africa/congo (Also www.globalministries.org/africa/partners/church-of-christ-in-congo.html).

[10] Rajaonarivony, J. Issues Facing United and Uniting Churches within the African Context with special reference to the Church of Jesus Christ in Madagascar, in *Living Today Toward Visible Unity*, Tom Best (ed) (Geneva: WCC Publication, 1988), 98.

Council for World Mission (CWM) and the Communauté d'Eglises en mission (CEVAA) and the Quaker Peace and service.[11]

The FJKM is the largest Protestant church in the country with a membership around 3½ million, 1,200 pastors and more than 5,795 congregations.[12] It has adopted the Presbyterian Synodal polity. Congregations are grouped into regional synods which meet at least once a year. The National Synod gathers every four years and the National Council of eighty members meets twice a year. The offices of the church are situated in the capital, Antananarivo. The FJKM has three theological colleges, and one theological faculty. It owns 552 schools. In its involvement in the fight against poverty the church gives high priority to evangelism, Christian education, and development in the training of its leaders. With its three departments, eight branches, different units, one orphanage, one printing house, development department, and permanent committees (such as finance, patrimony, national affairs and fight against injustice and corruption, fight against HIV-AIDS, etc.), the church witnesses to Jesus Christ in the national context.[13]

At the national level, the church maintains close contact with the Lutheran Church with which FJKM has been in partnership since 1913 through the Federation of Protestant Churches. Together with the Roman Catholic, the Anglican and the Lutheran churches, the FJKM founded the Christian Council in 1980, a significant expression of Christian solidarity and integrity in the country.[14] In recent times the church has become embroiled in the political crisis and conflict in Madagascar which has led to some of its leaders facing victimization and arrest. However, at this point in time, the situation seems to be a lot more stable.

The United Church of Christ in Zimbabwe

The United Church of Christ in Zimbabwe (UCCZ), founded in 1893, grew out of the work of the American Board of Foreign Mission of what is now the United Church of Christ (USA). The Global Ministries of the UCC (USA) continues to work closely with this partner church in the many facets of its ministry in Zimbabwe, even though the UCCZ became autonomous in 1973. The denominational membership today is approximately 30,000 people in 47 churches and several preaching points and worship groups.[15] It is composed of local churches, councils, conferences and the General Synod. It is active in evangelism, rural development, education and health care. Three vibrant evangelistic and revivalist movements contribute much to the life and witness of the church: the Volunteers (men's association), *Ruwadzano* (women's association) and the Youth Fellowship.[16]

The UCCZ has worked ecumenically on important efforts in Zimbabwe and is responsible for many schools and several health institutions in the country. The church's mission is to promote Christian living and to relate humankind to the larger body of Christ through teaching, healing, stewardship, preaching, and farming. The church revolves around the core values of hard work and self-reliance, and works to eradicate poverty and disease through technical and vocational life skills, training for survival, and integrated participatory community-based development.[17] The UCCZ looks to the word of God in the scriptures and to the presence and power of the Holy Spirit for its creative and redemptive work in the world. It affirms

---

[11] See:www.oikoumene.org/en/member-churches/church-of-jesus-christ-in-madagascar-fjkm.
[12]All information above from www.oikoumene.org/en/member-churches/church-of-jesus-christ-in-madagascar-fjkm.
[13] See www.oikoumene.org/en/member-churches/church-of-jesus-christ-in-madagascar-fjkm.
[14] See FJKM official website:www.fjkm.mg/. Another English website that provides much the same information as above is www.reformiert-online.net/adressen/detail.php?id=13205&lg=eng.
[15] Above information taken from www.oikoumene.org/en/member-churches/united-church-of-christ-in-zimbabwe.
[16] See: www.globalministries.org/africa/partners/united-church-of-christ-in-1.html.
[17] See their official website www.uccz.org/.

the responsibility of the church in each generation to make this faith its own in the reality of worship, in honesty of thought and expression, and in purity of heart before God.[18]

United Church of Zambia

The United Church of Zambia (a combination of Congregationalist, Methodist and Presbyterian Reformed Churches) owes its beginnings to the work of the London Missionary Society, the Church of Scotland Mission, the Union Church of the Copperbelt and the Copperbelt Free Churches. Prompted by concern about the needs of the masses in the Copperbelt, stimulated by the work of the Mindolo Ecumenical Institute and the All Africa Church Conference, and by the persuasion of Dr Kenneth Kaunda (the first President of the Republic of Zambia), these churches were destined to come together.[19]

In the Copperbelt, mining began in the early 1920s. Christians from various areas went to work in the mining towns, and interdenominational worship began in both the African and European housing areas. Helped by the fact that they were already co-operating in education and welfare, the Church of Scotland, the Methodist Missionary Society, and the London Missionary Society came together in African areas to form the Union Church of the Copperbelt. Shortly after this, the congregations of the European areas came together in the Copperbelt Free Church Council. By 1945, the way had been prepared for the union of the London Missionary Society and the Church of Scotland Mission in Northern Rhodesia. These congregations, along with the Union Church of the Copperbelt, joined to form the Church of Central Africa in Rhodesia. In 1958, the act of union took place. In 1965, the church united with the Methodist Church and the Church of Barotseland to form the United Church of Zambia. It was my joy and delight to preach at their Jubilee Service on 18th January 2015 with over 30,000 people in attendance at the Hero's Stadium in Lusaka. It is the largest Protestant church in Zambia today with over 3 million members, over 250 pastors and 1,060 congregations, and it continues to grow rapidly.[20]

The UCZ maintains good relations with the Methodist Church in Great Britain, the Church of Scotland, the United Church of Canada, Global Ministries of the Presbyterian Church (USA) and the Board for World Ministries of the United Church of Christ (USA), and CEVAA.[21]

United Congregational Church of Southern Africa

The Congregational Church was established in Southern Africa by the London Missionary Society (LMS) which started work in Cape Town in 1799. Within a few years, mission stations had been established throughout the Cape Province, in present-day Namibia, Botswana and Zimbabwe. At the invitation of the LMS, the American Board of Commissioners for Foreign Missions (ABCFM) came to South Africa in 1835 and commenced work in Natal and Mozambique. During the nineteenth century, English-speaking congregations were also established in the major centres of South Africa. After the withdrawal of the LMS from the Cape, the churches it had established, together with the English-speaking congregations, formed the Congregational Union of South Africa in 1859. This church united in 1967 with the Bantu Congregational Church (ABCFM) to form the United Congregational Church of Southern Africa, incorporating the work of the two bodies in South Africa, Botswana, Mozambique, Namibia and Zimbabwe. A further merger took place in 1972 when the UCCSA was reconstituted to include the congregations of the South African Association of the Disciples of Christ.[22]

---

[18] www.oikoumene.org/en/member-churches/united-church-of-christ-in-zimbabwe.

[19] Steven Pass, *The Faith Moves South: A History of the Church in Africa* (Malawi: Assemblies of God Press, 2006), 213.

[20] Consult the following websites:www.oikoumene.org/en/member-churches/united-church-of-zambia.

[21] See the following websites for more information: *http://uczsynod.org/about/ucz-history/and* www.actalliance.org/about/actmembers/the-united-church-of-zambia.

[22] For information here see: *www.oikoumene.org/en/member-churches/united-congregational-church-of-southern-*

Theologically, the UCCSA traces its roots back to the Reformation teachings of John Calvin. It also stands in the radical Anabaptist tradition that developed on the European continent and in England during the sixteenth and seventeenth centuries. The UCCSA governs itself in the belief that each local church is a 'gathered' company of Christian believers, whose only credal statement is the biblical affirmation: 'Jesus is Lord'. Each local church retains the right to govern itself in all matters that affect its life and work, but is inter-dependent on all other churches in the denomination, as they voluntarily pool resources and work to do together what they cannot do apart. The UCCSA is divided into regional councils composed of ministers and lay delegates from each local church. The regional councils have been organized to form synods in the different countries in which they are situated: Botswana, Mozambique, Namibia, South Africa and Zimbabwe. The highest governing body of the church is the assembly, which meets biennially and consists of ministers and lay delegates elected by the regional councils and synods. It is presided over by a president who serves for two years. An executive committee which is representative of the synods is in charge in between meetings of the assembly.

Until the implementation of the Bantu Education Act in 1953, the UCCSA and its precursors were responsible for widespread educational work in Southern Africa. Since 1954 it has maintained one private school in South Africa, the historic Inanda Seminary, near Durban. The church is still responsible for two high schools in Botswana and two in Zimbabwe. Ministers are trained at the University of the Western Cape, Fort Hare University, Natal University and the Evangelical Seminary of South Africa, the United Theological College in Zimbabwe, Ricatla Seminary in Mozambique, and Paulinum Seminary in Namibia.

Itself the product of church union, the UCCSA is deeply committed to ecumenical endeavour. It is a founding member of the South African Council of Churches and the Church Unity Commission and is fully involved in their activities. It is equally active in the Christian Councils of Botswana, Mozambique, Namibia and Zimbabwe.[23]

Placing primary emphasis on the role of the local church as the place where mission is practised, the UCCS has identified 'five marks of mission' as a tool for locating mission in the local church: Proclamation (Tell), Teaching and Nurturing (Teaching), Loving Service (Tend), Transforming Society (Transform), and Stewardship of Creation (Treasure).[24] Since its formation, the UCCSA has also placed great emphasis on justice and peace, this can be seen in its commitment to the poor and oppressed and their community empowerment programmes.[25]

Uniting Presbyterian Church in Southern Africa

The Uniting Presbyterian Church in Southern Africa (UPCSA) was formed and constituted in 1999 as the outcome of the union between the Reformed Presbyterian Church in Southern Africa and the Presbyterian Church of Southern Africa. These two churches shared the same origin, dating back to the nineteenth century when Britain took over the Cape Colony. Their distinctive characters were that the Presbyterian Church in Southern Africa was constituted among soldiers and settlers who arrived in the Cape in 1820. The Reformed Presbyterian Church, on the other hand, was a product of Scottish missions intended for the indigenous Africans, which started at Lovedale Mission in Alice.[26] It became autonomous in 1923. Efforts to bring these two churches together have a long history which basically is a mirror reflection of the history of South Africa's macrocosm. Clearly, the transition to democracy in the 1990s gave impetus to the union process, so the link of union to democracy in South Africa is symbolic and related.[27]

---

africa.

[23] See: *www.oikoumene.org/en/member-churches/united-congregational-church-of-southern-africa.*

[24] See:*www.uccsa.co.za/?mission.html.*

[25] See:*www.uccsa.co.za/?justice.html.*

[26] Notes from an unpublished Paper written by Graham Duncan.

[27] The Basis of Union Document spells this out very clearly in the General Assembly Papers of the then PCSA.

In 2003 the UPCSA formulated the following Vision Statement: A church which is one: 'In obedience to its sovereign Lord; In celebrating its living heritage as a Reformed Church in Southern Africa; In celebrating its cultural diversity; In addressing injustices and poverty in church and society; and In providing a model of racial reconciliation.'[28] Taking serious consideration of its African context, and being a church in three countries (South Africa, Zambia and Zimbabwe), the UPCSA set the following mission priorities: evangelism, stewardship focusing on training, and HIV/AIDS, with a special focus on the care of widows and orphans. Indeed, with the union willed by God as the church does believe, 'the burning bush that was not consumed' is the source of its fiery zeal for mission as a church of Christ.

In 2012, the UPCSA revised its Vision and Mission Statements. Its new vision is: 'To be a reconciled community of Christians exercising a prophetic witness to Christ in the world'. And its mission reads thus: 'We will proclaim our Triune God in Southern Africa through: Bearing witness to the saving love of Jesus Christ; Building vital reforming congregations for worship, ministry and discipleship; Visibly proclaiming the Kingdom of God through unity, justice, peace and love. The following mission priorities were adopted at the 2012 General Assembly: Evangelism; Supporting the development of missional congregations; Health, well-being and securing justice; Engaging in reconciliation and unity; and Stewardship.'[29]

It is said that to be truly reformed is to be ecumenical. The UPCSA has over the years remained faithful to this expression. It is affiliated to the World Council of Churches, the World Communion of Reformed Churches, Council for World Mission, South African Council of Churches, the Council of Churches in Zimbabwe and Zambia, and the Church Unity Commission. It also has very strong ties with partner churches abroad, for example, the Presbyterian Church (USA) and the Church of Scotland.

Uniting Reformed Church in Southern Africa

In 1994, the Uniting Reformed Church in Southern Africa (URCSA) was established through the union of the former Dutch Reformed Mission Church (DRMC) and the Dutch Reformed Church in Africa (DRCA). Both churches were the fruit of the mission work done by the Dutch Reformed Church in South Africa. Shortly after their arrival in 1652, the Dutch introduced slavery in the Cape and started a slave school to further the Christian religion, Dutch language and culture. The Dutch Reformed Church of the time had no organized mission activity and accommodated all racial groups. The baptism of slaves was left to the will of their masters. Very few baptized slaves were, however, confirmed as members of the church. In due course various mission organizations from abroad started working in South Africa, which led to a number of denominations amongst the indigenous people and slaves. This motivated the DRC to start its own independent mission work in 1824. Although the 1829 Synod formally rejected discrimination on the basis of skin colour, in practice people of colour were discriminated against, particularly at worship services and Holy Communion. The Synod of 1857 decided to allow separate services for coloured members 'because of the weakness of some'. The next logical step was the formation in 1881 of the DRMC as a separate church for the converts of the DRC's mission work. In each province of South Africa separate churches for Blacks and Coloureds were formed. All the coloured congregations eventually joined the DRMC, and the black churches the DRCA. Both remained under the control of the DRC for decades.[30]

In 1966, the DRMC decided in favour of structural unity between the churches of the DRC family. The DRCA put a similar emphasis on unification in 1975. It took another 19 years for that ideal to be partially fulfilled. The DRC did not join the union of the DRMC and the DRCA. The name of the URCSA (in the continuous tense) and its logo (an incomplete circle) reflect the church's emphasis on and hope for the re-unification of the DRC family and the wider family of God.

---

[28] The 2003 General Assembly Papers (UPCSA) reports this in the Assembly Priorities and Resources Committee Report.
[29] See 2012 General Assembly Papers and *www.upcsa.org.za/upcsa-home-mission.html.*
[30] Information in this section can be found on the URCSA website: http://urcsa.org.za.

In the process of unification, the Confession of Belhar with its strong emphasis on unity, reconciliation and justice was adopted in 1986 by the DRMC. This is very much the motivating power by which the URCSA lives. In addition, URCSA's confessional bases are the Apostles', Nicene and Athanasian Creeds, with the Canons of Dordt, the Confession Belgica and the Heidelberg Catechism. As a community of believers who are called together by the word of God and by his Holy Spirit, those who form the Uniting Reformed Church in Southern Africa are part of the church of Jesus Christ. Their mission is to effect the renewal of creation through the proclamation and witness of the kingdom of God as co-workers and followers of Christ through the power of the Holy Spirit.

The URCSA is divided into seven regional synods, including Namibia and Lesotho. Congregations are grouped together in presbyteries. The general synod determines the church's policy, and the regional synods reflect these policies in their various activities. URCSA's witness to humankind and the world is primarily expressed through its congregations. The congregation serves God, by witnessing and fighting against all forms of injustice; by calling upon the government and the authorities to serve all the inhabitants of the country, by allowing justice to prevail. URCSA's vision is 'Dynamic in Unity, Reconciliation and Justice'. As part of living out the latter, the URCSA is currently involved with unity and reconciliation talks with the Dutch Reformed Church (and family) under the facilitation of the author of this article.

Some Common Features of United Churches in Africa

Extracting from what has been said above, it can be established that United (Uniting) Churches have the following in common: mission, unity, theology and ecumenical interest. I shall illustrate this by linking them up in this section.

United (Uniting) Churches usually embrace a broad perspective of Christian mission which speaks of a 'turning to the world' approach.[31] There is a focus beyond the church which relates to the kingdom of God; and it is this imperative that drives these churches into unity and witness. As they join forces they seek to address the problems in the world. This is reflected, for example, in the vision and mission statement adopted by the Church Unity Commission (CUC, in South Africa) in June 2000. The CUC is committed to:

- seek agreement on the ministry of oversight which will make possible the full reconciliation of our ministries and a relationship of full communion;

- hold the churches to their commitment to work together for the spread of the gospel, for justice, peace and freedom, and the spiritual and material well-being of all people; to seek to become a fellowship in Christ which is not divided by tradition, nation, culture, class and colour; to pursue means whereby, under the guidance of the Holy Spirit, our churches in each place may act together in worship, witness and service.

- encourage and facilitate the ministry of reconciliation across the divisions of tradition, nation, culture, class, gender and colour both within and between our churches;

- invite other churches to share with us in the quest for fuller Christian unity;

- involve individual members of our churches in the realization of these aims.

This statement, however, speaks not only about 'turning to the world' in mission but also about uniting the church so that it may more effectively fulfil its mission in the world. It can be seen from the above that United and Uniting Churches have their mission directed in two ways: first to the world, to impact it with the love of Christ and second to work towards the oneness of the church. It is in the latter aspect that they

[31] See my unpublished PhD dissertation for a comprehensive discussion on mission in Jerry Pillay, *The Church and Development: Towards a Theology of Development* (University of Cape Town, 2000), 52-62.

differ from most other churches. These two aspects are related to the one mission of the church: the kingdom of God. Edinburgh 1910 suggested, without spelling it out, that authentic unity could not be had without authentic mission, without an open window towards the world. A WCC meeting in Switzerland recognized that it was inconceivable to divorce the obligation of the church to take the gospel to the whole world from its obligation to draw all Christ's people together; both were viewed as essential to the being of the church and the fulfilment of its function as the body of Christ. Listening to God's word and listening to each other belong together, however; and we can have the first if we are also prepared to have the second.

United and Uniting Churches offer a more directed focus to the mission of the church. What are some aspects of this focus on the church's mission? First, it acknowledges that it is the mission of the church to shape a new identity for society. The quest for a new identity is part of a serious effort to discover new values. South African society has been divided by apartheid; in such a context, a United Church consisting of people of different colour and culture presents itself as a witness to healing and reconciliation. Mission thus becomes very contextual.

Second, United and Uniting Churches embrace a holistic view of mission. The biblical focus of this view on the kingdom of God draws its attention not only to the unity of the church, but also to addressing injustices in the world. Its focus is not limited to the 'mere saving of souls' or to 'church planting'. In this sense it can also offer a collective and strengthened prophetic voice and role in society.

Third, this view of mission promotes values which in turn engender a deep sense of a shared life, a sense of community. The moral imperative confronting the church in promoting new values is to bring people into an authentic relationship with God and with one another, to nurture a community that 'breaks bread together' in the African sense of the term. For when bread is shared in our communities, it is a symbolism which expresses shared life in all its dimensions. Therefore, one of the challenges confronting the church is to be a radically inclusive community, revisiting the New Testament idea of *koinonia* as a model for shared existence. Such shared existence is also realized in the sharing of human and material resources.

Fourth, in South Africa, United and Uniting Churches, by virtue of their very existence, help in the building of a new nation; and in helping to build the new nation we will also learn how to express our unity in Christ.

Fifth, such churches are visible as a force for unity and change. By its ecumenical commitment, such a church demonstrates the possibility of bringing together people and faith structures which are diverse and which point the way to a common commitment.

Sixth and finally, such a view stands as a visible call to other denominations to heed Jesus' call that 'they may all be one'. Whilst the above points are not necessarily unique to United and Uniting Churches, they are, however, found in these churches in a more focused and concentrated form.

Conclusion

The Faith and Order Commission report in 1974 made the point that more negotiations for church unity were going on in Africa than in any other continent. The fact that Christianity is now shifted to the global South makes it even more appropriate for Africans to pave the way for church unity expressed in the formation of United Churches. Whilst this may be happening, it is on a very small, slow scale. Kalu puts it well when he says: 'The irony of our age is that church unity is more talked about than consummated.'[32] As expressed in the brief overview of some of the united churches and their commitment to mission, unity,

[32] Kalu, Church unity and religious change in Africa, in *Christianity in Independent Africa* (ed. Edward Fasholé-Luke), London: Rex Collings, 1978, 164.

theology and ecumenism in this study, it is clear that in our changing world we need a greater vision for United and Uniting Churches.

Bibliography

John Baur, *2000 Years of Christianity in Africa: An African History 1962-1992* (Nairobi: Paulines Publications 1994).

David B. Barrett (ed), *African Initiatives in Religion* (Nairobi: East African Publishing House, 1971).

Tom Best (Ed.), *Living Today Toward Visible Unity* (Geneva: WCC Publication, 1988).

Paul Gifford, *African Christianity Its Public Role* (Indiana: Indiana University Press, 1998)

Richard Gray, *Black Christians and White Missionaries* (London: Yale University Press, 1990).

Adrian Hastings, *African Christianity* (UK: The Camelot Press Ltd, 1978).

Edward Fasholé-Luke (ed), *Christianity in Independent Africa*, London: Rex Collings, 1978).

David Maxwell (ed), *Christianity and the African Imagination: Essays in Honour of Adrian Hastings* (Boston: Brill, 2001).

Isabel Apawo Phiri and Dietrich Werner (eds), *Handbook of Theological Education in Africa* (South Africa: Cluster Publications, 2013).

Websites

www.seiyaku.com/customs/crosses/congo.html

www.oikoumene.org/en/member-churches/africa/democratic-republic-of-congo.

www.united-church.ca/partners/global/africa/congo (www.globalministries.org/africa/partners/church-of-christ-in-congo.html)

www.oikoumene.org/en/member-churches/church-of-jesus-christ-in-madagascar-fjkm

www.united-church.ca/partners/global/africa/congo (www.globalministries.org/africa/partners/church-of-christ-in-congo.html)

www.oikoumene.org/en/member-churches/church-of-jesus-christ-in-madagascar-fjkm

www.oikoumene.org/en/member-churches/church-of-jesus-christ-in-madagascar-fjkm

www.fjkm.mg/

www.reformiert-online.net/adressen/detail.php?id=13205&lg=eng.

www.oikoumene.org/en/member-churches/united-church-of-christ-in-zimbabwe

www.oikoumene.org/en/member-churches/united-church-of-zambia

http://uczsynod.org/about/ucz-history/ and www.actalliance.org/about/actmembers/the-united-church-of-zambia

www.oikoumene.org/en/member-churches/united-congregational-church-of-southern-africa

www.globalministries.org/africa/partners/united-church-of-christ-in-1.html

www.uccz.org/

www.oikoumene.org/en/member-churches/united-church-of-christ-in-zimbabwe.

http://upcsa.org.za

http://urcsa.org.za

(34) Baptist Churches in Africa

Hany Longwe

The Baptist Union is a denomination where the local church is paramount. They do not speak of themselves as 'The Baptist Church', but rather as members of a local congregation or convention, and so on. They prefer to speak of themselves as convention, union, fellowship, assembly, association or churches, for example: Baptist Convention of Angola, Baptist Union of Gambia, Baptist Fellowship of Zambia, African Baptist Assembly, Association of Baptist Churches in Rwanda and Free Baptist Churches of Burundi. This is in reference to local Baptist churches that are characterized mainly by their emphasis upon voluntary association, congregational form of local churches or congregational form of church government and religious liberty.

History of Baptists in Africa

In 1792 black British Baptist ex-soldiers from Nova Scotia in Canada established the oldest Baptist congregation in Africa, the Regent Road Baptist Church, in Freetown, Sierra Leone. In 1822 Lott Carey, along with six other freed slaves from the USA, planted a second congregation in West Africa, Providence Baptist Church in Monrovia, Liberia. In spite of their modest early beginnings, Baptist work grew, not only in West Africa but also on the continent as a whole, albeit that the growth was slow.

Nigeria is the third country where Baptists developed the denomination in West Africa before World War I. In 1850, Thomas Bowen, a Southern Baptist Convention (USA) missionary, arrived at Badagry from where he proceeded inland to Abeokuta with the aim of reaching Ighoho. Two years later he was able to establish work there among the Yoruba.[1] The Yoruba spread the gospel of Jesus Christ to other parts of Nigeria and West Africa. The Nigerian Baptist Convention boasts of having 10,000 churches across the country, while the Mambilla Baptist Convention has 261. This makes Nigeria the most productive Baptist field in Africa.[2] Baptists are found in every country in West Africa except for Mauritania.

In 1843, the first Baptists arrived in Equatorial Africa. This West Indies Baptist Mission, many of whose members were freed Jamaican slaves who wanted to take the gospel of Jesus Christ to their African homeland, began work on the island of Fernando Po.[3] However the Spanish terminated the work in 1845. The first Baptist church in Cameroon was formed in 1849. German colonial rulers made it difficult for missionaries to work together, which led some local Baptists to work independently.[4] By 2012 there were over 1,532 Baptist congregations in Cameroon.

In 1880, American Baptists established themselves in the Democratic Republic of Congo. At the decision of the Livingstone Inland Mission these Baptists took over all the mission stations on the Congo River and then began to develop new stations of their own. In 1886 the black American Baptist missionaries arrived to further Baptist work in the Congo.[5] The Norwegian Baptists entered northern Congo and were followed by the American Mennonite Baptists in 1919 or 1920. There are over 5,300 Baptist churches in the Democratic Republic of Congo according to Baptist World Alliance statistics.

---

[1] Baptist World Alliance Heritage and Identity Commission, "Who are the Baptists? – Africa," www.bwa-baptist-heritage.org/hst-afr.htm.
[2] Baptist World Alliance – Statistics, https://www.bwanet.org/about-us2/statistics.
[3] Hildebrandt, *History of the Church*, 132.
[4] Hildebrandt, *History of the Church*, 163.
[5] Hildebrandt, *History of the Church*, 168.

In 1921, an independent Baptist mission from the USA entered Central African Republic and it was followed by another from Sweden. Central African Republic is now home to over 750 Baptist churches.

Baptists had a weak start in South Africa and a late entry in East Africa. In 1823 English Baptists established the first Baptist congregation in the Republic of South Africa among English settlers. Later in the century, German settlers also formed their own Baptist churches. In 1887 the mainly white churches formed the Baptist Union of South Africa. The Union also included the early African Baptist churches established by the work of the German Baptists and the National Black American Baptists. They were later incorporated into the Union as separate associations called the Banthu Baptist Church. About 1888, work began among the people of mixed race, and in 1903 among people of Asian origin. The Union later included the Afrikaanse Baptist Kerk, the Indian Baptist Mission and the National Indian Baptist Association. In 1987 the black Baptist Convention withdrew its associational status from the Baptist Union to form an independent group called the Baptist Convention of South Africa.[6] In 2004 there were five bodies of Baptists in the Republic of South Africa: Baptist Convention (then Banthu Baptist Church), Baptist Union, Baptist Mission, Baptist Association and Afrikaanse Baptiste Kerk. There are over 820 Baptist churches throughout the Republic of South Africa.

In 1818, in an attempt to enter the Congo, Baptists from England arrived in Angola. The comparative weakness of the Roman Catholic mission and Portuguese colonial rule in the interior provided the opportunity for the Baptists to be the first Protestant denomination to open many stations in the northern part of Angola from 1878.[7] Today, Angola has nearly 600 Baptist congregations.

The English Baptist Joseph Booth began Baptist work in Malawi. Booth was instrumental in establishing three Baptist missions in Malawi: the Baptist Industrial Mission in 1895, the Providence Industrial Mission in 1900, and the Seventh Day Plainfield Mission in 1901.[8] Southern Baptists of America influenced the establishment and government registration of the Baptist Convention of Malawi in 1970.[9] There are approximately 2,600 Baptist churches in Malawi.

Although Baptists entered Mozambique in 1921, it was only in 1968 that the United Baptist Church, now the largest Protestant body in the nation, emerged. Baptists are also present in Zambia with nearly 3,000 churches and in Zimbabwe with just over 480 churches. There is a sizeable community of over 55 Baptist churches on the island of Madagascar.

In East Africa, Baptists were first in Burundi in 1928 and Rwanda in 1939. In 1956, they were in Kenya and Tanzania, from where they established work in other neighbouring countries. In 1950, Baptist work began in Ethiopia, which now has over fifty churches. There are approximately 2,500 churches in Uganda, 3,000 churches in Kenya and over 3,300 in Tanzania.

Baptists have a small presence in Egypt. An Egyptian, Seddick W. Girgis, was instrumental in establishing a community of Baptists that numbered 500 by the end of 2010.[10] Only recently have Baptists increased their presence in South Sudan, mainly through assistance from Uganda, Kenya and the USA. In spite of the political situation, the Baptist Convention of South Sudan has approximately 1,000 members. Nevertheless, Baptist presence and activities are still very weak in the rest of North Africa, where Islam now dominates where in ancient times Christianity flourished. Despite the strong efforts of goodwill from other religions, denominations and other institutions over many decades, the denial of freedom to practise

---

[6] Louise Kretzschmar, *Privatization of the Christian Faith: Mission, Social Ethics and the South African Baptists.* Legon: Legon Theological Studies Series (1998), 28.

[7] Steven Paas, *The Faith Moves South: A History of the Church in Africa*, Zomba: Kachere Series (2006), 83.

[8] Hany Longwe, *Christians by Grace – Baptists by Choice: A History of the Baptist Convention of Malawi.* Mzuzu: Mzuni Press; Zomba: Kachere Series (2011), 30.

[9] Longwe, *Christians by Grace*, 68.

[10] "Who are the Baptists? – Africa", www.bwa-baptist-heritage.org/hst-afr.htm.

religion is prevalent in this part of Africa as in many other parts of the world.[11] This has affected not only Baptists, but all religious witness, whether Christian or otherwise.

In many African countries, Baptists are in the minority, and in a few, they exist only as individuals but not as congregations. The saying 'To be a Baptist is to be a missionary'. has been demonstrated in many ways and illustrated by the fact that Baptist witness in many areas in Africa was started by laypeople who had moved out on their own to settle, trade or work in other areas. Baptists are zealous for evangelistic outreach and to a great extent the growth of Baptist work in Africa can be attributed to this passion.[12] Like other Baptists, African Baptists have certain common features that stem from their historical background and theological heritage.

Baptist Distinctiveness

Baptists in Africa express some evidence of Anabaptist influence in spirit and thought blended with a moderate Calvinism. Although the Anabaptist movement may have been nothing more than an episode in sixteenth-century Germany, no other reformation movement so symbolized the break between the medieval and the modern worlds. Its influence outweighed the number of its adherents. Their rejection of the Constantinian state and church relationship, their emphasis on believer's baptism, their belief in religious and civic liberty, and their stress on mission and social ethics more significantly influenced the Baptist tradition than did the Separatists in which African Baptists are rooted.[13]

If properly understood, the Anabaptist concept of church, with all its ramifications, provides a clue to the essence of Anabaptism. The implementation of the believers' church is what separated Anabaptists from the Magisterial Reformers. Since then, several developments have occurred among Baptist churches. Baptists find guidelines for the church and Christian life in the New Testament alone. They do not see any justification of state churches even in the Old Testament. They acknowledge the legitimacy of the state as God-given but deny its jurisdiction in matters of religion. People should not be coerced to join the church. Baptists insist that the state must recognize both its limitations and responsibilities. Although there are variations of interpretations, Baptists believe that the demand for religious liberty is nothing less than a biblical principle inherent in the gospel.[14]

The foundation of Baptist ecclesiology is congregational polity. The local church is fully the church, the body of Christ, and not a branch of a national association. The local churches are competent to determine a strategy of missions in their locality, and to appoint their ministers and other officers. The meeting of the whole local church remains the first authority for all decision making. Nonetheless, the congregational government has been marred and distorted by an individualism that insists on the independence of the local congregation rather than practising its interdependence. In interdependence, co-operation and the combination of talents and gifts is stressed. This is seen in the New Testament and in the seventeenth-century English Baptist churches where constant movement of apostles, preachers, messages of encouragement and letters between the churches testified to interdependence. The positive aspects of congregational government are that it prevents the misuse of power by the church leaders, propagates the growth of maturity and responsibility on the part of the members, and affirms the principle of freedom in Christ. However, when congregational government is misunderstood, it can retard progress and promote

[11] Tony Cupit, "Religious Freedom and the Baptist Perspective," www.bwanet.org/Ministries/Human%20Rights/rfreedom.htm.

[12] B. Uche Enyioha, "Baptist Presence in Africa", in *All Africa Baptist Theological Educators' Conference*, Ibadan: All Africa Baptist Fellowship (2000), 69. See also Longwe, *Christians by Grace*, 73-238.

[13] Kretzschmar, *Privatization of the Christian Faith*, 333.

[14] Earl E. Cairns, *Christianity through the Centuries*, Grand Rapids: Zondervan (1996), 299.

the exploitation and oppression of the leadership. This happens when the congregations choose to disregard the position and responsibility placed on the leadership.[15]

Beyond the local church, Baptists organize themselves into voluntary associations. Early Baptists met for fellowship, evangelistic co-operation, and clarification of their belief and practice. These associations later developed into national organizations. Each local church or congregation is free in its policies, and indeed duty-bound by the concerns of the gospel, to enter into covenant relationship with other Christians, both locally, nationally and internationally to support mission work.

Being a church also means a coming together of people who have personally confessed their sins and acknowledged Jesus as Saviour and Lord of their life, received baptism, and continued the life of discipleship of being learners of God's Word. Baptists believe that baptism is a commitment to follow Christ and that a call to repentance and a 'born again' experience is at the heart of Christ's call to discipleship. The church is composed of believers who are priestly, meaning that they relate to and act for God.

According to the doctrine of the priesthood of all believers that Baptists cherish, no minister is mediator between God and people. Baptists have always believed that the vertical relationship also implies a horizontal expression of all believers being priests and servants to one another. As a result, there is no distinction in terms of function between the clergy and laity. This means that the individual ultimately must answer only to God and not to human authority, without overlooking the shared nature of the Christian priesthood. The priesthood of all believers has as much to do with the individual believer as it has with the church, with Christ as the great high priest. Like all other Baptists worldwide, Baptists in Africa, being marked by such diversities of cultures, racial identities, and ways of expressing theological convictions, have difficulty agreeing on the precise language for describing the doctrine of the priesthood of all believers.

Since the individual ultimately must answer only to God, Baptists also believe in freedom of conscience in defence of religious freedom, that is, no authority or religion can force anyone to believe. Soul liberty is at the centre of their understanding of human nature before God, and at the same time soul liberty is the force that affirms the principles of Christ alone, faith alone, grace alone and Scripture alone. This liberty allows not only Baptists, but also other individuals, to make choices about faith and commitment, unfettered by outside agencies. Baptists are a diverse people with no overarching rule demanding common thought or practice of such freedom. Yet there is unity among them because freedom from both outside and inside orders has meant freedom to develop in each situation a style of being a church that they believe best serves the interests of the Kingdom of God.

Contribution to Social Witness

Baptists in Africa have generally been lukewarm on social and political issues mainly due to the Baptist tenet of separation of church and state, which has sometimes been carried to extremes. They have not been fully active in matters of social, economic or political empowerment of people although these areas of concern cannot be totally divorced from Christianity. The total indifference displayed by Baptists in Africa on the issues that impinge on the lives of the people cannot be part of authentic Baptist heritage. They have not been in the forefront of the fight against apartheid and such issues as corruption, prostitution and women and child abuse. That has not left a good image of Baptists in Africa. They have failed to serve as effective agents of change.[16] Some reasons why Baptists have had a lesser role in social reform than other

[15] Louise Kretzschmar, "Authentic Baptist Leadership in Africa", in *All Africa Baptist Theological Educators' Conference*, Ibadan: All Africa Baptist Fellowship (2000), 43-44.
[16] Enyioha, "Baptist Presence in Africa," 71.

denominations include: evangelism priority, separation of church and state, individualism and the theological liberalism of much of the social gospel.[17]

North of the Zambezi River, sub-Saharan Africa's encounter with Christianity has been different from that of the people south of the Zambezi and especially south of the Limpopo where apartheid imposed racial divisions. Baptists in these two regions of the sub-Sahara have at times responded by variously participating in social revolt, withdrawing from social involvement and being part of the nonconformist movements. At the same time they have not been spared from constant temptations to abuse their faith to satisfy political and economic interests. Since many of their adherents are uncritical, uninformed and intellectually and theologically poor, Baptist churches experience at first hand these temptations of abuse of power within their own ranks. However some Baptists have drawn on their rich theological heritage to escape from the limitations of their background or group interests and develop new religious perceptions and structures. This is appropriate for the promotion and facilitation of social well-being of all peoples of Africa.[18]

One of the limitations to Baptists' meaningful contributions to social witness, apart from their numbers in different countries, is the congregational structures of church government. Though Baptists, while insisting on local autonomy, do have a national 'convention', this is a comparatively weak structure, with very limited possibilities of leadership speaking for the church. The Executive Committee can make statements as the Executive Committee, but the 'resolutions or statements are not binding'. In Baptist churches therefore, social involvement more often takes an individual rather than a corporate form, with the local congregation's support if the initiative is viewed as a corporate responsibility. Because of their very strong doctrine of separation of church and state, Baptist churches are usually not keen on public comment on social and political issues.[19]

Religious freedom and freedom of conscience force individual Baptists or groups to challenge personally the social issues at hand. They have had to work through other organizations to achieve reform. Many join special interest groups to confront moral problems. This method appeals to Baptists because they can choose the areas in which to make their contribution. Yet they have often had problems in these groups because, in an organization composed of member denominations rather than individuals, the corporate body may take a stand contrary to the position of an individual.[20]

Some leaders have created meeting spaces within their church buildings and homes for those fighting for social changes. They support groups that are fighting for an end to any form of oppression. Their homes can become nerve centres for the exchange of information and for counselling those oppressed. The individual Baptists or groups help with prayer, advice and practical assistance, and give assistance to those who suffer by bringing them into touch with relevant bodies such as the Red Cross and legal aid institutions. In the case of Baptists, the individual attitude is a typical Baptist attitude. It is not the national leadership who is supposed to act, but individuals who are committed to their faith based on the whole biblical message and are willing to take up a minority position. Many uncritical and uninformed Baptist members may be more willing to go along with the *status quo*. This does not make many Baptist adherents leaders for social change or willing supporters for action against social oppression.[21]

However, several Baptist national leaders have been leaders for social change, with or without the support of their local churches. They have done this as individuals, not under instructions from the conventions or unions. Though some church members may question the individuals' actions, and others

[17] Don A. Sanford, *A Choosing People: The History of Seventh Day Baptists*, Nashville Broadman (1992), 33-34.
[18] All Africa Baptist Fellowship, Mission Statement, www.aabfellowship.org/aabf/index.php/items/3-vision-mission
[19] Klaus Fiedler, "The 'Smaller' Churches and the Big Government," in *Church, Law and Political Transition in Malawi 1992-94*, eds. Matembo S. Nzunda and Kenneth Ross, Gweru: Mambo-Kachere (1997), 158-159.
[20] Don A. Sanford, *A Choosing People*, 331.
[21] Fiedler, "The 'Smaller' Churches and the Big Government," 162-163.

may not be happy with the positions taken, at the end the congregations have supported the leaders' actions. Because of the Baptist understanding of congregational church government, the congregation's support may be more relevant. The Baptist leader either accepts or refuses any position in the social movement.[22]

In times of national and international disasters, Baptists in Africa have been involved in all kinds of relief work. They have distributed food items to people in need, especially during drought. They have been involved not only in providing relief items, but also in disseminating practical information needed during endemic outbreaks such as Ebola. Baptist churches in the area have had televised public service announcements nationwide on the outbreak, and local evangelists have distributed pamphlets to outlying villages. Like other concerned Christians, they have prayed, gathered and handed out food items and financial support to some of the victims. With the help of overseas partners, Baptists have supported the government's efforts in the fight against such pandemics as Ebola.[23]

In an attempt to address the HIV/AIDS problem, many African Baptists have introduced 'True Love Waits' programmes to bring people together and spread the message of biblical purity to school and college youths and communities. 'True Love Waits' encourages the young to abstain from sexual intercourse until they marry. Through the efforts of trained leaders in churches and communities touched by the problem of sexual activity among the young, 'True Love Waits' can fight HIV/AIDS and other sexually transmitted diseases as well as unplanned pregnancies and a number of emotional, social, psychological and spiritual problems by helping young people change their attitudes and behaviour regarding sexual expression. The programme uses a proven verbally-based, culturally appropriate teaching approach to carry the message. In Uganda, the programme is said to have contributed to the reduction of the HIV/AIDS infection rate.

Baptists as Managers under God

Baptists believe and teach that God owns everything including a person's right to existence. Therefore, human beings are just stewards or managers of God's property. One day they will have to report on how they have used that which has been entrusted to them. For one reason or another, people have not managed resources well: as a result there are many poor and marginalized people throughout the world, many of whom are in Africa. Every Baptist is called to serve the poor and marginalized. Since God is concerned, every individual should be concerned about life holistically.

Many Baptists in Africa are female and they follow the paths that have been laid down for them. Although some seek out broader forms of witness and Christian service, Baptist women in Africa generally hold meetings and Bible studies and participate in evangelistic work. They hold sewing and cooking classes through which they seek out new members. Women are also engaged in welfare work and visit the sick and troubled. The social witness is not fostered by the church leadership, and it is not even noticed.[24]

Women's services dictated in part by culture and skills taught by the church agencies have frequently been of use only in a subordinate and domestic role. The training has concentrated on subjects like cooking, sewing, nursing and homemaking. Female elders play an active role as congregational advisers, settling disputes and supervising morals among women and girls. Even before the church era, women played the leadership roles like midwives, village elders, clan chiefs, religious leaders and mediators in family, village and clan disputes. The subordination of women to men in the home, church, school and

[22] Fiedler, "The 'Smaller' Churches and the Big Government," 164.
[23] Baptist Press, "Ebola Kills 6 in Baptist Woman's Family," www.bpnews.net/bpnews?id=43477.
[24] Kretzschmar, *Privatization of the Christian Faith*, 250-251.

society in general has been interpreted as the will of God. Though they live on the margin of life, they minister to others, male and female.

Early missionaries developed programmes for medical care of the people. Baptists have built hospitals, medical care centres, facilities for nutrition programmes, maternity homes and HIV/AIDS programmes. In some countries they have mobile clinics on land, lakes and rivers. They have also used the programmes as practical ways of witnessing for Christ.

Another early input of Baptists was the introduction of literacy classes in local churches. Later they built primary and secondary schools, then theological training institutions. Baptists have used their educational institutions as means of witnessing especially to young people. Only recently have Baptists introduced universities.

All Africa Baptist Fellowship

Many Baptist churches in Africa are members of the All Africa Baptist Fellowship (AABF), one of the six regions of the Baptist World Alliance (BWA), existing as an expression of the cohesion of Baptists in the Lord Jesus Christ. AABF has more than 50 member bodies in five sub-regions: North Africa, West Africa, Central Africa, East Africa and South Africa. Each of these has fellowships for youth, women and men.

Baptist growth in Africa can be attributed to their zeal for evangelistic outreach. Together they have done very well in providing medical care, but have not been outspoken on social witness.

Bibliography

All Africa Baptist Fellowship, Mission Statement, www.aabfellowship.org/aabf/index.php/items/3-vision-mission (accessed 4 December, 2014).

Baptist Press, 'Ebola Kills 6 in Baptist Woman's Family': www.bpnews.net/bpnews?id=43477 (accessed 3 October, 2014).

Baptist World Alliance Heritage and Identity Commission, 'Who are the Baptists? – Africa': www.bwa-baptist-heritage.org/hst-afr.htm (accessed 4 December, 2014).

Baptist World Alliance – Statistics, https://www.bwanet.org/about-us2/statistics (accessed 4 December, 2014).

Cairns, Earl E. *Christianity through the Centuries*. Grand Rapids: Zondervan, 1996.

Cupit, Tony. 'Religious Freedom and the Baptist Perspective': www.bwanet.org/Ministries/Human%20Rights/rfreedom.htm (accessed 12 December, 2014).

Enyioha, B. Uche, 'Baptist Presence in Africa', in *All Africa Baptist Theological Educators' Conference*, Ibadan: All Africa Baptist Fellowship, 2000.

Fiedler, Klaus, 'The "Smaller" Churches and the Big Government', in *Church, Law and Political Transition in Malawi 1992-94*, eds. Matembo S. Nzunda and Kenneth Ross, Gweru: Mambo-Kachere, 1997.

Hildebrandt, Jonathan. *History of the Church in Africa: A Survey*, rev. Achimota: African Christian Press, 1990.

Kretzschmar, Louise. 'Authentic Baptist Leadership in Africa', in *All Africa Baptist Theological Educators' Conference*, Ibadan: All Africa Baptist Fellowship, 2000.

Kretzschmar, Louise. *Privatization of the Christian Faith: Mission, Social Ethics and the South African Baptists*. Legon: Legon Theological Studies Series, 1998.

Longwe, Hany. *Christians by Grace – Baptists by Choice: A History of the Baptist Convention of Malawi*. Mzuzu: Mzuni Press; Zomba: Kachere Series, 2011.

Paas, Steven. *The Faith Moves South: A History of the Church in Africa*. Zomba: Kachere Series, 2006.

(35) ANABAPTIST CHURCHES IN AFRICA

Allen Goddard

Introduction

The story of those who were pejoratively called 'rebaptizers' or Anabaptists in Swiss, German and Dutch parts of Europe during the sixteenth century is characterised by 'believers' churches' which practised Jesus' love of one's enemy, with some exceptions, during a century of sectarian violence and civil wars.[1] The first Anabaptists understood the gospel message and how to be the church as *one calling and way of life* because of Jesus Christ and Christianity's *beginnings.*[2] Anabaptists continue to interpret Jesus' message of peace and Jesus' cruciform way of making peace, as *one* experience in the apostles' witness to Christ at the *beginnings* of the New Testament Church. Anabaptists' strong rejection of magisterial involvement in or control of the church, or missionary activity – our clear separation from state powers – also expresses an understanding of *the ending,* the *eschaton*, the *goal* of time and history. For Anabaptists, the church actively anticipates this time, when the crucified Lamb finally brings to submission all earthly powers and *ends* sin, war, death and sorrow, when the new creation, already come, is finally accomplished in Jesus' eternal healing of all nations. This essay first surveys the century of *beginnings of Anabaptist witness* on African soil.[3] The discussion then skips to the present, to consider the ecclesial and missiological challenges being faced by African Anabaptists today. The essay concludes with the Anabaptist invitation to peace-making as the heart of Christian witness, *in between* our very distinctive *beginnings* and *the Ending,* the goal of history, whose 'today' all Christians everywhere may live out together as we pray, 'May your Kingdom come…'[4]

Beginnings in Matabeleland and the Congo Basin

After four centuries of western missionary endeavour in Africa, Anabaptists were among the last arrivals, coming at first in 1898 to southern Matabeleland, Southern Rhodesia (today Zimbabwe). This area had been twice-conquered, once by King Lobengula of the amaNdebele[5] in the 1880s, and then after the death of Lobengula, by the British in 1896. In July 1898, Brethren in Christ (BIC) missionaries from Pennsylvania, Jesse and Elizabeth Engle, Hannah Frances Davidson and Alice Heisey, took up 3,000

---

[1] Three experiences have formed my growing commitment to the Anabaptist tradition: discovering Anabaptist role models who helped me object to conscription in the South African Defence Force, on grounds of conscience, during P.W. Botha's national state of emergency in 1986, conversations with Alan and Eleanor Kreider in Manchester, and participating in Mennonite worship and church life in the London Mennonite Centre till 1991. As a Mennonite Church does not exist in South Africa, my Anabaptist commitment continues in membership of our neighbourhood Methodist Society, and in the Anabaptist Network of South Africa. An introduction to the Anabaptist story is Walter Klaasen's *Anabaptism: Neither Catholic nor Protestant* (Kitchener, ON: Pandora Press, 2001).

[2] Theology presented in this essay has been shaped by essays on Anabaptist missiology and history in Wilbert Shenk, ed., *Anabaptism and Mission* (Scottdale, PA: Herald Press, 1984).

[3] For simplicity I have adapted all historical narratives in this essay from John Lapp and Arnold Snyder, eds., *Anabaptist Songs in African Hearts: Global Mennonite History Series: Africa* (Intercourse, PA: Good Books, 2006).

[4] An introduction to peace-making as the missional heart of the Church's witness is Alan Kreider, Eleanor Kreider, and Paulus Widjaja, *A Culture of Peace: God's Vision for the Church* (Intercourse, PA: Good Books, 2005).

[5] The Northern Ndebele people (Zimbabwean Ndebele: *amaNdebele*) are a Bantu nation and ethnic group in Southern Africa, who share a common Ndebele culture and Ndebele language.

hectares of land given by Cecil Rhodes as part of his drive to settle the British colony with white farmers and missionaries.

Deep mistrust was felt by the now leaderless amaNdebele for the host of incoming Protestant, Catholic and Anabaptist settlers, but this did not deter the BIC missionaries from quickly identifying with African people through *ilimo*, a Nguni village tradition of sharing manual labour. After working with the people, missionaries would preach, pray or invite the amaNdebele to Matopo Mission (today Matobo) to attend a Sunday School. In October 1898, Miss Davidson and Miss Heisey opened their first school for boys at Matopo, which taught Bible literacy and agricultural skills. Ten Matopo school boys committed to follow Christ in the first year. Together with Mlobeki Moyo, the first African BIC evangelist, these boys were baptized in the Ginqa River in August 1899.

BIC missionaries, like all nineteenth-century westerners, shared such paternalistic ideas of the Victorian age as the 'heathen' and 'winning souls'. However, the missionaries' practice of *ilimo,* their decision not to build missionary compounds but to welcome Africans into their homes, and their agricultural assistance, in an area devastated by recent wars, fostered trust and increasingly easy partnerships with African evangelists and amaNdebele communities. By 1908, Mlobeki Moyo, together with the Rev. Harvey, Mrs Emma Frey and the Rev. Henry Steigerwald, had established a second mission station at Mtshabezi. The centre included a church, a school for fugitive girls escaping arranged polygamous marriages, a boys' day school, vegetable training gardens and a poultry-raising project. In 1923, the pastor and teacher Manhlenhle Kumalo was sent south-west from Mtshabezi, where he was joined in 1924 by Bishop and Mrs Steigerwald, to pioneer a third mission centre at Wanezi. Martha Kaufman was to pioneer the first BIC community health services here, and the Rev. J.H. Frey established the Wanezi Bible Institute here in the 1930s, which was to train thousands of BIC pastors and lay workers.

BIC missionary work spread to Chief Macha's region north of the Zambezi (today Zambia) in 1907 when Miss Davidson, Miss Adda Engle, Ndabambi Moyo and Gono Sibanda left Matopo to pioneer schools and clinics among the baTongo people north of the Zambezi. *Nkosazana Debison,* as Hannah Frances Davidson was affectionately called, the pioneer nurse at Matopo, was now instrumental in starting nine outstations and schools from Macha, and for translating the New Testament into siTonga. She is remembered for tireless medical service that would eventually come to fruition in 1951 in the birth of the Macha Mission Hospital. Her fluency in siNdebele, siTonga and biblical Greek and her obvious love for the people meant that by the 1930s and 1940s the churches of the Macha Region were full of followers of Christ whose lives 'did more preaching than what they were able to say about their love for God and His saving grace'.[6]

Whereas Dutch Reformed and Anglican church planters of Southern Africa were closely identified with colonial establishments, BIC missionaries laboured at first almost entirely free of colonial patronage. This allowed for an early devolution of power to national leadership, so that in 1919 at Mtshabezi, African leaders were first invited to attend the annual Council of the BIC Board. In the following year African pastors, deacons and evangelists asked for an African representative to sit on the Council Executive. The missionaries responded by inviting *two* African representatives to serve the Executive as the first BIC African Overseers under the Bishop. Thus, Manhlenhle Kumalo and Nyamazane Dube began serving the Executive immediately as Overseers of the churches East and West of the Mzingwane River. In 1930, when the BIC council demarcated three church districts with Matopo, Mtshabezi and Wanezi at the centre of each, Ndebenduku Dlodlo was elected as third Overseer to the Executive Board, instead of a missionary, to oversee the founding District of Matopo.

Anabaptist presence in the Belgian Congo (today Democratic Republic of Congo) commenced in 1911 when Mennonites from the USA, Lawrence and Rose Haig, and the Congolese evangelist, Mutombo from

---

[6] A quote from R.M. Sichala's *Keep the Light Burning* cited in *Anabaptist Songs,* 55.

Luebo in south-western Congo, established 'chapel farms' for orphaned children at Kalamba Mukenge and Djoko Punda along the southern Kasai tributary of the Congo River. Two Anabaptist denominations from the USA, the Central Conference of Mennonites and the Defenseless Mennonite Church supported this work because the people of Kasai had been displaced by Arab slave traders one generation earlier. A joint mission committee of these two Mennonite conferences, the Congo Inland Mission (CIM), was established in January 1912. By 1917 the first seventeen Christians, mainly Mennonite school matriculants, were baptised at Djoko Punda.

In the early 1920s, Aaron Janzen, a Mennonite Brethren missionary with CIM working at Nyanga among the Pende people of East Kasai, moved away northwest to pioneer a strictly Mennonite Brethren mission centre at Baphende in the Kikwit area of the Kwilu River. He established farms and schools. So, by the mid-1920s there were two branches of Anabaptist presence in the southern Congo basin, one supported by CIM and the other an indigenous Congolese Mennonite Brethren initiative of the Janzens and their African colleagues.

By 1930, CIM reported 800 Mennonite church members and 6,675 scholars, with translation work for a Bible in Giphende underway. In the same year a Congolese team working with Ernestina Janzen of the Mennonite Brethren published Matthew, Luke and Acts in Kituba, a labour that continued after Janzen's death in 1937, until the New Testament was completed in 1943.

In 1933, a second independent Mennonite Brethren centre of activity commenced with the Rev. H.B. Bartsh in the Bologo and Dengese regions, and these, together with Mennonite Brethren stations on the Kwilu River, were amalgamated under the administration of the North American Mennonite Brethren (ABMB) in 1943. CIM and ABMB missionaries deliberately settled in areas that lacked basic services, so as to practically demonstrate the good news of Christ. 'This spirit of self-sacrifice is embedded in the collective memory of Congolese Christians.'[7]

As in Matabeleland, the beginnings of Mennonite witness in Belgian Congo centred on winsome partnerships with African evangelists, translators and teachers, with a focus on practical demonstration of Jesus' message, through agriculture, education and health. A perception of 'psychological dependency' by the Congolese on CIM and ABMB missionaries would only arise between the 1940s and Zaïre independence in 1960 when North American and Belgian state subsidies were increasingly used to fund Mennonite hospitals and schools. Nevertheless, as in Southern Africa, the beginnings of Anabaptist witness in the Congo basin bears a resemblance to the earliest Anabaptist tradition of the Radical Reformation, because Christ's socially transforming message of peace was gladly accepted by people previously displaced in internecine wars.

Anabaptist Beginnings in East Africa

After travels in Northern Tanganyika (today's Tanzania) with Emille Sywulke of the Africa Inland Mission, Orie Miller of the Mennonite Central Committee (MCC) and Elam Stauffer of the USA's Eastern Mennonite Board of Missions and Charities (EMBMC) decided to commence church planting at the village of Shirati in the Mara district, between Mt Kilimanjaro and Lake Victoria – the far north-western corner of Tanganyika. Elam and Elizabeth Stauffer and John and Ruth Moseman commenced in 1934 with Zedekiah Kisare, a local interpreter. Their vision matched the remoteness of their location, and reflected EMBMC's goal, to establish churches that would support local people through education and health care as independently as possible of the colonial administration. Between 1935 and 1938 five missionary stations including Bukiroba, Mugango, Bumangi and Nyabasi, with two hospitals, were already at work in this

[7] Erik Kumedisa, "Mennonite Churches in Central Africa" in *Anabaptist Songs,* 59.

remote lowland and midland region, directed by EMBMC missionary couples, the Stauffers, Mosemans, Shenks, Festers and Hursts.

Tanganyika's remote Mennonite mission centres resembled those of Congo and Matabeleland – churches, schools and medical clinics surrounded by networks of satellite outstations supporting scores of small churches, schools and agricultural demonstration farms. These African Mennonites and their North American missionary partners welcomed the 'East African Revival' which swept through the Great Lakes region during the 1940s. By 1954, Shirati Hospital was well established and started its pioneering leprosy work and research among the region's most marginalized people.

In Ethiopia, Mennonite presence began with an offer of economic assistance by the Mennonite Relief Committee (MRC) when Ethiopians had defeated an Italian army of occupation in 1945. At a time when Emperor Haile Selassie prohibited missionary activity in all Ethiopian Orthodox regions of the country, he invited former United Nations relief workers, Paul Hooley and Samuel Yoder of MRC, to Nazareth, south of Addis Ababa, to convert an abandoned cotton gin establishment into a hospital and community development centre. By 1947 MRC's 40-bed Haile Mariam Mambo Memorial Hospital, named after an outspoken outpatient, was fully functional, with an outpatient facility and nurses' training school.

After an audience with the Emperor, Mennonite missionaries Dorsa Mishler and Daniel Sensening received permission to evangelize a non-Ethiopian Orthodox area, and were assigned to the Muslim region of East Ethiopia near Deder. They built a school and clinic there in 1950. Meanwhile, at an MRC-established school at Bedeno near Nazareth, a group of ten Ethiopians converted to follow Christ and were taken in secret to Addis Ababa to be baptised, to avoid attention regarding the Imperial ban. Bati Ensermo and Badi Tessew, among this first group of 'rebaptized' Ethiopians, became two of the most fearless and fruitful Ethiopian evangelists, despite censure from the authorities. Thus the beginnings of Ethiopian Anabaptist witness conformed to the 'believers' church' pattern of missionary practice in place since the Radical Reformation. The Mennonites clothed the message of Jesus Christ in their labours of practical assistance, this time to a nation devastated by military occupation and civil war.

Most Recent Beginnings in the West and South

A Ghanaian baptized in the London Mennonite Fellowship, George Thompson, began church planting in southern Ghana in 1956, assisted by US missionaries. One generation later, mission work by maturing Ghanaian congregations led to the birth of three Mennonite churches in neighbouring Togo, between 1993 and 1996. Mennonite partnerships with other denominations have also resulted in a growing Mennonite presence in Nigeria, Benin, Côte d'Ivoire, Liberia, Senegal and Mali. This intentional commitment to partnerships in beginning Anabaptist witness in new parts of Africa has shaped work from the 1960s in South Africa's former Transkei region, Botswana, Swaziland, Lesotho, and in South Africa itself since 1994. Because of the saturation of missionaries and churches in the region, and the challenge of avoiding complicity with the apartheid regime, MCC, Mennonite and Brethren in Christ conferences from North America consciously decided *not* to plant new churches there, but to work alongside or within established churches in service or support roles. Thus an Anabaptist presence in Southern Africa has steadily grown, through relief work, agricultural development, advocacy for refugees and vulnerable women and children, pastoral ministry in churches, Bible training for African Independent Church pastors, and most recently, through MCC's peace education programme and the Mennonite Church Canada-initiated Anabaptist network in South Africa.[8]

[8] These insights come from working alongside MCC colleagues, James and Joan Alte and Mennonite Church Canada colleagues, Karen and Andrew Suderman. For in depth discussion of South African Mennonite witness see Andrew G. Suderman, "Mennonite Experience in South Africa: An Alternative Imagination", *Mennonite Quarterly Review* (April 2015): 253-274. Also see www.anisa.co.za for more on the work of ANiSA.

In Between *Beginnings* and the *Ending*

African Anabaptists have been sorely tested in our commitment to Jesus' message of peace by our Radical Reformation tradition of living peaceably in the church. The African Anabaptist story *between* our distinctive missionary *beginnings* and *the Ending* we live towards in Jesus' in-breaking Kingdom of peace has also challenged us to introduce peace in many violent conflicts. Our continent's liberation from colonial powers was marred by millions of deaths though debilitating liberation wars. During that period, trust with African Mennonites was sometimes broken as mission boards suddenly recalled missionaries, for example on the eve of independence in Belgian Congo and Rhodesia. In the early post-colonial era, there were sometimes destructive conflicts between rebellious African Anabaptist leaders and national and global Anabaptist structures. More recently, bloodshed has flared up again in Rwanda, Burundi, South Africa, the Democratic Republic of Congo (DRC), in the Horn of Africa and in North, East, Central and West Africa.

Between our beginnings in Jesus, the Radical Reformation and African missionary beginnings and where we stand today, African Anabaptists have often been tempted to look away from Christ who we believe is ever-present through the Holy Spirit in situations of conflict. African Anabaptists have sometimes failed but more often succeeded in responding peacefully in these situations.

Since 2006, Mennonite and BIC church membership in Africa has passed half a million members in sixteen countries. Today, Mennonite Churches are found mostly in Central, East and West Africa, while BIC churches are grouped more in the south. The present challenge of Anabaptists throughout Africa is to stand where Jesus stands: to feed the hungry and bring restorative justice to perpetrators and victims of violence, especially prisoners; to rescue child soldiers and child brides; to bring hope to refugees, for example in Kenya; to grieve with the sole survivors of genocide or to create a home and livelihood for street children and prostitutes, for example in Lagos, Accra or Cape Town; to change the hearts of South Africa's wealthy white elites through Jesus' compassion so that restitution for the homeless, hungry and destitute poor can be made; or to bring peaceful interventions into situations of xenophobic violence. There is also the growing challenge to future Christian witness and mission in Africa of increasingly authoritarian government regulation, backed by self-serving hegemonic global corporations.

African Anabaptists' distinctive *beginnings* in the Radical Reformation require us also to renew our understanding of *our ending,* Jesus' finally accomplished eternal reign of *peace,* which comes forward to meet us on African soil in the *present,* each 'today', as we continue in Jesus' prayer, 'Your kingdom come…' When Jesus' message, example and continuing presence enable us, beginning in our churches, to resist violence and so discover surprising possibilities that Jesus opens up through love of enemies, we will be best equipped to face these present and future challenges. African Anabaptists, together with our Orthodox, Catholic, Protestant and African Initiated Church brothers and sisters, welcome Jesus' reign of peace to break into our churches. They like to be the church *together,* turning violent history into the sacrificial witness of *peace-making.* In this way we will all be true to our *beginnings* and we will be living truly 'today' towards our one eternal peaceful *ending.*

Bibliography

Lapp, John and Arnold Snyder, eds., *Anabaptist Songs in African Hearts: Global Mennonite History Series: Africa* (Intercourse, PA: Good Books, 2006).

Klaasen, Walter, *Anabaptism: Neither Catholic nor Protestant* (Kitchener, ON: Pandora Press, 2001).

Kreider, Alan, Eleanor Kreider, and Paulus Widjaja, *A Culture of Peace: God's Vision for the Church* (Intercourse, PA: Good Books, 2005).

Shenk, Wilbert, ed., *Anabaptism and Mission* (Scottdale, PA: Herald Press, 1984).

Further Reading

For general introductions to Anabaptist faith and mission see Gerald J. Mast and J. Denny Weaver, *Defenseless Christianity: Anabaptism for a Nonviolent Church* (Pietermaritzburg: Anabaptist Network in South Africa, 2013) and C. Arnold Snyder, *Following in the Footsteps of Christ: The Anabaptist Tradition* in the *Traditions of Christian Spirituality Series,* Philip Sheldrake, ed. (Maryknoll, NY: Orbis, 2004). A more substantial introduction to Anabaptist history, theology and mission is C. Arnold Snyder, *Anabaptist History and Theology* (Kitchener, ON: Pandora Press, 1995). For in depth studies of Anabaptist presence in Africa see Jim Bertsche, *CIM/ AIM: A Story of Vision, Commitment and Grace* (Elkhart, IN: AIMM, 1998) and *The Jesus Tribe: Grace Stories from Congo's Mennonites, 1912-2012,* Rod Hollinger-Janzen, Nancy J. Myers, and Jim Bertsche, eds. (Elkhart, IN: Institute of Mennonite Studies, 2012). Winsome Anabaptist perspectives on the contemporary challenge of post-Christendom to Christian mission worldwide are found in Alan Kreider and Eleanor Kreider, *Worship and Mission After Christendom* (Milton Keynes: Paternoster: 2009).

(36) QUAKERS IN AFRICA

Esther Mombo

Introduction

Writing about Quakers in Africa is a task that cannot be covered in a short article such as this. But it is important to note two things from the onset. First, 46% of Quakers in the world live in Africa and the majority of them are in Kenya which has eighteen yearly meetings.[1] Second, in Africa the different Quaker traditions of programmed, unprogrammed, Evangelical and conservative meetings converge. The major groups include programmed and Evangelical and these are found in Eastern Africa, Rwanda and Burundi. The programmed meetings are aligned with the Friends United Meeting (FUM) and the Evangelical Friends Church International (EFCI). Both the programmed and Evangelical Quaker meetings in Africa emphasize the centrality of Christ and obedience to the teachings of Scripture and the meetings will employ pastors. All the different Quaker meetings gather together internationally at 'The Friends World Consultative Council' (FWCC). This umbrella body has regional headquarters in Nairobi and in the USA.

The History of the Religious Society of Friends

'The Society of Friends' (Quakers), as it came to be known, was founded during the period of seventeenth-century English Puritanism.[2] George Fox (1624-1691), the founder of Quakerism, went through a religious experience as he wrote afterwards in 1647:

> There is one, even Christ Jesus, that can speak to thy condition; and when I heard it, my heart did leap for joy... and this I knew experimentally.[3]

This experience laid a firm foundation for a personal faith, and also shaped the nature of his ministry, which was to 'turn people to the witness of God within them, though they were in darkness'.[4] Fox and his followers did not develop a system of doctrine or creed since they believed that Christ was the 'Inward Teacher', 'the true Light that lightest every man who cometh into the world'. And therefore there was no need for religion to deviate from the teachings.[5] Every person had the potential to receive this Light and in Fox's own words 'there was that of God in every person'.[6]

By laying emphasis on the 'Inner Light', the Quakers sought to deal with the theological, social and gender barriers which encompassed their society. The Quakers challenged hierarchical language and other forms that stratified the context of their day, including serving in the army.[7] These distinctive Quaker perceptions have been influential in formulating Quaker practices in different historical contexts – and Africa is no different.

---

[1] A yearly meeting is the highest organization in a Quaker tradition and it can cover a region or a country. Some countries have more than one yearly meeting while others have one yearly meeting.

[2] Hugh Barbour, *The Quakers in Puritan England,* New Haven: Yale University Press, 1964. 8. Godfrey Davies, *The Early Stuarts 1603 – 1660*, Oxford: Clarendon, 1937. XIX.

[3] Nickalls, *Journal of George Fox,* 11.

[4] Ibid, 35.

[5] Ibid, 13.

[6] Ibid, 335.

[7] Quaker Peace Testimony.

Quakers and Foreign Missionary Movements

Traditionally Quakers had relied on travelling ministers, men and women, to do missionary work. They refrained from organised mission work because it was incompatible with the basic Quaker dependence on the leading of the Spirit and the fear that it would lead to the development of structures involving a 'hireling ministry' (paid ministry). But with eighteenth-century Evangelicalism in Britain and the 1860s revivals in America, Quakers were caught up in the spirit of foreign missions and they began to go out to preach and do philanthropic work. In 1800, the first Quakerism had spread to the Gambia through the work of Hannah Kilham (1774-1832) from the Tottenham meeting.[8] She founded a girl's school and translation work which was later handed over to the United Methodists.[9] In 1868, British Quakers founded the Friends Foreign Mission Association (FFMA) in London and it established mission work in Madagascar, and in 1896, FFMA set up an industrial mission on the island of Pemba off the East Coast of Kenya which was a free slave colony.[10] The North American Quakers did not become involved in mission until early 1900, arriving in Kenya in 1902. Kenya became a base out of which Quakers spread in the eastern part of Africa. Some of the missionaries founded Quaker meetings in Rwanda and in later years in Burundi. From Burundi, the Quakers founded the meetings in the Democratic Republic of Congo. The stories of Quakers in other parts of Africa was continued either through individual missionaries or people who did not consider themselves as missionaries but who were Quakers and wanted to set up a meeting house.

The methodologies of the founding work in Africa depended on the type of Quakers but, overall, we can observe that Quakers are associated with education, health, vocational training, and evangelism, women's and peace work. There is no room to look at each of the above but two areas are of interest. First, the role and place of women. Second, the peace work in a continent that has continued to struggle with conflict situations on all fronts.

Women and Pastoral Ministry

The Religious Society of Friends (Quakers) has a reputation for being a religious group which lays emphasis on the 'priesthood of all believers', a non-hierarchical approach without ordained ministers, leading to equal participation among the adherents. The consequence of this ought to be equality between men and women with ministry open to both. Because of the diverse nature of Quakers in Africa an example from Eastern Africa is a reflection of the role and place of women in the leadership of meetings. The number of women pastors is lower than that of men and this is despite the fact that women were included in theological education when Friends Theological College (originally known as Friends Bible School) opened its doors to the first students.[11] In 1943, Rasoah Mutua joined the first eight men to study theology. After training, she became a preacher, speaking mostly in women's meetings but also in mixed groups. She travelled extensively in East Africa and later was distinctive in offering spiritual services to women in prison. She was a pioneer woman but after her, very few women received training. In the 1950s and the 1960s, no women were enrolled at the institution as there was no room for them, either at the institution or in the churches. The college opened up again for women in the middle of the 1970s.[12] Friends Theological College has continued to be a training school for men and women in pastoral ministry, but the numbers of

---

[8] The Religious Society of Friends had regular monthly meetings at the Tottenham house

[9] H.G. Agbet, *West Africa History,* 57.

[10] Henry T. Hodgkin, *Friends Beyond the Sea,* London: Headley, 1916. 64, 114.; *The Past Calls to the Present: Friends in Madagascar 1867 – 1967,* London: Friends Service Council, 1967.

[11] Friends Theological College, (Friends Bible Institute) is the only Quaker Institution of its kind in Africa training pastors for programmed meetings. It was started in 1943 at Lugulu under the leadership of Jefferson Ford, assisted by Joeli Litu and James Sangole.

[12] Esther Mombo, The role and place of women among Quakers in Kenya. Edinburgh 1999, chapter 8.

women both in training and in ministry have been fewer than those of men, even though the number of women in the Quaker meetings is higher than that of men.

The reasons for this disparity include the gap between the Quaker ideals and the realities of practising those ideals. The role and place of women has been influenced more by the context and setting of Quakers in Africa than by Quaker thought. In a patriarchal society, women traditionally are not given positions of authority. Furthermore, the understanding of religious authority is based on gender rather than on calling and training. Finally, the interpretation and understanding of ministry is based on exclusion rather than inclusion. Although these notions of ministry are being challenged socially and theologically, the realities of Quaker women's ministry are changing at a slow pace. While there are women who are in training or are theologically trained, they face discrimination when it comes to service in the meetings. It is not only in pastoral ministries that women face discrimination and exclusion but also in other aspects of leadership, for example, as clerks in meetings.

Quaker Peace Network in Africa

Among the distinctive features of Quakerism is the peace testimony which is traced back to the founder George Fox. The peace testimony is based on the belief that there is that of God in every person.[13] Peace-making is engraved in Quaker faith and practice. For Quakers, peace-making is not a profession but an attitude of life in which human beings should be treated as equals, and that which destroys human beings should be condemned. Throughout the history of Quakers, there have been many different organizations dealing with peace-making.

The African context continues to experience conflict on different fronts, including political, social, religious and economic, which affect the whole of human life. The Quaker Peace Network in Africa brings together the different peace initiatives in conflict areas. The history of the Quaker Peace initiatives is traced back to 1998.[14] But even before this, due to conflict in different parts of Africa, there were initiatives of Quaker meetings on peace-building. One of the early ones was an initiative created by the Cape Town monthly meeting in South Africa during the apartheid era called the 'Alternative to Violence Project' (AVP) which responded to the apartheid injustices of forced removal of people. The AVP developed into a peace centre in Cape Town, but also laid seeds for peace initiatives in other parts of Africa.

In the middle of the 1990s, the genocides in Rwanda and Burundi challenged the Evangelical Quaker traditions that had been there for over fifty years. The situation called for a peace initiative to deal with the displaced peoples and to walk alongside those who had been affected by the genocide. The Africa Great Lakes Initiative (AGLI), in collaboration with Friends World Committee of Consultation Africa Section (FWCC-AS), intervened in the crisis which was not only within Rwanda and Burundi but had spread to places where different groups had settled. In Burundi, another initiative was created known as Ministry for Peace and Reconciliation under the Cross (MIPAREC). In the Democratic Republic of Congo, the Friends church (CEEACO) took the lead on peace initiatives' activities to deal with the situations of political conflicts affecting that country.

In 2000, the Kenyan Quakers sought to look at peace issues in relation to the contexts of domestic violence, human rights violations, HIV/AIDS and tensions within and among different communities. Out

---

[13] Peace Testimony: A declaration from the Harmless and Innocent people of God called Quakers against all plotters and fighters in the world.

[14] Three Quaker policy organizations namely Friends Committee on national legislation (FNLC) in the US, the Quaker United Nations Office (QUNO) and Quaker Peace and Social Witness (QPSW) came together for sharing and consultation on peace issues (quakersintheworld.org).

of workshops for Quaker leaders by the Change Agents for Peace programme of Norway, a peace manual was prepared, named Mulembe.[15]

The events in Kenya in 2007-2008, the post-election violence, called for local peace initiatives to work among different ethnic communities and alongside survivors of conflict. The Kenyan Quakers borrowed ideas from the peace initiatives in the African Great Lakes Regions (AGLI) which they contextualized, and they created their own initiatives known as Friends Church Peace Teams (FCPT). In addition to the FCPT, in 2009, the Kenyan Quakers began to develop a peace curriculum for school.[16]

The result of these initiatives has been the creation of peace houses in the different countries, Rwanda, Burundi and the DRC, where there had been conflict. These houses continue to be centres of training for peace-building. In Kenya, the FCPT has formulated a peace curriculum to be taught in school to help young people engage with living at peace with their neighbours. It also aims to create a different method of dealing with conflict.

The peace initiatives in Africa have been supported by other international Quaker organizations with material assistance and capacity-building. Despite the initiatives that have been mentioned, they are like a drop in the ocean as issues of social injustice appear to be on the rise. While the initiatives have done work on both race and ethnic issues for co-existence, the religious scenes in different parts of the continent are of concern which calls for more peace initiatives on interfaith issues, over and above ethnicity and race.

Conclusion

In this short reflection, I have tried to show how the Religious Society of Friends was founded in Britain and, through missionary organizations, spread to Africa. I have indicated how the role and place of women has been influenced more by the African context than Quaker thought. I have also indicated how the peace testimony has been affected by situations of conflict and the initiatives of African Quakers to deal with issues of conflict.

Bibliography

Hugh Barbour, *The Quakers in Puritan England,* New Haven: Yale University Press, 1964.
Godfrey Davies, *The Early Stuarts 1603 – 1660*, Oxford: Clarendon, 1937. XIX.
Henry T. Hodgkin, *Friends Beyond the Sea,* London: Headley, 1916
Esther Mombo, *The role and place of women among Quakers in Kenya.* Edinburgh 1999
The Past Calls to the Present: Friends in Madagascar 1867 – 1967, London: Friends Service Council, 1967
www.quakersintheworld.org/quakers-in-action/306

[15] Mulembe means peace and is a common greeting in western Kenya, which has a big populations of Quakers in Eastern Africa of the programmed tradition.
[16] Initiative of Kenyan Friends, Friends United Mission (Africa) and George Fox University (Oregon USA). The curricular is aimed at helping learners to live and promote tolerance for diversity.

(37) WESTERN MISSION CLASSICAL PENTECOSTAL CHURCHES IN AFRICA

Joshua H.K. Banda

Introduction

This paper highlights the contribution of Western Mission Classical Pentecostal Churches in Africa to the development and advancements of Christianity. It sketches historical origins, enunciates attendant distinctives, takes a brief look at new Pentecostal churches in Africa and the challenges faced, and observes the milestones and impact on social developments achieved. Examples have been limited to the two leading western classical Pentecostal denominations, Assemblies of God (AG) (of US origin) and Pentecostal Assemblies of Canada (PAOC) (of Canadian origin).

Terminology

While attempting to classify Pentecostal expression into five different types, namely Classical, Indigenous, Independent Neo-Pentecostal, and Pro-charismatic churches as well as the charismatic renewal, Donald Miller and Tetsunao Yamamori cautioned rightly that the 'applicability' of these expressions of Pentecostalism 'becomes more nuanced when set in the context of different strains of Pentecostalism'.[1] This paper adopts a specific usage of the term 'Western Mission Classical Pentecostal Churches' with the understanding that the classification is used widely and is also contextually established in related scholarly literature as referring to Classical Pentecostal Churches which have their origin notably in western missionary outreach to the African continent.

Historical Origins

The Western Mission Classical Pentecostal movement traces its historical origins to the Azusa Street Revival in Los Angeles of the early years of the twentieth century.[2] Hollenweger and Synan noted that this worldwide Pentecostal movement which, after the above mentioned revival, sent out missionaries to fifty nations within two years, has built up and operated churches in Africa for most of the twentieth century.[3] Allan Anderson cites the Assemblies of God as one of the leading examples of classical Pentecostal churches that 'have become vibrant and rapidly expanding African churches throughout the continent',[4] operating in most of the sub-Saharan region.[5] Dempster, Klaus and Petersen mention the Apostolic Faith Mission, the Church of God, the Pentecostal Protestant Church and the Full Gospel of God, which have

---

[1] Miller, Donald E/Yamamori, Tetsunao *Global Pentecostalism: the New Face of Christian Social Engagement.* London: University of California Press (2007), 25.

[2] McClung L. Grant Jr. (ed) Azusa Street and Beyond: Pentecostal Missions and Church Growth in the Twentieth Century, South Plainfield, NJ: Logos 1986, 3.

[3] Hollenweger J Walter, Vinson Synan, The Holiness – Pentecostal Tradition, Charismatic Movements in the Twentieth Century, Grand Rapids and Cambridge 1997, 84-106.

[4] The Assemblies of God is the largest Pentecostal Fellowship in the world with a Worldwide growth that has surpassed 64 million members- https://paoc.org/family/who-we-are/associate-organizations- Accessed 26 June, 2015.

[5] Anderson Allan Evangelism and The Growth of Pentecostalism in Africa http//www.artsweb.bham.ac.uk/aanderson/publications/evangelism_and_the_growth_of_pen_htm Accessed 15 February 2015.

featured mainly in South Africa.[6] Another predominant Classical Western Mission Pentecostal Denomination is the Pentecostal Assemblies of Canada (PAOC).

While comparatively smaller statistically than the Assemblies of God (1:11 by number of respective congregations within North America when compared with the Assemblies of God – USA),[7] the PAOC has been instrumental in the establishment of thousands of indigenous denominations across Africa, totalling far more than their sending congregations at home.

Since the early 1950s, PAOC missionary efforts have been stronger in Central, Southern and East African regions, resulting in several thousands of nationally-led denominational organizations, such as the Pentecostal Assemblies of God in Zambia, which has slightly over 1,800 church congregations (1.2 million members and adherents). In the Southern Africa region, there are over 4,000 indigenous congregations associated with the PAOC in at least nine of the fifteen Southern African Development Community (SADC) countries.[8]

In East Africa, PAOC saw the establishment of significant congregations like the Nairobi Pentecostal Church (established in 1959) which, in 2003, re-registered as an autonomous entity, namely Christ is the Answer Ministries (CITAM), currently under the leadership of David Oginde, who succeeded Boniface Adoyo as overseer. CITAM has focused on the planting of contemporary city churches in key suburbs of Kenya, targeting younger people and largely middle-aged professionals. CITAM has witnessed significant numerical growth and financial stability, to the extent of fully taking 'ownership' of the Pan African Christian University which began under the auspices of PAOC as Pan African Christian College.

CITAM's indigenous fellowship, the Pan African Christian College (PAG) Kenya, has remained concentrated in the rural parts of the country and appears to have been negatively affected by leadership succession challenges that may have slowed down the growth.

In 2004, PAOC-associated national churches, in partnership with their PAOC Africa Field Office, formed a continental fraternity, namely, the Pentecostal Assemblies of Africa (PAOA), and framed under what they termed the Kampala Agreement, which reads:

> That we recognize ourselves as a co-operative Fellowship of Pentecostal Assemblies of precious faith throughout Africa, many of whom have had some form of relationship with the PAOC, whose purpose is to collaborate together for the purposes of fulfilling the great commission, the training of men and women for the ministry, the maintaining of doctrinal purity in our respective national churches or church, meeting the social needs of the people in our respective countries, providing the necessary forum for the fellowship of the ministers and the saints from our respective countries.[9]

The Assemblies of God, on the other hand, had by 2015 spread its work to at least fifty African countries, combining their missionary efforts under the banner of the Assemblies of God Africa Alliance (AAGA). These efforts have resulted in the establishment of 79,106 indigenous churches, holding 18,341,975 believers under the leadership of 89,991 pastors in the fifty countries of engagement. AAGA also holds a total of 257 training centres, some of them staffed by nationals with the support and complement of 404 western missionaries under the Assemblies of God World Mission Department

[6] Dempster W. Murray, Klaus D. Byron and Petersen Douglas, *The Globalization of Pentecostalism: A Religion Made to Travel.* Oxford: Regnum, 1999, 165.

[7] The PAOC have 1,100 churches across English- and French-speaking Canada, representing approximately 235,000 people who attend services conducted in more than 40 different languages across Canada. The number of credential holders and ministry leaders is estimated at 3,500 (https://paoc.org/family/who-we-are - accessed 26th June, 2015.

[8] These countries are: Angola, Democratic Republic of Congo, Malawi, Mozambique, Namibia, Seychelles, South Africa, Zambia, Zimbabwe.

[9] Minutes and Founding documents of the Pentecostal Assemblies of Africa, 2004.

(AGWM).[10] Reflecting a typical outreach-focused motif of classical western Pentecostal mission approaches, Assemblies of God Africa Regional Director, Gregory Berg, reported:

> When we look across the continent of Africa, we see incredible opportunity and open doors. As Assemblies of God missionaries sent from the USA, we pioneer in areas where the church has not been established, we nurture national churches where the church is in its infancy, and we partner with powerful national churches where growth and maturing has come.[11]

Prominent in the history of the Assemblies of God is their instrumentality in the formation of the World Assemblies of God Fellowship (WAGF) which William Molenaar noted as follows:

> The WAGF (originally called World Pentecostal Assemblies of God Fellowship) was established on August 15, 1989, at the International Decade of Harvest Conference. Founding delegates represented various national pentecostal churches that were historically and theologically connected to the AG and in fraternal relationship with each other.[12]

Citing a South American missionary example, Molenaar observed that most national churches which were members of the WAGF 'emerged from the missionary efforts of the AG USA'.[13] However, he pointed out that it is important to note that some national churches began separately from the AG USA. The *Assembléias de Deus* in Brazil, were recorded as the largest of the national churches, whose beginning is traced to 1911, three years before the founding general council of the AG USA in Hot Springs, Arkansas.[14]

Classical Pentecostal Distinctives

Grant McClung wrote that the classical Pentecostal movement owes its initial success to some fifteen causes[15] that the movement had bound itself to from inception and which in summary are:

1. A world conditioned to expect the supernatural.
2. Christians previously prepared to expect manifestation of the spirit.
3. Emphasis upon experience rather than doctrine or church government.
4. Pentecostals' self-image as a revitalization movement within the Christian Church.
5. An early thrust towards nominal Christians and lethargic believers rather than to the unconverted.
6. An appeal to the lower strata of the American society.
7. Taking the initiative in going to the people rather than waiting for them to come.
8. The use of mass meetings to create a sense of belonging to a community.
9. The effective use of newspapers, periodicals, to disseminate the Pentecostal message.
10. A democratic tendency, which attracts people of all classes with no discrimination.
11. Emphasis upon divine healing.
12. Meeting psychologically felt needs of people.

---

[10] http://agwmafrica.org/ - Accessed 26 June, 2015.
[11] http://agwmafrica.org/ - Accessed 26 June, 2015.
[12] William Molenaar, The World Assemblies of God Fellowship: United in the Missionary Spirit, http://worldagfellowship.org/wp-content/uploads/2011/12/History_of_World_-AG_Fellowship.pdf, 2, Accessed 24 June, 2015.
[13] Molenaar, 2.
[14] Molenaar, 2.
[15] McClung L. Grant Jr. (ed) *Azusa Street and Beyond: Pentecostal Missions and Church Growth in the Twentieth Century,* South Plainfield, NJ: Logos 1986, 3.

13. The conviction of early adherents that God had raised them up for a special work.
14. A tremendous spirit of sacrifice.
15. The principle of establishing indigenous churches.

The Classical Pentecostals' perception of the preaching of the word in evangelism was, and continues to, be that 'signs and wonders should accompany it, and that divine healing in particular was an indispensable part of Pentecostal evangelistic methodology'.[16] Emphasis on healing has been a major attraction for Pentecostalism, in many cultures of the world, and especially in Africa.[17]

Grant McClung has posited that divine healing is an 'evangelistic door-opener' for Pentecostals.[18] The numerous healings accounted for by Pentecostal Evangelists 'attested that God's Word was true and the result was a rejection of other methods of healing and many were persuaded to become Christians'.[19]

New Pentecostal Churches in Africa

Allan Anderson calls attention to the fact that many older missionary churches arose in western contexts of set liturgies, theologies, highly educated and professional clergy, and patterns of church structures and leadership with strongly centralised control. He observes that this often contributed to the feeling in the developing world that these churches were 'foreign' and that people first had to become westerners before becoming Christians.[20] Anderson notes that in the 1970s, partly as a reaction to what he identified as the 'bureaucratization process in establishing churches',[21] new independent Pentecostal and charismatic churches began to emerge all over Africa.[22] Most of the new independent Pentecostal and charismatic churches were influenced by the Pentecostal and charismatic movements in Europe and North America and by established Pentecostal mission churches in Africa. It must be noted that these new churches were independent of foreign churches and had an African foundation.[23] The young vibrant leaders that founded these new churches emerged in the context of interdenominational and evangelical campuses and school Christian organisations, with large followings. Initially, these new churches were non-denominational, but as they expanded[24] in recent years, most of them have developed denominational structures with many of their prominent leaders being 'episcopized'.[25] Noteworthy are leaders like Ezekiel Guti whose Zimbabwe Assemblies of God Africa (ZAOGA) hailed as a 'semi-autonomous group' that was expelled from the Apostolic Faith Mission (AFM) in 1959 following a struggle with missionaries and an elder male faction of the black leadership.[26]

It has been noted that the group subsequently joined the South African Assemblies of God of Nicholas Bhengu in association with the Pentecostal Assemblies of Canada. However, they were expelled, after which they formed their own organisation, the Assemblies of God Africa (AOGA), in 1967.[27]

Another of the prominent indigenous leaders that have emerged within Africa is William F. Kumuyi, who founded the Deeper Christian Life in 1973 in Nigeria. Kwabena Asamoah-Gyadu refers to them as

[16] Anderson Allan, Evangelism and the Growth of Pentecostalism in Africa, 2.
[17] Anderson, Evangelism, 2.
[18] Anderson, Evangelism, 2.
[19] Anderson, Evangelism, 2.
[20] Anderson, Evangelism, 2.
[21] Anderson, Evangelism, 2.
[22] Anderson, Evangelism, 2.
[23] Anderson, Evangelism, 2.
[24] Anderson, Evangelism, 2.
[25] Kwabena Asamoah – Gyadu African Pentecostal/Charismatic Christianity: An Overview.
[26] http://what-when-how.com/religious-movements/zimbabwe-assemblies-of-god-africa-religious-movement Accessed 24 June 2014.
[27] http://what-when-how.com.

leaders of 'multitudinous mega-independent new Pentecostal churches like Mensa Otabil, founder of the International Central Gospel Church in Ghana, and the likes of David O. Oyedepo, founder of Word of Faith Mission International or Winners Chapel in Nigeria'.[28] In this respect, Allan Anderson proposes that we cannot understand African Christianity today without also understanding this latest movement of revival and renewal.[29] Anderson also holds that most of Pentecostalism in Africa is 'more obviously an enculturated adaptation than a foreign imposition, with inevitable exceptions'.[30] This requires further reflection.

Challenges of the Pentecostal Churches

Allan Anderson contends that it is becoming increasingly difficult to define 'Pentecostal' precisely, adding, 'If we persist with narrow insights of the term, we will escape reality'.[31] Kwabena Asamoah-Gyadu observes that in Africa, the forerunners of Pentecostalism were 'indigenous prophet figures, many who were hounded out of historic missionary denominations for pursuing spiritualities sometimes scandalously seen by church authorities as belonging to the occult'.[32] He highlights William Wade Harris of the Gold Coast (now Ghana), Garrick Sokari Braide of the Niger Delta, Simon Kimbangu of the Congo and Isaiah Shembe of South Africa as prominent prophet figures that emerged[33] in the aforementioned regard.

This development gave rise to the emergence of the prophetic movement that birthed the popular spiritual, Aladura or Zionist Churches referred to collectively as 'African Independent Churches' or 'African-Initiated Churches' (AICs). The most prominent feature of AICs was the administration of healing sessions.[34] However, it is noted that many of them 'strayed into therapeutic methods that were not Christian'.[35] In view of this, it has become contentious to regard these older AICs as 'Pentecostal without qualification'.[36] It is also argued that the early Pentecostal missionaries from Europe and North America were generally 'authoritarian, often creating dependency and sometimes they were even racist'.[37]

A major criticism raised against the new vibrant Pentecostal and charismatic churches is that they propagate a 'prosperity gospel', the 'faith' or 'word' doctrine from the independent charismatic movements of North America, mainly taught and preached by Kenneth Hagin and Kenneth Copeland.[38]

Anderson argues that this form of the 'health and wealth' gospel appears to reproduce some of the worst features of the system of capitalism in Christian guise.[39] On the other hand, there are also voices to argue that it is the collapse of African economies around the 1980s which can be argued to be the main cause of the dependency syndrome of the new African Pentecostal churches on the USA.[40]

In Anderson's view, Paul Gifford, now held as a leading proponent of this subject, views the external Pentecostal dependency phenomenon as a form of neo-colonialism promulgated by American 'prosperity preachers', 'a sort of "conspiracy theory"'.[41] But Anderson contends that to identify these new churches in

---

[28] Kwabena, African Pentecostal/Charismatic Christianity, 2.
[29] Anderson, Evangelism, 9.
[30] Anderson, Evangelism, 7.
[31] Anderson, Evangelism, 2.
[32] Kwabena, African Pentecostal/Charismatic, 2.
[33] Kwabena, African Pentecostal/Charismatic, 2.
[34] Kwabena, African Pentecostal/Charismatic, 2.
[35] Kwabena, African Pentecostal/Charismatic, 2.
[36] Kwabena, African Pentecostal/Charismatic, 3.
[37] Kwabena, African Pentecostal/Charismatic, 3.
[38] Anderson, Evangelism, 11.
[39] Anderson, Evangelism, 11.
[40] Anderson, 11-12.
[41] Anderson, 12.

a wholesome way with the 'prosperity gospel' is a generalization, which mainly fails to appreciate the reconstructions and innovations made by the new African movements in adapting to a radically different context, just as the AICs did some years before.[42]

Milestones and Impact of Pentecostal Churches

All said and done, Western Mission Classical Pentecostal missionary efforts are rightly associated with what are seen generally as 'vibrant and expanding African churches throughout the continent'.[43] Kwabena observes that Pentecostalism is the fastest growing stream of Christianity in the world today, adding that 'the movement is re-shaping the 21st century'.[44] It is noted particularly that classical Pentecostal churches have thrived in Africa because they have preached a message that was readily accepted by ordinary African people. As a result, churches were 'rapidly planted'.[45]

Anderson observes that, from a theological point of view, these new churches are Christocentric and share an emphasis of the spirit with other Pentecostals.[46] It is also acknowledged that in keeping with their indigenization policy, the Pentecostals recognised charismatic leadership and indigenous church patterns wherever they arose and in most cases, leadership was not kept long in the hands of western missionaries.[47] And while Anderson indicates that the 'three self'[48] formula for indigenisation (self-governing, self-supporting, self-propagating) was automatically and easily achieved by many Pentecostal movements long before this goal was realised by older western mission churches,[49] it ought to be observed that much struggle for 'control' – particularly of financial budgets – has been a blot from which many lessons must be drawn.

Conclusion

On the whole, classical western Pentecostal mission efforts must be seen side by side with the spontaneous and rapid emergence of strong numerous indigenous African churches that are positively impacting national and international social, economic and political affairs. Most of the successes and failures recorded have been scored in a 'learning by doing' fashion, not necessarily deliberately planned for. As Gary McGee wrote:

> The first twenty years of Pentecostalism are mostly 'chaotic in operation'. Reports filtering back to the West to garnish newsletters would be full of optimistic and triumphalistic accounts of how many people were converted, healed and had received spirit baptism, seldom mentioning any difficulties encountered or the inevitable cultural blunders made.[50]

Similarly, Willem Saayman observed:

---

[42] Kwabena, African Pentecostal/Charismatic.
[43] Kwabena, African Pentecostal/Charismatic.
[44] Kwabena, African Pentecostal/Charismatic.
[45] Kwabena, African Pentecostal/Charismatic.
[46] Anderson, Evangelism.
[47] Anderson, Evangelism.
[48] Self-governing, self-supporting, self-propagating.
[49] Anderson, Evangelism.
[50] McGee, Gary, "Pentecostal Missiology: Moving beyond triumphalism to face the Issues," *Pneuma: The Journal of the Society of Pentecostal Studies*, 16:2 (1994): 208-211.

> Most Pentecostal movements 'came into being as missionary institutions' and their mission work was 'not the result of some clearly thought out theological decision, and so policy and methods were formed mostly in the crucible of missionary praxis.'[51]

Numerical and infrastructural growths continue to be notable as the churches draw masses of people from all levels of society – the poor, the middle class and the wealthy.

In the section considering African trends of Pentecostalism and their impact, Davis Martin refers to what he terms 'indigeneity, africanization and autonomous space'[52] as he corroborates his evidence with Ruth Marshall-Frattani's Nigeria-focused evidence. He indicates that Marshall-Frattani draws parallels between Latin America and Africa identifying the Assemblies of God as one layer of 'denominational mission churches…and their indigenous counterparts, drawn from the literate and semi-illiterate poor'.[53] Martin states that the other layer identified by Marshall-Frattani consists of a 'trans-denominational charismatic movement, appealing primarily to the young and the mobile and having a strong base in the universities'.[54] The potential and national impact inherent in these strata of persons in respective societies is quite significant – that is also an argument why their further theological education is so important.

Bibliography

Anderson, Allan. *Zion and Pentecost: The Spirituality and Experience of Pentecostal and Zionist/Apostolic Churches in South Africa*. Tshwane: University of South Africa Press, 2000

Anderson, Allan. 'Signs and Blunders: Pentecostal Mission Issues at "Home and Abroad" in the Twentieth Century', *Journal of Asian Mission* 2:2, September (2000): 193-210

Anderson, Allan, 'Christian Missionaries and "Heathen Natives": The Cultural Ethics of Early Pentecostal Missionaries', *Journal of the European Pentecostal Theological Association,* XXII (2002): 4-29

Barrett, David B. and Todd M. Johnson, 'Annual Statistical Table on Global Mission: 2002', *International Bulletin of Missionary Research* 26:1, January (2002): 22-23

Bosch, David J. 'Church Growth Missiology', *Missionalia* 16:1 (April1988): 13-24

Bueno, Ronald N. 'Listening to the Margins: Re-historicizing Pentecostal Experiences and Identities', in *The Globalization of Pentecostalism: A Religion made to Travel edited by* Dempster, MW, Klaus, BD and Petersen. D, 268-88. Oxford: Regnum, 1999

Clearly, Edward L. and Steward-Gambino, Hannah, eds. *Power Politics and Pentecostals in Latin America.* Boulder CA: Colorado Westview Press, 1994

Cox, Harvey, *Fire from Heaven: The Rise of Pentecostal Spirituality and the Reshaping of Religion in the Twenty-first Century*. London: Cassell, 1996

Dempster, M.A., Klaus, B.D. and Petersen, D, eds. *Called and Empowered: Global Mission in Pentecostal Perspective.* Peabody: Hendrickson, 1991

Faupel, D. William.*The Everlasting Gospel: The Significance of Eschatology in the Development of Pentecostal Thought.* Sheffield: Sheffield Academic Press, 1996

Gifford, Paul. *African Christianity: Its Public Role*. London: Hurst, 1998

Hastings, Adrian. *The Church in Africa 1450-1950.* Oxford: Clarendon, 1994

Hodges, Melvin L. *The Indigenous Church*. Springfield: Gospel Publishing House, 1953

Hollenweger, Walter J. *The Pentecostals.* London: SCM Press, 1972

Klaus, Byron D. and Loren O. Triplett, 'National Leadership in Pentecostal Missions'. In *Called and Empowered: Global Mission in Pentecostal Perspective*edited by M.A. Dempster, B.D. Klaus and D.

---

[51] Anderson, Evangelism.

[52] Martin, David. *Pentecostalism: The World Their Parish: Blackwell Publishing*, Oxford, 2002, 139-144.

[53] Martin, David. Pentecostalism, 139.

[54] Martin, David. Pentecostalism, 140.

Petersen, 225-241.Peabody: Hendrickson, 1991

Kwabena J. Asamoah-Gyadu. *Contemporary Pentecostal Christianity:* Interpretations form an African Context. Oxford: Regnum Books International, 2013

Kwabena J. Asamoah-Gyadu. 'Traditional missionary Christianity and new Religious movements in Ghana' (MTh thesis). Accra: University of Ghana, 1996

Kwabena J. Asamoah-Gyadu. 'The Church in the African State: The Pentecostal/Charismatic Experience in Ghana', *Journal of African ChristianThought* 1:2 (1998): 51-57

Land, Steven J. *Pentecostal Spirituality: A Passion for the Kingdom.* Sheffield: Sheffield Academic Press, 1993

Lewis W. Paul. *All the Gospel to All the World: 100 years of Assemblies of God Missiology*. Springfield: Assemblies of God Theological Seminary, 2014

Martin, David. *Pentecostalism: The World Their Parish.*Oxford: Blackwell Publishing, 2002

Martin, David. *Tongues of Fire.* Oxford: Blackwell Publishing, 1990

Maxwell, David. *Christians and Chiefs in Zimbabwe.* Edinburgh: Edinburgh University Press, 1999

Maxwell, David. 'Witches, Prophets and Avenging Spirits: The Second Christian Movement in North-East Zimbabwe', *Journal of Religion in Africa* 25:3 (1995): 309-35

McClung, L. Grant. 'Truth on Fire: Pentecostals and an Urgent Missiology', in *Azusa Street and Beyond: Pentecostal Missions and Church Growth in the Twentieth Century*, edited by L. Grant McClung,Jr.,47-54. South Plainfield, NJ: Logos, 1986

McClung, L. Grant. 'Spontaneous Strategy of the Spirit: Pentecostal Missionary Practices', in *Azusa Street and Beyond: Pentecostal Missions and Church Growth in the Twentieth Century*, edited by L. Grant McClung, Jr., 71-81. South Plainfield, NJ: Logos, 1986

McGavran, Donald A. 'What makes Pentecostal churches grow?' In *Azusa Street and Beyond: Pentecostal Missions and Church Growth in the Twentieth Century,* edited by L. Grant McClung, Jr.,121-123.South Plainfield, NJ: Logos, 1986

McGee, Gary B. 'Pentecostals and their Various Strategies for Global Mission: A Historical Assessment', In *Called and Empowered: Global Mission in Pentecostal Perspective*edited by M.A. Dempster, B.D. Klaus and D. Petersen, 203-224.Peabody: Hendrickson, 1991

McGee, Gary B. 'Pentecostal Missiology: Moving beyond triumphalism to face the issues', *Pneuma* 16:2 (Fall 1994): 275-282

McGee, Gary B. '"Power from on High": A Historical Perspective on the Radical Strategy in Missions', In *Pentecostalism in Context* edited by Wonsuk Ma and Robert P. Menzies, 317-336. Sheffield: Sheffield Academic Press, 1997

Menzies, Robert P. *Empowered for Witness: The Spirit in Luke-Acts.* Sheffield: Sheffield Academic Press, 1994

Míguez Bonino, José, 'Pentecostal missions is more than what it claims', *Pneuma* 16:2 (Fall 1997): 283-288

Miller, Donald, E. and Yamamori, Tetsunao. *Global Pentecostalism: The new face Of Christian Social Engagement.* Los Angeles, CA: University of California Press, 2007

Miller, Donald, E. *Reinventing American Protestantism in the New Millennium.* Berkeley, CA: University of California Press, 1997

Pentecostal Assemblies of Canada, https://paoc.org/family/who-we-are – (Accessed 26 June, 2015)

Pate, Larry D. 'Pentecostal Missions from the Two-Thirds World', In *Called and Empowered: Global Mission in Pentecostal Perspective*edited by M.A. Dempster, B.D. Klaus and D. Petersen,242-258. Peabody: Hendrickson, 1991

Penney,John Michael. *The Missionary Emphasis of Lukan Pneumatology.* Sheffield: Sheffield Academic Press, 1997

Pomerville, Paul A. *The Third Force in Missions*. Peabody: Hendrickson, 1985

Pomerville, Paul A. *Introduction to Missions: an independent-study textbook.* Irving, TX: ICI University Press, 1987

Saayman, Willem A. 'Some reflections on the development of the Pentecostal Mission model in South Africa', *Missionalia* 21:1 (April1993): 40-56

Sepúlveda, Juan. 'To overcome the fear of syncretism: A Latin American Perspective', In *Mission Matters* edited by L. Price, J. Sepúlveda and G. Smith, 157-168. Frankfurt am Main: Peter Lang, 1997

Sepúlveda, Juan. 'Indigenous Pentecostalism and the Chilean Experience', In *Pentecostals after a Century: Global Perspectives on a Movement in Transition* edited by Allan Anderson and Walter J. Hollenweger, 111-134. Sheffield: Sheffield Academic Press, 1999

Wagner, C. Peter. *Look Out! The Pentecostals are Coming.* Carol Stream: Creation House, 1973

Wagner, C. Peter, 'Characteristics of Pentecostal Church Growth', In *Azusa Street and Beyond: Pentecostal Missions and Church Growth in the Twentieth Century,* edited by L. Grant McClung, Jr.,125-132.South Plainfield, NJ: Logos, 1986

Walls, Andrew F. 'Of Ivory Towers and Ashrams: Some reflections on theological Scholarship in Africa', *Journal of African Christian Thought* 3:1 (June 2000): 1-5

William Molenaar, The World Assemblies of God Fellowship: United in the Missionary Spirit, http://worldagfellowship.org/wp-content/uploads/2011/12/History_of_World_-AG_Fellowship.pdf (Accessed 24 June, 2015)

Wilson, Everett A. *Strategy of the Spirit: J Philip Hogan and the Growth of the Assemblies of God Worldwide 1960-1990.* Carlisle: Regnum, 1997

Zimbabwe Assemblies of God Africa, Religious Movement, http://what-when how.com/religious-movements/zimbabwe-assemblies-of-god-africa-religious-movement- (Accessed 24 June 2014)

(38) Indigenous Classical Pentecostal Churches in Africa

Opoku Onyinah

The Pentecostal movement in its various forms constitutes the fastest growing group within Christianity on the African continent.[1] It started with the manifestation of the spirit in the lives of some persons, often referred to as 'prophets', and churches that sprang up from the historic churches. The Classical Pentecostal Churches therefore emerged on the African religious landscape as a second strand of the movement that emphasises the spirit-related elements of the Bible, movements that experience the gifts of the Holy Spirit, most often prominently including *glossolalia* or 'speaking in tongues' (Acts 2:4). Many of these Classical Pentecostal Churches have purely African roots and these are referred to as the Indigenous Classical Pentecostal Churches. However, the fact that there had been considerable European influence in the introduction of Classical Pentecostalism in Africa cannot be totally ignored, and as Kalu contends, 'many of the early classical Pentecostal groups came into Africa on the invitation of the indigenous Christians.'[2]

Significant among the Indigenous Classical Pentecostal Churches which are presented in this paper are The Church of Pentecost (Ghana), Christ Apostolic Church (Ghana), the Apostolic Church (Ghana and Nigeria), the Apostolic Faith Mission (South Africa), and Deeper Life Bible Church (Nigeria).[3] These are discussed in terms of their origins, growth and development.

The Church Of Pentecost (Ghana)

Origins

The Church of Pentecost traces its beginning to the activities of James and Sophia McKeown, both of Northern Ireland, who arrived in the then Gold Coast, in 1937, on the ticket of the Apostolic Church of the UK. McKeown was invited by Peter Anim and his movement, the then Faith Tabernacle Church, which later became Christ Apostolic Church. However, McKeown and Anim parted company in 1939 due to some theological differences. McKeown continued to work as a missionary of the UK Apostolic Church until 1953 when church practices and constitutional disputes caused his dismissal from the Apostolic Church of the UK.

Following McKeown's separation from his parent church in the UK, he was invited to lead the indigenous group, which had taken on a new name, the Gold Coast Apostolic Church. In 1957, when Ghana attained independence, the name was changed to the Ghana Apostolic Church. Thus, for some time, the two apostolic churches were operating side by side in Ghana: the Apostolic Church, Ghana (the original one from the UK) and the Ghana Apostolic Church. This situation prevailed until 1962 when the President of Ghana, Kwame Nkrumah, intervened in a legal battle between the two churches. As a result of the outcome of Nkrumah's ruling, the Ghana Apostolic Church (McKeown's group) was asked to change its name. It was then that a new name, 'The Church of Pentecost', was adopted. The origin of the Church of Pentecost, therefore, can be traced from the events of 1953, when James McKeown was dismissed from the

[1] Opoku Onyinah, "The Move of the Spirit Around the World," *Transformation* 22, no. 9 (2013). 9ff.
[2] Ogbu Kalu, *African Pentecostalism: An Introduction.* Oxford: University Press (2008), Viii.
[3] These churches are also in the Francophone part of Africa. For example, the Assemblies of God are very strong in Burkina Faso and Congo. For reading about African Pentecostalism, see Ogbu Kalu, *African Pentecostalism*, and Allan Anderson, *An Introduction to Pentecostalism*. Cambridge: Cambridge University Press (2014), 112-135.

Apostolic Church of the UK.[4] In 1971, the Church of Pentecost affiliated with Elim Pentecostal Churches of the UK; it is a mutual accord that still continues.

Growth and Development

The Church of Pentecost (CoP) was listed as the largest Protestant Christian denomination in Ghana by the last empirical church survey of the Ghana Evangelism Committee.[5] The church is spread all over Ghana in 13,288 congregations and has a membership of 2,078,166.[6] It is also actively operational in 85 other nations, where 2,456 assemblies or congregations have been established with a membership of 209,185. Two nations, Côte d'Ivoire and Benin, have reached autonomous status.[7]

Right from the beginning, McKeown's major contributions to the growth and development of the Church included his ability to provide selfless leadership, his personal integrity and his ability to put the Bible into practice. He emphasised the need for the church to be self-reliant in finance, governance and the propagation of the gospel. For Larbi, 'these principles helped to place the organization on a sound footing morally, financially, and in terms of its strong and uncompromising evangelistic drive. These principles have since defined the ethos of the church. McKeown played the role of a facilitator par excellence'.[8] Allan Anderson is right in his assessment that 'to all intents and purposes this was an autochthonous Ghanaian church'.[9]

The church has made remarkable progress in the area of manpower development. It has set up the Pentecost Theological Seminary, which offers theological education to pastors and church leaders, ensuring their being grounded in sound Pentecostal doctrine. The Pentecost Social Services (PENTSOS) Directorate runs a network of schools, farms, clinics and a fully-fledged hospital – the Pentecost Hospital at Madina, Accra – and these cater for the social needs of the members and the society at large. The church has also set up the Pentecost University College, contributing to the provision of high-level education in the country. A multi-complex convention centre has also been set up at Gomoa Fetteh, where churches and other organisations hold residential retreats, conferences, conventions and other religious programmes.

The church has the General Council as its highest decision-making body, but also has an International Executive Council, consisting of nine members, that runs its day-to-day activities. The centralised hierarchical administrative system also ensures internal controls and makes for better reporting system. The affairs of the church are run from its headquarters in Accra.

The Church of Pentecost lays much emphasis on the need for individuals to experience the baptism of the Spirit. This experience, coupled with the church's advocacy of the importance of African indigenous worship, has caused the growth of the church in Ghana, Africa and other parts of the world.

---

[4] For further discussion of this, see E. Kingsley Larbi, *Pentecostalism: The Eddies of Ghanaian Christianity*. Accra: CPCS (2001), 210-242.

[5] Ghana Evangelism Committee, *National Church Survey: Facing the Unfinished Task of the Church in Ghana.* Accra: Ghana Evangelism Committee (1989), 16-19.

[6] The State of the Church Address delivered by the Chairman of The Church of Pentecost at the 14th Extra-ordinary Council Meeting on 7th May 2014, 26 (unpublished paper).

[7] The Church of Pentecost, International Mission Report (January-December, 2013), 7.

[8] E. Kingsley Larbi, "Sustaining the Growth," in *James McKeown Memorial Lectures: 50 Years of the Church of Pentecost,* ed. Opoku Onyinah (Accra: The Church of Pentecost, 2004): 143.

[9] Allan Anderson, *An Introduction to Pentecostalism.* Cambridge: Cambridge University Press (2004), 117.

Christ Apostolic Church (Ghana)

Origins

The Christ Apostolic Church was founded by Peter Newman Anim in June 1939 at Asamankese. The church traces its roots to the True Faith Prayer Group formed by Peter Anim, which became the Faith Tabernacle Church in 1922. The founder had Presbyterian Thological training from Basel. In 1917, he took an interest in a religious periodical, 'The Sword of the Spirit', a magazine of the Faith Tabernacle Ministry, Philadelphia, edited by Pastor A. Clarke. The magazine emphasized faith healing and holiness, a religious ideology that appealed to Anim, and based on his new conviction, he founded the Faith Tabernacle Church. A major event in the history of the church that increased the faith of Anim and also added more people to the group took place in May 1923 during a revival meeting when people in Asamankese saw what was believed to be the glory of God in the form of a 'pillar of fire' on top of the church building. In his search for deeper religious experience, Anim got in touch with a magazine called 'The Apostolic Faith', published by the Pentecostal movement based in Portland, Oregon, USA, in which teachings on speaking in tonguess were espoused. Anim later separated from the Faith Tabernacle Church in 1930 and adopted the name 'The Apostolic Faith' community. In 1932, the Apostolic Faith experienced 'the Holy Ghost outpouring', an event referred to as the 'glossolalic phenomenon', which publicized the organization. The group affiliated with the Apostolic Church of Bradford in 1935 and adopted their name.

Growth and Development

The Church has a membership of over 217,810 nationwide and internationally, with over 2,496 branches across the length and breadth of Ghana. It has also opened branches in Côte D'Ivoire, Chad, Togo, Germany, Israel, Italy, USA and the UK.[10]

The church has a centralized system of administration with the General Council as the highest decision making body and an Executive Council that is responsible for the day-to-day administration of the church. Other councils include the Ministerial Council, the Territorial Council, the Area Council, the Circuit Council and the Local Council. The affairs of the church are run from its headquarters in Accra under the current Chairman, Apostle Dr Stephen Amoani.

The church is involved in social activities as its contribution to the development of the nation. In the light of the church's social responsibility, it has instituted a 'mission week', which is observed every year to raise funds to support the needy in society. Those who benefit from the fund include widows, orphanages in the country, the handicapped and the needy in society. The church has also set up a sorghum farm at Lassi, Atebubu. In the educational sector, the church has established a business college at Dormaa, preparatory and junior high schools at Berekum, a primary school at Akim Oda and New Jejeti Station in the Eastern Region, Bethel preparatory and junior high schools and the Christ Apostolic University College (CAUC) in the city of Kumasi.

The Apostolic Church (Ghana)

Origins

The revival which was followed by the mighty visitation of the Holy Spirit, and which broke out in Wales in 1904-1905, led to the springing up of many Pentecostal groups worldwide. These groups believed that the gifts of apostles, prophets, evangelists, pastors and teachers mentioned in Ephesians and the nine gifts

[10] The Christ Apostolic Church International Annual Administrative Report (2008) (unpublished paper). I am very grateful to Pastor Samuel Ofori of the Church of Pentecost for collecting and gathering material for me.

of the Holy Spirit spelt out in 1 Corinthians 12:1-11 should operate in the church. One such group, the Apostolic Church, was born in 1915 in Penygroes, North Wales.

The desire to know more about spiritual truths and seek spiritual awakening compelled some Christians to write for literature from various missions abroad. The leader of a group of Christians in Asamankese who were organized under the name 'The Faith Tabernacle Church', Peter Newman Anim, got in contact with the Apostolic Church in Bradford and requested that a delegation be sent to visit them. As a result, in 1935, Pastor George Perfect, a British Missionary who had been posted to Nigeria, was directed to visit the Christian group at Asamankese. They experienced the baptism of the Holy Spirit and needed instruction and guidance. Eventually, the group accepted to become a member of the Apostolic Church and Peter Anim was ordained as the first African pastor of the Apostolic Church of the then Gold Coast, now Ghana.

On 2nd March 1937, Pastor James McKeown arrived in the then Gold Coast as the first resident missionary. Barely six months after his arrival, a controversy broke out between him and the members. The Faith Tabernacle Church held on to a doctrine of 'no medication' and therefore when Pastor James McKeown contracted malaria fever and was taken to hospital, the Anim group broke affiliation with the Apostolic Church to form the Christ Apostolic Church. Other members who accepted McKeown arranged for him to move to Winneba to continue the ministry of the Apostolic Church of the Gold Coast. Three years later, the headquarters were transferred to Cape Coast and in 1948, they were again moved to Accra.

In 1953, the church was to experience another split when Pastor James McKeown was dismissed by the Apostolic Church in UK and was compelled to establish the Church of Pentecost.

Growth and Development

Today, there are more than 1,500 local churches in Ghana, and the church was also established in Togo, Benin, Burkina Faso, La Côte D'Ivoire, and the USA. In 1985, the Church in Ghana attained autonomy and its affairs are now steered by a presidential board headed by a president who is responsible to the National Council, the highest decision-making body of the church.

The church is involved in the provision of social services, running 48 pre-schools, 47 primary schools, and 31 junior secondary schools.

The Apostolic Church (Nigeria)

The outbreak of the revival in Wales in 1904-1905 had tremendous effects on many parts of the British Isles and was followed by a mighty visitation of the Holy Spirit which fell simultaneously on many parts of the world, during which many received the baptism of the Holy Spirit with signs following. This led to the birth of the Apostolic Church in 1915, as noted above. Daniel Powell Williams became the first President in 1913. Penygroes was the governmental centre, Glasgow was the financial centre and Bradford was the missionary centre.

The Apostolic Church has always operated with the aim of establishing indigenous churches of equal standing to the founding group. Since 1922, many nations have become autonomous with their own council and missionary board, including the Apostolic Church of Nigeria.

Origins

In 1918, the year of an influenza epidemic, a group that broke away from their various denominations came together to form the Diamond Society because of prosecution by their churches for practising divine healing. The group was to affiliate with the Faith Tabernacle Church in 1921. Through their encounter with and reading of apostolic literature, they entered into correspondence with the Apostolic Missionary Centre in Bradford, and on September 3rd, 1931, three missionary delegates, namely pastors D.P. Williams, Matthew Robert Payne and W.J. Williams arrived in Lagos and ministered in the principal towns of the western part of Nigeria. The group then changed their name to become the Apostolic Church, and in June 1932, Pastors G. Perfect (apostle) and I. Vaughan (prophet) arrived in Nigeria as their first resident missionaries.

In less than ten years after the affiliation, tension arose when the Nigerians discovered that the missionaries were in the habit of taking drugs, especially quinine. This led to a split in the church. Those who opposed the missionaries formed the Nigerian Apostolic Church and later changed their name to Christ Apostolic Church. Those who supported the missionaries continued under the name the Apostolic Church of Nigeria.

Growth and Development

According to the 1999 Apostolic Church World Conference statistics, Nigeria has the largest number of church members with over 4.5 million people in membership. The church is now physically present all over Nigeria. A national temple, touted as the largest church in the world, was dedicated to the glory of God in Olurunda, Ketu, in Lagos, on the 6th December 2011, with a seating capacity of about 100,000 worshippers at a time.[11] The affairs of the church are run from its headquarters in Olurunda-Ketu, Lagos.

To train the pastors and other church leaders, in 1946 the church set up the Apostolic Church Bible School which in October 2003 was renamed Apostolic Church Theological Seminary by the executive council of the church. On 7th March 2011, the Apostolic Church of Nigeria founded the Samuel Adegboyega University in Ogwa, in the Edo State of Nigeria.

The church is also involved in other forms of social services, such as sending funds to orphanages and other charitable organizations in Nigeria.

The Apostolic Faith Mission (South Africa)

Origins

The origin of the Apostolic Faith Mission (AFM) in South Africa can be traced to the ministry of five American missionaries who arrived in the country in May 1908 from Indianapolis, USA. They included John G. Lake, Thomas Hezmalhalch, their wives and A. Lehman. They had been baptized in the Holy Spirit in the Azusa Street Mission and had links with Dowie's Zion City, but had no links with any missionary organization in their home country. They headed to Johannesburg, where one Mrs Goodenough met them and gave them a place to stay in her house. From there, they began their first services from a rental hall in Doornfontein, Johannesburg, on 25th May 1908. As the young church grew, the missionaries moved to their central tabernacle in Bree Street, Johannesburg.

By 1909, the church had spread to the Orange River Colony. It was initially a multiracial church attracting both Boers and Blacks. In the 1950s and 1960s, however, the church was divided into four groups: the white parent church, and black, coloured and Indian daughter churches, in line with the apartheid system.[12] In 1996, the various groups came together to become one unit with the newly elected president, Isak Burger, apologizing for the past treatment of the non-white membership.

---

[11] 'The Apostolic Church', in thechristiancentre.org.uk/apostolic-church/apostolic-history, accessed 29th September, 2014 at 4.00pm.

[12] Matthew S. Clark, "Two Contrasting Models of Mission in South Africa: The Apostolic Faith Mission and the Assemblies of God," *Asian Journal of Pentecostal Studies* 8, no. 1 (2005): 144-145.

Growth and Development

This denomination has been described as 'one of South Africa's biggest classical Pentecostal denominations'.[13] The AFM places church planting and growth as a priority and as a result has spread to all parts of South Africa. It has a membership of about 1.2 million people, making it the fifth largest religious group in the country, representing about 7.6% of the total population. It has established more than 2,000 assemblies or local congregations.

The highest decision-making body is the triennial General Business Meeting, which elects national officers to run the day-to-day affairs of the church: president, deputy president, general secretary and general treasurer.

The AFM Theological Seminary, which is responsible for offering theological training for the church, is run from four campuses: Soshanguve Campus in North Pretoria, Covenant Campus in Durban, Kuils River Campus in Cape Town, and Aukland Park Campus in Johannesburg.

Deeper Life Bible Church (Nigeria)

Origins

The Deeper Life Bible Church started as a weekly Bible study group.[14] The founder, William Folorunso Kumuyi, a former Mathematics lecturer at the University of Lagos, started a Bible study group meeting at his residence at the university flat with fifteen members from different Christian denominations. By 1975, the group had witnessed tremendous growth in membership to about 3,000 when they organized their first retreat.

In 1978, Kumuyi attended a Bible School in Kenya, and his contacts and interactions with other Africans in that institution led to his invitation for a crusade in that same year. In 1979, he started a Bible study class in Kumasi in Ghana with thirty members. In November 1982, the Bible study groups began to organize worship services on Sundays, making it a church rather than a group.

Growth and Development

The church now has over 800,000 members in Nigeria alone, who worship in about 5,000 churches there. There are about 3,000 churches in other countries with missionaries sent to forty countries in Africa.

Practices that have significantly contributed to the growth of the church include Sunday worship services, home caring fellowships,[15] Monday evening Bible study that is transmitted live all over the world by satellite and the internet, and Thursday evening prayer meetings for healing and miracles.

To offer theological training to the church, the International Bible Training Centre (IBTC), which was formerly based only in Lagos, has now been decentralised to all the countries where there are church branches.

The church also engages in a variety of welfare activities, including the training of women in housekeeping skills and skills for economic improvement and the provision of health facilities for maternal and antenatal services.

---

[13] Anderson, "Introduction to Pentecostalism," 108.

[14] Anderson, "Introduction to Pentecostalism," 161.

[15] Groups of 15 members who meet on Sunday evenings at 5.30pm to take care of the spiritual and material needs of members.

Pentecostalism and Development

The early Pentecostals' concept of development can be inferred from the philosophy of Pastor James McKeown, the founder of the Church of Pentecost. His philosophy was 'just to evangelise',[16] and make the people know God.[17] He said, 'Once we have a strong church of people who really know Jesus and the Holy Spirit, then everything else will follow.'[18] McKeown's view was typical for the Pentecostals of the period, as indicated in the writings of some Pentecostal missiologists, such as Melvin Hodges and Paul Pomerville.[19] Hodges, for example, stresses that 'when the evangelical community gathers strength, the Christians themselves show concern for the betterment of their own people'.[20] Thus, the implication of McKeown's philosophy was that he was not going to build schools or hospitals or provide finance. The people who knew God were going to provide finance, build schools and hospitals and serve their nations in diverse ways. Thus early Pentecostals did not put major emphasis on social services. However, currently, as presented above, classical Pentecostal churches are actively involved in the establishment of schools, hospitals and politics. For example, the Assemblies of God general superintendent in Malawi, Dr Lazarus Chakwera, stood down to stand as one of the presidential candidates in Malawi's 2013 general election, although he did not win. The Rev. Dr Frank Chikane, the current president of the Apostolic Faith Mission of South Africa, became Director-General of the President, Thabo Mbeki, in 1991.[21] The current scholarly debate on the Pentecostal concept of development is often presented in the context of the uncertainties and crises of present day social, economic and political life. The focus is 'on the congruence between neo-liberalism and the Pentecostalist drive towards personal salvation and the creation of (what they call) new 'godly' arenas of influence and power'.[22] However, Pentecostals have always aimed at transformation in Christ, which leads to offering a better service to humanity. All other services are bridges to salvation in Christ. The Pentecostal concept of development needs to be understood from this view point.

Conclusion

It is obvious from all that has been discussed that classical Pentecostal denominations have become a prominent part of Christianity on the African continent. They have influenced Christianity on the continent, bringing life to western mission churches and bringing to birth many charismatic churches. Pentecostalism in its various forms offers the new face of African Christianity and determines the future of the church in Africa.

Bibliography

Allan Anderson, *An Introduction to Pentecostalism* (Cambridge: Cambridge University Press (2004).
Kwabena Asamoah-Gyadu, 'African Pentecostal/Charismatic Christianity: An Overview',

---

[16] Cf. Hans W. Debrunner, *A History of Christianity in Ghana*. Accra: Waterville Publishing House (1967), 325.
[17] Christine Leonard, *A Giant in Ghana: 3000 Churches in 50 Years - The Story of James McKeown and the Church of Pentecost*. Chichester: New Wine Press (1989), 75-76.
[18] Leonard, "Giant in Ghana," 76.
[19] Melvin L. Hodges, *The Indigenous Church*. Springfield: Gospel Publishing House (1953), 10; Paul A. Pomerville, "The Pentecostal Growth," in *Azusa Street and Beyond: Pentecost Missions and Church Growth in the Twentieth Century*, ed. L. Grant McClung, (South Plainfield: Logos, 1986), 150-55.
[20] Melvin L. Hodges, "A Pentecostal's View of Mission Strategy," in *Azusa Street and Beyond: Pentecost Missions and Church Growth in the Twentieth Century*, ed. L. Grant McClung (South Plainfield: Logos, 1986), 88.
[21] Anderson, "Introduction to Pentecostalism," 109.
[22] Dena Freeman, "Foreword," in *Pentecostalism and Development: Churches, NGOs and Social Change in Africa* (New York: Palgrave Macmillan, 2012), vii. The book discusses Pentecostalism and development.

www.lausanneworldpulse.com/464?pg=all.
Matthew S. Clark, 'Two Contrasting Models of Mission in South Africa: The Apostolic Faith Mission and the Assemblies of God', in *Asian Journal of Pentecostal Studies 8*, no. 1 (2005), 144-145.
Kingsley E. Larbi, *Pentecostalism: The Eddies of Ghanaian Christianity.* Accra: CPCS (2001).
Kingsley E. Larbi, 'The Church of Pentecost: Sustaining the Growth', in *James McKeown Memorial Lectures: 50 Years of the Church of Pentecost,* ed. Opoku Onyinah (Accra: The Church of Pentecost, 2004).
Ogbu Kalu, *African Pentecostalism: An Introduction.* Oxford: University Press (2008).
Opoku Onyinah, 'The Move of the Spirit Around the World', *Transformation 22* (2013), 9-46.
Ghana Evangelism Committee, *National Church Survey: Facing the Unfinished Task of the Church in Ghana.* Accra: Ghana Evangelism Committee (1989).
The State of the Church Address delivered by the Chairman of The Church of Pentecost at the 14th Extra-ordinary Council Meetings on 7th May, 2014 (unpublished paper).
The Church of Pentecost International Mission Report (January-December, 2013) (unpublished paper).
The Christ Apostolic Church International Annual Administrative Report (2008).
http://ir.knust.edu.gh/bitstream/123456789/332/1/fulltxt.pdf, accessed 29.10.15.
thechristiancentre.org.uk/apostolic-church/apostolic-history, accessed 29.9.14.

(39) Neo-Pentecostal Churches in Africa ('Prosperity Churches')

Kudzai Biri

Introduction

Pentecostalism has become a vibrant global phenomenon that has attracted the imagination of many. In this article, I give an overview of this form of Christianity in Africa. However, there is a need to clarify terminology. There is an ongoing contest in scholarship with regard to the labelling of Neo-Pentecostals in Africa. They are known by several appellations that include 'new churches', 'new religious movements' or 'prosperity churches', or are simply referred to as 'Pentecostals'. This confusion is also caused by the fact that some Neo-Pentecostals deny the label 'Pentecostals' as misguided. An example is that of the popular Nigerian-based tele-pastor of Christ Embassy, Christian Oyakhilome.[1] In spite of this, it is important to note that Neo-Pentecostal churches are vibrant and continue to mushroom in Africa. Under the claims of guidance by the Holy Spirit, Pentecostalism embodies multiple characteristics that are not only static but also controversial.

This article will not focus on the origins of Pentecostalism and its expansion into Africa (see Gifford, Maxwell, Kalu[2]). What is important in these writings is the significance of Africans as important players in the expansion of Pentecostalism in Africa, enriching it by co-opting indigenous elements of spirituality, culminating in a brand, 'African Pentecostalism', that has become a unique global phenomenon.

I argue that the 'reverse mission' is evidence of ministries that are materially equipped to finance the ever-expanding movements which in turn highlight some of the reasons that Neo-Pentecostals are regarded as 'prosperity churches'. While I am aware that the label is controversial, I do not intend to further the debate whether it is an accurate label or not, but to examine the basis of the labelling. It is therefore important to critique the Neo-Pentecostals against the background of that designation.

'Prosperity Churches': A Critical Analysis of Neo-Pentecostalism

Prosperity is the hallmark of Pentecostal churches in Africa. Zimbabwe Assemblies of God Africa (ZAOGA) of Ezekiel Guti, the Redeemed Church of God (RCG) in Nigeria, and the International Central Gospel Church of Mensa Otabil in Ghana are known for their vast resources and wealth. Poverty is demonised. In Zimbabwe, the United Families International Church of Emmanuel and Ruth Makandiwa preached about miracle money, miracle shoes, miracle babies, which is also a phenomenon in Nigerian Pentecostalism. Allan Anderson argues that the gospel of prosperity is an import from America.[3] Togarasei says that the prosperity message is understood especially in Southern Africa because of continued poverty.[4] Biri argues that in Zimbabwe these Neo-Pentecostals have become major stakeholders in partnering with

---

[1] Christian Oyakhilome is also the founder of a Nigerian-based Pentecostal church, Christ Embassy.
[2] See for example Paul Gifford, "Prosperity: A New and Foreign Element in African Christianity," *Religion* 10, no. 2 (2004): 160-184; David Maxwell, *African Gifts of the Spirit: Pentecostalism and the Rise of Zimbabwean Transnational Religious Movement.* London: James Currey; Harare: Weaver Press; Athens: Ohio University Press (2006); Ogbu Kalu, *African Pentecostalism: An Introduction*, Oxford: Oxford University Press (2008).
[3] Allan Anderson, *An Introduction to Pentecostalism*. Cambridge: Cambridge University Press (2004).
[4] Lovemore Togarasei, "The Pentecostal Gospel of Prosperity in African Contexts of Poverty: An Appraisal," *Exchange, 40* (2011): 336-350.

the government in developmental projects and this is true of Zambia, Ghana and many other countries.[5] Gifford adds that 'enchanted religious imaginations that are construed as militating against development on several scores lead to an emphasis on development'.[6] I argue that, while there are seeds of truth in that North America has influenced Pentecostalism in Africa, there is a need to pay attention to the traditional African cosmology that places emphasis on health and well-being and the 'here and now' by defying all negative vicissitudes of life through the consultation of religious functionaries. In other words, Pentecostals demonise African Traditional Religions (in many respects) but contradictorily continue to source from the traditional cosmologies in terms of beliefs and practices in their quest to amass resources. Gifford refers to this Pentecostal practice as 'dominion theology' as they claim dominion in all facets of life as the right of God's children,[7] the 'born again'.

The emphasis on material prosperity by Neo-Pentecostals in Africa should also be understood within the context of negating the missionary gospel that emphasises riches in heaven. I call this paradigm and radical shift in post-colonial Africa, a re-assertion and affirmation of Africa's intangible heritage – the religio-cultural beliefs which after subjection to suppression, demonization and other forms of attack by western missionaries, reappears in new forms and continues to be expressed in different forms and ways by Neo-Pentecostals (consciously or unconsciously). There is a need to note the differences that run in these ministries and denominations in spite of the fact that most of them are 'penny-capitalist'.[8] Also, of positive note, Anderson says:

> Pentecostal liturgy has social and revolutionary implications in that it empowers marginalized people, to overcome barriers of race, social status and education.[9]

Health and Well-being: The Trademark of African Pentecostalism

The quest for health and well-being is within the matrix of the prosperity gospel. Prosperity is deliverance from powers of darkness in order to realise total salvation, physically and spiritually. Deliverance, healing and prayer are central tenets in Pentecostal beliefs and practice in order to realize 'salvation'. Many Pentecostals in Africa have established healing schools to deal with cases beyond western medicines and are diagnosed as spiritual. Examples include Christ Embassy in South Africa, ZAOGA in Zimbabwe and the Synagogue Church of All Nations (SCOAN) in Nigeria. While success is explained on the progress of the individual, it extends to the family and the nations, thus the increasing interaction between Pentecostal leaders and politicians.[10] In countries like Zimbabwe, Uganda and Nigeria, Pentecostals have influenced decisions in the country, especially on moral issues which saw the denunciation of same-sex relationships. However, the major criticism is that Pentecostals fail to critique the ailing economies of their nations that are largely run by corrupt politicians. This failure to critique corruption when they have influence is regarded by Kalu as weak political theology[11] and by Biri as a manifestation of the corruption that is also

---

[5] Kudzai Biri, "Religion and Emerging Technologies in Zimbabwe: Contesting for Space?," *International Open and Distance Learning Journal 1*, no. 1 (2013): 19-27.
[6] Paul Gifford, *Christianity, Development and Modernity in Africa*. London: Hurst (2015), 1.
[7] Paul Gifford, *Christianity, Politics and Public Life in Kenya*. London: Hurst and Company (2009).
[8] David Maxwell, "Catch the Cockerel Before Dawn: Pentecostalism and Politics in Post-Colonial Zimbabwe," *Africa, 70*, no. 20 (2002): 249-277.
[9] Anderson, "An Introduction," 19.
[10] Afe Adogame, "The Politicisation of Religion and the Religionisation of Politics in Nigeria," in *Religion, History and Politics in Nigeria: Essays in Honour Of Ogbu Kalu*, eds. Ogbu Kalu, Chima J. Korieh, G. Ugo Nwokeji and Obioma Nnaemeka (Lanham: University Press of America, 2005): 125-139.
[11] Kalu, "African Pentecostalism," page numbers missing!

inherent within Pentecostalism when they shield corruption and emphasise prayer for leaders as a panacea for challenges in Africa.[12] However, the significance of their political theology is their affirmation of mother Africa and the emphasis on the empowerment of the black race. Ota Mensabil of Ghana, Guti and Tudor Bismarck of Zimbabwe are examples of Pentecostal leaders who forcefully espouse pan-African ideas in their theologies. Prosperity of individuals is marked by prosperity of the nations. The leaders are able to reach out to many people through different forms of media. It is therefore important to briefly consider the use of religious media by Pentecostals in order to propagate the gospel and advance their religious ideologies.

New Religious Media and Technologies

Gerrie ter Haar notes that the electronic media is a characteristic of modern Pentecostal movements in Africa under its strong tradition of oral culture.[13] This has enabled them to evangelise and connect with the outside world, facilitating mutual exchange which has enriched African Pentecostalism within the global framework. Deliverance and prayer sessions are communicated through the media. They have used religious media to convey the gospel message and market the founders of denominations and ministries as a way to lure people to the healing schools. In Nigeria, SCOAN of Temitope Bolugun Joshua has Global Network, Christ Embassy has Love World, ZAOGA has Ezekiel TV among many others as they market themselves and compete for clientele. Biri notes:

> Pentecostals claim to be experts in divine healing, prophecy and many other areas of specialisation. This differentiation is basically effective competition when they solicit people to join their churches, especially through advertisements on television, posters and pamphlets.[14]

Pentecostals use different forms of media to communicate and this competition partly explains why some figures such as TB Joshua and Odeyepo of Nigeria, Mensa Otabil and Kusi Boateng of Ghana and Ezekiel Guti of Zimbabwe emerge as spiritual mentors.

Godfather/mother Phenomenon: Fuelling the Rise of New Religious Movements

Another aspect in Pentecostalism is the concept of godfathers/mothers who provide counselling and guidance to their 'sons/daughters'. There are men and women that have emerged to be 'mothers' and 'fathers' of other Pentecostals. The claims are that they are imbued with God's wisdom and experience in the ministries and therefore they can provide mentorship especially on spiritual matters. This phenomenon has not received the special attention that it deserves. I argue that it is one that leads to formation of new denominations if the sons/daughters feel they are mature spiritually. Hollenweger points out that continued breakaways are the greatest weakness of Pentecostalism .[15] Mentorship of members might be the reason for renewal and growth in African Christianity as many who are mentored feel they are equipped to establish ministries. Some leaders are popular. In Zimbabwe, Ezekiel Guti has the title of African apostle and spiritual father even beyond African borders, in the Bahamas, America and the USA. In Ghana, Victor Kusi Boateng is one such for some Zimbabwean Pentecostal leaders. This is facilitated by international and trans-national connections that have characterised Pentecostalism in Africa.

---

[12] Biri, "Religion and Emerging Technologies in Zimbabwe: Contesting for Space?," *International Open and Distance Learning Journal 1*, no. 1 (2013): 19-27.
[13] Gerrie ter Haar, *Half Way to Paradise: African Christians in Europe*. Cardiff: Cardiff Academic Press (1998), 176.
[14] Biri, "Emerging Technologies," 12.
[15] Walter Hollenweger, *The Pentecostals*. Peabody: Hendrickson (1972).

I am aware that the concept of spiritual mother is not popular probably due to the patriarchal nature of both Pentecostalism and the dominance of male scholarship. In this study, I acknowledge the concept and the popularity especially in Zimbabwe and the fact that in many countries, couples are co-founders and become mentors. Also, interdenominational ministries are established by women or the women's ministries run by 'first ladies',[16] therefore women remain pivotal in Pentecostalism.

Criticisms of Neo-Pentecostal Churches

Criticism focuses on a number of issues deriving from the structures and theology of the denominations but this is not treated exhaustively in this article. Some scholars think there is lack of emphasis on the cross because of celebrating the founders of denominations who have become authoritarians[17] and 'living saints'.[18] Some of the churches are corrupt especially on the abuse of money because there appear to be no democratic and accountable structures. In Nigeria, it has been argued that, if you want to be rich, start a Pentecostal church or sell oil. In Zimbabwe, corruption is a major challenge and temptation because most of the leaders are establishing private schools and pre-schools as private properties and questions are often raised with regard to the sources of the money. The love of money has led to the question of whether these are men/women of God or men/women of gold.[19] Ukah dismisses the messages of prosperity as a charade[20] although that offhand dismissal is suspect. Nwosuh sees the prosperity gospel as a subtle denial of the reality of suffering pain and failure in Christian mystery which does not appropriate the mystery of the cross.[21]

In addition to the above criticism, the other problem is that of the continuous abuse of power by leaders. Many followers cannot critically question their authority. Hence, one finds examples like the South African End Time Message Church where in 2014, congregants were told to drink petrol and eat grass on the orders of the so-called man of God. In Zimbabwe, the media are awash with cases of sexual abuse of women by male leaders who take advantage of their status and unquestioned authority. Again, women and children constitute the bulk of those victimized. There is a need to point out that all these criticisms levelled against Neo-Pentecostals may not be universally binding in that I argue that there are a lot of variations in terms of practices in relation to the theology of prosperity.

In spite of this criticism, Anderson notes that the emergence of these churches indicates that there are unresolved questions such as healing, success and the holistic dimension of salvation.[22] He further says: The here and now problems being addressed by the new Pentecostal and charismatic churches are problems that still challenge the church today.[23] Asamoah-Gyadu adds:

---

[16] Kalu, "African Pentecostalism," 12.

[17] Kudzai Biri, *African Pentecostalism and Cultural Resilience: The Zimbabwe Assemblies of God Africa*. Unpublished DPhil, Department of Religious Studies, Classics and Philosophy, University of Zimbabwe, 2013.

[18] Hillary Achunike, *The Influence of Pentecostalism and Catholic Priests and Seminarians in Nigeria*. Onitsha: Africana First Publishers (2004).

[19] Kudzai Biri and Clemence Makamure, *Man of God or Man of Gold?: A Critique of Pentecostalism and the Message of Prosperity in Zimbabwe*, forthcoming.

[20] Asonzeh Ukah, *African Pentecostalism, Features Promises and Problems*, Lagos: African Heritage Publishers (2007).

[21] "Christianity without Memory: An Evaluation of Pentecostalism in response to Emeka Nwosuh", in: Ezra Chitando, Masiiwah Ragies Gunda, Joachim Kügler (eds): *Prophets, Profits and the Bible in Zimbabwe*, University of Bamberg Press 2013

[22] A: Anderson, *African Reformation, An Initiated Christianity in the 20th Century*, Asmara: Africa World Press (2001).

[23] Anderson, "African Reformation," 280.

> Africa within the last half century emerged as a hot bed of contemporary pentecostalism in both its classical and neo-pentecostal versions… The growing attention to the new brand of pentecostalism is testimony to its current significance in African Christianity.[24]

In spite of some valid criticism of some features within the Neo-Pentecostal churches they have indeed influenced and altered the face of African Christianity and placed African Neo-Pentecostals on the global map.

Conclusion

I have pointed out that Pentecostalism in Africa is a unique phenomenon within global Christianity. The movement continues to grow and to influence many facets of life and hence has changed the face of Christianity in Africa. The theology of prosperity is central in these Neo-Pentecostal churches. In spite of the vibrancy of Pentecostalism, there are also negative criticisms levelled against it, especially regarding prosperity and the unquestioned authority and status of the founders or leaders. In spite of criticisms against Pentecostals, they have remained a resilient and vibrant force on the religious landscape, affecting the public face of African Christianity and changing its social role.

Bibliography

Afe Adogame, The Politicisation of Religion and the Religionisation of Politics in Nigeria in *Religion, History and Politics in Nigeria: Essays in Honour Of Ogbu Kalu*, eds., Ogbu Kalu, Chima J. Korieh, C. and G. Ugo Nwokeji and Obioma Nnaemeka, U (Lanham, MD: University Press of America, 2005).: 125-139. Allan Anderson, *An Introduction to Pentecostalism*. Cambridge: Cambridge University Press (2004).

Kudzai Biri, 'Religion and Emerging Technologies in Zimbabwe: Contesting for Space?' *International Open and Distance Learning Journal 1*, no. 1 (2013): 19-27.

Paul Gifford, 'Prosperity: A New and Foreign Element in African Christianity', *Religion 10*, no. 2 (2004), 160-184

Paul Gifford, *Christianity, Development and Modernity in Africa*, Bonn, Leipzig, 2015

Ogbu Kalu, *African Pentecostalism: An Introduction*, Oxford, Oxford University Press, 2008

David Maxwell, *African Gifts of the Spirit: Pentecostalism and the Rise of Zimbabwean Transnational Religious Movement.* London: James Currey; Harare: Weaver Press; Athens: Ohio University Press (2006),

Lovemore Togarasei, 'The Pentecostal Gospel of Prosperity in African Contexts of Poverty: An Appraisal', *Exchange40* (2011), 336-350.

[24] Kwabena Asamoah-Gyadu, "From Prophetism to Pentecostalism: Religious Innovation in Africa and African Religious Scholarship," in *African Traditional Religions in the Study of Religion in Africa*, eds. Afe Adogame, Ezra Chitando and Bolaji Bateye (Farnham, UK: Ashgate, 2012), 2-3.

(40) INTERDENOMINATIONAL CHURCHES IN AFRICA

Robert Kwasi Aboagye-Mensah

Introduction

Interdenominational churches are a continent-wide phenomenon. They bring together Christians who feel led to worship in churches that are not tied to any particular denomination. There are two broad types: the interdenominational type in which the traditions of the various denominations are identifiable and the non-denominational type in which denominational interests may not necessarily play any part in church life. If it is interdenominational, pastoral oversight is usually provided by pastors from the denominations whose members belong to the congregation. The reasons for the rise of interdenominational and non-denominational churches vary as stated below. This article focuses on examples taken from such churches from Central and West Africa, specifically from Zambia and Ghana.

African-Initiated Interdenominational Church

Christianity came to sub-Saharan Africa under the banner of denominational labels. In order to manage, control and contain their denominational antagonism, each denomination from Europe initially settled among particular ethnic groups. Each denomination believed firmly that its teaching was the right one and therefore did everything possible to ensure that its converts did not come in contact with people from other denominations.

However, in the early 1920s, something dramatic and unique happened in Zambia. African Christians from different ethnic backgrounds came to the Copperbelt in Zambia to work as migrant mining labourers. They came from all over Burundi, Rwanda, Malawi, Tanzania, Zimbabwe, and other places in Central Africa. When these African Christians met there 'they found that their old denominational labels meant hardly anything at all'.[1] What mattered to them was that they were Christian, with the message of the Saviour in their minds and hearts, and were ready and eager to walk with it.

Some of these African Christians were already evangelists and leaders in their previous denominations before they arrived at the Copperbelt. So they organized themselves into a church to minister to their own spiritual and physical needs. They named their church the Union Church of the Copperbelt (UCCB). The church was officially inaugurated in 1925, and they set up their own Board of Elders to organize its work. Through successful fund-raising activities, they had money to pay their evangelists and opened a school. They shared the gospel not only with their fellow miners, but also with the 'Lamba people in the neighbouring villages round about'.[2]

A.C. Cross gives us some insight into how the UCCB was organized. He writes, 'A self-supporting, self-governing Native Church has grown up and it is carried on by the Church on its own initiative and responsibility, not only among the mining employees, but also in the un-evangelised villages of the surrounding native district. A body of elders ably governs the Church. These elders arrange the Church's evangelistic programme and instruction of converts besides the ordinary services of the Church. In the pastoral work they are particularly successful, and one has often been struck with the spiritual sagacity they have displayed in dealing with difficult cases of discipline or the restoration of the erring members.'[3] Some

---

[1] Denis M'Passou, *Mindolo A Story of the Ecumenical Movement in Africa*, Lusaka: Multimedia Publications, 1983, 2.
[2] M'Passou, Mindolo A Story of the Ecumenical Movement in Africa, 4.
[3] Cited in M'Passou, A Story of the Ecumenical Movement in Africa, 5; see A.C. Cross, *In World Dominion VII*, 412.

of the educated Africans who were given responsible jobs on the mines 'used their education not only for personal advancement, but also to further the Kingdom of God on the Copperbelt. After working hours they conducted ecumenical Bible study, made pastoral visits and administered church business'.[4]

In 1932, as a result of a serious industrial crisis, the missionary bodies sent out a team led by the Rev. Merle Davis to find out how they could assist the Union Church. Consequently, in 1933, the London Missionary Society sent the Rev. R.J.B. Moore to the Copperbelt. With the help of African Christians in the Union Church, such as Elli Chola, established located the headquarters of Union Church at Mindolo, 'since Mindolo was the centre of these mining towns and already it had been used as a meeting place for the Union Church of Copperbelt'.[5] By the end of 1935, they had acquired a lease of the land and built a mission station on the land.

In 1935, there was another labour unrest at the Copperbelt, due to an increase in taxation. Six Africans were killed as a result of the riots that followed. As part of finding a long-term solution to this problem, in 1945 the missionaries of the London Missionary Society and those of the Church of Scotland agreed to merge and form one church, which they named the *United Church of Central Africa in Rhodesia.* The Union Church of the Copperbelt was absorbed into this new church. The merger thus brought to an end the first ever purely African-initiated interdenominational church in Africa.

However, the vision that those Africans had did not die with the merger. Mindolo remains the epicentre of African ecumenism. First, to reactivate the vision of the early Africans, in September 1958, Mindolo Ecumenical Foundation (MEF), was launched at Mindolo which was the headquarters of the Union Church. So far, MEF continues to affect African churches in various ways, including running youth leadership training programmes, and journalism courses. Secondly, the first-ever 'All-Africa Church Conference' was held at Ibadan, Nigeria, 10th-19th January 1958. At that conference, the idea of establishing a pan-African ecumenical organization, 'All Africa Conference of Churches' (AACC), was conceived, as the churches' witness in the social, economic and political arena. It was initially located at MEF, because Mindolo was the birth-place of African ecumenism. 'So from 1959 the All Africa Conference of Churches (AACC) had its Secretariat at Mindolo Ecumenical Foundation. Dr Donald M'timkulu, the first General Secretary of the AACC, and his staff started from Mindolo from 1960 until 1963, when he resigned and became Principal of Mindolo Ecumenical Foundation. His successor, Mr Samuel H. Amissah, also operated from Mindolo Ecumenical Foundation until the new organization later decided to move to Nairobi, Kenya, in 1965.'[6] Thus, the conception of AACC that began in Ibadan in January 1958, and was born at MEF in 1959, was later fully baptized and confirmed at Kampala, Uganda, in 1963 and in 1965 permanently located at Nairobi in Kenya, from where it continues to reach out to all African countries and the rest of the world. Now MEF is jointly owned by the All Africa Conference of Churches and the Council of Churches in Zambia.

European-Initiated Interdenominational Church

In 1935, the idea of forming what is now known as Accra Ridge Church began as a response to the needs of a few Anglican Low Church British expatriate Christians who were 'not used to the incense burning and other rituals at the Cathedral services',[7] which is a High Church practice. It was therefore decided that in order to make them feel at home, both in the use of the English language and in simple liturgy, a new congregation be set up at the Ridge area where most Europeans lived. In 1936, the congregation was

[4] M'Passou, *Mindolo A Story of the Ecumenical Movement in Africa*, 6.
[5] M'Passou, *Mindolo A Story of the Ecumenical Movement in Africa*, 8.
[6] M'Passou, *Mindolo A Story of the Ecumenical Movement in Africa*, 97.
[7] Mrs. Marion Odamtten, "In the Beginning of the Accra Ridge Church", cited in *Accra Ridge Church 70th Anniversary Souvenir 1936-2006*, 11.

officially recognized with only twelve members. The construction of a chapel that began in 1945, and completed in 1946, was dedicated by the then Anglican Bishop of Accra, Bishop Aglionby.

Dr E.A. Sackey, a Methodist, was the first African to join the church in 1948 through an invitation from his British colleague, Mr Prockter.[8] The membership of the church started growing steadily. In 1946, the membership was about 70; and in 1968, it had gone up to 270. In 1986, membership had risen to 2,646, and by 2007, it had shot up to 4,000 and is still growing.[9]

In terms of governance, Accra Ridge Church (ARC), like the other interdenominational churches in Africa, has its own constitution. What is unique about ARC is that the Chairman of the Council is a lay person, and not an ordained minister, and together with the Secretary and Treasurer, they constitute the officers of the Church Council.[10]

Christian Council-initiated Interdenominational Churches

In 1957, the Ghana Church Union Committee was set up by the Christian Council of Ghana. Membership of the Committee was made up of the foundational members of the Council, namely, the Methodist Church Ghana, the Anglican Diocese of Accra, the Presbyterian Church of Ghana and the Evangelical Presbyterian Church of Ghana. The main objective was to 'enter into negotiation and formulate concrete proposals that would facilitate a merger as one church by the deadline of 1975-1976'.[11] By 1971, the much-anticipated organic union body was named Church of Christ, Ghana.

Unexpectedly, in 1977-1978, the idea did not materialize due to 'apparently insurmountable problems'.[12] However, the twenty years of preparation in worshipping together, witnessing together and working together among the negotiating churches gave birth to 'multiple interdenominational congregations served by several Ministers belonging to the participating churches'.[13] Indeed, the formation of some interdenominational churches started in the 1960s in anticipation of the organic union, as mentioned above.

A few examples may suffice to illustrate the point. In 1967, as a result of 'house-to-house evangelism and "crusades" embarked upon by some students of the then Trinity College, Legon, in the mid-1960s',[14] the Trinity United Church was formed and later located at the Trinity Theological Seminary (formally Trinity College, Legon) campus. In 1964, the Ghana Police Church, Accra, was established by 'a group of policemen and some enthusiastic civilians and their families who met regularly in their homes for Christian fellowship' and they all belonged to the 'mainstream Protestant Churches, namely, Presbyterian, Methodist, and Anglican'.[15] Another example is the founding of the Legon Interdenominational Church (LIC). The reason for the establishment of LIC is that, in the 1970s, church services on the University of Ghana campus were held in the hall chapels during the semester. Whenever the university was on recess, campus residents either had to make their way into town on Sundays to worship, or else put worship on

---

[8] Dr. E.A. Sackey, "A Brief History of the Accra Ridge Church", in *Accra Ridge Church Golden Jubilee Souvenir 1936-1986,* 7.

[9] Victoria Oddoye, "A Brief History of the Accra Ridge Church", Accra Ridge Church Golden Jubilee Souvenir, 1936-1986, 9. A.F. Lokko, Chairman of Council, "Welcome Address and Brief History of the Church", in *Accra Ridge Church 70th Anniversary Souvenir 1936-2006,* 13.

[10] See *Accra Ridge Church Constitution 199* for details.

[11] James Anquandah, *AGENDA Extraordinaire, 80 Years of The Christian Council of Ghana, 1929-2009*, Asempa Publishers, Christian Council of Ghana, 2009 (12-13).

[12] James Anquandah, *AGENDA Extraordinaire,* 3.

[13] James Anquandah, *AGENDA Extraordinaire,* 4.

[14] *Orientation Guide for New Members, Trinity United Church, Legon, booklet,* 5.

[15] Frank Twum-Baah, Chaplain/Chief Superintendent of Police, in 50th Anniversary of The Ghana Police Church, Accra brochure, 5.

hold until students returned for the next session. Through the initiative and commitment of the late Prof. Alan Duthie, the Rev. Prof. Joshua Kudadjie, Dr Frederick Phillips and Prof. Kwadzo Senanu, 'a place was found on campus where Christians from all denominations could gather together in worship during the term as well as during the vacation. Their aim was to share fellowship and to encourage one another to put their Christian faith into action wherever they found themselves'.[16]

The next example is the Tema Joint Church. On 10th September 1977 representatives from the Tema Ecumenical Committee, consisting of Evangelical Presbyterian, Presbyterian, Methodist, Lutheran, Salvation Army, African Methodist, Episcopal Zion representatives, and some from Roman Catholic Church traditions witnessed the dedication of the church and social centre which came to be known as the Joint Church Centre. It was built with funds donated by Protestant Churches in West Germany. It was meant to support co-operation among churches, to facilitate the worship of the Triune God by workers and management, and to support Christian mission to the work places, particularly in the industries in Tema.

However, it was not until August 1992 that, through the Tema Industrial Chaplaincy and a determined group of Christians from various denominational backgrounds, that the Tema Joint Church congregation was established. 'The motivating factor was the desire for an ecumenical English-speaking congregation and shorter services'.[17] It started with about thirty members and at its 20th Anniversary celebration in 2012 membership had gone up to over 950, including children, and it is still growing in membership and the impact of its services is felt within and outside the church.

Theological Profiles

All the interdenominational churches in Central Africa and West Africa maintain the theological stance of the denominations from which they emerged. They take the Holy Bible as the divinely inspired word of God; and believe in the Triune God as stated in the Apostles' Creed and the Nicene Creed. However, in terms of liturgy for worship on Sundays each interdenominational church has developed its own liturgy to fit its particular form of worship.

Church Organization and Social Witness

Each interdenominational church has its own constitution that clearly states who they are, what they do, and how they govern themselves. They all have various groups and organizations within each church that play significant roles in the churches' social witnessing, development and *diakonia*. For instance, most of them, if not all, have Women's Fellowships (Ladies Fraternity for Tema Joint Church); Men's Fellowships (Men's Fraternity for Tema Joint Church), Choirs, Youth Fellowships, Bible Study groups, Boys and Girls Brigades, Girls Fellowships, Outreach Fellowships, Evangelism Groups, etc. All these para-church organisations have very active young people, giving hope for their future continuity.

Through these groups the interdenominational churches offer social services or witness to various and varied needy individuals and organizations. For example, the Tema Joint Church Ladies Fraternity periodically visits and donates money and other items to a Roman Catholic orphanage, 'Sisters of Charity Home' at Ashaiman, a deprived community near Tema. The active witnessing and the evangelistic outreach of these organizations have contributed tremendously towards the phenomenal growth of the interdenominational churches in Ghana.

---

[16] Unpublished Paper on the "Brief History of LIC", p.1. See, *Legon Interdenominational Church (LIC) Constitution December 2010,* for more information on how the Church is structured and organized.

[17] Information card, 2. See also, *The Joint Church 20th Anniversary Souvenir Brochure and Thanksgiving Service, Sunday, 5th August 2012, and The Joint News, Volume 3, Issue 4, December 2012,* for details about the church and its activities and achievements.

In Ghana, most of these churches had been financially supporting the work of the Christian Council of Ghana (CCG) as their contributions had enabled the CCG to fulfil its obligations to the churches and the nation. They also actively participate in the life and ministry of the Council by having their representatives serving on the various committees and organizations of the Council.

Conclusion

As stated in the introduction, space and time will not permit us to include all the interdenominational churches in Africa in this article. For instance, we have Interdenominational Churches in Kenya and South Africa that are not covered here. It will suffice to say that they all give a central place to the Bible as the Word of God, create modes of worship that suit their particular needs, and encourage teaching and witnessing to their faith.

Bibliography

James Anquandah, *AGENDA Extraordinaire, 80 Years of The Christian Council of Ghana, 1929-2009*, Asempa Publishers, Christian Council of Ghana, 2009

Denis M'Passou, *Mindolo A Story of the Ecumenical Movement in Africa*, Lusaka: Multimedia Publications, 1983

Victoria Oddoye, 'A Brief History of the Accra Ridge Church', Accra Ridge Church Golden Jubilee Souvenir, 1936-1986

(41) Evangelical Churches and Movements in Africa

James Nkansah-Obrempong

Introduction

This article looks at evangelical churches and the evangelical movement in Africa. It provides a brief history of evangelical churches and the evangelical movement; it outlines the theological characteristics of evangelical churches and the movement and shows how they have contributed to and influenced spiritual growth, national development and improved the social, political and economic lives of the people within these churches and the movement. It also addresses how the churches and the movement have promoted *diakonia* within the national evangelical churches and other Christian communities.

The word 'evangelical' derives from the word 'evangel' that means 'gospel' or 'good news'. By definition, an evangelical church is one that is wholly committed to the preaching of the gospel of Jesus Christ as the only means of human salvation and that holds to the authority of the Holy Scriptures for faith and life. For such a church, the preaching of the whole gospel and evangelization and the preaching of the word of God is central to its mission and practice. The evangelical movement is an extension of the churches at the continental level that is committed to extend the Kingdom of God by making disciples of all nations and promoting the gospel of Jesus Christ throughout the entire globe and fostering Christ-centred transformation within church and wider society.

A Brief History of Evangelical Churches

The origins of these evangelical churches are linked with missionary activities of western mission agencies which came to Africa from the seventeenth century onward to evangelize Africa. Churches were planted as indigenous people expressed faith in Jesus Christ. These churches were established to nurture the new Christians and to give them opportunity to worship God. Different mission agencies came to different African countries, and through evangelization of the people, established churches in these countries. Most of these evangelical churches bear the DNA of the mother churches in the west that gave birth to them. So, we have evangelical churches spread over the entire continent of Africa. There have been some indigenous evangelical churches that have developed like the Aladura Churches in West Africa and the Zionist Churches in South Africa and more recently the Neo-Pentecostal and neo-charismatic churches that are springing up all over Africa. While these Pentecostal and charismatic churches are local initiatives by Africans, most have collaboration and partnerships with other charismatic and Pentecostal churches in Europe and North America.

Characteristics of African Evangelical Churches

Evangelical churches in Africa are trans-denominational and found within Protestantism. There are over 100 million evangelical believers in Africa who come from diverse denominational backgrounds such as Reformed, Baptists, Wesleyans, Pentecostals, Charismatics, Anabaptists, Anglicans and Lutherans spread across the entire continent. These churches subscribe to the salient elements of the Christian faith, namely: personal conversion or salvation from sin which comes to every human being freely and simply by faith in Jesus Christ who shed his blood for sin, and regeneration by the Holy Spirit. Evangelical churches uphold the authority of the Old and New Testament Scriptures as God's word and revelation to humanity, and they see the Scriptures as the primary authority for faith and practice. They affirm biblical inspiration and the infallibility of the Bible. They believe in the triune nature of God who exists eternally as Father, Son and Holy Spirit, each distinct and divine, and all involved in the redemption of humanity and creation. Evangelical churches provide a prophetic voice and challenge the *status quo*: they are relevant and speak to the issues and challenges facing them, and are strongly committed to evangelism and social action by addressing the socio-political and economic life of people in their countries.

These churches have played a seminal role in the spiritual growth and spread of Christianity in Africa. Through their unrelenting zeal to preach the gospel and to evangelize Africa, Christianity has been growing by leaps and bounds on the continent and today Africa boasts of being one of the leading Christian continents.

The Role of Evangelical Churches in Africa

Evangelical churches in Africa have played seminal roles in fighting for social and religious freedom, as well as economic and democratic space in many African countries where there have been injustices and religious, economic and political oppressions. Besides fighting for human dignity and freedom from oppression, these churches have engaged in transformative projects such as schools, hospitals, vocational training centres, and community development projects that have empowered many marginalized communities in Africa and have benefited and bettered the lives of many people in their countries. Evangelical churches continue to engage in these activities, 'by engaging in them, many marginalized people have experienced economic and social transformation.

Most of these evangelical churches are members of a continental body called the Association of Evangelicals in Africa[1] which provides the platform and support for them, and through national evangelical fellowships to foster *koinonia* among the various churches and other Christian communities.

The Historical Background of the Evangelical Movement in Africa

The Evangelical movement as an organized institution in Africa started with the formation of the Association of Evangelicals in Africa (AEA). Until this time, there was no organized and vibrant evangelical movement on the continent.

AEA was formed on 26th February 1966 at Limuru, Kenya, during a meeting of 102 evangelical Christian leaders from twenty-three African nations and missionaries from other countries led by its first African General Secretary, the late Rev. Dr Byang Henry Kato. The meeting had been convened as a result of the need felt by the evangelicals for a permanent association which would help build a united movement of the Body of Christ to promote evangelical unity, fellowship, and Christian witness in Africa.

AEA is one of the seven regional movements which make up the World Evangelical Alliance (WEA) and subscribes to the overall vision of WEA: to extend the kingdom of God by making disciples of all nations by Christ-centred transformation within society. AEA exists to foster Christian unity, provide identity, voice and platform for some 100 million evangelical Christians in Africa.

The movement's vision is to unite Evangelicals in Africa for holistic ministries that make a difference and its mission is to mobilize and empower Evangelical churches and mission agencies for total transformation of Africa through evangelization and effective discipleship. In order to realize the vision and mission, the Association is guided by the following six core values: partnership in the gospel; prayer for the transformation of individuals and communities; transformational engagement in society;

[1] See: http://www.aeafrica.org/

proclamation of the gospel in word, deed and life; stewardship of God's creation (resources); Christ-like character in service and leadership.

AEA National Evangelical Fellowships (NEFs)

In its half-century of existence, AEA has grown into a continental family of over 100 million evangelicals consisting of 36 National Evangelical Fellowships (NEFs) that are made up of numerous local churches across the continent of Africa. There are 34 Associate Members who consist of para-church organizations, and eleven Special Members representing local churches in countries where there are no National Evangelical Alliances. AEA works closely with these National Fellowships by providing an evangelical platform for the Association to respond effectively to spiritual, religious, socio-political and economic issues facing the church in Africa as integral to its mission.

We must point out that there are many evangelicals in Africa who are not members of the AEA, but they hold the tenets of evangelical theology. Most of these Christians are in the mainline denominations in Africa such as Anglican, Methodist, Presbyterian and Lutheran and in some of the charismatic and Pentecostal churches, which have their own national councils and associations that address their needs and concerns.

Theology and Characteristics of the Evangelical Movement

The evangelical movement in Africa sees itself as the custodian of evangelical theology or orthodoxy. There are certain characteristics of evangelical theology. These include the centrality of the gospel, faith in Christ as the means of salvation, faithfulness and obedience to God's word and acceptance of its authority for doctrine and practice, and the presence and power of the Holy Spirit in effecting transformation in peoples' lives. Evangelical theology simply is a Trinitarian theology. John Stott reiterates this notion of the evangelical faith in one of his publications:[2]

Evangelical theology upholds:

- Biblical revelation and the authority of Scripture for faith and practice.
- Commitment to the centrality of the Cross of Christ for humanity's and creation's redemption.
- Recognition and acceptance of the ministry of the Holy Spirit in the church to effectively apply the blessings of God to his people.

In summary, evangelical Christianity upholds these three fundamental ideas: the word, the cross, and the Holy Spirit. Any evangelical will uphold these fundamental truths of the Christian faith. Evangelicals in Africa have always upheld these basic tenets of the Christian faith and have defended them. These tenets of the Christian faith have social, political and economic implications for Christian engagement in society. However, some brands of African evangelicalism have not done so well on social, political and economic issues that affect people. Some of these groups tend to dichotomize the physical and the spiritual dimensions of human life. While there are successes that can be celebrated by evangelicals in Africa, we are yet to see any noticeable transformation in evangelical Christianity, especially in its impact on society.

African evangelicals since the early 1970s have tried to develop an African evangelical theology that is truly biblical and truly African. This has been a rewarding phenomenon, but very a difficult project. The challenge lies in being faithful to scripture and taking seriously the African cultural, religious, socio-economic and political contexts. Christianity's impact on the socio-economic and political lives of the African people depends on how well evangelical theology addresses these critical issues facing the African

[2] John Stott: *Evangelical Truth: a personal plead for unity, integrity and faithfulness,* 1999, 25-30.

continent. The AEA has endeavoured to provide and promote holistic ministries to address some of these critical issues facing the Africa Church through its commissions and projects.

More recently, with the new hermeneutics gaining ground in Africa, African women theologians are raising some fundamental theological issues relating to women's experiences that they feel the current theological discourse does not pay attention to. These are causing concerns for evangelical theologians, calling them to take seriously gender issues, as well as concern for the marginalized – such as the poor, children, and the destitute in society. Such concerns have pushed evangelicals to develop a vibrant theology that addresses human needs as well as engaging the intellectual realities of modern Africa.

The Association of Evangelicals in Africa's Commissions and Projects

To achieve this holistic, transformational ministry, AEA created eleven Commissions and five projects to address these different needs of the church. The Commissions were all based at the headquarters in Nairobi at their inception but for effectiveness in their work they were later decentralized to different countries in Africa, bringing the work and presence of the Commissions closer to the evangelical fellowships in the regions where AEA serves. Some of the Commissions are more active than others, but they are all working to address specific issues that Africans face.

The eleven Commissions include the following: Communications Commission (CC) in Côte d'Ivoire; Evangelism and Missions (EMC) in Nairobi; Ethics, Peace and Justice (EPJC) in Zimbabwe; Pan Africa Women Alliance (PACWA) in Burkina Faso; Relief and Development (ARDC) in Uganda; Theological and Christian Education (TCEC) in Nairobi; Youth and Sports (YSC) in Nairobi; Prayer and Church Renewal (PCRC) in Nairobi; Stewardship and Accountability (SAC); Evangelical Focus on Children (EFOC); and Information Technology (ITC).

Through its Theological and Christian Education Commission, AEA created two projects that include two graduate-level theological institutions, namely, the Nairobi Evangelical Graduate School of Theology (NEGST), now called Africa International University for Anglophone Africa, and the Bangui Evangelical School of Theology (BEST), also known as Faculté de Théologie Evangélique de Bangui (FATEB) for francophone Africa. Both theological institutions offer undergraduate and graduate programmes up to doctoral level. AEA theological institutions serve the church and the wider Christian community, training and equipping pastors, teachers, evangelists, missionaries, administrators, and laymen and women for the c church in Africa. Due to its interdenominational stance, it has trained Christian leaders from all the mainline, Pentecostal and charismatic churches in Africa and abroad. These two institutions have trained most African church leaders who are heads of churches and leading national church bodies, such as the National Council of Churches in Kenya (NCCK), heads of denominations and presidents of universities, all across Africa.

The second project of the TCEC is the Christian Learning Material Centre (CLMC) that was established to develop Christian materials to meet the educational needs of the African Church. Since its inception in 1983, CLMC has continued to produce Sunday school and Christian materials to help the church in Africa to disciple and train its members and build them up to maturity. This has helped bridge a gap and also produce materials that are culturally relevant for discipling Christians in Africa that are not western in origin and most often are not appropriate as teaching material for the African context.

The third project of the TCEC is the Accrediting Council for Theological Education in Africa, now called the Association for Christian Theological Education in Africa (ACTEA). It was founded in March 1976 to create a forum for evangelical theological schools in Africa, to assist them in areas of common need, to accredit theological institutions in Africa to ensure quality evangelical theological education and training for the African Church. Since its inception, ACTEA has accredited fifteen theological colleges and seminaries across Africa, including the Christian Service University in Ghana, Scott Christian University and the Nairobi Evangelical Graduate School of Theology in Nairobi, and many others. This has improved the quality of theological education in Africa.

AEA encourages and assists emerging indigenous mission organizations in Africa through its Commission on Evangelism and Missions by providing them with a platform for fellowship and exchange of ideas and strategies in missions. It encourages research on the unreached peoples in Africa and serves as a liaison between missionary sending agencies and receiving fields. It also stirs up evangelism at the grass root level by encouraging the formation of evangelism departments in the local churches, which in turn belong to the National Evangelism Committees.

The Ethics, Peace and Justice Commission of the AEA holds the portfolio of educating the church in matters of ethics, peace and social justice. They have advocated for religious tolerance, democratic space, equity and socio-economic development for all in many African countries where there is oppression and injustice.

The Pan African Christian Women Alliance (PACWA) exists as the women's commission of AEA to empower women to become all that God made them to be and encourage their full participation in every sphere of life as individuals, in families, in the church and in society. PACWA provides a forum through which Christian women work to fulfil their God-given mandate of reaching the whole world with the whole gospel of Jesus Christ.

PACWA empowers women through evangelism and discipleship, adult education programmes and training in holistic ministry and practical skills which include spiritual, physical, social and economic dimensions. PACWA is passionate about restoring the true dignity and self-worth of women who have been victims of gender-based violence and abuse. Through advocacy, PACWA seeks to push for policies, social structures that favour justice, equity, social and economic development for all.

The African Relief and Development Commission (ARDC) works to empower and transform society through relief, rehabilitation and development. It was created to serve the evangelical constituency and wider society in Africa to engage in meaningful and effective holistic ministries aimed at reducing human suffering.

ARDC is a Christian response to caring, collaboration and transformational development in Africa, and a continental movement of evangelical churches and Christian agencies committed to discipling nations for Christ through collaborative action.

Over the years, ARDC has enabled evangelical churches to develop a positive attitude and involvement in relief, development, and social transformation. ARDC has carried out interventions responding to needs of member alliances and communities affected by armed conflicts, wars, floods, famine, and other forms of natural or man-made disasters.

In 1987, AEA began expressing serious concern for the plight of children in Africa at its 4th General Assembly in Zambia. At its 6th General Assembly in Nigeria in 1993, AEA's Evangelical Focus on Children Commission (EFOC) was established. EFOC networks and collaborates with children's organizations in Africa to address the issues of children. EFOC seeks to raise children's profile in all Christian institutions and society; protect the rights of children; promote a holistic child ministry in evangelism and social concerns; produce or facilitate the production of good Christian education materials for children; and educate society on the proper place of children in the human community.

The AEA's Information Technology Commission was established to use modern technology for the dissemination of information and sharing of resources among the members and partners of AEA, and throughout the greater evangelical church. In a vision to serve and empower the dispersed global church, the IT Commission is to create a global digital infrastructure to build modern-day networks and systems providing a digital forum to help increase effectiveness in communication, exchange of information and promotion of partnership and collaboration among Christians and ministries on the web.

Conclusion

AEA has a strong commitment to missions and social engagement through its eleven commissions and five projects. The Nairobi Office is the headquarters of the movement and provides support services to the operational arms (commissions and projects), National Alliances, Associates and other global partners. AEA remains faithful to its vision of uniting the Body of Christ through capacity enhancement for effective holistic ministries for the transformation of Africa.

The Association has had six General Secretaries since its inception: the Rev. Kenneth Downing (1966-1970), the Rev. Dr Byang Henry Kato (1973-1975), the Rev. Dr Tokunboh Adeyemo (1977-2001), Mr Daniel Bitrus (2002-2005), the Rev. Dr Judy Mbugua (2005-2009) and the current General Secretary, Aiah Foday-Khabenje (June 2009 to the present).

As part of its commitment to foster unity and *diakonia* within the wider Christian community, Evangelicals in Africa through their global body, the World Evangelical Alliance, and their counterparts, the WCC and the Roman Catholic Church, jointly produced a text on *Evangelism in Multi-Religious Contexts*. This document has become very useful to Evangelicals in Africa as we seek to minister and share the Christian faith in a multi-religious context. This document, together with the *Cape Town Commitment: A Confession of Faith and a Call to Action*, are two important documents that should continue to shape and provide direction for African evangelicals as they engage in the world and do mission in a pluralistic society.

Bibliography

www.aeafrica.org

www.worldevangelicals.org/members/aea.htm

www.teasa.org.za

http://mb-soft.com/believe/text/evangeli.htm

https://www.oikoumene.org/en/resources/documents/wcc-programmes/interreligious-dialogue-and-cooperation/christian-identity-in-pluralistic-societies/christian-witness-in-a-multi-religious-world

Breman, Christina Maria. *The Association of Evangelicals in Africa*. Zoetermeer, Holland: Boekencentrum,1996.

Stott, John. *Evangelical Truth: A Personal Plea for Unity, Integrity, and Faithfulness*. Downers Grove, Ill. IVP, 2003

The Lausanne Movement. *The Cape Town Commitment: A Confession of Faith and a Call to Action*. Peabody: MA, Hendrickson Publishers, 2011.

Tidball, Derek. *Who are the Evangelicals?: Tracing the Roots of the Modern Movements*. London: Marshall Pickering, 1994.

(42) Independent Churches in Africa (AICs)

Thomas Oduro

The history of African Independent Churches dates back to the first century AD when according to Coptic Orthodox traditions, John Mark, a Jew who was born in Cyrene, one of the Pentapolis in North Africa, established Christianity in Alexandria. 'Traditional Coptic sources hold that "the Coptic Church is based on the teachings of St Mark who brought Christianity to Egypt during the reign of Emperor Nero in the first century, a dozen of years after the Lord's ascension…"'[1] This belief is so entrenched in the history of the Coptic Church of Egypt that in 1978 Pope Shenouda III, then the Coptic Patriarch of Alexandria, convened an assembly of twenty prominent AIC leaders in Cairo[2] to form the Organisation of African Instituted Churches (OAIC), an ecumenical council of African Instituted Churches.

Next in the line of churches believed to have been founded by Africans with a strong Afrocentric emphasis was the ancient Ethiopian church that was established by Egyptian Copts. 'The story of this church provides fascinating parallels and inspiration to parts of the AIC movement to emerge in the nineteenth century, particularly for those who see Ethiopia as the model of African dignity, independence and prestige'.[3] AICs can, therefore, be categorized into two main genres: early AICs and post-reformation AICs; the latter are the ones that this article is mainly about.

Activities of western Protestant missions and missionaries in sub-Saharan Africa from the nineteenth century onwards were successful; not only did they plant many denominations, they built and operated schools, hospitals, clinics and agricultural ventures. Many African languages were written. The Bible was translated into some African languages. Christianity, thus, got a firm footing in Africa.

Despite the success story of western missionaries in Africa, many African Christians drew people's attention to the need to establish African churches. These have been called precursors of AICs. Some of them robustly and plainly critiqued western missionaries and called for the Africanization of the church. David Brown Vincent, a Nigerian who later changed his name to Mojola Agbebi, in his Africanization campaign, stated emphatically that 'The foreigner is not fitted to construct an African Church'.[4] Other precursors[5] quietly ministered among Africans without openly critiquing western missionaries but incidentally taught African Christians that they too could minister in an African milieu.

Following the examples set by the precursors, many Africans began establishing their own form of Christianity which was different from the mainline African Christianity planted by western missionaries. The new form of Christianity was called African Independent Churches (AICs) by some western scholars and missiologists. They are so-called 'because they are African-initiated, are indeed indigenous, and – with some important exceptions – have carried on their life and ministry quite independently of mission-planted denominations, of local and national councils… which are themselves all emanations of western missionary endeavours'.[6] In most cases, the independence of the AICs was intentionally carried out in

---

[1] Thomas C. Oden, *The African Memory of Mark: Reassessing Early Church Tradition* (Downers Grove, Illinois: IVP Academic, 2011), 36.

[2] Allan H. Anderson, *African Reformation: African Initiated Christianity in the 20th Century* (Asmara: Africa World Press, Inc., 2001), 162.

[3] Anderson, *African Reformation*, 46.

[4] Adrian Hastings, *The Church in Africa 1450-1950.* (Oxford: Clarendon Press, 1994), 495. See also Anderson, *African Reformation*, 47-51.

[5] Deji Isaac Ayegobyin and S. Ademola Ishola, *African Indigenous Churches: An Historical Perspective* (Bukuru: Africa Christian Textbooks, 2013), 39-54.

[6] David A. Shank, "African Independent Churches, African Theology and Western Co-workers in the Missio Dei" in David A. Shank (ed), *Ministry in Partnership with African Independent Churches* (Elkhart, Indiana: Mennonite Board

reaction to some missionary policies, practices and interpretation of Scripture. Some African Christians became disgruntled with western missionaries' attempt to blend Christianity with western civilization, thus making African Christians conform to western Christianity, culture and lifestyles, as stated by Paul Makhubu, an AIC leader in South Africa.

> Some white missionaries, instead of teaching Christianity, promoted and taught white civilization. The blacks were stripped of their customs, and in exchange were forced into a culture they could never embrace.[7]

Many African beliefs, worldviews, cultures, personalities, values and concepts were either derided, dissuaded, discarded or labelled 'superstitious'. The use of African music, songs, liturgies, choreography, exuberance and costume in the church was discouraged and to some extent banned.[8] Africans who were trained in western educational institutions and seminaries were perceived fit to lead only Africans since it was difficult for some western missionaries to serve under African leaders.[9] Even though some scholars rebuff the reactionary theory and situate it to the initial emergence of the AICs,[10] there were many AICs that were established from the first quarter of the twentieth century in reaction to western missionaries' concept of Christianity.[11] No matter how the AIC phenomena is perceived, it is a fact that the 'AICs...seek the Africanization of Christianity in outlook, form and scope, distinct from and without administrative connections with foreign mission-based organizations'.[12] Other non-reactionary factors such as the translation of the Bible into African languages, the religious activities of African precursors of AICs, passion for a purer form of Christianity, the desire for a pragmatic Jesus and sheer ambition to be idolized[13] were prominent in the establishment of African Independent Churches. The complexity of the nature and ministry of the AICs earned them descriptions such as 'nativistic', 'tribal', 'neo-pagan', 'Ethiopian', and many others.[14] However, many scholars used the title 'African Independent Churches' (AICs) to describe the phenomena.

Over the years, some scholars have replaced the word 'Independent' in the AIC acronym with 'Initiated', 'Indigenous', and 'Instituted' but these are all varieties of their independence. The use of the word 'independent' is, however, the core description and understanding not only of their history and theology but also of their liturgies; it is the very reason for their existence. As a result, some AICs are not inhibited to 'repeat the Western pattern of some of the older churches in their doctrine, worship, polity, and to a large extent in their ethos'.[15] No matter how one regards the independence of the AICs, they 'fully

---

of Missions, 1991), 5.

[7] Paul Makhubu, *Who are the Independent Churches ?*(Braamfontein: Skotaville Publishers, 1998), 24.

[8] For examples of reactions against western missions, read Harris W. Mobley, *The Ghanaian's Image of the Missionary: An Analysis of the Published Critiques of Christian Missionaries by Ghanaians (1897-1955).* Leiden: E. J. Brill, 1970.

[9] Ted Olsen, "Bishop Before His Time," *Christian History*, Issue 79 (Vol. XXII, No. 3) 10-11, 13, 15. See also, Wilbert R. Shenk, *Henry Venn – Missionary Statesman* (Ibadan: Orbis Books, 1983), 112, 113.

[10] See Anderson, *African Reformation*, 27-29.

[11] In South Africa, according to Paul Makhubu, the Tomlinson's Report in 1955 listed thirty reasons for breakaways from white churches to form African Independent Churches. Most of the reasons were reactionary in nature. See, Paul Makhubu, *Who are the Independent Churches?* (Johannesburg: Skotaville Publishers, 1988), 20-38.

[12] John S. Pobee and Gabriel Ositelu II, *African Initiatives in Christianity: The growth, gifts and diversities of indigenous African churches – a challenge to the ecumenical movement* (Geneva: WCC Publications, 1998), 4.

[13] See, Kofi Asare Opoku, "A Brief History of Independent Church Movement in Ghana since 1862" in *The Rise of Independent Churches in Ghana,* Asempa Publishers (ed) (Accra: Asempa Publishers, 1990): 12-21; Allan Anderson, *African Reformation*, 31-33; Ayegobyin and Ishola, *African Indigenous Churches*, 11-16.

[14] Afe Adogame& Lazio Jafta, "Zionists, Aladura and Roho: African Instituted Churches" in Ogbu U. Kalu, ed. *African Christianity: An African Story* (Asmara, Eritrea: African World Press Inc., 2007), 272-274.

[15] Harold Turner, *African Independent Church II: The Life and Faith of the Church of the Lord (Aladura)* (Oxford:

deserve their name; they are nobody's puppets'.[16] As a result, they do not seek approval from any western church to develop their own doctrines, liturgies and mission; they are neither afraid nor embarrassed to be distinct from all other churches or Christian communions.

The African nature of AICs prompted Harold Turner to define AICs as 'a church which has been founded in Africa, by Africans and primarily for Africans'.[17] Other scholars later modified the definition as, churches initiated or founded by Africans for Africans.[18] Initially, such definitions seem legitimate but when one considers the spread of the AICs beyond the borders of Africa and the multiculturalism of their membership,[19] one realizes that the AICs are not homogenous religious organizations founded in Africa for Africans.

Growth of the AICs

The growth and spread of African Independent Churches has been phenomenal. Though it is difficult to compute the exact number of AICs in Africa, 'there are at least 10,000 different AIC denominations across the continent'.[20] Philip Jenkins observes:

> Every Easter, more than a million ZCC (Zion Christian Church) pilgrims gather for several days of celebrations at Zion City, the church's chief shrine in South Africa. To put it in perspective, the crowd gathered at the ZCC's pilgrimage is larger than that which greets the Pope in St Peter's Square on Easter morning.[21]

African Independent Churches can be found in about forty-three countries in Africa. In some countries, they form the largest population of Christians, as stated by Jenkins in 2002:

> Only about 30% of Botswana's church members belong to familiar denominations like Anglicans, Methodists and Roman Catholics. Seven per cent more adhere to Pentecostal groups, while the remainder, almost two-thirds of Christian believers, belongs to AICs. In this region at least, independent groups continue to grow quickly, while membership in the mission churches stagnates.[22]

Some AICs can be described as 'mega-denominations' since they have millions of congregants. Some of the mega-AICs are Zion Christian Church (ZCC) in South Africa, founded in 1924 by Engenas Lekganyane,[23] the Aladura group of churches and their appendages,[24] and the Church of Jesus Christ on Earth by His Special Envoy Simon Kimbangu (*Eglise du Christ sur la Terre par le Prophète Simon Kimbangu* (EJCSK)). It was established by Prophet Simon Kimbangu of the Democratic Republic of Congo in 1921.

Clarendon Press, 1967), xvi.

[16] Philip Jenkins, *The Next Christendom: The Coming of a Global Christianity* (Oxford: Oxford University Press, 2002), 68.

[17] Harold Turner, *Religious Innovation in Africa* (Boston: G. K. Hall & Co., 1979), 92.

[18] See Jenkins, *The Next Christendom*, 52. See also, Anderson, *African Reformation*, 45.

[19] Pobee and Ositelu II, *African Initiatives in Christianity*, 52.See also, Afe Adogame, *The African Christian Diaspora: New Currents and Emerging Trends in World Christianity* (London: Bloomsbury Academic, 2013), 70, 71.

[20] Thomas Oduro, Hennie Pretorius, Stan Nussbaum and Bryan Born, *Mission in an African Way: A Practical introduction to African Instituted Churches and their sense of mission* (Wellington, South Africa: Christian Literature Fund, 2008), 10.

[21] Jenkins, *The Next Christendom*, 68.

[22] Jenkins, *The Next Christendom*, 69.

[23] Read more about Zion Christian Church, Anderson, *African Reformation*, 98-106.

[24] Adogame, *The African Christian Diaspora*, 67

Today, the Kimbanguist Church is not only present in Congo (country of origin) but also in other countries in Africa, as in Angola, Congo/Brazzaville, Zambia, Central Africa, Burundi, South Africa, Nigeria, Kenya, Cameroon, Gabon, Senegal and Côte d'Ivoire, and other continents, as in Belgium, France, the Netherlands, Switzerland, Spain, Finland, Germany, England, Sweden, Ireland, Italy, Portugal, Canada, Brazil and the United States. Statistics gathered n 1981 put at more than five million the number of Kimbanguists around the world.[25]

Factors in Growth

The ability of leaders of the African Independent Churches to integrate African worldviews, personalities and concepts into their brand of Christianity attracts many people – including Christians from western mission churches and non-Christians – to them. The AICs are places where African worshippers feel at home because the worship styles, interpretation of scripture, emphasis on healing, interpretation of dreams and concept of *ecclesia* are not strange to them. Hannah Botsie, for instance, left the Methodist Church of Ghana to become a member of the Divine Healer's Church at Winneba, Ghana, because:

> In the Methodist Church there was no healing, our dreams were never interpreted; we never had messages (i.e. prophetic messages). Nothing was done to heal us of our diseases and no word at all was said about our future. There was nothing spiritual about the Methodist Church.[26]

In Africa, where most events are considered to have spiritual connotations and ramifications, practising a high sense of spirituality seems to be the *raison d'être* of the AICs. No wonder they are called 'spiritual churches' in Ghana, Kenya and Nigeria.[27]

Their emphasis on prayer and fasting and its resulting efficacy equip their members to wage spiritual warfare against the forces of darkness and to seek protection from God. As a result, AIC leaders claim to be spiritual stalwarts. 'Politically, we are harmless; economically, we are feeble; socially, we are downtrodden; but spiritually, we are more than giants.'[28] They claim to be in close communion with the Holy Spirit even to the extent of 'catching' songs,[29] receiving directives to where and when they should missionize,[30] from the Second Person of the Trinity. Therefore, their followers approach them for solutions to what they perceive as spiritual challenges.

Their worship styles are vibrant and vigorous. 'When black people worship, it is with the entirety of their being. Singing and dancing go together… They become emotionally involved, especially in the Zionist and Pentecostal churches.'[31] Women are not marginalized in AICs; their claim to being called into pastoral ministry and to lead denominations is respected. The use of their spiritual giftedness is also highly

---

[25] "Histoire du Kimbanguisme," Translated from French. www.kimbanguisme.net/histoire/histoire1.htm (accessed 26 January 2015).
[26] Robert W. Wyllie, *Spiritism in Ghana: A Study of New Religious Movements* (Missoula, Montana: Scholars Press, 1980), 128.
[27] Ayegboyin & Ishola, *African Indigenous Churches*, 18. Note: the term "Spiritual Churches" was initially used to ridicule the AICs but it has now become normative.
[28] Wyllie, *Spiritism in Ghana*, 105.
[29] Thomas Oduro, "Church Music in the Life of African Christian Communities", in Roberta King, et al. *Music in the Life of the African Church* (Waco, Texas: Baylor University Press, 2008), 81-99. See also, J. Akinyele Omoyajowo. *Cherubim and Seraphim: The History of an African Independent Church* (Lagos: NOK Publishers International, 1982), 61.
[30] Thomas A. Oduro, "'Arise, Walk through the Length and Breadth of the Land': Missionary Concepts and Strategies of African Independent Churches" in *International Bulletin of Missionary Research*, Vol. 38, No. 2, April 2014, pp. 86-89.
[31] Makhubu, *Who Are the African Independent Churches?* 25.

patronized.[32] In fact, AICs put a greater premium on the giftedness of women than their gender. Therefore, the AICs are churches where women receive the dignity they deserve among humanity.

Receiving divine healing is a central point of attraction of the African Independent Churches. Ayegboyin and Ishola have rightly observed that:

> Indeed, sickness is by far the most common reason which people give for attending AICs. Testimonies of healing, soundness and miracles are heard from many about their answered prayers. In quite a number of cases those concerned claim that they first went to the hospitals, and or consulted traditional leaders.[33]

AIC leaders, at times, heal without the use of elements[34] while in most cases they use many elements to heal.[35] AICs believe that Jesus Christ, being 'the same yesterday, today and tomorrow',[36] still heals. They do not relegate healing to the time of Jesus Christ and the apostles. They believe also that there is no disease that is beyond the healing power of Jesus Christ so they neither panic nor doubt whenever they are called to pray for the sick to be healed. In fact, they habitually invite people who are sick to come to Jesus for healing in their congregations.

The growth of the AICs does not depend only on their attempts to make Christianity look African; it also depends, to a larger extent, on a conscious commitment to evangelism and mission. Engaging in a conversation with people with problems – depression, fear of demons, marital problems, single-parenthood, drug addiction, unemployment, nightmares, constant miscarriages and child mortalities, fear of the future, etc. – and inviting them to come to Jesus for a solution is the commonest evangelistic strategy. Some AICs invite members to testify to what God has done for them whenever they meet to worship. Testimonies tend to build the faith of the audience and expand their theological perceptions. Furthermore, testimonies are disseminated to non-members with the purpose of inviting them to join AIC congregations. Some AICs in Nairobi, Kenya, strategically choose to worship near bus terminals and open spaces just to attract people who, under normal circumstances, would not dare to listen to them.

Initially, the uniqueness of the ministries of the AICs caused many members of western mission-founded churches to defect from their mother churches to join them. There was, thus, a great concern of leaders of some western mission-founded churches either to find the causes of the stupendous growth of the AICs or to devise some means to reclaim their members.

Persecution of the AICs

David Barrett has rightly observed that 'The history of modern African religious movements reveals a remarkably long list of movements and prophets that have fallen foul of colonial and other governments in Africa and have suffered persecution.'[37] The growth and spread of African Independent Churches is ironic when one considers the persecution some AIC forerunners endured at the hands of some colonial and African rulers for fear of instigating popular uprising due to their massive numbers of followers. The best-known ones are the burning of Kimpa Vita (1684-1706), also known as Donna Béatrice, and her son in the

---

[32] Philomena Njeru Mwaura, "Gender and Power in African Christianity: African Instituted Churches and Pentecostal Churches" in Ogbu U. Kalu (editor), *African Christianity: African Story* (Eritrea: Africa World Press Inc., 2007), 359-388. See also the ministry of prophetess Agnes Okoh in, Thomas Oduro, *Christ Holy Church International: The story of an African Independent Church* (Lagos: Greater Heights Publishers, 2009), 71-98.

[33] Ayegboyin and Ishola, *African Indigenous Churches*, 19.

[34] Oduro, *Christ Holy Church International*, 122, 123.

[35] Anderson, *African Reformation*, 199, 200.

[36] Hebrews 13:8

[37] David Barrett, *Schism and Renewal in Africa: An Analysis of Six Thousand Contemporary Religious Movements* (Nairobi: Oxford University Press, 1968), 72.

Kongo kingdom at the command of King Pedro of Portugal and at the request of the Catholic Capuchin missionaries,[38] and the extradition of William Wade Harris from Ivory Coast to Liberia, his home country, after a successful evangelistic stint in Ivory Coast and western parts of Ghana.[39] Some AIC leaders who followed the footpaths of the precursors were equally persecuted by some colonial governments who were alarmed at their numerous followers and popular message. The popularity of Prophet Simon Kimbangu, after raising a dead girl back to life, caused some uncomfortable political ripples in the administration of the Belgian colonial rulers. Consequently, he was arrested, tried and imprisoned for thirty years until he died.

The adherence of some AIC movements to directives of their leaders rather than the orders of some colonial governments became fertile grounds for persecutions. The Bulhoek massacre in May 1921 in which the colonial government of South Africa assembled 800 policemen to forcefully evict the Israelites (followers of prophet Enoch Mgijima), from the holy village of Ntabelanga at Kamastone, in which nearly 200 Israelites were killed, is a clear example. The Israelites congregated at Ntabelanga at the instruction of Mgilima who prophesied an impending millennium. Mgilima and other Israelites were jailed.[40] Prophetess Nontetha Nkwenkwe, a Xhosa who was born about 1875 and grew up at a place near King William's Town in South Africa, was an illiterate widow with ten children to care for. She was a herbalist and seer before God called her to begin a prophetic movement. Her followers refused to kill locusts in defiance of a law passed by the colonial government.

> According to her followers, Nontetha before she was arrested, had predicted that an invasion of locusts would sweep through the region. She proclaimed God had sent them as a punishment and decreed that none be killed. When a swarm of *voetganger* locusts descended on the area in September and October 1923, government officials ordered the people to kill them… When Nontetha's followers refused to kill the locusts, officials had a legal pretext for disrupting the movement.[41]

Prophetess Nkwenkwe was arrested and jailed in 1922. She was later released but banned from preaching. She disregarded the ban so she was labelled insane, 'a sufferer of dementia praecox or paranoia' and committed to mental hospitals at Fort Beaufort (1923) and at Pretoria in 1924 till she died on 20 May 1935.[42] Some Christians from western mission-founded churches also persecuted the AICs. Such persecutions emanated from their perception of the AICs.

> There was a time (and even today) when it was taught in the Established Churches that the Independent Churches are sects, Dissident churches, churches of ill-disciplined people, and therefore it was necessary to be careful not to mix oneself too much with these churches; if these lost sheep want to return to the fold let them repent and rid themselves of their dirty linen of independency.[43]

This Madagascan perception of AICs was also shared by many members of western mission-founded churches in other parts of Africa. Consequently, the uniforms, flags, colours, style of singing, liturgies,

---

38 Anderson, *African Reformation*, 47-51.

39 Ayegboyin and Ishola, *African Indigenous Churches*, 39-46.

40 Robert R. Edgar and Hilary Sapire, *African Apocalypse: The Story of Nontetha Nkwenkwe, a Twentieth-Century South African Prophet* (Johannesburg: Witwatersrand University Press, 2000), 23. See also, "A History of the Bulhoek Massacre," www.sahistory.org.za/topic/history-bulhoek-massacre.(accessed 5 February 2015)

41 Edgar and Sapire, *African Apocalypse,* 29.

42 Edgar and Sapire, *African Apocalypse*, 25-87. Attempts by the government to proscribe Nkwenkwe's moved failed. Her followers formed the Church of Nontetha.

43 Rev. Dr. Ratovonarivo, "The Independent Churches in Madagascar: A Brief Survey" in *African Independent Churches in the 80s,* Sam Babs Mala, ed. (Lagos: Gilbert, Grace and Gabriel Associates, 1983), 52.

doctrines, beliefs, choreographies, intellect, hermeneutics, homiletics and even worship styles of AICs have been ridiculed in various forms and degrees. Electronic and print media have been used extensively to vilify and demonize AICs and their leaders in many countries. African Independent Churches have, undoubtedly, been persecuted more severely than any Christian communion in Africa. The plight of the AICs can be likened to that of the Anabaptists in sixteenth-century Europe.

Contributions of the AICs to African Christianity

African Independent Churches can be said to have dramatically reformed the trend and perception of Christianity in Africa and of Africans when one considers the type of Christianity that was in place before their emergence. Theologically, they have inculcated African traditional concepts of God to give Africans a better understanding of God. They have accomplished this through the lyrics of their hymnodies, gospel songs and prayers.

Through the healing ministries of the AICs, Africans no longer perceive God as a transcendent God who should be approached through many human intermediaries for the forgiveness of sins and the efficacy of prayers. The intensity of their fasting and prayers, spiritual retreats, and their emphasis on living a spiritual life which is concomitant with being acceptable to God, have enabled Africans to retrieve their high sense of spirituality. AICs have reformulated the Christology of Africans. Jesus is no longer perceived only as a great moral teacher and a saviour but also a leader who pragmatically meets the needs of those who seek him. The Holy Spirit is now perceived as one who not only heals and regenerates but one who equips Christians to engage in battles with spiritual forces. African Christians no longer dread the mention of the name of the evil one and his cohorts or dismiss their reality as a figment of one's mind. By the testimonies of the AICs, African Christians believe that they are capable of resisting and overpowering Satan and his demonic alliances.

Liturgically, AICs have proven to Africans that God accepts contextual worship. During the consecration of the second bishop of the Cape Coast diocese of the Church of the Province of West Africa (the Anglican Church), John Pobee observed the enthusiasm of the congregation when they sang and danced to songs which emanated from the AICs. He later commented,

> The atmosphere accorded well with African style – spontaneous dancing, singing, and enthusiasm at public meetings. What is interesting is that an historic church like the Anglican Church was called and was able… to borrow from the music and style of the African Independent Churches.[44]

Pobee's observation is not peculiar to the Anglicans in Cape Coast. Many African Christian communities – including the ones established by western missionaries – now worship God by using their traditional choreographies, costumes, mother tongues, worldviews, cultural matrix, leadership concepts, rhythms, songs and instruments.

Missiologically, the AICs, though without mission professors, mission institutions, and mission committees, have spread, not only in African countries where they began, but beyond their countries of establishment to other African countries. AICs have planted many congregations in almost every continent of the world. Their missionary concepts and strategies are different from traditional western missionary concepts.[45] The spread of the AICs to other continents and African countries have made them the trailblazers of mission in reverse. Now, African Christians know that they can establish their congregations in foreign lands without necessarily receiving help from any church in the West.

---

[44] Pobee and Ositelu II, *African Initiatives in Christianity*, 1.
[45] Thomas A. Oduro, "'Arise and Walk….'", 86-88.

Socially, AICs have widened the understanding and scope of the *ecclesia* in Africa. The persecutions they endured and the lack of support from western Christians made them see themselves as the only ones to determine the qualitative, quantitative and financial growth of their churches. Following the trend of the AICs, African Christians now perceive the church as their own institution. As a result, Christianity is no longer referred to in Africa as 'the white man's religion'. Members of AICs see themselves as members of an extended African family – caring for one another as if they were genetic siblings.

Economically, AICs – though mostly poor and without receiving financial aid from the West – have built agricultural, health and educational institutions. AICs have proven to other Africans that the African Church can use her scarce resources to improve the economy of her immediate environment, just as western mission-founded churches, with some support from the West, have done in Africa.

Pastoral Training and Ecumenism

African Independent Churches use many pedagogies to train their leaders and members.[46] They also congregate in ecumenical bodies, the largest being the Organisation of African Instituted Churches (OAIC).

Conclusion

The emergence, meteoric growth, persecutions and contributions of African Independent Churches have enriched the story of Christianity in Africa and the world. It is not strange, therefore, that Pobee and Ositelu have stated emphatically, 'There is no way we can talk of world Christianity, much less Christianity in Africa, without taking account of this genre of AICs.'[47] Indeed, the AICs are 'the signature tune of African Christianity'.[48] Without taking account of them, it is difficult to either understand or appreciate African Christianity and its ramifications.

Bibliography

Adogame, Afe. *The African Christian Diaspora: New Currents and Emerging* Trends in World Christianity. London: Bloomsbury Academic. 2013

Adogame, Afe & Jafta, Lazio. 'Zionists, Aladura and Roho: African Instituted Churches' in Ogbu U. Kalu, ed. *African Christianity: An African Story,* edited by Ogbu U. Kalu, 271-287. Asmara, Eritrea: African World Press Inc., 2007.

Anderson, Allan H. *African Reformation: African Initiated Christianity in the 20th Century.* Asmara: Africa World Press, Inc., 2001.

Ayegboyin, Deji Isaac &Ishola, S. Ademola. *African Indigenous Churches: An Historical Perspective.* Bukuru: Africa Christian Textbooks, 2013.

Barrett, David, *Schism and Renewal in Africa: An Analysis of Six Thousand Contemporary Religious Movements.* Nairobi: Oxford University Press, 1968.

---

[46] See Thomas Oduro, "Theological Education in African Independent Churches: A Plethora of Pedagogies" in Isabel Apawo Phiri and Dietrich Werner (editors), *Handbook of Theological Education in Africa* (Oxford: Regnum Books International, 2013), 423-432.

[47] Pobee and Ositelu II, *African Initiatives in Christianity*, 5.

[48] Lamin Sanneh. "World Christianity and the new Historiography: History and Global Interconnections" in Wilbert R. Shenk (editor), *Enlarging the Story: Perspectives on Writing World Christian History* (Maryknoll, New York: 2002), 109.

Edgar, Robert R, and Sapire, Hilary. *African Apocalypse: The Story of Nontetha Nkwenkwe, a Twentieth-Century South African Prophet*. Johannesburg: Witwatersrand University Press, 2000.

Hastings, Adrian. *The Church in Africa 1450-1950*. Oxford: Clarendon Press, 1994.

Jenkins, Philip. *The Next Christendom: The Coming of a Global Christianity.* Oxford: Oxford University Press, 2002.

Makhubu, Paul. *Who are the Independent Churches?* Braamfontein: Publishers, 1998.

Mobley, Harris W. *The Ghanaian's Image of the Missionary: An Analysis of the Published Critiques of Christian Missionaries by Ghanaians (1897-1955).* Leiden: E. J. Brill, 1970.

Mwaura, Philomena Njeru. 'Gender and Power in African Christianity: African Instituted Churches and Pentecostal Churches' in *African Christianity: African Story,* edited by Ogbu U. Kalu, 359-388. Eritrea: Africa World Press Inc., 2007.

Oden, Thomas C. *The African Memory of Mark: Reassessing Early Church Tradition.* Downers Grove, Illinois: IVP Academic, 2011.

Oduro, Thomas A. '"Arise, Walk through the Length and Breadth of the Land": Missionary Concepts and Strategies of African Independent Churches', *International Bulletin of Missionary Research*, Vol. 38, No. 2 (April 2014): 86-89.

______. 'Church Music in the Life of African Christian Communities', in *Music in the Life of the African Church.* Roberta King with Jean Ngoya Kidula, James Krabill and Thomas A. Oduro., 81-99. Waco, Texas: Baylor University Press, 2008.

______. *Christ Holy Church International: The story of an African Independent Church.* Lagos: Greater Heights Publishers, 2009.

______. 'Theological Education in African Independent Churches: A Plethora of Pedagogies' in *Handbook of Theological Education in Africa,* edited by Isabel Apawo Phiri and Dietrich Werner, 423-432. Oxford: Regnum Books International, 2013.

Oduro, Thomas A, Pretorius, Hennie, Nussbaum, Stan and Born, Bryan. *Mission in an African Way: A Practical introduction to African Instituted Churches and their sense of mission.* Wellington, South Africa: Christian Literature Fund, 2008.

Olsen, Ted. 'Bishop Before His Time', *Christian History*, Issue 79, Vol. XXII, No. 3: 10-11, 13, 15.

Omoyajowo, J. Akinyele. *Cherubim and Seraphim: The History of an African Independent Church.* Lagos: NOK Publishers International, 1982.

Opoku, Kofi Asare. 'A Brief History of Independent Church Movement in Ghana since 1862' in *The Rise of Independent Churches in Ghana,* edited by Asempa Publishers, 12-21. Accra: Asempa Publishers, 1990).

Pobee, John S. and Ositelu II, Gabriel. *African Initiatives in Christianity: The growth, gifts and diversities of indigenous African churches – a challenge to the ecumenical movement.* Geneva: WCC Publications, 1998.

Ratovonarivo, Rev. Dr 'The Independent Churches in Madagascar: A Brief Survey' in *African Independent Churches in the 80s,* edited by Sam Babs Mala, 46-57. (Lagos: Gilbert, Grace and Gabriel Associates, 1983

Sanneh, Lamin. 'World Christianity and the new Historiography: History and Global Interconnections' in *Enlarging the Story: Perspectives on Writing World Christian History,* edited by Wilbert R. Shenk. Maryknoll, New York: 2002.

Shank, David A. 'African Independent Churches, African Theology and Western Co-workers in the Mission Dei' in *Ministry in Partnership with African Independent Churches,* edited by David A. Shank, 3-21. Elkhart, Indiana: Mennonite Board of Missions, 1991.

Shenk, Wilbert R. *Henry Venn – Missionary Statesman.* Ibadan: Orbis Books, 1983.

Turner, Harold. *African Independent Church II: The Life and Faith of the Church of the Lord (Aladura).* Oxford: Clarendon Press, 1967.

______. *Religious Innovation in Africa.* Boston: G. K. Hall & Co., 1979.

Wyllie, Robert W. *Spiritism in Ghana: A Study of New Religious Movements.* Missoula, Montana: Scholars Press, 1980.

Internet Articles

'Histoire du Kimbanguisme'. Translated from the French: www.kimbanguisme.net/histoire/histoire1.htm (accessed 5 February 2015)
'A History of the Bulhoek Massacre': www.sahistory.org.za/topic/history-bulhoek-massacre (accessed 5 February 2015).

(43) United Aladura Churches (UAC) – White Garment Churches in Africa

Rufus Okikiola Ositelu

Introduction

The United Aladura Churches (White Garment Churches) form the largest movement among the African-Initiated Churches. It was established in 1930. The members always wear white and no shoes in the temples (church buildings). It has about five thousand (5,000) churches all over the world and three thousand (3,000) in Nigeria alone. The Aladura Communion has an estimated population of fifty million members worldwide. Within this communion is found United Aladura Churches (UAC), an ecumenical umbrella organisation, founded in 2004 with its headquarters in Nigeria and branches all over the world. It has about 35 million members, 15,000 pastors and 12,000 parishes (congregations).

The Self-Understanding of the United Aladura Churches

In the Preamble of the UAC Constitution, the United Aladura Churches' motto is stated: 'The true light now shines' (1 John 2:8). Its vision is to encourage growth, purity, identity and unity of the White Garment/Aladura Churches. Its mission is stated as to facilitate and build the capacity of member churches towards living and sustaining a Christian lifestyle, thus upholding the status of White Garment/Aladura Churches in the African continent and beyond. According to its value statements, the UAC promote visible unification of White Garment/Aladura Churches, transparency of action, accountability and open-mindedness, culminating in living exemplary lives. It is governed by the Board of Trustees (BOT) of the United Aladura Churches (UAC) which includes seven senior church leaders. These include Most Elder Apostle Solomon Alao (C&S), The Most Rev. Dr Rufus Ositelu (TCLAW), Archbishop John Ogunsile (TCLAW), Pastor Emmanuel Oschoffa (CCC), Superior Evangelist S.O. Banjo (CCC), Bishop S.A. Ademosu (FCDM) and Bishop C.O. Kaiyewu (FCDM).

The Background and Self-Understanding of Cherubim and Seraphim Churches (C&S)

There are over 350 stand-alone church organizations within the Cherubim and Seraphim Church Movement (C&S) group of churches. In a bid to fortify its unity, the Cherubim and Seraphim Unification Church has ratified the election of its fourth supreme head, Prophet Solomon Adegboyega Alao. Before, he was the General Superintendent of Sacred Cherubim and Seraphim Church, the position he has held since 1995 after the demise of Prophet Jacob Adeolegan Omole, who became the fourth General Superintendent of the church in 1982.

The Background and Self-Understanding of the Church of the Lord (Aladura) Worldwide (TCLAW)

The Church of the Lord (Aladura) Worldwide (TCLAW) has its international and spiritual headquarters in Nigeria, West Africa, with parishes in Sierra Leone, Ivory Coast, Liberia, Ghana, Togo, Republic of Benin, UK, Germany, Luxembourg, Spain, Australia, New Zealand and the USA. TCLAW has about 3,600,000 members in Nigeria and 8,200,000 members worldwide. It has about 4,000 pastors, twelve provinces, 100 dioceses and 3,800 parishes. The church is a member of diverse organizations, including the World

Council of Churches, All Africa Conference of Churches, the Christian Council of Nigeria, and United Aladura Churches.

The Yoruba word 'Aladura' means 'Prayer Fellowship' or 'The Praying People'. The members of the Aladura churches believe in the power of praying and fasting (Yoruba is a major language of the south-western region of Nigeria). The founder of the Church of the Lord (Aladura), the late Prophet Dr Josiah Olunowo Ositelu (also written as Oshitelu), received his calling in 1925 and founded the Church the same year, and the independent church was inaugurated in 1930, in Ogere. Prophet General Dr Josiah Olunowo Ositelu (1900-1966) was the founder and first primate of the 'Church of the Lord (Aladura) Worldwide', one of the first-generation African Initiated and Independent Churches. The current Pope is His Eminence, the Most Reverend Dr Rufus Okikiolaolu Olubiyi Ositelu. He is the Archbishop and Metropolitan of the Arch-Province of Nigeria, and the incumbent and the Fourth Primate of the 'Church of the Lord (Aladura) Worldwide (TCLAW)' organization. He is also the Pope of the Aladura Communion Worldwide (ACW) consisting of all White Garment churches (Aladura Churches). Primate Ositelu is the son of the late Prophet General Dr Josiah Olunowo Ositelu and Archbishop (Mrs) Susannah Adewunmi Ositelu, popularly called 'Mama Aladura or Mama Kekere'.

The six tenets of the church as explained by the incumbent Primate – The Most Reverend Dr Rufus Ositelu – are:

Biblical-in-Pattern – in the sense that, in all matters of faith, conduct and doctrine, our Supreme Court of Appeal should always be the Holy Bible, and whenever we come to a crossroads or at a road-block in our deliberations, our next reaction must be: 'Let us read/hear what the Bible says on this.' Thus, the Holy Bible is our Spiritual Constitution.

Pentecostal-in-Power – in the sense that the Spirit of Jesus Christ is the Guide and Administrator of the Church through which the Church is guided, directed, filled, influenced, administered and managed. The Spirit of Jesus Christ shall quicken, inspire and stir everyone up, always to glorious and godly deeds.

Evangelical-in-Mission – in the sense that we carry the gospel of Christ to the nooks and crannies of the world, and to preach, witness and propagate the Good News to all, and to make disciples of all nations unto the Lord Jesus Christ, irrespective of background, race or gender.

Ecumenical-in-Outlook – in the sense that we embrace and encourage brotherly and sisterly love among believers, and not to forsake the assembly of the saints.

Prophetic-in-Ministry – in the sense that this is the genesis and pillar on which The Church of the Lord (Aladura) Worldwide (TCLAW) is anchored. The gifts of prophecy, dream, vision, revelation, speaking in tongues, healing, signs and wonder, teaching and administration are bestowed on the Church.

Social-in-Responsibility – in the sense that we believe that the Church should be a blessing to the communities where it is situated and the inhabitants of the state in general.

The major concerns of the church in the 21st century are to train more efficient church workers, and to expand its social contributions to the society at large. The church's seminary – Aladura Theological Institute (ATI) – has now been affiliated with Lagos State University (LASU) and offers diploma, graduate and postgraduate degree courses in Theology and Christian Education.

The Background and Self-Understanding of Celestial Church of Christ (CCC)

The Celestial Church of Christ is a spiritual, worldwide, united, indivisible Holy Church which came into the world from heaven by DIVINE ORDER on 29th September 1947 in Porto Novo, Republic of Benin, through the founder of the church, the Late Reverend Pastor Prophet Samuel Bilehou (sometimes written as Bilewu) Joseph Oshoffa (sometimes written as Oschoffa, Osofa) who, in addition to being the founder, was also the first Pastor (Head) of the church. The church is well known with parishes and dioceses all over the world, with its international headquarters in Nigeria. The movement has continued to grow since Oshoffa's death, but has also suffered setbacks, the most immediate being severe difficulties related to the matter of succession.

Some elements in the self-understanding and some challenges of the Celestial Church of Christ will be described in the following six points:

a) Schism in the Leadership of the Church – Several individuals have been claiming the leadership of the church since the death of its founder. Among them are Josiah Kayode Owodunni, Alexander Abiodun Bada (late), Paul Suru Maforikan, G. Bolanle Shonekan, just to mention a few.

b) Re-unification Effort – Efforts are being made to unify all the different factions of the church. Following the evidently negative and less progressive effects which partnership has had and is still having on the intractable leadership crisis in Celestial Church of Christ worldwide, through family-related loyalties and allegiance of shepherds and parishioners to human leaders (pastors), it became expedient for shepherds and parishioners to hold their total loyalty and allegiance to our Lord Jesus Christ alone and evolve a project that will bring us together in the same vineyard under ONE shepherd.

This development became necessary in order for such shepherds and parishioners to avail themselves of the opportunity to come together as an independent and unbiased body to fight on a common ground termed GLOBAL UNIFICATION OF THE CELESTIAL CHURCH OF CHRIST.

This project started with a clear mission to do the utmost to reconcile whatever differences that might be existing amongst the leadership of the church and unify the various factions so as to enable the church to properly promote the divine mission of winning souls for Christ. The project is not unmindful of the serious lacuna existing in the church constitution and the discretion of the spiritual tenets of the church by those who may not wish the church well; it is hoped that these shortcomings would be addressed as the project progresses.

The Celestial Church of Christ (CCC) unification and reform group, Nigeria and the Diaspora, consists of the universal unification group under Prophet Johnson Shodipe; the CCC northern elders' forum under Evangelist Akin Arikawe; the administration group under Michael Akinsoji; the CCC unification and renaissance mission under Prophet Emmanuel Asebiomo expressly to chart a new course of unity under one pastor (leader). Debo Oladimeji in a caption, 'CCC set to vanquish demon of disunity', reported on the situation of leadership in the Celestial Church of Christ (CCC) and efforts so far made to move the church forward. Excerpt:

> On April 30, 2013 the Celestial Church of Christ (CCC) unification and reform group, Nigeria and the Diaspora, published an advert in the Guardian Newspaper which made many members of the church eager to know more about CCC which has been without a true Pastor (Head) since the demise of the Pastor and Founder of the church, Rev. Samuel Oschoffa, 27 years ago… Emmanuel Asebiomo added that the effort they are making now is to bring the church together and that God has made it possible for them to formulate a new administrative structure, recommended a financial guideline, and drafted a new Nigerian Constitution to replace the Constitution Oschoffa left behind. Another member of the unification committee, Evangelist TundeAbai of CCC Igbekeleolu Parish, who has been a member of the church for over 35 years said that the Supreme Court, Nigeria held in the case of A.A. Bada and Owodunni that the present Constitution did not give room for easy succession of the late Pastor and Founder. And since he did not name a particular person who was to succeed him in that Constitution, the next step was that the spirit appoint his successor… He added that people are now tired of 'hooliganism' within the church. We are working towards a situation where the Spirit of God will descend to appoint a Pastor (Leader) for us…

c) Beliefs – Although the church takes elements from Yoruba thought, it also has strong similarities to the 'purification movements' against paganism that are relatively common in African Christianity and

Islam. Oshoffa believed he had a mission to combat 'Satan', 'fetish priests' and other 'powers of darkness'. The name of the group comes from the Bible, Deuteronomy 26:15: 'Look down from thy Holy habitation, from heaven, and bless thy people Celestial and the land which thou hast given us, as thou didst swear to our father, a land flowing with milk and honey.' The name signifies that they deem themselves as celestial or a representative of the heavenly on Earth.

d) Tenet and Mode of Worship – The church under the absolute dictatorship of the Holy Spirit is hereby emphasized: the name of the church 'Celestial Church of Christ' was revealed by the Holy Spirit through a prophet who was held in trance for seven days. The rules and regulations are written in the booklet of 'Tenets and Admission into the membership of Celestial Church of Christ'. The mode of worship includes the setting of the altar, and the seat therein, the number of candles used for various types of services and the seating arrangement in particular. It should be noted that the seating arrangements were revealed through a prophetess who under the influence of the Holy Spirit in the wilderness on Friday 5th October 1947, sketched the seating arrangement using oranges.

The Services of the Church – There are different orders of service laid down in the Celestial Church of Christ for different occasions such as Marriage, Funeral, Naming Ceremony, Mass in Remembrance of the dead, etc. The order for the respective occasion is strictly as revealed by the Holy Spirit and as set out in the booklet entitled 'Order of Service'.

e) Holy Rites or Sacraments – There are a number of Holy Rites or Sacraments within the form of worship in Celestial Church of Christ that are of utmost importance. Members shall avail themselves of the opportunity to partake in these rites or sacraments: Baptism, Holy Communion, Annual Washing of Feet, Annual Pilgrimage to Imeko in Ogun State, Nigeria, at Christmas Eve, Annual Harvest Thanksgiving Service, and Holy Mary's Day.

f) Membership – All persons who earnestly, sincerely desire to be saved looking for salvation and therefore accept Jesus Christ as the son of God and Holy conversion by taking up such duties and privileges as entailed in the fellowship and the Ten Commandments are welcome into the fold. Celestial Church of Christ is an inclusive congregation, anyone with the desire to observe the Tenets and Mode of Worship is welcome.

g) Lingering Fractionalization – According to Superior Evangelist Lagun Adesanya who is the Shepherd-in-Charge of the Celestial Church of Christ (CCC) Valley of El-Bereka Parish, Mushin, Lagos, in an interview to the Guardian newspaper, spoke on the obstacles to unification in Celestial Church and lingering fractionalization of the CCC worldwide, the impediments to the unification and the way forward, and said: 'Declaring anyone "Pastor" (Head of the CCC) is contempt of court... Judgement of the Supreme Court has to be respected... Problems in the church are caused by selfishness and love of money (the root of all evils)... The solution is for us to follow the guidance of the Supreme Court, which said: "Sit down, formulate a new constitution." That is what we should have done since June 2000 when judgement was given. They put it aside and are doing their own will... You see, to them the word pastor means money. But they misread the constitution. It says, "The pastor shall hold in trust the income on behalf of the workers." The money does not belong to the pastor. Now, it is winner takes all. Once you are pastor, all the money is yours. That is why there is no progress in the church...' The church unfortunately is also known for having suffered from all kinds of allegations of fraud within its own ranks.

The Background and Self-Understanding of Fellowship of Christ Disciples Ministry (FCDM)

The Independent Group Churches (FCDM) are diverse small churches whose founders were former members of the C&S, TCLAW or CCC groups. The United Aladura Churches (UAC) has been a blessing to this group. The UAC has also been the motivating factor in bringing them together under a new group name: 'Fellowship of Christ Disciples Ministry (FCDM)'.

This 'Independent' group is not a registered name but an adopted name. The churches under this group were not working together as a group prior to their membership in the UAC. But through the 'Love, Unity and Administration' existing within the UAC, they were motivated and encouraged to take a new group name: 'FCDM', which has now been registered with the Corporate Affairs Commission (CAC) in Abuja, Federal Capital Territory (FCT) of Nigeria. The membership of this group within the United Aladura Churches (UAC) actually brought the member churches of this group out of their obscurity, for none of them was known nationally before their membership in UAC. And their membership as a group within UAC actually brought them together and encouraged them to work with one another and got them to register their group with the Corporate Affairs Commission (CAC) in Abuja, Nigeria as 'Fellowship of Christ Disciples Ministry (FCDM)'. Before the registration of this group as FCDM, the group was known as 'Independent Group' with the acronym 'Ind'.

Two prominent leaders of the Disciples of Christ (Independent Aladura Churches) are:

Bishop S.A. Ademosu of the 'Mount Jieawowrrar All Saints Church Aladura Worldwide', situated in Odogbolu, Ogun State, Nigeria.

Bishop C.O. Kaiyewu of the 'Universal Church of God's Anointing', situated at 53, Balogun Street, Shomolu, Lagos, Nigeria.

Concern for Education

The African Initiatives in Christianity have diverse concerns for education. Some of them have seminaries or theological institutions of diverse standards. Their greatest challenge is funding, particularly for books and infrastructure. Some of them do not have theological institutions and their Ministers of Religion learn by observation. Help in these areas would highly be appreciated.

Bibliography

Rufus Okikiolaolu Olubiyi Ositelu, *African Instituted Churches: Diversities, Growth, Gifts, Spirituality and Ecumenical Understanding of African Initiated Churches*. Reihe: *Beiträge zur Missionswissenschaft / Interkulturellen Theologie* (Münster: LIT Verlag, 2002).

(44) PARA-CHURCH MISSION NETWORKS AND ORGANIZATIONS IN AFRICA (IFES)

Kuzipa Nalwamba

Introduction

This is a descriptive outline of the International Fellowship of Evangelical Students (IFES) and its contribution to mission as a para-church mission organisation. I begin by outlining, broadly, the founding history and missional impetus. Secondly, I present the mission ethos and strategy of IFES and its subsequent spread to and development in Africa, highlighting the opportunities and challenges presented by some public issues in Africa. Finally, I conclude by offering what I consider to be the specific contribution of IFES to the shaping and development of African Christianity, specifically highlighting its ecumenical contribution and its contribution in public life.

A Brief Historical Background and Overview of IFES

Kenneth Latourette attributes the inspiration that led USA churches' engagement in foreign missionary activities to student-initiated activities.[1] Their impact on foreign missionary endeavours lay in their provision of personnel. David Howard also credits student-initiated groups with influencing foreign missionary activity in American churches, beginning with the 'Haystack Prayer Meeting' that began in 1806. He also recounts the work of the 'Cambridge Seven' in Britain and the Student Volunteer Movement (SVM) of 1886-1887 and the Student Foreign Missions Fellowship (SFMF) which later merged with, and became, the missionary department of the Intervarsity Christian Fellowship (IVCF) in America. The mission impetus of the IVCF has become enshrined in a mission conference that has been held at Urbana University since 1948. A parallel commission conference takes place under the auspices of the Fellowship of Christian Unions (FOCUS) in Kenya and and has been held tri-annually since 1988.[2]

The Founding of IFES, its Missional Strategy and Ethos

IFES was founded in 1947 at Harvard University in the USA by leaders from ten Christian student movements in the world, namely, Australia, the Netherlands, the UK, Canada, China (a newcomer at the time), France, New Zealand, Norway, Switzerland and the USA. They met to confer on the draft constitution at an international conference. The Chinese evangelical student fellowship suggested the formation of a worldwide student movement that became IFES. The dream of those gathered at the conference was to see a clear evangelical witness established in every university in the world. That commitment is still at the heart of IFES ministry and is the basis of its '2020 Living Stones' vision which galvanises the worldwide fellowship around its four distinctives, namely:

1. IFES is an international, interdenominational fellowship of national movements.
2. IFES is an evangelical movement.
3. IFES is committed to student leadership.
4. IFES is committed to the objectives of evangelism, formation and mission.[3]

---

[1] Kenneth Scott Latourette, *These Sought a Country*, New York: Harper & Bros. (1950), 46.
[2] See, www.intervarsity.org/bible-studies, http://intervarsity.org/bible-studies/inductive-bible-study-hints.See also http://commission2014.info/.
[3] See, http://intervarsitylink.org/about-us/what-ifes.

IFES in Africa: Its Development and Spread on the Continent

IFES in Africa can be said to have developed on the wave of enthusiastic missionary initiatives from America and Europe. To that effect, we can surmise that IFES in Africa has its roots in the nineteenth-century missionary movement inspired by the missionary-oriented student groups that emerged in America and led to the advance of strong inter-college contacts that became the international fellowship that became IFES.

In Africa, IFES exists in two regions, divided along colonially defined linguistic lines: the first region covers both English- and Portuguese-speaking Africa (IFES-EPSA) where IFES is present in twenty-four countries and at a pioneering stage in four others, namely, Saõ Tomé, Somaliland, Somalia and Cape Verde Islands and Principe. The second region is French-speaking Africa, where IFES is present in thirteen French-speaking countries. The only French-speaking African countries that remain unreached by IFES are Djibouti, Seychelles and the Comoros Islands. The Africa region does not include North African countries which belong to the Middle East and North Africa (MENA) region.

The year 1955 saw the beginning of evangelical student work in Africa. At the beginning, British graduates from the Inter-Varsity Christian Fellowship went to many parts of Africa. In Nigeria, Freddy Crittenden, a former Oxford student leader who had served as a missionary in Africa returned to Britain to enthuse African students who were studying there to return and serve student ministry in Africa. He also mobilized British Christian academics to go and teach in tertiary institutions in Africa to encourage the growth of student witness on the continent.

In Ghana, Tony Wilmot, an Oxford graduate who had worked in both Ghana and Nigeria as a businessman, was keen about the vision of establishing student groups in English-speaking Africa. Wilmot travelled extensively, visiting universities and tertiary institutions to bring that vision to fruition. Students who became active members in turn spread the vision to other campuses. Students were mobilised through annual camps that nurtured student leaders and infused the vision to spread evangelical student work continent-wide. IFES work spread on the wave of this enthusiasm to East and West Africa.

The gradual spread on the continent led to the formation of the Pan-African Fellowship of Evangelical Students (PAFES) in 1958. Members include the University of Kumasi and University of Legon in Ghana, Nairobi University in Kenya, University of Monrovia in Liberia, University of Fourah Bay in Sierra Leone and the University of Salisbury (now Harare), Rhodesia (now Zimbabwe), and the University of Ibadan, in Nigeria.

In 1960, IFES appointed Alonzo Fairbanks, an Afro-American as PAFES's first travelling secretary. Although Fairbanks was based in Ibadan, he travelled across Africa. John Holmes, once a lecturer in Ghana, joined the PAFES staff team in 1962. Tony Wilmot continued to serve as a volunteer support as a kind of adjunct staff.

In 1962, the first PAFES conference took place in West Africa at Winneba in Ghana. Delegates were drawn from the University of Ibadan, Zaria College of Arts and Science and Lagos University. In 1965, an elected committee took over the affairs of PAFES from IFES. Daniel Jonah, a lecturer from Sierra Leone, was the first chairman of PAFES. In 1966, David Gitari of Kenya was appointed as the first general secretary of PAFES. Gottfried Osei-Mensah from Ghana was appointed PAFES travelling secretary for West Africa.

The first student conference for West Africa under the auspices of PAFES was held in Nigeria in September 1966 at Ijabcol Teachers' Training College in Shagamu. Delegates were drawn from Sierra Leone, Ghana, Senegal, Tchad, Congo, Kinshasa (now Democratic Republic of Congo) and Nigeria. It was during this West African PAFES conference that the need to form national student fellowships was first mooted. Ghana Fellowship of Evangelical Students (GHAFES) was born in 1966 and Nigeria Fellowship of Evangelical Students (NIFES) closely followed in 1968.

The work of IFES in Africa was therefore born out of the missionary zeal of young Africans and European and American graduates inspired by their leaders to opt for professions according to a concern for the missionary contribution they could make through them. From these efforts, a number of national movements emerged, many of which were initially funded using the IFES pool fund.

IFES: A Catalyst for Ecumenism in Africa?

Anecdotally, many graduates who have been in IFES fellowships confirm that they were afforded an opportunity to consider their denominational tenets of faith in the light of other denominations. In some cases, though, groups splintered because of doctrinal differences and new groups emerged. Despite that, the interdenominational character of student groups has made meaningful fellowship and mutual accountability possible in the Church in Africa. The camaraderie developed during student days has potential to galvanise the church as an agent of change in society.

Because denominations were imported into Africa, they can be transcended.[4] Mission stations that determined denominational affiliation in Africa were often determined by colonial jurisdictions. It is not unusual to have a campus fellowship with members ranging from Roman Catholic to mainline Protestant to Pentecostal and newer charismatic churches. In recent years, however, the proliferation of church-based groups on campuses has tempered the interdenominational character of IFES.

IFES and Public Life in Africa

Evangelicalism's world-denying character has often excluded social action.[5] The post-colonial context compelled IFES to reflect on issues of poverty, governance, corruption, and ethnicity among others.[6] The 1980s and 1990s saw the changes that ushered in multi-party democracy in many African countries. IFES graduates were among political candidates and others inspired some civil society movements that shaped some of those changes.[7] In the wake of HIV/AIDS and the recent Ebola crisis, IFES rallied together and pooled resources. On the issue of gender balance, IFES has a long way to go. That said, female students, who are mainly sidelined in many churches, take some leadership roles, albeit still somewhat confined in campus fellowships.[8]

---

[4] See Paul Gifford, *African Christianity: Its Public Role*, Indianapolis: Indiana University Press (1998), 183. See also John Weller & Jane Linden, *Mainstream Christianity to 1980 in Malawi, Zambia and Zimbabwe*, Gweru: Mambo Press (1984) and Joseph M. Kapolyo, *The Human Condition: Christian Perspectives through African Eyes*, Downers Grove: IVP Academic (2005).

[5] See John Stott, Ibid, p.28, 29. See also www.lausanne.org/content/covenant/lausanne-covenant.

[6] The IFES-EPSA and Francophone Africa IFES regions published topical Bible Studies and Essays on Poverty, Christian political involvement in societal issues alongside other 'regular' materials. See, http://ifesworld.org/en/regions/epsa-english-and-portuguese-speaking-africa.

[7] See Paul Gifford, *African Christianity: Its Public Role*, Indianapolis: Indiana University Press (1998) and see also, Isabel A. Phiri, President Frederick Chiluba and Zambia: Evangelicals and Democracy in a 'Christian Nation', In Ranger T.O (ed), *Evangelical Christianity and Democracy in Africa*, Oxford: Oxford University Press (2008), 197-206.

[8] See Kuzipa Nalwamba, "'For Such a Time as This': My Reflections on Serving as First Woman General Secretary of Zambia Fellowship of Evangelical Students", In Isabel Apawo et. al., *Her-Stories: Hidden Histories of Women of Faith in Africa*, Pietermaritzburg: Cluster Publications, 2002, 371-388. See also Kuzipa Nalwamba and Aggrey Mugisha, *Champions of Change: Making a Difference Where you are*, Nairobi: IFES-EPSA, 2005.

Conclusion

In this reflection, I present IFES as a student ministry that came to Africa on the wave of the nineteenth-century missionary surge. Its growth and development in Africa has been linked with the founding values and ethos as an evangelical, interdenominational and student-initiated ministry committed to evangelism, mission and *formation* within a worldwide fellowship of those committed to sharing its resources. I have presented a qualified account of the contribution of IFES' work to ecumenicity of the church in Africa, and outlined its efforts to grapple with societal issues from a Christian standpoint. The adaptation of western models of mission and ministry and the dearth of female leadership remain developmental issues in IFES in Africa.

Bibliography

(2005). In K. &. Nalwamba (Ed.), *Champions of Change: Making a Difference where you are.* Nairobi: IFES-EPSA.

Asamoah-Gyadu, J. (2013). *Contemporary Pentecostal Christianity: Interpretations from an African Perspective.* Eugene, OR: Regnum.

Freeman, A. (1999). Count Nicholas Ludwig von Zinzendorf:. *Journal of Ecumenical Studies, Summer-Fall*, 1-17.

Gifford, P. (1998). *African Christianity: Its Public Role.* Indianapolis: Indiana University Press.

Howard, D. (1970). *Student Power in World Missions* (1979 ed.). Downers Grove, IL: IVP.

Kapoloyo, J. (2005). *The Human Condition: Christian Perspectives through African Eyes.* Downers Grove, IL: IVP Academic.

Larson, H. (1994). Responding to the Challenge of the Transitions. In J. Lewis, Crossman, M, and Hoke, S (Eds.), *World Mission: An Analysis of the World Chrsitian Movement* (pp. 5-23-5-32). Pasadena, CA: William Carey Library.

Latourette, K. S. (1950). *These Sought a Country.* New York: Harper & Bros.

Lewis, A. (1962). *Zinzendorf, the Ecumenical Pioneer: A Study in the Moravian Contribution to Christian Mission and Unity.* Norwich: SCM Press.

Lowman, P. (1983). *The Day of His Power: A History of the International Fellowship of Evangelical Students.* Leicester: Inter-Varsity Press.

MacLeod, A. (2007). *C. Stacey Woods and the Evangelical Rediscovery of the University.* Downers Grove, Il: Intervarsity Press.

Nalwamba, K. (2002). 'For Such a Time as this': My Reflections on Serving as First General Secretary of the Zambia Fellowship of Evangelical Students. In I. Phiri, Govinden, B.D, and Nadar, S (Eds.), *Her Stories: Hidden Histories of Christian Women in Africa* (pp. 371-). Pietermaritzburg: Cluster Publications.

Phiri, I. (2008). President Frederrick Chiluba and Zambia: Evangelicals and Democracy in a 'Christian Nation'. In T. Ranger (Ed.), *Evangelcals and Christian Democracy in Africa* (pp. 95-129). New York: Oxford University of Press.

Ranger, T. (2008). Introduction: Evangelical Christianity and Democracy in Africa. In T. Ranger (Ed.), *Evangelical Christianity and Democracy in Africa* (pp. 3-35). New York: Oxford University Press.

Shedd, C. (1932). *Two Centuries of Student Christian Movements.* New York: Associated Press.

Steer, R. (2010). *Basic Christian: The Inside Story of John Stott.* Downers Grove, IL: IVP.

Stott, J. (2009). *Christian Mission in the Contemporary World.* Downers Grove, IL: IVP.

Weller, J and Linden, J. (1984). *Mainstream Christianity to 1980 in Malawi, Zambia and Zimbabwe.* Gweru: Mambo Press.

(45) The Seventh Day Adventist Church in Africa

Mary Getui

The roots of the Seventh Day Adventist Church (SDA) date back to 1863 in the USA. The church sprang up in the aftermath of the great disappointment of 1844 when the second advent of Christ, as expected by the Millerite Adventists, did not happen. The three names associated with the birth of the SDA Church are Hiram Edison, Joseph Bates and Ellen G. White. By the turn of the nineteenth century, Seventh Day Adventism had spread to Europe, Australia, South and West Africa. East Africa was reached in the early part of the twentieth century. The SDA presence is worldwide, with about 30% of the membership in Africa.

The missionary tide has changed. The SDA Church in Africa is playing a key role in the diaspora. Members of the SDA Church from various parts of Africa 'travel with the SDA message' and continue practising their faith by attending and opening new churches in America, Europe and Australia.

Generally, the SDA Church in Africa abides by the tenets of the world church, hence this article will only highlight where applicable the African situation or context, with focus on the theological profile, structure, contribution to social responsibility and development and a highlight on some challenges.

Theologically, the SDA Church draws from 28 Bible-based fundamental beliefs summarised as follows:

1. *The Word of God*: The Holy Scriptures, Old and New Testaments, are the written Word of God.
2. *The Godhead*: There is one God: Father, Son, and Holy Spirit.
3. *God the Father*: Is the Creator, Source, Sustainer, and Sovereign of all creation.
4. *God the Son*: Became incarnate in Jesus Christ. He became also truly human.
5. *God the Spirit*: Draws and convicts human beings, sent by the Father and extends spiritual gifts to the church, empowers it to bear witness to Christ, and in harmony with the Scriptures, leads it into all truth.
6. *Creation:* God is Creator. In six days the Lord made 'the heaven and earth' and established and rested on the seventh day of the first week, the Sabbath, as a perpetual memorial of His completed creative work. The first man and woman were made in the image of God as the crowning work of Creation, given dominion over the world, and charged with responsibility to care for it. When the world was finished, it was 'very good'.
7. *The Nature of Man*: Man and woman were made in the image of God. They disobeyed God; they denied their dependence upon Him and fell from their high position under God. Their descendants share this fallen nature and its consequences. But God in Christ reconciled the world to Himself and by His Spirit restores in penitent mortals the image of their maker. Created for the glory of God, they are called to love Him and one another, and to care for their environment.
8. *The Great Controversy*: Humanity is involved in a great controversy between Christ and Satan. This conflict originated in heaven when Satan led into rebellion a portion of the angles. He introduced the spirit of rebellion into this world when he led Adam and Eve into sin. To assist His people in this controversy, Christ sends the Holy Spirit and the loyal angels to guide, protect and sustain them in the way of salvation.
9. *The Life, Death, and Resurrection of Christ*: In Christ, God provided the only means of atonement for human sin. The death of Christ is substitutionary and expiatory, reconciling and transforming. The resurrection of Christ proclaims God's triumph over the forces of evil and assures final victory over sin and death.
10. *The Experience of Salvation*: In infinite love and mercy, God made Christ, who knew no sin, to be sin for humanity, so that in Him humanity might be made the righteousness of God. The Holy

Spirit renews minds, writes God's law of love in the hearts, and gives the power to live a holy life, and have the assurance of salvation now and in the judgement.

11. *Growing in Christ*: Jesus' victory gives humanity victory over evil. The Holy Spirit indwells and empowers for constant daily communion in prayer, feeding on His word, meditating on it and on His providence.
12. *The Church*: The Church is the community of believers who confess Jesus Christ as Lord and Saviour.
13. *The Remnant and Its Mission*: The universal church is composed of all who truly believe in Christ, but in the last days, a time of widespread apostasy, a remnant has been called out to keep the commandments of God and the faith of Jesus Christ, and heralds the approach of His Second Advent.
14. *Unity in the Body of Christ*: The church is one body with many members, called from every nation, kindred, tongue, and people. All are equal in Christ. This unity has its source in the oneness of the triune God.
15. *Baptism*: Baptism is a symbol of union with Christ, the forgiveness of sins, and the reception of the Holy Spirit. It is by immersion in water and is contingent on an affirmation of faith in Jesus and evidence of repentance of sin. It follows instruction in the Holy Scriptures and acceptance of their teachings.
16. *The Lord's Supper*: The Lord's Supper is a participation in the emblems of the body and blood of Jesus as an expression of faith in Him. Preparation for the Supper includes self-examination, repentance, and confession. The Master ordained the service of foot-washing to signify renewed cleansing, to express a willingness to serve one another in Christ-like humility, and to unite hearts in love. The communion service is open to all believing Christians.
17. *Spiritual Gifts and Ministries*: God bestows upon members in every age spiritual gifts. Given by the agency of the Holy Spirit, who apportions to each member as He wills, the gifts provide all abilities and ministries needed by the church to fulfil its divinely ordained functions. When members employ these spiritual gifts as faithful stewards of God's varied grace, the church is protected from the destructive influence of false doctrine, grows with a growth that is from God, and is built up in faith and love.
18. *The Gift of Prophecy:* One of the gifts of the Holy Spirit is prophecy. This gift is an identifying mark of the remnant church and was manifested in the ministry of Ellen G. White – the Lord's messenger. Her writings are a continuing and authoritative source of truth which provide for the church comfort, guidance, instruction, and correction. They also make clear that the Bible is the standard by which all teaching and experience must be tested.
19. *The Law of God*: The great principles of God's law are embodied in the Ten Commandments and exemplified in the life of Christ; and through the agency of the Holy Spirit, they point out sin and awaken a sense of need for a Saviour. Salvation is all of grace and not of works, but its fruit is obedience to the Commandments. This obedience develops Christian character and results in a sense of well-being.
20. *The Sabbath:* The Creator, after the six days of Creation, rested on the seventh day and instituted the Sabbath for all people as a memorial of Creation. The fourth commandment of God's unchangeable law requires the observance of this seventh-day Sabbath as the day of rest, worship and ministry, in harmony with the teaching and practice of Jesus, the Lord of the Sabbath. The Sabbath is a day of delightful communion with God and one another. It is a symbol of redemption in Christ, a sign of sanctification, a token of allegiance, and a foretaste of the eternal future in God's kingdom. The Sabbath is God's perpetual sign of His eternal covenant between Him and His

people. Joyful observance of this holy time from evening to evening, sunset to sunset, is a celebration of God's creative and redemptive acts.

21. *Stewardship*: Human beings, entrusted by God with time and opportunities, abilities and possessions, and the blessings of the earth and its resources, are responsible to Him for their proper use. God's ownership is acknowledged by faithful service to Him and fellow humankind and by returning tithes and giving offerings for the proclamation of His gospel and the support and growth of His church.
22. *Christian Behaviour*: Members are called to be a godly people who think, feel, and act in harmony with the principles of heaven, who will be involved only in those things which will produce Christlike purity, health and joy, in amusement, entertainment and dress. The body is the temple of the Holy Spirit; it is to be cared for intelligently. Along with adequate exercise and rest, members should adopt the most healthful diet possible and abstain from the unclean foods identified in the Scriptures, and also alcoholic beverages, tobacco, and the irresponsible use of drugs and engage only in whatever brings thoughts and bodies into the discipline of Christ, who desires wholesomeness, joy, and goodness.
23. *Marriage and the Family*: Marriage was divinely established in Eden and affirmed by Jesus to be a lifelong union between a man and a woman in loving companionship. A marriage commitment is to God as well as to the spouse and should be entered into only between partners who share a common faith. Divorce is permissible only for adultery. Parents are to bring up children to love and obey the Lord. By their example and their words, they are to teach them that Christ is a loving disciplinarian, ever tender and caring, who wants them to become members of His body, the family of God. Increasing family closeness is one of the hallmarks of the final gospel message.
24. *Christ's Ministry in the Heavenly Sanctuary:* There is a sanctuary in heaven – the true tabernacle which the Lord set up. In it, Christ ministers, making available to believers the benefits of His atoning sacrifice offered once for all on the cross. He was inaugurated as our great High Priest and began His intercessory ministry at the time of His ascension. In 1844, at the end of the prophetic period of 2,300 days, He entered the second and last phase of His atoning ministry. It is a work of investigative judgement which is part of the ultimate disposition of all sin, typified by the cleansing of the ancient Hebrew sanctuary on the Day of Atonement. In that typical service, the sanctuary was cleansed with the blood of animal sacrifices, but the heavenly things are purified with the perfect sacrifice of the blood of Jesus. The investigative judgement reveals to heavenly intelligences who, among the dead, are asleep in Christ and therefore, in Him, are deemed worthy to have part in the first resurrection. It also makes manifest those among the living who are abiding in Christ, keeping the commandments of God and the faith of Jesus, and in Him, therefore, are ready for translation into His everlasting kingdom. This judgement vindicates the justice of God in saving those who believe in Jesus. It declares that those who have remained loyal to God shall receive the kingdom. The completion of this ministry of Christ will mark the close of human probation before the Second Advent.
25. *The Second Coming of Christ*: The second coming of Christ is the blessed hope of the church – the grand climax of the gospel. The Saviour's coming will be literal, personal, visible, and worldwide. When He returns, the righteous dead will be resurrected and, together with the righteous living, will be glorified and taken to heaven, but the unrighteous will die. The almost complete fulfilment of most lines of prophecy, together with the present condition of the world, indicates that Christ's coming is imminent. The time of that event has not been revealed, and therefore, members are exhorted to be ready at all times.
26. *Death and Resurrection*: The wages of sin is death. But God, who alone is immortal, will grant eternal life to His redeemed. Until that day, death is an unconscious state for all people. When

Christ appears, the resurrected righteous and the living righteous will be glorified and brought up to meet their Lord. The second resurrection, a resurrection of the unrighteous, will take place a thousand years later.

27. *The Millennium and the End of Sin*: The millennium is the thousand-year reign of Christ with His saints in heaven between the first and second resurrections. During this time the wicked dead will be judged; the earth will be utterly desolate, without living human inhabitants but occupied by Satan and his angels. At its close, Christ with His saints and the Holy City will descend from heaven to earth. The unrighteous dead will then be resurrected and, with Satan and his angels, will surround the city – but fire from God will consume them and cleanse the earth. The universe will thus be freed of sin and sinners for ever.
28. *The New Earth*: On the New Earth, in which righteousness dwells, God will provide an eternal home for the redeemed and a perfect environment, for here God Himself will dwell with His people, and suffering and death will have passed away. The great controversy will be ended, and sin will be no more. All things, animate and inanimate, will declare that God is love, and He shall reign for ever. Amen.

It is important to recognize the contribution made by Africa, way back in 1931, towards having these beliefs summarised in an organized structure. In the volume *Seventh Day Adventists Believe,* it reads '… in response to an appeal from the church leaders in Africa for a statement which would help government officials and others to a better understanding of our work', a committee of four, including the President of the General Conference, prepared a statement encompassing 'the principle features'[1] of belief.

The administrative structure of the church starts at the local church, and proceeds to the district, the station, the conference/mission/field, union, division, to the General Conference. The General Conference serves as the headquarters. It is based in Silver Springs, Maryland, USA. Of the thirteen administrative divisions in the world, three are in Africa, namely East-Central Africa, Southern Africa-Indian Ocean and West-Central Africa with headquarters in Kenya, South Africa and Ivory Coast, respectively.

The General Conference session takes place every five years. While it is an open forum for SDA adherents, the General Conference Executive Committee, drawn from the top leadership of the SDA Church worldwide, deliberates on key issues. The Annual Council handles and builds towards the General Conference Session. There are also advisory departments, committees and commissions that handle appropriate matters.

While the SDA Church emphasizes evangelism where the twenty-eight fundamental beliefs are the focus, the church is engaged in initiatives for social witness, development and *diakonia* that relate to these beliefs. These initiatives aim at the edification of church members and non-members. They can be termed 'intra-outreach' and include education, health literature and health evangelism, social services, media evangelism and special ministries.

The church runs education institutions from basic to tertiary. In Kenya, the University of Eastern Africa, Baraton, was the first private university to be granted a charter in 1985 as was Babcock University in Nigeria. In the tertiary institutions, secular and theological programmes are on offer. These institutions provide trained human resources for service in the church and in the wider society.

The church has also invested in health facilities – clinics, dispensaries and hospitals. Of notable mention is the Benjamin S. Carson Sr School of Medicine at Babcock University in Nigeria, which is named after the renowned neurosurgeon. It was inaugurated in 2012.

Colporteur or literature evangelism is an outstanding feature of the SDA Church. Volunteers sell and distribute literature ranging from the Bible to books on health, family and other life issues. The literature is

[1] Seventh Day Adventists Believe, page V.

in both international and local languages. To facilitate literature evangelism, the church has set up publishing and printing facilities such as the Africa Herald Publishing House in Kenya.

The Adventist Development and Relief Agency (ADRA) and the Seventh Day Adventist Welfare Services are agencies that can be termed as the 'intra-outreach' development arms of the church. They operate internationally and across Africa, responding to war, disaster situations, and engaging in health and education initiatives.

The SDA Church operates several radio and television channels such as Adventist World Radio and Hope Channel that reach or are based in Africa. They offer a wide range of programmes, some specific for the SDA audience and others for consumption by the general public.

The church also concentrates on 'in-reach' programmes. Some of these include the Sabbath School. This is a weekly Bible study session at church, where members, divided according to age, discuss a designated quarterly theme, with specific topics for each day of the week that members are expected to apply to the individual and the context.

The annual camp meeting is another 'in-reach' programme. Just as for Sabbath School, the theme is universal, but the application is contextual. A camp meeting is also an opportunity to focus on other issues such as health, family life and stewardship. The different age groups as well as special needs groups also have designated programmes. A recent development is, where those congregations that can afford it, invite international speakers and guest choirs.

Involvement of the laity is another aspect that has contributed to the growth of the SDA Church. Given that clergy are few and have large flocks and geographical areas to cover, the church officers, from elders to those in charge of and engaged in various departments and programmes of the local church, play a key role in running the weekly, and especially Sabbath church programmes. The laity, in their financial giving of tithes and other offerings such as church building, make a significant contribution towards church growth and development. The Adventist Lay Service Industries (ASI) consists of lay professionals and business people whose objective is to train lay people to go into mission as the context dictates. Far-flung areas have been reached through provision of motorbikes. This could be termed 'mission within'.

The various categories in the church, such as those of age, gender and position, participate in activities of their own initiative or those organized by the church hierarchies. The children, youth, Adventist Men Organization and the Women Ministry gather for camps, retreats and conferences. The shepherdesses (the pastors' wives) also have and run programmes specific to their needs. One such event is the East and Central Division Youth Congress and Students Retreat held in December 2014 at the University of Eastern Africa, Baraton, Kenya which attracted about 1,000 participants. The theme was 'Turning Cities Upside Down: Training our Youth for Evangelism in the 21st Century'. Across the continent, The Vocational Bible School (VBS) is a big attraction for children during school holidays.

The SDA Church in Africa is thriving numerically but has to cope with some challenges.

A major challenge is culture-related, for example, the practice of polygamy, early marriages and spiritism. In responding to some of these issues, conferences are held and publications are released. The publication *The Church, Culture and Spirits – Adventism in Africa*, is a response to spiritism. It should be pointed out, however, that critique of African culture that could lead to appreciation and application of edifying African cultural values and practices has not been given due attention.

Another challenge for the church in Africa is that, while the numbers are growing, the 'wallet contribution' is not so much. Even so, through 'inter-outreach', the church in Africa contributes quarterly through the '13th Sabbath' offering. This fund supports projects in a specific region of the world church.

The world church, including Africa, has been challenged and has hearkened to the need to reinvent itself in order to address emerging issues such as HIV and AIDS, the environmental crisis, technology, gender and urban ministry, among others.

This brief survey is an indication that the SDA Church is one of the main denominational families that is making a major impact in Africa, and is contributing to the development of the SDA Church worldwide.

Bibliography

Alalade, A. Adekunle, *Limiting Factors of the Success of the Seventh-day Adventist Church in Africa. The Nigeria Case Study*, Ibadan, Agbo Aero Publishers, 2008.

Damsteegt, Gerard P. *Foundations of the Seventh-day Adventist Message and Mission*. Grand Rapids, William B. Eerdmans Publishing Company, 1977.

Donkor, Kwabena (Ed), *The Church, Culture and Spirits, Adventism in Africa* The Biblical Research Institute, General Conference of Seventh – day Adventists, Silver Spring MD, 2011.

Froom, Leroy Edwin, *Movement of Destiny*, Washington D. C., Review and Herald Publishing Association, 1971.

General Conference of Seventh day Adventists, *Church Heritage Manual A Course in Church History Highlighting Significant Details of Interest to the Youth of the Seventh – day Adventist Church*, General Conference Youth Department, 2002.

General Conference of Seventh Day Adventists *Seventh – day Adventists Believe*, Pacific Press Publishing Association, Silver Spring, MD, 2005.

Getui, Mary N. *The Establishment and History of the Activities of the Seventh – day Adventist (SDA) Church Among Abagusii of Western Kenya 19912 – 1985*, Master of Arts Thesis, University of Nairobi, 1985.

Ng, G.T. 'The Shifting Landscape of Adventist Mission' in *The Adventist World*, The International Paper for Seventh – day Adventists, January 2014.

Nwaomah, Sampson M. *The Church in Lucan Narratives, Model for Christian Mission in Africa*, Ibadan, Positive Press, 2012

Schwarz, R.W. *Light Bearers to the Remnant*, Mountain View; Pacific Press Publishing Association, 1979.

Part IV

National Surveys of African Christianity

(46) Christianity in Algeria

Harald Suermann

Religion	Pop 2010	Pct 2010	Pop 2025	Pct 2025	Gr Pct 1970 2025
Christians	64,600	0.2%	77,100	0.2%	1.2%
Independents	53,900	0.1%	65,000	0.1%	1.3%
African initiated	53,700	0.1%			
Orthodox	1,500	0.0%	1,300	0.0%	-0.8%
Protestants	4,000	0.0%	3,600	0.0%	-0.7%
Roman Catholics	5,000	0.0%	7,000	0.0%	2.2%
Pentecostals/Charismatics	21,600	0.1%	25,000	0.1%	1.0%
Evangelicals	2,600	0.0%	4,000	0.0%	2.8%
Muslims	35,481,000	98.5%	45,049,000	98.2%	1.6%
Chinese folk-religionists	11,900	0.0%	15,000	0.0%	1.6%
Buddhists	5,600	0.0%	8,000	0.0%	2.5%
Baha'is	3,500	0.0%	5,000	0.0%	2.5%
Jews	590	0.0%	600	0.0%	0.1%
people professing no religion	469,000	1.3%	710,000	1.5%	2.8%
Total population	**36,036,000**	**100.0%**	**45,865,000**	**100.0%**	**1.6%**

Source: Centre for the Study of World Christianity (CSGC), Boston, Gordon-Conwell TS

Algérie a 38,7 millions d'habitants (2014), dont 3500 de catholiques.[1] Les églises protestantes comptent entre 20.000 et 100.000 adhérents.[2] Des organisations estiment qu'il y a 380.000 convertis au Christianisme en Algérie.[3] Mais ces chiffres sont difficilement vérifiables. Le nombre de chrétiens coptes est estimé entre 1.000 et 1.500.

La constitution de 1989 déclare l'islam comme religion d'état. Des pratiques contraires à l'islam sont interdites et le président doit être musulman. La liberté religieuse est garantie, l'Église catholique romaine est officiellement reconnue par l'État. L'Église Protestante d'Algérie, une confédération des 39 églises protestantes, est enregistré par l'état. Les prêtres de nationalité algérienne ont le droit d'être payés par l'État. Pour les chrétiens d'autres nationalités les fêtes chrétiennes sont des jours fériés.[4]

---

[1] « Catholic Church in Algeria [Catholic-Hierarchy] », http://catholic-hierarchy.org/country/dz.html.

[2] « Algeria 2014 International Religious Freedom Report », www.state.gov/documents/organization/238660.pdf.

[3] Duane Alexander Miller et Patrick Johnstone, « Believers in Christ from a Muslim Background: A Global Census », *Interdisciplinary Journal of Research on Religion* 11, n° Article 10 (2015), https://tspace.library.utoronto.ca/handle/1807/30108.

[4] « Algeria 2014 International Religious Freedom Report ».

L'antiquité

Au 3e siècle le christianisme se répandît en Algérie. Des évêchés furent fondés dans les grandes villes. St. Augustin fut évêque de Hippo Regius, aujourd'hui Annaba. Mais l'Islam a supplanté le christianisme depuis le 7e siècle.

L'héritage colonial

En 1830 la France commença la conquête d'Algérie qui fut très violente. En même temps une politique de colonie de peuplement fut mise en place. La transformation du pays servit uniquement les intérêts des Français. En 1830 seize aumôniers et un prêtre syrien arrivèrent avec les militaires et célébrèrent une messe et un Te Deum pour la résurrection de l'Église d'Afrique.[5]

Mais peu après le nombre des aumôniers fut réduit. Les relations entre la hiérarchie catholique en Algérie et l'État français furent tendues encore longtemps. Le 24 décembre 1831 une nouvelle cathédrale à Alger fut dédiée à saint Philippe. Elle était une mosquée. Pour une assistance humanitaire on fit appel à une congrégation religieuse, les sœurs de saint Joseph de l'Apparition, nouvellement fondée en France. Le 4 août 1838 l'évêché d'Alger fut érigé, suffragant de l'archevêché d'Aix-en-Provence. Le premier évêque fut Mgr Antoine-Adolphe Dupuch, qui poussât son clergé dans la voie missionnaire et le fit apprendre l'arabe dans un embryon de séminaire qu'il créa. Le Ministre de la Guerre lui rappela que le clergé n'avait à s'occuper que de la population catholique. Le 9 novembre 1845 il donna sa démission.

Son successeur fut Louis-Antoine Augustin Pavy. À la suite de la révolution de 1848 et du coup d'État de Louis-Napoléon, une foule de personnes furent exilées en Algérie. Le nouvel évêque fonda 158 paroisses, un petit et un grand séminaire ainsi que des écoles. Il rappela les chrétiens à leurs devoirs, mais il resta distancé par rapport au dialogue avec les musulmans. Il les qualifiait d'infidèles et pensait comme beaucoup que les indigènes ne seront français que quand ils seront chrétiens. Des tentatives de mission auprès des musulmans furent rapidement arrêtées par le gouvernement.

En 1866 Alger fut érigé en archevêché avec ses suffragants Oran et Constantine. Après la mort de Mgr Pavy en 1867 Mgr Charles-Martial Allemand-Lavigerie fut nommé archevêque. Il voulût faire de la terre algérienne le berceau d'une nation chrétienne, « d'une autre France; répandre les lumières d'une civilisation dont l'Évangile est la source et la loi, les porter au-delà du désert jusqu'au centre de ce continent plongé dans la barbarie; relier ainsi l'Afrique du Nord et l'Afrique centrale à la vie des peuples chrétiens… ».[6] Une épidémie de choléra et la sécheresse en 1867 exigèrent son engagement humanitaire et social. À l'occasion il fonda la congrégation des Pères Blancs (La société des Missionnaires d'Afrique) et des Sœurs Blanches (Sœurs missionnaires de Notre-Dame d'Afrique). Il leur demanda de se faire arabe avec les Africains, parler arabe, se vêtir comme les autochtones et être à leur service. Il décréta qu'il n'ordonnera personne ne comprenant pas parfaitement l'arabe et ne s'expliquant pas convenablement dans cette langue.[7] Le 2 juillet 1872 Mgr Lavigerie consacra une grande église de pèlerinage au nord d'Alger, la basilique Notre Dame d'Afrique. Après sa mort l'Église catholique fut tentée de se replier sur elle-même.

En 1930 l'église célébra le centenaire de la « résurrection de l'Église d'Afrique » avec de nombreuses publications. Malgré le caractère laïc et anticlérical de la France, la christianisation et la colonisation

---

[5] André. Nozière, *Algérie : les chrétiens dans la guerre* ([Paris]: Cana, 2001), 23; Denis Gonzalez, « L'Eglise d'Algérie: enracinement, épreuves et conversions, de 1830 à nos jours », in *Histoire des chrétiens d'Afrique du Nord : Libye-Tunisie-Algérie-Maroc*, éd. par Henri Teissier et Antoine. Chatelard (Paris: Desclée, 1991), 118.

[6] Alexandre Pons, *La nouvelle Église d'Afrique ou Le catholicisme en Algérie, en Tunisie et au Maroc depuis 1830* (Tunis, 1930), 123-124; Karima Direche-Slimani, *Chrétiens de Kabylie (1873-1954): une action missionnaire dans l'Algérie coloniale* ([Saint-Denis]: Bouchène, 2004).

[7] Léon Cristiani, *Le cardinal Lavigerie: un grand bienfaiteur de l'Afrique (1825-1892)* (Paris: Ed. France-Empire, 1961), 53.

marchèrent ensemble. La tentative de lui donner une âme chrétienne et par conséquence française fut au centre de la politique coloniale.[8] En décembre 1905 une loi entra en vigueur en France qui sépare État et Église et assure la liberté de conscience. Elle laisse ses biens à l'Église mais l'État ne la reconnait pas et ne salarie ou ne subventionne aucun culte. En Algérie, les séminaires ainsi que les écoles fermèrent leur portes. La Trappe de Staouéli fut vendue. Plus tard les finances de l'archevêché d'Alger furent confisquées. C'est la ruine. La guerre de 1914 exigea encore plus du diocèse. L'Église fut occupée à sa survie. Elle suivit l'exemple de l'église en France et ainsi le fossé entre chrétiens et musulmans se creusa davantage.[9]

À cette époque Charles de Foucauld (1858-1916) choisit la vie contemplative dans le désert algérien pour imiter Jésus de Nazareth par l'amour. Il apprit la langue de la population et vivait avec elle. Il fut assassiné en 1916, mais plus tard plusieurs congrégations furent fondées dans son esprit.

Mgr Augustin-Fernand Leynaud (archevêque d'Alger 1916-1953) se mit à la reconstruction de l'Église et obtint la restitution d'immeubles diocésains ainsi que la réouverture du séminaire. Il fit construire des églises ou les fit restaurer. Les œuvres se multiplièrent. En 1939 la Deuxième Guerre mondiale éclata.

Les « Pères Blancs » fondèrent en 1940 le Centre d'études Berbères (CEB), et les « Sœurs Blanches » peu après le Centre d'études Berbères pour les femmes (CEBF). Les deux centres étaient en avance sur leur temps en faisant des recherches sur la culture indigène qui n'était pas considérée jusque là comme digne de recherche.[10]

L'Église protestante fut également très tôt présente en Algérie.[11] Une ordonnance royale du 31 octobre 1839 institua un poste pastoral de l'Église protestante à Alger pour servir les colons. L'ordonnance ne distinguait pas entre l'Église luthérienne et réformée et par la suite il y eut des disputes entre les deux églises. En 1867 un décret organisa l'Église protestante unie d'Algérie avec de consistoires mixtes à Alger, Oran et Constantine. L'Église protestante d'Algérie disparut en 1905 quand les églises et l'État ont été séparés en France. Les consistoires se scindèrent en deux.[12]

Les protestants voulurent instaurer des structures pour développer une mission évangélique parmi les autochtones, mais l'État français était contre toutes activités missionnaires qui pourraient attiser l'hostilité de l'Islam envers l'occupant. Mais en avril 1831 la société anglaise Church Mission to the Jews envoya le premier missionnaire évangélique en Algérie. Il s'adressa particulièrement aux juifs, mais aussi aux protestants pauvres souvent étrangers. La Société des Missions Évangéliques de Paris tenta d'établir des missions à plusieurs reprises mais dut abandonner le projet.[13]

Après l'armistice de la Deuxième Guerre Mondiale en 1945 la population indigène d'Algérie se souleva mais la rébellion fut réprimée.[14] L'Église catholique considéra le soulèvement comme injuste. Mgr Emile-Jean-François Thiénard, évêque de Constantine, accusa les rebelles d'être ingrats bien que la France

---

[8] Nozière, *Algérie : les chrétiens dans la guerre*, 24.

[9] Henri Teissier et Antoine. Chatelard, éd., *Histoire des chrétiens d'Afrique du Nord : Libye-Tunisie-Algérie-Maroc* (Paris: Desclée, 1991), 130-132.

[10] Marie-Josée Dor et Jean Fisset, « Pères Blancs et Soeurs Blanches, Tunisie et Algérie : Fondation, développement, travaux apostoliques », in *Histoire des chrétiens d'Afrique du Nord : Libye-Tunisie-Algérie-Maroc*, éd. par Henri Teissier et Antoine. Chatelard (Paris: Desclée, 1991), 183.

[11] Jacques Pannier, « Les Protestants Français et l'Algérie: Quatre épisodes », *Bulletin de la Société de l'Histoire du Protestantisme Français (1903-)* 79, n° 2 (1930): 146-203, www.jstor.org/stable/24290001.

[12] André Encrevé, *Protestants français au milieu du XIXe siècle: les réformés de 1848 à 1870*, Histoire et société, no 8 (Genève: Labor et Fides, 1986), 578-581; Jean Volff, « Une Église protestante unie en Algérie », *Revue d'histoire et de philosophie religieuses* 87 (2007): passim; Zohra. Ait Abdelmalek, *Protestants en Algérie. Le protestantisme et son action missionnaire en Algérie aux XIXe et XXe siècles* (Lyon: Olivétan, 2004), 14-84, http://books.google.com/books?id=uMHYAAAAMAAJ.

[13] Le grand nombre des sociétés missionnaires protestantes en Algérie: Zohra Ait Abdelmalek, *Protestants en Algérie: le protestantisme et son action missionnaire en Algérie aux XIXe et XXe siècles* (Lyon: Olivétan, 2004), 30-136.

[14] Gonzalez, « L'Eglise d'Algérie: enracinement, épreuves et conversions, de 1830 à nos jours », 134.

s'engage à leur profit pour une vie meilleure. Mgr Leynaud, évêque d'Alger, le confirma dans une homélie pour la fête de Saint Augustin. La hiérarchie catholique venait tous de France. Les évêques faisaient partie de la conférence épiscopale française et ils étaient payés par le gouvernement français. L'archevêque d'Alger éait membre d'office de l'assemblée des cardinaux et archevêques de France.[15] La plupart des prêtres ne s'occupait que des Européens[16]. La présence chrétienne et française ait équivalente, les valeurs chrétiennes considérées comme supérieures de celles de l'Islam. Pendant la période de la colonisation les Français ne se mêlèrent pas à la population indigène.[17] Dans les années 1950 quelques membres de l'Église critiquèrent cette attitude considérée comme l'expression du sentiment de supériorité des Européens, parmi eux en 1952 le président de l'Action Catholique d'Alger. L'archevêque d'Alger critiqua en 1952 que les prêtres étaient insensibles envers la population indigène.[18] Le clergé était divisé.

La société de missionnaires d'Afrique, fondée par le cardinal Lavigerie, s'occupait de la population locale. Elle était active surtout en Kabylie, mais eut aussi des postes à Alger et à Constantine. Depuis 1954 ils n'avisèrent plus la conversion de musulmans, mais offrirent des services sociaux comme écoles, dispensaires, etc. Les Petits Frères et Sœurs de Jésus, inspirés par Charles de Foucauld, partagèrent leur foi avec les plus pauvres en prières et partage.[19] L'Action Catholique plaida pour une cohabitation fraternelle. Dans sa dernière lettre pastorale en 1953, Mgr Leynaud aborda cette idée, en s'éloignant de ses idées antérieures. L'Action Catholique constata que la société algérienne avait immensément besoin de libération.[20] En hiver 1952/1953 les scouts chrétiens et musulmans commencèrent à coopérer et fondèrent en 1953 l'« Association de la jeunesse algérienne pour l'action sociale ».[21] La lutte pour la libération commença le 1er novembre 1954. Elle fut un défi pour l'Église divisée et elle la mit devant la question de savoir si la colonisation française était le garant de la présence de l'Église.[22]

L'archevêque Mgr Léon-Étienne Duval prit une position très nettement en faveur de la population algérienne lors de la lutte de libération. Sa devise était l'amour universel de Dieu, qu'il rappela à tout le monde. Elle comprenait aussi la population algérienne. Sur la base de la doctrine sociale il demanda avec le reste de l'épiscopat algérien dans une lettre adressée au gouvernement français de s'attaquer à la terrible famine en Algérie. En 1955 il parla lors d'une assemblée des cardinaux et archevêques à Paris de la misère des maghrébins en France, 1961 il demanda l'aide pour les français de retour en France et appauvris. Il rappela aux droits de l'homme face à la torture et demanda un procès équitable en toutes circonstances.[23] Pendant la lutte de libération il demanda le droit à l'autonomie pour les Algériens sans pourtant proposer une solution[24]. Il joua un rôle pilote en ce temps et Mgr Georges Louis Mercier, évêque de Laghouat et Mgr Paul-Pierre-Marie-Joseph Pinier, évêque de Constantine et Hippone le suivirent. Mgr Mercier attira l'attention sur le fait que la population indigène de la Kabylie s'appauvrissait tandis que les Français devinaient de plus en plus riches à cause du pétrole.[25] L'évêque d'Oran, par contre, se tut sur ces

[15] Nozière, *Algérie : les chrétiens dans la guerre*, 26-27.
[16] Henri Teissier, *Chrétiens en Algérie: un partage d'espérance* (Paris: Desclée de Brouwer, 2002), 55-56.
[17] Nozière, *Algérie : les chrétiens dans la guerre*, 24-25.
[18] Nozière, *Algérie : les chrétiens dans la guerre*, 27-29.
[19] Nozière, *Algérie : les chrétiens dans la guerre*, 30-31.
[20] Nozière, *Algérie : les chrétiens dans la guerre*, 32-37.
[21] Nozière, *Algérie : les chrétiens dans la guerre*, 37-40.
[22] Gonzalez, « L'Eglise d'Algérie: enracinement, épreuves et conversions, de 1830 à nos jours », 135.
[23] Nozière, *Algérie : les chrétiens dans la guerre*, 47-57; Gonzalez, « L'Eglise d'Algérie: enracinement, épreuves et conversions, de 1830 à nos jours », 135-137.
[24] Nozière, *Algérie : les chrétiens dans la guerre*, 57-77; voir aussi Darcie S. Fontaine, « Decolonizing Christianity » (Diss. Thesis, Rutgers, The State University of New Jersey, 2011), 313-346, https://rucore.libraries.rutgers.edu/rutgers-lib/33651/PDF/1/.
[25] Nozière, *Algérie : les chrétiens dans la guerre*, 92-102; Gonzalez, « L'Eglise d'Algérie: enracinement, épreuves et conversions, de 1830 à nos jours », 137.

événements. Il fut un partisan fervent de l'Algérie française.[26] Les protestants français, petits en nombre, furent également divisés en ce qui concerne leurs positions dans la lutte de libération en Algérie. Une grande partie prit position en faveur des Algériens ou servirent leurs intérêts.[27]

Le temps de la république

En 1962 deux événements majeurs furent d'une grande importance pour les catholiques d'Algérie: L'Algérie devint indépendante le 1er juillet 1962 et le 11 octobre le concile Vatican II fut ouvert. Pour l'Église catholique en Algérie commença la période dans laquelle elle dut faire ses preuves comme église décolonisée, qui dut apprendre à vivre en pays d'Islam sans la protection d'une puissance européenne. Le concile Vatican II dut donner des directives pour l'Église catholique dans les pays nouvellement décolonisés.[28]

Après la retraite des Français du pays le nombre des chrétiens devint très petit. Les femmes chrétiennes mariées à un Algérien et les quelques convertis algériens de l'époque coloniale formèrent la majorité des catholiques. À ce groupe stable s'ajoutèrent les chrétiens vivant en Algérie temporairement pour diverses raisons.[29] Ce groupe n'eut pas besoin le nombre des églises comme au temps colonial, dont une partie était d'anciennes mosquées. Beaucoup d'églises furent transformées ou retransformées en mosquées.[30]

Cette nouvelle situation présenta pour l'Église catholique ainsi que pour l'Église protestante un grand défi. Elles étaient une petite minorité majoritairement étrangère. Quelle identité et quelle tâche pour l'Église en Algérie ? Déjà avant l'indépendance un certain nombre de chrétiens se voua au service de la population autochtone. Un cercle d'étude formé de catholiques et de protestants posa la question de savoir si l'église en Algérie devait être une église d'ambassade, repliée sur elle-même ou une église du pays. Et on ne voulut pas être une église du concordat comme en Tunisie. On se donna la réponse à la question « quelle église en Algérie pour quels fidèles ? »: « C'est en s'acclimatissant culturellement que l'Église cessera d'être et d'apparaître sociologiquement étrangère. Être algérienne est la condition concrète de son universalité ».[31] Dans la suite il fallut faire des pas concrets.

En 1964 Mgr Duval devint cardinal et il obtint très peu après la nationalité algérienne comme de nombreux prêtres et laïcs. Mais la relation entre État et Église devait encore être réglée. Les droits de l'homme, la liberté religieuse inclue, en furent le fondement et la séparation entre l'État et l'Église était encore en vigueur.[32]

L'Église catholique en Algérie se comprenait comme signe dans la société musulmane et comme témoin des questions et des problèmes de cette société.[33] La fondation du Centre d'études Diocésain d'Alger en

---

[26] Nozière, *Algérie : les chrétiens dans la guerre*, 102-120.

[27] Geoffrey Adams, *The call of conscience: French Protestant responses to the Algerian War, 1954-1962*, Editions SR, v. 21 (Waterloo, Ont: Published for the Canadian Corporation for Studies in Religion = Corporation canadienne des sciences religieuses by Wilfrid Laurier University Press, 1998), passim.

[28] Raymond Facélina, « Une théologie en situation : approche méthodologique », *Revue des Sciences Religieuses* 48, n° 4 (1974): 311-21, doi:10.3406/rscir.1974.2711; Fontaine, « Decolonizing Christianity ».

[29] Jean Landousies, « Chrétiens et musulmans en Algérie », *Islamochristiana* 17 (1991): 116; Denis Gonzalez, « L'Église dans l'Algérie indépendante », in *Histoire des chrétiens d'Afrique du Nord : Libye-Tunisie-Algérie-Maroc*, éd. par Henri Teissier et Antoine Chatelard (Paris: Desclée, 1991), 235.

[30] Landousies, « Chrétiens et musulmans en Algérie », 104-105.

[31] Oissila Saaidia, « Le cas algérien, entre continuité historique et changement », in *Les relations Églises-État en situation postcoloniale : Amérique, Afrique, Asie, Océanie, XIXe-XXe siècles : actes de la 20e session du CREDIC (Chevilly-Larue, 27-30 août 2002)*, éd. par Philippe Delisle, Mémoire d'Églises (Paris: Éditions Karthala, 2003), 144-145.

[32] Saaidia, « Le cas algérien, entre continuité historique et changement », passim.

[33] Landousies, « Chrétiens et musulmans en Algérie », 117.

1966 fut une autre étape dans l'inculturation. Il forma les chrétiens dans la culture arabo-musulmane, avait focus sur la théologie et le pastoral, et arrangea des rencontres avec les musulmans. Il fut part du réseau des institutions qui travailla sur la culture algérienne et berbère ou sur les taches théologiques ou pastorales.[34] Le centre publia la revue de presse Maghreb – Proche et Moyen-Orient. À Oran on fonda des centres semblables.[35] Beaucoup de publications théologiques sur la vocation chrétienne en société musulmane apparurent.

Dans les années 70 la base des activités de l'église en Algérie fut modifiée. Toutes les associations furent dissoutes en 1972. L'Église catholique demanda la reconnaissance de deux de ses associations: L'Association Diocésaine d'Algérie (ADA) responsable des biens et les activités des quatre diocèses d'Alger, Oran, Constantine et Laghouat, et l'Association des Communautés Religieuses Catholiques d'Algérie (ACRA) avec le même but pour les congrégations. En 1974 les deux associations furent reconnues. Les deux associations furent aussi propriétaire des écoles, des centres de formation, des dispensaires, etc., mais en 1975 les services de santé et en 1976 l'enseignement furent nationalisés. Leur statut fut actualisé en 1988.[36]

En 1972 l'Église réformée d'Algérie fusionna avec l'Église Méthodiste Épiscopale et les autres Églises et Missions protestantes pour constituer l'Église Protestante d'Algérie.

L'Église catholique, souvent par le biais de la commission Justicia et Pax, parla au public par ses bulletins, et après 1990, l'année où la liberté de la presse fut développée, par la presse publique, pendant la première guerre du Golfe aussi par la radio et la télévision[37].

La crise de la société algérienne 1992-1998

En 1990 le multipartisme fut introduit en Algérie et des élections législatives furent prévues pour 1991, mais elles furent suspendues le 16 janvier 1992. Cela provoqua une crise avec plus de 100.000 morts. Toutes les écoles étrangères furent fermées et presque toutes les familles étrangères, la plupart chrétiennes, quittèrent le pays. Les épouses chrétiennes des Algériens aussi que les chrétiens proche-orientaux comme les coptes partirent. Seule la population européenne établie depuis longtemps et des étudiants d'Afrique subsaharienne restèrent. La communauté de chrétiens diminua d'environs 20.000 à quelques 1000 membres en 1993/1994.[38] En 1993 on commença à prendre des otages et on somma les non-musulmans de quitter le pays. Des étrangers furent assassinés. Malgré cette situation les prêtres et les religieux et religieuses restèrent dans le pays. Les évêques d'Algérie s'adressèrent aux chrétiens du pays le 2 janvier 1994 en décrivant la crise[39]. Le 8 mai 1994 le père Henri Vergès âgé de 64 ans et la religieuse Paule-Hélène Saint-Raymond, âgée de 67 ans, furent assassinés en quittant la bibliothèque fondée par l'archevêque d'Alger pour aider les jeunes à faire leurs devoirs et pour leur apprendre l'informatique. D'autres meurtres suivirent: quatre Pères Blancs en Kabylie le 27 décembre 1994; les sœurs Bibane Leclerc et Angèle-Marie Littlehohn; sept moines trappistes de Tibhirine enlevés le 21 mai 1996;[40] Mgr

---

[34] Gonzalez, « L'Église dans l'Algérie indépendante », 236; Jacques Levrat, *Une expérience de dialogue: les centres dd'étude chrétiens en monde musulman*, Studien ; 9 (Altenberge: Christl.-Islam. Schrifttum, 1987), 22-47.

[35] Landousies, « Chrétiens et musulmans en Algérie », 117-118.

[36] Landousies, « Chrétiens et musulmans en Algérie », 116-117; Gonzalez, « L'Église dans l'Algérie indépendante », 234,237.

[37] Landousies, « Chrétiens et musulmans en Algérie », 118-119.

[38] Teissier, *Chrétiens en Algérie*, 39-40.

[39] Islamochristiana 20, 1994, 212.

[40] Teissier, *Chrétiens en Algérie*, 40-42; A. Louf, « Le drame d'un amour porté jusqu'à l'extrême. Homélie pour la veillée de prière (Mont-des-Cats, 29 Mai 1996) », *Collectanea Cisterciensia* 58 (1996): passim; Giovanni Marchesi, « Algeria : il martirio di sette monaci trappisti », *La Civilità Cattolica* 147 (1996): 62-71; Pierre Miquel, « Les sept dormants de Tibhirine. (Pentecôte 1996) », *Collectanea Cisterciensia* 58 (1996): 199-200; L. Wehbé, « A mes frères de

Pierre Claverie, évêque d'Oran, avec son chauffeur le 1er août 1996.[41] Les moines et l'évêque étaient très populaires. Tous les assassinés reçurent l'occasion de quitter le pays, mais ils voulurent rester impuissants parmi les impuissants, suivant la théologie qu'ils avaient développée depuis l'indépendance: signe de l'amour de Dieu et accompagnateurs des pauvres. Ils ne purent pas se mettre à l'abri comme les étrangers sans trahir leurs idéaux. Cette crise des martyrs fut interprétée théologiquement comme le passage du vendredi saint au dimanche de Pâques.[42] Ainsi l'Église est devenue algérienne[43] ayant la confiance profonde de la population, la base d'un vrai dialogue.

Après 1998

Quand la crise fut largement surmontée, un grand nombre de travailleurs étrangers et des étudiants d'Afrique subsaharien ne revinrent et le nombre des chrétiens augmenta. Depuis ce temps-là aussi des groupes néo-évangéliques tentèrent des missions spécialement en Kabylie.

À l'occasion de l'année 2001, à laquelle l'ONU donna le thème « Dialogue entre les Civilisation », un grande colloque international sur le philosophe Augustin eut lieu du 1er au 7 avril à Alger et à Annaba, où Saint Augustin fut évêque.[44] Le Haut Conseil Islamique en collaboration avec l'université de Fribourg et l'Institutum Patristicum Augustianum à Rome et avec le concours de l'archevêque d'Alger, Henri Teissier, l'organisa. Le but était de réconcilier les Algériens avec leur passe pré-musulman. Ce colloque eut des effets positifs sur l'Église et les Chrétiens dans le pays: Leur confiance en eux fut fortifiée par le fait que le pays avait un si grand philosophe et théologien. Ce fut un signe d'acceptance de la foi chrétienne dans le pays.

Depuis la fin du millénaire l'Algérie est considérée comme une terre de mission par les néo-évangéliques. Les conversions se multiplient et de nouveaux lieux de culte émergent partout, accompagnés par la réclamation de la liberté de culte et de religion. Cela se passa surtout en Kabylie. Les autorités algériennes ont réagi plutôt par des mesures de répression. En 2004 et 2008 un débat de société au sujet de la liberté de culte eut lieu, dans lequel les convertis prirent la parole publiquement. Ces groupes de missionnaires entrèrent souvent masqués comme œuvre éducative et caritative ou ONG et ils sont très divers et non-liés entre eux. Jusqu'en 2006 les églises néo-évangélique se fédérèrent à l'Église Protestante d'Algérie.[45] L'État répondit à ce défi par la promulgation d'une loi interdisant la mission en 2006. Cette loi

---

l'Atlas : Témoignage d'un moine Arabe », *Collectanea Cisterciensia* 58 (1996): 217-223.

[41] Pierre Claverie, *Lettres et messages d'Algérie* (Karthala Editions, 1996); Jean-Jacques Pérennès, *Pierre Claverie: un Algérien par alliance*, L'histoire à vif (Paris: Éd. du Cerf, 2000).

[42] Gabriel Piroird, « L'Église d'Algérie et Notre-Dame de l'Attente », *Nouvelle revue théologique* 119 (1997): 503-519, www.nrt.be/docs/articles/1997/119-4/347-L%27%C3%89glise+d%27Alg%C3%A9rie+et+Notre-Dame+de+l%27Attente.pdf.

[43] Claude Rault, « La misión de la Iglesia en Argelia, hoy », *Misiones extranjeras* 205 (2005): 176-179.

[44] Elisabeth Tworek, « Auf den Spuren von Augustinus: Algerien bekennt sich zu seiner vorislamischen Zeit », in *Augustinus Afer: saint Augustin, africanité et universalité : actes du colloque international, Alger-Annaba, 1-7 avril 2001*, éd. par Pierre-Yves Fux et al. (Fribourg, Suisse: Editions Universitaires, 2003), 475-481; Jan Heuft, « Beispiel Algerien », in *Möglichkeiten christlich-islamischer Zusammenarbeit bei der Umsetzung der Menschenrechte und dem Aufbau von Zivilgesellschaften : Dokumentation einer Internationalen Fachtagung 11. bis 14. März 2002, Berlin*, éd. par Internationales Missionswerk missio <Aachen> (Aachen: Internationales Missionswerk missio, 2005), 79-80; les actes: Pierre-Yves Fux, Jean-Michel Roessli, et Otto Wermelinger, *Augustinus afer : saint Augustin : africanité et modernité : actes du Colloque international Alger-Annaba, 1-7 avril 2001*, Paradosis (Fribourg: Éditions Universitaires, 2003).

[45] Karima Dirèche, « Mondialisation des espaces néo-évangéliques au Maghreb. Controverses religieuses et débats politiques », *Méditerranée. Revue géographique des pays méditerranéens* 116 (2011): passim, http://mediterranee.revues.org/pdf/5390; Karima Dirèche, « Dolorisme religieux et reconstructions identitaires Les conversions néo-évangéliques dans l'Algérie contemporaine », *Annales. Histoire, Sciences Sociales* 64e année, n° 5

exige la permission du préfet régional pour célébrer un service divin et interdit la production des médias qui portent atteinte à la foi musulmane. Elle prend des mesures sévères contre le prosélytisme.[46] En 2008 plusieurs ieux de culte évangéliques en Kabylie furent fermés, le pasteur méthodiste et président de l'Église Protestante d'Algérie, en Algérie depuis 1963, fut expulsé pour raison de sécurité et un grand nombre de convertis furent arrêtés.

Les églises catholique et protestantes sont défiées par les activités des néo-évangéliques; elles étaient très discrètes, s'abstenaient de prosélytisme et menaient un dialogue islamo-chrétien discret.

Beaucoup de ressortissants d'Afrique sub-sahélienne sont venus récemment. Ils sont étudiants, immigrants ou travailleurs immigrés. Beaucoup sont catholiques, ainsi l'église devient-elle plus vivante avec une communauté plus grande. Des catéchistes d'origine sub-sahéliens participent largement à la pastorale auprès des ressortissants subsaharienne et de travailleurs immigrés d'Asie.

Le 24 mai 2008 Mgr Ghaleb Moussa Abdallah Bader fut nommé évêque d'Alger. Il est Jordanien et le premier évêque arabe à Alger, un pas vers l'inculturation arabe de l'Église locale. Mais il fut nommé nonce au Pakistan le 23 mai 2015. Dans la même année 2008 un Algérien converti au protestantisme présida pour la première fois l'Église Protestante d'Algérie. Cela donne à cette Église un autre légitimité dans l'appartenance nationale.

Bibliographie

Adams, Geoffrey. *The call of conscience: French Protestant responses to the Algerian War, 1954-1962.* Editions SR, v. 21. Waterloo, Ont: Published for the Canadian Corporation for Studies in Religion = Corporation canadienne des sciences religieuses by Wilfrid Laurier University Press, 1998.

Ait Abdelmalek, Zohra. *Protestants en Algérie. Le protestantisme et son action missionnaire en Algérie aux XIXe et XXe siècles.* Lyon: Olivétan, 2004. http://books.google.com/books?id= uMHYAAAAMAAJ.

Ait Abdelmalek, Zohra. *Protestants en Algérie: le protestantisme et son action missionnaire en Algérie aux XIXe et XXe siècles.* Lyon: Olivétan, 2004.

« Algeria 2014 International Religious Freedom Report ». Consulté le 2 mars 2016. www.state.gov/documents/organization/238660.pdf.

« Catholic Church in Algeria [Catholic-Hierarchy] ». Consulté le 2 mars 2016. http://catholic-hierarchy.org/country/dz.html.

Claverie, Pierre. *Lettres et messages d'Algérie*. Karthala Editions, 1996.

Cristiani, Léon. *Le cardinal Lavigerie: un grand bienfaiteur de l'Afrique (1825-1892).* Paris: Ed. France-Empire, 1961.

Dirèche, Karima. « Dolorisme religieux et reconstructions identitaires Les conversions néo-évangéliques dans l'Algérie contemporaine ». *Annales. Histoire, Sciences Sociales* 64e année, n° 5 (2009): 1137-62.

______. « Évangélisation en Algérie : débats sur la liberté de culte ». *L'Année du Maghreb*, n° V (1 novembre 2009): 275-84. doi:10.4000/anneemaghreb.596.

______. « Mondialisation des espaces néo-évangéliques au Maghreb Controverses religieuses et débats politiques ». *Méditerranée. Revue géographique des pays méditerranéens* 116 (2011): 59-65. http://mediterranee.revues.org/pdf/5390.

Direche-Slimani, Karima. *Chrétiens de Kabylie (1873-1954): une action missionnaire dans l'Algérie coloniale.* [Saint-Denis]: Bouchène, 2004.

(2009): 1137-62; Karima Dirèche, « Évangélisation en Algérie : débats sur la liberté de culte », *L'Année du Maghreb*, n° V (1 novembre 2009): 275-84, doi:10.4000/anneemaghreb.596; Nadia Marzouki, « Conversion as Statelessness: A Study of Contemporary Algerian Conversions to Evangelical Christianity », *Middle East Law and Governance* 4, n° 1 (1 janvier 2012): 69-105, doi:10.1163/187633712X626053.

[46] Marzouki, « Conversion as Statelessness », 76-81.

Dor, Marie-Josée, et Jean Fisset. « Pères Blancs et Soeurs Blanches, Tunisie et Algérie : Fondation, développement, travaux apostolique ». In *Histoire des chrétiens d'Afrique du Nord : Libye-Tunisie-Algérie-Maroc*, édité par Henri Teissier et Antoine. Chatelard, 163-94. Paris: Desclée, 1991.

Encrevé, André. *Protestants français au milieu du XIXe siècle: les réformés de 1848 à 1870*. Histoire et société, no 8. Genève: Labor et Fides, 1986.

Facélina, Raymond. « Une théologie en situation : approche méthodologique ». *Revue des Sciences Religieuses* 48, n° 4 (1974): 311-21. doi:10.3406/rscir.1974.2711.

Fontaine, Darcie S. « Decolonizing Christianity ». Diss. Thesis, Rutgers, The State University of New Jersey, 2011. https://rucore.libraries.rutgers.edu/rutgers-lib/33651/PDF/1/.

Fux, Pierre-Yves, Jean-Michel Roessli, et Otto Wermelinger. *Augustinus afer : saint Augustin : africanité et modernité : actes du Colloque international Alger-Annaba, 1-7 avril 2001*. Paradosis. Fribourg: Éditions Universitaires, 2003.

Gonzalez, Denis. « L'Eglise d'Algérie: enracinement, épreuves et conversions, de 1830 à nos jours ». In *Histoire des chrétiens d'Afrique du Nord : Libye-Tunisie-Algérie-Maroc*, édité par Henri Teissier et Antoine. Chatelard, 117-38. Paris: Desclée, 1991.

______. « L'Église dans l'Algérie indépendante ». In *Histoire des chrétiens d'Afrique du Nord : Libye-Tunisie-Algérie-Maroc*, édité par Henri Teissier et Antoine. Chatelard, 234-44. Paris: Desclée, 1991.

Heuft, Jan. « Beispiel Algerien ». In *Möglichkeiten christlich-islamischer Zusammenarbeit bei der Umsetzung der Menschenrechte und dem Aufbau von Zivilgesellschaften : Dokumentation einer Internationalen Fachtagung 11. bis 14. März 2002, Berlin*, édité par Internationales Missionswerk missio <Aachen>, 76-88. Aachen: Internationales Missionswerk missio, 2005.

Landousies, Jean. « Chrétiens et musulmans en Algérie ». *Islamochristiana* 17 (1991): 99-129.

Levrat, Jacques. *Une expérience de dialogue: les centres détude chrétiens en monde musulman*. Studien ; 9. Altenberge: Christl.-Islam. Schrifttum, 1987.

Louf, A. « Le drame d'un amour porté jusqu'à l'extrême. Homélie pour la veillée de prière (Mont-des-Cats, 29 Mai 1996) ». *Collectanea Cisterciensia* 58 (1996): 197-98.

Marchesi, Giovanni. « Algeria : il martirio di sette monaci trappisti ». *La Civilità Cattolica* 147 (1996): 62-71.

Marzouki, Nadia. « Conversion as Statelessness: A Study of Contemporary Algerian Conversions to Evangelical Christianity ». *Middle East Law and Governance* 4, n° 1 (1 janvier 2012): 69-105. doi:10.1163/187633712X626053.

Miller, Duane Alexander, et Patrick Johnstone. « Believers in Christ from a Muslim Background: A Global Census ». *Interdisciplinary Journal of Research on Religion* 11, n° Article 10 (2015). https://tspace.library.utoronto.ca/handle/1807/30108.

Miquel, Pierre. « Les sept dormants de Tibhirine. (Pentecôte 1996) ». *Collectanea Cisterciensia* 58 (1996): 199-200.

Nozière, André. *Algérie : les chrétiens dans la guerre*. [Paris]: Cana, 2001.

Pannier, Jacques. « Les Protestants Français et l'Algérie: Quatre épisodes ». *Bulletin de la Société de l'Histoire du Protestantisme Français (1903-)* 79, n° 2 (1930): 146-203. www.jstor.org/stable/24290001.

Pérennès, Jean-Jacques. *Pierre Claverie: un Algérien par alliance*. L'histoire à vif. Paris: Éd. du Cerf, 2000.

Piroird, Gabriel. « L'Église d'Algérie et Notre-Dame de l'Attente ». *Nouvelle revue théologique* 119 (1997): 503-19. www.nrt.be/docs/articles/1997/119-4/347-L%27%C3%89glise+d%27Alg%C3%A9rie+et+Notre-Dame+de+l%27Attente.pdf.

Pons, Alexandre. *La nouvelle Église d'Afrique ou Le catholicisme en Algérie, en Tunisie et au Maroc depuis 1830*. Tunis, 1930.

Rault, Claude. « La misión de la Iglesia en Argelia, hoy ». *Misiones extranjeras* 205 (2005): 176-79.

Saaidia, Oissila. « Le cas algérien, entre continuité historique et changement ». In *Les relations Églises-*

État en situation postcoloniale : Amérique, Afrique, Asie, Océanie, XIXe-XXe siècles : actes de la 20e session du CREDIC (Chevilly-Larue, 27-30 août 2002), édité par Philippe Delisle, 143-54. Mémoire d'Églises. Paris: Éditions Karthala, 2003.

Teissier, Henri. *Chrétiens en Algérie: un partage d'espérance*. Paris: Desclée de Brouwer, 2002.

Teissier, Henri, et Antoine. Chatelard, éd. *Histoire des chrétiens d'Afrique du Nord : Libye-Tunisie-Algérie-Maroc*. Paris: Desclée, 1991.

Tworek, Elisabeth. « Auf den Spuren von Augustinus: Algerien bekennt sich zu seiner vorislamischen Zeit ». In *Augustinus Afer: saint Augustin, africanité et universalité : actes du colloque international, Alger-Annaba, 1-7 avril 2001*, édité par Pierre-YvesFux, Jean-Michel Roessli, Otto Wermelinger, et Michael von Graffenried, 475-781. Fribourg, Suisse: Editions Universitaires, 2003.

Volff, Jean. « Une èglise protestante unie en Algérie ». *Revue d'histoire et de philosophie religieuses* 87 (2007): 71-76.

Wehbé, L. « A mes frères de l'Atlas : Témoignage d'un moine Arabe ». *Collectanea Cisterciensia* 58 (1996): 217-23.

(47) CHRISTIANITY IN ANGOLA

Luciano Chanhelela Chianeque

Religion	Pop 2010	Pct 2010	Pop 2025	Pct 2025	Gr Pct 1970 2025
Christians	19,906,000	93.8%	32,359,000	95.1%	3.3%
Independents	878,000	4.1%	1,320,000	3.9%	2.8%
African initiated	501,000	2.4%			
Protestants	5,354,000	25.2%	9,245,000	27.2%	3.7%
Pentecostal	2,300,000	10.8%			
Congregational	850,000	4.0%			
Adventist	608,000	2.9%			
Brethren	500,000	2.4%			
Baptist	382,000	1.8%			
Reformed, Presbyterian	279,000	1.3%			
Methodist	213,000	1.0%			
Roman Catholics	12,508,000	58.9%	20,000,000	58.8%	3.2%
Pentecostals/Charismatics	4,488,000	21.2%	6,000,000	17.6%	2.0%
Evangelicals	3,939,000	18.6%	5,542,000	16.3%	2.3%
adherents of traditional African religions	903,000	4.3%	1,000,000	2.9%	0.7%
Muslims	213,000	1.0%	340,000	1.0%	3.2%
Baha'is	2,100	0.0%	3,500	0.0%	3.4%
Buddhists	1,700	0.0%	2,200	0.0%	1.9%
Hindus	390	0.0%	500	0.0%	1.7%
Chinese folk-religionists	170	0.0%	200	0.0%	1.2%
people professing no religion	194,000	0.9%	310,000	0.9%	3.2%
Total population	**21,220,000**	**100.0%**	**34,016,000**	**100.0%**	**3.2%**

Source: Centre for the Study of World Christianity (CSGC), Boston, Gordon-Conwell TS

Introduction

Angola is situated in the south-west part of Africa, specifically in the Southern Africa region. Before the colonizers arrived from Portugal in 1482, the cluster of people in Angola lived together in harmony. The country, called Angola today, was governed by tribal kingdoms like Mbakongo, Ndongo, Mbundu, Kwanyama, Nganguela, Cokwe and others. Some of these kingdoms paid tribute to those who were stronger than them. It is true that those tribes who were not so strong paid tribute to those stronger than them, and this was considered normal in those societies. The current borders of Angola, decided by Europeans in 1885, do not represent the true reality of our people. Some of these tribes and kingdoms spread to other neighbouring countries. Before colonial rule, the tribes and kingdoms had their social structures in place. They developed rudimentary agriculture, hunting and fishing, as is still being done today. The education system worked, using the local social structures called *Onjango* for the education of boys and *Ochiwo* for girls. The education used here was holistic. Usually it was done from the senior people of a village to the younger generation orally. These structures taught mathematical calculations, moral values, ethics and professions through experience. Through the elders, who had knowledge of healing powers of traditional medicines, an efficient health structure was in place. Amongst the tribes of Angola, the largest is Mbundu, representing almost half the entire population.

According to the history of this country, Christianity in Angola began officially in 1491, with a Catholic mission station built in the São Salvador area (Zaire Province). João I, Manikongo of the powerful Kongo Kingdom and his son Afonso I, were converted to Christianity. The two of them were well-known figures, reigning from 1509 to 1543.[1]

> In 1878, the first Protestant missionaries, British Baptists, arrived in Angola. In 1880, they were followed by Congregationalists from the ex-American Board for Missions who arrived in Benguela. They then headed to the centre of Angola, establishing mission stations in Bailundo, Camundongo, Chilesso, Chissamba, Elende, Dondi, Galangui, Lobito, Huambo and Kuito. In 1885, Methodist missionaries arrived from America and set up their missions in Luanda, Quessua and Malanje. In 1897, the Angola Evangelical Mission was established in Cabinda, and the North Angola Mission started in 1925, in Uíge. In contemporary Angola, the Ovimbundu people are one of the most heavily Christianised groups.[2]
>
> Religious affiliation in Angola was difficult to define because many who claimed membership in a specific Christian denomination also shared perceptions of the natural and supernatural order characteristic of indigenous religious systems.[3] Sometimes the Christian sphere of the life of a community was institutionally separate from the indigenous sphere. In other cases, the local meaning and practice of Christianity were modified by indigenous patterns of belief and practice.
>
> Although Roman Catholic missions were largely staffed by non-Portuguese missionaries during the colonial era, the relevant statutes and accords provided that foreign missionaries could be admitted only with the approval of the Portuguese government and the Vatican, and on condition that they be integrated with the Portuguese missionary organization. Foreign Roman Catholic missionaries were required to renounce the laws of their own country, submit to Portuguese law, and furnish proof of their ability to speak and write the Portuguese language correctly. Missionary activity was placed under the authority of Portuguese priests. All of this was consistent with the Colonial Act of 1930, which advanced the view that Portuguese Catholic missions overseas were 'instruments of civilization and Portuguese national influence'. In 1940, the education of Africans was declared the exclusive responsibility of missionary personnel. All church activities, education included, were to be subsidized by the state. In reality, Protestant missions were permitted to engage in educational activity, but without subsidy and on condition that Portuguese be the language of instruction.[4]
>
> The important Protestant missions (or their predecessors) in place in the 1960s had arrived in Angola in the late nineteenth century. Thus, they had been at work before the Portuguese managed to establish control over the entire territory. Their early years, therefore, were little affected by Portuguese policy and practice. Before the establishment of the New State (*Estado Novo*) in Portugal in 1926, the authorities kept an eye on the Protestant missions but were not particularly hostile to them. Settlers and local administrators were often hostile, however, because Protestant missionaries tended to be protective of what they considered their charges. In those early years and later, Protestant missionaries were not only evangelists but also teachers, healers and counsellors – all perhaps in a paternal fashion but in ways that involved contact with Africans in a more sustained fashion than was characteristic of Roman Catholic missionaries and local administrators. Protestant missionaries worked at

[1] http://en.wikipedia.org/wiki/Jo%C3%A3o_I_of_Kongo

[2] Lawrence Henderson, *The Church in Angola: A River of Many Currents* (Cleveland: Pilgrim Press, 1990).

[3] A major part of the following paragraphs is taken from https://en.wikipedia.org/wiki/Christianity_in_Angola.

[4] http://en.wikipedia.org/wiki/Portuguese_Empire.

learning the local languages, in part to communicate better with those in their mission field, but above all in order to translate the Old Testament and New Testaments into African tongues.

> Protestant missionaries were much more likely than administrators and settlers to know a local language. Roman Catholic missionaries did not similarly emphasize the translation of the Bible and, with some exceptions, did not make a point of learning a Bantu language.[5]
>
> Because specific Protestant denominations were associated with particular ethnic communities, the structure of religious organization was linked with the structure of these communities. This connection was brought about in part by the tendency of entire communities to turn to the variety of Protestantism offered locally. The conversion of isolated individuals was rare. Those individuals who did not become Christians remained to a greater or lesser extent adherents of the indigenous system; unless they migrated to one of the larger towns, persons of a specific locality did not have the option of another kind of Christianity. Those members of a community who had not yet become Christians were tied by kinship and propinquity to those individuals who had converted. On the one hand, indigenous patterns of social relationships affected church organization; on the other hand, the presence of Christians in the community affected the local culture to varying degrees. Christians who could quote Scripture in the local languages contributed phrases to it that others picked up. The attributes of the Christian God as interpreted by the specific denomination sometimes became attached to the high god of the indigenous religious system and typically made that deity more prominent than previously.[6]

The involvement of the Protestant churches in the languages of their mission areas, their medical and other welfare activity, and their ability to adapt to local structures or (in the case of the Methodists among the Mbundu) to be fortuitously consistent with them gave Protestants much more influence than their numbers would suggest. For example, the leaders of the three major nationalist movements in the 1960s – the MPLA, UNITA, and the FNLA – had been raised as Protestants, and many others in these movements were also Protestants, even if their commitment diminished over time.

The Future for Angola?

In an article entitled 'Theological Education in Angola and Mozambique', I pointed out that there is a need for a new model of theological education, which at the same time is proactive, preventive and curative: one that redefines and rediscovers according to the perspective of the kingdom of God. I went further to argue for a new orientation of theological education which better empowers the gifts and ministries of fellow Christians to serve as agents for the kingdom of God, which can be seen in their daily life, and in the propagation and teaching of the Word of God. I also argued for a theological education that is closer to the people, empowering them so that they may be less vulnerable and susceptible to all sorts of distorted and false doctrines and teaching. Lastly, I emphasized that doing quality theological education was and always has been a major responsibility of the churches themselves. It is possible to get churches recommitted to a higher quality of theological education, and our responsibility is to make it better every day.[7]

I still believe that we need to revisit our Christianity in Angola and come up with the kind that embraces all its sons and daughters, regardless of their social status, sexual orientation or political affiliation. Here I look to Matthew 25 for direction and the correct answers are there: 'If you have done it to one of these little children, you have done it to me.'

Our churches are not going to overcome stigma and discrimination regarding those members challenged with HIV and AIDS-related illness in our communities if we are not able to look our fellow Christians in

---

[5] http://en.wikipedia.org/wiki/Public_administration.

[6] http://en.wikipedia.org/wiki/Christian_denomination.

[7] Luciano Chianeque, "Theological Education in Angola and Mozambique," in *Handbook of Theological Education in Africa,* edited by Isabel Phiri and Dietrich Werner, 218-222 (Oxford: Regnum Books International, 2013).

the eye and learn with them what we do not yet know. Christianity in Angola has to leave behind the self-pity approach in order to earn the government's favour. It is true that the Portuguese government treated Protestants in a hostile way or simply tolerated them, and they did with them what they wished. Today, our Constitution says that all denominations are equal before the law.

Christianity in Angola has a long way to go. First and foremost, those who announce it need to be completely transformed by the word they preach. These should be a catalyst. This is a big challenge. Many other challenges remain. How can we open up universities that are not going to penalize students who are Seventh Day Adventists, for instance? How can we work for the Kingdom of God and not for our own denominations? Who are we serving? How do we make our common testimony relevant for our current society in Angola? How do we distribute power? Finally, how are we influencing government officials, those who are our colleagues, family members and friends?

Bibliography

Chianeque, L. 'Theological Education in Angola and Mozambique.' In *Handbook of Theological Education in Africa,* edited by Isabel Apawo Phiri and Dietrich Werner, 218-222. Oxford: Regnum Books International, 2013.

Chianeque L. 'A Comparison of the Angolan Diaspora with Their Biblical Counterparts in the Post Exilic Period.' Unpublished Masters′ thesis. University of Durban-Westville, 2000.

Drucker, P. F. *Administrando em Tempos de Grande Mudança.* São Paulo: Thomson Pioneira, 996.

Henderson, L. W. *The Church in Angola: A River of Many Currents.* Cleveland: The Pilgrim Press, 1992.

Johnson-Hill, J. *Seeds of Transformation: Discerning the Ethics of a New Generation.* Pietermaritzburg: Cluster Publications, 1998.

(48) Le Christianisme au Benin

Simon Dossou et Omer Dagan

Religion	Pop 2010	Pct 2010	Pop 2025	Pct 2025	Gr Pct 1970 2025
Christians	4,162,000	43.8%	6,776,000	48.6%	3.3%
Independents	1,224,000	12.9%	1,680,000	12.1%	2.1%
African initiated	1,122,000	11.8%			
Protestants	805,000	8.5%	1,500,000	10.8%	4.2%
Pentecostal	434,000	4.6%			
Methodist	190,000	2.0%			
Roman Catholics	2,138,000	22.5%	3,700,000	26.5%	3.7%
Pentecostals/Charismatics	1,792,000	18.8%	2,800,000	20.1%	3.0%
Evangelicals	731,000	7.7%	1,201,000	8.6%	3.4%
adherents of traditional African religions	2,889,000	30.4%	3,308,000	23.7%	0.9%
Muslims	2,421,000	25.5%	3,800,000	27.3%	3.1%
Baha'is	12,500	0.1%	17,000	0.1%	2.1%
adherents of new religious movements	1,400	0.0%	2,000	0.0%	2.4%
people professing no religion	23,400	0.2%	34,000	0.2%	2.5%
Total population	**9,510,000**	**100.0%**	**13,937,000**	**100.0%**	**2.6%**

Source: Centre for the Study of World Christianity (CSGC), Boston, Gordon-Conwell TS

L'implantation du christianisme au Bénin1 ne fut pas chose aisée. Les premiers missionnaires qui y sont venus pour évangéliser des populations fortement ancrées dans leurs croyances religieuses n'ont pas eu la tâche facile. Traditionnellement, n'étaient tolérées que les pratiques du culte des ancêtres. Les missionnaires européens ont dû s'employer de toutes leurs forces pour occuper le terrain. Par rapport à la statistique, aujourd'hui le Bénin compte un grand nombre de confessions religieuses au point où il est difficile d'en donner un chiffre exact. D'après Albert de Surgy[2], de neuf Eglises dénombrées en 1955, on est passé à 36 Eglises en 1980, puis à plus de 81 en 1986 et à 96 en 1994.

Tout dernièrement, le projet ACERB (Action pour la recherche et la croissance des Eglises au Bénin) a dressé une liste de 430 églises présentes au Bénin[3].

De façon générale, on peut classer les Eglises qui forment le champ du christianisme de la manière suivante:

1- L'Eglise catholique; elle est la plus importante sur le plan statistique et de par son influence sociale. Au troisième recensement de la population[4], on estime qu'environ 26% des béninois sont catholiques.

[1] Ce texte a été écrit conjointement par Rev Dr Omer Dagan, Professeur d'Histoire de l'Eglise à l'Université Protestante de l'Afrique de l'Ouest, Porto-Novo, Bénin et le Prof. Simon Dossou, CETA, Lomé, Togo.
[2] L. OGOUBI, *Les religion dans l'espace public au Bénin*, l'Harmattan, Paris, 2008, 44.
[3] Collectif, *l'Histoire des Eglises Protestantes et Evangéliques du Bénin*, Annuaire Evangélique, 2003, 97.
[4] Ibid, 98.

Selon le journal des Missions[5] la première mission catholique s'est installée officiellement au Bénin en 1861.

2- Les Eglises protestantes, celles qui plongent leurs racines dans le protestantisme du XVIème siècle et implantées par les missionnaires anglais et américains. Cet ensemble est formé surtout de l'Eglise Protestante Méthodiste du Bénin (1843) et d'autres confessions telles que: L'église Evangélique des Assemblées de Dieu, dont l'œuvre a démarré en 1960, pour connaître une explosion sans pareil en 1985, grâce au travail du missionnaire français Jacques HALEPIAN.

3- Enfin, les églises dites indépendantes, celles fondées après les indépendances par des béninois, suite à des visions et des révélations personnelles. Elles sont congrégationalistes et ne sont attachées à aucune autre Eglise. C'est le cas de l'église dite du christianisme céleste.

Les premiers efforts du catholicisme

Selon Henri LABURET, cité par le père Barthélemy ADOUKONOU[6], la première tentative d'évangélisation du Dahomey, remonte au XVè siècle, vers les années 1486. En effet, en 1493, le pape Alexandre VI, avait confié le soin aux navigateurs de développer des relations avec les peuples, leurs souverains en les évangélisant. Par sa bulle « *le Portugal aura le droit de trafiquer tout le long des Côtes occidentales de l'Afrique* »[7]. C'est dans ce cadre que le roi d'Allada reçoit la visite du Portugais Joao Alfonso. Sans tarder, dès 1658 il va dépêcher à Madrid un ambassadeur du nom de Bans, pour solliciter des missionnaires prédicateurs afin de créer un Fort (ouvrage destiné à protéger un lieu), capable de concurrencer Ouidah. Peu de temps après, il reçut deux missionnaires catholiques accompagnés de deux officiers ayant la charge d'installer une factorerie. Mais cette mission ne fit pas un long moment.

Il fallait attendre 1659, pour voir certains capucins envoyés par le roi d'Espagne s'installer à Jekin pour évangéliser et convertir les populations au christianisme. Ce sont les missionnaires catholiques portugais, jésuites et capucins, qui les premiers prendront donc contact avec les côtes du Golfe de Guinée. Dès le milieu du XVème siècle, des bateaux portugais se lancèrent dans l'exploration de la Côte de Guinée. Tandis que leur mission première était la recherche de richesses, leur mission secondaire exigeait d'eux la promotion du christianisme comme frein à l'Islam, leur plus grand rival commercial et religieux. Grâce à la marine portugaise, la première manifestation catholique au Dahomey a été celle des marchands et des prêtres d'un ordre religieux.

Mais le roi, effrayé par le soulèvement des populations; sous l'action conjuguée des féticheurs et des marchands d'esclaves va refuser le baptême. Il jura de renvoyer les missionnaires qui, plus tard moururent empoisonnés sur le chemin de leur retour vers la côte.

Quelques années après, une Brésilienne du nom de Venosa de Jésus, va s'installer à Agoué pour construire en 1835 une première chapelle. Malheureusement celle-ci sera détruite par un incendie et le lieu devenu plus tard le cimetière des chrétiens.

Bref, si le catholicisme a été la première à chercher à implanter le christianisme au Bénin, elle ne fut cependant que la deuxième Eglise à y parvenir. Les méthodistes sont arrivés avant que le Vatican n'ait pu relancer un nouvel effort en 1861; ils précéderont ainsi de 19 années l'Eglise Romaine.

---

[5] Journal des Missions, N° 60.075 (1967-1968), Bibliothèque du Défap, Paris, 240.

[6]B. ADOUKONOU, *jalons pour une théologie africaine: essai d'une herméneutique chrétienne du vodoun,* Paris, Dessain et Tolra, 1980, 305.

[7] Grand Larousse Encyclopédique, tome 1, Paris, éd. Larousse1960, 232.

L'implantation du Méthodisme

Le processus de l'installation de la mission Wesleyenne au Dahomey a été une longue histoire. Selon B. HEGEMAN[8] la mission morave sur la Côte de l'Ouest africain a eu un sérieux impact au Dahomey. En 1768, douze chrétiens moraves originaires d'Europe centrale débarquèrent près de la Côte des Esclaves à la Côte d'Or, aujourd'hui le Ghana. Ils arrivèrent à Acrra en tant que missionnaires laïcs issus du mouvement morave piétiste allemand. Tout comme les premières missions des Capucins, ce mouvement fut décimé par la mort. A partir de 1780, les britanniques vinrent dans le Golfe de Guinée pour implanter le christianisme et par suite remédier aux effets désastreux de la traite des esclaves africains. Pour accueillir des esclaves émancipés ou libérés, ils établirent de nouveaux ports à Freetown, en Sierra Leone et, plus tard au Libéria où ils fondèrent des villes libres.

Les débuts de la Mission Méthodiste au Dahomey

L'implantation du méthodisme au Dahomey-Bénin a été l'œuvre incontestable du Rév. Thomas Birch FREEMAN, né le 29 Novembre 1809 à Twyford en Angleterre. Fils d'un ancien esclave noir et d'une mère anglaise, il a passé bon nombre d'années de son enfance et de son adolescence dans des conditions pénibles.

Sur le plan de la vocation, il fut admis comme prédicateur laïc en 1835 et s'est engagé dans la mission Wesleyenne en 1837, pour être consacré pasteur au mois d'octobre de la même année. Après son mariage avec mademoiselle Elisabeth BOOT en Novembre 1837, le pionnier Freeman s'embarqua pour l'Afrique.

Une fois arrivé au Dahomey, Freeman s'empressa d'aller voir le représentant du roi d'Abomey à qui il exposa le but de son déplacement, surtout son désir d'avoir un entretien avec le roi Guézo. Le 6 Mars 1843, dès son arrivée dans la cours royale, Freeman eut plusieurs entrevues privées avec le roi Guézo en présence de quelques notables.

Durant tout l'entretien, Freeman comprit qu'il avait été vraiment conduit par Dieu en venant visiter cet homme que personne ne pouvait approcher auparavant, sans provoquer sa colère. Selon Paul WOOD LAINE[9], l'œuvre d'évangélisation au Dahomey va commencer à Ouidah en 1854, grâce aux services de l'africain Joseph Dawson. Pendant les années suivantes, l'œuvre des méthodistes Wesleyens s'est répandue de lieux en lieux le long de la côte Dahoméenne. Elle se développait avec un succès appréciable au cœur de la population maritime. Mais, elle va souffrir de l'état de guerre permanent dans la région, des rivalités commerciales européennes, de la résistance Dahoméenne, de la mort fréquente chez les missionnaires et de la colonisation.

En effet, la France avait conquit la côte de Dahomey. Le méthodisme subissait de plus en plus une guerre d'usure. Tout en jouissant d'une forte croissance de 1842 à 1860, les méthodistes furent persécutés sur plusieurs autres années. Avec la conférence de Berlin de 1885, l'empire Britannique renonça soudain à ces revendications coloniales sur le Dahomey. Le méthodisme britannique devait maintenant survivre dans un environnement français hostile sans aucune considération ni sympathie politiques. A la fin de la guerre franco-dahoméenne en 1894, le méthodisme était au Dahomey une institution vaincue. Le catholicisme devint la religion quoique non officielle associée aux conquérants blancs.

Pour faciliter les relations avec l'administration française et permettre à la mission de continuer l'évangélisation, un accord a été trouvé avec la Société des Missions Evangéliques de Paris (SMEP). Suite à cet accord, des pasteurs français d'obédience protestante seront envoyés au Dahomey pour remplacer les anglais.

---

[8] B. HEGEMAN, *Between Glory and Shame, A historical and systematic study of education and leadership training models among the Baatonu in North Benin*, Pays-Bas, 2000, 13

[9] P. WOOD LAINE

Le méthodisme va progressivement s'étendre à l'échelle de la nation et vers les années 1913 on pouvait la regrouper en trois grandes zones:

La Mission du Bas Dahomey formée des circuits de Porto-Novo, de Cotonou et de Grand-Popo.

La Mission du Moyen Dahomey regroupant le circuit de Dassa-Savalou et le circuit de Savè-Kilibo.

Et la Mission du Haut Dahomey qui englobait tout le Nord du Dahomey.

Le moyen d'une telle extension a été la prédication fidèle de l'Evangile à tous les Hommes. En donnant ses premiers cadres intellectuels à la nation, elle a influencé positivement la vie politique, socio-économique et culturelle de tout le peuple. Depuis 1993, l'Eglise Protestante Méthodiste du Bénin a pris son destin en main avec son autonomie et malgré la crise qu'elle connaît elle est présente sur la scène nationale. Aujourd'hui, l'Evangile s'est répandu dans tout le pays, grâce à la contribution active, aussi bien des missionnaires étrangers que des pasteurs autochtones. Selon les statistiques de 2011[10] l'EPMB couvre toute l'étendue du territoire béninois avec une population de 250.000 fidèles environ répartis dans 476 temples desservis.

Origine et Naissance de l'Eglise du Christianisme Céleste au Bénin

Dès les années 1940, plusieurs mouvements messianiques se sont développés dans les milieux atteints par l'évangélisation en Afrique. En dehors du catholicisme et du méthodisme, l'église du christianisme céleste en sera l'une des religions populaires au Bénin et en Afrique de l'Ouest.

L'église du christianisme céleste (ECC) a été fondée en 1947 à Porto-Novo dans l'ancien Dahomey (actuel Bénin) par Samuel Biléou Joseph OSHOFFA.

En effet, originaire du Nigéria, les grands parents de Samuel Biléou que sont Ojopola et Koshina, avaient immigré d'Abéokuta à Dassa au Bénin où ils s'étaient installés en tant que fermiers. Suite aux nombreuses attaques des chasseurs d'esclaves, leurs trois enfants furent pris en captivités et amenés à Ajasè (Porto-Novo). Tous furent vendus à l'homme blanc. Mais, Joseph Oshoffa le père de Samuel Biléou Oschoffa, seul avait été revendu aux marchands européens installés à Ajasè à cause de sa santé fragilité[11].

Quelques années plus tard, Samuel Biléou nait le 18 mai 1909 à Porto-Novo, de père menuisier et de mère vendeuse de tissus, Fohoun. Il ne sera qu'un survivant parmi les fils de cette famille qui en avait déjà perdu plusieurs auparavant. De par son nom Biléou yorouba dont l'intention est *« s'il te plait de rester ici-bas, reste. Dans le cas contraire, retourne au Seigneur. Quant à moi, je t'avais consacré à l'Eternel avant même ta naissance»*[12], Samuel fut effectivement un enfant consacré à Dieu.

En 1909, quand il eut sept ans, son père tint sa promesse et le confia à un catéchiste méthodiste, M. Moise Gnansounou pour assurer son éducation. Celui-ci le garda jusqu'à l'âge de 13 ans avec son fils Nathanael Gnansounou. Puis il le confia au Pasteur David Hodonou LOKO. A l'école protestante de Porto-Novo, Samuel Biléou fit ses études primaires jusqu'au cours moyen II. Son éducation était rude et n'ayant pas de force physique pour se défendre et continuer, Samuel dut quitter pour rejoindre son père dans son métier de menuisier. Il obtint sa libération après quatre années d'apprentissages. Samuel était aussi un talentueux trompettiste. Il se débarrassera du travail épuisant de menuiserie un an après la mort de son père en 1939 pour se consacrer définitivement à la fanfare municipale où il était Trompettiste, puis il se livra au commerce du bois d'ébène.

A partir de novembre 1946, Samuel Biléou se mit à parcourir les villages de la vallée du fleuve l'Ouémé à la recherche de bois d'ébène mais jamais sans sa Bible. En effet, avant cette époque, et avec la proximité du Nigéria, la configuration du paysage religieux du Bénin avait changée. En plus du catholicisme et du méthodisme, une paroisse de l'église Bodawa, une séparatiste du méthodiste s'était rattachée à l'United

---

[10] Actes et Décisions du Synode Général tenu à Pobè, janvier 2011

[11] Cours de missiologie du Professeur Valentin DEDJI, UPAO, 2012.

[12] Entretien avec quelques fidèles de L'Eglise du Christianisme Céleste à Pobè, juillet 2010.

Native Africain Church du Nigéria et s'était installée. En 1930, la session Dahoméenne de l'église méthodiste africaine Eleja fut fondée aussi à Porto-Novo. Samuel, méthodiste et trompettiste eut le temps de visiter toutes ces communautés et bien d'autres.

Dans sa recherche de bois d'ébène, un jour de mai 1947, Samuel Biléou se retrouva dans la forêt après avoir traversé le fleuve Ouémé. Son piroguier se prit de violentes coliques et aussitôt il fut guéri de ses maux par l'imposition des mains de Samuel. Troublé par cette action instantanée, il prit peur et l'abandonna seul entre l'eau et la forêt. Ne sachant ni nager ni conduire une pirogue, Samuel demeura sur place en attendant un secours éventuel. Il priait ardemment et ne vivait que d'eau et de miel.

Le 22 mai 1947, Samuel fut terrifié par un grand évènement. Il eut l'éclipse du soleil qui le bouleversa et pendant qu'il priait les yeux fermés, il entendit distinctement une voix qui lui disait: grâce, grâce. Quant il ouvrit les yeux, il vit « un singe blanc ailé assit devant lui sur son séant. Il avait deux dents à la mâchoire supérieure et deux autres à la mâchoire inférieure. A sa droite, il vit un petit serpent marron avec un cou épais. Un peu à l'écart, se fut un oiseau avec des ailes pointues et des plumes colorées. Cet oiseau ressemblait à un paon, il faisait la roue. Cependant cet incident ne dura que quelques minutes »[13]. Tous les animaux disparurent et il resta dans sa solitude. Il ne pouvait vivre désormais que de la prière et de la lecture de sa Bible.

Le cours d'eau se mit à crue et faillit emporter son embarcation. Samuel Biléou se jeta alors dans la pirogue qui fut entrainée par le courant d'eau jusqu'à proximité du village d'Agonguê, dans la sous préfecture d'Adjohon. La nouvelle de sa disparition ayant été sue, tout le monde pris peur à sa vue La population pensait que c'était un revenant. Mais il pria pour un mourant avec force et confiance et ce dernier se leva pour s'asseoir. Un de ces compatriotes nommé Yessoufou, celui qui l'avait rencontré le premier courut annoncer la nouvelle à Porto-Novo. Comment un homme semblable à un fou, les cheveux ébouriffés, le menton embroussaillé peut-il ressusciter les morts ?

Dès son retour à Porto-Novo, Oshoffa était devenu une curiosité, et la foule le suivait partout où il allait. Le 29 Septembre 1947, Samuel Oshoffa rendit visite à son ami, Mr Frédéric Zenouvou et sa femme. De la communauté des Chérubins Séraphins, Mr Frédéric Zenouvou l'invita pour une séance de prière. Oshoffa y entra pour rendre grâce à Dieu. Une fois en prière, il eut une vision dans laquelle, il vit un être humain d'une clarté resplendissant et dont les pieds ne touchaient pas le sol. Cet homme lui chargea d'une mission spéciale: fonder une religion dont les membres n'adoreraient que Dieu. Cette église devrait être la dernière barque pour amener les hommes au salut » dira t-il.

Les défilés récurrentes à son domicile l'amène à demander de l'aide au commandant du cercle. Mais celui-ci refusa d'intervenir en le conseillant d'inviter les gens par circulaire à venir écouter les visions plutôt que de les renvoyer. Finalement, Oshoffa obtempéra le 8e jour sous la direction du Saint-Esprit. Ainsi Samuel Biléou Oshoffa fonda l'église du christianisme céleste. Ce nom fut spirituellement révélé à un certain Alexandre YANGA à la fin d'une transe de sept (7) jours. Cette église est reconnue par l'Etat Béninois et autorisée par décision numéro 2252 A.P.A. du 5 octobre 1965 au Journal Officiel du Dahomey. sous le numéro 28 du 1er Novembre 1965.

Doctrine et pratiques cultuelles de l'ECC

L'Eglise marche avec obéissance et amour. Elle se veut à la fois de l'émanation directe de l'Esprit et de la parole de Dieu telle qu'elle fut donnée d'entendre dans la Bible et la synthèse des religions traditionnalistes (catholique et méthodiste) et le pentecôtisme de type Aladura (groupe de prière). L'attachement à l'efficacité de la prière comme expérience de la puissance de l'Esprit, l'omniprésence des dons de prophétie et de guérison, la considération de Marie, la mère de Jésus comme la première personne obéissante de la terre, la suprématie du prophète, l'ascétisme et la liturgie officiellement inspirée avec des

[13] D'après les informations recueillies chez quelques dignitaires de la religion, pélerinage à la plage de Sèmè en 2010.

chants rythmés et dansés accompagnés d'une prédication démonstrative et dramatisée, font de l'ECC une église hétérogène et dominée par la vision d'un monde de combat entre les démons et les anges de Dieu. Elle participe non seulement à cette culture évangélique qui pourchasse les démons du paganisme africain mais aussi aux rites de fécondité, de protection et bien d'autres connus dans le monde traditionnel africain.

Selon les textes fondateurs, l'Eglise est considéré comme la manifestation terrestre de la véritable église de Dieu composée d'anges et d'archanges. Et bien qu'il existe une myriade d'anges, chacun d'eux a une tâche bien spécifique. Saint Michel est le distributeur de rôle sous la puissance de Jésus-Christ en dehors des archanges (Ap. 7:1 et 9: 15). Sur cette base, l'ECC est fortement hiérarchisée et séparée en deux groupes distincts: les leaders ou ceux qui gouvernent et les visionnaires. La vision est l'élément déterminant de cette religion.

L'église du christianisme céleste est une église particulière. Elle ne fait ni parti de l'Eglise catholique romaine ni des Eglises issus de la Réforme ni des religions traditionnelles. Mais malgré ce fait et malgré ses divisions répétées, l'Eglise du christianisme céleste connait une croissance inquiétante sur le plan locale et internationale.

Bref aperçu sur l'Eglise des Assemblées de Dieu du Bénin

L'Eglise des Assemblées de Dieu (ADD) tire ses origines dans le mouvement pentecôtiste apparu aux Etats-Unis en 1901. Ce mouvement fait suite à la mission du baptiste John Smith (1570-1612) dont l'élément principal d'objet de prédication est le baptême par immersion. Mais avant de revenir sur les ADD il serait intéressant de dire un mot sur les Eglises dites Evangéliques ou pentecôtistes évoluant an Bénin ou même dans d'autres pays. Comme le dit Cédric Mayrargue[14], *« elles ne se situent pas dans une perspective de dialogue interreligieux ou d'ouverture œcuménique. Elles font preuve, au contraire d'une certaine intransigeance, dans les discours comme dans les comportements »*. Il est dans ce cas là difficile de pouvoir avoir des relations franches et honnêtes avec elles. Ceci fait que les Eglises issues des missions de la fin du XIXè dans plusieurs pays ne peuvent pas créer des conseils chrétiens avec elles sans risque de voir les tentatives des divers groupuscules évangéliques de les marginaliser à terme. En effet, dans ces groupes, *« les pasteurs stigmatisent et diabolisent les autres cultes[15] »*.

Les ADD du Bénin qui sont en général de ce courant évangélique commencent à se démarquer de certains aspects d'intransigeances et d'anti-œcuméniques et peuvent maintenant se faire former dans les mêmes institutions théologiques que tout le monde.

En Afrique de l'ouest, cette Eglise s'installera au Burkina Faso. Selon François AHOLOUKPE[16], c'est avec les missionnaires américains que la mission du Burkina va progresser pour pénétrer le Bénin par le Nord-Ouest précisément par la région Atacora en 1945.

En effet, grâce au missionnaire américain Artur Wilson, la mission reçut l'autorisation du gouverneur français Robert Legendre de s'installer sur le territoire Dahoméen le 30 Septembre 1947. Une année plus tard, en 1948, le Pasteur Charles PETROSKY et mademoiselle Hélène ISELIN vinrent apporter leur aide et leur soutien à l'œuvre déjà entamée par leur confrère à Natitingou. Il faut dire qu'avant les Assemblées de Dieu, l'on notait déjà la présence des chrétiens catholiques et protestants surtout méthodistes au Bénin. Les missionnaires durent aussi compter avec la concurrence de l'Islam et des religions traditionnelles. Les

---

[14] Parmi les Eglises dites évangéliques, il y a celles qui se réclament d'un pentecôtisme pur et dur et qui de ce fait ne sont pas prêtes à appeler d'autres groupes comme issus du mouvement de la première pentecôte de l'ère chrétienne. Voir Cédric Mayrargue in: *Dynamiques religieuses et démocratisation au Bénin. Pentecôtiste et formation d'un espace public. Thèse de doctorat en Science Politique, 13 Décembre 2002 Inédit, 356*

[15] On peut voir le même article sur *http:/tel.archives-ouvertes.fr/tel-00298180/document du 17/3/2015, 356*

[16] F. AHOLOUKPE, l'Eglise Evangélique des Assemblées de Dieu du BENIN, Mémoire de licence, UPAO, 2011, Inédit.

premiers fidèles des Assemblées de Dieu selon nos enquêtes furent les chrétiens catholiques et méthodistes du sud, affectés à diverses fonctions au nord.

En 1949, un certain accord sera signé entre les églises existantes sur le territoire béninois. Le territoire sera reparti et chaque dénomination ou mission aura son champ d'action. Le Nord-Ouest a été concédé à la SIM[17]. En principe l'ensemble de l'Atacora était désigné comme zone de mission des Assemblées de Dieu (AD). Lors de la répartition définitive en 1949 entre protestants, les AD ne reçurent que la région du nord de l'Atacora. Mais, il y eut des dissensions au sein des communautés formant la SIM, au sujet des différentes règles de discipline et l'accord qui répartissait la limite des églises selon leur champ de mission a été remis en cause. En 1950, la ville baatonu de Kouandé a été gagnée par l'Envangile.

Avec l'arrivée de Daniel Bila PASGO et de Azaria SORGHO du Burkina-Faso, la mission s'étendit de Natitingou à Tanguiéta pour atteindre Boukoumbé. Cette avancée a été possible grâce à l'action d'une femme du nom de Hélène ISELIN. La mission de mademoiselle Hélène ISELIN consistait en la formation des jeunes. Les jeunes filles étaient initiées à la couture et au tricotage. Quelques années plus tard, une école de catéchètes fut ouverte et dirigée par cette dernière. Dans cette école, elle donnait aussi les cours de français.

De la mission à l'Eglise des Assemblées de Dieu

Le 07 Décembre 1956, à Tanguiéta, s'est tenue la première convention de la mission au cours de laquelle une constitution fut présentée et adoptée. Le premier comité formé à cet effet était composé d'un Togolais, d'un Béninois et d'Américains. Ainsi, l'Eglise africaine des Assemblées de Dieu du Togo-Dahomey est née. Mais le 03 Décembre 1965, suite à la délimitation des frontières, l'Eglise connut une scission. Il eut d'une part l'Eglise des Assemblées de Dieu du Togo et d'autre part l'Eglise des Assemblées de Dieu du Dahomey. Le 16 Décembre 1991, l'Eglise protestante des Assemblées de Dieu du Dahomey devient par un changement de nom, l'Eglise évangélique des Assemblées de Dieu du Dahomey (EEAD).

Dès la fin de l'époque coloniale, les AD[18] avaient quatre missions majeures avec plus de 1500 adultes et enfants actifs dont 600 d'entre eux étaient autochtones baatonu[19].

En 1960, les campagnes d'évangélisations aux abords des voies, les chants de louanges et les séances de prières étaient les principales activités des AD. La ville de Cotonou a été gagnée avec l'église de Jéricho. A Porto-Novo, l'œuvre fut commencée par le missionnaire français Pierre ROCHARD en 1967. On note le passage du Pasteur béninois Paul ZINSOU en Juillet 1971 puis du missionnaire américain Robert SMITH. En 1977, quand le pasteur Paul ZINSOU quitta l'Eglise, il fut remplacé par son collège David MENSAH. Il ouvre 21 églises à Porto-Novo. Dans le Zou, c'est en 1970 que l'Eglise n'a pu s'implanter par la perspicacité du pasteur Gabriel ABISSI, natif de la région. Vers 1986, l'évangéliste français Jacques HALPIAN arrive dans le Borgou-Alibori. Il commença l'œuvre dans la ville de Parakou avec l'appui des pasteurs nationaux dont Pierre TASSO, Adam SOBABE. Aujourd'hui les villes de Nikki, Boko, N'Dali, Kandi sont touchées. L'œuvre dans le Mono-Coffo quant à elle, a été la conséquence d'une crise entre les Eglises apostolique et pentecôtiste. Les fidèles de ces communautés soucieux de maintenir leur foi furent appel à l'Eglise des Assemblées de Dieu qui répond favorablement en la personne du missionnaire PIKIN. Ces événements se sont déroulés en 1970 et durèrent trois années. D'autres pasteurs furent affectés et l'Eglise s'installa définitivement.

Aujourd'hui l'Eglise des Assemblées de Dieu s'installe progressivement même dans les coins les plus reculés du Bénin. L'Eglise compte plus de deux cent cinquante (250) pasteurs et des centaines de fidèles ou laïcs.

---

[17] Soudan Interior Mission

[18] Assemblée de Dieu

[19] B. HEGEMAN, *Between Glory and Shame, A historical and systematic study of education and leadership training models among the Baatonu in North Benin*, Pays-Bas, 2000, 43

En conclusion, le christianisme au Bénin vit dans un pluralisme religieux dû au fait que depuis toujours le lien de sang semble plus fort que toute autre idéologie. Ainsi dans une même famille peuvent se retrouver côte à côte un protestant, un catholique, un musulman, un pentecôtisme et même un adepte de la religion endogène[20]. La croyance ou la non croyance sont des manifestations propres à chaque personne et leurs expressions ne sont pas assez fortes pour diviser les familles. Le christianisme longtemps considéré comme la religion du « colonisateur » reprend sa place entière dans le paysage religieux car chacun veut s'assumer dans sa propre foi. En laissant de côté les querelles de chapelle dues à certains extrémismes passagers, la religion a toujours eu un rôle fédérateur au Bénin empêchant de ce fait jusqu'ici, les guerres à connotation religieuse qu'on connait ailleurs sur le continent africain. Le christianisme y joue un grand rôle qu'il faut encourager partout.

Bibliographie

F. AHOLOUKPE, l'Eglise Evangélique des Assemblées de Dieu du BENIN, Mémoire de licence, UPAO, 2011, Inédit

Collectif, *l'Histoire des Eglises Protestantes et Evangéliques du Bénin*, Annuaire Evangélique, 2003

B. HEGEMAN, *Between Glory and Shame, A historical and systematic study of education and leadership training models among the Baatonu in North Benin*, Pays-Bas, 2000

L. OGOUBI, *Les religion dans l'espace public au Bénin*, l'Harmattan, Paris, 2008

[20] Les religions traditionnelles africaines sont plutôt appelées religions endogènes de nos jours.

(49) Christianity in Botswana

James N. Amanze

Religion	Pop 2010	Pct 2010	Pop 2025	Pct 2025	Gr Pct 1970 2025
Christians	1,431,000	69.9%	2,084,000	78.8%	2.5%
Independents	838,000	40.9%	1,356,000	51.2%	3.3%
African initiated	808,000	39.4%			
Orthodox	80	0.0%	100	0.0%	1.5%
Protestants	220,000	10.7%	350,000	13.2%	3.1%
Pentecostal	53,600	2.6%			
Adventist	41,200	2.0%			
Lutheran	32,900	1.6%			
Congregational	29,300	1.4%			
Roman Catholics	83,800	4.1%	87,000	3.3%	0.3%
Pentecostals/Charismatics	902,000	44.0%	850,000	32.1%	-0.4%
Evangelicals	101,000	4.9%	121,000	4.6%	1.2%
adherents of traditional African religions	588,000	28.7%	520,000	19.7%	-0.8%
Baha'is	16,200	0.8%	22,000	0.8%	2.1%
Muslims	5,400	0.3%	6,700	0.3%	1.5%
Hindus	2,700	0.1%	6,000	0.2%	5.4%
Buddhists	1,100	0.1%	1,200	0.0%	0.6%
Jews	410	0.0%	400	0.0%	-0.1%
Sikhs	240	0.0%	400	0.0%	3.6%
Chinese folk-religionists	110	0.0%	200	0.0%	4.1%
people professing no religion	3,200	0.2%	5,200	0.2%	3.3%
Total population	**2,048,000**	**100.0%**	**2,646,000**	**100.0%**	**1.7%**

Source: Centre for the Study of World Christianity (CSGC), Boston, Gordon-Conwell TS

Introduction

This article examines the introduction of Christianity in Botswana, its development and current status. Apart from discussing the historical development of Christianity in the country, the article also discusses the nature of the ecumenical movement in Botswana and the church's contribution to the socio-economic development of the Batswana as a people.

The Introduction of Christianity in Botswana

Christianity was introduced into Botswana in the first half of the nineteenth century by a number of missionaries belonging to different missionary societies who brought the Bible as the most effective means of salvation of humankind. From its humble beginnings in a few ethnic groups, missionary work has spread to almost every corner of the country, with churches and ministries mushrooming in all villages, towns and cities. According to sources at hand, it is estimated that 70% of the country's citizens identify themselves as Christians.[1] The Constitution of Botswana, which was adopted at independence in 1966, provides freedom of religion and the government generally respects this right in practice and seeks to protect it fully. However, for the sake of public order, the 1972 Societies Act requires that, in order to operate legally, all churches should be registered with the Registrar of Societies in the Ministry of Labour and Home Affairs through the Department of Civil and National Registration.[2] In the past, religious organisations were required to have a minimum of ten persons in order to be registered as churches. However, this number has been increased to 250 to curb the abuses perpetrated by some unscrupulous self-styled foreign and national pastors who in the past decade have established churches whose primary objective is to make money, through what has come to be known as 'the prosperity gospel'.

According to Hon. Dr Alfred Madigele, Assistant Minister of Health, there are more than 1,500 registered churches in the country, while more are still seeking registration.[3] If we add a similar number of religious societies, which are operating illegally, we can safely conclude that there were not less than three thousand churches and ministries in the country with a population of only 2,038,587 people in 2014[4]. Botswana is thus home to many churches which differ from one another in a number of ways, particularly in their belief systems, doctrines, church practice, religious experience, spirituality and church structures. On the basis of the above differences, churches in Botswana can be grouped into three major categories or typologies, namely: mainline churches, Pentecostal/charismatic churches and African Independent Churches. Each of these categories has its own identity and peculiarities, which make it different from other types of churches. It might be of interest to look at each of these in turn.

In the first instance, the mainline churches, also known as mission churches or historic churches, claim to belong to mainstream Christianity. They were introduced in Botswana largely from Europe and America in the nineteenth and twentieth centuries. This category of churches consists of the following: Roman Catholic, Anglican, Methodist, United Congregational Church in Southern Africa (formerly London Missionary Society or LMS), Lutheran, Dutch Reformed Church and Seventh Day Adventists. The early missionaries who were responsible for their introduction were Robert Moffat, David Livingstone, John Mackenzie, James Good, James Hepburn and Roger Price (London Missionary Society); Heinrich Backeberg, Ferdinand Zimmermann and Heinrich Christoph Schulenberg (Lutheran Church); H. Gonin and Pieter Brink (Dutch Reformed Church); Bishop Meysing and Fr Rittmuller (Roman Catholic Church); and Arthur Kretchma (Seventh Day Adventists), to name but a few. By their nature, the mainline churches can be considered as replicas of the mother churches overseas. The doctrines of each denomination, church practice, forms of worship, spirituality, aims and objectives, church structures, as well as church leadership, resemble those found in the mother churches in Europe and America. In 1998, the author estimated that more than 30% of the Christians in the country were members of the mainline churches, and

---

[1] Freedom of religion in Botswana, http://en.wikipedia.org/wiki/Freedom_of_religion_in_Botswana (accessed 23 August 2015).

[2] See Republic of Botswana-Governmental portal, Ministry of Labour and Home Affairs (MLHA), http://www.gov.bw/en/ministries--authorities/ministries/ministry-of-labour--home-affairs-mlha/ (accessed on 23 August 2015) where details regarding the requirements for the registration of religious organisations has been discussed in full.

[3] *Daily News,* Online, Gaborone, 29th January 2015.

[4] Population, see http://countryeconomy.com/demography/population/botswana, pg1 (accessed 24 August 2015).

this number has since increased tremendously as a result of population growth and individual conversions to Christianity.[5]

In the past decade, however, practically all mainline churches have been losing members to the revival charismatic churches which promise instant healing miracles and unimaginable riches which the believer can harvest by giving 'seed' money in the form of donations to men of God. Their liturgical services are also very entertaining and have thus become centres of great attraction to many people because they are accompanied with a great deal of modern music, healing testimonies, speaking in tongues, prophecy and the promise of health and wealth here and now. In order to counter this threat and ensure their survival, a number of mainline churches are, to a certain extent, Pentecostalising themselves while at the same time keeping their identity. This is the case in the Roman Catholic Church, which has created space for charismatics to hold separate church services themselves within the church at appropriate times during the week,[6] for, as the saying goes, 'If you cannot beat them, join them.' It is hoped that this action will keep people with a charismatic orientation in the church where their spiritual needs can be fully met.

This point naturally introduces us to the second category of churches in Botswana which is the Pentecostal-charismatic churches. Their origin is traced back to the religious revival that began in the USA at the beginning of the twentieth century and spread throughout the world. They were introduced into Botswana in the 1930s through the activities of migrant labourers who came into contact with Pentecostal churches during their stint in the mines in South Africa. They picked up momentum in the 1960s through the activities of Pentecostal missionaries from the USA and local preachers. They now constitute a religious force to reckon with and have moved from the periphery of Christianity to the centre, forming as it were the fourth force in Christendom. Theologically, the Pentecostal movement is based on the Pentecostal experiences that took place in Jerusalem on the day of Pentecost (Acts 2:1-47). Pentecostals claim that they too have received the same gifts that the apostles received on the day of Pentecost. They also believe that they can receive other gifts of the Holy Spirit such as power faith healing, prophecy and the interpretation of tongues, as described in 1 Corinthians 12 and 14. Doctrinally, many Pentecostal churches do not adhere to a specific creed but place a great deal of emphasis on the works of the Holy Spirit. Pentecostals claim that true Christians are only those who have experienced 'baptism in the Holy Spirit', and that such people constitute a 'community of saints' of 'born again' Christians. Faith healing by prayer and the laying on of hands is considered an integral part of the gospel based on the belief that 'deliverance' from sickness is provided for in the atonement and is the privilege of all believers.[7]

In recent years, the Pentecostal ideology has been pushed further by the 'charismatic revival movement' which has engulfed many African countries. It is seen in the form of ministries which have come to be popularly known as 'Fire Churches'. Their success is attributed to a complex number of factors which include rising levels of poverty, the promise of miraculous healing through faith, prosperity in business undertakings, the healing of incurable diseases, the perceived failure of modern scientific ways of healing in hospitals, ecstatic forms of worship, spirit possession, speaking in tongues and the intellectualized nature of Christian spirituality in mainline churches in faith and practice. At present, the pendulum of Christian expression and expansion is on the side of the 'Fire Churches' which are drawing thousands of people into their fold and are known to make a lot of money from people who attend their services. Unfortunately, much of the money earned in this way is used for the personal luxurious life of 'prosperity gospel preachers', or siphoned out of the country, leaving local people poor.

---

[5] James N. Amanze, *African Christianity in Botswana* (Gweru: Mambo Press), 35.

[6] See James N. Amanze & John Hamathi, "Charismatic Renewal in the Roman Catholic Church in Botswana: A Case Study of the Interaction between Religions of Authority and Religions of Spontaneity" in *Swedish Missiological Themes* 99, No. 1 (2011): 57-78, where this has been discussed in detail.

[7] See James N. Amanze, *Botswana Handbook of Churches* (Gaborone: Pula Press, 1994), where the characteristics of these churches have been discussed and described in depth.

As a result, in recent years, the government of Botswana has put in place measures that it hopes will put an end to the abuses perpetrated by both foreign and national 'prosperity gospel preachers' who, from a government perspective, 'abuse God, the people and push their agendas'.[8] In this regard, the 1972 Societies Act which in the past required a minimum of ten people to register a religious organisation, now demands 250 people. It is envisaged that this measure will curb the proliferation of churches in the country by making it difficult to start and register new churches.[9]

Having discussed the second category of churches in Botswana, it is now time to move on to the third category, the African Independent Churches. Their history is traced back to the second half of the nineteenth century and is closely associated with the emergence of new religious movements in South Africa, categorized by B.G. Sundkler into two opposite categories: 'Ethiopian' and 'Zionist'.[10] Many of these churches have been formed by breaking away from mainline churches, Pentecostal churches and other African Independent Churches as a result of leadership disputes, financial irregularities, doctrinal differences, corruption of church leaders, a desire to make money from their followers, an urge for spiritual renewal, faith healing and other motives. During the colonial period, their introduction into Botswana from South Africa and Zimbabwe met with stiff resistance from the missionaries, tribal chiefs and British colonial authorities. African Independent Churches in Botswana have much in common. They have been instituted by Africans to believe and worship God in African ways. They are called African Independent Churches because they are free of western control and leadership. They also have an all-African membership, drawn from all economic and social groupings, but especially the working class and the marginalised. Many of them place a great deal of emphasis on the importance and significance of African culture, much of which has been integrated into their doctrines, spirituality, worship, ethical conduct and church practice.[11]

At present, however, the impact of African Independent Churches has declined considerably. They are not as visible as they used to be, at least until the middle of the first decade of this century, when many used to flock to them for faith healing. Their place is now being slowly filled by 'Fire Churches', which have become centres of faith healing. One of the most interesting phenomena in recent years has been the rise to prominence and influence of Prophet T.B. Joshua of the Synagogue Church of all Nations (SCON) in Nigeria. Many Batswana travel to Nigeria on a daily basis seeking healing from the man of God who claims to have direct access to God. The same is true of Pastor Chris Oyakhilome of Christ Embassy who daily draws thousands of Batswana to his ministry in Nigeria for anointing and healing. This phenomenon has rendered African Independent Churches, whose main centre of attraction is faith healing, rather obsolete. Thus their future is in abeyance.

The Churches and the Ecumenical Movement

It has been noted above that Christianity was introduced into Botswana along tribal lines. This became a source of conflict among the different churches that were introduced in the country. For many years, churches were operating independently and in competition with one another. In some instances, they were involved in running battles against one another which made the idea of co-operation among the churches rather impossible. The turn of events took place during the 1960s when Botswana faced a severe five-year drought. This forced the churches to work together to provide relief to church members and others outside

[8] Yvonne Ditlhase, "Wolves in sheep's' skin" in *The Midweek Sun Online*, www.the.midweek.Sun.co.bw/news 4425-wolves-in-sheep (accessed on 20 August2015).

[9] Yvonne Ditlhase, "Wolves in sheep's skin"…. accessed on 20/8/2015.

[10] See B. G. Sundkler (1961), *Bantu Prophets in South Africa* (London: Oxford University Press), 38-64.

[11] See James N. Amanze, *African Christianity in Botswana* (Gweru: Mambo Press, 1998), for a detailed discussion of the theology of the African Independent Churches.

the jurisdiction of the churches without discrimination. Such initiatives were taken by the mainline churches, particularly the Anglican Church and the missionaries of the London Missionary Society, now the Congregational Church in Southern Africa. The drought also prompted the World Council of Churches to send Z.K. Matthews to Southern Africa in 1964 on a fact-finding mission. While in Botswana, he advised the churches to work together in order to obtain financial assistance from the WCC to combat the effects of the drought. This led to the formation of the North Bechuanaland Christian Council in 1965. This eventually led to the formation of the Botswana Christian Council (now the Botswana Council of Churches – BCC) in May 1966. The BCC is thus the brainchild of the mainline churches, and the majority of its membership consists of such churches, with a few from the African Independent and Pentecostal churches. The BCC has contributed tremendously to the socio-economic development of Botswana, in health, education, the provision of clean water to remote rural dwellers, and in the fight against HIV and AIDS.

Apart from this important organisation, there is also the Evangelical Fellowship of Botswana (EFB) whose membership consists of the majority of the Pentecostal and charismatic churches. For many years, this organisation was working in isolation and not interested in what they called the 'social gospel' pursued by the mainline churches. Emphasis was placed on evangelism and Christian spirituality. With the passing of time, however, there has been a paradigm shift in the work of the EFB. Pentecostal churches are now also involved in the 'social gospel' by engaging themselves in socio-economic activities that promote the welfare of Batswana as a whole.

In addition to the above, mention should also be made here of the Organisation of African Independent Churches Southern Region whose membership consists of the majority of African Independent Churches. This organisation was formed with the assistance of the Coptic Church in Egypt in the early 1980s, to promote the interests of the African Independent Churches which were, to a large extent, marginalised by both the mainline and Pentecostal churches. Last, but not least, it is important to note here the ecumenical work of the Ministers' Fraternals which are found in practically all the villages, towns and cities of Botswana. Membership of these Fraternals involves pastors in a given locality working together to promote the ecumenical agenda. In form and structure, they are the epitome of 'receptive ecumenism' since they act on a 'give and take' principle in their ecumenical engagements without any particular church imposing their ecumenical agenda on the other. All in all, the ecumenical movement in Botswana has given rise to a new religious order based on mutual co-operation, respect and understanding, and a sense of collective identity among Christians based on the knowledge that, though they differ in a number of fundamental points, they are essentially one as the Body of Christ.[12]

The Role of the Churches in Socio-economic Development

Before concluding this paper, it should be stated here that churches in Botswana have been catalysts and agents of socio-economic change from the time of their inception to the present. In the first instance, churches in Botswana, both individually and ecumenically, have contributed greatly in the field of health by building clinics and hospitals. Church hospitals such as the Deborah Retief Memorial Hospital (DRC), the Seventh Day Adventist Hospital in Kanye (SDA), the Livingstone Hospital in Molepolole (Church of Scotland Presbyterian), St Peter's Hospital in Mmadinare (Anglican) and the Ramotswa Clinic (Roman Catholic), have played a significant role in the provision of health services in Botswana till now.

In the field of formal education, a number of churches have established and run a several schools. St Joseph College in Gaborone and Mater Spei Secondary School (Roman Catholic) in Francistown and

[12] See James N. Amanze, "From Denominational Pluralism to Church Unity," in *Aspects of the history of the Church in Botswana*, eds. Fidelis Nkomazana & Laurel Lanner (Pietermaritzburg: Cluster Publications, 2007),15-49, where this process has been discussed in detail.

Moeding College (UCCSA) at Otse, to name a few, have contributed tremendously to the educational system of the country. Ecumenically, the mainline churches have contributed a great deal towards the socio-economic development of the country by establishing in Selebi-Phikwe the Urban Industrial School (to train young people in secretarial, accounting and administration skills), Amogelang Primary School (to cater for drop-outs), and the Building and Carpentry School for young adults, to minimize levels of unemployment and crime in the city. Ecumenically, the mainline churches have also encouraged people to embark on income-generating projects, such as horticulture, poultry, sewing and other economic activities designed to eradicate poverty.

Conclusion

In conclusion, this paper has dealt with the origins and development of Christianity in Botswana from the time of its arrival in the mid-nineteenth century to the present. Apart from reflecting on Christianity's historical development, the paper has also discussed ecumenical relations among the churches and the role of Christianity in the socio-economic development in Botswana. All in all, Christianity in Botswana has been a real blessing to the people, both spiritually and materially. However, in recent years, the introduction of the 'Fire Churches' seems to have tarnished the good image that the church had enjoyed for many years. There is a deep-felt perception that the 'gospel of prosperity' is doing people more harm than good. This has forced the government to change its policy of registration in order to protect the people from unscrupulously zealous self-styled men of God. They promise people unimaginable wealth and instant healing miracles which quite often amount to nothing but the sheer exploitation of the masses.

Bibliography

Amanze, J.N. *Botswana Handbook of Churches.* Gaborone: Pula Press, 1994.

Amanze, J.N. *African Christianity in Botswana.* Gweru: Mambo Press.

Amanze, J.N. *Ecumenism in Botswana: The Story of the Botswana Christian Council.* Gaborone: Pula Press, 2006.

Chirenje, J.M.A. *History of Northern Botswana 1850-1910.* London: Associated University Press, 1977.

Lagerwerf, L. *They Pray for You: Independent Churches and Women in Botswana.* Leiden: Interuniversitair Instituut voor Missiologie en Oecumenica, 1982.

Nkomazana, F. & Lanner, L (eds.). *Aspects of the History of the Church in Botswana.* Pietermaritzburg: Cluster Publications, 2007.

Sales, J. *The Planting of the Churches in Southern Africa.* Michigan: W.B. Eerdmans, 1971.

Sundkler, B.G.M. *Bantu Prophets in South Africa.* London: OUP, 1961.

Sales, J. 'Brief History of Christianity in Botswana.' Unpublished International History Conference Paper, Gaborone, University of Botswana, 1973.

(50A) CHRISTIANITY IN BURKINA FASO

Philippe Ouedraogo

Religion	Pop 2010	Pct 2010	Pop 2025	Pct 2025	Gr Pct 1970 2025
Christians	3,483,000	22.3%	6,529,000	27.3%	4.3%
Independents	77,800	0.5%	133,000	0.6%	3.6%
African initiated	43,400	0.3%			
Protestants	1,633,000	10.4%	2,850,000	11.9%	3.8%
Pentecostal	1,353,000	8.7%			
Evangelical churches	123,000	0.8%			
Roman Catholics	2,229,000	14.3%	3,838,000	16.1%	3.7%
Pentecostals/Charismatics	1,673,000	10.7%	3,000,000	12.6%	4.0%
Evangelicals	1,571,000	10.0%	2,501,000	10.5%	3.1%
Muslims	8,435,000	54.0%	13,227,000	55.3%	3.0%
adherents of traditional African religions	3,633,000	23.2%	4,000,000	16.7%	0.6%
Baha'is	2,700	0.0%	5,000	0.0%	4.2%
adherents of new religious movements	540	0.0%	1,000	0.0%	4.2%
people professing no religion	78,000	0.5%	141,000	0.6%	4.0%
Total population	**15,632,000**	**100.0%**	**23,903,000**	**100.0%**	**2.9%**

Source: Centre for the Study of World Christianity (CSGC), Boston, Gordon-Conwell TS

Introduction

The purpose of this paper is to survey the history of Christianity in Burkina Faso and its impact on the socio-economic life of the Burkinabe. This revealed religion co-exists peacefully alongside others, such as the traditional belief systems and Islam. Such co-existence since the beginning is an added value to the vitality and dynamism of Christianity in Burkina Faso. This may be considered a good example to the rest of the world.

I will briefly introduce the country and its religious aspects, then develop from there to set the background to better understand and appreciate the role Christianity is playing in this predominantly Muslim country.

Burkina Faso, the Country

Burkina Faso is a landlocked country in West Africa. It has a tropical climate of the Sudano-Sahelean type, characterized by a long dry season from October to April and a short wet season from May to September.

The impact of climate change, the poverty of the farmland, and inappropriate agricultural technology are disadvantages that slow down the efforts of hardworking peasants. The climate is very unstable across the country. Both the government and civil society, such as churches, NGOs and individuals, are heavily committed to expressing solidarity and working to improve the lives of the population.

How Christianity Came to Burkina Faso from the West Africa Region[1]

The first initiative for evangelizing West Africa, and later Burkina Faso, came from the Roman Catholic Church. In the mid-nineteenth century, the church in Europe was facing hostility from the modern world. Religious congregations were being suppressed and even driven away from France.[2] This situation is similar to the stories related in the New Testament, especially in the book of Acts. Such hostility can be interpreted today as God's providence for the gospel of Jesus Christ to reach Burkina Faso. It was also the time of the discovery of African territories by explorers. It was in these circumstances that the nineteenth century became a period of evangelization and colonization, both activities being often parallel and intermixed.

In 1867-1868, according to the Missionaries of Africa, there was a great famine in Algeria that left many orphans. Bishop Lavigerie in 1867 asked for 'the right to bring up those children who had no fathers nor mothers nor tutors'.[3] This was the first task which he assigned to the White Fathers and White Sisters. Missionary works at that time consisted mainly of schools and medical care, with a vision of reaching south of the Sahara Desert. In January 1899, Bishop Hacquart founded Ségou in a place where he had been four years before. Immediately afterwards he went in his travels to Moogo, in Mossi country.[4] He travelled through Ouagadougou in 1899 without stopping there. He thought that Koupela was more promising and it was there that the first mission was established in 1900, in what later became the country of Burkina Faso. After his tragic death on 4th April 1901 his Vicariate was divided in two: Sahara and Sudan. In June 1901 the mission of Ouagadougou was founded, with its first superior Father Templier. The Mossi were evangelized from Koupela and Ouagadougou. Bishop Bazin with other missionaries and lay Christians worked to build clinics, schools and churches. With words and deeds they marked the beginnings of the church in Burkina Faso. Sisters were called to help reach the women. The early and forced marriage of girls was a serious social issue at that time. The French colonial system, which was anti-clerical, made life difficult for the missionaries. In order to avoid this opposition, missions were established in other African countries under British, Belgian and German control. While the first missionaries reached West Africa at great cost, it needs to be pointed out, as Fage, Roberts, and Roland have argued, that some of the most notable Christian advances in the region were made in the absence of foreign missionaries, and the future development and maturity of the indigenous churches was largely dependent on the elimination of foreign control and paternalism.[5]

In Senegal and French West Africa as a whole, missionary education was discouraged and at times forbidden, and until the World War II mission schools played an almost negligible role compared with the state system.[6] In Madagascar, a convinced anti-clerical, Victor Angagneur, was governor-general from 1905 to 1910. Immediately on arrival he took steps which resulted in the closure of about four-fifths of the mission schools. Open-air religious meetings were prohibited, and in 1913 the separation of church and state in Madagascar was formally decreed. Only in French Equatorial Africa did the missions succeed in retaining a substantial role in education. The first missionaries from evangelical churches (Assemblies of God) came later, about 1919, to explore the land and to settle, and from January 1921 they had a similar experience in Ouagadougou and made a commitment to mission to Burkina Faso. Both missions played

---

[1] This section has been further discussed in Philippe Ouedraogo, *Female Education and Mission: A Burkina Faso Experience* (Oxford: Regnum Books, 2014), 29-30.
[2] Salles Part III Vol. 6.
[3] Salles Part III Vol. 6.
[4] Salles Part III Vol. 6.
[5] J. D. Fage, A. D. Roberts & Anthony Oliver Roland, *The Cambridge History of Africa Vol. 7 c. 1905-c. 1940* (Cambridge: Cambridge University, 1986), 140.
[6] Fage, Roberts & Roland, *The Cambridge History of Africa,* 179.

significant roles in evangelizing Burkina Faso during the French colonial period. Education and the compassion of God for the needy were part of both missions' strategy.

The Case of the Assemblies of God Church[7]

According to the testimony of the missionaries related in the documentary title 'The Mossi Land', it all started with a prophetic word received during the origins of Pentecostalism in early 1906 in a prayer meeting in the USA to go to the Mossi Land. For the American missionaries, evangelizing the Mossi Empire[17] was a priority because it is the largest ethnic group, well organized around the traditional King, and the language used was Mooré, spoken by the Mossi. To reach that goal the missionaries, both from America and France, gave the best of themselves to such an extent that some lost their lives through sickness in the first two weeks after their arrival in the country.

The first Assemblies of God Church missionaries arrived in the country on 1st January 1921 and were received by the Mossi King NaabaKoom II, who gave them land to establish their mission at Gounghin, today ex-Sector 8 of Ouagadougou.[8] The first missionaries developed functional educational programmes for literacy and evangelism and economic development. Being in a French colony the language was a challenge for the Americans. The native pastors requested that the missionaries contact the church in France and recruit a French missionary who could open a school in Upper Volta. Pastor Harold Jones made several visits and contacts in France and West Africa because it was difficult for an American missionary to open a primary school in a French territory. The churches' prayers were answered when at last Pastor Pierre Dupret and his wife first arrived in Dakar in 1946, then Ivory Coast in 1947, Guinea in 1948 and reached Upper Volta on 19th February 1948.[9] Formal education began in 1948. Within the spiritual mission of the church, evangelism and discipleship were high on the agenda, based on the commission Jesus Christ gave to his disciples known as 'the Great Commission' (Matt. 28:19-20). Non-formal education was thus one of the church's strategies for fulfilling its mission.

The first believers received from the missionaries a basic training in literacy, often using the sand on the ground as a teaching aid to learn how to read and write before the Mooré alphabet was printed.[18] Later, portions of Scripture were printed on a single sheet to assist in memorizing the Scriptures. One verse that comes to mind is 'Believe in the Lord Jesus, and you will be saved – you and your household' (Acts 16.31). It was among the texts which new Christians would have memorized. Such non-formal education took different forms of delivery but was essential to the local communities of believers. Portions of the Bible were translated by the missionaries with the help of natives. Soon a printing press was used to print church literature. Pastor John Hall and others made a great contribution by translating the entire Old Testament and writing Bible studies, hymn books, dictionaries and other resources in Mooré. Later Bible books were translated and printed, and a complete Bible in Mooré was made available through the Bible Alliance in the 1980s. In 2007 the study reference Bible with the new alphabet in Mooré was made available to the church after years of hard labour.

Women, in turn, learned how to read and write with the help of the American female missionaries who trained them in special classes, at the mill, or on the way to the well to fetch water. Small Bible schools started in different regions, and the main towns and villages in the Mossi Empire received the first African evangelists, who reached places such as Yako, Ouahigouya in the North, Koudougou in the Centre West, Kaya in Centre North and Tenkodogo in the East. All these different regions welcomed missionaries who

[7]See also Ouedraogo, *Female Education and Mission,* 44-46.
[8] K.M. Kabré, "Historique de l'enseignement Évangélique au Burkina Faso [The History of Evangelical Education in Burkina Faso]," Paper presented at the first conference of the Alliance of Evangelical Schools in Burkina Faso (AESEB), 7-9 October 2009.
[9] Kabré, "Historique de l'enseignement Évangélique au Burkina Faso."

were stationed there at the beginning of their field work to support the training of the new believers and church-planting initiatives.

Time and space does not allow covering all aspects of Christianity in Burkina Faso, sufficing to summarize that among the Evangelical and Pentecostals, the AG, the Deeper Life, the International Centre for Evangelism (CIE) churches are spread in all regions, especially in the main town of the region. In terms of size the AG has the lead, followed by the Evangelical Church of SIM in the East and the Christian Alliance Church in the West. The Federation of Churches and Missions has thirteen members including the above church names. Other smaller groups have joined the Council of Evangelical Churches Ministries and Missions of Burkina Faso (CEMMEB) which operates mainly from the capital, while there are still churches that are not members of either Federations.

In addition to the spread of the gospel, Christianity in Burkina Faso maintained a holistic approach and influences the socio-economic life of the people. Both the Roman Catholic and Evangelical/Pentecostal churches are active in all levels and types of education, health, peace building initiatives, advocacy, economic growth, governance and church capacity building to only mention a few sectors of intervention. Christianity in Burkina Faso has a voice and contributes to being the light and salt of the nation.

Bibliography

Fage, J. D., A. D. Roberts & Anthony Oliver Roland. *The Cambridge History of Africa Vol. 7 c. 1905 – c. 1940*. Cambridge: Cambridge University Press, 1986.

Kabré, K.M. 'Historique de l'enseignement Évangélique au Burkina Faso [The history of Evangelical education in Burkina Faso].' Paper presented at the first conference of the Alliance of Evangelical Schools in Burkina Faso (AESEB), 7-9 October 2009.

Ouedraogo, Philippe. 'The Legacy of Christianity in West Africa, with Special Reference to Burkina Faso', *Comparative Education*, 46, no. 3 (2010): 391-405.

Ouedraogo, Philippe. *Female Education and Mission: A Burkina Faso Experience.* Oxford: Regnum Books, 2014.

(50B) CHRISTIANITY IN BURKINA FASO

Kinda Tegwende Leonard

Le Burkina Faso, localisation et caractéristiques sociodémographiques

Le Burkina Faso couvre le territoire de l'ancienne colonie française de l'Afrique occidentale française, créée en 1919 et jadis dénommé Haute Volta. Situé au cœur de l'Afrique de l'Ouest, il est entouré par le Mali au Nord et à l'Ouest, le Niger au Nord-Est, la Cote d'Ivoire, le Ghana, le Togo et le Benin au Sud. Il s'étend sur une superficie de 274 200 km². Après les indépendances, le Burkina Faso a connu une succession de régimes d'exception et des régimes républicains plus ou moins démocratiques. La quatrième république culmine vers sa fin.

Selon le recensement général de la population et de l'habitat (RGPH)[1], le Burkina Faso comptait 14 017 262 habitants avec presque 52% de personnes de sexe féminin. Le taux de croissance annuelle de la population est d'environ 3%; les officiels estiment la population à environ 18 millions[2].

Une soixantaine de groupes sociolinguistiques couvre le pays; les plus importants en nombre sont les mossis (majoritaires et présents dans l'ensemble du pays), les bobos, les gourmantchés et les peulhs. Presque 2/3 de la population burkinabé a moins de 30 ans. 4 personnes sur 5 habitent en milieu rural. Une très forte majorité de la population pratiquent l'agriculture et de l'élevage.

En 2009, 28,2% de la population générale est déclarée alphabétisée. Le taux brut de scolarisation (TBS) était à 81,3% en 2012-2013 pour l'école primaire, et à 25,7% en 2012-2013 pour le secondaire[3].

Le revenu par tête est de USD 673. 46,7% de la population vit en dessous du seuil de pauvreté.

La population burkinabé est composée de musulmans (60,53%), d'animistes (15,34%), de catholiques (19%), de protestants (4,17%) et autres.

Pénétration et développement des religions monothéistes

Hormis l'Egypte et l'Ethiopie qui ont connu le Christianisme très tôt, l'Afrique, dans sa grande majorité, fut pendant des siècles le terreau des religions traditionnelles. Chaque famille ou chaque groupe ethnique avait des divinités qui faisaient l'objet d'adoration et de supplication pour des sujets divers allant de la purification et du pardon en passant par la protection de l'individu et de la communauté, de la production et de la reproduction… C'est à partir du XVe siècle que le Burkina ex Haute Volta connait les religions monothéistes.

L'Islam

L'Islam est la première religion monothéiste apportée au Burkina par les colporteurs musulmans[4]; cette pénétration restera confinée à la partie Ouest du pays. A la fin du XVIIIe siècle l'Islam est introduit dans la cours royale du Mogho-Naba, Empereur des mossis (plus grand groupe ethnique du Burkina jusqu'à l'heure actuelle) mais sans engendrer une large adhésion. C'est à partir du XIXe siècle que l'Islam commencera à toucher la plupart des groupes ethniques. Les migrations et les conquêtes y ont fortement contribué; certains groupes ethniques nomades en provenance du Sénégal, de la Guinée ont contribué à

---

[1] MEF, RGPH 2006, Rapport définitif, juillet 2008.
[2] OCHA – Burkina, Plan de réponse stratégique 2014-2016, Janvier 2014
[3] INSD, Annuaire statistique 2012, Edition 2013
[4] Wikipedia.org/wiki/Islam_au_Burkina_Faso consulté le 22/04/2015

l'implantation de l'Islam au Burkina Faso. Entre temps, l'Islam perçu comme un allié contre certaines chefferies animistes locales hostiles à la présence française a bénéficié du soutien de la force coloniale; issus pour la plupart du sunnisme, on rencontre au Burkina Faso les salafistes, les tidjania, et d'autres groupes minoritaires[5]. La communauté musulmane couvrant l'ensemble du territoire burkinabé est organisée en diverses associations quelques fois conflictuelles mais toutes engagées dans un prosélytisme actif, des œuvres sociales en matière d'hydraulique, de santé, d'éducation... plus ou moins prosélytiques.

Le Christianisme romain

Les premiers missionnaires, catholiques, sont arrivés au cours du premier trimestre de l'année 1899. Apres une exploration sommaire, une première mission, aujourd'hui la première paroisse catholique fut installée à Koupéla (zone Centre-Est) le 22 janvier 1900. Par la suite, d'autres missions sont installées à Ouagadougou en juin 1901, à Réo (zone du Centre-Ouest) en 1912, à Toma (zone de l'Ouest) en 1913, à Manga (zone du Centre- Sud) en 1920. Le 07 juillet 1920 Ouagadougou est érigé en évêché avec à sa tête Mgr Thevenoud Joanny qui coiffait aussi le nord de la Gold Coast (actuel Ghana). Déjà le 15 avril 1922 fut créée la Congrégation des Sœurs de l'Immaculée Conception (SIC) et en 1925 un premier centre de formation de catéchistes est ouvert à Guilongou, dans la périphérie de Ouagadougou. Des séminaires destinés à la formation des prêtres sont ouverts à Pabré (à une dizaine de kilomètres de Ouagadougou en 1933 et à Koumi (aussi à une dizaine de kilomètres de Bobo Dioulasso) en 1934. Parallèlement à l'Evangélisation, les missionnaires catholiques s'engagent dans des actions de promotion de la dignité de l'être humain, de l'agriculture, de l'élevage, de l'éducation, de la santé[6]... La mission catholique est ainsi partie pour la conquête du pays qui est actuellement découpé en 12 diocèses, des millions de fidèles, un nombre respectable d'infrastructures religieuses mais aussi de développement économique, éducatif et socio sanitaires.

Le Christianisme protestant

Les premiers missionnaires protestants, d'origine américaine et canadienne, sont arrivés au Burkina Faso à partir de 1921. Il s'agit par ordre d'arrivée la Mission des assemblées de Dieu en 1921, l'Alliance Missionnaire (CAMA) en 1923, la SIM (Soudan Interior Mission) en 1930, la WEC (Worldwide evangelical crusade) en 1931 et d'autres missions plus récentes. Ils vont affronter d'une part l'adversité de la nature et les maladies tropicales, d'autre part l'inimitié des autres religions; toutefois, ils garderont le courage pour répondre à l'appel du Seigneur. Ils vont utiliser toutes les stratégies possibles d'évangélisation: porte – à – porte, d'évangélisation publique dans les marchés, exorcisme... Très tôt les églises protestantes vont faire face aux défis de la formation du clergé par la création des écoles de formation pastorale. Pendant longtemps, l'Ecole Biblique des Koubri, créée par les assemblée de Dieu demeurera l'unique centre de formation. Recrutant à partir de la seule vocation sans aucune autre forme de qualification particulière, le futur pasteur y sera alphabétisé en langue nationale Moore et par la suite suivra, pendant 3 ans une formation biblique adaptée donc au niveau de l'ensemble des apprenants. A l'heure actuelle, une dizaine de dénominations dispose de leur centre de formation dont 3 établissements dispensent un enseignement du niveau supérieur. Les églises du Burkina peuvent être regroupées en deux blocs à savoir les églises membres de la FEME et les églises non membres de la FEME.

Les églises membres de la FEME

Le 01 Aout 1961, l'Eglise des Assemblée de Dieu en Haute Volta, la Mission des Assemblée de Dieu en Haute Volta, la Mission de Haute Volta, la Mission Evangéliques de l'Afrique Occidentale et la Soudan Interior Mission vont créer ensemble la Fédération des Eglises et Missions Evangéliques (FEME) avec

[5] www.planete-burkina.com/religions_burkina.php accédé le 24/04/2015
[6] www.mafrwestafrica.net/content/view/12/64/lang.fr/ accédé le 22/04/2015

Ouagadougou pour Siege[7]. Au fil du temps, les différentes Missions d'évangélisation d'obédience évangéliques/pentecôtistes vont s'y affilier. Plus ancien regroupement d'églises et de missions d'obédience pentecôtiste, la FEME comprend actuellement une douzaine d'Eglises et Missions.

La FEME a créé au début des années 1970 son organe chargé des questions de développement dénommé Office de développement des Eglises Evangéliques (ODE); il a célébré il y a quelques années son quarantenaire.

La FEME est actuellement la plus forte représentation des églises pentecôtistes au Burkina; elle est membre de l'Alliance Evangélique Mondiale (AEM).

Les églises non membres de FEME

A côté de cette forte communauté pentecôtiste dans sa très large majorité existent des églises non affiliées desquelles certaines ont opté pour seul référence le leader charismatique et fondateur de l'Eglise. Elles sont assez nombreuses et dispersées généralement dans les villes les plus importantes du Burkina. Jusqu'à preuve du contraire aucune n'est affiliée ni à l'Organisation des Eglises Indépendantes d'Afrique (OEIA), ni à une autre organisation régionale ou mondiale.

L'Association des Eglises Evangéliques reformées du Burkina (AEERB) est la seule Eglise non membre de la FEME et qui a souscrit à l'œcuménisme. L'AEERB a été créée à la fin des années 1970 et reconnue officiellement le 28 octobre 1986 par un groupe de fidèles dissident des assemblées de Dieu. Son premier président fut le feu Rev. Sombepouiré Lazare KINDA. Organisation confessionnelle d'obédience reformée, l'AEERB s'est engagée en faveur de la justice sociale et a multiplié des actions au profit des pauvres et des couches vulnérables. Le rapport d'évaluation de sa demande d'adhésion au COE en 2004 l'a qualifiée d'église de pauvres engagée pour les plus pauvres. Les efforts de développement déployés par l'AEERB lui valent des partenariats avec des missions diplomatiques et des institutions spécialisées des Nations Unies au Burkina Faso. En 1989, l'AEERB est reconnue comme une organisation non gouvernementale de droit burkinabé. Elle se reconnait membre de l'Eglise Universelle regroupant des femmes et des hommes qui ont cru à la Sainte Trinité et ont été baptisés au nom du Père, du Fils et du Saint Esprit. Elle reconnaît la Bible comme autorité souveraine, Parole de Dieu et Témoin de l'Amour de Dieu pour la création. Elle adhère aux confessions de foi de l'Eglise primitive (Nicée Constantinople) et aux confessions reformées historiques.

L'AEERB est convaincue que la nature humaine est composite; d'où la nécessité de s'en occuper de manière holistique. Elle espère l'accomplissement de l'unité des chrétiens, telle que voulue par Dieu; aussi est-elle disposée à prendre part à toute initiative susceptible d'y aboutir. Elle perçoit la coopération interreligieuse comme un facteur de préservation et de promotion de la paix.

L'AEERB est membre de l'Association des Conseils Chrétiens et Eglises d'Afrique de l'Ouest (FECCIWA), d'ACT Alliance, de la Conférence des Eglises de Toute l'Afrique (AACC) et de la Communion Mondiale des Eglises Reformées (WCRC), et du Conseil œcuménique des églises (WCC).

L'engagement social des Eglises

Les églises dans leur ensemble sont astreintes à certains impératifs imposés par Yahvé aux enfants d'Israël (la responsabilité d'accueillir l'étranger, la responsabilité de soutenir la veuve et l'orphelin…) et de Jésus à tous les chrétiennes et chrétiens. Ce qui fonde la dimension sociale du Christianisme. Au Burkina Faso, l'action sociale des églises est perceptible dans ce grand ensemble. Apres les visées prosélytiques des premiers instants, l'exigence en matière de professionnalisme conditionnant l'efficacité des actions et la nécessité de d'entrer en partenariat avec d'organisations de la société civile s'est imposée. Ainsi certains départements des œuvres sociales des églises sont devenus des références pour les organisations du

[7] www.ode-burkina.org/bibliothequeenli/index.html accédé le 24/04/2015

système des Nations Unies, pour des organisations non gouvernementales internationales, pour le gouvernement et même pour les populations locales. On peut citer entre autres l'Organisation catholique pour le développement et la solidarité (OCADES-CARITAS), l'Office de développement des églises évangéliques (ODE) crée par la FEME, l'Association DIGNUS créée par l'AEERB, le CREDO (Christian relief and Development Organisation) pour l'Assemblée évangélique de Pentecôte), l'ACCEDES pour l'Eglise de l'Alliance Chrétienne… les secteurs d'intervention couverts vont de l'éducation aux droits humains, en passant par la promotion de la bonne gouvernance, le développement rural, la santé, l'éducation… La contribution des églises au développement social et économique est importante et appréciée à sa juste valeur par tous les acteurs.

Les Eglises et le dialogue inter religieux

Le dialogue inter religieux est essentiel au Burkina. Ce dialogue est perceptible au plan social où dans beaucoup de familles des pratiquants de plusieurs religions vivent en harmonie. Le respect est de mise lors des évènements sociaux.

Au plan institutionnel, le dialogue inter religieux a une longue histoire au Burkina. Depuis longtemps, l'Eglise catholique a développé une approche particulière du dialogue inter religieux; elle se focalise sur le comportement et les attitudes publics des membres du clergé et de tout représentant de l'église catholique vis-à-vis des autres. Du coté des églises protestantes, la principale initiative est celle mise en route par le Program for Christian Muslim Relation; cette initiative vise d'une part à permettre aux leaders des organisations chrétiennes de mieux appréhender l'identité des autres religions, actuellement l'Islam, en vue d'une coexistence pacifique et d'autre part, à instaurer un dialogue continu entre les représentants des différentes religions. Apparemment le dialogue marche, mais il est souvent mis à mal par certains groupes extrémistes de part et d'autres[8]. Conscient de certaines menaces, le gouvernement du Burkina a mis en place en 2014 un observatoire des faits religieux dans les medias[9]. En considérant l'évolution du contexte global et la croissance rapide de la population musulmane au Burkina, il s'impose de rechercher une approche plus adaptée et plus efficace de ce dialogue.

---

[8] www.lefaso.net/spi.php?article49538 accédé le 22/04/2015

[9] www.lefaso.net/spip.php?article62979 accédé le 19/04/2015

(51) CHRISTIANITY IN BURUNDI

Innocent Iyakaremye

Religion	Pop 2010	Pct 2010	Pop 2025	Pct 2025	Gr Pct 1970 2025
Christians	8,737,000	92.3%	14,427,000	95.1%	3.4%
Independents	224,000	2.4%	450,000	3.0%	4.8%
African initiated	206,000	2.2%			
Orthodox	1,900	0.0%	3,500	0.0%	4.2%
Protestants	2,132,000	22.5%	3,628,000	23.9%	3.6%
Anglicans	850,000	9.0%			
Pentecostal	755,000	8.0%			
Adventist	189,000	2.0%			
Holiness	185,000	2.0%			
Baptist	63,600	0.7%			
Roman Catholics	5,602,000	59.2%	9,500,000	62.6%	3.6%
Evangelicals	1,500,000	15.8%	1,912,000	12.6%	1.6%
Pentecostals/Charismatics	1,370,000	14.5%	2,000,000	13.2%	2.6%
adherents of traditional African religions	509,000	5.4%	421,000	2.8%	-1.3%
Muslims	194,000	2.1%	300,000	2.0%	2.9%
Hindus	7,800	0.1%	10,000	0.1%	1.7%
Baha'is	7,500	0.1%	10,000	0.1%	2.0%
people professing no religion	5,600	0.1%	8,200	0.1%	2.5%
Total population	**9,461,000**	**100.0%**	**15,177,000**	**100.0%**	**3.2%**

Source: Centre for the Study of World Christianity (CSGC), Boston, Gordon-Conwell TS

Introduction

This chapter gives an overview of Christian history in Burundi starting from the first arrival of Catholic missionaries in 1879 to the present time. The exploration also highlights some critical relationships between Christian denominations during church planting. Attention is moreover paid to the rivalry and conflicts between Christianity and other faith religions. Finally, the involvement and impact of Christianity in Burundian social life are discussed.

Background to the Arrival of Christianity in Burundi

The first attempt to introduce Christianity as a new religion in Burundi was done in 1879 by the *Pères Blancs* (Missionaries of Africa), a Catholic missionary society founded in 1868-1869 by the French

Cardinal Lavigerie.[1] They wanted to open an entry point at Rumonge, on the east coast of Tanganyika Lake, from where they would control the whole country. However, they failed because of the death of four of them in 1881, mostly due to the weather conditions. Other trials of installation that followed also remained ephemeral until the end of the nineteenth century.[2] At this time, Mwezi-Gisabo IV was the *mwami* (king). He resisted the new religion in the beginning but later accepted and facilitated the mission's expansion, and eased missionaries' work until his death in 1908.[3]

In spite of the King's support, however, there was resistance from the population and hatred from traditional religion leaders who were feeling invaded, threatened and despised by the new religion. Nevertheless, this resentment diminished little by little due to the missionaries' humanitarian support for the people. In order to reconcile the situation, some people opted to observe both Christianity and traditional religion.[4] But still, as will be told below, the expansion of Christian missions was slow until the 1930s, where it boomed quite impressively.

As to Protestant missions, Gahama[5] suggests that their activities went unobserved until World War I, though the German Society of Missions of Neukirchen had five posts at Rubura (1911), Kogabami (1912), Banga (1912), Muyebe (1914), and Kibimba (1914). After World War I, American missions sought to take over these missions. Threatened by American financial and technical capacities that would help them to display their power, both the Belgian administration that had replaced German colonial administration and the *Pères Blancs* stood against this and decided instead to give them to the Belgian society of Protestant missions that had already been in Congo for some time. Other Protestant missions that were already in the country continued working, and others came, including John Haley of the Free Methodist Church, and the Mission Libre Suédoise (Pentecostal), that had both started their activities in Burundi in 1935.[6]

Strategies, Struggles and the Success of Expansion

In the laborious work of missionaries, strategies were developed to convert as many people as possible. One very important strategy was to target local leaders, as recommended to missionaries by Lavigerie in 1878. According to him, the most important strategy in a violent society divided into a multitude of patriarchal tribes is to gain the mind of the leader. He recommended the missionaries focus on this strategy, since once the leader was converted all the others would follow. Thus converting one leader is more strategic than labouring on hundreds of poor people approached in isolation.[7]

The second strategy was the installation of missions in very meticulously chosen places, especially where there was population density and where local leaders and other opinion-formers were concentrated.[8]

The third strategy was a careful teaching of Christianity, also recommended by Lavigerie. Three levels of teaching were provided, after which an exam was administered. There was the level of *Abanyarwandiko*

---

[1] Therese M. Ludovic Musaniwabo, *La Premiere Evangelisation du Burundi Sous le Règne de Mwezi et Sous la Conduite de Monseigneur Gerbon 1879-1912* (Paris: Louvaij-la-neuve, 1985), 17.

[2] Musaniwabo, *La Premiere Evangelisation du Burundi,* 2.

[3] Musaniwabo, *La Premiere Evangelisation du Burundi,* 3.

[4] Musaniwabo, *La Premiere Evangelisation du Burundi,* 3-4.

[5] Joseph Gahama, *Le Burundi Sous Administration Belge: La Période du Mandat 1919-1939.* Deuxième édition revue et corrigée (Paris: Karthala, 2001), 235.

[6] E. Gerald Bates, *A Soul Afire: A Saga of Visionary Leadership. The Life of J.W. Haley* (Indianapolis: Women's Ministries International, 1993), 30; Corneille Nkurunziza, *Responding to the HIV and AIDS Epidemic in the Context of Unjust Social Structures: A Challenge to the Burundian Pentecostal Churches' Theology of Mission.* Masters Thesis, University of KwaZulu-Natal, School of Religion, Philosophy and Classics, Pietermaritzburg, 2010, 62.

[7] Gahama, *Le Burundi Sous Administration Belge,* 228. See also Musaniwabo, *La Premiere Evangelisation du Burundi,* 4.

[8] Gahama, *Le Burundi Sous Administration Belge,* 221-124.

(applicants), to whom a few notions of religion were taught. There were also *Abanyamudali* (catechumens), who received the fundamental principles of Catholicism. Others were *Abanyamasakaramentu,* to whom all the details of Catholicism were revealed. A glossary called *Amajambo ya Mungu* (Word[s] of God) was also used between 1920 and 1936. These teachings lasted at least four years and people would be refused baptism if their morals were doubted or not approved of, especially those in polygamous unions. In addition to this long process of teaching that consumed at least three days a week were attendance at mass, occasional works in the mission, and the attendance of literacy courses.[9]

The fourth strategy was the Africanisation of Christianity. Rutayisire[10] explains here that missionaries in Burundi were integrating indigenous people as catechists and incorporating traditional values into the missional project as the best way to reach a very large number of people and to subdue traditional religion.

In addition to these four main strategies, missionaries were bringing material support, as mentioned above, and had opted for peaceful entry, unlike the Arabs and Muslims who had sought to forcibly invade the country and had failed.[11]

But these strategies did not yield much fruit, because there was always resistance from local leaders and other influential people. It needed one very important opportunity to see the situation change radically. This was the trust of colonial administration in Christianity and the preference of local leaders with Christian principles for it during the administrative restructuring. Conversion levels developed from a low base in 1922 when only two chiefs were converted. By 1925, out of 255 leaders (chiefs and their deputies), only 30 (11.8%) to 40 (15.7%) were Christians or in preparation to baptism. However, the survey conducted in 1933 discovered that, out of 682 leaders (chiefs and their deputies), 82.7% had joined the Christian religion as Christians (360) or as catechumen (204)![12]

The explosion in the conversion of the leaders was then also reflected in the rest of the population. Up till 1930, 8,701 people were reached after 51 years of work of the Catholic Church. This was multiplied by four (365,000 people) over the next ten years, in contrast to natural population growth which was only 2-3%. Impressed by this increase, missionaries called it a miracle and sign of God's presence in Burundi.[13] The rejected religion, Christianity, and especially the Catholic Church, now became a powerful and influential religion.

But analysts do not attribute this success of the Catholic Church only to administrative restructuring. Gahama suggests this success was aided by the reconciliatory role that missionaries were playing between the colonial administration and the local population, the close collaboration between missionaries and the colonial administration which resulted into leaving all the state schools into the hands of missionaries, the inherent predisposition of Christian in the Barundi, the crisis of legitimacy of traditional beliefs and power, and the lack of a substantial rival, since Protestants and Muslims were not influential.[14]

Meanwhile, as already alluded, Protestant missions were not having the same success. For example, in 1937, while the Catholic Church had registered 254,000 members,[15] all the other Christian missions (Mission Baptiste Danoise, Mission Libre Suédoise, Friends Africa Gospel Mission, and Seventh Day

---

[9] Gahama, *Le Burundi Sous Administration Belge,* 225.

[10] Paul Rutayisire, "L'africanisation du Christianisme et la Pratique Missionnaire en Référence a la Christianisation du Burundi (1897-a937) ", in *Eglise et Histoire de l'eglise en Afrique: Acte du Colloque de Bologne 22-25 Octobre 1988,* ed. Giuseppe Ruggieri (Paris: Beauchesne, 1988), 97-119.

[11] Musaniwabo, *La Premiere Evangelisation du Burundi,* 2-3.

[12] Gahama, *Le Burundi sous Administration Belge,* 229.

[13] Gahama, *Le Burundi sous Administration Belge,* 229.

[14] Gahama, *Le Burundi sous Administration Belge,* 234

[15] Gahama, *Le Burundi sous Administration Belge,* 219.

Adventist mission) had 949 members in total[16] – that is, 268 times less. This dominance of the Catholic Church in Burundi has remained until now, where 85% of its people claim to be Catholics.[17]

It is noteworthy that, in addition to having significant disparities in the number of members, Christian missions in Burundi had difficulty in co-existing with each other. But the colonial administration's favouritism played an important role in creating the problem. The situation of the Protestant churches was observed after World War I when the former German missions were taken over by the Belgian Society of Protestant Missions. The King's commissioner, Alfred Marzorati, thus divided the country into two zones. The east zone he gave to the Belgian mission that he favoured; while the west zone was left to the Seventh Day Adventist mission.[18]

As to the separation between Catholic and Protestant missions, Cardinal Lavigerie had from the beginning prevented missionaries from establishing Catholic missions close to Protestant missions.[19] Gahama[20] also records how, after these conflicts arose from the early European presence in Burundi, the German Resident, Schimmer, divided the country into two zones from the north to the south, leaving the east zone to Catholic missions and the west zone to Protestant missions. However, the Belgian colonial administration was not able to mediate the two Christian confessions. Instead, they sought to make the Catholic Church the national religion, favouring it at all levels while mistreating Protestant churches.[21] Bates wrote in this regard that in 1935,

> Most of the chiefs were either Roman Catholic or pagan and directed many kinds of persecution at the Protestants. Protestants were beaten or imprisoned. Missionaries incensed by the flagrant injustice of these actions, in some cases appealed to the colonial authorities and even had some local chiefs removed... In those early days, the various groups of Protestants worked closely together, maintaining an informal country-wide network of communication which helped to encourage them and co-ordinate their entry as a force to be reckoned with.[22]

The actors in the conflict between the two confessions were not only missionaries but also lay members, especially those in leadership. Finally, all the Protestant missions, regardless of their countries of origin, ended up having strict conditions to be established, whereas Catholic missions had no limitations and were allowed to disturb Protestant mission stations.[23] The Protestant network mentioned in the above quotation refers to the Protestant Council created in 1928 in order to resist such oppression.[24] Therefore, although Christianity is dominant in Burundi today, such expansion has passed through difficult, conflicting times.

Christianity's Relationship with Other Religions

We now explore the relationship between Christianity and other religions, specifically Islam and traditional religion. Muslims in Burundi were composed of two groups: (1) Asians and (2) the Swahili, the Islamised Blacks from the current Democratic Republic of Congo (DRC) and Tanzania. Following their school of

---

[16] Gouvernement Belge, *Rapport Présenté par le Gouvernement Belge au Conseil de la Société des Nations, au Sujet de l'administration du Ruanda-Urundi Pendant l'année 1937.* Bruxelles: Etablissements Généraux d'Imprimerie (1938), 96-98.

[17] Nicasius Achu Check, "Conflict in the Great Lakes Region: Revisiting the Case of Burundi," *Africa Insight.* 37, no.1 (April 2007), 44-62, 58.

[18] Gahama, *Le Burundi sous Administration Belge,* 236.

[19] Musaniwabo, *La Premiere Evangelisation du Burundi,* 40.

[20] Gahama, *Le Burundi sous Administration Belge*, 236.

[21] Gahama, *Le Burundi sous Administration Belge,* 237, 241.

[22] Bates, *A Soul a Fire,* 33.

[23] Gahama, *Le Burundi sous Administration Belge*, 241.

[24] Gahama, *Le Burundi sous Administration Belge,* 237

doctrine, there were three groups, the Ibadites (Arabs of Oman and Mesquite), the Shiites Ishmaelite (Indians), and Sunnites (Swahili).[25]

Resentment between Christians and Muslims started at the very beginning of the mission in 1879, especially at Bujiji where two members of the London Missionary Society stayed for six months without working because of the presence of Arab traders of ivory and slaves.[26] But Muslims had also tried to enter Burundi and Rwanda forcibly, which contributed significantly to their difficulties in becoming established in these countries. In 1886, Mohammed bin Khalfsan el Balwani, called Rumaliza, opened fire at Uzige but could not penetrate further because of the strong Burundian army. They therefore remained on country's periphery trading, making sporadic entries into it.[27]

Later, the German colonial administration decided to limit Muslims' (Arabs and Indians) access to the country. In 1905, it imposed on them a residence permit, delivered by the Usumbura (current Bujumbura) military post. When the Belgians took over in 1924, open war was directed against Muslims, whereas the Catholic Church was now allowed to install its missions close to Muslim positions, as a way to limit their expansion. The Swahili language that Muslims used was banned in schools, which also contributed to reducing the population's trust in Muslims.[28]

Apart from this – the co-operation between the Catholic Church and the colonial administration to combat Muslims – another sign of faith conflict was observed in the treatment given to the young King Mwambutsa. By the simple fact of being circumcised in March 1929, he was suspected of having Muslim tendencies. The missionary Gorju therefore threatened not to marry him to his newly converted fiancée, Therese Kanyonga, and wrote a letter on 23rd March 1929, preventing the resident missionary from letting Mwambutsa enter their church.[29]

Because of these limitations, in 1936, statistics of Muslims on the increase started showing a decline. Two different sources show that they were 6,341 in 1931, 8,220 in 1934, 8,936 in 1936, 8,336 in 1937, and 7,179 in 1939.[30] However, the literature displays other factors which would also have played a role in the Muslims' problem of expansion. Gahama notes here that they did not do much to expand their religion as Christians did. They were mostly involved in trading activity.[31]

Besides Islam, the other faith in Burundi is the traditional religion. With reference to Article 22 of the Versailles Treaty, the colonialists undertook to civilise the mandated colonies. Gahama observes that, in this context, civilising Burundi would mean transforming its traditional society into a western-style one. Therefore, the circular of the Minister of Colonies 15th January 1918 recommended the colonialists to abolish barbaric customs, which included any practice and behaviour whose significance was unknown by the colonialist.[32]

Likewise, missionaries were viewing many local practices and types of behaviour as barbaric and satanic. Rutayisire extensively elaborates on how, according to the missionary P. Van der Burgt, originally from the Netherlands, all the cultural elements of Burundians were in one way or another related to local religious practices and cults that he called sorcery.[33] He thus banned all sorts of cultural lifestyles, including the local name of God, *Imana,* the female's haircut style, *amasunzu,* local necklaces and

---

[25] Gahama, *Le Burundi sous Administration Belge,* 239-240.
[26] Musaniwabo, *La Premiere Evangelisation du Burundi,* 40.
[27] Gahama, *Le Burundi sous Administration Belge,* 238.
[28] Gahama, *Le Burundi sous Administration Belge,* 238.
[29] Gahama, *Le Burundi sous Administration Belge,* 231.
[30] Gahama, *Le Burundi sous Administration Belge,* 239; Gouvernement Belge, *Rapport Présenté par le Gouvernement Belge,* 99.
[31] Gahama, *Le Burundi sous Administration Belge,* 239.
[32] Gahama, *Le Burundi sous Administration Belge,* 240.
[33] Rutayisire, "L'africanisation du Christianisme," 99.

jewellery, and the invocation of spirits, although missionaries of liberal tendency later integrated some of these cultural elements into Christian practices or replaced them with trusted ones.[34]

However, the ceremony of *umuganuro* was not tolerated. This was the sorghum-sowing ceremony in which people from all over the country would gather at the King's residence to sow sorghum grains in two of his fields. These ceremonies had two important parts: the visible part in which all the people participated, and the hidden part that would take place by night. It is this latter part that diverged significantly from Christian principles because, while the drummers were performing with their latest energy, the King and his close chiefs were performing sexual rituals together with women. This ceremony was therefore abolished. Instead, from 1929, a prayer for blessing the sowing season was added to the church's agenda as an alternative, and beans and peas were included.[35]

Conflict between Christianity and traditional religions were moreover observed in people's resistance to a foreign faith. In addition to the reticence of local leaders and the population, especially in the beginning as already mentioned, open conflicts were also perceived. 'Thus Gahama and Musaniwabo respectively describe how chiefs in the north of Usumbura attacked new Christian converts.'[36] Divisions were also observed in families in which some members were converted to Christianity.[37] This seemed like the accomplishment of Matthew 10:34-38 of Christ having come not to bring peace but a sword and divisions.

It is thus noteworthy that, from the start, the relationship between Christianity and other faith religions was almost always characterised by rivalry and conflict. Currently, its relationship with Islam seems neutral. Although traditional religion is now not expanded and public, Christianity still does not tolerate co-existence with it, be it in the Catholic Church, the Protestant mainline churches, or newly initiated revival churches.

The Involvement and Impact of Christian Religion in Burundians' Lives

The involvement and impact of Christian religion in Burundian lifeare significant. Two levels are explored here. At social and developmental levels, we mentioned that, right from the beginning, missionaries used social action as one means of gaining the trust of the population and their leaders, and evangelising. This included the direct distribution of material aid, such as clothes, food, school fees and house materials. Their interventions also involved starting health facilities, formal schools and informal education centres, as well as the formation of community associations such as co-operatives, trade unions, and saving-credit groups.[38]

For example, the first school in Burundi was started by missionaries in 1902.[39] In 1937, the Catholic Church had 140 schools centres supported by colonial administration (*libres subsidiées*), of which 21 were for boys, 8 were for girls, and 111 were mixed, with 9,355 students in total.[40] They also had 102,269 students in 729 totally private schools. Since Protestant missions were not receiving much support from the secular administration, they focused on private schools. The Church Missionary Society had 340 students, the Mission Baptiste Danoise 920 students, the Friends Africa Gospel Mission 1425 students, and the Mission Libre Suédoise 1,003 students. However, available literature specifies that education during the colonial period was not necessarily conceived for the benefit of local people but more especially to serve

[34] Rutayisire, "L'africanisation du Christianisme," 99.

[35] Gahama, *Le Burundi sous Administration Belge,* 356-367.

[36] Gahama, *Le Burundi sous Administration Belge*, 369.

[37] Musaniwabo, *La Premiere Evangelisation du Burundi,* 34-35.

[38] P. Jean Perraudin, *Naissance d'une Eglise: Histoire du Burundi Chretien* (Ngozi, Burundi, 1963), 108-110, 189-195; Gaëtan Feltz, "Histoire des mentalités et histoire des missions au Burundi," ca. 1880-1960, in *History in Africa*, Vol. 12 (1985), 51-63, 57-58; Aude Laroque, *Historiographie et Enjeux de Memoires au Burundi* (PhD thesis, Université Pantheon-Sorbonne, Department of History, Paris, 2013), 77.

[39] Laroque, *Historiographie et Enjeux de Memoires au Burundi*, 77.

[40] Gouvernement Belge, *Rapport Présenté par le Gouvernement Belge*, 103.

the colonial administration and evangelisation.[41] Education was very basic – only a few students, meticulously selected on the basis of their ethnic groups, could enter secondary school. In 1960, there was only one university in the Belgian Congo and Rwanda-Urundi.[42] But the situation has changed, as specified below.

At a political level, the Catholic Church was particularly involved in politics and leadership during the colonial period. This was done through the principle of converting local leaders first and the masses later. The church also collaborated closely with the colonial administration to the point that, during administrative reorganisation under the Belgian colony, a life based on Christian principles was the major criterion for recruiting local leaders. This opportunity empowered much of the Catholic Church by giving all local leaders and those who desired leadership positions an incentive to flock to this church. Missionaries, therefore, started playing a role as intermediaries between local leaders and the colonial administration, and as advisors of colonial leaders in cases where important decisions needed to be taken.[43] Meanwhile, Protestant churches were still being marginalised. Moreover, both Catholic and Protestant churches were denied complete freedom in 1984 by president Jean Baptiste Bagaza, until 1987 when he was overthrown by Pierre Buyoya.[44]

It is also important to acknowledge the work of the National Council of Churches of Burundi. This was founded in 1989 under the name 'Conseil National des Eglises du Burundi or CNEB'. It had been known previously under the name of the Alliance of Burundi Protestant Churches in 1970 and the Protestant Missionary Alliance of Rwanda-Urundi in 1935. CNEB members include the various Anglican dioceses (Bujumbura, Gitega, Makamba, Buye and Matana), the United Methodist Church, the Free Methodist Church, the Union of Baptist Churches, the Evangelical Church of Friends (Quakers), and the Church of Jesus Christ on Earth by His Special Envoy Simon Kimbangu.[45] Co-operation between these churches has given them the power and the courage to take initiatives that would otherwise be hard to take alone. For example, since 2004 after the mass violation of human rights in Burundi, the CNEB collaborated with DanChurchAid in humanitarian action against landmines, delivering Mine Risk Education (MRE), and helping the community to minimise the risks of landmines.[46] When the country was preparing for presidential elections of June 2015, CNEB, together with FECCLAHA (*Communauté des Eglises et des Conseils Nationaux des Eglises de la Région de Grands Lacs*), made their call to the government and opposition parties, urging them to always seek and do what would promote peace in the country.[47]

However, the poor record of the Protestant churches' involvement in social development in Burundi, as mentioned above, was not only a colonial and political issue but was also theologically motivated to a certain degree. Nkurunziza explains at length that, when Swedish Pentecostal missionaries came to Burundi in 1935, their intention was 'to convert Burundians to Swedish-like Pentecostalism'.[48] In this Pentecostalism, as he explains, the gift of the Holy Spirit surpasses and replaces any other source of capacity and skills. Therefore, higher education was not considered as necessary; and even the training of pastors was limited to four weeks' biblical training.

---

[41] Laroque, *Historiographie et Enjeux de Memoires au Burundi*, 244-260.
[42] Gahama, *Le Burundi sous Administration Belge*, 259-260.
[43] Gahama, *Le Burundi sous Administration Belge*, 217, 227, 232.
[44] "Burundi", Worldmark Encyclopedia of Nations. 2007." *Encyclopedia.com.* Retrieved from www.encyclopedia.com (accessed 2 September. 2015).
[45] World Council of Churches (WCC). *A Handbook of Councils and Churches Profiles of Ecumenical Relationships.* Geneva: WCC (n.d.).
[46] DanChurchAid's SALW Awareness Raising and Risk Education: Mine Action and Armed Violence Reduction. Burundi: GICHD/CIDHG (2012).
[47] ECCLAHA, *Appel pour le Retablissement de la Paix au Burundi* (Nairobi: ECCLAHA, 2012).
[48] Nkurunziza, *Responding to the HIV and AIDS epidemic*, 64.

Another point to consider is the response of Christian churches to HIV and AIDS. Ingiyimbere[49] analyses the pastoral messages and letters of the Catholic bishops in relation to this issue, and finds that although the Catholic Church made efforts to address the pandemic in supporting those affected, it was very reticent at the start and confused HIV infection with being guilty of the sin of immorality, which limited its efforts in giving support to those needing it. Likewise, Nkurunziza[50] has analysed locally composed songs by Burundians under the inspiration of Pentecostal theology – the songs actually bought, used, and appreciated by members of all Protestant churches – and found that they also underpinned the notion of HIV being the result of immoral behaviour, a form of retributive theology. Through these few glimpses, therefore, it is apparent that, in spite of the numerical expansion of Christianity in Burundi as well as the efforts of Christian churches in helping the country, there is still a long way to go in applying a life-giving theology.

Conclusion

This article has given a picture of Christianity in Burundi from its arrival to the present. It suggests that, before Christianity arrived, there was a traditional religion which was the main factor in the population and leaders' resistance to the new faith, especially at the beginning. It has not been possible to explore all the major current issues, such as gender and environment, in relation with Christianity in Burundi. Further research is needed to clarify some of these issues in order to fully appreciate the impact of Christianity on Burundians' life.

Bibliography

Achu, Nicasius. 'Conflict in the Great Lakes Region: Revisiting the Case of Burundi.' *Africa Insight* 37, no.1 (April 2007): 44-62.

ECCLAHA. *Appel Pour le Retablissement de la Paix au Burundi.* Nairobi: ECCLAHA, 2012.

Feltz, Gaëtan. 'Histoire des Mentalités et Histoire des Missions au Burundi, ca. 1880-1960.' *History in Africa*, Vol. 12 (1985): 51-63.

Gahama, Joseph. *Le Burundi Sous Administration Belge: La Période du Mandat 1919-1939.* Deuxième édition revue et corrigée. Paris: Karthala, 2001.

Ingiyimbere, Fifèle. 'Le VIH-SIDA et l'Eglise Catholique au Burundi. '*Ethique et Société: Revue de Réflexion Morale. HIV/SIDA et Santé Publique* 4, no 3 (2007): 255-271.

Laroque, Aude, 'Historiographie et Enjeux de Mémoires au Burundi.' Thèse de Doctorat, Université Pantheon-Sorbonne, 2013.

Musaniwabo, Therese M. Ludovic. *La Première Évangélisation du Burundi Sous le Règne de Mwezi et Sous la Conduite de Monseigneur Gerbon 1879-1912*. Paris: Louvaij-la-neuve, 1985.

Perraudin, P. Jean. *Naissance D'une Église: Histoire du Burundi Chrétien.* Ngozi, Burundi, 1963.

Rutayisire, Paul. 'L'africanisation du Christianisme et la Pratique Missionnaire en Référence a la Christianisation du Burundi (1897-a937).' In *Eglise et Histoire de L'église en Afrique: Acte du Colloque de Bologne 22-25 Octobre 1988,* édité par. Giuseppe Ruggieri, 97-119. Paris: Beauchesne, 1988.

World Council of Churches (WCC). *A Handbook of Councils and Churches' Profiles of Ecumenical Relationships*. Geneva: WCC (no date).

---

[49] Fifele Ingiyimbere, "Le VIH-SIDA et l'Eglise Catholique au Burundi." *Ethique et société: Revue de réflexion morale. HIV/SIDA et santé publique* 4, no 3 (2007), 255-271.

[50] Corneille Nkurunziza, "Locally Composed Songs as Expression of Genuine Contextual Theology? The Case of Songs on HIV and AIDS in Burundian Pentecostal Churches." *Journal of Theology for Southern Africa* 142 (2012), 58-79.

(52A) CHRISTIANITY IN CAMEROON

Sadrack Djiokou

Religion	Pop 2010	Pct 2010	Pop 2025	Pct 2025	Gr Pct 1970 2025
Christians	12,007,000	58.3%	18,436,000	62.4%	2.9%
Independents	1,450,000	7.0%	2,500,000	8.5%	3.7%
African initiated	1,372,000	6.7%			
Orthodox	1,200	0.0%	1,500	0.0%	1.5%
Protestants	4,112,000	20.0%	6,503,000	22.0%	3.1%
Reformed, Presbyterian	2,581,000	12.5%			
Lutheran	394,000	1.9%			
Pentecostal	305,000	1.5%			
Baptist	259,000	1.3%			
Adventist	159,000	0.8%			
Roman Catholics	5,018,000	24.4%	7,400,000	25.1%	2.6%
Pentecostals/Charismatics	2,178,000	10.6%	2,750,000	9.3%	1.6%
Evangelicals	1,209,000	5.9%	1,713,000	5.8%	2.4%
adherents of traditional African religions	4,219,000	20.5%	4,800,000	16.3%	0.9%
Muslims	4,133,000	20.1%	5,976,000	20.2%	2.5%
Baha'is	54,400	0.3%	72,000	0.2%	1.9%
adherents of new religious movements	11,900	0.1%	9,200	0.0%	-1.7%
Chinese folk-religionists	790	0.0%	1,000	0.0%	1.6%
Buddhists	370	0.0%	1,000	0.0%	6.8%
Jews	54	0.0%	100	0.0%	4.2%
people professing no religion	164,000	0.8%	235,000	0.8%	2.4%
Total population	**20,591,000**	**100.0%**	**29,530,000**	**100.0%**	**2.4%**

Source: Centre for the Study of World Christianity (CSGC), Boston, Gordon-Conwell TS

L´histoire du Christianisme au Cameroun est aussi diversifiée que le Cameroun lui-même. Ce pays est considéré comme l´Afrique en miniature, de par sa géographie et ses composantes humaine, linguistique et culturelle. Ecrire l´histoire de la chrétienté au Cameroun relève finalement d´une intelligence de synthèse qui n´est pas facile de produire d´un trait ou sous une forme linéaire. Mais le message chrétien central basé sur le Christ lui-même reste l´élément unificateur des tendances chrétiennes dans ce pays et permet une synthèse historique que nous essayerons de faire ici. Par ailleurs, ayant travaillé comme Secrétaire général du Conseil des Eglises Protestantes à Yaoundé, ville-capitale qui regroupe toutes les tendances chrétiennes présentes au Cameroun, la tâche devient une passion qui me rapproche de nouveau des activités communes menées dans le cadre de ce Conseil avec ce qu´on a appelé les « grandes tendances chrétiennes protestantes » du Cameroun regroupées au sein du CEPCA.

Les premières missions sur le territoire

La mission chrétienne au Cameroun est avant tout le résultat d´un courage missionnaire historique, qu´il est juste de saluer au commencement de cet article. Il s´agit des gens qui ont quitté le « chez eux », pour se mettre à l´aventure, dans des conditions aussi bien difficiles qu´incertaines, pour proclamer au monde le message de Jésus-Christ, et ce, jusque dans les fin-fonds des forêts africaines et autres zones difficiles d´atteinte, en courant toutes sortes de risques, dus aussi bien aux escarpements de la nature, qu´aux maladies inconnues, en passant par des rencontres des peuples résistants et faisant face aux difficultés de communication et de compréhension entre les acteurs en présence, sans oublier les contraintes liées aux obligations de collaboration entre missionnaires et colons. Bien que la chrétienté se soit établie sur le continent africain dès les premières heures de sa diffusion dans le septentrion, elle n´a pas connu d´expansion, dû à l´absence dans les cultures africaines d´idées de prosélytisme, comme le remarque Jean Marc Ela parlant du christianisme éthiopien :

> « Vassalisé par l´Egypte et ne disposant pas de ressources matérielles nécessaires à son auto-expansion, le christianisme éthiopien s´en est tenu, par choix ou par résignation, à la traditionnelle tolérance africaine qui, en matière de religion, n´encourage point le prosélytisme. »[1]

Les premiers qui auront le courage de s´aventurer au nom de l´Evangile de Jésus-Christ sur les côtes camerounaises en 1841, seront les nommés Dr Prince et Rev. John Clarke, qui s´installeront pour une courte durée à Douala, où ils organiseront le travail d´évangélisation chez leurs frères de race. Ces derniers faisaient partie d´un groupe d´anciens esclaves des Amériques libérés, principalement de la Jamaïque, et qui avaient décidé de retourner dans leur continent d´origine où leurs parents avaient été pris en esclavage, afin de proclamer aux nations la dignité et la libération du Christ. Ils arrivent dans les confins du golfe de Guinée dans les années 1841-1844. Le Cameroun n´était alors qu´un conglomérat de chefferies claniques, dont les Portugais avaient découvert les côtes en 1472 déjà, et en passant le fleuve du Wouri auquel ils avaient donné le nom de « Rio dos Cameroes »[2] (rivières de crevettes) qui donnera ensuite son nom au pays. Ces deux seront suivi par le courageux et talentueux Joseph Merrick de la Jamaïque lui aussi, pour le compte, comme les deux premiers, de la Mission Baptiste de Londres. Après un court séjour à Douala, Merrick s´installe à Bimbia, près de Limbé, localité qui portera par la suite le nom de Victoria, avant de recouvrer son vrai nom vers les années 90. Ce dernier se mettra rapidement au travail, en commençant par l´étude des langues locales dont le *duala* et dont il commencera l´écriture, puis la mise sur pied d´un projet d´alphabétisation pour les populations locales. Merrick est considéré comme le tout premier missionnaire effectivement installé au Cameroun. Ce dernier sera suivi en juin 1845 par Alfred Saker, venu lui aussi pour le compte de la Mission Baptiste de Londres. Ce dernier s´installera à Douala, et c´est avec lui que la mission évangélique au Cameroun prendra un véritable essor, avec la création de plusieurs lieux de culte et d´enseignement religieux, à travers de cours bibliques, d´ateliers de formation artisanale et imprimerie. Son épouse Emilie s´engagera dans le travail de santé par la mise sur pied d´un établissement de formation d´infirmières et d´assistantes médicales. Avec le couple Saker, l´évangélisation ira de pair avec le travail de développement et d´apprentissage, dans les domaines divers comme l´alphabétisation, l´artisanat, l´école et la santé. Le concept de l´Evangile pour tout l´homme sera en application, ce qu´on appellera plus tard l´ « évangélisation holistique ». Avec la signature en juin 1884 d´un contrat de protectorat avec l´Allemagne sur le Cameroun, la Mission baptiste de Londres sera contrainte de quitter le pays au cours de la même année, pour céder la place à la mission allemande de Bâle.

---

[1] Ela. Jean-M., le *Cri de l´homme africain*, (Paris: Karthala, 2009)19

[2] Lire à ce sujet l´ouvrage d´Engelbert Mveng : Histoire du Cameroun, (Paris: Présence Africaine, 1963); Voire aussi Slageren, Jaap van, *Les origines de l´Eglise Evangélique du Cameroun, Missions européennes et christianisme autochtone*, (Yaoundé: édition CLE 2009), Nouvelle édition

L´Allemagne, à présent « protectrice » de ce qu´on appellera désormais le « Kamerun », favorisera le travail de la Mission de Bâle contre toute autre mission sur le pays, notamment la mission baptiste. Les missionnaires bâlois vont donc entreprendre un travail colossal de répandre l´évangile dans le pays, principalement sur le littoral, avant d´entamer leur montée vers le Grassfield (les montagnes de la région Ouest du Cameroun) dans les années 1903. Ils accompagneront leur travail, comme leurs prédécesseurs baptistes, d´enseignement à l´alphabétisation des indigènes, la formation artisanale et l´implantation d´écoles qui commenceront à former les premiers « intellectuels » camerounais, à l´instar de Modi Din, Kouo Issedu, Ekollo (1912). Les premiers évangélisés de la Mission baptiste feront appel à la Mission Baptiste allemande en vue de garder le contact à l´étranger et assurer la continuité du travail missionnaire de cette tendance dans le pays, mais qui ne connaitra plus un élan particulier dans son développement.

Le départ de la Mission de Bâle du Cameroun sera tumultueux, dû au départ précipité des allemands du Cameroun, du fait de la défaite de l´Allemagne á la première guerre mondiale et la première insurrection nationaliste au Cameroun contre les allemands.[3] Une tendance de former l´apartheid au Cameroun avait quelque peu hantée l´esprit des allemands qui voulaient exproprier les populations duala de la zone centrale du plateau du Deido. Le roi des duala, d´une main forte et bien déterminé, commença la résistance avant d´être lâchement exécuté par pendaison, ainsi que son secrétaire, après un procès éclair, au petit matin du 8 Août 1914. Le pasteur Modi Din sera lui, déporté et plusieurs nationalistes mis au silence, alors que toute résistance devait être réprimée dans le sang. Mais la Mission de Bâle sera contrainte de quitter le Kamerun en 1917, avec l´échec allemande à la guerre, comme précédemment indiqué.

Comme tous les autres territoires coloniaux allemands, le Kamerun sera placé sous le mandat de la Société des Nations (SDN), prédécesseur des Nations Unies (ONU) actuelles, qui en donnera mandat à la France et à la Grande Bretagne pour administrer le pays.[4] En faveur de cette situation, la France en profite pour débarquer ses missionnaires de la Société des Missions Evangéliques de Paris dès 1917, côté protestant. Côté catholique, comme nous le verrons plus bas, ce fut l´ère de toutes les facilités pour les missionnaires catholiques au Cameroun, d´où la rapidité d´implantation de cette église venue cinquante ans après les protestants. Ces derniers (protestants) se contenteront de consolider les acquis des missions précédentes, et renforceront les œuvres de formation et de nouveaux centres missionnaires seront tout de même créés, au fur et à mesure que le travail de colonisation française et anglaise sur le pays suivait son cours vers l´intérieur. La mission évangélique suivait la mission coloniale, et quelques fois la précédait dans la conquête des territoires et l´exploitation des richesses pour le compte de la métropole et au détriment des populations locales, dont seuls quelques élites étaient formés pour servir les causes de la colonie ou de la mission. Vincent Mulago s´interrogera alors, aux vues de ce qui se passera entre missionnaires et colons et la manière dont les Africains s´empresseront malgré tout à embrasser massivement un tel christianisme :

> « Est-ce un succès complet que ce magnifique mouvement vers le christianisme en Afrique ? Ce que nous voyons fleurir est-il enraciné dans l´âme de l´Africain ou est-ce simplement une expression de l´européanisation générale du continent noir ? »[5]

Pendant ce temps, les premiers pasteurs issus de la mission londonienne se mettaient au travail, poussés par leur unique foi en Jésus-Christ, qu´ils avaient appris à connaître et à aimer. Malgré les conditions difficiles de travail, la marche à pied sur des distances impossibles, ils œuvraient sans relâche pour la

[3] Voire: Kengne Pokam, E., *Les églises chrétiennes face à la montée du nationalisme camerounais*, (Paris: L´Harmattan, 1987)

[4] Cf. Owona, Adalbert : La naissance du Cameroun (1884-1914) Online, www.peuplesawa.com

[5] Mulago, Vincent, « Nécessité de l´adaptation missionnaire chez les Bantu du Congo », In : *Des prêtres noirs s´interrogent*, Paris, Présence Africaine et coll. « Rencontres », le Cerf, (1956) 21

bonne cause de l´Evangile, dans un dénuement qui n´avait pour motivation que la foi qui les poussait à aller vers l´avant. Le fossé entre les missionnaires et les pasteurs locaux dits indigènes était grand. Mais le courage missionnaire qui avait marqué au départ l´arrivée des Merrick et Saker devenait la marque même de leur engagement dans le champ de mission intérieure. La volonté de constituer une église locale forte et fidèle à l´Evangile du Seigneur n´avait pas de prix.

Les premières velléités à l´autonomie des églises

La mission française travaillera durant quarante ans à former les germes d´une église chrétienne camerounaise dont la structure suivra essentiellement la structure des églises de leur pays d´origine, sans tenir compte des composantes locales considérées comme primaires et païennes, et donc impropres à l´Evangile. Tout ce qui relèvera de la tradition locale sera interdit dans les communautés chrétiennes naissantes. La structure de travail mise en place dans la gestion de l´ensemble du travail missionnaire au Cameroun sera conforme à la volonté coloniale de contrôler les communautés afin de faciliter la visibilité sur les tendances politiques dans le pays et éviter ou mater toute velléité à l´indépendance. Une conférence missionnaire sera ensuite mise sur pied pour servir cette cause. Comme nous pouvons le lire sur le Site de présentation de l´Eglise Evangélique du Cameroun :

> « La Conférence des missionnaires, uniquement pour les Blancs, justifiée par l'impossibilité pour les ouvriers autochtones de s'autogérer. Cette institution et son contenu engendrent les premiers conflits, parce qu'en fait, les missionnaires ne considèrent pas le clergé local comme des collègues. Cependant, les lois et règlements administratifs leur confèrent une existence juridique. »[6]

Cette reconnaissance juridique poussera, à la demande du clergé local, vers les années 1950, à commencer à œuvrer pour l´autonomie des tendances locales, qui aboutira à la proclamation effective de l´autonomie des Eglises issues du travail missionnaire depuis Merrick, notamment, l´Eglise Evangélique du Cameroun (EEC), considérée à ce jour comme la plus grande Eglise protestante au Cameroun, une église essentiellement francophone, l´Union des Eglises Baptistes du Cameroun (UEBC) essentiellement produit de la mission Baptiste, tout comme la Presbyterian Church in Cameroon (PCC)[7], dont la formation avait été confiée à la Mission de Bâle après le travail effectué par les anglophones de la Mission baptiste londonienne, tout comme la Cameroon Baptiste Convention (CBC)[8] qui elle se constituera dès 1954 en une convention baptiste séparé des « non » baptistes que seront les presbytériens cités précédemment. Les autonomies acquises par ces églises en 1957 venaient en prélude à l´indépendance du pays qui sera proclamée trois ans plus tard pour la partie francophone du Cameroun en 1960 et quatre ans plus tard pour le côté anglophone en 1961. Les deux parties du Cameroun/Cameroon ne connaitront leur unification que le 20 mai 1972.

Mais dès avant ces autonomies presque massive des églises au Cameroun, l´histoire verra naître vers les années 1930 une tendance indigène d´une église « adaptée » au contexte local, issue surtout de la mission baptiste de Londres, que les missionnaires nommeront du nom de « Native Baptist Church », sous la houlette du très motivé et charismatique Lotin à Same, qui composera plus d´une centaine de cantiques chrétiens encore exécutés avec entrain à ce jour. Cette église acquerra son indépendance sous le nom de l´Eglise Baptiste Camerounaise (EBC).

Ce sera aussi le cas de l´Eglise Protestante Africaine (EPA), qui sera contrainte dans les années 1934 à s´organiser en une église indépendante pour la promotion des liturgie et langue locales pour le culte et qui

---

[6] Cf. www.eeccameroun.org

[7] Voire Site: www.pcc.cm

[8] On peut consulter à ce sujet le Site: www.cbc-cm.org

passera par plusieurs changement de noms, pour aboutir à celle qu´elle porte aujourd´hui. Mais elle reste l´une des plus petites églises dans l´échiquier des églises protestantes au Cameroun, à côté de l´Eglise Presbytérienne Camerounaise (EPC) dont elle est considérée comme une des scissions, issues toutes les deux de la Mission Presbytérienne Américaine installée au Cameroun dans les années 1921, essentiellement dans le sud forestier du Cameroun. Cette mission aura principalement travaillée sur la base d´une évangélisation par l´éducation, dans la création d´écoles de formation d´élites pour la mission, pour répandre l´esprit presbytérien dans le champ de la mission évangélique et qui consistera en d´autonomies des synodes et la gestion à la base des communautés locales par des presbytes. L´EPC garde encore une étroite collaboration avec la Mission américaine, devenue entretemps la Presbyterian Church USA.

Pendant ce temps, la Sudan Mission faisait sa percée dans la partie nord du Cameroun en 1923, suivi de la Mission Norvégienne en 1925, qui marquera l´entrée des luthériens dans le territoire camerounais, à partir de la région du nord essentiellement conquis par l'Islam dès 1715[9], à l´initiative de Adoulphus Eugene Gunderson, citoyen américain d'origine norvégienne. Ce dernier, qui allie les luthériens norvégiens et américains, réunira autour de lui des personnes engagées pour la cause du Christ dans le but d´apporter l´Evangile dans l´Adamaoua camerounais déjà fortement islamisé par des chefs musulmans venus du Mali via le Nigéria, dont le fameux conquérant et lamido Moddibo Adama[10] qui donnera son nom à cette localité du Cameroun. L´Eglise issue de ce travail conjoint des missionnaires aussi bien norvégiens, américains que danois, formera l´Eglise Evangélique Luthérienne au Nord-Cameroun (aujourd´hui Eglise Evangélique Luthérienne au Cameroun (EELC), anciennement au Cameroun et en Centrafrique (EELCRCA)) qui acquerra son autonomie vers les années 1960, après une décision 10 ans auparavant de la part des différentes missions, d´unir les forces dans un travail commun qui devrait ainsi aboutir à une église locale autonome. Toujours est-il que, comme toutes les églises issues de la mission, elle restera la copie des Eglises d´envoi, qui garderont une main mise aussi bien sur la structure que sur la gouvernance de l´église, dont la véritable « indépendance » ne suivra qu´avec le temps.

Il en sera de même de l´Eglise Fraternelle Luthérienne au Nord Cameroun, résultat du travail de la Mission Fraternelle Luthérienne d´Amérique, présente au Cameroun dans les années 1920. Cette mission s´installera dans la partie la plus au nord du Cameroun, à la croisée de chemins entre le Nigéria, le Cameroun et le Tchad. Elle sera l´œuvre des missionnaires pionniers que sont Revne et Kaardal. Ils auront travaillé dans les mêmes conditions que les missionnaires de la Sudan Mission, dans un environnement très islamisé, mais sans une véritable collaboration directe, ce qui aboutira à la création de l´Eglise Fraternelle Luthérienne au Cameroun (EFLC), reconnue en 1969 comme une Eglise autonome. La Mission procédera seulement vers les années 1957 à la formation des premiers collaborateurs locaux, qui ne bénéficieront que de quelques résidus de connaissances bien rudimentaires. Ce n´est que quelques années plus tard que les premières formations auront véritablement lieu et où quelques locaux bénéficieront de formations plus approfondies dans une école biblique offrant quelques notions de théologie.

Terrain d´unité des Eglises protestantes du Cameroun

Si la diversité des cultures et traditions au Cameroun explique aussi la diversité des églises et mouvements religieux, le désir des Camerounais de travailler à trouver des secteurs d´œuvres communes date dès avant même les premières heures des indépendances des églises issues de la mission, dans l´optique de défendre les intérêts des protestants dans ce qu´on appelait à l´époque l´Afrique Equatoriale Française, regroupant les pays comme le Tchad, le Cameroun, la République Centrafricaine, le Gabon et le Congo. En 1941, une

[9] Cf. Sa´ad, A. *The Lamibe of Fombia*. A political History of Adamawa 1809-1903, (Zaria: Ahmadou Bello University Press, 1977).

[10] Cf. Kirk-Green, A.H.M., Adamwa, *Past and Present. An Historical Approach to the Development of a Northern Cameroons Province*, (London: Oxford University Press, 1958).

fédération est mise sur pied pour tenter de coordonner les activités d´évangélisation et le fonctionnement des œuvres d´accompagnement que sont les écoles et les centres de santé, dispensaires ou hôpitaux dans cette vaste zone d´Afrique centrale. Les Camerounais s´en séparent par la suite pour créer la Fédération des Eglises et Missions du Cameroun (FEMEC)[11] en 1969, avec en son sein des églises citées précédemment, qui acceptent de se mettre ensemble pour coordonner leurs activités et éviter toute idée de concurrence déloyale dans le champ de mission et de conquête de nouveaux membres. Les Eglises sont au départ définies par leur situation géographique et répondant aux secteurs définis par les anciens missionnaires. Elles ont tendance à être vues comme des églises ethniques que seul le mouvement des populations sur l´ensemble du territoire aidera à dépasser, les membres d´église particulière ayant tendance de « transporter » leurs églises dans les nouveaux lieu de leur installation et de les ouvrir aux « autres », d´où le dépassement des « frontières » établies naturellement par la mission. Chaque église se veut nationale. On peut le voir dans les changements de noms de plusieurs d´entre elles au cours de leur évolution, pour prendre un caractère national. La FEMEC se donnera donc pour but de coordonner en quelques sortes ces présences et éviter tout frottement entre les églises œuvrant pour la même cause. La Fédération apparaît aussi comme une volonté de l´Etat camerounais d´avoir un seul interlocuteur protestant plutôt qu´une panoplie de groupuscules plus ou moins importants, d´autant plus que l´Etat devra considérer les églises comme des partenaires de développement, notamment dans le domaine de l´éducation et de la santé. Ces domaines relevant du secteur de travail d´un Etat, l´Etat camerounais se considérera redevable aux églises qui l´appuient dans ces secteurs, et donc devront bénéficier de quelques subventions financières qu´il faudra gérer dans un cadre coordonné que représentera la fédération. Avec l´évolution des concepts de travail, la FEMEC cèdera la place au CEPCA (Conseil des Eglises Protestantes du Cameroun), à la suite d´une réforme interne qui aboutira le 1er Avril 2005 au changement de nom, sans que les buts essentiels connaissent une évolution particulière, dont le désir d´unité des protestants du Cameroun.

En dépit de la nouvelle organisation (CEPCA), les Eglises gardent leur grande autonomie, et menacent même de se concurrencer mutuellement, en affaiblissant ainsi l´organisation dans ses buts, pour finir à en faire une caisse de résonnance et d´intérêts liés aussi bien aux subventions de l´Etat qu´aux aides étrangères. Le Conseil se contentera d´organiser chaque année la « Semaine du Protestantisme Camerounais », y compris quelques actions sporadiques dans le but d´unir en quelques sortes les chrétiens protestants du Cameroun, comme la semaine de l´unité des chrétiens du Cameroun. On retiendra tout de même un succès important dans l´histoire de cette organisation, c´est la fête du cent-cinquantenaire de l´arrivée de l´Evangile au Cameroun, dont toutes les églises issues de la mission avaient ensemble fêté avec entrain en 1994 dans les temples et lieux publics du pays. Dans l´entretemps, chaque Eglise fait son bonhomme de chemin avec plus ou moins ses crises de fonctionnement interne.

L´Eglise catholique romaine

L´Eglise catholique romaine a une forte assise dans la Cameroun. Implantée dans le pays une cinquantaine d´années après les premiers missionnaires protestants en 1890, l´évolution de cette église romaine au Cameroun a été fulgurante, essentiellement grâce à la France catholique dont les ressortissants devaient être bénéficiaires de facilités en terme de déplacements et d ´investissements dans l´assemble du pays. Mais les premiers missionnaires catholiques au Cameroun seront les Pères Pallottins allemands, qui débarqueront dans le pays dans la nuit du 24 au 25 octobre 1890, et prendront en main la première préfecture apostolique du Cameroun créée dans la même année.[12] De toute évidence, la France favorisera

[11] Messina, J.P., Slageren, J.v., *Histoire du christianisme au Cameroun : des origines à nos jours*, (Yaoundé: édition CLE, 2005) 252-256

[12] Voire: Messina, J.-P., *L´Eglise catholique face à l´indépendance du Cameroun sous administration française* (1949-

par la suite des missionnaires français au détriment d´autres congrégations religieuses dans le pays. Le continent africain sortait à peine de trois décennies d´esclavage éhonté, ayant connu une division arbitraire des grandes puissances à l´issue du Congrès de Berlin (1884-1885), l´Eglise « romaine » se donnera pour but, animée qu´elle était par la question de l´émancipation des noirs, de venir annoncer la liberté chrétienne, combattre les injustices et donner aux victimes de l´esclavage, qu´elle avait pourtant soutenue auparavant, et dans un contexte colonial dont elle avait été elle-même par ailleurs l´une des promotrices, le sentiment de justice et d´éveil des consciences locales. L´éducation et la santé vont constituer ses axes majeurs dans l´accomplissement de ses tâches missionnaires pour l´évangélisation de l´ensemble du pays. L´Eglise catholique au Cameroun va s´investir dans de nombreuses écoles et centres de formation et de nombreuses structures de formation sanitaire. Elle passe pour être la plus grande église chrétienne du Cameroun et représente environ 30% de la population du pays, devant les protestants, 20%. Le pays compte environ 20% de musulmans.

Les Eglises orthodoxes et anglicanes

Les orthodoxes sont au Cameroun depuis 1951 avec l´arrivée des commerçants grecs. Ceux-ci s´ouvriront peu à peu aux Camerounais dès les années d´indépendance du pays, d´où la contrainte d´adopter la langue française dans la liturgie qui se développera elle aussi lentement. Quant à l´Eglise anglicane, c´est en Avril 2003 qu´elle fondait son premier diocèse au Cameroun, cette Eglise est membre du Conseil des Eglises Protestantes au Cameroun.

Le mouvement pentecôtiste

Le mouvement des églises indépendantes, qui entretemps prospèrent dans les grandes villes du pays, ont su non seulement exploiter les « manquements » des églises issues de la mission, comme l´absence d´une spiritualité mouvementée et l´attachement à la vie intense de prière etc. mais aussi, elles ont bénéficié de la tragique pauvreté des populations pour prêcher un évangile de la prospérité et du miracle, tentant ainsi de répondre aux attentes d´une population confrontées à une situation de précarité sociale et économique, et aussi de profonde détresses dues aux nombreux problèmes de santé, de fécondité, de nutrition et de chômage.[13] La notion de guérison et de la grâce sera au centre des prédications, y compris l´évangélisation par la musique d´ambiance qui font danser même les plus handicapés du groupe. Celles-ci ne lèsent pas sur les moyens pour attirer autant de fidèles que possible, et les campagnes d´évangélisation sont organisées, des tracts distribués pour amener des gens, surtout les membres d´églises dites historiques, à changer pour un milieu dit plus « spirituel » et plus ouvert aux actions du Saint-Esprit à guérison immédiate. Ce sont essentiellement des églises sentimentales, où les « cœurs sont touchés » pour des raisons plus ou moins explicites. Des élites chrétiens ne sont pas du reste, compte tenu de la prédication sur des thèmes de l´épanouissement personnel et la promotion de l´enrichissement individuel face à un Dieu qui ne veut pas la mort du pécheur, mais qu´il se convertisse et vive une vie abondante, une vie de richesses aussi bien matérielles que spirituelles. Parmi les plus importantes, on compte l´Eglise du Plein Evangile arrivée au Cameroun vers les années 70. La plupart de ces églises pentecôtistes dites de « réveil » sont créées par des pasteurs ou missionnaires d´origine européenne ou américaine. Mais il existe aussi des églises de réveil d´obédience africaine, dont La Vraie Eglise de Dieu du Cameroun de Nestor Toukéa ou celle de Fomun, entre autres. Les années de crise économique et financière que traverse le Cameroun, et leur cortège de

---

1960), (Yaoundé: édition CLE, 2010) 23

[13] Lire l´intéressant article du journal français „Libération“ du 26 février 2016, 24-25

chômeurs, ont été favorable à l´éclosion de ces mouvements souvent taxés par les églises de mission de sectaires, et le sont encore de nos jours, d´où les difficultés d´une collaboration sincère entre ces églises.[14]

Témoignage évangélique par les œuvres

Dès le départ, les missionnaires n´avaient cesse d´accompagner leur travail d´évangélisation par d´activités concrètes, soit de formation ou de guérison des malades, non par la prière plutôt qu´au sein des structures sanitaires qu´ils mettaient sur pied, y compris la construction d´écoles et de centre de formations diverses. Les églises, devenues indépendantes, trouveront dans le secteur des œuvres leurs activités de prédilection, dont l´autre but était de montrer leur grandeur et importance aussi bien aux yeux de l´Etat qu´au yeux des églises-sœurs. On compte actuellement sur l´échiquier camerounais plus de très nombreuses écoles maternelles et primaires de type confessionnel, ainsi que d´écoles secondaires, de centres de santé comme des hôpitaux sur l´ensemble du territoire camerounais, sans oublier des centres de formation techniques professionnelles, entre autres. La tendance cette dernière décennie est celle de la création de structures universitaires. Le pays en compte actuellement une dizaine dont la grande Université Catholique d´Afrique Centrale (UCAC), tout comme l´Université Protestante d´Afrique Centrale (UPAC) dont le début remonte à l´année d´indépendance du pays. En effet, la Faculté de Théologie Protestante est connue comme la première institution universitaire du Cameroun dont l´inauguration a été faite par le tout premier président de la République naissante du Cameroun, Amadou Ahidjo, en 1960, année d´accès du Cameroun à l´indépendance.

En conclusion

Comme on peut le constater, le Cameroun est un pays fortement christianisé, en dépit d´une grande présence musulmane dans le pays. Il est important de noter l´exemplarité de cohabitation entre musulmans et chrétiens dans ce pays où la croyance en Dieu semble bien aller de soi, en même temps que les uns et les autres se respectent dans leurs choix religieux. La liberté du culte y est non seulement assurée par la loi du pays, mais aussi elle va de soi dans les comportements individuels, de sorte que des Camerounais n´auront aucun problème de partir d´une religion à une autre, ou d´une communauté chrétienne à une autre. Seul l´Etat se donne pour tâche de réguler la présence de lieux de cultes et de fermer ceux d´entre eux qui n´auront pas reçu d´autorisation officielle d´implantation.

Bibliographie

Criaud, Jean, *Le geste des spiritains, Histoire de l´Eglise au Cameroun*, 1916-1990, Publication du Centenaire, Yaoundé (1990)

Fath, S., „*Les nouveaux christianismes en Afrique*" In: Afrique contemporaine, (2015), N°252.

Karé, Lode, *Appelés à la liberté. Histoire de l´Eglise Evangelique Luthérienne du Cameroun,* Ansteleveen, Impocep (1990)

Keller, Werner, *The history of the Presbyterian Church in West Cameroon*, with additional chapters by Brustsch, J.R & Schnellbach, Presbook, Victoria (1969)

Kengne Pokam, E., *Les églises chrétiennes face à la montée du nationalisme camerounais*, L´Harmattan, Paris (1987)

[14] On peut lire les publications: Maud Lasseur: „Pluralisme religieux, entre éclatement et concurrence", in: *Politiques Africaines* (2011) N°23; - Sébastien Fath, „Les nouveaux christianismes en Afrique" in: *Afrique contemporaine*, (2015), N°252.

Kirk-Green, A.H.M., Adamwa, *Past and Present. An Historical Approach to the Development of a Northern Cameroons Province*, Oxford University Press, London (1958).

Gongo, L., *Histoire des forces religieuses au Cameroun.* De la Première Guerre mondiale à l´indépendance, Paris, Karthala, (1982)

Lasseur, M., „*Pluralisme religieux, entre éclatement et concurrence*", Politiques Africaines (2011) N°23

Messina, J.P., Slageren, J.v., *Histoire du christianisme au Cameroun : des origines à nos jours*, CLE, Yaoundé (2005)

Maud Lasseur: „*Pluralisme religieux, entre éclatement et concurrence*", Politiques Africaines (2011) N°23

Mveng, Engelbert, *Histoire des églises chrétiennes a Cameroun*: les origines, Presse universitaire UCAC, Yaoundé (1990)

Ngongo, Louis, *Histoire de forces religieuses au Cameroun*, Karthala, Paris (1982)

Ossama, N, *L´Eglise du Cameroun* : Schéma historique (1890-2000), UCAC, (2011)

Sa´ad, A. *The Lamibe of Fombia. A political History of Adamawa* 1809-1903, Ahmadou Bello University Press, Zaria (1977).

Sébastien Fath, „*Les nouveaux christianismes en Afrique*" In: Afrique contemporaine, (2015), N°252.

Slageren, Jaap van, *Les origines de l´Eglise Evangélique du Cameroun, Missions européennes et christianisme autochtone*, CLE, Yaoundé, (2009), Nouvelle édition

(52B) CHRISTIANITY IN CAMEROON

Samuel Désiré Johnson

Introduction

In this chapter we describe the evolution of the Christian landscape in Cameroon – from the nineteenth century to the present. Christian mission and the Muslim conquest took place in the beginning 'from the top' – that is, by the conversion or sensitization of the traditional chiefs; in turn, these persons used their power and authority to convert their subjects. It must also be pointed out that there were organizations and individuals coming from outside the country to promote their religion. Today, we are seeing more and more the evangelization or Islamization 'from the bottom'. This is a phenomenon that one may call a 'second religious globalization'.[1] This is essentially an effort carried out by Cameroonians themselves, some of them even in co-operation with foreign religious organizations. The religious landscape has changed completely in relation to what it was at the beginning of Christian evangelization and the Muslim conquest: 'Cameroon is experiencing a real shake-up in its religious context, which is characterized, not only by a multiplication of worship-related associations, but also by the slow decay of the ethno-regional areas taken over by the large historic Christian and Muslim organizations.'[2] Great mobility now characterizes the various religious movements. We are seeing the creation of many worship-related or religious associations (including NGOs) throughout the whole country, which no longer depends on historic Christian and Muslim organizations.

The Mutation of the Religious Landscape in Christianity

The evangelization of Cameroon took place due to the action of western missionary societies in collaboration with local participants. The communities that resulted are, on the administrative level, managed as branches of the western churches, even if, for their identity, they have a local identity which characterizes and distinguishes them from their mother churches.[3] In general, the churches are planted in the national territory, either in relation to the missionary strategy defined by the western missions, or according to regulation by the colonial authorities. Even though the south of the country has had a Christian missionary presence since the middle of the nineteenth century, Christianity did not arrive in the north until 1920 (Protestants) and 1946 (Catholics). The French administration, guided by a kind of pragmatism, at first tried to discourage the planting of Christian missions in the north.[4] After independence, the Muslim religious authorities also curbed the expansion of Christianity in the north, by refusing to offer land (for the construction of churches), by persecuting Christians and sometimes by burning their churches.[5]

---

[1] In my opinion, the first religious globalization corresponds to the revival of Islam and to the western missionary endeavour of the nineteenth century.

[2] Maud Lasseur, *Cameroun: Les Nouveaux Territoires de Dieu*, in *Afrique Contemporaine 2005/3 (No. 215)*, p.93 (this quotation and the following, my translation).

[3] S.D. Johnson, *La Formation d'une Eglise Locale au Cameroun. Le cas des Communautés Baptistes (1841-1949)* (Paris: Karthala, 2012).

[4] For example, the French missionary Maurice Farrely working for the SMEP, had been expelled from the north when trying to evangelize the *Kirdi* peoples. Later the French administration would soften its position.

[5] Ahidjo, the president of the republic of Cameroon, called on by Pastor Jean Kotto, then President of the FEMEC

The first development in the religious landscape, on the Christian side, took place at the beginning of the 1960s, with the arrival in French-speaking Cameroon of the Pentecostal movements. Before this, Pentecostal churches had been planted only in English-speaking Cameroon.[6] According to J.F. Bayard, it was the reunification of the British and French parts of the country that fostered the multiplication of Pentecostal movements that he calls 'sects'.[7] However, the presence of the Pentecostal movements did not decisively modify the religious landscape of Cameroon. It was still dominated by the so-called historic churches. The Pentecostal churches were despised by the established churches, who ignored them. They were, in fact, supported in this by the government which was suspicious of any movements that it did not control. The Pentecostals even suffered a degree of persecution.[8]

On the Catholic side, we must mention the birth of the Charismatic renewal which is (out of all proportion) the counterpart of the Protestant Pentecostal movement. This movement was characterized by the creation of ecumenical prayer groups in Catholic circles, groups which are not controlled by the hierarchy of the official Roman Catholic Church, and in which lay people play a major role.[9]

The second development took place at a geographical level. The Christian churches moved out of their historic areas, to be planted in zones where they had not been present before. This was particularly through the creation of communities, due to the mobility of business people or civil servants. Because they found themselves in a region where their denomination had not previously existed, they created a prayer cell which grew little by little and became a community linked with their denomination. The church leadership was then asked to send a worker (pastor or evangelist) to finish planting the denomination. This is how churches such as the EEC and the UEBC, which were found mostly on the coast and in the west, reached cities such as Yaoundé and Mbalmayo in the centre and Bertoua in the east. In the same way, the EPC, which historically had been planted in the south, moved its area of oversight to be planted on the coast and in other areas.

The third development in the religious landscape of Cameroon began in the 1990s, following the adoption of laws on public liberties. We then saw a genuine religious democratization. Evangelization became an individual enterprise: 'This spatial expansion... found new vigour... new Churches begin to penetrate the capitals of the administrative departments then the villages. Today, independent Churches start essentially within large urban centres... from which they spread out into the back-country.'[10] As reported by the local media, new churches now sprouted like mushrooms. They seemed to be more active than the so-called historic churches in the area of evangelization. At the same time, there has been a notable change in the organization of churches. While the historic churches are structured within a denomination (Baptists, Reformed, Lutherans, Catholics, etc.), the new churches are individual enterprises led by a guide who has called himself 'pastor', 'apostle' or 'prophet'. We are seeing more and more senior

---

(Council of Protestant Churches), put an end to these exactions. However, that did not keep some Muslim religious and administrative leaders from intimidating Christians.

[6] The very first Pentecostal denomination –*The Apostolic Church in Cameroon* – was planted in Cameroon in 1949. (See Maud Lasseur, *Islam et Christianisme en Movement: Mobilités Géographiques et Changements Religieux au Cameroun*, in *Espace Populations Société* [En ligne], 2010/2-3, http//eps.revues.org/4079, p.181).

[7] J.-F. Bayard, "Les Rapports entre les Eglises et l'Etat au Cameroun de 1958 à 1971," in *Revue Française D'études Politiques Africaines,* No. 80 (1972):79-104.

[8] It must be said that during this period Churches were forbidden to get involved in *politics*, which meant to say things that criticized the action of the government. The fact that they used English did not facilitate the situation. The government systematically refused to grant them an authorization.

[9] Father Pierre Meinrad Hebga, Jesuit priest and exorcist can be considered the founder of the *Charismatic renewal* movement in Cameroon. He discovered this movement while teaching at John Carroll University in Cleveland, Ohio at the beginning of the 1970s. Upon returning to Cameroon, he started the ecumenical community of believers EPHPHATA, which is dedicated to praise and intercession.

[10] Maud Lasseur, *Islam et Christianisme en Mouvement,* 187.

executives from the civil service or private companies discovering a pastoral vocation. They become the 'owners' of a church without having any theological or pastoral training. Their professional activity often serves as a means of recruiting members for their church.[11] The desire for doing evangelization with the goal of creating new communities does not seem to concern them. Generally, these new churches have only one building where the main leader officiates, assisted by henchmen who are completely submissive. Furthermore, the community is managed as a personal possession, administratively, doctrinally and financially.

The fourth and final development which, in my opinion, seems to be the most radical, is the use of television and the internet for evangelization. Since the arrival of cable television, Cameroon has been flooded by American, European, Asian and African channels that broadcast religious programmes all day long. Sermons and other evangelization with sessions of delivery from evil spirits are broadcast. One no longer needs a physical community in order to have a worship service. One can, from home or office, worship via a screen, with a pastor and Christians located thousands of kilometres away that one doesn't know. Theological classes and other types of religious training are accessible by the internet. The doctrinal and academic quality of this training remains quite doubtful.

Conclusion

We have tried to describe the developments that have appeared in the Christian religious landscape of Cameroon, which are also observable within Islamic religion. We have moved from evangelization and Islamization planned and controlled by recognized political and religious authorities, to an evangelization and Islamization brought about by individuals who, even though they represent globally recognized religious movements, act autonomously. We have also noted that the religious landscape has changed fundamentally at the geographic level. We have moved from the former division between a Christian south and a Muslim north to a total break-up of ethno-regional religious territories. Christian churches are now found in the remote areas of north Cameroon, just as mosques (sometimes several of them in the same neighbourhood) are found in the most isolated zones in the south. The same thing can be observed concerning the various Christian denominations which are no longer confined to their historic ethno-regional boundaries. The mosque is no longer a unifying factor; there are so many that there are doctrinal tendencies. Even though charity works such as schools and dispensaries were a Christian specialty, today one sees charity works multiply on the Muslim side, which often worries some Christian churches. These churches suspect Muslims of using them for proselytizing (what they themselves did for a long time). The administration that regulated religious implantation and practice in Cameroon seems to have now lost all control. Worship-related organizations are now planting in an anarchic manner. In addition to the presence on the ground of uncontrolled worship-related associations, the arrival of cable television and the internet makes it possible for foreign preachers to reach Cameroonian populations. The content of these sermons is not always under any form of control, which over time, in our humble opinion, could become a genuine threat to social peace in Cameroon.

Bibliography

Bayard, J. F. 'Les Rapports entre les Eglises et l'Etat au Cameroun de 1958 à 1971.' *Revue Française D'études Politiques Africaines* 80 (1972): 79-104.

Johnson, S. D. *La Formation d'une Eglise Locale au Cameroun. Le Cas des Communautés Baptistes (1841-1949).* Paris: Karthala, 2012.

[11] Sometimes certain employees feel compelled to belong in order to not displease their hierarchic chief who is privately serving as the pastor.

Lasseur, Maud. 'Cameroun: Les nouveaux territoires de Dieu.' *Afrique Contemporaine* 3, no. 215 (2005): 93-116.

Lasseur, Maud, 'Islam et Christianisme en Movement: Mobilités Géographiques et Changements Religieux au Cameroun,' Espace populations société, En ligne], 2010/2-3, http//eps.revues.org/4079 (accessed 27 May 2015).

(53) Christianity in Cape Verde

Max Ruben Ramos

Religion	Pop 2010	Pct 2010	Pop 2025	Pct 2025	Gr Pct 1970 2025
Christians	466,000	95.1%	552,000	94.4%	1.1%
Independents	33,800	6.9%	43,000	7.4%	1.6%
African initiated	1,700	0.4%			
Protestants	17,500	3.6%	25,000	4.3%	2.4%
Adventist	8,700	1.8%			
Holiness	7,700	1.6%			
Roman Catholics	454,000	92.6%	507,000	86.7%	0.7%
Pentecostals/Charismatics	36,000	7.3%	45,000	7.7%	1.5%
Evangelicals	9,800	2.0%	13,000	2.2%	1.9%
Muslims	13,500	2.8%	18,000	3.1%	1.9%
adherents of traditional African religions	5,500	1.1%	7,000	1.2%	1.6%
Baha'is	750	0.2%	1,000	0.2%	2.0%
Jews	62	0.0%	65	0.0%	0.3%
people professing no religion	4,300	0.9%	6,500	1.1%	2.7%
Total population	**490,000**	**100.0%**	**585,000**	**100.0%**	**1.2%**

Source: Centre for the Study of World Christianity (CSGC), Boston, Gordon-Conwell TS

The historical, social, political and cultural accommodation of Christianity in Cape Verde is inseparable from the process of European colonization. The occupation, settlement and spatial organization of this archipelago by the Portuguese in the 1460s established a slave regime. Europeans, Portuguese in particular, and enslaved Africans deported from the neighbouring Guinea Coast constituted its population. Although Cape Verde was only officially inscribed in the proclaimed *Respublica Christiana* with the papal bull of 1533, establishing the Diocese of Santiago, churches were being constructed from 1450 and clergymen were sent to the territory as a prerogative granted by the Pope to the King of Portugal.[1] Catholic missions were supported by the slave trade and priests participated in the human traffic by commercializing slaves and using them for domestic tasks.

Among slaves, conversion to Christianity was compulsory and, as happened in other African countries, they simultaneously attended the Catholic mass and African religious practices. At the start, the presence of the Catholic Church was restricted to two islands, Santiago and Fogo. This Catholicism was characterized by irregular contact between Catholic priests and enslaved Africans in those islands, a transitory and seasonal presence in the rest of the islands, and a scarcity of clergymen in the archipelago. This scenario started to change from 1866 onwards with the establishment of the first Catholic seminary in the island of

[1] Maria Emília Santos and Maria João Soares, “Igreja, Missionação e Sociedade”, in *História Geral de Cabo Verde, Vol. II*, coord. Maria Emília Santos (Lisboa, Praia: Centro de Estudos de História e Cartografia Antiga – Instituto de Investigação Científica Tropical, Instituto Nacional de Investigação Cultural, 2001): 359-508, 364.

São Nicolau, dedicated to graduate local priests and civil servants. During the 1940s and 1950s, the islands experienced a consolidation period of the Catholic catechism following two events that marked a definitive turning-point of Catholicism in Cape Verde: the signature of a Concordat in 1940 and the Missionary Agreement in 1941.[2] The first became a pivotal political instrument by reinforcing the role of the Catholic Church in the public sphere of Cape Verdean society.

The second event opened the archipelago to three Catholic missions: the Congregation of the Holy Spirit, the Salesians and the Capuchins. During this time, one of the most interesting Christian movements emerged from the rural areas of Santiago Island: the *rabelados*.[3] This religious movement emerged in the 1940s as an insurgence against new practices introduced by priests of the Congregation of the Holy Spirit, which intended to ban some practices taken as legacies from African funeral traditions and religious practices of the Santiago Catholic liturgy.[4] The constitution of the *rabelados* community, led by charismatic leaders such as Nhonhô Landim or Nhô Fernando, combined the insurgence against the church and the colonial state. Conflicts of this nature extended in various ways during the post-independence period. The *rabelados* way of life, with its millenarian, prophetic and 'anti-modern' approach and the persecution it suffered, illuminates the overlapping of the religious and political struggles of colonialism. Led by Spiritans and colonial authorities during those decades, this persecution was an attempt to control religion in the public sphere, and it also targeted the Protestant church already established in the islands, with big temples in the core of the villages and cities, the Church of the Nazarene. This church, born in the USA, was established at Cape Verde in the 1900s by João José Dias, a Cape Verdean migrant in t USA, at a time when others religions, except Catholics, were prohibited.[5]

In 1936, Nazarene missionaries from the USA followed Dias. Despite early persecution, the Church of the Nazarene spread to all the islands, gained prestige among the civil authorities and the Cape Verdean society, and became the best-known Protestant church in the islands. In the 1950s, American Nazarene missionaries organized the Nazarene Seminar in the island of São Vicente, where many local pastors were trained. Many exercised their pastorate in Cape Verde; others were sent off as missionaries abroad. In 2009, one of these pastors, Eugénio Rosa Duarte, was elected General Superintendent of the Church of the Nazarene.

Throughout the twentieth century, other Christian denominations emerged in the archipelago: in 1933, the Seventh Day Adventist Church, led by another Cape Verdean migrant from the USA, António Gomes;[6] in the 1950s, the Evangelical Baptist Church, led by Manuel Ramos[7]; and, in 1958, the Jehovah's Witnesses. More recently, with the independence of the country in 1975, another phase of Christianization began with the emergence of other Christian churches. Two of them, the New Apostolic Church and the

---

[2] Cf. Frederico Cerrone, *História da Igreja de Cabo Verde* (Mindelo: Gráfica do Mindelo, 1983): 47.

[3] See Edith Lasierra Muñiz, and Bargados, Alberto López, *Fidjos de Rabelado: Arte y lógicas de contestación en la isla de Santiago de Cabo Verde* (Barcelona: Bellaterra, 2012).

[4] Cf. Muñiz and Bargados, "Fidjos de Rabelado", 42-43.

[5] See Francisco Xavier Ferreira, *Primórdios do Evangelho em Cabo Verde* (Edição do autor, 1972); João Mateus Monteiro, "The Church of the Nazarene in Cape Verde: a Religious Import in a Creole Society". PhD Thesis (New Jersey, Drew University, 1997); Filomena Ramos Lima,. "História da Igreja do Nazareno – Uma Igreja Centenária em Cabo Verde (1901 – 2001) – Uma Perspectiva Educacional". Dissertação de Mestrado – (Faculdade de Letras da Universidade do Porto, 2009). The proclamation of the Portuguese Republic in 1910 allowed, a few months later in February 1911, the introduction of the laws that ensured religious freedom. In the same year, the Christian Rationalist doctrine started to be diffused in the archipelago, mainly in São Vicente Island, gaining sympathy and followers in the Catholic circle. See João Vasconcelos, *Histórias do Racionalismo Cristão em São Vicente, de 1911 a 1940* (São Vicente: Comissão Organizadora da Comemoração do 1° Centenário do Racionalismo Cristão em Cabo Verde, 2011).

[6] See Karl Marx Monteiro, *O que dizer dos Adventistas em Cabo Verde? – Um estudo de caso* (Praia: Tipografia Santos, 2012).

[7] See Manuel Ramos, *A Origem dos Baptistas em Cabo Verde* (Mindelo: Gráfica do Mindelo, 1996).

Church of Jesus Christ of Latter-day Saints, were established at Cape Verde in the 1980s. From the 1990s onwards, the South-South missionary enterprise was established, with the arrival of the Assembly of God, God is Love Pentecostal Church and the Universal Church of the Kingdom of God, from Brazil; Deeper Life Bible Church and Redeemed Christian Church of God from Nigeria; and the Bom Deus Church from Angola.

According to the census of 2010, the vast majority of Cape Verdeans identify themselves as Christians, in particular with the Catholic Church. Recently, this church saw its influence in the public sphere reinforced with the signature of a Concordat in 2013 between the Cape Verdean state and the Vatican City, and with the recent appointment of the first Cape Verdean cardinal, the bishop of the Santiago Diocese, Arlindo Furtado. The alliance between the state and the Catholic Church, increasing the institutional privileges of the latter, was contested in some religious and secular Cape Verdean circles. But the authorities justified it as the recognition to the role of the Catholic Church in the constitution of Cape Verdean identity. These facts testify to the status that is given to the Catholic Church and to Christianity in general, despite its controversial implications for the process of building the secular state.

Bibliography

Cerrone, Frederico. *História da Igreja de Cabo Verde*. Mindelo: Gráfica do Mindelo, 1983.

Ferreira, Francisco Xavier. *Primórdios do Evangelho em Cabo Verde*. Edição do autor, 1972.

Lima, Filomena Ramos. 'História da Igreja do Nazareno – Uma Igreja Centenária em Cabo Verde (1901 – 2001) – Uma Perspectiva Educacional.' Dissertação de Mestrado – Faculdade de Letras da Universidade do Porto, 2009.

Monteiro, João Mateus. 'The Church of the Nazarene in Cape Verde: a Religious Import in a Creole Society.' PhD Thesis, New Jersey, Drew University, 1997.

Monteiro, Júlio. *Os rebelados da ilha de Santiago, de Cabo Verde*. Lisboa: Centro de Estudos de Cabo Verde, 1974.

Monteiro, Karl Marx. *O que dizer dos Adventistas em Cabo Verde? – Um estudo de caso*. Praia: Tipografia Santos, 2012.

Muñiz, Edith Lasierra and Alberto López Bargados. *Fidjos de Rabelado: Arte y lógicas de contestación en la isla de Santiago de Cabo Verde*. Barcelona: Bellaterra, 2012.

Ramos, Manuel. *A Origem dos Baptistas em Cabo Verde*. Mindelo: Gráfica do Mindelo, 1996.

Santos, Maria Emília and Maria João Soares. 'Igreja, Missionação e Sociedade', in *História Geral de Cabo Verde*, Vol. II, coord. Maria Emília Santos (Lisboa, Praia: Centro de Estudos de História e Cartografia Antiga – Instituto de Investigação Científica Tropical, Instituto Nacional de Investigação Cultural, 2001): 359-508.

Vasconcelos, João. *Histórias do Racionalismo Cristão em São Vicente, de 1911 a 1940*. São Vicente: Comissão Organizadora da Comemoração do 1° Centenário do Racionalismo Cristão em Cabo Verde, 2011.

(54A) Le Christianisme en Republique Centraficaine

David Koudougueret

Religion	Pop 2010	Pct 2010	Pop 2025	Pct 2025	Gr Pct 1970 2025
Christians	3,198,000	71.9%	4,535,000	76.3%	2.4%
Independents	811,000	18.2%	1,120,000	18.8%	2.2%
African initiated	764,000	17.2%			
Protestants	719,000	16.2%	950,000	16.0%	1.9%
Dunker	414,000	9.3%			
Lutheran	107,000	2.4%			
Pentecostal	95,700	2.2%			
Evangelical churches	53,900	1.2%			
Disciples	28,900	0.7%			
Roman Catholics	1,386,000	31.2%	1,950,000	32.8%	2.3%
Evangelicals	1,268,000	28.5%	1,778,000	29.9%	2.3%
Pentecostals/Charismatics	842,000	18.9%	1,220,000	20.5%	2.5%
adherents of traditional African religions	611,000	13.7%	550,000	9.3%	-0.7%
Muslims	595,000	13.4%	800,000	13.5%	2.0%
Baha'is	10,800	0.2%	14,000	0.2%	1.8%
people professing no religion	30,200	0.7%	42,800	0.7%	2.3%
Total population	**4,445,000**	**100.0%**	**5,942,000**	**100.0%**	**2.0%**

Source: Centre for the Study of World Christianity (CSGC), Boston, Gordon-Conwell TS

Les ouvriers de la première heure

Le premier contact connu du christianisme avec la République Centrafricaine remonte à l'année1884 lorsque le Pasteur anglais Georg Grenfell de la Baptist Missionary Society (BMS) effectue une expédition exploratoire qui le conduit jusqu'au-delà des rapides de Bangui. La seule donnée disponible relative à cette expédition semble être le tracé du fleuve Oubangui sur une carte.

Le christianisme centrafricain naîtra aux abords de ce fleuve dix années plus tard, en 1894,avec comme pionniers et ouvriers de première heure les intrépides missionnaires spiritains sous l'impulsion de Mgr Philippe Prospère Augouard, Vicaire Apostolique de l'Oubangui-Chari, avec résidence à Brazzaville. Ces derniers constitueront la seule présence chrétienne dans le paysage religieux centrafricain pendant près d'un quart de siècle.

Deux premières bases missionnaires furent implantées au départ: Saint Paul des Rapides à proximité du premier poste administratif colonial, et Sainte Famille de Bessou, au voisinage du poste de Fort de Possel.

Quinze années plus tard deux autres bases seront installées un peu loin des rives de l'Oubangui: Notre Dame des Borossés en 1910 et Saint Joseph de Bambari en 1912.

La scène de pénétration du christianisme en Centrafrique présentait de nombreux défis parmi les quelles croyances ancestrales, certaines pratiques néfastes en vigueur dans les sociétés traditionnelles, les fléaux naturels, les séquelles de l'esclavage, surtout l'esclavage domestique, et la colonisation avec ses pratiques déshumanisantes de portage, de pagayée, de travaux forcés, d'imposition des populations et surtout un pillage organisé des ressources locales au travers des sociétés concessionnaires étrangères.

Les instruments choisis par les premiers missionnaires pour la pose des premières bases de la christianisation du pays étaient l'éducation, l'œuvre médicale, le rachat d'esclaves, l'accueil et l'hébergement des enfants (garçons et filles), l'amitié, l'évangélisation, le catéchuménat, la libération des pratiques ancestrales dévalorisant/dévaluant la personne humaine, un projet de vie différent de celui proposé par les systèmes traditionnels et coloniaux en vigueur dans le pays, ainsi que la pastorale de l'économie (agriculture et élevage).

Une première mission protestante baptiste américaine indépendante, conduite par le pasteur William Clarence Haas, en provenance du Congo Belge a séjourné à Rafai, à l'extrême Est de décembre 1915 à juin 1916. L'essentiel du travail de cette mission a consisté à établir des contacts, s'approprier les premiers éléments du répertoire culturel (lexèmes et morphèmes) qui lui seront très utiles lors du prochain séjour.

Expansion et couverture nationale

Le paysage religieux sera fortement modifié à partir de 1921.En effet, aux bases missionnaires catholiques déjà établies viendront se joindre des dizaines d'autres avec la pénétration de sept missions protestantes dont cinq américaines et deux européennes:la Mid-Africa Mission(MAM),[1] une mission baptiste, et la Mission Evangélique de l'Oubangui-Chari (MEOC)[2]initiées respectivement par William Clarence Haas et James Gribble, pénètrent en 1921 et installent leurs premières bases, la première à Fort Sibut au Centre, Fort Crampel au Nord et à Bangassou à l'Est et la seconde à Bassai, près de Bozoum au Nord-Ouest. La Mission Örebro, une mission baptiste de la Suède, pénètre en 1923 et choisit Bania, dans l'Ouest pour y poser sa première base. L'Africa Inland Mission,une mission évangélique conduite par John Buyse, entre en 1924 et établits a première base à Zémio, à l'extrême Est. La Mission Elim, une mission pentecôtiste avec Oscar Berntz-Land, en provenance de Suisse, implante une base dans la région d'Alindao, à l'Est, en 1927. La Sudan Mission[3] des USA, de tendance évangélique conduite par Gunderson, pénètre par le Cameroun et opte pour Aba, à l'Est pour installer sa base en 1930. En 1939, une autre mission américaine, la Central Africa Pioneer Mission, une autre mission pentecôtiste avec le couple Boyson, entre et établit sa station à Carnot, à l'Ouest.

Ces bases missionnaires contribueront à l'expansion rapide du christianisme sur toute l'étendue du territoire. Un quart de siècle plus tard on pouvait dénombrer une quarantaine de stations missionnaires protestantes et une vingtaine de stations catholiques éparpillées sur la quasi-totalité du territoire.

Les missions protestantes, sans perdre de temps, comme les catholiques, se lancent dans les contacts, les relations d'amitié, l'évangélisation, le catéchuménat, l'éducation formelle et non formelle, la pastorale de développement et de promotion humaine: écoles primaires dont certaines avec internat, œuvres médicales, écoles professionnelles, promotion féminine, etc.

La naissance des premières communautés chrétiennes est suivie du lancement des premières institutions de formation biblique et théologique dès les années 1930. De ces institutions de formation de base sortiront des évangélistes et prédicateurs. Les premiers catéchistes et prédicateurs formés sont envoyés dans les villages pour y implanter des postes d'évangélisation qui deviendront les premières églises locales.

Chez les catholiques, les écoles des catéchistes, les petits séminaires verront le jour. Les premiers grands séminaristes sont envoyés au Cameroun. Un premier prêtre centrafricain, Barthélemy Boganda est formé et ordonné en 1938.

---

[1] Cette appellation changera en 1953 pour devenir BaptistMid-Missions.
[2] Deviendra plus tard Mission Evangélique des Frères.
[3] Prendra plus tard la dénomination de Mission Evangélique Luthérienne.

L'introduction des presses vers la fin de cette période par les différentes missions et la production d'une littérature abondante en langues locales, en Sango et en français pour l'alphabétisation, l'instruction des chrétiens, la formation des premiers leaders des communautés, a été une grande contribution à la lutte contre l'analphabétisme, l'élargissement de l'horizon des populations et la promotions des langues locales et de la langue sango. Les premiers recueils de chants, la littérature biblique. Un premier Nouveau Testament en sangosera publié en 1935.

Sur la route de la liberté

Les années qui suivront la seconde guerre mondiale seront déterminantes pour la vie de la nation centrafricaine. Une quinzaine de nouvelles bases missionnaires, dont sept catholiques et huit protestantes verront le jour.

Toutes les missions vont procéder au renforcement des capacités des leaders autochtones en réaménageant les curricula des institutions de formation biblique et théologique.

Mais la figure dominante de cette période est celle de Boganda, le premier prêtre centrafricain, autorisé par son Evêque à s'investir dans la politique de son pays en vue de barrer la route au communisme et au socialisme. Il se présente aux législatives françaises et est élu à deux reprises comme député puis comme président du pays en 1958 avec l'appui massif de la population.

Il est le grand artisan de l'indépendance de la République Centrafricaine obtenu sans effusion de sang. Sa foi et ses convictions chrétiennes ont joué un rôle de premier plan dans son engagement et sa lutte politiques ayant conduit le pays à la liberté.

L'action politique de Boganda a eu comme répercussions des voies qui se sont déliées pour dénoncer les abus commis sur certaines bases missionnaires. Elle donnera lieu aux premiers schismes dans l'Eglise Protestante: les dénominations « Comité Mission Baptiste » avec le pasteur Simon-Pierre Boymandja et « Eglise Protestante Africaine » avec le pasteur Ayama ont vu le jour suite à l'exclusion de certains leaders par la Baptist Mid Mission à cause de l'appui apporté par ces derniers à la politique de Boganda.

La période post-indépendance

Boganda meut dans un accident d'avion en 1959. Une année après, le pays accède à l'indépendance, ce qui marque un tournant décisif aussi bien dans la vie nationale que dans la vie et les relations entre les différentes missions et les églises qui en sont issues.

Du côté protestant on assiste à la mise en réseaux des églises sous formes d'unions et d'associations: l'Eglise issue de l'œuvre de l'Africa Inland Mission se constitue en Eglise Evangélique Centrafricaine en 1960. Celle issue de la Mission Örebro se regroupe en Union des Eglises Baptistes de l'Ouest en 1962. L'Association Nationale des Eglises Baptistes voit le jour en 1964 et regroupe en son sein toutes les églises issues de l'œuvre de la Baptist Mid-Mission. L'Eglise Evangélique Luthérienne se forme en 1965. L'Union des Eglises Evangéliques des Frères voit le jour en 1968. L'Union des Eglises Evangéliques Elimse crée en 1973.

Un changement important intervient dans le leadership de l'Eglise Catholique: Mgr Joachim Ndayen en devient premier archevêque autochtone en 1968/1969.

L'Alliance des Evangélique en Centrafrique voit le jour en 1974 et regroupe en son sein plus de trois quarts de ces grands ensembles protestants à l'exception de ceux gardant des relations étroites avec la BaptistMid-Missions et la Mission Evangélique des Frères.

Des écoles, instituts et facultés de théologie sont initiées dans le but de former des cadres et renforcer les capacités du leadership chrétien.

Le christianisme dans les multiples crises centrafricaines

La République Centrafricaine a connu une série de crises pendant la période postindépendance dont les plus graves sont celles de 1979, 1982, 1996, 2002-2003 et 2013-2015. La contribution des leaders religieux à tous les niveaux de la résolution de ces conflits est inestimable. L'on peut relever l'implication de l'Archevêque de Bangui dans la résolution des tensions liées aux mutineries en 1996, les différentes lettres pastorales initiées par la Conférence Episcopale de Centrafrique, la conduite du dialogue politique inclusif par le Président de l'Alliance des Evangéliques de Centrafrique, le travail de la Plate-Forme Religieuse (Catholique, Musulman et Protestant) dans la crise née en 2013 avec les mouvements politico-militaires.

Une des particularités des années 2013 est l'introduction et le foisonnement des groupes charismatiques et pentecôtistes dans le paysage religieux centrafricain.

Un fait qui mérite d'être relevé est l'existence d'une certaine superposition des croyances chrétiennes et ancestrales dans la vie d'un certain nombre de pratiquants du christianisme et cela dès les premières heures. Ce qui est perceptible dans certaines occasions et dans les crises que traverse le pays. Des chrétiens n'hésitent pas à recourir à ces croyances et pratiques ancestrales en période de crise.

Bibliographie

Dongombé, Doyari Célestin, *L'Oubangui-Chari et son évangélisation dans le contexte de la politique coloniale française*, Paris, L'Harmattan, 2012.

Gnoka, Michel, *La problématique des confessions de foi des églises protestantes en République Centrafricaine*, Mémoire de Maîtrise en Théologie, Bangui: FATEB, 1983.

Godart, Louis &Zoubé, Cyprien, *De l'esclavage à la liberté*, Bangui: Saint Paul, 1987.

Hamilton, A. Benjamin, *Gribble's Dream...God's Design*, Winona Lake, BMH Books, 1987.

Kalck, Pierre, *Barthélemy Boganda, 1910-1959, élu de Dieu et des centrafricains, Saint-Maur-des-Fossés*, Editions Sépia, 1995.

Kalck, Pierre, *Histoire de la République Centrafricaine*, Paris: Editions Berger-Levrault, 1974.

Koudouguéret, David, *Les applications de la doctrine de la séparation ecclésiastique par la BaptistMid-Missions en République Centrafricaine*, Mémoire de Maîtrise en Théologie, Bangui: FATEB, 1984.

Ngarasso, Nicolas, *Pour une stratégie missionnaire (Avec référence spéciale à la Coopération Evangélique Mondiale et Centrafricaine)*, Mémoire de Maitrise en Théologie, Bangui: FATEB, 1983.

Ngouka Honoré, *La problématique des rapports mission-église en République Centrafricaine,* Mémoire de Maîtrise en Théologie, Bangui: FATEB, 1983.

Pénel, J. Dominique, Barthélemy Boganda, écrits et discours, 1946-1951: la lutedecisive, Paris; L'Harmattan, 1995.

Siango, Basile, Barthélemy Boganda, premier prêtre oubanguien fondateur de la République Centrafricaine, Pierrefitte-sur-Seine, Bajag-Méri, 2004.

Strong, Poly, *Burning Wicks, The Story of Baptist Mid-Missions*, Cleveland: Baptist Mid-Missions, 1984.

Toso, Carlo, *Centrafrique, un siècle d'évangélisation*, Bangui: Conférence Episcopale Centrafricaine, 1994.

Zarndé, René, *Dépendance ou indépendance*, Mémoire de Maîtrise en Théologie, Bangui, FATEB, 1983.

(54B) Le Christianisme en Republique Centraficaine

Jimi Zacka

La Pénétration du Christianisme en Centrafrique

Les missions catholiques s'implantèrent très tôt en Centrafrique, avec la fondation en 1893 de la mission de Saint Paul des Rapides (Spiritains) par Prosper Augouard, nommé vicaire apostolique de l'Oubangui en 1890. À partir de cette mission, les catholiques prirent contact avec plusieurs populations en remontant l'Oubangui et ses affluents et projetant la fondation de missions à l'intérieur du pays. Cependant l'hostilité des populations ne leur permit de fonder une deuxième mission, la mission Saint Joseph de Bambari, qu'en 1920.

C'est à cette époque seulement que commencèrent à arriver les missions protestantes : la Baptist Mid-Mission en 1915 suivie de la Brethren Mission, de la Mission Évangélique de l'Oubangui Chari (MEOC) devenue la Mission évangélique des Frères en 1921. La Swedish Baptist Mission arriva dans le Sud-Ouest du pays en 1923 suivie de la Swiss Pentecostal Missionary Society.[1]

La pénétration des églises protestantes dans l'intérieur du pays s'effectua tardivement, entre 1930 et 1950. Pour les besoins de l'évangélisation, les missionnaires catholiques et protestants réalisèrent d'importantes recherches linguistiques comme le dictionnaire français-banda du père Tisserand (1931). Les missionnaires protestants américains de la Mid mission et de la MEOC privilégièrent le sango et contribuèrent à sa diffusion dans l'ensemble du pays. À partir de l'Indépendance, les églises évangéliques autonomes centrafricaines se multiplièrent par un processus de scissions et de dissidences d'avec les églises européennes ou américaines, contribuant à un développement rapide des adhésions et des conversions.

État Actuel du Christianisme en Centrafrique

Un Christianisme morcelé[2]

Le recensement de 2003 fait apparaître, pour une population totale de 3 151 072 habitants, des résultats instructifs : 85% de la population est composée des chrétiens des diverses appartenances, 10,1% de musulmans et 4,9% d'animistes et autres religions, parmi lesquelles les religions syncrétiques locales (kimbangiste, Nzapa Ti Zandé, Christianisme prophétique en Afrique…), les Bahaï.

La présentation de ces chiffres réduit les pratiques religieuses traditionnelles et la spiritualité qu'elles expriment depuis des siècles sur des modes variés selon les régions et les cultures. Au-delà de leur diversité, elles manifestent généralement la croyance à des esprits multiples, à des forces qui animent le monde et dans lesquelles les âmes des ancêtres viennent se fondre. Elles agissent sur le quotidien des gens et il convient de les écouter, de pactiser avec elles et de se prémunir contre leurs éventuelles mauvaises intentions à l'égard des vivants. Les religions monothéistes (religions du Livre) que sont l'Islam et le christianisme sont comparativement relativement récentes et ces éléments religieux antérieurs n'ont pu être effacés facilement, quels que soient les efforts des nouvelles religions pour ôter ce qui n'est pas compatible

[1] Pierre Kalck, *Histoire de la RCA,* 1992, p.253
[2] Rapport de l'Observatoire Pharos 9.02.2015

avec leurs dogmes. C'est pourquoi des mélanges, des syncrétismes, des cohabitations inattendues existent entre religions traditionnelles, Islam et christianisme.

Reste que la Centrafrique est très majoritairement chrétienne avec une spécificité: les catholiques ne représentent que 35% des chrétiens, tandis que les églises pentecôtistes, prophétiques et évangéliques sont largement majoritaires dans la famille « protestante », conduisant à une très grande variété des dénominations.

Deux grandes alliances existent aujourd'hui : l'Alliance des Evangéliques en Centrafrique (AEC) présidée par le pasteur Guérékoyamé et l'Alliance Pentecôtiste, mais certaines églises indépendantes (Prophétique en Afrique, Kimbanguiste, etc.) n'appartiennent jusque-là à aucune alliance. Les trois principales dénominations membres de l'AEC (qui se retrouvent dans presque toutes les régions du pays, dans 15 des 16 préfectures à l'exception du Nord-est, où la seule véritable présence chrétienne est celle de l'Eglise catholique) sont :

- la Communauté des Églises Apostoliques
- l'Association des Églises de la Coopération Évangélique
- l'Association des Églises Baptistes Évangéliques Centrafricaines

Les autres dénominations importantes sont:

- l'Union des Églises Évangéliques des Frères qui a son fief au Nord, mais s'est implantée au centre, au centre-est et à l'Ouest (non membre de l'AEC).
- l'Association Nationale des Églises Baptistes (ANEB) qui se retrouve au centre, au centre-Est, au Nord et au Sud-est.
- l'Association des Églises Évangéliques Elim qui se concentre dans le Sud-est et le Sud et qui fut la première église pentecôtiste à s'installer dans le pays en 1927.
- l'Association des Églises Évangéliques Luthériennes qui se localise à l'Ouest.
- l'Union Fraternelle des Églises Baptistes qui se localise au Nord, une partie du Nord-Est,
- à l'Ouest, au Sud et au Sud-est.
- l'Église Évangélique Baptiste, qui se situe à l'Ouest et au Sud-ouest.
- la Communion des Églises Baptistes Indépendantes (non membre de l'AEC) qui se situe au centre, au centre-est et au Sud-est.
- l'Union des Églises Baptistes, qui est installée au Sud-est et au centre-est.
- l'Association des Églises Adventistes du 7ème Jour.

L'impact des Églises de Réveil en Centrafrique

Le succès des églises de réveil, de guérison et de délivrance est le phénomène marquant observé depuis les années 1990. Il répond à une demande croissante, de la part des populations, de recours spirituels face aux incertitudes et aux dangers du monde moderne. Ainsi, parfois, une seule chapelle composée de quelques dizaines de croyants, portant un nom distinct et dirigée par un pasteur, peut former, à elle seule, une église.

Cette affluence vers ces églises résulte d'une part, du rapport direct que ces églises établissent entre l'individu et le divin, chacun pouvant donc choisir de prier Dieu à la manière dont il l'entend ; et d'autre part, du fait que les adeptes peuvent suivre à tout moment un nouveau pasteur qu'ils trouveront, par exemple, plus charismatique. Parallèlement, toute personne peut s'ordonner pasteur, sans avoir besoin de la reconnaissance d'une autorité religieuse ou d'un diplôme.

Ainsi, malgré un nombre d'implantations largement supérieur, les nombres de fidèles des églises de réveil est bien moindre que celui des églises instituées. En effet, ces dernières (églises catholiques, églises baptistes ou évangéliques), réparties depuis un siècle sur l'ensemble du territoire, sont institutionnalisées.

Néanmoins, ici aussi, les fidèles des églises de réveil sont largement issus des rangs de l'Église catholique. Celle-ci fut victime, selon ces nouveaux convertis, de son formalisme, de son arrogance, et de ce qui est considéré comme une intellectualisation de la parole de Dieu.

Par conséquent, afin de reconquérir de nouveaux fidèles, l'Eglise catholique tente de renouveler son « offre religieuse » à travers un nouveau mouvement : le Renouveau charismatique. Sa dénomination relève du champ lexical pentecôtiste ; de même que ses méthodes se rapprochent de celles en cours dans ces églises.

Grâce à des campagnes d'évangélisation, la mise en exergue des charismes, et de l'organisation de séances de louanges et de prières, l'Église catholique essaie de remobiliser ses anciens fidèles et d'en acquérir de nouveaux. En dénonçant, à son tour, certaines pratiques, très critiquées aussi par les « *born again* », telle que la lecture de la Bible uniquement effectuée par le prêtre, ce nouveau mouvement tente de proposer une voie médiane.

Si certains convertis, déçus des dérives de quelques pasteurs, choisissent de tester ce nouveau mouvement, celui-ci ne fait pas que des adeptes du côté des catholiques. Ces derniers appréhendent en effet la remise en cause du dogme et de la hiérarchie.

Conclusion

Quoi qu'il en soit, un nouveau paysage du christianisme se dessine actuellement en Centrafrique. À côté des implantations plus anciennes des Églises historiques ou missionnaires, on note la prolifération de nouvelles communautés chrétiennes.

Aujourd'hui, les enjeux missiologiques insistent sur deux notions au contenu voisin : celle de contextualisation (côté protestant) et celle d'inculturation (côté catholique) du christianisme ; ils dissocient le christianisme de la culture occidentale qui l'a longtemps véhiculé, et cherchent à lui donner un christianisme purement centrafricain. Ainsi, les cérémonies cultuelles s'appuient sur les coutumes locales ; les instruments de musique et les danses centrafricains sont introduits dans la liturgie. Ces tentatives, dont la mise en œuvre n'est pas toujours acceptée ni facile, n'ont cependant pas empêché le développement du syncrétisme chrétien.

Par ailleurs, la vitalité de ces Églises concurrentes constitue évidemment un obstacle important à la christianisation devant la marée montante de l'islam. De même, de nombreux observateurs misent sur la capacité des Églises, en tant qu'agents de la société civile, à participer à la rénovation du pays dont elles font partie. Mais cet espoir est tempéré par les crises traversant de nombreuses Églises centrafricaines, dont les problèmes ne sont pas sans rapport avec ceux du reste de la société civile. De manière plus tragique, on a remarqué l'impuissance des Églises dans les crises récentes en République centrafricaine.

(55) Christianity in Chad

Jean-Arnold de Clermont

Religion	Pop 2010	Pct 2010	Pop 2025	Pct 2025	Gr Pct 1970 2025
Christians	4,252,000	35.7%	6,712,000	35.2%	3.1%
Independents	585,000	4.9%	852,000	4.5%	2.5%
African initiated	509,000	4.3%			
Protestants	1,308,000	11.0%	2,100,000	11.0%	3.2%
Evangelical churches	750,000	6.3%			
Brethren	393,000	3.3%			
Roman Catholics	1,760,000	14.8%	2,900,000	15.2%	3.4%
Evangelicals	1,468,000	12.3%	2,309,000	12.1%	3.1%
Pentecostals/Charismatics	786,000	6.6%	1,000,000	5.2%	1.6%
Muslims	6,554,000	55.1%	11,417,000	59.9%	3.8%
adherents of traditional African religions	972,000	8.2%	770,000	4.0%	-1.5%
Baha'is	98,700	0.8%	150,000	0.8%	2.8%
Chinese folk-religionists	3,800	0.0%	5,000	0.0%	1.9%
Buddhists	1,800	0.0%	3,000	0.0%	3.6%
people professing no religion	12,900	0.1%	18,500	0.1%	2.4%
Total population	**11,896,000**	**100.0%**	**19,075,000**	**100.0%**	**3.2%**

Source: Centre for the Study of World Christianity (CSGC), Boston, Gordon-Conwell TS

En 1910 on ne comptait aucun chrétien au Tchad. Ils seraient aujourd'hui 22,8% de la population[1], soit 2'925'000, dont 1'283'000 protestants, 847'000 catholiques et 795'000 chrétiens 'indépendants'.

Cette progression en un siècle tient aux missions protestantes arrivées dès 1917. Les missionnaires venaient des pays du Sud (Ex Congo français ou Congo belge.) où des œuvres étaient déjà installées. Les pays d'origines des premiers missionnaires étaient l'Amérique du Nord, le Canada, l'Australie, la Nouvelle Zélande, les pays nordiques, la Suisse et l'Allemagne et en moindre pourcentage la France, jusqu'aux années 1960.Les Églises du Tchad ont vécu une extension assez rapide, manifestant un dynamisme remarquable surtout parmi les populations d'origines animistes, parmi lesquelles il y a eu de nombreuses conversions.

Les premières missions s'implantant au Tchad, ont pu chacune décider d'un 'secteur' d'évangélisation dans ce grand pays. Depuis les années 1960-70, d'autres missions se sont implantées, cette fois surtout françaises et européennes, elles ont créé nombre d'églises. Il faut remarquer que la plupart des églises de la 'seconde vague' ont été aussi des églises évangéliques. Le Tchad est un pays qui a encore peu d'églises dites 'd'initiatives africaines'.

[1] *World Christian Encyclopedia*, vol 1, ed by D. Barrett, G. Kurian, T. Johnson, 2nd ed., Oxford Unity Press, 2001, 181.

Néanmoins les églises nombreuses, ont un peu de peine à réellement travailler ensemble. Il faut saluer des actions positives, telle 'l'Entente des Églises et Missions Évangéliques du Tchad'(EEMET). Une autre initiative est celle de l'Alliance des Eglises Evangéliques de Pentecôte du Tchad (AEEPT). A ce jour les responsables de la plupart des églises regrettent de devoir lutter, contre une tendance au retour des membres d'églises vers les traditions africaines, voire une orientation à un certain syncrétisme entre pratiques évangéliques et pratiques traditionnelles. Les enseignants et théologiens s'appliquent à corriger ces dérives. Les ambitions musulmanes (une mosquée dans chaque village du Tchad) influencent le pays. Les tchadiens en général et les chrétiens également sont aussi attirés par cette religion montante. C'est un problème quotidien des églises. Il faut toutefois noter que la constitution tchadienne est délibérément laïque.

Du côté catholique, les missions sont arrivées peu après les protestantes. Mais la mission du Tchad était sous la responsabilité du vicariat catholique de Khartoum. Dès 1929, les catholiques français s'inquiétant de l'implantation protestante déclarèrent y envoyer une mission. L'église catholique dispose aujourd'hui de 6 diocèses, et d'un vicariat apostolique.

Les Eglises tant catholiques que protestantes sont toutes impliquées dans le domaine de l'éducation avec, notamment, pour les protestants, une croissance ininterrompue d'écoles protestantes depuis la dernière décennie du XXe siècle et qui prennent en charge aujourd'hui plus de 5% des enfants scolarisés dans le pays. Il faut noter l'édification du premier lycée-collège Évangélique à N'Djaména créé en 1964, et géré aujourd'hui par l'église, qui enseigne près de 1200 élèves, dont un bon nombre sont musulmans et notés comme les autres sur des devoirs de religion et de Bible.

Les activités sociales des églises sont assez récentes hormis, dès le départ, des dispensaires et écoles primaires comme moyen d'évangélisation. Depuis les années 1970, les engagements des missionnaires et des églises se sont développés dans d'autres secteurs (agriculture, nutrition, santé, microcrédit, orphelinat, etc...). Les églises s'engagent dans un certain nombre de secteurs médicaux et des membres formés s'engagent au Tchad, souvent dans le cadre des activités sociales des églises.

Il faut mentionner nombre d'Instituts Bibliques en langues vernaculaires, d'Instituts Bibliques en langue française et deux écoles de théologie, qui forment au niveau de la licence de théologie.

Un même dynamisme se manifeste dans le domaine de l'action sociale et de l'évangélisation

Les Eglises sont très attentives aux relations interreligieuses et participent chaque année à une 'journée de prière pour la paix, la cohabitation pacifique et la concorde nationale'.

Perspectives d'avenir.

Les églises devront faire face à deux problématiques:

Les tendances internes à l'Islam à l'échelle sous régionale et internationale mettront-elles en danger la coexistence aujourd'hui pacifique des deux religions? Ceci ajouté au mouvement de renouveau dans l'arabisation du pays qui fait craindre, dans l'inconscient collectif des chrétiens, une « islamisation » du Tchad. Il y a donc là des points de tension à surveiller.

L'autre défi de l'Eglise est de pouvoir faire entendre sa voix dans l'espace public. Il lui faudrait, pour cela, se pourvoir d'une vision du monde biblique et chrétienne qui lui soit propre, en cohérence avec ses fondements, ses valeurs et sa foi. Dotée de cette ossature, elle pourra se positionner de façon pertinente en développant une force de proposition dans les différents problèmes de société touchant le pays. C'est aujourd'hui ce qui lui manque face aux visions dominantes du monde en présence. Car, entre matérialisme à l'occidentale et Islam (qui, au-delà d'être une simple spiritualité, propose une vision du monde cohérente), l'Eglise du Tchad peine à se faire entendre.

(57A) CHRISTIANITY IN THE DEMOCRATIC REPUBLIC OF CONGO[1]

Lubunga W'ehusha

Religion	Pop 2010	Pct 2010	Pop 2025	Pct 2025	Gr Pct 1970 2025
Christians	62,834,000	95.3%	100,160,000	95.8%	3.2%
Independents	17,814,000	27.0%	27,850,000	26.6%	3.0%
African initiated	14,706,000	22.3%			
Orthodox	12,600	0.0%	16,000	0.0%	1.6%
Protestants	12,315,000	18.7%	19,300,000	18.5%	3.0%
Pentecostal	2,467,000	3.7%			
Reformed, Presbyterian	1,710,000	2.6%			
Baptist	1,533,000	2.3%			
Methodist	1,400,000	2.1%			
Evangelical churches	1,368,000	2.1%			
Disciples	1,034,000	1.6%			
Adventist	796,000	1.2%			
Anglicans	500,000	0.8%			
Mennonite	431,000	0.7%			
Congregational	403,000	0.6%			
Roman Catholics	35,807,000	54.3%	55,500,000	53.1%	3.0%
Pentecostals/Charismatics	20,548,000	31.2%	32,500,000	31.1%	3.1%
Evangelicals	4,480,000	6.8%	7,137,000	6.8%	3.2%
adherents of traditional African religions	1,561,000	2.4%	2,000,000	1.9%	1.7%
Muslims	916,000	1.4%	1,370,000	1.3%	2.7%
Baha'is	267,000	0.4%	420,000	0.4%	3.1%
Hindus	93,300	0.1%	150,000	0.1%	3.2%
adherents of new religious movements	5,300	0.0%	10,000	0.0%	4.3%
Buddhists	3,500	0.0%	6,000	0.0%	3.6%
Jews	370	0.0%	400	0.0%	0.5%
people professing no religion	259,000	0.4%	420,000	0.4%	3.3%
Total population	**65,939,000**	**100.0%**	**104,536,000**	**100.0%**	**3.1%**

Source: Centre for the Study of World Christianity (CSGC), Boston, Gordon-Conwell TS

[1] In this essay I have often used the Democratic Republic of Congo along with the old name "Kongo", which comes from the former Kingdom of Kongo through which Christianity entered the country.

Introduction

The development of Christianity in the Democratic Republic of Congo (hereafter DRC) is closely linked with the history of the country. The ever-changing political landscape of the DRC has played a tremendous role in Christianity as it stands today. From the time of Portuguese explorers to the current global world, each era has put its mark on Christianity in the DRC. This essay aims at surveying the development of Christianity in three major epochs of the history of the country: the pre-colonial, colonial and post-colonial.

The Pre-Colonial Era

Portuguese Missionaries

The DRC was first exposed to Christianity by Portuguese missionaries who came to the country following the visit of the Portuguese explorer, Diego Cao, who reached the mouth of the River Kongo in 1482. The Kingdom of Kongo was located along the coastal part of the Atlantic Ocean, extending on both sides of the River Kongo, from Angola to Kabinda and part of Congo Brazzaville. Its population was estimated at two and a half million.[2] Diego Cao found that people of the Kingdom of Kongo were friendly and he strove to establish a relationship between the two monarchies[3] by making several expeditions to the Kingdom of Kongo. His fourth expedition of 1491 is considered as decisive in the Christian history of Kongo because it brought into the Kingdom the Roman Catholic missionaries. The chief of the coastal province of Soyo, Mani Soyo, was the first to be baptised and two months later the King himself, Nzinga Nkuvu, the Mani Kongo, was baptised and renamed Joao I, in honour of the King of Portugal, Joao II.[4]

Christianity flourished during the reign of Mvemba Nzinga, one of the sons of King Nzinga Nkuvu, renamed Afonso after baptism, who converted to Christianity with his mother. The King himself backslid after a short while because he was opposed to burning his fetishes and the preaching against polygamy, but Prince Afonso was a dedicated Catholic. After the death of King Nzinga Nkuvu in 1506, Afonso, assisted by the Portuguese, fought and defeated another son and all his enemies and established a Christian kingdom. During his reign, more missionaries came to Kongo and Alfonso sent many people to be trained as priests, government officials and medical workers. Among people sent by Afonso was his son Henrique who became a priest and eventually the first Catholic bishop from Kongo in 1518.[5] The Christian King Afonso wanted his son to strengthen Christianity in the kingdom but he was not allowed to serve his own people. Since the Portuguese opposed the creation of a diocese in Kongo, Bishop Dom Henrique was sent to work in Tunisia, fell ill, and eventually went to Rome where he died in 1526.[6]

After the death of King Afonso I in 1543, the kingdom declined, as well as Christianity. Subsequent kings were no longer interested in Christianity and the Portuguese became more interested in settling in Angola than in the Kongo. Slowly, people returned to their traditional beliefs, while the Portuguese invested more of their time in the slave trade than in evangelization.[7] Despite the support and personal involvement of the royal family, this early Christianity started to decline, to disappear altogether by 1790.

---

[2] Jonathan Hildebrandt, *History of the Church in Africa: A Survey* (Denver, Co: Academic Books, 1990), 62.

[3] Nimi a Nzima, ruler of Mpemba Kasi (Congo Kingdom), made an alliance with Nsaku Lau, the ruler of the neighbouring Southeastern Mbata Kingdom. These kingdoms made an alliance to co-exist and helped to ensure the succession of their ally's lineage in their territories.

[4] Adrian Hastings, *The Church in Africa 1450-1950* (Oxford: Clarendon Press, 1994), 73.

[5] John K. Thornthon, "Afro-Christian Syncretism in the Kingdom of Kongo," *Journal of African History* 54 (2013): 53-77, 62.

[6] Daywel èZiem, "Henrique, Dom, C. 1495 to C.1526 Roman Catholic Kongo (D.R. Congo)." *Dictionary of African Christian Biography.* www.dacb.org/stories/demrepcongo/henrique_dom.html (accessed 17/02/2015).

[7] Hildenbrandt, *History of the Church in Africa,* 68.

Early Enculturation of the Gospel

People who received the gospel in the Kingdom of Kongo tried to adapt it to their own culture. This indigenisation was often accompanied with syncretism, as in the case of a young Kongolese woman, Dona Beatrice Kimpa Vita (1684-1706). In 1704, when she turned 20, Dona Beatrice Kimpa Vital declared that she met Saint Anthony in a dream and was charged with a message of restoring the Kingdom of Kongo. She moved to the old capital city, Saõ Salvadore, where she preached her message and made a number of converts. There were three major points in her message: first, Saint Anthony was the patron of all saints, and people should pray only to him. Secondly, she announced impending punishment because Jesus was angry with the Kongolese people. They needed to ask for mercy. Thirdly, Saint Anthony was about to deliver good things to his devotees.[8] This last point included having black saints instead of white ones, thereby contradicting the teaching of Capuchin missionaries. She changed the story of the Nativity and declared that Jesus was black as well as Kimpa Vita's mother, and had been born in Kongo. She even modified the prayer of *Ave Maria* and *Salve Regina and*, adding her own words. Her teaching was considered heretical by the Roman Catholic Church. As many people were being drawn to her in the ruins of the old capital of Kongo, she was arrested and burned as a witch and heretic in 1706.[9]

The Colonial Era

The expedition of Henry Morton Stanley, an American journalist sent to find David Livingstone, who was considered as lost in the heart of Africa, should be mentioned as the most important event that opened the door for the re-evangelization of the Kongo by both Catholics and Protestants. In his endeavour to verify if Lualaba was the source of Nile, Stanley followed the River Kongo from its source in Katanga Province to the Atlantic Ocean to the west, about 2,000 miles, for a trip which lasted from 1874 to 1877 during which as many as 90% of his support team perished. He was the first European to cross the country from east to west and his report indicated that the country was densely populated and rich in resources – if somebody were ready to invest money. The publication of the report of this expedition in Europe caused, on the one hand, the Belgian King Leopold II to fight and obtain the Kongo as his personal domain, the Free State of Kongo, at the Congress of Berlin in 1885. On the other hand, British Baptists, touched by the plight of the unreached people in the interior of Kongo that Stanley met in his expedition along the River Kongo, were prompted to send missionaries to the country. I will show how these two movements contributed to the development of Christianity in the DRC.

Belgian and Roman Catholic missionary work

As argued earlier, early Portuguese Christianity had died out towards the end of the eighteenth century in the DRC, moving to Angola where it continued its mission. Catholic missionaries from the neighbouring French colony of Brazzaville were the first to establish some mission work in the River Kongo region in 1866.

After what has been termed the 'Scramble for Africa',[10] King Leopold II of Belgium inherited the Kongo as his own domain, the Free State of Kongo, in 1885, but he had been funding Stanley to explore and develop the country since 1877. Since King Leopold II was a Roman Catholic, at first he wanted only Belgian Roman Catholic missionaries to work in his territory. Therefore, the work started by French Roman Catholics was to be taken over by Belgian Roman Catholics. Moreover, King Leopold II 'distrusted

---

[8] For more details see, John K. Thornton, *The Kongolese Saint Anthony: Dona Beatriz Kimpa Vita and the Antonian movement, 1684-1706* (Cambridge: University Press, 1998).

[9] Hastings, *The Church in Africa 1450-1950,* 107.

[10] Thomas Pakenham, *The Scramble for Africa 1876-1912* (London: Weidenfeld and Nicolson, 1991). This book describes how Europeans rushed to divide up the African continent into pieces for their colonisation and enrichment.

French and Portuguese missionaries as being likely to further their respective countries' colonial aspirations'.[11] King Leopold II soon realised that the DRC was such a big territory that Belgian Roman Catholics alone could not reach the whole country. He therefore allowed other Europeans, even Protestant missionaries, to establish their mission work in the country, as I discuss below. But because King Leopold II was a Catholic, he especially encouraged the Catholic Church to expand in the Congo.

After the cession of the Congo Free State to the Belgian government in 1908, the Roman Catholic Church remained the prominent religion of the Belgian colony. As a favoured religion, the Roman Catholic Church occupied urban cities and was given free lands by the government to pursue their mission in the Congo. In 1914, more different Roman Catholic bodies were at work in the Belgian Congo than in any other political entity in Africa south of the Sahara. These included Jesuits, priests of the Sacred Heart of Jesus, Trappists, Premonstratensians, Redemptionists, the Mill Hill Fathers, Benedictines and Capuchins, Dominicans and Salesians, Brothers of Christian Schools, Brothers of Charity of Gand, the Marists Brothers, the Sisters of Charity of Gand, the Sisters of Our Lady of Namur, the White Sisters and Franciscan Missionaries.[12]

The colonial government favoured Roman Catholic missionaries by giving them financial assistance and making laws which helped the work of the Catholic Church. As a result, the Catholic Church was quite strong by 1960 and its membership very large.

It should be noted that, when King Leopold II took possession of the country, he was not interested in building schools. The whole of the education system and all health facilities came from Catholic and, to a lesser part, Protestant mission work.

Protestant Missionaries

After the publication of Stanley's report on the Kongo, a group of British Baptists decided to create what they called the Livingstone Inland Mission (LIM), because Stanley gave the name of Livingstone to the Kongo River. Its objective was to establish mission stations from the coast to Stanley Pool. The first missionaries of the LIM began working in the DRC in 1878. They progressed up the river, building small mission posts which later on would be transformed into full mission stations with schools and health facilities. After seven years of hard work and multiple challenges caused by sicknesses, the lack of roads and ignorance of local languages, LIM decided in 1884 to hand over its pioneer work of seven active mission stations (actually, ten in total, some having been abandoned before) to the American Baptist Mission Union (ABMU). Together with LIM, the Baptist Missionary Society (BMS) of England was also pioneering some work in the same area. Later, in 1884, the society got a ship which allowed them to reach their target of Stanley Pool while creating more stations along the Kongo River.

After a successful beginning by the Baptists from England and America, more American missions joined the work in the DRC. The main reasons for attracting more Americans was that King Leopold II was confident that Americans would not try to take his Kongo Free State away from him as some Europeans (France, Germany and Portugal) had attempted. It is said that King Leopold II 'formed a marriage of convenience with the British Baptists, to whom he gave tax concessions and land grants in return for their support'.[13]

During the colonial period (1908-1960), more Protestant mission work was started in the Congo. In 1910, the Africa Inland Mission (AIM) became the first Christian organisation to start work in Congo from the east. At an early stage, other missionary organisations used the permission given to AIM to enter the east under the aegis of the AIM. But during the colonial period, more churches entered the country through

[11] Elizabeth Isichei, *A History of Christianity in Africa; From Antiquity to the Present* (Grand Rapids, MI: W.B Eerdmans, 1995), 188.
[12] Hildebrandt, *History of the Church in Africa,* 167.
[13] Isichei, *A History of Christianity in Africa,* 188.

the east, such as the Swedish Evangelical Free Church, Assemblies of God, Norway's Free Evangelical Mission, the British Pentecostal Union Mission, and the African Mission and Evangelization Society.[14]

One major achievement of the Protestant church in Congo was that Protestant missionaries (especially Americans and Swedish) working there saw and reported to the world the atrocities being committed by King Leopold II to those citizens who did not meet the quota of red rubber and ivory. The news spread and more confirmation was brought to the public so that world opinion forced the Belgian government to take the Congo Free State away from King Leopold II.[15]

Although Protestant churches were active in building schools, hospitals and clinics, most of them struggled financially to run their institutions because, until 1948, only Roman Catholics were given subsidies for education. In order to address their problems with the government, they organised what was called the Congo Protestant Council (CPC), though not all Protestant missions joined it. Its first meeting was held in Kinshasa in 1902. First, it was decided to meet after two years, but after 1940 the Council had annual meetings.[16] Many Congolese agree that the CPC was more a gathering for missionaries, while deep divisions were maintained between different denominations. The United Church of Christ in Congo had yet to come onto the scene (after independence). But it is important to think of independent churches that emerged during the colonial regime.

African Independent Churches

In the DRC, the Kimbanguists remain the most popular and best organised independent church. Simon Kimbangu, the church's founder, was born in 1989 in the village of Nkamba, in the province of Lower Kongo, where he was baptised with his wife and became a member of the Baptist Church in July 1915.[17] In 1921, he professed to have had a divine commission for the people of the DRC. He healed a critically ill woman called Nkiantondo, followed by several miracles. This attracted great crowds to Nkamba, which is now the Holy Jerusalem of the Kimbanguists. Besides this crowd of followers, Kimbangu's colleagues, *Bangunza* or prophets, taught that one day the black people would overthrow the colonial regime. But his followers maintain that Kimbangu had always advocated obedience to the civil authorities. Kimbangu insisted on monogamy and abstinence from alcohol and narcotics. He became a threat to the Belgian administration.[18]

The Belgian government persecuted and arrested Kimbangu in September 1921 and he was kept in prison until his death in 1951. His movement was forsaken by both Catholics and Protestants and the church went underground for many years, during which the wife of Kimbangu, Mary Muilu, was considered as the spiritual leader. The church was recognised on the eve of Independence in 1959 as *Eglise de Jésus Christ sur la Terre par le prophète* Simon Kimbangu (EJCSK). It would become a strong community after Independence.

The Post-colonial Era

Christianity in the DRC changed tremendously after Independence. The Catholic Church could no longer remain dominant, though many leaders who led the country after Independence had graduated from Catholic schools. The religious landscape began to change rapidly as Protestant churches and Kimbanguists were allowed to expand. Independence broke all the boundaries of missionary fields and

[14] Hildebrandt, *History of the Church in Africa,* 167.
[15] Isichei, *A History of Christianity in Africa,* 435.
[16] Viola L. Smith, *Bâtir Sur le Roc* (Kinshasa: MediaSPaul, 1966), 265.
[17] Hastings, *The Church in Africa 1450-1950,* 508.
[18] Isichei, *A History of Christianity in Africa,* 199-200.

privileges given to the Roman Catholic Church. Although the Catholic Church continued to increase and reform under the leadership of Cardinal Malula, it was no longer as prominent as it had been.

When President Mobutu Sese Seko introduced his policy of 'authenticity' in the early 1970s as a recovery or return to traditional African values, Christianity in Zaire was deeply affected. In 1972, he made it obligatory that all Christian names be replaced with African ones. He put a ban on religious broadcasting, church youth groups and religious publications. He also nationalised the Catholic university, the Lovanium and Protestant University of Kisangani. After 1972, only three Christian churches were allowed to operate, namely, the Protestants (who became *Eglise du Christ au Zaire,* ECZ, or the United Church of Christ in Zaire), the Roman Catholics and the Kimbanguists. Churches that were not affiliated to ECZ continued to operate illegally in the country.[19] Cardinal Malula, despite leading the enculturation and modifying Catholic rituals and attires to reflect African values, became very critical of the despotism of Mobutu's regime, which led him to have frequent trouble from the government.

Mobutu's decision to have one Protestant Church, ECZ, had a positive effect among Protestants. The strong unity of the Protestant Church was due first to political pressure from Mobutu's regime which wanted just a few unified bodies as religious interlocutors with the government. On the other hand, the momentum generated by the synergy of working together as one body has consolidated the unity of Christianity in a way that had never before been experienced, not even during the missionary era.

As for the Kimbanguist movement, the post-colonial era marks the end of its clandestine operation and the start of its blossoming. After official recognition by the government on the eve of Independence in 1959, the leadership was given to Joseph Diangienda Kuntima, the youngest son of the prophet Kimbangu who had died in 1951. His senior brother, Solomon Dialungana Kiangani, succeeded him until his death in 2001. His son, Simon Kimbangu Kiangani, succeeded him and was the current spiritual leader at the time of writing. The church has spread to other African countries as well as overseas, and has earned esteem and recognition all over the world. The Kimbanguist Church is the first independent church to be given full affiliation in the World Council of Churches since 1969.

Alongside their father, the two former spiritual leaders have, after their death, been connected in a surprising and highly problematic way with the Christian doctrine of the Trinity in recent Kimbanguist belief and preaching. It is not surprising that the former name of 'Church of Christ' by the prophet Kimbangu is no longer used. This anti-Christian development of Kimbanguist doctrine, considering Simon Kimbangu and his sons to be forming the divine Trinity, has weakened ecumenical co-operation between the Kimbanguists and other Christian churches (ECC and Catholics). Some scholars hold this belief to be only 'symbolic', while the current leadership of the church seems to uphold this teaching as fundamental to Kimbanguism. It is an ongoing debate which has been followed up by the WCC and its members.

Current Trends in Christianity and Conclusion

While Christianity in the DRC is still dominated by the three major bodies, Catholics, Protestants and Kimbanguists, the current trend is towards diversification and division. The charismatic movement, which started in the form of small prayer groups, developed rapidly into a full charismatic flow that drew members from major established churches. There seems to be no brake on its diversification since new forms and congregations are steadily being born without restriction. The terrain is favourable to the proliferation of these prophetic and miracle-driven movements since the country experiences a weakened political leadership after years of wars and tribal conflicts. There is no authority controlling this new form of Christianity, and people are being attracted and galvanized by unconventional forms of worship, the performance of miraculous signs, and the promise of instantaneous healing, wealth and well-being without

[19] Isichei, *A History of Christianity in Africa,* 344.

any effort. Curiously, adherents of the new movements are recruited from all social strata of society, especially among urban citizens where these Christian stars have a receptive audience.

The movement provides an opportunity for those marginalised by the mainline churches (women and people without theological training) to assert their charisma and occupy leadership positions in the 'body of Christ'. The architects of this new trend are to be found among Nigeria's bishops and prophets as well as some TBN broadcasters. Every preacher of this movement is doing their best to imitate Christian stars and present the message of a quick fix for all the problems of poverty and sickness. In a country that has been torn apart by years of war and in which the rate of unemployment is estimated at over 60% of its population; it is therefore understandable that hungry and desperate people accept this 'new form of liberation'. It is hard to gauge the future of this movement. Sexual orientation was not a big issue among Christians a few years ago but now, with exposure to global media, the voices of those who feel discriminated against because of their sex orientation are being raised. They will likely find a more receptive ear in the new pluralistic religious landscape than in the mainline churches.

The major result of this trend is that the three major Christian organisations, Catholics, Protestants and Kimbanguists, live under threat and are showing real signs of working together and of ecumenical co-operation for survival. Can this lead to a more religiously tolerant society? Further diversification is predictable; so the future of Christianity in the DRC lies in the capacity to be flexible and accommodating without compromising one's faith.

Bibliography

Hastings, Adrian. *The Church in Africa 1450-1950.* Oxford: Clarendon Press, 1994.

Hildebrandt, Jonathan. *History of the Church in Africa: A Survey.* Denver, Co: Academic Books, 1990.

Isichei, Elizabeth, *A History of Christianity in Africa; From Antiquity to the Present*. Grand Rapids, MI: W.B Eerdmans, 1995.

Smith, Viola L. *Bâtir Sur le Roc.* Kinshasa: MediaSPaul, 1966.

Thornton, John K. 'Afro-Christian Syncretism in the Kingdom of Kongo,' *Journal of African History* 54 (2013): 53-77.

Thornton, John K. *The Kongolese Saint Anthony: Dona Beatriz Kimpa Vita and the Antonian Movement, 1684-1706.*Cambridge: University Press, 1998.

(57B) CHRISTIANITY AU REPUBLIC OF CONGO-BRAZZAVILLE

Fred O. Biyela

Religion	Pop 2010	Pct 2010	Pop 2025	Pct 2025	Gr Pct 1970 2025
Christians	3,645,000	89.6%	5,402,000	90.3%	2.7%
Independents	520,000	12.8%	730,000	12.2%	2.3%
African initiated	434,000	10.7%			
Orthodox	440	0.0%	600	0.0%	2.1%
Protestants	456,000	11.2%	580,000	9.7%	1.6%
Congregational	374,000	9.2%			
Pentecostal	40,500	1.0%			
Roman Catholics	2,763,000	67.9%	4,160,000	69.5%	2.8%
Pentecostals/Charismatics	845,000	20.8%	1,200,000	20.1%	2.4%
Evangelicals	212,000	5.2%	245,000	4.1%	1.0%
adherents of traditional African religions	196,000	4.8%	220,000	3.7%	0.8%
Muslims	57,200	1.4%	85,000	1.4%	2.7%
Baha'is	26,300	0.6%	45,000	0.8%	3.6%
adherents of new religious movements	17,000	0.4%	26,000	0.4%	2.9%
Chinese folk-religionists	290	0.0%	500	0.0%	3.7%
Buddhists	180	0.0%	300	0.0%	3.6%
people professing no religion	124,000	3.1%	204,000	3.4%	3.4%
Total population	**4,066,000**	**100.0%**	**5,983,000**	**100.0%**	**2.6%**

Source: Centre for the Study of World Christianity (CSGC), Boston, Gordon-Conwell TS

À cheval sur l'équateur en Afrique centrale, le Congo-Brazzaville couvre une superficie de 342.000 km^2. Estimée à environ 4,5 millions d'habitants, la population congolaise est chrétienne à 89,9%, dont 62% de catholiques, 12,7% de protestants (notamment ceux de l'Église Évangélique du Congo), 13% de fidèles des nombreuses Églises prophétiques ou de réveil.[1] Loin d'opérer une étude exhaustive du christianisme au Congo-Brazzaville, cette contribution dresse en quatre temps forts un aperçu chronologique des Églises chrétiennes dans la tumultueuse histoire politique de cet État laïc.

Premières Missions Chrétiennes durant L'Occupation Européenne (1483-1945)

L'ancien royaume du Kongo, duquel deux pays tirent leur nom, recouvrait une partie des territoires actuels du Congo-Brazzaville, de la RDC, de l'Angola et du Gabon. Ce royaume, qui déclina au 18e siècle, connut

[1] D'après les statistiques religieuses datées de 2010, établies par le *Center for the Study of Global Christianity* du *Gordon-Conwell Theological Seminary* (Bernard Coyault, « Figures prophétiques... », 92-93). Cependant, Bernard Coyault prévient contre toute « illusion fixiste de mono-appartenances » dans le contexte du Congo-Brazzaville (*Ibid.*).

une première évangélisation de missionnaires catholiques européens après que le navigateur portugais Diego Cão franchit l'embouchure du fleuve Congo en 1483. Le roi Nzinga Nkuwu fut baptisé en 1491 sous le nom de João 1er. De nouveaux convertis opérèrent, par la suite, une résistance contre l'occupation portugaise. Des prophètes comme Francisco Kassola en 1632, Kimpa Vita en 1704, furent à l'origine des premiers mouvements syncrétiques.[2] La contestation s'amplifiait devant les atrocités dont se rendaient complices les missionnaires : traite négrière, méthodes rappelant la Croisade et la Contre-réforme, répression des « hérétiques » brûlés vifs, proscription des traditions locales jugées « fétichistes » ; autant de circonstances propices à l'interruption de l'évangélisation européenne.

Les missionnaires chrétiens revinrent à partir de la seconde moitié du 19e siècle ; leur évangélisation prit corps jusqu'aujourd'hui. Il en est ainsi des religieux de la Congrégation du Saint Esprit arrivés peu après le début de la colonisation française.[3] C'est le 25 août 1883 que monseigneur Hyppolyte Carrie fonda la première mission catholique à Loango. La mission protestante commença en 1909 avec l'œuvre des missionnaires suédois de la Svenska Missionsförbundet.[4] Ces derniers donnèrent naissance à l'actuelle Église Évangélique du Congo (EEC), la plus importante confession religieuse au Congo-Brazzaville après l'Église catholique romaine. En 1937, l'Armée du Salut s'installa dans le Congo français avec un succès rapide. En effet, les croyances locales attribuaient à ce mouvement protestant la vertu de protéger ses adeptes contre toute agression sorcellaire. Outre la construction des édifices religieux et la formation catéchétique des fidèles, l'évangélisation catholique et protestante s'accompagna d'actions sociales telles que les constructions d'écoles ou de dispensaires et bien d'autres œuvres caritatives.

Les Églises Chrétiennes dans le Contexte de la Décolonisation (1945-1963)

Avec l'autonomie progressive des colonies françaises d'Afrique, l'action sociale catholique et protestante renforça la société civile : création en 1951 d'un syndicat chrétien, fondation en 1952 de l'hebdomadaire catholique *La Semaine africaine*, le plus ancien organe de presse du Congo-Brazzaville. En outre, ces Églises historiques produisirent malgré elles des figures prophétiques marquées par le messianisme Kongo des 17e et 18e siècles. Pasteur de l'Église Évangélique du Congo, Daniel Ndoundou créa au sein de son institution le mouvement *Nsikumusu* (Réveil) en 1947[5], un mouvement dont l'influence reste perceptible dans plusieurs Églises chrétiennes du Congo-Brazzaville, particulièrement au regard de l'offre thérapeutique et du retour au passé musical Kongo. Catéchiste catholique, Victor Malanda fonda le mouvement *Croix-koma* à la fin des années 1950 (officiellement en 1964), avant d'être excommunié par Mgr Théophile Mbemba, le premier archevêque congolais[6]. L'excommunication du catholique Victor Malanda tranche avec l'attitude des missionnaires protestants qui intégrèrent le *Nsikumusu* de Daniel Ndoundou au sein de leur Église. En matière d'inculturation, l'Église Évangélique du Congo a donc pris une longueur d'avance sur l'Église catholique qui aura attendu l'application des réformes du concile Vatican II.

Il convient aussi de souligner le rôle considérable des mouvements prophétiques autonomes, avec d'illustres prophètes en quête de liberté politique et d'émancipation religieuse. C'est le cas du

---

[2] Martial Sinda, *Le messianisme congolais....*

[3] La colonisation française commença en 1880 lorsque Pierre Savorgnan de Brazza signa un traité avec le roi Makoko.

[4] Bernard Coyault, « Figures prophétiques... », 11.

[5] *Ibid.*

[6] Prophétique, le mouvement Croix-koma reflète un certain messianisme. Son prophète est considéré comme un libérateur de la nation congolaise : « Dieu a choisi le prophète Malanda pour que chaque Congolais retrouve la liberté. Le prophète Malanda est au Congo ce qu'est le général de Gaulle à la France ; d'où le choix de la croix de Lorraine [symbole de la Résistance de 1940-1945] comme emblème du mouvement *Croix-koma* » (entretien avec Ta Malela, le leader actuel de *Croix-koma*, Nkankata le 3 février 2013).

matsouanisme apparu en 1945, et du « Christianisme prophétique en Afrique » (ou Église de Zéphirin) fondé en 1947 ; deux mouvements politico-religieux au parcours différent. D'une part, le matsouanisme, qui opéra un boycott fiscal, fut durement réprimé par l'administration coloniale. Durant la cruelle répression dite des « Trois francs », des miliciens se livrèrent à d'impitoyables exactions et à des viols massifs dans le département du Pool dévolu au résistant André Matsoua. D'autre part, le « Christianisme prophétique en Afrique » connut, à partir de 1953, un essor et bénéficia du soutien de nouvelles autorités congolaises. Aussi l'Église de Zéphirin apparaissait-elle comme « une religion d'État » du fait de sa « collusion avec les hommes politiques du Moyen-Congo »[7] qui remportèrent des élections législatives et municipales grâce à ses adeptes.

Les Églises Face au Régime Marxiste-Léniniste (1963-1991)

L'euphorie de l'indépendance se heurta vite aux restrictions de la révolution socialiste de 1963 avec son lot de dérives : monopartisme, exécutions publiques d'opposants, nationalisation des écoles chrétiennes, confiscation de biens d'Églises, arrestations arbitraires, tortures et assassinats d'hommes d'Église parmi lesquels le cardinal Émile Biayenda. Ce dernier fut enlevé et tué le 22 mars 1977 peu après Marien Ngouabi, le chef de l'État assassiné le 18 mars de la même année.[8] Le meurtre du cardinal Biayenda, qui entretenait de bonnes relations avec le président Ngouabi, relèverait plus d'une vengeance ethnique que d'un acte anticlérical. Des proches du président assassiné auraient accusé le cardinal d'avoir neutralisé les « pouvoirs » du chef de l'État qu'il avait rencontré quelques heures avant le putsch[9] ; une audience présidentielle pourtant programmée deux mois à l'avance. Outre la violence due à la militarisation du champ politique, le régime communiste restreignit la liberté de culte, au point qu'en 1978, l'État ne reconnut que sept confessions religieuses dotées d'un statut légal : l'Église catholique, l'Église Évangélique du Congo, l'Armée du salut, l'Église kimbanguiste, l'Église du « Christianisme Prophétique en Afrique », le Conseil islamique du Congo et un mouvement religieux japonais dénommé Terinkyo. Certaines des Églises non reconnues plongèrent dans la clandestinité, tandis que d'autres, comme le mouvement « Louzolo Amour », s'érigèrent en associations d'entraide mutuelle. Ce contexte totalitaire favorisa l'unité des chrétiens tous exposés aux mêmes persécutions. C'est ainsi que naquit le Conseil Œcuménique des Églises du Congo (COEEC) composé de l'Église catholique, l'Église Évangélique du Congo, l'Armée du Salut et l'Église kimbanguiste.[10] La première rencontre œcuménique se tint du 20 au 23 Janvier 1970, à l'occasion de la semaine de prière pour l'unité des chrétiens. Depuis lors, le Conseil Œcuménique des Églises du Congo poursuit chaque année des activités fédératrices. Les chorales, par exemple, organisent régulièrement des concerts de chants religieux dans les paroisses des différentes Églises.

Par ailleurs, le pape Jean-Paul II se rendit dans ce pays marxiste en mai 1980, une visite qui suscita une sorte de coexistence pacifique entre les Églises et les gouvernants du « Congo populaire », jusqu'à l'ouverture démocratique des années 1990. C'est dans ce contexte qu'en 1987, 77 Églises demandèrent leur reconnaissance auprès du ministère de l'Intérieur. Ce nombre augmenta jusqu'à 354 en 1990, à l'orée de la Conférence nationale.[11]

---

[7] Philippe Moukoko, *Dictionnaire général ...*, 186.

[8] Le prédécesseur de Marien Ngouabi, Alphonse Massamba-Débat, fut exécuté le 25 mars avec nombreux de ses partisans. Signalons, par ailleurs, qu'un procès de béatification et de canonisation du cardinal Émile Biayenda a été ouvert dans les années 1990.

[9] Abraham Okoko-Esseau, « The Christian Churches ... », 151.

[10] Depuis le début des années 2000, les kimbanguistes ne font plus partie du Conseil œcuménique des Églises pour des raisons doctrinales.

[11] Abel Kouvouama, « Conférence nationale ... », 391. La plupart des Églises chrétiennes obtinrent leur statut légal et

Rôle des Églises Chrétiennes dans L'Ouverture Démocratique (1991-2016)

Souveraine, la Conférence nationale du Congo postcolonial se déroula du 25 février au 10 juin 1991, avec notamment la participation des confessions religieuses. Présidée par un jésuite et évêque catholique, monseigneur Ernest Kombo, cette Conférence nationale fut un événement politico-religieux à plus d'un titre. En effet, le retour du pluralisme politique résulte d'intenses négociations entre l'État et le Conseil Œcuménique des Églises du Congo qui, le 10 août 1990, se prononça clairement pour la démocratie dans une lettre adressée au président de la République Denis Sassou Nguesso. Un autre document signé le 9 novembre 1990 s'intitule *« Lettre des responsables des Églises chrétiennes du Congo aux fidèles sur l'engagement politique ».*[12]

En outre, les Églises chrétiennes se sont impliquées dans la gestion des crises consécutives au processus démocratique, avec une décennie de guerres civiles entre 1992 et 2002 : médiation entre les camps du président Pascal Lissouba et de l'opposition, organisation de séances de prière œcuméniques pour la paix en présence des plus hautes autorités nationales, initiatives des commissions « Justice et paix ». En revanche, une rébellion armée revendique le message de l'Évangile. Il s'agit des *Nsilulu* du pasteur Ntumi, un mouvement prophétique apparu en 1998 dans le contexte d'une guerre cruelle qui a fait plusieurs victimes civiles dans le département du Pool et dans les quartiers sud de Brazzaville. Certaines études inscrivent les *Nsilulu* dans le messianisme Kongo. Mais d'autres, sans en exclure la portée messianique, considèrent ce mouvement armé comme une création de l'État visant à justifier la répression, voire l'invasion des forces gouvernementales et de leurs milices alliées dans un département acquis à l'opposition.[13]

Plus récemment, les Églises ont timidement participé au débat sur le changement constitutionnel qui a permis au chef de l'État de briguer un nouveau mandat en mars 2016. Dans leur message de Noël 2014, les évêques catholiques se sont opposés à toute révision constitutionnelle et ont proposé que « l'alternance au pouvoir devienne une règle intangible et immuable pour la démocratie congolaise ».[14] Le pouvoir en place les a accusés de prendre parti. Les réactions et le mutisme des Églises consécutifs à cet épisode ont révélé, parmi les ecclésiastiques, une divergence d'appréciation de la situation sociopolitique.

Cette synthèse a dressé une esquisse de la participation ecclésiale à la vie politique du Congo-Brazzaville depuis les premières missions chrétiennes jusqu'à l'ouverture démocratique propice à de fortes recompositions religieuses. Aussi l'investissement politique du champ religieux et l'implication des Églises chrétiennes dans l'arène politique participent-ils de la fluidité entre religion et politique au regard de l'État contemporain en Afrique.

Bibliographie

Bazenguissa-Ganga, Rémy, Ibéa Atondi, Etanislas Ngodi, et Patrice Yengo, « Les "écuries". Les formes d'engagement des urbains dans la guerre électorale du Congo-Brazzaville (1997-2009) », *in* Bazenguissa-Ganga, Rémy et Sami Makki, eds., *Sociétés en guerres. Ethnographies des mobilisations violentes*, Paris : Maison des sciences de l'homme, 2012, 57–92.

Coyault, Bernard, *Figures prophétiques et chants révélés dans le réveil évangélique du Congo*, thèse de doctorat, Paris, EHESS, 2015.

Kouvouama, Abel, « Conférence nationale et modernité religieuse au Congo », *in* CURAPP, *Questions Sensibles*, Paris : P.U.F., 1998, 387–412.

---

s'organisèrent autour de diverses fédérations ecclésiales.

[12] Joseph Tonda, « De l'exorcisme ...», 266.

[13] Rémy Bazenguissa-Ganga *et al.*, « Les "écuries"...», 86.

[14] http://www.lasemaineafricaine.net/index.php/vie-de-leglise/10927-message-de-noel-des-eveques-du-congo, consulté le 9 juin 2016.

Moukoko, Philippe, *Dictionnaire général du Congo*-Brazzaville, Paris, Montréal : L'Harmattan, 1999.

Okoko-Esseau, Abraham, "The Christian Churches and Democratisation in the Congo", *in* Gifford, Paul, ed., *The Christian Churches and the Democratisation of Africa*, Leiden : Brill, 1995, 148–167.

Sinda, Martial, *Le messianisme congolais et ses incidences politiques : kimbanguisme, matsouanisme, autres mouvements*, Paris : Payot, 1972.

Tonda, Joseph, « De l'exorcisme comme mode de démocratisation. Églises et mouvements religieux au Congo de 1990 à 1994 », *in* Constantin, François et Christian Coulon, eds., *Religion et transition démocratique en Afrique*, Paris : Karthala, 1997, p 259-284.

(58) LE CHRISTIANISME EN COTE D'IVOIRE

Simon K. Dossou

Religion	Pop 2010	Pct 2010	Pop 2025	Pct 2025	Gr Pct 1970 2025
Christians	6,511,000	32.3%	10,387,000	36.2%	3.2%
Independents	1,397,000	6.9%	2,160,000	7.5%	2.9%
African initiated	1,334,000	6.6%			
Orthodox	50,100	0.2%	66,000	0.2%	1.9%
Protestants	1,869,000	9.3%	2,800,000	9.8%	2.7%
Pentecostal	988,000	4.9%			
Holiness	412,000	2.0%			
Baptist	221,000	1.1%			
Methodist	166,000	0.8%			
Roman Catholics	3,469,000	17.2%	5,450,000	19.0%	3.1%
Pentecostals/Charismatics	2,011,000	10.0%	3,000,000	10.4%	2.7%
Evangelicals	1,737,000	8.6%	2,323,000	8.1%	2.0%
Muslims	8,555,000	42.5%	12,170,000	42.4%	2.4%
adherents of traditional African religions	4,951,000	24.6%	6,000,000	20.9%	1.3%
Baha'is	29,200	0.1%	37,000	0.1%	1.6%
Buddhists	9,500	0.0%	11,000	0.0%	1.0%
adherents of new religious movements	4,700	0.0%	8,000	0.0%	3.7%
Hindus	1,500	0.0%	2,000	0.0%	1.9%
people professing no religion	69,600	0.3%	102,000	0.4%	2.6%
Total population	**20,132,000**	**100.0%**	**28,717,000**	**100.0%**	**2.4%**

Source: Centre for the Study of World Christianity (CSGC), Boston, Gordon-Conwell TS

Introduction

La Côte d'Ivoire est considérée comme un pays très religieux à tel point qu'on y rencontre l'Eglise Catholique qui est la plus vieille arrivée dans le pays. L'Eglise Méthodiste y est arrivée un peu dans le sillage de la prédication du prophète Harriste. En dehors des églises catholiques et méthodistes arrivées presqu'à la fin du 19è et au début du 20è siècle, il y a un grand nombre de communautés chrétiennes souvent appelées évangéliques ou pentecôtistes qui se partage le terrain de la foi chrétienne dans le pays.

Dans les lignes qui suivent, nous présentons ces églises en trois volets: Catholique, Méthodistes et Evangéliques.

L'Eglise Catholique en Côte d'Ivoire

L'Eglise catholique a connu des tentatives d'arrivée depuis 1637 avec les Pères Capucins bretons. Ils essaient de s'installer à Assinie mais sans succès[1].

Les débuts de la mission d'évangélisation catholique

LES PREMIERS PAS

C'est véritablement avec la colonisation française que les missionnaires catholiques ont eu la possibilité de commencer un travail d'évangélisation à proprement parler. En effet, le 11 janvier 1895, le gouverneur de la colonie de la Côte d'Ivoire adresse au Supérieur « de la Société des Missions Africaines (SMA) une lettre dans laquelle il se préoccupe de la possibilité d'établir des missions » dans cette partie de l'Afrique de l'Ouest[2]. Son souci est relayé à la Congrégation pour la Propagande de la Foi qui répond favorablement en créant la Préfecture apostolique de la Côte d'Ivoire le 25 Juin 1895 avec pour responsable le père Matthieu Ray. En attendant l'arrivée de ce dernier sur le terrain, il est immédiatement suppléé par les pères Hamard et Bonhomme[3]. C'est ainsi que ces derniers se sont vus confier la direction de l'école publique dans laquelle ils ne tardent pas à introduire les prières et le catéchisme dans le programme. Dans le même élan, plusieurs écoles ont été ouvertes dans plusieurs localités comme Grand-Bassam, Assinie, Bonoua, Dabou etc. Selon les missionnaires comme d'ailleurs selon l'administration coloniale, « le véritable avenir de la Côte d'Ivoire chrétienne est dans les écoles »[4], car pensent-ils, c'est leur seul moyen d'apostolat par excellence, selon Pierre Trichet cité par E. Gnagoran.

LES ECUEILS A LA MISSION

En ces débuts de la mission l'enthousiasme seul ne suffit pas pour faire avancer l'œuvre d'évangélisation. Dès Avril 1899, une épidémie de fièvre jaune vient frapper les missionnaires. Plusieurs d'entre eux dont le Préfet apostolique le Père Matthieu Ray succombèrent à la maladie. Jusqu'en 1904, la fièvre jaune a sévi, tuant pendant cette période près d'une vingtaine de prêtres et religieuses. Plusieurs écoles sont fermées et même détruites par la mission elle-même pour éviter d'éventuelles contaminations.

Dans la même période, l'administration coloniale rompt les relations qui existaient entre elle et la mission dans le cadre des écoles. Toutes les subventions ont été supprimées rendant le travail très difficile pour la mission catholique. Ainsi, le 1er janvier 1904, toutes les indemnités aux écoles privées sont supprimées. Les missionnaires décident de réorienter le travail d'évangélisation en faisant plus de visites dans les villages. Les conversions à la foi chrétienne se sont multipliées et le nombre d'églises locales a augmenté de façon notable. Cette situation, restée ainsi jusqu'au début de la première guerre mondiale a fait que l'église catholique en 1914, ne gérait que 3 écoles sur les 12 qu'elle comptait avant la reprise en main de ces dernières par les pouvoirs publiques dix ans plus tôt. Par contre, le nombre de chrétiens à doubler, voire tripler à partir de 1915 surtout « après la prédication du prophète Harris »[5].

---

[1] Ernest Gnagoran YAO BI: Côte d'Ivoire: Un siècle de catholicisme, Histoire de la Côte d'Ivoire, Editions du CERAP Abidjan 2009.
Ce livre présente plusieurs éléments intéressant notre sujet ici et nous y puiserons l'essentiel des informations

[2] Ernest Gnagoran Yao Bi: Op cit, 17

[3] Idem: 18

[4] Ibidem 19

[5] Op.cit 25

L'essor de la mission jusqu'à ce jour

Avec la fin de la première guerre mondiale, la mission catholique à hâte de renouer avec ses écoles mais l'administration tarde à donner les autorisations de réouverture. Ainsi à partir de 1926, l'église ouvre de nouvelles écoles dans plusieurs localités du pays car elle avait la possibilité de dispenser des cours de catéchisme aux élèves en dehors des heures officielles de cours décrétées par l'administration. C'était une bonne opportunité pour se faire des chrétiens. A l'époque, « être chrétien, c'est être détenteur d'un certain pouvoir, c'est avoir une promotion sociale »[6].

En raison de la rude concurrence avec l'église du prophète Harris et le protestantisme naissant à l'époque, l'église catholique utilisait ses écoles comme des lieux incontournables de son expansion évangélique. L'occupation de l'espace a porté ses fruits de telle sorte que, quelques années plus tard, l'objectif de Mgr Moury, appuyé par les pères Garcia, Gaulé, Person, Gandon et plusieurs autres a été largement atteint. Il crée un organe de presse, des mouvements d'action catholique chargés de la diffusion et de l'expansion de la religion chrétienne.

Pour consolider tout ce travail mis en route, des écoles de catéchistes ont été créées en plusieurs endroits et le nombre des élèves s'est accru très rapidement. La création du bulletin « La Côte d'Ivoire Chrétienne » en novembre 1937 était à la fois une presse de propagande catholique mais aussi une alternative à la fermeture du bulletin « Notre Voix », organe d'un parti d'alliance socialo-communiste, qui critiquait sans ménagement la religion, l'Eglise et la mission[7].

Les mouvements d'action chrétienne comme le scoutisme en 1938, et la Jeunesse ouvrière catholique (JOC) en 1939 sont créés. Cette dernière à l'origine, avait pour vocation de « christianiser le monde ouvrier en y combattant les erreurs matérialistes, en apportant le mieux être dans les foyers, en recréant la fraternité chrétienne au bureau, à l'atelier et au chantier etc. »[8].

Le travail des catéchistes a été salué avec beaucoup d'enthousiasme par tous les missionnaires car sans eux, le nombre de fidèles ne pourrait pas augmenter comme on le constate sur le terrain. Dans le même temps, on constate le coup de pouce important que donnent les différents gouverneurs à l'œuvre d'expansion catholique au 'détriment des autres confessions religieuses'[9]. Ces représentants de l'administration coloniale se croyaient investis d'une mission de civilisation que les missionnaires catholiques appuyaient volontiers eu égard au soutien qu'ils recevaient d'eux. Pendant très longtemps, plusieurs ont critiqué cette collaboration trop voyante entre l'église catholique et l'administration. Sans être la même chose de nos jours, plusieurs semblent voir les avatars du passé

Au début de l'année 2000, les statistiques présentent l'église catholique selon les chiffres suivants: prêtres diocésains: 485, prêtres missionnaires: 298, religieux: 369, religieuses: 1016, catéchistes: 12049, paroisses: 267, nombres de catholiques: 2 964 058. Depuis lors il s'est ajouté à toutes ces composantes de nouveaux visages, de nouveaux lieux de cultes, etc. Le constat est: Bien que les 2 premiers prêtres ivoiriens n'aient été ordonnés qu'en 1947, ils sont un très grand nombre de nos jours. On ne doit pas ignorer qu'au milieu de toute cette embellie de chiffres, il y a aussi beaucoup d'érosion dans cette église, due à la prolifération des groupes évangéliques, pentecôtistes et autres prêcheurs de tout bord.

L'église catholique dans la société ivoirienne

Depuis l'appel du pape Jean-Paul II le 12 Mai 1980 qui dit « Soyez vous-mêmes… vous pouvez, vous qui êtes si fiers de vos possibilités, donnez au monde la preuve que vous êtes capables de résoudre vous-mêmes vos problèmes propres… mais en veillant à orienter tout cela dans la bonne direction »[10], l'église

---

[6] Op.cit 38
[7] Op.cit 42
[8] Op cit 43
[9] Op ; Cit 47
[10] Op.cit 108

catholique a fait de grands pas dans le cadre de sa triple autonomie. Ainsi elle a mis tout en œuvre pour son autonomie culturelle, en personnel et financière.

En effet, aujourd'hui, l'église catholique à l'instar des autres communautés chrétiennes de la Côte d'Ivoire fait tout pour intégrer les valeurs culturelles africaines dans l'expression de la théologie, dans la manière d'adorer avec les instruments de musique traditionnelle, avec des compositions de chants religieux sur des airs connus dans la société. Plusieurs groupes d'étude biblique se réunissent sous forme des groupes traditionnels de l'arbre à palabre. L'habit liturgique s'inspire beaucoup des traditions locales. L'adaptation des enseignements aux valeurs proches des sensibilités africaines contribue beaucoup à l'affermissement de la foi des chrétiens.

Le clergé resté longtemps composé de missionnaires étrangers à commencer à s'enrichir de nationaux dans tous les domaines. Comme signalé plus haut, de deux prêtres ivoiriens en 1947, l'église catholique en compte un très grand nombre aujourd'hui. Elle jouit presque d'une autonomie en personnel. Cependant, il faut continuer à encourager les vocations sacerdotales et ne pas laisser tomber la formation des formateurs.

Pour faire face aux charges liées aux personnels, l'église catholique a besoin de mobiliser ses fidèles en vue d'une autonomie financière. Pendant longtemps, les chrétiens étaient habitués à voir tout venir des missionnaires étrangers pour les besoins de leurs paroisses. Le clergé a lancé de vigoureux appels pour une participation financière conséquente des fidèles. Ainsi, les mentalités ont changé et les chrétiens participent financièrement à la vie de leur paroisse et de l'église. « Ils n'ont plus de réticence ni de complexe à s'engager dans les services nécessaires à la promotion de leur institution »[11]. Afin que les écoles appartenant à l'église ne souffrent pas trop des retards de subventions de l'Etat pour payer les enseignants, il est vivement souhaité que les chrétiens puissent donner un coup de main dans ce domaine là aussi à travers leurs dons. Cela n'est pas le cas en ce moment car plusieurs pensent que les écoles sont des activités génératrices de revenus qui devraient même soutenir l'œuvre d'évangélisation. Mais tout compte fait, l'église catholique se bat pour atteindre son autonomie financière, ne serait-ce que dans les domaines les plus vitaux.

Sur le plan sociopolitique, l'église catholique évoque tous les problèmes qui concernent le vécu des populations. Ainsi, à travers des lettres pastorales, des prédications et autres prises de position, elle a abordé des questions touchant au combat pour l'émancipation des populations et la promotion humaine, l'institution du mariage chrétien et la monogamie. Elle s'est prononcée sur la règlementation de la dot qu'elle trouve que son abus fait perdre son sens à cette coutume respectable et livre pieds et poings liés, les jeunes filles parfois aux riches vieillards. Elle plaide aussi pour l'abolition du matriarcat qu'elle trouve comme une coutume injuste et sans fondement. Elle continue jusqu'à ce jour à jouer un rôle de veilleur et de prophète dans une société où le monde a tendance à oublier la volonté de Dieu.

L'eglise Methodiste en Cote D'ivoire

Pendant que la mission catholique était sur le terrain, il apparaît une autre mission qui vient de l'inspiration de l'œuvre du mulâtre Thomas Birch Freeman (1809-1890) missionnaire anglais qui a travaillé du Cape Coast (Ghana) jusqu'au Nigeria. C'est ainsi que l'Eglise Méthodiste en Côte d'Ivoire est considérée comme l'œuvre des pionniers méthodistes organisés par ce missionnaire.

L'Eglise Méthodiste en Côte d'Ivoire qui a fêté son centenaire en 2014 est aujourd'hui un porte flambeau de l'évangélisation dans le pays et un instrument évangélique dans le cadre du développement socio-économique.

Un bref parcours de la vie de cette église permet de mesurer le chemin parcouru malgré les difficultés qu'elle connaît aussi.

[11] Ibid 116

DES DEBUTS DIFFICILES

Du fait de son appartenance à ce qui était considéré comme colonie française, l'église méthodiste a eu du mal à s'installer en Côte d'Ivoire. En effet, les négociants anglais de la Sierra Leone et du Liberia employaient plusieurs de leurs ouvriers en Côte d'Ivoire où ils avaient des comptoirs. Ces ouvriers, chrétiens, méthodistes pour la plupart, se réunissaient en communautés de prières et s'autogéraient sans pasteurs ni catéchistes depuis les années 1860. Avec le temps, ils auraient bien voulu s'organiser en communautés fortes mais entre 1860 et 1914, « la méfiance, le refus et l'interdiction du colonisateur ont freiné toute expansion de la mission méthodiste qui était de surcroit affaiblie par son caractère disparate. Ainsi en ce temps-là, le terme catholique était synonyme de français et le terme protestant résonnant comme subversif »[12]. Pour avoir l'autorisation de s'installer officiellement dans les colonies françaises pour l'exercice du culte méthodiste, la Wesleyan Mission Society (WMS) a été obligée de s'affilier à la Société des Missions de Paris (SMP). Malgré cela, la mission méthodiste était interdite de mettre en place des établissements d'enseignement général. Pendant longtemps, la mission méthodiste en Côte d'ivoire a été obligée de dépendre de la Gold Coast pour ses activités. C'est seulement en 1914, que la Côte d'Ivoire a été érigée en circuit durant le synode de la même année.

PLUSIEURS A LA TACHE AU DEBUT DE L'EGLISE METHODISTE EN COTE D'IVOIRE

En plus des communautés de prières, entre 1913 et 1915, le prédicateur William Wade Harris entrepris une vaste campagne d'évangélisation sous l'égide de l'église méthodiste épiscopale du Liberia dont il était membre. Il parcourut le long du sud côtier de la Côte d'Ivoire et invita ces auditeurs à se tourner vers le Christ en abandonnant l'adoration des dieux traditionnels. Son message a été reçu par les populations visitées et plusieurs se sont convertis à la foi chrétienne. Ne pouvant pas s'installer là pour consolider le travail entamé, ce sont d'autres personnes qui ont continué son œuvre. Des gens se réclamant de lui ont créé ce qui est devenu plus tard l'Eglise du Prophète Harris ou Eglise Harriste qui existe jusqu'à ce jour. Plusieurs convertis après la prédication de Harris ont constitué la base de l'Eglise méthodiste en Côte d'Ivoire. Brimades, spoliations ont continué jusqu'à ce que le pasteur William John Platt, surintendant général de l'église méthodiste à Porto-Novo au Dahomey (aujourd'hui Bénin) vienne ouvrir une enquête sur les différentes exactions. Dans une lettre du 16 Août 1924 qui est un genre d'appel pathétique à des jeunes pasteurs français ou francophones à venir aider l'église méthodiste en pleine expansion en Côte d'ivoire, les pasteurs Paul Wood Lainé et Antoine Lethel avec l'accord de William John Platt, ont réussi à décider plusieurs jeunes pasteurs à s'engager pour la mission dans ce pays. Ainsi, du Dahomey, de Gold Coast, de France plusieurs pasteurs sont arrivés pour booster le travail d'évangélisation. En l'espace de quelques années, les circuits de Grand-Bassam, de Dabou, d'Abidjan, de Grand-Lahou ont été créés et on connu un accroissement rapide de chrétiens méthodistes.

Le premier pasteur méthodiste Ivoirien est Reverend Martin MEL consacré en 1946, malheureusement décédé très tôt en 1949.

---

[12] Lors du centenaire de l'Eglise méthodiste en Côte d'Ivoire en 2014, le Bishop Benjamin BONI de l'Eglise Méthodiste Unie Côte d'Ivoire (EMUCI) a fait l'historique de la mission méthodiste en Côte d'ivoire, dans un No Spécial appelé LE METHODISTE. Ainsi, de 1860 à ce jour, l'église a été présentée à travers l'histoire. On y lit, ses succès et ses échecs durant sa vie de plus de 100 ans en réalité.

L'Eglise Méthodiste, des années 1940 à ce jour

Avec l'appel lancé en 1924 par Paul Lainé et consorts, la mission méthodiste en Côte d'ivoire a connu un développement rapide. Parmi les grands événements de cette église on peut retenir:

1946: Consécration du premier pasteur Ivoirien

1958: La Côte d'Ivoire qui faisait partie du District Daho-Togo-Côte d'Ivoire est érigé en District distinct rattaché à la Conférence Méthodiste de grande Bretagne

1963: Rev Pasteur Samson NANDJUI est élu premier Chairman du District de Côte d'Ivoire

1974-1982: 2è Chairman, Rev Pasteur Lambert Auguste ACKAH

1983-1985: 3è Chairman, Rev Pasteur, Emmanuel YANDO

09 Février 1985: Le District est érigé en église autonome sous le nom: Eglise Protestante Méthodiste de Côte d'Ivoire (EPMCI) avec comme premier président le Rev pasteur Emmanuel YANDO (1985-1990)

1990-1998: 2è Président de l'EPMCI Rev Pasteur Lambert Akossi N'CHO

1998-2005: 3è Président de l'EPMCI Rev Pasteur Benjamin BONI

23 Décembre 2001: Décision d'intégration de l'EPMCI à L'Eglise Méthodiste Unie (EMU)

04 Octobre 2003: Célébration de l'intégration de l'EPMCI à L'EMU

13 Mars 2005: Investiture du premier Bishop de l'EMUCI Bishop Benjamin BONI

L'Eglise Méthodiste dans la société ivoirienne

L'Eglise Méthodiste a connu des dissidences internes dans son parcours comme cela a été le cas avec presque toutes les églises protestantes issues de la Réforme du XVIè siècle. Cependant, l'essentielle de l'œuvre évangélique est dirigée aujourd'hui par l'Eglise Méthodiste Unie Côte d'Ivoire qui a à sa tête Bishop Benjamin BONI.

En Côte d'ivoire, tous les acteurs politiques ont toujours eu un grand respect pour l'œuvre méthodiste à cause de sa rigueur dans la gestion. Les œuvres les plus représentatives sont:

LES ASSOCIATIONS

La vie associative de l'église méthodiste est caractérisée par plusieurs mouvements et associations très actifs pour l'animation de la vie spirituelle des fidèles. C'est ainsi qu'on rencontre au niveau des Districts, des circuits, des secteurs et des églises locales, l'Ecole du Dimanche, les Scouts, l'Association Chrétienne des élèves et étudiants protestants créée en 1958, l'Union de la jeunesse protestante créée en 1963, l'Union des femmes méthodistes en 1963. Le Directoire musical national est créé en 1975.

LES ŒUVRES DE TEMOIGNAGES

Les œuvres de témoignages sont des activités créées par l'église pour soutenir l'évangélisation mais qui entrent dans le cadre des institutions sociales. les principales sont: L'hôpital méthodiste de Dabou créé en 1968 et ses annexes, la Maison protestante de l'étudiant (MAPE) créée en 1968 avec le centre d'accueil protestant pour les étudiants de toute nationalité et de toute religion, le foyer de jeunesse, la fraternité du port, le centre John Wesley pour l formation continue etc.

LES INSTITUTIONS DE FORMATION

La formation scolaire et universitaire a commencé très tôt avec l'évangélisation du pays. Les écoles méthodistes dont les premières remontent à 1926 comprennent aujourd'hui 18 écoles préscolaires, 39 écoles primaires, 7 établissements secondaires et l'université méthodiste fondée en 2006 avec plusieurs unités de formation dont Sciences Juridiques Administratives et politiques, Sciences Economiques et de Gestion, Unité des langues, des lettres et des civilisations

Les realisations socio- economiques et autres

Les réalisations socio-économiques sont des activités génératrices de revenus dont le but est de pourvoir aux besoins financiers de l'église. On y compte l'immeuble Alliance ayant 6 niveaux à usage commerciale créé en 1986, des magasins de commerce à Abidjan, des plantations d'hévéaculture et de palmiers à huile.

Sur le plan statistique, l'EMUCI compte aujourd'hui: 1060 églises locales, 1 373 069 fidèles, 17 districts, 189 pasteurs en activité en 2013, 300 catéchistes, 9 607 prédicateurs laïques.

L'EMUCI est membre de plusieurs organisations œcuméniques dont le Conseil Œcuménique des Eglises (COE), la Conférence des Eglises de Toute l'Afrique (CETA) etc.

L'Eglise méthodiste s'est toujours investie dans la recherche de la paix aux côtés des autorités politico-administratives de la Côte d'Ivoire. Cet engagement l'a souvent contrainte à démentir son accointance avec les régimes au pouvoir à certain moment de l'histoire du pays. Il lui est aussi arrivé de se retrouver en froid avec certains politiques qui estiment qu'elle est trop proche d'une certaine opposition. Mais, elle reste une église incontournable sur l'échiquier national.

Les autres confessions religieuses en Côte d'ivoire

Si l'Eglise catholique et méthodiste sont les plus représentatives sur le plan de la chrétienté en Côte d'ivoire, il existe plusieurs autres qui se partagent le paysage religieux. L'Islam aussi est bien présent dans le pays pour l'exercice de la foi sans oublier les adeptes de la religion traditionnelle.

L'Eglise Harriste en Côte d'ivoire

Après l'arrivée de l'église catholique en Côte d'Ivoire, survient un prédicateur venu du Libéria du nom de William Wade Harris Wury né aux environs de 1860 d'une famille non chrétienne. Il fréquente l'école de la mission méthodiste et est baptisé dans cette confession pendant qu'il était chez son oncle Rev John C. LowRie. Il a travaillé tour à tour comme garçon membre d'équipage de vaisseaux anglais et allemands qui faisaient la ligne Liberia –Lagos et Gabon, puis comme moniteur d'école et enseignant. Il est ensuite devenu interprète officiel du gouvernement du Liberia en 1899. Il était du côté de la légalité quand il décide de s'associer aux anglais blancs contre le gouvernement local. Il a été incarcéré en 1910 et dans sa prison, il dit avoir reçu la visite d'un ange qui lui demande d'aller évangéliser ses frères. Une fois libéré, il commença son travail sur place puis longea la côte jusqu'en Côte d'ivoire où il prêcha aussi. Il travaille dans une zone où l'église catholique était déjà sans grand succès auparavant. Il a été arrêté et jeté en prison plusieurs fois pour de brefs séjours. Mais en janvier 1915, Harris et les trois femmes qui l'accompagnaient dans sa mission ont été expulsés alors que le travail avait commencé à prendre un grand essor. Partis de Côte d'Ivoire, par trois fois, ils ont tenté de revenir continuer leur prédication mais ils en ont été empêchés par les autorités coloniales. Il n'a jamais condamné la polygamie car il la considérait comme faisant partie de la vie africaine.

En 1924, les missionnaire méthodistes ont reconnu le travail de Wade Harris en Côte d'Ivoire et ont tenté de récupérer les chrétiens qu'il avait baptisés. Ils l'ont réussi avec des méthodes de duplicité que l'histoire n'a pas acceptées. Plusieurs de ses fidèles sont devenus soit catholiques soit méthodistes.

Harris meurt au Liberia des suites de maladie en Avril 1929, épuisé et sans argent.

Son œuvre est restée vivace surtout parce qu'elle a connu un succès incroyable même après le départ du prophète de la Côte d'Ivoire. Une église harriste à été créée en 1931 suite à la visite en 1928 du leader Ebrié Jonas Ahui, qui avait été consacré par le prophète et qui avait reçu sa bible, sa croix et le dernier message écrit de Harris. L'Eglise Harriste compte environ 200 000 membres de nos jours sans compter les adeptes qui sont en Sierra Leone, au Ghana et dans d'autres pays dont la France.

L'Eglise Harriste de Côte d'Ivoire dirigée par son actuel président Félix TCHOTCHMEL est membre du Conseil Œcuménique des Eglises (COE). Elle a quelques dissensions internes comme plusieurs églises protestantes mais son encrage dans le paysage chrétien de Côte d'ivoire est certain et positif.

Les Eglises Evangéliques et Pentecôtistes

L'église catholique qui est la plus ancienne en Côte d'Ivoire partage de nos jours l'espace spirituel avec les protestants méthodistes, les harristes et un grand nombre de dénominations issues des mouvements évangéliques et pentecôtistes nés en grande partie des Etats-Unis au début du 20 è siècle. Il existe aussi plusieurs autres églises d'origine africaine comme le christianisme céleste très offensif dans sa forme de recrutements de ses fidèles, ainsi que les Aladura qui sont même membres de la CETA et du Conseil Œcuménique des Eglises (COE).

L'ACTIVITE EVANGELIQUE EN COTE D'IVOIRE

Les églises dites évangéliques ne datent pas de très longtemps en Côte d'Ivoire. Cependant, le nombre de leurs fidèles a évolué assez rapidement aussi bien dans ce pays qu'à travers le monde. Les plus représentatives sont: l'Eglise des Assemblées de Dieu, les Adventistes du 7è jour etc.

En règle générale, les évangéliques sont d'abord des chrétiens protestants qui se réclament de la Réforme du 16è Siècle. Le terme évangélique décrit les mouvements de réveil piétistes des 18è et 19è siècle. A cette époque là, on est d'abord évangélique avant d'être méthodiste, baptiste ou autres.

En 2010, on compte environ 523 millions de pentecôtistes dans le monde et 210 millions d'évangéliques.

En Côte d'Ivoire, on compte environ 450 dénominations et 25 fédérations ou confédérations protestantes évangéliques[13]. En dehors des Assemblées de Dieu et quelques autres qui ont une assise nationale, la plupart de ces dénominations n'ont qu'un seul lieu de culte et une petite poignée de fidèles venant d'autres communautés. Parfois ces derniers s'empressent de retourner dans leur communauté d'origine après quelque temps. Leurs initiateurs se donnent, sans aucun critère reconnu, des titres qu'ils estiment valorisant sur le plan social: « bishop, apôtre, docteur prophète, etc ». Souvent, ils n'ont aucune formation biblique ou reçoivent au rabais sur le tas une formation théologique de façon expéditive. Il faut cependant reconnaître que certains d'entre ces initiateurs ont une formation de marketing qui leur donne la possibilité de se faire un monde fou en l'espace de quelques années. Vu, « le bazar » que plusieurs de ces églises créent sur le « marché spirituel », l'administration fait des contrôles de temps à autres et ferme certaines d'entre elles.

Le message que véhiculent certaines de ces églises est celui de la consolation, de la prospérité, d'un Christ capable de résoudre tous les problèmes ici bas. En effet, il n'est pas rare que la plupart de ces fondateurs d'églises y arrivent partant de presque rien. Du jour au lendemain, ils deviennent riches et visibles dans la société qui les a toujours ignorés auparavant. Le nom de certaines de ces églises est le « cliché » de ce que pensent ou rêvent leurs fondateurs. Ainsi on rencontre des églises de nom de: « église de la consolation, église des gagnants, église des champions, église des rachetés, église Dieu peut tout etc. ». A cause de leur tendance à faire l'apologie du bien-être sur terre et à encourager leurs fidèles à s'enrichir au tant que possible sur terre, leur prédication à été qualifiée d'évangile de prospérité. Eux-mêmes démontrent leur prospérité en roulant dans de grosses voitures, portant des habits de grand prix et

[13] Plusieurs documents ont été consultés pour avoir les informations concernant les évangéliques et pentecôtistes en Côte d'Ivoire. On peut les consulter tels qu'indiquer dans la bibliographie.

menant une vie ostentatoire de luxe. Ce qui fait dire à certains critiques que derrière le rideau de théologie de la rédemption ou de la prospérité, se cachent des enjeux économiques importants et une lutte pour la reconnaissance sociale. Parmi ces personnes qui réussissent de cette façon ce cache une connexion à plusieurs réseaux importants et parfois internationaux qui sont des opportunités d'affaires économiques et financières permettant de mobiliser des ressources financières considérables. Certains d'entre eux sont soupçonnés d'être des relais de puissances étrangères qui ont des agendas cachés.

Malgré leur appartenance à des regroupements connus, plusieurs d'entre eux sont jaloux de leur ascension personnelle et n'ont aucun esprit œcuménique ou de partage de prérogative. Il y en a qui sont réfractaires à toute contradiction à leur point de vue.

En Côte d'Ivoire, Il n'est pas rare de les voir évoluer seul même tout en cherchant à débaucher les chrétiens de leurs églises d'origine, catholique, méthodiste ou harriste qualifiées à un moment donné « d'églises mortes ».

Sur le marché de la spiritualité, bien des chrétiens trouvent la solution à leurs problèmes en fréquentant ces lieux de culte car tous ne sont pas « des charlatans ».

Leur engagement sociopolitique se fait souvent en fonction de l'intérêt qu'ils peuvent en tirer. Ils peuvent être soit très engagés derrière un politique soit totalement indifférents à la vie politique de leur pays.

Enfin, leurs rapports avec les musulmans et les adeptes de la religion traditionnelle sont très flous. Cela dépend de l'intérêt qu'ils peuvent en tirer bien que la tendance générale est au rejet de tous les autres qualifiés de sataniques.

Conclusion

Le christianisme se présente en Côte d'Ivoire comme une religion généralement acceptée partout. Mais c'est surtout au Sud et au Centre du pays qu'il semble majoritaire. Il est connu de tous que l'islam est arrivé dans l'extrême nord du pays depuis le 16è siècle et qu'il a toujours mené une vie sans problème avec les autres religions. C'est la raison pour laquelle les relations islamo-chrétiennes en Côte d'Ivoire sont généralement considérées comme cordiales même s'il y a toujours une méfiance avec certaines composantes chrétiennes dont les groupes pentecôtistes extrémistes.

L'Eglise en Côte d'Ivoire est considérée comme un ferment de développement du pays depuis les débuts jusqu'à ce jour. Les nationalistes y voient cependant un genre de complicité négative avec les puissances étrangères comme cela a été le cas depuis l'arrivée du catholicisme presque en même temps que les colons français. L'église doit faire un effort pour rester impartiale dans un pays où l'on prône la laïcité sous toutes ses formes.

Bibliographie

DAGAN O. GB.: De la Réforme Protestante du XVIème Siècle au Méthodiste. Bibliothèque Nationale, Porto-Novo, Benin, 2015

FASSINOU M.et al.: Histoire de l'Eglise Protestante Méthodiste du Bénin 1843-1993 Imprimerie CNPMS, Porto-Novo, 1993

FASSINOU M.: De grandes figures de l'Eglise Protestante Méthodiste Du Dahomey-Togo au Bénin. Des origines à nos jours (1843-2009) Bibliothèque Nationale Bénin 2008

Ernest Gnagoran YAO BI: Côte d'Ivoire: Un siècle de catholicisme, Histoire de la Côte d'Ivoire, Editions du CERAP Abidjan 2009

SANNEH L.: West African Christianity, The religious Impact, Orbis Books 1983, NY

YAO BI E.NG: Côte d'Ivoire: Un siècle de catholicisme, Les Editions du CERAP, Abidjan 2009

Revue: Débats, courrier d'Afrique de l'Ouest, Christianisme multiforme en Afrique de l'Ouest, No 56-57, Juillet-Août, 2008
Revue le Méthodiste: Edition Spéciale Centenaire, Août 2014, Abidjan
Revue Guérir: Abidjan, Octobre 2013

Websites

www.dacb.org/stories/liberia/f-legacy_harris.html
https://fr.wikipedia.org/wiki/Église_harriste

(59) Le Christianisme a Djibouti

Michael Schlick

Religion	Pop 2010	Pct 2010	Pop 2025	Pct 2025	Gr Pct 1970 2025
Christians	14,500	1.7%	18,500	1.8%	1.6%
Independents	260	0.0%	420	0.0%	3.3%
African initiated	260	0.0%			
Orthodox	6,000	0.7%	7,300	0.7%	1.4%
Oriental Orthodox	4,300	0.5%			
Protestants	660	0.1%	800	0.1%	1.3%
Roman Catholics	7,200	0.9%	9,500	0.9%	1.9%
Pentecostals/Charismatics	530	0.1%	700	0.1%	1.9%
Evangelicals	300	0.0%	420	0.0%	2.4%
Muslims	805,000	96.9%	968,000	96.5%	1.2%
Baha'is	720	0.1%	1,000	0.1%	2.2%
Hindus	330	0.0%	440	0.0%	1.9%
people professing no religion	10,000	1.2%	15,200	1.5%	2.8%
Total population	**831,000**	**100.0%**	**1,003,000**	**100.0%**	**1.3%**

Source: Centre for the Study of World Christianity (CSGC), Boston, Gordon-Conwell TS

Bien que Djibouti (indépendant depuis 1977)[1] soit un tout petit pays de 23000m², faisant partie de la Ligue arabe, dont l'Islam (essentiellement sunnites d'obédience chaféite) est la religion d'Etat depuis le 15 septembre 1992, la diversité du paysage chrétien et son rayonnement sont surprenants. Le pluralisme religieux sur le territoire est connu depuis toujours.[2]

Trois communautés chrétiennes sont aujourd'hui bien présentes et visibles.[3] Le christianisme orthodoxe, monophysite d'Ethiopie, historiquement lié à celui d'Egypte, l'Eglise Catholique Romaine et l'Eglise Protestante, lié à la Fédération Protestante de France, sont reconnues comme Eglises par les autorités publiques.[4] Un petit groupe de chrétiens, notamment de nationalité éthiopienne, appartenant à l'Eglise Néo Apostolique dépendant de l'Allemagne, demande la reconduite de son statut en tant qu'Eglise chaque année auprès de l'Etat Djiboutien.

[1] Pour avoir un aperçu historique sur Djibouti nous recommandons: Philipe Oberlé et Pierre Hugot, *Histoire de Djibouti, Des origines à la République*. Djibouti: Présence Africaine Edition, 1985

[2] En ce qui concerne cette question, nous pouvons renvoyer le lecteur à l'étude de Colette Dubois, *Djibouti au regard de ses timbres-poste (1893-1977). Image d'altérité, images de propagande*, Paris, ARESAE-INALCO, 1998.

[3] L'Eglise Orthodoxe Grecque, qui fut la première communauté chrétienne à édifier une église à Djibouti, est aujourd'hui inexistante, faute de membres.

[4] L'histoire de l'implantation des églises chrétiennes, dites de tradition, est bien documentée dans l'ouvrage de Colette Dubois et Pierre Soumille, *Des chrétiens à Djibouti en terre d'islam (XIXe-XXe siècles)*, Paris: Edition Karthala, 2004.

L'Eglise Orthodoxe d'Ethiopie

L'Eglise Orthodoxe d'Ethiopie, visible par son lieu de culte depuis les années 1980, a décidé de prendre soin des croyants orthodoxes sur place. Elle est à la foi sous l'authorité de Abba Jacob et de Abouna Matthias[5], qui envoie des prêtres à Djibouti.[6] L'Eglise Orthodoxe est aujourd'hui fréquentée par environ 9500 fidèles, venant de la Syrie, de l'Inde, de l'Egypte, de l'Erythrée et de l'Ethiopie. L'action sociale se résume à quelques aides aux réfugiés à travers le centre culturel éthiopien, avec le soutien de l'ambassade de l'Ethiopie.

L'Eglise Catholique

L'Eglise Catholique, sur le territoire depuis les années 1880, compte aujourd'hui environ 6000 âmes[7], principalement dans la capitale. Elle réunit des expatriés, pour une grande partie des ressortissants français, notamment militaires. Devenue diocèse en 1955 et rattaché au Saint-Siège[8], elle assure une présence au-delà de Djibouti-ville. Elle contribue depuis toujours généreusement au développement du pays à travers l'éducation et des œuvres sociales.[9] La diaconie est davantage l'expression de la communauté et non seulement de l'évêque ou des prêtres.[10] L'Eglise catholique souligne également l'aspect communautaire au niveau de l'expression spirituelle et cultuelle.[11] D'autres secteurs d'activité du Diocèse de Djibouti sont portés par des religieuses.[12]

Depuis 1979 Caritas de Djibouti est lié à Caritas International. Son engagement est très diversifié sur tout le territoire.[13] Elle travaille davantage avec les associations locales.

Les relations entre la Cathédrale, le Temple et l'Eglise orthodoxe éthiopienne sont fraternelles. En revanche les relations sont un peu réservé quant aux communautés éthiopiennes pentecôtistes et charismatiques non institutionnalisés, mais pourtant bien existantes à Djibouti[14], suite à une forte migration des populations depuis de nombreuses années.[15] Certaines de ses communautés sont rattachés à des Eglises en Ethiopie, qui à leur tour semblent pour une part être soutenues par des oeuvres missionnaires des Etats Unis.[16]

L'Eglise Protestante Evangélique de Djibouti-EPED

L'EPED, liée à la Fédération Protestante de France-FPF[17], ne s'est établi que très tardivement, vers les années 1960 à Djibouti.[18] Elle n'a jamais été une mission au sens classique du terme. Ainsi n'est-elle pas le

[5] Abune Mathias est le 6ème Patriarche de l'Eglise éthiopienne orthodoxe.
[6] L'Eglise compte actuellement 6 prêtres, 3 diacres, 9 consacrés pour l'enseignement et 10 femmes consacrées.
[7] Selon une estimation de Mgr Giorgio Bertin.
[8] Dubois, Des chrétiens à Djibouti.
[9] Trois écoles primaires, un centre d'apprentissage technique, plusieurs centres d'alphabétisation, l'Ecole de la Nativité (préscolaire, primaire et collège), tenue par les Sœurs Franciscaines.
[10] Les rapports quinquennaux aux archives de l'évêché de Djibouti, écrit par les évêques successives, documentent minutieusement le travail effectué depuis les débuts.
[11] Entretien avec le Père Matthieu Kasinzi le 4 fevrier 2015
[12] Il s'agit des Sœurs de St Joseph de Tarbes du Kenya, Des Sœurs de Mère Térésa et des Sœurs de la Consolata.
[13] Caritas participe activement à des œuvres sociales telles que: L'aide alimentaire, l'aide sanitaire, l'aide aux « enfants des rues », l'éducation et l'alphabétisation, l'aide aux migrants, l'urgence humanitaire, lutte contre la sécheresse, etc.
[14] La plus ancienne Eglise est « Living Word Church », communauté pentecôtiste sans affiliation avec l'Ethiopie
[15] Pour la question de l'implication de l'EPED dans l'accueil des réfugiés: Dubois, Des Chrétiens à Djibouti, 288-292.
[16] Sources orales
[17] EPED est membre de la FPF à travers La Communauté d'Eglises Protestantes Francophones-Ceeefe et le Service de Mission-Defap

résultat d'une « conquête », mais plutôt la réponse à une réalité et le résultat d'une entraide et de bienveillance. Les Protestants doivent avoir leur place dans le paysage religieux à condition qu'ils fassent preuve de discrétion. La population musulmane contesterait et se relèverait contre tout prosélytisme.[19] L'EPED réunit des chrétiens venant des dénominations et des cultures multiples. L'éventail confessionnel intra protestant dépasse celui du Conseil Œcuménique Des Egiles (COE) et constitue un véritable laboratoire pour l'Evangile. Malgré la petite taille de l'EPED[20], son rayonnement dans le pays est incontestable à travers ses actions éducatives et sociales.[21] Selon la déontologie du protestantisme français, elle cherche davantage à impulser et innover des idées et des projets, qu'à mener des actions à grande échelle.[22]L'EPED joue un rôle pacificateur en accueillant quelque fois des protestants rattachés plus ou moins à des œuvres missionnaires, visant à amener le Christ auprès des autochtones. Ces mouvements sont multiples et se distinguent par leurs stratégies missionnaires. Etant donné que la situation politique et religieuse dans beaucoup de pays musulmans rend toute présence missionnaire impossible, Djibouti attire davantage. Le rôle de l'EPED, qui n'est décidemment pas dans une démarche prosélyte, est aussi d'accueillir certains de ces chrétiens, qui sont dans un ordre dispersé, et de les mettre dans un rapport compatible avec la législation du pays.

Red Sea Mission-RSM

La RSM, depuis 1975 (avant l'indépendance 1977) en République de Djibouti, à la particularité d'être le seul mouvement missionnaire protestant, établie en tant que tel, dans la région. Dès le départ l'organisme se considère comme multidénominationnel. La RSM opère sur le territoire dans le domaine du développement à travers plusieurs projets.[23]

Conclusion

Dans un climat global ou l'extrémisme religieux prend des formes destructrices, il est désirable que la présence chrétienne dans ce pays musulman continue à être un exemple réussi, montrant que le vivre ensemble non seulement est possible, mais au contraire aide à construire un monde paisible et respectueux. L'avenir reste pourtant incertain. Que sera Djibouti demain ?[24]

Bibliographie

Colette Dubois et Pierre Soumille, *Des chrétiens à Djibouti en terre d'islam (XIXe-XXe siècles)*, Paris: Edition Karthala, 2004

---

[18] Dubois, Des chrétiens à Djibouti, 243-263.

[19] Lors d'une rencontre le 6 juin 2014, Ali Aref, ancien gouverneur de Djibouti, qui était à l'initiative de la donation du terrain sur le Boulevard de la République (centre ville) pour la construction du temple, nous rappelle l'importance d'un lieu de prière pour chaque communauté, afin de promouvoir le vivre ensemble en paix.

[20] La fluctuation de la population protestante est très importante. On peut néanmoins compter moyennement sur 150-200 personnes proche du temple.

[21] Depuis 1984 le centre de formation de l'EPED à proposé des formation professionnel notamment aux jeunes femmes venant des milieux défavorisés.

[22] Exemple: La réhabilitation de toute l'infrastructure de l'EPED a été organisé sous forme d'un chantier-école sur 5 ans.

[23] Formation professionnelle (école de langue), bibliothèque, infirmerie, microcrédit etc.

[24] Concernant la situation politique actuelle nous renvoyons sur une interview du chef de l'Etat: François Soudan, « Ismaïl Omar Guelleh, La France ne nous considère pas » *Jeune Afrique* n° 2822 (2015): 29-32.

Philipe Oberlé et Pierre Hugot, *Histoire de Djibouti, Des origines à la République*. Djibouti: Présence Africaine Edition, 1985

(60A) Christianity in Egypt – Orthodox Perspectives

Wedad A. Tawfik

Religion	Pop 2010	Pct 2010	Pop 2025	Pct 2025	Gr Pct 1970 2025
Christians	7,576,000	9.2%	8,508,000	7.8%	0.8%
Independents	125,000	0.2%	203,000	0.2%	3.3%
African initiated	122,000	0.1%			
Orthodox	7,208,000	8.8%	7,700,000	7.1%	0.4%
Oriental Orthodox	7,205,000	8.8%			
Protestants	493,000	0.6%	605,000	0.6%	1.4%
Roman Catholics	195,000	0.2%	170,000	0.2%	-0.9%
Pentecostals/Charismatics	584,000	0.7%	720,000	0.7%	1.4%
Evangelicals	402,000	0.5%	500,000	0.5%	1.5%
Muslims	73,986,000	90.2%	99,729,000	91.5%	2.0%
Baha'is	2,000	0.0%	2,500	0.0%	1.5%
Chinese folk-religionists	1,600	0.0%	2,000	0.0%	1.4%
Hindus	1,200	0.0%	2,000	0.0%	3.6%
Buddhists	760	0.0%	1,000	0.0%	1.8%
Jews	91	0.0%	100	0.0%	0.6%
people professing no religion	473,000	0.6%	695,000	0.6%	2.6%
Total population	**82,041,000**	**100.0%**	**108,939,000**	**100.0%**	**1.9%**

Source: Centre for the Study of World Christianity (CSGC), Boston, Gordon-Conwell TS

A Brief History[1]

Christianity in Egypt dates back to the very beginnings of Christianity itself, even to the escape of the Holy Family to Egypt from King Herod, in fulfilment of the Old Testament prophecy: 'Out of Egypt I called my son' (Matt. 2:15). There were also some figures from Alexandria who had good knowledge of Christianity, as we read in the Book of Acts about Apollos of Alexandria, who was 'an eloquent man and mighty in the Scriptures'. He had been instructed in the way of the Lord, and taught accurately the things of the Lord (Acts 18:24-27).

Nevertheless, the foundation of the Church of Alexandria is ascribed to Mark the evangelist. After his journeys and service with Paul and Barnabas and Peter, he finally evangelized in Alexandria.

Mark founded the Church of Alexandria (the See of St Mark), known as the Coptic Orthodox Church.[2] But his life ended as a martyr at the hands of the heathen and his blood flowed over the streets of

[1] For a more extensive overview see Samir Fawzi Girgis, "Of the Copts' Heritage", Volume I [in Arabic] (Cairo: St. John the Beloved Publishing House, 2004).

[2] The word Copt refers to the Egyptians in general, for it is derived from Aegyptos derived from the old Egyptian term Het-Ka-Ptah, meaning "the house of the spirit of Ptah", referring to Memphis the capital at that time. From the word Aegyptos came the English word Egypt. According to some, the Egyptians are the descendants of Mezraim, the son of

Alexandria, irrigating the seeds of faith. That was on 8th May AD 68. From this beginning, martyrdom became a characteristic of the Coptic Church.

A Suffering Church

Coptic Church history is both glorious in her illustrious figures, and tragic in her suffering. The pride of the Coptic Church is the Cross, represented in the persecutions that began in AD 68 with the martyrdom of Mark, followed by persecution at the hands of the Roman rulers and most of the following rulers of Egypt. The Christians of Egypt suffered severely under the Roman rulers Severus (AD 204), Decius (AD 250), Valerian (AD 251), and Diocletian (AD 284-303). This made the Copts take the year of the reign of Diocletian in AD 284 as the beginning of their Coptic Calendar, to commemorate the faith of the martyrs. Historians witness to the Coptic Church as preserving the light of the Christian faith for centuries, in spite of incredible oppression and persecution.[3]

Christianity spread all over Egypt within half a century from the coming of Mark to Alexandria, as is evident from the texts of the New Testament that were discovered in many parts of Egypt. It is the fulfilment of the Old Testament prophecies, as written in Isaiah 19:19: 'In that day there will be an altar to the Lord in the midst of the land of Egypt, and a pillar to the Lord at its border.'

Egypt under Muslim Rule

A new era began in the seventh century with the Arab invasion of Egypt. New types of persecution began and were faced by the Copts with the same steadfastness of faith. They proved loyal to their faith and country, in spite of all the hardships and tribulations.

The Miracle of Coptic Culture

Coptic culture is deep-rooted, dating back to Egypt's Pharaohs. It continued miraculously for 2,000 years in spite of all attempts at marginalization and destruction. All countries that occupied Egypt, whether Roman or Byzantine, Turkish or Arab, tried hard to destroy Coptic culture and identity, but all of them failed, for it was built on steadfast faith and adherence to Coptic identity. With this culture, the Copts contributed to Egyptian history in spite of all the pressures they endured. The miracle is that it is a culture of a people who have faced enormous challenges throughout the past twenty centuries, and who still face them today, continually offering sacrifices of the blood of thousands of their martyrs so that they may not surrender their existence, their land or their church.

The Contribution of the Coptic Church to World Christianity

Nobody can speak of the contribution of the Coptic Church to world Christianity without tracing it to its early centuries, for any present contribution is based on and derives from these roots. The Copts follow in the steps of their fathers.

The most significant contributions of the Coptic Church to world Christianity are the Catechetical School of Alexandria and the Monastic Movement.

Ham, the son of Noah. Consequently, all Christians and even the Moslems are also considered Copts.

[3] Montague Fowler, *Christian Egypt: Past, Present, and Future* (Book II. Ch. i.) (London: Church Newspaper Company Limited, 1901), 189.

The Catechetical School of Alexandria

The Catechetical School of Alexandria was founded to counter the heathen school that was there with its pagan philosophies. The first great scholar who headed the School was Pantaenus, who died in AD 200 and was succeeded by Clement of Alexandria, followed by Origen, then Dedymos. Many of the early church fathers either graduated from or headed it. It was revived in 1893 by Pope Cyril V, in Cairo. It developed at the hands of great Coptic scholars, like St Habib Gerguis. By this time, numerous branches had been opened in Alexandria, Cairo and in other districts of Egypt, and abroad in the USA (Los Angeles), Germany and Australia. It is now situated within the Patriarchate area.

Another academic postgraduate school, the Institute of Coptic Studies, was founded over sixty years ago, in 1954. Its aim is to promote studies in the various branches of Coptic culture. It prepares graduates for service in the church and academic work in the various branches of Coptic culture: theology, history, the Coptic language, art, hymnology, etc. It awards a Diploma of Coptic Studies in these branches after two years of study, following which a graduate prepares a thesis under the supervision of the professors of the Institute, ending with the thesis being examined and the successful researcher being awarded the MA degree, and afterwards the PhD degree for the researcher's dissertation. It encourages research work, and plays a distinguished role in the field of theology and ecumenism. It has an irregular scholarly magazine, besides the various publications of its professors.

The Monastic Movement and Asceticism

This is the second outstanding contribution of the Coptic Church to world Christianity. From the fourth century onwards, Egyptian Christianity was characterized by its emphasis upon the ascetic life, and the neighbourhood of Alexandria started being filled with monasteries, which grew more numerous as time went on.[4]

Monasticism began in Egypt and had its influence in the formation of the Coptic personality through the teachings and writings of the great church fathers of Egypt. It began at the end of the third century and flourished in the fourth century. The first anchorite was St Paul the hermit (228-343), but the first who founded a monastic community was St Anthony (251-356) who is known throughout the world as the father of monasticism. Afterwards St Pachomius (292-346) founded the cenobite system of monasticism with its rules. The third was St Shenouda, who founded the White Monastery in Upper Egypt, following the Pachomian system, but more strictly. Many other prominent figures were involved, like St Makarius the Great.

From Egypt, monasticism spread elsewhere into the world. St Basil, for instance, who organized the monastic movement in Asia Minor, visited Egypt in 357 and derived benefit from it. St Jerome also visited Egypt in 400, writing in detail of his experience of Egyptian monasticism. In the sixth century, St Benedict established monasteries after the example of the system of St Pachomius. There were also Coptic missions to northern Europe, like St Maurice the commander of the Thebes Legion who left Egypt to serve in Rome, but ended up evangelizing the mountain inhabitants of Switzerland. There is a small town and a monastery there, both bearing his name where his holy body lies with some of his books and belongings.

The monastic movement witnessed some decline due to persecution, but its revival came at the hands of Pope Shenouda III, through the restoration of old monasteries and the building of new ones, and the ordaining of many monks and nuns. There are now over two thousand of them, in dozens of monasteries.[5]

---

[4] Otto F.A. Meinardus, Christian Egypt: Ancient and Modern, 2nd Revised Edition (Cairo: The American University in Cairo Press, 1977), 164.

[5] Famous monasteries at present include: four in Wadi Natrun, namely: monasteries of St. Makarius, St. Bishoy, Baramous, and Surian; one near Alexandria is St. Minas Monastery; various in Middle and Upper Egypt, that of St. Samuel, Al Moharraq, St. Paul, St. Anthony and the White monasteries. These are inhabited

Throughout history, the monks have played a key role in Christianity. Great theologians from among the monks had their influence on world Christianity alongside lay theologians, and their writings still have influence. The popes and bishops of the Coptic Church are chosen from among the monks. Recent popes who have been influential include the late Pope Kyrillos (Cyril) VI, and the late Pope Shenouda III. The 110th patriarch, known as Cyril IV, also known as the Reformer,

was one of the most significant milestones in the history of the Coptic Church. He sought to consolidate the Coptic Church in Egypt and was committed to raising the educational standard of the Copts, through establishing schools.[6]

More Contributions of the Coptic Church to World Christianity, Past and Present

- Her great theologians defended the faith against heresies and left a treasure of theological and ascetic literature, which greatly influenced Christian theology and asceticism. Among these were St Athanasius the Apostolic (bishop 328-373), who played an important role at the Council of Nicaea and left a treasury of writings. St Cyril of Alexandria of the fifth century was a great defender of the Incarnation and also left important theological writings.
- Her present fathers and scholars still follow the same path and defend the faith against heresies and atheism. Recently, Metropolitan Bishoy and Bishop Raphael, besides some clergy and scholars, have continued this tradition through a series of seminars, lectures and writings.
- The translation by the Copts of the Scriptures into Coptic in the second century was a major contribution. The world's museums and libraries contain copies of these translations.
- They were the first to invent the method of chiselling into wood for blind students (fifteen centuries before Braille).
- The first private Arabic printing presses were founded by Pope Cyril IV around 1855.[7]
- Coptic art is distinctive, be it painting, architecture or textiles.

The Modern History of Christianity in Egypt

The standing of the Copts began to improve in early nineteenth century with the rule of Mohammed Ali. The unity of the nation, including Christians and Muslims, became more apparent, and it was able to face the extremists in the 1919 Revolution. The church has always separated itself from politics.

However, in the next few decades persecution resumed due to extremist Islamic movements, such as the Salaphees and the Muslim Brothers who ruled Egypt for one year, a period characterized by many violent practices. Thanks to God that their rule ended after a year through the revolution of 30th June 2013, in which all the people rose up, supported by the army. They ousted the president, and a new president (El Sisi) was elected showed himself to be wise, loyal and brave, not discriminating against the Copts. He has been trying hard with the help of the army to put an end to terrorism in Egypt. We pray that he succeeds.

In February 2015, a harsh new act of terrorism was perpetrated against the Copts by the terrorist Islamic movement ISIS. They brutally beheaded twenty-one Egyptian Coptic labourers in Libya and broadcast the whole crime on t social media, defying the whole world and alleging that they were defending Islam. The truth of this was contradicted by their preceding murder of dozens of the Egyptian army and police.

---

by hundreds of monks.

[6] Otto Friedrich August Meinardus, *Two Thousand Years of Coptic Christianity* (Cairo: American Univ in Cairo Press, 2002), 69-70.

[7]Meinardus, *Two Thousand Years of Coptic Christianity,* 70.

In spite of all such brutal acts, the Copts hold fast to their faith, trusting that the Lord never forsakes his people in Egypt. God's care of the Copts appears in the blessings with which God strengthens them. An example is the repeated apparitions of the Holy Virgin Mary, beginning in April 1968 in her church in Zeitoun District for years. This apparition was witnessed by millions of Christians and people of all religions and nationalities, and was broadcast by Egyptian TV and published in the worldwide press. Similar apparitions were repeated in other churches and districts, even in Upper Egypt in Assiut and in Guiza, Cairo. This is taken by the Copts as a comforting sign of God's support for them in their days of tribulation and suffering, giving them hope and refreshing their souls.

As for the number of the Copts at present in Egypt, there are no accurate statistics, for the trend is to avoid religious classification. But it is estimated at over twenty million out of a total population of approximately ninety million, in addition to those living overseas.

Various Denominations in Egypt[8]

The largest denomination in Egypt is the Coptic Orthodox Church, while there are also other Orthodox churches, and the two main Catholic and Protestant churches.

The Orthodox Churches

THE COPTIC ORTHODOX

This is the largest denomination, representing about 90% of the Christians in Egypt. The present Patriarch, the 118th of the See of St Mark, is HH Pope Tawadros II, succeeding the late Pope Shenouda III, a great figure who did much for the church, world Christianity and church unity. The present Patriarchate is based in St Mark's Cathedral in Cairo, and has another seat in Alexandria. It has numerous dioceses all over Egypt and abroad, headed by bishops, of whom the Holy Synod is presided over by the Pope. A lay council helps manage church finances and forms a link between the clergy and the Holy Synod. The Seminary and the Postgraduate Institute of Coptic Studies are the church's main educational institutions.

OTHER ORTHODOX CHURCHES INCLUDE:

- The Greek Eastern Orthodox Church, dating back to the first century, with churches in Cairo and Alexandria, and some ecclesiastical and private schools.[9]
- The Oriental Armenian Orthodox[10] and Syrian Orthodox Churches, with churches, educational institutions and social activities.

The Roman Catholic Churches, presided over by the Pope of Rome[11]

***The Patriarchate of Alexandria for the Coptic Catholics*:** This dates back to 1219. They have a cathedral and some churches all over Egypt, besides a seminary.
Other Catholic churches include:
Greek, Armenian, Syrian, Maronite, Chaldean and Latin Catholic Churches.

[8] Youssef Sabri, "Introduction to the Personal Status Laws," Lectures to the Seminary.
[9] Fowler, *Christian Egypt: Past, Present, and Future*, 224-228.
[10] Fowler, "Christian Churches & Missions in Egypt," in *Christian Egypt: Past, Present, and Future*, Book II Ch. iv, 273.
[11] Fowler, "Christian Churches & Missions in Egypt", Ch. iii, 232-234.

Protestant (Evangelical) Churches

There are over 150 traditions. They work through the 'Evangelical Nile Synod', a mother body that manages many churches and institutions.

OTHER EVANGELICAL CHURCHES IN EGYPT[12]

The twentieth century witnessed the coming of missionaries to Egypt from the West and spreading all over the country. The present churches include: Presbyterian, which is the largest, Episcopal (Anglican) Church,[13] Reformed, Apostolic Grace Church, Apostolic Church (including the Baptist), Pentecostal, Plymouth Brethren and Adventists. Many other evangelical churches have been founded by other missionaries or independent movements.[14]

Efforts for Church Unity and Relations with Muslims

Since the 1970s, the late HH Pope Shenouda III encouraged dialogue with other churches, including the Roman Catholic, Eastern Orthodox and Anglican, as well as with Muslims. His ecumenical efforts were distinguished. Pope Tawadros II followed the same path, commencing with exchange visits with the Roman Catholic and Russian Eastern Orthodox Churches. The Coptic Orthodox Church was among the first churches to join the World Council of Churches. Its bishops and theologians have always participated effectively and actively in WCC meetings and efforts for unity.

Internally, a Council of all churches of Egypt was founded in 2013 to bring together all churches together in one Spirit in Christ, and to promote amicable relations with Muslims. It works alongside the Middle East Council of Churches, which has always played a great role in fostering church unity and deep relations with the Islamic countries of the region.

Exchange visits between church leaders and Al Azhar (the official Islamic institution) focus on feasts and special events. Sharing common national events is encouraged, especially among youth from both sides. The Youth Bishopric of the Coptic Orthodox Church and the Ministry of Youth take the lead, celebrating such events together. At a state level, the trend is the same. For instance, a large celebration was held for the second millennial anniversary of the Coming of the Holy Family to Egypt, escaping from King Herod. This reveals the readiness of most Egyptians to strengthen their co-existence.

Bibliography

El Masry, Iris Habib. *The Story of the Coptic Church.* Alexandria: St George Church, Sporting, 1983.

Fowler, Montague. *Christian Egypt: Past, Present, and Future.* London: Church Newspaper Company, Limited, 1901.

Gabra, Gawdat, *Be Thou There: The Holy Family's Journey.* Cairo, AUX Press, 2001.

Gabra, Gawdat. *Coptic Monasteries: Egypt's Monastic Art & Architecture.* Cairo: AUC Press, 2002.

Gerguis, Samir Fawzi, ed. *Of the Copts' Heritage, Volume I [in Arabic].* Cairo: St John the Beloved Publishing House, 2004.

Malaty, Tadros Y. *Introduction to the Coptic Orthodox Church.* Alexandria: St George Church, 1993.

---

[12] Adib Salama, *History of the Evangelical Church in Egypt* (Cairo: Dar Al Thakafa, 1982), 50-93; 113- 140; 321-328; Eissa Diab, *Introduction to the History of the Evangelical Churches and their theology* (Lebanon: Arabic Baptist Theological School, 2009) 115-120. www.st-tekla.org.
George Onsy, "Map of the Christian Denominations in Egypt", January 2015.

[13] Meinardus, "Christian Egypt: Ancient and Modern", 572-573.

[14] Fowler, "Christian Egypt: Past, Present, and Future", 274-277.

Meinardus, Otto F.A. *Christian Egypt: Ancient and Modern.* Cairo: The American University in Cairo Press, 1977.

Meinardus, Otto F.A., *2000 Years of Coptic Christianity.* Cairo: The American University in Cairo Press, 1999.

Middle East Council of Churches. *A Guide to the Churches of the Middle East.* Cairo: MECC, 1999.

The Holy Synod sub-committee presided by His Holiness Pope Shenouda III. *The Holy Family in Egypt (first edition).* Cairo: St Minas Monastery, 2000.

The Oriental Orthodox Churches, Publications Committee. *The Oriental Orthodox Churches (Coptic, Syrian, Armenian): a historical overview (first edition).* (Cairo: The Oriental Orthodox Churches Publications Committee, 2006).

Youhanna, Menassa. *History of the Coptic Church [in Arabic].* Cairo: Al Mehabba Bookshop, 1983.

(60B) Christianity in Egypt – Evangelical Perspectives

Andrea Zaki

This paper provides a critical account of the history, participation, contributions and challenges of the Evangelical Church in Egyptian society. Despite the fact that this relationship is historic (more than 150 years), the priority here is given to the participation and challenges in the latter half of the twentieth century and its implications in the first decade of the third millennium.

Evangelical Church in Egypt – A History of More than a Century and a Half

In December 1850, a Hamayouni Firman (was a decree that granted Presbyterian church to freely worshiped, without any form of hinderance or annoyance) was issued in recognition of the Presbyterian Church in Egypt besides the Orthodox Church and the Catholic Church. The message that was provided by missionaries was based on some of the principles of theology and faith, which came as a result of the Reformation in the sixteenth century. When this movement came to Egypt, many Egyptians believed in it. In February 1863, there was the nomination of the first elders and deacons in Cairo; then a special church meeting was held in 1876 in the district of Azbakeya.

The Current Composition of the Evangelical Church in Egypt

The Evangelical church in Egypt currently includes eighteen denominations, the Synod of the Nile and seventeen other Evangelical churches; however, before the state, they are all represented by one entity, which is the Evangelical General Council.

The Evangelical Synod of the Nile

The origin of the word ‘synod’ goes back to the Latin *synodus*, which again goes back to the Late Greek *synodos*, which means ‘meeting’ or ‘assembly’. The first synod in Egypt began in 1898, and because of the breadth of its evangelistic work, it created four congregations. Over time, the Synod has expanded to become what it is in its current composition: eight congregations and four hundred local churches.

It is worth mentioning that the Synod represents the supreme authority of the local churches in a particular geographical area. In addition, the Synod helps local churches in the performance of their mission in the field of education, theological studies, medical institutions, pastoral work, media, services, development, women’s work, Sunday schools and other spiritual and social fields. Moreover, the Evangelical Presbyterian Church has a Faculty of Theology that is considered to be the largest in the Arab world amongst colleges of evangelical theology.

Other Evangelical Churches in Egypt

There are seventeen other evangelical churches other than the Synod, such as the Brethren Church, Open Brethren Church, Faith Church, God Church, Apostolic Church and Episcopal Church.

Denomination	*Number of Churches*
Brethren Church	240
Open Brethren Church	10
Reformed Church	103

Faith Church	42
God Church	13
Apostolic Church	164
Grace Apostolic Church	17
Grace Church	17
Christian Model Church	24
Christ Church	25
Baptist Church	20
First Baptist Bible Church	1
Pentecostal Church	55
Independent National Baptist Church	27
Preaching the Gospel Church	10
Episcopal Church	15
Dutch Message Church	1
Evangelical Synod of the Nile (mentioned above)	400
Total	***1184***

The Evangelical General Council in Egypt

The General Council represents the evangelical community before the state, and consists of the eighteen evangelical denominations in Egypt. According to the Hamayouni Firman, in December 1850, the representative of the Anglican Communion (currently the head of the church) has the right to consider all financial affairs, personnel and social issues. On 29th March 1991, the Evangelical General Council in Egypt agreed on the internal regulations of the Council, consisting of 17 articles, which were approved by the Interior Ministry. It is worth mentioning that the regulations in their first article identified the Congregation Evangelical General Council as representing all the evangelical denominations and subsidiary local churches before of the state.

The Main Contribution of the Evangelical Church to Egyptian Society

The Witness of the Church as a model for society

The Evangelical Church has offered unique community models with outstanding educational facilities, health and social work for over a century and a half. The importance of these community-based initiatives lies in the model for social service that they provide. In a society influenced by corruption, a good Christian social model of community and service can create a different atmosphere, emphasizing communication and support, building bridges. At a time when many tend to call for exclusion, these community-based initiatives, using an enlightened social model, can swim against the current and prove to be an effective Christian presence. Moreover, the Evangelical Church has never used a non-Arab worship style in the Arabic context. The church has focused on press, publishing and translation, and is present at theological, cultural, social and political levels.

Indeed, the church never felt isolated from society and its concerns. From the beginning, it has taken an active role in the development and enlightenment of the community without regard for religious affiliation, race or ethnicity. The Evangelical Mission in Egypt has focused on education, at both pre university and university level. In addition, it has worked hard on adult literacy as a way to free people from ignorance.

The church has always worked on the understanding that every human is created in the image of God and therefore has the right to live in dignity. The church has worked for better health through the establishment of hospitals and nursing schools. For the same reason, it supported the development of the poorest communities and raise their standard of living. This progress was accomplished through churches or civil society organizations that have evangelical roots.

In a similar way, the Coptic Evangelical Organization for Social Services (CEOSS) played a significant role in civil society in the period after the Egyptian Revolution 2011. CEOSS focuses on spreading democracy and education for democracy. It emphasizes the concept of citizenship and the role of the media by modelling public awareness and highlighting its significance in the spread of human and civil values. Another of CEOSS's major concerns is networking and focusing on societal dialogue among the different elements of civil society, especially the poor, women, people with disabilities and youth. CEOSS offers micro-credit systems which focus on developing the economic status of the poor and lower middle classes in order to overcome approaches based purely on charity and to promote empowerment and rights-based development.

Encouraging Civil Society

Although Egypt's civil society is weak, the promotion of it will contribute significantly to its presence on the ground. An active civil society promotes a pluralistic identity through diverse affiliations as it creates new common ground through voluntary work, and contributes to democratic practices. Because the church is part of the community, it needs to take initiatives and work hard to consolidate the values of democracy, volunteering, and to emphasize the importance of individuals as influencing the society to which they belong.

In the process of development, the church need not stop at providing aid and assistance, but needs to focus also on community cultural development to support a culture of co-existence and to consolidate the values of citizenship, pluralism and tolerance. No one can deny that, for more than 150 years, the church took an active political role in all the events the nation has passed through, because the church did not live in isolation from society, but it was part of it and it worked for its development.

Self-Realization through the Presence of 'The Other'

With the discourse on exclusion, the church emphasizes the importance of self-realization through the presence of 'the other' and through new community-based initiatives that emphasize the participation of everyone in planning, implementation and evaluation. Its new community initiatives in social, cultural and political fields which ensure the presence of 'the other' are important and relevant for an effective formulation of the positive presence of everyone in society.

Major Challenges Facing Christianity in Egypt

Intellectual Challenges

There are many intellectual challenges which contribute to increasing the gap within society in Egypt. These challenges include religious scepticism, which limits the national identity to religious identity and considers it to be the sole indicator of human identity. This contributes to curbing pluralism and creating an attitude of single loyalty. It also raises many doubts about the relationship between Christians and the West, and these doubts question Christians' patriotism.

On the other hand, the challenge of questioning the doctrine of 'the other' creates a kind of bitterness that lead to violence or withdrawal and marginalization. This doubt cannot be removed easily; in some cases, this negative mental image is amplified and turned into contempt of the doctrine of 'the other', evolving into rejection of 'the other', and in some cases even isolation. This doubt may take the form of pressure on the other to change religion, either legitimately or illegitimately. All this leads to rejecting 'the other', provoking sectarian strife and creating a huge gap in the community, making some Christians in

Egypt prefer isolation and confinement within their own communities rather than openness and integration with 'the other'.

There is also another problem in the social and cultural alienation that results from a sense of marginalization and exclusion over a long time. A constitution and laws as such are not responsible for this marginalization, but rather they are due to the unfair practices of some leaders and officials. It is also notable that there is an exclusion of culture and civilization of the Copts from the cultural reality in Egypt, in addition to the biased treatment of their heritage. This discrimination of their history and heritage has formed misconceptions and contributed to making co-existence a difficult vision. In return, this has made the Copts value their own heritage. Other groups consider only Egyptian Pharaonic culture and ignore the rest of the cultures that have emerged. These groups have called for the rejection of the Arabic language, considering it an alien language, which has led to further alienation.

Moreover, places of worship represent a major challenge for Christians in Egypt. Current laws are an obstacle to building places of worship for religious minorities; it should not be necessary to get a governor's approval and official permits to carry out repairs to places of worship already in place (city laws should apply). It is noticeable, for example, that the usual cause of sectarian violence in Egypt comes mostly when Christians try to build or repair their churches. However, a law for places of worship was drafted to ease the process, but it has yet to be presented to parliament. Although the government is sometimes co-operative, those affiliated to religious movements stand in the way.

When religious identity is the sole determining factor of political participation, it is natural that religious minorities would rebuild their identity in light of political and cultural turmoil. The rise of religious movements contributed to the shift from national affiliation and loyalty to religious affiliation and loyalty. Also, reducing identity to religious identity has reduced the concept of pluralism and the creation of a concept of unilateral loyalty.

In addition, the issue of freedom of belief, especially religious freedom, is one of the most complicated issues in the region, particularly in Egypt. There is a culture of extremism prevailing in the region. Freedom of belief should promote religious freedom (in theory and practice) in addition to the freedom of individuals to choose their beliefs.

Challenges by the Minority Mentality

In the 1990s, an important debate took place in Egypt and the Arab world about whether Christians in Egypt should be considered a minority. However, the term 'minority' used here refers to religious numerical data. With a quick glance at the characteristics of a minority mentality, we can summarize elements of this attitude as follows:

Divine Intervention and the Millennial Kingdom

The mentality of the minority tends to include apocalyptic dreams represented in the return of Christ and the Millennial Reign. The second coming of Christ will contribute to ending pressure, creating a new society with no religious minorities. Actually, this doctrine has serious political, social and cultural dimensions. Christ reigning on earth for a thousand years, as some believe, will provide an ideal model for a new government, based on divine right, which does not practise discrimination but achieves equality. This visionary dream of the Millennial Kingdom reflects the vision of religious concepts of political, social and cultural significance. It represents a trend of escaping from the pressures of the current situation and a move towards ideal future dreams. As soon as these minority thoughts and mentalities are transferred from the actual world itself to the other and other-worldly world, the celestial level, history stops completely and thought becomes limited and no longer subject to analysis or study.

IDENTITY

One of the most important contradictions that make up the minority mindset is a particular concept of religious identity. At a time when minorities need to push the community towards a common national identity, they instead resort to a narrow concept of religious identity. This contradiction creates a sort of hypocrisy that affects the credibility of national loyalty. On the other hand, minorities always fear the danger of a national meltdown, which makes them resolve to uphold their religious identity. This is what has happened in Egypt during the past few decades, as the Copts turned to isolation. This complex situation caused confusion and in some cases encouraged the religious affiliations of extremists to use their religious identity for political purposes.

(61) Christianity in Eritrea[1]

Tewelde Beyene

Religion	Pop 2010	Pct 2010	Pop 2025	Pct 2025	Gr Pct 1970 2025
Christians	2,162,000	46.1%	3,050,000	46.3%	2.3%
Independents	18,800	0.4%	32,000	0.5%	3.6%
African initiated	18,800	0.4%			
Orthodox	1,953,000	41.6%	2,781,000	42.2%	2.4%
Oriental Orthodox	1,950,000	41.6%			
Protestants	52,800	1.1%	95,000	1.4%	4.0%
Lutheran	42,800	0.9%			
Roman Catholics	154,000	3.3%	185,000	2.8%	1.2%
Pentecostals/Charismatics	123,000	2.6%	220,000	3.3%	3.9%
Evangelicals	31,500	0.7%	50,000	0.8%	3.1%
Muslims	2,411,000	51.4%	3,383,000	51.4%	2.3%
adherents of traditional African religions	35,500	0.8%	38,000	0.6%	0.5%
Baha'is	1,600	0.0%	2,400	0.0%	2.9%
Hindus	1,100	0.0%	1,600	0.0%	2.2%
people professing no religion	78,600	1.7%	111,000	1.7%	2.3%
Total population	**4,690,000**	**100.0%**	**6,585,000**	**100.0%**	**2.3%**

Source: Centre for the Study of World Christianity (CSGC), Boston, Gordon-Conwell TS

The Pre-Christian Context

Important for the understanding of Christianity in Eritrea are early historical relationships with Jewish traditions: According to these traditions, in pre-Christian Aksum, one group of people worshipped a serpent king *(Negus Arwye).* Along with this went the cult of a host of good and evil spirits and genii, associated with trees, springs and mountain tops. Again, tradition has it that the other group of people followed Mosaic Law. Today, several historians – Ethiopian, Eritrean and others – question, or outrightly dismiss, the historicity of the traditions relating to the Queen of Sheba and her son Menelik,[2] allegedly born out of a relationship of the queen with King Solomon, as both the initiators of Judaism and the founders of a tri-millennial dynasty. Without delving into the details of the debate, suffice it to highlight the role of the Queen of Sheba lore as the foundation of a thought system that shaped the identity, culture and traditions of the people, forged centuries of history and determined the course of key events. The embodiment in

---

[1] This is a shortened version of a longer essay on Christianity in Eritrea which is contributed to this volume and can be seen in full length in the digital collection on African Christianity in> www.globethics.net/web/anthology-african-christianity.

[2] See, for example: Bahru Zewde, *A History of Ethiopia, 1855-1991,* Addis Ababa: Ohio University Press-Addis Ababa University Press, 2001, 7; Id., *A Short History of Ethiopia and the Horn*, Addis Ababa: Department of History, Addis Ababa University, 1998, 57.

Ethiopian and Eritrean Christianity of such Old Testament practices as circumcision, ritual purity, dietary laws, the observance of the Sabbath and such persistent traditions as the one revolving around the Ark of the Covenant, believed to have been abducted from Jerusalem and preserved in Aksum, the origin of the clergy from Aaron, and the genealogical connections of the Christian population with the twelve tribes of Israel, may not necessarily mean that as large a people as the 'the other half' were of Jewish religion. It is however indicative of significant relations with ancient Israel, from which those traditions may have developed in the course of centuries.[3]

If, in addition to the above, one adds Aksum's cultural and commercial contacts with the Mediterranean world and the civilizations across the Red Sea, the overall picture that emerges in the early centuries AD is one of an eclectic religious microcosm, whose pantheon was shared by both local and foreign – i.e. South Arabian, Jewish, Greek and other – components.

Orthodox Tewahedo Christianity

History highlights

Authoritative historians believe that the eunuch referred to in the Acts of the Apostles (8:26-40), was not an Aksumite, as he was a servant of Candace, this being the name of a series of Meroïtic queens.[4] Nonetheless, when the Syrian young man Frumentius introduced Christianity to the court of King Ezana in the later 330s, small Christian enclaves were already present among the foreign traders and some of their native partners in Adulis and other coastal centres as well as in the towns along the caravan routes leading across the Eritrean plateau, into Aksum. Adulis, the main seaport of the kingdom, was soon to become one of the few suffragan dioceses under the metropolitan see of Aksum. Owing to St Frumentius' episcopal consecration by St Athanasius, Aksum became an ecclesiastical province of the Alexandrian patriarchate and followed in its footsteps in rejecting the Council of Chalcedon.[5] Some time later (in the eighth or ninth century?) a pseudo-canon, attributed to Nicaea, was formulated, stipulating that the metropolitan bishop had to be permanently an Egyptian by birth.[6] Between the fifth and sixth centuries, groups of Syrian missionary monks established monastic centres and carried out extensive evangelistic activities in various parts of both Tigray and Eritrea.

At the beginning of the eighth century, following the rise of Islam, Aksum lost its Eritrean coastal and maritime possessions to the Arabs and, under the pressure of the Beja, northern populations sweeping across Eritrea, the political fulcrum shifted southwards in the direction of today's central Ethiopia. Here the ancient rulers of Aksumite origin were replaced by a local dynasty of the Cushitic stock, the Zagwe, who ruled over the country from 1150 up to 1270, when the Amhara, speakers of a tongue of the Semitic cluster, established a dynasty that claimed its origin from King Solomon and the Queen of Sheba. The 'Solomonic dynasty' would maintain power, through various vicissitudes, up to the fall of emperor Haile Selassie in 1974.

---

[3] Cf. Edward Ullendorff, *Ethiopia and the Bible*, Oxford: Oxford University Press, 1968, 73-118, 131-145.

[4] Cf. Carlo Conti Rossini, *Storia d' Etiopia*, Bergamo: Instituto italiano d'arti grafiche, 1928, 145; Belaynesh Michael, "Candace," in Belaynesh Michael, Stanislas Chojnacki, Richard Pankhrust, eds., *The Dictionary of Ethiopian Biography*, Addis Ababa: Institute of Ethiopian Studies, 1975, 43.

[5] The Ethio-Eritrean Orthodox Tewahedo Church adheres to the Cyrillian formula, *"The one incarnated nature of God the Word,"* rejecting the term *monophysis* and preferring instead *miaphysis.* Cf. Aymro Wondemagegnehu-Joachim Motuvu, *The Ethiopian Orthodox Church,* Addis Ababa: Ethiopian Orthodox Mission, 1970, 98-99.

[6] Cf. Stuart Munro Hay, *Ethiopia and Alexandria. The Metropolitan Episcopacy of Ethiopia*, Warszawa-Wiesbaden: Bibliotheca Nubica et Aethiopica, 1997, 14-18.

The establishment of important Eritrean Orthodox Tewahedo Christian monasteries such as Debre Libanos in Shimezana and Debre Sina, near Keren, is attributed to members of Syrian missionary groups. It was at this time and in such Eritrean and Tigrean monastic centres that Christianity was first enculturated, the translation of the Bible, of patristic, theological, liturgical and monastic texts being the first most remarkable achievements in that connection.[7]

Territorial expansion in Ethiopia, through lengthy and bloody conflicts with Muslim and pagan forces, was systematically accompanied by the evangelization of new territories under the leadership of two powerful monastic leaders – Iyesus-Mo'a (ca. 1214-1293) and Tekle-Haymanot (ca. 1215-1313). The third great monastic leader, Ewstathewos (ca. 1273-1352) and his disciples expanded Christianity further in Tigray and today's Eritrea.[8] No less than 20 of the 22 monasteries still existing in the latter country were established by them. Though ostracized for over one hundred years for their strict observance of the Sabbath (in addition to Sunday), a practice that was condemned by both the Ethiopian court and the Egyptian metropolitans, the Ewstathean monasteries in Tigray and Eritrea made a substantial contribution to the liturgical, theological and literary movements which marked Christian history, particularly in the fourteenth and fifteenth centuries. Among other factors, it was through the heroic endurance of Filipos, the founder of Debre Bizen, the most important monastery in Eritrea established in 1373-1374, that the observance of the Sabbath received official ratification by King Zer'a-Ya'iqob at the Council of Debre Metmaq in 1451. Extensive land grants bestowed by the monarchs upon many monasteries in Eritrea, as elsewhere, enhanced their religious, social and political influence in society.

In the wake of Portuguese military intervention, a Roman Catholic mission was entrusted to the Jesuits (1555-1632). However, the conversion of Emperor Sesenyos (rl. 1607-1632), the forced imposition of Roman Catholicism as the state religion, and the 'Latinization' of the liturgy and of the whole Christian traditional system, triggered a chain of violent reaction by the entire Orthodox Tewahedo community and led to the final debacle of the 'Catholic Latin experiment'.[9] The Eritrean monasteries, along with the rest of Ethiopia, were in the forefront in the struggle for the defence of their Christian cultural identity and tradition.

During the colonial 'Scramble for Africa', while Ethiopia retained its sovereignty through Menelik II's (1844-1913) resounding victory over the Italians at the battle of Adwa in 1896, Eritrea was given over to the latter as a colony. In the early 1930s, the Italian colonial government undertook unsuccessful attempts to separate the Eritrean Orthodox community from Ethiopia, with an Eritrean metropolitan bishop directly dependent on the Coptic patriarchate in Egypt. This attempt having failed, following the occupation of Ethiopia in 1935, Italian efforts concentrated on severing Ethiopia's jurisdictional ties with the Coptic patriarchate. A synod was thus convened in Addis Ababa in 1937 by Marshal Rodolfo Graziani, in which the Ethiopian abbot Abune Abraham was appointed metropolitan bishop. Five bishops were also selected and consecrated, and for the first time Eritrea had its own bishop in the person of Abune Marqos, abbot of Debre Bizen. The Coptic patriarchate from Cairo excommunicated the new archbishop, the five bishops and all the clergy consecrated by them. After Haile Selassie's return from exile in 1941, relations with Egypt were restored and the excommunicated prelates and clergy pardoned and reinstated.[10] In the following years, by the emperor's own initiative, and in continuity with the appointment of the first

---

[7] Cf. Tewelde Beyene, "Evangelization and Inculturation in the History of Ethiopian Christianity," *Ethiopian Review of Cultures,* no. 6/7/ (1996-97), 5-20.

[8] After the fall of Aksum, before it was made a political entity by the Italians in the late nineteenth century, the area was called subsequently: *Ma'ekele-Bahr*, *Medre-Bahr*, *Mereb-Mellash*, with some other variations.

[9] Cf. Tewelde Beyene, "Hanno riconsacrato i nostri *Tabot*. Conflitti fra inculturazione e latinizzazione nella storia missionaria in Etiopia ed Eritrea", *Ad Gentes: Teologia e Antropologia della Missione*, no.17/2 (1913),148-177.

[10] Cf. Cesare Marongiu Bonaiuti, *Politica e religioni nel colonialismo italiano, 1882-1941*, Varese: Giuffrè, 1982, 72-90, 151-199; Paolo Borruso, *L'ultimo impero cristiano,* Milano: Guerini e Associati, 2002, 83-252.

legitimate Ethiopian bishops back in 1929, negotiations were resumed, leading to full autocephaly. In 1959, Abune Basylios, abbot of Debre Libanos in Shewa, was elected the first patriarch of Ethiopia-Eritrea.[11]

All through the revolutionary period (1974-1991), despite its atheistic orientation, the Marxist regime chose a policy of dictatorial-revolutionary control over, rather than the suppression of, the church in Ethiopia, as much as in Eritrea. The church's life, organization and activities were thus put under severe strain as a consequence of the regime's heavy-handed interference.

As an immediate result of the independence of Eritrea in 1991, the Eritrean Orthodox community also became ecclesiastically autonomous, seeking a formal legitimization of its status, not from Ethiopia but directly from the Patriarchate of Alexandria. Subsequent to the consecration of the first five Eritrean bishops, Abune Filipos, former abbot of Debre Bizen, was appointed the first Patriarch of the Eritrean church in May 1998.

Some aspects of Eritrea's Christian heritage

The depth of Christianity's impact on Ethiopian-Eritrean society has its roots in the ability to integrate local cultures with a variety of influences and to mould them into a harmonious blend leading, in turn, to a unique model of the Christian faith. As an illustration of this process, I select five areas of the Christian life and heritage common to both countries.

MONASTIC LIFE

Through a constant supply of evangelists, writers, theologians and saints, monasticism has, throughout the centuries, wielded an influence whose range extended to virtually all aspects of life. Until the rise of modern schools in the twentieth century, monasteries were the only educational centres offering a learning corpus that was essentially spiritual and ecclesiastical in content, with excursions into such subjects as computation and astronomy. Its completion may take a period of much more than a decade. As a function of monasticism's pivotal role in the church, Christian spirituality as such displays a vivid monastic imprint in its forms of private and public prayer, ascetic practices and religious expression. Monastic life exists in both the anchoretic and coenobitic forms, for both men and women. Introduced into Eritrea and Tigray by Syrian monks in the sixth century, coenobitism is rooted in the rule of St Pachomius as the main guideline, with Egyptian and Syrian hagiographic and ascetic sources as the basis of its spirituality.[12] The *Gedl*, or hagiography of the founder of the monastery and of other saints, composed by local monastic writers, is the literary *locus* where oriental Christian spirituality and local inspiration meet and blend to carve out the model of the indigenous monastic holy person.

After its thorough indigenization in the long post-Aksumite era, monasticism developed in two branches, or houses: the house of Ewstathewos in the north, i.e. mostly Tigray and today's Eritrea, and the house of Tekle-Haymanot in the south. The co-existence of the two houses were not always peaceful. Differences in theological issues, and claims for monastic seniority and regional rivalries were behind protracted tensions. In terms of monastic ideals, the difference between the two houses is one of emphasis on particular elements of spirituality, ascetic practice and organization. Common to both traditions are the *fuga mundi*, leading to the establishment of monastic settlements on inaccessible mountaintops and wooded heights, strict enclosure, private and common liturgical prayer, long and rigorous fastings, hospitality, study and manual work. In the vicinities of all monasteries, hermit monks (*bahtawyan*) live in simple huts

---

[11] Paolo *Borruso, L'ultimo impero Cristiano,* 253-262.

[12] Among the sources of monastic spirituality, the following may be mentioned: the *Collectio Monastica*, the *Patericon Aethiopice*, the *Asceticon*, the *Gerenticon*, normative and ritual rules *(ser'ate menqwesenna)* such as those of Pacomius and Anthony, and the three Syrian authors known as *Filkesyos*, *Mar Yes'haq* and *Menfesawi Aregawy*.

and caves, totally devoted to prayer and penance after the great traditions of St Paul of Thebes and St Anthony the Great. Among the hermits are found the *Nazrawyan* – easily recognized by their long and rough hair, the leather cloak they dress, and the long cruciform iron stick they carry – who, from time to time, leave their seclusion to preach penance to the people,. The history and the presence of female monasticism, comprehensive of both cloistered and non-cloistered nuns, is not less remarkable. Most probably as ancient as male monasticism, it grew under the aegis of, and in dependence upon, the former. This however did not prevent female monasticism from enlisting the leadership or the membership of nuns who left a lasting imprint on the spiritual and political history. At present, Ethiopia and Eritrea have more monks and nuns, monasteries and convents, than all the non-Chalcedonian and Orthodox churches put together. Far more numerous are the secular clergy, consisting of married priests, and therefore ineligible for episcopacy or second marriage in case of widowhood. Theologically less trained, but fully integrated into the economic and social life of the peasantry, these secular priests offer a highly relevant pastoral service.

LITURGICAL WORSHIP

It is believed that Frumentius, after his consecration in Alexandria, introduced the Coptic liturgy, which, before being translated into Ge'ez, was celebrated in Greek in the Aksumite churches and chapels. Subsequently, liturgy underwent an intensive local elaboration, to the extent that, today, the Ge'ez and the Coptic rites make up two autonomous branches of the Alexandrian liturgical family. Though difficult to assess with any degree of certainty as to when and how it took place, the embodiment of Old Testament Hebraic elements – such as the presence of the *Sancta Sanctorm* within the internal three-centric structural arrangement of the churches, the observance of the Sabbath, and several other practices – is impressive. It is much easier to explain the influence of the Syrian liturgy, since Frumentius and most of the missionary monks who came to the country several decades after him were Syrian in origin and culture. More input came from various oriental liturgies through the contacts that the monks had with the Christian communities in Jerusalem, since at least the early thirteenth century. The first half of the second millennium saw the confluence of a twofold movement: an inflow of numerous texts of the Coptic Church in Arabic translated into Ge'ez on the one hand and the contribution of local theologians composers of treatises and liturgical texts, on the other. The convergence between external influences and local input came to its height with the emergence of a distinctively Ethiopian-Eritrean liturgy. While in terms of contents and structure, the Mass shares much in the tradition of the Alexandrian and other eastern liturgies, unique to the Ethio-Eritrean tradition is instead the Divine Office. The cathedral services, steered by the *debtera*,[13] are solemnly celebrated in cathedrals or major churches on Sundays and major feasts. They include the *Waziema* or solemn Vigil Vespers that last four to five hours, the *Meweddes,* or office of the night, and the *Sebhate Negh*, corresponding to the Latin matins or lauds, directly connected with the *Meweddes.* They are then followed by the Eucharistic celebration. All such services consist of hymns, prayers, intercessions, psalms and antiphons. The *Tabot*,[14] on which the Eucharist is celebrated, is the focal

[13] A lay specialist in ecclesiastical subjects, holding an intermediate position between the clergy and the laity, with the main task of guiding the liturgical chant.

[14] The term *Tabot* derives from the Aramaic *tebuta* and, in Ge'ez as well as in other Semitic languages, means chest, case, coffer. By extension it came to indicate also ark, temple, sanctuary. The *Tabot* as such is a small rectangular tab of wood or, less frequently, of stone, corresponding to the sacred stone used by the Latins for the Eucharistic celebration. The average *Tabot* slab is approximately 3 to 5 cm. thick and 0,50 x 0,30cm. wide. Its surface and various sides are engraved with legends and symbols indicating the names of the Trinity, of Mary and the particular saint to whom a given church is dedicated. Consecrated by the bishop with solemn rituals, and placed in the innermost section of the church, it cannot be seen by any lay person. On particular occasions it is carried out for procession, enveloped in precious clothes, with cantors and *debteras* performing liturgical songs and dances before it. The most solemn of such

point of the whole liturgical service. The cathedral service, just as the Mass, is chanted entirely with the help of a notation (*meleket*) to remind the singers of the music to which each piece should be sung. The whole divine office is performed in the standing position, with the support of a long prayer stick (*meqwemiya*). Two musical instruments are used: the sistrum (*tzenatzel*) and the drum (*kebero*). Stick, drum and sistrum are all involved when, at regular intervals, chant is accompanied by holy dance. Tradition attributes the invention, by divine inspiration, of the liturgical music and dance to St Yared, a sixth-century priest. However, it has been realistically suggested that Old Testament Hebraic sources, pre-Christian and Christian Egypt, and the Eastern Christian world must have had a share in their origin. Yet, Yared may very well have had a central role in the re-elaboration, initial indigenization and development of a nucleus of the liturgical musical corpus. Beside the cathedral service, the *Office of the Hours* or *Monastic Hours* or *Horologion*, is celebrated not only in the monasteries or parish churches, but also privately by numerous pious Christians, cleric and lay alike. Besides the Missal (*Metzhafe Qeddassie*) and the ritual of the Sacraments, other liturgical books include the *Senkesar* or Sinaxary, the *Degwa* or antiphonary, the *Mewas'et* or collection of responsorials, the *Me'eraf* or hymnary, and the *Metzhafe Getzawye* or liturgical calendar. The latter, consistently with the Julian calendar, has a three-year cycle with 365 days and one leap year with 366 days. Due to the difference in computing the date of creation and of Christ' s birth, the calendar is seven years and eight months behind the common Christian era. The year consists of thirteen months, i. e. twelve with thirty days, and one (*Pagumen*) with five to six days.

LITERATURE

Until the nineteenth century, literature was religious and mainly Christian in content, with Ge'ez as the only literary language. Ge'ez script, originating from the *Sabaic* and developing with its own distinct characteristics, appeared in the north in the immediate pre-Christian Aksumite time in the form of epigraphy. Its development as a full-fledged literary language started with the introduction of Christianity, through the translation, from the Greek, of the Bible (the Septuagint for the Old Testament and the Syriac Lucianic for the New Testament) and of various patristic, liturgical and monastic texts. Along with the biblical books shared as canonical by the other Christian churches, there are other texts that are considered divinely inspired.[15] After an extended gap following the decline of Aksum, the thirteenth century ushered in a second most fertile literary period, reaching its peak in the fourteenth and fifteenth centuries. Among

---

celebrations is that of *Temqet*, the feast of Jesus' baptism. On the eve of the feast, the *Tabot* is taken to a riverside where the entire night is spent in prayers, hymns and liturgical dance, in an atmosphere strongly reminiscent of the place and the veneration enjoyed by the Old Testament Ark of the Covenant. In fact, the *Tabot*, venerated in every church, is a representation or, more accurately, a replica of the Ark of the Covenant containing the tables of the Law believed to be preserved in the mother Church of Aksum, the second Zion, since when, according to the *Kibre Neghest*, Menelik I, son of king Solomon and the Queen of Sheba, abducted it from Jerusalem. Being the centrepiece of the liturgical service, the basis of the claim to being the chosen people of God and the emblem of the community's spiritual and social unity, the *Tabot* is, with the Cross, the most treasured and venerated symbolic object in Ethiopia and Eritrea. Cf. Edward Ullendorff, *Ethiopia and the Bible*, Oxford: The British Academy, 1968, 77, 82-89, 122; Agostinos Tedla da Hebo, "Il Tabot: la sua importanza religiosa e giuridico-cultuale nella Chiesa Etiopica," ed. Habtemichael Kidane, *Orientalia Christiana Periodica*, 60 (1994), 131-157.

[15] There is no official statement of the Ethio-Eritrean Orthodox Churches concerning the canonicity of the Scriptures, but only references to authoritative biblical books. Today a distinction is made between *broader* and *narrower* canon. Due to a different method of counting, both of them have 81 books. The *narrower canon*, apparently influenced by western Churches, does not include the books whose authority is doubted by other Christian traditions. The *broader canon* has in addition a number of apocryphal and deutero-canonical books such as Enoch, Jubilees, the "Shepherd" of Hermas, Judit, Tobit, Ecclesiasticus. Cf. P. Brandt, "Bible Canon", in *Encyclopaedia Aethiopica*, I, pp. 371-373. Books such as Enoch and Jubilees are of paramount importance in biblical studies today, for their texts have survived in their entirety only in their Ge'ez version.

other things, the *Kibre Neghest* (Glory of the Kings) was elaborated in the north with the definitive appropriation of the Queen of Sheba story, and the earliest known examples of *qene*, a peculiar form of religious poetry, beginning to appear. Behind much of that spirited literary season there was, among other factors, the need to define the central contents and forms of the Orthodox faith vis-à-vis such controversial issues as the observance of the Sabbath and the rise of heretical movements such as *Stephanism* in the north and *Michaelism* in the south. In the sixteenth and seventeenth centuries, the Muslim onslaught on Christianity and the clash with the Jesuit missionaries gave new momentum to dialectical and apologetic theological compositions. Subsequently, the Anointing of Christ became the main focus of internal theological controversy, whereas the literary output increased its momentum in the fields of religious poetry and the translation of rituals and doctrinal treatises. In the nineteenth century, Ge'ez began to give way to Amharic in Ethiopia, and Tigrinya in Tigray and Eritrea, as literary languages. This development is in its full swing today – however, more in the secular than in the religious realm, for the Orthodox Church tends to rely heavily on the literary corpus accumulated in past centuries.

Painting

Born in the form of rock drawing, of which there exist numerous prehistoric exemplars in Eritrea, traditional pictorial art has been influenced to a lesser degree by African artistic traditions than by those deriving from the Christian Mediterranean and western Asian areas. The medieval definition of painting as the 'Bible of the illiterate' may be said to suit very well Eritrea's pictorial tradition. To instruct on the essential contents of faith, to convey the central tenets of theological truth, to arouse the urgency of asceticism as a means of purification towards an intimate union with God – here are the canons determining both the content and the style of traditional painting. This being the case, the artist is much more inclined to paint the content rather than the shape, 'to visualize dogmas and theological concepts, rather than offer a visual pleasure, to depict objective reality, more than to express personal impression'.[16] As a result, there is little concern for the interplay of colours, perspectives, and proportions. Instead, painting will be a display of essential traits, of the vividness of colours and flatness of background. The range of privileged themes is made up of biblical stories from both Testaments, the Trinity, Christology, the Eucharist, Mariology, Angelology and Hagiology, as well as great national sagas, with the ubiquitous Solomon and Saba cycles, and moments in the history of Christianity, and much more.

Popular religion

In the several centuries of its history, Christianity has permeated not only the church's and the Christian kingdom's institutions and their intellectual culture, but also the daily life and the whole existence of the huge, largely illiterate and generally peasant, masses of people. The central role of religion in traditional rural society has its most significant symbol in the location of the church, with its *Tabot*, on the highest hill dominating the village. The authority and veneration paid to the spiritual father (*Abbat Nefs*: father of the soul) in every traditional family represents the link between the church and the individual members of the community. Circumcision, baptism, marriage and funerals are the major events in which official and popular religion meets to mark the various stages of the faithful's existence. There are 250 fasting days a year, and a prodigious number of feasts, extra-liturgical devotions, votive offerings, processions and pilgrimages to numerous local and national shrines making up the fabric of the daily life of the people. The policy of moulding Christianity into the local culture, so wisely adopted by the evangelizers since the earliest centuries, has inspired a sense of continuity rather than of rupture, with the pre-Christian, mainly

[16] Kristen Stoffergen Pedersen, *Gli Etiopi*, Roma: Libreria Editrice Vaticana, 1988, 144.

Cushitic, religious substratum at the level of popular religion as much as it did at the intellectual and institutional levels. In that context, the exceptional veneration of the Virgin Mary could be a remote legacy of the ancient worship of a pagan goddess, perhaps the earth mother,[17] just as certain feasts celebrated once a month may go back to the ancient Semitic lunar calendar. The mountaintops where churches are erected, the trees surrounding the same churches, the healing waters and springs to which people flow in large numbers to cure their illnesses, are apparently legacies of ancient pagan beliefs connecting such locations with the presence of spirits and genies. The *Damiera*, the big bonfire lit on *Mesqel* (the feast of the Finding of the Holy Cross) at the end of the rainy season, may trace its roots back to most ancient pagan rituals around the productive cycles of the earth, the meaning of which may have changed at the time of King Dawit II (d. 1413), who received a fragment of the true Cross from the Coptic patriarch. While the above aspects were thoroughly Christianized, the same process had a by-product in the survival of a whole body of superstitious beliefs and practices in popular religion. Amulets, magic scrolls *(lelafe-tzedq),* rituals, symbols against evil spirits, the evil eye and the like, are widespread. In history, there are instances showing attempts by kings and church authorities to purify Christianity from such survivals of the pre-Christian substratum. Nevertheless, even today, some priests and *debteras* are still to be found writing magic scrolls and combining Christian exorcism with formulas and symbols of an equivocal nature. In spite of everything, one could hardly overstate the value and the critical importance of popular religion. Christianity has survived against all the odds, thanks not only to warrior Christian kings, to monastic theologians and writers, but also to its ability to control and weave together the myriad of strands of the life of the people – in other words, popular religion, with all its values and flaws.

Other Christian Churches

After the demise of the Jesuit mission in the seventeenth century, the Roman Catholic Church undertook a new and more promising course under the leadership of St Justin De Jacobis and his Lazarist successors in the Apostolic Prefecture (1839-1847), later the Vicariate (1847-1894), of Abyssinia. Through the perusal of the Ge'ez rite, and the formation of the native clergy, fervent communities flourished, in the midst of mounting persecutions, in the Akele-Guzay and Bogos provinces of Eritrea and in northern Ethiopia. In 1894, following the creation of the Italian colony of Eritrea, the new political territory was separated from the Apostolic Vicariate of Abyssinia to become the Apostolic Prefecture (1894) and Apostolic Vicariate (1911) of Eritrea, under the responsibility of the Capuchin friars.

In 1866, the first Protestant missionaries landed at Massawa – Carl Johan Carlsson, Per Erik Kjellberg and Lars Johan Lange, all sent by the Swedish Evangelical Mission to work among the Oromo of south-west Ethiopia. Given the difficulties faced by other missionaries in Ethiopia under emperor Twodros II, they were advised by the French consul in Massawa, Werner Munzinger, to settle among the Kunama and the Nara. With the arrival of more missionaries, mission houses were opened at Tandare, Oganna and Kulluku. However, the killings of some of the missionaries, the natural death of others, the upheavals and the raids that involved the area in those years, drove the missionaries to abandon the region in 1870 and to move to Monkullo (Massawa) and, later on, to Gheleb. It was only in 1897 that the missionaries could resume work among the Kunama, where they devoted themselves to the study of the language, translating books, and to teaching and preaching.

In spite of their meagre numbers, the Roman Catholic and the Evangelical churches have significantly marked the history and the development of the country through the editions and translations of the Bible, the dissemination of literacy and the promotion of modern schools and clinics. The intellectual class formed in their schools, with such prestigious figures as Weldeab Weldemariam of the Evangelical Church,

[17] Carlo Conti Rossini, *Etiopia e genti di Etiopia,* Firenze: Remporad, 1937, 173.

one of the fathers of the Eritrean independence, came to prominence in the political arena in the 1940s and 1950s onwards.

In conclusion, one pertinent question can be asked: how well is Christianity faring today, at a time when changes in Eritrea are as revolutionary and sweeping as elsewhere? The 1974 Ethiopian revolution and its independence in 1991 have opened entirely new scenarios, with opportunities, problems and challenges for the churches in Eritrea to face and meet. My argument is that, because of their long tradition, their role in shaping the history and the culture of the Eritrean people and the moral authority they still enjoy, both the Christian churches and Islam have a fundamental role to play in the new society now emerging in Eritrea. This is on condition that differences of whatever nature are nurtured, not as factors of conflict, but as sources of reciprocal enrichment, and the Eritrean government on its part be truly disposed to appreciate and value whatever the churches and other religions have to offer outside the precincts of the sanctuary.

Bibliography

Abir, Mordechai. Ethiopia. The Era of the Princes. London and Harlow: Longmans, 1968.

Arén, Gustav. Evangelical Pioneers in Ethiopia. Origins of the Evangelical Church Mekane Yesus. Stockholm-Addis Ababa: EFS Forlaget-Evangelical Church Mekane Yesus, 1978.

Beyene, Tewelde. La politica cattolica di Seltan Sagad I (1607-1632) e la missione della Compagnia di Gesù in Etiopia: precedenti, evoluzione e problematiche, 1589-1632. Roma: Pontificia Universitas Gregoriana, 1983.

Chaillot, Christine. The Ethiopian Orthodox Tewahedo Church Tradition. Paris: Inter-Orthodox Dialogue, 2002.

Chojnacki, Stanislas. Major Themes in Ethiopian Painting. Wiesbaden: Franz Steiner Verlag, 1982.

Cohen, Leonardo. The Missionary Strategies of the Jesuits in Ethiopia, 1555-1632. Wiesbaden: Harrassowitz Verlag, 2009.

Crummy, Donald. Priests and Politicians. Catholic and Protestant Missions in Orthodox Ethiopia, 1830-1868. Oxford: The Clarendon Press, 1972.

da Nembro, Metodio. La Missione dei Minori Cappuccini in Eritrea. Roma. Istituto Storico Cappuccini, 1953.

Ghebre-Medhin, Jordan. Peasants and Nationalism in Eritrea. Trenton: The Red Sea Press, 1989.

Grierson, Roderick R. & Stuart Munro Hay. The True Story of the Greatest Relic of Antiquity. The Ark of the Covenant, London: Weidenfeld and Nicolson, 1999.

Hablesellassie, Sergew et al., The Church of Ethiopia. A Panorama of History and Spiritual Life. Addis Ababa: Ethiopian Orthodox Church, 1997.

Hablesellassie, Sergew. Ancient and Medieval Ethiopian History to 1720. Addis Ababa: United Printers, 1972.

Iyob, Ruth. The Eritrean Struggle for Independence, 1943-1993. Cambridge: Cambridge University Press, 1997.

Kidane, Habtemichael. L'Ufficio Divino Della Chiesa Etiopica. Roma: Pontificio Istituto Orientale, 1998.

Longrigg, Stephen Hemsley. A Short History of Eritrea. Oxford: Clarendon Press, 1974.

Lusini, Gianfrancesco. Studi sul Monachesimo Eustazian., Napoli: Istituto Universitario Orientale, 1993.

Munro-Hay, Stuart. Ethiopia, The Unknown Land: A Cultural and Historical Guide. London-New York: I. B. Tauris, 2008.

O'Mahoney, Kevin. The Ebullient Phoenix. A History of the Vicariate of Abyssinia, 1839-1916. Asmara-Addis Abeba: Francescana Printing Press-United Printers, 1982-1992.

Ricci, Lanfranco. 'Le Letterature d' Etiopia.' In Storia delle letterature d' Oriente edited by Oscar Botto, 802-891, Milano: Vallardi, 1969.

Taddia, Irma. 'Le Istituzioni Monastiche del Sera'e (Eritrea): le Istituzioni Monastiche e la Struttura Della Proprietà Fondiaria,' Africa, 48 no. 3 (1993): 446-463.

Tamrat, Taddese. *Church and State in Ethiopia, 1270-1527.* Oxford: The Clarendon Press, 1972.
Trimingham, John Spencer S. *Islam in Ethiopia.* London: Frank Cass, 1976.
Ullendorff, Edward. *The Ethiopians. An Introduction to Country and People.* London-Oxford-New York: Oxford University Press, 1973.

(62) CHRISTIANITY IN ETHIOPIA

Bruk Ayele Asale

Religion	Pop 2010	Pct 2010	Pop 2025	Pct 2025	Gr Pct 1970 2025
Christians	52,153,000	59.6%	75,209,000	60.1%	2.5%
Independents	2,175,000	2.5%	2,990,000	2.4%	2.1%
African initiated	2,157,000	2.5%			
Orthodox	34,951,000	39.9%	51,400,000	41.1%	2.6%
Oriental Orthodox	34,950,000	39.9%			
Protestants	14,541,000	16.6%	19,301,000	15.4%	1.9%
Baptist	7,744,000	8.8%			
Lutheran/Reformed	5,576,000	6.4%			
Pentecostal	551,000	0.6%			
Roman Catholics	857,000	1.0%	1,458,000	1.2%	3.6%
Evangelicals	12,394,000	14.2%	19,017,000	15.2%	2.9%
Pentecostals/Charismatics	9,556,000	10.9%	14,500,000	11.6%	2.8%
Muslims	29,529,000	33.7%	43,678,000	34.9%	2.6%
adherents of traditional African religions	5,734,000	6.5%	6,007,000	4.8%	0.3%
Baha'is	23,900	0.0%	28,000	0.0%	1.1%
Jews	16,600	0.0%	17,000	0.0%	0.2%
Hindus	6,500	0.0%	8,500	0.0%	1.8%
Buddhists	1,400	0.0%	2,000	0.0%	2.4%
people professing no religion	96,900	0.1%	95,000	0.1%	-0.1%
Total population	**87,562,000**	**100.0%**	**125,044,000**	**100.0%**	**2.4%**

Source: Centre for the Study of World Christianity (CSGC), Boston, Gordon-Conwell TS

There are three major groups of denominations in Ethiopia, namely, the Ethiopian Orthodox *Tewahedo* Church (EOTC), Protestants and Roman Catholics. This brief article surveys the historical background of each of them proportionally, their current status, and the actual and potential relationships across the denominations.

The Introduction of Christianity and the Ethiopian Orthodox *Tewahedo* Church (EOTC)

There are three traditions describing the reception of Christianity in Ethiopia that historians argue about. These include: (1) the pre-Christian connection of Ethiopia with Jerusalem and the immediate introduction of Christianity through the Ethiopian eunuch (Act 8:27-40);[1] (2) the apostolic introduction by St Matthew

[1]Even if it is far from convincing, some scholars such as Edwin M. Yamauchi (*Africa and the Bible* [Grand Rapids, Michigan: Baker Academic, 2004], 161-181) argue that "the Ethiopian Eunuch was not from Ethiopia."

(and some other apostles), who came to preach the good news in Ethiopia, and who died and were buried there; and (3) the introduction of Christianity in the fourth century by two brothers, which happened by accident.[2]

Based on oral tradition and significant literary evidence, the EOTC and Ethiopian historians make strong claims for a long-standing historical relationship and religious ties between Ethiopia and Jerusalem, dating back to the time of King Solomon.[3] It is in this context that the visit of the Ethiopian eunuch to Jerusalem and his baptism by Philip, as told in Acts 8, is seen as the firstfruit of Ethiopian Christianity.[4] The EOTC believes that, even if Christianity was introduced at a very early period, both priestly ministry and sacramental services were introduced only in the fourth century with the arrival and ministry of St Frumentius.[5]

The apostolic ministry of St Matthew to Ethiopia, for which the EOTC makes no strong claims, has been mentioned by a number of writings dating to as early as Origen.[6] Pankhurst rightly notes the claim of the EOTC that Christianity first reached Ethiopia in the early apostolic period, and 'that "many" at that time "believed". The faith did not, however, become the state religion until the early fourth century'.[7] Scholars like Taddesse Tamrat[8] and John Baur[9] also agree with an early introduction of Christianity, not

---

[2] John Baur (*2000 Years of Christianity in Africa: An African Church History*, 2nd ed. [Nairobi: Paulines Pub, 2009], 35) however, adds up another one by taking out the second one here. He writes, "Ethiopian tradition knows three steps in the advent of Christianity: Philip's eunuch brought the faith, Frumentius the priesthood, and the Nine Saints monastic life."

[3] For detailed discussion see the *Kebre Negest,* an Ethiopian Epic from the fourteenth century AD. For an English translation of the text of this document, see E.A. Willis Budge, *The Kebra Nagast*, 1932, www.sacred-texts.com/chr/kn/.

[4] Eusebius of Caesarea, for instance, wrote, "But as the preaching of the Saviour's Gospel was daily advancing, a certain providence led from the land of the Ethiopians an officer of the queen of that country, for Ethiopia even to the present day is ruled, according to ancestral custom, by a woman. He, first among the Gentiles, received of the mysteries of the divine word from Philip in consequence of a revelation, and having become the first-fruits of believers throughout the world, he is said to have been the first on returning to his country to proclaim the knowledge of the God of the universe and the life-giving sojourn of our Saviour among men; so that through him in truth the prophecy obtained its fulfilment, which declares that 'Ethiopia stretcheth out her hand unto God' [Ps 67.11]" (Eusebius Pamphilius, *Church History, Life of Constantine, Oration in Praise of Constantine*, Series II, vol. 1 in *Nicene and Post-Nicene Fathers*, ed. by Philip Schaff, Book 2, ch.1, 1890, www.ccel.org/schaff/npnf201.iii.vii.ii.html).

[5] [EOTC], *The Ethiopian Orthodox Tewahedo Church Faith, Order of Worship and Ecumenical Relations*, 2nd ed. (Addis Ababa: Tinsae Publishing House, 1996), 7. However, this argument may raise some questions such as whether there was church structure before this time or whether there were just a few individual Christians. But even so, individual Christians would surely read the Scriptures and celebrate baptism and eucharist. As these are important issues to understand the status of the church in the first couple of centuries, until the commencement of the official priestly ministry by St Frumentius, such questions need further study.

[6] For detailed discussion see, Aymro Wondmagegnehu and Joachim Motovu, *The Ethiopian Orthodox Church* (Addis Ababa: The Ethiopian Orthodox Mission, 1970), 1. Here I must also highlight that Ethiopians do not have surnames and they are known by their given names, in this article Ethiopians are referred to by their given names.

[7] Richard Pankhurst, *The Ethiopians*, The Peoples of Africa series (Oxford: Blackwell Pub., 1998), 34. There are some scholars who insist that the introduction of Christianity into Ethiopia occurred only in the fourth century, among whom Paul P. Henze (*Layers of Time: A History of Ethiopia* [London: Hurst & Co., 2000], 32-34) and de Lacy O'Leary (*The Ethiopian Church: Historical Notes on the Church of Abyssinia*, [London: Society for Promoting Christian Knowledge, 1936], 19) are included. However, the discovery of Ge'ez manuscripts from as early as the fourth to sixth centuries AD reveals that Christianity had been well established before the translation of at least the discovered manuscripts ("Discovery of earliest Illuminated Gospel Manuscripts Found in Ethiopian Monastery", www.ninesaintsethiopianorthodoxmonastery.org/Sacred_Archaeological_of_Ethiopia.html/).

[8] Taddesse Tamrat, *Church and State in Ethiopia: 1270-1527* (Oxford: The Clarendon Press, 1972), 22.

[9] Baur, *2000 Years of Christianity in Africa*, 35.

through the eunuch or the apostles, but rather through merchants and travellers since Axum[10], at that early stage, had developed strong communications with the Greco-Roman world.

But the Ethiopian state, which was known as the Axumite Kingdom, in the mid-fourth century AD officially declared Orthodox Christianity as its official religion, where the last sixteen centuries were uniquely identified with its strong relationship of church and state as the 'Christian island of Ethiopia'.[11] Except for three external and one internal attempt to break the bond and threaten the relationship between state and Orthodox Church, the Ethiopian Christian Empire monopolized the history of the country from its official emergence in the fourth century until its demise in 1974.

One of the ways to see the shifts in the history of the Ethiopian Christian Empire would be to divide its history into periods of major moves, where five major eras can be traced: (1) the Axumite Empire, from the first half of the fourth century to about the eighth to tenth centuries, where Christianity was declared as a state religion; (2) the Zague Dynasty, eleventh to thirteenth century, a period of expansion of Christianity form the Semitic to the Cushitic group of people, where landmark cathedrals were built in a new centre, Lasta, Lalibela; (3) the Restored Solomonic Dynasty, from the second half of the thirteenth century to the early sixteenth century, where major church reform took place under the leadership of a famous king, Zere'a Yacob, and others; (4) the Gondorine Period, from the late sixteenth century to the eighteenth century, with significant fragmentation within Orthodox Christianity and repeated western missionary attempts; and (5) the emergence of modern Ethiopia since the mid-nineteenth century until the rise and fall of the last constitutional imperial monarch, Haile Selassie I, in the mid-twentieth century, when Orthodox Christianity finally became only one of the many religious groups in Ethiopia. In the midst of all these major eras, other considerable, though short, events took place as ferments and turning-points to the next era. Among those intrusions were: (1) the mysterious Queen Judith of the ninth century, who is believed to have come from a 'Falasha' origin and spread Judaism by severely damaging Christianity; (2) the powerful Adal conqueror Ahmed Gragn of the sixteenth century, who played a significant role in the expansion of Islam in Ethiopia with very lasting effects; and (3) an interlude of a failed attempt by Portuguese Jesuits to Catholicize Ethiopia in the early seventeenth century are notable with major consequences in shifting the gears of both the nation's religious and political future. Finally, (4) the short-lived *Lij* Eyasus' Islam-oriented reign on the threshold of the twentieth century is also noteworthy; a challenge from within.

Based on this central outline and the interludes, there have been shifts of centre and periphery, shifts of territorial boundaries, with the inclusion and exclusion of various ethnic and religious groups at various times, which fermented and shaped different dynamics in the current religio-political landscape of Ethiopia. In connection with the church-state relationship, three major shifts have been evident in Ethiopia in the fast-changing twentieth century, as compared with its history of three millennia. (1) The monarchy

---

[10] Axum or Aksum is an Amharic name for the city in the northern part of Ethiopia which was originally the capital of the Kingdom of Aksum and remains one of the oldest continuously inhabited places in Africa.

[11] This expression was repeatedly used by the last Ethiopian Emperor, Haile Selassie I, at his introductory message of Amharic Bibles printed during his reign and elsewhere. Eskil Forslund (*The Word of God in Ethiopian Tongues: Rhetorical Features in the Preaching of the Ethiopian Evangelical Church Mekane Yesus*, Studia Missionalia Upsaliensia LVIII [Uppsala: International Tryck AB, 1993], 29-30), for instance, quotes one of his speeches in noting the significance of the metaphor in using religion for political interest, as the expression illustrates that Ethiopia has been surrounded by an ocean of Islam, remaining a strong Christian Empire. Asefa Sori (*Profile of Religious Experience in Ethiopia*, 2009, www.religion.ucsb.edu/projects/summerinstitute/Reference%20files/religion%20in%20home%20countries/Ethiopia--Assefa.htm) defines the expression as an "old propaganda that was effectively used by various warlords to oppress those Ethiopians who did not subscribe to that faith [i.e. EOTC's faith]". He also noted that in recent years, the expression was revived among some Orthodox circles and they "directly relate it to the publication of the 2007 National Census result which by showing the Christian majority data (62.8%), strengthened the old notion 'Ethiopia an Island of Christianity', and [it is printed on] t-shirts, caps and banners [which are] used during [some public] celebration[s] meant to unequivocally tell the Muslims that you do not belong here."

was increasingly spiritualized, in a more legal way than ever before, by declaring it as eternally perpetual, which however – and ironically – led to its termination. (2) The outburst of the 1974 Ethiopian 'socialist/ communist' Revolution, another extreme marked as pursuing a non-religious 'socialist/ communist' nation, in essence drove church and state in Ethiopia apart. (3) By overthrowing the *Derg* regime, a new constitutional democracy was declared, with a secular state and religious freedom guaranteed by the 1995 constitution under The Ethiopian People's Revolutionary Democratic Front (EPRDF)-led government.

In the recent religio-political history of Ethiopia, the period of severe persecution of all religious groups by the brutal regime of Mengistu Haile Mariam from 1974 till 1991 is noteworthy.[12] A simple expression of the brutality can be seen from the murder of two church leaders by the military dictator, namely, the EOTC Patriarch, Abuna Theophilus, who was murdered in July 1979, and the Rev. Gudina Tumsa, the General Secretary of the Ethiopian Evangelical (Lutheran) Church Mekane Yesus.[13]

In fact, this was an unprecedented period in the separation of church and state, where the EOTC lost its dominance as a state religion and its ability to impose its power over the other emerging religious groups at various periods of the country's history.[14] Some major effects can be observed from such a huge shift between church and state in this period: (1) A kind of empathy arose among various denominations and sense of unity between all churches in Ethiopia for the first time, as they all were persecuted by the communist regime.[15] (2) The government was criticized since, in order to keep itself in power, it assigned puppet leaders at various levels of the church,[16] where some churches became merely the servants of the brutal regime.[17] (3) Despite severe persecution by the government, the sense of equality encouraged religious groups, other than the Orthodox,[18] to expand to some degree and claim their national identity.[19]

---

[12] For a summary of action against Christian Churches in general by the Derg, and for more description on the degree and extent of the persecution on each individual denomination, see Mikael Doulos, "Christians in Marxist Ethiopia," *Religion in Communist Lands* 14 (1986): 140-145.

[13] Øyvind M. Eide, *Revolution and Religion in Ethiopia: The Growth and Persecution of the Mekane Yesus Church 1974-85*, East African Studies (Oxford: James Currey; Athens: Ohio University Press; Addis Ababa: Addis Ababa University Press, 2000), 33, 178.

[14] Two main problems for such an assertion are (1) the unpredictability or inconsistency of the religious policy of the Derg regime and (2) the EOTC's persistence in persecuting other religious groups, though it was persecuted by the regime to a lesser degree.

[15] For a discussion on an attempt to create an ecumenical forum to react to the common threat of atheism, a result of the new Marxist-Leninist ideology, see Eide, *Revolution and Religion*, 127-128.

[16] The tension within the ETOC, until 1981, between those who felt that they must accept the *status quo* "in order to preserve the Church," and those who boldly rejected submission to the government, is clearly described by John Brown ("Religion and Revolution in Ethiopia," *Religion in Communist Lands*, 9 [1981]: 54-55). Brown ("Religion and Revolution," 55) further noted how the government bribed the church, to silence its voice: "The government has given the Church a large budget.... The Church is tolerated by the government provided that it does not criticize the revolution and supports the government's social policies."

[17] Two major incidents are noteworthy to show how the strategy of the Derg regime used religious institutions for its political purpose. First, after detaining and killing the Patriarch and killing, arresting, or retiring most of the bishops of the EOTC, a puppet Patriarch and new bishops, who could follow the government's instruction, were appointed on 1979, which resulted in "[f]rom now on the EOC was a vehicle of the regime" (Eide, *Revolution and Religion*, 166). Secondly, the government prepared an interreligious seminar in 1977 where "the political aim of the organizers was to mobilize the religious communities in a kind of united religious front behind the government" (Eide, *Revolution and Religion*, 165).

[18] In fact, this tendency of growth of other churches made the EOTC to view them "as threat, and communists have used this fear to provoke riots against evangelical Churches" (Brown, "Religion and Revolution," 52).

[19] For instance, it is argued that Islam evidently spread throughout Ethiopia during the Derg regime's religious policy (Harold G. Marcus, *A History of Ethiopia* [Berkley/Los Angeles/London: University of California Press, 1994], xii) where EOTC and Islam enjoyed relative freedom, as they willingly submitted to the government's political agenda by purportedly supporting state-assigned puppet leaders (Eide, *Revolution and Religion*, 164-65; Mulatu Wubneh and

Paradoxically, however, this was a period where religious groups were under tight control by the state at best (EOTC and Islam), or under extraordinary persecution at worst (especially Protestants), yet many denominations and religious groups were able to grow significantly in reaction to the persecution. Even the EOTC, despite the significant reduction of its political power along with such other benefits as access to resources, could see the significance of its relative separation from the state, especially in revitalizing its prophetic identity as a church.[20]

One of the major challenges the EOTC is facing currently is the paradox of keeping a balance between its precious traditions and the quest for internal reformation. EOTC is a very prestigious and unique church in keeping long-standing traditions in its distinctive liturgy, colourful ceremonial practices, ancient literature, an educational system and theological stands. In the meantime, it is called to respond to the contextual and contemporary questions and demands a new generation is posing. If the church is aware and alert enough to build itself on the younger generation, its legacy will be preserved for those that follow. As the biggest and the mother church of all Christian denominations in Ethiopia, the EOTC is wise to deliberately take the initiative in forming ecumenical relationships, so that its influence may extend from the churches to the entire nation. As the firstborn church of the nation, her leadership is still enormously needed.

Protestantism in Ethiopia

Protestant missionaries were introduced to Ethiopia from the seventeenth century by Peter Heyling in the north, the nineteenth century by Johann Krapf in central and western Ethiopia, and the twentieth century by Thomas Lambie in the south. In many cases, their arrival and their welcome were associated with 'the political and material aid which the Ethiopians now began to expect from Europe'.[21] As a result, most of the attempts by western missionaries either to reform the EOTC from within or to establish any kind of Protestant church were not successful in 'Ethiopia proper' (the Northern Amhara/Tigray-dominated Orthodox areas), until Menelik's expansion (reigned 1889-1913) to other ethnic groups since the end of the nineteenth century.

With a desire to modernize his empire, Emperor Tewodros (1855-1868) welcomed western missionaries, though the deal did not succeed. During the time of Menelik II, missionaries based themselves in some remote parts of the new territories. The modernist Emperor Haile Selassie decreed in 1944 that the country was 'divided into what was termed "Ethiopian Church Areas" and "Open Areas",'[22] where the 'Open Areas', predominantly non-Christian, referred to areas in which missionaries might preach and teach their own denominational faith. The focus of the missionaries was mainly evangelizing adherents in the areas where traditional religion was practised. Based on missionary backgrounds, various denominations were founded and expanded significantly during the reign of the last Emperor as indigenous churches.

It was largely because of their recent introduction and attachment to the West that Protestant churches were severely persecuted during the Derg regime, which ironically gave them the unique momentum to

---

Yohannis Abate, *Ethiopia: Transition and Development in the Horn of Africa*. Profiles: Nations of Contemporary Africa [Boulder, Colorado: Westview Press; London: Avebury, 1988], 126-128). For a well-researched and systematically articulated religious policy of the Derg regime, see Eide, *Revolution and Religion*, 162-174.

[20] Eide (*Revolution and Religion*, 167-168) argues that the persecution and the relative separation from the state helped the EOTC to revitalize itself in a number of ways, which included strengthening of internal organization, more emphasis on theological education, introduction of Sunday schools, renewed attitude to attend Church services in mass, and so on.

[21] Sergew Hable Selassie, "The Expansion and Consolidation of Christianity: c. 350 to 650 A.D," in *The Church of Ethiopia: A Panorama of History and Spiritual Life*, ed. Sergew Hable Selassie (Addis Ababa: B.S.P.E., 1970), 7.

[22] Forslund, *The Word of God in Ethiopian Tongues*, 37.

firmly establish their foundations and to expand beyond imagination. The extreme persecution and repression of this period prepared them to explode and spread like wildfire during the new democracy and freedom. With the rapid growth of recent decades, they have proved to be the third largest religious group, with increasing recognition as Ethiopians, coupled with the dropping of the term *mete,* a derogative name given to them during the Derg regime, meaning '(new) comers (from outside)', 'foreigners/outsiders', or those who did not belong here.

Even if the vast majority of Protestants in Ethiopia have come into a relative unity under the umbrella of the Evangelical Churches' Fellowship of Ethiopia (ECFE), the ever-growing fragmentation of churches remains one of the major challenges. It is surprising to see a lot of internal strife and division among many Protestant churches in Ethiopia, immediately after the end of the persecution era. A paradox which persisted in recent decades was an unceasingly high growth rate, on the one hand, and many serious quarrels within denominations, between leading denominational figures, and division based on non-confessional matters, in a more secular manner, on the other. The ethical and moral reputation the Protestant community built up during those hard days until the time of religious freedom is now at risk. Had the Protestants set aside their internal problems and focused on the broader agenda of the good news of Jesus Christ, they would have done much to influence this country where they are entrusted to lead the whole nation, even while they remain a relative minority. Doors are wide open for them not only to contribute the maximum they can but also to take the lead in directing the present and envisioning the future of this great country.

Roman Catholics in Ethiopia

Attempts by Jesuit missionaries in the fifteenth and sixteenth centuries to catholicize the Ethiopian Christian nation mark the explicit roots of Catholics in Ethiopia. However, these failed attempts instead developed animosity with the Ethiopian Orthodox Church.[23] After the expulsion of the Jesuits in the sixteenth century, the Roman Catholic Church again attempted missionary work in the eighteenth and nineteenth centuries, and with some difficulty gave birth to the current Catholic Church in Ethiopia. Even if their stay was very short-lived, the teachings of the Jesuits had immense consequences in fomenting a centuries-long bloody dispute in the history of the EOTC. Furthermore, the five-year Fascist Italian invasion (1935-1941) persecuted the church and massacred its clergy,[24] developing more hatred against the Roman Catholic Church. During this period, the EOTC played a significant patriotic role in taking sides in the struggle for liberation against the Fascist regime.

In their present stance, except for a major difference in 'their understanding of the primacy of the Bishop of Rome, the Ethiopian Catholic and Orthodox Churches have basically the same sacraments, the same prayers, the same devotion to the Blessed Virgin Mary and the angels and the saints, and the same traditions – in short, the same faith.'[25] As a result, the Catholics do not consider the EOTC as a mission field; rather, they strive for a genuine relationship and promote ecumenism.[26]

---

[23] On the failure of these attempts, the Catholics blame the strong nationalistic attachment between the EOTC and the Ethiopian states. As stated by the Ethiopian Catholic Church, "these missions eventually failed due to the national-religious attachment of the Ethiopians, in particular, the Coptic party, to their Monophysite doctrine, and the strict link between religious and political struggles" ("Ethiopian Catholic Church, The" www.ecs.org.et/index.php?option=com_content&view=article&id=175&Itemid=87#History).

[24] Sergew Hable Selassie, "The Period of Reorganization," in *The Church of Ethiopia: A Panorama of History and Spiritual Life*, ed. Sergew Hable Selassie (Addis Ababa: B.S.P.E., 1970), 35.

[25] "Ethiopian Catholic Church."

[26] Owen Lambert, "Ecumenism in Ethiopia," *African Ecclesiastical Review* 21 (1979): 172-179.

The Roman Catholic Church in Ethiopia is probably now known mainly for its shared liturgical and practical links with the EOTC[27] and its global dominance rather than its minimal demographic presence in the country, which is currently only about 0.7% of the national population.[28] However, its sizeable involvement and contribution in changing the lives of many Ethiopians through education, health, infrastructure and other development and relief activities made the presence of the Catholic Church influential and constructive in many parts of the country.[29]

Relationships among Denominations in Ethiopia

The relative openness of Emperor Haile Selassie I towards the Evangelicals after the Italian invasion (especially since 1941), the inclusive attack of the communist regime on all religions since 1974, and the current government's inclusion of religious equality in the constitution since 1991, has improved the relationship little by little, even if it has been very slow. From its inception, the Bible Society of Ethiopia (BSE) has, for example, been one of the ventures through which the relationships among all Ethiopian churches have been facilitated.[30] In other words, irrespective of their historic differences, Orthodox, Catholics and Protestants have become not only more and more tolerant towards each other, but also open to promoting relationships and ecumenism.

It is important to note that with all their unique identity, reflecting their respective missionary origins, Ethiopian Protestants and Catholics have largely been influenced by and adopted a number of EOTC traditions and practices, and have developed an Ethiopian identity.[31] One such prominent element is the Ethiopian calendar, where both Protestants and Catholics follow the EOTC calendar year, which is 'Ethiopian', and not the calendar of the West. All Ethiopian Christians, therefore, celebrate New Year, Christmas, Epiphany, Easter and other church festivals on different dates from the other global denominations, in unity with the EOTC, and adopting local tradition. Furthermore, unlike other Evangelicals, the Finding of the True Cross is also celebrated by many Ethiopian Evangelicals and Catholics with the EOTC.

Conclusion

In conclusion, the dynamics of the country in the last quarter of the twentieth century and the early decades of the 21st century finally marked Ethiopia as becoming a secular state where religious freedom of all religious groups was constitutionally guaranteed. After an era of religious persecution for about one and a half decades, a new period has dawned where all religious groups in Ethiopia can be seen as equals. This new era, however, does not merely invite but also strongly demands that all religious groups and their

[27] There are two liturgical rites practiced in the Ethiopian Catholic Church where from Addis Ababa to northward they follow the Ge'ez Rite, which is very close to that of the EOTC, whereas from Addis Ababa to southward, they celebrate the Latin Rite, adopted into various local languages.

[28] FDRE-PCC, *Summary and Statistical Report*, 143.

[29] For instance, the first university-college in Ethiopia had been founded by the Catholic Jesuits priests with an invitation by Emperor Haile Selassie I and named after him.

[30] Currently BSE has opened an office devoted to promoting ecumenism and maintaining strong cooperation both at higher and grass-root levels. The results from the efforts in the last couple of years have been highly appreciated as immensely fruitful and encouraging (Seleshi Kebede, Personal communication, 21 December, 2011).

[31] For a discussion on more common elements shared across all denominations and the major influences of the EOTC on other churches in Ethiopia, see Bruk A. Asale, "*1 Enoch* in *Jude* and in the EOTC 'Canon': Developing an Adequate Insight in Second Temple Literature (STL) in the Various Ethiopian Churches for a Better Understanding of Each Other and for the Promotion of Ecumenism and Mutual Cooperation," PhD Diss., University of KwaZulu-Natal, 2015, 257-260.

adherents, who are citizens of the nation, respond to the new developments and its challenges actively and responsibly in nation-building, to make a better place for all. This can be achieved if the current spirit of ecumenism and mutual respect among the various denominations in Ethiopia is nurtured by overcoming a history of conflict and animosity.

Bibliography

Arén, Gustav. *Envoys of the Gospel in Ethiopia: In the Steps of the Evangelical Pioneers 1898-1936*. Studia Missionalia Upsaliensia LXXV. Stockholm: EFS-förlaget, 1999.

______. *Evangelical Pioneers in Ethiopia: Origins of the Evangelical Church Mekane Yesus*. Studia Missionalia Upsaliensia XXXII. Stockholm: EFS-förlaget, 1978.

Asefa Sori. *Profile of Religious Experience in Ethiopia*. 2009. www.religion.ucsb.edu/projects/summerinstitute/Reference%20files/religion%20in%20home%20countries/Ethiopia--Assefa.htm (accessed on 17 October, 2012).

Aymro Wondmagegnehu and Motovu, Joachim. *The Ethiopian Orthodox Church*. Addis Ababa: The Ethiopian Orthodox Mission, 1970.

Bakke, Johnny. *Christian Ministry: Patterns and Functions within the Ethiopian Evangelical Church Mekane Yesus*. Studia Missionalia Upsalinsia xliv. Oslo: Solum Forlag A.S., 1987.

Baur, John. *2000 Years of Christianity in Africa: An African Church History*. 2nd ed. Nairobi: Paulines Pub, 2009.

Brown, John. 'Religion and Revolution in Ethiopia,' *Religion in Communist Lands*. 9 (1981): 50-55.

Bruk A. Asale. '*1 Enoch* in *Jude* and in the EOTC 'Canon': Developing an Adequate Insight in Second Temple Literature (STL) in the Various Ethiopian Churches for a Better Understanding of Each Other and for the Promotion of Ecumenism and Mutual Cooperation,' PhD Diss., University of KwaZulu Natal, 2015.

Doulos, Mikael. 'Christians in Marxist Ethiopia.' *Religion in Communist Lands*.14 (1986): 134-145.

Eide, Øyvind M. *Revolution and Religion in Ethiopia: The Growth and Persecution of the Mekane Yesus Church 1974-85*. East African Studies. Oxford: James Currey; Athens: Ohio University Press; Addis Ababa: Addis Ababa University Press, 2000.

[EOTC]. *The Ethiopian Orthodox Tewahedo Church Faith, Order of Worship and Ecumenical Relations*, 2nd ed. Addis Ababa: Tinsae Publishing House, 1996.

Ephraim Isaac. *The Ethiopian Church*. Boston: H. N. Sawyer Co., 1976.

Forslund, Eskil. *The Word of God in Ethiopian Tongues: Rhetorical Features in the Preaching of the Ethiopian Evangelical Church Mekane Yesus*. Studia Missionalia Upsaliensia LVIII. Uppsala: International Tryck AB, 1993.

Henze, Paul P. *Layers of Time: A History of Ethiopia*. London: Hurst & Co., 2000.

Jones, A.H.M. and Elizabeth Monroe. *A History of Ethiopia*. Oxford: Clarendon Press, 1935.

Kaplan, Steven. *The Monastic Holy Man and the Christianization of Early Solomonic Ethiopia* Studien zur Kulturkunde 73. Wiesbaden: Franz Steiner Verlag, 1984.

Lambert, Owen. 'Ecumenism in Ethiopia.' *African Ecclesiastical Review* 21 (1979): 172-179.

Marcus, Harold G. *A History of Ethiopia*. Berkley/Los Angeles/London: University of California Press, 1994.

Munro-Hay, Stuart. *Aksum: An African Civilisation of Late Antiquity*, 1991. www.dskmariam.org/artsandlitreature/litreature/pdf/aksum.pdf (accessed on 04 May, 2012).

Richard Pankhurst, *The Ethiopians*, The Peoples of Africa (Oxford: Blackwell Pub., 1998

O'Leary, de Lacy. *The Ethiopian Church: Historical Notes on the Church of Abyssinia*. London: Society for Promoting Christian Knowledge, 1936.

Prouty, C. & E. Rosenfeld. *Historical Dictionary of Ethiopia*, African Historical Dictionaries, no. 32. Metuchen, NJ: The Scarecrow Press, 1981.

Sergew, Hable Selassie. 'The Establishment of the Ethiopian Church.' In *The Church of Ethiopia: A Panorama of History and Spiritual Life*, ed. Sergew Hable Selassie, 1-6. Addis Ababa: B.S.P.E., 1970.
Sergew, Hable Selassie. 'The Expansion and Consolidation of Christianity: c. 350 to 650 A.D,' in *The Church of Ethiopia: A Panorama of History and Spiritual Life*, ed. Sergew Hable Selassie, 7-9. Addis Ababa: B.S.P.E., 1970.
Sergew, Hable Selassie, 'The Period of Reorganization,' in *The Church of Ethiopia: A Panorama of History and Spiritual Life*, ed. Sergew Hable Selassie, 31-42. Addis Ababa: B.S.P.E., 1970.
Taddesse Tamrat. *Church and State in Ethiopia: 1270-1527*. Oxford: The Clarendon Press, 1972.
Ullendorff, E. *Ethiopia and the Bible*. London: Oxford University Press, 1968.

(63) Le Christianism du Gabon (seulement L'Eglise evangelique du Gabon)

Jean Jacques Ndong Ekouaghe

Religion	Pop 2010	Pct 2010	Pop 2025	Pct 2025	Gr Pct 1970 2025
Christians	1,301,000	84.4%	1,799,000	85.0%	2.2%
Independents	257,000	16.6%	365,000	17.2%	2.4%
African initiated	245,000	15.9%			
Protestants	181,000	11.7%	260,000	12.3%	2.5%
Reformed, Presbyterian	125,000	8.1%			
Holiness	28,200	1.8%			
Pentecostal	19,600	1.3%			
Roman Catholics	833,000	54.1%	1,160,000	54.8%	2.2%
Pentecostals/Charismatics	148,000	9.6%	200,000	9.5%	2.0%
Evangelicals	44,500	2.9%	56,700	2.7%	1.6%
Muslims	159,000	10.3%	225,000	10.6%	2.3%
adherents of traditional African religions	50,200	3.3%	50,000	2.4%	0.0%
adherents of new religious movements	9,500	0.6%	11,000	0.5%	1.0%
Baha'is	630	0.0%	1,000	0.0%	3.2%
people professing no religion	21,500	1.4%	30,600	1.4%	2.4%
Total population	**1,542,000**	**100.0%**	**2,116,000**	**100.0%**	**2.1%**

Source: Centre for the Study of World Christianity (CSGC), Boston, Gordon-Conwell TS

En remontant son origine, l'Eglise Evangélique du Gabon, nous conduit a Boston aux USA en 1825. Une jeune société missionnaire appartenant a des milieux piétistes, l'American Board of Commissionners of Foreign Missions (ABCFM).

Dans le but d'annoncer l'Evangile en Afrique, le comite de la société a livra a des enquêtes et des préparatifs qui vont aboutir a un premier voyage d'exploration en 1833-1834 oïl le cap des palmes c'est-à-dire, 'actuel Liberia fut choisi. Ils ont pour l'objectif: former parmi les autochtones, des catéchistes, des maitres, des évangélistes et des Pasteurs.

Certaines difficultés surgiront au Liberia ou cap des Palmes. Les objectifs fixes par les missionnaires n'étant pas les mêmes que ceux des volons par rapport a leurs rapports avec les populations indigènes.

Pour ces motifs et d'autres encore, les missionnaires Wilson et Griswold s'embarquent le 17 Mai 1842 sur un voilier. Ils entrent en contact avec la population, ils arrivent finalement dans l'Estuaire du Gabon, 3a, ils y débarquent le 22 Juin 1842. Ils ont eu le sentiment, qu'ils talent conduits par la main de Dieu.

Au bout d'une semaine, le navire repart au cap des Palmes ramenant Griswold et Wilson étant resté.

Les décisions essentielles sont déjà prises. La station missionnaire sera établie au lieu même du débarquement sur une petite colline au dessus du village du roi Glass qui les a accueillis doit l'installation a Baraka: un ancien parc d'esclaves des portugais un 'baracao'. La station missionnaire Protestante s'y trouve toujours.

Des le milieu de juillet 1842 Wilson ouvre la première école avec un effectif de 15 élevés. Au cours de la première armée, arrivent:Monsieur Walker, Madame Wilson, Monsieur Griswold. Ils sont bien rejoints par Madame James et un petit groupe de chrétien du cap des palmes: l'actuel Liberia.

En 1843, il y avait déjà 3 écoles et plus de 60 élevés. Elles étaient tenues par des originaires du cap des Palmes de race Grebo.

Au début de 1843 les marins français débarquent et signent des accords avec les chefs locaux, et Glass devient un territoire français. Cependant, les missionnaires américains déclarent n'avoir pas été entraves dans leur travail, et leurs relations avec les autorités françaises ont été souvent amicales.

En 1849, en Septembre, trois stations étaient ouvertes: Baraka, Olendebenk (en amont de Donguila) et Nengue Nengue Wile qui est confluent du como et de la Bokoue, face a Kango a la frontière entre les Bakele et les Sekiani.

Les missionnaires avaient toujours les yeux fixes vers les Fang, une tentative fut faite, en 1854, mais en vain parce que la pénétration des zones de l'intérieur était difficile, pourtant en 1855 le contrat fut établi avec les villages Fang au nord de Nengue Nengue. Mais la mort de Monsieur Adams qui avait commence a étudier la langue Fang en 1856 et celle de son collègue Herrick mort en 1857 entrainent la fermeture de la station de Nengue Nengue.

Apres seize (16) ans de travail, l'Eglise de Baraka ne comptait en 1858 que douze membres, avec en majorité les originaires du cap des Palmes, it y avait pourtant eu une quarantaine de conversions. Certains étaient très tentes par la magie, l'immoralité, l'alcool et la pratique de l'esclavage domestique, le manque de persévérance dans la vie morale était l'obstacle essentiel a la constitution d'une Eglise stable. It est important de noter qu'a Baraka, it y avait une école des filles et des garçons.

En 1870, it y aura fusion de l'American Borad of Commissioners et la mission presbytérienne des Etats Unis. Elle s'était installe en 1850 dans l'ile de Corisco et en 1865 a Benito dans l'actuelle Guinée Equatoriale. Les contacts fréquents ont facilite la décision de fusionner en 1870 et de confier les postes de cette région aux presbytériens.

La mission presbytérienne des Etats unis a donc succède a l'American Board en 1870.

La partie nord du district de Benito fut érigée comme Eglise autonome en 1879. Elle s'appellera l'Eglise autonome de Batanga. C'est donc de la qu'est partie l'œuvre d'évangélisation de l'Eglise presbytérienne dans le sud Cameroun en milieu Boulou. Cependant, le fleuve Ogoоue va constituer une voie d'accès l'interieur du pays, ce qui favorisera la fondation d'une nouvelle station. En 1874 le Docteur Nassau s'installe a Mbila Mbila, malheureusement 2 ans l'absence du docteur Nassau, la station sera pillee. 11 déménagera donc pour la colline de Kangwe, en face de l'ile de Lambarene.

En 1888 une école fut construite a Andende, au haut de la colline « les Ameriki ». Il ya aussi eu dans l'estuaire la fondation de la station d'Angom Foulabifoun sur le como.

Il est a noter que Lambaréné se trouve au centre du Gabon en milieu Galoa, proche au Mpongwe parlant a peu près la même langue. Le Docteur Nassau fonde une nouvelle station a 80km en amont. Sur la rive droite de l'Ogooue Talagouga chez les fang. Les missionnaires étudient leur langue, les évangélisent grâce aux catéchistes Galoa. Suite a des inondations répétées la station est transporte a la première Ile de Ndjole en 1896, elle a subsiste jusqu'en 1944 ou elle est finalement transférée a Ndjole.

La présence française a apporte un appui a l'œuvre missionnaire cependant, l'administration française était réticente a regard des missionnaires américains dont les écoles enseignaient en anglais et en Myene. A cet des pour parlers vont s'engager en 1887 avec la société des missions évangéliques de Paris.

L'administration Française ayant désormais la main mise dans le territoire occupe auparavant par les américains. Les américains commencent par céder les territoires de leur mission pour la société des missions évangéliques de Paris:

En 1892, il va eu la cession de la station de Talagouga, en aval de Ndjole qui plus tard sera désormais a Ndjole. En 1893 cession de la station de Kangwe a la société des missions évangéliques de Paris. 1913 cession de la station de Baraka a la société des missions évangéliques de Paris.

La société des missions évangélique de Paris se mettra a fonder des stations a travers le Gabon pour assurer l'annonce de l'évangile. La station de Ngomo est fonde en 1898, celle de Samkita en 1900. En 1913, le Docteur SCHWEITZER, sous les auspi de la société des missions évangélique de Paris arrive a Lambaréné.

En 1922 fondation de la station d'Ovan le Pasteur Samuel GALLEY dans l'Ogooue-Ivindo, 1929 Fondation de la station d'Oyem dans le Woleu-Ntem. 1933 cession a la christian and missionary Alliance de la responsabilite de l'evangelisation du Sud Gabon (Eglise de l'Alliance chretienne et missionnaire). Le 30 Juin 1961, l'Eglise Evangelique du Gabon obtient a Port-Gentil son autonomie.

En 1967, lors d'un synode National tenu en Ogooue-Ivindo dans la Paroisse de Ntsengkele, l'Eglise Evangélique connaitra le début d'une longue crise qui fera naitre la scission dans l'Eglise Evangelique du Gabon,

une scission qui durera environ trente ans (30ans) une tentative de réconciliation par feu Président de la République Omar BONGO ONDIMBA en 1989 sera infructueuse car la trêve de paix sera rompue en 1992 avec la déclaration de Ndjole. Ainsi, l'Eglise Evangélique du Gabon, grâce a la médiation de la CEVAA par plusieurs missions et sur celle conduite par le feu Pasteur Henry HARRY, réunira définitivement l'Eglise Evangélique du Gabon, qui désormais optera pour un système rotatoire a la tete de l'Eglise Evangélique du Gabon qui a commence en 1997 et a bouclé le premier tour du système rotatoire en 2014, le système rotatoire qui a suivi l'ordre historique de la pénétration de l'évangile dans notre pays a savoir:

- L'Ogooue-Estuaire par le Pasteur Jean Noel OGOULINGUENDE.
- L'Ogooue-Ivindo par le Pasteur Jean Marie EMANE MINKO.
- Le Woleu-Ntem par le Pasteur Clement OBAME MEZUI.
- Le Ntem par le Pasteur ASSOUMOU EDZANG ONDO.

A ce jour, nous sommes au début du deuxième tour du système rotatoire par le Révérend Jean Jacques NDONG EKOUAGHE, élu le 30 Mars 2014

Bibliographie

Marie PERRIRAZ-RIHS, *missionnaire au Gabon* Geneve Nilliers-le-Bel: Labor et fides/ Societe biblique Frangaise [1969]

Expose du_Professeur_RATANGA 2010, BARAKA-M1SSION, siege de l'Eglise Evangelique du Gabon.

Conference sur *'la charte de l'Eglise Evangelique du Gabon de 1997'* le 16 Fevrier a Libreville par le Reverend Docteur KHUNDE TONA.

Rapport de la commission Constitutionnelle relatif au *maintien ou non du système rotatoire* du 5 juillet 2011

ZORN Jean-François, Le grand siècle d'une mission protestante. La mission de Paris de 1822 à 1914, Edition Karthala, Paris, 2012

(64) CHRISTIANITY IN GAMBIA

Chammah J Kaunda
(with a contribution by Ralphina Phillott-Almeida)

Religion	Pop 2010	Pct 2010	Pop 2025	Pct 2025	Gr Pct 1970 2025
Christians	75,300	4.4%	118,000	4.4%	3.1%
Independents	12,500	0.7%	20,700	0.8%	3.4%
African initiated	4,200	0.2%			
Orthodox	570	0.0%	700	0.0%	1.4%
Protestants	11,600	0.7%	18,000	0.7%	3.0%
Roman Catholics	47,600	2.8%	75,000	2.8%	3.1%
Pentecostals/Charismatics	16,200	1.0%	30,000	1.1%	4.2%
Evangelicals	4,600	0.3%	7,500	0.3%	3.2%
Muslims	1,501,000	88.7%	2,431,000	90.1%	3.3%
adherents of traditional African religions	92,800	5.5%	110,000	4.1%	1.1%
Baha'is	13,800	0.8%	22,000	0.8%	3.2%
Hindus	270	0.0%	400	0.0%	2.6%
people professing no religion	9,600	0.6%	16,100	0.6%	3.5%
Total population	**1,693,000**	**100.0%**	**2,698,000**	**100.0%**	**3.2%**

Source: Centre for the Study of World Christianity (CSGC), Boston, Gordon-Conwell TS

Introduction

Gambia is the smallest country in mainland Africa, bordered to the north, east and south by Senegal, with a small coast on the Atlantic Ocean in the west. Until 2015, when the country was declared an Islamic state,[1] it was a secular state, with religious freedom still enshrined in the constitution.

---

[1] Recently, Gambian President Yahya Jammeh declared Gambia an Islamic republic, saying the move marks a break with the colonial past. BBC News, "Gambia declared Islamic republic by President Yahya Jammeh," (12 December 2015), www.bbc.com/news/world-africa-35082343 (accessed 26 Dec. 15). He has stressed that the rights of the Christian minority would be respected and that women would not be held to a dress code. But many feel there is an ulterior political motive and are uncertain as to whether an Islamic state would ensure that the rights of all citizens and non-citizens are respected especially because of the history of human rights abuses. The 89-page report recently published under the title, "State of Fear: Arbitrary Arrests, Torture, and Killings," describes the human rights situation in Gambia since President Yahya Jammeh took power in 1994. It demonstrated how he has ruthlessly repressed all forms of dissent and how the State security forces and paramilitary forces have carried out unlawful killings and arbitrarily arrest, detain, and disappearance people, causing hundreds to flee the countries. Most of the human rights abuses documented in the report are from 2013 to 2015. See, the Human Rights Watch, "State of Fear Arbitrary Arrests, Torture, and Killings," https://www.hrw.org/sites/default/files/report_pdf/gambia0915_4up_0.pdf (accessed 26 Dec. 2015). Thus, the declaration brings uncertainty to the small Christian population in the Gambia. The global Christianity family is urged to pray for the peace and continuous religious tolerance in the Gambia.

Christianity arrived in Gambia with Portuguese sailors in 1456 when they sailed up-river and landed on James Island. In 2010, Christianity was 4.7%[2] in various denominations. The Christian community is situated mostly in the west and south among the Creoles or Akus who are the descendants of freed slaves brought to Gambia from Sierra Leone in 1787.[3] Christianity is fundamentally Roman Catholic with some Protestant groups including Anglicans, Methodists, Baptists, Seventh Day Adventists, Jehovah's Witnesses, and various small evangelical denominations. Islam is the majority religion, accounting for about 95.3% in 2010.[4]

The History of Christianity

Roman Catholic Church

The Catholic Church first came to Gambia through Portuguese sailors in 1456 who arrived on James Island. In 1849, a Catholic mission station was established in Bathurst on St Mary's Island (later named Bathurst). The Roman Catholic missionaries of the Order of the Holy Ghost (Spiritans) arrived in the country in 1822. But missionaries struggled to convert local people in Gambia. The work started growing only when freed slaves who were converts came to settle in Gambia after the creation of Bathurst. But tangible results came only in 1905 when the Irish Father (Giovanni) John Meehan arrived in the country. In 1931, he created the Vicariate Apostolic of Senegambia[5] and separated it from Dakar. In the 1950s, the church gave highest priority to the urban areas of Bathurst, Georgetown and Basse.[6] Missionary activities along the Alahein River valley were initiated by Fr Matthew Corrigan in 1958, but this was done from a base in Bathurst. Fr Andrew Carroll took over this work in 1960 and established himself in Kartong under two agreements: the first was that he directed evangelistic efforts exclusively at the 'pagan' Kalorn and did not try to convert Muslims. The second was that he was to establish an elementary school open to all children in the community which he began in 1961 while the church was raised in 1964. Over the years, mission work was extended to include eight other villages in this area.[7]

The Methodist Church

The Methodist Church is one of the oldest churches in Africa and has a history going back to 1821 when John Baker arrived at Tendaba and was shortly joined by John Baker from Sierra Leone. They were

---

[2] Pew Forum Center, "Table: Christian Population as Percentages of Total Population by Country," (December 19, 2011), www.pewforum.org/2011/12/19/table-christian-population-as-percentages-of-total-population-by-country/ (accessed 26 Dec. 15).

[3] Paul Jenkins and Lamin Sanneh, "Gambia," in *The Encyclopedia of Christianity, Volume 2,* eds. Erwin Fahlbusch et al, 378-399 (Grand Rapids: Wm. B. Eerdmans Publishing Co., 2001).

[4] Pew Research Center, "Table: Muslim Population by Country (January 27, 2011), www.pewforum.org/2011/01/27/table-muslim-population-by-country/ (accessed 26 Dec. 2015)

[5] Senegambia was a loose confederation in the late twentieth century between Senegal and the Gambia.

[6] For detailed discussion of the history of Christianity in the Gambia see, Fr. William Cleary, *Reaping a Rich Harvest: A History of the Catholic Church in The Gambia* (Banjul: Cathedral of Our Lady of the Assumption, 1990); Bakary Gibba, "The West Indian Mission to West Africa: The Rio Pongas Mission, 1850-1963," (PhD diss., University of Toronto, 2011), Bakary Gibba doctoral thesis is particularly informative as he goes into greater detail of the Anglican missionary work in the Rio Pongas and demonstrated how racism between the white and black missionaries hinder mission progress.

[7] For detailed documentation of missionary work of Roman Catholic going back to the sixteenth century, see, Peter Mark, *'Portuguese' Style and Luso-African Identity: Precolonial Senegambia, Sixteenth-Nineteenth Centuries* (Bloomington: Indiana University Press, 2002); Steven K. Thomson, "Christianity, Islam, and 'The Religion of Pouring': Non-linear Conversion in a Gambia/Casamance Borderland," *Journal of Religion in Africa* 42 (2012): 240-276.

encouraged to leave and concentrate their work in Bathurst.[8] They moved down to Banjul and established the first high school for boys. In 1935, the Wesley Church was built in Macoumba Jallow Street. Later, chapels and churches appeared in Serrekunda, Bakau, Georgetown and other areas of the Kombo St Mary District as well as in up-river districts.[9] They erected a chapel for the small Christian community called Bethesda in August 1821. The missionary work against slavery and other oppression was very important. Sanneh notes that the church 'joined the struggle against slavery, social repression and discrimination against women with all their hearts and minds, however meagre the means, however uncertain the future and however hazardous the path'.[10] The Methodist Church and Church of England took responsibility for the fate of the many freed slaves who had been brought to Gambia. Many of the Anglicans among them came from Sierra Leone, as the Church Missionary Society was active among the liberated Africans. In 1832, there was a station in MacCarthy Island with a resident assistant Methodist minister. The initial aim was to evangelize among the Fulas, an Islamic ethic group, but this was unsuccessful. Thus, they shifted attention to the freed slaves.[11] Early Methodist evangelistic strategy focused first on education, and schools were built. Methodist education was ecumenical and interfaith. Anglican and Muslim children were all enrolled in school from the start. The Methodists devoted themselves to educating Muslim children and affording them equal opportunities. This trend has continued up to the present as Methodist education still caters for all Gambians, irrespective of their religion, creed or ethnicity. However, education has not helped to bring about significant growth in church membership.[12] Second, Methodists also invested in health care as part of its evangelistic strategy. Third, in the 1970s, the Methodist Church prioritized agriculture as another part of its missionary strategy.

The Anglican Church

The Anglican Church in Gambia had a rough beginning. There were missions in West Africa before 1855, but all the missionaries either died or left because of disease. It was not until the Society for the Propagation of the Gospel in Foreign Parts (SPG) partnered with the Diocese of the West Indies that two missionaries, John Henry A. Duport and Hamble James Leacock, were able to make some headway in the country. The Anglican diocese of the Gambia and Rio Pongas finally made inroads in the country through the Aku. The Anglicans, together with the Roman Catholics and Methodists, found that evangelization of Gambian Muslims was next to impossible.[13] The Anglican Church in Gambia was established after erratic early stages, when the British colonial administration provided a series of chaplains for the West Indian garrison which was stationed in Bathurst. The station was founded in 1816, as a home for the resettlement of liberated slaves from the West Indies and USA. There was no fixed Anglican church building in Bathurst, even by 1861, when an expatriate chaplain, Robert Hughes, and his wife were posted from Sierra Leone by the then colonial governor. Anglican worship was held in the Garrison (now the Quadrangle site) or the military Officers' Mess. By 1871, a government census indicated that there were 291 Anglicans in Bathurst, predominantly among freed slaves, settlers, soldiers, colonial traders and administrators. This

---

[8] J Kofi Agbeti, *West African Church History: Church Missions and Christian Foundation: 1482-1919, Volume 1* (Leiden: E. J Brill, 1986), 51. This book also gives a good overview of the history of the church in Gambia.

[9] Rodney L. Prom, "The Inculturation of the Gospel: Implications for the Methodist Church the Gambia's Quest for Church Leadership," (MPhil. thesis, the University of Manchester, 2013), 76; Martha T. Frederiks, *We Have Toiled All Night: Christianity in The Gambia 1456-2000* (Zoetermeer: Uitgeverig Boekencentrum, 2003), 194. Martha T. Frederiks' book developed from her doctoral thesis is one of the most detailed works on Gambian Christianity.

[10] Prom, "The Inculturation of the Gospel," 77.

[11] Prom, "The Inculturation of the Gospel,"78.

[12] Prom, "The Inculturation of the Gospel," 84.

[13] Christine Elizabeth Curley, "Anglican Stagnation and Growth in West Africa: The Case of St. Paul's Church, Fajara, The Gambia," (MTh. thesis, Wycliffe College and the University of Toronto, 2012), 33.

sporadic trend continued until the 1880s, but unfortunately, the Anglican African chaplaincy was closed on the departure of the West Indian Regiment from Gambia in 1884.

But by 1899, a growing and vibrant family of African merchants existed. This group was economically stable and appealed to the Bishop of Sierra Leone for a permanent priest to be assigned to the Anglican community in Bathurst. They offered to guarantee a residence and a stipend for the priest. Thus, the first African Anglican priest in Bathurst came to Gambia.[14] The Church of England built the Anglican Cathedral of St Mary in 1901 and also proceeded to build schools and other places of worship. After 1935, this African Anglican Church became the centre of the new, amalgamated Diocese of The Gambia and Rio Pongas (Guinea), administered by its first bishop, an Englishman, John Charles Sydney Daly. This extended ecclesiastical authority of St Mary's Cathedral continued until the 1950s.[15]

Evangelical/Pentecostal Churches

The colonial government was conservative in its policy with regard to new churches in Gambia. As a result, Pentecostalism never became popular there.[16] Today, Gambia has a handful of evangelical churches that struggle to make their present felt. The Churches of Christ from Roseville, Michigan, established the first congregation in 1974 in Gambia. Abiding Word Ministry (AWM), which was established in 1988, is the earliest Pentecostal church in Gambia, though most of its members are not Gambians.[17] The Evangelical Church of Gambia (ECG) with its mission wing, House of Wisdom, with a focus on evangelising Muslims, is of South Korean origin, established in 1988.[18] It includes the Omega Training Institute (OTI) where people are trained in a vocational skill and equipped to start sustainable businesses. Others are Winners Chapel, called Living Faith Church (Nigeria), established in 1996, the Deeper Life Church (Nigeria), Assemblies of God (Canada), Church of God, Christian Mission Fellowship (Nigeria), and Lighthouse Chapel (Ghana). Most of these churches are of recent origin and have remained small, and most of the churches founded by Nigerian and Ghanaian denominations have attracted the majority of their followers among those country's migrants.[19]

The Gambia Christian Council

The Gambia Christian Council was founded in 1965 as 'a fellowship of churches and Christian organizations that worship one God in the Trinity of the Father, the Son and the Holy Spirit; accept as scriptures the Holy Bible consisting of the Old and the New Testament; have an established organization that teaches the Christian way of life and exercises discipline; are prepared to encourage their members to participate in ecumenical activities'.[20] It is an ecumenical association of Roman Catholic, Anglican, Methodist and other churches.

[14] Frederiks, *We have Toiled.*
[15] Ralphina Phillott-Almeida, "Christianity in Gambia: Historical Biography of St. Mary's Cathedral, Banjul," (Prepared for inclusion in the commemorative Programme for the Patronal Festival of St Mary's Cathedral that was held on 12th July 2015), Email: dietrich.werner@brot-fuer-die-welt.de (14 December 2015 15:48).
[16] Marloes Janson, *Islam, Youth and Modernity in the Gambia: The Tablighi Jama'at* (London: International African Institute and Cambridge University Press, 2013). 262.
[17] Frederiks, *We have Toiled,* 367ff.
[18] Curley, "Anglican Stagnation and Growth in West Africa," 43-44.
[19] Janson, *Islam,* 262.
[20] WCC, "The Gambia Christian Council," https://www.oikoumene.org/en/member-churches/africa/the-gambia/the-gambia-christian-council (accessed 26 Dec. 15).

Interfaith Relations

Despite having one of the highest percentages of Muslim populations in sub-Saharan Africa, Gambia celebrates its religious harmony and tolerance more than most African countries. It is one of the few countries where intermarriage between Muslims and Christians exist, protected by the law and socially acceptable. In some areas, Islam and Christianity are syncretized with African traditional religious worldview. For instance, Marloes Janson observes the Pentecostalization taking place among the Tablighi Jama'at youth who present themselves as 'born-again Muslims', influenced by Chrislam preachers from Nigeria.[21] The Chrislam is a new form of syncritsic religion which has integrated beliefs from both Islam and Christianity without taking side with either of them. It refers to a new form of interfaith religion. Janson did some brilliant research on Chrislam in Gambia which refers to a set of religious movements founded by Muslim leaders which were influenced by Pentecostalism in Nigeria. He concluded that there is a move toward 'Islamic Pentecostalism'.[22] These movements have borrowed many features from Pentecostal Christians and yet remain Muslim. In short, Gambian Christians seems to realise that they have more in common with Gambian Muslims than they have in common with western Christianity. The same is true of Gambian Muslims. They appear to believe that have more common with Gambian Christians than they have with Arabian Muslims.[23] The Gambian worldview unifies them. There is also an Inter-Faith Group for Dialogue and Peace established by various faiths and church denominations to engage in matters of common interest.[24]

Conclusion

Despite early predictions that Christianity would eventually be swamped by the Muslim majority, Christianity remains stable. The focus on evangelization and conversation in the nineteenth and the first half of the twentieth centuries seems to have been slowly replaced by a focus on reinforcing the faith and the concept of mission for socio-economic progress.

Bibliography

Access Gambia, 'Religion,' www.accessgambia.com/information/religion.html (accessed 26 Dec. 15).

Agbeti, J Kofi. *West African Church History: Church Missions and Christian Foundation: 1482-1919, Volume 1*, Leiden: E. J Brill, 1986.

Cleary, Fr William. *Reaping a Rich Harvest: A History of the Catholic Church in The Gambia*, Banjul: Cathedral of Our Lady of the Assumption, 1990.

Curley, Christine E. 'Anglican Stagnation and Growth in West Africa: The Case of St Paul's Church, Fajara, The Gambia,' MTh. Thesis, Wycliffe College and the University of Toronto, 2012.

Frederiks, Martha T. 'Mission or Submission?—From Mission History towards an Intercultural History of Christianity: Case-study The Gambia.' in *Mission Revisited: Between Mission History and Intercultural Theology,* edited by Küster, Volker, 81-92, Berlin: Lit Verlag, 2010.

Frederiks, Martha T. *We Have Toiled All Night: Christianity in The Gambia 1456-2000,* Zoetermeer: Uitgeverig Boekencentrum, 2003.

---

[21] Janson, *Islam,* 262.

[22] Janson, *Islam,* 262.

[23] This observation was made by Paul Gifford in African Christianity, see his recent book, *Christianity, Development and Modernity in Africa (London:* Hurst & Company, 2015).

[24] Access Gambia, "Religion," www.accessgambia.com/information/religion.html (accessed 26 Dec. 15); Arnold Hughes and David Perfect, *Historical Dictionary of The Gambia, fourth Edition* (Lanham, Maryland: Scarecrow Press, 2008), 187-188.

Gibba, Bakary. 'The West Indian Mission to West Africa: The Rio Pongas Mission, 1850-1963,' PhD diss., University of Toronto, 2011.
Hughes, Arnold and David Perfect. *Historical Dictionary of The Gambia, fourth Edition,* Lanham, Maryland: Scarecrow Press, 2008.
Jenkins, Paul and Lamin Sanneh. 'Gambia,' in *The Encyclopedia of Christianity, Volume 2,* eds. Fahlbusch. Erwin *et al*, 378-399, Grand Rapids: Wm. B. Eerdmans Publishing Co., 2001.
Mark, Peter. *'Portuguese' Style and Luso-African Identity: Precolonial Senegambia, Sixteenth-Nineteenth Centuries,* Bloomington: Indiana University Press, 2002.
Prom, Rodney L. 'The Inculturation of the Gospel: Implications for the Methodist Church the Gambia's Quest for Church Leadership,' MPhil. Thesis, the University of Manchester, 2013.
Thomson, Steven K. 'Christianity, Islam, and 'The Religion of Pouring': Non-linear Conversion in a Gambia/Casamance Borderland,' *Journal of Religion in Africa* 42 (2012): 240-276.

(65) CHRISTIANITY IN GHANA

Sylvia Owusu-Ansah

Religion	Pop 2010	Pct 2010	Pop 2025	Pct 2025	Gr Pct 1970 2025
Christians	15,573,000	64.0%	22,518,000	66.9%	2.5%
Independents	5,106,000	21.0%	7,630,000	22.7%	2.7%
African initiated	4,194,000	17.2%			
Orthodox	4,000	0.0%	6,000	0.0%	2.7%
Protestants	6,384,000	26.3%	8,900,000	26.4%	2.2%
Pentecostal	3,621,000	14.9%			
Methodist	900,000	3.7%			
Reformed, Presbyterian	825,000	3.4%			
Adventist	515,000	2.1%			
Anglicans	269,000	1.1%			
Baptist	132,000	0.5%			
Roman Catholics	3,053,000	12.6%	4,640,000	13.8%	2.8%
Pentecostals/Charismatics	8,931,000	36.7%	12,400,000	36.8%	2.2%
Evangelicals	4,787,000	19.7%	6,585,000	19.6%	2.1%
Muslims	4,817,000	19.8%	6,680,000	19.8%	2.2%
adherents of traditional African religions	3,804,000	15.6%	4,300,000	12.8%	0.8%
adherents of new religious movements	26,500	0.1%	35,000	0.1%	1.9%
Baha'is	14,000	0.1%	20,000	0.1%	2.4%
Hindus	4,900	0.0%	7,000	0.0%	2.5%
Chinese folk-religionists	700	0.0%	1,000	0.0%	2.4%
Buddhists	490	0.0%	700	0.0%	2.5%
Jews	440	0.0%	400	0.0%	-0.6%
people professing no religion	76,500	0.3%	116,000	0.3%	2.8%
Total population	**24,318,000**	**100.0%**	**33,678,000**	**100.0%**	**2.2%**

Source: Centre for the Study of World Christianity (CSGC), Boston, Gordon-Conwell TS

Introduction

Records have established that Christianity was first introduced to the then Gold Coast on 20th January, 1482, by a team of 600 men from Portugal led by Don Diogo d'Azambuja who first arrived in Elmina, near Cape Coast.[1] Upon arrival, he introduced the chiefs to the Christian faith with the promise of establishing

[1] Kofi Agbeti, *West African Church History* (Leiden: E.J. Brill, 1986), 4.

trade relationships between them. As a positive response to this offer, the chiefs 'granted the Portuguese a site on which a fort and a chapel were built'.[2] By the end of 1617, the Roman Catholics were the dominant Christian missionaries in the Gold Coast, even though their evangelisation did not yield enduring results. In 1637, the Dutch arrived on the Gold Coast and laid siege to and captured the Portuguese fort at Elmina, and also took over Fort St Anthony at Axim in 1642.[3] Other Europeans including the Danes, Swedes and Branden-Burgers settled on the coast and built forts such as the Danes' fort at Christiansburg near Accra, which later became the 'Government house of Ghana', now known as The Castle. Even though the main purpose of building these forts was commercial, chaplains were provided to administer spiritual succour to the inmates of the fort and some 'local Africans'.[4]

The Establishment of the Mission Churches

Substantial missionary activities began in the Gold Coast from December 1828 by four missionaries from the Basel Mission, namely, Karl F. Salbach, Gottlieb Holzwarth and Johannes Henke, all of German origin, and Johannes Gottlieb Schmidt, a Swiss.[5] They settled in Christiansburg but later relocated to the Akwapim ridge because of the favourable weather conditions there. The Rev. Joseph Rhodes Dunwell, the first Methodist missionary to the Gold Coast, arrived in 1835 and settled at Cape Coast in the Central Region. Dunwell's missionary trip to Ghana resulted from 'the indigenous Ghanaian request for Bibles for Christian Development'.[6] F.L. Bartels establishes that, 'together with the local Christian pioneers, although he lived among them for only six months, Dunwell sowed the seed which has grown into the mature plant of the Methodist Church, Ghana'.[7] Dunwell's contribution is very significant for the start of the Methodist Church in Ghana. However, the success story of the Wesleyans cannot be completely told without mentioning the selfless services rendered by the Rev. Thomas Birch Freeman, 'son of a black father and a white mother', towards the expansion of the Methodist Church.[8] In his time, missionary work spread to Kumasi, the second largest city of Ghana, popularly known as the Garden City. After it had gained autonomy from its western roots on 28th July 1961, the Methodist Church in Ghana experienced tremendous growth as it continued the tradition of its founder John Wesley in the winning and discipling of converts.

A little while after Dunwell had introduced Methodism to the eastern half of the Gold Coast, 'Andeas Riis went on a missionary journey from Christiansburg to Akropong to plan the foundations of the Basel Mission Church in the eastern half'.[9] Andreas moved to settle permanently in Akropong on 21st March 1831, which could be termed as the start of the work of the Basel Mission in Akropong.[10] Earlier, in 1828, the Basel Mission had started work at Osu and Nimgo at the Danish fort of Christiansburg in Accra.[11] Clarke notes that, in spite of the favourable weather in the Akropong in the Akwuapim Mountains, for various reasons, the Basel Mission had accomplished very little by 1840, while the death rate of missionaries and the rivalry between the Danish and British had not abated.[12] He explains:

---

[2] Agbeti, *West African Church History*, 4.
[3] Abgeti, *West African Church History*, 5.
[4] Agbeti, *West African Church History*, 6. "Fanti" is traditionally and popularly known by the indigenes as "Mfanste".
[5] Kingsley E Larbi, *Pentecostalism: The Eddies of Ghanaian Christianity* (Accra: Blessed Publications, 2001), 16.
[6] "The Methodist Church Ghana, from Autonomy to the Present", accessed 2 May 2015, www.methodistchurch-gh.org/index.php/the-church/autonomy-of-the-methodist-church-ghana
[7] F. L. Bartels, *The Roots of Ghana Methodism* (Cambridge: CUP, 1965), 1.
[8] "The Methodist Church Ghana, from Autonomy to the Present".
[9] Bartels, *Ghana Methodism*, 1965, 6.
[10] Bartels, *Ghana Methodism*, 1965, 6.
[11] Peter B. Clarke, *West Africa and Christianity* (London: Edward Arnold Publishers Ltd., 1986), 41.
[12] Clarke, *West Africa and Christianity*, 41.

> While the Basel Mission Committee had sent missionaries to the Gold Coast to 'open schools and in general live in brotherly love with the Africans', the Danish administration, on the other hand, demanded that the missionaries devote themselves exclusively to work among the Danish congregations at Christiansburg.[13]

Clarke maintains that the Danish authorities' decision to move the headquarters of the Basel Mission to Akropong in the Akwuapim Hills was favourable to the health of the missionaries but it also exposed them to 'political infighting'.[14] Gradually, the Basel Missionary committee gained roots in Akropong and its environs despite the death of its missionaries and political rivalries. Between 1828 and 1918, the Presbyterian Church had recorded the remarkable growth of 'a total Christian community of 30,000'.[15]

The German Bremen Society arrived in 1847 in the Trans-Volta Region. Roman Catholic missionaries came to the Gold Coast in 1881 and settled at Elmina. The first Fanti Roman Catholic priests ordained by Bishop Porter of Cape Coast were George Ansah from Elmina and Francis Menya from Pedu near Cape Coast. The African Methodist Episcopal Church came in 1898, followed by the Anglican Church in 1906. The African Methodist Episcopal (AME) Zion was formed (from the American Methodist Episcopal Zion Church) in 1720 in New York when the 'coloured' people separated from the Whites to form a Methodist Episcopal church in New York. The purpose of this separation was to allow the coloured people the freedom and liberty to 'exercise their spiritual gifts among themselves'.[16] After a while, there were similar separations between the Whites and the Coloureds in all mixed congregations, while in 1820, the separatist groups came together to form the African Methodist Episcopal Zion Church.[17] The missionary work of the church began in Liberia in 1876 by the Rev. Andrew Cartwright, who worked assiduously and sacrificially amidst financial constraints.[18] A more extensive and profound work was done by the AME Zion church in Ghana, supervised by two retired Wesleyan Methodist ministers, the Rev. Egyin-Asaam and Thomas Birch Freeman, the son of the veteran missionary of the Methodist Church in Ghana. Freeman opened the first AME Zion church in Ghana at Keta and later another at Cape Coast.[19] 'Suitable African young men were recruited for training in the United States.' The first to be recruited was Emmanuel Kwegyir-Aggrey who never returned after his studies, defeating the whole purpose of the offer of establishing trade relationships. Afterwards, Frank Arthur, formerly known as Frank Ata Osarn-Pinanko, was sent to America for training. Upon his return to the Cape Coast, the AME Zion church flourished. He was able to open churches at Winneba and Twifo.[20] Primary and secondary schools attached to the churches that had been opened were also established. Prominent among them was the Aggrey Memorial Secondary School, 'a co-educational unit at Cape Coast'.[21]

Another mission church worth noting is the Seventh Day Adventist Church. The Seventh Day Adventist Church was established in the Gold Coast in 1888 through the efforts of Francis I.U. Dolphijn, a Ghanaian staying at Apam.[22] The first missionaries, namely, Karl G. Rudolph and E.L. Sanford, were sent to Apam in the Central Region in 1893. The Gold Coast Mission of the Seventh Day Adventists was established in 1894 with its headquarters at Cape Coast. In 1914, W.H. Lewis, the first President of the Gold Coast Mission, chose Agona Asante as the missionary headquarters, 'after he had been heartily accepted by Nana Kwame Boakye I, chief of Agona'. In 1915, the pioneering work of the Asante region was begun by Lewis

[13] Clarke, *West Africa and Christianity*, 41.
[14] Clarke, *West Africa and Christianity*, 41.
[15] Larbi, *Pentecostalism*, 17.
[16] Agbeti, *West Africa Church History*, 143.
[17] Agbeti, *West Africa Church History*, 143.
[18] Agbeti, *West Africa Church History*, 143.
[19] Agbeti, *West Africa Church History*, 147.
[20] Agbeti, *West Africa Church History*, 150.
[21] Agbeti, *West Africa Church History*, 150.
[22] Seventh Day Adventist, "Central Ghana Conference," www.cgcsda.org/our-history (accessed 30 April, 2015).

and his team, and the work expanded to Ntonso, Wiamoase and Asamang. Pastor Clifford arrived at Agona in 1931, and in 1932 he assisted in establishing the Bekwai Training School.[23] The first black president of the Ghana Mission, Pastor C.B. Mensah, was elected in 1959. The church engages in a number of activities, like evangelism, constituency meetings, camp meetings, youth camps, church planting and establishing institutions.[24]

Evangelism through Educational and Medical Work

Medical Outreach Endeavours

The mission churches embarked on medical service as part of their evangelistic endeavours. World War I and the deportation of the Basel missionaries in 1917 led to a temporary closure of the hospital until Scottish missionaries arrived to continue the medical work and also provide health services for women and children at Abetifi.[25] Several other clinics were established in different parts of the country. Prominent among them was a '60-bed clinic at Agogo, Ashanti Region, in 1929'. Other clinics were opened by the Basel Mission at Dormaa Ahenkro in 1951 and Bechem in 1952. F.D. Harker and Mrs Margaret Benzies (Scottish missionaries) established the Akropong School for the blind in 1943 which was initially overseen by the Scottish Mission but later on handed over to a committee made up of representatives from the Presbyterian and Methodist churches and the Ministry of Education. All kinds of handiwork were taught in the school, such as basket and mat weaving, cane work and training in shorthand and typing. There was collaboration between the government and the mission churches in producing health facilities and services for Ghanaians. The major contribution made by mission churches towards medical work in Ghana is in providing a large number of Christian doctors and nurses, and providing training for African staff.[26]

Evangelism through Education

The western European Christian missions embarked on a number of projects as a catalyst for evangelism. One of the major ones was providing western education. Till the nineteenth century, the mission churches were the main providers of this through the schools they established. Education through the mission schools played a major role in the process of gaining independence in Ghana.[27]

African Initiated Christianity

Ghanaian Pentecostalism began with the ministries of three prophetic figures, namely, Prophet Wade Harris, Prophet Samson Oppong and Prophet John Swatson.[28] The Pentecostal experiences of *peaking in other tongues*, healing and miracles, casting out devils, and deliverance from fetishism and paganism were first introduced into Ghanaian Christianity by these prophets in the early 1900s. Before the appearance of these prophets, the only form of Christianity known to the people of Ghana was the one brought by the western mission churches. The ministries of these three prophetic figures marked the beginning of the 'spiritual' churches in Ghana.

---

[23] Evangelistic Training School and Seminary, www.cgcsda.org/our-history/ (accessed 30 April 2015).
[24] Seventh Day Adventist: Central Ghana Conference, www.cgcsda.org/our-history (accessed 30 April 2015).
[25] Larbi, *Pentecostalism,* 21.
[26] Hans W. Debrunner, *History of Christianity in Ghana* (Accra: Waterville Publishing House, 1967), 344.
[27] Debrunner, *Christianity in Africa*, 340.
[28] Larbi, *Pentecostalism,* 61.

Classical Pentecostal Churches in Ghana

Peter Newman Anim began the Faith Tabernacle Church in 1917. Anim's church was affiliated to the Apostolic Church in the UK in 1935 and, as a result, James McKeon was sent by the British church to assist him in 1937.[29] Anim's strict adherence to the doctrine of divine healing without compromise brought division between them when McKeon was attacked by sickness and had to resort to medication. When Anim parted ways with McKeon, he named his church Christ Apostolic. McKeon, however, continued to work for the UK Apostolic Church until he resigned in 1935 and began his own Gold Coast Apostolic Church. The three Pentecostal churches, Anim's Christ Apostolic Church, McKeon's Gold Coast Apostolic Church and the Apostolic Church of Gold Coast, affiliated to the UK Apostolic Church, were the three Pentecostal churches in Ghana during this period. The Apostolic Church of Gold Coast became the Apostolic Church of Ghana when they later gained autonomy from the UK church. McKeon's Gold Coast Apostolic Church later on became the Church of Pentecost. The last of the four main Classical Pentecostal churches in Ghana is the Assemblies of God Church.

The Assemblies of God was the first foreign Pentecostal body to begin in Northern Ghana. The church's first missionaries from America, the Rev. Lloyd and Margaret Shirer came to the northern region of the Gold Coast in 1931 and started work in Wagadugu. They returned to the USA and brought more missionaries to support this work. Some of them had health challenges and returned. Others died but Lloyd and Margaret continued to work for quite a long time until they finally decided to work under the Department of Social Welfare and Community Development. The Assemblies of God Church concentrated more on providing health facilities and in the development of literature, rather than on church planting, compared with the other Pentecostal churches.

The Rise of Charismatic Churches in Ghana

A great evangelical Pentecostal revival began in Ghana in the 1960s and early 1970s that resulted in the proliferation of several non-denominational groups known as 'fellowships' all over the country.[30] Examples of such non-denominational Bible study groups, prayer associations and fellowships are the Ghana Evangelical Society (GES), founded by Evangelist Enoch Agbozo, the Hour of Visitation Choir and Evangelistic Association (HOVCEA), founded by Evangelist Isaac Ababio, the Youth Ambassadors for Christ Association (YAFCA), founded by the Rev. Owusu Afriyie, and the National Evangelistic Association (NEA). Most of the members of these para-church organizations were drawn from the mission and classical Pentecostal churches. Some of these fellowships became the bedrock of the new independent or neo-Pentecostal churches.

Scripture Union is one of the oldest para-church groups training leaders, many of whom later joined the charismatic ministries, either as founders or as leading members. The leading charismatic churches in Ghana now are the Christian Action Faith Chapel founded by Bishop Duncan Williams, ICGC by Dr Mensah Otabil, Perez Chapel International by Bishop Charles Agyinasare, the Light House Chapel International by Bishop Dag Hayward Mills, and Gospel Light by Bishop Addae Mensah. There are several other charismatic churches in Ghana. Research by Kweku Okyerefo into the reasons for the astronomical growth of some Pentecostal and neo-Pentecostal churches in Accra shows that members are attracted to these newer churches because of the 'spiritual and material benefits individuals derive from Pentecostalism'.[31] Members of the Lighthouse and Royal House Chapels, the targeted churches for the

---

[29] Larbi, *Pentecostalism*, 107.

[30] Para-church groups refer to non-denominational fellowships, which trained a lot of leaders who later became head of some Charismatic Churches.

[31] Michael Perry Kweku Okyerefo, "Pentecostalism in the City of Accra: a Blossom on Functional Appeal and Urban Fecundity," *American Journal of Sociological Research* 1, no.1 (2011): (27-34) 30.

study, declared, among other things, that their reasons for joining the churches included 'being impressed by the lively church services, the feeling that one's spiritual needs are satisfied, experiencing God's presence in these churches, receiving the Holy Spirit, and the church's material assistance to members in time of need'.[32]

Apart from the charismatic experience within Pentecostal and neo-Pentecostal churches there are also the charismata within the western mission, or older, churches in Ghana. Members of the mainline – Roman Catholic, Methodist, Presbyterian, Evangelical Presbyterian, Baptist Convention and other churches – who have had an encounter or association with Pentecostal or Charismatic groups have transferred their experience to the mainline churches. Within the mainline churches are prayer groups and associations with a charismatic orientation referred to as charismatic renewal.

Conclusion

In the early nineteenth century, the mission churches started settling and gaining ground in the coastal areas. Notable among them were the Presbyterian Church of Ghana, Evangelical Presbyterian, Methodist Church, Anglican Church, and Roman Catholic Church. These churches combined evangelism with education and medical services. From the 1900s, what has come to be known as the Pentecostal/ Charismatic experience started in the country. Such ministries were marked by the supernatural, healing and deliverance from fetishism and demon possession.

Bibliography

Agbeti, Kofi. *West African Church History*. Leiden: E.J. Brill, 1986.

Asamoah-Gyadu, Kwabena. *African Charismatics*. Leiden: Koninklijke Brill, 2005.

Asamoah-Gyadu, Johnson. 'Renewal within African Christianity – A Study of Some Current Historical and Theological Developments within Independent Indigenous Pentecostalism in Ghana.' PhD Thesis, University of Birmingham, 2000.

Clarke, Peter, B. *West Africa and Christianity*. London: Edward Arnold Publishers Ltd., 1986.

Debrunner, Hans, W. *History of Christianity in Ghana*. Accra: Waterville Publishing House, 1967.

Larbi, Kingsley E. *Pentecostalism: The Eddies of Ghanaian Christianity*. Accra: Blessed Publications, 2001.

Okyerefo, Kweku Michael Perry. 'Pentecostalism in the City of Accra: a Blossom on Functional Appeal and Urban Fecundity'. *American Journal of Sociological Research* 1 no.1 (2011): 27-34.

Omenyo, Cephas Narh. *Pentecost outside Pentecostalism: A Study of the Development of Charismatic Renewal in the Mainline Churches in Ghana*. The Netherlands: Boekencentrum Zoetermeer, 2002.

---

[32] Okyerefo, "Pentecostalism in the City of Accra", 30-31.

(66A) Christianity in Guinea Bissau

Chammah J. Kaunda and Luciano Chianeque

Religion	Pop 2010	Pct 2010	Pop 2025	Pct 2025	Gr Pct 1970 2025
Christians	194,000	11.8%	300,000	13.0%	3.0%
Independents	40,300	2.5%	61,000	2.7%	2.8%
Protestants	25,100	1.5%	45,300	2.0%	4.0%
Evangelical churches	18,600	1.1%			
Roman Catholics	169,000	10.3%	245,000	10.6%	2.5%
Pentecostals/Charismatics	49,400	3.0%	80,000	3.5%	3.3%
Evangelicals	22,200	1.4%	38,000	1.7%	3.7%
Muslims	733,000	44.9%	1,099,000	47.8%	2.7%
adherents of traditional African religions	686,000	42.0%	870,000	37.8%	1.6%
Baha'is	280	0.0%	300	0.0%	0.5%
people professing no religion	20,700	1.3%	31,600	1.4%	2.8%
Total population	**1,634,000**	**100.0%**	**2,301,000**	**100.0%**	**2.3%**

Source: Centre for the Study of World Christianity (CSGC), Boston, Gordon-Conwell TS

Guinea Bissau is on the west coast of Africa, bounded to the west and south by the Atlantic Ocean, to the north by Senegal, and to the east and south by Guinea. Guinea Bissau came into contact with Europeans through Portuguese explorers in 1446. The Roman Catholic Franciscan order arrived in 1462. In 1532, the diocese of St James of Cape Verde was established. The diocese was responsible for mission work on the mainland but the process of evangelization was very slow. In May 1940, a Concordat[1] between the Holy See[2] and Portugal was signed. This resulted in the separation of Guinea Bissau mission work from Cape Verde that same year.[3]

The Protestant tradition came through the World Evangelical Crusade (now WEC International) from the UK in 1939.[4] They established themselves in Bolama, the old capital of Guinea Bissau, which was then an overseas province of Portugal. Soon after their arrival in the country, they made their first convert, Ms Guilhermina Barbosa, who was known as Mimi. From that date, the work of evangelization continued with the participation of missionaries from the US and Britain in the 1950s and 1960s. The missionary work reached the regional areas of Guinea Bissau, Bassora, Biombo as well as the archipelagos of Bijagós and

---

[1] René Metz defines a concordat as a formal agreement or a treaty between the Holy See and a sovereign state that defines the relationship between the Catholic Church and the state with regard to the mutually concerned matters. See his, *What is Canon Law?* (first edition) (New York: Hawthorn Books, 1960), 137.

[2] The Holy See is the ecclesiastical jurisdiction of the Catholic Church in Rome, the episcopal see of the Pope.

[3] John Pobee, "Guinea-Bissau," in *The Encyclopedia of Christianity, Volume 2* (E-I), eds. Erwin Fahlbusch *et al* (Michigan: Grand Rapids, 2001): 487-488.

[4] Hazel Willis, *Light Shines in the Darkness: The Story of the Evangelical Church of Guinea Bissau, 1940-1974* (Bulstrode, UK: WEC, 1996).

Cantio. Its work resulted in the creation of one the largest Protestant congregations, called the Evangelical Church. This work included medical service.[5]

The New Apostolic Church of Germany arrived in the country in the 1970s and also resulted in the emergence of the largest non-Catholic Christian tradition in Guinea Bissau.[6] The work of the New Apostolic Church in Guinea-Bissau continues to be in the care of the German District Church of North Rhine-Westphalia.

There is also a small Anglican community of the Province of West Africa and the small Guinea Bissau mission of the Seventh Day Adventist Church, which is part of the larger Sahel Union Mission consisting of a number of other West African countries.[7]

The armed struggle which started in 1963 confined evangelization to Bissau as the Christian activists were perceived as freedom fighters. Many of them were killed – for instance, in the north, Mr Mormoso, and in the south, Mr Victor Martins, who thus became Christian martyrs. During this period, many people migrated to the neighbouring countries of Guinea (aka Guinea-Conakry), Senegal and Gambia.[8]

After independence from Portugal in 1974, many Christians who had previously left the country started to return, which gave a different momentum to the work of evangelization. Missionaries started to come from all over the world: the USA, UK, Holland and Brazil.

Politically, the country became multi-party in 1990. With this change, the country saw the mushrooming of new political parties and opened up to the world to the point that new Christian denominations began to work there as well. These denominations are JOCUM (Youth with a Mission), Assemblies of God, the Baptist Church, and others. Today there are more than twenty-five Christian denominations.

Yet there is no ecumenical body in the country that can supervise all these denominations. However, the personal relationships between these church leaders are excellent on a personal level. When there is any need to speak with one voice, there is a problem within the existing denominations in the country. In 1999, civil war destroyed much of the mission work in the interior, forcing the workers to flee to the western part of the country. Despite these challenges, evangelistic work continues to thrive in the country and the Bible has been translated into three local languages.[9]

Bibliography

Davis, Jennifer. *The Republic of Guinea-Bissau: Triumph over Colonialism.* (New York: The Africa Fund, 1974).

Lobban, Richard Andrew and Peter Karibe Mendy. *Historical Dictionary of the Republic of Guinea-Bissau.* Lanham, Maryland: The Scarecrow Press, 1997.

Melton, J. Gordon. *Encyclopedia of Protestantism.* New York: Facts on File, 2005.

Pobee, John. 'Guinea-Bissau.' In *The Encyclopedia of Christianity, Volume 2* (E-I), edited by. Erwin Fahlbusch *et al.* 487-488. Michigan: Grand Rapids, 2001.

Urdang, Stephanie. 'Fighting Two Colonialisms: The Women's Struggle in Guinea-Bissau.' *African Studies Review* 18, no. 3 (Dec. 1975): 29-34.

---

[5] H. Willis, *Light Shines in the Darkness.*

[6] J. Gordon Melton, *Encyclopedia of Protestantism* (New York: Facts on File, 2005).

[7] Melton, *Encyclopedia of Protestantism.*

[8] Stephanie Urdang, "Fighting Two Colonialisms: The Women's Struggle in Guinea-Bissau," *African Studies Review* 18, no. 3 (Dec. 1975): 29-34.

[9] Pobee, "Guinea-Bissua."

(66B) A Realidade Crista Evangélica na Guiné-Bissau

Joaquim Correia

Historia

Maio de 1940, chega a Bissau a Besse Fricker Brierly uma menina Inglesa missionaria da WEC Internacional. Acompanhada pela Sra. Libânia, Cabo-verdiana, já de idade, costureira. Chegaram a Bolama a antiga capital da Guine, então província portuguesa. Começa a evangelização. A primeira convertida chama-se Guilhermina Barbosa, mais conhecida por Mimi.

Nos anos das décadas de 50 e 60 duas levas importas de missionários chegaram dos Estados Unidos e da Grã-Bretanha. Os frentes de evangelização se diversificaram, Bissau, a actual capital do pais da Guiné-Bissau, Bassorá no Norte com a etnia Balanta, Biombo também no Norte oeste com etnia pepel, arquipélago dos bijagós com a etnia bijago, Catio no Sul, com as etnias Sossos e balantas de fora.

Em 1963, começa a luta de libertação nacional, a evangelização ficou confinada em Bissau. No interior os Evangelistas eram confundidos com os activistas da luta de libertação. Alguns Evangelistas chegaram a ser barbaramente mortos, temos exemplo de Victor Martins no Sul da Guine e Formoso no Norte. Muitos se refugiaram nos países vizinhos, Senegal, Gambia e a Republica da Guine. A Única Escola bíblica que funcionou de ano de 1953 a 1956, em Lendem (Norte) fechou a sua porta. As igrejas se concentraram mais em Bissau e nas 4 outras pequenas cidades, onde não se verificavam constantes movimentações militares.

Pós-guerra

Vindo a Independência, 1974, muitos cristãos decidiram voltar as suas aldeias de origem, com isso muitos novas igrejas nasceram em aldeias, vilas e cidades do interior. Outra vez novos missionários começaram a chegar, dos Estados Unidos, Grã-Bretanha, Holanda e o Brasil. Em 1976, o Instituto Bíblico reabriu-se. Novos pastores e evangelistas locais voltarem a ser formados e o trabalho começou a se estruturar, pouco a pouco os nacionais começaram a assumir a liderança da igreja.

!990, um novo período da Igreja começara. O pais deixa a politica de um único partido e começaram a surgir mais partidos, com isso varias denominações começaram a chegar também. Ate 1990, só havia a Igreja Evangélica da Guiné-Bissau, fundada pela WEC Internacional. A maior denominação Evangélica da Guiné-Bissau ate a data presente. Depois, Chega a Missão JOCUM, A Igreja Assembleia de Deus, a Igreja Batista, e muitas outra igrejas independentes vindos dos países africanos, a Pentecoste e outras. Hoje o pais da Guiné-Bissau conta com mais de 25 denominações em fase de implantação.

Relação inter-denominacional

A relação entre os pastores de varias denominações evangélicas existentes no pais é excelente. Quando eles se encontram em qualquer evento, a dificuldade de distinguir quem é quem é enorme. Mas congregar as denominações numa única organização é quase impossível. Houve varias tentativas de congrega-las em torno de Aliança das Igrejas e Missões Evangélicas da Guiné-Bissau, mas nunca teve sucesso. Por exemplo, A Igreja Evangélica da Guiné-Bissau (IEGB) não faz parte da Aliança. Ela foi fundadora da Aliança, mas num dado momento, ela não se sentiu confortável na organização se retirou e ficou em torno do Conselho Nacional da Igreja Evangélica da Guiné-Bissau. E tem outras que nem fazem parte da Aliança e nem do Conselho nacional da Igreja Evangélica.

Quem Representa os Evangélicos perante o Estado da Guiné-Bissau quando for necessário?

Considerando que quando o pais obteve a sua Independência, a Igreja Evangélica, a Igreja Católica e a Igreja Muçulmana, como são chamadas por muitos guineenses, já existiam. Uma mesquita, um templo e a catedral católica de Bissau, são mesmo isentos de pagar luz e agua. As três Instituições religiosas são consultadas quando for necessário. A Igreja evangélica chegou a ter no palácio da Republica, um pastor para representar todos os religiosos junto ao presidente da república e como assessor do presidente para assuntos religiosos.

A Linha teológica

A WEC Internacional trabalhou na Guiné-Bissau há mais de meio seculo, Ela recebe missionários de varias denominações, desde as mais conservadoras a mais pentecostais. A linha de pensamento foi sempre, enfatizar o que nos une como evangélicos e deixas de lado tudo que nos separa. Respeito pela corrente teológica do colega. A Igreja Evangélica foi implantada neste princípio. Os crentes emprenharam isso no seu viver cotidiano e se tornaram conhecidos por este modo de viver. As novas denominações estão com dificuldade de enfatizar as suas características seus costumes denominacionais. Um pastor estrangeiro, pentecostal, chegou a dizer que os crentes de cada pais tem a sua maneira de se comportar e reagir as situações. Ele pregava numa cruzada Evangelística, num estádio e esperava ouvir os gritos de gloria Deus, aleluia, e raras vezes ele ouvia isso. Está evidente nos membros a fraca consciência denominacional e muito menos ainda, a nução das correntes teológicas existentes.

As Parcerias

A população Evangélica está na ordem de 2,5 a 3% no universo de 1.5 milhão de habitantes. Ainda tem muitas coisas para fazer. O povo é aberto ao evangelho. Mesmo nas aldeias de maioria muçulmana, verifica-se a conversão de pessoas a Cristo. Muitas igrejas são lideradas por obreiros leigos, sem qualquer preparo bíblico teológico. Existem poucas instituições para formação de obreiros. Praticamente os trabalhos voltados para o desenvolvimento de comunidades são inexistentes. Contudo a pobreza e as necessidades são gritantes. Conforme o comité nacional de luta contra VIH/SIDA, o índice de pessoas infectadas, em vez de diminuir esta a aumentar O número de crentes aumenta gradativamente, mas com fraca capacidade económica para suportar os encargos com trabalhos missionários.

Vimos a grande necessidade de valorizar a conexidade como a maior possibilidade de comunicação entre as igrejas com o objectivo de aumentar a comunhão entres irmãos, buscando cumprir a meta, que é tornar conhecido o nome do Senhor em todos os cantos do país. Isso só é possível graças a parcerias locais, nacionais e internacionais, principalmente com as organizações crista de desenvolvimento.

Discipulado e integração

Verifica-se a fraca compreensão do discipulado como um modo de ser da igreja e não, simplesmente, como um programa. Ser discípulo de Jesus é uma exigência. O evangélicalismo impõe uma prática de discipulado focado na salvação, santificação, no serviço e na caminhada cristã. Nas estruturas das igrejas, mesmo as ditas mais organizadas há uma necessidade da existência de:

1. Implantar a Instituição encarregue pelo Discipulado;
2. Publicação e distribuição de materiais que fundamenta a fé e Carácter Cristão para aplicação nas igrejas locais;
3. Manual de Implantação do Discipulado, para orientar os pastores e líderes locais sobre os programas de discipulado, nas igrejas;

4. Realizar workshops Nacional, Regional, Municipais e Local sobre discipulado.

Os Cristãos VIH/SIDA

Cada vez mais, eu vi que eh imperativo criar na Guiné-Bissau uma organização ecuménica de luta contra VIH/SIDA a fim ajudar as igrejas a ter posições bem definidas quanto o seguinte:

1. Aspecto Teologia e ética, 2. Zelar pelas pessoas vivendo com VIH/SIDA. 3. Educar e formar lideres, membros das igrejas e da sociedade em geral dentro de currículos estigma e estigmatizado, sexo e Sexualidade, Género e violência baseada no género, Amor, dignidade, compaixão, Confissão e arrependimento.

Bibliografia

Willis, Hazel – Lus Numia na Sukuru, missão Evangelica, Bubaque. Guine-Bissau, 1996
Mancindoe, Betty – Viagem a Terra Desconhecida, Wec Internacional, 1970
Lima, Ernesto – O Evangelho de Cristo Na Guine-Bissau, 2007
Blackman, Rachel – HIV e AIDS: começando a agir, Tearfund 2005

(69) Christianity in Kenya

Susan Murimi

Religion	Pop 2010	Pct 2010	Pop 2025	Pct 2025	Gr Pct 1970 2025
Christians	32,664,000	81.0%	48,104,000	82.1%	2.6%
Independents	6,825,000	16.9%	9,690,000	16.5%	2.4%
African initiated	5,249,000	13.0%			
Orthodox	656,000	1.6%	850,000	1.5%	1.7%
Eastern Orthodox	656,000	1.6%			
Protestants	17,018,000	42.2%	24,380,000	41.6%	2.4%
Anglicans	5,000,000	12.4%			
Pentecostal	3,133,000	7.8%			
Nondenominational	2,500,000	6.2%			
Reformed, Presbyterian	2,069,000	5.1%			
Baptist	1,462,000	3.6%			
Adventist	989,000	2.5%			
Holiness	474,000	1.2%			
Salvationist (Salvation Army)	463,000	1.1%			
Friends (Quaker)	361,000	0.9%			
Methodist	272,000	0.7%			
Roman Catholics	9,137,000	22.7%	13,620,000	23.2%	2.7%
Pentecostals/Charismatics	12,367,000	30.7%	19,700,000	33.6%	3.2%
Evangelicals	11,540,000	28.6%	16,722,000	28.5%	2.5%
adherents of traditional African religions	3,623,000	9.0%	4,600,000	7.8%	1.6%
Muslims	3,251,000	8.1%	4,760,000	8.1%	2.6%
Baha'is	427,000	1.1%	620,000	1.1%	2.5%
Hindus	206,000	0.5%	300,000	0.5%	2.5%
Jains	79,100	0.2%	115,000	0.2%	2.5%
Sikhs	37,400	0.1%	52,000	0.1%	2.2%
Jews	2,400	0.0%	2,500	0.0%	0.2%
Chinese folk-religionists	2,000	0.0%	3,000	0.0%	2.9%
Buddhists	1,300	0.0%	2,000	0.0%	3.0%
Zoroastrians	820	0.0%	800	0.0%	-0.1%
people professing no religion	33,900	0.1%	50,500	0.1%	2.7%
Total population	**40,328,000**	**100.0%**	**58,610,000**	**100.0%**	**2.5%**

Source: Centre for the Study of World Christianity (CSGC), Boston, Gordon-Conwell TS

Introduction

Kenya has been applauded as the 'haven of missions'.[1] But this haven was only to emerge in the early twentieth century which is late compared with other missionary activities in West and Southern Africa. Though there were Christian missionary activities as early as the fifteenth century, their impact was short-lived and Christianity had to be 'reintroduced' in the late nineteenth century. The Christian presence in Kenya may thus be broken into two phases: early Christian contacts from the fifteenth to eighteenth centuries, and the second phase of contacts starting from the late nineteenth century.

Early Christian Contacts

The earliest Christian contact was through Portuguese traders in the late fifteenth century. Their activities were restricted to the coast, hence missionary activity did not penetrate the hinterland.[2] The first encounter of the Portuguese with the coastal people was through Vasco da Gama in 1498 en route to India. Notably, Islam had already established itself on the east coast. Vasco da Gama put up a pillar in Malindi, which not only acted as a symbol of Portuguese[3] sovereignty, but also as the first symbol of Christianity on the coast. After him, other navigators came, accompanied by priests, chaplains and other Christian workers.[4]

Initially, the Portuguese operated from Malindi but later moved to Mombasa. This saw the beginning of the famous Fort Jesus in 1593. The fort was completed in 1595 but became a protracted and contentious issue between the Arabs and the Portuguese.[5] The name, however, is an indication of how Portuguese traders put themselves under the banner of Christianity. In spite of the odds, evangelization continued on the coast and, by 1600, the Christian community in Mombasa had grown to about 4,000 people.[6]

Unfortunately, with Portuguese influence extinguished along the coast, so was Christianity. The Portuguese are partly to blame for this, due to their crusading spirit against Islam. They vehemently condemned Islam, which served only to increase resentment against Christianity. In addition, double standards in their lifestyles did not commend the Christian message. As Nthamburi states, 'While Christianity had a chance during this period, that chance was lost through cruelty, oppression and indulging selfish passion'.[7] But based on the fact that most of those who had converted to Christianity were from African Traditional Religions and not Muslims, one feels there was a stronger underlying factor in the collapse of Christianity. The Portuguese had failed to integrate the gospel with the culture of the local people. Little wonder it could not last, as it had not genuinely taken root in African soil.

---

[1] Zablon Nthamburi, "The Beginning and Development of Christianity in Kenya", in *From Mission to Church, A Handbook of Christianity in East Africa,* ed. Zablon Nthamburi (Nairobi: Uzima Press, 1991), 13.

[2] John Baur, *2000 Years of Christianity in Africa* (Nairobi: Paulines Publications Africa, 2nd Revised Edition 1998), 86.

[3] The Portuguese were primarily interested in controlling trade; hence, their expeditions were occasionally atrocious. This by far discredited Christianity. Their atrocities were particularly brought to the fore in 1585 when one of them was killed in a jihad against the Portuguese. In 1587, they razed the island of Faza and brutally killed its inhabitants, including women and children, on a revenge mission. Their moral and ethical behaviour contradicted the Christian character they purported to ascribe to and propagate.[3] It is therefore not surprising that Christianity was slow in taking root on the coast. For instance, in 1505, Francisco d'Almeida invaded Kilwa, dethroned the Sultan and built a port to protect Portuguese interests. See Nthamburi, "The Beginning and Development of Christianity in Kenya", 2; Baur, *2000 Years of Christianity in Africa,* 87.

[4] Nthamburi, "The Beginning and Development of Christianity in Kenya", 1-2, 30; Baur, *2000 Years of Christianity in Africa,* 87.

[5] Baur, *2000 Years of Christianity in Africa,* 88; Nthamburi, "The Beginning and Development of Christianity in Kenya", 4.

[6] Nthamburi, "The Beginning and Development of Christianity in Kenya," 4.

[7] Nthamburi, "The Beginning and Development of Christianity in Kenya," 6.

The Second Phase of Christian Contacts

The second phase of Christian contacts in Kenya was given momentum by the arrival of Christian explorers on the East African coast from mid-nineteenth century. The first nineteenth century missionary in Kenya was John Ludwig Krapf, who arrived in Mombasa in 1844 under the Church Missionary Society (CMS). By this time, traces of Christianity that had been introduced in the late fifteenth century had disappeared, except for a few church buildings and Fort Jesus.[8] Johann Rebmann joined Krapf in 1846 and a CMS station was started at Rabai. Even with the presence of the missionaries, Christianity delayed in taking root. It was in 1851, seven years after Krapf's arrival at the coast that the first convert was baptized by Rebmann. Records show that the convert was a cripple and at the point of death.[9] This may serve to indicate that the general status of the earliest people to embrace Christianity were those on the margins of society.

In 1885, Africa was divided into spheres of influence between Germany and Britain through the Berlin Conference. Subsequently, missions tended to follow their parent administrations for protection purposes. In the same year, the Imperial British East African Association (IBEA) was founded for expansion of trade. It was granted a royal charter in 1888, thereby propelling the Protestant missionary activities as it provided protection. In 1895, the British Government took over from IBEA and declared British East Africa (later known as Kenya) as its protectorate.[10]

After Kenya had become a protectorate, closely followed by the construction of the railway up from Mombasa, the missionary movement underwent a radical change. The railway brought an influx of mission groups to the interior. These included the Gospel Missionary Society (GMS) in 1897, the Church of Scotland Mission (CSM) in 1898, the Holy Ghost Mission in 1899, the CMS in 1901, and the African Inland Mission (AIM) in 1901.[11] With such an influx, competition among the missions was bound to arise,[12] thereby creating a need to work out modalities of operation and co-operation. To avoid overlaps in their interests and activities, they agreed on a policy of 'comity', with each having its area of influence.[13]

The Roman Catholics had their areas of influence as well. These were mainly divided between three groups: the Holy Ghost Fathers who established a station at Limuru in 1899, the Consolata missionaries who arrived in 1902 and established a station at Kiambu, and the Mill Hill missionaries who arrived in 1903 and established mission stations in the Western Region.[14]

Apparently, the northern part of the country was hardly evangelized. Various reasons such as the semi-arid climate of the region and the nomadic life of its inhabitants may be attributed to this. In addition, security concerns had prompted the government to issue strict prohibitions against permanent missionary activities there.[15] By implication, then, geographical factors greatly determined how Christianity spread in Kenya.

---

[8] D. B. Barrett, G. K. Mambo, J. McLaughlin and M. J. McVeigh, eds., *Kenya Churches Handbook; The Development of Kenyan Christianity 1498-1973* (Kisumu: Evangel Publishing House, 1973), 30.

[9] Barrett et al eds., *Kenya Churches Handbook,* 21. There are discrepancies in sources over who baptised Mringe, the dying cripple. Nthamburi states that Krapf baptised him. What is important is that the two missionaries were working together at this point. See Nthamburi, "The Beginning and Development of Christianity in Kenya," 8.

[10] Barrett et al. eds., *Kenya Churches Handbook,* 22; See also Nthamburi, "The Beginning and Development of Christianity in Kenya," 10.

[11] Barrett et al. eds., *Kenya Churches Handbook,* 22.

[12] Nthamburi, "The Beginning and Development of Christianity in Kenya," 11.

[13] Barrett et al. eds., *Kenya Churches Handbook,* 23.

[14] Baur, *2000 Years of Christianity in Africa,* 257, Barrett et al. eds., *Kenya Churches Handbook*, 23, 31-33; Nthamburi, "The Beginning and Development of Christianity in Kenya," 14-16.

[15] See Baur, *2000 Years of Christianity in Africa,* 374-375.

The first few decades of Christianity in Kenya witnessed a proliferation of translations of scriptures into local languages.[16] These translations influenced the course and shape of Christianity perceptibly. Africans started reading the Scriptures and interpreting it for themselves, and at times differently, from the missionaries' understanding. An immediate outcome of this was the emergence of independent churches, especially in the 1920s and early 1930s.[17]

Christian Trends and Developments

First, since its inception, Christianity in Kenya has taken different trends in relation to the national and international contexts. One of the earliest developments was the 'Africanisation' of the church. Africans clamoured for religious independence in practice and leadership, and this led to a surge in the growth of African Independent Churches (AICs) with their Africanised approach to Christianity.[18]

Second, another major development has been an increased political involvement by the Kenyan church. Before independence, most of the mission churches had adopted a non-involvement policy towards local politics. This stance continued even after Independence during the reign of Kenyatta (1963-1978). The position however took a drastic turn during President Moi's term (1978-2002). The church took a leading role in castigating Moi's administration for its authoritarianism and autocracy. There arose strong prophetic voices such as the Rev. Dr Timothy Njoya, Bishop Henry Okullu, Archbishop David Gitari and the Rev. Mutava Musyimi who were mainly from the Protestant wing. Later the Roman Catholics joined the Protestants with the leading voice of Archbishop Ndingi Mwana Nzeki. Due to concerted calls by the church and other stakeholders for a pluralistic state, the constitution was amended to revert back to a multi-party state in 1991.[19] The church was equally involved in spearheading the drafting of a new constitution, a task dubbed as 'The *Ufungamano* Initiative'.[20] Unfortunately, the Christian voice that had been so much to

---

[16] For instance, the Giriama Old Testament was published in 1901. In the same year the Pokomo New Testament was also translated, followed closely by the translation of the Gospel of John into Kikuyu in 1903. The first Maasai Gospel was translated in 1905, with the Gospel of Mark being translated into Dholuo in 1911. By 1926 both the Kikuyu and Dholuo New Testament were complete. Barrett et al. eds., *Kenya Churches Handbook*, 22-24.

[17] A case in point was the *Aroti* (dreamers) or *Watu wa Mungu* (people of God) which emerged among the Kikuyu in 1927. Barrett et al. eds., *Kenya Churches Handbook*, 24; For further analysis of AICs in Kenya, see Francis K. Githieya, *The Freedom of the Spirit: African Indigenous Churches in Kenya* (Georgia: Scholars Press, 1997); F.B. Welbourn, *A Place to Feel at Home: A Study of Two Independent Churches in Western Kenya* (Nairobi: Oxford University Press, 1866); F.B. Welbourn, *East African Rebels: A Study of Some Independent Churches* (London: SCM Press, 1961).

[18] Barrett, David B. "The Expansion of Christianity in Kenya AD 1900-2000," in *Kenya Churches Handbook: The Development of Kenyan Christianity 1498-1973*, eds., D. B. Barrett, G. K. Mambo, J. McLaughlin & M.J. McVeigh (Kisumu: Evangel Publishing House, 1973), 170-171. Noteworthy, independent churches had started emerging as early as 1914. Johana Owalo had formed the Nomiya Luo Mission in 1914. See, Barrett et al, eds., *Kenya Churches Handbook*, 23.

[19] Kenya Demographic and Health Survey 2003 (Nairobi, July 2004), 1; B.A. Ogot, "Transition from Single-Party to Multiparty Political System 1989-93," in *Decolonization and Independence in Kenya 1940-93*, eds., B.A. Ogot & William Ochieng (Nairobi: East African Educational Publishers, 1996), 245. Moi's penchant for single-party is still evident in his speeches up till now. He blames the present woes of the country on multi-party politics. Reportedly he asserted, "I said when I was in leadership that multiparty politics would drive this country towards chaos and instability but people said Moi is resisting democracy. We are now seeing problems caused by multiplicity of parties." *The People Daily (*Wednesday, September 2, 2009), 20.

[20] 'Ufungamano' initiative was named after the jointly-owned building (Christian Leadership Center) by the NCCK and the Catholic Episcopal Conference. The initiative also brought together the Evangelicals, Muslims and the Hindus. The drafted constitution was however rejected. Paul Gifford, *Christianity, Politics and Public Life in Kenya* (London: Hurst & Company, 2009), 33-41.

the fore as the voice of the voiceless and in keeping the government in check started diminishing during the reign of President Kibaki (2002-2013).

Third, globalization has undoubtedly shaped the course and features of Christianity in Kenya. As movement and communication across the globe increased, denominational boundaries have also been rendered porous. Apart from a lingering North American influence,[21] there is a growing phenomenon of 'Nigerianization' of Kenyan Christianity. There has been an upsurge of Nigerian-originated churches. For instance, Winners Chapel under David Oyedepo has over sixty churches across the nation.[22] Similarly, choruses of Nigerian origin, characterized by the use of Pidgin English, are frequently sung in Kenyan churches.[23] It is this growing Nigerian influence on all facets of life that has been described by Larry Madowo, a Kenyan journalist, in stating that 'the Nigerian colonization of Kenya is here. You might not recognize it just yet because it is wearing sunglasses and acting up'.[24]

Fourth, another development observed by Aylward Shorter is that of growing secularism, as exhibited in the capital Nairobi. Shorter notes that, although church membership in Nairobi is on the rise, the numbers of the 'unchurched' is more than half the total population of Nairobi.[25] His observation is corroborated by a survey published by Daystar in 1989 which indicates that 80% of Nairobi's population claim to be Christian, yet only 12% of that population attends church on a weekly basis.[26] The scenario is also captured in the national survey done in 2001 by ACM-FTT Afriserve. The survey found that there was a growing nominalism and lethargy, based on the fact that, though Kenya claims to be 80% Christian, only 7% of the Christian population attend Protestant churches.[27] These trends raise a red flag to any observer of Kenyan Christianity. It is probably what led Shorter to claim that 'what happened in nineteenth-century Europe is happening all over again in Africa'.[28]

Christian Relations with Other Faith Communities

The relationship between Christianity and other religious expressions has been relatively harmonious. Other major faiths include Islam, Hinduism in its different variants, and the traditional religions. In pursuit of mutual understanding and harmonious co-existence, the Inter-religious Council of Kenya (IRCK) was registered in 1983. It seeks to bring together all faith communities in Kenya. Its activities are co-ordinated by the main religious bodies in Kenya.[29] The clamour for co-existence is particularly demonstrated during

---

[21] See Murimi for a further analysis on the Americanization of Kenyan Christianity; Murimi, "The Changing Face of Pentecostalism in Kenya Since 1910," 186-195.

[22] *The Standard*, "Thanksgiving for Bishop David Oyedepo on his 60th Birthday" (Sunday, September 28, 2014), 21.

[23] This was witnessed at NPC when two choruses with a Nigerian origin and accent were sung by the whole congregation. The choruses were *Oseyee Oseyee*, and *He has the Final Say*. The choir sang a song from South Africa titled; *Ichokwadi Mwari Varipo*. Observation, NPC Valley Road, Nairobi, 27 February 2013.

[24] Daily Nation, *"It's Nigeria, not China, that is slowly but surely colonizing us,"* (Tuesday, August 26, 2014), 6.

[25] Aylward Shorter and Edwin Onyancha, *Secularism in Africa. A Case Study: Nairobi City* (Nairobi: Pauline Publications,1997), 36

[26] Stan Downes, Robert Oehrig & John Shane, *Summary of the Nairobi Church Survey* (Nairobi: Daystar University College, 1989), 17-42.

[27] Central region has 7% attendance out of a national population of 12%, Coast has 5% attendance with a national population of 9%, Eastern region has 12% attendance with a national population of 15%, North Eastern has 0.13% attendance out of a national population of 4%, Nyanza has 6% out of 15% national population while Western has 5% attendance out of 12% national population. ACM-FTT Afriserve, *The Unfinished Task: A National Survey of Churches in Kenya* (ACM-FTT Afriserve: 2004), xiv, 12.

[28] Shorter, *Secularism in Africa,* 36.

[29] Such religious bodies include; Kenya Conference of Catholic Bishops (KCCB), National Council of Churches of Kenya (NCCK), Evangelical Alliance of Kenya (EAK), Organization of African Instituted Churches (OAIC-Kenya), Seventh Day Adventist Church (SDA), Supreme Council of Kenya Muslims (SUPKEM), National Muslim Leaders

national days where different faiths share podiums and offer prayers for the nation. For instance, the IRCK organized and invited all Kenyans to a national day of prayer in July 2014. The theme of the day was 'May we Dwell in Unity'.[30]

Though this has been the case, there have been signs of growing tension between Christians and Muslims. One of the contributing factors towards this tension is increased terrorist activities in Kenya. Since the bombing of Nairobi's American Embassy in 1998, there has been a string of terrorist attacks targeting Christians. These include the bombing of Hope FM broadcasting house in 2006, the Westgate Mall attack in September 2012, the Mandera bus attack in November 2013, among others. In the last two incidents, the attackers targeted non-Muslims. There have also been attacks on churches and church ministers by radicalized Muslims, particularly along the coast. This has led to some churches discontinuing their services for fear of attack. The police have also moved in to secure churches in Mombasa.[31] Recognition of *Kadhi* courts in the constitution of Kenya[32] has also contributed to the tension. The position of the church in Kenya is that all religions should be treated equally by law.

Towards Christian Unity

The surge of various mission groups (denominational and faith missions) on the Kenyan soil at the eve and dawn of the twentieth century meant that Christianity was introduced in various expressions based mostly on theological interpretations and ecclesial structures. The need for organic unity was thus pressing from the first decade of the Christian presence in Kenya. Initially, the various Protestant mission groups worked on a comity agreement in 1906, drawing up spheres of influence. The comity arrangement, however, did not work, setting off a greater search for Christian unity.[33]

In 1908, a meeting was held at Maseno, bringing together the CMS, AIM, CSM, Seventh Day Adventists and the American Friends to work out modalities of effective evangelism. This set in motion a battery of conferences. In 1909, a year earlier than the World Missionary Conference in Edinburgh, a united missionary conference was held at Kijabe in search of a united native church. The Methodists joined the earlier-mentioned mission groups.[34] In July 1913, a landmark conference in ecumenical development was held at Kikuyu, Thogoto. CMS, CSM, AIM, GMS and the Methodists put out a proposal for a federation of missions that would work towards eventual organic unity. For various reasons, and in particular opposition from the Anglican Bishop of Zanzibar, the proposal did not materialize. The argument was that Anglicans should not link themselves with non-episcopal denominations. This was after the Anglican Bishop of Mombasa had administered Holy Communion to all the delegates except the

---

Forum (NAMLEF), Shia Ithnashari Muslim Association (SHIA), and the Hindu Council of Kenya (HCK). Inter-religious Council of Kenya, www.intereligious.or.ke (accessed 28 January 2015).

[30] The theme was posted in an advert in the *Daily Nation*. It further stated, "A nation without God is a nation without a future! A nation without God is a nation without hope! A nation without God is a nation headed for destruction!" *Daily Nation* (Friday July 4, 2014), 31. IRCK also held inter-faith prayers on 26/9/2013 for the victims of the Westgate mall attack. It brought together top clerics of Christian, Hindu and Muslim faiths. www.bbc.com/news/world-africa-24347548 (accessed 28 January 2015).

[31] Daily Nation, *Police Move in to Secure Churches* (Monday, January 19, 2015), 9.

[32] *The Constitution of Kenya*, Chapter Ten, Part 3, Article 170 (Nairobi: National Council for Law Reporting, Revised edition 2010), 105.

[33] Thomas A. Beetham, "Co-operation Between the Churches," in *Kenya Churches Handbook: The Development of Kenyan Christianity 1498-1973*, eds., D. B. Barrett, G. K. Mambo, J. McLaughlin, M.J. McVeigh (Evangel Publishing House: Kisumu, 1973), 149-153.

[34] William B. Anderson, *The Church in East Africa 1840-1974* (Dodoma: Central Tanganyika Press, 1977), 70-72. Nthamburi, "The Beginning and Development of Christianity in Kenya," 21.

Quakers who do not acknowledge special sacraments.[35] The stage had nonetheless been set, which led to the formation of an Alliance of Protestant Missions in 1918, bringing together the five founding mission groups. The search continued and, in 1924, the Kenya Missionary Council (KMC) was formed which brought together all Protestant missions. A major drawback of the KMC was its exclusivity. Though it was formed on African soil, Africans were not fully represented. In the 1913 and 1918 conferences, there was not a single African Christian in attendance. Similarly, the Roman Catholic missionary societies were not members, making it a predominantly Protestant venture. In an attempt to deal with such shortcomings, the Christian Council of Kenya (CCK) was formed in 1943 and the KMC disbanded in 1944.[36] In 1966, CCK became the National Christian Council of Kenya. It later changed its name to National Council of Churches of Kenya (NCCK). Currently, NCCK has a membership of 27 denominations, nine associate members and six fraternal members. Its mission is to 'transform lives through ecumenism, capacity-building, advocacy and service delivery'.[37]

The foregoing is a clear indicator that there have been attempts towards ecumenical development in Kenya. Nonetheless, these initiatives have been encumbered by an atmosphere of suspicion, chiefly between Protestants and Roman Catholics. The Roman Catholics are not members of NCCK. The suspicion has also been among the Protestants which led to the formation of the Evangelical Alliance of Kenya (EAK) in 1975. The EAK brings together evangelical churches and para-church organizations in Kenya.[38] When formulating a document on fostering national unity in 1983, NCCK owned up to the fact that the reality of a united church was still elusive. It stated: 'It would be very hypocritical of us to talk about national unity without touching on the scandalous division of the churches in Kenya.'[39]

In spite of the suspicion, there has been a growing attitude of ecumenical co-operation among Christians of various traditions in Kenya. Co-operation has been witnessed in matters of Bible translation, general and theological education, student ministry, university chaplaincies, united congregations,[40] medical work and civic education, among others.[41] An area that deserves special mention in social work is the church's involvement in the fight against HIV and AIDS. Denominational and religious boundaries have been crossed through the formation of the Kenya Network of Religious Leaders Living with or Personally Affected by HIV and AIDS (KENERELA+).[42]

---

[35] F. B. Welbourn, *East African Christian* (Oxford University Press: London, 1965), 75-76; Jesse Mugambi, John Mbinda, Judith Vollbrecht, *Ecumenical Initiatives in Eastern Africa; AACC/AMECEA Joint Research Project* (Nairobi, AACC/AMECEA, 1982), 5; Agnes Chepkwony Abuom, "Mission Outpost 1943-1963," Crouch Margaret (ed.*), A Vision of Christian Mission. Reflections on the Great Commission in Kenya 1943-1983* (Nairobi: National Council of Churches of Kenya, 1993), 4.

[36] Abuom, "Mission Outpost 1943-1963", 4-5; Mugambi et al, *Ecumenical Initiatives in Eastern Africa*, 6-7.

[37] The National Council of Churches in Kenya, http//www.nnck.org/newsite2/index.php/about-ncck/membership-of-ncck

[38] EAK has a membership of 52 denominations and 7 key para-church organizations. Evangelical Alliance of Kenya, http://ww.eakenya.org/members (accessed (27 January 2015).

[39] NCCK, *A Christian View of Politics in Kenya: Love, Peace and Unity* (Nairobi: Uzima Press, 1983), 46. The NCCK had taken the task of expounding on Nyayo philosophy which consists of the principles of love, peace and unity.

[40] In 1960, the Anglicans, Presbyterians and Methodists created a United Church in Nairobi: Lavington United Church. This unity, however, is precarious with the Presbyterians taking the Methodists to court. See *Daily Nation* (6 February 2013).

[41] For an in-depth analysis on areas of ecumenical cooperation, see Nthamburi, "The Beginning and Development of Christianity in Kenya," 22-23.

[42] KENERELA+ is a regional chapter of the international network (INERELA+). It brings together religious leaders living with HIV/AIDS for fellowship, mutual empowerment, physical and structural support. Through the Network, religious leaders address issues of stigma and discrimination associated with HIV and AIDS. INERELA+ Positive Faith in Action, http://inerela.org (accessed 28 January 2015).

Conclusion

Such diversity notwithstanding, the church in Kenya has made remarkable strides towards ecumenical co-operation. There is however need for more in view of the growing tension between Christians and Muslims in Kenya.

Bibliography

Abuom, Chepkwony Agnes, 'Mission Outpost 1943-1963.' In *A Vision Of Christian Mission: Reflections on the Great Commission in Kenya 1943-1983*, ed. Margaret Crouch, 3-43. Nairobi: National Council of Churches of Kenya, 1993.

ACM-FTT Afriserve, *The Unfinished Task: A National Survey of Churches in Kenya* (ACM-FTT Afriserve: 2004).

Anderson, William B. *The Church in East Africa 1840-1974*. Dodoma: Central Tanganyika Press, 1977.

Barrett, D. B., G. K. Mambo, J. McLaughlin & M. J. McVeigh, eds. *Kenya Churches Handbook; The Development of Kenyan Christianity 1498-1973*. Kisumu: Evangel Publishing House, 1973.

Barrett, David B. 'The Expansion of Christianity in Kenya AD 1900-2000.' In *Kenya Churches Handbook: The Development of Kenyan Christianity 1498-1973*, eds. D.B. Barrett, G. K. Mambo, J. McLaughlin & M. J. McVeigh, 157-191. Kisumu: Evangel Publishing House, 1973.

Baur, John. *2000 Years of Christianity in Africa*. Nairobi: Paulines Publications Africa, 2nd Revised Edition 1998.

Beetham, A. Thomas. 'Co-operation Between the Churches.' *In Kenya Churches Handbook, The Development of Kenyan Christianity 1498-1973*, eds. D.B. Barrett, G. K. Mambo, J. McLaughlin & M. J., McVeigh, 149-153. Kisumu: Evangel Publishing House, 1973.

Daily Nation, April 10, 2013.

Daily Nation, 'Police Move in to Secure Churches', January 19, 2015.

Daily Nation, February 6, 2013.

Downes, Stan, Robert Oehrig & John Shane. *Summary of the Nairobi Church Survey*. Nairobi: Daystar University College, 1989.

Gifford, Paul. *Christianity, Politics and Public Life in Kenya*. Hurst & Company: London, 2009.

Githieya, K. Francis. *The Freedom of the Spirit: African Indigenous Churches in Kenya*. Scholars Press: Georgia, 1997.

Kaplan, Irving, et al. *Area Handbook for Kenya*. Washington D.C.: U.S Government Printing Office, 2nd edition, 1976.

Kenya Demographic and Health Survey, 2003. Nairobi, July 2004.

Madowo, Larry. 'It's Nigeria, Not China, that is Slowly but Surely Colonizing Us.' In *Daily Nation*, Tuesday, August 26, 2014.

Mbiti, John S. 'Diversity, Divisions and Denominationalism.' In *Kenya Churches Handbook: The Development of Kenyan Christianity 1498-1973*, eds., D. B. Barrett, G. K. Mambo, J. McLaughlin, M.J. McVeigh, 144-148. Kisumu: Evangel Publishing House, 1973.

Murimi, Susan. 'The Changing Face of Pentecostalism in Kenya Since 1910: An Examination of Historical, Religious and Cultural Dynamics.' Unpublished PhD Thesis, Akrofi-Christaller Institute of Theology, Mission and Culture, December 2013.

Mugambi, Jesse, John Mbinda & Judith Vollbrecht. *Ecumenical Initiatives in Eastern Africa; AACC/AMECEA Joint Research Project*. Nairobi: AACC/AMECEA, 1982.

NCCK. *A Christian View of Politics in Kenya: Love, Peace and Unity*. Nairobi: Uzima Press, 1983.

Nthamburi, Zablon. 'The Beginning and Development of Christianity in Kenya.' In *From Mission to Church, A Handbook of Christianity in East Africa*, ed. Zablon Nthamburi, 1-36. Nairobi: Uzima Press, 1991.

Welbourn, F.B. & B.A. Ogot. *A Place to Feel at Home: A Study of Two Independent Churches in Western Kenya*. Nairobi: Oxford University Press, 1866.

Welbourn, F.B. *East African Christian.* London: Oxford University Press, 1965.
Welbourn, F.B. *East African Rebels: A Study of Some Independent Churches*. London: SCM Press, 1961.

(70) CHRISTIANITY IN LESOTHO

James N. Amanze and Khosi Emmanuel Makubakube

Religion	Pop 2010	Pct 2010	Pop 2025	Pct 2025	Gr Pct 1970 2025
Christians	1,845,000	91.8%	2,218,000	93.4%	1.2%
Independents	215,000	10.7%	234,000	9.9%	0.6%
African initiated	207,000	10.3%			
Protestants	496,000	24.7%	560,000	23.6%	0.8%
Reformed, Presbyterian	279,000	13.9%			
Anglicans	111,000	5.5%			
Pentecostal	62,400	3.1%			
Baptist	13,700	0.7%			
Methodist	12,600	0.6%			
Roman Catholics	1,060,000	52.7%	1,280,000	53.9%	1.3%
Pentecostals/Charismatics	349,000	17.3%	380,000	16.0%	0.6%
Evangelicals	148,000	7.3%	177,000	7.5%	1.2%
adherents of traditional African religions	141,000	7.0%	120,000	5.1%	-1.1%
Baha'is	17,800	0.9%	26,000	1.1%	2.6%
Hindus	1,200	0.1%	1,600	0.1%	1.9%
Muslims	930	0.0%	1,400	0.1%	2.8%
people professing no religion	4,600	0.2%	6,700	0.3%	2.6%
Total population	**2,011,000**	**100.0%**	**2,373,000**	**100.0%**	**1.1%**

Source: Centre for the Study of World Christianity (CSGC), Boston, Gordon-Conwell TS

Introduction

Lesotho with an area of 11,720 square miles and an estimated population of 1.9 million people is a landlocked country surrounded completely by South Africa. It has a vibrant and fast growing Christian population which is estimated at 90% of the entire population in the country. It is dominated by three large Christian churches namely the Roman Catholic Church, the Lesotho Evangelical Church and the Anglican Church. Other Christian Churches operating in Lesotho today include the Seventh-Day Adventist Church, African Methodist Episcopal Church, the Dutch Reformed, Lesotho Methodist Church, and a variety of Pentecostal–charismatic Churches. There is also a strong body of African Independent Churches. The constitution of Lesotho and other laws and policies protect religious freedom and there are no established government requirements for churches to register, therefore, there are no penalties for not registering a church. Those who register, however, are required to produce a constitution and a leadership committee.[1]

[1] US Department of State, "Lesotho" http://www.state.gov.documents organisation assessed on 29/5/2016.

The History of Christianity in Lesotho

The history of Christianity in Lesotho is traced back to King Moshoeshoe who requested Christian missionaries to come to his country to start missionary work there. As a result of this request, three missionaries in South Africa namely Thomas Arbousset, Eugene Casalis and Constant Gosselin of the Paris Evangelical Missionary Society arrived in Lesotho in 1833 and established the first mission station at Moriya twenty five miles south west of Thaba Bosiu. From this humble beginning the church experienced tremendous growth with the arrival in the missionary field of Francois Coillard, Adolphe Mabille and Eugene Casalis the latter the son of Eugene Casalis.[2] This marked the beginning of missionary work in Lesotho. Eventually other churches joined this missionary venture. One of these was the Roman Catholic Church whose work is traced back to Bishop Allard and Father Joseph Gerard of the Congregation of the Oblates of Mary Immaculate, who visited Moshoeshoe in 1862. He gave them permission to set up a mission station at Roma about twenty miles South of Thaba Bosiu.[3] From there the church spread throughout the country. The extent of the expansion was such that it lead to the establishment of an independent diocese in 1961 with Maseru as its metropolitan.[4]

Apart from the above two churches, the Anglican Church has also made its presence felt in Lesotho. It was introduced at the invitation of King Moshoeshoe. It began its work in 1875 in Maseru and from there spread to other parts of the country.[5] This marked the beginning of the Anglican Church in Lesotho in a more permanent basis. Despite some difficulties as a result of wars in the country, congregations were established at a number of places such as Matsieng, Mafeteng, Maseru, Masite to name but a few. The Anglican Church in Lesotho is part of the Church of the Province of Southern Africa. It received its first African Bishop in 1976 in the person of Desmond Tutu.[6]

One of the main interesting features of Christianity in Lesotho is that many Christians still observe and practice some of their traditional cultural beliefs and rituals alongside Christianity. A number of things such as church music and traditional clerical attire to name a few have been introduced during church services.[7] This means that Christianity has been inculturated in many aspects of church life. The indigenization of the church is considered as one of the ways of entrenching Christianity in the bosom of mother Africa.

The Church and Socio-economic Development

One of the most important aspects of the Christian Churches in Lesotho is their contribution to the socio-economic development of the country. This contribution has taken place mainly in the field of education, health and income generating projects that can lead to poverty eradication. In this regard, different churches have contributed in different ways. For example, apart from building churches, the Lesotho Evangelical Church opened the Morija Printing Works in 1874. This led to the rapid expansion of the Word of God in Lesotho by enabling people to read the Bible for themselves. Apart from this, the LEC established industrial schools, as well as primary schools. A theological school was founded in 1889. Other institutions intended to boost the socio-economic development of the people include the Scot

[2] Sundkler, *A History*..., 380.
[3] Sales, *The planting*...,104.
[4] Gordon Haliburton…, 156.
[5] Haliburton, *Historical Dictionary,* 6.
[6] Haliburton, *Historical Dictionary,* 8.
[7] International Religious Freedom Report, U.S. Department of State, http//www. state.gov/j/drl/rls/irf/2005/5179.htm assessed on 29/5/2016.

Memorial Hospital, Tebeleng Hospital and Lesotho Training College. These institutions have continued to flourish to the present day.[8]

The Roman Catholic has also contributed tremendously to the socio-economic development of the country. In the course of its missionary work it has built teacher training colleges, High Schools, Secondary schools, vocational schools, hospitals, seminaries, convents, printing works and book shops. In 1945 Bishop Bonhomme of the Roman Catholic Church established Pius XII University College at Roma. This was the first institution of higher education in the High Commission Territories that is, Botswana, Lesotho and Swaziland. In 1964 the college became part of the University of Basutoland, Bechuanaland and Swaziland (UBBS). In 1975 the University was nationalised and renamed the National University of Lesotho (NUL).[9] UBBS contributed significantly to the establishment of the University of Botswana and the University of Swaziland in 1982.[10]

In the same vein, the Anglican Church has also contributed significantly in the socio-economic development of the country, of course, with varying degrees of success. The Anglican Church operates a number of schools and one hospital. In parternership with the Anglican Church in Durham, Great Britain, the church operates a number of projects ranging from tree planting to income generating small businesses. The church has also developed educational programmes that conscientise people of the dangers of the HIV and AIDS pandemic. One such programme is the Ha Mohatlane Community Centre in Berea District which provides vocational training.[11]

New Forms of Division in the Lesotho Church

The independence of Lesotho as a country in 1966 caused turbulences to the Church. New forms of injustice and inequality emerged. The road from colony to free and prosperous state was full of potholes. The change from mission to church was beset by new forms of dependence and corruption.[12] Eventually even the ecumenical fire was put out by new ways to continue old divisions.

During the 1960s the most significant role played by church leaders in the political arena was still that of the Roman Catholic missionaries and it was this continued involvement that requires attention in the lead up to Independence. The major political factor was the role of the churches and missionaries. From the early 1970s on, numerous Basotho church leaders began to play a larger political role.[13] The Catholic missionary priests resolved to support the Basotho National Party (BNP) which was founded through their support. They intensified their campaign against the Basotho Congress Party (BCP) and alleged communist threat. The Calvinists (Protestants) were perceived to be supporting the BCP and therefore, the Catholics strengthened their support for the BNP. Although they found ways to support the BNP financially and materially, their primary contribution was the well-developed Catholic infrastructure they allowed, and indeed allowed the party to use.[14] It was a major factor in rise of the BNP, for as Theresa Blanchet-Cohen points out:

[8] Haliburton, *Historical Dictionary,* 87.

[9] Scott Rosenberg, Richard F. Weisfelder, *Historical Dictionary of Lesotho*, Google Books, 41. https://books.Google.co.bw assessed on 29/5/2016.

[10] Haliburton, *Historical Dictionary,* 156.

[11] Rosenberg, *Historical Dictionary,* 41.

[12] Craig Hincks, *Quest for Peace,* 2009, 581.

[13] Ibid., 585.

[14] Ibid.

> With possible exception of the chiefs there was then no intermediary structure of government, no organization in Lesotho whose scope equaled that of the churches. The Colonial Administration, and later the political parties never developed a network of local ramifications as extensive as the missionaries.[15]

The schools and teachers were used to reach desired goal. The teachers of which some were the catechists had a tremendous influence on the community. Accordingly, paid time off given to some teachers to campaign on behalf of the party and increasingly the church severely punished the teachers with BCP sympathies. To this effect, a confidential letter from the Catholic Schools Secretary, states:

> Teachers who are officially members of the Congress and who are known as such must be given three months' notice in the course of this month of September...If however, the manager wishes to give reasons for his notice he is free to do so. But please do not tell any teacher that he is given notice because he is a Congress member.[16]

Some of the missionary attempts were frustrated. Some of the teachers refused to cooperate although that had cost them jobs. The alliance between the BNP and the missionaries was not that satisfying. Even Chief Leabua Jonathan who was the leader of BNP was perceived by the missionaries to be not as loyal as they thought he would be. On his part the BNP leader felt that he was suffocated by the missionary's expectations. The BNP leader wanted to win both Catholics and Protestants. This intention is made clear in his letter to a South African official that his close alliance with the Catholics would be maintained only as long as it remained politically suitable:

> You said you did not like the support which the Catholic Church is giving me. I became a Catholic because of circumstances which I explained to you, but at heart I am still a Protestant and I cannot let you down. When I control the Government after the elections we shall find a good way of dealing the Roman Catholic danger which we discussed at length with you. I also told you what its intention is in Basotoland. But at present, it is wise to use them to get the overwhelming support of the Catholics in this country.[17]

From an ecumenical point of few, the negative effects of the Catholic missionary involvement in politics would last for many years. The missionaries achieved their goal but in the process of winning, their image and integrity were seriously tarnished.[18] Not only that their reputation was tainted but that caused damage to the relations between the churches. Fr. Jean-Lous Richard lamented that whatever might have been the intentions of the Churches in involving themselves in political matters and especially in party politics, it remains that the relations between Churches were gravely exacerbated and that this this involvement pushed back any hope of seeing ecumenism becoming the dominant factor in church relations.[19]

The Church in Lesotho was faced with a profound challenge to fight against the injustice committed by the government and against the mistrust within itself. On one hand, they were forced to speak with one voice to condemn the brutalities of the BNP regime and on the other hand, the Protestants were blaming the Catholics that since it was their regime, they were not victimized. To the Lesotho Evangelical Church, this anti-Protestant bias of the government had been clear since near beginning. Already in March, a letter in the Protestant newspaper called *Leselinyana* had identified the strong denominational element in Lesotho political divisions:

---

[15] Theresa Blanchet-Cohen, 'The Corporate Structure of the Catholic Church in Lesotho: 1930-1956.' 1976, 250.

[16] Letter from the Schools Secretary, Rev. Fr. M. Gareau, to School managers in Maseru District, 19 September 1960, trans. from French.

[17] Letter from Leabua Jonathan to the Commissioner-General for the Sotho of South Africa, 18 November 1964.

[18] Craig Hincks, *Quest for Peace*, 2009, 586.

[19] Jean-Louis Richard, 'Background Information on Lesotho', 19 December 1983, 3.

> Clearly the state of emergency was declared because of the rivalry of Lesotho's political parties. But it has developed into a denominational war. Most of the misfortunes have befallen you members of this Church.[20]

The Ecumenical Movement in Lesotho

Ecumenical relation between Christians in Lesotho has dominated the history of Christianity for a long time. This led to the creation of the Christian Council of Lesotho (CCL) in 1965. Its membership consists of the major churches in Lesotho, namely the Lesotho Evangelical Church, Roman Catholic Church, Anglican Church, African Methodist Episcopal Church as well as some smaller churches. The CCL was formed in order to promote and enhance ecumenical cooperation among the Christian churches operating in the country. Another aim has been to protect human rights and promote peaceful conflict resolution in the country. It has also been engaged in development work particularly in the area of health, education and poverty eradication. The CCL established an agricultural training centre at Thaba-Khupa in order to train Basotho agriculturalists who would then go out into the villages to train others. Other economic projects include vocational schools for girls in Maseru, and a rural water supply project. The CCL has also been concerned with the provision of clean water to remote villages in the country.[21]

Despite mistrust between the Catholic Church and the Lesotho Evangelical Church, who were both members of the Christian Council of Lesotho, CCL was never deterred from performing its prophetic role for the past 50 years. An article in Work of Justice noted that the Heads of Churches have been able to speak prophetically, negotiate confidentially and move quickly in many moments of national crisis.[22] The Church in Lesotho has left a profound lesson that Basotho have capacity to solve their own issues without foreign intervention. Therefore, the political instability which Basotho are experiencing nowadays can also be solved this way provided that there is political will.

CCL started to celebrate the 50th Jubilee from 7th August 2015 and ended with the 26th - 27th May 2016 Annual General Meeting. The AGM delegates acknowledged the CCL achievements and challenges over the past 50 years. They emphasized the need for forgiveness, reconciliation, and remembering, not to become the prisoners of the painful past but to ensure that the past challenges do not recur. Moreover, they considered that as a moment to reflect on where CCL comes from and to move forward to building relationships and sustainable peace. However, they also highlighted the problems facing the Basotho nations such as lack of good governance, lack of rule of law, lack of economic justice and lack of respect for the human rights. They resolved that CCL shall continue to exercise its prophetic role as a prophetic voice to address the national issues.

The Role of the Church in Politics and Peace-making

Since independence the churches in Lesotho have played an active role in the political life of the country. For example, the two largest Christians denominations in the country have been in the forefront of political life. The Roman Catholic Church is associated with the Basotho National Party while the Lesotho Evangelical Church has been associated with Basutoland Congress Party and its offshoots. The differences between the two parties have over the years become a source of intense political conflict. This conflict, however, has been managed by the willingness of the churches to work together for the sake of the common good. As a result, the Christian churches have become the most effective players of conflict resolution and mediators in political conflict. For example, during the 2012 general elections the Lesotho

---

[20] 'Seeteetelane' (a nickname), 'Ho Kereke ea Evangeli lesotho', *Leselinyana*, 20 March 1970, 4.
[21] Rosenberg, *Historical Dictionary*, 41
[22] 'Churches and Politics in Lesotho,' *Work of Justice*, no. 30, September 1991, 5.

Council of Churches played a very important role to ensure that conflicts during elections, that characterised the political life of Lesotho in the previous years, should not repeat again. In this regard, as early as August 2011 church leaders assisted the government to come up with strategies that could lead to peaceful elections in 2012. The Christian Council of Lesotho with the political expertise of Archbishop Desmond Tutu in peace-making addressed political leaders on the importance of peaceful elections. In order to seal their deal and ensure commitment by political leaders, an election pledge was signed by all of them during which they committed themselves to accept the election results. This confirmed many peoples' views that relationship build between church leaders and politicians is the best thing that can lead to peaceful co-existence among people.[23]

The Role of the Church in the Fight against HIV and AIDS

Since 2002 the Christian Council of Lesotho has been involved in the fight against the HIV and AIDS pandemic. This has been done by developing home-based health care programs and creating scholarship programs for AIDS orphans to attend high school as well as providing nevirapine to pregnant women in order to reduce mother-to-child transmission of the HIV virus. The CCL helped the creation of the Private Health Association of Lesotho in 1973 an organisation that continues to provide health care services to the people of Lesotho to the present day.[24]

In conclusion, this paper has discussed Christianity tracing its beginning in the first half of the 19th century to the present day. The role of the churches in the socio-economic development of the country has also been discussed.

Bibliography

Baeta, Christian G. *'My Visit to Lesotho.'* All Africa Conference of Churches, Nairobi. April 1975.

Blanchet-Cohen, Therese. *'The Corporate Structure of the Catholic Church in Lesotho*, 1930-1956.' M.Phil. dissertation University College London, 1976.

Haliburton, Gordon, *Historical Dictionary of Lesotho*, New Jersey: The Scarecrow Press, 1977,

Hincks, Craig W. *Quest for Peace: An ecumenical History of the Church in Lesotho.* Maseru: Morija Printing Works.

Hogarth, Robin. '*The Spirit of Traditional African Gospel*, 1997.

Lapointe, Eugene. *An Experience of Pastoral Theology in Southern Africa: Inculturated and Committed Christian Communities*. Rome: Urbanaina University Press, 1986.

Mohono, Samuel A. *'Spiritual Maturity of Matitta and Schism.'* Unpublished typescript, n.d.

Richard, Jean-Louis. 'Background Information on Lesotho.' Unpublished typescript. 19 December 1983

Sales, Jane M. *The planting of the Christian churches in South Africa*, Grand Rapids, Michigan: William B.

Sundkler, Bengt & Christopher Steed, *A history of the Church in Africa*, Cambridge: Cambridge University Press, 2000.

[23] "UNDP works with churches to resolve election disputes," http://www.is.undp.org; assessed on 1/6/2016.

[24] Scott Rosenberg, Richard F. Weisfelder, Historical Dictionary of Lesotho, Google Books, 89-91.

(71) Christianity in Liberia

Samuel B. Reeves

Religion	Pop 2010	Pct 2010	Pop 2025	Pct 2025	Gr Pct 1970 2025
Christians	1,604,000	40.5%	2,499,000	43.6%	3.0%
Independents	637,000	16.1%	965,000	16.8%	2.8%
African initiated	565,000	14.3%			
Protestants	539,000	13.6%	863,000	15.1%	3.2%
Methodist	148,000	3.7%			
Lutheran	110,000	2.8%			
Pentecostal	107,000	2.7%			
Holiness	38,700	1.0%			
Anglicans	38,100	1.0%			
Adventist	38,000	1.0%			
Nondenominational	25,500	0.6%			
Roman Catholics	311,000	7.9%	550,000	9.6%	3.9%
Pentecostals/Charismatics	605,000	15.3%	920,000	16.1%	2.8%
Evangelicals	319,000	8.1%	535,000	9.3%	3.5%
adherents of traditional African religions	1,647,000	41.6%	2,158,000	37.7%	1.8%
Muslims	635,000	16.0%	940,000	16.4%	2.7%
Baha'is	11,100	0.3%	20,000	0.3%	4.0%
people professing no religion	60,400	1.5%	111,000	1.9%	4.1%
Total population	**3,958,000**	**100.0%**	**5,728,000**	**100.0%**	**2.5%**

Source: Centre for the Study of World Christianity (CSGC), Boston, Gordon-Conwell TS

Brief History

Liberia is Africa's oldest independent nation. Different from any other nation in Africa, Liberia was born in the womb of a church. Her declaration of independence was signed and the first sessions of both houses of legislature was held in the Providence Baptist Church on Broad and Center Streets, on July 26th 1847. Unlike most of Africa, Liberia was never colonized. Liberia is boarded on the west by Sierra Leone, north by Guinea, east by the Ivory Coast, and south by the Atlantic Ocean. It is interesting to note that all her neighbours have predominately non-Christian populations.

According to the National Census, Liberia has an estimated population of 3.5 million people. It is made up of 95% natives, 2.3% of American descent, while the remaining 2.7% are other nationals living and working in the country. The country has sixteen major ethnic groups divided into three language families. The Mande make up 47.2% of the population, the Kru 41.3%, and the West Atlantic 7.9%.

According to the 2008 National Census, 85.5% of Liberia's population practises Christianity.[1] Muslims comprise 12.2% of the population, largely coming from the Mandingo and Vai ethnic groups.[2] The vast majority of Muslims are Malikite Sunni, with sizeable Shia and Ahmadiyya minorities.[3] Traditional indigenous religions are practised by 0.5% of the population, while 1.8% subscribe to no religion.[4]

Since its existence, Liberia has been a land of rich cultures and traditions. The culture and tradition of the Liberian people are the connecting link that enables them to maintain their common identity and life.

The Dawn of Christianity in Liberia

The beginning of Christianity in Liberia is joined at the hip with the arrival of freed people of coloured (ex-slaves) from the Carolinas, Georgia and Virginia in the United States to Liberia. Following their emancipation, the American Colonization Society (ACS) was established to assist in their voluntary repositioning to the West Coast of Africa. The majority of them were Christians who looked forward to making their new home a place influenced by Christianity. Unfortunately, most of them remained on the coast. In the 1820s, the Baptist Church, and the Methodist and Protestant Missionary Societies were organized on board the ship *Elizabeth*, which brought the first settlers to Liberia.

The Growth of Christianity in Liberia

With regard to the spreading of the gospel throughout the nation, the Christians who brought it to Liberia were very slow in reaching the interior and proclaiming Jesus to the local population. For a very long time these pioneer missionaries restricted themselves to the coast, and remained socially, politically, religiously and culturally isolated from the rest of the country and its people.

Liberia does however have an undisputed Christian heritage. Because of this , before Independence, the capital city of Liberia was first called 'Christopolis'. meaning the 'City of Christ'. The name was later changed to Monrovia in honour of America's fifth president, James Monroe who, it is said, significantly contributed to the formation of the American Colonization Society which was responsible for the repatriation of emancipated slaves to Africa. In appreciation of his generosity, some 'unspiritually-minded' settler leaders changed the name of the capital city. Unlike other countries in Africa, Liberia celebrates a national holiday called 'Fast and Prayer Day', which is set aside to mobilize national prayers for the spiritual cleansing and healing of the nation (2 Chr. 7:14). This national day was born out of a political crisis between Liberia and the British colonial parents of Sierra Leone in the mid-1800s out of which Liberia, along with its political leadership, was delivered only by the power of prayer. Since then, this National Day of Fast and Prayer has been annually observed. The contents of the national anthem, the national flag, the pledge of allegiance, and the first constitution of Liberia (1847-1985) all point to the fact that Liberia's forefathers had assumed Liberia to be a Christian nation.

The Christian denominations in Liberia include the Lutheran, Baptist, Episcopal, Presbyterian, Roman Catholic, United Methodist, African Methodist Episcopal (AME) and AME Zion denominations, and a variety of Pentecostal churches. Some of the Pentecostal movements are affiliated with churches outside

---

[1] "International Religious Freedom Report 2010: Liberia". *United States Department of State. November 17, 2010.* Retrieved July 22, 2011.

[2] *Ibid.*

[3] The World's Muslims: Unity and Diversity. *Pew Forum on Religious & Public life. August 9, 2012.* Retrieved March 31, 2014.

[4] International Religious Freedom Report 2010: Liberia. *United States Department of State. November 17, 2010.* Retrieved July 22, 2011.

the country, while others are independent. There are also members of the Church of Jesus Christ of Latter-day Saints (Mormons) and Seventh Day Adventists. Christians live throughout the country.

In the Liberian church setting, people use the term *kwi* to imply a style of worship of a Christian church that is marked by reserve and decorum.[5] This is changing rapidly throughout the country. *Kwi* is a Liberian term used to connote westernization.[6] Services in churches considered to be non-*kwi* have more outward spiritualist expression, with dancing and even street processions in colourful costumes as key elements. Non-*kwi* churches also have self-proclaimed prophets who interpret dreams and visions, and prioritize a direct experience of the Holy Spirit. Liberia's educated elite have historically regarded the apostolic churches as churches of the uneducated and thus non-*kwi*.[7]

Currently, the church, with functioning and multiplying congregations is reproducing itself in a cross-cultural society. It is in the vanguard of spearheading indigenous missions throughout the country.

One would further expect that all of Liberia's people groups would by now be adequately evangelized and made disciples of Christ, but there are still unreached people groups in parts of the country. There are still challenges in mission endeavours and some of the country's people groups remain vulnerable to the rapidly and silently invading forces of Islam and other religious groups, which are scrambling for a place in Liberia. There is a need for a reliable national research statistic on the church in Liberia to help determine the extent of the harvest field and harvest force in the country. The church must put aside her denominational labels and religious restrictions, and combine its effort, expertise and resources to move this force and implement its mission. This will aid the acceleration of the gospel and mission opportunities throughout the length and breath of the nation.

Some Current Challenges

Today, the church has numerous challenges to deal with emerging from complicated, contradictory and unstable relationship between religion, law and human rights, including the country's turbulent history of civil, ethnic tensions, widespread impunity and corruption. These makes it difficult for the Church's prophetic voice to have positive impact on an ongoing efforts towards peace building and reconstruction . There's a need for God-fearing, honest, credible and accountable leaders in both the church and the larger society that will uphold the rule of law and restore the lost image of the nation. The church must continue to speak up and be a shining example against the vice of rampant corruption that continues to invade every sector of Liberian society due to the high rate of poverty and joblessness. The church must engage in a holistic gospel – meeting the whole needs of the whole person and the high illiteracy rate with a proper educational system. There is a need for sound theological education that will train and equip godly men and women for evangelism and promoting the propagation of biblical Christianity in the nation.

More than at any other time in the history of the church in Liberia, she has the most educated clergy, so she must invest in research in mission in order to have a genuine picture of the state of the church. The church must allow, teach, promote and strengthen partnership and networking among the churches and para-church organizations for mission mobilization.

A large number of foreign missionary groups work amenably and freely throughout the country. The constitution provides for freedom of religion, and the government generally respects this right in practice. Notwithstanding frequent interaction among religious groups, some tensions remain. Some societal abuses or discrimination based on religious belief or practice occur.

---

[5] Liberia Country Study, "The Christianity of Indigenous Africans", GlobalSecurity.org
[6] Culture of Liberia", EveryCulture.com
[7] Liberia Country Study, "The Christianity of Indigenous Africans", GlobalSecurity.org

Bibliography

Ayodeji Olukoju. *Culture and customs of Liberia* (Greenwood Publishing Group, 2006)

Caranda, Doughba C. II and William B. Harris. *Liberia's Legacy: 'Our Heritage' Yesterday, Today* (UK: SCP Third World Publisher, 1993)

Johnstone, Patrick and Jason Mandryk. *Operation World, 21st Century edition* (UK: Paternoster, 2001)

Glover, Robert Hall. *The Progress of World-wide Missions* (New York: Harper & Row, 1960)

Bowie, Richard W. *Light for the Nations: A Biblical Theology of Evangelization* (Singapore: Haggai Institute, 2000)

(72) Christianism en Libye

Harald Suermann

Religion	Pop 2010	Pct 2010	Pop 2025	Pct 2025	Gr Pct 1970 2025
Christians	163,000	2.6%	210,000	3.0%	1.7%
Independents	3,400	0.1%	6,000	0.1%	4.0%
African initiated	3,300	0.1%			
Orthodox	67,200	1.1%	75,000	1.1%	0.7%
Oriental Orthodox	51,000	0.8%			
Protestants	5,600	0.1%	6,600	0.1%	1.0%
Roman Catholics	85,000	1.4%	120,000	1.7%	2.3%
Pentecostals/Charismatics	7,900	0.1%	13,000	0.2%	3.4%
Evangelicals	2,600	0.0%	3,000	0.0%	1.1%
Muslims	6,062,000	96.7%	6,822,000	96.3%	0.8%
Buddhists	19,200	0.3%	25,000	0.4%	1.8%
Hindus	5,400	0.1%	7,000	0.1%	1.7%
Sikhs	2,200	0.0%	3,000	0.0%	2.2%
Chinese folk-religionists	1,700	0.0%	2,100	0.0%	1.5%
Baha'is	600	0.0%	800	0.0%	1.9%
adherents of traditional African religions	460	0.0%	600	0.0%	1.7%
Jews	120	0.0%	130	0.0%	0.5%
people professing no religion	10,900	0.2%	16,100	0.2%	2.6%
Total population	**6,266,000**	**100.0%**	**7,086,000**	**100.0%**	**0.8%**

Source: Centre for the Study of World Christianity (CSGC), Boston, Gordon-Conwell TS

La Libye compte 6,3 millions d'habitants, dont actuellement moins de 57.000 Catholiques. 50.000 Catholiques habitent dans le Vicariat Apostolique de Tripoli. Les trois autres vicariats apostoliques Benghazi, Misrata et Derna[1] sont vacants. Le plus grand groupe est celui des réfugiés subsahariens, suivis des étudiants subsahariens et des travailleur immigrés d'Asie et d'Europe. 60.000 Coptes vivent en Libye. Une paroisse copte-orthodoxe à Tripoli dépend du diocèse de Tunis. 80 Grecs-orthodoxes ont un évêque à Tripoli et deux prêtres, un à Tripoli et un à Benghazi. Des églises évangéliques existent à Tripoli et Benghazi, mais aussi ailleurs dans le pays, ainsi que des églises pentecôtistes à Tripoli et Misrata et ailleurs. Mais à l'heure de la rédaction de l'article, on n'est pas sûr du nombre de chrétiens ni du fonctionnement des institutions à cause de la guerre civile dans le pays.[2]

---

[1] Vacant depuis 1948.

[2] United States Departmen of State – Bureau of Democracy, Human Rights, and Labor, « Libya 2014. International Religious Freedom Report », 2014, www.state.gov/documents/organization/238680.pdf.

L'antiquité

Dans l'antiquité le christianisme s'étendit en Libye (Pentapole et Cyrénaïque) à partir de l'Égypte. L'Église était alors sous la juridiction du Patriarche d'Alexandrie. Le christianisme disparut avec la conquête islamique au 7e siècle.

L'époque coloniale

En 1911 le Royaume d'Italie déclara la guerre à l'Empire ottoman et occupa les villes côtières de la Libye. La même année Mgr Ludovico Antonnelli arriva en Libye et le 23 février 1913 érigea le Vicariat Apostolique de Libye. Les relations entre le pouvoir colonial et l'Église ne furent pas faciles à cause de l'anticléricalisme italien. Mgr Antonnelli eut six stations paroissiales avec une résidence. En 1919 Mgr Giacinto Tonizza lui succeda. Il développa l'infrastructure de l'Église en construisant la cathédrale ainsi que des jardins d'enfant, des écoles et des centres pastoraux. Mais il favorisa aussi le développement de l'Action Catholique.[3] Le 3 février 1927 le Vicariat Apostolique de Libye fut divisé en deux. Il changea son nom en Vicariat Apostolique de Tripolitaine, l'autre vicariat se nomma Vicariat Apostolique de Cyrénaïque. Pendant la période coloniale l'Église catholique eut aussi le devoir d'encourager les soldats envoyés de force.[4] Malgré cela l'Église catholique soigna toujours ses bonnes relations avec la population musulmane.[5]

La Libye indépendante

La Libye proclama son indépendance en 1951 et devint une monarchie constitutionnelle sous le règne du roi Idris al-Sanussi.

Muʿammar al-Qaddafi prit le pouvoir le 1er septembre 1969 et il décréta le 21 juillet 1970 la confiscation immédiate des biens des Italiens, y compris les biens des églises. À l'issue de négociations ardues six missionnaires catholiques purent rester au pays et deux lieux de culte furent concédés: Tripoli et Benghazi. Le vicaire de Tripoli put rester, tandis que le vicaire de Benghazi dut quitter le pays définitivement. La plupart des églises furent fermées malgré la garantie de la liberté religieuse par la constitution. La cathédrale de la capitale fut transformée en mosquée.[6] Après coup cet acte est justifié comme une « purification » de l'Église, qui était jusque là presque purement italienne. Aujourd'hui elle est internationale.[7]

En 1971 Pape Shenouda III établit de nouveau l'éparchie copte-orthodoxe de Pentapole occidental (Cyrénaïque) comme Archidiocèse de Tripoli. Trois églises copte-orthodoxes existent: à Tripoli, Benghazi et Misrata.

Du 2 au 5 février 1976 un congrès sur le dialogue islamo-chrétien eut lieu à Tripoli. Il fut interprété comme un signe que l'expulsion des Italiens n'avait pas visé l'Église comme telle. À la suite du dialogue pendant ce congrès l'église de Benghazi fut rendue aux chrétiens et devint plus tard siège du deuxième évêque. Finalement il déboucha sur des relations diplomatiques avec le Vatican en 1997. Mais ce congrès suscita aussi d'autres réactions. Quelques personnalités musulmanes et chrétiennes, intéressées au

---

[3] Filiberto Sabadin, « L'Église de Libye au XXe siècle », in *Histoire des chrétiens d'Afrique du Nord: Libye-Tunisie-Algérie-Maroc*, éd. par Henri Teissier et Antoine Chatelard (Paris: Desclée, 1991), 156.
[4] Sabadin, « L'Église de Libye au XXe siècle », 157.
[5] Sabadin, « L'Église de Libye au XXe siècle ».
[6] Filiberto Sabadin, « La situation actuelle en Libye », in *Histoire des chrétiens d'Afrique du Nord: Libye-Tunisie-Algérie-Maroc*, éd. par Henri Teissier et Antoine Chatelard (Paris: Desclée, 1991), 245.
[7] Giovanni Martinelli, « Libye », *Se Comprendre* 04/02 (2004): 3.

dialogue, jugèrent bon de mettre sur pied un autre type de rencontres. C'est de là que le G.R.I.C (Groupe de Recherche Islamo-Chrétien) est né.[8]

En 1977 al-Qaddafi proclama l'instauration de la Jamahiriya socialiste libyenne-arabe. L'Église put se remettre un peu. Les travailleurs immigrés, surtout des Philippines, de Pologne et de Corée, augmentèrent le nombre de fidèles. En 1988 des chrétiens arabes les remplacèrent.[9]

Depuis le début des années 80 les relations entre l'État libyen et le Saint Siège s'améliorèrent peu à peu. En 1986 Mgr Giovanni Martinelli fut jeté en prison pour dix jours suite au bombardement américain de Tripoli.[10] Pendant l'embargo suivant de l'attentat de Lockerbie (1988) le Saint Siège et la Libye entamèrent des relations diplomatiques le 10 mars 1997. Par la suite, le vicariat de Benghazi reçut un nouveau vicaire, Mgr. Sylvester Carmel Magro.

En mars 1989 le Conseil Pontifical pour le Dialogue Interreligieux et le Dawa Islamiyya (World Islamic Call Society) commencèrent des délibérations bilatérales et des dialogues. Les séances se tinrent en alternance entre Tripoli et Rome, commençant à Tripoli. En mars 2002 la 7e session eut lieu à Tripoli sous le titre « Dialogue des cultures au temps de la globalisation ».[11]

En 2003 le Pape Shenouda III fit pour la deuxième fois une visite en Libye. Il reçut l' « Algaddafi International Prize for human rights » comme 14e lauréat.[12] Dans la même année le Patriarche œcuménique Bartolomé I visita la Libye sur l'invitation du Collège du Dawa Islamiyya et fit un discours sur le dialogue interreligieux.[13]

Depuis 2004 l'État libyen est beaucoup plus intéressé au dialogue interreligieux et interculturel. En plus le vicaire de Tripoli et un prêtre copte-orthodoxe furent invités à parler à la télévision sur les relations entre l'Église et l'Islam en Libye.[14]

L'Église catholique en Libye était très engagée socialement. Dans le Vicariat de Tripoli 35 religieuses de sept congrégations travaillaient dans des centres pour handicapés, orphelins et personnes âgées. Dans le Vicariat de Benghazi quatre congrégations étaient engagées dans différents hôpitaux.[15]

En 2011 la guerre civile commença et al-Qaddafi fut tué le 20 octobre 2011. En 2014 des milices rivalisantes se firent la guerre. En décembre 2015 un traité de paix fut conclut. En novembre 2011 au début du « printemps arabe » en Libye la Conférence des Évêques de la Région Nord de l'Afrique (CERNA) exprima encore sa joie de la nouvelle liberté. L'évêque de Tripoli, Mgr Martinelli, admit que « la Libye n'a jamais été un pays fondamentaliste, et les Libyens ne sont pas hostiles aux chrétiens. » Il ressentit le désir d'une présence chrétienne dans le pays, tandis que Mgr Maroun Lahham, évêque de Tunis, fut scandalisé

---

[8] Jean-Paul Charnay, « Le Dialogue islamo-chrétien: Essai d'interprétation psycho-stratégique », *Politique étrangère* 41, n° 3 (1976): passim, www.jstor.org/stable/42669976; <Sr> Maria Mechthild, « Dialog der Kulturen und Religionen am Beispiel „Islam und Christentum". Zeugnis aus dem afrikanischen Kontext », *Ordenskorrespondenz* 44 (2003): 49; Jacques Lanfry, « Témoignage sur le séminaire de dialogue islamo-chrétien de Tripoli (1-6 février 1976) », *Islamochristiana*, n° 38 (2012): passim, http://cat.inist.fr/?aModele=afficheN&cpsidt=27501105.

[9] Sabadin, « La situation actuelle en Libye », 246-247.

[10] Giovanni Cubeddu, « Mediterraner Realismus », *30 Tage*, n° 03 (2004), www.30giorni.it/ articoli_id_3487_l5.htm.

[11] Risto Jukko, *Trinity in unity in Christian-Muslim relations: the work of the Pontifical Council for Interreligious Dialogue*, History of Christian-Muslim relations ; 7 (Leiden [u.a.]: Brill, 2007), 21.

[12] « Al-Gaddafi International Prize For Human Rights », www.gaddafiprize.org/WhoEn.htm.

[13] Patriarch Bartholomew, « Lecture of His All Holiness Ecumencal Patriarch Bartholomew at the Islamic College of Lybia » (Islamic College of Lybia, 9 novembre 2003), https://www.patriarchate.org/lecture?p_auth=vsdc0Xgx&p_p_id=101_INSTANCE_4xqHyd1IywNL&p_p_lifecycle=1&p_p_state=exclusive&p_p_mode=view&p_p_col_id=column-1&p_p_col_pos=1&p_p_col_count=2&_101_INSTANCE_4xqHyd1IywNL_struts_action=%2Fasset_publisher%2Fexport_journal_article&_101_INSTANCE_4xqHyd1IywNL_groupId=32008&_101_INSTANCE_4xqHyd1IywNL_articleId=1069100&_101_INSTANCE_4xqHyd1IywNL_targetExtension=pdf.

[14] Maria Mechthild, « Dialog der Kulturen und Religionen am Beispiel „Islam und Christentum". Zeugnis aus dem afrikanischen Kontext », 49.

[15] Martinelli, « Libye », 3.

par l'annonce du Conseil national de transition de fonder la future législation du pays sur la charia.[16] Depuis il y eut plusieurs attentats contre les chrétiens et des églises. En mars 2013 un attentat fut commis contre l'église copte-orthodoxe à Benghazi. Le 24 février 2014 sept coptes fut découverts morts sur la plage de Benghazi. Le 19 juillet 2014 un Philippin fut décapité parce qu'il n'était pas musulman. Le 24 décembre 2014 trois coptes d'une famille furent tués à Sirte.[17] En février 2015, 21 coptes furent kidnappés et décapités en direct devant les caméras. En avril 28 chrétiens éthiopiens subirent le même sort. Le 3 juin 2015, 86 chrétiens érythréens furent kidnappés.

Bibliographie

« Al-Gaddafi International Prize For Human Rights ». Consulté le 5 avril 2016. www.gaddafiprize.org/WhoEn.htm.

Charnay, Jean-Paul. « Le Dialogue islamo-chrétien: Essai d'interprétation psycho-stratégique ». *Politique étrangère* 41, n° 3 (1976): 219-39. www.jstor.org/stable/42669976.

Conférence des Évêques de la Région Nord de l'Afrique (CERNA). « Communiqué final Tunis novembre 2011 ». Consulté le 4 avril 2016. http://amisdiocesesahara.free.fr/cernacom1111.html.

Cubeddu, Giovanni. « Mediterraner Realismus ». *30 Tage*, n° 03 (2004). www.30giorni.it/ articoli_id_3487 _l5.htm.

Jukko, Risto. *Trinity in unity in Christian-Muslim relations: the work of the Pontifical Council for Interreligious Dialogue*. History of Christian-Muslim relations ; 7. Leiden [u.a.]: Brill, 2007.

Lanfry, Jacques. « Témoignage sur le séminaire de dialogue islamo-chrétien de Tripoli (1-6 février 1976) ». *Islamochristiana*, n° 38 (2012): 145-56. http://cat.inist.fr/?aModele=afficheN&cpsidt=27501105.

Maria Mechthild, <Sr>. « Dialog der Kulturen und Religionen am Beispiel „Islam und Christentum'. Zeugnis aus dem afrikanischen Kontext ». *Ordenskorrespondenz* 44 (2003): 49-52.

Martinelli, Giovanni. « Libye ». *Se Comprendre* 04/02 (2004): 1-4.

Patriarch Bartholomew. « Lecture of His All Holiness Ecumencal Patriarch Bartholomew at the Islamic College of Lybia ». Islamic College of Lybia, 9 novembre 2003. https://www.patriarchate.org/lecture?p_auth=vsdc0Xgx&p_p_id=101_INSTANCE_4xqHyd1IywNL&p_p_lifecycle=1&p_p_state=exclusive&p_p_mode=view&p_p_col_id=column-1&p_p_col_pos=1&p_p_col_count=2&_101_INSTANCE_4xqHyd1IywNL_struts_action=%2Fasset_publisher%2Fexport_journal_article&_101_INSTANCE_4xqIIyd1IywNL_groupId=32008&_101_INSTANCE_4xqHyd1IywNL_articlcId=1069100&_101_INSTANCE_4xqHyd1IywNL_targetExtension=pdf.

Sabadin, Filiberto. « La situation actuelle en Libye ». In *Histoire des chrétiens d'Afrique du Nord: Libye-Tunisie-Algérie-Maroc*, édité par Henri Teissier et Antoine Chatelard, 244-49. Paris: Desclée, 1991.

______. « L'Église de Libye au XXe siècle ». In *Histoire des chrétiens d'Afrique du Nord: Libye-Tunisie-Algérie-Maroc*, édité par Henri Teissier et Antoine Chatelard, 155-59. Paris: Desclée, 1991.

United States Departmen of State – Bureau of Democracy, Human Rights, and Labor. « Libya 2014. International Religious Freedom Report », 2014. www.state.gov/documents/organization/238680.pdf.« Al-Gaddafi International Prize For Human Rights ». Consulté le 5 avril 2016. www.gaddafiprize.org/WhoEn.htm.

[16] Conférence des Évêques de la Région Nord de l'Afrique (CERNA), « Communiqué final Tunis novembre 2011 », http://amisdiocesesahara.free.fr/cernacom1111.html.

[17] United States Departmen of State – Bureau of Democracy, Human Rights, and Labor, « Libya 2014. International Religious Freedom Report ».

(73) Christianity in Madagascar

Laurent Ramambason

Religion	Pop 2010	Pct 2010	Pop 2025	Pct 2025	Gr Pct 1970 2025
Christians	11,997,000	56.9%	19,080,000	60.1%	3.1%
Independents	982,000	4.7%	1,620,000	5.1%	3.4%
African initiated	889,000	4.2%			
Orthodox	25,400	0.1%	50,000	0.2%	4.6%
Protestants	6,851,000	32.5%	9,700,000	30.6%	2.3%
Lutheran	3,400,000	16.1%			
United churches	2,786,000	13.2%			
Anglicans	386,000	1.8%			
Adventist	179,000	0.8%			
Roman Catholics	5,167,000	24.5%	8,100,000	25.5%	3.0%
Evangelicals	1,666,000	7.9%	2,372,000	7.5%	2.4%
Pentecostals/Charismatics	1,343,000	6.4%	2,300,000	7.2%	3.7%
adherents of traditional African religions	8,518,000	40.4%	11,794,000	37.2%	2.2%
Muslims	445,000	2.1%	670,000	2.1%	2.8%
Baha'is	18,700	0.1%	27,000	0.1%	2.5%
Hindus	12,200	0.1%	20,000	0.1%	3.3%
Chinese folk-religionists	10,500	0.1%	17,000	0.1%	3.2%
Buddhists	5,300	0.0%	8,000	0.0%	2.8%
Jews	320	0.0%	300	0.0%	-0.3%
people professing no religion	72,500	0.3%	112,000	0.4%	2.9%
Total population	**21,080,000**	**100.0%**	**31,728,000**	**100.0%**	**2.8%**

Source: Centre for the Study of World Christianity (CSGC), Boston, Gordon-Conwell TS

The Portuguese discovered Madagascar and Brazil in 1500. That was eight years after the discovery of America and the completion of the *reconquista*, the defeat of Muslim armies in the Iberian Peninsula. In 1502, the Muslims faced conversion or expulsion. The conquering mood and practice of the discoverers have been identified as one of the reasons why Madagascar did not become an Islamic country like the Comoros and Indonesia. They engaged themselves in wiping out Muslim influence, on the one hand, and evangelizing, on the other.

Two centuries later, Islam was reported to have gained access to King Andrianampoinimerina (1787-1810), who invited to his palace eleven Muslims from the south-east. They taught literacy with Arabic characters and worked as soothsayers and astrologers. However, the King's son Radama I, opted for Latin characters to write the Malagasy language in 1823. Since then the national influence of Islam has been only academic until the 1980s. Then Muslims began to have access to national radio and the formerly rare sight of Malagasy women in burqas appeared more frequently in the capital.

In the 21st century, statistic providers differ in their reports about religion in Madagascar. The number of Muslims would vary from 2% to 10%. The percentage of Christians also varies from 45% to 60%, and the number of people following various sorts of primal religions from 40% to 90%.

It is important to learn more how the historic world church and Christians in Madagascar have contributed to mutual development. Since the beginning of the sixteenth century, Malagasy people have received and responded to the Christian faith in relation to five historic phenomena: the missionary movement, the translated Bible, the ecumenical movement, national life, and post-modernism.

The Missionary Movement

Jao de San Thomas, a Dominican, who died in 1585, is reputed to have been the first missionary to come to Madagascar. A plaque at the Catholic Church in Fort Dauphin in the south-east informs us that it was founded between 1613 and 1620 by two Jesuits, Pedro Freire and Luis Mariano. Many Catholic missionaries were reported to have come to this area until 1660, and they succeeded in baptizing more than 77 local people. After that, there was scarcely any mention of Catholic missions to Madagascar until 1837.

The London Missionary Society (LMS), founded in 1795, was one the flagships of the British missionary movement. Its missionaries, David Jones and Thomas Bevan, set foot on the island in 1818 as Protestant pioneers. They initiated a mission of remarkable success, enhanced by an indigenous missionary movement known as the *Isanenimbolan'Imerina,* formed fifty years later. Quaker missionaries came to support the LMS in Madagascar before the Friends Foreign Mission Association (FFMA) was organized in England in 1868. Other missionaries came from elsewhere. Lutheran missionaries from the Norwegian Missionary Society and the American Lutheran Free Church and Lutheran Board of Mission reached the island in 1866 and 1892 respectively. The arrival of the reformed Mission Protestante Française (MPF) coincided with French possession of the island in 1896. The MPF became the Evangelical Church of Madagascar in 1958. The LMS mutated into the Church of Christ in Madagascar and the FFMA into the Friends Malagasy Church in 1961.

The Translated Bible

The first Bible in Malagasy was just off the press when the persecution of Christians, which lasted for nearly thirty years, broke out in 1835. The Bible was almost the only source of strength and guidance for Christians as there were no missionaries left and churches were not allowed. In the late nineteenth century new insights came to some rural Bible readers when they faced various hardships. The lack of medical facilities and the reality of demon possession were pervasive in rural areas. The Jesus they read of in the New Testament healed people and cast out demons.

A revival movement emerged when a rural man, Rainisoalambo, experienced healing in 1893-1894. He initiated new ways of being Christian and proclaiming the good news. The movement known as *fifohazana* was reproduced and enhanced elsewhere by the effective leadership of Neny Ravelonjanahary from Manolotrony in 1927, Nenilava from Ankaramalaza in 1942, and Dadatoa Rakotozandry of Farihimena from 1946. Independently of one another, they led different movements of the same *fifohazana* pattern.

Leadership succession in the *fifohazana* was not through bloodline, nor election. It was by charisma, by the same way of reading the Bible and the same challenges in rural Madagascar. In other words, the Bible functioned as the mission *alma mater*, the mission matrix of the leaders. After the last leader had passed away, questions were raised about when the mission *alma mater* would raise new *fifohazana* leaders, fitting its matrix in Madagascar. The same question can be asked concerning the West and elsewhere. Will there be revival or would reform leaders like Luther arise?

Many people who joined *fifohazana* received deliverance and healing. However, the ministry of the *fifohazana* has never been carried out with the propaganda for healing and miracles. They do not call people for healing. Rather their 'shepherds', *mpiandry* in Malagasy, are known for their radical call for repentance and persistence in prayer. They cast out evil spirits and lay on hands for empowerment. The ministry of *mpiandry*, unlike that of pastors, was unremunerated from the very beginning. The movement was anti-idol, solving the problem syncretistic pastors struggled to face. Poverty was alleviated in *fifohazana* centres by common economic activities. Shelter and care were provided for the marginalized, mainly those with severe mental illness. While the reproduction of church ministers takes place in seminaries, theological colleges and through church education, that of the *mpiandry* of the *fifohazana* takes place in revival centres, called *toby.*

The Ecumenical Movement

The problem of unity first emerged after 1861 when the door opened for missionaries to return. This was a dilemma for Anglicans, who enjoyed the dominant position in Britain. They wanted to appoint a bishop in Madagascar; but they were fully aware that it was not fair to interfere with the work of the nonconformist LMS mission. Initially, the LMS made their opposition clear. However, the situation evolved in such a way that the Anglicans did eventually appoint their bishop and built a cathedral in the capital. In contrast to its dissolution in India into the Church of South India and the Church of North India, the Anglican Church refused to engage themselves in the movement towards corporate union among Protestant denominations in Madagascar.

Unlike the Anglicans, the Catholic missions had no qualms whatever about intruding into the field of the LMS. In 1865, they began their own work on Bible translation, inventing a name of Jesus different from the name already found in the Protestant Bible. It sealed a radical division between Catholic and Protestant. When French colonial power took over in 1896, the Catholics saw their time had come. They arrogated to themselves the right to choose and confiscate lands and properties. 'The Jesuit persecution caused the death of several Malagasy pastors, who were falsely accused as disloyal, and about a hundred village churches were seized by the priests,' wrote James Sibree on page seven of his book *Ten Years Review of Mission Work in Madagascar 1901-1910,* published in 1911. The new Catholic churches were built alongside Protestant ones. It explains why, in Imerina, nearly every village has two church buildings, one Protestant and one Catholic.

To follow up the 1910 Edinburgh meeting, missionary societies working in Madagascar formed the Inter-Missionary Conference in 1913. In 1950, the Lutheran churches merged to constitute the Malagasy Lutheran Church. The churches started by the British and French missionaries united into the Church of Jesus Christ in Madagascar (FJKM) in 1968. The difficult negotiations were monitored closely by the World Council of Churches and reported in the Ecumenical Review. It was seen as puzzling as it was the only union project making the sacraments optional; the Quakers, who did not recognize any sacrament, exercised a great deal of self-denial to make this church union possible. The Inter-Missionary Conference changed into the Federation of Protestant Churches in 1964. It is now the platform where the FJKM and the Malagasy Lutheran Church have inter-communion. The process of uniting the two churches has stalled since July 1987, when the Lutheran General Synod officially rejected the goal of organic unity.

The strain on relations between Protestants and Catholics began to ease on the eve of political independence. In 1959, a flood disaster prompted the Christians to come together and act under the guidance of an Ecumenical Social Council. In 1970, an Ecumenical Commission on Theology was formed. The National Council of Churches (FFKM) was inaugurated in 1979, a year after the agreement to have a common name for Jesus, *Jesoa*. The common name facilitated the ecumenical translation of the Bible which was published in 1991. Later, the Lutherans voiced their preference for the old Protestant pronunciation and convinced the Bible Society to re-use *Jesosy* in a new version of the Protestant Bible (!). Despite this backtracking, the FFKM is among the few national church councils in the world which included Catholics.

The mainline churches are known as 'senior' churches. The others, which are not Catholic, that is, the FJKM, Lutheran and Anglican, are termed 'junior' churches because they came later and have smaller memberships. They either split from the mainline churches or evolved from missions based overseas. Some of them co-operated with the 'senior' churches within the Malagasy Bible Society. Others would actively shun or criticize the mainline churches. In contrast, the historic *fifohazana* leaders refrained from starting new denominations, though they had the power to do so. However, the *Fifohazana Soatanana* had its own ecumenical problem. After the death of the first leader, the movement split into two groups. They are still separated, though their headquarters are located in the same town.

National Life

Madagascar is a nation constituted by eighteen main groups of people speaking the same language with various dialects. The Merina group is the largest. It is the most Christianized because the early missions successfully focused their work on Imerina. Coming from the periphery of politics and culture in Britain, the nonconformist LMS and Quaker missions occupied the very centre of politics and culture in Madagascar. In that context, the nonconformist roots of the LMS were tested on many occasions. The Merina were associated with Christianity by some ethnic groups. For that reason, Merina military success closed the doors on further Christianization. Colonial France came and defeated the Merina in 1896. They confiscated LMS properties, and steered education towards their own interests. Madagascar constitutes an example of the worst effects of French colonialism and post-independence possessiveness. The churches have failed to produce a satisfactorily patriotic political class. What they achieved since Independence has been to bring warring factions together round a table to solve major crises.

The early missions sowed the seeds of European civilization. They started the first school and college, created the Malagasy alphabet, translated the Bible, and carried out development projects. However, economic development has remained an unfulfilled dream for Malagasy people. The ruthless IMF/World Bank restructuring and wild devaluations from the 1980s have failed. They brought the economy to its knees with little prospect of rescue. Church education has not helped young people stand on their own feet and contribute to the economic development of the island. They fail to compete and win in an imposed hyper-capitalistic world.

Post-modernism

Madagascar was hit by a post-Christian mood in 1905 with the arrival of the French governor Victor Augagneur. He prohibited classes in church buildings and cut government subsidies to church schools. Open-air evangelism was discouraged, and public conferences and debates were organized to ridicule religion. The French doubt in 'grand narratives' was forced on the Malagasy. Freemasonry and secret societies gained members.

Changes in the churches in the West and the political situation in Madagascar served as forces to create a post-missionary situation. In the 1960s and 1970s, political independence and the numerical decline of the churches, among other factors, transformed the nature of the missionary societies. The LMS became the Council for World Mission in 1977 and shifted its head offices from London to Singapore in 2011. The FFMA ceased to be an independent body in 1927 and has been known as the Quaker Peace and Social

Witness since 2001. The MPF retracted to be a Département Evangélique Français d'Action Apostolique in 1970, keeping the money and properties of the mother missionary society in France. The Communauté Evangélique d'Action Apostolique, formed in 1971, unites the churches started by the missionary society overseas. It remains based in France.

The post-Christian mood was integrated into a philosophical framework, post-modernism, which believes truth to be plural. A mass conversion from 'exclusivist' to 'pluralist' religious outlooks gripped the West in the 1990s. The change took place while missionary Islam, with pre-modern values, hit the news on television. Additionally, self-styled prophets and people who are alleged to have gone to hell or heaven came back to tell stories that gripped people's imagination and attracted attention in Madagascar.

Are the churches, founded by the missionaries, following the downward turn of western churches? Opinions diverge – however, two remarks can be made. First, Malagasy diaspora Christians are increasing in the West, the Middle East and elsewhere. Their presence has a missionary function different from that of the missionaries, who came to their land in the nineteenth and first half of the twentieth century. The missionaries had funding, organizational, political, military and cultural domination. The Malagasy in the diaspora have very little, if any, of these means. Second, the co-operation of *fifohazana* with the churches, founded by the missionaries, is helping the churches avoid the declining trend of their mother churches in Europe and America. Every mainline church is, in fact, growing. *Fifohazana* constitutes a specific Malagasy contribution to world mission and 'doing church'.

Bibliography

Baubérot, Jean. ''L'anti-Protestantisme politique à la fin du XIXè siècle' 'in: *Révue d'histoire et de philosophie*, 52 (1972): 449-484.

Cousins, William. *A Brief Review of the L.M.S. Mission in Madagascar from 1861 to 1870*. Antananarivo: LMS, 1871.

Deschamps, Hubert. ''Conceptions, problèmes et sources de l'histoire de Madagascar'' *Journal of African History*, 1, 2 (1960), 249-256.

Ferrand, Gabriel. *Les musulmans à Madagascar et aux Iles Comores. Les Antaimorona* (Paris, Ernest Leroux, 1891). <http://aefek.free.fr/iso_album/biblio_ferrand_gabriel.pdf>

Goodall, Norman, *A History of the London Missionary Society 1895-1945.* London, New York, Toronto: Oxford University Press, 1954.

Huckett, William. *Ten Years' Review of Mission Work in Madagascar, 1911-1920*. Antananarivo: LMS, 1921.

Lovett, Richard. *The History of the London Missionary Society 1795-1895*. 2 vols. London: OUP, 1899.

Mantaux, Christian. 'Islam noir et blanc de la côte de Zenj à Madagascar', Fas.2, *Recherches et Documents*, N°12. Antsiranana: Institut Supérieur de Théologie et de Philosophie de Madagascar, 1992.

Mantaux, Christian. 'Islam noir et blanc de la côte de Zenj à Madagascar', Fas.1, in: *Recherches et Documents*, N°10. Antsiranana: Institut Supérieur de Théologie et de Philosophie de Madagascar, 1991.

Neill, Stephen. *Towards Church Union 1937-1952. A Survey of Approaches to Closer Union among the Churches.* London: SCM Press, 1952.

Peetz, Otto. *Friends' Mission work in Madagascar Up to 1927 and its Doctrinal Implications.* Oxford: Mansfield College, 1960.

Ralibera. *Fifohazan'ny mpianatry ny Tompo miray amin'i Soatanana*. 7th impression. Antananarivo: Volamahitsy, 1961.

Ramambason Laurent. 'Malagasy Christians amidst the Lubricating Blood of Grinding Economic Models: A Missiological Approach to Socio-economic Issues.' *Mission Studies*, Journal of the IAMS, Vol. XIII-1&2 (1996): 256-267.

Randrianaivo, Benjamin (ed.) *Fanazavana momba ny Fifohazana Ambatoreny-Soatanana.* Antananarivo: Industrie Graphique Tananarivienne, 1964.

Sibree, James. *Ten Years Review of Mission Work in Madagascar 1901-1910.* Antananarivo: LMS, 1911.
Thorogood, Bernard (ed.). *Gales of Change. Responding to a Shifting Missionary Context. The London Missionary Society 1945-1977.* Geneva: WCC Publications, 1994.
Thunem, A. *Ny Fifohazana eto Madagasikara.* Tananarive: Mission Norvégienne, 1935.

(74) CHRISTIANITY IN MALAWI

Isabel Apawo Phiri, Gertrude Kapuma and Chimwemwe Harawa

Religion	Pop 2010	Pct 2010	Pop 2025	Pct 2025	Gr Pct 1970 2025
Christians	11,732,000	79.4%	18,811,000	81.3%	3.2%
Independents	2,135,000	14.5%	3,600,000	15.6%	3.5%
African initiated	1,771,000	12.0%			
Orthodox	3,500	0.0%	3,500	0.0%	0.0%
Protestants	4,646,000	31.5%	7,550,000	32.6%	3.3%
Reformed, Presbyterian	1,643,000	11.1%			
Pentecostal	1,203,000	8.1%			
Adventist	532,000	3.6%			
Baptist	532,000	3.6%			
Anglicans	288,000	1.9%			
Evangelical churches	151,000	1.0%			
Holiness	86,900	0.6%			
Lutheran	80,000	0.5%			
Roman Catholics	4,692,000	31.8%	8,116,000	35.1%	3.7%
Pentecostals/Charismatics	3,183,000	21.6%	5,500,000	23.8%	3.7%
Evangelicals	2,647,000	17.9%	4,356,000	18.8%	3.4%
Muslims	1,981,000	13.4%	3,195,000	13.8%	3.2%
adherents of traditional African religions	949,000	6.4%	950,000	4.1%	0.0%
Baha'is	34,600	0.2%	55,000	0.2%	3.1%
Hindus	32,100	0.2%	50,000	0.2%	3.0%
Sikhs	750	0.0%	1,400	0.0%	4.2%
adherents of new religious movements	580	0.0%	800	0.0%	2.2%
Jews	270	0.0%	300	0.0%	0.7%
people professing no religion	39,900	0.3%	70,500	0.3%	3.9%
Total population	**14,770,000**	**100.0%**	**23,134,000**	**100.0%**	**3.0%**

Source: Centre for the Study of World Christianity (CSGC), Boston, Gordon-Conwell TS

Introduction

According to the 2008 Population and Housing census, there were about thirteen million people in Malawi, of whom about 83% were Christians, 13% Muslims, 2% belonged to other religions, and 2% did not belong to any religion at all.[1] Unfortunately, these statistics do not acknowledge the existence of African indigenous religions which influence the way Christianity and Islam is practised in Malawi. The purpose of this article is to give a brief survey of the growth of Christianity, from the time it was introduced before the formation of the British Central Africa Protectorate in 1891, which was renamed the Nyasaland Protectorate in 1907, and further renamed Malawi in 1964.

Historical churches

Christianity was brought to Malawi by various missionaries as a result of the missionary work of David Livingstone, who visited the area in 1859. After his death, missionaries from various backgrounds established pioneer churches in Malawi between 1861 and 1901. The historical churches can be divided into two groups: the so-called mainline churches and the smaller churches. The mainline churches include the following:

The Anglican Church was introduced into Malawi through the Universities' Mission to Central Africa (UMCA) in 1861. The UMCA was formed as a direct response to the call of David Livingstone for the introduction of Christianity and commerce into Central Africa to combat the Arab slave trade. But after three years of missionary work in the Shire Highlands, the station was abandoned due to conflict with local leaders. Nevertheless, the missionaries returned in 1879.[2] The church is now part of **the Church of the Province of Central Africa,** a member of the World Council of Churches, with fifteen dioceses in Botswana, Malawi, Zambia and Zimbabwe. Four of those dioceses are in Malawi, namely, Lake Malawi, Northern Malawi, Southern Malawi and Southern Malawi – Upper Shire.

The Church of Central Africa Presbyterian is found in Malawi, Zambia and Zimbabwe with five synods. Three of the synods are located in Malawi and are called Livingstonia Synod, Blantyre Synod and Nkhoma Synod. These synods were founded by three different missionary groups. In 1875, the Free Church of Scotland established the Livingstonia Mission in the North of Malawi. The Blantyre Mission in the South was established by the Church of Scotland in 1876. The Nkhoma Mission was founded by the Dutch Reformed Church Mission in 1889 in the Central Region of Malawi. The Livingstonia Mission joined with the Blantyre Mission in 1924 to form the CCAP, and in 1926, Nkhoma joined.[3] The Evangelical Presbyterian Church of Malawi is a Reformed Christian church in Malawi but not part of the CCAP. Statistics show that the CCAP is the largest Protestant denomination in Malawi. The Blantyre Synod was accepted as a member of the World Council of Churches in July 2014.

The Catholic Church in Malawi came through the missionary work, initially of the White Fathers who first arrived in Malawi in 1889 but, due to sickness and difficult working conditions, they abandoned the mission. When they returned in 1901, they established mission stations in Central Malawi. The Montfort Fathers followed and established missions in Southern Malawi. The Catholic Church in Malawi has two archdioceses in Lilongwe and Blantyre, and six in Chikwawa, Mangochi, Zomba, Dedza, Karonga and Mzuzu. Today, the Catholics are the largest Christian denomination in Malawi with over two million members – around a third of the Christians and a fifth of the total population. Their fast growth in Malawi is attributed to tolerance of the local culture, unlike the Protestant missionary groups.

---

[1] Population and Housing Census 2008, Main Report (Zomba: National Statistics Office, September 2009), 13. Some books put Islam around 35-45% of the population. See Valiant Moosa, *The History of Muslims in Malawi, Before and after Christianity to Modern Times* (Blantyre: Fattani, 2005), 8.

[2] Michael Gelfand, *Lakeside Pioneers: The Universities Mission to Central Africa and the Beginnings of Missionary Enterprise* (Oxford: Blackwell, 1964), 1-2.

[3] John Weller and Jane Linden, *Mainstream Christianity to 1980 in Malawi, Zambia and Zimbabwe* (Gweru: Mambo Press, 1984), 118-119.

The second category of the smaller historical churches was fostered by the British missionary Joseph Booth. Booth is linked with the establishment of the following churches: the Zambezi Industrial Mission (1892), the Nyasa Industrial Mission (1893), the Baptist Industrial Mission of Scotland (1898), the Seventh Day Adventist – Plainfield (1900), the South African General Mission (1901), and the Seventh Day Adventists Mission (1902).[4]

Booth is also associated with assisting Malawians to found churches such as the Providence Industrial Mission (PIM) by the Rev. John Chilembwe in 1900, the Watch Tower Movement in 1908 by Elliot Kamwana, and a series of Seventh Day Adventist missions in northern Malawi by Charles Domingo. In addition, there are other churches founded by Malawians, either who had studied in mission schools or who had gone to work in the mines in South Africa. Some of the churches include the Children of God (*Ana a Mulungu*) founded by Wilfred Gudu, the African Methodist Episcopal Church (MEC) which came to Malawi through Hanock Phiri in 1924, and the African National Church founded by Simon K Mkandawire, Paddy Nyasulu, Robert S Mhango and Levi Mumba in 1929.

In the 1930s, Pentecostal churches under various denominations such as the Assemblies of God, the Apostolic Faith Mission, and the Pentecostal Holiness, among others, began to enter the country. Pentecostalism emphasises the work of the Holy Spirit and a personal relationship with God.

The latest on the scene are the charismatic churches, such as Agape (1982), Faith of God (1984), Living Waters (1985), All for Jesus (1993), Flames of Victory (1993), Calvary Family Church (1994), The Vineyard (1994), New Christian Life, Fountain of Victory, Pentecostal Holiness, Bushiri Ministries and many others. At times, the categorisation of the Pentecostal and charismatic churches is very difficult, because some denominations show characteristics of both. By 2004, there were 211 Pentecostal and charismatic denominations in Malawi.[5] They concentrate on revivals, prayer, and healing or prosperity teaching.

Six per cent of Malawians belong to a Baptist church, of which there are many in Malawi. The majority of them belong to the following categories: the African Baptist Assembly, Malawi, Inc. with 787 congregations and 72,800 members, the Baptist Convention of Malawi (BACOMA) with about 1,300 municipalities and approximately 150,000 members, and the Evangelical Baptist Church of Malawi with about 300 churches and 19,000 members.[6]

Other important historic Protestant churches with a recent history include the following: a) The United Methodist Church in Malawi was begun in 1987 through the mission outreach of the neighbouring Zimbabwe Annual Conference.[7] The church was started by the Rev. Alufeyo Mpulula in Lilongwe at Gaga Village. The Rev. Daniel Mhone became the superintendent when it was declared a Provisional Annual Conference.[8] b) The Lutheran Church in Central Africa came to Blantyre in 1963. Missionary work expanded from the Southern Region of Malawi to the Central Region. It is a member of the Confessional Evangelical Lutheran Conference (CELC), a worldwide organisation of the Confessional Lutheran Church bodies. [9] The Evangelical Lutheran Church of Malawi was founded on 21st November 1982 by lay people who had become Lutherans while working in the neighbouring countries of Tanzania and Zimbabwe. It is

---

[4] For further information see also Harry Langworthy, *"Africa for the African:" The Life of Joseph Booth* (Blantyre: CLAIM, 1996).

[5] Report on UNESCO workshop on Monotheistic Religions in Malawi held at Grace Bandawe Conference Centre in Blantyre (19-20 October 2007), 29.

[6] https://de.wikipedia.org/wiki/Baptisten_in_Malawi (accessed 29 July 2015); Hany Longwe, *Christians by Grace – Baptists by Choice. A History of the Baptist Convention of Malawi, Zomba and Luwinga* (Zomba: Kachere Series) 2012.

[7] See more at: www.umcmission.org/Explore-Our-Work/Africa/Malawi#sthash.MGLQQbIK.dpuf.

[8] Interview with Rev Robert Mdoka, February 2015.

[9] En.wikipedia.org/wiki/lutheranchurch of central africa (accessed 29th July 2015).

now led by Bishop Joseph Bvumbwe.[10] c) The Brethren Church in Malawi began as an outreach ministry of Zimbabwe in 1983. Its current leader is Bishop Ephraim Disi. They have 55 congregations with a membership of 4,800 and 6,720 affiliates.[11]

Christianity and Development

Scholars of religion have noted the impact and significance of Christianity in Malawi and have written about its influence on the social, economic and political life of the nation.[12] In general, churches in Malawi work hand-in-hand with the government in the following areas:

- Education: schools at different levels, including tertiary education and vocational training.
- Health and healing: clinics, hospitals, home-based care, and spiritual healing.
- Mass media: printing, the provision of religious literature, private radio stations and TV, and media houses.
- Social action: development projects, human rights advocacy for access to clean water, sanitation, food security, etc.
- Politics: the church has worked hard to bring about a multi-party system of government and continues to play the role of a watchdog of democracy through PAC.[13]

Ecumenism

The Christian denominations have formed different associations to promote development, advocacy and civic education on national issues. The notable ones are as follows:

- **The Christian Council of Malawi** (January 1942) which brings together the following churches: Africa Evangelical Church, African Methodist Episcopal Church, Anglican Diocese of Lake Malawi, Anglican Diocese of Northern Malawi, Anglican Diocese of Southern Malawi, Anglican Diocese of Upper Shire, Baptist Convention of Malawi, Central Africa Conference of Seventh Day Baptists, Church of Africa Presbyterian, Church of Central Africa Presbyterian Blantyre Synod, Church of Central Africa Presbyterian Livingstonia Synod, Church of Central Africa Presbyterian Nkhoma Synod, Church of Nazarene, Churches of Christ, Evangelical Church of Malawi, Evangelical Lutheran Church of Malawi, Free Methodist Church, Independent Baptist Church, Providence Industrial Mission, Salvation Army and Zambezi Evangelical Church. The aim is to give churches the opportunity to speak with one voice in areas of health, advocacy, education, spirituality, youth and women's empowerment.
- **The Episcopal Conference of Malawi**: this brings together the seven dioceses of the Roman Catholic Church in Malawi.
- **The Evangelical Association of Malawi** (EAM) is an umbrella body for 108 churches and Christian organizations (58 evangelical churches and 50 Christian organizations). It caters for the smaller missions, such as the Zambezi Industrial Mission and the Nyasa Industrial Mission.

---

[10] www.nwswi.org/webfiles/fnitools/documents/history_of_our_companion_relationship.pdf (accessed 30th July 2015).

[11] www.bic-church.org/wm/explore/malawi.asp (accessed 29th July 2015).

[12] Kenneth R. Ross, *Christianity in Malawi: A Source Book* (Gweru: Mambo Press, 1996), 11.

[13] The Public Affairs Committee (PAC) is a civil society, interfaith organization made up of the main Protestant, Catholic and Muslim faith groups in Malawi. It operates in the areas of good governance and human rights. PAC is composed of the Malawi Council of Churches (MCC), Episcopal Conference of Malawi (ECM), Evangelical Association of Malawi (EAM), Muslim Association of Malawi (MAM) and Quadria Muslim Association of Malawi (QMAM). See www.pacmw.org/ (accessed 29 July 2015).

- **The Charismatic and Pentecostal Association of Malawi** (CHAPEL) brings together charismatic and Pentecostal denominations and some African Instituted Churches.
- **The Baptist Convention of Malawi** (BACOMA) caters for Baptist groupings in Malawi.

Another aspect of co-operation is the formation of inter-church associations. This came about from the consideration that the churches' role in development could best be played if they acted not as individual entities but together. Examples of this category include:

The Christian Service Committee (CSC) (1967) for relief operations (floods and refugees), welfare projects, such as school feeding, and development, including drilling boreholes, building school blocks, and the provision of food security, water and sanitation.

The Christian Hospitals Association of Malawi (CHAM) drawing membership from thirteen Protestant churches and the Catholic Church in Malawi.

The Christian Literature Association (CLAIM), created in 1968 by thirteen churches.

The Board for Theological Studies (BTS) currently has eight theological Institutions. The Board for Theological Studies brings together some theological institutions of different traditions aimed at teaching a common theology syllabus suitable for Malawi today.

MANERELA is a network of religious leaders living with or personally affected by HIV and AIDS.

The ecumenical work of the church is remarkable because it has been able to achieve a common goal. The unity of the churches helps denominations to reach out to those areas they cannot reach individually. It has become common now that pastors (ministers) within a community form what they call a 'pastors' fraternal'; the purpose of these is to help pastors work together.

Apart from the associations which are under the umbrella of the different churches, there are religious groups which are non-denominational, such as World Vision International, which concentrate on interdenominational Christian witness and development in different sectors. A popular ecumenical gathering are what are known as **interdenominational fellowship groups**. Adherents can have dual membership – to an established church and to the fellowship. These fellowships are also known as ministries. With the passage of time, some develop into churches. They concentrate on purely spiritual matters. Examples include the New Life for All Ministry, Life Ministry, and the Women's World Day of Prayer which invites Muslim women to participate as well.

Some mainline churches may not allow their members to go to such fellowships but at a practical level, this is difficult to control. One way of keeping their members within their churches is that most mainline churches have introduced religious ceremonies that may attract people. For example, the Roman Catholic Church has a charismatic wing which has adopted a charismatic type of worship which may include speaking in tongues. The CCAP has what it calls contemporary worship. This allows Christians to have the freedom of singing choruses and dancing to gospel music as is the case with Pentecostal and charismatic churches. This attracts many young people as they feel no longer restricted to a particular or traditional way of worship. Christians want lively worship services and one result of this has been the growth of many choirs in the church to supplement traditional hymns with other types of music. There is an increase in outreach by various denominations to meet the spiritual needs of their members. Another activity which is growing and becoming popular are nights of prayer services. Observations show that night prayers are patronised by the young, an indication that they have some needs which may be addressed by the churches.

At an international level, some churches in Malawi have joined organizations like the World Alliance of Reformed Churches, the Episcopal Conference of Eastern Africa (AMECEA), the Association of Theological Institutions in Southern and Central Africa (ATISCA), the World Council of Churches (WCC), the All Africa Conference of Churches (AACC), the Lutheran World Federation, and the Network for Congregational Theology (NETACT).

Challenges for Christianity in Malawi

In this section, we would like to highlight five major challenges faced by the churches in Malawi. The challenges are not presented in any particular order of importance. The first challenge is the role of women in the church. Women are often denied their rightful place in the church simply because of their gender. Even in the churches that have accepted women's leadership roles or ordination, the situation is not easy. Women continue to struggle for recognition and acceptance as equal partners. In this context, women's ordination is controversial. After many years of debating as to whether or not to allow women to administer the word and sacrament, the Assemblies of God ordained their first woman in 1994. Her ordination became possible because the church leadership recognized the call of God to women. This was followed by the Livingstonia and Blantyre Synods of the CCAP in 2000 and 2001 respectively. The Blantyre Synod has even appointed a women to the position of Synod Moderator, something that had always been a male preserve. The United Methodist Church in Malawi now allows the ordination of women. Debates continue in the Nkhoma Synod and in the Anglican Church on whether to allow women's ordination or not. In churches where women have not been given this opportunity, they have continued to participate fully in the church's other ministries. They are regarded as the backbone of many churches. They work hard in fund-raising activities, pastoral visitations, singing in choirs, entertaining visitors, teaching Sunday school and many other activities. They are very active in their own women's groups, helping themselves on their spiritual journey. Despite all the delays in allowing women to take leadership roles in the mainline churches, women in the Pentecostal and Charismatic movements have gone ahead to lead churches. Women have moved from the mainline churches and founded house churches which have become community churches. In these churches, women have assumed the highest positions as founders and even bishops. In other Pentecostal churches, the leadership of women is seen in the wife of the leader being given a title and called Pastor. 'The pastor's wife or first lady serves as a noble power for mobilising and deploying the female evangelical power.'[14] Examples of some of these churches founded by women are the Chilobwe Healing Centre (Mayi Nyajere, 1986), Revival Ministries (Mayi Gonthi, 1986), Blessed Hope Church and Ministries (Bishop Yami Mchika, 1992), Namatapa Miracle Centre (Mayi Chipondeni, 1992) and the Chisomo Worship Centre (Mayi Chapomba, 1998).

The second challenge is the role of youth in the churches. The missionaries who brought Christianity also promoted education, which helped many young people to go to school and gain knowledge, skills and jobs. But today the young are faced with many challenges such as dropping out from school, unemployment, early marriages and drugs, to mention just a few. In some of the churches, the young are not given the opportunity to participate in church activities, and in some cases the young find traditional church services boring. They want a vibrant church. Church leaders are not of one mind in finding solutions for youth involvement in the churches. It is evident that most of the young people who have participated in youth groups such as the Students' Christian Organization in Malawi (SCOM) have become responsible leaders in many sectors, including the church. This is because, in such groups, young people were given the chance to develop their gifts.

The third challenge currently facing the church in Malawi is the HIV and AIDS epidemic. The church has moved from preaching messages that promoted stigma to messages with life-affirming theologies. However, we still have some pastors who discourage their members from taking anti-retroviral treatment, claiming that they can effect miraculous healing through prayer alone. The presence of an umbrella body called Malawi Interfaith Aids Association (MIAA) is helping to mitigate this challenge. This body is also helping the faith community to be involved in advocacy when dealing with HIV and AIDS issues.

The fourth challenge is the relationship between Christianity and African culture. African people express their Christian faith through their culture, and it is difficult to separate the two. However, some

[14] Ogbu Kalu, *African Pentecostalism: An Introduction* (New York: Oxford University Press, 2008), 153.

African theologians have argued for a methodology that helps to avoid African cultural practices that are hazardous to human life and which do not promote human dignity. Examples of such cultural practices include witchcraft and sorcery, wife inheritance, property theft and child marriages.

The fifth challenge is secularization. The secular world respects the church in Malawi and expects its members to be exemplary. Alarming cases of gender-based violence, corruption, the misappropriation of church and public funds by some church leaders and some church members, all affect the credibility of the Christian teaching.

Despite this, the church is still strong in Malawi and it is called upon to address issues of the modern world such as gender affirmation and standing for the marginalised, youth culture, equal access to education, homosexuality and the promotion of human dignity.

The growth of the church with so many denominations and ministries is a clear indication that the people of Malawi would like to have the Word of God in their lives. This growth should serve to promote unity and foster a common goal, instead of wasting time in competition and making other denominations seem inferior. Disputes within and between churches may make the possibility of further ecumenical development impossible.

In partnering with the government on developmental issues, the church should continue to take its prophetic role of ministry seriously, without compromising its call. As watchdogs, the church is called to stand for peace and justice. It has to ensure that there is an equal distribution of resources in the country to all its citizens, and that there is a fair representation of people in all sectors, based on merit.

Bibliography

Gelfand, Michael. *Lakeside Pioneers: The Universities Mission to Central Africa and the Beginnings of Missionary Enterprise.* Oxford: Blackwell, 1964.

Langworthy, Harry. *'Africa for the African': The Life of Joseph Booth.* Blantyre: CLAIM, 1996.

McCracken, John. *Politics and Christianity in Malawi 1875-1940: The Impact of Livingstonia Mission in the Northern Province*. Blantyre: CLAIM, 2000.

Population and Housing Census 2008, Main report. Zomba: National Statistics Office, September 2009.

Report on UNESCO workshop on Monotheistic Religions in Malawi (unpublished) held at Grace Bandawe Conference Centre in Blantyre,19-20 October 2007.

Ross, Andrew. *Blantyre Mission and the Making of Modern Malawi.* Blantyre: CLAIM, 1996.

Ross, Kenneth R. *Christianity in Malawi: A Source Book.* Gweru: Mambo Press, 1996.

Tengatenga, James. *Church, State and Society in Malawi: The Anglican Case*. Limbe: Assemblies of God Press, 2006.

Weller, John and Jane Linden. *Mainstream Christianity to 1980 in Malawi, Zambia and Zimbabwe.* Gweru: Mambo Press, 1984.

(75) CHRISTIANITY IN MALI

Youssouf Dembele

Religion	Pop 2010	Pct 2010	Pop 2025	Pct 2025	Gr Pct 1970 2025
Christians	442,000	2.9%	519,000	2.2%	1.1%
Independents	15,000	0.1%	17,000	0.1%	0.8%
African initiated	14,200	0.1%			
Protestants	93,800	0.6%	120,000	0.5%	1.7%
Holiness	81,600	0.5%			
Roman Catholics	342,000	2.3%	400,000	1.7%	1.1%
Evangelicals	102,000	0.7%	140,000	0.6%	2.1%
Pentecostals/Charismatics	27,300	0.2%	50,000	0.2%	4.1%
Muslims	13,379,000	88.2%	21,352,000	90.1%	3.2%
adherents of traditional African religions	1,329,000	8.8%	1,800,000	7.6%	2.0%
Baha'is	1,100	0.0%	2,500	0.0%	5.4%
adherents of new religious movements	760	0.0%	1,500	0.0%	4.7%
people professing no religion	15,400	0.1%	27,500	0.1%	4.0%
Total population	**15,167,000**	**100.0%**	**23,702,000**	**100.0%**	**3.0%**

Source: Centre for the Study of World Christianity (CSGC), Boston, Gordon-Conwell TS

Introduction

Mali is one of the largest territories in West Africa. It is the cradle of great empires such as Ghana Empire (4th-11th centuries), Mali Empire (8th-16th centuries), and the Songhai Empire (8th-16th centuries). During the French colonization (late 19th to mid-20th centuries), the area came to be known as French Sudan. It became Mali after its independence from France in 1960.

Three major religious groups inhabit Mali: Malian traditional religions, Islam and Christianity. Traditional religions are natives of the land. They are part of the fabric of the Malian soul. Islam arrived in Mali in the eighth century, less than a hundred years after its birth in Arabia. It is now the religion of the great majority of Malians. The Christian presence in Mali started in the late nineteenth century. A minority of Malians adhere to it. This short presentation focuses on this Christian minority under three headings: a historical survey, Christian engagement, and living alongside the two other religious groups.

A Historical Survey of Christianity

There are the two first Christian families in Mali, namely, Catholicism and Protestantism. It was the Fathers of the Holy Spirit who were the first missionaries to enter the country. They constructed the first Catholic mission station in the small town of Kita in November 1888. The work of the Catholic missionaries fits neatly into five periods. The years 1888-1901 mark the beginning of the mission.

The second period, 1901-1921, was a difficult one. Due to sickness and the death of many of the Catholic missionaries, the Fathers of the Holy Spirit left in 1901. The White Fathers arrived the following year, in September 1922, and opened a mission at Sikasso, appointing three missionaries at Mandiakuy.[1] The start of World War I affected mission work. For seventeen years, no new mission station started while some existing ones closed.

During the third period, 1921-1947, though World War II broke out, the work of the mission was fruitful. New mission stations opened, some Malian priests were ordained and the first training institutions started.

The fourth period, 1947-1962, was one of the most productive for the future of the work. Two major events took place: the political independence of Mali and the beginning of the Second Vatican Council. This period witnessed the foundation of three Apostolic Prefectures. The number of missionaries increased and several new mission stations opened. Mgr Luc Sangare became the first Malian Archbishop of Bamako.

The fifth period, 1962-2015, witnessed local Christians assuming responsibility for evangelization and management. It was the period of the National Church.[2]

Protestant missionaries first explored Mali in 1913. Only after the signature of the Treaty of Saint-Germain-en-Laye on 10th September 1919 did the French authorities allow Protestant missions to settle in Mali. Four American missions made their entry: The Gospel Missionary Union (GMU, 1919), the Christian and Missionary Alliance (C&MA, 1923), The Evangelical Baptist Mission (EBM, 1951), and the United World Mission (UWM, 1954). The Protestant Church in Mali originated from the joint efforts of these four mission agencies. The churches planted by them formed four church denominations respectively under the names of the Christian Evangelical Church of Mali (ECEM, 1960), the Evangelical Protestant Church of Mali (EEPM, 1961), the Protestant Church of Kayes (EPRK, 1965), and the Federation of the Evangelical Baptist Churches (FEEB, 1971).

The founding missions and the church denominations came together in 1963 to form the National Association of Evangelicals in Mali (AGEMPEM).[3] Since the advent of democracy in Mali in 1991, several independent churches and Christian movements from Nigeria entered Mali. They came together in an Association called AMEN-REVEIL[4].

Christian Engagement

The two Christian families in Mali are involved in holistic ministry. They showed concern for the spiritual, physical, psychological and social needs of the people to whom they ministered.

Language Learning and Literacy Work

The missionaries started their ministry by learning the local languages. They reduced to writing the main local language, wrote grammar books, lexicons, collections of proverbs and stories, collections of local medicinal plants, and made great efforts to develop literacy primers. Some missionaries did valuable anthropological and sociological research on Malian society. They taught the new believers, children and adults, to read and write their mother tongue. They thus prepared the future readers of the Bible and other writings in the local languages.

---

[1] La commission nationale préparation centénaire, Cent ans: Eglise du Mali (15-20 November 1988): pp.45-46; Letters to our Friends. Missionaries of Africa: White Fathers. http://mafr.net/files/pdf/lettre11ang.pdf (Accessed 10 February 2016).

[2] La commission nationale préparation centénaire, *Cent ans: Eglise du Mali* (15-20 Novembre 1988): pp.43-49.

[3] Daniel Coulibaly, *Histoire de l'Eglise au Mali* (AGEMPEM: 2007), pp.10, 45-175.

[4] These movements and Churches are of Charismatic Trend.

Education and Church Leadership Training

Both church families devoted time and resources to the training of future National Church leaders. The Catholic Church and missions trained several lay leaders.[5] They created three training centres and four seminaries for the training of catechists, moderators and priests. The Catholic Church understood that education was part of her mission. Almost every parish had its own school. there are two high schools, and several professional schools.

The Protestant churches and missions managed two training centres in the Bamanan language for pastors. The Protestant churches and missions manage four Bible schools and a theological and missiological seminary for training pastors and other church leaders in French. They do not focus so much on schools. They did more in literacy, and professional training.

Health Centres

All the mission agencies were involved in running medical activities in the villages they settled in. They contributed to improving the health of the local population. There are now Catholic and Protestant hospitals serving Christians and non-Christians alike.

Poverty Alleviation and Development

The churches and missions were sensitive to the great poverty of the local people. They engaged in several activities to alleviate poverty. Several Christian NGOs are active in Mali to share Christian love.

The Church and Other Religions in Mali

Though Mali is predominantly Muslim, the church is constantly growing. It covers the whole country in spite of some opposition. Christians maintain friendly relationships with Muslims and followers of traditional religions, and share meals with people of other faiths during religious celebrations such as Christmas and Easter. They receive return hospitality during the feasts of the other faiths. Funerals and weddings are opportunities for Christians and people of other faiths to mourn and rejoice together. The occupation of two thirds of Malian territory in 2012 by rebels and Islamists did not specifically target the church. All the Christians left the area because they felt insecure but no single Christian was killed or injured during that time. The 2015 killing of three young people in Timbuktu, including two Christians, had nothing to do with their faith.

Bibliography

Coulibaly, Daniel. Histoire de l'Eglise au Mali. AGEMPEM: 2007.

Diakité, Drissa. La dynamique sociale des mouvements confessionnels. Août 1998. Not Published.

La commission nationale préparation centénaire. Cent ans: Eglise du Mali. 15-20 Novembre 1988.

Letters to our Friends. Missionaries of Africa: White Fathers. http://mafr.net/files/pdf/lettre11ang.pdf (Accessed 10 February 2016).

[5] The training was done through a programme entitled: Voir, Evaluer, Agir (See, Evaluate, and Act) in Daniel Coulibaly, Histoire de l'Eglise au Mali (AGEMPEM: 2007), p.41.

(77) Christianity in Mauritius

James Rodney Curpanen

Religion	Pop 2010	Pct 2010	Pop 2025	Pct 2025	Gr Pct 1970 2025
Christians	408,000	32.7%	434,000	33.3%	0.4%
Independents	15,600	1.2%	24,000	1.8%	2.9%
African initiated	9,700	0.8%			
Protestants	126,000	10.1%	125,000	9.6%	-0.1%
Pentecostal	111,000	8.9%			
Roman Catholics	284,000	22.7%	290,000	22.2%	0.1%
Pentecostals/Charismatics	292,000	23.4%	340,000	26.1%	1.0%
Evangelicals	115,000	9.2%	125,000	9.6%	0.6%
Hindus	561,000	45.0%	548,000	42.0%	-0.2%
Muslims	207,000	16.6%	214,000	16.4%	0.2%
Baha'is	22,500	1.8%	35,000	2.7%	3.0%
Chinese folk-religionists	16,400	1.3%	19,000	1.5%	1.0%
Buddhists	3,100	0.2%	3,500	0.3%	0.9%
Sikhs	2,700	0.2%	3,400	0.3%	1.5%
adherents of traditional African religions	2,500	0.2%	2,800	0.2%	0.9%
adherents of new religious movements	700	0.1%	850	0.1%	1.3%
people professing no religion	23,300	1.9%	42,500	3.3%	4.1%
Total population	**1,248,000**	**100.0%**	**1,304,000**	**100.0%**	**0.3%**

Source: Centre for the Study of World Christianity (CSGC), Boston, Gordon-Conwell TS

Introduction

It is commonly believed that the first Christian service held on the island of Mauritius may have been of Reformed tradition when the Dutch first landed in September 1598 to take possession. The Dutch named the island after one of its Princes, Maurice de Nassau. The Dutch never really settled on the island. In March 1616, the first Roman Catholic mass was celebrated by a priest on his way to Madagascar.[1] The next Catholic visit, followed by a permanent presence, would be in October 1721. This was also the era of French rule. A prominent historical figure of the church is Father Jacques Désiré Laval who concentrated his work among former slaves.[2] Mgr Jean Margeot became the first Mauritian RC bishop in 1969 and cardinal in 1988.

---

[1] Breejan Burrun. *Histoire Des Religions Des Iles Maurice et Rodrigues.* Vacoas: Editions Le Printemps Ltée (2002): 11

[2] Benjamin Moutou. *Les Chrétiens de l'ile Maurice.* Port Louis: Best Graphics (1996): 256-258

The British captured the island in 1810. From then on, other churches established themselves, beginning with the Anglicans. The Rev. H. Shepherd served as the chaplain. In 1825, the first assembly met in an old gunpowder mill, which later became St James Cathedral, inaugurated in 1850 by the Catholic Bishop of Colombo, Mgr James Chapman.[3] The Diocese of Mauritius was created in 1854.

The Spread of Christianity

The Rev. John Le Brun arrived as a London Missionary Society envoy in May 1814. He started the Evangelical Independent Church in 1818. He worked mainly amongst the coloured population by opening schools in various places over the island and became known as the 'Apostle of free education'. The church's first church building was St John's in Port Louis, inaugurated in 1851.[4] The Reformed presence was reinforced in 1851 by the Church of Scotland. Their first pastor was the Rev. Patrick Beaton. In 1876, there was a fusion of the Evangelical Independent Church and the Church of Scotland which fell under Scotland until it became the Presbyterian Church of Mauritius, constituted by an act of parliament in 1979.

The Swedenborg (New Jerusalem) church arrived in 1846. The Seventh Day Adventists (SDA) organized themselves as a church in September 1914 under the leadership of Pastor Paul Badaut from France.[5] The Chinese Christian Assembly, which met from 1953 in the Presbyterian church of Rose Hill, then later on in Port Louis, became the Chinese Christian Fellowship in 1981. Early efforts of the 1930s and 1940s gave birth to several evangelical churches established officially in the late 1970s. In 1967, Pastor Aimé Cizeron from the Assembly of God (AOG) in France launched the local branch, commonly known as Mission Salut et Guérison. Several dissident churches are offshoots of the AOG, such as La Voix de la Délivrance, Eglise de Pentecôte Unie, and le Centre Evangélique Charismatique, for example. Others, such as the Christian Charismatic Church or the Christian Revival Centre, started independently. L'Eglise Chrétienne was born following charismatic renewal within the Roman Catholic Church, and constituted itself as a church in 1977.[6]

Early collaboration between the churches was in the form of an auxiliary of the British & Foreign Bible Society under the presidency of the British governor Robert Townsend Farquhar. Most collaborative efforts fell within the twentieth century. The Presbyterians and Anglicans included the Roman Catholics to form an Ecumenical Working Group. After thirty-five years, it opened up to include the Assemblies of God and the Fellowship of Christian Churches (FCCM). Prison Fellowship Mauritius has a wider co-operation. In the 1980s, Christians rather than churches created faith-based organizations such as Youth For Christ, YMCA, Gideon's, Child Evangelism Fellowship and Scripture Union. Membership increased rapidly to include Campus Crusade, IFES, YWAM, the Haggai Institute and numerous others.

At the end of the twentieth and early 21st centuries, more recently established churches began to form associations. FCCM started in the 1990s. To avoid the term 'denomination', several churches formed a Federation of Evangelical Churches. Similarly, Pentecostals created the Federation of Pentecostal Protestant Churches, the Baptists also have formed a federation and it seems the trend will continue.

The Roman Catholic, Anglican and SDA have maintained a strong presence in the formal educational field. From its rich heritage, the Presbyterians are left with a pre-primary school in the village of Pointe aux Piments. However, recently a couple of schools have been opened by independent Evangelicals. Several

---

[3] Ghislain Emmanuel. *A History of the Anglican Diocese of Mauritius (1810-19730 with an addendum (1973-2000).* Rose Hill: Edition de l'Océan Indien (2014): 5-32.

[4] L. Rivaltz Quenette, *L'Oeuvre du Révérend Jean Le Brun à l'ile Maurice* (Moka: Institut Mahatma Gandhi, [1982] 2014).

[5] Breejan Burrun, *1914-2014: 100 ans de L'Eglise Adventiste à Maurice* Vol 1. (Rose Hill: Cube Printing Ltée, 2014), 51.

[6] Burrun, *Histoire Religion*, 29-47.

churches run educational and literacy programmes that complement formal schooling in their community neighbourhoods or in poverty-stricken areas.

Training for clergy is a concern of all denominations. Since 1987, the Presbyterian, Anglican and Roman Catholic churches have jointly dispensed biblical and theological TEE-style training through Formation Biblique et Théologique. The Mauritius Bible Institute, in partnership with Vose Seminary Australia, is run by the evangelicals. All the churches depend heavily on overseas training.

During the years 2000 to 2008, with the support of Southern African Churches in Ministry with Uprooted (SACMUP), the Presbyterians took up the concerns of the displaced population from the islands of Chagos and Diego Garcia. Today, the Protestant Evangelical Church (PEC) continues this mission. The Roman Catholics, Presbyterians and PEC have solid ministries of alleviating poverty and working with the homeless. Several Baptist and Pentecostal churches now also move into these fields of service. Youth for Christ worked for many years with drug addicts and alcoholics within an island-wide network that included Hindu and Muslim groups. Ministry against domestic violence had a few proponents earlier on (among the RCs and Presbyterian), but today includes many religious groups and associations driven by a government programme. The evangelicals and Pentecostals are still diffidently considering their roles in this area.

A major challenge facing Mauritian Christians this century is obviously an ecumenism that would include as many denominations as possible. There have been hesitant attempts to set up fellowships, all short-lived. Division occurs across doctrinal lines, but also with regard to social involvement, national or worldwide issues such as HIV and AIDS, or the pastoral role of women. For a population of 1.3 million, having more than a hundred separate churches and denominations calls for deep reflection. Another great challenge is how to relate to other religions, while still maintaining the mission to evangelise. Only the Catholics, Anglicans and Presbyterians form part of the Council of Religion constituted in 2001, and which includes Hindus, Muslims, Buddhists and Baha'is. Together with the University of Mauritius, this Council runs a certificate programme on Inter-Faith and Peace.

Bibliography

Burrun, Breejun. *Histoire des Religions des îles Maurice et Rodrigue*. Vacoas: Editions le Printemps Ltée, 2002.

Burrun, Breejun. *1914-2014: 100 ans de L'Eglise Adventiste à Maurice, vol 1.* Rose Hill: Cube Printing Ltée, 2014.

Emmanuel, Ghislain. *A History of the Anglican Diocese of Mauritius (1810-1973).*

Rose Hill: Edition de l'Océan Indien, 2014 (1975).

Moutou, Benjamin. *Les Chrétiens de l'île Maurice.* Port Louis: Best Graphics, 1996.

Operation World, Prayer Movement: Mauritius. Last modified February 15, 2015. www.operationworld.org/maur

Quenette, L. Rivaltz. *L'Oeuvre du Révérend Jean Le Brun à l'île Maurice*. Moka: Institut Mahatma Gandhi, 2014(1982).

Vanmeerbeck, Evariste. *Vie du Révérend Jean Le Brun, Fondateur de L'Instruction Gratuite à Maurice.* Moka: Institut Mahatma Gandhi, 2014(1865).

Wikipedia, *Demographics Mauritius*. Last modified February 15, 2015. http://en.wikipedia.org/wiki/Demographics_of_Mauritius

(78) CHRISTIANITY IN MOROCCO

Yelins Mahtat

Religion	Pop 2010	Pct 2010	Pop 2025	Pct 2025	Gr Pct 1970 2025
Christians	31,300	0.1%	29,800	0.1%	-0.3%
Independents	4,400	0.0%	7,600	0.0%	3.7%
African initiated	4,300	0.0%			
Orthodox	610	0.0%	600	0.0%	-0.1%
Protestants	5,200	0.0%	5,300	0.0%	0.2%
Roman Catholics	20,000	0.1%	15,000	0.0%	-1.9%
Pentecostals/Charismatics	4,000	0.0%	5,500	0.0%	2.2%
Evangelicals	3,700	0.0%	4,400	0.0%	1.2%
Muslims	31,999,000	99.7%	38,134,000	99.7%	1.2%
Baha'is	32,300	0.1%	38,000	0.1%	1.1%
Jews	2,700	0.0%	2,100	0.0%	-1.7%
people professing no religion	42,100	0.1%	50,400	0.1%	1.2%
Total population	**32,108,000**	**100.0%**	**38,255,000**	**100.0%**	**1.2%**

Source: Centre for the Study of World Christianity (CSGC), Boston, Gordon-Conwell TS

Introduction

Christianity reached the shores of North Africa about the year AD 100. The stories of Christian martyrs, theologians and popes testify to the vigorous presence of the Christian faith in this region.[1] Yet, Morocco in particular, compared with Egypt or Lebanon, has not kept tangible traces of Christianity. This fact is mostly obvious starting from the Muslim conquest of the region in the late seventh century. Medieval and modern times were a period of tension and conflict between the two faiths and were marked by piracy and maritime warfare. This climate of animosity allowed little for the presence of Christianity in Morocco. It is only at the end of the nineteenth century that its presence and impact became strongly visible. Later, during colonial times, the Christian population increased considerably and the spiritual needs of the new European settlers required the establishment of a significant number of churches, schools and hospitals. After Independence, the European population decreased dramatically and there was a massive exodus of Christians from Morocco. At the end of the twentieth century, Morocco has become a major transit and, later, terminal destination for sub-Saharan citizens. Nowadays, they constitute the great majority of church members and the new face of Christianity in this country.

---

[1] Steele, Francis. R. Not in Vain: The Story of North African Mission. Pasadena, California: William Carey Library, 1981. 10

Antiquity

Along with other reasons, the absence of translations of the Bible in Tamazight and the failure of the Christian faith to take root in the local culture might explain the surprisingly quick disappearance of Christianity from Morocco.[2] In fact, it is only after 1900 that the Bible was first translated into the tongue of Imazighen, the autochthonous inhabitants of North Africa. The historians who are acquainted with such iconic North African Christian martyrs as St Perpetua and St Felicity; such well-known theologians and churchmen as Cyprian, Tertullian and the illustrious St Augustine; and such popes as St Victor I (c. 186-198), St Miltiades (311-314), and St Gelasius (492-496) can hardly explain the rapid disappearance of Christianity in later times. Christianity found its way to Morocco via Spain during the Roman period. Certain Amazigh tribes were Christian. Archaeological findings testify to the existence of Christian communities in Roman urban centres such as Volubilis.[3] Yet, during Muslim rule in Morocco in particular, it is merely diplomatic representatives, traders, mercenaries and captives who constituted the small community of Christians there.[4]

Pre-colonial Times

With the second half of the nineteenth century, the tide began to turn. As western powers gained interest in North Africa, Morocco became more accessible to a Christian presence and Christian missionary work. Father José Lerchundi (1836-1896), a Spanish Franciscan missionary and an Arabic scholar, founded a Spanish-Arabic press and a school in Tétouan where he was stationed. He also edited a book of Arabic grammar and later founded a hospital and a secondary school in Tangier. Other women and men of brave character and a particular passion for the spread of Biblical teaching travelled to Morocco. They set for themselves the main task of preaching the message of the gospel to the local inhabitants. The most remarkable among them was Emma Herdman (1844-1899). She was a highly educated woman with an excellent training in the Bible and remarkable talent for languages. She arrived in Tangier in 1884.[5] She was active in co-ordinating a network of itinerant Moroccan converts who were preaching and telling the gospel in many northern coastal cities and mostly in Fes. About the same time, E.F. Baldwin, a Southern Baptist preacher and the first Northern African Mission (NAM) missionary arrived in Tangier in 1884. The Tulloch Memorial Hospital and Hope House, both in Tangier, testify to the work of the NAM.[6] Other NAM missionaries arrived a few years later. In 1896, the Gospel Missionary Union, which originated in Kansas, sent five men to the cities of Fes, Meknes and Larache. They dressed as Arabs and conducted sermons in the souks and the streets.[7] Besides their translation of parts of the New or Old Testaments in Arabic or Tamazight, these missionary groups distributed Bibles. They also offered, some more than others and at different times, medical care, industrial work and schooling to local people in need.[8]

---

[2] Teissier, Henri. Histoire des Chrétien d'Afrique du Nord. Paris: Desclée/Proost France, 1991. 54-64
[3] Baida, Jamaa, Vincent Feroldi. Présence Chrétienne au Maroc, XIX et XX siècles. Rabat: Editions et Impressions Bouregreg, 2005. 9
[4] Baida, Jamaa, Vincent Feroldi. Présence Chrétienne au Maroc, XIX et XX siècles. Rabat: Bouregreg, 2005. 10
[5] Isaacs, Albert A. A Biographical Sketch Relative to the Missionary Labors of Emma Herdman in the Empire of Morocco. London: S.W. Partridge and Co, 1900
[6] Steele. *Not in Vain.* 60
[7] Phillips, Dennis H. "The American Missionary in Morocco." The Muslim World, LXV-1. (1975): 1-20
[8] See J.L. Miège (1955), and also W.N. Heggoy (1960) for more data on Faith Missions in Morocco since the end of the nineteenth century.

Colonial Times

In March 1912, Morocco fell under the French and Spanish protectorates. Chaplains accompanied the invading French armies. The French *Fréres Mineurs*, a group of Franciscan voluntary army chaplains, arrived in Morocco during the French military campaign in 1908. During the second half of the nineteenth century, Morocco had already signed treaties to allow the Christian population religious freedom. The Moroccan-Spanish armistice agreement in 1860 had opened the door to the activities of the Catholic Church in Northern Morocco. The Franco-Spanish treaty regarding the right to religious freedom was signed on 27th November 1912.[9]

The French authorities under Hubert Lyautey's (1854-1934) command between 1912 and 1925 did not contribute to the progress of the missionary effort. The famous *politique musulmane* conducted by the French *résident général* avoided any interference with Moroccan spiritual affairs and thus put a brake on the propagation of the Christian faith. Lyautey's prohibition of missionary work amongst the Tamazight-speaking inhabitants of Morocco was met with disapproval in church circles.[10] The Catholic Church mainly targeted the European population while the non-official Faith Mission Protestants remained openly active in proselytism. In 1912, Franciscan nuns arrived and started offering their services to the less fortunate among the local population in infirmaries, girls' boarding schools, dispensaries, hospitals and schools.[11] Nonetheless, a few missionaries, namely, Father André Peyriguère (1883-1959) and Father Charles André Poissonnier (1897-1938), to name only two, preferred to maintain a respectful proximity to the inhabitants of peripheral Morocco away from political circles. Poissonnier, a Franciscan, lived close to the locals and offered medical help in his dispensary in the village of Tazert, near Marrakesh. Father Peyriguère, who explicitly opposed the use of Christianity for colonial purposes, set himself the task of healing the sick and assisting the needy in his dispensary in el-Kbab in the Middle Atlas. In 1940, Father Othon de Launay, a former officer, founded a dispensary in the ancient city of Meknes.[12]

In 1928, Mohammed ben Abdeljalil (1883-1962), a Muslim-born and well-educated young Moroccan converted to Christianity. Jean-Mohammed, as his name was after his conversion, was born to an elite family of Moroccan nationalists from the religiously prestigious city of Fes. This conversion was perceived in Moroccan circles not just as mere apostasy but as an act of treason. In Moroccan intellectual and militant circles, 'Christianization' was portrayed as a threat to national identity and unity, and was felt to be a parallel strategy to colonial rule. Further tension occurred as the so-called 'Berber' *dahir* was promulgated by the French authorities in 1930. It was perceived as a colonial divide-and-conquer strategy. In response, nationalists used Islamic slogans to mobilize the Moroccan public around questions of Muslim identity and Arab-Amazigh solidarity.[13] Inevitably, both Jean-Mohammed's conversion and the 'Berber' *dahir* cast shades of suspicion on Christian activity.

Opposition to missionary work was not limited exclusively to Moroccan militants. A few years before the World War II, the Christian community, including both secular and religious individuals and priests, set themselves apart from the official political line and encouraged more understanding and dialogue with Moroccans and Islam. In 1944, the ideas of Paul Buttin, a French lawyer and a businessman who arrived in Morocco in the 1920s, in his magazines *Terres d'Afrique* (1944) and *Méditerannée* (1946), sent an explicit call to the Muslim, Christian and Jewish populations to join in the human community and transcend nationalistic attitudes. He also, among other churchmen, denounced the injustice and cruelty of the colonial

[9] Baida, Feroldi. 35
[10] Baida, Feroldi. 49
[11] Le Maroc Catholique. No.10, 300-305 and No.11, 333-339, October and November, 1932.
[12] Baida, Feroldi. 93
[13] Ramon Lourido and Guy Martinet. Les Mutations de l'Eglise au Maroc au XXe Siècle in Histoire des Chrétiens d'Afrique du Nord. Henri Teisssier, director of study. Paris: Desclée. 151-152

authorities. The Catholic Church was by then in opposition to the superior attitude of the French central authorities and started a new phase of dialogue with Muslims.[14]

The Universal Declaration of Human Rights in 1948 expressed the high hopes of the international community in protecting fundamental human rights. The demands of nations for regaining their sovereignty became more urgent than ever before. In 1952, Mgr Lefèvre, appointed apostolic vicar in Rabat in 1947, had already published a letter where he recommended the Catholic Church in Morocco establish relationships of dialogue and justice.[15] This period witnessed the birth of magazines and study and research centres promoting Muslim-Christian encounters and reflection.

Post-colonial Times

Morocco gained its political independence in 1956. With the major exodus of Europeans, the Christian population significantly decreased. The Catholic Church abandoned proselytism in favour of serving the entire society. It opened its facilities exclusively to the Moroccan youth. Nowadays, there are fifteen schools (offering education to 12,000 students). In the years 1980-1981, a research and study centre, *La Source*[16], was opened in the capital Rabat to serve Moroccan researchers. The invitation which Hassan II addressed to Pope John Paul II and the latter's visit to Casablanca in 1985 prepared the ground for more encounters between Islam and Catholicism. In 2005, a cultural centre, including a library and an exhibition hall, was inaugurated in Beni Mellal, Southern Morocco. In 1977, an Islamo-Christian Research Group (GRIC) saw the light.

Starting from the 1990s, and thanks to the increase of Moroccan economic co-operation with sub-Saharan African countries, migrants, students and professionals started living in the country. The church regained the vibrant life it once had. There would, nowadays, be about 30,000 baptized foreign Christians in Morocco. Among them, 4,000 are practising Catholics, while 3,000 are practising Protestants affiliated with the official church (*Eglise Evangélique au Maroc*). In addition to that, non-official migrant churches, mostly Congolese and Nigerian, bring together 4,000 individuals.[17] Due to social pressure and the law against proselytism, Moroccan Christians are compelled to remain silent. According to various sources, their number would be about 5,000.[18]

Both official and non-official churches contribute to the vast diversity of religious denominations and practices. This Christian minority will set the stage for an ethnically and more religiously diverse Morocco.

Bibliography

Baida, Jamaa, Vincent Feroldi. *Présence Chrétienne au Maroc, XIX et XX siècles*. Rabat: Bouregreg, 2005

Coyault, Bernard. L'Africanisation de l'Eglise Evangélique au Maroc: Revitalisation d'une Institution Religieuse et Dynamique d'Individualisation in *l'Année du Maghreb*, 11 (2014)

Davis, Ila Marie. *A Gleam of Light: The Trials and Triumphs of a Century of Missionary Work in Morocco*. Kansas City: Gospel Missionary Union, 1989

---

[14] Baida, Feroldi. 103-105

[15] Lefèvre, Amédée L. L'Eglise du Maroc, Quelques Directives (1950-1957). Rabat: Faits et Idées, 1959. 28-35

[16] Later to become Institut Oecuménique de Théologie al Mowafaqa which was established in 2012 thanks to the joint initiative of the two official Churches, l'Eglise Catholique and l'Eglise Evangélique au Maroc. Ref. www.almowafaqa.com

[17] Coyault, Bernard. L'Africanisation de l'Eglise Evangélique au Maroc: Revitalisation d'une Institution Religieuse et Dynamique d'Individualisation in *l'Année du Maghreb*, no. 11 (2014). 81-103

[18] Morocco 2014 International Religious Freedom Report, ref.www.state.gov/documents/organization/ 238682.pdf (accessed Jan.,20 2016)

Heggoy, Willy Norman. *Fifty Years of Evangelical Missionary work in North Africa, 1881-1931*. Ph.D. thesis. The Hartford Seminary Foundation, 1960

Isaacs, Albert A. *A Biographical Sketch Relative to the Missionary Labors of Emma Herdman in The Empire of Morocco*. London: S.W. Partridge and Co, 1900

Lefèvre, Amédée L. *Eglise du Maroc, Quelques Directives (1950-1957)*. Rabat: Faits et Idées, 1959

Lourido Diaz, Ramon, Guy Martinet. *Les Mutations de l'Eglise au Maroc au XX Siècle* in *Histoire des Chrétiens d'Afrique du Nord*. Henri Teisssier (director of study). Paris: Descleé, 1991

Miège, Jean-Louis. *Les Missions Protestantes au Maroc (1875-1905)* in Hespres, Vol. 42. 1955. 1rst and 2nd quarter

Phillips, Dennis H. '*The American Missionary in Morocco*.' The Muslim World, LXV-1. (1975)

Steele, Francis. R. *Not in Vain: The Story of North African Mission*. Pasadena, California: William Carey Library, 1981

(79) CHRISTIANITY IN MOZAMBIQUE

Felicidade N. Chirinda

Religion	Pop 2010	Pct 2010	Pop 2025	Pct 2025	Gr Pct 1970 2025
Christians	12,572,000	51.7%	19,957,000	54.7%	3.1%
Independents	3,140,000	12.9%	4,800,000	13.2%	2.9%
African initiated	2,971,000	12.2%			
Orthodox	800	0.0%	800	0.0%	0.0%
Protestants	3,266,000	13.4%	5,400,000	14.8%	3.4%
Pentecostal	1,351,000	5.6%			
Baptist	458,000	1.9%			
Adventist	400,000	1.6%			
Reformed, Presbyterian	357,000	1.5%			
Holiness	243,000	1.0%			
Anglicans	135,000	0.6%			
Roman Catholics	5,291,000	21.8%	8,400,000	23.0%	3.1%
Pentecostals/Charismatics	4,694,000	19.3%	5,900,000	16.2%	1.5%
Evangelicals	2,487,000	10.2%	3,679,000	10.1%	2.6%
adherents of traditional African religions	7,411,000	30.5%	9,768,000	26.8%	1.9%
Muslims	4,186,000	17.2%	6,500,000	17.8%	3.0%
Hindus	38,600	0.2%	50,000	0.1%	1.7%
Chinese folk-religionists	4,400	0.0%	8,000	0.0%	4.0%
Baha'is	2,900	0.0%	5,000	0.0%	3.6%
Buddhists	2,100	0.0%	4,000	0.0%	4.4%
Jews	240	0.0%	200	0.0%	-1.2%
people professing no religion	104,000	0.4%	170,000	0.5%	3.3%
Total population	**24,321,000**	**100.0%**	**36,462,000**	**100.0%**	**2.7%**

Source: Centre for the Study of World Christianity (CSGC), Boston, Gordon-Conwell TS

Introduction

The interest in investigating the way in which Christianity was introduced and developed in Mozambique has gradually grown, mainly among foreign researchers. Their major interest has been to understand the relationship between the Roman Catholic Church and the Protestant Church, the decolonization process, regional integration in Southern Africa, and Church history during the liberation struggle and the post-Independence context in Mozambique.[1]

[1] Robert Neil Faris, "A Changing Paradigm of Mission in the Protestant Churches in Mozambique: A Case Study of

The Birth of Christianity and its Impact

Christianity was introduced to Mozambique in 1498, by Vasco da Gama, a Portuguese explorer.[2] Da Gama was on his trip of discovering the maritime route to India when, in January 1498, he arrived at the port of Inhambane in the south of Mozambique; in March that same year, he berthed at the port of Ilha de Moçambique, where the first Christian worship service and Holy Communion were held. This is considered to have been the beginning of Christianity in Mozambique. Islam had already been established in the region. The two religions lived in confrontation and hatred; therefore, the local people were forced to choose the religion that could protect them, by giving them their land and wealth.

It is a fact that the major Portuguese intention in Africa and India was commerce and trade in gold and spices. That is why twenty-three merchant-ships were sent to Vasco da Gama, during his presence on the east coast of Africa, so that he could establish a strong Portuguese presence in the region. Because of the way in which Christianity was introduced into the country, historians affirm that the Portuguese arrived with guns in one hand and with the Bible and the Cross in the other. The guns terrorized the population because they were used for coercion, for domination and for the destruction of people's lives, including their rich culture.[3]

In spite of the above, Mozambique owes to the Roman Catholic Church the introduction of Christianity. When missionaries like the Jesuits and Dominicans arrived, they established the first mission in 1560 and initiated evangelization of the natives in Zambezia, Manica, Sofala and Tete. They were successful in converting many people, including King Monomotapa. These conversions were undertaken through the efforts of Gonçalo da Silveira. This missionary used to be accompanied by soldiers in his evangelistic work, because of confrontations with Muslims. This fact caused suspicion and the population convinced King Monomotapa that da Silveira was a spy. In March 1561, da Silveira was assassinated under the orders of the King.[4] The spread of Christianity was thus full of betrayal, bloodshed and injustice, because the evangelistic work was mixed with greed for power and money, an image that damaged the Christian faith and relationships at that time.

As mentioned above, Catholicism remained for more than two hundred years the main Christian religion in Mozambique. However, in spite of all the privileges that the Roman Catholic Church enjoyed, it could not provide the native population with more than a rudimentary education.[5]

The Impact of Protestantism

During the second half of the nineteenth century, South Africa became a privileged destination for many people, including Mozambican citizens. The main reason that caused people to migrate to South Africa was the discovery of gold and diamonds, whose industry provided job opportunities to Mozambicans who became workers in the mines. The other reason was the war that devastated Southern Africa. Many immigrants were contacted by Protestant churches to be converted, and those who were converted

---

Eduardo Mondlane" (PhD Thesis 2007), 12.

[2] Antonio Garcia, SJ, "Pêro de Covilhã, o Primeiro Católico Europeu a Visitar Sofala" em *História de Moçambique Cristão,* 17-28; A.C. Saunders, *Historia Social dos Escravos e Libertos Negros em Portugal (1441-1555)* (Lisboa, Portugal: Temas Portugueses 1982), 75.

[3] Justo L González, "O Reino Vândalo da Africa" em *História Ilustrada do Cristianismo – A Era dos Reformadores até à Inconclusa-* 2 ed.rev. (São Paulo: Vida Nova, 2011), 230-231; Simão Chamango, "Chegada do Evangelho em Moçambique" (Maputo, 1987), 8.

[4] Jan Butselaar, "Os Portugueses em Moçambique" em Africanos, Missionários e Colonialistas, 20; António Garcia, "Pêro de Covilhã, o Primeiro Católico Europeu a visitar Sofala 1489 e, Gonçalo da Silveira, Proto- Mártir de Moçambique e da África Austral" em *História de Moçambique Cristão,* 17-32; 91-93.

[5] Faris "A Changing Paradigm of Mission in the Protestant Churches in Mozambique," 12.

introduced the Protestant faith to Mozambique. During their holidays or home visits, they started their own churches. Some of them were later followed by white missionaries who had started the historic churches. Others developed as African Independent Churches (AIC's).[6] The Portuguese colonial regime did not welcome the proliferation of Protestants. At the beginning, they considered those who attended these Protestant churches as ignorant people, so their activities were restricted to the south of Mozambique, and this was interpreted as these Protestant churches being pushed to the margins,[7] and when they started building schools, hospitals, agricultural settlements and providing theological training, the hatred only increased. Protestants were persecuted, imprisoned and assassinated[8] but, much of the time, the reasons were not disclosed. The Protestants recognized that working as individual churches was dangerous. Therefore, they agreed to work ecumenically, and in 1948 they launched the Christian Council of Mozambique.

Ecumenism

The Mozambicans received from the institutions under the Christian Council an education that provided them with an alternative identity. This identity identified them as human beings created in God's image, as Christians and as Mozambicans. The conditions were created for them to use artistically their vernacular languages in the fight against injustice with pride. Theological training challenged their inferiority complex. Ecumenism was also a tool by which the church interacted locally and internationally with others. African Christians learned how to listen and critically analyze and question social and religious issues. Critical analysis allowed them to understand their roles as peace-makers and to foresee the future of their country and the church. Many Mozambicans, women and men, gave their lives in order to liberate their country not only from colonialism, but also from oppression and injustice.

Mozambique became independent in June 1975, becoming a Popular Republic. After Independence, churches experienced new forms of marginalization. They had to face the Marxist-Leninist ideology in order to defend and to remain accountable for their Christian faith. Many Christians found themselves in a dilemma of loyalties between their faith and the political party, while others felt a strong sense of betrayal.[9] As usual in such crises, religion had to find its place in the new social order. This made church leaders unite their efforts in reflecting on the kind of relationship they needed to maintain with the state. The answer was given in Paul's letter to the Romans (13:1-7), and it reinforced the affirmation of the church reformers Luther and Calvin.[10] The church was also challenged by a new war between Mozambicans, when the National Movement of Resistance (RENAMO) was created, forcing the country to face a new war that lasted for sixteen years. This war was supported by the apartheid regime of South Africa and other countries from abroad. Mozambique's infrastructure and people's lives were destroyed; the country was bleeding and badly wounded. Many people had abandoned religion and the church, but they came back and

---

[6] Jan Butselaar, "Três Povos, Três Culturas" (8, 16); Patrick Harries "Cristianismo" em *Junod e as Sociedades Africanas* (Maputo: CIEDIMA, 2007), 75-95; Teresa Cruz e Silva, "A Missão Suiça, Religião e Sociedade" em *Igrejas Protestantes e Consciência Política no Sul de Moçambique: O Caso da Missão Suiça.* (1930-1974) (Maputo: CIEDIMA, 2001), 40.

[7] Charles Biber. "Cent Ans au Mozambique: Le Parcours d'une Minorité" (Lausanne, 1992), 9.

[8] Teresa Cruz e Silva, "Porquê Mataram Manganhela?" em *Zedequias Manganhela – Uma Biografia Contextualizada.* (1912-1972) (Maputo: Norprint 2014),114.

[9] Felicidade Naume Chirinda "Positive Impact of Autonomy and Identity Formation" in *Autonomy of the Igreja Presbiteriana de Moçambique – Pastoral Concern for Liberation.* (PhD Thesis, University of Pretoria, 2012), 79-84; Faris "A Changing Paradigm of Mission," 12.

[10] Félix Abena Mbembe, "Luther, Calvin et les enjeux de la cohabitation entre l'Église et l'État" en *Eglise et Pouvoir Politique en Afrique" Perspectives Théologiques et Historiques.* Simon K Dossou (éditor scientifique) (Éditions CLÉ, Yaoundé and CETA, Nairobi 2013),151-156.

a new revival was started, while the church continued to work ecumenically. So the Christian Council of Mozambique suggested its envoys meet with Renamo in the diaspora, while internally it was in dialogue with the government. The church worked tirelessly in mobilizing the community for prayer and worship, and in civic education for young people and adults. A ceasefire was achieved in 1990 followed by a long process of discussion that ended with the signing of a peace agreement at Sant'Egídio in Rome, which opened the door to co-operation between the Protestant and Roman Catholic churches. In 1994, the first democratic elections took place.[11] A new social order was established and the churches found their place in the secular state.

The Church Facing New Challenges and Opportunities

As demonstrated above, the number of new churches and Christian associations has increased in recent years. This compelled us to ask why this increase and what it meant for the development of Christianity in Africa.

The political changes after the 1992 Peace Agreement transformed the country from a centralized economy to a market one. This new situation created opportunities for civil society – that is, it increased involvement in social issues that had been reserved for the state. The churches gained a new vision and worked ecumenically as never before.[12] Thus, they were able to mobilize the whole community thoroughly, in order to continue the pacification of the country, as well as gathering and destroying the weapons (the *Transformação de Armas em Enxadas* [TAE] Project. In English "Transforming Guns into Hoes").This also mobilized society to embrace the new social order positively. The churches were also involved in health issues, especially the struggle against HIV and AIDS, malaria and tuberculosis, as well as in the defence of our planet, through their involvement in issues of climate change as well as in the Extractive Industry Programme, by preventing conflict between the companies and the population living in the surrounding areas. The Christian Council of Mozambique is a good example of the defence of the population's rights.[13]

These new trends helped the Protestant church to recognize and to affirm working together with the Catholic Church as well as with Muslims and Hindus. This is the example of the Electoral Observatory, composed of different religious institutions and national NGOs. While the churches were making efforts to reduce political intolerance, the RENAMO leader Afonso Dhlakama decided to go back to the bush in October 2013. The Christian churches, Muslim leaders and national NGOs were organized by the Electoral Observatory to initiate a new dialogue with Afonso Dhlakama. They travelled many times to Gorongosa in order to meet him. The dialogue was multi-faceted, because the team also met the Republic President Armando Guebuza, the leaders of the Mozambican Parliament, the senior leaders of Renamo in Maputo and the wider community, in order to mobilize them for peaceful participation in elections and for their monitoring. This is one of the powerful examples of how the new trends pressed the churches and religious leaders into exercising their pastoral care and counselling ministries.

During this critical period, religious leaders created another ecumenical faith-based organisation called the Council of Religions in Mozambique or COREM. One of its objectives has been to address the issue of physical health, such as the prevention of infant and mother deaths, malnutrition, child abuse, premature

---

[11] Iraê Baptista Ludinin, "Participação Política do Cidadão numa Sociedade em Mudança: desafio das abstenções nas eleições de 2008 e de 2009 em Moçambique" em *Moçambique Democrático Espelhado nas Eleições Autárquicas, Presidenciais, Legislativas e Assembleias Provinciais de 2008-2009* (Maputo, CIEDIMA, SARL 2012),14; Nicholas Otieno and Hugh McCullum, *Journey of Hope – Towards a New Ecumenical Africa* (Geneva: WCC Publications 2005), 84.

[12] Otieno and McCullum, "Journey of Hope," 87.

[13] Ludin, "Moçambique Democrático," 44.

marriages, concerns on education and other issues around physical, spiritual and psychological health. When President Armando Guebuza and Afonso Dhlakama signed the 'Hostilities Cessation Agreement' on 5th September 2014, religious leaders announced the creation of a network for reconciliation and peace: RRRP (Religious Network for Reconciliation and Peace). This new network challenged the religious community in Mozambique to demonstrate the relevance of its unity and willingness to address and assure reconciliation, peace and dignity for all citizens.

The Place and Role of Christianity in Mozambique Today

My experience as a theologian and clergywoman shows that Christianity in Mozambique is a blessing to society. My affirmation is sustained by the calls and appeals that are made by society in general, which urge the church to take the lead against violence, road accidents, murder, HIV and AIDS, land conflicts, kidnapping, human trafficking and the trafficking of human organs – besides other issues that dehumanize and humiliate human society. Such appeals include leadership accountability as an indispensable ingredient for reconciliation and peace, while they serve to remind religious leaders that they are an integral part of society and have to contextualize their theology.

Bibliography

Biber, C. *Cent Ans Au Mozambique: Le Parcous d'une Minorité.* Éditions du Soc, 1992.

Butsellar, J.V. *Africanos, Missionários e Colonialistas: Fundadores da Igreja Presbiteriana de Moçambique (1880-1896).* Maputo-Tempográfica, 1987

Chamango, S. 'Chegada do Evangelho em Moçambique'. Manuscrito não publicado, Maputo, 1987.

Chirinda, F.N. 'Autonomy of the Igreja Presbiteriana de Moçambique (IPM)- Pastoral Concern for Liberation.' PhD Thesis, University of Pretoria, 2012.

Chitando, E. 'Our Burning Issues – A Pan African Response.' Nairobi, 2013.

Cruz e Silva, T. *Igrejas Protestantes e Consciência Política no Sul de Moçambique: O Caso da Missão Suiça (1930-1974).* Maputo, CIEDIMA, 2001.

Direcção Nacional de Assuntos Religiosos. Unpublished Manuscript. Maputo, 2014.

Faris, Neil R. 'A Changing Paradigm of Mission in the Protestant Churches of Mozambique: A Case Study of Eduardo Mondlane.' PhD Thesis, University of Cape Town, 2007.

Garcia, A SJ. *História de Moçambique Cristão.* Volume 1. Lourenço Marques, 1972.

Gonçalves, J.J. *Protestantismo em Africa – Contribuição para o Estudo do Protestantismo na Africa Portuguesa.* Volume 2, Lisboa, 1960.

González, J.L. *História Ilustrada do Cristianismo – A Era dos Mártires até à Era dos Sonhos Frustrados.* Brasil: Vida Nova, 2011.

Harries, P. *Junod e as Sociedades Africanas – Impacto dos Missionários Suiços na Africa Austral.* Maputo: CIEDIMA, 2007.

Ludin, I.B. *Moçambique Democrático Espelhado nas Eleições Autárquicas, Presidenciais, Legislativas e Assembleias Provinciais de 2008-2009.* Maputo, CIEDIMA 2012.

Mbembe, F.A. 'Église et Pouvoir Politique en Afrique – Perspectives Théologique et Historiques'. Éditions CLÉ, Yaoundé and CETA: Nairobi, 2013.

Otieno, N. & McCullum, H. *Journey of Hope – Towards a New Ecumenical Africa.* WCC Publications, 2005.

Pereira, M.V e Chirinda, F.N. *Tempo de Mudar, Tempo de Agir – Mulheres Reflectindo Teologicamente sobre a Problemática do HIV e SIDA.* Pietermaritzburg: Círculo de Teólogas Africanas Conscientes, 2007.

Saunders, A.C. *História Social dos Escravos e Libertos Negros em Portugal.* Lisboa, 1982.

(80) CHRISTIANITY IN NAMIBIA

Maria Kapere

Religion	Pop 2010	Pct 2010	Pop 2025	Pct 2025	Gr Pct 1970 2025
Christians	2,002,000	91.2%	2,764,000	92.1%	2.2%
Independents	268,000	12.2%	343,000	11.4%	1.7%
African initiated	247,000	11.3%			
Protestants	1,457,000	66.4%	1,910,000	63.6%	1.8%
Lutheran	1,134,000	51.7%			
Reformed, Presbyterian	151,000	6.9%			
Anglicans	70,000	3.2%			
Pentecostal	32,200	1.5%			
Adventist	24,700	1.1%			
Roman Catholics	420,000	19.2%	510,000	17.0%	1.3%
Pentecostals/Charismatics	348,000	15.9%	445,000	14.8%	1.7%
Evangelicals	296,000	13.5%	357,000	11.9%	1.3%
adherents of traditional African religions	129,000	5.9%	130,000	4.3%	0.0%
Baha'is	10,500	0.5%	14,500	0.5%	2.2%
Muslims	7,500	0.3%	11,000	0.4%	2.6%
Jews	2,500	0.1%	3,800	0.1%	2.8%
people professing no religion	42,100	1.9%	78,800	2.6%	4.3%
Total population	**2,194,000**	**100.0%**	**3,002,000**	**100.0%**	**2.1%**

Source: Centre for the Study of World Christianity (CSGC), Boston, Gordon-Conwell TS

Introduction

Namibia is situated in the south-western corner of Africa. It shares borders with Angola in the north, South Africa in the south, Botswana in the east, Zambia and Zimbabwe in the north-east and the Atlantic Ocean to the west. Its total land area is about 824,295 sq km. It has a population of 2.4 million according to the population census of 2012.

The country is predominantly arid, a desert or semi-desert country, of which the Namib Desert in the west stretches the full length of the coastline from the Kunene River in the north to the Orange River in the south.

Namibia was occupied by the Germans from 1884 to 1915. During World War I, the South Africans took over from the Germans and administered the country as a mandate, until after World War II when it annexed the country.

The repressive apartheid laws were also enforced in Namibia by the South African government, and this led to discontent among the black and coloured populace, which eventually led to the formation of the liberation movement, the South-West Africa Peoples Organization (SWAPO) in 1961. Namibia gained independence from South Africa on 21st March 1990. Religious freedom is enshrined in the constitution.

The history of Christianity in Namibia started when a certain group of Namibians, mostly the Nama and Coloureds, crossed the Orange River from present-day South Africa and brought Christianity with them, having learned it from the Dutch.[1] They crossed the Orange River after 1652, settling in southern and central Namibia. The London Missionary Society (LMS) arrived in the area in 1812 and formed an interdenominational organization that included Anglicans, Methodists, Presbyterians and Congregationalists.

Their biggest achievement was the translation of the Bible into one of the Namibian languages, Khoekhoengowab (Damara-Nama). Lack of supplies and trouble with Namibians over grazing land led the LMS to request the Rhenish Mission Society (RMS), which consisted of various Lutheran and other Protestant churches in Germany, to take over their work.

The RMS had arrived in 1842 with the first German colonists and was carrying out an aggressive campaign to convert Namibians, dismissing African indigenous religions and culture as inferior to Christianity and western culture. Anglican mission work in Namibia can be traced back to 1860, while the Roman Catholic Church arrived in 1882. Both these churches encountered many difficulties, including German government prohibitions against working in the existing Lutheran mission fields. The first congregation of the Dutch Reformed Church was established in 1898 at Warmbad in southern Namibia.

From the 1920s, Namibian Christians began to create self-governing, self-supporting, self-propagating and self-theologizing churches. In 1946, the African Methodist Episcopal Church was established in Namibia as one of the African Initiated or Independent Churches (AICs). A variety of larger and smaller independent churches were established in Namibia. Examples are the messianic tradition of Chief Hendrik Witbooi (1890), the Ethiopian Church secessions (1923, 1955), and Zionist Prophetic Churches after 1955. Most of these groups are characterized by features typical of African Independent Churches (AICs). They were founded by means of a dynamic process of secession from mainline churches (Ethiopians) or Pentecostal churches (Zionists). Most of them centre on a specific leader or at times two leaders, and can thus be termed 'messianic' or 'prophetic'. The leaders of Ethiopian churches tend to be messianic while the leaders of the Zionist churches tend to be prophetic. Some of these churches are quite close to their mainline counterparts and have become strong and well-respected denominations in Namibia.

The first efforts of independent Christian leadership in Namibia are to be found in the work of catechists and evangelists who continued their ministries, after the departure of the missionaries (lay preachers and lay church planters). Several churches were built by indigenous leaders and tribal chiefs. Jonker Afrikaner built the first church in Windhoek in 1840, and preached to the Herero community. Some other Orlam chiefs followed his example in establishing the churches within their tribal areas, e.g. Chief Hendrik Hendriks of the Velskoendraers in 1846, and the Herero Chief Zeraua in 1864 at Otjimbingwe, who contributed 10,000 bricks for a new church building. This was a trend that resulted from Commando Church of Chief Hendrik Witbooi of Gibeon after 1890.

In 1971, during the struggle for liberation from South African administration, the country's churches rejected apartheid and the South African occupation of Namibia in the famous 'Open Letter of 1971'. Addressed to the South African Prime Minister, John Vorster, the letter demanded that South Africa co-operate with the United Nations to make Namibia an independent state.

The publication of the Open Letter broke the silence of the church on social and political issues and sparked a wave of protests throughout the country, including strikes by workers in Walvis Bay, Windhoek and Tsumeb, and brought Namibia to international attention. The letter clearly stated: 'If we, as the Church, remain silent much longer, we will become liable for the life and future of our country and its

[1] Paul John Isaak, *The Story of the Paulinum Seminary in Namibia*. Windhoek: Namibia Publishing House, 2013:pp. vii-xv

people.' Thus, the churches committed themselves to 'see to it that the Human Rights (Charter) be put into operation, that South West Africa (Namibia) may become a self-sufficient and independent state'. Church newsletters spread the message to the country and beyond. Thereafter, the churches provided institutionalized resistance to the South African regime: church buildings offered sanctuary, and pastors and laity formulated an ideology and action plan for liberation.

The Spread and Existence of Christianity in Namibia

With one of the world's biggest gemstone diamond deposits, large quantities of copper, zinc, uranium and salt, vast tracts of land ideal for cattle farming, and fish-laden coastal waters, from the 1840s Namibia attracted European settlers. With the coming of European settlers, the Germans in 1884 made the territory a colony known as South West Africa and began a sustained drive to subdue the indigenous communities through 'protection treaties', which granted German companies the right to 'develop' the area economically. The settlers grew rich, but the indigenous people became impoverished. Lutheran missionaries who arrived with the Germans attempted to Christianize Namibia based upon the strategy of the four Cs: Commerce, Christianity, Civilization and Conquest.

Such a history of the four Cs was brought its climax when, in 1904, Kaiser Wilhelm II sent a German commander, General Lother von Trotha, to crush the liberation struggle in Namibia by fair means or foul.

However, the Africans were conscious of the strategy of the four Cs and started to employ their own discourse based on African spirituality with its anthropological core value of *Ubuntu* ('I am because we are and, since we are, therefore I am'). Instead of rejecting Christianity outright, however, Namibians Africanized the religion by contextualizing the gospel, for example, by holding onto their faith in the Triune God.[2]

Recent Major Trends and Developments at a National Level for Christianity

Namibia remains a predominantly Christian country. The three Evangelical Lutheran churches the Evangelical Lutheran Church in Namibia (ELCIN), the Evangelical Lutheran Church in the Republic of Namibia (ELCRN) and the German Evangelical Church (GELC) – have the largest Christian membership. The Roman Catholic Church with 340,000, the Anglican Church with 200,000, the Seventh Day Adventist Church in Caprivi with a membership of about 30,000, the African Methodist Church with 80,000, and the Dutch Reformed Church with 35,000. There are about more than 200 Pentecostal and Charismatic churches with membership varying between two hundred to five thousand members each. The Namibian Christian Apostle and Prophet Association also applied for membership.

Christianity in Namibia is growing. New Pentecostal and Charismatic churches are being established daily, even to the despair of mainline and other Pentecostal churches.

However, the main challenge for the church in Namibia remains its prophetic mission. Before Independence, during the Liberation War and the struggle against colonialism, unity among the major churches in Namibia was solid, vibrant and prophetic. Leaders of the six member churches of the Council of Churches in Namibia (CCN) formed a united front and expressed themselves against oppression, discrimination and racial segregation with the contempt that it deserved.

The issue of social economic justice remains complex, challenging and critical. Issues like poverty, unemployment, especially youth, land, gender justice, HIV/AIDS, ethnicity, racism and tribalism are on the rise. Political tolerance is not practised. Many people are asking why the Voice of CCN has become quiet. CCN started a dialogue forum in late 2014 which became more vocal and visible in 2015. Reconciliation,

[2] Isaak, *The Story of the Paulinum Seminary in Namibia,* vii.

peace and reconstruction should be seriously reflected upon by the church and relevant strategies, with plans and actions mapped out and implemented.

Membership of CCN churches has grown from six at Independence to seventeen. Even the Association for Pentecostal and Charismatic churches in Namibia has become a member.

The Christian Leaders in Namibia are challenged to give direction, and it becomes inevitable that collaboration and co-operation amongst the denominations is enhanced.

Relations with Other Major Faith Traditions

According to the Constitution, Namibian remains a secular state (Article 1) where all persons shall have the right to freedom to practise any religion and to manifest such practice (Article 21). Historically, through the determined efforts of its people, Namibia gained its independence and immediately implemented a model constitution, guaranteeing fundamental human rights and freedoms as a sovereign, democratic, unitary and secular state.

By definition, a secular state is a concept whereby a state or country purports to be officially neutral in matters of religion and to treat all its citizens equally, regardless of religion, and claims to avoid preferential treatment for a citizen from a particular religion over other religions. Thus, in Namibia we have a very peaceful co-existence of the various faiths.

Such an atmosphere of peace and religious tolerance is illustrated by the fact that Namibians have adapted Christianity and African indigenous religious rituals by means of indigenous music, songs, artwork and forms of worship. Drumming, singing and dance have attracted people to Sunday services and church-sponsored youth gatherings. Such integration has particularly motivated Christian youth.

Furthermore, despite the fact that more than 90% of Namibians claim to be Christian, other major religions such as African Traditional Religion, Islam, Judaism, etc. are given equal status in Namibia.

Key Instruments which Churches in Namibia have Developed to Contribute to Christian Unity

At the outset, one must state as clearly as possible that, in Namibia, any discussion on unity has to be linked with ecumenism. Let me briefly explain. The story of Namibia as the product of unity and ecumenism must be told from both a political and a religious perspective. In modern history, since the twentieth century, the first steps that were taken for the birth of the Namibian nation as the product of ecumenism and the nation's coming together in unity is both religious and political.[3] From the beginning, Namibians have looked to and found solidarity from the broad ecumenical movements, namely, the World Council of Churches, other ecumenical church bodies and organisations, the United Nations and, in Namibia, from the South West African Peoples Organization (SWAPO). These broad ecclesiological and political ecumenical bodies have been courageous enough to support the liberation struggle and challenge the churches to redouble their efforts to seek unity among themselves and to ensure that Namibia would be free.

The search for unity and ecumenism started the process of conscientizing Namibian Christians as well as offering a window of opportunity for ecclesiological and political bodies to play a major role in the liberation of Namibia – and they have made a decisive contribution which in the end culminated in the UN supervised elections and, as a result, the long-awaited Namibian independence became a reality. The culmination of all these developments can be summed up in one sentence: ecclesiological and political

---

[3] Isaak, Paul John, 2012 "Cultural Dominance and Mental Slavery: The Role of German and African missionaries in Colonial Namibia" in *The German Protestant Church in Colonial Southern Africa: The Impact of Overseas Work from the Beginnings until the 1920s.* Edited by Lessing, Hanns, Bester, Julia, et al. Pietermaritzburg: Cluster Publications, 2012, 578-579.

unity and ecumenism made its day in Namibia because of the upholding of the biblical principle in Galatians 3:28: 'There is neither Jew nor Gentile, neither slave nor free, nor is there male and female, for you are all one in Christ Jesus.'

The key instrument that the Namibian Churches developed to promote and participate in Christian unity and ecumenism was the establishment of the Council of Churches in Namibia (CCN). In the early 1970s, the Namibian churches entered into a loose alliance, the Christian Centre, which had a dual role: to speak with a united and ecumenical voice against injustice on behalf of the voiceless, and to initiate enabling projects for the poor. This initiative was later revamped and its scope broadened and, as a result, CCN was formed in 1978.[4] CCN provided further opportunities for the various church denominations to come together to share their experiences and make joint statements on matters of common interest. CCN is an ecumenical organization, a reconciling, healing and caring fellowship of Christian churches, united in service to society with the objective of broadening ecumenism in Namibia.

CCN is an ecumenical body whose concerns extend from religious to social and educational matters. Core values of CCN include:

- Upholding the dignity of all people as created in God's image
- Being committed stewards of resources entrusted to them
- Networking and partnership with other stakeholders
- Promoting study of the Bible and obedience to Christ
- Standing for accountability, transparency, Christlike leadership and unity in diversity
- Commitment to reconciliation
- Advocating for justice, peace, fundamental human rights, freedom and human dignity for all, and
- Aspiring to be a sustainable Council

Currently, CCN is encouraging its member churches to establish ecumenical committees round the country. These forums are intended to enhance stronger relations among the churches at a local level to address social and economic challenges like moral and ethical decay in our societies – to help communities to help themselves through projects.

Common Instruments of Social Work

Churches and faith-based organizations (FBOs) play a critical role in the lives of Namibians. They shape and influence spiritual, social, health, cultural and the economic development of the individuals, families and communities they serve. Ninety per cent of the Namibian population is regarded as Christian. This implies that the churches have a ready audience, willing to attend church services. This indicates that the Namibian churches do have a niche to reach out to, positively influencing the behaviour and attitudes of its followers for the promotion of more equal and inclusive rights-based development. The church also reaches the rural and remote areas where other institutions do not.

The Council of Churches in Namibia started the Ecumenical Social Community Action Programme (ESCA) funded by the Helsinki Deaconess Institute in 2012, its mandate being to empower vulnerable and marginalized communities for self-reliance and engaging in activity for sustainable national development.

ESCA is initiated as a means through which the Council of Churches in Namibia (CCN) mobilizes Namibian domestic resources for more equal development through the application of participatory methods in vulnerable communities. It is raising awareness about the socio-economic challenges facing the Namibian people; and the role of the church in mobilizing resources for transformation through advocacy

[4] "The Council of Churches in Namibia (CCN) is an umbrella of all major churches in Namibia with 18 member churches representing about 1.5 million Namibians constituting 90 % of the population. (See www.ccnnamibia.org)

(Prophetic Voice) and community development. Training of clergy, youth, and women had been the focus for the past two years.

The Council has also signed a memorandum of understanding with the government. This enables communities to be supported to establish community projects for self-help.

Bibliography

Buys, Gerhard L., and Shekutaamba V.V. Nambala. *History of the church in Namibia, 1805-1990: An introduction*. Windhoek: Gamsberg Macmillan, 2003.

Horn, Nico. 'Religion and human rights in Namibia: focus: the foundations and future of law, religion and human rights in Africa.' *African Human Rights Law Journal* 8.2, 2008, 409-431.

Isaak, Paul John, 2012 'Cultural Dominance and Mental Slavery: The Role of German and African missionaries in Colonial Namibia' in *The German Protestant Church in Colonial Southern Africa: The Impact of Overseas Work from the Beginnings until the 1920s.* Edited by Lessing, Hanns, Bester, Julia, et al. Pietermaritzburg: Cluster Publications, 2012.

Paul John Isaak, *The Story of the Paulinum Seminary in Namibia*. Windhoek: Namibia Publishing House, 2013.

The Council of Churches in Namibia (CCN). www.ccnnamibia.org (Accessed 19 December 2015).

(81) CHRISTIANITY IN NIGER

Issiaka Aboubacar

Religion	Pop 2010	Pct 2010	Pop 2025	Pct 2025	Gr Pct 1970 2025
Christians	58,800	0.4%	88,200	0.3%	2.7%
Independents	17,000	0.1%	28,900	0.1%	3.6%
African initiated	11,300	0.1%			
Protestants	20,100	0.1%	32,000	0.1%	3.2%
Roman Catholics	21,400	0.1%	27,000	0.1%	1.6%
Pentecostals/Charismatics	26,700	0.2%	42,000	0.1%	3.1%
Evangelicals	18,400	0.1%	30,000	0.1%	3.3%
Muslims	15,561,000	95.5%	28,746,000	97.0%	4.2%
adherents of traditional African religions	653,000	4.0%	780,000	2.6%	1.2%
Baha'is	5,700	0.0%	10,000	0.0%	3.9%
Sikhs	3,800	0.0%	5,500	0.0%	2.5%
people professing no religion	9,900	0.1%	15,200	0.1%	2.9%
Total population	**16,292,000**	**100.0%**	**29,645,000**	**100.0%**	**4.1%**

Source: Centre for the Study of World Christianity (CSGC), Boston, Gordon-Conwell TS

Situation générale

Le Niger est un pays continental entouré par l'Algérie, la Libye, le Tchad, le Nigéria, le Bénin, le Burkina Faso et le Mali; le Niger couvre une superficie de 1.267.000 km².

Sur un total d'environ 5500 km de frontière dont près de 3000 sont rectilignes, le Niger n'a que quelques centaines de kilomètres de frontières naturelles constituées essentiellement par des affluents du fleuve Niger, avec le Burkina par la Sirba et la Tapoa, avec le Bénin par le Mékrou sur une centaine de kilomètres et le fleuve Niger lui-même sur 150km jusqu'au bassin du Lac Tchad. Le pays doit son nom[1] au cours d'eau qui l'arrose dans sa partie occidentale sur environ 550km.

Le relief du pays est essentiellement caractérisé par un ensablement constant et monotone. Le réseau hydrographique est pratiquement inexistant dans un pays dont la survie est fondamentalement liée à une pluviométrie malheureusement capricieuse. Le pays appartient donc à l'une des zones les plus chaudes du globe et connait deux types de climats:

- Un climat désertique sur la majeure partie de sa superficie
- Un climat tropical, à une seule saison des pluies, pluies qui commencent timidement au mois de Juin, s'intensifient à partir de Juillet pour atteindre leur maximum au mois d'Août.

[1] Donaint Pierre et Lancrenont François: Le Niger, 2edition, Paris, Puf, 1975, Collecion Que Suis-je ; 5

Données Démo Linguistiques

L'histoire des populations, notamment en Afrique, est un domaine du savoir particulièrement complexe. Ceci est dû en grande partie au fait que les études sont très lentes avec des résultats qui peuvent avoir évolués de façon notable avant leur publication.

Ceci étant, la population du Niger est estimée à 3.240.000 habitants en 1960, année de l'indépendance, puis est passée à 5.098.427 personnes au recensement général de 1977. Les résultats provisoires du dernier recensement effectué en 1988 indiquent, quant à eux, le chiffre de 7.249.956 habitants, soit une augmentation de plus de deux (02) millions d'individus en onze (11ans) »[2] mais de plus de seize millions d'habitants aujourd'hui. Cette population est également repartie à travers les huit régions que compte le pays: l'Agadez, le Diffa, le Zinder, le Tahoua, le Tillabéri, le Dosso, le Maradi et Niamey. Quant aux ethnies, il faut compter six (06) grands groupes: les Haoussas (53,5%), les Zarmas (14,7%), les Touaregs (10,6%), les Peulhs (10,4%), les Kanouris, les Bériběri, les Manga (4,6%), les Songhai (4%). Il convient d'ajouter aussi les Toubous (0,5%),les Gourmantché (0,3%), les Arabes (0,3%).

Les ethnies des communautés étrangères représentent 1,8% de la population. Signalons que la quasi-totalité de la population est composé de musulmans sunnites (98, 6%).

Croyances et pratiques religieuses avant l'arrivée du christianisme

Composé à 98,6% de musulmans, le Niger est reconnu comme l'un des pays les plus islamisés de l'Ouest Africain. Cela n'étonne guère pour peu qu'on a présent à l'esprit l'ancienneté du fait Islamique. Le premier contact de l'islam avec l'espace nigérien remonterait au « VIIe siècle, à l'expédition du conquérant musulman Ogba Ibn Nafi au Kawar en 666»[3], soit seulement 35ans après la mort du prophète Muhammad. Depuis lors, l'islam n'a cessé de gagner du terrain dans cet espace, comme cela s'observe actuellement.

Au Niger, les gens sont donc très croyants. La croyance en un Dieu unique, créateur et maître du monde et partagée par tous. Mais cette divinité est assistée par un messager et par des esprits des ancêtres, l'homme est le résultat de son passé dit-on. Ainsi des survivances animistes incompréhensibles (les esprits des services, les dieux de la nature et diverses puissances mystiques) s'infiltrent dans toute la vie et la dominent, ceux là ont insidieusement infiltrés l'islam

L'Islam est ainsi embarqué dans un syncrétisme religieux fait d'une fonction entre les pratiques religieuses officielles et des croyances traditionnelles superstitieuses.

Publiquement on prie et on jeûne, mais lorsqu'un évènement malencontreux survient, on se précipite chez les marabouts, le féticheur ou l'initié en magie noire[4].

Au total, les piliers de l'islam sont bien ancrés au Niger, mais la religion n'a pas assez pénétré les comportements quotidiens. Cela est dû au fait que la religion traditionnelle occupe une place de choix dans la vie des populations. C'est dans ce climat de croyances et de pratiques diverses qu'apparaîtront les missionnaires Chrétiens en vue de prêcher la bonne nouvelle de Jésus Christ.

Christianisation

Au Niger, en effet, comme nous l'avons dit ci-haut 98,6% de la population sont musulmans. Les premières communautés Chrétiennes (Catholique, Protestant) ont été crées grâce à des chrétiens provenant des pays limitrophes, Bénin, Burkina-Faso, Nigéria, Togo. Ceux-ci se sont installés dans le pays pour faire leur

[2] Marchés Tropicaux et Méditerranées, No 2243, du 4 Novembre 1988, 3028

[3] Cuoq, J.M.: Recueil des sources Arabes concernant l'Afrique Occidentale du VIIè Siècle. Clé, Yaoundé, Paris, 1975, 209

[4] C'est pourquoi certains ont tôt fait de dire que « l'islam noir, est un islam féticheur ou maraboutique »

commerce ou sont employés par les maisons de commerce étrangères qui opèrent dans le pays. Quelques ont travaillé dans l'administration ou dans les organisations internationales opérant dans le pays. Certains d'entre eux sont venus avec leur famille ou en ont fondé avec le temps. Etant chrétiens, ils ont fini par créer des lieux de culte pour adorer. Par les nationaux, ils sont considérés comme des fidèles étrangers d'une religion étrangère à la culture locale.

Pour les Nigériens, la question ne se pose même pas; « être Nigérien, c'est être nécessairement musulman ». Mais cela n'a pas empêché, au cours des ans, que s'instaurent de bons rapports avec les autorités locales, les populations grâces aux activités de promotion de la dignité des fidèles chrétiens. Ainsi, la présence du christianisme au Niger est de nos jours sans équivoque, il est caractérisé par une multitude d'Eglises libres et charismatiques. Parmi ces Eglises, nous pouvons citer l'Eglise Catholique, l'Eglise Baptiste, l'Eglise Evangélique Presbytérienne du Niger, ...

Le Catholicisme

Au début du XXe siècle, le Niger était une colonie sous le gouvernement de Dakar et Niamey n'était qu'un petit village sur la rive gauche du grand fleuve.

Des missionnaires avaient commencé à sillonner les grands espaces africains, mais en 1925, un officier français, le colonel Abadie constatait que, le Catholicisme ne comptait « aucun adhérent indigène au Niger. Il n'y a pas un missionnaire catholique sur tout le: territoire de la colonie »[5.] Ce n'est en effet qu'en Janvier 1931 que le P. François Faroud, de la société des missions africaines de Lyon (SMA), fonde la première « station » à Niamey, ainsi le premier acte de naissance de l'Eglise au Niger quatre vingt quatre ans (84) se sont déjà écoulés.

Longtemps, l'Eglise a été cachée par respect pour les musulmans. D'autant plus que les premières communautés Chrétiennes au Niger se sont constituées autour de chrétiens venus des pays voisins.

Le Protestantisme

L'histoire du protestantisme nigérien vient du Nigeria en 1934. La première personne contactée fut ABA MOUSSA, marabout du sultanat de Zinder (ancien capital du Niger) et originaire de cette même ville »[6]. Ainsi, avec les protestants, nous assistons à une nouvelle stratégie qui consiste à explorer le centre ouest du pays habité par des ethnies plus ouvertes au contact avec l'étranger. Ainsi dès sa naissance la mission protestante à découvert que l'évangélisation d'un milieu musulman est le contraire du prosélytisme, c'est-à-dire qu'on ne peut attendre des hommes qu'ils se convertissent à l'évangile si, préalablement, les églises ne sont converties à l'homme. C'est pourquoi les protestants ont vite compris que leur devoir ne consiste pas seulement à implanter des Eglises, mais aussi à proclamer l'amour de Jésus que donne l'Evangile à tout l'homme. C'est alors qu'ils se trouvent dans l'obligation de chercher des voies...pour apporter cette délivrance aux opprimés, aux pauvres et à tout le peuple. Ainsi, en militant toutes pour un christianisme unifié, les missions donnent une grande énergie quant à l'évolution et l'avenir du christianisme au Niger.

Cette unification religieuse se concrétise par la création de l'Alliance des missions Evangéliques du Niger (AMEN) qui regroupe toutes les Eglises protestantes du Niger. Le but de cette association est d'établir un dialogue qui tend vers la cohabitation, la vie commune, l'action commune et la reconstruction du pays. En se basant sur cette réalité qu'est la tolérance religieuse au Niger, le rapprochement des religions chrétiennes ne souffrira à priori d'aucun handicap. De ce fait, AMEN comme canal de

[5] https://www.google.com/search?q=Mgr+Michel+Cartat%C3%A9gui%2C+Ev%C3%AAque+de+Niamey+cit%C3%A9+par+l%27Agence+Fides du 25 Mars 2015.

[6] Pasteur Ladd Soumaila: Eglise Presbytérienne de la République du Niger (Une Eglise purement nationale)

rapprochement des religions chrétiennes constitue un atout en vue de renforcer le dialogue entre chrétiens et musulmans au Niger.

Eglise Evangélique Presbytérienne du Niger

> « L'histoire est un besoin qu'éprouve chaque groupe humain, à chaque moment de son évolution de chercher et de mettre en valeur dans le passé les faits, les évènements, les tendances qui préparent le temps présent, qui permettent de le comprendre et qui aide à le vivre disait Lucien Febre»[7].

Ainsi notre intention ici est de jeter un regard sur la jeune église qui est l'Eglise Evangélique Presbytérienne du Niger (EEPN). Il s'agit d'informer d'autres et les amener à vivre sous un angle réellement œcuménique la parole de Dieu qui s'y transmet par la joie du maître de la mission Jésus-Christ. C'est là la finalité que nous partageons avec toute l'Eglise chrétienne du monde et d'Afrique en particulier.

L'Eglise Evangélique presbytérienne du Niger (EEPN) est une jeune communauté issue du travail des ressortissants Togolais, Béninois et Ghanéens à Niamey.

Elle est reconnue officiellement comme association religieuse le 12 Novembre 1986. Cette reconnaissance est publiée dans le Journal Officielle de la République du 26 Décembre de la même année. L'EEPN est organisée d'après le système reformé et suit la logique théologique de l'Eglise Evangélique Presbytérienne du Togo (EEPT) qui est son inspiratrice. Aujourd'hui des responsables d'Eglises et d'organismes nationaux et internationaux ont tour à tour visité cette jeune communauté (par exemple la CEVAA, la Mission de Brême et autres…).

De nos jours cette Eglise compte quelques nigériens dont le premier a été baptisé le 23 Avril 2000 et grâce au soutien financier de la CEVAA est devenu Pasteur de cette Eglise aujourd'hui, formé à l'université de l'Afrique de l'Ouest[8] (campus de Porto-Novo / Bénin).

L'Eglise Evangélique Presbytérienne du Niger exerce son ministère pour le moment dans la capitale nigérienne (Niamey). Elle est actuellement située non loin du commissariat central de Niamey et à près de 1,5km de l'université Nationale de Niamey. Mais malgré cela, pour marquer sa présence au sein de la nation nigérienne, l'Eglise dispose d'un collège en construction sans doute ouvrira ses portes au cours de l'année Académique 2015-2016. La clôture du terrain octroyer a cette Eglise Par l'état pour les projets suivants: construction du siège de l'Eglise, pour l'alphabétisation et de formations professionnelles, Jardins d'enfants et primaires etc… est en chantier.

Conclusion

Au terme de cette brève histoire de la foi et du christianisme au Niger, nous pouvons dire que, malgré qu'elle constitue une minorité de la population nigérienne, la communauté chrétienne est tout de même manifeste. Elle n'a cessé de s'implanter dans le pays avec des missions de diverses origines. La naissance et l'évolution missionnaire de l'Eglise Evangélique Presbytérienne du Niger constituent le témoignage vivant que les paroles d'envoi du Christ dans Matthieu[9] sont bien comprises et qu'elles sont bien exécutées.

Il est primordial de noter que « dans l'Eglise du Niger ou au Niger le travail pour le développement est constitutif de l'évangélisation et de l'annonce du royaume de Dieu ». Dans les champs de Dieu, il faut être patient. Car le grain ne grandit pas une nuit. Il faut suivre, pendant de longues années, vivre le temps des

---

[7] Lucien Febre: Combat pour l'histoire, Ed. Armand Colin, Paris, 1992, 2è de couverture

[8] L'auteur de ce texte est ce théologien nigérien formé dans la vision œcuménique de l'Eglise du Christ.

[9] Matthieu 28:19 « « Allez, faites de toutes les nations des disciples, les baptisant au nom du Père, du Fils et du Saint-Esprit ».

semailles, le temps de la patience, de l'amitié vécue avec les gens, avec nos pères d'Islam, il faut souvent donc beaucoup de temps pour devenir des amis, partager sa foi avec eux, s'estimer profondément.

Cette pensée réconfortante donne une grande énergie à la jeune communauté Presbytérienne du Niger et à toute personne et organisme qui désire l'aventure d'ouverture avec elle dans ce vaste champ d'évangélisation qu'est le Niger.

Bibliographie

Cuoq, J.M.: Recueil des sources Arabes concernant l'Afrique Occidentale du VIIè Siècle. Clé, Yaoundé, Paris, 1975

Donaint Pierre et Lancrenont François: Le Niger, 2edition, Paris, Puf, 1975

(82) CHRISTIANITY IN NIGERIA

Helen Adekunbi Labeodan

Religion	Pop 2010	Pct 2010	Pop 2025	Pct 2025	Gr Pct 1970 2025
Christians	73,349,000	46.0%	108,760,000	46.6%	2.7%
Independents	28,708,000	18.0%	39,500,000	16.9%	2.2%
African initiated	27,421,000	17.2%			
Orthodox	42,200	0.0%	64,000	0.0%	2.8%
Protestants	47,430,000	29.8%	61,000,000	26.1%	1.7%
Anglicans	20,100,000	12.6%			
Pentecostal	7,795,000	4.9%			
Evangelical churches	6,000,000	3.8%			
Baptist	5,253,000	3.3%			
United churches	3,350,000	2.1%			
Methodist	2,700,000	1.7%			
Roman Catholics	21,092,000	13.2%	32,000,000	13.7%	2.8%
Pentecostals/Charismatics	48,302,000	30.3%	73,000,000	31.3%	2.8%
Evangelicals	32,461,000	20.4%	48,030,000	20.6%	2.6%
Muslims	73,275,000	46.0%	110,500,000	47.3%	2.8%
adherents of traditional African religions	12,251,000	7.7%	13,500,000	5.8%	0.6%
Baha'is	38,500	0.0%	55,000	0.0%	2.4%
Hindus	30,300	0.0%	40,000	0.0%	1.9%
adherents of new religious movements	16,700	0.0%	22,000	0.0%	1.9%
Buddhists	8,500	0.0%	12,000	0.0%	2.3%
Chinese folk-religionists	4,700	0.0%	7,000	0.0%	2.7%
Jews	1,200	0.0%	1,200	0.0%	0.3%
people professing no religion	451,000	0.3%	660,000	0.3%	2.6%
Total population	**159,425,000**	**100.0%**	**233,558,000**	**100.0%**	**2.6%**

Source: Centre for the Study of World Christianity (CSGC), Boston, Gordon-Conwell TS

A Survey of the History of Christianity in Nigeria

The 170-year-old story of Christianity in Nigeria has been told several times by different sources from different perspectives. Christians make up to 48.2% of the entire population of the country.[1] Nigeria has

[1] Deji Okegbile, "170 years of the Church in Nigeria – Beyond the Present", www.punchng.com

one of the largest Christian populations in Africa with over 70 million belonging to the church.[2] The basis for the first missionary movement were European expeditions and trade of the fifteenth century. A search for a sea route to the East Indies and India facilitated the early contacts of Europeans traders with the west coast of Africa, including Nigeria.[3] The Portuguese explorers were the first to make this journey to Nigeria. They visited Benin in 1477, meeting the King Ozoula who entered into alliances with the King of Portugal. Consequently, he allowed the Portuguese to build the trading post at Gwalo, Ughoton, and gave them some slaves as gifts. Thereafter, they convinced him to allow some of his sub-chiefs to be baptized in 1516. On the death of the King, however, Christianity vanished.[4]

In Warri, the Portuguese met the Olu of Warri in 1555. He was baptized and adopted a Portuguese name: Saint Sebastian. Later, his son Domingo was sent to Portugal for a period of ten years for a western education. He then came home with a Portuguese wife of high birth. Their son, Don Antonio, who later became Olu was said to have been educated in Christian theology in Portugal. When he ascended the throne, he spread Christianity among his subjects. The benefit from this association was that Warri rulers from 1570 till 1733 became professing Christians. A breakdown in trade relations always meant a break in mission;[5] the attempt by Portuguese missionaries at Christianizing the people of Benin and Warri failed woefully due to their interest in trade and commerce rather than in mission. Christianity was also made a 'palace religion'. Another reason alluded to was an insufficient knowledge of the religion on the part of people. Often the new religion conflicted with their traditional values. Only a shadow of this first attempt was left at the end of this contact.

An effective missionary work began in Nigeria on 24th September 1842 when Thomas Birch Freeman and two Fanti missionaries, Mr and Mrs William De-Graft, arrived in Badagry from the Wesleyan Methodist church. They bought a plot of land and began holding prayer meetings. Later they erected a small bamboo chapel and gathered the chiefs and people to explain the purpose of their coming.[6] They attended to the needs of the freed slaves who requested a missionary.[7] On 11th December that year, a Sunday, Freeman got to Abeokuta and paid homage to King Sodeke who was impressed with him. In the afternoon he held a service with the King in attendance.[8]

The second missionary society to enter the Yoruba Mission was the Church Missionary Society (CMS). Henry Townsend and Andrew Wilhelm arrived at the port of Badagry on 17th December 1842. Townsend, though from CMS did not disregard Freeman's guidance. Oduyoye confirmed that they worshipped together in the Methodist Church on Christmas Day before Townsend left for Abeokuta on 29th December. He was warmly welcomed by the same King Sodeke. Promising to open a station in Abeokuta, Townsend returned to London to be ordained bishop. He came back in 1844 as promised.[9] He returned to Badagry on 17th January, 1845, to move his team back to Abeokuta for missionary work. The team consisted of the

---

[2] Okegbile, "170 years of the Church in Nigeria."

[3] Akpenpuum Dzurgba, "A History of Christian Mission in Nigeria: a Developmental Approach." *Asia Journal of Theology* 5, No. 1 (1991): 186.

[4] David N.A Kpobi, 2005, "African Chaplains in Seventeenth Century in West Africa" in *African Christianity: An African Story*, ed Ogbu Kalu (Department of Church History, University of Pretoria: Pretoria), 141.

[5] Kpobi, "African Chaplains," 41.

[6] John Ferguson, *Some Nigerian Church Founders* (Ibadan: Daystar Press, 1971), 4.

[7] A good number of freed Yoruba slaves that were converted Christians requested specially for white missionaries to continue to minister to them and secondly to minister to their heathen brethren who had sold them into slavery. One such plea was from James Ferguson. Warraru, the king of Badagry at that time countersigned Ferguson's letter of appeal to Rev. Thomas Dove, a Methodist Minister in Freetown in a letter dated March 2, 1841 to send a missionary to Badagry.

[8] Ferguson, *Some Nigerian Church Founders*, 4.

[9] Deji Ayegboyin & F.K.U. Asonzeh, "Taxonomy of Churches in Nigeria; A Historical Perspective," *Orita,* 34, No.1-2 (2002): 68.

Rev. and Mrs Townsend, the Rev. and Mrs Gollmer, the Rev. and Mrs Crowther with their two children, and Mr Marsh, a catechist. The plan was obstructed, however, as a result of the death of King Sodeke. Thus, they waited at Badagry for eighteen months and seized the opportunity to establish the CMS church in Badagry, on 9th March, 1845. Townsend and Gollmer continued the study of Yoruba, while Crowther continued the translation of the Bible into Yoruba and began the translation of the Anglican Book of Common Prayer.

Later, they proceeded to Abeokuta in July 1846 where it flourished exceedingly. The relationship between the missionaries and the Egba rulers could best be described as a symbiotic one.[10] Oduyoye explained that Egba was so important to the missionaries because Abeokuta was a home to all and a city of refuge for those dispersed by war. Despite this seemingly cordial relationship, some of the Abeokuta people saw the overbearing attitude of the missionaries and developed a degree of distrust of them. They felt the white men came only to tap their lands' resources, force them to obey their foreign rules and, later, dominate them as they did in Lagos.[11]

The third missionary society in Nigeria was the Scotland Mission, known as the Presbyterian Church. The Scotland Missionary Society started its work in Nigeria in 1846 through the initiative and the willingness of the Jamaican Presbytery.[12] As from 1839, the Presbytery started to think about sending a mission to Africa. This was because the Negroes of the Presbytery began to have a great concern for indigenous peoples in Africa. After adequate information had been gathered about the continent of Africa, between 1839 and 1840, the Presbytery took a decision in 1841 to send missionaries to Africa.[13] They sent the Rev. Hope Masterdom Waddell, his wife and another Scottish couple to Calabar. They arrived on 10th April 1846.[14]

---

[10] The missionary activity helped in checking the intrusion of Dahomey because they might have captured Abeokuta if not for the military intervention of the British Government. However, this relationship did not eventually favour the Egbas as this made them to remain perpetually the subject of the British government and the missionaries. In spite of this, they enjoyed British support in many ways, including the ousting of Kosoko the king of Lagos in 1851, general development, prosperity in trade and politics of the Yoruba region.

[11] Adewale O.Ogunrinade and Friday Abu Ogbole, "Christianity in Nigeria before Pentecostalism," *Academic Journal of Interdisciplinary Studies* (MCSER-CEMAS-Sapienza University of Rome), Vol 2 No 2, July 2013. The presence of the British in Lagos led to the enthronement of Akintoye (after Kosoko had been deposed), who signed a treaty which made Lagos a protectorate of the British Government. The British had been poking into the affairs of the Yoruba people, the intertribal wars, and taking sides from Lagos to buttress this claim.

[12] The Scotland Missionary Society, which was formerly known as the Edinburgh Society since 1796 set up the Scottish Mission in Jamaica in 1824. Another missionary body known as the United Session of Scotland also started its ministry in Jamaica and through the merger of the two societies the joint Presbyterian Church in Jamaica was formed. For more explanation see J. Kofi Agbeti, *West African Church History: Christian Mission and Church Foundations 1842-1919* (Leiden: E.J. Brill), 1986.

[13] In line with the decision, as George Blyth and Peter Anderson (who were both Scottish Missionaries in Jamaica) were recuperating in England after falling ill in Jamaica, they met sea captains who advised them to look towards the direction of Old Calabar for a result-oriented missionary work. The two missionaries sent a letter to the chiefs of Old Calabar showing their willingness to come over for missionary purposes and the reply was enthusiastic. The Calabar chiefs were conceived that the presence of the white missionaries would increase their trade chances with other parts of the world and further give them and their children great avenues to be taught how to read and write faster. When they came, they (chiefs of Duke and Creek towns) encouraged the missionaries whom they accommodated to instruct their people and introduce the town people to legitimate trade, apart from trade in slaves.

[14] S.A. Fatokun, "Pentecostalism in South-Western Nigeria with Emphasis on the Apostolic Church, 1931-2001," Ph.D. Thesis submitted to the Department of Religious Studies, University of Ibadan, Nigeria.
Kofi Agbeti, *West African Church History: Christian Mission and Church Foundations 1842-1919* (Leiden: E.J. Brill, 1986).

Baptist mission work in Nigeria could be traced to the arrival of Thomas J. Bowen, on 5th August 1850 at Badagry.[15] Due to the wars in the Yoruba areas, the roads that led to Igboho were closed and he could only get as far as Abeokuta. For a period of eighteen months, Bowen stayed in Abeokuta as the guest of the King and the CMS and other missionaries there. So he used the opportunity to study the Yoruba language and vocabulary and, in 1862, published a book entitled, *Grammar and Vocabulary of the Yoruba Language*. He visited the King of Ketu who received him warmly. However, due to the intolerance of the King's chiefs, he was advised to leave. He proceeded to Ijaye and soon after that left for America,[16] but returned to Nigeria newly wedded. With him came also J.H. Lacy and his wife and J.S. Dennard and his wife. However, due to the scourge of malaria, the Lacys were sent back home while the Dennards died. The Bowens reached Ijaye and erected a chapel in 1854. They then moved to Ogbomoso where the work was successful. Apart from the Ijaye and Ogbomoso stations, other stations were established at Oyo, Shaki, Igboho and Ilorin with the help of other Baptist missionaries.[17] The Baptist Mission's story among the Yorubas and in Nigeria was a success. It resulted in the formation of the Nigerian Baptist Convention in 1919.[18]

The Catholic missionary re-establishment started in 1860. On 17th February 1862, Father Borghero visited Lagos and was overwhelmed by the great reception accorded him. Before this visit, he had chosen a place called Ouidah in Dahomey where a considerable number of repatriated slaves were settled, and he established a Roman Catholic community consisting of 'quasi-African Catholics'.[19] Brazilian Catholics, missionaries and peoples from Sierra Leone and Cuba who had been expelled from Lagos in 1851, all took advantage of the peace[20] in Lagos to return. These were the people who welcomed Father Borghero in 1862. He departed but returned in 1868 to set up a station as expected, but could not stay long. So he appointed Father Bouche as the superior of the station. However, Father Bouche also did not stay long there, and was replaced by Father Cloud. Father Cloud's contribution to the development of the agricultural settlement yielded good results. His vision was really in line with the general Roman Catholic educational policy of the time: to train children to make use of their intellects and hands. Father Cloud's initiative was boosted by a Roman Catholic layman called Sir James Marshall, an British trader and a supreme judge for Lagos and Cape Coast, who advised Cloud to ask the Governor of Lagos for a nine-mile strip of land at Topo along the coast near Badagry.[21] The land was granted on 26th July 1876 and Topo was given its first superior, under Father Poirer. Topo developed greatly.[22] More attention and credence were accorded the

---

[15] See Bowen's Diary, August 1850.

[16] Kurunmi, the chief of Ijaye, asked him to select any site of his choice for his mission. After choosing a site, he ran into a series of problems, which ranged from lack of money to build a house, to his poor state of health. Therefore, he went back to the United States of America.

[17] S.A. Fatokun, Pentecostalism.

[18] Thomas O'Conor High, *Outlined Notes on the Expansion of Baptist Work in Nigeria 1850-1939* (Ibadan: Caxton Press, 1970), 35.

[19] Patrick Grantley, *Mission to West Africa: The Story of the Society of African Mission (SMA) 1856-1907* (Rome: SMA, 1991),160.

[20] Lagos around this time was free from the violence of the wars that it had sustained, especially the 1851 bombardment by the British. Kosoko was deposed as king and Akintoye signed a treaty with the British to discontinue the slave trade and to allow safe and legitimate businesses to take place. This peaceful environment attracted many people who had fled Lagos to come back.

[21] Kofi Agbeti, *West Africa Church History*.

[22] In the arrangement, Topo was a free zone for local Nigerian families, who were offered residence there. The condition for staying there was to farm and the beneficiaries would pay back their rent in kind, and assist in clearing and cultivating farmland. This system was aimed at steering the youth from depending on clerical professions and the government alone. This achievement soon suffered a setback because of the drift of youth and children on the farmland from the settlement to towns such as Lagos and Porto-Novo. Despite this, the achievement of the settlements cannot be de-emphasized. This was because hundreds of acres of land were cleared and many thousands of coconut trees were

Catholic mission in Lagos in 1877-1878 when the construction of the Holy Cross Cathedral was started, to be completed in 1881. In all, the Catholic mission recorded enormous achievements because the fathers were supported by the local people. They were further assisted by the Catholic nuns, who were workers of the Franciscan Sisters of the Propagation of the Faith in Lyons.

The Holy Ghost Fathers is another Catholic order that came to Nigeria; the order came to Onitsha in 1885 to establish the Roman Catholic Church.[23] By 1889, Onitsha had been accorded as 'the Ecclesiastical Province' to oversee the whole of the eastern part of Nigeria. The Holy Ghost Fathers later established a station at Lokoja in 1884, and also founded the Ecclesiastical Province of Kaduna in 1911.[24]

The next mission to study is the Sudan Interior Mission. They sent three missionaries, namely, Walter Gowans, Thomas Kent and Rowland Bingham, to the northern region of Nigeria. After their initial efforts had been aborted, a subsequent attempt was fruitful in 1893 when some churches were established. The churches were christened the Evangelical Churches of West Africa (ECWA) in 1901. To assist the Sudan Interior Mission, the Sudan United Mission was formed. SUM was able to establish six churches.[25]

All the churches discussed above are referred to as historical, 'mainline', 'established' or 'mission' churches, as they have a line of history and traditions that predates their presence in Nigeria.[26] Apart from these was the establishment of the Ethiopian churches.[27] These were the Ebenezer Baptist Church, formed March 1888, the United Native African Church, 1891, the African Church Bethel, 1901, and the United African Methodist Church (Eleja) in 1917.

Furthermore, the emergence of independent churches in Nigeria in the late nineteenth century caused Nigeria to experience the contextualization of Christianity. These were the Christ Apostolic Church, The Cherubim and Seraphim Society, The Church of the Lord Aladura and Celestial Church of Christ. These are all referred to as African Indigenous Churches.[28] Consequently, they provided a springboard for the emergence of evangelical, charismatic and Pentecostal movements which are predominantly indigenous in Nigeria. This is another significant landmark in Nigerian Christianity which emerged in the twentieth century. They are classified into Classical Pentecostals, Charismatic Pentecostals and the Neo-Pentecostal Church.[29]

---

cultivated. In addition, herds of cattle and plantations of cassava were put in place and the crops thrived very well. This settlement further helped in establishing orphans and slaves who were previously unsettled. In addition, a convent was established in 1892 for girls. See for more explanation Joseph Parkes, "*The Church in Nigeria*," *New Catholic World* 226 (1983): 231.

[23] Parkes, "The Church in Nigeria," 231.

[24] Patrick Grantley, *Mission to West Africa.*

[25] Deji Ayegboyin & F.K.U. Asonzeh, "Taxonomy of Churches in Nigeria; A Historical Perspective," *Orita* 34, No.1-2 (2002).

[26] Deji Ayegboyin & F.K.U. Asonzeh, "Taxonomy of Churches in Nigeria."

[27] Ethiopianism was used during the colonial era as different forms of struggle against the European influence and most especially their leadership on church issues in Africa. This was coined for Africans from the text biblical: Ps 68:31. The literacy brought by the missions contributed immensely towards this. As the secular was into nationalism, the church before Nigerian independent was into Ethiopianism. For more explanation see Ayegboyin Deji & S. A Ishola, *African Indigenous Churches* (Jos: African Christian Text Books, 2013).

[28] They are also referred to as "African instituted churches", or "African Independent Churches" (AICs) established by Africans, for Africans, without the doctrine of the Europeans, unlike the Ethiopian churches that were founded by Africans for Africans but with the doctrines of the mission churches they seceded from.

[29] The Classical Pentecostal churches are Pentecostal churches that have their sources from Europe and America before Nigerian independence in 1960, while the Charismatic movement is a spiritual wave that is partly in the earlier wave of Pentecostalism in Nigeria. It historically demarcates Classical Pentecostalism from Neo-Pentecostalism. Neo-Pentecostal churches, however, are very recent Pentecostal churches which their leaders claim authority on through their charismatic qualities. See Ayegboyin Deji & F.K.U. Asonzeh, "Taxonomy of Churches in Nigeria; A Historical Perspective," 78-85 for more explanation.

Summary Data of Religious Demography

Nigerian churches officially came together under five main blocks of a national umbrella known as the Christian Association of Nigeria (CAN) in 1976. The five blocks are the Catholic Secretariat of Nigeria, the Christian Council of Nigeria, the Christian Pentecostal Fellowship of Nigeria/Pentecostal Fellowship of Nigeria, the Organisation of African Independent Churches and Tarrayar Ekelesioyoyin Kristi, a Nigeria/ Evangelical Church Winning All. Nigeria is seen to be home to the region's largest Christian population. Nigeria's large Christian community is diverse. Nearly sixty million are Protestants, about twenty million are Catholics, and more than 750,000 are 'other' Christians. All of Christianity's major groups have grown in Nigeria since the 1970s, but the growth of Pentecostal churches has been especially dramatic in recent decades.[30] Lagos is acknowledged as the most Pentecostal city in the world.[31]

Recent Major Trends and Developments

The first phase of Christianity introduced in the nineteenth century are the mainline churches, while the second phase came up in the early twentieth century through the African Indigenous Churches. The third and most recent phase is the Pentecostal or Charismatic Churches in the 1970s. This phase brought about preaching on spiritual manifestation, holiness and deliverance and, more recently, brought the theology of prosperity into the Nigerian Christian circle. In fact, this has drastically changed the face of Christian faith and has indeed affected the major beliefs and doctrines of the church as it began to lay more emphasis on materialism as against spirituality. Nevertheless, the mainline churches still mostly maintain the precepts of their foreign missions. However, this has made them to lose some members, especially youth, to the Pentecostals who seem livelier and profess to give solutions to every type of problems. With this in mind, the mainline churches started including things like praise and worship, speaking in tongues, special prayer programmes and vigils.

Islam has given a kind of unrest to Christianity in Nigeria.[32] It has faced several religious crises and in recent time combating with 'Boko Haram' has claimed thousands of lives.[33] This has called for inter-faith dialogue and special prayer meetings but not so far any reported physical combats between the two as a form of retaliation from Christians.

The General Contribution of Christianity to National Development

There is no doubt that Christianity has made significant contributions to Nigerian society in several ways. These are:

---

[30] Allan Anderson, *An Introduction to Pentecostalism: Global Charismatic Christianity* (Cambridge University Press, 2004), 159-161.

[31] Anderson, *An Introduction to Pentecostalism.*

[32] This also includes the registration of Nigeria as a member of the Organisation of Islamic Countries by Gen. Ibrahim Babangida's military administration. The national census has not asked questions about religion since 1963 because the proportion of Muslims and Christians in Nigeria is a sensitive political issue. In 1953, 21.4% of Nigeria's population was Christian, 45.3% was Muslim and 33.3% belonged to other religions, including African Traditional Religions. By 1963, the percentage of the population that belonged to other religions had declined by 15 points, nearly matching the 13.1-point increase for Christians. During this same period, the percentage of Muslims increased by less than 2 points. Christians have since increased in number and share to become about half of the population. For details see Pew Research Center's Forum on Religion & Public Life, "Spirit and Power: A 10-Country Survey of Pentecostals," 2006, www.pewforum.org/Christian/Evangelical-Protestant-Churches/Spirit-and-Power.aspx.

[33] The *Boko Haram* movement, as it's commonly known, means in Hausa: "Western education is a sin." It also calls itself *Jama'atu Ahlis Sunna Lidda'awati wal-jihad* meaning; People Committed to the Propagation of the Prophet's Teachings and Jihad. The terrorist group was generally said to have emerged in the year 2009.

Education and literacy

Foreign Christian missions pioneered western education in Nigeria. Their programmes include literacy development, classes for religious instruction, Sunday school and catechism, elementary and primary education, teacher training and secondary education, and theological education and training. Other branches of Christianity in Nigeria followed suit and have even gone to the extent of founding private universities which some mainline churches are already geared up for. Education was the most potent tool for the transformation of Nigerian society and also the most effective tool of evangelism.[34] Concomitantly, Christian missions pioneered Christian literature ministry and translation in Nigeria. They reduced African languages to writing, with grammar and syntax.

The health sector

By the end of the nineteenth century, hospitals were as effective as schools. By 1914, various missions had established hospitals like the CMS Iyi Enu Hospital near Onitsha, the Wesley Guide Hospital in Ilesha, the Baptist Hospital in Ogbomosho, and the Sacred Heart Hospital of the Society for African Missions in Abeokuta. Missionary involvement had, as its aim, the eradication of superstitious beliefs about different diseases. Other branches of Christianity in Nigeria started earlier have not hesitated to follow suit.

Economic development

Churches in Nigeria have contributed immensely to the economic development of the country through investment in different sectors of the economy such as agriculture, real estate, the capital market, shopping complexes and schools.[35] Their roles are also important for job creation.

Social formation and transformation

Christian missions in Nigeria had given transforming powers that inculcate morality, honesty, integrity, obedience and trust. This does not mean that we do not have wolves among sheep that have tarnished the image of Christianity and been bad examples. Nevertheless, a good number of churches still speak against them and in general against social vices.

Conclusion

The 170 years of the church in Nigeria have delivered a measure of spiritual, physical, educational, medical and social growth, especially the worldwide global applause of the indigenous Pentecostal and charismatic revival and renewal movements and missionary initiatives.

Bibliography

Agbeti. Kofi J. *West African Church History: Christian Mission and Church Foundations 1842-1919.* Leiden: E.J. Brill, 1986.

Ajayi, J.F. *Christian Mission in Nigeria, 1841-1891: The Making of a New Elite*. London: Longman Group Ltd,1965.

______. *A Patriot to the Core: Bishop Ajayi Crowther*. Ibadan: Spectrum Books Ltd, 2001.

Anderson, Allan. *An Introduction to Pentecostalism: Global Charismatic Christianity.* Cambridge: University Press, 2004.

---

[34] Babs Fafunwa, *History of Education in Nigeria* (London: George Allen & Unwin, 1980), 67.

[35] S.C. Nwite and A. Wilson, *Churches in Nigeria and Investment Strategies: Problems and Prospect. Book of Abstracts* (Second World Congress on Research and Development, Ibadan: University of Ibadan, 2010).

Ayandele, E.A. *The Missionary Impact on Modern Nigeria, 1842-1914, A Political and Social Analysis.* London: Longman Group Ltd, 1966.

Ayegboyin, Deji & Ishola, S. A. *African Indigenous Churches: An Historical Perspective.* Lagos: Greater Heights Publications, 1997.

Fafunwa, Babs. *A History of Education in Nigeria*. London, George Allen & Unwin, 1980.

Falk, Peter, *The Growth of the Church in Africa.* Jos: African Christian Textbooks, 1997.

Groves, C.P. *The Planting of Christianity in Africa.* London: Lutterworth Press, 1948-1958.

Isichei, Elizabeth. *A History of Nigeria.* London: Longman, 1983.

Sanneh, Lamin. *West African Christianity: The Religious Impact,* Maryknoll: Orbis, 1983.

(83) CHRISTIANITY IN RWANDA

Tharcisse Gatwa

Religion	Pop 2010	Pct 2010	Pop 2025	Pct 2025	Gr Pct 1970 2025
Christians	9,373,000	91.1%	13,211,000	91.9%	2.3%
Independents	1,008,000	9.8%	1,510,000	10.5%	2.7%
African initiated	918,000	8.9%			
Orthodox	1,500	0.0%	1,500	0.0%	0.0%
Protestants	3,310,000	32.2%	4,450,000	31.0%	2.0%
Anglicans	1,240,000	12.0%			
Adventist	732,000	7.1%			
Baptist	484,000	4.7%			
Pentecostal	463,000	4.5%			
Reformed, Presbyterian	271,000	2.6%			
Roman Catholics	4,734,000	46.0%	7,006,000	48.7%	2.6%
Evangelicals	2,060,000	20.0%	3,141,000	21.8%	2.9%
Pentecostals/Charismatics	1,949,000	18.9%	2,850,000	19.8%	2.6%
Muslims	518,000	5.0%	800,000	5.6%	2.9%
adherents of traditional African religions	360,000	3.5%	300,000	2.1%	-1.2%
Baha'is	20,000	0.2%	30,000	0.2%	2.7%
Hindus	540	0.0%	800	0.0%	2.6%
people professing no religion	21,900	0.2%	36,100	0.3%	3.4%
Total population	**10,294,000**	**100.0%**	**14,377,000**	**100.0%**	**2.3%**

Source: Centre for the Study of World Christianity (CSGC), Boston, Gordon-Conwell TS

The evangelisation of the Kingdom of Rwanda was initiated by the White Fathers[1] who arrived from Uganda in 1900. The first Protestant missions were from Bethel (by Bielefeld, Germany), who arrived from Tanganyika in East Africa, then the Seventh Day Adventist missionaries, the Anglicans, the Danish Baptists, the Methodists and the Pentecostals.[2] In the latter half of twentieth century came the Lutherans from Tanzania and many new religious groups, claiming an indigenous origin and leadership. In a single century, Christianity grew to be one of the most influential institutions of the land with more than 90% of a population estimated at twelve million, one of the most highly Christianised country in Africa.[3]

---

[1] The congregation was founded in 1868 in Algiers by a French prelate, Cardinal Lavigerie. The true name of the organisation is the *Missionary Society of Africa*. They adopted the name of White Fathers by imitation to Muslims aiming at reaching out to evangelise in those contexts.

[2] Butselaar & Twagirayesu, ed [1982], *Ce don que nous avons Reçu*. Bruxelles: Eglise Presbyterienne au Rwanda.

[3] The 2012 National census projected the population of Rwanda for 2014 at around 12 million. Similarly, Statistics published by the US government estimate the population of Rwanda in July 2013 at 12 million. Of these 56.5 % are roman Catholics; 26 % Protestants; 11.1% Seven-day Adventists; 4.6% Muslims and 1.7 no religious and others. If we

The Implantation of Missions in Rwanda

The Roman Catholic Church. On 2nd February 1900, Mgr Jean Joseph Hirth, a French national heading a team of three other European priests and many Baganda from Uganda, arrived in Nyanza, the headquarters of the monarchy. King Musinga allowed them to start the first mission stations in Save, in the south of the country, on 8th February 1900, followed by a chain of mission stations across the country – in Zaza (in the east, 1900), Nyundo (in the west, 1901), Rwaza (in the north,1903), Mibilizi (in the south-west, 1903), Kabgayi (in the centre, 1905), Murunda (in the west, 1909); Rulindo (in the centre, 1909), Kansi (in the south, towards Burundi, 1910). The first baptism was administered on 12th April 1903, Easter Sunday, to 26 catechumen (22 boys and four girls).[4] Two other baptisms took place on 15th August and 24th December 1903.[5] In 1917, King Musinga was forced to sign a bill granting religious freedom; in October that same year, Mgr Hirth ordained the two first Rwandan priests, Donat Rebero and Balthazar Gafuku.

The Protestants. German Protestant missionaries who first evangelised Rwanda were ministering among the German colonial officials in German East Africa to which Rwanda and Burundi then belonged. From Usambara, a delegation consisting of pastors Dr Ernst Johanssen and Ruccius, plus a number of Tanganyikans, arrived in August 1907; they met King Musinga who authorised the opening of stations in Zinga (in the east) and Kirinda (in the centre) that year. Rubengera opened in 1909, Kiteme on Ijwi Island (1910), Remera-Rukoma (1912), then Kigali, Cyangugu and Rukira. At the outbreak of World War I, the German missions had eleven stations.[6]

In 1921, the Germany missions were taken up by the small Société Belge des Missions Protestantes au Congo (SBMPC). They were joined by two young Adventists (1919) in Rubengera and Kirinda before they later moved to create their own stations in Gitwe and Rwankeri;[7] the Anglicans arrived from Uganda in 1922 and established a mission station in Gahini, in the east of Rwanda. They later extended to Shyira (in the north), Shyogwe (in the centre) and Kigeme (in the south). The Danish Baptist missionaries from Burundi started to evangelise from the south in 1928; the Swedish Pentecostals from eastern DRC started to evangelise from Gihundwe (in the south-west in 1940), while the American Methodists initiated a mission in Kibogora (in the west in 1941). Today, the Pentecostals and the Seventh Day Adventist Church are the fast-growing communities which have overtaken the Presbyterians and the Anglicans.

---

add up the Seven-day Adventists together, all Protestants together represent 37.1%. www.state.gov/ documents/organisation/222297.pdf, "Rwanda 2013 International Religious Freedom Report. Executive Summary accessed 24-01-2015.

[4]In accordance to the instruction of Cardinal Lavigerie, the catechumenate would last four years. It was exceptionally reduced to 3 years for the first baptism in Rwanda. Jean Van der Meersch [1993], *Le Catéchumenat au Rwanda de 1900 ànosjours*, Kigali: Pallotti Presses, p 43.

[5] 17 and 51 catechumen were baptised. Of the hundreds baptized in 1903, three would become priests: Donat Rebero, ordained 1917 [died 1926], Joseph Bugondo, ordained in 1919 [died 1942] and Jovita Matabaro, ordained 1920 [died 1973] [Rutinduka 2014:40].

[6] Blamed for the war in Europe, the Germans were defeated in Africa in 1916; they lost their colonies and the missionaries had to leave. Under the 1919 Versailles Treaty, Tanganyika was given to Britain whilst Rwanda and Burundi were given to Belgium.

[7] The first Seven Day Adventists in Rwanda were two young converts, David Delhove and Henry Monnier. These two started as officers in the Belgian colonial troops; they were allowed to settle and run the missionary stations abandoned by the German to locals in Rubengera and Kirinda. When the Belgian protestant missionary society was given the control over the German missions, Delhove and Monnier left to initiate Gitwe and Rwankeri. They later extended mission work in Mugonero [West].

Evangelism

In the 1930s, the Catholic Church experienced mass conversions known as *Irivuze Umwami* ('what the King says'). King Musinga, seen as a threat to evangelisation, had been dismissed in 1930. Exiled, he died in Moba, a site in the south-east of DRC; he was replaced by one of his sons, Rudahigwa, a Roman Catholic convert. Enthroned in 1931 by both Mr Voisin and Mgr Classe, respectively the Belgian governor of the colony and the head of the Roman Catholic Church,[8] Rudahigwa led the ruling elite to Christianity. His conversion made a psychological impact on the masses who followed his example. There was a common perception that the King had ordered his subjects to convert to Catholicism. Thus the population applied the phrase of the common knowledge: *Irivuze umwami ukoma yombi* ('what the King says, you applaud'). According to many views, the King never gave such an instruction, but the confusion persisted and the missionaries enjoyed it.

In reality, the missionaries had reached an agreement with the colonial administration on political reforms, aimed at removing from power the so-called 'old guides' (traditional chiefs). Baptism was one of the criteria for keeping the position of chief. The conditions for the chiefs to be baptized consisted of presenting a record number of postulants for catechism. Hence, for the chiefs, urging the population to convert became both a duty and a motive for political survival.

The Fathers were however excited by the ruling elite's conversion and the influence the church gained. In missionary literature, these conversions were known as 'the tornado', from an article published in *La Revue des Grands Lacs* in 1936; it was 'welcomed' as the greatest Catholic missionary achievement on the continent, a 'miracle, the hand of God on earth discovered by the Europeans', 'the Spirit that blows in tornadoes from above'.[9]

In the climax of the tornado, two major events deserve our attention: the baptism, in 1943, of the King, the queen and the queen mother; and a memorable ceremony during which, in October 1946, King Mutara III consecrated Rwanda to Jesus Christ and the Virgin Mary, a 'significant move of the Catholic Church', according to Father Muvala. The discourse of the consecration was an extraordinary piece of contextual theology. The King publicly recognised the Lordship of Jesus and the Virgin Mary over any national traditional religion or philosophy. The Catholic hierarchy continued to be influential in society and have direct influence in colonial and post-colonial politics.[10] And yet, the Catholic hierarchy was speaking of God from a top-down perspective.[11]

Church, Culture and Literacy

From the beginning, the missionaries took an interest in learning the language of the country, Kinyarwanda, along with the customs, social institutions, laws and rules. By 1911, four books were published in a mixture of the Kinyarwanda and Luganda languages, the *Ekitabu Kyo Kufutula Bigambo Bye Dini, Okuvaku Belemye Bwi Si Okugera mu Misi Wacu* ('the book that explains faith words from the creation up today'). The missionaries continued to use many imported concepts, like *Mungu* ('God' – instead of Imana); *Roho Mutagatifu* (instead of 'Holy Spirit', *Mwuka w'Imana*).[12] The missionaries codified the Kinyarwanda language; however imperfect it was, it still worked until the 1960s when Father Alexis Kagame made substantial improvement of the phonetics and orthography.

---

[8] The move was done in disrespect of the custom where Abiru, the guardians of the monarchical customs were sole competent to enthrone the King. Governor Voisin said: "Rudahigwa, as you were nominated by the kin of the Belgians, I proclaim you of Rwanda". Then Mgr Classe said: "Your name of the throne is Mutara III" [Gatwa 2004: 89].

[9] Rutayisire 1985:100

[10] Kalibwami; 1991; Linden 1977 & 1999; Gatwa 2005; Gatwa et Karamaga 1990; Rutinduka 2014; Rutayisire 2014

[11] Gatwa 2005:90

[12] Jean Van der Meersch [1993], *Le catéchuménat au Rwanda de 1900 à nos jours*. Kigali: Pallotti, 50.

At the time of Vatican II, the Catholic Church had four local bishops.[13] The hierarchy would deal with the republican institutions mostly run by political leaders who had graduated from the seminaries, including Gregoire Kayibanda (President 1962-1973), and the graduates of Indatwa College in Astrida.[14] The church's active role and influence in Rwandan politics with an ethos of closeness was extensively documented by many researchers.[15]

In 1963, the Dominicans from Canada created the first university in Rwanda which remained the only one until the 1990s. The church and its religious congregations run many organisations, social and charity activities under Caritas, schools under the Secretariat for Education, youth and lay organisations, newspapers including Kinyamateka (1933), the only Rwandan weekly for years, and Hobe, the journal for children created by Mgr Bigirumwami (1954). In 1988, the church started a radio station, *Radio Maria,* which broadcast from Kabgayi. From cultural and intellectual perspectives, much of the scholarly information and knowledge on past and present Rwanda were produced within the Roman Catholic Church by foreign and local clergy, including the most prominent Father Alexis Kagame.[16]

Protestant initiatives in evangelism include the 1925 Kirinda missionary conference that initiated the translation of the Bible in Kinyarwanda,[17] the establishment in 1930 of geographic limits for missions to avoid competition and rivalry, the formation in 1935 of the Alliance of the Protestant churches in Rwanda and Burundi and, finally, the formation in 1963 of the Council of Protestant Churches in Rwanda (CPR)[18] which co-ordinated various activities, including education, through its office of National Protestant Education, BNEP.

Speaking out for God from Personal Piety

In 1933, a spiritual revival emerged in Gahini, an Anglican missionary station. Influenced by the Keswick revival movement in England, the Rwandan movement was later known as the East African Revival; its

---

[13] Aloys Bigirumwami in Nyundo, Jean Baptiste Gahamanyi in Butare, Joseph Sibomana in Ruhengeri then Kibungo and the Swiss born André Perraudin in Kabgayi. Mgr Perraudin, as Primate of the Catholic Church from 1956 to 1976 sponsored the first Rwandan politicians including Grégoire Kayibanda. In 1976 Vincent Nsengiyumva took over both ecclesial and political leadership. Today, the Roman Catholic Church has 9 dioceses, more than 140 parishes for over 6 million believers. Much smaller, the Anglican Church has 11 diocèses for less than 1 million of believers.

[14] Created by the Colonial government for the education of the sons of the chiefs, the college was given to the Fathers of Charity for management.

[15] Linden 1977; 1999; Justin Kalibwami 1991; Rutayisire 1989 & 2014; Blackmann 1994; Gatwa 2005

[16] Father Alexis Kagame of the indigenous clergy started his intellectual activities in late 1930s; he was appointed by King Mutara III a member of the prestigious Abiru royal institution hence acceded to volume of royal corpus of cultural and traditional material. He defended a doctoral thesis of philosophy in 1951 in Rome on the Rwandan philosophy of being published in 1954]. Philosopher, ethno-historian, linguist he was a reference of knowledge in Africa, one of the editors of the General history of Africa by UNESCO. Other influential figures of the local clergy was Mgr Aloys Bigirumwami who collected and commented volumes of corpus of the Rwandan popular wisdoms under the title *Imihango n'Imigenzereze ya Kinyarwanda*, work that has become a reference to subsequent studies; Father Muzungu [See his three volumes, *Le Dieu des nos peres*]. Among foreigners, Canon De Lacger, Father Pages, Arnaux; Nothomb.

[17] The translation was sponsored by the United Bible Society and the British and Foreign Bible Society. Led by Rev Harold Guillebaud from the UK, the team published the NT in Kinyarwanda in 1931 and the whole Bible in 1957. The Catholics waited until 1967 when Father Alexis Kagame published the first translation of the New Testament. In 1981 both Protestant and Catholics initiated an ecumenical translation of the Bible completed in 2002; but in parallel, the Catholic conducted their own translation which was published in 1989.

[18] In 1962 Ruanda-Urundi obtained independence into two entities. The tense political context wouldn't allow to work cross the two borders; hence the Alliance of Protestant Churches split into the Alliance of Churches for Burundi and the Protestant Council for Rwanda.

focus was not the ruling elite as with the Catholics, but individuals. The missionaries attempted to emulate the Keswick teachings on the holiness of God, the new birth, repentance, faith, prayer, the Holy Spirit, sanctification, the public confession of sins, visions and prophecies, participating regularly in fellowship meetings, and walking in the light of the Holy Spirit. After a promising beginning, the movement declined in the 1950s, a development blamed on opposition coming from Catholicism, communism and nationalism.[19] It reappeared in the 1970s in an Anglican girls' school in Kigeme. From a Puritan perspective, the revival achieved a great deal: the *Abarokore* or 'born-again' involved in evangelisation insisted on the *ethnic togetherness*, while teams of evangelists sponsored by the Ruanda Mission toured East Africa, Europe, Asia and the Americas, forming a worldwide fellowship. Their attitude towards politics, on the other hand, was one of clear distance.

Catholics, Protestants, State Relations and Social Actions

The relations between missionaries and King Musinga regime were never very good. The King suspected the missionaries of thwarting his power and plotting to take away his authority, while the missionaries saw him as anti-missionary and western civilisation.

Between Catholics and Protestants, relations were never very good either. While the Catholics were influential in Rwandan politics, the Protestants were left on the sidelines but the constant internal quarrelling for power and leadership, particularly within the Anglican Church from the 1970s up to the 1990s, never helped to promote the credibility of the Protestants. However both Catholics and Protestants, separately, initiated many socio-economic activities to alleviate poverty and the suffering of the people. As from the beginning, about a hundred Catholic orders joined in supporting the mission work, providing both human and material resources. Religious orders helped to create or run schools on behalf of the Belgian colonial power.[20]

Protestants were both discriminated against but also had little ambition to promote general education. It was only in 1947 that the alliance of the Protestant churches in Ruanda-Urundi opened the first secondary school for primary school teachers in Shyogwe. The first Protestant high school opening up to university education started in 1965 in Kigali, by the Presbyterian Church of Rwanda, assisted by the Swiss churches. A centre of excellence, the College Officiel de Kigali (COK) was unfortunately nationalised in 1976 by the Habyarimana regime to host the Franco-African College of Statistics and Applied Economics (IAMSEA).

The Training of the Clergy

Lavigerie, a former professor of ecclesiastical history in the Paris Sorbonne University (1853-1860), applied the early church structure on the catechumenate. He was inspired by the Canon XVIII's conclusions of the Council of Trent and the Leon XIII (1878-1903) encyclical in which the Pope invited the universal church, in particular in Africa, to create seminaries. Mgr Hirth, a former assistant rector and professor of seminaries in Algiers and Jerusalem, had experience of seminaries. He created the first seminary in 1903 in Rubya, Tanzania; fifteen Rwandans (ten from Save and five from Zaza) were recruited; in 1904, they joined 43 other recruits from the rest of the Vicariate. Of these Rwandans, two, Donat Rebero and Balthazar Gafuku, persisted up to priestly ordination in 1917; they were the first Rwandan priests.

---

[19] Ntihinyuzwa: 354

[20] To mention but a few, the school of sons of chiefs, Indatwa in Astrida created in 1926 run by the Fathers of Charity; the technical school in Kicukiro, Kigali run by the Salesians; the Athenee Royale, Bujumbura, Burundi run by the fathers of Holy Spirit, etc.

In 1913, following the creation by Pope Pius X of the Kivu Vicariate, detached from Nyanza's and consisting of Rwanda, Burundi and Buha (west of Tanzania), a new seminary opened in Kabgayi. It was transferred to Nyakibanda in 1936 till the present. When Mgr Hirth retired in 1922, the Pope created two Vicariates, one for Rwanda, given to Mgr Leon Classe, and another for Burundi, given to Mgr Gorju. Rwanda and Burundi continued to train priests in Nyakibanda till 1952.[21] Between 1917 and 2012, the Kabgayi, then the Nyakibanda, seminaries had formed 1,054 priests.

Within the Protestant missions, clergy training was viewed with suspicion and even accused of a lack of faith. Exceptionally, the Presbyterian Church pioneered theological formation in sending candidates to train abroad, starting with Naasson Hitimana and Ildephonse Muzigamfizi, who trained in Cameroon from 1958. These two were ordained to ministry in 1963, 46 years after the first Roman Catholic ordination. Hitimana became the first African leader of the church. He pioneered the creation of the first ecumenical theological seminary in Butare in 1970, which has since trained about 700 pastors and church leaders. As from 2010, this institution was transformed into a fully-fledged university, the Protestant Institute of Arts and Social Sciences (PIASS). Within the Protestant family, the Seventh Day Adventist Church, after years of stagnation, revised with quality education under the Union's leadership of the Rev. Peck, E. Sembeba, Amon Rugerinyange and Hesron Byiringiro.[22]

Religiosity and Mariology

From 28th November 1981, another spiritual revival was sparked off in the Roman Catholic Church of Kibeho, south of Rwanda. Many school pupils claimed to have received messages from the 'Mother of the Word', i.e. the Virgin Mary. The visionaries invited the church hierarchy, public authorities and the populace to repent, devote, love and revere the 'Mother of God'. The Roman Catholic hierarchy was divided between the pros and the antis. Some questioned the poor academic background of the school children, their Biblical illiteracy and their moral standards, while others suspected political manipulations.[23] And yet, on 29th June 2000, Kibeho was officially recognised as a 'holy place of apparitions of the Virgin Mary'. It has become a pilgrimage destination for believers from the region and beyond.

The Church and the Genocide

The church hierarchies have been blamed to missing the opportunity to address ethnic discrimination and manipulation before and during the genocide.[24] Many observers trace the genocide ideology back to the 1959 episode, during which hundreds of the ruling Batutsi elite were killed and others sent into exile. While the discrimination of the Bahutu was overwhelming during the time of colonial rule, dominated by the colonial-missionary alliance with the Batutsi ruling elite, the situation was reversed during the republican era. In 1990, when the descendants of the 1959 refugees attacked Rwanda from Uganda, the regime exacerbated ethnic feelings against the Batutsi community within the country. Many killings were conducted in various places of Batutsi concentration. The paroxysm was the 1994 genocide that followed the death of Presidents Habyarimana of Rwanda and Ntaryamira of Burundi.[25]

---

[21] That same year Burundi opened its Superior Seminary in Burasira.

[22] Today the Seven Day Adventist Church has three universities, one for the whole central Africa, in Kigali, a second in Gitwe and a lay University in Kigali.

[23] Misago, later bishop of Gikongoro that covers Kibeho, remarked that some of the visionaries were regularly invited by the propagandists of the regime even seen in the private residences of the president of Rwanda [Misago 1991:366].

[24] Rutayisire 2014

[25] Gatwa 2005

The post-genocide era was characterised by a malaise created by both the loss of the Catholic Church's dominant position and criticism lodged against her misguided role and the absence of stance against the genocide.[26] The church hierarchy had kept silent or had spoken too little while hundreds of thousands of victims, including believers and members of the clergy, were being slaughtered across the country.[27]

In 1991, there was an AACC-inspired initiative, out of which the hierarchies on both sides formed a Contact Committee to mediate in the political crises between 1991 and early 1994. Though mixed results were achieved, the hierarchy missed the opportunity of capitalising on that to try to defuse the malaise. Some of the Protestant churches repented for the failure; but it was only in 1998 that the Catholic Church organised an extraordinary synod in dioceses in preparation for its centenary celebrations.[28] Interestingly, the approach run from below within ecclesial communities speaking up on the topic of ethnicism. One of the major findings was the need for a Gacaca (Rwanda's community courts which is loosly translated as "justice amongst the grass") but this was exploited by the government.[29]

A Spring of Revivalism

The religious life of the aftermath of the 1994 genocide was imbued with the arrival of new charismatic movements. The end of the genocide inspired many refugees to return from their long exile; streams of former refugees managed to join some local churches. But many others decided to start their own church. A new era of religious pluralism started. In less than ten years, more than 300 new religious movements were registered.[30]

The absence of ecclesiology, doctrine and theological training for these initiators, expressed in liturgical improvisation, added to the extraordinary variety of leaders' titles and became a matter of controversy. First, they practised a theology of deliverance, calling the people – both the authorities and the populace – to pray continuously for deliverance; to publicly confess and repent of the evil that had led to the genocide. Secondly, the new churches formed their own 'fora' (the Alliance of Evangelical Churches, AEC; the Federation of Born Again Churches and Organisations, FOBACOR). However, since 2000, these two convinced the older National Council, the Protestant Council of Rwanda (CPR) to form a body called 'Peace Plan'. Apostle Paul Gitwaza, leader of Zion Temple, one of the new churches, was elected in 2013 as its chair. He took over from retired Anglican, Archbishop Emmanuel Kolini. From 2011, 'Peace Plan' has organised annual crusades called *Rwanda Shima Imana* (Go Rwanda. Thank God!), to thank God for the country's renaissance.

In 2014, both Catholics and Protestants were able to co-operate in the elaboration of a declaration, confessing and repenting of missed opportunities of the past, as seen in the 1994 genocide against the Tutsi.[31] This move gave new hope for inter-church and church self-state dialogue.

---

[26] Blackmann 1994; Gatwa 2005; Rutayisire 2014

[27] Some exceptions include Pastor Athanase Rwamuhizi [a Presbyterian minister in Kugituntu parish]; Sr Félicité Niyitegeka of Nyundo, Father Munyaneza of Mukarange parish; Claver Nzabamwita and his wife Angelique Mushinzimana of Kiziguro, Mathias Kanamugire of Rukara; Cyprien Rugamba of the Emmanuel Community killed with his wife and children. Timothy Longman (2010), *Christianity and Genocide in Rwanda. African Studies 112*. NY: Cambridge University Press.

[28] Rutayisire 2014:3012, 3

[29] This traditional mechanism of conflict resolution within families and communities was rehabilitated by the government and used in the trial of the perpetrators of the genocide. As from 2001 up to 2012 the Gacaca community tribunals treated more or less 2 million cases.

[30] Gatwa & Rutinduka 2014, 246-249

[31] The process initiated by PEACE PLAN culminated in the June 2014 Musanze Church leaders' retreat which adopted the Declaration. The working group is chaired by the Anglican bishop of Kigeme, Augustin Mvunabandi.

Bibliography

Tharcisse Gatwa [2005], *Churches and Ethnic Ideology in Rwandan Crises 1900-1994* (Oxford and New Delhi: OCMS).

Tharcisse Gatwa and Laurent Rutinduka [2014], *Histoire du Christianisme au Rwanda des Origines à nos Jours* (Yaoundé: CLE).

Tharcisse Gatwa, 'Christianity in Rwanda', in Daniel Patté (ed), *The Cambridge Dictionary of Christianity*, (Cambridge and New York: Cambridge University Press, 2010), 1116-17.

Justin Kalibwami [1991], *Le Catholicisme et la Société Rwandaise 1900-1962* (Paris: Présence Africaine).

Augustin Mvuyekure [2003], *Le Catholicisme au Burundi 1922-1962: Approche Historique des Conversions* (Paris: Karthala).

Jean Van der Meersch [1993], *Le catéchuménat au Rwanda de 1900 à nos jours*. Kigali: Pallotti, 50.

Butselaar & Twagirayesu, ed [1982], *Ce don que nous avons Reçu*. Bruxelles: Eglise Presbytérienne au Rwanda.

http://www.state.gov/documents/organisation/222297.pdf, "Rwanda 2013 International Religious Freedom Report. Executive Summary accessed 24-01-2015.

(84) Christianity in Senegal

Simon Kossi Dossou

Religion	Pop 2010	Pct 2010	Pop 2025	Pct 2025	Gr Pct 1970 2025
Christians	703,000	5.4%	1,027,000	5.1%	2.6%
Independents	23,000	0.2%	34,000	0.2%	2.7%
African initiated	2,300	0.0%			
Protestants	13,300	0.1%	21,300	0.1%	3.2%
Roman Catholics	667,000	5.1%	1,000,000	5.0%	2.7%
Pentecostals/Charismatics	50,400	0.4%	75,000	0.4%	2.7%
Evangelicals	8,900	0.1%	13,000	0.1%	2.6%
Muslims	11,754,000	90.7%	18,492,000	92.3%	3.1%
adherents of traditional African religions	450,000	3.5%	450,000	2.2%	0.0%
Baha'is	24,900	0.2%	35,000	0.2%	2.3%
Buddhists	1,700	0.0%	2,200	0.0%	1.5%
adherents of new religious movements	1,000	0.0%	1,300	0.0%	1.7%
Chinese folk-religionists	410	0.0%	550	0.0%	1.9%
people professing no religion	21,600	0.2%	28,500	0.1%	1.9%
Total population	**12,957,000**	**100.0%**	**20,037,000**	**100.0%**	**2.9%**

Source: Centre for the Study of World Christianity (CSGC), Boston, Gordon-Conwell TS

Introduction

Dans l'Anthologie du Christianisme en Afrique, les Eglises du Sénégal, se retrouvent entre autres comme des minorités visibles mais croyantes en Christ vivant au milieu de populations majoritairement musulmane. Ainsi, parler des minorités visibles pose un problème d'équilibre qu'il n'est pas toujours facile d'établir. Cependant, cela constitue une richesse à l'échelle d'une nation.

Il est généralement admis de nos jours que le christianisme est en train de faire de grands bonds dans l'hémisphère Sud où se trouve le Sénégal. Dans ce pays comme dans plusieurs autres africains, les chiffres évoluent très rapidement à cause de la multiplication des lieux de cultes. Au Sénégal, ceci est dû à une religion musulmane assez tolérante dans le pays.

Après avoir présenté brièvement le pays, nous verrons les grandes communautés chrétiennes et leur rôle dans la vie socio-économique et politique du pays.

Le Senegal: Le Pays at Les Hommes

Le Sénégal est un pays d'une superficie de 196 722 Km2 avec une population d'environ 14 000000 d'habitants avec une forte densité de populations surtout dans les grandes villes. Les ethnies les plus nombreuses sont : Wolofs (46,3%), Peuls (21,8%), Sérères (14,7%), Diolas (3,7%), les Malinkés (3,0%) etc . On ajoute à ces populations locales, des Libanais, des Maghrébins, des européens dont un grand nombre de Français, des chinois et un grand important de populations africaines venues de plusieurs pays car le Sénégal abrite de nombreuses institutions internationales.

L'économie du pays est surtout basée sur la pêche, le tourisme et les services. L'agriculture est surtout basée sur l'arachide qui est devenue une spécialité locale par rapport à d'autres pays africains.

C'est dans cet environnement socio-économique que les chrétiens évoluent comme une minorité croyante. En effet, la population sénégalaise compte environ 95% de musulmans de traditions soufis, donc un islam tolérant en général. Les 5% restantes se partagent les autres manifestations de foi qu'elles soient chrétiennes ou non.

Le Christianisme au Senegal

Le Sénégal, est découvert par les portugais en 1445. Etant tous des chrétiens catholiques, ces portugais implantent leur religion dans les villes comme Gorée, Saint-Louis, Rufisque etc. C'est plus tard au 17è siècle que le Vatican va prendre directement le relais de l'évangélisation. Pendant longtemps, la religion chrétienne est restée celle des étrangers et les missionnaires n'ont pas réussi à s'attirer la bienveillance des populations locales comme il le fallait, bien que quelques natifs sénégalais soient devenus chrétiens.

En effet, l'islam qui est entré dans le pays par le biais des caravaniers a trouvé une terre d'accueil principalement à travers les puissants rois que sont les Toucouleurs El Hadj Omar TALL au Nord et Samory Touré au Sud.

La concurrence entre musulmans et chrétiens pour se faire des adeptes a tourné en faveur de l'islam car les leaders religieux du côté musulman étaient tous les marabouts sénégalais et non des arabes. Tandis que du côté des chrétiens, leurs leaders étaient presque tous des européens, ce qui donnait le sentiment aux sénégalais que le christianisme était une religion étrangère.

La foi chrétienne au Sénégal est portée par certaines églises qui sont plus ou moins le reflet des dénominations importées. Les principales Eglises ou communautés chrétiennes sont. :

L'Eglise catholique romaine

L'Eglise catholique au Sénégal a été prise en charge par le Vatican à partir du 17 è S. Mais c'est surtout à partir de 1819 qu'un essor des catholiques a été remarqué avec les sœurs de Saint Joseph de Cluny en France. Elles s'installent à Saint-Louis, ouvrent une chapelle et une école pour filles. La cathédrale de Saint-Louis sera construite et inaugurée en 1828. Plus tard ce sera l'Eglise de Gorée. C'est en 1840, que les premiers prêtres originaires de Saint-Louis vont être consacrés. En 1943, le premier collège secondaire catholique est fondé dans la même ville. Peu à peu le catholicisme gagne le pays, favorisé par les gouverneurs français, presque tous catholiques. Plusieurs congrégations monastiques comme les bénédictins, les franciscains et autres y sont arrivées d'Europe pour exercer leur vie de piété et mener plusieurs activités socio-économiques.

Aujourd'hui, le clergé catholique du Sénégal est majoritairement composé de Sénégalais et les vocations au ministère sacerdotal ne font pas défaut à cette église.

Comme on le constate avec les autres églises du pays, la cohabitation entre musulmans, chrétiens et adeptes d'autres religions est très paisible en général.

L'Eglise Protestante du Sénégal (EPS)

C'est en 1863 que le Directeur de la Société des Missions Evangéliques de Paris (SMEP), Eugène Casalis envoya au Sénégal un jeune Suisse du nom de Louis Jacques pour apprendre la langue et les mœurs des sénégalais. Celui-ci s'installa en Casamance et ouvrit aussitôt une station missionnaire comprenant une école. En 1867, trois sénégalais dont une femme appelée Salimata Ndiaye sont envoyés en France à l'Ecole

Protestante. En 1876, seule la femme revient de France car les deux autres hommes sont morts de fièvre jaune. Salimata nantie de son brevet devient monitrice à l'école des filles de Saint-Louis.

Dans la foulée, plusieurs missionnaires sont venus au Sénégal pour servir l'Eglise Protestante mais la mission n'a pas réussi à prendre parmi les autochtones. De 1924 à 1960, elle vivote car les missionnaires ne lui ont pas vraiment permis d'évoluer et est également restée l'église des étrangers venant de partout en Afrique et du monde. Tant bien que mal, l'EPS a continué à survivre au milieu de beaucoup d'incompréhensions internes jusqu'à la consécration de son tout premier pasteur sénégalais le 5 Décembre 1982, Samuel Vauvert Dansoko, de famille bambara. Ce dernier, parti pour des études théologiques complémentaires s'est installé aux Etat-Unis. L'Eglise a connu une crise majeure en 1996, ce qui a conduit l'autorité administrative à la fermer momentanément. Après plusieurs missions de réconciliations menées sous l'égide de la Conférence des Eglises de Toute l'Afrique (CETA) et de la Cevaa, Communauté d'Eglises en mission, le pasteur ivoirien Jonas ADOU y est envoyé en 2003 avec pour mission de la redynamiser. Celui-ci entreprend un travail de restructuration interne et fait former les responsables de femmes, de jeunes, leur donnant des capacités de devenir diacres, prédicateurs et anciens d'églises. Les activités ont sérieusement repris et il fait former trois pasteurs sénégalais dans les universités protestantes du Cameroun et du Bénin et qui sont déjà opérationnels sur le terrain. Deux autres lieux de culte ont été ouverts : Dieupeul à Dakar et Khor à Saint-Louis. Une autre paroisse est en projet en Casamance. Le Centre des œuvres sociales appelé Centre Liberté est construit avec à ses côtés une école maternelle et un cours primaire. Le pasteur Philippe Jean-Baptiste Mendy est l'actuel Modérateur de l'Eglise.

Eglise Luthérienne du Sénégal

L'Eglise Luthérienne du Sénégal est l'une des dernières nées des églises du monde œcuménique au Sénégal car elle a vu le jour en 1974 et à été officiellement reconnue comme association évangélique à but non lucratif, ni politique par les autorités du pays à travers un récépissé en date du 14 Février 1987.

Venu dans le paysage des églises protestantes du Sénégal, elle s'est développée assez rapidement et compte en ce moment plus d'une dizaines de paroisses et de champs d'évangélisation. Elle est ainsi présente dans six régions du pays dont : Thiès, Fatick, Dakar, Louga, Saint-Louis et Kaolack. Elle a trois départements : Formation théologique, développement communautaire et Action Sociale. Son personnel est majoritairement composé de sénégalais avec quelques missionnaires venus de l'extérieur.

La caractéristique principale de cette église est sa ferme volonté d'accompagner l'évangélisation par les œuvres de témoignage ou œuvres sociales. Ainsi, plusieurs jeunes gens et jeunes filles sont accompagnés pour leurs études et apprentissages à un métier. De même la petite enfance et le grand âge sont pris en compte selon les moyens de l'église.

Autres communautés de foi

Il est utile de signaler que malgré le caractère dominant de l'islam au Sénégal, il existe un grand nombre d'églises protestantes qui mènent leurs activités spirituelles à Dakar et environs. Ces églises sont l'émanation de communautés chrétiennes étrangères qui sont arrivées avec quelques fonctionnaires internationaux qui sont affectés dans le pays pour un temps. Une fois acceptées dans le pays, les membres de ces communautés continuent à maintenir la flamme allumée après le départ du fondateur officiel. Au nombre de ces églises ont peut citer : Eglise Baptiste de Dakar, Mission évangélique Foursquare au Sénégal, Mission Internationale de la vie, Eglise Evangélique de Dakar, Eglise Méthodiste de Grand Yoff, Eglise Méthodiste Unie Grand-Yoff et Nord-Foire Dakar, Eglise de la Grâce Internationale etc.

Le caractère parfois entreprenant de plusieurs de ces communautés plutôt pentecôtistes assimile leur méthode d'évangélisation au prosélytisme. Ceci a souvent créé des malentendus entre leurs responsables et des jeunes musulmans du pays engendrant parfois des troubles qui aboutissent à des pillages et incendies de lieux de cultes de temps à autres.

Si les églises évangéliques et pentecôtistes sont les plus touchées par ce genre de situations conflictuelles, il est arrivé que l'Eglise catholique n'y a pas été épargnée ces dernières années.

Cependant, le caractère pacifique de l'islam sénégalais n'a jamais été remis en cause par les chrétiens du pays.

Enfin, malgré l'hégémonisme de l'islam suivi du christianisme, il existe au Sénégal d'autres manifestations de la foi même très petites. C'est ainsi qu'on rencontre des adeptes des religions traditionnelles africaines surtout en Basse Casamance.

Tout en étant très insignifiant, il existe des personnes adeptes de la foi Bahaï, Bouddhiste que sont généralement des Asiatiques installés dans le pays depuis un certain nombre d'années.

Toutes ces religions contribuent à l'équilibre sociopolitique du pays car leurs dirigeants sont souvent consultés pour apporter leur point de vue par rapport aux situations cruciales engageant la vie des populations.

Conclusion

Au terme de cette brève présentation du christianisme au Sénégal, il est important de rappeler que ce pays est dirigé comme un Etat laïc malgré ses 95% de musulmans. C'est un islam très tolérant que les autres religions doivent cependant ménager à cause des idéologies importées qui sont susceptibles d'exacerber les tensions à la moindre occasion jugée contraire aux intérêts du plus grand nombre.

Bibliographie

BRIA I. et al (Editeurs): Dictionnaire Œcuménique de missiologie, Cerf/Labor et Fides/CLE 2003
DJEREKE J-C: Etre chrétien en Afrique aujourd'hui, CIPCRE, 2002
DOSSOU S.K.: Le Décalogue. CLE, 2002
KATO B.: Pièges théologiques en Afrique, CPE, 1981
SANNEH L.: West African Christianity, The religious Impact, Orbis Books 1983, NY
YAO BI E.NG: Côte d'Ivoire : Un siècle de catholicisme, Les Editions du CERAP, Abidjan 200
http://ambasenromevatican.over-blog.org/page/La_presence_de_lEglise_au_Senegal

(86) Christianity in Sierra Leone

Arnold C. Temple

Religion	Pop 2010	Pct 2010	Pop 2025	Pct 2025	Gr Pct 1970 2025
Christians	763,000	13.2%	960,000	12.2%	1.5%
Independents	167,000	2.9%	203,000	2.6%	1.3%
African initiated	64,100	1.1%			
Orthodox	570	0.0%	500	0.0%	-0.9%
Protestants	336,000	5.8%	361,000	4.6%	0.5%
Methodist	146,000	2.5%			
Holiness	58,000	1.0%			
Pentecostal	42,700	0.7%			
Roman Catholics	283,000	4.9%	400,000	5.1%	2.3%
Pentecostals/Charismatics	225,000	3.9%	270,000	3.4%	1.2%
Evangelicals	159,000	2.8%	181,000	2.3%	0.9%
Muslims	3,742,000	64.8%	5,367,000	68.2%	2.4%
adherents of traditional African religions	1,183,000	20.5%	1,400,000	17.8%	1.1%
Baha'is	13,500	0.2%	21,000	0.3%	3.0%
Hindus	3,000	0.1%	4,500	0.1%	2.9%
adherents of new religious movements	1,300	0.0%	2,000	0.0%	3.1%
people professing no religion	70,500	1.2%	120,000	1.5%	3.6%
Total population	**5,776,000**	**100.0%**	**7,874,000**	**100.0%**	**2.1%**

Source: Centre for the Study of World Christianity (CSGC), Boston, Gordon-Conwell TS

The Church in Sierra Leone started in 1792 with the coming of freed slaves to Freetown. They were members of the Methodists, Baptists and Countess of Huntingdon churches. They built chapels and organised congregations under local leadership. This group of settlers was later joined by another, known as Maroons, from Jamaica on 1st October 1800. They spent their first year building houses and their own chapel.

Sierra Leone became a British colony in 1808. The colony was in a strategic position from which to apprehend slave ships and enforce the ban on the slave trade. Within a period of fifty-six years of the ban, several ships loaded with slaves destined for the transatlantic market were intercepted and about 50,000 freed slaves brought to Freetown. These became known as 'Recaptives' or 'Liberated Africans'. The Church Missionary Society and the Wesleyan Methodist Missionary Society co-operated with the colonial government in providing education. They settled them in villages and demarcated the villages into parishes. In addition to the clergymen, schoolteachers were also appointed.

In time, the two groups of settlers and the 'Liberated Africans' became known as the Creoles. Together with seventeen ethnic communities, they form the population of Sierra Leone.

Seventeenth-Century Missionary Attempts

Even though present-day Christianity in Sierra Leone is derived from the events of 1792, it is worth noting that there were earlier missionary attempts in the seventeenth century. It is generally accepted that the first known Christian missionary to Sierra Leone was Father Balthasar Barreira, a Portuguese Jesuit who visited in 1605. His mission was unsuccessful and he left Sierra Leone in 1610. Other Jesuits and Capuchins made attempts but to no avail. Their mission was hampered by the growing British influence during the eighteenth century. The politics of Europe affected the work of mission in Sierra Leone in no small measure.

Activities from 1822 onwards saw the establishment of Roman Catholicism in Sierra Leone.

In 1822, Mother Anne-Marie Javouhey, the founder of the Sisters of St Joseph of Cluny, visited Sierra Leone and Gambia. She organised the 'Liberated African' Hospital. Unfortunately, it was the time of the yellow fever epidemic. She caught the fever herself and returned to France in September 1823.

Bishop Melchoir Marie Joseph De Marion Bresillac, a French missionary bishop, was the first Roman Catholic bishop of Sierra Leone, appointed in 1858. He arrived on 16th May 1859. Unfortunately, an epidemic broke out in Sierra Leone. Within a period of seven weeks of his arrival, the bishop and four priests died. They were buried at the Kissy Road Cemetery in Freetown, after funeral rites performed by a Methodist minister, replacing the Anglican bishop who had also died before the ceremony. The funeral service was well attended by Protestant Christians, bringing out in a very clear way the ecumenical spirit that characterised Sierra Leone Christianity.

Mainline Protestantism

The churches continued under local leadership until 1811, when the first expatriate Methodist missionary, the Rev. George Warren, and three school teachers were appointed and sent out by the British Conference.

With the establishment of the churches by the settlers' community and the involvement of the missionary societies, particularly the Church Missionary Society (CMS) and the Wesleyan Methodist Missionary Society (WMMS), the seed of mainline Protestantism was planted on the soil of Sierra Leone. It germinated and took root and growth started.

With the establishment of parishes, societies or congregations, the missions built schools along with churches. Wherever the missions spread, a western educational system was established. Schools became strategic in mission.

In addition to the many primary schools, secondary education was also provided. CMS established the Sierra Leone Grammar School (1845) and its female counterpart, the Annie Walsh Memorial School (1849). The Methodist Boys' High School (1874) and the Methodist Girls' High School (1880) were established by the Methodists. In 1922, the Roman Catholics established St Edward's Secondary School for boys and St Joseph's Convent which later became a secondary school for girls.

In 1814, the Church Missionary Society built an institution at Leicester village for the training of children in various trades and teaching. This later became Fourah Bay College in April 1827. It was granted university status in 1876 and affiliated to the University of Durham. When the institution was threatened by lack of funds, the Anglican Bishop Walmsley entered a collaborative scheme with the Wesleyan Methodist Missionary Society. It was this ecumenical initiative that saved the closure of Fourah Bay College.

Other denominations also established schools and, by the year 1904, out of 42 secondary schools in Sierra Leone, 28 were established and run by the churches. The trend is the same today as the church continues to have an impact on the education system.

Both in the days of colonial rule and now, as far as possible, the churches have worked in co-operation with the government and within government policy guidelines on education. They have also remained the proprietors of their schools while the government takes the responsibility for paying teachers' salaries and also makes grants towards the repair of buildings and equipment. However, this co-operation seemed to take control of the schools' curriculum away from the churches, with the result that Christian education no longer has a prominent place in the curriculum. It has become an optional subject and in some schools is not taught at all. This has become a matter of great concern for the churches, and they are now rethinking the nature of their co-operation with the government in education.

Socio-Political Action as Christian Pastoral Encounter

The missions were also engaged in medical work. The missionaries were themselves victims of the climatic conditions and attacks of malaria.

In response to the lack of proper medical care resulting in the high mortality rate, the Church Missionary Society established the Princess Christian Cottage Hospital in 1892, with a doctor and three nurses from England to serve the east end community of Freetown. In a similar vein, Mrs Medd, a trained nurse and wife of a Methodist missionary, ran a clinic on her veranda. This effort grew into the Wesley Guild Hospital in 1930, renamed the Nixon Memorial Hospital in 1950. The Roman Catholic Mission opened a general and maternity clinic in Serabu in the Southern Province in about the mid-1950s.

About 1969, the Baptist Mission established a dispensary in Mambolo, and an eye clinic in 1974. An extension of the ophthalmic clinic, including wards for the admission of patients, was undertaken in 1976. The mission also runs a rehabilitation centre where those who recover are taught agricultural methods and crafts to enable them to become useful in society and earn a living.

In 1968, the Methodists established a demonstration farm in Tikonko in the Southern Province with an extension service to over fifty villages in the Tikonko and Bumpe Chiefdoms. Unfortunately, his project was brought to an end by civil war in Sierra Leone (1991-2002).

With the establishment of the new Missionary Diocese of Bo within the Anglican Church in Sierra Leone in 1981, a health centre was built in Kangama in 1986. Before that, there was no medical work of the Anglican Church in the hinterland. The diocese encouraged a policy of each parish developing an agricultural project. The aim, according to Bishop Gbonda, was to improve the livelihood of the members so they would be better able to support the diocese through their parishes; a move towards self-reliance.

The missionary movement from Sierra Leone to other parts of West Africa can be linked with the economic growth of the colony. The Niger expedition, which was an economic venture, opened up travelling possibilities along the coast and contributed to the evangelistic thrust. In about 1839, some 'Liberated Africans' bought a slave ship from an auction mart and named it *Wilberforce,* after William Wilberforce. They made a journey to Badagry on 1st April, where they sold mainly British goods from Sierra Leone and returned with goods from Nigeria.

Following the success of that voyage, these 'Liberated Africans', through Thomas Will, one of their leaders, petitioned the government to permit them to be involved in a commercial venture in Badagry. With permission granted, they requested the Church Missionary Society and the Wesleyan Methodist Missionary Society to provide missionaries so that the Christian mission would be established alongside the commercial venture. Interestingly, Badagry had been a centre of slave trading in the past.

Both the Wesleyan Methodist Missionary Society and the Church Missionary Society showed interest in the expedition, as it provided an avenue for the expansion of mission. Those on the expedition included the Rev. J.F. Schon and the Rev. Samuel Adjai Crowther. They returned as envoys of peace and reconciliation to the very port from which they had been taken and sold as slaves. They had worked hard and purchased a condemned slave vessel which they had put together, and employed a navigator and proceeded to Badagry, not just out of economic interest but also with the intention of making the gospel known.

By the 1860s, there were Creole civil servants, traders and missionaries in the Gambia, Liberia, Ghana and Nigeria. There were fairly large Creole communities in Congo, Fernando-Po and the Cameroons. Wherever the Creole community was established and whatever the purpose, be it trade or government service, the mission of the church was established alongside it.

The Rev. W.H. During, a 'Liberated African' Methodist minister, was sent from Sierra Leone as a missionary to Kenya in 1880, and worked at the headquarters of the mission in Rivbe. He commanded great respect among the people and was nicknamed the *Mzungu-mweusi*, which is translated the black European.[1]

The Roman Catholic mission also developed an interest in the Mende land and opened a station in Serabu, in the Bumpeh Chiefdom, in February 1905. It was the fruit of effective pastoral ministry. While Chief Makavore of Bumpeh Chiefdom was imprisoned at Pademba Road Prison, in Freetown, for complicity in the 1898 Hut Tax War, the Roman Catholic Bishop, O'Gorman, visited him on frequent occasions. On his release, the chief was grateful and became a Roman Catholic. He then invited the bishop to send a missionary to the area. The bishop appointed Father Kuntzmann to Serabu and the Sacred Heart Parish was established there with a school attached to it.

The United Brethren in Christ Mission

From the start of its mission in 1839, the United Brethren in Christ have concentrated in the Mende and Sherbro areas of Sierra Leone. Mission agents combined trading with their mission work in order to be self-supporting. The mission also started a work among the Kono people in 1910.

The union among the Methodists, the Evangelical United Brethren and United Brethren in Christ in America in 1968 led to the Evangelical United Brethren Church becoming the 'United Methodist Church in Sierra Leone'.

American Wesleyans and the Baptist Convention

The work of the American Wesleyan Mission was a northern mission, started in Kunso in the Northern Region of Sierra Leone in 1889. At the request of the Chief of Masumbo, a station was opened and missionaries stationed there. By the year 1919, the mission was well established in the North.

The Rev. Gill, a missionary associated with the Baptists, started the mission at Mambolo. In spite of the fact that Mambolo was predominantly a Muslim village, the Baptist Church was enthusiastically welcomed by the Paramount Chief, who was also a Muslim. The Chief put about a hundred acres of land at the disposal of the mission. A co-educational secondary school was opened in September 1968 with five hundred pupils and a dispensary established.

The Rev. Hagan saw the need for co-operation in the mission field. He sought to have a united Baptist witness. He called a meeting of the various Baptist groups involved in work in Sierra Leone. Following a series of meetings, the Baptist Convention of Sierra Leone was inaugurated and the Rev. Joseph Saidu Mans was elected its first President.

The Rev. J. S. Mans retired as President of the Convention in 1994 and was succeeded by the Rev. Moses Kanu and later by the Rev. Tani Babington-Johnson.

---

[1] T. A. Beetham, "A Sierra Leone Missionary to Kenya", *Sierra Leone Bulletin of Religion* 1, no. 2 (1959) 56-57. Cf. *The Minutes of Conference United Methodist Free Church 1875-1891.*

The African Independent Churches

Independent prayer groups, founded mainly by women, preceded the African Independent Churches. One was founded by a respected member of the Freetown community, Mrs Martha Davies and nine women, including Mrs Jane Bloomer and Mrs Adela Jones. Their activities included singing, praying, the study of the scriptures and sharing of their experiences of God's presence and love manifested in his protection and providence. They met mainly on weekdays and Sunday afternoons. They did not consider themselves a church, but as a prayer group that supplemented the prayer ministry of the churches in Freetown.

One of their number, Mother Jane Bloomer, was ordained by the Bishop of the African Methodist Episcopal Church and she became the first woman to be ordained a minister in Sierra Leone.

The God is our Light Church that originated from Ghana was established in Sierra Leone in 1944 by Mr James Ngebuva Kajue (a Roman Catholic) and Mr Seineh Sesay. They became members of that church while they were attached to the Ghana Railway in Tekoradi as signalmen.

Apostle Adejobi was the influential person who took the Church of the Lord 'Aladura' from Nigeria to Sierra Leone. Several other such churches, from Nigeria, Ghana and those founded by Sierra Leoneans, were established in the 1950s and 1960s, and were popular among Christians in Sierra Leone.

Setbacks and Schisms

With more than two hundred years of mission to its credit, the mainline churches in Sierra Leone have not grown much. Several reasons are responsible for this state of affairs. There were cracks in the relationship between the western expatriate missionaries and the natives. Some of the missionaries demonstrated imperialistic tendencies and capitalised on existing ethnic divisions. That affected, and continues to affect, the growth of Christianity in Sierra Leone adversely and in no small measure.

Schisms and disunity are other major setbacks in the mission of the church in Sierra Leone and have played a vital role in the slow growth of the churches. Small as Sierra Leone is, it has more than fifty autonomous denominations. With a population of just about six million and the Christians forming just about 20% of it, the situation is ridiculous. It all boils down to concerns around issues of 'power'.

An Autonomous Methodist Church

As the spirit of nationalism pervaded the political arena following Independence in 1961 and the preparations for the 1967 elections, the Committee could no longer fail to see the wisdom of autonomy. It finally came in 1967. The Sierra Leone Synod of the Conference of the British Methodist Church became an autonomous Conference of the Methodist Church, Sierra Leone.

The inaugural conference was held in Freetown in January 1967 with representatives from each of the two Districts, and the Rev. W.E.A. Pratt was elected as President of Conference. The provincial district was later further divided into two, the Bo/Kenema district and the Kailahun/Kono district.

In the Conference of 2014, the nomenclature 'President' was changed to 'Bishop', and the Rt Rev. Arnold Temple inducted and installed his successor, the Rt Rev. Albert S. Beah as Bishop of the Methodist Church, Sierra Leone.

Pentecostals

The 1980s saw the emergence of new Pentecostal and Charismatic churches. This was influenced by several factors, including the seeming superficial worship of the mainline churches and the visit of American and European evangelists, including Reinhard Bonnke. Bible schools organised by Freetown Bible Center contributed to the new thinking. As the new churches mushroomed, there was in-fighting and attempts, even among themselves, to 'unchurch' each other. Sanity returned with leadership offered by Bishop Archibald Cole, Bishop Sam Jolly and others. The Pentecostal Fellowship of Sierra Leone was formed, with Bishops Cole and Jolly as President and Secretary respectively.

Ecumenical Initiatives

Inspired by the vision of Bishop Walmsley, the Anglican Bishop, a 'Denominational Co-operation' conference was held in Freetown in 1912. The original thrust was for co-operation in evangelism and Bible translation. The work of the continuation committee led to the formation of the United Christian Council in 1926. In 1950, it became the co-ordinating body for the churches in matters of education. This became a very effective national ecumenical instrument. It later changed its name to the Council of Churches in Sierra Leone.

The Council played a major role in galvanising the churches for a significant engagement in ending the civil war in Sierra Leone (1991-2002). It provided relief for refugees and displaced people, and took the risk in seeking out the rebel leader, Foday Sankoh, in the jungle and engaging him in peace talks. The church and their Muslim counterparts formed the Inter-religious Council and created a chance for reconciliation. The Bishop of the United Methodist Church, who was also the President of the Council of Churches, provided leadership in the Truth and Reconciliation Committee.

With the outbreak of the Ebola virus in Sierra Leone in 2014, the Council positioned itself and engaged positively with the government and relevant institutions in the effort of combating the disease.

Bibliography

Alie, Joe A. D. (1990), *A New History of Sierra Leone,* London: Macmillan Publishers Ltd.

Bane Martin. J. (1956) *Catholic Pioneers In West Africa,* Dublin: Clonmore and Raynolds, Ltd.

Forster, Raymond Samuel (1961) *The Sierra Leone Church, An Independent Anglican Church*, London: SPCK

Fyfe, Christopher (1962) A History of Sierra Leone, London: Oxford University Press.

Ingham E. G. (1894) *Sierra Leone after A Hundred Years,* London.

Johnson T. S. (1953) *The Story of a Mission: The Sierra Leone Church, First Daughter of CMS*, London: SPCK.

Kendall Elliott (1978) *The End of an Era: Africa and The Missionary*, S.P.C.K. London.

Marke Charles (1913) *Wesleyan Methodism in Sierra Leone,* London: Charles H. Kelly.

Olson Gilbert W. (1969) *Church Growth in Sierra Leone*, Grand Rapids, Michigan: William B. Eerdmans Publishing Company.

Pratt, Lewis J. *The Methodist Church, Sierra Leone- From a Mission to an Autonomous Conference*, (unpublished handbook).

Sanneh, Lamin (1983), *West African Christianity; The Religious Impact*, London: C. Hurst & Company Ltd.

Shyllon, Lesie E. T. (2008) *Two Centuries of Christianity in an African Province of Freedom – Sierra Leone, a case study of European influence and culture in Church development, Freetown: Print Sundries and Stationers.*

Stock, Eugene. (1899) *The History Of The Church Missionary Society: Its Environment, Its Men And Its Work,* (in four volumes) London: Church Missionary Society

Sumner, D. L (1963) *Education in Sierra Leone*, Freetown: Government Printing Press

Temple-Anono, ACee (2012) *Being the Church in Sierra Leone Today,* Freetown: Institute of Mission Study & Research

Turner, Harold W. (1967) *African Independent Church:* Vol. 1 *The Church of the Lord Aladura*, Oxford University Press.
Valcarcel, S. J. (n.d.) *A Short History of Baptists In Sierra Leone*, European Baptist Mission, Bad Homburg.
Avery W. L. (1972) 'Christianity in Sierra Leone' *African Research Bulletin* II, 2, pages 3-28
Beetham, T. A. (1959) 'A Sierra Leone Missionary To Kenya' *Sierra Leone Bulletin of Religion* 1, no. 2, pages 57-62.
Buxton Thomas F. V. (1913) 'The Creole in West Africa' *African Society*, XII.
Buxton T. F. 'The Vocational outlook of the Sierra Leone Creoles' *Sierra Leone Studies*, old series, No. 32, pages 52-57
Fyfe C. H. (June 1961) ' West African Methodists in the Nineteenth Century' *Sierra Leone Bulletin of Religion* III, 1. pages 22 – 29
Fyfe C. H. (July 1962) 'The Baptist Churches in Sierra Leone' *Sierra Leone Bulletin of Religion*, IV 2, pages 53-61)
Fyfe C. H. (December 1962), 'The Countess of Huntingdon Connexion in the nineteenth century' *Sierra Leone Bulletin of Religion,* Vol. 4. No. 2,
Hair P. E. H. (June 1963) 'Archdeacon Crowther and the Delta Pastorate 1892-1899' *Sierra Leone Bulletin of Religion, Vol.* 5. No. 1, pages 18-27.
Hair P. E. H. (December 1964) 'Freetown Christianity and Africa' Vol. 6 No. 2, pages 13-21
Hair P. E. H. (1966) 'Creole Endeavour and Self Criticism in Sierra Leone Church Missions' *Sierra Leone Bulletin of Religion,* VIII.1.
Hamelberg Edward (June 1964) 'The Jesuits in Sierra Leone 1605-1617. A Whirlwind of Grace' *Sierra Leone Bulletin of Religion,* Vol. 6 No. 1, pages 1-8.
Kup A. P. 'Jesuits and Capuchin Missions of the Seventeenth Century' *Sierra Leone Bulletin of Religion*, Vol. 5 No. 1 pp. 27-34
Markwei Martie (December 1967) 'The Rev. Charles Knight in Methodist History' *Sierra Leone Bulletin of Religion 2*, Vol. 9. No. 2, pp. 55-66.
Ndanema I. M. (1961) 'The Martha Davies Confidential Benevolent Association' *Sierra Leone Bulletin of Religion* Vol. 3 No. 2 pp. 64-67
Walls A. F. (June 1959) 'The Nova Scotian Settlers and their Religion' *Sierra Leone Bulletin of Religion* 1, pages 3-28.
Walls A. F. (June 1961) 'The Usefulness of School Masters...' *Sierra Leone Bulletin of Religion* Vol. 3, No. 1 pp. 28- 40.
Walls A. F. (1970) 'A Christian Experiment: The Early Sierra Leone Colony' in Cummings, *Studies in Church History,* Vol. 6 'The Mission of the Church and the Propagation of the Faith, Cambridge University Press, pages 107 – 129.

(87A) Christianity in Somalia

Bob Hedley

Religion	Pop 2010	Pct 2010	Pop 2025	Pct 2025	Gr Pct 1970 2025
Christians	4,500	0.0%	4,100	0.0%	-0.5%
Independents	400	0.0%	400	0.0%	0.0%
African initiated	400	0.0%			
Orthodox	1,800	0.0%	1,300	0.0%	-2.1%
Protestants	2,000	0.0%	2,200	0.0%	0.6%
Roman Catholics	100	0.0%	100	0.0%	0.0%
Evangelicals	550	0.0%	700	0.0%	1.6%
Pentecostals/Charismatics	450	0.0%	500	0.0%	0.7%
Muslims	9,558,000	99.8%	14,315,000	99.8%	2.7%
adherents of traditional African religions	7,000	0.1%	9,000	0.1%	1.6%
Hindus	5,400	0.1%	7,500	0.1%	2.2%
Baha'is	2,800	0.0%	3,600	0.0%	1.8%
people professing no religion	4,200	0.0%	5,000	0.0%	1.1%
Total population	**9,582,000**	**100.0%**	**14,344,000**	**100.0%**	**2.7%**

Source: Centre for the Study of World Christianity (CSGC), Boston, Gordon-Conwell TS

Somalia has an estimated population of about 11 million people. Most Somalis are Sunnis, based on Ash'ariyah theology and Shafi'I jurisprudence. There has been a history of Sufism, and in recent years Salafism has been growing. It is believed that Islam was introduced into Somalia very soon after the Hijra in 622 AD. The oldest mosque in Somalia is said to date from the seventh century. Many believe that conversion from Islam to another religion, or a different branch of Islam, is equivalent to apostasy (Arabic: *ridda*). Muslim scholars have different views on the punishment which should be meted out to apostates, basing their arguments on the Qu'ran and the Hadith. According to different interpretations, punishment will either be in the after-life, or should be dealt with by imprisonment, beating or the death penalty. There are also different prescriptions for men and for women, but generally a period of three days' imprisonment is allowed for the apostate to return to Islam. The death penalty is the common punishment meted out in many Islamic communities. As Islam is considered by many Somalis to be the 'religion of Somalis', any person converting to Christianity is considered to be an apostate, and deserving death. At the very least, a convert can expect to be 'considered dead' by their clan and family members, and shunned by them. Thus Somali Christians tend to keep a very low profile, and keep to themselves.

There is no record of Christian mission in Somalia before 1881, although Christian Ethiopians must have traded with Somalis before that. In the 1880s, present-day Somalia was taken from the various ruling sultans, and was divided between the British, who established a protectorate over what is known as Somaliland, and the Italians. (Other Somali groups were also present in modern-day Djibouti, north-east Kenya, and south-east Ethiopia.) During the colonial period, Christian missionary activity started to take place, with Christians carrying out diaconal work, as well as serving predominantly the expatriate community. The first Roman Catholic missionaries arrived in 1881, and began serving the expatriate community, establishing missions in Berbera, Mogadishu and Kismayo. Swedish Lutheran missionaries followed in 1889. The Swedish Lutherans record baptising 350 Somalis during their time in Somalia. At the end of World War I, the Italians forbade the Lutherans from operating in their territory, and expelled the Protestant missionaries. Somalia was established as a Vicariate Apostolic by the Holy See, and a cathedral was built in Mogadishu in 1928. The Catholic missionaries worked predominantly among the 'Bantu' Somalis, a minority ethnic group which descended from Bantu ex-slaves who were brought to Somalia as a work force for their Somali overlords.[1]

The Anglicans also had established work, predominantly in Somaliland. The work of the Anglican Church fell under the Anglican Diocese of Egypt. Mennonites and the Sudan Inland Mission both began social service projects in Somalia. By 1950, a population of about 8,500 Somali Christians was recorded.

In mid-1960, both (Italian) Somaliland and (British) Somaliland gained independence and joined together as Somalia, under an elected government. The first constitution was accepted in 1961. In it, Somalia is declared as an Islamic state. The government was overthrown in a military coup in 1969, following the execution of the second President, Abdirashid Ali Shermarke, and Siad Barre took power. Siad Barre promulgated 'scientific socialism' which, despite his assertions that it was compatible with Islam, alienated many Somali Muslims, particularly after the execution of ten Muslim leaders following a protest. A new constitution was put in place in 1979.[2]

Siad Barre did not allow the missionaries to proselytise, but did allow them to carry out humanitarian work. The Catholic Relief Services began work in Somali in the 1960s. Apostasy was still legally considered a crime.

On 16th March 1976, the Holy See consecrated Bishop Pietro Salvatore Colombo, OFM, as Bishop, and established the Catholic Diocese of Mogadishu on 20th November that year. The Roman Catholic Church carried out diaconal work through Caritas Somalia. In the same year, the Mennonites and SIM missionaries were expelled from Somalia.

Civil war broke out in 1988, and Somaliland declared independence from the rest of Somalia in 1991, an ambition which it is still pursuing. The Anglican Church in Hargeisa was destroyed by bombing in 1988. Puntland, situated to the south of Somaliland, was relatively stable.

The ensuing inter-clan chaos, often referred to as 'the period of the warlords' caused immense suffering. In response, the first UN humanitarian mission, United Nations Operation in Somalia (UNOSOM I), took place. In November 1992, in response to a widespread famine which claimed about 300,000 lives, the UN began a second mission, the Unified Task Force (UNITAF), from December 1992 until May 1993 under the title 'Operation Restore Hope', and this was replaced by a third UN mission (UNOSOM II). Christian relief agencies were active in the humanitarian aid efforts.

A multinational military force led by the US tried to restore peace by defeating the warlords, and capturing Mogadishu under the title of 'Operation Gothic Support'. Notable among the warlords were Mohamed Farrah Aideed and Ali Mahdi Muhammed.

Many Somali Christians tried to leave and be resettled in other countries. The number of Somali Christians recorded in 1990 had dropped to about 2,000. Christians still remained active in diaconal work. The Roman Catholic Church had established a hospital at Mela, and a Nursing School in Mogadishu. Bishop Pietro Salvatore was assassinated in the cathedral in Mogadishu on 9th July 1989, and Bishop

[1] Jason Mandryk, *Operation World: The Definitive Prayer Guide to Every Nation* (Illinois: InterVarsity Press, 2010), 575; David B. Barrett, *World Christian Encyclopedia: A Comparative Survey of Churches and Religions in the Modern World, AD 1900-2000* (Oxford: Oxford University Press, 1984), 672-673.

[2] See Janice Hamilton, *Somalia in Pictures* (Minneapolis: Twenty-First Century Books, 2007), 30-32; Mohamed, Iman Abdulkadir. 'Somali Women and the Socialist State.' *Journal of Georgetown University-Qatar Middle Eastern Studies Student Association*, 2015, 4.

Giorgio Bertini of Djibouti was consecrated as the Apostolic Administrator after that, and still holds that position. In 1990, the Catholic hospital at Mela was destroyed.

In 1991, Siad Barre's regime was overthrown, and the Islamic Courts Union was founded, to restore a semblance of peace in Somalia, under the banner of Islam. In July 2006, with US support, Ethiopia invaded Somalia and the Islamic Courts Union was ousted, and a transitional federal government was set up, which was sited first in Nairobi, and later in Baidoa. Many Somalis perceived the invasion by Ethiopian forces as a 'Christian' country attacking a Muslim state (despite Ethiopia having a secular government, and having a Muslim population of about 40%.) By December 2006, the Islamic Courts Union had been ousted from Mogadishu. In 2007, the African Union, supported by the United Nations, set up the African Union Mission in Somalia (AMISOM), consisting of troops from six other African nations and a police force from five others. Part of the youth wing of the Islamic Courts Union developed into the Islamist movement, Al-Shabaab, which controls large swathes of Southern Somalia, and has linked itself with Al-Qaeda. Al-Shabaab promotes a strict interpretation of Sha'riah, and considers as apostate any who do not follow their interpretation. They consider the US and its allies, especially Ethiopia and Kenya, as 'crusaders against Islam'. Needless to say, the situation of the Christian minority continued to worsen, with Al Shabaab encouraging people to spy and inform on their neighbours. Sr Leonella Sgorbati, a Consolata Sister, and the head of the Nursing School, was shot dead on 17th September 2006, just four days after she had returned from Kenya. In 2008, the Catholic Cathedral in Mogadishu was destroyed by Islamists. It is reported that, in Al-Shabaab-held areas, apostasy from Islam or being found to be a Christian, results in immediate execution.

Diaconal work in Somalia continues through Caritas Somalia and the ACT Alliance. There is a Somalia ACT forum, which includes Christian Aid, Norwegian Church Aid, the Lutheran World Federation and Diakonie Katastrophenhilfe, which is based in Nairobi. Finn Church Aid has also been active in Somaliland. Most ACT partners work through local Somali partners and, for security reasons, no Christian symbols are used on vehicles. There have been some moves from the Somalia Government to request 'Christian' organisations to start to rebuild Christian sites, not as churches, but as various diaconal institutions (such as a library on the site of the Anglican Church in Hargeisa). Other organisations, such as the American Friends Service Committee, work in peace-building, through local Somali organisations.

However, the new Provisional Constitution, adopted on 1st August 2012,[3] and which came into effect on 19th September 2012, has the following to say about 'religion':

Article 2 – State and Religion

1. Islam is the religion of the state.
2. No religion other than Islam can be propagated.
3. No law can be enacted that is not compliant with the general principles and objectives of Shari'ah.

Article 17 – Freedom of Religion and Belief.

1. Every person is free to practise his or her religion.
2. No religion other than Islam can be propagated in the Federal Republic of Somalia.

Christianity has been known as a 'minority religion' in Somalia, with the exact number of Somali Christians in Somalia currently unknown, but estimated to be between one hundred and one thousand.[4] Most are thought to belong to the Wesleyan Church of the Nazarene or the Roman Catholic Church. However, denominationalism has little meaning for such a small, persecuted minority. Many Somalis have

[3] The Federal Republic of Somalia. Provisional Constitution adopted August 1, 2012, Mogadishu, Somalia. Website: www.constitutionnet.org/vl/item/federal-republic-somalia-provisional-constitution-adopted-august-1-2012-sep-19-2012 (accessed 19 December, 2015).

[4] According to Christian Aid Missions, it is estimated that Christians in Somalia add to only 0.3% while evangelical Christianity is estimated to 0.0%. Website: www.christianaid.org/Interactive_World/countryPages/Somalia.aspx (accessed 19 December, 2015).

come into contact with Christians during the time they have lived overseas, as migrants or as refugees, as well as through the work of humanitarian aid agencies. As peace is restored to Somalia, some of the diaspora have started to return and perhaps there will be a more open and tolerant attitude to the Christians of Somalia in the future. For the time being, however, Somali Christians in Somalia have to continue to live in hiding.

Bibliography

Abdulkadir, Mohamed, I. 'Somali Women and the Socialist State.' *Journal of Georgetown University-Qatar Middle Eastern Studies Student Association*, 2015, 1-10.

Barrett, David B (ed.). *World Christian Encyclopedia: A Comparative Survey of Churches and Religions in the Modern World, AD 1900-2000*. Oxford: OUP, 1984

Christian Aid Missions, www.christianaid.org/Interactive_World/countryPages/Somalia.aspx. (accessed 19 December, 2015).

Hamilton, Janice. *Somalia in Pictures*. Minneapolis: Twenty-First Century Books, 2007.

Mandryk, Jason. *Operation World: The Definitive Prayer Guide to Every Nation*. Illinois: InterVarsity Press, 2010.

The Federal Republic of Somalia. Provisional Constitution Adopted August 1, 2012, Mogadishu, Somalia. Website: www.constitutionnet.org/vl/item/federal-republic-somalia-provisional-constitution-adopted-august-1-2012-sep-19-2012 (accessed 19 December, 2015).

(87B) Christianity in Somalia

Alex N. Kamwaria and Michael T. Katola

Introduction

The presence of Christianity in Africa began during the earthly ministry of Jesus Christ. A few accounts are cited to support this assertion. For example, the New Testament of the Bible mentions several events in which Africans were witnesses to the life of Christ and the ministry of the apostles. It is possible that the history of Christianity in Africa began when these Africans shared with other Africans what they had witnessed.

The history of Christianity in Somalia is very sketchy. Much of it can only be deciphered from archaeological data, references from Judeo-Christian culture, and written accounts. It is important to note that written accounts were delivered by scholars with no religious orientation. The purpose of this chapter is to articulate the evidence of evangelization of the Somali-speaking people, but not the land of Somalia. Specific statistics of conversion to Christianity or Islam are challenging to come by, partly because national censuses are either non-existent, not regularly undertaken or, if they existed at all, are out-of-date or inaccurate. The following section will mark out some descriptions which give evidence of the early existence of Christianity in Somalia.

The Pre-Colonial Era

The earliest written accounts of Somalia are found in the records of the Fifth Egyptian Dynasty, which dates back to 2000 BC. Somalia is described as the land of Punt and a source of highly sought-after frankincense and myrrh. The minority Muslim population lived peacefully with their co-religionists and paid tribute to the Aksumite monarch. However, this peaceful co-existence was disrupted in AD 1415, when King Negus Yakuno Amlak of Abyssinia conquered Seylac, killed many Muslims and forced the survivors and their mosques to be converted to Christianity and churches, respectively.[1] Within a few decades, Christianity had again disappeared from (Seylac) Somalia.

Later, in AD 1542, St Francis Xavier is recorded to have visited the island of Soqotra along the Gulf of Aden coast of northern Somalia.[2] In his letter to the Jesuit headquarters in Rome dated 20th September 1542, Xavier recounts his encounters with the inhabitants of the island. He described them as the converts of St Thomas, apparently totally illiterate, without any scriptures, totally no idea about the sacrament of baptism, having Lenten feasts parallel to those of the Monophysite Ethiopian Orthodox Church, proud of being Christians, and hostile to Yemeni Muslims. Their priests were also illiterate, though they were able to conduct daily prayers from memory in the Chaldean language which they did not understand. How long Christianity lingered in the Island is not known.

---

[1] Giorgio Bertin, *Christianity in Somalia.* (Muqdisho: Croce del Sud Cathedral. Manuscript, 1983), 9.

[2] Greville Stewart Parker Freeman-Grenville, *The East African Coast: Select Documents from the first to the early nineteenth century* (Oxford: Clarendon Press, 1962), 135-137.

The Colonial Era

When the British and Italian colonial forces entered Somalia, they met a people with intense xenophobia, full of ferocious pride in their own independence, and a vigorous martial tradition. In 1839, the British occupied the southern port of Aden. The early 1880s saw a notable increase in France and Italian interests in an area whose commercial opportunities had been considerably enlarged by the opening of the Suez Canal.

Hallet notes that one of the greatest obstacles to the spread of Christianity in Somalia was an outstanding Muslim called Muhammad Abdille Hassan.[3] He was popularly known to his followers by the Arabic honorific 'Sayyid' (Master) and to his opponents as the 'Mad Mullah'. He had spent his life travelling widely in search of knowledge, to Aden, Sudan and East Africa. He also toured Arabia from where he acquired membership of the new Islamic fraternity, the Salihiya, who were basically reformists. In Somalia, Abdille Hassan settled in Berbera, where he attracted the attention of many people by his preaching. Hallet presents Abdille Hassan as 'a brilliant propagandist in the Somali style, a master of language whose scathing satire and virulent invective have come to form part of the heritage of Somali literature'.[4] Using his oratory, pious and diplomatic skills, Abdille Hassan made over 3,000 radical followers, popularly known as 'Dervishes'. He felt strong enough to formally declare *jihad* against the so-called 'infidels'.

From 1899, Abdille Hassan made scathing attacks on his co-religionists (Catholics, Protestants and Ethiopian Christians), by referring to them as infidels who thrived on subversion and aggression. He particularly warned the Catholic missionaries of dire consequences for erecting a mission station outside his territory in Berbera. However, some local people paid no attention to his teachings and were outraged by his attacks on their traditional clan fraternities. Also, urbanised Somalis ignored him on the grounds that the British administration had established a modest system of administration that had greatly improved local security, and so created favourable conditions for flourishing commerce.[5]

Christian Missions in Somalia

As noted above, Christian mission attempts were made during the colonial period under British and Italian rules. There is no record of Christian mission in Somalia before 1881, although Ethiopian Christians must have interacted with Somalis before that. During the colonial period, Christian missionary activity started with Christians carrying out diaconal work, as well as serving predominantly the expatriate community. The first Catholic missionaries were the Consolata, who arrived in 1881 and dedicated themselves to institutional work. They began serving the expatriate community and established some missions in Berbera, Mogadishu and Kismayu.[6] Later, in 1927, the Holy See established a Vicariate Apostolate in Mogadishu. The following year, a cathedral was built in Mogadishu. Ten years later, they handed over to the Franciscan missionaries. Among those who embraced the Catholic faith were the Bantu who were regarded by other Somalis as belonging to a lower caste, and the ex-slaves who had been brought to Somalia to work for their Somali overlords.

The Swedish Lutheran missionaries followed the Consolata missionaries in 1889. They recorded baptising over 350 Somalis during their time in Somalia. The Anglicans followed by establishing mission work, predominantly in Hargeisa. They established a church under the jurisdiction of the Anglican Diocese of Egypt. Other Christian missionaries who carried out mission work through social service projects

---

[3] Robin Hallet, *Africa Since 1875: A Modern History* (Nairobi: East African Educational Publishers, 1993), 131.
[4] Hallet, *Africa Since 1875*, 133.
[5] Bengt Sundkler and Christopher Steed, *A History of the Church in Africa* (Cambridge: CUP, 2000).
[6] John Baur, *2000 Years of Christianity in Africa: An African Church History* (Nairobi: Paulines Publications Africa, 2001), 291.

include the Mennonites and the Sudan Inland Mission in Somalia. By 1950, Somalia's Christian population was roughly estimated to be 8,500.

Christianity in Independent Somalia

In mid-1960, Somalia gained independence under an elected government. The first Constitution of 1961declared Somalia an Islamic state. When Siad Barre took power in 1969, he promulgated scientific socialism which he claimed was compatible with Islamic doctrines. However, he was considerably hostile to some Somali Muslims, particularly after he executed ten Muslim leaders following a political unrest. In 1972, Barre directed that all the church property, except the Catholic cathedral at Mogadishu, be nationalised by the government. This reduced the number of missionaries in Somalia, with many Protestant missionaries leaving. By 1976, there were only seven Franciscan Friars, sixty-two Consolata Sisters, and one Bishop (Pietro Salvatore Colombo, OFM) in the Catholic Diocese of Mogadishu.[7] The diocese carried out its mission work through Catholic Relief Services that had begun its work since the 1960s in Somalia. A new constitution was put in place in 1979, in which the teaching of the Qu'ran was made compulsory in all schools, apostasy and proselytization to other religion prohibited, but humanitarian activities were allowed.

When the inter-clan war broke out in 1988, immense suffering was witnessed by many civilians. The Anglican Church that was established in Hargeisa was destroyed by bombing in 1988. Also, Bishop Colombo of the Catholic Diocese of Mogadishu was assassinated in the cathedral on 9th July 1989. In addition, the hospital at Mela and Nursing School in Mogadishu established by the Catholic Church were all bombed in 1990. The number of Somali Christians recorded in 1990 had dropped to about 2,000. All in all, the Consolata Sisters' charitable activities in the face of war were still highly appreciated, though carried out under anxious war conditions.

Recent years have been a particularly dark period for the Somali nation. The unresolved inter-clan wars have not been resolved. There has been no durable peace since the overthrow of Siad Barre's regime in 1991. Countless peace agreements have been promulgated and broken. Frequent attempts by the international community to rebuild Somalia have not been successful. For example, in 2006, a transitional federal government was set up, which was sited first in Nairobi, and later in Baidoa. However, war-lordism continued and hundreds of thousands of Somalis fled their country. In 2007, the African Union, supported by the United Nations, set up the African Union Mission in Somalia (AMISOM) consisting of troops from six African nations. The AMISOM was set up to pacify Somalia by ridding it of the Al-Shabaab that controlled large part of Southern Somalia. In such a scenario, the plight of Christians was worse. A Consolata Sister, Leonella Sgorbati and the head of the Nursing School in Mogadishu, was shot dead on 17th September 2006. Two years later, the Catholic Cathedral in Mogadishu was destroyed by Islamic Jihadists.

In September 2012, a new Government was elected to replace the transitional federal government, and a new constitution was developed. Though the constitution emphasises the freedom to practise religion, it specifies that no religion other than Islam may be propagated in the Federal Republic of Somalia. In addition, no law could be enacted that was not compliant with the general principles and objectives of Sha'ria.

Currently, Christian missionary activities for Somalia are carried out through Caritas Somalia and the Action of Churches Together (ACT) alliance, which includes Christian Aid, Norwegian Church Aid, Lutheran World Federation and Diakonie Katastrophenhilfe, which are all based in Nairobi. Other organisations include Finn Church Aid and the American Friends Service Committee, which work through

[7] Baur, *2000 Years of Christianity in Africa*, 291.

local Somali organisations. Most Christian missionaries work through local Somali partners, and for security reasons no Christian symbols are used on vehicles delivering aid to Somalia.

There have been some moves from the Somali government to request Christian organisations to start to rebuild Christian sites and institutions. Currently, the exact number of Christians in Somalia is unknown. Anecdotal sources estimate it to be between one hundred and one thousand. Most are thought to belong to the Wesleyan Church of the Nazarene and the Catholic Church. Many Somali refugees have come into contact with Christianity in their countries of refuge. With the restoration of peace by the AMISOM forces in Somalia, many refugees have started to go back to rebuild their lives. There is hope that the new republic of Somalia will be more open and tolerant to Christianity.

Conclusion

The above discussion demonstrates how the history of Christianity in Somalia is difficult to decipher. The religion is mentioned only in passing by all scholars of African church history since Christianity has only a negligible number of followers. Islam is the state religion of Somalia and Christians have not only been persecuted but killed. Evangelism is strictly outlawed and the few Christians in the country must keep their faith secret. It seems Christianity will have only slow growth in Somalia but written records show that the Bible is available in three of the five languages used in the country. Although displaying a Bible in the open can endanger the life of a Christian, the availability of it in local languages gives hope for the future of Christianity in Somalia.

Bibliography

Aram, B. I. 'Somali's Judeo-Christian Heritage: A Preliminary Survey.' *Africa Journal of Evangelical Theology* 22 (2) (2003): 3-28.

Baur, J., *Years of Christianity in Africa: An African Church History.* Nairobi: Paulines Publications Africa, 2000.

Bertin, G. *Christianity in Somalia.* Muqdisho: Croce del Sud Cathedral. Manuscript, 1983.

Bowers, P. 'Nubian Christianity: The Neglected Heritage.' *Africa Journal of Evangelical Theology* 4 (1) (1985): 3-23.

Brown, M. *Where Giants Trod: The Saga of Kenya's Desert Lake.* London: Quiller Press, 1989.

Burton, R.F. *First Steps in East Africa, or An Exploration of Harar.* Mineola: Dover Publications, 1987.

Cassaneli, L. V. *The Shaping of Somali Society: Reconstructing the History of a People, 1600-1900.* Philadelphia: University of Pennysylvania, 1982.

Freeman-Grenville, G.S.P. *The East African Coast: Select Documents from the first to the early nineteenth century.* Oxford: Clarendon Press, 1966.

Hallet, R. *Africa Since 1875: A Modern History.* Nairobi: East African Educational Publishers Ltd., 1993.

Magesa, L. *African Religion: The Moral Traditions of Abundant Life.* Nairobi: Paulines, 1998.

Mbiti, J.S. *African Religions and Philosophy.* London: Heineman, 1969.

Nkrumah, K. *Consciencism: Philosophy and Ideology for Decolonization.* London: Panaf, 1974.

Oliver, R. *The Cambridge History of Africa: From c.1050 to 1600* (Vol. 3). Edited by R. Oliver. Cambridge: Cambridge University Press, 1977.

Schlee, G. *Identities on the Move: Clanship and Pastoralism in Northern Kenya.* Nairobi: Gideon S. Were Press, 1994.

Sundkler, B. and Steed, C. *A History of the Church in Africa.* Cambridge: Cambridge University Press, 2000.

Zorc, R.D. and Osman, M.M. *Somali-English Dictionary* (third edition). Dunwoody: Kensington, MD, USA, 1993.

(88) Christianity in South Africa

Graham Duncan

Religion	Pop 2010	Pct 2010	Pop 2025	Pct 2025	Gr Pct 1970 2025
Christians	42,368,000	82.1%	48,167,000	82.4%	0.9%
Independents	20,411,000	39.5%	23,650,000	40.5%	1.0%
African initiated	19,637,000	38.0%			
Orthodox	30,400	0.1%	30,000	0.1%	-0.1%
Protestants	13,137,000	25.4%	14,800,000	25.3%	0.8%
Reformed, Presbyterian	3,247,000	6.3%			
Anglicans	2,798,000	5.4%			
Pentecostal	2,393,000	4.6%			
Methodist	1,474,000	2.9%			
United churches	1,080,000	2.1%			
Lutheran	642,000	1.2%			
Roman Catholics	3,493,000	6.8%	3,810,000	6.5%	0.6%
Pentecostals/Charismatics	24,342,000	47.2%	26,000,000	44.5%	0.4%
Evangelicals	5,183,000	10.0%	5,536,000	9.5%	0.4%
adherents of traditional African religions	3,656,000	7.1%	3,400,000	5.8%	-0.5%
Hindus	1,227,000	2.4%	1,300,000	2.2%	0.4%
Muslims	887,000	1.7%	950,000	1.6%	0.5%
Baha'is	245,000	0.5%	300,000	0.5%	1.4%
Buddhists	163,000	0.3%	180,000	0.3%	0.6%
Jews	72,600	0.1%	55,000	0.1%	-1.8%
Chinese folk-religionists	34,500	0.1%	38,000	0.1%	0.7%
Confucianists	20,600	0.0%	25,000	0.0%	1.3%
adherents of new religious movements	18,300	0.0%	23,400	0.0%	1.7%
Sikhs	10,900	0.0%	13,000	0.0%	1.2%
Spiritists	2,300	0.0%	2,500	0.0%	0.4%
Jains	2,100	0.0%	2,300	0.0%	0.7%
people professing no religion	2,914,000	5.6%	3,980,000	6.8%	2.1%
Total population	**51,622,000**	**100.0%**	**58,436,000**	**100.0%**	**0.8%**

Source: Centre for the Study of World Christianity (CSGC), Boston, Gordon-Conwell TS

Introduction

Any attempt to survey the church scene in South Africa is almost impossible due to problems in categorising churches using the same criteria – size, polity, liturgy, theology, ethos, history and mission – in one brief chapter. What is provided then are impressions offered by a reforming Catholic of the Presbyterian tradition who is a committed ecumenist. First, some general introductory comments are offered concerning the state of the church in South Africa since 1994, but necessarily taking account of earlier history. Second, a brief selective survey is given of the variety of dynamic traditions. Few details of membership are given except where this is necessary. These are readily available elsewhere. Suffice it to say that there are an estimated 7,000 churches in South Africa,[1] although Conradie[2] is probably correct in suggesting that, given the vast growth and disparity in definitions of what constitutes a church, such information 'is no longer very helpful'.

The Status Quo in South Africa

Contemporary Christianity in South Africa is marked by significant fragmentation among the established mainline churches, and stagnation or retrenchment within them, with exponential growth among the Pentecostal/charismatic churches. Fragmentation is a feature of those churches which were united in the struggle both for and against apartheid.

It is noteworthy that the Churches of European Origin (CEOs) are at the forefront of the ecumenical movement, yet they have made little impact on or relationship with the African Initiated Churches (AICs).[3] They themselves, through their long-term (fifty years-plus) involvement in the Church Unity Commission and even longer involvement with the SACC and its predecessors (going back to 1904), have signally failed to unite. Only two church unions have taken place since the last decade of the twentieth century. The same is true of their relationship with the Pentecostal churches which are particularly susceptible to political opportunism.[4]

The issue of fragmentation is universal,[5] as is attested in the World Council of Church's (1991) *Canberra Statement:* 'The scandalous divisions damage the credibility of their witness to the world in worship and service.'[6] Perhaps the greatest condemnation is that the churches 'have remained satisfied to co-exist in division'[7] in denial of Küng's assertion: 'The Church *is* one and therefore *should* be one.'[8] Mayson, speaking from a South African perspective, supports this view, attributing the situation to the quest for power by Christian institutions:

---

[1] Answers.com, www.answers.com/Q/How_many_churches_are_there_in_South_Africa (accessed 17 October 2014).

[2] Ernst Conradie, 'Why the Quest for Identity?' in *The Quest for Identity: In So-called Mainline Churches in South Africa,* edited by E. Conradie & J. Klaasen (Stellenbosch: Sun Press, 2014): 8-14, 11.

[3] Conradie, 'Why the Quest for Identity?', 9-19.

[4] Conradie, 'Why the Quest for Identity?', 11; Graham A Duncan, "State of the Union: The Uniting Presbyterian Church in Southern Africa, 1999-2004," *Studia Historiae Ecclesiasticae* XXXI no. 2, October 2011,189; John W de Gruchy, "The Quest for Identity in the So-called 'Mainline' Churches in South Africa," ed. Ernst Conradie & John Klaasen, *The Quest for Identity: In So-called Mainline Churches in South Africa* (Stellenbosch: Sun Press, 2014): 22.

[5] Graham A. Duncan, "Ever old and ever new, keep me travelling along with you": 21st-century Notae Ecclesiae specifically necessary for Churches in Southern Africa. *HTS* 67 (1) #851 (2011), *5.*

[6] World Council of Churches (WCC), 1991, *The Unity of the Church: Gift and Calling – The Canberra Statement,* WCC, Geneva, viewed 23 February 2010, from www.oikumene.org/en/ resources/documents/wcc-comissions/faith-and-order-commission/i-unity-the-church-and-its-mission/the-unity-of-the-church-gift-and-calling-the-canberra-statement.html (accessed 17 October 2010), 1.

[7] WCC, *The Unity of the Church,* 2

[8] Hans Küng, *The Church* (London: Search, 1968), 273.

> … linking themselves to the political and economic elites of their age, [which] has produced the disastrous confusion of conflicting churches… The modern concern for ecumenism shows no sign of uniting denominationalism.[9]

A predominant and enduring factor in church life is evidence of inherent racism[10] (from before the beginning of the ecumenical movement in South Africa since its inception in 1904). This is the greatest challenge to theology and the church in South Africa. What Willem Saayman says about the Dutch Reformed Church (DRC) can be ascribed to all CEOs, for they share a common history of mission in South Africa:

> What is abundantly clear in this day and age is that racism cannot be an abiding feature of any institution claiming to be Christian in its essence[11] (Saayman 2007:10).
>
> The DRC indeed has a racist past, but that is not the only past it has, and it is not the only institution or group of people in the new South Africa who have a racist past. Furthermore, a racist past can be dealt with and changed[12] (Saayman 2007:133).

Saayman is correct, but racism cannot be changed if it has not been dealt with first. Support comes from the International Federation of Christian Churches president Ray McCauley during the hearings of the Truth and Reconciliation Commission:

> We know that many Christians within our constituency, still to this day, find it hard to accept any responsibility for what happened in the past…

While many were prepared to admit that apartheid was a mistake, they were willing to offer only a half-hearted apology.

> That sort of confession, in my mind, is cheap and fails to get to grips with true confession which leads to repentance, which in turn leads to meaningful forgiveness, followed by restitution and reconciliation.[13]

Since 1994, racism has gone underground and is manifested in subtle ways with both Blacks and Whites asserting racism, using equity as a tool or a target. Virtually no South African church has responded positively and actually engaged and dealt with the issue, and it remains a subliminal expression of human and Christian disunity. The only exception is to be found in the struggle among the Dutch Reformed churches to appropriate the Belhar Confession as an instrument of belief and common witness.

Sub-issues related to racism are poverty (stewardship is largely regarded as looking after God's resources for our own benefit), gay marriage (where church decision-makers are united in contravention of

---

[9] Cedric Mayson, "Power Sharing and Secular Spirituality," in *Power Sharing and African Democracy: Interdisciplinary Perspectives*, ed. Cornel. du Toit (Pretoria: UNISA Press, 2010), 71-87, 73.

[10] David J. Bosch, Transforming *Mission: Paradigm Shifts in the Theology of Mission (*Maryknoll: Orbis, 1991), 530, n.7.

[11] Willem Saayman, *Being Missionary, Being Human: An Overview of Dutch Reformed Mission* (Pietermaritzburg: Cluster, 2007), 10.

[12] Saayman, *Being Missionary,* 133.

[13] SAPA 1997. "Whites must confess to support for apartheid policy", TRC hearing, East London, November 19. www.justice.gov.za/trc/media%5C1997%5C9711/s971119c.htm (accessed 17 January 2015); cf Lawrence Jones, "Divided Evangelicals in South Africa", in *Religious Resurgence and Politics in the Contemporary World,* ed. Emile Sahliyeh (Albany, NY: State University of New York Press, 1990), 107.

the freedom granted in the constitution, and separated by changing mores in society and possibly in their membership) and HIV/AIDS. With regard to HIV/AIDS, Storey raises an interesting possibility:

> Imagine, for instance, if some coalition of churches had taken on the AIDS pandemic with the same passion shown by the SACC against apartheid? Imagine if their local congregations had dropped some of the pointless activities that pass for church life and fashioned themselves as AIDS education centres, sanctuaries, hospices? You can be sure that the Mbeki government would have poured scorn and coals of fire on their heads, but such a coalition would have saved hundreds of thousands of lives among the 'least of these', which is what matters to God.[14]

This is a matter on which churches are united in theory but separated in administration, practice and especially finance.

De Gruchy sums up where many in the church find themselves in the church today, and perhaps explains why some church communities and denominations eschew unity: 'Many members are… more interested in whether or not their local congregation provides a meaningful home, and whether or not their church is truly serving their [own] needs.'[15] This is probably more true in congregations with little commitment to mission. De Gruchy further sees the need for the search for identity to be grounded in an ecumenical process. However, almost ten years earlier, he held the view that ecumenism was in trouble by noting 'a growing lack of ecumenical enthusiasm these past few years, and a growing spirit of denominationalism'.[16] This is the result of a failure of love which is a challenge for mission 'constrained by Jesus' love' (2 Cor. 5:14).[17]

Christian Traditions in South Africa

As stated above, no attempt will be made to cover all denominations. A judicious and representative selection is offered.

African Initiated Churches (AICs)

AICs arose out of a desire to express their response to mission Christianity (enculturation) in their own distinctive way, and as a rejection of imposed forms of worship, discipline, racism and remuneration. The Ethiopian type churches are an African phenomenon which arose in (especially, Southern) Africa during the last quarter of the nineteenth century, some of which were supported by American expressions of AICs, eg the American Methodist Episcopal Church. They did not totally reject mission Christianity as such, for they often maintained their previous forms of liturgy, polity, theology and liturgical dress. Numerous attempts have been made to categorise them. Two of the largest expressions of African indigenous Christianity are the Zion Christian Church (ZCC) and the Ama Nazaretha Church.

Churches of European Origin (CEOs)

At the present time, the churches of European origin are mainly black in membership and have, in general, adopted a broad approach to theology within their separate confessions of faith, although there is a trend

---

[14] Peter J. Storey, "Why in the World Would you Want to be a Methodist if you are not a Wesleyan?" in Emile Sahliyeh (ed.), *Rediscovering Wesley for Africa,* ed. Emile Sahliyeh (Pretoria: MCSA, 2006), 171.
[15] De Gruchy, "The Quest for Identity," 16.
[16] John W. de Gruchy, "Becoming the Ecumenical Church," in *Being the Church in South Africa Today,* ed. Barney N. Pityana & Charles Villa-Vicencio (Johannesburg: SACC, 1995), 12.
[17] Bosch, *Transforming Mission,* 286-291, 514, 519.

towards a more conservative evangelical, even literalist, disposition, particularly on matters such as same-gender civil unions and HIV/AIDS. This may be a symptom of South African society which, historically, was bypassed by the deep effects of the Enlightenment, the more recent sexual revolution of the 1960s, and the concurrent European 'Honest to God' debate.[18] At that time, the Constitution of the South African Republic was formed out of an exclusivist conformist paradigm, while the democratic South African constitution is derived from an inclusivist liberatory paradigm.

While it might be possible to get the impression that the CEOs are integrated, this is far from the truth. For them, this is an ongoing struggle as they try, with varying degrees of commitment and success, to overcome their apartheid history. The issues which led to secessions late in the nineteenth century are still problematic – race, stipend differentials, the training of ministers, white ministers serving only white congregations (with a slowly increasing number of black ministers serving white parishes), and differentials in approaches to youth work, discipline and language. The apartheid paradigm continues to define what services are offered to communities, while regular worshippers do not represent the demographics of the country. The conservative nature of these churches allows the status quo to be maintained and reinforced, supported by a false consciousness regarding social and political reality. One of the challenges posed in response by the CEOs to the government regarding their support for apartheid was that they themselves were practising ecclesiastical apartheid

The following church traditions could be considered as CEOs: Anglican Church of South Africa, Church of England in South Africa, United Congregational Church of South Africa, Methodist Church of Southern Africa, Uniting Presbyterian Church of Southern Africa, Baptist Union of South Africa, Baptist Convention of South Africa, Evangelical Lutheran Church of South Africa, Lutheran Church in South Africa (LCSA), Reformed Churches, Dutch Reformed Church (*Nederduitse Gereformeerde Kerk,* NGK), Hervormde Church (*Nederduitsch Hervormde Kerk,* NHK), Gereformeerde Kerk in Suid-Afrika ('DopperKerk'), Afrikaanse Protestantse Church (APK), Uniting Reformed Church in Southern Africa (*Verenigende Gereformeerde Kerk in Suid-Afrika*), the Roman Catholic Church, and Pentecostal churches.

The Non-Church Movement

There is also an increasing constituency of people who believe but do not belong, who are disenchanted with the institutional church. An example is the main Dutch Reformed churches which promoted an apartheid theology and now attempt to justify a democratically-based theology in a constituency which has not made the psychological/spiritual adjustment. In addition, a number of other reasons are cited:

> The challenge of secularism in some contexts, the tensions between public AND private forms of devotion in a politically volatile climate, the connection between liturgy and life, the ordination of women and the role of women in leadership positions, issues around homosexuality that often tend to tear congregations and churches apart, issues around indigenisation and cultural authenticity, and the ecological reformation of Christian worship amidst the rapid growth of churches proclaiming the prosperity gospel.[19]

This has led to disillusionment and confusion with the church as an institution, and many have retreated into a personal faith or ever smaller non-aligned communities of believers (cf. Uchimura Kanzō's non-church movement in Japan).[20] There is a danger here, however, where:

---

[18] John A.T. Robinson, *Honest to God* (London, SCM, 1963).
[19] Conradie, "Notions and forms of ecumenicity," 30.
[20] Hiroshi Shibuya & Chiba Shin, *Living for Jesus and Japan: The Social and Theological Thought of Uchimura Kanzō* (Grand Rapids: Eerdmans, 2013), 129-135.

> A major feature of the church scene today is the growing preoccupation of churches and denominations with their own identity, the search by each for a secure plot on which to build their designer-house in what they think is their distinctive and unique architecture of the spirit.[21]

Instruments for Promoting Christian Unity

We deal with two organisations. The CUC represents the CEOs, while the SACC has a broader constituency.

Church Unity Commission (CUC)

The Church Unity Commission was formed in 1968 and included the Anglican, Congregationalist, Methodist and Presbyterian churches. By 1974, all the member churches, who also belong to the South African Council of Churches, had accepted a Declaration of Intention to seek union.[22] The Commission, which never had a high profile, now has a lower profile than during the apartheid era. But the churches still tend to duplicate programmes and to act independently.[23] There has been a lack of consultation and co-operation at national and regional levels. In this respect, women have taken the lead. Local ecumenism is of critical importance. The adoption of the Declaration of Intention led to the formation of a number of united congregations involving two or more member denominations. In recent years, most enquiries have come from rural areas where declining white populations and spiralling costs make denominational congregations an unaffordable luxury.

Over the years, 'the emphasis in the work of the CUC has shifted from seeking agreement on doctrinal and ecclesiastical issues to promotion co-operation (sic) in mission'.[24] In 1982, mutual acceptance of members was achieved, and in 1995 mutual acceptance of ministers was accepted. Throughout its history, organic unity has been frustrated by the issue of the ministry of oversight (i.e. bishops). It has never been able to achieve a significant degree of racial integration:[25] 'black members could not be inspired at all, as the whole process seemed irrelevant to their existential dilemma.'[26] It is no longer clear what role the CUC has to play in the absence of a desire for organic union.

South African Council of Churches (SACC)

The role and impact of the South African Council of Churches has altered enormously since 1994: 'The 1980s were dominated by the ecumenism of struggle in which the South African Council of Churches... played the major role.'[27]After being in the vanguard of the struggle against apartheid, for which it received substantial moral and financial support internationally, which was transferred to government agencies with the advent of democracy, the situation changed rapidly. It was credited with adopting the policy of 'critical

---

[21] Keith Clements, *Ecumenical Dynamic: Living in More than one Place at the Same Time* (Geneva: WCC, 2013), 198.
[22] Joseph Wing, "Ten Years of Talks', *In Touch,* II, 11, May (1978), 21-32, 25.
[23] Donald G.L. Cragg, "Church Unity Commission (CUC). (Southern Africa)," *The Ecumenical Review* July 1, 54 (2002), 3. www.thefreelibrary.com/Church+Unity+Commission+%28CUC%29.+%28Southern+Africa%29.-a092136481 (accessed 23 December 2014).
[24] Church Unity Commission (CUC), *Report to Churches* (CUC: Port Elizabeth, 2006).
[25] Joseph Wing, 'Report to the Churches', *In Touch,* II, 16, August (1983), 4.
[26] Peter J. Storey, "Why in the World Would you Want to be a Methodist if you are not a Wesleyan?' in *Rediscovering Wesley for Africa,* ed. P. Malinga & N. Richardson (Pretoria: MCSA, 2006), 168.
[27] Donald G.L. Cragg, "Church Unity Commission (CUC). (Southern Africa," *The Ecumenical Review* July 1, 54 (2002), 3.

solidarity' with the government. However, Vellem[28] credits Charles Villa-Vicencio's *Theology of Reconstruction* (1992)[29] with this fabrication. Its policy represented 'critical engagement' and earned the disapproval of the ANC which then found a more compliant partner in the Pentecostal churches, especially Rhema under the leadership of Ray McCauley.

The SACC was not involved in the recent formation of the National Interfaith Leaders Council (NILC) in 2009, under McCauley's chairmanship. It claimed to have problems with the founding document of the NILC. According to the government, the NILC is a mass-based group of religious leaders from across the country, which reflects all the major faiths practised in South Africa.[30] This is symptomatic of 'the political marginalisation of the SACC'.[31]

> The strongest indication of Mr McCauley's status in South Africa's new order was his appointment to head up the newly created National Interfaith Leaders Council (NILC), a body meant to advise and aid the government on the delivery of social services – among other things. The leadership of the NILC, which abruptly displaced South Africa's Council of Churches, saw the former strong man dubbed the 'high priest of South Africa.'[32]

With regard to the problem of lack of integrity, those from the CEOs should interrogate their own actions and decisions, for there is also a problem of lack of consistency in theological stance which is not allowed to stand in the way of the moral religion trajectory since 1994 where a choice was made to 'downplay the national priority for decent work, focusing instead on narrower moral dilemmas such as abortion and same-sex marriage'.[33] The SACC has struggled with problems which emanate largely from their financial issues, and their integrity has been seriously compromised. The SACC has been accused of political irrelevance and ideological differences.[34] However, the SACC has felt it was being punished for its refusal to become a formal ally of the ruling party, its failed attempt to intervene over former president Thabo Mbeki's 'recall' last year, and its failure to endorse the ANC before this year's elections.[35]

The one area which has been suppressed is the contribution of Black Theology to ongoing church life. Charles Villa-Vicencio's *Theology of Reconstruction* (1992) was a theological attempt to maintain a 'white' hegemonic theology. It failed as the result of its adoption of and a commitment to a paradigm from an east European context. It failed to understand that the very conditions that birthed black theology had not been addressed. Liberation remains a global ecumenical challenge and a black liberation theology may still offer an alternative to 'the Constantinian model of the church',[36] a 'religion of empire'.[37]

---

[28] Vuyani S. Vellem, "Ecumenicity and a Black Theology of Liberation, in '*South African Perspectives on Notions and Forms of Ecumenicity,*'' ed. E.M. Conradie (Stellenbosch: SUN Press, 2013), 178.
[29] Charles Villa-Vicencio. *A Theology of Reconstruction: Nation Building and Human Rights* (Cape Town: David Philip, 1992).
[30] SACC Excluded from Interfaith Council, April 2009, www.iol.co.za/news/south-africa/sacc-excluded-from-interfaith-council-1.455696#.VJU9xsC3N_(accessed 20 December 2014).
[31] EM Conradie, "Notions and Forms of Ecumenicity: Some South African Perspectives', in *South African perspectives on notions and forms of ecumenicity*, ed. E.M. Conradie (Stellenbosch: SUN Press, 2013), 13-76, 16.
[32] Liston, "Inside the most Powerful Church in South Africa." www.independent.co.uk/news/world/africa/inside-the-most-powerful-church-in-south-africa-2006129.html (accessed 17 January 2015).
[33] Gerald West, "The ANC's Deployment of Religion in Nation Building: From Thabo Mbeki, to 'The RDP of the Soul' to Jacob Zuma," in *Power Sharing and African Democracy: Interdisciplinary Perspectives*, ed. C. du Toit (Pretoria: UNISA Press, 2010), 89-120, 116.
[34] K. Sosibo, "Council of Churches in Wilderness" (*Mail & Guardian* 23 March 2012) http://mg.co.za/article/2012-03-23-council-of-churches-in-wilderness (accessed 20 December 2012).
[35] M. Mataboge, "Why ANC Dumped Council of Churches" (*Mail & Guardian* 18 Sep 2009) http://mg.co.za/article/2009-09-18-why-anc-dumped-council-of-churches (accessed 20 December 2014).
[36] Vellem, "Ecumenicity and a Black Theology," 181.
[37] Vellem, "Ecumenicity and a Black Theology," 182.

Many South African churches demonstrate their commitment to ecumenism through membership of a number of regional, continental and international bodies such as the All Africa Council of Churches (AACC), the Association of Evangelicals of Africa, the World Council of Churches (WCC) and the World Communion of Reformed Churches (WCRC).

Conclusion

While there appears to be little that is positive in the South African church scene, it is important not to underestimate faithfulness within this deeply committed Christian country which is still coming to terms with the onset of democracy and the healing of the wounds of apartheid in all sections of the community. The situation is dynamic, as South African Christianity operates within a fluid context of relations with the state as well as among its constituent denominations. Despite repeated calls to the churches to call the government to account, there is a heavy price to be paid for doing so. The 'mainline' churches are either stagnant or declining in terms of numbers while the African Initiated and Pentecostal churches are expanding rapidly. To counter this, Vellem recommends a 'religion of creation'[38] grounded in a black theology of liberation based on inclusivity, justice, solidarity and the integrity of creation – the *shalom* of God.

There is a great need for the development of an ecumenical vision to which CEOs, AICs and Pentecostal churches can commit themselves (hopefully with other faith expressions), in order to offer a common vision of a truly rainbow nation.

Bibliography

Balia, D.M. *Black Methodists and White Supremacy in South Africa.* Durban: Madiba, 1991.

Bax, D. *The Presbyterian Church of Southern Africa: An Introduction.* Cape Town: Rondebosch United Church, 1997.

Bosch, D.J. *Transforming Mission: Paradigm Shifts in Theology of Mission.* Maryknoll: Orbis, 1991.

Conradie, E. and Klaasen, J. (ed.). *The Quest for Identity, in So-called Mainline Churches in South Africa.* Stellenbosch, Sun Press, 2014.

Conradie, E.M., ed. *South African Perspectives on Notions and Forms of Ecumenicity.* Stellenbosch: SUN Press, 2013.

De Gruchy, J.W. & de Gruchy S. *The Church Struggle in South Africa (25th anniversary edition).* Fortress: Minneapolis, 2005.

De Gruchy, J.W. 'The Contest for Reformed Identity in South Africa during the Church Struggle against Apartheid.' In *Reformed Churches in South Africa and the Struggle for Justice: Remembering 1960-1990,* edited by M.A. Plaatjies van-Huffel & R. Vosloo, 26-36. Stellenbosch: SUN Press, 2013a.

Duncan, G.A. 'State of the Union: The Uniting Presbyterian Church in Southern Africa, 1999-2004', *Studia Historiae Ecclesiasticae* XXXI (2005), 189-219.

Duncan G.A. 2011. ''Ever Old and Ever New, Keep Me Travelling Along with you:' 21st-century Notae Ecclesiae specifically necessary for churches in Southern Africa.' *HTS Teologiese Studies/Theological Studies* 67(1), Art. #851, 8 pages. doi.10.4102/hts.v67i1.851

Hexham, I and K. Poewe-Hexham. 'South African's Black African Charismatics.' In *The New International Dictionary of Pentecostal and Charismatic Movements*, Stanley M. Burgess and Eduard M. van der Maas, 227-238. (Rev. ed.) Grand Rapids, MI: Zondervan, 2003.

Jones, Lawrence. 'Divided Evangelicals in South Africa.' In *Religious Resurgence and Politics in the Contemporary World,* edited by Emile Sahliyeh, 107-110. Albany, NY: State University of New York,

[38] Vellem, "Ecumenicity and a Black Theology," 182.

1990.

Mogashoa, M.H. 'South African Baptists (1820-1948).' PhD thesis. Pietermaritzburg: University of Natal, 2004.

Muller, R. *African Pilgrimage: Ritual Travel in South Africa's Christianity of Zion*. London: Ashgate Press, 2013.

Pityana, B.N. and C. Villa-Vicencio (ed.). *Being the Church in South Africa Today.* SACC: Johannesburg, 2005.

Plaatjies- van, Huffel M.A. and R. Vosloo (eds). *Reformed Churches in South Africa and the Struggle for Justice: Remembering 1960-1990.* Stellenbosch: SUN Press, 2013.

Saayman, W. Being Missionary, Being Human: An Overview of Dutch Reformed Mission. Pietermaritzburg: Cluster Publications, 2007.

Thomas, D. *Christ Divided: Liberalism, Ecumenism and Race in South Africa.* Pretoria: South Africa, 2002.

(89) Christianity in Republic of the Sudan (Northern Sudan) and Republic of South Sudan[1]

Chammah J Kaunda

Northern Sudan

Religion	Pop 2010	Pct 2010	Pop 2025	Pct 2025	Gr Pct 1970 2025
Christians	6,126,000	60.9%	10,454,000	65.5%	3.6%
Independents	57,000	0.6%	92,000	0.6%	3.2%
African initiated	46,900	0.5%			
Orthodox	3,000	0.0%	3,000	0.0%	0.0%
Protestants	2,767,000	27.5%	3,900,000	24.5%	2.3%
Anglicans	1,554,000	15.5%			
Reformed, Presbyterian	833,000	8.3%			
Nondenominational	222,000	2.2%			
Pentecostal	87,300	0.9%			
Congregational	60,000	0.6%			
Roman Catholics	5,301,000	52.7%	7,300,000	45.8%	2.2%
Evangelicals	1,368,000	13.6%	1,856,000	11.6%	2.1%
Pentecostals/Charismatics	632,000	6.3%	840,000	5.3%	1.9%
adherents of traditional African religions	3,268,000	32.5%	4,500,000	28.2%	2.2%
Muslims	614,000	6.1%	920,000	5.8%	2.7%
Baha'is	620	0.0%	1,000	0.0%	3.2%
Chinese folk-religionists	480	0.0%	700	0.0%	2.5%
Buddhists	230	0.0%	400	0.0%	3.9%
Hindus	200	0.0%	300	0.0%	2.8%
people professing no religion	46,800	0.5%	74,000	0.5%	3.1%
Total population	**10,056,000**	**100.0%**	**15,951,000**	**100.0%**	**3.1%**

Source: Centre for the Study of World Christianity (CSGC), Boston, Gordon-Conwell TS

[1] This version relies on the work of Andrew C. Wheeler, "Christianity in Sudan," in *Dictionary of African Christian Biography,* www.dacb.org/history/christianity%20in%20sudan.html (accessed 08 December 2015). The original version of Wheeler was first published in Zablon Nthamburi, ed., *From Mission to Church: A Handbook of Christianity in East Africa* (Nairobi: Uzima Press, 1991).

South Sudan

Religion	Pop 2010	Pct 2010	Pop 2025	Pct 2025	Gr Pct 1970 2025
Christians	1,916,000	5.3%	1,947,000	3.8%	0.1%
Independents	19,300	0.1%	22,000	0.0%	0.9%
African initiated	19,300	0.1%			
Orthodox	97,000	0.3%	120,000	0.2%	1.4%
Protestants	758,000	2.1%	850,000	1.7%	0.8%
Anglicans	520,000	1.4%			
Nondenominational	210,000	0.6%			
Roman Catholics	1,081,000	3.0%	1,120,000	2.2%	0.2%
Evangelicals	394,000	1.1%	450,000	0.9%	0.9%
Pentecostals/Charismatics	137,000	0.4%	150,000	0.3%	0.6%
Muslims	32,810,000	90.9%	47,160,000	92.9%	2.4%
adherents of traditional African religions	1,007,000	2.8%	1,100,000	2.2%	0.6%
Baha'is	2,200	0.0%	3,000	0.0%	2.1%
Jews	2,200	0.0%	2,000	0.0%	-0.6%
Chinese folk-religionists	1,700	0.0%	2,000	0.0%	1.0%
Buddhists	800	0.0%	1,000	0.0%	1.5%
Hindus	700	0.0%	900	0.0%	1.7%
people professing no religion	374,000	1.0%	524,000	1.0%	2.3%
Total population	**36,115,000**	**100.0%**	**50,740,000**	**100.0%**	**2.3%**

Source: Centre for the Study of World Christianity (CSGC), Boston, Gordon-Conwell TS

Introduction

The history of the church in Sudan is divided into three main phases: first, 543-1504, the church in ancient Nubia. This period in the history of northern Sudan has perhaps been best served by scholars, both historians and archaeologists. Second, c. 1700-1885, Catholic missions to Nubia. This second phase, up to the time of the Mahdiyya has, not surprisingly, been a particular interest of Catholic mission historians. The third is a period from 1899 to the present day in which the modern evangelization of Sudan has taken place. This period is from the establishment of Anglo-Egyptian Condominium[2] to the present. This is focus of this brief chapter.

Christian Mission during the Condominium 1899-1955

Scholars argue that Byzantine missionaries brought Christianity to northern Sudan (then called Nubia) by about the end of the first century after Christ.[3] The Christian kingdom of Nubia prospered for about 600

[2] Condominium is a period from 1899 to 1955. In January 1899, an Anglo-Egyptian agreement restored Egyptian rule in Sudan but as part of a condominium, or joint authority, exercised by Britain and Egypt.
[3] S. Jakobielski, "Christian Nubia at the Height of its Civilization," in *General History of Africa – Volume III – Africa*

years before being raided by Islam. Modern Sudanese Christianity was reintroduced into South Sudan by British missionaries in the nineteenth century. Yet British imperial authorities restricted missionary activity to the south.[4] In order to briefly represent Christianity in the two countries of Sudan – North and South, this essay is divided into two major parts.

The Republic of (North) Sudan

As soon as the city of Omdurman fell in the Battle of Omdurman in 1898, in which Lord Kitchener defeated the Mahdist forces and killed the Khalifa, placing Sudan under British control, several missionary groups began to enter Sudan. But the Verona Fathers, one of the most enduring Christian missionary presences in the country, had already arrived in 1854 under the leadership of Denial Comboni who became the first Catholic Bishop of Central Africa.[5] The members of the Comboni missionary society,[6] together with the Sudanese Catholic converts who had escaped from Mahdi to Egypt, returned to work in Sudan. The Protestant missions were established by the New Zealand branch of the Sudan United Mission (SUM), a broad non-denominational missionary organization and the Anglican Church Missionary Society (CMS). Scholars argue that the missionary presence did not determine its success in establishing a Christian community until the indigenization of the churches during the 1960s and 1970s, after the expulsion of the missionaries.[7] The first task of these missionaries was to gather a small Christian community in Omdurman. Several key factors can be linked with the spread of Christianity in the Nuba Mountains.

The second form of witness that missions developed in northern Sudan was educational activity. The government did little to encourage modern western education. They were content to support the traditional Qu'ranic education of mosque and *khalwa*.[8] The Gordon Memorial College in Khartoum was established in 1902 with an aim of training clerks and craftsmen for government service. It has gone through transformation over the years and provides technical education, and was established in 1956 as Khartoum University when Sudan gained independence.[9]

The missionaries were responsible for modem education in Sudan, which was perceived as a way of civilizing the Sudanese people and also as a tool for evangelization. At the turn of the twentieth century, the Verona Fathers started two girls' schools, in Khartoum and Omdurman. The Church Missionary Society (CMS) started a Coptic all-girl school in Khartoum in 1902. These schools attracted both Christian and Muslim girls from Egypt and Sudan. The Presbyterians also started a boys' school in Khartoum in 1905. There are many other mission schools that laid the foundation of all contemporary primary and secondary education in the Sudan. Initially, the government sponsored some of the elementary schools, but this policy was abandoned in the 1920s in favour of the *khalwas*.[10]

The third evangelistic method that missionaries made use of was within the government restrictions of medical work. Both the Catholics and CMS maintained clinic work in Khartoum and Omdurman. The

---

from the Seventh to the Eleventh Century, eds. M. El Fasi and L. Hrbek, 194-223 (San Francisco: UNESCO, University of California Press. 1992).

[4] From Wikipedia, the free encyclopedia, "Christianity in Sudan," https://en.wikipedia.org/wiki/Christianity_in_Sudan#cite_note-5 (accessed 9 Dec. 2015).

[5] Sophie Ibbotson and Max Lovell-Hoare, *Sudan* (Bucks: Global Pequot Press, 2012).

[6] The Comboni missionary order originated from the charism of St. Daniel Comboni who believed that the time had come for the regeneration of the African people.

[7] Siri Lamoureaux, "Nuba Christianity: the Search for Security in the North," www.cedej-eg.org/IMG/pdf/Siri_Lamoureaux_editsSL_May2013.pdf (accessed 9 Dec. 2015).

[8] Khalwa refers to secluded retreats for initiates to the Sufi mystical orders that dominated Sudanese Islam. In the twentieth century it refers the schools for instructing the young in the *Qur'an*.

[9] Wheeler, "Christianity in Sudan."

[10] Wheeler, "Christianity in Sudan."

CMS hospital in Mahdist capital of Omdurman under Dr Edmund Lloyd was established with the objective of equipping Sudanese medical staff.[11]

It must be highlighted here that the presence of Christians in positions of power was perceived as an affront to Islamic authority. Thus, throughout the condominium and the independent period, there were major restrictions on Christian activities in most parts of northern Sudan, with the exception of the Nuba Mountains.[12] Andrew C. Wheeler noted that 'this has in part been due to official policy, and in part the natural antipathy of a predominantly Muslim population'. In the early 1990s, northern Sudan was perceived as a land of opportunity for education and employment for most South Sudanese until the independence of South Sudan in 2011. The large congregations that meet in northern towns which started as early as the 1940s consist mainly of southern migrants, with a few others from the Nuba Mountains. Before the independence of South Sudan, Christians in the north, as a minority, received strong support from the majority Christian community in the south. Despite the Comprehensive Peace Agreement (CPA), including Omar Bashir's own promises of cultural and religious diversity, it seems there were no legal systems that protect the interests of Christians in the new constitution.[13] In recent times, there have been increased threats, prejudice and discrimination against churches and Christian minorities in the north.

The Sudan United Mission in the Nuba Mountains

The Australian branch of SUM began sending missionaries to work in Sudan in 1914. From 1920, they concentrated on the eastern Nuba Mountains, which became the SUM field. The church established by SUM in 1913 is known as the Sudanese Church of Christ (SCOC) which became autonomous in 1962. The congregations are located in the capital city and in the Nuba Mountains.

The Church Missionary Society in Nuba Mountains

In 1929, Wilson Cash who was the then General Secretary of CMS, visited Sudan. This visit was the result of his vision of taking the gospel to the Nuba Mountains through medical and educational work. In 1933, the government invited CMS to help provide Christian and vernacular education in the western Nuba Mountains (SUM, as noted above, was working in the east). SUM and CMS translated the Bible into the Sudanese languages, and the New Testament has been published in Moro, Krongo, Otoro, Haibani, Nyirere and Koalib. But CMS work in the western Nuba Mountains was not as strong as SUM's in the eastern. Frequent changes in staff and a shortage of staff slowed down the work. Also, the strong emphasis on education meant that CMS was less active in evangelism than SUM. SUM's commitment to evangelism made them more active in Bible translation.[14]

The Nuba Churches in Khartoum and Omdurman

Today, the Sudanese Church of Christ and the Episcopal Church of Sudan have a number of congregations in the Nuba Mountains. But the greatest growth has taken place in Khartoum and Omdurman. The Omdurman Bible Training Institute (OBTI) was established in 1970 by Bishop Butrus Shokai. The Institute was later renamed after its founder as the Shokai Bible Training Institute.[15]

---

[11] Bengt Sundkler and Christopher Steed, *A History of the Church in Africa* (Cambridge: CUP, 2000).
[12] Wheeler, "Christianity in Sudan."
[13] Lamoureaux, "Nuba Christianity: the Search for Security in the North."
[14] Wheeler, "Christianity in Sudan."
[15] Shokai Bible Training Institute, "Shokai Bible Training Institute," http://khartoum.anglican.org/index.php?PageID=sbti (accessed 9 Dec. 2015).

The Republic of South Sudan

South Sudan is the youngest African country, and became an independent state on 9th July 2011, following a referendum that was passed with 98.83% of the vote in favour of creating a new state. The country had remained shut off from northern Sudan until the mid-nineteenth century with the establishment of the 'route through the Sudd in order to plunder ivory and slave traders, and to the ineffective and corrupt efforts at administration of Egyptian and Mahdist governors'.[16] Throughout the twentieth century, the relationship between the north and the south entrenched oppression and exploitation by the northern political administration. The creation of condominium government gave freedom to the north but at first had little or no effect on the socio-political life of the South, as repression continued by both British colonialist and northern Sudan. In the south, the English language, rather than Arabic, was encouraged as the official language, along with six other southern languages as the basis of instruction in elementary education. The southern policy was meant to protect missionary work against Muslim infiltration in the south, but the government had no interest in developing modern education, or any other form of socio-economic progress there.[17]

The story of the emergence of a Christian community in Southern Sudan must be seen against this backdrop of government policy. The aspirations of both Muslim and Christian communities are perceived by the Sudanese to be at the heart of post-Independence conflict in the Sudan. Religion is a highly political issue in Sudan, and its political context must always be kept in mind.

The condominium government prohibited missionary activities in northern Sudan, but they were encouraged in the south. The Catholics were most eager to embark on work there. By 1903, the 'spheres policy' committed the Verona Fathers to working in the Bahr-el-Ghazal region of south-western Sudan. They developed mission stations and the area remains staunchly Catholic. They also established trade and an elementary school. But the evangelistic work was not successful. The Verona Fathers gained permission in 1910 to open a station at Gondokoro where they consolidated a few believers who had been baptized fifty years before. This was later closed and further stations were opened at Rejaf East, and Juba on the Nile.

The American Presbyterian Mission established themselves after some delay in Doleib Hill near the mouth of the Sobat River in 1902. They emphasized evangelism through education and practical training and economic development.[18] In 1903, they founded a school which was approved by the government. The school developed and, in 1924, became a boarding school and the centre of a large network of several schools. In 1907, the mission bought a boat to help provide healthcare up the Sobat River to the Nuer people. This work resulted in the establishment of a hospital high up the Sobat River amongst the Nuer in 1923. Despite this success in practical work, progress in evangelism and church planting was slow. The first baptism took place only in 1913, and by 1923, the number of baptized believers was only about 200. The Presbyterian Church still remains the smallest among the three main churches of Southern Sudan.

CMS was the last of the three missions to begin work in the south. By 1905, it became urgent for CMS to become involved in mission work there before it was taken over by one of the other missions. In 1920, the South Sudan Mission was placed under the episcopal oversight of the Bishop of Uganda and became part of the CMS Elgon Mission. Bishop Leonard Kitching was consecrated the first Bishop of the Upper Nile Diocese, whose jurisdiction covered the whole Elgon mission area. After his death in 1935, the south of Sudan was restored to the Diocese of Egypt and the Sudan. CMS also gave attention to education and medical work but this was done among individual ethnic groups in the south. The revival that spread from

[16] For detailed discussion on the history of oppression and exploitation of the South by both British colonialists and Northern Sudan, see Wheeler, "Christianity in Sudan."

[17] Wheeler, "Christianity in Sudan."

[18] Wheeler, "Christianity in Sudan."

Uganda to the south of Sudan in 1941 resulted in the conversion of about 18,000 Christians. In that year, the first African clergy were ordained. Daniel Deng become the first Sudanese Anglican bishop in 1955.[19]

Active Churches in Northern Sudan and South Sudan

South Sudan Council of Churches (SSCC)

The comprehensive peace agreement (CPA) in 2005 eventually led to the separation of Sudan into two sovereign states, decided in the referendum of 2011. The Sudanese Council of Churches (SCC) decided to establish two separate ecumenical organizations for the two countries; the decision was reached at the SCC's 20th General Assembly from 3rd-7th July 2013 in Nairobi, Kenya.[20] The council for the Republic of South Sudan known as South Sudan Council of Churches (SSCC) and the other, for the Republic of Sudan, is known as Sudan Council of Churches (SCC). It is important to emphasise that the Church in South Sudan is a stakeholder and plays an important role in nation-building and also played an historic role in peace-making, and in preserving the heritage, civilization and values which underpin the concept of humanity. It has also recognized the need for a single body to embrace all the churches as a basis for clear consultation and co-operation in promoting Christian witness to the values of justice, peace, love and reconciliation, which are necessary for promoting stability and peace among the Sudanese people. The following are some of the active church traditions in South Sudan:

The Coptic Orthodox Church

With the establishment of the Anglo-Egyptian Condominium, the Coptic Church was reorganized in Sudan to care for the many Copts who now came to Sudan as government officials or as traders. In 1904, the foundations of the Coptic Cathedral were laid in Khartoum. Other churches were built to serve the Coptic communities in the Nile Valley and in Kordofan, including Omdurman, Atbara, Wad Medani, Gedaref, El Obeid and Kadugli. Today, there are two dioceses: the Diocese of Nubia Atbara and Omdurman stretches from the Egyptian border southwards and up the Blue Nile. The Diocese of Khartoum and Uganda stretches south of Khartoum to Uganda.

The Coptic Church is mainly concerned with the pastoral care of Copts working in Sudan, although in recent years there has been some evangelism amongst southerners and Nubans living in Khartoum. The Coptic community has always been active in education and they are amongst the most educated people in northern Sudan.

The Roman Catholic Church

In the north, until 1950, the Catholic population consisted mainly of expatriates or Catholic belonging to various Catholic religious orders. After 1950, and especially since the disturbances in the South, many Catholics from the south have settled in the north. Many of the Catholic communities in the north today are made up of southerners. Since 1960, northern Sudan has been divided into two vicariates, each with its own bishop. These are the Vicariate Apostolic of Khartoum and the Vicariate Apostolic of El Obeid. Like the other missionary-founded churches in northern Sudan, the Catholic Church is growing quickly, but this growth is mainly amongst southerners and Nubas who are moving to the towns.

---

[19] Adam Matthew Publications, "Church Missionary Society Archive," www.ampltd.co.uk/digital_guides/church_missionary_society_archive_general/editorial%20introduction%20by%20rosemary%20keen.aspx (accessed 9 Dec 2015).

[20] World Council of Churches, "South Sudan Council of Churches," https://www.oikoumene.org/en/member-churches/africa/south-sudan/sscc (accessed 9 Dec 2015).

Sudanese Church of Christ

This church has grown from the work of the Sudan United Mission. Today it has a Church in Nuba Mountains, Khartoum and Omdurman. It has also spread to all cities of northern Sudan. It has 37 local congregations with 87 pastors and evangelists all over the Sudan. It shares a Bible school at Melut with the Sudan Interior Church.

Sudan interior Church

This Sudan Interior Mission is one of the largest Protestant missions in the world. it mainly works in Nigeria and Ethiopia. In 1935, when the Italians invaded Ethiopia, all the SIM missionaries were expelled. Some of them came to Khartoum, hoping to keep in touch with Ethiopia, to ask the colonial government for permission to work in Sudan. They were allowed to work in parts of the Blue Nile and upper Nile provinces. In Khartoum they have maintained an active work with a lively Church, active youth and a bookshop. In1976, the name Sudan Interior Church was adopted for the Sudanese congregation.

Episcopal Church of Sudan

Nuba Mountains, though nearer to Southern Sudan than Khartoum, falls under Khartoum. As highlighted above, missionaries were banned from working in the Nuba Mountains to avoid educating and converting the Nuba people to Christianity. But later the government gave permission to the missionaries, but only to work in education and medical work. The work began in 1899 in Omdurman and spread to the southern region. Until 1974, the Diocese of Sudan was part of the Jerusalem archbishopric. It was restored to the jurisdiction of the Archbishop of Canterbury until the new Province, consisting of four new dioceses, was established in 1976.[21]

Other Churches in Northern Sudan and South Sudan

There are other churches which are yet to be admitted to SCC membership. These churches are the Ethiopian Orthodox, Armenian Church, Greek Catholic Church, Africa Inland Church, Presbyterian Church of Sudan, Sudan Pentecostal Church, Baptist Church, Brethren Church, Christian Brotherhood Church, Episcopal Methodist, Free Evangelical Church, Full Gospel Church, Great Commission Church, Kush Church, Lutheran Church of Sudan, Lutheran Evangelical Church, National Lutheran Church, New Apostolic Church, Reform Church, Sudanese Brethren Church, Sudan Pentecostal Church-Shigls, Sudanese Reform Church and Sudanese Brethren Church.

The Church in the Search for National Unity in South Sudan and Northern Sudan

The church in northern Sudan has been experiencing attacks which increased as the south voted for independence. The struggle for liberation in the south resulted in the emergence of a vibrant church based in the north. But the attacks and threats of attacks have continued, with the Sudanese government sanctioning destruction of some churches in Khartoum, Omdurman and the Nuba Mountains.[22] Some Christians have been killed in air raids by government forces.[23] But this has not dampened the spiritual

[21] Anglican Communion, "Province of the Episcopal Church of South Sudan & Sudan," www.anglicancommunion.org/structures/member-churches/member-church.aspx?church=sudan (accessed 9 Dec. 2015).

[22] World Watch Monitor, "Two Sudan Churches Destroyed, One for a 'Marketplace'," https://www.worldwatchmonitor.org/2015/10/4077326/ (accessed 9 Dec. 2015).

[23] Bos News Life, "Sudan Christians Mourn Murdered Believers; Church Destroyed," (July 7, 2014), www.bosnewslife.com/33294-sudan-christians-mourn-murdered-believers-church-destroyed (accessed 9 Dec. 2015). The report by Asylum Research Consultancy gives a detailed explanation about the situation in the Nuba Mountains:

fervour of the church in its evangelism, or in dedication and innovativeness in equipping its members in the businesses, hotels and industries of the north. The church is now a significant and permanent part of the northern religious landscape. This must be seen as relevant to the contemporary debate over the place of Islam and Christianity within northern Sudan.[24]

The church has always played a central role in South Sudan. It was a vital instrument in the peace agreement that led to the nation's independence . The Catholic Church succeeded in persuading church leaders in Rome to give a pastoral response to the oppression and repression in Sudan. In fact, churches such as the Catholic and Anglican have long played a role of provider of basic services such as education and health. In the violent period, the churches have helped the most vulnerable and provided immediate relief and means to help people rebuild their lives and the country. The post-independent civil war in South Sudan has also brought together the religious and political identities of most South Sudanese. The churches in South Sudan have remained steadfast in their commitment to providing immediate relief for the hundreds of thousands of internally displaced people and to the ultimate goal of peace and reconciliation in South Sudan.

Conclusion

This chapter has looked at Christianity in South Sudan and northern Sudan, and several factors were observed that led to the establishment of the church. Some of these were the British colonial policy of separation and related education policies, health and education, material support and transnational connections to higher education and training, literacy and Bible translation. Later factors include conflict-related social and political identity and insecurity.[25]

Bibliography

Gray, Richard. *A History of the Southern Sudan 1839-1889.* Oxford: OUP, 1961.

Jakobielski, S. 'Christian Nubia at the Height of its Civilization.' In *General History of Africa – Volume III – Africa from the Seventh to the Eleventh Century,* eds. M. El Fasi and L. Hrbek, 194-223. San Francisco: UNESCO, University of California Press, 1992.

Sanderson, L. Passmore and Neville Sanderson. *Education, Religion and Politics in Southern Sudan 1899-1964.* Khartoum and London: Ithaca Press and Khartoum University Press, 1981.

Sundkler, Bengt and Christopher Steed. *A History of the Church in Africa.* Cambridge: Cambridge University Press, 2000.

Wheeler, Andrew C. 'Christianity in Sudan.' In *Dictionary of African Christian Biography,* www.dacb.org/history/christianity%20in%20sudan.html (accessed 8 December 2015).

see Asylum Research Consultancy, Mountains, "Situation in Khartoum and Omdurman," (9 September 2015 – COI up to 18 August 2015) www.refworld.org/pdfid/55efe85e4.pdf (accessed 9 Dec 2015).

[24] Wheeler, "Christianity in Sudan."

[25] Lamoureaux, "Nuba Christianity: the Search for Security in the North."

(90) Christianity in Swaziland

Sonene Nyawo

Religion	Pop 2010	Pct 2010	Pop 2025	Pct 2025	Gr Pct 1970 2025
Christians	1,046,000	87.6%	1,283,000	89.2%	1.4%
Independents	572,000	47.9%	694,000	48.2%	1.3%
African initiated	558,000	46.7%			
Protestants	144,000	12.1%	205,000	14.3%	2.4%
Pentecostal	35,400	3.0%			
Anglicans	24,800	2.1%			
Evangelical churches	23,400	2.0%			
Holiness	19,200	1.6%			
Methodist	12,300	1.0%			
Lutheran	9,400	0.8%			
Adventist	8,100	0.7%			
Roman Catholics	56,000	4.7%	60,000	4.2%	0.5%
Pentecostals/Charismatics	597,000	50.1%	700,000	48.7%	1.1%
Evangelicals	137,000	11.5%	206,000	14.3%	2.7%
adherents of traditional African religions	118,000	9.9%	120,000	8.3%	0.1%
Muslims	7,800	0.7%	9,000	0.6%	1.0%
Baha'is	5,400	0.5%	6,300	0.4%	1.1%
Hindus	1,800	0.2%	2,100	0.1%	1.0%
people professing no religion	14,200	1.2%	17,800	1.2%	1.5%
Total population	**1,193,000**	**100.0%**	**1,438,000**	**100.0%**	**1.3%**

Source: Centre for the Study of World Christianity (CSGC), Boston, Gordon-Conwell TS

Early Beginnings

The advent of Christianity in Swaziland begins with a dream. King Somhlolo dreamt of strange people that had long hair hanging down from their heads, resembling tassels. They emerged from the sea, carrying two objects, a *umculu* (scroll) and a *indilinga* (round object/coin).[1] The King was instructed by a voice in the dream that he should accept the scroll and reject the round object, and also not to hurt these people.[2] It is on record that King Somhlolo had heard, from his representatives at the Zulu court, that the son and heir of

[1] Sonene Nyawo, "The Early Encounter between Swaziland and the Western Missionaries: The Establishment of the Evangelical Church in Swaziland, 1982-1950." M.A. Thesis, University of Natal, Pietermaritzburg (2004), 81.

[2] Joshua Mzizi, "Church and State in Swaziland is Somhlolo's Dream a Scandal for Swazi Hegemony" in Religion and Politics in Swaziland, ed. Simangaliso Kumalo (Bloemfontein: SUN Media, 2013), 236.

Sekonyela, chief of the Mantatees, had been instructed by the missionaries, and was staying with them at the Mpharane mission station.[3] Sobhuza then decided to send a delegation to Mpharane to request a missionary to reside at his royal kraal and instruct his son and successor Mswati. 'It was just before taking this decision that the Swazi King had had his dream of the *umculu* and the *indilinga.*[4] Unfortunately, because of financial constraints, the missionaries could not attend to Sobhuza's request promptly. Nonetheless, on his death bed, the dying king made his son and successor promise that he would pursue his father's vision.[5] The Swazi accepted this dream as a revelation by national ancestors about the unknown future of the nation in the midst of some external threats.

The Realisation of the King's Dream

In pursuit of this historic dream, young King Mswati II, after his installation as King of Swaziland, sent his two headmen, Majuba Mndzebele and Mkonkoni Kunene, in 1838 to fetch the missionaries to bring the *umculu* to Swaziland. The Swazi generally longed for the missionaries because 'they heard that the missionaries were white people who were preaching the Word of *Mvelinchanti* (God), and they evidently took it from the *umculu*'.[6] After a considerable delay, in 1844, the Wesleyan Missionary Conference, held at Grahamstown, accepted King Mswati's request, and decided to send missionaries to Swaziland. Eventually, the Rev. James Allison and the Rev. Richard Giddy, with two Basotho evangelists, decided on an exploratory visit to Swaziland before establishing a permanent settlement. They got a friendly reception from a gathering of 'notables' at Lozitha Royal Palace which included the young King Mswati II, Queen Mother Tsandzile, the King's uncle Prince Mbukwane, and about 200 chiefs and Tindvunas.[7] At the King's instruction, they were designated some land at the southern portion of the Swazi domain, known as Dlovunga. Having received orders to help the missionaries in any way possible in the construction of the buildings, the local people completed a chapel and a large house for living accommodation, surrounded by a high fence, within a week. Also, they laid out a garden where they planted 150 fruit trees.[8] The two white missionaries ultimately left for South Africa, taking along with them two young Swazi men, Job and Barnabas, to be trained as teachers. The entire scenario of the first missionaries coming to Swaziland leads Kasanene, amongst other scholars, to the conclusion that 'unlike the most African countries, missionaries did not come to Swaziland on their own initiative; they were invited by the Swazi authorities and received an enthusiastic welcome when they arrived. All this was because of Sobhuza's dream'.[9]

While Allison was in South Africa to raise enough funds for the second expedition and final settlement amongst the Swazi, Job and Barnabas, who had graduated as teachers and African evangelists, became aggressive in the task of converting the Swazi to Christianity and teaching them to read and write.[10] However, the lifestyle of the converts who accepted Christianity soon changed, and they were estranged from the rest of the community: 'they changed their way of dressing, those who had been polygamous chased away all their wives except one, they did not take part in beer parties or other traditional gatherings, and they boycotted Swazi national ceremonies and rituals.'[11]

---

[3] Rogers Cazziol, *A Comparative study of Christian Missions in Swaziland*. Ph.D. Thesis, University of Natal, 1989, 96.

[4] Cazziol, *A Comparative Study of Christian Missions*, 96

[5] Loskini Mabundza, The Influence of Christianity on the Swazi. M.A. Thesis, Canadian Nazarene College, 1976, 37.

[6] James Matsebula, *A History of Swaziland*. Cape Town: Longman, 1972, 16.

[7] Cazziol, *A Comparative Study of Christianity on the Swazi Missions*, 98.

[8] James Matsebula, *A History of Swaziland* (2nd edition), 1987, 35.

[9] Peter Kasanene, *Religion in Swaziland*. Braamfontein: Skotaville, Publishers, 44

[10] Matsebula, J.S.M., *A History of Swaziland*, 36

[11] Joshua Mzizi," Impediments to Religions Tolerance in Swaziland: A Historical Survey" in *UNISWA Research*

The smooth progress of missionary work was disturbed by some internal disputes within the royal family over some royal cattle.[12] Three rebellious chiefs and some people within the Kunene clan fled to the mission station seeking refuge, and Allison refused to surrender them to Mswati's commanders. On 14th September 1846, the mission station was attacked, but with Mswati's orders not to harm the missionaries or any of the assistants, they were spared.[13] However, this caused terror amongst the people and an estimated 1,000 Swazis fled to Pietermaritzburg following the missionaries; hence the area became known as Mahamba or 'the runaways'.[14] This voluntary flight put an end to mission work in Swaziland for at least 35 years,[15] while Mswati II was King.

The Establishment of Early Mission Churches in Swaziland

It was during King Mbandzeni's reign, beginning in 1880, that Christianity made inroads in Swaziland again. Under pressure from the concessionaires, Mbandzeni realised the importance of the education once offered by the missionaries. On his own initiative, in May 1880, he invited the Rev. Jackson to Swaziland to build a mission station at Usuthu in Luyengo that would have educational and industrial buildings. His sole aim was to send his nine children for an education. With the invitation of the Rev. Jackson, 'doors were once more opened for missionary competition, and a scramble for Swazi souls began'.[16] Amongst these missionaries were the Rev. Msimango and the Rev. Mangena, Swazi ministers who had fled from Mahamba mission for the Wesleyan Methodist Church. In 1887, the Berlin Lutheran Missionary Society followed, but 'did not commence active missionary work until 1902 when they were joined by the Rev. Johannes Mndziniso, a Swazi Lutheran Church Minister'.[17] In 1890, the South African General Mission (the present AEC) began its work in Bethany, under the Rev. Dudley Kidd and John Baillie. The Scandinavian Alliance Mission (SAM) which gave birth to the Evangelical Church came next, led by Miss Malla Moe and started work at Bulunga in 1892. The Church of the Nazarene began planting churches in Swaziland about 1911 when Harmon Schmelzenbach arrived at Endzingeni. Roman Catholicism began in 1913, with the arrival of Servite missionaries who established a mission in Mbabane. All the western missionaries that settled in Swaziland pioneered formal education in Swaziland and their first priority was to establish schools for Swazi children and also health facilities for the people. They used education as the most effective tool for evangelization.[18]

After the formation of mission churches, there were many Pentecostal and charismatic churches that mushroomed, together with Zionist churches that blended Swazi traditional understanding with Biblical teachings. Very soon, even though Swaziland was not an officially Christian nation, everyday practices point to Christianity's overriding popularity. Most Swazis identify themselves as Christians, a claim easily seen by even a brief time spent in the kingdom, where many churches populate town and countryside and the media produce a ubiquitous background of gospel music, preaching and instructions on living a godly

---

Journal, Vol 12 (1998), 43-54 (47).

[12] Matsebula, *A History of Swaziland*, p.16. When Malambule handed the reigns of government to the young Mswati, he appropriated some of the royal cattle for himself and hid them. When Mswati found this out later, he sent his men to demand the return of the cattle and to punish Malambule. Malambule fled with his brothers Ndlela and Fokotsi to the south of the country to seek refuge among the Kunene clan. When Mswati sent his regiments to attack this clan for giving protection to the refugees, they fled to the mission station.

[13] Kasenene, *Religion in Swaziland*, 45.

[14] Matsebula, *A History of Swaziland*, 36.

[15] Kasenene, *Religion in Swaziland*, 46.

[16] Kasenene, *Religion in Swaziland*, 47.

[17] Kasenene, *Religion in Swaziland*, 47.

[18] Sonene Nyawo, "Multi-Faith Religious Education in Swaziland: A Response to Globalisation." A paper presented at the Annual BOLESWA TRS Conference, University of Swaziland, Kwaluseni, 27th February-1st March 2010, 4.

life.[19] Likewise, the International Religious Freedom (IRF) report,[20] Religious Intelligence Country Profile[21] and similar aggregate reports assume a Christian majority, suggesting that about 40% of the population affiliate with syncretistic indigenous Christian Zionist churches, 20% are Roman Catholic, with other Christian denominations including Anglicans, Methodists, Evangelicals and new Pentecostal-charismatic style ministry churches making up 30%. Less than 10% of the population consists of Muslims, Jews, Mormons and Baha'is.

Christian Ecumenical Organisations in Swaziland

The high proliferation of churches in Swaziland eventually resulted in doctrinal differences, hence the establishment of ecumenical organisations that aimed to reconcile the divided Christian churches and forge real unity. As rightly noted by Amanze, church unity in the ecumenical context does not necessarily entail uniformity of doctrine, worship and governance. Instead, it denotes unity in reconciled diversity in which there are neither fierce divisions nor paternalistic relationships among the different Christian denominations.[22]

There are therefore three ecumenical church bodies in Swaziland, namely, the Swaziland Conference of Churches, the Council of Swaziland Churches, and the League of African Churches. The three ecumenical organizations have had different aims and objectives since their establishment. The Swaziland Conference of Churches (SCC) was formed in 1929 by individual European missionaries belonging to the numerous mission churches and agencies that had set up mission stations in Swaziland. The overriding aim of SCC has been to foster and promote co-operation and fellowship among the various mission churches engaged in Christian evangelism in Swaziland.[23] SCC experienced a split in 1976 when liberal member churches withdrew their membership to form the Council of Swaziland Churches (CSC). While the Swaziland Conference of Churches aims primarily at church planting and the conversion of non-Christians, the Council of Swaziland Churches strives to address social concerns in Swazi society, such as poverty, underdevelopment, and social injustice.[24]

Unlike SCC and CSC, which were founded by former mission churches, the League of African Churches in Swaziland (LACS) was formed by King Sobhuza II (1889-1982) in liaison with African clergy belonging to African Independent / Initiated Churches in the early 1940s. The King and leading African clergymen created LACS mainly in response to concerted attempts by the then British colonial government – in collusion with some European missionaries – to ban Zionist Christian Churches in Swaziland.[25] Given Sobhuza II's pioneering, legitimizing and mentorship role in the formation and consolidation of the

[19] Sonene Nyawo and Casey Golomski, C. "Christians' Cut: Ecumenical Perspectives on Male Circumcision in Swaziland's HIV Epidemic." A paper to be presented at an Ecumenical Conference, hosted by The Journal of Southern African Studies, University of Botswana, 2015, 4.
[20] International Religious Freedom (IRF) Report: Swaziland. 2012. Washington: Bureau of Democracy, Human Rights, and Labor, U.S. Department of State. www.state.gov/j/drl/rls/irf/2012/af/208202.htm, accessed 12 February 2015.
[21] Religious Intelligence Country Profile (2011) http://web.archive.org/web/200806261100027 [accessed 10 September, 2014].
[22] James Amanze, *The Origin and Development of the Ecumenical Movement in Botswana: 1965 – 1994*. Gaborone: Department of History and the Department of Theology and Religious Studies, University of Botswana. (1994), 56.
[23] Cazziol, *A Comparative Study of Christianity on the Swazi Missions*, 98.
[24] Ndlovu Hebron, The Royal Easter Ritual and Political Actions in Swaziland. Ph.D Dissertation, McMaster University (1994), 87.
[25] Nyawo, Sonene, Hebron Ndlovu, David Nhlabatsi, and Patrick. Mkhonta. The League of African Churches in Swaziland: Challenges and Prospects: A Study Commissioned by the University of Swaziland. Kwaluseni: University of Swaziland (2011), 24.

organization, the constitution of LACS recognizes Ingwenyama (the King) of Swaziland as its lifelong Patron, and provides that the annual meeting of LACS be held at [Lobamba]Ludzidzini Royal Residence.[26]

Sundkler, in his survey of the history of Zionist and Apostolic churches in Swaziland confirms that LACS was the brainchild of King Sobhuza II who spearheaded its formation in order to unite the Indigenous African Churches, especially the Zionist churches which were notorious for being disorganized and prone to proliferation.[27] The King also sought to protect LACS from all possible threats. The aims of LACS are to promote fellowship and unity among African Initiated Churches as well as to forestall further proliferation of African Initiated Churches in the country. Since its inception, LACS has been credited with rendering unequivocal support for Swazi cultural nationalism; it fully supports Swazi sacred kingship and other sacred traditions such as the sacred *Incwala* ceremony[28], while the SCC and the CSC shunned or adopted a critical stance toward them[29]

Sundkler further notes that LACS reciprocated the King's intervention on its behalf by creating the annual Good Friday Ceremony in which all Christians belonging to Indigenous African Churches celebrate the Easter Ceremony with the King, the Queen Mother, and members of the Swazi royal family and senior politicians. The observation that the most notable achievement of LACS has been the creation of the Good Friday Ceremony is also shared by Kuper (1986),[30] Cazziol (1987)[31] and Kasenene (1987).[32]

In conclusion, Christianity in Swaziland came by royal invitation, and it spread after the death of King Somhlolo through missionary expansion and African initiative. As a result, Swaziland built its socio-economic and political ideology upon culture and the Bible; thus making culture and religion an intricate and intertwined web.

Bibliography

Amanze James, *The Origin and Development of the Ecumenical Movement in Botswana: 1965 – 1994.* Gaborone: Department of History and the Department of Theology and Religious Studies, University of Botswana,1994.

Cazziol, Rogers, *The Swazi Zionists: An Indigenous Religious Movement in Southern Africa.* Kwaluseni: University of Swaziland 1987.

Kasanene Peter, *Religion in Swaziland.* Braamfontein: Skotaville, Publishers, 1993.

Kuper Hilda. (1986). *The Swazi: A South African Kingdom.* New York: Holt.

Matsebula James, *A History of Swaziland.* Cape Town: Longman, 1972.

Matsebula James, *A History of Swaziland* (2nd edition), Cape Town: Longman, 1987.

Mzizi, Joshua, 'Church and State in Swaziland is Somhlolo's Dream a Scandal for Swazi Hegemony' in Religion and Politics in Swaziland, ed. Simangaliso Kumalo Bloemfontein: SUN Media, 2013.

Mzizi, Joshua, 'Impediments to Religions Tolerance in Swaziland: A Historical Survey' in *UNISWA Research Journal,* vol 12, 1998, 43-54.

Nyawo Sonene and Golomski, Casey. 'Christians' Cut: Ecumenical Perspectives on Male Circumcision in Swaziland's HIV Epidemic.' A paper to be presented at an Ecumenical Conference, hosted by The Journal of Southern African Studies, University of Botswana, 2015.

---

[26] Nyawo, Ndlovu, Nhlabatsi, and Mkhonta. The League of African Churches in Swaziland, 16.

[27] Sundkler Bengt, *Zulu Zion and Some Swazi Zionists.* Oxford: Oxford University Press (1976), 75.

[28] Incwala is a national rite of passage celebrated annually around December and January. It is sacred and spiritual festival which acts as culmination of the Swazi system of beliefs regarding the veneration of the Ancestors as part of national life.

[29] Rogers Cazziol, *The Swazi Zionists,* 54.

[30] Hilda Kuper *The Swazi: A South African Kingdom.* New York: Holt (1986), 220.

[31] Rogers Cazziol, *The Swazi Zionists,* 47.

[32] Peter Kasenene, "Ecumenical Progress in Swaziland." PhD Thesis, University of Cape Town (1987), 68.

Nyawo Sonene, 'Multi-Faith Religious Education in Swaziland: A Response to Globalisation.' A paper presented at the Annual BOLESWA TRS Conference, University of Swaziland, Kwaluseni, 27th February-1st March 2010.

Nyawo, Sonene, Hebron Ndlovu, David Nhlabatsi, and Patrick. Mkhonta. 'The League of African Churches in Swaziland: Challenges and Prospects.' A Study Commissioned by the University of Swaziland. Kwaluseni: University of Swaziland 2011.

Sundkler Bengt. *Zulu Zion and Some Swazi Zionists*. Oxford: OUP, 1976.

Thesis and Dissertations on the subject

Cazziol. Rogers. 'A Comparative study of Christian Missions in Swaziland.' PhD., Thesis, University of Natal, 1989.

Kasenene, Peter. Ecumenical Progress in Swaziland. PhD Thesis, University of Cape Town, 1987.

Ndlovu. Hebron. 'The Royal Easter Ritual and Political Actions in Swaziland.' PhD., Dissertation, McMaster University, 1994.

Nyawo, Sonene. 'The Early Encounter between Swaziland and the Western Missionaries: The Establishment of the Evangelical Church in Swaziland, 1982-1950.' M.A. Thesis, University of Natal, Pietermaritzburg, 2004.

Mabundza, Loskini, 'The Influence of Christianity on the Swazi.' M.A. Thesis, Canadian Nazarene College, 1976.

Online Articles

International Religious Freedom (IRF) Report: Swaziland. 2012. Washington: Bureau of Democracy, Human Rights, and Labor, U.S. Department of State. www.state.gov/j/drl/rls/irf/2012/af/ 208202.htm, accessed 12 February 2015.

Religious Intelligence Country Profile (2011) http://web.archive.org/web/20080626110027 [accessed 10 September, 2014]

(91) CHRISTIANITY IN TANZANIA

Laurenti Magesa

Religion	Pop 2010	Pct 2010	Pop 2025	Pct 2025	Gr Pct 1970 2025
Christians	25,303,000	55.4%	41,939,000	58.2%	3.4%
Independents	998,000	2.2%	1,700,000	2.4%	3.6%
African initiated	239,000	0.5%			
Orthodox	13,100	0.0%	13,300	0.0%	0.1%
Protestants	13,955,000	30.6%	19,300,000	26.8%	2.2%
Lutheran	5,601,000	12.3%			
Anglicans	3,318,000	7.3%			
Pentecostal	1,799,000	3.9%			
Baptist	1,035,000	2.3%			
Nondenominational	762,000	1.7%			
Adventist	619,000	1.4%			
Moravian	587,000	1.3%			
Roman Catholics	12,826,000	28.1%	20,600,000	28.6%	3.2%
Evangelicals	7,541,000	16.5%	10,962,000	15.2%	2.5%
Pentecostals/Charismatics	4,906,000	10.7%	7,500,000	10.4%	2.9%
Muslims	14,221,000	31.2%	22,420,000	31.1%	3.1%
adherents of traditional African religions	5,327,000	11.7%	6,405,000	8.9%	1.2%
Hindus	389,000	0.9%	620,000	0.9%	3.2%
Baha'is	191,000	0.4%	310,000	0.4%	3.3%
Chinese folk-religionists	23,800	0.1%	35,000	0.0%	2.6%
Sikhs	13,500	0.0%	20,000	0.0%	2.7%
Buddhists	10,200	0.0%	15,000	0.0%	2.6%
Jains	9,900	0.0%	13,000	0.0%	1.9%
Jews	290	0.0%	300	0.0%	0.1%
Zoroastrians	140	0.0%	150	0.0%	0.7%
people professing no religion	160,000	0.4%	255,000	0.4%	3.1%
Total population	**45,649,000**	**100.0%**	**72,033,000**	**100.0%**	**3.1%**

Source: Centre for the Study of World Christianity (CSGC), Boston, Gordon-Conwell TS

Introduction

Tanzania lies on the east coast of Africa, between 28 and 41 degrees longitude and 1 and 12 degrees latitude south. It borders the Indian Ocean to the east, Lake Victoria, Kenya and Uganda to the north,

Rwanda and Burundi to the north-east, Lake Tanganyika and the Democratic Republic of Congo (DRC) to the west, Zambia to the south-west, and Lake Malawi (or Nyasa), Malawi, and the Ruvuma River and Mozambique to the south. Its total land area is 945,087 square kilometres or 364,900 square miles, inclusive of the offshore the Island of Zanzibar.[1]

The United Republic of Tanzania (*Jamhuri ya Muungano wa Tanzania* in Kiswahili, Tanzania's national language) came into existence following a political union in 1964 between the mainland, Tanganyika, and Zanzibar. According to the 2012 national census, Tanzania has a total population of approximately 45 million people, with 43.6 million on the mainland and 1.4 in Zanzibar. The population is divided almost equally between genders. The great majority of the people (approximately 80%) live in rural areas, although there is now a rapid movement to urban centres.[2]

Official surveys by religious affiliation were outlawed in Tanzania since 1967. Therefore, apart from imprecise estimates by private observers, sociologists and religious leaders, there is no accurate data about this. Indications are, however, that Muslims, Christians and adherents of African Indigenous Religion comprise about 90% of the population, each with approximately 30%. The remaining 10% is made up of various other faiths, including African Initiated/Independent churches (AICs). Buddhism, Hinduism and Sikhism originated mainly from India and the Far East, and their membership is practically confined to the people of these ethnicities. Whereas there is an uneven mixture of these religions in mainland Tanzania, Zanzibar is 98-99% Muslim.[3]

Early Christian Missions

The denominations to which most Tanzanian Christians belong include the Roman Catholic, Anglican and Lutheran churches. There also exist, in smaller numbers, the Salvation Army, the Seventh Day Adventists, the Church of Jesus Christ of Latter Day Saints, the African Inland Mission/Church, the Mennonite Church and the Jehovah's Witnesses. Apart from the earlier Pentecostal missions in the country, such as the Assemblies of God, the Swedish Free Mission, the Pentecostal Assemblies of God and the Pentecostal Evangelistic Fellowship, there are now a growing number of new Evangelical and Pentecostal groups, many originating from overseas. In the last fifty years, there have also arisen a number of African Initiated Churches (also known as African Independent or African Founded Churches, or AICs). All these are found in varying degrees of influence across the country.

Although some Catholic Dominican and Augustinian friars had done some missionary work in Zanzibar by the very end of the sixteenth century in the wake of the Portuguese exploration of the East Coast of Africa, results were meagre. Christianity soon disappeared there until the mid-nineteenth century.[4] Under the umbrella of the Anglican Church Missionary Society (CMS) from London, Johann Ludwig Krapf arrived in Zanzibar in 1844, to be joined shortly by Johann Rebmann. Krapf's interests, however, lay among the Oromo of Ethiopia, so that he almost immediately moved his operational headquarters to Rabai Mpya in Kilifi, Kenya. There he composed the first-ever Swahili-English dictionary and translated various books of the Bible into Kiswahili, exceptional legacies for mission work, even for Tanzania. Although Rebmann visited the Kilimanjaro region, he did not engage in any significant evangelizing there.

---

[1] http://geography.about.com/library/cia/blctanzania.htm.

[2] The United Republic of Tanzania. *Tanzania in Figures 2012* www.nbs.go.tz/takwimu/references/ Tanzania_in_figures2012.pdf (accessed 12 February 2015) and http://ccs.ukzn.ac.za/files/madulu.pfd

[3] John Baur, *2000 Years of Christianity in Africa: An African Church History* (Nairobi: Paulines Publications Africa, second edn. 2009), 439.

[4] Lucas Malishi, *A History of the Catholic Church in Tanzania* (Dar es Salaam: Tanzania Episcopal Conference, 1990), 11-13.

Missions with an Enduring Impact[5]

Protestant Missions

The beginning of Christian missions in Tanzania with a lasting impact may be dated to the 1860s. In 1864, Bishop William Georg Tozer and Dr Edward Steere of the London-based Universities Mission to Central Africa (UMCA) arrived in Zanzibar in response to the appeals of the traveller David Livingstone. Tozer and Steere began their work by redeeming and baptizing slaves. Soon they were joined by others, including some women missionaries. The UMCA established a college and printing press in Zanzibar. The mission quickly moved northwards to the Usambara region, at Magila near Tanga. Other mission stations were later established at Masasi and Likoma Island in Lake Nyasa, as well as other places in southern Tanzania.

In the wake of the German occupation of coastal Tanzania after the 1884-1885 Berlin Conference that agreed on the partitioning of Africa among the European powers of the day, missionaries of the German Lutheran Evangelical Missionary Society (EMS) for East Africa, or Berlin III (later to be renamed the Bethel Mission) came to Tanzania. Johann Jacob Greiner arrived in Dar es Salaam at Kigamboni in 1887. Despite resistance from the Arabs, the Bethel Mission expanded to Kisarawe and beyond. Three years later, August Kramer established a mission and school in Tanga. Within a few years, more stations were opened in several areas around the Usambara Mountains and elsewhere in the country. In 1910, Ernst Johansen arrived in Bukoba, northwest of Lake Victoria, and established mission stations there.

Evangelists from the Berlin Missionary Society, or Berlin I, settled at Ipagika or Pipagika near Lake Nyasa in 1891. They quickly spread out towards Mbeya and Iringa in the Southern Highlands region. Then, in 1893, another group of German missionaries from the Leipzig Mission Society, took up residence in Old Moshi, Machame, and elsewhere in the Kilimanjaro, Pare and Meru regions in north-eastern Tanzania.[6] At almost the same time, the Moravians, also from Germany, settled in the Rungwe area north of Lake Nyasa, and soon moved further north to Rukwa around Lake Tanganyika and Unyamwezi in the Tabora region.

The Lonon- Missionary Society, to which Livingstone belonged, had missionaries in Nassa on the east of Lake Victoria by 1887. They were replaced there by the American-founded African Inland Mission/Church (AIM/AIC) in 1897. The Seventh Day Adventists (SDA), also of American origin, arrived in Tanzania in 1903. From Dar es Salaam, they spread to Pare and north-westwards to Mara and Shinyanga around Lake Victoria. By the beginning of the twentieth century, Anglican and Lutheran missions were already present in many parts of the country.[7]

Catholic Missions

Priests of the Catholic Congregation of the Holy Ghost Fathers (HGF) arrived in Zanzibar in 1863. Like the Anglicans, they also evangelized ransomed slaves. In 1868, they established a mission station at Bagamoyo. From there they built other stations in the neighbouring Morogoro area. Some HGF went northward and worked among the Chagga people around Mount Kilimanjaro. Another group of Catholic

---

[5] Carl-Erick Sahlberg, *From Krapf to Rugambwa: A Church History of Tanzania* (Nairobi: Evangel Publishing House, 1986) provides an excellent presentation on this subject.

[6] These German-founded Lutheran churches entered into an alliance in 1938 called the Federation of Lutheran Churches in Tanganyika. In 1964, it became the Evangelical Lutheran Church in Tanzania (ELCT). The Church has 22 Dioceses: North Western, North Eastern, Pare, Northern, North Central, Karagwe, Central, Southern, Konde, South Central, Ulanga /Kilombero, Eastern and Coastal, Mbulu, Iringa, Dodoma, East of Lake Victoria, Mara, Meru, South Western, Morogoro, South East of Lake Victoria, and South Eastern. www.elct.org

[7] At the moment, the Anglican Dioceses in Tanzania are: Central Tanganyika, Dar es Salaam, Kagera, Kibondo, Kondoa, Lweru, Mara, Masasi, Morogoro, Mount Kilimanjaro, Mpwapwa, Newala, Rift Valley, Ruaha, Rorya, Ruvuma, Shinyanga, South-West Tanganyika, Southern Highlands, Tabora, Tanga, Tarime, Victoria Nyanza, Western Tanganyika, Zanzibar, Kiteto, and Lake Rukwa. See www.episcopalchurch.org/anglican.province/anglican-church-tanzania

missionaries, the White Fathers (WF) arrived in Zanzibar in 1878, and in the 1890s successively established posts at Bukumbi near Mwanza and in the Tabora, Kabanga and Karema regions, the latter two near Lake Tanganyika. At the same time, another group of WF arrived in Bukoba from Uganda and founded stations at Rubya, Kagondo and Kashozi. Their female counterparts, the White Sisters, joined them in 1902.

Arriving in Tanzania in January 1888, the Roman Catholic Benedictine Friars (OSB) and Sisters settled at Pugu near Dar es Salaam. The Order had to withdraw briefly on account of political complications, but they returned to Kurasini the following year. They expanded their missions southwards to the Lindi, Masasi and Iringa regions (at Lukuledi, Nyangao, Peramiho and Tosomaganga). Later they set up other stations at Ndanda, Mahenge, and in Dodoma at Bihawana. By the 1890s, they were working in Kibosho and Kilema (Kilimanjaro) and Tanga. Carl-Erik Sahlberg notes that, by 1914, the Catholic Church had established six main administrative centres on the Tanzanian mainland: Kilimanjaro and Bagamoyo (under HGF), Dar es Salaam (OSB), Tabora, Karema and Bukoba (WF).[8]

Under widespread anti-German feeling after World War I, German missionaries, both Catholic and Protestant, had to leave the country practically en masse. However, by 1930, they had returned to most of their former stations. Other groups also arrived during this period: the Passionists (to Dodoma), the Pallotines (Singida and Mbulu), the Maryknoll Fathers (Shinyanga), the Rosminians (Tanga) and the Salvatorians (Nachingwea). After World War II in 1945, the German missionaries again were compelled to leave and were replaced by the Swiss.

Newer and Indigenous Missions

New missions (apart from the Lutherans, Catholics and Anglicans) arrived in the country from the 1950s with Dar es Salaam as the launching ground. Among them were the Presbyterians (1950) who went to Tanga, the Salvation Army (1953) in Mbeya, Tarime and Moshi, and the Mennonites, north-east of Lake Victoria, in Musoma, Shirati and their vicinity. Between 1950 and 1960, the Baptists founded stations in Mbeya, Tanga, Kigoma, Masasi, Mbozi, Mwanza, Moshi and Arusha. The Greek Orthodox Church came in 1963. This church is small in Tanzania and is concentrated in towns across the country, serving almost exclusively immigrants of Greek origin.

There are not many AICs in Tanzania. Only a few have made their presence felt: Watch Tower (1919), Last Church of God and His Christ, or Ba-Ngemela after its leader (1925), in the Mbeya region, African National Church (1935), Holy Spirit Church (1953) in Bukoba, Maria Legio of Africa (1960) in north-eastern Tanzania, and Zion Tabernacle Church or Hema ya Sayuni (mid-1940s) in the Kilimanjaro region.[9]

In contrast with the missionary churches, most of whose official stance was to discourage African spiritual customs and practices like polygamy, initiation rites, and belief in witchcraft, many AICs were founded precisely to align belief in Jesus Christ with African spirituality. Although they are often described as reactions against mission Christianity, T.O. Ranger points out helpfully that 'most offer solutions which they believe to be positively good instead of resting content with negative criticism of the missions'. Their characteristics include, but transcend, the usual categorization of the politically-oriented 'Ethiopian' or spiritually-leaning 'Zionist' churches to include also those based on 'a whole series of African answers' to African problems.[10]

---

[8] Currently, the Catholic Church in Tanzania consists of 34 dioceses: Arusha, Bukoba, Bunda, Dar-es-Salaam, Dodoma, Geita, Ifakara, Iringa, Kahama, Kayanga. Kigoma, Kondoa, Kondoa, Lindi, Mahenge, Mbeya, Mbinga, Mbulu, Morogoro, Moshi, Mpanda, Mtwara, Musoma, Mwanza, Njombe, Rulenge-Ngara, Same, Shinyanga, Singida, Songea, Sumbawanga, Tabora, Tanga, Tunduru-Masasi, and Zanzibar. See www.catholic-hierarchy.org/country/dtz2.html

[9] T.O. Ranger. *The African Churches of Tanzania* (Nairobi: East African Publishing House, 1972).

[10] Ranger, *The African Churches of Tanzania,* 4-5.

Church Activities

The churches' situation after World War II facilitated the formal development of indigenous leadership in all the Christian denominations. The period also marked the expansion of evangelization around the country with an inevitably African, albeit muted, flavour. After the 1960s, the churches in Tanzania began to make the transition from European-focused to Africa-centred mission in terms of self-government, self-support and self-propagation.

Most missions, with the conspicuous exception of the Pentecostals who seemed suspicious of involvement in 'secular' affairs, had from the start placed an emphasis on investing in schools and healthcare facilities wherever they went. The Catholics were especially disposed to educational work, seeing it as a prime way of getting converts: 'Where it is impossible to carry on both the immediate task of evangelization and your educational work,' declared English Cardinal Arthur Hinsley on a visit to Tanganyika in the 1920s, 'neglect your churches in order to perfect your schools.'[11] Missionaries had from the beginning also emphasised the training of local church leaders.

Among the Wahaya of Bukoba and along the Kagera River, for example, much of the evangelization work was done by indigenous converts. Notable among them were Andrea Kajerero, Zakaria Ikate, Abraham Mpandakyaro and Josiah Kibira. Others included Canon Cecil Majaliwa, Deacon John Swedi and Sub-deacon George Farajallah who had already been ministering in various places under the UMCA since the 1870s. There were also Pastor Yakobo Ng'ombe with the Lutherans in the Tanga region in the 1920s, and Evangelists Tugulmiwe Wikungu and Yohannes Kipamila (Moravian) in the early 1900s in Urambo and Rungwe. Among the Catholics were Doctor and Catechist Adrien Atiman in Karema.

Thus, from the 1950s, Africans were beginning to be missionaries to themselves and audaciously building local, not missionary, churches, with previous encouragement. Bishop C.A. Chambers (CMS) of Central Tanganyika had intimated that, 'The future hope of Tanganyika [Christianity] lies in a sufficient supply of earnest, well-equipped Africans, who will go out to their brethren and preach and teach and live Christ.'[12] The same sentiments had been echoed in the Catholic Church by Popes Benedict XV (in *Maximun Illud*, 1919) and Pius XI (*Rerum Ecclesiae*, 1926). To this end, Cardinal Lavigerie's WFs had established a seminary at Kipalapala in Tabora in 1925, the Benedictines at Peramiho and Ndanda, and the HGF in Moshi and Morogoro. Consequently, in 1958, the presidency of the Lutheran Church in northern Tanganyika was given to the indigenous churchman, Pastor Stefano Moshi. Among the Catholics, Laurian Rugambwa was consecrated Bishop for Rubato (1953), Charles Msakila for Karema (1960), and Joseph Kilasara for Moshi (1960). Also in 1960, Rugambwa was made Cardinal, the first-ever black African.

Ecumenical and Interreligious Relations

From the outset of mission work in Tanzania, the Anglican churches (UMCA and CMS), on the one hand, and the Lutheran churches (Berlin, Bethel, Leipzig, and Moravian), on the other, collaborated. They often assisted one another in pastoral activities, even establishing certain infrastructure projects together. In Morogoro in 1911, both groups set up a joint school to counter Muslim influence there. The SDA and AIM churches, however, have tended to shun such collaboration. So has the Catholic Church, particularly before the Second Vatican Council (1962-65), refusing to join the World Council of Churches in 1948. This stance was reflected in Catholic missionary work in Tanzania. The Pentecostal churches have in general also not been enthusiastic about ecumenical co-operation.

Except the SDA and PAG, most of the Protestant churches are members of the Christian Council of Tanzania (CCT), based in Dodoma. The Catholic Church co-operates with the Council in various projects

[11] Sahlberg, *From Krapf to Rugambwa*, 134.
[12] Sahlberg, *From Krapf to Rugambwa*, 128.

of mutual interest as a form of practical ecumenism. For example, the churches have a joint medical committee and present common broadcast programmes on national radio. In terms of spiritual ecumenism, there are joint prayers among all Christian churches during the Week of Prayer for Christian Unity every January. Far-reaching ecumenical initiatives, such as the shared training of ministers, common catechetical programmes or intercommunion, however, though desirable, are not yet a reality.

As already mentioned, apart from the intuition of a few visionary individuals, like Father (later Bishop) William Vincent Lucas (UMCA) in Masasi, Pastor Traugott Backman (Moravian) in Rungwe, and Pastor Bruno Gutmann (Leipzig Mission) in Kilimanjaro, who held a deep respect for indigenous customs and actively sought to integrate them into Christian belief and practices, little or no attempt has been made by the mission churches to enter into serious formal dialogue with African religion. In fact, those who tried faced opposition from their missions and were accused of 'heathenizing' Christianity.[13]

Relations between Christian missions and Islam in Tanzania have been characterized by suspicion on both sides, despite the fact that, for decades, Christians and Muslims had lived cordially side-by-side. The situation seems to have worsened since the 1980s.[14] Relations with the civil administration have also often been ambiguous. Since Independence, and especially after the 1967 Arusha Declaration that attempted to turn the country into a socialist state, the uncertain relationship between the Christian churches and the state, continues in different forms.[15]

Yet, involvement by the churches in the social life of the nation has been significant and is often openly sought by the state. Up to 1961, most of the literate individuals were products of mission schools, and the churches, as we have noted already, also provided most of the health care infrastructure. Christian churches established development projects of one kind or another in various places: carpentry, animal husbandry, farming of different crops, and so on. Girls and women especially benefitted from mission social work through education and mother-and-child care, advancing their status in society. Women missionaries who accompanied their male counterparts were instrumental in this evolution, as do their indigenous counterparts today. Thanks also to the churches, the Kiswahili language spread throughout the country.

Contemporary Developments

The most conspicuous developments in the Christian churches in Tanzania since Independence have taken place within the churches themselves, in terms of growth in numbers, theology, models of worship, and justice and peace activities. Even if in the past there were inevitably elements of African spirituality in Christian practice among African Christians, this was hidden because it was generally disapproved of as 'heathen'. Converts were required to abjure African religiosity altogether as a primary condition of membership of the churches. With the rise of an educated African clergy, however, this blanket censure came to be seen as unacceptable. The development of African theology with its double emphasis on 'enculturation' and 'liberation' has been instrumental in this transformation.

African theology has also inspired changes in the symbols and style of worship in the main mission churches, if not in the Pentecostal churches. Moreover, in most churches, there is increasing appreciation of lay ministries, awareness of care for the environment and a wider involvement in matters of justice and peace. If 'there is growing recognition that the African Church has an increasing global voice and that there

---

[13] Sahlberg, *From Krapf to Rugambwa*, 78-79. Also Klaus Fiedler, *Christianity and African Culture: Conservative German Protestant Missionaries in Tanzania, 1900-1940* (Leiden: E.J. Brill, 1996). For Lucas see www.dacb.org/stories/tanzania/lucas_williamv.hotml

[14] Frans Wijsen and Bernadin Mfumbusa, *Seeds of Conflict: Religious Tensions in Tanzania* (Nairobi: Paulines Publications, 2004).

[15] John C. Sivalon, *Kanisa Katoliki na Siasa ya Tanzania Bara 1953 hadi 1985* (Peramiho: Benedictine Publications Ndanda, 1992).

are distinctive cultural, religious and human values that Africa can offer to the world',[16] it is also due to the assiduous efforts being undertaken by the Christian churches in Tanzania.

Bibliography

Baur, John. *2000 Years of Christianity in Africa: An African Church History*. Nairobi: Paulines Publications Africa, second edn. 2009.

Fiedler, Klaus. *Christianity and African Culture: Conservative German Protestant Missionaries in Tanzania, 1900-1940*. Leiden: E.J. Brill, 1996.

Malishi, Lucas. *A History of the Catholic Church in Tanzania*. Dar es Salaam: Tanzania Episcopal Conference, 1990.

Ranger, T.O. *The African Churches of Tanzania*. Nairobi: East African Publishing House, 1972.

Sahlberg, Carl-Erick. *From Krapf to Rugambwa: A Church History of Tanzania*. Nairobi: Evangel Publishing House, 1986.

Sivalon, John C. *Kanisa Katoliki na Siasa ya Tanzania Bara 1953 hadi 1985*. Peramiho: Benedictine Publications Ndanda, 1992.

Wijsen, Frans and Bernadin Mfumbusa. *Seeds of Conflict: Religious Tensions in Tanzania*. Nairobi: Paulines Publications, 2004.

[16] Baur, *2000 Years of Christianity*, 428.

(92) Christianisme du Togo

Simon K. Dossou, Charles Klagba and Dake Trimua

Religion	Pop 2010	Pct 2010	Pop 2025	Pct 2025	Gr Pct 1970 2025
Christians	2,962,000	46.3%	4,402,000	47.1%	2.7%
Independents	204,000	3.2%	300,000	3.2%	2.6%
African initiated	119,000	1.9%			
Protestants	913,000	14.3%	1,172,000	12.5%	1.7%
Pentecostal	386,000	6.0%			
Reformed, Presbyterian	360,000	5.6%			
Baptist	85,600	1.3%			
Methodist	63,500	1.0%			
Roman Catholics	1,673,000	26.2%	2,550,000	27.3%	2.9%
Pentecostals/Charismatics	781,000	12.2%	1,000,000	10.7%	1.7%
Evangelicals	508,000	7.9%	688,000	7.4%	2.0%
adherents of traditional African religions	2,221,000	34.8%	3,194,000	34.2%	2.5%
Muslims	1,158,000	18.1%	1,700,000	18.2%	2.6%
Baha'is	31,800	0.5%	31,000	0.3%	-0.2%
adherents of new religious movements	3,200	0.1%	3,500	0.0%	0.5%
people professing no religion	15,500	0.2%	21,500	0.2%	2.2%
Total population	**6,391,000**	**100.0%**	**9,352,000**	**100.0%**	**2.6%**

Source: Centre for the Study of World Christianity (CSGC), Boston, Gordon-Conwell TS

Il est reconnu qu'à côté des églises traditionnellement reconnues comme historiques au Togo, il existe un grand nombre de dénominations chrétiennes qui opèrent sur toute l'étendue du territoire national.

Introduction – Les Eglises dites historiques

On parle d'églises historiques ou missionnaires lorsqu'on évoque les toutes premières missions chrétiennes arrivées dans le pays. La plupart y sont arrivées avant même la colonisation formelle du pays. Ainsi en est-il de l'Eglise Méthodiste arrivée en 1843, l'Eglise Ewe devenue successivement Eglise Evangélique du Togo puis Eglise Evangélique Presbytérienne du Togo en 1848, puis l'Eglise Catholique arrivée en 1860. L'Eglise des Assemblées de Dieu (ADD) pour sa part est arrivée seulement en 1936.

L'Eglise Méthodiste du Togo (Charles Klagba)

Dès la fin du XVIIe siècle, le mouvement anti-esclavagiste a permis au Gouvernement Anglais d'établir sur la Côte Ouest africaine une colonie-refuge pour esclaves libérés sur un point de l'Afrique qui avait été particulièrement dépeuplé. Bientôt quelques centaines d'anciens esclaves débarquèrent dans la nouvelle

Colonie. L'Acte d'Emancipation voté par les deux Chambres du Parlement Anglais le 1er Août 1834 libérait huit-cent rachetés, au frais du Gouvernement, montant: *Vingt millions de livres sterling versés aux propriétaires des esclaves libérés.*

Dès la fondation de la Colonie de Sierra-Léone, des Aumôniers (Pasteurs de l'Eglise Anglicane) avaient accompagné les anciens esclaves à Freetown. L'Eglise Méthodiste commença l'envoi de missionnaires à partir de 1811. Malheureusement plusieurs ont péri en peu de temps par défaut de précautions sanitaires indispensables à la santé des Européens, et ignorées à cette époque: 5 décès en 12 ans. Cependant, l'évangélisation se poursuivit sans arrêt.

En 1834, la Société des Missions Méthodistes avait décidé de commencer une œuvre missionnaire en Gold Coast qui n'était pas encore une colonie, mais un représentant du Gouvernement Anglais chargé de protéger les sociétés commerciales y résidait. Là encore hélas, les tristes expériences des premières années de travail missionnaire de la Sierra-Léone se renouvelèrent: 5 missionnaires avaient péri en *quatre ans*.

L'œuvre de Thomas Birch Freeman

C'est alors que s'était offert à la Société missionnaire, un jeune homme, fils d'une Anglaise et d'un noir, habitant l'Angleterre: Thomas Birch Freeman. Luttant déjà contre l'esclavage à *vingt 20* ans, il avait exactement *24 ans* quand avait été voté l'Acte d'Emancipation. Le cœur de Freeman n'a pas été moins ému en apprenant successivement la mort des missionnaires méthodistes de Sierra-Léone et ceux de Gold Coast. C'est pourquoi il avait senti l'appel de Dieu à aller travailler sur la terre d'Afrique, dont son père était originaire. Il lui semblait, qu'étant donnés ses origines, il pourrait supporter plus facilement que les autres le climat de la Côte occidentale. Les membres du Comité Missionnaire avaient pensé de même et l'avaient accepté comme candidat au Saint Ministère en 1835. Marié avec Elisabeth Boot le 5 novembre 1837, il avait pris départ sur un voilier pour l'Afrique avec sa femme. Arrivés à Cape Coast le 3 janvier 1838, Freeman devenait veuf le mois suivant. Néanmoins il avait entrepris et avait poursuivi sans relâche, pendant dix-neuf années, de prodigieuses activités dans les pays du Golfe du Bénin.

Mission au Nigéria, au Dahomey et au Togo

Sur invitation des anciens esclaves Egbas revenus chez eux au Nigeria, Freeman s'est rendu à Abéokuta en Septembre 1842, et avait installé le Pasteur Graft. Mais cette ville vivait sous la menace constante de l'armée du Dahomey. Aussi sur son chemin de retour, Freeman a décidé-il de se rendre à Abomey en vue d'obtenir la confiance du Roi Guezo pour la sécurité de son œuvre au Nigéria. Après deux mois d'attente à Ouidah, il avait été enfin reçu par le Roi, successivement à Cana et à Abomey du 13 au 20 Mars 1843. Ayant obtenu de Guezo l'autorisation d'évangéliser dans le royaume, il était retourné en Gold Coast.

Le début de l'ère chrétienne et du méthodisme au Togo

De Ouidah pour rejoindre la Gold Coast, l'infatigable Freeman, a marqué un arrêt à Aného en Mars 1843. Le Révérend Thomas Birch Freeman a rendu visite au Roi Georges Akouété Zankli Lawson 1[er.] Suite à leurs entrevues, le Roi lui a donné son plein accord d'ouvrir un lieu de culte dans son Palais royal à Aného, ancienne capitale du Togo. Le tout premier culte chrétien et méthodiste au Dieu Trinitaire, le Père, le Fils et le Saint-Esprit, a été célébré le 28 Mars 1843 au Palais royal. Cette date marque le début de l'ère chrétienne et du méthodisme au Togo. Pendant son séjour à Aného, il a rendu aussi visite au Roi des Adjigos, Quam Dessou et a organisé plusieurs campagnes d'évangélisation en plein air sur la place qui porte encore aujourd'hui son nom: Flanmani. Par la suite, la plupart des activités de Freeman s'étaient limitées en Gold Coast où, admis à la retraite en 1886, il est mort le 12 Août 1890 à Accra.

L'Eglise Méthodiste du Togo (EMT) est la plus ancienne des Eglises du Togo. Dès son implantation, l'Eglise Méthodiste au Togo elle était son appellation, était rattachée de 1843 à 1978 à de vastes régions ecclésiastiques dénommées Districts, rattachés tous à l'Eglise mère, l'Eglise Méthodiste en Grande Bretagne. Il y avait:

- le District Gold Coast-Nigeria-Dahomey-Togo,
- le District Dahomey-Togo-Côte d'Ivoire et le dernier était
- le District Dahomey-Togo.

En effet, de 1843 à 1878 l'Eglise Méthodiste au Togo faisait partie du District Gold-Coast-Nigéria-Dahomey-Togo, et avait pour Chef-lieu: Cape-Coast. Pendant ces temps, des missionnaires-adjoints venaient de Ouidah. Ils étaient chargés de superviser chaque quinzaine, l'implantation méthodiste à Aného.

Pendant cette période, Aného était déjà érigée en station principale et avait comme Chef-lieu de circuit méthodiste, Ouidah pour le Daho-Togo.

De 1878 à 1898 il y avait le District Nigéria-Dahomey-Togo, qui avait pour Chef-lieu: Nigéria. Au cours de cette période, le premier Temple méthodiste au Togo a été construit et inauguré en 1898.

De 1898 à 1925 l'Eglise naissante du Togo a fait partie du District Dahomey-Togo qui avait pour Chef-lieu: Porto-Novo.

De 1925 à 1957 elle a fait parie du District Dahomey-Togo-Côte d'Ivoire avec pour Chef-lieu: Porto-Novo. Enfin de 1957 au 10 septembre 1978, l'Eglise au Togo a fait partie du District Dahomey-Togo avec pour Chef-lieu: Cotonou.

Il faut noter qu'en 1957, a été créé le communauté méthodiste du Togo dont le Chef-lieu était Aného, puis transféré après à Lomé. Signalons qu'en 1965, le District Daho-Togo disposait de douze (12) pasteurs consacrés dont trois étaient originaires du Togo.

En 1972, le District Daho-Togo est devenu l'Eglise Protestante Méthodiste Daho-Togo.

Quelques années plus tard, la région synodale du Togo a été séparée de l'Eglise Protestante Méthodiste du Bénin le 10 Septembre 1978 pour devenir un District autonome sous la juridiction de la Conférence de la Grande-Bretagne avec l'investiture du nouveau Président et Surintendant Général du District en la personne du Rév. Pasteur Stéphan James Ahluivi Lawson, Ancien Secrétaire Général associé de la Conférence des Eglises de Toute l'Afrique (CETA). Au lendemain de cette proclamation solennelle, l'Eglise s'était organisée sur la base de la Constitution conçue depuis 1960 pour les Eglises d'Outre-mer de l'Afrique Occidentale.

Le 28 Mars 2000, l'Eglise Méthodiste du Togo (EMT) a changé son statut de District qu'elle était depuis sa séparation du Dahomey en 1978, pour devenir une Eglise autonome vis-à-vis de l'Eglise mère (Eglise Méthodiste de Grande Bretagne).

Elle est désormais érigée en Conférence qui est l'Organe suprême (*Assemblée Générale*) de l'Eglise. L'Eglise dispose aujourd'hui d'une Constitution et d'un Règlement Intérieur qui régulent le fonctionnement de tous les organes centraux et décentralisés, ainsi que les commissions et institutions spécialisées. Le Conseil de la Conférence est l'organe d'exécution et de décisions de l'Eglise entre deux Conférences biennales.

L'Eglise Méthodiste du Togo (EMT) dispose d'une Administration Centrale, de six (6) Districts (Lomé, Lacs, Yoto, Bas-Mono, Missionnaire-Atakpamé, Missionnaire-Tsévié) dirigés par des Surintendants Généraux. Les Pasteurs et les Evangélistes sont les principaux ouvriers de l'Eglise et sont assistés dans leur ministère par des prédicateurs laïcs et d'autres ouvriers laïcs.

L'Eglise dans la Cité

Le principe qui guide l'Eglise dans le domaine de sa présence dans la sphère publique est la **solidarité critique** vis-à-vis de tous les acteurs de la vie sociale économique et politique. L'objectif visé est de rendre la cité, le Togo vivable à tous les citoyens et citoyennes quels qu'ils soient et où qu'ils se trouvent.

Les Finances de l'Eglise

Les finances de l'Eglise sont organisées autour des trois champs d'engagement missionnaire: l'**edification**, le temoignage, le **service**. Les finances dans l'Eglise, avant d'être une affaire matérielle, sont d'abord une affaire spirituelle. La façon dont les ressources financières sont rassemblées, réparties et gérées dénote la maturité spirituelle d'une Eglise. Il s'agit d'être des co-gestionnaires fidèles et honnêtes des ressources que Dieu a données à travers ses fidèles.

L'Eglise Méthodiste du Togo est une Eglise en pleine expansion et compte environ quatre vingt dix mille (90 000) membres.

L'Eglise Evangélique Presbytérienne du Togo (Dake TRIMUA)

Le Topos

Nous n'avons pas la prétention de faire l'Histoire de l'Institution EEPT, et nous ne le pouvons pas vue l'étendue du champ et le temps qui nous est consacré pour ce sujet. Permettez-nous donc de vous donner simplement les Arcanus (arcanes), c'est-à-dire les repères chronologiques de la Naissance, l'Evolution, l'Affirmation et les perspectives de notre commune Institution Ecclésiastique: l'EEPT.

Denominations

La Dénomination EEPT a connu plusieurs mutations, métamorphoses, si vous préférez, dues à l'Article 2 des Statuts de la Mission-mère d'Allemagne. Cet article stipule: nous citons: « La Société comprend des Fidèles de Confession Luthérienne et réformée. Pour la propagation du Royaume de Dieu parmi les païens, elle se conforme aux préceptes du Seigneur Jésus-Christ, Mat. 20, 18-20. Elle le fait avec la conviction que la différence de confession, qui chez nous a des racines historiques ne doit pas être transplantée dans le monde païen, mais que grâce à l'annonciation de l'Evangile sous l'égide du Seigneur et de son Esprit, les Eglises se constituent chez les païens avec leur dénomination de manière spécifique » (Fin de citation).

En terme clair, la Liberté est laissée aux Eglises qui naissent en champs de misions, de choisir leur dénomination (appellation). Les premières communautés naissantes, étant embarrassées, s'appelaient 'Bremen -Tɔwo, ou Bremen Mission'. Or, il se trouve que ces communautés sont situées dans une ère géographique et linguistique définie: Les Ewe.

- L'appellation passe dès lors de Bremen Mission à Ewe-Mission; à Ewe Kristo Tɔwo (Les chrétiens Ewe);
- Ewe Kristo Hame (Eglise Ewe), appellation qui durera longtemps jusqu'en 1957. Là on constate que la Chrétienté a dépassé la sphère Ewe et englobe les autres ethnies du Togo, ce qui a impliqué de passer à la dénomination:
- Eglise Evangélique du Togo (EET) Togo Nyanyui Hame.

A partir des années 1960 (indépendances), l'univers religieux togolais était bombardé par l'émergence de nouvelles sensibilités religieuses, difficiles à gérer; ce qui avait conduit le Président feu Eyadema à délimiter les tendances religieuses au Togo au nombre de Catholique, Protestant Evangélique, méthodiste, Assemblée de Dieu; Baptiste, Pentecôtiste; le reste devant se fondre dans les six Eglises reconnues. Avec la Démocratie instaurée (1990) et la libéralisation de l'expression religieuses, le Togo se trouve littéralement envahi par des sensibilités religieuses incontrôlables, avec un pluralisation des 'dénominations' divers. Au Synode de Vogan en 1992, l'EEPT fut obligée pour éviter toute confusion de noms, de reprendre l'épithète 'Presbytérien' qu'il avait laissé, pour redevenir 'Eglise Evangélique Presbytérienne du Togo – EEPT'.

Panorama Historique

Périodicités (Grandes Périodes)

Quatre grandes périodes historiques (Périodicités) marquent l'EEPT:
1847 – 1914: MISSION de BREME (Période pré-coloniale et coloniale).
1914 – 1929: Eglise Ewe Autonome (Régime Français).
1929 – 1959: MISSION de PARIS (collaboration).
1959 : à nos jours: Indépendance, Affirmation responsable de l'EEPT.

Dates – Clefs (EEPT) et Evénements

1822 Fondation de la Société des Missions Evangéliques de Paris (SMEP)
1835 Idée de création d'une Société Missionnaire Allemande.
1836 Fondation de la 'Norddeutsche Gessellschaft' par les 'Amis de la Mission (Société de Mission de l'Allemagne)' à Hambourg.
1847 Semence de l'Evangile à PEKI: Blengo en Côte de L'or, par Lorenz Wolf de la Mission de Brême, après des tentatives missionnaires sans succès en Nouvelle Zélande et en Inde Orientale; l'objectif était d'atteindre le Gabon.
1848 Début de l'œuvre scolaire en Allemand à Péki.
1851 Transfert du siège de la Mission de Brême (M B) de Hambourg à Brême au Nord de l'Allemagne d'où la société portera le nom de 'Mission de Brême = Bremen Mission'
1859 Arrivée du linguiste Bernard Schlegel qui fixe la langue Ewe et sa grammaire, pour la traduction de la Bible en Ewe et l'œuvre scolaire (documents en Ewe).
Il est considéré comme le Père de la langue Ewe qui fait entrer cette langue dans l'ère Guttemberg.
1876 Ebauche d'une constitution Ecclésiastique Ewe par Dr ZAHN, alors Inspecteur de la Mission de Brême.
1884 Signature du Protectorat sur le Togo par Nachtigal G et Mlakpa I.
1885 Conférence de Berlin (Allemagne Ouest) et balkanisation de l'Afrique en territoires coloniaux entre les puissances européennes.
1893 Création de la première paroisse en terre togolaise, après la Conférence de Berlin; ce fut à Tove, devenu Mission Tove, Berceau de l'EEPT; grâce à l'Evangéliste Albert Kwami Koko BINDER, le 14 avril, venant de Kéta.
1895 Création de la paroisse de Lomé-Afegame par Andreas AKU.
1895 Paroisse d'Agu
1900 Début du 20e siècle mouvementé avec les deux Guerres Mondiales et la Crise économique. C'est aussi le siècle des découvertes et des inventions. L'appétit colonial était accentué avec des travaux forcés, des pressions et répressions; période de traumatisme, de névrose et d'exploitations iverses du Continent Africain.
1907 le 20 septembre, Ordonnance du Gouverneur Allemand J. Gref ZECK 'interdisant Tout accès au Nord à toute personne y compris, les Togolais, depuis Sokodé jusqu'à Mangu'. Raison: insécurité totale dans la région. L'action d'évangélisation était alors bloquée.
1912 Istallation à Kamina (15 km environ d'Atakpame), d'un Téléphone Sans Fil (TSF) reliant directement le Togo à Berlin; afin de contrôler les mouvements des troupes de guerres d'Europe.
1914-1918: Déclenchement des hostilités de la Première Guerre Mondiale, départ massif des missionnaires pour défendre les drapeaux de leurs Nations. La jeune Eglise Ewe du Togo se trouvait brutalement sevrée, sans missionnaire, sans formation pour la relève, sans finances: seul le couple Bürgi, de nationalité Suisse, était toléré à rester au Togo. Très fatigué, Bürgi et son

épouse rentraient définitivement en Suisse en 1921.
Pratiquement, l'Eglise Eve du Togo avait commencé son autonomie forcée avec le départ des missionnaires en 1914. De 1914 à 1918, sept (7) catéchistes furent consacrés Pasteurs pour combler le vide et soutenir

1922 (18-22 mai) Premier Synode Général de l'Eglise Ewe (Kpalimé)

Décisions importants:

1. Adoption de la Constitution Ecclésiastique, Ebauche de l'Inspecteur de la Mission de Brême; ZAHN (1875).
2. Election du Modérateur; Confirmation de A. AKU à ce poste. (Il assurait l'intérim).
3. Election du Secrétaire Synodal: Robert BAETA.
4. Réaffirmation de l'Unité de l'Eglise Ewe entre le Togo et le Ghana par delà les frontières coloniales.
5. Lettre d'Appel à la S. M. E. P.:
   - Aider à récupérer les biens séquestrés de l'Eglise par le Gouvernement Colonial Français; l'Eglise ayant des représentants légaux auprès du Gouvernement.
   - Organisation du Système Scolaire sur le modèle de la France.

1927-1928 Voyage d'enquête au Togo du missionnaire Ch. MAITRE venant du Cameroun pour voir la possibilité d'envoi des missionnaires Français au Togo; rapport à la S.M.E.P.

1929 Arrivée du missionnaire Ch. CARRIERE: réorganisation des Ecoles

1930 Arrivée du missionnaire Pasteur Gustave CUENOD pour reprendre l'Eglise Ewe comme champ de mission par la S.M.E.P. placé à l'Ecole Biblique de Gobe, 2 demoiselles; Doyimont (internat des filles à Agu; Giugler, dispensaire d'Agu); toutes venaient du Sénégal.

1931 Révision et adoption de la Constitution Ecclésiastique;

1931 Décès du Modérateur A. AKU; remplacé par Pasteur MALLET.

1932 Nouvelle révision et adoption de la Constitution et Discipline de l'Eglise au Synode de Kpalimé. Début de Conflit d'autorité entre l'Eglise/Institution; Eglise et Mission de Paris; qui gouverne et dirige qui ? Le problème est d'ordre politique et religieux:
- Une Eglise autonome structurée avec sa Constitution, sa discipline, sa Bible, sa Liturgie, ses Cantiques, ses dirigeants.
- Une Société Missionnaire (S.M.E.P.) qui veut mettre en cause l'autonomie de cette Eglise en la considérant comme Champ de Mission.
- La France avait peur de l'autonomie de l'Eglise; dans un territoire dirigé comme une colonie, alors que le Togo est placé simplement sous tutelle; n'a jamais été colonisé; le Cameroun de même, les deux territoires classés dans la Catégorie B.

1932 Premier voyage d'exploration du missionnaire G. CUENOD dans le Nord-Togo; revient avec quelques jeunes kabyè placés en Formation comme catéchiste à Gobe.

1937 Début d'évangélisation du Nord-Togo par les catéchistes formés: Ch. LOMDO à Pya; AJOM J. à Landa, PATCHSSI et NUPABI à Kara. Salomon KUTA de Kassi-Landa ayant commencé l'Evangélisation itinérante dans la région. Les autres comme: Kpalyom T. ABITCHAO, Samuel BATANATA rejoindront les premiers pionniers pour enraciner l'Evangile dans le Nord.

1939-1945: Deuxième Guerre Mondiale. Jacques DELORD, arrivé au Togo pour la Mission en 1940 est bloqué par la guerre au Séminaire transféré définitivement à Atakpamé en 1938.

1945 J. DELORD arrive à Kara pour la mission.

1946 Installation de J. DELORD avec sa famille à Kudé pour l'affermissement de l'œuvre missionnaire; début de soins médicaux par Françoise DELORD, Centre Médical de Farendè.

1956 Accueil du missionnaire Charles HEIN des Etats-Unis de l'Eglise Réformée pour l'évangélisation dans l'Akébou, avec résidence à Atakpamé, quartier Doulassa.

1957 Eglise Evangélique Ewe (Ewe Kristo Hame) devient Eglise Evangélique du Togo-EET.

1958 Autonomie politique du Togo
1959 Indépendance de l'EEPT
1960 (27 avril) Indépendance politique du Togo
1961 Début d'Evangélisation de la Région de l'Est-Mono à partir de Notsè (base à Naolo) par la Mission de Brême sous la direction de Eric VIERING.
1963 Coup d'Etat Sanglant au Togo
1963 Déclaration de la 'Position de l'Eglise vis-à-vis de la politique' (Synode d'Amlamé).
1963 Création de la Commission de Réflexions Théologique (CRTH)
1964 Année d'Evangélisation: les douze (12) thèses du Renouveau: 'Tout l'Evangile à Tout L'Homme'.
1967 Lancement de l'Evangélisation dans le Ouatchi par L'EET et l'Eglise Méthodiste du Togo (EMT).
1967 Création du Centre Agricole Expérimentale avec élevage à Dayes Afeyeyeme.
1969 Inauguration de l'Hôpital Bethesda d'Agu-Nyogbo.
1970 Déclaration de Foi de l'EET (Synode de Sodo).
1972 Prise en charge des salaires de l'enseignement confessionnel catholique et Protestant (Subvention de l'Etat).
1974 Changement de prénoms importés au Togo (décision personnel de Eyadema); suppression de Etienne.
1975 Position de l'EET sur 'le Statut des Chrétiens Polygames' dans l'Eglise; sont chrétiens à part entière.
1976 Le Centre de Formation des Jardinières d'Enfants (CFJE) de Kpalimé, propriété de l'EET est cédé à l'Etat Togolais.
1978 Suppression des 'Sectes' au Togo par décret de l'Etat: six (6) confessions religieuses chrétiennes reconnues officiellement: Eglise Evangélique du Togo (EET), Eglise Méthodiste du Togo (EMT), Eglise Catholique Romaine (ECR), Eglise Baptiste du Togo (EBT), Eglise Protestante des Assemblées de Dieu (EPAD), Eglise Pentecôtiste du Togo (EPT). Les autres sensibilités religieuses chrétiennes doivent se fondre dans les six reconnues.
1980 Création du Partenariat Togo-Allemagne-Ghana (TAG)
1984 Réorganisation de l'EET en six (6) Régions Ecclésiastiques, avec un Inspecteur pour chaque région et un Inspecteur Général qui coordonne toutes les Régions Ecclésiastiques. J. HUNLEDE fut le premier Inspecteur Général, succédé à son décès par D. E. TRIMUA.
1986 Première Consultation de TAG à Béthania
1990 Début de la Démocratisation au Togo.
1991 20 juin, début de la Conférence Nationale Souveraine. Election du Premier Ministre (Maître KOFFIGOH).
1992 Eglise Evangélique du Togo (EET) devient Eglise Evangélique Presbytérienne du Togo (EEPT) au Synode de Vogan.
1993 Centenaire de l'EEPT à Mission Tove: adoption du Logo avec la date de 1893 Naissance de l'Eglise à Mission Tove.
1995 Evaluation de l'Institution EEPT dans tous ses rouages avec recommandations pour une redynamisation de l'Eglise.
1998 Mise en place de la 'Commission de Pilotage de Redynamisation de l'EEPT (COPIREEPT): Quatre (4) Axes de le Redynamisation:
1- Constitution; 2- Administration; 3- Pastorale Sociale; 4- Ressources Humaines et Financières.
2000-2004: L'EEPT traverse une crise endogène et exogène sur tous les plans: Constitutionnel, Administratif, Pastoral, Humaine et Financière.

- Inharmonie au niveau de la Direction Générale.

- Méfiance au sein du Corps Pastoral.
- Faible collaboration entre les Catéchistes.
- Collaboration apparente entre les Presbytres.
- Conflit d'autorité à l'intérieur de chaque corps.
- Irrespect et insoumission caractérisent certains responsables d'Eglise à l'égard de leur chef hiérarchique.
- Faible contrôle des Finances, qui favorise l'évaporation des fonds financiers dans la nature; ce qui met l'institution dans une paupérisation anthropologique et à la dépendance avancée et humiliante de l'Extérieur.

L'historien constate que l'EEPT a atteint sa vitesse de croisière sous la Modérature du Rév. Pasteur AYIVI, aux plans:

- Structurel (infrastructures)
- Théologique
- Spirituel
- Ethique
- Fonctionnel
- Moral.

Après feu Modérateur AYIVI, l'Institution Eglise a amorcé sa baisse de régime vers un déclin sans freins ni amortisseurs jusqu'à ce jour.

Conclusion

L'EEPT, en tant qu'institution, est née et demeure 'démocratique' et a: dans sa Constitution et dans son Fonctionnement: Paroisse-District, Région, Bureau Exécutif, Comité Synodal, Synode National de la basse sphère à la haute sphère et vis-versa. Les Mandatures sont définies (2 au plus) et les votes aux bulletins secrets; après pré-sélection par le corps pastoral. Trois (3) candidats ayant plus de voix sont présentés au Synode pour Election, qui prévoit, en cas de non majorité absolue d'un candidat au premier tour, d'autres tours à la majorité simple. Le Modérateur élu ne sera installé qu'après avoir collaboré avec le sortant pendant trois (3) mois au plus.

Le nouveau Modérateur sera alors officiellement intronisé et prend les commandes pour un mandat renouvelable une fois (soit 2 mandats). Les Inspecteurs sont proposés par le Bureau Exécutif et nommés par le Comité Synodal qui les présente au Synode.

Enfin, la force et le secret de l'EEPT se trouvent dans sa vision d'une Eglise nationale, une et indivisible, son élan prophétique, la consolidation de son arsenal pastoral, ce qui doit la pousser à bannir toute tendance raciste et régionaliste pour la pérennisation de son harmonie et la viabilité de son action pastorale sociale.

L'Eglise Catholique du Togo (Simon Dossou)

En 1860, la Congrégation Romaine de la Propagation de la Foi a créé le vicariat apostolique du Dahomey (aujourd'hui Bénin) attribuée à la Société des Missions Africaines de Lyon (SMA). Le père Borghero, responsable de la nouvelle mission s'établit à Ouidah en 1861 et se mit à explorer Grand-Popo (Bénin) et Aneho (Togo). C'est le début très lointain de l'Eglise catholique au Togo. C'est seulement le 12 Avril 1892 que le Vatican érigea le Togo en préfecture apostolique, qu'il confia à la Société du Verbe Divin de Steyl, qui est une société allemande[1] dont le siège est cependant au Pays-Bas.

[1] Ces informations peuvent être consultées dans N.L.GAYIBOR (dir) in Histoire des Togolais. Elles sont systématisées

Dans son développement, l'église catholique au Togo est devenue vicariat apostolique le 16 Mars 1914, divisé et confié à la Société des Missions Africaines de Lyon le 15 Mars 1923. Le 18 Mai 1937, la préfecture de Sokodé (Nord Togo) a été érigée puis est devenue Préfecture de Lomé le 14 Juin 1938 puis celui d'Archidiocèse le 14 Septembre 1955. Dans son évolution, l'église catholique a créé d'autres diocèses que sont: Atakpamé le 29 Septembre 1964 puis ceux d'Aneho et de Kpalimé en 1994.

Le clergé catholique au départ était composé en majorité d'européens C'est progressivement que des nationaux y sont entrés. Si les togolais y sont majoritaires de nos jours, il y a un bon nombre de prêtres missionnaires. En effet, le diocèse de Lomé en 2015 compte 177 prêtres diocésains et 66 prêtres missionnaires soit plus du tiers du total. La Conférence des évêques du Togo est composée de Sept évêques en pleine activité et de 2 évêques émérites. L'église est administrée par ces évêques et prêtres épaulés par 341 religieuses, 76 religieux non prêtres et 2060 catéchistes.

L'Eglise a plusieurs institutions et œuvres qui constituent ses œuvres de témoignage dont les plus importantes sont: Grand Séminaire Interdiocésain Saint Jean- Paul II, Grand Séminaire de Philosophie Benoit XVI, Séminaire Propédeutique Saint Paul, Université Catholique de l'Afrique de l'Ouest, Direction Nationale de l'Enseignement Catholique et Direction des Œuvres Pontificales Missionnaires, Commission Nationale « Justice et Paix », Radio Maria-Togo, Télévision Catholique (TVC), les Aumôneries, etc.

L'Eglise Catholique s'est beaucoup investie dans les questions politiques du Togo, particulièrement depuis les années 1990. Elle a sorti plusieurs lettres épiscopales pour prendre position officiellement contre la politique gouvernementale. Il lui est tout de même arrivé de s'investir dans la recherche de la paix dans le pays en offrant évêques, prêtres et laïques engagés pour présider ou accompagner des institutions de contre-pouvoir et de management de la vie sociale. Plusieurs observateurs n'ont pas hésité à dire que l'Eglise catholique a toujours eu un comportement de concurrence feutrée avec les autres anciennes églises que sont l'EEPT et l'EMT. Ces dernières s'en plaignent parfois dans des cercles non officiels.

Les Eglises venues après la Colonisation

Outre les églises dites historiques, Plusieurs autres communautés chrétiennes opèrent au Togo depuis de longues dates. Ces dernières années le nombre s'est considérablement accru. Nous en donnons ici quelques informations.

L'Eglise des Assemblées de Dieu du Togo (ADD)

En 1936, le champ des églises opérant au Togo s'est élargi avec l'arrivée de l'Eglise des Assemblée de Dieu qui est une mission issue du Pentecôtisme fondé aux Etats-Unis d'Amérique (USA) en 1906 par l'évangéliste William Seymour.

C'est à partir du Burkina Faso (ex- Haute Volta) que quelques missionnaires des ADD sont entrés au Togo en 1921 pour leur première exploration. Mais c'est surtout en 1936 que les premiers missionnaires américains se sont installés à Dapaong au Nord Togo. Leur travail a été appuyé par des missionnaires originaires de la Haute-Volta. L'évangélisation du Nord Togo a connu un grand succès du fait qu'aucune œuvre d'évangélisation n'était faite là où ils ont commencé leur activité. La première station missionnaire fut installée en 1940 par le Rev et Mme Paul Weidman venus de Tenkodogo (Haute Volta), qui sont repartis un an plus tard après la démolition de leur case par les intempéries. C'est seulement en 1947 qu'un autre couple de missionnaire du nom de Brown est revenu continuer le travail entamé par le premier mais maintenu en vie par les autochtones du Nord Togo devenus chrétiens. Les premiers jeunes à aller se faire former comme pasteurs arrivèrent à l'Institut Biblique de Koubri en Haute Volta à pied après presque 300 Km de marche dans les années 40. A partir des années 50, des autochtones formés sont associés à l'œuvre

---

dans le fascicule, Archidiocèse de Lomé (TOGO) Annuaire 2015, p.5

d'évangélisation qui a connu un essor presque partout au Nord Togo dont Dapaong, Bassar, Mango, Sokodé etc.

C'est le 1er Juin 1960 que l'Eglise des ADD fut implantée à Lomé, puis à Kpalimé (Togo) en 1962. Après les indépendances du Togo et du Dahomey (Bénin), les églises des ADD du Togo et du Bénin sont devenues autonomes à partir de 1965 en raison des contraintes que créait la traversée des frontières pour aller d'un pays à l'autre en vue des assemblées trimestrielles, annuelles et autres manifestations communes. Depuis son autonomie, cette église a eu deux présidents autochtones dont le premier élu en 1965 était Rev Pasgo Bila Daniel l'un de ceux qui étaient allés se faire former en Haute-Volta au tout début. Le deuxième président en poste en ce moment (2015) est le Rev Djakouti Mitré, élu en 1987 à la retraite du premier[2]. L'Eglise des ADD a développé des œuvres de témoignage dans tout le pays avec une Caisse de micro-crédit très bien appréciée de beaucoup de gens.

Autres Eglises dans le paysage chrétien du Togo

Plusieurs églises de tendance pentecôtiste se sont installées au Togo à la faveur de ce que disait un ministre du gouvernement: « le Togo ne dispose d'aucune réglementation spécifique pour encadrer l'exercice du culte sur son territoire. Laissant donc un espace très libéral au nom du principe selon lequel: lorsqu'il n'y a pas de restrictions, la liberté reste absolue, dans lequel s'engouffrent aussi bien vrais pasteurs qu'aventuriers de tout acabit »[3].

En l'espace de quelques décennies, le Togo a sur son territoire, des églises qui ont pour noms entre autres: le Christianisme Céleste, mondialement connu et qui est né au Dahomey (Bénin) vers la fin des années 40s précisément le 29 Septembre 1947, les Témoins de Jehovah, plusieurs églises de tendance pentecôtiste dont Praise Chapel, Winner Chapel, Topa Church et bien d'autres d'origine anglophone (ghanéenne, nigériane, libérienne, américaine) qui vont proliférer et draineront un grand nombre de fidèles et de curieux en quête de sensation spirituelle ou d'œuvres miraculeuses. De fait, ces églises taxées ironiquement d'annoncer « l'évangile de prospérité », se multiplient et s'installent partout sans demander aucune autorisation d'exercice de culte ou commencent leur œuvre d'évangélisation en attendant qu'ils obtiennent une éventuelle autorisation. On compte plus de 4000 micro- dénominations sur toute l'étendue du territoire. Les églises historiques voient ce développement se produire sous leurs yeux sans pouvoir les canaliser sur le plan théologique car la plupart de leurs membres viennent des anciennes églises, catholiques et protestantes.

En conclusion, le Togo se révèle comme un pays où les chrétiens forment un grand nombre des croyants du pays, sans oublier que l'islam aussi progresse aux côtés des religions traditionnelles africaines qui ont toute pour nom le vaudou.

Bibliographie

Marguerite J. et Matthieu D. FASSINOU, Histoire de l'Eglise Protestante Méthodiste du Bénin, Joseph A. DJIVO, 1993

Nicoué Lodjou GAYIBOR, Histoire des Togolais, Vol. 2, Tome 2, PUL, Lomé

M. DIDEH, l'Eglise Protestante Méthodiste du Bénin: Togo des origines jusqu'à nos jours, Mémoire de Maîtrise en Théologie, Yaoundé, Faculté de Théologie Protestante, 1984

---

[2] La plupart de ces informations se recoupent avec celles qui se retrouvent ailleurs dont sur le net cf http://eadtogo.org/index.php?option=com_content&view=article&id=229&Itemid=29

[3] Ces mots viennent de Mr Gilbert BAWARA, alors Ministre de l'Administration territoriale cf http://news.icilome.com/?idnews=803019 en date du 13/8/2015

Salomon Kuassi LOKO, l'Implantation et Evolution de l'Eglise au Togo, Mémoire pour l'obtention du Diplôme d'Etudes de Théologie, Porto-Novo, 1998
Robert CORNEVIN, La Mission Méthodiste in Histoire du Togo
Robert CORNEVIN, Le Togo des origines à nos jours, Paris, 1988, Académie des Sciences d'Outre-mer
John PRITCHARD, Methodists and their Missionary Societies, Ashgate Methodist Studies, 2014
Il est l'actuel Président de l'Eglise Méthodiste du Togo.

(93) Christianity in Tunisie

Harald Suermann

Religion	Pop 2010	Pct 2010	Pop 2025	Pct 2025	Gr Pct 1970 2025
Christians	23,800	0.2%	20,900	0.2%	-0.8%
Independents	2,100	0.0%	2,100	0.0%	-0.1%
African initiated	2,000	0.0%			
Orthodox	240	0.0%	200	0.0%	-1.2%
Protestants	850	0.0%	1,100	0.0%	1.6%
Roman Catholics	20,000	0.2%	17,000	0.1%	-1.1%
Pentecostals/Charismatics	2,200	0.0%	2,000	0.0%	-0.7%
Evangelicals	610	0.0%	750	0.0%	1.4%
Muslims	10,583,000	99.5%	12,261,000	99.5%	1.0%
Baha'is	2,100	0.0%	2,600	0.0%	1.4%
Jews	1,900	0.0%	2,000	0.0%	0.4%
Chinese folk-religionists	170	0.0%	200	0.0%	1.1%
Buddhists	80	0.0%	100	0.0%	1.5%
people professing no religion	28,600	0.3%	33,000	0.3%	1.0%
Total population	**10,639,000**	**100.0%**	**12,320,000**	**100.0%**	**1.0%**

Source: Centre for the Study of World Christianity (CSGC), Boston, Gordon-Conwell TS

La Tunisie a aujourd'hui 11 millions d'habitants. Selon la constitution, l'Islam est religion d'État, mais le gouvernement permet la pratique d'autres religions. Le chef d'État doit être un musulman. Les activités missionnaires comme la distribution de matériel religieux sont interdites. 22.000 des 30.000 chrétiens sont des étrangers. Le statut de l'Église catholique est réglé clairement depuis 1964, quand le gouvernement tunisien et le saint Siège ont conclu une convention. La convention stipule que l'Église catholique peut posséder sept églises mais qu'elle peut demander la permission pour d'autres chapelles dans des lieux où c'est nécessaire. L'Église catholique est libre d'action dans les établissements de formation, les actions sociales, etc. Aujourd'hui on compte à Tunis et sa banlieue quatre églises catholiques, deux églises protestantes (accueillant des évangéliques), une église orthodoxe grecque et une église orthodoxe russe. Il y a aussi des églises catholiques à Hammamet, Sousse, Gabès et Sfax.

L'antiquité

Le christianisme se répandit très vite. À Carthage vit l'apologiste Tertullien. Le concile de Carthage (418) condamna le pélagianisme. En 439 les Vandales et les Alains fondèrent un royaume. Ce royaume dura jusqu'en 533. Il propagea l'arianisme. Après la conquête islamique le pays fut rapidement arabisé et le christianisme disparut.

Le temps colonial

En 1843 déjà, le vicariat apostolique fut établi en Tunisie avant la soumission de la Tunisie (1881-1883). Après l'établissement du protectorat le Vicariat devint en 1884 Archevêché de Carthage. Le premier évêque fut Charles-Martial-Allemand Lavigerie. Au 19e siècle les fidèles de l'Église catholique furent des étrangers. Les Frères des Écoles Chrétiens, les Pères Blancs et les Sœurs de St. Joseph de l'Apparition fondèrent des œuvres éducatives et caritatives.[1]

En 1881 commença l'histoire de l'Église réformée en Tunisie avec l'arrivée de Jocelyn Bureau, mais qui ne fut pas encore ordonné. En 1889 le temple actuel de Tunis fut dédicacé; d'autre suivirent à Gabès et à Sousse.[2]

En 1927 l'Institut des Belles Lettres Arabes (I.B.L.A.) fut fondé. C'est un centre important jusqu'à aujourd'hui de la langue arabe et des études islamologues. Il est spécialisé dans la culture tunisienne. Depuis 1937 il publie la Revue de l'I.B.L.A. En 1949 l'Institut Pontifical d'Études Arabes (IPEA) fut fondé. L'I.B.L.A. se concentra sur la culture tunisienne et la littérature arabe moderne, tandis que L'IPEA devint le centre de formation pour le personnel de l'église au niveau universitaire. Le but était de former un clergé ouvert au monde islamique. L'IPEA fut transféré à Rome en 1964.[3] Beaucoup de personnalités sont sorties de cet institut qui ont pris des initiatives importantes de dialogue avec l'islam à Rome ou dans la francophonie lors du Concile de Vatican II et après: le P. Joseph Cuoq qui constitua au niveau du saint-siège une structure de dialogue et dirigea le sous-secrétariat pour les relations avec l'islam après le concile et le P. Robert Casper, qui a fondé le Groupe de Recherche Islamo-Chrétien (G.R.I.C.) à Tunis en 1977. Dès le début, le groupe rechercha un dialogue académique approfondi, dans lequel on se prononça sur les convergences comme aussi sur les divergences. Musulmans et chrétiens étaient en nombre égal. Dans les années 80 le G.R.I.C. était en crise et sa dissolution fut envisagé en 1991.[4]

En 1930 le congrès eucharistique eut lieu à Carthage. Le fait que la France soit représentée officiellement fut contesté par les nationalistes tunisiens ainsi que par quelques représentants de l'Église catholique. Le futur président Habib Bourghiba voyait le congrès comme une nouvelle croisade.[5] Ce congrès fut le sommet symbolique de la colonisation avec la coopération avec l'Église catholique. Mais il y eut aussi des prêtres et des évêques qui conduisirent l'Église avec une main heureuse dans le temps de l'indépendance de la Tunisie.

En 1953 Mgr Maurice Perrin arriva à la tête du diocèse. Pendant la crise franco-tunisienne (1950-1954) il se montra modéré. Il essaya de comprendre les Tunisiens et leurs aspirations à l'indépendance. Il savait que l'avenir de l'Église se déciderait dans les années précédant l'indépendance. Mgr Michel Hervé-Bazin,

---

[1] F Grazzini, « L'Église en Tunisie », in *Histoire des chrétiens d'Afrique du Nord : Libye, Tunisie, Algérie, Maroc*, éd. par Henri Teissier (Paris: Desclée, 1991), 139.

[2] « Notre histoire », *Eglise Réformée de Tunisie*, 2 février 2013, www.ertunis.com/un-peu-dhistoire/.

[3] Grazzini, « L'Église en Tunisie », 141; Marie-Josée Dor et Jean Fisset, « Pères Blancs et Soeurs Blanches, Tunisie et Algérie : Fondation, développement, travaux apostoliques », in *Histoire des chrétiens d'Afrique du Nord : Libye-Tunisie-Algérie-Maroc*, éd. par Henri Teissier et Antoine. Chatelard (Paris: Desclée, 1991), 181-183; Jacques Levrat, *Une expérience de dialogue: les centres d'étude chrétiens en monde musulman*, Studien ; 9 (Altenberge: Christl.-Islam. Schrifttum, 1987), 486-63; Gérard Demeerseman, *André Demeerseman, 1901-1993: à Tunis, soixante ans à l'Institut des Belles Lettres Arabes, IBLA*, Histoire des mondes chrétiens (Paris: Karthala, 2014).

[4] Gabus, « L'expérience du dialogue islamo-chrétien dans le cadre du GRIC », *Islamochristiana* 19 (1993): 117-24; Serain, « Le Groupe de recherches islamo-chrétien (G.R.I.C.) », *Chemins de Dialogue* 15 (s. d.): 207-9; Mokdad Arfa Mensia, « Une expérience privilégiée de dialogue : le GRIC », in *Muslim-Christian perceptions of dialogue today : experiences and expectations*, éd. par Jacques Waardenburg (Leuven; Paris: Peeters, 2000), 183-200.

[5] Grazzini, « L'Église en Tunisie », 141; Pierre Soumille, « L'Église catholique et l'État tunisien après l'indépendance: le « modus vivendi » du 9 juillet 1964 », in *Les relations Eglises-Etat en situation postcoloniale : Amérique, Afrique, Asie, Océanie, XIXe-XXe siècles : actes de la 20e session du CREDIC (Chevilly-Larue, 27-30 août 2002)*, éd. par Philippe Delisle, Collection Mémoires d'Eglises (Paris: Editions Karthala, 2003), 189.

un de ses trois vicaires généraux, publia l'hebdomadaire diocésain La Tunisie Catholique. Cet hebdomadaire traita aussi des questions de l'Islam et des musulmans et tenta ainsi d'ouvrir les yeux des fidèles pour la majorité de la société. Mgr. Hervé-Bazin fut responsable des œuvres ecclésiales et des écoles catholiques. André Demeerseman, Père Blanc, élève du Père Henri Marchal et membre de la direction de l'I.B.L.A. favorisa les activités missionnaires sans œuvre ni conversion.[6] En tant que vicaire général il ne se prononça pas ouvertement pour l'indépendance de la Tunisie, mais s'engagea pour les intérêts des tunisiens. Il plaida toujours pour un équilibre des intérêts. Il fut responsable pour les religieux. André Collini fut le troisième vicaire général responsable des prêtres et les fidèles.[7]

Bien que la hiérarchie catholique fût consciente de la période transitoire difficile, on continua les activités religieuses comme si de rien n'était. Là où il avait des Européens on continua même les constructions.[8] De son côté l'archevêque montra sa bonne volonté et fit enlever la statue du cardinal Lavigerie devant l'entrée de la ville.[9] Il arrêta les constructions des chapelles dans de lieux où il n'y avait plus d'Européens. L'Hebdomadaire reçut le nouveau nom de « l'Écho du diocèse de Carthage ».

La grande mutation commença avec le départ forcé des Franciscaines missionnaires de Marie en 1956 qui travaillaient dans l'« Hôpital de la libération », et avec le départ volontaire des Assomptionnistes, qui vendirent leur Collège Maurice Caillous de la Marsa à la Mission Culturelle Française.[10]

À la veille de l'indépendance la Tunisie comptait 3,4 millions d'habitants, dont 255.000 non-musulmans. 60.000 étaient juifs, la grande majorité du reste catholiques, dont 100.000 vivaient à Tunis. Ils étaient presque tous des étrangers. Il existait 78 paroisses avec 100 églises et chapelles, servies par 228 prêtres, donc 153 diocésains.[11]

L'Église dans la Tunisie indépendante

L'indépendance de la Tunisie en 1956, la guerre de Bizerte en 1961, la nationalisation des propriété foncières des colons et l'introduction de l'économie planifiée réduisirent le nombre des chrétiens en Tunisie. En 1959 certaines activités ecclésiales furent défendues et des bâtiments furent expropriés.[12]

Le 19 juin 1959 le président tunisien Habib Bourghiba fit une première visite au Vatican. Le pape Jean XXIII le reçut dans sa bibliothèque privée. Habib Bourghiba réclama un accord direct entre le Vatican et la Tunisie, car les accords du temps colonial étaient obsolètes. La deuxième visite eut lieu le 23 septembre 1962 à la veille du Concile Vatican II. Mais ce ne fut qu'après la visite du ministère des affaires étrangères tunisien le 16 février 1963 que l'on décida d'ouvrir des pourparlers sur le statut de l'Église catholique en Tunisie.[13] En 1964 un nouvel accord fut conclu, qui régla le « modus vivendi » entre la République tunisienne et le Saint Siège.[14]

---

[6] Oissilia Saaïdia, « Henri Marchal, technique d'apostolat auprès des Musulmans », in *L'altérité religieuse: un défi pour la mission chrétienne, XVIIIe-XXe siècles : actes du colloque de l'Association francophone œcuménique de missiologie et du Centre de recherches et d'échanges sur la diffusion et l'inculturation du christianisme, tenu à Torre Pellice (Italie) du 29 août au 2 septembre 1999*, éd. par Françoise Jacquin et al. (Paris: Karthala, 2001), 121-37.

[7] Soumille, « L'Église catholique et l'État tunisien après l'indépendance: le « modus vivendi » du 9 juillet 1964 », 159-160.

[8] Soumille, « L'Église catholique et l'État tunisien après l'indépendance: le « modus vivendi » du 9 juillet 1964 »., 161-162.

[9] Elle fut transportée chez les Pères Blancs à Carthage, puis démontée en 1964 lors du départ des Pères Blancs.

[10] Soumille, « L'Église catholique et l'État tunisien après l'indépendance: le « modus vivendi » du 9 juillet 1964 », 161-163.

[11] Soumille, « L'Église catholique et l'État tunisien après l'indépendance: le « modus vivendi » du 9 juillet 1964 », 161.

[12] Soumille, « L'Église catholique et l'État tunisien après l'indépendance: le « modus vivendi » du 9 juillet 1964 », 163-164.

[13] Soumille, « L'Église catholique et l'État tunisien après l'indépendance: le « modus vivendi » du 9 juillet

Le nouvel accord prévoyait que le Saint Siège transfère des lieux de culte sans compensation (109 églises et presbytères), sept églises restèrent en possession de l'Église catholique. En revanche l'État reconnaît le culte de l'Église catholique, qui s'exerce librement, mais discrètement. Des prêtres peuvent entrer au pays et obtenir un permis de séjour. Le titre d'évêque fut refusé, l'archevêché de Carthage fut dégradé entant que prélature territoriale de Tunis. Les communiqués officiels devaient être présentés aux autorités publiques.

Ces changements furent douloureux pour l'Église catholique. Beaucoup de prêtres durent quitter le pays. Mais la conquête la plus importante fut que l'Église pouvait exercer son culte librement. Ce fut un nouveau départ pour l'Église catholique, qui doit maintenant servir le pays et n'est plus une église coloniale protégée.[15] En 1968 le premier synode eut lieu, pendant lequel on réfléchit sur la place de l'Église et son rôle dans la société tunisienne. Prêtres et religieux doivent chercher un travail dans les institutions tunisiennes, surtout dans le système de santé publique, de formation et social. Ainsi les prêtres et religieux ne sont plus des maîtres, mais doivent servir la société.[16] En 1988 le deuxième synode eut lieu, qui confirma le chemin de l'Église catholique dans la société musulmane.[17]

Dans les années 90 les relations entre l'État et l'Église catholique se débloquèrent encore plus. Le 30 mai 1992 le Jordanien Fouad Twal fut nommé évêque de Tunis, un signe visible que l'Église catholique n'est pas une affaire européenne, mais que le christianisme est aussi lié à la culture arabe. Le 31 mai 1995 la prélature territoriale devint diocèse. En avril 1996 le pape Jean-Paul II visita la Tunisie et parla surtout des droits de l'homme.

Après les attentats du 11 septembre 2001 le gouvernement tunisien prit quelques mesures pour améliorer la sécurité. En ce contexte le dialogue interreligieux et interculturel gagna une plus grande importance. Du 20 au 21 janvier 2003 un colloque sur l'avenir du dialogue interreligieux eut lieu à l'université de az-Zitouna à Tunis. La plus grande importance du dialogue interreligieux apporta aussi à l'Église un plus grand respect. Son engagement dans le social constitue un espace privilégié pour la rencontre entre chrétiens et musulmans. Les dix écoles de l'Église catholique avec 6000 élèves et l'hôpital favorisent ces rencontres.[18]

En 2003 de grands changements eurent lieux pour les églises. Le déménagement de la Banque Africaine de Développement d'Abidjan à Tunis apporta des milliers de Africains prospères dans les années suivantes. Ils étaient surtout chrétiens comme aussi les étudiants subsahariens qui poursuivirent leurs études depuis un certain temps en Tunisie. Les églises se remplirent et les Africains façonnèrent la liturgie, surtout par de nouveaux chorals. En cette année arrivèrent des membres de l'Institut du Verbe Incarné, une congrégation argentine, ce qui changea le ton des cérémonies religieuses en Tunisie. Les Sœurs Blanches, traditionnelles et culturellement françaises, durent changer leur façon de célébrer la liturgie, mais aussi leur théologie de même que le clergé.[19]

1964 »Soumille, « L'Église catholique et l'État tunisien après l'indépendance: le « modus vivendi » du 9 juillet 1964 », 165-167 concernant les déliberations 167-179.

[14] XXX (Name), « l'Église en Tunisie. Le modus vivendi du 9 juillet 1964 », *Annuaire de l'Afrique du Nord.* 3 (1964): 63-71, http://aan.mmsh.univ-aix.fr/Pdf/AAN-1964-03_18.pdf.

[15] Fulvio Grazzini, « L'Église en Tunisie après l'indépendance », in *Histoire des chrétiens d'Afrique du Nord : Libye, Tunisie, Algérie, Maroc*, éd. par Henri Teissier (Paris: Desclée, 1991), 225; Soumille, « L'Église catholique et l'État tunisien après l'indépendance: le « modus vivendi » du 9 juillet 1964 », 179-187.

[16] Grazzini, « L'Église en Tunisie après l'indépendance », 226-227.

[17] Grazzini, « L'Église en Tunisie après l'indépendance », 233.

[18] Fuad Twal, « Tunisie », *Se Comprendre* 04/02 (2004): 6-7.

[19] Katia Boissevain, « Migrer et réveiller les Églises : Diversification des cultes chrétiens en Tunisie », *L'Année du Maghreb*, n° 11 (23 décembre 2014): part. 22-26, doi:10.4000/anneemaghreb.2253; Katia Boissevain, « Des conversions au christianisme à Tunis », *Histoire, monde et cultures religieuses*, n° 28 (1 décembre 2013): 47-50, www.cairn.info/resume.php?ID_ARTICLE=HMC_028_0047.

L'an 2003 apporta aussi de grand changement pour les églises protestantes. Les protestants, principalement Français, Suisses, Belges, Américains ou Anglais possédaient deux églises à Tunis. Aujourd'hui elles sont devenues évangéliques et non-denominationales. Une multitude des cultes et des services y sont célébrés.[20] En 2006 la Redeemer Church of Champions fut fondée par la séparation des autres églises protestantes. Elle est originaire du Nigeria et affiliée aux Assemblées de Dieu. Elle est missionnaire et pentecôtiste.[21]

Le 8 septembre 2005 Mgr Maroun Elias Nimeh Lahham devint évêque de Tunis, après que son prédécesseur soit devenu coadjuteur du patriarche latin de Jérusalem. En 22 mai 2010 le diocèse devint archidiocèse. Deux ans plus tard Mgr Lahham devint également évêque auxiliaire du patriarche latin de Jérusalem. En 2011 commença la révolution en Tunisie dite « Printemps arabe ». En 2014 la nouvelle constitution entra en vigueur. Elle garantit la liberté religieuse, y compris être athée et changer la religion. Le 21 février 2013 Ilario Antoniazzi devint nouvel archevêque de Tunis. En 2014 la Banque Africaine de Développement est retournée à Abidjan. Il faudra observer l'effet sur les congrégations chrétiennes en Tunisie.

Bibliographie

Arfa Mensia, Mokdad. « Une expérience privilégiée de dialogue : le GRIC ». In *Muslim-Christian perceptions of dialogue today : experiences and expectations*, édité par Jacques Waardenburg, 183-200. Leuven; Paris: Peeters, 2000.

Boissevain, Katia. « Des conversions au christianisme à Tunis ». *Histoire, monde et cultures religieuses*, n° 28 (1 décembre 2013): 47-62. www.cairn.info/resume.php?ID_ARTICLE=HMC_028_0047.

———. « Migrer et réveiller les Églises : Diversification des cultes chrétiens en Tunisie ». *L'Année du Maghreb*, n° 11 (23 décembre 2014): 105-21. doi:10.4000/anneemaghreb.2253.

Demeerseman, Gérard. *André Demeerseman, 1901-1993: à Tunis, soixante ans à l'Institut des Belles Lettres Arabes, IBLA*. Histoire des mondes chrétiens. Paris: Karthala, 2014.

Dor, Marie-Josée, et Jean Fisset. « Pères Blancs et Soeurs Blanches, Tunisie et Algérie : Fondation, développement, travaux apostoliques ». In *Histoire des chrétiens d'Afrique du Nord : Libye-Tunisie-Algérie-Maroc*, édité par Henri Teissier et Antoine. Chatelard, 163-94. Paris: Desclée, 1991.

Gabus. « L'expérience du dialogue islamo-chrétien dans le cadre du GRIC ». *Islamochristiana* 19 (1993): 117-24.

Grazzini, F. « L'Église en Tunisie ». In *Histoire des chrétiens d'Afrique du Nord : Libye, Tunisie, Algérie, Maroc*, édité par Henri Teissier, 139-42. Paris: Desclée, 1991.

Grazzini, Fulvio. « L'Église en Tunisie après l'indépendance ». In *Histoire des chrétiens d'Afrique du Nord : Libye, Tunisie, Algérie, Maroc*, édité par Henri Teissier, 225-34. Paris: Desclée, 1991.

Levrat, Jacques. *Une expérience de dialogue: les centres d'étude chrétiens en monde musulman*. Studien ; 9. Altenberge: Christl.-Islam. Schrifttum, 1987.

« Notre histoire ». *Eglise Réformée de Tunisie*, 2 février 2013. www.ertunis.com/un-peu-dhistoire/.

Saaïdia, Oissilia. « Henri Marchal, technique d'apostolat auprès des Musulmans ». In *L'altérité religieuse: un défi pour la mission chrétienne, XVIIIe-XXe siècles : actes du colloque de l'Association francophone œcuménique de missiologie et du Centre de recherches et d'échanges sur la diffusion et l'inculturation du christianisme, tenu à Torre Pellice (Italie) du 29 août au 2 septembre 1999*, édité par Françoise Jacquin, Association francophone œcuménique de missiologie, Jean-François Zorn, et Centre de recherches et d'échanges sur la diffusion et l'inculturation du christianisme (France), 121-37. Paris:

[20] Boissevain, « Migrer et réveiller les Églises », paragr. 29-30; Boissevain, « Des conversions au christianisme à Tunis », 50-57.

[21] Boissevain, « Migrer et réveiller les Églises », sect. 36-40; Boissevain, « Des conversions au christianisme à Tunis », 57-60.

Karthala, 2001.
Serain. « Le Groupe de recherches islamo-chrétien (G.R.I.C.) ». *Chemins de Dialogue* 15 (s. d.): 207-9.
Soumille, Pierre. « L'Église catholique et l'État tunisien après l'indépendance: le « modus vivendi » du 9 juillet 1964 ». In *Les relations Eglises-Etat en situation postcoloniale : Amérique, Afrique, Asie, Océanie, XIXe-XXe siècles : actes de la 20e session du CREDIC (Chevilly-Larue, 27-30 août 2002)*, édité par Philippe Delisle, 155-202. Collection Mémoires d'Eglises. Paris: Editions Karthala, 2003.
Twal, Fuad. « Tunisie ». *Se Comprendre* 04/02 (2004): 6-7.
XXX (Name). « l'Église en Tunisie. Le modus vivendi du 9 juillet 1964 ». *Annuaire de l'Afrique du Nord.* 3 (1964): 63-71. http://aan.mmsh.univ-aix.fr/Pdf/AAN-1964-03_18.pdf.

(94) Christianity in Uganda

Christopher Byaruhanga

Religion	Pop 2010	Pct 2010	Pop 2025	Pct 2025	Gr Pct 1970 2025
Christians	27,860,000	84.0%	45,301,000	84.7%	3.3%
Independents	1,141,000	3.4%	1,706,000	3.2%	2.7%
African initiated	821,000	2.5%			
Orthodox	29,300	0.1%	35,000	0.1%	1.2%
Protestants	14,026,000	42.3%	22,400,000	41.9%	3.2%
Anglicans	12,450,000	37.6%			
Pentecostal	966,000	2.9%			
Adventist	342,000	1.0%			
Roman Catholics	13,649,000	41.2%	22,000,000	41.1%	3.2%
Pentecostals/Charismatics	7,197,000	21.7%	11,800,000	22.1%	3.4%
Evangelicals	6,322,000	19.1%	10,273,000	19.2%	3.3%
Muslims	3,982,000	12.0%	6,445,000	12.0%	3.3%
adherents of traditional African religions	778,000	2.3%	900,000	1.7%	1.0%
Hindus	273,000	0.8%	420,000	0.8%	2.9%
Baha'is	96,700	0.3%	170,000	0.3%	3.8%
Chinese folk-religionists	4,400	0.0%	7,000	0.0%	3.2%
Jews	3,400	0.0%	3,600	0.0%	0.4%
Jains	3,100	0.0%	5,000	0.0%	3.2%
Buddhists	2,000	0.0%	3,000	0.0%	2.6%
Sikhs	1,700	0.0%	2,600	0.0%	2.9%
Zoroastrians	0	0.0%	0	0.0%	0.0%
people professing no religion	146,000	0.4%	240,000	0.4%	3.4%
Total population	**33,149,000**	**100.0%**	**53,497,000**	**100.0%**	**3.2%**

Source: Centre for the Study of World Christianity (CSGC), Boston, Gordon-Conwell TS

Introduction

The introduction of Christianity in Uganda began with a sketch map of Equatorial Africa that was sent to England in 1856 by Johannes Rebmann. Convinced by what this map showed, in 1857 the Royal Geographical Society sponsored an exploratory expedition to Central Africa by Captain Richard Burton and John Speke. According to Speke, Uganda was a field open to Christianity if England would not neglect his discovery. Speke had conceived the idea of making Uganda the base of the missionary enterprise in Central Africa in the 1860s, but his idea was never supported by any missionary society in Britain.

While Uganda became known to Britain geographically through the expedition of Speke, the discovery of her people was through Henry Morton Stanley. Stanley's expedition across Africa was sponsored by *The New York Herald* and London's *Daily Telegraph* newspapers. It was during this time that Stanley visited Uganda and introduced King Mutesa to Christianity. As a result, Mutesa requested Stanley to invite Christian missionaries to Uganda.[1] Stanley's letter was received warmly in Britain, and three days after its publication, £5,000 was offered to the Church Missionary Society (CMS) to organise a mission to Uganda.

On 27th April 1876, CMS sent seven missionaries to Uganda, but only two of them, namely, the Rev. C.T. Wilson and Shergold Smith, arrived at Mutesa's court on 30th June 1877. Unfortunately, Smith was killed in December and Wilson remained alone for a year until Alexander Mackay joined him. CMS was not alone in its interest in Stanley's advocacy of Uganda as a field of missionary enterprise because, at this time, 'becoming a missionary and conquering innumerable souls to Christianity was a necessity and a duty'.[2] The Roman Catholics, who had been planning the evangelization of the east Africa region for many years, sent priests of the order known as the White Fathers from Algiers. They were sent out by the Society of Notre Dame d'Afrique and arrived in Uganda on 23rd February 1879.

To avoid conflict, Cardinal Lavigerie had ordered the White Fathers not to open any station close to an Anglican one. However, it was practically impossible for Lavigerie's instructions to be carried out in Uganda because it was the public policy of the country that all foreigners' activities should be carried out at the King's court. The restriction on the missionaries' activities enabled the King not only to participate in the reading classes but also to keep the missionaries' activities under his control. The rival versions of Christianity in Uganda, although 'a scandal to the Christendom',[3] fitted well into the traditional factionalism of court life. Both Anglican and Catholic missionaries soon attracted a lively interest among the pages at the King's court.

The Spread of Christianity outside the King's Court

The death of Mutesa, a king who was neither in favour of nor against Christianity on 9th October 1884, was a disturbing event in the life of the infant church in Uganda. At the beginning of his reign, Mwanga was faced with three factions, which eventually became identified with three different religious parties. First, there was the older generation of chiefs who had held power in the kingdom for some time, and they were upholders of the traditional religion. Secondly, there was the younger generation of future leaders (pages) who were divided into two groups, namely, Roman Catholics and Anglicans. Thirdly, there was the Muslim party, under the leadership of the Arabs.

The 1880s were also the era of the European 'Scramble for Africa'. In Mwanga's opinion, the missionaries were part of the great force of Europeans who would one day overrun his kingdom. Mwanga, therefore, decided to assert his authority over all the Christians. His turning against the Christians led to the death of the first three Christian converts on 31st January 1885 and the death of an Anglican Bishop, James Hannington, on 29th October 1885. Hannington's death led to the death of Joseph Mukasa Balikuddembe,[4] a Catholic, on 15th November 1885. Balikuddembe was killed for daring to criticize Mwanga for the murder of the Anglican bishop. In May and June 1886, a large massacre of Christians, both Catholic and Anglican, took place. Those killed were accused of disobedience. The martyrs walked to their deaths

---

[1] Henry M. Stanley, *Through the Dark Continent,* Vol. I (London: Sampson Low, Marston, Searle & Rivington, 1878), 325.

[2] Mario Cisternino, *Passion for Africa: Missionary and Imperial Papers on the Evangelization of Uganda and Sudan 1848-1923* (Kampala: Fountain Publishers Ltd, 2004), 239.

[3] Zablon Nthamburi (ed.), *From Mission to Church: A Handbook of Christianity in East Africa* (Nairobi: Uzima Press, 1995), 84.

[4] Joseph Mukasa Balikuddembe was the first Ugandan Catholic martyr.

singing religious songs and praying for their executioners. Their courage inspired many people who saw them happily march to their execution centre, so they began to seek instruction from the remaining Christians.

The storm of persecution having blown over, the Christians were convinced that there was no future for the church in Uganda unless the Christians themselves secured political and military power. The missionaries' attitude toward the political establishment also changed. Up to this time, they had been happy to work within the framework of the existing political system with no intention of having it changed. After the persecutions, the missionaries and the African Christians concluded that the infant church in Uganda could no longer be protected by the existing political system. They needed to secure political and military power. Christians began to organize themselves into a standing army. It was at this time that many Christians were called into new positions of power at the King's court. Mwanga's change of attitude toward the Christians helped Christianity to spread much more widely. But by 1888, Mwanga became scared that the new generation of leaders was becoming too powerful. His suspicion came true when in September 1888 he was overthrown by the young generation of leaders which included Muslims. However, he was later reinstated by the Christians. Although Mwanga was happy that he had been reinstated, he himself was hardly a 'king' any longer.[5] The real power was now in the hands of the Christian chiefs. But within Christianity itself the rift between the Catholic and Anglican converts was growing worse every day.

In 1893, the Anglican Bishop Alfred Robert Tucker and the Catholic Bishop Jean Joseph Hirth verbally agreed to divide the country into two spheres of Christian influence. The Anglicans were to work in eastern Uganda and the Catholics in western and northern Uganda. Later, the verbal agreement was interpreted as merely a setting forth of the two bishops' intentions. Such was the state of affairs when, in April 1894, the British government formally declared a Protectorate over Uganda.[6] It allowed the presence of other Catholic religious groups in Uganda besides the White Fathers.

The Spread of Christianity outside Buganda

The spread of Christianity into the three kingdoms of western Uganda took nearly twenty years. From 1894, the western kingdoms of Uganda, namely, Toro, Bunyoro and Ankole, had come to terms with British colonialism. As in central Uganda, so in the west, kings and chiefs irresistibly became Anglican. In 1894, Kasagama, the King of Toro, asked for missionaries to be sent to Toro and CMS immediately sent four catechists. In 1895, the White Fathers also sent Catholic missionaries to batoro people of Toro Kingdom in southwestern Uganda. At the end of the 1890s, CMS began to train *batoro* catechists who eventually spread the gospel outside the King's palace.

While, in Toro, Christianity came as part of an attempt by Kasagama to recreate his father's kingdom with the help of the British administration, in Bunyoro it was as a response of the traditional leaders to the military defeat of King Kabalega by the British. In 1896, Byabachwezi, who was acting as the King's deputy, requested missionaries. In response to Byabachwezi's request, the Rev. A.B. Fisher visited Bunyoro and left two catechists behind. The Anglican mission in Bunyoro was found in Hoima. As in Buganda, in Hoima the missionaries lived next to the royal court. The White Fathers, who had begun working at Bukumi in 1895, opened a mission at Hoima in 1901. A Catholic outstation was quickly established in Masindi. Although, in Bunyoro, leadership was also in the hands of the Anglicans, there was

[5] Cisternino, *Passion for Africa*, 245.

[6] For a detailed account on why Britain decided to declare a Protectorate over Uganda, see Christopher Byaruhanga, *Bishop Alfred Robert Tucker and the Establishment of the African Anglican Church* (Nairobi: WordAlive Publishers, 2008), 114-129.

less animosity between the two traditions; a situation that helped the Catholics to quickly gain a numerical advantage over the Anglicans.

In Ankole, Christianity came as part of the King's desire to increase his influence over his subjects. But Ankole's first contact with Christianity was in 1888 and 1889 during the Christian exile. The first serious attempt, but an unsuccessful one, to send catechists to Ankole was made in 1898. In 1899, the Rev. H. Clayton visited Ankole and left behind a few catechists and, by 1901, a little reed church had been built. The baptism of a few leading chiefs, including the Mugabe (King), took place at the end of 1902. As a result, Anglicanism became the religion of the King and the Bahima. In the same year, the White Fathers arrived in Ankole. Instead of trying to compete with the Anglicans for the allegiance of the *Bahima* (pastoralists), the White Fathers went straight to the *Bairu* (agriculturalists).

The Ugandan Catholic and Anglican evangelists were inspired by the sacrifice of the Uganda martyrs to offer themselves as missionaries. For instance, in Ankole, Kigenzi and Kisoro, two men stood out for their excellent work in the spread of Christianity: Apollo Kivebulaya (an Anglican) and Yohana Kitagana (a Catholic).

Unlike central and western Uganda, eastern Uganda lacked the cultural cohesiveness that was common in other parts of present-day Uganda. However, it was due to Semei Kakungulu's conquest[7] that Christianity came to eastern Uganda, with the exception of Busoga. Unlike other parts of Uganda, there was the imposition of Kiganda culture and Luganda became the language of the church in the east. The imposition of Kiganda culture caused Christianity to remain a foreign religion in the east for a long time.[8]

The first Anglican evangelists to the north were from Banyoro. They were invited by Rwot (chief) Awic to Acholi in 1903. Awic was not only suspicious of European values but was also not interested in Christianity. In Lango, it was Odora of Aduku who actively promoted Anglicanism in the area. However, in both Acholi and Lango, the usual CMS strategy of using chiefs was not applied because the colonial administration in the area insisted on a rigid separation of church and state. In order to reinforce this separation, the colonial administration burned down churches that were built too close to government headquarters. The colonial policy of separation of church and state reinforced the Acholi and Langi prejudices against Christianity. The north of Uganda was assigned to the Verona Fathers, an Italian society founded by Bishop Daniel Comboni. The Catholics struggled to make an impact there.

It was Bishop Willis who negotiated with the Africa Inland Mission to send Anglican missionaries to West Nile and form congregations that were part of the Native Anglican Church. For the Catholics, it was the Verona Fathers who evangelized West Nile. Christianity made a greater impact in West Nile than in other parts of northern Uganda. In 1929, the Anglican Bible Churchmen's Missionary Society (BCMS) started working in Karamoja. They were later joined by the Verona Fathers. The Verona Fathers soon overtook the Anglicans through their effective schools and relief work. Unlike West Nile where Christianity has made a greater impact, in Karamoja Christianity has remained peripheral to this pastoral society.[9]

Consolidation of the Church in Uganda

The Anglican Church was never an official established church in colonial Uganda. However, it had a privileged position both in terms of its relationship with the local rulers and the British administration. The

[7] Nthamburi, *From Mission to Church*, 92. Semei Kakungulu compensated "for his political failure in Buganda by carving out for himself a kingdom in Eastern Uganda.

[8] It was in the 1950s that the Ateso Bible and Prayer Book were produced. A few years ago the Catholic priests started to conduct worship in the vernacular among the Jopadhola.

[9] Roland Oliver, *The Missionary Factor in East Africa* (London: Longman, Green and Co., 1952), 182-183.

Catholic Church had no such political role in the colonial state.[10] Despite continuing political discrimination, by appealing among the peasantry due to the official British policy of religious neutrality that allowed them to evangelize freely throughout the country, Catholics made impressive progress. As a result, Catholics came to form the majority of Christians in Uganda.

The continuing success of the Anglican and Catholic missions in the spread of Christianity in the colonial era was partly due to the introduction of a formal system of schooling, scientific medicine and colonial economy. Formal western education in Uganda was pioneered by the CMS, the White Fathers and the Mill Hill Mission. With the introduction of formal education, one began to see the formation of the new Ugandan society that had a territorial basis. The kind of Christianity that emerged had two branches: one producing the upper and middle class and another producing the lower class.

Both Catholic and non-Catholic missionaries played a great role in the introduction of scientific medicine in Uganda, having realized that Africans lived in very poor health conditions. Like education, medical work became an integral part of their missionary strategy.[11] To the spiritual, educational and medical services, the CMS and Roman Catholic missionaries added direct economic work as an integral part of the mission of the church in Uganda.

The mission stations stood out as centres of new standards of living within the surrounding areas. African converts were encouraged to engage in the growing of cash crops such as coffee and cotton, which had been introduced by the Protectorate government. The missionaries used local leaders in their campaigns and urged them to play an important role in the economic development of their people. Many of them took this advice seriously.

During the colonial era, the common argument of the Christian missionaries was that the spiritual experience that was noted among the Christians in Uganda was to be encouraged by growth in responsibility in terms of organizing an African church ministry. On 31st January 1891, the first six catechists were commissioned by the Anglican Bishop Tucker. In 1893, he ordained the first six African deacons, some of whom he also ordained priests in 1896. Bishop Tucker and the Catholic Bishop Henri Streicher were of the view that the church that can produce martyrs can also produce priests. It was Bishop Streicher who did much to encourage priestly vocations in the Catholic Church. The first two Ugandans to be ordained in the Catholic Church in 1913 were Bazilio Lumu and Viktoro Mukasa. In 1939, the Catholic Church in Uganda produced the first African Catholic bishop of modem times, Joseph Kiwanuka.

African Pentecostal churches are the latest development in Uganda's church history. At first, Pentecostals were denied permission by the colonial government to operate because they were received with scepticism and apprehension. Some Christians in the mainline churches who became Pentecostal were excommunicated. However, later in 1960, the colonial government authorized the Pentecostal churches to start operating freely in Uganda. Since 1960, the Pentecostal churches have not only grown tremendously but also demystified the pastoral ministry. Despite the challenge of these new churches, the Anglican and Catholic Churches continue to retain the allegiance of an overwhelming majority of Ugandans.

The Rise of Nationalism

In the 1950s, it was the Anglican schools that were the breeding ground for rising nationalism. There were varied church responses to this in Buganda and Uganda at that time. Sometimes the Anglican hierarchy was suspicious of Buganda nationalism. While the majority of church leaders were in support of Ugandan

[10] The Bishop of Uganda stood third in order of precedence at official functions, after the Governor and the King of Buganda.

[11] Byaruhanga, "The Church of the Province of Uganda" in Ian S. Markham, J. Barney Hawkins IV, Justyn Terry and Leslie Nunez Steffensen (eds.), *The Wiley-Blackwell Companion to the Anglican Communion* (Oxford: John Wiley & Sons, Ltd, 2013), 225.

nationalism, a few of them remained suspicious of it. However, by the end of the 1950s, the entire Anglican Church hierarchy was being forced by events to reconsider their attitude toward Ugandan nationalism. But even with the change of attitude toward Ugandan nationalism, the hierarchy of the Anglican Church was often attacked for identifying itself too closely with the colonial authorities.

The Anglican Church lost a lot of support from Buganda in those years due to the ambiguity of the relationship between the church hierarchy and the colonial government. Catholics too were under attack in these years from traditionalists. After long years of being passive in political matters, as independence approached, the Catholic hierarchy increasingly saw the Democratic Party as a suitable party for Catholics to support.

Christianity in Independent Uganda

There was an assumption that the growth of the church in Uganda would suffer greatly once the colonial power had departed. This did not happen. On the contrary, the growth of the church since 1962 when Uganda became independent has been extraordinary by any standards. In the year 2000, Philip Jenkins projected the number of Christians in Uganda would be twenty-four million in 2025.[12]

Uganda remained a British protectorate until 9th October 1962, when it became an independent country, with the King of Buganda as President and Milton Obote as Prime Minister.[13] On the eve of Independence, there were three major political parties formed in Uganda: the Uganda People's Congress (UPC) led by an Anglican, the Democratic Party (DP) led by a Catholic, and the Kabaka Yekka (KY). An alliance between the UPC and KY increased the chances of the UPC of winning elections. With the failure of DP to gain power in 1962, the Catholic Church was forced back into its pre-Independence role as the church without political power. In 1962, religion was a strong factor in Ugandan politics , a situation that has remained the case until today. Due to the strain in relations between Anglicans and Catholics, mainly due to politics, the Uganda Joint Christian Council (UJCC) was formed in 1963. When Bishop Joseph Kiwanuka became the Catholic Archbishop of Kampala, his Anglican counterpart, Archbishop Leslie Brown, approached him on the question of co-operation. As a result, in 1963 the bishops of the two church traditions agreed to form the UJCC, which was inaugurated in 1964. Since then, the Council has been joined by other churches. The sub-committees of the UJCC concerned with education, social welfare, mass communication and medicine were established. Remarkable developments in co-operation in Uganda have been realized in such areas as theology, religion and religious education, leading to the introduction of the same Baptismal Formulary in Luganda for Anglican and Catholics, and a joint syllabus in religious education for primary and secondary schools and teacher training colleges.[14]

Generally, the political situation in Uganda since 1962 has forced the Catholic Church to adopt a much more critical stance toward successive governments. Both Archbishop Kiwanuka and his successor Cardinal Emmanuel Nsubuga have had occasion to speak out strongly on the abuse of human rights, speaking not only for Catholics but for all oppressed Ugandans. The Anglican Church, by contrast, has reflected all the tensions and disunity which have characterized Ugandan society as a whole. The fact that a Protestant-dominated party came to power at Independence meant that a close relationship between the Anglican Church and the state was bound to continue. The Pentecostal churches have tended to be apolitical.

---

[12] Philip Jenkins, *The Next Christendom: The Coming of Global Christianity* (Oxford: Oxford University Press, 2000), 91.

[13] In 1966, Obote took full control of the government.

[14] For a detailed account of the work of the Uganda Christian Joint Council, see Byaruhanga, *The History and Theology of the Ecumenical Movement in East Africa* (Kampala: Fountain Publishers, 2015), 163-167.

The Church in Uganda under the Military Regime

On 25th January 1971, while the president of Uganda, Milton Obote, attended a Commonwealth meeting in Singapore, Idi Amin led a coup d'état and took control of the country, declaring himself president. The coup is reported to have been backed by Israel and Britain. Amin's victory over Obote's regime was initially greeted with widespread support, both within Uganda and by the international community. Britain, Israel and the USA were quick to recognize Amin as the rightful leader of Uganda. Those in opposition to Obote originally welcomed the coup and Amin's government. However, this changed when Amin himself began solidifying his absolute control over the nation. Amin presided over the most dictatorial regime which post-Independence Uganda has had. Although, originally, Amin had found support from Christian states, he soon turned to Islamic states when his demands for large increases in military assistance were rebuffed by Israel and Britain. Amin agreed to officially turn Uganda into a Muslim state after Saudi Arabia and Libya agreed to provide the money necessary to enforce conversion to Islam.

Amin started to view the churches as potential centres of opposition, and over the next few years, many Christians, both Anglicans and Catholics, were killed for various 'offences'. For instance, a preacher who read over the radio a psalm which mentioned Israel, was shot in 1972. Amin accused the Anglican Archbishop Janani Jakaliya Luwum of treason and had him and two cabinet ministers, both committed Christians, arrested and killed on 16th February 1977.[15] Archbishop Luwum is recognized as the first martyr of the second century of Christianity in Uganda. This latest in a long line of atrocities was greeted with international condemnation, but apart from the continued trade boycott initiated by the USA in July 1978, verbal condemnation was not accompanied by action. Amin did not only kill high-ranking persons in society but also ordinary citizens from targeted ethnic groups and districts.

Religious conflicts were another characteristic of the Amin regime that had its origins in the nineteenth century. After rediscovering his Islamic allegiance in the effort to gain foreign aid from Libya and Saudi Arabia, Amin began to pay more attention to the formerly deprived Muslims in Uganda, a move which turned out to be a mixed blessing for them. Muslims began to do well in what economic opportunities yet remained, the more so if they had relatives in the army. Construction work began on Old Kampala Hill, the site of Kampala's most prominent mosque. Many Ugandan Muslims with a sense of history believed that the Muslims defeated by Christians in 1889 were finally being redressed. Christians, in turn, perceived that they were under siege as a religious group.

Amin's rule had many lasting negative consequences for Uganda: It led to a low regard for human life and personal security, widespread corruption, and the disruption of economic production and distribution.

The Church under Museveni's Regime

After Amin's regime, political developments in Uganda have gone full circle, from parliamentary democracy to years of dictatorships and military rule, and back to a parliamentary democracy during President Yoweri Museveni's regime. In January 1986, Museveni successfully seized control of the country and democratic presidential elections were held in 1996. During Museveni's regime, the church has increased in importance and influence. Many Ugandans have thrown their energies and resources behind the church. In the case of the Catholic Church, this has been a period of enthusiastic church building, the growth of parishes, dioceses and the creation of new provinces.

[15] February 16 was declared a public holiday in Uganda by President Yoweri Museveni on February 16, 2015.

Bibliography

Byaruhanga, Christopher. *Bishop Alfred Robert Tucker and the Establishment of the African Anglican Church*. Nairobi: WordAlive Publishers, 2008.

Byaruhanga, Christopher. *The History and Theology of the Ecumenical Movement in East Africa.* Kampala: Fountain Publishers, 2015.

Lugumba, S. M. E. and J. C. Ssekamwa. *A History of Education in East Africa 1900-1973.* Kampala: Kampala Bookshop Publishing Company, 1973.

Nthamburi, Zabulon ed. *From Mission to Church: A Handbook of Christianity in East Africa.* Nairobi: Uzima Press, 1995.

Oliver, Ronald. *The Missionary Factor in East Africa.* London: Longman, Green and Co., 1952.

Ward, Kevin. 'Eating and Sharing: Church and State in Uganda', *Journal of Anglican Studies* 3, no. 1 (June 2005): 99-119.

(95) Christianity in Zambia

Teddy Chalwe Sakupapa

Religion	Pop 2010	Pct 2010	Pop 2025	Pct 2025	Gr Pct 1970 2025
Christians	11,997,000	86.2%	19,586,000	89.5%	3.3%
Independents	2,629,000	18.9%	3,650,000	16.7%	2.2%
African initiated	848,000	6.1%			
Orthodox	7,400	0.1%	8,000	0.0%	0.5%
Protestants	4,745,000	34.1%	7,500,000	34.3%	3.1%
United churches	1,144,000	8.2%			
Adventist	1,096,000	7.9%			
Pentecostal	865,000	6.2%			
Reformed, Presbyterian	641,000	4.6%			
Baptist	274,000	2.0%			
Anglicans	264,000	1.9%			
Holiness	168,000	1.2%			
Brethren	142,000	1.0%			
Evangelical churches	70,900	0.5%			
Roman Catholics	4,559,000	32.8%	7,651,000	34.9%	3.5%
Pentecostals/Charismatics	3,290,000	23.6%	5,330,000	24.3%	3.3%
Evangelicals	2,576,000	18.5%	4,220,000	19.3%	3.3%
adherents of traditional African religions	1,479,000	10.6%	1,600,000	7.3%	0.5%
Baha'is	243,000	1.7%	400,000	1.8%	3.4%
Muslims	141,000	1.0%	220,000	1.0%	3.0%
Hindus	17,900	0.1%	25,000	0.1%	2.2%
Chinese folk-religionists	8,500	0.1%	12,000	0.1%	2.4%
Buddhists	4,000	0.0%	6,000	0.0%	2.8%
Jews	1,700	0.0%	1,700	0.0%	0.0%
Sikhs	260	0.0%	400	0.0%	2.8%
people professing no religion	24,300	0.2%	41,000	0.2%	3.5%
Total population	**13,917,000**	**100.0%**	**21,892,000**	**100.0%**	**3.1%**

Source: Centre for the Study of World Christianity (CSGC), Boston, Gordon-Conwell TS

Introduction

This contribution offers a descriptive profile of Christianity in Zambia. It is specifically argued that, while there is a noticeable presence of other religions in Zambia, such as Islam and the Bahai faith, Christianity is the dominant religious influence in the country. Be that as it may, I contend that Zambian Christianity may be best described as a mosaic of various Christian expressions. Structurally, I begin with a historical overview of the introduction of missionary Christianity in Zambia and the subsequent shift from mission to church. The second part discusses the changing face of Christianity in Zambia and highlights the challenges and opportunities presented by this development. Finally, I conclude with a discussion of the public role of Christianity in Zambia.

A Brief History of Mainstream Christianity in Zambia

The southern African nation of Zambia (formerly Northern Rhodesia) has a population in excess of thirteen million people and is generally considered to be a *de facto* Christian nation.[1] Christianity is largely an outcome of the nineteenth-century missionary movement.[2] Comparatively, Zambia was the last field in south-central Africa to be reached by missionary societies from the north. Its landlocked position seems to have rendered it inaccessible to 'missions' for a long time. Towards the end of the nineteenth century, a number of missionary societies began to make inroads into the country. The Plymouth Brethren missionary Frederik Arnot is said to have been the first Christian missionary to settle within the borders of present-day Zambia, following his arrival at Lealui in 1882.[3] In terms of missionary societies, it was the London Missionary Society (LMS) that made earlier attempts to establish missions in Zambia.[4] Since 1877, the LMS had been struggling against all odds to establish a station in the southern end of the Lake Tanganyika area. Before this, the LMS missionary explorer David Livingstone had already visited the Bemba Chief Chitimukulu in 1867.

The LMS eventually set up mission stations among the Mambwe people at Nyamukolo and Fwambo, in 1884 and 1887 respectively.[5] In what was then called Barotseland (now Western Province), Francois Coillard of the Paris Evangelical Mission established a mission at Lealui in 1887 following successful approval by the Lozi King, albeit during a period of political upheaval within the kingdom.[6] The positive reception that Coillard enjoyed in Barotseland was due to a great extent to the catalytic presence of Sotho evangelists and teachers in his team. In correspondence with Coillard, the Primitive Methodist Missionary Society undertook a long and difficult journey to Barotseland but the King would not allow them to settle there. They finally managed to establish a mission at Nkala in Ila land in 1893.

Although the Roman Catholic Church (RCC) had made preliminary contact with the people of Zambia as early as 1730, it formally established its first mission post in Zambia in 1891 near Mambwe-Mwela in the north of the country.[7] This was largely a result of the missionary work of the White Fathers. In late 1899, the Dutch Reformed Church of South Africa started missionary work at Magwero in eastern Zambia.[8] In 1900, the Church of Scotland established a mission in northern Zambia. The Anglican Church established its first significant mission station at Msoro near Chipata in the east in 1911 and assigned the Malawian Leornad Kamungu to its charge.

---

[1] See 2010 census. Details available at www.zamstats.gov.zm/census/cen.html

[2] See Teddy Sakupapa, "Local Ecumenism in the Zambian Context," In: *South African Perspectives on Notions and Forms of Ecumenicity*, edited by E. Conradie (Stellenbosch: Sun Press, 2013), 158.

[3] Charles P. Groves, *The Planting of Christianity in Africa, Vol 3 1878-1914* (London: Lutterworth Press, 1965), 137.

[4] Bwalya Chuba, *A History of Early Christian Missions and Church Unity in Zambia* (Ndola: Mission Press, 2005), 20.

[5] See Peter Bolink, *Towards Church Union in Zambia: A Study of Missionary Cooperation and Church Union Efforts in Central Africa* (Franeker, Neth: T. Waver, 1967), 33-36.

[6] See Philippe Burger et al (eds.), *The Spread of the Gospel in Barotseland: From Paris Mission to the United Church of Zambia* (Paris: Defap, 2010), 10.

[7] See Hugo Hinfelaar, *History of the Catholic Church in Zambia* (Lusaka: Bookworld Publishers, 2004), 1.

[8] Gerdien Verstraelen-Gilhuis, *From Dutch Mission Church to Reformed Church in Zambia: The Scope for African Leadership and Initiative in the History of Zambian Mission Church* (Netherlands: Franeker, 1982), 45.

The above-named mission societies and others soon proliferated in the country and gradually spawned a number of churches. These included the Roman Catholic Church, the United Church of Zambia (UCZ), the Reformed Church in Zambia (RCZ), the Anglican Church in Zambia, and the Church of Central Africa Presbyterian (CCAP), among others.[9] The Catholic Church is the largest single denomination, while the UCZ is the biggest Protestant church in the country. With reference to the UCZ, Gifford notes that this church 'is a remarkable ecumenical venture that is almost unique in Africa'.[10] It was formed in 1965 as a union of the United Church of Central Africa in Rhodesia (UCCAR), the Church of Barotseland and the Methodist Church, thus bringing together Congregational, Presbyterian/Reformed and Methodist Christian traditions (Chuba 2005:143). Contrary to what one would expect in a former British colony, the Anglican Church is much smaller in Zambia. The RCZ is most widespread in the eastern part of the country but continues to make inroads in other areas. Other larger Protestant churches include the Seventh Day Adventists, the Salvation Army and the Baptist Convention of Zambia. Many of these churches have further developed their missionary heritage of schools and health institutions, although some such institutions have been surrendered to government control.

In retrospect, it may be argued that, while missionary Christianity contributed immensely to African society through the introduction of western medical systems and the establishment of schools, its hostile approach to African culture and religion has been a subject of much criticism by several commentators. One strong criticism in this regard is that missionary endeavours were difficult to disengage from colonial intent. Nevertheless, some argue to the contrary – that, in some cases, missionaries were prepared to fight the colonial administration 'if it seemed... that the rights of the African were being infringed or betrayed'.[11]

The Emergence of Pentecostalism in Zambia

From the foregoing, it may be argued that the history of mission work in Zambia is integral to an adequate account of the history of Christianity in the country generally, and that of mainstream Christianity in particular. Mainline churches retained their dominance on the Zambian religious scene until the 1970s when other forms of Christianity began to appear. African Independent Churches (AICs) were among the first wave of an attempt to Africanise Christianity within the Zambian context. Some of these include Alice Lenshina's Lumpa Church, founded during the 1950s, and Emilio Mulolani's Catholic Church of the Sacred Heart of Jesus (also known as Ba Mutima). Lenshina had been a Christian at the Lubwa Mission of the Church of Scotland in north-eastern Zambia. Her prophetic and millenarian movement led the opposition to the newly independent regime of Kenneth Kaunda in 1964, resulting in a 'civil war' between her followers and Kaunda's party. Mulolani had been a Roman Catholic who had earlier been a student at Kipalapala major seminary. These and other AICs are no longer prominent in Zambia. Enculturation that has resulted in the appropriation of indigenous symbols in the liturgy is more evident within the Catholic Church. The healing sessions of Emmanuel Milingo (once Archbishop of Lusaka) were indicative of an

[9] For a history of some of these churches see Bolink, *Towards Church*; Burger et al (eds.), *The Spread*; Brian Garvey, *Bembaland Church: Religious and Social Change in South Central Africa, 1891-1964* (Leiden, 1994); Bwalya Chuba, *Mbeleshi in a History of the London Missionary Society* (Gaborone, Pula Press, 2000); Hinfelaar, *History*; Verstraelen-Gilhuis, *From Dutch Mission.*

[10] Paul Gifford, *African Christianity: Its Public Role* (Indianapolis: Indiana University Press, 1998), 183.

[11] Stephen Neil, *Colonialism and Christian Missions* (London: Lutterworth Press, 1966), 309. Cf. Henry Meebelo, *Reaction to Colonialism: A Prelude to the Politics of Independence in Northern Zambia 1893-1939* (Manchester: Manchester University Press, 1971), 27.

attempt to take seriously African religious experience. Milingo's approach was considered unconventional and it led to his transfer out of Zambia to a new assignment in Rome.[12]

Another significant development in Zambian Christianity was the emergence of Pentecostalism during the early 1970s, largely due to the influence of classic European and North American Pentecostalism (such as the Pentecostal Assemblies of God and the Church of God), as well as Pentecostal missions and independent ministries. The latter included the German evangelist, Reinhard Bonnke, American evangelists like Jimmy Swaggart and Kenneth Copeland and others in Africa. Various Christian student fellowships contributed to the spread of Pentecostalism, serving as a platform where young students encountered this expression of the Christian faith. Youth ministries in schools and tertiary institutions, under the auspices of Scripture Union, the Zambia Fellowship of Evangelical Students, Campus Crusade, Navigators and others, left a Pentecostal influence that is residual within Zambian Christianity.

Alongside this was the charismatic ferment which affected many churches in Zambia as an outgrowth of the global charismatic movement.[13] The initial impact of these Pentecostal expressions was in the form of charismatic worship which soon led to factions in congregations between Pentecostal-inclined (mostly youth) members and so-called 'traditionalists'. The ensuing strife eventually culminated in breakaways in mainline churches. Significant examples include the UCZ and the RCZ who experienced major breakaways, which resulted in the formation of Bible Gospel Church in Africa (BIGOGA) and Grace Ministries in 1993 and 2001 respectively. The 1990s particularly witnessed the proliferation of new Pentecostal churches, particularly those with no links with classic Pentecostalism.

In its many forms and expressions, Pentecostalism has fast become the representative face of Christianity in Zambia.[14] It has indeed become a prominent feature of Zambia's religious landscape. However, one must be cautious not to downplay the vitality and growth within mainline churches too. Cheyeka and others are thus correct when they argue against the tendency to generalise interpretations of the significance of Pentecostalism in Zambia.[15]

From the perspective of mainline churches, there is a noticeable shift from questioning charismatic worship (which dominated the late 1990s) to the recent dynamic that has led to the unabashed 'Pentecostalisation of Christianity' in Zambia. The notion of this 'Pentecostalisation of Christianity' has been described by Ghanaian theologian Asamoah-Gyadu as an attempt by mainline churches in Africa to accommodate some Pentecostal elements.[16] This seems to be the case in the local Zambian context where several mainline churches are appropriating elements of Pentecostalism in their liturgies and practice of ministry.

The rapid growth of the Pentecostal phenomenon in Zambia may be attributed to a number of factors. The Pentecostal message with its emphasis on the power of God to miraculously and mystically transform all life situations – including the healing of diseases, ensuring prosperity and solving believer's daily problems – has indeed been attractive to many. Such a message is compelling and seductive for people whose decreasing quality of life and multiple life struggles are a daily experience. Even more significant is

---

[12] See Hugo Hinfelaar, *Bemba-speaking Women of Zambia in a Century of Religious Change (1892-1992)* (Leiden: E.J. Brill, 1994), 171-175.

[13] For a history of charismatic Christianity in Zambia see Austin Cheyeka, "Towards a History of the Charismatic Churches in Post-Colonial Zambia," in *One Zambia, Many Histories: Towards a History of Post-Colonial Zambia*, eds. Jan-Bart Gewald, Marja Hinfelaar and Giacomo Macola (Leiden: E.J. Brill, 2008), 144-163.

[14] David Gordon, *Invisible Agents: Spirits in a Central African History* (Ohio: Ohio University Press, 2012), 187.

[15] Austin Cheyeka, Marja Hinfelaar & Bernhard Udelhoven. "The Changing Face of Zambia's Christianity and its Implications for the Public Sphere: A Case Study of Bauleni Township, Lusaka," *Journal of Southern African Studies* 40, no. 5 (2014): 1031-1045.

[16] Kwabena Asamoah-Gyadu, *African Charismatics: Current Developments within Independent Indigenous Pentecostalism in Ghana* (Leiden: Brill, 2005), 30.

the ability of Pentecostalism in Zambia to appropriate both the indigenous and contemporary Zambian/African cultures' anthropocentric focus. Pentecostalism has thrived on the fertile ground of Zambian traditional cosmologies by appropriating notions of salvation within the framework of their inherently religious and anthropocentric cosmology. Further, salvation is holistically conceived. Akin to Mbiti's description of salvation in African Traditional Religion, salvation in Zambian traditional cosmologies 'has to do with physical and immediate dangers that threaten individual or community survival, good health, and general prosperity or safety'.[17] Accordingly, material blessings (children, good health, shelter, etc) are deemed a stamp of divine approval.

Ecumenism in the Zambian Context

Zambia has three so-called church mother bodies, namely, the Council of Churches in Zambia (CCZ), the Evangelical Fellowship of Zambia (EFZ) and the Zambia Episcopal Conference (ZEC). The CCZ is composed of ecumenically inclined Protestant churches. The EFZ is made up of evangelical churches including a variety of Pentecostal/Charismatic churches, while ZEC is the administrative body of the Roman Catholic Church. These three bodies especially collaborate on issues that require the common witness of churches.[18] Within the field of theological education, most mainline churches (e.g. Roman Catholics, UCZ, RCZ, Anglicans and Baptists) run sizeable seminaries and university colleges. Nevertheless, these largely remain a denominational enterprise as there is very little collaboration in theological education among these institutions. Established Pentecostal churches such as the Pentecostal Assemblies of God also offer training programmes for pastors in their denominational Bible colleges. The need to develop theological education synergies among theological institutions in Zambia remains crucial.

In view of the fragmented theological education scenario portrayed above, Theological Education by Extension in Zambia (TEEZ) – an ecumenical venture established for the purpose of preparing all God's people for works of Christian service through non-residential theological training – holds much promise in bringing theological education closer to churches, particularly churches of Protestant mission origin. The Mindolo Ecumenical Foundation (MEF), established in 1959, is yet another significant ecumenical venture in Zambia. It was originally founded with the aim of serving the Christian church and the community. It was established as a centre of study and worship and for consultation on the unity and renewal of the church and its responsibility in society.[19] MEF also served as the headquarters of the All Africa Conference of Churches in the early 1960s.

The Public Role of the Church

As the most dominant religious influence in the country, Christianity has been a significant factor in national social and political matters before and after the independence struggle against British colonialism. Already, in 1924, the Northern Rhodesia missionary conference campaigned against the tax system which was imposed on Africans by the British colonial authorities. It later also allied itself with local opposition to the Federation.[20] This notwithstanding, some of the local people involved in the nationalist struggle

---

[17] John Mbiti, "Some Reflections on African Experience of Salvation Today", in *Living Faiths and Ultimate Goals: A Continuing Dialogue*, ed. S.J Samartha (Geneva: World Council of Churches, 1974), 108-119.

[18] Joe Komakoma (ed.), *The Social Teachings of the Catholic Bishops and Other Christian Leaders in Zambia: Major Pastoral Letters and Statements, 1953-2001* (Ndola: Mission Press, 2003).

[19] Denis M' Passou, *Mindolo: A Story of the Ecumenical Movement in Africa* (Lusaka: Multimedia Publications, 1983), 26-28.

[20] John Weller & Jane Linden, *Mainstream Christianity to 1980 in Malawi, Zambia and Zimbabwe* (Gweru: Mambo Press, 1984), 191-200.

questioned certain missionary attitudes despite having been beneficiaries of missionary education. Kenneth Kaunda, a son of an African minister and who later became Zambia's first President, is an example of this critical stand. Kaunda noted thus:

> In my days at Lubwa [mission], I had begun to question certain things in the life of the mission which seemed incompatible with the teaching of Christ in the Bible. I could not see why the European missionaries should have special seats in church and why the Rev. Paul Mushindo [an African] went about on foot or on a cycle while the missionaries rode around in cars.[21]

At the same time, there were missionaries such as the Methodist minister Colin Morris who earned the confidence of many Zambian Christians and the close friendship of Zambia's future President Kenneth Kaunda as a result of his 'political outspokenness'[22] in support of the liberation struggle.

By the early 1960s, many missions had become churches. The role of churches in a decolonised Zambia which had been honed during the struggle for independence became quite evident in the subsequent years of nation-building. The churches would not only respond but also contribute to shaping social, economic and political developments in the ensuing transitions. For instance, churches opposed the United National Independence Party (UNIP) government's attempt to introduce 'Scientific Socialism' into the Zambian educational system via the nationwide educational reform between 1976 and 1982. The churches were concerned about the exclusion of religious education from the proposed curriculum, and the proposal to convert church buildings into classrooms in an attempt to overcome the dearth of school space.[23]

In 1991, Zambia changed from being a one-party state into being a multi-party democracy. Churches made a significant contribution by way of civic education during that historic transition. They conscientized citizens through church-owned media and joint statements that underscored the importance of civil society and democracy.[24] The Kaunda government was persuaded to return to multi-party politics and to hold elections in 1991. Churches were further involved in monitoring the elections which ousted Kenneth Kaunda's UNIP and ushered in a newly-formed party, the Movement for Multiparty Democracy (MMD), under the presidency of Frederik Chiluba.

On 29th December 1991, barely two months after taking over the presidency, Chiluba declared Zambia a Christian nation.[25] Later in 1996, the declaration was included in the preamble of the Zambian Constitution. In a joint statement, the CCZ, EFZ and ZEC only cautiously welcomed the declaration of Zambia as a Christian nation, while lamenting the lack of consultation in the process. They further raised concern that the declaration should not compromise freedom of conscience and worship.[26] There were therefore divergent views regarding both the declaration and the enshrining of the same in the constitution. This notion of a Christian nation has in recent times attracted scholarly work on Christianity in Zambia and its role in Zambian politics.[27] Engaging with some of these studies, Cheyeka and others argue that, in practice, the declaration is first and foremost a moral discourse, at least from the perspective of Pentecostals and evangelicals in Zambia.[28]

---

[21] Kenneth Kaunda, *Zambia Shall Be Free* (New York, 1963), 146.

[22] John V. Taylor & Dorothea Lehmann, *Christians of the Copperbelt: The Growth of the Church in Northern Rhodesia* (London: SCM Press, 1961), 157-158.

[23] Komakoma, '*The Social Teachings*,' 107-133.

[24] Komakoma, '*The Social Teachings*,' 140-196.

[25] Austin Cheyeka, *The Politics and Christianity of Chilubaism 1991-2011* (Ndola: Mission Press, 2010), 26-30.

[26] Komakoma, '*The Social Teachings*,' 264.

[27] Gifford, *African Christianity*; Isabel Phiri, "President Frederick Chiluba and Zambia: Evangelicals and Democracy in a 'Christian Nation'", in *Evangelical Christianity and Democracy in Africa*, ed. T.O. Ranger (Oxford: Oxford University Press, 2008). See also Gifford, *African Christianity*, 197-206.

[28] Cheyeka *et al.* "The Changing Face…," 1034.

Conclusion

In this contribution, I have described the growth of Christianity in Zambia from missionary times to the contemporary period which has seen the emergence of many forms of Christian expressions. Such growth shows, as Walls argues, that 'Modern African Christianity is not only the result of movements among Africans, but it has been principally sustained by Africans and is to a surprising extent the result of African initiatives'.[29] I have further demonstrated that Christianity in Zambia holds an important place in society and that the churches – particularly the mainline churches – have engaged government on critical social issues. Although the contribution of Pentecostal churches to social issues is rather clumsy, it is not completely absent. Ecumenical co-operation between churches notwithstanding, there is a need for further collaboration beyond the question of social ethics.

Bibliography

Bolink, Peter. *Towards Church Union in Zambia: A Study of Missionary Cooperation and Church Union Efforts in Central Africa*. Franeker, Neth: T. Waver, 1967.

Burger, Philippe *et al*, eds. *The Spread of the Gospel in Barotseland: From Paris Mission to the United Church of Zambia*. Paris: Defap, 2010.

Cheyeka, Austin Marja Hinfelaar and Bernhard Udelhoven. 'The Changing Face of Zambia's Christianity and its Implications for the Public Sphere: A Case Study of Bauleni Township, Lusaka.' *Journal of Southern African Studies* 40, no. 5 (2014): 1031-1045.

Cheyeka, Austin. *The Politics and Christianity of Chilubaism 1991-2011*. Ndola: Mission Press, 2010.

Cheyeka, Austin. 'Towards a History of the Charismatic Churches in Post-Colonial Zambia.' In *One Zambia, Many Histories: Towards a History of Post-Colonial Zambia*, edited by Jan-Bart Gewald, Marja Hinfelaar and Giacomo Macola, 144-163. Leiden: E.J. Brill, 2008.

Chuba, Bwalya. *A History of Early Christian Missions and Church Unity in Zambia*. Ndola: Mission Press, 2005.

Chuba, Bwalya. *Mbeleshi in a History of the London Missionary Society*. Gaborone: Pula Press, 2000.

Garvey, Brian. *Bembaland Church: Religious and Social Change in South Central Africa, 1891-1964*. Leiden: Brill, 1994.

Gifford, Paul. *African Christianity: Its Public Role*. Indianapolis: Indiana University Press, 1998.

Gordon, David. *Invisible Agents: Spirits in a Central African History*. Ohio: Ohio University Press, 2012.

Hinfelaar, Hugo. *History of the Catholic Church in Zambia*. Lusaka: Bookworld Publishers, 2004.

Hinfelaar, Hugo. *Bemba-speaking Women of Zambia in a Century of Religious Change (1892-1992)*. Leiden: E.J. Brill, 1994.

Kaunda, Kenneth. *Zambia Shall Be Free*, New York: Frederick A. Praeger, 1963.

Komakoma, Joe, ed. *The Social Teachings of the Catholic Bishops and Other Christian Leaders in Zambia: Major Pastoral Letters and Statements, 1953-2001*. Ndola: Mission Press, 2003.

Meebelo, Henry. *Reaction to Colonialism: A Prelude to the Politics of Independence in Northern Zambia 1893-1939*. Manchester: Manchester University Press, 1971.

Neil, Stephen. *Colonialism and Christian Missions.* London: Lutterworth Press, 1966.

Omenyo, Cephas. 'Agenda for a Discussion of African Initiatives in Christianity: The West African/Ghanaian Case.' *Missiology: An International Review* 39, no. 3 (2011): 373-390.

Passou, Denis M. *Mindolo: A Story of the Ecumenical Movement in Africa*. Lusaka: Multimedia Publications, 1983.

[29] Andrew Walls, *The Missionary Movement in Christian History: Studies in the Transmission of Faith* (Maryknoll, NY: Orbis Books, 1996), 89. Cf. Cephas Omenyo, "Agenda for a Discussion of African Initiatives in Christianity: The West African/Ghanaian Case," *Missiology: An International Review* 39, no. 3 (2011): 373-390.

Phiri, Isabel. 'President Frederick Chiluba and Zambia: Evangelicals and Democracy in a 'Christian Nation.'' In *Evangelical Christianity and Democracy in Africa*, edited by T.O. Ranger, 95- 129. Oxford: OUP, 2008.

Taylor, John V. and Dorothea Lehmann. *Christians of the Copperbelt: The Growth of the Church in Northern Rhodesia*. London: SCM Press, 1961.

Verstraelen-Gilhuis, Gerdien. *From Dutch Mission Church to Reformed Church in Zambia: The Scope for African Leadership and Initiative in the History of Zambian Mission Church*. Netherlands: Franeker, 1982.

Walls, Andrew. *The Missionary Movement in Christian History: Studies in the Transmission of Faith*. Maryknoll, NY: Orbis Books, 1996.

Weller, John and Jane Linden. *Mainstream Christianity to 1980 in Malawi, Zambia and Zimbabwe*. Gweru: Mambo Press, 1984.

(96) Christianity in Zimbabwe

Molly Manyonganise

Religion	Pop 2010	Pct 2010	Pop 2025	Pct 2025	Gr Pct 1970 2025
Christians	11,575,000	82.8%	17,113,000	88.3%	2.6%
Independents	5,900,000	42.2%	9,180,000	47.4%	3.0%
African initiated	5,761,000	41.2%			
Orthodox	5,100	0.0%	5,400	0.0%	0.4%
Protestants	3,293,000	23.6%	4,420,000	22.8%	2.0%
Adventist	951,000	6.8%			
Pentecostal	670,000	4.8%			
Methodist	389,000	2.8%			
Anglicans	381,000	2.7%			
Baptist	277,000	2.0%			
Lutheran	210,000	1.5%			
Reformed, Presbyterian	120,000	0.9%			
Salvationist (Salvation Army)	101,000	0.7%			
Roman Catholics	1,743,000	12.5%	2,600,000	13.4%	2.7%
Pentecostals/Charismatics	6,275,000	44.9%	8,000,000	41.3%	1.6%
Evangelicals	1,055,000	7.5%	1,486,000	7.7%	2.3%
adherents of traditional African religions	2,074,000	14.8%	1,800,000	9.3%	-0.9%
Muslims	95,800	0.7%	140,000	0.7%	2.6%
Baha'is	41,500	0.3%	54,000	0.3%	1.8%
Hindus	19,400	0.1%	20,000	0.1%	0.2%
Jews	12,200	0.1%	12,000	0.1%	-0.1%
adherents of new religious movements	1,700	0.0%	1,700	0.0%	0.0%
Spiritists	600	0.0%	600	0.0%	0.1%
Chinese folk-religionists	420	0.0%	440	0.0%	0.3%
Buddhists	200	0.0%	200	0.0%	0.1%
people professing no religion	153,000	1.1%	228,000	1.2%	2.7%
Total population	**13,974,000**	**100.0%**	**19,370,000**	**100.0%**	**2.2%**

Source: Centre for the Study of World Christianity (CSGC), Boston, Gordon-Conwell TS

Introduction

This chapter looks at Christianity in Zimbabwe. The purpose of such an endeavour is to bring out how Christianity came to Zimbabwe and how it has developed over time. However, it should be noted that doing this is a challenging task because the history of Christianity in Africa in general is complex. The reason is that Christianity did not arrive in Africa in general, or in Zimbabwe in particular, as a uniform entity, as it was clothed in different attire, namely, Catholicism and Protestantism. Over the years, it has taken on new forms and it continues to be regenerated.

The Arrival of Christianity in Zimbabwe

The arrival of Christianity in Zimbabwe dates back to the sixteenth century when Goncalo da Silveira arrived at the Mutapa court. He was a Jesuit. Various reasons have been put forward to explain why Silveira was sent to Mutapa State. For instance, Silveira's coming there needs to be understood in the broader context of the history of Portuguese settlement in Southern Africa from 1505 to 1560. The main purpose for this settlement was for trade in gold and ivory. Their other intention was to expel the Arabs who were already in control of that trade. It is in this context that a mission was undertaken to Mutapa State with the sole aim of converting its Emperor. His conversion was crucial to the Portuguese since they believed that once he was a Christian, he would influence his people to become Christians too. Apart from the above, Silveira's mission was perceived as one that would benefit both Portugal and the Church of Rome. For example, Portugal would have a monopoly over trade in the Eastern Coast and its enemies (especially the Arabs) would have suffered.[1] On the other hand, the Roman Catholic Church would have widened its missionary horizons. From Ukah's perspective, 'the Portuguese missionaries resorted to a 'church-state' model of planting Christianity by targeting local chiefs and hoping that, once these chiefs had converted, their people would follow suit.'[2] What is evident from the above analysis is that, from the outset, when Christianity came to Zimbabwe, it was closely linked with politics. However, Silveira's activities were short-lived as he was murdered at the command of the King after Arab traders had influenced him to turn against Silveira. After his death, a new Order of Catholics was sent to the Mutapa court.

Catholics of the Dominican Order arrived at the Mutapa Court in the seventeenth century. These came together with a Portuguese battalion which was dispatched by the Portuguese government to avenge Goncalo da Silveira's death. According to Verstraelen, the Portuguese missionaries were withdrawn in 1667 because of political upheavals.[3] The major successes of the Catholic missionaries during this period were that they were able to build some churches in Manyika (Manicaland) and Mazowe[4] at places such as Masapa, Dambarare, Ruhanje and Bukutu.[5] However, most scholars are generally agreed that, by the time they had withdrawn from Mutapa State, the Portuguese missionaries had failed to make a visible mark on the local inhabitants in terms of spreading Christianity. Gundani argues that, apart from the churches they built, 'there is nothing to suggest the growth of what could possibly be called a church beyond small

---

[1] S.I.G. Mudenge, *Christian Education at the Mutapa Court: A Portuguese Strategy to Influence Events in the Empire of Munhumutapa* (Harare: Zimbabwe Publishing House, 1986), 5.

[2] A. Ukah, "African Pentecostalism: Features, Promises and Problems," *Institute of Ethnography and African studies,* Working Papers, No. 79 (2007): 3.

[3] F.J. Verstraelen, *Zimbabwean Realities and Christian Responses: Contemporary Aspects of Christianity in Zimbabwe* (Gweru: Mambo Press, 1998), 3.

[4] Verstraelen, *Zimbabwean Realities and Christian Responses,* 3.

[5] P.H Gundani, "Iberians and the African Clergy in Southern Africa," in *African Christianity: An African Story*, ed O.U. Kalu, 172-186 (New Jersey: Africa World Press, 2007), 153.

groups of Portuguese traders and settlers, their *mestizo* children, and the slaves that obeyed them'.[6] In the same vein, Matikiti argues that, 'although many Catholic churches were planted, they had all disappeared by the time Protestant missions arrived in the nineteenth century'.[7] The major reason for the failure has been given as the close identification of the missionaries with the Portuguese government. Furthermore, converting emperors had one problem in that it produced a popular religion while at the grassroots level the people were not converted. The fact that the rulers embraced Christianity did not make their subjects become Christians, as was expected by the Portuguese missionaries. The emperors themselves were not genuine Christians. They converted for political benefits, namely, to get help from Portuguese mercenaries. Furthermore, the Portuguese failed to realize how little real contact these Mutapa princes had with Christianity.[8] At the end of the day, no genuine Christians could be seen in the whole empire. A second attempt to Christianise Zimbabwe was to be seen in the nineteenth century.

Nineteenth-Century Mission Christianity in Zimbabwe

The nineteenth century marks the second phase of Christian mission in Africa in general, and Zimbabwe in particular. This was a result of the evangelical revival in Europe which started in the eighteenth century. The revival spilled over into foreign lands, leading to the establishment of missionary societies. The zeal for missionary work was stimulated by the combination of evangelicalism (living according to the gospel) with evangelism (preaching the gospel). This kind of Christianity has been referred to as 'mission' or 'missionary' Christianity. In the first twenty years of colonialism, twenty different missionary groups established themselves in Zimbabwe. In order for these churches to avoid competing for converts, the Southern Rhodesia Missionary Conference was held in 1903 with the aim of defining spheres of influence for each church so that each denomination would be restricted to one area within the country for evangelism. These boundaries were blurred after Zimbabwe's independence such that mainline church missionaries were free to establish their churches across the country. While several Christian missions were established in Zimbabwe during this time, this chapter restricts itself to looking at those it considers to be the major ones.

In the nineteenth century, two forms of missionary Christianity were introduced in Zimbabwe, namely, Catholicism and Protestantism. After its failure in the sixteenth century, Catholicism was reintroduced in Zimbabwe in 1879 when the Jesuits arrived in Matabeleland. They found the London Missionary Society (LMS) already in the area. The LMS introduced the Jesuits to Lobengula who valued them only as technicians and refused them permission to establish a mission station. In 1885, the Jesuits withdrew from Matabeleland only to come back in 1890 with the Pioneer Column. This saw the introduction of Catholicism in Mashonaland and Manicaland.

Apart from Catholicism, Protestant Christianity was also introduced in Zimbabwe in the nineteenth century. The LMS was the first to engage in missionary work in Matabeleland in 1859. Through the influence of Robert Moffat, Mzilikazi granted the Society permission to build a mission station at Inyati with a second mission station established in 1870 at Hope Fountain. The LMS and the Catholics encountered various challenges in Matabeleland which led to the failure of their mission endeavours.

Another form of Protestant Christianity to come to Zimbabwe in the nineteenth century is Methodism. Methodism came in two forms, specifically Wesleyan Methodists from Europe in 1891 and the United Methodists from North America in 1897. While Wesleyan Methodists were dominant in Mashonaland, the

---

[6] Gundani, "Iberians and the African Clergy in Southern Africa," 156.

[7] R. Matikiti, *Christian Theological Perspectives on Political Violence in Zimbabwe: The Case of the United Church of Christ in Zimbabwe*. PhD Thesis. University of Zimbabwe, 2012, 119.

[8] H. Bhila, "Trade and Early Missionaries in Southern Zambezia," in Christianity South of the Zambezi, Vol. 2, ed M.F.C. Bourdillon, 25-42 (Gweru: Mambo Press, 1977), 31.

United Methodists were prominent in Manicaland. Also prominent in both Manicaland and Mashonaland was the Anglican Church whose bishop, George Knight-Bruce, was granted permission to tour Mashonaland by Lobengula in 1888. Mission stations were later to be established in Mashonaland and Manicaland through his efforts and those of other Anglican missionaries. Other churches to establish mission stations in Zimbabwe were the Dutch Reformed Church (1891), the Salvation Army (1891), the American Board of Commissioners for Foreign Missions (ABCFM), now known as the United Church of Christ (UCCZ) (1893), Seventh Day Adventists, and the Church of Sweden (1902), among others. As mission Christianity was slowly taking root in Zimbabwe, another form of Christianity, Pentecostalism, was also introduced in Zimbabwe.

The Pentecostal phenomenon in Zimbabwe dates back to the pre-Independence era. Pentecostal churches like the Apostolic Faith Mission in Zimbabwe (AFM), Zimbabwe Assemblies of God Africa (ZAOGA) and many others were formed at that time. For years, Pentecostals were viewed as a weird form of Christianity and were always looked down upon. They were usually referred to as *chechi dzemweya* (churches of the spirit) or *chechi dzevanochema* (churches of those that cry). However, in the current epoch, Pentecostalism has been fast emerging as a dominant brand of Christianity in Zimbabwe. Togarasei says that Christian historians are now agreed that Pentecostalism was introduced in Zimbabwe in 1915 by Zacharias Manamela who was a migrant worker from South Africa and first preached in Shurugwi.[9] However, there are other accounts which point to Paul Kruger as having been instrumental in bringing the Apostolic Faith Church to Zimbabwe. As a result, in its formative stages, AFM was referred to as *Chechi yekwa Kruger* (Kruger's Church). Pentecostal churches continue to be formed in Zimbabwe with some becoming prominent while others remain on the margins. While some secede from other Pentecostal churches, others are coming out of Protestant churches.

In recent years, there has emerged in Zimbabwe a typically new Pentecostal phenomenon which I have termed 'Prophetic Pentecostalism'. Some scholars would classify these as New Pentecostal Churches (NPCs). Prophetic Pentecostalism in this chapter refers to a new form of Christianity currently sweeping across Zimbabwe which has its anchor in prophecy. Basing its argument on Joel 2:28, this kind of Pentecostalism believes that God is still speaking to his people today. Founders of these churches allege that traditional Pentecostalism stifled the voices of the prophets. Examples of these churches are United Family International Church (UFIC) which was founded in 2010 by Emmanuel Makandiwa who broke away from AFM in Zimbabwe, Spirit Embassy – founded by Uebert Angel (2007), Kingdom Embassy – founded by Passion Java, and Walter Magaya's Prophetic Healing and Deliverance (PHD) Ministries, also breaking away from AFM in 2012. Most of the 'prophetic' Pentecostal churches (PPCs) emerged during Zimbabwe's socio-economic and political crises. 'Prophets' Makandiwa, Angel, Java, Magaya and many others have convinced their followers that they can predict their future as well as diagnose the causes of their misfortune. We see in their activities a close affinity with the African Initiated Churches, or *mapositori*[10] as they are called in Zimbabwe, in that, while the classical Pentecostals rejected the foretelling and forthtelling by white-garmented churches in Zimbabwe by viewing it as synonymous with the traditional practice of divination, these newly-formed churches have embraced the practice. They have also made sensational claims of performing miracles of raining gold and money. Also central to their teachings is the doctrine of fatherhood. This doctrine stipulates that each of them should submit to a spiritual father.[11] In this case, Makandiwa and Angel have Ghanaian Victor Kusi Boateng as their spiritual father; Angel is

---

[9] Lovemore Togarasei, *The History of Pentecostal Christianity in Zimbabwe* (forthcoming).

[10] Mapositori is a term that was originally used to describe members of white garmented churches in Zimbabwe. Currently, it is loosely used to refer to members of all African Independent Churches including Zionists.

[11] Ezra Chitando, Molly Manyonganise, and Obert B. Mlambo, "Young, Male and Polished: Masculinities, Generational Shifts and Pentecostal Prophets in Zimbabwe," in *Prophets, Profits and the Bible in Zimbabwe*, ed. E. Chitando, M.R. Gunda and J Kugler, 153-170 (Bamberg: University of Bamberg Press, 2013), 161.

the spiritual father to Java while Magaya's spiritual father is the famous Nigerian 'prophet' T.B. Joshua. While the use of the term 'father' is not new in Christian churches, its use in these PPCs has taken on new forms. For Chitando, Manyonganise and Mlambo, this doctrine needs to be understood within the wider contestations in masculinities as the prophets seek domination in terms of both space and power.[12]

Closely linked to Pentecostalism are African Initiated Churches (AICs). Zimbabwe has witnessed a phenomenal growth of these churches. Daneel has produced a detailed account of the origins and activities of AICs in Zimbabwe in his various volumes on the subject (Daneel 1971, 1976, 1987 and 1988). In Zimbabwe, African Independent Churches continue to emerge, owing largely to leadership wrangles. In recent years, the economic challenges that have bedevilled the country have given rise to the formation of these churches as disgruntled members who feel deprived seek to form their churches in which they are able to control the financial activities. Most open spaces in Zimbabwe's urban areas have been turned into sacred shrines where the newly-formed AICs meet. It is really difficult to maintain a register of these churches because of the rate at which they are sprouting. While the cracks in the churches have been blamed largely on leadership wrangles, in recent years there has been a lot of political influence which has caused turmoil.

The Ecumenical Movement in Zimbabwe

Churches in Zimbabwe have sought collaboration through a number of umbrella bodies. These are the Zimbabwe Council of Churches (ZCC) – formed in 1964, the Zimbabwe Catholic Bishops' Conference (ZCBC) which emerged in 1969, the Evangelical Fellowship of Zimbabwe (EFZ) – formed in 1962, and the Union for the Development of Apostolic Churches (UDACIZA) – formed in 1993, which represents AICs. From these ecumenical bodies, the Heads of Christian Denominations was formed, through which the church in Zimbabwe has been able to engage in the socio-political life of the country. For example, in pre-independent Zimbabwe, the ZCC and the ZCBC (formerly RCBC) actively challenged the colonial government to cease its oppressive tendencies against black people. During the liberation struggle, Christian bodies, especially the ZCBC through the Catholic Commission for Justice and Peace, spoke against the excesses of the war.

After Independence, the ecumenical bodies led their respective churches to support the government in most of its developmental projects. The concentration on development led the church to ignore the flaws of the black government. In other words, the church muted its prophetic voice. When people's lives began deteriorating due to the adoption of the Economic Structural Adjustment Programme (ESAP) in 1991 at the recommendation of the International Monetary Fund (IMF), as well as the general dictatorial tendencies of the ZANU PF government, the church sought to speak out. After the 2000 land reform programme, the church condemned the violence that ensued. From this period, we have witnessed the active participation of the church in politics. The ecumenical bodies have issued individual as well as joint pastoral statements directed at those in political power. The most notable of the joint pastoral statements were both published in 2006: *A Call to Conscience* as well as the National Vision Discussion Document (NVDD), entitled *The Zimbabwe We Want: Towards a National Vision for Zimbabwe: A Discussion Document*. The church was breaking its silence and had chosen to speak on behalf of the voiceless. Apart from speaking, the church bodies also engaged in voter education, gender justice programmes, election monitoring, advocacy, social welfare, national healing and reconciliation, among other programmes.

[12] Chitando, "Young, Male and Polished," 161.

Conclusion

This chapter has highlighted the development of Christianity in Zimbabwe from the sixteenth century to the present day. It has discussed the major types of Christianity in Zimbabwe, namely, missionary Christianity and Pentecostalism, as well as AICs. Despite their differences, the chapter has shown how, through the ecumenical movement in Zimbabwe, these churches are coming together to speak with one voice against the oppressive tendencies of the politicians as well as to respond to other socio-economic challenges that are bedevilling Zimbabwe.

Bibliography

Baur, J. *2000 Years of Christianity in Africa: An African Church History*, second edition. Nairobi: Paulines Publications, 1994.

Bourdillon, M.F.C., ed. *Christianity South of the Zambezi,* second edition. Gweru: Mambo Press, 1977.

Copplestone, J.T. *History of Methodist Missions*. New York: The Board of Global Ministries, 1973.

Dachs, S.A., ed. *Christianity South of the Zambezi*, Vol.1. Gweru: Mambo Press, 1973.

Daneel, I. *Quest for Belonging: Introduction to a Study of African Independent Churches.* Gweru: Mambo Press, 1987.

Mudenge, S.I.G. *Christian Education at the Mutapa Court: A Portuguese Strategy to Influence Events in the Empire of Munhumutapa.* Harare: Zimbabwe Publishing House, 1986.

Soderstrom, H. *God Gave Growth: The History of the Lutheran Church in Zimbabwe, 1903-1980*. Gweru: Mambo Press, 1984.

Zvobgo, C.J.M. *A History of Christian Missions in Zimbabwe, 1890-1939*. Gweru: Mambo Press, 1996.

Part V

African Christianity and Ecumenism

(97) History of African Ecumenism and Inter-Church Co-operation

James Amanze

Introduction

This chapter gives an account of how the ecumenical movement began in Africa from 1900 to the present day. It argues that the missionary factor was the bedrock of ecumenism as a result of the conflict that emerged among the missionary bodies and the need to achieve co-operation and unity among them for the advancement of the gospel in Africa. It discusses the various ecumenical initiatives that were carried out by churches in Africa which culminated in the creation of national Christian councils and various regional ecumenical bodies which have been instrumental in fostering unity among the Christian churches and people of other faiths. The chapter also examines the various achievements that the ecumenical movement has made in Africa, the challenges that it faces today, and it looks into the future of African ecumenism.

The Missionary Factor as the Bedrock of Ecumenism

Africa is a home to numerous religions, which today compete with one another for membership. The religions that make headlines are Christianity and Islam but, over and above these, there are other religions such as Hinduism, Bahai, Buddhism, Judaism, Sikhism and, in recent years, there is a great deal of talk about Satanism. Underlying all these religions are African Traditional Religions which are considered as the indigenous religions of Africa whose presence goes back to time immemorial. The relationship between these religions has over the centuries been one of conflict rather than co-operation. The nineteenth century was a great period of Christian expansion in Africa whereby a number of missionary societies under the inspiration of their mother churches overseas planted churches practically everywhere on the continent. The dilemma, however, is that the church came to Africa already divided into different denominations, bearing labels such as Roman Catholic, Anglican, Methodist, Lutheran, Seventh Day Adventist, Pentecostal, Charismatic, and then African Independent Churches. Colonialism exacerbated these divisions and made the life of the African people unbearable. This is the context in which the ecumenical movement was born across Africa.

Gabriel Setiloane, in 'The ecumenical movement in Africa: From mission to moratorium', has noted that the ecumenical movement and co-operation in Africa has its roots in the missionary factor. According to Setiloane, at the beginning of the missionary era there was mutual assistance among the missionaries born out of solidarity in the face of a strange and unfriendly environment. Writing about missionary work in Southern Africa, Setiloane has noted that it was customary for missionaries, of whatever nationality, who went north of the Orange River to make their way first to Kuruman where Robert Moffat of the London Missionary Society was based in order to receive guidance as to which of the tribes would accept them and their services.[1] This seems to have been the case in a number of African countries.

Unfortunately, with the passing of time, this co-operation turned into conflict as the missionaries competed for converts and engaged in 'empire-building'. These conflicts led to divisions in the mission field not only among the missionaries themselves but also among their converts. In some instances, such

---

[1] Gabriel Setiloane, 'The Ecumenical Movement in Africa: From Mission Church to Moratorium', in *Resistance and Hope: South African Essays in Honour of Beyers Naudé,* eds. Charles Villa-Vicencio and John de Gruchy. (Grand Rapids, MI: Eerdmans, 1985), 137.

conflicts led to open war between Christian communities, as was the case in Uganda where Anglicans and Roman Catholics fought running battles at Namirembe, Kampala, at the beginning of the missionary work there.[2] Interestingly, it was these missiological conflicts among Christian denominations that created the need for ecumenical dialogue. Thus mission and ecumenism are two sides of the same coin. Soon the missionaries realised that, if *Missio Dei* were to succeed in Africa, it required reconciliation, unity and co-operation among its bearers. Andrew R. H. Thompson, in 'Communities of the Spirit: The Missiology of Roland Allen in the Twenty-first Century', has noted that one of the most fundamental points of *Missio Dei* is that the witnessing community should display values of reconciliation, peacefulness and egalitarianism in the midst of a world that undermined or rejected those values. This is because the mission of the church is the proclamation of God's reconciling mission in the lives of people and communities everywhere. It takes place wherever the life and ministry of the church constitute a genuine testimony to the kind of reconciled, loving relationships that God desires for his creation.[3] It is in this respect that ecumenism cannot be conceived outside the mission of the church in Africa.

The Genesis of African Ecumenism and the Creation of National Christian Councils

Numerous essays and books have been written which chronicle the genesis of co-operation and unity in African Christianity, and yet it is important to refresh our memories here. Jamie Lynn Hollis, in 'Ecumenism: Moving towards multi-faceted global conversion', has noted that 'the word ecumenical not only means working across denominational divides… but also includes the concept of working together, united across other divides that exist in the global church… The visibly united church must, through the grace of God, work across and through not only denominations but also cultures, languages, contexts, political lines, economic divides, disciplines, strengths, weaknesses and quirks'.[4] In this regard, ecumenical co-operation and unity mean that the whole church is called to take the whole gospel to the whole world.[5]

It is important to note that, though historically the beginning of the modern ecumenical movement is traced back to the 1910 Edinburgh Conference, there had been other initiatives long before that date.[6] It has been noted above that the ecumenical movement was triggered by divisions occurring between missionaries and agencies working in the same neighbourhood, country and region from different denominational backgrounds. These divisions severely undermined the credibility of that which they wanted to witness, that is, the love of God in Christ for all humanity. Although such conflicts were addressed at the local, national and regional levels through comity agreements, it was still felt that there was a need for a global partnership in Christian mission.[7] It was this need that called for the holding of the Edinburgh Conference in 1910.

In *A History of the Ecumenical Movement in Africa*,[8] the author has indicated that, in Africa as a whole, attempts to promote co-operation and unity in African Christianity predates the 1910 Edinburgh Conference, in which case it could be argued that the African continent was both the precursor and catalyst of ecumenical efforts initiated elsewhere. In this regard, African Christianity contributed significantly towards the efforts of uniting global Christianity. This is supported by events in the mission field in Africa

---

[2] James N. Amanze, *A History of the Ecumenical Movement in Africa* (Gaborone: Pula Press, 1998), 124-126, where the conflict between Roman Catholics and Anglicans in Uganda led to a civil war.

[3] Andrew R. H. Thompson, 'Communities of the Spirit: The Missiology of Roland Allen in the Twenty-first Century', in *Edinburgh 2010: Youth Perspectives,* ed. Kirk Sandvig (Pasadena, CA: William Carey, 2010), 16.

[4] Jamie Hollis, 'Ecumenism: Moving Toward a Multi-Faceted Global Conversation', in *Edinburgh 2010: Youth Perspectives*, ed. Kirk Sandvig (Pasadena, CA: William Carey, 2010), 88.

[5] Hollis, 'Ecumenism', 88.

[6] Amanze, *A History of the Ecumenical Movement*, 154.

[7] Hollis, 'Ecumenism', 88.

[8] Amanze, *A History of the Ecumenical Movement,* where this has been discussed in detail.

for, at the very beginning of the twentieth century, attempts at church unity were under way in Malawi (1900), Congo (1902), South Africa (1904), Kenya (1908), Tanzania (1911), Nigeria (1911), Sierra Leone (1912) and Zambia (1914) to name but a few countries.[9] Later, the ecumenical movement accelerated under the inspiration of ecumenical institutions that were put in place as a result of the 1910 Edinburgh Conference such as the International Missionary Council, Life and Work, and Mission and Order. Their activities, which ultimately led to the formation of the World Council of Churches on 23rd August 1948, inspired African church leaders to form National Christian Councils that have become the backbone of the ecumenical movement in African Christianity today.

It appears that the African people have had no serious difficulties in embracing ecumenical co-operation compared with their counterparts in Europe and America. Setiloane has indicated that signs of ecumenical co-operation, tolerance, mutual acceptance and co-operation between churches are more evident in African than elsewhere in the world. In Africa, denominational barriers are criss-crossed with amazing ease, especially at the congregational level.[10] This is evidenced by the fact that in many southern African cities, towns and villages, churches have established fraternal organisations of ministers and pastors whose membership is open to all denominations. This enables different member churches to discuss practical issues affecting their lives and the opportunity to pray together for church unity during which pulpit exchange is also practised. According to Setiloane, this and other forces at work in the African soul continue to reduce the divided nature of the church as it came from abroad.[11] There are indications that the African people are easily able to relate with one another on ecumenical issues, especially at the grassroots level because of their philosophy of humanity variously known as *Ubuntu, umunthu* or *botho*. This is characterised by strong human ties. Human beings are not considered as islands but as a network of people bound together by their Master Creator. On this matter, D.G.S. M'Timkulu, cited by Setiloane, puts it succinctly:

> The social ties binding the African Christian to his extended family and clan have always been stronger than the forces of separation that arise from membership in different denominations. The important family occasions like births, marriages, funerals and clan festivals bring together in one place of worship relatives with different confessional backgrounds. On these occasions, they not only share in common acts of worship with gay disregard of denominational differences, but they also take part in symbolic acts of family and clan unity that have their roots in the traditional past.[12]

It will be seen from the above that the people of Africa are open to ecumenical co-operation despite the difficulties created by their mother churches in Europe and America. Various efforts made by the local churches to achieve church unity have quite often been aborted because of opposition from the mother churches because of the bitterness of separation that took place in ecclesiological circles as a result of the sixteenth-century Protestant Reformation.

Towards the Formation of Continent-wide Ecumenical Organisations

One of the most interesting aspects of African ecumenism is that, from its humble beginnings in the 1900s, it eventually lead to the formation of continent-wide ecumenical organisations that brought African ecumenism out of the closet to an international level, giving it not only a specific shape but also some impetus unprecedented in the history of Christianity in Africa. Chief among these are the All Africa

[9] Amanze, *A History of the Ecumenical Movement* .
[10] Setiloane, 'The Ecumenical Movement in Africa', 246.
[11] Setiloane, 'The Ecumenical Movement in Africa', 246.
[12] Setiloane, 'The Ecumenical Eovement in Africa', 147.

Conference of Churches (1963), the Association of Evangelicals of Africa and Madagascar (AEAM – 1966), the Symposium of Episcopal Conferences of Africa and Madagascar (SECAM), and the Organisation of African Independent Churches (OAICs – 1982).[13]

Yemba has indicated that the emergence of these pan-African ecumenical organizations changed the configuration of the ecumenical movement in order to meet the challenges the African world faces today.[14] Since space does not allow us to discuss all the pan-African ecumenical organisations noted above, this section of the chapter will focus on the role played by the All Africa Conference of Churches (AACC), which is a fellowship of 169 national churches in 39 African countries, enjoying a congregational membership of more than 120 million Christians.[15] The inauguration of the AACC on 20th April 1963 under the theme 'Freedom and unity in Christ' ushered in a new era in African ecumenism. At the time of its inception, there was a general euphoria that its formation signalled the end of an era characterized by denominationalism which was seen as a cancerous destroyer of genuine Christianity, and the beginning of an authentic African Christian era in which different denominations, and the different churches and missions established in Africa were coming to a close.[16] M'Timkulu described it as 'undoubtedly the single most historic event that has taken place within the life of the churches in Africa during the twentieth century'.[17]

The Achievements of the Ecumenical Movement in Africa

The original dream of the ecumenical movement in Africa was the quest for 'organic church unity'. To this end, various attempts were made by the churches in Southern, Central, East and West Africa to form a 'United Church of Africa'. However, such attempts ended in utter failure. It is true that in 1964 unity of some kind among the churches was achieved in Zambia between the Methodists, the Paris Evangelical Missionaries, the Baptists and the United Church of Canada Mission to the Copperbelt, which formed the 'United Church of Zambia', but such attempts proved unsuccessful in other parts of Africa because of resistance from mother churches.[18] At present, this dream seems unattainable since many churches seem to be going back to denominationalism in order to protect their identity and ensure their survival.

Having said this, it should however be noted that not everything has been lost. It has been observed, for example, that over the years the church in Africa has acted as a 'watchman' in the midst of the nations, prophetically witnessing to the divine demands for truth, justice, peace and fighting to end all forms of oppression, discrimination, injustice and corruption.[19] In this regard, the ecumenical movement in Africa has played a crucial role in the development of the African people spiritually, politically, economically and culturally. At the time of the inauguration of the AACC, the theme of the first Assembly was similar to that adopted later in the same year by the Organisation of African Unity (now the African Union) which was 'Unity and Freedom'. What was even more interesting is that, at the same time, the first Pan-African Youth Conference held its meeting under the theme 'Freedom under the Cross'. These themes were not a mere coincidence but they encapsulated in a strategic way the agenda and vision of the churches and the

[13] https://www.oikoumene.org/resources/documents/faith-and-order (accessed 21 May, 2014).
[14] https://www.oikoumene.org/resources/documents/faith-and-order (accessed 21 May, 2014).
[15] Nicolas Otieno. *For a New Africa: With Hope and Dignity* (Geneva: WCC Publications, 2004), 7.
[16] Jesse .N. K. Mugambi, 'Some lessons from a century of Ecumenism in Africa', in *Visions of Authenticity: The Assemblies of the All Africa Conference of Churches 1963-1992,* ed. Efiong Utuk, (Nairobi: AACC, 1997), 31.
[17] Andrea Karamaga, 'General Secretary's Report to the 10th General Assembly', Kampala, 4th June 2013, 12.
[18] Setiloane, 'The Ecumenical Movement in Africa', 146.
[19] Michael Kinnamon and Brian E. Cope, *An Anthology of Key Texts and Voices* (Geneva: WCC Publications, 1997), 244.

continent as a whole. They were aimed at uniting and liberating the continent of Africa from the thrall of colonialism. Such ecumenical action led to the liberation of most African countries.[20]

One of the most tangible examples of how the ecumenical movement contributed towards the liberation of the African people was the fight against apartheid in South Africa. Agnes Abuom, in 'Africa and the ecumenical movement', has noted that one of the achievements of the ecumenical movement in Africa was indeed the fall of apartheid in South Africa. According to Abuom, the establishment by the WCC of its Programme to Combat Racism in South Africa helped the world to see the oppression of Africa with new eyes and named apartheid for what it was. She writes:

> The moral and ethical claims of solidarity were not just informed by the human rights regime but by the naming of apartheid as a sin against God and humanity. Nelson Mandela affirmed this theological thinking during his profound message to the World Council of Churches Assembly held in Harare in December 1998.[21]

Abuom has noted that freedom and independence in South Africa was, in part, the result of the acts of solidarity between the global moral community and the local ecumenical movement.[22] In this regard, in the context of South Africa, one of the achievements of the ecumenical movement was the Kairos Document which was written by an ecumenical group of theologians at the height of apartheid in 1985. The document argued that the moment of truth (*kairos*) had come when the churches were challenged by God to take a decisive action to liberate its people. What it is important to note is that the document generated a great deal of discussion and excitement not only in South Africa but also in other parts of the world. It assisted the oppressed South African community to fight for its freedom by arguing that true reconciliation and genuine peace cannot be achieved without justice.[23]

The ecumenical movement in Africa has also been concerned with issues of peace and has thus been involved in peace-making processes. Karamaga has observed that the African context has always been characterised by volatility, going back to colonial times and the movement for independence that followed. Of particular interest in this regard were the struggles for self-determination in many parts of Africa. But even after independence, a number of African countries faced internal upheavals that required political action to achieve peace. As a result, issues of conflict resolution have been at the top of the ecumenical movement's agenda. For example, since its formation, the AACC has been engaged in promoting peace in Africa which has been recognised even by non-Christian organisations. A good example was the request that was made by the government of the Sudan, asking the AACC to facilitate negotiations with the freedom fighters in the South that culminated in the signing of the peace agreement in 1972 which allowed Sudan to enjoy peace for eight years before war broke again. According to Karamaga, the AACC ministry of mediation and peace-making has been experienced in all parts of Africa throughout its fifty years of existence.[24] Peace-making interventions in places where there has been political conflict in Africa have also been made by National Christian Councils.[25]

One of the issues that has bedevilled the people of Africa is poverty. It is considered one of the factors that has hampered the economic growth and development of Africa. The majority of the African people

---

[20] All Africa Conference of Churches: Message of the Golden Jubilee Assembly, Kampala, Uganda, 3rd-9th June 2013, 1.

[21] Agnes Abuom, 'Africa and the Ecumenical Movement.' In *For a New Africa: With Hope and Dignity*, ed. Nicholas Otieno, (Geneva: WCC, 2004), 20.

[22] Abuom, 'Africa and the Ecumenical Movement', 21.

[23] Kinnamon and Cope, *An Anthology*, 245.

[24] Karamaga, 'General Secretary's Report', 22.

[25] For example, the Botswana Council of Churches' intervention and peace-making efforts when conflict broke out between Botswana and Namibia over Sedudu Island. See James N. Amanze, *Ecumenism in Botswana: The story of the Botswana Christian Council* (Gaborone: Pula Press, 2006).

live in absolute poverty. As recently as 2009, out of 24 nations identified as having low human development, 22 of them were said to be in Africa. Valentine Mokiwa, at the 10th General Assembly of the AACC which was held in Kampala in June 2013, described the situation as 'disheartening, paining, shameful and unbecoming'.[26] The ecumenical movement in Africa has addressed this problem by opting to take action on behalf of the poor. During the 10th General Assembly, Mokiwa conscientised the people by saying that 'the church cannot stay indifferent on this matter. The church must decide to take sides with those whose rights are stolen, the underprivileged and the oppressed'.[27] In this regard, a number of National Christian Councils and other ecumenical organisations, throughout the ecumenical movement, have taken initiatives to uplift the life of the poor by using different strategies aimed at the eradication of poverty.

With this in mind, the ecumenical movement in the 21st century has focused on supporting African debt campaign initiatives such as Africa Jubilee 2000. National campaigns against debt and structural adjustment programmes culminated into a pan-African consultation in Dakar, Senegal, in December 2000. This consultation came up with a declaration entitled 'Africa: From resistance to alternatives'. It advocated a total and unconditional cancellation of all African debt. This demand was based on the undisputed economic, social, moral, legal and historical arguments that the debt was fundamentally a human, social and political problem and not a financial or technical issue, as the World Bank and the IMF attempted to demonstrate.[28]

Mention should also be made here of the ecumenical efforts in Africa to fight against HIV and AIDS. This pandemic has been considered by the ecumenical movement as one of the most horrifying forms of violence on the African continent. In this vein, throughout the HIV and AIDS pandemic period, ecumenical organisations, in co-operation with the WCC, equipped and accompanied the African churches in their struggle against this scourge. The WCC, for one, facilitated a number of initiatives in different churches and institutions which helped them to educate the masses regarding the cause of HIV and AIDS and how to prevent the condition since there was no cure. Armed with this knowledge and with the help of anti-retroviral drugs, a number of people in Africa today have managed to prolong their lives.

Theologically, the ecumenical movement spearheaded by the AACC has taken seriously the issue of peaceful co-existence between Christians and Muslims on the continent. Interfaith dialogue between these two faiths has been tackled earnestly in recent years in close collaboration with the programme for Christian-Muslim relations in Africa (PROCUMURA).29

Challenges Facing African Ecumenism Today

Despite the fact that many gains have been made by the ecumenical movement in the spiritual, social, economic and political spheres, there are still a number of challenges that people in Africa face today. Such challenges have been succinctly captured by the message of the Golden Jubilee Assembly in Kampala in the following words:

> We still have situations of poor governance, some countries still have bad and autocratic leadership, corruption is still a major obstacle to development in some African countries, there is misuse of state resources by some leadership at the expense of the poor, religious conflicts, resource-based wars fanned by outside powers but promoted by greedy local leaders, the unethical and indiscriminate extraction of natural resources such as crude

[26] Address of the Most Rev. Valentine Mokiwa at the 10th General Assembly, Kampala, Uganda, 4th June 2013, 3.
[27] Address of the Most Rev. Valentine Mokiwa, 4.
[28] www.wcc-coe.org/wcc/africa/index-e.html (accessed 9 June, 2014).
[29] Karamaga, 'General Secretary's Report', 19.

> oil, minerals, timber... by multinational companies without real benefit to the citizens... the brain drain, xenophobia, homophobia, Afrophobia, climate injustice, food insecurity and many more.[30]

In addition to the challenges noted above, Yembahas observed that there was a degree of ecumenical lethargy in the churches of Africa, often because people were preoccupied with their own individual concerns rather than institutional survival and identity. Each church is defensive about its own identity.[31] This legacy, inherited from the colonial period, has kept countries and peoples of the former colonies bound to the countries and peoples of their respective civilpowers. This has become a serious obstacle towards achieving genuine ecumenism. It is important to note that many church denominations in Africa today tend to identify themselves with three commonwealth bodies: the anglophone, francophone and lusophone. The implication of this is that, since many Christian denominations are affiliated to these bodies, such an affiliation is an obstacle to the evolution of authentic African expressions of Christianity among the churches for fear that to deviate from the norms of their mother churches overseas will lead to reprisals and reprimands.[32] It has been observed though that while, in cultural and practical experience, African Catholics, Anglicans, Lutherans, Methodists and others have more in common with each other than with their counterparts in Europe and North America, the patterns of economic relationships that they have with them make it difficult for African ecumenism to evolve across confessional lines.[33]

Looking into the Future

The ecumenical movement in Africa has not only been looking into the past in order to correct the wrongs created by colonialism, ethnicity and other negative influences affecting African societies, but it has also been looking into the future. In this regard, reference should also be made to the ecumenical activities of the AACC as the epitome of African ecumenism. During the Golden Jubilee in Kampala in June 2013, the AACC pledged to continue fostering actions in collaboration with the African Union for the attainment of a continent which is more solidly integrated economically, politically and spiritually by committing itself to the preservation and maintenance of God's creation. As a forward-looking ecumenical organisation, the AACC pledged and committed itself to promote and consolidate ecumenical action in three areas, namely: (a) protecting human life by ensuring that no life is lost through war, hunger, disease and poor facilities for expectant mothers; (b) promotion and enhancement of human life by ensuring holistic growth for everyone by emphasising education, good living conditions, proper shelter and all that promotes abundant life for all; and finally (c) helping the African people to celebrate the fact that the centre of gravity of Christianity has shifted from the northern hemisphere to the southern, something that requires new theological reflection – in order to dispel ignorance, heretical teachings, and the proliferation of schisms within the body of Christ – and theological education that is Christocentric and pragmatic, informed by and expressed in African life and thought.[34]

As part of its efforts to prepare for the future, the ecumenical movement, of which the AACC is the most visible and representative ecumenical institution on the continent, saw the need to prepare the leadership of the growing church. To this end, the AACC has in recent years devoted time and space to equipping young theologians on the continent with leadership skills and theological knowledge. This led to the creation of the Theological Institute by the Theological Department of the AACC. Such institutes

[30] All Africa Conference of Churches: Message of the Golden Jubilee Assembly, 1.
[31] https://www.oikoumene.org/en/resources/documents/wcc-commissions/faith-and-order (accessed 21 May, 2014).
[32] Mugambi, 'Some lessons from a century of Ecumenism ', 18.
[33] Mugambi, 'Some lessons from a century of Ecumenism ', 18.
[34] All Africa Conference of Churches: Message of the Golden Jubilee Assembly, 2-3.

prepare young theologians for future leadership on the continent. Two such institutes were held in Maputo, Mozambique, in 2008 and Kampala, Uganda, in June 2013.

At the same time, in recent years the AACC decided to revitalise the network of theological associations in each sub-region namely: ATISCA, ATIEA, WAATI and ASTHEOL. This led to the foundation of the All Africa Academy of Theology and Religious Studies (AAATRS) in Nairobi in December 2012.

Conclusion

This chapter has discussed the ecumenical movement in Africa from the beginning of the 1900s to the present day. The religious background which gave rise to the ecumenical movement has been discussed. It has been noted that the ecumenical movement was a result of the conflicts that emerged in the mission field. Various attempts made by Africans to foster and enhance the ecumenical spirit have been discussed. The achievements that the ecumenical movement has brought to Africa have been noted. We conclude by noting that the ecumenical movement has been faced with a number of challenges that have prevented it from achieving organic church unity as the ultimate goal. Attempts have also been made to look into the future.

Bibliography

Abuom, Agnes, 'Africa and the Ecumenical Movement.' In *For a New Africa: With Hope and Dignity*, edited by Nicholas Otieno. Geneva: WCC, 2004.

All Africa Conference of Churches: Message of the Golden Jubilee Assembly, Kampala, Uganda, 3rd-9th June 2013.

Amanze, James N., *A History of the Ecumenical Movement in Africa.* Gaborone, Botswana: Pula Press, 1998.

Amanze, James N., *Ecumenism in Botswana: The story of the Botswana Christian Council.* Gaborone: Pula Press, 2006.

Karamaga, Andrea, 'General Secretary's Report to the 10th General Assembly', Kampala, 4th June 2013.

Kinnamon, Michael, and Cope, Brian E., *An Anthology of Key Texts and Voices.* Geneva: WCC Publications, 1997.

Mokiwa, Valentine, The 10th General Assembly, Kampala, Uganda, 4th June 2013.

Mugambi, Jesse K., 'Some Lessons from a century of Ecumenism in Africa.' In *Visions of Authenticity: The Assemblies of the All Africa Conference of Churches 1963-1992,* edited by Efiong Utuk,. Nairobi: AACC, 1997.

Setiloane, Gabriel, 'The Ecumenical Movement in Africa: From Mission Church to Moratorium.' In *Resistance and Hope: South African Essays in Honour of Beyers Naudé* edited by Charles Villa-Vicencio and John de Gruchy, 137-147. Grand Rapids, MI: Eerdmans, 1985.

Sandvig, Kirk (ed.), *Edinburgh 2010: Youth Perspectives.* Pasadena, CA: William Carey, 2010.

(98) ETHNICITY AND AFRICAN DENOMINATIONALISM – A CASE STUDY ON KENYA

Joseph Wandera

Introduction

This chapter analyzes Anglican discourses on ethnicity, mainly within the Anglican Church of Kenya but also in the larger region, especially Tanzania and Sudan. The chapter employs a critical discourse analysis in order to show that there is significant social differentiation within the Anglican Church of Kenya which revolves around perceptions of marginalization in the church. These discourses threaten cohesion within it, and thereby its identity and mission. The chapter presents key signifiers of ethnic-based tension in the church, focusing on the election of bishops, appointment of clergy and laity into positions and promotions into higher ranks within church ministry. Based on an analysis of the discourses, the chapter argues that there is an urgent need for intervention for the church to be more cohesive and true to its identity and mission. Although this chapter focuses on Kenya, with some reference to Anglicanism in Tanzania and Southern Sudan, the findings illuminate issues that have a particular resonance for the rest of the Anglican Church in Africa.

The issue of ethnicity has dominated the politics of democratization and nation-building in many African countries. In Kenya, there is a general perception among citizens that ethnic undercurrents play a major role for accessing job appointments in public services and other entitlements. Politicians and the common *wananchi* (citizens) in Kenya frequently lament about how negative ethnicity is affecting national development. The establishment of the National Cohesion and Integration Commission in Kenya points to this concern for more cohesion among Kenyans in order for sustainable development to be realized.[1]

There have been significant scholarly reflections on how ethnicity plays out in Kenyan politics, economics and other sectors of public life.[2] However, there is scanty extensive academic literature on how ethnicity plays out in church life.[3] Such lack of scholarly reflections on this question can be dangerous for various reasons: it can shift attention too far from the overall ethnic framework within which the African Anglican Church is working; it can encourage the blurring of relevant distinctions and differentiations within the Anglican community itself, and the accomplishments of Kenyan Anglicanism may be overvalued, while real challenges are downplayed or ignored.

This chapter discusses the existence of social differentiation within the Anglican Church of Kenya by analyzing a religious discourse. More specifically, the main research question is: how are Anglicans discussing negative ethnicity? What are they saying about it? What is the implication of Anglican discussions on ethnicity for cohesion within the church?

---

[1] Claire Elder, Susan Stigant and Jonas Claes, 'Elections and Violence in Kenya: Making prevention stick': www.usip.org/sites/default/files/PW101-Elections-and-Violent-Conflict-in-Kenya-Making-Prevention-Stick.pdf (accessed 28 May, 2015).

[2] See, for example, John Lonsdale, 'Moral Ethnicity and Political Tribalism', 131-150; Occasional Paper 11 (Roskilde, Denmark: Department of International Development Studies, Roskilde University, 1994) http://rossy.ruc.dk/ojs/index.php/ocpa/article/view/3608/1790 (accessed 28 May, 2015); Felicia Yieke, 'Ethnicity and Development in Kenya: Lessons from 2007', *Kenya Studies Review,* Vol. 3,no. 3, December (2011), 5-16.

[3] For an exception, see Douglas W. Waruta, 'Tribalism as a Moral Problem in Contemporary Africa', in *Moral and Ethical Issues in African Christianity*: Exploratory Essays in Moral Theology, eds. Jesse N.K. Mugambi and Anne Nasimiyu-Wasike, 119-136 (Nairobi: Initiatives Publishers, 1992), 112-30.

The main approach in religious studies has been to study religion as a system of symbols that exists independently of actors, thus *sui generis*.[4] However, in recent times, scholars of religion are increasingly paying attention to individual actors, or to a significant extent, the dialectical relation between systems and actors.[5] In this contribution, I focus on individual religious actors within a discourse. The main objective is to gain insight into the relationship between religious discourse and (the lack of) social cohesion. Based on analysis of the discussion about negative ethnicity, I argue that the discourse on ethnicity in the Anglican Church rotates round key themes such as concerns about marginalization in Church leadership and perceived lack of access to material development and information. These discourses lend themselves to considerable fragmentation of the faithful within the Anglican Church along ethnic lines. The chapter concludes by advocating an immediate response to these inequalities, real or perceived, in order to establish a more cohesive Anglican Church that can effectively fulfil its mission.

The method used in this chapter is analyzing a religious discourse. The aim is to acquire insight into the symbolic power of language as a precondition of explaining existing social differentiation. The main premise is that the way individuals speak about others creates and recreates their own social reality and how they view others. In other words, the constitution of society comes within the articulation of differences, which is given generalized symbolic meaning, though only within specific symbolic systems. In that sense, discourse (language) is a form of social practice and an agent of social transformation.

I use Norman Fairclough's critical discourse analysis by gathering data through focus discussion groups involving staff and students of the Faculty of Theology, St Paul's University, Kenya.[6] All the student participants chosen randomly were at varying stages of their Bachelor of Divinity studies. Most of the respondents were Kenyans. However, three of the participants were non-Kenyans, two Southern Sudanese and one Tanzanian. The majority of the participants were male, with only two females. All except two in the focus groups were ordained ministers. One was a suffragan bishop. There were two lay participants, both women. To supplement data gathered from focus group discussions, I also interviewed individually lecturers in the faculty of theology. In addition to primary data gathered through focus group discussions and interviews, this chapter makes use of secondary data from two biographies of Kenyan Anglican bishops and the wider literature. All the data was analyzed using Fairclough's 'polymethodic' approach, namely the analysis of text and language, the analysis of discursive practice and social practice.

A theory that I found relevant for this chapter and which I adopted is the discussive constructivist paradigm towards understanding ethnicity. The main argument of this theory is that of ethnicity as an 'imagined community', a social and historical construct and a product of human action, in which such commonalities and shared values as speech, language and political organization and activities are woven into the psyche and consciousness of people who believe they share the same identity.[7]

This chapter has three sections: an overview of the history of Anglicanism in Kenya, the emergence of ethnic identities in the Anglican Church, and the themes emerging out of discourse analysis on ethnicity, along with a conclusion and recommendations.

Anglicanism in Kenya: An Overview

The Anglican Church of Kenya (ACK), known as the church of the Province of Kenya (CPK) until 1998, is the oldest Protestant church in Kenya. Its history dates back to 1844, when the first missionary from the

---

[4] Clifford J. Geertz, *The Interpretation of Cultures* (New York: Basic, 1973), 470.

[5] Talal Asad, *Genealogies of Religion. Discipline and Reasons for Power in Christianity and Islam* (Baltimore, MD: John Hopkins University Press 1993).

[6] Most of the focus group discussions and interviews were conducted at St Paul's University, 7th-30th April 2015.

[7] Crawford Young, *Ethnicity and Politics in Africa* (Boston, MS: Boston University African Studies Center, 2002), 1-102.

Church Mission Society (CMS), Dr Johann Ludwig Krapf, arrived in Mombasa. With a present membership of over five million, the ACK is also the largest Protestant church in the country. Unlike other mainline churches, for example, the Presbyterian, Methodist and Reformed, which have a huge presence in Kenya, the ACK has a national presence. Compared with other Protestant traditions, the Anglican Church of Kenyan can claim to be more multi-ethnic both in its composition and in its spatial presence.

The ACK has a strong heritage of civic engagement, \especially since the 1990s, when individual clerics such as Bishops Henry Okullu, David Gitari and Alexander Muge, joined by clergy from other traditions, such as Timothy Njoya from the Presbyterian Church and Catholic Bishop Nding'i Mwana wa Nzeki, the ACK led churches in the call for multi-party politics in Kenya. During this period, these individual clerics played a constructive and important role in the development of a broad-based movement for political change.

Nevertheless, the discourses that we will examine show that the local Anglican Church also has its internal problems that contribute to its slipping into another mode of engagement: that of sectarian competition for an ethnic-based symbolic presence. While ACK leadership and ordinary Christians may continue to make a constructive contribution to public life, their efforts may also be limited by their desire to see their respective symbols dominate the public sphere.

Ethnic Identities in the Anglican Church of Kenya

Despite its long history, national and multi-ethnic composition and civic engagement highlighted in the preceding section, the ACK faces the challenge of negative ethnicity within its ranks. Private and public discourses in the church are framed around claims of ethnic marginalization.

The term 'ethnicity' is a broad concept best defined by identifying its key aspects. It is characterized by '... a myth of a common ancestry, a common past, a link with a homeland, a sense of group solidarity and elements of common culture which entails a common cult, customs and language.'[8] In most cases, the term is taken to be synonymous with 'tribalism'.

Ethnic identities play both a positive and negative role in Africa in general and Kenya in particular. It is because of the recognition of this dual nature of ethnicity that Koigi Wa Wamwere argues that there is a distinction between ethnicity and negative ethnicity.[9] Berman rightly argues that 'Ethnicity in Africa has some vital and positive elements such as "ethnic morality"' – that '... complex web of social obligations that define people's rights and responsibilities, and that protect people when they are most vulnerable and alone', 'which subordinates... one's behaviour to certain moral imperatives when dealing with other group members'.[10]

On the positive side, for example, translation provides the gateway to eradicating obsolete linguistic, cultural, artistic divides within church and society. Thus, as it moves, translation crosses lines of difference, sometimes blurring those differences. The globally acclaimed liturgical revisions in the Anglican Church of Kenya which took place in the early 1990s, producing a new prayer book of liturgies that were 'both thoroughly Biblical and authentically African, both faithful to Anglican tradition and contextually creative' is an example of the positive role of ethnic diversity in the church.[11]

---

[8] John Hutchinson and Anthony D. Smith (eds.) *Ethnicity: Oxford Reader* (Oxford: OUP, 1996), 25.

[9] Koigi wa Wamwere, *Towards Genocide in Kenya: The Curse of Negative Ethnicity* (Nairobi: Mvule Africa Publishers, 2008), 22.

[10] Bruce Berman Dickson Eyoh and Will Kymlicka, 'Ethnicity and Democracy in Historical and Comparative perspective', in *Ethnicity & Democracy in Africa*, eds. Bruce Berman and Will Kymlicka, (Athens, OH: Ohio University Press, 2004), 4.

[11] David Gitari, 'Preface', in *Modern Services* (Nairobi: Uzima, 1991).

In the present revised Anglican liturgy, familiar objects such as fish, cattle, sheep and crops are used in the framing of it. All these images are familiar within most Kenyan communities. The understanding is that what is significant in one community might not be significant in another, but that all of us have something significant.

Translating the gospel into people's ethnic languages enables better understanding than when this is done in a national language such as Swahili. There is recognition that, in the African setting, it is through an African reading of the Scriptures, particularly in African languages, and by paying attention to the resonances of the biblical categories in the African primal world-view, that the impact of the gospel can be experienced afresh.[12]

However, when not done well, translation can accentuate difference rather than efface it. That ethnicity points to aspects such as shared language, beliefs, religion, race or colour that makes people unique and distinct from others.

This contribution, however, is mainly interested in the negative effects of ethnicity in the Anglican Church of Kenya. The study is also an attempt to respond to two interrelated stimuli: first, the current socio-religious situation in Kenya that is characterized by private and public debate about negative ethnicity and the region at large, and second, the scholarly commitment of a recent conference at St Paul's University, Limuru. Regarding the former, in the last decade we have witnessed increased incidents of credal conflicts and incidents of violence. There is need, therefore, not just for interfaith conversation aimed at arresting the situation but also intra-faith discussions on the same question. Another reason for this contribution was a conference held 17th-18th May 2010 at St Paul's University, Kenya. This important academic event was a scholarly attempt at responding to the 2007-2008 post-election violence in Kenya. Among the emerging themes from that conference was the role of training institutions in addressing the challenge of ethnicity.[13]

Bishops' Discourses on Ethnicity in Kenya

As pointed out above, the pervasive nature of negative ethnicity and the attendant discourses around it is evident in various discourses. I would like to use two illustrative rather than exhaustive discourses as a peg and hang on it some of the questions raised. The first is an exchange between three Anglican bishops published in their biographies – those of David Gitari (1937-2013) Henry Okullu (1929-1999), and Manasses Kuria (1929-2005), and the second discussions with Anglican seminarians and faculty at St Paul's University, Limuru.

The context of the bishop's discussions of ethnicity was the circumstances surrounding the succession of Kenya's first Anglican Archbishop, Festo Olang (1914-2004). In a biography of Archbishop Kuria, Musalia writes: 'Another explanation of Archbishop Olang's retirement was one that linked him with accusations of nepotism and tribalism, especially referring to a case in which he had employed his own son as a driver.'[14] Here Manasseh Kuria, Kenya's second Anglican Archbishop, reflects on the question of 'tribalism' as it emerged during the succession of Festo Olang, his predecessor. He indicated that, although the retirement dates of Olang was due, his involvement in acts of nepotism caused fellow bishops and the laity to look forward to his retirement with some sense of urgency, and in fact rejected his formal request for a legal extension of his tenure.

---

[12] Kwame Bediako, *Jesus and the Gospel in Africa: History and Experience* (Maryknoll, NY: Orbis Books, 2004), 104.
[13] Diphus Chosefu Chemorion, C. B Peters and Esther Mombo (eds.), *Contested Space, Ethnicity and Religion in Kenya* (Limuru, Kenya: Zapf Chancery, 2013).
[14] Martha Wangari Musalia, *Archbishop Manasses Kuria – A Biography: Strong in the Storms* (Nairobi: Word Alive, 2001), 62.

According to biographies of Kuria, Okullu and Gitari, the question of ethnicity once again resurfaced during Olang's succession. Against the widespread expectation, among some, that Okullu, then Bishop of Maseno South, on account of his age, education and experience would succeed Olang, Manasseh Kuria was elected as Kenya's second indigenous Anglican Archbishop.

The contested nature of Olang's succession is captured in Okullu's autobiography, published in 1997:

> The third element that was used to block my election was tribalism. The Kikuyu factor was very strongly enforced by the political tribalism in which Charles Njonjo was the prime mover.[15]

Okullu, a Luo by tribe, names his fellow Anglican Bishop Gitari, a Kikuyu, as having participated in a plan to prevent him from ascending to the highest clerical office in the Anglican Church of Kenya.

> Gitari surprised me by saying that since Olang (from Western Kenya) had been Archbishop, 'This time you from Western Kenya are to be prepared to work with an Archbishop from Central Province.'[16]

In his recently published autobiography, published in 2014, Archbishop Gitari responds to Okullu's allegations:

> I told the bishop [Okullu] very frankly that Bishop James Mundia and the Luhyas could not support his candidature because of the ongoing boundary row at Maseno South. Then I told him that predominantly Kikuyu dioceses could also not support him as they believed he had a deep prejudice against Kikuyus... I never told Okullu that 1980 was the turn for a Kikuyu to be elected Archbishop. I have never been a tribalist in my service to the church and the nation.[17]

From the above-cited discourses on ethnicity, it is evident that it is a subject that pervades private and public discussions among Anglicans, not least bishops, in Kenya. The discussion also points to the contested nature of ascending to the highest clerical offices within the Anglican Church and the bitter divisions that this process brings about.

As indicated earlier, these two cases are not isolated. The ethnic question has continued to overshadow elections in the Anglican Church of Kenya (see for example, Kyalo, Paul).

Locating Ethnic Divisions within the Anglican Church of Kenya

It is important to consider the origins of these strong ethnic identifications in a church which biblically, canonically and constitutionally is supposed to be an open and all-embracing community. According to Phiri, 'To a large extent, Africans experienced the gospel not just as a liberating and reconciling tool but also as a tool of colonialism, racism, classism, *exclusivism* [italics mine] and schism.'[18] This view is corroborated by Kenyan church historian Esther Mombo who traces ethnic-based discourses way back to the introduction of mission societies in Africa:

---

[15] John Okullu, *Quest for Justice: An Autobiography of Bishop John Henry Okullu*. (Kisumu: Shalom, 1997), 131.
[16] Okullu, *Quest for Justice*, 131.
[17] David Gitari, 'Troubled but not destroyed' (Nairobi: Archbishop David Gitari Foundation, 2014), 70.
[18] Isabel Phiri, 'Life in Fullness: Gender Justice: A Perspective from Africa', *Journal of Constructive Theology* Vol. 8, no. 2, (2002): 79.

> The mission societies divided themselves into various ethnic regions. Anglicans organized themselves around dioceses but following the British pattern of districts[19]

According to some scholars, the construction of African ethnicity was further promoted and aided by the processes of translation:

> Christian mission and mission education that created standardized print versions of 'tribal' languages from related vernacular dialects, created a literature intelligentsia and, with translations of the Bible, provided them with potent literacy resources for the imagining of ethnic history and culture.[20]

So while, as argued earlier in this contribution, translation played a positive role in the life of the church in terms of making the gospel more accessible to the people of God, it also had limits and ironically helped construct a strong ethnic consciousness among Christians, effectively destroying church unity.

The fragmentation of the African community along ethnic lines was also exacerbated through the colonial policy of 'divide and rule'. British colonial policy in Kenya confined the earliest political associations in Kenya within the borders of ethnically defined administrative districts. The most critical division and debate leading up to independence was between the Kenya African National Union (KANU), under the leadership of Jomo Kenyatta, and the Kenyan African Democratic Union (KADU), under the leadership of, among others, Daniel Arap Moi. KANU was led by and was primarily perceived to represent Kenyatta's Kikuyu and Odinga's Luo, Kenya's most populous ethnic groups. KADU emerged in reaction to KANU, as a coalition of smaller ethnic groups.

It is often generally agreed that, even more than the colonial administration, the post-independence political leadership in Africa and Kenya in particular has exploited ethnic differences in order to maintain political power.

These ethnic-based political organizations seem to have played out in the Anglican Church of Kenya as well.

The effects of the appearance of ethnicity in Kenyan society is that individuals began to view themselves as being different from others in the same community with whom they did not share certain characteristics. Discourses around ethnicity took place not only among the church hierarchy but also among ordinary clergy and the laity.

Emerging Themes on Negative Ethnicity

The reality of negative ethnicity in the church

Consistent with the textual discourse cited above from the three biographies, the focus group discussions I had with students and faculty at St Paul's showed a real concern about negative ethnicity in the Anglican Church. All the respondents agreed that this was a major problem in the church in dividing worshippers along ethnic lines, by – for example – privileging some while disenfranchising others within church leadership and appointments.

Although most of the participants were Kenyan clergy, one participant from Southern Sudan also narrated how negative ethnicity has played out in his diocese. The exception were participants from Tanzania who agreed that the phenomenon '… is there but not much', attributing this to the legacy of Tanzania's founding President Julius Nyerere, who did much to build nationhood beyond sectarian lines.

[19] Esther Mombo, oral interview, 27th April 2015.

[20] Bruce Berman and Will Kymlicka, *Ethnicity & Democracy in Africa* (Athens, OH: Ohio University Press, 2004), 5-6.

According to participants, negative ethnicity in the Anglican Church is visible in a variety of sectors including appointment and promotion to positions of leadership within the church, the role of church in secular political processes, the division of dioceses and the posting of clergy.

Ordination, appointment and the transfer of clergy

A participant stated that one sometimes needed to have a 'God father' in order to be ordained in the Anglican Church. Participants discussed how appointment to positions of leadership in the Anglican Church was conducted not on the basis of merit but ethnic bias. A participant from Southern Sudan narrated how a duly elected bishop could not be consecrated because 'he did not come from the right tribe'. After exactly eleven months [after his election], the Archbishop decreed that the election was invalid and a new election had to be conducted. Another participant from Kenya explained: 'Out of the eight archdeacons in this particular diocese, seven are from the Bishop's tribe... that is why others are contemplating breaking away.' From the above, it was clear that ethnicity was used as a basis for the ordination, appointment and deployment of clergy at various hierarchical levels within the Anglican Church. In some contexts, where members of certain ethnic groups had perceptions of being marginalized, ethnic resurgence could take the form of demands for inclusion through threatening or actually breaking away from a diocese. The mobilization of ethnic identities thus represents a strategy for gaining access to – and the capture of – the church's resources. Mirroring secular society, most Anglican clerics and the faithful perceive the creation of a diocese as an opportunity for battling over the division of the 'church cake'. However, the most tragic consequence of this pervasive and patronizing framework of Anglican ministry has been a largely subservient clergy and laity whose prophetic voice is chronically castrated.

According to participants in the focus group, the transfer of clergy from one parish to another is sometimes based on ethnic consideration. According to one participant, those close to the bishop are deployed to parishes in urban areas *kwa mafuta* (i.e. fatty or juicy) parishes, while those perceived not to be close to the bishops serve in peripheral parishes where raising money to support their ministry is a headache. The consideration of the material benefits available in a given parish, combined with the clergy's ethnic identification, determined deployment.

Ethnic bias in offering or not offering positions in the church was not limited to ministerial positions but also extended to lay offices such as the Mothers' Union, Kenya Anglican Youth Organization, the accounts offices and administrative roles. A lay female participant explained how she failed to be appointed to the position of Mothers' Union co-ordinator in her diocese because she did not belong to the bishop's tribe. 'It was given to someone who was a relative of the bishop.'

The consideration of ethnicity in offering a position to an individual, or not, is closely tied to spatial realities in a given diocese. Thus, a participant explained how Anglicans choose whether or not to attend KAYO conferences on the basis of where the event is being held in a given year. The same consideration, according to this participant, plays out in the election of the KAYO General Secretary. 'To be elected as KAYO General Secretary, where one comes from is always an issue,'

The church and politics

Participants discussed how the ACK was influenced by political processes. Accordingly, during the election of the Archbishop, the members of the Electoral College held prior meetings to deliberate on how they would vote. Eventually they voted, based on perceptions of which candidate supported a particular political party and who among the contestants would best secure the interests of their 'ethnic' group in national politics.

The influence of the political processes on perceptions about church elections was also evident in the language employed in the focus groups. For example, one participant spoke of 'the tyranny of numbers' to describe how ethnic numerical strength was used to advantage in church election processes. The 'tyranny of numbers' was a hypothesis that was generated by Kenya's political scientist Mutahi Ngunyi, during the countdown to the 2013 general election, with the conclusion that Raila Odinga and his 'CORD Alliance' had lost the 2013 election to Uhuru Kenyatta's Jubilee Alliance the moment voter registrations ended on 18th December 2012. Uhuru went on to win the election and Jubilee won a majority in both houses. In contrast to this, numerous opinion polls indicated otherwise. One participant in the focus group noted that 'those people who are in the political arena are the same people who are in the church'. While political leadership in Tanzania helped bring cohesion in the church in Tanzania beyond ethnicity, in Kenya there was an opposite effect. The analysis of the discussion corroborates a point made by Paul Gifford in relation to the church's role in politics in Kenya and its inability to be trusted by the general populace as an objective arbitrator during the 2007-2008 post-election violence: 'The common perception that the churches had allowed themselves to be co-opted foreclosed any role like that of the early 1990s.'[21] For many keen observers today, the ACK might, unlike the 1990s, be guilty of complicity in social fragmentation of Kenyan society and, not least, fragmentation within itself along ethnic lines.

Facing the Challenge of Negative Ethnicity

From the foregoing, the challenge to ethnicity within the Anglican Church is real. As indicated, discussions on this issue centre round issues of leadership and perceived material benefits by those in leadership – to the disadvantage of those on the periphery. The 'othering process' within the Anglican Church is framed round ethnicity, with terms such as 'insider' or 'outside', 'our own' or 'the other'. This othering process can be more complex than just ethnic. For example, in his autobiography, Gitari writes:

> The death of Bishop Magua caused a crisis in the diocese of Mount Kenya South. The process to elect a new bishop was set in motion but five members of the Electoral College from Muranga District refused to participate in the election... The Christians of Muranga had figured out that if the election of a bishop were held, then a candidate from Kiambu would succeed the late Magua, who also hailed from Kiambu, because seven out of the twelve electors were from Kiambu.[22]

Among the dioceses in Western Kenya, the othering process has also played out between sub-tribes and clans, with each seeking to outdo the other in the affairs of the dioceses. One participant asked, 'Why must every tribe have a diocese?' 'Why must the former Western Province have seven dioceses?' – pointing to the complexity of the othering processes.

The challenge of ethnicity is also based on perceptions of material benefits and access to local and international information if one of 'our own' should become a bishop. In this scenario, the election of leaders is first and foremost based on the criteria of their 'being our own' and only secondarily on their calling and competence.

Analysis of Social Practice

In terms of social practice, Fairclough notes that the text/discourse has ideological and power relations.[23] In the same frame, Stuart Hall has pointed out that discourse is placed, positioned, situated, and all knowledge is contextual.[24] Therefore, it is important to consider the subject positions of the participants. The

---

[21] Paul Gifford, 'Christianity Co-opted', in *Religion and Politics in Kenya*, ed. Ben Knighton, (New York: Palgrave, 2009), 216.
[22] David Gitari, 'Troubled but not destroyed' (Nairobi: The Archbishop David Gitari Foundation, 2014), 70.
[23] Norman Fairclough (ed.), *Discourse and Contemporary Social Change* (Bern, Switzerland: Lang, 2007).
[24] Stuart Hall, 'Ethnicity: Identity and Difference', in *Becoming National: A Reader,* eds. Geoffrey Eley and Ronald Grigor Suny, 339-351., (Oxford and New York: Oxford University Press, 1996).

assumption is that discourse cannot be neutral and is ever open to various interpretations. In this frame, participants' language use is constituted by and constitutes a particular social reality. The participant's language use could be aimed at making and remaking the existing social reality.

5.1 'People perceive that if we elect this person into this position then we are going to be politically affected.'

A participant used the term 'perceive' in describing people's sentiments on the role of ethnicity in election of a bishop. Other participants were more blunt in their framing of statements reporting them as reality.

5.2 'I have no problem if people in leadership positions are from the same community if it is done on merit.'

At least one participant appeared to defend the election of a bishop from the same community in church positions, arguing that merit should be the main consideration. From this perspective, history, language and culture define ethnicity. Ethnicity is made by the context in which identity and subjectivity are constructed. This approach to ethnicity comes from the re-conceptualization of identity as a process of identification. Identity is not stable but fluid, changing in historical contexts. If identity is a dynamic process, its stability can only be certain through a narrative of self.

Conclusion

The Anglican Church in Kenya and, to some extent, in the wider region of East Africa, has been vocal on a number of issues within and outside the Anglican Communion. The church also has a strong history of civic engagement. However, from the perspective of the participants in this study, the church faces other pressing local questions that greatly threaten its identity and effectiveness. Although the question of negative ethnicity has precedents in colonial history, this unfortunate legacy has been internalized and localized in the church through tendencies by both clergy and laity leading to the creation of boundaries among adherents. The discourses analyzed above point to the fact that negative ethnicity is a major challenge in the Anglican Church today. This reality mimics the ethnic narrative in the rest of the region. Although the contribution focuses mainly on the Anglican Church of Kenya, it also makes use of data and findings from Tanzania and Sudan, thus showing the relevance of the Kenyan case study to the wider East African region. From the discourses studied, the phenomenon of negative ethnicity is seen through the appointment to church positions, transfers, the creation of dioceses and the influence of political processes on church elections. The author recommends that church leadership needs to address this problem as a matter of urgency in order to have a more cohesive church that is effective in its mission. It is important that ethnic diversities in the church be managed in such a way as to be channelled positively into the mission of the church. The challenge of the Anglican Church is how to appeal to Christian values to inform and transform social relationships.

Bibliography

Asad, Talal. *Genealogies of religion*: *Discipline and Reasons for Power in Christianity and Islam*. Baltimore, MD: John Hopkins University Press 1993.

Hutchinson, John, and Smith, Anthony D. (eds.). *Ethnicity: Oxford Reader*. Oxford: OUP, 1996.

Gifford, Paul. 'Christianity Co-opted.' In *Religion and Politics in Kenya*, edited by Ben Knighton, 201-221. New York: Palgrave, 2009,

Hall, Stuart .'Ethnicity: Identity and Difference.' In *Becoming National: A Reader*, edited by Geoffrey Eley and Ronald Grigor Suny, 339-351. Oxford and New York: Oxford University Press, 1996.

Phiri, Isabel. 'Life in Fullness: Gender Justice: A Perspective from Africa.' *Journal of Constructive Theology* Vol. 8, no. 2, (2002): 69-82.

Yieke, Felicia. 'Ethnicity and Development in Kenya: Lessons from 2007.'*Kenya Studies Review* Vol. 3, no. 3, December (2011): 5-16.

Young, Crawford. *Ethnicity and Politics in Africa*. Boston, MS: Boston University African Studies Center 2002.

Waruta, Douglas W. 'Tribalism as a Moral Problem in Contemporary Africa.' In *Moral and Ethical Issues in African Christianity,* edited by Jesse N. K. Mugambi and Anne Nasimiyu-Wasike , 112-130. Nairobi: Initiatives Publishers, 1992.

(99) History of National Christian Councils in African Christianity

Agnes Abuom

Introduction: Understanding the Nature and Purpose of Christian Councils

The theme of this chapter is approached both from a general perspective and informed by personal encounters with many National Christian Councils (NCCs) in Africa during my studies and work as a resource person and senior ecumenical leader. The role and history of National Christian Councils of Churches in African Christianity is largely rooted in decades of missionary agencies' work and ecumenical endeavours in sharing resources through the instrument of Round Tables in recent times.[1] To-day, Africa has about forty National Christian Councils[2] and they can be categorized into three groups, namely: the first-generation NCCs which include those councils that have celebrated a centenary and golden jubilees (for example, NCCs in South Africa, Ghana, Sierra Leone, Rwanda, Tanzania, Kenya, Nigeria, Zimbabwe and Uganda); the second group, which is the majority – those councils that were formed soon after many African countries became independent; and finally, the third category consists of the ones that came into existence in the 1970s and thereafter which include the NCCs of Madagascar, Swaziland, Angola, etc.[3] The historical moment of their formation and the context within which NCCs operate has had a great bearing on the evolving role and nature of the respective National Christian Councils in African Christianity. This chapter seeks to illustrate how NCCs in Africa have evolved through the different phases of their existence, and how their contribution has affected the search for unity and co-operation in order to overcome the scandal of division. The three major pillars of co-operation and fellowship of these churches are the concerns for ecumenical unity, for mission and evangelism, and for the provision of diaconal services. This chapter therefore argues that, in their contribution to African Christianity, NCCs have contributed in all these three dimensions which have therefore, in one way or another, become markers of the NCCs' contribution in different countries and at various epochs. But it is most important to note that the continuing and overarching role of these councils was mainly to provide platforms where different confessional families could engage on issues and concerns of common interest or divergent views, including those relating to doctrinal matters.

---

[1] Round table meetings have been used by different mission agencies. The WCC Round Table is an instrument that was developed by the WCC in consultation with development partners and churches. It is used to convene funding and implementing partners to discuss and agree on common programmes of action and resources. See the WCC *Manual for Ecumenical Project Management: A Guide for planning, monitoring and Evaluation*: https://www.oikoumene.org/en/resources/documents/wcc-programmes/justice-diakonia-and-responsibility-for-creation/ecumenical-solidarity/manual-for-ecumenical-project-management (accessed 12 December, 2015).

[2] See the (incomplete) list of National Christian Councils on the AACC website: www.aacc-ceta.org/index.php/members/national-christian-councils (accessed 12 December, 2015).

[3] Huibert Van Beek, *A Handbook of Churches and Councils: Profiles of Ecumenical Relations.* (Geneva: WCC Publications, 2006).

Spiritual and Ecclesial Foundations for the Ecumenical Movement

> 'My prayer is... that all of them may be one, Father, just as you are in me and I am in you. May they also be in us so that the world may believe that you have sent me'.[4]

By invoking this prayer of Jesus which sees the unity of humanity in the church as a witness to the Trinitarian reality, we encounter the imperative of ecumenism as a missionary task and frontier within and outside the church. First and foremost, National Christian Councils are a manifestation of the ecumenical movement which is born within and not outside the church but, secondly, according to this biblical passage, there is also a process at work by which the whole of humanity is drawn together by the witness of the church to the unity already experienced in the prayer of Jesus. So the ecumenical journey of African Christians in coming together in council begins with a sense and act of prayer. In the Christian tradition, there is a deeper yearning for the whole of humanity to rediscover her authentic identity in the household of God. For example, the Lord's Prayer has proved to be the most authentic ecumenical instrument and inspiring spiritual vision, both of the church and of the councils. It is prayed across all Christian confessions – Orthodox, Roman Catholic, Protestant and Pentecostal. This prayer sends ripples of unity during every private moment and public presence of the church in the world. The Lord's Prayer binds and limits divisive forces, not just in the world but also among churches. To pray, as we do, and to address God as 'Our Father' has great ecumenical significance – a significance which goes beyond the unity of the denominations within the Christian Church in National Councils of Churches, and transcends and embraces the unity of all humankind.

The formation and establishment of many National Christian Councils in Africa goes back to the work of the National Missionary Councils which in some countries were their forerunners. Mission agencies found themselves in competition for space and people. In order to address this and other challenges of the day, they decided to form Mission Councils across Africa.[5] We should point out that some African Christian Councils are unique in that they embrace membership of the Catholic and Orthodox churches, which is not the practice in many regions. The Uganda Joint Christian Council, the Swaziland Council of Churches and the Sudan Christian Council are examples of those also having Orthodox and Roman Catholic membership, while the Sudan Christian Council also has the Pentecostal Church as a member. We should not also lose sight of the fact that mission agencies, while being aware of the need for unity, were primarily interested in the effectiveness of evangelism and also the need to confront the social issues of the day, such as the need for education, health and the solving of labour disputes, all of which implied the need for creating a united front vis-à-vis the regional or national political and economic powers. In spite of that, Missionary Councils and National Councils have continued to provide places for regular meetings of member churches, for joint prayer and action as well as the co-ordination and sharing of experiences and ideas.

Historical Milestones in the Formative and Contemporary Period of the Development of National Christian Councils

A number of councils in Africa predate the global ecumenical movement. This is the case, for example, in South Africa, Ghana, Nigeria and Kenya where churches perceived the need to create common platforms for ministry at quite an early stage. In most cases, these councils were instrumental in contributing to the

---

[4] John 17:20-21.

[5] On the history of NCCs and Mission Councils, see also WCC, *National Councils of Churches*: www.oikoumene.org/en/about-us/organizational-structure/related-bodies/national-councils-of-churches (accessed 11 December, 2015).

liberation of Africa during the decolonization process. During World War II, a number of churches were headed already by African leadership because of the impact of the war on the work of mission agencies. This was the case, for instance, in Tanzania which was earlier known as Tanganyika, where – owing to the war – the missionaries had had to relocate. The mission societies had produced a crop of Africans who could read and interpret the Bible. Therefore quite a substantial number of early Christian African leaders actively joined in the decolonization process and led political movements. A significant contribution of Christian councils which is not often clearly mentioned also consists of the evolution of African Instituted Churches (AICs) which opposed the mission agencies' approach to ministry as an instrument of spreading western civilization and culture, and criticized examples of obvious incongruence between the teaching and living of the biblical message. In this area, we observe Christianity in Africa taking on a liberative dimension and diverging from the original 'mother' churches in protest, thereby initiating new Christian communities today known as African Instituted Churches. Initially, these churches were not granted membership of National Christian Councils until after the 1970s.[6] In Kenya and in places like Congo, these churches were part of the protest against the political establishment of the day to declare independence through letters of protest and political witness to the colonial administration.

The first generation of councils had functional departments of theology to reflect on matters of faith, while councils at the same time also provided platforms for sharing and addressing common issues, such as education and health. But issues of the unity of the church did not emerge as pivotal in several NCCs, as expected, apart from some crucial countries like Zambia where the unity of the church really became a central issue, resulting in the United Church of Zambia. In East Africa, there were joint activities between Kenya and Tanzania in the area of media, also one could observe united congregations in Kenya for English-speaking and Kiswahili-speaking people (Lavington United and Bahati respectively). Other forms of relevant contributions by councils at this time related to the formation of major common theological colleges like St Paul's College in Limuru. A series of meetings were held in East Africa for building and creating a church union, but in the end there still was no united church. However, the Newspaper *ROCK/Target*, which was owned by both Kenyan and Tanzanian Christian Councils, became the 'voice of the voiceless' before the phrase gained currency. It was this newspaper that the WCC used for its Assembly News during the Nairobi assembly in 1975. Major contributions of NCCs in pre-independent Africa consisted of playing the role of convenors as there were few places or opportunities for Christians to meet and discuss common issues of church and society. The convening role of the NCCs in providing platforms for dialogue paved a way for Christians from different parts of a country to get to know each other and even appreciate the different viewpoints in the various confessional families. As Christians increasingly got to know each other, they also began to work together. The NCCs thus provided a major service by facing up to and overcoming some of the colonial heritage which had marked African Christianity. This is because in the planting of the faith in Africa, colonial governments allocated different denominations and mission agencies to specific geographical regions and, historically, there was hardly any chance for Christians from different denominations to interact properly except in certain areas like East Africa when there was the East African Revival which affected more than five countries. Given the political mood and increasing insecurity in some countries, no individual denomination or church could speak up on some of the thorny issues single-handedly. So the NCCs provided a single but important voice.

It is worth noting that several African Christian Councils, although national in character, have forged alliances across geographical boundaries.[7] In 1963, the All Africa Conference of Churches (AACC) was established before the formation of the Organization of African Unity, the forerunner of the African Union.

[6] There are some studies on this related to Zimbabwe, South Africa and DR Congo.

[7] See, for instance, the Fellowship of Christian Councils and Churches in West Africa (FECCIWA); https://en.wikipedia.org/wiki/Fellowship_of_Christian_Councils_and_Churches_in_West_Africa (accessed 12 December, 2015).

This also encouraged NCCs to work together on major social and political issues of concern, and to provide leadership as churches got involved in the struggle for liberation as well as in pioneering critical social innovation. It can be argued that this was a higher level of the search for unity by the churches in Africa which started in debates, going as far back as the 1950s. The AACC has provided an umbrella for all the NCCs, and enabled them to share views and challenges across geographical regions and, in addition, providing a continental platform upon which councils and churches could discuss ecclesial, political, economic and social matters.[8] Examples of regional ecumenical councils in Africa are the formation of the Fellowship of Churches and Councils in the Horn of Africa and Great Lakes (FECCLAHA), the Fellowship of Churches and Councils of Eastern and Southern Africa (FECCESA), and the Fellowship of Churches and Councils in West Africa (FECCIWA). These have emerged as regional ecumenical platforms, engaging both councils and churches in respective geographical regions and bringing them together on pertinent issues affecting them. Each in the past has focused on one issue, for instance, 'peace' for FECCLAHA, 'liberation and economy' for FECCESA, and 'governance and disarmament' for FECCIWA. The agenda-setting by these councils and churches has also been the basis of a more global ecumenical interaction.

National Councils of Churches in the Post-Independence Period

As indicated above, the councils began the process of nation-building alongside the nationalist governments in the 1960s and continued throughout the 1990s when states in Southern Africa attained independence, to serve as the voice of the people. In the meantime, front-line states like Zambia, Botswana, Tanzania, etc. hosted thousands of refugees which called for the provision of basic social services.

The role and contribution of councils can be framed along the following pillars: National Christian Councils have articulated the commitment of churches for education, as in several cases in Africa, churches still provide up to half the educational institutions, and the percentage is even higher in some countries. Through National Christian Councils, churches have also ensured that the religious education curriculum runs in tandem with its own beliefs and faith understanding. National Christian Councils have also played a critical role in policy-making, trying to influence national plans for education. Several councils have also significantly contributed to capacity-building of Christians through the provision of scholarships – most of which in the past came through the World Council of Churches. Theological education and leadership formation in some countries is an issue which is discussed and shaped as a joint venture of councils and member churches.

The relevance of National Christian Councils is also underlined by the fact that a new understanding of healing and wholeness was initiated by them, as health institutions were often started by councils and were only handed over to governments or specialized Christian Health Associations which remain associated with the Christian councils and which are platforms of churches which still manage health facilities. With new forms of diseases and challenges such as HIV and AIDS, it has often been the Christian Councils which have pioneered a new Biblical understanding of healing and human dignity.

The socially innovative role of National Christian Councils is further underlined by the fact that they often provided the opportunity for Christian engagement with society through church and society programmes. An example in point is Ghana where the Urban Rural Mission Unit in the National Council has provided the space and avenues for churches in independent Africa to meet the social challenges of their contemporary social context. As long as African secular civil society organizations were at their embryonic stage, NCCs provided a very active and unique ecumenical opening for the churches' participation in social work. Although many a National Christian Council did not embrace the Roman

[8] See next Chapter of this publication on History and Profile of AACC by Edison Kalengyo.

Catholic Church, youth departments often worked with the World Student Christian Federation (WSCF), and through Student Christian Movements reached out to the younger generation in ways which were all-encompassing and inclusive as broad-based ecumenical platforms. In brief, National Christian Councils in Africa played an important role in complementing new independent government efforts, especially on socio-economic issues, and provided skill training and vocational education centres where there were few employment opportunities.

The late 1980s and 1990s were a period of a second liberation, and again the National Christian Councils provided platforms for churches to work together in working for democratization and human rights at a time when repression was intense and civil society organizations could hardly speak at all. Through the role of a convenor, civic and voter education, including advocacy for human dignity, became priority agendas for National Christian Councils, besides undertaking traditional *diakonia* interventions. Acting and speaking together by churches in joint councils was so critical because the impact of the Cold War meant that Africa was divided between the western and eastern blocs, and despotic rulers got away with the violation of human rights and the elimination of its advocates. In spite of individuals, such as Archbishop Luwum of Uganda, being killed, the prophetic ministry of the church through National Christian Councils continued. During the 1970s and through to the 1990s, Africa experienced many conflicts culminating in the Rwandan genocide in 1994, and at one time, Africa was the leading continent in the number of conflicts. It should also be observed that in countries where there were different races as in Kenya, Zimbabwe and South Africa, national councils worked together with churches for peaceful and cohesive community and race relations. African churches, organized in common national councils, could engage together in the vanguard, searching for peace through healing and reconciliation work. This is evidenced by the work in Sudan and the new nation of South Sudan. Another issue that the councils have enabled the church to address and appreciate is the issue of gender and the empowerment of women. Although this was not as strong in the earlier years, many national councils are enabling churches and Christians to better understand the place of men and women in church and society, particularly inasmuch as the process in this issue has been rather slow, especially in reinterpreting the biblical texts.

The role and contribution of the churches in councils becomes the more meaningful if these national councils are the sole (and a lonely) voice in countries where there are no other prophetic voices, as has been the case in several instances on the African continent. It is equally important to note that, without the member churches, the councils alone could not weather the storms, be this during colonial times, during the post-independence period, or even in the struggle for the second liberation.

Challenges in the Role of National Christian Councils

Over the decades, the national councils have faced major challenges and some nearly closed down until the AACC intervened in order to salvage them. It is essential to observe that only a few types of council have continued the search for Christian unity in the traditional form of conciliar unity. By focusing on social and economic development, a number of councils became centres of capacity-building for member churches, and even begun to slide into the member churches' development departments. And as resources for mission and theology dwindled after a while, these departments then fizzled out. In several countries, including those keen on church union, the work of Faith and Order became much less known, compared with relief and development work. Of course, the NCCs remained crucial instruments of development but also in providing advocacy as they interacted with the government, as long as they received funds for doing so. It is important also to state, however, that the initial and continuing role of National Christian Councils in matters of mission and evangelism still continues but with more emphasis on joint weeks of prayer, liturgy and capacity-building. Today, member churches of councils are under pressure from the new brand of charismatic Christianity whose understanding of ecumenism and church unity presents a paradigm shift, although a certain number of them also seeks to participate in broad ecumenical platforms. The powerful influence of the prosperity gospel from North America and the push for churches to function as civil society entities has been a challenge for NCCs. Churches which have been pillars of conciliar ecumenism are struggling as councils absorb the concept and operational style of NGOs and actors in civil society.

The Changing Role and Contribution of National Christian Councils

When the drums change the rhythm, the dance steps have to change as well.[9]

The councils have undoubtedly contributed to the growth, self-understanding and brand of African Christianity and churches, including the growth of ecumenism in Africa. Their role has been building, nurturing and strengthening capacity, and providing platforms for a united voice and action. In some instances, they have pioneered innovation in society, at the same time moving churches to the frontiers of mission and evangelism. Times have changed, however, and many countries have now become far more pluralistic, leading to society having to grapple with new theological and ethical questions that demand more attention and new approaches. The drums remain the same but the rhythm has changed and so must the dance. The imperative of the search for and vision of the unity of the church and the unity of humankind remains the foundation and leading vision of National Christian Councils in Africa. The fragility of many types of councils, however, requires a repositioning in order to remain the moral conscience and critical voice of the churches in a given national context, and to enable ordinary Christians to be alive and alert to what it means to be Christian in Africa and the world today. The time when councils carried out huge programmes with large numbers of staff is long over, and current contexts dictate a change in organizational capacity and role while retaining the vision and mandate.

Therefore a few more roles that councils can maximise and build upon include:

Undertaking studies on relevant subjects – galvanizing, mobilizing people and gathering them round issues of church and society that deepen faith and strengthen participation in society. Such studies could be theological or social. Councils remain a vital moral conscience of society in the quest for a language that will make such studies viable for propagating faith, service and mission.

Convening and accompanying roles – where churches and communities of faith begin to engage ecumenically with a vision of the unity of church and humankind within their respective historical contexts. In this respect, councils should continue to accompany ecumenical formation processes and the nurturing of leadership that fosters change. Another equally critical area of accompaniment is the true liberation of oppressed sectors of society, especially women's liberation which remains an unfinished task, even in the church.

Creating safe spaces for encounters – between and with different stakeholders like the universities, NGOs and churches – with the aim of eradicating spiritual, cultural and material poverty and developing a critical and holistic understanding of poverty and illness. Councils are uniquely placed to further the cause of young men and women by providing them safe spaces for their own reflection on matters of faith and issues affecting them in society. Indeed, the future of National Christian Councils is dependent on relevant strategies and methods that affirm the dignity of all, and especially of young people as members of the broader ecumenical movement across the confessional families.

Enhancing platforms for interfaith dialogue and collaboration – on the imperative of justice and peace: Councils and churches should not lose sight of the looming danger of nuclear war and the potential for nuclear proliferation as more countries acquire this facility without supervision, especially in the light of increased conflicts. Through these dialogue platforms, councils should encourage regional approaches to

[9] African proverb communicated by André Karamaga.

peace, healing and reconciliation since conflicts need a regional conflict management system. Other issues that might be approached from an interfaith perspective include climate change and the use of natural resources made available by God.. Interfaith platforms are as essential today as before in facilitating appreciation for diversity and plurality in the many components of Christian faith and other faiths.

Networking and Creating Linkages – Councils are themselves networks and are best suited for networking with scholars and institutions of higher learning in order to provide scholarships for Christianity which is relevant, as the currently dominant western scholarship and approach to faith may not serve the today's challenges in Africa. A Caribbean church leader – the, now late, Myles Munroe – bemoans the fact that our cemeteries are full of knowledge, buried and inaccessible to present and future generations – while the councils are able to facilitate documentation, profiling and sharing best ecumenical practices and stories. So much happens but little or none of it is properly shared, let alone documented for future reference and improvement, including avoiding the reinvention of the wheel.

Interaction and complementarity – African councils have contributed and continue to play a role on the regional and global ecumenical scene, in order to ensure agreement on principles of complementarity among all ecumenical players, in affirming the common vision of the movement and ensuring synergy on issues and concerns of advocacy internationally.

Prophetic ministry – advocacy that enables churches to be the voice, ears and instruments of those on the margins in mission, justice, peace, healing and reconciliation as well as maintaining dialogue with those at the centre of power.

Promoting inclusive ecumenism – playing the role of facilitators and co-ordinators for encounters. National Christian Councils should fully co-operate with the Global Christian Forum where all organized Christian confessional families are represented.

We can conclude with the affirmation: Christian Councils have a place and role in African Christianity, especially for facilitating the rooting of the faith and enabling internalization of Christianity as an African faith within the global community of faiths.

Bibliography

All Africa Council of Churches. www.aacc-ceta.org/index.php/members/national-christian-councils (accessed 12 December, 2015).

Fellowship of Christian Councils and Churches in West Africa (FECCIWA). https://en.wikipedia.org/wiki/Fellowship_of_Christian_Councils_and_Churches_in_West_Africa (accessed 12 December, 2015).

Van Beek, Huibert H. *A Handbook of Churches and Councils: Profiles of Ecumenical Relations.* Geneva: WCC Publications, 2006.

World Council of Churches. 'Manual for Ecumenical Project Management: A Guide for Planning, Monitoring and Evaluation.': https://www.oikoumene.org/en/resources/documents/wcc-programmes/justice-diakonia-and-responsibility-for-creation/ecumenical-solidarity/manual-for-ecumenical-project-management (accessed 12 December, 2015).

World Council of Churches. 'National Councils of Churches.' www.oikoumene.org/en/about-us/organizational-structure/related-bodies/national-councils-of-churches (accessed 12 December, 2015).

(100) The History and Profile of the AACC

Edison Kalengyo

Introduction

The All Africa Conference of Churches (AACC) is a continental ecumenical organization inaugurated on 20th April 1963 in Kampala, Uganda, as a fellowship of Christian churches and related organizations. Today it includes 143 member churches and 31 associate members,[1] all in 41 African countries.[2] The vocation of the AACC is to foster and sustain fellowship and unity among churches for common witness and service.

The material that follows below is drawn from the All Africa Conference of Churches' Post-Jubilee Assembly Programmatic Thrusts 2014-2018.[3] AACC has its vision as: 'Churches in Africa together for Life, Truth, Justice and Peace (John 10:10).' The AACC's mission stipulates: 'The All Africa Conference of Churches is a fellowship of churches and institutions working together in their common witness to the gospel by:

- Mobilizing to faithfully live the message of God's love;
- Nurturing a common understanding of the faith;
- Interpreting and responding to challenges to human dignity; and
- Acting prophetically in Word, Life and Service for healing.'

In obedience to God and the imperatives of the gospel, AACC is committed to operate honestly and with integrity, and in a spirit of love. In its service for the churches, AACC is pro-active and engages in discernment for positive transformation. It is committed to ecumenical vocation and focuses on result-oriented programmes strategically designed to address specific issues emerging on the continent.

It is fair to say that, strategically, AACC is the prophetic presence and witness of the churches in Africa. It is an ecumenical instrument facilitating synergy amongst its members, with the people of Africa. AACC further mobilizes its constituency to speak with one voice on issues affecting the people of the African continent.

The AACC, being a church-based organization, has determined that theology rather than ideology forms the basis of its programmes. To this end, all the programmatic work of AACC is informed by theology. Relevant contextual theological reflection focused on the needs of the growing church in Africa has come to be the basis of all the programmes and activities of AACC.

The beginning of the All Africa Conference of Churches

The historic meeting that took place in Ibadan, Nigeria, 10th-19th January 1958, will forever remain in the annals of the All Africa Conference of Churches as the decisive meeting at which the idea of forming a continental ecumenical body by the churches in Africa was conceived. Notable here is the role played by the Nigerian Christian Council and the International Missionary Council (IMC). The official invitation to

---

[1] Associate members consist of National Christian Councils of Churches, Sub-Regional Fellowships, Lay Centres, Institutes of Theology and the Organisation of African Instituted Churches.

[2] These statistics are drawn from updated AACC directories for member churches and associate members as at May 2015. The directories are not published.

[3] As reproduced in the AACC Post-Jubilee Assembly Programmatic Thrusts (2014-2018), 4.

that meeting came from the Nigerian Christian Council. In his forward to a report written about this meeting, George W. Carpenter states,

> Representatives of church bodies in twenty-five African countries attended the conference – a much more widely representative gathering of Africans than had ever before come together for any purpose.[4]

These church representatives included, among others: African bishops, superintendents, seasoned church leaders and elders of the church. This was the first time that prominent church leaders drawn from the continent met and talked to each other face-to-face. Actual attendance at the conference was 195. Of these, 96 were representatives of churches in Africa: 74 African men, 16 African women, and six Europeans representing the white churches of Southern Africa. In addition to these, there were 48 missionaries from countries outside Africa. Also in attendance were 45 staff members, consultants and visitors from Europe and North America. Additionally, there was a unique representation of the Asian community – six Asians as delegates from the Ghana Assembly expressing their solidarity with this historic meeting.[5]

In his opening address, Sir Francis Ibiam, Chairman of the Conference, was very lucid about the significance of the All-Africa Church Conference.[6] First, the conference would provide an opportunity to get to know one another. Second, those gathered together would discover their common difficulties and problems, and find out how best to solve them. Third, the conference would help

> … to bring all the churches in Africa together in an effort to build up the great countries of the African continent in Jesus Christ who is the foundation of all things, so that Africa shall no longer be branded as the dark continent but become a continent from which emanates light, truth and righteousness, knowledge, wisdom and understanding, goodness and prosperity, honour and blessing, because the continent of Africa will have learned to put God first.[7]

The All-Africa Church Conference in Ibadan was organised around the main theme of 'The Church in Changing Africa' with the following specific sub-themes:

1. The Church, Youth and the Family
2. The Church and Economic Life
3. The Church and Citizenship
4. The Church, African Culture and Islam
5. The growing Church

According to Carpenter, 'The most remarkable feature of the Conference is that here for the first time the African Church found its voice.'[8] Unlike in the past, when missionaries spoke and represented the people of the continent of Africa, as noted by Carpenter, this was not the case at the Ibadan conference, adding:

---

[4] International Missionary Council. *The Church in Changing Africa', All Africa Church Conference Report, Ibadan, Nigeria, January 10-19, 1958* (New York: International Missionary Council, 1958), 5.
[5] Statistics drawn from the 'The Church in Changing Africa', All Africa Church Conference Report, 6.
[6] International Missionary Council, *The Church in Changing Africa*, 9.
[7] International Missionary Council, *The Church in Changing Africa*, , 9-10.
[8] International Missionary Council, *The Church in Changing Africa*, 7.

It was most heartening to see the African churchmen and churchwomen themselves come forward one after the other, speaking capably, confidently and effectively; and to watch the growing sense of personal responsibility, initiative and commitment with which they dealt with the issues before them.[9]

The resolve of those who attended the conference in Ibadan is well captured in the final paragraph of the 'Message to the churches of Africa' from this conference:

The continent of Africa will see unparalleled events and changes during the rest of this century, welcomed by some, feared by others. We pray that the Christian Church of Africa will play its role as champion, teacher, counsellor and shepherd during these crucial years. We are humbly aware of our responsibilities to God and to this continent, and dedicate ourselves anew to their performance, trusting that we shall be led and supported by our fellow-Christians throughout Africa and the world.[10]

This resolve was followed by the formation of a Provisional Committee. Its terms of reference were clarified in a resolution that was unanimously adopted by the Conference on 18th January 1958 as follows:

That this Conference name a committee here to consult with the Christian Councils of Africa, church bodies and other agencies concerned with the witness for Christ in Africa, in order to give consideration to the implementation of the report of this Conference and particularly as to the appointment of a Continuation Committee and / or a regional secretary. It is suggested that the General Chairman of this Conference and the Chairman of the Steering Committee be members of the committee.[11]

Pursuant of this resolution, the following were chosen as members of this committee:[12]

Sir Francis Ibiam – Nigeria
Esther L. Coker – Sierra Leone
Jean Keller – Cameroun
Jean Lubikulu – Belgian Congo
Henry Makulu – Northern Rhodesia
Julio J. Miguel – Angola
Stefano Moshi – Tanganyika
Alan S. Paton – South Africa
T. Rasendrahasina – Madagascar
George W. Carpenter – USA

Birth of the All Africa Conference of Churches

While admittedly the idea of forming a continental ecumenical organisation for Africa was conceived at the Ibadan meeting in Nigeria, 1958, the actual birth of the All Africa Conference of Churches took place in Kampala, Uganda, on 20th April 1963 at the historic First Assembly of the All Africa Conference of Churches. As to the composition of this Assembly, it was stated:

This was the most representative meeting of church leaders ever held in Africa. Over four hundred delegates, observers and consultants came from over one hundred churches from forty countries in Africa, as well as from sister churches and Christian councils in four continents. Distinguished heads of Protestant, Anglican and Orthodox communions and independent churches were there, along with parish ministers, laymen, women and youth delegates from all over Africa.[13]

---

[9] International Missionary Council, *The Church in Changing Africa*, 7.
[10] International Missionary Council, *The Church in Changing Africa*, 16.
[11] International Missionary Council, *The Church in Changing Africa*, 17.
[12] International Missionary Council, *The Church in Changing Africa*, 17. For further reading see, 'Drumbeats from Kampala', Report of the First Assembly of the All Africa Conference of Churches, 6-7.
[13] 'Drumbeats from Kampala', 4.

The main theme of the Kampala Assembly was 'Freedom and Unity in Christ'. There were sub-themes as follows:

1. Freedom and Unity in the Family
2. Freedom and Unity in the Church
3. Freedom and Unity in Society
4. Freedom and Unity in the Nation

A number of significant decisions were taken at the First AACC Assembly in Kampala. Notable were the following key developments:

1. Establishment of the post of a General Secretary. S.H. Amissah was appointed as the first AACC General Secretary (1964-1971).
2. The AACC Constitution was adopted, clarifying the functions of AACC and its structures with detailed provisions for membership.[14]
3. Mindolo Ecumenical Foundation in Kitwe, Zambia, became the home of the AACC secretariat. The secretariat moved from Mindolo to Nairobi in 1965.

The All Africa Conference of Churches has continued to grow over the years as demonstrated in the various subsequent assembly reports.[15] These assemblies were held in various countries under various themes that reflected the continental needs of the time as follows:

1. Second AACC Assembly held in Abidjan, Cote d'Ivoire, 2nd-12th September 1969, on the theme 'Working with Christ in Africa Today'.
2. Third AACC Assembly held in Lusaka, Zambia, 12th-14th May 1974, on the theme, 'Living No Longer for Ourselves but for Christ'.
3. Fourth AACC Assembly held in Nairobi, Kenya, 31st July-12th August 1981, on the theme 'Following the Light of Jesus Christ'.
4. Fifth AACC Assembly held in Lomé, Togo, 18th-25th August 1987, on the theme 'You shall be My Witnesses'.
5. Sixth AACC Assembly held in Harare, Zimbabwe, 25th-29th October 1992, on the theme 'Abundant Life in Jesus Christ'.
6. Seventh AACC Assembly held in Addis Ababa, Ethiopia, 1st-10th October 1997, on the theme 'Entering the 21st Century with Hope'.
7. Eighth AACC Assembly held in Yaoundé, Cameron, 22nd-27th November 2003, on the theme 'Come, Let us Rebuild'.
8. Ninth AACC Assembly held in Maputo, Mozambique, 7th-12th December 2008, on the theme 'Africa, Step Forth in Faith'.
9. Tenth AACC Assembly (which was also the Jubilee Assembly) held in Kampala, Uganda, the place of the birth of AACC, 3rd-9th June 2013, on the theme 'God of Life, Lead Africa to Peace, Justice and Dignity'.

The Programmatic Work of the All Africa Conference of Churches

The AACC has been of service to its constituency through its programmatic work over the years. Four broad areas of focus can be identified as follows:

1. Peace and Advocacy.
2. Theology, Ecumenical and Interfaith Relations.

[14] For the full AACC Constitution, see 'Drumbeats from Kampala', 61-65.

[15] For a summary of the various assemblies, see further Christopher Byaruhanga, *The History and Theology of the Ecumenical Movement in East Africa* (Kampala: Fountain Publishers, 2015), 185-202.

3. Empowerment, Diakonia and Development.
4. Family Life and Gender Justice (a new programme promoting family values and dignity for all, especially the most vulnerable).

Peace and Advocacy

Over the years, the AACC has played a critical role in preventing conflicts in fragile situations in Africa. Since its inception in 1963, the AACC has been keen to intervene in fragile situations to ensure peace and prevent conflict. This has been because the church in Africa has had a deep concern about the enormous and unnecessary loss of life and the accompanying lack of dignity that conflict has caused on the continent and elsewhere. The church in Africa recognizes that conflict undermines the dignity of people who are created in God's image (Gen. 1:27). As a membership organization made up of many churches in many countries across Africa, AACC is mandated to accompany individuals, communities and nations, whenever they are in difficulty. AACC's engagement has been undergirded by the following understandings:

1. **That mediation and dialogue cost less than open conflict** – the AACC holds that, whereas the beginning of open conflict can be witnessed, its end and the subsequent consequences cannot be predicted or predetermined.
2. **Conflict resolution** and **reconciliation** – the AACC sees this as a means through which the peaceful ending of conflict and the promotion of justice is achieved. In this endeavour, the AACC has been using negotiation, mediation and ecumenical diplomacy as important tools through which grievances are processed for the rebuilding of trust for forgiveness to take place.
3. **Peace-making** – the AACC undertakes this in situations where conflict has already been witnessed or where symptoms of conflict exist. AACC's interventions are aimed at conflict transformation and thus focuse upon forestalling future conflict. AACC primarily seeks to establish some means of ethical agreements among conflicting parties. Further to this, AACC seeks to achieve some level of, if not full, reconciliation among adversaries in the hope that a new mutual understanding may emerge and thus drive the parties towards the path of healing. In this regard, the Eminent Persons' Ecumenical Programme for Peace in Africa (EPEPPA) is AACC's main instrument for engagement in conflict resolution and peace-making. It serves as a mechanism for Early Warning, Rapid Response, Conflict Analysis and Mediation. Through this programme, AACC has so far deployed missions to Liberia, Kenya, Cote D'Ivoire, Madagascar, Sudan, South Sudan, Central African Republic and Mozambique, among others, in the years 2007-2014. The AACC has been inviting credible personalities from African society, interfaith leaders and the international community to play this important role of eminent persons.
4. **Peace Consolidation** – where AACC seeks to take action to identify and support structures which will strengthen and solidify peace in order to avoid a relapse into conflict. AACC's programme on *Supporting Democratic Transitions* is aimed at assisting in the consolidation of peace. The AACC holds that, in spite of the shortcomings of governance and justice systems based on the principles of democracy, they remain the best way of safeguarding peace and human dignity. In this regard, AACC has accompanied the people in the Great Lakes and Horn of Africa regions in building their capacity for effective engagement in the electoral processes. The AACC has also accompanied National Christian Councils to observe elections in Sierra Leone, Nigeria, Liberia, Ghana, Cameroon, South Africa, Mozambique, Zambia, South Sudan, Uganda, Kenya and Tanzania, among others.

A number of examples in which the AACC has been a major facilitator for conflict prevention and peace consolidation can be cited. Here are just a few of them:

South Africa

The AACC was founded in a period during which many African states were struggling to regain their political liberation from their colonizers, especially against apartheid and Portuguese colonization. Therefore, like many other church organizations around the world, the AACC played an important role in undermining the apartheid regime and the falsified gospel that supported it.

For instance, Archbishop Desmond Tutu was elected as the President of the AACC, 1987-1997. This election was not only aimed at recognizing his immense value to the church in Africa, it was also aimed at providing a platform for one of the fiercest opponents of the apartheid regime to amplify this opposition. This contribution of the AACC was publicly acknowledged by President Nelson Mandela who came to express it personally on 13th December 1998 during the World Council of Churches (WCC) General Assembly held in Harare, Zimbabwe, where he thanked both the AACC and WCC for their contribution.

Sudan/South Sudan[16]

In 1966, the AACC was invited by the Government of Sudan to assist it mediate with Anya Nya, the Sudanese Liberation movement which spearheaded the struggle for justice, peace and human dignity in the whole of Sudan. This resulted in the 1972 Addis Ababa Peace Agreement which held for ten years until 1983.

In 1990, the AACC was invited to mediate between the two conflicting factions of SPLM/SPLA.

In 1992-1997, the AACC facilitated numerous talks including 'the people-to-people talks' that immensely influenced the agenda for the liberation struggle. The build-up from these talks is what facilitated the signing of the CPA in 2005 and South Sudan's self-determination in 2011.

Following the violent split of the SPLM/A in December 2013, the AACC has been instrumental in facilitating the involvement of churches and the people of South Sudan in the conflict resolution talks led by IGAD in Addis Ababa and also within South Sudan.

Liberia

Before the 2011 referendum and general elections, Liberian churches called on the AACC to express their concern about the increasingly polarized political situation in Liberia which they saw as a precursor for violence, if not contained early enough. This caused the AACC to dispatch a team of eminent persons to Liberia, 6-12 August 2011.

The delegation held talks with the government, political parties, politicians, civil society organizations and religious leaders, with the aim of dissuading them from holding radical political positions and instead seeking to resolve their differences through dialogue, thus guaranteeing peace.

Mozambique

The AACC and the local churches (both Protestant and Catholic) played an important role as non-official mediators in Mozambique's civil war of 1977-1992. Churches were particularly important in establishing and sustaining communication channels with the protagonists. This was the case because they were trusted and respected for their ministry of presence within the suffering that was going on. It was the mediation by the church that precipitated the breakthrough in the Mozambique peace process.

In recent past, the AACC used personal contacts with the government and the Renamo leadership to insist on resolving differences through dialogue rather than war when signs of conflict were discerned as the country started gearing up for its 2014 general election. The AACC argued that war was not only costly, but would also undermine the many gains that had been made since the end of the 1977-1992 civil

---

[16] For details of this, see Samuel Kobia, *Dialogue Matters: The Role of Ecumenical Diplomacy in the Run-Up to the Independence of South Sudan* (Nairobi: Zapf Chancery Publishers, 2013).

war. In follow-up to the AACC's concern, a team of peace-makers from Mozambique visited the AACC headquarters to deepen their understanding on how they could avert the looming conflict.

Further, the AACC sent a team of election observers to the October 2014 general elections.

Great Lakes Region

AACC has for years been an active mediator between the countries of the Great Lakes Region, a role that has been acknowledged by key players in the region.

Kenya

In February 2013, the AACC facilitated a visit to Rwanda by 100 Kenyan community elders from the Kikuyu and the Kalenjin communities to see the negative effects of ethnicity as the country prepared for its 2013 general election. The AACC also sought to expose the elders to the mediation and restoration process that the Rwandan people had used to overcome the effects of the 1994 genocide as well as to bring about healing. The AACC was remembering that ethnicity had played a significant role in fanning the conflict that emerged after the results of the 2007 Kenyan general election and in which these two communities were the main actors.

The elders acknowledged the lessons they had learned and committed themselves to speak to their people about the need for peaceful co-existence.

Interfaith Missions

Central African Republic (CAR) – in April 2014, the AACC made a solidarity visit to CAR and held talks with religious leaders from the Christian and Muslim faiths, as well as political leaders and civil society groups. The AACC established that the conflict in CAR was purely political but with ethnic and religious implications. The AACC has also established that the people of CAR have not lost hope for peace and the reconstruction of their nation. The AACC endeavours to continue engaging Christian and Muslim faith leaders, the political class and the entire CAR nation to realize that war brings only pain.

Nigeria – in June 2014, the AACC, in collaboration with the Programme for Christian Muslim Relations in Africa (PROCMURA), organised a Seminar for Christian and Muslim leaders (imams, bishops and lay Muslims and Christians) and a Young People's Forum. Both meetings had participants from Kaduna State of northern Nigeria and were both aimed at sharing experiences and identifying ways through which the religious communities of the State, and the wider community in northern Nigeria, could resist provocation by extremist groups, whatever their origin.

The final memorandum by the young people saw them commit to work for peace in their own environments, and never to yield to provocation from religious extremists.

On the other hand, religious leaders made firm commitments to take the message of peace and restraint to their respective communities as seen in the seminar's communiqué.

Theology, Ecumenical and Interfaith Relations

It is widely acknowledged that there is a noticeable shift in the centre of gravity of global Christianity from the global North to the global South. This remarkable numerical growth of confessing Christians in Africa is largely due to mission strategies of churches in Africa centred around the readiness and willingness of the faithful to share their faith in Christ Jesus with those around them and beyond.

But there are also enduring challenges for the growing churches of Africa. First, the need for them to work together has never been more critical than in our time. Most churches in particular regions of Africa reflect the political, ethnic and denominational divides of those regions. Each church seems to have its vision and mission agenda. There is uneven distribution of both human and material resources, even among churches in the same region or locality. Regrettably, in some cases, churches in the same area will carry out their mission activities in a negative or competitive spirit rather than being complementary. In such situations, it becomes difficult for the churches to speak with one voice on social and political issues that concern their individual or respective congregations.

The AACC, through its Theology Programme, brings the gospel imperative of unity to bear on the mission of the churches in Africa. This is in line with the affectionate prayer of Jesus Christ for the church when he prayed 'that they may all be one, just as you, Father, are in me, and I in you, that they also may be in us, so that the world may believe that you have sent me' (John 17:21 NIV). When churches work together, they bring their congregations along with them, which in turn leads to strong communities.

Second, the majority of the numerous Christian churches lack well resourced and equipped leaders with the capacity to offer much-needed leadership. It is no exaggeration to state that the one single outstanding challenge for churches in Africa is that of leadership development. AACC is committed to the nurturing of a unique generation of ecumenically grounded church leaders able to reflect theologically on contextual issues prevailing on the continent. The revitalized regional theological networks with their member institutions and the All Africa Academy of Theology and Religious Studies (AAATRS) are among the AACC avenues for leadership training and development. AACC is working hand-in-hand with the following regional theological networks: Association of Theological Institutions in Southern and Central Africa (ATISCA), Association of Theological Institutions in Eastern Africa (ATIEA), West African Association of Theological Institutions (WAATI), and Association des Institutions Théologiques d'Afrique Francophone (ASTHEOL). AACC accompanies these regional theological networks to meet every two years. The All Africa Academy of Theology and Religious Studies that was launched in December 2012 had its first congress in Nairobi, Kenya, 19th-22nd February 2015 on the theme 'African theology of life with dignity'.

Third, the reality of the existence of faiths other than Christianity demands that Christian communities need to understand and appreciate those of other faiths in order to foster a spirit of peaceful co-existence. Peace is a prerequisite for all humankind undertakings. This is especially so for the churches whose Master and Lord Jesus Christ is both our peace and the giver of peace (Eph. 2:14; John 14:27). Christians have no choice other than to embrace peace among themselves and those of other faiths. That too is intrinsic to the Christian mission.

Lastly, the spiritual landscape of Africa demands contextual theological reflection and education that address the specific needs and challenges in Africa today. Theology made in Africa is what will support the growing church in Africa. Theological reflection that leads to the generation and preservation of knowledge is a strong pillar of a growing church. Theological education and reflection is to the churches what blood is to the human body – a separation of the two inevitably leads to death, and that should not be allowed to happen to the church in Africa.

AACC promotes authentic and contextual theological reflection that enables the churches in Africa to sustain and nurture a generation of ecumenically grounded church leaders in line with Jesus Christ's mission of unity, peace and dignity for humankind. AACC achieves this through:

- Promotion of regional theological networks as centres of contextual theological reflection. Such reflections inform the church's decisions and actions regarding her mission on the continent.
- Promotion of the All Africa Academy of Theology and Religious Studies as a continental centre for theological reflection.
- Production and provision of credible contextual theological materials as resources to the churches and theological institutions.
- Exposure of young theologians to the ecumenical and spiritual landscapes of the African continent as part of the ecumenical formation of the younger generation of theologians for leadership

responsibility in the church and the ecumenical movement, through internships and theological institutes that have proved essential in leadership development for the church in Africa.

- Fostering an understanding and appreciation of people of other faiths among young theologians, theological educators and students: building them up as models and agents of peaceful co-existence with people of other faiths in their localities. This will specifically enhance Christian-Muslim relationships on the continent.
- Strengthening the work of the Theology Advisory Committee. Its membership is drawn from networking organisations such as ATISCA, ATIEA, WAATI, ASTHEOL, Circle of Concerned Women Theologians, ETE and PROCMURA, among others. The Advisory Committee on theology serves to provide coherent interpretations and prescribe interventions on matters of theological concern.
- Transforming the AACC Library and its Archives into a continental and global centre of information and research on ecumenism while serving as a model and training centre for theological institutions, churches and national councils on the continent and beyond.
- Strengthening the worship and spiritual life of the community of believers at the AACC secretariat in Nairobi – anchoring the spiritual life of the community in the Lord Jesus Christ who is the chief proponent of unity and peace.

Empowerment, Diakonia and Development

Here AACC accompanies churches in their diaconical work of eradicating structural injustice that negates Christ's promise of fullness of life through impacting knowledge, poverty eradication, the improvement of economic well-being and ecological sustainability on the African continent. This AACC does so through:

1. **Economic justice and poverty eradication programmes** which facilitate consultations and networking among key players in churches and the National Councils of Churches (NCCs) to strategise approaches undertaken to address poverty in Africa. AACC also engages other stakeholders working on Sustainable Development Goals.
2. **Leadership skills development for churches and National Councils of Churches (NCCs).** Through this, AACC builds institutional and individual capabilities, especially the managerial competence of its churches, NCCs and Civil Society Organisations (CSOs). This is informed by the need for the responsible, transparent and accountable stewardship of resources as important ingredients for the transformation of the continent. From time to time, AACC carries out organizational assessment of NCCs on request in the context of operations and governance structures to better position the councils in their duties.
3. **Food security and climate change in Africa.** Here AACC serves as a platform for awareness raising, advocacy, building linkages and constructive engagement with churches, CSOs and other stakeholders to effectively articulate and present the voice of the African continent in international dialogue on food security and climate change in Africa

Challenges

The first challenge confronting AACC is financial sustainability in the face of ever-dwindling donor funds. There has not been a significant demonstration of financial ownership of AACC by her member churches. For many years, budgetary support for AACC from member churches has stagnated at 0.1%. AACC needs to devise ways of mitigating this. Deliberate steps need to be taken to enhance internal revenue. The second critical challenge is one of localization. By this I mean the understanding and ownership of the AACC at the grassroots level of its membership. The situation becomes worse when it comes to young people.

AACC is not only irrelevant but largely unknown among the young people of its member churches. There will need to be an increase in deliberate efforts to enhance the visibility of AACC and its activities at its grassroots membership if AACC is to remain relevant to its constituency. This will in turn enhance the ownership of AACC by its constituency. This enhanced ownership in my view will result in direct financial support for AACC that will enable it to carry on its programmatic work.

Conclusion

The AACC, for all intents and purposes, remains the only ecumenical organization in Africa with a continental mandate and credibility. Its clear vision and mission is timeless; its contribution to the life of the churches in Africa invaluable. Those at the helm of the leadership of AACC need to be constantly reminded of this so that the great potential of this continental ecumenical body is exploited to the full for the benefit and the dignity of the peoples of Africa.

Bibliography

AACC Post-Jubilee Assembly Programmatic Thrusts (2014-2018).

Byaruhanga, Christopher. *The History and Theology of the Ecumenical Movement in East Africa.* Kampala: Fountain Publishers, 2015.

'Drumbeats from Kampala', Report of the First AACC Assembly.

International Missionary Council. *The Church in Changing Africa', All Africa Church Conference Report, Ibadan, Nigeria, January 10-19, 1958.* New York: International Missionary Council, 1958

Kobia, Samuel. *Dialogue Matters: The Role of Ecumenical Diplomacy in the Run-Up to the Independence of South Sudan.* Nairobi, Zapf Chancery Publishers Africa, 2013.

'The Church in Changing Africa'. *All-Africa Church Conference Report*, Ibadan, 1958 Meeting. New York, International Missionary Council, 1958.

Unpublished AACC directories for member churches and associate members as at May 2015.

(101) History and Profile of OAIC

John Njeru Gichimu

Introduction

The Organization of African Instituted Churches (OAIC) is an umbrella organization for African Independent Churches (AICs) on the continent. Its head office is located in Nairobi, Kenya. This chapter examines the identity of AICs and their mobilization towards the formation of the OAIC; the movement's early struggle to define its own identity, rooted in the key concept of 'founding visions'; the development of programmes to express this concept practically; and the recent transformation of OAIC through reorganization and continued self-questioning, to its present position as an African Christian body in close contact with village level communities, yet able to contribute significantly to international debates.[1]

Identity

The terms 'African Independent' or 'African Instituted Churches' (AICs) are used synonymously for a large number of heterogeneous faith communities across sub-Saharan Africa. AICs are essentially 'home-grown' churches, often among the poorest communities. The OAIC understands an AIC to be a church that acknowledges Jesus Christ as Lord, and which has separated by seceding from a mission church or an existing African independent church, or has been founded as an independent entity under African initiative and leadership.[2] The first AICs were formed as Christian movements to preach the gospel and to protect African values and forms of society against the impact of colonialism, and against any negative or overly restrictive aspects of missionary-founded churches. They saw their churches as prophets of a new, reformed and more humane form of society that was both African and Christian, replacing the colonialism that had deprived African people of their initiative, freedom and sense of self-worth.

Although AICs date back to the nineteenth century, they began to be founded in considerable numbers from the 1920s onwards. For simplicity, they can be grouped into three broad categories:

- *Nationalist* – those churches that were founded as part of a broader movement to seize political power from the Europeans, and which saw recovering ownership of their churches and their country from the hands of foreigners as part of their divine calling. 'Nationalist' is an outsider's term; members of these churches more usually call themselves *Ethiopian* (Southern Africa), *African* (West Africa), or simply *Independent* (East Africa). Unfortunately, these terms are ambiguous when employed outside their immediate context. Pending agreement among AICs themselves on an appropriate term,, we continue to call them *Nationalist.*
- *Spiritual* – churches in which the power and gifts of the Holy Spirit are central, and which are close to African culture. These churches often created alternative 'counter-communities' of the Holy Spirit in opposition to colonial or missionary models of society. Other names of these churches are *Aladura* (West Africa), *Roho* or *Akurinu* (East Africa), *Zionist* or *Apostolic* (Southern Africa).

---

[1] In preparing this chapter, I wish to acknowledge the assistance of the Rev. Nicta Lubaale, OAIC General Secretary, Prof. Victor Molobi of the University of South Africa, Dr John Padwick, who served with OAIC, 1978-1985 and again 1993-2010, and the Rev. Dr Thomas Oduro of Good News Theological Seminary, Ghana.

[2] Slightly modified from David B. Barrett's definition, in *Schism and Renewal in Africa: An Analysis of Six Thousand Contemporary Religious Movements* (Nairobi: Oxford University Press, 1968), 50.

- *African Pentecostal churches* – founded after political independence, influenced by the global Pentecostal movement, and strongly oriented towards the future but retaining roots in African culture.

Mobilization: OAIC origins and the First and Second General Assemblies

In John 17:20-26, Jesus prays for the unity of believers, 'that they may all be one. As you, Father, are in me and I am in you, may they also be in us, so that the world may believe that you have sent me'.

The AICs' desire to come together to form councils has a long history. Initially, AICs were unwilling to join the so-called 'mainline' church councils which were generally hostile to their formation and even their very existence. This led AICs to work for their own councils from as early as 1913, but with limited success, and at a local level. In 1978, this desire found international expression when the OAIC was founded in Cairo with support from the ecumenical churches.[3]

The 'quest for belonging' by the African Independent Churches had resulted in several initiatives after 1930 to relate to the ancient African and Orthodox churches of Egypt and Ethiopia. When, in 1976, the Coptic Church under Pope Shenouda III consecrated Bishop Antonious Markos as Bishop of African Affairs, to be stationed in Nairobi, part of his brief was to develop relationships with AICs. Independently, the Anglican Consultative Council and the Archbishops of the Anglican province of Africa had also become interested in these churches. In Nairobi, Bishop Markos met experienced Anglican researcher David Barrett, who enabled the Bishop to contact dozens of Kenyan AICs and to arrange visits to AICs in DRC, and in West and Southern Africa.[4] In 1978, twenty AIC leaders were invited to Egypt by Pope Shenouda to visit the roots of African Christianity.[5] The leaders were genuinely interested in the Coptic tradition, particularly as an African and non-western source of legitimacy for their own churches. Visits to the Egyptian 'Biblical sites' and to monasteries in the eastern and western deserts strengthened AIC leaders' understanding of the African roots of Christianity. One South African commented, 'We thank God that we have come to a black church, a church that goes back to the first black Apostle of Jesus Christ.'[6]

The gathering (subsequently called the 'First OAIC General Assembly') proceeded to form a continent-wide association of AICs with the name Organization of African Independent churches.[7] Primate Adejobi of the Church of Lord (*Aladura*) from Nigeria became Chairman, and Bishop Markos Organizing Secretary.[8] Other committee members were the General Secretary, Bishop I. Mokoena, South Africa – St John's Mission; His Eminence J.K.N. Diangienda, DRC – Kimbanguist Church; and Ntate S.A. Muhono, Lesotho – Moshoeshoe Berean Bible Readers' Church. This committee was charged with convening a second OAIC Conference.[9] Assembly resolutions focused on the development of programmes described as 'Spiritual Teaching and Training'. This term embraced Bible teaching, leadership training, training for Sunday School and youth work, and the promotion of theological training for qualified leaders – all in a form acceptable to AICs of diverse traditions and often with members of little formal education.[10]

---

[3] David B. Barrett and John Padwick, *Rise Up and Walk* (Nairobi: Oxford University Press, 1989), 13, 40.

[4] Barrett was the chief editor of the *World Christian Encyclopedia* 1st edition. (Nairobi: Oxford University Press, 1982).

[5] Barrett and Padwick, *Rise Up and Walk,* 40.

[6] Njeru Wambugu, '*(1943-2008*). *The Organization of African Instituted Churches: An Introduction and Brief History*', (Nairobi: OAIC, 1996).

[7] In 1985, the word 'Instituted' replaced 'Independent' which had proved unacceptable to the Kenyan government during the process of registration. See Wambugu, 'The Organization of African Instituted Churches'.

[8] David A. Shank, 'Mission Relations with the Independent Churches in Africa', *Missiology,* Vol. XIII, (1985): 37-38.

[9] Barrett and Padwick, *Rise Up and Walk,* 41.

[10] Shank, 'Mission Relations with the Independent Churches', 38. An 'African Independent Churches Service', to provide a variety of help for member churches, was also agreed, along lines originally proposed for the All Africa

Significant funding for the Assembly came from European and North American ecumenical churches, expressing the then widespread concern to find ways of bringing AICs into the wider Christian family, and a recognition that earlier attempts to do this had largely failed.

The OAIC held its Second General Assembly in 1982 at the conference centre of the All Africa Conference of Churches (AACC) headquarters in Nairobi. The meeting of 48 leaders addressed the serious task of facing the problems of independence in the African church scene.[11] The Assembly adopted a constitution, and resolved to set up a General Secretariat in Nairobi. Although the Second General Assembly was held on ecumenical premises, and largely financed by ecumenical partners, it decided at this stage not to seek affiliation with any other Christian body, expressing simply a willingness to co-operate with such bodies. The OAIC needed to become properly conscious of its own identity before seeking closer relations with larger, well established associations of churches.[12]

The Challenge of Grassroots Theological Education

The Cairo meeting had focused on training and theological education, and the first programme to begin was Theological Education by Extension. This was the second option, after an initial funding proposal for a theological institution for AICs sent to WCC was rejected.[13] In 1980, the United Presbyterian Church (USA) seconded to the OAIC two TEE programmers experienced with such work in Chile – the Rev. Agustin and Mrs (later Rev.) Rosario Battle.[14] Two Kenyan TEE enablers were trained initially as part of a pilot project. By 1996, the programme had trained twenty-one Trainers of Trainers (TOTs) – six were women – from Tanzania, DRC, South Africa, Ghana, Cameroon, Madagascar and Kenya. Many of the TEE texts were produced by trainees on the course. Initially, there was no formal syllabus – texts were written in response to expressions of need from the churches. TEE proved to be an excellent tool for mobilizing isolated AICs and introducing them to the wider AIC community and the catholicity of the church. Its participatory methodology recognized from the start the principle of listening to and valuing voices from the grassroots as equals to those of theological professionals.

Nevertheless, an evaluation of the programme by Prof. Douglas Waruta of the University of Nairobi in 2000 underlined as a critical issue the task of ensuring that the 'content of theological education [is] commensurate to the identity and integrity of African instituted churches' – thus indirectly recognizing the existence of AIC theology, and the difficulty of determining its key elements across the variety of AICs, especially since AIC theology in general is oral and not written.[15]

Developing Appropriate 'Development' Education for AICs

Some AICs distrusted any programme aimed at improving living standards as 'un-spiritual', believing that 'development' had an external agenda and threatened the integrity of African communities; others, often under pressure from national governments, welcomed it as part of the modernising agenda; yet other

---

Conference of Churches, but never implemented by the AACC. This service eventually became integrated into the Research and Communications programme of the OAIC.

[11] Sam Babs Mala (ed.), *African Independent Churches in the 80s* (Nairobi: OAIC, 1983), 3.

[12] Mala, *African Independent Churches,* 3-4.

[13] Wambugu, (*1943-2008*), *The Organization of African Instituted Churches'.*

[14] Augustin and Rosario Battle, 'Theological Education by Extension Training for African Independent Churches: Second Anniversary report', in *African Independent Churches in the 80s,* ed. S. Babs Mala (Nairobi: OAIC, 1983).

[15] Douglas Waruta, 'Evaluation Report on: TEE and its future in AICs', 2000. An earlier evaluation was done by Rosario Battle in 1988 under the supervision of CORAT-Africa. See 'TEE Programme Report: OAIC Third General Assembly held 23rd-30th August 1997' at Limuru Conference Centre, Kenya. Rosario Battle's evaluation of 1988 was never presented to the OAIC Executive.

churches thought 'development' should be used primarily to improve church structures rather than the lives of people in the community. The second programme Rural Development by Extension (OAIC/RDE), under Dr Roger Sharland, was not started until 1990, and had to define itself carefully. Its training focused on empowering people with grassroots practical skills, in agriculture, agro-forestry, health, environment, handicrafts, etc. Advice was given on small-scale institutional projects (nursery schools, carpentry workshops, clinics, village polytechnics, etc.) and on the use of appropriate technology. The general objective of the programme was to reach the 'poorest of the poor', especially smallholders and women.

A pilot project was started in Kenya, in which churches were asked to identify two co-ordinators, one man and one woman, to be trained as TOTs and then to return to work in their church and community. Although seminars subsequently were held in Tanzania and Ghana, the programme was slow to move beyond East Africa. On the positive side, it was noted that some churches had begun to grapple with the meaning of development. Moreover, as early as 1991, RDE offered teaching on HIV and AIDS – well in advance of many other church programmes. Nevertheless, the programme was challenged for not being distinct *conceptually* from other contemporary models of grassroots development, having insufficient roots in AIC thought and practice, and was subsequently replaced.

Founding Visions

This term refers to the original AIC founders' understanding of the world and of the gospel that they had embraced, which had moved them to act as African Christians in that world. Such visions were crystallized in the formation of AICs, in their traditions, teachings and ways of life, and have been passed down (and modified) by subsequent generations. Such visions initially empowered AIC members (and still do) to critique and to stand against dominant models of society and development.

The concept of founding visions emerged from the process of clarifying AIC values vis-à-vis these dominant models, and was first articulated at an OAIC workshop in Johannesburg in 1996.[16] It has assisted AIC members working in practical programmes to identify the sources of the values which motivate them in their sacrificial service to the community.[17] It also lies behind recent attempts by the theological programme to encourage AICs to recover their founding visions, and to reflect upon them in the light of contemporary challenges, so that their ministries and mission may be more effective, and the gospel of Jesus Christ communicated afresh to new generations and cultures. The concept of 'founding visions' has thus become a significant link between the OAIC's theological and more practical programmes.

Third General Assembly 1997, Limuru, Kenya

This was the most representative meeting of AICs in history and clearly established their identity as a self-conscious community of Christians. The meeting renewed the OAIC Executive Committee (elected at the previous General Assembly back in 1982). The leader of the Eternal Sacred Order of the Cherubim and Seraphim churches from Nigeria, Baba Aladura Dr Otubu, was chosen as Chairman, and the Rev (later Archbishop) Njeru Wambugu of the National Independent Church of Africa – Kenya was confirmed as General Secretary. The Assembly also started the revision of the OAIC constitution, so that power and

[16] In a paper presented by N. Lawford, 'Imunde, 'The Vision of the Founders: Towards a Theology of Development for African Independent Churches in Africa', Background Paper No. 1, OAIC Johannesburg Theology of Development Workshop 28th November-8th December 1996: 'Imunde's term was "founders' vision", subsequently changed by the OAIC to "founding vision" to take away the implied emphasis on individual founders.'

[17] John Padwick and Nicta Lubaale, 'Harnessing Popular Visions for Social Transformation: The Experience of the OAIC in its Work with African Independent Churches', in Gerrie Ter Haar, *Religion and Development: Ways of Transforming the World* (London: Hurst, 2011), 315-30.

decision-making might be transferred to the regions – already in existence but not hitherto formally recognized. These were: West Africa (Anglophone), West Africa (Francophone), Nigeria, DRC, Southern Africa, Madagascar, East Africa, and North Africa.[18]

The Assembly was preceded by a consultation with the World Council of Churches on how AICs could contribute to the forthcoming WCC General Assembly in Harare – marking a significant shift towards alignment with (and subsequent membership of) the world ecumenical movement. One emerging issue was the conflict between the AICs' long-established practice of standing on their own feet and of seeking assistance from outside (as smaller and poorer AICs now wanted to do). How to move into relationships of interdependence with richer or more powerful bodies remains relevant to the present day.

Building Community Support Systems

As in the mid-1990s, AICs' suspicion of 'development' had driven the OAIC to the articulation of the 'founding visions', so in the next few years the urgency of countering the spread of HIV and AIDS led the OAIC to re-evaluate AICs' relationships with and commitment to their local communities.

RDE (Rural Development by Extension) was renamed 'Programme for Participatory Development' (PPD), recognizing the change in direction and its use of participatory methodologies.[19] RDE had often found itself going over the heads of church leaders in order to reach people in the villages. The new goal was to build the churches' abilities to work with their local communities, so that together they could plan and carry out development themselves. This involved capacity-building of the churches through the training of development facilitators; management training for church leaders; and civic and political education.[20]

Though, in 1997, HIV and AIDS had been recognized as a programme in its own right under the Rev. Nicta Lubaale, in practice, both the PPD and the HIV and AIDS programmes worked closely together. A number of new approaches characterized the programmes' evolution. First, senior church leaders were facilitated to look critically at theological issues and any risky cultural practices leading to the transmission of HIV, enabling them to becoming *owners* of their cultures and teachings, the better to direct and control them. Next, leaders were facilitated to uncover critical issues in the church and wider community underlying the disease's spread. These included issues of governance (the dominance of men in structures of power); theology and culture; and poverty, health and nutrition. The process required listening to social peer groups (women, youth, children and men). Alongside this, the programmes sought to value already existing community and church structures, and to build on their social and spiritual capital in order to help them engage with emerging realities. The immediate aim was to secure support for the most vulnerable children and orphans, but the new approach had a wide impact on OAIC practice.

This gave rise to the name 'BUCOSS: Building Community Support Systems'. Through BUCOSS, leaders were mobilised in twelve countries, and 125 TOTs and 1,247 community-level enablers trained. Its major achievement was the emergence of strong community-level responses to the pandemic.[21]

In 2004, a conference, 'Reclaiming Our Space', was held in Pretoria to celebrate and communicate AICs' achievements in their ministry in HIV and AIDS, their ability to act effectively in the community

---

[18] OAIC, 'Organization of African Independent Churches Second Conference Nairobi, Kenya 1982, Conference Papers'.

[19] Organisation of African Instituted Churches: Report of the Programme for Participants for the year 2000.

[20] OAIC, 'OAIC HIV/AIDS & Development Programme: An Introduction', Nairobi, n.d. but c. 2005. In East Africa, support and training for small business and micro-enterprise groups continued.

[21] See OAIC, *Our Lives Our Initiatives: Initiatives on HIV/AIDS from African Independent Churches and Community Organizations in Uganda and Kenya* (Nairobi, 2005).

(their *agency*: 'the ability to act to bring about change rather than being acted upon as a patient'[22]), and to value their particular heritage at this critical period in African history – thus starting the continuing process of encouraging AICs to 'reclaim their space' in African forums and decision-making. A key expression at the conference was 'critical solidarity'. This term describes OAIC's relationships, and those of its facilitators and trainers, with member churches and participating communities. 'Critical solidarity' requires long-term commitment to a church or community and recognition of its strengths and values, while remaining free to critique its weaknesses and failures.

The Reorganization of the OAIC

For a number of years, the OAIC Secretariat sought to transform the organization to be more responsive to the needs of member churches, and able to draw on the founding visions while engaging effectively with the challenges produced by rapidly changing local and global environments.[23] From 2005 to 2007, under the leadership of the new General Secretary, the Rev. Nicta Lubaale, the OAIC worked to translate the lessons learned into a long-term strategy, 'Visions for a Better World', approved in 2009.[24] This process was informed by a profound reflection on the freshly clarified vision and values of the organization:

OAIC Vision Statement

The people of Africa transformed by the good news of Jesus Christ:

- Blessed by the Spirit of God,
- Building on their cultures,
- Living abundant life in community for their children and the world.

The effect of this paradigm shift can be seen in all the current programmes (Just Communities, Theology, Livelihoods and Health) but is illustrated here with examples from the first two.

Just Communities

This programme was launched in September 2010. AICs' struggles for social justice are based on *Ubuntu,* an understanding that the well-being of all is the basis on which each person can stand in welfare and community with others. Well-being is impossible however unless the institutions of society – the family, economy, politics, government, culture and so on – can be transformed into the fulness of life which Christ has provided (John 10:10).

The key aims of the programme are grounded by Proverbs 13:23: 'The field of the poor may yield much food, but it is swept away through injustice.' Just communities enable AICs to harness their voices and speak out on issues of social justice and governance. It starts with recognizing the resourcefulness of the people. It requires a deeper understanding of the causes of poverty and injustice, and a capacity to question and challenge institutions (particularly in areas of public policy formulation and accountability for public

[22] Amartya Sen, *Development as Freedom* (New York: Anchor Books, 1999).

[23] The link between founding visions and practical engagement with socio-political challenges is indicated by an introduction to the OAIC's Vision and Mission: 'The OAIC is motivated by the AIC members and millions of Africans who look forward to a society in which all can enjoy well-being. These visions are rooted in an African philosophy of life in which care, reciprocity, acceptance, openness and equality are core values. AICs are a Christian outworking of these African values and they remain important in the AICs' ability to mobilize people to engage with the challenges facing contemporary African societies: www.oaic.org/?page_id=51 (accessed 5 May, 2015).

[24] OAIC, 'OAIC Visions for a Better World: Abundant Life for All in Community', Strategic Framework, 2009-2013.

services and resources) on the basis of how well they enable everyone to live life in dignity.[25] It draws on OAIC's earlier experience in facilitating workshops at the village level in which participants with no technical background were enabled (for example) to recognize the impact of Structural Adjustment Programmes in their own experience.[26] The methodology has also been used with groups of other or mixed faiths.

Theology Programme

How can OAIC facilitate the living and working out of its vision by AICs (that is, the *mission* of the AICs to the world) through *theology and theological education*? An OAIC concept paper of 2005, 'Facilitating AICs to articulate their theologies in the global context', had addressed the challenges that had led to the fossilization of the original TEE programme. The paper proposed a working definition of theology in the AIC setting: 'Theology is people making sense of God in the midst of their histories, cultures and contemporary struggles for survival.'[27] A consultation on this paper held in Nairobi in 2009 examined the OAIC's vision from a theological perspective, highlighting its positive valuation and critique of African culture as the inescapable, God-given, historical context for the reception and interpretation of the gospel, and the creation of the original AIC theologies ('the Founding Visions'). It recognizes the power of the gospel to continuously transform people, theologies and churches so that the challenge of the gospel remains fresh and focused on contemporary realities. It led to an affirmation of the church as *movement* – of the people of God called by him and empowered by his Spirit to undertake new initiatives in mission. This mission is to be seen especially in the building of *Ubuntu* (i.e. *shalom*), a humane society without poverty, exploitation or disease, and in the articulation and communication both within Africa and globally of this vision of the human community under God.

This challenge has focused on recent developments in the Programme of Theology, defining key tasks (among others) as:

- Facilitating the articulation, communication and renewal of AIC founding visions and the development of AIC theologies.
- Enhancing the AIC understanding and practice of mission, especially in cross-cultural and urban settings, and among young people.
- Sharpening and re-focusing OAIC distance-education methodology and practice.
- Facilitating the strategic growth of AIC theological institutions.
- Promoting the positive teaching of AIC theologies and AIC issues in non-AIC theological institutions.[28]

In this consultation and another in 2013,[29] theological experts from conventional theological institutions and other churches were invited to participate and to offer their critique with solidarity. The process of developing an appropriate framework for theological education in AICs continues. It raises issues – not for the first time but still urgent – around the identity of AICs as a heterogeneous community of churches; how to develop a training framework relevant to this multi-tradition community; the exploration of theological themes significant to the AICs (e.g. the work of the Holy Spirit at work in the church and wider community, and the role in this work of prophecy, dreams and visions). It requires a curriculum to be

---

[25] Brochure: OAIC Just Communities.

[26] In this case, through the creation of 'time lines' developed from people's own experience.

[27] *Facilitating AICs to Articulate their Theologies in the Global Context: A Concept Paper for the OAIC Department of Theology*, 2.

[28] Consultation on AIC Theology and Ministerial Formation, Nairobi, 1st-3rd December 2009.

[29] OAIC Theological Education Consultative Meeting at CORAT-Africa, Nairobi, 2013.

developed for people who are at the same time sources of that curriculum. Unless the uniqueness of AICs is well reflected in the framework, the curriculum and writing of materials will not meet the requirements.

Ecumenical and Interfaith Engagement

OAIC has consistently worked with other Christian churches and organizations, evangelical and ecumenical. Through these various partnerships, OAIC seeks to share AIC insights and values, as well as learn from other Christian traditions. The organisation is involved in the WCC as a regional ecumenical organisation in a working partnership with the WCC and is now recognised as the World Christian Communion. The OAIC is actively participating in the work and leadership of the Global Christian Forum and has been a participant in the annual Conference of Secretaries of Christian World Communions. In 1996, OAIC became an associate member of the All Africa Conference of Churches (AACC). OAIC's connections also include partnerships with several European and North American agencies. The organization has also developed good working relationships with a number of African evangelical faith-based organizations and fellowships. At a continental level, OAIC's national chapters and regions have well-established partnerships with their national ecumenical bodies. For example, the OAIC Nigeria Chapter is an active member of the Christian Association of Nigeria. The Kenya Chapter is also highly involved with several Kenyan ecumenical groups including the National Council of Churches of Kenya (NCCK), the Ufungamano Inter-Religious Forum, and the Inter-Religious Council of Kenya (IRCK). The OAIC is a founding member of the Africa Council of Religious Leaders.

Making Our Voices Heard at Continental and Global Levels

On occasion, the OAIC has hosted international conferences to articulate popular responses to contemporary issues (e.g. 'Growing the Harvest: Rethinking Agriculture food security in sub-Saharan Africa' at Limuru in 2012).[30] The OAIC has brought the voices of the people from rural and urban settings across Africa to global forums as the organisation engages with multilateral agencies such as the UN and the World Bank.[31]

Conclusion

In 1978, AICs were largely out of touch with the ecumenical churches, and had no voice to represent them. In recent years, their visions and particular values – often those held most strongly by some of the poorest and less educated communities of Africa – have been heard globally through the OAIC's presence in a variety of forums. The development of the OAIC as an organization has been marked by continuing tensions: enabling the local (and often traditional) visions of the AICs to engage with contemporary realities, and with the experience and wisdom of the wider church, and keeping open channels of communication between grassroots voices and visions and the wider community at local, national and international levels, articulating these voices in such a way that they can be heard to be relevant far beyond their village origins. It has been a challenging journey of continual self-critique and courageous initiatives.

---

[30] Refer to the unpublished Conference report *Growing the Harvest: Rethinking Agriculture Food Security in sub-Saharan Africa*, by Alice Wainaina (18th-20th September 2012). Consult the OAIC website for more information.

[31] The OAIC participated in the process that shaped the statement *Ending Extreme Poverty: A Moral and Spiritual Imperative*.

Bibliography

Barrett, David B. *Schism and Renewal in Africa: An Analysis of Six Thousand Contemporary Religious Movements*. Nairobi: Oxford University Press, 1968.

Barrett, David B. and Padwick, Timothy J. *Rise up and Walk*. Nairobi: Oxford University Press, 1989.

Consultation on AIC Theology and Ministerial Formation. Nairobi, 2009. www.oaic.org.

Facilitating AICs to Articulate their Theologies in the Global Context: A Concept Paper for the OAIC. Department of Theology, Nairobi, 2005.

Haar, Gerrie Ter (ed). *Religion and Development: Ways of Transforming the World.* London: Hurst, 2011.

Imunde, Lawford N. 'The Vision of the Founders: Towards a Theology of Development for African Independent Churches in Africa.' Background Paper No. 1, OAIC Johannesburg Theology of Development Workshop, 28th Nov. - 8th Dec. 1996.

Mala, Sam Babs (ed). *African Independent Churches in the 80s*. Lagos: Gilbert, Grace and Gabriel Associates, 1983.

OAIC, *Our Lives Our Initiatives: Initiatives on HIV/AIDS from African Independent Churches and Community Organizations in Uganda and Kenya.* Nairobi: 2005. www.oaic.org.

OAIC, 'OAIC HIV/AIDS & Development Programme: An Introduction'. Nairobi, c. 2005. www.oaic.org.

OAIC, Just Communities. Nairobi, 2010. www.oaic.org.

OAIC, Theological Education Consultative Meeting. Nairobi, 2013. www.oaic.org

OAIC, Visions for a Better World, *Abundant Life for All in Community: Strategic Framework, 2009-2013.*

Organisation of African Instituted Churches: Report of the Programme for Participatory for the year 2000. Nairobi.

Sen, Amartya, *Development as Freedom*. New York: Anchor Books, 1999.

Shank, David A., 'Mission Relations with the Independent Churches in Africa', *Missiology,* Vol. XIII, (1985): 37-38.

TEE Programme Report: OAIC Third General Assembly held 23rd-30th August 1997', Nairobi.

Wambugu, Njeru. '(1943-2008), The Organization of African Instituted Churches: An Introduction and Brief History'. Nairobi, OAIC, 1996.

Waruta, Douglas. 'Evaluation Report on TEE and its future in AICs'. Nairobi, 2000. www.oaic.org.

(102) THE ROMAN CATHOLIC CHURCH AND AFRICAN ECUMENISM

Peter Uche Uzochukwu

Introduction

In many African countries today, inter-church relationships are fraught with mistrust. While the mainline churches tend to dismiss the new independent churches as dislocated and immature, the latter, for their part, tend to perceive the former as foreign (pro-West), too rigid and lacking in African concern, content as well as relevance. Each of them vehemently tries to outshine the other in winning public space and reckoning. So, the fear of losing the battle for socio-economic space in society, and the other conjectured fear of being swallowed up by another church in the event of Christian unity, tend to prevent many African churches from any meaningful engagement in ecumenism. The ecumenical movement in this continent is, therefore, in dire need of a strategy or tool that can help churches overcome such fears. To succeed in Africa, the ecumenical process must, therefore, be one that can assist the churches first to develop, in their particular Christian traditions, open-minded profiles and then a mechanism for mutual enrichment among the churches. Such ecumenical drives must assure participating churches that their particular identities will be preserved (even enhanced) as they jointly pursue their fuller collective reality as one Church of Christ.

The current chapter locates such a needed strategy in the Catholic Church's effort at reshaping its self-understanding as the *Family of God*, an image it proposed in 1994, as an ecclesiological tool for homogenising its African region. The chapter highlights the import of that spectacular ecclesiological insight; underscoring its strategic value as the much-needed panacea for ecumenism in Africa.

After highlighting the evolution and content of the preferred model of church for Africa, we shall next stress the model's special ecumenical features; and then argue, in the next two steps, the strategic importance of the *Family of God* model of church as the most apt platform or framework for promoting Christian unity in Africa. What follows, in the next three sub-sections, are the result of such repositioning; then some evaluatory remarks, after which this chapter will draw a tentative conclusion that, once every church achieves some level of inclusiveness and mutual enrichment in its internal structures; and once the churches embrace one another as distinct units of the same one family of God, their journey towards complete unity has begun.

Evolution and Content of an Ecumenically Enabling Catholic Ecclesiological Initiative for Africa

In its Special Assembly for Africa (1994), the global Synod of Bishops of the Catholic Church set out to formulate, for its African members, a pertinent model of ecclesiology (namely: the church as the *Family of God*) which they believe could promote the church's enculturation and evangelisation drives in the new millennium and, most importantly, enhance ecclesiastical cohesion in the African region of the church. This preferred model of church takes its inspiration from the teaching of the Second Vatican Council and aims at building on the great value African cultures place on the sense of family. To actually formulate it, the Synod delved into biblical, patristic theological and cultural resources.

After depicting the church as the 'household' of God in which his family lives, the Second Vatican Council taught that it is God's plan to populate his family (the church) with human families.[1] Furthermore,

---

[1] Second Vatican Council, 'Dogmatic Constitution on the Church, *Lumen Gentium*', in *Decrees of the Ecumenical Councils, Vol. 2, Trent to Vatican II*, ed. Norman P. Tanner (Washington, DC: Georgetown University Press, 1990),

the Council taught that the church is a family of God[2] that is kept together by a common bond[3] and fraternal unity.[4] Deepening this teaching, John Paul II later taught that the human family is both a communion of persons and a domestic church.[5] For him, since the church is the *Body of Christ*, it is kept united by its one head, namely Jesus Christ. Finally, he likens the human family to the Trinity,[6] its originator; describing the family as the cradle of human life and unity since it forms the basis for the unity which God ordained for humanity. According to John Paul II, the family shares in the life and mission of the church.[7] These insights came to the fore at the 1994 Special Assembly for Africa of the Synod of Bishops.

As it sought for a relevant tool that could promote strong cohesion among its local communities operating in varied socio-cultural spheres of life in Africa, the Synod arrived at the *Family of God* model of church. Presenting the result of the Synod's deliberations, Pope John Paul II had first to confirm that the family and its values occupy a fundamental and widespread position in the life of Africans.[8] African cultures, he noted, embody an acute sense of solidarity and community life. In Africa particularly, he further noted, the family remains the foundation on which the social edifice is built.[9] Indeed, community of life in African society is expressed in and through the extended family system.[10] The document does not merely extol the family-like way of life in Africa; it also proposes a family-like form of being for the church and in her approach towards evangelisation.[11] By extension, the document proposes family-like dialogues in promoting Christian unity. As we shall shortly argue, this teaching has the potency to homogenize Catholic ecclesiological practices in Africa (and beyond) and then predispose the entire church for wider ecumenical engagement. For want of space, I discuss, in the next few paragraphs, two relevant features of the family way of life that make it a highly efficient tool for promoting Christian unity in Africa.

No. 6. Henceforth, this document will be referred to as *LG*. Again, the church is not only regarded as Christ's body but also a new communion of kinship in which all members are regarded as members of each other. (Second Vatican Council, 'Pastoral Constitution on the Church in the Modern World, *Gaudium et Spes*', in *Decrees of the Ecumenical Councils, Vol. 2,* No. 32). For other aspects of the church's theology of family, see *LG* Nos. 6 and 51, and *GS* Nos. 40 and 92.

[2] *LG* Nos. 28 and 32 present the Second Vatican Council's foundational teaching on the church as family.

[3] *LG* No. 32.

[4] Second Vatican Council, 'Decree on Ecumenism, *Unitatis Redintegratio*', in *Decrees of the Ecumenical Councils, Vol. 2, N*o.2. Henceforth, this document will be cited as *UR*.

[5] John Paul II, 'On the Role of the Christian Family in the Modern World, *Familiaris Consortio*, 22nd November 1981', in *Vatican II: More Post Conciliar Documents,* Vatican Collections, 2, ed. Austin Flannery (Northport, NY: Costello, 1982), 815-98, No..21. Henceforth, this document will be cited as *Familiaris Consortio*.

[6] John Paul II, ''The Family is the Cradle of Life': address to the *Pro Familia* Institute of Brescia, Italy, 23rd April 1994, in *L'Osservatore Romano,* weekly edition in English, No. 21, 25th May 1994, 2. For him, the family, just like the human person, bears the likeness of God because it is a community of individuals who are united by common destiny and love.

[7] John Paul II, '*Familiaris Consortio*, Nos. 49 and 50.

[8] John Paul II, *The Church in Africa: Post-Synodal Apostolic Exhortation, 'Ecclesia in Africa.'* (Nairobi: Paulines Publications Africa, 1995), No. 43. Henceforth, this document will be cited as *The Church in Africa.*

[9] *The Church in Africa,* No. 80.

[10] *The Church in Africa,* No. 43. This is a system whereby relationships of all degrees of sanguinity, marriage or other social affinity, maintain a very close relationship with one another as members of the same family.

[11] *The Church in Africa*, No. 57.

Special 'Ecumenical' Features of the Family Way of Life

In the following sub-themes (entitled: Unity in diversity and Unifying mutual enrichment), we try to highlight two features of the family as reasons we consider the family way of life an appropriate framework, or foundation, for promoting Christian unity.

Unity in diversity

The family is a system of intimate and multi-layered relationships based on oneness established between members who, in themselves, retain their distinct natures as individuals. It is the bedrock of loving communion within human community.[12] From the Christian perspective, the family represents a specific expression (though an approximation) of the Trinitarian communion, by which the three persons of the Trinity, Father, Son and Holy Spirit, share one being while still existing as three distinct persons. This is the prototype of unity in diversity, which is mirrored in the family. Likewise, members of the human family live in oneness (based, in this case, on their common root and destiny) while respecting the distinctiveness of the individuals and sub-groups that make it up. We consider this unity in diversity – the bedrock of Christian unity.

To nurture this feature, the family is also equipped with inherent mechanisms for resolving disputes as well as reconciling estranged parties within its fold.[13] In Africa, the family not only galvanizes the unity of its members, but it seeks to foster relational ties with other families, and even tribes.[14] The mode of living in the family entails an interplay of unconditional love, mutual growth and the healthy interdependence of members. The family promotes voluntary fusion and deep cordiality as well as harmony and unity among its members.[15] Indeed, the family's dialectical and dynamic form of communion can provide the churches with naturally appealing principles for their ecclesiological and ecumenical considerations. Little wonder then that some churches in Africa found it so easy to start immediately to incorporate some family features in their ministries and liturgy.[16] The unifying and galvanising roles of the family can constitute, if co-opted in the churches, viable principles of ecclesiological and ecumenical regeneration.[17]

[12] Nicholas Fogliacco, 'The Family: An African Metaphor for Trinity and Church', in *Inculturating the Church in Africa: Theological and Practical Perspectives,* eds. Patrick Ryan and Cecil McGarry (Nairobi: Paulines Publications Africa, 2001), 128.

[13] Such mechanisms include family meetings and other occasions like ancestral rituals, funerals, marriage ceremonies, engagement rites, sacrifices, initiation-rituals, etc., where members of the family, led by their elders and heads, gather to discuss and resolve issues. John Mutiso-Mbinda, 'African Background for Community Building', *African Ecclesiastical Review* Vol. 19, no. 5 (1977): 301. See Emmanuel Orobator, 'A Church in Dialogue as the Family of God', in *What Happened at the African Synod?* ed. Cecil MacGarry (Nairobi: Paulines Publications Africa, 1995), 41.

[14] One of the most solemn forms of social pact, through which such extension of ties is achieved, is the blood pact. Symposium of the Episcopal Conferences of Africa and Madagascar. *The Church as Family of God, Instrumentum Laboris and Pastoral Letter* (Accra: SECAM Publications, 1998), 65-70. Henceforth, this document will be cited as *Symposium, IL.*

[15] One of the clearest manifestations of these cultural values in Africa is the practice of commensality, i.e. the cultural practice of sharing meals together. Symposium, *IL,* 59.

[16] Citing two cases; that of a Protestant pastor (Willy Mnyagwata) and that of a Catholic diocese (the Diocese of Kasayi Zaire), Kabasele F. Lumbala demonstrates how easily churches in Africa started incorporating components of family life into their ecclesial and liturgical lives. He recounts how Mnyagwata integrated the role of 'elders by blood' in a Christian rite of reconciliation in his church, and how the diocese in Zaire assigned some liturgical roles to families of those to be ordained and those to be professed in their rituals for ordination and religious profession. Kabasele F. Lumbala, 'The Church as Family in Africa', *Concilium* (1995): 96.

[17] Francis A. Sullivan, like many other theologians, is convinced that one way the church can build on what has been established in the Council is by stepping up its efforts to embrace a variety of perspectives to dialogue-in-love. Francis A. Sullivan, *Creative Fidelity: Weighing and Interpreting Documents of the Magisterium* (New York: Paulist, 1996), especially 1-11.

Another striking element of the family unity in diversity feature is its ability to hold the tension within its fold even in the face of religious pluralism found among some of its members. In some African traditional settings, for instance, each family or kinship system has its own particular deity to which it collectively pays homage. Yet individual members are allowed to pay allegiance to different deities (outside the family deity) according to their own needs.[18] This inclusiveness in religious practice allows individual members of the same extended family to enjoy their distinctiveness while upholding family unity and common identity. Using the case of a 'kin-focused religion' in West Africa, Wiel Eggen opines that religion in Africa thrives on a deep awareness and respect for one another's destiny. He insists that religious hostility or division, traceable to over-centralization of religious systems, or religious absolutism, has little place in African religious traditions.[19] These innate factors of some African families are viable ingredients for promoting unity among African churches since we have the background that does not extend human antagonism to the realm of the gods.

As we have seen, the family's ability to retain this unique feature of unity in diversity,[20] is strengthened by its inherent mechanisms for group management, conflict resolution and reconciliation.[21] These and other numerous family values can be relied upon in trying to satisfy the contemporary yearning for borderless, participatory and healing communities.[22] They obviously led the Catholic Church into adopting the *Family of God* model of church as a tool for promoting its internal ecclesiastical cohesion in the African region.

Unifying mutual Enrichment

The average African family embraces not only a variety of degrees of consanguinity[23] but also an expansive network of relationships and co-existences of individual members (some of whom belong to different religious traditions); yet its unity is not hampered. An outstanding feature of the African family matrix is the interdependency of many households who mutually build each other up towards one formidable family lineage. These elements of mutual complementarity could hold the key to the future development of the contemporary ecumenical movement in Africa. Up to now, some church members still perceive ecumenism as an uncanny development in Christianity that is capable of misleading them into betraying their particular traditions. They feel that, by venturing into any ecumenical collaboration, their own 'genuine' elements of Christianity will be mixed up together with the 'not so genuine' elements which they perceive the other churches to have. On the other hand, family members are given to making up for

[18] Symposium, *IL,* 58.

[19] Wiel Eggen, 'Mawu Does Not Kill: On Ewe Kinship-Focused Religion', in *Exchange,* Vol. 31, no. 4 (2002): 342-61, 359. Eggen argues that kin-based traditional religions have no absolutizing tendencies, and so they promote harmony and complementarities among a variety of religious perspectives.

[20] Symposium, *IL,* 61.

[21] African families and communities have traditional rites for reconciliation which can be good resources for reconciling divided Christian communities in Africa. The Igbo people of south-eastern Nigeria, as Uzukwu points out, term such ritual 'Igba-ndu', meaning binding life together or – in religious terminology – making a covenant of peace between quarrelling parties. Elochukwu E. Uzukwu, *A Listening Church: Autonomy and Communion in African Churches* (Maryknoll, NY: Orbis Books, 1996), 86-87. In Igboland (eastern Nigeria), many Christian churches are increasingly drawing from this traditional tradition in settling disputes. Its features include anointing with oil, celebrating Christian services or the drinking of holy water to seal a common bond or to establish new life together between hitherto warring parties.

[22] Elisabeth Raiser, 'Inclusive Community', in *A History of the Ecumenical Movement, Volume 3, 1968-2000,* eds. John Briggs, Mercy Amba Oduyoye and Georges Tsetsis (Geneva: WCC Publications, 2004), 243-77, 243.

[23] This includes various layers of consanguineous relationships between grandparents and grandchildren; parents and children; siblings and step-families; uncles, aunts and cousins, as well as between in-laws and other social affinities. Catholic Bishops' Conference of Nigeria, *The Church in Nigeria, Family of God on Mission: A Pastoral Exhortation to the Clergy, Religious and Lay Faithful on the First National Pastoral Congress* (Enugu: CIDJAP Press, 2004), No. 55.

whatever is lacking in each other for the sake of their common destiny. So, in a special way, the *Family of God* model can provide the churches and ecclesial communities with a generally acceptable framework for building each other up and embracing one another.[24] Such convictions obviously led some mainline churches in Nigeria to take initiatives in the 1970s and 1980s towards the establishment of 'ecumenical institutes'[25] in the cities of Ibadan, Lagos and Enugu. These institutes were run by pooling together lecturers from various Christian denominations. Such moves were an emulation of the earlier efforts by some Protestant churches that also began some joint programmes for education, health care, urban ministries and the training of pastors in eastern Nigeria.[26] These developments led to a lot of cross-fertilisation of ideas and mutual enrichment among the Christian denominations. Unfortunately, such efforts were not sustained, probably due to the lack of a full-blown development of this motivational insight – the family of God.

For their part, many African churches adopt the principles of the African family matrix in promoting their ecclesial outfits. For instance, Christian Pentecostal communities progressively feature family elements and values, such as the titles of 'brothers' and 'sisters', family-like fellowships, mutual interfaces etc., while many institutional outfits of the African Initiated Churches are becoming increasingly structured in the forms of close-knit groups or communions built around some charismatic figures.[27]

Thus, to achieve the realisation of the full reality of the One, Holy, Catholic and Apostolic Church,[28] churches seem to have no other option than to complement one another. This could be one of the greatest sources of motivation for the churches in re-awakening their dormant ecumenical vision and zeal. Thus, the 1994 Synod of Bishops' efforts in embracing the separated churches and ecclesial communities as *households of faith*[29] remains a very promising move. This insight may not be new in Christianity but could be very catalytic in heightening the ecumenical momentum of our time.

Our goal in highlighting the *Family of God* model of the church is to encourage the churches to jointly embark upon the process of mutual enrichment of one another in order to realise their full (but not an all-absorbing) unity in the one Church of Christ. So, introducing this family principle of mutual complementarities into the ecumenical journey of the churches will surely help them overcome their hitherto prevailing fear of being swallowed up by one another. This is more timely since it has been argued that separation among the churches has not destroyed their essential unity.[30] Mutual edification, if embraced, could result into churches embracing each other's basic Christian tenets and structures, in their

[24] According to surveys conducted by the Faith and Order Movement, church union negotiations show increasing embrace of the organic pattern of unity among the uniting churches who are often referred to as 'family' or 'family of churches'. Thomas F. Best and Church Union correspondents, 'Survey of Church Union Negotiations 2003-2006', *The Ecumenical Review* Vol. 58, issue 3-4, (2006): 298. See Edwin Izuchukwu Okonkwo, *Praying in Communion with the Saints* (Enugu, Nigeria: SNAAP Press, 2011), 44-45. According to these scholars, many of these negotiations feature the urge to give specific and, especially, organic patterns to Christian unity, which we argue that the family model can provide.

[25] Anthony Chike Idigo, *Ecumenism in the Wake of the New Evangelisation in Nigeria* (Enugu, Nigeria: SNAAP Press, 2002), 23.

[26] Idigo, *Ecumenism in the Wake,* 23. Such included moves to expound commonly the basic Christian (Nicene) Creed and the two sacraments of baptism and the eucharist by the Methodist, Baptist, Presbyterian and Anglican churches in Nigeria.

[27] Laurenti Magesa, 'African Ecclesiologies', in *Dictionary of Third World Theologies,* eds.Virginia Fabella and R.S. Sugirtharajah (Maryknoll, NY: Orbis Books, 2000), 71.

[28] John Paul II, 'On Commitment to Ecumenism, in *Ut Unum Sint', Origins* 25 (1995): 50-72, No. 78. Henceforth, this document will be cited as *Ut Unum Sint.*

[29] Symposium, *IL,* 124-27.

[30] Henk Witte, 'Building Ecumenical Community at the Local Level: A Case Study', in *Of All Times and of All Places: Protestants and Catholics on the Church Local and Universal,* eds. Leo J. Koffeman and Henk Witte (Zoetermeer, Netherlands: Meinema, 2001), 216.

legitimate differences, while being open for mutual transformation.[31] There is thus no doubt that the idea of mutual complementarity (which this notion of the church as the family of God embodies) can lead the churches to rediscover the common heritage of early Christianity and help them grow together towards unity as units or households within the same family of God.

Church as Family of God: New Catholic Self-Repositioning, New Ecumenical Vigour in Africa

A new wave of Ecumenical re-awakening in African Catholicism

Before the 1965 promulgation of the decree on ecumenism *Unitatis Redintegratio*,[32] the Catholic Church never officially belonged to any national, regional or even the World Council of Churches. Forty years later, however (as Brian Farrell also noted in his 2005 assessment of the impact of the decree on the life of the church), 'the Catholic Church is now a member of seventy of the existing 120 national councils of churches, and takes part in three out of seven regional councils of churches, and in seven regional councils associated with the World Council of Churches'.[33] Farrell's survey further notes that the Catholic Church has become 'a member of fourteen national Christian councils or councils of churches in Africa, three in Asia, ten in Oceania, twelve in the Caribbean, twenty-five in Europe, one in North America, and five in South America'. As it pertains to the joining of national Christian associations in Africa, while some Catholic churches took early steps in pioneering and becoming full members (as in Nigeria where Catholic and Anglican church leaders jointly pioneered the formation, on 27th August 1976, of the Christian Association of Nigeria with the Catholic Cardinal Ekandem as its first president), others merely joined an already existing national councils of churches (as the South African Catholic Church did only in 1995[34]). Again, Catholic dioceses in Nigeria, as in many other African countries, now have commissions both for ecumenism and also (fully or partially) trained personnel dedicated to the task of promoting Christian unity in their localities. Regarding ecumenical dialogue, Farrell's report further reveals that 42 out of 83 Catholic Bishops' National Conferences did declare, in their responses to the survey inquiry, that the Catholic

---

[31] As Cassidy noted, the situation by which the spiritual richness of the Eastern monastic tradition 'flowed over into' the western church, in spite of the churches' separation, could be described as one of such instances of mutual edification among the churches. Edward Idris Cassidy, *Ecumenism and Interreligious Dialogue: Unitatis Redintegratio, Nostra Aetate* (New York, NY: Paulist Press, 2005), 17. Another instance of inter-church growing together relates to the evolution of issues of conciliarity and primacy among Anglican and Catholic churches. Anglican-Roman Catholic International Commission, *The Final Report, Windsor, September 1981* (London: SPCK, 1982), 98. Such emerging realities include 'new forms of regional primacy' in both traditions like the elective presidencies of Roman Catholic Episcopal conferences and certain elective primacies in the Anglican Communion. *The Final Report, Windsor,* 76.

[32] Second Vatican Council, 'Decree on Ecumenism, *Unitatis Redintegratio*', in *Decrees of the Ecumenical Councils, Vol. 2, Trent to Vatican II*, ed. Norman P. Tanner (Washington, DC: Georgetown University Press, 1990), No. 8. Henceforth, this document will be cited as *UR*..

[33] Bishop Brian Farrell, 'Ecumenism Today: The Situation in the Catholic Church': www.vatican.va/roman_curia/pontifical_councils/chrstuni/documents/rc_pc_chrstuni_doc_20041121_farrell-ecumenismo_en.html (accessed 12 July, 2015). This was a presentation made by Brian Farrell, as Secretary of the Pontifical Council for Promoting Christian Unity, to the international meeting held near Rome to mark the 40th anniversary of the promulgation, on 21st November 1964, of the Second Vatican Council's Decree on Ecumenism *Unitatis Redintegratio*.

[34] The Catholic Church in Southern Africa became a full member of the South African Council of Churches (SACC) only in 1995. Although the Second Vatican Council, which ended in 1965, had given an express mandate for the Catholic Church to join the ecumenical movement, the South African Catholic Bishops' Conference (SACBC) preferred to maintain only observer status in SACC for the thirty years that followed such a mandate. SACBC, *Directory on Ecumenism for Southern Africa* (Pretoria, South Africa: Department for Ecumenism and Inter-Religious Dialogue, 2003). Henceforth, this document will be cited as *DESA*.

Church, in these localities, now has permanent structures of dialogue with other churches and communities present in their territories; and that 38 among them have mixed commissions of dialogue.[35]

Drawing heavily here from a pan-African empirical survey, which the present scholar conducted in 2005 while researching for his, now published, doctoral dissertation, one can affirm that Vatican II ecumenical teaching and directories did usher in among African Catholics an unprecedented awakening to the drive towards Christian unity. For instance, as a respondent from Kenya states, the fact that Kenyan Catholics do now come together and agree to erect common structures for ecumenism is, on its own, a positive sign of ecumenical growth.[36] The situation is not different in Uganda where, as was reported, 'we (Christians) are now able to act freely together in social events; where there is equal respect for church leaders and church properties, and there is growing understanding of each other's beliefs and practices.'[37] Again, the Catholic Church in Tanzania has come out to join other churches in commonly using the Swahili version of the Bible translated by non-Catholics without making any distinction or discrimination.[38] The same obtains in a diocese in Ghana where, as was reported, 'the only version of the Bible available in the vernacular is produced by Protestants, but Catholics appreciate it, in spite of its overtly Protestant orientation'.[39] On the other hand, one observes among Catholics a growing appreciation of other Christians more than in earlier times. Indeed, 'in the past', according to one of the respondents from Mali, 'Protestants were regarded as heretics by Catholics but now that has changed.'[40] Such initiatives do constitute a form of *dialogue of life*, which has the capacity to endorse the needed ecumenical culture in Africa.

Specifically, ecumenical growth in contemporary African Catholicism can be witnessed in three broad areas of life in Africa, namely: human development; socio-cultural rituals for life-enhancement; and sharing in Christian resources. A few insights can suffice here.

Once issues of human development arise, churches quickly put aside their differences. In some cases, the Catholic Church tends to take the lead once a common threat to dignified human existence crops up in society. For instance, after the war in the DR Congo, the Catholic diocese of Basankusu (working with Jesuit Refugee Services), joined the reconstruction of a Protestant hospital in Baringa. In like manner, through some open youth programmes (such as education, sports, reading and video clubs, Bible-sharing, evangelisation), for which the Salesian Fathers of Don Bosco are well known, the Congolese Catholic Church not only promotes community development, but it also fosters ecumenical thought and culture among the members of the churches concerned.[41] In such circumstances, the need to promote human development often overrides denominational differences.

In Africa, life-enhancement rituals are non-denominational. So African Christians tend to overlook their denominational differences in matters regarding the marking (or accomplishment) of vital stages in human life cycles. From this background, marriages or the death of members often serve as occasions for Christians across denominational boundaries to cherish one another. Thus, funerals and wake-keepings are often embarked upon as legitimate opportunities for praying together and for providing mutual consolation among Christians of various traditions.[42]

---

[35] Farrell, 'Ecumenism Today: The Situation in the Catholic Church': www.vatican.va/roman_curia/pontifical_councils/chrstuni/documents/rc_pc_chrstuni_doc_20041121_farrell-ecumenismo_en.html (accessed 12 July, 2015).

[36] Respondent from Kenya, *Doctoral Research Questionnaire*, Kenya: 2005, 6. I prefer to uphold the anonymity of the respondents, whose expert opinions may not necessarily be the official teaching of their bishops or dioceses.

[37] Respondent from Uganda, *Doctoral Research Questionnaire,* Uganda: 2005, 10.

[38] Respondent from Tanzania, *Doctoral Research Questionnaire*, Uganda: 2006, 3.

[39] Respondent from Ghana, *Doctoral Research Questionnaire* Ghana: 2006, 3

[40] Respondent from Mali, *Questionnaire de recherche doctorale,* Mali: April, 2005, 11.

[41] Respondent from Cameroun, *Questionnaire de recherche doctorale,* Cameroun: May 2005, 10.

[42] Respondent from DR Congo, *Questionnaire de recherche doctorale,* March, 2006, 6.

On the other hand, the issue of sharing in the Christian heritage is becoming a welcome development among some emerging Catholic groups or movements. In a Catholic diocese of the Central African Republic, some religious movements or pious associations, like the Community of the Beatitudes and the Charismatic renewal movement, took some ecumenical initiatives, under the guidance and support of the local church, and organized common prayers with other Christians.[43] In some parts of Ghana, representatives of four main historical churches (Catholic, Anglican, Methodist and Presbyterian) started to meet, four times a year, to discuss issues of common interest such as Christian morality, the sacraments, funerals and marriage. They also embarked on some socio-cultural projects, like the Vocational Technical School, which they now jointly own and run.[44] Likewise, an ecumenical translation of the Bible and the common use of such versions of the Scriptures also help to make young Christians of different traditions feel more united with each other.[45] Renewal movements in various churches are increasingly imbibing inclusivity (or non-discrimination) in their forms of prayers and evangelical exercises. This posture, which the Charismatic renewal movement, among others, embodies in the Catholic Church, often helps to bring Christians of various traditions together in various parts of Africa.[46]

At this juncture, it needs to be stated that most of the ecumenical structures, namely, commissions for ecumenism (assisted by experts and, where possible, a secretariat at global, national and diocesan levels) and even ecumenical directories, ecumenical institutes, church organs like pastoral councils, ministries and facilities, etc., are still either too weak or non-functional. To sustain the tempo of ecumenical revival in Africa, we contend that uninformed or prejudiced mindsets or behaviour (in the words of John Bluck) need to be addressed, or else they make nonsense of any global policy.[47] Also, African church leaders and the few experts in ecumenism need to teach more about the life-based and praxis-oriented values, structures and symbols of Christian unity that are available in the *Family of God* approach.

Development of Local Ecumenical Directories: A vital working tool for Roman Catholic participation in African ecumenism

The Second Vatican Council's decree on ecumenism, *UR*[48] and the Directory for the Application of Principles and Norms on Ecumenism,[49] which are the global norms on ecumenism for Catholics, make provisions for local adaptations and complementarity. Thus, to address their differing contexts effectively, bishops at various local or regional levels are urged by Revised Directory (henceforth *RD*), 'to issue practical norms for the needs and opportunities presented by diverse circumstances in the light of the prescriptions of the supreme Church authority' (*RD* 39 §2). Diocesan commissions are, likewise, enjoined to adapt the decisions of episcopal conferences to their contexts (*RD* 44 and 84) just as Catholic centres of

---

[43] Respondent from a diocese in Central African Republic, June 2006, 9.

[44] Respondent from Ghana, *Doctoral Research Questionnaire,* Ghana, August 2006, 5.

[45] Respondent from Cameroun, *Questionnaire de recherche doctorale,* Cameroun, May 2005, 3. See also another respondent from Cameroun, in reply to *Questionnaire de recherche doctorale,* Cameroun, 2005, 6.

[46] Respondent from DR Congo in reference to *Questionnaire de recherche doctorale*, DR Congo, 2006.

[47] John Bluck, *Everyday Ecumenism: Can You Take the World Church Home?* Risk Books Series, No. 35 (Geneva: WCC Publications, 1987), 3.

[48] According to the Second Vatican Council's decree on ecumenism, the local church hierarchy can (unless where the statutes of the Bishops' Conference or the Holy See state otherwise), use its discretion in adapting to its local context certain elements in the general policy on sharing in the spiritual heritage of Christians, *Communicatio in Sacris. UR*,. n. 8.

[49] Article No. 18 of the *Directory for the Application of Principles and Norms on Ecumenism* identifies some factors that call for and, indeed, make imperative the adaptation of the general Catholic policies on ecumenism, to the contexts of the various regions and situations, namely, the diversity of nations, differences of relationships between the Catholic Church and other churches or ecclesial communities on the levels of ecclesiology, collaborations and dialogue. Pontifical Council for the Promotion of Christian Unity. *Directory for the Application of Principles and Norms on Ecumenism* (Vatican City: s.n., 1993). Henceforth this document shall be cited as Revised Directory, or *RD.*

formation or institutes of education are asked to adapt the curriculum and programmes of their ecumenical formation to the actual situations of life of persons and groups undergoing training with them (*RD* 5, 44, 56 and 84).

Acting on these provisions, and being fully convinced that the local African context has its own local ecumenical needs (for which local tools are needed), many dioceses in Africa have issued their own ecumenical directives.[50] Taking, as a case in point, SACBC's local directory on ecumenism issued in 2003 under the title *Directory on Ecumenism for Southern Africa* (*DESA*), I shall under this sub-section, attempt to highlight the importance of such vital[51] ecumenical tools in Africa. Then I shall also, in the next few paragraphs, point out areas of continuity and discontinuity between the global Catholic document (*RD*) and its local African complements (in this case, *DESA*). Thereafter, I shall investigate how far *DESA* succeeded in exposing the particular ecumenical needs of the area. Then the quality or efficiency of *DESA*'s measures in addressing local needs will be analyzed. Our evaluation of *DESA* will focus on the need for such localized efforts to embrace larger African Catholic communions within a contextualised global Christian perspectives.

A correlation of the directives and policies of *DESA* and *RD* reveals that the former (which is younger) essentially preserves the universal Catholic ecumenical policies and praxis earlier produced by *RD* (an older document). Apart from its profuse references to *RD*, *DESA* also draws insights from a number of Second Vatican Council documents.[52]

From the perspective of regional African Catholicism, however, it contains little or nothing of the larger African authoritative insights; not even from *Ecclesia in Africa* (rightly described as the most authoritative ecclesiastical document on African Catholicism within the time in question).[53] Again, *DESA* lacks inputs from either the Symposium of Episcopal Conferences of Africa and Madagascar (SECAM), or other local authorities in Africa. As such, one can argue that the central features of the continent's ecumenical experiences may have been lost on the Southern African document, which actually fails to draw from, or plug into, its surrounding regional ecumenical contingencies or experiences. Indeed, the generous leaning on *RD*[54] tends to present *DESA* as unduly focusing more on global Catholic interest or ideal with little

---

[50] Various local churches in Africa (namely, dioceses, vicariate apostolate / apostolic prefectures, and Episcopal conferences) have, in one way another, responded to the mandate of the Second Vatican Council by issuing some directives on ecumenism. One of the earliest among them was issued in June 1965 at the plenary meeting of the Zambia Episcopal Conference, whose directives to the clergy and laity of the country centred on intercommunion and sacramental or non-sacramental sharing with non-Catholic churches: Adrian Smith, 'Ecumenism in Zambia', *African Ecclesiastical Review* Vol. 9, no. 2, (1967): 103. From the replies to our empirical survey, we discovered that a sizeable number of local churches in Africa have issued some documents on the lines of an ecumenical directory, while the majority has not. We could lay our hands only on *DESA*, the directory from the Southern African Catholic Bishops' Conference (SACBC).

[51] South African Catholic Bishops' Conference (SACBC), *DESA*.

[52] Such documents include: *Unitatis Redintegratio*, *UR* (*DESA*, No. 8), *Dignitatis Humanae* (see *DESA*, No. 4.1.5) and *Lumen Gentium* (see *DESA*, No. 4.1.5). It also reflects in the Holy See documents like the 1981 document from John Paul II, On the Role of the Christian Family in the Modern World, *Familiaris Consortio* (see *DESA*, Nos. 7.1; 7.3; 7.9) and the *Rite for Christian Initiation* (see *DESA*, Nos. 4.1.6.1).

[53] John Paul II variously describes *Ecclesia in Africa* (EIA) as a document with very far-reaching objectives. According to him, it is of 'decisive importance' (*EIA*, No. 1), of 'fundamental' relevance (*EIA*, No. 8) and of 'profound significance' (*EIA*, No. 19), first, for the church in Africa, as well as the universal church. Thus, it is difficult to understand why the opportunities offered in such an important document (which surprisingly features only once in *DESA*, and that is in the Preamble) could not be explored in the latter for the benefit of a more culturally relevant (yet universally authentic) local Catholic ecumenical model.

[54] With references to a total of 107 different articles from the 1993 Directory for the Application of Principles and Norms on Ecumenism, *DESA* is able to raise its 80 paragraphs of directives and recommendations. A thorough elucidation and local adaptation of *RD*, which *DESA* hopes to achieve by so doing, entails more than a recapitulation of

attention to local realities. With regard to approach, emphasis or orientation, however, while *RD* inductively pursues global ideals, *DESA,* for its part, could be said to be deductively addressing some local ecumenical exigencies of the Catholic Church in Southern Africa.

African cultures, according to Pope John Paul II's exhortation, are blessed with an immense sense of solidarity and community life expressed in extended family systems etc., which should be preserved as part of a priceless cultural heritage.[55] One of the best ways to preserve this is to apply and institutionalise them in the life of the church, so that Christianity can take deeper root in this part of the world. Apparently motivated by African family values, articles 7.10 and 7.12 of *DESA* urge that full use be made of opportunities afforded in the ecumenical celebration of mixed marriages, and that special consideration be given to spouses in such marriages, who may wish to approach the sacraments together. Such locally inspired directives can help to strengthen the drive towards incorporating, within the ecumenical thrust of African Christianity, typical African communitarian institutions, symbolisms and norms like the extended family as well as other ties or bonds of social solidarity. Nevertheless, *DESA's* provision in this direction is insufficient.

Two of the greatest ecumenical challenges facing African churches, which are sorely missed in *DESA,* have to do with re-establishing mutual trust, or the healing of past memories,[56] among innumerable numbers of independent churches, and developing an effective ecumenical training programme. Indeed, mutual trust is a critical factor in deepening any relationship between two persons; hence forgiveness and reconciliation stand out as key factors in African ecumenism. Again, the kenotic spirit and skills entailed in Christian reconciliation cannot be imbibed simply from institutional mandates or theological dialogues, provided for in such directories. Rather, a sound and holistic ecumenical formation (both in classrooms and in real-life ecumenical contexts), is sorely needed. Such hardly yet exists anywhere in Africa and sadly does not seem to be well provided for in DESA. For instance, concerning ecumenical formation, while *DESA* nn. 3.4 and 3.5 instruct that it should be given to lay members and future priests, it seems, however, to make no clear provision for the training of serving clerics, let alone experts, or even bishops (whose impact on local ecumenism can have highly definitive results).

RD; it also involves a creative reading and application of *RD,* in such a way that can even enrich the general Catholic ecumenical tradition.

[55] *EIA,* No. 43.

[56] In the case of South Africa, for instance, it is obvious that many Christian denominations share in one form of guilt or another regarding the roles they played or omitted to play during the apartheid era. Jurgens Hendriks and Johannes Erasmus, 'Interpreting the New Religious Landscape in Post-Apartheid South Africa', *Journal of Theology for Southern Africa,* No. 109 (2001): 65. See also D. Louw, 'The Healing Power of Forgiveness', in *Meeting the Future: Christian Leadership in South Africa*, eds. Duncan Buchanan and Jurgens H. Hendriks (Randburg, South Africa: Knowledge Resources, 1995), 149-156. In one case, quoting the church's resolution in a 1960 consultation. J.W. Hofmeyr, J.A. Millard and C.J.J. Froneman accuse the Dutch Reformed Church of having supported the apartheid policy as 'the only realistic solution for race relations in South Africa'. See J.W. Hofmeyr, J.A. Millard, C.J.J. Froneman (eds.), *History of the Church in South Africa: A Document and Source Book* (Pretoria, South Africa: University of South Africa, 1991), 216. Tristan Borer, in the same vein, presents the Catholic Church, under the auspices of SACBC, as having dragged its feet both in joining the South African Council of Churches (SACC), and in bringing itself to overtly condemn apartheid or declare the apartheid regime illegitimate. For further reading, Tristan Anne Borer, *Challenging the State: Churches as Political Actors in South Africa 1980-1994* (Notre Dame, IN: University of Notre Dame Press, 1998). Later in this work, this scholar also accuses SACC of having refrained from an outright condemnation of the new reformed apartheid constitution. T.A. Borer, *Challenging the State,* 80. So, in one way or the other, Christian bodies did not fully meet each other's expectations which, somehow, may still remain a barrier to smooth post-apartheid relationships. Thus, they need to embrace the option of asking for (or giving) pardon and forgiveness in the new dispensation, if their ecumenical advances to one another are not to be marred by old prejudices and grudges.

Overall, the current effort at raising local ecumenical directories remains not only a very useful means of exposing the interplay between local and universal exigencies and demands in the same church. It is also a way of exploring the church's rich diversity, whilst promoting its global catholicity. Such local African ecumenical directories could form the basis for a unique African contribution to the global ecumenical enterprise.

New thinking and forms of cohesion and co-belonging in Africa

Promoting ecumenism in and through the 'family of God' promises to make the following ecumenical inroads: evolving an inclusive ecclesiology and inserting the principles of Christian unity within the ambience of human reality. It also entails, in our view, the grounding of ecumenism in the living experience of Christians. By this provision, Catholics seem to have been awakened to the call to embrace Christian unity as a vital condition of Christian, as well as human, life.

Today, there have consequently emerged structural bonds (in the forms of pan-African Bishops' Conferences (or SECAM), Pan-African Roman Catholic Clergy Conference, the pan-African Congress for Catholic Laity, etc.), binding Catholic members, thoughts and structures in Africa together in a spirit of inter-connectedness and cohesion. Furthermore, as the global Catholic Church currently prepares for the Synod on the Family, theologians in Africa have also evolved a common platform for galvanizing African input at the Synod. It holds then, by extension, that global ecumenical movements can succeed, in the African Church and Christianity, suspicious as it is of the historical subjugation, paternalism, and haughtiness of western Christianity,[57] if it adopts home-grown African apparel and indigenous accessories such as those found in the *Family of God* model.

Within this approach, ecumenical structures, operational frameworks and values, as well as inter-church relationships, can be fed with the basic principles and values of the family institution. In a sense, just as evangelisation is said to be lifeless unless families radiate holiness,[58] so also, ecumenism would be sterile unless it promotes existential unity at the centre of which is the family – the acclaimed heart of human community. In the *Family of God* model, the church seems to have discovered a commonly acceptable and flexible framework for unity.

Evaluation

Every system has its own shortcomings. In the next paragraphs, therefore, we shall briefly identify as well as try to divest the African family matrix of its negative tendencies. First, as the Synod notes, families in Africa are faced with some challenges such as exclusivism, tribalism and parochialism, as well as the lack

[57] According to a recent survey of church leaders and institutions in the various regions of Africa, the western church and Christianity played a key role in facilitating colonialism, bigotry and slavery in Africa, and therefore cannot absolve itself of complicity in the historical injustices against Africans. So local African Christians are not so keen in partnering with any global ecumenical strategy unless proper forgiveness is sought from Africa and African interests and values incorporated in such a strategy. All Africa Conference of Churches, 'Report of the Study on African Ecumenical Engagement with the Consultation Process: Towards a Joint EU-Africa Strategy': www.aprodev.eu/files/Africa_ACP/EU Africa/Report%20of%20the%20Study%20on%20Joint%*20EU-Africa%20Strategy%20(3).pdf*. See also European Centre for Development Policy Management (2007) Outline for the Joint EU-Africa Strategy as Endorsed by the Ministerial Troika Meeting of 15th May 2007: http://europafrica.org (accessed 12 June, 2007); NEPAD (2001) *The New Partnership for Africa's Development* (Pretoria: NEPAD); NEPAD (2003) *A Summary of NEPAD Action Plans* (Pretoria: NEPAD); W. Rodney, *How Europe Underdeveloped Africa* (Dar-es-Salaam, Tanzania: Tanzanian Publishing House, 1973).

[58] This is stated in Camillo Ruini's letter, as the vicar of the Pope, to families in 1994. Camillo Ruini, 'Unless Families Radiate Holiness, the New Evangelization is Lifeless', in *L'Osservatore Romano,* weekly edition in English, No. 23, 8th June, 1994, 7.

of some Christian ideals in the African approach to marriage and family.[59] The goal here is to analyse the weakness of the family (both as an institution and as a way of living), in the bid to strengthen and reposition it for better service towards the goal of Christian unity.

Africans tend to pay undue allegiance to blood relationships in such a way that they can go to the extreme of denying justice to non-relatives; claiming that 'blood is thicker than water'.[60] This misconception of the true purpose of family-relatedness, which arises from a somewhat exclusive understanding of love, justice and solidarity, leads to the vices of nepotism, tribalism and ethnicism in Africa. So does the other extreme, seen in the statements of Albert Obiefuna, who argues that a fellow Christian is more a brother or sister than a blood relative who is non-Christian.[61] Both conceptions employ the same exclusivist logic of 'We and They', and are thus guilty of the same error, namely, exclusion. Both cases end up erecting, rather than breaking down, barriers. Such notions of the family contradict the universal ethos of Christ's love, which Christianity preaches and, if not corrected, can weaken the foundation of any ecclesiology or ecumenism that is based on them.

One can argue that the tendency of the family system to condone nepotism and favouritism[62] can present the family model as less suitable for ecumenism since it can lead churches into taking closed and particularist postures[63] in ecumenical interactions. As a panacea, the values of objective solidarity[64] for which the African family is known, should rather be highlighted instead. A Christian approach, in correcting such negative traits, is to immerse the African family in the Christian mysteries of the Trinity and the Incarnation. Exemplifying the universal love of God the Father, Jesus Christ died to save and reconcile all. The Holy Spirit, who is generated from the Father and the Son, bring new life and growth wherever God wills. In a move that accords a higher value to the human family, into which he himself was also born at the Incarnation, Christ announced, for all, a new birth from on high (John 3:3) that is brought about by the power of the Holy Spirit (John 3:5). Through Christ himself, the visible boundaries of the biological family expand to include all human beings (Eph. 2:13-14; 3:16). So now, irrespective of their biological family lineage, tribal or racial background, all believers in Christ have been adopted as God's children (Rom. 8:23; Gal. 4:5). These insights can reinforce the ecumenical value of the African Christian family.

The Christian family in Africa, thus inserted in the transcendent and universal love of the Christian God[65] becomes a veritable symbol for the unity of Christians. Indeed, instead of condoning ethnicism and exclusivism, such a transformed sense of the family rather helps to correct the said negative tendencies in the African family and empowers Christians to rise above the particularist tendency of the biological family.[66]

---

[59] *The Church in Africa,* No. 50.

[60] Catholic Bishops' Conference of Nigeria, *The Church in Nigeria*, No. 54.

[61] Albert K. Obiefuna, 'Presenting the Church as a Family to Christians in Africa: A Presentation to the th General Congregation of the Synod of Bishops' Special Assembly for Africa', *L'Osservatore Romano* (weekly edition in English, No. 17, 27 April, 1994), 9.

[62] Mercy Amba Oduyoye, 'The African Family as a Symbol of Ecumenism', *The Ecumenical Review* Vol. 43, issue 4, October (1991): 465-478.

[63] André Birmelé (ed), *Local Ecumenism: How Church Unity is Seen and Practised by Congregations* (Geneva: WCC Publications, 1984), 35.

[64] Benedict XVI, *Africa's Commitment (Africae Munus): Post Synodal Exhortation of his Holiness Pope Benedict XVI* (Nairobi: Paulines Publications Africa, 2011), No. 91.

[65] African Christians appreciate the universal nature of Christian love, which recognizes all human beings as not only lovable and equal but also interrelated: Eunice Kamara, 'Love as the Basis of Universalism', *African Ecclesiastical Review* Vol. 36, (1994): 380.

[66] Lawrence Nwankwo, 'From Power Christianity to Christianity that Empowers: Towards a Theology of Empowerment in the Nigerian Context.' Doctoral Dissertation, Faculty of Theology, K.U. Leuven, Leuven, 2004, 360 and 445.

All said and done, the fact that this proposal on the church as *Family of God* resonates well with the African context is unmistakable. Within a few months after its official articulation in the 1994 Synod, elements of family began immediately, as stated above, to spring forth in the ecclesial and liturgical life of local African communities of the church. Another reason the *Family of God* model (profiled with the African extended-family principles) enjoys widespread acceptance among the churches is that it presents the Church of Christ in a flexible mould, which can easily be embraced by the churches without fear of losing their distinctiveness. Thus, divested of its negative tendencies, the *Family of God* model of the church can help the churches realise their contemporary ecumenical dreams. What needs to be stated here, however, is that Catholic ecumenical growth and inter-church engagement seem to be uneven in some national or regional contexts in Africa; in some places it is very robust while in others it appears to be very weak. Again, in some areas, we see the Catholic Church fully joining in some inter-church ecumenical ventures, while in other areas, it is not involved.

This is due to various reasons bordering on differences in the ecumenical zeal and commitment on the part of some local ordinaries or episcopal conferences (under whose direct guidance local or regional ecumenism falls squarely on the Catholic Church). Other reasons include rough ecumenical terrain, unappealing or unclear objectives in some ecumenical circles, and the amorphous nature, as well as the un-ecumenical stance of some independent churches – and not forgetting fluctuations in ecumenical momentum.

Conclusion

From the foregoing, it is clear that the *Family of God* model of Church has really had an effect on African Catholicism in a positive ecumenical manner. No doubt therefore that a further theological harnessing of the rich resources available in this model, first by the Catholic Church, and then by the Christian denominations and communities in Africa, can further promote new self-understanding and ecumenical repositioning in view of greater ecumenical growth among the churches. Also, a good embrace of this model by the churches will surely help them to develop ingenious and enduring capacities for promoting Christian unity in Africa. In fact, if African Christianity really hopes to generate a unique voice and momentum within the global ecumenical movement, it has to be along these lines. Thus, this presentation is convinced that anchoring Christian unity in the (family) existential realm of Christians could hold the key to unlocking the ecumenical regeneration of African Catholicism and Christianity. It could also be one of the best contributions Africa could make to the contemporary global ecumenical drive.

Bibliography

All Africa Conference of Churches, 'Report of the Study on African Ecumenical Engagement with the Consultation Process Towards a Joint EU-Africa Strategy.' www.aprodev.eu/files/Africa_ACP/EUAfrica/Report%20of%20the%20Study%20on%20Joint%20EU-Africa%20Strategy%20(3).pdf (accessed 12 June, 2007).

Best, F. Thomas, and Church Union correspondents, 'Survey of Church Union Negotiations 1992-1994.' *The Ecumenical Review* Vol. 47, (1995): 70-130.

______. 'Survey of Church Union Negotiations 1994-1996.' *The Ecumenical Review* Vol. 49, (1997): 223-61.

______. 'Survey of Church Union Negotiations 2003-2006.' *The Ecumenical Review* Vol. 58, issue 3-4, (2006): 297-385.

Birmelé, André (ed.), *Local Ecumenism: How Church Unity is Seen and Practised by Congregations.* Geneva: WCC Publications, 1984.

Anglican-Roman Catholic International Commission, *The Final Report, Windsor, September 1981.* London: SPCK, 1982.

Bluck, John, *Everyday Ecumenism: Can You Take the World Church Home?* Risk Books Series, No. 35. Geneva: WCC Publications, 1987.

Benedict XVI, *Africa's Commitment (Africae Munus): Post Synodal Exhortation of his Holiness Pope Benedict XVI.* Nairobi: Paulines Publications Africa, 2011.

Cassidy. Edward Idris, *Ecumenism and Interrreligious Dialogue: Unitatis Redintegratio, Nostra Aetate.* New York: Paulist Press, 2005.

Catholic Bishops' Conference of Nigeria, *The Church in Nigeria, Family of God on Mission: A Pastoral Exhortation to the Clergy, Religious and Lay Faithful on the First National Pastoral Congress.* Enugu, Nigeria: CIDJAP Press, 2004.

Eggen, Wiel, 'Mawu Does Not Kill: On Ewe Kinship-Focused Religion.'*Exchange* Vol. 31, no. 4, (2002): 342-61.

Fogliacco, Nicholas, 'The Family: An African Metaphor for Trinity and Church.' In *Inculturating the Church in Africa: Theological and Practical Perspectives,* edited by Peter Kayandogo and Cecil McGarry, 120-58. Nairobi: Paulines Publications Africa, 2001.

Idigo, Chike, *Ecumenism in the Wake of the New Evangelisation in Nigeria.* Enugu, Nigeria: SNAAP Press, 2002.

John Paul II, 'On the Role of the Christian Family in the Modern World, *Familiaris Consortio*, 22nd November 1981', in *Vatican II: More Post Conciliar Documents*, 815-898. Vatican Collections, 2, Austin Flannery (ed). Northport, NY: Costello, 1982.

______. 'The Family is the Cradle of Life'. Address to the *Pro Familia* Institute of Brescia, Italy, 23rd April 1994', in *L'Osservatore Romano,* weekly edition in English, No. 21, 25th May 1994, 2.

______. *The Church in Africa: Post-Synodal Apostolic Exhortation, 'Ecclesia in Africa'.* Nairobi: Paulines Publications Africa, 1995.

______. 'On Commitment to Ecumenism, *Ut Unum Sint',* in *Origins* 25 (1995): 50-72.

Kamara, Eunice, 'Love as the Basis of Universalism.' *African Ecclesiastical Review* Vol. 36, (1994): 379-90.

Lumbala, Kabasele F. 'The Church as Family in Africa.' *Concilium* (1995): 93-98.

Magesa, Laurenti, 'African Ecclesiologies.' In *Dictionary of Third World Theologies,* edied by Virginia Fabella and R.S. Sugirtharajah. Maryknoll, NY: Orbis Books, 2000.

Mutiso-Mbinda, John, 'African Background for Community Building.' *African Ecclesiastical Review* Vol. 19, (1977): 299-306.

Nwankwo, Lawrence. 'From Power Christianity to Christianity that Empowers: Towards a Theology of Empowerment in the Nigerian Context.'. Unpublished doctoral dissertation, Faculty of Theology, K.U. Leuven, Leuven, 2004.

Obiefuna, K. Albert, 'Presenting the Church as a Family to Christians in Africa: A Presentation to the Fourth General Congregation of the Synod of Bishops' Special Assembly for Africa.' *L'Osservatore Romano,* weekly edition in English, No. 17, 27th April 1994, 9.

Oduyoye, Mercy A, 'The African Family as a Symbol of Ecumenism.' *The Ecumenical Review* Vol. 43, issue 4, October (1991): 465-478.

Okonkwo, Izuchukwu Edwin, *Praying in Communion with the Saints.* Enugu, Nigeria: SNAAP Press, 2011.

Orobator, Emmanuel, 'A Church in Dialogue as the Family of God.' In *What Happened at the African Synod?* Edited by Cecil MacGarry, 33-50. Nairobi: Paulines Publications Africa, 1995.

Raiser, Elisabeth, 'Inclusive Community.' In *A History of the Ecumenical Movement 1968-2000,* Volume 3, edited by John Briggs, Mercy Amba Oduyoye and Georges Tsetsis, 243-277. Geneva: WCC Publications, 2004.

Rodney, W., *How Europe Underdeveloped Africa.* Dar-es-Salaam, Tanzania: Tanzanian Publishing House, 1973.

Ruini, Camillo, 'Unless Families Radiate Holiness, the New Evangelization is Lifeless.' In *L'Osservatore Romano,* weekly edition in English, No. 23, 8th June, 1994.

Second Vatican Council, 'Decree on Ecumenism, *Unitatis Redintegratio.*' In *Decrees of the Ecumenical Councils, Vol. 2, Trent to Vatican II*, edited by Norman P. Tanner, 908-920. Washington, DC: Georgetown University Press, 1990.

Second Vatican Council, 'Dogmatic Constitution on the Church, *Lumen Gentium.*' In *Decrees of the Ecumenical Councils, Vol. 2, Trent to Vatican II*, edited by Norman P. Tanner, 849-900. Washington, DC: Georgetown University Press, 1990.

South African Catholic Bishops' Conference (SACBC), *Directory on Ecumenism for Southern Africa* Pretoria, South Africa: Department for Ecumenism and Inter-Religious Dialogue, 2003.

Sullivan, A. Francis, *Creative Fidelity: Weighing and Interpreting Documents of the Magisterium.* New York: Paulist Press, 1996.

Symposium of the Episcopal Conferences of Africa and Madagascar: *The Church as Family of God, Instrumentum Laboris and Pastoral Letter.* Accra, Ghana: SECAM Publications, 1998.

Uzukwu E. Elochukwu, *A Listening Church: Autonomy and Communion in African Churches.* Maryknoll, NY: Orbis Books, 1996.

Witte, Henk, 'Building Ecumenical Community at the Local Level: A Case Study.' In *Of All Times and of All Places: Protestants and Catholics on the Church Local and Universal*, edited by Leo J. Koffeman and Henk Witte, 207-231. Zoetermeer, Netherlands: Meinema, 2001.

(103) Evangelicals and African Ecumenism

David N.A. Kpobi

Introduction

Evangelicalism and ecumenism are often considered to be two different strands of Christianity although they are simply descriptions of two approaches to the practice of Christianity and are not necessarily opposed to one other. Evangelicals and ecumenists are indeed united in their zeal to propagate the gospel of Jesus Christ and to proclaim him as Saviour of the world. The two approaches are driven by the underlying conviction that give rise to different emphases in the practice of the faith. In this chapter, we focus on relations between these two groups as an aspect of the development of Christianity on the African continent. The chapter is divided into four main parts:

1. Ecumenism in Africa.
2. Evangelicalism in Africa.
3. Evangelicals and the Ecumenical Movement in Africa.
4. Diffusion of the Evangelical-Ecumenical Tension.

Ecumenism in Africa

If ecumenism is to be understood as the efforts of the churches in working together for the proclamation of the gospel, then the ecumenical spirit cannot be said to have been lacking in Africa before the advent of the ecumenical movement of the nineteenth century.[1] Mission in Africa was from the very beginning carried out by different mission organisations representing various Christian confessions, and the denominations were indeed co-operating with each other in many ways. The participation of the African Church in the movement may have been largely obscured by the prevailing understanding that the entire continent was a mission field at the time and that mission co-operation was hardly considered as an ecumenical effort. It is therefore perhaps not wrong to locate the cardinal impulses of ecumenism in Africa at the beginning of the twentieth century, specifically at the World Mission Conference held in New York in 1900. It was this meeting that first brought together various mission organisations working in Africa to find ways of co-ordinating their work on the continent. Ten years later, the famous World Mission Conference in Edinburgh (1910) focused much on Africa and decided not to separate mission and ecumenism. The ecumenical spirit in mission that surfaced at Edinburgh found its way into the meetings of churches on the continent, particularly among youth. Even before Edinburgh, mission societies in Southern, Eastern and Central Africa had started organising joint conferences to consider doing mission together.[2] The next World Mission Conference, at Le Zoute in 1926, was therefore significantly convened under the theme,

---

[1] The origin and use of the term 'ecumenism' is discussed in a number of publications. Among these, one may consult the following: W.A. Visser 't Hooft, 'The Word Ecumenical – Its History and Use', in *A History of the Ecumenical Movement 1517-1948*, 3rd edition, eds. R. Rouse and S. Neill (Geneva: WCC Publications, 1986), 735-740; and David N.A. Kpobi, *Mission in Ghana – The Ecumenical Heritage* (Accra: Asempa Publishers, 2008), 9-12.

[2] This included the Nyasaland (Malawi) United Missionary Conference of 1904 in Blantyre, the East Africa Missionary Conference of 1909 in Nairobi, and the meeting of the Alliance of Protestant Missions in Nairobi in 1913. See Jesse N. K. Mugambi, 'The Ecumenical Movement and the Future of the Church in Africa', in *The Church in African Christianity – Innovative Essays in Ecclesiology*, eds. Jesse N. K. Mugambi and L. Magesa (Nairobi: Initiative Publishers, 1990), 11.

'The Christian Mission in Africa' and was specifically focused on getting the churches and mission organizations to develop a common strategic plan for mission in Africa. In West Africa, this ecumenical spirit resulted in the formation of the Christian Council of Ghana in 1929.[3] Many other activities helped to propel the ecumenical vision in Africa after these, but it was indeed the formation of the World Council of Churches in 1948 that provided the greatest impetus for the growth of an active and vibrant ecumenical movement in Africa. The inauguration of the All Africa Conference of Churches in 1963 was perhaps the greatest indication of Africa's desire to be a visible part of the worldwide ecumenical movement.

It was no surprise that the growth of ecumenism on the African continent inevitably led to the formation of various other associated bodies to promote different aspects of the ecumenical dream. The Ecumenical Association of Third World Theologians (EATWOT) was formed at a meeting of third world theologians in Dar-es-Salaam, Tanzania, in 1976 and included a number of African theologians. In 1980, African theologians also met in Yaoundé, Cameroon, to form the Ecumenical Association of African Theologians (EAAT) which was a significant indication of how much the ecumenical spirit had become accepted on the African continent. The main motivation for the emergence of these associations has been to provide the ecumenical theological accompaniment needed by the churches in their work in Africa. It is important to note that African Roman Catholic theologians were often part of such meetings and have continued to be since. The Roman Catholic organisation, Symposium of Episcopal Conferences of Africa and Madagascar (SECAM) has demonstrated much commitment in co-operating with Protestant communions on the continent.

Evangelicalism in Africa

'Evangelical' is derived from the Greek *euangelion* that was translated 'gospel' or 'good news', and which became the standard word for the church's mission. The term has however undergone much evolution in meaning over the centuries and became quite important during the Protestant Reformation of the sixteenth century. The reformer, Martin Luther, used the word with reference to its essential meaning as the core of the Christian message as contained in scripture. He was supported by other reformers like Calvin and Zwingli who espoused *sola scriptura,* and by the mid-seventeenth century both Lutheran and Reformed leaders had accepted the label 'evangelical'. Even the Roman Catholic Church referred to the Reformers as such. The Protestants did not however remain united for long, as evidenced by the rise in the eighteenth century of the evangelical revival or Great Awakening. The evangelical revival began in England as a reaction to the dominance of ritualistic forms of worship in the Anglican Church and the gradual erosion of the spiritual fervour that had characterised the reformation movement. The movement soon spread to the colonies in North America and created a diversified spiritual experience that was responsible for many rifts and misunderstandings among Christians. In the nineteenth century in particular, the term 'evangelical' was reserved for those Christians who resisted what was considered to be liberalising theological tendencies within the Protestant churches. At that time, the term 'evangelical' came to be associated with fundamentalism although it was only some versions of the movement that could be so described. Evangelicalism on the African continent may not be separated from the evangelical awakening of the eighteenth century in the sense that it was this revival movement that eventually produced many of the mission organisations that succeeded in introducing an enduring Christian presence on the continent. The 1846 meeting of 'Evangelicals' in London signalled a new attempt to salvage the *sola scriptura* credentials of the movement. Significantly, this meeting resulted in the founding of the British Evangelical Alliance in 1846 which later led to the founding of the World Evangelical Alliance (WEA) in 1951,[4] originally

[3] Kpobi, *Mission in Ghana – The Ecumenical Heritage,* 102-14.

[4] The name was later changed to World Evangelical Fellowship (WEF) and back again to WEA.

consisting of individual evangelical Christians and later becoming more of a fellowship of evangelical churches.

The end of this century saw the founding of a number of Protestant mission organisations, beginning with the London Baptist Missionary Society in 1792. Others soon followed, all with the single objective of extending mission work beyond Europe and North America.[5] These mission societies were explicitly evangelical and non-denominational in character, and those that moved into Africa came along with the spiritual fervour of the evangelical movement. The churches they founded were therefore nurtured with the ideals of the movement. Later developments, however, indicate that this spirit was not sustained and that many African churches acquired other orientations that would cause another evangelical revival (Pentecostalism) on the African continent in the twentieth century.

The twentieth century presented its own challenges to the Christian world, and the church in Africa did not escape this impact. The post-independence years did not turn out to be exactly what many African Christians had hoped for in terms of co-operation between African churches and the new political leadership. The expected impact of the churches was hardly cultivated by the politicians, leading to some Christians calling on the churches to focus more on evangelistic activities and less on social service. These calls arose particularly among Christians who were inclined toward the 'evangelical' wing of the churches. Some of these church leaders therefore began to establish 'evangelical fellowships' consisting of Christians from various denominations to concentrate on spreading the evangelical Christian faith in Africa outside the structure of the churches. The earliest of these fellowships were formed in West Africa, namely, the Sierra Leone Evangelical Fellowship (1959), the Evangelical Federation of Upper Volta (1961), and the Evangelical Association of Ivory Coast (1962).

Evangelicals and the Ecumenical Movement in Africa

However, the Association of Evangelicals in Africa (AEA) would eventually become the foremost gathering of Evangelicals on the continent. The formation of the AEA has been said to have been provoked by the first pan-African theological consultation held at Emmanuel College in Ibadan, Nigeria, in January 1966 under the theme of 'Biblical Revelation and African Beliefs' which was addressed, among others, by two eminent African theologians, Bolaji Idowu of Nigeria and John Mbiti of Uganda.[6] The consultation was held under the auspices of the AACC and dealt with topics including gods, ancestors, the spirit world, the traditional priesthood and sacrifice in the African context. A suggestion at the end of the consultation for churches in Africa to pursue an 'African Christian Theology', in which attention would be given to the primal religions, received a sharp response from the leaders of the growing evangelical movement. The evangelical movement had been planning their own consultation and found justification in responding to the 'liberal' views from the AACC. The evangelical consultation was held at Limuru, Kenya, in February 1966 where the AEA was formally inaugurated.[7] This important meeting was attended by over one hundred evangelical Christian leaders from twenty-three African nations. The meeting had been convened primarily to bring unity and co-ordination to the work and activities of evangelical Christian leaders on the continent. It was also planned as a direct counter-move to the growing ecumenical movement on the continent which

[5] The best-known ones were London Missionary Society (1795), Edinburgh and Glasgow Missionary Society (1796), Netherlands Missionary Society (1797), Church Missionary Society (1799), Wesleyan Methodist Missionary Society (1813), Basel Evangelical Missionary Society (1815), and the North German (Bremen) Missionary Society (1836).

[6] The proceedings and presentations at this conference were edited and published by Kwesi Dickson and Paul Ellingworth under the title, *Biblical Revelation and African Beliefs* (London: Lutterworth Press, 1969). Other prominent speakers at this consultation included Vincent Mulago, Harry Sawyerr and Stephen Ezeanya.

[7] The association was originally named the Association of Evangelicals of Africa and Madagascar (AEAM) and bore that name until 1993 when it was changed, probably because there was no need to separate Madagascar from Africa.

was considered not to be in the best interests of the rapid evangelisation of the continent. One of the objectives of the AEA therefore has been to 'mobilize and empower evangelical churches and mission agencies for total transformation of Africa through evangelisation and effective discipleship'.[8] As at the end of 2014, the AEA was made up of thirty-six National Evangelical Fellowships and para-church organisations.9

The AEA was founded with much active support from the World Evangelical Association based in London which considered the activities of the World Council of Churches in Africa, represented by the All Africa Conference of Churches, as promoting liberal theology and fostering syncretism in African Christianity. The WEA was unhappy with scholarship grants to Africans by the WCC to study theology in known liberal universities and seminaries in the West. They contended that such African scholars often promoted a theology that was moving Africans away from the centrality and authority of the Bible and encouraging the growth of syncretistic African Initiated Churches (AICs). The WEA consciously pursued an attitude of non-co-operation with the global ecumenical movement and was eager that their African collaborators shared this. Besides the WEA, two other international evangelical mission organisations had influenced the formation of the AEA in 1966. The USA-based Interdenominational Foreign Mission Association (IFMA) and the Evangelical Foreign Mission Association (EFMA) had in 1962 jointly established an 'Africa Evangelical Office' in Nairobi to 'protect' evangelical churches from ecumenical influences.[10]

The WEA found support among a number of African scholars, including the Nigerian Byang Kato who became a leading advocate for evangelical theology in Africa.[11] Kato and others, including Tokunboh Adeyemo, worked hard to gain a following from among theologians and ordinary Christians in Africa. Kato did not hide his objection to what he and others considered as the undue influence exerted on African theological students in western universities to imbibe western-formulated doctrines that were inimical to the growth of the church in Africa. One of his statements to this effect was typical of such abhorrence:

> It is unrealistic to expect so many students from the Third World to digest Aquinas, Tillich or Cone and return home unaffected.[12]

In furtherance of the objectives of the AEA, its General Assembly meeting in January 1973 chose the theme of 'Christian Education Strategy', making it a platform for Byang Kato to launch his African Evangelical theology as a counter-teaching to the liberal theology of the AACC. Kwame Bediako observes that for Kato 'the rationale for the existence of the AEAM consisted in its being an "evangelical" counterblast to the "ecumenical AACC"'.[13] Kato and his colleagues had been incensed by the meeting of the International Mission Conference of the WCC held in Bangkok in 1972-1973 where participants focused on what they described as 'liberating' Third World churches from 'old-fashioned' missionary theology. Kato and others were predictably alarmed at the proposals from this meeting which they saw as an imposition of ecumenical theology on African churches. In addition, Kato who became the first General

---

[8] Association of Evangelicals in Africa – www.aeafrica.org (10 accessed December, 2014).

[9] www.aeafrica.org (10 accessed December, 2014).

[10] See David M. Howard, *The Dream that will not Die: The Birth and Growth of the World Evangelical Fellowship 1846-1985* (Exeter, UK: Paternoster, 1986), 67.

[11] Byang Kato was born in Nigeria and became General Secretary of Evangelical Church of West Africa (ECWA). In 1973, he was appointed General Secretary of AEAM, and the following year 1974 became Vice President of the World Evangelical Fellowship.

[12] Byang Kato, *Theological Pitfalls in Africa* (Kisumu, Kenya: Evangel Publishing House, 1975), 140.

[13] Kwame Bediako, *Theology and Identity: The Impact of Culture upon Christian Thought in the 2nd Century and Modern Africa* (Oxford: Regnum, 1992), 396. Bediako also discusses in detail Kato's position on the evangelical-ecumenical divide, 391-407.

Secretary of AEA, intended to fight against what he and others considered to be the promotion of the study of African religions and Islam by African universities. In his *Theological Pitfalls in Africa*, Kato devoted three chapters to discussing ecumenism and ecumenical theology and the dangers that this posed to the development of true 'Biblical Christianity' in Africa. He condemned what he saw as 'poisonous elements' in the WCC's 'theology of ecumenism'.[14] He accused the ecumenical movement, represented in Africa by the AACC, of making it too easy to accommodate all kinds of theological positions, explaining that, as far as he was concerned, the only reason for studying the primal religions of Africa was to expose its idolatry and falsity, and not to treat it as *praeparatio evangelica* as the AACC was doing.

The Pan African Christian Leadership Assembly (PACLA)

Given the frosty relationship that was developing between Evangelicals and the ecumenical movement in Africa, it was not surprising that other measures were adopted by both sides to promote their objectives. One of the measures adopted by AEA was to organise the Pan African Christian Leadership Assembly (PACLA) in Nairobi in December 1976. The genesis of PACLA is closely related to the famous International Congress on World Evangelisation held in 1974 in Lausanne, Switzerland. Forty-five Christian leaders from Africa attending this congress used the opportunity to hold a pan-African meeting to plan for the rapid evangelisation of the African continent. Calling themselves 'Concerned Evangelicals', their main objective was to push forward their agenda of evangelical Christianity for Africa as a counter-movement to the theology of the AACC and the WCC.[15]

The group appointed Bishop Festo Kivengere of Uganda and Michael Cassidy of African Enterprise (AE) to ensure that such a meeting became a reality. Gottfried Osei-Mensah from Ghana, who was a member of the Lausanne Committee, joined this team and took over the organisation of the conference.

PACLA was in session for ten days in Nairobi, 9th-19th December 1976, financed among others by grants from the Billy Graham Evangelistic Association, African Enterprise and World Vision. In all, there were 737 delegates attending from forty-eight African countries. Eight objectives were set for this meeting but we highlight here the seventh of these which more or less captures both the spirit and intention of the meeting:

> To clarify the contribution under God which the African Church, as part of the worldwide body of Christ, can make in the cause of Christian world mission.[16]

The organisers invited representatives of the AACC and other 'liberals' to the meeting, including John Mbiti and John Gatu, in spite of objections from some evangelical leaders, including Kato. One workshop group was devoted to a discussion of 'Ecumenism in Africa'.[17] The other topics and subjects discussed at this meeting encompassed everything relating to the preaching of the true gospel in Africa and all aspects of mission as they affected the African continent at the time.[18] The speakers included such stalwarts of the evangelical movement as Billy Graham and John Stott. Indeed, John Stott made a presentation on 'Theological Tension Points in Ecumenical-Evangelical Relationships'. Some participants also criticized the AACC emphasis on Christian-Muslim dialogue which, in their view, was taking up much of the time that could otherwise be more usefully employed in winning converts to the church. Moreover, such

[14] Kato, *Theological Pitfalls,* 140-41.
[15] Michael Cassidy and Gottfried Osei-Mensah, *Together in One Place:The Story of PACLA* (Nairobi: Evangel Publishing House, 1978), 31.
[16] Records of the Pan African Christian Leadership Assembly (PACLA) Collection 172 held in the archives of the Billy Graham Center, Wheaton, IL.
[17] 'Programme of the Pan African Christian Leadership Assembly', schedule for Tuesday, 14th December 1976.
[18] Cassidy and Osei-Mensah, *Together in One Place*, 1978.

dialogue had not produced much result in terms of reducing or ending conflicts among Christians and Muslims on the continent.

By the end of the meeting, the Evangelicals were strongly resolved to continue to pursue the establishment of 'Biblical Christianity' in Africa. The story of PACLA, including the history and proceedings, was published jointly by Gottfried Osei-Mensah and Michael Cassidy in 1978.[19]

Diffusion of the Evangelical-Ecumenical Tension

Evangelical-ecumenical tensions in Africa have subsided considerably in our day. The latter part of the twentieth century and much of the twenty-first have seen the lessening of tension between African Evangelicals and other Christians on the continent. A close look at relationships among the various traditions gives the impression of more tolerance and desire for co-existence. What could be the reasons behind this changing state of affairs? What has changed? The response to this question is both simple and complex.

In the first place, the last twenty-five to thirty years have seen the rise of the Pentecostal and charismatic movement in much of Africa which has been one of the greatest challenges to the existence of the mainline western-founded churches. In most cases, the attraction of these newer churches lay in their tendency to combine elements of evangelicalism with American mega-church practices. This was a development that attracted many youth from the older churches and even caused a number of local evangelical fellowships to become churches. It also resulted in the older churches adopting 'evangelical' attitudes and practices alongside their orthodox ones. Many of the older churches are now responding to the growing quest for spirituality among both the young and old in Africa, and thereby denying Evangelicals any reason to continue to accuse them of lacking 'spiritual warmth' and vitality. The evangelical movement therefore now lacks sufficient reason to consider historic mission Christianity as a real threat to the spread of Christianity in Africa. It appears therefore that the 'hostility' that once characterised relationships between evangelical and liberal Christians is being steadily diminished. In the same vein, ecumenical formation which, in Africa, was historically rooted in the youth movements and lay training centres of Protestant denominations is experiencing a steady decline. Again, the WCC has in recent times devoted much resource to reaching out to Evangelicals and Pentecostals as well as to Roman Catholics.[20] Whilst this has been interpreted by some Evangelicals as an attempt to broaden the ecumenical movement, many others have welcomed it, if cautiously.

No one need be surprised at these developments since the signals had been present all along. We have indicated earlier that the fact that a continent-wide assembly like PACLA was organised in 1976 was an indication of the lack of confidence in the efforts of the AACC in evangelising the continent, and particularly the fact that the objectives of PACLA were strikingly similar to what the AACC claimed to have been trying to do on the continent. It was significant, therefore, that the second PACLA meeting held in 1994 was jointly sponsored by the AACC, AEA and Africa Enterprise (AE), This was the clearest indication that the main players in Christian mission in Africa were beginning to read the signs of the times and were embarking on 'a translation of such signs into new insights of what it means to be the church as a living organic community of faith'.[21] We also agree with Detlef Kapteina that the invitation of so-called 'liberal theologians' to the first PACLA meeting was already a strong signal against 'Kato's rather

[19] Cassidy and Osei-Mensah, *Together in One Place*, 1978.

[20] The Global Christian Forum, first organised in Nairobi (6th-9th November 2007) was one such initiative of the WCC. Participants included historic Protestants, Roman Catholics, Orthodox, Pentecostals and Evangelicals of many different shades.

[21] Nicholas Otieno, *Journey of Hope – Towards a New Ecumenical Africa* (Geneva: WCC Publications, 2005), 23.

polemical and defensive criticism against non-evangelical African theologians',[22] and an indication of some willingness within the evangelical camp to seek a more conciliatory working relationship with others.

We would also cite the project that produced the *Africa Bible Commentary* which was an initiative of the AEA but which was embraced and promoted as a laudable project by non-Evangelicals on the continent. Indeed, the concern expressed by the General Editor, Tokunboh Adeyemo, in his General Introduction to it, regarding the quality of the church in Africa, was shared by both Evangelicals and other Christians on the continent.[23]

Finally, Africans today find themselves having to live more and more in multi-faith environments requiring co-existence with religions they might have considered strange or unacceptable. It is therefore no longer convenient or even wise for Christians to separate themselves into Evangelicals, Protestants, Pentecostals, etc. Therefore, we would reiterate what is arguably the greatest challenge facing the church in Africa today, namely, harnessing the various expressions of Christian theology on the continent, subjecting them to serious reflection and employing them to create a community that is positively responsive to the gospel. Uniformity in theology can in no way be the aim of such a process. Solidarity in mission, if it succeeds in sifting the chaff from the real stuff, should enrich and not impoverish Africa's experience of God.

Bibliography

Adeyemo, Tokunboh (ed.), *Africa Bible Commentary*. Nairobi: Word Alive Publishers, 2006.

Association of Evangelicals in Africa. www.aeafrica.org (accessed 10 December, 2014).

Bediako, K., *Theology and Identity: The Impact of Culture upon Christian Thought in the 2nd Century and Modern Africa*. Oxford: Regnum, 1992.

Cassidy, Michael and Osei-Mensah, Gottfried, *Together in One Place: The Story of PACLA*. Nairobi: Evangel Publishing House, 1978.

Dickson, Kwesi. A. and Ellingworth, Paul (eds.), *Biblical Revelation and African Beliefs*. London: Lutterworth Press, 1969.

Howard, David, *The Dream that will not Die: The Birth and Growth of the World Evangelical Fellowship 1846-1986*. Exeter, UK: Paternoster, 1986.

Kapteina, Detlef, 'The Formation of African Evangelical Theology.' *African Journal of Evangelical Theology,* Vol. 25, no. 1, (2006): 61-84

Kato, Byang, *Theological Pitfalls in Africa.* Kisumu, Kenya: Evangel Publishing House, 1975.

Kpobi, David N. A., *Mission in Ghana: The Ecumenical Heritage.* Accra: Asempa Publishers, 2008.

Mugambi, Jesse N.K., and Magesa, Laurenti (eds.), *The Church in African Christianity – Innovative Essays in Ecclesiology*. Nairobi: Initiative Publishers, 1990.

Otieno, Nicholas, *Journey of Hope – Towards a New Ecumenical Africa.* Geneva: WCC Publications, 2005.

Rouse, Ruth, and Neill, Stephen C. (eds.), *A History of the Ecumenical Movement 1517-1948*, 3rd edition. Geneva: WCC Publications, 1986.

Visser 't Hooft, W.A., 'The Word Ecumenical: Its History and Use.', In *A History of the Ecumenical Movement 1517-1948*, (3rd edition), edited by Ruth Rouse, and Stephen Neill, 735-740.. Geneva: WCC Publications, 1986.

[22] Detlef Kapteina, 'The Formation of African Evangelical Theology', *African Journal of Evangelical Theology,* Vol. 25, no. 1, (2006), 78.

[23] Adeyemo had stated that 'the Church in Africa was a mile long in terms of quantity but only an inch deep in terms of quality': Tokunboh Adeyemo (ed), *Africa Bible Commentary* (Nairobi: Word Alive Publishers, 2006), viii.

(104) PENTECOSTALS AND AFRICAN ECUMENISM

Fidelis Nkomazana

Introduction

This chapter examines Pentecostal ecumenical fellowships, alliances and councils in Africa, as well as their activities and contributions to the growth of Christianity. In response to the spirit of ecumenical understanding, co-operation and unity in addressing issues of common interest, Pentecostals in Africa have been forging relationships and ties at national, regional, continental and international levels. The discussion touches on national ecumenical associations and there are thirty-six of these bodies across the continent. At a continental level, these national associations have given rise to the Association of Evangelicals in Africa, an important umbrella body for all Pentecostal national bodies and churches, charismatics and para-church organizations. Other wider ecumenical relations, such as the All Africa Conference of Churches, Accrediting Council for Theological Education in Africa, and Association of Pentecostal Theological Education in Africa, will also be examined. At the international level, Pentecostal churches and these national umbrella bodies are affiliated to the World Pentecostal Fellowship, which will be discussed in the closing pages of this chapter.

Pentecostal National Ecumenical Associations

From the 1970s onwards, we began to see Pentecostals in Africa developing relationships with national ecumenical bodies in order to promote unity, dialogue and co-operation, and to foster common ecumenical action within Pentecostal churches, and with other churches and religious faiths. Some of these national bodies include the Evangelical Alliance of Angola, Evangelical Fellowship of Botswana, Association of Evangelicals in Eritrea, Evangelical Churches Fellowship of Ethiopia, Evangelical Alliance of Kenya, Evangelical Association of Malawi, Association Evangelica de Moçambique, Evangelical Fellowship of Namibia, Evangelical Fellowship of Sierra leone Evangelical Alliance of South Africa, Swaziland Conference of Churches, Tanzania Evangelical Fellowship, Evangelical Fellowship of Uganda, and Evangelical Fellowship of Zambia, to name just a few.

These developments have taken place over time and continue to manifest themselves at various stages and settings. Pentecostal churches continue to respond to new challenges posed by globalization and the technological advances of the 21st century through these ecumenical bodies. The growth of these bodies has not only increased the level of interaction and dialogue between Pentecostal churches and other religious faiths, but has also helped the church to cross old boundaries and stand together in order to transform and serve society. To appreciate these developments, three examples of national ecumenical bodies are discussed in detail below.

The Evangelical Fellowship of Botswana (EFB)

After independence, Botswana witnessed the establishment of Pentecostal relationships with ecumenical organizations, which created an atmosphere of understanding, mutual respect and tolerance. Through ecumenical co-operation, Pentecostals solved many differences and challenges.[1]

---

[1] James Amanze, *The Origin and Development of the Ecumenical Movement in Botswana, 1965-1994* (Gaborone: Pula Press, 1994), 1-4.

Four major ecumenical organizations – the Botswana Council of Churches (BCC), Evangelical Fellowship of Botswana (EFB), the Organization of African Initiated Churches (OAIC), and Ministers' Fraternal (MF),[2] were from the 1960s founded with the aim of bringing co-operation and unity to bear on addressing national religious, political and social issues. In the past, doctrinal differences had contributed towards the marginalization of Pentecostals and AICs by the older mission churches. This had compelled church leaders to adopt a new approach through close co-operation in order to address issues of national and common interest.[3]

The BCC, the oldest of the umbrella organizations, was mainly founded by mainline churches in 1966. The EFB, an umbrella organization for all Pentecostals and other 'Bible Believing', evangelical or 'born again'-types of churches in Botswana, was established in 1973.[4] The OAIC, which brings together African Independent Churches, was formed in 1978. The fourth umbrella organization is the MF, an important ecumenical forum for all Christian ministers in Botswana, responsible for organizing fellowship forums and a platform for all umbrella organizations for sharing ideas, learning and acting together on national issues. The MF is strategically placed to address issues, such as organizing joint national worship services, intended to transcend denominational differences and boundaries. Pentecostals have played a leading role in the activities of the MF to the extent that the current chairman of the organization, Mr Sam Makgaola, is a Pentecostal from the Assemblies of God.[5]

The goals of the different dialogues represented by MF are modest but significant, resulting in the mutual learning, sharing and understanding of the faith, identifying areas of doctrine and church life which need fuller exploration, and looking for ways of co-operating in various fields. The BCC, EFB, OAIC and MF have stood together and presented a united voice on critical issues such as human rights, land and abortion. The four organizations have organized joint conferences and workshops on various issues. In 2005 and 2006, the leadership of the three umbrella organizations participated in conferences and workshops that were organized by the BCC to discuss the national Vision 2016 initiatives of 'Building a Moral and Tolerant Society', and subsequently forwarded their contribution to the Vision 2016 Council. The broad ecumenical composition of the MF is a remarkable achievement because it brings together leaders from Pentecostal, mainline and African Independent Churches. Its ecumenical aim is to develop a united Christian witness and streamline the efforts of different churches in carrying out national responsibilities. It views itself as a fellowship of churches and Christian organizations which seek to encourage ecumenism and promote democracy, peace and justice through healing, reconciliation, economic development and empowerment of the disadvantaged, as well as through reflection on theological issues.

The formation of these umbrella organizations has helped different religions and denominations to cross religious boundaries to meet and mix with people of other faiths. The old religious order of mistrust, competition and conflict among the churches, before the early 1960s, was being challenged to give way to a new religious order based on mutual co-operation, respect, understanding and a sense of common identity among Christians, despite their many fundamental differences. This provides an opportunity for a environment conducive to interaction, discovery, encounter and exchange between different faiths. While Pentecostalism's involvement in interfaith encounters is in the best national and broader faith interests, radical Pentecostals are totally against the existence of such an ecumenical objective of creating dialogue and uniting all Pentecostals with other religions and churches.[6]

---

[2] James Amanze, *Ecumenism in Botswana: The Story of the Botswana Christian Council* (Gaborone: Pula Press, 2006), 344-54.

[3] James Amanze, *Botswana Handbook of Churches* (Gaborone: Pula Press, 1994), 192, 221.

[4] Amanze, *Botswana Handbook of Churches*, 32-33.

[5] Amanze, *Botswana Handbook of Churches*, 26, 42-43, 221, 192.

[6] Interviewed Apostle D. D Monnakgosi, Mogoditshane, Botswana, March, 2007.

By 2002, the EFB had grown to 42 churches with over 500 local churches and groups around the country,[7] with the objective of providing ecumenical dialogue, unity, networking, advocacy, discipleship, gender equality and economic empowerment, and leadership development through education, research, conferencing and information dissemination.[8]

The EFB is made up of local committees under the leadership of the EFB National Executive which manages the central office. Via this office, the EFB communicates issues of importance to all its member churches countrywide. EFB strictly adheres to the events listed in its annual calendar; and from among the most important events of the calendar year are the annual conference and joint crusades to address HIV and AIDS and other issues of national concern such as poverty, unemployment and democracy. The current EFB projects include a proposed hospice for counselling services and facilities for the terminally ill.

The Pentecostal Fellowship of Nigeria (PFN)

While PFN was founded in 1985 and inaugurated in 1986 in Lagos, as the Pentecostal umbrella organization uniting all Pentecostal and charismatic churches and organizations believing in the Pentecostal experience as stated in Acts 2:4, ecumenical efforts in Nigeria date back to the 1930s, when Joseph Babalola of Faith Tabernacle led a revival that converted 1,000 people. In 1932, his movement initiated ties with the Pentecostal Apostolic Church of Great Britain after coming into conflict with the colonial authorities, but this association collapsed over the use of modern medicine.[9] In 1974, the Pentecostal umbrella organization, Grace of God Ministry, was founded in eastern Nigeria. In the 1980s, Pentecostals became active in the Christian Association of Nigeria (CAN), which was founded in 1976, initially including only Catholics and mainline Protestants, but by 1988 it had incorporated churches associated with the PFN and the Organization of African Initiated Churches. At about that time, the CAN youth wing organized prayer campaigns against the proposal to introduce Sha'riah law in Nigeria. This development resulted from the decision in 1986 by General Babangida to make Nigeria a member of the Organization of the Islamic Conference, which triggered numerous Pentecostal protests. Pastor Benson Idahosa, an influential Pentecostal leader of evangelical student revivals and founder of the church of God Mission International in 1972, threatened to call for a Christian boycott of newspapers favouring Islamization. In 1987, Sheikh Abubakar Gumi, a leading Muslim cleric, publicly declared that Muslims would never allow non-Muslims to assume political leadership in Nigeria. In response, Pentecostals through PFN rallied together for action.[10] In brief, the objectives of PFN were advocacy for national peace and unity, gender equality, empowerment and the protection of women and children.

The Evangelical Fellowship of Zimbabwe (EFZ)

The EFZ, an umbrella organization of Pentecostals and Charismatics in Zimbabwe, was founded in 1962 and represents denominations, churches, para-church movements and individual Christians of evangelical persuasion. It has grown to a membership of over 300 churches and over 4.5 million members. It provides a platform for joint action and the co-ordination of the activities of the member bodies. It focuses on leadership development, evangelism, theological reflection, education, the need for the church to be a prophetic voice, relief and development. Its vision is presented as 'A fellowship of Evangelicals fulfilling the Great Commission to impact the nation in all aspects of life' and its mission as 'To mobilize, empower and network evangelicals for the accomplishment of the Great Commission in Zimbabwe'. The vision and the mission of the EFZ are anchored in following core values and areas of operations: Christ-centredness;

---

[7] Interviewed Sam Makgaola of the Assemblies of God, August, 2006.

[8] Interviewed Pastor Emmanuel Ngwako, EFB offices, Gaborone, August, 2007.

[9] Alan Anderson, *An Introduction to Pentecostalism: Global Charismatic Christianity* (Cambridge: CUP, 2004), 86-87.

[10] Pew Research Center, 'Historical Overview of Pentecostalism in Nigeria': www.pewforum.org/2006/10/05/historical (accessed 9 December, 2015).

engagement and development; mission and world evangelism; church planting, discipleship and prayer; women's, youth and child ministry; hospitality and conferences; research and development through monitoring, evaluation, research and documentation; peace and justice through peace-building, conflict resolution and management; democratic government and social integration; election monitoring; humanitarian relief and development through child protection, HIV and AIDS, shelter, water and sanitation; emergencies and disaster preparedness; gender equlity through economic development and empowerement , women's social, political, economic and ministry development.[11] These activities gave birth to various projects on social justice, conflict mediation and resolution, prostitution and gender-based violence, orphanages, empowerment and the fight against HIV and AIDS. On some of these, the EFZ and the Zimbabwe Christian Council, an umbrella organization for mainline churches, joined efforts to promote ecumenicity on certain national projects.

Other Forms of Pentecostal Expressions of Ecumenism in Africa

Para-Church Organizations

Another important ecumenical development in Africa has to do with the growth of para-church organizations, most of which are inclined to Pentecostal theology and practice. Zimbabwe alone has over 41, some of the largest being Scripture Union and Prison Fellowship International.

Prison Fellowship International (PFI)

PFI was founded in the USA in 1976 by Charles Colson and expanded internationally in 1979. Today it works in more than 125 countries in Africa and around the world as the largest association of national Christian missionaries working within the criminal justice sys.[12] PFI has two Africa Regional Directors, Mr Samuel N'tcho (Ivorian), representing Francophone Africa and Mr Enocent Silwana (Zambian), representing Anglophone Africa. At the PFI Board of Directors, the African region is represented by Charles Cofie from Ghana and Mrs Ida Drameh from Gambia, secretary and member of the Board of Directors respectively.[13]

Scripture Union Africa (SU)

Scripture Union (SU) is an international,interdenominational evangelical Christian organization, which works with churches throughout Africa and the world to make God's Good News known to children, young people and families; to encourage them to become followers of God through regular Bible reading and prayer, and also to link up with their local church. It was founded by Josiah Spiers in London on 2nd June 1867. He adopted a new approach to sharing Christ with children by teaching hymns and choruses and telling stories at their level of understanding.

From the 1940s, SU began to grow throughout the world. National Scripture Union organisations are autonomous and are affiliated to Scripture Union International. This also gives each national SU a level of independence in the way of contextualising its mission so that its work is appropriate to the context, culture and situation of the people it seeks to serve. SU is found in almost every African country with its regional headquarters in Nairobi, Kenya. It spread to Zimbabwe in 1945.[14] Among other things, SU has been

---

[11] Evangelical Fellowship of Zimbabwe, 'Vision – a fellowship of evangelical, impacting the nations in all aspects of life': http//efzimbabwe.org (accessed 9 December, 2015).

[12] Prison Fellowship International, 'What We Do: The Problem, Spreading the Gospel, Rescuing Children and Restoring Justice', http://pfi.org (accessed 9 December, 2015).

[13] Prison Fellowship International, 'What We Do'.

[14] Scripture Union Africa, 'Children and Youth Following Jesus, filled with hope and transforming the families and

involved in HIV education, research and information dissemination in schools and universities, with the vision of an AIDS-free generation through evangelism. In many Africa countries, the activities of the organization focuses on schools ministry, the production and distribution of Bible guides, prayer ministry, camps, values education, sports ministry, work with people with special needs, capacity-building and partnerships, training and leadership development.

By 1985, Scripture Union International had developed its aims, statement and working principles, which African Scripture Union groups have over the years been implementing through leadership training, development and partnership with the local church and schools in order to empower youth through coaching, mentoring and providing life skills as they grow to mature adults. The organisation is primarily a volunteer organisation with only a small number of full-time staff training, encouraging and co-ordinating ministry workers round the world.[15]

Pentecostalism and Wider African Ecumenism

Relationships between Pentecostals and the All Africa Conference of Churches as well as the experiences of the Cameroonians and South Africans are a good example here.

Pentecostals and All Africa Conference of Churches (AACC)

While there are initiatives for creating dialogue and co-operation between the Pentecostal associations and AACC, there is a growing suspicion between these two ecumenical bodies. For instance, AACC is not happy with some Pentecostals who have embraced the prosperity gospel teaching, which the organization regard as controversial, especially the extent to which they emphasize this teaching which is seen as exploiting the ignorance and emotions of the poor. Speaking at the ecumenical platform of the World Social Forum in Nairobi, Kenya, the Rev. Dr Nyansako-ni-Nku, President of the AACC, a fellowship of mainline Protestant, Orthodox and indigenous Christians, for instance, criticized this teaching and regarded the Pentecostals as a 'disease' spreading across Africa. He specifically directed his remarks at a type of Pentecostal prosperity preacher, whom he said exploited people in the name of the gospel and became richer, while the congregations became poorer.[16] The emergence of the National Association of Evangelicals and the World Evangelical Fellowship (now Alliance), however, continue to create a rich history of ecumenical collaboration between Pentecostals and other Christians, fellowships, federations and councils. The WCC has also been holding talks with Pentecostals internationally to improve relationships and co-operation between Pentecostals and other Christians.[17]

The Cameroonian Experience

Relationships between Pentecostals and mainline churches in Cameroon also leave something to be desired. The mainline churches excluded Pentecostals from their activities and interactions. Pentecostals, on the other hand, resorted to making provocative statements against the mainline churches. The situation was characterized by mutual accusations.[18] The sources of division were, first, on baptismal practices, that

---

nations of Africa': www.ScriptureUnion.org.ZW/history-and-background.php (accessed 9 December, 2015).

[15] www.su-africa.org (accessed 5 October, 2015).

[16] World Religions News, 'African Church Leader Warns of "disease" of Pentecostalism': http://archives.adventistreviews.org/article/955/archives/issue-2007-1503 (accessed 9 December, 2015).

[17] WCC, 'A worldwide fellowship of churches seeking unity, a common witness and Christian service': www.oikoumene.org/en/church-families/pentecostal-churches (accessed 9 December, 2015).

[18] Priscille Djombone, 'Manifestations of Ecumenism in Africa Today: A Study of the Mainline and Pentecostal

is, whether this be by total immersion or by infant baptism. The second source of open rivalry between the two family churches was on training. Mainline churches insisted on training for many years in scholarly exegesis, critical and historical Biblical methods, while Pentecostals saw that as a waste of time, believing that the Holy Spirit led the preacher. While the Pentecostals have in recent years changed their approach to training and have introduced their own theological institutions, they have remained fundamentalist in their approach to the Bible. The third source of conflict is the role of the Holy Spirit, whom the Pentecostals see as leading believers in reading the Bible, and they accuse the mainline churches for ignoring him. While dialogue remains difficult, the decision of some Pentecostals, such as the Full Gospel Mission, to join the ecumenical body for the mainline churches has contributed towards creating a more conducive ecumenical environment.[19]

The South African Experience

The history of Pentecostalism in South Africa has shown that it is inherently ecumenical in nature and practice. From 1975, Frank Chikane, a member of the Apostolic Faith Mission, the largest Pentecostal denomination in South Africa, participated in numerous interdenominational organizations – such as the Student Christian Movement, Reinhard Bonnke's Christ for All Nations evangelistic ministry, which closely worked with Pentecostal churches for the expansion of Christianity in Africa – and became General Secretary of the South African Council of Churches, an umbrella body for all churches. He also became politically engaged in fighting against apartheid, performed the important role of mediator on political issues in co-operation with Pentecostal and other Christian ecumenical bodies for a common policy. The impact on society was huge.[20]

Pentecostalism and the International Ecumenism of Evangelical/Pentecostals

The other important African ecumenical organizations that have contributed immensely to creating networks, dialogue and partnerships within the continent as well as internationally are the Association for Evangelicals in Africa, the Accrediting Council for Theological Education in Africa and the Association of Pentecostal Theological Education in Africa.

The Association of Evangelicals in Africa (AEA)

AEA is a continental umbrella association for evangelical Christians promoting dialogue, fostering unity and common ecumenical action. Its mission is to mobilize and empower evangelical churches and mission agencies for the total transformation of Africa through evangelization and effective discipleship, and thus increasing the level of interaction between Pentecostal and other Evangelical churches. Its vision therefore is to unite Evangelicals in Africa for holistic ministries that make a difference. It exists to equip, connect and unite Evangelical churches in Biblical theology and transformative mission for the establishment of God's kingdom.

AEA has about 150 million individual Christian associates in Africa. It has its headquarters in Nairobi and is currently putting up massive buildings, which were due to open in 2017.[21] It was formed in Kenya in 1966 by 102 evangelical Christian leaders from twenty-three African nations and missionaries from other countries. Its purpose was to establish a permanent association promoting evangelical unity, fellowship and

Churches in Cameroon', *International Journal for the Study of the Christian Church,* Vol. 8, no. 4, (2008): 355-68.
[19] Djombone, 'Manifestations of Ecumenism', 364-67.
[20] Pew Research Center, 'Historical Overview of Pentecostalism in South Africa'.
[21] Association of Evangelicals in Africa, 'A Symbol of African Evangelical Unity': www.aeafrica.org/news/view.htm (accessed 9 December, 2015).

Christian witness in Africa. In its half-century of existence, the AEA has grown into a continental family of over 100 million Evangelicals consisting of thirty-six National Evangelical Fellowships that are made up of numerous local churches. There are thirty-four associate members who consist of para-church organizations and eleven special members representing local churches in countries where there are no National Evangelical Alliances. Within the AEA is the Pan African Christian Women Alliance (PACWA) Women's Commission, bringing together African women to strategize on conflict prevention, management, resolution and issues vital to Evangelicals in Africa.[22]

The Accrediting Council for Theological Education in Africa (ACTEA)

ACTEA is the ministry of the Theological and Christian Education Commission of the Association of Evangelicals in Africa (AEA). It was started in 1975, seeing the need for the Association for Evangelical Theological Schools in Africa. It provides theological strategy for Evangelicals in Africa. Due to the Pentecostal attitude of 'no theology but the Bible', these churches were characterized by an inability to engage theologically at the academic level or appreciate the importance of theological education for sound interpretation and effective evangelistic tasks.[23] ACTEA was granted membership of the AEA Theological and Christian Education Commission in 1990. Its mission is basically for accreditation. Its objectives are to promote quality evangelical theological education in Africa by providing support services, facilitating academic recognition, fostering networking through enhancing excellence, quality and relevance in theological education. The provision of support services involves the provision of directories of theological schools and TEE in Africa, bulletins, Africa prayer networks, the Africa Newsletter, along with documents on conferences, library services, staff training seminars and workshops. Fostering networking involves linking schools and theological educators across Africa and beyond, facilitating institutional collaboration, the sharing of resources and best practice, and consolidating reflection on challenges facing theological education. Accreditation is all about facilitating academic recognition. It seeks to enhance, assess and sanction every aspect of theological programmes for post-secondary and higher levels in Africa.

As a quality assurance institution, ACTEA has the mandate of promoting quality and relevant evangelical theological education in Africa through networking, the provision of various services and accreditation. Its Standards and Guides meet internationally acknowledged standards of quality. The ACTEA accreditation process is self-evaluating, followed by peer review assessments.[24]

The Association of Pentecostal Theological Education in Africa (APTEA)

APTEA is an interdenominational Pentecostal association giving oversight to Pentecostal theological education in Africa. Due to its ecumenical approach, it welcomes non-Pentecostal institutions into membership. It was formed on 21st February 2011 in Nairobi when Pentecostal church leaders and theological educators from across Africa and partners from the USA were brought together to establish an association to network and set standards for APTEA. It is a member of the World Alliance for Pentecostal Theological Education (WAPTE), which is the education arm of the Pentecostal World Fellowship (PWF), an international body that sets and monitors standards for endorsement, accreditation and teacher certification for its members. Its aim is to increase awareness of education programmes in Africa with the intention of achieving efficiency and excellence in Pentecostal mission through the recognition of academic programmes, faculty development, institutional enrichment and scholarly research and writing; approval of standards and procedures for endorsement and accreditation, provision of teacher certification

---

[22] Pew Research Center, 'Historical Overview of Pentecostalism in Nigeria'.

[23] Phillippe Emedi, 'ACTEA and Quality Assurance in Evangelical Theological Education in Africa', in *Handbook of Theological Education in Africa,* eds. Isabel Phiri and Dietrich Werner, (Pietermaritzburg, South Africa: Cluster Publishing, 2013), 1066, 1068.

[24] Emedi, 'ACTEA and Quality Assurance', 1064-74.

and promotion of contextual scholarly research and writing; and to encourage the sharing of resources and promoting faculty enrichment. It plays a critical role as an instrument for ecumenical co-operation among African Pentecostal Christians and other African associations of theological education in pursuance of academic excellence.[25] The major hindrance is that there are few Africans found in strategic leadership of the main organization of the Pentecostal World Fellowship which is mainly dominated by educators from the West. There is therefore a crucial need to Africanize APTEA for relevance at every level.[26]

Past Pentecostal perception of scholarship and spirituality led to theological education being seen as a secular discipline. Pentecostal tradition in Africa inherited a model of ministerial formation that was based on profound suspicion and indifference towards scholarship and academic theological education. In the past, distrust of academic theological education resulted in a lack of adequately qualified personnel to run institutions in Africa. Pentecostals in Africa had inherited a western model of theological education resulting from a type of theological education and ministerial formation producing ministers after the model of the West. Africans became a vulnerable target for fundamentalist models of education produced by Bible colleges uncritically established and exported to Africa producing Christians that had no relevance to Africa in terms of culture or epistemologies.[27]

Finally, it must be observed that, while APTEA is an excellent initiative, there is a need to ensure contextualization of research and scholarship on current trends in theological education, through the support and promotion of development of local leaders, consultations, networking and close working relationships, and the sharing of resources and collaboration on matters of mutual concern for Pentecostal churches and theological institutions in Africa.

The World Pentecostal Fellowship (WPF)

At a global level, the majority of African Pentecostals have joined the WPF as against the World Evangelical Alliance. WPF, which has about sixty global member organizations, is a fellowship of Pentecostal churches and denominations from across the world. Its mission is to unite and mobilize the global Spirit-filled family in completing the Great Commission of Jesus Christ. It also nurtures an environment of co-operation and flexibility among the Pentecostal mission organizations worldwide. It recognizes the diversity of historical and experiential backgrounds of the various Pentecostal enterprises and promotes their global networks. The WPF is therefore a global co-operation and fellowship of Pentecostal theological associations, bringing together Pentecostal theological institutions and educators seeking to enrich ecumenical networks of Pentecostal denominations. Twenty-three world conferences in eighteen major cities affecting global Christianity have so far been held. It was at the first conference in Zurich in 1947, that a resolution to establish an organization similar to the World Council of Churches was reached and acted upon. This meeting was organized by a Swiss pastor, Leonard Steiner, assisted by David du Plessis, a South African church leader. Since then the conference has been conducted every three years in various major cities around the world. In 2001, the conference was in Los Angeles, California, which was convened in celebration of the Azusa Street Revival. It was at the 2004 conference that the WPC formally took the name World Pentecostal Fellowship. In 1982 and 2004, the conferences were held in Nairobi and Johannesburg, which closely linked WPF with Africa.

Pentecostal churches and organizations that conform to the PWF statement of faith apply for membership to the Advisory Committee of the Fellowship. The statement of faith of the WPF is both Evangelical and Pentecostal in belief and practice.

---

[25] Chammah J. Kaunda, 'African Pentecostalism Coming of Age: The Association for Pentecostal Theological Education in Africa from an Ecumenical Perspective', in *A Handbook of Theological Education in Africa,* 1050-58.
[26] Kaunda, 'African Pentecostalism Coming of Age', 1050-58.
[27] Kaunda, 'African Pentecostalism Coming of Age', 1050-58.

Conclusion

The chapter has examined the significance of Pentecostal ecumenical movements in Africa. The growth and increase of these ecumenical bodies have led to greater networking, relationships within Pentecostalism, dialogue, greater understanding, unity, co-operation and an impact on society. African Pentecostal/Evangelical associations not only present an excellent agenda for dialogue, networking and co-operation with other regional and international ecumenical organizations, but also point to better leadership development and training programmes in the future.[28] The growth of this ecumenical co-operation will increase the level of interaction between Pentecostals and other theological institutions, which will result in the sharing of resources and a willingness to partner and learn from each other.

Bibliography

Amanze, J., *The Origin & Development of the Ecumenical Movement in Botswana, 1965-1994*. Gaborone: Pula Press, 1994.

______. *Botswana Handbook of Churches*. Gaborone: Pula Press, 1994.

______. *Ecumenism in Botswana: The Story of the Botswana Christian Council*. Gaborone: Pula Press, 2006.

Martin, D., and Mullin, P. (eds.), *Strange Gifts: A Guide to Charismatic Renewal*. Oxford: Blackwell, 1984.

Anderson, A., *An Introduction to Pentecostalism: Global Charismatic Christianity*. Cambridge: CUP, 2004.

Strohbehn, U., *Pentecostalism in Malawi: A History of the Apostolic Faith Mission in Malawi*. Zomba, Malawi: Kachere, 2005.

Phiri, I. A., and Werner, D. (eds.), *Handbook of Theological Education in Africa*. Pietermaritzburg, South Africa: Cluster Publishing, 2013.

[28] World Council of Churches, 'Pentecostal Churches'. www.oikoumene.org/en/church-families/pentecostal-churches (accessed 9 December, 2015).

(105) The Contribution of African Student Christian Movements to African Ecumenism

Chammah J. Kaunda and Albert Billy Bangirana

Introduction

African Christianity highlights the significant Christian student organisations which have contributed greatly to the development of Christianity. These organisations serve to buttress faith principles among young people at a stage marked by numerous life challenges. They are also powerful examples of political movements which influenced black politics and contributed to independence in many African countries. The aim of this chapter is to describe different Christian student organisations working in different parts of Africa and to assess their contribution to African Christianity with regard to strengthening ecumenism in Africa.

Denominational Christian Student Associations

Catholic Student Associations

The Association of Catholic Tertiary Students (ACTS)[1] is a movement for tertiary students, which exists at institutions for higher education within South Africa. Each ACTS branch has to be affiliated to the local School Representative Committee (SRC) and is to be a prophetic presence, challenging the life of the institution. It is a student-driven organisation, empowering students to lead within the church, within institutions of higher education and within society as a whole. Only full-time students may be members; however, this requirement does not apply at Universities which offer distance learning such as UNISA.

The Nigeria Federation of Catholic Students (NFCS)[2] is an association that forms an umbrella for all groups, societies, faculty associations, etc. of all Catholic students in the University of Nigeria, Nsukka. The motto of NFCS is 'Living the Faith'. NFCS also affiliates the Catholic Law Students Association of Nigeria (CALSAN), covering all Nigerian universities, and the Catholic Law Students Association (CLASA) of the University of Benin.

These Christian student organisations provide spiritual, academic and social welfare and fraternity to the Catholic student population of Africa. They are also involved in youth structures within various dioceses, thus contributing to the development of youth in the local church.

Seventh Day Adventist Tertiary Student Ministry[3]

The Seventh Day Adventist Church (SDASA) is a voluntary, faith-based organisation of students established in 1967. It vision is to empower students and mobilize professionals for the healing of the nations through engagement with students in universities and other tertiary education campuses in Africa. The SDASA is registered in South Africa as an nonprofit organisation under the Social Development Act of 2001. It covers the geographic area of Botswana, Lesotho and Swaziland. The SDASA empowers students through facilitating their growth and development. In addition, the association mobilizes

---

[1] acts.sacbc.org.za/wp-content/uploads/2012/03/ACTSidentity.pdf (accessed 5 October, 2015).

[2] http://nfcscganunn.org/home/# (accessed 5 October, 2015).

[3] www.sdasa.co.za/about.html (accessed 5 October, 2015).

professionals and entrepreneurs to use their skills, abilities and expertise for professional contributions in order to enhance best practice within the Seventh Day Adventist Church.

Chi Alpha Campus Ministries (XA)

The Chi Alpha Campus Ministries (XA) (usually known as Chi Alpha Christian Fellowship on campus, but sometimes University Christian Fellowship or 'Schoolname' Christian Fellowship, and occasionally Christians in Action) is an Assemblies of God USA Christian ministry for college students around the world. It began as a ministry to college students in 1947 through the inspiration of J. Robert Ashcroft. The Fellowship does not seem to have made headway in Africa with the exception of Zambia and South Africa. Students from Assemblies of God in Zambia (POAG) at the University of Zambia, and from Assemblies of God Churches (AOG) in South Africa at the University of KwaZulu-Natal, have formed Chi Alpha.[4] XA's mission is to reconcile students to Jesus Christ, thereby transforming the university, the market-place, and the world. The fellowship functions with a fivefold philosophy: being a community of worship, prayer, fellowship, discipleship, and mission.[5]

Ecumenical Student Movements

The World Student Christian Federation (WSCF) – Africa Region

The WSCF is an association of sovereign national Student Christian Movements (SCM) forming the youth and student arm of the global ecumenical movement, and at the same time the oldest form of Christian student movements in Africa. It is non-governmental organization (NGO) which has working relationships with UNESCO and consultative status with the United Nations. The ecumenical movement was very much initiated by pioneers rooted in the ecumenical Christian student organizations which in most cases include Orthodox, Protestant, Catholic and Anglican students. The Africa Region with a regional office in Nairobi, Kenya, consists of thirty Student Christian Movements in over 27 countries.[6] Having started as a movement in 1895, 'WSCF has been uniting and promoting co-operation among Christian Movements and Associations of students and members of the academic community throughout the world.'[7] The movement provides opportunities for Christian formation, witness, ministry and ecumenical dialogue across cultures, gender, ethnicity and race – through engaging students in Bible study, theological reflection and social analysis of the political and economic situation in Africa, and enabling them to formulate action from Christian perspective. Its mission is to empower students in critical thinking and the constructive transformation of our world.

It is important to note that a number of renowned church leaders, and leaders in ecumenical bodies such as the World Council of Churches, the All Africa Conference of Churches, the National Council of Churches, and some renowned political leaders, were themselves members of certain ecumenical student movements unified by the WSCF. Some of the notable personalities in this case are: Stephen Bantu Biko, an anti-apartheid activist in South Africa in the 1960s and 1970s and a student leader who founded the Black Consciousness Movement; Oliver Reginald Tambo, a South African anti-apartheid politician and revolutionary who served as President of the African National Congress from 1967 to 1991; Samuel Kobia, a theologian who served as the first Kenyan General Secretary of the World Council of Churches, 2004-2009; Edouard Chivambo Mondlane, the founding President of the Mozambican Liberation Front (FRELIMO); Kwame Nkrumah, who led Ghana to independence from Britain in 1957 and served as its

---

[4] David M. Gordon, *Invisible Agents: Spirits in a Central African History* (Athens, OH: Ohio University Press, 2012).
[5] www.chialpha.com/About-XA/worldwide-chi-alpha.html (accessed 5 October, 2015).
[6] http://wscfglobal.org/?page_id=11039 (accessed 5 October, 2015).
[7] www.wscf-africa.org/index.php?option=com_content&view=article&id=19&Itemid=27 (accessed 5 October, 2015).

first prime minister and president; Mwalimu Julius Nyerere, a Tanzanian statesman, who served as the first president of Tanzania; Isabel Apawo Phiri (Associate General Secretary of WCC); Fulata Mbano-Moyo (WCC's Programme Executive for Women in Church and Society); Mercy Amba Oduyoye, an African theologian from the Methodist Church known for her work in African women's theology and the founding of the Circle of Concern African Women's Theologians (and former Associate General Secretary of WCC); André Karamaga (General Secretary of All Africa Conference of Churches) and Ellen Johnson Sirleaf, the 24th of President of Liberia and the first elected female head of state in Africa, among others

Youth for Christ Africa (YFC)

Youth for Christ is a worldwide Christian movement working with young people round the globe. It works with local churches and other like-minded partners for evangelism amongst young people in order to develop them as lifelong followers of Jesus characterised by godliness in lifestyle, devotion to the word of God and prayer, boldness in evangelism, and commitment to social involvement. YFC is found in over 39 African countries and its primary focus is on 'Generation 21' (or G21 – those aged below 21). The movement has its regional office in islands of the Indian Ocean – which include Madagascar, Mauritius, Réunion, Seychelles, the Comoros Islands, Mayotte and Rodrigues; East Africa – which consists of Burundi, Ethiopia, Kenya, Rwanda, Tanzania and Uganda; Francophone Africa – which consists of Benin, Burkina Faso, Cote d'Ivoire, Guinea, Mali, Niger, Senegal and Togo; Southern Africa – which consists of Botswana, Lesotho, Mozambique, Namibia, South Africa, Swaziland, Angola, Malawi, Zambia and Zimbabwe; and West Africa (Anglophone) – which consists of Gambia, Ghana, Guinea-Bissau, Liberia, Nigeria and Sierra Leone.

YFC believes that G21 is the generation that will bring transformation in Africa. YFC is implementing G21 through a variety of ministries, such as prayer triplets, abstinence programmes, children's homes, radio and television programmes, and many others. G21 is a call to be God's catalyst in faithfully developing a pan-African generation of young people who will be characterised by prowess in spiritual warfare, boldness in evangelism, passion in social involvement, and godliness in leadership, thus reflecting an exemplary Christian life. The following two examples can be given:

In South Africa,[8] YFC bases its ministry activities on the following 'four pillars':

- Godliness in lifestyle
- Devotion to the word of God and prayer
- Passion for sharing the love of Christ
- Commitment to social involvement

All YFC centres in South Africa are similar but not exactly the same. This is primarily due to the felt needs of the different communities and town centres which exist. The outreach endeavours and social involvement initiatives are tailored specifically to the young people in each locale. This means that some centres may have ministry projects, other centres do not, while some centres may run similar ministry projects differently. The ministry activities include but are not limited to: spiritual development (evangelism and discipleship), camps and conferences, equipping youth leaders and workers for effective youth ministry, schools andprisons ministries, children and youth at risk, which include equipping leaders and young people with skills for HIV / AIDS prevention and awareness, life skills, peer education and job creation.

In Kenya, YFC has a vision to evangelize and disciple young people to become Kenya's godly future leaders. Their current ministries include weekly Berean Bible clubs in schools, music teams whose main focus is evangelism, and the Taraja Home for former street boys which focuses on discipleship, education and vocational training.

---

[8] http://yfc.org.za/ministries-projects (accessed 5 October, 2015).

Youth Alive, where everyone is somebody and Jesus is Lord[9]

Youth Alive Ministries (YAM) is an interdenominational Christian youth development organization that communicates the gospel message to young people in Southern Africa. It is one of the oldest and most successful youth organizations in Soweto that has played a major role in character and leadership development of young people since its establishment in 1959. Youth Alive provides discipleship, leadership development and community outreach through its various projects and activities, including youth clubs, camps, training, mentorship, educational support and seminars. Youth Alive celebrated its fiftieth Anniversary in 2010 which brought renewed energy and vision to both former and current members to take it to the next level. The urge to revamp the currently dilapidated Dube Centre building to suit future youth needs, more focused programmes and staff capacity-building is a key priority in taking the organization forward.

Evangelical Student Movements

International Fellowship of Evangelical Students (IFES) – Africa Region

IFES is a confederation of evangelical Christian student movements in Africa which encourage evangelism, discipleship and mission among students.[10] The fellowship promotes and unites collaboration among evangelical associations of students throughout the continent. IFES has local autonomous student movements in over forty African countries. To mention few, such include in Benin: Groupe Biblique des Elèves et Etudiants du Bénin; Cameroon: Groupes Bibliques des Elèves et Etudiants du Cameroun; Ethiopia: Evangelical Students' and Graduates' Union of Ethiopia (EvaSUE); Ghana: GHAFES Ghana; Kenya: FOCUS Kenya; Malawi: Student Christian Organisation of Malawi (SCOM); Madagascar: Union des Groupes Bibliques de Madagascar; Zambia: ZAFES Zambia; Angola: GBECA Angola and South Africa: Students' Christian Organization of South Africa. The vision of IFES is to build students into 'communities of disciples, transformed by the gospel and impacting the university, the church and society for the glory of Christ'.[11] The IFES promotes an interdenominational approach to evangelism, and has six strategic priorities: communicating the good news of Jesus Christ, strengthening leadership and formation, promoting student-graduate integration, building sustainable support, and engaging with the university.

Campus Crusade (CRU)

Campus Crusade Christ International (CCCI), which changed its name to Cru (a shortening of 'Crusade') in 2011, is an interdenominational evangelical Christian organization which was started in 1951 by Bill and Vonette Bright. They pursued their passion for ministry by starting Campus Crusade for Christ (in the USA) at the University of California in Los Angeles. From its humble beginnings working among college students, Cru has since grown into one of the largest international Christian ministries in the world, reaching beyond students to serve inner cities, the military, athletes, political and business leaders, the entertainment industry, and families.[12] The Brights spent more than half a century building and leading Cru to its current size of more than 27,000 staff members and 225,000 volunteers working in 190 countries worldwide and over 37 countries in sub-Saharan Africa.[13] Africa is divided in three regions, each with its

---

[9] www.youthalive.co.za (accessed 5 October, 2015).

[10] Douglas Johnson, *A Brief History of the International Fellowship of Evangelical Students* (Lausanne, Switzerland: IFES, 1964): http://ifesworld.org/en (accessed 5 October, 2015).

[11] http://ifesworld.org/en/our-vision (accessed 5 October, 2015).

[12] John G. Turner, *Bill Bright and Campus Crusade for Christ: The Renewal of Evangelicalism in post-war America* (Chapel Hill, NC: University of North Carolina Press, 2008).

[13] www.cru.org/about/our-leadership/our-founders.html (accessed 21 October, 2015).

area leaders: Southern and Eastern Africa, West Africa, and Francophone Africa. Cru is referred to by a different name in different African countries. For example, in Ghana, it is called Great Commission Movement of Ghana; in Nigeria, it is called Great Commission Movement of Nigeria; in Kenya, it is called Life Ministry, and in South Africa, it is called Campus Crusade for Christ South Africa.

Cru helps members to fulfil the Great Commission in the power of the Holy Spirit by exposing people to the claims of Jesus Christ, winning people to faith in him, building them up in their faith and sending them to win and disciple others, and helping the Body of Christ through evangelism and discipleship. Cru movements aim to multiply, build and send Christ-centred disciples who launch spiritual movements in faith, growth and fruitfulness.[14]

Conclusion

There are many more other Christian student organisations in Africa which are not mentioned in this brief chapter which has assessed the contribution of African student Christian movements to African ecumenism. These movements prioritise the welfare of young people and their future. They take joy in training young people in professional skills for sustainability and faith-based values, transcending denominational parameters. Notably, some – such as Youth Alive, Youth for Christ and Scripture Union (discussed in previous chapter) – value the integral development of all their members, irrespective of their denominational affiliation. More especially, Catholic organisations, such as ACTS and NFCS, have cautiously embraced students from other religious traditions though they still limit leadership to baptised Catholics. Further, it is important to note that ecumenical student associations are not as popular as they used to be. Many students prefer their denominational student movement, causing some of these associations to lose their ecumenical flavour.

To this effect, we have made the following observations regarding these associations: first, they usually use the approach to ministry based on their denominational orientation. This means that if the association is evangelical, its objectives and mission will reflect the broader framework within which evangelical churches function. Second, many of these organisations seems to be struggling to remain socially relevant in the different contexts of Africa as some still function with the colonial missionary paradigm despite the fact that they are led by Africans. Third, some of the African Christian student movements like WSCF and SCM have strong impact and a historic role in building up a new generation of African Christians engaged ecumenically and beyond their own denominational borders; however, the SCM type of ecumenism, has often reached beyond the historical mainline churches. Fourth, it seems to us that there is a need for some of these organisations to strive to transcend their parochialism and begin to find ways of co-operating with one another without losing their uniqueness. These may enable them to introduce a new discourse, one that can allow for ecumenical reinterpretation of the role of the Bible in student formation in the current African context.

Bibliography

ACTS, 1999, 'Association of Catholic Tertiary Students the Identity of Acts': acts.sacbc.org.za/wp-content/uploads/2012/03/ACTSidentity.pdf (accessed 5 October, 2015).

CCCSA, 2015, 'Campus Crusade for Christ South Africa': www.cccsa.org.za/about-us (accessed 21 October, 2015)

Chi Alpha, 2014. 'Africa', www.chialpha.com/About-XA/worldwide-chi-alpha.html (accessed 5 October, 2015).

[14] www.cccsa.org.za/about-us (accessed 21 October, 2015).

CRU, 1994, 'Bill and Vonette Bright: Founders of Campus Crusade for Christ International': www.cru.org/about/our-leadership/our-founders.html (accessed 21 October, 2015).

Gordon, David M., *Invisible Agents: Spirits in a Central African History.* Athens, OH: Ohio University Press, 2012.

IFES, 2014, 'International Students of Evangelical Fellowship': http://ifesworld.org/en (accessed 5 October, 2015).

Johnson, Douglas, *A Brief History of the International Fellowship of Evangelical Students*. Lausanne, Switzerland: IFES, 1964.

NFSC, 2013-2015, 'The Nigerian Federation of Catholic Students UNN': http://nfcscganunn.org/home/# (accessed 5 October, 2015).

SDASA, 2014, 'The Seventh Day Adventist Student Association': www.sdasa.co.za/about.html (accessed 5th October 2015).

SU, 2013, 'Scripture Union Africa': www.su-africa.org (accessed 5th October 2015).

The World Student Christian Federation (WSCF), 2015, 'African Region': www.wscf-africa.org/index.php? option=com_content&view=article&id= 19&Itemid=27 (accessed 5 October, 2015).

Turner, John G., *Bill Bright and Campus Crusade for Christ: The Renewal of Evangelicalism in post-war America*. Chapel Hill, NC: University of North Carolina Press, 2008.

WSCF Global, 2015, 'Africa': http://wscfglobal.org/?page_id=11039 (accessed 5 October, 2015).

Youth Alive, 2012, 'Welcome to Youth Alive, where everyone is somebody and Jesus is Lord': www.youthalive.co.za (accessed 5 October, 2015).

Youth for Christ South Africa, n.d., 'Ministry/Project': http://yfc.org.za/ministries-projects (accessed 5 October, 2015).

(106) AFRICAN CONTRIBUTIONS TO GLOBAL ECUMENISM

Setri Nyomi

Introduction

The ecumenical movement is inspired by the line in Jesus' High Priestly prayer that indicates: 'I ask… that they may all be one. As you, Father, are in me and I am in you, may they also be in us, so that the world may believe that you have sent me.' Believers who catch this passion of the Lord Jesus Christ for his followers to be one and therefore commit to the unity of the church are those who are described as ecumenical. This is not a cheap commitment to having everyone in the same household and then everyone lives happily ever after. It entails a costly following of the Lord Jesus Christ in a manner in which all in the *oikos* can have a fair share of the gifts and opportunities offered within the household – regardless of race, gender, economic or social status or which part of the world they come from. This is what brings justice to the core of what is entailed in Christian unity. This also means our understanding of what it means to belong to the *oikos* needs to be examined so that doctrinal errors do not lead anyone astray.

Africans who catch the vision expressed in the high priestly prayer, live into it with an understanding of that value of being together in the same *oikos* – the *Ubuntu* spirit which radically holds that we are in the community together – we belong together – not as individuals or even as separate denominational entities. Following the Lord Jesus Christ includes living by this spirit of oneness. It is in this spirit that Africans have been contributing to global ecumenical engagement right from the early years and the early centuries of Christianity.

In this chapter, we explore some of these contributions, beginning from the early years of Christianity and the African churches which have lived in this way for centuries. This is followed by a brief examination of Africa in the context of the 1910 Edinburgh Missionary Council which is widely seen as the beginning of the modern ecumenical movement. The closing section is devoted to some of the developments towards organic church unions, identify some ideas and issues that have been contributed to the ecumenical movement from Africa.

Africa's main resources are its peoples, and the vision and ideas they have brought to the 'ecumenical table'. Therefore we end by exploring the contributions of some visionary and influential individuals as well as the organizations and associations that have inspired and strengthened the global ecumenical movement. These lists cannot be exhaustive. They represent many other communities and individuals who have made tremendous contributions to the global ecumenical movement. We choose to name even the partial list in this chapter because African contributions can never be faceless. They represent real people.

African Contributions in the Early Years of Christianity

The discussion between the Ethiopian eunuch and the 'stranger' who joined him in his chariot marked the first record of African engagement in global ecumenism (Acts 8:26-39).[1] The African is portrayed as the recipient in this encounter. And at face value, one would not attribute any contribution to him. However, a deeper reading of that account shows clearly that the Ethiopian's contribution to that conversation was

---

[1] See the emphasised communal nature of early Christian faith in the Middle East and African origins of Christianty, Jacquelyn Winston 'Listening to the African Witness', in Christianity in Early Africa: Ancient Traditions, Proufound impact, *Church History* issue 105, (2013): 4-5.

profound. His deep questions contributed to an understanding of the gospel's power to reach across geographical, cultural and social differences, if we are willing to engage ecumenically. His first question on the meaning of the Isaiah passage helped bring out an application of insights. While his second question, 'What is there to prevent me from being baptized?' may have broken through the misunderstanding of Philip in this encounter to engage in a discussion across cultural, geographic and, one could say, credal boundaries. Even if Philip had any doubts that an African could be included on the 'ecumenical table', this question may have shattered those doubts. This, then, is the first record of African contributions to global ecumenism.

In the 1900 or so years that followed this event, Africans have made further contributions to global ecumenism. Names such as Clement, Tertullian (160-225), Origen (185-254), Athanasius (c. 296-373), Cyril, Cyprian and Augustine (c. 354-c. 430) are well-known personalities in church history.[2] They crossed boundaries and made significant contributions in their time to Christian unity and in addressing the issues of their day. They were Africans – mainly from North Africa. Because they wrote in Greek or Latin, their Africanness is often ignored. Instead, they have been identified more with the languages in which they wrote – Greek or Latin. A brief review of the impact of four of these would suffice in establishing the fact that a whole host of African patriarchs have contributed to the growth of Christianity and the ecumenical movement.

Clement is known to have had a passion for Christian unity. As leader of the church in Rome around the turn of the first century AD, he went out of his way to write a letter to the church in Corinth to address divisive tendencies in it, urging its members to unite. This spirit of rising above division in the Christian Church today continues to be an inspiring force within the modern ecumenical movement.

Origen can be described as one of the first biblical scholars who challenged biblical literalism in the third century of the Christian era. He consistently pointed to finding the significant meaning behind biblical truths and inspired the acceptance of the Old Testament as part of Christian scriptures. Many scholars in the modern ecumenical movement move away from biblical literalism in a manner that mirrors the works of Origen. Origen was also a controversial character since some of his thinking and writings were identified as heretical. The church in Rome as well as in Alexandria had misgivings about his orthodoxy. While these questions may remain blemishes on his legacy, there is no doubt that Origen did make a significant contribution to the church ecumenical.

Born in Alexandria, Athanasius can be credited with the leadership of the early church which resolved some difficult and divisive issues. He became noted as the main defender of Trinitarianism against Arianism. One abiding legacy of his impact is the Nicene Creed which is widely used in the ecumenical movement today. While the version which the ecumenical movement uses today is a 381 revision of what was first developed in 325 in Nicaea, it is true that the process was begun and largely developed under the leadership of Athanasius. He died in 373, about eight years before the Niceno-Constantinopolitan Creed was developed. In this particular area, this son of Africa has indeed preserved Christian unity in a manner that few patriarchs have been able to match.

Augustine of Hippo is probably the patriarch of African origin most quoted by scholars in western Christianity. His origins and ministry location can be traced to modern Tunisia and Algeria. Augustine has left the church with many legacies which cannot be enumerated here. The most notable ones include:

- His stand against slavery as an issue of justice and how, through his influence, many slaves were freed in the Roman empire.
- His view that the church is one, although with two expressions – the visible aspect and the invisible. The visible aspect consists of those who can be clearly seen within the church as an institution. These may include those who are genuine (the wheat) and those who are not (the tares). The

[2] Jacquelyn Winston 'Listening to the African Witness' (2013).

invisible aspect consists of persons of all eras (living or dead) whose souls are destined for heaven. He indicated that the latter cannot be determined by human judgement and may not even be known for certain by human observers.

- Augustine advocated pacifism – except where silence or the pacifist stance leads to a greater evil. Therefore his stance is very close to what has become labelled as the 'Just war' position.

These and other patriarchs of African origin have left legacies that continue to affect modern ecumenism, especially in the areas of Christian unity, justice and uniting to overcome heresy.

The Coptic Church and the Ethiopian Orthodox Tewahedo Church

There is very little information on African contributions for most of the first two millennia of Christian history. However, there can be no doubts that the contributions of Africans to world Christianity were there and that Christian traditions in Ethiopia remain among the oldest in the world.[3] At the very least, we have evidence of two African churches which for centuries have stood as strong forces in their witness even in the face of major challenges and persecution.

The Coptic Church has been in continuous existence since the very first century of Christianity. It is believed that the gospel writer, Mark, took the good news to Egypt where the Coptic Church began. Its leaders have been avid defenders of Christian orthodoxy. As noted earlier, under the leadership of Pope Athanasius, the church in Alexandria defended the faith against heresy and came up with uniting instruments of the faith. The Coptic Church has kept its ecumenical commitments down the centuries. In the twentieth century, this was demonstrated by the fact that it was a founding member of the World Council of Churches, the All Africa Conference of Churches and the Middle East Council of Churches.

The Ethiopian Orthodox Tewahedo Church has been in continuous existence since the fourth century. Its history has close associations with the Coptic Church throughout the centuries.[4] It gained autonomy from the Coptic Church only in the twentieth century. It is not known what happened to Christianity in the land known as Ethiopia between the conversion of the Ethiopian eunuch recorded in Acts 8 and the early fourth century. From the beginning, this church too has been ecumenically engaged, and this commitment continued into the era of modern ecumenism. The Ethiopian Orthodox Church is a founding member of the World Council of Churches and the All Africa Conference of Churches.

Both the Coptic Church and the Ethiopian Orthodox Tewahedo Church have contributed to leadership in ecumenical organizations – including, for example, presidents of the World Council of Churches. Both churches were present as observers at the Second Vatican Council, and both are active in the family of Oriental Orthodox Churches. They have also been active participants in dialogue between the Oriental Orthodox Churches and some Christian world communions – for example, with the World Alliance of Reformed Churches – now the World Communion of Reformed Churches.

The 1910 Missionary Council in Edinburgh

It is common practice to trace modern ecumenism to the 1910 World Missionary Council in Edinburgh. It is strange that in spite of the remarkable contributions of Africans to the history of Christianity, the organizers did not think of inviting any African to the Council.

The absence of Africans at the 1910 Edinburgh World Missionary Council is an inexplicable tragedy that still leaves many questions without answers. Is it possibly because of a racist attitude that prejudiced

---

[3] See Tekletsadik Belachew 'From Abba Slama to King Lalibela', in Christianity in Early Africa: Ancient Traditions, Proufound impact, *Church History* Issue 105, (2013): 18-23.

[4] Christine Chaillot, *The Ethiopian Orthodox Tewahedo Church Tradition. A Brief Introduction to Its Life and Spirituality* (Paris: Inter-Orthodox Dialogue, 2002).

both organizers and participants against the participation of Africans? What is even more baffling is the fact that there seemed not to be any notice of this remarkable absence of Africans nor was there any known criticism of this, either in the Council or in the decades that followed. It seemed to have been taken for granted.

In spite of this lapse, it is interesting to note that, during that Missionary Council, a good number of country reports were on missionary activities in Africa. Africa was a subject and there were many discussions and outcomes that had Africa as their focus. Undoubtedly, the ideas that emerged around Africa may have been affected by African thinking, and this would have been enhanced if Africans had been present. We are therefore forced to limit any direct African impact on the 1910 Edinburgh Missionary Council to the five Americans (four men and one woman) of African descent (Afro-Americans) who *were* present. While none of them was born on the continent of Africa, they may in some way be associated with African contributions.

It needs to be pointed out that, during that era, there were a number of articulate African church agents who could have contributed much to the Missionary Council. These included Archdeacon Crowther of Sierra Leone and Nigeria (son of Bishop Samuel Adjayi Crowther), Bishop James Johnson of Sierra Leone and Nigeria, John Tengo Jabavu of South Africa, and James Kwegyir Aggrey of the then Gold Coast.

The fact that the 1910 Missionary Council did not include any African reflects a lost opportunity for the modern ecumenical movement. This is because the centuries before then as well as the ten decades since 1910 have clearly demonstrated that Africa and Africans have contributed tremendously to the ecumenical movement in terms of ideas, issues and visionary personalities.

United and Uniting Churches in Africa

Churches which have entered into unions in many parts of the world have done so as an expression of living out the high calling of the ecumenical movement. They have been an inspiration to the ecumenical movement. African churches are included among such churches.

Most churches which came into being as a result of European or North American missionary activities also experienced the side-effect of being organized along ethnic lines. For practical reasons, church mission agencies evangelized to particular ethnic communities, and so, even if the work expanded to other tribes within a particular geographical area, the churches often had a sense of predominance in one or two ethnic groups. This was not the original intention of the mission agencies.

The desire for Christian unity led to a number of church unity initiatives on the continent of Africa. Moves towards the organic unity of churches gained momentum in countries such as Malawi, Zambia, Ghana, Nigeria and the Democratic Republic of Congo. Not all of them led to success. But they did bring together churches in a greater faithfulness to the Lord of the church whose High Priestly prayer recorded in John 17 desired that all may be one. Here are some success stories:

1. The Church of Central Africa – Presbyterian (CCAP) with three Synods in Malawi, and one each in Zambia and Zimbabwe, is a good expression of African Christian commitment to organic church unity. As early as 1911 (less than one year after the Edinburgh Missionary Council), serious unity talks began between two Presbyterian churches in Malawi which were brought by two different missionary bodies representing two different churches in Scotland. In 1924, this became a reality and, two years later, another church originating from the Dutch Reformed Church in South Africa joined. Thus, in 1926, the Church of Central Africa – Presbyterian was born in Malawi. Later, in 1965 and 1984, the Harare Synod and the Zambia Synod joined.
2. The United Church of Zambia (UCZ) came into being in 1965. The very coming together of several churches to unite in one church in Zambia is a testimony to the value of Christian unity. That church continues to keep the ecumenical touch burning in Zambia and on the continent of Africa.

3. The Church of Jesus Christ in Madagascar (FJKM) is the result of the unity of three churches in Madagascar in 1968. It continues to inspire Christian unity today.
4. Eglise du Christ au Congo (ECC): This is an interesting formation, slightly different from other church unions. From the 1930s, the churches in what is now the Democratic Republic of Congo have been seeking to form a stronger bond with one another. The normal path of a National Council of Churches led to stronger ties until, by 1970, it became realized in a federation which is understood as an organic union. This marked the birth of the ECC. Each member church retained its identity, but they are together in the ECC as one body.
5. The Uniting Reformed Church of Southern Africa (URCSA) in the history of South Africa, where many churches divided along racial lines. Some of the organic church unions therefore mark the coming together of churches in response to the Christian calling to be one, as well as expressions of faith to overcome the legacy of apartheid. In 1994, the Dutch Reformed Mission Church and the Dutch Reformed Church in Africa united to form URCSA. Currently, there are serious conversations to further overcome the legacy of apartheid so that there is a stronger union that involves more of the Dutch Reformed Church family in South Africa.
6. The Uniting Presbyterian Church of Southern Africa became a reality in 1999 when the Reformed Presbyterian Church in Southern Africa and the Presbyterian Church in Southern Africa entered into union. This coming together in obedience to God is also an expression of putting the legacy of apartheid behind and building a community above racial divisions.

These are just a few examples of organic unions in Africa.[5] This spirit will continue to inspire the ecumenical movement all over the world. In addition to this, many countries work together through the National Councils of Churches and Christian associations.

Issues and Ideas Contributed to the Global Ecumenical Movement by Africa and Africans

Africans have been contributing issues and ideas to the 'ecumenical table' for a long time. The following are some of the ideas and issues that have come strongly to the ecumenical agenda because of or inspired by Africa and African voices.

1. Mission and Evangelism: African churches have often seen this as the core calling of churches. Therefore, they have sought to strengthen this in many ecumenical forums. Many African church leaders have indicated clearly that any mission of the church or any evangelization can be strengthened if churches rise above competition, come together and present the gospel together. This has led to the formation of mission and evangelism departments in a number of National Councils of Churches. The emphasis of engaging in mission and evangelism together has therefore brought a direct impact on the quest for church unity. In addition, new insights into mission thinking have been brought into the ecumenical movement by African theologians and missiologists. John de Gruchy and Tinyiko Maluleke, both of South Africa, are two examples of such visionaries who have dared to challenge traditional mission models and paradigms.
2. Redefinition of Mission Relationships: The history of the Christian churches has been characterized by top-down power relationships in which churches which sent missionaries, or which financially support churches which resulted from their mission work, often exerted power over the churches they brought into being. This typically meant that many African churches were seen as subordinate to churches in Europe and North America. By questioning this within the ecumenical movement, there was created an awareness of these problematic power relationships. In the 1960s, African ecumenical leaders such as the Very Rev. John Gatu called for a moratorium in the

[5] See World Council of Churches 'United and Uniting Churches'. https://www.oikoumene.org/en/church-families/united-and-uniting-churches (accessed 24 June 2016).

sender-receiver model of mission and church relationships. He and others raised critical questions about these power relationships. While the work of healing is not yet complete, the ecumenical movement has come a long way from what it was in the 1960s. There is still much room for improvement.

3. Religion and Culture: In the past, African cultures were denigrated and looked down on. For decades, the efforts of many African ecumenists led to a rethinking of what God's incarnation in the world meant for different communities. This line of questioning has led to renewed interest in the dialogue between different cultures and the Christian faith, and a reclaiming of the dignity of cultures which had been looked down on in the past.
4. Dismantling Colonialism: Churches worked together in many African countries to support the independence movements that overthrew European colonial powers in many African countries in the mid- to late twentieth century.
5. Exposing and Dismantling Racism and Apartheid: Racism, especially apartheid, remained a blight on the African scene for many decades. African churches brought attention to the viciousness and church-divisive nature of apartheid within the ecumenical movement very powerfully through bodies such as the World Council of Churches and the then World Alliance of reformed Churches. In 1969, the World Council of Churches initiated the Programme to Combat Racism in which churches all over the world were engaged in the fight against racism and apartheid. Many Africans gave leadership to this effort. Another example of African leadership in this area is what happened within the World Alliance of Reformed Churches. In 1982, it was the South African delegates to the World Alliance of Reformed Churches General Council in Ottawa, Canada, that led the General Council to declare *status confessionis* on apartheid and to declare that any theological justification of it as heresy. This led to a new phase in the fight against racism and apartheid.
6. Gender Justice: Sexism and gender-based injustice is a major problem in many parts of the world, including Africa. African voices have always been present in exposing this evil, and in giving expression to the transformation that needs to take place. They have constantly pointed this out powerfully, even in their own contexts. The voices of Justice Annie Jiagge and Professor Mercy Amba Oduyoye (both of Ghana), Dr Brigalia Bam of South Africa, and Dr Rose Zoe Obianga of Cameroun are just a few of those which would not allow the ecumenical movement to remain silent. Their actions, together with the actions of many women and men who remain active in the ecumenical movement today, will continue to make a difference in this area of the ecumenical movement.
7. Economic Justice: Africa is seen in many circles as a very poor continent. However, for many decades, African ecumenists have been pointing towards a different reality – systemic injustice that has ensured the impoverishment of Africa and other contexts considered to be in the global South. The movements to expose this evil and to ensure the ecumenical movement develops life-giving actions have been inspired by the powerful voices of those who live on the margins – many of whom are in Africa. The process that led to the Accra Confession of the World Alliance of reformed Churches (WARC) as well as the process of AGAPE within the World Council of Churches are largely inspired by Africans. For example, under the auspices of the World Alliance of Reformed Churches, it was when African ecumenical leaders gathered in Kitwe, Zambia, in 1995 that they issued a strong call for action on economic injustice. The Accra Confession which is a major resource for ecumenical action was developed in Accra, Ghana, during the 24th General Council of WARC in 2004. This area takes on board both economic and climate justice.

8. Theology of Reconstruction: By the 1990s, a paradigm shift in doing theology that was relevant in the context of Africa had emerged. This was named the Theology of Reconstruction.[6] It posits that, while liberation is necessary in many contexts, the African context is called upon to pay attention to reconstruction that would lead towards a more holistic theological reflection on the continent – a reflection that would lead towards reclaiming the God-given dignity and life-affirming place that God has given Africans. This is a contribution to the ecumenical movement that benefits Africans and peoples on other continents.
9. Responses to Challenging Situations on the Continent: As serious conflicts led to major community upheavals, African churches worked with their counterparts in other regions of the ecumenical movement in order to respond. These included responses to armed conflicts, to refugees, to the consequences of bad governance and dictatorships, and to natural as well as to human-caused disasters.
10. Ecumenical Theological Education: Africa has fostered this through the national councils of churches as well as continental and sub-regional associations of theological institutions.
11. Attention to Young People: The youth movement in Africa has been very vibrant and has made their quota of contributions, including written resources, over the years. This is not surprising because, in both the twentieth and 21st centuries, African churches are filled with young people.
12. Interfaith Dialogue: In many African communities, people of different religions live in community together. African ecumenical engagement has therefore given much value to ecumenical dialogue.

African Personalities that have Influenced and Inspired the Ecumenical Movement

There are many African personalities who have influenced and inspired different instruments within the ecumenical movement. Here we name just a few of them.

1. In the area of initiatives for the formation of ecumenical instruments, prominent names among those who contributed to the ecumenical movement include Sir Francis Akanu Ibiam of Nigeria, Bishop Josiah Kibira of Tanzania, Professor D.G.S. M'timkhulu, and the Rev. Sam Amissah of Ghana. These four contributed greatly to the formation of the All Africa Conference of Churches and its early years. They were also active in the global ecumenical movement.
2. African leaders in the ecumenical movement who became presidents of the World Council of Churches include Justice Annie Jiagge of Ghana, Archbishop Walter Makhulu of South Africa, Dr Aaron Tolen of Cameroun, Pope Shenouda III of Egypt, Patriarch Abune Paulos of Ethiopia, Dr Agnes Abuom of Kenya, Dr Simon Dossou of Benin, and Rev. Dr Mary-Anne Plaatjies van Huffel of South Africa. Dr Agnes Abuom also became the Moderator of Central Committee of the World Council of Churches in 2013.
3. Leaders of the anti-apartheid movement include Archbishop Desmond Tutu, the Rev. Dr Allan Boesak, the Rev. Frank Chikane, and Dr Brigalia Bam – all of South Africa.
4. General Secretaries and Associate General Secretaries of global ecumenical bodies: as the world entered the 21st century, the ecumenical movement found itself face-to-face with four Africans as General Secretaries of major world ecumenical organizations: the Rev. Dr Samuel Kobia of Kenya (General Secretary of the World Council of Churches), the Rev. Dr Ishmael Noko of Zimbabwe (Lutheran World Federation), Dr Musimbi Kanyoro of Kenya (World Young Women's Christian Association), the Rev. Dr Setri Nyomi of Ghana (World Alliance of Reformed Churches which, under his leadership, then became the World Communion of Reformed Churches), Prof. Isabel Apowa Phiri (Associate General Secretary of the World Council of

[6] Jesse N. K. *Mugambi, From Liberation to Reconstruction*: *African Christian Theology after the Cold War* (Nairobi: East African Educarional Publishers, 1995).

Churches), and Prof. Mercy A Oduyoye (former Associate General Secretary of the World Council of Churches).

5. Those who infused the ecumenical movement with creative African reflections and actions include Prof. John Mbiti (Kenya), the Very Rev. John Gatu (Kenya), Bishop John Henry Okullu (Kenya), Prof. Mercy Amba Oduyoye (Ghana), Prof. Kwesi Dickson (Ghana), the Rev. José Chipenda (Angola), Prof. Russel Botman (South Africa), Prof. Kwame Bediako (Ghana), Dr Brigalia Bam (South Africa), Prof. John S. Pobee (Ghana), Prof. Isabel Phiri (Malawi), Ms Omega Chilufya Bula (Zambia), Dr Jesse Mugambi (Kenya), Dr Effiong Utuk (Nigeria), Bishop Mvume Dandala (South Africa), and the Rev. Dr André Karamaga (Rwanda).
6. Gender Justice: Justice Annie Jiagge, Prof. Mercy Amba Oduyoye, Dr Brigalia Bam, Ms Rose Zoë Obianga, Ms Omega Bula, and Dr Nyambura Njoroge, and Dr Fulata Lusungu Moyo.

These are just a sampling of a fraction of the African personalities that have contributed to the ecumenical movement. A list of this kind risks the inadvertent omission of many others who should have been included. The list is indeed not exhaustive. There are countless others who contributed to the ecumenical movement at local, national, sub-regional, continental and global levels. African contributions are never simply individual affairs. All these, both named and unnamed, have been able to contribute to the ecumenical movement because of their communities – including their spouses, children and families.

Ecumenical Organizations and Associations which Reflect African Contributions to the Ecumenical movement

The All Africa Conference of Churches (AACC) is Africa's premier ecumenical organ. From its main offices in Nairobi, Kenya, and regional office in Lomé, Togo, it continues to play a leading role in mobilizing African churches in ecumenical engagement. Complementing the AACC are sub-regional fellowships such as the Fellowship of Council of Churches in Southern Africa, the Fellowship of Churches and Councils in West Africa, and the Fellowship of Churches and Councils in the Great Lakes Region of Africa.

The Ecumenical Association of Third World Theologians – EATWOT: this is association of men and women committed to the struggle for the liberation of Third World peoples. While it includes people from all over the world, it is significant to note that it was born in Africa – Dar-es Salaam, Tanzania, in 1976. It has also benefited from African leadership in its history. It has fostered ecumenical reflections across confessional lines including Roman Catholics, Protestants and indigenous churches. It has also included people of faiths other than Christian.

The Organization of African Instituted Churches brings together churches on the continent of Africa which do not have their origins in external missionary efforts. This body, based in Nairobi, supports the African Instituted Churches and is a major resource in contributing to global ecumenism.

The Circle of Concerned African Women Theologians is a body of visionary women who have engaged in critical discussion through which their members have been empowered as instruments of transformation in their contexts. Through the insightful publications of its members, the ecumenical movement in Africa and beyond has been enriched.

The Project for Christian-Muslim Relations (PROCMURA) is an organization that has mediated the peaceful co-existence of Christians and Muslims in Africa. Its pro active stance in fostering dialogue between the two religions has helped to bring understanding and has prevented the misuse of religious sentiments for injustice or violence.

Youth and Student movements: the African continental and national branches of students and youth ecumenical organizations have also contributed much to the worldwide ecumenical movement. Bodies such as the World Student Christian Federation, Student Christian Movement, Fellowships of Evangelical

Students, and other youth and student Christian organizations have been instruments of mobilizing young Africans to contribute to the ecumenical movement.

Another expression of the ecumenical movement in Africa is the Associations of Theological Education which seek to strengthen the theological education that is offered on the continent.

In addition, African contributions within global ecumenical bodies such as the World Council of Churches, World Communion of Reformed Churches, Lutheran World Federation, World Methodist Council, Anglican World Communion, World YWCA and World YWCA are immeasurable.

Conclusion

The question, 'What are African contributions to global ecumenism?' is a deep one and, unless one limits its scope, one would have a long and rather unfocused article. Here we have chosen to focus in a manner that gives readers a quick basis for affirming that, from the very beginning of Christian history, until now African contributions have been very notable.

Africa also includes those in the diaspora. But within the scope of this article, we can only acknowledge that many Africans in the diaspora have also contributed to the global ecumenical movement.

In the 21st century in which Africa is identified as one of the areas in which Christianity is growing, it is good to know that Africa and Africans continue to play significant roles in ecumenism.

Bibliography

Bediako, Kwame, *Christianity in Africa: The Renewal of Non-Western Religion*. Maryknoll, NY: Orbis Books, 1995.

Chaillot, Christine, *The Ethiopian Orthodox Tewahedo Church Tradition. A Brief Introduction to Its Life and Spirituality*. Paris: Inter-Orthodox Dialogue, 2002.

Kobia, Samuel, *The Courage to Hope: The Roots for a New Vision and the Calling of the Church in Africa* (Risk Book Series). Geneva: WCC Publications, 2003.

Maluleke, Tinyiko S., 'Christianity in a Distressed Africa. A Time to Own and Own Up'. *Missionalia* Vol. 26, no.3, December (1998): 324-340.

Mugambi, Jesse N. K., *From Liberation to Reconstruction: African Christian Theology after the Cold War*. Nairobi: East African Educarional Publishers, 1995.

Njoroge, Nyambura J., and Musa W. Dube (eds.) *Talitha Cum! Theologies of African Women*. Pietermaritzburg, South Africa: Cluster Publications, 2001.

Nyomi, Setri (ed.), *Ecumenical Youth Movement in Africa.* Nairobi: AACC, 1993.

Oden, Thomas C., *How Christianity Shaped the Christian Mind: Rediscovering the African Seedbed of Western Christianity*. Downers Grove, IL: IVP, 2010.

Oduyoye, Mercy A, *Hearing and Knowing: Theological Reflections on Christianity in Africa*. Maryknoll, NY: Orbis Books, 1986.

Sanneh, Lamin, *Whose Religion is Christianity? The Gospel beyond the West*. Grand Rapids, MI: Eerdmans, 2003.

Van Beek, Huibert, *Handbook of Churches and Councils: Profiles of Ecumenical Relationships*. Geneva: WCC Publications, 2006.

(107) AFRICAN CHURCHES AND THE WORLD COUNCIL OF CHURCHES

Chammah J. Kaunda and Isabel Apawo Phiri

Introduction

We consider that the time this chapter is being written to be an exceptionally favourable one when the current moderator of the World Council of Churches' (hereafter, WCC) Central Committee is from one of WCC's founding member churches in Africa – the Anglican Church of Kenya. Dr Agnes Aboum was elected by 150-member Central Committee at its 10th Assembly in Busan, South Korea, held 30th October-8th November 2013. She is the first woman moderator and first African ever to hold this position in the whole of the WCC existence.

The main object of this short chapter is to give a concise appraisal of some of the areas through which African Churches (hereafter, ACs) have engaged with WCC since its inauguration in 1948. The sections proceed by appraising WCC member churches in Africa, followed by WCC Presidents from Africa, then WCC staff from African member churches, and finally, WCC programmes initiated by ACs.

WCC Member Churches in Africa

While at the start of the modern ecumenical movement and in the years that led to establishment of the WCC, Africa was still regarded as a 'mission field' with little or no ecclesial identity of its own,[1] it is important to emphasise that ACs have actively participated in the WCC since the inaugural assembly in Amsterdam, 1948. In his compiled volume, *A Handbook of Churches and Councils,* Huibert van Beek documents that the Church of the Province of South Africa, the Methodist Church of Southern Africa, the United Presbyterian Church in Southern Africa, the Anglican Church of Kenya, the Ethiopian Orthodox Tewahedo Church (Oriental) and the Anglican Church of Tanzania were among the 147 founding WCC member churches.[2]

The period between the 1950s and 1960s marked the beginning of a new phase of ACs' participation in the WCC with their entry into membership of the WCC. This was a period that marked the end of the colonial mission period and the start of the post-colonial mission era as both nations and churches we gained independence from the so-called 'mother' churches in Europe and North America. This sovereignty gave them complete autonomy to chisel their destinies and many of them applied for membership with the WCC. Even the African Initiated Churches (AICs), which were regarded as separatist or sects, applied for WCC membership. The first to apply and be accepted was the Kimbanguist Church from Democratic Republic of Congo in 1968. Van Beek gives information on 96 churches in 37 countries as being current members of the WCC at the time of his *Handbook's* publication in 2006.[3] This information, including the one on the WCC website, does not include churches that have recently been accepted into membership. For example, the Blantyre Synod of the Central Africa Presbyterian Church has been accepted and the Dutch Reformed Church (DRC) re-admitted.

---

[1] WCC, 'Africa', https://www.oikoumene.org/en/member-churches/africa (accessed 6 November, 2015).
[2] Huibert van Beek, *A Handbook of Churches and Councils: Profiles of Ecumenical Relationships* (Geneva: WCC Publications, 2006).
[3] van Beek, *A Handbook of Churches and Councils*, 112- 220.

WCC Presidents from Africa

The WCC elects regional presidents at each assembly to serve as representatives in their respective regions. The role of the president is to promote ecumenism and to interpret the work of the WCC. They also voice the concerns of the WCC's member churches in the region to the Council's leadership. These presidents also serve as members of the Central Committee, the body responsible for carrying out the policies approved by the Assembly. According to the WCC's constitution, the presidents are 'persons whose ecumenical experience and standing is widely recognized by the member churches and among the ecumenical partners of the World Council in their respective regions and ecclesial traditions'.[4] With the exception of the first two assemblies – Amsterdam, Netherlands, 1948 and Evanston, USA, 1954, during which ACs were not adequately represented, the rest of the assemblies have had a WCC president for Africa – as follows: at the New Delhi Assembly, India, 1961, Sir Francis Ibiam, an elder in the Presbyterian Church of Nigeria, was called as the first WCC president for Africa. At the Uppsala Assembly, Sweden, 1968, the Rt Rev. Dr Alphaeus Hamilton Zulu, the first black bishop of the Anglican Southern Africa Diocese of Zululand and Swaziland, was elected. The Nairobi Assembly, Kenya, 1975, elected as the first African woman WCC President, Justice Annie Jiagge of the Evangelical Presbyterian Church, Ghana. She was also elected as moderator (chair) of the WCC's Commission on the Programme to Combat Racism. At the Vancouver, Canada, Assembly, 1983, the Most Rev. Walter Paul Kotso Makhulu of the Church of the Province of Central Africa (Botswana) was elected as WCC Africa president. At the 7th Assembly, Canberra, Australia, 1991, Dr Aaron Tolen of the Presbyterian Church of Cameroon took on the mantle. At the 8th Assembly, Harare, Zimbabwe, 1998, Dr Agnes Abuom of the Anglican Church of Kenya became the Africa president for the WCC. The Rev. Dr Simon K. Dossou of the Protestant Methodist Church of Benin was elected at 9th Assembly, Porto Alegre, Brazil, 2006. And at the 10th Assembly, Busan, South Korea, 2013, Dr Mary-Anne Plaatjies van Huffel of the Uniting Reformed Church in Southern Africa was elected. These women and men have been instrumental in promoting and contextualising the WCC's revolutionary theological and social ethical vision of justice and equitable social order.

WCC Staff from African Member Churches

African churches have also collaborated with WCC through individuals who have served as staff in WCC. There has been WCC staff from various member churches in Africa who have contributed to shaping the Council's global vision. Some of the African staff of the WCC are as follows:

Archbishop Desmond Tutu from the Anglican Communion of Southern Africa was appointed Vice-Director of the Theological Education Fund (TEF) of the WCC, at Bromley, UK, from 1972 to 1975. He was designated as Associate Director because his responsibility was specifically to fund-raise for theological education in Africa. Prof. John Mbiti, a priest from the Anglican Church Kenya, was appointed the first African Director at the Ecumenical Institute of the World Council of Churches at the Château de Bossey in Geneva which he served from 1974 to 1980.[5] Dr Brigalia Bam, an Anglican from South Africa, served the Council as Executive Programme Secretary for the Women's Department. Prof. John S. Pobee from the Anglican Church of Ghana was a predecessor of Archbishop Tutu as Africa Region Associate Director of TEF which has been renamed as the Programme on Theological Education (PTE) and later became the executive director of the Theological and Ministerial Formation Programme of the WCC from

[4] WCC, 'Constitution and Rules of the World Council of Churches (Porto Alegre, Brazil, February 2006): Constitution': www.oikoumene.org/en/resources (accessed 6 November, 2015).

[5] Jacob K. Olupona, 'A Biographical Sketch', in *Religious Plurality in Africa: Essays in Honour of John S. Mbiti*, Jacob Olupona and Sulayman Nyang (eds.), (Berlin: Mouton de Gruyter, 1993), 1-10.

1992 until 1998.[6] Prof. Mercy Oduyoye, a Methodist theologian from Ghana, was the first African to become Deputy General Secretary of WCC in 1989. The Rev. Dr Samuel Kobia from the Methodist Church in Kenya was first appointed as Executive Secretary for Urban Rural Mission of WCC. In 2003, Kobia served as director and special representative for Africa of WCC. He was elected as the first African General Secretary of WCC in August 2003, and held office from 2004 to 2009.

Mr William Temu, a Roman Catholic from Tanzania, served as Africa Desk then Director of Management. Evelyn Appiah (Ghana) was Executive Secretary of the Stream of Lay Participation towards Inclusive Community. Rev. Fr Kwame Labi from Ghana was WCC programme executive for Urban and Rural Mission. Dr Agnes Abuom, an Anglican from Kenya, was in WCC youth education. Mr Melaku Kifle, Ethiopian Orthodox, was Executive Secretary – Refugees Affairs. The Rev. Clement Janda (Sudan) worked in WCC's international affairs department. Mr Richard Murigande (Rwanda) was Executive Secretary – Africa Desk. The Rev. Dr André Karamaga from the Presbyterian Church of Rwanda served as the African Vice-President of the WCC and later led the remobilisation of the Christian community in Rwanda after the tragic genocide in 1994; Dr Rogate Mshana, a Lutheran from Tanzania, was Programme Executive, Economic Justice, then for a while Director – Justice, Diakonia and Responsibility for Creation Programme. Dr Nigussu Legesse, Ethiopian Orthodox Church, was Programme Executive in charge of African relations and was responsible for South Sudan. Mrs Sydia Nduna, an Anglican from Zambia, was WCC Programme Executive for Migration and Social Justice. Dr Fulata Lusungu Mbano-Moyo, a Presbyterian from Malawi, is Programme Executive – Women in Church and Society (its name was changed to Just Community of Women), while Ms Semegnish Asfaw Grosjean of the Ethiopian Orthodox Church is WCC's Programme Executive for International Affairs. Dr Sue Parry, a Baptist from Zimbabwe, is Consultant – Health and Healing. Dr Amélé Adamavi-Aho Ekué, a Togolese/German professor of Ecumenical Social Ethics and former dean of the Ecumenical Institute of WCC, currently serves as the Programme Co-ordinator of Ecumenical Theological Education. The Rev. Fr Dr Lawrence Lwuamadi, a Roman Catholic priest from Nigeria, is a professor of Ecumenical Biblical Hermeneutics at the Ecumenical Institute of the WCC. Prof. Paul Isaak from the Lutheran Church of Namibia served as professor of ecumenical missiology from 2007 to 2012 at the Ecumenical Institute of the WCC. Prof. Dr Isabel Apawo Phiri, a Presbyterian from Malawi, was appointed as WCC Associate General Secretary for Public Witness and Diakonia in 2012. Ms Lona Wilson Lupai, from South Sudan, is one of the longest-serving programme assistants.

WCC Programmes Initiated by the ACs

The WCC, through the Assembly mandate that it has been receiving from the members churches in Africa, has continued to take initiatives in developing programmes. There have been a number of WCC programme initiatives in Africa, but here we aim to give only a concise appraisal of some of these programmes.

The Programme to Combat Racism – PCR

In the 1960s, the WCC first general secretary, Willem A. Visser 't Hooft, initiated a conversation that apartheid should be regarded as a heresy. At the Council's 4th Assembly in Uppsala, Sweden, 1968, many delegates from global South member churches demanded that the WCC should give priority to the

[6] For a detailed discussion on the contributions of Tutu, Pobee and Njoroge to the development of ecumenical theological education in Africa, see Chammah J. Kaunda, 'Imagining a Just and Equitable African Christian Community: A Critical Analysis of the Contribution of Theological Education Fund/Ecumenical Theological Education (1910–2012).' Doctoral thesis, University of KwaZulu-Natal, 2013.

elimination of institutionalized racism. This resulted in the creation of the WCC Programme to Combat Racism (PCR) which was launched in 1969 in response to the Uppsala mandate. In the 1970s and 1980s, PCR played a controversial role in international debate about white minority rule in South Africa. The WCC also set up a special fund, which was given to racially oppressed groups in order to strengthen their organizational capability. The programme also confronted WCC member churches in South Africa for contributing to the perpetuation of institutionalised racism through their own policies. This resulted in some churches globally relinquishing membership with WCC because they felt the Council was supporting terrorists – the Africa National Congress (ANC). Yet the contribution that the programme made was enormous and even international organisations and politicians in South Africa have recognised WCC for its contribution to end apartheid there.

The Ecumenical HIV and AIDS Initiative in Africa (EHAIA)[7]

The EHAIA is a WCC programme which started in 2002 in response to a request by the WCC member Churches in Africa with other ecumenical partners. They requested the Council to join them in fighting the HIV pandemic in Africa. The programme has been promoting HIV competence among churches, and calls for theological institutions to include HIV in their curricula. It has also been working to deal with the core religious and cultural issues that contribute to the pandemic. At the 10th Assembly in Busan, 2013, EHAIA was given a mandate to expand beyond Africa and become active internationally, sharing its African experiences and expertise.

In 2012, the EHAIA reflected on its impact and demonstrated how many churches in Africa have become 'HIV-competent' in that they have started expressing attitudes that are more accommodating to HIV-positive people and are involved in the fight against HIV. It was reported that many church leaders have been attending EHAIA workshops and many theological institutions have now integrated HIV into their curricula due to EHAIA's initiatives. There is also an impressive and voluminous literature which has been produced on theological, religious and cultural perspectives on HIV and gender.

The EHAIA has also contributed to breaking some African taboos on sexuality and gender within both church and society. The contextual Bible studies methodological approach has been adopted and has enabled the EHAIA staff to bring out new perspectives on issues of gender and HIV.

The Ecumenical Disability Advocates Network (EDAN)

The WCC has a long history of involvement with people with disability which goes back to 1971 when the Commission on Faith and Order acknowledged that the unity of the church cannot be achieved without inclusion of persons with disabilities. The 5th Assembly, Nairobi, Kenya, 1975, issued a statement on 'The Handicapped and the Wholeness of the Family of God' which affirmed that 'the church's unity includes both the "disabled" and the "abled"'.[8] The 8th Assembly in Harare, Zimbabwe, 1998, became a springboard for the creation of the Ecumenical Disability Advocates Network (EDAN). EDAN is based in Nairobi, Kenya, under the leadership of Dr Samuel Kabue as its Programme Executive. The main goal of EDAN has been that of advocacy. It advocates 'the inclusion, participation and active involvement of persons with disabilities in sphere of the church and society'.[9] The programme is hosted by the All Africa

---

[7] For a detailed discussion, see WCC, 'Ecumenical HIV and AIDS Initiatives and Advocacy (EHAIA)', 2015: https://www.oikoumene.org/en/what-we-do/ehaia (accessed 7 November, 2015).
[8] A detailed history of EDAN is given in WCC, 'WCC Work on Persons with Disabilities: History': www.wcc-coe.org/wcc/what/jpc/hist.html (accessed 6 November, 15).
[9] For more information, see EDAN, 'Ecumenical Disability Advocates Network (EDAN)', (2015): www.edan-wcc.org (accessed 6 November, 15).

Conference of Churches (AACC) but functions with an international ethos through volunteer co-ordinators in all regions where the WCC operates.

The Ecumenical Pharmaceutical Network (EPN)

The Ecumenical Pharmaceutical Network (EPN) was established by the WCC and now operates independently in Nairobi, Kenya. The history of EPN dates back to 1981 when the Christian Medical Commission (CMC) of the WCC decided to provide advice and consultations on pharmaceutical issues in the health programmes of churches in Africa. CMC, with the support of a steering committee called Pharmaceutical Advisory Group (PAG), organised a consultation in Geneva to discuss issues related to pharmaceutical service delivery in Africa. They appointed a pharmaceutical adviser who provided technical assistance to the churches on medicine management and the rational use of medicines in different pharmaceutical programmes. The Pharmaceutical Adviser was finally relocated to Nairobi in 1997, and the church-based organizations that received support became a network. This resulted in the creation of EPN which has over eighty members from over thirty countries around the world, and was registered as a non-government organization in Kenya in 2004. The current Executive Director of EPN is Dr Mirfin Mpundu. EPN strengthens church health systems by focusing on promoting access to and the rational use of medicines, HIV and AIDS care and treatment, the professionalization of pharmaceutical services and sharing information.[10]

Ecumenical Theological Education (ETE)

The WCC initiative in theological education in Africa cannot be over-emphasized. Since the inception of the Theological Education Fund, which was started by the International Missionary Council (IMC) and its successors, the Programme on Theological Education (PTE) and the Ecumenical Theological Education (ETE), African Christianity has benefited from this relationship with the renewal and reformation of theological curricula, scholarships for staff development and the production of theological literature for theological education and the church.

First, the programme gave an opportunity for African scholars/leaders who worked as staff, such as Archbishop Desmond Tutu, Prof. John Pobee and Dr Nyambura Njoroge, to develop into global ecumenical voices. It also provided a platform for a South and North theological dialogue to which African scholars contributed African perspectives on theological education and theological thinking. This needs to be strengthened.

Second, the programme exposed African scholars to new trends in global Christianity which enabled them to add their own theological voice in the global ecumenical family. It also enabled African theological institutions to rethink their theological curricula. In early 2002, the ETE called for integrating and mainstreaming HIV and gender in theological curricula; this has helped most institutions to undergo transformation and remain up-to-date in their theological educational philosophies.

Third, the ecumenical scholarship fund on the African continent has helped many African theologians to become what they are today. The programme supported the theological education of renowned African theologians on the continent such as Isabel Apawo Phiri, Musa Dube, Philomena Mwaura, Fulata Mbano-Moyo, Ezra Chitando and many others who have made huge contributions to the ecumenical movement, theological education and African Christianity generally. The documentation of the impact of African scholars who have been supported through ecumenical scholarship remains to be done.

---

[10] For more information, see, ENP, 'History', (2015): www.epnetwork.org/en/about-us-5 (accessed 6 November, 15).

Fourth, through ecumenical scholarships, African theologians have been able to produce literature for the church and theological education on current issues such justice and peace, poverty, the economy, education, gender, climate change, migration and HIV, and give a unique African theological voice in ecumenical theological debates round the world. These works have begun to influence the way theological education is being done in Africa by encouraging theological institutions to bring current contextual issues to the forefront in the way theological students are equipped.

Conclusion

The argument has been put forward that the presence and participation of ACs in the WCC has contributed to the paradigm shift in the Council's social thought as oriented to reconceptualise 'the programmes dealing with development, social justice, racism and conflict resolution, but also evangelism, theological education, formation of the laity etc.'[11] We submit that most of the areas mentioned remain in need of more empirical research in order to glean insights into the impact the WCC has made on African Christianity through engagement with African churches.

Bibliography

'Ecumenical Disability Advocates Network (EDAN).' www.edan-wcc.org (2015), (accessed 6 November, 2015).

Ecumenical Pharmaceutical Network, 'History.' www.epnetwork.org/en/about-us-5 (2015), (accessed 6 November, 2015).

Kaunda, Chammah J., 'Imagining a Just and Equitable African Christian Community: A Critical Analysis of the Contribution of Theological Education Fund/Ecumenical Theological Education (1910-2012).' Unpublished doctoral thesis, University of KwaZulu-Natal, 2013.

Oduyoye, Mercy A, 'Africa', in *A History of the Ecumenical Movement, 1968 to 2000*, Volume 3, edited by John Briggs, Mercy Oduyoye and Georges Tsetsis, 469-93. Geneva: WCC Publications, 2004.

Olupona, Jacob K., 'A Biographical Sketch', in *Religious Plurality in Africa: Essays in Honour of John S. Mbiti*, edited by Jacob Olupona and Sulayman Nyang, 1-10. Berlin: Mouton de Gruyter, 1993.

van Beek, Huibert, *A Handbook of Churches and Councils: Profiles of Ecumenical Relationships.* Geneva: WCC Publications, 2006.

WCC, 'Africa.' https://www.oikoumene.org/en/member-churches/africa (accessed 6 November, 2015).

WCC, 'Constitution and Rules of the World Council of Churches (as amended by the 9th Assembly, Porto Alegre, Brazil, February 2006).' www.oikoumene.org/en/resources (accessed 6 November, 2015).

WCC, 'Ecumenical HIV and AIDS Initiatives and Advocacy (EHAIA).' https://www.oikoumene.org/en/what-we-do/ehaia (2015), (accessed 7 November, 2015).

WCC, 'WCC Work on Persons with Disabilities: History.' www.wcc-coe.org/wcc/what/jpc/hist.html (accessed 6 November, 2015).

[11] WCC, 'Africa'.

(108) NOTIONS AND FORMS OF ECUMENICITY IN AFRICA

Ernst M. Conradie

Introduction and Context

The University of the Western Cape in South Africa has embarked on a three-year project on 'Ecumenical Studies and Social Ethics' in which the interface between 'ecclesiology' – i.e. matters of 'Faith and Order', and 'Ethics', i.e. matters of 'Life and Work' and of 'Church and Society' – is investigated in the African context. The underlying question is how the 'and' that connects what the church is and what the church does should be understood. There is a widely acknowledged tension, also in the African context, in which the emphasis is placed on either the one or the other. The project culminated in a conference hosted in June 2015 on 'Ecclesiology and Ethics: The State of Ecumenical Theology in Africa'.

In one of the think tanks that constitute the project, the very meaning of the adjective 'ecumenical' was explored. What notions and forms of ecumenicity may be identified, for example, in the South African context? In a contribution to the volume of essays that was subsequently published, I identified and described some 23 distinct ways in which the term 'ecumenicity' can and has been understood in different historical epochs and contexts.[1]

In this brief contribution, I will merely list these notions of ecumenicity without any discussion, and then reflect on possible forms that 'being ecumenical' may take in the wider African context.

1. The whole inhabited world (*oikoumene*)
2. Ecumenicity and catholicity (the spread of the church throughout the inhabited world)
3. The recognition of seven church councils as 'ecumenical' since Nicaea (325)
4. The conciliar movement amidst major ecclesial schisms
5. Mission and evangelism in an ecumenical spirit
6. Faith and Order: Mutual recognition of the one faith that Christians have in common
7. Life and Work: Theological reflection on social issues
8. Ecumenical theological education
9. Worship and celebrating the liturgy together
10. Ecumenism from above? A fellowship of churches or what do ecumenical structures, offices and bureaucrats do?
11. Church and Society: The dominance of the social agenda of the church
12. Ecclesiology and Ethics: Bridging a widening gap in the ecumenical movement
13. Ecumenicity as 'dialogue' with other living faiths
14. A 'wider ecumenicity'? (including the whole of humankind)
15. The whole household of God as the global political economy
16. The planetary household
17. The universe story: At home on earth!
18. A return to Nicene Christianity
19. Bilateral conversations on matters of faith and order
20. A sense of belonging to Christian world communions within confessional traditions

[1] See Ernst M. Conradie, 'Notions and Forms of Ecumenicity: Some South African Perspectives', in *South African Perspectives on Notions and Forms of Ecumenicity*, ed. Ernst M. Conradie (Stellenbosch, South Africa: SUN Press, 2013), 13-76.

21. Ecumenism as *ad hoc* collaboration
22. Inter-denominational reform and de-form movements
23. The search for more inclusive ecumenical structures (e.g. the Global Christian Forum)

A few comments on the logic behind this list may be helpful. The sequence is more or less in a historical order but is also organised in terms of wider and narrower definitions of the *oikoumene*. The first notion of ecumenicity was a secular one and inclusive in terms of the known 'inhabited world' of the time (including North Africa). The definitions then become increasingly narrowed towards the Council of Nicaea (3 above) and the diverging confessional traditions contesting the proper interpretation of Nicaea (4). It becomes even narrower after Edinburgh 1910 to refer to five dimensions of the modern ecumenical movement (5-9). Since the establishment of the global ecumenical structure of the World Council of Churches in 1948 (10), there has been a tendency (according to some critics) to allow the dominance of the social agenda of the church (11), inviting questions around ecclesiology and ethics (12). However, there is also a subsequent tendency to widen the meaning of ecumenicity to include dialogue with other living faiths (13), the unity of humankind (14), the political economy (15), the planetary household (16) and the universe (17). In response, others have called for a return to Nicene Christianity and thus for a far narrower, less amorphous notion of ecumenicity (18). This has become even narrower in terms of bilateral conversations (19), confessional world communions (20) and *ad hoc*, local forms of ecumenism (21). Yet others would again seek to widen the definition to focus on para-church reform movements (22) or more inclusive but also more tentative and fragile ecumenical structures (23).

Ecumenicity in Africa

Each of the notions of ecumenicity described above has been articulated in the African context by African spokespersons and has had an impact on African Christianity.[2] Each has therefore also had a contested reception so that it is impossible and inappropriate to generalise. For instance, all five the dimensions of the modern ecumenical movement are relevant to the quest for church unity in Africa. Instead, I will offer a number of observations to capture some of the underlying tensions pertaining to the ecumenical movement in the African context:

First, there can be no doubt that the tension between ecclesiology and ethics[3] also characterises ecumenical relations in Africa. One may observe that matters of 'ethics', i.e. the social agenda of the church and the prophetic witness of the church amidst socio-political developments, typically dominate nation-wide and continent-wide ecumenical gatherings. Notwithstanding the much celebrated African religiosity, such a focus on 'ethics' often leads to a form of self-secularisation and politicisation. By contrast, matters of 'ecclesiology' typically come to the forefront at local ecumenical gatherings, e.g. in the form of a liturgy for ecumenical services, planning for funerals and occupying positions of ecclesial authority, not to mention attempts to secure a larger share of the religious market for a particular brand of Christianity.

Second, it may be noted that the divide between ecclesiology and ethics also permeates contemporary African Christian theology. Discourse on enculturation and indigenisation typically focuses on positions of leadership and ordination, liturgical innovation, hymnody and an African interpretation of the Christian faith. By contrast, black theology and theologies of liberation and reconstruction tend to focus on issues of 'ethics'. The same applies to African women's theology although ordination and the position of women occupying positions of ecclesial leadership at the local level are also addressed.

---

[2] For a discussion of African ecumenism, see the section on recommended reading below.
[3] See the volume edited by Thomas F. Best and Martin Robra, *Ecclesiology and Ethics: Ecumenical Ethical Engagement: Moral Formation and the Nature of the Church* (Geneva: WCC Publications, 1997).

Third, there is some widespread resistance in Africa against what may be called 'ecumenism from above', i.e. a focus on official ecumenical structures and ecumenical gatherings as the primary form of ecumenical fellowship. The dysfunctional structures of the South African Council of Churches provide an illustration of what is at stake. One may argue that such pan-African structures are necessary in order to identify and discuss common problems in Africa, especially related to 'ethics'. However, given geographical distances and the soaring cost of international travel in Africa, such structures and gatherings are extremely expensive to maintain. As a result, African ecumenism remains dependent on financial resources from beyond its borders. Nevertheless, there seem to be ample funds available amongst churches within Africa – as church building projects, the thriving gospel music industry and the opulence of ecclesial tycoons amply illustrate. Yet there seems to be little enthusiasm for channelling such funds into ecumenical structures.

Fourth, the contrast with European ecumenical relations may be instructive. In most countries in Europe, one finds either a (former) state church or a situation where more than 80% of Christians in a particular country belong to two or at most three churches. With some exaggeration, one may observe that one almost needs to travel out of one's own country to encounter other main branches of Christianity. The model of ecumenical bureaucracy that was developed in Europe implied that ecumenical offices often become nothing but the international desk of a denomination or a national council of churches. By contrast, in most African countries (Egypt and Ethiopia may provide exceptions), one finds a wide variety of confessional traditions due to the legacy of colonialism and foreign mission. Again exaggerating, but only a little, one may find more denominational variety within one block of streets in an African city than in some countries in continental Europe (the UK, and to some extent the Netherlands, may be exceptions).

Fifth, one may observe that ecumenical fellowship is alive and well at a local level across Africa even where national structures are difficult to maintain. This is illustrated by ecumenical co-operation that one finds in organising funerals, local charities, activist organisations, trade union meetings, sports teams and school committees alike. Even where religion plays no overt role (e.g. in sport), there is a need to deal with religious diversity. At the local level, people seem perfectly able to live with such ecclesial (but not always religious) diversity most of the time.

A sixth observation pertains only to South Africa – where it is often observed that 10 o'clock on Sunday remains the 'most divided hour' of the week. Such divides are mainly in terms of race and class, and may be understood as the long-term effect of the social engineering and town planning associated with segregation and apartheid. This is exacerbated by entrenched forms of denominationalism amidst a quest to establish a sense of identity. Since denominational differences amongst so-called mainline churches are mainly derived from Europe, it is not always clear to the laity what is at stake. However, it is also true that such differences are internalised after a few generations in terms of ecclesial structures and rituals so that members feel at home in their own denominational settings. Admittedly, this situation is being eroded by competition over ecclesial market share with a plethora of newly established independent, evangelical and Pentecostal churches, each jostling for adherents.

A final observation pertains to new forms of ecumenism that are emerging beyond the official ecumenical structures. Here one may mention grassroots forms of ecumenism associated with funerals, vigils, *stokvels*, music groups and women's prayer groups. Indeed, if there is a sense of crisis with respect to large ecumenical structures or at the level of church leadership, grassroots ecumenism in villages and urban communities alike seems to be alive and well in most African countries. The laity are not perturbed by denominational differences or leadership tussles and are perfectly able to co-operate, share and enjoy fellowship whenever there is a need and in response to any threat or challenge. Such local collaboration is not only found with respect to events that are overtly religious in nature. This is best illustrated by protest marches, trade unions and political movements. In the past, religious leaders have often played a significant role in this regard and were seen to be acting in unison at the front of marches in the struggle against apartheid.[4]

One may also mention *ad hoc* forms of ecumenism that seem to attract thousands of participants. These include events such as the Pan-African Christian Leadership Assembly (PACLA, 1976) and the South African Christian Leadership Assembly (SACLA, 1979). It also includes gospel festivals often held at large sports stadiums. Three features of such gospel festivals may be noted. First, these gatherings are undoubtedly inter-denominational even though they attract mainly Christians from an evangelical or Pentecostal persuasion and not necessarily those from so-called mainline churches. Second, they are also non-denominational in the sense that they signal the demise of denominations. Third, they are based on *ad hoc* forms of collaboration with very specific targets and follow-up plans (also in terms of addressing social needs). What they lack in terms of the institutionalisation of a movement they make up in terms of mustering considerable energies over the short term. One would need to have one's ears close to the ground to pick up various other emerging forms of ecumenicity at a local level in South Africa and elsewhere in Africa.

Conclusion

The discussion of the notions and forms of ecumenicity above suggests some fluctuation between attempts at an inclusive widening or a qualitative narrowing of what being ecumenical might entail. Given the recent developments that challenge the parameters of the modern ecumenical movement as represented by the World Council of Churches and its affiliates, it is understandable that some are searching for more inclusive ecumenical structures. Such efforts are born from a growing awareness of the shifting centre of gravity in global Christianity. This may be understood geographically, given secularisation in the global North and a shift in the number of Christian adherents towards countries of the global South, and more recently also towards the East. Added to this is the shifting of the centre of gravity away from mainline churches towards free-standing local (usually evangelical) churches, charismatic groups, numerous neo-Pentecostal churches and a wide variety of indigenous churches, for example in the Southern African context.

Bibliography

Amanze, James N., '100 years of the Ecumenical Movement in Africa: A Historical Appraisal of its Successes and Failures in the Twentieth Century', *Journal of Theology for Southern Africa,* Vol. 105 (1999): 1-15.

Best, Thomas F., and Robra, Martin (eds.), *Ecclesiology and Ethics: Ecumenical Ethical Engagement, Moral Formation and the Nature of the Church.* Geneva: WCC Publications, 1997.

Conradie, Ernst M. (ed.), *African Christian Theologies in Transformation.* Stellenbosch, South Africa: EFSA, 2004.

______. (ed), *South African Perspectives on Notions and Forms of Ecumenicity.* Stellenbosch, South Africa: SUN Press, 2013.

Guma, Mongezi, and Milton, Leslie (eds.), *An African Challenge to the Church in the 21st Century.* Johannesburg, South Africa: SACC, 1997.

Lombaard, Christo (ed.), *Essays and Exercises in Ecumenism.* Pietermaritzburg, South Africa: Cluster Publications, 1999.

Mugambi, Jesse N.K. (ed), *The Church and the Future in Africa: Problems and Promises.* Nairobi: AACC, 1997.

---

[4] For a discussion, see Molefe Tsele, 'African Ecumenism within the Context of NEPAD.', In *African Christian Theologies in Transformation*, ed. Ernst M. Conradie, (Stellenbosch, South Africa: EFSA, 2004), 111-18.

Oduyoye, Mercy A, 'Africa', in *A History of the Ecumenical Movement, 1968-2000*, Volume 3, edited by J. Briggs, Mercy Amba Oduyoye and G. Tsetsis, 469-94. Geneva: WCC Publications, 2004.
Pityana, Barney N., and Villa-Vicencio, Charles (eds.), *Being the Church in South Africa Today*. Johannesburg, South Africa: SACC, 1995.

(109) African Christianity and Partnership with European Churches

Fidon Mwombeki

The Beginnings

African Christianity is mainly a product of European mission work, after Africa was 'discovered' and colonized by Europe, with one of the goals being its Christianization. I however do not share the popular opinion that mission was a tool for colonization, but the other way round. The link between the two cannot be denied since, as we often observe, the church is a part of society, and what happens in society is reflected in the church as well.[1] Most of the time, missions worked in the colonies of their home countries.

It is no wonder that, until now, links with Africa in many aspects are with or through Europe – be it air travel to anywhere in the world, telecommunication, economic ties, etc. Africa has not succeeded in releasing itself from the cords Europe tied from the time of colonialism, including church relations.[2] Most of the churches in Africa have European missionary roots, until the recent wave of American-based charismatic movements. Their theologies are shaped by European denominational controversies, which Africans have adopted, sometimes without even understanding why.

From Mission Fields to Daughter Churches to Sister Churches

During the independence movements against colonialism, indigenous leaders of what have so far been called Protestant 'mission fields' or 'mission churches' fought for church independence too, many of which gained independence close to the time of political independence. One can see the debate during all international missionary conferences since Edinburgh 1910, where the concern of equality of partnership has been the issue.[3]

However, there was a clear difference between the independence of the church from the political independence of countries. There were formal independence celebrations when the colonial leaders left, when new flags were flown, and a radical break with the colonialists was made. Until now, however, links with the former missions continue and churches in Africa celebrate jubilees of the arrival of the first missionaries, and never the end of the missionary era. Conversely, no country celebrates the arrival of the first colonialist, but they do celebrate their departure – on Independence Day! In church contexts, missionaries were not usually expelled, and there was no real break with relations with missions abroad. What changed was leadership. The leaders of the now-independent churches wanted to maintain links and relationships with the missions with great respect. Many missionaries remained and continued to work under new leadership. Later, the number of missionaries diminished, not because of expulsion but due to financial constraints in their sending missions.

These mission fields slowly became 'daughter churches', continuing to benefit from relationships with missions, including different forms of grants and support until now. The grants target mainly diaconic and

---

[1] The WCC was formed in the same year as United Nations (UN) – in 1948 – and the All Africa Conference of Churches in the same year as the Organization for African Union (OAU, renamed African Union-AU) in 1963.

[2] Globalization (and global dominance of America) has opened up links with other continents, especially Asia, but the primary links are still with Europe.

[3] See, for example, Lothar Bauerochse, *Miteinander Leben und Lernen: Zwischenkirchliche Partnerschaften als Ökumenische Lerngemeinschaften* (Erlangen, Germany: Verlag der Evangelische Lutherische Mission, 1996), especially chapter 1.

developmental structures and institutions. Schools, hospitals, orphanages, offices of the churches, car-pools and printing facilities, were established even in remote areas where the colonialists never penetrated. These are based on the financial systems established by missions, but they were foreign to the normal lives of the people in Africa. After the missionaries had left, missions continued to finance these institutions, including payment systems of church workers and pension schemes. These have proven to be difficult for independent young church to take over and finance.

As a result, African churches have continued to be dependent on their 'mother churches' for heavy financial investments, including expensive administrative structures. This is, however, again reflected also in broader society, whereby even colonial countries continue to finance a big chunk of the budgets of their former colonies. The structures established by colonialism such as cities, universities, parliaments, cabinets, elections and governance structures, cannot easily be financed by local resources.

Partnership?

The idea of partnership is theological.[4] Based on our understanding of Scripture – that we are all brothers and sisters in Christ, and church is a spiritual entity which does not depend on worldly power – what is needed is a partnership of equals before God. But is such partnership possible in this unequal world?

The roles of African and European churches were from the beginning defined by history. Europe is the initiator of ideas and the wealthier partner, while Africa is a receiver! But these roles are not considered theologically correct.

After serving in ecumenical context several years, I regret to have to admit that these roles are not easily changed. I realize that it is very difficult for Europeans to change their role as giver and learn to receive (from Africans), just as it is difficult for African churches to change and learn to give (to Europeans). Because of these traditional roles, African churches have not assumed their equal share of responsibility in ecumenical affairs, just as European churches would not like to be seen as recipients.

Attempts to Forge an Equal Partnership

There have been several attempts to enhance equality in partnership since it is the wish of both partners. This is the attempt of many forms of partnership, e.g. between church districts, congregations, institutions, etc. There have been several forms of structural change in missions to reflect this understanding.[5] The goal of restructuring is to put into practice the theological conviction that no church is too poor to give something, and no church is too rich to receive from others, and all churches are equal. However, since the financial burden of running missions as well as global ecumenical bodies is still carried mostly by European churches, and the financial contributions of African churches are next to negligible, it remains only a theologically correct feeling. And I have to say, African churches have the capacity to do more, if they shed the enslavement of the role of being a happy receiver.

There have been structures deliberately placed within missions to negotiate with their African church partners on equal terms.[6]

---

[4] See Bauerochse, 156-65.

[5] Several mission organizations have transformed themselves into global partnership of equals between the former 'daughter churches' and European churches over several decades. See Kai Funkschmidt, *Earthing the Vision: Strukturreformen in der Mission unterssucht am Beispiel von CEVAA (Paris), CWM (London) und UEM (Wuppertal)* (Frankfurt am Main, Germany: Verlag Otto Lembek, 2000).

[6] See e.g. Eila Helander and Wilson Niwagila, *Partnership and Power* (Erlangen, Germany: Verlag der Evangelische Lutherische Mission, 1996). Many mission supporters in certain countries of Europe unite and form round tables to deal with issues with their partners . African churches have no such possibility of co-ordinating with each other before

An Intrinsically Unequal Parnership

I would like to highlight some areas which I believe demonstrate the continuing inequality in partnership between African and European churches.

Structural level

What annoys the African church leaders most is the fact that, in European churches, African churches are not regarded the same as other European churches. In very few cases have European churches signed partnership agreements with churches in Africa. Many of the missions which started the African churches are no longer independent institutions but departments within European churches, mainly called 'ecumenical departments'. Communication between African churches and European churches takes place within these departments and the top leadership of African churches. When an African bishop visits a European church, a former 'mother church', an African bishop is received by a head of ecumenical department, sometimes not even a pastor, with a 'courtesy call' to the office of the fellow church leader. But official talks are conducted by the ecumenical department. I am aware that, when dealing with other church leaders from Europe or America, that the bishop of the European church takes a lead.

There is a clear similarity with society at large. In political relations, European countries have two separate ministries dealing with foreign countries. For European and other richer countries, the ministry of foreign affairs is responsible. But for African and other poorer continents, it is a lower-regarded ministry, normally called 'development co-operation' which is responsible. In general, foreign ministers of European countries, let alone heads of countries, do not visit Africa. It is normally the minister responsible for 'development co-operation' who comes as a donor. Topics of discussion are not the mutual exchange of ideas and formulating common strategy on something, but listening to the needs of the poor country and stating the conditions of support, or inspecting whether these conditions have been met. And African countries must do all they can not to offend the donors, whose action can have serious financial repercussions to the government. Are churches any different?

Theological level

I am not sure there is a genuine feeling of equality at the theological level. I time and again hear and see indications of feelings of superiority and inferiority on the theological side. I do not think that the theological ideas of Africans are taken as seriously as those of European theologians. During debates on theologically contentious issues, I very often hear comments from European theologians and leaders which demonstrate feelings of superiority. At the same time, African churches are frustrated by the trivialization of the issues they want to bring to discussion in global venues. The issues of spirits of the dead (though unresolved in Europe as well), polygamy, witchcraft and superstition, are not taken seriously by European churches. But they use money and power to make sure the issues they raise are indeed taken up by African churches, or else…

The money factor

It is always said: let us keep money out of the partnership. It never happens. This is because money is simply a medium of exchange. There is nothing discussed more in the churches, both in Europe or in Africa, than money. Let us be honest: money is always central to any interaction. We may imagine we have partnerships which do not have financial aspects. Who pays, who gives, who receives, who reports to whom, what are the conditions of getting money, and the attitude and style of reporting requirements, are all major aspects of partnerships. Proper reporting and accountability are simply good stewardship, within

---

meeting one particular mission organization. The power relations are clear.

one church or between churches. I find it unfair for African churches to use political correctness in the idea of partnership to avoid financial accountability, which they should have even within their own churches.

The back-donor factor

But there is a new development in Europe which strongly influences the partnership between European and African churches, i.e. the back donor. As the churches and former missions have less and less money, the role of the para-church development agencies is reshaping the partnership. The areas of co-operation are more and more determined not by the churches, but by the 'specialized ministries'. These are essentially agencies established, backed and originally financed by churches in Europe after the World War II. Therefore money is more available for humanitarian and development activities, which the missions started and financed for decades[7] since the idea of separation between mission and development is foreign to African churches.

Specialized ministries are financed largely by private donations and governments as 'back-donors'. These back-donors have demands and conditions for project funding which the 'specialized ministries' pass on to the recipient African churches. Since the African churches need the money to serve their people, they are forced to accept these conditions which are sometimes strange. For example, African churches have always seen people from their partner churches in Europe as fellow missionaries in one global mission. But through these development agencies, with conditions from their donors against excluding non-believers, churches sometimes are forced to accept employees from Europe who have no affinity with church. I remember seeing one such person who was provocatively washing his car in front of the church during Sunday service who, when confronted, responded that attending a church service was not in his job description, and he was free to use his time as he wished. And since the partnership follows the same pattern as governments in Europe, there are cases where churches in Africa are forced not to bring faith matters into the partnership, or are asked to put aside their ethical convictions, because they are excluded by the 'back-donors'.

Changing dynamics

All relationships are in some way influenced by economic power, whether in a small village or at a global level. No matter what European countries may criticize China for (human rights, hacking, environmental concerns, economic espionage), it cannot pass any resolutions or take any action against China. It is simply too important for European economic survival. As long as Africa is economically weak in relation to Europe, the African churches continue to think along the same lines as their governments. As long as European countries deal with Africa at the level of 'development co-operation' and not 'foreign relations', the churches find it difficult to escape the *Zeitgeist*.

But the dynamics are changing. More and more African churches no longer depend on European churches to run their affairs. Most churches would survive a donation moratorium, which was not the case in the 1970s.[8] More and more partnerships will be based on aspects other than economics. Indeed, some church social and developmental services would suffer much in the event of a moratorium, but most church ministries are not any longer supported from abroad.

The question before us is whether the traditional donor-recipient roles are changing after so many years of discussion and the desire for equal partnership. In my experience, both sides have serious problems in embracing the changing circumstances and adapting positively. I do not see African churches doing their

---

[7] Konrad Raiser, 'Foreword', in *Christianity, Poverty and Wealth: The Findings of 'Project 21,* ed. Michael Taylor,*'* (London and Geneva: SPCK and WCC, 2003), ix.

[8] Eugeniah Ombwayo Adoyo, *Mission and Moratorium in Africa: The issues underlying the proposal for a missionary moratorium, and the implications of its failure for the future of mission/church relationships in Africa (with special reference to English-speaking Africa)* (Oxford: Oxford Centre for Mission Studies, 1990).

fair share in global ecumenical responsibilities as much as they are capable of. And I do not see the European churches ready to be just like others, not being the dominant donor. It is even more difficult for them to be humble enough to receive. I lead an organization which is focusing on transforming these roles, but I see how difficult it is to change.[9] For example, at the local level of partnership between church districts in Germany and an African church, partnership groups in Germany are totally surprised when they hear that a delegation from Africa will pay its own airfares. They have no problem about being asked for such items. This change is difficult for both partners.

As African churches are feeling more economically independent, they also feel freer to express what they think and even challenge their European partners theologically. Since it has always been the role of the donor to threaten ending a partnership if the African Church does not behave, the tables are turned when an African church gives an ultimatum to a European church to explain its theological position on some matter, or else the African Church will end the partnership! This is new! And no European church is used to facing an ultimatum from an African church.

Bibliography

Adoyo, Eugeniah Ombwayo, *Mission and Moratorium in Africa: The issues underlying the proposal for a missionary moratorium, and the implications of its failure for the future of mission/church relationships in Africa (with special reference to English-speaking Africa).* Oxford: Oxford Centre for Mission Studies, 1990.

Bauerochse, Lothar, *Miteinander Leben und Lernen: Zwischenkirchliche Partnerschaften als Ökumenische Lerngemeinschaften.* Erlangen, Germany: Verlag der Evangelische Lutherische Mission, 1996.

Funkschmidt, Kai, *Earthing the Vision: Strukturreformen in der Mission unterssucht am Beispiel von CEVAA (Paris), CWM (London) und UEM (Wuppertal).* Frankfurt am Main, Germany: Verlag Otto Lembek, 2000.

Helander, Eila and Niwagila, Wilson, *The Partnership and Power.* Erlangen, Germany: Verlag der Evangelische Lutherische Mission, 1996.

von Local, Brunhild, *Von Fremdheit und Freundschaft.* Wuppertal, Germany: United Evangelical Mission, 2011.

Taylor, Michael, *Christianity, Poverty and Wealth: The Findings of 'Project 21'.* London and Geneva: SPCK and WCC, 2003.

[9] Brunhild von Local, *Von Fremdheit und Freundschaft* (Wuppertal, Germany: United Evangelical Mission, 2011).

(110A) African Christianity and Partnership with Asian Churches

Manoj Kurian

Introduction

The perspectives of this chapter are influenced by the personal and institutional transformation processes[1] which followed the challenge of responding to the call of churches in sub-Saharan Africa given to the WCC at the 8th Assembly in Harare (1998), to accompany African churches in facing and overcoming the HIV and AIDS pandemic. The magnitude of suffering I witnessed transformed me as much as the enormous sense of hope and solidarity which we experienced in working closely with individuals, churches and communities in Africa who enabled and allowed us to overcome hopelessness and desperation. We realised in the WCC that those who are vulnerable and facing tremendous challenges are in fact precious resource persons and teachers of hope, resilience and love, and not just recipients of services. Our story as WCC staff is not unique. There are a myriad examples of the transformative power in relationships between African and Asian Christianity in the twentieth and 21st centuries which are affecting global Christianity and the nature of ecumenism. Today, a third of the world population of over seven billion people are Christians, making it the religion with the largest following in the world. More than a century ago, in 1910, about two-thirds of the world's Christians lived in Europe, as they it had been for a millennium. Nowadays, only about a quarter of all Christians live in Europe (26%) while more than a third live in the Americas (37%). The share of the Christian population in sub-Saharan Africa has shot up from 9% in 1910 to 63% in 2010, while in Asia-Pacific, it rose from 3% to 7%.[2] Until the turn of the twentieth century, only a small proportion of the population of sub-Saharan Africa and Asia was Christian. This meant that their meagre presence contributed to low levels of documented contacts between the Christian communities in both continents. The meteoric rise of Christian populations in sub-Saharan Africa, as well as its impressive expansion in Asia-Pacific, has ensured that about one in every four Christians in the world lives in sub-Saharan Africa (24%), and about one in eight lives in Asia and the Pacific (13%). This reality makes it vital for us to understand the history, the dynamics, the possibilities and the challenges of relationships between African and Asian Christianity. How can Christian faith positively influence the rapidly expanding and deepening ties in trade, commerce and culture between the two continents? Grappling and dealing with this relationship is vital to ensure the dynamic presence and the transformative power of Christianity yet to be realized in the world in the years ahead.

But as a first step, it is essential to review briefly the historical context of Afro-Asian relationships.

The Historical Context of Afro-Asian Relationships

The Silk Road, Spice and Incense Routes connected Asia, Africa and Europe for over 3,000 years. These land and maritime routes were channels, central to trade and cultural interactions between the three continents. These very routes also ushered the spread of Christian (Nestorian), Manichaean, Buddhist and, later, Islamic religions into various regions of Asia and Africa.

---

[1] The author is a medical doctor from Asia trained in public health who, after joining the WCC in 1999, was responsible for the 'Health and Healing' programme of the WCC and had to sense the full weight of the immense challenge of facing and overcoming the HIV and AIDS pandemic on the African continent and beyond.

[2] *Global Christianity: A Report on the Size and Distribution of the World's Christian Population*, Pew Research Center's Forum on Religion and Public Life, Boston 2011.

In the centuries before 1500, some of the world's great civilizations, such as Kush (in present-day Sudan), Aksum (in present-day Ethiopia and Eritrea) and Great Zimbabwe, flourished in Africa. During the Roman period and perhaps earlier, the south-east African coast, extending from Kenya to as far south as Tanzania, was called 'Azania' by the Greeks and Romans. This has been recorded in the first century BC classic travelogue, 'The Periplus of the Erythraean Sea'.[3] Rhapta, the southernmost metropolis known in the Roman world, is described in the book. 'Azania' was known as 'Zesan' to the Chinese, as documented in Weilüe ('A Brief History of Wei'), a Chinese historical text written by Yu Huan between AD 239 and 265. In the second century AD, a map of Azania, attributed to Claudius Ptolemy, places Rhapta near a river identified today as Rufiji in Tanzania. Ptolemy identified the settlers of the area as Rafiji, which is similar to the name of the modern people in the area, the Wa-Rufiji.[4]

From the first to the fifth century AD, the influence of the kingdom of Aksum extended far beyond the coast of modern Ethiopia and Eritrea. They were not bound to the Byzantine Roman Empire and avoided allying with them to prevent conflicts with the Persians. The Aksumite coins were heavily based on contemporary Byzantine gold and copper issues, but adapted the designs to their advantage, asserting the use of Christian symbolism. This emphasised Aksum's competing right to Christian kingship in the fifth century, assuming the hegemony over the non-Byzantine Christian peoples of Arabia, the Persian Empire and East Africa. Byzantium possessed far greater military and economic resources, but was also geographically distant from this Christian diaspora, and was unable to exert real political control over them. As a consequence, the kings of Aksum used their position on the lucrative eastward trade routes to claim their place in Christendom.[5] The nation sought to assert its right as the Christian protector in Arabia as demonstrated by the events of AD 524, when Aksum sent military aid to the Christians of Himyar in response to persecution by the Himyarite state (present-day Yemen). In 1940, a hoard of 140 Kushan Empire gold coins dated between the first century BC and the first century AD was found in the Debre Damo monastery in northern Ethiopia.[6] The Kushan Empire extended across present-day northern India, Pakistan and Afghanistan, and the find indicates the rich trade links between the African and Asian continents during the early Christian era. Aksumite coins and pottery have also been excavated in the Indian subcontinent and Sri Lanka, providing added evidence of this relationship.[7] But with the rise of the Arabs in the seventh century and their monopoly of the route to India, with their massive maritime networks, the influence of the Kingdom of Aksum declined. The economic decline meant that Aksumite gold coinage was no longer viable in the East and become scarce in India from the sixth century onwards. As a lasting tribute to this African influence, Indians continued to use Aksumite coins in material and cultural traditions, adapting the decorative elements and continuing to mint Indian copies and versions of Aksumite coins.[8]

---

[3] Wilfred H Schoff *The Periplus of the Erythraean Sea: Travel and Trade in the Indian Ocean,* (translated and annotated from the ancient Greek), by a merchant of the first century (New York, London, Bombay and Calcutta: Longman Green, 1912), https://zethio.files.wordpress.com/2014/04/the-periplus-of-the-erythraean-sea.pdf (accessed 20 June, 2016).

[4] Felix Chami, University of Dar-es-Salaam, Metropolis of Rhapta and Azania, https://www.academia.edu/15058889/Metropolis_of_Rhapta_and_Azania (accessed 20 June, 2016).

[5] David W. Phillipson, *Foundations of an African Civilisation: Aksum and the Northern Horn, 1000 BC-AD 1300* (Eastern Africa Series), James Currey (British Institute of East Africa, 2014).

[6] Walter de Gruyter, *Aufstieg und Niedergang der Roemischen Welt*: Principat, Part 2, Volume 9 (Berlin: De Gruyter, 1978). Details on the Kushan gold coin hoard found c. 1940 in the Debre Damo monastery.

[7] Ramasubha Krishnamurthy, 'Aksumite Coins of Ethiopia from Karur, Tamil Nadu' (Studies in South Indian Numismatics 8 (1999),, 58-64.

[8] R. Day, *Imitation in Aksumite Coinage and Indian Imitations of Aksumite Coins* (Rosetta 9.5: 16-22, 2011). www.rosetta.bham.ac.uk/colloquium2011/day_coins.pdf (accessed 20 June, 2016).

But the dynamism of Africa was not linked with one kingdom. Africa continued to relate closely to Asia, even with these seismic geopolitical changes. At least from the seventh century, the inhabitants of the East African coast (Bantu- and Cushitic-speaking communities) created a cosmopolitan culture along the Swahili coast that was deeply involved in trade round the Indian Ocean, including the Persian Gulf. The name 'Swahili', from the Arabic word *sahil* meaning 'shore', was later applied to nearly forty trading towns which developed along eastern coastal Africa. Persian, Arab, Indian and Chinese merchants made their way to towns on the islands of Zanzibar and Pemba, Shanga, Manda, Pate and Malindi (Kenya), Mogadishu (Somalia) and Kilwa (Tanzania), the Comorian archipelago and Mahilaka (Madagascar), Chibuene and Inhambane (Mozambique), using the force of the monsoon in their search for profits.[9] The seasonal trade winds enabled them to carry goods from East Africa to South Asia from April to September, and to then return between November and February. The ships' captains and crews found a ready home in the cosmopolitan and, after the ninth century, Islamic world of the East African coast. The traders were hosted by the maritime communities in the ports that dotted the African coastline of the Indian Ocean. The city-states traded with inland kingdoms like Great Zimbabwe to obtain gold, ivory and iron. It is clear that the city-states had no authority over the nation's hinterland, and traded with them as equals. Archaeological evidence shows that communities living deep inland, such as those in Palapye, in present-day Botswana in the seventh century, had major iron industries, processing iron ore, most probably for export to places like India, South-East Asia, and China. At the same time, the East African city-states were buying items from Asia. Many residents of these city-states and the communities in interior Africa could afford and were willing to buy cotton, silk, glass and porcelain objects with their exports. Archaeological evidence of these purchases is found both in the Swahili city-states and communities deep in Botswana, Zimbabwe and Tanzania.[10]

In the spring of 1331, the great Moroccan traveller and writer Mohammed Ibn Battuta travelled south along the East African coast from Aden to Mogadishu, Mombasa and Kilwa. The writings of his journey reveal dynamic, hospitable and prosperous regions, inhabited by indigenous Africans who were predominantly Muslim – both Sunni and Shia.[11]

The maritime expedition to the West by the Admiral Zheng He (1371-1433), in the early part of the Ming Dynasty, demonstrated the great importance of the maritime routes in connecting Africa and Asia through the centuries. Zheng He commanded seven maritime expeditions almost a century before the Portuguese reached India. During Zheng He's fifth, sixth and seventh voyages (1417-33), the Ming fleet visited South-East Asia, India, Arabia and the east coast of Africa, where they called in at towns in what are now Somalia and Kenya, almost reaching the Mozambique Channel. Recently, scientists have unearthed a 600-year-old Chinese coin on the Kenyan island of Manda. The coin was issued by Emperor Yongle of the Ming Dynasty, who reigned 1403-1425, to whom Admiral Zheng He reported.[12] This find adds to the list of Chinese coins found in Africa- which includes the North Song Chinese coin, minted between 1017 and 1021, recovered from Kuumbi cave in Zanzibar, and two Northern Song Chinese coins dated 1080 and 1040, found in Harla, Ethiopia, in 2011.[13]

---

[9] Paul J. J. Sinclair and Thomas Hakansson, *The Swahili City State Culture, A Comparative Study of Thirty City State Cultures*, 463-81, ed. Mogens Herman Hansen (Royal Danish Academy of Sciences, Copenhagen, 2000).
[10] Unearthing the origins of East Africa's lost civilization, http://edition.cnn.com/2015/10/19/africa/kilwa-rhapta-felix-chami (accessed 20 June, 2016).
[11] Said Hamdun, Noel King, *Ibn Battuta in Black Africa* (Princeton, NJ and New York: Markus-Wiener Publishing, 1994), 13-25.
[12] Field Museum, 'Ancient Chinese coin found on Kenyan island', in Science Daily, 13th March 2013, www.sciencedaily.com/releases/2013/03/130313131900.htm (accessed 28 January, 2016).
[13] The Extended East Route is the African part of the Silk Route, Marco Vigano, 2011,https://www.academia.edu/2566792/Northern_Song_coin_finds_in_Harla_Ethiopia_point_to_newly_found_silk_

Towards the close of the fifteenth century, Vasco da Gama found a route to Asia by sailing from Portugal around Africa, eventually reaching India with the help of a Swahili navigator named Majid from Malindi in present-day Kenya. European countries had been buying Asian goods for years from middlemen and were using more difficult routes. In 1499, da Gama returned to Portugal with great success and wealth. The Portuguese government took an immediate interest in the Swahili city-states, and moved to gain control over the Indian Ocean trade. The city-states had never needed forts or huge armies, and they were unprepared for the Portuguese onslaught. With the control of the sea routes across the Indian Ocean passing to the expanding European powers, the Swahili city-states and the African trading communities rapidly declined.

Among all the trade from Africa, through the centuries, the slave trade was one component. In the year 1500, Africans and persons of African descent formed a minority of slaves in the world. With European colonization, rapid expansion of the sugar trade and plantations in the New World, and the explosive increase in the transatlantic slave trade, by the year 1700, Africans and persons of African descent formed the majority of the world's slave population. Patrick Manning calls 'African Slavery a phenomenon of the modern world'.[14]

But it would be inaccurate and an insult to humanity to paper over the history of the Oriental and African components of the slave trade. The demand for slave labour at times drew fierce competition between Arabs and East Indians. Such rivalry accelerated with the arrival of the Portuguese in the Indian Ocean region in the late fifteenth century and led to increased kidnappings of Africans from the interior of the continent (extending west of Lake Tanganyika), with ever-increasing numbers of men, women and children being dispersed across the regions of the Indian Ocean.

But it is also flawed to see the historical African presence in Asia from the exclusive perspective of slavery. Africans came to India as early as the fourth century AD. They flourished as traders, artists, rulers, architects and reformers between the fourteenth century and seventeenth century. They are called Habshi/Siddi – distinct communities descended from Bantu peoples from South-East Africa. They rose to prominence on the western coast of India. Some of them brought their traditional music and Sufi Islam with them. Africans were an integral part of several Indian sultanates, and some of them even started their dynasties. Along the western coast of India, African communities built a chain of fortifications, controlling sea access from Daman, in the north, down to the island of Janjira, south of Bombay. There, beginning in the early seventeenth century, Habshi/Siddi sailors-turned-rulers established a royal lineage that reigned for nearly 300 years.

Those who arrived enslaved from Africa to the Indian subcontinent were integrated into Indian society. Some of them rose to the highest echelons of society. Jamal-ud-Din Yaqut was a slave-turned-nobleman who was a close confidante of Razia Sultana (the first female monarch of the Delhi Sultanate in India, 1200-1240), and who is thought to have been her lover.[15]

The most notable person of African descent who was originally a slave in Indian history, is Malik Ambar (1549-1626)[16] who was born in Harar, Ethiopia. Due to poverty, he was sold into slavery as a child. He was educated in Baghdad, before being sent to India to serve Chengiz Khan (who himself was a freed African slave), the Regent Minister of the Sultan of Nizam Shahi in Ahmednagar. Upon the Khan's death in 1594, Ambar was freed and soon launched himself into one of the most formidable careers in the political history of the Deccan. He eventually rose to become the Prime Minister of the Ahmadnagar

---

routes_from_China_to_the_Horn_of_Africa (accessed 20 June, 2016).

[14] Patrick Manning, *Slavery and African Life: Occidental, Oriental, and African Slave Trades* (Cambridge: CUP, 1990), 29-32.

[15] Fatima Mernessi, *The Forgotten Queens of Islam* (Minneapolis, MN: University of Minnesota Press, 1997), 97.

[16] Malik Ambar, 'Military guru of the Marathas', in *The Hindu*, 12th October 2008, www.thehindu.com/todays-paper/tp-features/tp-sundaymagazine/article1437711.ece (accessed 28 January, 2016).

Sultanate. He became famous for his military campaigns against the Mughal Empire and the Sultanate of Bijapur, and successfully developed guerrilla warfare against much larger armies. He was an excellent administrator, developing a systematic revenue settlement for major regions of the Deccan, and a builder who developed canal systems in the area round Ahmednagar. He is deeply respected in India and his impressive mausoleum in Khuldabad, Maharashtra, stands to this day.[17]

In conclusion, from ancient times until the sixteenth century, the relationship between Africa and Asia was mostly on a level. In most parts of Africa during that period, societies had become highly developed. They often had complex systems of participatory government, or were established powerful states that covered large territories and had extensive regional and international links. There was an exchange of peoples across the continents, which also involved a high level of cultural and religious integration and social mobility.

Mutual Solidarity in the Struggle for Dignity and Liberation

The Political context

The transatlantic slave trade led to the loss of millions of lives and the departure of millions of those who could have contributed to Africa's future. The economies of African societies were devastated by the trade and were increasingly unable to follow an independent path of development. Asian communities also suffered, albeit to a lesser extent, to the slave trade and later, to varying levels of servitude and indentured labour. One also has to note the presence of destructive indigenous collaboration, driven by greed as well as need, amongst communities in Asia and Africa, with colonial forces, to exploit their people and their neighbouring peoples. The heritage of colonial rule and the reality of some modern leaders and governments that are still not accountable to their people have contributed to the continuation of this disruption. The common yoke of colonial exploitation brought opportunities for collaboration and mutual inspiration amongst African and Asian communities.

The South African Experience

In this context, the Asian presence in South Africa from the seventeenth century is an outstanding example. As early as 1654, slaves from South-East Asia – predominantly from Java (present-day Indonesia), Dutch Malacca (in present-day Malaysia), and those from India (Bengal, the Coromandel and Malabar coast), were introduced to the Cape of Good Hope by the Dutch colonizers and traders. Over the following years, they were followed by slaves from various other South-East Asian regions, exiled political dissidents and Muslim religious leaders who opposed the Dutch presence in what is now Indonesia. Over time, the Indonesian slaves intermarried with various other groups from South and South-East Asia, Madagascar, and native African groups, and currently constitute the 'Cape Malay' community which numbers around 200,000 people.

Indentured labourers arrived in South Africa from South and North-East India between 1860 and 1911 during the British colonial period. Gujarati traders also arrived in the region through long-established Indian Ocean economic networks. Currently, the population of Indian origin numbers 1.3 million, approximately 2.6% of the South African population. A vast majority of the Asians have lost their links with their ancestral land and have long considered South Africa their permanent home. In spite of their long historical presence, persons of Indian origin were regarded as temporary residents until permanent citizenship was granted to them in 1961. Anti-Indian rhetoric which in the past had been expressed openly, as in the 1949 African riots against Indians who were perceived to be privileged, continues to be subtly

[17] Richard M. Eaton, 'Malik Ambar', in *A Social History of the Deccan, 1300-1761* (Cambridge: CUP, 2005).

experienced in post-apartheid popular culture and the press, augmenting South African Indians' sense of vulnerability.[18] In spite of these challenges, Asian's continues to play a critical role in all sections of the society today. They have also played a vital role in the anti-apartheid movement. The extent to which Indians should consider themselves as part of an Indian diaspora and be linked with India as a diasporic homeland is a subject of debate in the Indian public sphere. Fatima Meer, in a speech at the 2003 'Non-Resident Indian Day', contested the idea that Indians in South Africa should feel part of a larger Indian diaspora: 'Diaspora is a word I abhor… We, Indian South Africans, have had to struggle hard to claim our South Africanness, and that is something that we jealously guard. We are not a diaspora of India in South Africa because we claimed South Africa for our own.'[19]

While half of South African Indians are Hindu, one in four is Muslim and the rest Christian. The Cape Malay are predominantly Muslim. Asians in South Africa form a dynamic component of the 'rainbow nation' and are active in inter-religious discourse and collaboration.

South Africa is also the mother who nurtured and launched two of the greatest freedom fighters of the world in recent times – Mohandas Karamchand Gandhi and Nelson Mandela. In Gandhi's life, the struggle for the liberation of both continents is personified. He arrived in South Africa in 1893 at the age of 24 as a newly qualified lawyer on a temporary assignment to act on behalf of a local Indian trader in a commercial dispute. The short stint turned into a 21-year stay, with spells in India and England. By the time Gandhi left South Africa for the last time in 1914, he had already earned the title 'Mahatma' (or Great Soul) for his work in securing significant legal concessions for the local Indian population in South Africa. During his time in South Africa, he developed the strategy known as 'Satyagraha' (truth-force), in which campaigners mobilized mass civil disobedience and went on peaceful marches and presented themselves for arrest in protest against unjust laws. This form of action was to become one of the great political tools of the twentieth century, influencing the civil rights movement in the USA and the African National Congress in the early years of its struggle against apartheid in South Africa. Nelson Mandela was inspired by Gandhi's ideals and teachings, and noted that it played a significant role in the transformation of South Africa and in overcoming apartheid. Mandela noted: 'India is Gandhi's country of birth; South Africa his country of adoption. He was both an Indian and a South African citizen.'[20]

Through his family, Gandhi always remained in Africa. In 1917, Gandhi's son Manilal (1892-1956) returned to South Africa to assist in printing the 'Indian Opinion', a Gujarati-English weekly publication and was a social activist all his life. He was jailed several times by the British colonial government after protesting against unjust laws. Of his three children, Arun and Ela are social-political activists and recognised leaders in South Africa today.

International Afro- Asian Solidarity

In the post-colonial period, African and Asian leaders started to collaborate strategically in the international arena. The historic Bandung Conference (Asian-African Conference), held in April 1955, brought representatives from twenty-nine governments of Asian and African nations to Bandung in Indonesia. The conference's stated aims were to promote Afro-Asian economic and cultural co-operation and to oppose colonialism or neo-colonialism by any nation. They discussed peace and the role of the Third World in the

---

[18] Edward Ramsamy, 'Between Non-racialism and Multiculturalism: Indian Identity and Nation Building in South Africa', *Journal of Economic and Social Geography* Vol. 98, Issue 4, (2007): 468-81.

[19] Fatima Meer, *Speech to the plenary session with the Ministry of External Affairs*, 9th January 2003: proceedings of the First Pravasi Bharatiya Divas, 9-11th January 2003,: http://indiandiaspora.nic.in/ppbd.htm (accessed 9 February, 2016).

[20] Nelson Mandela shared a special bond with India, and had striking similarities with Gandhi (Press Trust of India), Published in Deccan Chronicle, 7th December 2013, www.deccanchronicle.com/131206/news-current-affairs/article/nelson-mandela-gandhi-south-africa-had-strong-indian-connections (accessed 9 February, 2016).

Cold War, economic development and decolonization. The core principles of the Bandung Conference were political self-determination, mutual respect for sovereignty, non-aggression, non-interference in internal affairs and equality. As the decolonization process was still ongoing, the delegates at the conference took it upon themselves to speak for other colonized peoples (especially in Africa) that had not yet established independent governments. The conference was an important step in the genesis of the Non-Aligned Movement.

U Kyaw Than, General Secretary of East Asia Christian Conference from 1968 to 1974 (the precursor to the Christian Conference of Asia), stated that the Afro-Asian spirit of Bandung had inspired the first Asia Christian meeting in Prapat in Sumatra, Indonesia. The meeting was key to the establishment of the first regional Asian ecumenical organisation in 1959 and also contributed to the creation of the All Africa Conference of Churches in 1958.[21]

The relationships between Asia and Africa have also helped to lift up voices against oppression and exclusion within their societies, such as caste discrimination. Caste discrimination is a global human rights issue, which is particularly widespread throughout South Asia (India, Pakistan, Bangladesh, Sri Lanka and Nepal). Similar forms of discrimination also exist in South Asian diaspora communities, Japan, Yemen and some African countries such as Senegal, Nigeria, Mauritania, Niger, Mali and Kenya. The International Dalit Solidarity Network (IDSN) was founded in the year 2000 to advocate for Dalit human rights and to raise awareness of Dalit issues nationally and internationally. It is a good example of a global platform which brings regional, national and international players together round specific human rights issues and to speaks and act for oppressed communities.[22]

The Christian mission context

THE LINKS WITH COLONIAL EXPANSION

Christian mission had, in many instances, been made use of by colonisers. In the role of the coloniser, Christians saw it as their moral duty to civilise those they encountered. Part of their civilising programme was western education, which often translated to the colonised adopting the coloniser's language, culture and worldview whilst losing one's own. In many colonised regions, local knowledge on healing was scorned as missionaries worked against traditional healers, associating them with indigenous faiths and superstitions, and as impediments to the missionary enterprise. These actions drove traditional medicine underground.[23]

In many instances, the colonised were dispossessed of their land, cultures, livelihoods and industry. They were often reduced to fuelling the industrial revolution of the colonial powers. The conversion of millions to the Christian faith in sub-Saharan Africa and Asia could not protect them from the brutal impact of colonisation and economic globalisation, and corresponded with the further impoverishment of those societies. Conquering and proselytizing mission by Roman Catholic and Protestant missionaries also inflicted deep wounds on the already existing smaller Christian communities, especially on the Malabar coast of India.[24]

---

[21] Listening to the voice of Afro-Asian people: *Bandung Spirit Revisited*. Afro-Asian Mission Conference in Bangalore 15th April 2005, http://english.cri.cn/2238/2005-4-15/33@228231.htm (accessed 9 February, 2016).

[22] The International Dalit Solidarity Network: http://idsn.org

[23] Mulweli F. Mulaudzi, 'Synergy between indigenous knowledge systems, modern health care systems and scientific research – A Vision for the 21st Century', *Health as Gesundheit* Vol. 6, no. 4, (2001): 14-20.

[24] K.M. George, Mission for Unity or Unity for Mission? An Ecclesiological Perspective on Orthodox Mission, Vol. 17, (Oxford: Regnum, 2013).

THE GOSPEL OF JUSTICE AND PEACE

There were, however, many Christian missionaries who challenged the oppressive practices of traders and Conquistadors. Traders and the British East India Company saw independent missionaries as a threat to their unscrupulous activities, as the missionaries raised the concerns of indigenous people and therefore their passage to India was often refused. The great Baptist missionary and social reformer William Carey (1761-1834) had to find his way to India via the Danish trading post of Tranquebar (today's Tharangambadi) on a Danish vessel. He went on to translate the Bible into Bengali, Oriya, Assamese, Arabic, Hindi and Sanskrit, and opened Serampore, the first college to offer Christian theological education in Asia.

The efforts of David Livingstone (1813-1873), the Scottish missionary, explorer and doctor, helped chart the way into the interior of the African continent, contributing to the 'Scramble for Africa'. But he also helped publicise the horrors of the slave trade, and mobilised public opinion which hastened the abolition of slavery. There were other prophetic Christian voices such as those of the Quakers, one of the earliest Christian opponents to slavery, who petitioned the British Parliament in 1784, pleading the case for ending slavery.[25] The healing ministry also provided an alternative to the dominant narrative of colonisation. The selfless and sacrificial work of Christian missionary health personnel, establishing health care centres in remote rural regions, which had been neglected by the colonial administrations, is a very inspiring testimony and a message of hope. The churches assisted health care provision through its infrastructure but also through contributions to the development and training of health professionals. Christianity provided the roots of vibrant volunteerism, and a sense of calling and vocation to those involved in the church-related health services. The faith communities and many of their church leaders who were close to the people, started to mobilize against the excesses of colonialism, the impact of economic globalisation and unjust trade practices. In the field of health, church-related organisations have pioneered in successfully working against the unfair pricing of medicine and campaigning for health for all, and to provide credible and affordable alternatives to commercial health care providers.

The key to transformative mission in Africa and Asia has been the empowerment of indigenous Christians to own, interpret and live the message of Jesus in their contexts. The missionaries who enabled converts to take ownership of the message and equipped them for independent thinking and action with the ability to question injustice, succeeded in planting the seeds of Christ's message far and wide.

CHRISTIAN SELF-UNDERSTANDING IN THE AFRICAN AND ASIAN CONTEXT

The most significant impact of the rapid expansion of Christianity in the twentieth century was that Christianity became a global religion. Indigenous Christians in Asia and Africa, along with others from the global South, were increasingly able to see their faith through their own eyes to interpret and live the message of Christ in their own contexts. The rise of Liberation Theology and contextual interpretations of Christianity united theologians in the global South. The Ecumenical Association of Third World Theologians (EATWOT) and the Circle of Concerned African Women Theologians are significant movements in modern Christianity which expand the foundational dimensions of Christianity. They brought the message of Christ closer and more meaningfully to people and equipped theologians from the global South to deal with existential issues such as gender relations, sexuality, violence and disease. The writings and thinking of African and Asian theologians form mutually informative signposts for the journey of faith for millions of Christians, helping them to relate their faith, to deal with complex realities, overcoming extensional and relational challenges.

---

[25] Society of Friends, London Yearly Meeting, *Meeting for Sufferings: The Case of our Fellow-Creatures, The Oppressed Africans,* Respectfully Recommended to the Serious Consideration of the Legislature of Great Britain, by the People Called the Quakers (London, 1784), 3.

The third International Missionary Council (IMC) conference held at Tambaram (in Madras or present-day Chennai, South India) in 1938, was a historic landmark in Christian mission history, when the predominantly western Christian mission enterprise turned truly international. An analysis of the participation in the two conferences held 28 years apart, reveals this transformation of Christian mission. In the first World Missionary Conference held in Edinburgh (1910), of the 1,215 official delegates, only 19 came from the non-western world, of which all but one participant was from Asia (India) and one participant who was indigenous African (Ghana). But at the third International Missionary Council conference held at Tambaram (1938), 26 out of the 471 delegates – i.e. more than half of them – were from younger churches in Asia, Africa and Latin America. The African delegation included the theologian C.G. Baeta from Ghana, Albert Lutuli and Miss Mina Soga from South Africa, and Thompson Douglas Samkange, a Zimbabwean Methodist minister.[27]

The event had a great impact on international missions and ecumenism, encouraging common witness and deepening unity among churches. The biography of Thompson Douglas Samkange reveals that, on attending the Tambaram conference, he was inspired by the zeal for unity and self-reliance of Asian Christians. He also used the occasion to meet with Indian leaders such as Gandhi and Nehru, and also deepened his friendship with other African delegates. Thompson Douglas Samkange was already a noted church leader and a leading voice for African Christian unity in 1938. In 1928, he had co-organized the Southern Rhodesia Native Missionary Conference. On his return from the Tambaram Conference to Zimbabwe (erstwhile Southern Rhodesia), he renewed his commitment to African leadership in church and state. Passionately committed to a unity that superseded divisions of race, tribe, region, social status or religious affiliation, Samkange helped to found the Southern Rhodesia Bantu Congress in 1938, uniting existing associations in a national political movement. Under his leadership, the Congress aspired to generate mass membership and demanded full democratic rights, which became the hallmarks of later nationalist movements.[28]

The reawakening of the modern ecumenical movement and the creation of the World Council of Churches has played a dynamic and critical role in bringing the churches and Christians of Africa and Asia together. The ecumenical movement also strengthened ties between the indigenous churches of Africa and Asia which did not have parent mission bodies to facilitate such links. This is illustrated by the informal meeting of Orthodox Churches of Africa and Asia that took place on the sidelines of the inaugural Assembly of the World Council of Churches in Amsterdam in 1948. The informal meeting between indigenous churches on both continents, perhaps the first in a thousand years, was convened by His Grace Abuna Theophilus of the Ethiopian Orthodox Church, who later became the Patriarch of the church. The Coptic Orthodox Church from Egypt, The Ethiopian Orthodox Church in Egypt and the Malankara Orthodox Syrian Church from India (all from the Oriental Orthodox family), were the first three Orthodox churches to join the modern ecumenical movement as founding members of the World Council of Churches in Amsterdam in 1948. The other Orthodox churches joined the ecumenical movement only at the WCC's General Assembly in New Delhi in 1961 and at the following Central Committee meeting in Paris in 1962.[29]

---

[26] Carl F. Hallencreutz, 'Tambaram Revisited', in *International Review of Mission,* Vol. LXXVIII, no. 307, July (1988): 353-54.

[27] Joshua Kalapati, *Edinburgh to Tambaram: A Paradigm Shift in Missions or the Horizons of Mission Broadened?* (Dharma Deepika, Chennai, January, 2010).

[28] Terence Ranger, *Are We Not Also Men? The Samkange Family and African Politics in Zimbabwe, 1920-1964* (1995, a collective biography of Thompson Samkange and of two of his sons, Sketchley and Stanlake), (London: Heinemann / Evanston, IL: Northwestern University Press, 1970).

[29] Geevarghese Mar Osthathios, *Dictionary of the Ecumenical Movement* (WCC and Eerdmans 2002); A History of the Ecumenical Movement, 1948-1968, Volume 2 (Geneva: WCC Publications, 1968).

The formation of the regional ecumenical Councils in Africa (the All Africa Council of Churches: AACC) and Asia (initially called the East Asia Christian Conference and currently the Christian Conference of Asia: CCA) in 1958 and 1959 respectively, also played a significant role in uniting churches on both continents. The continental platforms also provided many venues for Afro-Asian interactions and collaboration.

Formation, Service and Transformation

True relationships only can develop when we share with each other, our joys, pain, challenges, dreams and aspirations, in a spirit of mutual respect, love and concern. This sharing forms the basis of working together with the intention of sharing resources, experiences and talents, to overcome many challenges, to establish the reign of God each day!

Though there is tremendous room for development in building closer relationships between the churches and people of Africa and Asia, there are numerous examples that indicate that this is already happening. I will present a few, which is in no way a comprehensive listing.

Institutional linkages providing experiential learning and training

The following institutions are examples of Christian, church-related institutions or initiatives or those founded by Christians following foundational values of Christianity.

The Institute for the Healing of Memories

The Institute for the Healing of Memories was founded by the veteran anti-apartheid campaigner and monk, Father Michael Lapsley, in Cape Town, South Africa. Fr Lapsley was seriously injured by a letter bomb dispatched by the apartheid regime but turned his personal tragedy into a clarion call for peace and forgiveness. The Institute seeks to contribute to the healing journey of individuals, communities and nations. They work primarily in South Africa and also have operations globally by offering healing of memories workshops, seminars and talks all over the world. In Asia, the Institute for the Healing of Memories has been instrumental in conducting programmes in Indonesia, Timor-Leste, Korea, Japan and Sri Lanka.[30]

The Jamkhed International Institute for Training and Research in Community Health and Development

The Comprehensive Rural Health Project, Jamkhed (CRHP), based in rural Maharashtra, India, has been working among the marginalized and rural poor. The project was founded in 1970 by the renowned Christian doctor couple, Drs Raj and Mabelle Arole, to bring health care to the poorest of the poor. At the core of this comprehensive community-based approach is its embracing of equity for all, using health care as a means of breaking the cycle of poverty. CRHP has been a leader in public health and development in rural communities in India and around the world, and its work has been recognized by WHO and UNICEF, and has been introduced to 178 countries across the world. Since the opening of the Training Centre in 1994, thousands of local and international representatives of NGOs, governments and health care professionals have been trained in the CRHP approach. Many of the professionals who have benefitted are from Africa.[31]

---

[30] The Institute for the Healing of Memories, www.healing-memories.org (accessed 9 February, 2016).

[31] The Comprehensive Rural Health Project, Jamkhed (CRHP), www.jamkhed.org (accessed 9 February, 2016).

Universities and Theological Institutions

Theological institutions and universities, in Africa and Asia have had a long history of receiving students and faculty from other continents, promoting an Afro-Asian exchange of experience and training. Notable examples are the University of KwaZulu-Natal in South Africa and the United Theological College in Bangalore. They provide in-depth training and life-changing experiences for theologians, clergy and laity on critical theological and existential challenges. The key topics on which collaborative work and training are conducted are contextual Bible studies, HIV and AIDS, Dalit Studies, Gender Relations, Violence and Human Sexuality.

Afro-Asian Church initiatives

THE KOREAN CHURCH AS A PARTNER IN AFRICA

Korean missions are an extraordinary phenomenon in Christian mission today. There are an estimated 17,000 missionaries from South Korea spread all over the world in more than 173 countries. There are also examples where individual churches such as the Presbyterian Church in Korea, have established large Universities – with comprehensive educational institutions offering education in the arts, sciences and medicine in African countries such as Ethiopia and Malawi. The missions raise many challenges related to issues such as partnerships and linkages with existing church structures, responsiveness to local needs, and cultural and language adaptation. But not unlike earlier missions from the West, they are expected to develop and adapt in years to come. But their commitment to the gospel, expertise and the level of investment of these Asian churches in Africa is not in question and is deeply appreciated by local communities.[32]

RELIGIOUS ORDERS OF THE ROMAN CATHOLIC CHURCH

In the Catholic Church, the number of clergy and religious sisters belonging to religious orders has dropped everywhere except in Asia and Africa. In Asia alone, religious orders have 206,831 individual priests, brothers, religious sisters and bishops (not including diocesan clergy, lay missionaries and catechists). In Africa, religious orders have 90,101 individual priests, brothers, religious sisters and bishops (not including diocesan clergy, lay missionaries and catechists).[33] These dedicated pastors and religious sisters are also playing a key role in the mutual development and enrichment of churches and communities in Africa and Asia.[34] The tremendous role of the vast networks of religious orders in Africa and Asia, and the actual connections and relationships are difficult to quantify. This will require much more research. Catholic religious orders are often transnational, and many of the newer orders begun in the twentieth and 21st centuries originate and are staffed predominantly by priests, brothers and religious sisters from the global South. Hence, it is reasonable to attribute a significant level of Afro-Asian relationship in the context of religious orders. To illustrate the possibility, consider one religious order, the Missionaries of Charity, founded in Kolkata in 1950 by Mother Theresa. This India-based organisation operates 517 missions in more than a hundred countries. In Africa, the Missionaries of Charity have a presence in 42 of the 54 countries.[35] The Order consists of over 4,500 religious sisters and is supported by thousands of volunteers

---

[32] Richard M. Verreynne, *Rethinking Missions in Africa – Partnership with Korean Churches – Appreciating the Korean Church as a Missionary Partner in Africa* (2008), http://wrfnet.org/resources/2008/09/rethinking-missions-africa-partnership-korean-churches (accessed 9 February, 2016).

[33] Catholic Church Statistics 2014, Agency for Pontifical Missionary Work, 19 October 2014.

[34] 'Faithful are growing fastest in Africa', Vatican Insider, in *La Stampa,* 28 May 2014, www.lastampa.it/2014/05/28/vaticaninsider/eng/the-vatican/figures-on-church-life-are-out-faithful-are-growing-fastest-in-africa-dRthMlMuMpaKfO5MmB8DrJ/pagina.html (accessed 08 February,2016).

[35] Volunteering for Mother Teresa's Missionaries of Charity,

with donations from ordinary people. They care for refugees, ex-prostitutes, the mentally ill, sick and abandoned children, people living with HIV and leprosy, the aged, and convalescents. They also have schools run by volunteers to educate street children and run soup kitchens.

Ecumenical training programmes

National, regional and international ecumenical institutions (including the WCC and its Ecumenical Institute at Bossey, Switzerland) are engaged with various group training programmes and courses, which give opportunities for the young, laity and clergy of Africa and Asia to come together, earn from each other and chart a common ecumenical future with other individuals from all regions.[36] There are examples of various specific ecumenical programmes dealing with gender, HIV, peace and reconciliation, and health and healing which have helped design and develop frameworks and guidelines for training and formation. An example of such a process that engaged African and Asian experiences was conducted by the World Council of Churches in collaboration with AACC, CCA and the Christian Medical Association of India. The Afro-Asian Mission Consultation on the Ecumenical Response to the Challenge of Healing Ministries was held in Bangalore, India, in November 2004. The meeting developed a tool for use in congregations focusing on 'Healing, Reconciliation and Power'.[37]

Looking to the Future

After a gap of a few centuries, we are experiencing tremendous growth in trade and an increase bilateral relations between Asia and Africa. A key difference today, predating the sixteenth century, is that Christian communities currently hold a prominent role in both continents. As commercial, cultural and religious interaction expands between Africa and Asia, what will the relationships be based on? Will the values of mutual respect, dignity, equity and justice take pre-eminence? How can Christian values influence the ethical and moral standing of these relationships? As indigenous churches develop and become stronger in Africa and Asia, how will they relate to other churches and different religious groups? How can we as Christian communities ensure inclusivity and encourage ecumenical and interreligious relations as the centre of gravity of Christianity increasingly shifts south? As communities and societies in Africa and Asia become wealthier and their governments more powerful, will the churches and people of God stand with the poor, vulnerable and sick? Will the followers of Jesus in Africa and Asia stand for the rights and dignity of the least amongst us? How can we strengthen ecumenical instruments and institutions to foster greater collaboration between the two continents? How can we continue to develop relationships between the churches and people of Africa and Asia, to ensure that we hold the trajectory for the establishment of the reign of God amongst us?

Bibliography

Amaladoss, M. (Michael), 'Cross-inculturation of Indian and African Christianity.' *African Ecclesiastical Review* Vol. 32, no. 3, June (1990: 157-168.

Appelbaum, Patricia, 'Visions of a Better World: Howard Thurman's Pilgrimage to India and the origins of African American non-violence.'*The Christian Century* Vol. 129, no. 11, May (2012): 38-39.

---

www.motherteresa.org/07_family/volunteering/ v_cal.html#2a (accessed 10 February, 2016).

[36] Ecumenical Institute at Bossey, https://institute.oikoumene.org/en (accessed 10 February, 2016).

[37] Healing, Reconciliation and Power: A Tool for Use in Congregations, developed from the Afro-Asian Mission Consultation, 2004, http://difaem.de/uploads/tx_bfactorpublikationen/healing_reconciliation_power_02.pdf (accessed 10 February, 2016).

De Souza, Teotonio R., *The Afro-Asian Church in the Portuguese Estado da India.* Bern, Switzerland: Evangelische Arbeitsstelle Oekumene Schweiz, 1988.

Eaton, Richard M. *A Social History of the Deccan, 1300-1761: Eight Indian Lives*. Cambridge: CUP, 1990.

Ehret, Christopher, *The Civilizations of Africa: A History to 1800.* Charlottesville, VA: University of Virginia Press, 2002.

Hallencreutz, Carl F., 'Tambaram Revisited.'*International Review of Mission* Vol. LXXVIII, no. 307, July (1988): 353-54.

Hamdun, Said and King, Noel. *Ibn Battuta in Black Africa.* Princeton, NJ: Markus Wiener Publishers, 1975.

Holeka, Matouš, 'Reading the Bible in various streams of Liberation Theology: Latin American Theology, South African Black Theology and Indian Dalit Theology.' *Communio Viatorum* Vol. 56, no. 2, (2014): 169-196.

Khalidi, Omar, 'African Diaspora in India: The Case of the Habashīs of the Dakan.' *Hamdard Islamicus* Vol. 11, no. 4, Winter (1988): 3-22.

Llewellyn-Jones, R., 'Africans in the Indian Mutiny.' *History Today* Vol. 59, Issue 12, December (2009): 40-47.

Malieckal, Bindu, 'India's Luso-Africans: The Politics of Race, Colonialism, and Gender in early modern Portugal and post-colonial Goa.', In *Religion and Politics in a Global Society: Comparative Perspectives from the Portuguese-speaking World*, edited by Paul C. Manuel, Elynna Lyon and Clyde Wilcox, 47-72. New York, Toronto and Plymouth, UK: Lexington Books, 2013.

Manning, Patrick, *Slavery, and African Life: Occidental, Oriental, and African Slave Trades.* Cambridge: CUP, 1990.

Obeng, Pashington, 'Religion and Empire: Belief and Identity among African Indians of Karnataka, South India.' *Journal of the American Academy of Religion* Vol. 71, no. 1, March (2003): 99-120.

Phillipson, David W., *Foundations of an African Civilization: Aksum and the Northern Horn 1000 BC-AD 1300.* Addis Ababa: Addis Ababa University Press, 2012.

Ramsamy, Edward, 'Between Non-racialism and Multiculturalism: Indian identity and Nation Building in South Africa.' *Journal of Economic and Social Geography*, Vol. 98, Issue 4, September (2007):, 468–481.

Ranger, Terence, *Are We Not Also Men? The Samkange Family and African Politics in Zimbabwe* 1920-1964. London: James Currey, 1995.

Schoff, Wilfred H., *The Periplus of the Erythraean Sea: Travel and Trade in the Indian Ocean*, (translated and annotated from the ancient Greek) by a merchant of the first century, Longman Green & Co., New York, London, Bombay, Calcutta, 1912. https://zethio.files.wordpress.com/2014/04/the-periplus-of-the-erythraean-sea.pdf (accessed 20 June, 2016).

Sinclair, Paul J. J., and Hakansson, Thomas. ''The Swahili City-State Culture.' In *A Comparative Study of Thirty City-State Cultures*, edited by Mogens Herman Hansen, 463-81. Copenhagen: The Royal Danish Academy of Sciences, 2000.

Verreynne, Richard M., *Rethinking Missions in Africa:Partnership with Korean Churches – Appreciating the Korean Church as a Missionary Partner in Africa* (2008). http://wrfnet.org/resources/2008/09/rethinking-missions-africa-partnership-korean-churches (accessed 9 February, 2016).

Widyatmadja, Josef P., *Spirituality of Common Future: Asia-Africa Beyond Globalization: The spirit of Bandung and a New World Order*. Hong Kong: Christian Conference of Asia, 2002.

______ (ed.), *Asia Africa spirit and Struggle amid Globalization: Towards a Common Future: Asia Africa search and Struggle for Global Justice*. Papers presented in the Asia-Africa Forum 2005 organized by CCA-URM in Jakarta, Indonesia, 11th-15th April 2005, to commemorate the fiftieth anniversary of Bandung Conference 1955 (Christian Conference of Asia Urban Rural Mission, Hong Kong, 2005). http://vakindia.org/archives/Vikalp-April2005.pdf (accessed 20 June, 2016).

(110B) AFRICAN CHRISTIANITY IN PARTNERSHIP WITH ASIAN CHURCHES

Augustine Chingwala Musopole

Introduction

Africa and Asia have had long contacts all along its eastern boundary along the Indian Ocean. There was much trade going on between the Middle East, India, China and the East African coast. It was along these trade routes that Christianity also spread to India and China. Traders, using sailboats, followed the flow of monsoon winds in the Indian Ocean and the Arabian Gulf. The Arabs traded along the East African coast long before the presence of the Europeans disturbed them and took control of their major trading posts of Zanzibar, Pemba and Kirwa.

A Christian Presence on the East African Coast

Vasco da Gama, a Portuguese explorer, arrived on the East African coast in 1498 in search of an alternative sea route to the Empire of Prester John and to India. In 1503-1504, the Portuguese took over Zanzibar to be part of the Portuguese Province of Ethiopia and Arabia. Due to the weakness of the Portuguese presence, Zanzibar came under the Sultanate of Oman in 1698, but a century later, in 1890, it fell to British suzerainty.

Even though Christianity has Asian origins, it has also deep roots in African religiosity and spirituality.[1] North African Christianity contributed much to the development of western Christianity and theology while Christianity in Ethiopia remained orthodox and isolated. Christianity was brought initially on the East African coast by Portuguese missionaries to the empire of Mwenemotapa. The first Roman Catholic missionary was Fr Gonçalo da Silveira, SJ (1526-1561). He arrived in the empire of Mwenemotapa in 1560, but was murdered the following year at the instigation of Arab Muslim traders there. The Catholics were followed by the Anglicans who entered into the region in 1861, following the appeal of David Livingstone at Oxford University. David Livingstone wanted missions to engage in the spread of Christianity, civilization and commerce with a view to the abolition and eradication of the slavery carried out by Arabs on the east coast. Livingstone characterized this scourge as 'the open sore' of Africa. When the initial attempt to establish a mission in the Shire Highlands of present-day Malawi failed, the mission was moved to Zanzibar. The second wave of the Christian missions to Africa was confronted with the problem of slavery on both the Atlantic and Indian Ocean coasts. The irony is that it was these converted slaves who founded African Christianity on both coasts, the faith which is now spreading throughout Africa at an unprecedented speed.

African Christianity and Islam

The relationship between African Christianity and Islam goes back to the time of Muhammad when he was being persecuted in Mecca and some of his follower had fled to Ethiopia where they were taken care of by

---

[1] A debatable view has been put forward by African scholars that Christianity has African religious roots; leading the way among these scholars was Yosef Ben Jochannan, an Egyptologist. See his, 'The African Origin of Christianity, https://www.youtube.com/watch?v=KhzgO4UeshY (accessed 7 October, 2015).

the Christians there, leading Muhammad to issue instructions that Christians should be treated as friends and not as enemies.[2] However, over time, Christianity and Islam clashed over the issues of African slavery and control over trade along the East African coast. However, during this time of encounter between Africa and Asia, there was no partnership between the nascent African Christianity and Asian churches since both were new and were referred to in ecumenical circles as 'the younger churches'.

Afro-Asian Solidarity

Politics and trade have had much to do with the spread of Christianity all over the world. It would have been expected that the churches could have followed the lead of African and Asian political leaders in coming together to seek political and economic collaboration among themselves to resist neo-colonialism and being sucked into Cold War politics. This was the agenda of the Bandung Conference of 1955. 'The Africa and Asia nations also pledged to mutually support their economic development, vowing to rely on themselves instead of Western foreign aid... The Bandung Conference inspired the creation of the Non-Aligned Movement in 1961. Members of this Movement eventually became known as the Third World.'[3] However, in spite of the churches of Africa forming for themselves a platform of dialogue and collaboration in the All Africa Conference of Churches, their commitment to the Afro-Asian collaboration was not worked on as was expected. Even after the Christian population had shifted to the south, a south-to-south Christian relationship still does not take central emphasis in the agenda of the All African Conference of Churches..

The All Africa Conference of Churches (AACC)

A visit to the offices of AACC in Nairobi for information on any visible partnership between African Christianity and Asian churches was most disappointing for both of us at the lack of any information on this subject. The officer concerned could not even recall any collaboration with the Christian Council of Asia (CCA), let alone with the churches of Asia. While there were many partnerships with Europe and the USA, and also with the Caribbean Council of Churches as per their official records, and details of who was invited to their Assemblies, none could be found on relations with Asian churches in any reports since the AACC was founded in 1963 till now. There was no mention of the Asian fraternal delegation or even of a simple message of good wishes from the churches.

However, of late, attempts have been made for the two continental regions to reach out to each other. For instance, the Presbyterian Church in Taiwan has entered into partnership with the Evangelical Church of Mekane Yesus in Ethiopia, and with the Nkhoma Synod of the church of Central Africa Presbyterian in Malawi. In the case of Malawi, the partnership was discontinued when Malawi switched diplomatic relations from Taipei to Beijing. Rather than partner with a national entity, some partnerships are devolved as missionary functions at a congregational or presbytery level, with the tacit approval of the national offices. It seems that it is the Asian churches that are taking the initiative in establishing the partnership. This may be due to economic imbalances and skilled expertise being exchanged between the Asian and African churches.

---

[2] See John Baur, *2000 Years of Christianity in Africa: An African Church History*, 2nd edition (Nairobi: Paulines Publications Africa, 2009).
[3] George McTurnan Kahin, 'The Asian-African Conference: Bandung, Indonesia', (April, 1955), http://history.state.gov/milestones/1953-1960/bandung-conf (accessed 7 October, 2015).

The Role of Global Conferences

Global communions and conferences have tended to provide opportunities for the meeting of African and Asian Christians for mutual fellowship, discussions of some common problems and issues, and for mutual understanding. While individuals from both Africa and Asia may be acknowledged as leaders in such conferences, partnership remains at the level of occasional interaction and does not translate into programmatic partnership, and too often such interactions have not gone beyond conference deliberations and papers.[4] Nonetheless, such leadership relations might also have had some impact in promoting partnership between church-related bodies. There is a need for an Afro-Asian theological solidarity that promotes contextual theologies.[5]

African and Asian Songs

Two songs seem to have linked Africa and Asia indelibly. These songs are, 'I have decided to follow Jesus', whose reputed author is the Indian Sadhu Sundar Singh (1889-1929); and the other is 'Kumbaya, my Lord, kumbaya', a Creole song from West Africa meaning 'Come by me, Lord, come by me'. These are very popular songs both in Africa and Asia. In Africa, the song, 'I have decided to follow Jesus' has been given what is called a jiving or twisting melody, and young people dance to it every time they sing it.

Music is possibly the one area in which African Christianity is able to promote partnership with Asian churches. African songs are beginning to make inroads into Asian religiosity and spirituality. Some of the African songs that Asians have chosen at the various meetings, especially during World Council of Churches General Assemblies, were taken back home and taught in church. One person who has done most to make possible what I call 'ecumenism in song' is the Asian musicologist Prof. Ito Lohof at Tainan Theological College and Seminary and the Asian Institute for Liturgy and Music. He is the editor of the current hymnal of the Presbyterian Church in Taiwan in which he included eighteen African songs. The other musicologist who has helped spread African songs was Tom Colvin (1925-2000), a Scottish missionary to Malawi and Ghana. It seems to me that music is one of the most effective ways in which partnership can be forged to mutually enhance spiritualities, as well as translations of our theological expression and understanding.

Ecumenical Association of Third World Theologians (EATWOT)

If there is one organization in which African and Asian theologians have partnered and collaborated, it is EATWOT. It was constituted in Dar-es-Salaam in 1976. The initial idea for such an association was conceived by African Roman Catholic students studying in Louvain, Belgium. Its precursor was a colloquium in the 1950s organized by some African priests studying in Rome. Its proceedings were published as 'African Priests Question Themselves'. Therefore, that vision was expanded in the 1970s to embrace the global South, namely, Asia, Latin America, and minority groups in North Africa, especially black theologians. EATWOT provided a platform on which African and Asian theologians could interact and learn from one another, and hence advance theological partnership. The EATWOT global assemblies

[4] Of late, African church leaders have headed some of these church communion bodies and ecumenical organizations; for instance, Sam Kobia was General Secretary of the WCC; Setri Nyomi was the General Secretary of the World Reformed Council of Churches; Ishmael Noko was General Secretary of the World Lutheran Federation; Musimbi Kanyoro was General Secretary of the YWCA; and Mercy Oduyoye was once Deputy General Secretary of the WCC, a position that Isabel Phiri has been holding. In their own way, each has helped African Christianity to improve its partnership with Asian churches – possibly not directly, but rather indirectly.

[5] In its MTh programme, Tainan Theological College and Seminary provides a good model, aimed at the promotion of contextual theologies.

met in each continent, hosted by the regional continental associations. K.C. Abraham, one of their presidents, edited a book in which differences and commonalities were discussed. Africa shared with Asia its concern for the incorporation of African Traditional Religions and culture into its theological agenda, which has led to the theology of enculturation; while Asia shared its ancient multi-religiosity, and multicultural heritage with their ancient religio-philosophical systems, a religious population, and extreme poverty scenarios.

Theological and Missionary Partnerships

Tainan Theological College and Seminary in Taiwan has, in the last ten years, attempted to promote a coming together of African and Asian students for an experience in contextual theologies at a Master of Theology level. This was the brainchild of the Rev. Dr Hwang Po-ho who was then principal and Dr M.P Joseph teaching at Chang Jung Christian University in India, with the active support of western partners and the Presbyterian Church of Taiwan for scholarship support. The programme has proved revolutionary, according to their testimonies, in helping students to think contextually in their theology as they carry out their tasks in the parishes. While Asian churches in Taiwan and South Korea are reaching out to partner African churches, Africa's response has been rather lukewarm. In the Roman Catholic Church, Indian priests in some religious orders are working with the African Church, for instance, the Society of the Divine Word (SVD),[6] the Paulines,[7] and etc.

Conclusion

If we subject the African and Asian Christian partnership to a SWOT[8] analysis, it would expose more weaknesses than strengths, more opportunities than threats. The following are some of the factors that are contributing to this state of affairs: (a) western political hegemony which has oriented African Christianity towards the West; (b) the economic and theological power of western Christianity from which African Christianity is only beginning to liberate itself as it seeks to define its selfhood; (c) slow self-authentication and self-understanding of both African and Asian churches; (d) the Cold War divide and rejection in appreciating the socialist and communist message in relation to human liberation, in contradiction to exploitative capitalistic hegemony; (e) preoccupation with each continent's issues and problems, leading to a narrow vision of both global history and mission; (f) a focus on cultural and linguistic identities rather than appreciation of commonalities and differences for mutual spiritual growth.

Bibliography

Jochannan, Yosef Ben, 'The African Origin of Christianity.' https://www.youtube.com/watch?v=KhzgO4UeshY (accessed 7 October, 2015).

Baur, John, *2000 Years of Christianity in Africa: An African Church History*, 2nd edition. Nairobi: Paulines Publications Africa, 2009.

Kahin, George McTurnan, 'The Asian-African Conference: Bandung, Indonesia' (April 1955). http://history.state.gov/milestones/1953-1960/bandung-conf (accessed 7 October, 2015).

McGahan, Florence, "Paulists." *The Catholic Encyclopedia*. Vol. 11. (New York: Robert Appleton, 1911). http://www.newadvent.org/cathen/11587c.htm (accessed 7 October, 2015).

---

[6] See Society of the Divine Word www.svd-ca.com/WhoWeAre.htm (accessed 7 October, 2015).

[7] SeeFlorence McGahan, "Paulists." *The Catholic Encyclopedia*. Vol. 11. (New York: Robert Appleton, 1911). http://www.newadvent.org/cathen/11587c.htm (accessed 7 October, 2015).

[8] Acronym for Strengths, Weaknesses, Opportunities and Threats.

(111) African Christianity and Partnership with North American Churches

David D. Daniels

Introduction

The wide ecumenical arena in which African and North American Christianity operate has a long history, even preceding the advent of the ecumenical movement itself. Ecumenical relationships between the churches in Africa and North America have been important in the witness of Christianity on both continents. The ecumenical arena is the setting where churches in Africa and North America confront church-dividing issues regarding race, church order and doctrine. The long ecumenical history, broadly defined, captures the exchanges between Christians in Africa and North America as well as partnerships between churches.

Four historical periods basically frame this rich history of ecumenical encounters. The first period is marked by the presence of African-born Christians in North America. Since Egyptian, Nubian, Ethiopian, and Congolese Christianity precede the rise of Christianity in North America, African Christians carried to North America by the forced migration of the transatlantic slave trade shaped the first period of the early relationship between African and North American Christianity. The second period in the relationship begins during the late eighteenth and early nineteenth centuries with the migration of Afro-American and Afro-Canadian Christians to Sierra Leone. The third period opens with the mass European colonization of Africa that emerged from the Berlin Conference of 1884-1885, extending to the 1960s with the demise of colonialism in much of Africa, save Southern Africa. The fourth period commences with the Mission Moratorium as well as the Pentecostal explosion to the present day.

Phase I (Early 1600s to 1790s)

African Christianity's long history of interacting with North American churches reaches back to the formation of the Thirteenth Colonies along the east coast of North America during the 1600s. Congolese Christianity is a discernible religious current during this era, pouring into the streams of early diasporic African Christianity in North America. North Americans of European descent recognized Christianity as a religion that had Congolese and Angolan adherents in both Africa and North America during colonial North America. Congolese Christianity can be interpreted as a contributing factor in the emergence and development of northern Christianity during the seventeenth and eighteenth centuries.[1]

Congolese and Angolans navigated Christianity in North America in a particular way because of the history of Congolese Christianity, itself a product of the encounter between traditional Congolese religion and Roman Catholicism during the late fifteenth to the early eighteenth centuries, especially Portuguese Roman Catholicism.

Ira Berlin contended:

---

[1] Jeroen Dewulf, 'Emulating a Portuguese Model: The Slave Policy of the West India Company and the Dutch Reformed Church in Dutch Brazil (1630-1654) and New Netherlands (1614-1664) in Comparative Perspective', *Journal of Early American History* Vol. 4, (2014): 3-36; David D. Daniels, 'Congolese Christianity in the Americas of the 17th and 18th Centuries', in *Polycentric Structures in the History of World Christianity*, ed. Klaus Koschorke (Wiesbaden, Germany: Harrassowitz Verlag, 2014), 215-26.

> In the long history of North American slavery, no other cohort of black people survived as well and rose as fast and as high in mainland society as the Atlantic creoles. The experience of the charter generations contrast markedly with what followed… [They] entered a society not markedly different from those they had left [in Central Africa]. There, in New Netherlands, the Chesapeake, Louisiana, and Florida, they made a place for themselves, demonstrating confidence in their abilities to master a world they knew well. Many secured freedom and a modest prosperity, despite the presumption of racial slavery and the contempt of their captors.[2]

The Congolese and Angolans played a pivotal role in constructing the religious landscape of North America.

Protestantism among Congolese and Angolans in the Americas emerges during the seventeenth century in Dutch North America. The historian Alfloyd Butler noted that the first mass Protestant conversion of Africans in North America occurred in South Carolina during the early eighteenth century. He identified the critical presence of enslaved Angolan and Congolese who brought their Roman Catholicism with them from Africa as a major factor in the mass conversion. A 1739 letter from South Carolina noted:

> Amongst the Negroe Slaves there are a people brought from the Kingdom of Angola in Africa; many of these speak Portugueze (which Language is as near Spanish as Scotch is to English), by reason that the Portugueze have considerable Settlement, and the Jesuits have a Mission and School in the Kingdom and many Thousands of the Negroes there profess the Roman Catholic Religion.[3]

The revivals of the 1740s produced a new era with the first mass conversion of Africans to Christianity in British North America and of African peoples to Protestantism. Many of the congregations among Afro-Americans will identify with Africa in their name: Ethiopian Church of Jesus Christ (renamed First African Baptist), Abyssinia Baptist Church, Bethel African Methodist Episcopal, First African Presbyterian, St Thomas African Episcopal, and African Union Church (also called Union Church of Africans).[4]

Phase II (1790s to 1880s)

During the second period, Afro-Canadian and Afro-American Christianity related to Africa through missions, emigration, colonization and Ethiopianism. During the 1790s, Afro-American Christians who had migrated to Canada, specifically Nova Scotia, relocated to Sierra Leone and joined in the formation of Freetown Colony. According to scholars such as Ogbu Kalu and Lamin Sanneh, these Nova Scotian Christians inaugurated the modern missionary enterprise in Africa. They are followed by Afro-American missionaries such as Lott Carey and a group of twenty-eight others who emigrated to Sierra Leone as well as Afro-American missionaries and émigrés who would later settle in Liberia. These Nova Scotian and Afro-American Christians initiated the earliest western non-white missionary activity in Africa.[5]

White western missionaries from the USA and Canada arrived in Southern Africa during the early nineteenth century. Other white North American missionaries including Lydia Ann Beers and William H.

[2] Ira Berlin, 'From Creole to African: Atlantic Creoles and the Origins of African-American Society in Mainland North America', in *The William and Mary Quarterly,* Third Series 53:2 (April 1996), 282.

[3] 'Account of the Negroe Insurrection in South Carolina', in *Stono: Documenting and Interpreting a Southern Slave Revolt*, ed. Michael Mark Smith, (Columbia, SC: University of South Carolina, 2005), 14.

[4] Alfloyd Butler, *Africanization of Christianity* (New York: Carlton Press, 1980); Henry H. Mitchell, *Long-Hidden Realities of the First Years.* (Grand Rapids, MI: Eerdmans, 2004), 83.

[5] Ogbu Kalu, *Clio in a Sacred Garb: Essays on Christian Presence and African Responses, 1900-2000* (Trenton, NJ: Africa World Press, 2008), 164; Lamin Sanneh, *Abolitionists Abroad: American Blacks and the Making of Modern West Africa* (Cambridge, Massachusetts: Harvard University Press, 1999); Leroy Fitts, *Lott Carey: First Black Missionary to Africa* (Valley Forge, PA: Judson Press, 1978); Sylvia M. Jacobs (ed.), *Black Americans and the Missionary Movement in Africa* (Westport, CT: Greenwood Press, 1982).

Clarke would serve in places such as Liberia and Lagos Colony, respectively. Before the modern missionary enterprise, Thomas Thompson served on the Gold Coast from 1752, sponsored by the Society for the Propagation of the Gospel in Foreign Parts; he had previously served as a missionary in New Jersey Colony.[6]

Studies of the nineteenth century demonstrate the complexity of the relationship between the North American Christianity and Africa. While a few Afro-American and white North American Christians viewed Africans in Africa favourably, Africans were regularly described as 'heathenish' and Africa as the 'dark continent'. The relationship between Afro-American émigrés and their descendants – Nova Scotians in Sierra Leone and Americo-Liberians in Liberia – with the local peoples was often marked by discrimination, condescension and prejudice. Along with white North Americans, Scotians were accused of participating in the Europeanizing of the African.[7]

Phase III (1880s to 1960s)

The negative thinking about Africa and Africans helped Europeans in their legitimising of the partitioning of Africa. This process ushered in a new era in the history of Christianity in Africa and complicated the relationship between African and North American Christianity. Many white-led North American denominations such as the Southern Baptist Convention with African missions became seen as allies of European colonialism in Africa. Only a small number were perceived as disruptive of the colonial system.[8]

During the early phase of this third period, a small group of African-led congregations entered alliances with Afro-American denominations; their congregations broke away from white western missionary control. These congregations initiated the transition from mission churches to autonomous churches in Africa. In their protest against 'European cultural domination and control of decision-making in the church', these African Christians were identified as 'Ethiopianists' because of their advocacy of African pastoral leadership and religious self-determination.[9]

While most African independent congregations remained autonomous or formed African-led denominations, some congregations joined Afro-American denominations such as the African Methodist Episcopal Church, the African Methodist Episcopal Church Zion, and the National Baptist Convention, Inc. Later, others would join Afro-American denominations such as the African Orthodox Church and the Church of God in Christ. In some cases, these denominations would be accused by the European missionaries and colonial authorities of being anti-colonial as well as advocates of an 'Africa for the Africans' ideology.[10]

A new phase emerges from the increasing presence of educated Afro-Americans missionaries who were the 'equals' of the white colonists within the structures of the early to mid-twentieth-century colonial Africa as well as those missionaries who served as critics of colonialism such as William Henry Sheppard. Others who challenged colonialism included Afro-American Christians such as C.C. Boone who called for political freedom for the Congo, for instance, in 1909, as well as African Christian leaders such as John Chilembwe who sought political freedom for his people in East Africa.[11]

---

[6] Adrian Hastings, *The Church in Africa 1450-1950* (Oxford: OUP, 1994, 2004 rpt.), 178; Baker J. Cauthen (ed.), *Advance: A History of Southern Baptist Foreign Missions* (Nashville, TN: Broadman Press, 1970).
[7] Sandy Martin, *Black Baptists and African Missions: The Origins of a Movement, 1880-1915* (Macon, GA: Mercer University Press, 1989).
[8] Jonathan S. Barnes, *Power and Partnership: A History of the Protestant Mission Movement* (Eugene, OR: Pickwick Publications, 2013), 46-88.
[9] Kalu, *Clio in a Sacred Garb,* 165-69.
[10] Kalu, *Clio in a Sacred Garb,* 168-72.
[11] William E. Phipps, *William Sheppard, Congo's African American Livingstone* (Louisville, KY: Geneva Press, 2002); Martin, 189.

The African Methodist Episcopal Church was especially perceived by some European colonial leaders as a subversive group in Southern Africa. Additionally, African Methodist Episcopal Church leaders outlined a religious agenda that called for the uniting of 'the oppressed peoples' of the West such as Afro-Americans, Amerindians, Jews and the Irish, as well as 'people of colour' in Cuba, Puerto Rico and Philippines within the imperial grip of the USA, along with those under European domination in Africa, India and China.[12]

During the late nineteenth and early twentieth centuries, various conferences convened African and Afro-American Christians around issues related to their relationship and strategies to address the African situation. These ranged from the 1893 Chicago Conference on Africa where delegates included Yakub Pasha, an Egyptian, Monolu Massaquoi, a Vrai prince, and Henry McNeal Turner, an Afro-American bishop within the African Methodist Episcopal Church, to the First Pan-African Conference in 1900, which was held in London, UK. These became venues for race-based organizations.[13]

The education of Africans like John Chilembwe in Afro-American colleges would foster transatlantic relationships between African and Afro-American Christians. Chilembwe would return to East Africa and open an industrial mission modelled after Afro-American institutes; the mission received support from the National Baptist Convention, Inc., a denomination founded and governed by Afro-Americans. The Phelps Stokes Fund, a major funder of Afro-American education during the early twentieth century, would also fund the education of Africans in Africa, using the Christian industrial education model inaugurated at the Hampton Institute and made famous through the success of the Tuskegee Institute.[14]

Mark Christian Hayford of the Gold Coast (later part of Ghana) and Mojola Agbebi of Lagos Colony (later of Nigeria), were African Christians who travelled from Africa to the USA, introducing American audiences to the African situation during the early 1900s. In this case, Hayford delivered the lecture, 'West Africa and Christianity', at Rochester Theological Seminary, predominantly a white Baptist institution.. After organizing the African Baptist Union of West Africa in 1898, Agbebi toured the USA in 1903, presenting the West African church to a North American audience. This Baptist Union would include congregations in what would become present-day Nigeria, Ghana, Sierra Leone and Cameroon. Both Agbebi and Hayford would raise funds in North America to support the operation of their African-led Baptist denominations.[15]

Other African-born Christians such as Charles Manuel Grace of the Cape Verde Islands and Laura Kofi of the Gold Coast would establish religious movements in the USA during the 1910s and 1920s, respectively. Kofi and her successors would establish a transatlantic religious relationship between USA and West Africa, creating a context for religious exchanges.[16]

In 1942, the Federal Council of Churches in the USA, an ecumenical body which was the precursor of the National Council of Churches in the USA, sponsored a major conference where the platform included

---

[12] Lawrence S. Little, *Disciples of Liberty: The African Methodist Episcopal Church in the Age of Imperialism, 1884-1916* (Knoxville, TN: University of Tennessee Press, 2000), 64.

[13] Christopher Robert Reed, *Black Chicago's First Century,* Vol. 1: 1833-1900 (Columbia, MO: University of Missouri Press, 2005), 372-78.

[14] George Shepperson and Thomas Price, *Independent African*: *John Chilembwe and the Origins, Setting and Significance of the Nyasaland Native Rising of 1915* (Edinburgh: Edinburgh University Press, 1958).

[15] Mark C. Hayford, 'West Africa and Christianity: A Lecture Delivered at the Rochester Theological Seminary, New York, USA, September 28th, 1900' (Baptist Tract and Book Society, 1903); Mojola Agbebi, 'The West African Problem,' in *Papers on the First Interracial Problems (1911),* ed. Gustav Spiller, paper contributed to the first International Race Congress.

[16] Marie W. Dallam, *Daddy Grace: A Celebrity Preacher and His House of Prayer* (New York: New York University Press, 2007); Richard Newman, 'Warrior Mother of Africa's Warriors of the Most High God: Laura Adorkor Kofey and the African Universal Church', in *This Far By Faith: Readings in African-American Women's Religious Biography*, eds. Judith Weisenfeld and Richard Newman, (New York: Routledge, 1996), 110-23).

the call to end western colonialism and imperialism. This was adopted by the Federal Council, which included approximately thirty predominately white mainline denominations. By this act, these white American denominations joined some of the Afro-American denominations in advancing the role of the church as a protest organization, advocating for the end of European Africa.17

Phase IV (1970s to the Present)

In 1971, John G. Gatu, an East African clergyman who served as the General Secretary of the Presbyterian Church in East Africa, called upon North American churches to comply with a five-year moratorium on North American and other western Christian missionaries to Africa. As colonialism ended in most of Africa, save Southern Africa, Gatu called for an end to western hegemony in African denominations. He sought an opportunity for African Christians to rethink and reformulate the church and her mission in Africa without western interference or its agenda in the revisioning. This Mission Moratorium would give the African Church an opportunity to become a fully self-governing, self-propagating, self-funding and self-theologizing Christian community. The Mission Moratorium demanded that North American churches relate to African churches as peers, switching a relationship of dependency and western domination to one of interdependency and mutuality. In 1974, at the Third Assembly of the All Africa Conference of Churches, which had been founded in 1963 and was deemed to become the pre-eminent ecumenical body of churches in Africa, endorsed the Mission Moratorium. Since North American mainline denominations, ranging from Reformed Presbyterian, Lutheran, Methodist and Baptist to the United Church of Canada, were the primary audience, they became the key North American agents in this changing of ecclesial postures.[18]

Although never fully implemented, the call for a mission moratorium in the early 1970s was a watershed moment in African Christianity when the Protestant leadership shifted from European missionaries to African clergy, and when the last vestiges of European colonialism were dislodged from African Christianity, which was thrust into the newly emerging post-colonial reality. Initially, in the post-colonial era, western missionaries held some remaining control. The Moratorium raised expectations that African Christianity would be totally liberated from western control. During the 1970s, African Christianity accelerates the decolonization of Christianity in Africa and mounted an African Christianity that in significant ways was a break from the missionary-founded Christianity of the colonial era.

The African Pentecostal explosion during the post-1960s era fostered transnational linkages between the congregations of African Christian immigrants in North America with African-founded denominations such as the Church of Pentecost, the Presbyterian Church of Ghana, and the Redeemed Christian Church of God, as well as the Cherubim and Seraphim. For instance, the Redeemed Christian Church of God is the largest among the African immigrant denominations in North America with over 500 congregations in the USA and eighty in Canada.[19]

Between the 1960s and early 1990s, Southern African Christians found sectors within North American Christianity, including Martin Luther King, Jr., which supported the freedom struggle in Southern Africa,

---

[17] David Hollinger, *After Cloven Tongues of Fire: Protestant Liberalism in Modern American History* (Princeton, NJ: Princeton University Press, 2013), 67-69; Mark Hulsether, 'Shifting Perspectives on Africa in Mainline Protestant Social Thought: The Case of Christianity and Crisis Magazine', in *Freedom's Distant Shores: American Protestants and Post-colonial Alliances with Africa*, ed. R. Drew Smith, (Waco, TX: Baylor University Press, 2006), 11-36.

[18] Morrell F. Swart, *The Call of Africa: The Reformed Church in America Mission in the Sub-Sahara, 1948-1998* (Grand Rapids, MI: Eerdmans, 1998), 208-18.

[19] Jehu J. Hanciles, *Beyond Christendom: Globalization, African Migration, and the Transformation of the West* (Maryknoll, NY: Orbis Books, 2008), 276-302; David D. Daniels, 'African Immigrant Churches in the United States and the Study of Black Church History', in *African Immigrant Religions in America*, eds. Jacob Olupona and Regina Gemignani (New York: New York University Press, 2007), 47-60.

ranging from Angola and Mozambique to Southern Rhodesia and apartheid South Africa. Leaders such as Desmond Tutu and Allan Boesak would tour North America offering a theological critique of apartheid. Campaigns were mounted to divest from South African corporations; signs were displayed stating: 'Free South Africa.'[20]

New theological voices emerged in Africa during this period that found interlocutors within North America; these African theologians ranged from John Mbiti to Allan Boesak to Mercy Oduyoye. Within North America, theologians of the stature of James Cone, Letty Russell and John Douglas Hall engaged these African theologians.[21]

During the early part of the 21st century, the partnership between African Christianity and North American Christianity again became strained. The relationship had been strained by debates over gender, and specifically the ordination of women clergy, and over sexual orientation, especially the ordination of gays and lesbians, the consecration of gay clergy as bishops, and same-sex marriage. From these tensions have emerged new ecclesial formations where some congregations in North America, especially within the Anglican communion, have assigned themselves to Anglican dioceses in Africa.[22]

In this period, contemporary relationships are also marked by renewed alliances that focus on justice, peace and the sustaining of creation. Partnerships were forged to address the HIV/AIDs crisis theologically as well as through the initiatives of health care ministries. Campaigns to end poverty in Africa were mounted with micro-enterprise ministries, and other economic ventures were launched.

Conclusion

Changes in ecumenical posture define how African Christianity has related to North American churches since the rise of colonialism on the North American continent until the early 21st century. The role of Congolese Christianity, as a feature in the rise of North American Christianity, began the relationship between Christianity on both continents in a way that shows the influence flowing from African Christianity to North American Christianity. The role of the Nova Scotian and Afro-American Protestant missionaries and immigrants to West Africa during the late 1700s and early 1800s illustrate the pivotal role of 'New World Africans' upon the emerging modern Protestant missionary enterprise. White North American dominance in African missions is clearly a later development in the relationship between African and North American Christianity; it must be situated within its proper historical context in order to be appropriately classified. The shift in relationship prompted by the Mission Moratorium as well as African Pentecostalism created a new era in the African and North American ecumenical reality.

Bibliography

Baldwin, Lewis, 'Martin Luther King, Jr., a "Coalition of Conscience", and Freedom in South Africa.' In *Freedom's Distant Shores: American Protestants and Post-colonial Alliances with Africa*, edited by R.

[20] Lewis Baldwin, 'Martin Luther King, Jr., a "Coalition of Conscience", and Freedom in South Africa', in *Freedom's Distant Shores: American Protestants and Post-colonial Alliances with Africa Freedom's,* ed. Drew Smith (Waco, TX: Baylor University Press, 2006), 53-82; Columba Aham Nnorum, 'African American Churches and the Evolution of Anti-apartheid Activism', in *Long March Ahead: African American Churches and Public Policy in Post-Civil Rights America*, ed. R. Drew Smith (Durham, NC: Duke University Press, 2004), 193-216; Renate Pratt, *In Good Faith: Canadian Churches Against Apartheid* (Waterloo, Ontario: Wilfrid Laurier University Press, 1997).

[21] Dwight N. Hopkins, *Black Theology USA and South Africa: Politics, Culture, and Liberation* (Maryknoll, NY: Orbis Books, 1989); Rosemary Radford Ruether, *Introducing Redemption in Christian Feminism* (Sheffield, UK: Sheffield Academic Press, 1998).

[22] Willis Jenkins, 'Episcopalians, Homosexuality, and World Mission', *Anglican Theological Review* Vol. 86, No. 2, (2004): 293-316.

Drew Smith, 53-82. Waco, TX: Baylor University Press, 2006.
Barnes, Jonathan S., *Power and Partnership: A History of the Protestant Mission Movement*. Eugene, OR: Pickwick Publications, 2013.
Berlin, Ira, 'From Creole to African: Atlantic Creoles and the Origins of African-American Society in Mainland North America.' *The William and Mary Quarterly* Vol. 53, no. 2, April (1996): 251-288.
Butler, Alfloyd, *Africanization of Christianity*. New York: Carlton Press, 1980.
Cauthen, Baker J. (ed.), *Advance: A History of Southern Baptist Foreign Missions*. Nashville, TN: Broadman Press, 1970.
Dallam, Marie W., *Daddy Grace: A Celebrity Preacher and His House of Prayer*. New York: New York University Press, 2007.
Daniels, David D., 'African Immigrant Churches in the United States and the Study of Black Church History.' In *African Immigrant Religions in America*, edited by Jacob Olupona and Regina Gemignani, 47-60. New York: New York University Press, 2007.
______., 'Congolese Christianity in the Americas of the 17th and 18th Centuries.', In *Polycentric Structures in the History of World Christianity*, edited by Klaus Koschorke, 215-226. Wiesbaden, Germany: Harrassowitz Verlag, 2014.
Dewulf, Jeroen, 'Emulating a Portuguese Model: The Slave Policy of the West India Company and the Dutch Reformed Church in Dutch Brazil (1630-1654) and New Netherlands (1614-1664) in Comparative Perspective.' In *Journal of Early American History* Vol. 4, (2014): 3-36.
Fitts, Leroy, *Lott Carey: First Black Missionary to Africa.* Valley Forge, PA: Judson Press, 1978.
Hanciles, Jehu J., *Beyond Christendom: Globalization, African Migration, and the Transformation of the West*. Maryknoll, NY: Orbis Books, 2008.
Hastings, Adrian, *The Church in Africa 1450-1950*. Oxford: OUP, 1994, 2004.
Hollinger, David. *After Cloven Tongues of Fire: Protestant Liberalism in Modern American History.* Princeton, NJ: Princeton University Press, 2013.
Hopkins, Dwight N., *Black Theology USA and South Africa: Politics, Culture, and Liberation.* Maryknoll, NY: Orbis Books, 1989.
Hulsether, Mark, 'Shifting Perspectives on Africa in Mainline Protestant Social Thought: The Case of the Christianity and Crisis Magazine.' In *Freedom's Distant Shores: American Protestants and Post-colonial Alliances with Africa*, edited by R. Drew Smith, 11-36. Waco, TX: Baylor University Press, 2006.
Jacobs, Sylvia M. (ed.), *Black Americans and the Missionary Movement in Africa.* Westport, CT: Greenwood Press, 1982.
Jenkins, Willis, 'Episcopalians, Homosexuality, and World Mission.' *Anglican Theological Review,* Vol. 86, no. 2, (2004): 293-316.
Kalu, Ogbu, *Clio in a Sacred Garb: Essays on Christian Presence and African Responses, 1900-2000.* Trenton, NJ: Africa World Press, 2008.
Little, Lawrence S., *Disciples of Liberty: The African Methodist Episcopal Church in the Age of Imperialism, 1884-1916*. Knoxville, TN: The University of Tennessee Press, 2000.
Martin, Sandy, *Black Baptists and African Missions: The Origins of a Movement, 1880-1915*. Macon, GA: Mercer University Press, 1989.
Mitchell, Henry H., *Long-Hidden Realities of the First Years.* Grand Rapids, MI: Eerdmans, 2004.
Newman, Richard, 'Warrior Mother of Africa's Warriors of the Most High God: Laura Adorkor Kofey and the African Universal Church.' In *This Far By Faith: Readings in African-American Women's Religious Biography*, edited by Judith Weisenfeld and Richard Newman, 110-123. New York: Routledge, 1996.
Nnorum, Columba Aham, 'African American Churches and the Evolution of Antiapartheid Activism.' In *Long March Ahead: African American Churches and Public Policy in Post-Civil Rights America*, edited by R. Drew Smith, 193-216. Durham, NC: Duke University Press, 2004.

Pratt, Renate, *In Good Faith: Canadian Churches Against Apartheid.* Waterloo, Ontario: Wilfrid Laurier University Press, 1997.

Phipps, William E., *William Sheppard, Congo's African American Livingstone*. Louisville, KY: Geneva Press, 2002.

Reed, Christopher R., *Black Chicago's First Century,* Vol. I: 1833-1900. Columbia, MO: University of Missouri Press, 2005.

Ruether, Rosemary Radford, *Introducing Redemption in Christian Feminism.* Sheffield, UK: Sheffield Academic Press, 1998.

Sanneh, Lamin, *Abolitionists Abroad: American Blacks and the Making of Modern West Africa.* Cambridge, Massachusetts: Harvard University Press, 1999.

Shepperson, George and Price, Thomas. *Independent African*: *John Chilembwe and the Origins, Setting and Significance* of *Nyasaland Native Rising of 1915*. Edinburgh: Edinburgh University Press, 1958.

Smith, Michael M. (ed.), *Stono: Documenting and Interpreting a Southern Slave Revolt*. Columbia, SC: University of South Carolina, 2005.

Swart, Morrell F., *The Call of Africa*: *The Reformed Church in America Mission in the Sub-Sahara, 1948-1998*. Grand Rapids, MI: Eerdmans, 1998.

(112) African Christianity and Partnership with Latin American Churches

Luciano Chanhelela Chianeque

Introduction

The Church of our Lord Jesus Christ, it has been said, was born in Jerusalem as a *community* of believers of whom the majority were fishermen and domestic workers, and which later only grew in numbers (as narrated in the book of Acts). This growth of the young church aroused some suspicion from the existing majority religion of that time, the Jewish community which centred round the Old Testament and lived in Palestine. A situation emerged between the two faith communities by which the Jews began to persecute the young Christian community heavily. In its struggle for survival, the Christian community was forced to seek refuge in some of the neighbouring countries, in what today is known as Greece. While remaining bound up with the Hebrew culture of their original country, Christians also had to acquaint themselves with the culture of the new host country Greece, and particularly to a new way of thinking, namely, *philosophy*. As the young church understood the command to go forth in mission, it came also to Italy. Here again it was faced with a new way of life, particularly a new style of governing, so it had to adapt again to new realities and accommodate itself to the *emperor* theology.. Many centuries later, due to the industrial revolution, the church in Europe was challenged and had to struggle with many social ills in Europe which caused a major part of the church to migrate from Europe to the other side of the Atlantic in America. There the church yet again had to adjust itself as it encountered a new world of *business* and economic success. As one can see from these simple examples, the church – due to its process of accommodation to different cultural setting in various hoist countries – was formed according to different leading paradigms, i.e. it was first a community shaped by a 'philosophy-model', then by an 'emperor-model', and finally by a 'business-model'.

African Christianity today, one may say, is also a result of old struggles, old influences and old intrigues among the so-called mother churches in Europe, America and Latin America. While the historic churches in Africa have become independent in terms of official structures of decision-making and have founded councils of churches, in which the historic churches often play a major role, the old hegemonic language still plays a major role in terms of mentality and a sense of dependence. However, as Africans, we also should remain filled with deep gratitude and appreciation to all those missionary churches which acquainted us with our Christian heritage and also paved the way towards independence from colonialism. It is remarkable how many missionaries have made sacrifices so that we in later generations could be enlightened by the grace, love and mercy of Jesus Christ. We are convinced that the historic efforts of missionaries, their sacrifices and their love cannot be repaid by us, but only Almighty God himself will reward them in his kingdom in his own way. Thus, African Christianity, despite all the struggles and negative influences of the past, is today an entity in its own right and able to make its own decisions, test new governing rules, and learn as a church to be self-propagating and self-sustaining. Here one should talk in terms of providing a real partnership – and everybody knows that partnership in its most demanding form is possible only among equals. Therefore this needs to apply also to the relationships with the sending churches as they send out missionaries or fraternal workers, Therefore the promotion of a real and balanced, integrated partnership between churches, agencies and choirs has a huge potential for coming to life again, and for better relations being promoted between churches in Europe and the established churches on the African soil.

In the church, there are always some tensions between conservatives and liberals about the hidden issue of who is to become the leading voice in the religious community in a given country.

At the beginning, there were hidden issues which were not so noticeable until the 1960s, when the struggle with regard to human rights, women's rights and all sorts of other rights became a dominant concern. In the 1970s, churches in Africa were influenced by the Azusa Street Revival which in principle was a genuine and positive experience of renewal. But it also has had an ambivalent character since in several cases it brought with it the influence of a kind of 'business spirit'. For understanding African Pentecostalism, we need always to remember that African Christianity often saw itself as inferior and, either explicitly or implicitly, had its identity formed by patterns of relationship which were based on concepts of being dominant and inferior – that is, a pattern of relationship subtly interpreted in terms of a master-servant relationship. It is from this background that many people on the African continent decided to appoint and ordain themselves as pastors and start their own churches as they could not stand and accept the fact that in their own country they found white masters ruling them – and even in their own church it seemed to be the same story. so they decided to create their own African Pentecostal and Independent churches.

The Latin American Experience

Once Europeans had discovered the western hemisphere and church leaders had determined that its residents were indeed human beings, both Spanish and Portuguese monarchs justified their claims to colonies and commercial monopolies in terms of bringing Christianity to the 'heathen'. The monarchs codified this rationalization in the 1494 Treaty of Tordesillas that divided the non-European world between the colonial powers for commerce, colonization and religious conversion. Pope Alexander VI confirmed the treaty. For roughly the next three centuries, evangelization in a colonial mindset dominated church activities and church-state relations. The monarchs provided financial and political assistance. Conversion, often not much more than just baptism and mandatory weekly masses, was largely the work of Franciscan and Dominican religious orders, and later the Company of Jesus (Jesuit missionaries). During the colonization of the Caribbean, Bartolomé de Las Casas (1474?–1566), a former conquistador turned into a true missionary, and later became a blistering critic of Spanish practices. In his political tract 'A Short Account of the Destruction of the Indies', he described the conquest quite frankly and critically as sadistic brutality, torture, enslavement and murder of indigenous peoples. He called on the king to restrain the conquest, to reverse Indian slavery, and to regulate Spanish-Indian relations. Spain's colonial rivals (e.g. England) and rebellious dominions (e.g. the Dutch) reprinted the book widely, often with Albrecht Dürer's (1471–1528) fanciful and terrifying engravings to mobilize popular opinion against the Spaniards. As Protestant northern Europe gained ascendancy over the Catholic South in global geopolitics, the influence of this text continued to grow, and its negative portrayal of Spaniards and the church still colours popular perceptions in the 21st century, both in Latin America as well as in Africa.[1]

Religious leaders undertook efforts to restrain the conquistadors and colonists and to impose religious orthodoxy by instituting the Inquisition in Spain's possessions. Because they were felt to have an incomplete understanding of religious doctrine, indigenous people, except in cases of bigamy and cannibalism, were not subject to the Inquisition. In its efforts to evangelize the indigenous people and the arriving African slaves, the church used its most powerful symbols, frequently announcing new martyrs, saintly behaviour, and miracles. The most famous of these, the 1531 apparition of the Virgin of Guadalupe

[1] Laura Heikes, 'Úna Perspectiva Diferente: Latin Americans and the Global Missions Movement', *Missiology: An International Review* Vol. 31, no.1, January (2003), 72-3.

in Mexico, created an indigenous Mexican mythology in which an Indian, Juan Diego, was chosen by the Virgin to carry her message to a Spanish bishop.[2]

The Roman Catholic Church in Latin America has long been criticized for helping to maintain an anachronistic social system and economic underdevelopment, low levels of education, a rigid class system, a lack of interest in economic achievement and support of traditional order. Catholics themselves admit that few creative thinkers have come from Latin America, and that theologically and administratively the Catholic Church has conformed to patterns drawn chiefly from southern Europe. Yet, today, no institution in Latin America is changing more rapidly, and in directions that have important implications, not only for defining new relationships between Christianity and the values of society, but also for the role that the church will play in the region's development.

Like many cultural changes, however, this transformation of the Catholic Church has been neither as abrupt nor as total as casual observers have often reported. Just as the church was never as monolithic or reactionary as its critics claimed, recent reform movements have not totally captured the Catholic community or followed a single, unified path. Rather, the church is in a continuous transition which has greatly intensified in the last decade, building on a long tradition of division and dissent that dates as far back as the early sixteenth century, when Father Bartolomé de las Casas provoked a debate over the indigenous policy of the Spanish conquerors.[3]

One reason for the success of Pentecostalism in Latin America is that it has very successfully absorbed Latin American culture. The music, for example, which one can hear in Pentecostal churches, has the same rhythms which people enjoy outside church. In fact, within only one century, Pentecostalism has become indigenous, or 'Latin Americanized', to a much greater extent than Roman Catholicism has become in its four centuries of presence in Latin America.

Another factor for the success of Pentecostalism lies in the great emphasis on faith healing, as many Latin Americans who grow up in a Catholic environment convert to Pentecostalism due to a health crisis. The healing ministry is one of the propelling motors of the Pentecostal boom.

At the same time, Pentecostal preachers tend to sound very similar to their congregants: they are close to the language of the people. They are themselves often non-literate and they speak to their flock in the same way that people in Latin American speak to each other. They also tend to look like their congregants. Therefore, in Guatemala, many Pentecostal preachers are Mayan, and in Brazil they are Afro-Brazilian. By contrast, in the Catholic Church, most priests are part of the elite. They are either white or *mestiços* (persons with both European and Native South American blood), and many are actually from Europe.[4]

Partnership with Africa?

Historically, from what we know, the majority of the so-called mission churches in Africa were planted by European or American missionaries, but recently Pentecostalism has emerged also as an indigenous movement in Africa, which has also appealed to the poor and to outsiders. More recently even African Pentecostalism has also begun to appeal to middle-class professionals, such as doctors and lawyers, who have formed their own denominations in Brazil and Guatemala, amongst other countries. The emphases on

---

[2] Fr. William Saunders, 'Saint Juan Diego and Our Lady', in *Catholic Education Resource Centre*. http://www.catholiceducation.org/en/culture/catholic-contributions/saint-juan-diego-and-our-lady.html (accessed 25 June, 2016).

[3] William Saunders, 'Saint Juan Diego and Our Lady,' in *Arlington Catholic Herald*. http://www.catholiceducation.org/en/culture/catholic-contributions/saint-juan-diego-and-our-lady.html (accessed 25 June, 2016).

[4] William Saunders, 'Saint Juan Diego and Our Lady.'

'inner healing', individual responsibility and prosperity theology are especially appealing to these more affluent Pentecostals.

Many of the poor people in Africa are especially attracted by prosperity theology, also known as the 'Health and Wealth' gospel, as it gives people hope that they can move upwards, regardless of their situation. People are told that, with sufficient faith and active petition to God, eventually the things and dreams that you want for your life will be yours. That, indeed, is a very powerful message for someone who otherwise has very little.

Competition from Pentecostal churches has definitely made the Latin American religious landscape more robust. In addition to contributing to a certain renewal within the Catholic Church, it has also affected mainline Protestant churches – such as the Presbyterian and Methodist churches – which, like the Catholics, now also offer their own version of Pentecostalism.

The New Movement

Africa has been suffering from different influences with regard to the situation of Christianity and other religions in their context. In the case of Portuguese-speaking Africa, Neo-Pentecostalism has invaded many of the formal spaces of the so-called mainline churches. The new Brazilian church called Igreja Universal do Reino de Deus (Universal Church of the Kingdom of God) is taking its members from all denominations to form and claim its space and place in Africa. Its success is based on the peculiar mixture between biblical and African practices of cure and magic in its style of piety. African minds are vulnerable and tempted by these types of worship and adoration rather than having to focus on morals or values which are void of any actual practical action.

There is a strong Pentecostal belief in miracles and the prosperity gospel, but not so much about work – and it is stated that this message can render the believer a blessing and thus eternal life. Africa is rich, as many people say, but in reality the majority of Africans are also very poor, and if there is anything which promises them some real change in life here and now, they readily follow. Outsiders are often irritated and amazed by the ways in which people are called to give to the Lord, so that they may receive God's favours, and how easily people are caught and attracted by such messages. The church, as we stated earlier, seems to be transformed into a business model. This happens with both church leaders (and what they are trying to get from people) as with politicians. Therefore we come back to our assumption at the beginning that in church history one can see a peculiar transformation from the church which, having been founded as a community, conforms to a 'philosophy'-model, to an 'emperor-model', and finally to a 'business-model'. We should give thanks to God that he is righteous, and therefore the powers of this world will not prevail over against his church.

Conclusion

The important relationships, contributions and forms of partnership between trends in Latin American Catholicism and Evangelical movements within African Christianity will continue to assume a crucial significance in African Christianity as they contribute to social change and conscientization. Latin America is underdeveloped, not only because it does not produce enough, but because the majority of the people cannot and do not know how to participate in national life. In this context, which provided a major challenge which cannot be postponed indefinitely, Catholics and the Evangelical Church may have a formative role in Latin America.

The future of the partnership between churches in Latin America and those in Africa will be shaped not only on the basis of common challenges in terms of poverty, marginalization, the struggle for self-realization, competitions and faith healing, but even more on a true sense of Christian brotherhood, where the strengthening of each other, a sense of mutual recognition, which many churches in Africa are missing from their funding partners, is going to be a reality. It is interesting to see that the Universal Church of the Kingdom of God has dealt with the issue of nationhood differently from the so-called missionary churches in Europe and North America. Latin American Christianity is definitively as vibrant as the forms of Christianity which one can find in Africa. Living in the meantime in a global religious market, both forms of Christianity have to work together to offer people attractive religious options, and they need each other in genuine mutual partnership.

Bibliography

Heikes, Laura 'Úna Perspectiva Diferente: Latin Americans and the Global Missions Movement.' *Missiology: An International Review* Vol. 31, no. 1, January (2003): 69-85.

Jenkins, Philip *The Next Christendom: The Coming of Global Christianity*. New York: Oxford University Press, 2002.

Nolen, Steve, 'Partnering with Latin American Churches to Complete the Great Commision.' *Global Missiology* Vol. 1, no. 7, (2009). http://ojs.globalmissiology.org/index.php/english/issue/view/1 (accessed 24 June, 2015).

Smith, Dwight P., 'Slaying the Dragons of Self Interest: Making International Partnership Work.' *Evangelical Missions Quarterly* Vol. 28, no. 1, January (1992): 18-23.

(113) AFRICAN CHRISTIANITY IN PARTNERSHIP WITH CARIBBEAN CHURCHES

George Mulrain

Introduction

From the time of the Caribbean's early history of slavery, there was the tendency among people of the region to affirm the culture of Europe over and above that of Africa. Especially where the Christian Church was concerned, its preachers and teachers overtly or implicitly suggested that, to be acceptable in the sight of the God revealed in Jesus Christ, one had to adopt a stance that was as distant as possible from anything African. Such was the impact of a context in which people of dark skin colour were relegated to the lower echelons of society. However, down through the centuries with the passage of time, the inhabitants of the Caribbean region soon began to engage themselves in a process of evaluation. They reassessed Africa's contribution to history and rejected ideas that had been gaining popularity among critics in the North that Blacks were inherently an inferior race.

During the 1970s when Black Power, with its 'black is beautiful' slogan, was being proclaimed in the USA, in South Africa and in other parts of the world, there was a move within churches of the Caribbean to examine the curricula of Christian education programmes. The aim was to determine whether Christians were being educated to appreciate their Caribbean culture as having divine approval rather than being described as devilish or demonic. Well might Europeans have been seeing the culture of Africa in a negative light, but that ought not to be so among Africans or people of African descent. The message needed to be effectively communicated that all cultures are God-given and that the culture of Africa was no less sacred than that of Europe.

From the latter part of the twentieth century and into the 21st, corrective measures were being implemented so that the people of the Caribbean could appreciate that the various facets of their culture did have their origins with the Creator. Despite the significant African presence in churches across the region, it must be acknowledged that it would take many years before notions of European superiority were eradicated from people's thinking. In the meantime, there were signs that, in the attempt to forge a Christian culture that was genuinely indigenous, as well as a brand of Christianity that was equally indigenous, the people of the Caribbean were duty-bound, because of their heritage, to espouse a partnership with African Christianity.

The Nature of African Christianity

Caribbean understandings of what African Christianity was all about had to do with how they perceived the worship life of Africa. Indeed, there was the idea of vibrant worship characterized by lively singing, movement, dance and dramatization. This was because the liturgy associated with African Traditional Religion included dancing, the offering of sacrifices and spirit possession. Such religious components were seen, for example in *vaudou* (Haiti), *santeria* (Cuba), *pukkumina* (Jamaica) and *shango* (Trinidad and Tobago). However, it was noted that the expression of African Christianity was not to be confined to worship but embraced all spheres of life, including the sense of belonging to a community.

On a personal note, I have found the African cultural emphasis upon community to be very helpful in my ministry. I always remember participating in the naming ceremony for the child of one of my Ghanaian friends, and was impressed by how, as part of the ritual, the newborn was handed round the circle and each adult present called the child by name. Since then, whenever I baptize an infant, I seize the opportunity to walk through the congregation with the child to emphasize that 'this little one' is now an integral part of the community of faith.

In addition to worship, efforts to address sickness through prayer and anointing with oil are respected within African Independent Churches as a pointer in the direction as recommended by the Scriptures.[1] The trait of hospitality is perhaps a most effective demonstration of an important aspect in the life of African people in general and Christian people in particular, recommended as it is in the letter to the Hebrews.[2]

Quite apart from community, healing and hospitality, an ingredient often overlooked when considering the nature of African Christianity is African theology. This is a theology that embraces a cosmology or worldview that includes belief in a Supreme Spiritual Being (God) and in a series of lesser spiritual beings, some of whom are nature spirits and some ancestral spirits. There is the notion that spiritual beings are everywhere present and interact with mortal beings, sometimes through dreams and visions, and on those special occasions during worship where persons are deemed to be spirit-possessed. This lends support to the contention of African Christians that it is false to compartmentalize life into sacred and secular since, in reality, all life is sacred, lived as it is in the presence of the Supreme Being and the lesser spiritual beings.

Emergence of the Partnership between African Christianity and the Caribbean Churches

For centuries, then, it was Europe that set the pattern as to what within the Caribbean region constituted Christian practice, including worship. From the sixteenth century through to the nineteenth, once-free Africans had been captured and brought to the Caribbean to work as slaves on the sugar plantations. Their European overlords insisted that they desist from practising their traditional religion or any semblance of it. They were to adhere to Christianity as understood by the people of Europe. The French 'Code Noir',[3] which determined how Africans captured as slaves were to be treated, stipulated that all slaves brought into the colonies were to be baptised into the Catholic faith. This led to a fear on the part of descendants of Africa to overtly practice any ritual that they might have cherished while they were at home in Africa. One result of this insofar as religion was concerned was the creation of what might be referred to as a system of dual membership, wherein the individual, during the day, would worship in accordance with what was expected by the authorities, but, under cover of darkness, he or she dared to give expression to typically African behaviour. Understandably, this resulted in syncretism in worship and led to the emergence of Christian groups that reflected both Euro-Christian and Afro-Christian understandings of the faith. It is this sort of blending that led eventually to a partnership between African Christianity and the Caribbean churches.

The partnership about which we speak was to be expected, given that, from the very beginning, in Roman Catholic, Anglican, Methodist, Moravian, Seventh Day Adventist and other churches within the region, those of African descent were in the majority. There are of course churches whose names suggest a definite link with Africa. There is the Ethiopian Orthodox Church which established itself in Jamaica in 1970. There is the African Methodist Episcopal Church which is present in English-speaking Caribbean territories such as Barbados, the US Virgin Islands, Trinidad, Jamaica and Guyana; in Spanish-speaking countries like the Dominican Republic; in Francophone territories like Haiti, and in Dutch-speaking places like Suriname. But because, historically, many of the denominations within the Caribbean received liturgical and administrative patterns that emanated from Europe and North America, the African flavour, although slowly establishing itself, still remained somewhat superficial.

The African contribution to the partnership is more pronounced in churches that historically do not have denominational ties with churches in the North, but which might be regarded as home-grown or

[1] Jas 5:13-16.
[2] Heb 13:1-2.
[3] A decree passed by King Louis XIV in 1685.

indigenous. There are Revival churches which emerged in Jamaica during the 1860s.[4] Their worship includes hymn singing, the recitation of psalms, drumming, handclapping, prayers, Bible readings, 'spiritual' dancing leading to spirit possession, preaching, visions, the lighting of candles, the bearing of crucifixes, the burning of incense and the sprinkling of blood. Healing is important, hence the use of healing techniques such as prayer, fasting, the laying-on of hands, bush baths, anointing with oil, and exorcism. According to Dr Dale Bisnauth: 'The whole purpose of the revivalist service is to induce the spirits to possess the worshippers, also to receive revelations through dreams and visions. The emphasis of revivalism is clearly on personal spiritual growth and development. The movement, therefore, shares the ethos of the Protestant thrust in the Caribbean up to recent times.' Bisnauth maintains that 'Revival churches constitute the Africanisation of Protestantism'.[5]

The African contribution to the partnership is also seen in the Spiritual Baptist churches which are to be found in places like Trinidad and Tobago, Barbados and Saint Vincent.[6] These churches emerged in the early 1900s and faced persecution. For example, in 1913 they were declared illegal in St Vincent, no doubt because of the noisy nature of their worship. They went underground but the police persecuted them until a lessening of the harshness in the 1930s and the repeal of the law in 1965. They were also declared illegal in Trinidad and Tobago. This was in 1919. However, in 1951, legislation was passed to allow them to worship in their own way. The Spiritual Baptists faced fewer problems in Barbados where they were given permission to worship relatively free of persecution.

Spiritual Baptist churches are in many respects similar to the Revival churches of Jamaica. Their altars are decorated with candles, flowers, crucifixes and religious pictures. When they meet together for worship, it is not confined to indoors because they are committed to witnessing on the streets. When ceremonies take place indoors, the ritual includes sprinkling water in the corners of the church to ensure purification of the worship space, handclapping, the ringing of a hand bell and preaching. There is emphasis placed on baptism by immersion which may take place in a river or at the seaside. Dreams and visions are important. So too are healing and possession by the Holy Spirit. Liturgically, theirs is a syncretistic blend of Yoruba religion, Roman Catholicism, Anglicanism and Pentecostalism.

Conclusion

My contention is that there is definitely a partnership developing between African Christianity and Caribbean churches. As mentioned above, it is being reflected particularly in terms of how worship services are conducted. There is a growing willingness on the part of Christian churches in the region to be as expressive in terms of movement and dance as their African counterparts. As far as theology is concerned, much is shared in common. Along with African Christians, Caribbean churches have a Trinitarian understanding of God. However, there are doctrinal issues that are not spelt out officially but espoused and internalised by people of African descent, for example, the belief that there is ongoing communication between the physical and spiritual worlds, notably through dreams, visions and spirit possession. European Christianity has not offered much teaching on such things as the Scriptural reference to our 'struggle not against enemies of blood and flesh, but against the rulers, against the authorities, against the cosmic powers of this present darkness, against the spiritual forces of evil in the heavenly places'.[7] By contrast, African Christianity is better equipped because the ordinary members of the church

---

[4] The 1860s is regarded as that special time in Jamaica's history when the country experienced a great religious revival.
[5] Dale Bisnauth, *History of Religions in the Caribbean*, (Trenton, New Jersey: African World Press, 1996), 179.
[6] Eudora Thomas, *A History of the Shouter Baptists in Trinidad and Tobago,* (Ithaca, N.Y.: Calaloux Publications, 1987).
[7] Ephesians 6:12.

are aware of the powers of evil in their ongoing experience and of the need to be well prepared to combat such negative forces.

The other noticeable benefit accruing from this partnership between African Christianity and the Caribbean churches is a greater emphasis upon the ministry of healing. Whereas, in the past, Christians within the region tended to be dismissive of indigenous healers, today there is more willingness to consider that herbal remedies and ritual treatment for various types of illnesses might very well be options approved by the Holy Spirit alongside the patented offerings of western medical science. Serious attention is now being given by churches across the denominations to healing services that focus on prayer and anointing with oil.

In the final analysis, Caribbean churches have merely scratched the surface. There are greater depths of spirituality to be realized. However, as the partnership develops, and the people of the Caribbean realize that blessings come not only from Europe and North America but from Africa as well, the Holy Spirit will certainly enable a deepening of the faith and practice among the churches within the region.

Bibliography

Barrett, Leonard E. *The Sun and the Drum: African Roots in Jamaican Folk Tradition.* London: Heinemann, 1976.

Bisnauth, Dale. A *History of Religions in the Caribbean*, Trenton, New Jersey: African World Press, 1996.

Burnett, David. *World of the Spirits: A Christian Perspective in Traditional and Folk Religions.* Oxford Monarch Books, 2005.

Chilcote, Paul W. *Making Disciples in A World Parish: Global Perspectives on Mission and Evangelism.* Eugene, Oregon: Pickwick Publications, 2011.

Erskine, Noel L., *Decolonizing Theology, A Caribbean Perspective.* Trenton, NJ: Africa World Press Inc, 1998.

Gregory, Howard (ed.) *Caribbean Theology: Preparing for the Challenges Ahead.* Kingston, Jamaica: University of the West Indies Press, 1995.

Kilson, Martin L. and Rotberg, Robert I. *The African Diaspora: Interpretive Essays.* Cambridge: Harvard University Press, 1976.

Moorish, Ivor. *Obeah, Christ and Rastaman: Jamaica and its Religion,* Cambridge, James Clarke, 1982

Mulrain, George. 'African Cosmology and Caribbean Christianity.' In *At the Crossroads: African Caribbean Religion and Christianity,* edited by Burton Sankeralli , 46 – 66. Trinidad: CCC, 1995.

Mulrain, George. *Caribbean Theological Insights: Exploring Theological Themes Within The Context of The Caribbean Region.* Bahnhofstrasse, Saarbrücken: Blessed Hope Publishing, 2014.

Mulrain, George. 'The Caribbean.' In *An Introduction to Third World Theologies,* edited by John Parratt, 163-181., Cambridge: Cambridge University Press, 2004.

Spencer, William D. *Dread Jesus,* London: SPCK, 1999.

Taylor, Patrick, Case, FredErick I. *The Encyclopedia of Caribbean Religions,* (Vol. 1 A-L). Urbana, Chicago and Springfield: University of Illinois Press, 2013.

Thomas, Eudora, *A History of the Shouter Baptists in Trinidad and Tobago.* Ithaca, N.Y.: Calaloux Publications, 1987.

Titus, Noel. *Conflicts and Contradictions: the Introduction of Christianity to the Sixteenth Century Caribbean,* London, Minerva, 1998.

Williams, Lewin L., *Caribbean Theology,* New York, Peter Lang, 1994

(114) African Christianity and Partnership with Middle Eastern Churches: The Palestine Kairos Document

Edwin Arrison

This chapter seeks to explain the significant role played by the South African churches and the world church against apartheid in South Africa, and why the South African church community is now well placed to support Christians in Palestine struggling for an end to apartheid as expressed through the Israeli Occupation. In 2017, Palestine commemorates both the centenary of the British-imposed Balfour Declaration and the fiftieth anniversary of the 1967 occupation by Israel of the West Bank and the Syrian Golan Heights.

Introduction

In 1994, South Africa emerged from the nightmare of apartheid. The words used to describe apartheid by the UN and international church bodies were words such as 'crime against humanity', evil, inhuman, heresy, etc.

When Nelson Mandela was inaugurated as President of the new South Africa in May 1994, he used the words 'never, never and never again…' in his inaugural speech.[1] Those who were present and who listened carefully would have recognised the words 'never again…' but this time it was placed firmly within an African context and also given greater and triple emphasis.

However, before this speech could be made, apartheid first had to be defeated by humanity.

Sections of the South African church were particularly active against apartheid, especially in the thirty years before its demise, led by people such as Desmond Tutu, Allan Boesak, Frank Chikane, Beyers Naudé and Denis Hurley. This was extremely important, as the apartheid government always justified its policy on the basis that they were the last bastion of Christianity against Communism. The presence of Christian leaders in the struggle against apartheid was therefore particularly important.

At a global level, Archbishop Trevor Huddleston also led the global anti-apartheid movement from London, and the Rev. Barney Pityana headed up the Programme to Combat Racism (PCR) at the World Council of Churches (1988-1992), succeeding Baldwin Sjollema.

There was another reason why this church involvement in the thirty years before apartheid fell was important: the fact that, by 1960, the ANC and other liberation movements had given up on the idea of a purely non-violent struggle and formed an underground military movement called *Umkhonto we Sizwe*, the Spear of the Nation.

The mainline churches could not with any authenticity express their displeasure at such a move (which they did) without appearing to be hypocritical, since many of them were supplying chaplains to the apartheid army. It simply had to find creative ways of becoming involved in non-violent action against apartheid to retain, first, its credibility in South Africa but, more importantly, the credibility of the gospel. The fact that many of the churches had links with the global church meant that the message against apartheid could also be expressed on global platforms.

From 1960 to 1990, much of the world church attention was focused on the issue of apartheid in South Africa, especially the theological justification for it provided primarily by Dutch Reformed Church theologians in South Africa. This probably reminded some European theologians too much of the

---

[1] See Nelson Mandela 'Statement of Nelson Mandela at his Inauguration as President', *African National Congress,* www.anc.org.za/show.php?id=3132 (accessed 25 June, 2016).

theological support given to Nazism by most of the church in Germany, and the resistance to that by the Confessing Church.

Besides, theologians and church leaders, ordinary Europeans, Americans, Africans and other citizens of the world showed their displeasure of apartheid by boycotting South African goods and sport, advocating sanctions and divestment despite the fact that their government leaders, particularly Reagan, Thatcher and Kohl, were reluctant to do so.

Sadly, even some churches were reluctant to heed the call for sanctions against South Africa. Despite the fact that Archbishop Tutu headed up the Anglican Church in Southern Africa, the Church of England synods during the 1980s consistently voted against sanctions and divestment in South Africa, claiming that it would hurt 'the Blacks' more. Ordinary Christians and other citizens were, however, not convinced by these arguments and mobilized against apartheid, even on the streets of major cities of the world.

What is therefore happening today in Israel and Palestine reminds South African and other theologians of the church struggle against apartheid. This memory is what Kairos theologians called a 'dangerous memory' when we celebrated the thirtieth anniversary of the 1985 Kairos Document in South Africa (see further below). It was at this conference that a call was made for the intensification of Boycott, divestment and Sanctions (BDS) against Israel.[2]

Besides the memory of apartheid, the reality on the ground has been investigated by a South African research body (the Human Sciences Research Council), and its research found that the situation in the West Bank today can be compared with apartheid in South Africa.[3] The Russell Tribunal on Palestine, meeting in Cape Town in 2011 under the leadership of Stéphane Hessel, found that not only the West Bank situation can be compared with apartheid, but also what is happening in Israel today – since something like fifty laws discriminate between Jewish Israelis and Arab Israelis.[4] Both Desmond Tutu and Jimmy Carter have also described the situation in both the West Bank and Israel as apartheid.

The ideology of apartheid challenges the fundamental belief that all human beings are created equal, in the image of God, and are equally loved by him. In order to show its displeasure at this heresy, the world church had no option but to clearly distance itself from it. But this was not easy and many 'church theologians' tried a milder approach to end apartheid, but ultimately the Kairos moment was felt so strongly that, by 1988, most church leaders took part in the 'Standing for the Truth' campaign and even called for prayer for the downfall of apartheid.

Again, it is not easy for many to recognise the situation in Israel and Palestine today as apartheid, but most South African theologians have identified it as such.

Background of the Church Struggle against Apartheid

For readers who are unaware of the worldwide church focus on the issue of South African apartheid, it is worth recounting some of the salient events over a thirty-year period.

---

[2] See Kairos Southern Africa, 'Kairos SA 30th Anniversary Conference Ttatement: Dangerous Memory and Hope for the Future', https://kairossouthernafrica.wordpress.com/2015/08/20/kairos-sa-30th-anniversary-conference-statement (accessed 25 June, 2016).

[3] See Virginia Tilley 'Report: Israel practicing Apartheid in Palestinian Territories' in *Human Sciences Research* Council, www.hsrc.ac.za/en/media-briefs/democracy-goverance-and-service-delivery/report-israel-practicing-apartheid-in-palestinian-territories (accessed 25 June, 2016).

[4] See Russell Tribunal on Palistine (RToP), www.russelltribunalonpalestine.com/en/sessions/south-africa/south-africa-session-%E2%80%94-full-findings/cape-town-session-summary-of-findings (accessed 25 June, 2016).

The Cottesloe Consultation (1960) in Johannesburg

In December 1960, the World Council of Church convened a consultation on the church and apartheid in a Johannesburg suburb called Cottesloe. This was primarily in response to the Sharpville massacre that had taken place the preceding March, where white policemen shot and killed black protesters, most of them in the back.

It is interesting to note that this was also the year that Chief Albert Luthuli received the Nobel Peace Prize. He was the leader of the African National Congress (ANC) but also a Christian leader in South Africa.

At the Cottesloe Consultation, Beyers Naudé began to emerge as what Eberhard Bethge described as the 'Dietrich Bonhoeffer of South Africa'.[5] He was an Afrikaner leader and was being groomed to either become the Moderator of the Dutch Reformed Church or even Prime Minister of apartheid South Africa. He could not justify apartheid theologically (not even a mild version of it) and decided to leave the white Dutch Reformed Church and join the black Dutch Reformed Church. He also became the leader of the Christian Institute of South Africa.

'The Message to the people of South Africa' (1968)

By 1968, the Christian Institute published a document called 'The Message to the People of South Africa' in which it distanced the gospel of Jesus Christ from apartheid. This was widely read and accepted and was the precursor to what was to happen in the 1970s, particularly the church's support for the Black Consciousness Movement.

The banning of Beyers Naudé and other church and theological figures:

Dr Beyers Naudé established the Christian Institute in 1963, after he had resigned from the Dutch Reformed Church. By 1977, Beyers Naudé and others such as Brian Brown were served with banning orders and the Christian Institute was closed down by the apartheid regime.

Desmond Tutu became the General Secretary of the South African Council of Churches in 1978, a post he held until 1984.

The Establishment of the Programme to Combat Racism of the WCC (1970)

In 1970, the WCC established the Programme to Combat Racism, with a major focus on apartheid in South Africa. Even though it was seen as controversial by some, this body adopted the 'Lusaka Statement' in 1987, which called upon the churches to support the liberation movements with humanitarian aid.

Expulsion of the Dutch Reformed Church by the WARC (1982)

By 1982, the World Alliance of Reformed Churches adopted the statement that 'Apartheid is a heresy', and expelled the white Dutch Reformed Church from its membership, and at the same time elected Alan Boesak as its moderator.

Launch of the South African Kairos Document: 1985[6]

The Kairos Document was the 'straw that broke the camel's back' and built on statements against apartheid, but went further by analysing the way in which, particularly the English-speaking missionary

---

[5] See De Gruchy John, 'Beyers Naudé: South Africa's Bonhoeffer? Celebrating the Centenary of the birth of Beyers Naudé - 1915-2015', *Stellenbosch Theological Journal* Vol. 1, no 1, (2015): 79–98.

[6] South African Histoey Online, 'Challenge to the Church: A Theological Comment on the Political Crisis in South Africa: The Kairos Document, 1985' http://www.sahistory.org.za/archive/challenge-church-theological-comment-political-crisis-south-africa-kairos-document-1985#sthash.V65DU0HC.dpuf (accessed 24 June, 2016).

church leadership, carefully approached the issue of apartheid, thereby leading Christians to a notion of 'false reconciliation' and 'false peace'.

Adoption of the Belhar Confession[7] *by the Dutch Reformed Mission Church (now called the Uniting Reformed Church of Southern Africa – URCSA): 1986*

Because of its confessional nature, and its link with the white Dutch Reformed church, the 'coloured' section of the Dutch Reformed Church adopted the Belhar Confession in 1986 and urged the white Dutch Reformed church to do the same. More than twenty years after the end of apartheid, it has still not done so on a national level even though some of its regional synods have urged the national church to take this step.

I highlight the development of all these church statements and actions in order to:

1. Explain the similar ways in which churches across the world were both supportive of the struggle against apartheid while some saw it as controversial and wanted to proceed cautiously;
2. To argue why the situation in Israel and Palestine is reminiscent – with some interesting differences – of what happened in South Africa during the church struggle against apartheid; and,
3. Underline why I believe that the church in South Africa is well placed to stand in solidarity with the people of Palestine, and to explain the situation in Palestine to the world church.

There is, however, one important difference: the majority of South Africa's population was Christian, while the majority of the people of Israel and Palestine are Jewish or Muslim. The small but significant Christian population of Israel and Palestine therefore holds the key to global Christian involvement towards creating a just solution in Israel and Palestine. They have now done this through the publication of the Palestine Kairos Document – and the world church is once again asked to respond to this new Kairos.

South African Christians, because of their experience against apartheid, are therefore ideally placed to lead this global solidarity movement with both the Christians and, ultimately, with all the people of Palestine and Israel.

The Israel-Palestine 'Sharpville' Moment (2008)

In 2008, Israel invaded Gaza and killed more than 2,000 Palestinians. In 2014, Israel repeated this and once again killed more than 2,000 Palestinians, this time mostly civilians.

The Palestine Kairos Document (2009)

At the adoption of the Palestine Kairos Document[8] in Bethlehem in December 2009, a letter of support from Archbishop-emeritus Desmond Tutu was read out. Delegates expressed great appreciation for this letter, coming as it did from South Africa. The South African delegation, consisting of the writer of this article, Edwin Arrison, Dr Stiaan van der Merwe and the Rev Solomuzi Mabuza, together with some members of the Ecumenical Accompaniment Programme in Palestine and Israel (EAPPI), was also warmly welcomed and several references were made to the South African Kairos Document and the South African church struggle against apartheid. A call to support BDS (Boycott, Divestment and Sanctions) was also made at the adoption of the Palestine Kairos Document.

Another message of support was read by the delegates of the All Africa Conference of Churches. It was recognised that, while there was strong support coming from Europe and the USA, support from the African Church would prove to be especially significant over the coming years.

---

[7] See The Belhar confession letter, http://www.upcsa.org.za/docs-archive/belhar_confession_with_letter.pdf (accessed 24 June, 2016).

[8] See 'Kairos Palestine', www.kairospalestine.ps (accessed 24 June, 2016).

Concerns about the African Church

Some concerns about the role of the African Church were expressed in both public and private.

The major concern was that African Christians were coming to Israel on pilgrimage to visit 'dead stones' but they rarely interacted with the 'living stones', i.e. Arab Palestinian Christians, living in the land where Jesus was born, died and rose again, and where our most sacred texts were written. A group called 'Kairos Nigeria' has now arisen in Nigeria to counter this narrative about Israel and Palestine within the Nigerian church context.

One of the South African delegates, the Rev Moss Nthla, on a visit to the Palestinian Christians in August 2008, discovered that something he had done a few years earlier was directly detrimental to his Palestinian sisters and brothers. He was completely unaware that planting a tree in what the Israelis called the 'South Africa Park' was actually a former Palestinian village called Lubya. It was only on his visit in 2008 that he discovered how the Jewish National Fund was playing on the Judeao-Christian link and using it to undermine the story of Palestinian Christians and other Palestinians. Soon after this visit, a film was made by Dr Heidi Grunebaum, a South African Jew, about the village of Lubya.[9]

The Intensification of Support for Palestine from Christians in South Africa since 2009

The three delegates returning from the launch of the Palestine Kairos Document returned to a South African ecumenical movement that was both weak and divided.

However, in April 2010, Kairos Southern Africa drafted a statement in support of Kairos Palestine and more than sixty South African church leaders and theologians signed this statement.[10] This was the first major statement by the South African church on the question of Palestine.

Desmond Tutu, even though he was retired, is the one South African church leader who has consistently supported Kairos Palestine.

In 2011, he opened the Russell Tribunal on Palestine in Cape Town in the presence of the Anglican Archbishop of Cape Town, Thabo Makgoba. Allan Boesak also gave a testimony at this session of the Russell Tribunal.

Various church leaders' delegations have visited Palestine, and at the end of 2012, a church leaders' delegation from South Africa released a statement calling their experience of apartheid in Palestine and Israel as having a sense of being tormented by the reminder of being in an apartheid state.[11]

Dr Mitri Raheb again visited Cape Town in 2013 to deliver the Steve de Gruchy lecture. This put him in touch with the well-known South African theologian, John de Gruchy who, in his morning meditations at the Kairos 30th anniversary celebrations, referred to the Gospel of Mark as 'the first Palestine Kairos Document' because of the words in the first chapter of Mark: 'The time is now.'[12]

In 2013, South Africa hosted a event initiated by Sweden called the 'Moving Mountains Global Youth Event' where young people from at least eight African countries attended and pledged to do all they could to support the struggle for justice in Palestine through their churches.

Two Anglican diocesan synods (Natal and Saldanha Bay) have adopted resolutions on Israel and Palestine at their respective synods. While this is only a small start, it is likely that other synods will follow

---

[9] See Village under the Forest, https://www.uwc.ac.za/Announcements/Pages/The-Village-under-the-Forest.aspx (accessed 24 June, 2016).

[10] See 'A South African Christian response to the Palestinian Kairos Document', www.voltairenet.org/article164794.html (accessed 24 June, 2016).

[11] See South African Church delegation to Palestine, http://marthiemombergblog.com/tag/south-african-church-delegation-to-palestine (accessed 24 June, 2016).

[12] Mark 1:15.

and ultimately a Provincial Synod is likely to do the same. This will be a powerful signal for the rest of the South African church to follow.

In 2014, after the latest Gaza war, the biggest march in democratic South Africa was held in Cape Town on 9th August 2014. Archbishop-emeritus Desmond Tutu and the current moderator of the Uniting Reformed Church of Southern Africa, Dr Mary-Anne Plaatjies van Huffel, addressed this mass gathering of support for the people of Gaza.

Finally, Kairos Southern Africa has now initiated an art project called 'Via Dolorosa' to paint 8m x 2m paintings of the fourteen Stations of the Cross from a Palestinian perspective. Once this project is completed, the painting will travel throughout the world, allowing Christians across the world to reflect on the suffering of the Palestinian people in the light of the Passion Story, and to make decisions about how to engage with that situation, which has been described by Mitri Raheb as one of 'empire'.

Conclusion

This chapter begins to show how the 'Kairos moment' of South Africa in 1985 has inspired the Palestine Kairos Document of 2009 and how this has now reinspired sections of the South African church community, particularly Kairos Southern Africa, to draw comparative theological lines between apartheid in South Africa and the occupation of Palestine by the state of Israel, a state that is often lauded by many Christians throughout the world. It pre-empts the possibility that the world church will once again be awakened to the reality of evil and how theology may be used to justify oppression of one people by another. While South African apartheid was a form of localised racism, the occupation of Palestine can only be seen as a form of globalised racism and a global theology of Christian Zionism that informs much Christian thinking about the state of Israel. The narrative of Israel as an apartheid state is therefore an important first step in distancing the world church from the theological justification of the oppression of the Palestinian people.

Bibliography

Not much of the work contained in this chapter is contained in books, but the following will help readers to understand the reason for the work being done in South Africa:

Ateek, Naim, *A Palestinian Christian Cry for Reconciliation*. Maryknoll, NY: Orbis Books, 2008.
Boesak, Alan, *Kairos, Crisis, and Global Apartheid*. New York: Palgrave MacMillan, 2015.
Braverman, Mark, *Fatal Embrace*. Austin, TX: Synergy Publications, 2010.
De Gruchy, John, *The Church Struggle in South Africa*. London: SCM Press, 2004.
Nolan, Albert, *God in South Africa*. Grand Rapids, MI: Eerdmans, 1988.
Raheb, Mitri, *Faith in the Face of Empire*. Bethlehem, Palestine: Diyar Publishers, 2014.
Tutu, Desmond, *God is not a Christian*. Johannesburg, South Africa: Rider, 2011.

(115) The Future and Challenges of African Ecumenism

André Karamaga

Introduction

The Christian faith is, and remains, contagious in such a way that those who adhere to it adapt it and integrate it into their context, but they cannot really live according to it and enjoy it without transmitting it to others. It is this imperative of transmitting the faith received and contextualized in conjunction with socio-cultural dynamics that we call Christian mission.

Considered up to now as a mission field, Africa has a major challenge in re-examining its responsibility vis-à-vis the Universal Church of Christ which is deepening its roots on the continent.

The Church in Africa, for which we need to explore the way it could be one, according to Jesus' prayer, has a special profile which has never existed anywhere else. In some African countries, the number of denominations is estimated to be more than 5,000.

It is also worth mentioning that the church (or churches) which considers itself as invested of the mission to change situations is not immune from the influence and conditioning of that same situation. Obviously, whether it is in Africa or elsewhere, this responsibility of making sure the Church of Christ develops and has a future primarily rests on Christian men and women, and specifically on those of them who are at various levels of responsibility in the church. Indeed, they must remain aware of the fact that we belong to the church and that this Church that we consider ours and wrongly refer to as 'our Church', doesn't belong to us at all. The Church belongs to Christ, its head and its Lord who, because of his grace and his infinite love, has associated us with his ministry of shepherd and preacher of the gospel of salvation. Consequently, any church leader, at whatever level, has to take their responsibility seriously, not only out of respect for Christ, but also because of the ministry (service) and the mandate we have voluntarily subscribed to in response to our vocation (calling).

We will then try in the following pages to understand the dynamics and the basis of our responsibility, oriented towards a better future based on values of the gospel which, once they are rooted in our cultural universe, can only generate hope and dignity.

The African Church is not an entity separate from the Universal Church. One of its main responsibilities, which we will try to understand, is to contribute to life, to the testimony and the credibility of the Universal Church, which is the body of Christ, the African Church is organically and spiritually part and parcel of it.

The Chances of the African Church

How can we then refer to the ethical implications of spirituality, which undoubtedly are now part and parcel, not only of the life but also of the survival of African populations, without letting comparison about the shortcomings block us, as if our failure could justify another?

Moreover, when there is an effort to situate the church in Africa in the context of the global Church, one realizes that the roots of the African Church can be traced back to the period before Christianity. For instance, how can the fact that the Israelites spent more than four hundred years in the African continent at a period where material and cultural exchanges among different regions of the continent were frequent, not be taken into account? Can the reality of these exchanges between the African peoples and the Israelites explain the fact that there are striking similarities between African monotheism and the biblical one? I will come back to such concerns later on.

In any case, the stay of the Israelites in Africa is not an episodic detail, since it is associated with the founding of the Israelites through the hospitality granted to Joseph when he was sold as a slave. This successful reception and integration culminated in his promotion to the rank of Prime Minister (Gen. 41:37-49). Indeed, if the benediction and reconciliation which occurred in Africa between the sons of Jacob did not take place, it would have been impossible, later on, to talk about the Israelites as a people and as a nation.

In the year 721 BC, when Samaria, the capital of Israel, was conquered by the Assyrians, and later, in 587 BC, Jerusalem, the capital of Judah, by the Babylonians, the Israelites were scattered not only in Europe, but also in Northern Africa[1]

Young person Schaaf and Kwame Bediako (1994) have indicated that during the four centuries before Jesus-Christ, the Jews settled in the whole of the Near East, in Egypt, in Northern Africa, in Sudan up to Ethiopia.'[2] Let us also underline the fact that the Old Testament, the whole of the holy books of the Israelites which later became the Holy Scriptures for Christians, was translated from Hebrew into Greek in Alexandria, in Egypt, during the third century BC as the first missionary translation of the Bible called 'the Septuagint'.

Moreover, according to the story recounting what happened on the day of Pentecost, Africans were also present at this crucial time of what the history of the church considers as the birthday of the church (Acts 2:9-11). The story of the Ethiopian eunuch, baptized by Philip (Acts 8: 26-40), and that of Simon of Cyrene, known for having carried Jesus' cross (Mark 15:21) are proof of the presence of Africa at the beginning of Christianity. The rapid expansion of the faith which conquered the north of Africa up to Ethiopia, producing such eminent theologians as Tertullian and St Augustine, are well stated by historians. Indeed, in the fourth century AD, 20% of Christians during that time were Africans. It is well known that this rapid expansion of Christianity in Africa was seriously affected by the arrival of Islam in the seventh century AD.

The One God, the Basis of Unity

Some stories of the evangelization of Africa give the impression that God was imported into Africa by western missionaries. This impression is even stronger when African Christianity is considered as a new faith incarnated in an empty space which was waiting to be filled with a new, universal and timeless religion. This conception is not only misleading, but is also insufficiently informed about Africa and Christianity. For, on one hand, Africa and its inhabitants should not be considered as empty vessel that some foreigners came to fill, without foundations or references to their spiritual experience. On the other hand, the Christian faith is neither a set of doctrines that are out of time, nor an experience of life that can be handed out of a specific geographical or socio-historic context.

After a long debate carried on during the twentieth century, often based on lack of information and sometimes on prejudice, there are two aspects of the truth of traditional religion that we can consider as obvious: on one hand, there is the belief in one transcendent God that can be found in every corner of the African continent. This belief which is experienced and carried by successive generations since the mists of time, is confirmed by the existence in each African language of a name used to refer to God, with

[1] John Stevenson, *A Survey of the Old Testament: The Bible Jesus Used* (Hollywood, CA: Redeemer Publishing: 2008).

[2] Ype Schaaf and Kwame Bediako. *On their Way Rejoicing: The History and Role of the Bible in Africa* (Carlisle, UK: Paternoster Press, 1994).

connotations which give an idea of the conception people have of him. This fact shows the striking similarities between monotheistic Judaism and Christianity.

Thus, it is not possible to recognize the reality of monotheism in the African spiritual landscape and still refer to the African Traditional Religion as 'animism'. Let us be reminded that this expression 'animism' was introduced by Edward Tylor who was trying to describe Mexican beliefs which, according to him, were reduced to the submission of the diffuse forces which govern the universe.[3]

If we take as our starting-point the view that the debate over the recognition of African monotheism is closed, a debate which, in other respects, was linked with the way Africans were implicitly viewed, we can affirm that this monotheism constitutes an extraordinary opportunity for the church in Africa.

Whether it is today or in the past, when people speak about God, they don't always realize that they are referring to the Supreme Being who preceded us, not only in time and space, but also as existing within the African people they are talking about. As for Africa, people go to the extent of expressing their impatience in continually hearing speeches from those who try to convince them of the existence of God, while they already believe in this God. Evangelization in Africa does not consist in proving the existence of God, but by showing the signs and the tangible manifestations of God's presence. And according to the message transmitted by Jesus Christ to the disciples of John the Baptist when they came to confirm if he was really the one sent from God; Jesus underlined the fact that, when God is in a nation, things change and victory of life over death becomes a reality (Matt. 11:1-6).

More importantly, faith in the one transcendent God is shared not only by Christians and aspects of some African Traditional Religions, but also with Muslims. And this is not a detail of no importance, since the demarcation line between these three forms of faith which conquered African spirituality is largely unclear.

Indeed, at both demographic and geographic levels, the co-existence of the aspects of these three faiths is a striking reality. For instance, it is not a rare occurrence to find Christians, Muslims and aspects of traditional religion living together in the same family and sharing in their daily life.

Is not this belief in one God shared by the majority of Africans really an opportunity which can serve as the basis of peace, harmony and strong unity?

In order to seize this opportunity, all African Christians and Muslims must broaden their vision beyond Africa in order to help the world abandon its present tendency of seeking to transform religion into an ideology and changing it into an instrument of hatred and violence.

The Church Inherited by Africa

Those who look at statistics and numerical progression indicators say that Africa is increasingly becoming the new cradle of world Christianity.[4]

We can highlight a number of dynamics which seem to determine the configuration of situations on this continent whose populations have been considered as 'incurably religious', an expression introduced by the Kenyan theologian, John Mbiti.[5]

African Christianity is characterized by diversity of expression and of ecclesial organization which have never been observed anywhere else. There are, on the one hand, the various congregations of the Catholic Church and those of the Orthodox family and, on the other hand, the Protestant variety of churches.

First, Christianity in Africa is diverse because of the various origins of its denominations. For example, in the same country, a Baptist church from America has a different ecclesial organization from a Baptist

[3] (Sir) Edward Burnet Tylor, *Primitive Culture* (two vols), (London: John Murray, 1871).

[4] See Lamin Sanneh and Joel A. Carpenter (eds.), *The Changing Face of Christianity: Africa, the West, and the World* (Oxford: OUP, 2005).

[5] John S. Mbiti, *African Religions and Philosophy* (London: Heinemann, 1969).

church of Scandinavian origin. Thus, in a given country, it is not rare to find four or five churches of the same confession operating as administratively different entities from each another.

But the diversity in African Christianity is determined not only by geographical origins. It is even more obviously seen in churches referred to as 'independent', founded by African preachers which, for the most part and for various reasons, are different from the denominations founded by foreign missionaries.

Nevertheless, schematically, African Christianity can be classified under four categories depending on the origin and the history of the tendencies which form it:

1. The first category is made up of denominations which were imported into the continent by former slaves which were liberated and brought back to some of the coastal countries of West Africa. During their stay in the countries where they were taken as slaves, several Africans turned to Anglicanism, Methodism or Presbyterianism. When they came back to the continent, these Africans founded Anglican, Methodist or Presbyterian churches, which today are mainly active in Sierra Leone, the Gambia and Liberia.
2. The second category is made up of denominations which are the result of missionary work from the eighteenth century, including the Catholic Church working closely with the Orthodox Church.
3. The third category is composed of churches referred to as indigenous (independent), working together through the Organization of African Instituted Churches (OAIC), with its headquarters in Nairobi, Kenya.
4. The fourth category is that of Pentecostal ecclesial communities whose number is steadily increasing in a spectacular way. These churches, which call themselves Evangelical, also have an alliance which gathers them together and which has its headquarters in Nairobi, Kenya.

There is no clear demarcation between these four categories. A lot of Africans find it strange to make a distinction between Christians called ecumenical and others called evangelical! Should the true Christian not be both ecumenical and evangelical?

The Challenge of New 'Christian' Denominations

If we have decided to dedicate a separate section to these new groups which identify themselves as 'churches', it doesn't mean that we refuse to recognize them as such, as part of African Christianity. We don't have the right to judge or harbour a prejudice about the viability or the inadequacy of this or that community which claims the identity or the status of church. But the real question to ask is what would be the attitude to adopt vis-à-vis a new religious movement which emerges in this or that context. Such a question is not new. The Christian memory keeps vivid the story of the wisdom of Gamaliel concerning the new Christian groups after the launch of the Christian movement.

'Men of Israel, consider carefully what you intend to do with these men. Some time ago, Theudas appeared, claiming to be somebody and about four hundred men rallied to him. He was killed, all his followers were dispersed, and it all came to nothing. After him, Judas the Galilean appeared in the days of the census and led a band of people in revolt. He too was killed, and his followers were scattered. Therefore, in the present case I advise you: Leave these men alone! Let them go! For if their purpose and activity is of human origin, it will fail. But if is from God, you will not be able to stop these men; you will only find yourselves fighting against God.' (Acts 5: 35-39).

Currently, spiritual groups of all varieties, whose number goes beyond understanding, have emerged and claim to be churches. In Angola, for example, there are more than 800 groups which have requested to be recognized as churches with a legal entity.

In his book, 'Le Saint-Esprit interroge les esprits' (The Holy Spirit is Interrogating the Spirits), Masamba Ma Mpolo recounts how this kind of movement is experienced in DRC and specifically in its capital Kinshasa where, he argues, gatherings and prayer groups – organized in homes, bars and drinking dens, in streets and public markets – are swarming, and where preacher-evangelists are even setting themselves up in buses.[6] Many people wonder how to react to this phenomenon which follows the rule of the free market of everything, including illusion.

Where are We Coming from?

The fact that, in most cases, missionaries had forbidden the integration of African cultural elements in Christian liturgy and in the life of the church, had created a reaction after African churches gained their autonomy. Mission were put on the same level as colonization, until people forgot the eminent role played by some missionaries in the endorsement of African languages and in the fight against illiteracy.

This reaction differed depending on where the situation was observed and analyzed, whether it was in local communities or places of reflection such as theological institutions.

It was also the period where theological students started writing their papers on the value of traditional structures of the group of origin (for example, the notion of God amongst different groups of people, the role of initiation, and comparison between marriage in a given ethnic group and in the Bible, etc.).

In theological conferences, themes such as polygamy, funeral rites and even traditional religion as a coherent set of beliefs, have been studied seriously and sometimes in an openly 'apologetic' way in their favour. There is, nevertheless, this striking fact: nobody dare translate these reflections in conferences and in theological training institutes with a clear desire to endorse African culture into specific decisions to integrate this or that element considered as positive in the structured life of the church.

Even deeper, in theological faculties as well as in various conferences and seminars, reflections on the enculturation of the gospel reached conclusions which maybe could explain the hesitation of Africans to introduce their cultural values into the liturgy and the life of the church. Indeed, from the moment when African cultures ceased to be seen as primitive, people realized that these cultures served as support and source of the life that our ancestors managed to maintain and transmit to successive generations from time immemorial. But people also understood that religion is the pivot of culture, and we cannot define culture without taking into account its religious dimension.

For Africa, traditional religions wrongly considered as 'animism', proved to be a coherent monotheism which presented striking similarities with the monotheism of the Bible. Even though this was an uplifting discovery, it came as a major blow to the 'enculturation approach' of the gospel we mentioned briefly above. The main issue was how to integrate this or that African value into the life of the church without falling into the trap of syncretism, which was considered by some missionaries as the worst of sins, because it is true that every element and every cultural value undoubtedly has a religious dimension. It is because of this fear of syncretism that the church of Africa has continued welcoming and receiving inspiration from people and communities imbued with cultural values and elements, which it has not dared integrate into its life. Everybody knows the consequence of this confusion that we may consider to be the worst type of syncretism. On the one hand, there is the risk of having Christians who are living a double life: they celebrate in church, but they use African approaches to solve the problems of daily life. On the other hand, there is the risk of having individuals and communities who choose to continue considering their cultural origins negatively, a situation that becomes a tragic battle, denying oneself. An African proverb says that a person can run away from something that is running after them, but nobody can run away from what is inside them.

The choice – or rather, the fear – of going to the limit of the enculturation process of the gospel in Africa for fear of syncretism hides another reality: we forget that the model of Christianity that we

[6] Masamba, Ma Mpolo, Jean, *Le Saint-Esprit interroge les esprits: Essai de relecture et pistes psycho-pastorales de la spiritualité en Afrique: Cas de la République démocratique du Congo* (Cameroun: Éditions Clé, 2002).

internalized is undoubtedly a syncretistic one. Nevertheless, if this enculturation process of the gospel in Africa somehow lost momentum, the journey never ended. The present question is to ask ourselves where we are at this time in our journey towards church unity.

Where Are We?

The question about where we are in the enculturation process of the gospel in Africa has to be preceded by two admissions:

- The first one is to recognize that the church became implanted in Africa and it has become an undoubted reality in spite of its defying complexity.
- The second one is to recognize that Africa, which is progressively becoming the main pillar of world Christianity, will certainly put its mark on this the faith which is in the process of configuration, one way or another. The generations which are going to follow therefore have a huge responsibility, especially our generation which has witnessed radical changes.

After these two admissions, allow me to ask the questions I have been asking myself since I started reflecting on the enculturation process of the gospel in Africa:

1. Have there been in other places and at other times of the history of the church concerns similar to the ones we are having about the enculturation of the gospel in any given context? For example, who were the theologians who accompanied the missionary work of Paul (apart from Paul himself) to implant the gospel in the cultures of the peoples that this apostle evangelized?
2. Do we have the right to call into question the fact that our respective churches which are present and active, even in the midst of our tragedies, are not yet really African?
3. Do our churches really feel the value of the efforts and strategies that we invest in, in order to implant the gospel message in our cultures?

These questions become even more complicated when we realize that the expression 'enculturation' has become a synonym for 'incarnation'. Enculturation is not different from the incarnation of Christ at the centre of our realities. If such is the case, would it be legitimate to pretend to incarnate Christ and his gospel, while the initiative is God's in his total Sovereignty?

We have here fundamental questions that we bring back to the table, but not for aggravating the loss of momentum of the enculturation process, which will determine the future of ecumenism in Africa.

It is in the depth of this battle that God and his gospel come to meet us and, just as Jacob did, we would not let him go until he blesses us.

Where Are We Heading?

We have just positioned ourselves and we didn't have the time to position our churches vis-à-vis the battle between life and death for the survival and the dignity of our countries and our continent. Any African entity, and especially any church, which takes the promise of the gospel to give life in abundance to every human being seriously, does not have the right to overlook the seriousness of the battle between life and death that our populations are facing. We can no longer continue managing the contradiction between the 'life in abundance' promised by the gospel and the abundance of misery which is killing our people in a continent which has now become the cradle of today's Christianity.

Considering the seriousness of the situation, our cultural references themselves lose their viability and their raison d'être. Can we really celebrate God joyfully when our children have come to the point of taking the risk to be thrown into oceans while trying to run away from their continent? What cultural value is there behind the desperate action of a mother who kills her child in order to fill her body with a certain amount of drugs that she expects to sell once she reaches the other side of the sea? We are therefore at the forefront of this battle, and this is where the gospel meets us to help us resist the multiple forces of death which threaten us.

The light brought by Jesus in the enculturation process of the gospel in our context consists of starting at the points of reference which have guided our ancestors and our contemporaries to live together. For instance, Jesus would tell Africans, 'Your ancestors told you that it is strictly inconceivable to kill a woman, even in time of war, because a woman is the bearer of life and fertility, as for me, I tell you, not only that you should not kill a woman, but also that the sacredness of life and the integrity of creation must be respected'. Drawing from this message with faith and conviction, the African Church can definitely solve the sufferings imposed on women in war and acts of genocide which put our dignity to shame.

Ecumenism – or the Imperative of Unity

The unity of the church is not an option to take or to leave. It is a non-negotiable imperative tightly linked with the vocation and the essence of the church in remaining faithful to its Lord.

> 'My prayer is not for them alone. I pray also for those who will believe in me through their message, that all of them may be one, Father, just as you are in me and I am in you. May they also be in us so that the world may believe that you have sent me' (John 17:20-21).

A cry from the heart, a wish or a prayer? These words – considered as Jesus' in the gospel according to John – carry a message which goes beyond a purely organizational strategy given by a master who is about to release his students into society for them to implement what they have learnt. The one who is pouring out his heart before his father to magnify the imperative of unity, is also God, to whom all Christian prayer is addressed. We thus have here an interesting situation whereby the one who has the power to fulfil prayer emphasizes, in the form of a request, what he is ready to give, the basis of his intimate relationship with his father. This is therefore a choice whose weight and gravity go hand-in-hand with our faithfulness to Christ and to the mandate of unity that he is giving us to be witnesses of his kingdom of peace, love and justice in this divided world.

Having clarified this, let's come back to the situation in Africa in order to try to see if we can consider the fragmented landscape that our present Christianity offers. We are faced with the dilemma of a glass which is half-filled which some will see, negatively, as half-empty, while others will see, positively, as half-full! In other words, African Christianity offers an image with two contradicting faces.

An understandable pride

On the one hand, there is the image of a giant, when one looks at Christianity's exceptional numerical growth and its dynamism based both on its youth and the intensity of its strikingly vibrant spirituality. This image settles more and more into our subconscious to such an extent that it creates a certain pride and a feeling that we are now part of a spiritual movement which will influence, one way or the other, the future and the fate of Africa and world Christianity.

This pride is reinforced and even turns into joy and celebration when members of the Christian family trust us and give to any of us major responsibility.

Justifiable worries

The image of the giant applied to the African Church in the context of world Christianity can be based on relatively understandable considerations.

I even heard a preacher explain that the African Church is becoming more and more as though the parable of the mustard seed was being realized, the seed which a man took and planted in his field and which grew to become a big tree so that the birds of the air come and perch in its branches (Matt. 13: 31).

These images are wonderfully encouraging as they counterbalance, in a way, the Afro-pessimism that many people experience today, including some Africans who have no hopeful points of reference.

But let us also take into account the fact that there are people who depart from these two optimistic images to take the reflection further and see things from a critical perspective.

It is true that the African Church has become numerically huge, such that we have the right to be proud and grateful for it. For many, it represents an inexhaustible reservoir of faith in life and of strength in the fight for survival. In that sense, it is comparable with that big tree that the weak lean on and from which they sing together, like the birds of the air which glorify the Lord in their own way, as the parable says.

But don't we have the right to twist the parable in order to demand from the big tree that it may produce fruit in abundance so that the birds do not have to sing on an empty stomach? In that case, we can be sure that the songs of praise and commitment to build love, peace and dignity as a sign of the kingdom of God in this world will take over the songs of flight to a faraway sky that our multiple youth choirs, throughout the continent, are singing.

Still, we have the duty to take into consideration people who consider our gigantic church to be a giant with clay feet! This type of worry is fundamentally based on the situation of fragmentation we mentioned above.

What is more frightening in the case of Africa is the confusion between ethnic groups and Christian denominations. If, just as we said, this is not specific to Africa, let's recognize that taking such a challenge with other fragilities linked with history can lead to unpredictable consequences.

In other words, since Africa has more than 2,600 ethnic groups and Christian denominations formed in many cases according to ethnic entities, how can we think of the unity of the church which is supposed to be a ferment of African unity and the unity of mankind? Let's quickly acknowledge that this question becomes more complicated with the emergence of multi-party systems, when it is possible to find a group which has its own language, its own denomination and its own political party!

Based on the previous considerations, will it still be possible to consider our multiple diversities so trapped and so entangled with one another as an opportunity for the church in Africa? I remain convinced about it for the following reasons:

Primarily, the church is neither a given denomination nor a local church, nor even the family setting, as Paul took the liberty of stating it:

> Greet Priscilla and Aquila, my fellow-workers in Christ Jesus. They risked their lives for me. Not only I but all the churches of the Gentiles are grateful to them. Greet also the church that meets at their house (Rom. 16:3-5).

The church first and foremost consists of individuals so varied and diverse that. This in itself requires the need for harmony and understanding within such diversity. These individuals come from all ethnic and social categories, including children, young people, women, the sick, the poor, the rich, etc. Hence, the image of the church as a body is vital:

> The body is a unit, though it is made up of many parts; and though all its parts are many, they form one body. So it is with Christ. For we were all baptized by one Spirit into one body – whether Jews or Greeks, slaves or free – and we all given the one Spirit to drink (1 Cor. 12:12-13).

Conclusion

We can't find a better theology that is so clear and specific as the basis of management of the diversities of the multi-dimensional identities which are emerging today and which settle while opposing each other, be it in Africa or elsewhere. And it is in this perspective that we should base our approach and our strategies on Christ and his Spirit in order to break egoisms and denominational barriers to liberate them from their imprisonment at the individual, ethnic or national level. And this is not actually something that is theoretical, since we have examples of churches in Africa which have taken the plunge.

New ecumenical vision for the church in Africa must be at the top of our ecclesiological agenda.

Bibliography

Abuom, Agnes, 'Africa and the Ecumenical Movement.' In *For a New Africa: With Hope and Dignity*, edited by Nicholas Otieno. Geneva: WCC, 2004.

All Africa Conference of Churches, 'The Message of the Golden Jubilee Assembly, Kampala, Uganda', 3th 9th June 2013.

Amanze, James N. *A History of the Ecumenical Movement in Africa,* Gaborone: Pula Press, 1998.

Ma Mpolo, Masamba J., *Le Saint-Esprit interroge les esprits: essai de relecture et pistes psycho-pastorales de la spiritualité en Afrique: cas de la République démocratique du Congo*. Cameroun: Éditions Clé, 2002.

Mbiti, John S., *African Religions and Philosophy*. London: Heinemann, 1969.

Mugambi, Jesse K. 'Some Lessons from a Century of Ecumenism in Africa.' In *Efiong Utuk, Visions of Authenticity: The Assemblies of the All Africa Conference of Churches 1963-1992.* Nairobi: AACC, 1997.

Otieno, Nicholas (ed.), *For a New Africa: With Hope and Dignity*. Geneva: WCC Publications, 2004.

Sanneh, Lamin and Carpenter, Joel A. (eds.) *The Changing Face of Christianity: Africa, the West, and the World*. Oxford: Oxford University Press, 2005.

Setiloane, Gabriel. 'The Ecumenical Movement in Africa: From Mission Church to Moratorium.' In *Resistance and Hope: South African Essays in Honour of Beyers Naudé*, edited by Charles Villa-Vicencio and John de Gruchy, 137-147. Grand Rapids: Wm. B. Eerdmans, 1985.

Schaaf, Ype and Bediako, Kwame M. *On their Way Rejoicing: The History and Role of the Bible in Africa.* Carlisle, U.K.: Paternoster Press, 1994.

Stevenson, John. *A Survey of the Old Testament: The Bible Jesus Used*. Hollywood: Redeemer Publishing, 2008.

Tylor, (Sir) Edward B. *Primitive Culture*. (2 vols.). London: John Murray, 1871.

Part VI

Issues and Themes in African Christianity

(116) LEADERSHIP FORMATION AND EDUCATION IN AFRICAN CHRISTIANITY: HISTORICAL PERSPECTIVE[1]

Chammah J. Kaunda

Introduction

Leadership formation underscores the educational essence of theological institutions across denominational alliances in African Christianity. The key responsibility of theological education is to develop contextually shaped leadership with the competence and maturity required to function in the ever-changing African religious landscape. This article argues that theological institutions in Africa should be more deliberate in this purpose. It acknowledges that the current concern for leadership formation and education in African Christianity can only be understood against the background of the wider international developments in mission. Beginning with Edinburgh 1910, through to the integration of the International Missionary Conference (IMC) and World Council of Churches.[2] This background is necessary to understanding the development of leadership formation and education.

Historical Foundations, Development and Transformation

First, the history of Christian missions in Africa is the history of leadership formation and education. The dream of enhancing this in Africa was conceived in Edinburgh 1910, which had already called for gender-sensitivity in this endeavour. Scholars have demonstrated that in the aftermath of the conference, mission agencies remained beholden to a time-honoured patriarchal ideology.[3] It can also be argued that whereas leadership formation and education was perceived as necessary to give indigenous clergy confidence and pride as Africans, nevertheless it was also an instrument to develop docile leaders that could easily be controlled.

Second, leadership formation and education remained a major concern of the IMC at a conference held in Jerusalem in 1928. The catch-phrase at Jerusalem was, 'transfer of the responsibility and authority to the younger churches'.[4] Even at the IMC in Tambaram in 1938, the issues received major attention and a full section of the conference was dedicated to the issue of theological training in the 'younger churches'. In response to the IMC Tambaram 1938 recommendation, extensive studies were conducted in Africa from 1950 to 1953 in order to gain insights on what could be done to improve the quality of leadership formation

---

[1] This article is adapted from my doctoral thesis which was supervised by Prof Isabel Phiri and Prof Roderick Hewitt. The thesis gives a detailed discussion on the development o f theological education and ministry formation in Africa from Edinburgh 1910 to 2012. See Chammah J. Kaunda, 'Imagining a Just and Equitable African Christian Community': A Critical Analysis of the Contribution of Theological Education Fund/Ecumenical Theological Education (1910-2012)' Unpublished PhD Thesis (University of KwaZulu-Natal, Pietermaritzburg, 2013).

[2] Willem A. Visser 'THooft (ed.), *The New Delhi Report: The Third Assembly of the World Council of Churches 1961* (New York: Association Press, 1962), 56.

[3] More insightful articles on the question of theological education and ministry formation in Africa can be found in Dietrich Werner, David Esterline and Namsoon Kang (eds.), *Handbook of Theological Education in World Christianity:* Theological Perspectives, Ecumenical Trends, Religious Surveys (Oxford: Regnum Books International, 2010). For the argument on sidelining of women in ministry formation in African Christianity see, Klaus Fiedler, *The Story of Faith Missions: From Hudson Taylor to Present Day Africa* (Cumbria: Regnum Books International, 1994).

[4] International Missionary Council. *The Life of the Church: International Missionary Council Meeting at Tambaram, Madras, December 12-29, 1938, Tambaram Series Volume 4.* (London: Oxford University Press, 1939).

and education in Africa. The objectives of the survey were as follows: (i) to investigate the current state of theological education throughout Africa, (ii) to report on the trends and tendencies as they affect the recruiting, training and supporting the ministry of the church, and (iii) to make suggestions on the future development of African ecumenical theological education.[5] The survey was done in these three parts. The first was done by Stephen Neill in 1950 and covered East and West Africa.[6] The second was done by Searle Bates (Chairman)[7] and others in 1953 and covered Angola, Belgian Congo, French West Africa, French Equatorial Africa, Liberia, Mozambique and Ruanda-Urundi. The third was done by Norman Goodall and Eric W. Nielsen in 1953 and covered the then Union of South Africa, Southern and Northern Rhodesia and Nyasaland.[8] A critical evaluation of these reports reviews three aspects of leadership formation and education for missionaries: a) It was reserved for the ordained ministry to support a clergy-centred church. In many cases, it also became a tool for producing an elite professional class who were incapable of responding adequately 'to the needs of the masses, [being] preoccupied [instead] with position and privilege at the expense of dynamic, corporate ministry'.[9] b) It was perceived as an antidote against denominationalism and academic departmentalism. c) Whereas the Jerusalem Council of 1921 had made a shift in its ideology concerning other world faiths, these reports completely neglected the religious plurality in Africa.

Third, the formation of the Theological Education Fund (TEF) by IMC in Accra, Ghana, in 1958, with its successful transformation as the Programme for Theological Education and Ecumenical Theological Education, was strategic in the improvement of leadership formation and education in African Christianity. TEF had three mandates. The first mandate (1958-1965) attempted to raise scholarship, strove for academic excellence and scientific standards in theological education, and focused on the notion of 'indigenisation', in order to strengthen indigenous theological education. During this mandate, the All Africa Conference of Churches (AACC) was inaugurated in Kampala, Uganda, in April 1963. It has been argued that founding 'of the AACC marked the end of the missionary era and the beginning of the autonomy of African Churches.'[10] In the second mandate (1965-1970), under James Hopewell, TEF expressed both continuity and discontinuity with its first mandate. In the tradition of the first mandate, it had tried to strengthen ministerial training in 'the younger churches.' Yet, the situation was far more complex, involving the task of nation-building after colonialism and the need to achieve an authentic African self-hood.[11] Moreover, 'the consequences of neo-colonialism were just as clear in the world economy as they were in the world mission and education'.[12] Accordingly, TEF emphasized the missionary

---

[5] Dyron Daughrity, 'Bishop Stephen Neill, the IMC and the State of African Theological Education in 1950', *Studies in World Christianity*, 18, no. 1, (2012): 41-64.

[6] Stephen Neill, *Survey of the Training of the Ministry in Africa Part 1: Report of a Survey of Theological Education in East and West, with Special Reference to the Training of the Ordained Ministry, Undertaken in April to July, 1950, Under the Auspices of the International Missionary Council* (London and New York: International Missionary Council, 1950). WCC-TEF Archives, Box 26.31.39, Genève.

[7] Searle Bates, Christian G Baëta, Frank Michaeli and Bengt G. M. Sundkler, *Survey of the Training of the Ministry in Africa Part 1: Report of a Survey of Theological Education in Angola, Belgian Congo, French West Africa, French Equatorial Africa, Liberia, Mozambique and Ruanda-Urundi, Undertaken in June to December, 1953* (London and New York: International Missionary Council, 1954). WCC-TEF Archives, Box 26.31.40, Genève.

[8] Norman Goodall and Eric W. Nielsen, *Survey of the Training of the Ministry in Africa Part III: Report of a Survey of Theological Education in the Union of South Africa, Southern and Northern Rhodesia, and Nyasaland, Undertaken in September to December 1953* (London and New York: International Missionary Council, 1954), WCC-TEF Archives, Box 26.31.44, Genève.

[9] Ross F. Kinsler, *The Extension Movement in Theological Education* (Pasadena: William Carey Library, 1981), 8.

[10] AACC, 'All Africa Conference of Churches', (2012). www.aacc-ceta.org/en/about-us.html (accessed 1 June 2015).

[11] TEF, *Ministry in Context: The Third Mandate Programme of the Theological Education Fund (1970-77)* (Bromley: Theological Education Fund, 1972), 12.

[12] Christine Lienemann-Perrin, *Training for a Relevant Ministry: A Study of the Theological Education Fund* (Madras

orientation and thrust which called for leadership formation and education that leads authentic encounter between Christian faith and socio-cultural experiences within the context.

For the first time, a recommendation from TEF linked the church's self-understanding of its mission with its appropriation and assimilation of the Christian gospel with the cultural milieu of the people. In the third mandate, Archbishop Desmond Mpilo Tutu served on the executive as the first African Region Director of TEF (from 1972 to 1974). Contextualization came to be perceived as 'a theological necessity demanded by the incarnational nature of the Christian faith'.[13]

The Current Historical Period – 1975-2015

First, TEF was officially integrated into the WCC in 1977 and renamed Programme for Theological Education (PTE) after several months of study. PTE as the successor focused on 'ministerial formation,' 'which was interpreted in the broadest sense to include all the people of God,' ordained and non-ordained, recognized by the churches for the practise of ministry in its multiple forms and theological meanings.[14] At the Fifth Assembly of the WCC, held for the first time on African soil in Nairobi, Kenya, in 1975, under the theme 'Jesus Christ Frees and Unites', the report on 'Education for Liberation and Community' was presented. It stressed that 'the threats to human survival now looming call for changes in the world far beyond minor reforms in the present system'.[15] Five elements were identified as emerging: comprehensive concept of ministry; holistic approach, formation and education; contextualization; ecumenical dimension; global solidarity.

Second, the theme of the consultation was 'Theological Education in Africa: Quo Vadimus?' Its theme sought to deal with the question of the future of leadership formation and education under four major themes: (i) theology, theological education, and the church; (ii) continuity and change; (iii) ecumenical perspectives and dimensions; (iv) funding.[16]

Third, the Kuruman Moffat Mission Consultation in 1995 came after PTE had been transformed in 1992 to the Ecumenical Theological Education (ETE) as a way to align theological education with the vision of the WCC. Kuruman identified four generalised aspects[17] of the renewing vision of African Christianity: holistic vision, healing vision, communal vision and an ecumenical vision. These aspects were too general and lacked specific strategies for the church to use in order to focus on present challenges in Africa.[18]

Fourth, the next critical stage was the consultation held in Kempton Park, Gauteng, South Africa, 17-22 September 2002. It considered the question: 'What kind of theologies and ethical value system inform and help shape the church, Christianity and ecumenism in Africa?'[19] The notable commitments of this

---

and Genève: WCC, 1981), 125.

[13] TEF, *Ministry in Context,* 19.

[14] WCC, *Central Committee Minutes of the Twenty-Ninth Meeting, Genève, Switzerland, 10-18 August 1976* (Genève: World Council of Churches, 1976), 1.

[15] WCC, *Workbook for the Fifth Assembly of the World Council of Churches, Nairobi, Kenya, 23 November – 10 December 1975* (Genève: World Council of Churches, 1995), 41.

[16] John S. Pobee and Joshua N. Kudadjie (eds.), *Theological Education in Africa: Quo Vadimus?* (Genève: World Council of Churches, 1990).

[17] For the critique of these aspects see Dietrich Werner, 'Viability and Ecumenical Perspectives for African Theological Education in Africa: Legacy and New Beginnings in Ecumenical Theological Education/World Council of Churches', *Missionalia,* 38, no. 2, (August 2010): 275-293.

[18] John W. de Gruchy, 'Renewal Out of Africa: A Report on the African Consultation on the Viability of Ecumenical Theological Formation, Moffat Mission, Kuruman, 1-6 August, 1995', *Ministerial Formation,* 71 (1995): 5-10.

[19] Nyambura J. Njoroge, 'WCC Activity Report', *Theological Education and Ecumenical Formation, Johannesburg, South Africa, Documents – Conference (16-22 Sep 2002)*: 1-7 at 2. WCC-ETE Archives, uncategorized, file: 6, Genève.

consultation were, first, the Circle of Concerned African Women Theologians had received encouragement for the participation of women in theological education and research and for their voices to be heard more. Second, the commitment to take on board concerns such as violence, HIV and other dread diseases, gender issues, the New Partnership for Africa's Development (NEPAD) and ecumenism had become a major concern of the ETE-based initiative for mainstreaming HIV and AIDS in theological education in Africa. This programme is now carried forward by the Ecumenical HIV and AIDS Initiative in Africa (EHAIA). Third, the commitment to address the concerns of people with disabilities (by incorporating sign language subjects in theological curricula) has been vigorously applied by the Ecumenical Disability Advocates Network (EDAN) in cooperation with the ETE/WCC.[20] Fourth, was the commitment to support and encourage the networking of all TEE efforts to share materials and standardize qualifications.[21]

Fifth, the Ninth AACC General Assembly in Maputo, Mozambique, in 2008 under the theme 'Africa, Step Forth in Faith' was crucial in revitalising the vision for leadership formation and education. Four imperatives emerged: (i) the search for unity, (ii) the restoration of human dignity, (iii) the quest for peace, and (iv) ecumenical formation.[22] These imperatives remain critical in Africa, especially with the threats of religious extremism and homophobia.

Sixth, in the post-Maputo era (2009-2014), there have been various initiatives in transforming leadership formation and education. There are some notable trajectories, trends and achievements. First was the critical involvement of the AACC as a piloting instrument for the continental synchronization of theological education, in order to enhance its prophetic voice in communities overwhelmed by traumatic existential challenges. Second, there has been a revitalization of African associations of theological education since 2009. Third, the publication of the significant *Handbook of Theological Education in Africa* was a milestone in ecumenical co-operation in leadership formation and education. This 1,110-page volume under the editorial leadership of Isabel Phiri and Dietrich Werner, published in 2013 by Regnum Studies in Global Christianity and Cluster Publications in South Africa, brought together over one hundred scholars across denominations in Africa and the global ecumenical family.[23] Fourth is the current book project on an *Anthology of African Christianity* – a research project of WCC from 2013 to 2016, which is collaborative research to give a concise description of all major African Church families and traditions and a coherent picture of the current state and trends in African Christianity. This project is significant as it presents information on African Christianity's various facets, traditions, rapid processes of change, how Christianity is being expressed in indigenous forms, and its contribution to social and political development on the continent.

The seventh significant development came from the three joint conferences of academic societies in religion and theology of Southern Africa. The first conference took place in June 2009, hosted by the Faculty of Theology at Stellenbosch University. The ETE-WCC, in joint co-operation with the South African Missiological Society (SAMS) also gave its support. The second conference took place in June 2012, hosted by the School of Religion, Philosophy and Classics at the University of KwaZulu-Natal. The third is the recent launch of the first congress of the All Africa Academy of Theology and Religious Studies (AAATRS) of the AACC in February 2015. The AAATRS brought together African scholars across denominational affiliations and marked a new creative stage in the search for authentic leadership formation and education.

---

[20] See, Werner et al. (eds.), *Handbook of Theological Education in World Christianity.*

[21] See, Werner et al. (eds.), *Handbook of Theological Education in World Christianity.*

[22] Tharcisse Gatwa, 'All Africa Conference of Churches 9th General Assembly Theological Institute Maputo, 1-12 December 2008', *Report,* 1(2008): 1-38.

[23] For various articles on trends and perspectives in leadership formation and education please refer to Isabel Phiri and Dietrich Werner (eds), *Handbook of Theological Education in Africa* (Regnum: Regnum Studies in Global Christianity and Pietermaritzburg: Cluster Publications, 2013).

The eighth significant development is through the AACC process of mentoring younger African theologians through the methodology of African Theological Institute which was introduced at the Maputo Assembly in 2008 under the theme: 'Africa Step Forth in Faith'. The Institute also held its activities before and during the AACC 10th Assembly in 2013, which addressed the theme 'God of life, lead Africa to peace, justice and dignity'. These initiatives have continued to strengthen contextual theological reflections and programmes for theology, interfaith dialogue and ecumenism. The institutes have provided opportunities for young African theology students to engage and work for African ecumenical initiatives. It has given them opportunities for exposure to understand the place of African Christianity in global Christianity and to understand current theological trends on issues related to the future of African Christianity.

Ninth, there have been some significant milestones: a) the consolidation of the plans to launch a two-year Masters in Social Transformation (MST) at the Université Protestante au Congo, focusing on the issues of disabilities;[24] b) there has also been a serious focus on how to improve theological education for AIC leaders with regard to the theological education by extension programme;[25] c) the AATEEA Conference held in Ghana in October 2010 under the theme 'equipping and mobilizing all God's people for human transformation and ecological restoration: the role of TEE,' was another significant 'moment' in the development chain of African theological education; and d) is that which emerged from the consultation of the World Conference of Associations of Theological Institutions (WOCATI) held 4th-8th July 2011, in Johannesburg in South Africa.

There are other similar initiatives in Africa. I have focused on these because of their ecumenical significance. It can be argued that these initiatives are explicit pointers to the continuous struggle within African Christianity to find a dynamic ideological basis to undergird leadership formation and education for African Christianity for an African continent in search of socio-political and economic transformation.

Conclusion

The need for sound leadership formation and education has become more acute in contemporary African Christianity. This is precisely because the continent is facing new challenges that demand rethinking the ideological underpinning of leadership formation and education, because how the community of faith nurtures and equips its leaders determines its longevity and effectiveness. Leadership formation and education is crucial because it determines the future of the church. It is about shaping, moulding, nurturing and equipping leaders with new trans/contextual consciousness, in order to get a deeper understanding and appreciation of their personal, contextual and global experiences. As Christianity in Africa marches on an irreversible path towards an indefinable future, leadership formation and education must become the main priority on its agenda. The religio-social landscapes are so changing that it will take capable leadership to lead the church into the next phase of transformation. The ever-shifting religio-social landscapes have revolutionised human understanding of the socio-political and economic function of the Church so much that most of the previously cherished assumptions and paradigms that undergirded leadership formation and education have become obsolete. The question is no longer about proving the existence of God or mind games in theologizing but how human apprehension of God can transform the heart and nurture and develop insights and skills essential for the practice of socially responsive pastoral ministry.

---

[24] Phiri and Werner, *Handbook of Theological Education in Africa.*

[25] OAIC, 'Organization of African Instituted Churches: Consultation on AIC Theology and Ministerial Formation, Karen, Nairobi, 1-3 December 2009', *Consultation* (December 2009), 1-31.

Bibliography

Bates, Searle, Christian G. Baëta, Frank Michaeli and Bengt Sundkler. *Survey of the Training of the Ministry in Africa Part 1: Report of a Survey of theological education in Angola, Belgian Congo, French West Africa, French Equatorial Africa, Liberia, Mozambique and Ruanda-Urundi, Undertaken in June to December, 1953*. London and New York: International Missionary Council, 1994. WCC-TEF Archives, Box 26.31.40, Genève.

Daughrity, Dyron. 'Bishop Stephen Neill, the IMC and the State of African Theological Education in 1950.' *Studies in World Christianity* 18, no. 1, (2012): 41-64.

de Gruchy, John W. 'Renewal Out of Africa: A Report on the African Consultation on the Viability of Ecumenical Theological Formation, Moffat Mission, Kuruman, 1-6 August, 1995.' *Ministerial Formation* 71 (1995): 5-10.

Fiedler, Klaus. *The Story of Faith Missions: From Hudson Taylor to Present Day Africa*. Cumbria: Regnum Books International, 1994.

Gatwa, Tharcisse. 'All Africa Conference of Churches 9th General Assembly Theological Institute Maputo, 1-12 December 2008' *Report* (2008): 1-38.

Goodall, Norman and Eric W. Nielsen. *Survey of the Training of the Ministry in Africa Part III: Report of a Survey of Theological Education in the Union of South Africa, Southern and Northern Rhodesia, and Nyasaland, Undertaken in September to December 1953*. London and New York: International Missionary Council, 1954. WCC-TEF Archives, Box 26.31.44, Genève.

International Missionary Council. *The Life of the Church: International Missionary Council Meeting at Tambaram, Madras, December 12-29, 1938, Series Tambaram Series, 4*. London: Oxford University Press, 1939.

Kinsler, Ross F. *The Extension Movement in Theological Education*. Pasadena: William Carey Library, 1981.

Lienemann-Perrin, Christine. *Training for a Relevant Ministry: A Study of the Theological Education Fund.* Madras and Genève: WCC, 1981.

Neill, Stephen. *Survey of the Training of the Ministry in Africa Part 1: Report of a Survey of Theological Education in East and West Africa, with Special Reference to the Training of the Ordained Ministry, Undertaken in April to July, 1950, Under the Auspices of the International Missionary Council*. London and New York: International Missionary Council, 1950. WCC-TEF Archives, Box 26.31.39, Genève.

Njoroge, Nyambura J. 'WCC Activity Report,' *Theological Education and Ecumenical Formation, Johannesburg, South Africa, Documents-Conference,* 16-22 Sep 2002. WCC-ETE Archives, uncategorized, file: 6, Genève, 1-7.

OAIC. 'Organization of African Instituted Churches: Consultation on AIC Theology and Ministerial Formation, Karen, Nairobi, 1-3 December 2009,' *Consultation* (December 2009): 1-31.

Pobee, John S. and Joshua N. Kudadjie (eds.). *Theological Education in Africa: Quo Vadimus?* Genève: World Council of Churches & Accra: Asempa Publishers, 1990.

TEF. *Ministry in Context: The Third Mandate Programme of the Theological Education Fund (1970-77).* Bromley: Theological Education Fund, 1972.

Visser 't Hooft, Willem A. (ed.). *The New Delhi Report: The Third Assembly of the World Council of Churches 1961.* New York: Association Press, 1962.

WCC. *Workbook for the Fifth Assembly of the World Council of Churches, Nairobi, Kenya, 23 November – 10 December 1975*. Genève: World Council of Churches, 1975.

WCC. *Central Committee Minutes of the Twenty-Ninth Meeting, Genève, Switzerland, 10-18 August 1976.* Genève: World Council of Churches, 1976.

Werner, Dietrich, David Esterline, Namsoon Kang & Joshva Raja (eds.). *Handbook of Theological Education in World Christianity: Theological Perspectives, Ecumenical Trends, Regional Surveys.* Oxford: Regnum Books International, 2010.

Werner, Dietrich. 'Viability and Ecumenical Perspective for African Theological Education: Legacy and New Beginnings in Ecumenical Theological Education/World Council of Churches.' *Missionalia* 38 no. 2 (August 2010): 275-293.

(117) Phenomenology and the Politics of Naming in African Christianity

Eliot Tofa

Introduction

This chapter is on phenomenology and the politics of naming in African Christian Ministries (ACMs). The point is that the rapid proliferation of ACMs has not only precipitated a radical departure in the naming of Christian churches but has transformed the face of Christianity in Africa today. To this end, the chapter submits that the 'idioms and new ideas of missions had a tremendous influence on the prophetic, spiritual African churches',[1] and by so doing 'helped to ensure that they would emerge as Christian churches rather than as re-statements of African religion'.[2] The adoption of designations (such as prophet, man/woman of God, pastor, bishop, senior pastor, spiritual father, general overseer, and academic titles such as professor, doctor, etc.) are often adopted as a marketing strategy for ACMs as part of an authentic representation of the message of Jesus Christ and that of his *true* followers.

Naming of Christian Churches: A Historical Perspective

The birth of naming within ACMs is understood as a nuanced response to a changing religious landscape and a need for self-definition. Today, some of these churches have gone beyond borders, adopting 'symbols, techniques and ideas which they find to be more appropriate or useful in coping with (the) new and wider world that was intruding upon them, an encounter that occurred at several levels of African religious systems.'[3] For that reason, traditional titles (such as bishop, reverend, deacon, priest, etc.) commonly used in the so-called mainline churches – Roman Catholic and Protestant – have not only been adopted but broadened to include distinctive family titles (relational), such as *baba* (father), *amai* (mother), high reverend, spiritual father, and academic titles such as professor, doctor, prophet and so on. This chapter, therefore, briefly highlights some of the common titles, explaining why naming is important in African Christianity and how this informs the character as well as nature of Christianity on the continent.

On the Politics of Naming in African Initiated Churches

A name is a label that defines what these ACMs represent – who they are – and is used as a marketing strategy. The naming of these churches is therefore highly politicised. The names of ACMs, in the author's view, are not only a marketing strategy but are 'idioms' of 'the experience of prophecy, the desire for spiritual healing, the desire to eradicate witchcraft, the experience of spiritual possession, and the passion for creating holy places.'[4] To illustrate this point, let us take a look at some of the names of ACMs and designation(s) of the founding superintendents:

- Amazing Grace Christian Assembly in Ghana – Pastor
- Bread of Life in Swaziland – Prophet
- Charismatic Redeemed Ministries International in Malawi – Apostle (aka General Overseer)

---

[1] O.T. Ranger, 'African Initiated Churches', in *Transformation*, 24, no. 2, (2007): 65.
[2] Ranger, 'African Initiated Churches', 65.
[3] R. Strayer, 'Mission History in Africa: New Perspectives on an Encounter.' *African Studies Review* Vol. 19 (1976):1-15, 2.
[4] Ranger, 'African Initiated Churches', 65.

- Destiny International Christian Center in Swaziland – Reverend
- Zion Christian Church, Moria – Reverend Bishop Dr
- Turn Right Ministries Inc – Rev Doctor Bishop, Pastor, Overseer, Prophet
- Aladura – Pope Living Testimonies for Jesus Bible Ministry in Ghana, with branches in Europe, the United States of America and the Middle East – Minister
- *Guta RaJehovah* in Zimbabwe – *Mai* (Shona for 'mother')
- Jesus Calls Worship Centre in Swaziland – Apostle
- *Johanne Marange* Apostolic Church in Zimbabwe, Democratic Republic of Congo, Botswana, South Africa, Zambia, Malawi, etc. and the United States of America – High Priest
- *Johane Masowe wechishane* in Zimbabwe – *Madzibaba* (Shona for 'father')
- Winners Chapel (aka Living Faith Church) in Nigeria, with branches across the world – Reverend
- Redeemed Christian Church of God in Nigeria with several branches in Africa – Botswana, Lesotho, Mozambique etc. and beyond – President/Pastor
- Synagogue Church of All Nations in Nigeria – Man of God
- Turning Point International Christian Centre in South Africa – Minister
- Zion Christian Church Mutendi/Nehemiah in Zimbabwe – Bishop

The names given above are certainly a summary of a holistic interpretation that founders, followers or potential followers attach to the name. This is also true for descriptions of designations and positions in 'mushrooming' ACMs. When one looks at such names of churches and designations of the leader, it is conspicuous that names are of great significance. From the titles such as *baba* (father) or *amai* (mother), it appears African culture has contributed significantly in the naming of these churches. The thrust of the discussion is that founders of ACMs carefully consider options before settling for any given name, drawing from indigenous cultures as well as parent churches. The names, among other things, revolve around:

- The significance of the cross – Calvary Worship Centre, Jesus Calls Worship Centre, etc;
- Christian living – Light of Life, Turning Point, Amazing Grace, etc.
- Aspirations – Bread of Life, Redeemed Christian Church, etc.
- Sacred days – Johanne Masowe Wechishanu (of the fifth day or simply of Friday)
- Mountains – Zion, the City of David, e.g. Zion Christian Church

The names can border on 'factionalism', as suggested in naming churches after individual persons such as Mutendi/Nehemiah, Jesus, etc. On the other hand, it appears the founder's perception of the flora and fauna, certain scriptural texts, their mission and the desire for deliverance (not for everyone who has faith in Jesus but only for immediate church members) influences the naming of these voluntary organizations. Take Eagle's Wings, for example. The eagle appears about thirty-three times in the Bible with different symbolism: love, care, strength and majesty to express God's compassion for humankind (Ex. 19:4 – 'You have seen what I did to the Egyptians and how I bore you on eagles' wings and brought you to Myself'; Deut. 32:11-12 – 'As an eagle stirs up its nest, hovers over its young, spreading out its wings, taking them up, carrying them on its wings. So the Lord alone led him, and there was no foreign god with him'); fortitude and unwavering (Jer. 4:13 – 'Behold, he shall come up like clouds, and his chariots like a whirlwind. His horses are swifter than eagles. Woe to us, for we are plundered!'; Is. 40:31: '... but those who hope in the Lord will renew their strength. They will soar on wings like the eagles; they will run and not grow weary, they will walk and not be faint.') In the New Testament, very few passages mention the eagle (Matthew 24:28) but it is one of the allegorical beasts used to refer to the Gospel of John by early church fathers.[5] This is because of the incisive nature of the gospel. The belief was that the gospel, like an eagle, is so penetrating that it rises above all else. The eagle is a bird known for its fortitude, rising above the storm, and it has a penetrating view. It suffices to say that, by naming a church Eagle's Wings, for

[5] Paton J. Goag. *Introduction to the Synoptic Gospels.* Edinburgh: T & T Clark, 1895.

example, this persuades followers to have the strength to sail through daily challenges and rise up with Jesus Christ. This is, however, my judgement based on the attributes of the eagle given above.

In the same vein, some ACMs are not only a City of God (Guta RaJehovah/Mwari) but are expressive of the total salvation of believers in the present – Winners Chapel. Inasmuch as some names remind followers of the redemptive death of Christ on the cross, Calvary Worship Centre, and some call believers prospective converts to repentance by having faith in the living Christ in Sword and Spirit (Eph. 6:10:17); with total allegiance and without backsliding. This is a kerygmatic message to followers – Jesus calls believers to faithful repentance, serve him and emulate his life in their faith and practice. Notably, when these churches go beyond borders, making disciples from all nations, they include phrases such as 'international church' – '*Synagogue Church* of all nations', 'house', etc. In short, the naming of these churches reflects the forces of globalisation. This is evident in the use of electronic media (like Facebook, Twitter, radio, YouTube, the MultiChoice's digital satellite DStv service in Africa for tele-evangelism, etc.), print media (billboards, car stickers,[6] pamphlets and magazines), and rock/ building paintings[7] in reaching a wider audience.

As for the designation of founders and offices, it is evident that the titles are heavily influenced by both the Old and New Testaments: priest (Lev. 21:10; Num. 35:25; Ezk 7:5, etc.); prophet (1 Sam. 9:6-10; 2 Kgs 1:2-4; 4:18-37; Hag. 1:13 etc.); pastor (1 Pet. 5:1-5; 1 Tim. 3:2; Heb. 3:20) and bishop (Phil. 1:1) etc. In turn, the founders see themselves as messengers of God and shepherds of the churches, holding uncontested positions in some cases, e.g. the title 'priest'. Priests were from the house of Levi and priesthood was hereditary. In this context, the naming of some ACMs is a political move intended to create uncontested terrains. In addition, some of the common designations cited above are taken from the Bible: for example, deacon (1 Tim. 3: 8-12); pastor (Eph. 4:8,11); evangelist (Acts 21:8; Eph. 4:11; 2 Tim. 4:5); prophet (Is. 43:27; Num. 24:4, etc.); overseer (2 Chr. 2:18; 2 Chr. 34:13; 1 Tim. 3:1-7); intercessor (1 Sam. 12:23; Rom. 8:34; Acts 12:5; Eph. 6:16-18 etc.) and stewards (Luke 12:35-38; 1 Cor. 4:4-5), etc. In short, the designation of names is kerygmatic, calling adherents and potential converts to total submission to the gospel and serving the church.

Conclusion

From the above discussion, one could reach the conclusion that the naming of ACMs has changed through time and is constructed around certain beliefs, concerns as well as aspirations. It is highly political! On the other hand, it appears stiff competition from rival communities influences the politics of naming in these churches – a marketing strategy! For that reason, each Church claims to represent an authentic version of Christianity, using terminology like: 'This is the turning point in your Christian journey' – Turning Point International Christian Centre, 'We are already saved' – Redeemed Church of God or 'We have been commissioned by Jesus/God to preach the true gospel' – Christ Embassy, and so on. Such concerns possibly explain why some founders claim to have had a direct encounter with Jesus himself or God[8] in this or the other world. The title used, in some cases, reminds followers of uncontested terrains – that the office of the leader is hereditary. There can be no contenders for priesthood for it rests within the family.[9]

---

[6] For example, the most common sticker on cars in Swaziland is 'We are sons and daughters of love, let love lead' (John 15:12-14).

[7] For example, bridge painting such as 'Jesus is coming in 2023' in Ezulwini, Manzini, Swaziland or 'Jesus is Lord Barber Shop', etc.

[8] For example, Johanne Marange, the founder of the Marange church claims to have been transported to heavenly places where he had a direct encounter with God/Jesus.

[9] This has been one of the major causes of secessionism in most African Initiated churches; for example, the current leadership wrangles in the Johannes Marange Church or Rueben Mutendi's Zionist Church.

Overall, titles such as *mai/baba* argue that, in their configuration, some ACMs are certainly 'reverting' to indigenous religions systems of thought, the pool from which they recruit new converts. Arguably, the naming and practices of ACMs are expressive of an amalgamation of indigenous and Christian symbols as these churches adapt to an ever-changing religious landscape.

Bibliography

Bourdillon, M. F. C. *Where are the Ancestors?* Harare: University of Zimbabwe, 1994.

Bourdillon, M. F. C. *Religion and Society: A text for Africa*. Gweru: Mambo Press, 1997.

Goad, P. J. *Introduction to the Synoptic Gospels*. Edinburgh: T & T Clark, 1895.

Daneel, M. L. *Old and New in Southern Shona Independent Churches: Background and Rise of the Major Movements,* Volume 1. Paris and The Hague: Mouton, 1971.

Daneel, M. L. *Old and New in Southern Shona Independent Churches: Church Growth – Causative Factors and Recruitment Techniques,* Volume II. The Hague and Paris: Mouton, 1974

Dube, L, Shoko, T. & Hayes, S. *African Initiatives in Healing Ministry*. Pretoria: UNISA Press, 2011.

Killingray, D. 'Passing on the Gospel: Indigenous Churches in Africa.' *Transformation* 28, no. 2, (2011): 93-102.

Isichei, E. *A History of Christianity in Africa: From Antiquity to the Present*. Michigan: William B. Eerdmans Publishing Company, 1995.

Oduro, T. 'Theological education and Training: Changes of African independent churches in Ghana.' *Journal of African Instituted Church Theology* 2, no. 1, (2006): 1-15.

Ranger, O. T. 'African Initiated Churches.' *Transformation* 24, no. 2, (April 2007): 65-71.

Strayer, R. 'Mission History in Africa: New Perspectives on an Encounter.' *African Studies Review* Vol. 19, (1976): 1-15.

Sundkler, B. *Bantu Prophets in South Africa*. South Africa: International Institute Studies, 1961.

Tofa, Eliot. 'In Jesus' Name You Are Free': HIV, ARVS and Healing Space in African Initiated Churches.' *UNISWA Research Journal* Vol. 27, (2011), 70-85.

(118) Women in African Christianity

Hazel O. Ayanga

Introduction

The gospels, and the Bible in general, indicate that women have always been part of the Christian church. In some accounts, women were the first people to receive and proclaim the good news of the risen Christ. There is also significant evidence of women's involvement and activity in the early Christian church. It is suggested that perhaps the major form of involvement was in house churches. However, as Christianity grew and expanded to various parts of the world, the role of women has consistently diminished. Church historians attest to this, pointing out that, by the fifth century, women's visible activity in the church began to be curtailed by the development of a hierarchy of leadership that was predominantly male. Women were excluded from the priesthood. Thus a situation was created in which men were predominantly in the pulpit while women filled the pews. This is the organization that the Christian missionaries carried with them to Africa and other mission fields. Western Christian missionaries were greatly influenced by the ideas and teachings of early church fathers and theologians. These include Tertullian, Augustine, Chrysostom, and reformation leaders like Martin Luther, among others. They were all agreed on the subordination of women and the inability of women to hold any leadership positions, both in and out of the church. They carried these persuasions to the mission field as well. Nevertheless, women played and continue to play a pivotal role in African Christianity and in Christian mission.[1]

Historians record many women of faith in Christian antiquity.[2] Some of the early church fathers and theologians came to faith because of the examples of their mothers and other women. Augustine finally became a Christian as a result of the prayers and teaching of his mother, Monica. John Chrysostom's mother played a pivotal role in his Christian upbringing. Ironically, these church leaders have little or nothing positive to say about women.

The Missionary Era

John Baur, in his *2000 Years of Christianity in Africa: An African Church History,* published in 1998, recognizes the place of women in African Christianity by saying that 'the co-operation of women was the greatest innovation in evangelization'.[3] Although many early missionaries were men, several brought their wives and children along to the mission fields. Although these women did not participate in activities like church planting, they initiated and participated in activities that were later to have far-reaching effects on women in general and the Church in Africa in particular. Missionary women were not just interested in the spiritual welfare of women in Africa. They took keen interest in their social status and welfare. To help improve the status of women, many missionary women were involved in the provision of medical facilities

---

[1] For detailed historical examples both from Africa as well as Asia see: Christine Lienemann-Perrin, Atola Longkumer, and Afrie Songco Joye (eds.), 'Putting Names with Faces: Women's Impact in Mission History.'(Nashville, TN: Abingdon Press, 2012), 389; See also a related review: *International Review of Mission*, Volume 102, Issue 2, November (2013), 264–266,

[2] "Catherine Kroeger. "The Neglected History of Women in the Early Church." *Christian History Institute.* https://www.christianhistoryinstitute.org/magazine/article/women-in-the-early-church/ (accessed 29 March, 2016)

[3] John Baur, *2000 Years of Christianity in Africa: an African Church History.* Nairobi: Paulines Africa, 1998, 107.

and the establishment of girls' schools. This includes women like Lula Schmelzenbach[4] of the Nazarene Mission in Swaziland and Twyla Ludwig[5] of the Church of God (Anderson, Indiana) who worked at the Kima Mission where she single-handedly started a girls' school and taught women to cook and sew.[6] For missionary women, as for the African women among whom they ministered, leadership in the church was not an option. They concentrated on perfecting 'women's roles' as defined by their denominations and church tradition. Catholic sisters were also involved in this work. Baur records that they were often able to do and go where the monks and Fathers would not go. These included the Missionary Sisters of the Precious Blood who worked among the Zulu, and the Missionary Sisters of Africa who started work in North Africa around 1869, and the Sisters of St Joseph who sent Sr Anne Marie Javouhy to Senegal about 1819.[7] In all these activities, women still had to be under the leadership of their male counterparts.

But women found an avenue for service and greater participation in associations and movements. The Mothers' Union for women in the Anglican Communion,[8] the Women's Guild in the Presbyterian Church[9] and *Chigwirizano cha Amayi a Chikristu* in Malawi and the Women's Ministries of the Church of God are examples of women's participation in African Christianity. These and other similar organizations and movements gave African women an avenue for self-expression and, indeed, for the development of leadership skills. They gave women an opportunity not only to *do* something but also to *be* something or somebody. Many of the movements, like the Mothers' Union, started off as support groups for women, offering some kind of basic education for them. However, these organizations continued to encourage women to play service roles rather than church leadership roles *per se*. Some of the mother churches were both cynical and unsupportive of these organizations and their activities. Indeed, in some cases, the oversight of these women's associations was taken over by men. There was the fear that these movements would become churches within their churches and thus challenge both the unity and the leadership hierarchies of the larger church.[10]

But women continued to be church in the best way they knew how – and within the confines of the strictly patriarchal framework in which they existed. They cleaned the church buildings, they taught Sunday school and they made tea for visitors and members as need arose. They arranged the flowers and were ushers during the Sunday services. They supported one another by creating prayer cells and prayer groups. In some cases they created prayer partner cells where two or three met either weekly or monthly and prayed for their own specific needs.[11] They comforted each other and in some cases formed widows' associations to help widows to be firm against some of the cultural practices that were deemed harmful and unfair to them.[12] Those whose husbands were in church ministry assisted them as best they could, without being too forward or obtrusive. Thus, women in the African Church served and supported the men without

---

[4] She published the biography of her husband, providing also a lot of details on her own work: Lula Schmelzenbach, *Missionary Prospector: A Life Story of Harmon Schmelzenbach – Missionary to South Africa* (Kansas City MO: Beacon Hill Press, 1936) – See more at: www.whdl.org/content/missionary-prospector-life-story-harmon-schmelzenbach-missionary-south-africa#sthash.d3zQvZBb.dpuf.

[5] See: Twyla I. Ludwig, Watching the Cooking Pot (Prestonsburg, KY: Reformation Publishers, , 2010).

[6] Dana Lee Robert *American women in Mission: A Social History of their Thought and Practice*. (Georgia: Mercer University Press, 1997), 238.

[7] Baur, 2000 Years of Christianity, 184.

[8] See: www.mothersunion.org/media-centre/our-history.

[9] See: http://pceaheadoffice.org/WOMANS_GUILD.html.

[10] Isabel Apawo Phiri. *Women, Presbyterianism and Patriarchy: Religious Experience of Chewa Women in Malawi*. (Blantyre: Christian Literature Association in Malawi, 2000), 80.

[11] This was something I witnessed in my home. My mother had several women as prayer partners. They would meet on different days of the week for this purpose.

[12] These included polygamy, wife inheritance and female circumcision among others.

necessarily participating in leadership or decision-making processes. It was understood that they could do this without formal theological education.

Women in African Initiated Churches

Whereas women in general stayed within the established churches and denominations, the spirit of unrest that swept through the African Church during the missionary period resulted in some women leaving to form their own churches or to join those formed by others. This unrest was the result of general dissatisfaction with European control and governance of both church and state. The fact that women were not formally trained in theology meant that they could not be ordained, and thus were excluded from ordained ministry as well as from other leadership roles. Opportunities for self-expression were also limited. The emergence of churches initiated by Africans for Africans seemed to provide the much longed-for space for women to be truly themselves. It gave them the opportunity to be both African and Christian. Women play prominent roles in these churches although very few are led by women. A few exceptions include the Cherubim and Seraphim church of West Africa. This African church was co-founded by Moses Orimolade and Captain Christiana Abiodun Akinsowon.[13] The latter finally took over the leadership of the entire movement. But this did not go down well with her male counterpart. He, together with others, tried to convince her to be the head of all the women in the movement rather than be seen as the topmost leader of both men and women.[14] Others include the Christian Catholic Apostolic Stone Church in Zion of South Africa which gives women the space to be leaders and to exercise full authority in the church. Gaudencia Aoko co-founded the Legio Maria Church in Kenya with Simeon Ondetto, in 1963. But by 1968, women were already being sidelined from the leadership of the church. This led Aoko to found her own church of the same name. The Legio Maria (Legion of Mary) is unique in that it is the largest existing African Initiated church with roots in the Roman Catholic Church.[15] Women in these and other African Initiated Churches are recognized as healers and prophets, as well as providers of pastoral care and ministry to the poor and vulnerable in society. They have continued to be church in vibrant and exuberant ways that were not open to them in western and missionary churches.

African Women and Theological Education

During the missionary era and several decades after, theological training for women was viewed as neither important nor necessary. This was mainly because such training was aimed at producing candidates for ordained ministry and women's candidature was not a consideration. In many of the African Initiated Churches, formal theological training was not a basic requirement even for the men in leadership positions. The leading and direction of the Holy Spirit were the main requirement. But with access to western education made available by missionaries, women in the African Church began to desire much more than the mere basics. They sought to understand and interpret the message of the gospel for themselves and from a woman's perspective. Opportunities to pursue higher education became more and more available to African women after the political independence of their various countries. In a survey[16] done by Mercy

---

[13] Brigid M. Sackey, *New Direction in Gender and Religion: The Changing Status of Women in African Independent Churches.* (Oxford: Lexington Books, 2006).

[14] Mercy Amba Oduyoye, *Daughters of Anowa: African Women and Patriarchy.* (Maryknoll, New York: Orbis Books, 1995).

[15] http:www.britannica.com/EBchecked/topic/364890/Legio Maria; see also: https://en.wikipedia.org/wiki/Legio_Maria.

[16] Mercy Amba Oduyoye. 'Theological Education for Women in Africa' in *Transforming Power: Women in the Household of God. Proceedings of the Pan-African Conference of the Circle of Concerned African Women*

Amba Oduyoye in 1996, it is noted that women's access to theological education in Africa was often slow and sometimes painful. Oduyoye notes that, by 1978, roughly two decades after the political independence of many African nations, women admitted to departments of religion in public universities in Anglophone Africa were still few.[17] But these institutions represented the most equal opportunities for women to pursue higher education in theology and religious studies. In some of these institutions, the enrolment of women in these departments has slowly overtaken that of men. For example, in Moi University in Eldoret, Kenya, the current Master of Arts in Religion programme has three women and only one male student. Although Theological Institutions were slow to admit women in their own right, they have continued to increase the numbers of women admissions over time.

The voices of women in decision-making and leadership positions have thus remained muted because of the lack of opportunities in the training that would equip them with both knowledge and necessary skills. Women still fill the pews while the men still occupy the pulpits. Women in church have generally been recipients of theology rather than initiators of theology based on their own lived experiences. Women at the grassroots continue to be church without having a say in some of the very basic and personal aspects of their lives. It is this lack of voice for women that the Circle of African Women Theologians has sought to address since its inception.

The Circle of Concerned African Women Theologians

The Circle of Concerned African Women Theologians (the Circle) formally came into existence in 1989 in Accra, Ghana. However, there were other meetings and associations prior to the inauguration of the Circle. These associations both inspired and supported the Circle. They include the Ecumenical Association of Third World Theologians (EATWOT) and the meeting of African Women Theologians held in Ibadan, Nigeria, in 1980.[18] Under the charismatic leadership of Mercy Amba Oduyoye, the Circle sought to be the voice of African Christian women at the grassroots level. To this end, research and publication was and still is one of the major pillars and activities of the Circle. Indeed, the main objective of the Circle is 'to write and publish theological literature written by African women from their own experience of religion and culture on this continent'.[19] Several publications attest to the achievement of this objective.[20] Today the Circle boasts of several national chapters and regional representation in Eastern Africa, West Africa, Central and Southern Africa. There is also representation in Egypt.

Conclusion

Women have always been active participants in African Christianity. Generally, their participation has not been in the public domain and therefore not publicly acknowledged. Nevertheless, women have been the foundation of the African Church by living their faith and leading by example rather than by word alone. They have given the church in Africa a theology of life, born out of their lived experience as African Christian women living in Africa with all its complexities and challenges.

---

*Theologians,*ed. Mercy Amba Oduyoye (Accra: Sam Wood, 1997), 65.

[17] Oduyoye, "Theological Education for Women in Africa"

[18] Oduyoye, *Transforming Power*, 1.

[19] Musimbi Kanyoro in her keynote speech in Oduyoye, *Transforming power*, 11.

[20] Each region has at least two publications, in addition to those that come out of the Pan African conferences.

Bibliography

Baur, John. *2000 Years Christianity in Africa: an African Church History.* Nairobi: Paulines Africa, 1998.

Getui, Mary and Obeng Emmanuel (eds). *Theology of Reconstruction: Exploratory Essays*. Nairobi: Acton, 1999.

Lienemann-Perrin, Christine, Longkumer, Atola and Joye, Afrie Songco (eds). *Putting Names with Faces: Women's Impact in Mission History.* Nashville, TN: Abingdon Press, 2012.

Ludwig, Twyla I. *Watching the Cooking Pot.* Prestonsburg, KY: Reformation Publishers, 2010.

Kroeger, Catherine. "The Neglected History of Women in the Early Church." *Christian History Institute.* https://www.christianhistoryinstitute.org/magazine/article/women-in-the-early-church/ (accessed 29 March 2016).

Oduyoye, Mercy A. *Daughters of Anowa: African Women and Patriarchy*. Orbis Books, Maryknoll, New York, 1995.

______. "Theological Education for Women in Africa," in *Transforming Power: Women in the Household of God. Proceedings of the Pan-African Conference of the Circle of Concerned African Women Theologians,* edited by Mercy Amba Oduyoye. Accra: Sam Wood, 1997.

Phiri, Isabel Apawo. *Women, Presbyterianism and Patriarchy: Religious Experience of Chewa Women* in *Central Malawi.* Blantyre Christian Literature Association, 2000.

Robert, Dana L. *American Women in Mission: a Social History of their Thought and Practice*. Georgia: Mercer University Press, 1997.

Sackey, Brigid M. *New Direction in Gender and Religion: The Changing Status of Women in African Independent Churches.* Oxford: Lexington Books, 2006.

Schmelzenbach, Lula. *Missionary Prospector: A Life Story of Harmon Schmelzenbach – Missionary to South Africa.* Kansas City MO: Beacon Hill Press, 1936.

(119) African Church Women's Organizations

Molly Longwe

Introduction

This chapter focuses on the agency of African churchwomen organizations as an enduring missionary legacy in the growth and development of African Christianity. It would not be far-fetched to call women organizations 'the face of the African Church' or 'a church within a church'. This is because of the way they have displayed their visibility and their strong character. As Brigalia Bam notes, 'A very significant feature of the role of women in the life of some churches in South Africa is the *Manyano* phenomenon… These groups form a powerful presence in many churches.'[1] While women's organizations in Africa number as many as there are churches and denominations in Africa, this chapter will focus on only a few significant groups and organizations. They are called by various names in the different churches or denominations, according to their languages. For instance, the Women's *Manyano* of the Methodist Church of Southern Africa[2] or the Women's Fellowship of the Evangelical Lutheran Church in Zimbabwe.[3] In Malawi, the terms *Chigwirizano,*[4] *Umanyano,* and *Mvano* refer mostly to Presbyterians (and in other smaller churches); *Umodzi wa Amayi* are the Baptists; *Amayi a Dorika* are the Seventh Day Adventists; *Amayi a Chifundo, Legio Maria* and *Amayi a Tereza* are the Roman Catholic groups;[5] and the Mothers' Union of the Anglican Church (same as in South Africa).[6]

Three issues are reflected in this chapter: how African churchwomen's organizations make a unique contribution to the development and expansion of African Christianity; the reasons for the success story of women's organizations' and the challenges and way forward for these organizations as they continue to grow and serve the church.

Women's Organizations: Tool for Church Development and Expansion

Little did the western missionary women of the late nineteenth and early twentieth centuries know what their untiring work among African women would yield! It was not their expectation that their efforts would yield such great results. To their amazement, they saw Bible study groups, prayer groups and sewing clubs slowly blossoming and forming into women's national organizations. Some organizations struggled, due to resistance and opposition from their colonial mother bodies, such as the Mothers' Union of the Anglican Church in South Africa;[7] while others were being watched very closely by the male church authorities, like

---

[1] Brigalia Bam, 'Women and the Church in (South) Africa: Women are the Church in (South) Africa' in *On Being Church: African Women's Voices and Visions*, eds. Isabel Apawo Phiri and Sarojini Nadar (Geneva: World Council of Churches, 2005), 13.

[2] Their website is www.methodist.org.za/organisations/women-manyano.

[3] The Church's website is www.elcz.co.zw/churchorgans.html.

[4] The Church's website is www.kga.org.za/.../ccap-church-of-central-africa-presbyterian.

[5] Rachel, Nyagondwe-Fiedler, "Pastors' Wives and Patriarchy: Experiences of Church Women in Malawi," in *On Being Church: African Women's Voices and Visions,* eds. Isabel A Phiri and Sarojini Nadar (Geneva: World Council of Churches, 2005), 173-183.

[6] Their website is www.mothersunionsa.org or www.anglicannews.org/.../mothers-union...

[7] Beverley G Haddad, 'The Mothers' Union in South Africa: Untold Stories of Faith, Survival and Resistance' in *Her-Stories: Hidden Histories of Women of Faith in Africa*, eds. Isabel A Phiri, Devakarsham B Govinden, and Sarojini Nadar (Pietermaritzburg: Cluster Publications, 2002), 101- 117.

Chigwirizano, of Nkhoma Synod of the Presbyterian Church of Central Africa in Central Malawi.[8] Scholars acknowledge that through these organizations, churches in Africa have expanded tremendously as a result of the evangelistic programmes which they carried out through direct evangelism, pastoral care and social work, and through the young women's work as discussed below.

Expansion through Evangelism

A few examples suffice here to illustrate that women have contributed tremendously to the development of the church in Africa through their agency and evangelism. Writing on the development of the Baptist Convention of Malawi (BACOMA), Hany Longwe points out that discussion on evangelism and church growth is incomplete without acknowledging the role of women (and youth) and their influence on those processes. Longwe attributes the growth of the Baptist women's organization, *Umodzi wa Amayi*, and of BACOMA as a whole, to the evangelistic revivals of the 1970s and the 1980s and hints that 'when BACOMA talks of numerical gains, the majority were women, because it was the majority of women who responded to the preaching of the Word'.[9] Similarly, in her work, Rachel Banda examines the role of the Baptist women's organization in the development of BACOMA, especially in Southern Malawi from 1961-2001. She argues that, although there was a high level of foreign missionary influence in the life of the indigenous church, it was the local women who played the major role.[10] In the same vein, the Good Women Association of Nigeria of the Christ Apostolic Church is renowned for their evangelistic seminars, retreats and conferences. Dorcas Akintunde notes that due to their numerous outreach programmes, many converts joined the church. Women were involved in house-to-house evangelism and distributed tracts in market places and other centres within their communities.[11]

Expansion through Pastoral and Social Work

Providing pastoral work for the needy within their churches and communities has also been recognized as one of the achievements of women's organizations in African Christianity. One example is that of the achievements of the Good Women Association of Nigeria. Akintunde highlights the remarkable impact of the association on the ministry of the Christ Apostolic Church (CAC) through women's pastoral work. This includes caring for the poor, the sick, the aged and widows; prison ministries; health and education ministries.[12] Through the Association's School of Midwifery, Akintunde reports that the ministry of the midwives in particular made significant contributions to the growth and expansion of Christ Apostolic Church in Nigeria. The Faith Home Centres run by CAC provide spiritual refuge and a haven of hope to both women and men. Adult literacy programmes to cater for the majority of women who can read and write have been an ongoing focus, not only in CAC but in many women's groups in Africa. The CAC girls

---

[8] Isabel Apawo Phiri, *Women, Presbyterianism and Patriarchy: Religious Experience of Chewa Women in Central Malawi,* A Kachere Monograph (Blantyre: CLAIM, 1997).

[9] Hany H Longwe, *Christians by Grace – Baptists by Choice: A History of the Baptist Convention of Malawi.* Kachere Theses no. 19, Mzuni Books no. 3, (Zomba/Mzuzu: Kachere Series/Mzuni Press, 2011), 239-312.

[10] See Rachel Nyagondwe Banda, *Women of Bible and Culture: Baptist Convention Women in Southern Malawi*, Kachere Theses no. 7, (Zomba: Kachere Series, 2005), 18-88.

[11] Dorcas O Akintunde, 'The Achievements and Hurdles of the Good Women Association of Nigeria (1943-2001)' in *Her-Stories: Hidden Histories of Women of Faith in Africa*, eds. Isabel Apawo Phiri, Devakarsham B Govinden, and Sarojini Nadar (Pietermaritzburg: Cluster Publications, 2002), 93. See also Reinhard Ludwig Frey, *History of the Zambia Baptist Association 1905-2005*, Kachere Theses no. 18 (Zomba/Mzuzu: Kachere Series/Mzuni Press, 2009), 239-312.

[12] Akintunde, 'The Achievements and Hurdles of the Good Women Association of Nigeria (1943-2001)', 91-95.

have not been left out of the Association's caring ministry. This is evidenced by the emphasis placed on the education of the girls through the establishment of girls' schools.

Space for Passing on the Legacy to Young Women

In their quest to maintain the traditional structures of passing on African values, many women's organizations created space to cater specifically for the needs of young women, especially as they enter adulthood.[13] Another aim was to nurture young women in their faith through these rites. Much to the dismay of the western missionary teachers, some women's organizations struggled to have Christianized rites of passage. Articles in the volume *Rites of Passage in Contemporary Africa*, edited by James L. Cox, show this tension.[14] This was due to the westerners' lack of understanding of the importance of religion and rituals in African culture. As Oduyoye notes, 'African rituals have an import that is at once psychological, spiritual, political, and social' because of their integrated worldview.[15] For instance, the major significance of puberty rites in most African ethnic groups is that a young person becomes a member of his or her community, and therefore takes on adult responsibilities, including marriage and bearing children. However, inasmuch as African Christianity has been commended for the enculturation of these rites, African women theologians have argued for a hermeneutic of 'suspicion' of these rites. They note that even in their Christianized form, most of the teaching encourages the subordination of women.[16] Rosemary Edet, for example, notes the ambiguity of childbirth rituals. She points out that while the rituals are occasions of thanksgiving, joy and celebration, and give the mother a sense of accomplishment and inclusiveness, they also impart ritual impurity and guilt to the act of bringing forth new life by imposing some taboos.[17]

Women's Organizations: Reasons for a Success Story

While African churchwomen through women's organizations are hailed for their unique contribution to the development and expansion of Christianity in Africa, the Circle of Concerned African Women Theologians (the Circle) must also be hailed for bringing the voices of African churchwomen to the fore for theological analysis.[18] For instance, Mercy Oduyoye regards the volume, *Her Stories*, edited by Isabel Apawo Phiri, Devakarsham Betty Govinden and Sarojini Nadar, as the Circle's first attempt 'to sweep the rooms for our religious communities until they have retrieved the lost coin'.[19] Through their stories, a variety of

[13] Some of the rites that an individual goes through in life are pregnancy, birth, naming, puberty, marriage, death and burial.

[14] James L. Cox (ed.), *Rites of Passage in Contemporary Africa: Interaction between Christian and African Traditional Religions* (Cardiff: Academic Press, 1998). See also Molly Longwe, *Growing Up: A Chewa Girls' Initiation,* Kachere Theses no. 15, (Zomba: Kachere Series, 2006); Phiri, *Women, Presbyterianism and Patriarchy*; Rachel Nyagondwe-Fiedler, *Coming of Age: A Christianized Initiation among Women in Southern Malawi* (Zomba: Kachere Series, 2005).

[15] Mercy A Oduyoye, 'Women and Ritual in Africa', in *The Will to Arise: Women, Tradition, and the Church in Africa*, eds. Mercy Amba Oduyoye and Musimbi R. A Kanyoro (Pietermaritzburg: Cluster Publications, 2006), 9.

[16] For example, see *The Will to Arise: Women, Tradition, and the Church in Africa*, eds. Mercy Amba Oduyoye and Musimbi R. Kanyoro (Pietermaritzburg: Cluster Publications, 2006).

[17] Rosemary N. Edet, 'Christianity and African Women's Rituals', in *The Will to Arise*, 32.

[18] The Circle emerged as a platform for African women's theologies; where women's experiences, perspectives and theological reflections are brought to light with the aim of bringing 'dignity, liberation and fullness of life, especially to the women in Africa', see Nyambura J. Njoroge, 'Preface', in *Talitha cum! Theologies of African Women*, eds. Nyambura J. Noroge and Musa W. Dube (Pietermaritzburg: Cluster Publications, 2001), viii.

[19] Mercy Amba Oduyoye, 'Preface: Naming Our Mothers', in *Her Stories: Hidden Histories of Women of Faith in Africa* eds. Isabel Apawo Phiri, Devarakshanam Betty Govinden and Sarojini Nadar (Pietermaritzburg: Cluster Publications, 2002), xi.

experiences of women of faith in Africa are analyzed from women's perspectives. Nyambura Njoroge draws attention to the pioneering African Christian women, 'the unsung heroines, who after "hearing and knowing" the word of God from missionaries went out their own way to become missionaries among their own people'.[20]

This success of the women's organizations resonates well with Mary McClintock Fulkerson's observation that faith traditions create 'subject positions' or roles that hinder or limit women instead of liberating them. McClintock Fulkerson argues that in such cases 'the faith of a woman can enable her to resist such powerful oppressive messages and help her find the strength to preach and lead others and exercise a high degree of autonomy.'[21] Thus, African churchwomen's organizations are a reality of this resistance to the patriarchal church. The women have been successful by creating spaces for themselves to function in accordance with their gifting and full human potential as God originally intended. Their success is seen as a means for the women's self-expression, leadership skills development, spiritual development, and space for ecumenism as discussed below.

A Form of Self-Expression

Dignity and a sense of belonging are features that women's organizations have given to African women. In analyzing the beginnings and development of women's organizations in Africa, African women theologians acknowledge how the women's organizations have been space for self-expression as children of God. Remarking about the Anglican Mothers' Union in South Africa, Haddad states that 'these churchwomen's organizations are an indigenous expression of African women's spirituality.'[22] Women's spirituality must also be seen as a characteristic of the traditional spirituality of African people, whose concern for spiritual power from a mighty God to overcome certain spirit-world based evils that threaten life, often results in an extensive and extended time of prayer for healing and deliverance.

Women created for themselves safe space for prayers, Bible study, and freedom to use their God-given gifts. As women fellowship together and share their lives together, it gives them a sense of belonging to the church of God. While culturally African women are recognized through their motherly and wifely roles, the women are able to serve their God through their organization, although with clerical control in some church traditions.[23] Speaking about the *Manyano* Women's Movement of the Methodist Church in South Africa, Lyn Holness observes that the uniform also gives the woman a 'sense of identity, of being somebody in her own right.'[24] Nyagondwe adds that the issue of identity is much more important to the women than the meanings of the uniforms or of the colours. In addition, the uniform gives the women a sense of unity and belonging.[25] Thus, dressed in her uniform, a woman assumes dignity, self-confidence and a sense of pride, not just within her organization but within a patriarchal society. Phiri notes that once a woman wears her uniform, it gives her a certain amount of power and authority, especially when they go out witnessing and preaching.[26]

---

[20] Nyambura J. Njoroge, 'Reclaiming Our Heritage of Power: Discovering Our Theological Voices', in *Her Stories,* 42-43.

[21] Cited in Elaine Graham, Heather Walton and Frances Ward (eds.), *Theological Reflection: Methods*. (London: SCM Press, 2005), 150.

[22] Haddad, 'The Mothers' Union in South Africa', 101.

[23] See, for example, Phiri, *Women, Presbyterianism and Patriarchy*, 71-90 and Haddad, 'The Mothers' Union in South Africa', 104.

[24] Lyn Holness, 'Women's Piety and Empowerment: An Observer's Understanding of the Methodist Women's *Manyano* Movement', *Journal of Theology for Southern Africa* No. 98, (July 1997): 26.

[25] Nyagondwe Banda, *Women of Bible and Culture*, 111.

[26] Phiri, *Women, Presbyterianism and Patriarchy,* 83.

Space for Leadership Talent Development

If one glances at the organizational structures and the many activities of the women's organizations, one cannot fail to notice talented and strong leadership. Having been denied access to positions of leadership within the male dominated church, women have created spaces for themselves to exercise and develop their leadership roles among women. Speaking about Chewa women, Phiri argues that while the Christian message of new life in Christ attracted large numbers of African women to the church, the same message resulted in the women losing the leadership roles that they enjoyed in their traditional religious cultures.[27] However, looking at the success story of these organizations, it shows that the women did not remain passive, bemoaning their loss. Instead, they found alternative ways of continuing and utilizing their leadership roles in the new context which the missionary women had introduced to them, although restricted to women's organization. Njoroge notes that it was the training and development of women's leadership through their organizations that equipped them to participate in the emerging ecumenical movement, theological education, church leadership and even the ordained ministry.[28]

Another aspect of leadership roles in women's organizations is that of pastors' wives. It has been noted that being the spouse of a minister is considered as another opportunity for African women to serve in a leadership position in the church in Africa. For instance, Njoroge observes that it was the missionaries' wives who consequently introduced the same leadership pattern in mission churches for the pastors' wives.[29] In some church traditions, the leadership of the pastors' wives in the women's organizations is clearly stated, while in others it is not prominent. For instance, in the Baptist Convention of Malawi, the major responsibility of pastors' wives is reflected in their leadership role in the women's organization.[30] Pastors' wives are involved in teaching women during weekly meetings; inducting new members until they qualify to wear the uniform, and carrying out pastoral duties among the churchwomen. Longwe observes that a pastor's wife's leadership in pastoral care and visitation at the local church level sometimes takes on more importance than that of her husband. Some pastors' wives could be prepared more for this work of ministry in case they have an opportunity for theological education.[31]

Space for Spiritual Development

Women's organizations are not only renowned for their outreach programmes but also provide space for spiritual development of their members. Through their organizations, women ground themselves in the scriptures. Bible study and prayer is the major activity in their weekly meetings. For one to become a member of an organization, one has to undergo some training of at least three months, which includes learning and memorizing Bible verses. A strong advocacy for strict Christian values for the women and their families is one of the objectives of most of the women's organizations. Women are also encouraged to teach their children Christian values.[32]

---

[27] Phiri, *Women, Presbyterianism and Patriarchy*. Musopole also speaks of Ngoni women who, armed with spears, fought and guarded their villages, see Anne Nachisale Musopole, 'Sexuality and Religion in a Matriarchal Society', in *The Will to Arise: Women, Tradition, and the Church in Africa*, eds. Mercy Amba Oduyoye and Musimbi R. A. Kanyoro (Pietermaritzburg: Cluster Publications, 2006), 197.

[28] Nyambura J. Njoroge, 'Reclaiming Our Heritage of Power: Discovering Our Theological Voices', in *Her Stories*, 42-43.

[29] Njoroge, 'Reclaiming Our Heritage of Power', 43.

[30] Molly Longwe, 'A Paradox in a Theology of Freedom and Equality: Experiences of Pastors Wives (*Amayi Busa*) in the Baptist Convention of Malawi (BACOMA)', PhD Thesis, University of KwaZulu-Natal, 2012, Chapters 6 and 7. See also Rachel Nyagondwe Banda, *Women of Bible and Culture*, 117.

[31] See Longwe, 'A Paradox in a Theology of Freedom and Equality', chapters 6.

[32] Phiri, *Women, Presbyterianism and Patriarchy*, 88.

Space for Ecumenism

While the women's weekly meetings provide space for growth at local level, many groups have national, continental and international meetings within their various denominations.[33] Of interest here are the ecumenical groups to which many of them also subscribe for fellowship and prayers. Two examples are the Pan African Christian Women's Alliance (PACWA), the product of the Association of Evangelicals of Africa and Madagascar. The second one is the World Day of Prayer under the World Council of Churches (WCC). Njoroge observes that the women's quest for cooperation in prayer and social-economic issues paved the way for unity, and entry into the twentieth-century ecumenical movement.[34]

Women's Organizations: Challenges and the Way Forward

African churches recognize the tremendous contribution of women's organizations to the church in Africa. Similarly, African women theologians acknowledge the women's impact that through their energetic and resilient faith and spirituality, women permeate Christianity in Africa 'with a form and character that is indeed worthy of recognition'.[35]

However, the growing influence of women's organizations elicits fear in some churches. This was seen in the case of Nkhoma Synod where Phiri noted that the women were often reminded to keep the unity between the church and the women's organization, and accord church leaders due respect. An elder was therefore appointed to attend all the weekly meetings with the view of controlling what they discuss and reporting their discussions to Session and the General Assembly.[36] This is viewed as an example of the extent of patriarchy in the church. However, women theologians have also been critical of the way these women's organizations use and abuse their power. Without realizing it, they also promote patriarchy by oppressing and marginalizing other women and men when they take positions of leadership.[37]

It is the concern of the women theologians that both women and men should seek new ways of forming the present-day church. The question that we may ask is: To what extent are the women's organizations empowering women? This is especially with regard to the ordained ministry, since women have shown their leadership skills and are the ones who form the majority of church membership. Another concern is that not many of the women leading in these organizations have any theological education. This is especially evident in their conservative ways of interpreting the Bible. There is a need for women to challenge patriarchal models of misinterpretation because they are the ones who suffer. For this to happen, more and more women have to rise to the challenge of becoming theologically trained and well versed in their sacred texts. These organizations provide safe space where transformation in the church can take place, given the right tools. Young women should also be encouraged to study life-affirming theologies with the intention of coming back to their organizations and leading Bible studies more freely.

Conclusion

The success stories of churchwomen's organizations in African Christianity show how these women have exhibited dynamic leadership skills and spiritual growth, both at congregational and ecumenical levels. Since more and more church traditions are now ordaining women ministers, women need to take seriously the challenge of theologically equipping themselves. This will equip them to take on leadership roles in

---

[33] For example, the Baptist Union of Southern Africa (BWUSA) is a regional meeting under the Baptist World Union of Africa.

[34] Njoroge, 'Reclaiming Our Heritage of Power', 43.

[35] Phiri, Govinden and Nadar, 'Introduction' in *Her-Stories: Hidden Histories of Women of Faith in Africa*, 2.

[36] Phiri, *Women, Presbyterianism and Patriarchy*, 87-92.

[37] Phiri, *Women, Presbyterianism and Patriarchy*, 85-86.

churches and other church organizations, as well as teaching roles in theological institutions and universities.

Bibliography

Akintunde, Dorcas Olubanke. 'The Achievements and Hurdles of the Good Women Association of Nigeria (1943-2001).' In *Her-Stories: Hidden Histories of Women of Faith in Africa*, edited by Isabel Apawo Phiri, Devakarsham Betty Govinden & Sarojini Nadar, 84-100. Pietermaritzburg: Cluster, 2002.

Brandel-Syrier, Mia. *Black woman in Search of God*. London: Lutterworth, 1962.

Cox, James L., ed. *Rites of Passage in Contemporary Africa: Interaction between Christian and Traditional Religions*. Cardiff: Academic Press, 1998.

Frey, Reinhard Ludwig. *History of the Zambia Baptist Association, 1905-2005*. Kachere Theses no. 18. Zomba: Kachere Series, 2009.

Haddad, Beverley G. 'The Mothers' Union in South Africa: Untold Stories of Faith, Survival and Resistance.' In *Her-Stories: Hidden Histories of Women of Faith in Africa*, edited by Isabel A. Phiri, D. Betty Govinden, and Sarojini Nadar, 101-177. Pietermaritzburg: Cluster, 2002.

Holness, Lyn. 'Women's Piety and Empowerment: An Observer's Understanding of the Methodist Women's *Manyano* Movement.' *Journal of Theology for Southern Africa* 98, (July 1997): 21-31.

Longwe, Hany H. *Christians by Grace – Baptists by Choice: A History of the Baptist Convention of Malawi*. Kachere Theses no. 19, Mzuni Books no. 3. Zomba/Mzuzu: Kachere Series/Mzuni Press, 2011.

Longwe, Molly. *Growing Up: A Chewa Initiation*. Kachere Theses no. 15, Zomba: Kachere Series, 2006.

______. 'A Paradox in a Theology of Freedom and Equality: Experiences of Pastors Wives (*Amayi Busa*) in the Baptist Convention of Malawi (BACOMA).' PhD diss., University of KwaZulu-Natal, 2012.

Mia Brandel-Syrier. *Black Woman in Search of God*. London: Lutterworth, 1962.

Mombo, Esther. '*Harahamisi* and *Jumaa*: The Development of the Women's Meetings in East Africa Yearly Meetings of Friends (Quakers).' In *Her- Stories: Hidden Histories of Women of Faith in Africa,* edited by I. A. Phiri, D. B. Govinden and S. Nadar, 59-83. Pietermaritzburg: Cluster, 2002.

Nadar, Sarojini. 'On Being Church: African Women's Voices and Visions' in *On Being Church: African Women's Voices and Visions* edited by Isabel A Phiri and Sarojini Nadar, 16-28. Geneva: World Council of Churches, 2005.

Njoroge, Nyambura J. 'Preface.' In *Talitha Cum! Theologies of African Women,* edited by Nyambura J Njoroge and Musa W Dube, vii-viii. Pietermaritzburg: Cluster Publications, 2001.

______. 'Reclaiming Our Heritage of Power: Discovering Our Theological Voices.' In *Her Stories: Hidden Histories of Women of Faith in Africa* edited by Isabel Phiri, Devakarsham Betty Govinden & Sarojini Nadar, 39-57. Pietermaritzburg: Cluster Publications, 2002.

Nyagondwe-Fiedler, Rachel. 'Pastors' Wives and Patriarchy: Experiences of Church Women in Malawi.' In *On Being Church: African Women's Voices and Visions,* edited by Isabel A Phiri and Sarojini Nadar, 173-183. Geneva: World Council of Churches, 2005.

______. *Coming of Age. Zomba: A Christianized Initiation Among Women in Southern Malawi.* Zomba: Kachere Series, 2005.

______. *Women of Bible and Culture: Baptist Convention Women in Southern Malawi*. Zomba: Kachere Series, 2005.

Oduyoye, Mercy Amba. 'Preface: Naming Our Mothers.' In *Her Stories: Hidden Histories of Women of Faith in Africa* edited by Isabel Phiri, Devakarsham Betty Govinden & Sarojini Nadar, xi-xii. Pietermaritzburg: Cluster Publications, 2002.

Oduyoye, Mercy Amba and Musimbi R Kanyoro (eds.). *The Will to Arise: Women, Tradition and the Church in Africa*. Pietermaritzburg: Cluster Publications, 2006.

Phiri, Isabel Apawo. *Women, Presbyterianism and Patriarchy: Religious Experience of Chewa Women in Central Malawi*. A Kachere Monograph. Blantyre: CLAIM, 1997.

______. 'The Church and Women in Africa.' In *The Wiley-Blackwell Companion to African Religions* edited by Elias Kifon Bongmba, 256-268. Oxford: Blackwell Publishing, 2012.

Phiri, Isabel A., Govinden, Devakarsham B. and Nadar Sarojini'Introduction.' In *Her Stories: Hidden Histories of Women of Faith in Africa* edited by Isabel Phiri, Devakarsham Betty Govinden & Sarojini Nadar, 1-13. Pietermaritzburg: Cluster Publications, 2002.

(120) The Role of Youth in Shaping African Christianity

Malebogo Kgalemang

Introduction: Defining Youth

The question of 'What, or who, is youth?'[1] has historically been addressed along various disciplinary enquiries. The young has been variously defined sociologically as two varying age ranges: generally, fourteen to thirty-five years for some countries or fifteen to twenty-four years according to the UN. Rajui Assaad and Farzaneh Rourdi-Fahim note this age-range is characterised by a few transitions from childhood dependency to the independence of adulthood.[2] Furthermore, this period is marked by enthusiasm, dreams and ambitions.[3] Assaad and Rourdi-Fahim observe that these 'set the stage for adult life, such as education, marriage, and entrance into the job market'.[4] Yet the young are sensitive to transformations in the economy, as their activities, prospects and ambitions are dislocated and redirected.[5]

Anthropology defines the young as a 'historically constructed social category, as a relational concept and youth as a group of action forming an especially sharp lens through which social forces are focused in Africa'.[6] In many African societies, initiation schools mark the stage into youth as an important stage or a rite of passage. For example, in traditional Botswana culture, the initiation school for boys and girls gave them adulthood rights and responsibilities, such as getting married, owning property and participating in public debates.

Christianity is the fastest growing religion in Africa. Sub-Saharan Africa is apparently home to 'almost one in four of the world's Christians'.[7] It is expected, according to the Pew Research Report on religion, that Africa will become the continent with the largest number of Christians by a wide margin. The Pew Report on religion further states that sub-Saharan Africa's share of the global Christian population may rise from 24% in 2010 to 38% in 2050.[8] But what does this mean for the population of the young? Commencing from the universal, in 2010, Christians were only slightly older, with a average age of thirty, than the age of the overall population (with the average age of 28).[9] This means the age breakdown of the world's population is not distinct from that of the world's Christian population. The Pew Report on religion gives an example of the world's population younger than 15, as about 27% of the world's people overall. The following section explores particular Christian youth organisations and discusses the role youth play in shaping African Christianity.

---

1 Deborah Durham, 'Youth and the Social Imagination in Africa: Introduction to Parts 1 and 2', *Anthropological Quarterly*, 73, no. 3, Part 1 (Jul. 2000): 113-120.

2 Ragui Assaad and Faszaneh Roudi-Fahimi, 'Youth in the Middle East and North Africa: Demographic Opportunity or Challenge?' Washington, DC. *Population Reference Bureau*, 2007.

3 Assaad & Roudi-Fahimi, 'Youth in the Middle East', 114.

4 Assaad & Roudi-Fahimi, 'Youth in the Middle East', 115.

5 Assaad & Roudi-Fahimi, 'Youth in the Middle East', 115.

6 Durham, 'Youth and Social Imagination', 114.

7 Sherrill Jacobs. 'Church Business Goes Digital in Africa.' www.thisisafricaonline.com/Business/Church-business-goes-digital-in-Africa (accessed 20 February 2015).

8 Pew Research Report: Pew Templeton Global Religious Future Project. www.globalreligiousfutures.org/ www.pewforum.org/data/ (accessed 20 February 2015).

9 Pew Research Report. www.globalreligiousfutures.org.

The Role of Youth in Shaping African Christianity

Africa, particularly sub-Saharan Africa, has a significant number of Christian youth organizations. The majority of these are evangelistic in nature and orientation. Good examples include *Youth for Christ International in Africa, Youth with a Mission* and *The African Christian Youth Development Foundation.* In general, Christian youth organizations cater for the various needs of youth. The overarching drive is catering for the spiritual needs of the young which is addressed through the preaching of the gospel of Jesus Christ. However, Christian organizations are not limited to meeting the spiritual needs of the young. The majority of youth organizations explored below also cater for the material and social needs of the young. However, the way the young are shaped by Christian youth organizations differs from one African country to another and even from one denomination to another. Whereas, in some countries, Christian youth organizations are essential to the development of the young, in others they are not visible. However, Christian youth organizations are much more numerous than can be discussed in this paper. This is because almost every church denomination and congregation has its own youth department and organization. Below, I briefly present Christian youth organizations on the African continent.

Young Women's Christian Association (YWCA)[10]

Originally formed in Britain, but currently headquartered in Switzerland since 1965, YWCA is the oldest Christian youth non-profit organization. YWCA is found in at least twenty-five member associations in sub-Saharan Africa. The latest addition is the Rwandan Young Women's Christian Movement in 1995, which has since been legally recognised by the government of Rwanda in 2005. With goals to transform communities and empower women, YWCA began strictly as a Christian movement shaped by a Christian ethos. It has since taken a holistic role to help shape and establish young women. YCWA developed the following focus areas: young women's leadership; sexual and reproductive health and rights, HIV and AIDS and violence against women. The holistic approaches were equally important in nurturing women.

Youth for Christ International

Youth for Christ International is an organization present in at least thirty-six African countries. Its main goal is the evangelisation of youth. This evangelization has high spiritual approaches through its movement called 'Generation 21',[11] which is characterised by cultivating skills in spiritual warfare, boldness in evangelism, passion in social involvement and godliness in leadership. It also features the greatest change in accommodating the young, their aspirations and desires. Though evangelistic, the organization is also holistic in approach. It is committed to social, mental and physical development in tackling issues and challenges facing the young. Youth for Christ International, for example, has created HIV and AIDS programmes, and vocational skills, etc.[12] It has abandoned traditional modes of reaching the young, opting for what the young prefer. These include the use of blogs, Twitter and various other modes of reaching the young. Its pioneering work in Africa is concentrated in the following Nigerian cities: Akure, Asaba, Kadune, Owerri and Lagos, with its headquarters in South Africa since the 1940s.

Youth with a Mission

Youth with a Mission is an inter-denominational, non-profit, Christian, missionary organization. Though it caters for all Christian ages, its primary focus is on youth. Its purpose is to 'make God known' to the young. One of the means through which it makes God known is its ministry of helps, the Mercy Ministry. This has a number of relief and development programmes. It champions young people's interests and

---

[10] Young Women's Christian Association (YWCA), www.worldywca.org (accessed 14 August 2015).
[11] Youth For Christ International in Africa, http://africa.yfci.org/ (accessed 16 August 2015)
[12] Youth Rise: Nigeria. http://youthrise.org/projects/youth-rise-nigeria (accessed 16 August 2015).

provides space for them to spearhead its vision and ministry. Hence, its purpose is to train the young and support them by creating spaces for them to flourish and develop.

The African Christian Youth Development Foundation

The African Christian Youth Development Foundation is a Nigeria-based youth organization that seeks to advance the glory of God and the Kingdom of Christ. It has a holistic approach that seeks to promote education and relieve poverty among Christian youth in Africa. It uses 'subtle' Christian political activism to challenge and change the rules and practices that generate poverty. In addition, it has an interfaith or pluralistic approach to 'building bridges of trust and understanding among the different faith traditions and cultures in communities where the young live and work'.[13] It nurtures the spiritual life of young Christians, such that they become worthy ambassadors of the Lord Jesus Christ, in the process equipping young Christians to minister effectively to the young.

One of its key goals is to cultivate ethical living. This is practised through an invitation to people to examine their lives and to act on the pressing moral, ethical and spiritual issues and challenges of our time. It encourages the inclusion of faith and values perspective in public discourse.

The Catholic Youth Network for Environmental Sustainability in Africa (CYNESA)

The Catholic Youth Network for Environmental Sustainability in Africa (CYNESA) is a movement inspired by St Pope John Paul's 1990 message for the World Day of Peace. In the message, he made an urgent call to upscale ecological awareness: 'Today the ecological crisis has assumed such proportions as to be the responsibility of everyone… Its various aspects demonstrate the need for concerted efforts aimed at establishing ties and obligations that belong to individuals, peoples, states, and the international community.'[14] Young Catholics in Eastern Africa took this mantle and actively networked with five other countries: Burundi, Democratic Republic of Congo, Tanzania, Zambia and Zimbabwe for addressing environmental challenges from Christian perspectives.

CYNESA's mission seeks to respond to the 'twin challenges of environmental degradation and climate change in an effective, co-ordinated manner, culturally sensitive and spiritually grounded'.[15] The goals of CYNESA are delineated along three objectives. Fist, it aims at education and awareness creation, in which the aim of CYNESA is preparing a 'toolkit on climate change that draws from Scripture'.[16] It is also informed by Ignatian Spirituality, scientific research and Catholic social teaching. The second objective is developing networking and advocacy training. The latter seeks to build 'relationships with like-minded partners; to train young Catholics in advocacy on environment sustainability, and to link initiatives on the continent'.[17] Thirdly, it promotes and supports context-based plans for young people to act in their parishes, schools and within their youth movements. It provides training, resources and consultation to parish communities to assist in the development of youth ministry initiatives. In regard to the environment and the young, it provides specific programmes to children, teens and families in youth ministry.

Scripture Union (SU)

Scripture Union, commonly abbreviated as SU, is one of the oldest Christian youth organizations in the world. It was founded in Britain by an American student and spread worldwide to over 130 countries, with

---

[13] African Christian Youth Development Foundation. www.acydfoundation.cfsites.org (accessed 16 August 2015)
[14] The Catholic Youth Network for Environmental Sustainability in Africa (CYNESA). www.http://cynesa.org/ (accessed 14 August 2015)
[15] Catholic Youth Network, (CYNESA) www.http://cynesa.org/.
[16] Catholic Youth Network, (CYNESA) . www.http://cynesa.org/.
[17] Catholic Youth Network, (CYNESA) www.http://cynesa.org.

about sixty member countries in the African region and sub-region. Its African headquarters are in Nairobi, Kenya.

SU is a non-denominational Christian youth organization that operates in post-primary schools in some African countries while it is also predominantly involved in primary schools in other African Countries. It was a movement that had a 'variety of specialist ministries'.[18] It works with churches to present the good news of Jesus Christ to children, youth and families. Its vision has targeted children and youth following Jesus, and filled them with hope and trust in God. One of its other objectives was to promote Bible reading among children of all ages in primary and high school, with a view to 'furthering personal discipleship, Christian community and social concern'.[19] Young Christian readers of the Bible were to be made aware of the reality and presence of God. Scripture Union has been an excellent evangelising organization that reaches both primary and high school with the gospels, thereafter encouraging them to be active in their churches or to find churches if they did not have one. Because of its lengthy existence in a number of countries, it has developed excellent rapport with host governments. According to J. Kwabena Asamoah-Gyadu, SU also became 'coterminous with conservative evangelism'.[20]

All Africa Conference of Churches (AACC) and Youth Empowerment

The All Africa Conference of Churches is a fellowship of Christian churches that holds its general assembly every eighteen months. Each assembly is preceded by a 'Youth Pre-Assembly Event'[21] which reflects the value AACC place on the young. At its Ninth Assembly, Bernard Okok-Obuoga discussed six hallmark areas for youth empowerment towards effective, sustainable and responsible leadership on the continent. Only four will be covered in this section.

First, leadership and organizational structures will play an effective role with a strong voice of the All Africa Youth and Students Assembly (AAYSA) towards sustainable and transparent working relationships. Lobbying, advocacy and networking is the second important hallmark for 'positive socio-economic transformation that responds to local realities and the needs of the people'.[22] Since a world is as effective as its educational development, education towards effective youth leadership is pertinent. Therefore, youth empowerment can take 'the form of training and exposure for strengthening skills'.[23] AACC facilitates this through exchange programmes between the AACC youth and those from African sub-regions. Fourthly, the integration of young people into the mainstream activities of ecumenical organizations is another important hallmark of empowerment towards effective leadership. The AACC sought to separate the 'AACC Women's Desk from the Youth Desk'[24] who will also be integrated into the 'activities and leadership of the church'.

Conclusion

Clearly, more Christian youth organizations are active in some sub-Saharan Africa countries than this section can fully explore. Given the advancement of social networks, the youthfulness of the African

[18] James N. Amanze, *A History of the Ecumenical Movement in Africa.* (Gaborone: Pula Press, 1999), 243.
[19] Amanze, *A History,* 244.
[20] J. Kwabena Asamoah-Gyadu, *African Charismatics: Current Developments within Independent Indigenous Pentecostalism in Ghana* (Leiden; Boston: Brill, 2005), 102-103.
[21] Bernard Okok-Obuoga, 'Youth Empowerment for Effective Leadership' in *Africa Step Forth in Faith: The 9th AACC General Assembly Report, Maputo 2008*: All Africa Conference of Churches.
[22] Okok-Obuoga, 'Youth Empowerment', 56.
[23] Okok-Obuoga, 'Youth Empowerment', 56-57.
[24] Okok-Obuoga, 'Youth Empowerment', 56-57.

population and the challenges facing the young, Christian youth organizations and the church will continue to play a vital role in shaping and being shaped by the young in sub-Saharan Africa.

Bibliography

Amanze, James N. *A History of the Ecumenical Movement in Africa.* Gaborone: Pula Press, 1999.

Anderson, Allan H. *African Reformation: African Initiated Christianity in the 20th Century.* Trenton, NJ: African World Press, 2001.

Asamoah-Gyadu, J. Kwabena. *African Charismatics: Current Development within Independent Indigenous Pentecostalism in Ghana.* Leiden; Boston: Brill, 2005.

Clarke, Gerald. 'Faith Matters: Faith-Based Organizations, Civil Society and International Development.' *Journal of International Development* Vol. 18, Issue 6 (2006): 835-848.

Okok-Obuoga, Bernard. 'Youth Empowerment for Effective Leadership.' In *Africa Step Forth in Faith: The 9th AACC General Assembly Report.* 2008.

(121) African Church Men's Organizations

Kennedy Owino

Introduction

The purpose of this chapter is to give a brief overview and description of the various church men's organizations in Africa, highlighting some examples of such organizations in particular denominations. Because it is difficult to speak of men's organizations in Africa without making links to ongoing studies on men and masculinity in Africa, I will concur with van Klinken who argues that 'the question of how men and masculinities are addressed, contested and transformed in local churches calls for an in-depth qualitative research…'[1] The hope, therefore, is that this brief survey will contribute to ongoing discussions among scholars, and also establish the need for further qualitative research on church men's organizations within critical studies of men and masculinity in Africa.

Church Men's Organizations in Africa

Christianity in Africa is diverse, coming with a variety of expressions in church denominations. Hence, church men's organizations are numerous and they number as many as there are churches and denominations. The paradox, however, is that an increased interest in the studies of men and masculinity in the past three decades has surprisingly not given enough attention to church men's organizations as part of its enquiry, with the exception of a few qualitative studies.[2] In several ways, applying a critical approach to studies of men and masculinity to examine reasons for increased growth in men's organization and associations in various church denominations in Africa can be attributed to the quest for what it means to be a Christian man within changing social religious contexts. Towards this goal, men are seen to respond to complex societal changes. Such responses are evident from conversations within men's organizations, either directly or indirectly, and to a wide extent focus on a belief that Christian men have a 'divine responsibility' from God for the local church, their homes and community.

Within this understanding, men are constantly negotiating new ways of being Christian men and are continually reminded of the need to stand against emasculation. The need to constantly protect and defend what it means to be a Christian man remains central in most of the church men's organizations. Of importance to note within this quest to defend what is perceived as an 'ideal' Christian man are: how Christian men have responded to concerns on gender inequalities, the empowerment of women which has contributed to contemporary shifts in gender roles and relations, concerns around issues of sexuality, and social and economic shifts that have brought changes in family organizations. Hence, with all their diversities, church men's organizations have become associations *of* men and a space *for* men who seek to equip and empower men to be better Christian men in their families, at their workplace and in the community at large.

---

[1] Adriaan S. Van Klinken, *Transforming Masculinities in African Christianity: Gender Controversies in Times of AIDS.* (Burlington: Ashgate, 2013), 21.

[2] See for example qualitative research on men by Ezra Chitando in Zimbabwe – 'A New Man for a New Era? Zimbabwean Pentecostalism, Masculinities, and the HIV Epidemic', *Missionalia* 35, no. 3, (2007): 112-127; by Van Klinken in Zambia – 'Transforming Masculinities in African Christianity' 2013; and Kennedy Owino in South Africa – 'Godly Manhood': Evangelical Constructions of Masculinities in a South African Context – A Case Study of the Mighty Men's Conference (MMC), 2014.

Terminologies, Naming and General Activities of Church Men's Organizations

Generally, different church denominations in Africa have applied varied terminologies to refer to their church men's organizations. These include, but are not limited to, terms such as Men's Groups, Men's Associations, Men's Ministry, Men's Fellowships, Men's Forums, Men's Society and Father's Fellowships. In some case, particular names are given to men's organizations in various church denominations, typifying what they intend their men to be – for example, 'Men for His Master', 'Men of Truth', 'Men of Valour', 'Men for Faith', 'Fathers of Honour' or 'Mighty Men'. Such names do not specifically include the term 'African', but are designed to inculcate particular values, behavioural expectations and characters which call men to strive and live to a particular desired standard. In most cases, concepts such as 'godly manhood', or 'Christlike men', 'the man as priest, prophet and king' are applied to typify notions of 'biblical manhood' as an alternative image of 'ideal' forms of Christian church men, against what the church does not expect of men, often described in the language of 'irresponsible manhood', or 'weak men'. Emphasised strongly in most of the church men's organizations is the key concept of 'responsible manhood', but this is often understood within the contours of a traditional definition of manhood which has risks of propagating the norms of patriarchy. The conservative notion of who a man is expected to be is grounded in the idea of his primary responsibility as the head in marriage, who provides for the needs of the family and thereby provides leadership in all areas of life.

As a space seeking to address men and their roles in church, at home and in the workplace, church men's organizations use different methods to motivate men to become faithful and responsible. The majority of these men's organizations outline their mission and vision as beginning with the need to address and meet men's spiritual and religious development and growth within their specific church denominations. Events that can bring men together for the purpose of enhancing their spiritual, mental, social and physical growth include men's monthly meetings, men's breakfast meetings, men's weekends, men's retreats and camps, men's business summits and men's conventions. These meetings tend to cover a wide range of themes addressing concerns around fatherhood, issues on marriage, gender and sexuality, a quest for purity and integrity, the need for mentoring young men to be godly Christian men and the various ways men can be effective in the church.

In some cases, men have crossed church denominational boundaries and regularly gather together in the form of men's interdenominational conferences. This depicts the difference between men's movements and church men's organizations. An analysis of men's movements shows that different church men's organizations, irrespective of their church affiliation, come together for specific reasons. Examples of such men's movements are evident with the Promise Keepers (PK) – South Africa[3] and the Mighty Men's Conference (MMC),[4] also found in South Africa and other countries in Africa. Such men's movements adhere to conventional Christian beliefs about who men 'should be' and are often established within perceptions of social 'crises' of masculinity among Christian men, thereby calling men to a journey of retreat towards rediscovering themselves and their 'divine mandate' in society.[5] Other men's movements still hold international affiliations yet take the form of organizations seeking to improve the lives of other men. An example of this is the Full Gospel Business Men's Fellowship International (FGBMI) in South

---

[3] See Lahoucine Ouzgane and Robert Morrell (eds), *African Masculinities: Men in Africa from the late Ninetieth Century to the Present* (Hampshire: Palgrave Macmillan, 2005); Angus Buchan and the Promise Keepers, https://www.discerningtheworld.com/2009/11/11/angus-buchan-and-the-promise-keepers/ (accessed 31 January, 2016).

[4] See Angus Buchan's Movement in Owino, 'Godly Manhood': Evangelical Constructions of Masculinities', 2015.

[5] See for example Michael A Messner. *Politics of Masculinities: Men in Movements.* (London: Sage Publications, 1997).

Africa, which is also found in other African Countries.[6] Its mission is stated as an 'International Fellowship of Men doing the Business of the Gospel, Fully.'

Some Examples of Church Men's Organizations in Africa

The Young Men's Guild of the Methodist Church

The Young Men's Guild (YMG) is an organization of African laymen within the Methodist Church of Southern Africa (MCSA), founded in 1920.[7] Madise points out that the establishment of the mining industry in South Africa was a major catalyst behind the emergence of this church men's organization in the mining compounds of Kimberley (in the Northern Cape) and Benoni (near Springs), where young men sought new ways to address their spiritual needs.[8] The YMG branded themselves as an organization described as 'The Young Men's *Manyano*', or 'The Sons of Wesley'. With the passing of time, the organization became known as 'The Young Men's Guild' (*Umanyano Lododana*) or the *Amadodana*,[9] following the submission of its constitution for approval by the 1929 Conference.[10] Their emergence can be linked with a variable Apostolic Band after the pattern of the Holy Club of Oxford which inspired the Wesleys with a gripping call to evangelise, a passion to save souls and a zeal to propagate the gospel of Jesus Christ.[11] With its official uniform adopted in 1938 through the District Synod, the YMG is known for its transformation of the rigid form of worship in the Methodist Church, with regular gatherings of men's conventions. Its motto is 'One Heart, One Way'.[12] The organization has a general mandate of:[13]

1. Calling sinners to repentance and to acceptance of the saving faith in Jesus Christ.
2. Spreading Scriptural Holiness in the land by calling Christians to a 'way of life' that is compatible with their profession of religion as propounded by the early Christian church…thereby promoting a life of abstinence from all forms of unrighteousness such as evil, drinking, and sexual sins.
3. Bringing every young man and woman into the fold of the Christian church for wholehearted and active service in the church.

The Anglican Men's Association

The Anglican Men's Association is an association or organization of men in various Anglican churches in Africa formed with the view of bringing Anglican men into fellowship with one another. For example, the Kenyan Anglican Men's Association (popularly known as KAMA) emerged from what was initially known as Father's Association or the Father's Union or the Men's Association, following various gatherings of Anglican men across different dioceses in the Province of Kenya. In Kenya, it is widely held that Father's Union was started by the late Archbishop Manasses Kuria in order to meet the needs of men

[6] See the vision, mandate and the core values of the Full Gospel Business Men's Fellowship International (FGBMFI) at www.fgbmfi.org.za/ (accessed 31 January 2016).
[7] Ezekiel E. Mahabane, 'The Young Men's Gild' in A. E. F Garrett (ed), *South African Methodism: Her Missionary Witness* (Cape Town: Methodist Publishing House, 1965), 107-109.
[8] Mokhele Madise, 'The Centenary of *Amadodana* in the Methodist Church of Southern Africa: Development and Influence of this Movement', *Studia Historiae Ecclesiasticae* 39, Suppl.1, (2013): 353-363.
[9] '*Amadodana*' is an IsiXhosa and IsiZulu word meaning young men. In English the name would be the 'Young Men's Guild', an order of men's organisation in the Methodist Church. For detailed historical origin and development of this men's organisation see Madise, 'The Centenary of *Amadodana* in the Methodist Church of Southern Africa', 2013.
[10] Mahabane, 'The Young Men's Gild', 108.
[11] Mahabane, 'The Young Men's Gild', 107-108.
[12] Madise, 'The Centenary of *Amadodana* in the Methodist Church of Southern Africa', 2013.
[13] Mahabane, 'The Young Men's Gild', 108-109.

and to strengthen their fellowship in the church.[14] It was only in July 2001, under the leadership of the retired Archbishop Dr David M. Gitari, that the fellowships that were referred to as Father's Union were officially registered by the Provincial Synod as the Kenya Anglican Men's Association (KAMA).[15]

Under the motto, 'But as for me and my household, we will serve the Lord' (Josh. 24:15b), KAMA addresses the role of men in the church in respect to concerns around church leadership, community leadership, political leadership and men in development work. The department organizes breakfast planning meetings where thematic issues such as men and their role in mentorship are discussed. They discuss and formulate remedies for other contemporary issues that affect men and the church, like matters of youth, HIV & AIDS and environmental degradation.[16] Similar men's organizations exist in the Anglican Church of Southern Africa by the name 'Anglican Men's Fellowship' in different dioceses;[17] in Ghana it has the same name, 'Anglican Men's Fellowship', and in Nigeria, the 'Men's Fellowship.'

Adventist Men's Organization

The Adventist Men's Organization is a department within the Seventh Day Adventist Church concerned with nurturing men for service to God, family and the community. Various Adventist churches have autonomous men's organizations with different mottos. For example, the Adventist men's organization at Jomo Kenyatta University Seventh Day Adventist Church in Kenya seeks to "nurture men for the purpose of building a solid foundation for the church, the homes and the communities".[18] The Adventist Men's Organization of the Seventh Day, Bantama Church in Ghana, for instance, has the motto 'The just man walketh in his integrity; his children are blessed after him' (taken from Prov. 20:7). The Bantama Adventist Men's Organization was, therefore, established primarily to promote programmes and activities designed to foster the spiritual, intellectual, social, moral and physical well-being of students, the working class, businessmen, professional men and many more.[19]

The bottom line in Adventist men's organizations is to be able to get men into small groups, meeting together regularly, ideally on a weekly basis. Men's ministry is about building relationships with God and other men. Similar Adventist men's organizations can be found in Zimbabwe, Zambia and in other countries in Africa.

The Presbyterian Church Men's Fellowship

The Presbyterian Churches in Africa have men's organizations in the form of men's fellowships. For example, the Presbyterian Church Men Fellowship (PCMF) of the Presbyterian Church of East Africa

[14] Alfred Sheunda Keyas, 2005. 'Kuria, Manasses', *Dictionary of African Christian Biography*, www.dacb.org/stories/kenya/kuria_manasses.html.

[15] All Saints' Cathedral Diocese, Kenyan Anglican Men's Association, http://allsaintscathedraldiocese.org/index.php/departments/missions/kama.html; Anglican Diocese of Mount Kenya South, KAMA, http://ack-mtkenyasouth.org/diocese/kama.

[16] Anglican Church of Kenya. Kenyan Anglican Men's Association (KAMA), www.ackkcodioc.org/node/64.

[17] The Anglican Women's Fellowship (Mothers Union) has been more actively involved in the Church compared to its men. This led to the creation of the 'Church Men's Society' and the Network of St Bernard Mizeki Guild as an entity separately for men to do welfare and express their faith Southern Africa (see Delene Mark, Ignatius Swart, and Austen Jackson, 'The Anglican Church and Social Welfare in Post-apartheid South Africa, in *Welfare, Religion and Gender in Post-apartheid South Africa*, eds. Ignatius Swart, Amanda Gouws, Per Petterson, Johannes Erasmus and Fouwien Bosman (Stellenbosch: SUNMEDIA, 2012), 165-184.

[18] Seventh Day Adventist Church, *The Adventist Men Organization*. https://jkusda.adventistafrica.org/amo (accessed 31 January 2016).

[19] Seventh Day Bantama Church, Bantama Adventist Men's Organization, www. bantamasdachurch.org/ adventist-mens-organization-a-m-o/ (accessed 31st January 2016).

(PCEA) in Kenya brings together men under the motto 'Working for the Lord'.[20] The PCMF seeks to restore the family to God's original intentions, within its philosophy specified as, 'We believe in Men being the best as God intended'.[21] The Presbyterian Church of Africa (PCA) in South Africa, Malawi, Zambia and Zimbabwe have the Young Men's Christian Association (YMCA) as an active group of men within their churches.[22] Men within the Uniting Presbyterian Church in Southern Africa (UPCSA) have a men's association, the Uniting Presbyterian Men's Fellowship (UPMF). Its mission is to build Christ-centred and Spirit-filled men within the denomination and, at large, to became a moral regeneration tool for men in society.[23]

The Catholic Men's Association

The Catholic Men's Association (CMA) are at the same time referred to as Catholic Men's Organization (CMO) and operates alongside the association of Catholic women called the Catholic Women's Organization (CWO).[24] The men's association is a lay movement for all men in the Catholic Church, with its origins dating back to 1947 when it was formed by the Catholic Men of Italy, under the guidance and instruction of Cardinal Giuseppe Pizard of Italy.[25] In 1948, Pope Pius XII welcomed the CMA foundation and declared it a Catholic Church Association.[26] As an organization for laymen within the Roman Catholic Church, the CMO operates as a religious organization found in various countries of Africa, including Nigeria, Kenya, South Africa and Zambia. Among Catholic men, the figure of St Joachim (an ancient saint)[27] is used in some contexts as a model of Catholic manhood and a religious ideal of masculinity, intended to motivate Catholic husbands and fathers to model their lives around his 'love, faithfulness, obedience, devotion, diligence, goodness and openness of husband and wife to one another'.[28] Generally, the CMA seeks to increase men's commitment to the church and its Catholic faith and teachings.

The United Congregational Church of Southern Africa

Not much is written about the men's organization in the United Congregational Church of Southern Africa (UCCSA). Nonetheless, it is recognised by its motto, 'The Solders for Christ'.[29] The men's organizations

---

[20] Presbyterian Church of East Africa, *Presbyterian Church Men Fellowship,* www.pceaheadoffice.org/ PCMF.html (accessed 31 January 2015).

[21] Presbyterian Church of East Africa, *Presbyterian Church Men Fellowship,* www.pceaheadoffice.org/ PCMF.html (accessed 31 January 2015).

[22] The Presbyterian Church of Africa. www.presbyterianchurchofafrica.co.za/ (accessed 31 January 2016).

[23] Uniting Presbyterian Church in Southern Africa, www.upcsa.org.za/docs-ga2012/Split_papers/petitions.pdf (accessed 31 January 2016).

[24] Anthony B. C. Chiegboka, 'Challenges of Catholic Men in the Church and the World', *African Journal Online* 1, no. 2, (2009), www.ajol.info/index.php/jrhr/article/view/87328/77044 (accessed 31 January 2016).

[25] Catholic Men Association of Kenya-Makupa Parish-Mombasa, https://www.facebook.com/.../Catholic-Men-Association.../17925611546... (accessed 31 January 2016).

[26] In 1983, CMA was first nationally introduced in Kenya through the Diocese of Nakuru by missionaries from Austria. The Association was nationally inaugurated on 17th August 2000, at the Holy Family Minor Basilica in Nairobi, in a memorable Eucharistic celebration presided over by Rev. Raphael Ndingi Mwana N'zeki, Archbishop of the Archdiocese of Nairobi. See Catholic Men Association of Kenya. https://www.facebook.com/.../Catholic-Men-Association.../17925611546... (accessed 31 January 2016).

[27] According to apocryphal Christian traditions, Joachim is the father of Mary who is the mother of Jesus. See Adriaan S. van Klinken, 'St. Joachim as a Model of Catholic Manhood in Times of AIDS: A Case Study on Masculinity in an African Christian Context', *Cross Currents* Vol. 61 no. 4, (2011, December): 467-479.

[28] Van Klinken, 'Transforming Masculinities in African Christianity', 62.

[29] Steve de Gruchy, 'Some Historic Roots and Contemporary Routes of the United Congregational Church of Southern Africa (UCCSA)', https://fwnw.com/407795435 (accessed 31 January 2016).

vary from one congregation to another, with different names applied to refer to the organization, ranging from Men's Group to Men's Forum and Men's Ministry.

Church Men's Organization in some Pentecostal and African Instituted Churches

In the majority of Pentecostal churches in Africa, men's organizations are referred to as Men's Ministries, Men's Groups or Men's Fellowships. For example, in South Africa, the Pentecostal Holiness Church Men's Ministry, is a fellowship which seeks to help men become dedicated to God, motivated for ministry, and mobilized for action.[30] In Zambia, we have the well-known Northmead Pentecostal Assemblies of God Church whose men's ministry is called Men of Truth, working towards raising men to 'biblical manhood.'[31] Similar groups of men's ministry and men's fellowships exist in other Pentecostal denominations such as the Apostolic Faith Mission in South Africa, the Assemblies of God, and the Full Gospel Church. Such men's groups are not only limited to Classical Pentecostal churches but are also found in Neo-Pentecostal and emerging Charismatic churches.

Church men's organizations also exist in some African Instituted Churches like the Zion Christian Church. The all-male *Mokhukhu* organization which initially developed under the leadership of Edward Lekganyane as a church choir, wearing military-style khakis, police-style hats, and the star badge, is a good example of a men's organization in an African Instituted Church.[32] This group engages in dancing, singing and praying three times a week.

Challenges and Way Forward for Church Men's Organizations in Africa

The restructuring of the corporate world in most African countries in the past three decades has in various ways brought shifts in gender roles, leaving many Christian men 'vulnerable' within their traditional understanding of who an ideal Christian man is supposed to be. Given the emphasis made on gender equality, socio-economic and political shifts have mainly contributed to an increased entry of women who were previously appreciated as 'home-makers' into the labour market. In real-life situations, notable changes are currently destabilising the conventional notions and beliefs of what an 'ideal' Christian man should be. The effect of this is that notions of a Christian man, as the head in marriage and provider of primary needs in the home and a leader at work, are to a wide extent disrupted. Faced with such changing contexts in which men find themselves, church men's organization must not remain religious spaces that seek to re-establish 'lost' traditional understandings of masculinity based on the assumed erosion of the authority of Christian men at home and at work. The priority of these men's organizations should not be seeking to safeguard and 'save men' from the tensions of emasculation. Rather, they must seek to equip men towards what it means to be a Christian man in a changing contemporary context. Archbishop Thabo Makgoba of the Anglican Church of Southern Africa in this case gives a charge, challenging men towards a fresh reflection of what it means to be a Christian man in today's world – 'especially in being actively part of the solution'.[33] To be part of this desired solution, church men's organizations should aim to use this religious space to bring transformation by engaging men towards fresh reflection on alternative forms

[30] Men's Ministries PHCSA, Constitution of the Men's Ministries of Pentecostal Holiness Church in South Africa 2010 – 2015, www.phcsa.co.za/wp-content/uploads/2015/02/Mens-Ministry-Manual.pdf (accessed 31 January 2016).
[31] Van Klinken, 'Transforming Masculinities in African Christianity.'
[32] See Marcus Ramogale and Sello Galane, 'Faith in Action: Mokhukhu of the Zion Christian Church', www.folklife.si.edu/resources/festival1997/faithin.htm (accessed 31 January 2016).
[33] Thabo Makgoba, Archbishop Thabo Makgoba's Charge to the Provincial Synod of the Anglican Church of Southern Africa. http://archbishop.anglicanchurchsa.org/2010/09/archbishop-thabo-makgobas-charge-to.html (accessed 02 February 2016).

of being men. In a similar way, Lesejane cautions against resistance to change and transformation often led by men:

> Without offering much evidence, it can be argued that such resistance is based on men fearing the loss of their privileged positions in the life and power systems of society. For men, the oppressive (to women) teachings and practices are maintained in the church to protect the interests of men, accumulated over the centuries, using varying texts, traditions and interpretations thereof.[34]

Alternative interpretations of who a Christian man should be are therefore crucial in church men's organizations. These should address, among other concerns, religious assumptions that God divinely created men with masculinity(ies); the dangers of 'soft patriarchy' in Christian homes which embrace aspects of violence and abuse against women and children. Such organisations should seek to help men embrace the challenge of Jesus Christ who is highly esteemed as an ideal model for masculinity in most church men's organization who is in actual fact a counter-model to the ideals of a Christian man that as ever currently being promoted.

Bibliography

All Saints' Cathedral Diocese. 'Kenyan Anglican Men's Association.' http://allsaintscathedraldiocese.org/index.php/departments/missions/kama.html

Anglican Diocese of Mount Kenya South. KAMA, http://ack-mtkenyasouth.org/diocese/kama (accessed 28 January, 2016).

Anglican Church of Kenya. 'Kenyan Anglican Men's Association (KAMA).' www.ackkcodioc.org/node/64 (accessed 30 January, 2016).

Buchan, Angus and the Promise Keepers. https://www.discerningtheworld.com/2009/11/11/angus-buchan-and-the-promise-keepers/ (accessed 31 January, 2016).

Catholic Men Association of Kenya-Makupa Parish-Mombasa. https://www.facebook.com/.../Catholic-Men-Association.../17925611546... (accessed 31 January, 2016).

Chiegboka, Anthony B. C. 'Challenges of Catholic Men in the Church and the World.' *African Journal Online* 1, no. 2 (2009). www.ajol.info/index.php/jrhr/article/view/87328/77044 (accessed 31 January, 2016).

Chitando, Ezra. 'A New Man for a New Era? Zimbabwean Pentecostalism, Masculinities, and the HIV Epidemic.' *Missionalia* 35, no. 3, (2007): 112-127.

de Gruchy, Steve. 'Some Historic Roots and Contemporary Routes of the United Congregational Church of Southern Africa (UCCSA).' https://fwnw.com/407795435 (accessed 31 January, 2016).

Full Gospel Business Men's Fellowship International (FGBMFI). www.fgbmfi.org.za/ (accessed 31 January, 2016).

Keyas, Alfred Sheunda. 'Kuria, Manasses,' *Dictionary of African Christian Biography*. www.dacb.org/stories/kenya/kuria_manasses.html (accessed 29 January, 2016).

Lesejane, Desmond. 'Through Men, by Men, for Men: Christianity and the Quest for Gender Equality.' *Agenda,* Special Focus, 2005, 78-79.

Madise, Mokhele 'The Centenary of *Amadodana* in the Methodist Church of Southern Africa: Development and influence of this Movement.' *Studia Historiae Ecclesiasticae* 39, Suppl.1 (2013): 353-363.

Mahabane, Ezekiel E. 'The Young Men's Gild.' In *South African Methodism: Her Missionary Witness,* edited by A. E. F Garrett, 107-109. Cape Town: Methodist Publishing House, 1965.

---

[34] Desmond Lesejane, 'Through Men, by Men, for Men: Christianity and the Quest for Gender Equality', *Agenda* Special Focus (2005) 78-79.

Makgoba, Thabo. Archbishop Thabo Makgoba's Charge to the Provincial Synod of the Anglican Church of Southern Africa. http://archbishop.anglicanchurchsa.org/2010/09/ archbishop-thabo-makgobas-charge-to.html (accessed 02 February 2016).

Mark, Delene, Swart, Ignatius and Jackson, Austen 'The Anglican Church and Social Welfare in Post-apartheid South Africa, in *Welfare, Religion and Gender in Post-apartheid South Africa*, eds. Ignatius Swart, Amanda Gouws, Per Petterson, Johannes Erasmus and Fouwien Bosman, 165-184. Stellenbosch: SUNMEDIA, 2012.

Men's Ministries PHCSA. 'Constitution of the Men's Ministries of Pentecostal Holiness Church in South Africa 2010 – 2015.' www.phcsa.co.za/wpcontent/uploads/2015/02/ Mens-Ministry-Manual.pdf (accessed 31 January, 2016).

Messner, Michael. *Politics of Masculinities: Men in Movements.* London: Sage Publications, 1997.

Ouzgane, Lahoucine and Robert Morrell, eds. *African Masculinities: Men in Africa from the Late Nineteenth Century to the Present*. Hampshire: Palgrave Macmillan, 2005.

Owino, Kennedy. ''Godly Manhood': Evangelical Constructions of Masculinities in a South African Context – A Case Study of the Mighty Men's Conference (MMC).' Doctoral thesis, University of KwaZulu-Natal, 2014.

Presbyterian Church of East Africa. 'Presbyterian Church Men Fellowship.' www.pceaheadoffice.org/PCMF.html (accessed 31 January, 2015).

Presbyterian Church of Africa. www.presbyterianchurchofafrica.co.za/ (accessed 31 January, 2016).

Ramogale, Marcus and Sello Galane. 'Faith in Action: Mokhukhu of the Zion Christian Church.' www.folklife.si.edu/resources/festival1997/faithin.htm (accessed 31 January, 2016).

Seventh Day Adventist Church. 'The Adventist Men Organization.' https://jkusda.adventistafrica.org/amo (accessed 31 January, 2016).

Seventh Day Adventist Bantama-Church. 'Bantama Adventist Men's Organization.' www. bantamasdachurch.org/adventist-mens-organization-a-m-o/ (accessed 31 January, 2016).

Uniting Presbyterian Church in Southern Africa. www.upcsa.org.za/docs-ga2012/Split_papers/petitions.pdf (accessed 31 January, 2016).

Van Klinken, Adriaan S. 'St Joachim as a Model of Catholic Manhood in Times of AIDS: A Case Study on Masculinity in an African Christian Context.' *Cross Currents* 61, no. 4, (2011, December): 467-479.

______. *Transforming Masculinities in African Christianity: Gender Controversies in Times of AIDS.* Burlington: Ashgate, 2013.

(122) SUNDAY SCHOOL MOVEMENTS IN AFRICAN CHRISTIANITY

Jan Grobbelaar

Origin of a Movement

The origin of Sunday schools seems to be debatable. Already in the sixteenth century, St Charles Borromeo had organized a Sunday school in the district of Milan to teach needy children. There are also other early cases of Sunday schools, for example, those established by the Rev. Joseph Alleine, a Yorkshire clergyman, in the seventeenth century.[1] Traditionally, the English Anglican evangelical Robert Raikes (1735-1811) is credited as the pioneer of the Sunday school movement. The growing number of poor and illiterate children working long hours in factories as a result of the industrial revolution, as well as the growing number of young people in prison, distressed him.[2] Since it was the only day they did not work, he started with a school on a Sunday in 1780 to provide education for these needy children. He started in the kitchen of Mrs Merideth's home, across from the prison in Sooty Alley, in Littleworth, one of the worst slum districts in the city of Gloucester.[3] Although Sunday schools were a semi-secular institution where children were taught reading, spelling and writing, it was done with the Bible as their textbook to 'keep them from turning to a life of crime'.[4]

Denominations and non-denominational organizations replicated Sunday schools widely and the movement grew rapidly. In 1785, it spread to Wales and a year later to Ireland.[5] Quickly, this led to the formation of independent regional and interdenominational societies. In 1785, the Society for the Establishing and Maintaining of Sunday Schools in Great Britain was established by William Fox and in 1803 it was replaced by the London Sunday School Union.[6] It is estimated that by 1786, 250,000 children were attending Sunday schools,[7] and by 1789, 300,000 children were already attending Sunday school in England.[8] The popularity of Sunday schools was hugely influenced by Raikes who, as the then editor and proprietor of the *Gloucester Journal*, gave much publicity to its cause.

The movement did not only grow in the UK but also began to spread to Europe and the USA. Sunday schools started in Germany in 1786 and in 1836 it was established in the Netherlands.[9] In Europe, many

---

[1] Nam Soon Song, 'Sunday School Revisited: An Alternative to Christian Education of the Church Today?', *Religious Education*, 108.2 (2013): 2.

[2] James Estep, Roger White and Karen L. Estep (eds.), *Mapping out Curriculum in your Church: Cartography for Christian Pilgrims* (Nashville, TN: B&H Publishing Group, 2012), 79.

[3] Dirk Coetsee and Jan Grobbelaar, 'A Church where Children are Welcome: A New Paradigm for Children's Ministry in Africa', in *Handbook of Theological Education in Africa,* eds. Isabel Apawo Phiri and Dietrich Werner (Pietermaritzburg: Cluster Publications, 2013), 804. Cf. Song, 'Sunday School Revisited', 5.

[4] Estep, White and Estep (eds.), *Mapping out Curriculum*, 79.

[5] Pertti Luumi and Ulrich Becker, 'Sunday School', in *Encyclopedia of Christianity Volume 5,* eds. Erwin Fahlbusch, Jan Milic Lochman, John Mbiti, Juroslav Pelikan and Lukas Vischer, Translation ed. Geoffrey W. Bromiley (Grand Rapids, MI: Eerdmans, 2008), 230.

[6] Luumi and Becker, 'Sunday School', 229.

[7] Joseph Kofi Antwi, "Integrating Indigenous Akan Educational Patterns into Christian Education in the Presbyterian Church of Ghana." (Unpublished MPhil thesis, Kwame Nkrumah University of Science and Technology, 2011): 44.

[8] Dirk J Viljoen, 'Die dooplidmaatbediening van die Nederduitse Gereformeerde Kerk 1962 tot 1990, met toespitsing op die kategeseenjeugaksies,' (Unpublished DD thesis, University of Pretoria, 1994): 20.

[9] Dawid W. De Villiers, 'Die Kategese in die Nederduitse Gereformeerde Kerk in SA: 'n Prinsipiële, Historieseen Praktiese Ondersoek van die Kategese in die Nederduitse Gereformeerde Kerk in SA': unpublished DD thesis, University of Stellenbosch, 1957, 257.

Sunday School Unions were also formed, for example, in the Netherlands (1865), Finland (1888) and Norway (1889).[10] It seems as if the first Sunday school in the USA was held by William Elliot in 1785 at Oak Grove, Virginia.[11] According to De Villiers, it was the Methodist church that took the Sunday school to the USA, in 1785.[12] From Virginia, Sunday schools sprang up in rapid succession in South Carolina, Maryland, Rhode Island, New York and Pennsylvania.[13] The goal of these Sunday schools was to teach children reading, writing and moral consciousness.[14] In 1791, a new Sunday school society, the First Day Society, a group of clerics and merchants, was organized in Philadelphia.[15] In 1821, the American Sunday School Union was founded.[16]

According to Thomas, 'it was the goal of the original Sunday school to offer an education to those that may otherwise do without. Yet the very nature of what its founders were hoping for was spiritual transformation as well as secular education of reading and writing'.[17] Religious education and evangelisation was from the beginning part and parcel of Sunday schools. When compulsory state education was established in the 1870s in both Britain and America, reading and writing became the responsibility of the weekday schools and religious education became the sole focus of the Sunday schools.

Origins in Africa

The growth and intention of the Sunday school movements made it inevitable that Sunday schools became part of the foreign missionary endeavour. The extension of the Sunday school to Africa during the nineteenth century was largely dependent upon foreign missionary societies working in different countries in Africa.[18] Mumo states: 'Sunday schools were introduced in Africa as a component of the Christianity the western missionaries propagated.'[19]

In his study on Christian Education in the Baptist Convention of South Africa, Matshiga concurs: 'Over the years, missionaries who were in charge of Convention churches were very helpful in ensuring that Christian education took place.'[20] Nduka is even of the opinion that 'tribute must be paid to the efforts and sacrifices of those in the West for the immense contribution of organising and popularising Sunday school. It would have been hard for Africa to benefit if these people had not sacrificially pursued this calling'.[21] In

---

[10] Luumi and Becker, 'Sunday School', 229.

[11] Elmer Towns, 'Sunday School', in *The Popular Encyclopaedia of Church History,* eds. Ed Hindson and Dan Mitchell, (Eugene, OR: Harvest House Publishers, 2013): 318.

[12] De Villiers, 'Die Kategese in die Nederduitse Gereformeerde Kerk in SA', 257.

[13] Towns, 'Sunday School', 318.

[14] Religious Studies Department, Centenary College of Louisiana, *A Brief History of the Sunday School*: www.centenary.edu/religion/dotto/rel203/Sunday%20school.ppt (accessed 5 February 2015).

[15] Towns, 'Sunday School', 318.

[16] Luumi and Becker, 'Sunday School', 229.

[17] Darren W. Thomas, 'The Role, History, and Decline of the Sunday School', in 'An Analysis of Sunday School Factors Leading to Effective Assimilation in Selected Baptist Churches in Georgia': unpublished EdD thesis, Southern Baptist Theological Seminary, 2005: 3eridan.websrvcs.com/clientimages/36689/historyofthesundayschool.pdf (accessed 29 January 2015).

[18] Edwin Wilbur Rice, *The Sunday-school Movement 1780-1917 and the American Sunday-school Union 1817-1917* (New York: Arno Press and New York Times, 1971).

[19] Peter M. Mumo, 'Sunday Schools as the Foundation of Christian Nurture and their Relevance for Theological Education in Africa', in *Handbook of Theological Education in Africa*, eds. Isabel Apawo Phiri and Dietrich Werner, (Dorpspruit, South Africa: Cluster Publications, 2013), 795.

[20] Dumile J. Matshiga, 'Christian Education in the Baptist Convention of South Africa with special reference to churches in the Transvaal: A Practical Theological investigation': unpublished PhD thesis, University of Pretoria, 2001: ii.

[21] O.C. Nduka, *Growing a Healthy Sunday School in African Churches* (Abia State, Nigeria: Assemblies of God Press,

many cases, Sunday schools were the first step towards the establishment of day schools, usually referred to as mission schools.[22]

However, the establishment of Sunday schools was not the starting-point of giving religious education to children and youths in Africa. Mumo states:

> Different cultures have always had different ways of imparting religious education to children and other members of society… Africans likewise had an elaborate system of imparting religious and other forms of education. The entire African way of life was interlaced with different types of education. There were proverbs and wise sayings which had a profound message to pass to society on all aspects of life. Rites of passage were loaded with education dealing with all aspects of life such as morality, spirituality, relationships and life skills.[23]

More formal Christian education on African soil had already started in the first century, with the establishment of the first African church in Alexandria, Egypt. From the histories of the North African church fathers such as Tertullian (c. 155-c. 240), Origen (185-254), Cyprian (c. 200-258), Athanasius (296-373), Augustine (354-430) and Cyril of Alexandria (c. 376-444), it is clear that education played a vital part in their own development, and they very much emphasised the important role of education for children.[24]

The Ethiopian church was another pioneer of Christian education in Africa. In AD 316, Frumentius and Edesius, two Phoenician brothers from Tyre, accompanied their uncle Metropius on a voyage on the Red Sea to Ethiopia. They were sold as slaves to the king of Aksum in Ethiopia. They soon gained the King's favour and he appointed them to responsible positions. Just before his death, the king set them free. The widow queen insisted that they stay in the service of the court to help educate her young son Erazanes until he was old enough to become king. The brothers used their influence to spread the gospel in Ethiopia and some of the local people accepted Christ as their Saviour. When Erazanes came of age, the brothers were released from their commitment. Edesius went back to Tyre and was ordained as priest. Frumentius travelled with him only up to Alexandria, where he stayed behind. Here St Athanasius consecrated him as bishop of the church in Ethiopia.

The Missionary Period

It took more than a millennium before the rest of Africa was introduced to Christianity on a significant scale. Many mission stations were planted and, because the missionaries understood the multi-dimensional nature of salvation, they did not establish only churches, but in many cases, also health care facilities, for example, hospitals or mobile clinics, and dispensaries, as well as schools and other educational institutions.[25] As a tool of evangelism and faith formation, most of the missionary societies implemented a Sunday school programme at various mission stations. In an article on the educational impact of the Presbyterian mission in Eastern Nigeria, Taylor wrote:

> To the Efik, adult and child, there was often little difference between day school and Sunday school. The mission did see them differently, and used the latter for ecclesiastical purposes. If diary entries are to be

---

2004), 78.

[22] Luumi and Becker, 'Sunday School', 230.

[23] Mumo, 'Sunday Schools as the Foundation', 63.

[24] Coetsee and Grobbelaar, 'A Church where Children are Welcome', 806.

[25] Justus G. Mbae, 'Keynote Address. Conference on Education as a Tool for Evangelization and Development in the Modern World', in *African Ecclésial Review* Vol. 54, no.1 and 2, (2012): 6.

> believed, Sunday schools attracted staggeringly huge crowds who enjoyed the singing and drama productions as well as the opportunity to reinforce their reading skills.[26]

Originally, these Sunday schools were established where there were already some converts present. However, later on, Sunday schools started as the first missionary involvement in new areas, and only after that were churches planted.[27] As part of this missionary movement, it seems that the first Sunday school in Southern Africa was established by missionaries in Cape Town in the late eighteenth century.[28] Greyling is of the opinion that the first Sunday school in South Africa was established in 1841 in Pietermaritzburg by the missionary Daniël Lindley.[29] The first official Sunday school at the Cape was founded, according to De Villiers, on 26th May 1844 in a Dutch Reformed congregation in Cape Town, which was pastored by the Rev. Abraham Faure. During his studies in England, Faure had been exposed to the Sunday school movement.[30] At its beginning, the Cape Town Sunday school was attended by 125 children, but in only six months it grew to 400 children.[31] By 1894, 706 congregations had Sunday schools and more than 21,000 children attended.[32] In 1915, SANSSA, the South African National Sunday School Association, a South African unit of the World Sunday School Association, was established in Port Elizabeth.

Sunday schools were mainly attended by children, even from as young as three years of age. Although efforts were made to extend these classes to adults, only a few newly-converted adults attended.[33] In most parts of Africa, Sunday schools were and still are primarily for children, although it seems that different churches in different parts of Africa, for example in Nigeria, later on broadened the Sunday school movement to adults.[34] In the early years, no standard curriculum was used and the lessons taught were prepared from the Bible and the teachers were mainly the wives of missionaries.[35] Through the years, the emphasis has always been on the Bible, and a wide variety of Biblical content. Scripture verses to memorise were used and taught with the use of different teaching techniques.[36]

Main Avenue

Gradually, Sunday school became the main avenue in African churches for nurturing children in the Christian faith. According to Mumo, 'nearly all Church denominations and local churches in Africa have a Sunday school programme'.[37] Despite some struggles and differences in development, the questions asked

---

[26] William D Taylor, 'The Presbyterian Educational Impact in Eastern Nigeria', *Journal of Religion in Africa,* 14:3 (1983): 228.
[27] Mumo, 'Sunday Schools as the Foundation', 795.
[28] Nkonsenhle Zwide Nxumalo, 'An Examination of Nine Sunday Schools in the Manzini area of Swaziland with Reference to the Relationship between Church Growth and a Vibrant Sunday School Programme': unpublished DTh thesis, South African Theological Seminary, 2014, 45.
[29] E. Greyling, *Die Sondagskool van die Nederduitse Gereformeerde Kerk,* 2nd and revised edition (Bloemfontein, South Africa: Sondagskool Boekhandel, 1965), 18.
[30] De Villiers', Die Kategese in die Nederduitse Gereformeerde Kerk in SA', 258.
[31] E. Greyling, *Die Sondagskool van die Gefedereerde Nederduitse Gereformeerde Kerke in Suid-Afrika* (Bloemfontein: Sondagskool Boekhandel, 1955), 18.
[32] Erna Oliver, 'Sunday School: Past and Present', *Studia Historiae Ecclesiasticae,* Vol. 32, no. 1, (2006): 121.
[33] Mumo, 'Sunday Schools as the Foundation', 795.
[34] Foluke Bosede, 'Trends in Christian Education in Anglophone West Africa: Nigeria', *Christian Education Journal,* 3:10 Supplement (2013): 66.
[35] Mumo, 'Sunday Schools as the Foundation', 795.
[36] Ray Johnston, *Help! I'm a Sunday School Teacher* (El Cajon, CA: Youth Specialities Books, 1995), 72.
[37] Mumo, 'Sunday Schools as the Foundation', 793.

in different parts of Africa are to a great extent very similar.[38] Existing differences between churches are mostly based on church polity.[39]

In general, the focus of Sunday schools was the spiritual formation of children. The objectives of the Sunday school can be summarised as follows:[40]

- To bring children to Christ and impart a personal knowledge of God to them;
- To provide Bible teaching to gain understanding of God's word;
- To develop a vibrant Christian life by relating Bible teachings to daily life;
- To develop appreciation for and loyalty to their Christian heritage; and
- To prepare them for church membership.

To reach the above-mentioned goals, Sunday schools were very much fashioned on the western day school model. Instead of providing primary education to children in a society which is excluding them from the educational system, Sunday school has become the primary tool for faith transmission to children inside the church. What has not changed is the educational paradigm. 'The Sunday school… is a carbon copy of a standard public school… The style, the strategy, even the classes, are based on the public school matrix. The children hardly notice any difference.'[41]

The problem with keeping this school-oriented approach intact is that faith formation very easily becomes only an intellectual exercise. The transfer of knowledge in a classroom setting away from everyday real life, is seen as the (only) vehicle to faith formation and life transformation. 'The result is a fragmented life where spiritual growth becomes a temporary, isolated process determined by a one-hour information download once a week, measured by performance in cognitive examinations and rewarded with certificates and graduations. With this type of 'educational' foundation, it is difficult to bring adult church members to an integrated life of faith and commitment to God and his Kingdom.'[42] What is more, this approach separates the generations into homogeneous groups with the noble motivation that each group's needs can best be ministered to on its own cognitive level, in its own language and style. This fragmentation usually influences the whole life of the church. In the process, children and parents, including almost all other adults, are separated from each other. The result is that children are excluded from the total life of the church and become marginalized in the faith family.

May be the biggest hurdle to overcome to change this educational paradigm to more effective faith-transformation for children is the way Africans, in general, think about children and ministry with children. In this regard, Tioye states:

> As for children's ministry, it is somewhat seen as a second-class ministry. Children ministry is not recognized as a ministry as such, but rather a gathering to prevent disturbing adults' worship. Children have value in a general perspective, but when it comes to the priorities of the church, children are overlooked and underrated; the perception is sometimes negative. Most of the time adults see children as troublesome, difficult to manage, noisy, egocentric, and the like.[43]

---

[38] Victor B. Cole, 'Guest Editorial: Trends in Christian Education in Africa – An Overview', *Christian Education Journal,* Vol. 10, Supplement (2013): 49. Cf. Fortuna N. Tioye, 'Trends in Christian Education in Francophone West Africa', *Christian Education Journal,* Vol. 10, Supplement (2013): 53.
[39] Tioye, 'Trends in Christian Education', 56, 59.
[40] Tioye, 'Trends in Christian Education', 57.
[41] Coetsee and Grobbelaar, 'A Church where Children are Welcome', 807.
[42] Coetsee and Grobbelaar, 'A Church where Children are Welcome', 807.
[43] Tioye, 'Trends in Christian Education', 54.

Still a Struggle

Through the years, this educational paradigm also created other problems for the Sunday school in Africa. According to Nxumalo, 'Much of Africa still struggles with the basic necessities needed to run a good Sunday school programme.'[44] After describing what Christian education should be, Semenye makes the following remark: 'When we examine the Christian education that is offered in East Africa, it does not measure up to what has been described above…'[45] This situation was partially the result of the fact that the role of the Sunday school in obtaining the noble goals of Christian Education, was not really recognised in the extensive research on Christian Education done in Africa during the last half of the twentieth century.[46]

The Sunday school classes are mostly large, with the average class size between twenty and thirty children, and sometimes up to ninety.[47] One reason is that the enrolment rate is very high. 'In a study conducted in African Instituted Churches, Kenya, it was found that, in many churches, Sunday schools have higher enrolments than other educational and even church services.'[48] Another reason for these big classes is limited infrastructure or the absence of good facilities.[49] Furthermore, there are not enough well-trained volunteer teachers available. Many of the available volunteers have no acquaintance with teaching children and the training available for them is mostly à la carte.[50] The training is mostly not relational-based and an excellent child-friendly teaching methodology is absent.

Right from the beginning, the lack of a proper and relevant curriculum that meets the needs of learners in Africa, was a major problem for Sunday schools. According to Nduka, Sunday school material was more standardised during the early 1900s as a result of efforts made by John H. Vincent and B.F. Jacobs of the American Sunday School Union.[51] Although the intention was good, the result was that the curriculum and the materials used became more and more western-based.[52] Mould observes from an ecumenical perspective:

> During the 19th century and well into the 20th century, in the modern missionary movement, it was standard practice for the sending churches to transplant their various forms of Christian education with little or no change, for churches being founded or aided in other lands and continents. Typically, Western teaching materials were exported. Even with translations, adaptations and attempts at curriculum by Western missionaries, none of them tasted or taught like a home-grown product. The marks of Western acculturation were too evident, the hard facts and nuances of a different local culture too great, to allow best learning to occur.[53]

The result of this approach was that

> Many of the African teachers find it difficult to use some Western lessons, even if they read English. Western materials often rely on the teacher being able to read a lesson written as if the teacher were talking to the students, then, without memorizing it word for word, remember the main ideas and present it to the students in

---

[44] Nxumalo, 'An Examination of Nine Sunday Schools', 46.
[45] Lois Semenye, 'Trends in Christian Education in East Africa', *Christian Education Journal,* Vol. 10, Supplement (2013): 74.
[46] Nduka, *Growing a Healthy Sunday School*, 253.
[47] Tioye, 'Trends in Christian Education', 58.
[48] Mumo, 'Sunday Schools as the Foundation', 795.
[49] Cf. Nxumalo, 'An Examination of Nine Sunday Schools', 46; Mumo, 'Sunday Schools as the Foundation', 798; Tioye, 'Trends in Christian Education', 58; and Semenye, 'Trends in Christian Education in East Africa', 75.
[50] Nxumalo, 'An Examination of Nine Sunday Schools', 46; Mumo, 'Sunday Schools as the Foundation', 798; Tioye, 'Trends in Christian Education', 58; and Semenye, 'Trends in Christian Education in East Africa', 76.
[51] Nxumalo, 'An Examination of Nine Sunday Schools', 45.
[52] Tioye, 'Trends in Christian Education', 56.
[53] Ralph N. Mould, 'Indigenous Curriculum Development – on an Ecumenical Basis', *International Review of Mission,* 60, no. 240, (1971): 462-463.

> similar fashion. African teachers often prefer to use their own words to express the lesson, and are not practiced in rephrasing written words as their own. Western materials are often too long for African Sunday schools, where reading speeds are often slower. More and more Western materials are based around group activities that require space, tables and equipment, but African teachers seldom have access to these.[54]

Another consequence of this use of western-based materials is that 'the African worldview is ignored or given in negative light'[55] while many themes and topics are not relevant to the African context with no practical importance for African children.[56]

Positives

In spite of the above-mentioned struggles, Cole is of the opinion that Sunday school is improving by leaps and bounds.[57] One of the factors for this improvement is the invaluable complementing work of para-church organizations, for example, Youth for Christ, Navigators, Life Ministry, Child Evangelism Fellowship, Scripture Union, Christian Union, Fellowship of Christian Unions, and Association of Evangelicals. They enhance spiritual growth through developing materials, training workers, evangelisation and disciple-making across Africa.[58] Taken on their own, Sunday schools also had a major and positive influence on the lives of many children. 'Generations of church leaders all over the world can trace their spiritual roots to a Sunday school class and a devoted teacher somewhere in their childhood. This is as true in Africa as in any other part of the world.'[59] At the end of his study on the Sunday school, Mumo came to the following conclusion: 'Sunday schools are an important organ of the Church in Africa. Despite the haphazard way they are run and the challenges they encounter, they still remain robust. They continue to enrol large numbers and give Christian nurture to millions of Africans.'[60]

Therefore, the churches in Africa have to invest in the faith formation of all these children. Maybe the challenge is not to try and do a better job of Sunday schools by building more facilities, by training more volunteer staff or by developing more relevant learning materials. Instead, we should critically rethink the underlying paradigm of Sunday schools and create a paradigm shift[61] to a way of doing ministry with children in which they are welcomed and fully included in the whole life of the local church, experiencing a more integrated faith formation process.

Bibliography

Antwi, Joseph Kofi, 'Integrating Indigenous Akan Educational Patterns into Christian Education in the Presbyterian Church of Ghana': unpublished MPhil thesis, Kwame Nkrumah University of Science and Technology, 2011.

Bosede, Foluke, 'Trends in Christian Education in Anglophone West Africa: Nigeria'. *Christian Education Journal,* Vol. 10, Supplement (2013): 63 -72.

[54] Every Child Ministries, 'Establishing African Sunday Schools': www.ecmafrica.org/projects/find-project-by-country/dr-congo-projects/sunday-school-ministries (accessed 30 January, 2015).
[55] Mumo, 'Sunday Schools as the Foundation', 799.
[56] Tioye, 'Trends in Christian Education', 58; and Semenye, 'Trends in Christian Education in East Africa', 77.
[57] Cole, 'Guest Editorial', 50.
[58] Cole, 'Guest Editorial', 50; and Semenye, 'Trends in Christian Education in East Africa', 75.
[59] Coetsee and Grobbelaar, 'A Church where Children are Welcome', 807.
[60] Mumo, 'Sunday Schools as the Foundation', 801.
[61] Cf. Tioye, 'Trends in Christian Education', 53; and Coetsee and Grobbelaar, 'A Church where Children are Welcome', 803-07.

Coetsee, Dirk and Jan Grobbelaar, 'A Church where Children are Welcome: A New Paradigm for Children's Ministry in Africa', in *Handbook of Theological Education in Africa*, edited by Isabel Apawo Phiri and Dietrich Werner, 803-17.Pietermaritzburg: Cluster Publications, 2013.

Cole, Victor B., 'Guest Editorial: Trends in Christian Education in Africa – An Overview'. *Christian Education Journal,* Vol. 10, Supplement (2013): 47-52.

De Villiers, Dawid W., 'Die Kategesein die Nederduitse Gereformeerde Kerk, in SA: 'n Prinsipiële, Historieseen Praktiese Ondersoekvan die Kategesein die Nederduitse Gereformeerde Kerk in SA': unpublished DD thesis, University of Stellenbosch, 1957.

Estep, James, Roger White and Karen L. Estep (eds.), *Mapping out Curriculum in your Church: Cartography for Christian Pilgrims.* Nashville, TN: B&H Publishing Group, 2012.

Every Child Ministries, 'Establishing African Sunday Schools'. www.ecmafrica.org/projects/find-project-by-country/dr-congo-projects/sunday-school-ministries (accessed 30 January, 2015).

Greyling, E., *Die Sondagskool van die Gefedereerde Nederduitse Gereformeerde Kerke in Suid-Afrika.* Bloemfontein, South Africa: Sondagskool Boekhandel, 1955.

Greyling, E., *Die Sondagskool van die Nederduitse Gereformeerde Kerk.* 2nd and revised edition. Bloemfontein, South Africa: Sondagskool Boekhandel, 1965.

Johnston, Ray, *Help! I'm a Sunday School Teacher.* El Cajon, CA: Youth Specialities Books, 1995.

Luumi, Pertti and Becker, Ulrich, 'Sunday School'. In *Encyclopedia of Christianity Volume 5,* edited by Erwin Fahlbusch, Jan Milic Lochman, John Mbiti, Juroslav Pelikan and Lukas Vischer. Translation editor, Geoffrey W Bromiley, 229-31. Grand Rapids, MI: Eerdmans, 2008.

Matshiga, Dumile J., 'Christian Education in the Baptist Convention of South Africa with Special Reference to Churches in the Transvaal: A Practical Theological Investigation': unpublished PhD thesis, University of Pretoria, 2001.

Mbae, Justus G., 'Keynote Address. Conference on Education as a Tool for Evangelization and Development in the Modern World'. *African Ecclésial Review,* Vol. 54, no.1 and 2, (2012), 4-13

Mould, Ralph N., 'Indigenous Curriculum Development – on an Ecumenical Basis', *International Review of Mission,* Vol. 60, Issue 240, (1971): 462-477

Mumo, Peter M., 'Sunday Schools as the Foundation of Christian Nurture and their Relevance for Theological Education in Africa'. In *Handbook of Theological Education in Africa,* edited by Isabel Apawo Phiri and Dietrich Werner, 793-802. Dorpspruit, South Africa: Cluster Publications, 2013.

Nduka, O.C., *Growing a Healthy Sunday School in African Churches.* Abia State, Nigeria: Assemblies of God Press, 2004.

Nxumalo, Nkonsenhle Zwide, 'An Examination of Nine Sunday Schools in the Manzini Area of Swaziland with Reference to the Relationship between Church Growth and a Vibrant Sunday School Programme': unpublished DTh thesis, South African Theological Seminary, 2014.

Oliver, Erna, 'Sunday School: Past and Present'. *Studia Historiae Ecclesiasticae,* 32, no.1, (2006), 117-134.

Religious Studies Department, Centenary College of Louisiana, 'A brief history of the Sunday school': www.centenary.edu/religion/dotto/rel203/Sunday%20school.ppt (accessed 5 February, 2015).

Rice, Edwin Wilbur, *The Sunday-school Movement 1780-1917 and the American Sunday-school Union 1817-1917.* New York: Arno Press and New York Times, 1971.

Semenye, Lois, 'Trends in Christian Education in East Africa'. *Christian Education Journal,* Vol. 10, Supplement (2013), 73-79.

Song, Nam Soon, 'Sunday School Revisited: An Alternative to Christian Education of the Church Today?' *Religious Education,* Vol. 108, issue 2, (2013),180-192.

Taylor, William D., 'The Presbyterian Educational Impact in Eastern Nigeria'. *Journal of Religion in Africa,* Vol. 14, Fasc 3 (1983), 223-245.

Thomas, Darren W., 'The Role, History, and Decline of the Sunday School'. In 'An Analysis of Sunday School Factors Leading to Effective Assimilation in Selected Baptist Churches in Georgia': unpublished EdD thesis, Southern Baptist Theological Seminary, 2005: 3eridan.websrvcs.com/clientimages/36689/historyofthesundayschool.pdf (accessed 29 January, 2015).

Tioye, Fortuna N., 'Trends in Christian Education in Francophone West Africa'. *Christian Education Journal,* Vol.10, Supplement (2013), 53-62.

Towns, Elmer, 'Sunday School'. In *The Popular Encyclopaedia of Church History: The People, Places, and Events that Shaped Christianity,* edited nby Ed Hindson and Dan Mitchell . Eugene, OR: Harvest House Publishers, 2013.

Viljoen, Dirk J., 'Die Dooplidmaatbedieningvan die Nederduitse Gereformeerde Kerk 1962 tot 1990, met Ttoespitsing op die Kategeseen Jeugaksies': unpublished DD thesis, University of Pretoria, 1994.

(123) URBAN AND RURAL MODELS OF SMALL CHRISTIAN COMMUNITIES (SCCS): A CASE STUDY ON EASTERN AFRICA

Joseph G. Healey

Introduction

A background paper for the 'International Consultation on Rediscovering Community' at Notre Dame, Indiana in the USA in December, 1991 compiled over 3,500 different names, titles, terms and expressions for Small Christian Communities (SCCs) and Basic Christian Communities (BCCs) worldwide.[1] The term 'Small Christian Communities'[2] is mainly used by the Catholic Church and many varieties of the term 'small groups' and 'small prayer groups' are used by the other Christian Churches. In Eastern Africa there are two distinct models or paradigms of church expressed through small communities: the Protestant/Pentecostal Model and the Catholic Model. Both are very creative and are found in both urban and rural areas. Due to the data available, this article is mainly about the Catholic experience.

The Protestant/Pentecostal Model

There are many varieties of small groups, small prayer groups, small communities and church small groups/small group Christian Churches in Eastern Africa that can be classified as follows:

- Bible Study Groups, Café Churches, Fellowship Groups, House Cell Fellowships and House Churches in the Anglican (Episcopalian) Church.
- Home Group Fellowship Small Groups that operate like Fraternal Communities in the Baptist Church.
- Small Cell Groups in the Mormon Church and Seventh Day Adventist (SDA) Church.
- Cell Churches, Cell Groups, Devotional Groups, Fellowship (called *Ushirika* in Swahili) Groups, Home Cells, Home Churches and Spiritual Growth Groups in the Pentecostal churches.
- District Groups in the Presbyterian Church.
- Church Homes in the United Church of Christ.

The cornerstone of most of these small groups[3] or small prayer groups is the Bible. Most common is weekly Bible Study following an organized reading and study plan. At times there is Bible Sharing and Bible Reflection. Devotional small groups are increasing. Fellowship is very important, especially in the African context, including emphasis on community building, singing and socializing together.

---

[1] Joseph Healey, 'Evolving A World Church From the Bottom Up: An Analysis and Interpretation of 3,500 Different Names, Titles, Terms, Expressions, Descriptions and Meanings for and about Small Christian Communities/Basic Christian Communities in the World with 11 Case Studies From Six Continents', Background Paper for the International Consultation on 'Rediscovering Community – International Perspectives', University of Notre Dame, South Bend, Indiana, USA, 8-12 December, 1991, Notre Dame: Photocopied Paper, 33 pages. Sections of this paper were published in Agatha Radoli (ed.), *How Local is the Local Church? Small Christian Communities and Church in Eastern Africa*, Eldoret: AMECEA Gaba Publications, *Spearhead* 126-128, 1993. pp. 59-103 and the *Newsletter of Latin American/North American Church Concerns (LANACC)*.

[2] In Eastern Africa we capitalize the terms 'Small Christian Community' (SCC), 'Small Christian Communities' (SCCs) and Basic Christian Communities (BCCs) because it is a key pastoral priority in our parishes and dioceses and the official pastoral policy of the Catholic bishops.

[3] A very helpful resource is the Small Groups Website that is a ministry of *Leadership Journal.* It has many Training Tools and Bible Studies. www.smallgroups.com (accessed 17 February, 2015).

The rapid development of Evangelical and Pentecostal churches in Africa has witnessed the growth of the cell group model. In Nairobi, Kenya, they are described as 'a cell group of faithful living in the same vicinity'.[4] They evangelise the world by multiplying new groups. These small groups, especially in urban areas, often follow the systematic teaching plan of a dynamic pastor or charismatic leader with many printed resources and electronic resources like large video screens in the church.

Catholic Model

Today, there are over 180,000 Small Christian Communities (SCCs) in the Catholic Church in the nine AMECEA[5] countries in Eastern Africa. Tanzania has over 60,000 SCCs and Kenya has over 45,000 SCCs. SCCs are a 'New Way of Being (Becoming) Church' and a 'New Model of Church' in Eastern Africa. These SCCs 'are not a movement in the Catholic Church, but the church on the move' to distinguish them from various movements like the Charismatic Movement and the Marian Movement. SCCs are not a programme or project, but a way of life. They are directly integrated into the pastoral structure and leadership of the parish. Three helpful 'descriptions' gathered over the years of both urban and rural SCCs in the Catholic Church in Eastern Africa are:

- An SCC is a small neighbourhood, parish-based group that is a pastoral model of church that transforms the parish into a communion of communities and an instrument of evangelization.
- An SCC is a small group of around fifteen people who meet weekly, usually in their homes, to reflect on the Bible especially the Gospel reading for the following Sunday, and connect it to their daily lives.
- An SCC is a caring, sharing, faith-reflecting, praying and serving community in which ongoing Christian formation and pastoral outreach takes place.

Historical Perspective of the Catholic Model

The very beginning of Small Christian Communities (SCCs) in the Catholic Church in Eastern Africa (and the whole of English-speaking Africa) can be traced back to the joint pastoral and missionary efforts of the American Maryknoll missionaries in three rural parishes in the Luo-speaking Deanery (Nyarombo, Ingri and Kowak Parishes) in North Mara in Musoma Diocese in north-western Tanzania in 1966. Then these small communities spread to Masonga and Tatwe that are also Luo-speaking parishes.

The Maryknoll missionaries focused on the formation of small natural communities that were neighbourhood groups of Luo-speaking people in the rural areas. By 1968, Nyarombo Parish had 28 small communities, Ingri Parish had 22, and Kowak Parish had 25. As many as 80% of the local Catholics participated in these small communities.

In the late 1960s, Dutch Missionary of Africa Father J. Brouwer, MAfr,, developed the plan of the town parish of Tabora in Tabora Archdiocese, Tanzania, that had six wards. Each ward had small groups of

---

[4] 'Small Christian Community – a Cell Group of Faithful Living in the Same Vicinity', *The Nairobian*, 8-14 August, 2014, 4.

[5] AMECEA is an acronym for 'Association of Member Episcopal Conferences in Eastern Africa.' It is a service organisation for the National Episcopal Conferences of the nine English-speaking countries of Eastern Africa, namely Eritrea (1993), Ethiopia (1979), Kenya (1961), Malawi (1961), South Sudan (2011), Sudan (1973), Tanzania (1961), Uganda (1961) and Zambia (1961). The Republic of South Sudan became independent on 9 July, 2011, but the two Sudans remain part of one Episcopal Conference. Somalia (1995) and Djibouti (2002) are Affiliate Members. AMECEA is one of the eight Regional Episcopal Conferences of SECAM (Symposium of Episcopal Conferences of Africa and Madagascar).

Christians that consisted of 10-12 families. These SCCs met regularly to pray, read the Bible, discuss their problems and explore how they could best live their Christian lives.

In 1969, Small Christian Communities started in St Charles Lwanga Catholic Church, Regiment Parish in an urban area of Lusaka Archdiocese, Zambia. German Missionary of Africa Father Andreas Edele, MAfr started SCCs in the parish through a three-year visitation of parishioners in their homes.

Thus, experiences of SCCs at the grassroots existed in both rural and urban areas before the famous AMECEA Study Conference on 'Planning for the [Catholic] Church in Eastern Africa in the 1980s' in Nairobi, Kenya, in December, 1973. This conference stated: 'We have to insist on building church life and work on Basic Christian Communities in both rural and urban areas. Church life must be based on the communities in which everyday life and work take place: those basic and manageable social groups whose members can experience real inter-personal relationships and feel a sense of communal belonging, both in living and working.'[6] This pastoral policy was in the context of the statement: 'We are convinced that in these countries of Eastern Africa it is time for the Church to become truly local, that is, self-ministering, self-propagating and self-supporting.'[7]

The AMECEA Study Conference on 'Building Small Christian Communities' took place in Nairobi, Kenya, in July 1976. The key statement was: 'Systematic formation of Small Christian Communities should be the key pastoral priority in the years to come in Eastern Africa.'[8] This is the single most important statement made about SCCs.

Findings in Evaluating SCCs in the Catholic Church in Eastern Africa

Building the Church as Family of God: Evaluation of Small Christian Communities in *Eastern Africa* by Joseph Healey is a free online ebook containing 633 pages as of 2nd August 2015 on the Small Christian Communities Global Collaborative Website.[9] This book systematically evaluates SCCs in the Catholic Church in Eastern Africa only. A search shows that the word 'urban' is mentioned 71 times and the word 'rural' 62 times. Some findings were:

Research on the composition and characteristics of the members of SCCs in Eastern Africa include these factors: age, cultural preferences, economic status (poor/rich), education, employment, ethnicity (one ethnic group/many), gender, geography (urban, urban/rural [called peri-urban in Zambia], rural/urban, rural), living/housing situation, marital status (single/engaged/married), political affiliation, etc. While the overwhelming majority are Catholics, there are some SCC members from other religious denominations. A major challenge is how to creatively integrate these differences.

Depending on location, Muslims and members of African Religions living in the neighbourhood also participate in these SCCs. In the SCCs of the villages in rural areas in Eastern Africa, Catholic and members of African regions live side-by-side and share many aspects of everyday life. In urban areas that are predominantly Muslim, tensions sometimes arise, but most people want to live peacefully together.

Today, some situations in Africa lead to the instability or even the disappearance of SCCs/BCCs. On the one hand, war and political instability force people – especially in rural areas – to leave their home or even the country. On the other hand, the situation of economic instability and poverty force people to spend most of their time searching for the basic necessities of life to survive. Then many Catholics have not

---

[6] 'Guidelines for the Catholic Church in Eastern Africa in the 1980s.' *African Ecclésial Review (AFER)*, Vol. 16, no 1 and 2, (1974): 10.

[7] 'Guidelines for the Catholic Church:' 12.

[8] AMECEA Study Conference on 'Building Small Christian Communities: Conclusions.' *African Ecclésial Review (AFER)*, Vol. 18, no. 5 (October, 1976): 250.

[9] www.smallchristiancommunities.org/images/stories/pdf/Build_new.pdf (accessed 2 August, 2015).

enough time to participate in the SCC/BCC activities. SCCs/BCCs require a minimum of peace and stability to really be the 'Church in the Neighbourhood'.

Today, Galatians 3:28 is rewritten in our SCCs in Kenya to read: 'There is neither Kikuyu nor Luo, there is neither Christian nor Muslim, there is neither Catholic nor Protestant, there is neither married or unmarried, there is neither rich nor poor, there is neither educated nor uneducated, there is neither city dweller nor rural dweller, there is neither Kenyan nor foreigner (expatriate), there is not male and female; for you are all one in Christ Jesus.'

In Eastern Africa we can refer to SCCs as the homestead of God in rural areas and the household of God in urban areas. SCCs are household churches. SCCs are small households of faith. SCC Twinning can also take place on the local level, for example, twinning between a SCC in an urban area and a SCC in a rural area of a diocese.

A special challenge is to respond creatively to the changing sociological patterns in the neighbourhoods in urban areas in Ethiopia. A new style of SCCs is needed for Catholics who are scattered and move frequently in cities such as Addis Abba. Ethiopian Bishop Lesanu-Chrostos Matheos states: 'We have a difficulty in setting up SCCs in urban areas – people are a minority, scattered and not neighbours.'[10]

On the growing challenge of how to develop SCCs in urban areas, Tanzanian Bishop Method Kilaini points out:

> The challenge of Dar es Salaam Archdiocese is to unite the Catholics from all those diverse origins with different status into one cohesive church. To have these people who are uprooted from their cultural home setting and are in an anonymous milieu keep their personal respect reinforced by mutual support in doing good. To give them a new clan and a new tribe whose cohesion is based on faith, love and care. In other words, to give them an extended family in the city that they left at home in the village.[11]

Especially in urban areas, Africans of different Christian denominations and religious faiths live side-by-side. In the traditional African spirit of community, unity and hospitality, neighbourhood Catholic SCCs are inclusive. Christians of other denominations participate in the following: social activities such as the celebrations of marriages, graduations, year-end parties and national patriotic events; visiting the sick; bereavement; and outreach programmes such as community health care, visiting people with HIV/AIDS, visiting prisoners and self-help campaigns to fix up the neighbourhood.

One can expect that factors such as urbanisation and secularism/secularisation influence the changing styles and patterns of SCCs in Eastern Africa. In some parishes of the city periphery and the housing estates, there is a half-developed form of SCCs that is sometimes called a 'block system' or 'cell sytem'. The geographical parish area is divided into neighbourhood areas. People of such 'blocks' or 'cells' meet in one of their homes, pray together, share their experiences, organise neighbourly help, report to the parish council. The priests realise they need these blocks for the administration of the parish, but do not develop them further into genuine, fully-fledged SCCs.

Italian missionary Father Daniel Moschetti, MCCJ's insight is that SCCs are a fitting ecclesiology for the cities in Africa:

---

[10] Lesanu-Chrostos Matheos' comment during the Second Theological Colloquium on Church, Religion and Society in Africa (TCCRSA II). Theme: 'The Church We Want: Theological Voices From Within and Outside the Church at the Service of Ecclesia in Africa.' Hekima College Institute of Peace Studies and International Relations. Nairobi, Kenya, 7 August, 2014.

[11] Method Kilaini. 'Small Christian Communities: Sharing the Tanzania Pastoral Experience.' Mwanza: Printed Paper, 2014: 4. The Swahili version is 'Jumuiya Ndogo Ndogo za Kikristo (JNNK): Uzoefu wa Kichungaji wa Tanzania.' www.smallchristiancommunities.org/images/stories/pdf/small_christian.pdf (accessed 2 August, 2015).

> This leads to a measure of decentralization to neighbourhood household groups. This model of being a church-community befits the human situation of the city and slum-dwellers because it creates a network of solidarity and mutual trust.[12]

SCC members themselves describe how their small communities offer security and support in the midst of the unrest, crime and violence of Nairobi city life.

An interesting example of SCCs responding to the contemporary signs of the times is the changes in the languages used in SCC Bible services and meetings due to population shifts in urban areas in Africa. Kenyan Consolata seminarian, Walter Kisikwa Ingosi, IMC, narrates an important case study involving a critical incident when two non-Gikuyu-speaking families moved into an all Gikuyu-speaking area of St John the Baptist Parish in Nairobi Archdiocese. He explains how, after much discussion in their meetings, the St Maria Goretti SCC members 'were willing to solve it [the language issue] once and for all by allowing all their meetings to be done in Kiswahili. They acknowledged what had taken place and asked forgiveness from the two families. This was a very important decision that brought everyone home. They were able to decide themselves and join together in a way that will unite them together'.[13]

There is a lot of discussion about the breakdown of the family structure in our contemporary society in Africa (and more so in western society). There are large numbers of single parent homes in urban centres like Nairobi. The husband/father is often a 'missing person'.[14] In the absence of men in the slums and informal settlements of many Nairobi parishes, single mothers are elected the leaders of their SCCs.

Truly, the Small Christian Communities are an important 'answer' to the many questions on the New Evangelisation. We have seen it in the busy urban Kariobangi Parish in Nairobi. The very active and well organised 72 SCCs help over 75,000 Catholics in the parish. The Small Christian Community was the success story for the methodology of St Paul and our contemporary experience in Eastern Africa shows we have to revive it again all over the world if we want to remain a vibrant and witnessing Church today.

Key factors in the growth of SCCs in both urban and rural areas in Eastern Africa include: moving from inward-looking prayer groups to authentic SCCs that are outward-looking and mission-minded; Eastern Africa SCCs that are a pastoral, parish-based model; the importance of Bible Sharing, Bible Reflection and practical action in the life and ministry of SCCs; the active involvement and participation of lay people in this new model of church that emerges from the grassroots up; using the Pastoral Spiral ('See', 'Judge' and 'Act') as a new paradigm for promoting justice and peace in Africa today.

Eastern Africa SCCs have developed a more enculturated model that is deeply involved in evangelisation. A key challenge is the question: 'What are the different human problems in Africa that we should reflect on in our SCC meetings in the light of the Gospel?' based on St John Paul II's Apostolic Exhortation, *The Church in Africa*, No. 89. As a new model of church, SCCs emphasise deeper biblical reflection and more regular use of the Pastoral Spiral to influence more effectively the pastoral and social life around them. As facilitators of reconciliation, justice, and peace, SCC members can be very important in the transformation of the Catholic Church in Africa and in the transformation of the religious, social, economic, political and cultural life of African society.

New Directions of SCCs in Eastern Africa

An ongoing challenge for SCCs is to constantly read the signs of the times and to respond creatively to the religious, social, economic, political and cultural shifts and trends in Eastern Africa. This means

[12] Daniel Moschetti. *Urban Ministry in Africa: Need for New Models*. Eldoret: AMECEA Gaba Publications, *Spearhead* Nos. *145-147*, 1997: 64.
[13] Walter Ingosi. 'A Challenge of Using Different Languages in a SCC.' Nairobi: Unpublished Paper, 2013: 4.
[14] Healey, *Building the Church as Family of God*: 201.

strengthening the 'Lights' (more emphasis on justice and peace concerns) and correcting the 'Shadows' (too many SCCs have become fund-raising projects).

The vitality and growth of SCCs is seen in their new expressions. For example, in the last five years Youth Small Christian Communities (YSCCs) have developed especially in urban areas in Eastern Africa with two main types: Parish-based and school-based/campus-based (such as university students in dormitories/residence halls/hostels). Due to African cultural traditions, African youth normally do not speak in public in front of adults, so youth do not usually actively participate in adult SCCs in Eastern Africa. Thus, it is crucial to form specific youth SCCs that give young people a specific identity, voice and role and to encourage them to plan their own discussions, reflections and activities.

In the light of important meetings and events on family and marriage in the next few years, a new challenge is how Small Christian Communities can promote Christian values in our families and marriages in Eastern Africa.

As we move into the future we continue to create the path by walking. The way forward is open-ended and exciting for the growth of SCCs. New priorities will emerge. With the help of the Holy Spirit, may the Christian Churches in Eastern Africa respond boldly and creatively.

Bibliography

African Proverbs, Sayings and Stories Website. www.afriprov.org (accessed 17 February, 2015).

AMECEA Plenary. *Building Christian Communities, African Ecclésial Review (AFER)*, Vol. 18, no. 5.Eldoret: AMECEA Gaba Publications, 1976.

AMECEA Plenary. *Planning for the Church in Eastern Africa in the 1980s, African Ecclésial Review (AFER)*, 16, no 1 and 2. Eldoret: AMECEA Gaba Publications, 1974.

AMECEA Website. www.amecea.org (accessed 17 February 2015).

Final Documents of the Third Extraordinary General Assembly of the Synod of Bishops on 'The Pastoral Challenges of the Family in the Context of Evangelization' including the *Report of the Synod* and the *Message.* Vatican Website, 2014. www.vatican.va/roman_curia/synod/index.htm (accessed 17 February, 2015).

Flynn, Kieran. *Communities for the Kingdom: A Handbook for Small Christian Community Leaders.* Eldoret: AMECEA Gaba Publications, *Spearhead* nos. 181-182, (2007).

Francis, Pope. Post-Synodal Apostolic Exhortation, *The Joy of the Gospel*. Nairobi: Paulines Publications Africa, 2013 and Vatican Website, 2013.

Healey, Joseph M. M, 'Twelve Case Studies of Small Christian Communities in Eastern Africa,' in *How Local is the Local Church? Small Christian Communities and Church in Eastern Africa*, edited by Radoli, Agatha, 59-103. Eldoret: AMECEA Gaba Publications, 1993.

______. 'Evolving A World Church From the Bottom Up: An Analysis and Interpretation of 3,500 Different Names, Titles, Terms, Expressions, Descriptions and Meanings for and about Small Christian Communities/Basic Christian Communities in the World with 11 Case Studies From Six Continents,' Background Paper for the International Consultation on 'Rediscovering Community – International Perspectives,' University of Notre Dame, South Bend, Indiana, USA, 8-12 December, 1991, Notre Dame: Privately printed, 1991.

______. *Building the Church as Family of God: Evaluation of Small Christian Communities in Eastern Africa*, Eldoret: AMECEA Gaba Publications – CUEA Press Double *Spearhead* Nos. 199-200 (Print Version 2012 and 1st Reprint 2014).

______. *Building the Church as Family of God: Evaluation of Small Christian Communities in Eastern Africa*. Free Online Ebook on the Small Christian Communities Global Collaborative Website. www.smallchristiancommunities.org/images/stories/pdf/Build_new.pdf (accessed 2 August, 2015).

Healey, Joseph and Donald Sybertz. *Towards an African Narrative Theology*. Nairobi: Paulines Publications, 1996 and Maryknoll, NY: Orbis Books, 1997.

Healey, Joseph and Jeanne Hinton (eds.), *Small Christian Communities Today: Capturing the New Moment.* Maryknoll, NY: Orbis Books, 2005; Nairobi: Paulines Publications Africa, 2006; and Bangalore: Claretian Publications, 2006.

Instrumentum Laboris for the Synod of Bishops XIV Ordinary General Assembly, *The Vocation and Mission of the Family in the Church and the Contemporary World*, Vatican: Liberia Editrice and Nairobi Paulines Publications Africa, 2015. www.vatican.va/roman_curia/synod/documents/rc_synod_doc_20150623_instrumentum-xiv-assembly_en.html (accessed 17 February, 2015).

John Paul II, Post-Synod Apostolic Exhortation, *The Church in Africa* (*Ecclesia in Africa),* Nairobi: Paulines Publications Africa, 1995.

Lineamenta of the Synod of Bishops XVI Ordinary General Assembly. *The Pastoral Challenges of the Family in the Context of Evangelization*, Vatican: Liberia Editrice and Nairobi: Paulines Publications Africa, 2015. www.vatican.va/roman_curia/synod/documents/rc_synod_doc_20141209_lineamenta-xiv-assembly_en.html (accessed 17 February, 2015).

Morgan, Alison, 'September, 2014 Notes' on Roger Walton, *Disciples Together – Discipleship, Formation and Small Groups*, London: SCM Press 2014, retrieved on 27 February, 2015, www.alisonmorgan.co.uk/Walton2014.pdf (accessed 17 February, 2015).

Small Christian Communities Global Collaborative Website and 'Facebook Page.'www.smallchristiancommunities.org (accessed 2 August, 2015).

Small Groups Website. www.smallgroups.com (accessed 17 February, 2015).

(124) Pastoral Theology: Its Role and Relevance in African Christianities

Herbert Moyo

Introduction

Actions speak louder than words. The church can be described by academics and theologians in books and articles, but it is the life of the church through overtly pastoral religious practices and the general life of Christians that makes the church visible in society. Pastoral theology is the theological praxis of the church as the body of Christ. It seeks to interact with the socio-economic, religious and political realities of specific contexts. Pastoral theology is the theological and doctrinal foundation and justification for the pastoral praxis of African Christianities. The continuous critical reflection on the continuous pastoral practices of Christianities is the foundation of the relevance of pastoral theology.

Pastoral theology is the discourse on the praxis of God and the praxis of human beings in the socio-economic, religious and political context. Christianity in Africa has so many types and styles that it becomes fair to talk of African Christianities instead of African Christianity. Pastoral theologies vary according to the different strands of Christianities. However, in general, pastoral theology concerns itself with the inherent presence of Christianity in the everyday life of Christians. Pastoral theology drives the visibility of Christianity at significant points of the lives of individuals and communities, both in joy and sorrow. In fact, in most African settings, pastoral theology is synonymous with the functions of a pastor as he or she responds to the pastoral needs of individuals, groups and communities.[1] This chapter argues that pastoral theology is the heartbeat of African Christianities, as pastors act as diviners or spirit mediums, responding on behalf of God (and the church) to the challenges and joys of communities as the shepherding arm of Christianity. I will describe pastoral theology to lay the ground for a discussion on the role of the pastoral theology which can be personified by the role of the pastor. The chapter describes the African context in general and how it interplays with the understanding of the role and relevance of pastoral theology in African Christianities.

Defining Pastoral Theology

Pastoral theology is concerned with the holistic care of humanity and the environment from a theological perspective. Mwaura says, 'Pastoral theology… discusses the duties, obligations and the functions of the priest in the care of souls.'[2] In addition to this understanding, I would say it is the care for all creation by pastors and all believers as espoused by the concept of the priesthood of all believers. Pastoral theology is the action-reflection dialectic in the shepherding ministry of the church. It is central in African Christianities as it makes Christianity relevant to the contextual needs of people. Pastoral theology contextualizes and enculturates pastoral care, producing a hybrid suitable for specific contexts.[3]

---

[1] W. Drum. 'Pastoral Theology' in *The Catholic Encyclopedia* (New York: Robert Appleton Company, 1912). http://www.newadvent.org/cathen/14611a.htm (accessed 9 February, 2015).

[2] Philomena Njeri Mwaura, 'Healing: A Pastoral Concern', in *Pastoral Care in African Christianity*, eds. D. W. Waruta and Hannah W. Kinoti (Nairobi: Acton Publishers, 2000), 72.

[3] See Roderick R. Hewitt, *Church and Culture: An Anglo-Caribbean Experience of Hybridity and Contradiction* (Pietermaritzburg: Cluster Publications, 2012), 50-84.

Mwaura adds pastoral theology '... can best be understood when it is integrated into the cultures, times, circumstances and actual situations of a particular people'.[4] This understanding calls for theological reflection on the contextual pastoral needs and dynamics in a variety of socio-economic, cultural, religious and political situations of the location of the church. 'Pastoral theology is the continued reflection of the Church on the unchanging truth of doctrine in view of its being lived in faith, hope, and charity, and in view of giving direction to all of the pastoral activity of the Church. Pastoral theology studies doctrine in order to uncover its significance for the human person and build up the one, holy, catholic, and apostolic Church.'[5]

Pastoral theology in African Christianities can be classified into six operational models of pastoral care, with different denominations emphasizing certain models over others. The following are the basic classifications: pastoral care (PC) as performance of miracles and exorcisms; PC as homiletics, liturgy and worship; PC as prophetic social action for socio-economic and political transformation; PC as healing (there are different forms of healing ministries but the basic understanding is that the church must do healing); PC as socialization (personal interaction)[6] and PC as religious and civic education. Currently, in African Christianities, the most prominent models of pastoral care are healing and the performance of miracles to solve the problems of church and pastoral clients. Churches that perform miracles are fast-growing compared to those that heal through the western type of hospitalization. To sum up this section, pastoral theology is the praxis of the pastoral care ministry of the church as it demonstrates the mystery of the saving power of the Christian God over other gods.

The Role of Pastoral Theology in African Christianities

Pastoral theology and social construction

African Christianities cannot be ignored by either politicians or economists in determining the direction of society. Pastoral care is, in some cases, part of the many problems of society, but it is also part of the solution. Pastoral theology interrogates different socio-economic and political challenges from a Christian perspective.

Pastoral theology determines the nature of the pastoral voices that are heard in African Christianities. The role of pastoral theology in social construction is to develop an authentic Christian pastoral voice within the diverse Christianities that can positively contribute to socio-economic and political development and/or stability.[7] The challenge is that there are many voices that claim to be authentic pastoral voices, and this confuses society, since there are no tools for authenticating the voices that they come across. On the one hand, the pastoral voice of the church is believed to bring new life through conversion and transformation of individuals and communities. The prophetic pastoral voice is expected to speak the truth to political establishments, thereby bringing peace and justice where there is strife and war. On the other hand, pastoral voices can lead to war and suffering, in cases such as in Nigeria where religious strife exist

[4] Mwaura, 'Healing: A Pastoral Concern', 72; See also John Mbiti, *African Religions and Philosophy* (London: Heinemann, 1969) and Thomas Oden, *Pastoral Theology: Essentials of Ministry* (San Francisco: Harper and Row, 1983), x.

[5] Ave Maria University, "What is Pastoral Theology?" www.avemaria.edu/MajorsPrograms/GraduatePrograms/MTSinPastoralTheology/WhatisPastoralTheology.aspx. (accessed 20 February, 2014).

[6] Emmanuel Y. Lartey, *In Living Color: An Intercultural Approach to Pastoral Care and Counselling* (London and New York: Jessica Kingsley Publishers, 2003), 55-59.

[7] Herbert Moyo, 'Religion and African Indigenous Knowledge Systems: Healing and Communal Reconstruction in African Communities', *Alternation* Special Edition No. 11, (2013): 207-236.

between Christians and the Boko Haram militants.[8] At times, the pastoral voice can speak unreasonably in the name of God. For example, it is irresponsible for the pastoral voice to say that sick people with chronic illnesses should stop taking scientifically proven medications because they have been healed by the Holy Spirit. Hence, the lack of analysing the nature of the pastoral voice can at times lead to war, human suffering and death.

In Africa, there is no problem of unbelief. However, there is the challenge of the authenticity of the pastoral voices that people are being asked to believe. This is especially true of African Christianities where church leaders speak with many contesting voices at times, for instance, against tried and tested means of healing chronic diseases such as HIV, tuberculosis and diabetes. The role of pastoral theology is to come up with life-affirming pastoral practices and proclamations.

Celebrating the God of life and standing up for dignity and justice through pastoral theology

Pastoral care as prophetic social action for socio-economic and political transformation is social activism by pastoral care-givers. Christianity in Africa is a key factor in civil society and can be regarded as one of the most vibrant assets, energies and tools for engaging social and political developments on the African continent. In this case, pastoral theology in African Christianities becomes concerned with social action, with pastoral care-givers becoming social activists.[9]

Africa is riddled with unfavourable political developments that impact negatively on the socio-economic sphere of humanity. Corruption, partisan politics, political violence, rigged elections, genocides, tribalism, ethnic wars and civil wars are very common in most parts of Africa. The above scenarios usually result in the abuse of human rights, economic meltdown, and mass movements of people as internally displaced people and as refugees. Pastoral care-givers advocate prophetically against questionable political developments through ecumenical structures and individual prophetic pastors. According to the World Council of Churches, 'Christians have been called by God to fulfil a mission in the world, and obedience to this call means full participation in the life of the world.'[10] Christians have a responsibility to be concerned about the structures of society as well as the morality of individuals who make up society.

The church '... seeks a responsible society in which there is a genuine respect for persons, freedom, peace, justice for all, and a due restraint of power... defending basic rights and dignity...'[11] The African political realm is affected by tribalism, ethnic wars, racism, political intolerance and the inherent mentality of a one-party state system. In this realm, pastoral theology has the role of being the conscience of society. Through pastoral theology, the church should play a role of bringing about tolerance, agreements, the harmonizing of competing claims, persuasion and co-operation for the sake of influencing the quality of life in society. In fact, '... the presence and ministry of the church influence the quality of life in society. As one formative influence, the church may awaken and renew the social conscience within society. Such influence upon the common life will have indirect consequences for policies of the state'.[12] Through pastoral theology the church should use its wealth and heritage of ethical teachings to speak prophetically in defence of human dignity, human rights and human welfare.

Through *diaconia*, the church responds to government failure by providing hospitals, schools and hospices, sourcing drugs, food parcels and entrepreneurial initiatives. The church therefore seeks to bring

---

[8] Goodluck Jonathan, 'Why Nigeria has not Defeated Boko Haram' *Premium Times*, 28 September 2014. https://www.premiumtimesng.com/news/ headlines/168771-why-nigeria-has-not-defeated-boko-haram-jonathan.html (accessed 15 November, 2014).
[9] Lartey, 'In Living Color', 57-58.
[10] WCC 1967:110.
[11] WCC1967:111.
[12] WCC 1967:112.

the heavenly values of equity to the kingdom of the world. 'The model of pastoral care implied in this approach has been described as prophecy to structures or speaking truth to power.'[13]

Pastoral theology and the healing ministry of the church

African Christianities have a mandate to heal society of any possible iniquity and sickness. The African context is premised on physical, emotional, spiritual, psychological, communal and relational wellness.[14] Wellness and health from an African perspective is holistic. For example, there is a need for continued healing in coming to terms with different sexualities,[15] such as homosexuality, trans-gender, bisexuality and intersex. Christianities should begin to stumble by being inclusive rather than to stumble on the side of excluding others, to err by loving rather than to err by hurting. Pastoral theology espouses the healing of broken relationships.

African Traditional Religion is rooted in the realm of the supernatural. Christianity has also been placed in that realm. In the African worldview, religion is set apart mainly for responding to situations beyond human capabilities. It is in situations such as death, incurable diseases, bad luck and spiritual challengesthat people turn to religion for answers. Christianity is therefore to fill the gap of ATRs by responding to challenges through supernatural acts.

In the realm of the supernatural, the most common reference is made to questions of sickness and prosperity. Healing for the sick is central in the quest for religious intervention. The future of pastoral theology in African Christianities therefore lies in its ability to respond to the socio-economic and healing needs of Africans. Having challenges based on diseases such as HIV and AIDS, tuberculosis and malaria, churches can only do well in responding to these.

Popular, growing African pastoral ministries are founded on healing. These churches perform miracles and spiritual healing in the name of Jesus. Miraculous healing crusades, camps and sessions are held, where people profess to have been miraculously healed. For example, in the time of HIV and AIDS, on many television channels across sub-Saharan Africa, images of people living with HIV being 'miraculously healed' are being aired. In some instances, people living with HIV form their own queue, carrying placards that indicate their specific health challenge. The 'man of God'[16] will then touch the person living with HIV and declare him or her delivered in 'the name of Jesus'.[17] In many instances, people are given holy water or holy pieces of string or wool to use as tangible sources of healing.

Pastoral ministries that do not promote miraculous healing do not attract a big following. The growth of African Christianities is determined by healing. This is understandable, since for Christianity to be comfortable in Africa, it has to resonate and enculturate with ATRs. The beliefs and practices of ATRs seek to secure health and eliminate pain and suffering. 'Salvation in ATRs is to a very large extent earthbound: health, prosperity and longevity in this world.'[18] In agreement, Laurenti Magesa says,

> … so from beginning to the end, from birth to death, African religion stresses and orients its adherents, directly or symbolically, towards the 'abundance of life' motif. Thus birth, all the rites of passage marking different

---

[13] Lartey, *In Living Color*, 58.

[14] See Mwaura, 'Healing: A Pastoral Concern', 72-100.

[15] Herbert Moyo, 'Caught between a Rock and a Hard Place: The Politics of Homosexuality and the Response of the Evangelical Lutheran Church in Zimbabwe (ELCZ)', *Journal of Gender and Religion in Africa* Vol. 18, No. 1, (July 2012): 155-167.

[16] It is mostly and popularly men who perform such miracles, hence the popular phrase 'man of God', with little said about 'woman of God'.

[17] Ezra Chitando and Charles Klagba, *In the Name of Jesus! Healing in the Age of HIV* (Geneva: WCC Publications, 2013), 2.

[18] Chitando and Klagba, *In the Name of Jesus!*, 6.

> stages in the development of the vital force, and indeed earth itself as the culmination of life, receive special attention in African Traditional Religious activity.[19]

Ogbu Kalu is of the view that the issue of health and healing is a very important aspect of religious life in Africa, and in explaining the growth of both AICs and Pentecostalism on the continent. Healing is the heartbeat of pastoral care. It releases the energy for participatory worship that integrates the body, spirit, and soul.[20]

Pastoral Care as Socio-Economic Transformation

Amongst the AICs, the quest for material success and prosperity ranks second to healing in many sprouting ministries in Zimbabwe and South Africa. The growth of Pentecostal churches and AICs is also located in spiritualization of materialism. In Zimbabwe, prophets such as Emmanuel Makandiwa of the United Family International Church, Eurbert Angel[21] of Spirit Embassy, and Walter Magaya of Prophetic Healing Deliverance Ministries (popularly known as PHD Ministries) perform miracles to give people material gain. There is popular miracle money where the prophet prays that one gets money and the following day there is money in the bank account of the church member. People give to the church ('seeding') in order to receive tenfold from the 'man of God'. Prophets pray for people to have homes, money, motor vehicles, businesses, designer clothes and employment. If there is witchcraft preventing prosperity, the prophets can exorcise such evil spells in the name of Jesus.

In the pastoral healing mission of the churches, the question of who approves what is becoming urgent. In seeking to become responsible, there are situations that could result in a high level of irresponsibility. If, in the process of healing, the church discourages adherents from taking tried and trusted forms of medication, then this becomes irresponsible and criminal on the part of the church. For example, there are people who have stopped taking antiretroviral drugs because of claims that they have been miraculously healed. People then develop drug-resistant strains of HIV. This has also happened to people with other forms of chronic illness, such as hypertension and diabetes. In such cases, the church should be prophetic to itself. Through scientific means, the state has also been questioning the voice of the church. So, who authenticates the pastoral voice of the church in the ongoing healing mission where these have displayed a level of irresponsibility?

Pastoral Care as Care

People in many parts of Africa are wounded both physically and emotionally and they need healing. So a key function of pastoral theology is to create an understanding of a God who cares for humanity and the environment. The relevance of pastoral theology cannot be over-emphasized in Africa's context of multiple forms of wounds – caused by perpetual wars in some parts of Africa, the salient scourge of HIV and AIDS which is vicious in Africa, poverty and bad governance.

---

[19] Laurenti Magesa, *African Religion: The Moral Tradition of Abundant Life* (Nairobi: Pauline Publications Africa,1998), 250.

[20] Ogbu Kalu, *African Pentecostalism: An Introduction* (New York: Oxford University Press, 2008), 263.

[21] This prophet's original name before being called by God was Eurbert Mudzamiri. After his calling to serve God, he resorted to a new identity.

The Relevance of Pastoral Theology in African Theologies

The primary focus of pastoral theology is precisely the 'living relevance' of doctrine in contemporary Africa. It is not divorced from the globalized world, but is still unique from the rest of the world in its own way, thereby requiring uniquely African interpretations of the gospel message. Pastoral theology is the theoretical soul of the praxis of pastoral care. Pastoral theology enables continuous reflection on the practices of the pastoral ministry of the church. Pastoral theology is the theoretical basis for bringing the word of God to the socio-economic and political realities of given pastoral contexts to inspire a spirit of liberation. In addition, Lartey says pastoral theology is also based '... on a socio-economic and political analysis of a specific social context. Such analysis is undergirded by historical criticism and theological reflection. Its aim is the transformation of societies and persons'.[22] So the relevance of pastoral theology in African Christianities is that it is a tool through which pastoral care-givers engage in the praxis of practical care. As a result, it can be argued that pastoral theology is the science of pastoral care that renders all 'branches of theology, whether theoretical or practical, purpose in one way or another to make priests the ministers of Christ, and the dispensers of the mysteries of God'.[23] These branches include '... the apologetic, dogmatic, exegetic, moral, juridical, ascetical, liturgical... pastoral theology teaches the priest his part in this work of Catholic and Christian tradition of revealed truth...'[24]

Furthermore, the life of the church is premised on pastoral theology in activities such as teaching/educating, healing, guiding, liturgy/worship, administration of sacraments as per denominational dogma, catechumen classes for denominational indoctrination, reconciling and repairing injured morals, empowering, nurturing and liberating.[25] Pastoral theology needs to continue to reflect on the nature and direction of pastoral duties and responsibilities in African Christianities. This will enable continued refinement of pastoral praxis in Africa from a contemporary globalized Africa.

Conclusion

This chapter defined pastoral theology from an African perspective. The definition was followed by a discussion on the role of pastoral theology in African Christianities. The third section of the chapter discussed the relevance and need for pastoral theology in African Christianities. It can be concluded that pastoral theology is the reflection aspect of pastoral practices of the church in different contexts. This kind of action and reflection needs to continue to guide and inform the pastoral life of African Christianities.

Bibliography

Ave Maria University: *What is Pastoral Theology?* www.avemaria.edu/MajorsPrograms/Graduate Programs/MTSinPastoralTheology/WhatisPastoralTheology.aspx (accessed 20 February, 2014).

Chitando, E. and Klagba, C. *In the Name of Jesus! Healing in the Age of HIV.* Geneva: WCC publications, 2013.

Drum, W. 'Pastoral Theology'. In *The Catholic Encyclopedia*. New York: Robert Appleton Company, 1912, www.newadvent.org/cathen/14611a.htm (accessed 09 February, 2015).

Hewitt, R. R. *Church and Culture: An Anglo-Caribbean Experience of Hybridity and Contradiction.* Pietermaritzburg: Cluster Publications, 2012.

Jonathan, G. 'Why Nigeria has not Defeated Boko Haram.' *Premium Times*, 28 September 2014

[22] Lartey, 'In Living Color', 58.

[23] MLA citation. Walter Drum, 'Pastoral Theology', *The Catholic Encyclopedia,* Vol. 14 (New York: Robert Appleton Company, 1912), www.newadvent.org/cathen/14611a.htm (accessed 9 February, 2015).

[24] www.newadvent.org/cathen/14611a.htm.

[25] See, Lartey, 'In Living Color', 60-68.

https://www.premiumtimesng.com/news/headlines/168771-why-nigeria-has-not-defeated-boko-haram-jonathan.html (accessed 15 November, 2014).

Kalu, O. U. *African Pentecostalism: An Introduction.* New York: Oxford University Press, 2008.

Lartey, Y. E. *In Living Color: An Intercultural Approach to Pastoral Care and Counselling.* London and New York: Jessica Kingsley Publishers, 2003.

Magesa, L. *African Religion: The Moral Tradition of Abundant Life*. Nairobi: Paulines Publications Africa, 1998.

Mbiti, J. *African Religions and Philosophy*. London: Heinemann, 1969.

Moyo, H. 'Caught between a Rock and a Hard Place: The Politics of Homosexuality and the Response of the Evangelical Lutheran Church in Zimbabwe (ELCZ).'*Journal of Gender and Religion in Africa* Vol. 18, no. 1, (July 2012): 155-167.

Moyo, H. 'Religion and African Indigenous Knowledge Systems: Healing and Communal Reconstruction in African Communities.' *Alternation* Special Edition No. 11, (2013): 207-236.

Mwaura, N. N. 'Healing as Pastoral Concern.' In *Pastoral Care in African Christianity*, edited by D. W. Waruta and Hannah W. Kinoti, 72-100. Nairobi: Acton Publishers, 2000.

Oden, T. *Pastoral Theology: Essentials of Ministry*. San Francisco: Harper and Row, 1983.

(125) Human Sexuality in African Christianity

Ezra Chitando

Introduction

The theme of human sexuality has been a consistently problematic one since the arrival of the Christian faith in Africa. It has generated considerable debate, creativity and controversy. At stake has been whether churches in Africa have been realistic in their engagement with African understandings of human sexuality. Although the more recent debates over homosexuality threaten to dominate the discussion of it in Africa, it is only a fraction of the larger issue. Human sexuality has been an integral part of the story of African Christianity. Across different epochs and geographical contexts, churches have sought to address human sexuality in Africa.

This chapter summarises the key issues that have characterised the debate on human sexuality in Africa. In the first section, the chapter highlights the major issues that have emerged in the African churches' encounter with human sexuality. The second section draws attention to the trends and patterns that can be observed from the African churches' engagement with it. In the third section, the chapter offers some suggestions on how African churches can be more effective in their response to human sexuality.

African Christianity and Human Sexuality: Major Issues

One of the earliest areas of confrontation between missionaries and African Christians in many parts of the continent was around perceptions of African sensuality and sexuality. The dominant paradigm among missionaries was that African dances were too suggestive and that African men in particular had an insatiable sexual appetite. Furthermore, the prevailing notions of what was acceptable behaviour in the missionaries' home countries had an effect on their assessment of African sexual practices.[1]

The negative attitude towards African marriage practices was also felt in addressing polygamy. Most missionaries contended that the practice of African men in marrying more than one wife was un-Christian. In some instances, this gave rise to African Independent/Indigenous/Initiated/Instituted Churches (AICs), many of whom appealed to the Hebrew Bible to support the practice. In addition, there were also underlying social, cultural and economic reasons that were behind polygamy.[2] Other issues relating to sexuality/marriage and missionaries included the payment of bridewealth (dowry), the role of indigenous spirituality in marriage practices, and others. Most missionaries insisted on upholding western values which they mistook for gospel values. Even as the churches have enculturated and indigenised the gospel, the tension between African values and 'biblical' values continues to be experienced.[3]

Most churches in Africa are now led by Africans, particularly after the decolonising 1960s (some churches Africanised their leadership during their struggles for independence). Nevertheless, they continue to struggle with issues of human sexuality. This became patently clear in the churches' response to HIV and AIDS. When the epidemic broke out in the mid-1980s, the global Christian community struggled to

[1] R. J. Priest, 'Missionary Positions: Christian, Modernist, Postmodernist', *Current Anthropology* 42 (2001): 29-68.
[2] Julius K. Muthengi, 'Polygamy and the Church in Africa: Biblical, Historical, and Practical Perspectives', *Africa Journal of Evangelical Theology* Vol. 14, no. 2, (1995): 55-78.
[3] See for example, Onesimus Ngundu, 'Mission Churches and African Customary Marriage: A History of Church Marriages and a Case for an African Christian Customary Marriage Ceremony', *African Journal of Evangelical Theology* Vol. 30, no. 1, (2011): 35-53.

address the theme of sex and sexuality in an open and empowering way. Shame, secrecy and silence dominated the churches' response to HIV and AIDS.[4] Donald Messer elaborates on this when he writes:

> Christians often get tongue-tied when speaking publicly about human sexuality. Christian leaders, so steeped in shame and often lacking in scientific or medical understanding and terminology, typically sidestep the important and life-saving realm of sex education. Too embarrassed to be forthright and honest, they leave the educational work to others who may or may not share their same relational values or ethics of responsibility.[5]

The struggle to address human sexuality by churches in Africa has come out more forcefully in the debate on homosexuality in Africa. Without deliberately setting out to cause harm or pain, many churches in Africa have come across as deeply and irretrievably homophobic. They have struggled to contribute to a more nuanced understanding of sexuality and social justice.[6] This is predominantly the result of an inherited theological conservatism and a refusal to be open to new knowledge and information regarding the complex nature of human sexuality.

Alongside the challenge posed by homosexuality, African churches have struggled to articulate progressive theologies around HIV prevention, especially in relation to the issue of condoms. Although attitudes had mellowed by the end of the first decade of the 21st century, many church leaders remained uneasy in mentioning condoms as an effective HIV prevention strategy.[7] In addition, the theme of comprehensive sex education and information proved divisive, with many church leaders resisting it being taught for adolescents and young people. Their main fear has been that introducing sex education to adolescents and youth will make them more adventurous and contribute towards them becoming sexually active at an earlier age.

African Christianity and Human Sexuality: Emerging Issues

There are a number of factors that can help to account for the attitudes of African churches towards the theme of human sexuality. Although a longer narrative is required to do justice to them, in this chapter I draw attention to the major issues. First, the influence of missionary Christianity on African Christianity needs to be acknowledged. Although African theologians have expended considerable energy in arguing for Africanisation and localisation of the gospel message, the effects of the missionaries remain discernible. This is particularly true in relation to responses to human sexuality. African Christianity has largely upheld the missionary attitudes towards human sexuality. The tendency to avoid discussing the subject, or approaching it from a 'hyper-spiritual' stance, remains pronounced.

Second, the impact of missionary Christianity and colonialism on African structures, institutions and approaches needs to be recognised. African structures and institutions were effective in addressing sex and sexuality in their own context. Consequently, there were rites of passage, sacred specialists and counsellors who equipped young people with knowledge relating to sex and sexuality. Although sex was associated with mystery and awe, connected as it was with spirituality,[8] it was also demystified through song and dance. Indigenous approaches to human sexuality tended to be more embracing of its power and

---

[4] See for example, Ezra Chitando, *Living with Hope: African Churches and HIV/AIDS,* Volume 1 (Geneva: World Council of Churches, 2007).

[5] Donald E. Messer, *Breaking the Conspiracy of Silence: Christian Churches and the Global AIDS Crisis* (Minneapolis: Fortress Press, 2004), 42.

[6] Marc Epprecht, *Sexuality and Social Justice in Africa: Rethinking Homophobia and Forging Resistance* (London: Zed Books, 2013).

[7] See for example, Gillian Patterson, ed., *HIV Prevention: A Global Theological Conversation* (Geneva: Ecumenical Advocacy Alliance, 2009).

[8] Laurenti Magesa, *African Religion: The Moral Traditions of Abundant Life* (Maryknoll, NY: Orbis Books, 1997).

complexity. For example, among the Shona people of Zimbabwe, there were poems to celebrate sex (although it was mainly the woman who was expected to praise the man's sexual prowess). However, the missionaries discouraged such 'sex positive' approaches to life, leading to the general demonization of sex among most indigenous people.

Third, there is an underlying, robust defence of an imagined, pristine African culture. It is striking that most church leaders will justify the general refusal to address human sexuality in its complexity by appealing to 'traditional African culture'. They claim that this culture upholds the sacredness of sex and sexuality. They argue that, as custodians of African culture, they cannot support 'un-African' and 'western' practices such as homosexuality. This ideological commitment to African culture can be understood within the context of African Christianity's quest for autonomy. It is tied to the continent's experiences with missionary Christianity and colonialism. Most African church leaders, like their politicians, do not want to be lectured to by people from the global North. They react very strongly as they want to resist patronising attitudes by their former colonisers.

Fourth, the Bible is featured quite prominently in African Christian responses to human sexuality. There is a deliberate effort to uphold 'biblical standards' in relation to shaping human sexuality. Literal interpretations of the Bible are quite dominant in African Christianity. This has been pronounced in the response to homosexuality. Many church leaders in Africa are staunchly opposed to homosexuality because they are convinced that the Bible is unequivocal in its denunciation of it.[9] The role of the Bible in shaping attitudes towards human sexuality in African Christianity needs to be explored in greater detail.

African Christianity and Human Sexuality: Some Proposals

The HIV epidemic has highlighted the urgent need for African Christianity to approach human sexuality with a greater degree of openness and realism. By the time churches had offered more effective responses, too many lives had been lost. There is a need to accept this basic truth: human beings are sexual beings. In many instances, sex does take place within the kind of relationships churches do not approve of – between unmarried people, across generations and between people of the same sex. There is a need for African churches to realise that young people are now accessing information, including information on sex and sexuality, from diverse sources. In order for churches to remain effective, they need to provide life-saving, accurate and relevant information on human sexuality in all its complexity.

In order for African Christianity to address the complexity of human sexuality more comprehensively, theological institutions in Africa must invest heavily in equipping their students and graduates with the relevant knowledge and skills. Considerable ground has already been covered in mainstreaming HIV and AIDS in the curricula of theological institutions and university departments of religious studies and faculties of theology. However, there is a need for addressing the theme of human sexuality in greater detail and to acknowledge its importance. Without suggesting that this becomes the most dominant theme on the agenda of contemporary theological education in Africa, one can still challenge theological educators to take human sexuality more seriously.

African Christianity will be able to cover more ground in addressing human sexuality by interacting more closely with the publications of the Circle of Concerned African Women Theologians (the Circle). The Circle has been highly creative and consistent in addressing the theme of human sexuality in its writings. It has explored the relevance of such concepts as pleasure in the understanding of sexuality in Africa. It has also challenged the patriarchal tendencies controlling women's sexuality and have called for women's full liberation. Scholars such as (in no particular order) Isabel A. Phiri, Musa W. Dube,

[9] See, for example, Masiiwa Ragies Gunda, *The Bible and Homosexuality in Zimbabwe* (Bamberg: Bamberg University Press, 2010).

Nyambura J. Njoroge, Musimbi R. Kanyoro, Mercy Amba Oduyoye, Fulata Moyo, Sarojini Nadar, Madipoane Masenya and others, have encouraged African male church leaders to take women's experiences seriously. This has also included the call to challenge sexual and gender-based violence and promote women's health and well-being.[10]

In the light of the foregoing, African Christianity will need to embrace less conservative interpretations of the Bible if it is to do justice to the complexity of human sexuality. This is not to suggest that African Christianity completely abandons its sense of identity. It is only to propose that more diverse and dynamic interpretations of the Bible be embraced in the face of rapid social transformation. Old questions need new answers, even as new questions need answers too! In this regard, African Christianity must approach the Bible in new and creative ways as it seeks to respond to human sexuality in all its complexity and diversity.

Conclusion

Human sexuality continues to challenge African Christianity in many ways. In this paper, I have outlined the historical factors that have shaped African Christianity's response to human sexuality. I have also proposed some steps that must be taken to ensure that African Christianity addresses human sexuality in a broader, more relevant and effective way.

Bibliography

Chitando, Ezra. *Living with Hope: African Churches and HIV/AIDS*. Volume 1. Geneva: World Council of Churches, 2007.

Dube, Musa W. and Musimbi Kanyoro, eds. *Grant Me Justice: HIV/AIDS and Gender Readings of the Bible*. Pietermaritzburg: Cluster Publications, 2004.

Epprecht, Marc. *Sexuality and Social Justice in Africa: Rethinking Homophobia and Forging Resistance*. London: Zed Books, 2013.

Gunda, Masiiwa Ragies. *The Bible and Homosexuality in Zimbabwe*. Bamberg: Bamberg University Press, 2010.

Magesa, Laurenti. *African Religion: The Moral Traditions of Abundant Life*. Maryknoll, NY: Orbis Books, 1997.

Messer, Donald E. *Breaking the Conspiracy of Silence: Christian Churches and the Global AIDS Crisis*. Minneapolis: Fortress Press, 2004.

Muthengi, Julius K. 'Polygamy and the Church in Africa: Biblical, Historical, and Practical Perspectives.' *Africa Journal of Evangelical Theology* Vol. 14, no. 2, (1995): 55-78.

Ngundu, Onesimus. 'Mission Churches and African Customary Marriage: A History of Church Marriages and a Case for an African Christian Customary Marriage Ceremony.' *African Journal of Evangelical Theology* Vol. 30, no. 1, (2011): 35-53.

Patterson, Gillian (ed.). *HIV Prevention: A Global Theological Conversation*. Geneva: Ecumenical Advocacy Alliance, 2009.

Priest, R. J. 'Missionary Positions: Christian, Modernist, Postmodernist.' *Current Anthropology* 42, (2001): 29-68.

---

[10] See for example, Musa W. Dube and Musimbi Kanyoro, eds., *Grant Me Justice: HIV/AIDS and Gender Readings of the Bible* (Pietermaritzburg: Cluster Publications, 2004).

(126) Secularisation and African Christianity

Scott Everett Couper

Introduction

The acceptance of faith by the Ethiopian eunuch demonstrates Christianity's origins have roots in Africa. The writings of Augustine of Hippo and others demonstrate Africa to be a fount of Christian theology. Yet, Christianity's later seventeenth-century introduction to sub-Saharan Africa by western 'historic mainline' mission agencies and European colonisation rendered African Christianity greatly diminished due to the West's pejorative views of African culture. Modernisation, pluralism, urbanisation and formal education and the West's imposed divorce of African culture and orthodox Christian theology and the resulting emasculation of traditional African spirituality has rendered mainline African Christianity particularly susceptible to the threat of secularisation in the post-modern world. The author surveys Southern African history and highlights the thought of Steve Biko in arguing that African Indigenous Churches (AICs) have, since the turn of the twentieth century, best resisted white supremacy by countering the estrangement of African Christianity from indigenous culture. The flawed manner in which the West introduced Christianity in sub-Saharan Africa renders mainline African Christianity vulnerable to bureaucratisation and institutionalisation, and thus increasingly irrelevant to Africans. Furthermore, Pentecostalism in Africa harbours the seeds of secularisation with its western Protestant emphasis on a temporal and realised soteriology (health, wealth and individualism). The author argues that, for mainline African Christianity to halt its decline and resist secularisation, it must learn from the AICs' resistance to white supremacy and better graft itself onto an African consciousness, thus becoming more relevant, and must challenge and contest Pentecostal terrestrial soteriology.

Definitions and Parameters

'Secularism' has been understood by Christian polemicists to be any 'spirit' opposed to Christianity, regardless of its source or content; such an understanding is 'so broad to be useless'.[1] Hence, for the purposes of this chapter, a definition and parameters of 'secularisation' must be articulated. The word 'secularisation' derives from the Latin word *saeculum*, meaning 'the age' or 'the world'.[2] 'Secularisation' is a symptom of the modern world (the term not having been used before the nineteenth century) and post-modern world (the term being widely used only in the twentieth century). Generically, it is the *process* of

---

[1] Jerald Brauer, 'Secularism', in *A Handbook of Christian Theology: Definition Essays on Concepts and Movements of Thought in Contemporary Protestantism* (New York: Meridian Books, 1958), 339. For example, Benno van den Toren arguably uses a polemic lens to define 'secularisation' (24-30). While, van den Toren eruditely qualifies and specifically defines secularisation and accurately articulates that which it is *not* (5), the *Zeitgeist* of his paper, and especially the abstract, blurs all the lines so carefully articulated. The paper alludes to the 'so broad to be useless' definition of secularisation by including as examples: declining church membership (4), the use of traditional healers (3) and religious convictions circumscribed to the private sphere (3). By failing to distinguish between advocating for living-out Christian values in the public realm and the public realm adopting and enforcing Christian values, van den Toren almost advocates for theocracy (22 and 28); Benno van den Toren, 'Secularisation in Africa: A Challenge for the Churches', *Africa Journal of Evangelical Theology* Vol. 22, no. 1, (2003): 3-30.

[2] Karen Armstrong, *Fields of Blood: Religion and the History of Violence* (London: The Bodley Head, 2014), 2-3. Armstrong cites: Wilfred Smith, *The Meaning and End of Religion: A New Approach to the Religious Traditions of Mankind* (New York, 1962), 33.

becoming more 'of the world' and less 'religious, sacred or spiritual', and thus it is the process of becoming less 'subject or bound by religious rules'.[3] Arguably, the forces fomenting secularisation in the world, and thus in African Christianity, are, primarily, modernisation and pluralism, and, secondarily, rural to urban migration and formal (modern) education.[4]

When using the term 'secularisation' in this chapter as related to African Christianity, a key differentiation must be made between the secularisation of individuals (private) and social institutions (public).[5] Prominent Egyptian scholar Abdelwahab Elmessiri (1938-2008) made this distinction using the terms 'comprehensive' and 'partial' secularisation.[6] 'Comprehensive secularisation' is the process whereby:

> ...the utmost efforts [are made] to restrict religion, absolute values and metaphysics from *all walks of life* ...[because] a rationalistic/materialistic viewpoint sees... the universe... devoid of any sanctity or mystery (Couper's emphasis).[7]

'Partial secularisation' confines itself to the realms of politics and perhaps economics' – that is, it expresses a 'separation of church and state'.[8] While modernisation, pluralism, urbanisation and formal education inevitably and irreversibly foster 'partial secularisation', they do not necessarily foster 'comprehensive secularisation'.

This chapter does not accede to a [Max] Weberian (1864-1920) thesis, otherwise known today as the 'Secularisation Thesis', that societies (and thus Africans) are being increasingly 'comprehensively' (in the sense of publicly *and privately*) secularised – that is, that they believe in 'secularism' as an ideology. Till now, scholars have constantly argued for or against this thesis. The notable Peter Berger (b. 1929) has at different times in his career argued for, and later against, it. That Africans may leave mainline for schismatic denominations, syncretisticly visit a *sangoma* (a traditional healer) while also attending church, participate in a lifestyle not historically compatible with orthodox Christianity (e.g. in polygamy or homosexuality), or leave the Christian faith altogether and practise an existential spirituality does *not* constitute 'secularisation'. In short, individuals who change or fuse religious practices are *not* increasingly secular.

A [Émile] Durkheimian (1858-1917) thesis asserts that society can undergo 'partial' secularisation' (public and state) while its constituent individuals may not (private and religion). This is also known as 'compartmentalisation'. Societies are composed of macro-social systems and institutions (instrumentalities) that include laws (courts), economies (markets), polities (governments) and social services (hospitals and schools). This chapter affirms that while individuals may not be increasingly secularised, their instrumentalities – within modern democratic states that protect the rights of all its

---

[3] Judy Pearsall, ed. *The Concise Oxford Dictionary*, 10th edition (Oxford: Oxford University Press, 1999), 1295. A crucial distinction must be made between the words 'secularisation' which is a *process* and 'secularism' which is an *ideology*. This chapter relates primarily to secularisation as a process. Michael Horton, 'The Secularisation Thesis', in 'Secularising Religion', *Modern Reformation* Vol. 22, no.5, (2013): 26.

[4] van den Toren, 'Secularisation in Africa', 3. Horton, 'The Secularisation Thesis', 26.

[5] One author refers to this distinction as 'differentiation' of the secular sphere from the religious sphere. Technically, this 'differentiation' is in and of itself a manifestation of secularisation. However, for the purposes of this short chapter, this study does not examine secularisation in such a nuanced fashion. Nonetheless, differentiation, or 'partial secularisation' is *not* indicative of a secularist (as an ideology) threat. John Coffey, 'Secularisation: Is It Inevitable?' www.jubilee-centre.org/secularisation-is-it-inevitable-by-john-coffey/ (accessed 27 September 2015).

[6] Nasir Sanaullah, 'Arab Islamic Response to Secularism: A Case Study of Dr. Abdelwahab Elmessiri', *Journal of Humanity & Islam* Vol. 3, no. 1, (2013): 13.

[7] Abdelwahab Elmessiri and Aziz Al Azmah, *Secularism under the Microscope* (Beirut: Dar al Fikr, 2000), 67.

[8] Elmessiri, 'Secularism under the Microscope', 120 and Abdelwahab Elmessiri, 'The Partial Secularization and the Comprehensive Secularization', (Cairo: Dar al Shorouk, 2002), 220.

diverse citizens, no matter their creed or lack thereof – are, or should be. Due to the advent of plural societies, Christianity should no longer control the world as it did before the Renaissance, Reformation and Enlightenment. In short, a heterogeneous religious or spiritual constituency that participates in 'partial secularisation' (and is thus anti-theocratic) is not synonymous with one that is undergoing 'comprehensive secularisation' (and thus the abandonment of public *and private* spiritual and religious values and practices). Populations are not necessarily becoming more ideologically secular as a result of 'the collapse of religious hegemony', though 'partial secularisation' has occurred.[9] For example, advocacy supporting the abandonment of draconian punitive legislation against homosexuality in Malawi is *not* an example of 'comprehensive secularisation' (it is rather 'partial secularisation'), as heterosexuals will still have strong negative spiritually-based sentiments against the practice and such disdain will govern their private behaviour, and thus they remain 'religious'.[10] This chapter, rightly or wrongly, sympathises with what John Mbiti declared the case: Africans are notoriously spiritual.[11] The question is: Will this always remain the case?

In a 1972 address entitled 'The Church as Seen by a Young Layman', Steve Biko (1946-1977) addressed elderly black *abafundisi* (ministers). In it, Biko asserted:

> In most cases, religion is intricately intertwined with the rest of the cultural traits of society. In a sense, this makes the religion part and parcel of the behavioural pattern of that society and makes the people bound by the limits of that religion through a strong identification with it. Where a people are subjected to a religion that is removed from their cultural make-up, then elements of disgruntlement begin to be noted, and sometimes open defiance is soon displayed. Hence, one can make the claim that most religions are specific, and where they fail to observe the requirements of specificity, then they must be sufficiently adaptable to convey relevant messages to different people in different situations.[12]

As one surveys the historical points of interface between Christianity and indigenous Africans, we observe, though certainly not without exception, a pervasive irrelevance of Christianity to its converts and adherents. Ironically, the introduction of Christianity itself initiated a process of secularisation in Africa with its distinction between the sacred and profane that previously did not exist in African Traditional Religions. Yet, this irrelevance is largely due to the manner, or brand packaging, of Christianity by those who introduced a western acculturated form of the religion and, seeing it as normative, imposed it on indigenous Africans without the required flexibility alluded to by Steve Biko. This irrelevance led to, for missionaries, disappointing conversion rates, the initiation and growth of separatist or dissenting movements (the so-called 'Ethiopian,' independent, or African initiated churches, AICs) and syncretistic faith practises that combine African traditional spirituality and Christianity. Therefore, the decline in numbers and influence of mainline or orthodox Christianity (inaccurately termed 'secularisation' by many) is actually a long-held historical pattern of Africans recognising Christianity's irrelevance to their spiritual and cultural consciousness, and their proverbial 'voting with their feet' and leaving the historic mission churches. Therefore, the decreased societal influence of orthodox Christianity is *not* due to the 'comprehensive secularisation' of Africans *per se*, but rather due to mainline Christianity's failure to be culturally and thus spiritually relevant to Africans.[13] In short, African Christians are taking their 'notorious'

---

[9] Coffey, 'Secularisation: Is it Inevitable?' 3.
[10] Faith Karimi, 'Amnesty: Malawi Suspends Anti-gay Laws', Cable News Network (CNN) 6 November 2012. http://edition.cnn.com/2012/11/06/world/africa/malawi-antigay-laws/index.html (accessed 30 September, 2015).
[11] John Mbiti, *African Religions and Philosophy* (London: Heinemann, 1969), 1 and 262.
[12] Steve Biko, 'The Church as Seen by a Young Layman' in *Steve Biko: I Write What I Like* (Johannesburg: Picador Africa, 2004), 59-60.
[13] A similar point has rightfully been made regarding theories of economic and social development in Africa. Mustapha Kurfi, 'Secularisation and Development in Africa: A Terrific Façade', *Global Journal of Human Social*

spirituality elsewhere. Furthermore, because of AICs' religious and cultural relevance in Africa, they are best resisting any nominal 'comprehensive secularism' that will soon, if it has not already, encroach on the African continent. If mainline Christianity desires Africans to resist 'comprehensive secularisation' (and remain within its fold), it would do well to note Biko's analysis and AICs' lessons regarding acculturation and spiritual relevance.[14]

Resisting Ecclesiastical White Supremacy

In his seminal text, *Introduction to African Religion*, John Mbiti rightly asserts that Christianity is indigenous to Africa.[15] The narrative of Philip and the unnamed Ethiopian in Acts 8 is evidence that the Christian faith is endemic to Africa. Tradition holds that St Mark brought the faith to Egypt in AD 42. Likewise, the writings of Clement of Alexandria, Origen, Athanasius, Cyril, Tertullian, Cyprian and Augustine of Hippo demonstrate that the development of Christian systematic theology has its roots in Africa (as does, ironically, the origins of western civilisation).[16] Yet, with the arrival of Jan van Riebeeck and the Dutch settlers in 1652, Christianity as it was introduced to sub-Saharan Africa had a distinct western European veneer. One of the first converts to Christianity, a Khoikhoi girl named Krotoa, and then – following her baptism – 'Eva', demonstrates the degree to which western Christianity has perhaps been irrelevant. Eva's new faith did not sufficiently help her navigate within the limited space she found herself in, and she died succumbing to prostitution and alcoholism.[17]

The first missionary sent to Southern Africa, George Schmidt (1709-1785), baptised Vehettge Magdalena Tikhuie (d. 1800), or 'Lena', at Genadendal in 1742. But Dutch opposition caused Schmidt to abandon the Moravian mission in 1744, leaving Lena a remnant until the mission was later reconstituted. Lena's leadership of the mission by default is a rare example of indigenous Christian autonomy.

Beginning with the Baptist Missionary Society (Baptist) in 1792, the London Missionary Society (Congregational) in 1795, the Church Missionary Society (Anglican) in 1799, and the American Board of Commissioners for Foreign Missions (Congregational) in 1810, mission societies rigidly instilled a westernised Christianity on African converts. The iconoclast Johannes van der Kemp (1747-1811) preached to Khoikhoi and black Africans. Two contemporary young mystical Xhosa prophets, Nxele-Makanna (1790-1820) and Ntsikanna (1780-1821), heard excerpts of van der Kemp's sermons and incorporated Christian theology into traditional African spirituality.[18] Ntsikanna proved more orthodox, becoming arguably the first modern African theologian who contextually wrote hymns, poems and liturgy. He represented 'a genuinely new birth of Christian insight within African culture and society'.[19]

From the mid-1800s, indigenous Christians in Southern Africa began to exhibit greater confidence and interrogated the new faith. Rivalry within the Anglican Church erupted between Bishop William Colenso (1814-1883) and the metropolitans in Cape Town and London. Colenso's troubles began when he endeared himself to the indigenous perspectives of his protégé William Ngidi over issues of biblical scholarship and

---

Science: Sociology and Culture Vol. 13, no. 6, (2013): no pages indicated.

[14] Justin Ukpong, 'Christology and Inculturation: A New Testament Perspective' in *Paths of African Theology*, ed. Rosino Gibellini, (Maryknoll, New York: Orbis Books, 1994), 40-61.

[15] John Mbiti, *Introduction to African Religion* (Oxford: Heinemann International Literature and Textbooks, 1975), 182-3.

[16] Rosino Gibellini, ed. 'African Theologians Wonder…and Make Some Proposals' in *Paths of African Theology*, 1-2.

[17] Jane McKinnon, 'Krotoa' in *A Tapestry of Lives: Cape Women of the 17th Century* (Cape Town: Kwela Books, 2004), 63-82.

[18] Noel Mostert, *Frontiers: The Epic Struggle of South Africa's Creation and the Tragedy of the Xhosa People* (New York: Knoph, 1992), 424-91.

[19] Adrian Hastings, *The Church in Africa, 1450-1950* (New York: Oxford University Press, 1994), 219.

Zulu traditional customs such as polygamy.[20] In 1879, Colenso's domestic antagonists, the missionaries of the American Zulu Mission, adopted the 'Umsunduze Rules', banning practices such as *ukulobolisa* (bride price). These rules caused irrevocable damage to Christian relations and served as a catalyst to at least two future American Board break-away churches.

At the start of the twentieth century, many black African Christians began to exert greater initiative. Frustration with western cultural norms and white supremacy within ecclesiastic polities led many black African clergy to secede from the mission churches that had ordained them. Nehemiah Tile (d. 1891) and James Dwane (1848-1916) broke from the Methodist Church in 1884 and 1896, respectively. Mpambani Mzimba (1850-1911) broke with the Presbyterian Free Church of Scotland in 1898. Enoch Mgijima (1858-1929) broke from the Wesleyan Methodist Church in 1910. Simungu Shibe (dates unknown) and Gardiner Mvuyana (1886-1925) broke from the Congregationalists in 1898 and 1917, respectively.[21] At the same time, 'dissenting Zionist ministers in Johannesburg were participants in a transnational sphere of evangelical practice that highly prized individual autonomy and self-determination in religious matters'.[22] One mystical prophet, Isaiah Shembe (1870-1935), with Wesleyan, Baptist, Apostolic Faith Mission and secondhand Lutheran influences, initiated a new church (Nazareth Baptist Church) and faith (Shembe) in 1910 that intimately connected with the African consciousness.

Resisting 'Comprehensive Secularism'

Towards the conclusion of Steve Biko's 1972 message to his older clerical audience, he advised:

> In order to be able therefore to change the churches, we have to first gain ascendance over them in that white model, then thereafter turn that model into one we cherish, we love, we understand, and one that is relevant to us.[23]

In other words, Biko argued for Africans not to mimic western models of ecclesiastic governance but urged their indigenisation. Second, Biko advised in his conclusion:

> The second area in which we must focus our attention is a thorough understanding of Black Theology... Christianity can never hope to remain abstract and removed from people's environmental problems. In order to be applicable to people, it must have meaning for them in their given situation. If they are an oppressed people, it must have something to say about their oppression.[24]

Since the advent of imported Christianity through colonialism during the modern era, Africans have always countered the effects of white supremacy with secession, dissent and independence. Yet, a new

[20] Livingstone Ngewu, 'John William Colenso and the Enigma of Polygamy' and Jonathan Draper, 'The Trial of Bishop John William Colenso' in *The Eye of the Storm: John William Colenso and the Crisis of Biblical Inspiration*, ed. Jonathan Draper (Pietermaritzburg: Cluster Publications, 2003), 293-325.

[21] William Wilcox, 'The American Zulu Mission in Its Relation to the African Congregational Church' and Frederick Bridgman, 'Ethiopian Movement and Other Independent Factions Characterised by a National Spirit', in *The South African Deputation Papers: Presenting Some Aspects and Problems of the Work of the Two South African Missions of the American Board* (Printed for the American Zulu Mission, Natal and the East Central African Mission, Rhodesia, 1904), 9-12 and 29-30, respectively.

[22] Joel Cabrita, 'Revisiting 'Christian Independency': Urban Moderns and the Pursuit of Self-Perfection in Early Twentieth-Century Johannesburg', unpublished draft paper (work in progress). See also: Robert Houle, *Making African Christianity: Africans Reimagining Their Faith in Colonial South Africa* (Bethlehem: Lehigh University Press, 2011).

[23] Biko, *The Church as Seen by a Young Layman*, 63.

[24] Biko, *The Church as Seen by a Young Layman*, 64.

ideological hegemony possibly approaches: 'comprehensive secularism'. If mainline African Christianity wishes to remain at the forefront of the opposition to 'comprehensive secularism', and therefore remain 'notoriously spiritual', then it must respond to 'comprehensive secularism' as effectively as AICs responded to white supremacy. Mainline Africans must fuse traditional polities and spiritualities into Christianity, thus making the faith more relevant to its continental constituency. If mainline African Christianity fails, its now diminishing remnant will seek further relevance in syncretistic schisms or 'comprehensive secularism'.

Secularisation *in* African Christianity

While the majority of this chapter focuses on secularisation *and* (that is, as separate and opposed to) African Christianity, a word must be related to secularisation *within* (that is, as a component part of) African Christianity. To this, Steve Biko comments on two forms of secularisation within African Christianity – bureaucratisation and institutionalisation:

> It must be noted that the Church in... Africa as everywhere else, has been spoilt by bureaucracy. No more is it just an expression of the sum total of [African's] religious feelings; it has become, in fact, highly institutionalised, not as one unit but as several powerful units, differing perhaps not so much on scriptural interpretation as in institutional aims... This bureaucracy and institutionalisation tends to make the church removed from important priorities and to concentrate on secondary and tertiary functions like structures and finances, etc. And because of this, the Church has become very irrelevant and in fact an 'ivory tower', as some people refer to it.[25]

Secularisation in the form of bureaucratisation and institutionalisation is a manifestation of the manner in which the West introduced Christianity to sub-Saharan Africa. First, as mentioned earlier, the West imposed a new culture on Africans. Christianity brought 'new styles of clothing, new customs, new forms of customs, new forms of etiquette', the former ways 'were described as being pagan and barbaric'.[26] Second, and closely related to the threat of secularisation within African Christianity from the outset, the West introduced Christian division to Africa. John Mbiti notes: 'Another major problem facing Christianity in Africa is the large number of church divisions, denominations, groups and sects. Many of these were imported from abroad.'[27] The West brought a fractured and factionalised faith, separated not so much by belief but more by style (internal western Christian culture) and polity (itself highly western). The competition within areas for constituencies by Lutherans, Congregationalists, Methodists, Presbyterians and Anglicans mirrored the balkanisation initiated at the Berlin Conference (1884-1885) of African geo-political areas and constituencies into colonial nation-states.

Again, the secularisation of African Christianity in the form of bureaucratisation and institutionalisation has historically been best countered by AICs who, for good or bad, do not emphasise an allegiance to western cultures of administration and formal education, nor even to autochthonous hierarchies. Rather than procedures and protocols, AICs emphasise the indwelling of the Holy Spirit and the 'cult of personality' (perceived as a conduit of the Holy Spirit). AICs, such as the Zionists and Shembe, are therefore perceived by most Africans to be more intimate and relevant to their lives. Mainline African Christianity, unless it has allowed sufficient cultural flexibility, is thus viewed by most Africans to be alien: western, codified and rarefied.[28] Those Africans who remain within the historic mainline mission churches become, like western Europeans, more 'comprehensively secularised'.

---

[25] Biko, 'The Church as Seen by a Young Layman', 61-2.
[26] Biko, 'The Church as Seen by a Young Layman', 60.
[27] Mbiti, *Introduction to African Religion*, 184.
[28] Mbiti, *Introduction to African Religion*, 185.

Strongly related to Steve Biko's warning to African Christianity not to mimic western Christianity's institutional paradigms, as imported by mainline historic missions, is an extrapolated thesis derived from Max Weber which argues that rationalism and materialism (consumerism) within Protestantism (in particular, Reformed and Calvinist Protestantism) fosters secularisation *within* African Christianity. Weber explains:

> Protestants especially seem to promote rationalism and materialism as a means to find prosperity. Wealth and worldly prosperity have been interpreted by Protestant groups to indicate the blessing and grace that God has bestowed upon them. This love for the material and worldly possessions that has been identified with Protestants will eventually distract attention away from religion.[29]

The explosive exponential growth of Pentecostalism (originally derived from North America) within Africa is the greatest evidenced-based argument that 'comprehensive secularisation' is not taking hold in Africa. However, Lovemore Togarasei postulates that Pentecostalism is a Trojan horse harbouring 'comprehensive secularisation' (as its foci are on health, wealth and individualism, otherwise known as the 'prosperity gospel'). Modern Pentecostalism's soteriological concerns relate primarily to the proximate and worldly rather than the ethereal and eternal.[30] Togarasei highlights His People Christian Church in Johannesburg that uses secular symbols and practices that tap into values of social reconstruction and economic achievement...' His People Church in Johannesburg offers secular music styles and media to engender immediate pleasure and entertainment. Togarasei cites the Zimbabwe Assemblies of God Africa [in] Africa, the United Family International Church and the Christ Embassy as ministries that focus on healing (a very present soteriological emphasis). Pentecostal preachers in Zimbabwe, such as Uebert Angel and Emmanuel Makandiwa, preach and demonstrate a theology extolling wealth by owning luxury vehicles and offering 'modern, well-adorned institutions in architecture, furnishings and... administrations', such as at the Celebration Church.[31] In short, a growing African Christianity is in fact emulating the trajectory of secularisation *within* Protestant Reformed Christianity through its mainline historic missions and a recently morphed version of Pentecostalism.

Conclusion

Africans are 'notoriously spiritual'. Yet, nothing is absolute, not even Africans' seemingly inherent proclivity for the sacred. To resist 'comprehensive secularism', mainline African Christianity should not be seduced to reverting back – back to some half-contrived primordial 'roots'.[32] Rather, African Christianity should contest 'comprehensive secularism' with its present and future dynamic *African* consciousness. While contesting white supremacy, Congregationalist lay preacher and the first black African Nobel Peace Prize-winner Albert Luthuli warned:

> This exultation of an almost obsolete way of life, tribalism, was a studied effort by [white supremacists] to gain acceptance by Africans of a reactionary policy of the [white supremacists], a 'back to tribalism', African 'policy.' It would be more correct to call [their policy] a caricature of tribalism, for *fortunately* irreparable

[29] Jaco Beyers, 'The Church and the Secular: The Effect of the Post-secular on Christianity', *HTS Theological Studies 70*, no.1, Art. #2605 (2014): 8.

[30] Lovemore Togarasei, 'Modern/Charismatic Pentecostalism as a Form of 'Religious' Secularisation in Africa', *StudiaHistoriae Ecclesiasticae* 41, no. 1, (2015): 56-66.
van den Toren (2003) and Horton (2013) also make excellent cases that secularisation occurs *within* Christianity *and* African Traditional Religions.

[31] Togarasei, 'Modern/Charismatic Pentecostalism', 60-1.

[32] Van den Toren, 'Secularisation of Africa: A Challenge', 25.

> damage has been done to tribalism by our two hundred years of contact with an aggressive civilisation, itself subjected to the dynamic forces of a highly scientific and technological age and a dynamic revolutionary religion, Christianity (Couper's emphasis).[33]

African Christianity's future is brighter than its past. 'Comprehensive secularisation' will fail to take hold in Africa if mainline African Christianity charts a course forward rather than back and remains loyal to its dynamic African consciousness. Perhaps the best means to contest 'comprehensive secularism' is for mainline churches to partner with AICs, receiving the gifts of a Christianity fused with an African consciousness while sharing the gifts of education and administration, and to partner with Pentecostal churches so as to challenge and contest 'comprehensive secularisation' originating from a temporal and materialist western spirituality.

Bibliography

Armstrong, Karen. *Fields of Blood: Religion and the History of Violence.* London: The Bodley Head, 2014.

Biko, Steve. 'The Church as Seen by a Young Layman.' In *Steve Biko: I Write What I Like.* Johannesburg: Picador Africa, 2004.

Beyers, Jaco. 'The Church and the Secular: The Effect of the Post-secular on Christianity,' *HTS Theological Studies* Vol. *70*, no.1, Art. #2605 (2014): 1-12.

Brauer, Jerald. 'Secularism,' in *A Handbook of Christian Theology: Definition Essays on Concepts and Movements of Thought in Contemporary Protestantism.* New York: Meridian Books, 1958.

Cabrita, Joel. 'Revisiting 'Christian Independency': Urban Moderns and the Pursuit of Self-Perfection in Early Twentieth-Century Johannesburg,' unpublished paper.

Coffey, John. 'Secularisation: Is It Inevitable?' www.jubilee-centre.org/secularisation-is-it-inevitable-by-john-coffey/ (accessed 27 September, 2015).

Elmessiri, Abdelwahab and Aziz Al Azmah. *Secularism under the Microscope.* Beirut: Dar al Fikr, 2000.

Elmessiri, Abdelwahab. *The Partial Secularization and the Comprehensive Secularization.* Cairo: Dar al Shorouk, 2002.

Gibellini, Rosino (ed.). 'African Theologians Wonder…and Make Some Proposals.' In *Paths of African Theology*, edited by Rosino Gibellini, 1-8, Maryknoll, New York: Orbis Books, 1994.

Hastings, Adrian. *The Church in Africa, 1450-1950.* New York: Oxford University Press, 1994.

Horton, Michael. 'The Secularisation Thesis,' in 'Secularising Religion.' *Modern Reformation* 22, no. 5, (2013): 26-41.

Houle, Robert. *Making African Christianity: Africans Reimagining Their Faith in Colonial South Africa.* Bethlehem: Lehigh University Press, 2011.

Karimi, Faith. 'Amnesty: Malawi Suspends Anti-gay Laws,' Cable News Network (CNN), 6 November 2012. http://edition.cnn.com/2012/11/06/world/africa/malawi-antigay-laws/index.html (accessed 30 September, 2015).

Kurfi, Mustapha. 'Secularisation and Development in Africa: A Terrific Facade.' *Global Journal of Human Social Science: Sociology and Culture* Vol. 13, no.6, (2013): no pages indicated.

Luthuli, Albert. 'Back to Tribalism is Unrealistic,' *Golden City Post*, 18 October 1959.

Mbiti, John. *African Religions and Philosophy.* London: Heinemann, 1969.

______. *Introduction to African Religion.* Oxford: Heinemann International Literature and Textbooks, 1975.

McKinnon, June. 'Krotoa' in *A Tapestry of Lives: Cape Women of the 17th Century.* Cape Town: Kwela Books, 2004.

Mostert, Noel. *Frontiers: The Epic Struggle of South Africa's Creation and the Tragedy of the Xhosa*

[33] Albert Luthuli, 'Back to Tribalism is Unrealistic', *Golden City Post*, 18 October 1959, 7.

People. New York: Knoph, 1992.

Ngewu, Livingstone. 'John William Colenso and the Enigma of Polygamy' and Draper, Jonathan. 'The Trial of Bishop John William Colenso' in *The Eye of the Storm: John William Colenso and the Crisis of Biblical Inspiration*, edited by Jonathan Draper, 293-325. Pietermaritzburg: Cluster Publications, 2003.

Pearsall, Judy (ed.). *The Concise Oxford Dictionary*, 10th edition. Oxford: Oxford University Press, 1999.

Sanaullah, Nasir. 'Arab Islamic Response to Secularism: A Case Study of Dr. Abdelwahab Elmessiri.' *Journal of Humanity & Islam* Vol. 3, no. 1, (2013): 9-16.

Togarasei, Lovemore. 'Modern/Charismatic Pentecostalism as a Form of 'Religious' Secularisation in Africa.' *Studia Historiae Ecclesiasticae* Vol. 41, no. 1, (2015): 56-66.

Ukpong, Justin. 'Christology and Inculturation: A New Testament Perspective.' In *Paths of African Theology*, edited by Rosino Gibellini, 40-61. Maryknoll, New York: Orbis Books, 1994.

van den Toren, Benno. 'Secularisation in Africa: A Challenge for the Churches.' *Africa Journal of Evangelical Theology* Vol. 22, no. 1, (2003): 3-30.

Wilcox, William. 'The American Zulu Mission in Its Relation to the African Congregational Church' and Bridgman, Frederick. 'Ethiopian Movement and Other Independent Factions Characterised by a National Spirit.' In *The South African Deputation Papers: Presenting Some Aspects and Problems of the Work of the Two South African Missions of the American Board* (Printed for the American Zulu Mission, Natal and the East Central African Mission, Rhodesia, 1904), 9-12 and 29-30, respectively.

(127A) The Prosperity Gospel in African Christianity

Lovemore Togarasei

Introduction

One major characteristic of African Christianity of late is the prominence of the 'prosperity gospel'. Although this gospel was initially associated with Pentecostal churches, with the 'pentecostalisation'[1] of African Christianity, this gospel is now found even in some mainline and evangelical churches, in one form or another. But what is this gospel of prosperity? What is its history and what are its major tenets? How has it been received in Africa by both its followers and critics? This article addresses these questions. It is based on various works that have been published on the subject of the prosperity gospel in the past few years.

The Prosperity Gospel: Definition

The prosperity gospel is known by a number of names: 'dominion theology',[2] 'faith gospel',[3] 'faith formula theology'.[4] 'name it and claim it', or 'health and wealth gospel'.[5] Basically, the teaching of this gospel is that God wants believers to prosper physically, materially and spiritually. Thus, according to this gospel, getting rich is seen as God's will and an outward manifestation of his blessings. One only needs to have faith in God through Jesus and blessings will follow. Several scriptures are cited in support of the gospel of prosperity (Deuteronomy 8:18; Malachi 3:10; John 10:10).

A Brief History of the Prosperity Gospel

The roots of the prosperity gospel can be traced back to American prosperity preachers such as E.W. Kenyon, Oral Roberts, William Branham and Kenneth Copeland. Sufficient work has been done in tracing this history (Gifford 1998 and Chilenje 2013). Suffice it to say that, by the 1960s, the prosperity gospel had become a major feature on the American Christian landscape. This gospel came to Africa through American evangelists and through African Pentecostals trained in American Bible schools. For example, the Fire Convention conference was held in Harare, Zimbabwe, in 1986, and several prosperity preachers from America and Europe spread the prosperity gospel there. African preachers who had accepted the prosperity gospel also helped spread it through establishing Bible colleges that emphasized this gospel. Examples are the All Nations' Bible Seminary of Benson Idahosa in Nigeria, and Africa Multination for Christ College (AMFCC) of Ezekiel Guti in Zimbabwe. We also need to highlight the role played by

---

[1] 'Pentecostalisation' here means adopting Pentecostal-like characteristics with Pentecostalism marked by the centrality of the Holy Spirit manifested in signs like speaking in tongues.

[2] A. Corten and R. Marshal-Fratani, 'Introduction', in *Between Babel to Pentecost: Transnational Pentecostalism in Africa and Latin America*, eds. A. Corten and R. Marshal-Fratani (London: Hurst and Company, 2001): 5.

[3] Paul Gifford, *African Christianity: Its Public Role* (London: Hurst and Company, 1998), 62.

[4] J. Kwabena Asamoah-Gyadu, *African Charismatics: Current Developments with Independent Indigenous Pentecostalism in Ghana* (Leiden: Brill, 2004), 203.

[5] Adré Droogers, 'Globalisation and Pentecostal Success', in *Between Babel and Pentecost: Transnational Pentecostalism in Africa and Latin America,* eds. Adré Droogers and Ruth Marshall-Fratani (London: C. Hurst and Co., 2001), 41-61.

books, pamphlets and other publications by prosperity preachers, in spreading the prosperity gospel in Africa.

The Major Tenets of this Gospel

The prosperity gospel emphasizes that God has good plans for every individual. God did not intend human beings to suffer and so prepared only good for them. All that is required of individuals is to have faith in God through Jesus Christ, a faith that unlocks the entrance to all the good prepared for them by God. Thus, the prosperity gospel does not despise wealth. God did not create human beings to be poor. The Old Testament provides proof texts for this gospel. For example, a favourite text on wealth is Deuteronomy 8:18, 'You shall remember the Lord your God, for it is he who gives you power to get wealth…' (RSV). The prosperity gospel also has a political theology of its own. Advocates of the prosperity gospel believe that, if Africa is to prosper, it needs God-fearing leaders. Thus, as a God-fearing born-again leader, the late President of Zambia, Frederick Chiluba, declared the country a Christian nation in 1991, stating, 'Since Zambia had entered into a covenant with God, the nation would be blessed to the point where it would stop borrowing from others and become a lender of resources instead.'[6] The prosperity gospel discourages borrowing, arguing that since God owns all that is in the world, believers can claim this ownership too and should therefore not owe anyone.

These tenets are emphasised by nearly all prosperity gospel preachers in Africa.[7] The prosperity gospel in African Christianity teaches Africans optimism, underlining the fact that God has great plans for the continent. All that the continent has to do is to surrender in faith to God, to obey God's commands – and prosperity will follow. Tithing is central to the unlocking of God's blessings in prosperity gospel theology, as well as other forms of offering to God.

Prosperity Gospel Attractions in Africa

Despite some negative appraisals, this type of gospel continues to attract many followers. What could be the attractions? A number of reasons could be given.

Pentecostal churches that promote the prosperity gospel became popular in Africa in the 1990s. This was the time when the Bretton Woods institutions were promoting economic structural adjustment policies in many African countries. The failure of these policies left a number of African countries impoverished, with many companies retrenching workers. It can be argued that people lost confidence in socio-economic policies and the ability of governments to improve their lives. In the midst of this came the prosperity churches offering divine solutions in the name of the prosperity gospel. Integrating the gospel with the African belief that human events are controlled by spiritual powers, the charismatic churches found a number of followers. The prosperity gospel resonated with the traditional African anthropology that emphasises those in right relationships with God and that the ancestors are blessed with abundant life, physically, materially and spiritually. Prosperity gospel preachers therefore offered a Christian version of the traditional African understanding of prosperity and well-being.

---

[6] Simon Coleman, *The Globalisation of Charismatic Christianity: Spreading the Gospel of Prosperity* (Cambridge: Cambridge University Press, 2000): 33.

[7] Nimi Wariboko, 'Pentecostal Paradigms of National Economic Prosperity in Africa', in *Pentecostalism and Prosperity: The Socio-Economics of the Global Charismatic Movement*, eds. Katherine Attanasi and Amos Yong (New York: Palgrave Macmillan, 2012), 35-62; Lovemore Togarasei, 'The 'Birth' of a Prophet: Andrew Wutawunashe's Break from the Reformed Church in Zimbabwe', *Exchange: Journal of Missiological and Ecumenical Research* 35, no. 2, (2006): 215-225.

Traditional African religion has rituals for honouring ancestors. Among the Shona people of Zimbabwe, families (or tribes) conduct libations that are meant to seek or maintain divine (ancestral) favours and blessings. In such rituals, the ancestors are symbolically given food and drink to the accompaniment of praise poetry, on the understanding that, when honoured, ancestors will bless the families and individuals with health and wealth. Asonzeh Ukah also observes the use of praise poetry among the Yoruba of Nigeria in a bid to seek divine favours.[8] As Nimi Wariboko says, 'Favors from the gods in (African) traditional societies are not limited to the care of souls, but they also include blessings of fecundity, riches and a long and healthy life.'[9] Wariboko goes on to say that the western binary approach of separating the spiritual from the material, making God concerned with the spiritual only, is not in line with traditional African beliefs. Thus the prosperity gospel concurs with the African belief that a good standing with God results in material and physical blessings.

The gospel of prosperity also found fertile ground in Africa because of the poverty and suffering that people experience. A number of African governments have failed to supply people with the basics of life, including health care, food and water. The gospel of prosperity then came, promising a miraculous supply of these needs. In fact, the gospel of prosperity thrives in contexts of poverty. In these contexts, prosperity should not be thought of only in terms of money and material abundance. This is true for a few of the rich Pentecostals, but for the majority of African Pentecostals, prosperity refers to the ability to afford the basics of life: to live a healthy life, to afford basic food, to be able to send children to school and to live in happy marriages. When they talk about prosperity, the majority of African Pentecostals talk about having *sadza /palichi/ nshima/ ugali* (staple food) on the table.

Debates on the Prosperity Gospel in African Christianity

The prosperity gospel raises debates as to whether or not it is biblical, contributing to the social and economic development of its followers, influenced by an American understanding of the gospel, or in line with indigenous notions of prosperity.

Those who think it is biblical base their arguments on several Biblical texts. For example, Old Testament stories of the success and prosperity of Abraham are used together with New Testament texts like 3 John 2 ('Beloved, I pray that you may prosper in all things and be in good health, just as your soul prospers', NKJV). However, those against the prosperity gospel also find many texts in the Bible to support their position. For example, they find in Jesus and Paul lives of simplicity, quite contrary to what prosperity preachers teach.

As to whether the gospel contributes to the social and economic development of believers, again, there are different voices. There are those who believe that the prosperity gospel (with its emphasis on offerings and tithes as the ingredients for success) is bent on milking believers' hard earnings for the benefit of the pastors. But there are also many, especially the followers of this gospel, who think that the prosperity gospel is good for individual and social development. Even among scholars, a growing number think the gospel of prosperity contributes to Africa's social and economic development.[10]

---

[8] Asonzeh Ukah, *A New Paradigm of Pentecostal Power: A Study of the Redeemed Christian Church of God in Nigeria* (Trenton: World Press, 2008): 34.

[9] Wariboko, 'Pentecostal Paradigms of National Economic Prosperity in Africa', 41.

[10] See for, example, Lovemore Togarasei, 'The Pentecostal Gospel of Prosperity in African Contexts of Poverty', *Exchange: Journal of Missiological and Ecumenical Research* Vol. 40. Issue 2, (2011): 336-350 and The Centre for Development and Enterprise South Africa, 'Under the Radar: Pentecostalism in South Africa and its Potential Social and Economic Role', in *Pentecostalism and Prosperity: The Socio-Economics of the Global Charismatic Movement*, eds. Katherine Attanasi and Amos Yong (New York: Palgrave Macmillan, 2012), 63-85.

Concerning its origins in Africa, Paul Gifford believes the prosperity gospel is mainly influenced by the USA, and serves to comfort those who are already wealthy, by describing wealth as a sign of divine grace.[11] He therefore does not see the contribution of the gospel to the social development of the majority of the people in Africa. While it cannot be denied that the prosperity gospel was influenced by American evangelists, it is important to note its local appropriation. Rosalind Hackett has cautioned Pentecostalism scholars against over-emphasising the external influence on African Pentecostalism.[12] She notes that indigenous beliefs and practices also play a role in shaping Pentecostalism in Africa. This is very true of the gospel of prosperity. It fits in well with the traditional African emphasis on health and prosperity. African indigenous religion emphasizes that, when one's relations with the ancestors are good, then one's health and economic prosperity are assured.

Conclusion

We should end by pointing out that the prosperity gospel raises different reactions from different people on the continent. Be that as it may, its promise of wealth and health in contexts of poverty and limited health facilities gives hope and a positive mindset to Africans. It encourages believers to develop entrepreneurial skills for survival in contexts that offer very limited formal opportunities for one's sustenance. It is clear that the Bible does not celebrate poverty, and therefore to describe this gospel as unbiblical is rather unfortunate. Lastly, there are also prosperity preachers who have taken it to the extreme, especially for personal gain, and this should be condemned.

Bibliography

Chilenje, V. 'The Challenges of the Prosperity Gospel for Reformed/Presbyterian Churches in the 21st Century'. In *In Search of Wealth and Health: The Prosperity Gospel in African, Reformed Perspective*, edited by Hermen Kroesbergen 10-26. Wellington: Christian Literature Fund, 2014.

Coleman, S. *The Globalisation of Charismatic Christianity: Spreading the Gospel of Prosperity*. Cambridge: Cambridge University Press, 2000.

Corten, A. and Marshal-Fratani, R.. 'Introduction'. In *Between Babel to Pentecost: Transnational Pentecostalism in Africa and Latin America*, edited by Andre Corten and Ruth Marshal-Fratani, 1-20. London: Hurst and Company, 2001.

Dada, A. O. 'Prosperity Gospel in Nigerian Context: A Medium of Social Transformation or an Impetus for Delusion?' *ORITA: Ibadan Journal of Religious Studies* 36, nos.1 and 2, (2004): 95-105.

Droogers, A. 'Globalisation and Pentecostal Success'. In *Between Babel and Pentecost: Transnational Pentecostalism in Africa and Latin America*, edited by Adré Corten and Ruth Marshal-Fratani, 41-61. London: Hurst and Company, 2001.

Gifford, P. *African Christianity: Its Public Role*. London: Hurst and Company, 1998.

Hackett, R. 'The Prosperity Gospel in West Africa'. In *Religion and the Transformation of Capitalism*, edited by Richard H. Roberts, 199-214. London: Routledge, 1995.

Asamoah-Gyadu, Kwabena J. *African Charismatics: Current Developments with Independent Indigenous Pentecostalism in Ghana*. Leiden: Brill, 2004.

Kroesbergen, H. 'The Prosperity Gospel: A way to Reclaim Dignity?.' In *In Search of Wealth and Health: The Prosperity Gospel in African, Reformed Perspective*, edited by, Hermen Kroesbergen, 78-88. Wellington: Christian Literature Fund, 2013.

---

[11] Gifford, *African Christianity*.

[12] Rosalind Hackett, 'The Prosperity Gospel in West Africa', in *Religion and the Transformation of Capitalism*, ed. R. Roberts (London: Routledge, 1995), 199-214.

Mate, R. 'Wombs as God's Laboratories: Pentecostal Discourses of Femininity in Zimbabwe.' *Africa*, 72, no. 4, (2002): 549-568.

The Centre for Development and Enterprise South Africa, 'Under the Radar: Pentecostalism in South Africa and its Potential Social and Economic Role'. In *Pentecostalism and Prosperity: The Socio-Economics of the Global Charismatic Movement*, edited by, Katherine Attanasi and Amos Yong, 63-85. New York: Palgrave Macmillan, 2012.

Togarasei, L. 'The 'Birth' of a Prophet: Andrew Wutawunashe's Break from the Reformed Church in Zimbabwe.' *Exchange: Journal of Missiological and Ecumenical Research*, Vol. 35, no. 2, (2006): 215-225.

Togarasei, L. *'The Pentecostal Gospel of Prosperity in African Contexts of Poverty.' Exchange: Journal of Missiological and Ecumenical Research* Vol. 40, issue 2, (2011): 336-350.

Ukah, *A New Paradigm of Pentecostal Power: A Study of the Redeemed Christian Church of God in Nigeria.* Trenton: World Press, 2008.

Wariboko, N. 'Pentecostal Paradigms of National Economic Prosperity in Africa'. In *Pentecostalism and Prosperity: The Socio-Economics of the Global Charismatic Movement*, edited by, Katherine Attanasi and Amos Yong, 35-62. New York: Palgrave Macmillan, 2012.

(127B) The Prosperity Gospel and Economic Growth in African Christianity

Moji Ruele

Introduction

This paper explores the socio-economic implications of the prosperity gospel in the lives of African Christian in the 21st century. For the purposes of this chapter, the prosperity gospel or theology is used to mean that God wants to bless Christians spiritually, physically and materially. The paper starts by defining the main concepts used in the paper such as Pentecostalism, the prosperity theology and economic growth. It then goes on to discuss some of the methods used by African Pentecostals, before showing how economic crises in many parts of Africa have contributed to the emergence of African Pentecostal churches.

Defining Prosperity Theology and Economic Growth by African Christian Pentecostalism

In order to understand how prosperity theology plays a role in economic growth in the case of African Pentecostalism, it is important first to understand and define the following terms: Pentecostalism in general, prosperity and economic growth. Pentecostal is a nomenclature corresponding with the name of the Jewish feast of Pentecost, which took place fifty days after Passover (Greek: *Pentekonta*). As described in the New Testament book of Acts, which is central to Pentecostal spirituality, Jesus' followers gathered together following his death (around the time of Passover), resurrection and ascension; on the Day of Pentecost, 'they were all filled with the Holy Spirit and began to speak in tongues as the Spirit gave them utterance' (Acts 2:4 RSV). Prosperity means to live in abundance, or to flourish, spiritually and materially. In public discourse, the term 'prosperity' is often understood to refer to material goods, by assuming that material well-being can be accurately assessed by one common currency. Thus, money or material wealth becomes the measure of abundance (or scarcity), that takes place in human history.[1] According to Gerardo Marti, 'prosperity theology' as a term therefore has a historical dimension.[2] Specifically, prosperity theology developed amid the progressive globalization of modern capitalism. Economic growth as understood in this context can best be defined largely as a matter of good stewardship of the world's resources. It is a matter of using human skills, knowledge and experience together with the natural resources of animal, vegetable and mineral so as to achieve a greater output of the means of meeting human needs out of a given input of the means of production. By doing this, we get a more effective material basis for men and women to better our lives, and to be adequately fed, clothed and housed, and to be freed from the grind for survival. Economic growth, like any other economic or political aim, cannot be regarded as an end in itself. It is a means of giving us greater resources which can be used in ways which promote God's glory. The understanding in Pentecostalism is that this is in line with God's purposes, that men should enjoy the good things of this world, receiving them as his gifts and using them to his glory.[3]

---

[1] Douglas A. Hicks, 'Prosperity, Theology, and Economy' in *Pentecostalism and Prosperity: The Socio-Economics of the Global Charismatic Movement,* eds., Katherine Attanasi and Amos Yong (New York: Palgrave Macmillan, 2012), 240.

[2] Gerardo Marti, *Hollywood Faith: Holiness, Prosperity, and Ambition in a Los Angeles Church* (New Brunswick, N.J.: Rutgers University Press, 2012), 132.

[3] John F. Sleeman, *Economic Crises: A Christian Perspective* (London: SCM Press, 1976), 137-139.

Prosperity theology, therefore, is fundamentally about how we understand God's action in relation to human actions, which requires us to reflect upon how God acts in the world. What is the relationship between human prosperity and divine and human actions? Prosperity theology tends to emphasize entrepreneurial initiatives which can certainly enhance a sense of human agency or ability to shape one's own economic future.

The Pentecostals' Methods for Economic Growth and Prosperity

This section offers an overview of some of the methods used by the African Pentecostals in pursuit of economic growth and prosperity. The aim is to show the relation between some of the approaches, frameworks and strategies used by African Pentecostal churches to attain prosperity, in response to economic deprivation, poverty and economic crises. In what follows I briefly discuss five approaches used by Pentecostals in promoting the economic message of prosperity.

The Prosperity Model

The first is the Prosperity Model which presents a comprehensive picture of individualization and summarizes profound structural shifts in advanced capitalist structures, the welfare state, and corporate-backed commercialization (which are all aspects of globalization). Ulrich Beck sketches the model of individualization and summarizes how, amid increasing economic uncertainty, broad societal transformation leaves some individuals with greater economic development out of their own particular life course. He calls this approach an individualization thesis with chronic indeterminacy of risk and risk-taking, which must be followed by all Pentecostals, including African Pentecostals.[4] As an approach, the Prosperity Model encourages individuals to take risks in order to attain economic growth and prosperity in their lives.

The Covenant Paradigm

The second model is the Covenant Model that argues that God blesses nations, either according to the covenant of giving, or in response to the covenant of good efforts. According to this theory, the individual's prosperity, which starts with ceaseless sacrificial giving of money or time and effort to the church, will lead to prosperity, economic growth and national development. In the Covenant Model, irrespective of the overall state of the national economy in many African countries, poverty is perceived as a religious problem caused either by a lack of faith, or a failure to trust in whatever God promises. Therefore, all poor people who live according to the covenant and faith in God will become prosperous and gain economic growth, whereas those who do not will become poor.[5]

The Spiritualist Paradigm

The third model is the Spiritualist/Scriptural Model also known as the Spiritualist Paradigm. It often emphasizes spiritual warfare as the necessary first step to national prosperity. It is perhaps the earliest paradigm to emerge in the peneumatological imagination of African Pentecostals as it confronted both western modernizing cultures associated with globalization and African traditional cultures, which they regarded as demonic. It is also based on an exchange model in which God and Satan act in history. The success or failure of individual and national actions therefore depends on fidelity to Jesus Christ. According to this model, the demands of faithfulness to Jesus Christ include strict obedience to biblical

---

[4] Ulrich Beck, *Risk Society: Towards a New Modernity* (London: Sage Publications, 1992), 13.

[5] Amos Yong, 'Salvation, Society, and the Spirit: Pentecostal Contextualization and the Political Theology from Cleveland to Birmingham, from Springfield to Seoul', *Paxpneuma: The Journal of Pentecostals & Charismatics for Peace and Justice* Vol. 5, no. 2, (2009): 22-34.

commandments, and the rejection of African Traditional Religions and repudiation of certain indigenous cultural practices believed to be demonic. The key to development, therefore, is intercessory prayer and deliverance (exorcism) to redeem the land – in this case the African continent. Spiritualist pastors and congregants believe political and economic powers have both an outer form and an inner spiritual dynamic that animate their manifestation and uphold them.[6]

The Excellence Model

Fourth is the Excellence Model which encourages one to have a strong work ethic and to strive for excellence in everything. The Excellence Model builds upon the prosperity gospel by adding to it the perspective of human capability development and Afrocentric sentiments. If Africans are sowing and reaping material blessings, they must do so according to the proponents of this model, with the best machinery and organization.[7]

The Missional and Contextual Arguments

Fifth is the Missional Argument also known as the Contextual Argument. This method uses sermons that teach people to give in abundance and that money is not evil. According to Akoko, this changed the thinking of a lot of Pentecostals who started establishing businesses in response to the economy that was in crisis.[8]

The African Economic Crisis as a Context for the Growth of African Christian Pentecostal Churches

Since the end of the era of colonialism, many African countries have regrettably been going through a serious economic crisis that has left few untouched and retarded progress significantly. This crisis has given rise to compounding poverty, misery and unemployment, and at the same time ferments fear, doubt and uncertainty is due to increases in social insecurity. Causes of the crisis are many, complex and very difficult to identify – not just by the ordinary man, but even by academics.[9]

Post-colonial government efforts in Africa to control the crisis have also yielded few dividends in specific terms, though there has been much official rhetoric and contradictory claims of recovery in progress. The traditionally established churches (such as the Roman Catholic, Anglican, Methodist, Baptist, Lutheran and many others) have also been worried about the crisis. They have made their own spiritual contribution in explaining its causes and how to fight it. They have often expressed this through sermons in churches and in pastoral letters. However, they have neither succeeded in convincing their members nor the population at large on the practical relevance of their options and strategies.[10]

Since then, the most existential task facing Africans in general has been economic development to reverse the crisis. For African Pentecostal Christians, this raises the urgent question: what is the Pentecostal churches' understanding and teaching on the continent's economic predicament?

Part of the answer to this question was the rise and spread of Pentecostalism during this period of economic crisis in many parts of Africa. This was coupled with mass defections from the established churches to new Pentecostal churches, which could be interpreted as a public sign of dissatisfaction by

[6] Yong, 'Salvation, Society, and the Spirit', 22-34.
[7] Yong, 'Salvation, Society, and the Spirit', 22-34.
[8] Mbe Robert Akoko, *'Ask and You shall be Given.' Pentecostalism and the Economic Crisis in Cameroon* (Leiden: African Studies Centre, African Studies Collection, 2007), 13.
[9] Piet Konings, 'Plantation Labour and Economic Crises in Cameroon', *Development and Change* 26 no. 3, (1995): 525-549.
[10] Pierre Titi Nwel, 'The Churches and the Democratic Upheaval in Cameroon 1982-1993', in *The Christian Churches and Democratization of Africa*, ed.,Paul Gifford (Leiden: E.J. Brill, 1995), 168-187.

African Christians. Many Pentecostal African Christians felt that the way the established churches have gone about addressing the spiritual and material needs of their followers in Africa was not helpful. Such increasing disillusionment shows that a surging number of Christians do not consider it enough for mainline churches to make critical statements about the worsening economic situation. They also condemned the few who lived in obscene opulence while the majority wallowed in poverty and misery.[11] During the time of economic crisis, many parts of Africa have witnessed the proliferation and flourishing of Pentecostal groups, particularly in English-speaking areas. Some of these groups are the Apostolic churches, Full Gospel Mission, Church of Christ, Church of God, True Church of Christ, Assemblies of God, Africa Bible Church, Christian Missionary Fellowship International, Winners Chapel, Deeper Life Bible Church, Arm of God Church, New Generation, Celestial Frontiers Millennial Church, United Pentecostal Church, Bethel World Outreach Ministry, Living World Church, Universal Church of the Kingdom of God, Living Faith Worldwide Church – and many others.

Based on the ever-increasing numbers of African Pentecostal Christian churches, it is becoming clear that the African Christian landscape is very different from a century ago when the historic mission churches – Catholic, Anglican, Methodist, Baptist and Lutheran – dominated the scene in fighting for economic growth and prosperity. As already indicated, available examples indicate that considerable changes have now taken place with the arrival of the Pentecostal churches in many parts of Africa. In South Africa, for example, the Apostolic Faith Mission is numerically stronger than the Dutch Reformed Church. The Church of the Pentecost is probably Ghana's largest Protestant body. Indeed, in Ghana, Kenya, South Africa, Uganda, Zambia and Zimbabwe, 'born again' churches are so numerous and their leaders so influential that they may just be considered 'mainstreams', 'mainline' or as established as Anglicans and others.

An Application of African Christian Pentecostal Methods for Economic Growth and Prosperity

In order to apply African Pentecostal methods for economic growth and prosperity, one must first recognize that the most existential task facing Africans in general is economic development and prosperity. For African Pentecostals, prosperity theology emerges neither as a tool for the exploitation of workers nor a class pursuit of higher status. It is a practical process towards religious life to the demands of life, particularly with regard to economics.[12] Each of the Pentecostals, both on the African continent and the world over, adopts to a method of life figuring out how to acquire prosperity or a method of practical adaptation (developing practical ways of functioning in a particular society) as an economic message for the accumulation of wealth, in order to attain prosperity and fight poverty. Many of these methods have been used for a long time to persuade Pentecostals that God provides a solution to every problem, depending on the faith of the individual or people in general.

Below I make an attempt to show how these methods are applied by some African Christian Pentecostals. It is important to note that, generally, the processes of Bible reading and the application of the above-mentioned approaches and frameworks are very much dependent on the people's circumstances . As such, the African Pentecostal interpretation of the Bible and the application of this model is a result of their actual situation, due to prevailing socio-economic and political conditions. This context influenced their biblical exegesis. The socio-economic and political chaos that characterized post-colonial Africa became the springboard and a possible space for application of the above-mentioned methods. Below, I make an effort to blend these methods and frameworks within the African context described above.

---

[11] Mbe Robert Akoko, *'Ask and You shall be Given.' Pentecostalism and the Economic Crisis in Cameroon* (Leiden: African Studies Centre, African Studies Collection, 2007), 13.

[12] Gerardo Marti, *Hollywood Faith: Holiness, Prosperity, and Ambition in a Los Angeles Church* (New Brunswick, N.J.: Rutgers University Press, 2012), 132.

First, I start with the Prosperity Model, which is seen by many Pentecostals as a specific and pragmatic method to address economic crises in general. Amos Yong notes that prosperity theology has the potential to contribute to African economic growth and prosperity.[13] He posits a mentality that has the potential to transform global economies, suggesting that economic theory has the potential to focus on a new form of renewal economics. Christian missionary work, understood within this framework, is that there is not only the forgiveness of sins but also spiritual healing and deliverance for people from the powers and the forces that oppress them, such as economic factors. Thus it involves not only health and spiritual well-being, but wealth. It also engenders hope in impoverished situations; it may motivate actions that could gradually overcome poverty. The prosperity gospel message also puts emphasis on members achieving high levels of prosperity. It associates failure to thrive with the devil's machinations. People who use this method also appeal to the Bible to support teaching and preaching on wealth. Akoko singles out Cameroon as an example, where African Pentecostals have placed much emphasis on this method as a way of responding to the economic crisis bedevilling their country.[14] This view is shared by Jua, who notes that, when an individual or a group is deprived of certain things considered important to society such as education, nourishment or money (as is the case in many parts of Africa), two religious doctrinal alternatives could be used to help overcome deprivation.[15]

Secondly, I discuss the Covenant Model through which Christians demonstrate their faith in God to turn round their bad economic circumstances, by giving financial and other material resources to the church. The covenant model/paradigm is based on the agricultural metaphor of sowing and reaping: sow tithes and offerings (among other elements of a self-sacrificial way of life) into the church and reap a bumper harvest of wealth.

Thirdly, the Spiritualist Paradigm sees African economic crises as demonic forces. The underlying factor under this model or theory is that the continent has been mortgaged to evil forces, and needs to be bought back by persistent and fervent prayer. It sees national poverty as spiritual, and economic wisdom begins by seeking God's deliverance from powers, principalities and rulers (Eph. 6:12) who foul up the economies of Africa. Pastors who believe in this model (such as Emeka Nwankpa) argue that spiritual forces, demons and the devil hold back Africa's economic development. Therefore, they pray and cast out these powers.[16]

Fourthly, the Excellence Model is based on a strong work ethic. An African Pentecostal pastor identified with this model is Bishop David Oyedepo of Winners Chapel (Ota, near Metropolitan) Lagos. His Afrocentric perspective situates the task of economic development within a pan-African context. As an example of how he applies this method, he delivers his Afrocentric message in ways that transcend narrow identification. His method also has transnational and transracial appeal, because it is couched in the typical born-again rhetoric of destiny (*telos*). In applying this method, he claims God has given him a special task for African nations and African Pentecostals, to conquer their poverty and recover their dignity. He encourages his followers to pursue excellence. There is no doubt that his message harbours salient features of the prosperity gospel model but his ego goes beyond crass, vulgar wealth and health to the extent that it embraces a teleological conception of Africans, based on a vision of professional excellence. This pastor argues that African Pentecostals can uplift Africa to her glorious destiny when they execute their work at a

---

[13] Amos Yong, 'A Typology of Prosperity Theology: A Religious Economy of Global Renewal or a Renewal Economics?' in *Pentecostalism and Prosperity: The Socio-Economics of the Global Charismatic Movement,* ed., Katherine Attanasi & Amos Yong (New York: Palgrave Macmillan, 2012), 15-33.

[14] Mbe Robert Akoko, *'Ask and You shall be Given.' Pentecostalism and the Economic Crisis in Cameroon* (Leiden: African Studies Centre, African Studies Collection, Vol. 2, 2007).

[15] Nantang Jua, 'Cameroon: Jump-Starting Economic Crises', *Africa Insight,* Vol. 21, no. 3, (1991): 162-170.

[16] Emeka Nwankpa, *Redeeming the Land* (Achimota, Ghana: African Christian Publishers, 1995), 7.

First World level of excellence.[17] Through this method, African Pentecostal sermons also quote popular verses such as 'Blessed are the poor'. In response to dwindling funding of local churches, they often quote: 'Jesus came to bring abundant life and prosperity.' In Jesus' teaching, the exorcism of evil spirits needs to be followed by receiving the Holy Spirit (Matt. 12:43-45). Thus, with deliverance comes faith that can move mountains and make possible what is otherwise impossible (Matt. 17:20-21) so that, 'Whatever you ask for in prayer with faith, you will receive' (Matt. 21:22). On numerous occasions, the synoptic evangelists affirm that Jesus healed all the sick who came to him (Matt. 4:36; Mark 1:34, 6:56; Luke 6:19, 9:11; Acts 5:16, 8:7, 28:9). The Prosperity Model thus involves not just wealth; it involves health *and* physical well-being.[18]

Going back to the Old Testament, the Prosperity Model advocates suggest that God not only called Abraham the 'father' of God's chosen and elect people, but also blessed him abundantly in every way: socially, economically and materially. Joseph's many-coloured robe foreshadowed his later prosperity as second-in-command over the whole of Egypt. Job's faithfulness was rewarded, not only with the full restoration of his health but also with double the prosperity that he had had before his calamity. In each instance and many others, the Bible portrays God's desire to bless his people with spiritual, physical and material abundance.[19] Above all, the operation of these purposes is sustained and advanced by the ethos of professional excellence. Thus, the Excellence Model is a triangle of nationalism (the Afrocentric view), professionalism (human capacity-building), and the prosperity gospel's orientation to development.[20]

Fifthly, the missional argument and contextual argument interface with the global economy through investing in development efforts or entrepreneurial projects. In applying both the missional and contextual argument to the African context, Amos Yong outlines and frequently quotes scriptural texts such as 3 John 2: 'Beloved, I pray that all may go well with you and that you may be in good health, just as it is well with your soul.' This prayer is understood by African Pentecostals as having three dimensions of blessings: the spiritual, the physical and life in totality.[21]

According to Kalu, the Scriptures, from this perspective, have promised salvation for souls (both now and in the after-life), divine healing for the body, and material prosperity for physical beings. Christ's ministry, understood within this prosperity framework, operates at each of these levels, as well as emphasizing material prosperity. It also teaches that there is not only forgiveness of sins, but also spiritual healing and deliverance of people from the physical and material powers and forces that oppress them.[22]

Conclusion

In approaching this paper, I started by defining its main concepts such as the prosperity gospel, before briefly outlining and discussing five examples of the methods of Pentecostalism. I have attempted to show

---

[17] Nimi Wariboko, 'Pentecostal paradigms of National Economic Prosperity in Africa', in *Pentecostalism and Prosperity: The Socio-Economics of the Global Charismatic Movement,* eds., Katherine Attanasi and Amos Yong (New York: Palgrave Macmillan, 2012), 36-59.

[18] Gary S. Greig & Kevin N. Springer (eds), *The Kingdom and the Power: Are Healing and the Spiritual Gifts Used by Jesus and the Early Church Meant for the Church Today? A Biblical Look at How to Bring the Gospel to the World with Power* (Ventura, California: Regal Books, 1993).

[19] H.L. Bosman, I.G.P. Gous and I.J.J. Spangenberg (eds.), *Plutocrats and Paupers: Wealth and Poverty in the Old Testament* (Pretoria: Van Schaik, 1991).

[20] Jean-Francois Medard 'Les eglises protestantes au Cameroun, entre tradition autoritaire et ethnicité', in *Religion et Transition Democratique en Afrique*, eds., F. Constantine and C. Coulon (Paris: Karthala, 1997), 17.

[21] Amos Yong, 'A Typology of Prosperity Theology: A Religious Economy of Global Renewal or a Renewal Economics?', in *Pentecostalism and Prosperity: The Socio-Economics of the Global Charismatic Movement,* eds., Katherine Attanasi and Amos Yong (New York: Palgrave Macmillan, 2012), 15-33.

[22] Ogbu U. Kalu, *African Pentecostalism: An Introduction* (New York & Oxford: Oxford University Press, 2008), 9.

how the African economic context creates a breeding ground for the spread of Pentecostalism, before showing in conclusion how such methods are applied in that context. When making an application of the five methods used by African Pentecostals, it becomes very clear that they all agree that the African context which is characterized by economic crisis, corruption and mismanagement requires some form of moral regeneration and spiritual uplift. They also see poverty as demonic, evil and blasphemous. Therefore it requires some form of spiritual intervention as well as relevant biblical exegesis.

Bibliography

Akoko, Mbe Robert. *'Ask and You shall be Given.' Pentecostalism and the Economic Crisis in Cameroon.* Leiden: African Studies Centre, African Studies Collection, Vol. 2, 2007.

Beck, Ulrich. *Risk Society: Towards a New Modernity.* London: Sage Publications, 1992.

Bosman, H.L., Gous, I.G.P. andSpangenberg, I.J.J. *Plutocrats and Paupers: Wealth and Poverty in the Old Testament.* Pretoria: Van Schaik, 1991.

Greig, Gary S. and Springer, Kevin N., (eds.) *The Kingdom and the Power: Are Healing and the Spiritual Gifts used by Jesus and the Earthly Church meant for the Church Today? A Biblical look at how to Bring the Gospel to the World with Power.* Ventura, California: Regal Books, 1993.

Hicks, Douglas A. 'Prosperity, Theology, and Economy.' In *Pentecostalism and Prosperity: The Socio-Economics of the Global Charismatic Movement,* edited by Katherine Attanasi and Amos Yong, 239-251. New York: Palgrave Macmillan, 2012.

Kalu, Ogbu U. *African Pentecostalism: An Introduction.* New York and Oxford: Oxford University Press, 2008.

Konings, P. 'Plantation Labour and Economic Crises in Cameroon.' *Development and Change* Vol. 26, no. 3, (1995): 525-549.

Jua, N. 'Cameroon: Jump-Starting Economic Crises.' *Africa Insight* Vol. 21, no 3. (1991): 162-170.

Marti, Gerardo. *Hollywood Faith: Holiness, Prosperity, and Ambition in a Los Angeles Church.* New Brunswick, N.J.: Rutgers University Press, 2012.

Medard, F. 'Les Eglise Protestantes au Cameroun, Entre Tradition Autoritaire et Ethnicité.' In *Religion et Transition Democratic en Afrique,* edited by F. Constantine and C. Coulon. Paris: Kathala, 1997.

Nwankpa, Emeka. *Redeeming the Land.* Achimota, Ghana: African Christian Publishers, 1995.

Nwel, Pierre Titi. 'The Churches and the Democratic upheaval in Cameroon 1982-1993.' In *The Christian Churches and Democratization of Africa,* edited by Paul Gifford, 168-187. Leiden: E.J. Brill, 1995.

Sleeman, John F. *Economic Crisis: A Christian Perspective.* London: SCM Press, 1976.

Yong, Amos. 'A Typology of Prosperity Theology: A Religious Economy of Global Renewal or a Renewal Economics?' In *Pentecostalism and Prosperity: The Socio-Economics of the Global Charismatic Movement,* edited by Katherine Attanasi and Amos Yong, 15-33. New York: Palgrave Macmillan, 2012.

Yong, Amos. 'Salvation, Society, and the Spirit: Pentecostal Contextualization and the Political Theology from Cleveland to Birmingham, from Springfield to Seoul.' *Paxpneuma* Vol. 5, no. 2, (2009): 22-34.

Wariboko, Nimi. 'Pentecostal paradigms of National Economic Prosperity in Africa.' In *Pentecostalism and Prosperity: The Socio-Economic of the Global Charismatic Movement,* edited by Katherine Attanasi and Amos Yong, 36-59. New York: Palgrave Macmillan, 2012.

(128) THE IMPACT OF EUROPEAN RACISM ON CHRISTIANITY IN AFRICA[1]

Linda Naicker

Introduction

The origins of European racism can be traced to the nineteenth century when a pioneer in the study of comparative anatomy and skull analysis, Professor Johann Blumenbach, developed the idea that the people of Europe belonged to one race.[2] Blumenbach claimed that Europeans represented the highest racial type within the human species. This newly established racial order set the stage for racial formation in European colonies and was used to justify European domination, paternalism and imperialism. These scientific and scholarly developments in Europe coincided with missionary expansion into Africa and other newly discovered continents and promulgated dispossession, discrimination and subjugation through racial prejudice in all spheres of life. This article traces the development of European racism and examines its impact on Christianity in Africa from the nineteenth to the twenty-first century.

The Roots of Racism in Africa

In his book 'Origin of Species', published in 1859, British naturalist Charles Darwin asserted that a species' ability to survive was determined by a natural selection of inherited variations. Darwin's species thesis led to the development of race theory, in which Africans were placed in the category of inferior intermediates in the chain of human existence.[3] The fields of sociology, psychology, anthropology, theology, biology and medicine became instruments to prove the inferiority of various race groups in comparison to the white race and maintain patriarchal dominance over colonized peoples. Influential scientists in the field of eugenics[4] provided a scientific brand of racism which determined variables of phenotype, intelligence and ability to achieve, in terms of civilization or culture, based on genetics.[5] This led to the treatment of Africans as sub-human and justified European domination and exploitation.[6]

The science of eugenics was contested in the twentieth century, with scientists finding little evidence of the existence of biologically different race groups. Scientists found that the average genetic difference between two randomly selected individuals is 0.2% of all the genes and that the physical traits used to

---

[1] 'Racism' is defined as a social group or cultural entity that denies the dignity of another group and leads to the ultimate assertion that this group is superior and demonstrates a desire to dominate. See World Council of Churches, 'Program to Combat Racism' https://wwwaluka.org/struggle/collection/WCC.

[2] Gill Sutton, 'The Layering of History: A Brief Look at Eugenics, the Holocaust and Scientific Racism in South Africa', *Yesterday and Today*, no. 1, (May 2007): 22-23.
'Race' can be defined as a social phenomenon in which contested systems of meaning serve as the connection between physical features and personal characteristics. See Ian F. Haney-Lopez, 'The Social Construction of Race', in *Critical Race Theory*, eds. Richard Delgado and Jean Stefancic (Philadelphia: Temple University Press, 2000), 63.

[3] G. Sutton, 'The Layering of History', ', 22-23.

[4] The science of eugenics was developed as an off-shoot of the Darwinian Theory in Britain in the 1800s. Sir Francis Galton coined the term to mean 'well-born'. He claimed that biologically-determined leadership qualities were inherent traits of the British ruling class. See Linda Naicker, 'The Role of Eugenics and Religion in the Construction of Race in South Africa', *Studia Historiae Ecclesiasticae* Vol. 38, no. 2, (December 2012): 209-220.

[5] Naicker, 'The Role of Eugenics and Religion in the Construction of Race in South Africa', 211.

[6] Naicker, 'The Role of Eugenics and Religion in the Construction of Race in South Africa', 212.

distinguish individuals are determined by 0.1% of all the genes, proving that there is only one race – the human race.[7]

Before the eighteenth and nineteenth centuries, European involvement with Africa was largely transitory, with limited control of foreign lands. The dawn of the Industrial Revolution made Europe the master of manufacturing and gave new impetus for overseas exploration. Europeans in Africa and other newly discovered regions now began to think in terms of domination and colonialism, and consequently began to extend their settlements.[8] Europe's involvement with Africa became characterised by aggression, in the forms of political belligerence, destroying ancient kingdoms, tearing down societies, vigorously imposing European forms of thought and education on African peoples and imposing a European brand of Christianity on African people.

Christianity and Racism in Africa

According to Villa-Vicencio, for the most part the missionary endeavour coincided with the European age of expansion. The history of missionary expansion followed the same plan as the history of colonization. Churches in Africa and other European colonies became colonial stations for churches in Europe.[9] The prevailing sentiment was that European civilization and Christianity were indistinguishable.

The denigration suffered by Africans on the basis of race is well documented, particularly by proponents of Black and African Theologies, as is the belief that, in many ways, eighteenth and nineteenth-century Christianity collaborated with colonial oppressors in disparaging Africans.[10] The ruthless attack on the African psyche was intended to denigrate the African person and despoil the African heritage. In the words of Archbishop Tutu:[11]

> The worst crime that can be laid at the door of the white man (who, it must be said, has done many a worthwhile and praiseworthy thing for which we are always thankful) is not our economic, social and political exploitation, however reprehensible that might be; no, it is that his policy succeeded in filling most of us with a self-disgust and self-hatred. This has been the most violent form of colonialism, our spiritual and mental enslavement, which we have suffered from, that can only be called a religious or spiritual schizophrenia.

There exists a plethora of literature that shows the association between the colonial mission to Africa and the Christian mission to Africa.[12] Explorers, missionaries and traders became representatives of European colonial interests in Africa, resulting in Africa's vulnerability to colonization and domination. By 1914, with the exception of Ethiopia and Liberia, Africa had been partitioned and occupied by the imperial powers of Britain, France, Germany, Portugal, Belgium, Spain and Italy.[13] Christianity came to Africa at the price of African people's freedoms, traditions and communities.

---

[7] Haney-Lopez, 'The Social Construction of Race', 164.

[8] Stephen Neil. *A History of Christian Missions.* (Harmondsworth: Penguin, 1986), 211-214.

[9] Charles Villa-Vicencio, *Between Christ and Caesar: Classic Contemporary Texts on Church and State* (Cape Town: David Philip, 1986), 170.

[10] See Desmond Tutu, 'Black Theology and African Theology – Soulmates or Antagonists' in *A Reader in African Theology*, ed. John Parrat (Cambridge: Cambridge University Press, 1987), 37-44.

[11] Tutu, 'Black Theology and African Theology – Soulmates or Antagonists', 37.

[12] See John Parrot, *A Reader in African Christian Theology*, (Cambridge: Cambridge University Press, 1987).

[13] A. Adu Boahen (ed.), *General History of Africa VII: Africa under Colonial Domination 1880-1935* (London: James Curry, 1990), 320; J. F. Ade Ajaji (ed.), *General History of Africa: Africa in the 19th Century until the 1880s* (London: James Curry, 1998), 300-320.

The Christian Response to European Racism in Africa

At its 2nd Assembly in 1954, the World Council of Churches (WCC) conveyed the conviction that any form of segregation based on race, colour or ethnicity is contrary to the gospel. It called its member churches to work towards the abolition of segregation and discrimination within their own life and society. The Geneva Conference on Church and Society in 1966 raised a strong voice against the sin of racial arrogance and oppression. At the 4th WCC Assembly in Uppsala in 1969, the WCC identified racism practised by the white-skinned against the darker-skinned as one of the world's basic problems and a blatant denial of the Christian faith. The WCC therefore set the Programme to Combat Racism (PCR) in motion worldwide. The PCR is regarded as one of the most significant expressions of faith in world Christianity. Its objectives included providing financial aid to racially oppressed groups and organizations, supporting victims of racial injustice and promoting social justice.[14]

The 1950s signified a new era in church and political life in Africa, when African people demanded freedom from their colonial oppressors. By 1961, eighteen countries had received independence. This prompted the churches in Africa to form an ecumenical body to deal collaboratively with their new responsibilities. The All-Africa Conference of Churches (AACC) was established in 1963 and was tasked with dealing with the challenges of racism, civil war, the refugee problem and other pertinent issues facing the African continent.[15] At their 3rd Assembly in Lusaka, Zambia, in 1974, the issue of the liberation of Africa was discussed. The general secretary of the AACC, Burgess Carr, explained that those who resorted to the use of violence against oppressive regimes in South Africa, Rhodesia and Portugal were not condemned for their actions.[16] Portugal relinquished its rule over Mozambique and Angola in 1975 and in 1980 Robert Mugabe's socialist liberation movement took power in Rhodesia after a landslide election victory.[17] The question then became whether South Africa would attain independence next.

Africa's Last Bastion of White Supremacy

South Africa became the last country whose racial policy was based on white supremacy. Christian concern grew rapidly as structural racism heaped tyranny on the lives of the country's black majority population by the white minority population. For example, a missionary policy document published by the Dutch Reformed Church in 1935 stated that Afrikaners fear equality between black and white and the consequent racial fusion such equality may engender. The document went on to state that Blacks and Coloureds must develop apart from Europeans. The policy laid the foundation for the Dutch Reformed Church's stance on race relations in South Africa.[18]

The National Party, consisting of a large number of Dutch Reformed Church leaders, came into power in 1948. Historians maintain that, to an extent, the racist ideology of the Dutch Reformed Church had its roots in the convictions of a secret Afrikaner group, the Broederbond. The Broederbond believed that the Afrikaner nation was placed in Southern Africa by God.[19] By 1933, the Broederbond had over 1,000 members, with the principle influence being wielded by a small group of academics steeped in neo-

---

[14] Jeremiah Manari, 'Special Projects of the WCC: The Project on Women and the Programme to Combat Racism', in *Essays and Exercises in Ecumenism,* ed. Christo. Lombaard (Pietermaritzburg: Cluster Publications, 1999), 307-325.

[15] James Amanze, 'Some Large Ecumenical Organizations of the African Continent', in *Essays and Exercises in Ecumenism,* ed. Christo Lombaard (Pietermaritzburg: Cluster Publications, 1999), 137-149.

[16] J. Adonis and Joan A. Millard, 'Christianity in South Africa since 1948', in *A History of Christianity in South Africa,* eds. J. W. Hofmeyr and Gerald J. Pillay (Pretoria: HAUM Tertiary, 1994), 280.

[17] Shubane Khehla 'The Black Consciousness Movement: The Soweto Uprising of 1976', in *New History of South Africa,* eds. Hermann Giliomee , Bernard Mbenga (Cape Town: NB Publishers, 2007), 359-361.

[18] Adonis and Millard, 'Christianity in South Africa since 1948', 254.

[19] Adonis and Millard, 'Christianity in South Africa since 1948', 254.

Calvinist thought. Many politicians were members of the Broederbond as well as the Dutch Reformed Church (DRC). Shubane states that a 1934 Broederbond pamphlet declared, 'The Afrikanerdom shall reach its ultimate destiny of domination in South Africa... Brothers, our solution for South Africa's troubles [are] not that this or that party shall gain the upper hand, but that the Afrikaner Broederbond shall rule South Africa.'[20]

A Dutch Reformed Church synod in 1946 found that the Broederbond was not in conflict with the Bible or Christian principles. In 1947, a DRC congress took place in Johannesburg, the proceedings of which were published in a booklet entitled 'Kerk en Stad' (Church and State), giving guidelines for the white Dutch Reformed Church's policy towards other racial groups. The congress highlighted the need for segregation of white and black as well as the conviction that the church must take the lead role in drafting a workable racial policy. The document was finalized in 1951 under the title, 'Rapport oor die Skriftuurlike Gronde van Rasse-apartheid' ('Report on the Scriptural Basis for Racial Apartheid').[21]

Christianity can legitimise racist ideology, show disinterest in the face of racism or act as a mechanism of radical transformation. Many South African clergy, including the likes of Ambrose Reeves, Trevor Huddleston, Beyers Naudé, Desmond Tutu and Allan Boesak raised their voices against the racist ideology of the South African government. The WCC's Programme to Combat Racism was highly controversial among the churches in South Africa. It supported reflection and action among churches in Southern Africa and provided direct humanitarian support to liberation movements.[22]

The Kairos Document,[23] released in 1985, produced by a number of theologians, lay people and clergy, was signed by 150 people. It appealed to Christian churches to oppose civil authority, raise their voices against apartheid and stand in solidarity with the poor and oppressed. It criticized white Christian privilege for not defending oppressed people being tortured by the apartheid state. The document went on to name the Dutch Reformed Churches as being the most prominent proponent of the apartheid government's racial policies.

Two documents published in the late 1980s, 'A Relevant Pentecostal Witness' and 'The Road to Damascus', called upon South African Christians to reject injustice and hypocrisy which is contrary to the gospel.[24] South Africa obtained freedom from the oppression of apartheid in 1994.

The legacy of South Africa's racist past has far-reaching consequences for its future. Economic injustice is rife and the issue of land distribution is still a source of tension. Political corruption, unemployment, a weakening health care system and lack of service delivery have negative effects on the country, most especially on the poorest of the poor. While the nation is no longer legally defined by race, race is still a thorny issue. Notable amongst South Africa's problems is the xenophobic violence by South Africans against foreigners from other parts of the continent. This is testament to the bitterness and division that is still prevalent in South African society.

The churches and ecumenical organizations need to take a collective stand to deal with what can only be referred to as a devastating crisis. Just as they made a concerted effort to eradicate institutionalized racism in Africa, so too there needs to appear a moment of truth, a *kairos*, a point of reckoning, where xenophobic violence becomes unequivocally targeted and eradicated. What is most clear with regard to xenophobic violence in South Africa is that discrimination produces social chaos and life-threatening mayhem. The

---

20 Shubane, 'The Black Consciousness Movement: The Soweto Uprising of 1976', 289.

21 Adonis and Millard, 'Christianity in South Africa Since 1948', 254.

22 See The World Council of Churches, 'Programme to Combat Racism, Struggle for Freedom', https://www.aluka.org/struggle/collection/WCC (accessed 1 April, 2015).

23 Kairos Theologians. *The Kairos Document: Challenge to the Churches: A Theological Comment on the Political Crisis in South Africa,* Revised Second Edition, (Braamfontein: Skotaville, 1986).

24 Theological Education by Extension College, *Exploring our African Christian World: Workbook A* (Turffontein, 2011), 1-15.

fundamental values of equality, dignity and opportunity for all human beings must become the social norm in Africa and, most especially, in post-apartheid South Africa.

Conclusion

The historical development and impact of racism on African Christianity and the Christian response to it points the way for how we must address all forms of oppression in God's world. Wherever racism, xenophobia, inhumanity, indignity and exploitation exist, the church must take a stand. The words of liberation theologian Allan Boesak still ring true today, as they did a decade before the last racist regime in Africa fell:

> Violence, greed and the demonic distortion of human values continue to destroy God's world and God's people. Economic exploitation is escalating, rather than abating, and economic injustice is still the dominant reality in the relationship between rich and poor.[25]

Bibliography

Adonis, J. and Millard, J. 'Christianity in South Africa Since 1948.' In *A History of Christianity in South Africa,* edited by J. W. Hofmeyr and Gerald J. Pillay, 251-295. Pretoria: HAUM Tertiary, 1994.

Ajayi, A. *General History of Africa: Africa in the 19th Century until the 1880s.* London: James Curry, 1998.

Amanze, J. 'Some Large Ecumenical Organizations of the African Continent.' In *Essays and Exercises in Ecumenism,* edited by Christo Lombaard, 137-149. Pietermaritzburg: Cluster Publications, 1999.

Boahen, A. *General History of Africa VII: Africa under Colonial Domination 1880-1935.* London: James Curry, 1990.

Boesak, A. *Black and Reformed: Apartheid, Liberation and the Calvinist Tradition.* Johannesburg: Skotaville Publishers, 1984.

Haney-López, I.F. 'The Social Construction of Race.' In *Critical Race Theory,* edited by Richard Delgado and Jean Stefancic, 164-175. Philadelphia: Temple University Press, 2000.

Henriot, P. 'Adjusting in Africa: For Whose Benefit?' Paper delivered at Trocaire Conference, Dublin, 30 October 1998.

Kairos Theologians. *The Kairos Document: Challenge to the Churches: A Theological Comment on the Political Crisis in South Africa.* Revised Second Edition. Braamfontein: Skotaville, 1986.

Manari, J. 'Special Projects of the WCC: the Project on Women and the Programme to Combat Racism.' In *Essays and Exercises in Ecumenism,* edited by Christo Lombaard, 307-325. Pietermaritzburg: Cluster Publications, 1999.

Naicker, L. 'The Role of Eugenics and Religion in the Construction of Race in South Africa.' *Studia Historiae Ecclesiasticae* Vol. 38, no. 2, (2012): 209-220.

Neil, S. *A History of Christian Missions.* Harmondsworth: Penguin, 1986.

Nel, R. 'Mixing African colours into the Paradigm Shifts in Theology and Mission.' *Missionala* 39, no. 1/2 (2011): 114-129.

Oden, T. *Africa Shaped the Christian Mind: Rediscovering the African Seedbed of Western Christianity.* Downers Grove: Intervarsity Press, 2008.

Parrat, J. *A Reader in African Christian Theology.* Great Britain: Cambridge University Press, 1987.

[25] Alan Boesak *Black and Reformed: Apartheid, Liberation and the Calvinist Tradition* (Johannesburg: Skotaville Publishers, 1984), 154.

Shubane, K. 'The Black Consciousness Movement: The Soweto Uprising of 1976.' In *New History of South Africa,* edited by Hermann Giliomee and Bernard Mbenga , 346-395. Cape Town: NB Publishers, 2007.

Sutton, G. 'The Layering of History: A Brief Look at Eugenics, the Holocaust and Scientific Racism in South Africa.' *Yesterday and Today,* no. 1, 2007, 22-30

Theological Education by Extension College. *Exploring our African Christian World: Workbook A,* Turffontein, 2011.

Tienou, T. 'Authentic African Christianity.' In *A Reader in African Christian Theology,* edited by John Parrat, 91-98. Cambridge: Cambridge University Press, 1987.

Tutu, D. 'Black Theology and African Theology – Soulmates or Antagonists?' In *A Reader in African Theology,* edited by John Parrat, 36-44. Cambridge: Cambridge University Press, 1997.

Villa-Vicencio, C. *Between Christ and Caesar: Classic Contemporary Texts on Church and State.* Cape Town: David Philip, 1986.

World Council of Churches. 'Programme to Combat Racism – Struggle for Freedom – South Africa.' https://www.aluka.org/struggle/collection/WCC (accessed 1 April, 2015).

(129) DECENT WORK AND AFRICAN CHRISTIANITY

Rowanne Sarojini Marie

Introduction

Work is central to the well-being of people. In addition to providing needed income within households, work can also pave the way for broader social and economic advancement, thus strengthening individuals, their families and communities. Both individual and social identity is conditioned by work, which is indispensable for the survival and security of people.

The subject of 'decent work' and African Christianity is a broad one which cannot be adequately addressed here. However, the purpose of this chapter is to highlight some of the key areas in which this important topic is being considered. It is essential to commence with an understanding of the notion of 'work'.

Notions of 'Work'

Generally, society tends to refer to 'work' as 'paid employment'.[1] Because of technological innovations, the character and nature of work is going through a deep transformation such that new types of work are rising to prominence.[2] In addition to technological advancements which change the character of work, the aspect of culture with different people considering different activities to be work, creates confusion about what work really means. In many societies, when we say that someone is 'working' we are not merely indicating that a person is involved in a particular kind of activity, but we are also implicitly ascribing value to that person. 'To work is good; not to work is bad. A person who does not work is less valued in a society.'[3] Thus, for example, we hear deprecatory remarks about people who are 'only housewives' or 'only domestic helpers'. Since paid work gives access to monetary power, and hence to independence, it becomes a door to active participation in the home and society at large.

Work can be defined as 'the carrying out of tasks which enable people to make a living within the environment in which they find themselves,'[4] or a set of activities that are associated with performing one's paid occupation, thus providing money for the purchase of goods and services.[5] Miroslav Volf, who writes from a theological perspective, describes work as honest, purposeful and methodologically specified social activity whose primary goal is the creation of products or a state of affairs that can satisfy the needs of working individuals or the co-creators.[6] Such human activity, which includes both paid and unpaid activity, must ensure compatibility with human dignity, which remains at the core of work activities.[7] Added to these various notions, Caroline Moser[8] makes us aware that work is much more than paid roles, enabling us to understand the multi-faceted nature of work. She proposes that work can be divided into three spheres:

---

[1] Rowanne Sarojini Marie, 'Towards a Gendered Theology of Work', *Journal of Theology for Southern Africa,* no. 149 (2014): 126-141.
[2] Marie, 'Towards a Gendered Theology of Work', 127.
[3] Miroslav Volf, *Work in the Spirit: Toward a Theology of Work* (Oregon: Wipf and Stock Publishers, 2001), 4.
[4] Tony J. Watson, *Sociology, Work and Industry* (London: Routledge, 1980), 83.
[5] Carol J Auster, *The Sociology of Work, Concepts and Cases* (California: Thousand Oaks, 1996), 1.
[6] Volf, '*Work in the Sprit',* 11.
[7] Darryl Cosden, *A Theology of Work: Work in the New Creation* (Eugene: Wipf and Stock Publishers, 2006), 179.
[8] Caroline Moser, *Gender Planning and Development: Theory, Practice and Training* (London: Routledge, 1993).

productive, reproductive and community. Productive work is defined by Moser as the production of goods or services rendered for income or subsistence, while reproductive work includes tasks such as cooking, cleaning, washing, looking after children; and finally community work is voluntary or unpaid work.[9] Having broadly described the notion of work, how then do we understand the notion of 'decent work'?

Understanding 'Decent Work'

The notion of 'decent work' 'is based on the understanding that work is not only a source of income but more importantly a source of personal dignity, family stability, peace in community, and economic growth that expands opportunities for productive jobs and employment.'[10] The concept was introduced and promoted by the International Labour Organization (ILO)[11] in 1999, who summed up as its priorities the need to promote opportunities for women and men to obtain decent and productive work, in conditions of freedom, equity, security and human dignity.

The three 'rights' as pointed out by the ILO are the right to work, rights in work and the right to adequate social protection. In this regard, the ILO advocates that decent work is not confined to wage employment, but extends to self-employment, home-working and other income-generating activities.[12] The strategic objectives of the ILO are listed as full employment, workers' rights, social protection and social dialogue.[13]

The ILO emphasised that within its overall 'decent work' strategy, 'social protection' is a critical component. The absence of social protection results in neither work nor lives being decent. 'Social protection seeks to protect workers at their workplaces in the formal and informal economy against unfair, hazardous and unhealthy working conditions.'[14] While social protection is a basic human need, there are some groups that are particularly vulnerable and disadvantaged in Africa, for example, migrant workers and their families,[15] people living with or affected by HIV and AIDS,[16] women and children[17] as well as people in the informal economy. It is these groups of people who experience weakened productive potential due to the absence or inadequacy of social protection.

An important underlying value within the decent work paradigm is that labour is not a commodity and should therefore not be considered as one more product on the market upon which a cost worth is placed. The fact that work involves human life makes one consider the moral and ethical values of work since it engages much more than material components.[18] The notion of 'decency' does not have a uniform standard

---

[9] Moser, '*Gender Planning and Development'*, 31.
[10] Draham P. Ghai (ed.), *Decent Work: Objectives and Strategies* (Geneva: International Labour Office, 2006).
[11] International Labour Organisation, 'Decent Work Agenda 1999', www.ilo.org/global/about-the-ilo/decent-work-agenda/lang--en/index.htm (accessed 10 November, 2014).
[12] ILO, *'Decent Work Agenda 1999'*, 1.
[13] Juan Somavia. 'The ILO Decent Work Agenda as the Aspiration of People', in *Philosophical and Spiritual Perspectives on Decent Work,* ed. Dominique Peccoud (Geneva: International Labour Office, 2004), 5.
[14] International Labour Organisation, 'Decent Work Agenda 2007-2015', www.ilo.org/public/english/standards/relm/rgmeet/11afrm/dg-thematic.pdf (accessed 25 February, 2015), 8.
[15] See Roswitha Golder, 'Towards a Theology of Work from the Perspective of Women Migrants', in *Dignity of Work: Theological and Interdisciplinary Perspectives,* ed. Kenneth Mtata (Minneapolis: Lutheran University Press, 2011), 79-88.
[16] See Veikko Munyika, 'The Impact of the HIV and AIDS Epidemic on the World of Work and Development', in *Dignity of Work: Theological and Interdisciplinary Perspectives,* ed. Kenneth Mtata (Minneapolis: Lutheran University Press, 2011), 99-108.
[17] Decent Work for Africa's Development, Tenth African Regional Meeting, Addis Ababa, 2003 Report of the Director-General, International Labour Office, www.ilo.org/public/english/standards/relm/rgmeet/index.htm (accessed 1 March, 2015).
[18] Dominique Peccoud (ed.), *Philosophical and Spiritual Perspectives on Decent Work* (Geneva: ILO Publications,

and evolves in different societies embracing flexibility. However, at its basic core is the 'value' that is attached to human life. Due to the diverse nature of 'decency' it becomes essential to search for a 'global ethic' which provides the hermeneutical keys to move from one value discourse to another, thus locating those core universal values that seem to be compatible with one another.[19] Therefore, *decent* work seeks to challenge the dual nature of work, where in some parts of the world workers attain high levels of material welfare, while in other places, gross violations of human rights such as child labour, slavery and forced labour are still being practised.

African Notions of 'Decent Work'

The African continent is said to have potential for growth and development. It is also a continent scourged by poverty and inequality, since the gap between the poorest and the richest in Africa is also one of the widest in the world.[20] The unemployment and underemployment challenge on the continent continues to contribute to the vicious cycle of poverty which is perpetuated by a deficit of 'decent work'.

As in most cultures and traditions around the world, work in the Africa context is held in high esteem, carrying significance economically, socially and spiritually. A work ethic is 'the attitude of a group or society towards work', and embedded in African thinking is the notion that work is good and remains higher on the society scale of values than play or leisure.[21]

In order to analyse the work ethic in traditional African society, one must do so in the context of religion and traditional values. An African is a very religious person. In fact, the African human is said to be 'incurably religious', so it becomes difficult to divorce any aspect of life, including work, from religion.[22] Whatever values, virtues or ethics are ultimately discovered, they are based on the religious inclination of an African.

Kenneth Mtata argues that there is a significant connection between our work and faith practices, as he develops an 'African theology of work'.[23] He states, 'Work is one significant area of contact between faith and the world and as such must form an important topic not only for faith communities.'[24] In traditional African societies, work was carried out by groups of people who worked together, usually with the household constituting a production unit, resulting in much work being done in a shorter space of time.[25] In the African context, there is a deep connection between the world of work and the spiritual world. 'Whether the hunter had good dogs, the farmer had many cattle to plough the field, or one had a great voice to sing, in order to be successful, in one's work, Africans believed in the final capital that came from the supernatural, be they Ancestors or God or other benevolent powers.'[26] The understanding that work is the co-operation between human beings and the spiritual world is deeply entrenched in traditional African

---

2004), 5.

[19] Konrad Raiser, 'Conflicting Values: Dialogue of Cultures on Decent Work', in *Philosophical and Spiritual Perspectives on Decent Work* (Geneva: ILO Publications, 2004), 17.

[20] Decent Work for Africa's Development, Tenth African Regional Meeting, Addis Ababa, 2003. Report of the Director-General, International Labour Office, www.ilo.org/public/english/standards/relm/rgmeet/index.htm (accessed 1 March, 2015).

[21] Ezekial Ajibade, 'African Traditional Work Ethics and the Challenges of Decent Work Agenda', www.academia.edu/6139384 (accessed 20 September, 2015).

[22] See Ajibade, 'African Traditional Work Ethics and the Challenges of Decent Work Agenda', www.academia.edu/6139384 (accessed 20 September, 2015).

[23] Kenneth Mtata, 'An African Theology of Work: A Lutheran Perspective', in *Dignity of Work: Theological and Interdisciplinary Perspectives,* ed. Kenneth Mtata (Minneapolis: Lutheran University Press, 2011), 35-49.

[24] Mtata, 'An African Theology of Work', 7.

[25] Mtata, 'An African Theology of Work', 37.

[26] Mtata, 'An African Theology of Work', 38.

thinking. Hence the concept of decent work in the African context cannot be separated from religious dialogue. Such dialogue, together with deeper reflection on the concept of decent work, becomes a key building-block for development strategies aimed at combating poverty, social exclusion, unemployment and underemployment that plagues Africa. The ILO, as well as other organizations, are convinced that decent work remains at the core of addressing such needs, thereby having potential to lead to a socially inclusive and economically dynamic African development framework.[27]

Christian Convergence and 'Decent Work'

The immense need for a convergence between the decent work agenda and the Christian tradition becomes more evident and critical.[28] Such convergence has potential to open up opportunities for dialogue between politicians, practitioners and theologians. Examining the pillars upon which the decent work agenda is built, Martinot-Lagarde states that each of these pillars touches on theological and anthropological questions, which are centred on the notion of human dignity.[29] The fundamental rights are expressed as: no forced labour, the eradication of the worst forms of child labour, freedom of association, collective bargaining and no discrimination, all of which are enabling and provide the basis for social improvement.[30] He links this understanding with the story of Exodus which speaks of the value of freedom, where the freeing of the Israelites from the domination of the Egyptians led to a process of liberation.[31] He comments that freedom of association is central to the way we understand the faith and that forcing children to work in inhumane conditions not only deprives them of their personal future, but of that of the whole of society.[32] The Christian tradition must respond to the notion of 'decent work' understanding the necessity for convergence.[33] An example of such convergence is that of the World Council of Churches partnering with the International Labour Organization (ILO) to facilitate dialogue between the Christian and Muslim leaders in Egypt to address issues of social justice, specifically as this relates to honest work and youth employment.[34] One of the key features of such a partnership was to raise the awareness of community leaders to give a better understanding of the work agenda, resulting in all participating stakeholders implementing processes that led to the specific creation of employment for young people.

Similarly, in South Africa, the ILO partnered with the International Poverty Centre for Inclusive Growth (IPC-IG) under the auspices of the United Nations Development Programme (UNDP) to find synergies between social security interventions and public employment programmes as an important contribution towards achieving the Decent Work Agenda (DWA).[35] The Eleventh Africa meeting report of the ILO declares that decent work is not a motto, it is a movement which strives towards the dignity of decent work

---

[27] *Decent Work for Africa's Development*, Tenth African Regional Meeting, Addis Ababa, 2003 Report of the Director-General, International Labour Office, www.ilo.org/public/english/standards/relm/rgmeet/index.htm (accessed 1 March, 2015).

[28] Pierre Martinot-Lagarde, 'Theology of Work, Opportunities and Challenges', in *Dignity of Work: Theological and Interdisciplinary Perspectives,* ed. Kenneth Mtata (Minneapolis: Lutheran University Press 2011), 71-78.

[29] Martinot-Lagarde, 'Theology of Work, Opportunities and Challenges', 72.

[30] Martinot-Lagarde, 'Theology of Work, Opportunities and Challenges', 73.

[31] Martinot-Lagarde, 'Theology of Work, Opportunities and Challenges', 73.

[32] Martinot-Lagarde, 'Theology of Work, Opportunities and Challenges', 74

[33] Martinot-Lagarde, 'Theology of Work, Opportunities and Challenges', 74.

[34] The project agreement title is: 'Advancing peace through social justice' and is spearheaded by the WCC in conjunction with the ILO. Such convergence led to the establishment of an interfaith platform for social justice issues in Egypt.

[35] Rudi Dicks, et al, 'Achieving a Decent Work Agenda in South Africa: A New Growth Strategy', National Labour and Economic Development Institute (NALEDI), 2011, www.global-labour-university.org/fileadmin/GLU_conference_2011/papers/Rudi_Dicks.pdf (accessed 1 September, 2015).

for a decent life.[36] It is clear that such an agenda becomes possible only by strengthened co-operation and mutual reinforcement by national governments and other key role-players such as the 'World Bank, the IMF and the European Union, particularly in terms of the follow-up to the Africa Union Extraordinary Summit on Employment and Poverty Alleviation in Africa'.[37] Such partnerships become further reinforced by aligning with the religious sector for greater benefit (as illustrated by the example in Egypt).

Interreligious dialogue becomes an effective and important tool for building peace and justice, and it is to this end that organizations such as the ILO have been facilitating the spirit of interreligious dialogue as part of continuing exploration of the meaning of work and social justice.[38] Together with civil society partners and other faith-based organizations, it is imperative for Christianity to identify common values and goals. Through these discussions, they are positioned to form a deeper understanding of work and social justice, thus intensifying the exploration for universal decent work values.

Conclusion

'Decent work' is a human right and is an issue of social justice which must be prioritized within the discourse of African Christianity. In addition to the need to create jobs with extended social protection, is the need to promote social dialogue. To combat the evil of 'indecent work', it is imperative that African Christianity partners with organizations which prioritise the decent work agenda. The important ingredients in this discourse are 'social dialogue' and convergence that is driven by religion, and Christianity in particular. In addition, and of importance, is an ongoing quest for an 'African ethic' of values which seeks a common framework for promoting and understanding decent work.

Bibliography

Auster, Carol J. *The Sociology of Work, Concepts and Cases.* California: Thousand Oaks, 1996.

Cosden, Darryl. *A Theology of Work: Work in the New Creation.* Eugene: Wipf and Stock Publishers, 2006.

Dicks, Rudi, et al. 'Achieving a Decent Work Agenda in South Africa: A New Growth Strategy. National Labour and Economic Development Institute (NALEDI), 2011', www.globallabouruniversity.org/fileadmin/GLU_conference_2011/papers/Rudi_Dicks.pdf (accessed 1 September, 2015).

Ezekiel Ajibade, 'African Traditional Work Ethics and the Challenges of Decent Work Agenda.' www.academia.edu/6139384 (accessed 10 April, 2015).

Ghai, Draham P. *Decent Work: Objectives and Strategies*. Geneva: International Labour Office, 2006.

Golder, Roswitha. 'Towards a Theology of Work from the Perspective of Women Migrants.' In *Dignity of Work: Theological and Interdisciplinary Perspectives,* edited by Kenneth Mtata, 79-88. Minneapolis: Lutheran University Press, 2011.

ICT Church and Labour Project Research Group. 'Workers, the Church and Alienations of Religious Life', In *The Three-fold Cord: Theology, Work and Labour, edited by* Gerald West and James Cochrane, 253-278. Pietermaritzburg: Cluster Publications, 1991.

International Labour Office, 'Decent Work for Africa's Development, Tenth African Regional Meeting, Addis Ababa, 2003, Report of the Director-General.' www.ilo.org/public/english/standards/relm/rgmeet/index.htm (accessed 1 March, 2015).

International Labour Organization, 'Decent Work Agenda 1999.' www.ilo.org/global/about-the-ilo/decent-work-agenda/lang--en/index.htm (accessed 10 November, 2014).

[36] The Decent Work Agenda in Africa: Eleventh African Regional Meeting, Addis Ababa, 2007, ILO: Geneva.

[37] See The Decent Work Agenda in Africa: Eleventh African Regional Meeting, Addis Ababa, ILO: Geneva, 2007:27

[38] Juan Somavia, 2012. *Convergences, Decent work and social justice in religious traditions*, ILO: Geneva, 2012,10.

International Labour Organization, 'Decent Work Agenda 2007-2015.' www.ilo.org/public/english/standards/relm/rgmeet/11afrm/dgthematic.pd (accessed 25 February, 2015).

Marie, Rowanne Sarojini. 'Towards a Gendered Theology of Work.' *Journal of Theology for Southern Africa,* No. 149 (2014): 126-141.

Moser, Caroline. *Gender Planning and Development: Theory, Practice and Training.* London: Routledge, 1993.

Mtata, Kenneth (ed.), *Dignity of Work: Theological and Interdisciplinary Perspectives.* Minneapolis: Lutheran University Press, 2011.

______. 'An African Theology of Work: A Lutheran Perspective.' In *Dignity of Work: Theological and Interdisciplinary Perspectives,* edited by Kenneth Mtata, 35-49. Minneapolis: Lutheran University Press, 2011.

Martinot-Lagarde, Pierre. 'Theology of Work, Opportunities and Challenges.' In *Dignity of Work: Theological and Interdisciplinary Perspectives,* edited by Kenneth Mtata, 71-78. Minneapolis: Lutheran University Press, 2011.

Munyika, Veikko. 'The Impact of the HIV and AIDS Epidemic on the World of Work and Development.' In *Dignity of Work: Theological and Interdisciplinary Perspectives,* edited by Kenneth Mtata, 99-108. Minneapolis: Lutheran University Press, 2011.

Peccoud, Dominique (ed.) *Philosophical and Spiritual Perspectives on Decent Work.* Geneva: ILO Publications, 2004.

Somavia, Juan. 'The ILO Decent Work Agenda as the Aspiration of People.' In *Philosophical and Spiritual Perspectives on Decent Work,* edited by Dominique Peccoud, 3-11. Geneva: International Labour Office, 2004.

Volf, Miroslav. *Work in the Spirit: Toward a Theology of Work.* Oregon: Wipf and Stock Publishers, 2001.

Watson, T J. *Sociology, Work and Industry.* London: Routledge, 1980.

(130) MIGRATION IN AFRICAN CHRISTIANITY

Rose Nyirimana Mukansengimana

Introduction

African people are renowned for their strong religious beliefs that contributed to making the continent a fertile ground for the spread of Christianity. On the other hand, it has been argued that Christianity has made African culture even more openly religious.[1] Consequently, as Christianity seemed to lose ground in the land where it originated, the church in Africa has not ceased to grow – to the extent that many believe that the centre of Christianity has now moved to Africa. It is, however, observed that this continent has often experienced challenging situations that threatened the welfare of the people, forcing them to migrate tovarious parts of the world. It is important to note that most immigrants are Christians on the move, carrying their religious identity to new contexts. This chapter looks into the actual or potential impact of African migration on the spread of Christianity. It contends that the waves of migration affecting African people and the resulting movement of African Christians constitute an opportunity for Christianity to expand. After a brief description of the concept of migration, the chapter explores God's attitude toward the migration of his chosen people. This will shed light on what may be God's design for the contemporary African Christian migrants.

The Concept of Migration: A Theological Dimension

Migration refers to different types of human movements. Carrol differentiates between migrants who move to other places of their own volition, usually seeking lengthy or permanent residence, and refugees who flee their country out of fear of persecution or those who run away from armed conflicts.[2] Migration is a universal and a timeless phenomenon. As Aboagye-Mensah asserts, 'Migration as a movement of people from one place to another within and across geographical, ethnic, cultural and religious boundaries, is an integral part of human existence.'[3] Basing his view on the Bible, Aboagye-Mensah argues that 'migration is as old as human beings'.[4] Indeed, in biblical traditions, migration is often willed by God or used by him to fulfil divine purposes.

God and Migration in Scripture

While God's ability to be with the chosen people wherever they go may be understood to be a result of God's omnipresence, sometime scripture describes God as a migrating God. In the exodus story, God is reported to be on the move with the people. As they leave Egypt, God leads the way in a pillar of cloud by day and escorts them in a pillar of fire by night (Ex. 14:21-22). Later in the wilderness, the same cloud covering the tabernacle moved with the people, leading the way and instructing them when to set out and

---

[1] Harvey C. Kwiyani, *Sent Forth: African Missionary Work in the West.* (Maryknoll: Orbis Books, 2014), 23.

[2] Daniel M. Carroll, *Christians at the Border: Immigration, the Church, and the Bible*. (Grand Rapids: Baker Academic, 2008), 21.

[3] Robert K. Aboagye-Mensah 'Perspective and Biblical Migration and Mission', in *Babel is everywhere! Migrant Reading from Africa, Europe and Asia*. eds, Asamoah-Gyadu, Adrea Frochtling and Andrea Kunz-Luncke. (Frankfurt am Main: Peter Lang. 2013), 15.

[4] Aboagye-Mensah, 'Perspective and Biblical Migration and Mission', 15

when to settle (Num. 9:15-24). Moreover, God, who was understood to be seated on the mercy seat covering the Ark, would accompany the people as the Levites carried the Ark. When God told Moses, 'My presence will go with you…' (Ex. 33:14) it was as if God meant this literally.

In the New Testament, God is described as a migrant in the person of Jesus, the Word that was with God and came to dwell in a new environment (John 1:1-14). Not only did Jesus live among us as a migrant, he also experienced migration with his family to Egypt. This migration is understood to have been planned by God who used it to accomplish his divine will (Matt. 2:14-15).

Migration Willed by God

The God of the Old Testament wants people to migrate. In the creation story, for instance, God wants mankind to fill the earth (Genesis 1: 28). Obviously, migration was a prerequisite for accomplishing this plan. In the story of the tower of Babel, humanity attempted to resist the plan and to stay in one place. God intervened and forced them to migrate (Genesis 11:8). The promises given to Abraham are subject to his willingness to migrate (Genesis 12:1-2). It was as migrants that Abraham and his descendants could fulfil God's plan to bless the nations. God may not be the root cause of all situations that forced the people to leave their locations and migrate to other places, but once these situations happened, God used the resulting migration to accomplish his divine will.

Migration Used by God

The Joseph narrative makes it plain that Joseph was made a migrant as a result of the evil plans of his brothers. Yet Joseph's migration was used by God to bless the Egyptians and to preserve the house of Jacob. Jacob's family arrived in Egypt as economic migrants. God used their presence to reveal his identity, attributes and character to both the Israelites and to all the nations who heard all that he did in Egypt. Later, forced migration of Israel under the Assyrians and the Babylonians seems to have served the same purpose of God's self-revelation to the Israelites and to their host nations.

In the New Testament, Jesus insists twice that the work he left to his followers will be accomplished only through migration. The so-called Great Commission of Matthew 28:18 spells out what Jesus expects his followers who remain on earth to do, making disciples by baptizing and teaching. Going to all the nations was the prerequisite for doing this. The need to migrate is re-emphasized in Acts 1:8 where Jesus repeats that his followers are to be witnesses from Jerusalem to the ends of the world.

However, succumbing to fear, they decided to stay in the same place. God, who wanted them to go out, overcame this fear at Pentecost. They were given the boldness to speak fearlessly, and the ability to speak the languages of all the surrounding nations. They were equipped for migration. It appears, however, that the disciples were not ready to leave the comfort of their place. They were ready to be witnesses but within Jerusalem (Acts 2:42-47). It was when their comfort was broken by persecution that they were forced to migrate, preaching the word all over Judea, Samaria and all over Asia (Acts 8:1-10).

This abrupt persecution that forced the believers into the life of migrants became an opportunity to fulfil the Great Commission. Carroll argues that 'migration is not only about the reasons and mechanics of the move to another place; it is about life in that new setting'.[5] The migration of Christians is therefore a life of proclamation in a new setting. Christian settlement in new places results not only in personal uplifting but also in the foundation of churches in new places. The persecution that caused migration did not originate from God but he used migration as an instrument to promote the growth of Christianity. There is no reason God could not do the same with today's many situations of migration.

[5] Carroll, *Christians at the Border*, 71.

The Impact of African Waves of Migrations on Christianity across the Globe

In recent centuries, Africa has been experiencing huge trajectories of mass emigration, involving a significant number of Christians. The major causes for such movements have their roots in 'failed leadership, patrimonial political culture, civil wars and drought'.[6] While the visible reasons are rooted in existential concerns having not much to do with religion, the migration phenomenon has caused African Christianity to move beyond the continent and to become global in nature, with the establishment of churches across America, Europe and Asia. There seems to be a theological dimension in the phenomenon of migration.

Those who find a 'theological dimension' in the waves of migration see in migration God's given opportunity for taking the gospel to the far ends of the globe. Carroll argues that all of us have a certain way of looking at ourselves and the world in which we live; meaning that each individual has a set of lenses through which we interpret the reality that surrounds us and our identity and role in that context.[7] It is not strange therefore that some see behind the African migration a commission to take the gospel into distant places.

African Migration and Church Growth in the Diaspora

Kwiyani argues that African immigrant congregations which started appearing in the West in the 1970s have in the past twenty years multiplied greatly all across the Americas, Europe and Asia.[8] He asserts that by the time he produced his work in 2014, the two largest churches in Europe were African-led, founded by Nigerians. These are the Blessed Embassy of the Kingdom of God located in Kiev, Ukraine, with 30,000 members, and the Kingsway International Christian Centre located in London with 12,000 members, almost entirely African. There are other African immigrant congregations in Germany, Canada, the USA, etc.[9]

Haugen also observes a sizable number of African churches founded by immigrants in the Chinese city of Gwangzhou. Despite the state-sanctioned institutions imposed on foreign religions, the 'underground Pentecostal churches led by Africans attract a large number of African migrants…'[10] Hence, in recent years, Christianity in Africa has been a mobile faith sending out missionaries. In Kwiyani's judgement, 'It is as if God has preserved God's Church in Africa while it was dying out in Europe and North America, and now, God is calling the church out of Africa to reinvigorate world Christianity'.[11]

Major Characteristics and Challenges of African Migrant Churches

African migrant congregations in the diaspora are described as vibrant communities that respond to immigrant conditions by providing a conducive spiritual environment for experiencing God in the midst of urban chaos, poverty, racism, confusion, anomie and alienation. It is also argued that in cities across

---

[6] Ogbu M. Kalu, 'The Andrew Syndrome: Models in understanding Nigerian Diaspora', in *African Immigrants Religions in America,* eds. Jacob K Olupona, and Regina Gemignani (New York: University Press, 2007), 61-85.
[7] Carroll, *Christians at the Border,* 63-64.
[8] Kwiyani, *Sent Forth,* 18.
[9] Kwiyani, *Sent Forth,* 18.
[10] Heidi O. Haugen 'Take over Asia for God: The Public Face of African Pentecostal Churches in China', In *The Public Face of African New Religious Movements in Diaspora: Imagining the Religious Other*, ed. Afe Adogame (Farnham, England: Ashgate Publishing Limited 2014), 105.
[11] Kwiyani, '*Sent Forth', 17.*

America, faith-based community organizations meet the needs of immigrant communities by offering social services that state and local government often fail to provide.[12]

However, immigrant life is not prestigious. Most of the time, immigrants are looked down upon and discriminated against in their host communities. It is in reaction to such challenges that many African immigrants seek to maintain their cultural identities through developing communal links, religious institutions and social support structures. Immigrant churches then seem to focus more on helping their members to cope with the new environment, rather than doing a purely missionary ministry. They often care for the emotional, psychological, spiritual and material needs of their members, and encourage them to preserve their Christian identity in new cultures. This is what Akinade alludes to, stating: 'I argue for a death-refusal stance of African spiritual sensibilities even when they are being open to an intrusive, and corrosive, wider world. And this resilience has enabled African churches to flourish in the new cultural environments'.[13] This focus on the needs of migrants often overshadows the drive to reach out to the 'nations'. This may explain the low representation of the local members in many African immigrant churches.

But the focus on the socio-economic and cultural situation of immigrants is not the only factor affecting immigrant churches. Sometimes they are not warmly welcomed in the host community, as is the case in China[14] and in Brazil.[15] In Brazil, the African migrant church, particularly the recent spread of a so-called 'Yoruba tradition', is perceived as competing with other Afro-Brazilian religious communities.[16] 'The consequence of this competition is a growing demarcation between *terreiros* (religious communities) and less willingness to co-operate.'[17]

Moreover, there is a challenge arising from generational conflict. In this case, Mossiere observes that migrant youth usually possess the ability to adapt better to new environments. Youth embrace more easily the norms found in new places, which they often find to be relatively modern compared to those of their home context advocated by their parents. He goes on to argue that more often than not, inter-generational relationships are driven by the language issue, such as when older members want to maintain their home tongue in worship services, while youth seek to adopt the language of their social environment. The problem may even lead the church to split or simply disappear.[18]

Conclusion

This chapter has argued that the migration of God's people, regardless of its causes, has often been an important tool that God has used to reach out to the nations. The chapter proposes that the frequent waves of migration in Africa that involve a significant number of African Christians could be viewed as an opportunity given to African Christianity to impact the world. In order to exploit fully this opportunity,

---

[12] Jacob K. Olupona, and Regina Gemignani, eds. *African Immigrants Religions in America*. (New York: University Press, 2007), 16.

[13] Akintunde Akinade, 'Non-Western Christianity in the Western World: African Immigrant Churches in the Diaspora', in *African Immigrants Religions in America,* eds. Jacob K. Olupona, and Regina Gemignani (New York: University Press, 2007), 96.

[14] Haugen, 'Take Over Asia for God', 107

[15] Bettina E. Schmidt, 'The Discourse about 'Africa' in Religious Ritual goes global', in *The Public face of African new religious movements in Diaspora: Imagining the religious other*, ed. Afe Adogame (Farnham, England: Ashgate Publishing Limited 2014), 32.

[16] Bettina, 'The Discourse about 'Africa' in Religious Ritual goes global', 29-44.

[17] Bettina, 'The Discourse about 'Africa' in Religious Ritual goes Global', 29-44.

[18] Geraldine Mossiere, 'Juggling Multiple Identities to Overcome Minority Status: Young Congolese Pentecostals in Montreal (Quebec)', in *The Public face of African New Religious Movements in Diaspora: Imagining the Religious Other*, ed. Afe Adogame (Farnham, England: Ashgate Publishing Limited 2014), 147-162.

however, there is a need for the African immigrant churches to revisit their routine of catering mainly for immigrant members and to adopt deliberate strategies for reaching out to the host communities. On the other hand, the impact of the migrant churches depends much on the willingness of the churches in the host communities to embrace the migrant churches for better collaboration.

This chapter has portrayed Africa as a new cradle of Christianity. Hence, it urges African scholars and interested Christian bodies like the WCC and AACC[19] to recognise the importance of this topic within the African continent, because 'No serious study of Africa can ignore Christianity and the role it has come to play in Africa'.[20] The chapter advises African scholars to explore not only how African Christianity has transformed other continents but also how the 'explosion' of African Christianity is transforming the African continent as well. Kwiyani's grandfather's wisdom can be our inspiration: 'Until the lions can tell their stories, the story of the hunt will always glorify the hunter.'[21] In other words, the story told from a secondhand source will always be biased and incomplete.

Bibliography

Aboagye-Mensah, K. Robert. 'Perspective and Biblical Migration and Mission', in *Babel is everywhere! Migrant Reading from Africa, Europe and Asia*, edited by J. Kwabena Asamoah-Gyadu, Adrea Frochtling and Andrea Kunz-Luncke, 15-24. Frankfurt am Main: Peter Lang. 2013.

Akinade, Akintunde. 'Non-Western Christianity in the Western World: African Immigrant Churches in the Diaspora.' In *African Immigrants Religions in America,* edited by Jacob K. Olupona, and Regina Gemignani, 89-101. New York: University Press, 2007.

Carroll, Daniel M. *Christians at the Border: Immigration, the Church, and the Bible*. Grand Rapids: Baker Academic, 2008.

Haugen, O. Heidi. 'Take over Asia for God: The public face of African Pentecostal Churches in China.' In *The Public face of African new religious movements in Diaspora: Imagining the religious other,* edited by Afe Adogame, 105- 123. Farnham, England: Ashgate Publishing Limited, 2014.

Kalu, M. Ogbu. 'The Andrew Syndrome: Models in understanding Nigerian Diaspora.' In *African Immigrants Religions in America*, edited by Jacob K. Olupona, and Regina Gemignani, 61-85. New York: New York University Press, 2007.

Manchala, Deenabandhu. 'Migration: An opportunity for Broader and Deeper Ecumenism.' In *Theology of Migration in Abrahamic Religions,* edited by Elaine Padilla and Peter Phan, 155-171. Macmillan: Palgrave Macmillan 2014.

Mossiere, Geraldine 'Juggling multiple identities to overcome minority status: Young Congolese Pentecostals in Montreal (Quebec).' In *The Public face of African New Religious Movements in Diaspora: Imagining the Religious other*, edited by Afe Adogame, 147-162. Farnham, England: Ashgate Publishing Limited 2014.

Olupona, Jacob K. and Gemignani, Regina (eds.), 'Introduction.' In *African Immigrants Religions in America*, 1-24. New York: University Press, 2007.

Schmidt, Bettina E. 'The discourse about "Africa".' In religious ritual goes global,' in *The Public face of African New Religious Movements in Diaspora: Imagining the Religious other*, edited by Afe Adogame, 29-44. Farnham, England: Ashgate Publishing Limited, 2014.

[19] The details on the role played by some Christian bodies such the WCC, the CICARWS, the CCM and many others in response to migration from at least 1956 to 2005 are provided by Manchala in his article : Migration: 'An Opportunity for Broader and Deeper Ecumenism''.

[20] Akinade, 'Non-Western Christianity', 9

[21] Kwiyani, *Sent Forth, 30.*

(131) MARTYRS AND WITNESSES OF FAITH IN AFRICAN CHRISTIANITY

Ssekabira Vincent and Brigitte Rabarijaona

Introduction

Martyrdom is central to the Christian faith. Indeed, Christian history begins with the life and death of Jesus Christ. Its history continues with the formation of the early Christian church, Emperor Constantine's Holy Roman Empire and the great schism into Eastern and Western Christianity. Its first martyr is Jesus himself. The history of Christianity focuses on the life, death and resurrection of one person, Jesus Christ, the Son of God.

Jesus Christ stated publicly and without fear that he spoke with the authority of God. This claim angered the religious authorities in Palestine and they handed Jesus over to the Roman authority as a revolutionary. He was tried, condemned, and put to death through crucifixion.[1]

'Martyr' is a transliteration of the Greek and is a legal term meaning 'witness'. It refers to a person who has firsthand knowledge of a fact or an event and was often used to refer to a followere of Christ. According to Sauer and Howell, the terms martyr and martyrdom are enshrined within the definition of a Christian who voluntarily suffers death as the penalty for witnessing to and refusing to renounce his faith, or a tenet, principle or practice belonging to it.[2] Biblical law requires the testimony of at least two witnesses to establish the guilt of an offence.[3] In the case of a charge of murder, and presumably any capital offence, it was a duty of the witnesses to cast the first stone.[4] The story of Susanna may express a polemic against hasty judgments and hence care in the examination of witnesses.[5] False witness is prohibited.[6] Sometimes God is brought in as a witness and judge.[7] The biblical legal aspect is well-documented by articles of various scholars like M. Greenberg,[8] John L. McKenzie[9] and F.W. Danker.[10]

'Martyr' is used in relation to Christ himself in the New Testament. The mission of Paul after his conversion had a lasting impact in spreading the message of the work of Jesus, his death and resurrection. Gentiles and Jews had equal access to the Christian faith. However, the church remained small and was persecuted, particularly under tyrannical Roman Emperors, under whom being a Christian was an illegal act. Christians became martyrs. The term moved from just being a legal term, a 'witness' in court, to being

---

[1] On Jewish authority, he was condemned for 'blasphemy'; before the Roman authorities they presented it as political and him as 'revolutionary.'

[2] Christof Sauer and Richard Howell (eds), *Suffering, Persecution and Martyrdom: Theological Reflections Vol 2* (Kempton Park: AcadSA Publishing, 2010), 42.

[3] See Deut 19:15; Num 35:30. The rule is illustrated in the trial of Naboth (1 Kgs 21:10, 13). Nothing is said in the Bible regarding qualification of witness.

[4] Deut 17:6-7.

[5] Charles George Herbermann, et al. eds., *The Catholic Encyclopedia: An International Work of Reference on the Constitution, Doctrine, and History of the Catholic Church* (New York: The Encyclopedia press, inc, 1908).

[6] Ex 23:1.

[7] Mal 3:5.

[8] George Arthur Buttrich (ed.), 'Witness', *The Interpreter's Dictionary of the Bible*, Vol. IV (R-Z) (Nashville: Abingdon Press, 1962), 864.

[9] See John L. McKenzie, 'Witness', *Dictionary of the Bible*, Macmillan, New York, 1966, 933-935.

[10] Geoffrey W. Bromiley (ed.) , 'Witness', *The International Bible Standard Encyclopedia*, Vol. IV (Q-Z) (Grand Rapids, Michigan: William B. Eerdmans, 1988), 1086-1087.

a 'witness' to the truth of Jesus Christ to the extent of pouring out one's blood. The Christian martyrs acted as an inspiration of courage and determination in the way one lived a Christian life.

Martyrs and Witnesses of Faith in Anglophone Africa – Examples from Uganda and Congo

Marsh and Kingsworth speak of the Buganda martyrs that were killed largely for their Christian faith, also because of their refusal to engage in sodomy as demanded of them by King Kabaka Mwanga of the Buganda Kingdom.[11]

Oduyoye observes that, faced with persecution, the early Christian church in Northern Africa chose martyrdom and thus a new way of life.[12] Martyrdom's theological base was absolute loyalty to God, which made participation in the imperial cults and local kingships unthinkable.

Anderson recounts the martyrdom of Simon Kimbangu from Congo, the founder of the Kimbanguist Church. He was imprisoned in 1921 by the Belgian Government and died in prison in 1951. In Uganda, one example of recorded Christian martyrdom was the execution of 31 Buganda martyrs at Namugongo, on Ascension Thursday, 3rd June 1886. The Christians were martyred for their faith under the order of Buganda Kabaka Mwanga.[13] These Buganda martyrs were killed largely for their beliefs and aspirations for a new way of social organization and form of life. Faupel notes that the Ugandan martyrs were resigned to die for Jesus Christ. Those who were executed on 3rd June 1886 were not the first Ugandan martyrs to be executed and tortured for being Christians. Faupel also narrates the death of two Ugandan Basoga who were martyred for their faith on 27th May 1886.[14]

Other African martyrs include those African Christians who were massacred in the seventeenth century in the Kingdom of Monomotapa, present-day Mozambique, under Portuguese domination.[15] Zimbabwe also had martyrdom where thirteen mission workers of the Elim Pentecostal Church died on the night of 23rd June 1978, as they had lived for their faith.[16]

During the period of the struggle for Kenya's independence,[17] the Christian faith was put to the test by the Mau Mau. Duiker and Speilvogel narrate that the Mau Mau was an amorphous organization whose members were primarily from the Agikuyu community and who sought independence for Kenyans from British colonial rule.[18]

James Hannington, a missionary bishop, was killed by King Mwanga as he was travelling to Uganda. The first native martyr in Uganda was a Roman Catholic, Joseph Mukasa Balikuddembe. On 3rd June 1886, a group of 32 men and boys (22 Roman Catholic and ten Anglican) were burned at the stake. Most of them were young pages in Mwanga's household, from their head-man, Charles Lwanga, to the thirteen-year-old Kizito.

---

[11] Zoe A. Marsh and G. W. Kingsworth, *An Introduction to the History of East Africa. 3rd ed* (Cambridge: Cambridge Press, 1966), 28, Figure 1, Column 2.

[12] Mercy Amba Oduyoye, *Hearing and Knowing: Theological Reflections on Christianity in Africa* (New York: Orbis Books, 1991), 20-21.

[13] John F. Faupel, *African Holocaust: The Story of the Uganda Martyrs* (London: Geoffrey Chapman, 1969), 198-206.

[14] Faupel, *African Holocaust,* 198-206.

[15] Alfred John Wills, *An Introduction to the History of Central Africa, 2nd ed.* (London: Oxford University Press, 1967), 38-43.

[16] William Purcell, *Martyrs of our Time* (London: A.R. Mowbray and Co. Ltd, 1983), 141-142.

[17] Richard Frost, *Race against Time: Human Relations and Politics in Kenya before Independence* (London: Transafrica Press, 1978), 28, 149.

[18] William J. Duiker and Jackson J. Spielvogel, *World History* (Minneapolis: West Publishing Company, 1994), 254-257. Also included is Oliver Roland and J. D. Fage, *A Short History of Africa* (Middlesex: Penguin Books Ltd., 1972).

The Uganda martyrs are a group of 23 Anglican and 22 Catholic converts to Christianity in the historic kingdom of Buganda, now part of Uganda, who were executed between November 1885 and January 1887. The Catholic Church beatified these martyrs to its faith in 1920 and canonized them in 1964.

Kabaka Mwanga II succeeded to Uganda's throne in 1884. A year later, he ordered the execution of Yusufu Rugarama, Makko Kakumba and Nuwa Serwanga, who had converted to Christianity. Encouraged by his prime minister, on 29th October 1885 he had the incoming Anglican Bishop James Hannington assassinated on the eastern border of his kingdom.

Martyrs and Witnesses of Faith in Francophone Africa – the Case of Madagascar/Martyrs et Témoins de la foi en Afrique Francophone – L'example de Madagascar

Le christianisme est venu en Afrique avec la colonisation: les colons sont venus avec la Bible dans une main et le fusil dans l'autre. C'est par ce cliché que se résume l'arrivée 'systématique' du christianisme en Afrique au dix-neuvième siècle. En Europe, on dit que le christianisme est venu par défaut par la conversion des empereurs des premiers siècles. En tout cas, on ne peut pas nier le fait que le christianisme a eu des trajectoires différentes dans ces deux continents. Ce qui les rapproche c'est l'enjeu politique qu'elles revêtent. Il est vrai qu'il y a des églises chrétiennes africaines plus anciennes que la colonisation comme celles de l'Éthiopie et du Soudan,[19] l'époque coloniale reste un tournant majeur pour le christianisme en Afrique.

Quand on parle de religion, on touche à un élément identitaire important. Il n'est alors pas étonnant si le christianisme n'a pas toujours été accueilli à bras ouverts par les africains qui avaient déjà leurs religions.[20] Résistance et adhésion allaient ainsi de pair à cette époque. Résistance pour ceux qui voyaient leur identité et leur intérêt menacés par cette religion nouvelle, et adhésion pour ceux qui ont été touchés par le message de l'évangile. De la résistance naît la persécution, et de l'adhésion naît un témoignage de foi qui va jusqu'à payer de sa propre vie. Nous allons alors par cet article essayer de donner un aperçu de cette situation en prenant le cas de Madagascar avant d'analyser la portée et les enjeux de ces témoignages de foi pour l'église de l'époque et d'aujourd'hui.

La Résistance au Christianisme, le Cas de Madagascar

Le premier contact de Madagascar avec le christianisme n'avait pas de lien direct avec la colonisation. Ce fut des missionnaires dominicains qui ont essayé timidement de l'introduire dans le nord de Madagascar en1585. Mais le christianisme n'a pas tenu le coup face à la religion traditionnelle de la région et l'influence de l'islam qui commençait aussi à cette époque.[21] D'autres « tentatives » missionnaires ont eu lieu: au début du dix-septième siècle par des prêtres Jésuites qui étaient assez maladroits dans leur relation avec l'autorité de la côte ouest Malagasy.[22] Une autre vague de missionnaires catholiques est venue suite à

---

[19] Ces églises datent du quatrième siècle de notre ère. Cf. Stéphane Ancel, Eloi Ficquet, « L'Eglise orthodoxe tewahedo d'Ethiopie et ses enjeux contemporains » in *L'Ethiopie contemporaine,* ed. Gérard Prunier (Paris: Karthala, 2007): 185-236.

[20] On parle ici de 'religions', au pluriel, car il n'y a pas une seule religion africaine. Mbiti dit: « We speak of African Traditional Religions in the plural because there are about three thousand African peoples (tribes), and each has its own religious system », see John Mbiti, *African Religions and Philosophy,* (Oxford; Portsmouth: Heinemann, 1990), 1. Il faut toutefois noter que dans la deuxième édition de cet ouvrage, Mbiti lui-même parle aussi de la religion africaine au singulier pour souligner le potentiel d'unité dans cette diversité des religions en Afrique. Mbiti, *Religions and Philiosphy,* xiii.

[21] Bruno Hübsch, « Ny nifandraisan'I Madagasikara voalohany tamin'ny fivavahana kristianina » (Taonjato faha 17 sy faha 18), in *I Madagasikara sy ny fivavahana kristianina,* Collectif (Fianarantsoa: Ambozontany, 1992), 163-184.

[22] Hübsch, 'Ny nifandraisan'I Madagasikara', 169.

la création de la congrégation « De Propagande Fide » en 1622.[23] Portugais et français se relayaient dans ce cadre mais n'ont pas pu aller plus loin puisque l'envoi de missionnaires le lien avec le commerce et la traite d'esclaves posait des problèmes. Il fallait alors attendre l'arrivée des missionnaires protestants anglais de la LMS (London Missionary Society) en 1818 pour mieux comprendre le christianisme. Ces missionnaires – pasteurs et artisans – ont commencé par séduire le pouvoir royal Merina[24] qui cherchait à avoir des alliés afin de réussir à conquérir tout le pays. En échange de la facilitation de l'acquisition d'armes depuis l'Angleterre, le roi Radama I (1810-1828) leur a permis de construire des écoles et enseigner. Cela rendait services aux missionnaires qui commençaient à réunir autour d'eux les plus brillants élèves malagasy qu'ils ont par la suite engagés dans la traduction de la Bible qui commença en 1820.

A la mort de Radama I, la reine Ranavalona I prit la relève. Cette dernière commençait à se méfier de la proximité des missionnaires britanniques avec l'administration royale mais pour des raisons diplomatiques, elle ne les a pas empêché de faire leur travail. D'où l'autorisation de baptiser une vingtaine de personnes converties au christianisme en 1831. La ferveur de ces nouveaux chrétiens a fait que leur nombre grandisse significativement. Leurs rassemblements attiraient de plus en plus de monde. Cela était vu d'un mauvais œil par la reine qui trouvait sa position menacée.

Dans la culture malagasy, le roi ou la reine était considéré-e comme un dieu avec toute l'adoration et le respect qui lui sont dus. Toute activité rassemblant un certain nombre de personnes était vue par l'autorité royale comme une provocation, voire une concurrence. C'est cela qui sera l'enjeu principal de la persécution du christianisme à cette époque. Ce fut l'autorité royale et non le peuple qui devenait résistante. Ainsi, en 1832, la reine commençait à s'en prendre aux chrétiens autochtones, sans encore inquiéter les missionnaires,[25] diplomatie oblige! Les missionnaires continuaient donc à prêcher l'Autre royaume et ses principes. L'entourage de la reine devenait sensible à ce genre de discours qu'il considérait comme une incitation à s'opposer à l'autorité royale, et à vénérer des ancêtres étrangers. Se sentant déstabilisées, ils ont alors commencé à inciter le peuple à réagir contre ce mouvement naissant. Pendant ce temps, les églises continuaient à se remplir et les rencontres dans des endroits secrets se multipliaient.

En 1835, la persécution se radicalisait, la répression des chrétiens et chrétiennes devenait de plus en plus violente. Cela a duré jusqu'en 1861, date de la fin du règne de Ranavalona I. Les missionnaires qui ont essayé de protéger les chrétiens en accueillant les rencontres chrétiennes chez eux ont été contraints de quitter le territoire. Il y eut alors des chrétiens et chrétiennes qui ont fait machine arrière en reniant leur foi, ceux-là ont eu un allègement de peine. En revanche, ceux qui sont restés fermes et prêts à mourir pour leur foi devenaient de plus en plus fervents. La parution de la Bible en malagasy, le 21 juin 1835, leur servait de tremplin. Ils continuaient à se voir en cachette pour prier, lire, et méditer les Saintes Ecritures. Il leur était toutefois difficile de limiter les infiltrations dans leurs rassemblements. L'autorité royale était régulièrement informée de tout leur plan, et les dirigeants de ces rencontres ont été dénoncés. Des centaines de chrétiens ont été dépouillés de leurs biens et jetés en prison.

Ce fut dans ces circonstances que les premiers martyrs ont été tués en 1837. Refusant de renier sa foi après plusieurs semaines de prison, et une nuit entière de torture, la jeune Rasalama, âgée de vingt sept ans, une des premières jeunes élèves des missionnaires, était tuée, percée de lance le 14 août 1837. D'autres ont été brûlés vifs, décapités, jetés du haut d'une falaise, ou réduits à l'esclavage. Leurs Bibles ont été collectées puis brûlées à la place publique. Quelques unes ont pu être cachées en lieu sûr et servaient d'outil pour nourrir la foi des rescapés qui ont réussi de fuir ou de se cacher dans des grottes. En 1856, les

[23] Fondée par le Pape Grégoire XV en 1622 pour la propagation du catholicisme, cette congrégation a changé de nom et est devenu « Congrégation pour l'Évangélisation des Peuples ».

[24] Peuple de la partie nord des hautes terres centrales de Madagascar.

[25] Micheline Rasoamiaramanana, « Ny nitsipahan'ny fanjakana teto Madagasikara ny fivavahana kristianina », in *I Madagasikara sy ny fivavahana kristianina,* Collectif (Fianarantsoa: Ambozontany, 1992), 217-240.

missionnaires repartis ont pu faire venir en cachette 1500 Bibles. Cela renforçait de plus en plus la foi des chrétiens qui réalisaient qu'ils n'étaient pas abandonnés.

En 1838, quelques chrétiens malagasy ont réussi à fuir à l'île Maurice puis en Angleterre grâce à l'aide d'anciens missionnaires. Ceux-là sont devenus des missionnaires à leur tour.

Quels Enjeux pour la Persécutions et Quels Avantages Pour les Martyrs?

Nous pouvons en tirer que comme au temps de la première église, la persécution n'a fait qu'élargir les territoires du christianisme et renforcer la foi des rescapés. Grâce au témoignage des martyrs, le christianisme malagasy a survécu à cette épreuve sanguinaire. Madagascar n'était pas le seul pays à être passé par ces moments de résistance. Il y eut des histoires similaires dans d'autres pays d'Afrique et nous savons que les persécutions continuent de faire des martyrs jusqu'à nos jours. Depuis le temps des apôtres, les enjeux de la persécution ne changent pas, il s'agit de politique et de leadership.

Si la reine Ranavalona avait une stratégie moins violente et plus élaborée, elle aurait pu empêcher le christianisme de se répandre. Le fond du problème ne se trouve pas dans le fait que les chrétiens vénèrent un ancêtre étranger ou servent un autre royaume car nous savons que le respect des anciens et des dirigeants reste de mise en Afrique. Il ne s'agit pas non plus d'empêcher une quelconque concurrence entre le Dieu des chrétiens et le ou la demi-dieu qui est le roi ou la reine, ces derniers savent pertinemment qu'ils restent de humains limités. Les raisons des persécutions ne sont pas religieuses, elles se trouvent plutôt dans la crainte de ne pas pouvoir maîtriser le développement du mouvement des chrétiens et de perdre le contrôle de l'influence de leurs dirigeants. C'est pourquoi, au delà d'une démarche de foi et de piété, certains empereurs et rois, occident comme en Afrique, n'ont pas hésité à se convertir au christianisme. Cela pour des raisons purement politiques: garder une place influente, maîtriser les situations, et continuer à asseoir le pouvoir. C'est ce qui s'est passé à Madagascar à la mort de Ranavalona I en août 1861.[26] A peine arrivé au pouvoir, son successeur, le roi Radama II, a aussitôt autorisé les chrétiens à se réunir en publique. Ceux qui ont fui ont pu revenir sur les hautes terres, les missionnaires ont été autorisés à revenir, et des églises ont été bâties en mémoire des martyrs. Le règne de Radama II fut de courte durée (1861-1863). Assassiné en mai 1863, son épouse, Rasoherina (1863-1868) lui succéda, suivie par Ranavalona II (1868-1883). Ces deux dernières ont continué la politique de Radama II, accordant une liberté au christianisme qui est même devenu une religion d'état. Ranavalona II a troqué les idoles royales contre la Bible qui trônait au palais. Elle s'est fait baptisé avec son premier ministre le 29 février 1869. Le christianisme est alors devenu une religion d'Etat. Une église fut construite dans l'enceinte du palais. Par la suite, des milliers de gens se firent baptiser.[27] Cette politique a permis à l'autorité royale de contrôler les allées et venue des missionnaires et des chrétiens et avoir le dernier mot sur l'organization de l'église.

Face à ce retournement de la situation se pose la question de savoir si un tel christianisme politique rend encore service à l'Eglise et à l'évangile. Les martyrs et témoins de la foi ont-ils donné leur vie pour de telles 'paix' et 'entente' de façade ? Paix et entente artificielles qui n'ont pas pu empêcher les colons de prendre possession des terres africaines. De nos jours, les persécutions revêtent une autre forme: le système politique et économique mondial imposant une « laïcité » aveugle, ne laissant aucune place aux plus faibles. Les martyrs et témoins de la foi de nos jours seraient alors ceux qui sont prêts à risquer leur vie pour instaurer plus de justice et d'équité politique, économique, écologique… et religieux.

---

[26] Françoise Raison-Jourde, « Fifehezan'ny fanjakana ny fiangonana sy adim-pivavahana », in *I Madagasikara sy ny fivavahana kristianina,* Collectif (Fianarantsoa: Ambozontany, 1992), 277-298.

[27] Raison-Jourde, 'Fifehezan'ny fanjakana', 279.

Conclusion

The examples of martyrdom, referred to above in short case studies from Uganda, Congo and Madagascar, point to the fact that living witnesses of faith, including those who gave their lives to Christ, are an integral part of African Christianity and its history, in many parts of the African continent. A comprehensive study on martyrs and other extraordinary witnesses to faith still needs to be written. What has become clear in this initial survey is a key conviction common to many facets of Christian faith on the African continent – that to be a Christian is to identify oneself with Jesus' example of suffering, self-denial and self-sacrifice in doing God's will (Matt. 16:24-27; 23:12-12; John 12:25-26). There is a need to take up one's cross daily (Luke 9:23). In some cases, this can lead to explicit martyrdom (as in the case of Coptic Christians beheaded in Libya in 2015). In this sense, martyrdom is part of being a Christian. But the end, as is confessed in many hymns and faith statements in Africa, is not the final victory of death, but the final victory of God's eternal justice as revealed in the resurrection of Jesus Christ.

Bibliography

Anderson, Allan *African Reformation: African Initiated Christianity in the 20th Century.* Eritrea: Africa World Press, Inc., 2001.

Anderson, William B. *The Church in East Africa: 1840-1974.* Tanzania: Central Tanganyika Press, 1977.

Austin, Bill R. *Austin's Topical History of Christianity.* Wheaton, Illinois: Tyndale House Publishers, 1983.

Boer, Harry. *A Short History of the Early Church.* Grand Rapids, Michigan: William B. Eerdmans Publishing Co, 1976

Bromiley, Geoffrey W. (ed.), 'Witness'. *The International Bible Standard Encyclopedia*, Volume 4: Q-Z. 1086-1087. Michigan: William B. Eerdmans, 1988.

Buijtenhuijs, Robert. *Essays on Mau Mau: Contributions to Mau Mau Historiography.* Leiden: African Studies Centre, 1982.

Collins, Robert O., (ed.), *Problems in the History of Colonial Africa: 1860-1960.* Engelwood Cliffs: Prentice-Hall, Inc., 1970.

Contran, Neno, MCCJ. *They are a Target: 200 African Priests Killed.* Nairobi: Paulines, 1996.

Cruden, Alexander. *Cruden's Complete Concordance to the Old and New Testaments.* Grand Rapids, Michigan: Zondervan, 1949.

Curtin, Philip, Feierman, Steven, Thompson, Leonard and Vansina, Jan. *African History.* Essex: Longman Group UK Ltd, 1978.

Davidson, Basil (ed.), *The African Past: Chronicles from Antiquity to Modern Times.* Boston: Little Brown, 1964

Dowley, Tim (ed.), *Lion Handbook: The History of Christianity.* Herts, UK: Lion, 1977

Duiker, William J. and Spielvogel, Jackson J.. *World History.* Minneapolis: West Publishing Company, 1994.

Faupel, John F. *African Holocaust: The Story of the Uganda Martyrs.* London: Geoffrey Chapman, 1969.

Ferguson, Everett, (ed.), *Encyclopaedia of Early Christian History.* New York: Garland Publishing House, 1990.

Freedman D. N., (ed.), *The Anchor Bible Dictionary. Volume 1.A-C.* New York: Doubleday, 1992.

Frost, Richard. *Race against Time: Human Relations and Politics in Kenya before Independence.* London: Transafrica Press, 1978.

Gatu, G John. *Joyfully Christian Truly African.* Nairobi: Acton Publishers, 2006.

González Justo L. *The Story of Christianity:. The Early Church to the Dawn of the Reformation* (Vol. 1). San Francisco: Harper, 1984.

Buttrich, George A. (ed.) 'Witness', *The Interpreter's Dictionary of the Bible*, (Volume 4), R-Z, Nashville: Abingdon, 1962.

Herbermann, Charles George et al. (eds.), *The Catholic Encyclopedia: An International Work of Reference on the Constitution, Doctrine, and History of the Catholic Church, Volume 4,* New York: The Encyclopedia press, inc, 1908.

Irvin, Dale T. and Sunquis, Scott W. t. *History of the World Christian Movement: Earliest Christianity to 1453* (Volume 1). Maryknoll, New York: Orbis Books, 2005.

Isichei, Elizabeth. *A History of Christianity in Africa: From Antiquity to the Present.* London: Society for Promoting Christian Knowledge, 1995.

Karanja, John K. *Founding an African Faith. Kikuyu Anglican Christianity: 1900-1945.* Nairobi: Uzima Press, 1999.

King, Marie Gentert. *Foxe's Book of Martyrs.* New Jersey: Fleming H. Revell, 1968.

Marsh, Zoë. A. and Kingsworth, G. W.. *An Introduction to the History of East Africa. 3rd ed.* Cambridge: Cambridge Press, 1966.

Mbiti, John S. *African Religions and Philosophy.* Nairobi: Heinemann, 1969.

______. *Bible and Theology in African Christianity.* Nairobi: Oxford Press, Eastern Africa, 1986.

McKenzie, John L. 'Parable.' In *Dictionary of the Bible*, 635. London: Geoffrey Chapman, 1966.

Ng'ang'a, Mbugua J. 'Agikuyu Christian Martyrs: An Exploratory Study of the Faith of Selected Agikuyu Christian Martyrs During the Mau Mau Period in Kenya (1952-1960).' MA Thesis, South African Theological Seminary, 2011.

Oduyoye, Mercy A. *Hearing and Knowing: Theological Reflections on Christianity in Africa.* New York: Orbis Books, 1991.

Oliver, Roland and Atmore, Anthony. *Africa Since 1800: Fifth Edition.* Cambridge: Cambridge Press, 2005.

Oliver, Roland and Fage, John D. *A Short History of Africa.* Middlesex: Penguin Books Ltd, 1972.

Pearsall, Judy, (ed.), 'Role', *The Concise Oxford Dictionary*, (10th Edition), New York: Oxford Press, 1999.

Purcell, William. *Martyrs of Our Time.* London: A.R. Mowbray and Co. Ltd, 1983.

Sauer, Christof and Howell, Richard (eds.), *Suffering, Persecution and Martyrdom. Theological Reflections Vol 2.* Kempton Park: AcadSA Publishing, 2010.

Stevenson, James. *A New Eusebius: Documents Illustrative of the History of the Church to AD 337.* London: SPCK, 1975.

(132) African Spirituality and African Christianity

Francisca Hildegardis Chimhanda

Introduction

The spirituality of a people can be understood as the driving force or innate capacity for maintaining an authentic God-human-cosmos reciprocal and mutual relationship. It is what causes human beings to overcome their limitations in knowing and responding to God. From this perspective, African Christian spirituality is seemingly embedded in cultural and Christian values for attaining the creation and baptismal dignity of the *imago Dei/Christi* (image of God/Christ; cf. Gen. 1:26-27; Rom. 8:17; Gal. 4:6). But African Christian spirituality is complex and therefore defies simplistic definition. However, there are commonalities and divergences in African culture(s) and Christian spirituality. This is because what unites African culture and Christian traditions (God/Christ) is greater than what divides them. This chapter on African spirituality concentrates on the commonalities rather than the divergences.

African Christian spirituality is culturally and historically conditioned. It is thus dynamic and this posits a challenge for its relevance in responding to current contextual issues. The latter include Christian monotheism in relation to ancestral belief, post-colonial challenges (including land ownership, re-distribution, good stewardship, and environmental sustainability), and gender equality. We will draw practical examples of African Christian spirituality from the Shona people of Zimbabwe[1] and the Roman Catholic Church.

A creative dialogue of culture and the gospel shows that there is mutual influencing of enculturation, evangelisation and the incarnation. This is justified by acknowledging that, prior to Christian evangelisation, Africans knew God through their experience of the transcendent. Christianity introduced the concept of special revelation of God in and through Christ, and thus reinforced African spirituality and expanded the view.

Pope John Paul II explains the mutual influencing of the incarnation, evangelization and enculturation as follows:

> The purpose of evangelization is 'transforming humanity from within and making it new'. In and through the Only Son, the relations of people with God, one another and all creation will be renewed. For this reason the proclamation of the Gospel can contribute to the interior transformation of all people of good will whose hearts are open to the Holy Spirit's action.[2]

Pope Francis[3] is emphatic that God is the gospel, who is 'a source of newness'.

---

[1] The Shona people of Zimbabwe are grouped into five major Shona dialects – Karanga, Zezuru, Manyika, Korekore and Ndau.

[2] Pope John Paul II, *Post-Synodal Apostolic Exhortation, Ecclesia in Africa* [EA], 42, http://w2.vatican.va/content/john-paul-ii/en/apost_exhortations/documents/hf_jp-ii_exh_14091995_ecclesia-in-africa.html (accessed 16 July, 2015).

[3] Pope Francis, in the Apostolic Exhortation *Evangelii Gaudium*(EG), 10-11, http://w2.vatican.va/content/francesco/en/apost_exhortations/documents/papa-francesco_esortazione-ap_20131124_evangelii-gaudium.html (accessed 11 September, 2015).

African Christian Spirituality

It appears that the key to unlocking African Christian spirituality is the Great Commandment to 'Love God… and your neighbour as yourself' (Matt. 22:34-39; Mark 12:28-31; Luke 10:25-27). In the African Bantu Shona religious worldview, 'neighbour' includes the environment[4] and *Ubuntu* ethic (which in Shona is '*unhu*' meaning personhood). Consequently, salient features of African Christian spirituality to be examined include belief in God or the Supreme Being,[5] *Ubuntu* ethic or the attainment of full humanity,[6] and belief in unity between the spiritual and the physical environments.[7]

African Belief in the Supreme Being

In the critical dialogue of culture and the gospel, Shona Christians located God at the apex of the ancestral mediation ladder[8] in cases of petition for rain, harvest thanksgiving, peace and deliverance from drought, disease and pestilence. The Shona area spirits are known as *Mhondoro* (lion spirits) and these are proto-ancestors in the dynasty of chiefs. At the foot of the ancestral mediation ladder are *vadzimu* (family spirits) who also have living mediums (men and women). They have called the Christian God, *Mwari.* Although the Shona pray to *Mwari* and the ancestors, they do not equate *Mwari* with the ancestors. The Shona assign to *Mwari* prerogatives of *Musiki* (Creator) and, in particular, *Musikavanhu* (Creator of human beings) and ultimate giver and source of all life and redemption.[9]

For the Shona, *Mwari* is elusive, neither male nor female, and is a universal God, who gives rain and sunshine and 'fruitful seasons' to all people (Matt. 5:45; Acts 14:15-17). The Shona understand the environment as a catholic (universal) space for encounter with the gracious God. Consequently, the forests are holy and things found in it (mushrooms, wild fruits, honey, medicinal herbs, trees and shrubs, etc.) are to be made available to everyone by picking them sparingly and in such a way as to promote continued growth and propagation.

If traditionally the Shona considered *Mwari*a a remote god, only interested in national issues, Christianity introduced or reinforced the immanence and dynamic agency of God in and through Christ. Shona Christians have internalised this concept as attested by theophoric names, for example *Tinashe* (God amongst us), that is Emmanuel (Matt. 1:23), *Simbarashe* (power of God) and *Ngonidzashe* (mercy of God). The suffix '*-she*' stands for Chief, also called *Mambo*. Shona Christians have called God and Christ *Ishe* and *Mambo,* respectively.

---

[4] Francisca Chimhanda, 'The Liberation Potential of Shona Culture and the Gospel: A Post-Feminist Perspective.' *Studia Historiae Ecclesiasticae*, Vol. XL (2014): 308.

[5] Vincent Mulago, 'Traditional African Religion and Christianity.' In *African Traditional Religion and Christianity,* ed. Jacob K. Olupona (New York: Paragon House, 1991) 119-134.

[6] Luke Lungile Pato, 'Being Fully Human: From the Perspective of African Culture and Spirituality', *Journal of Theology for Southern Africa,* issue 66, (1997): 53-61.

[7] John Pobee, *Skenosis: Christian Faith in an African Context* (Gweru: Mambo Press, 1992), 66; Pato, 'Being Fully Human', 56.

[8] Francisca Chimhanda, *Christ the Ancestor: Shona Christianity and the Roots for Feminist Liberative Praxis* (Saarbrücken: VDM Verlag, 2011), 82; Michael Bourdillon, *The Shona Peoples: An Ethnography of the Contemporary Shona, with Special Reference to their Religion* (Gweru: Mambo Press), 24.

[9] Chimhanda, *Christ the Ancestor,* 82-84; Nisbert Taringa', 'African Metaphors for God: Male or Female?', *Scriptura* Vol. 86, (2004): 174-179.

African Ancestral Belief

African ancestral belief posits God and the environment in anthropomorphic existential analogy. Pope Francis concurs with this view in alluding to 'human ecology'.[10] For the Shona, land is mother, the big breast that feeds its children to satiety and the great womb from which people come (at birth) and return (at death).[11] For Christianity, the environment is our mother who 'opens her arms to embrace us… sustains and governs us… and… produces various fruits with coloured flowers and herbs'.[12] Sacramentally, God is in creation but transcends it. Ontologically, the earth and all that is in it is God's (Ps 24:1-2). African ancestors are not gods. The historical Bantu migration shows they became owners of the land by default (through conquest and occupation). *Ivhu* (soil) is personified as the ancestors, and their living descendants are *vana vevhu* (children of the soil). This is biblical and, to a certain extent, Christian. In the second creation myth in Genesis, Adam is created from dust (Gen. 2:7).

The chief's lordship over the land can be best understood in terms of servant leadership and stewardship over God's graces (Gen. 1:28-30). Good stewardship is shown in the Shona practice of *Zundera Mambo* (the community works in the chief's field and proceeds are used to provide for *vanhu vaMwari* – (the widow, orphan, stranger and the mentally and physically challenged). This is also echoed in sacramental Christology that portrays the encounter with Christ in the distressing disguise of the poor, sick, prisoners, etc. (Matt. 25:35-46). The *Zundera Mambo* concept can provide a correction to post-colonial Africa in general, and Zimbabwe in particular, where the leaders have succumbed to dictatorship and massive looting of the national coffers. This has produced a minority of black elites and made the poor majority poorer.

Ancestral spirituality is a powerful tool in curbing ecological disaster. It means that land is communal and a priceless heritage. Consequently, the present generation has a responsibility to preserve the environment and pass it on to future generations.

Ubuntu spirituality

As shown above, *Unhu* (*Ubuntu*) spirituality is concerned with the attainment of full humanity or newness of life. Christian parallels to this include the attainment of 'eternal life', 'fullness of (life) God' (Eph. 3:19) and 'life… abundantly' (John 10:10). Four pillars of *Unhu* are elaborated below.

Unhu (Personhood)

Becoming 'fully human' is a process that takes place from before birth to life after death. Communal ontology and epistemology as aspects of African Christian spirituality mean that both the person and church need to exist with and for others. Life is celebrated in a series of rites of passage. According to the Shona, in this process *unhu* can be enhanced or diminished. In the liberation struggle against colonialism, political slogans like *ivhukuvanhu* (land to the people) implied that the colonial oppressors had no *unhu* or were not human. This was because, from the outset, they regarded Blacks as non-persons, when they acquired vast tracts of already inhabited ancestral land.

Shona communal identity is undergirded by totemism. *Mutupo* (totem – animal or part of it) and *chidavo* (praise names) are used in greeting, thanking, and for correct burial and inauguration of the dead as the powerful protective ancestors. Thus, it is the whole family, clan and ancestors that are greeted,

---

[10] Pope Francis encyclical *Laudato Si(LS)*, 5 http://w2.vatican.va/content/dam/francesco/pdf/encyclicals/documents/papa-francesco_20150524_enciclica-laudato-si_en.pdf (accessed 13 November, 2015).

[11] Francisca Chimhanda, 'Land is our Mother: A Shona Bantu Feminist Perspective', in *Tradition: Fixed and Mobile: Essays in Honour of Rev. Prof. Rodney Moss*, eds. Itumeleng D. Mothoagae and Anselm Laurence Prior (Pretoria: UNISA, 2013), 123-149.

[12] Pope Francis, LS, 1.

thanked and praised. In the Roman Catholic tradition, Pope John Paul II asserts that African ancestral veneration is 'a preparation for belief in the Communion of the Saints'.[13]

But in corporate personality, there is the risk that the individual's unique dignity and rights can be compromised, in what Gordon Chavhunduka calls 'extended patience'.[14] This is the case, for example, with substitute and pledged, levirate marriages that impinge on the dignity and rights of the girl-child and widows. Alternatively, the individual can be a liability to the whole extended family, as in the case of murder.

Umwe (Togetherness)

Traditionally, among the Shona, *umwe* was shown in the practice of *humwe* (families, village community and neighbouring village communities join in common tasks like ploughing, weeding, harvesting etc.). Today, with urbanisation and the erosion of the extended family, *humwe* practice has almost died out. However, the *humwe* concept is used in projects like running children's homes (in particular for HIV and AIDS orphans) and educating children from poor families.

Ushamwari (Friendship)

Although African religion does not proselytise, it is inclusive of all people beyond the boundaries of the family, clan and tribe. This orientation is captured in the Shona adage: 'Friendship is greater than consanguine relationships.'

Kugamuchira Vayeni (Hospitality)

The Shona put a high value on hospitality. This is evidenced by the fact that they have a time of day called *Ruvhunzavayeni* (dusk – when 'visitors' begin to arrive and 'ask' either for direction to their destination or to be put up). The *Zundera Mambo* practice described above is an element of Shona hospitality.

Conclusion

This chapter has shown how African Bantu Shona spirituality is rich in life-affirming elements critical to the God-human-cosmos interrelationship. The creative dialogue of culture and the gospel exposed the mutual influencing of evangelisation, enculturation and the incarnation. The great commandment of love and the Bantu ethic of being fully human were recognised as the key for unlocking African Christian spirituality. African Christian spirituality was acknowledged as dynamic and, therefore, offering the possibility of responding to current social, economic and political issues, for the ultimate purpose of the attainment of fullness of life for humanity (including a sustainable environment), all to the greater glory of God.

Bibliography

Bourdillon, Michael. *The Shona Peoples: An Ethnography of the Contemporary Shona People, with Special Reference to their Religion*. Gweru: Mambo Press, 1976.

Chavhunduka, Gordon. 'Traditional Medicine and Christian Beliefs'. *Christianity South of the Zambezi* Vol. 2, (1977): 131-146.

Chimhanda, Francisca. *Christ the Ancestor: Shona Christianity and the Roots for Feminist Liberative Praxis.* Saarbrucken: VDM Verlag, 2011.

[13] Pope John Paul II, *EA*, 43.

[14] Gordon L. Chavhunduka, 'Traditional Medicine and Christian Beliefs', *Christianity South of the Zambezi,* Vol. 2, (1977), 131-146.

______. 'Land is our Mother: A Shona Bantu Feminist Perspective.' In *Tradition: Fixed and Mobile: Essays in Honour of Rev. Prof. Rodney Moss*, edited by Itumeleng D. Mothoagae and Anselm Laurence, 123-149. Prior Pretoria: UNISA, 2013.

______. 'The Liberation Potential of Shona Culture and the Gospel: A Post-Feminist Perspective.' *Studia Historiae Ecclesiasticae*, Vol. XL (2014): 305-328.

Mulago, Vincent. 'Traditional African Religion and Christianity.' In *African Traditional Religions in Contemporary Society,* edited by Jacob K. Olupona, 119-134. New York: Paragon House, 1991.

Pato, Luke L. 'Being Fully Human.' *Journal of Theology for Southern Africa,* no. 97, (1997): 53-61.

Pobee, John S. *Skenosis: Christian Faith in an African Context.* Gweru: Mambo Press, 1992.

Pope Benedict XVI. *Africae Munus: Apostolic Exhortation on the Church in Africa in the Service of Reconciliation, Justice and Peace.* World Media Publication, 2011.

Pope Francis. *Apostolic Exhortation 'Evangelii Gaudium'*(EG), 10-11, http://w2.vatican.va/content/francesco/en/apost_exhortations/documents/papa-francesco_esortazione-ap_20131124_evangelii-gaudium.html (accessed 11 September, 2015)

Pope Francis. http://w2.vatican.va/content/dam/francesco/pdf/encyclicals/documents/papa-francesco_20150524_enciclica-laudato-si_en.pdf (accessed 13 November, 2015).

Pope John Paul II. *Post-Synodal Apostolic Exhortation 'Ecclesia in Africa.'* http://w2.vatican.va/content/john-paul-ii/en/apost_exhortations/documents/hf_jp-ii_exh_14091995_ecclesia-in-africa.html (accessed 16 July, 2015).

Taringa, Nisbert. 'African Metaphors for God: Male or Female?' *Scriptura* Vol. 86 (2004): 174-179.

(133) African Church Choirs and the Role of Music in Africa

Felix Muchimba

Introduction

Singing is an integral part of the African culture and lifestyle. Music has always played a central role in African education, communication, celebration and entertainment. Hence, singing occupies a leading role in the existence of Africans. As a matter of fact, one cannot imagine most public activities in Africa unaccompanied by music.

The role that African choirs play in contemporary Africa is multi-faceted. It is diverse in the sense that choirs' functionalities range from informal to formal community activities, and from traditional to civil gatherings. Often these gatherings serve as conduits of civic and social development as well as being places of worship and political participation. Such gatherings and activities may also fulfil the task of community mobilization. Therefore, the songs composed and sung by the choirs have to fulfil and reflect these functionalities and also bring a sense of unity, solidarity and community to the those present.

The Role of Music in Spiritual Empowerment in Africa

The primary role of the choir is to support and enhance the congregation in singing worship songs. A well-rehearsed choir will make the worship of the congregation 'come alive' by breathing life into the text as it sings with clear understanding and insight into the words and their meaning. Consequently, the texts shape the faith of those involved in worship. It is for this reason that the choir plays an integral function in worship, guiding the gathered assembly in prayer and praise through song.

Music is one of the most obvious learning activities emphasizing the process of 'learning by doing' or better still 'learning by singing'. People tend to remember things better when they are sung. The hymnal is a valuable aid in teaching the Bible since much of the hymnal is scripture set to music. The choir is more than a musical organization in which songs are rehearsed and learned; it is a Bible-teaching tool. Even in New Testament days, it seems that songs had an admonishing or teaching function. This is made clear especially when we compare Colossians 1:28, 'We proclaim him, admonishing and teaching everyone with all wisdom, so that we may present everyone perfect in Christ' with Colossians 3:16:

> Let the word of Christ dwell in you richly as you teach and admonish one another with all wisdom, and as you sing psalms, hymns and spiritual songs with gratitude in your hearts to God.

Choirs are also a tool for teaching theology as some of the fundamental doctrines of Christian faith have been incorporated into some of our greatest hymns. In most parts of rural Africa, where people are illiterate, choir music plays a major role in teaching Christian doctrine and practice. Christian music is always music with a message and good choir music is that which functions by reinforcing and emotionalizing the message of the words. Hymns also help in the interpretation of the Scriptures because the songs are able to take Biblical teaching from its original cultural setting, interpret it and apply it to the current context.

Furthermore, because the words in the hymns include praising and thanking God for His love toward Christians, teaching Christians how they should live, focusing on the future and asking for God's help and guidance as they live each day, they can assist the church in worship.

In this way,biblical truths can be a great resource of comfort and help during trying and difficult times. It is for this reason that Church choirs in Africa remain a great resource in times of celebrations such as weddings and during times of bereavement, funerals and burials as a source of hope and comfort. Africans retain their faith in God and find comfort and strength in the songs they sing. Indeed, choirs offer a means of catharsis, and listening to these songs and having them in our mind's storehouse is a precious treasure as these hymns can bring much comfort and peace to the spirit and soul. It is little wonder that today there are many songs being sung by African choirs that reflect the African spirituality in terms of trusting God to meet their daily needs and healing their diseases in the midst of harsh economic conditions – songs that may not be appreciated by western friends who do not know what abject poverty feels like.

The Role of Music in Community Building in Africa

Christopher I. Ejizu explains what constitutes an African Community (notwithstanding the fact that in our post-modern world 'community' is being redefined):

> The sense of community and human living are highly cherished values of traditional African life... Traditional Africans share the basic instinct of gregariousness with the rest of human-kind. Families and members of kin-groups from minimal to maximal lineages, generally live together and form community. Africans share life intensely in common. For traditional Africans, community is much more than simply a social grouping of people bound together by reasons of natural origin and/or deep common interests and values. It is both a society as well as a unity of the visible and invisible worlds; the world of the physically living on the one hand, and the world of the ancestors, divinities and souls of children yet to be born to individual kin-groups. In a wider sense, African traditional community comprehends the totality of the world of African experience including the physical environment, as well as all spirit beings acknowledged by a given group.[1]

Community-building is developing authentic relationships between people. Music has the unique opportunity to build community and help participants develop a sense of belonging. Muchimba observes, '... in African worship everyone participates in some way by singing, dancing, ululating, playing an instrument, or by clapping hands. When Africans make music, a spirit of community is created...'[2]

Music is indeed a potent symbol of identity. Like language, it is one of those aspects of culture, which can readily serve the aspect of 'ethnic identity'. People gather where the music is, and celebrate the human experience together humbly as a participatory experience where everyone is part of the activity. It is here where the central heartbeat of a community is formed, providing ongoing contact, shared interests and the opportunity for social interaction and fun. Amy Izushima and Alicia Ramirez state, 'Music, then, has many functions, like the energy, that gives birth to what is almost a soundtrack to life. It is the social, emotional, and cognitive vehicle of society, reflecting the imprint of our present identity and the always-evolving identity.'[3] In African society, various rites of passages and ceremonies are marked by music and celebrations which give the participants a sense of community and identity. Each participant at such ceremonies is acknowledged as a significant contributor to the magic of the moment. Hence, the participant's sense of appreciation and significance within the community is enhanced, especially through the songs that reflect such a belief. In connection with this, Muchimba states, 'Music also serves as a

---

[1] Christopher I. Ejizu 'African Traditional Religion and the promotion of community-living in Africa' www.afrikaworld.net/afrel/community.htm (accessed 11 November, 2014).

[2] Felix Muchimba, *Liberating the African Soul – Comparing African and Western Music and Worship Styles* (Colorado Springs: Authentic, 2007), 38.

[3] The Suvvy Musician Blog Home base for music careers & entrepreneurship 'The future and role of music in modern society' www.savvymusician.com/blog 'The-future-and-role-of-music-in-modern-society' (accessed 5 December, 2014).

powerful symbol of social interaction and identity, and Africans share keen feelings as to what kind of music belongs to them. It is little wonder that in the days of slavery, African Americans used 'Black Music' as a major symbol of group identity.'[4]

Furthermore, music in Africa is a primary contributor to values that create supportive and responsive family relationships. It reinforces the formal religious structure that helps African families cope with life and social stresses, such as economic and various inequalities in the community. John Allan states that music is often used to strengthen resolve in moments of crisis within a given community.[5] Allan further states that music can be a very powerful tool in providing a vehicle of expression for the less articulate in society.[6] Within a community, choral music can also serve to provide solace and solidarity, a positive self-image, emotional and spiritual release. Most choirs in Africa are mainly made up of young people and, within these choirs, songs are composed and sung that teach youth values, morals, and human ethics.

The Role of Music in Political Witness in Africa

The relationship between choral music or music in general and politics is evident in many cultures because music has been employed to present a particular political message. It can certainly motivate people towards political goals, and it can connect people to ideas and thoughts that they never would have realized without hearing the words spoken. For example:

> In 1970s Nigeria, Fela Kuti invented Afro Beat music as a way to protest the oil company regime of Nigeria. His song 'Zombie' became a global hit that railed against Nigeria's military dictators. In South Africa, the indigenous Mbatanga music helped bring about the end of apartheid and it spread a message of peace and reconciliation in that nation. The reason this works is because music gets people thinking, talking, and doing.[7]

Hill shows how music has an intrinsic power to propagate political ideologies as compared to a political pamphlet. Music can be both entertaining and educative and informative. Unlike a stirring speech, its echo could last beyond the starting-point of the pulpit. Music is not like a manifesto which is often full of political and economic jargon, familiar and appealing only to the enlightened minds. Music can easily be memorized by anyone, repeated and disseminated even by the less educated. In this way, "A pamphlet, no matter how good, is never read but once, but a song is learned by heart and repeated over and over"[8]

Over the years in Africa, as any other part of the world, music has been used as a means to communicate political messages that may not be acceptable across the political divide. Indeed, such music has provided the means to transmit political messages that would otherwise not have been expressed in common political language or speech. In some societies, politicians have made attempts to control its use because of the influence it has on individuals in the community regardless of their social status. This is more so when those in power feel threatened or exposed by the messages being conveyed in the songs. Within the context of politics, choral music can be an agent of change – an implicit or explicit commentary on power.

---

[4] Muchimba, '*Liberating the African Soul*', 80.

[5] John Allan '*Music, Movement and Silence in Worship*' in Harold Rowdon (ed), *Declare his Glory, Congregational Worship Today* (Carlisle: Partnership Periodicals, 1998), 78.

[6] Allan, 'Music, Movement', 91.

[7] Barrett Martin 'Music and the Politics of Resistance' www.huffingtonpost.com/barrett-martin/music-and-the-politics-of_b_4087557.html (accessed 10th November, 2014).

[8] Ron Eyerman and Andrew Jamison, *Music and Social Movements: Mobilizing Traditions in the Twentieth Century* (Cambridge: University Press, 1998), 59.

Conclusion

Music has been around for thousands of years and it appeals to everyone. Choral music and African society have always been intimately related. Music has always played an important role in teaching and communication in general as one listens to the lyrics and understands what is being said in the song. Music reflects and creates religious, social and political conditions that facilitate change in these three disciplines of African life.

In Africa, music is crafted by composers to educate, inform and entertain the listeners. As people are educated, the hope is that they will perceive the world within the light of the lyrics – to better themselves and their communities. Hence, music transforms not only those who perform it but especially those who listen to it. Religious, social and political beliefs, once embodied fully and convincingly in the lyrics of the singers, have the power to influence others to make a change.

Bibliography

Allan, John. 'Music, Movement and Silence in Worship' In *Declare his Glory, Congregational Worship Today* edited by Harold Rowdon, 63-78. Carlisle: Partnership Periodicals, 1998.

Ejizu, Christopher I. 'African Traditional Religion and the Promotion of Community-living in Africa'. www.afrikaworld.net/afrel/community.htm (accessed 11 November, 2014).

Eyerman, Ron and Jamison, Andrew. *Music and Social Movements: Mobilizing Traditions in the Twentieth Century.* Cambridge: University Press, 1998.

Martin, Barrett 'Music and the Politics of Resistance'. www.huffingtonpost.com/barrett-martin/music-and-the-politics-of_b_4087557.html (accessed 10 November, 2014).

Muchimba, Felix. *Liberating the African Soul – Comparing African and Western music and worship styles.* Colorado Springs: Authentic, 2007.

The Suvvy Musician Blog Home base for music careers & entrepreneurship 'The future and role of music in modern society'. www.savvymusician.com/blog 'The-future-and-role-of-music-in-modern-society' (accessed 5 December, 2014).

(134A) The African Christian Family Life

Priscille Djomhoue et Paulin Poucouta

Les anthropologues considèrent la famille comme la cellule la plus fondamentale des groupes sociaux. Elle est le socle social, économique, juridique, et religieux de la vie d'un peuple : « une société sans famille est comme un fruit sans noyau », comme dit le proverbe africain.

Mais la famille s'organise différemment selon les cultures et selon les convictions religieuses. Qu'en est-il de l'Afrique? Nous nous proposons de présenter la famille africaine, puis la famille africaine chrétienne. Aujourd'hui, face à la crise qui secoue la société, ne convient-il pas de s'investir dans la ré-évangélisation des familles?

La Famille Africaine

La famille large

En Occident on parle de famille nucléaire pour désigner la cellule constituée du père, de la mère et des enfants, et on utilisera l'expression « famille élargie » pour désigner les autres membres à qui on est d'une manière ou d'une autre liés par le sang. En Afrique, par contre, les liens familiaux de mari, femme et enfants sont aussi importants que ceux qui nous unissent aux grands parents, tantes, oncles, cousins et autres. Comme le relève si bien Setri Nyomi et Kasonga Wa Kasonga[1], l'expression « famille élargie » n'a pas d'équivalent dans la plupart des langues africaines. De plus, en Afrique lorsque deux personnes se marient, elles acquièrent l'une envers l'autre, la responsabilité des relations sanguines. Les cérémonies de mariages traditionnels, encore pratiqués aujourd'hui, incluent des rites symboliques qui consolident les liens familiaux indestructibles.

Jean Gaston Roland résume bien ces caractéristiques de la famille africaine : «La famille africaine traditionnelle est très étendue. Elle ne se réduit jamais au père, à la mère et leurs enfants, vivant à part dans l'intimité d'un appartement séparé.»[2]

On comprend pourquoi le mariage traditionnel n'engage pas uniquement deux personnes, mais deux familles. D'ailleurs, autrefois, les parents initiaient les rencontres entre les jeunes gens ou alors arrangeaient tout simplement des mariages pour eux. Certes, cette pratique disparait progressivement, mais cela ne supprime pas l'influence culturelle du processus qui légitime le mariage. Même si les futurs mariés se choisissent, ce sont les membres de leurs familles respectives qui prennent les contacts nécessaires avant l'organisation des différentes cérémonies.

Les personnes âgées

Les personnes âgées occupent une place importante dans la famille africaine. En effet, les enfants leur doivent respect et assistance. De nombreux pays n'ont ni des structures qui s'occupent des personnes âgées ni des assurances pour régler les questions financières. C'est pourquoi, à un certain âge, les parents ou grands-parents sont pris en charge et récupérés par la famille jusqu'aux derniers moments de leur existence.

---

[1] Setri Nyomi, Kasonga Wa Kasonga, *Guide des familles chrétiennes d'Afrique au vingt et unième siècle,* Nairobi, CETA, 2002, p. 86.

[2] Jean Gaston Roland, « la famille africaine et l'éducation », http://jeangastonrostand.centerblog.net/1-la-famille-africaine-et-education, consulté le 6 janvier 2015.

Les enfants

Les enfants sont considérés comme le bien le plus précieux de la famille. De nombreux proverbes le soulignent. Tous les enfants ont les mêmes droits : ceux issus du couple, ceux venus de la famille de l'homme et de celle de la femme. En même temps que les valeurs culturelles et traditionnelles, ils partagent avec l'ensemble de la famille les valeurs chrétiennes, la vie de foi et d'adoration. L'éducation de l'enfant concerne l'ensemble de la famille. C'est pourquoi, les vacances passées auprès des grands parents ou d'un oncle au village permettent à l'enfant d'en apprendre plus sur sa culture et ses traditions. En ville, les membres de la famille qui sont sans emplois peuvent assurer périodiquement la garde des enfants, ce qui est bénéfique aussi bien pour l'enfant que pour eux.

Homme et femme

Si la famille est large, elle se structure néanmoins autour du couple, l'homme et la femme. Les rôles entre les deux époux sont répartis selon les coutumes diverses d'un continent pluriel dans ses us. Néanmoins, presque partout, le père est le chef incontesté de la famille. Il la dirige et veille à la discipline des différents membres. Il a la responsabilité de nourrir les siens. Il est le garant de la tradition. Dans les familles matrilinéaires, c'est l'oncle maternel, le frère de la maman qui détient cette autorité.

La femme, elle, est essentiellement celle qui donne la vie et l'entretient. Elle se doit d'être une bonne ménagère, une épouse fidèle, une mère féconde. Elle donne la vie, l'entretient et éduque. Sa situation socio-juridique est quasiment limitée inférieure à celle de l'homme. Certes, aujourd'hui, la situation a énormément évolué, principalement grâce à l'école, à l'emploi et aussi à l'évangélisation. Pourtant, les représentations traditionnelles, elles, restent fortement ancrées dans les esprits autant des hommes que des femmes.

La Vie Familiale Chrétienne en Afrique

Le mariage chrétien

En Afrique, le mariage chrétien se moule quelque peu sur la configuration culturelle de la famille. Ainsi, le mariage se célèbre en trois étapes : le mariage traditionnel, le mariage civil et le mariage religieux.

Le mariage traditionnel s'organise selon les coutumes de chaque tribu. Néanmoins, presque partout, la cérémonie du mariage traditionnel est précédée de contacts entre les familles du futur couple. Ces rencontres se déroulent en plusieurs étapes : les futurs conjoints rendent visite à leurs belles familles respectives pour se faire connaître ; puis les parents du jeune homme vont visiter plusieurs membres de la famille de la jeune fille, en commençant pas ses parents, puis les grands parents et les oncles et tantes. Ces visites permettent aux membres des différentes familles de faire connaissance et d'échanger des présents. A la fin de la phase des visites, les familles déterminent la date du mariage traditionnel, qui sera scellé par divers rites.

Quant au mariage civil, il est contracté devant une autorité établie par l'Etat. Il est reconnu par les pouvoirs civils. Les deux familles considèrent également cette étape comme un autre moment de rencontre.

Le mariage religieux, lui, arrive à la fin de ces cérémonies parce que l'Église, dans plusieurs pays, exige l'acte de mariage civil comme pièce nécessaire à la bénédiction nuptiale. L'acte du mariage civil doit porter nécessairement la mention : régime matrimonial monogamique accepté. C'est ici que l'on établit l'une des différences fondamentales entre le mariage chrétien et le mariage non chrétien. Mais la réalité est tout autre : il existe aujourd'hui des polygames chrétiens. Beaucoup sont engagés dans les Églises même si les pasteurs et les prêtres refusent de bénir leur union et les excluent de la participation à la sainte cène ou à la communion eucharistique.

Ces trois étapes du mariage posent le problème de leur coût financier qui peut dissuader les jeunes à s'engager. L'Église ne doit-elle pas aider à harmoniser ces trois formes de célébration, tout en gardant à chacune son sens originel ?

La famille chrétienne, un lieu œcuménique

Les Africains attachent une importance capitale aux relations familiales, par de-là les disparités idéologiques, sociales et religieuses. C'est pourquoi la famille est souvent occasion de rencontres œcuméniques. Tous les événements de la vie mettent ensemble les membres de la famille.

Ainsi, la naissance d'un enfant est toujours une occasion de réjouissance pendant laquelle toute la famille se donne le devoir de faire un geste symbolique. Il s'agit de rende visite au nouveau-né et à ses parents ou d'envoyer un cadeau si on est très éloigné. C'est ainsi qu'on accueille le bébé et qu'on l'intègre dans la famille. Son baptême sera l'occasion de rassembler les différents membres de la famille. Même les non- chrétiens ou adeptes d'autres religions y prennent part. Ce qui favorise la cohabitation religieuse.

De même, les deuils sont occasion de retrouvailles des différents membres de la famille et des voisins, toutes confessions religieuses confondues.

Les défis de la culture traditionnelle

Pourtant, la famille chrétienne rencontre de nombreux défis liés à la tradition. Ainsi, la société africaine accorde une grande valeur à la procréation. Ce fait constitue un défi pour les couples chrétiens qui n'ont pas d'enfant. Plusieurs hommes se voient obligés, sous la pression de leurs familles, de contracter un second mariage parce que la première épouse « n'a pas été capable de procréer ». Cela d'autant plus que jusqu'à une certaine époque, on estimait, traditionnellement, que la stérilité est féminine : ainsi, lorsque l'enfant ne vient pas, la femme est la coupable. Mais l'évolution de la science et l'incitation faite aux couples à consulter un médecin ont permis de dissiper ce malentendu. Alors, lorsqu'il est établi cliniquement que l'homme n'est pas capable de procréer, il arrive que la famille de la femme lui recommande d'être infidèle, afin d'offrir une progéniture à son mari. Ces deux attitudes menacent constamment l'unité et l'harmonie du couple chrétien. Ils s'éloignent alors de l'Église qui n'encouragent ni l'adultère ni la polygamie.

Ailleurs, on remédie à la stérilité par l'adoption. En Afrique, la réalité de la famille large devrait aider à apporter une solution au problème douloureux. En effet, élever et éduquer l'enfant d'un autre membre de la famille paraît tout à fait normal. Pourtant, la société et la famille posent un méprisant sur les couples sans enfants. Ce qui affecte même les couples chrétiens.

De même, la dot initialement conçue comme un symbole, un échange de cadeaux et approfondissement des relations entre familles s'est dénaturée. Elle freine l'engagement de nombreux jeunes. De plus, elle dévalorise la dignité de la femme considérée comme une marchandise. Il convient alors de travailler à restituer à la dot sa valeur symbolique initiale.

Les défis des transformations socio-culturelles

Comme partout dans le monde, en Afrique aussi, la famille subit les contrecoups des mutations socio-culturelles. Les tensions socio-politiques se répercutent de manière insidieuse sur la cellule familiale. Les nouvelles valeurs culturelles qui résultent de l'ouverture facilitée par la télévision, internet et les autres médias constituent aussi un défi dans la mesure où elles divisent très souvent les membres de la famille qui se sentent bousculées dans leurs habitudes et leurs repères. Cette déstructuration pénalise l'ensemble de la famille, mais particulièrement les enfants, les personnes âgées et les femmes.

En effet, aujourd'hui, les enfants et les jeunes ont perdu le statut de rois qu'il avait dans la tradition africaine. Parfois, ils sont parfois instrumentalisés dans les conflits, exploités dans les plantations ou utilisées comme domestiques. D'où l'importance d'investir dans la formation des jeunes et des enfants. En maints endroits, les personnes âgées sont exclues et subissent de nombreux sévices sous la fallacieuse accusation de sorcellerie. Les femmes sont également les principales victimes de la violence lors des conflits ou dans les foyers, mais aussi de nombreuses discriminations[3]. Sans céder aux modes, il faut réaffirmer plus fermement et défendre la dignité des femmes. Enfin, la misère croissante, les nouvelles formes d'existence et l'égoïsme ambiant ont parfois raison de la solidarité traditionnelle.

Devant tous ces défis, on comprend l'appel de Marcus Ndongmo à « sauver la famille africaine »[4].

Conclusion: Évangéliser la Famille Africaine

En effet, dans une société où les valeurs morales s'effritent, la famille chrétienne doit être le lieu où l'on retrouve la joie de vivre, où se réveillent, se renforcent et se purifient les valeurs d'unité, de cohésion, de responsabilités partagées, de confiance, et surtout de profonde et réelle fidélité. Ce qui passe par une évangélisation permanente qui repose sur la parole de Dieu[5], en l'occurrence les quatre piliers que proposent les Actes des Apôtres : l'enseignement des apôtres, la fraction de pain, la prière et la communion fraternelle (Ac 2, 42-47). En somme, selon le mot du Cardinal Albert Joseph Malula, « Si nous voulons christianiser la société africaine, nous devons commencer par la famille qui en est la cellule »[6].

Bibliographie

De Saint Moulin, Léon : *Œuvres complètes du Cardinal Malula vol.7 : textes concernant la famille. Théâtre et chants*, Kinshasa, Facultés catholiques de Kinshasa, 1997.

Gaston Roland, Jean: « la famille africaine et l'éducation », http://jeangastonrostand. centerblog.net/1-la-famille-africaine-et-education, consulté le 6 janvier 2015.

Ndongmo M. : *Sauver la famille africaine*, Yaoundé, PUCAC, 2008.

Nyomi, Setri/Wa Kasonga Kasonga: *Guide des familles chrétiennes d'Afrique au vingt et unième siècle,* Nairobi, CETA, 2002.

Ngalula, Tshianda J. : *Dieu dénonce et condamne les violences faites aux femmes*, Kinshasa, Éditions Mont Sinaï, 2005.

[3] Cf. J. Ngalula Tshianda, *Dieu dénonce et condamne les violences faites aux femmes*, Kinshasa, Éditions Mont Sinaï, 2005.

[4] M. Ndongmo, *Sauver la famille africaine*, Yaoundé, PUCAC, 2008.

[5] Cf. Setri Nyomi, Kasonga Wa Kasonga, *Guide des familles chrétiennes d'Afrique au vingt et unième siècle,* p.19-20.

[6] Léon de Saint Moulin, *Œuvres complètes du Cardinal Malula vol.7 : textes concernant la famille. Théâtre et chants*, Kinshasa, Facultés catholiques de Kinshasa, 1997, p. 63.

(134B) THE AFRICAN CHRISTIAN FAMILY LIFE

Kapya Kaoma

Introduction

As a child, I remember embarrassing my father in the presence of fifth graders. My father was teaching a class on the 'family' as understood in the West: father, mother and children. Since we lived within the school premises, my father invited me to his class. He then asked me the following question, 'How many are you in your family?' As a first grader, then, I failed to answer his question; something that did not only embarrass me but also confused me. With indignation, he answered his own question – telling the class that we were six. 'Well, that's not true. We are more than that,' I thought as I left his classroom. As an African, my *ulupwa* (family) is made up of all my relatives as well as those who share my *mukowa* (*totem*), and not just my biological siblings as my father told his class. Our home was filled with people, and many more visited us nearly every month. We were all told they were *ulupwa* (family) since we shared the same *mukowa* (totem). We were repeatedly reminded that *ifikolwe fyesu* (ancestors) were also part of the family.

My childhood encounter was again repeated during my time in England. As a single person then, people asked me whether I had a family. Yes, I had a family – though not married – I had both small and big fathers (*batata mukalamba nabatata mwaice*), both big and small mothers (*bamayo mukalamba na bamayo mwaice*), sisters, brothers, etc. – they made our family. People would remind me that they wanted to know whether I was married and had children. All I would say is, 'No, I am not married but I have a family.' I am sure they thought I was too backward in my outlook – little did they know that I sought to teach them about the diversity of families in the world. It is from this perspective that African Christian family life should be addressed.

The concept of Christian family life presupposes the existence of African Christianity. The question is: Can we speak of African Christianity or Christianities? What is the relationship between the Roman Catholic, the Anglican, the Pentecostal theology and the theology of African Initiated Churches? In the light of marriage, are plural marriages and customary marriages Christian? And how can Christian family life appear in contemporary Africa amidst so many denominational theologies and socio-economic and political challenges?

In order to address these questions, I seek to define family life within the African framework. Whereas some Christians link the family to marriage and procreation (father, mother and children), and others to community, in this chapter I argue that the Christian family life needs to model the concept of the family of God. This model suggests a radical concept of Christian family life since it invites Africans into loving relationship with other members of God's family.

The Colonial Transformation of the African Family

As a teacher, my father was taught to view the family as father, mother and children. Yet at home, the family was something wider that we were born into. His students did not accept his interpretation either; they were part of the bigger 'family' of many fathers, mothers, uncles, cousins, aunties, sisters, brothers and so on. Whereas 'the biological factor is necessary in constituting kinship relations,' in African cosmology, other societal factors can 'equally form new relations that are akin to blood ties'.[1]

---

[1] Peter Assenga, 'The African Family Spirit: A Nexus of Justice, Peace and Reconciliation', *African Ecclesiastical*

One example is the concept of *Mukowa*. All those who shared our *mukowa* (totem) were equally part of the family. This is because in Bantu cosmology, identity is established 'through *mukowa*. Totems symbolize belongingness; they define and interconnect families, clans and kingdoms… What genealogies are to westerners, totems are to the Bantu'.[2] In fact, when two people meet, their first obligation is to establish their relatedness through *mukowa*. In Chishinga, Ushi and Bemba cosmologies, 'people who share the same *mukowa* cannot get married no matter how distant they might be'.[3] This understanding moves the family from the sexual realm to that of relationships.

African family life in the face of colonialism

In 1960, Anne Barnett wrote, 'In Africa today, the Christian home and family life are being subjected to severe tests. Past customs are discarded and new situations are encountered for which there has been little preparation.'[4] Reflecting on the September 1959 Christian Council of Kenya's conference on the Christian family, Barnett outlines some issues churches faced then. Polygamy, bride price, the upbringing of children, sex education, Christian home life and family planning were among the many issues the conference addressed – albeit from the western worldview. To Barnett, African cosmology was dying; hence Africans needed a new way of living. Barnett, however, did not define what constitutes the Christian home and family life – apart from monogamy and children.

After fifty-fives years, the issues the church sought to address are still alive. Yet the context is different. Barnett wrote, when Africa was under colonial rule, and her statement about the 'past customs' being 'discarded' was not entirely true, since many Africans experienced modernity from a traditional cosmological perspective.

How then can Christian family life be understood? In the last decade or so, 'defending traditional family values' is repeatedly used from the USA to Russia to Africa. Yet what constitutes the 'traditional family' is assumed rather than defined. While the African 'traditional family' includes all relatives, in the West the term refers to the nuclear family. For example, Daniel Aleshire writes, 'It was one of those good and tough days of our family – particularly for four year-old Jonathan and his mother.'[5] Like my father, Aleshire's understanding of the family is limited to his wife and child. To explain the diversity of families, Thomas E. Breidenthal proposes a shift from family to household. To him, what constitutes a household is 'a very high degree of familiarity,' which is found in all households. Breidenthal writes,

> Christian marriage is not the only form of Christian householding, if only because marriage and family life is not the only form that human life together takes. The range and variety of Christian households is wide and rich, and in affirming the natural goodness of life together, Christian faith must begin affirming this diversity. This does not mean every form of householding is acceptable, because not every living arrangement stands up to the demands of justice and love.[6]

Review Vol. 51, issue 1-2 (March-June 2009): 52-77, 59.

[2] Kapya J. Kaoma, *God's Family, God's Earth: Christian Ecological Ethics of Ubuntu* (Zomba, Malawi: Kachere Series, 2013), 73.

[3] Kaoma, *God's Family, God's Earth,* 74. See also Karla O. Poewe, 'Matriliny in the Throes of Change: Kinship, Descent and Marriage in Luapula, Zambia, Part One', *Africa: Journal of the International African Institute* Vol. 48, no. 3 (1978), 210. In other African cultures, however, marriage between people who share the same totem is encouraged.

[4] Anne Barnett, 'Christian Home and Family Life in Kenya Today', *International Review of Mission,* Vol. 49, issue 196 (October 1960): 420.

[5] Daniel Aleshire, 'Family Life and Christian Spirituality', *Review and Expositor*, 86 (1989), 209-214.

[6] Thomas E. Breidenthal, *Christian Households: The Sanctification of Nearness* (Cambridge, Mass: Cowley Publications, 1997), 93.

Although he accepts same-gender households, he argues that polygamy is not appropriate for Christian households.

If demands for justice and love are the basis for Christian households, Breidenthal's rejection of polygamy while accepting same-sex relationships is another example of how western Christianity favours its values over those of others. Africans, on the other hand, are likely to accept polygamy over same-gender households. Regardless, the exportation and imposition of the limited 'nuclear family' as a default Christian family has led to the disintegration of the African family – leading to many social problems such as street children, destitution and various forms of violence – from domestic to sexual.

The African Christian family life

The question of Christian family life assumes the existence of a distinct Christian definition of the family. In Africa, this distinct element is linked with the colonial or missionary era. In the colonial cosmology, the African traditional concept of the family was demeaned and abandoned in favour of the nuclear family: father, mother, and children. This shift followed a shift from the land-based to the urban-based economy. Since rural life depended on the land, the African traditional family worked to secure one's wellbeing. In the money economy, however, an individual's meagre income was just enough to sustain one's life – forcing Africans to ignore their obligations to their kin.

Besides, in matrilineal communities such as the Chishinga and Bemba cultures, maternal uncles were said to be responsible for their sisters' children. Yet colonial governments only recognized wife and biological children as the man's 'family' members. Since missionaries shared this limited understanding of the family, they confirmed and somehow sacralized it. They divided the African family into two; the father, mother and children became primary members, while the rest, including one's own parents and siblings, were now 'extended family' members. One's primary responsibility was to the first; responsibility to the extended family was deemed secondary.

It is critical to realize that the concepts of 'extended family' and 'nuclear family' were of a colonial and missionary origin. As Peter Assenga contends, the Chagga of Tanzania lack these concepts since an 'African belongs to a web of relations far beyond the nuclear family'. One 'is born into a community of relatives (not only a household consisting of a father and a mother, with or without siblings)'.[7] As a family member, an African is socialized to put 'others before one's own needs'.[8] This understanding is in line with the teaching of Jesus. In the Kingdom of God, we don't have extended family brothers and sisters – rather, we are all primary members of God's family.

African Christian Family Life – Is it about Marriage?

Discussions on the family in Africa have conflated the family with marriage. Generally, heterosexual marriage is perceived as the African family. This is understandable since the Christian family life is associated with the story of Adam, Eve and their children. In the Christian Bible, this assumption is linked to the Holy Family – Joseph, Mary and Jesus. Although Jesus grew up in the socio-cultural context in which the family went beyond father, mother and children, missionaries presented the heterosexual and monogamous marriage in the Church as the Christian family.

In many African societies, however, the family and marriage are two distinct institutions. Whereas marriage was part of the family, it was not the family per se. Among the Bemba, Chishinga and Ushi people of Zambia, *ulupwa* (family) is not '*in'ganda yandi*' (implying marriage). Whereas sex or marriage

[7] Assenga, 'The African family spirit', 62.
[8] Assenga, 'The African Family Spirit', 69.

constitutes *'in'ganda',* it does not define the family. On the contrary, marriage builds and expands family life since it brings two families together.

In line with Breidenthal above, belongingness defines and, to some extent constitutes, an African family. Just as a married person belongs to the family of both the living and the living dead (ancestors), so does the single mother, the divorcee, a child, and the single person. For instance, the Chishinga people say, *eko nafuma, kwaliba abantu* (where I come from, there are people) or *nalikwata abantu* (I have people). Usually, these words are meant to be a reminder to others that if something wrong happens to that person, his or her people will seek justice on one's behalf. In fact, the bigger the family, the bigger the respect one is accorded. Aptly stated, the family is bigger than the household; though every household is part of the family. Thus the Christian family life is inclusive – divorcees, single parents, widows, and people of various sexual orientations and gender identities are all members of this family.

Belonging to the family also implies wider socio-economic, religious, and cultural obligations and benefits. When disaster strikes, for example, all family members are equally affected. In this ethical system, the 'I' is minimized while the 'we' is maximized; sharing is both an individual and community virtue to which every individual ought to aspire. Whereas western civilization disconnected Africans from their families, in reality, Africans belong to a much bigger family than the church has accepted.

Apart from arguing that the African family life revolves around the ethics of *Ubuntu,* Desmond Tutu writes that if we accept:

> … that we do belong together, that our destinies are bound up in one another's, that we can be free only together, that we can survive only together, that we can only be human together, then a glorious world would come into being where all of us lived harmoniously together as members of one family, the human family, God's family.[9]

Similarly, Bujo argues that one 'becomes a person only through active participation in the life of the community'.[10]

In theological terms, the Christian family life is a kenotic process through which we empty ourselves (*kenosis*) for the sake of others in the world of violence, greed and selfishness. To live is to exist within the web of sacred communal relationships with one's kin, ancestors and the Supreme Being.

Is African Christian family life possible?

It is important to note that conflating marriage with family carries hetero-normative assumptions of patriarchy. It places masculinity at the centre of the family – raising gender justice issues as well as leading to the oppression of women and those who choose not to marry. For instance, can Christian family life exist in the absence of males, as is usually the case in contemporary Africa? Fulata L. Moyo writes:

> The increasing reality of female-headed households… and the religio-cultural teaching of men as heads of the family as well as the research finding that HIV/AIDS is more prevalent in societies which have gender imbalances, raise many questions for faith-based communities in Africa today. How do we define men as household heads in families of widows, and divorced and single mothers? How can faith-based communities transform the concept of headship so as to encourage mutuality and communion of partners who complement each other?[11]

---

[9] Desmond Tutu, *God Has a Dream: A Vision of Hope for Our Time* (New York: Doubleday, 2004), 23-24.

[10] Benezet Bujo, *Foundations of an African Ethic: Beyond the Universal Claims of Western Morality* (New York: The Crossroad Publishing Company, 2001), 87. For the ecological implication of the family of God, see Kaoma, *God's Family, God's Earth,* 92-114; *The Creator's Symphony: African Christianity, The Plight of Earth and the Poor* (Dorpspruit, Pietermaritzburg, Cluster Publications, 2015).

[11] Fulata Lusungu Moyo, 'Religion, Spirituality and Being a Woman in Africa: Gender Construction Within the

Moyo's point is critical to the understanding of family life. With the increasing number of child-headed households due to wars, terrorism, AIDS and other disasters across the continent, where do we place child headed-households? How is the family to be conceived in the absence of both parents? How about sexual minorities?

The family is a social unity in which life is lived, shared and experienced. Being human means being connected to the wider family. Yet the African family transcends the physical – it connects one with the ancestors as well as with those to come and with the Creator. Since African family life is 'collective', possessing *Ubuntu* (to be truly human) means upholding traditional values of care for all members of one's family.

Towards an African Christian Family Life: Some Observations

Scholars in Africa, especially Roman Catholic theologians, have wrestled with the question of family life. Is the church's teaching on family life in line with the African life-world? What do we do with those who are married to more than one wife or husband? And what is the role of the African family in the life of religious brothers, nuns or celibate priests? In addition, are those who belong to other churches still part of the Christian family? If the family is *ecclesia domestica* (domestic church), what is the place of single people in the Christian family life?[12]

Brian Hearne explores these questions in detail. Accepting that the African family is becoming narrower each passing year, he proposes the church community as 'the new extended family, where the bond of grace sets up not only new relationship but also new kinship patterns, transcending ethnic, national and racial boundaries'.[13] Christian family life, he argues, ought to be 'geared towards the common wellbeing of both women and men and is based on more inclusive beliefs and teachings, especially acknowledging that both women and men are created in the image of God'.[14]

Hearne's argument seeks to replace the African traditional family life with the western Christian definition of the family. I propose a different route – Christianity needs to become African if it is to transform the continent. African Christian family life needs to revisit its traditional understanding of life in which families were intricately connected. Regardless, the emphasis placed on the nuclear family paints an heretical picture of Christianity. Christianity is a communal religion and no isolated Christian exists – we are one family, and one body of Christ. This understanding is closer to the African understanding of the family than to the western one.

Consequently, to replace African family life with western Christian family life will not fully address the crisis of Christian family life on the continent. This is because an African Christian is not fully planted in the western worldview but lives between the two worlds – that of ancestors and that of post-colonial Africa. To this end, Christian family life ought to revolve round the concept of the family of God which has wider application than the western understanding of the family. In God's family life, we are all members, regardless of our socio-economic or religious differences. Since the Triune God is the Creator, sanctifier and sustainer of this family life, all Africans are full members as well as participants in the common life of the people of God. Unlike in the hetero-normatively defined family, in God's family, grandmothers, single mothers, fathers, sexual minorities as well as children all find acceptance. This concept puts greater responsibility on all Christians – we are called to care for all of God's people and especially the least of these (Matt. 24). As Jesus said, 'Whoever does God's will is my brother and sister

---

African Religio-cultural Experiences', *Agenda: Empowering Women for Gender Equity* No. 61 (2004): 75.

[12] Brain Hearne, 'Christian Family Life: Some Pastoral Priorities', *African Ecclesiastical Review* Vol. 24, no. 5, (1982): 290.

[13] Hearne, 'Christian Family Life', 290.

[14] Moyo, 'Religion, spirituality and Being a Woman in Africa', 76.

and mother' (Mark 3:35; Matt. 12:48). Note that Jesus did not say they are extended family members but his siblings.

In addition, the concept of the family of God confronts the narrow definition and application of the Christian family life. It calls us to care not just for our brothers and sisters of the nuclear family, but for strangers and the outcasts; it has no Jew or Gentile, male or female and it is not sexually defined. To become the centre of love, peace and dignity, family life must become inclusive of all humanity and all Creation.

African Christian family life ought to be a place of peace and harmony. It ought to address all forms of violence that demean and destroy life. The over-empowering of males over women, and the boy child over the girl child are issues that African Christian family life ought to address. As God's family, both male and female, have a special role to play in the family. Here, African customs as well as Christian teachings which demean women or sanction violence against women must be confronted. Moreover, Christian family life should address the issue of 'girl child rape' (child marriages) that continues to destroy African girls.

Furthermore, the Christian family life ought to confront the violence associated with sexual minorities. The Church can aid the acceptance as well as the protection of our fellow human beings who do not fit into our colonial-gender-defined roles. Besides, the church needs to explore ways of providing pastoral care to inter-sex children, and their families.

Finally, the Christian family participates in the life of the justice-loving God. Our narrowly defined family life is in contrast to the African family life as well as to the gospel of Christ. A good African Christian family ought to uphold the positive values of both traditional life and the Christian faith – it must participate in the *missio Creatoris Dei* (the mission of the Creator God). These religious values form and inform how Christian family life is upheld – it calls us to love our neighbours as ourselves while looking out for the Earth and the least of Jesus' brothers and sisters. And there are billions of them.

Bibliography

Aleshire, Daniel. 'Family Life and Christian Spirituality.' *Review and Expositor*, Vol. 86 no. 2, (1989): 209-214.

Assenga, Peter. 'The African Family Spirit: A Nexus of Justice, Peace and Reconciliation.' *African Ecclesiastical Review* Vol. 51, issue 1-2, (March-June 2009): 52-77.

Barnett, Anne. 'Christian Home and Family Life in Kenya Today.' *International Review of Mission* Vol. 49, issue 196, (October 1960): 420-426.

Breidenthal, Thomas E. *Christian Households: The Sanctification of Nearness*. Cambridge, Mass: Cowley Publications, 1997.

Bujo, Benezet. *Foundations of an African Ethic: Beyond the Universal Claims of Western Morality*. New York: The Crossroad Publishing Company, 2001.

Hearne, Brain. 'Christian Family Life: Some Pastoral Priorities.' *African Ecclesiastical Review* Vol. 24, no. 5, (1982): 289-299.

Kaoma, Kapya J. *God's Family, God's Earth: Christian Ecological Ethics of Ubuntu*. Zomba, Malawi: Kachere Series, 2013.

Kaoma, Kapya J. *The Creator's Symphony: African Christianity, The Plight of Earth and the Poor.* Dorpspruit, Pietermaritzburg: Cluster Publications, 2015.

Moyo, Fulata L. 'Religion, Spirituality and Being a Woman in Africa: Gender Construction Within the African Religio-cultural Experiences.' *Agenda: Empowering Women for Gender Equity* No. 61 (2004): 72–78.

Poewe, Karla O. 'Matriliny in the Throes of Change: Kinship, Descent and Marriage in Luapula, Zambia, Part One.' *Africa: Journal of the International African Institute* Vol. 48, no. 3, (1978): 205-218.

Tutu, Desmond. *God Has a Dream: A Vision of Hope for Our Time.* New York: Doubleday, 2004.

(135) Gender Justice in African Christianity

Lilian Cheelo Siwila

Introduction

In almost all spheres of life, research on gender has become more pronounced. As such, it is no longer possible to do theology without relating our theological engagement to gender pedagogies. Despite the discussion that the concept of gender still raises within church circles, there are still some forms of resistance to gender justice. From an African Christian perspective, issues of gender are in some cases said to be a foreign imposition, associated with feminism. Yet the concept of gender is as old as humanity. Historically, humanity has always lived in gendered frameworks, even though this is not usually acknowledged. For African women theologians, the issue of gender has been part of their agenda right from the inception of the Circle of Concerned African Women Theologians (the Circle). In their fight against patriarchy, African women theologians have always been aware of the need for an all-inclusive theology that brings both men and women into the fight against gender injustice within religio-cultural and patriarchal circles. This chapter demonstrates how African women theologians have responded to gender justice by calling for a theology of partnership with male theologians. Using a selected number of male theologians who are also called friends of the Circle, the chapter shows how the proposed partnership by African women theologians has helped to promote gender justice within African Christianity.

Dealing with the Backlog of Mission Biases on Gender

A brief background on missionary perception on gender can assist in demonstrating the development of gender discourses within African Christianity. Missionaries who introduced the gospel to Africa operated within a patriarchal framework that was embedded in their patriarchal culture and that of a Christian heritage. Therefore, despite the participation of women in mission work, male missionaries still emerged as superiors and the gospel was still presented in a patriarchal framework. This meant that the kind of African theology which emerged as a reaction to mission work was also formulated around patriarchal ideologies.

It is these ideologies that justified the exclusion of women from participating in theological education and church activities such as ordination. This is because most of the ecclesial duties were still under male influence as such offices as ordination were still viewed as a male space. Gender roles in terms of maleness and femaleness were so distinct that both parties almost found it a taboo to cross over and perform roles that were defined for 'the other'. The idea that some of these roles are socially constructed was not usually entertained, since the roles themselves were seen as societal norms. From an African theological perspective, the concept of enculturation was a reaction to the missionary way of addressing culture and paved the way for discussions on gender justice. At first, African theology was criticised by African women theologians for the way in which it embraced enculturation. Women theologians felt that African male theologians failed to address women's struggle for gender justice. Despite this critique, the presence of enculturation created space to address mission and colonial identities within African Christianity that were also affecting issues of justice.

Following these perceptions, it is evident that African theologians at first found it difficult to include issues of gender in their articulation of an African Christianity. Women's concerns continued to be sidelined, both in the church and in theological education. From an academic perspective, most of the literature that was written during this period carried patriarchal biases rooted in both African and western worldviews. This patriarchal bias was also found in the church, where the liturgy remained male-oriented to the disadvantage of women. Maluleke argues that:

> ... for a long time African Theology has been at peace with the patriarchy inherited from both western and African cultures. The logic of patriarchy has been internalised in such a way that even when dealing with issues of oppression and exclusion African theologians could not easily make the connection. Ideologically and spiritually, African Theology remained largely beholden to chauvinist ideas when it came to gender relations.[1]

It was not until the emergence of African women theologians[2] that a paradigm shift in discussions on gender issues arose among African theologians. African women theologians emphasised the need for gender justice in all spheres of life. Although the Circle emphasised the liberation of women, they were aware that this could not be possible without involving men in this fight. Therefore, right from the inauguration of the Circle, scholars such as Oduyoye advocated a two-pronged theology that calls for the participation of male theologians in the fight against gender injustice.[3] Oduyoye has always argued that African women theologians are not against male theologians. Instead, their fight is against patriarchy and cultural practices perpetuated by some men in the name of preserving culture.[4] From this background, this chapter hopes to address the role played by male theologians in promoting gender justice within the work of African women theologians.

African Male Theologians' Contribution to the Project of Gender Justice

From the time the Circle of Concerned African Women Theologians was inaugurated in 1989, African women theologians have always advocated for an all-inclusive theology.[5] African women theologians have also been aware that the fight against gender injustice can not be achieved without involving male theologians. Discussing the contribution of male theologians to the Circle project, Oduyoye singles out the contribution of John Pobee to the first conference of African women theologians, which saw the birthing of the Circle. Pobee, who was then Executive Secretary for the WCC Theological Education programme, adopted the vision of the Circle as his own project. He helped to raise funds for the 1989 Pan-African Conference.[6] Phiri and Siwila observe that African women theologians' partnership with African male theologians has always been part of the Circle's agenda.[7] It is from such accounts that the Circle has journeyed with male theologians in its search for gender justice within African Christianity.

Apart from the account provided by Oduyoye on Pobee, there are other African male theologians who have been involved in gender advocacy as part of the Circle project, especially in the fight against HIV and

---

[1] Tinyiko Maluleke, 'An African Theology Perspective on Patriarchy', *The Evil of Patriarchy in Church, Society and Politics* (a paper presented at a consultation hosted by Inclusive and Affirming Ministries, the University of the Western Cape and the Centre for Christian Spirituality, Cape Town, 2009), 33.

[2] The Circle of Concerned African Women Theologians was born in 1987 through its founding member Mercy Amba Oduyoye. One of the main objectives for its inception was the need for women to find their voices in African Christianity, both in the Church and in academic circles. In this way, women have managed to challenge the patriarchal ideologies through their writings. For further reading see Isabel Apawo Phiri, 'Major Challenges for African Women Theologians in Theological Education (1989-2008)', *Studia Historiae Ecclesiasticae* XXXIV, No. 2, (2008): 63-81.

[3] Mercy Amba Oduyoye, *Talitha Cum! Proceedings of the Convocation of African Women Theologians* (Ibadan: Daystar, 1989).

[4] Mercy Amba Oduyoye, *Introducing African Women Theologians* (London: Sheffield Academic Press, 2001).

[5] Oduyoye, *Talitha Cum!* 1989.

[6] Mercy Amba Oduyoye, 'The Story of the Circle', *Ecumenical Review* Vol. 53, no 1, (January 2001), 97-100.

[7] Isabel Apawo Phiri and Lilian Siwila, 'The Circle of Concerned African Women Theologians: Transforming Theological Education', in *Handbook of Theological Education in Africa,* eds. Isabel Phiri and Dietrich Werner (Pietermaritzburg: Cluster Publications, 2013), 698.

AIDS and gender-based violence. However, it was not until the 2007 Pan-African Circle Conference which was held in Yaoundé, Cameroon, that male theologians were officially recognised as friends of the Circle. This was a five-day conference, attended by 130 participants, who included women theologians, ordained women serving in local congregations, partners of the Circle and male theologians.[8] One of the goals of the conference was to facilitate dialogue between male and female theologians in working together to address issues such as HIV and AIDS and gender justice.[9] In response to male theologians' involvement in gender justice, Phiri states that there is a serious and deliberate critical engagement from a number of male theologians on issues raised by women theologians. This paradigm shift became more pronounced on issues such as HIV and AIDS and gender-based violence.[10] The Circle's Yaoundé report states that the conference was ground-breaking in that it was the first Circle conference where male theologians were invited to take a prominent role in dialoguing with the Circle members on masculinity and HIV and AIDS.[11]

The outcome of the participation of the male theologians at the Circle conference was a book project on masculinity which was published by WCC/EHAIA. The presence of male theologians in the Circle conference also created a space for these male scholars to discuss issues of masculinity from a gendered perspective. It also helped to challenge the essence of African Christianity, to create space for dialogue on gender justice.

Projects that have Contributed to Gender Justice through the Work of the Circle

Although a number of male theologians have taken the initiative to address gender justice through different means, it is important to point outthe work of two projects. The Ecumenical HIV and AIDS Initiative in Africa (EHAIA), in collaboration with the World Council of Churches (WCC), created a strong partnership with the Circle in the fight against HIV and AIDS. The partnership between the Circle and the WCC through EHAIA has demonstrated in many ways male involvement in the Circle, through scholars such as Ezra Chitando.[12] The male scholars working in this field have addressed the call for gender justice through their research on masculinity. Scholars such as Chitando have focussed on different forms of masculinities that either promote or are a threat to gender justice. He uses the concept of masculinities to show how patriarchy and religio-cultural practices contribute to gender injustice.[13] As Kanyoro argues, culture is a double-edged sword which can also be used as the main form of justification for oppression and injustice, especially to those whom culture defines as 'the other' or the 'outsider', who in most cases are the women.[14] Chitando further observes that some of the religio-cultural patriarchal beliefs and taboos that are imposed on women in the name of culture also make women silent about the oppression that they experience. This is because both religion and culture can also present themselves as enemies of gender

[8] 'Yaoundé Circle report', compiled by Isabel Apawo Phiri, 2007.

[9] Phiri, 'Yaoundé Circle Report'.

[10] Phiri, 'Major challenges for African women theologians', 63-81.

[11] Phiri, 'Yaoundé Circle Report'.

[12] Chitando is one of the male theologians who has been actively involved in the work of the Circle through research and publication. His focus on gender justice is concentrated around HIV and AIDS and masculinities. Some of the publications that have been published in relation to the Circle and gender justice by EHAIA can be obtained from www.wcc-org/wcc/what/mission/ehaia-docs-ehtml – EHAIA documents – World Council of Churches.

[13] For further reading see Ezra Chitando and Notando Hadebe (eds.), *Compassionate Circles: African Women Theologians Facing HIV* (Geneva: WCC Publications, 2009).

[14] Musimbi Kanyoro, *Introducing Feminist Cultural Hermeneutics: An African Perspective* (Cleveland: Pilgrim Press, 2002).

justice.[15] The collaboration between the Circle and EHAIA has led to a number of research projects around issues of gender justice, especially in relation to HIV and AIDS.[16]

Another project that has been instrumental in partnership with the Circle in promoting gender justice is the Tamar Campaign under the Ujamaa Centre at the University of KwaZulu-Natal. Through the use of contextual Bible study, Gerald West is one of the African male (biblical) scholars who has made a significant contribution to the fight against gender-based violence.[17] His contribution to the Circle project on gender justice led to the launch of the Tamar Campaign during the 2007 Yaoundé Pan-African conference. Although many African women theologians have been involved in the Tamar Campaign, even before its launch, the 2007 partnership still remains significant. This is because it was here that the Tamar Campaign was owned as part of the Circle project. West's work becomes significant in that it brings out a male perspective in the fight against gender-based violence, using the Bible as a resource among ordinary readers in local communities.

The Way Forward for Gender Justice in African Christianity

Following the two examples stated above, it is evident that African Christianity has also played a role in advocating for gender justice through the involvement of male theologians in the work of the Circle. Maluleke, however, warns that male theologians should not just join the women theologians, but they need to be 'born again.'[18] This calls for a challenge to respond to issues that affect women and the urge to promote gender equity and partnership that inform transformation. At the same time, gender justice should not just be seen as a form of inclusivity. This is one of the critical misconceptions that has been commonly used in misrepresenting the definition of gender. Under this concept, gender is conceptualised as a way in which society uses equity in terms of statistics to create gender balance. Therefore, gender representation is used to show gender justice. If numbers were used to qualify gender justice, then most African churches would be free of the oppression of women, since women are the majority in the church in Africa.[19] Yet the opposite happens: the majority find themselves being ruled over by the minority. According to Millennium Development Goal 3, gender equality should be seen in terms of equal representation, equal value and treatment for both men and women.[20] Therefore, as African male theologians engage on issues of gender justice, a more in-depth understanding of gender is needed. This will help African Christianity to be more effective in its conceptualisation of gender equity that is authentically African. This will also call for new forms of theology that not only advocate for equal representation but also for justice for all.

---

[15] Ezra Chitando, *Troubled but Not Destroyed: African Theology in Dialogue with HIV and AIDS* (Geneva: WCC publications, 2009).

[16] Chitando and Hadebe, *Compassionate Circles* (2009). This was one of the volumes published by EHAIA in partnership with the Circle.

[17] For more information on Contextual Bible Study see the Ujamaa website at www.ujamaa.ukzn.ac.za.

[18] Tinyiko S. Maluleke, 'The 'Smoke Screens' called Black and African Theologies: The Challenge of African Women Theology', *Journal of Constructive Theology* Vol. 3, no. 2, (1997): 39-63. Also Laurent Magesa, 'The Challenge of African Women Defined Theology for the 21st Century', in *The Challenges and Prospects of the Church in Africa: Theological Reflections of the 21st Century,* eds. Nahashon W. Ndung'u and Philomena N. Mwaura (Nairobi: Paulines Publications Africa, 2005), 88-101.

[19] Brigalia Bam, 'Women and the Church in (South) Africa: Women are the Church in South Africa' in *On Being Church: African Women's Voices and Visions* Geneva, eds. Isabel Apawo Phiri and Sarojini Nadar (Geneva: World Council Churches, 2005), 11.

[20] www.ippf.org/our-work/what-we-do/advocacy/millennium-development-goals (accessed 07 January 2015).

Conclusion

African Christianity has entered another era in doing theology. As a result of this, gender issues are now emerging in different forms. While we talk about gender as the socialisation of men and women, today gender is also talked of in terms of identity leading to homosexuality. This calls for a need to address the issue of gender justice from an African Christian male perspective. African women theologians have provided a platform for this kind of engagement. This is because the call to break the chain of gender injustice in African Christianity cannot be over-effective without placing emphasis on a partnership of equals between men and women.

It is therefore important to appraise the works of African male theologians who adhered to the call for a two-pronged theology in an effort to promote gender justice. Henriot calls for a church that seeks to say something to today's African context.[21] Oduyoye further adds that a church is only a church when it seeks justice.[22] Therefore, the challenge for African Christianity to embrace gender justice also involves the re-evaluation of the prophetic presence of gender in our theological debates, as well as a reconsideration of what it means for the church to be at the intersection between power relationships and gender.

Bibliography

Bam, Brigalia. 'Women and the Church in (South) Africa: Women are the Church in South Africa.' In *On Being Church: African Women's Voices and Visions*, edited by Isabel Apawo Phiri and Sarojini Nadar, 8-16. Geneva: World Council of Churches, 2005.

Chitando, Ezra. *Troubled but Not Destroyed: African Theology in Dialogue with HIV and AIDS.* Geneva: WCC Publications, 2009.

Chitando, Ezra and Hadebe, Nontando (eds). *Compassionate Circles: African Women Theologians Facing HIV.* Geneva: WCC Publications, 2009.

Henriot, Peter J. 'Grass Root Analysis: The Emphasis on Culture.' In *Liberation Theologies on Shifting Grounds,* edited by Georges de Schrijver, 335-350. Leuven: Leuven University Press, 1998.

Kanyoro, Musimbi. *Introducing Feminist Cultural Hermeneutics: An African Perspective.* Cleveland: Pilgrim Press, 2002.

Magesa, Laurenti. 'The Challenge of African Women Defined Theology for the 21st Century.' In *Challenges and Prospects of the Church in Africa: Theological Reflections of the 21st Century.* Edited by Nahashon W. Ndung'u and Philomena N. Mwaura, 88-101. Nairobi: Paulines Publications Africa, 2005.

Maluleke, Tinyiko. 'Dealing Lightly with the Wound of my People?' *Missionalia*, Vol. 25, no. 3, (1997): 324-343.

______. 'An African Theology Perspective on Patriarchy.' In *Inclusive and Affirming Ministries. The Evil of Patriarchy in Church, Society and Politics.* A paper presented at the consultation hosted by Inclusive and Affirming Ministries, the University of the Western Cape and the Centre for Christian Spirituality, Cape Town, 2009.

Mwaura, Philomena Njeri. 2005. 'Gender and Power in African Christianity: African Instituted Churches and Pentecostal Churches.' In *African Christianity: An African Story*, edited by Ogbu U. Kalu, 410-445. Pretoria: University of Pretoria.

Oduyoye, Mercy. *Introducing African Women's Theologies.* London: Sheffield Academic Press, 2001.

______. 'The Search for a Two-Winged Theology: Women's Participation in the Development of Theology in Africa.' In *Talitha Qumi! Proceedings of the Convocation of African Women Theologians*

[21] Peter J. Henriot, 'Grass Root Analysis: The Emphasis on Culture', in *Liberation Theologies on Shifting Grounds,* ed. Georges de Schrijver. (Leuven: Leuven University Press, 1998), 348.

[22] Mercy Amba Oduyoye, 'Ecclesiology in African Women's Perspective', in *On Being Church: African Women's Voices and Visions,* eds. Isabel Apawo Phiri and Sarojini Nadar (Geneva: World Council of Churches, 2005), 152.

1989 (second edition), edited by Mercy Amba Oduyoye and Rachel M. Kanyoro, 31- 56. Accra-North: Sam-Woode Ltd., 2001a.

______. 'Ecclesiology in African Women's Perspective'. In *On Being Church: African Women's Voices and Visions,* edited by Isabel Apawo Phiri and Sarojini Nadar, 146-156. Geneva: World Council of Churches, 2005.

Phiri, Isabel A. 'Major Challenges for African Women Theologians in Theological Education (1989-2008). *Studia Historiae Ecclesiasticae*, XXXIV, no. 2, (2008): 63-81.

(136) African Philosophy and African Christianity[1]

Julius Gathogo

Introduction

African Philosophy is expressed in almost the entire life of an African life. *Ubuntu* is one of the concepts that express it well, despite some of its shortcomings. This chapter sets out to show that the concept of *Ubuntu* (humanness) is an aspect of African hospitality; and in turn, African hospitality and *Ubuntu* are expressions of African Philosophy. The paper demonstrates the wealth of African songs and proverbs in building on African hospitality, and hence African Philosophy. These theologies of reconstruction, in African Christianity, are driven by the need to re-write our own stories; hence reconstruct our past histories, in order to genuinely move forward; and this can be seen as the key to addressing the concerns of our contemporary Africa. The biblical Nehemiah's rebuilding project, following his discovery that the wall of the city of Jerusalem was in ruins after years in Babylonian captivity (refer to the book of Ezra-Nehemiah), serves as an inspiration to these post-exilic theologies. In view of this, the chapter demonstrate the reconstructive impact of *Ubuntu* in the post-colonial Africa.

In view of this, the vital role of African Christianity in the reconstruction of post-colonial Africa, within ideals of African philosophy (*Ubuntu* and hospitality), can be seen especially when we mull over the fact that African cultural practices and philosophical outlook is the raw material for African Christianity. The African philosophical world is a religious world. Christianity in Africa finds itself enriched by the ideals seen in *Ubuntu* philosophy, which is an aspect of African hospitality.

Religion and Philosophy in Africa

In his authoritative book, *African Religions and Philosophy*, John Mbiti discovered that religion and philosophy in Africa are intertwined. In other words, religion and culture, which in Africa are hard to distinguish, express the philosophy of the African people. He noted thus, 'Religion is the strongest element in traditional background, and exerts probably the greatest influence upon the thinking and living of the people concerned.' And while religion can be discerned in terms of beliefs, ceremonies, rituals and religious officiants, 'philosophy is not easily distinguishable'.[2] Mbiti thus uses 'philosophy' to refer to 'the philosophical understanding of African peoples concerning different issues of life'.[3] He goes on to say:

> Philosophy of one kind or another is behind the thinking and acting of every people, and a study of traditional religions brings us into those areas of African life where, through word and action, we may be able to discern the philosophy behind. This involves interpretation of the information before us, and interpretation cannot be completely free of subjective judgement. What, therefore, is 'African Philosophy', may not amount to more than simply my own process of philosophising the items under consideration: but this cannot be helped, and in any case I am by birth an African. Philosophical systems of different African peoples have not been formulated, but some of the areas where they may be found are in the religion, proverbs, oral traditions, ethics and morals of the

---

[1] This is a revised version of an article that first appeared as 'African Philosophy as Expressed in the Concepts of Hospitality and *Ubuntu*', *Journal of Theology for Southern Africa*, 130 (March 2008), 39-53.

[2] John S. Mbiti, *African Religions and Philosophy* (Nairobi: EAEP, 1969), 1.

[3] Mbiti, *African Religions and Philosophy*, 1.

> society concerned… 'African philosophy'… refers to the understanding, attitude of mind, logic and perception behind the manner in which African peoples think, act or speak in different situations of life.[4]

While rightly acknowledging that African religion permeates all the spheres of life, Mbiti however fails to appreciate the same with regard to African hospitality. For in Africa, an ideal person is primarily hospitable. This hospitality is ideally extended to all people: friends, foes, and/or strangers. It is also extended to all areas of life. Thus, in looking at *Ubuntu* (humanness and/or respect for human dignity) as an aspect of African hospitality, one realises that the post-colonial Africa cannot fail to uphold human dignity after stints under the pre-colonial *unyama* or *ubulwane* (that is, animal like behaviour).

What is African Philosophy?

In view of the above, an understanding of what African philosophy is can best be premised on the fact that every human mind works on the principles that are philosophically hinged even though they might not be clear to an individual. If philosophy is defined as love (or reasoning about) wisdom (of the people), then every person has philosophy in him or her, even though one may not be conscious of it, or may never know how to articulate it. To this end, every human society has a philosophy both in the strict and loose sense of the word; for indeed, people's thought systems and actions constitute a philosophy.[5] It is by this premise that the phrase 'African Philosophy' is defined.

In attempting to define 'African philosophy', it is critical to underline the two major schools of philosophical thought that lay a claim in defining it. That is, 'ethno-philosophical school'; and 'professional school'. A brief look at them will suffice. Ethno-philosophy holds that an African philosophy indeed exists; and that it is not a phenomenon that is being created, established or developed. Rather, it is something that needs revelation and interpretation.[6] To this end, ethno-philosophers make a bold statement to their European counterparts that Africans possess a system of thought that reveals a system of philosophy of religion and of cosmology similar to that of Europeans. As a matter of fact, ethno-philosophy came into existence in 1945 following the publication of Placide Tempels' book, *Bantu Philosophy*.[7] This school of philosophy was given the name 'ethno-philosophy' because it attempted to translate African ethnic thought into categories and language of western philosophy. Some of the categories are ontology, substance, essence, and being; while its chief proponents are John Mbiti of Kenya, Alexis Kagame of Rwanda, Tempels, and Marcel Griaule of France. All in all, different ethno-philosophers portray diverse views to qualify and distinguish this philosophy. In particular, Mbiti employs the notion of time,[8] Griaule, the notion of Nommo,[9] and Kagame, the notion of being.[10]

The second category is the 'professional school' of African philosophy. It was started in the 1960s by professionally trained philosophers, all of whom studied philosophy at European universities, and later taught it at African universities.[11] They include Kwasi Wiredu of Ghana, Odera-Oruka of Kenya, and Peter Bodunrin of Nigeria. Accordingly, this school of thought has many elements in common with western philosophy. That is, its mode of argumentation and criticism, plus its insistence that logic, in its strict and academic meaning, is the only tool of philosophising. Again, its emphasis is individualistic, as opposed to

---

[4] Mbiti, *African Religions and Philosophy*, 1-2.
[5] James N. Mburu, *Thematic Issues in African Philosophy* (Nairobi: Acacia, 2003), 1.
[6] Mburu, *Thematic Issues in African Philosophy,* 8.
[7] Placide Tempels, *Bantu Philosophy* (Translated by Rev. Colin King), (Paris: Presence Africaine, 1959, 1969).
[8] Mbiti, *African Religions and Philosophy.*
[9] Marcel Griaule, *Conversations with Ogotommeli* (Translated Dieu d'eau) (London: Oxford University Press, 1965).
[10] Alexis Kagame, *La Philosophie Bantu Compare* (Paris: Presence Africaine, 1976).
[11] Mburu, *Thematic Issues in African Philosophy,* 4.

collective thoughts. It is mainly a personal reflection on specific issues and concepts that are problematic to an individual.[12] Odera-Oruka denies its link with western philosophy when he says:

> There is a tendency to accuse African philosophers such as P. Hountondji,[13] Kwasi Wiredu,[14] Peter Bodunrin[15] and myself of subjecting the criteria of what constitutes African philosophy to the canons of Western philosophy. And according to these accusers, such criteria are embodied in the demand that philosophy must be scientific, foundational, critical, analytical, and systematically reflective. These, we are told, are the characteristics of a western philosophy. And African philosophy would fail to demonstrate its identity if it were to be anchored on such characteristics.[16]

Ethno-philosophers such as Mbiti, Kagame and others, however, insist that African philosophy consists of a body of logically coordinated thought on the nature of the universe, of existence, of humanity, and of the things that surround humanity. This logically coordinated thought is obtained from the interpretation of basic cultural beliefs.[17] To this end, this chapter is in working agreement with ethno-philosophers, that there is a distinct African philosophy, which is expressed in the belief systems among the Africans from time immemorial. Hence, this chapter considers African philosophy as that which is articulated through general acts of hospitality or *Ubuntu*; political ideologies such as Negritude and African Socialism, among others; proverbs that attempt to shed light on the universe, human beings; African stories that attempt to explain the origins of life and death; African rituals that attempt to explain the rites of passage such as birth and marriage; African traditions such as beliefs and attitudes; and African arts such as dance and song.

What is African Hospitality?

Basically, African hospitality can be defined as that extension of generosity, giving freely without strings attached. It can also be seen as 'an unconditional readiness to share'.[18] This sharing has to be social and religious in scope. In view of this, it can be simply seen as the willingness to give, to help, to assist, to love and to carry one another's burden without necessarily putting profit or rewards as the driving force. Oduyoye and Olikenyi link hospitaity with African philosophy when they contend that it shapes and defines the being and the existence of an African person (ontology). In particular, Olikenyi explains that African hospitality, which he contends is a vital aspect of existence in Africa, is one of the few facets of ancient African culture that is still intact and strongly practised today by most Africans in spite of all the forces of recent external influence or even internal pressure.[19] He quotes Uzukwu, who develops this view further when he says:

---

[12] Mburu, *Thematic Issues in African Philosophy,* 5.
[13] See Paulin Hountondji, *African Philosophy: Myth and Reality* (Bloomington: Indiana University Press, 1983).
[14] Kwasi Wiredu, *Philosophy and African Culture* (Cambridge: Cambridge University Press, 1980).
[15] See Peter Bodunrin, 'The Question of African Philosophy', *Philosophy* Vol. 56, No 216, Cambridge University Press, (1981): 161-179.
[16] ee Henry Odera-Oruka, *Practical Philosophy* (Nairobi: East African Educational Publishers, 1997), 167-168; see also Henry Odera-Oruka, *Trends in Contemporary African Philosophy* (Nairobi: Shirikon Publishers, 1990).
[17] See Mbiti, *African Religions and Philosophy.*
[18] A. Echema, *Corporate Personality in Igbo Society and the Sacrament of Reconciliation* (Frankfurt am Main: Peter Lang, 1995), 35.
[19] Gregory I. Olikenyi, *African Hospitality: A model for the Communication of the Gospel in the African Cultural Context* (Nettetal: Steylerverlag, 2001), 102.

> Despite the destabilization of traditional life by colonialism, foreign world views, technology and modern living… African hospitality has held rather well to the extent that it could be described as a way of being an African.[20]

In Oduyoye's view, hospitality is 'inherent in being African, as well as in adhering to a religion that derives from the Bible…' It is 'given a religious meaning, and linked with the ancestors, Christ and God.'[21] Similarly, Moila sees African hospitality as that which embodies the entire philosophy of African peoples. To begin with, he defines it as simply African cultural and moral values, which are not theoretical, but a way of life.[22] This indicates that the understanding of hospitality is as wide as that of the concept of religion in African permeating all spheres of African life.[23]

While defining African hospitality as the brotherhood or sisterhood 'between the members of the same family group and/or of the same clan,' Moila goes on to say that:

> Each member of the same family group is bound to offer food and shelter to any member of his or her group who needs it. However, it is also an African custom to offer hospitality even to strangers. Hospitality is perceived and practised by Africans as open-handed, instinctive and the most natural thing in the world.[24]

By saying that hospitality as practised by Africans is 'instinctive and the most natural thing in the world', Moila is alluding to the fact that African hospitality is more unique in comparison to other versions that are practised in many other parts of the world, especially in Europe and North America.

> On the whole, the study of hospitality, in Africa today, is crucial considering that it is not seen as a mere academic issue that is simply exercised by 'arm-chair' practitioners; but rather, as a reconstructive and practical element in post-colonial Africa that remains a common denominator to all regardless of our educational backgrounds. To this end, it can be exploited positively to build better relationships among various peoples living in continental Africa. It can also be used to conscientize people on the need to work hard so that they can have something to be hospitable with. Clearly, revisiting this element of culture (hospitality) is critical in our times; for indeed, it is an idea whose time has come. Clearly, it is in tandem with St Paul's words in Roman 15:7 'welcome one another as Christ has welcomed you'.

Ubuntu Philosophy

In the social domain, *Ubuntu* philosophy can best illustrate African hospitality. As an aspect of African hospitality, *Ubuntu* enriches African philosophy by its clear and concise way in which it expresses the thinking of the ideal African person (*Muntu*). In various publications, it is critical to underline that *Ubuntu* has been referred to as *Ubuntu* philosophy. Why? It embodies the positive thinking of the Africans. Nevertheless, this reference takes us back to our introductory definition of 'African Philosophy'. In other words, can we talk of 'African philosophy'? Are Africans capable of philosophising in quite the same way as we talk of Greek philosophy or Indian philosophy or Chinese or even European philosophy? Is the traditional African mind capable of philosophising? And must African philosophy be on a par with western philosophy?

This debate, however, started over 200 years ago when the renowned German idealist, G.F. Hegel (1770-1831), in his famous *Philosophy of History* ignored Africa, as he argued that Africans were

---

[20] Uzukwu quoted in Olikenyi, *African hospitality:* 102.
[21] Mercy A. Oduyoye, *Introducing African Women's Theology*. (Sheffield: Sheffield Academic Press, 2001), 94.
[22] Moeahabo Phillip Moila, *Challenging Issues in African Christianity* (Pretoria: CB Powell Bible Centre, 2002), 1.
[23] Compare Mbiti, *African Religions and Philosophy*, 1-2.
[24] Moila, *Challenging Issues in African Christianity,* 2.

incapable of philosophising. Seen from that perspective, he felt that they deserved no place in his research on philosophy through the history of the peoples of the world. Similar, such racial biases are evident in the works of Lucien Levy-Bruhl's, *The Notebooks on Primitive Mentality*; J.C. Carothers', *The Mind of Man*; and Dietrich Westermann's, *The African Today*.[25] In acknowledging *Ubuntu* as one of the expressions of African philosophy, we are puzzled that a philosopher of Hegel's status could pass a wholesale judgement on the African mind. Hence an attempt at correcting Hegel's error. For indeed, there is no tenable logical basis for his polemical position, which denied traditional Africans, philosophy, culture, history or even religion.

In defining *Ubuntu* as an aspect of African hospitality or as a philosophy, it is important to stress that the concept is described differently among the various African communities. For instance, it is called *Unhu* among the Shona of Zimbabwe; *Ubuntu* among the Nguni speakers of Southern Africa; *Utu* among the Swahili speakers of East Africa; and *Umundu* among the Kikuyu of Kenya. Basically, it is both a philosophical and a religious concept that defines the individual in terms of his or her relationships with others. In the African context, it suggests that the person one is to become, by behaving with humanity, is an ancestor worthy of respect or veneration. In other words, those who uphold the principle of *Ubuntu* throughout their earthly lives will be rewarded or promoted in death by becoming ancestors. In turn, they will achieve a unity with those still living.[26]

African Philosophical Concepts and African Christianity

As noted, African philosophical concepts such as *Ubuntu* which is an aspect of African hospitality enriches African Christianity, especially in its emphasis on respect and love for 'the other'. By 'the other' is meant the love of one's neighbour, the love for those who are not like us, the underprivileged, the marginal, the minorities, the poor, the rich and others. This resonates well with the eight beatitudes that were uttered by Christ as recorded in Matthew 5:3-12, during the Sermon on the Mount. This is especially the case when we consider the fifth beatitude: 'Blessed are the merciful: for they will be shown mercy.' Certainly, *Ubuntu* philosophy is a spiritual foundation of African societies. It is a unifying vision or worldview enshrined in the Nguni maxim *Umuntu ngumuntu ngabantu*, that is, 'a person is a person through other persons'.[27] This *Ubuntu* concept is also found in other African communities, even though there are different vocabularies and phrases that are used to describe it; and it will suffice to illustrate it by citing a few examples. The Kikuyu idiom, which says that, *Mundu ni mundu ni undu wa andu,* means that, 'a human being is a person because of the other people'. The same can be said of the Sotho whose idiom says that, *Motho ke motho ka batho ba bang* with a similar translation to those of other African communities. It is also the same as *Munhu munhu nekuda kwevanhu* among the Shona of Zimbabwe. This African motto articulates a basic respect and compassion for others – as its bottom line. It can be interpreted as both a factual description and a rule of conduct or social ethic. It both describes human being as 'being-with-others' and prescribes what 'being-with-others' should be all about. As such, *Ubuntu* has a certain Africanness and religious commitment in the welfare of fellow human beings that is manifestly African in essence.

As an African philosophy, *Ubuntu* expresses the African sense of community. That is, instead of, 'I think, therefore I exist' (*cogito, ergo sum*) of the French philosopher René Descartes, the African asserts, 'I am because we are' or 'I am related, therefore, I am' (*cognatus ergo sum* or an existential *cognatus sum, ergo sumus,* meaning *I am related, therefore we are*).[28] This compares with Mbiti's summary of the

[25] See Cletus N. Chukwu, *Introduction to Philosophy in an African Perspective* (Eldoret: Zapf Chancery, 1995), 301ff.
[26] Kwesi. A. Dickson, *Theology in Africa*, (Marykholl: Orbis Books TTCL, 1984), 198; cf. Mbiti, *African Religions and Philosophy*, 83.
[27] Augustine Shutte, *Ubuntu: An Ethic for a New South Africa.* (Pietermaritzburg: Cluster Publications, 2001), 46.
[28] *cf.* Julius Gathogo, *The Truth About African Hospitality: Is there Hope for Africa?* (Mombasa: The Salt, 2001), 21.

philosophy underlying the African way of life, thus: 'I am, because we are; and since we are, therefore I am.'[29] The Akan of Ghana would say, 'I belong by blood relationship; therefore I am.'[30] Indeed, this parallels the concretisation of the Being (*Sein*) as Being-with in the *Dasein* Analytic in Martin Heidegger's 'Philosophy of Being'.[31]

In seeing *Ubuntu* as that which expresses the African sense of community, we are driven to appreciate that *Ubuntu* philosophy, just like African Christianity, addresses holistic living, and especially contemporary issues. In other words, what can one say about *Ubuntu* and clan systems, blood relatives, women, corruption and reconstruction? Why do we find many acts of *unyama* or *ubulwane* (animal-like behaviours) in a continent that is a hundred percent *Ubuntu*? The same question can be posed in another way: why do we find corruption, xenophobia, racism, ethnic animosities, gender disparities and other vices in a continent that boasts of being the most Christian in the 21st century? Seen in this way, Africa's humane philosophies speak from the same continuum with African Christianity. Indeed, their ideals of human fellowship and communality are basically the same. Put differently, African philosophies and African Christianities are not opposed to one another; rather, they enrich one another. In the light of the post-colonial reconstruction of Africa, African Christianity and African philosophies will be critical in rebuilding the declining or broken African walls in terms of governance, education, economy, leadership, ecology and gender relations. As in the words of Nehemiah 2:18, African philosophies resonate well with the call: 'Let us start [re]building.'

To this end, Charles Villa-Vicencio contends that South Africa would do well in establishing a 'heritage, which proclaims a message about human nature which provides an alternative to both western notions of individualism and ideological Marxist perceptions of collectivism'.[32] In view of this, Villa-Vicencio for example, sees the reconstruction of post-apartheid South African society as needing the people to transcend both the individualism and collectivism in order to form an all-inclusive and all-encompassing community. This, to him, is the ideal notion of *Ubuntu.*

Facilitating a process of reconstruction means being willing to reason out together as human beings who value other persons; and therefore being willing to work towards a better society that not only respects human dignity; but more importantly a holistic and prosperous society for all. For as Robert Schreiter notes, reconstruction is 'a different kind of liberating theology, because the opportunity for it is so rare'.[33] For whether we are in Somalia, Democratic Republic of Congo, Liberia, Rwanda, South Africa, Eastern Europe, Chile, Argentina or elsewhere – it is a moment of grace that should not be bypassed.'[34]

Conclusion

The chapter has attempted a definition of African philosophy. It revisited the two major African schools of philosophical thoughts that lay a claim to defining philosopy. That is, 'ethno-philosophical school'; and 'professional school'. And by dialoguing with both concepts of *Ubuntu* and hospitality, the chapter demonstrates that African philosophy is essentially one of the definite components of African culture. In this sense, African philosophy cannot be construed as that which represents the entire constituents of what is comprehensible as African culture. Indeed, they are not synonymous. Some interrelations however exist

[29] Mbiti, *African Religions and Philosophy*: 108.
[30] Joseph Healey and Donald F. Sybertz, *Towards An African Narrative Theology* (Nairobi: Paulines, 1996), 62.
[31] Martin Heidegger, *Sein und Zeit, Marx Niemeyer Verlag Türbingen* (Siebzehnte Auflage, 1993), 117-125.
[32] Charles Villa-Vicencio, 'Telling One Another Stories: Toward a Theology of Reconciliation', in *The Reconciliation of Peoples: Challenge to the Churches*, (New York: Orbis Books, 1997), 164.
[33] Robert J. Schreiter, *The New Catholicity: Theology between the Global and the Local* (Maryknoll, New York: Orbis Books, 1999), 110.
[34] Schreiter, *The New Catholicity: Theology between the Global and the Local*, 110-112.

between both concepts; and by critiquing *Ubuntu* in not fully 'including' African women in its schema of its all-embracing humanisation, the chapter has in turn demonstrated the task of African philosophy as that of scrutinising and evaluating the standards of African culture with its implied values.

Following the ideals of African Christianity as seen in Jesus' call for the love of 'the other' (Mark 12:31), African philosophies will be critical in, not only combating xenophobia, corruption, gender imbalances, and ethnic decisions but, more importantly, in facilitating the social reconstruction of Africa. For in recalling ancient hospitality and philosophies as an 'agenda' of our time, this points to the fact that the ancestral resources are critical in the reconstruction of our beloved continent. Certainly, this is the time to rewrite our history and reinterpret it in a relevant fashion. Clearly, these African philosophical resources have something to bequeath to Christianity in Africa and to the rest of the world.

Bibliography

Bodunrin, P. 'The Question of African Philosophy,' *Philosophy* Vol. 56, No 216, Cambridge University Press, (1981): 161-179.

Chukwu, C. N. *Introduction to Philosophy in an African Perspective*. Eldoret: Zapf Chancery, 1995.

Echema, A. *Corporate Personality in Igbo Society and the Sacrament of Reconciliation*. Frankfurt am Main: Peter Lang, 1995.

Gathogo, J. *The Truth About African Hospitality: Is there Hope for Africa?* Mombasa: The Salt, 2001

Griaule, M. *Conversations with Ogotommeli* (Translated Dieu d'eau). London: Oxford University Press, 1965.

Healey, J and Sybertz, D. *Towards An African Narrative Theology*. Nairobi: Paulines, 1996.

Heidegger, M. *Sein und Zeit, Marx Niemeyer Verlag Türbingen* (Siebzehnte Auflage, 1993.

Hountondji, P. *African Philosophy: Myth and Reality*. Bloomington: Indiana University Press, 1983.

Kagame, A. *La Philosophie Bantu Compare*. Paris: Presence Africaine, 1976.

Mbiti, J. S. *African Religions and Philosophy*. Nairobi: EAEP, 1969.

Mburu, J. N. *Thematic Issues in African Philosophy*. Nairobi: Acacia, 2003.

Moila, M. P. *Challenging Issues in African Christianity*. Pretoria: CB Powell Bible Centre, 2002.

Odera-Oruka, H. *Practical Philosophy*. Nairobi: East African Educational Publishers, 1997.

Oduyoye, M. A. *Introducing African Women's Theology*. Sheffield: Sheffield Academic Press, 2001.

Olikenyi, G. I. *African Hospitality: A model for the Communication of the Gospel in the African Cultural Context*. Nettetal: Steylerverlag, 2001.

Schreiter, R. J. *The New Catholicity: Theology between the Global and the Local*. Maryknoll, New York: Orbis Books, 1999.

Tempels, P. *Bantu Philosophy* (Translated by Rev. Colin King). Presence Africaine, Paris, 1959, 1969.

Wiredu, K. *Philosophy and African Culture*. Cambridge: Cambridge University Press, 1980.

PART VII

THE PUBLIC ROLE OF AFRICAN CHRISTIANITY

(137) African Christianity and Development: The Case of ACT Alliance[1]

Isaiah Kipyegon Toroitich

ACT Alliance Understanding of Development

When ACT Alliance was founded in 2010, it committed itself, among other things, to be engaged in high quality and effective transformational development programmes that contribute towards positive change in people's lives.[2] The Alliance's understanding of transformational development is drawn from its theological affirmation that all persons are created in the image of God, with the right and potential to live just, humane, and dignified lives in sustainable communities.[3]

This conceptualisation and understanding of development, which was also espoused strongly by ACT International and ACT Development,[4] therefore calls for working more towards a transformation that protects the dignity of communities. ACT Alliance finds its inspiration from the Christian faith, which challenges all to reject conditions, structures and systems that perpetuate poverty, injustice and violation of human rights.[5]

ACT Alliance also uses the Rights-Based Approach (RBA) to development, which is about deliberately and explicitly focusing on achieving the minimum conditions required for people to live with dignity. It does so by exposing the root causes of vulnerability and marginalisation, while empowering people to claim and exercise their rights and fulfil their responsibilities. RBA recognises poor people as having inherent rights essential to livelihood security – rights that are validated by international standards and laws. As Action Aid describes it, people are denied their human rights, not through mere omission, forgetfulness or lack of effort, but due to unequal power relations.[6] RBA thus involves the transformation of power relations, by empowering rights holders and strengthening the accountability and capacity of duty bearers.

In its approach and conceptualisation of development, ACT has twelve key concepts that undergird its development policy and practice: participation, empowerment, capacity development, non-discrimination, gender equity, cultural and spiritual sensitivity, reaffirming human rights, advocacy, promoting peace, reconciliation and right relationships, effective communication, environmental sustainability, and over-consumption and lack of sharing.[7] These twelve concepts broaden the methodology of implementing development work for ACT Alliance, its members and partners, to include development practice and development policy. This enables ACT Alliance to integrate its programmatic work with advocacy at all levels. In addition, as a humanitarian network, ACT Alliance has integrated its development work and

---

[1] ACT Alliance is a network of 146 churches and church-based organisations from protestant and orthodox traditions, undertaking humanitarian, development and advocacy work in 140 countries.

[2] ACT Alliance, "ACT Alliance – Action by Churches Together Founding Document," www.actalliance.org/resources/policies-and-guidelines/legal-documents/ACT-founding-doc-ENG.pdf

[3] ACT Alliance, "Our Understanding of Development," www.actalliance.org/resources/policies-and-guidelines/our-understanding-of-development/Our_Understanding_of_Dev_ACTD-ACTA_ENGLISH_Jan2013.pdf

[4] ACT International and ACT Development were the predecessors of ACT Alliance. The two were merged in 2010 to form the unified ACT Alliance.

[5] ACT Alliance, "Founding Document."

[6] Action Aid, "Human rights-based approaches to poverty eradication and development," www.actionaid.org/sites/files/actionaid/the_rights_based_approach.pdf.

[7] ACT, "Our Understanding of Development."

advocacy with its disaster risk reduction work. This is elaborated in the Alliance's understanding of 'linking relief, rehabilitation and development' (LRRD).

In the spirit of LRRD, ACT Alliance recognises that implementation of a humanitarian response should not only meet immediate humanitarian needs but do so in a manner that ensures capacity and supports general conditions for recovery and long-term development.[8] The integrated approach also demands linking work at the grassroots to national, regional and international levels. In both cases, the Alliance recognises and emphasises the centrality of communities.

According to ACT Alliance's Global Strategy 2015-2018,[9] economic power is gradually shifting from the global North to the growing economies in the global East and the South. Emerging economies, such as China, India, Brazil and others, play new roles as donors and in international trade, while they face growing inequalities within their own countries.

Several countries and regions are plagued by protracted resource conflicts, war-lordism, large displacements and shrinking space for civil society organisations, adding to the already growing complexity of emergencies and sustainable development. Climate change, population growth, rapid and unplanned urbanisation as well as food and water insecurity, leave communities increasingly at risk of crisis. Extreme weather events are reported to intensify and cause increasingly climate-induced displacement.

In a sense, these analyses and discussions have affected how ACT Alliance understands and does development, all over the world, but specifically in Africa, where a majority of its members operate.

ACT Alliance in Africa

By the middle of 2015, approximately ninety member organisations of ACT Alliance worked in Africa. These include organisations whose origin is Africa, and others which do not come from Africa but either run or support development projects on the continent. Much of the work done by ACT Alliance in Africa is in the sub-Saharan region. In Africa, as in all other parts of the world, the members of ACT Alliance have organised themselves into national and regional forums, which are platforms that bring together members working within a specific country or region. Churches have a central role in the work of the Alliance, given the Alliance's primary identity as a church-based network.

To explore the work of ACT Alliance in Africa, it is necessary to begin by examining the context, in terms of development issues, of the continent. Africa is still grappling with high levels of poverty, which ranks as one of its key challenges. According to Martin, while Africa's recent economic performance has been quite impressive, the economic growth has not delivered corresponding benefits in terms of poverty reduction. He attributed this discrepancy to, among other things, the failure of African economies to generate sufficient productive employment.[10]

Most of ACT Alliance's development work focuses on poverty eradication. The Alliance acknowledges that poverty is mainly driven by a myriad of root causes, including historical and current injustices, inequality, bad governance, corruption, and destruction of the environment.[11] In undertaking development

[8] ACT Alliance, "ACT Alliance Response to an Emergency: Policy, Guidelines and Tools, and Annexes," www.actalliance.org/resources/policies-and-guidelines/act-response-mechanisms/act-alliance-response-to-emergencies/Response_to_Emergencies_ApprDraft_Dec11.pdf

[9] ACT Alliance, *Full Life and Dignity for All: Global Strategy 2015-2018, a Framework for Action*. Geneva: ACT Alliance, 2014.

[10] Pedro Martins, "Growth, Employment and Poverty in Africa: Tales of Lions and Cheetahs," http://siteresources.worldbank.org/EXTNWDR2013/Resources/8258024-1320950747192/8260293-1320956712276/8261091-1348683883703/WDR2013_bp_Growth_Employment_and_Poverty_in_Africa.pdf.

[11] ACT, "Our Understanding of Development."

work, therefore, ACT Alliance and its members support the empowerment of communities affected by poverty and oppressive structures to claim their rights, whilst seeking the transformation of values and structures that lead to over-consumption and lack of sharing of the available resources.

For the purpose of this paper, four examples where ACT Alliance has undertaken development work in Africa will be highlighted. The cases will only be briefly described, without giving detailed analysis. The cases are: strengthening women's participation in Mali; peace and development in South Sudan; economic justice and development in Southern Africa; and mobilisation for environment and climate justice.

Strengthening Women's Participation in Mali

In Mali, ACT member, Norwegian Church Aid (NCA), together with five local organisations, have been working on the issue of governance, with a focus on the role of women in leadership structures. This is in a context where women do not have the opportunity to take up leadership roles, in spite of their contribution to society. In 2005, NCA and its partners in Mali conducted a baseline survey which confirmed that only 10% of parliamentarians, 6.5% of municipal councillors, and less than 1% of mayors were women.[12] It was particularly clear in Mali's northern regions of Kidal, Gao and Timbuktu that women were unable to exercise their right to engage in political processes. This project further engaged in expansive consultation processes with women, to gain their views on the question of political participation.

Consequently, the primary interventions under this project were to mobilise women into leadership roles, develop strategic partnerships with organisations that worked on governance and women's rights, raise public awareness and ultimately support women who were ready and willing to vie for elective positions in government at all levels. The immediate opportunity to measure the success of this project was in the 2009 general elections in Mali.

As part of the strategy, the programme mobilised women into groups, reaching over 30,000 women in the region. This was followed by capacity strengthening of the women who were members of the groups, on issues such as democracy, human rights, decentralised governance, women leadership and advocacy. It is within this group that women political candidates were identified and nurtured.

By the end of 2009, this initiative had resulted in a 54% increase in the number of women seeking elective positions, and a 42% increase in the number of women elected as councillors. In addition, the project had also contributed to a greater level of acceptance of women in decision making, and their right to participate politically.[13]

Mali, as a predominantly Muslim country, is an important case for ACT Alliance, which is a Christian network. It showcases the Alliance's commitment to the principle of impartiality – responding to human suffering irrespective of race, gender, belief, nationality, ethnicity or political persuasion.

Other parts of Africa where ACT Alliance members have engaged in issues related to women and governance include Kenya, where the National Council of Churches and the Anglican Development Services – Kenya, in partnership with international and national organisations, worked with election processes as well as the constitutional review process.

Peace and Development in Sudan and South Sudan

As a big credit to the work of churches during the conflict in Sudan (before the birth of South Sudan), Stein Villumstad,[14] then the regional representative for Norwegian Church Aid in Eastern Africa, reported that

[12] ACT Alliance. *Clapping with Both Hands: Promoting Gender Equality."* www.actalliance.org/resources/publications/ACT_Gender_Good-Practice-Report_%202012.pdf.

[13] ACT Alliance, "Clapping with Both Hands."

[14] Stein Villumstad, *Social Reconstruction of Africa: Perspectives from Within and Without* (Nairobi: Acton

throughout the more than two-decades-long war and conflict there were only two recognisable entities in the south: the churches and the Sudanese People's Liberation Movement/Army (SPLM/A). He further gave a strong profile of the role of organisations such as the World Council on Religion and Peace, All Africa Conference of Churches and others in peace and conflict resolutions efforts in Sudan. Practically all the members of ACT Alliance in Kenya, Ethiopia and Uganda contributed in one way or another to peace-building and conflict resolution in Sudan, particularly in the process leading to the Comprehensive Peace Agreement (CPA) between the government of Sudan and the People's Liberation Movement/Army in 2005.

The CPA, and the processes surrounding it, led to the creation of the new country, South Sudan, which was a dream-come-true for many people. Unfortunately, the new country has been bedevilled by many challenges, including continued insecurity and a tumultuous political and humanitarian situation.

Organisations like the Lutheran World Federation (LWF), a global member of ACT Alliance, have carried out humanitarian and development work in South Sudan right from the start, in conjunction with churches and related organisations. LWF has specifically worked to support refugees and internally displaced people fleeing conflict and violence in South Sudan. In conformity with ACT's selection of South Sudan as a priority country for the strategic period 2011-2014, a number of other organisations, both regional and international, have invested significantly in development programmes and in the humanitarian response and peace and reconciliation efforts. They include DanChurchAid (DCA), Norwegian Church Aid (NCA), Inter-Church Organisation for Development Co-operation (ICCO), Christian Aid (CA), Sudan Council of Churches (SCC), World Renew and Swiss Church Aid.

In terms of long-term development work, DanChurchAid has implemented mine-clearing projects and helped local communities and authorities dispose of explosive remnants of war, including mines and unexploded artillery shells. According to DCA,[15] landmines and Explosive Remnants of War (ERW) pose a serious danger to civilians and humanitarian actors in South Sudan, and especially to internally displaced people (IDPs). These weapons make it nearly impossible for communities to pursue their daily lives and livelihoods. Following the recent political violence that erupted in late 2013 and led to the displacement of over 700,000, the need for education on disposal of landmines and other ordinances increased drastically, particularly because the displaced people often found themselves in unfamiliar areas, which may have land mines.

Through the implementation of the project activities, DCA provided life-saving risk education in Awerial County, Lakes State, where over 85,000 displaced civilians had taken refuge.[16] In addition to this, the DCA project provided briefings to UN and NGO staff that were engaged in humanitarian assistance in the area. DCA has implemented Mine Action activities from its regional base in Juba since 2012 and thus has a solid base in South Sudan.

In Darfur, Sudan, ACT Alliance, in partnership with Caritas Internationalis, has undertaken a large scale, multi-sectoral humanitarian programme since July 2004. According to a joint report of the two networks, the Darfur programme is unique because it has pooled human and financial resources from both networks into one organisational management structure, and because of its vastness, with over US$120 million being raised and expended between 2004 and 2014. It is estimated that the beneficiary population has been as high as 500,000 people in the initial years and in recent years, around 350,000 people.[17]

Publishers, 2001).

[15] DanChurchAid, "Mine Action Activities Extended at a Crucial Moment," https://www.danchurchaid.org/news/news/mine-action-activities-extended-at-a-crucial-moment-chf-gives-further-funding-for-dca-s-work-in-south-sudan.

[16] DanChurchAid, "Mine Action."

[17] ACT Alliance & Caritas Internationalis, *A History of the Joint ACT-Caritas Darfur Programme*, Geneva, ACT

Other instances where ACT Alliance and church communities and leaders played a key role in peace and development in Africa include the conflict between Ethiopia and Eritrea, the truth, justice and reconciliation process in post-apartheid South Africa and the conflict situation in Sierra Leone. In all these cases, national, regional and international faith-based organisations (FBOs) took up the responsibility to midwife reconciliation.[18]

Economic Justice and Development

Anglican Development Services – Kenya, for the last ten years or more, worked on economic justice issues including fair trade, international debt, justice for coffee farmers and the cash crop value chain. In partnership with other FBOs and NGOs, the organisation advocated for the halting of the proposed Economic Partnership Agreements (EPAs), a free trade area agreement that would lead to an unfair and unbalanced opening up of the African market to goods and services from the European Union.[19] This advocacy and campaigning for economic justice also forged good programming partnerships between ACT members operating in Kenya and their many partners, such as the establishment of the Kenya Small Coffee Growers Association (KESCOGA), which supports the capacity of small scale coffee farmers. An evaluation of the KESCOGA project found that the initiative had made a significant contribution in providing new insights into what had been going on in the coffee industry in Kenya from a historical perspective.[20]

In Southern Africa, ACT Alliance members Economic Justice Network, Church of Sweden, and church councils in SADC region, under the umbrella of the Southern African Regional Forum (SARF), have for the last six years been organising the Alternative Mining Indaba, which is a public forum to discuss issues related to mining and how it affects communities. Alternative Mining Indabas are organised in parallel with the annual international Cape Town Mining Indaba, which brings together mining companies, business and governments to strategize. At the Alternative Mining Indaba, people from all over the world, representing communities that are affected by mining, share testimonies, research and exchange ideas on human rights and justice in the context of extractive industries.[21]

This initiative has grown and become a well-recognised annual forum for people and communities, as well as civil society and churches working on mining and extractive industries. It has further become a strong advocacy tool, enabling ACT members, churches and partners to engage with governments and multi-national companies. In this regard, in 2012, ACT members played a key role in the mediation and negotiations that led to the end of the high-profile dispute at the Lonmin platinum mine in Marikana, South Africa.[22]

Still on the question of economic justice and development, members of ACT Alliance in Mozambique implemented a microcredit project, which led to the promotion of equality through savings and credit unions targeted at women. The microfinance project was supported by ACT member, the Primate's World Relief and Development Fund. From the onset, the project aimed at reducing household poverty, while at the same time giving women the opportunity to run a financial institution that catered for their needs.

Alliance 2015.

[18] Villumstad, "Social Reconstruction of Africa."

[19] Ongwen, Oduor, *"Engaging Economic Partnership Agreements: Critical Issues for Africa"* (Nairobi: Beacon, 2007).

[20] NORAD, "Small Scale Coffee Farmers Project: Evaluation Report," www.norad.no/globalassets/import-2162015-80434-am/www.norad.no-ny/filarkiv/ngo-evaluations/15a-evaluation-of-the-beacon-coffee-advocacy-initiative-2008-kenya.pdf.

[21] ACT Alliance, *Strength in a Changing world: ACT Alliance Annual Report* (Geneva: ACT Alliance, 2012).

[22] ACT Alliance, *Strength in a Changing World.*

The project area covered Nampula, Nacala and Pemba regions of Mozambique, where women had little or no access to banking facilities. It was inspired by a group of women in 1996, who wanted a loan to support their cassava cake business. These women became the very first 47 members of the microcredit initiative. By 2012, the initiative had 4,500 members, and a majority of the loans taken by the women were used to set up businesses, or expand existing ones.[23]

The success of this project has been attributed to the integration of key development policy and best practice, such as empowerment and capacity building, gender equality, rootedness and a keen understanding of the local context.[24]

Mobilising for Environment and Climate Justice

Africa is among the regions of the world that is most affected by the impacts of climate change, and is extremely vulnerable to environmental degradation. For most members of ACT Alliance in Africa, just like for many churches and faith-based organisations, engagement with climate change policy and politics increased significantly in 2006, when the 12th Conference of the Parties (COP 12) to the United Nation Framework Convention on Climate Change (UNFCCC) was held in Nairobi, Kenya. COP 12 ushered in a new era of mobilisation, led by organisations such as the All Africa Council of Churches, ecumenical movements in Africa, and ACT members active in Kenya, including Christian Aid, Norwegian Church Aid, Bread for the World, Anglican Development Services – Kenya and Church of Sweden.

Since then, ACT Alliance in Africa has followed the negotiations under the UNFCCC and engaged in national and regional level advocacy towards governments in Africa and regional bodies such as the African Union and Southern Africa Development Community. The approach that the Alliance has used in Africa is primarily around mobilisation and advocacy, as well as the implementation of community programmes that address climate change adaptation and mitigation.

One of the most significant contributions of ACT Alliance was in 2011, when the continent hosted another Conference of the Parties; this time the 17th session (COP 17) in Durban, South Africa. Throughout the year, members of the Alliance in Eastern and Southern Africa participated in key mobilisation activities, including several high profile events like the international faith leaders' conference on climate justice and sustainable peace in Africa.

In addition, a convoy of 160 youth from Africa, supported by a few young people from the global ecumenical family, made its way from Nairobi to Durban in a climate justice caravan. The caravan, which was under the banner 'We Have Faith, Act Now for Climate Justice' mobilisation, targeted youth and faith communities and leaders with key activities such as awareness raising, capacity-building and political sensitisation towards COP 17.

It was received by the Archbishop Emeritus Desmond Tutu and the petitions collected were handed over to the UNFCCC Executive Secretary, Christiana Figueres.

The members of ACT and other ecumenical partners have consistently worked towards highlighting the vulnerability of Africa to the impacts of climate change, and to call on governments and the international community to look at climate change from justice, moral and ethical perspectives. Climate change has since remained firmly on the agenda of the churches and many ACT members in Africa continue to prioritise it in their work.

In Ethiopia, for example, the Lutheran World Federation's Department for World Service implemented several projects that assisted communities to better prepare for droughts that occur as a result of a changing climate. The project supported pastoralist communities in Oromia region, Dawe District, to harvest rain

---

[23] ACT Alliance, *Clapping with Both Hands: Promoting Gender Equality* (Geneva: ACT Alliance, 2012).

[24] ACT Alliance, *Clapping with Both Hands*.

water, as a protective measure against drought.[25] By 2009, the project had constructed three large ponds with a capacity of 15, 35 and 18 million litres respectively. This ensured that there was water during the dry period, and that communities would not need to migrate in search of water.

Conclusion

The ACT Alliance's strategic direction indicates that the Rights-Based Approach to development will continue to be central in the Alliance's work. The economic inequality, conflicts and fragility of states and weak governance structures require continued engagement with both rights holders and duty bearers.[26] Churches and organisations whose work is mandated by churches have significant influence and leverage towards decision makers and communities. Therefore, in Africa, the ecumenical movement needs to continue supporting transformation of power relations at all levels. As shown by the examples of work undertaken by ACT Alliance in Africa, churches in Africa are often in a unique position to challenge decision makers and accompany communities. This dual role is central to the prophetic mission of the ecumenical movement in Africa.

The cases above also show that insecurity is a challenge for many humanitarian and development actors in many parts of Africa, calling for a focus on the security of personnel, particularly local and national staff. In spite of this, locally-rooted organisations such as churches and community-based organisations, including members of ACT Alliance, are often well positioned to operate.

Addressing humanitarian and development issues in Africa is increasingly seen primarily as the role of Africans themselves. ACT Alliance and other ecumenical organisations should prioritise support for preparedness, innovation and capacity in Africa. It is expected that the situation of communities in African countries, particularly those affected by conflicts and protracted emergencies, will remain dire. Given the changing development and humanitarian funding landscape, there is a need to mobilise resources, including within the continent, to ensure that these communities are served. This will continue to be a challenge for churches and networks, including ACT Alliance. In this regard, advocacy is required in order to ensure financial and technical support for local and national level initiatives.

Bibliography

ACT Alliance, 'ACT Alliance – Action by Churches Together Founding Document,' www.actalliance.org/resources/policies-and-guidelines/legal-documents/ACT-founding-doc-ENG.pdf (accessed 4 July 2015).

ACT Alliance, 'Our Understanding of Development': www.actalliance.org/resources/policies-and-guidelines/our-understanding-of-development/Our_Understanding_of_Dev_ACTD-ACTA_ENGLISH_Jan2013.pdf (accessed 7 July 2015).

ACT Alliance, 'ACT Alliance Response to an Emergency: Policy, Guidelines and Tools, and Annexes,' www.actalliance.org/resources/policies-and-guidelines/act-response-mechanisms/act-alliance-response-to-emergencies/Response_to_Emergencies_ApprDraft_Dec11.pdf (accessed 20 July 2015).

ACT Alliance. *Full Life and Dignity for All: Global Strategy 2015-2018, a Framework for Action.* Geneva: ACT Alliance, 2014.

ACT Alliance. 'Clapping with Both Hands: Promoting Gender Equality': www.actalliance.org/resources/publications/ACT_Gender_Good-Practice-Report_%202012.pdf (accessed 10 July 2015).

[25] ACT Alliance, *Tacking Climate Change, Communities Making a Difference* (Geneva: ACT Alliance, 2009).

[26] ACT Alliance, *Full Life and Dignity for All: Global Strategy 2015-2018, a Framework for Action* (Geneva: ACT Alliance, 2014).

ACT Alliance & Caritas Internationalis. *A History of the Joint ACT-Caritas Darfur Programme.* Geneva: ACT Alliance 2015.

ACT Alliance. *Strength in a Changing World: ACT Alliance Annual Report*. Geneva: ACT Alliance, 2012.

ACT Alliance. *Tacking Climate Change, Communities Making a Difference*. Geneva: ACT Alliance, 2009.

Action Aid, 'Human Rights-Based Approaches to Poverty Eradication and Development': www.actionaid.org/sites/files/actionaid/the_rights_based_approach.pdf (accessed 10 July 2015).

DanChurchAid, 'Mine Action Activities Extended at a Crucial Moment': https://www.danchurchaid.org/news/news/mine-action-activities-extended-at-a-crucial-moment-chf-gives-further-funding-for-dca-s-work-in-south-sudan (accessed 14 July 2015).

Martins, Pedro. 'Growth, Employment and Poverty in Africa: Tales of Lions and Cheetahs': http://siteresources.worldbank.org/EXTNWDR2013/Resources/8258024-1320950747192/8260293-1320956712276/8261091-1348683883703/WDR2013_bp_Growth_Employment_and_Poverty_in_Africa.pdf (accessed 13 July 2015).

NORAD, 'Small Scale Coffee Farmers Project: Evaluation Report', www.norad.no/globalassets/import-2162015-80434-am/www.norad.no-ny/filarkiv/ngo-evaluations/15a-evaluation-of-the-beacon-coffee-advocacy-initiative-2008-kenya.pdf (accessed 7 July 2015).

Ongwen, Oduor, 'Engaging Economic Partnership Agreements: Critical Issues for Africa'. Nairobi: Beacon, 2007.

Villumstad, Stein. *Social Reconstruction of Africa: Perspectives from Within and Without.* Nairobi: Acton Publishers, 2001.

(138) Development, the Bible and the Role of the African Church[1]

McGlory Speckman

Introduction

This chapter primarily reflects on two aspects of development, namely, its definition and biblical concepts thereof. Secondarily, it briefly outlines the role played by the African Church in development. It argues that the ambivalent role of the church in respect of development is partly caused by the church's misaligned understanding of development, and partly by the lack of a biblical concept of development. The conclusion suggests that a closer look at the practice of the African Indigenous Churches and Pentecostal Churches be undertaken in future studies as this offers a different and interesting perspective of the African Church's role in development.

It is almost four decades since the World Council of Churches identified the church as an important grassroots vehicle for development.[2] Yet Africa, which at one point was thought to be 'notoriously religious',[3] is one of the few continents that are known to be lagging behind in many aspects of development. This ironic situation may, in part, be ascribed to a misaligned definition of development which impacts on the criteria for evaluating developmental projects and, in part, to the church's lack of a biblical concept of development. The church's zeal for development seems to have been affected by a drying up of funds from the former European mission agencies while the African Indigenous Churches (AICs) and Pentecostal Churches offer an interesting perspective. Hence, for the purposes of this contribution, my broadening of the definition of the church. My primary aim is to reflect on the aspects of definition and biblical concepts while the secondary aim is to briefly reflect on the role played by the African Church in development.

Definitions of Development in Retrospect

The term 'development' is both elusive and contested. Conservative sociological definitions associate it with a 'quantum jump'[4] from the old and traditional to the modern.[5] The latter had elements of imperialism which entailed shedding one's culture in favour of western culture, exchanging traditional technology for modern technology and aspirations towards economic growth.[6] Outside its sociological context, the term defined the church's missionary activities that led to conversions and transformed individuals from a

---

[1] By "African Church" is meant the African Indigenous Churches and the Pentecostal Churches operating in Africa. "Church" here refers to the churches that have been established by the missionaries and are often referred to as the "mainline churches".

[2] This is reflected in the booklets commissioned and published between 1981 and 1993 which I came across in Geneva, Switzerland in 1994. A much earlier book which was also among the collection of the WCC was by Peter Sartorius (1975), *Churches and rural development: guidelines for action*, Geneva: Commission on the Church's participation in development, WCC. It also placed similar confidence in the church.

[3] Mbiti 1990. *African Religions and Philosophy*. Port Harcourt: Heinemann, 1

[4] Jolly, R 1977:22 "Changing views on development". In Nossin, JJ (ed). *Surveys for development: a multidisciplinary approach,* Amsterdam, Elsevier, 19-48.

[5] Coetzee, JK. 1989, *Development is for people*. Johannesburg: Southern Books.

[6] Ibid. 20-22

'heathen' to a 'Christian' status as development.[7] This was based on the jump of the 'heathen' – voluntarily or by coercion, from the traditional (African) to the western way of life, this being regarded as 'civilisation' or, in the Xhosa language of South Africa, *ukugqobhoka*.[8] Interestingly, the term in Mndende means 'the one with a hole'. In other words, it refers to an 'empty shell'. This is how some traditional Africans view western forms of religion.

In the aftermath of World War II (1948), 'development aid' was introduced in terms of the Marshall Plan,[9] ostensibly to assist nations who had suffered economic losses as a result of the war. Critics of the manner in which such aid was administered, who were initially based in Latin America, responded with a 'dependency theory' whose analysis revealed that 'aid' was, in fact, leading to dependency.[10] The Alternative Theory of Development (ATD) which focused on the power of the people and transformation of socio-economic structures, evolved out of this (Korten 1990, initially confined to People-Centred Development).[11] It basically emphasized the power within individuals and communities which could be utilised to bargain for improvements and transformation of living conditions.[12] More importantly, it portrayed the focus on economic growth which manifested in the form of 'community development' or 'self-help schemes' as they were known, as being 'reductionist'.[13] It was upon this that the Asset-based Approach to development built its case,[14] taking the potential of the community further to an auditing and listing of assets.[15] For a while, this was thought to be the ultimate radical approach. The School of Theology and Religion at the University of KwaZulu Natal, for example, under the leadership of Steve de Gruchy (RIP), embraced the Asset-based Approach, offering a postgraduate course on it which, from 2003, was co-ordinated by Clint Le Bruyns. Some educationists at the University of Pretoria saw it as a potential approach for nurturing the young.[16] A very important contribution of this approach was the exposure of the fact that the previous approaches (no matter how well-intentioned), started from a point of deficiency.[17] However, this has not led to a paradigm change. Nor was it sustainable in underdeveloped communities.

While the church had not consciously embraced the Alternative Theory, its practice had been ambivalent. On the one hand, it organised and administered funds for 'self-help' schemes while on the other, it preached a 'pie in the sky theology'.[18] This is in contrast to what the World Council of Churches

---

[7] Mndende, N. 2014. "African Traditional Religion". In: Lewis, C. & Sherbok, D. (eds) 2014. *Sensible Religion.* Surrey: Ashgate; Pato 1997 Pato, LL. 1997. "Being fully human from the perspective of African culture and spirituality". *JTSA* 97:53-61, Evans, BF. 1979. Campaign for Human Development: church involvement in social change. *Review of Religious Research*, 20(3):264-278.

[8] Mndende, ibid. 182.

[9] Rositter 1985:15-16, cited in Speckman, MT. 2007. *A biblical vision for Africa's development?* Pietermaritzburg: Cluster Publications, 3-4.

[10] Ekins, P. 1992. *A new world order: grassroots movements for global change*. New York: Routledge; Cardoso, FH. 1979. *Dependency and development in Latin America*. Berkeley: University of California.

[11] Korten (1990) Korten, DC. 1990. *Getting to the 21st century: voluntary action and the global agenda*. West Hartford: Kumaria Press, later developed his own model which was based on four phases: relief (1950s -1960s), community development (1970s-1980s), policy analysis (1980s-1990s) and People Centred Development (1990s to the 21st century).

[12] Korten, ibid., Desroches, J. & George, J. 1984. *A People Centred Development*. New Delhi: Commonwealth Publishers.

[13] Speckman, ibid., 25.

[14] Speckman, ibid. cf Kretzman, JP & McKnight, JL 1993 *Building communities from Inside Out: a path toward finding and mobilising a community's assets.* Chicago: ACTA.

[15] Eloff, I and Ebersohn, L. 2001: 150, "The implications of an asset-based approach to early intervention", *Perspectives in Education*, 19(3): 147-157.

[16] Eloff & Ebersohn, ibid.

[17] Kretzman & McKnight, ibid., 1-2, Eloff & Ebersohn, ibid. 149-150.

[18] In the course of his research, the Church Historian, H. Mogashoa, stumbled over documents of the Baptist missionaries in South Africa which taught people not to bother about earthly riches while they prepared for heavenly

meant by 'sustainable development'. It also misses the point made by Pope John Paul VI (1979) who defined development as enabling the 'release of a God-given potential' in each individual while not totally excluding economic growth. Instead of reflecting on how to facilitate the release of potential and the extent to which the church's structures and teaching free the individual to participate in a transformed life, the church preoccupies itself with polemical clauses such as 'triumphalist theology' or 'prosperity gospel', while criticising other churches' approaches to a 'holistic' ministry.

Plausible as the ATD approaches might be, they have not, in recent decades, demonstrated corresponding success at grassroots level. Instead, they seem to almost exclusively appeal to a limited audience, the academics. The model is difficult to implement as it offers nothing to the majority who need immediate material benefits. Even in countries such as India where the concept advocated by Latin American intellectuals initially bore much fruit and generated refined definitions of development,[19] attention currently seems to be turning to a robust industrialisation.[20] Despite India being one of the leading Third World countries in development, parts of it are like the former East Germany before the fall of the Berlin Wall (1989) – modest to substandard infrastructure and visible poverty which contrasted sharply with a high sense of ethical values, intellectual prowess and responsible citizenship. On African soil, the *Ujamaa* system of Tanzania (1967-1985), fashioned along similar lines, produced similar results during the presidency of Nyerere which was in time reversed by reality on the ground. The latter two situations are not directly linked to the Christian faith or church doctrine but they illustrate what is to be expected in a context where there is no dialogue between ideology and reality.

While there may be some truth in the statement that Jesus called on his disciples to sacrifice,[21] it is only partially so. The church lacks a balance between, for example, the words appropriated by Jesus in Luke 4:16-20, sometimes known as his 'Liberation Manifesto' and other statements ascribed to him, for example, '... that they might have life, and have it abundantly' (John 10:10 NIV) on which some churches base their prosperity gospel. The missionaries who established churches (and themselves) in Africa led a self-sufficient life, sponsored by overseas missionary agencies, such as the United Society for the Propagation of the Gospel (USPG), in the big compounds they owned, often in the midst of dispossessed and poor communities. There are Roman Catholic, Lutheran, Anglican, Methodist, etc. mission stations throughout Africa, most of which have become defunct since the withdrawal of funding for overseas missions. It has to be mentioned however, that despite some of the mission stations being run like manors by some missionaries, they remained the centre of life where people received education and some technical skills. It would seem that the ambivalence is caused by the church's misaligned definition of development, if it ever had one.

Given the above, I define development as the facilitation of 'a process of releasing an individual's potential (Pope John Paul XVI 1979) so as to enable him/her to contribute to the welfare of the *politeia*/city'.[22] It should be noted that this definition goes beyond Pope John Paul VI's and that it captures the spirit of the Alternative Theory, the Bible and Vatican II (on the common good) and the recognition of the fact that an individual's welfare is integrally tied to that of the city and vice versa. The difference between this and traditional understandings is that it creates a link between the spiritual and material needs which seemingly is what attracts African Christians to the Pentecostal and African Indigenous Churches.

---

riches. Same documents appealed for second-hand clothing from overseas churches.

[19] cf Desroches & George, ibid.

[20] See the industrialisation policies of 1977 and subsequent years. May's (2006:10) optimism based on a link between work, assets and markets changes nothing as none of these belong to the poor either.

[21] Bonhoeffer, D 1963 Bonhoeffer, D. 1963. *The cost of discipleship*. New York. Macmillan cf Matt. 8:19-20, Luke 14:26-27).

[22] Winter, WB. 1994. *Seek the welfare of the city: Christians as benefactors and citizens*. Michigan: Eerdmans cf Jeremiah, 29:7.

Biblical Concepts of Development

It has to be stated at the outset that 'development' is not a biblical term.[23] However, this does not mean that the Bible is devoid of any concept of development. Depending on the tools used, it is possible to find concepts in the following clusters: i) miracle narratives in the gospels and Acts ii) teaching in the gospels, Acts and Pauline letters, namely, Romans, 1 Corinthians and 2 Thessalonians iii) preaching in the gospels and Acts.

I have argued elsewhere[24] that some biblical texts function well in a context of development. That was based on results obtained through the employment of the contextual-developmental approach which I had devised for the reading of Acts 3:1-10. The employment of the same approach in the reading of John 5:1-10 produced comparable results.[25] In terms of these, a few things define development in the *modus operandi* of Jesus and the early church. These include i) psychological emancipation ii) physical transformation iii) response by taking a step forward and iv) taking advantage of the new-found independence. Each of these manifests in a different way in different contexts, for example, in 1 Corinthians 12, the sudden realisation that each member has a role to play in the body is psychological emancipation; a shedding of whatever inhibits one from playing that role may be both physical and psychological and doing something about it equals both a step forward and taking advantage of the new-found independence.

The gospels almost invariably portray a Jesus who frees individuals from the power of sin, sickness and disability (Matt. 8:3, 16; Mark 1:41-42; 8:23-25; Luke 6:10) so they may tend for themselves and their families. This is deduced from the stories found in the non-Jewish religious background of the time (Luck 1986) which provide a *topos* for the interpretation of biblical narratives. The Acts of the Apostles has both the freeing of the individual for the same purpose (Acts 3, 16) and the teaching of Paul about the need for the healthy to work so they may earn (Acts 20:16). Romans (12:1-2) refers to the need for a transformed mind, an encouragement for a psychological emancipation which echoes John 5:1-10, the transformation of the man who had been lying at Bethsaida for 38 years, waiting for someone to help him into the healing water. 1 Corinthians contains teaching on the role of each individual in the Body (1 Cor. 12:12-40). 2 Thessalonians, on the other hand, contains an admonishment of the healthy and idle who are dependent on others for food and everything (2 Thess. 3:6-10). When these are read against the Graeco-Roman background albeit of Aristocratic prejudices, according to some experts in Roman social history (e.g. Saddington), a sharp contrast between the Jewish practice of almsgiving and well-motivated warnings against giving to beggars in the City States, becomes glaring.[26] The latter attitude resonates with the approaches of the Alternative Theory of Development.

If Jesus and the subsequent leaders of 'The Way' had not intended the above, his interaction with the beggars would have been characterised by charity and more charity, as there were many that looked up to him.[27] The miracle narratives instead invariably convey the message that a transformation of the mind and body create capacity for self-sufficiency. I have made the point elsewhere that this was the intended

---

[23] Speckman, MT 2001 "For Nolan's sake, let us move on: a plea for a developmental approach in contextual theology". In Speckman, MT & Kaufmann, LT (eds) 2001, *An agenda for contextual theology in South Africa: Essay in honour of Albert Nolan.* Pietermaritzburg: Cluster Publications.

[24] Speckman, ibid., p. xxviii.

[25] Speckman, ibid. 221.

[26] Speckman, MT 1997, Beggars and Gospel in Luke-Acts: some emerging trends in the light of theories of human development in SA. Neotestamentica 32(2):309-337; Speckman, MT 2007.

[27] In Plautus we read: "To give to a beggar is to do him an ill-service" (*Trinnimus* 339) because giving once leads to having to give daily. In other words, the beggar will never be able to fend for himself/herself.

message of the miracle narratives as it was the case in the pleas of those who approached the healers and sages of the first century in the Common Era.[28]

The New Testament thus offers various concepts of development, most of which are based on the respective approaches of Jesus, the early church and Paul.[29] According to the narratives, Jesus transformed body and mind as a way of removing the obstacles to development. Paul, not being always able to do the same, focused on a psychological emancipation in the hope of freeing the body for action. In between, Peter, John and others emulated Jesus with healing miracles and economic redistribution (Acts 2:42-47; 3:1-10; 4:32-35; 14:8-10).

Development in the African Church

It would be incorrect to claim that the church in Africa is not involved in development work. The literature produced by donors and young African scholars affirms this.[30] In some cases, it is even involved in spite of itself. However, much of what it is doing differs from what I have stated above as my understanding of development. Hence I described its position as being ambivalent. The mainline churches often serve as conduits for income-generating community development projects on the one hand while on the other, they preach that Christians should not worry about the riches of this world and that they should look up to the 'birds of the air' which are provided for by the unseen Father (Matt 6:26-32). Either the original authors of the verses quoted were limited by their contexts which they could not transform, or the church today needs to urgently find an appropriate model of development.

The African Church on the other hand, appears to be offering something different although it may not be based on any developmental theory. As already stated above, it sees no tension between the spiritual and the material. On the contrary, anecdotal evidence from the African Indigenous Churches and Pentecostal Churches indicates that the latter is perceived as an outflow or a spinoff of the former. Africans, always wishing to appease the spirits so they may be blessed, find a natural home in the spiritual churches although, in order for them to be seen as 'civilised' people, they retain membership of the mainline churches. The discourse on enculturation between African theologians and the mainline churches (1970s-1990s) revealed that some people were 'devout Christians by day and African traditionalists by night'[31] in pursuit of a combination of needs. Some, especially professionals, choose Pentecostal churches because they offer both the spiritual and the material needs without them having to fall back on 'heathen' practices. There are numerous records of healings performed, successful prayers for employment, prayers for fertility, and in one case, a 'dead' person being raised back to life.[32] I tried to show above that the ministries of Jesus and the early church had a similar effect.

Despite the above, it would appear that the mainline churches seem not to be in a theological space to reflect on why their younger counter-parts are having a competitive edge ahead of them. They have not, for example, provided a credible reason why an African believer who worships in a Pentecostal Church should not interpret John 10:10 as meaning that life in its fullness incorporates their daily bread, money for electricity, monthly bond for their house and happiness at home... and that all these things have to be prayed for, followed by hard work – either as a self-employed person or someone else's employee. It

[28] Speckman, MT 2007: 134-35.

[29] A limited number of miracles by Peter and his companions in the Acts of the Apostles resembles those of Jesus. In addition, Acts 4 shows that the miracle in Acts 3:1-10 led to the challenge of the social structures and authorities.

[30] Kabuaya, B. 2013, *Transforming Africa: The role of the church in developing political leaders*. PhD thesis. Unisa. http://hdl.handle.net/10500/11871; Chu, IS. 2014, *The Church and development in Africa.* USA: Pickwick Publications.

[31] Dwane, S 1980 Lecture notes on African and Black Theologies. Fedsem.

[32] Speckman, MT 2007:97-99.

appears, instead, that they are stuck in the past where a limited form of development (community development) only took place with funding received from Europe.

Conclusion

The definitions as well as biblical concepts of development provided above shed light on what development is about and the extent to which the concept is undergirded by the scriptures. However, it has also become clear in the above reflection that the mainline churches have been slowed down in their developmental programmes by the erosion of overseas funds. African Indigenous and Pentecostal churches, on the other hand, need no external funding but seem to have a manner of drawing out the inner energy of believers, as did Jesus, to generate income and finance themselves as well as the church. The spirits are invoked in the process in order to connect the individual with the supernatural world, thus 'claiming' the material benefits awaiting them. This is a perspective future research in development and religion in Africa should explore.

Bibliography

Bonhoeffer, D. 1963. *The cost of discipleship.* New York. Macmillan

Cardoso, FH. 1979. *Dependency and development in Latin America.* Berkeley: University of California

Chepkwony, A. 1991. 'Development involvement of churches in Eastern and Southern Africa', *Scriptura* 39: 9-14

Chu, IS. 2014, *The Church and development in Africa.* USA: Pickwick Publications

Coetzee, JK. 1989, *Development is for people.* Johannesburg: Southern Books

Dwane, S. 1980, Lecture notes on African and Black Theologies. Fedsem

De Gruchy, S. 2007. Telephonic conversation about the Master's module on Theology and Development at UKZN

Desroches, J. & George, J. 1984. *A People Centred Development.* New Delhi: Commonwealth Publishers.

Ekins, P. 1992. *A new world order: grassroots movements for global change.* New York: Routledge.

Eloff, I and Ebersohn, L. 2001. 'The implications of an asset-based approach to early intervention', *Perspectives in Education,* 19(3): 147-157.

Evans, BF. 1979. Campaign for Human Development: church involvement in social change. *Review of Religious Research,* 20(3):264-278

John Paul VI, 1979. 'Encyclical, Populorum Progression'. Translated and cited in: Henry, CFH and Hancock, RL (eds) 1979. *The ministry of development in Evangelical Perspective.* Pasadena: William Carey

Kabuaya, B. 2013, *Transforming Africa: The role of the church in developing political leaders.* PhD thesis. Unisa. http://hdl.handle.net/10500/11871

Kretzman and McKnight 1993. *Building communities from Inside Out: a path toward finding and mobilising a community's assets.* Chicago: ACTA.

Korten, DC. 1990. *Getting to the 21st century: voluntary action and the global agenda.* West Hartford: Kumaria Press.

Luck, G. *Arcana Mundi: Magic and the occult in the Greek and Roman worlds: a collection of ancient texts.* Baltimore: Longman, John Hopkins.

May, J. 2006. 'Assets, Markets and Entitlement'. In: Clark, DA (ed.) *Elgar companion to development studies.* Cheltenham: Edward Publishing Ltd.

Mbiti, JS. 1990. *African Religions and Philosophy.* Port Harcourt: Heinemann.

Mndende, N. 2014. 'African Traditional Religion'. In: Lewis, C. & Sherbok, D.(eds) 2014. *Sensible Religion.* Surrey: Ashgate

Mogashoa, MH. 2000. 'Black Baptists merely loaned leadership: an historical survey of native leadership in the Baptist Church in South Africa (1869-1994)'. In: Nthane, J, Ndala, WG and Mogashoa, MH (eds). *Leading your church towards holistic growth*. Johannesburg: Baptist Convention (33-69)

Mutambara, E. 1992. 'Church and development in Zimbabwe: a woman's perspective'. In: Koegelenberg, R (ed). *Church and development: an interdisciplinary approach*. Stellenbosch: Ecumenical Foundation of South Africa (126-146)

Nyerere, JK, 1970. Ujamaa: The basis for African socialism. Michigan. Jihad Productions

Pato, LL. 1997. 'Being fully human from the perspective of African culture and spirituality'. *JTSA* 97:53-61

Saddington, D. 1997. Lecture on the reception of beggars in the City States. Unisa

Sartorius, P 1975. *Churches and rural development: guidelines for action*, Geneva: Commission on the Church's participation in development, WCC

Speckman, MT. 2007. *A biblical vision for Africa's development?* Pietermaritzburg: Cluster Publications

Winter, WB. 1994. *Seek the welfare of the city: Christians as benefactors and citizens*. Michigan: Eerdmans.

World Council of Churches (1983-1994) Publications on development

(139) CHRISTIANISME ET LES ECOLES EN AFRIQUE: CAS DE L'AFRIQUE CENTRALE

Levi Ngangura Manyanya

De très bonne heure, les premiers missionnaires protestants et catholiques se sont engagés dans l'action sociale en Afrique central,[1] dans des pays où les infrastructures scolaires étaient presque inexistantes. Ce qui est assez étonnant puisqu' ils étaient originaires des pays d'Amérique ou d'Europe où une tradition de séparation nette entre Eglise et Etat existait déjà. Comment peut-on interpréter leur changement d'approche en arrivant en Afrique centrale ou comment l'ont-ils fait ? Quelle vision sous-tend cette particularité de l'engagement des églises chrétiennes dans la formation de l'élite africaine ? Pour essayer de répondre à ces questions, nous commencerons par une analyse liminaire de la doctrine de l'Eglise en matière d'éducation et un bref aperçu sur le système éducatif traditionnel en Afrique centrale. Puis, nous poursuivrons cette analyse en insistant sur le rapport qui existe entre enseignement profane en Afrique centrale et évangélisation. Enfin, nous terminerons notre propos par dégager l'apport de l'action sociale de l'Eglise en Afrique centrale.

La doctrine de l'Eglise en matière d'éducation

Bien que les églises chrétiennes (protestantes et catholiques) gèrent actuellement des écoles et des universités en Afrique centrale, l'enseignement profane n'était pas, à l'origine, considéré comme faisant partie de la mission du christianisme naissant. Dès ses origines, et pendant plusieurs siècles encore, l'Eglise ne semblait pas avoir explicitement l'aspiration d'organiser les écoles pour l'enseignement profane. Même si en Matthieu 28,19, les apôtres avaient reçu l'injonction d'aller auprès de toutes les nations et de les enseigner, cet ordre de Jésus avait été compris par les premiers chrétiens, selon les avis des spécialistes actuels, comme fondamentalement l'évangélisation apostolique.

Ce n'est que plus tard – spécialement au Moyen-âge – que l'Eglise, devenue le principal corps stable de la société, s'adonne à l'enseignement; et là encore, il s'agissait en premier lieu d'un enseignement corporatif, et ensuite, peu à peu, d'un enseignement profane.[2] Cela voudrait donc dire que la formation de ses clercs fut quasi naturellement la préoccupation majeure de l'Eglise mais, progressivement, l'instruction des laïcs dans différents domaines du savoir l'intéressa dans le but évangélique. Ainsi, au fil des temps, l'Eglise s'est retrouvée, en fin de compte, en possession des écoles non pas en raison d'une vocation enseignante destinée aux profanes, vocation clairement définie au départ, mais presque par conjoncture naturelle, les faits ayant créé la fonction.

Certes, on ne pourrait pas contester à l'Eglise son droit presque inné de fonder les écoles lorsqu'on tient compte de ses visées universalistes, la conscience qu'elle a une mission pédagogique, l'indépendance qu'elle proclame ou la personnalité dont elle jouit.[3] Mais l'Eglise n'a pas le droit exclusif de fonder et de diriger des écoles, l'Etat ou la famille peut aussi s'en prévaloir. Naturellement, l'éducation des enfants revient avant tout aux parents. C'est un devoir quasi sacré que les parents exercent eux-mêmes ou par d'autres personnes de leur choix. Pourtant, tout le monde est en même temps conscient de limites de certains parents pour assurer une éducation publique de leurs enfants. C'est pourquoi, d'aucuns reconnaissent à l'Etat le droit et le devoir de s'occuper de la question scolaire.

---

[1] En parlant de l'Afrique centrale, cette étude se fonde essentiellement sur l'histoire et les expériences des anciennes colonies belges. Il s'agit notamment de la République démocratique du Congo, du Rwanda et du Burundi.

[2] Voir BUSUGUTSALA GANDAYI GABUDISA, *Politiques éducatives au Congo-Zaïre: De Léopold II à Mobutu*, Paris: L'Harmattan (1997), 17-18.

[3] BUSUGUTSALA, *Politiques éducatives au Congo-Zaïre*, 19.

Pour revenir au droit de l'Eglise de fonder des écoles, il conviendrait de voir comment la doctrine de l'Eglise en matière d'éducation s'est développée chez les catholiques et les protestants. Même s'il n'y a pas de grandes divergences entre eux, on notera, du côté catholique, que la déclaration du Concile de Vatican II, telle que consignée dans *Gravissimum Educationis Momentum*,[4] s'ouvre sur le droit à l'éducation de chaque personne humaine en se fondant sur la dignité humaine. Le Concile affirme que la tâche de dispenser l'éducation revient en premier lieu à la famille qui requiert l'aide de toute la société. Quant aux responsabilités de l'Eglise en cette matière, le Concile proclame tout d'abord la compétence de l'Eglise pour donner une éducation. Il affirme ensuite la mission d'annoncer aux humains les voies du salut et de les aider à atteindre le plein épanouissement de la vie. Puis, il indique que l'Eglise est une mère tenue à assurer à ses enfants une éducation qui imprégnera toute leur vie de l'esprit du Christ. Enfin, l'Eglise doit aider tous les peuples à promouvoir la perfection complète de la personne humaine pour le bien de la société terrestre et pour la construction d'un monde humain.

S'agissant des protestants, les réformateurs s'accordent presque tous sur le fait que les fidèles doivent être formés. La formation étant l'une des voies appropriées pour leur permettre de mieux faire lire la Bible, comprendre les enseignements de la foi chrétienne et contribuer ainsi au développement du monde. C'est ainsi que la formation des fidèles fut, pour les réformateurs, un moyen ou une pratique, voire une nécessité pour la mise en œuvre du principe de la primauté de la Bible (*Sola Scriptura* en latin).

En effet, en 1530, au cours d'une prédication, Martin Luther élabore une recommandation importante aux termes de laquelle il oblige les parents d'envoyer leurs enfants à l'école.[5] Généralement, la réforme de Martin Luther est bien connue pour sa lutte contre les indulgences, et particulièrement l'impact de ses thèses, mais on n'insiste pas assez sur sa vision des écoles. Or, pour lui, une formation d'élite semble aussi bien importante qu'une formation solide de base. On sait aussi qu'il a toujours insisté dans sa vie sur l'opportunité de créer dans chaque ville ou village une école pour les garçons et une autre pour les filles.[6]

Bref aperçu sur le système éducatif traditionnel en Afrique centrale

En Afrique centrale, l'organisation des écoles de type occidental – du moins sous la forme que nous les connaissons aujourd'hui – coïncide avec l'arrivée des missionnaires protestants et catholiques au XIXe siècle. Mais cela ne signifie pas que l'Afrique précoloniale était dépourvue d'un système éducatif qui préparait la jeunesse à la vie. Bien au contraire, une éducation dite traditionnelle visant à enraciner la personne dans son milieu de vie était d'usage et l'affaire de tous les membres de la communauté. Ainsi la société elle-même était une école où les jeunes gens apprenaient tous les jours non seulement le savoir et le savoir-faire mais aussi le savoir-être. En famille ou dans son entourage, avec la participation entière de la communauté, la jeune fille ou le jeune garçon apprenait les métiers ménagers ou tout ce qu'il pourra, une fois devenu adulte, transmettre à son tour aux générations futures.

Assurément, dans ce système éducatif, les jeunes filles et les jeunes garçons n'étaient pas préparés pour les mêmes fonctions.[7] Par exemple, la jeune fille devait assister sa mère ou ses grandes sœurs dans les travaux ménagers pendant que le jeune garçon était avec son père ou ses grands-frères au travail. En règle générale, cette division du travail selon le sexe attribuait aux hommes les travaux de défrichage des

---

[4] Le concile de Vatican II, convoqué par le pape Jean XXIII, est devenu le symbole de l'ouverture de l'Eglise au monde moderne; la première réunion de ce concile eut lieu 11 octobre 1962 et la dernière le 8 décembre 1965.

[5] Cf. LALA Unsi Libay, « L'enseignement protestant congolais: Hier, aujourd'hui et demain » in *Revue du CRIP* n° 1 (2002), 252.

[6] LALA, « L'enseignement protestant congolais », 252.

[7] Voir Yves-Valentin KANEZA HABIYAMBIRE, Efficacité de l'enseignement primaire aux pays de la Communauté Economique des Pays des Grands Lacs (CEPGL): Questions approfondies sur le Rwanda, Thèse de Doctorat, Université de Bourgogne, 2011, 87-91.

champs, la construction, les soins du bétail, la forge, la culture, la fabrication des objets en bois, etc. Quant aux femmes, elles s'occupaient ordinairement des travaux ménagers, des tâches agricoles estimées légères mais réclamant plus de patience (comme le semis ou le sarclage), les soins de petits animaux domestiques, etc.

Aujourd'hui, on peut encore noter quelques mérites en faveur du système d'éducation traditionnelle en Afrique. Ce système était par exemple intimement lié aux besoins réels de la communauté où la formation s'effectuait.[8] Mais, à l'heure de la mondialisation, il ne semble plus approprié pour répondre aux problèmes actuels de l'éducation dans les pays africains. On pourrait lui reprocher entre autres faiblesses le maintien de l'inégalité entre filles et garçons avec la grande estime aux garçons.

Les premières écoles missionnaires comme pilier au service d'évangélisation

En arrivant en Afrique centrale dans un contexte colonial, les missionnaires chrétiens considérèrent immédiatement les écoles comme un moyen privilégié pour évangéliser les Africains et une voie stratégique pour réduire progressivement la résistance des peuples autochtones. Ils implantèrent, certes, des postes missionnaires ici et là, mais ils devaient également et rapidement former des autochtones pour une communication efficace ou comme auxiliaires de l'administration coloniale.

Dans des pays presque sans routes, les premiers missionnaires éprouvaient de grandes difficultés pour se déplacer de villages en villages. Au premier moment, ils ne pouvaient le faire qu'à pieds ou alors sur des litières ou des « *tipoy* » pour de longues distances. C'est pourquoi, de premières petites écoles commencèrent à se former autour des stations missionnaires et les premiers élèves furent en majorité recrutés parmi les domestiques des missionnaires et leurs proches.

L'enseignement dépendant étroitement de l'œuvre de l'évangélisation, les classes étaient ouvertes à tout le monde sous la supervision d'un missionnaire ou d'un catéchiste. Toutefois, comme les infrastructures d'accueil faisaient défaut, d'autres écoles furent parfois organisées sous de grands arbres, voire dans des chapelles des paroisses.[9]

La vocation de ces écoles était essentiellement l'apprentissage de la lecture, l'écriture, l'évangélisation avec un accent sur les bonnes manières de vivre, l'hygiène et, souvent, l'apprentissage des métiers. Ce système scolaire offrait à vrai dire un enseignement utilitaire, l'enseignement religieux étant à son centre, malheureusement avec une appréciation souvent négative de la culture des autochtones.

Lors de cette première phase, les écoles fonctionnaient généralement [2]dans une situation de grande précarité. Outre les difficultés liées au manque des manuels scolaires, des infrastructures, du personnel enseignant qualifié ou des langues d'enseignement, les premières écoles des missionnaires étaient également exposées à la réticence des autochtones. Elles n'avaient pas en effet suscité une adhésion massive comme c'est le cas aujourd'hui. Pour les Africains, les écoles paraissaient à l'origine comme des « établissements étrangers » c'est-à-dire implantées par des étrangers ou mises au service d'une philosophie extérieure. C'est pourquoi les Africains les appelaient souvent des « écoles des Blancs » et, pendant de très longues années, les Africains furent très méfiants vis-à-vis de ces écoles venues de l'Occident. Cela ne va pas sans dire que pour ramener des enfants à l'école et les y maintenir il fallait déployer des efforts considérables. Dans certains villages, un bon nombre d'enfants n'ont fait à l'origine que des apparitions éphémères à l'école. La tâche était encore particulièrement difficile pour la scolarisation des jeunes filles ou des garçons issus des familles jouissant des privilèges coutumiers de « gardiennes de la tradition ». Il fallait souvent, en différents lieux, faire usage des forces pour convaincre les parents et les enfants à accepter la scolarisation de type occidental.

---

[8] Tharcisse GATWA et André KARAMAGA, *Les autres Chrétiens rwandais: La Présence protestante*, Kigali, éditions Urwego (1990), 79.

[9] Ce sont les écoles appelées « chapelles-écoles » et qui évoluaient sous la responsabilité d'un enseignant-catéchiste.

Si déjà avant les indépendances, les écoles organisées par des missions chrétiennes mettaient un accent particulier sur l'enseignement religieux, elles n'étaient pas pourtant les seules institutions qui assuraient la formation aux jeunes. On pouvait aussi compter, dans certaines contrées et selon la législation en cours, différents types d'écoles. Tout d'abord, nous pouvons mentionner les écoles créées ou organisées par des missions chrétiennes (catholiques ou protestantes) avec des programmes agréés par l'Etat. Une charge importante de telles écoles étaient couvertes par des subventions gouvernementales à condition que leurs programmes soient agrées par l'Etat et que l'inspection assurée par l'Etat continue à donner un avis favorable. Puis, on connaissait quelques écoles officielles – en nombre très réduit sans doute – créées par le Gouvernement qui en assumait en même temps toutes les charges. Enfin, les écoles libres non subsidiées et organisées par des tiers (des missions chrétiennes ou non). C'est parmi ces dernières que l'on peut également compter à l'époque des écoles ayant un caractère confessionnel, comme les petits ou grands séminaires, les instituts de théologie, etc.

Il s'avère aussi indispensable de noter que dans certains pays africains, le pouvoir colonial ne traitait pas les écoles organisées par les missions chrétiennes de la même manière. Par exemple, en R.D.Congo, le roi Léopold II accorda, aux termes d'une convention signée avec le Saint-siège le 26 mai 1906, beaucoup d'avantages matériels, moraux et financiers aux missions catholiques en matière éducative. Les missions protestantes s'étaient vues purement et simplement exclues de cette convention qui accordait aux missions catholiques le droit d'acquérir des concessions allant de 100 à 200 hectares à titre gratuit en propriété perpétuelle n'importe où elles veulent s'implanter. De même, en 1925-1926 les écoles catholiques reçurent du gouvernement colonial, de façon généralisée des subsides sans égales par rapport aux écoles protestantes.[10]

Action sociale des Eglises et professionnalisation de l'enseignement après les indépendances

Tout le monde sait que l'enseignement vise d'une façon générale à assurer aux apprenants la formation dans tous les domaines (physique, intellectuel, moral, civique, spirituel, etc.). Mais encore vers les années 1960 où plusieurs pays africains accèdent aux indépendances, il se posait toujours l'épineux problème d'insuffisance de cadres autochtones et le peu d'écoles disponibles étaient organisées par les Eglises (catholiques et protestantes) en Afrique centrale. L'enseignement paraissait, jusque là, aux yeux de plusieurs observateurs, comme le monopole presque exclusif des Eglises protestantes et catholiques. Celles-ci étaient encore essentiellement constituées d'étrangers et ne prenaient d'importantes décisions que sous l'influence des missionnaires. Souvent, on reproche aux premiers missionnaires et aux Eglises de n'avoir pas à l'origine encouragé aux Africains d'envoyer leurs enfants dans les établissements officiels. Les Eglises avaient tendance à n'accorder leur confiance qu'à l'enseignement issu de leurs propres écoles. C'est ainsi que les querelles occidentales entre missions et de fois l'esprit d'intolérance ou un manque de collaboration entre Eglises en Occident se retrouvaient sur le terrain africain; elles n'avaient alors pas permis aux écoles de jouer pleinement leur fonction spécifique d'instrument nécessaire pour l'unité nationale.

Par ailleurs, face à la demande accrue des cadres dans les pays africains à peine sortis de la colonisation, des débats divers sur des questions scolaires eurent lieu et des gouvernements ont fait appel aux initiatives privées. Avec de nouvelles politiques scolaires, les églises chrétiennes continuèrent non seulement à créer d'autres écoles, mais se mirent également à diversifier les sections et les options à telle enseigne que des écoles devenaient un véritable noyau de développement des villages. Les écoles ne se concentraient plus seulement à la formation des instituteurs, mais aussi à la formation des agents médicaux, des agents des

[10] Thomas MUNAYI Muntu-Monji, « Les Missions protestantes et la question scolaire au Zaïre (1890-1960) » in *Bulletin de Théologie Africaine*, Vol vi, n° 11 supplément (1984), 161.

bureaux administratifs ou des jeunes intéressés par de divers métiers. Elles contribuaient en même temps à dessiner une image positive des églises ou à les placer même au « centre de la vie du village ». Puis, pour résoudre le problème de manque de cadres suffisants et compétents, les églises chrétiennes vont, au fil de temps, décider de s'engager dans l'organisation de l'enseignement du niveau universitaire.

L'essor des écoles organisées par les Eglises en Afrique centrale est remarquable. Actuellement, les cadres ayant fréquenté des écoles organisées par les Eglises se comptent en grand nombre. Ces écoles forment aujourd'hui, presque dans chaque pays un réseau important dont personne ne peut se passer si elle envisage mener une action de grande envergure dans le domaine éducatif.

Mais qu'est ce qui fait leur spécificité ? A vrai dire, les traits essentiels qui distinguent les écoles organisées par les Eglises chrétiennes en Afrique centrale ne se trouvent pas dans un mode de constitution des organes scolaires inconnu des autres types d'écoles. Même si ces Eglises restaient souvent, ou restent encore, confrontées à bien des difficultés liées à l'environnement socio-politique et économique, la spécificité de leurs écoles réside avant tout dans la vision et les valeurs qui sous-tendent leur action. Depuis leurs origines, les Eglises chrétiennes travaillent pour l'émergence des leaders du changement, des cadres qui regardent l'avenir avec confiance et optimisme. Cela signifie que les églises chrétiennes visent un enseignement qui assure la formation intégrale pour tous; qui incarne des valeurs morales et spirituelles dans la formation; qui promeut une formation diversifiée, sans oublier les écoles technique et professionnelles. Un tel type d'enseignement suscite chez l'apprenant un esprit de respect, de tolérance, de justice inspiré par les valeurs chrétiennes; il contribue également à la formation des cadres assumant leurs responsabilités avec initiative et détermination. Puis, il situe de plus en plus l'apprenant au centre de sa formation pour le développement efficient de ses aptitudes, cultive la fonction critique de la société, valorise les compétences professionnelles et la collaboration avec tous les partenaires éducatifs (parents, Église, gouvernement, enseignants). Enfin, il met à la disposition du personnel et des apprenants des outils et des supports pédagogiques et se préoccupe des conditions de travail de l'apprenant ainsi que de l'éducateur, etc.

Bibliographie

BAUR, John, *2000 Years of Christianity in Africa: An African Church History*, Second Revised Edition (Nairobi, Paulines Publications Africa, 2001).

BUSUGUTSALA GANDAYI GABUDISA, *Politiques éducatives en Congo-Zaïre: De Léopold II à Mobutu* (Paris, L'Harmattan, 1997).

GATWA, Tharcisse et KARAMAGA, André., *Les autres Chrétiens rwandais. La présence protestante* (Kigali, Editions Urwengo, 1990).

KANEZE HABIYAMBERE, Yves Valentin, *Efficacité interne de l'enseignement primaire aux pays de la Communauté Economique des Pays des Grands Lacs (CEPGL): Question approfondies sur le Rwanda*, Thèse de doctorat en Sciences de l'Education, Université Bourgogne, 2011 (thèse inédite).

LALA Unsi Libay, « L'enseignement protestant congolais: hier, aujourd'hui et demain », in *Revue du CRIP* 1 (2002) 249-263.

MOKONZI BAMBANOTA, Gratien, *De l'école de la médiocrité à l'école de l'excellence* (Paris, L'Harmattan, 2009).

NGOY BOLIYA, Daniel et MUNAY MUNTU-MONJI, Thomas, « L'enseignement supérieur et Universitaire congolais: historique, situation actuelle et perspectives d'avenir », in *Revue du CRIP* 1 (2002) 265-288.

SYLLA, Khadim, *L'éducation en Afrique. Le défi de l'excellence* (Paris, L'Harmattan, 2004).

(140) THE FINANCIAL STABILITY AND SELF-RELIANCE OF AFRICAN CHURCHES

Evangelos Thiani

The last fifty years have been a time of many changes in religious demographics. The research done on global Christianity has shown a lot of interesting discoveries regarding the rise of Christianity in the global South in the period between 1970 and 2020, and it is expected that this trend will continue. According to the 2013 report, released by the Center for the Study of Global Christianity at Gordon-Conwell Theological Seminary in Massachusetts,[1] 41.3% of all Christians were from Africa, Asia or Latin America. By 2020, this figure is expected to be 64.7%'. In Africa alone, Christianity is expected to grow 'from 143 million in 1970 (38.7% of the continent's population), to 630 million by 2020 (49.3%)'.[2] This growth is shown across the board in all major Christian denominations in Africa: Roman Catholic, Protestant and Orthodox.[3] According to this report, Christianity in Africa has grown at an annual rate of 3.02% as shown by the religion's data:

> In 1910, only 9% of Africa's population was Christian, and 80% of Christians lived in just four countries: Ethiopia, South Africa, Egypt and Madagascar. By 1970, Africa's Christian percentage had risen to 38.7%, many of whom were converts from ethno-religions in SSA. In 2010, the Christian percentage was 48.3%, and by 2020 it is expected to reach 49.3%.[4]

While the global South is growing in Christian numbers, the global North is experiencing the opposite, a decline that is expected to continue.[5] The *Pew Forum* found that 'more than 1.3 billion Christians live in the global South (61%), compared with about 860 million in the global North (39%)'.[6] This is proof enough that the global South Christianity in general has to wake up and create very strong foundations that will stand firm during the expected shift of Christianity. Africa in this case must be ready to be considered a Christian resource centre, sending future missionaries to the rest of the world. It is for this very reason that Africa must turn round and stop relying on the global North for anything, including missionaries, finance, research, theological education, strategies and all other resources because, if the same demographic pattern in the global South and global North continues, then Christianity will have a very difficult time in the future, being in the hands of people who will not be able to sustain it.

Moratorium and Partnership in African Missions

The African Church has shown a lot of potential in sustaining herself financially, but at the same time she has kept herself linked with her mother churches in Europe and America, and to some extent she has been unable to break from her dependency syndrome. Just as African nations strove for independence in the mid-1900s, so the African Church has struggled since then to fight the tendency to remain a 'big baby', that is, still depending on her mother churches, even after she has grown to maturity. This was made

---

[1] Centre for the Study of Global Christianity, *Christianity in its Global Context, 1970-2020: Society, Religion, and Mission* (South Hamilton, MA: Gordon-Conwell Theological Seminary, June 2013) hereafter Gordon-Conwell report 2013.

[2] Gordon-Conwell report 2013, 7-9.

[3] Gordon-Conwell report 2013, 22-33.

[4] Gordon-Conwell report 2013, 22.

[5] Pew Research Center, *Global Christianity: A Report on the Size and Distribution of the World's Christian Population* (Pew Forum on Religion & Public Life, December 2011) hereafter Pew report 2011.

[6] Pew report 2011, 13.

especially clear by the 'Moratorium on Missions' campaign instigated by the All Africa Conference of Churches (AACC) leadership and some of its member churches in the 1970s. The major proponent of this campaign was the Rev. Dr John Gatu, a minister of the Presbyterian Church of East Africa (PCEA) in Kenya, who was General Secretary of the National Council of Churches in Kenya and the Moderator of his church, and the Rev. Canon Carr Burgess, a minister of the Episcopal, and later Anglican, Church of Liberia, who was the General Secretary of AACC at that time.[7]

It all started in a 1971 missionary conference in Milwaukee, USA, where Gatu was invited to present a paper. In his paper, he called for the Africanization of the African Church by having western missionaries let the Africans fund and lead their church in their own ways and methods, as well as letting the Africans make the decisions of their church without any western or foreign influence. For Gatu, all the problems of the African churches could only be resolved if western missionaries withdrew from Africa. Let the Africans manage their own churches – that was his plea, and he believed the Africans to be capable of doing so. Gatu was angered by the fact that African church leaders considered going abroad like a fishing trip which they would take for fund-raising, a practice which, he explained, he regarded as shameful for the capable African Church that had turned her bishops, general secretaries, moderators and Presidents into 'good ecclesiastical beggars' by always singing the tune of poverty in the churches. Encountering the trend of always expecting others to decide about withdrawing funding and personnel, and always remaining dependent on the mentality of church leaders who would take what they could get from western partners, Gatu insisted that the Africans must themselves decide on their own affairs. He pointed out that they therefore needed to liberate themselves from what kept them from becoming an active missionary church. He pleaded for this transformation of colonial mentalities, knowing that not many African church leaders would at first accept his new way of thinking, but he still maintained it would be the only way to become an authentic African Church.[8] The 'Moratorium Debate' went beyond this missionary conference in Milwaukee. It was a major theme of discussion at the 1973 World Mission Conference held in Bangkok, Thailand, at the third AACC Assembly, held in Lusaka, Zambia 1974, and at the 5th WCC Assembly held 1975 in Nairobi, Kenya. As Mugambi explains, the 'Moratorium issue… became a theme of heated debate and controversy throughout the ecumenical movement during the 1970s, especially in Africa and the North Atlantic'.[9]

In the third AACC General Assembly held in Lusaka in 1974, Gatu was invited to address the same issue. Canon Burgess Carr at this stage had adopted a campaign deemed necessary for the African churches to attain self-reliance and authenticity in reclaiming their dignity, as he termed it. In his address to the Assembly, Carr explained that, 'self-reliance is actually a means toward achieving selfhood,' adding that 'the Church in Africa can never be itself so long as it depends primarily on foreign money, personnel, and decisions influence. For it is still true that 'he who pays the piper calls the tune'.[10] He thus asked the African churches to act upon a rediscovery and perhaps a redefining of their identity as African Christians. Carr explained to the Assembly that some African churches were ready to go on to self-dependency immediately, but also recognized the fact that others needed more time before letting go of foreign aid and foreign missionary personnel.[11] He encouraged those who thought it impossible, to look at the African

[7] cf. P. Wakatama, "Moratorium" in John Corrie (ed.) *Dictionary of Mission Theology: Evangelical Foundations* (Downers Grove, IL: InterVarsity Press, 2007), 246-248.

[8] John Gatu, "A call for the Africanisation of the Church in Africa", Unpublished presentation paper to the Mission Festival in Milwaukee, USA in October 1971; John G. Gatu, *Joyfully Christian Truly African* (Nairobi: Acton Publishers, 2006), 132-178.

[9] J.N.K Mugambi (ed), *The Church and the Future in Africa: Problems and* Promises (Nairobi: All Africa Conference of Churches, 1997), 199-200.

[10] AACC June 1975 Report, "The Moratorium Debate: What is being said and done" (unpublished report from the AACC Archives).

[11] AACC June 1975 Report, "The Moratorium Debate".

Instituted Churches (AICs) which were founded by Africans, run by Africans and were also supported by funds received from Africans. As he later told the National Council of Churches of Christ in the USA, Carr believed that, for the Moratorium to succeed, it would need a comprehensive Africanization of the structures, orders and programmes of churches in order to contain African values and priorities.[12] In his definition of what the Moratorium on missions was all about, Carr explained to the assembly:

> It means that African churches must now find ways of financing and manning their own institutions and halt dependency upon foreign financial and administrative structures. [Such] structures prevent the Church in Africa from being itself, [and] from fulfilling its mission in the African context. When the Church in Africa becomes self reliant, then it would be able to be authentically African and yet remain a wholesome part of the universal Church. Only then would it be able to determine its own priorities and fulfil her mission in Africa and the world. Some Churches in Africa have always been self-reliant. Others are ready to take up this option today. And there are still others which cannot be expected to become self reliant immediately – for these, it will take time. But for all the Churches in Africa, one thing is clear: the moment of truth has come: no longer are they prepared to continue to receive foreign aid continuously. The aid they receive from now on will be not to ensure their dependency but to accelerate their self-reliance.[13]

After Lusaka, a taskforce was formed at the AACC headquarters in Nairobi, Kenya, to advise the African churches on how to attain selfhood, independency and self-sustainability, and it was resolved that AACC was to help her member churches in the future to do the following: to be self-supporting through encouraging investment and other projects that could generate income in African church properties; to train church workers in planning, administration and stewardship; to encourage post-theological training for church workers; to facilitate the exchange of ideas among churches in Africa especially on how to become self-supporting and how to fund-raise and, finally, to help churches start projects aimed at community development.[14] This taskforce report complemented, and gave even more strength to, the findings of the Ministry for Social Justice Work Group reports given in Lusaka, Zambia, in May 1974.[15]

The Moratorium call 'asking the mission boards in Europe and North America to withdraw their money, personnel, and influence, in order to allow, and where necessary, force the churches locally to take a break from dependency',[16] was received with mixed reactions locally, regionally and internationally. The strongest reactions came from the mission agencies and mother churches offering the aid and personnel that the Africans were proposing to cut-off.[17] Such churches and mission agencies mainly did not understand why their generosity and patronage would be rejected or seen as harmful while it was considered a very Christian-based and acceptable gesture.[18] Furthermore, they saw the Moratorium as a danger to the catholicity of the church and thus counted it as an isolationist agenda, but never as an end to the dependency syndrome created in the African Church by well-meant Christian programmes from

---

[12] Carr Burgess, "The Mission of the Moratorium", address to the National Council of Churches of Christ in the USA, Executive Committee of the Division of Overseas Ministry – Jan 10 1975 (Unpublished paper from the AACC Archives).

[13] Carr Burgess, "The Moratorium: A search for self-reliance and authenticity" (Nairobi: *AACC Bulletin*, Department of Information, June 1974), p.1. Cf. Efiong Utuk, *Visions of Authenticity: The Assemblies of the All Africa Conference of Churches 1963-1992* (Nairobi: All Africa Conference of Churches, 1997), 107-113.

[14] AACC, Self-Reliance Moratorium Task Force report of July 1976 (unpublished notes from AACC Archives).

[15] cf. The AACC Ministry for Social justice Work Group III Report to the AACC Third General Assembly in Lusaka Zambia, 11th-24th May 1974.

[16] Mugambi, *The Church and the Future in Africa*, 199.

[17] cf. E.M. Uka, *Missionary go Home? A Sociological Interpretation of An African Response to Christian Mission* (Frankfurt: Peter Lang, 1989); James A. Scherer, *Missionary, Go Home! A Reappraisal of the Christian World Mission* (Eaglewood Cliffs, NJ: Prentice-Hall, 1964).

[18] Cf. J.N.K Mugambi, *Christian Theological & Social Reconstruction* (Nairobi: Acton Publishers, 2003), 213.

western churches and mission agencies. It was only later that some missionaries, as in obvious example of Glenn Schwartz, would confess that the mother churches and mission agencies abroad kept the African churches dependent with money, personnel and decision-making.[19]

Partnership Response after the Moratorium Call

After reviewing the Moratorium call, some African churches decided not to follow it, their main fear being how to pay their clergy and continue their development projects that had been entirely funded from abroad. Such churches opted for a review of their relationship with their foreign donors; most of them calling it a 'partnership'. Although the term 'partnership' was used even before the Moratorium call, it was only after the 1970s Moratorium debate that excessive use of this term could be observed in church-based projects in Africa getting funding from the global North. The use of this term will later be proved to be simply a term used to continue the old system of the global North churches offering the global South funding, personnel and major decisions guidelines.[20]

While western missionaries believed they were partners with African churches, the Africans believed differently. This was observed during a mission conference in Canada, when Professor Elmer explained having asked the participants what 'partnership' meant for them: for the Canadian members it meant 'mutuality, sharing, respect, co-operation, collaboration and so on', while for those from the global South it meant 'another way for the White man to control' the African churches.[21] Jonas Dah, in an article, has explained that one of the major hindrances of real partnership was that the receiving churches in the South were not offered opportunities to offer something back to their partners in the North. Therefore the South never addressed the donors as equal partners, as the relationship was primarily defined as consisting of giving from one end and receiving at the other end, with the rules always being by the ones offering. This was aggravated by examples that some partners in the North used disturbing pictures and messages in their fund-raising campaigns which degraded the South, the South being shown to 'a large extent (as consisting of) those people with torn dresses, houses that depict slum conditions or barely huts with leaves or grass roofs, emaciated or bony-looking persons, those with ulcers or some deformation, etc.'.[22]

True partnership, however, is supposed to be a proper two-way activity, where both persons and groups partnering have something to offer to each other with their common goal leading which is 'to accomplishing great things for the Kingdom of God'.[23] Lederleitner therefore pleads not to cut off foreign funding where it is absolutely needed for meaningful joint projects, but that churches engaged in a partnership relationship should work on avoiding 'sinful behaviours' of distorted partnership, i.e. practices which deepen dependency and neglect mutual accountability. For a better way of practising partnership in mission and development, Lederleitner recommends that there should be biblical founded accountability and contextualized accounting processes on both sides relating to money and other resources offered in a partnership. She also asks that dignity and mutuality should be fostered, as well as processes that will help to offer capacity building and sustainability to the partners. Such actions, Lederleitner insists, have to be

---

[19] cf. Glenn J. Schwartz, *When Charity Destroys Dignity: Overcoming Unhealthy Dependency in the Christian* Movement (Lancaster, PA: World Mission Associates, 2007), xxv; Robert D. Lupton, *Toxic Charity: How Churches and Charities Hurt Those They Help and How to Reverse it* (New York, NY: HarperOne, 2011) 15-16.

[20] Mary T. Lederleitner, *Cross-Cultural Partnership: Navigating the Complexities of Money and Mission* (Downers Grove, IL: InterVarsity Press, 2010); David F. Hesselgrave. *Planting Churches Cross-Culturally: North America and Beyond, second edition* (Grand Rapids, MI: Baker Academics, 2000); Jonas N. Dah (ed.), *Mission in a Post Missionary Era: Papers Presented at the Consultation on Mission at the Presbyterian Church Centre Kumba* (Kumba: Presbyterian Church in Cameroon, 2008).

[21] Lederleitner, *Cross-Cultural Partnership:* foreword.

[22] Dah, *Mission in a Post Missionary Era,* 89.

[23] Lederleitner, *Cross-Cultural Partnership*, 21.

initiated at the beginning of the partnership and not just at a later stage. The partners must let the process of partnership grow with grace and patience in the pace of the church they are assisting, knowing that it is a great investment that will take the church being helped to the greatest heights God would like to take them.[24] In a similar direction, Dah explains that partnership in mission is the task of all Christians wherever the church is and that both the South and North have a lot to offer to each other as equal parties. Power-sharing among partners and participation of both ends in decision-making is an integral element in mutual partnership as well as openness, trust and elimination of prejudices. Honest and trustful partnership includes sharing, not only to include material resources like 'money, personnel and things', but also non-material resources like theologies, liturgies, songs, lifestyles and new forms of spirituality.[25] For an enlarged concept of partnership to be acted out, Dah recommends the following three principles:

1. The initiative and leadership will come from the people of the area itself knowing their talents, culture and socio-political conditions;
2. The local people must be helped to contribute and make their voices heard in the setting of priorities;
3. The nature of the participation in mission will have to take into consideration the universality of the church.[26]

Selfhood Response after the Moratorium Call

Those churches that took the Moratorium call seriously would later enjoy the fruits of their decisions, which led them to attaining a higher degree of selfhood. An example in point is the Presbyterian Church in Eastern Africa (PCEA) in Kenya, which asked their mother church and all mission agencies to stop funding them for five years. They formed an African structure for their church and methods of fund-raising that would work for them, naming this initiative *Jitegemea* (Swahili for self-reliance). Before their five years of the Moratorium on foreign missions funding, personnel and influence were over, they were already self-sustaining, offering a perfect example of how African churches could sustain themselves fully without any foreign help. Some examples of what they put into practice included paying their clergy regularly and starting a pension fund for them, building churches and business centres, buying church vehicles, and even offering their mother church in Scotland funds to resuscitate a house for homeless children in Edinburgh with KShs 200,000 (about US$30,000 at that time).[27]

African Churches' Efforts in Funding their Activities

While many African churches have no problem in uplifting the spiritual life of their flock, and thus there is a considerable rise in numbers of adherents of the Christian faith in Africa, the major challenge has been in how to raise funds that will sustain African churches. The African Instituted Churches (AICs) in Africa have been at the forefront in establishing ways of raising funds locally. Most of them have done this since their inception and proved for sure that African churches do not need to rely on foreign help unless it is of absolute necessity. In most instances, the AICs have had their clergy continue working and raising their funds from other non-ministerial jobs.[28] This is imitating the tent-making ministry culture of St Paul, who

---

[24] Lederleitner, *Cross-Cultural Partnership*, 101-144. Cf. Daniel Rickett, *Making Your Partnership Work* (Enumclaw, Washington: WinePress, 2002).

[25] Dah, *Mission in a Post Missionary Era,* 90-92.

[26] Dah, *Mission in a Post Missionary Era,* 91.

[27] Schwartz, *When Charity Destroys Dignity,* 12-13, 18-19.

[28] cf. Paul Makhubu, *Who are the Independent Churches. Black Theology Series Volume 7.* (Johannesburg: Skotaville Publishers, 1988).

took care of his needs and those of his companions in his missionary journeys without asking for anything from the congregations he formed and ministered to, as he confesses when he says: 'You yourselves know that these hands of mine have supplied my own needs and the needs of my companions. In everything I did, I showed you that by this kind of hard work we must help the weak, remembering the words the Lord Jesus himself said: 'It is more blessed to give than to receive''[29] (Acts 20:34-35 NIV; cf. Acts 18:1-4). A good number of African churches have used what Kiiru suggests below and in most cases a combined effort of all the following four efforts have proved to be very successful in the life of African churches:

1. Getting the most from church members in terms of offerings, tithes and donations;
2. Identifying some close friends who have ties with the church or ministry both locally and overseas;
3. Encouraging the sale of services and products which meet the needs of the congregations and local community;
4. Establishing income-generating activities and viable investment projects.[30]

Giving to the church through Sunday collection baskets as St Paul asked the Corinthians ('On the first day of every week, each one of you should set aside a sum of money in keeping with your income, saving it up, so that when I come no collections will have to be made' (1 Cor. 16:2 NIV)), is a very common practice of raising church funds in Africa. Other methods have been fund-raising and auctioning of business or farm products set in different times of the year in many churches. In some instances, the local clergy ask that fund-raising be made for specific work and request the people to give willingly, like Moses asked the Israelites (cf. Ex. 25:1-9, 35:4). The Africans, like the Israelites, give in amazing ways. Pledging to give a certain amount of money per month or per year is also catching up with many African Christians, while others pay monthly or annually a set amount for each individual or family, mainly termed as CESS (a local tax system). In recent times, African families that feel blessed come to church and give an offering in front of the congregation, and in return the local clergy prays and blesses such families. These thanksgiving offerings are becoming increasingly popular in African churches and in some instances they have been proved to produce more funds in churches than any other forms of fund-raising, probably because it is a gift given willingly (compare the biblical saying, 'Each of you should give what you have decided in your heart to give, not reluctantly or under compulsion, for God loves a cheerful giver' (2 Cor. 9:7 NIV)). Other African churches have of late invested in buying properties that they rent for business premises, rental houses, and offices; either on land originally intended for parish buildings only, or on newly acquired lands intended for set investments. Some African churches are buying these investments with funds raised in the many ways already described, or in some other instances through bank loans.

A new phenomenon in Africa, borrowed from the early twentieth century American Pentecostal and Evangelical traditions and other faith movements, is fast developing. The so-called 'prosperity gospel' or 'prosperity theology' states that, if one offers to God material things like money, property or other things of worth through the church or her clergy, then God will offer them 'divine healing, the riches of this world, and happiness without suffering'.[31] The clergy in the churches preaching this theology emphasize giving in order to receive, asking their followers to name and claim what they desire and want God to offer them through faith. Some African Christians, wanting to protect their wealth, and those who don't have wealth wanting to attain the same, flock into such churches. Material gain and wellness prophecies are promised to

---

[29] cf. Thomas Oduro et al., *Mission in an African Way: A Practical Introduction to African Instituted Churches and their Sense of Mission* (Wellington: Christian Literature Fund and Bible Media, 2008), 155-170; Christopher R. Little, *Mission in the Way of Paul: Biblical Mission for the Church in the Twenty-First Century. Studies in Biblical Literature Volume 80* (New York/Oxford: Peter Lang Publishing, 2005). Robert L. Plummer and John Mark Terry, *Paul's Missionary Methods: In His Time and Ours* (Downers Grove, IL: InterVarsity Press, 2012).

[30] Kiiru, *Mobilizing & Managing Resources,* 237.

[31] J.N. Saracco, 'Prosperity Theology' in John Corrie (ed.) *Dictionary of Mission Theology: Evangelical Foundations* (Downers Grove, IL: InterVarsity Press, 2007), 322.

all who want it, claim it and who 'plant a seed' (offer money or other forms of wealth) in the church. The mainline churches are losing many members, although many of their members have double membership. And several mainline churches also feel tempted to start fund-raising, using such theologies of divine healing and blessing related to giving. The mainline churches have always explained that suffering and evil as well as poverty are to be taken in perseverance and faith, knowing that we are only passersby in this world and thus should focus on the future of eschatological life, where all pains and sorrows will be put to an end. On the other hand, the proponents of the gospel and theology of prosperity are teaching that God will offer material wealth, wellness and health only to His faithful servants, first in this world and secondly also in the next life. As could be expected, many African Christians wanting to be part of the double inheritance of life and its goodies in the now-and-not-yet Kingdom of God, opt for the second option, following the promises of the Prosperity Gospel.

Globalization has opened another door of the expansion of these theologies through the internet, radio and television programs that are broadcasted internationally, regionally and locally, and hence the magnitude of its exposure and followers is growing on a daily basis. Prosperity theologies frequently also use biblical texts wrongly to convince their listeners. The commonly used scriptural texts in these theologies include Mark 10:29-30 (emphasizing sowing and reaping), and Mark 11:23-24 and Genesis 1 (emphasizing the power of words spoken in faith). Unfortunately, 'the challenge of the prosperity gospel is that people are attracted to its message of wealth and health, and do not recognize that the message is not biblical', as Chilenje has explained.[32] Some of the clergy in such churches have started in very small and open spaces, rented or borrowed premises, but within no time they become millionaires and billionaires, owning big premises and lands where their mega-churches and new businesses are started, some of them owning posh cars and their own television airtime in national and regional networks. Such immense financial growth and stability on the positive side shows that Africans can sustain their churches without any outside help, but on the other, negative, side, the problematic nature of some of the theologies involved can be viewed as stealing in the name of God from those who are needy and poor.[33]

A major problem of churches handling money is the unfortunate lack of transparency and accountability in those receiving and handling the funds (and this applies not only in Africa but elsewhere as well).[34] We should remind ourselves of the biblical approach applied by St Paul when he sent Timothy to collect the Corinthian church funds. This is something to keep in the minds of all involved in electing church treasurers and accountants, as the spiritual uprightness of persons involved in handling finances is emphasized in Biblical teaching:

> For Titus not only welcomed our appeal, but he is coming to you with much enthusiasm and on his own initiative. And we are sending along with him the brother who is praised by all the churches for his service to the gospel. What is more, he was chosen by the churches to accompany us as we carry the offering, which we administer in order to honour the Lord himself and to show our eagerness to help. We want to avoid any criticism of the way we administer this liberal gift. For we are taking pains to do what is right, not only in the eyes of the Lord but also in the eyes of man. In addition, we are sending with them our brother who has often proved to us in many ways that he is zealous, and now even more so because of his great confidence in you. As for Titus, he is my partner and co-worker among you; as for our brothers, they are representatives of the churches and an honour to Christ (2 Cor. 8:7-23 NIV).

---

[32] Victor Chilenje, "The challenge of the prosperity gospel for Reformed/Presbyterian churches in the 21st century", in Hermen Kroesbergen (ed.), *In Search of Health and Wealth: The Prosperity Gospel in African, Reformed* Perspective (Wellington: Christian Literature Fund, 2013), 10.

[33] cf. Kroesbergen, *In Search of Health and Wealth*; Saracco, 'Prosperity Theology' 322-326.

[34] cf. L. Scott, "Money" in John Corrie (ed.) *Dictionary of Mission Theology: Evangelical Foundations* (Downers Grove, IL: InterVarsity Press, 2007), 244-246; Daniel D. Busby, "Spending Church Money" in Berkeley, *Leadership Handbook of Management & Administration,* 527-536.

The African Church and Cultural Methods of Sustainability

Many African churches and faith-based organizations (FBOs) have managed to have their own local leaders and local missionaries within their countries, regions and even internationally and, even better, contextual theologies have been an ongoing venture in African theology all across the continent. The African church leadership should understand that raising money is a theological element that is imperative for the African Church to be termed local. Promoting ways of eradicating financial dependencies and deficiencies should be a theological vision as well as on the church's sustainability agenda.

Wherever possible, the African Church should strive to contextualize her methods of raising church funds. Africans have always been proud of their dignity, but when it comes to money, they seem to lose it. African dignity and work ethic should be instilled in all financial initiatives of the church, and henceforth the African Church should seek financial aid only when in extreme need.

Participatory community and economic development has been applied and practised in Africa since the 1960s, when the Africans realized the time had come to build up their liberated countries. As Mulwa puts it: 'People should, of necessity, participate in decisions that affect their lives. This serves to instil local responsibility as well as enhancing their sense of dignity and worth. It is believed that people will give their total support to initiatives that they helped to create.'[35] Raising funds through locally accepted African ethics such as the ethics of *ubuntu* (fraternity) and of *harambee* (solidarity) could offer the African Church even greater financial stability. As Turaki says, 'In traditional African thought, it is almost impossible to think of a human being in isolation. Humans are always conceived of in relationship with others.'[36] Generosity in African traditional society 'promoted the well being of the community and the welfare of the individuals in that community,'[37] while it was practised in a way that discouraged dependency on the neighbours or the extended family members. Using the African philosophies of solidarity would therefore mean bringing people of the same faith together as a family and community, to practise generosity by uniting their small contributions that would come together to a significant amount communally. The funds raised thereby would be dignifying, knowing that they originated from the local church and that everyone in the church participated in their own small way. A person of *ubuntu* and *harambee*, therefore, is one who shares, participates and who thinks of the well-being and growth of the community, and in this way, the spiritual community: the church.[38]

Conclusion

The African Church is growing on a day-to-day basis and, with time, Africa will bring back the old glory of African Christianity found in North Africa in the first six hundred years of Christianity. The African Church must enhance and support her own activities and make herself a comprehensively indigenous church by becoming self-supporting, self-governing, self-propagating and self-theologizing. Financial or economic sustainability has been defined as promoting ways that will supply the church with her needs today, and help her continue using positive strategies and locally identified resources, without compromising the future. The church in Africa must pioneer new ways of raising funds from its local context in order to sustain herself and, at the same time, eliminate all unbiblical and unethical methods of raising funds, like certain ways promulgated by prosperity gospel theology. Those appointed to serve as

---

[35] Francis W. Mulwa, *Demystifying Participatory Community Development: Beginning from the People Ending at the People*, revised edition (Nairobi: Paulines Publications Africa, 2013).
[36] Yusufu Turaki, *Foundations of African Traditional Religion and Worldview* (Nairobi: WordAlive Publishers Limited, 2006), 109.
[37] Hannah Wangeci Kinoti, *African Ethics: Gikuyu Traditional* Morality (Nairobi: CUEA Press, 2013), 123.
[38] cf. Stan Chu Ilo, *The Church and Development in Africa: Aid and Development from the Perspective of Catholic Social Ethics* (Nairobi: Paulines Publications Africa, 2013).

church finance officers and leaders should have proper managerial skills to bring in effectiveness and efficiency which will eliminate all misappropriation of funds.

Bibliography

AACC Ministry for Social justice Work Group III Report to the AACC Third General Assembly in Lusaka Zambia, 11th-24th May 1974. Unpublished notes from AACC Archives, May 1974.

AACC Report, 'The Moratorium Debate: What is being said and done'. Unpublished report from the AACC Archives, June 1975.

AACC Self-Reliance Moratorium Task Force Report'. Unpublished notes from AACC Archives, July 1976.

Bediako, Kwame. *Theology and Identity: The Impact of Culture Upon Christian Thought in the Second Century and in Modern Africa.* Eugene, OR: Wipf and Stock Publishers, 1999.

Berkley, James D. *Leadership Handbook of Management & Administration.* Revised and Expanded edition. Grand Rapids, MI: Baker Books, 2007.

Bevans, Stephen B. *Models of Contextual Theology, revised and expanded edition.* Maryknoll, NY: Orbis Books, 2002.

Burgess, Carr. 'The Mission of the Moratorium', address to the National Council of Churches of Christ in the USA, Executive Committee of the Division of Overseas Ministry – Jan 10 1975. Unpublished paper from the AACC Archives, January 1975.

______. 'The Moratorium: A search for self-reliance and authenticity'. Nairobi: *AACC Bulletin*, Department of Information, June 1974.

Centre for the Study of Global Christianity, *Christianity in its Global Context, 1970-2020: Society, Religion, and Mission.* South Hamilton, MA: Gordon-Conwell Theological Seminary, June 2013.

Corrie, John. *Dictionary of Mission Theology: Evangelical Foundations*. Downers Grove, IL: InterVarsity Press, 2007.

Dah, Jonas N. *Mission in a Post Missionary Era: Papers Presented at the Consultation on Mission at the Presbyterian Church Centre Kumba*. Kumba: Presbyterian Church in Cameroon, 2008.

Efiong, Utuk. *Visions of Authenticity: The Assemblies of the All Africa Conference of Churches 1963-1992.* Nairobi: All Africa Conference of Churches, 1997.

Gatu, John G. 'A call for the Africanisation of the Church in Africa'. Unpublished presentation paper to the Mission Festival in Milwaukee, USA in October 1971;

______. *Joyfully Christian Truly African*. Nairobi: Acton Publishers, 2006.

Hesselgrave, David F. *Planting Churches Cross-Culturally: North America and Beyond, second edition.* Grand Rapids, MI: Baker Academics, 2000.

Ilo, Stan Chu. *The Church and Development in Africa: Aid and Development from the Perspective of Catholic Social Ethics*. Nairobi: Paulines Publications Africa, 2013.

Kiiru, Macmillan. *Mobilizing & Managing Resources: Foundations, Principles &* Strategies. Nairobi: Evangel Publishing House, 2010.

Kinoti, Hannah Wangeci. *African Ethics: Gikuyu Traditional Morality*. Nairobi: CUEA Press, 2013.

Kraft Charles H. and Tom N. Wisely. *Readings in Dynamic Indigeneity*. Pasadena, CA: William Carey Library, 1979.

Kroesbergen, Hermen. *In Search of Health and Wealth: The Prosperity Gospel in African, Reformed* Perspective. Wellington: Christian Literature Fund, 2013.

Lederleitner, Mary T. *Cross-Cultural Partnership: Navigating the Complexities of Money and Mission.* Downers Grove, IL: InterVarsity Press, 2010.

Little, Christopher R. *Mission in the Way of Paul: Biblical Mission for the Church in the Twenty-First Century. Studies in Biblical Literature Volume 80*. New York/Oxford: Peter Lang Publishing, 2005.

Lupton, Robert D. *Toxic Charity: How Churches and Charities Hurt Those They Help and How to Reverse it.* New York, NY: HarperOne, 2011.

Makhubu, Paul. *Who are the Independent Churches. Black Theology Series Volume 7.* Johannesburg: Skotaville Publishers, 1988.

Mugambi, J.N.K. *The Church and the Future in Africa: Problems and* Promises. Nairobi: All Africa Conference of Churches, 1997.

______. *Christian Theological & Social Reconstruction*. Nairobi: Acton Publishers, 2003.

Mulwa, Francis W. *Demystifying Participatory Community Development: Beginning from the People Ending at the People*, revised edition. Nairobi: Paulines Publications Africa, 2013.

Oduro, Thomas, Hennie Pretorius, Stan Nussbaum and Bryan Born. *Mission in an African Way: A Practical Introduction to African Instituted Churches and their Sense of Mission*. Wellington: Christian Literature Fund and Bible Media, 2008.

Plummer, Robert L. and John Mark Terry. *Paul's Missionary Methods: In His Time and Ours.* Downers Grove, IL: InterVarsity Press, 2012.

Rickett, Daniel. *Making Your Partnership Work*. Enumclaw, Washington: WinePress, 2002.

Scherer, James A. *Missionary, Go Home! A Reappraisal of the Christian World Mission*. Eaglewood Cliffs, NJ: Prentice-Hall, 1964.

Schreiter, Robert J. *Constructing Local Theologies*. Maryknoll, NY: Orbis Books, 1985.

Schwartz, Glenn J. *When Charity Destroys Dignity: Overcoming Unhealthy Dependency in the Christian* Movement. Lancaster, PA: World Mission Associates, 2007.

Turaki, Yusufu. *Foundations of African Traditional Religion and Worldview.* Nairobi: WordAlive Publishers Limited, 2006.

Pew Research Center, *Global Christianity: A Report on the Size and Distribution of the World's Christian Population*. Pew Forum on Religion & Public Life, December 2011.

Uka, E.M., *Missionary go Home? A Sociological Interpretation of An African Response to Christian Mission*. Frankfurt: Peter Lang, 1989.

(141) AFRICAN CHURCHES AND GOOD GOVERNANCE IN AFRICA

Titus Ogalo Pacho

Introduction

The issue of governance is at the centre of the biggest challenges Africa is facing today. Bad governance, including corruption, has become a cancerous growth in many African countries. It has seen proceeds from natural resources and revenue from taxation being diverted to serve a few individuals to the detriment of the many, instead of developing common goods such as education, health services and infrastructure. The 1989 World Bank report on sub-Saharan Africa, for instance, characterized the crisis in the region as a 'crisis of governance'.[1] Therefore, the question of governance becomes one of Africa's most important needs. Even though Africa is not one country, many countries on the continent have common problems related to governance, coupled with a startling lack of accountability among politicians, church leaders, civil servants and other individuals, amounting to widespread moral decay. However, the details, nuances and practical dynamics of the problem can vary from place to place. The church cannot afford to be quiet on the issues of governance. Both church leaders and the congregations are citizens who are affected directly or indirectly by those responsible for governance. In what follows, I shall examine the concept of good governance in the context of African churches and their role in promoting or hindering it. I do not mean to suggest this section exhausts the discourse but it serves as an introductory discussion on the topic. What ought to be the role of African churches in the realm of good governance? To answer this question, we need to understand first the concept of good governance and distinguish it from its opposite – bad governance.

The Concept of Good Governance

While there might not always be a common view of what governance entails, it operates at every level of human interaction including household, community, national, regional and global levels. A fundamental element of governance includes an interactive process by which individuals and institutions, public and private, manage their common affairs. It permeates economic, social, and environmental spheres.

Good governance is in itself a normative principle which determines what *ought* to be done in connection with governance issues. It holds that individuals and institutions are obliged to perform their functions in a manner that promotes good values of efficiency, public honesty, transparency, and responsiveness to society.[2] The United Nations Development Programme (UNDP) describes good governance as, among other things, participatory, transparent and accountable, effective and equitable, and it promotes the rule of law. It ensures that political, social, and economic priorities are based on broad consensus in society and that the voices of the poorest and the most vulnerable are heard in decision-making over the allocation of development resources.[3] In considering good governance, democracy which refers to the legitimacy of government is an important component.[4] The above parameters can be viewed as the 'principles of good governance' although they might not be exhaustive. Conversely, bad governance

---

[1] World Bank, *Sub-Saharan Africa, From Crisis to Sustainable Growth* (Washington DC: World Bank, 1989).

[2] Chowdhury, N. and C.E. Skarstedt, "The Principle of Good Governance, A Draft Working Paper" (Oxford, 2005), 4.

[3] UNDP, "Reconceptualizing Governance: Discussion Paper 2" (New York: Management Development and Governance Division, Bureau for Policy and Programme Support, 1997).

[4] Lewis Akpogena, "The Church and Good Governance" (2012).

could entail, but may not be limited to, oppressive systems, rules and policies; corruption; political or social instability and conflict, unjust structures; and ineffective structures and systems.

Role of African Churches in Good Governance

African churches can serve as role models of best practice of good governance if they adhere to its principles. They should intervene in political and economic matters and advocate human rights protection, human freedom, dignity and socio-economic justice. Once they practise the principles of good governance themselves, they can have the moral authority to offer viable opposition to oppressive and corrupt governments while emphasizing values of good governance, servant leadership, transparency, responsibility, honesty, accountability, justice, love, integrity, generosity, industriousness and self-giving even amidst intimidation.

In many parts of Africa, Christianity has always been a factor in Africa's democratic processes.[5] African churches have a moral duty to contribute to the development of a social, economic, political and cultural order that facilitates the growth and fulfilment of every person. This order should be extended to the natural environment so that humans are to exercise responsible and caring stewardship of the earth and its resources. The view that the church can have no authority in the operation of the state is contrary to the objectives and vision of progressive society. It is clear in the Bible that besides Joseph being a man of God, he also served as a prime minister in Egypt; Moses was a liberator who led the people out of bondage to their Promised Land; and Daniel played a role in politics while in exile.[6]

Although Christianity cannot be equated with any system of government, it must remain critical of all social orders.[7] It is part of Christian witness within the political sphere to evaluate all the political systems prophetically from the perspective of the reign of God.[8] It is the prophetic duty of African churches to discern whether the systems that govern a country are in alignment with that of the kingdom of God. The establishment of a democratic order will not usher in the kingdom of God, but it is considered the best form of government that human beings are able to construct given the constraints of our ability and the extent of our fallibility.[9] Larry Diamond emphasises that Africa will not develop economically unless it develops institutionally a capacity for democratic governance.[10] In situations where democracy is limited and civil society is underdeveloped, the churches are sometimes the only civil organisations that can inspire and support a movement towards true democracy and development of a civil society which can counteract and change a monopolising one-party system which usually abuses power.[11]

It is the duty of the church to be committed to the holistic mission of combining preaching the gospel and administering the sacraments with a deep commitment to social justice. The church has always embraced a theological position for social justice but it should refrain from delving into partisan politics which divide rather than unite. 'The church must be the unifier not divider, to shepherd the flock despite different political orientations.'[12] The role of the church in the promotion of social justice is quite biblical as evidenced by the whole credo of the book of the prophet Amos, and even by the generality of the

---

[5] Munetsi Ruzivo, "A Mapping of the Church Groups in Zimbabwe," in *The Role of the Church in the Struggle for Democratic Change in Zimbabwe* (2008), 4.

[6] Edwin Mwase, "Church and Politics are Inseparable" *Sunday Mail* (29 July to 4 August, 2012), D3.

[7] John W. Gruchy. "Theological Reflections on the Task of the Church in the Democratisation of Africa," in *The Christian Churches and the Democratisation of Africa,* edited by Paul Gifford (New York: E.J. Brill, 1995), 48.

[8] Gruchy, "Theological Reflections on the Task of the Church in the Democratisation of Africa," 48.

[9] Gruchy, "Theological Reflections on the Task of the Church in the Democratisation of Africa," 48.

[10] Larry Diamond, "The Second Liberation," *Africa Report* 32, no. 6 (1992), 41.

[11] Frans J. Verstraelen, *Zimbabwean Realities and Christian Responses* (Gweru: Mambo Press, 1998), 75.

[12] World Council of Churches (WCC), "Churches in Africa Hope for Good Governance and Stable Democracy" (2013).

teaching of Jesus Christ himself.[13] However, 'neither justice nor freedom can flourish without the development of appropriate social structures'.[14] The role of African churches in enabling this to happen is part of the church's mission. African churches must therefore develop appropriate strategies based on a sound theological reflection to promote democracy and good governance, first among themselves and second in particular contexts and Africa in general. This role places the church as 'the conscience of society and the heartbeat of morality'.[15] African churches must emphasize and promote the kingdom values for democracy and good governance through seminars, training, workshops, sermons, press release, sensitization and community mobilization.[16]

Five trajectories may help the African churches to play their role in the democratisation process and good governance, namely, prophetic, personalist, covenantal, liberal and socialist.[17] The prophetic trajectory arises out of the experience of liberation, affirms human equality and seeks social justice. Theological reflection on democracy must of necessity continually return to this prophetic source of Christian faith which finds its focus in Jesus and his proclamation of the reign of God. The personalist trajectory focuses on an understanding that human beings are created in the image of the triune God. This agrees with the concept of *Ubuntu* where personal identity is relational rather than individualist.[18] It is therefore the role of African churches to emphasize human sociality, interdependence of persons and the common good which are central to democracy. The covenantal trajectory reminds people that they have a covenant with God and all their actions are therefore accountable to God. It stresses the need for human responsibility before God and towards others on the basis of God's reign in Jesus Christ. This leads to a strong emphasis on accountability not only to an electorate but also to God. The liberal trajectory focuses on the promotion of human rights based on their God-given dignity, which implies that all human beings are created the same and are endowed with the same physical and spiritual components.[19] The socialist trajectory is mainly concerned with economic justice and democracy. It emphasises that there can be no democracy without economic justice and responding to the plight of the poor. The above trajectories bring about a Christian theological contribution to the democratisation process and good governance.

When governments in Africa act or speak contrary to their own laws and international norms and standards, it is important for the churches to remind them of their responsibilities.[20] They must speak out boldly in cases of corruption, abuse of office and bad governance as 'guardians of public ethics and morality and to hold the government accountable to its citizens and to the law'.[21] The churches should also speak against draconian laws that are enacted to oppress citizens at the expense of a few powerful leaders' who act and speak with immunity. Furthermore, Africa churches should remind governments that they are not masters, but servants of the people who elected them to serve the electorate.

Nevertheless, African churches themselves face challenges in democracy and good governance. First, there is the problem of contradiction. African church leaders have often been told by secular leaders to clean the huge backlog of injustices, corruption, leadership struggles, poor succession plans, tribalism and mismanagement of resources before they dare to speak against the issues in politics and governance.[22]

---

[13] Mwase, "Church and Politics are Inseparable," D3.

[14] Gruchy, "Theological Reflections on the Task of the Church in the Democratisation of Africa," 47.

[15] Mwase, "Church and Politics are Inseparable," D3.

[16] Lewis Akpogena, "The Church and Good Governance" (2012).

[17] Gruchy, "Theological Reflections on the Task of the Church in the Democratisation of Africa," 53-54.

[18] Gruchy, "Theological Reflections on the Task of the Church in the Democratisation of Africa," 53.

[19] Pacho, *Critical and Creative Education for the New Africa,* 135.

[20] Nicholas Mkaronda et al., eds. *Prophetic Witness in Zimbabwe: Critical Voices Emerging in Times of Crisis* (Harare: Ecumenical Support Services), 2003.

[21] Mkaronda, *Prophetic Witness in Zimbabwe: Critical Voices Emerging in Times of Crisis,* 77.

[22] Lewis Akpogena, "The Church and Good Governance" (2012).

African churches therefore ought to demonstrate a good example of good governance so that they can have the moral authority to challenge bad governance in other sectors. Second, we live in religiously pluralistic societies. Modern democracy began with the rejection of the church's temporal power and the affirmation of religious tolerance. This does not mean that churches do not have a vital contribution to make to the renewal of democracy both at the level of values and functionality.[23] Third, 'the affinity of Christian faith to democratic values' has been severely compromised by the 'historical distance of churches towards democracy'.[24] The church has too often been ambivalent about human equality, freedom, rights and justice. Theological reflection must, of necessity, critically examine the extent to which Christian belief has become perverted, and the extent to which the praxis of the church has been unfaithful to the gospel. At the same time, theological reflection needs to exercise a critique of democracy and the democratisation process in terms of the norms of justice, equality and freedom.[25]

Conclusion

The churches in Africa have a moral obligation to address governance issues on the continent. To accomplish this task, they must first and foremost embrace the principles of good governance themselves and address their own internal governance problems if they are going to have moral authority and relevance in addressing the subject on the continent, and in their respective regions, countries and communities. African churches must be the prophetic voice to the continent. Their role in good governance can be more effective and productive if they live what they preach by practically proclaiming and demonstrating the principle of good governance in their policies, values, processes, behaviour and institutions. They should help combat the problem of bad governance at all levels of society in Africa, perhaps by emphasizing values of good governance, transparency, responsibility, honesty, accountability, justice, industriousness and self-giving. From the beginning of the Christian movement, the role of the church in society has not only been to proclaim the message of the reign of God, but to seek to be a sign of that reign within its own ecclesial life and structures. Today there is much debate on whether or not the church should itself be more democratic in its own structures. The issues are complex because for some, hierarchy is of the essence of the church whereas for others the goal is an egalitarian community. We need to recognise that from the beginning, the idea of participation has been central to all forms of church government. This is symbolised most dramatically by the sacrament of baptism which declares that all those who are baptised, irrespective of gender, social class, or ethnicity, are united as equals within one body and share together in the mission of the church in the world.[26] However, since a human project cannot be achieved in isolation but demands collective responsibility, promoting a culture of good governance in Africa should be the collective responsibility of all stakeholders at the individual, household, community, national, regional and global levels.

Bibliography

Akpogena, Lewis, *'The Church and Good Governance'*. January 31, 2012. www.thenigerianvoice.com/news/81424/1/the-church-and-good-governance.html(accessed 24 January, 2015)

Chowdhury, N. and C.E. Skarstedt. *'The Principle of Good Governance*, A Draft Working Paper.' In the CISDL 'Recent Developments in International Law Related to Sustainable Development Series.' Oxford, United Kingdom, 2005.

[23] Gruchy, "Theological Reflections on the Task of the Church in the Democratisation of Africa," 49.

[24] Wolfgang Huber, "Christianity and Democracy in Europe," *Emory International Law Journal* 6 (1992), 35.

[25] Gruchy, "Theological Reflections on the Task of the Church in the Democratisation of Africa," 49.

[26] Gruchy, "Theological Reflections on the Task of the Church in the Democratisation of Africa," 55.

Diamond, Larry. *'The Second Liberation.' Africa Report* 32, no. 6 (1992),

Gruchy, John W. 'Theological Reflections on the Task of the Church in the Democratisation of Africa.' In *The Christian Churches and the Democratisation of Africa,* edited by Paul Gifford, 47-60. New York: E.J. Brill, 1995.

Huber, Wolfgang. 'Christianity and Democracy in Europe.' *Emory International Law Journal* 6, 1992.

Mkaronda, Nicholas, et al., eds. *Prophetic Witness in Zimbabwe: Critical Voices Emerging in Times of Crisis.* Harare: Ecumenical Support Services, 2003.

Mwase, Edwin. 'Church and Politics are Inseparable.' *Sunday Mail*, 29 July to 4 August, 2012, D3.

Pacho, Titus O. *Critical and Creative Education for the New Africa.* Bern: Peter Lang AG, 2013.

Ruzivo, Munetsi. 'A Mapping of the Church Groups in Zimbabwe.' In *The Role of the Church in the Struggle for Democratic Change in Zimbabwe,* 2008, 4-14.

UNDP. '*Reconceptualizing Governance: Discussion Paper 2*.' New York: Management Development and Governance Division, Bureau for Policy and Programme Support, 1997.

Verstraelen, Frans J. *Zimbabwean Realities and Christian Responses*. Gweru: Mambo Press, 1998.

World Bank. *Sub-Saharan Africa, From Crisis to Sustainable Growth.* Washington DC: World Bank, 1989.

World Council of Churches (WCC). '*Churches in Africa Hope for Good Governance and Stable Democracy.*' May 17, 2013. www.thenigerianvoice.com/news/113770/1/churches-in-africa-hope-for-good-governance-and-st.html (accessed 24 January 2015).

(142) AFRICAN CHURCHES, CONFLICT RESOLUTION, RECONCILIATION AND PEACE-BUILDING ON THE CONTINENT

Samuel Kobia

Introduction

The idea of conflict resolution and reconciliation in the international community gained greater currency in the last decade of the twentieth century and into the beginning of 21st century. But it can be correctly argued that reconciliation is not a new concept for the church. A gospel imperative, reconciliation is intrinsic to the ministry of the church. Nevertheless we shall start this article by describing a simple theoretical framework against which the involvement of the African churches in conflict resolution, reconciliation and peace-building is to be considered. Then we shall look at a theological basis for the churches' involvement in which some imperatives will be spelt out. Given that conflicts occur within specific socio-cultural contexts, it will be shown that there is also a cultural imperative that informs, however indirectly, the churches' work in conflict resolution and reconciliation. Before highlighting a selection of actual situations in which African churches have been involved, we shall consider three types of conflicts to which churches have responded. The conclusion identifies key challenges to the churches' ministry of reconciliation.

Theoretical Framework

A major finding of researchers on socio-political determinants is that conflicts are prevalent in poor and weakly-institutionalized countries. Given its weak economic performance in the post-independence period and her high conflict prevalence, determinants of conflict in Africa are of particular interest. According to the Armed Conflict Database (ACD) measure of civil conflict (based on a threshold of 1,000 battle deaths) findings suggest that about 8.5% of country/years in Africa since 1950 are conflict years compared to around 5% of country/years in the rest of the world over the same period.

Suggestions offered in trying to explain this situation include: conflict in Africa is viewed as a reflection of its poverty, thus lowering the cost of fighting; conflict is the product of rent-seeking for natural resources; conflict is a reflection of polities that are ethnically polarized with weak institutions for conflict resolution. The last argument is based on the observation that Africa's modern political geography reflects a rather arbitrary division of territory by colonial powers, thus creating a particular challenge for nation-building and effective peaceful states.

The standard economic approach to political violence looks for factors that explain the costs and benefits of using violence to achieve specific ends, particularly in the form of either remaining in power or mounting an insurgency. Benefits from using violence are frequently couched in terms of capturing resources either directly, as in the capture of territory, or through winning political power. Conflicts can also be the product of long-standing grievances between groups. Moreover, ethnic polarization can be said to be positively correlated with conflict.

In 1992, the then UN Secretary General, Boutros Boutros-Ghali, defined peace-building as 'action to identify and support structures, which will tend to strengthen and solidify peace in order to avoid a relapse into conflict'.[1] In effect then, peace-building is a term that describes interventions that are designed to

---

[1] UNSG, 1992 report, An Agenda for Peace, paragraph 21.

prevent the start or resumption of violent conflict by creating an atmosphere of sustainable peace, and puts in place processes that ensure peace is maintained at all times. Peace-building activities address the root causes or potential causes of violence, create a societal expectation for peaceful conflict resolution and stabilize society politically and socio-economically.

The Theological Basis for the Church's Involvement in Conflict Resolution, Reconciliation, and Peace-Building

Conflict resolution is conceptualized as the methods and processes involved in facilitating the peaceful ending of conflict and retribution. In most instances, the church would be interested in peace-making, which usually takes place when there is already conflict or symptoms of conflict and thus used to bring the conflicting parties to a state of inaction. Peace-making is practical conflict transformation focused upon establishing equitable power relationships robust enough to forestall future conflict, often including the establishment of means of agreeing on ethical decisions within a community, or among parties that had previously engaged in inappropriate (i.e. violent) responses to conflict.

The involvement of the church in conflict resolution, reconciliation, healing and peace-building is founded on the gospel imperative in that according to Jesus, Blessed are the peace-makers, for they will be called children of God' (Matt. 5:9). This is reaffirmed by Paul in 2 Corinthians 5:18-20. '... All this is from God, who reconciled us to himself through Christ, and has given us the ministry of reconciliation…'; and in Hebrews 12:14, 'Pursue peace with everyone, and the holiness without which no one will see the Lord'. James also emphasizes that, '… a harvest of righteousness is sown in peace for those who make peace' (James 3:18).

The biblical basis of peace-making, peace-building and reconciliation is not limited to the New Testament. We are entreated to 'seek peace and pursue it' (Psalm 34:14). And Isaiah foresees the eschaton when 'nation shall not lift sword against nation… neither shall they learn war any more' (Isaiah 2:4). The African churches' work on peace and reconciliation is complimented by the cultural imperative for peace.

In Africa, traditional conflict resolution processes are part of a well-structured, time-proven social system that is geared towards reconciliation, and improvement of social relations. The methods, processes and regulations are deeply rooted in the customs and traditions of the African people. The processes strive to restore a balance, to settle conflict, to eliminate disputes and to anticipate and stop or pre-empt conflict. Localized dispute resolution processes remain a key tradition within the African community. The church in Africa, being an integral part of modern African society, embraces these processes and is recognized as a mediator of conflicts and a peace-builder who is admonished to always be truthful.

Mapping of Conflicts in Africa

There are two types of conflicts in Africa: those that are to do with historical injustices, and those to do with contemporary issues and trends.

These conflicts can be classified as open or latent.

Open conflicts

Open conflicts involve open struggle or clashes between opposing forces. These can end up in prolonged fighting, battle or war. Examples include Libya (2009 to the present), Egypt (2010), Nigeria (2009 to the present), Mali (2009 to the present), Chad (2006), Central Africa Republic (2010 to the present), Democratic Republic of Congo (1996 to the present), South Sudan (1959-1972;1973-2005; 2013 to the present), Sudan (1959-1972; 1973-2005), Somalia (1992 to the present) and Northern Uganda (1987-2006).

Latent conflicts

Latent conflicts are conflicts in their own right, or the first phase of an open conflict. Latent conflict exists whenever individuals, groups, organizations, or nations have mistrusts that develop to differences that bother one or the other. However, these differences are not great enough to cause one side to act to alter the situation but could easily lead to an open conflict at the slightest of provocations. These include: Morocco-Western Sahara (1970s to the present); Algeria (2010); Kenya (1992-2014), Eritrea (1987 to the present) and Ethiopia (1987 to the present); Burundi (1994 to the present), Rwanda (1994 to the present); Madagascar (2004 to the present); Mozambique (2000 to the present) and South Africa (1994 to the present).

Specific Interventions

The church in Africa has undertaken mediation roles in countries such as Sudan/South Sudan, Mozambique, Democratic Republic of Congo, Rwanda, Burundi, Kenya, Ghana, S. Africa, and Uganda. For the purposes of this paper, we shall use Sudan/S. Sudan and Kenya as our case studies with a particular focus on interventions by the All Africa Conference of Churches (AACC) and the National Council of Churches in Kenya (NCCK) respectively.

Before presenting the case studies, it is important to make a quick mention of three situations where churches have intervened and mediated successfully. In 1994, in South Africa, communities were involved in violent conflicts along political lines: ANC supporters versus Inkatha supporters in Johannesburg. The South African Council of Churches initiated dialogue, but the most effective was the mediation by the then Presiding Bishop of the Methodist Church in Southern Africa, Mvume Dandala. At a high risk to his own safety, Dandala played a mediation role running over many months but eventually his efforts brought together the warring parties and peace was restored.

In Uganda, the activities of the Lord's Resistance Army from 1987 resulted in abductions and killings of hundreds of villagers. The Uganda Joint Christian Council initiated a conflict resolution programme which had a good measure of success. Moreover, the efforts of the Catholic Church, and those of Bishop Okello of the Anglican Church, led in the late 1990s/ 2000s to useful peace talks and the release of many abducted girls and women.

Thirdly, in 1995 a conflict ignited by a dispute over the price of a chicken at a market-place in the northern part of Ghana led to an ethnic war between Konkombas and Nanyumbas. Over several months, fighting between members of the two tribes resulted in the death of scores of innocent citizens. The Ghana Council of Churches, with technical assistance from Nairobi Peace Initiative-Africa, established mediation processes that led to signing of a peace pact whose ceremony was attended by the president of the country. Chiefs of the respective communities were also involved. Once peace was restored, the chiefs continued to nurture reconciliation using traditional and cultural approaches. Till now, the two communities have lived in peace and harmony.

Sudan/South Sudan

The 1972 Addis Ababa Peace Agreement brokered by AACC and WCC was the first ever mediated agreement in resolving the Sudanese conflicts. The Agreement was reached between the government of Sudan and Anyanya I[2], the Southern Sudanese liberation movement initiated to fight for freedom, justice and democracy in Sudan. The full account of the process leading to the signing of the Addis Ababa

[2] Anyanya (also Anya-Nya) was a southern Sudanese separatist rebel army formed during the First Sudanese Civil War (1955-1972)

Agreement has been well documented in the *Mediation of Civil Wars in Africa*,[3] and *Too Many Agreements Dishonoured*.[4]

Following the split in 1990 in the Sudan Peoples Liberation Movement and Army (SPLM/A), the churches in Kenya undertook to resolve the conflict between the concomitant factions. The NCCK and the People for Peace of the Catholic Church in Kenya, with technical assistance from Nairobi Peace Initiative – Africa, mediated for eight months. Among the achievements of this process were: the release of prisoners of war held by the two factions; an agreement on the democratization of the movement; the recognition by SPLM/A of the role of traditional leaders in conflict resolution and reconciliation; the acceptance by SPLM/A of the churches' role in monitoring any future human rights violations by the SPLM/A.

In 1995, the WCC and Caritas International formed the Sudan Ecumenical Forum (SEF) which became the main platform and framework through which the major ecumenical partners would accompany the SCC and the New Sudan Council of Churches (NSCC). The SEF basic ethos was that the Sudan churches should occupy the centre of all that was done in the name of Sudan, and that the Sudan churches, through the SCC and the NSCC, would determine the agenda of SEF.

Through this framework, the Sudan churches embarked on people to people grassroots peace processes which contributed significantly to the eventual signing in 2005 of the Comprehensive Peace Agreement (CPA) in Nairobi, Kenya.

In the run-up to the Sudan Referendum and eventually the Independence of South Sudan, churches in Sudan, with the accompaniment of AACC and WCC, engaged in high-level advocacy and diplomacy to help in securing a peaceful atmosphere for the referendum and independence.

Kenya

Since Kenya experienced the 'ethnic conflicts' or 'land clashes' of 1992 in the Rift Valley in the build-up towards the first multi-party general elections, similar conflicts have occurred in different parts of the country, most notably in the election years of 1997 and 2007. The latter would have far-reaching consequences with many victims left homeless, landless, destitute, injured, abused or dead. The NCCK was among the first organizations to respond to the 1992 violence in the Rift Valley and Western Kenya through a series of interventions under the *Land Clashes Project* later renamed *Relief and Rehabilitation Project, the Peace and Reconciliation Project, the Community Peace-building and Development Project* and finally, *Community Peace-building and Reconciliation Project.*

The project had a three-stage operation: emergency assistance to the internally displaced families in the camps; addressing the resettlement needs of the 'victims'; thirdly, focusing more on re-integration and healing of the 'clash victims' in which relationship and peace-building among the affected communities took centre stage under 'Good Neighbourliness' seminars.

NCCK's overall goal has remained to have communities in the Rift Valley co-exist harmoniously and to reduce the level of violence in the affected areas. 'Good Neighbourliness' has since become the leitmotif and a connecting point. In this context, a 'neighbour' refers to persons who were members of a community other than one's own. Secondly, kinship developed out of intermarriage became a starting-point to strengthen good neighbourliness. 'Good Neighbourliness' consisted of a series of community-level workshops, conducted in remote villages where conflict had occurred. These have targeted all sectors of the community, across the conflict divide and included a broad range of actors such as women, youth and elders. The guiding philosophy has been that reconciliation would only be achieved through constructive dialogue, mutual co-operation and respect for the rights of individuals and communities.

---

[3] Hezkias Asefa: Mediation of Civil Wars, Approaches and Strategies.

[4] Abel Alier: Southern Sudan: Too Many Agreements Dishonoured (Sudan Studies) Jan 1, 1999.

One of the major specific outcomes of the 'Good Neighbourliness' seminars was the establishment of localized platforms that would meet on a monthly basis to analyze the local peace situation and to plan an appropriate strategic response. They also constantly monitored incidences of violence within their locality and co-ordinated other local activities with NCCK and other stakeholders. Good Neighbourliness seminars have since become platforms where communities dialogue and reflect on their experiences. This is a very effective peace-building method.

Challenges

There are three main challenges to the church's mission in conflict resolution, reconciliation, healing and peace-building: to live and act in faith, hope and love; to overcome the fear of speaking truth to power; the capacity to bring about hope to those living lives of hopelessness and despair.

The churches could address these by embracing a ministry of presence where violence, poverty, suffering and pain is found; developing and adopting an integral and holistic approach to healing and reconciliation based on the realization that the consequences of conflict are not only vertical but also horizontal; regaining basic biblical principles and understanding reconciliation and forgiveness; and giving content, sharpness and clarity to reconciliation.

Bibliography

Ajayi, A. T and Buhari, L. O; Methods of Conflict Resolution in African Traditional Society; African Research Review, Vol. 8 (2), Serial No. 33, April, 2014:138-157

Bates, Robert: (2008), 'The Logic of State Failure: Learning from Late-Century Africa', Conflict Management and Peace Science, 25, 297.314.

Besley, T and Reynal-Querol, M; (2012) The Legacy of Historical Conflict Evidence from Africa; http://thred.devecon.org/papers/2012/2012-014_Besley_The-Legacy-of.pdf

Kiptoo, William; (2013); Rebuilding Relationships Through Good Neighbourliness Seminars in the Rift Valley, Kenya www.beyondintractability.org/kiptoo-rebuilding

Kobia, Samuel: (2013); Dialogue Matters: The Role of Ecumenical Diplomacy in the run-up to the independence of South Sudan; APF Chancery Publishers Africa Ltd; Limuru..

Kobia, Samuel: Reconciliation and the Healing of Memories; Lecture at a Public Seminar; Irish School of Ecumenism, Dublin, 30 April 2007.

Kobia, Samuel: Churches' Responsibility for World Peace and Reconciliation; Speech at the WCC Seminar at Oulu City Library, 27 may 2005.

Komuhangi, J; (2006) Report on FES Dialogue on Conflict and Peace Building in Eastern Africa: Planting Seeds for Justice, Lasting Peace and Sustainable Development.

Murdock, George P (1959), Africa: Its People and their Culture History, McGraw-Hill Book Company, New York.

Nyukuri, B. K; (1997): *The Impact of Past and Potential Ethnic Conflicts on Kenyan's Stability and Development.* A paper prepared for the USAID Conference on Conflict Resolution in the Greater Horn of Africa; Department of History and Government University of Nairobi.

Opondo, E.O; (2006) Making Choices for Peace: Aid Agencies in Filed Diplomacy; Paulines Publications Africa, Nairobi.

Orobator, A.E; (2013) Practising Reconciliation, Doing Justice and Building peace: Conversations on Catholic Theological ethics in Africa; Paulines Publications Africa, Nairobi.

SECAM; (2001); Peace, Fruit of Reconciliation; Paulines Publications Africa, Nairobi.

ZELEZA, PAUL TIYAMBE; (undated); Introduction The Causes & Costs of War in Africa: From Liberation Struggles to the 'War on Terror'; www.ohioswallow.com/extras/9780821418093 _intro.pdf

(143) CLIMATE CHANGE AND FOOD SECURITY: A CHALLENGE FOR AFRICAN CHRISTIANITY

J.N.K. Mugambi

1. Introduction

The connection between climate and food supply has been recognized and appreciated in all cultures, across generations, as a matter of common sense. Through cultural creativity, innovation, invention and adaptation, humans found ways and means to survive as long as they lived within the natural climate rhythms, and within the capacity of the natural ecologies to replenish year after year, season after season. Climate science confirms that since 1850 the natural climate cycles have continually deviated from the normal seasonal rhythm on a global scale, to the extent that flora and fauna have lost their natural capacity to adjust – in all climate zones on Planet Earth. It is this human disruption that has been identified as one of the major factors responsible for this climate variability, through the emission of increasing amounts of greenhouse gases into the atmosphere. At the same time, natural environments have been destroyed through urbanization, transport infrastructure, mining, plantation agriculture, and so on.[1]

Religion, especially Christianity, has welcomed and embraced this technological 'advancement', including environmental degradation, as an integral outcome of 'progress'. As early as 1910, the World Missionary Movement was enthusiastic about such industrial progress, then considered advantageous for the spread of Christianity outside Europe and North America. The two devastating world wars that followed (1914-18 and 1939-45) were to demonstrate the immense capacity of humans to annihilate each other, with environmental impacts that will continue for centuries. Africans have contributed least in destruction of the global environment, but they have suffered most. Christianity was introduced as 'Good News', but not everything associated with the missionary enterprise could be described as such. Africans welcomed biblical scriptures whole-heartedly, but response to the rest of the missionary initiatives evoked mixed responses across Africa, to the extent that Africa has the largest number of independent churches in the entire history of Christianity.[2]

Within the modern ecumenical movement, some visionaries have raised awareness about the destructive tendencies of science and technology, but their voices have been more peripheral than central. Preoccupation has been more with matters of 'Faith and Order', on the one hand, and 'Mission and Evangelism', on the other. In ecumenical circles, the relation between 'church' and 'society' remained more an 'academic' discourse than a practical 'vocation'.[3] The theme of the First Assembly of the World Council of Churches – convened at Amsterdam in 1948 – was 'Man's Disorder and God's Design'. This theme was a cryptic recognition among ecumenist theologians that human intelligence had been deployed more for destructive ends, than for constructive ones, with regard both to culture and the environment.

Despite the ecological crisis that has loomed since the 1940s, it is interesting that none of the ten Assemblies of the WCC (between 1948 and 2013) had 'Environment' or 'Ecology' as the main theme. Yet in Christian missionary outreach, Jesus is proclaimed as the herald of 'Life in Abundance'. From the WCC

---

[1] John Houghton, *Global Warming: The Complete Briefing,* Fourth Edition, Cambridge: CUP, 2010.

[2] Allan Anderson, *African Reformation,* Trenton, New Jersey: Africa World Press, 2001.

[3] The late Professor Charles Birch was among those ecumenists most vocal on environmental stewardship. In his Address to the Fifth WCC Assembly at Nairobi in November 1975 he proclaimed the oft-quoted challenge: "The Rich must live more simply, so that the Poor may simply live." This challenge is yet to be heeded, in view of increasing economic inequality between and within nations.

Sixth Assembly at Vancouver (1983) emerged a phrase that remained in vogue for a while, but soon faded into oblivion: 'Justice, Peace and Integrity of Creation'. There were inconclusive debates on the meaning of 'The Integrity of Creation', and on the relationship between this phrase and the struggles for Justice and Peace, especially in Africa, the Caribbean and the Pacific.[4] On the basis of sound research, the WCC sub-unit on Church and Society, and the WCC Working Group on Climate Change issued several statements coinciding with secular international conferences. The purpose was to raise awareness on the theological and ethical dimension of political, economic decisions made at such conferences relating to environment and ecology.[5]

It is impossible for 'life in abundance' to be enjoyed by the majority in a global context where the global environment has been so degraded as to threaten the survival of the larger proportion of humankind, and where global inequality increases in inverse proportion year after year. Those few with the least capacity for ecological adaptation continue with profligate destruction of the environment, while the many with least capacity for coping continue to suffer marginalization. Oxfam has documented this extreme global inequality in its 2015 Report released during the World Economic Forum at Davos, Switzerland, in January 2016 – with the implication that reducing poverty remains more a wish than an attainable goal.[6] As Professor Charles Birch pleaded in December 1975 during his Address to the Fifth WCC Assembly, '…the rich must live more simply, so that the poor may simply live'.[7] While a few have great capacity for adaptation, and can offer 'charity' and 'sympathy' for the majority, the fact is that we humans as a species have only one planet on which to survive, or perish. Archbishop Desmond Tutu advises:

> We often hear that we do not inherit the earth from our fore parents but are borrowing it from our children. This is not correct. We are stealing it from them! We cannot pay back all the resources we are devouring in order to feed our growth economy. Nor can we bring back all the species whose extinction we are bringing about.[8]

Pleas from the less industrialized nations have been for justice, and equity, but the responses from the most industrialized have been pity, empathy and condescension. Empathy is not part the vocabulary of climate change negotiations. Climate change has rendered subsistence agriculture unsustainable, especially in tropical Africa, Asia, South America and the Pacific – where the majority of people live. The low coastlands, islands and atolls are at risk of submersion by rising sea levels, and the fate of the peoples living there remains in doubt. Pope Francis in his encyclical *Laudato Si* reminds all people of goodwill to take care of creation, because the life of flora and fauna depends on the sustenance of an ecological balance for the global ecology as a whole.

> We know it is impossible to sustain the current level of consumption of more developed countries and the wealthiest sectors of society, where the habit of wasting and throwing away reaches unprecedented levels. Already they have exceeded certain maximum limits of exploitation of the planet, without the problem of poverty having been resolved.[9]

---

[4] During the 1980s there was much campaigning against nuclear power, partly because of the Cold War that was raging; partly because of the risks associated with it, and partly because of its expensive outlay. Poor nations were discouraged to opt for it, but the rich nations continued undeterred.

[5] For example, www.climatejusticeonline.org/wp-content/uploads/WCC-climate-change-booklet.pdf.

[6] www.democracynow.org/2016/1/21/the_1_economy_the_worlds_richest.

[7] Charles Birch, "Creation, Technology and Human Survival", in *Ecumenical Review,* Geneva: WCC, January 1976, pp. 66-79.

[8] Archbishop Desmond Tutu, Sermon preached at Copenhagen Cathedral, 28 October 2014, http://reliefweb.int/videos/single/noedhjaelp/hJW70nSKDTQ.

[9] *Laudato Si,* 27, www.hillheat.com/files/Laudato_Si_formatted_translation.pdf.

The preliminary observations in this introductory section provide some background for the rest of this essay.[10] Food security and ecological stewardship are intricately related. If every human generation could add more to nature than it consumes, Planet Earth would become a paradise for future generations. Conversely, if each generation continues to plunder nature, humans will become an endangered species, as a result of their own self-destruction, as Professor Jared Diamond has illustrated.[11]

2. Historical Context

African Christians in the 21st century live a paradoxical existence, in a continent that, reportedly, has the fastest growing adherence to Christianity, and at the same time is the most impoverished, the most dehumanized and the most humiliated. Is this adherence to Christianity a response to the impoverishment, dehumanization and humiliation? Or is it a renewal of traditional African religiosity, expressed in Christian idioms?[12] History might perhaps hint at some clues. For several centuries Europe suffered imperial oppression under Roman rule. The Council of Trent (1545-63) declared the Reformers and their teachings anathema. This declaration was reiterated at the First Vatican Council (1869-70). The Second Vatican Council (1962-65) did not revoke the excommunication, but Pope John XXIII could say about the Protestants that they are 'our separated brethren', since the Lord's Prayer was common to both Roman Catholics and Protestants.[13] The Christians of western and northern Europe, together with their siblings in North America, having achieved freedom from the Roman and Ottoman Empires, appropriated the Christian ethos for scientific and technological modernization of their societies.

Christianity, having been spread across western and northern Europe by Roman priests, notable among them Francis of Assisi, Augustine of Canterbury and others, became normative for both élite and commoner. Roman missionaries and priests introduced literacy and literature, and this Roman literary background remains integral to European academia. Monasteries and abbeys remain an essential part of European cultural history.

In turn, Protestant and Catholic missionaries, following their compatriot discoverers, explorers, traders, adventurers and conquerors, went abroad and established mission stations in the colonies. These mission stations became the nuclei of the African Christianity we document at the beginning of the 21st century. The European missionary legacy in Africa is now archival. Hardly anything remains of the missionary past, which fits in squarely with the present expressions of African Christianity. Whatever remains of it is in the foreign languages, liturgies and vestments. The modern Christian missionary enterprise is a beneficiary, and an agent of the industrialization and urbanization whose by-product is the ecological disaster now recognized as a global crisis.

This fact was affirmed at the World Missionary Conference at Edinburgh in 1910, and reaffirmed at the Centenary in 2010. In the name of 'Progress', natural habitats were destroyed and replaced with centres of 'modernity'.[14] African traditions were archived as remnants of bygone generations. While African converts were taught the virtues of the European Reformation and Renaissance, they were also taught to despise their cultural roots and their traditional wisdom. They were taught to discard the techniques through

---

[10] For authoritative impact of Climate Change globally see *IPCCC Fifth Assessment Report,* 2013.

[11] Jared Diamond, *Collapse: How Societies Choose to Fail or Succeed,* http://aloki.hu/pdf/0402_205209.pdf.

[12] Principles to guide responsible stewardship of Creation see The Earth Charter, www.unesco.org/education/tlsf/mods/theme_a/img/02_earthcharter.pdf.

[13] The phrase "separated brethren" and similar expressions have been used severally in the history of Catholicism. Despite the call for unity, African Christianity is much more diverse and much more fragmented than expressions of Christianity in any other region and at any other period. See "Separated Brethren" Term Before Vatican II (1962-1965)", ["Separated Brethren" Term Before Vatican II (1962-1965)].

[14] See Daryl Balia and Kirsteen Kim, eds, *Edinburgh 2010: Witnessing Christ Today,* Oxford: Regnum, 2010.

which their ancestors had navigated their survival for many generations, and through many landscapes. The 21st century has begun with the reaffirmation of the African cultural and religious heritage, expressed in a broad variety of languages and academic disciplines. This essay outlines the resulting ecological crisis, with reference to geography and climatology, concluding with some Christian theological insights derived from doctrinal and biblical syntheses. African Christian theology, having come of age, heralds the African Christian Reformation, rooted in the long African cultural heritage that predates many cultures on other continents, and provoked by the imperial and missionary legacy dating from the European voyages of 'Discovery, Expansion and Empire'.[15]

3. Africa's Place in Global Ecology

As human beings, we depend on our environment for survival. If we care for our environment it will care for us. If we mess up our environment it will mess us up in return. The greatest challenge for leaders in each generation is to be the vanguard of ecological rehabilitation, so that future generations in their turn will build on the measures taken now. Environmental degradation is not restricted within national and regional boundaries; it is trans-border and trans-continental. The consequences of irresponsible exploitation of the environment in a particular country at a particular time will cross to other countries, regions and periods. Owing to this complexity of environmental degradation, it is essential for all environmental rehabilitation to be locally based, but internationally co-ordinated. Adaptation to climate change is not a luxury, and should not be a hobby or charitable activity. It is a necessary strategy to restore ecological balance for the sake of the present and future generations on this planet.

Since 1850, some nations have contributed more than others towards the current ecological crisis. The nations suffering most are the ones that contributed the least damage. Adaptation will have to be local, but commitment to rehabilitation will have to be global, as a matter of necessity for the survival of all. Adaptation is a matter of equity, not charity. The demands of African nations on the industrialized nations for corrective action to rehabilitate the environment have often been interpreted as calls for 'help'. But the restoration of the environment cannot be confined within national, regional or continental borders. Restoration of tropical ecology is a global challenge, considering that the winds carrying pollutants perpetually cross the Equator twice a year in the annual seasonal cycles. Africa is the only continent that lies evenly within the tropics and, because of this planetary position, the continent is affected twice a year by seasonal shifts of the Inter-Tropical Convergence Zone (ITCZ).[16]

Africa is the only continent with two vast tropical deserts, the Sahara in the north and the Kalahari in the south. Although the equatorial zone strides across the continent from the Atlantic to the Indian Oceans, the continent of Africa has more arid and semi-arid than arable wetland. Thus Africans have to invest much more for agricultural production than other continents, especially in the arid and semi-arid regions north and south of equatorial Africa. The national boundaries are such that some African nations have to invest much more than others for basic necessities essential for survival, including water, food, wood, energy, shelter and transportation.

There are several major rivers on the continent, but most sections of these rivers are not navigable. Most of the larger rivers are shared by a variety of nations. The rivers and their tributaries originate in one nation and drain in another, passing through several more. Thus the management of river catchments and river basins is trans-national, and can be achieved only with effective trans-border co-operation. Such is the situation with the Nile (Kenya, Uganda, Rwanda, Congo, Ethiopia, Sudan, South Sudan, Egypt, Tanzania), the Congo (Congo Republic, Zambia, DR Congo, South Sudan, Central African

[15] See Isaac M.T. Mwase and Eunice Kamaara, eds., *Theologies of Liberation and Reconstruction,* Nairobi: Acton, 2012; W.D. Hussey, *Discovery, Expansion and Empire,* Cambridge University Press, 1954.
[16] http://geography.about.com/od/climate/a/itcz.htm.

Republic, Angola, Uganda Rwanda, Burundi), the Zambezi (Angola, DR Congo, Zambia, Malawi, Zimbabwe, Mozambique), and the Niger (Nigeria, Burkina Faso, Mali, Niger, Cote′ d'Ivoire, Sierra Leone, Guinea, Liberia).[17] When the rainfall feeding these rivers declines, the river volume also declines. Most Africans depend on rain-fed agriculture for their survival.[18]

4. The Impact of Industrialization on Africa's Ecology

If ecological balance could be maintained, human habitation could be sustained without endangering any of the co-existing species. But when the relationships between humans and other species are distorted, some of the species have either to migrate to other environments, or they risk becoming extinct. In Madagascar there was a large bird called the dodo, which could neither fly nor run fast. Sailors from Europe en route to Asia found that it had good meat, and its eggs were also big and nutritious. They hunted the bird and collected its eggs. By the year 1800, it had become extinct. Human survival in Africa is at great risk, unless we can learn to balance our existential relationships among ourselves, with other human beings, with other species and also, with future generations. This challenge is emphasized in the *Earth Charter* launched in 1992 during the United Nations Conference on Environment and Development (UNCED) at Rio de Janeiro, Brazil.

Those environments that are easier to live in may support larger populations, up to a limit. When that limit is passed, survival becomes threatened for the species that live there. For illustration, let us consider Kenya's ecology. Other African countries can also be studied using the same principle. About 80% of Kenya is arid or semi-arid. The large area of semi-arid lands south of the Sahara Desert is called the Sahel, in which northern Kenya is located. The remaining 20% of Kenya is divided into two segments by the Great Rift Valley (which begins in Lebanon and ends in southern Malawi). On each side of the Great Rift Valley there are high mountain ranges, which attract moisture brought by the seasonal winds from the Indian Ocean. The ranges include the Mount Kenya Range; the Aberdare Range; the Mau Escarpment Range; the Mount Elgon Range and the Kilimanjaro Mountain.[19]

Researchers report that Mount Kilimanjaro has lost 80% of its permanent icecap since 1912. Proportionally, Mount Kenya has lost even more icecap than Mount Kilimanjaro during the same period. The permanent icecaps on these mountain ranges have for millennia supplied fresh water through the seasonal thawing. The forests on these mountain ranges have kept the environment cool, and for millennia they have stored the rain runoff in the humus piled underneath. The water stored on the slopes slowly seeped into the rivers and streams with a steady flow for most of the year. Today, most of the rivers and streams are almost dry between September and March. When the long rains fail in April and May, the volume on the rivers and streams remains low. Such was the crisis in 2008-2009, when hydro-based electricity had to be rationed nationally. Likewise, the peak of Mount Kilimanjaro, highest mountain in Africa and one of the highest in the world, has lost most of its permanent ice during the twentieth century, adversely affecting the local ecology in Tanzania and Kenya. The people of East Africa who depended on these mountain ranges are now food-insecure. The permanent ice caps guaranteed stable seasonal predictability, regular rainfall and predictable weather patterns. From the perspective of the local inhabitants in each ecological zone, global warming is experienced as a great threat to their survival. They are not aware of the debates and UN negotiations about the reduction, per capita, of carbon dioxide emissions, but they know that they and their descendants are food-insecure. Increasing temperatures have

---

[17] www.unep.org/dewa/vitalwater/article36.html.

[18] www.grida.no/publications/vg/africa/page/3126.aspx.

[19] http://na.unep.net/geas/getUNEPPageWithArticleIDScript.php?article_id=90.

led to the melting of mountain glaciers on Africa's major mountains.[20] Similar ecological disaster has been observed on the Ruwenzori mountain range in Uganda, where the permanent icecap has shrunk and the line of vegetation has risen considerably during the twentieth century, with disastrous consequences for the local populations.[21]

In October 2009, the UN Food and Agriculture Organization issued an alarm that Lake Chad had shrunk more than 90% – from 25 000 square kilometres in 1963 to less than 1500 square kilometres – between 1963 and 2001, due to climatic variability, climate change and population pressure over those decades. putting at risk the livelihoods of more than 60 million people in Nigeria, Cameroon, Central African Republic, Chad, Niger and Nigeria. The rivers draining into Lake Chad have declined in volume, the most important factor being reduced precipitation. By 2009, the decline in fish production was at least 60%; in addition there had been massive degradation of pasturelands, leading to a shortage of animal feed, estimated at 45% in some places in 2006, and a reduction in livestock and biodiversity.

This humanitarian disaster represented by the shrinking Lake Chad in Central Africa should be urgently addressed, according to the FAO. This lake was once one of the world's largest bodies of water. If water continues to recede at the current rate, Lake Chad could disappear within decades, according to NASA climate forecasts. The thirty million people living in the region are being forced into sharper competition for water. The drying-up of the lake and the deterioration of the production capacity of its basin have adversely affected local socio-economic activities. Degradation of water and land resources is a significant factor in migrations and conflicts.[22]

4. Successes and Failures of Science and Technology in Ecology Management

Global warming is an ecological reality, confirmed in the series of five official Reports of the United Nations Framework Convention on Climate Change (UNFCCC). It is also widely acknowledged that the rapid rate of global warming is induced largely by industrialization through the use of fossil fuels, particularly petroleum and coal, since the invention of the internal combustion engine. The luxury enjoyed by the industrialized countries in the Organization of Co-operation and Development (OECD) has been at the expense of the global environment. Global warming is caused mainly by emissions of exhaust gases from the machines which facilitate the necessities and luxuries especially in the industrialized nations. The exhaust gases cause a 'greenhouse' effect over the atmosphere, interfering with the natural ecology that would otherwise regulate itself. Human beings are challenged to work with nature, not against it. Science and technology, especially since 1850, has endeavoured to work against nature.

From the perspective of applied ethics, the impact of science and technology is both positive and negative. Positively, science and technology are manifestations of the human capacity to tame nature and appropriate its goods for the enhancement of comfort. Negatively, science and technology has no limits for human enquiry and experimentation. Thus the scientists and technologists, especially in the North Atlantic region, insist on their freedom to conduct research and to probe all aspects of reality – without restriction or sanction. This sanction-free approach to human enquiry is both a blessing and a curse.

Positively, human beings are endowed with curiosity, which urges them to enquire and explore far beyond their familiar immediate environment. Through that enquiry and exploration, culture is developed. Negatively, the urge of human beings to transcend themselves sometimes becomes an end in itself, rather than a disposition towards self-actualization. Technological competition between nations has led to many wars which have destroyed civilizations. Today, too much knowledge, effort and money is invested

---

[20] www.grida.no/publications/vg/africa/page/3104.aspx.
http://na.unep.net/geas/getUNEPPageWithArticleIDScript.php?article_id=90.
[21] http://epicureandculture.com/rwenzori-mountains-global-warming/.
[22] www.fao.org/news/story/en/item/36126/icode/, www.unep.org/dewa/vitalwater/jpg/0281-lakechad-EN.jpg.

in the development of weaponry, at a time when the majority of people in the world need the basic necessities for their survival. Responsible leadership requires that we focus our attention on priorities that ensure the survival of the most vulnerable communities: the basic necessities, such as food, water, shelter, health and transportation, and education.

The *Earth Charter,* launched in June 1992 during the UN Conference on Environment and Development (UNCED) at Rio De Janeiro, Brazil, provides the basis for global commitment for the peoples of all nations to take responsibility for ecological rehabilitation at local, national, regional and international levels:

> We must decide to live with a sense of universal responsibility, identifying ourselves with the whole Earth community as well as our local communities. We are at once citizens of different nations and of one world in which the local and global are linked. Everyone shares responsibility for the present and future well-being of the human family and the larger living world. The spirit of human solidarity and kinship with all life is strengthened when we live with reverence for the mystery of being, gratitude for the gift of life, and humility regarding the human place in nature.[23]

Sir John Houghton, former Chairman of the Intergovernmental Scientific Panel responsible for the compilation of the UNFCCC Reports, has proposed three principles to guide the corrective measures necessary for the long-term measures humankind must embark upon to reverse the current ecological crisis:

> There are three principles that are frequently put forward as those that should govern such action. First, there is the *Precautionary Principle* that is included in the Climate Convention and that states that that the lack of full scientific certainty should not prevent appropriate action being taken. The second is that *polluters should pay* for the damage of their pollution, a well-known principle that has been built into environmental legislation for a long time. It can be applied, for instance, through the taxation of pollution or through the setting up of trading arrangements. The third principle, the most difficult to apply, is that of equity – *inter-generational equity* and international equity. At the moment, 55% of carbon dioxide emissions are produced by the richest one-sixth of the world's population, the United States alone being responsible for 25%. Just 3% is emitted by the poorest one-sixth of the world. There is obviously great inequity here.[24]

- *The Precautionary Principle:* All industrial activity should be done taking great precaution not to endanger ourselves, other peoples, other species and future generations. We must think of others, not only about ourselves. The resources from which we derive our luxuries are finite. We are not the only nation, race, religion or gender entitled to them. Even future generations are entitled.
- *The Polluter Pays Principle:* We must take responsibility for the historical emissions that have brought the world to this ecological global crisis. Our economic policies should include contributing towards the rehabilitation of local ecological zones that have been destroyed by our historical emissions.
- *Inter-generational Equity Principle:* It is essential for vulnerable communities to adapt themselves to the changing ecological conditions now threatening human survival. Policies and programs for adaptation to global warming will be local, but all nations, especially members of the OECD (which are responsible for most of the historical emissions that have brought about this global ecological crisis) will have to do their part, taking into consideration the most vulnerable in their midst – fellow humans, other species and future generations.

---

[23] www.earthcharterinaction.org/invent/images/uploads/echarter_english.pdf.

[24] www.jri.org.uk/resource/climatechangeoverview.htm; See also Sir John Houghton, *Global Warming: The Complete Briefing,* Fourth Edition, Cambridge University Press, 2009.

5. The Decline of Staple Food Production

Throughout the twentieth century, Africa's fragile ecology was severely disturbed. The forested slopes of most mountain ranges were cleared for large-scale and small-scale agriculture, with disastrous consequences. Before this disruption, the original natural habitat had sustained lush flora and fauna, which, for millennia, supplied staple food for the peoples that had co-existed with other species. The disruption caused by human settlement during the twentieth century has resulted in great shortage of staple foods at the beginning of the third millennium, caused largely by land-use policies and activities, which destroyed the ecological balance in each of these habitats. Before the disruption, each drop of rain would flow cleanly down the rivers and streams, which would be crystal clear. Today a drop of rain runoff it takes almost equal volume of fertile soil with it. Consequently, much of the fertile volcanic soil on the mountain ranges of Kenya has been washed downstream into the Indian Ocean and Lake Victoria. We are unable to feed ourselves because of our own mishandling of our habitats.

The claim that environmental degradation is caused by 'over-population' is not convincing, in view of the fact that there are countries with high population density but without deforestation, including some European countries, Japan and South Korea. According to UN Statistics for 2014, three out of the top twenty countries with the highest percentage of forest cover are also ranked very highly ranked in the UN Human Development Index (HDI) – Finland (73%), Japan (69%) and Sweden (69%). These facts confirm that it is possible for a nation to enjoy a high standard of living while at the same time caring for the environment.[25]

A report issued by the Food and Agriculture Organization (FAO) shows that African nations engaged in export of cash crops have high rates of undernourishment. There is evidence also that in those countries undernourishment is most prevalent in cash crop-producing areas. These facts raise the question of the justification for land use policies that do not raise the quality of life of producers. Other than exploitation, there is no justification for a population to be forced into growing cash crops on the land where basic food used to be grown, then to be fed on 'Food Aid' procured through food subsidies from the former imperial powers. The campaign for the abolition of food subsidies has raged for many years in the World Trade Organisatiion (WTO) and other forums. Poor nations are discouraged from offering subsidies to their peasant farmers, because of the likely adverse impact on the export of subsidized food in the countries where cash crop farming is the main preoccupation of peasant smallholders. During the Tenth WTO Ministerial Conference in Nairobi, Kenya (December 2015), after intense lobbying, an agreement was reached for export subsidies to be abolished for all sectors including agriculture. It remains an open question whether the nations used to these subsidies will comply, considering that the agreement is voluntary rather than legal. There are no specified penalties for nations that do not comply.[26]

Prevalence of under-nourishment in key export countries
of traditional cash crops – Country Proportion of undernourished in total population

Ethiopia	37.1	Fruit and vegetables
Former Sudan*	36.0	Cotton and other textile fibres (inclusive of South Sudan)
Tanzania	33.0	Tobacco
Zimbabwe	30.5	Tobacco
Mozambique	29.3	Tobacco
Cote d'Ivoire	20.5	Coffee, tea, cocoa; fruit and vegetables
Malawi	20.0	Tobacco

[25] www.blatantworld.com/data/the-most-forested-countries-in-the-world-by-total- of-land/; https://data.undp.org/dataset/HDI-Indicators-By-Country-2014/5tuc-d2a9.
[26] www.dawn.com/news/1227554; https://www.wto.org/english/news_e/news15_e/mc10_19dec15_e.htm.

Kenya	15.7	Coffee, tea, flowers; fruit and vegetables; tobacco
Cameroon	13.3	Coffee, tea, cocoa
Nigeria	7.3	Coffee, tea, cocoa
Ghana	<5.0	Coffee, tea, cocoa
Tropical Africa	24.8	

[www.wageningenur.nl/upload_mm/7/b/b/a16b98bc-948d-41f0-8e58-6e1bd8070297_2014-015%20Achterbosch_WEB.pdf]

In July 2014, the Food and Agriculture Organization (FAO) released a list of the thirty-three countries in need of food assistance, twenty-six of them in Africa: Central African Republic, Zimbabwe, Burkina Faso, Chad, Djibouti, Eritrea, Guinea, Liberia, Malawi, Mali, Mauritania, Niger, Sierra Leone, Cameroon, Congo, Côte d'Ivoire, DR Congo, Ethiopia, Madagascar, Mozambique, Senegal, Somalia, South Sudan and Uganda. Again, this list shows that Africa's agricultural production has not increased since 1960, although agricultural land has been alarmingly degraded. The rapid growth of Africa's population is not matched with corresponding local production of basic foods. At the same time, land continues to be used for purposes other than basic food production as listed above, including flowers, rubber, sugar, lumber, and so on. A nation incapable of feeding its population will risk political instability and external interference. Food subsidies from industrialized nations are sent as 'Food Aid' to Africa, a continent with more than enough land to feed its citizens.[27]

6. Theological Reflection

a) The missionary background

David Livingstone was one of the leading campaigners for replacing the 'illegitimate slave trade' with 'legitimate agricultural trade'. His slogan was 'Christianity, Civilization and Commerce'. Malawi became one of the earliest British colonies to embark on Livingstone's model, which Christian missionaries replicated in other colonies. Thus Christian mission stations became the earliest centres where Africans were taught how to grow, on unviable small plots, the cash crops whose yield was primarily for exporting to cities of the colonial power. At the same time, settlers from colonial countries took vast stretches of land for large-scale production of the same agricultural commodities with the same markets in Europe, competing with the African peasant growers. Co-operatives could not compete with the settlers' large-scale production. Consequently, African peasants remained poor – on their own land. This cash crop policy remained entrenched in tropical Africa, even after national sovereignty had been achieved. A few African nations nationalized the settlers' farms (such as Tanzania and Zimbabwe), but nationalization did not make these large-scale farms more profitable. An agricultural economy based on the production and marketing of luxury-food commodities cannot feed a national population. It may enrich a few farmers with access to luxury markets, but the peasant producers will always be at the mercy of corporate producers and their sales agents.[28]

The colonial policy of exploiting African nations as sources of cheap labour and raw commodities has not changed. Since the trade in raw commodities is in strong foreign currencies, African countries have continued to be the net losers. The Economic Partnership Agreements (EPA) between the European Union and African, Caribbean and Pacific Countries (ACP) will not reverse this inequity, owing to the dominant

[27] www.fao.org/3/a-i3899e.pdf.

[28] www.pambazuka.net/en/category.php/features/77990.

power of the EU in its dealings with the regional blocs in the African, Caribbean and Pacific regions. Ecological rehabilitation is not a priority in EPAs, not being profitable in the short term. Ecological damage under old colonial policies took many decades, and will take centuries to correct, even if it is at all possible.[29]

Christian mission stations became centres and models for environmental destruction, as missionaries destroyed the local habitat in order to replicate their temperate ecology in tropical Africa. Exotic flowers, herbs, shrubs, trees and crops were introduced from Europe, and Africans were discouraged from growing their traditional foods. European cuisine became normative among African converts. Although traditional African cuisine was cheaper and much more healthy, African Christians were indoctrinated into believing that the missionary cuisine was superior. This teaching was consistent with the disparagement of anything African, and the elevation of everything European. Christianity was inculcated in African converts as 'European' Christianity, with its variants in the specific denominations that came to particular parts of Africa. In tropical Africa the 'wedding cake' has become the symbol of a 'Christian' wedding – a delicacy that is not part of any African menu.[30]

The Europeanization of Africa was intended to be comprehensive; those who rejected it were condemned as rebels. African Independent Churches in various African colonies were voices of protest, and were condemned as both religious and political movements of rebellion. Consistently, African Independent Churches became the religious aspect of revolt against colonial domination, alongside the political movements that were banned in much the same way that the European Reformation and Renaissance were two sides of the same coin: the revolt against Roman Catholicism.[31]

b) Doctrinal creeds

i) The Apostle's Creed: The Christian faith affirms that the universe and everything therein is God's creation. This is the first article of the Apostles' Creed whose first affirmation is: 'I believe in God Almighty, Maker of heaven and earth.' This affirmation is an echo of Psalm 24:1-2: 'The earth is the LORD's and all that is in it, the world, and those who live in it; ² for he has founded it on the seas, and established it on the rivers' (NRSV). Church doctrine, especially under the influence of the European Reformation, has tended to undervalue the significance of this first article of the Apostles' Creed. In practice, what does it mean to affirm that God Almighty is the 'Maker of heaven and earth'? Did God create the world and retire (deism), or is God still actively involved the programme of creation (theism)? What is the role of human beings in the divine programme of creation? Is it responsible leadership for human beings to continually destroy the ecology that makes life possible on earth? These are theological questions, as much as they are ethical and technological.[32]

ii) The Nicene Creed: The Creed of Nicaea is even more explicit: 'We believe in one God, the Father of all, Creator of all things visible and invisible.' In the Nicene Creed, the attribute of divine progeny replaces that of divine omnipotence. God is the 'Father of all' and 'Creator of all things visible and invisible'. It might appear as though the Nicene Creed differs radically from the Apostles' Creed. The difference between the two is not in content, but in language. Both these creeds, in their First Article, emphasize that human beings are creatures, and must not conduct themselves as if to usurp God's authority as Creator. In Luke 10:21-24, Jesus Christ refers to God as 'Father, the Lord of heaven and earth'.

---

[29] http://trade.ec.europa.eu/doclib/docs/2009/september/tradoc_144912.pdf.

[30] J.N.K. Mugambi, "Christianity and the African Cultural Heritage" [epository.up.ac.za/bitstream/handle/2263/21579/021_Chapter20_p516-542.pdf?sequence=25].

[31] Karl Holl, *The Cultural Significance of the Reformation,* op. cit.

[32] J.N.K. Mugambi, "Creation and Salvation in Theologies of Reconstruction", in E.M. Conradie, ed., *Creation and Salvation: A Companion on Recent Theological Movements,* Münster: LIT Verlag, 2012, Ch. 11, pp. 325-39.

> [21] At that same hour Jesus rejoiced in the Holy Spirit and said, 'I thank you, Father, Lord of heaven and earth, because you have hidden these things from the wise and the intelligent and have revealed them to infants; yes, Father, for such was your gracious will.[d] [22] All things have been handed over to me by my Father; and no one knows who the Son is except the Father, or who the Father is except the Son and anyone to whom the Son chooses to reveal him.'

These affirmations are derived from the first chapter of the book of Genesis, in which the origin of everything is attributed to God. It is through God's authority that everything comes into being: God speaks, and it is done. Human beings are not responsible for bringing themselves into the world. They are God's creatures, just like all others. The verses in Genesis 1 are a great poem expressing the omnipotence of God, and the finitude of human beings and other parts of God's creation. Creatures have neither power, nor authority. Their existence is dependent on the authority of the divine Creator.

iii). St Paul's Creed: St Paul, addressing the Colossians, affirms that Jesus is one with God the Creator:

> **15** He is the image of the invisible God, the firstborn of all creation; **16** for in[a] him all things in heaven and on earth were created, things visible and invisible, whether thrones or dominions or rulers or powers – all things have been created through him and for him. **17** He himself is before all things, and in[b] him all things hold together. (Col. 1:15-17)

In this affirmation, St Paul is emphasizing that we human beings are finite, in contrast with the infinite Creator. The ecological crisis we suffer is the result of the human usurpation of divine providence, to the point that in our culture we conduct ourselves as if we were divine. This is blasphemy, with disastrous consequences. Sir John Houghton – as a scientist and as a Christian – reminds us that scientific enquiry and technological innovation do not exempt us from moral responsibility and spiritual discernment. As creatures that are endowed with intelligence and the capacity for tool-making, we have the capacity to become co-workers to improve creation, rather than to degrade it. From the perspective of the creeds cited above, the ecological destruction we continue to inflict on Planet Earth is our responsibility as humans, and it is our duty to rehabilitate the earth for future generations. John Houghton encourages us to shun despair:

> Lack of will is not a new problem, of course, for humans. It is largely a moral and spiritual problem, one that St Paul presented in his letter to the Romans (Rom. 7:18) in the New Testament, commenting that he had not completely solved it for himself in his own experience. People often say to me, 'The problem is so big, it will never be solved; you're not going to get anywhere; the politicians will never agree; greedy people will never change their ways.' So why am I optimistic?[33]

John Houghton gives three reasons for optimism, which he explains on the basis of his vocation as a meteorologist and as a negotiator within the UN Framework Convention on Climate Change, representing the UK when he was Chief Meteorologist:

> *First,* I have experienced the scientific community, many hundreds of scientists from a wide range of countries, ideologies, disciplines and backgrounds, come together with great commitment to agree a scientific assessment of likely climate change. *Secondly,* the necessary technology is available, or is becoming available and industry is beginning to see climate change as an issue that provides great opportunities for technical advance. And thirdly, I am a Christian, and I believe that God is committed to his creation, a commitment he has demonstrated by sending Jesus into the world to be the saviour of the human race. In delegating to humans the care of his creation, God has not left us to do it on our own. That he is there to help us with the great task has been a great source of strength to me in my work with the IPCC. I felt this particularly strongly as a few of us met for prayer during the very demanding IPCC Plenary in

[33] John Houghton, www.jri.org.uk/resource/climatechangeoverview.htm.

Shanghai. *Finally* let me comment again on the need for commitment. If human communities are to be fulfilled and creative, they not only need goals related to economic performance but also moral and spiritual goals. Care for the overall health of the planet is such a goal. Scientists are already working hard and in concert to provide better information about likely climate change, governments in the FCCC have begun to set the necessary framework for change, and business and industry are beginning to recognize the need for action and the opportunities for innovation in new technologies. It is up to all of us as world citizens to support the action being taken, and contribute to it.[34]

7. What We Ought to Do

Is there any hope? What must we do? Yes, there is hope, and there are many things we can do – individually, collectively, nationally and internationally. Here are some of the strategies we can adopt:

a) Arable Land Recovery: Recover as much arable land as possible from the semi-arid areas. More than two thirds of the Netherlands was recovered from the sea. The people built little walls to keep the sea water out during low tides, and eventually a very large area was recovered for very productive farming. We must commit ourselves to convert our semi-arid areas into fertile farmland. We can do it. Libya has done it. South Africa has done it. Peru has done it. Australia has done it. California has done it. China has done it. India has done it. We can do it. Perhaps we should say with Obama, 'Yes, we can. Yes we can.' But this initiative can best succeed if individuals take initiatives. Government can provide incentives to encourage individuals to harvest fertile land from semi-arid areas. But we must not expect Government as an institution to embark on such projects. If we follow that route we shall end up with 'white elephants'.[35]

b) Staple Foods: Diversify our staple foods. Each ecological zone has carbohydrate, protein and vitamin foods best suited for them. We must work with nature, never against nature. Maize is not an East African crop. It came from Central America, and was introduced to Africa by the Portuguese during the sixteenth century. Rice came from Asia. Wheat and barley came from Europe. We have never been able to grow enough of these exotic cereals, because our region is not ecologically suitable for them. Our ecological zone is the natural home for bananas, sweet potatoes, yams, cassava, arrowroots and various millets. We need to develop these crops, and make them our staple diet. They are nutritious, and they are healthy. Vegetable proteins are healthy, and they grow well in our ecological zone. Animal proteins should also be diversified. Cattle may be prestigious to grow and eat. But are they economical to keep as livestock? We need to think very creatively and innovatively.[36]

c) Food Shelf-Life: Prolong the shelf-life of all our staple foods. A large percentage of the harvest of our foods is lost because of its very short shelf-life. We must learn how to keep our harvests fresh, nutritious and suitable for human consumption for as long as possible. Refrigeration is an option, but a very expensive one. Drying is another option, which is much cheaper, because we have much solar energy in our region. A third option is to keep the harvest on the farm for as long as possible, provided that it does not hinder the growing of the next crop. Yams intercrop with trees, and one harvests only what is needed, leaving the rest in the soil until another ration is required. Seasoning is another option,

[34] www.jri.org.uk/resource/climatechangeoverview.htm.

[35] Jesse N.K. Mugambi and G. Kebreab, *Fresh Water to Eradicate Poverty: Understanding the Issues,* Norwegian Church Aid, 2006. https://www.kirkensnodhjelp.no/en/about-nca/publications/reports/; Mary Tiffen et. al, *More People, Less Erosion: Environmental Recovery in Kenya,* London: Overseas Development Institute, 1994.

[36] Frances Moore Lappé, *Food First: Beyond the Myth of Scarcity,* Ballantine, 1981; William Byron, ed., *The Causes of World Hunger*, Paulist Press, 1983.

which is complicated by the risk of chemical poisoning. We need to develop methods of food preservation conducive to our own habitats, and simple enough for all of us to apply.[37]

d) Community Education: Educate everyone to rely on our own products rather than on imported subsidized foods. This can be done successfully if we begin from our own homes, and integrate it into our curriculum.[38]

e) Food Policies: Enact national food policies, which will require every ecological zone in Africa to become a source of staple foods not only for the people of that area, but for this region. Movement of foods from one area to another should be encouraged, so that we begin to diversify our staple foods, using varieties grown within this region rather than imported from abroad.[39]

f) Energy from Renewable Sources: Embark on a deliberate policy to generate most electricity from renewable sources, particularly solar, wind and geothermal steam. On 25th July 2015, Germany generated 78% of its national electricity output from solar panels and wind turbines. The national borders of Germany are between latitudes 47 and 55 degrees north.[40] If Germany can generate so much electricity from solar panels so far north of the Equator, Africa – most of it located within the tropics – can certainly generate much, much more, electricity from the sun and from the regular seasonal winds. With much success, Kenya has begun diversifying its energy generation from hydro-electric power generation to solar panels, wind turbines and geothermal steam turbines.[41]

g) Cost Reduction: At the regional level, each region in Africa should be able to feed its own population with staple foods grown within that region. Such a policy will reduce transport costs and wastage in transit.[42] Africa is the only continent that mostly consumes what it does not produce, and mostly produces what it does not consume. Wealth can never be created and accumulated under such policy and practice. Wealth is created through the production of what people consume, importing the deficit while at the same time consuming what they produce and exporting the surplus. Wealth is the net difference between these equations.[43]

h) Green Belts: Nobel Laureate Professor Wangari Maathai campaigned for the greening of Africa through afforestation at domestic, local, national and regional levels.[44] Africa can, and should, feed its population with food grown within the continent, on the basis of the strategy outlined above. Heeding the challenge and campaign of Wangari Maathai, the Great Green Wall of Africa is an example of the commitment of African peoples and nations to constructively respond to the ecological crisis of which they are more the victims than the perpetrators. It is a stretch of territory greened with planted trees, covering 7,775 kilometres in length and fifteen kilometres wide, from the Atlantic Ocean to the Red Sea, through eleven nations, along the edge of the Sahara Desert. The nations involved are Mauritania, Senegal, Mali, Burkina Faso, Niger, Nigeria, Chad, Sudan, Ethiopia, Eritrea and Djibouti. Each nation within the strip is responsible for the afforestation of that section. The purpose is to create a natural barrier against the

---

[37] http://siteresources.worldbank.org/INTARD/Resources/MissingFoods10_web.pdf.

[38] Jesse N.K. Mugambi, "Responsible Leadership in Education and Development", in Christoph Stückelberger and J.N.K. Mugambi, eds, *Responsible Leadership: Global and Contextual Ethical Perspectives,* Nairobi: Acton, 2007; Globethics.net Series Vol. I, pp. 79-96.

[39] www.kilimo.go.tz/MAFAP/MAFAP-brochure-eng-WEB.pdf.

[40] On Germany see http://thinkprogress.org/climate/2015/07/29/3685555/germany-sets-new-renewable-energy-record/.

[41] On domestic solar units in Kenya see www.bloomberg.com/features/2015-mkopa-solar-in-africa/; file:///Users/mugambi/Downloads/24_Kenya-policy-report-note.pdf.

[42] www.fao.org/docrep/w0078e/w0078e03.htm.

[43] www.economist.com/blogs/feastandfamine/2012/05/food.

[44] Wangari Maathai, *Unbowed: A Memoir,* New York: Knopf, 2006; Greenbelt Movement, http://pats-eduent.net/xpeople_6maathai.pdf.

southward spread of the Sahara Desert. Co-operation in this long-term project is an illustration of the great potential for African nations to work together for the common good of global humanity.[45]

8. A Message of Hope

Yes, we can feed ourselves. Yes, we can. Let us not wait for other people to come to Africa to throw their surplus foods and clothes at us, as if we are incapable of feeding and clothing ourselves with food grown on our own fertile soils and fabrics woven on our looms. We can feed and clothe ourselves. Yes we can – especially if we live up to the imperatives of *The Earth Charter* with its emphasis on the necessity for all of us humans to work together to make the earth better than we found it, in consideration of other people, other species, and future generations.[46] African Christians cannot rehabilitate their continent on their own, since they share it with others, and in view of the fact that climate change as experienced by us today is the consequence of generations of environmental pollution, originating elsewhere. Ecological rehabilitation is the task for all people who care for the present and future generations. This insight is part of African wisdom.

Tragically, the twenty-first Conference of Parties to UNFCCC at Paris, France (December 2015) postponed remedial action to 2020, which will be nearly fifty years after the first UN Conference on Environment and Development (UNCED) at Stockholm, Sweden, in 1972.[47] Hardly any politician who participated in the Stockholm negotiations will be alive then, and if alive, hardly any of them will have any influence on policy. For the sake of winning elections, the present generation of politicians in industrialized nations has reneged on the responsibility to act now, leaving the people of Africa, the Caribbean and the Pacific (ACP) to fend for themselves – even though they are more victims than perpetrators in the deteriorating global macro-climatic indicators.[48]

The Beatitudes of Jesus remind us again that God's reign prevails, even when human adversity seems overwhelming (Matt. 5:1-12). Life in abundance will come, not from charity and patronage, but through retributive justice (John 10:10). It would be prudent and wise for us all to add more to nature than we extract from it. This is the way to become co-workers with the Creator (I Cor. 3:9) and the way to fulfil our aspirations as creative creatures.

The Interfaith Summit hosted by the Archbishop of Uppsala, Sweden, issued a manifesto urging political leaders of the most powerful nations to hasten consensus based on the Kyoto Protocol. The Manifesto was timed in anticipation of the 2009 Fifteenth Conference of the Parties. In one paragraph, the Manifesto states:

> We urge political and religious leaders to bear responsibility for the future of our planet and the living conditions and habitat preservation of new generations, assured in this of support and co-operation from the faith traditions of the world. The climate crisis is a fundamental spiritual question for the survival of humanity on Planet Earth. At the same time, we know that the world has never before been more capable of creating sustainable development. Humanity possesses the knowledge and technology. Popular commitment to doing what can and must be done is growing. We are challenged to review the values, philosophies, beliefs and moral concepts which have shaped and driven our behaviours and informed our dysfunctional relationship with our natural environment.[49]

---

[45] https://www.thegef.org/gef/great-green-wall.
[46] www.unesco.org/education/tlsf/mods/theme_a/img/02_earthcharter.pdf.
[47] www.britannica.com/topic/environmentalism.
[48] Archbishop Tutu's Message at COP 15, https://www.youtube.com/watch?v=tuu6tOE8gKc.
[49] Uppsala Inferfaith Climate Summit Manifesto https://www.svenskakyrkan.se/interfaithclimatesummit/inenglish.

During the UN Copenhagen Climate Conference (COP 15), Archbishop Rowan Williams preached a sermon at Copenhagen Cathedral on 13th December 2009, in which he emphasized:

> We meet as people of faith in the context of this critical moment in human history; and so we are not here just to plead or harangue, let alone to encourage panic and terror. We are here to say two simple things, to ourselves, our neighbours and to our governments. First: don't be afraid, but ask how the policies you follow and the lifestyle that you take for granted look in the light of the command to love the world you inhabit. Ask what would be a healthy and sustainable relationship with this world, a relationship that would in some way manifest both joy in and respect for the earth. Start with the positive question – how do we show that we love God's creation? Second: don't separate this from the question of how we learn to trust one another within a world of limited resources. In such a world there can be no trust without justice, without the assurance of knowing that my neighbour is there for me when I face insecurity or risk… How shall we build international institutions that make sure the resources get where they are needed… Love casts out fear; and the promise that makes sense of all this is the promise we heard in the reading from St Paul's letter to the Romans: if we allow God to teach us trust and if we learn to live in trust and confidence, the whole created order feels the effects. The 'slavery' imposed on the created order by human sinfulness and selfishness gives way to liberation; human freedom and the fulfilment of the destiny of the world around are manifested together, and the result is glory.[50]

It is worthwhile to conclude this paper with the prayer of Pope Francis in *Laudato Si,* May 2015:

> God of love,
> show us our place in this world
> as channels of your love for all the creatures of this earth,
> for not one of them is forgotten in your sight.
> Enlighten those who possess power and money
> that they may avoid the sin of indifference,
> that they may love the common good,
> advance the weak, and care for this world in which we live.
> The poor and the earth are crying out.
> O Lord, seize us with your power and light,
> help us to protect all life, to prepare for a better future,
> for the coming of your Kingdom of justice, peace,
> love and beauty. Praise be to you! Amen.[51]

Bibliography

Abrecht, Paul, ed, *Faith Science and the Future,* Fortress Press, 1979.

Anderson, Allan: *African Reformation,* Trenton, New Jersey: Africa World Press, 2001.

Birch, Charles, 'Creation, Technology and Human Survival', in *Ecumenical Review,* Geneva: WCC, January 1976, pp. 66-79; *Regaining Compassion- for Humanity and Nature,* New South Wales University Press, 1993.

Byron, William, *The Causes of World Hunger,* Paulist Press, 1983.

Conradie, E.M., ed., *Creation and Salvation: A Companion on Recent Theological Movements,* Münster: LIT Verlag, 2012.

[50] Dr Rowan Williams, "Perfect Love Casts Out Fear", Sermon at Copenhagen Cathedral 13 Dec. 2009, http://rowanwilliams.archbishopofcanterbury.org/articles.php/765/act-for-the-sake-of-love-archbishop-preaches-in-copenhagen-cathedral.

[51] www.hillheat.com/files/Laudato_Si_formatted_translation.pdf.

Hallman, David, ed., *Ecotheology: Voices from North and South,* Wipf and Stock, 2009.
Houghton, John, *Global Warming: The Complete Briefing,* Fourth Edition, Cambridge: CUP, 2010.
Lappé, Frances Moore, *Food First: Beyond the Myth of Scarcity,* Balantine Books, 1981.
Maathai, Wangari, *The Green Belt Movement: Sharing the Experience and the Approach,* New York: Lantern Books, 2006.
Mugambi, Jesse N.K. et. al., *Fresh Water to Eradicate Poverty,* Norwegian Church Aid, 2006.
Pope Francis, *Laudato Si: On Care of Our Common Home,* Vatican, May 2015.
Rasmussen, Larry, *Earth Community, Earth Ethics,* New York: Orbis, 1997.
Tiffen, Mary et. al, *More People, Less Erosion,* London: Overseas Development Institute, 1994.
UNESCO, *The Earth Charter,* www.unesco.org/education/tlsf/mods/theme_a/img/ 02_earthcharter.pdf

(144) The African Union and All Africa Conference of Churches

Bethuel A. Kiplagat

Setting the Stage

The All Africa Conference of Churches was inaugurated on 20th April 1963 in Kampala and a month later, on May 25, 1963, the Organisation of African Unity came into being in Addis Ababa. The All Africa Conference of Churches is a fellowship of 172 member churches and Christian Councils in 43 countries. The African Union (AU) covers the whole continent of 54 member countries except Morocco which suspended its membership because the organization recognized the Western Sahara Liberation Front. The two organisations celebrated their Golden Jubilee in 2013 in Addis Ababa and Kampala.

The African Union celebrated the Jubilee by launching a new vision for the continent, called Agenda 2063. The agenda is to be people-driven and owned. The Chairman of the African Union approached the Secretary General of AACC to organize a consultation for inter-faith organization that is Muslim, Christian, Sikh, Bahai, Hindu and African Traditional Religion to deliberate on the draft Agenda 2063. The Consultation was held on 5-6 November 2014 at the Headquarters of AACC in Nairobi. There were 93 participants, and I had the privilege of attending the Consultation. The report of the Consultation was tabled at the February Summit of the African Union.

The Agenda 2063 "The Africa we want" draws its inspiration and spirit from pan-Africanism as it 'seeks to galvanise and unite in action all Africans and the diaspora around the common vision of a peaceful integrated and prosperous Africa, driven by its citizens and taking its rightful place in the world' and it continues to argue for 'an inclusive growth and sustainable development'. Politically united and based on the ideals of pan-Africanism the vision unfolded here is for an Africa of good governance, respect for human rights, justice and the rule of law.

AACC is in a unique and privileged position to contribute significantly to the Agenda 2063 and the future of Africa and the world. Apart from the AU, I do not think there is another continental organization with such an extensive network and experience in dealing with the problems of the continent over these many years. Where did it start?

We have to go to Ibadan in Nigeria where it all begun with the holding of the first Pan-African Church Conference on January 10-19, 1958, attended by 195 delegates, the majority of whom were Africans. Race was still a factor in those days and in fact the report gave the racial breakdown of the delegates as follows: 'Racially, the conference consisted of 96 Negros, 92 Whites, and seven Asians.' George W. Carpenter who was the organizer of the conference wrote in a glowing and paternalistic manner when he observed Africans 'speaking capably, confidently and effectively and to watch the growing sense of personal responsibility, initiative and commitment with which they dealt with the issues before them'.

The conference came up with two important recommendations and a prophetic statement about the future of Africa. A decision was made to set up a Provisional Committee to explore the best ways and means of providing links between and among the Churches and this is what led finally to the establishment of a continental body to carry on with the work of the Church. Islam came up for discussion out of a concern that it was gaining more ground and spreading across the continent, and the reason for the perceived growth was noted as follows:

1. Islam is presented as the religion of the coloured people and Christianity the religion of the Whites. Further, a Muslim missionary approaches the African as a brother, a fellow sufferer from oppression and exploitation.

2. Islamic teaching and practice of equality between race and colour groups and its emphasis on the brotherhood of man are also attractive to sensitive Africans.

The delegates were concerned and felt that the issue of Islam is sensitive and should be approached prayerfully and with humility. The church needed to be equipped in order to share the good news with the Muslim brother or sister and neighbour. To this end, a suggestion was made to establish a movable study centre on Islam in Africa. But, instead of a movable study centre, the Islam in Africa Project was created with the objective of initiating dialogue between Muslims and Christians in Africa, and this has given birth to the Programme for Christian-Muslim Relations in Africa (PROCMURA) with its headquarters based in Nairobi. PROCMURA works very closely with AACC as a sister organization. PROCMURA has been on the ground for the last 56 years and has acquired deep knowledge of Islam in Africa. The African Union, being aware of the experience of PROCMURA with Islam in Africa, invited Dr Johnson Mbilah, the Secretary General, as key advisor to the workshop on 'Radicalisation, Violent Extremism, Deradicalisation, Counter Radicalisation and Counter Violent Extremism in Brazzaville for the Economic Community of Central African States'. Given the impact of religious radicalization on the continent of Africa, PROCMURA's work is cut out for the coming decade, and the African Union will rely on its experience and knowledge to combat the problem of the regionalization of politics.

The Challenge

Africa was on the move. The spirit of freedom was in the air. The message to the churches recognized and rejoiced in the advance of countries towards self-government but warned of the difficulties ahead, and this is what they said:

> The continent of Africa will see unparalleled events and changes during the rest of this century, welcome by some, feared by others. We pray that the Christian Church of Africa will play its role as champion, teacher, counsellor and shepherd during these crucial years. We are humbly aware of our responsibilities to God and this continent, and dedicate ourselves anew to their performance, trusting that we shall be led and supported by our fellow Christians throughout Africa and the World.

What an insight to discern what lay ahead. Changes came, and in the avalanche of independence, within a very short time from 1957 to 1965, Africa was liberated – except the Portuguese colonies, and countries where there were sizable European communities, such as South Africa, Southern Rhodesia and Namibia, and these were to take several decades before they were liberated.

There was no time to settle and enjoy the hard-won freedom before the continent was plunged into a serious crisis. In January 1963, news came that the recently elected President of Togo was assassinated. For the next two decades, there were coups and counter-coups and assassinations of heads of states and political leaders. There were at least twenty-three heads of states assassinated between 1963 and 1980. The last one was Murtala Mohamed of Nigeria. The countries that suffered most were Liberia, Ghana, Nigeria, Burundi and Ethiopia. Coups led to civil wars or internal conflicts. Over thirty countries have suffered from internal conflicts and some of these wars are still raging. The wars caused major dislocation of people, internally displaced and refugees. These were part of the events predicted by the Ibadan message. Did the church act as a counsellor and shepherd at this critical period of African history? They were there in refugee camps, and did not shy from giving support to the liberation struggle, thus complementing the efforts of the Organisation of African Unity.

The coups, civil wars and assassination of leaders are one part of the picture. The question we need to ask is, what was the agenda, the vision articulated and expressed by the pan-African conferences starting in 1900 (London) and culminating in 1945 (Manchester), before being moved to Africa in 1958 (All African Peoples Conferencein Accra).

The New Agenda

The Agenda was tabled at the first gathering of Africans from the continent and the diaspora, at the London Conference of 1900, and Agenda included:

- The struggle against racism
- Colonies of Africa and West Indies to be granted self-rule
- Political and other rights for Afro-Americans

The Agenda was further expanded to include a call for a united front for Africans in the diaspora and Africa as they struggled for their liberation. There was the call for the exploitation of the resources of Africa for the benefit of the people. The idea of integration of markets was also included as part of the vision. Even the idea of the United States of Africa was mooted.

The first pan-African conference on the continent of Africa took place in independent Accra, Ghana, in 1958, attended by delegates from independent African countries and political leaders that were still struggling for independence. The 1958 conference in Accra strategised and articulated the road map for the realization of the great dream, namely:

- The total liberation of the whole continent of Africa.
- The struggle against racism and the elimination of racism in Africa.
- The call for political unity of the continent starting at regional level.
- Commitment to the development of Africa

This may seem to have been a tall order, but with independence of Ghana, morale was upbeat: freedom was not only possible but was coming. Unity was paramount to sacrifice in the process of decolonization.

Putting the Accra conference and previous pan-African conferences into the geo-political context, one can see that this was a mirror image of the famous Berlin Conference in 1885 when the great powers carved up the whole continent of Africa, creating their individual spheres of influence. Africa was divided into fifty-two states under Britain, France, Germany, Italy, Portugal and Spain. The reason given was to avoid conflicts among these powers over resources – minerals and human. Africa was thus divided, colonized and its people subjected to racial discrimination.

Accra therefore planned to roll back what had been done to the continent – through decolonization and the dismantling of racist structures, thus uniting Africa and creating an integrated economy.

To a very large extent, the tide has been reversed. Apart from two islands, Mayotte being one of them, the whole continent has been liberated politically. The creation of the Organisation of African Unity and what has become the African Union is the first step towards a United States of Africa. Already, regional organisations – such as East African Community, the Common Market for South and East Africa and the Economic Community of West Africa – are on the road to economic and monetary integration. The year 1994 was an important milestone with the election of Nelson Mandela as the first black President of South Africa and with it the crumbling of the racist edifice of apartheid South Africa. That is not all.

The people of Africa longed for freedom, peace and dignity. The era of one-party states and military dictatorships is behind us. There are signs of hope on the horizon towards the process of the democratization of the continent. This process was given a major boost by events that took place outside Africa. The coming down of the Berlin Wall, and the subsequent collapse of the centralized one-party communist regimes of Eastern Europe, events which ushered in the collapse of the ideological walls which had been fertile ground for undemocratic regimes, whose leaders were never subject to the will of people. Competitive politics are now the practice in nearly all the countries of Africa. The Boku Haram of Nigeria, Al-Shabaab of Somalia, Al-Qaeda of Maghreb and the impact of the Arab Spring has halted the process of democratization of the continent. Let us hope that this is a temporary hiccup. What about Africans in the diaspora? They were not to be left behind.

With the wind of change blowing across Africa, it crossed over also to the New World, to the West Indies and America. Caribbean nationals did not have to struggle so hard when Britain peacefully handed over power to the indigenous people.

Freedom did not come easily; the Afro-Americans had to struggle. There were marches, sit-ins and civil disobedience. In their struggle, they were demanding:

- Meaningful civil rights legislation
- The elimination of racial segregation in public schools
- Laws prohibiting racial discrimination in employment

The high point of their struggle was the historic march on Washington and the famous speech of Martin Luther King: 'I have a dream'. In his speech, he longed for the day when his children 'will not be judged by the colour of their skin but the content of character', ending his speech with the words of the Negro spiritual, 'Free at last, Free at last, Thank God we are free at last'. The March on Washington for Jobs and Freedom took place on August 28, 1963.

Their struggle was not in vain, and King's dream was and is being realized. In 1964, the American congress enacted what had been termed a landmark piece of legislation – the Civil Rights Act of 1964, that outlawed discrimination based on race, colour, religion, sex or national origin. The legislation ended segregation in school, the workplace and public accommodation. And there the foundation and groundwork was laid for an Afro-American to assume the highest office of the USA. King's dream has been fulfilled but that is phase one and more work lies ahead over the next fifty years.

Africa has begun the journey of the next fifty years with the launching of AGENDA 2063 and this was done at the Jubilee celebration in the 2013 in Addis Ababa. In order to achieve the objectives of Agenda 2063, the African Union is mobilizing the participation and inputs of key stakeholders in Africa and in diaspora. It is for this reason that AACC was approached to organize an inter-faith workshop on the Agenda. The workshop was opened by Mr Mandla Madonsela, the representative of the Chairman of the African Commission. The vision is inspired by the spirit of Pan-Africanism and African Renaissance, which will 'contribute to self-determination freedom progress and collective prosperity'. Mr Mandla Madonsela shared with the participants eight key points which will drive the realization of Agenda 2063. Among these points are to:

- Galvanise and unite all Africans and the diaspora in the common vision of a peaceful, integrated and prosperous Africa.
- Harness the continental endowments embodied in its people, history, cultures, natural resources and George-political position to effect equitable and people-centred growth and development.
- Offer policy space for individual sectorial and collective actions to realize the continental vision.

The AACC should take the advantage offered by the AU which is giving space to civil society to contribute effectively to the realization of Agenda 2063. Fortunately, AACC has observer status with the AU. The relationship was formalized by the signing of Memorandum of Understanding between the two organizations on March 14, 2013 in Addis Ababa.

The objective of the Memorandum states:

> The objective of this memorandum is to strengthen co-operation between the Parties to facilitate the development and integration agenda of African Union. Subject to the terms of the present Memorandum of Understanding and consistent with all the Commission policy, both parties seek to share knowledge and resources (both human, in kind and monetary) in order to pursue an alliance focused on supporting the cause of socio-economic development, good governance, conflict prevention, and resolution across the African continent.

The doors of the Commission are wide open and it is up to the AACC to set up its own specific agenda where it can make an important contribution towards the achievement of the objectives set out in Agenda 2063. How can AACC creatively use the extended network and human resources it has, not only in Africa but also in the diaspora? What contribution can Africans from the diaspora make to the realization of the great dream of the founding fathers of pan-Africanism, namely, the creation of a United States of Africa which will welcome them where they can feel at home? Let me pitch in what I believe the AACC can contribute.

The most important asset which we have is not so much the past but the present and the future. Let us learn the lessons and experiences of the past but not allow it to dominate or dim the present or the future. God has given us the gift of imagination and dreams. Martin Luther King had his dream and it has been realized. Let the church, the All Africa Conference of Churches, dream dreams – but dreams should not be limited, so let us come out with impossible dreams and, fifty years on, we shall be greatly surprised that it has indeed been realized.

Bibliography

Report of the Consultation with African Faith Based Organisations on African Agenda 2063 – AACC

The Church in changing Africa – Report of the All Africa Conference of Churches, Ibadan, Nigeria January, 1958 (Only one original copy at AACC Archives)

10th General Assembly & Golden Jubilee Celebrations Report – AACC Report

Memorandum of Understanding between African Union Commission (AUC) and All Africa Conference of Churches (AACC)

Vision of Authenticity – The Assemblies of the All Africa Conference of Churches 1963-1992 Efion Utuk, All Africa Conference of Churches Nairobi – Kenya

The Scramble for Africa – Thomas Pakenham

What is it to us? Quotation and Questions from the All Africa Christians Youth Assembly, Nairobi – Kenya, December 27th, 1962-January 7th 1963, Freedom Under the Cross

Africa's Moment – Jean Michael Severino and Oliver Ray, Policy Press

On Pan-Africanism – Saheed A. Adgamobi

The Pan-African Congress

Pan Africanism – Colin Legum, Frederick A. Praeger

I attended the All African Conference of Churches – Kampala 1963

Participated at the Conference – Students & Youth, Freedom under the Cross.

First hand practical knowledge of Issue affecting the continent

Work experience – Church State, Private Sector, NGO

Workshop on 'Radicalisation, Violent Extremism, Deradicalisation, Counter Radicalisation and Counter Violent Extremism in ECCAS' December 1-3, 2014 – Brazzaville, Republic of Congo

(145) The AU Agenda 2063 and the Role of African Churches in Development

Obiora F. Ike

'I am black and beautiful, daughters of Jerusalem...
The sons of my mother disliked me,
They made me to work in their fields.
Yet my own fields – I could not take care of.'
(Song of Songs 1:5-6)

African Christianity is as Old as Christianity Itself

Christianity in Africa is not a recent arrival. It came to Africa during the time of the Apostles and can claim to be 'the new homeland of Jesus' (Pope John Paul II). Recent statistics show that Christianity has established her message beyond dispute in many countries within the continent of Africa and has become a force to be reckoned with. During his visit in November 2015 to Kenya, Uganda and the Central African Republic, the head of the Catholic Church described Africa as the 'Continent of Hope' (Pope Francis in Nairobi, Kenya, addressing young people, 27th November 2015), a description which contradicts the daily reality of the harsh conditions, sufferings and challenges which confront the peoples of the continent, even as we write. African Christianity has made the Bible its own. A large number of religious men and women devote their lives to the message of the churches. It is estimated that in 2063, Africa shall have the largest numbers of Christian missionaries compared with any other continent. In the ongoing dearth and absence of spirituality worldwide, Africa is moving forward to becoming a 'spiritual reservoir for the world' (Edward Blyden) and, in the words of Pope Benedict XVI, 'the spiritual lung of Christendom' (message at the Second Africa Synod, Rome, October 2009).

Jesus Christ himself as a baby found refuge with his foster father Joseph and mother Mary in Egypt (Matt. 2:13-15) because Herod the King slaughtered many innocent children in his bid to kill the infant child Jesus out of envy. Records show that Africa stayed close to the person and message of Christ, even to the extent of his cross being carried to Golgotha By Simon of Cyrene, an African from today's Benghazi in Libya (Mark 15:21).

Besides the work of Mark the evangelist who brought the faith to Egypt and from thence to the rest of North Africa, the pillars of Christendom rest on the great Augustine of Hippo, Clement of Alexandria, Athanasius, and even of Origen who wrote his history of early Christianity on African soil, all of whom bear testimony to the 2,000 years of Christian culture. Many stories in the Bible depict the relationship of Africa to Jesus. The Acts of the Apostles records the highly-placed administrator in the kingdom, an Ethiopian eunuch who received baptism from Philip the Apostle and travelled to his country to spread the Good News in those parts (Acts 8:26-40). To this day, history indicates that the Ethiopian Coptic Church has a claim to be the lead over Jerusalem, Rome and Antioch as the historically least interrupted of all Christian traditions since Apostolic times.

At a time when other continents wallowed in paganism and resisted the Christian message, as happened under Caesar in the ancient Roman Empire, the message of Christ found its way into Africa and was joyfully received. Development and civilization in Africa, particularly since the 19th and 20th century, is inconceivable without the history and impact of the Christian message and the work of Christian missionaries.

A Continent Constantly Ravaged but Never Extinguished

History shows that the African continent with all her beauty and glory has experienced the wickedness of other continents, especially of Europe, which devastated her 'gardens' and forced her to work in the gardens of other people, making 'the black and beautiful' (as the Song of Songs quoted above), who share equality and dignity as human beings under the Fatherhood of God, live in slavery, horrific poverty and injustice. What the European colonizers failed to understand was how much the African had to suffer from the invasion of Africa that placed a whole continent into a position of inferiority. The effects of that inglorious past of slavery, colonialism and ongoing marginalization stand as a blot on the continent until today.

It seems that in the present era, the joyful face of Africa has become the sorrowful face of the 'black mother', who cries over so many of her children who languish in misery. The reality on the ground is that of a continent ravaged, leaving millions of victims of injustice, exploitation and oppression – many of them young children and women, victims of famine and fraternal wars. It is in this context that the project of renewing the mission and identity of the church in Africa in service to integral education, reconciliation and human development, corresponds to the Africa Union Agenda 2063 and finds its *Sitz im Leben* and raison d'être.

John Baur, a Swiss missionary who worked in East Africa for several years and made the continent his home, narrates the continuity of the Christian presence in Africa. In one of his publications, he states: 'The Church had been flourishing on the northern shores of the continent for six hundred years before Islam was born... The subsequent history of Christian presence in Africa is, for many centuries, like a trickling stream through the desert. Yet God's providence never let it dry up and in our days it has become a great flood watering the whole continent.'[1]

The Role of African Christian Churches in Development

The foundation of most of the African churches was laid during the colonial period, 1880-1960. This era brought to Africa many of the modern tools for evangelization and a new method of human development through education, the apostolate of the schools, social and health services and the various economic and political infrastructures which have helped in decolonization and sustained the continent's access to modernization and the benefits of globalization. What would have happened if the missionary enterprise of the nineteenth and twentieth centuries had not taken place?

Jesus Christ stated as his mission: 'I came that they may have life and have it more abundantly' (John 10:10). This mission is also the agenda for the role of African churches in development. Development is integral and includes social, economic, political, religious, technological, cultural and personal dimensions. Development implies the promotion and preservation of life, the enhancement of life, support for life and the fight to save life against all forms of the 'culture of death' which technology and the blind drive for development bring.

The churches have a role to play in development in Africa. Together with Agenda 2063,[2] there is a need to respond to the problems of the continent. These include working to heal the many divisions ravaging the continent and promoting a culture of unity, peace and development. They also include issues of religious peace and inter-religious dialogue, ecumenical dialogue within the churches and with the state; the application of Christian social principles in governance, leadership and family. These principles and values elucidate the values of solidarity and community, environmental consciousness, respect for Mother Earth

---

[1] John Baur, "2000 Years of Christianity in Africa- an African Church history", published by Paulines Kenya, 1994, 17.

[2] See „The Future we want for Africa". African Union Agenda 2063: http://agenda2063.au.int/.

and the responsible use of created goods, protection and respect for property including its equitable distribution, the value of work and its promotion through the use of skills, self-help initiatives, poverty eradication projects in agriculture and its allied products. Furthermore, the role of the churches in development go beyond the pulpit with a specific concern for the less privileged through health care programmes, protection and working for the aged, building up the young, protection of life for the unborn and respect for life at all stages.

The churches' legitimacy must be measured on its stand for life. African churches become relevant in the AU's Agenda 2063 if they challenge all elements that contradict the dignity and guarantee of life, whether in business, politics or economics. The Christian churches play a role in educating people to a culture of subsidiarity thinking and democracy founded on participation, respect of competencies and division of power, the rule of law and its respect by the high and the low. This role is promoted through massive education of the young and the aged towards justice, the integrity and preservation of creation, ecological practices, health and well being, the integral development of society and the human person. If the churches are to remain relevant, then they must teach, practise and work for the common good of all, while pointing to this need in wider society.

The AU Agenda 2063 Applied to Questions for the Christian Churches

With the benefit of hindsight and with envisioning of the next fifty years, using the AU Agenda 2063[3] as criteria, the challenges of the present – which impact on both the Christian churches, religious groups in general, the larger society and particularly the young who are the future – include the problems of secularism, urbanization, acculturation, westernization, modernization, globalization, relativism and growing individualism and its attendant alienation, especially evident in the cities of modern Africa. The questions which logically arise are the following:

First, how can religion, religious values and traditions, morality and the Christian message stand up to the 'Signs of the Times' in 2063, retaining its values as 'the light of the world and the salt of the earth'? (Matthew 5).

Secondly, how can the message of Christianity be authentic and convincing to the world of the African 'Areopagus' displaying a disunited Christendom with seemingly unending divisions and fragmented denominations, all claiming authority in the name of Christ? The constant influx of new sects, growing numbers of independent African churches, Pentecostal movements, American-style one-man-show preachers, and the occasional manifestation of 'dubious claims and deceit in some for monetary gain' over a poverty-stricken believing populace looking for healing and salvation, calls into question the role of the African churches in the unity and development of Africa.

Thirdly, how can African Christians feel at home in the 'European garb' of their culturally influenced churches at a time when the themes of enculturation hold sway with demands for culturally rooted authenticity, 'back to basics' movements and the need for a deeper incarnation of the gospel into the African personality?

Fourthly, how can the African churches, true to the message of Christ, construct and reconstruct an integral vision of development of the whole person? How can African churches in collaboration with the agents of the state, build up the development of the human family in Africa, founded on principles of justice, equity, mutual respect, the biblical concepts of mercy and forgiveness, healing, inclusion, the guarantee of freedom and human rights? How can these essential Christian values be made the charter for orientation in the formation of all agents of youth, schools, government institutions, and civil society? The AU Agenda needs to be communicated in harmony with the evangelization and social teaching of the

---

[3] See popular version: http://agenda2063.au.int/en/sites/default/files/agenda2063_popular_version_05092014_EN.pdf.

churches and brought into contact with initiatives of the World Council of Churches, the Second Vatican Council, the Ecumenical Association of African Theologians, and the Bishops' Conferences of the various regions and countries within the continent.

Finally, and indeed seriously, taking into consideration the divisions inherited from the past which has led to senseless wars ravaging the continent – how can we rediscover and emphasize the role African churches can play for healing, sanctifying, leading and teaching in prophetic service and exemplary leadership of the peoples of Africa.

The answers to these questions constitute the role of the African churches alongside the Agenda 2063 of the Africa Union in the development of the African woman and man. It remains an agenda which is open for participation by the churches, as it is the churches who know that such an agenda to be achieved is possible only under the powerful presence of the Holy Spirit who 'makes all things new'. The challenge and the role of the African churches in development is through the renewal of their own mission and identity in service to integral education, reconciliation and human development. Only a renewed church can truly contribute to the AU Agenda. Agenda 2063 is a sure path for a proper partnership of and with the Christian churches in Africa.

(146) Public Theology in African Churches[1]

Nico Koopman

Introduction

Christian faith enjoys its highest levels of growth on the continent of Africa. Africa is a continent with immense public challenges. It is perhaps the continent where we struggle more than on any other to provide every inhabitant with water and food, health care and housing, education and employment, safety and security, peace and prosperity, well-being and wellness in body, soul and spirit.[2]

On this continent, reflection on the theme of Christian faith and public life is crucial. 'Public Theology' is the name that we might consider to describe this reflection upon faith and public life.

Public Theology – An Unavoidable Tautology

Public Theology is used in a variety of ways.[3] In this essay, the notion of Public Theology is used simply as an indispensable facet, aspect, emphasis, approach, perspective in theology. Public Theology as a crucial facet of theology has a threefold focus. The first focus entails reflection upon the inherent public contents, nature and thrust of the Christian faith. The Christian faith is public because it witnesses to the triune God, the Creator who made and sustains all reality, and the Saviour who reconciles and saves all reality, and the Holy Spirit who renews and accompanies all creation. It is for the fulfilment of the new reality that Christ lived and died, and rose and will return.

Secondly, Public Theology focuses on the inherent public rationality and reasonability of Christian faith. Jesus commands us to love God also with our minds. Anselm of Canterbury describes Christian faith as a faith that seeks understanding, *fides quaerens intellectum*. He argues that we believe in order to understand, that we are challenged continually to strive to understand what we believe, and that we are called upon to give a rational account of the hope that lives within us.

Thirdly, Public Theology is a crucial facet of theology that focuses upon the public significance, meaning, impact and implications of the Christian faith. It seeks to bring the Christian faith into dialogue with the questions and plights of human beings in all walks of life, and with the plights of the rest of creation. Public Theology assists our efforts to discern the liberating and dignifying meaning of Christian faith for our situation, especially the plights and pain of the vulnerable, the destitute, the poor, the wronged and the marginalized.

To reflect upon these questions is supposed to be the task of all theology. However, since we always run the risk of neglecting this public dimension in our theological labour, it is crucial that we in the meantime employ this disturbing tautology – to continuously remind us of the public nature, public rationality and public significance of our faith, and about the public calling of churches.

---

[1] Originally written under the title: Public Theology in African churches. Christocentric, Trinitarian and dignifying.

[2] For a discussion of the public challenges of Africa, see N Koopman, Human dignity in Africa: A Christological approach, in *Scriptura: International Journal of Bible, Religion and Theology in Southern Africa*, 2010, 240-249.

[3] For a very illuminating article on the origins and various uses of the notion of Public Theology see DJ Smit, The Paradigm of Public Theology – Origins and Development, in H Bedford-Strohm, F Hohne and T Reitmeier (eds), *Contextuality and Intercontextuality in Public Theology*. Proceedings from the Bamberg conference 23 – 25 June 2011. Munster: Lit Verlag, 11-23.

Public Theology – An Indispensable Facet of all Theologies

This humble and reserved understanding of Public Theology has many benefits. It helps us to recognize that all theology is in fact Public Theology. The notion of Public Theology is, therefore, not in competition with theologies like Liberation Theology, Black Theology, Feminist Theology, Queer Theology, Sexual Theology, Disability Theology, Eco-Theology, African Theology and African Womanist Theology. Public Theology as described above is a crucial facet of all these theologies – to such an extent that one could even speak of a Liberationist Public Theology, a Black Public Theology, a Feminist Public Theology, a Queer Public Theology, a Sexual Public Theology, a Disability Public Theology, an Eco-Public Theology, an African Public Theology, an African Womanist Public Theology. All these theologies are actually in a variety of ways dealing with the threefold question regarding the public contents, rationality and significance of Christian faith. The notion of Public Theology reminds and inspires these theologies, and other theologies, to deepen this threefold public focus.[4]

This less pretentious approach to Public Theology also means that we do not establish a new theological discipline or sub-discipline. Understanding Public Theology as an indispensable facet and emphasis of all theology means that theological disciplines are challenged to view their task in a fresh light. Each one of them is challenged to discern their contribution to a better understanding of the public contents, rationality and significance of the Christian faith.

Public Theology – Seeking Dignity in the Public Arena

Public Theology focuses upon the public contents, rationality and significance of Christian faith in all the public, terrains, areas, domains, environments of life, from the most intimate to the most global and cosmic dimensions of life. These include the lives of individuals, marriage, family, circles of friends, culture, work, churches, broader society – which includes political life, economic life, ecological life, civil society, public discourse and public opinion-formation.

In all these spheres of life, Public Theology strives to enhance the acknowledgement, affirmation and actualisation of dignity for all. One of the most recent bills of rights on the continent of Africa, namely, the Bill of Rights of the Constitution of the Republic of South Africa, describes a life of dignity as one of the healing of the wounds of the nation, justice and freedom. Churches and other religious communities do have a distinctive contribution to make to materializing healing, justice and freedom.

Public Theology – Christocentric and Trinitarian

The word 'theology' in Public Theology is of importance. This word suggests that the involvement of churches and theology in pubic life is a theological involvement. From the perspective of faith in the triune God contributions are made. No attempt is made to function as economists or political scientists. No room is made for the accusation that public theologians are social scientists with a religious interest.

Public Theology can be described as a Trinitarian theology. A Trinitarian approach assures that we drink from the rich wells and insights of the Christian tradition. A Trinitarian approach deals with all the

---

[4] Two African scholars recently wrote dissertations about this creative relationship between Public Theology and Black Theology, and Public Theology and Liberation Theology, respectively. See V Vellem, *The symbol of liberation in South African public life: A Black Theological Perspective* (Unpublished PhD dissertation, Pretoria University, 2007);N Tenai *The poor and the public. A critical evaluation of Public Theology from a Black Theological perspective*(Unpublished PhD dissertation Stellenbosch University, 2011).For a helpful discussion of the relationship between Black Theology and Public Theology see V Vellem, Allan Aubrey Boesak – A black public theologian from the belly of a kgodumodumo, in P Dibeela, P Lenka-Bula and V Vellem (eds.), *Prophet from the South. Essays in honour of Allan Aubrey Boesak*(Stellenbosch: Sun Press, 2014), 268-276.

loci of the Christian confession of faith and dogmatics, i.e. theology (the doctrine of God), Christology, Pneumatology, doctrine of creation and providence, anthropology, soteriology, ecclesiology, eschatology, etc.

The Trinitarian approach to Public Theology that I support is a Christocentric approach. This means that we reflect upon the triune God in the light of the culmination of God's revelation, i.e. in the light of Jesus Christ. Based on the description of Christ's Person and work in terms of the notion of his threefold office we can speak of a threefold Public Theology, namely, a Prophet Public Theology, a Priestly Public Theology and a Royal Servant Public Theology. All these three approaches contribute to developing a theological response to the immense challenges of Africa.[5]

Public Theology – Prophetic

The Heidelberg Catechism Question 31 describes the prophetic office of Christ as follows: '... our Prophet and Teacher who fully reveals to us the secret council and will of God concerning our redemption...'

In what he calls a contemporary hermeneutic, interpretation and understanding of the prophetic office, Methodist theologian, Geoffrey Wainwright[6] argues that the ongoing discernment of the will of God might illuminate the quest in contemporary societies, which are experiencing an information explosion, to develop *sapientia*, wisdom, amidst so much *scientia* and information. And in a context of meaninglessness and purposelessness, the ongoing discernment of God's will provides *telos*, purpose and meaning.

In the prophetic discourse of Public Theology in Africa, we might view our prophetic practices as witness about and participation in the life of Christ, the Prophet, who reveals the truth, the will of God, as a truth of our justification by Christ, and as a truth that entails our calling to seek justice in the world. The prophetic quest is therefore a quest for the truth of our justification and salvation in Christ, which is expressed in justice in the world, which is served by *sapientia* and discernment.

On the basis of this understanding of prophetic Christology, ecclesiology and ethics, one might venture to suggest five modes of prophetic speaking that might serve the prophetic calling of the church well.

Building upon, adjusting and appropriating the work of James Gustafson about the public speaking of churches, I have constructed five interdependent and complementary modes of prophetic speaking.[7] These are prophetic speaking as envisioning, criticism, story-telling, technical analysis and participation in policy-making.

Envisioning entails the spelling out of the ideal picture of a new society. The vision informs about a new and better reality. The vision also inspires to a new lifestyle, new practices and new habits and virtues. The vision of a new life transforms persons and systems, individuals and societies to reflect the values and the goods of a new society. A society of dignity that comes to expression in justice and freedom is the vision that South Africans, from a variety of religious and secular backgrounds, agree upon. This vision is expressed in the Bill of Rights of the 1996 South African Constitution.

Prophetic *criticism* refers first of all to self-criticism. Where churches fail to embody the vision of a new and transformed society, we offer self-criticism. Churches also offer courageous public criticism where

---

[5] This last part of the essay draws upon a recent publication of mine. See N Koopman Public Theology and the public role of churches in South Africa today. Insights from the confession of the threefold office of Christ, in AH Cole (ed), *Theology in service to the church*(Eugene, Oregon: Wipf and STOCK Publishers, 2014), 139-152.

[6] G Wainwright, G Wainwright, *For our salvation. Two approaches to the work of Christ* (Grand Rapids: William B. Eerdmans Publishing Company, 1997), 133-135.

[7] For an extensive discussion of these five modes of prophetic speaking see N. Koopman, Modes of prophecy in a democracy?, in: Bedford-Strohm, H and De Villiers, DE (eds.) *Prophetic witness. An appropriate contemporary mode of public discourse? Theology in the public square/Theologie in der Offenlichkeit* Band 1. Berlin: Lit Verlag, 2011, 181-192.

individuals, leaders and institutions betray this vision. Where the visionary task entails annunciation, the task of criticism entails denunciation. Where visionaries announce the liberating new, critics denounce the persistence of the oppressive old.

Prophetic *story-telling* refers to the telling of stories of pain and oppression. Story-tellers give voice especially to the pain and cries of the marginalized, outcasts and silenced people and creatures of society. Story-telling also tables the hopeful and inspiring stories of victory and liberation.

Technical analysis implies that, with the help of appropriate experts, thorough analyses are made of complex public problems and challenges. This technical discourse facilitates more credible and adequate responses by churches to complex and sophisticated public challenges.

Policy discourse refers to the participation of churches in the quest to make, implement and monitor policies that will enhance the plight of the most vulnerable in society. This discourse, however, implies that we need to move from merely offering broad visions for public life. We also should also avoid providing blueprints for policies. But churches need to provide parameters for policy-making that are less broad than visions, and less specific than blueprints. The notion of 'middle-axioms' that was developed in 1937 by the Life and Work section of the later World Council of Churches might still prove helpful in this regard.[8]

Public Theology – Priestly

The Heidelberg Catechism Question 31 describes the priestly office of Christ as follows:

> '... our only High Priest, who by the one sacrifice of his body has redeemed us, and ever lives to make intercession for us with the Father ...'

In his contemporary hermeneutic for the priestly office, Wainwright[9] argues that Christ the Priest replaces our pain and suffering, which are expressed in alienation, with reconciliation, and he replaces our sin and guilt, which are expressed in estrangement, with atonement. Christ restores us to divine communion and to communion with each other. Wainwright[10] spells out the concrete and public forms that cry out for this reconciliation, atonement and restored communion:

Oppression is political alienation, for the disenfranchised are deprived of the privileges and responsibilities that go with the human vocation to live in society; poverty is economic alienation, for the impoverished are cut off from their share in the fruit of the earth that humankind is charged by God to cultivate; sickness is physical alienation, and a troubled mind is psychological alienation, and both remove the sufferers from the flourishing existence which God envisioned for his human creatures; slavery is alienation of identity, the profoundest infraction of the dignity of every child of God; bereavement displays death as the alienation of humankind from the life of communion for which it was made.

Jesus Christ, the Public Priest, entered into this human condition of alienation and estrangement. This estranged humanity is the humanity that Christ assumed and, in the words of Hans Us von Balthasar,[11] 'what had not been assumed would not have been healed'.

For African churches who seek to develop priestly public theologies, the recommendations offered by Wainwright might be very helpful in our context of so many manifestations of alienation and estrangement.

Public Theology challenges, invites and inspires churches to overcome political alienation. Many African countries have good democratic visions and policy documents in place. However, we need to work

---

[8] For a discussion of the potential of middle axioms see N Koopman, Churches and public policy discourses in South Africa, in *Journal of Theology for Southern Africa*, 136, March 2010, 41-56.

[9] G Wainwright, *For our salvation*, 150-153.

[10] G Wainwright, *For our salvation*, 150.

[11] Quoted by G Wainwright, *For our salvation*, 151.

for social solidarity, social cohesion and the joint building of social capital. We have sound macro-economic policies and practices in place, but the benefits do not reach the poor, and we still have the biggest gap between rich and poor in the world. Beside our noble human rights principles of access to basic necessities, millions are still excluded from physical and mental health care. We still hurt each other on the basis of racial, national, tribal, gender and socio-economic identities, and on the basis of identity of sexual orientation, age and disability. We even hurt nature.

The priestly office calls us to work to overcome these alienations, hurts and violations of dignity, and so to work for the actualization of dignity, health, healing and for restitutive reconciliation and reconciling justice.

Public Theology – Royal Servant

The Heidelberg Catechism Question 31 describes the kingly office of Christ as follows:

> … our eternal King, who governs us by his Word and Spirit, and defends and preserves us in the redemption obtained for us.

Wainwright[12] argues that the Royal Servant office teaches contemporary societies about authority, freedom, power and hope. In a world that seeks autonomy and, in the process, aims to become deistic and eliminate any idea of divine action and rule, the plea is not to burn down the house of authority, and not to bring down the Scriptures, creeds, liturgies and institutions of the admittedly imperfect historic church.

In a society hungry for cultural freedom and an absolute right of self-expression, this office calls for recognition that my neighbour is, negatively put, the limit of my freedom, and, positively put, a personal call to service. He lastly mentions that this office assures us of ultimate hope in the exalted Lord and King.

In the African context, this office might be employed to decontaminate imperialistic notions of power that seem to threaten the idea of the servant power that is characteristic of power in the democratic vision with its central words like *minister*, which literally means servant, and the word *president* which means the one that presides, that one serves as an example amongst the servants, the servant *per excellence*. More than that, the *Christocracy* tells of a Lord, a King who is Shepherd and the most humble of servants. Simultaneously, this office calls disciples to fulfil their calling as citizens to a public life of respecting authority, and living responsibly, in the church and in all walks of life.

The Royal Servant calling also entails that the life of freedom be defined as a life of freedom from bondage and freedom for a life of service. This view of freedom provides appropriate guidelines and parameters for developing a human rights culture, specifically to advance freedom and justice rights, and also to obey the call to freedom and justice responsibilities.

The Royal Servant office also prompts a life of hope. Hope can be described in a threefold manner. Hope is realistic hope because it is founded on the biggest reality of all, namely, the cross and resurrection, ascension and *parousia* of Jesus Christ, which is the fulfilment of the promises of God. Against this background, hope is responsive hope. Hope therefore pays attention, functions pro-actively, and is expressed in actual involvement in the matters of life. Hope is resilient hope. Despite the most difficult circumstances Christian hope perseveres with patience and fortitude.

Based on this calling, churches of authority and hope are moral communities for the formation of disciples and citizens of character and virtue. According to American theologians, Bruce Birch and Larry Rasmussen,[13] an etymological study of the word ‘character’ indicates that character has to do with the engraving of particular principles into a person. They refer to the Greek roots of the word, which means

[12] G Wainwright, *For our salvation*, 169-171.

[13] B Birch and L Rasmussen, *Bible and ethics in the Christian life* (Minneapolis: Augsburg Press, 1989), 124.

engraving tool and, by extension, the marks made by an engraving tool. Character, hence, has the notion of values, which are engraved into a person, over time, so that they become assimilated, incarnated, and embodied in the person. Character, like the virtues, therefore, develops over time in communion with God and other human beings.

Social and political scientists in various parts of the world argue that democracies with human rights cultures that serve the common good cannot become a reality without leaders and citizens of civic virtue and character. Societies hunger for people of public and civic virtue: public wisdom in contexts of complexity, ambiguity, tragedy and *aporia* (anxiety or perplexity); public justice in context of inequalities and injustices on local and global levels; public temperance in context of greed and consumerism amidst poverty and alienation; public fortitude amidst situations of powerlessness and inertia; public faith amidst feelings of disorientation and rootlessness in contemporary societies; public hope amidst situations of despair and melancholy; public love in societies where public solidarity and compassion are absent.

Public Theology – Growing in Africa

The notion of Public Theology as described above is growing in African churches, and in African academic settings.

The Beyers Naudé Centre for Public Theology (BNC) co-operates with various churches to explore with these churches the liberating, transformative and dignifying potential of congregational practices for all facets of public life. This collaboration is entitled Congregations and Public Life. The public meaning and significance of practices like prayer, worship, hymns, baptism, holy communion, diaconal services, witnessing, catechesis, church administration, church buildings, budgeting, fund-raising, etc. are jointly explored. The BNC cooperates with, amongst others, the Uniting Reformed Church of Southern Africa, the Dutch Reformed Church, the Anglican Church of Southern Africa, the Methodist Church, the Moravian Church in South Africa, the Rhenish Church in South Africa, the Volkskerk of Africa, a variety of Charismatic and Pentecostal churches in especially black townships in South Africa, and with ecumenical bodies like the Consultation of Church Leaders in the Western Cape and the South African Council of Churches. The BNC played a major role in the development of a framework for co-operation between the Consultation of Churches in the Western Cape and the Western Cape government. At the request of the SACC, the BNC facilitated the development of a theological response to the international arms trade from a South African perspective.

The BNC and the Mkar Centre for Public Theology and Development in Nigeria co-operate with research and joint conferences, in which pastors of the Reformed Church in Nigeria are involved. Dr Olo Ndukwe[14] of Nigeria wrote a dissertation on the Social Ethics and Public Theology of John Howard Yoder and its potential relevance for the Nigerian context. He heads a Centre for Public Theology in Nigeria. Earlier in this essay, reference was made to the dissertations on Public Theology by a South African theologian, Vuyani Vellem, and a Kenyan theologian, Noah Tenai. In his public theological work, Moravian theologian, Karel August, strongly developed the notion of public church.[15]

Various theological institutions in Africa are now members of the Global Network for Public Theology that was established in Princeton in 1997, and that consists of theological institutions for Public Theology from all continents.

It is also important to note some churches and institutions do not use the notion of Public Theology explicitly, but they do address the three sets of questions of Public Theology described early in this essay.

---

[14] See O Ndukwe, *An evaluation of John Howard Yoder's social ethics from an African perspective* (Unpublished PhD dissertation, Stellenbosch University, 2006).

[15] See K August, *The Quest for being Public Church: The South African Challenge to the Moravian Church in Context 1737-2004* (RSA: The Moravian Printing Works, 2005).

Conclusion

The beautiful and wealthy continent of Africa where so much ugliness and poverty exist, can, by the grace of the triune God, be transformed into a continent that flourishes. Churches and theology, specifically public churches that are guided by a Prophetic, Priestly and Royal Servant Public Theology that reminds of the public contents and thrust, the public rationality and reasonability, and the public significance and impact of Christian faith, can play an indispensable role in this regard.

Bibliography

Bedford-Strohm, H, Hohne, F and Reitmeier, T (eds), *Contextuality and Intercontextuality in Public Theology*. Proceedings from the Bamberg conference 23 – 25 June 2011. Munster: Lit Verlag, 11 – 23.

Bedford-Strohm, H and De Villiers, DE (eds.) *Prophetic witness. An appropriate contemporary mode of public discourse? Theology in the public square/Theologie in der Offenlichkeit* Band 1. Berlin: Lit Verla, 2011, 181 – 192.

D'Costa, Gavin 2005. *Theology in the Public Sphere: Church, Academy and Nation*. Malden, Mass: Blackwell Publishers.

Graham, E 2013. *Between a rock and a hard place. Public Theology in a Post-Secular Age.* London: SCM Press.

Hansen, LD (ed.) 2007. *Christian in Public: Aims, Methodologies and Issues in Public Theology.* Stellenbosch: Sun Press.

Hansen, LD and Koopman, NN (eds.) 2014. *International Journal of Public Theology*, Vol.8, No.4. Special Issue. South Africa 20 years after democracy. Leiden/Boston: Brill.

Koopman, NN 2007. Guest editor, *Journal of Reformed Theology*, Vol.1, No.3, focusing on Public Theology. Leiden/Boston: Brill.

Kim, S2011. Theology in the Public Sphere. Public Theology as a catalyst for open debate. London: SCM Press.

Mathewes, C 2007. *A Theology of Public Life*. Oxford: University Press.

Rasmusson, Arne. 1994. *The Church as Polis: From Political Theology to Theological Politics as Exemplified by Jurgen Moltmann and Stanley Hauerwas*. Lund: University Press.

Stackhouse, M 2014. *Shaping Public Theology. Selections from the writings of Max Stackhouse.* Grand Rapids/Cambridge: Eerdmans Publishing Co. Paeth, SR, Breitenberg, H jr/ Lee, Hak Joon (eds.).

Storrar, WF and Morton, AR (eds.) 2004. *Public Theology for the 21st Century. Essays in honour of Duncan B. Forrester.* London/New York: T&T Clark.

Conradie, E (ed.) 2007. *Essays in Public Theology by Dirk Smit.* Stellenbosch: Sun Press.

Von Sinner, R *The churches and democracy in Brazil. Towards a Public Theology focused on citizenship.* Eugene, Oregon: Wipf & Stock.

(147) HEALING AND HEALTH IN AFRICAN CHRISTIANITY

Chammah J Kaunda and Isabel A Phiri

Introduction

The health and healing ministry of the church is rooted in the ministry of Jesus Christ. While acknowledging that the scope of some African churches' understanding of health and healing seem rather narrowed to miracles and physical healing, nevertheless most churches display strong beliefs in healing through prayer and various rituals. The believers are invited for prayers for good health and for relief from illness and pain. Healing is perceived as central to what it means to be a church in the context of human struggle for just access to health care. There is healing through prayer/intercession, through religious rituals, pilgrimages for healing to some renowned prophets such as T.B. Joshua in Nigeria, and also through some related forms of religious interventions.[1] Healing in some churches in Africa seems to 'fulfil certain functions not met by modern medicine' but to some extent also resonate with the Old and New Testaments, which have more commonality with 'African traditional practices than with modern medicine'.[2] The pertinent question for African Christianity is: How can reconceptualised traditional healing practices be broadened in scope in contemporary Africa amidst unjust access to health care, socio-political, economic, and ecological struggle?

Health and Healing in Traditional Africa

It is not possible to discuss health and healing in African Christianity without considering the traditional African conception of health and healing. In fact, some scholars see more in common between African traditional practices of healing and African Christianity than with modern medicine.[3] In traditional African society, the search for health and healing is deeply entrenched in religious beliefs and practices and manifest in greetings, in the kind of food people eat and every aspect of life. African Traditional Religions have been called religious traditions of wholeness or health or abundant life as termed by Laurent Magasa.[4] The onus of a search for health and healing is not merely on individuals but on the whole community. In African thought, an individual cannot achieve health alone, because health is embedded in cosmic relationships and can only be achieved through restoring harmony in these vital relationships. In actual fact, the sickness of an individual is an indication of a deeper communal malaise.

The community knew that dealing with the symptom is only a temporal solution. True healing requires the re-establishment of rightness in relationships.[5] This was the concern of African Traditional Religions. Health and healing in this system of thought was more than a physical cure but a process of re-aligning the patient with the origin of the influences so as to re-balance the disorder (sickness). It was about restoring

---

[1] Sheila S. Walker, "Witchcraft and Healing in an African Christian Church," *Journal of Religion in Africa* (1979): 127-138; Willem Berends, "African Traditional Healing Practices and the Christian Community," *Missiology: An International Review*, *21*, no. 3 (1993): 275-288.

[2] Berends, "African Traditional Healing," 275.

[3] Berends, "African Traditional Healing," 275.

[4] Laurenti Magesa, *African Religion: The Moral Traditions of Abundant Life* (Maryknoll, New York: Orbis Books 1997), 65.

[5] Newell S. Booth, "Tradition and Community in African Religion," *Journal of Religion in Africa,* 9, no, 2 (1978): 81-94 at 91.

the patient's balance in the universe which makes the process of healing a course of growth for the whole community 'towards ever greater and more complex wholeness'.[6] Thus, health and healing has to do with growth in just social ordering, equal political participation, fair economic access, and religious inclusion. This is a framework within which traditional Africa approached health and healing on the premise of bondedness.

The African religious conception of health and healing is steeped in tradition; it comes and flows from God through the ancestors to the whole community. Sickness or illness was understood as a breach in spiritual or social harmony, either internal or external.[7] There was a belief in some African societies that human beings are multi-dimensional beings (they are more than their physical bodies) with different levels which function together as a whole – communal or social, moral, physical and spiritual, and if any of these aspects are out of balance, the person is said to be sick – physically or spiritually.[8] Every individual in the community had a moral responsibility to keep these aspects balanced so as to ensure an uninterrupted flow of life from God into the community. It was imperative for members of the community to avoid altering these rhythms and patterns as their actions had direct implications on the wellbeing of the whole community.[9] Bondedness is the key to understanding traditional African community of life that 'whatever happens to the individual happens to the whole group, and whatever happens to the whole group happens to the individual'.[10] In this worldview, where interconnectedness and interdependence are central guiding principles of the symbiotic community, *everyone* is responsible for health and healing for the whole community.[11]

The African sense of community refers to the critical interlink of human beings (living, dead and unborn), natural environment and spiritual world in essential ways so that unity is indissoluble.[12] This means that individuals could not regard even their 'own life as purely personal property or concern. It is the group which is the owner of life, a person being just a link in the chain uniting the present and future generations. For that reason one's health is a concern for the community, and a person is expected to preserve this life for the good of the group'.[13] In this worldview, being healthy means that sound and harmonious relationships among human beings, the natural and the spiritual worlds are kept in intricate balance. The individual and the community must always be consciously of the symbiotic chain of relationships that constitute the category which is defined as 'life'. In short, to be in good health is to be at one and peace with all dimensions of life in the cosmos, to be within it and to interiorise the universe in its fullness within one's being. The universe and an individual are indivisible. The fullness of the universe is within an individual inasmuch as an individual is within the universe. Sickness involves the entire system of cosmic relationships within which the individual is but a tiny link in the chain of life. There is no such

---

[6] Rosemary Gordon Bridges: *Metaphor for Psychic Processes* (London: Karnac Books, 1993), 158.
[7] Magesa, *African Religion,* 65.
[8] Shana Davis, "Traditional African Healing: Medicine & Africa," in African Code, www.africanholocaust.net/news_ah/traditionalhealing.html (accessed 15 Dec. 15).
[9] Harvey J. Sindima "Community of Life: Ecological Theology in African Perspective," (1990) www.religion-online.org/showarticle.asp?title=2327 (Accessed 15 Dec. 15).
[10] John Mbiti, *African Religions and Philosophy* (London, Ibadan, Nairobi: Heinemann, 1969), 109.
[11] Chammah J Kaunda, "Towards an African Theological Education for Gender Justice and Peace: An African Theological Reflection on the Concept of Just-Peace," *Journal of Gender and Religion in Africa,* 18, no. 1 (2012): 137-153.
[12] See, Munyaradzi F. Murove, ed. *African Ethics: An Anthology of Comparative and Applied Ethics* (Scottsville: University of KwaZulu-Natal Press, 2009). See especially articles by Munyaradzi F. Murove.
[13] Peter Kasenene, "African ethical theory and the four principles," in *Cross-Cultural Perspectives in Medical Ethics, second edition,* eds. Robert Veatch, 347-357 (Sudbury, MA, Jones and Bartlett, 2000), 349.

thing as a solitary adventurer, the individual's action 'vibrates to the rhythm of the power of the universe and of the generations'.[14]

The implications are that failure to maintain harmonious relationships within oneself and every member of the community of life which extends to nonhuman creation and to do what is necessary to live in reconciliation in order to strengthen the community bonds, especially through justice and peace results in disorder/sickness.[15] Thus, the African sense of health and healing was based on sound relationships which should be kept in harmony. Without harmonious relationships, health and healing cannot flow in the community. Harmonious living (which includes ultimate community values such as justice, peace, hospitality, love, equality, respect and so on) was a precondition for health and healing which are prerequisites for progress and human development. The function of religion was perceived as that of enabling human beings to align their actions and understand their position in the universe and thereby continue to enjoy health and wellness which are essential characteristics of God. All moral values were based on an understanding that the good is that which promotes the well-being and wholeness of an individual and the community. Thus, African tradition's quest for health and healing was based on enabling an individual and the community members' recognition of their complex interconnectedness and their place on the earth, bringing their actions into equilibrium with the cosmos. Since the African concept of health and healing was holistic, bringing the reintegration of cosmic relationships through nurturing harmonious relationships, it remains quite difficult to understand fully the extent to which some African churches have absorbed this worldview into their healing traditions. In what follows, we look at the missional implications for healing and health ministry for churches in Africa today.

Towards a Missional Theology of Health and Healing in the African Church

From our analysis above, it is clear that health and healing are socio-relational issues rather than merely individual physical processes. This means that health and healing must be perceived within a socio-relational framework rather than in physical wholeness. Recent health issues have demonstrated the socio-relational nature of health and healing. HIV and AIDS and, more recently, the Ebola outbreak in West Africa are clear examples of the socio-relational nature of disease that affects individuals, lovers, couples, families and entire communities around the world and have profound political and economic implications. These diseases affect not just an individual but the entire universe. The Ebola tragedy demonstrated how interdependent and vulnerable human beings have become. The virus started spreading from West Africa to other countries through those who came in contact with it and crossed the borders to other countries. The airports were closed in some countries and others imposed a ban on Ebola-affected countries. Given the socio-relational nature of health and healing, the ministry of the church is intrinsically communal in which the community of believers are called alongside (*paraclete*) those suffering, into mutual transformation through justice and reconciliation.

This is what Jesus accomplished through his life, ministry, death and resurrection in which he transformed the worlds of human understanding of suffering. On the cross, Jesus became the symbol of human suffering because of sin (a breach in cosmic harmony). The effect of brokenness in the human and divine relationship was re-enacted by Jesus on the cross, as demonstrated in his loud cry, 'Why have you forsaken me?' (Matt. 27:46). The fall of humanity in Genesis 3 caused an imbalance in cosmic relational equilibrium. Jesus re-enacted this experience of brokenness in cosmic relational balance. Thus, his resurrection was the re-establishment of cosmic relational harmony. It was inevitable that the resurrection

---

[14] Alassane Ndaw, "Unity and Value in African Thought," in *Facts and Value: Philosophical Reflections from Western and Non-Western Perspectives*, eds. MC Doeser and JN Kraay, 171-175 (Dordrecht: Martinus Nihoff Publishers, 1986), 173-174.

[15] Magesa, *African Religion,* 65.

was to happen in Trinitarian socio-community of the Father and the Holy Spirit.[16] The argument here is that the resurrection was wrought through relationship, and this serves as the paradigm of authentic healing and thus provides the archetype of the human search for wholeness and health. Similar to the African worldview, health and healing within a Trinitarian perspective confronts the narrow definition and application of Christian health and healing as a merely physical cure. It underpins health and healing on cosmic reconciliation so that all recognize God's vision for universal wholeness and justice. This means that while healing processes could include praying with and for the sick, confession and forgiveness, the laying-on of hands, anointing with oil, and spiritual gifts of healing as outlined in 1 Corinthians 12, it cannot be reduced to such miraculous interventions. Healing demonstrates Trinitarian *shalom* – the God who is whole. This wholeness is a result of Trinitarian pilgrimage of love and justice.

Conclusion

This chapter argues that the Church has been a healing instrument since its inception. Given this tradition, contemporary mission cannot be done effectively without engaging in the ministry of healing and health. The following conclusions can be drawn from the discussion above:

- The mission of God in the world is a healing mission. God is in the world to bring about cosmic healing and reconciliation.
- Health is an attribute of God. The Trinitarian God exists in radical wholeness and health which he seeks to share within cosmic relationships. Thus, health and healing are deeply entrenched in the concept of salvation.
- Healing is a process of relational growth. It is a dynamic holistic process rather a merely physical cure.
- The church is an agent of God's mission of healing in the world. The church is called to be a healing community through which the power of God's healing can be mediated in the world. This means the role of the church is twofold: first, healing through religious ritual. Second is advocating for a proper health care system that includes the struggle for infrastructural development, adequately equipped medical personnel, justice, fairness, accountability and accessibility.

The church must become an instrument in searching for innovative ways to promote and advocate for access to quality health care for all. The members can be encouraged to live healthy lifestyles and consider ways in which mutual access to medical aids can be secured together.

Bibliography

Berends, Willem. 'African Traditional Healing Practices and the Christian Community.' *Missiology: An International Review, 21*, no. 3 (1993): 275-288

Booth, Newell S. 'Tradition and Community in African Religion,' *Journal of Religion in Africa,* 9, no, 2 (1978): 81-94.

Colbert, Don. *What Would Jesus Eat?: The Ultimate Program for Eating Well, Feeling Great, and Living Longer*. Nashville: Thomas Nelson, 2005.

Davis, Shana. 'Traditional African Healing: Medicine & Africa,' in African Code, www.africanholocaust.net/news_ah/traditionalhealing.html (accessed 15 Dec. 2015).

Dube, Musa W.S. 'Praying the Lord's Prayer in a global economic era.' *The Ecumenical Review* 49, no. 4 (1997): 439-450, 446.

[16] God the Father raised Jesus (Acts 2:24, 32; 3:15, 26; 4:10; 5:30; 10:40; 13:30, 33, 34, 37; Rom. 4:24; 6:4; 10:9; 1 Cor. 6:14; Gal. 1:1; Col. 2:12). God the Holy Spirit raised Jesus from the dead (Rom/ 4:1; 8:11).

Kasenene, Peter. 'African ethical theory and the four principles,' in *Cross-Cultural Perspectives in Medical Ethics, second edition,* eds. Veatch, Robert, 347-357. Sudbury, M.A. Jones and Bartlett, 2000.

Kaunda, Chammah J. 'Towards an African Theological Education for Gender Justice and Peace: An African Theological Reflection on the Concept of Just-Peace,' *Journal of Gender and Religion in Africa,* 18, no. 1 (2012): 137-153.

Keum, Jooseop ed. *Together Towards Life: Mission and Evangelism in Changing Landscapes.* Geneva: WCC, 2013.

Magesa, Laurenti. *African Religion: The Moral Traditions of Abundant Life*. Maryknoll, New York: Orbis Books 1997.

Mbiti, John *African Religions and Philosophy*. London, Ibadan, Nairobi: Heinemann, 1969.

Mugambi, Jesse NK and Mika Vähäkangas. *Christian Theology and Environmental Responsibility.* Nairobi: Acton, 2001.

Murove, Munyaradzi F. ed. *African Ethics: An Anthology of Comparative and Applied Ethics*. Scottsville: University of KwaZulu-Natal Press, 2009.

Ndaw, Alassane. 'Unity and Value in African Thought.' In *Facts and Value: Philosophical Reflections from Western and Non-Western Perspectives*, eds. MC Doeser and JN Kraay, 171-175. Dordrecht: Martinus Nihoff Publishers, 1986.

Sindima, Harvey J. 'Community of Life: Ecological Theology in African Perspective.' (1990), www.religion-online.org/showarticle.asp?title=2327 (Accessed 15 Dec. 15).

Swartley, Willard M. *Health, Healing, and the Church's Mission: Biblical Perspectives and Moral Priorities.* Downers Grove: IVP Academic, 2012.

Walker, Sheila S. 'Witchcraft and Healing in an African Christian Church.' *Journal of Religion in Africa* (1979): 127-138.

World Council of Churches. 'Healing and Wholeness: The Churches' Role in Health, CMC, Genf 1990, i-iv. 1-40.' http://difaem.de/fileadmin/Dokumente/
Publikationen/Dokumente_AErztliche_Mission/healing (Accessed 15 Dec. 2015).

(148) African Christianity, Public Health and Epidemics

Susan Parry

'I have come that they might have life, and have it abundantly' (John 10:10).

'For I was hungry and you gave me food, I was thirsty and you gave me something to drink, I was a stranger and you welcomed me, I was naked and you gave me clothing, I was sick and you took care of me, I was in prison and you visited me... just as you did it to one of the least of these who are members of my family, you did it to me' (Matt. 25:35, 36, 40).

The threefold mission of Jesus as recorded in Matthew 4:23-25 was 'to preach, to teach and to heal.' This has been at the forefront of the Christian expansion in Africa and elsewhere. Health services followed on or accompanied the establishment of churches and missions in the early days, from humble beginnings to the development of full-scale hospitals, health training institutions and multiple outreach services, predominantly for the poor and most marginalised in inaccessible areas.

Currently, faith-based organisations (FBOs) are among the major health providers in developing countries, and acknowledged to be providing 30-70% of health services in sub-Saharan Africa.[1] Whilst government health services are principally found in urban areas and along major transport routes, FBO health care facilities are most often located in the under-served areas, providing compassionate care to the marginalised, the poor and the vulnerable. Their services are not in competition with government services but are complementary and non-partisan. Whilst they are commonly recognised as providing the backbone of the rural health care provision, these same health care facilities are frequently not included in national statistics nor are their health providers included in policy and strategic decisions.

The Christian Health Associations

Over time, in many countries across Africa, the various Christian health service providers, principally Catholic and Protestant, chose to collaborate by forming national umbrella organisations that would coordinate the activities of the various Christian health institutions and health programmes, form joint procurement of drugs to reduce costs, and would liaise with their governments advocating for an enabling environment and for direct support (financial and personnel). In addition, these ecumenical organizations would provide administrative and technical support to all member units, especially those in inaccessible areas to provide holistic, quality, affordable and accessible health services with a preferential treatment option for the poor. Thus, proper collaboration was ensured in providing health needs that complemented government national efforts, as well as availing mechanisms for sharing and scaling up innovations. An example is the Christian Health Association of Malawi (CHAM) which currently operates 180 health facilities and twelve training colleges located throughout the country, providing 37% of health care and training up to 80% of the national health workers.[2]

---

[1] Olivier J, Tsimpo C, Gemignani R, et al. Understanding the roles of faith-based health care providers in Africa: review of the evidence with a focus on magnitude, reach, cost, and satisfaction. *Lancet 2015; published on-line July 7. http:// dx.doi.org/10.1016/S0140-6736(15)60251-3.* Bandy, G, Crouch, A, Haenni, C et al. Building from common foundations: the World Health Organization and faith-based organizations in primary health care. World Health Organization, Geneva; 2008.

[2] Christian Health Association of Malawi. Web site: www.cham.org.

In 2007, the Africa Christian Health Associations' Platform (ACHAP) was formed to act as a continent-wide umbrella organisation for the many Christian health associations.

Primary Health Care

In 1968, the World Council of Churches identified, following several studies, that church health facilities were focused primarily on curative and palliative medical care, a top-down approach, which made little sustainable improvement in the overall health of the populations being served. They concluded that there was a need to focus more on prevention, with community engagement to help communities be more responsible for their own health, coupled with a renewed focus on addressing the social determinants of health, development and empowerment, a bottom-up approach. Working examples were identified and shared and thus the WCC Christian Medical Commission was one of the prime movers towards what is now universally known as 'community-based primary health care'. This led to a unique collaboration between WCC and WHO, and a non-state relationship which has persisted to this day. The contribution of the churches in the evolution in thinking and practice of primary health care is a lasting contribution to public health.[3]

Public Health

Public health refers to all organized measures to *prevent* disease, *promote* health, and *prolong life* among the population as a whole. The focus is on entire populations, not on individual patients or diseases.[4]

The philosophy of primary health care stressed an integrated approach to preventative, curative and promotion of health services both for the community and for the individual.

In the 1970s, Christian communities began to train village health workers to educate communities on basic health, hygiene and sanitation. They were also trained to recognise common conditions and treat with basic medical supplies or refer where necessary. Small health centres were established to provide low cost patient care, as well as provide facilities for routine antenatal services and early childhood health services. In these new decentralised health care systems, many mission hospitals began to play an essential role by acting as intermediaries between local village health services and the centralised state supported hospitals.[5]

The emergence of epidemics is where the Christian community and Christian health services have been most challenged and have effectively risen to the challenge. The following represent the best-known epidemics affecting Africa in the recent past.

Cholera

Cholera is an acute, diarrheal illness caused by infection of the intestine with the bacterium *Vibrio cholerae*. It tends to be found and spread in places with inadequate water treatment, poor sanitation, and inadequate hygiene. In 2008-2009, the deterioration of sanitary and water supplies around the cities, and a declining the health infrastructure in Zimbabwe led to an outbreak of cholera of epidemic proportions, affecting 52 out of 62 districts in all ten provinces resulting in 98,424 cases and 4,276 deaths.[6] It was

---

[3] Litsios. S, 'The Christian Medical Commission and Development of WHO's Primary Health Care Approach,' American Journal of Public Health. November 2004, 94(11): 1884-1893. www.ncbi.nlm.nih.gov/pmc/articles/PMC1448555/.

[4] World health Organisation: www.who.int.

[5] Kurian. M. 'Transformation of Mission and Healing in the 20th Century,' Oct 2015 *Ecumenical Review*, forthcoming.

[6] World health Organisation. 2009. www.who.int/csr/don/2009_06_09/en.

described by *Médecin Sans Frontières* as 'the worst in years'.[7] In addition to suffering, cholera is well known for causing widespread fear and, as in most epidemics, common rumours and beliefs need to be considered and not underestimated or overlooked. In this case, religious believers had both negative and positive responses. A large sect (Johanne Masowe) resisted the community health educators during the outbreak and many infected members failed to seek treatment. Others sought treatment secretly from cholera treatment camps and were reported to have repented afterwards to the sect leaders.[8] In this crisis, as in other similar health challenges, many Pentecostal and other 'tent ministries' promoted 'divine healings' and encouraged adherents to put their faith in God and not in medications. Whilst miracles may happen, blind faith that is not supported by scientific proof is very dangerous, particularly in epidemics, and where people have ceased treatment, it has cost many their lives.[9]

On the other hand, leading Christian denominations supported health education campaigns by devoting Sunday worship time to health education. The priests and pastors ensured no crowding in pew benches, the 'Peace sign' was replaced by a non-touch gesture, and the common communion cup was removed. Community volunteers were trained, creating volunteer networks, and church assets (church halls, schools and health institutions) were made freely available, especially for health education purposes. By involving the communities to be proactively engaged, and to assume some responsibility, they were empowered, not only to deal with cholera but future epidemics as well.

When drugs were in critical supply, the Ecumenical Pharmaceutical Network in Kenya facilitated supplies to be trucked across Africa to the Zimbabwe Church Health Association – in solidarity.[10]

HIV and AIDS

Coming to terms with HIV and AIDS and the resulting impact, and developing appropriate effective responses was a hard learning curve, especially for faith-based responders. HIV challenged the way we think and operate, and our traditional way of dealing with contentious or challenging issues. It flourished in a milieu of stigma and discrimination, increasing the isolation and suffering of those living with the disease.[11] In the early days of the epidemic, the mid-1980s to the late 1990s, the faith community was seen to be negative, especially where attitudes, based on fear, ignorance and prejudice, led to harsh moral judgements on those affected. It was accused of obstructing the efforts of the secular world in the area of prevention and of reducing issues of HIV to simplistic moral pronouncements, making churches places of exclusion rather than places of refuge and solace. Whilst in many instances these accusations were justified, it was not always or everywhere. Many congregations and parishes were at the forefront of care and support. A great number of these initiatives did not wait for funding in order to begin; they just responded and demonstrated real compassion in a world of deep suffering.

Theological reflection has been extensive, revisiting many of the beliefs of the time, re-examining interpretations of scripture in the era of HIV as to whether they were life-affirming or life-threatening. The faith community was the first to initiate home-based care initiatives and support groups and community care-givers, described by UNAIDS as 'the backbone of effective HIV care and support programmes'.[12] It

---

[7] Naafs. Jolanda 'Cholera in Zimbabwe. Kept quiet, not solved.' www.globalmedicine.nl 2009.

[8] Mukuruva. C.T; Community-based Emergency Management: A *Case Study* on a *Cholera Outbreak in Zimbabwe*: a Thesis Submitted to for the Degree of Master of Public Health (MPH), *2012*. http://aut.researchgateway.ac.nz/bitstream/handle/10292/4681/MukuruvaCT.pdf?sequence=6.

[9] Chitando, Ezra and Charles Klagba. Eds., *In the Name of Jesus! Healing in the Age of HIV*. WCC, 2013.

[10] Ecumenical Pharmaceutical Network. Annual Report 2009.

[11] Susan Parry, '*Beacons of Hope. HIC Competent Churches: a framework for Action.*' Geneva. World Council of Churches Publication (2008).

[12] UNAIDS. www.unaids.org/en/resources/presscentre/featurestories/2013/september/20130909caregivers.

also purposely and meaningfully involved people living with HIV, particularly religious leaders living with HIV, to confront stigma and inform responses. The church has also been in the forefront of addressing many of the social determinants that drive the epidemic as well as involvement in advocacy for access to services and treatment, including the neglected area of treatment for children.[13]

The crucial role of the faith-based organisations in the collaborative response is now well recognised and acknowledged. Worldwide, the World Health Organisation estimated in 2004 that one in five organisations engaged in HIV programming is faith-based, and the Catholic Church alone is said to be responsible for providing up to one quarter of that entire care.[14] The extensive networks of support groups and responders to HIV that have been established over the years, are quite unprecedented and the lessons learned have informed responses to other emerging epidemics, such as Ebola.[15]

Ebola

In the initial weeks following the 2014 Ebola outbreak, the lack of accurate information and the media frenzy precipitated fear and panic that resulted in irrational responses and widespread stigma, discrimination and rejection. Mixed responses came from the religious communities, particularly when draconian measures were instituted that conflicted with cultural values, traditions and religious practices. Once they became involved, faith leaders played a transformational role, using every opportunity to raise awareness, de-stigmatise, encourage and accompany communities through the crisis.[16] Their historical continuous presence through war and peace, their accompaniment through significant life events and their voice on behalf of the people earned them the trust and respect of local communities. Throughout the crisis, they continued to provide essential services, particularly in keeping hospitals open to deal with all the non-Ebola cases. Many paid with their lives. A critical role they also played was in promoting the 'safe and dignified burial protocols', and in accompanying the grieving through this process.

In July 2015, the President of Liberia awarded the Liberian Council of Churches the highest distinction: the 'Grand Commander, Order of the Star of Africa' for their sustained response to Ebola through concerted prayer and community action.

The faith leaders played an essential role in social mobilization and behaviour change. However, when the UN agencies arrived, they failed to make use of the capacity or local knowledge of the faith responders until very much later. This delay was costly in terms of lives.

The Way Forward

A number of events are converging at this particular time in history. For a long while, the UN, most international agencies and governments have held preconceptions and prejudices that associate faith-based humanitarian services with proselytization and have failed to engage with them. There is thus an under-appreciation of the extent of the faith-based presence, capacities, local knowledge, socio-cultural

---

[13] Caritas. www.caritas.org/what-we-do/health/haart-for-children
Ecumenical Advocacy Alliance: www.e-alliance.ch/en/s/.

[14] Susan Parry, '*Beacons of Hope. HIC Competent Churches: a framework for Action.*' (2008).
Vitillo RJ. Role of faith in the global response to HIV and AIDS. Panel discussion on spirituality, religion and social health – in conjunction with World Health Assembly; May 19th, 2005.

[15] Parry S, '*Ebola and HIV: Faith based response – A presentation of the evidence, lessons learned and recommendations for future action'.* Religion and Sustainable Development Conference: Building Partnerships to end extreme poverty. World Bank, Washington DC, 7th-9th July 2015.

[16] Featherstone. A, '*Keeping the Faith. The role of Faith leaders in the Ebola response.*' Study carried out in Sierra Leone and Liberia for CAFOD, Christian Aid, Islamic Relief and Tearfund (July 2015).

understanding and their links with the community. Moreover, there is a lack of understanding that faith-based organisations provide essential complementary services to governments, and that their non-partisan service is both a *mandate* and an *expression* of their faith, rather than a means to proselytization.[17]

Ebola clearly demonstrated that a technical approach alone will not rapidly and effectively contain a disease that essentially requires behavioural change, and the faith communities are highly effective at community mobilization through their multiple networks and channels.

The World Bank President, Jim Yong Kim, has stated that the eradication of extreme poverty by 2030 will not happen without the involvement of the faith communities and that, further, 'Our alliance with faith leaders to end extreme poverty is rooted in our understanding that we need prophetic voices to inspire us just as we need evidence to guide us.'[18]

The world has recently adopted the Sustainable Development Goals – the 2030 Agenda – which focuses not only on the poor and developing countries but on all countries. There is an energy and enthusiasm to start working now on these goals and to find the most effective way of doing so. 'Faith communities, omnipresent in Africa, can be part of the solution if included as full partners, engaging their powerful communications networks and local knowledge.'[19]

This is thus a *kairos* moment for the church. Secular agencies want to engage but do not know how to, and are trying to overcome some of the barriers that have existed. The faith community is more than civil society. It provides more than health services and humanitarian support. Faith compels us to recognise the dignity of all and treat each with compassionate holistic care and love – it is our mandate – we must simply claim that space.

Bibliography

Bandy, G, Crouch, A, Haenni, C et al. *Building from common foundations: the World Health Organization and faith-based organizations in primary healthcare*. World Health Organization, Geneva; 2008.

Chitando, Ezra and Charles Klagba. Eds., *In the Name of Jesus! Healing in the Age of HIV*. WCC, 2013.

Litsios. S, 'The Christian Medical Commission and Development of WHO's Primary Health Care Approach,' *American Journal of Public Health*. November 2004, 94(11): 1884-1893

Mukuruva. C.T; Community-based Emergency Management: A Case Study on a Cholera Outbreak in Zimbabwe: a Thesis Submitted to for the Degree of Master of Public Health (MPH), 2012.

Parry, Susan. '*Beacons of Hope. HIC Competent Churches: a framework for Action.*' Geneva. World Council of Churches Publication (2008).

[17] Parry S, '*Ebola and HIV: Faith based responses*'.

[18] www.worldbank.org/en/news/speech/2015/04/09/global-faith-leaders-and-world-bank-group-president-jim-yong-kim-on-call-and-commitment-to-end-extreme-poverty.

[19] Marshall K, Smith S, *Religion and Ebola: learning from experience.* The Lancet Faith-based health care. July 2015. Article published on-line July 7, 2015. http://dx.doi.org/10.1016/S0140.6736(15)61082-0.

(149) Healing and Reconciliation as a Pastoral Mandate in African Christianity

Charles B. Manda

'Never break the pot that keeps you together.'[1]

Introduction

Mbiti alleges that 'Africa is severely wounded by the roughness of ugly struggles in political, social, economic, and religious spheres. These deep wounds from ruthless blows on the body, the mind, and the soul, affect the whole society'.[2] Latey adds, 'As human beings, we find ourselves broken and bruised in so many ways and we find ourselves in need of physical, emotional, psychological and spiritual restoration.'[3] This brief essay explores the meaning of healing and reconciliation in the African context and how pastoral ministry in African Christianity can use them to enhance the restoration of individuals and relationships that are broken and bruised in so many ways. The article concludes with what I call a 'to-do list' to enhance pastoral ministry in African Christianity.

Healing in the African Context

The traditional African worldview is that suffering is caused by sins and misdeeds that offend the gods and ancestors, or by being out of harmony with society.[4] Ward adds that 'for African people life is a continuum of social, cosmic, personal and communal events. When one breaks the moral codes of society then the ties between oneself and community are also fragmented'.[5] For example, in the case of illness, it is not the individual who is seen as needing healing but the broken relationships which needs to be healed. Mbiti adds: 'To be human is to belong to the whole community, and to do so involves participating in the beliefs, ceremonies, rituals and festivals of that community.'[6] For this reason, 'healing must be facilitated by the community'.[7] Mbiti notes that 'African people perform many rituals which are directed at ensuring good health, healing, preventing danger to health, curing barrenness, removing impurities in people and homesteads, and protecting people, animals and crops'.[8] These rituals seek to prevent death, to delay death,

---

[1] John S. Mbiti, 'Peace and Reconciliation in African Religion', *Dialogue & Alliance,* Vol. 24, no. 1, Spring/Summer (2010) www.upf.org/resources/speeches-and-articles/3226-js-mbiti-peace-and-reconciliation-in-african-religion (accessed 20 November, 2015).

[2] John S. Mbiti, "Peace and reconciliation in African Religion," Dialogue *& Alliance,* Vol. 24, No. 1: Spring/Summer 2010, www.upf.org/resources/speeches-and-articles/3226-js-mbiti-peace-and-reconciliation-in-african-religion (accessed 20 November 2015).

[3] Emmanuel Y. Latey, *In Living Color: An Intercultural Approach to Pastoral Care and Counselling* (2nd Ed). (London: Jessica Kingsley Publishers, 2007), 62.

[4] Aloysius Lugira, *African Religion: World Religions* (revised edition) (New York, Facts On File, Inc, 2004), 13.

[5] Edwina Ward, "Similarities and Differences in Cross-Cultural Pastoral Supervision," *Journal of Theology for South Africa* (July 2002), 51-64.

[6] John S. Mbiti, *African Religions and Philosophy* (Nairobi, Heinemann Educational Books Ltd, 1969), 2.

[7] Vhumani Magezi, "Community Healing and the Role of Pastoral Care of the Ill and Suffering in Africa," *In die Skriflig* 40, no. 3 (2006),505-521, 506.

[8] John S. Mbiti, *Introduction to African Religion* (2nd ed.) (Oxford: Heinemann Educational Publishers, 1975),139.

or to ward it off.[9] However, Jesse Mugambi stresses, 'when a person dies, he or she does not go to either heaven or hell or to another world, rather a person changes form from physical mode of existence to a spiritual (ghostly) one'.[10] Thus, in traditional African worldview, death is a rite of passage.

Reconciliation in the African Context

Emmanuel Latey sees reconciliation as involving bringing together again parties that have become estranged or alienated from each other.[11] In the African cosmology, reconciliation means restoration of relationships in the community. The community includes: ancestors, the living, the living-dead, and those yet to be born.[12] When these relationships are broken, ritual actions may relieve the problems and sufferings of human life. This relief may come either by satisfying the offended gods or by resolving social conflicts, which requires a remedy in order to bring back the wholeness of life to the people.[13] Therefore, rituals become vehicles that help facilitate the reconciliation and renewed commitment to the community's values and life.

To-Do List for Pastoral Ministry

Miroslav Volf[14] and Cori Wielenga[15] argue that, although churches are the presumed instruments of peace, in the face of violent conflict, they are instead often impotent, at best, or perpetrators of violence, at worst. Volf argues further that talking about reconciliation from the pulpit is not enough, but that the social meaning of reconciliation needs to become a reality in church practice. One may ask: How does reconciliation become a reality in African Christianity?

Making Public Spaces Intimate

It is vital that pastoral ministry creates safe spaces for people to share their stories. By 'making public spaces intimate', Van der Merwe and Pumla Gobodo-Madikizela mean bringing our most intimate hurts into the public space, so that 'the talking about the hurts' triggers something in the audience with which they identify, which they receive and respond to.[16] Anyone who attended the healing fishbowl at Busan, South Korea during the World Council of Churches (WCC) Conference in 2013 would agree with me about the power of 'making public spaces intimate' as participants shared their experiences from their hearts. Fr Michael Lapsley, an Anglican priest and founder of the Institute for the Healing of Memories (IHOM), facilitated the fishbowl, both in the plenary and small group sessions chaired by Dr Nyambura Njoroge. He had people sit in a circle. The idea of the circle resonates with African worldview. I still remember my Systematic Theology 101 class at the University of KwaZulu-Natal, where Professor Anthony Balcomb taught us that Africans think in circles. This means they include everyone in what they do because the one you exclude becomes your enemy. Indeed, Fr Lapsley invited everyone into the circle, regardless of their pain, experience, race, sexual orientation, gender, and all the other schisms that divide

---

[9] Mbiti, *Introduction to African Religion*, 139.
[10] J.N.K. Mugambi, *African Heritage and Contemporary Christianity* (Nairobi: Longman Kenya, 1989), 51.
[11] Latey, *In Living Color*, 65.
[12] Lugira, "*African Religion,"* 13.
[13] Thorpe, S.A., *African Traditional Religions: An Introduction* (Pretoria: University of South Africa, 1991), 24-25.
[14] Miroslav Volf, *The End of Memory: Remembering Rightly in a Violent World* (Grand Rapids: Eerdmans, 2006).
[15] Cori Wielenga, "Shattered Stories: Healing and Reconciliation in the South African Context," *Verbum et Ecclesia* 34, no. 1 (2013), 6, Art. #747, 8 pages. http://dx.doi. org/10.4102/ve.v34i1.747 (accessed 26 Nov. 15).
[16] Van der Merwe, "*Narrating our Healing*," 47.

and conquer the church. Although surrounded by the audience in both sessions, members of the smaller community, i.e. the circle, shared from their hearts one at a time. When one finished telling his or her story, they left the circle to allow others to come in. The space gave people permission to face and confront their pain. In her book, *Trauma and Recovery,* Judith Herman argues that 'remembering and telling the truth about terrible events are prerequisites both for the restoration of the social order and for the healing of individual victims'.[17] She adds, 'When the truth is finally recognised, survivors can begin their recovery.'[18] Since African Christianity ministers to a majority of people who believe that the 'restoration of the social order'[19] brings healing, people who 'think in circles', and people who use oral tradition, the pastoral ministry would facilitate healing and reconciliation by adapting the healing fishbowl method of the WCC and apply it in their contexts.

Wielenga argues that healing and reconciliation take place in the mutuality of the sharing, and such sharing has the potential of bringing recognition of the sameness of the other that shatters long-held assumptions. Sharing stories involves not only listening to the other but having an opportunity to share one's own stories as well.[20] Thus Wielenga challenges the churches to learn from organisations that are involved in 'making public spaces intimate' for people to share their stories. In particular, Wielenga draws our attention to the work of IHOM and African Enterprise, which have experience in facilitating healing in multiracial congregations. I bear testament to the work of IHOM, because I have been part of the facilitating team since 2008. I have also travelled with Fr Lapsley, in South Africa, Europe, Asia and America, during which time I have listened to hundreds of stories from church, religious and non-religious people alike. I still remember facilitating two workshops in the Anglican Diocese of KwaZulu-Natal in 2013, which the bishop and over fifty clergy and their spouses attended. In almost all workshops across the globe, I have observed the tension between silence and disclosure that was palpable amongst participants at the beginning of the workshop. However, the creation of public intimate space permitted people to share their painful and challenging experiences, which ministers of religion usually hide and suffer in silence.

Koinonia Encounters

Wielenga suggests that churches 'plan to have story-sharing encounters around a meal or a *braai* fire at the church on a regular basis'.[21] She challenges congregations that reach out to impoverished communities to take the time to hear stories from the community and share their own stories which have the potential of transforming the encounter from the problematic one of the 'rich' congregation patronising the poorer one to a mutual sharing and learning experience.[22] For Wielenga, this is the way forward to minister healing and reconciliation in and across divided congregations and communities. African Christianity can take advantage of the fact that a majority of its congregants live in rural communities of Africa where reading and writing may be problematic. Nevertheless, storytelling or African oral tradition continues to flourish as a medium of transmitting intergenerational knowledge from one generation to another. Therefore, storytelling is a valuable tool to utilise.

---

17 Judith L. Herman, *Trauma and Recovery: The Aftermath of Violence – from Domestic Abuse to Political Terror* (New York: Basic Books, 1992), 1.
18 Herman, *Trauma and Recovery,* 1.
19 Herman, *Trauma and Recovery,* 1.
20 Wielenga, "*Shattered Stories,*" 7.
21 Wielenga, "*Shattered Stories,*" 7.
22 Wielenga, "*Shattered Stories,*" 7.

Publishing Relevant Children's Stories

Frederick Douglass once said, 'It is easier to build strong children than to repair broken men [sic].'

His words resonate with the Malawian proverbs: *Mmela mpoyamba* (Charity begins at home) or *kuwongola mtengo mpoyamba* (literally translated: If you want to grow a tree that is straight, do so while it is still young, otherwise it is difficult when it is old). The thinking in these Malawian proverbs correlates with the Bible verse:

> Train up a child in the way s/he should go, and when s/he is old s/he will not depart from it (Prov. 22:6, RSV).

The sense here is that African Christianity flourishes in an environment where the oral tradition flourishes. According to Lugira, the African oral tradition, with its myths, legends, stories, and proverbs, instils the important elements of religion and culture in the minds and hearts of the African people. These stories, myths and tales teach Africans from early childhood about the ethics and beliefs of their community, why things are as they are, how life is lived, the power and majesty of God, etc.[23] While some churches like Pentecostals, missionary and African versions of the missionary churches teach Sunday school to children, it is an opportunity for African Christianity or theological education to publish children's stories, Sunday school materials or educational curricula for schools and theological institutions that teach social, moral and spiritual values, love and tolerance of the other, embedded in African indigenous knowledge systems. We should not only gather children around the fire, the table, Sunday school, etc, and tell them about why animals do not talk, or why chickens do not have breasts, or *The Adventures of Tintin*; we need to tell or read to them stories about the social, moral and spiritual values of their culture, community and God. This lays a foundation for them upon which to build their moral values, faith in God and the confidence they need to face daily challenges.

Conclusion

This paper explored healing and reconciliation concepts as understood in the African context with the hope that the pastoral ministry could derive lessons from them as it executes its mandate of facilitating healing and reconciliation in African Christianity. The findings show that the term healing has varied meanings, depending on the context it is used in. While healing may mean curing the disease in the medical model, in the African context healing comes as a result of restoration or reconciliation of broken relationships, making these two concepts to be interdependent. The paper recommends a to-do list which has implications for the role the pastoral ministry in African Christianity can play to bring about healing, not only to the individual, but also to his or her support systems.

Bibliography

Andreason, Stuart 'Urban Planning and Sustainable Economic Development', http://stuartandreason.com/?p=133 (accessed 28 December 2015).

Herman, Judith Lewis. *Trauma and Recovery: The Aftermath of Violence from Domestic Abuse to Political Terror.* New York: Basic Books, 1992.

Latey, Emmanuel Y. *In Living Color: An Intercultural Approach to Pastoral Care and Counselling* (2nd ed). London: Jessica Kingsley Publishers, 2007.

Lugira, Aloysius M., *World Religons*: *African Traditional Religion* (third edition), New York: Chelsea House Publishers 2004. Magezi, Vhumani. 'Community Healing and the Role of Pastoral Care of the Ill and Suffering in Africa.' *In die Skriflig* Vol. 40, no. 3, (2006): 505-521.

---

[23] Lugira, "*African Religion*," 33.

Mbiti, John S. *African Religions and Philosophy.* Nairobi: Heinemann Educational Books Ltd, 1969.

______. *Introduction to African Religion* (Second edition). Oxford: Heinemann Educational Publishers, 1975.

______. 'Peace and Reconciliation in African Religion.' *Dialogue & Alliance,* Vol. 24, No. 1 (Spring/Summer 2010), www.upf.org/resources/speeches-and-articles/3226-js-mbiti-peace-and-reconciliation-in-african-religion (accessed 26 November, 15).

Mugambi, J.N.K. *African Heritage and Contemporary Christianity*. Nairobi: Longman Kenya, 1989.

Thorpe, S.A. *African Traditional Religions: An Introduction.* Pretoria: University of South Africa, 1991.

Van der Merwe, Chris & Pumla Gobodo-Madikizela. *Narrating our Healing: Perspectives on Working through Trauma.* Newcastle: Cambridge Scholars Publishing, 2008.

Volf, Miroslav. *The End of Memory: Remembering Rightly in a Violent World.* Grand Rapids: Eerdmans, 2006.

Ward, Edwina. 'Similarities and Differences in Cross-Cultural Pastoral Supervision.' *Journal of Theology for South Africa*, No. 116, July (2003): 51-64.

Wielenga, Cor., 'Shattered Stories: Healing and Reconciliation in the South African Context,' *Verbum et Ecclesia* 34, no.1, (2013).), Art. #747, 8 pages. http://dx.doi. org/10.4102/ve.v34i1.747 (accessed 26 November, 15).

(150) The Role of Churches and NGOs in Civil Society – A South African Case Study[1]

R.A. Koegelenberg

Introduction

The best way to reflect on the role of churches and NGOs in civil society in Africa is to focus on a specific context or case study – in this case, the developments in South Africa – that could highlight some of the trends and challenges. The South African experience may not be applicable to all other countries or regions of Africa, although there may be broad similarities in the process from a liberation struggle for independence to the post-transition political developments in new democracies.

It is impossible (and almost irresponsible) to reflect on the similarities and fundamental differences between churches and NGOs in a short paper. Their roles in civil society may sometimes be similar – like responding to specific challenges facing citizens in society, e.g. in delivering social services; responding to the needs of local communities; or strengthening the voice of marginalised groups in advocacy.

But there are also fundamental differences, which could best be illustrated by an example: when former Archbishop Tutu led a march of a broad coalition of civil society and political organisations to the previous, undemocratic Parliament, he was confronted by a government official who asked: Where did you get your mandate from? His response to this implied lack of legitimacy was 'from God'. The rationale for the church's role in civil society is its understanding of being part of God's mission (in all its facets) in this world – in the first place, it is not dependent on democratic or grassroots support.

In this contribution, I will reflect on the following five points:

- First, the meaning of the concept of civil society and a brief and selective overview of the changing context and role of non-governmental organisations (NGOs) from the time of the opposition to apartheid, through a period of transition, to a constitutional democracy;
- Secondly, reaching the milestone of twenty years of democracy provides an opportunity to review achievements and failures. Many observers conclude that South Africa is at a crossroads, or even within a deep crisis (as a failing state) – what went wrong? The crisis manifests itself in two ways: (i) in the political culture – a former liberation movement that cannot distinguish its party interests from the responsibility of the government or state in constitutional democracy; and (ii) in economic terms – the poverty, inequality and unemployment evident in a rich country;
- Thirdly, the conflict or disconnect between government policies and reality: the policies on the role of civil society and the experience of decreased funding available for church-based programmes and NGOs delivering social services;
- Fourthly, the important role of churches and NGOs 'to give life to the constitution';
- Finally, I shall offer a few concluding remarks on the relationship between churches and NGOs, the unintended consequences of international donor policies on civil society, and the importance of international dialogue to address some of the challenges.

---

[1] This is a shortened and edited version of a paper delivered at the colloquium on "Religion and Civil Society in South Africa and Germany", hosted by the "Forschungszentrum Internationale und Interdisziplinäre Theologie" (FIIT) in Heidelberg, 11-14 September 2014.

The Concept of Civil Society

Churches and non-governmental organisations (NGOs)[2] are two important components of the broader civil society in South Africa. There are many different definitions of civil society. According to Taylor: 'The essential elements of civil society are ordinary citizens coming together in community around issues of common interest or need.'[3]

De Gruchy defines civil society as 'that network of non-governmental organisations (NGOs), churches and other religious communities, trade unions, the media and voluntary associations, which in modern democratic societies provides the means whereby people can participate in pursuing social goals and protecting particular interests... a strong civil society is necessary if democratic transition from authoritarian rule is to be sustained'.[4]

In defining civil society in relation to the function of the state or government, Friedman emphasises that:

> Civil society is the realm in which citizens acquire a voice enabling them to ensure that government responds to their needs and is accountable to them[5]... Citizens do not band together in civil society to avoid the state – they do so to ensure that they have a voice in government decisions. The government needs civil society if it is to respond to citizens' desires and needs – civil society needs government to protect its freedom to associate and to implement the will of citizens expressed by the competing demands and proposals by organisations that give voice to citizens' concerns... an organization which provides a voice for as many citizens as possible... ensures maximum citizen participation in decisions – the prime rationale of democracy.[6]

According to Friedman, it is a weakness in South African civil society at the moment that it has a 'shallow base'– not really representing the majority of poor citizens – which hinders its influence in decision-making: 'civil society has often been reduced to making suggestions which government decision-makers are free to ignore'.[7] Since 1994 the new political leadership has been more interested in placing its stamp on society than in listening to independent voices.[8]

The Changed Political Context and its Effect on Civil Society

Taylor gives a good summary of the changing conditions that affect civil society in his paper 'Struggles against systems that impoverish: South African civil society at the crossroads'.[9]

In the era of the struggle against apartheid: the United Democratic Front (UDF) was formed in 1983 with 400 diverse organisations representing almost three million members. 'The aim of the UDF, through uniting different organisations such as trade unions, was to make South Africa ungovernable – thereby crippling the apartheid system.'[10]

---

[2] Most of the literature distinguishes non-governmental organisations (NGOs – indicating well-established organisations with formal management structures) from community-based organisations (CBOs – smaller networks within local communities), or civil society organisations (CSOs – referring to a range of smaller or larger NGOs), or faith-based organisations (FBOs – referring to church-based or religiously linked, or religiously initiated organisations); or registered non-profit organisations (NPOs) – which all belong to the diversity of organisations that together constitute "civil society".

[3] J. Taylor, 2012, 4.

[4] J. de Gruchy, 2014, 104.

[5] S. Friedman & E. McKaiser, 2009, 12-13.

[6] Ibid. 13, quoted from S. Friedman & M. Robinson, 2007, 643-668

[7] Ibid. 20.

[8] Ibid. 23.

[9] See the good overview by James Taylor, 2012, 4.

[10] Ibid. 5.

Before 1980, support to civil society organisations (CSOs) often 'came via the church, political or trade union organisations. They had international links that created channels through which flowed relationships of solidarity and small amounts of funding'.[11] Local communities and role players were trusted and had the discretion to use the funding as they saw fit.

During the 1980s, representatives of international funding agencies started shifting more funding to non governmental organisations (NGOs) but, with the increase in funding, the regulatory framework also changed – it required new systems and formal funding contracts. The years between 1980 and 1990 were the heyday of the NGO sector, which received substantial funding from international partners – and this played a key role in the transition towards democracy.[12]

In the period of transition and reconstruction (from the 1990s): the role of NGOs changed from opposition to apartheid towards building a new democratic dispensation:

> The focus shifted from fighting for the rights of citizens to developing practical means of meeting human rights and needs. Now highly skilled NGOs were active in developing models of effective service in all areas of society... Those that participated in the struggle... started to explore what it means to lead a normal life as a member of a democratic society. Many of the people's struggle organisations disbanded or took on new roles in the democratic processes.[13]

Civil society and NGOs at the crossroads*:* over the last decade, new challenges have developed, placing civil society and NGOs at a crossroads: the relationship between NGOs and the state has become more complex. Initially, their role became less political – as non-profit organisations (NPOs), they did not act politically, but focused on the delivery of programmes (assisting the government).

The relationship between NGOs and government changed to one of increasing tension: many community-based organisations (CBOs) supported the struggle and recognised the frustration of people who lacked access to basic services – and they held the government accountable for this. The challenge was then how to interact with a democratic, legitimate government. Increasingly, NGOs were challenged as not having the legitimacy of being mandated by the people and were accused of being agents implementing foreign agendas.[14]

Over the last few years, the tension between NGOs with a human-rights focus has intensified: NGOs that challenged bad governance on national and provincial levels through court orders (for example, to ensure that schools receive handbooks or basic facilities) are repudiated by government representatives because they 'mess up the good story there is to tell about South Africa'. This tension was recently underlined by the legal procedures initiated by the South African Litigation Centre to try to force the South African government to arrest president Omar al-Bashir of Sudan during an African Union summit in South Africa.[15]

Nevertheless, it is widely recognised by many authors that religious institutions, churches and civil society networks played an important role in the struggle against apartheid and the process of democratisation and nation-building (from 1990 onwards).[16]

Coinciding with the milestone of twenty years of being a constitutional democracy, several authors have reflected on the country's positive achievements – but also on the fundamental challenges that endanger the vision for building a new society. What are the factors that have caused this crisis – what's gone wrong?[17]

---

[11] Ibid. 5.
[12] Ibid. 6.
[13] Ibid. 6.
[14] Habib 2003, quoted in Taylor 2012, 7
[15] See article by Habib, *Sunday Times*, 21 June 2015, 13.
[16] See contributions of T. Kuperus (2011); J. Taylor (2012); M. du Preez (2013); A. Boraine (2014).
[17] See M. du Preez (2013) and A. Boraine (2014).

Reviewing Twenty Years of Democracy: Crossroads

The nature of the crisis is captured well by Neville Alexander:

> Our real concerns are the palpable signs of social breakdown all around us: the ever more blatant examples of greed and corruption involving public figures, who are expected to be the role models for youth; the unspeakable abuse of children, of the aged and of women; the smug dishonesty, indiscipline and slothfulness of those who are paid to render public services; the lack of respect for life-preserving rules… the violence in so many communities… in short, the mayhem and apparently suicidal chaos that ordinary people experience in their daily lives. These things are our everyday reality.[18]

Acknowledging the positives

In his book *A Rumour of Spring*, Max du Preez highlights the following truth: 'We South Africans – the political parties, government, business, civil society – have hugely underestimated the real impact and legacy of colonialism and apartheid.'[19]

He affirms this point before reflecting on the positives (the silver lining) of the new South Africa: the importance of our new constitution, which guarantees our freedoms and basic rights and is a blueprint for how we ought to behave as a nation. He refers to a speech by Judge Cameron in which he emphasised the value of the constitution: 'It is a practicable, workable charter. And it has proved itself modestly but practically effective as a basis for the democratic exercise of power in our half-broken, half-fixed country.'[20]

Du Preez also highlighted that 'We are free as any nation in the world to say what we want, do what we want, go where we want and to associate with whom we want… South Africa is still one of the most open societies in the world… Our media are diverse and freer from legal restriction than in most societies… The rule of law still reigns supreme… Our faith communities are strong and there is an almost complete absence of religious intolerance'.[21]

Our academic institutions are doing well: 'Our top five universities are also the top five on the continent… our sport teams punch far above their weight… our economy has grown substantially… Our tax revenue grew by 491% between 1994 and 2010 (from R114 billion to R674 billion).[22]

In terms of 'the delivery of services', he quotes Frans Cronjé: 'The ANC may be accused of many things… but the data we have published is unambiguous that the ANC and the government it leads deserve considerably more credit for improving the living standards of poor and black South Africans than it has received.'[23]

What went wrong? What is the nature of the crisis?

I restrict my reflections on the nature of the crisis to two factors:

- First, a general dissatisfaction about the lack of respect shown from the leadership of the ruling ANC for critical engagement with citizens and civil society institutions;
- Secondly, the nature of the economic crisis facing many South Africans.

---

[18] N. Alexander, 2013, 39-40.
[19] M. du Preez, 2013, 7.
[20] Ibid. 41.
[21] Ibid. 42.
[22] Ibid. 43.
[23] Ibid. 46 – This is also the thrust of government's own assessment in the "Twenty Year Review" by the Presidency, The Presidency, 2014, 164.

ANC POLITICAL CULTURE: CAPTIVE IN STRUGGLE MODE AND SELF-ENRICHMENT

Former Archbishop Desmond Tutu has expressed his dissatisfaction with the entrenched culture in the ANC and its leadership in several public statements. Giving the Nelson Mandela annual lecture in 2004, during Mbeki's presidency and his denial of the HIV/AIDS national crisis, he reflected on 'What are our failures and challenges?' and remarked:

> We want our society to be characterized by vigorous debate and dissent where to disagree is part and parcel of a vibrant community, that we should play the ball not the person and not think that those who disagree, who express dissent, are ipso facto disloyal or unpatriotic. Unthinking, uncritical, kowtowing party line-toeing is fatal to a vibrant democracy.. It is lucrative to be on a party list. The rewards are substantial and if calling into question party positions jeopardises one's chances to get on the list then not too many are foolhardy and opt for silence to become voting cattle for the party.[24]

He further emphasised: 'We were involved in the struggle because we believed we would evolve a new kind of society. A caring, a compassionate society. At the moment many, too many, of our people live in gruelling demeaning, dehumanising poverty. We are sitting on a powder keg. We really must work like mad to eradicate poverty.'[25]

In his recent forward to a new book by Alex Boraine ("What's gone wrong? On the brink of a failed state"), he concluded: 'For the ANC members, their ultimate loyalty is not the country or the state. No, their loyalty is to the party. The party is *über alles.*'[26]

The same sentiment is expressed by Jay Naidoo, a former leader of the largest trade union (COSATU) and a member of President Mandela's cabinet. In his reflection on 20 years of democracy, Jay Naidoo asked:

> Are our lives better 20 years into democracy? The answer is a decisive 'yes'. We have made progress.... We are a constitutional democracy... Could we have achieved more? Again an unequivocal 'yes'... our leaders are inaccessible and out of touch... We are a nation on the ropes... South Africa's leaders have let us down. Our politicians show contempt for their public office – being elected seems to instil in them the notion that they are somehow born to rule over us, that citizens are subjects... They gave up on us, and in turn we have given up on them. An endless litany of scandals has left us exhausted... The quadruple evils of joblessness, poverty, rising inequality and corruption are sinking South Africa... if we do not create concrete pathways out of poverty for the next generation, we are sowing the seeds of our own destruction.'[27]

The danger of a political elite that uses political power for self-enrichment is evident in two areas: corruption, and the explosion of the public service, where loyal cadres of the party are awarded with highly paid positions.

Croucamp emphasised: 'The political, moral and economic crisis in society is evident from the fact that the tentacles of tender-entrepreneurship (abuse of procurement procedures) manifests in a tight network of opportunistic relationships (between party officials, business entrepreneurs, members of Parliament/ Executive) that is maintained through corruption and access to state funding – and legitimised through the quest for economic empowerment – both on national and provincial levels.'[28]

---

[24] Tutu, 2004, 56.
[25] Ibid. 33.
[26] Boraine, 2014, xiii.
[27] J Naidoo, *Sunday Times*, 20/04/2014, 21.
[28] See P. Croucamp, 2014, "Separate Zuma from ANC flock", in *Die Burger*, 2 September, 12.

In his latest book on South Africa, Johnson concludes: 'After 20 years… an extremely serious situation had been reached by 2014… South Africa is heading fast for another investment crisis.'[29] The culture of enrichment through political office is best illustrated in the extended networks of President Zuma's family: he is head of the Masibambisane Rural Development Trust (MRDI), the Jacob Zuma Foundation and the Jacob Zuma RDP Education Trust, to which companies that wanted government favours were wise to contribute.[30] 'The Zuma era has brought about the sweeping criminalisation of the South African State.'[31]

He also highlights the explosion in the public sector: under ANC rule, the number of the ministers and senior state bureaucrats increased dramatically: 'Whereas in 1973 there were 18 ministers and directors-general, in May 2014 this has increased to 35 ministers, 38 deputy ministers, 159 directors-general – and additional 7,782 directors'[32] on highly paid salaries.

This does not mean that NGOs and churches have no weaknesses, or that that they are necessarily responding better to the needs in society. There is a long and critical tradition in re-assessing the strengths and weaknesses of NGOs.[33]

POVERTY IN A RICH COUNTRY: INEQUALITY AND UNEMPLOYMENT

In a previous paper 'Poverty in a rich country: South Africa',[34] I dealt with the question of whether economic growth created a new opportunity to address the challenge of social inequality (social justice, more equity). Two important considerations were highlighted, namely, the legacy of colonialism and apartheid, and the kind of economic and socio-development since South Africa's transition to democracy in 1994.

The Legacy of Colonialism and Apartheid

The close link between political power and economic dominance in the history of South Africa has been well documented by Sampie Terreblanche.[35] He also highlighted the increase in unemployment of the labour force between 1970 (20%, 1.9 million) and 1995 (40%, 4.8 million) – shortly after the transition to democracy.

Poverty in South Africa is characterised by three factors: first, 'the gulf between rich and poor', that is, the inequality expressed in the Gini co-efficient (a measure of inequality and poverty[36]), almost the highest in the world; secondly, the fact that poverty in South Africa exists as a direct consequence of deliberate economic and political policy (apartheid legacy); and thirdly, that it affects the human dignity of poor people.[37]

According to Terreblanche,[38] the turning-point in South Africa's history occurred in 1986, when a combination of political developments resulted in pressure from the Soviet Union on the ANC to negotiate, as well as pressure from western countries on the South African government of the time to negotiate. This cleared the way to start negotiations for a political settlement in South Africa.

---

[29] R. Johnson, 2015, 17.
[30] Ibid. 36.
[31] Ibid. 45.
[32] Ibid. 113.
[33] See the whole edition of "Der Überblick, 2001. Zeitschrift für ökumenische Begegnung und internationalen Zusammenarbeit", Quartalschrift des kirchlichen Entwicklungsdienstes; September 2001: NGOs: Protest in wessen Namen? (provided by Renate Wilke-Launer, former editor).
[34] My unpublished paper, Brot für die Welt conference, Berlin, 8 and 9 April 2013.
[35] See S J Terreblanche, 2002, 373.
[36] See: https://en.wikipedia.org/wiki/Gini_coefficient
[37] F. Wilson & M. Ramphela, 1989, 4.
[38] S.J. Terreblanche, 2012, 7-16.

New economic trends after 1994?

Did the transition to democracy change the patterns of unemployment, poverty and inequality that were the key features of the economic legacy of apartheid?

With the transition to democracy in 1994, new trends emerged. In the Presidency's (2008a) review, the changing structure of the economy is evident in the changing figures of employment in certain sectors. According to this report, there was a reduction in employment from 1994-2004 in the sectors that traditionally had employed the largest number of unskilled workers: mining (-29%), agriculture (-12.1%) and manufacturing (-1.7%).[39]

The criticism that the economic policy of South Africa since 1994 has produced 'jobless growth' has been contradicted by some studies. Bhorat has shown the shift to new sectors where higher skills are demanded.[40] Landman and others have shown a decrease in the percentage of poverty – even if the numbers of poor people have increased.[41] Van der Berg has concluded that poverty has declined since 2000, but that inequality has remained high.[42]

According to David Williams, South Africa's post-apartheid economic reforms have slowed and 'stalled'. He called South Africa 'a stalled state':[43] investors and the business sector have lost confidence, based on concerns 'about crime, corruption, labour market issues and political populism'.

Mills and Herbst further observed: 'South Africa's economy has remained schizophrenic, often characterized as both Third and First World. By 2011, 14.1 million South Africans were receiving a state welfare grant, this figure having increased from 3.5 million over a decade. The number of registered individual taxpayers in South Africa numbered 5.9 million in 2009/10, and the number of businesses 1.9 million.'[44]

The ANC government used South Africa's comparative advantage (natural resources), as well as a more efficient tax-collection system, to generate resources for the redistribution of wealth through an extension of the welfare system (especially child-care grants and pensions). At the same time, they transformed and rapidly extended the civil service (previously white): the greatest job gains in South Africa have occurred in the public sector!

Du Preez pointed out that, in 2012, about 1.4 million employees of the public service cost about R380 billion. According to the state treasury, 11.5% of South Africa's GDP is spent on state salaries – which is even higher when the employees of state-owned entities (such as SAA, ESKOM, Transnet) are included, raising it to approximately 14 per cent: 'This makes South Africa's civil service the most expensive in the world'[45] – in comparison with Russia (3.7%), Brazil (4.6%) and Nigeria (4%).

Mills pointed to a recent Stats SA Labour Force Survey that showed an increase of 42,000 civil service jobs in the year 2011, although 91,000 jobs were lost in the private sector. In an era when technological improvements should have made governments leaner, such a shift represents an ideological choice.[46]

---

[39] The Presidency, 2008a, "Towards a fifteen-year review, synthesis report – a discussion document", Policy Coordination and Advisory Services (PCAS), Table 24, 97-98.

[40] H. Bhorat, 2006, "The possible state of unemployment and job creation by 2014", unpublished paper, Economic Policy Forum; EFSA Institute for Theological and Interdisciplinary Research, Lanzerac, Stellenbosch, 27 July 2006.

[41] Landman, J.P., Bhorat, H., Van der Berg S., Van Aardt, A., 2003, "Breaking the grip of poverty and inequality in South Africa 204-2014 – trends issues, and future policy options", Development Forum Series, EFSA Institute for Theological and Interdisciplinary Research, Stellenbosch.

[42] S. van der Berg, 2006, 'Dimensions of poverty', unpublished paper (slide 28), economic policy forum EFSA Institute for Theological and Interdisciplinary Research, Lanzerac, Stellenbosch, 30 August 2006.

[43] As cited in *Africa's Third Liberation, the New Search for Prosperity and Jobs* (ed.) G. Mills and J Herbst, 2012, 59-60.

[44] Ibid., 60-61.

[45] M. du Preez, 2013, 92.

[46] See Mills G., 'Economy needs a big dose of tough love – the interests of the unemployed must be put ahead of the

According to Mills and Herbst, this redistributive model is unsustainable.[47]

Moeletsi Mbeki agrees with this interpretation:[48] 'The (black) elite fought for democracy to achieve political equality; to achieve economic equality, it adopted a policy of wealth redistribution... But the downside to such an approach is that it diverts resources from investment to consumption... the scramble for wealth redistribution has also become a main driver of corruption.'

Conclusion: post-apartheid government economic policy has driven South Africa to the wrong kind of economic growth. The large corporations that dominated the economy (especially in mining and minerals) were allowed to internationalise their businesses, while there was no requirement to invest in South Africa. Government allowed them to shift capital abroad without increasing domestic investment.[49] This has led to a decline in the manufacturing and productive sectors. This growth is not sustainable. Economic policy in SA should focus on supporting industrial development and employment creation.

What went wrong with South Africa's transformation process between 1986 and 2012?

Terreblanche concluded: 'It is time for us as South Africans to acknowledge, in all sincerity, that the transformation has been a disappointing one – a huge failure, in fact. We replaced the immoral and inhumane system of apartheid with an immoral and inhumane politico-economic system.'[50] The political 'side' of the new dual system is pathetically inefficient and corrupt, while the economic 'side' is too powerful, too self-centred and too globally-oriented.

Neville Alexander put it differently: 'The demise of apartheid as a political-ideological system... did not lead to the kind of society that many of us... had imagined a post-apartheid South Africa would be... apartheid capitalism was succeeded by post-apartheid capitalism... There was no revolution; at best, what we got was no more than regime change.'[51]

Conflict between Policy and Reality

There is a conflict between government policy (emphasising co-operation and partnership), and the reality experienced by NGOs – as manifested in the funding crisis for NGOs delivering social services.

The Diagnostic Review and the 'National Development Plan 2030'

On 11th May 2010, President Zuma appointed the National Planning Commission – a committee of experts in different fields of society – to analyse the key challenges that South Africa is facing. A 'diagnostic report' was released on 9th June 2011 entitled *Combating poverty and inequality as key objectives*, which identified nine major challenges confronting South Africa: too few people work; the very poor quality of school education for black children; infrastructure is poorly located, inadequate and under-maintained; spatial divides hinder inclusive development (leaving the apartheid legacy intact); the economy is unsustainably resource intensive; the public health system cannot meet demand or sustain quality; public services are uneven and often of poor quality (especially at local, municipal level); corruption levels are high (in public service and society); South Africa remains a divided society.

On 15th August 2012, the Commission handed over the National Development Plan 2030 to the President and the country. On the release of the National Planning Commission's 2030 report, Mr Cyril Ramaphosa, Chairperson of the Commission, stated: 'We need to work together if we are to ensure that it

---

short-term pain of the employed', *Mail & Guardian*, 17-23 June, 2011, 27.

[47] Ibid. Summary, 61.

[48] Mbeki, M. (ed.), *Advocates For Change. How to Overcome Africa's Challenges*, 2011, 8-9.

[49] S. Mohamed, "Negative Trends in the South African Economy", in Moeletsi Mbeki, 2011, 15.

[50] S.J. Terreblanche, 2012, 124.

[51] N. Alexander, 2013, 41.

is a future our country deserves… it is a plan for the country. Responsibility for implementation lies with all of us: government, business, trade unions, civil society and citizens. No single social force, not even government, can implement the plan on its own. It requires a joint effort, constant dialogue and partnerships throughout society.'[52] On 6th September 2012, the cabinet adopted the Plan as the framework for South Africa's future development. The objectives of the Plan are the elimination of poverty and the reduction of inequality through specific programmes.

Partnership and co-operation between government and civil society?

Both the Diagnostic Review and the NDP 2030 are quite radical in acknowledging the failures and challenges facing South Africa in 'creating a better life for all'. In the NPD, there are key passages dealing with the importance of co-operation between the state and other sectors (civil society) to promote active citizenship.[53]

With regard to civil society's role: 'Civil society leaders represent citizens on issues closest to their hearts… they form an integral part of a vibrant democracy that involves people in their own development.'[54]

The emphasis on partnerships with civil society, especially with regard to NGOs delivering social services, is clearly spelled out in the 'policy on funding of Non-Profit Organisations' of the National Department of Social Development (DSD).[55]

For civil society and the religious sector, the danger is that the notion of 'real partnerships' with other sectors remains nothing more than lip service to an ideal. Although there is a general appeal 'to work together', the experience in civil society, as well as in the business and religious sectors, is that the government acts as if it has the sole mandate to implement programmes (event though it lacks the capacity).

Sampie Terreblanche is more outspoken in his chapter 'The fairy-tale optimism of the NDP versus the likelihood that the Poverty, Unemployment and Inequality (PUI) problem will be perpetuated'.[56]

The reality of decreased funding: a crisis for NPOs and NGOs

Substantial unspent budgets by key national departments (Health, Social Development, Education, Housing, etc.) are returned to the National Treasury annually as a result of bad management and the unwillingness to enter into functional partnerships with other sectors.

This is also reflected in the national crisis of NGOs and non-profits (NPOs), where state subsidy for welfare projects falls short and many face closure, or have already been forced to close. The lack of transparent and proper consultations between the Department of Social Development and NPOs has clearly

---

[52] *Mail & Guardian*, 17 August 2012, Opinion contribution.

[53] The NDP emphasises: "South Africa needs leaders that work together. Just as the transition from apartheid was a win-win solution rather than a short-sighted power struggle, the fight against poverty and inequality will have benefits for all – black and white … To successfully implement this plan, the country needs partnerships across society working together towards a common purpose. The Presidency, 2011. The National Development Plan 2030: Our Future – Make It Work, 57.

[54] Ibid. 58.

[55] "Government alone cannot address all the challenges facing society without the involvement and participation of all sectors of society … Many of our achievements have been possible because of the co-operation that we have with civil society organisations". See Department of Social Development (DSD): Draft policy on financial awards to service providers, 2013.

[56] S. J. Terreblanche, "Lost in Transformation", p.119. He concludes: "the main problem with the NDP is that it has not considered the historical trends of the past 130 years and it does not consider *the structural nature* of the PUI problem, the role that political and economic structures played from 1886 to 1994, and after 1994, in creating and perpetuation the PUI problem".

demonstrated the unequal levels of power in this relationship: there are roughly 100,000 NPOs who between them deliver almost 60% of all welfare services the government is obliged to deliver. In the case of child welfare services, NPOs provide closer to 90% of the services that are delivered.[57]

This situation became aggravated in 2012: many welfare groups, fulfilling many of the state's obligations, are being crippled by its inefficiency and indifference. Government funding is failing non-profit organisations serving children, the elderly, disabled and vulnerable people living in poverty. The government is constitutionally bound to deliver these services, but the non-profit organisations carry out most of the work. Inadequate funding levels for services rendered and late disbursements cause a lot of damage to NGOs. State subsidies for older persons in NGO homes are totally inadequate – they have remained unchanged for the last 20 years.[58]

Apart from the crisis in these 'service-delivering civil society networks' (which include many religious and church-based networks and NGOs), the transition to democracy in South Africa has had other negative consequences, exacerbated by the international financial crisis: well-established church networks (such as the South African Council of Churches) are in a severe financial crisis, while others have been forced to close already (e.g. the Institute for Democracy in South Africa: *Idasa*).[59]

Although management decisions could have contributed to these crises, the fact is that strong civil society institutions that could make a substantial contribution to the national debate on the kind of society South Africans want to build for the future are disappearing at a very crucial time of our country's history.

A strong democracy also needs strong civil society institutions and networks that are sustainable (in core staff and functions) in order to make a meaningful contribution. The costs in failing to create the democratic space and sustainable non-partisan civil society institutions could be extremely high in the long term. In South Africa, churches have elaborate social programmes that reach many beneficiaries, whereas the state cannot reach everybody.[60]

The Constitution: The Role of Churches and NGOs

Churches and NGOs have a crucial role to play in South Africa's relatively young democracy. Reflecting on 'What does it mean that we have a constitutional state?', Judge Edwin Cameron concluded:

> The Constitution is not self-executing. It needs us to give it life – us, the citizens and inhabitants of South Africa, young and old, male and female, rural and urban, township and suburb dwellers. The Constitution creates the practical structures that enable the rest of us – you and me, together with principled, honest leadership, a committed government, an active citizenry and vigorous civil society institutions – to perfect our future.[61]

In analysing the Constitution (especially the Bill of Rights) with regard to freedom and equality, Amy Meyer concludes:

> In South Africa, with such socio-economic extremes, many citizens are not politically empowered or aware, and are thus marginalized from real involvement in the decisions that affect them. The right, as it stands, is therefore

[57] See article by Ann Crotty, "Meeting with government further frustrates NPOs', *Business Report*, August 30, 2011, 16.
[58] See article by Heidi Swart, "Welfare groups fight for survival", *Mail & Guardian*, May 18-24, 2012, 19.
[59] See Carol Paton's report, "Idasa leaves a gap as it succumbs to lack of funding", *Business Day*, 28 March, 3.
[60] See NRASD presentation to President Mbeki that led to a formal Memorandum of Understanding (2005) to cooperate in social programmes.
[61] E. Cameron, 2014, 276.

> only protecting people from being excluded from voting. It does not necessarily create the space for citizens to realise this right. [62]

This is especially with regard to the socio-economic rights found in our Bill of Rights: the right to a healthy environment (section 24); the right to housing (section 26); the right to health, food and social security (section 27) and the right to education (section 29) – these provide 'strong evidence that we prescribe an inclusive society'.[63]

The former Minister of Finance, Trevor Manuel, focusing on the challenges of poverty and inequality, emphasised that 'the concern that we should all express is the risk that for many... the constitutional promise is now either extinguished or deferred'.[64] Although we now have a model constitution with democratic values and fundamental human rights, regular democratic elections, etc., the danger is that one can 'tick all the boxes' of the 'form' of democracy without realising the 'substance' of a constitutional democracy.[65] Key to realising this substance of democracy is meeting the demand for real participation.[66]

It is not only with regard to socio-economic rights that the Constitution is under threat, but also in terms of guaranteeing basic human rights to foreigners in South Africa. During the recent xenophobic violence that was unleashed against foreigners, it was often the NGOs like Lawyers for Human Rights that defended their expulsion from the Central Methodist Church in Johannesburg or gave them access to legal counsel.[67] At the same time, numerous churches and other faith groups supported the foreigners with food parcels and tried to protect them at community level.

Max du Preez highlights the crucial role for civil society:

> The question we should ponder is whether we are going to live up to our real potential in the next few decades; whether we are going to develop and prosper; whether we're going to succeed in bringing social and economic justice to all citizens... Visionary political and business leadership and a lot more civic activism are preconditions. We'll need leaders in all sectors of our society to forge a new social contract that most citizens will buy into.[68]

Steven Friedman elaborates on the challenge for civil society in democracy – not to focus on engagement with government alone:

> The task for civil society is to move beyond a reliance on direct engagement with the government to a strategy which stresses more the need to deepen roots in society. Actively defending the freedoms which make that possible is a core civil society concern – its immediate future may thus depend on how energetically and effectively it unites behind the institutions and rights which make civil society possible... As always, civil society and democracy feed off each other: neither will flourish unless the other does too... it is therefore of critical importance that they form more effective coalitions amongst themselves.[69]

---

[62] Ibid. 19.
[63] Ibid. 20
[64] T. Manuel on the role of civil society in sustaining our constitutional democracy, in *Daily Maverick*, 12 November 2014.
[65] Ibid. 2.
[66] Ibid. 2, citing Michelle Bachelet's Nelson Mandela Memorial Lecture in 2013.
[67] *The Economist*: "South Africa's migrants – nice words, harsh deeds", 4 June 2015.
[68] M. du Preez, 2013, 269.
[69] S. Friedman & E. McKaiser, 2009, 47-48.

Are the churches and NGOs succeeding in playing this critical role in our constitutional state?

There are a few studies that focus on evaluating the role of the churches and NGOs/CSOs within the democratic dispensation that emerged in 1994.

In a contribution by Frans Cronje, he refers to the critical role of NGOs and the danger if the state should attempt to limit their role:

> By 2014 civil society had also begun to turn against the government. Civil society organisations routinely challenged new government policies in court on issues ranging from policing to education… (there is a) danger of controlling civil society formations by monitoring or de-registering them.[70]

In her research, Tracy Kuperus asked the question: 'Does the political involvement of churches in a democratic South Africa differ significantly from the apartheid era?... Do churches and interdenominational organizations, as key civil society actors, help or hinder the consolidation of democracy in South Africa?'[71] The results are mixed: 'Some argue that civil society can be a stumbling block to strengthen democracy (when they only serve selective interests), others argue that it contributes to democratic consolidation.'[72]

In her essay, she focused on the 'public policy advocacy role' in four case studies in South Africa: (NG Kerk, SACC, Rhema and ZCC),[73] whilst acknowledging that this forms only a selective part of the role of Christian churches. One of the interesting results highlighted in this contribution is the perceived diminishing role of mainline churches (and the SACC as a beacon in the struggle against apartheid) versus the strengthening of Evangelical and Charismatic churches (which were almost neutral in terms of opposition to apartheid).

With regard to the SACC: with its 27 member churches, it took a leading role in the struggle against apartheid – and produced the 'Message to the people of South Africa' which declared that apartheid was an unjust political policy and contrary to the biblical message of reconciliation.[74] It supported the Freedom Charter and its role was appreciated in the ANC. After the transition to democracy, its influence diminished rapidly – competing more and more with other Pentecostal and charismatic churches. Its 'critical solidarity' with government (selective support) and its 'watchdog role' (evaluating and criticising) of government contributed to its being side-lined by the ANC leadership.[75]

In evaluating the role of the different churches, Kuperus concluded: 'As civil society actors, churches and church leaders can play a positive role in democratisation *only if* they maintain an autonomous voice vis-à-vis the government.'[76]

The transition to democracy impacted directly not only on the formation and role of NGOs, but also on the traditional role of the SACC and numerous new and changing ecumenical initiatives. Ernst Conradie gives an overview on these ecumenical developments and concludes: 'It is at least evident from these rather confusing developments that the relationship between church, party, government and state calls for constant clarification. Many churches that supported the liberation movement in South Africa nowadays recognise the need to maintain their autonomy from any political structure.'[77]

---

[70] F. Cronje, 2014, 171.
[71] T. Kuperus, 2001, 279.
[72] Ibid. citing L. Diamond and E. Gyimah-Boadi.
[73] Dutch Reformed Church, South African Council of Churches, Rhema Bible Church, Zionist Christian Church.
[74] John W de Gruchy, *The Church Struggle in South Africa*, 2nd ed., Grand Rapids Eerdmans, 1986, 120.
[75] T. Kuperus, 2001, 293.
[76] Ibid. 299.
[77] E. Conradie. 2013. 15.

Concluding Remarks

In his book *The Role of Civil Society in a Failing State,* Alex Boraine[78] refers to the prominent role of NGOs in challenging the government of the day on fundamental policies: the role of the Treatment Action Campaign (TAC) to force President Mbeki's government to start a treatment programme for HIV and AIDS; the Right2Know (R2K) coalition to oppose new legislation to control free access to information (the so-called Protection of State Information Bill); Corruption Watch and the Social Justice Coalition.[79] He concludes: 'Civil society was important under the apartheid state; it is equally important under a failing state.'[80]

The church is part of broader civil society, and often collaborates with civil society or NGO/CBO initiatives – it is often the church that enables civil society to function by providing the enabling space (physical and intellectually), the prophetic vision that enables civil society initiatives and networks to do their work. We have seen this in South Africa and in Germany (e.g. the Leipzig democracy demonstrations in the former Eastern Germany).

Crucial in many of these new initiatives is the fact that prominent church leaders like Archbishop Thabo Makgoba (Anglican) and the churches provide the space and support for these public campaigns to defend basic rights. Thus, the history of co-operation between churches and NGOs is repeating itself. This revived the model that was followed in the struggle against apartheid: church leaders act as custodians of the struggle to realise the rights of the marginalised. It is an omission in the book by Boraine that he pays no attention to the role of the churches… being a former church leader himself (turned politician).

Friedman has pointed out that democracy and civil society need one another to flourish. In a sense, the same applies to the relationship between churches and NGOs. Where they share common values and explore collaboration, they are more effective and together strengthen the role of civil society.

Formal collaboration and co-operation between ecumenical or church networks, NGOs and governments are a fundamental part of civil society today. 'Being church' could refer to international networks (globally), synod or regional networks, the local congregation, or even specific services (such as food services) of a local congregation. The ecumenical church always has been a global (catholic, universal) institution – long before 'globalisation' became a social and economic concept.[81]

One of the interesting case studies in this regard has been the formal Memorandum of Understanding (MOU) since 1999 between the Catholic Church (Caritas Internationalis) and UNAIDS (the United Nations Programme on HIV/AIDS). Despite fundamental differences in the social teachings of the Catholic Church and UNAIDS (e.g. the distribution and usage of condoms), they co-operate closely and respect their differences. This is reflected in the statement by UNAIDS director Michel Sidibé in 2009:

> The Church's uncompromising position on the need for social justice – to do what is right – and on the inherent dignity of individuals, inspires us to campaign for universal access to comprehensive HIV prevention, treatment, care and support as a moral imperative.[82]

Formal co-operation between churches and NGOs in the North and the South is necessary to counter some of the negative developments in international development co-operation: current policies of donors have a direct impact on the survival chances of NGOs and many church-based social programmes in the

---

[78] A. Boraine, 2014, 109.
[79] Ibid., 112-113.
[80] Ibid., 114.
[81] See my paper on "Poverty and Civil Society in a global perspective" – the role of church initiated networks, unpublished paper 2013.
[82] See M. Czerny, "Global Catholic responses to AIDS since the discovery of HIV", in S. Bate & A. Munro, *Catholic Responses to AIDS in Southern Africa*, 165.

South. Not only is there a substantial decrease in available funding, but the conditions attached to some of the grants are counter-productive and sometimes have serious, unintended, negative (and unethical) consequences.

One example will suffice. Germany is one of the main donors of the Global Fund to fight HIV and AIDS, malaria and TB – contributing annually approximately 200 million euros to the Global Fund's budget. In the financial management of this grant, the minimising of financial risk plays a key role. One consequence of this needs to be spelled out: where the funds are mostly needed (in poor rural areas of South Africa) there are no formal partners that can benefit from the grant (e.g. the largest African Independent Churches), since their financial systems are not sophisticated enough to manage these funds.

The effect of a risk-management approach is intensified and aggravated by a 'results-based' approach that has become popular in the 'evaluation industry': the quest for accountability and the measurement of results through linear logical frameworks (base-line studies; measuring inputs, outputs and impact). Thus in South Africa (and other parts of the world) the Country Co-ordinating Mechanisms (CCMs) increasingly formulate 'easily measurable targets' (called 'key population groups') to ensure that they can prove 'impact', or 'value for investment' (maximum impact with small amount of funding). The intention of such an approach may be good, but the unintended consequences are bad – it does not build long-term relationships of trust or capacity within the target communities (the moment donor funding stops, the programmes disappear). It also raises fundamental ethical issues.

How does one explain to a child who has lost both parents that you cannot support him/her any longer with food, clothes, supervision by care-workers – because the South African National AIDS Council (SANAC) has decided that the infection rate is higher in another district – and the funds should be shifted?

We are at a very challenging political point in South Africa today, where the formal structures and procedures of a constitutional democracy are misused to trample on the core values of our democracy. The effect is to prevent and obstruct accountability, responsibility and transparency with regard to the Executive (the Cabinet, e.g. the case of the weapons procurement scandal and the Nkandla upgrading scandal involving R250 million of public funds for a private residence of the president).

In his Easter message of 2014, Anglican Archbishop Thabo Makgoba emphasised: 'It is vital that our political leaders start to focus on value-based decisions as they lead South Africa into the future. The question of leadership stands out as a key determinant of our future... Governance is navigated by our decisions and our decisions are navigated by our values... Governance has to do with how we exercise power, not lord it over others. Governance is how we lead, not how we order... acting to provide humanity with a contextual framework in how we build relationships of trust with others.' [83]

In his contribution on 'Economic Policy and Theological Reflection in South Africa', Piet Naudé concludes that 'theology should not give up on its proven strength of providing critical perspectives on society... Providing a social vision might be the prime Christian contribution to shaping policy'.[84]

Bibliography

Alexander, N. 2013. Thoughts on the new South Africa, Jacana Media.

Bate S C & Munro A (Eds.). 2014. Catholic Responses to AIDS in Southern Africa, Southern African Catholic Bishops' Conference, Pretoria.

Bhorat, H, 2006. 'The possible state of unemployment and job creation by 2014', unpublished paper, economic policy forum, *EFSA Institute for Theological and Interdisciplinary Research*, Lanzerac, Stellenbosch, 27 July 2006.

Boraine, A. 2014. What's gone wrong? On the brink of a failed state. Jonathan Ball.

[83] T. Makgoba, 2014, The Sunday Independent, 20 April 2014, 19.

[84] P. Naudé, 2014, 470.

Cameron, E. 2014. Justice: a personal account, Tafelberg.
Conradie, E. (ed.). 2013. South African perspectives on notions and forms of ecumenicity, Sun Media, Stellenbosch – a publication of the EFSA Institute.
Cronje, F. 2014. A time traveller's guide to our next ten years, Tafelberg.
Crotty, A. Meeting with government further frustrates NPOs, Business Report, August 30, 2011, p 6.
De Gruchy, J W. 1986. The church struggle in South Africa, 2nd ed., Grand Rapids, Eerdmans.
De Gruchy, J W. 2014. A Theological Odyssey – my life in writing; Beyers Naudé Centre Series on Public theology, Stellenbosch University, Sun Press.
Department of Social Development (DSD), The. 2013. Draft Policy on financial awards to service providers. Confidential draft – accessed by author, who is a member of the review panel.
Du Preez, M. (ed). 2011. Opinion pieces by South African thought leaders, Penguin Books
Du Preez, M. 2013. A rumour of spring: South Africa after 20 years of democracy, Zebra Press.
Der Überblick, 2001. Zeitschrift für ökumenische Begegnung und internationalen Zusammenarbeit, Quartalschrift des kirchlichen Entwicklungsdienstes; September 2001: NGOs: Protest in wessen Namen? (Provided by Renate Wilke-Launer, former editor).
Focus, The Journal of the Helen Suzman Foundation, Issue 73, Social Inclusion, August 2014
Friedman, S & McKaiser E (Eds.). 2009. Civil Society and the post Polokwane South African state: assessing civil society's prospects of improved policy engagement; Centre for the Study of Democracy, Rhodes University/University of Johannesburg, commissioned by the Heinrich Böll Foundation
Friedman, S. 2014. Way forward lies with policy changes, not project roll-outs, in: Business Day, 1/06/2014, accessed 6/09/2014 from: www.bdlive.co.za/opinion/columnists/2014/06/07
Habib, A. 2013. South Africa's suspended revolution – hopes and prospects, Wits University Press, Johannesburg.
Habib, A. The Sunday Times, Bashir should be in the dock – but so should Bush and Blair, 21 June, 2015, p 13
Johnson, R. 2015. How long will South Africa survive? The looming crisis, Jonathan Ball, Johannesburg.
Koegelenberg, R. 2013. Unpublished paper, Brot für die Welt conference, Berlin, 8 & 9 April 2013
Koegelenberg, R. 2013. Poverty and Civil Society in a global perspective, unpublished paper, conference hosted by the Dutch Reformed Church in Helderberg, Somerset West, 21 August 2013.
Kuperus, T. 2011. The political role and democratic Contribution of Churches in Post-Apartheid South Africa, in: Journal of Church and State vol. 53 no.2 pp 278-306
Landman, JP, Bhorat, H, Van der Berg S, Van Aardt, A. 2003. 'Breaking the grip of poverty and inequality in South Africa 204-2014 – trends issues, and future policy options', *Development Forum Series, EFSA Institute for Theological and Interdisciplinary Research*, Stellenbosch.
Makgoba, T. 2014. The Sunday Independent, 20 April 2014, p 19.
Manuel, T. 2014. Daily Maverick, 12 November, Op-Ed: The role of civil society in sustaining our constitutional democracy
Mbeki M (ed), 2011. Advocates for Change, How to overcome Africa's challenges, Picador Africa.
Meyer, A. 2014. Social Inclusion and the Constitution: a Deconstruction, in: Focus, the Journal of the Helen Suzman Foundation, Issue 73, August 2014 p. 16-20.
Mills, G. & Herbst, J., 2012, Africa's Third Liberation, the new search for prosperity and jobs, Penguin Books
Mills, G, Economy needs a big dose of tough love – the interest of the unemployed must be put ahead of the short-term pain of the employed, Mail & Guardian, 17-23 June, 2011, p. 27.
Naidoo, J. 2014. South Africa burns while our politicians tune out in a daze, Sunday Times, 20/04/2014, p 21.
Naudé, B. 1996. The Church, transition and transformation in South Africa, in: Studies and Reports by the EFSA Institute for Theological & Interdisciplinary Research, Stellenbosch.

Naudé, P. 2014. Economic Policy and Theological Reflection in South Africa: an Overview and Assessment after Twenty Years of Democracy, in: International Journal of Public Theology 8 (2014) 445-470, Brill, Leiden

Paton, C. Idasa leaves a gap as it succumbs to lack of funding, Business Day, 28 March, p.3.

Swart, H. Welfare groups fight for survival, Mail & Guardian, May 18-24, 2012, p.19

Presidency, The. 2003. *Towards a ten year review, synthesis report on implementation of government programmes*, Policy coordination and Advisory Services (PCAS)

Presidency, The. 2008a, *Towards a fifteen year review, synthesis report – a discussion document,* Policy coordination and Advisory Services (PCAS)

Presidency, The. 2008b. '*Towards an anti-poverty strategy for South Africa, draft discussion document,* Policy coordination and Advisory Services (PCAS)

Presidency, The. 2011. National Planning Commission, *The National Development Plan 2030: our future – make it work.*

Presidency, The. 2014. *Twenty Year Review South Africa, 1994-2014*, 11 March 2014.

Robinson M and Friedman S. 2005. *Civil society, democratisation and foreign aid in Africa.* Institute of Development Studies (IDS), IDS Discussion Paper 383.

Taylor, J. 2012. *Struggles against systems that impoverish: South African Civil Society at the Crossroads* (see www.pria.org/civil-scoiety-at-crossroads-/2451).

Terreblanche, SJ, 2002. *A history of inequality in South Africa, 1652-2002*, University of Natal Press, Scottsville.

Terreblanche, SJ, 2012. *Lost in Transformation, South Africa's search for a new future since 1986.*

Tutu, D. 2004. Nelson Mandela Annual Lecture, p 32. www.nelsonmandela.org/uploads/files/NMF_Lecture_Book_small.pd, accessed on 6/09/2014.

Van der Berg, S, 2006, 'Dimensions of poverty', unpublished paper, economic policy forum *EFSA Institute for Theological and Interdisciplinary Research*, Lanzerac, Stellenbosch, 30 August 2006

Wilson, F & Ramphela, M, 1989, *Uprooting poverty: the South African challenge*, Report for the Second Carnegie Inquiry into Poverty and Development in Southern Africa, David Phillip, Cape Town.

(151) RELIGIOUS EXTREMISM AND THE UNITY OF NATIONS IN AFRICA[1]

Hans Spitzeck

Introduction

The phenomenon of religious extremism deserves special attention. 'Religious extremism' can be defined as a set of religious ideas and socio-political strategies favouring one segment of the population and denying the dignity and rights of minorities or opponents by religious exclusion. In many cases, religious extremism relies on an idealized tradition of a particular religion by narrowing it down to simplified rules and laws. Religious extremism is a descriptive concept applied from outside. It is widely used as a *terminus technicus*. Various questions are raised: Are secular concepts of the nation and state adequate to deal with the challenges posed by Al Shabaab[2] and Boko Haram?[3] How is religion being mobilized within the dynamics of power struggle? How can the politicization of religion and the religionisation of politics in contemporary Africa[4] be understood and countered? To answer these questions, an interdisciplinary approach is appropriate which begins methodically with the concept of social conflict.[5]

Political Islam and Religious Extremism

Political Islam opposes western patterns of social life. It strives to unite all Muslims and to overcome differences in teaching and separation by non-theological factors. It is not one homogeneous system of thought or a homogeneous movement. On the contrary, there exists a political tradition in Islamic societies that opposes western influence and counters the disorder caused by weak and corrupt Muslim leaders. Such postures took shape after the occupation of Egypt by Napoleon Bonaparte in 1798 and expanded after the collapse of the Ottoman Empire and the abrogation of the caliphate in 1924. Today, opposition to the sovereignty of the people constitutes the uniting element of extremist thinking within political Islam.

Nigeria suffers a political crisis because of socio-religious conflicts. The vicious cycle of violence is not coming to an end. Nigeria's is not a religious conflict, but a complex mixture of local conflicts involving access to land, goods and political power, based mainly on ethnic affiliation. The federal government is not able to solve the problem and the introduction of Sha'riah law in twelve northern states with their predominantly Muslim populations has not calmed the situation. During colonial times, the British

---

[1] This is a shortened version of a more elaborated essay under the title: Hakuna Baraka – Religious Extremism and the Unity of Nations in Africa which was presented to the all African Academy of Religious and Theological Studies, held in AACC, Nairobi 19-21 February 2015.

[2] *Ash-Shabāb* is an Arabic term meaning "the young". The full name of the movement is *Harakat al Shabab al-Mujahideen (HSM)*, English: Mujahideen Youth Movement.

[3] Boko Haram is a Hausa expression and means "Western education is forbidden". The groups denominate officially as *Jama'atu Ahlis Sunna Lidda'Awati Wal-Jihad*, which means "People Committed to the Prophet's Teachings for Propagation and Jihad".

[4] We owe the expression "politicisation of religion and the religionisation of politics" to Johnson Mbillah, General Secretary of the *Programme for Christian Muslim Relations in Africa – PROCMURA*. Mbillah introduced it in the analysis of the 2013 crisis in the Central Africa Republic. Meanwhile African political leaders like the President of Tanzania Jakaya Kikwete refer to it. Cf. PROCMURA (Ed.), Briefing on the Tanzania Christian and Muslim Religious Leader's Conference, 6 to 9 October 2014.

[5] This approach to the relationship between faith and conflict is taken from Hans G. Kippenberg, "Keine Frage des Glaubens (No issue of faith)", *Welt-sichten Magazin*, no. 10 (2012): 28-31.

governed the northern part of Nigeria by indirect rule through the Fulani aristocracy that had formerly ruled the Sokoto caliphate. Today, both Christians and Muslims claim to constitute the majority of the population. Therefore political considerations require that Christian and Muslim representation in government be balanced.

When Goodluck Jonathan, a Christian, assumed the presidency in 2010, this factor ignited the conflict that developed subsequently with Boko Haram. 'Boko Haram' is the designation used by journalists to denounce the movement's avoidance of western values and its fundamental opposition to the democratic status quo. The name Boko Haram means 'western education is forbidden' or 'westernization is a sacrilege'; *haram* is the Arabic word for 'unclean' or 'forbidden', and *boko* is a Hausa expression, referring to the Latin alphabet and western education generally. The official name of Boko Haram is *Jama'atu Ahlis Sunna Lidda 'Awati Wal-Jihad* (People Committed to the Prophet's Teachings for Propagation and Jihad). It is a Sunni Islamic group advocating strict adherence to Islamic law (*Sha'riah*). The movement began with a religious school and community centre in Maiduguri, the capital of Borno State, which attracted poor people and unemployed youth. Right from the beginning, the centre declared its intention to create an Islamic state and voiced its condemnation of state corruption. It used the infrastructure of a Wahhabist organization, the Izala Society,[6] which had enjoyed the support of the government of Borno for a long period.

In 2009, the police attacked Boko Haram's headquarters in Maiduguri and killed 700 of its followers, including the leader Mohammed Yusuf. By doing so, it violated human rights. Yusuf was succeeded by Abubakar Shekau who transformed the group into a Salafist jihadist group by strengthening its operational capabilities. In 2011, it attacked the headquarters of the United Nations mission in Nigeria and a police station in Abuja by means of suicide bombings. Such incidents in Nigeria were unprecedented. Since then, Boko Haram has carried out many violent operations, mainly in the north-east of Nigeria. On 14th May 2013, Nigeria declared a state of emergency in three north-eastern states. Since then the military has been fighting Boko Haram with troops on the ground and with air strikes. Meanwhile, Boko Haram has shifted from hit-and-run tactics to the occupation of territory.

Since 2009, Boko Haram has killed more than 5,000 civilians, with the level of violence increasing in recent years. During the first half of 2014, the number of killings totalled 2,000. The group boasts a military strength of 9,000 fighters and has attracted international attention with its kidnapping of 276 school girls in April 2014. In August 2014 it declared that the territory under its control in north-east Nigeria constitutes an integral part of the Islamic caliphate and thus is no longer part of the Nigerian state. Boko Haram claims an unspecified territory in north-east Nigeria with operations in Cameroon and Niger as well. The Nigerian authorities and the Nigerian military have been unable to end the crisis. Negotiations with Boko Haram have failed. The challenge to the unity of Nigeria continues. A political solution is not in sight.

In Nairobi, Kenya, the Westgate shopping mall was attacked on 21st September 2013. The attack continued until 24th September with the building, meanwhile, set on fire. The attack resulted in more than sixty deaths and more than 175 people wounded. The Islamist group al-Shabaab claimed responsibility for the attack as revenge for the Kenyan military's deployment in Somalia. The target and the reasons given for the attack were unambiguous. The Westgate mall had functioned as an upmarket shopping centre and had served as a symbol of the liberal western lifestyle. It attracted youngsters from affluent families who frequented it for leisure and conspicuous consumption.

During colonial times, the Muslim community in Kenya had succumbed to economic decline and political irrelevance. Today, the Swahili communities of the coast and the Somali population in the north-

---

[6] The Izala Society (Jama'at Izalatil Bidiawa Iqamatus Sunnah) is a conservative Muslim brotherhood which follows a strict interpretation of Islam opposed to the traditional forms of Islam in Nigeria.

east – both of them Muslim – are living in the two poorest provinces of Kenya. In 1992, the Swahili Imam Sheik Khalid Balal founded the Islamic Party of Kenya (IPC), among the first expressions of radical Islam in the country. With the attacks of al-Qaeda on the US embassies in Nairobi and Dar es Salam in 1998, terror had become an instrument of resistance in Somalia and Kenya. The Mombasa Republican Council (MRC), which included Christians, meanwhile advocated independence for the coastal strip of Kenya, though by non-radical means. Later a segment of the movement broke away and formed al-Hidschra, the Kenya branch of al-Shabaab.

After the Westgate massacre, the Kenyan government intensified its operations against terrorism. Soldiers and police looted the Somali neighbourhood of Eastleigh in Nairobi and raped numerous Somali women. Additionally, the authorities revoked the citizenship of various Kenyan Somalis, rendering them refugees in their own country. This action intensified the ardour of extremists. Violence in the coastal region stems from various grievances. Kenya's body politic is characterized by various cultural and economic tensions. Religious affiliation of the coastal population is Islamic, while people from the highlands are Christians. Al-Shabaab exploits these divisions which cause the internal tensions of Kenya. Exactly who attacked the Westgate mall is still not known.

In the Central African Republic (CAR), President Bozizé was overthrown in 2013. The population in the northern and eastern parts of the country is mainly Muslim while Christians in the west and south comprise about 50% of the entire population. From 2006 onwards, the conflicts of Chad and Darfur spilled over into the CAR by means of a mobilised Muslim population. In 2011, the USA sent 100 military advisors to fight the Lord's Resistance Army which had relocated from Uganda to the CAR. In 2012, the armed conflict escalated. In August of that year, the Séléka was formed as a coalition of the *Union des forces démocratiques pour le rassemblement* (UFDR) and the *Convention des patriotes pour la justice et la paix* (CPJP) for the purpose of overthrowing the government. Séléka is a Sango word meaning 'alliance'. Séléka's aim was to administer Islamic law (*Sha'riah*) in the country. In March 2013, President Bozizé was overthrown by a coup d'état organized by the Séléka rebels. Michel Djotodia, one of the leaders of the rebels, became the first Muslim president of the CAR. His administration was unable to prevent the country from the ensuing chaos. On the 25th July, the Archbishop of Bangui, the President of the Islamic Community, Imam Layama, and the President of the Alliance of Evangelicals visited the Prime Minister Tiengaye, calling unanimously for peace initiatives in response to the rising tensions. They were keenly aware of the risk of the religious radicalization of the conflict.

Djotodia tried to dissolve the Séléka militia in September 2013, but most of its members refused to disband. The Séléka had already become engaged in an armed conflict with the Anti-balaka militias,[7] which had been formed originally in the 1990s as village self-defense forces. In November, the country faced a rapidly escalating cycle of violence, characterized by massive killings. Anti-balaka forces killed Muslim civilians and forced thousands of Muslims to flee. They committed multiple atrocities and several massacres against the mostly Muslim Fula ethnic group. The African Union sent troops to halt the impending genocide. On 11th January 2014, Michael Djotodia and his prime minister resigned and Catherine Samba-Panza was elected as interim president. In February 2014, the United Nations deployed more troops to the country for peace-keeping purposes. On 23rd July 2014, following Congolese mediation efforts, Séléka and anti-balaka representatives signed a ceasefire agreement in Brazzaville.

Instruments of State, Civil Society and Religious Communities in Africa

It has become virtually de rigueur to address the root causes of poverty while disregarding social exclusion effected by public policy. Religious conflicts in Africa are surface manifestations of more deeply

[7] Anti-balaka means "anti-machete" or "anti-sword" in the local Sango and Mandja languages.

entrenched socio-political conflicts. Even if those conflicts can be traced to colonial times, the state always has the option of addressing them and restoring justice. Social exclusion and the political neglect of the people's will undermine the unity of the nation. Democratic participation opens up doors to development and sustainable peace. Without economic justice, African nations will not realize stability. Security and peace are the results of socio-political processes of integration, not of military or police action.

It is important to dissect the intentions of the political and religious extremist. 'Overcoming violence becomes possible when the intended enemy or victim refuses to accept his/her role in a relationship marked by violence.'[8] Samuel Kobia explains this insight: 'The culture of violence follows the logic of domination and oppression, of victory and defeat. In order to maintain itself, it needs an enemy or a victim, for through the fear or suffering of the victim the dynamic of violence is affirmed and renewed.'[9] All police action must be exercised cautiously in order to avoid impunity and to avoid the violation of human rights.

The peaceful transformation of conflicts requires active civil society engagement in a twofold task: firstly, to engage in civic education and to monitor compliance with human rights standards including freedom of religion and, secondly, to contribute to the transformation of structural injustices. Development work by religious communities must involve the general populace regardless of its religious affiliation. Development projects promoted by churches and Muslim organizations must address the causes of poverty and religious extremism. A study carried out in Nigeria has shown that 'community development with a strong focus on the participation of all local actors is able to bond people together, beyond identities such as faith and tribal affiliation or attempts at political participation'.[10]

On 24th September 2014, more than 120 Muslim scholars sent an open letter to Ibrahim Awwad Al-Badri, alias 'Abu Bakr Al-Baghdadi', leader of the Islamic State.[11] This open letter was an important initiative to counter religious extremism, with relevance for Africa as well. It provides an example of how to address misleading teaching and forbidden action within the Muslim community.

In practical terms, inter-religious dialogue, encounter and co-operation are good instruments to overcome religious divides. In vast sectors of African society, there are initiatives to become better acquainted with each other. Once again, there is a twofold challenge: knowing the other requires knowing oneself. Civic education must include religious information and avert the politicization of religion and the religionisation of politics. In order for inter-religious councils to effectively engage with these issues, they must be included on the Agenda of Africa for the purpose of isolating and overcoming religious extremism.

Consideration of these issues leads to core theological challenges: How does one understand the co-existence of Christianity, Islam and other religions in Africa? Which concept of God is commensurate with the Holy Scriptures in the context of Africa? The answers to these questions must correspond with the traditions and realities of the African continent.

God is the source of life. 'Surely it is good to know that God (in the Christian tradition) created all of us (not only Christians) in his image, thus investing us all with infinite worth. God initiated a covenant relationship with all humankind, exemplified in the covenant with Noah by which God promised to not destroy his creation again with water.'[12] This covenant provides a theological foundation for the rejection of religious extremism with its tendency to subject followers of other religions to its understandings.

To worship God and to respect life are two sides of the same coin. In Africa, harmony is attributed to God. 'At any stage of life there are regulations and practices intended to restore broken harmony and,

---

[8] Samuel Kobia, *Dialogue Matters, The Role of Ecumenical Diplomacy in the Run-Up to the Independence of South Sudan*, Limuru, Kenya (2013), 7. By this Samuel Kobia builds on a concept of Konrad RAISER.

[9] Kobia, *Dialogue Matters,*7.

[10] Andrew Gwaivangmin, Wolfgang Kaiser, *Signs of Hope, Development Conflict and Religion in Northern Nigeria* (RURCON / EED, Jos, Nigeria / Bonn, Germany 2010), 35.

[11] See the key components of the statement from No. 3–6 of the Executive Summary, www.lettertobaghdadi. com.

[12] Desmond Tutu, *God is not a Christian, Speaking truth in times of crisis*, London (2013), 7.

therefore, restore good relationships with God.'[13] In a nutshell, all theology must be a learning theology, providing answers to today's questions in the context of Africa's realities.

There is no blueprint that provides guidance for engagement with religious extremism. Every single case must be addressed in its specific context. Nevertheless, political processes occur in an international context. Thanks to electronic media, the most remote areas in North Africa, in the Middle East and beyond can accompany the processes that impinge on extremism. The interdependence of political processes must not be underestimated. We remember the symbolic power of the attack on the twin towers of the World Trade Center in New York or the Mohamed cartoons in a Danish newspaper. Huntington's Clash of Civilizations is a misleading theory. It ignores religious heterogeneity as a predominant social reality throughout the world and fosters international conflict along religious lines. It is not a strategy adequate to counter religious extremism.

The German scholar, Winrich Kühne, draws attention to the financing mechanisms of jihadist groups. Al Shabaab is involved in the trafficking of *quat* to Europe, the Taliban profit from the cultivation of opium in Afghanistan, and al-Qaeda in the Islamic Maghreb (AQIM) is engaged with contraband trade. Only by mobilising organized crime and international financing do religious extremists obtain the means by which to buy sophisticated weaponry.[14] Any policy designed to counter extremism must of necessity address its economic aspects.

Conflicts in Africa must be solved by Africans. The African Union (AU) has a leading role in the maintenance of stability in Africa with the unity of its member nations. Human security is a number one priority. The internationalization of regional conflicts is not in Africa's interest. All military action against terror will fail unless it goes hand in hand with a feasible political, social, economic and cultural project based on dignity. Without trust and public support, it is not possible to overcome violence and its root causes.

Ideologically, the Lord's Resistance Army in Uganda – latterly in Central African Republic – and Boko Haram are not the same. But, politically, both have challenged the unity of the respective nation states. They have applied the mechanism of guerrilla war with determined leaders who do not hesitate to exercise violence.

Religious communities have a shared responsibility to work for and maintain peaceful co-existence. Personal encounter, conceptual dialogue and practical co-operation pave the way to flourishing inter-religious relationships in the context of social, political, economic, cultural, and theological considerations.

Conclusions

This essay argues that the African Union must recognize the important role that religions play with regard to the peace and development of the continent. In 2010 the Citizens and Diaspora Directorate of the AU Commission initiated a conference in Abuja, Nigeria that brought together Africa's religious leaders to deliberate on how the AU can work to promote peace on the continent. A structured partnership between the African Union, as the main regional continental organization, and the religious communities on the continent is a promising means by which to counter the religionisation of politics.

---

[13] André Karamaga, "African and Christian Concepts of God", in *God of Life*, ed. Edison M. Kalengyo (All Africa Conference of Churches, Nairobi 2013), 37.

[14] Winrich Kühne, Vom Terror zum Kalifat (From Terror to Caliphate), in *IPG Journal*, 15.09.2014, www.ipg-journal.de/kommentar/artikel/vom-terror-zum-kalifat-581/.

Bibliography

Czada, Roland, Thomas Held, and Markus Weingardt, *Religions and World Peace, Religious Capacities for Conflict Resolution and Peacebuilding*, Baden-Baden, 2012.

Gwaivangmin, Andrew, Kaiser, Wolfgang, *Signs of Hope, Development Conflict and Religion in Northern Nigeria*, eds. RURCON / EED, Jos, Nigeria / Bonn, Germany, 2010.

Kalengyo, Edison M., ed., *God of Life*, All Africa Conference of Churches, Nairobi, 2013.

King, Martin Luther, *Why we can't wait*, New York: Harper & Row, 1964.

Kippenberg, Hans G. 'Keine Frage des Glaubens (No issue of faith)', in *Welt-sichten Magazin*, no. 10 (2012): 28-31.

Kobia, Samuel, *Dialogue Matters, The Role of Ecumenical Diplomacy in the Run-Up to the Independence of South Sudan*, St Paul's University, Limuru, Kenya, 2013.

Kühne, Winrich, 'Vom Terror zum Kalifat (From Terror to Caliphate)', in *IPG Journal*, 15.09.2014 (www.ipg-journal.de/kommentar/artikel/vom-terror-zum-kalifat-581/).

Miguez Bonino, José, 'Totalitarianism', in *Dictionary of the Evangelical Movement*, Geneva / Grand Rapids 1991, 1011-1012.

Miller, Larry, 'Terror in the Name of God, An Existential Challenge to Religious Believers', in *Fides Et Libertas, The Journal of the International Religious Liberty Association*, 2013, http://passthrough.fw-notify.net/download/405521/www.irla.org/assets/public/files/fides/Fides_2013.pdf.

PROCMURA, *Briefing on the Tanzania Christian and Muslim Religious Leader's Conference*, 6 to 9 October 2014.

Tutu, Desmond Mpilo, *God is not a Christian, Speaking truth in times of crisis*, ed. John Allen, London, Sydney, Auckland, Johannesburg: Rider, 2013

Werkner, Ines-Jacqueline, Oliver Hidalgo, eds., *Religionen – Global Player in der internationalen Politik? (Religions – Global Players in International Politics?),* Wiesbaden, 2014

(152) RELIGION AND DEVELOPMENT IN AFRICAN CHRISTIANITY[1]

Steve de Gruchy (+)

The call for Christians to be involved in some form of development action is perhaps best summarized by the powerful statement from James that, 'just as the body without the spirit is dead, so faith without works is also dead' (Jas 2:26). This reminder that the Christian faith is not just about intellectual assent, but about a life lived in compassionate service to others, especially the vulnerable, sums up much of the Biblical witness from Moses and the Jubilee laws through to Jesus and the message of the Kingdom of God. This approach emerged as a key message in the vast array of writings calling the church in Africa to be involved in issues of national reconstruction and social development during the 1980s and 1990s.[2] Although Julius Nyerere penned these words decades ago, and in the sexist language of his time, we may take them as representative of this approach:

> I am suggesting to you that unless we participate actively in the rebellion against those social structures and economic organizations which condemn men to poverty, humiliation and degradation, then the Church will become irrelevant to man and the Christian religion will degenerate into a set of superstitions accepted by the fearful. Unless the Church, its members and its organizations, express God's love for man by involvement and leadership in constructive protest against the present conditions of man, then it will become identified with injustice and persecution. If this happens, it will die – and, humanly speaking, deserve to die – because it will then serve no purpose comprehensible to modern man.[3]

It would seem that faith, without the works of development, is not only dead, but deserves to die.

Whose Faith? Whose Works?

There is, however, an unasked question lying at the heart of this approach that hides a key set of issues facing the Church in Africa as it seeks to be engaged in social development, namely, 'whose faith and

---

[1] The article in this form was first published under the title: "Of Agency, Assets and Appreciation: Seeking Some Commonalities between Theology and Development" in: Beverley Haddad (ed), Keeping Body and Soul Together: Reflections by Steve de Gruchy on Theology and Development (Pietermaritzburg: Cluster Publications, 2015), 66-86. It is reprinted here with permission.

[2] See for example: Joseph Agbasiere and Boniface Zabajungu (eds), *Church Contribution to Integral Development* (Eldoret, Kenya: AMECEA Gaba Publications, 1989); Renier Koegelenberg (ed), *Transition and Transformation: A Challenge to the Church* (Cape Town: EFSA, 1994); Barney Pityana and Charles Villa-Vicencio (eds), *Being the Church in South Africa Today* (Johannesburg: SACC, 1995); Renier Koegelenberg (ed), *The Reconstruction and Development Programme: The Role of the Church, Civil Society and NGOs* (Cape Town: EFSA, 1995); Isabel Phiri, Kenneth Ross and James Cox (eds), *The Role of Christianity in Development, Peace and Reconstruction: Southern Perspectives* (Nairobi: All Africa Conference of Churches, 1996); Liz Carmichael "Creating Newness: The Spirituality of Reconstruction" in Len Hully, Louise Kretzchmar, and Luke Pato (eds), *Archbishop Tutu: Prophetic Witness in South Africa* (Cape Town: Human and Rousseau, 1996), 182- 198; McGlory Speckman, "For Nolan's Sake Let's Move On: A Plea for a Developmental Dimension in Contextual Theology" in McGlory Speckman and Larry Kaufamnn, *Towards an Agenda for Contextual Theology* (Pietermaritzburg: Cluster, 2001), 390-406; Jesse Mugambi, "From Liberation to Reconstruction" in Emmanuel Katangole (ed), *African Theology Today* (Scranton: The University of Scranton Press, 2002), 189 -206; Sipho Mtetwa, "Imperatives for Ecumenical Movement Participation at the WSSD 2002: Issues of Life and Death for Africa" in *Bulletin For Contextual Theology* 8, 2/3 (2002), 6-10.

[3] Julius Nyerere, "The Church and Society" in *Freedom and Development* (Dar Es Salaam: Oxford University Press, 1973), 215.

whose works are we talking about?' The assumption underlying much of our theologizing about development is that Christians must *do* good things for those who are poor, less privileged, marginalized or helpless. These poor people are in need of our good works. *We,* who truly believe, need to roll up our sleeves, practise what we preach, and get involved in helping those who need help.

However, I am convinced that underlying this approach is the assumption that there is a divide between Christians and the needy that is similar to the divide between actors and beneficiaries, agents and clients, doctors and patients, and ultimately the subjects and objects of history. This is what leads me to ponder: 'whose faith and whose works?' What about the faith of the poor, and more importantly, what about *their* works? How is it that we have come to understand the parables of the good Samaritan and the sheep and goats, and the message of James as being aimed at a class of people who can *do*, whereas we do not understand it as part of the message for the class of people who are perceived to be needy, to be 'not able to do', to be simply *beneficiaries* of the good deeds of others? And in making this fundamental assumption of being 'not able to do', are we not simply mirroring the power dynamics that lie at the heart of the experience of poverty, and hence reinforcing the very problem we think we are solving?

This approach strikes me as foolhardy for two important reasons, the second one of which is the central concern of this essay. But first, it is clear – from a purely descriptive point of view – that it is simply wrong to make the assumption that poor people are 'not able to do'. Poor people are always engaged in strategies and struggles for survival, adaptation and freedom. The insights of James Scott[4] and Jean and John Comaroff,[5] three scholars who have attracted the interest of South African theologians,[6] have drawn attention to precisely this matter of acknowledging the agency of the poor. This theme has been taken up by (South) African theologians in a range of ways, as noted by Tinyiko Maluleke:

> I suggest that we are being called to a humble but careful observance of the struggles of Africans to be agents against great odds, not by ignoring or discounting the odds, but by confronting them. Africans have always been agents, never 'simply victims, wallowing in self-pity'; they have always exercised their agency in struggles for survival and integrity. However, their agency has not always been recognised let alone nurtured. Speaking from a South African perspective, my sense is that there is a new wave of awareness of the agency of ordinary, marginalized Africans. In fact, at their best and most creative, African theologies have always proceeded on some gut-feeling and almost stubborn insistence that Africans were agents and no mere doormats trampled upon by civilisers, missionaries and colonialists.[7]

The point is well made. At the same time, however, Maluleke's reference to *nurturing* this agency leads us to speak of another reason why we would be foolhardy to ignore the agency of the poor. This second, more prescriptive reason is the central concern of this essay, namely, that the gospel addresses the poor also with a call to translate their faith into works, and that this is crucial for the church's involvement in social development everywhere, and especially in sub-Saharan Africa. This means recovering the theological vision of the *vocation* of the poor themselves, as a key element for a contemporary theology of development. To do this we need to build upon the descriptive and interpretative task that helps us uncover

---

[4] James C. Scott, *Domination and the Arts of Resistance: Hidden Transcripts* (New Haven and London: Yale University Press, 1990).
[5] Jean Comaroff and John L. Comaroff, *Of Revelation and Revolution, Volume I, Christianity, Colonialism and Consciousness in South Africa* (Chicago: University of Chicago Press, 1991).
[6] A helpful discussion of the implications of these insights for South African theology is found in Gerald West, *The Academy of the Poor: Towards a Dialogical Reading of the Bible*, Second edition (Pietermaritzburg: Cluster Publications, 2003). See especially Chapter Two, 15-45.
[7] Tinyiko Maluleke, "The Rediscovery of the Agency of Africans: An Emerging Paradigm of Post-Cold War and Post-Apartheid Black and African Theology" in *Journal of Theology for Southern Africa* 108 (2002), 22.

this agency in the past. (Maluleke speaks of '(a) acknowledging, (b) valorizing and (c) interpreting') – but also to encourage it as a key element in the future (thus Maluleke adds, '(d) enhancing'[8]).

To recover a theological vision of vocation, my sense is that we need to move beyond an isolated focus on identity, which has tended to dominate African theology in the past while, and seek to integrate issues of identity with a focus on agency. I am mindful of the fact that the theological concern with the identity of the poor is deeply rooted in the struggle against the European colonial and Christianizing enterprise and, in South Africa, Zimbabwe and Namibia, against apartheid. Against the overwhelming political, economic and ideological apparatus that was ranged against ordinary people, all of which sought to strip Africans of their identity, we can appreciate the political power of the appropriation of such simple theological truths such as, 'I am a child of God. I bear his image. His Son died on the cross for me. He loves me as I am.' No-one made this more a central theological theme in the struggle against apartheid than Desmond Tutu:

> Yes, you are a God-carrier. God dwells in you. He dwells in me. That is why it is such a blasphemy for God's children to be treated as if they were things, uprooted from their homes and dumped in arid resettlement camps… Those who are victims of injustice and oppression would not have to suffer from a slave mentality by which they despised themselves and went about apologising for their existence. They would know that they matter to God, and nothing anybody did to them could change that fundamental fact about themselves.[9]

Today, this kind of faith conviction may provide a powerful bulwark against the dehumanizing experiences of domestic violence, HIV infection, homophobia and unemployment.

The Vocation of the Poor

This conviction is of course absolutely true, but it is not the whole truth. One of the inherent problems embedded in it, rather ironically in the face of the colonial project, is that it can be a message of passivity. It claims a status before God by virtue of one's *being*. It says nothing about one's *doing*. And yet the issue of doing is crucially important for one's identity, particularly for the poor. Bryant Myers puts it like this:

> When the poor accept their marred identity and their distorted sense of vocation as normative and immutable, their poverty is complete. It is also permanent unless this issue is addressed and they are helped to recover their identity as children of God, made in God's image, *and their true vocation as productive stewards in the world God made for them…*
>
> Who we are is a question of both being and doing… I believe that poverty mars both parts of the identity of the poor. The result of poverty is that people who are poor no longer know who they are (being) nor do they believe that they have a vocation of any value (doing).[10]

It is important to recognise that in both creation accounts from which the affirmation of identity is traditionally drawn, the truth of being made in the image of God (Gen. 1:27) or being filled with God's own breath of life (Gen. 2:7) is immediately coupled with the theme of *vocation*, the calling to be responsible actors in this world newly created by God (Gen. 1:28; 2:15). This understanding of vocation is at the heart of the theological understanding of labour as a constitutive part of what it means to be truly human, in the use of our gifts and talents to be co-workers with God in the world. From this is drawn the critique of alienated labour under slavery, feudalism, capitalism and communism, and the vision of human

---

[8] Maluleke, "The Rediscovery of the Agency of Africans", 22.
[9] Desmond Tutu, *Hope and Suffering* (Grand Rapids, Michigan: Eerdmans, 1985), 140.
[10] Bryant Myers, *Walking with the Poor* (Maryknoll, NY: Orbis, 1999), 76. Italics added for emphasis.

beings working in harmony with God and the earth to create a better life, characterized by justice and peace.[11]

Drawing from these same roots, and standing in this same trajectory, James reminds us that faith without works is dead. Thus any vision of Christian involvement in social development cannot have as its assumption, as so much of it unfortunately does, the faith and works of Christians and the Church over and against those who are poor and needy; but has to affirm, enhance and appreciate the *faith works*[12] of the poor themselves. This is the message of the gospel for the poor, that they are both made in the image of God and called to be actors in the drama of creation and salvation itself. They are not, and cannot be, simply passive objects of history, but are invited to be the subjects of their own history.

One of the most influential attempts to move this kind of concern for the vocation of the poor from a purely descriptive level to a prescriptive programme for action is the work of the Brazilian educationist, Paulo Freire, as captured in his book concerning adult education, *The Pedagogy of the Oppressed*. Deeply influenced by his Roman Catholic faith and his partnership with the World Council of Churches, Freire promotes *humanization* as the good to which society should struggle, indeed as 'the people's vocation'.[13] Dehumanization is the process in which people are treated as 'things', as objects in other people's worlds, and because there is a fundamental relationship between ends and means, the struggle for humanization must itself be humanizing. As he warns us, 'to discourse on humanism and to negate people is a lie'.[14]

> The oppressed have been destroyed precisely because their situation has reduced them to things. In order to regain their humanity they must cease to be things and fight as men and women. This is a radical requirement. They cannot enter the struggle as objects in order later to become human beings.[15]

What makes us 'human beings', for Freire, is that we communicate, that we have a *word*. 'Dialogue imposes itself as the way by which [people] achieve significance as human beings. Dialogue is thus an existential necessity.'[16] Thus the deepest act of dehumanization, of treating people as things, is to strip them of their word, to censor, to refuse to communicate, to shun dialogue. *Anti-dialogical action* is the antithesis of liberating praxis[17] and needs to be replaced with *dialogical action,* for 'dialogue, the encounter among men and women to name the world, is a fundamental precondition for their humanization'.[18] Dialogical action implies that the 'oppressed' (an admittedly wide and contested term for Freire) cannot be passengers on the journey, but find their own sense of freedom via their agency in the struggle for freedom. And because this is dialogical action, this agency is not simply expressed through action, in some sort of politburo-led, revolutionary cannon-fodder way, but also through reflection. For Freire it is crucial that the insights, perspectives, rituals and symbols of the poor contribute to the very vision of the future that is being sought. Action and theory thus find expression in liberating praxis:

---

[11] The Roman Catholic Church has a well-established theological tradition with regards to the humanizing role of labour. See especially John Paul II, *On Human Work: Encyclical Laborem Exercens* (Pretoria: Southern African Catholic Bishops' Conference, 1981).

[12] I take this term from the title of a book by Jim Wallis, *Faith Works: Lessons on Spirituality and Social Action* (London: SPCK, 2002).

[13] Paulo Freire, *Pedagogy of the Oppressed*, Revised Edition (London: Penguin, 1996), 25.

[14] Freire, *Pedagogy of the Oppressed*, 72.

[15] Freire, *Pedagogy of the Oppressed*, 50.

[16] Freire, *Pedagogy of the Oppressed*, 69.

[17] Freire, *Pedagogy of the Oppressed*, 119-148.

[18] Freire, *Pedagogy of the Oppressed*, 118.

> It is when the majorities are denied their right to participate in history as Subjects that they become dominated and alienated. Thus, to supersede their condition as objects by the status of Subjects – the objective of any true revolution – requires that the people act, as well as reflect, upon the reality to be transformed.[19]

Freire's concept of dialogical action is not without the problems inherent in moving from a descriptive theory to a prescriptive programme. He is, after all, wanting to be a teacher rather than a journalist, and that implies a likely conflict around just what is taught, and how it is taught. The vocation of the teacher and the vocation of the poor are not necessarily in harmony! His pedagogical method works hard at these issues, seeking to get beyond the reality of hegemony and ideology; but any concept of 'dialogue' has to be extremely sensitive in order to be sufficiently adequate to deal with all the implications of power represented in the teacher-pupil relationship, even (especially!) when these pupils are adults. Scott's notion of 'hidden transcripts', referred to above, reminds us that the authentic voice of the poor is not readily accessible simply through correct pedagogy. It is not even easily accessible through nuanced and committed scholarship, as pointed out by Gayatri Spivak's in her tortuous but classic essay, 'Can the Subaltern Speak?'[20] In the face of precisely these concerns, Gerald West has sought to develop such a sensitive and programmatic notion of dialogue for Christians in his book, *The Academy of the Poor: Towards a Dialogical Reading of the Bible.*[21]

Having laid out the contours of a theological vision of the vocation of the poor, therefore, what I propose to do here is to build on this project by engaging with three key themes that are at the cutting edge of 'secular' development theory, and that engage with this vision. It is clear to me that much of the writing and thinking about the involvement of the church in Africa in social development is long on Biblical mandate, exhortation and liberatory passion, but it is rather weak in the area of such theory. We lack a coherent vision of development that will enable us to talk with, and walk alongside, African civil society as it seeks to engage in transforming the worlds in which we live. My hope is to reflect on *agency, assets* and *appreciation* as significant commonalities between theology and development.

Of Agency

An extremely influential thinker in contemporary development theory is Amartya Sen, the Nobel-Prize winning, Bangladeshi economist. Sen has drawn his thinking on poverty, famine, economics and development over the past two decades to a climax in his book, *Development as Freedom*.[22] In this book he advances the fundamental argument that freedom is both the primary end, and the principal means of development. He argues that freedom is, firstly, the goal of development, a 'good thing in itself'.[23] In page after page, he advances clear empirical evidence and economic theory to support his contention that development is nothing other than 'the process of expanding human freedoms'.[24] For Sen, freedom is not the opposite of 'oppression', but is rather opposed to *unfreedom,* a word he defines to include the full range of hindrances to human flourishing or 'capability deprivation'. Freedom thus includes 'elementary capabilities like being able to avoid such deprivations as starvation, undernourishment, escapable morbidity and premature mortality as well as the freedoms that are associated with being literate and

[19] Freire, *Pedagogy of the Oppressed*, 111.
[20] Gayatri Chakravorty Spivak, "Can the Subaltern Speak?" in Cary Nelson and Lawrence Grossberg (eds), *Marxism and the Interpretation of Culture* (Urbana and Chicago: University of Illinois Press, 1988), 271-313.
[21] Gerald West, *The Academy of the Poor: Towards a Dialogical Reading of the Bible*, Second edition (Pietermaritzburg: Cluster Publications, 2003).
[22] Amartya Sen, *Development as Freedom* (New York City, Random House, 1999), 282.
[23] Sen, *Development as Freedom*, 18.
[24] Sen, *Development as Freedom*, 36.

numerate, enjoying political participation and uncensored speech and so on'.[25] With this understanding of 'human capabilities' and the impact that freedom must have on the poor for it to be real freedom, Sen moves far beyond liberal notions of freedom, including those proposed by John Rawls.[26]

Secondly, and perhaps of more importance to Sen and to us in this essay, freedom is also the primary *means* of development. For him, freedom is 'a principal determinant of individual initiative and social effectiveness. Greater freedom enhances the ability of people to help themselves and also to influence the world, and these matters are central to the process of development'.[27] He notes that this affirms the 'agency aspect' of the individual, and his work supports what he calls an 'agent-oriented view':

> In terms of the medieval distinction between 'the patient' and 'the agent' this freedom-centred understanding of economics and of the process of development is very much an agent-oriented view. With adequate social opportunities, individuals can effectively shape their own destiny and help each other. They need not be seen primarily as passive recipients of the benefits of cunning development programmes. There is indeed a strong rationale for recognizing the positive role of free and sustainable agency – and even of constructive impatience.[28]

This insight leads Sen to stand firmly against the dominant neo-liberal paradigm that places economic concerns at the pinnacle of development strategies,[29] and to argue for the pre-eminence of political freedoms and liberal rights over economic growth.[30] Sen advances three reasons for this, namely, that political freedoms are of *direct importance* to human living; have an *instrumental role* in helping people get a hearing in expressing their claims to attention, and have a *constructive role* 'in the conceptualization of needs', including economic needs. This third reason has echoes of Freire's understanding of 'praxis'. Here Sen argues that freedom creates the space in which dialogue can occur, so that people can be agents in shaping not only the struggle for development, but the very vision of what that 'development' might be:

> Political and civil rights, especially those related to the guaranteeing of open discussion, debate, criticisms and dissent, are central to the process of generating informed and reflected choices. These processes are crucial to the formation of values and priorities, and we cannot, in general, take preferences as given independently of public discussion, that is, irrespective of whether open debates and interchanges are permitted or not.[31]

Sen recognises, like Freire, that if agency means anything, then it is not just a question of mindless action, but also of a contribution at the level of theory to 'values and priorities' so that the preferences for political, social and economic life can be shaped by all the citizens, including the poor, and not just the dominant elites: 'The reach and effectiveness of open dialogue are often underestimated in assessing social and political problems.'[32]

Sen illustrates and advances these insights when he considers the particular agency of women in social change. He is concerned that a focus simply on the sufferings and deprivations of women which society must somehow correct, misses the point that what is at stake here is the *agency* of women. This agency has a role to play in dealing with the 'iniquities that depress the well-being of women', but more importantly, 'the limited role of women's active agency seriously afflicts the lives of all people – men as well as

---

[25] Sen, *Development as Freedom*, 36.
[26] See John Rawls, *Political Liberalism* (New York: Columbia University Press, 1993).
[27] Sen, *Development as Freedom*, 18.
[28] Sen, *Development as Freedom*, 11.
[29] See his clear rejection of the view which "sees development as a 'fierce' process, with much 'blood, sweat and tears' – a world in which wisdom demands toughness". Sen, *Development as Freedom*, 35.
[30] Sen, *Development as Freedom*, 148.
[31] Sen, *Development as Freedom*, 153.
[32] Sen, *Development as Freedom*, 153.

women, children as well as adults'.[33] Sen provides economic data to underscore his claim that the enhanced agency of women increases their own life expectancy, through claims within the household to better nutrition and health care,[34] reduces the mortality rates of children as well as reducing fertility rates through the influence that comes with education and literacy,[35] and relates directly to a reduction in violence crimes in a given society.[36] He writes:

> The changing agency of women is one of the major mediators of economic and social change, and its determination as well as consequences closely relate to many of the central features of the development process...
>
> Nothing, arguably, is as important today in the political economy of development as an adequate recognition of political, economic and social participation and leadership of women. This is indeed a crucial aspect of 'development as freedom'.[37]

David Korten of the People-Centred Development Forum shares many of the concerns of Amartya Sen in his important book, *Getting to the 21st Century: Voluntary Action and the Global Agenda,*[38] especially the priority of political over economic concerns on the development agenda, and the agency of the poor. For Korten, like Sen, these two are intrinsically linked. He is convinced that the dominant development paradigm, with its growth-at-any-cost approach, has exacerbated the three major crises of the end of the twentieth century, namely, poverty, environmental stress, and communal violence. This dominant development paradigm 'equates human progress with growth in the market value of economic output and subordinates both human and environmental considerations to that goal'.[39] Against this, a new vision of transformation is needed, one that is shaped by the concerns of justice, sustainability and inclusiveness. For Korten, this is the agenda of 'a people-centred development vision', which sees development as a 'people's movement more than as a foreign-funded government project'.[40]

> The people have been expected to put their faith and resources in the hands of government. In return governments have promised to bestow on the people the gift of development. This promise has proven to be a chimera born of false assessment of the capacity of government and of the nature of development itself.[41]

One of the upshots of this growing recognition is the emerging development role of civil society. But this is itself problematic. Korten surveys the plethora of organisations that make up civil society, and notes how many so-called development NGOs are serving agendas that do not promote people-centred development. One of the fundamental problems with civil society organisations is that they are at heart 'third-party organisations'; they exist to meet the needs of people other than themselves.[42] People's Organisations (POs), on the other hand, are 'first-party organisations' and it is they who do and must play the central role in people-centred development. Self-reliant co-operatives, landless associations, irrigator

---

[33] Sen, *Development as Freedom*, 191.
[34] Sen, *Development as Freedom*, 193ff.
[35] Sen, *Development as Freedom*, 195ff, 198ff.
[36] Sen, *Development as Freedom*, 200ff.
[37] Sen, *Development as Freedom*, 202ff.
[38] David Korten, *Getting to the 21st Century: Voluntary Action and the Global Agenda* (West Hartford: Kumarian Press, 1990).
[39] Korten, *Getting to the 21st Century,* 3.
40 Korten, *Getting to the 21st Century*, 5.
41 Korten, *Getting to the 21st Century*, 95.
42 Korten, *Getting to the 21st Century*, 96.

associations, burial associations, credit clubs, labour unions, trade associations and political interest groups are among some of the collectives that may be POs.[43]

One of the crucial elements that they bring to the fore is that of citizens' voluntary action, a central part of Korten's vision as the title of his book suggests.

> If transformation is to come, it must come as a consequence of voluntary action, an act of human commitment to collective survival driven by a vision that transcends the behaviours conditioned by existing institutions and culture. We must look to people's movements as the key to transformational change in the current era.[44]

Korten does not use the terms 'agent' or 'agency', but many of his insights into volunteerism and citizens' action parallel the thinking of Freire and Sen around this concept, for it is in embracing such action that people become agents in their own development struggles. This agency aspect becomes clearer in Korten's well-known typology of 'four generations of voluntary development action'[45] in which he charts a movement from relief and welfare; through small-scale, self-reliant local development; and sustainable systems development; to the fourth generation, namely, *people's movements*. Thus, for Korten, fourth generation strategies look beyond those of the first three. 'Their goal is to energize a critical mass of independent, decentralized initiatives in support of a social vision'.[46]

Of Assets

Sen and Korten, each in their own way and drawing on their own experiences and insights, have provided a framework for understanding the agency of the poor in development, and have thus rooted our theological vision of vocation within a wider discourse. Their thinking on this theme has enriched our understanding of development by providing ways in which we can understand and interpret development theory and praxis congruent with our faith. As we acknowledge the importance of the agency of the poor in development, so we must move on – to ask what it is that the poor contribute to the process, and therefore to a consideration of *assets* and the insights of John Kretzmann and John McKnight in their paradigm-shifting workbook, *Building communities from the inside out: A path toward finding and mobilizing a community's assets.*[47]

Kretzmann and McKnight resonate with much of what we have noted above, when they point out that a key challenge in the task of development is to avoid building a dependency syndrome between poor, needy people with lots of problems, and non-poor providers of services with lots of solutions. This kind of relationship leads to less and less confidence, dignity and empowerment for those who are on the margins of society, and so works counter to any real development of people and communities. They call this kind of approach, a 'needs-driven dead end', and propose in its stead the alternative path of 'capacity-focused development'. The traditional solution, or needs-driven approach, sees communities as simply full of problems. Here we are confronted with images of needy, problematic and deficient people living in needy, problematic and deficient villages, slums or neighbourhoods. There is clearly some truth in this picture, but the traditional approach takes this to be the whole truth.

Many poor people come to accept this image of themselves, as needy people whose well-being depends upon being a client of service providers. They become consumers of welfare help, rather than producers of

---

43 Korten, *Getting to the 21st Century*, 100.

44 Korten, *Getting to the 21st Century*, 105.

45 Korten, *Getting to the 21st Century*, Chapter Ten, "From relief to people's movement" 112ff.

46 Korten, *Getting to the 21st Century*, 127.

47 John Kretzmann and John McKnight, *Building Communities from the Inside Out: A Path Toward Finding and Mobilizing a Community's Assets*, Centre for Urban Affairs and Policy Research, Northwestern University (Chicago: ACTA Publications, 1993).

their own solutions. Their agency is undermined. The whole approach is guaranteed to create dependency, weaken the internal resources of a community, and lead to helplessness and despair. Problems in a community are not seen as symptoms of a deeper problem – the inability of a community to solve its problems. The more outsiders try to deal with the symptoms, the more the real problem is made worse!

The simple truth that Kretzmann and McKnight identify is that you cannot build a community on what people do not have. Successful community development grows out of policies and activities based on the capacities, skills and assets of poor people and their neighbourhoods. It is important to clarify at the start that this does not mean that these communities do not need additional resources, or that they are 'best left alone' in some kind of warped understanding of 'self-help'. What it does mean is that outside resources will be much more effective if local people are themselves investing and mobilizing their own resources, and are able to set the agenda for outside help on the basis of their strengths rather than weaknesses. The assets of poor communities 'are absolutely necessary, but usually not sufficient' to meet the challenges of development.[48]

There are three kinds of assets in a village or neighbourhood, namely, individuals (their skills, gifts and financial resources), associations (the resources represented by churches, clubs, and local organisations, etc.) and institutions (libraries, schools, police stations, etc). For Kretzmann and McKnight the task of a community-builder is to map these assets, and then to seek ways to build relationships among and between them, so as to strengthen the community's own capacity to enhance its well-being. Thus the 'three simple, interrelated characteristics' of the approach are that it is asset-based, in the sense that any development strategy starts with what is present rather than with what is absent in the community; internally-focused, with its stress upon 'the primacy of local definition, investment, creativity, hope and control';[49] and relationship-driven, in that the challenge faced by community-builders is to constantly build and rebuild the networks within the asset-base of the community.

Kretzmann and McKnight's model has drawn on the 'strong neighbourhood-rooted tradition of community organizing, community economic development and neighbourhood planning'[50] within the USA. Nevertheless, it exhibits some crucial affinities around the concept of *assets* with the Sustainable Livelihoods Framework (SLF), a widely used approach for understanding poverty in the third world. The SLF was first promoted by the World Commission on Environment and Development (WCED) in 1987, and since then the approach has received widespread support and use amongst development organizations such as the Institute for Development Studies (IDS) at Sussex University, the Overseas Development Institute (ODI), the British government's Department for International Development (DIFD), the International Institute for Sustainable Development (IISD), the People-Centred Development Forum (PCD Forum), Oxfam and, importantly, the United Nations Development Programme (UNDP).[51]

We cannot here provide a comprehensive analysis of the framework as a whole,[52] and will simply reflect upon some key elements around our theme of *assets.* The SL approach recognises that poor and vulnerable people are *agents in* rather than *clients of* their development, and it does so by working with the already existing portfolio of assets of the household and the community, as well as the livelihood strategies that are already in place. Along with Kretzmann and McKnight, it recognises that you cannot build a community

[48] Kretzmann and McKnight, *Building Communities*, 8.
[49] Kretzmann and McKnight, *Building Communities*, 9.
[50] Kretzmann and McKnight, *Building Communities,* 9.
[51] United Nations Development Programme, *Sustainable Livelihoods Unit Home Page*, www.undp.org/sl/Overview/an_overview.htm
[52] For a comprehensive analysis see my essay, "The Contribution of Universities to Sustainable Development" in Robert Fincham, Susse Georg and Eskild Holm Nielsen (eds), *Sustainable Development and the University: New Strategies for Research, Teaching and Practice* (Pietermaritzburg: Brevitas, 2005), 53-74. See also Chapter Seven in this volume.

on what people do not have. Working with the assets and relationships that already exist in development efforts, 'a key objective is to remove the constraints to the realization of potential. Thus people will be assisted to become more robust, stronger and better able to achieve their own objectives'.[53]

At the household and community level, the SLF draws our attention to the portfolio of five key livelihood assets that people have access or entitlement to. These are:

> *Human Capital*, the skills, knowledge, good health, and ability to labour. It is the foundational asset that is necessary, though not sufficient, for positive livelihood outcomes.
>
> *Social Capital*, the social resources upon which people draw in pursuit of their livelihood objectives. It includes networks and connectedness, more formal group membership and trust, reciprocity and exchange.
>
> *Natural Capital*, the natural resources that are available to households and communities in pursuit of their livelihoods. It includes everything from intangible public goods, such as the atmosphere, to direct resources such as trees and plants.
>
> *Physical Capital,* the infrastructure and producer goods that are required to support livelihoods. Infrastructure is only an asset insofar as it helps the poor to meet their needs.
>
> *Financial Capital,* the money that is available to the household, in a range of forms such as cash, livestock, jewellery, or the regular inflows of money. This is the most versatile asset, as it can be converted into other assets, and it can contribute directly to livelihood outcomes like purchasing food or medicines, or through leveraging social and political influence.

The SL Framework does not make a distinction between the micro and the macro levels of development activity. 'The SL approach, by using both participatory and policy (cross-sectoral) tools, highlights the inter-linkage between livelihood systems at the micro level and the macro policies which affect these livelihoods'.[54] As Butler and Greenstein put it, the SL approach emphasizes,

> the importance of macro level policy and institutions to the livelihood options of communities and individuals. It also stresses the need for policy development and planning to be informed by lessons learnt and insights gained at the local level. This will give local people a stake in policy and increase overall effectiveness.[55]

The SLF does this through its concept of the 'vulnerability context'. Apart from this typology of the portfolio of assets available to poor households and communities, the articulation of this 'vulnerability context' in which households and communities exist, is the other extremely helpful contribution of the SLF to our discussion about assets. This is an immediate recognition that we are dealing with people who are at risk, not because they are stupid or lazy, but because their portfolio of assets and their livelihood strategies are subject to a range of influences that prescribe and determine the opportunities and choices that they have for their livelihood strategies. We suggest that there are three key elements that make up this wider context of livelihoods.

> *Shocks, Stresses, Seasonality*, such as civil war, stock-market collapse, a live-stock disease such as foot and mouth, a flood, drought or even the onset of freezing weather.

[53] Mark Butler and Ran Greenstein, *Sustainable Livelihoods: Towards a Research Agenda for the Church Land Programme* (Johannesburg: Community Agency for Social Enquiry, 1999), 46.
[54] UNDP, *Sustainable Livelihoods*, 6.
[55] Butler and Greenstein, *Sustainable Livelihoods,* 46.

Policy, Laws, Institutions, referring to the *intentional* structures, institutions, formations and contracts that are set in place to regulate social and communal life.

Culture, Religion, Customs. It is clear that in most African contexts, the portfolio of livelihood assets, the livelihood strategies, and the desired livelihood outcomes are deeply influenced by these elements, and any strategy that desires to enhance such livelihoods ignores them at its peril.

These three elements of the wider vulnerability context make the important link between the micro and macro levels of development. It is vital to see the asset portfolio of the local household or community in relationship to the institutions, organizations, policies, legislation, culture, religion and customs that shape livelihoods. These provide the reality in which the community resides, and which therefore has a direct link to the household, and the asset portfolio. Out of the vulnerability context, with the three elements mentioned above shaping and constraining their possible responses, people make use of their asset portfolio to pursue livelihood strategies. The result of this is a range of livelihood outcomes that could include more income, increased well-being, reduced vulnerability, improved food security and a more sustainable use of the natural resource base.[56] Robert Chambers and Gordon Conway argue that a livelihood is sustainable when it,

> can cope with and recover from stress and shocks, maintain or enhance its capabilities and assets, and provide sustainable livelihood opportunities for the next generation; and which contributes net benefits to other livelihoods at the local and global levels and in the short and long term.[57]

One of the issues that emerges in our reflection on the SLF that is of importance for this essay, concerns the role and place of religion. Within the framework, religion is moved out of the household and community level and into the 'vulnerability context', with the assumption that it serves as a wider constraining net in which people construct their livelihood strategies. We are bound to ask if this is an adequate representation of reality, particularly in Africa. Is it not possible that religion, faith or spirituality functions as part of the asset portfolio; that it is something that people 'have' which they actively utilize in their livelihood strategies? Some may argue that this is present in the categories of human capital and social capital. One may, however, question if this highlights the role of religion and religious assets in the most appropriate way. For example, Kretzmann and McKnight have no hesitation in recognizing that some of the key assets in any community are the local religious institutions:

> Each particular religious institution offers a unique configuration of specific resources which can be utilized in the process of community building. Yet every religious institution, whether large or small, urban or rural, Protestant, Catholic, Jewish, Muslim, Buddhist, or other always offers certain common sets of resources which can be mobilized effectively to assist in community renewal.[58]

---

[56] For further information on the SLF see Robert Chambers and Gordon Conway, *Sustainable Rural Livelihoods: Practical Concepts for the 21st Century.* Institute of Development Studies Discussion Paper 296. (University of Sussex, Brighton: IDS Publications, 1992); Czech Conroy, "Preface" and "Introduction" in Czech Conroy and Miles Litvinoff, *The Greening of Aid: Sustainable Livelihoods in Practice* (London: Earthscan Publications, 1988), xi-xiv; Robert Chambers, "Sustainable Rural Livelihoods: A Key Strategy for People, Environment and Development" in Conroy and Litvinoff, *The Greening of Aid*, 1-17; Koos Neefjes, *Environments and Livelihoods: Strategies for Sustainability.* (Oxford: Oxfam, 2000), 58- 112; People-Centred Development Forum, "Principles of Sustainable Livelihoods", http://iisd.ca/pcdf/1995/ princsl.htm.

[57] Chambers and Conway, *Sustainable Rural Livelihoods,* 7.

[58] Kretzmann and McKnight, *Building Communities*, 143.

This insight opens the way for us to begin to think of religion in itself as an asset for people, and especially for poor people, and even more especially for poor African people. I believe that this is a creative way in which we can understand the work of Beverley Haddad in her research amongst poor women in Vulindlela, KwaZulu-Natal.[59] She makes the point that,

> In planning programmes of development action, faith as an integral part of women's lives must be acknowledged as a community resource. Networks of religious women such as the *manyano* movement are a key site of survival practice and a place where poor and marginalized women are taking control of their lives. This movement accounts for one of the largest religious groupings of indigenous African women in South Africa. Through these churchwomen's prayer groups, poor and marginalized women find courage, strength and resources to persevere in the face of near death.[60]

Likewise, Jim Cochrane has drawn attention to religious health assets, which he labels as 'a kind of endogenous resource that may be leveraged for dealing with health crises as part of public health policy and practice'.[61] Through a contextual grounding of his theory in a case study of the historically black settlement of Imizamo Yetho, Hout Bay, Cape Town, he makes clear that these assets are not just those of large, rich and powerful institutions, but are rooted in the lives of the poor and marginalized.

Of Appreciation

Clearly, the relationship between faith, agency and assets presents itself with many creative possibilities in our desire to understand and be engaged in social development. Yet it does pose the question as to how we are to proceed, and what the role of 'outsiders' is within the process. An insight into the changed nature of the approach of outsiders towards the poor due to a growing awareness of their agency and assets can be gained by following the shift from Rapid Rural Appraisal (RRA) to Participatory Rural Appraisal (PRA) to Participation Learning and Action (PLA). The first approach, RRA, was an investigative method used by outside experts to quickly gauge the development needs of a given community through on-the-spot field work. This was itself an innovation, namely, the idea that it was better to send someone to go and look at the situation on the ground (however quickly), than simply to sit in a government office and make plans on paper!

However, as the RRA approach was applied, it began to be shaped by a range of concerns, key of which was the recognition, by development activists, of the value of the insights and wisdom of the poor who were the subjects of the appraisal. The PRA approach grew out of this, and the 'rapid' was replaced with 'participatory', signalling a conscious desire to both spend more time amongst the people in the community in an attempt to really try and understand 'what is going on', and to encourage the active participation of the poor in the process of appraisal itself. A whole range of creative exercises was developed to facilitate this process.[62]

The success of PRA tools and exercises meant that use was found for it in urban areas, and so the 'rural' part of the title seemed redundant. Furthermore, the concept of appraisal continued to carry within itself a clear distinction between the subjects and objects of research, a distinction that fails to recognise that both

---

[59] Beverley Haddad, *African Theologies of Survival: Intersecting Faith, Feminisms and Development* (Unpublished PhD thesis, Pietermaritzburg, University of Natal, 2000).

[60] Beverley Haddad, "Theologising Development: A Gendered Analysis of Poverty, Survival and Faith" in *Journal of Theology for Southern Africa* 110 (2001), 16.

[61] James Cochrane, "Religion in the Health of Migrant Communities: Cultural Assets or Medical Deficits?" Paper delivered at Health and Migration in Southern Africa Conference, Cape Town, January 2003.

[62] See Robert Chambers, *Rural Appraisal: Rapid, Relaxed and Participatory,* Institute of Development Studies Discussion Paper 311 (University of Sussex, Brighton: IDS Publications, 1992).

development facilitators and poor people are engaged in a mutual learning process. Again, this process of participatory learning is not for its own sake, but for the goal of social, cultural and economic transformation of poverty. Thus the term 'action' was added, to create 'Participatory Learning and Action' (PLA). This movement from RRA to PRA to PLA, is responsive to the growing recognition of the role of the agency and assets of the poor in development, for as Bryant Myers notes, 'from the results of a properly done PLA exercise the poor can discover how much they really do know, what resources and skills they already have, and how resourceful they have been in the past'.[63]

Indeed, these tensions between the RRA, PRA and PLA approaches raise to prominence the vital relationship between giving priority to the agency and assets of the poor on the one hand, and the way in which non-poor outsiders can engage with the poor in the mutual struggle for justice in such a way that this agency and these assets are not compromised. For the very act of compromising the agency and assets is itself an act of injustice. Now we begin to come full circle in this essay, for this was the issue we noted in our reflection on Paulo Freire and his educational method, namely, the tension between the vocation of the teacher and that of the pupil, expressed now as the tension between the vocation of the poor and the vocation of the development agent.

This search for a process by which the agency and the assets of the poor can be enhanced in dialogue with outsiders, has given rise in some quarters to what is known as 'Appreciative Inquiry' (AI), and which bears some resemblance to the work of Freire and others in adult education. The fact that this approach has been adopted by, amongst others, the International Institute for Sustainable Development (IISD) to enhance its use of the SLF, should alert us to the congruence between it and the focus on the agency and assets of the poor. Neil Ford of the IISD makes precisely this point when he points out (in language remarkably similar to that of Kretzmann and McKnight) that the dominant model of development practice is a problem-centred one that 'can often disempower the community it is meant to help, by conditioning local people to view their village as a place full of problems that only outsiders can solve, and needs that only government can meet'.[64] The SLF, on the other hand, helps people understand their strengths, analyse their options, plan effectively and participate more equally; and AI becomes the way in which development agencies can facilitate this.

> Appreciative inquiry starts from a fundamentally different – and more positive – point. It is designed to help local people identify their achievements. This process can be very empowering for people who have always considered themselves poor and disadvantaged. When they look for their strengths, they are often amazed to discover how resilient, adaptive and innovative they are. They have to be – poverty is a cruel and unforgiving circumstance. By focusing on their strengths they can use the 'positive present' to build a shared vision of a better future, one that is grounded in reality. Appreciative inquiry creates a development pathway based on what is right rather than what is wrong.[65]

The AI approach makes creative use of memory and visioning around four stages, namely: *discovering*, which explores and appreciates what has been good in the past and what works at present;[66] *dreaming* about what might be if the good could be expanded into the future; *dialogue* amongst the participants to construct a vision of what can be achieved; and *delivery* of the vision through action. The circle continues, as this action itself becomes the focus of discovery. As with the Asset-Based approach and the SLF, Appreciative Inquiry does not minimize the problems that beset a community. Quite clearly the process

---

[63] Myers, *Walking with the Poor*, 174.

[64] Neil Ford, "Foreword" in Charles Elliot, *Locating the Energy for Change: An Introduction to Appreciative Inquiry* (Winnipeg: IISD, 1999), vi.

[65] Neil Ford, "Foreword", vi.

[66] This seems similar to the focus of contemporary African theology as noted by Maluleke above. See "The Rediscovery of the Agency of Africans".

takes place within and seeks to overcome experiences which threaten 'the good'. However, instead of being incapacitated by the overwhelming sense of deficit, AI is driven by what Charles Elliot calls the 'heliotropic principle', which states that 'organizations operate like plants: they move toward what gives them life and energy'.[67]

The outsider, who seeks to assist through the AI approach, will therefore approach poor people and communities exhibiting some of the following characteristics:

- An assumption of health and vitality
- A desire to connect through empathy
- A sense of personal excitement, commitment and concern
- An intense focus to listen with the right side of the brain
- Generative questioning, pointing toward clues and guiding
- Belief in the community and its story
- Tolerance for ambiguity, generalization and dreams
- A passion for dialogue and a dislike of monologue.[68]

I am surely not alone in wishing that this list were simply the job description of the ordained clergy in my church! And, of course, by implication, of all baptized Christians!

Theological Themes

This intuitively positive reaction to the approach of Appreciative Inquiry suggests that we may have succeeded in our task. This was to explore the commonalities between the *secular* language of agency, assets and appreciation and *theological* themes so that as Christians we can begin to understand, interpret and engage with development practice alongside other role players in African civil society. In doing this we have done two things: we have explored these three themes in some depth, and noted how central to current development thinking they are; and we have seen how the three themes share a common vision, namely, the affirmation of the humanity and vocation of the poor, their role in the struggle for humanization, the gifts they bring to this struggle, and the role of the non-poor outsider in affirming this humanity, role and gifts.

We began by being reminded of James' strident words: 'Faith without works is dead' (2:26). Throughout this essay we have been reminding ourselves that this is not only a word for the non-poor, a call – as it were – to charitable acts towards the unfortunate poor who have no works of their own (and, by implication no faith). It is also a word for the poor. They too gain dignity when addressed by the fullness of the gospel. It is not enough that they have faith. Faith without works is dead. The gospel calls them to engage in the works of love, peace and justice in the struggle for their own humanization. This, as Freire reminds us, is the 'true generosity' that must be at the heart of any contemporary theology of development:

> True generosity consists precisely in fighting to destroy the causes which nourish false charity. False charity constrains the fearful and subdued, the 'rejects of life,' to extend their trembling hand. True generosity lies in striving so that these hands – whether of individuals or entire peoples – need be extended less and less in supplication, so that more and more they become human hands which work, and working, transform the world.[69]

---

[67] Charles Elliot, *Locating the Energy for Change: An Introduction to Appreciative Inquiry* (Winnipeg: IISD, 1999), 43.

[68] David Cooperider and Suresh Srivastva quoted in Myers, *Walking with the Poor*, 177.

[69] Freire, *Pedagogy of the oppressed*, 27.

(153) THE BASIC INCOME GRANT IN NAMIBIA – A MODEL FOR DEVELOPMENT IN AFRICA

Claudia and Dirk Haarmann

Introduction

This chapter examines the role of a universal basic income grant in poverty alleviation and development. The basis is the worldwide first Basic Income Grant pilot project implemented in Otjivero, Namibia, where, for a period of two years, every person in the settlement received an unconditional cash grant of N$100 (about €10) per month. The impact analysis of the pilot shows the potential of such a grant in addressing poverty, e.g. malnutrition and food insecurity, but also in fostering local economic development through redistribution. The chapter therefore argues that a universal, unconditional cash grant is an effective tool in development policy, not only in Namibia, but also in other countries.[1]

The second part of the chapter focuses on the role of the church in the project and how contextual theology influenced her advocacy work and vice versa, that is, how the pilot project enriched contextual theology.

Namibian Case Study

Namibia is a country rich in natural resources like gold, diamonds, uranium and fish. It is one of the least densely populated countries in the world, but the small population of 2.2 million people is very diverse, consisting of eleven different language groups. Namibia gained its independence in 1990. The years of colonialism and apartheid have created a system of structural inequalities along racial, class, language and gender lines. Despite efforts of the new government, these inherent social and economic imbalances have remained largely intact. A Gini co-efficient of 0.743[2] as the measure of income inequality illustrates that a small class holds most of the wealth while the majority of Namibians still live in poverty.[3] A recent study found that 42% of Namibia's population is undernourished (New Era, 8th June 2015), making it one of the eight African countries ranked at the highest level of undernourishment. The HIV prevalence rate stands at 16% and maternal deaths have doubled in the last fourteen years and are currently at 449 per 100,000 births.[4] These indicators give an idea of the poverty and hardship experienced by the majority of people in Namibia.

---

[1] The chapter draws on the research results of the BIG pilot project and the first year report: *Making the difference! The BIG in Namibia, a* research and report jointly done by several researchers and authors, namely Claudia Haarmann, Dirk Haarmann, Herbert Jauch, Hilma Shindondola-Mote, Nicoli Nattrass, Ingrid van Niekerk and Michael Samson. For further details and background of the research see, www.bignam.org/Publications/BIG_Assessment_report_08b.pdf (accessed 10 September 2015).

[2] A score of 0 would indicate a perfectly equal distribution of income amongst the population, while a score of 1 would indicate that one person would own everything and the rest nothing. Countries like South Africa and Brazil have Gini-coefficients at 0.578 and 0.55 respectively.

[3] The United Nations Development Programme. *The Real Wealth of Nations: Pathways to Human Development. Human Development Report 2010* (New York: UNDP, 2005), 154, http://hdr.undp.org/sites/default/files/reports/270/hdr_2010_en_complete_reprint.pdf (accessed 12 September 2015).

[4] Kerry Cullinan, "Namibia: Health Authorities Tackle Maternal Mortality," (2005), http://allafrica.com/stories/201002230101.html (accessed 29 September 2015).

The BIG Proposal in Namibia

The Basic Income Grant is an unconditional universal cash transfer that had originally been proposed by a Namibian government-appointed Tax Consortium, NAMTAX. NAMTAX reviewed the country's tax system to determine structural changes for economic growth. In its recommendations, NAMTAX pointed to the necessity to reduce poverty and income inequality in order to achieve sustainable economic development. NAMTAX found that by far the best method of addressing both would be a universal income grant (NAMTAX 2002a), which then became known as the Basic Income Grant (or BIG). The NAMTAX Commission made the proposal, based on financial calculations proving the affordability of such a grant within the macroeconomic framework of the Namibian economy.

At the time, only a few newspaper articles supported the proposal as 'good news for the poor', but while Government had been keen on taking on recommendations of the NAMTAX commission on the income revenue side, like the proposed capital gains tax, there was silence on the BIG.

The BIG Coalition

In 2004, concerns in the country about the widespread poverty, the high inequality and silence on the BIG proposal grew. The Evangelical Lutheran Church, under the leadership of Bishop Kameeta, spearheaded the setting up of a Coalition to promote a BIG for all Namibians. The BIG Coalition consisted of six umbrella bodies in Namibia, namely, the Council of Churches (CCN), the National Union of Namibian Workers (NUNW), the Namibian NGO Forum (NANGOF), the Namibian Network of AIDS Service Organisations (NANASO), the National Youth Council (NYC) and the Church Alliance for Orphans (CAFO).

For the first two years, the Coalition embarked on an extensive lobby campaign based on research and economic modelling. However, even detailed economic models and tax effort analyses could not convince Government to introduce a basic income, and the debate did not move forward. While some in Government supported a BIG right from the beginning, critics claimed that a BIG would lead to dependency and laziness and pointed to the fact that a BIG had never been implemented anywhere in the world.

When, at the end of 2006, a delegation of the BIG Coalition attended an international symposium on basic income in Cape Town, the delegation realised that, in other countries, researchers had already discussed a BIG for decades without it ever being implemented. The understanding grew that something drastic and different needed to be done, since Namibia would not have the time to spend years debating it without any actual impact on people's lives. It was then that the BIG Coalition decided to move from words to action, for deeds speak louder than words. The idea of the worldwide first pilot project of a universal cash grant was born. It is, however, noteworthy that this understanding had grown among the Namibian delegation and some academics from South Africa, who had a similar experience. In fact, it did not find the support of the majority of the gathering. Despite the scepticism which the proposal received, it stimulated the debate at the conference and Namibia's BIG Coalition's chairperson Bishop Kameeta, who had motivated the new idea in the plenary, was termed 'the butt-kicker' of the conference.

The idea of the pilot was rooted in the experience of the liberation struggle in Southern Africa, where, for example, English medium schools or township clinics often challenged the oppressive regime to revise otherwise ideologically hardened positions. Furthermore, it drew on the experience of pilot projects in other policy areas like the treatment of AIDS patients, where a successful pilot project led to the implementation of national programmes. For example, pilot projects in Haiti, Rwanda and South Africa demonstrated that antiretroviral treatment could be provided effectively to poor people – even to those living in deep rural areas. The pilots helped change national and international policy, thereby paving the way for the dramatic global roll-out of anti-retrovirals (ARVs). The BIG Coalition hoped that, by putting into operation a BIG pilot project, government leaders and others could see how the BIG could be transformed into a national programme. In 2007, the BIG Coalition decided to implement a pilot project to move the policy debate forward and to evaluate and document the impact of a Basic Income Grant on poverty and on sustainable economic livelihoods of individuals as well as on the community.

The Situation before the BIG

After careful examination of several villages in Namibia, the Otjivero settlement, including the Omitara 'town' in the Omitara District, in the east of the country was chosen. Otjivero-Omitara was selected for its manageable size and accessibility, for its characteristics of the community reflecting the many population groups in Namibia, and for its extreme poverty situation. Otjivero mirrored many poor communities in Namibia. Furthermore, Otjivero was known for its bad reputation amongst the local farmers as an apparent hotbed of criminal activities. Otjivero-Omitara is located some 100 kilometres east of Windhoek. People (mainly laid off farm workers) started settling in the squatter camp Otjivero about 5 km away from Omitara in 1992.[5] After Independence in 1990, despite the commercial farmers' objections, people were no longer forcefully removed and could settle on this government-owned land. A feature of the area is the proximity to a large dam that supplies water to Windhoek and surrounding areas. Unusually, the people in Otjivero had access to a free water supply, but the area was impoverished, with no access to land and the people prone to diseases, such as TB and HIV/AIDS, with most of them living in shacks made out of plastic, wood and zinc. The settlement struggled to subsist as a viable community. The relatively small settlement has very little space for people to cater for their economic survival, since all around cattle and hunting farms have fenced in the estates, leaving nothing to the majority of the people but the mere place to put up a shack. Over time, the Government built a school and a clinic, but there has been persistent conflict with the surrounding commercial farmers because of illegal hunting, trespassing and the collection of firewood. The statement of Wilhelmina Gawises, a single mother of three children exemplifies the desperation and abject poverty people in Otjivero faced on a daily basis:

> There is a problem of unemployment and we don't have money to travel to Gobabis and Windhoek to look for work. I have three children, aged 10, 13 and a 7-month-old baby. Now I don't know where their father is and I have no job or money to send them back to school. I and my three children depend on my unemployed parents for food and accommodation. Sometimes I wish I was dead because I cannot stand this type of life any more. I am supposed to provide and protect my children and parents but I am failing to do that. Life is very difficult here, we live in poverty with no hope for the future.

If a BIG had a positive impact in this hostile and hazardous environment, the success certainly could be replicated at least equally well elsewhere.

The pilot implemented the following policy: every resident under the age of 60 living in Otjivero received N$100 each month from January 2008 until December 2009, 930 residents receiving this grant without any condition. The money for children and youth up to the age of 21 was paid out to a person designated as their 'primary care-giver' which by default was the mother.

The BIG Coalition fund-raised for the pilot project within Namibia and internationally and received donations from individuals, congregations, churches, and both national and international organisations. This immense support enabled the BIG Coalition to run the two-year pilot project.

---

[5] In the remainder of the article we will refer to Omitara-Otjivero simply as Otjivero, as this is the name by which the Pilot Project has become known.

The Impact of the BIG in Otjivero

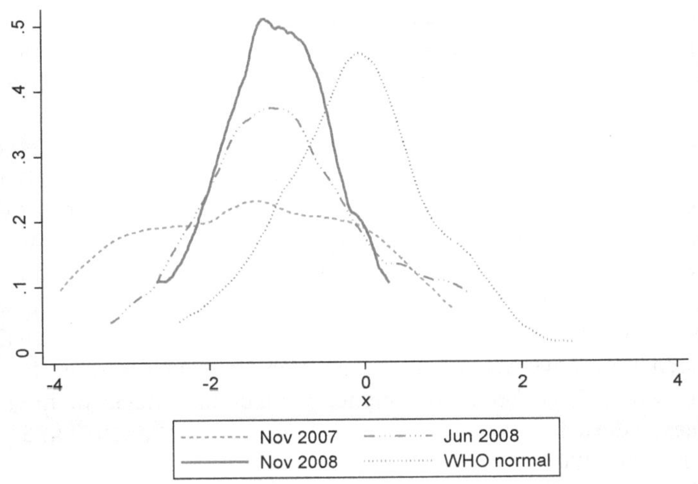

Graph 1: Weight for age scores according to WHO standard – before and after BIG (for children in households without significant in-migration)

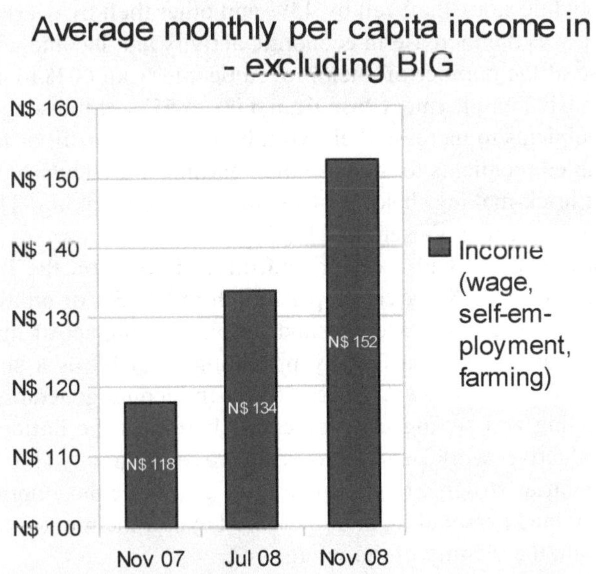

Graph 2 Average monthly per capita income in N$ – excluding BIG payments

With the introduction of the BIG, household poverty dropped significantly. Using the food poverty line of the Namibian government, 76% of residents fell below this line in November 2007. Within one year, with the BIG, this number was reduced to 37% amongst households not affected by migration, the rate even decreased to 16%. These statistics reveal the direct and fast impact of a cash grant on food security.

The BIG resulted in a huge reduction of child malnutrition. Using a WHO measurement technique, the data shows the significant improvement of children's weight-for-age in a short period of time. In November 2007, 42% of children in Otjivero were underweight. Six months later, this was reduced to 17% and to 10% after ten months.

HIV-positive residents had huge difficulties in accessing ARVs, due to food insecurity and the prohibitive cost of travel to the next hospital. The BIG enabled them to afford nutritious food and gain access to medication. This was further enhanced by the government's decision to make ARVs available in Otjivero, freeing residents from the need to travel to the next town.

Before the introduction of the BIG, almost half of the school-going children did not attend school regularly. Pass rates stood at about 40% and drop-out rates were high. Many parents were unable to pay the school fees. After the introduction of the BIG, more than double the number of parents paid school fees (90%) and most of the children now have school uniforms. Non-attendance due to financial reasons dropped by 42% and this rate would have been even higher without the effects of migration towards Otjivero-Omitara. Drop-out rates at the school fell from almost 40% in November 2007 to 5% in June 2008 and further to almost 0% in November 2008.

The residents used the settlement's health clinic much more regularly after the introduction of the BIG. Residents now paid the N$4 payment for each visit and the income of the clinic increased fivefold.

Further, the BIG contributed to the reduction of household debt, with the average debt falling from N$1,215 to N$772 between November 2007 and November 2008. Savings increased during that period, which was reflected in the increasing ownership of large livestock, small livestock and poultry.

The BIG made a positive impact in the crime situation. Overall crime rates – as reported by the local police station – fell by 42% while stock theft fell by 43% and other theft by nearly 20%.

The most striking finding was the increase in economic activity and income amongst residents. The data collected showed a decrease of the number of unemployed people from 60% to 45%. To put it differently: since the introduction of the BIG, employment rose from 44% to 55% of those aged 15 and above.

Thus the BIG enabled recipients to increase their work both for pay, profit or family gain as well as self-employment. The grant enabled recipients to increase their earnings, particularly through starting their own small businesses, including brick-making, baking of bread and dress-making. The BIG contributed to the creation of a local market by increasing households' buying power.

This increase in economic activity had a major and direct impact on the income situation. Personal incomes rose from an average of N$118 per capita per month to N$152, or on average by 29% in just one year without taking the BIG payment into account and despite the impact of migration into the area and into the households. The research observed that by providing the BIG as a small source of secure and reliable income, people were able to engage more effectively in income-generating activities and were able to take small risks by investing and setting up businesses. It refutes the notion and critique that people would withdraw from productive work when receiving 'free money'. This is an important finding especially in times when countries struggle to stimulate local economic development. The stimulus created by the BIG resulted in a sustained personal income increase beyond the money given from the outside and led to economic activity within the vicinity of the village.

The introduction of the Basic Income Grant reportedly reduced the dependency of women on men for their survival. The BIG gave women a measure of control over their own sexuality, freeing them to some extent from the pressure to engage in transactional sex.

The empirical evidence refuted the criticism that the BIG would increase alcoholism. The community committee tried to curb alcoholism by raising awareness within the community and by reaching an agreement with local pub owners not to sell alcohol on the day of the pay-out of the grants.

The Reciprocal Influence of the BIG on Development and Theology

As outlined in the introduction, the churches – especially the Evangelical Lutheran Church in the Republic of Namibia (ELCRN), played a crucial role in the BIG Coalition. The ELCRN hosted the BIG Coalition and led the practical implementation of the Pilot Project. Bishop Kameeta was the Chairperson of the Coalition and later became the first Minister of Poverty Eradication in the Namibian Government, undoubtedly because of his role as Chairperson of the BIG. While the Coalition was by no means a faith-based group but a broad civil society coalition, it is worthwhile to look at how contextual theology shaped the churches' involvement in the advocacy work towards a BIG and in turn how the pilot project shaped theology at the same time. The policy which shaped the policy enriched the theology at the same time.

In the tradition of Ernesto Cardinal and applying the methods of Gerald West, a central part of the church's campaign was to read biblical texts with the experience of the Basic Income Grant pilot project. In the light of the BIG, texts like the 'feeding of the five thousand', 'the healing at the pool', Psalm 23 and the Exodus story with the special focus on the manna, were interpreted with a different perspective.

The manna story can serve as one example of such an interpretation: In Exodus 16 it is described how the Israelites when travelling through the desert, unable to grow food, hungry and without hope, received manna. Each person was given the amount to cover their needs, without strings attached. It kept people moving and enabled them to journey through the desert, from slavery to the Promised Land.

This contextual reading opened the eyes that a cash grant can be compared to manna: it has been given to everybody, without strings attached, in the faith that it will be put to good use. In the situation of the Israelites, nobody would have said, don't give them manna, they will become lazy and dependent – so why are people saying it about a cash grant?

Likewise, one can also ask: Why did God not give them palm trees with dates or today it would maybe translate into a textile factory to create jobs? Some development experts would surely argue that this would be more sustainable and cost-effective, easier to implement, than manna… The intention and logic behind the manna is however clear: God wanted his people to move on, he gave them something to nourish them, they could pick it up, get out of slavery and move on – like the BIG in a poor and food-insecure community or a cash grant during the drought. The immediate need of food and nourishment was taken care of. But at the same time, it did not make people stationary or dependent on further interventions from outside like fertilizer or foreign machinery bought from development aid. Instead, the option to spend the grant according to their own needs and plans, the reliability and security of monthly payments enabled people to take the future in their hands, make plans and become independent.

Like the manna, the cash grant is given to everybody, creating a community without jealousy but with a deeper sense of solidarity towards each other. This was surely important also for the Israelites in the desert. Imagine the Israelites would have been divided by some officials installed by Moses into those who were to receive bread and those who are not? The same is true for communities in poverty or during a drought. Everybody is affected, everybody gets support without having to prove or do anything. The cash grant did not divide the communities but put everybody on the same footing. The community where the BIG was implemented stressed this point again and again. The fact that everybody received the grant created a new sense of community, unity and solidarity in contrast to jealousy and stigmatisation.

Coming back again to the role of the church in the BIG Coalition and the underlying thinking: the reading of the Exodus story revealed the potential of combining and applying contextual theology and development practice. By keeping them in dialogue with each other and by learning from each other, a new understanding of the Bible texts as well as new development practice emerged. The churches were able to apply their reading of the Bible in this situation and act creatively and innovatively.

This interpretation of the biblical text served as a signpost for the churches how to do development work, and the experience with the BIG encouraged the churches to go against traditional approaches based on the principles of charity rather than social justice.

The contextual Bible studies with the experience of the BIG pilot enhanced the theology of the churches and changed their perspective in the development debate and practice. And conversely, development practice was enriched by theology. Just to give an example: two years ago, the Senator of Sao Paulo in Brazil, from the workers' party, asked at an international conference on development in Munich, how the churches in Namibia would interpret the manna story and its implications for development practice round the world. He explained that he was fully aware that the conference was not a theological one, but he had learned about the story, and that would really be of interest for him and his political work in Brazil. This was indeed a new experience for many development experts. And as odd as it might have seemed to some, it showed that theology in development is not a one-way street. Rather to the contrary, the 'by their fruits theology' was also recognized and brought into the debate. However, it required the churches to learn more about development, to learn how to do social action research, learn concepts of poverty, development, social transformation, advocacy, etc. and have the tools for project design, implementation and management. There was a clear need for that, as there was a huge discrepancy between many theological and developmental declarations and their practical implementation.

Conclusion

The BIG pilot in Namibia aimed to illustrate the impact of a universal grant as an immediate measure of poverty alleviation through redistribution. The results established the effectiveness of a BIG not only in fighting poverty, in providing food security and decreasing malnutrition, but most interestingly in kick-starting local economic growth in a rural setting and fostering social development. Although circumstances differ substantially in the various parts of Africa, the BIG pilot provides an important example in the ongoing debate about usage of universal grants in development policy. In more and more cash-based societies, a BIG enables people to improve their living conditions in an independent and self-determining way. The experience of the pilot is evidence that the majority use the money wisely, not only for their immediate needs, but for productive and long-term goals as well. Moreover, the BIG is an important tool for injecting much-needed cash into rural communities for sustainable development.

The BIG campaign also showed the important role of churches in development. However, to be meaningful, there is a need to become a community of true agents and visionaries in development based on the concept of equality, justice and love. Or, to stay in biblical language, the churches need to reject so-called development approaches that come with thorns and thistles but rather to engage with those that bear fruit.

Bibliography

Cullinan, Kerry. 2010. 'Namibia: Health Authorities Tackle Maternal Mortality.' http://allafrica.com/stories/201002230101.html (accessed 7 September 2015).

Haarmann, Claudia, Dirk Haarmann, Herbert Jauch, Hilma Shindondola, Nicoli Nattrass, Ingrid Niekerk, and Michael Samson. *Making the difference! The BIG in Namibia.* Basic Income Grant Pilot Project Assessment Report, April 2009, Windhoek, Namibia: Desk for Social Development, 2009.

Haarmann, Claudia and Dirk Haarmann. 'The developmental impact of a Basic Income Grant.' in *The Basic Income Grant in Namibia: Resource Book,* eds. C. Haarmann, and D. Haarmann, 31–42. Windhoek: the Desk for Social Development (DfSD), 2005.

NAMTAX, 2002a. 'NAMTAX report Appendix 4: Income Redistribution and Poverty Relief – A Universal Income Grant combined with Indirect Tax Increases.' (2005), www.ippr.org.na/Non-IPPR%20research/Namtax%20Second%20Section%2015Dec20021.doc (accessed 7 September 2015).

NAMTAX, 'The Namibian Tax Consortium Report on Taxation in Namibia. December 2002.' 2002b, www.ippr.org.na/Non-IPPR%20research/Namtax%20first%20section15Dec20021.doc (accessed 7 September 2015).

Schlechter, Deon. '42.3 percent of Namibians are undernourished.' *New Era* (2010) https://www.newera.com.na/2015/06/08/42-3-percent-namibians-undernourished (accessed 12 September 2015).

The United Nations Development Programme. *The Real Wealth of Nations: Pathways to Human Development. Human Development Report 2010* (New York: UNDP), 154, http://hdr.undp.org/sites/default/files/reports/270/hdr_2010_en_complete_reprint.pdf (accessed 12 September 2015).

(154) THE RELEVANCE OF BODY THEOLOGY FOR DEVELOPMENT IN AFRICAN CHRISTIANITY

Gerald O. West

Introduction

The Ujamaa Centre for Community Development and Research (Ujamaa Centre) began doing 'Contextual Bible Study'[1] work on the biblical story of Tamar, the daughter of King David, in 1996.[2] While King David is a familiar figure in Christian churches and faith-based organisations, his daughter, who was raped within his household by his son is less well known. Tamar has been deliberately marginalised in the formal liturgical life of the church, with her story hardly ever being read on a Sunday within church lectionaries.

The Ujamaa Centre does its Contextual Bible Study (CBS)[3] work within community-based organisations that invite the Ujamaa Centre to work with them as they struggle to use their faith resources – like the Bible – for the transformation of their communities. In this sense, our work with the story of Tamar can be considered as a contribution to community development, with a focus on the body.

Our first community-based invitation to work with this text came from a cross-sector of rural and urban African women who asked the Ujamaa Centre to work with them on the pressing issue of gender violence. The work that was done together then has generated a series of CBS on what has become known as the Tamar Campaign, focusing on gender violence, and also a series of CBS focusing on men, in what has become known as a Redemptive Masculinities series.[4]

Since 1996, the Tamar CBS has been taken up all over the world, particularly in contexts where the Bible continues to be a local community-based resource. Major international ecumenical networks like the World Council of Churches (WCC) and the related Ecumenical HIV and AIDS Initiative in Africa (EHAIA), and significant continental African ecumenical organisations like the Fellowship of Christian Councils and Churches in the Great Lakes and Horn of Africa (FECCGLAHA) have adopted the Tamar CBS as part of their own gender programmes. In addition, the Ujamaa Centre has trained trainers from these and many other faith-based organisations, enabling them to use CBS methodology for the construction of their own 'local' CBS and theological resources.[5]

Central to the CBS work of the Ujamaa Centre is a 'theory of change' that draws deeply on the praxis cycle. From the praxis cycle the Ujamaa Centre has come to understand how and why its CBS work enables local faith-based formations to use the Bible for survival, liberation, and fulness of life – to resist the forces of death and to align with the God of life. This essay elaborates on what we in the Ujamaa Centre have so far discerned about our theory of change, using the Tamar CBS as an example.

---

[1] Gerald O. West, *Contextual Bible Study* (Pietermaritzburg: Cluster Publications, 1993).

[2] Gerald O. West and Phumzile Zondi-Mabizela, "The Bible Story That Became a Campaign: The Tamar Campaign in South Africa (and Beyond)," *Ministerial Formation* 103(2004).

[3] 'CBS' is more than an abbreviation; the Ujamaa Centre has been asked by some of the communities we work with not to call what we do 'Bible study', because, they insist, what we do "is not what we do in church".

[4] http://ujamaa.ukzn.ac.za/.

[5] www.fecclaha.org/index.php?option=com_k2&view=item&layout=item&id=57&Itemid=197.

A Theory of Change

The Ujamaa Centre's theory of change is founded on the foundational tenet of liberation theology: the epistemological privilege of the poor.[6] The knowledge of the poor is vital to any project of social transformation. Development cannot be done without the presence of the poor themselves. They are the agents of their own development and they have assets. And among these assets is religion.[7] Faith, and faith-based resources like the Bible are potential assets which the poor (and other marginalised sectors) can deploy in projects of social transformation.

So in engaging with gender-based violence, it is the presence and participation and knowledge of the habitual victims of gender-based violence – women – that provide the starting-point of social transformation. Their epistemology is fundamental to an analysis of gender violence and provides the necessary 'logic' for the forms of action that they might choose to take as part of a transformative project.

For these reasons, the Ujamaa Centre favours organised communities of poor and marginalised women in its gender-based work. The use of the term 'organised' is deliberate. The organised poor and marginalised are central to our theory of change. By being 'organised', poor and marginalised sectors have already constructed their own safe and sequestered sites, and have already begun to assemble their own discourse concerning their oppression and marginalisation. They have already forged a vocabulary for talking about their realities (including their bodies), and they are in (partial) control of their own space.

Here the Ujamaa Centre's praxis is informed by the work of James Scott. The organised marginalised have 'a shared interest in jointly creating a discourse of dignity, of negation, and of justice'. 'They have, in addition,' Scott continues, 'a shared interest in concealing a social site apart from domination where such a hidden transcript can be elaborated in comparative safety.'[8] As Scott indicates, a safe social site enables an articulation. Put differently, the question posed by Gayatri Spivak, of whether or not the subaltern *can* speak,[9] should be recast as a question which takes space seriously. A more appropriate question would be: '*Where* can the subaltern speak?' For as Scott so eloquently argues, subordinate classes are less constrained at the level of thought and ideology than they are at the level of political action and struggle 'since they can in secluded settings speak with comparative safety'.[10] Human dignity, even in the most damaged and denigrated subaltern, demands some form of 'speaking'.[11] *How* the subaltern speaks depends almost entirely on local 'sectoral' control of space.

This is why women's faith-based groups are such important sites for dealing with gender-based violence. These are sites that have already been established by women in the face of patriarchy, with particular faith-based symbols and rituals playing a significant role in securing these sites.[12] CBS work only takes place in such sites when and if the Ujamaa Centre is invited by those who control particular sites to enter their site and to collaborate with them.

---

[6] Per Frostin, *Liberation Theology in Tanzania and South Africa: A First World Interpretation* (Lund: Lund University Press, 1988), 6.

[7] Steve de Gruchy, "Of Agency, Assets and Appreciation: Seeking Some Commonalities between Theology and Development," in *Keeping Body and Soul Together: Reflections by Steve De Gruchy on Theology and Development*, ed. Beverley G. Haddad (Pietermaritzburg: Cluster Publications, 2015).

[8] James C. Scott, *Domination and the Arts of Resistance: Hidden Transcripts* (New Haven and London: Yale University Press, 1990), 114.

[9] Gayatri C. Spivak, "Can the Subaltern Speak?," in *Marxism and the Interpretation of Culture*, ed. Gary Nelson and L. Grossberg (London: Macmillan, 1988).

[10] Scott, *Domination and the Arts of Resistance*, 91.

[11] Gerald O. West, "Newsprint Theology: Bible in the Context of HIV and AIDS," in *Out of Place: Doing Theology on the Cross-cultural Brink*, ed. Jione Havea and Clive Pearson (London: Equinox Publishing, 2011).

[12] Beverley G. Haddad, "The Manyano Movement in South Africa: Site of Struggle, Survival, and Resistance," *Agenda* 61(2004).

Such sites are already full of resources, full of assets. The constraint on marginalised African women is not their lack of assets, but how some of these assets, like the Bible, have been used by the dominant patriarchal structures and systems that govern their lives. The Bible is interpreted by institutional patriarchy, including the church, as consisting of a singular voice and conveying a singular message. This is where and why the Ujamaa Centre is invited to work with such women's groups. The resources of biblical scholarship enable the Bible to be read as a text with divergent and even contesting voices. We read unfamiliar biblical texts – those texts excluded from or on the margins of public ecclesiastical practice. And we re-read familiar biblical texts in unfamiliar ways, re-locating well-worn texts within their literary and socio-historical contexts and so rendering them alive in new ways. The resources of biblical scholarship enable the detail of the Bible to be visible, unconstrained by the dominant theological frameworks of institutional religion (or the naive and uncritical notions of religion prevalent in 'secular' development agencies).

The story of Tamar in 2 Samuel 13:1-22 is a good example. This text has little or no presence in the public life of the church anywhere in the world. Most lectionaries do not include this portion of the Bible in their set readings for a formal Sunday service. In our experience with this biblical text among women we regularly find that they are unaware that this story in the Bible. And though this story is a 'text of terror',[13] it has demonstrated a remarkable capacity to evoke the voice of a biblical woman and the kindred voices of contemporary women who share her experience of violence and abuse. As the Ujamaa Centre has often been told, 'If this story is in the Bible we will not be silent'. Recovering Tamar's voice – a remarkably articulate voice – has provided additional vocabulary – sacred vocabulary – with which contemporary women can tell their own embodied stories and work together to bring about the transformation of the patriarchal systems that both construct and condone gender-based violence.

The very decision to extract this part of the story from the larger story of David and his male dynasty within Samuel and Kings is significant. This part of the story may well have had an independent existence prior to its co-option by the dominant male narrative and its insertion into the story of great male leaders. The story told in 2 Samuel 13 may well be a part of a hidden, disguised narrative told among women. By identifying Tamar's voice as significant and sacred, we recover a part of the tradition that has struggled to be heard.

In identifying this scriptural voice and offering it to local communities of African women, we offer a potential site for the doing of what James Cochrane has referred to as 'incipient theology'.[14] As organised groups of church women – women of faith – gather together in safe spaces they control, the Tamar CBS offers an articulation of body theology. Tamar breaks the silence of abuse and speaks, both before the abuse and after it. Her words have the potential to set in motion a 'crystallization' whereby the other members of the group recognise 'close relatives' of their own experience, connecting them to a 'single power grid'.[15] James Scott is here describing a common experience among marginalised sectors, as they together construct a vocabulary with which to talk about shared realities. What we recognise within the Ujamaa Centre is that this experience is a form of body theology. What is present but inchoate and incipient within the bodies of individual women is catalysed by the Tamar CBS, and slowly the women forge a way of talking about what is in their bodies. As both James Scott and John Holloway have argued, the dignity of being human demands an attempt to articulate what is held within the body.[16] And as

---

[13] Phyllis Trible, *Texts of Terror: Literary-Feminist Readings of Biblical Narratives* (Philadelphia: Fortress, 1984), 37-63.

[14] James R. Cochrane, *Circles of Dignity: Community Wisdom and Theological Reflection* (Minneapolis: Fortress, 1999), 111.

[15] Scott, *Domination and the Arts of Resistance*, 223-24.

[16] http://libcom.org/library/dignitys-revolt-john-holloway See also John Holloway, "Dignity's Revolt," in *Zapatista! Reinventing Revolution in Mexico*, ed. John Holloway and Elíona Peláez (London: Pluto, 1998).

Philippe Denis reminds us, 'the elaboration of the painful experience and its validation through empathetic listening' enables a narrative of the embodied traumatic experience to take shape.[17]

The dignity of Tamar, present in her gracious and caring attitude to her brother, present in her analysis and articulation of why her brother should not 'force' her, present in her refusal to be silenced after she has been raped, invokes and kindles the dignity of contemporary women who have come to connect with her story in the Bible. Tamar's 'discourse', evident in both what she says and does, offers additional resources for the articulation of contemporary incipient women's theologies, which, when corporately constructed within a safe and sacred space, offer resources with which to confront the dominant forces of patriarchal control of the Bible, the church, and society at large. Body theology then becomes public theology.

In terms of our theory of change, the participatory CBS 'processes' and 'products' (see below) provide an array of additional assets or resources which organised groups of women can combine with the assets they already have and with which they can work for social transformation.

Social Change

In the late 1980s, the South African biblical scholar Itumeleng Mosala argued that a 'critical' reading of the Bible enabled a critical 'reading' of context.[18] Put negatively, Mosala is concerned that 'unstructural understanding of the Bible may simply reinforce and confirm unstructural understanding of the present'.[19] CBS is a response to this recognition, offering a critical-structural-systemic pedagogical framework with which to re-read the Bible. The dominant framework within which the Bible is read by the church, civil society, and even development agencies, is as a book with a singular voice and a singular message focused on the singular individual. Biblical scholarship knows a quite different 'text'. For biblical scholarship, the Bible is a geographically, historically and ideologically diverse text. Indeed, most biblical texts are constituted by distinct redactional layers, each of which has its own distinctive social location and ideology.[20]

Contextual Bible Study offers such detail to communities of the poor and marginalised, but in a manner that is pedagogically enabling. There are various ways of describing CBS praxis, but one way of conceptualising our work is to recognise a series of interconnected 'movements' that shape the collaborative interpretative-reading process.

The overarching movement is that of 'See-Judge-Act', a process formed in the worker-priest movement in Europe in the 1930-40s.[21] This movement begins within the organised formations of the poor and marginalised as they analyse ('See') their context, 'from below'. This analysis of their 'reality' is then brought into dialogue with the 'prophetic' voices of the Bible (and theology), enabling 'the God of life' to address ('Judge') their lived social reality. Through this dialogue with the Bible 'the shape of the gospel'[22] – namely, to bring good news – is used to plan a series of actions ('Act') that will bring about

---

[17] Philippe Denis, "Storytelling and Healing," in *A Journey Towards Healing: Stories of People with Multiple Woundedness in Kwazulu-Natal*, ed. Philippe Denis, Scott Houser, and Radikobo Ntsimane (Pietermaritzburg: Cluster Publications, 2011), 11.

[18] Itumeleng J. Mosala, *Biblical Hermeneutics and Black Theology in South Africa* (Grand Rapids: Eerdmans, 1989).

[19] Mosala, *Biblical Hermeneutics and Black Theology*, 32.

[20] See for example Norman K. Gottwald, *The Hebrew Bible: A Socio-Literary Introduction* (Philadelphia: Fortress, 1985).

[21] James R. Cochrane, "Questioning Contextual Theology," in *Towards an Agenda for Contextual Theology: Essays in Honour of Albert Nolan*, ed. McGlory T. Speckman and Larry T. Kaufmann (Pietermaritzburg: Cluster Publications, 2001), 76-77; Gerald O. West, *Biblical Hermeneutics of Liberation: Modes of Reading the Bible in the South African Context*, Second Edition ed. (Maryknoll and Pietermaritzburg: Orbis Books and Cluster Publications, 1995), 188-93.

[22] Albert Nolan, *God in South Africa: The Challenge of the Gospel* (Cape Town: David Philip, 1988).

transformation of their social reality, so that all who live in this reality may have life, and have it abundantly (John 10:10).

Within this overarching movement, there is another movement, from 'community-consciousness' to 'critical-consciousness' to 'community-consciousness'. The 'See' moment of social analysis generates a particular contextual concern that becomes the 'theme' for the Bible study – a theme such as sexual gender-based violence. The engagement with the Bible (the Judge component) begins with a community's 'thematic' interaction with the biblical text being used ('community-consciousness'), allowing every participant to share their particular understanding of the chosen text. This moment not only makes it clear to the participants that the Bible study belongs to them, but also offers a reception history of that text's presence in a particular community, their own community. The Bible study then moves into a series of re-readings of the text, slowing down the process of interpretation, using the resources of socially-engaged biblical scholarship ('critical-consciousness'). The particular sets of 'critical' tools that are used by biblical scholarship are offered to the participants as additional resources with which to engage the biblical text, through a series of questions related to the biblical text. After a series of 'critical-consciousness' questions, the Bible study moves back into 'community-consciousness', as the participants appropriate (en-Act) the biblical text for the particular social project of transformation identified in the 'See' moment.

With respect to the particular critical resources of biblical scholarship, there is another layer of movement. The movement begins within the 'See' moment with an initial thematic 'in-front-of-the-text' engagement with the text ('community-consciousness'), bringing the generative contextual theme of the community workshop into dialogue with a particular biblical text. The interpretative process then slows down, entering the 'critical-consciousness' moment via a literary engagement with the text. Though a form of 'critical' engagement, the choice to begin critical engagement 'on-the-text' is deliberate because it offers an egalitarian entry point to 'critical-consciousness', enabling all participants to engage with the detail of the text. In most cases, literary engagement leads 'behind-the-text' to a socio-historical engagement with the text, as participants probe the world that produced the text, seeking for lines of connection between both the literary dimensions and the socio-historical dimensions of the text and their contextual realities, seeking lines of connection between contemporary communities of faith and struggle and 'biblical' communities of faith and struggle. While these dimensions of the biblical *text* are the focus of these second and third moments, the process moves in the fourth moment back 'in-front-of-the-text' (into 'community-consciousness'), as the participants now appropriate this critically re-read and reconstituted text for their particular project of social transformation ('Act'). Together, as the Tamar CBS examples that follow in the next section illustrate, these concentric and intersecting movements constitute 'the Contextual Bible Study process'.

Implicit within these CBS processes, facilitation 'practices' are vital to CBS community-based work, enabling both 'group process' – the active participation of each participant – and the CBS process – the slow but steady procession through the three movements of CBS process.[23] Part of the 'conversion' of the socially engaged biblical scholar is becoming 're-schooled' as a facilitator, collaborating with other community-based facilitators so as to enable participatory transformation. CBS begins and ends under the control of a particular local community, who use the resources of the CBS, along with a range of their own resources (and the resources of other agencies who may be invited to participate in the community-based initiative), to plan for and implement community-based action.

---

[23] Anne Hope and Sally Timmel, *Training for Transformation: A Handbook for Community Workers*, 4 vols., vol. Book 1 (Gweru: Mambo Press, 1984).

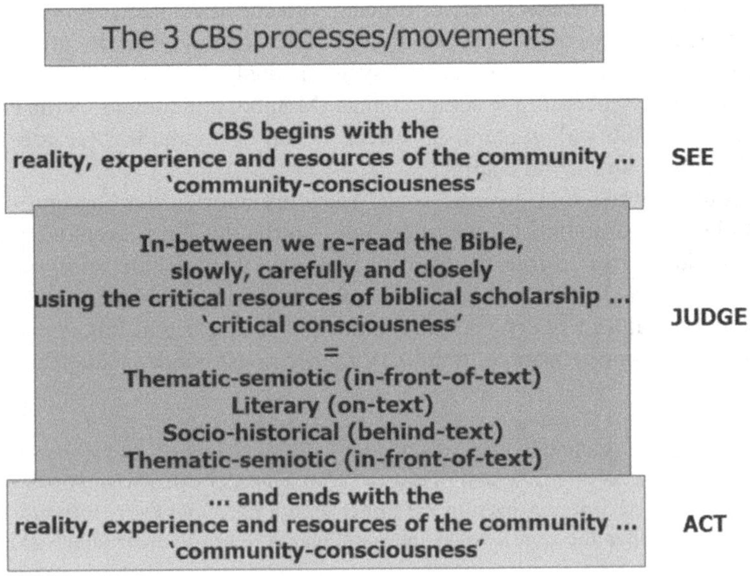

CBS processes are focused on generating a critical-structural-systemic interpretation of the Bible, reinforcing and providing additional critical tools to the capacities already present in an organised community-based group. As Mosala made clear, such structural interpretative resources are crucial, not only to a reading of the Bible, but also to a reading of reality. The unstructural-individual focus of the dominant forms of Christianity are the default orientation within the church, civil society, and development agencies. And yet religion and the Bible are far more complex, requiring a more critical engagement. CBS offers a more critical engagement with the Bible, and in so doing provides an array of additional tools for a particular community-based group to engage both with a significant faith resource – the Bible – as well as with the structural-systemic dimensions of their realities, and so too, of the potential areas of social change with these realities.

Religious Change

What Mosala is saying, in other words, is that social change requires religious change. This is a central tenet of the Ujamaa Centre's theory of change. Religion cannot be left 'as is' while development work is done. In order for development work to be done, religion, which is part of the very fabric and scaffolding of life for millions of Africans, must be transformed, otherwise it gets in the way of social transformation. CBS is about religious change.

The emphasis on the concept 'contextual' within 'Contextual Bible Study' is a recognition that religion must serve context. 'True service submits itself to the cause which it serves, deeming that cause holy.'[24] This is why the notion of the 'shape' of the gospel was so important to the struggle against apartheid in South Africa. Albert Nolan argued that what was determinant of the Christian faith (and indeed any faith)

[24] Stephen Donaldson, *The Last Dark* (London: Gollancz, 2013), 444.

was that its 'shape' ought to be 'good news for the poor' (Luke 4:18).[25] The significance of faith for social change is that it should offer a particular shape or trajectory to social change that is good news for the poor and marginalised. And just as CBS offers a set of tools for a structural-systemic interpretation of the shape of scripture, so it offers a set of tools for a structural-systemic analysis of South African reality and a set of tools for a structural-systemic trajectory for social change. Method, not content, is the crucial concern here; CBS does not offer fixed biblical content, it offers a set of methods that are useful for biblical interpretation, social analysis, and social change.

Among the contextual realities that demand social transformation is the ongoing problem of violence against women and children. Colonialism, apartheid, and patriarchy have wreaked a vortex of havoc on African women and children. And while the Bible has voices that collude with and even inspire these destructive forces, the Ujamaa Centre has been working with 2 Samuel 13:1-22, an unfamiliar text in the liturgies and lectionaries of almost every Christian church, but a text that has demonstrated its capacity through CBS processes to empower women in their struggle against gender violence. The CBS we use has the following shape:

> 2 Samuel 13:1-22 is read aloud, preferably dramatically. After the text has been read a series of questions follow.
> *1. Read 2 Samuel 13:1-22 together again in small groups. Share with each other what you think the text is about.*
> Each small group is then asked to report back to the larger group. Each and every response to question one is summarized on newsprint. After the report-back, the participants return to their small groups to discuss the following questions.
> *2. Who are the main characters in this story and what do we know about them?*
> *3. What is the role of each of the male characters in the rape of Tamar?*
> *4. What does Tamar say and what does Tamar do? Focus carefully on each element of what Tamar says and does.*
> When the small groups have finished their discussion, each group is invited to present a summary of their discussion. After this report-back the smaller groups reconvene and discuss the following questions.
> *5. Are there women like Tamar in your church and/or community? Tell their story.*
> *6. What resources are there in your area for survivors of rape?*
> Once again, the small groups present their report-back to the plenary group. Creativity is particularly vital here, as often women find it difficult or are unable to articulate their responses. A drama or a drawing may be the only way in which some groups can report.
> Finally, each small group comes together to formulate an action plan.
> *7. What will you now do in response to this Bible study?*
> The action plan is either reported to the plenary or presented on newsprint for other participants to study after the Bible study.

Questions 2, 3 and 4 are 'critical-consciousness' questions, slowing down the reading process by inviting a re-reading of the literary features of the text (and through them opening up space to explore behind-the-text). On either side of these questions that explore the detail of the text are questions that embed the CBS in 'community-consciousness'. Among these questions each does its own critical work. Question 2 moves the CBS from the spontaneous and varied responses of the participants to a more considered focus on the detail of the text. A focus on character is one form of analysis that anyone can do, and yet it is a form of critical analysis, enabling a recognition of the literary dimensions of the text. Question 3 builds on this preliminary literary analysis, using the theme of gender violence to give shape to how the characters are analysed. Participants are enabled, via this question, to recognise the relational

[25] Nolan, *God in South Africa: The Challenge of the Gospel*, 17. For what this would look like in terms of inter-faith relations see Matthew C. Palombo, "Interfaith Praxis in South African Struggle for Liberation: Toward a Liberatio-Political Framework for Muslim-Christian Relations" (University of Johannesburg, 2014).

dimensions of patriarchy. Patriarchy is not about individual 'bad men'; it is about the structural-systemic systems that support male power. Question 3 probes this matrix of male power. Question 4 then shifts the focus from male power to female agency. Tamar is a 'victim' of rape; but she is much more than this, she is an articulate agent who talks back to power and acts against power. Through her speech and action male power is both delineated and resisted.

More recently, we have constructed a variation on this CBS where we take up the challenge of the many women we have worked with, to do work with 'their men' around notions of masculinity. The advent of HIV and AIDS and the more recent roll-out of ARVs (antiretroviral drugs) has enabled men to take responsibility for their sexuality and their masculinity. The Ujamaa Centre has been invited into this space, where we have worked with local communities in a quest for redemptive forms of masculinity. At the moment its form is somewhat flexible, but a relatively stable version of it is as follows:[26]

1. Have you heard this text (2 Sam. 13:1-22) read publically... on a Sunday? Share with each other if and when and where you have heard this text read.
2. Who are the main characters in this story and what do we know about them?
3. What is the role of each of the male characters in the rape of Tamar?
4. How would you characterize Amnon's masculinity in this text? Consider:
What prevents Amnon initially from acting on his love for Tamar (v. 2)?
What is it that changes Amnon's love (v. 1) to sickness/lust (v. 2), and then enables him to act on his sickness/lust (vv. 4-6)?
How does he react to Tamar's arguments (v. 14)?
How does he behave after he has raped Tamar (vv. 15-17)?
5. What kind of man does Tamar expect or hope Amnon to be? What kind of man could Amnon be according to Tamar? What kind of man does Tamar want? Consider:
What does she say (vv. 12-13,16), and what do each of the things she says tell us about her understanding of what it means to be 'a man'?
What does she do (v. 19), and what do each of things she does tell us about her understanding of what it means to be 'a man'?
6. What are the dominant forms of masculinity in our contexts (in various age groups), and what alternative forms of masculinity can we draw on from our cultural and religious traditions?
7. How can we raise the issue of masculinity in our various gender and age-groups?

Questions 2 and 3 are the same as in the Tamar CBS and accomplish similar critical capacity building. Question 4 in what we have called the Redemptive Masculinity version is another critical question, probing notions of 'masculinity' in this biblical story (and providing resources for an analysis of masculinity in contemporary South African society). Question 4 also juxtaposes Amnon and Tamar, deconstructing the dominant stereotypes about male self-control and rationality. In this biblical story it is Tamar who is self-controlled and rational and Amnon who is emotional. Question 5 too is a critical question, allowing each of the elements of Tamar's argument to deconstruct dominant notions of masculinity and to reconstruct alternative masculinities.

These two Contextual Bible Studies inhabit the dialogical space between the epistemology of our primary dialogue partners – women who have experienced abuse – and the detail of the text made apparent through the critical capacities of biblical scholarship. Each CBS has the capacity to explore the personal-psychological and the social-structural dimensions of each of their respective areas of focus, namely, gender violence and masculinity. In both cases the sets of critical-consciousness questions are followed by a set of community-consciousness questions, where participants are able to apply and practise the critical

---

[26] In this case I have not included the facilitator guidelines as I have done in the previous case. Here I include the questions only.

tools they have acquired through the critical consciousness questions. If the CBS site is a safe and sacred space, the resources of the CBS processes combine with the resources that the community-based group already has, to plan for and implement forms of action for social change.

CBS is not about knowing one's Bible better. CBS is about changing an unjust world, using the Bible as a potential 'weapon'[27] of struggle. CBS is also uniquely placed to recognise and participate in the intersections between the related struggles of the poor and marginalised.

Intersecting Struggles

The Bible is already a significant resource in many African communities. CBS comes alongside this community-based resource and 'redeploys' it for social transformation, liberating it from it the dominant and normative theological paradigm, a paradigm that emphasises the personal and individual dimensions of faith. The poor and marginalised already know the God of life, but their Bibles are more ambiguous. The dominant theologies of our time tend to draw on those trajectories within the Bible that blame the poor for being poor, blame the unemployed for being unemployed, blame the HIV-positive for being HIV-positive, blame the abused for being abused, blame the disabled for being disabled, etc.[28] CBS recovers other biblical trajectories, those that situate the poor, the unemployed,[29] the HIV-positive,[30] the abused, the disabled, etc. within particular social and theological structures and systems, enabling these 'blamed' sectors to understand the structures and systems that marginalise them. And by so doing, CBS releases the blamed/stigmatised, both theologically and socially, enabling them to reassert their dignity and to work for structural and systemic change.

The theological system that is used to individualise and blame the woman abused by gender violence is the same theological system that is used to individualise and blame the unemployed person and the HIV-positive person. CBS 'reveals' this theological system, exposing it as just one theological system, not 'the' theological system. CBS deconstructs the dominant theological systems of our churches and offers other more redemptive theological systems, following other trajectories in the Bible.

The very act of interpreting the Bible in other ways develops social and interpretative resilience among the poor and marginalised. Social resilience resides in the recognition that individuals are not to blame for the social ills that confront them, enabling them to resist the systems that underlie the social ills. Interpretative resilience resides in the capacity CBS offers to the poor and marginalised to re-read the Bible for themselves, enabling them to resist dominant interpretations. CBS builds capacity for faith-based resilience.

Psycho-social resilience has been recognised as a substantive resource in trauma theory. The work of the Ujamaa Centre indicates that building the capacity of marginalised sectors to interpret the Bible from and for their own experience, recognising that there are contending biblical theological trajectories or voices, nurtures the 'interpretative resilience' of those struggling to live abundant lives in the context of gender violence (and other forms of oppression) in a context like South Africa.

---

[27] Takatso Mofokeng, "Black Christians, the Bible and Liberation," *Journal of Black Theology* 2(1988): 40.

[28] Gunther H. Wittenberg, *Resistance Theology in the Old Testament: Collected Essays* (Pietermaritzburg: Cluster Publications, 2007), 61-79.

[29] Gerald O. West and Sithembiso Zwane, ""Why Are You Sitting There?" Reading Matthew 20:1-16 in the Context of Casual Workers in Pietermaritzburg, South Africa," in *Matthew: Texts@Contexts*, ed. Nicole Duran Wilkinson and James Grimshaw (Minneapolis: Fortress Press, 2013).

[30] Gerald O. West, "The Poetry of Job as a Resource for the Articulation of Embodied Lament in the Context of Hiv and Aids in South Africa," in *Lamentations in Ancient and Contemporary Cultural Contexts*, ed. Nancy C. Lee and Carleen Mandolfo (Atlanta: Society of Biblical Literature, 2008).

Conclusion

CBS is a resource for recognising and reading the neglected dimensions of the Bible, those that focus on the structural and systemic dimensions of life. While social activists and development agencies are adept at analysing society in structural and systemic terms, they tend to revert to a default one-sided and individualistic understanding of the Bible. CBS confronts those who would do development among the 'faith-ful' to analyse faith more fully, and in particular to understand the Bible as a complex and contested text.

But CBS is not simply another tool for development practitioners to wield in their work. CBS requires the presence of the poor and marginalised to activate and authenticate it. Their bodies are integral to the process of social transformation, and this includes their embodied faith. Tamar tells her story of gender violence in 2 Samuel 13:1-22. CBS offers a safe and sacred framework for millions of contemporary Tamars to tell their stories and to work together for social transformation. Others, including development practitioners, are welcome to participate, but only if they are willing to reconsider their one-sided and individualistic notions of religion.

Bibliography

Cochrane, James R. *Circles of Dignity: Community Wisdom and Theological Reflection*. Minneapolis: Fortress, 1999.

Cochrane, James R. 'Questioning Contextual Theology.' In *Towards an Agenda for Contextual Theology: Essays in Honour of Albert Nolan*, edited by McGlory T. Speckman and Larry T. Kaufmann, 67-86. Pietermaritzburg: Cluster Publications, 2001.

de Gruchy, Steve. 'Of Agency, Assets and Appreciation: Seeking Some Commonalities between Theology and Development.' In *Keeping Body and Soul Together: Reflections by Steve De Gruchy on Theology and Development*, edited by Beverley G. Haddad, 66-86. Pietermaritzburg: Cluster Publications, 2015.

Denis, Philippe. 'Storytelling and Healing.' In *A Journey Towards Healing: Stories of People with Multiple Woundedness in Kwazulu-Natal*, edited by Philippe Denis, Scott Houser and Radikobo Ntsimane, 5-17. Pietermaritzburg: Cluster Publications, 2011.

Donaldson, Stephen. *The Last Dark*. London: Gollancz, 2013.

Frostin, Per. *Liberation Theology in Tanzania and South Africa: A First World Interpretation*. Lund: Lund University Press, 1988.

Gottwald, Norman K. *The Hebrew Bible: A Socio-Literary Introduction*. Philadelphia: Fortress, 1985.

Haddad, Beverley G. 'The Manyano Movement in South Africa: Site of Struggle, Survival, and Resistance.' *Agenda* 61 (2004): 4-13.

Holloway, John. 'Dignity's Revolt.' In *Zapatista! Reinventing Revolution in Mexico*, edited by John Holloway and Elíona Peláez, 159-98. London: Pluto, 1998.

Hope, Anne, and Sally Timmel. *Training for Transformation: A Handbook for Community Workers*. 4 vols. Vol. Book 1. Gweru: Mambo Press, 1984.

Mofokeng, Takatso. 'Black Christians, the Bible and Liberation.' *Journal of Black Theology* 2 (1988): 34-42.

Mosala, Itumeleng J. *Biblical Hermeneutics and Black Theology in South Africa*. Grand Rapids: Eerdmans, 1989.

Nolan, Albert. *God in South Africa: The Challenge of the Gospel*. Cape Town: David Philip, 1988.

Palombo, Matthew C. 'Interfaith Praxis in South African Struggle for Liberation: Toward a Liberatio-Political Framework for Muslim-Christian Relations.' University of Johannesburg, 2014.

Scott, James C. *Domination and the Arts of Resistance: Hidden Transcripts*. New Haven and London: Yale University Press, 1990.

Spivak, Gayatri C. 'Can the Subaltern Speak?' In *Marxism and the Interpretation of Culture*, edited by Gary Nelson and L. Grossberg, 271-313. London: Macmillan, 1988.

Trible, Phyllis. *Texts of Terror: Literary-Feminist Readings of Biblical Narratives*. Philadelphia: Fortress, 1984.

West, Gerald O. *Biblical Hermeneutics of Liberation: Modes of Reading the Bible in the South African Context*. Second Edition ed. Maryknoll and Pietermaritzburg: Orbis Books and Cluster Publications, 1995.

West, Gerald O. *Contextual Bible Study*. Pietermaritzburg: Cluster Publications, 1993.

West, Gerald O. 'Newsprint Theology: Bible in the Context of HIV and AIDS.' In *Out of Place: Doing Theology on the Cross-cultural Brink*, edited by Jione Havea and Clive Pearson, 161-86. London: Equinox Publishing, 2011.

West, Gerald O. 'The Poetry of Job as a Resource for the Articulation of Embodied Lament in the Context of HIV and AIDS in South Africa.' In *Lamentations in Ancient and Contemporary Cultural Contexts*, edited by Nancy C. Lee and Carleen Mandolfo, 195-214. Atlanta: Society of Biblical Literature, 2008.

West, Gerald O., and Phumzile Zondi-Mabizela. 'The Bible Story That Became a Campaign: The Tamar Campaign in South Africa (and Beyond).' *Ministerial Formation* 103 (2004): 4-12.

West, Gerald O., and Sithembiso Zwane. ''Why Are You Sitting There?' Reading Matthew 20:1-16 in the Context of Casual Workers in Pietermaritzburg, South Africa.' In *Matthew: Texts@Contexts*, edited by Nicole Duran Wilkinson and James Grimshaw, 175-88. Minneapolis: Fortress Press, 2013.

Wittenberg, Gunther H. *Resistance Theology in the Old Testament: Collected Essays*. Pietermaritzburg: Cluster Publications, 2007.

(155A) ROLE AND RELEVANCE OF THEOLOGY FOR THE FUTURE OF AFRICAN CHRISTIANITY

James Kombo

Background to Study

The Pew Research Center has just released the first-ever formal demographic projections using data on age, fertility, mortality, migration and religious switching for multiple religious groups around the world. Both the data and the results released totally change the texture of theology as we face the 2050 mark. Although the Pew Research Center makes seven conclusions, four are particularly significant for this present study:

1. **Islam is the fastest-growing major religion. The determinants for this trend are the** highest fertility rate and the youngest population. On account of this, the Muslim population is expected to increase from 1.6 billion people (23% of the world's population as of 2010) to 2.76 billion people (30% of all people in 2050). By 2050, Muslims will nearly equal Christians, and the two are expected to be roughly equal in numbers by 2070.
2. The world's Christian population is expected to remain steady (at about 31%), but the regional distribution of Christians is forecast to change significantly. **Nearly four in ten Christians (38%) are projected to live in sub-Saharan Africa in 2050**, this being an increase from the 24% who lived there in 2010. Note also that the number of the world's Christians living in Europe has fallen from 66% in 1910 to 26% in 2010. The indications are that there will be a further decline to about 16% in 2050.
3. The number of religiously unaffiliated people is increasing in the United States and Europe, and the growth is projected to continue. Conversely however, the overall percentage of the **unaffiliated is expected** to ***decrease*** **between 2010 and 2050 (from 16% to 13%).** This overall drop is attributed to the relatively old age and low fertility rates of large populations of religious 'nones'(those religiously unaffiliated) in China and Japan.
4. **Christians will decline from more than three-quarters of the population in 2010 in the USA to two-thirds in 2050**. The determinants of this are relative rise in religious 'nones', Muslims, Hindus and others.[1]

Previously, scholars of African Christianity have observed that the African Church has in the last few years been growing exponentially at a time when the church in the northern continents is visibly shrinking.[2]

---

[1] Pew Research Center, The Future of World Religions: Population Growth Projections, 2010-2050, 2 April 2015. www.pewforum.org/2015/04/02/religious-projections-2010-2050/#projected-growth-map downloaded on 3 April, 2015.

[2] Scholarship on World/Global Christianity is generally agreed on this trend. Some of the kingpins of this persuasion include Philip Jenkins (*The Next Christendom: The Rise of Global Christianity*, New York: Oxford University Press, 2002; *The New Faces of Christianity: Believing the Bible in the Global South*, New York: Oxford University Press, 2006), Lamin Sanneh (*Whose Religion is Christianity?: The Gospel Beyond the West*, Grand Rapids: Eerdmans, 2003; *The Changing Face of Christianity: Africa, the West, and the World* (co-edited with Joel A. Carpenter). Oxford: Oxford University Press, 2005; *Translating the Message: The Missionary Impact on Culture*. Maryknoll, New York: Orbis Books, 1989) Andrew Walls (*The Missionary Movement in Christian History*. Maryknoll, New York: Orbis Books, 1996; *The Cross-Cultural Process in Christian History: Studies in the Transmission and Appropriation of Faith*. Maryknoll, New York: Orbis Books, 2002), Kwame Bediako (*Jesus and the Gospel in Africa: History and Experience*, Maryknoll, NY: Orbis Books, 2004; *Theology and Identity: The Impact of Culture upon Christian Thought*

Further predictions have indicated that 'Africa has become, or is becoming, a Christian continent in cultural as well as numerical terms, while on the small scale the West has become, or is rapidly becoming, a post-Christian society'.[3] Philip Jenkins repeats the same sentiment although with a different accent as follows: 'All too often, statements about what "modern Christians accept" or what "Catholics today believe" refer only to what that ever-shrinking remnant of western Christians and Catholics believe. Such assertions are outrageous today, and as time goes by they will become ever further removed from reality.'[4]

It is now on record that the total sub-Saharan African population will grow at a faster pace than in any other region in the next forty years, and that this population is expected double from 823 million in 2010 to 1.9 billion in 2050. This population growth will catapult both Christianity and Islam to the point that both faiths will have doubled their adherents in 2050. Christianity will continue to be sub-Saharan Africa's largest religious group, thanks to fertility, age structure, religious switching, as well as migration, growing from 517 million in 2010 to more than 1.1 billion in 2050, but there follow three important considerations: 1) The Muslim population will in this period grow faster than the Christian population (170% vs. 115%), rising from 248 million to 670 million; 2) the African Traditional Religions and the religiously unaffiliated will in the intervening period, rather than diminishing, record modest growth; and 3) **nearly four in ten Christians (38%) are projected to live in sub-Saharan Africa in 2050**, this being an increase from the 24% who lived there in 2010, thus confirming Africa as the undisputed centre of gravity for the Christian faith.

Theology Responding to African Christianity

With these demographics, one expects to see a fairly robust and agenda-setting theology in response both to the data and the identity of Christianity. Perhaps we could borrow from the experience of Christianity in its formative years in the second and third centuries. At that time, three things dominated the early church's theological agenda: i) there was remarkable focus on articulation, teaching and promulgation of orthodoxy and standards of faith; ii) then there was greater emphasis on the institution of church leadership with particular emphasis on definition of the office of bishop as the primary protector and defender of the faith; and then iii) there was heightened focus on the necessity of centres for academic theology. Theology for Africa, in my opinion, should present the burgeoning African Christianity with these dynamics for its own Christianization in the next four decades.

Theology for Africa must seek to inspire greater appreciation for doctrinal grounding, catechesis and worship

Note that sub-Saharan Christianity is largely touted as 'a thousand miles wide and one inch deep',[5] and now an even more complex situation arises: the reality of the ever-increasing Muslim population in the same region, on the one hand, and the rise in the population of adherents of African Traditional Religions and the religiously unaffiliated, on the other. In this situation, one sees the major theological task of the

---

in the Second Century and in Modern Africa (Oxford, Oxford UK: Regnum, 1999 [1992]) and David Barrett (*World Christian Encyclopedia: A Comparative Survey of Churches and Religions in the Modern World Volume I: The World by Countries: Religionists, Churches, Ministries.*

[3] Lamin Sanneh, *Whose Religion is Christianity? The Gospel Beyond the West.* Eerdmans Publishing, Grand Rapids, MI, 2003: 36.

[4] Philip Jenkins, *The Next Christendom. The Coming of Global Christianity.* Oxford University Press, Oxford, 2002:3.

[5] Those who think this way have not merely focused on the negative energies of the African Christianity. Generally the observation is that this is a blossoming Christianity that is weak in doctrinal grounding and devoid of discipleship. Some of the negative trends which have become part of African Christianity include the "Man of God" syndrome, "Cash for Christ" phenomenon, bossy and bully leadership, and to some degree, a *crossless Christianity* that preaches a *crossless Christ.*

church as formulating and teaching Christian doctrine in a manner which offers opportunity for deep, reflective, consistent and relevant interaction with both the African as currently presented, on the one hand, and in a manner that is consistent with the roots of Christianity in the early church, on the other. In this task, one sees focus on orthodoxy as a priority – recognition of false ideas, controversies, and internal inconsistencies. The need for strong pillars of orthodoxy is important primarily because of malignant controversies and internal inconsistencies within the African Church; and then in a secondary sense the need to challenge Africa's present reality which manifests increasing interest in Islam as well growing numbers among the African Traditional Religions and the religiously unaffiliated. This follows a lesson from the first Egyptian churches: although these churches successfully spread the good news in the Coptic language and planted robust churches throughout the interior of Egypt, the church in the region was tremendously weakened and reached near collapse, not on account of the onslaught of Islam or the growing interest in folk religions but by the emergence of false teachings and crippling internal theological controversies right from within itself.

One direction of holding this conversation is pinning it on the practical axis of advocacy for *catechesis*, on the one hand, and reconsideration for winning anew the largely ignored historical *creeds* of the church on the other. This strategy creates a culture and an environment in which the church is doing its catechesis around essential theological ideas and therefore becoming theologically astute while it at same time points the sub-Saharan African Church to its roots among the church fathers in the early church. In other words, the strategy is a demand on the church's commitment to methodological instructions in sound teaching that addresses both the historical and contemporary scandals of the church and society.

Note that *catechesis* and the *creeds* can very easily and inadvertently be an afterthought, particularly among African Pentecostals and charismatics, and even a blind spot, if the agenda is not raised high in the African Christian consciousness. However, at this time in the history of African Christianity, we must embrace the place of *catechesis* and win anew the early church's *creeds* as theological strategies for establishing the identity of the sub-Saharan African Church, and linking it with the early church, deepening the Christian faith among the converts, stimulating the mind with Christian content and satisfying the heart with the meat that is the gospel. The essence of this is knowing God and, as John Calvin wrote, 'To know God is to be changed by God; true knowledge of God leads to worship.'

If the *catechesis* and the *creeds* are about knowing God, and therefore about his worship, then one would as well conclude that by theology focusing the African Church along the paths of *catechesis* and the *creeds*, it is in fact stating the future of the African Church as essentially worship. The best example of what happens when proper worship is pushed to the periphery is well captured in Kuzimierz Bem's article 'Christianity Cannot Survive the Decline in Worship':

> Around the year 1510, a delegation of Christians from Sudan, which had been recently overrun by Muslim conquest, went to the Christian Ethiopian court and begged the emperor to send them bishops and priests. The Christians remaining in Sudan needed clergy to lead worship, administer the sacraments, and teach the people. But the emperor refused, sending them away empty-handed. With no Christian worship, within 100 years Christianity in Sudan became extinct and forgotten until the twentieth century.[6]

Theology for Africa then must guide the African Church towards a balance between *logos* and *praxis*, doctrine and devotion, word and spirit. There must not be a *theologia dogmatica* within the African context that is separated from *theologia vitae spiritualis*. Theology in this context must then indicate that the interest is not merely assenting to *creeds* and opening up to the possibility for *catechesis*, but more importantly, an engagement with the word that leads to experience with the infinite – a personal encounter

---

[6] Kuzimierz Bem, 'Christianity Cannot Survive the Decline in Worship', www.faithstreet.com/onfaith/2015/01/23/christianity-cannot-survive-the-decline-in-worship/35932. Downloaded on 2 May, 2015.

with God's word and a zeal for the glory of God. This engagement must be 'robust, faithful, engaging' but at the same time its focus 'must be the God revealed to us in Jesus Christ, God's free, abundant, deep grace and love shown for us on the cross.'[7]

Theology for Africa should prioritize the formation of leadership for itself, the wider African society and the African migrant communities of the diaspora

Leadership of the church injects completely new dynamics – nobody has prepared African church leaders for the dynamics raised by the findings of the Pew Research Center. Indeed, since Ali Mazrui's idea of Africa's triple heritage, there has not been a real follow-up on the status and actual proportions of the population of Africa's faiths (Christianity, Islam and African Traditional Religions) going forward. How is the African Church to respond to the need for reliable leaders for contemporary Africa, let alone forming dependable church leaders that will match the reality of contemporary sub-Saharan Africa church? It appears that the African Church has yet to respond to this question. As a matter of fact, the African Church is still unaware of these trends and is promoting a leadership that is a replica of what is available in the larger African society in which 'the high ideals of democracy, of an independent judiciary and economic growth gave way to autocratic rule, either in one party states or military dictatorships, where repression, injustice, human rights abuses, mal-administration, misappropriation of public funds and other resources, as well as corruption became the order of the day'.[8] Kretzschmar and Heifitz particularly speaking both to the African Church and the society write:

> Among the growing calls for the 21st century to be the African century, all Africans, including African Christians, need to pay serious attention to one of the vital components that will effect genuine transformation, namely, that of authentic leadership. Given the situation in Africa today, plagued as many countries are with leadership problems in government, business, churches, and civil society as a whole, there can be little doubt in our minds of the vital importance of the issue of leadership for our continent.[9]

There is every justification therefore for theology to focus for the start on leadership – a leadership that is 'expected to live by example, be socially and environmentally responsible, be ethical and moral, have a certain degree of humbleness, aim to serve and inspire others, promote leadership based on respect and love, not fear'.[10] Theology for Africa takes this position because we are well instructed by Linthicum that: 'Without leadership development, everything you have done will pass away. But with it, the future is constantly being created anew for the people of your community.'[11] The reality of African Christianity is that it desperately needs a critical manpower who will not only be capable of creating the future for the African Church and society, but a leadership that will steer the church in a generation where the demographics of religion will increasingly be driven by fertility, age structure, religious switching and migration.

---

[7] Kuzimierz Bem, 'Christianity Cannot Survive the Decline in Worship.'

[8] PGJ Meiring, "Leadership for reconciliation: A Truth and Reconciliation Commission perspective." Downloaded on 16 Feb, 2015 in www.ve.org.za/index.php/VE/article/viewFile/1235/1677.

[9] Kretzschmar, L 2002: "Authentic Christian leadership and spiritual formation in Africa", *Journal of Theology for Southern Africa* 113 (July 2002): 41ff. See also Heifitz, R A 1999. *Leadership without easy answers*. London: Harvard University Press, 51ff.

[10] Mwambazambi, K. & Banza, A.K., 2014, 'Developing transformational leadership for sub-Saharan Africa: Essential missiological considerations for church workers', Verbum et Ecclesia 35(1), Art. #849, 9 pages. http://dx.doi.org/10.4102/ ve.v35i1.849, 6.

[11] Linthicum, R.C., 1991, *Empowering the poor: Community organizing among the city's 'Rag, tag and bobtail*, Marc, Monrovia, 93.

PACLA II,[12] a follow-up to PACLA I and convened in Nairobi, agonized with the idea of church leadership and networking with specific interest on the theme 'Developing Godly Leaders for Africa'. The question raised by PACLA II was how Africa in its multifaceted crises was to focus on the task of building networks and developing godly leaders capable of dealing with its questions in every sphere of life. Among the issues identified and raised at PACLA II for in-depth consideration were leadership emergence, selection, development and succession. Note that this agenda has not included the present reality of sub-Saharan Africa in relation to Islam, the African Traditional Religions and the religiously unaffiliated. At the theological and ministerial formation level, I do not see significant activity towards the achievement of the PACLA II ideals. Consequently, the PACLA II agenda risks stagnation; meanwhile, significant time will be lost as theology struggles to grapple with the implications of the Pew Research Center's conclusions for the leadership of the church in sub-Saharan Africa.

What PACLA II envisioned for the church appears to have been the concern of Irenaeus. He, however, held the conversation within the confines of what he saw as the job description of the Bishop – leader *par excellence*. For him, the bishop represented a leadership that ably addressed the orthodoxy-heresy onslaught. The holder of this office did not only exhibit the much-needed traits of transformational leadership[13] in respect to defining orthodoxy that resonated both with the church's own life and experience as well as with its future, but he also modelled Spirit-led worship, administered the sacraments, and taught his congregations.[14] The clearest articulation of Irenaeus' idea of a church leader is captured in his *Adversus Haereses* 3.3.3:

> When the blessed apostles had founded and built up the Church, they handed over the ministry of the episcopate to Linus. Paul mentions this Linus in his Epistle to Timothy. Ancletus succeeded him. After him Clement received the lot of the episcopate in the third place from the apostles. He had seen the apostles and associated with them, and still had their preaching sounding in his ears and their tradition before his eyes – and not he alone, for there were many still left in his time who had been taught by the apostles. In this Clement's time no small discord arose among the brethren in Corinth, and the Church in Rome sent a very powerful letter to the Corinthians, leading them to peace, renewing their faith and declaring the tradition which they had recently received from the apostles… To this Clement there succeeded Evaristus. Alexander followed Evaristus; then, sixth from the apostles, Sixtus was appointed; after him, Telephorus, who was gloriously martyred; then Hyginus; after him, Pius; then after him, Anicetus. Soter having succeeded Anicetus, Eleutherius does now, in the twelfth place from the apostles, hold the inheritance of the episcopate. In this order, and by this succession, the ecclesiastical tradition from the apostles, and the preaching of the truth, have come down to us. And this is

[12] To understand Pan African Christian Leadership Assembly (PACLA), one has to go back to the 1974 International Congress on World Evangelization held in Lausanne, Switzerland. At the meeting, 45 Christian leaders from Africa broke into a group that discussed the possibility of a Pan African meeting of church leaders to discuss the challenges of the burgeoning Christian community on the continent. This group nominated Bishop Festo Kivengere of Uganda and Michael Cassidy of Africa Evangelistic Enterprise to explore what could be done. In February 1975, the Kenyan leaders put together an informal meeting to begin thinking through the concept. This *ad hoc* committee chaired by Osei-Mensah invited representatives from the rest of Africa to larger meeting in Nairobi. After about a year of planning, PACLA I was held in Nairobi Kenya, December 9-19, 1976. For an in-depth analysis of PACLA, refer to www2.wheaton.edu/bgc/archives/GUIDES/172.htm.

[13] Mwambazambi, K. & Banza, A.K., 2014, 2-5.

[14] Mwambazambi and Banza argue that "spirituality is an important aspect of leadership which also determines whether someone's leadership is good or bad." Spirituality in this case as explained by Mihai (2009:1) "is more about how people identify themselves, how they view the world, interact with others, and make decisions." (Mihai, J., 2009, 'Spirituality and leadership: Would an organization benefit from spiritual leaders?', Spirituality in Higher Education Newsletter 1(4), 1–2).

> most abundant proof that there is one and the same vivifying faith, which has been preserved in the Church from the apostles until now, and handed down in truth.[15]

The new leadership of the African Church, like the succession of bishops in Irenaeus' mind, must direct itself and its audience towards a new and a different identity away from borrowed convictions, rootless beliefs and mere religiosity well informed by current demographics. Lewis Sperry Chafer, the founder of Dallas Theological Seminary, once said: 'Men, give them something to believe.' This is the yearning of the African Church – it is looking for something to believe, a different thing, the truth that it has ownership in. The worshipers are waiting for guidance, they must be pointed away from mere pietistic and charismatic forms of Christianity which neglects wisdom, discernment and holiness and knows far less about the Bible and the faith than one would hope. Theology therefore must show direction in forming leadership that will guide the African Church and its diaspora down this already beaten path.

Spaces for theological and ministerial formation have decreased significantly in recent decades

One would have expected that with the understood phenomenal growth of Christianity in Africa within the last few decades, there would be a corresponding expansion of theological and ministerial formation and specialization in areas of theological interest. At least, this is the pattern we see in the patristic period of the early church. During this period, the church responded to the needs of the church by opening up Alexandria which specialized in Greek philosophy and produced Clement, Origen, Didymus; then there was Antioch which emphasized the moral example and humanity of Christ as well as interpretation of Scripture in the light of the historical context, and producing such theologians as Diodore of Tarsus, John Chrysostom, the Cappadocian Fathers, and then the Western North Africa which in fact was the centre for Latin theology, and was more practical than their philosophically-minded Greek counterparts. Some of the well-known products of this school include Cyprian, Tertullian and Augustine.

This, however, is not the case here. The past two decades, 1990s and 2000s, were phenomenal for the rise of Christian university in the majority of Africa. During this period, practically all the renowned degree-granting theological colleges and seminaries in East Africa, for instance, transformed themselves into private Christian universities. The table below shows ten institutions in this category:

Theological College/Seminary	University and year of change of status
1. Scott Theological College	Scott Christian University (1997)
2. Pan Africa Christian College	Pan Africa Christian University (2008)
3. Nairobi Evangelical Graduate School of Theology	Africa International University (2010)
4. Nairobi International School of Theology	Africa Leadership University (2010)
5. Kenya Highlands Bible College	Kenya Highlands Evangelical University (2011)
6. Bishop Tucker Theological College	Uganda Christian University (1997)
7. Lutheran Theological College Makumira	Tumaini University (1996)
8. St Paul's Theological College	St Paul's University (2007)
9. Kaaga Rural Training Centre and Methodist Training Institute consecutively	Kenya Methodist University (2006)
10. Graduate School of Theology, under the name, Catholic Higher Institute of Eastern Africa (CHIEA).	Catholic University of East Africa (1992)

[15] Irenaeus, *Against Heresies*, Book 3, Chapter 3 Verse 3. Translated by Alexander Roberts and William Rambaut. From *Ante-Nicene Fathers*, Vol. 1. Edited by Alexander Roberts, James Donaldson, and A. Cleveland Coxe. (Buffalo, NY: Christian Literature Publishing Co., 1885.) Revised and edited for New Advent by Kevin Knight.

Note the following features: a) the institutions listed constitute what used to be East Africa's premier theological and ministerial schools from the 1960s-1990s then dedicated only to theological training and ministerial formation; b) all the listed institutions have since transformed into multi-faculty private Christian universities; c) the institutions continue to receive financial and material support from founding missions although the bulk of their support is locally generated from tuition fee collection; d) for all practical purposes, theology in all the new universities is no longer the institutions' flagship programme and therefore does not occupy a privileged position, other programmes have taken over; e) the phenomenon which indicates that theology is no longer a flagship programme and that it is steadily diminishing in prominence in the institutions is true for the protestant universities as it is for the Anglicans, the Catholics and the evangelicals; f) Kenya seems to be more affected than its neighbours; for instance, out of the ten institutions listed, eight are Kenyan.

The shift of domicile of theology from the theological college to the university is in my opinion a boon to the discipline. For the first time, theology in Africa can be said to have attained independence from the prying eyes of the missions abroad. Here, then, is another unnoticed but major shift: now theology has local initiatives as its major support base. The other important gain is what Dietrich Warner sees as the strategic role and accountability of theology to the society.[16] With this role highlighted, theology does not only ascend to its own platform but its position attains higher levels of recognition and transparency – that theology programmes in the universities are themselves accredited by the national regulatory bodies is itself a statement of endorsement by society; and now theology is respected as a significant contributor to the national grid and as an academic discipline in its own right. This has happened because it is understood that the environment in the university encourages quality assurance, inspires research and emboldens engagement with new knowledge. But there is a warning. The presence of theology in universities means that there has to be some engagement on how or in what form theology is to exist in universities. First, there is the increasing pressure of Islam and other religions to be balanced against the missionary agenda of theology; and then there is increasing secularization of the universities as environments for ideological discourses. These questions are being raised in the context of Europe where theology has always been in the universities; we too must raise them in the context of Africa.

Five conclusions, however, can be made from this shift: 1) that the African academy is experiencing a positive change of attitude towards theology and a clear break with the past thus admission of theology into its ranks. 2) It appears that this positive disposition to theology now means that the discipline is no longer functioning in a protected environment and therefore has to compete with other disciplines on the same footing. 3) For the first time, theology is really becoming independent from mission headquarters abroad and is adjusting to the dynamics of new and local forms of support. 4) Part of this adjustment has manifested in marked recession of academic theology in comparison to its global performance in previous years. 5) With time, and as the fledging universities solidify denominations, universities are increasingly doing in-house theological training. This approach means a complete remodelling of theology: less emphasis on academic rigour and a greater interest in enabling the faithful to understand the faith more fully and to equip them more diligently for witness to their faith in Christ.

Concluding Remarks: What Does the Church Do with the New Demographics?

This paper highlights three main things it sees as the areas the church in sub-Saharan Africa must pay attention to in the next few decades: 1) Greater appreciation for orthodoxy, catechesis, and worship; 2) prioritization of leadership formation; and 3) creating spaces for theological and ministerial formation.

[16] Dietrich Werner, "The future of theology in the changing landscapes of universities in Europe and beyond." www.globethics.net/web/the-future-of-theology-in-europe/mission.

Whereas this agenda is buoyed by a similar position taken by the patristic church, the recently released research conclusions by the Pew Research Center offer a particularly compelling justification. Its research indicates unprecedented growth rate of the Muslim population in sub-Saharan Africa by 2050; confirms that, in the intervening period, nearly four in ten Christians (38%) are projected to live in sub-Saharan Africa in 2050; then it reveals that African Traditional Religions are likely to experience some nominal growth in the next four decades. Although, on the whole, the African Christian situation appears optimistic, the global picture is rather pessimistic. The Pew Report indicates that 'people are leaving Christianity in droves. About 106 million Christians are expected to switch affiliation from 2010 to 2050 while only about 40 million people are expected to enter Christianity'.[17] This is the state of things for the church in sub-Saharan Africa. Theology must do something about this state of things. Perhaps in thinking through new trends, it may be important to listen to the counsel of the General Secretary of WCC, Dr Olave Fykse Tveit. For him:

> Theology is an imperative for ecumenism. And ecumenism is an imperative for doing theology today. Theological reflection today requires attitudes, a culture and structures of mutual accountability of theology within the wider ecumenical context. We all need to be challenged by others. And we also need to be able to challenge others in an accountable way. Ecumenical sensitivity and competence in theology and theological education widen the horizons of denominational theology. Proper Christian theology relates to, reflects and nurtures the mission of the church to serve the one humanity and the one creation, building a culture of a just peace day by day. Denominational identity and reference do not have to be contrary to ecumenical theology and theological education, but there is no future for any denominational identity or theology without solid ecumenical accountability and global responsibility.[18]

Bibliography

Barrett, David. *World Christian Encyclopedia: A Comparative Survey of Churches and Religions in the Modern World Volume I: The World by Countries: Religionists, Churches, Ministries*.

Bediako, Bediako. *Jesus and the Gospel in Africa: History and Experience*, Maryknoll, NY: Orbis Books, 2004.

______. *Theology and Identity: The Impact of Culture upon Christian Thought in the Second Century and in Modern Africa.* Oxford, Oxford UK: Regnum, 1999.

Bem, Kuzimierz. 'Christianity Cannot Survive the Decline in Worship', www.faithstreet.com/onfaith/2015/01/23/christianity-cannot-survive-the-decline-in-worship/35932. Downloaded on 2 May, 2015.

Heifitz, R A. *Leadership without easy answers*. London: Harvard University Press, 1999.

Irenaeus, *Against Heresies*, Book 3, Chapter 3 Verse 3. Translated by Alexander Roberts and William Rambaut. From *Ante-Nicene Fathers*, Vol. 1. Edited by Alexander Roberts, James Donaldson, and A. Cleveland Coxe. (Buffalo, NY: Christian Literature Publishing Co., 1885.) Revised and edited for New Advent by Kevin Knight.

Jenkins, Philip. *The Next Christendom: The Rise of Global Christianity*. New York: Oxford University Press, 2002.

______. *The New Faces of Christianity: Believing the Bible in the Global South*, New York: Oxford University Press, 2006.

---

[17] Pew Research Center, The Future of World Religions.

[18] Olave Fykse Tveit, "The future of theology in the changing landscapes of universities in Europe and beyond", Oslo Consultation, 6 June 2012. https://www.oikoumene.org/en/resources/documents/general-secretary/speeches/keynote-address-on-theology-and-unity-in-oslo-consultation.

______. *The Changing Face of Christianity: Africa, the West, and the World* (co-edited with Joel A. Carpenter). Oxford: Oxford University Press, 2005.

Kretzschmar, L. 'Authentic Christian leadership and spiritual formation in Africa', *Journal of Theology for Southern Africa* 113 (July 2002)

Linthicum, R.C., *Empowering the poor: Community organizing among the city's 'Rag, tag and bobtail,* Marc, Monrovia, 1991.

Meiring, PGJ. 'Leadership for reconciliation: A Truth and Reconciliation Commission perspective.' Downloaded on 16 Feb, 2015 in www.ve.org.za/index.php/VE/article/viewFile/1235/1677.

Mwambazambi, K. & Banza, A.K., 2014, 'Developing transformational leadership for sub-Saharan Africa: Essential missiological considerations for church workers', *Verbum et Ecclesia* 35(1), Art. #849, 9 pages.

PACLA. www2.wheaton.edu/bgc/archives/GUIDES/172.htm.

Pew Research Center, The Future of World Religions.

Pew Research Center, The Future of World Religions: Population Growth Projections, 2010-2050, 2.4.15 www.pewforum.org/2015/04/02/religious-projections-2010-2050/#projected-growth-map accessed on 3 April 2015.

Sanneh, Lamin. *Whose Religion is Christianity? The Gospel Beyond the West.* Grand Rapids: Eerdmans, 2003

______. *The Cross-Cultural Process in Christian History: Studies in the Transmission and Appropriation of Faith*. Maryknoll, New York: Orbis Books, 2002.

______. *Translating the Message: The Missionary Impact on Culture*. Maryknoll, New York: Orbis Books, 1989.

Tveit, Olave Fykse. 'The future of theology in the changing landscapes of universities in Europe and beyond', Oslo Consultation, 6 June 2012. https://www.oikoumene.org/en/resources/documents/general-secretary/speeches/keynote-address-on-theology-and-unity-in-oslo-consultation

Walls, Andrew. *The Missionary Movement in Christian History*. Maryknoll, New York: Orbis Books, 1996.

Warner, Dietrich. 'The future of theology in the changing landscapes of universities in Europe and beyond.' www.globethics.net/web/the-future-of-theology-in-europe/mission.

(155B) ROLE AND RELEVANCE OF THEOLOGY FOR THE FUTURE OF AFRICAN CHRISTIANITY: A SOUTH AFRICAN RESPONSE

Ian Nell

Introduction

It is a privilege to react to the insightful contribution of James Kombo on the role and relevance of theology for the future of African Christianity. I want to structure my own contribution in the following way: I will be making use of Kombo's three basic statements on the role of theology in Africa, but I want to reframe his arguments by making use of a theo-dramatic approach. By making use of this approach I hope to illustrate some of my own convictions concerning the future of theology from a South African perspective.

Kombo links the three components that he uses as framework for his article in an interesting way to the formative years of the church during the second and third centuries, of which a great deal took place on African soil. According to Kombo[1] there were three related aspects that dominated the early church's agenda and he translates them into three challenges for the decades to come and describes them as follows: a) theology for Africa should seek to inspire greater appreciation for doctrinal grounding, catechesis and worship, b) theology for Africa should prioritise formation of leadership for itself, the wider African society and the African migrant communities in the diaspora and c) spaces for theological and ministerial formation have decreased significantly over the last two decades.

Through my own reframing, I hope to pay respect to his contribution and want to reflect and think along with him concerning the challenges. The choice for a theo-dramatic framing relates to the following convictions: for dialogue and reflection on the role of theology, especially in the light of the historical relationship between North/West and South/East, we need 'bridging theories' that can link these worlds to each other. The so-called action turn and the innovative metaphor of drama as epistemological starting-point reinforce theo-drama as a 'bridge theory' that can stimulate meaningful discourse on the challenges that we face. By making use of three categories from the world of drama, namely, stage, plot and characters, I want to structure my reflection concerning the challenges for theology in South Africa.

Stage

I start with the stage and connect with Kombo's third point that relates to the meaning of creating spaces for theological and ministerial formation. De Gruchy and Chirongoma[2] worked in their contribution to *The Routledge Companion to the Christian Church*[3] with four images from Africa, helping us to understand the unique history of the 'South African stage'. The images are earth, water, fire and wind. Each of these elements points to an influence from the past that is still important for reflection on the role and relevance of theology in South Africa.

---

[1]James Kombo. "Role and Relevance of Theology for the Future of African Christianity," in *Anthology of African Christianity*, ed. Dietrich Warner and Isabel Phiri. (Dorpspruit: Cluster, 2015.) Forthcoming.

[2] Steve de Gruchy and Sophie Chirongoma. "Earth, Water, Fire and Wind: Elements of African Ecclesologies," in *The Routledge Companion to the Christian Church*, ed. Gerard Mannion and Lewis S. Mudge. (New York: Routledge, 2007, 291-305).

[3] Gerard Mannion and Lewis S. Mudge (Eds). *The Routledge Companion to the Christian Church* (New York: Routledge, 2007).

- *Earth* – points to the long history of the Christian faith on African soil as well as the role of traditional African religions.
- *Water* – relates to the western influences that missionaries and colonists brought with their ships to the shores of Africa.
- *Fire* – refers to the struggle of African believers to stay Christian and loyal to Africa amidst the dehumanisation in colonial attire they experienced.
- *Wind* – relates to the presence of the Spirit in Africa in the forms of Pentecostalism, revival movements and emerging forms of being church as a reaction to the *missio Dei* (mission of God) on this fascinating continent.

As a first extension of Kombo's third point, it is important for institutions that act as 'spaces for formation' to take seriously the unique contextual challenges posed by the four images or symbols. In this regard De Gruchy[4] refers in another publication to the fact that we cannot avoid thinking about and reflecting within a South African context on topics such as 'religious pluralism, climate change, globalization and poverty, war and violence, refugees and xenophobia, HIV and AIDS, TB, malaria and cholera, rape and domestic violence, and the like'.

In Kombo's[5] reference to spaces for formation, he discusses the specific situation in East Africa and shows in what ways well-known colleges and seminaries were transformed into private universities. In South Africa one finds another dynamic at work. Since the dawn of democracy in 1994 there are quite a number of faculties of theology that had close relations with specific denominations that were transformed into departments of religious studies and incorporated into faculties of humanities. At the moment there are only four faculties of theology left in South Africa, located at the Universities of Stellenbosch, Pretoria, Bloemfontein and Potchefstroom.

According to Dreyer,[6] a number of other spaces for theological formation developed during the past twenty years in South Africa. It relates, inter alia, to a number of changes that took place in higher education in the country. Today, one finds seventy-eight privately registered higher education institutions and another twenty-two that were granted provisional registration for accreditation. From this number there are twenty that provide programmes for theological studies.

To summarise, concerning spaces for theological formation, one finds them in public as well as private institutions and although there was a reduction in the number of public institutions, there was also a considerable increase in the development of private institutions for theological formation. However, there is still a serious shortage concerning these spaces for formation if one looks at the tremendous growth of the Charismatic churches as well as the African Initiated Churches. Hendriks and Erasmus[7] discuss the dramatic way in which these groups grew during the last decades and their growing future importance concerning the role and relevance of the Christian faith in South Africa. This fact also calls for serious reflection, as Werner[8] discussed in a recent document related to his work at the World Council of Churches.

---

[4] Steve de Gruchy. "Theological Education and Missional Practice: A Vital Dialogue," in *Handbook of Theological Education in World Christianity: Theological Perspectives, Ecumenical Trends and Regional Surveys*, ed. Dietrich Werner et al. (Oxford: Regnum Books International, 2010: 42–50).

[5]Kombo, "Role and Relevance", 8.

[6] Jaco Dreyer. "South Africa," in *The Wiley-Blackwell Companion to Practical Theology*. (Chichester: Blackwell, 2012:508-509).

[7] Jurgens J. Hendriks and Johannes C. Erasmus. "Religion in South Africa: The 2001 Population Census Data," *Journal of Theology for Southern Africa*121, no. 1 (2005): 88-111.

[8] Dietrich Werner. "Theological Education in the Changing Context of World Christianity: An Unfinished Agenda," *International Bulletin of Missionary Research* 35, no. 2(2011): 92-100.

Plot

Kombo[9] places considerable emphasis on the importance of the dogmatic grounding of theology with the emphasis on creeds and confessions. He discusses this point in the light of a number of challenges posed to the content of the Christian faith in Africa. According to Vanhoozer,[10] creeds and confession are the 'local performances' of the plot of the gospel. These local performances of the gospel are, according to Kombo,[11] under threat – relating it to the popular saying 'a thousand miles wide and one inch deep' as well as the ever-increasing Muslim population on the continent. As an answer to this he is convinced that 'one sees the major theological task of the church as formulating and teaching Christian doctrine in a manner which offers opportunity for deep, reflective, consistent and relevant interaction with both the African as presently presented on the one hand and in a manner that is consistent with the roots of Christianity in the early church on the other hand'.

With this proposal one cannot disagree, but what makes the situation in South Africa and maybe also in other parts of Africa quite complex, relates to the fact that theological formation also faces a number of other challenges linked to the plot of the gospel. In this regard I will only briefly refer to the following five challenges within the South African context:

- A first challenge is the so-called lack of integration of the theological curriculum because of specialisation and fragmentation. According to Conradie[12] this challenge is related to the fact that it has an impact on the product of theological formation in the sense that one often finds leaders that have excellent academic qualifications, but lack spiritual wisdom, maturity and ministry competence.
- The second challenge relates to the problematic role that government played since 1994 by expecting tertiary institutions to be accredited according to a certain set of standards if they want to provide theological qualifications to people interested in furthering their studies and career. According to Dunsmuir and McCoy[13] this also describes the problematic discourses on the way that theological education has to fit in with secular underpinnings of higher education.
- A third challenge speaks to the cultural domination of the West and specifically the Eurocentric hegemony when one reflects on the 'script' of the drama. Therefore, according to Higgs[14] we need a reconstruction of theology specifically for Africa in which African indigenous knowledge systems should find their rightful place.
- A fourth challenge relates to the expectations concerning gender roles in Africa. According to Trisk,[15] relevant theological education in South Africa should be engendered. This should be put into practice by mainstreaming gender studies and transforming the structures of theological institutions.

[9] Kombo, "Role and Relevance", 3.

[10] Kevin J. Vanhoozer. *The Drama of Doctrine: A Canonical-linguistic Approach to Christian Theology*(Westminster: John Knox Press, 2005).

[11] Kombo, "Role and Relevance", 3.

[12] Ernst Conradie. "Is the Re-integration of Theological Education Viable?," in *Contested Issues in Training Ministers in South Africa*, ed. Marilyn Naidoo (Stellenbosch: Sun Press, 2015: 13-26).

[13] Craig Dunsmuir and Michael McCoy. "Accreditation and Ministerial Formation: Serving Two Masters?," in Naidoo (ed), *Contested Issues,* 27-42.

[14] Phillip Higgs. "The African Renaissance and the Decolonisation of Theological Education," in Naidoo (ed), *Contested Issues,* 43-56.

[15] Janet Trisk. "Choosing the Better Part: Engendering Theological Education?." in Naidoo (ed), *Contested Issues,* 57-68.

- A last challenge can be linked to the difficult process of managing diversity in theological education. According to Naidoo,[16] a deeper question ought to be asked and that is whether South Africans will manage to 'unthink' older categories of citizenship and refine them. According to her, this is very important if we want to move further than race categories and political bondage.

These challenges belong to the agenda of reflection on the different components of the plot regarding the role and relevance of theology for the future of Africa. Such reflection could be further supported if we pay attention to some of the questions that Guder[17] poses in a more global setting concerning theological education. He asks:

> How does theological formation equip churches to engage critically the Christendom legacy which so profoundly shapes western Christianity? How does theological formation take seriously the broad consensus that the gathered community (or 'local congregation') is the primary agent of God's mission in the world? How will theological institutions equip congregations, through the ministry of their graduates to lead their lives 'worthy of the calling to which they have been called' (Eph. 4:1)? How does the witness of particular congregations testify to the global scope of God's love and the global calling of his gathered and sent people? How does the vital dialogue of theological education and missional practice contribute to the church's witness to its God-given unity, in all of its cultural and contextual diversity?

This brings one to the last component of a theo-dramatic approach concerning reflection on the role and relevance of theology from a South African perspective, and this relates to the role of the actors or characters in the drama.

Characters

The actors are of special importance concerning the performance of the theo-drama in local contexts. Kombo's[18] remark on the formation of leadership in this regard emphasises an important point: 'Leadership of this church injects completely new dynamics – nobody has prepared the African church leaders for the dynamics raised by the findings of Pew Research Center.' In this regard he asks some questions:

> How is the African church to respond to the need for reliable leaders for the contemporary Africa, leave alone forming dependable church leaders that will match the reality of the contemporary sub-Saharan Africa church? It appears that the African church is yet to respond to this question. As a matter of fact, the African church is still unaware of these trends and is promoting a leadership that is a replica of what is available in the larger African society in which the high ideals of democracy, of an independent judiciary and economic growth gave way to autocratic rule, either in one party states or military dictatorships, where repression, injustice, human rights abuses, mal-administration, misappropriation of public funds and other resources, as well as corruption became the order of the day.

Without going into the dynamics of the questions and remarks of Kombo, I find the three suggestions by De Gruchy and Ellis[19] for a new generation of leaders very meaningful to answer some of his questions.

---

[16] Marilyn Naidoo. "Dealing With the Other: Managing Diversity in Theological Education," in Naidoo (ed), *Contested Issues,* 69-84.

[17] Darrell Guder. "Theological Formation for Missional Faithfulness after Christendom: A Response to Steve de Gruchy," in *Handbook of Theological Education in World Christianity: Theological Perspectives, Ecumenical Trends and Regional Surveys*, ed. Dietrich Werner et al. (Oxford: Regnum Books International, 2010:51-55).

[18] Kombo, "Role and Relevance", 4.

[19] Steve de Gruchy and Willem Ellis. *Christian Leadership in 'Another Country': Contributing to an Ethical Development Agenda in South Africa Today* (Amsterdam: Rozenburg, 2008:9-20).

They are of the opinion that leaders should keep their eyes on three things to play their roles with conviction in a dramatically changing context: power, collaboration and a dialogical pedagogy.

Power, according to De Gruchy and Ellis,[20] relates to 'relationship differences in terms of key factors such as race, age, gender, nationality, language and professional status' and will have a direct influence on a next generation of leaders. To tackle these tough issues it will be necessary to collaborate. Therefore, it is important to counter the temptation of individualism and models of teamwork should be developed and collaborative endeavours be enhanced. To address the previous two aspects, a dialogical pedagogy is a prerequisite. This means, inter alia, that 'the teachers need to learn, and the learners need to teach'.[21] Wisdom and knowledge develop through conversations and dialogue where we are prepared to learn from one another. All three of these aspects speaks to Kombo's[22] call for the formation of leaders for the new challenges that were addressed above.

Conclusion

By making use of these three concepts of stage, plot and character within a theo-dramatic framework, I have tried to support and enhance the thoughts of Kombo. I believe that these aspects should also be on the agenda of concerned people reflecting on the role and relevance of the Christian faith in Africa in the 21st century.

Bibliography

Conradie, Ernst. 'Is the Re-integration of Theological Education Viable?' In *Contested Issues in Training Ministers in South Africa*, edited by Marilyn Naidoo, 13-26. Stellenbosch: Sun Press, 2015.

De Gruchy, Steve. 'Theological Education and Missional Practice: A Vital Dialogue.' In *Handbook of Theological Education in World Christianity: Theological Perspectives, Ecumenical Trends and Regional Surveys*, edited by Dietrich Werner, 42-50. Oxford: Regnum, 2010.

De Gruchy, Steve and Sophie Chirongoma. 'Earth, Water, Fire and Wind: Elements of African Ecclesologies.' In *The Routledge Companion to the Christian Church*, edited by Gerard Mannion and Lewis S. Mudge, 291-305. New York: Routledge, 2007.

De Gruchy, Steve and Willem Ellis. *Christian Leadership in 'Another Country': Contributing to an Ethical Development Agenda in South Africa Today*. Amsterdam: Rozenburg, 2008.

Dreyer, Jaco. 'South Africa.' In *The Wiley-Blackwell Companion to Practical Theology*, 508-509. Chichester: Blackwell, 2012.

Dunsmuir, Craig and Michael McCoy. 'Accreditation and Ministerial Formation: Serving Two Masters?' In *Contested issues in training ministers in South Africa*, edited by Marilyn Naidoo, 27-42. Stellenbosch: Sun Press, 2015.

Guder, Darrell. 'Theological Formation for Missional Faithfulness after Christendom: A Response to Steve de Gruchy.' In *Handbook of Theological Education in World Christianity: Theological Perspectives, Ecumenical Trends and Regional Surveys*, edited by Dietrich Werner et al., 51-55. Oxford: Regnum Books International, 2010.

Hendriks, Jurgens J and Johannes C Erasmus. 'Religion in South Africa: The 2001Population Census Data'. *Journal of Theology for Southern Africa*121, no. 1 (2005): 88-111.

Higgs, Phillips. 'The African Renaissance and the Decolonisation of Theological Education'. In *Contested Issues in Training Ministers in South Africa*, edited by Marilyn Naidoo, 43-56. Stellenbosch: Sun Press, 2015.

[20] Steve De Gruchy and Willem Ellis, *Christian Leadership*, 19.
[21] Steve De Gruchy and Willem Ellis, *Christian Leadership*, 19.
[22] Kombo, "Role and Relevance", 3.

Kombo, James. 'Role and Relevance of Theology for the Future of African Christianity'. In *Anthology of African Christianity*, edited by Dietrich Warner and Isabel Phiri. Dorpspruit: Cluster, 2015. Forthcoming.

Mannion, Gerard and Lewis Mudge (Eds). *The Routledge Companion to the Christian Church*. New York: Routledge, 2007.

Naidoo, Marilyn. 'Dealing with the Other: Managing Diversity in Theological Education.' In *Contested Issues in Training Ministers in South Africa*, edited by Marilyn Naidoo, 69-84. Stellenbosch: Sun Press, 2015.

Trisk, Janet. 'Choosing the Better Part: Engendering Theological Education?' In *Contested Issues in Training Ministers in South Africa*, edited by Marilyn Naidoo,57-68.Stellenbosch: Sun Press, 2015.

Vanhoozer, Kevin J. *The Drama of Doctrine: A Canonical-linguistic Approach to Christian Theology*. Westminster: John Knox Press, 2005.

Werner, Dietrich. 'Theological Education in the Changing Context of World Christianity: An Unfinished Agenda.' *International Bulletin of Missionary Research*35 no. 2 (2011): 92-100.

Part VIII

Resources for the Study of African Christianity

Isabel Apawo Phiri, Dietrich Werner and Roderick Hewitt

Adamo, David Tuesday, *African and Africans in the New Testament*. (Lanham, Maryland: University Press of America. Inc, 2006).

Adeyemo, Tokunbo (ed). *The African Bible Commentary*. (New York: WordAlive Publishers/Zondervan, 2006).

Adogame, Afe, Roswith Gerloff, and Klaus Hock, (eds). *Christianity in Africa and the African Diaspora: The Appropriation of a Scattered Heritage*. (London and New York: Continuum, 2008).

Adogame, Afe. *The African Christian Diaspora: New Currents and Emerging Trends in World Christianity*.(London/ New Delhi/ New York/Sydney: Bloomsbury Academic, 2013).

Amanze, James N (ed.) *Biblical Studies, Theology, Religion and Philosophy*. (Eldoret: Zapf Chancery. 2010).

Amanze, James N. *A History of the Ecumenical Movement in Africa*. (Gaborone: Pula Press, 1999).

Anderson, Allan H. *African Reformation: African Initiated Christianity in the 20th Century*. (Trenton, NJ: African World Press, 2001).

Appiah-Kobi, Kofi and Sergio Torres, (eds.), *African Theology En Route: Papers from the Pan-African Conference of Third World Theologians*, (Maryknoll: Orbis, 1983).

Ault, James (ed.) *African Christianity Rising: Two Part Documentary Film* Series Stories from Ghana (77: 00) Stories from Zimbabwe (73: 00). James Ault Production, 2012. 4 DVDs http://jamesault.com/documentaries/africaproject/.

Baëta, C.G. (ed.). *Christianity in Tropical Africa*. (Oxford: Oxford University Press, 1968).

Barrett, David B. *Schism and Renewal in Africa*. (Nairobi: Oxford University Press, 1968).

Baur, John *2000 Years of Christianity in Africa: An African Church History*, (Nairobi: Paulines Publications, 1994).

Bediako, Kwame *Christianity in Africa, The Renewal of a Non-Western Religion* (Edinburgh: Edinburgh. University Press/Maryknoll, NY: Orbis Books, 1995).

Bediako, Kwame, *Theology and Identity: the Impact of Culture upon Christian Thought in the Second Century and in Modern Africa*. (Cumbria: Regnum Books, 1992).

Bengt Sundkler and Christopher Steed, *A History of the Church in Africa*. (Cambridge: Cambridge University Press, 2000).

Bitek, Okot, p', *African Religions in Western Scholarship*. (Nairobi: Literature Bureau, 1971).

Byamugisha, Gideon., *Breaking the Silence: How can Religious Institutions talk About Sexual Matters in their Communities*, (Kampala: Tricolour Designers and printers, 2000).

Bond George, Walton Johnson, & Sheila S. Walker. *African Christianity: Patterns of Religious Continuity*. (New York: Academic Press, 1979).

Bongma, Elias (ed.), *African Religions: The Wiley-Blackwell Companion*. (Oxford: Wiley-Blackwell, 2012).

Bonk Jonathan (ed). *Dictionary of Africa Christian Biography*. (Boston: Boston University Press).

Burton, Keith Augustus. *The Blessing of Africa*. (Illinois: IVP Academic, 2007.

Chitando Ezra and Sophia Chirongoma (eds). *Justice Not Silence: Churches facing sexual and gender based violence* (Stellenbosch: Sun Press, 2013).

Chitando, Ezra *Acting in Hope: African Churches and HIV/AIDS*. (Geneva: WCC, 2007).

Comaroff, Jean and John L. Comaroff, *Of Revelation and Revolution: Christianity, Colonialism and Consciousness in South Africa*, vol. 1. Chicago: University of Chicago Press, 1991.

Cox, Harvey. *Fire from Heaven: The Rise of Pentecostal Spirituality and the Reshaping of Religion in the Twenty-first Century*. (Reading, MA: Addison-Wesley, 1995).

Cox, James (ed.) *Rites of passage in Contemporary Africa, Interaction between Christianity and African Traditional Religions*. (Cardiff: Academic Press, 1998).

Cox, James L. and Gerrie Ter Haar, eds. *Uniquely African? African Christian Identity from Cultural and Historical Perspectives*. (Trenton and Asmara: Africa World Press, 2003).

Daneel Marthinus L. and Robert Dana L. *The African Initiatives in Christian Mission* Series . Pretoria: UNISA Press.

Daneel, Marthinus L. *Quest for Belonging: Introduction to a Study of African Independent Churches.* Gweru: Mambo Press, 1987.

De Gruchy, John. *The Church Struggle in South Africa. (*Cape Town: David Philip, 1979).

Dickson, Kwesi. *Theology in Africa*. New York: Orbis, 1984).

Dickson, Kwesi A. and Paul Ellingworth *eds. Biblical Revelation and African Beliefs.* (New York: Orbis Books, 1969).

Daughrity, Dyron B. *The Changing World of Christianity: The Global History of a Borderless Religion,* (New York: Peter Lang, 2010).

Douglas E. Thomas, *African Traditional Religion in the Modern World.* (London: MacFarland and Company, 2005).

Dube, M. W. (ed). *Other Ways of Reading: African Women and the Bible*. (Atlanta: SBL & Geneva: WCC, 2001).

Dube, Musa W. and Musimbi Kanyoro (eds). *Grant Me Justice: HIV/AIDS & Gender Readings of the Bible*. (Pietermaritzburg: Cluster Publications, 2004).

Dube, Musa W. Andrew M. Mbuvi, and Dora Mbuwayesango, (eds). *Postcolonial Perspectives in African Biblical Interpretations*. (Atlanta: Society of Biblical Literature, 2012).

Ellis, Stephen and Gerrie ter Haar. *Worlds of Power: Religious Thought and Political Practice in Africa. (*Oxford: Oxford University Press, 2004).

Éloi Messi Metogo, (ed). *African Christianities* Concilium. (London: SCM Press, 2006).

Engelke, Matthew. *A Problem of Presence: Beyond Scripture in an African Church*. (Berkeley: University of California Press, 2007).

Fiedler, Klus. Gundani, Paul. and Mijoga, Hilary., eds. *Theology Cooked in an African Pot.* (Zomba: ATISCA, 1998).

Fiedler, Klus. *The Story of Faith Missions. (*Regnum/Oxford, 1994).

Gehman, Richard. *African Traditional Religion in Biblical Perspectives.* (Kampala: East African Publication Publishers 1989).

Gifford, Paul. *Christianity, Development and Modernity in Africa*. Oxford: Oxford University Press, 2016).

Gifford, Paul. *African Christianity: its Public Role*. (London: Hurst and Company, 1998).

Haddad, Beverley G. (ed). *Religion and HIV and Aids: Charting the Terrain*. (Pietermaritzburg: University of KwaZulu-Natal Press, 2011).

Hastings, Adrian, *The Church in Africa 1450-1950* (Oxford: Clarendon Press, 1994).

Hastings, Adrian. *A History of African Christianity 1950-1975.* (Cambridge: Cambridge University Press, 1979).

Healey, Joseph and Donald Sybertz. *Towards an African Narrative Theology*. (Limuru: Paulines Publications Africa, 1996).

Idowu, Bolaji. *Towards an Indigenous Church.* (London: Oxford University Press, 1965).

Isichei, Elizabeth. *A History of Christianity in Africa from Antiquity to the Present.* (New Jersey: William B. Eerdmans Publishing Company, 1995).

Kabue, Samuel, Mombo Esther, Kalgalo, Joseph and Peter, C.B. (eds.) *Disability, Society, and Theology Voices from Africa.* (Limuru: Zapf Chancery, 2011).

Kalu, Ogbu U. *Clio in a Sacred Garb: Essays on Christian Presence and African Responses, 1900-2000.* (NJ: Africa World Press, 2008).

Kalu, Ogbu. (ed). *African Christianity: An African Story*. (Pretoria: University of Pretoria, 2005).

Kalu, Ogbu. *African Pentecostalism: An introduction*. (New York: Oxford University Press, 2008).

Kanyoro, Musimbi R. A., and Nyambura J. Njoroge. eds. *Groaning in Faith: African Women in the Household of God.* (Nairobi: Acton, 1996).

Kanyoro, Musimbi R. (ed.) . *Feminist Cultural Hermeneutics: An African Perspective,* (Cleveland: The Pilgrims press, 2002).

Katongole, Emanuel M. *A future for Africa: Critical Essays in Christian Social Imagination*. (Scranton: The University of Scranton Press, 2004).

Kato, B. H. *Theological pitfalls in Africa.* (Evangel Publishing House, 1987).

Kofi, Appiah-Kubi and Torres Sergio (eds). *African Theology En Route: Papers from the Pan-African Conference of Third World Theologians,* (Accra/New York: Orbis Books, 1979).

Maxwell, David and Ingrid Lawrie, (ed). *Christianity and the African Imagination: Essays in Honour of Adrian Hastings.* (Leiden and Boston: Brill, 2013).

Mbiti, J. S. *Concepts of God in Africa.* (London/Nairobi: S.P.C.K/Acton Press., 1970/2012).

Mbiti, John S. *Bible and Theology in African Christianity*. (Nairobi/Oxford: Oxford University Press, 1986).

Mbiti, John S. *Introduction to African Religion* 2nd edition. (Oxford: Heinemann Educational Publishers, 1991).

Mbiti, John S. *African Regions and Philosophy* (Garden City, NY: Anchor Books, 1970).

Mugambi, J.N.K. *From Liberation to Reconstruction. African Christian Theology after the Cold War,* (Nairobi: East African Educational Publishers, 1995).

Mukonyora, Isabel, James L. Cox, and Frans J. Verstraelen, eds., *Re-Writing the Bible: The Real Issues*. Gweru: Mambo Press, 1993).

Njoroge, Nyambura J. and Musa W. Dube. eds. *Talitha Cum: Theologies of African Women.* (Pietermaritzburg: Cluster, 2001).

Nasimiyu, A. Wasike and J.N.K. Mugambi, *Moral and Ethical Issues in African Christianity,* (Nairobi: Acton Press, 1992).

Nyamiti, Charles. *African Tradition and the Christian God.* (Eldoret: Gaba Publications).

Nthamburi, Zablon. The African Church at the Crossroads- A Strategy for Indigenization. (Nairobi: Uzima Press, 1991).

Oden, T.C. *How Africa Shaped the Christian Mind.* (Downers Grove, Ill.: IVP, 2007).

Oduyoye, Mercy A. *Hearing and Knowing: Theological Reflections on Christianity in Africa*. (New York: Orbis Press, 1993).

Oduyoye, Mercy A. *Daughters of Anowa.* (Maryknoll, New York: Orbis, 1995).

Oduyoye, Mercy. A. & Kanyoro, Musimbi R. A. (eds.), *The Will to Arise: Women Tradition, and the Church in Africa,* (Maryknoll: Orbis Books, 2001).

Oduyoye, Mercy. *Introducing African Women's Theology,* (Cleveland: Pilgrim Press: 2001).

Okoth, Assa. *A History of Africa 1855-1914.* (Nairobi: East African Educational Publishers, 1979).

Olupona Jacob and Sulayman S. Nyang (eds.) *Religious Plurality in Africa: Essays in honour of John S. Mbiti.* (New York/Berlin: Mouton de-Guyter 1993).

Olupona Jacob K. and Sulayman S. Nyang (eds). *Religious Plurality in Africa: Essays in Honour of John S. Mbiti*, (Berlin/ New York: Mouton de Gruyter, 1993).

Parrinder, Geoffrey E. *African Traditional Religion*. (London: S.P.C.K., 1968).

Parratt John (ed.) *A Reader in African Theology*, (London: SPCK 1997).

Phiri, Isabel Apawo and Sarojini Nadar (eds.), *On Being Church: African Women's Voices and Visions*. (Geneva: Geneva, 2005).

Phiri, Isabel Apawo, Devarakshanam Betty Govinden and Sarojini Nadar (eds). *Her-Stories: Hidden Histories of Women of Faith in Africa.* (Pietermaritzburg: Cluster, 2002).

Phiri, Isabel Apawo and Sarojini Nadar. (eds). *African Women Religion and health: Essays in Honour of Mercy Amba Oduyoye.* (Maryknoll: Orbis, 2006).

Phiri, Isabel Apawo and Werner, Dietrich (eds) *Handbook of Theological Education in Africa.* (Oxford/Pietermaritzburg: Regnum Books International/Cluster Publication, 2013).

Ranger, O. Terrence (ed). *Evangelical Christianity in Africa.* (Oxford: Oxford University Press, 2008).

Russell. H. *The Missionary Outreach of the West Indian Church: The Jamaican Baptist Missions to West Africa in the Nineteenth Century.*(New York: Peter Lang Publishers, 2000).

Sanneh, Lamin. *Encountering the West: Christianity and the Global Cultural Process: The African Dimension.* (Maryknoll, NY: Orbis Books, 1993).

Sanneh, Lamin. *Translating the Message: The Missionary Impact on Culture* (Maryknoll, NY: Orbis, 1989).

Sanneh, Lamin. *Whose Religion is Christianity: The Gospel Beyond the West. (*Grand Rapids and Cambridge: William B. Eerdmans, 2003).

Schaaf, Ype. *On Their Way Rejoicing: The History and Role of the Bible in Africa.* (Carlisle: Paternoster Press, 1994).

Setiloane, Gabriel. M. *African Theology: An Introduction.* (Skotaville Press, Johannesburg, 1986).

Sundkler, Bengt and Steed, Christopher, *A History of the Church in Africa* (Cambridge: Cambridge University Press, 2000).

Taylor, John V. *The Primal Vision: Western Christendom and the African View of Life*. (Philadelphia: Fortress Press, 1963).

The Wipf and Stock African Christian Studies Series: http://wipfandstock.com/catalog/series/view/id/1/

Turner, Harold W. *Religious Innovation in Africa: Collected Essays on New Religious Movements.* (Boston, MA: G.K. Hall, 1979).

Walls, Andrew F. *Missionary Movement in Christian History: Studies in the Transmission of Faith.* (Maryknoll, NY: Orbis Books, 1996).

West, Gerald O. Dube Musa W. (eds) *The Bible in Africa: Transactions, Trajectories and Trends.*(Leiden and Boston: BRILL, 2000).

Yorke, Gosnell L.O.R. (ed.) *Bible Translation and African Languages. (*Nairobi: Acton, 2004).

Also published by Regnum

Orthodox Handbook on Ecumenism:Resources for Theological Education
Kalaitzidis, Fitzgerald, Hovorun, Pekridou, Asproulis, Werner & Liagre (Eds)
2014 / 978-1-908355-44-7 / 962pp (hardback) (paperback 978-1-908355-41-6)

We highly recommend the publication of this new Orthodox Handbook for Teaching Ecumenism edited by a group of orthodox theologians in collaboration with WCC Program, the Conference of European Churches, Volos Academy for Theological Studies in Greece, and Holy Cross Greek Orthodox School of Theology in Brookline, Massachusetts. This Handbook which is part of a broader ETE project of publishing resource books for theological education and teaching ecumenism in different settings is in many ways a historic publication. While this Handbook is written by Orthodox authors and is addressed primarily to the Eastern Orthodox, I am sure that it will be useful also for a broader constituency.

Olav Fykse Tveit, World Council of Churches, General Secretary

Asian Handbook for Theological Education and Ecumenism
Hope Antone, Wati Longchar, Hyunju Bae, Huang Po Ho &
Dietrich Werner (eds)
2013 / 978-1-908355-41-6 / 675pp
The Asian Handbook for Theological Education and Ecumenism signals an investment towards the future of the ecumenical movement in Asia. Being a region with limited available resources and extreme diversity, education and training is widely thought to be a significant way of opening a new future of common witness and sharing in various areas. The release of this tremendously rich resource book, right in time of the occasion of the 10th assembly of the World Council of Churches, will open new dimensions of exploring new ways of community life, common witness, mutual enrichment and guidance of Asian churches through the new era of ecumenism.

Kim Young-Ju, National Council of Churches in Korea, General Secretary

Handbook of Theological Education in Africa
Isabel Apawo Phiri & Dietrich Werner (Eds)
2013 / 978-1-908355-45-4 / 1110pp (paperback)
This Handbook of Theological Education in Africa is a fascinating witness to the explosive status quo of Theological Education. The historical and regional (inter alia) surveys open our eyes and ears to see and hear how fast it has taken root historically, geographically, and ecum-enically. The landscape of African Theological Education has changed drastically during the final twenty to thirty years of the last century. There is very much to appreciate about it and what has been achieved. We have grounds to make us rejoice, and for which to thank the Lord.

John Mbiti, Theologian and Philosopher

This Handbook of Theological Education in Africa has something for everybody.
Mercy Oduyoye, Director of Institute of Women in Religion and Culture in Accra, Ghana